COMPACT OXFORD THESAURUS FOR U

Compact Oxford Thesaurus
for University and College Students

FIRST EDITION

Edited by
Sara Hawker
with Maurice Waite

OXFORD
UNIVERSITY PRESS

OXFORD
UNIVERSITY PRESS

Great Clarendon Street, Oxford OX2 6DP

Oxford University Press is a department of the University of Oxford.
It furthers the University's objective of excellence in research, scholarship,
and education by publishing worldwide in

Oxford New York

Auckland Cape Town Dar es Salaam Hong Kong Karachi
Kuala Lumpur Madrid Melbourne Mexico City Nairobi
New Delhi Shanghai Taipei Toronto

With offices in

Argentina Austria Brazil Chile Czech Republic France Greece
Guatemala Hungary Italy Japan Poland Portugal Singapore
South Korea Switzerland Thailand Turkey Ukraine Vietnam

Oxford is a registered trade mark of Oxford University Press
in the UK and in certain other countries

© Oxford University Press 2007

Database right Oxford University Press (maker)

First published 2007

British Library Cataloguing in Publication Data

Data available

Library of Congress Cataloging in Publication Data

Data available

Typeset in Frutiger and Parable
by Asiatype, Inc
Printed in Italy
by Legoprint S.p.A.

ISBN 978-0-19-921629-1

2

Contents

Introduction

The *Compact Oxford Thesaurus for University and College Students* is a completely new text that has been tailored to meet the particular requirements of those in higher education, following market research with a wide spectrum of university and college students. In its selection and arrangement of senses and synonyms, and its extensive use of example sentences, the thesaurus is designed to help students write and express themselves more fluently, more accurately, and with greater confidence in college assignments as well as in letters and job applications. The centre section, *Effective Writing for College and Career*, has been specially written to provide additional practical guidance on the use of the thesaurus, enabling students to make the best possible use of the information a thesaurus contains to improve their writing.

Both the main part of the thesaurus and the centre section are directly informed by evidence of how the English language is actually used today, drawing on the analysis of hundreds of millions of words of real English contained in the Oxford English Corpus. This analysis enables us to provide better-matching and more useful sets of synonyms than ever before. Extra help with choosing the right word is given in boxed notes throughout the main text. These offer clear information about words that are often confused (such as *affect* and *effect* or *imply* and *infer*). There are also notes on sensitive vocabulary, giving guidance about certain terms which should be avoided in careful writing. You can access more information about how to improve your writing and use a thesaurus to the best advantage, as well as interactive tests, in the Online Resource Centre (www.oup.com/uk/dictionaries/cotfs).

The thesaurus has an attractive two-colour design and a clear, open layout, with each new section of an entry starting on a new line. This makes it especially easy both to locate the word or sense you are looking for and to find a suitable synonym.

The editor would like to thank Catherine Soanes for her invaluable help with the central section of the thesaurus. Anne McGee, Phyllis Creme, and Colleen McKenna, from the Centre for the Advancement of Learning and Teaching at University College London, also provided valuable advice on this section.

Guide to the thesaurus

The *Compact Oxford Thesaurus for University and College Students* is designed to be as straightforward and easy to use as possible. This section provides details on how the entries are structured, the treatment of different types of English, and the abbreviations used. You will find more information in the **Vocabulary solutions: how to use a thesaurus** section in the centre of the book.

▶ STRUCTURE OF ENTRIES

Here is an explanation of the main types of information in the thesaurus.

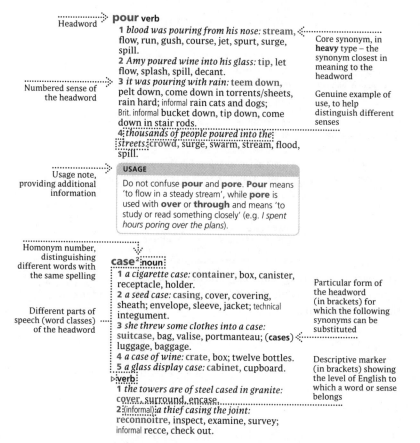

Headword ⋯⋯⋯⋯▷ **pour** verb

1 *blood was pouring from his nose:* stream, ◁⋯⋯⋯⋯ Core synonym, in flow, run, gush, course, jet, spurt, surge, spill.

heavy type – the synonym closest in meaning to the headword

2 *Amy poured wine into his glass:* tip, let flow, splash, spill, decant.

Numbered sense of the headword ⋯⋯▷ **3** *it was pouring with rain:* teem down, pelt down, come down in torrents/sheets, rain hard; informal rain cats and dogs; Brit. informal bucket down, tip down, come down in stair rods.

Genuine example of use, to help distinguish different senses

4 *thousands of people poured into the streets:* crowd, surge, swarm, stream, flood, spill.

Usage note, providing additional information ⋯⋯▷ **USAGE**

Do not confuse **pour** and **pore**. **Pour** means 'to flow in a steady stream', while **pore** is used with **over** or **through** and means 'to study or read something closely' (e.g. *I spent hours poring over the plans*).

Homonym number, distinguishing different words with the same spelling ⋯⋯

case² noun

1 *a cigarette case:* container, box, canister, receptacle, holder.

Particular form of the headword (in brackets) for which the following synonyms can be substituted

2 *a seed case:* casing, cover, covering, sheath; envelope, sleeve, jacket; technical integument.

Different parts of speech (word classes) of the headword ⋯⋯

3 *she threw some clothes into a case:* suitcase, bag, valise, portmanteau; **(cases)** ◁⋯⋯⋯ luggage, baggage.

4 *a case of wine:* crate, box; twelve bottles.

5 *a glass display case:* cabinet, cupboard.

▷**verb**

1 *the towers are of steel cased in granite:* cover, surround, encase.

Descriptive marker (in brackets) showing the level of English to which a word or sense belongs

2 (informal) *a thief casing the joint:* reconnoitre, inspect, examine, survey; informal recce, check out.

read verb

1 *he was reading the newspaper:* study, scrutinize, look through; pore over, be absorbed in; run your eye over, cast an eye over, leaf through, scan, flick through, skim through, thumb through; formal peruse.

2 *he read her a passage from the letter:* read out/aloud, recite, declaim.

3 *I can't read my own writing:* decipher, make out, make sense of, interpret, understand.

4 *how do you read the situation?* interpret, understand, explain, analyse, construe, take, see.

5 *he read modern history at university:* study, take; N. Amer. & Austral./NZ major in; informal do.

□ **read something into something** *officials cautioned against reading too much into the statistics:* infer from, extrapolate from, assume from, deduce from, conclude from, attribute to; read between the lines.

> WORD LINKS
>
> **legible** clear enough to read
> **illegible** not clear enough to read
> **literacy** the ability to read and write
> **illiteracy** the inability to read and write

Descriptive marker showing the level of English for which the following synonym is appropriate

Combined synonym group standing for both read out and read aloud

Descriptive markers showing the regions of the world in which the following synonym is used

Phrase for which the following synonyms can be substituted

Words that are associated with the headword but are not actual synonyms

---

incessantly adverb

she talked incessantly about her problems: constantly, continually, all the time, non-stop, without stopping, without a break, round the clock, {morning, noon, and night}, interminably, unremittingly, ceaselessly, endlessly; informal 24-7.
OPPOSITES: occasionally.

Curly brackets, showing that the words they contain form one complete synonym

Word (or words) meaning the opposite of the headword: most have entries of their own where a wider choice can be found

---

premeditation noun

advance planning, forethought, pre-planning, intent, criminal intent; Law malice aforethought.
OPPOSITES: impulse.

Descriptive marker showing the specialist field or area of activity in which the following synonym is used

---

quote verb

1 *he quoted a passage from Shakespeare:* recite, repeat; take, extract, copy out.

2 *she quoted one case in which a woman had died:* cite, mention, refer to, name, instance, specify, identify; point to, present, put forward.

▷ noun. See QUOTATION.

Cross-reference (in small capitals) to another word in the thesaurus

▶ TYPES OF ENGLISH

Most of the entries, senses, and synonyms in this thesaurus are part of standard English. This means that they are words we use in every kind of situation, from writing a college assignment or formal report to emailing or chatting with friends. Some words, however, are suitable only for certain contexts, or are usually only found in certain types of writing. Where this is the case, a descriptive marker called a label is used to indicate what type of English the word belongs to.

This thesaurus uses three different types of descriptive label:

- **register** labels refer to a particular level of use in the language, indicating whether a word or phrase is informal, formal, literary, and so on. The register labels used in the thesaurus are listed below. You will find more information about choosing the right word for different written or spoken contexts in the section called Vocabulary solutions: how to use a thesaurus in the centre of the book.

- **geographical** labels show that a word or phrase belongs to a variety of English used in a particular part of the world. Most of the words and phrases used in standard British English will be the same as those in other varieties, but there are some that are only found in one type of English (for example, the normal word in American English for rubbish is garbage). These kinds of words are labelled with the appropriate geographical marker.

  Note that the label Brit. means that a word or phrase is typically found in British English, but is not found in American English, though it may be used in other varieties, such as Australian English. The labels US and N. Amer., on the other hand, mean that a word or phrase is typically found in US or North American English (North America = the US *and* Canada), but is not standard in British English, though it may be found elsewhere.

- **subject** labels are used to show that a word is associated with a particular subject field or specialist activity, such as Law, Music, or Computing.

Register labels

- **formal:** normally only used in writing, especially official documents (e.g. abode or cognizant)
- **technical:** normally used only in technical language, though not restricted to a particular subject field (e.g. occlude or frangible)
- **literary:** found only or mainly in works of literature (e.g. foe or slay).

Note, however, that this type of language is often deliberately used in the media to create a particular tone or effect.

- **informal:** normally only used in speaking, writing, or email to friends (e.g. barmy or gawp)
- **dated:** no longer used by most English speakers but still used by older people (e.g. cad)
- **historical:** only used today to refer to something that is no longer part of modern life (e.g. alms)
- **old use:** old-fashioned language, not in ordinary use today, though sometimes used to give an old-fashioned effect and also found in the literature of the past (e.g. comely or spirituous)
- **humorous:** used with the intention of sounding amusing or playful (e.g. transmogrify or delectation)
- **euphemistic:** used instead of a ruder or more direct term (e.g. tired and emotional instead of 'drunk')
- **derogatory:** used with the deliberate intention of expressing a low opinion of someone or insulting them (e.g. crony)
- **rare:** not in normal use today or in previous times (e.g. osculate, meaning 'to kiss')

When you are writing for university or college, you are unlikely to encounter situations in which it would be appropriate to select a synonym that belongs to the last seven types of English, but it is nevertheless useful to have a broad understanding of these categories. This type of vocabulary may also be effective or useful in creative writing.

▶ ABBREVIATIONS USED IN THE THESAURUS

Austral.	Australian
Brit.	British
N. Amer.	North American
N. English	Northern English
NZ	New Zealand

Trademarks

This thesaurus includes some words which have, or are asserted to have, proprietary status as trademarks or otherwise. Their inclusion does not imply that they have acquired for legal purposes a non-proprietary or general significance, nor any other judgement concerning their legal status. In cases where the editorial staff have some evidence that a word has proprietary status this is indicated in the entry for that word by the label trademark, but no judgement concerning the legal status of such words is made or implied thereby.

Aa

aback adverb
□ **take someone aback**
surprise, shock, stun, astonish, startle,
take by surprise, stagger, astound;
dumbfound, nonplus, stop someone in
their tracks; throw, unnerve, disconcert,
unsettle; informal flabbergast, knock
sideways; Brit. informal knock for six.

abandon verb
1 *the party abandoned policies which had
made it unelectable:* renounce, relinquish,
dispense with, set aside, disclaim, disown,
disavow, discard, wash your hands of, have
done with; give up, drop, jettison; informal
ditch, scrap.
2 *fans invaded the pitch and the match
was abandoned:* discontinue stop, end,
terminate, halt, bring to a halt, break off,
cancel.
3 *he abandoned his wife and children:*
desert, leave, leave high and dry, turn
your back on, cast aside; jilt, strand, leave
stranded, leave in the lurch, throw over;
informal walk out on, run out on, dump,
ditch.
4 *the skipper gave the order to abandon
ship:* vacate, leave, depart from, withdraw
from, quit, evacuate.
5 *a vast expanse of territory was abandoned
to the invaders:* relinquish, surrender, give
up, cede, yield, leave.
▷ noun *she sings and sways with total
abandon:* lack of inhibition, lack of
restraint, wildness.

abandoned adjective
1 *a home for abandoned children:* deserted,
cast aside; literary forsaken.
2 *an abandoned tin mine:* unused, disused,
neglected, idle; deserted, unoccupied,
uninhabited, empty.
3 *a wild, abandoned dance:* uninhibited,
unrestrained, wild, reckless, unbridled,
impulsive, impetuous.

abase verb *I watched my colleagues abasing
themselves before the dean:* humble,
humiliate, demean, lower, degrade, debase,
cheapen; (**abase yourself**) grovel, kowtow,
bow and scrape, toady, fawn; informal crawl,
suck up to someone.

abashed adjective *Harriet looked
slightly abashed:* embarrassed, ashamed,
shamefaced, remorseful, conscience-
stricken, mortified, humiliated, chagrined,
crestfallen, sheepish, red-faced.

abate verb
1 *the storm had abated:* subside, die
down/away/out, lessen, ease, let up,
decrease, diminish, moderate, decline,
fade, dwindle, recede, tail off, peter out,
taper off, wane, ebb, weaken, come to an
end.
2 *nothing abated his crusading zeal:*
decrease, lessen, diminish, reduce,
moderate, ease, soothe, dampen, calm,
tone down, allay, temper.
OPPOSITES: intensify, increase.

abatement noun
1 *the storm still rages with no sign of
abatement:* subsiding, dying down/away/
out, lessening, easing off, let-up, decrease,
moderation, decline.
2 *noise abatement:* decrease, reduction,
lowering.

abbey noun monastery, convent, priory,
friary, nunnery.

abbreviate verb *'network' is often
abbreviated to 'net':* shorten, reduce, cut;
abridge, condense, contract, compress,
pare down, prune, shrink, telescope;
summarize, abstract, precis, synopsize,
edit.
OPPOSITES: lengthen, expand.

abbreviated adjective shortened,
reduced, cut, abridged, condensed, concise,
compact, succinct; summary, thumbnail;
formal synoptic.
OPPOSITES: long.

abbreviation noun short form,
contraction, acronym, initialism;
diminutive.

abdicate verb
1 *the king abdicated in 1936:* renounce the
throne, stand down, step down, resign,
retire, bow out.
2 *Ferdinand abdicated the throne:*
relinquish, renounce, give up, surrender,
vacate, cede; formal abjure.
3 *the state abdicated all responsibility for
their welfare:* disown, reject, renounce,
give up, refuse, relinquish, repudiate,

a

abandon, turn your back on, wash your hands of.

abdication noun
1 *Edward VIII's abdication:* renunciation of the throne, resignation, retirement.
2 *an abdication of responsibility:* disowning, renunciation, rejection, refusal, relinquishment, repudiation, abandonment.

abdomen noun stomach, belly, intestines, gut; informal tummy, middle, insides, guts, pot, paunch.

> WORD LINKS
> **abdominal**, **ventral** relating to the abdomen

abdominal adjective *he had severe abdominal pain:* gastric, stomach, intestinal, visceral; technical enteric, duodenal, ventral.

abduct verb *she was abducted by two men and held for 36 hours:* kidnap, carry off, seize, capture, run away/off with, make off with, spirit away, hold hostage, hold to ransom; informal snatch.

aberrant adjective *these illnesses can involve psychosis and aberrant behaviour:* abnormal, atypical, anomalous, irregular, deviant, rogue; strange, odd, peculiar, uncommon, freakish.
OPPOSITES: normal, typical.

aberration noun *economists said the figures were a statistical aberration:* anomaly, departure from the norm, deviation, abnormality, irregularity, variation, freak, rarity, oddity, peculiarity, curiosity; mistake.

abet verb *several villagers were accused of aiding and abetting the smugglers:* assist, aid, help, lend a hand, cooperate with, collaborate with, work with, collude with, be in collusion with, be hand in glove with; side with, support, back, encourage, promote; connive at.
OPPOSITES: hinder.

abeyance noun *the project was left in abeyance for the time being:* suspension, a state of suspension, a state of uncertainty; (**in abeyance**) pending, suspended, deferred, postponed, put off, put to one side, unresolved, up in the air; informal in cold storage, on ice, on the back burner.

abhor verb *he abhorred sexism in every form:* detest, hate, loathe, despise, regard with disgust, shrink from, recoil from, shudder at; formal abominate, execrate.
OPPOSITES: love, admire.

abhorrence noun hatred, loathing, detestation, revulsion, disgust, repugnance, horror, aversion, odium; formal execration, abomination.

abhorrent adjective *many will have committed offences that other prisoners find abhorrent:* repugnant, hateful, loathsome, despicable, abominable, execrable, detestable, repellent, repulsive, revolting, disgusting, distasteful, horrible, horrifying, awful, heinous, reprehensible, obnoxious, odious, nauseating, offensive, contemptible.
OPPOSITES: admirable.

abide verb
1 *he expected everybody to abide by the rules:* comply with, obey, observe, follow, keep to, hold to, conform to, adhere to, stick to, stand by, act in accordance with, uphold, heed, accept, go along with, acknowledge, respect, defer to.
2 *I can't abide the smell of cigarettes:* tolerate, bear, stand, put up with, endure, take; informal stomach; Brit. informal stick.
3 *at least one memory will abide:* continue, remain, survive, last, persist, linger, stay, live on.
OPPOSITES: flout, disobey.

abiding adjective *he had an abiding respect for her:* enduring, lasting, persisting, long-lasting, lifelong, continuing, remaining, surviving, standing, durable, everlasting, perpetual, eternal, unending, constant, permanent, unchanging, steadfast, immutable.
OPPOSITES: short-lived, ephemeral.

ability noun
1 *the manager had lost his ability to motivate the players:* capacity, capability, power, faculty, facility; means.
2 *he is a player of exceptional ability:* skill, talent, expertise, aptitude, skilfulness, savoir faire, prowess, mastery, accomplishment; competence, proficiency; adeptness, dexterity, adroitness, deftness; informal know-how.

abject adjective
1 *many families are living in abject poverty:* extreme, acute, great, severe, dreadful, terrible, appalling, awful, dire, atrocious; wretched, miserable, hopeless.
2 *an abject apology:* obsequious, grovelling, fawning, servile, cringing, sycophantic, submissive, craven.

ablaze adjective *several vehicles were ablaze:* on fire, alight, aflame, in flames, flaming, burning, blazing.

able adjective
1 *he will soon be able to resume his duties:* capable of, competent to, equal to, up to, fit to, prepared to, qualified to; allowed to, free to, in a position to.
2 *an able student:* intelligent, clever, talented, skilful, skilled, accomplished, gifted; proficient, good, adroit, adept; capable, competent.
OPPOSITES: incompetent, incapable.

able-bodied adjective *every able-bodied man was required to serve in the armed forces:* healthy, fit, in good health, robust,

strong, sound, sturdy, vigorous, hardy, hale and hearty, strapping, lusty.
OPPOSITES: infirm, frail.

abnormal adjective *the illness is recognizable from the patient's abnormal behaviour:* unusual, atypical, untypical, non-typical, unrepresentative, anomalous, aberrant, irregular, unexpected, unfamiliar, unconventional, surprising, unorthodox, singular, exceptional, extraordinary, out of the ordinary, uncommon; strange, odd, peculiar, freakish, curious, bizarre, queer, eccentric; deviant, unnatural, perverse, perverted; informal weird, funny.
OPPOSITES: normal, typical.

abnormality noun
1 *babies born with physical or mental abnormalities:* malformation, deformity, flaw, defect, irregularity.
2 *the abnormality of his behaviour was a cause for concern:* unusualness, atypicality, irregularity, anomalousness, aberrance, aberration; strangeness, oddness, peculiarity.

abolish verb *the law was abolished in 1961:* put an end to, get rid of, scrap, end, stop, eradicate, eliminate, quash, axe; cancel, annul, dissolve; rescind, repeal, revoke, overturn; discontinue, remove, drop, jettison; formal abrogate; informal do away with, ditch.
OPPOSITES: retain, create.

abolition noun scrapping, ending, eradication, elimination; cancellation, annulment, dissolution; revocation, repeal, rescindment, discontinuation, removal; formal abrogation.

abominable adjective *the uprising was suppressed with abominable cruelty:* atrocious, appalling, awful, terrible, dreadful, loathsome, detestable, hateful, odious, despicable, contemptible, diabolical, horrifying, shocking, nauseating, repugnant, disgusting, revolting, repellent, abhorrent, reprehensible; nasty, unpleasant, obnoxious, vile.
OPPOSITES: admirable.

abomination noun *in both wars, internment was an abomination:* atrocity, disgrace, horror, obscenity, outrage, evil, crime, monstrosity; anathema.

aboriginal adjective *the area's aboriginal inhabitants:* indigenous, native; original, earliest, first; ancient, primitive; Anthropology autochthonous.

abort verb
1 *the pregnancy was aborted:* terminate, end.
2 *the organism can cause pregnant ewes to abort:* miscarry, have a miscarriage.
3 *the crew aborted the take-off:* terminate, stop, end, discontinue, halt, call off; informal pull the plug on.

abortive adjective *a series of abortive attempts at political reform:* unsuccessful, failed, fruitless, vain, thwarted, futile, useless, unavailing, ineffective, ineffectual, to no effect, to no avail, unproductive, inefficacious.
OPPOSITES: successful.

abound verb
1 *cafes and bars abound in the narrow streets:* be plentiful, be abundant, be numerous, proliferate, be thick on the ground.
2 *a stream which abounded with trout and eels:* be full of, overflow with, teem with, be packed with, be crowded with, be thronged with; be alive with, be crawling with, be overrun by/with, swarm with, bristle with, be thick with; informal be stuffed with, be jam-packed with, be chock-a-block with, be chock-full of.

about preposition
1 *a book about ancient Greece:* regarding, concerning, with reference to, referring to, with regard to, with respect to, respecting, relating to, on, touching on, dealing with, relevant to, connected with, in connection with, on the subject of, in the matter of, apropos, re.
2 *two hundred people were milling about the room:* around, round, throughout, over, through, on every side of.
▷ **adverb**
1 *there were babies crawling about in the grass:* around, here and there, to and fro, back and forth, from place to place, hither and thither, in all directions.
2 *I knew he was about somewhere:* near, nearby, around, hereabouts, not far off/away, close by, in the vicinity, in the neighbourhood.
3 *apparently, the car cost about £15,000:* approximately, roughly, around, round about, in the region of, circa, of the order of, something like; or so, or thereabouts, there or thereabouts, more or less, give or take a few, not far off; Brit. getting on for.
□ **about to**
just going to, on the point of, on the verge of, on the brink of; ready to, all set to, preparing to, intending to, soon to; informal within an ace of.

about-turn noun (Brit.) *the government was forced to make an about-turn over the bill:* volte-face, U-turn, reversal, retraction; change of heart, change of mind.

above preposition
1 *light filtered through a tiny window above the door:* over, higher than; on top of, on, upon, atop.
2 *those above the rank of Colonel:* superior to, senior to, over, higher than, more powerful than; in charge of, commanding.
3 *you must be above suspicion:* beyond, not open to, not vulnerable to, out of reach of; immune to, exempt from, not liable to.
4 *an increase above the rate of inflation:*

a

greater than, more than, higher than, exceeding, in excess of, over, over and above, beyond, surpassing, upwards of.
OPPOSITES: below, under, beneath.

▷ adverb
1 *in the darkness above, something moved:* overhead, on/at the top, high up, on high, up above, up in the sky, high above your head, aloft.
2 *the two cases described above:* earlier, previously, before, formerly.

▷ adjective *the above example was chosen to illustrate the underlying problem:* preceding, previous, earlier, former, foregoing, prior, above-stated, aforementioned, aforesaid.

▫ **above all**
primarily, before everything, first of all, most of all, chiefly, most importantly, in the first place, first and foremost, mainly, principally, predominantly, especially, essentially, basically, in essence.

▫ **above yourself**
ever since her promotion she'd been getting above herself: conceited, proud, arrogant, self-important, cocky; haughty, disdainful, supercilious; informal stuck-up, high and mighty, uppity, big-headed, swollen-headed.

above board adjective *the proceedings were completely above board:* legitimate, lawful, legal, licit, honest, fair, open, trustworthy; informal legit, kosher, on the level.

abrade verb *the paintwork had been abraded over the years by the weather:* wear away, wear down, erode, scrape away, corrode, eat away at, gnaw away at.

abrasion noun
1 *he had abrasions to his forehead:* graze, cut, scratch, scrape, gash, laceration, injury, contusion; sore.
2 *the metal is resistant to abrasion:* erosion, wearing away/down, corrosion.

abrasive adjective
1 *don't use abrasive kitchen cleaners:* corrosive, corroding; caustic, harsh, coarse.
2 *her abrasive manner won her few friends:* harsh, caustic, acerbic, curt, brusque, sharp, cutting, severe, hard, tough, stern; insensitive, unfeeling, unsympathetic, inconsiderate, rough, callous.

abreast adverb
1 *they walked three abreast:* in a row, side by side, alongside, level, beside each other, shoulder to shoulder.
2 *try to keep abreast of current affairs:* up to date with, up with, in touch with, informed about, acquainted with, knowledgeable about, conversant with, familiar with, au fait with; formal au courant with.

abridge verb shorten, cut, cut down, edit, truncate, pare down, prune; abbreviate, condense, compress, reduce, shrink;

summarize, sum up, abstract, precis, synopsize, give a digest of, put in a nutshell.

abridged adjective *an abridged text of his speech:* shortened, cut, cut down, condensed, abbreviated, potted; concise, summary, outline, thumbnail; bowdlerized, censored, expurgated.

abridgement noun summary, abstract, synopsis, precis, outline, digest, résumé.

abroad adverb *he regularly travels abroad:* overseas, out of the country, to/in foreign countries.

abrupt adjective
1 *the car came to an abrupt halt | I was surprised by the abrupt change of subject:* sudden, unexpected, without warning, unanticipated, unforeseen, precipitate, surprising, startling; quick, swift, rapid, hurried, hasty, immediate, instantaneous.
2 *he spoke in a very abrupt manner:* curt, brusque, blunt, short, sharp, terse, brisk, crisp, gruff, rude, discourteous, uncivil, unceremonious, offhand, rough, harsh; informal snappy.
3 *he tends to write in abrupt, epigrammatic paragraphs:* disjointed, jerky, uneven, disconnected, inelegant.
4 *an abrupt slope:* steep, sheer, precipitous, sharp, sudden; perpendicular, vertical.
OPPOSITES: gradual, gentle.

abscess noun ulcer, sore, cyst, boil, blister, pustule, carbuncle, whitlow, wen; inflammation, infection.

abscond verb *176 detainees absconded:* run away, escape, flee, make off, take flight, take off, decamp; bolt, make a break for it, take to your heels, make a quick getaway, beat a hasty retreat, run for it, make a run for it; disappear, vanish, slip away, steal away, sneak away; informal cut and run, skedaddle, scarper, vamoose; Brit. informal do a bunk, do a runner.

absence noun
1 *he felt that everything had changed during his absence from school:* non-attendance, non-appearance; absenteeism, truancy; leave, holiday, sabbatical; Brit. playing truant; N. Amer. vacation.
2 *the absence of anything to eat:* lack, want, non-existence; unavailability, deficiency, dearth; need.
OPPOSITES: presence.

absent adjective
1 *she was absent from work:* away, off, out, non-attending, truant; off duty, on holiday, on leave; informal AWOL.
2 *when carbohydrates are absent from the diet, protein is used for energy:* missing, lacking, unavailable, non-existent.
3 *she looked up with an absent smile:* distracted, preoccupied, inattentive, vague, absorbed, abstracted, unheeding,

oblivious, absent-minded, dreamy, far away, in a world of your own, lost in thought, in a brown study; blank, empty, vacant; informal miles away.
OPPOSITES: present, attentive.
▷ **verb** *Rose absented herself from the occasion:* stay away, be absent, withdraw; retire, take your leave, remove yourself.

absent-minded adjective forgetful, distracted, preoccupied, inattentive, vague, abstracted, unheeding, oblivious, in a brown study, wool-gathering; lost in thought, pensive, thoughtful, brooding; informal scatterbrained, miles away.

absolute adjective
1 *there was absolute silence in the house* | *an absolute disgrace:* complete, total, utter, perfect; out-and-out, outright, entire, pure, decided; thorough, thoroughgoing, undivided, unqualified, unadulterated, unalloyed, unmodified, unreserved, downright, undiluted, consummate, unmitigated, sheer, arrant, rank.
2 *everything I have told you is the absolute truth:* definite, certain, positive, unconditional, categorical, unquestionable, incontrovertible, undoubted, unequivocal, decisive, conclusive, confirmed, infallible.
3 *no one dare challenge her absolute authority:* unlimited, unrestricted, total, supreme, unconditional, arbitrary; ultimate.
4 *an absolute monarch:* autocratic, despotic, dictatorial, tyrannical, authoritarian, autonomous, sovereign; omnipotent.
5 *absolute moral standards:* universal, independent, non-relative, non-variable.
OPPOSITES: partial, qualified, limited.

absolutely adverb *you're absolutely right:* completely, totally, utterly, perfectly, entirely, wholly, fully, quite, thoroughly, unreservedly; definitely, certainly, positively, unconditionally, categorically, unquestionably, undoubtedly, without doubt, without question, unequivocally; exactly, precisely, decisively, conclusively, manifestly, in every way/respect, one hundred per cent.

absolution noun
1 exoneration, discharge, acquittal; release; freedom; formal exculpation.
2 (Christianity) forgiveness, pardon; formal remission.

absolve verb
1 *this fact does not absolve you from responsibility:* exonerate, discharge, acquit, vindicate; release, free, relieve, liberate, clear, exempt; formal exculpate; informal let off.
2 (Christianity) *I absolve you from your sins:* forgive, pardon.
OPPOSITES: blame, condemn.

absorb verb
1 *a sponge-like material which absorbs water:* soak up, suck up, draw up/in, take up/in, blot up, mop up, sop up.
2 *she absorbed the information in silence:* assimilate, digest, take in.
3 *the company was absorbed into the new concern:* incorporate, assimilate, integrate, take in, subsume, include, co-opt, swallow up.
4 *she was totally absorbed by the performance:* engross, grip, captivate, rivet, hold, involve, enthral, spellbind, fascinate, interest, intrigue, engage, occupy, preoccupy.

absorbent adjective *absorbent kitchen paper:* porous, spongy, sponge-like, permeable, pervious, absorptive.

absorbing adjective *an absorbing and informative book:* interesting, fascinating, captivating, gripping, engrossing, compelling, compulsive, enthralling, riveting, spellbinding, intriguing, thrilling, exciting; informal unputdownable.
OPPOSITES: boring, uninteresting.

absorption noun
1 *the absorption of water:* soaking up, sucking up.
2 *the company's absorption into a larger concern:* incorporation, assimilation, integration, inclusion.
3 *her absorption in the music:* involvement, immersion, raptness, captivation, fascination, engagement, occupation, preoccupation.

abstain verb
1 *he abstained from wine:* go without, deny yourself, forgo, refrain from, desist from, forbear from; give up, renounce, avoid, eschew; refuse, decline; informal cut out.
2 *most pregnant women abstain, or drink very little:* be teetotal, take the pledge; informal be on the wagon.
3 *262 voted against, 38 abstained:* not vote, decline to vote.

abstemious adjective *he seems to have led an abstemious life:* self-denying, restrained, self-restrained, moderate, temperate, abstinent, self-disciplined, sober, austere, ascetic, puritanical, spartan.
OPPOSITES: self-indulgent.

abstinence noun *I started drinking again after six years of abstinence:* teetotalism, temperance, sobriety, abstemiousness, abstention; self-denial, self-restraint.

abstract adjective
1 *abstract concepts such as love or beauty:* theoretical, conceptual, notional, intellectual, metaphysical, philosophical, academic.
2 *abstract art:* non-representational, non-pictorial.
OPPOSITES: actual, concrete.

a

▷**verb**

1 *the staff abstract material for an online database:* summarize, precis, abridge, condense, compress, shorten, cut down, abbreviate, synopsize.

2 *a scheme to abstract more water from the river:* extract, pump, draw off, withdraw, remove, take out/away; separate, isolate.

▷**noun** *an abstract of her speech:* summary, synopsis, precis, résumé, outline, abridgement, digest, summation.

abstracted adjective *she seemed abstracted and unaware of her surroundings:* preoccupied, distracted, absent-minded, in a world of your own, with your head in the clouds, daydreaming, dreamy, inattentive, thoughtful, pensive, lost in thought, deep in thought, immersed in thought, wool-gathering, in a brown study, musing, brooding, absent; informal miles away.
OPPOSITES: attentive.

abstraction noun

1 *his style of writing focuses on facts rather than abstractions:* concept, idea, notion, thought, theory, hypothesis.

2 *she sensed his momentary abstraction:* preoccupation, distraction, absent-mindedness, dreaminess, inattentiveness, inattention, wool-gathering; thoughtfulness, pensiveness.

abstruse adjective *he was unable to follow the abstruse arguments put forward:* obscure, arcane, esoteric, recherché, rarefied, recondite, difficult, hard, puzzling, perplexing, cryptic, complex, complicated, involved, over/above your head, incomprehensible, unfathomable, impenetrable, mysterious.

absurd adjective *what an absurd idea!* preposterous, ridiculous, ludicrous, farcical, laughable, risible, idiotic, stupid, foolish, silly, inane, imbecilic, insane; unreasonable, irrational, illogical, nonsensical, pointless, senseless; informal crazy, hare-brained; Brit. informal barmy, daft.
OPPOSITES: reasonable, sensible.

absurdity noun preposterousness, ridiculousness, ludicrousness, risibility, idiocy, stupidity, folly, foolishness, inanity, insanity; irrationality, illogicality, pointlessness, senselessness.

abundance noun *the island boasts an abundance of wildlife* | *the abundance of fish in the waters:* profusion, wealth, host, cornucopia; plenty, quantities, scores, multitude; plentifulness, profuseness, copiousness; formal plenitude; informal millions, lots, heaps, masses, stacks, piles, loads, tons, oodles.
OPPOSITES: lack, scarcity.

abundant adjective *an abundant supply of food:* plentiful, copious, ample, profuse, rich, lavish, liberal, generous, bountiful, large, huge, great, bumper, overflowing, prolific, teeming; in abundance; informal galore.
OPPOSITES: scarce, sparse.

□ **be abundant**
abound, be plentiful, be numerous, be in abundance, proliferate, be thick on the ground.

abuse verb

1 *the judge abused his power:* misuse, misapply, misemploy; exploit, take advantage of.

2 *he was accused of abusing children:* mistreat, maltreat, ill-treat, treat badly; molest, interfere with, indecently assault, sexually abuse, sexually assault; injure, hurt, harm.

3 *he faces a misconduct charge for abusing the referee:* insult, be rude to, swear at, curse, call someone names, taunt, shout at, revile, vilify, slander, cast aspersions on; Brit. informal slag off.

▷**noun**

1 *the abuse of power* | *the scheme is open to administrative abuse:* misuse, misapplication, misemployment; exploitation, corruption.

2 *the abuse of children:* mistreatment, maltreatment, ill-treatment; molestation, interference, indecent assault, sexual abuse, sexual assault; injury, hurt, harm.

3 *human rights abuses:* injustice, offence, crime, wrong; wrongdoing, misconduct.

4 *he hurled abuse at the driver:* insults, obscenities, expletives, curses, swear words; swearing, cursing, name-calling; invective, vilification, vituperation, slander.

abusive adjective *he was fined for making abusive comments to officials:* insulting, rude, offensive, obscene, vulgar; disparaging, belittling, derogatory, disrespectful, uncomplimentary, pejorative; scurrilous, defamatory, slanderous, libellous; informal bitchy.

abut verb *the eight US states abutting the Great Lakes:* adjoin, be adjacent to, border, neighbour, join, touch, meet, reach, be contiguous with.

abysmal adjective *some of the teaching was abysmal:* very bad, dreadful, awful, terrible, appalling, atrocious, disgraceful, deplorable, shameful, lamentable, woeful, laughable; informal rotten, pathetic, useless, lousy, dire, the pits; Brit. informal chronic, shocking, hopeless.

abyss noun chasm, gorge, ravine, canyon, rift, crevasse, hole, gulf, pit, cavity, void, bottomless pit.

academic adjective

1 *an academic institution:* educational, scholastic, instructional, pedagogical.

2 *he has a distinctly academic turn of mind:* scholarly, studious, literary, well read, intellectual, clever, erudite, learned, educated, cultured, bookish, highbrow, donnish, cerebral; informal brainy.

3 *the debate has been largely academic:* theoretical, conceptual, notional, philosophical, hypothetical, speculative, conjectural, suppositional, putative.
OPPOSITES: practical.

▷**noun** *a group of Russian academics:* scholar, lecturer, don, teacher, tutor, professor, fellow, man/woman of letters, thinker, bluestocking; formal pedagogue; informal egghead, bookworm.

academy noun school, college, university, institute, seminary, conservatory, conservatoire.

accede verb (formal) *he acceded to the government's demands:* agree to, consent to, accept, assent to, acquiesce in, comply with, go along with, concur with, yield to, give in to, give way to, defer to, surrender to.

accelerate verb
1 *the car accelerated down the hill:* speed up, go faster, gain momentum, increase speed, pick up speed, gather speed, put on a spurt.
2 *inflation started to accelerate:* increase, rise, go up, leap up, surge, escalate, spiral.
3 *the university accelerated the planning process:* hasten, speed up, quicken, step up, advance, expedite, promote, give a boost to, stimulate, spur on, precipitate.
OPPOSITES: decelerate, delay.

acceleration noun
1 *the acceleration of the industrial process:* hastening, speeding up, quickening, stepping up, advancement, boost, precipitation.
2 *an acceleration in the divorce rate:* increase, rise, leap, surge, escalation.

accent noun
1 *a Scottish accent:* pronunciation, intonation, enunciation, articulation, inflection, tone, modulation, cadence, timbre, manner of speaking, delivery; brogue, burr, drawl, twang.
2 *the accent is on the first syllable:* stress, emphasis, accentuation, force, prominence; beat.
3 *the accent is on comfort:* emphasis, stress, priority; importance, prominence.
4 *a circumflex accent:* mark, diacritic, diacritical mark.

▷**verb** *fabrics which accent the background colours in the room:* highlight, focus attention on, draw attention to, point up, underline, underscore, accentuate, spotlight, foreground, play up, bring to the fore, heighten, stress, emphasize, feature.

accentuate verb *the simple outfit accentuated her long legs* | *you should accentuate the positive:* highlight, focus attention on, draw attention to, point up, underline, underscore, accent, spotlight, foreground, play up, bring to the fore, heighten, stress, emphasize.

accept verb
1 *he accepted a pen as a present* | *we do not accept personal cheques:* receive, take.
2 *he accepted the job immediately:* take on, undertake, assume, take responsibility for.
3 *she accepted an invitation to lunch:* say yes to, reply in the affirmative, agree to.
4 *she was accepted as one of the family:* welcome, receive, embrace, adopt.
5 *he accepted Ellen's explanation:* believe, regard as true, give credence to, credit, trust; informal buy, swallow.
6 *we have agreed to accept his decision:* go along with, agree to, consent to, acquiesce in, concur with, assent to, comply with, abide by, follow, adhere to, act in accordance with, defer to, yield to, surrender to, bow to, give in to, submit to, respect; formal accede to.
7 *he accepts that he made a mistake:* admit, acknowledge, concede, allow, own, recognize.
8 *she will just have to accept the consequences:* reconcile yourself to, resign yourself to, get used to, adjust to, learn to live with, make the best of, face up to; tolerate, endure, put up with, bear, take, submit to.
OPPOSITES: refuse, reject.

USAGE

Do not confuse **accept** with **except**. **Accept** means 'to agree to receive or do something', while **except** means 'not including; apart from' (*they work every day except Sunday*).

acceptable adjective
1 *an acceptable standard of living:* satisfactory, adequate, reasonable, quite good, fair, decent, good enough, sufficient, sufficiently good, fine, not bad, all right, average, tolerable, passable, middling, moderate; informal OK, so-so, fair-to-middling.
2 *a most acceptable present:* welcome, appreciated; pleasing, agreeable, delightful, desirable, satisfying, gratifying, to your liking.
3 *the risk had seemed acceptable at the time:* bearable, tolerable, allowable, admissible, sustainable, justifiable, defensible.
OPPOSITES: unacceptable.

acceptance noun
1 *the acceptance of an award:* receipt, receiving, taking, obtaining.
2 *the acceptance of responsibility:* undertaking, assumption.
3 *her acceptance as one of the family:* welcome, favourable reception, adoption.
4 *his acceptance of Matilda's explanation:* belief, credence, trust, faith.
5 *their acceptance of the decision:* compliance with, acquiescence in, consent to, concurrence with, assent to, agreement with.
6 *a mood of resigned acceptance:* tolerance, toleration, resignation.

accepted adjective *he wasn't handsome in the accepted sense:* established, traditional, acknowledged, recognized, orthodox; usual, customary, common, normal, general, prevailing, accustomed, familiar, popular, expected, routine, standard, stock; literary wonted.

access noun
1 *the building has a side access:* entrance, entry, way in, means of entry; approach, means of approach, ingress.
2 *they were denied access to the stadium:* admission, admittance, entry, right of entry; entrée.
3 *students have access to a photocopier:* the use of, permission to use.
▷ **verb** *the program used to access the data:* retrieve, gain access to, obtain; read.

accessible adjective
1 *the village is only accessible on foot | an easily accessible reference tool:* reachable, attainable, approachable; obtainable, available; informal get-at-able.
2 *his accessible style of writing:* understandable, comprehensible, easy to understand, intelligible; informal user-friendly.
3 *Professor Cooper is very accessible:* approachable, friendly, agreeable, obliging, congenial, affable, cordial, welcoming, easy-going, pleasant.

accession noun
1 *the Queen's accession to the throne:* succession; assumption of, inheritance of.
2 *accession to the Treaty of Rome was effected in 1971:* assent, consent, agreement; acceptance, acquiescence, compliance, concurrence.
3 *recent accessions to the museum:* addition, acquisition, new item, gift, purchase.

accessorize verb *she accessorized her designs with spectacular jewellery:* complement, enhance, set off; accompany, decorate, adorn, ornament, trim.

accessory noun
1 *camera accessories such as tripods and flashguns:* attachment, extra, addition, add-on, adjunct, appendage, appurtenance, supplement; Brit. fitment.
2 *fashion accessories:* adornment, embellishment, ornamentation, decoration.
3 *she was charged as an accessory to murder:* accomplice, partner in crime, associate, collaborator, fellow conspirator; henchman.

accident noun
1 *he was involved in an accident at work:* mishap, misadventure, unfortunate incident, misfortune, mischance; disaster, tragedy, catastrophe, calamity.
2 *there was a serious accident on the motorway:* crash, collision, pile-up, smash, bump, road traffic accident, RTA; derailment; Brit. informal shunt.
3 *it was pure accident that he had come across them:* chance, coincidence, twist of fate, freak, hazard; fluke, bit of luck, serendipity; fate, fortuity, fortune, providence, happenstance.

accidental adjective
1 *an accidental meeting | the damage might have been accidental:* chance, unexpected, unforeseen, unanticipated, unplanned, coincidental, adventitious, random; fortuitous, lucky, serendipitous, fluky; unlooked-for, unintentional, unintended, inadvertent, unpremeditated, unthinking, unwitting.
2 *the location is accidental and contributes nothing to the poem:* incidental, unimportant, by the way, subsidiary, subordinate, secondary, peripheral, tangential, extraneous, extrinsic, irrelevant, non-essential, inessential.
OPPOSITES: intentional, deliberate.

accidentally adverb *we met accidentally:* by chance, by accident, by a twist of fate, as luck would have it, fortuitously, by a fluke, by happenstance, coincidentally; unexpectedly, unintentionally, inadvertently, unwittingly.

acclaim verb *the play has been widely acclaimed by critics:* praise, applaud, commend, approve, welcome, pay tribute to, speak highly of, compliment, celebrate, sing the praises of, heap praise on, wax lyrical about, eulogize, lionize, admire, hail; formal laud; informal rave about.
OPPOSITES: criticize.
▷ **noun** *she has won acclaim for her commitment to democracy:* praise, applause, tributes, accolades, acclamation, plaudits, compliments, congratulations; approval, approbation, admiration, commendation.
OPPOSITES: criticism.

acclaimed adjective *an acclaimed Australian novelist:* celebrated, admired, esteemed, well thought of, well received, acknowledged; eminent, great, renowned, distinguished, prestigious, illustrious, pre-eminent.

acclamation noun praise, applause, tributes, accolades, acclaim, plaudits, compliments, congratulations; approval, admiration, approbation, commendation.
OPPOSITES: criticism.

acclimatization noun adjustment, adaptation, habituation, accommodation, acculturation; familiarization.

acclimatize verb *they gradually acclimatized to the heat:* adjust, adapt, accustom yourself, habituate yourself, accommodate yourself, acculturate; get used, become inured, reconcile yourself, resign yourself; familiarize yourself; find your feet, get your bearings, become seasoned.

accolade noun
1 *he received the accolade of knighthood:* honour, privilege.
2 *the hotel won a top accolade from the inspectors:* award, tribute, commendation, praise, testimonial, compliment, pat on the back; salutes, plaudits, congratulations, bouquets.

accommodate verb
1 *refugees were accommodated in army camps:* lodge, house, put up, billet.
2 *the cottages accommodate up to six people:* hold, take, have room for.
3 *our staff will make every effort to accommodate you:* help, assist, aid, oblige; meet the needs/wants of, cater for, fit in with, satisfy.
4 *she tried to accommodate herself to her new situation:* adjust, adapt, accustom, habituate, acclimatize, acculturate, get accustomed, get used, come to terms with.
5 *the bank would be glad to accommodate you with a loan:* provide, supply, furnish, grant.

accommodating adjective
it's good of you to be so accommodating: obliging, cooperative, helpful, eager to help, adaptable, amenable, considerate, unselfish, generous, willing, hospitable, neighbourly, kind, friendly, pleasant, agreeable; Brit. informal decent.

accommodation noun
1 *they were living in temporary accommodation:* housing, lodgings, living quarters, quarters, rooms; home, residence, place to stay; shelter, a roof over your head; formal abode, dwelling; informal digs.
2 *there was lifeboat accommodation for 1,178 people:* space, room, seating; places.
3 *an accommodation between the two parties was reached:* arrangement, understanding, settlement, accord; deal, bargain, compromise.
4 *their accommodation to changing economic circumstances:* adjustment, adaptation, habituation, acclimatization, acculturation.

accompaniment noun
1 *a musical accompaniment:* backing, support, background, soundtrack.
2 *the wine makes a superb accompaniment to cheese:* complement, supplement, addition, companion, accessory.

accompany verb
1 *he accompanied her to Paris:* go with, escort, travel with, keep someone company, partner, chaperone, attend; show, see, usher, conduct; tag along with.
2 *the illness is often accompanied by nausea:* occur with, co-occur with, coexist with, go with, go together with, go hand in hand with, appear with, attend by.
3 *he accompanied the choir on the piano:* back, play with, play for, support.

accomplice noun
partner in crime, associate, accessory, confederate, collaborator, fellow conspirator; henchman; informal sidekick.

accomplish verb
the planes accomplished their mission: fulfil, achieve, succeed in, bring about/off, carry out/through, execute, effect, perform, do, discharge, complete, finish, conclude, realize, attain.

accomplished adjective
she is an accomplished pianist: skilled, skilful, expert, masterly, virtuoso, master, consummate, proficient, talented, gifted, adept, adroit, deft, dexterous, able, good, competent, capable, efficient, experienced, seasoned, trained, practised, professional, polished; informal great, mean, nifty, crack, ace.

accomplishment noun
1 *the reduction of inflation was a remarkable accomplishment:* achievement, attainment, feat, act, move; coup.
2 *drawing was another of her many accomplishments:* talent, skill, gift, ability, forte; achievement.
3 *a poet of considerable accomplishment:* expertise, skill, skilfulness, talent, adeptness, adroitness, deftness, dexterity, ability, prowess, mastery, competence, capability, proficiency, aptitude, artistry, art; informal know-how.

accord verb
1 *the national assembly accorded him more power:* give, grant, present, award, vouchsafe; confer on, bestow on, vest in, invest with.
2 *his views accorded with mine:* correspond, agree, tally, match, concur, be consistent, harmonize, be in harmony, be compatible, be in tune, correlate; conform to; informal square.
▷**noun**
1 *a peace accord:* pact, treaty, agreement, settlement, deal, entente, concordat, protocol, contract, convention.
2 *the two sides failed to reach accord:* agreement, consensus, unanimity, harmony, unison, unity; formal concord.
□ **of your own accord**
voluntarily, of your own free will, of your own volition, by choice; willingly, freely, readily.
□ **with one accord**
unanimously, in complete agreement, with one mind, without exception, as one, of one voice.

accordance noun
□ **in accordance with**
the ballot was held in accordance with trade union rules: in agreement with, so as to conform with, in conformity with, in line with, true to, in the spirit of, observing, following, heeding.

a

according adverb
□ according to
1 *conditions were atrocious, according to one worker:* as stated by, as claimed by, on the authority of, in the opinion of.
2 *cook the rice according to the instructions:* as specified by, in accordance with, in compliance with, in agreement with, as per.
3 *salary will be fixed according to experience:* in proportion to, proportional to, commensurate with, in relation to, relative to, in line with, corresponding to.

accordingly adverb
1 *they appreciated the danger and acted accordingly:* appropriately, correspondingly, suitably.
2 *accordingly, he returned home to Yorkshire:* therefore, for that reason, consequently, so, as a result, as a consequence, in consequence, hence, that being the case; formal thus, ergo.

accost verb *reporters accosted him in the street:* speak to, call to, shout to, hail, address; approach, confront, detain, stop, waylay; informal buttonhole, collar.

account noun
1 *a detailed account of the incident:* description, report, statement, explanation, exposition, delineation, portrayal; record, log, chronicle, history; narrative, story, tale; view, impression, version; blog, weblog.
2 *the firm's quarterly accounts:* financial record, ledger, balance sheet, financial statement; (**accounts**) books.
3 *I pay the account off in full each month:* bill, invoice; debt, charges; informal tab.
4 *his background is of no account:* importance, import, significance, consequence, substance; formal moment.
▷ verb *her visit could not be accounted a success:* consider, regard as, reckon, hold to be, think, look on as, view as, see as, judge, adjudge, count, deem, rate.
□ account for
1 *they must account for the delay:* explain, answer for, give reasons for, rationalize, justify.
2 *excise duties account for over half the price of Scotch:* constitute, make up, comprise, form, compose, represent.
□ on account of
because of, owing to, as a consequence of, due to, thanks to, by/in virtue of, in view of.
□ on no account
never, under no circumstances, not for any reason.

accountable adjective
1 *the government was held accountable for the food shortage:* responsible, liable, answerable; to blame.
2 *the game's popularity is barely accountable:* explicable, explainable; understandable, comprehensible.

accoutrements plural noun equipment, paraphernalia, things, apparatus, tackle, implements, materials, outfit, regalia, impedimenta, trappings, accessories; formal appurtenances; informal kit, gear, stuff, bits and pieces.

accredit verb
1 *he was accredited with being one of the world's fastest sprinters:* recognize as, credit with.
2 *the discovery of distillation is usually accredited to the Arabs:* ascribe, attribute.
3 *professional bodies accredit these research degrees:* authorize, recognize, approve, certify, license.

accredited adjective official, recognized, authorized, approved, certified, licensed.

accretion noun
1 *the accretion of sediments in coastal mangroves:* accumulation, formation, collecting, cumulation, accrual; growth, increase.
2 *the city has a historic core surrounded by recent accretions:* addition, extension, appendage, add-on, supplement.

accrue verb
1 *financial benefits will accrue from restructuring:* result, arise, follow, ensue; be caused by.
2 *interest is added to the account as it accrues:* accumulate, collect, build up, mount up, grow, increase.

accumulate verb
1 *investigators have yet to accumulate enough evidence:* gather, collect, amass, assemble, cumulate; stockpile, pile up, heap up, store up, hoard, lay in/up.
2 *his debts were accumulating:* build up, increase, grow, multiply, accrue; run up

accumulation noun mass, build-up, pile, heap, stack, collection, stock, store, stockpile, reserve, hoard; amassing, gathering, cumulation, accrual, accretion.

accuracy noun *we have confidence in the accuracy of the statistics:* correctness, precision, exactness; fidelity, faithfulness, truth, truthfulness, veracity, authenticity, realism, verisimilitude.

accurate adjective
1 *accurate information | an accurate representation of the situation:* correct, exact, right, error-free, perfect, precise; factual, fact-based, literal, faithful, true, truthful, true to life, authentic, realistic; formal veracious; Brit. informal spot on.
2 *an accurate shot:* well aimed, on target, unerring, sure, true; deadly, lethal.

accusation noun *there were accusations of bribery:* allegation, charge, claim, assertion, imputation; indictment, arraignment.

accuse verb
1 *four people were accused of assault:*

charge with, prefer charges against, indict for, arraign for.
2 *they accused the government of electoral fraud:* blame for, lay the blame on, hold responsible for, hold accountable for; condemn for, criticize for, denounce for; informal point the finger at.
OPPOSITES: absolve, exonerate.

accustom verb *he had accustomed himself to living in darkness:* adapt, adjust, acclimatize, habituate yourself, accommodate yourself, acculturate; reconcile yourself, become reconciled, get used to, come to terms with, learn to live with, become inured.

accustomed adjective *the money would not have kept Nicholas in his accustomed lifestyle:* customary, usual, normal, habitual, regular, routine, ordinary, typical, traditional, established; literary wonted.

acerbic adjective *he is known for his acerbic wit:* sharp, forthright, astringent, abrasive, caustic, trenchant, mordant, cutting, biting, searing, scathing; sarcastic, sardonic.

ache noun
1 *a stomach ache:* pain, cramp, twinge, pang; gnawing, stabbing, stinging, smarting; soreness, tenderness, irritation, discomfort.
2 *the ache in her heart:* sorrow, sadness, grief, anguish, pain, agony, torture, hurt.
▷**verb**
1 *my legs were aching:* hurt, be sore, be painful, be in pain, throb, pound, twinge; smart, burn, sting; Brit. informal play up.
2 *her heart ached for poor Philippa:* grieve, sorrow, be in distress, be in anguish; bleed.
3 *Marie ached for his affection:* long, yearn, hunger, thirst, hanker, pine, itch; crave, desire.

achieve verb *they developed a strategy for achieving their environmental goals:* attain, realize, bring off/about, accomplish, carry out/through, fulfil, execute, perform, engineer, pull off, conclude, complete, finish; earn, win, gain, acquire, obtain, get, secure, reach.

achievement noun
1 *the achievement of a high rate of economic growth:* attainment, realization, accomplishment, fulfilment, implementation, execution, performance; conclusion, completion.
2 *they felt justifiably proud of their achievement:* accomplishment, attainment, feat, performance, act, action, deed, effort, exploit; work, handiwork.

Achilles heel noun *the cost of the process may prove to be its Achilles heel:* weakness, weak point, weak spot, shortcoming, failing, imperfection, flaw, defect, chink in someone's armour.
OPPOSITES: strength.

aching adjective
1 *an aching back:* painful, achy, sore, stiff, tender, uncomfortable; hurting, in pain, throbbing, pounding, smarting, burning, stinging.
2 *an aching heart:* sorrowful, sad, miserable, grieving, distressed, anguished, grief-stricken; heavy.

acid adjective
1 *a juicy fruit with a slightly acid flavour:* sour, tart, bitter, sharp, acidic, acrid, pungent, vinegary, acetic.
2 *acid remarks:* acerbic, sharp, bitter, caustic, abrasive, astringent, harsh, sarcastic, sardonic, cutting, biting, stinging, trenchant, mordant, scathing, wounding, hurtful, unkind, vitriolic, venomous, spiteful; informal bitchy, catty.
OPPOSITES: sweet, pleasant.

acknowledge verb
1 *the government acknowledged that the tax was unfair:* admit, accept, concede, grant, allow, confess, own, recognize.
2 *few people acknowledged my letters:* answer, reply to, respond to.
3 *he did not acknowledge Colin, but hurried past:* greet, salute, address; nod to, wave to, raise your hat to, say hello to.
OPPOSITES: reject, ignore.

acknowledged adjective *he was one of the acknowledged experts in this field:* recognized, accepted; approved, accredited, confirmed; declared, confessed, avowed.

acknowledgement noun
1 *there was acknowledgement of the need to take new initiatives:* acceptance, admission, concession, recognition, confession.
2 *Travis gave a smile of acknowledgement:* greeting, welcome, salutation.
3 *she left without a word of acknowledgement:* thanks, gratitude, appreciation, recognition.
4 *I sent off the form, but there was no acknowledgement:* answer, reply, response.

acolyte noun *he found himself surrounded by eager acolytes:* assistant, helper, follower, disciple, supporter, votary; derogatory minion, underling, lackey, henchman; informal sidekick, groupie, hanger-on.

acquaint verb *new staff should be acquainted with fire exit routes:* familiarize, make familiar, make aware of, inform of, advise of, apprise of, let know, get up to date; brief, prime; informal fill in on, bring up to speed on.

acquaintance noun
1 *he was no more than a business acquaintance:* contact, associate, colleague.
2 *she had prospered from her acquaintance with him:* association, relationship, contact.

a

3 *the pupils had little acquaintance with the language:* familiarity with, knowledge of, experience of, awareness of, understanding of, comprehension of, grasp of.

acquainted adjective *she was acquainted with the traditional customs:* familiar, conversant, at home, up to date, au fait; abreast of, well versed in, knowledgeable about, well informed about; informed about, apprised of; formal cognizant of, au courant with; informal up to speed, clued in.

acquiesce verb *she acquiesced in his decision:* accept, consent to, agree to, allow, assent to, concede; comply with, cooperate with, give in to, bow to, yield to, submit to; informal go along with.

acquiescence noun consent, agreement, acceptance, assent, leave; compliance, concession, cooperation; submission.

acquiescent adjective compliant, cooperative, obliging, agreeable, amenable, tractable, persuadable, pliant, unprotesting; submissive, yielding, biddable, docile.

acquire verb *he had acquired shares in the company:* obtain, come by, get, receive, gain, earn, win, be given; buy, purchase, procure, possess yourself of, secure, pick up; informal get your hands on, get hold of, land.
OPPOSITES: lose.

acquisition noun
1 *the gallery's Bronze Room will house a new acquisition:* purchase, buy, accession, addition, investment, possession.
2 *the acquisition of funds:* obtaining, gaining, earning, winning, procurement, collection.

acquisitive adjective greedy, avaricious, covetous, possessive, grasping, rapacious, mercenary, materialistic; informal money-grubbing.

acquisitiveness noun greed, avarice, cupidity, covetousness, possessiveness, rapaciousness, rapacity, materialism.

acquit verb
1 *the jury acquitted her:* clear, exonerate, find innocent, absolve; discharge, release, free, set free; informal let off.
2 *the boys acquitted themselves well:* behave, conduct yourself, perform, act.
OPPOSITES: convict.

acquittal noun *the acquittal of the defendants:* exoneration; discharge, release, freeing.
OPPOSITES: conviction.

acrid adjective *the acrid smell of smoke:* pungent, bitter, sharp, strong, sour, harsh, unpleasant; stinging, burning.

acrimonious adjective *they had a heated and acrimonious discussion:* bitter, angry, rancorous, hostile, bad-tempered, ill-tempered, caustic, harsh, sharp, cutting; vicious, vitriolic, venomous, nasty, spiteful.

acrimony noun bitterness, anger, rancour, resentment, ill feeling, ill will, bad blood, animosity, hostility, enmity, antagonism, spleen.
OPPOSITES: goodwill.

act verb
1 *the Government must act to remedy the situation:* take action, take steps, take measures, move; react.
2 *he was acting on the orders of the party leader:* follow, act in accordance with, obey, heed, comply with; fulfil, meet, discharge.
3 *an estate agent acting for a prospective buyer:* represent, act on behalf of; stand in for, fill in for, deputize for, take the place of.
4 *Alison began to act oddly:* behave, conduct yourself, react.
5 *the scents act as a powerful aphrodisiac:* operate, work, function, serve.
6 *the drug acted directly on the blood vessels:* affect, have an effect on, work on; have an impact on, influence.
7 *he acted in a highly successful film:* perform, play a part, take part, appear.
8 *we laughed, but most of us were just acting:* pretend, play-act, put it on, fake it, feign it.
▷ noun
1 *acts of kindness* | *a criminal act:* action, deed, feat, exploit, move, gesture, undertaking, operation; achievement, accomplishment.
2 *the act raised the tax on tobacco:* law, decree, statute, act of Parliament, enactment, edict, dictum, ruling, measure; bill.
3 *the first act of the play:* section, subsection, division, part, segment.
4 *a music hall act:* performance, turn, routine, number, sketch, skit.
5 *it was all just an act:* pretence, show, front, facade, masquerade, charade, posture, pose, affectation, sham, fake.

acting noun *the theory and practice of acting:* drama, the theatre, the stage, the performing arts, dramatics, dramaturgy, stagecraft, theatricals.
▷ adjective *the bank's acting governor:* temporary, interim, caretaker, pro tem, provisional, stopgap; deputy, stand-in, fill-in.
OPPOSITES: permanent.

action noun
1 *her action saved the child's life* | *there is no excuse for their actions:* act, deed, move, exploit, feat, undertaking, manoeuvre; behaviour, conduct, activity.
2 *he called for tougher action to protect teachers:* measures, moves, steps, operations.

3 *a man of action:* energy, vitality, vigour, forcefulness, drive, initiative, spirit, liveliness; activity; informal get-up-and-go.
4 *the action of hormones on the pancreas:* effect, influence, working; power.
5 *he missed all the action while he was away:* excitement, activity, happenings, events, incidents; informal goings-on.
6 *twenty-nine men died in the action:* fighting, hostilities, battle, conflict, combat, warfare; engagement, clash, encounter, skirmish.
7 *a civil action for damages:* lawsuit, legal action, suit, case, prosecution, litigation, proceedings.

activate verb *Mark pressed the button which activated the machine:* operate, switch on, turn on, start up, set going, trigger, set in motion, actuate, boot up; trip.

active adjective
1 *despite her age she's still very active:* energetic, lively, sprightly, spry, vital, dynamic; busy, occupied; mobile; informal on the go, full of beans.
2 *an active member of the union:* hard-working, busy, industrious, diligent, tireless, contributing, effective, enterprising, involved, enthusiastic, keen, committed, vigorous, devoted, zealous.
3 *the watermill was active until 1960:* operative, working, functioning, functional, operating, operational, in action, in operation; live; informal up and running.
OPPOSITES: listless, passive.

activity noun
1 *there was a lot of activity in the area:* action, movement, commotion, hustle and bustle, hurly-burly, liveliness, life, stir; events, incidents, happenings; informal toing and froing, comings and goings.
2 *the school offers a wide range of activities:* pursuit, occupation, interest, hobby, pastime, recreation, diversion, entertainment.
3 *the companies have begun joint marketing activities in the US and the UK:* project, scheme, venture, undertaking, enterprise, act.

actor, **actress** noun performer, player, thespian; film star, matinee idol, star, starlet; informal ham; Brit. informal luvvy.

actual adjective *the estimate was much less than the actual cost | those were his actual words:* real, true, genuine, authentic, verified, attested, confirmed, definite; existing, existent, physical, concrete, factual, de facto, bona fide.
OPPOSITES: notional.

actuality noun *the journalistic debate about actuality and fiction:* reality, fact, truth, real life.

actually adverb *I looked upset but actually I was very excited:* in reality, in fact, as a matter of fact, really, in truth, if truth be told, to tell the truth.

actuate verb
1 *the sprinkler system was actuated by the fire:* activate, operate, switch on, turn on, start up, set going, trigger, trip, set in motion.
2 *the defendant was actuated by malice:* motivate, prompt, stimulate, move, drive, influence, spur on, impel.

acumen noun *a gullible young man with little or no business acumen:* shrewdness, astuteness, acuity, sharpness, sharp-wittedness, brains; judgement, understanding, awareness, sense, common sense, discernment, wisdom, wit, sagacity, perspicacity, insight, perception, penetration; informal nous, savvy, know-how.

acute adjective
1 *residents are facing an acute shortage of drinking water:* severe, critical, drastic, dire, dreadful, terrible, awful, grave, bad, serious, desperate, dangerous; old use parlous.
2 *acute stomach pains:* sharp, severe, excruciating, agonizing, racking, searing.
3 *his acute mind:* astute, shrewd, sharp, sharp-witted, incisive, discerning, perceptive, perspicacious, penetrating, insightful, piercing, discriminating, quick, quick-witted, agile, nimble, clever, intelligent, brilliant, canny, sagacious, wise, judicious; informal smart, quick off the mark, quick on the uptake, savvy.
4 *an acute sense of smell:* keen, sharp, highly developed, very good, sensitive.
OPPOSITES: mild, dull.

acutely adverb *Lucy looked acutely embarrassed:* extremely, very, exceedingly, markedly, severely, intensely, deeply, profoundly, keenly, painfully, desperately, tremendously, enormously, thoroughly, heartily, terribly.

adage noun *it is vital for every pilot to remember the old adage 'safety first':* saying, maxim, axiom, proverb, aphorism, dictum, precept, motto, saw, truism, platitude, cliché, commonplace; rare apophthegm.

adamant adjective *they asked again, but he was adamant:* determined, resolved, resolute, firm, unshakeable, immovable, inflexible, unwavering, unswerving, uncompromising, steadfast; stubborn, unrelenting, unyielding, unbending, rigid, obdurate, intransigent, dead set.

adapt verb
1 *we've adapted the hotels to suit their needs:* modify, alter, change, adjust, convert, redesign, restyle, refashion, remodel, reshape, revamp, rework, rejig, redo, reconstruct, reorganize; customize, tailor; improve, amend, refine; informal tweak.

a

2 *he has adapted well to his new home:* adjust, acclimatize yourself, accommodate yourself, habituate yourself, become habituated, get used, orient yourself, get your bearings, find your feet, acculturate; assimilate, integrate, blend in, fit in; reconcile yourself, come to terms.

adaptable adjective
1 *an adaptable workforce capable of acquiring new skills:* flexible, versatile, cooperative, accommodating, amenable; resilient.
2 *an adaptable piece of furniture:* versatile, modifiable, convertible, adjustable; multi-purpose, all-purpose.

adaptation noun
1 *the adaptation of old buildings:* conversion, alteration, modification, redesign, remodelling, revamping, reconstruction.
2 *his adaptation to their way of life:* adjustment, acclimatization, accommodation, habituation, acculturation; assimilation, integration.

add verb
1 *the front porch was added in 1751:* attach, build on, join, append, affix, connect, annex; include, incorporate.
2 *they added all the figures up:* total, count up, compute, reckon up, tally; Brit. tot up.
3 *her decision just added to his misery:* increase, magnify, augment, intensify, heighten, deepen, amplify; exacerbate, aggravate, compound, reinforce; add fuel to the fire, fan the flames.
4 *she added that she had every confidence in Laura:* go on to say, state further, continue, carry on.
OPPOSITES: subtract.
□ **add up** (informal) *the situation just didn't add up:* make sense, stand to reason, hold up, hold water, ring true, be convincing.
□ **add up to**
1 *the subsidies added up to £1700:* amount to, come to, run to, make, total, equal, number.
2 *the recent riots add up to a deepening crisis:* amount to, constitute; signify, signal, mean, indicate, denote, point to, be evidence of, be symptomatic of, spell.

addendum noun appendix, codicil, postscript, afterword, tailpiece, coda, supplement; adjunct, appendage, addition, add-on, attachment; rider.

addict noun *a heroin addict:* user; informal junkie.

addicted adjective
1 *he was addicted to tranquillizers:* dependent on; informal hooked on.
2 *she became addicted to the theatre:* devoted to, passionate about, obsessed with, fixated on, a slave to; informal hooked on, mad about, crazy about, fanatical about.

addiction noun
1 *his heroin addiction:* dependency, habit.
2 *a slavish addiction to fashion:* devotion to, dedication to, obsession with, passion for, mania for, infatuation with, enslavement to.

addictive adjective *crack cocaine is highly addictive:* habit-forming; compulsive.

addition noun
1 *the soil is improved by the addition of compost:* adding, incorporation, inclusion, introduction.
2 *an addition to the existing regulations:* supplement, adjunct, addendum, appendage, add-on, extra; rider.
□ **in addition**
1 *conditions were harsh, and in addition some soldiers fell victim to snipers:* also, additionally, as well, what is more, furthermore, moreover, into the bargain, to boot.
2 *there were eight presidential candidates in addition to the General:* besides, as well as, on top of, over and above; informal plus.

additional adjective *beach towels are provided without additional charge | additional workers are needed:* extra, added, supplementary, supplemental, further, auxiliary, ancillary; more, other, another, new, fresh.

additionally adverb *the organization relied additionally on a vast network of informers:* also, in addition, as well, too, besides, on top of that, moreover, further, furthermore, what is more, over and above that, into the bargain, to boot.

additive noun *the marmalade is free from any artificial additives:* added ingredient; preservative, colouring; Brit. informal E-number.

addled adjective *his brain was addled with hallucinogenic drugs:* muddled, confused, fuddled, befuddled, muzzy, dazed, disoriented, disorientated; informal woozy.

address noun
1 *our officers called at the address yesterday morning:* house, flat, apartment, home, residence.
2 *the president's address received lukewarm applause:* speech, lecture, talk, discourse, oration, monologue; sermon, homily.
▷ verb
1 *the preacher addressed a crowded congregation:* talk to, give a talk to, speak to, make a speech to, give a lecture to, lecture, hold forth to; preach to, give a sermon to.
2 *she addressed my father as 'Mr Stevens':* call, speak to, write to.
3 *correspondence should be addressed to the Banking Ombudsman:* direct, send, communicate, convey.
4 *the minister failed to address the issue of subsidies:* deal with, tackle, get to

grips with, apply yourself to, confront, get down to, turn your hand to, take in hand, undertake, concentrate on, focus on, devote yourself to.

adduce verb *facts and figures have been adduced to bolster the argument:* cite, quote, name, mention, instance, refer to; put forward, present, offer, advance.

adept adjective *an adept negotiator:* expert, proficient, accomplished, skilful, talented, masterly, consummate, virtuoso; adroit, dexterous, deft, artful; brilliant, marvellous, formidable, outstanding, first-rate, first-class, excellent, fine, splendid; informal great, top-notch, ace, mean, crack.
OPPOSITES: inept.

adequacy noun
1 *questions were raised about the adequacy of the existing services:* satisfactoriness, acceptability; sufficiency.
2 *he had deep misgivings about his own adequacy:* capability, competence, ability, aptitude, suitability; effectiveness, fitness; formal efficacy.

adequate adjective
1 *he lacked adequate financial resources:* sufficient, enough, requisite.
2 *the company provides an adequate service:* acceptable, passable, reasonable, satisfactory, tolerable, fair, decent, quite good, moderate, unexceptional, unremarkable, undistinguished, ordinary, average, middling; informal OK, so-so, fair-to-middling.
3 *the workstations were small but seemed adequate to the task:* equal to, up to, capable of, suitable for, able to do, fit for, sufficient for.

adhere verb
1 *paint will not adhere well to a greasy surface:* stick, cling, bond, attach; be stuck, be fixed, be glued.
2 *they adhere scrupulously to Judaic law:* abide by, stick to, hold to, comply with, act in accordance with, conform to, submit to; follow, obey, heed, observe, respect, uphold, fulfil.

adherent noun *he was a strong adherent of monetarism:* follower, supporter, upholder, defender, advocate, partisan, disciple, devotee, votary; member; believer, worshipper.
OPPOSITES: opponent.

adhesive noun *a spray adhesive:* glue, fixative, gum, paste.
▷ adjective *adhesive mortar:* sticky, tacky, gluey, gummed; viscous, viscid.

ad infinitum adverb *the tradition will be maintained ad infinitum:* forever, for ever and ever, evermore, always, for all time, until the end of time, in perpetuity; perpetually, eternally, endlessly, interminably, unceasingly, unendingly; Brit. for evermore.

adjacent adjective
1 *they were given adjacent rooms:* adjoining, neighbouring, next-door.
2 *a building adjacent to the Italian embassy:* next to, by, by the side of, abutting, contiguous with, bordering on, beside, alongside; attached to, touching; close to, near.

adjoin verb *my office adjoined the doctor's surgery:* be next to, be adjacent to, border on, abut, be contiguous with; join, connect with, touch.

adjoining adjective *the two women had adjoining bedrooms:* connecting, interconnecting, adjacent, neighbouring, next-door; contiguous; attached, touching.

adjourn verb
1 *the hearing was adjourned:* suspend, break off, discontinue, interrupt, prorogue.
2 *sentencing was adjourned until June 9:* postpone, put off/back, defer, delay, hold over; shelve.
3 *they adjourned to the sitting room for liqueurs:* withdraw, retire, retreat, take yourself; formal repair.

adjournment noun suspension, discontinuation, interruption, postponement, deferment, deferral, stay, prorogation; break, pause, recess.

adjudge verb *he was adjudged guilty of the offence of obstruction:* judge, deem, find, pronounce, proclaim, rule, hold, determine.

adjudicate verb *the case was adjudicated in the High Court:* judge, try, hear, examine, arbitrate; pronounce on, give a ruling on, pass judgement on, decide, determine, settle, resolve.

adjudication noun judgement, decision, pronouncement, ruling, settlement, resolution, arbitration, finding, verdict, sentence.

adjudicator noun judge, arbitrator, arbiter; referee, umpire.

adjunct noun *surveys are a useful adjunct to other methods of data collection:* supplement, addition, extra, add-on, accessory, accompaniment, complement; attachment, appendage, addendum.

adjust verb
1 *Kate had adjusted to her new life:* adapt, become accustomed, get used, accommodate yourself, acclimatize yourself, orient yourself, reconcile yourself, habituate yourself, acculturate, assimilate; come to terms with, blend in with, fit in with, find your feet in.
2 *he adjusted the brakes:* modify, alter, regulate, tune, fine-tune, calibrate, balance; adapt, rearrange, change, rejig, rework, revamp, remodel, reshape, tailor, improve, enhance, customize; repair, correct, rectify, overhaul, put right; informal tweak.

a

adjustable adjective alterable, adaptable, modifiable, convertible, variable, multiway, versatile.

adjustment noun
1 *new teachers face a challenging period of adjustment:* adaptation, accommodation, acclimatization, habituation, acculturation, assimilation, naturalization.
2 *the car will run on unleaded petrol with no adjustment:* modification, alteration, adaptation, regulation, rearrangement, change, reconstruction, customization, refinement; repair, correction, overhaul, improvement.

ad-lib verb *she ad-libbed half the speech:* improvise, extemporize, speak impromptu; play it by ear, make it up as you go along; informal wing it.
▷ **adverb** *she spoke ad lib:* impromptu, extempore, without preparation, without rehearsal, extemporaneously; informal off the cuff, off the top of your head.
▷ **adjective** *a live, ad-lib commentary:* impromptu, extempore, extemporaneous, extemporary, improvised, unprepared, unrehearsed, unscripted; informal off-the-cuff.

administer verb
1 *the union is administered by a central executive:* manage, direct, control, operate, regulate, conduct, handle, run, organize, supervise, superintend, oversee, preside over, govern, rule, lead, head, steer; be in control of, be in charge of, be responsible for, be at the helm of; informal head up.
2 *paramedics administered drugs:* dispense, issue, give, provide, distribute, hand out, dole out; apply.
3 *a gym shoe was used to administer punishment:* inflict, mete out, deal out, deliver.

administration noun
1 *the day-to-day administration of the company:* management, running, direction, control, command, charge, conduct, operation, leadership, government, governing, superintendence, supervision, regulation, overseeing.
2 *the previous Labour administration:* government, cabinet, ministry, regime, executive, authority, directorate; parliament, congress, senate; rule, term of office, incumbency.
3 *the administration of anti-inflammatory drugs:* provision, issuing, issuance, dispensing, distribution; application.

administrator noun *hospital administrators say the cutbacks would force the maternity ward to close:* manager, director, controller, head, chief, leader, governor, supervisor; informal boss.

admirable adjective *the player has done an admirable job for the team:* commendable, praiseworthy, laudable, meritorious, creditable, exemplary, honourable, worthy, deserving, respectable, worthwhile, good, sterling, fine, masterly, great.
OPPOSITES: deplorable.

admiration noun *his patience and good nature commanded widespread admiration:* respect, approval, approbation, appreciation, regard, esteem; commendation, acclaim, applause, praise, compliments, tributes, accolades, plaudits.
OPPOSITES: scorn.

admire verb *I admire your courage:* respect, approve of, think highly of, rate highly, hold in high regard/esteem, applaud, praise, commend, acclaim.
OPPOSITES: despise.

admirer noun *he was a great admirer of Henry James:* fan, devotee, enthusiast, aficionado; supporter, adherent, follower, disciple.

admissible adjective *the tape recording was admissible as evidence:* valid, allowable, allowed, permissible, permitted, acceptable, satisfactory, justifiable, defensible; legitimate, lawful, legal, licit.

admission noun
1 *membership entitles you to free admission:* admittance, entry, entrance, right of entry, access, right of access, ingress; entrée.
2 *a written admission of liability could have serious consequences:* confession, acknowledgement, acceptance, concession.

admit verb
1 *Paul admitted that he was angry:* confess, acknowledge, own, concede, grant, accept, allow; reveal, disclose, divulge.
2 *he admitted three offences of reckless driving:* confess to, plead guilty to, own up to.
3 *he unlocked the door to admit her:* let in, allow to enter, permit to enter, usher in, show in, receive, welcome.
4 *he was admitted as a scholar to Winchester College:* accept, take on, receive, enrol, enlist, register, sign up.
OPPOSITES: deny, exclude.

admittance noun *people were unable to gain admittance to the hall:* entry, right of entry, admission, entrance, access, right of access, ingress; entrée.

admonish verb
1 *he was severely admonished by his father:* reprimand, rebuke, scold, reprove, reproach, upbraid, chastise, chide, berate, criticize, take to task, read the Riot Act to; formal castigate; informal tell off, haul over the coals, bawl out, rap over the knuckles, give someone hell; Brit. informal tick off, have a go at.
2 *she admonished him to drink less:* advise, counsel, urge, exhort; warn; formal enjoin.

admonition noun

1 *a breach of the rules which led to an admonition:* reprimand, rebuke, reproof, remonstrance, reproach, criticism, recrimination, censure, strictures; formal castigation; informal telling-off, dressing-down, rap over the knuckles; Brit. informal rollicking, ticking-off.
2 *an admonition to proceed carefully:* exhortation, warning, piece of advice, recommendation.

adolescence noun teenage years, teens, youth; pubescence, puberty.

adolescent noun *an awkward adolescent:* teenager, youngster, young person, youth, boy, girl; juvenile, minor; informal teen.
▷ **adjective**
1 *an adolescent boy:* teenage, pubescent, young; juvenile; informal teen.
2 *they looked less than amused at such adolescent behaviour:* immature, childish, juvenile, infantile, puerile.
OPPOSITES: adult, mature.

adopt verb

1 *this approach has been adopted by many big banks:* choose, take up, follow, pursue.
2 *she was recently adopted as the Labour candidate for the constituency:* select, choose, pick, vote for, elect, settle on, decide on, opt for; name, nominate, appoint.
3 *they adopted local customs:* espouse, take on/up, embrace, assume.
OPPOSITES: abandon.

adorable adjective *I have four adorable Siamese cats:* lovable, appealing, charming, cute, sweet, enchanting, engaging, endearing, delightful, lovely, beautiful, gorgeous, winning, fetching; Scottish & N. English bonny.

adoration noun

1 *the girl gazed at him with adoration:* love, devotion; admiration, high regard, awe, idolization, worship, hero-worship, adulation.
2 *the Mass begins our day of prayer and adoration:* worship, glory, glorification, praise, thanksgiving, homage, veneration, reverence.

adore verb

1 *he adored his mother:* love, love dearly, be devoted to, dote on, hold dear, cherish, treasure, prize, think the world of; admire, hold in high regard, look up to, idolize, worship; informal put on a pedestal.
2 *the people had come to pray and adore God:* worship, glorify, praise, revere, venerate, pay homage to.
OPPOSITES: hate.

adorn verb *the public rooms were adorned with tapestries:* decorate, embellish, ornament, bedeck, deck, deck out, dress, trim, swathe, wreathe, festoon, garland, emblazon; grace, beautify.

adornment noun decoration, embellishment, ornamentation, ornament, enhancement, beautification; accessories, frills, trimmings, finishing touches.

adrift adjective

1 *their empty boat was spotted adrift:* drifting, unmoored, unanchored.
2 *the pipe of my breathing apparatus came adrift:* loose, free; detached, unsecured, unfastened, untied, unknotted, undone.

adroit adjective *he showed himself to be an adroit politician:* skilful, adept, dexterous, deft, able, capable, skilled, expert, masterly, masterful, master, practised, polished, slick, proficient, accomplished, gifted, talented; quick-witted, quick-thinking, clever, sharp, cunning, wily, resourceful, astute, shrewd, canny; informal mean, ace, smart, savvy.
OPPOSITES: inept, clumsy.

adroitness noun skill, skilfulness, prowess, expertise, adeptness, dexterity, deftness, ability, capability, mastery, proficiency, accomplishment, artistry, art, facility, aptitude, flair, finesse, talent; quick-wittedness, cleverness, sharpness, cunning, astuteness, shrewdness, resourcefulness, savoir faire; informal know-how, savvy.

adulation noun *he is remarkably unspoilt by all the adulation he has received:* hero-worship, idolization, adoration, admiration, veneration, devotion, glorification, praise, flattery, blandishments.

adult adjective

1 *an adult woman:* mature, grown-up, fully grown, full-grown, fully developed, of age.
2 (euphemistic) *an adult movie:* pornographic, obscene, dirty, rude, sexually explicit, erotic; informal blue.

adulterate verb *essential oils that have been adulterated can cause harmful side effects:* make impure, degrade, debase, spoil, taint, contaminate; doctor, tamper with, dilute, water down, weaken; informal cut, spike, dope.
OPPOSITES: purify.

adulterous adjective

1 *an adulterous relationship:* extramarital.
2 *his adulterous wife:* unfaithful, faithless, disloyal, deceiving, deceitful; informal cheating, two-timing.
OPPOSITES: faithful.

adultery noun infidelity, unfaithfulness, disloyalty; extramarital sex; affair, liaison.
OPPOSITES: fidelity.

advance verb

1 *the battalion advanced rapidly:* move forward, proceed, press on, push on, push forward, make progress, make headway, gain ground, approach, come closer, draw nearer, near.

a

2 *the court may advance the date of the hearing:* bring forward, put forward, move forward.
3 *the move advanced his career:* promote, further, forward, help, aid, assist, boost, strengthen, improve, benefit, foster.
4 *our technology has advanced in the last few years:* progress, make progress, make headway, develop, evolve, make strides, move forward, move ahead; improve, thrive, flourish, prosper.
5 *the hypothesis I wish to advance in this article:* put forward, present, submit, suggest, propose, introduce, offer, adduce, moot.
6 *a relative advanced him some money:* lend, loan, put up, come up with; Brit. informal sub.
OPPOSITES: retreat, postpone, hinder.
▷**noun**
1 *the advance of the aggressors:* progress, forward movement; approach.
2 *a significant medical advance:* breakthrough, development, step forward, step in the right direction, quantum leap; find, finding, discovery; invention.
3 *the writer is going to be given a huge advance:* down payment, retainer, prepayment, deposit, money up front.
4 *he kept making sexual advances:* pass, proposition.
▷**adjective**
1 *an advance party of settlers:* preliminary, first, exploratory.
2 *clients on our mailing lists will receive advance notice of all events:* prior, early; beforehand.
□**in advance** beforehand, before, ahead of time, earlier, previously; in readiness.

advanced adjective
1 *advanced manufacturing techniques:* state-of-the-art, new, modern, up to date, up to the minute, the newest, the latest; progressive, avant-garde, ahead of the times, pioneering, innovatory, sophisticated.
2 *advanced further-education courses:* higher-level, higher, tertiary.

advancement noun
1 *the advancement of computer technology:* development, progress, evolution, growth, improvement, advance, furtherance; headway.
2 *employees must be offered opportunities for advancement:* promotion, preferment, career development, upgrading, a step up the ladder, progress, improvement, betterment.

advantage noun
1 *one of the advantages of an online business is that it can earn you money while you sleep:* benefit, value, good point, strong point, asset, bonus, boon, blessing, virtue; beauty, usefulness, convenience informal plus.

2 *they appeared to be gaining the advantage over their opponents:* upper hand, edge, lead, whip hand; trump card; superiority, dominance, ascendancy, supremacy, power, mastery.
3 *there is no advantage to be gained from delaying the process:* benefit, profit, gain, good; informal mileage, percentage.
OPPOSITES: disadvantage, drawback.

advantageous adjective
1 *the arrangement is advantageous to both sides:* beneficial, of benefit, helpful, of assistance, useful, of use, of value, of service, profitable; expedient, in someone's interest.
2 *at the end of the war, farmers were in a relatively advantageous position:* good, fortunate, lucky, favourable; superior, dominant, powerful.
OPPOSITES: detrimental, disadvantageous.

advent noun *the advent of digital technology:* arrival, appearance, emergence; dawn, birth, rise, development.

adventure noun
1 *stories of astonishing miracles and heroic adventures:* exploit, escapade, deed, feat, experience; stunt.
2 *they set off in search of adventure:* excitement, stimulation, thrills; risk, danger, peril, hazard, uncertainty.

adventurous adjective
1 *an adventurous traveller:* daring, daredevil, intrepid, bold, fearless, brave, unafraid, venturesome, unshrinking, dauntless; informal gutsy, spunky.
2 *a long and adventurous journey:* exciting, thrilling; risky, dangerous, perilous, hazardous.
OPPOSITES: cautious.

adversary noun opponent, rival, enemy, antagonist, combatant, challenger, contender, competitor, opposer; opposition, competition; literary foe.
OPPOSITES: ally, supporter.

adverse adjective
1 *the company made a profit of around 10 per cent, in spite of the adverse economic climate:* unfavourable, bad, disadvantageous, inauspicious, unpropitious.
2 *the drug's adverse side effects:* harmful, dangerous, injurious, detrimental, deleterious.
3 *the military feared an adverse response from the public:* hostile, unfavourable, antagonistic, unfriendly, ill-disposed, negative.
OPPOSITES: favourable, beneficial.

USAGE

Do not confuse **adverse** with **averse**. **Adverse** means 'harmful' or 'unfavourable'. **Averse** is typically used with 'to' and means 'very unwilling to', for example *I'm* *not averse to helping out* (i.e. *I'm willing to help out*).

adversity noun *they remain steadfast in the face of adversity:* misfortune, bad luck, trouble, difficulty, hardship, distress, disaster, suffering, sorrow, misery, woe, pain, trauma; mishap, misadventure, accident, upset, reverse, setback, crisis, catastrophe, tragedy, calamity, blow; vicissitudes, hard times, trials and tribulations.

advertise verb *the car was advertised as 'the fastest sports car in the world':* publicize, promote, market, call attention to, make public, make known, announce, broadcast, proclaim, trumpet; informal push, plug, hype.

advertisement noun notice, announcement; commercial, promotion, blurb, write-up; poster, leaflet, pamphlet, flyer, bill, handbill, handout, circular, brochure, sign, placard; informal ad, advert, push, plug, puff.

advice noun *the charity offers support and advice to victims of crime:* guidance, counselling, counsel, help, direction; information, recommendations, guidelines, suggestions, hints, tips, pointers.

advisable adjective *it is advisable to book a table in advance:* wise, sensible, prudent, recommended, a good idea, desirable, preferable, best; expedient, politic, advantageous, beneficial, profitable, in your interests.
OPPOSITES: inadvisable.

advise verb
1 *they advise the government on issues affecting small businesses:* counsel, give guidance to, guide, offer suggestions to.
2 *he advised caution:* recommend, suggest, urge, encourage, advocate; formal enjoin.
3 *you will be advised of the requirements:* inform, notify, give notice, apprise, warn, forewarn; acquaint with, make familiar with, make known to; informal fill in on.

adviser noun counsellor, mentor, guide, guru, consultant, confidant, confidante; coach, teacher, tutor.

advisory adjective *she agreed to serve the committee in an advisory role:* consultative, consultatory, advising.
OPPOSITES: executive.

advocacy noun *his outspoken advocacy of the agreement has won him no friends:* support for, backing, promotion, championing; recommendation.

advocate noun *she was a powerful advocate of children's rights:* champion, supporter, upholder, backer, promoter, proponent, exponent, spokesman, spokeswoman, spokesperson, campaigner, fighter, crusader; propagandist, apostle, apologist.
OPPOSITES: critic.
▷ **verb** *heart specialists advocate a diet low in cholesterol:* recommend, prescribe, advise, urge; support, back, favour, subscribe to, uphold, champion, campaign on behalf of, speak for, argue for, lobby for, promote.

aegis noun *the negotiations were conducted under the aegis of the UN:* auspices, protection, backing, support, patronage, sponsorship, charge, care, guidance, guardianship, trusteeship, agency, umbrella.

aeons plural noun *the age of piracy was stamped out aeons ago:* ages, an age, an eternity, a long time, a lifetime; years; informal donkey's years; Brit. informal yonks.

aesthetic adjective *the design was not considered to be very aesthetic:* artistic, tasteful, in good taste; graceful, elegant, beautiful, attractive, pleasing, lovely, exquisite.

affability noun friendliness, amiability, geniality, congeniality, cordiality, warmth, good humour, good nature, kindliness, kindness, courtesy, courteousness, civility, approachability, amenability, neighbourliness.

affable adjective *Tom turned out to be a polite, affable man:* friendly, amiable, genial, congenial, cordial, warm, pleasant, nice, likeable, personable, charming, agreeable, sympathetic, good-humoured, good-natured, kindly, kind, courteous, civil, gracious, approachable, accessible, amenable, sociable, outgoing, gregarious, clubbable, neighbourly, welcoming, hospitable, obliging.
OPPOSITES: unfriendly.

affair noun
1 *what you do is your affair:* business, concern, matter, responsibility, province, preserve; problem, worry; Brit. informal lookout.
2 (**affairs**) *the police launched an investigation into his financial affairs:* transactions, concerns, activities, dealings, undertakings, ventures, business.
3 *the board admitted responsibility for the affair:* event, incident, happening, occurrence, episode, eventuality; case, matter, business.
4 *his affair with Anthea was over:* relationship, love affair, romance, fling, flirtation, dalliance, liaison, involvement, intrigue, amour.

affect[1] verb
1 *climate change will affect the lives of millions:* make a difference to, have an effect on, have an impact on, impinge on, influence, act on; change, alter, modify, form, shape.

a

2 *the experience affected him deeply:* move, touch, make an impression on, hit hard; upset, trouble, distress, disturb, shake.

> **USAGE**
>
> Do not confuse **affect** and **effect**. **Affect** is a verb whose chief meaning is 'to make a difference to'; **effect** is used both as a noun meaning 'a change which is the result of something' (*the substance has a painkilling effect*) and as a verb meaning 'to bring something about' (*the prime minister effected many policy changes*).

affect² **verb**
1 *Paul affected an air of injured innocence:* pretend, feign, fake, simulate, make a show of, make a pretence of, sham; informal put on.
2 *she had affected what she considered to be a posh English accent:* assume, take on, adopt.

affectation noun
1 *he had always hated affectation:* pretension, pretentiousness, affectedness, artificiality, posturing, posing; airs, airs and graces.
2 *nothing would shake his affectation of calm:* facade, front, show, appearance, pretence, simulation, posture, pose.

affected adjective *she talked in a very affected way:* pretentious, artificial, contrived, unnatural, stagy, studied, mannered, ostentatious; insincere, unconvincing, feigned, false, fake, sham, simulated; informal phoney, put on.
OPPOSITES: natural.

affecting adjective *their fumbling onstage shyness is oddly affecting:* touching, moving, emotive, emotional, heart-warming; poignant, sad, upsetting, haunting.

affection noun *they greeted each other with obvious affection:* fondness, love, liking, tenderness, warmth, devotion, attachment, friendship; warm feelings.

affectionate adjective loving, fond, tender, warm, adoring, devoted, caring, doting, warm-hearted, soft-hearted, friendly; demonstrative; informal touchy-feely, lovey-dovey.
OPPOSITES: cold.

affiliate verb *the college is affiliated with the University of Wisconsin:* link, associate, federate, ally, unite, combine, join up; connect to, attach to.

affiliated adjective associated, allied, related, federated, connected, linked; in league, in partnership.

affiliation noun association, connection, alliance, link, attachment, tie, relationship, fellowship, partnership, coalition, union, federation, confederation.

affinity noun
1 *she has a natural affinity with animals and birds:* empathy, rapport, sympathy, accord, harmony, relationship, bond, fellow feeling, like-mindedness, closeness, understanding; liking, fondness; informal chemistry.
2 *there is a semantic affinity between the two words:* similarity, resemblance, kinship, relationship, association, link, analogy, correspondence; formal similitude.
OPPOSITES: aversion, dissimilarity.

affirm verb
1 *he affirmed that they would send military assistance:* declare, state, assert, proclaim, pronounce; guarantee, pledge, give an undertaking.
2 *the referendum affirmed the republic's right to secede:* uphold, support, confirm, ratify, endorse.
OPPOSITES: deny.

affirmation noun
1 *an affirmation of faith:* declaration, statement, assertion, proclamation, pronouncement.
2 *the poem ends with an affirmation of pastoral values:* confirmation, endorsement, ratification.
OPPOSITES: denial.

affirmative adjective *an affirmative answer:* positive, assenting, consenting, favourable.
OPPOSITES: negative.
▷**noun** *she took his grunt as an affirmative:* agreement, acceptance, assent, acquiescence, concurrence.

afflict verb *she was afflicted with chronic health problems:* trouble, burden, cause suffering to, beset, oppress; torment, plague, blight, bedevil, rack, curse.

affliction noun
1 *this herb is reputed to cure a variety of afflictions:* disorder, disease, complaint, ailment, illness, indisposition; literary malady.
2 *he bore his affliction with great dignity:* suffering, pain, trouble, torment, misery, hardship, misfortune, adversity.

affluence noun wealth, prosperity, fortune; riches, money, resources, assets, substance, means.
OPPOSITES: poverty.

affluent adjective *she was the only child of a very affluent family:* wealthy, rich, prosperous, well off, moneyed, well-to-do; propertied, of means, of substance; plutocratic; informal well heeled, rolling in it, made of money, loaded.
OPPOSITES: poor, impoverished.

afford verb
1 *I can't afford a new car:* pay for, bear the expense of, spare the price of; run to, stretch to, manage.

2 *it took more time than he could afford:* spare, allow yourself.
3 *the rooftop terrace affords beautiful views:* provide, supply, furnish, offer, give.

affront noun *the paintings, in his view, were an affront to public morality:* insult, offence, slight; outrage, atrocity, scandal; informal slap in the face, kick in the teeth.
▷ **verb** *she was affronted by his familiarity:* insult, offend, mortify, pique, wound, hurt; put out, irk, displease, vex, gall; outrage, scandalize, disgust; informal put someone's back up.

aficionado noun *jazz aficionados regard it as perhaps the greatest album ever made:* connoisseur, expert, authority, specialist, pundit; enthusiast, devotee; informal buff, freak, nut, fiend, maniac, fanatic, addict.

afoot adjective & adverb *there are some changes afoot:* in preparation, in progress; in the air/wind, brewing, looming, in the offing, on the horizon; happening, going on.

afraid adjective
1 *she suddenly felt very afraid:* frightened, scared, terrified, fearful, petrified, scared to death, terror-stricken, terror-struck, frightened/scared out of your wits; intimidated, alarmed, panicky, anxious, worried; informal scared stiff, in a cold sweat; N. Amer. informal spooked.
2 *don't be afraid to ask awkward questions:* reluctant, hesitant, unwilling, disinclined, loath.

after preposition
1 *he made a speech after the performance:* following, subsequent to, at the close/end of, in the wake of.
2 *the village was named after a Roman officer:* in honour of, as a tribute to.
3 *animal studies after Bandinelli:* in the style of, in the manner of, in imitation of.
OPPOSITES: before, preceding.

> WORD LINKS
> **post-** forming words meaning 'after in time or order', such as *postgraduate* ('relating to study undertaken after completing a first degree') or *post-natal* ('happening after childbirth')

after-effect noun *the city's inhabitants are still suffering from the after-effects of the war:* repercussion, aftermath, consequence.

aftermath noun *the authorities were unable to cope with the aftermath of the disaster:* repercussions, after-effects, consequences, effects, results.

afterwards adverb *we all celebrated afterwards at a pub:* later, later on, subsequently, then, next; at a later time/date, in due course.

again adverb *her spirits lifted again:* once more, afresh, anew.

□ **again and again** repeatedly, over and over again, time and time again, many times; often, frequently, continually, constantly.

against preposition
1 *a number of delegates were against the motion:* opposed to, in opposition to, in disagreement with, unsympathetic to, hostile to, averse to, antagonistic towards, inimical to, resistant to, at odds with; informal anti.
2 *he was swimming against the tide:* counter to, in opposition to, contrary to, in the opposite direction to.
3 *his age is against him:* disadvantageous to, a drawback for, unfavourable to, damaging to, detrimental to, prejudicial to, harmful to, injurious to, deleterious to.
OPPOSITES: in favour of, pro.

age noun
1 *her hearing had deteriorated with age:* elderliness, old age, senescence; your advancing/advanced/declining years.
2 *the Elizabethan age:* era, epoch, period, time.
3 (**ages**) (informal) *I haven't seen him for ages:* a long time, an eternity; informal ages and ages, donkey's years; Brit. informal yonks.
▷ **verb**
1 *Cabernet Sauvignon ages well:* mature, mellow, ripen.
2 *he had aged in the last few years:* grow old, look older, decline.

aged adjective *an aged man with grizzled hair:* elderly, old, older, advanced in years, senior, senescent, ancient, in your dotage, long in the tooth, past your prime; informal getting on, over the hill.
OPPOSITES: young.

agency noun
1 *an advertising agency:* business, organization, company, firm, office, bureau.
2 *the infection is caused by the agency of insects:* action, activity, means, effect, force, power, vehicle, medium.

agenda noun *a meeting with a fixed agenda:* list of items, schedule, programme, timetable, line-up, list, plan.

agent noun
1 *the sale was arranged through an agent:* representative, intermediary, negotiator, broker, go-between, middleman, proxy, emissary, envoy; spokesperson, spokesman, spokeswoman.
2 *a travel agent:* agency, business, organization, company, firm, bureau.
3 *a CIA agent:* spy, secret agent, undercover agent, operative, fifth columnist, mole; N. Amer. informal spook.
4 *the agents of destruction:* instrument, producer, author, perpetrator; catalyst.
5 *a cleansing agent:* medium, means, instrument, vehicle; substance.

a

agglomeration noun *the suburb is an agglomeration of houses, shops, and offices:* collection, mass, cluster, pile, heap; accumulation, build-up; miscellany, jumble, hotchpotch, mixed bag.

aggravate verb
1 *the new law could aggravate the situation:* worsen, make worse, exacerbate, inflame, compound; add fuel to the fire/flames, add insult to injury, rub salt in the wound.
2 (informal) *you don't have to aggravate people to get what you want:* annoy, irritate, exasperate, put out, provoke, antagonize, get on someone's nerves, try someone's patience; Brit. rub up the wrong way; informal bug, hack off; Brit. informal wind up.
OPPOSITES: alleviate, improve.

aggravation noun
1 *the recession led to the aggravation of unemployment problems:* worsening, exacerbation, compounding.
2 (informal) *no amount of money is worth the aggravation:* nuisance, annoyance, irritation, trouble, difficulty, inconvenience, bother; informal hassle, aggro.

aggregate noun
1 *the specimen is an aggregate of rock and mineral fragments:* compound, amalgam, mixture, mix, combination, blend; collection, mass, agglomeration, assemblage.
2 *he won with an aggregate of 325:* total, sum total, sum, grand total.
▷adjective *an aggregate score:* total, combined, gross, overall, composite.

aggression noun *an act of aggression:* hostility, aggressiveness, belligerence, pugnacity, force, violence; bellicosity, militancy, warmongering.

aggressive adjective
1 *he's very aggressive:* violent, confrontational, antagonistic, pugnacious; quarrelsome, argumentative.
2 *an aggressive foreign policy:* warmongering, warlike, warring, belligerent, bellicose, hawkish, militaristic; expansionist; informal gung-ho.
3 *the company owes its success to an aggressive sales force:* forceful, assertive, vigorous, energetic, dynamic; bold, audacious; informal pushy, in-your-face.
OPPOSITES: peaceful.

aggressor noun attacker, assailant, assaulter; invader.

aggrieved adjective
1 *the manager looked aggrieved at the suggestion:* resentful, affronted, indignant, disgruntled, upset, offended, piqued, vexed, irked, irritated, annoyed, put out; informal peeved, miffed, riled, nettled.
2 *the aggrieved party:* wronged, injured, harmed.
OPPOSITES: pleased.

aghast adjective *she winced, aghast at his cruelty:* horrified, appalled, shocked, dismayed, stunned, staggered.

agile adjective
1 *she was as agile as a monkey:* nimble, lithe, supple, limber, acrobatic, light-footed, light on your feet, fleet-footed; informal nippy.
2 *she had an agile mind:* alert, sharp, acute, shrewd, astute, perceptive, quick-witted.
OPPOSITES: clumsy, stiff.

agitate verb
1 *any mention of Clare agitates my grandmother:* upset, perturb, fluster, ruffle, disconcert, unnerve, disquiet, disturb, worry, distress, unsettle; informal rattle, faze.
2 *she agitated for the appointment of more women:* campaign, battle, fight, struggle, strive, push, press.
3 *agitate the water to disperse the oil:* stir, whisk, beat.

agitated adjective *I could see that he was agitated:* upset, flustered, disconcerted, unnerved, perturbed, anxious, worried, unsettled; nervous, jumpy, edgy, on edge, tense, keyed up; informal rattled, in a flap, in a state, jittery.
OPPOSITES: calm, relaxed.

agitation noun
1 *she was wringing her hands in agitation:* anxiety, distress, concern, alarm, worry, nervousness.
2 *there was widespread agitation for social reform:* campaigning, battling, fighting.

agitator noun troublemaker, rabble-rouser, agent provocateur, demagogue; revolutionary, firebrand, rebel, insurgent, subversive; informal stirrer.

agnostic noun sceptic, doubter; unbeliever, disbeliever, non-believer; rationalist.

ago adverb *my husband died nearly fifteen years ago:* in the past, before, earlier, back, since, previously.

agog adverb *everyone was agog to hear what he would say:* eager, excited, impatient, keen, anxious, avid, in suspense, on tenterhooks, on the edge of your seat, waiting with bated breath.

agonize verb *all the way home she agonized about what she should do:* worry, fret, brood, upset yourself, rack your brains, wrestle with yourself, be worried/anxious, fuss.

agonizing adjective *he died after suffering months of agonizing pain:* excruciating, acute, severe, extreme, intense, harrowing, racking, searing.

agony noun *he was screaming in agony:* pain, torment, torture, anguish, suffering, trauma.

agrarian adjective *Brazil is rapidly diversifying its agrarian economy:* agricultural, farming; rural.

agree verb
1 *I agree with you:* be of the same opinion, concur, see eye to eye, be in sympathy, be united, be as one.
2 *they had agreed to a ceasefire:* consent to, assent to, accept, approve, give your approval to, allow, acquiesce in; formal accede to.
3 *the plan and the drawing do not agree with each other:* match, match up, accord, correspond, conform, coincide, fit, tally, be in harmony/agreement, be consistent/equivalent; informal square.
4 *they agreed on a price:* settle, decide, arrive at, negotiate, reach an agreement, come to terms, strike a bargain, make a deal, shake hands.
OPPOSITES: disagree, differ.

agreeable adjective
1 *an agreeable atmosphere of rural tranquillity:* pleasant, pleasing, enjoyable, pleasurable, nice, to your liking, appealing, charming, delightful.
2 *an agreeable companion:* likeable, charming, amiable, affable, pleasant, nice, friendly, good-natured, sociable, genial, congenial.
3 *we should get together for a talk, if you're agreeable:* willing, amenable, in accord/agreement.
OPPOSITES: disagreeable, unpleasant.

agreement noun
1 *all heads nodded in agreement:* accord, concurrence, consensus; assent, acceptance, consent, acquiescence, endorsement.
2 *an agreement on military cooperation:* settlement, deal, understanding; compact, treaty, covenant, pact, accord, concordat, protocol.
3 *there is some agreement between my view and that of the author:* correspondence, consistency, compatibility, accord; similarity, resemblance, likeness; formal similitude.
OPPOSITES: disagreement.

agricultural adjective farm, farmed, agrarian, cultivated; rural.
OPPOSITES: urban.

agriculture noun farming, cultivation, husbandry, land/farm management; agribusiness, agronomy.

ahead adverb
1 *he peered ahead, but could see nothing:* forwards, towards the front.
2 *he had ridden on ahead:* in front, at the head, in the lead, at the fore, in the vanguard, in advance.
3 *she was preparing herself for what lay ahead:* in the future, in time, in time to come, at a later date, later on, in due course, next; formal henceforth.
4 *they are ahead by six points:* leading, winning, in the lead, in front, first.
OPPOSITES: behind.
□ ahead of
1 *Blanche went ahead of the others:* in front of, before.
2 *we have a demanding trip ahead of us:* in store for, waiting for.
3 *the motorway was finished two months ahead of schedule:* in advance of, before, earlier than.
4 *in terms of these amenities, Britain is ahead of other European countries:* more advanced than, further on than, superior to, better than.

aid noun
1 *with the aid of his colleagues he prepared a manifesto:* assistance, help, support, backing, cooperation; a helping hand.
2 *humanitarian aid:* relief, charity, financial assistance, donations, contributions, subsidies, handouts, subventions; debt remission.
OPPOSITES: hindrance.
▷ verb
1 *he provided an army to aid the King of England:* help, assist, come to someone's aid, give assistance, lend a hand, be of service.
2 *lavender essence can aid restful sleep:* facilitate, promote, encourage, help, further, boost; speed up, hasten, accelerate, expedite.
OPPOSITES: hinder.

aide noun assistant, helper, adviser, right-hand man; adjutant, deputy, second, second in command; subordinate, junior, underling, acolyte.

ailing adjective
1 *I went to see my ailing mother:* sick, unwell, ill, sickly, poorly, weak, in poor/bad health, infirm, invalid, debilitated, indisposed, below par; Brit. off colour; informal laid up, under the weather.
2 *the country's ailing economy:* failing, debilitated, in poor condition, weak, poor.
OPPOSITES: healthy.

ailment noun *a mysterious stomach ailment left me very shaky:* illness, disease, disorder, complaint, affliction, infirmity; literary malady; informal bug, virus; Brit. informal lurgy.

aim verb
1 *he aimed the rifle:* point, direct, train, sight, line up.
2 *she aimed at the target:* zero in on, fix on, draw a bead on.
3 *undergraduates aiming for a first degree:* work towards, set your sights on, try for, strive for, aspire to, endeavour to achieve; formal essay.
4 *this system is aimed at the home entertainment market:* target, intend, direct, design, tailor, market, pitch; destine.

a

5 *we aim to give you the best possible service:* intend, mean, have in mind/view; plan, resolve, propose, design.
▷ **noun** *our aim is to develop gymnasts to the top level:* objective, object, goal, end, target, design, desire, desired result, intention, intent, plan, purpose, raison d'être, object of the exercise; ambition, aspiration, wish, dream, hope.

aimless **adjective** *he led an aimless existence:* purposeless, directionless, goalless, without purpose, meaningless.
OPPOSITES: purposeful.

air **noun**
1 *hundreds of birds hovered in the air:* sky, atmosphere; heavens; literary ether.
2 *he upended his glass with an air of defiance | the place had an air of neglect:* appearance, look, impression, aspect, aura, manner, expression, tone.
3 (**airs**) *he'd no patience with women putting on airs:* affectations, pretension, pretentiousness, affectedness, posing, posturing, airs and graces; Brit. informal side.
▷ **verb**
1 *this is a chance for you to air your views:* express, voice, make public, articulate, state, declare, give expression/voice to, ventilate; have your say.
2 *the windows were opened to air the room:* ventilate, freshen, refresh, cool.
3 *the film was aired nationwide:* broadcast, transmit, screen, show, televise, telecast.

WORD LINKS
aerial existing or taking place in the air

airily **adverb** *the doctor dismissed his troubles airily:* lightly, breezily, casually, nonchalantly, heedlessly, without consideration, flippantly.
OPPOSITES: seriously.

airing **noun**
1 *the airing of different views:* expression, voicing, articulation, declaration, communication.
2 *I hope the BBC gives the play another airing:* broadcast, transmission, screening, showing, telecast.

airless **adjective** *a hot, airless room:* stuffy, close, stifling, suffocating, oppressive; unventilated, badly ventilated.
OPPOSITES: airy, ventilated.

airtight **adjective** *an airtight container:* sealed, hermetically sealed, closed/shut tight.

airy **adjective**
1 *the conservatory is light and airy:* well ventilated, fresh; spacious, uncluttered; light, bright.
2 *an airy gesture:* nonchalant, casual, breezy, flippant, insouciant, heedless.
OPPOSITES: airless, stuffy.

aisle **noun** passage, passageway, gangway, walkway.

akin **adjective** *something akin to gratitude overwhelmed her:* similar, related, close, near, corresponding, comparable, equivalent; analogous.
OPPOSITES: unlike.

alacrity **noun** *she accepted the invitation with alacrity:* eagerness, willingness, readiness, enthusiasm, keenness.

alarm **noun**
1 *the girl spun round in alarm:* fear, fright, panic, anxiety, apprehension, trepidation, nervousness, distress, agitation, consternation, perturbation.
2 *a smoke alarm:* siren, danger/warning signal.
▷ **verb** *the news had alarmed her:* frighten, scare, panic, agitate, upset, disconcert, shock, dismay, disturb, unnerve, distress; informal spook; Brit. informal put the wind up.

alarming **adjective** *our countryside is disappearing at an alarming rate:* worrying, disturbing, distressing, upsetting, disconcerting, disquieting; frightening, unnerving, shocking; informal scary.

alarmist **adjective** *the newspapers were filled with alarmist propaganda:* scaremongering, pessimistic.

alcohol **noun** liquor, strong/alcoholic drink, drink, spirits; informal booze, the hard stuff, the demon drink, the bottle.

WORD LINKS
alcoholism, **dipsomania** addiction to alcohol
temperance, **teetotalism** the practice of never drinking alcohol

alcoholic **adjective** *alcoholic drinks:* intoxicating; strong, hard; informal stiff; old use spirituous.
▷ **noun** *he is an alcoholic:* dipsomaniac, drunk, drunkard, problem drinker, alcohol-abuser, person with a drink problem; sot; informal lush, alky, soak, wino.

alcove **noun** recess, niche, nook, inglenook, bay.

alert **adjective**
1 *police have asked neighbours to keep alert:* vigilant, watchful, attentive, observant, wide awake; on the lookout, on your guard/toes, on the qui vive; informal keeping your eyes open/peeled.
2 *he was over eighty, yet he was as mentally alert as a man half his age:* quick-witted, sharp, bright, perceptive, wide awake, on your toes; informal on the ball, quick on the uptake, all there, with it.
OPPOSITES: inattentive.
▷ **noun**
1 *the army called for a state of alert:* vigilance, watchfulness, attentiveness, alertness.
2 *a flood alert has been issued:* warning, notification, notice; siren, alarm, signal, danger/distress signal.

▷ **verb** *police were alerted by a phone call:* warn, notify, apprise, forewarn, put on your guard, put on the qui vive; informal tip off.

alias noun *he is known under several aliases:* assumed name, false name, pseudonym, sobriquet; pen/stage name, nom de plume/guerre.
▷ **adverb** *Cassius Clay, alias Muhammad Ali:* also known as, aka, also called, otherwise known as.

alibi noun *we've both got a good alibi for last night:* defence, justification, explanation, reason.

alien adjective
1 *alien cultures:* foreign, non-native.
2 *an alien landscape:* unfamiliar, unknown, strange, peculiar; exotic, foreign.
3 *a vicious role alien to his nature:* incompatible with, conflicting with, contrary to, in conflict with, at variance with.
4 *alien beings:* extraterrestrial, unearthly.
OPPOSITES: native, familiar.
▷ **noun** *an illegal alien:* foreigner, immigrant, incomer; émigré.

alienate verb *his homosexuality alienated him from his conservative father:* estrange, divide, distance, put at a distance, isolate, cut off; set against, turn away, drive apart, drive a wedge between, disunite, set at variance/odds.

alienation noun *she shared my deep sense of alienation:* isolation, detachment, estrangement, distance, separation, division.

alight¹ verb
1 *he alighted from the train:* get off, step off, disembark; pile out.
2 *a swallow alighted on a branch:* land, come to rest, settle, perch.
OPPOSITES: board.

alight² adjective
1 *the bales of hay were alight:* burning, on fire, in flames, blazing, ablaze, aflame.
2 *her face was alight with laughter:* lit up, glowing, bright, shining, radiant.

align verb
1 *the desks are aligned in straight rows:* line up, put in order, put in rows/columns, place, position, situate, set, range.
2 *he aligned himself with the workers:* ally, affiliate, associate, join, side, unite, combine, join forces, form an alliance, team up, band together, throw in your lot, make common cause.

alike adjective *all the doors looked alike:* similar, much the same, indistinguishable, identical, uniform, interchangeable; cut from the same cloth, like peas in a pod; informal much of a muchness.
OPPOSITES: different.

▷ **adverb** *great minds think alike:* similarly, the same, in the same way/manner/fashion, identically.

alimony noun *his ex-wife has been trying to track him down for alimony:* financial support, maintenance, support; child support.

alive adjective
1 *he was last seen alive on Boxing Day:* living, live, breathing; animate; informal alive and kicking.
2 *the old traditions have been kept alive:* surviving, existing, in existence, existent, active, functioning, in operation.
3 *the thrills that kept him really alive:* animated, lively, full of life, alert, active, energetic, vigorous, spry, sprightly, vivacious, exuberant, ebullient, zestful, spirited; informal full of beans, chirpy.
4 *teachers need to be alive to their pupils' backgrounds:* aware of, conscious of, mindful of, responsive to, sensitive to, familiar with, interested in, awake to.
OPPOSITES: dead, inanimate.

all determiner
1 *all the children went:* each of, each/every one of, every single one of; every, each and every.
2 *the sun shone all week:* the whole of the, the complete, the entire.
3 *in all honesty | with all speed:* complete, entire, total, full; greatest possible, maximum.
▷ **pronoun**
1 *all are welcome:* everyone, everybody, each/every person.
2 *all of the cups were broken:* each one, the sum, the total, the whole lot.
3 *they took all of it:* every part, the whole/total amount, the whole lot, the entirety.
▷ **adverb** *he was dressed all in black:* completely, fully, entirely, totally, wholly, absolutely, utterly; in every respect, in all respects.

> **WORD LINKS**
>
> **omni-, pan-** forming words meaning 'relating to all, including all', such as *omniscient* ('knowing everything') and *pan-African* ('including the whole of the African continent')

allay verb *the report attempted to allay public fears:* reduce, diminish, decrease, lessen, assuage, alleviate, ease, relieve, soothe, calm, take the edge off.
OPPOSITES: increase, intensify.

allegation noun *he made allegations of corruption against the administration:* claim, charge, accusation, assertion, declaration, statement, contention, argument.

allege verb *he alleged that he had been assaulted:* claim, assert, declare, state, contend, argue, affirm, attest.

alleged adjective *the alleged conspiracy:* supposed, claimed, purported, ostensible, so-called; unproven.

allegedly adverb *he allegedly stabbed the girl:* reportedly, supposedly, reputedly, purportedly, ostensibly, apparently, by all accounts, so the story goes.

allegiance noun *those wishing to receive citizenship must swear allegiance to the republic:* loyalty, faithfulness, fidelity, obedience, adherence, homage, devotion.
OPPOSITES: disloyalty, treachery.

allegorical adjective *an allegorical painting:* symbolic, metaphorical, figurative, representative, emblematic.

allegory noun *the book is a political allegory:* parable, fable; metaphor, symbol, emblem.

allergic adjective *she was allergic to nuts:* hypersensitive, sensitive, sensitized.

allergy noun *she developed an allergy to feathers:* hypersensitivity, sensitivity, allergic reaction.

alleviate verb *he couldn't prevent her pain, only alleviate it:* reduce, ease, relieve, take the edge off, deaden, dull, diminish, lessen, weaken, lighten, allay, assuage, palliate, soothe, help, soften, temper.
OPPOSITES: aggravate.

alley noun passage, passageway, alleyway, back alley, backstreet, lane, path, pathway, walk.

alliance noun
1 *a defensive alliance:* association, union, league, confederation, federation, confederacy, coalition, consortium, affiliation, partnership.
2 *an alliance between medicine and morality:* relationship, affinity, association, connection.

allied adjective
1 *a group of allied nations:* federated, confederated, associated, in alliance, in league, in partnership; unified, united, integrated, amalgamated.
2 *agricultural and allied industries:* associated, related, connected, interconnected, linked; similar, like, comparable, equivalent.
OPPOSITES: independent.

allocate verb *the authorities allocated 50,000 places to refugees:* allot, assign, distribute, apportion, issue, give, grant, award.

allocation noun
1 *the efficient allocation of resources:* distribution, assignment, apportionment, allotment.
2 *our annual allocation of funds:* allowance, allotment, quota, share, ration, grant, slice; informal cut.

allot verb *an extra £3 billion has been allotted to the health service:* allocate, assign, apportion, distribute, issue, give, grant; earmark for, designate for, set aside for; hand out, dish out, dole out.

allow verb
1 *the police allowed him to go home:* permit, let, authorize, give permission/authorization/leave, grant someone the right, license, enable, entitle; consent, assent, give your consent/assent/blessing, sanction, acquiesce in, agree, approve; informal give the go-ahead, give the thumbs up, OK, give the OK, give the green light.
2 *allow an hour or so for driving:* set aside, allocate, allot, earmark, designate, assign.
3 *income rose by 11 per cent, allowing for inflation:* take into consideration, take into account.
4 *he allowed that the penalty seemed too harsh for the crime:* admit, concede, grant, accept, agree, acknowledge.
OPPOSITES: prevent, forbid.

allowable adjective *the maximum allowable number of users:* permissible, permitted, allowed, admissible, acceptable, legal, lawful, legitimate, licit, authorized, sanctioned, approved, in order; informal OK, legit.
OPPOSITES: forbidden.

allowance noun
1 *your baggage allowance:* quota, allocation, permitted amount, share, ration, portion, slice.
2 *the elderly receive a heating allowance every winter:* payment, sum of money, contribution, grant, subsidy; maintenance, financial support.
3 *a tax allowance:* concession, reduction, decrease, discount.
□ **make allowances for**
1 *you must make allowances for delays:* take into consideration, take into account, bear in mind, have regard to, plan for, get ready for, cater for, allow for, make provision for, prepare for.
2 *she made allowances for his faults:* excuse, make excuses for, forgive, pardon, overlook.

alloy noun mixture, mix, amalgam, blend, compound, combination, composite.

all right adjective
1 *the tea was all right:* satisfactory, acceptable, adequate, fairly good, passable, reasonable; informal so-so, OK.
2 *thank goodness you're all right:* unhurt, uninjured, unharmed, unscathed, in one piece, safe, safe and sound; well, fine, alive and well; informal OK.
3 *it's all right for you to go now:* permissible, permitted, allowed, allowable, admissible, acceptable, in order; informal OK.
OPPOSITES: unsatisfactory.

▷ **adverb**
1 *the system works all right:* satisfactorily, adequately, fairly well, passably, acceptably, reasonably; informal OK.
2 *it's him all right:* definitely, certainly, unquestionably, undoubtedly, indubitably, undeniably, assuredly, without a doubt, beyond any doubt, beyond the shadow of a doubt.

allude verb *we will allude briefly to the main points of the debate:* refer to, mention, touch on, suggest, hint at, imply, make an allusion to.

allure noun *the allure of Paris:* attraction, lure, draw, pull, appeal, enticement, temptation, charm, seduction, fascination.

alluring adjective *her voice was soft and alluring:* enticing, tempting, appealing, inviting, captivating, fetching, seductive; enchanting, charming, fascinating.

allusion noun *his poetry is full of classical allusions:* reference, mention, suggestion, hint.

ally noun *they are close political allies:* associate, colleague, friend, confederate, partner, supporter.
OPPOSITES: enemy, opponent.
▷ **verb**
1 *the Catholic powers allied with Philip II:* unite, combine, join up, join forces, band together, team up, collaborate, side, align yourself, form an alliance, throw in your lot, make common cause.
2 *he allied his racing experience with business acumen:* combine, marry, couple, join.

almighty adjective
1 *I swear by almighty God:* all-powerful, omnipotent, supreme, pre-eminent.
2 (informal) *the silence was broken by an almighty roar:* very great, huge, enormous, tremendous, colossal, massive, mighty; very loud, deafening, ear-splitting, ear-piercing, thundering, thunderous.

almost adverb *lunch is almost ready:* nearly, about, more or less, practically, virtually, all but, as good as, close to; approaching, bordering on, verging on; informal pretty much.

alone adjective & adverb
1 *she was alone in the house:* by yourself, on your own, all alone, solitary, single, solo; unescorted, without a partner; Brit. informal on your tod.
2 *he managed alone:* unaided, unassisted, without help/assistance, single-handedly, solo, on your own.
3 *she felt terribly alone:* lonely, isolated, solitary, deserted, abandoned, forlorn, friendless.
4 *a house standing alone:* apart, by itself/ yourself, separate, detached, isolated.
5 *you alone can inspire me:* only, solely,

just; and no one else, and nothing else, no one but, nothing but.

aloof adjective *an aloof and somewhat austere figure:* unfriendly, unapproachable, detached, distant, unsociable, remote, formal, stiff, austere, withdrawn, reserved, unforthcoming, uncommunicative; informal stand-offish.
OPPOSITES: friendly.

aloud adverb *he read the letter aloud:* audibly, out loud, for all to hear.
OPPOSITES: silently.

already adverb *she had already suffered a great deal:* by this/that time, by now/then, before now/then, until now/then, up to now/then; formal thus/so far.

also adverb *he's also very good at sport:* too, as well, besides, in addition, additionally, furthermore, further, moreover, into the bargain, on top of that, to boot.

alter verb
1 *Eliot was persuaded to alter the passage:* change, make changes to, make alterations to, adjust, make adjustments to, adapt, amend, modify, revise, revamp, rework, rearrange, reorder, redo, restyle, rejig, refine, vary, transform; informal tweak.
2 *the state of affairs had altered:* change, become different, undergo a change, develop, evolve.

alteration noun *he made an alteration to the text:* change, adjustment, adaptation, modification, revision, amendment; rearrangement, reordering, restyling, rejigging, reworking, revamping.

altercation noun *I had an altercation with the ticket collector:* argument, quarrel, squabble, fight, disagreement, difference of opinion, falling-out, dispute, disputation, wrangle, war of words; Brit. row; informal run-in; Brit. informal barney, bust-up, slanging match.

alternate verb
1 *his moods alternated between aggression and despair:* change, occur in turn/ sequence, rotate, follow one another.
2 *the narrative alternates personal observation with historical fact:* give turns to, take in turn, rotate, take in rotation, interchange.
▷ **adjective**
1 *she attended on alternate days:* every other, every second.
2 *place the leeks and pasta in alternate layers:* interchanging, alternating, occurring in turns.

alternative adjective
1 *an alternative route:* different, other, another, second, possible, substitute, replacement; standby, emergency, reserve, backup, auxiliary, fallback.
2 *an alternative lifestyle:* unorthodox, unconventional, bohemian, non-standard,

a

unusual, uncommon, out of the ordinary; radical, revolutionary, nonconformist, avant-garde, offbeat.
▷ **noun** *there are a number of alternatives available:* option, choice, other possibility; substitute, replacement.

alternatively adverb *alternatively, you may telephone us direct if you wish:* on the other hand, as an alternative, or; otherwise, instead.

although conjunction *although the sun was shining it wasn't that warm:* in spite of the fact that, despite the fact that, notwithstanding (the fact) that, even though/if, for all that, while, whilst.

altitude noun *we are now flying at an altitude of 40,000 feet:* height, elevation.

altogether adverb
1 *he wasn't altogether happy:* completely, totally, entirely, absolutely, wholly, fully, thoroughly, utterly, perfectly, one hundred per cent, in all respects.
2 *we have five offices altogether:* in all, all told, in total.
3 *altogether it was a great evening:* on the whole, overall, all in all, all things considered, on balance, on average, for the most part, in the main, in general, generally, by and large.

> **USAGE**
>
> Note that **altogether** and **all together** do not mean the same thing. **Altogether** means 'completely' or 'in total', while **all together** means 'all in one place' (*it was good to see my family all together*) or 'all at once' (*they came in all together*).

altruism noun *they supported the measures not out of altruism but out of self-interest:* unselfishness, selflessness, public-spiritedness, compassion, kindness; charity, benevolence, beneficence, philanthropy, humanitarianism.
OPPOSITES: selfishness.

always adverb
1 *he's always late:* every time, each time, at all times, all the time, without fail, consistently, invariably, regularly, habitually, unfailingly.
2 *she's always complaining:* continually, continuously, constantly, forever, perpetually, incessantly, ceaselessly, unceasingly, endlessly, the entire time; informal 24-7.
3 *the place will always be dear to me:* forever, for evermore, until the end of time, eternally, for eternity.
OPPOSITES: never, seldom, sometimes.

amalgamate verb *the two departments were amalgamated:* combine, merge, unite, integrate, consolidate; join together, join forces, band together, link up, team up, go into partnership; fuse, blend, meld.
OPPOSITES: separate.

amalgamation noun combination, union, blend, mixture, fusion, synthesis, composite, amalgam.

amass verb *he amassed a large fortune:* gather, collect, assemble; accrue, accumulate, cumulate; stockpile, store up, lay in/up, garner; informal stash away.

amateur noun *the crew were all amateurs:* non-professional, non-specialist, layman, layperson; dilettante.
▷ **adjective**
1 *an amateur sportsman:* non-professional, non-specialist, lay; dilettante.
2 *their efforts were very amateur:* incompetent, inept, unskilful, inexpert, amateurish, clumsy, maladroit, bumbling.
OPPOSITES: professional.

amaze verb *the size of the place amazed her:* astonish, astound, surprise, stun, stagger, nonplus, shock, startle, stupefy, stop someone in their tracks, take someone's breath away, dumbfound; informal bowl over, flabbergast; Brit. informal knock for six.

amazed adjective *the girl still looked amazed:* astonished, astounded, surprised, stunned, staggered, shocked, startled, stupefied, thunderstruck, taken aback, dumbfounded, dumbstruck, at a loss for words, speechless; informal flabbergasted; Brit. informal gobsmacked.

amazement noun astonishment, surprise, shock, stupefaction, incredulity, disbelief, speechlessness, awe, wonder, wonderment.

amazing adjective *an amazing sight greeted our weary eyes:* astonishing, astounding, surprising, stunning, staggering, shocking, startling, stupefying, breathtaking; remarkable, extraordinary, incredible, unbelievable.

ambassador noun
1 *the American ambassador:* envoy, plenipotentiary, emissary, representative.
2 *he's a great ambassador for the sport:* representative, promoter, champion, supporter, campaigner.

ambience noun *the relaxed ambience of the cocktail lounge:* atmosphere, air, feel, feeling, character, quality, impression, flavour, look, tone, aura, climate, mood; informal vibe.

ambiguity noun *we can detect no ambiguity in this section of the Act:* ambivalence, equivocation; inexactitude, vagueness.

ambiguous adjective *the judge agreed that the law was ambiguous:* equivocal, ambivalent, open to debate/argument, arguable, debatable; inexact, unclear, vague, confusing.
OPPOSITES: clear.

ambition noun
1 *we need men and women with ambition:* drive, determination, enterprise, initiative, eagerness, motivation, enthusiasm, zeal, commitment, a sense of purpose; informal get-up-and-go.
2 *her ambition was to become a model:* aspiration, goal, aim, intention, objective, object, purpose, intent, plan, desire, wish, design, target, dream.

ambitious adjective
1 *a talented and ambitious young journalist:* aspiring, aspirational, motivated, determined, forceful, enterprising, enthusiastic, energetic, zealous, committed, power-hungry; informal pushy, go-ahead, go-getting.
2 *an ambitious programme of social reform:* large-scale, extensive, wide-ranging, far-reaching, grand; difficult, challenging, hard; unrealistic.

ambivalent adjective *the public has a rather ambivalent attitude toward science:* equivocal, uncertain, unsure, doubtful, undecided, in two minds, inconsistent, contradictory; indecisive, inconclusive, irresolute, torn, in a dilemma, on the horns of a dilemma, in a quandary, sitting on the fence, hesitating, wavering, vacillating, equivocating, blowing hot and cold; informal iffy.
OPPOSITES: unequivocal, certain.

amble verb *they ambled along the riverbank:* stroll, saunter, wander, meander, walk, go for a walk, promenade; informal mosey; Brit. informal mooch, pootle.

ambush noun *the soldiers were killed in an ambush:* surprise attack, trap; dated ambuscade.
▷ **verb** *twenty youths ambushed their patrol car:* pounce on, waylay, surprise, attack by surprise, lay a trap for, set an ambush for, lie in wait for.

ameliorate verb *any move that ameliorates the situation is welcome:* improve, make better, better, make improvements to, help, benefit; relieve, ease, mitigate.
OPPOSITES: worsen.

amenable adjective
1 *an amenable child:* compliant, accommodating, biddable, manageable, controllable, tractable, pliant, malleable, acquiescent, complaisant, cooperative, easily handled.
2 *many cancers are amenable to treatment:* susceptible, receptive, responsive.
OPPOSITES: uncooperative.

amend verb *the rule was amended to apply only to non-members:* revise, alter, change, modify, qualify, adapt, adjust; edit, copy-edit, rewrite, redraft, rephrase, reword, rework, revamp.

amends plural noun
□ make amends atone, make restitution, make good; (**make amends to**) compensate, recompense, indemnify, make it up to; (**make amends for**) atone for, make up for, expiate.

amenity noun *the older type of housing lacks basic amenities:* facility, service, convenience, resource, benefit, advantage.

amiable adjective *the amiable young man greeted me enthusiastically:* friendly, affable, good-natured, pleasant, agreeable, likeable, genial, good-humoured, congenial, cordial, charming, easy to get on/along with, companionable, sociable, personable.
OPPOSITES: unfriendly.

amicable adjective *the meeting was relatively amicable:* friendly, good-natured, cordial, civilized, harmonious.
OPPOSITES: unfriendly.

amid preposition
1 *the jeep was concealed amid pine trees:* in the middle of, surrounded by, among, amongst.
2 *the truce collapsed amid fears of a revolt:* in an atmosphere of, against a background of; as a result of.

amiss adjective *an inspection revealed nothing amiss:* wrong, awry, faulty, out of order, defective, unsatisfactory, incorrect; inappropriate, improper.
□ not come/go amiss be welcome, be pleasant, be useful.
□ take something amiss be offended, take offence, be upset.

amity noun (formal) *this will bring greater amity between our peoples:* friendship, harmony, understanding, accord, cooperation, goodwill, cordiality, warmth; formal concord.
OPPOSITES: enmity.

ammunition noun *police seized arms and ammunition:* bullets, shells, projectiles, missiles, rounds, shot, cartridges; munitions.

amnesty noun *an amnesty for political prisoners:* pardon, reprieve; release, discharge; informal let-off.

amok adverb
□ run amok *stone-throwing protesters were running amok:* go berserk, get out of control, go on the rampage, rampage, riot, run riot.

among, amongst preposition
1 *you're among friends:* surrounded by, in the company of, amid, in the middle of.
2 *a child was among the injured:* included in, one/some of, in the group/number of.
3 *he distributed the proceeds among his creditors:* between, to each of.

a

amoral adjective *an amoral attitude to sex:* unprincipled, without standards, without morals, unethical.
OPPOSITES: moral, principled.

> **USAGE**
>
> **Amoral** and **immoral** do not mean the same thing. **Amoral** means 'without morality', while **immoral** means 'not following accepted standards of morality' (*killing and torture are immoral*).

amorous adjective *she rejected his amorous advances:* lustful, sexual, amatory, erotic, ardent, passionate.

amorphous adjective *an amorphous grey mass:* shapeless, formless, structureless, indeterminate, nebulous.

amount noun
1 *the event raised a substantial amount of money:* sum, quantity.
2 *the diary should include details of the amount and type of food eaten:* quantity, volume, mass, bulk, weight.
□ **amount to**
1 *the bill amounted to £50:* add up to, come to, run to, be, make, total; Brit. tot up to.
2 *their actions amounted to a conspiracy:* constitute, be tantamount to, be the equivalent of, be equal to.

ample adjective
1 *there is ample time for discussion:* enough, sufficient, adequate, plenty of, more than enough, enough and to spare.
2 *an ample supply of wine:* plentiful, abundant, copious, profuse, rich, lavish, liberal, generous, bountiful, large, huge, great.
3 *she stood with her hands on her ample hips:* broad, wide, full, plump, voluptuous.
OPPOSITES: insufficient.

amplify verb
1 *speakers amplify the sound:* make louder, raise, turn up, increase, magnify.
2 *these notes amplify information contained in the statement:* expand, enlarge on, elaborate on, add to, supplement, develop, flesh out, add detail to.
OPPOSITES: lower.

amulet noun lucky charm, charm, talisman, mascot.

amuse verb
1 *he made faces to try to amuse her:* entertain, make laugh, divert, cheer up, cheer, please, charm, delight; informal tickle.
2 *he amused himself by writing poetry:* occupy, engage, busy, employ, distract, absorb, engross, hold someone's attention; interest, entertain, divert.
OPPOSITES: bore.

amusement noun
1 *his eyes twinkled with amusement:* mirth, merriment, hilarity, glee, delight; enjoyment, pleasure.
2 *I read the book for amusement:* entertainment, pleasure, leisure, relaxation, fun, enjoyment, interest, diversion; informal R & R.
3 *a wide range of amusements:* activity, entertainment, diversion; game, sport.

amusing adjective *behind that incident there lies an amusing story:* entertaining, funny, comical, witty, hilarious, droll, diverting.
OPPOSITES: boring.

anaemic adjective
1 *his anaemic complexion:* colourless, bloodless, pale, pallid, pasty, wan, ashen, grey, sallow, whey-faced.
2 *the team gave a thoroughly anaemic performance:* feeble, weak, insipid, bland; lame, tame, lacklustre, spiritless, ineffective, ineffectual.

anaesthetic noun narcotic, painkiller, painkilling drug; sedative, analgesic.

analgesic adjective *an analgesic drug:* painkilling, pain-relieving, narcotic; palliative.

analogous adjective *sleep had always been regarded as being in some way analogous to death:* comparable, similar, like, corresponding, parallel, related, equivalent, akin.
OPPOSITES: unrelated.

analogy noun similarity, parallel, correspondence, likeness, resemblance, correlation, relation, kinship, equivalence; formal similitude.
OPPOSITES: dissimilarity.

analyse verb *we need to analyse the results in more detail:* examine, study, scrutinize, evaluate, investigate, explore, research, review; break down, interpret, anatomize, dissect.

analysis noun *an analysis of the causes of the rising crime rate:* examination, study, evaluation, investigation, breakdown, scrutiny, review, interpretation, dissection.

analytical, **analytic** adjective *a more analytical approach was needed:* systematic, logical, scientific, methodical, organized, ordered, orderly, rigorous.
OPPOSITES: unsystematic.

anarchic adjective *postmodern society is increasingly anarchic:* lawless, without law and order, in disorder/turmoil, unruly, chaotic, turbulent.
OPPOSITES: ordered.

anarchist noun insurgent, rebel, subversive, revolutionary, insurrectionist.

anarchy noun lawlessness, disorder, chaos, turmoil, revolution, insurrection, mobocracy.
OPPOSITES: government, order.

anathema noun *racial hatred was anathema to her:* abhorrent, repugnant, hateful, repellent, offensive.

anatomy noun
1 *the anatomy of the brain:* structure, form.
2 *a detailed anatomy of a society and its institutions:* analysis, examination, study, evaluation, investigation, survey, review.

ancestor noun
1 *he could trace his ancestors back to King James I:* forebear, forefather, predecessor, antecedent, progenitor, primogenitor.
2 *the instrument is an ancestor of the lute:* forerunner, precursor, predecessor.
OPPOSITES: descendant, successor.

ancestry noun ancestors, forebears, forefathers, progenitors, antecedents; family tree; lineage, genealogy, roots.

anchor verb
1 *the ship was anchored in the bay:* moor, berth, be at anchor.
2 *the fish anchors itself to the coral:* secure, fasten, attach, affix, fix.

ancient adjective
1 *the ancient civilizations of the Mediterranean:* early, old, prehistoric; primeval, primordial, primitive; bygone, of long ago.
2 *an ancient custom:* old, age-old, time-worn, time-honoured.
3 *you make me feel ancient:* antiquated, aged, elderly, decrepit, antediluvian, in your dotage; old-fashioned, out of date, outmoded, passé; informal out of the ark; Brit. informal past its/your sell-by date.
OPPOSITES: recent, contemporary.

ancillary adjective *the school has eleven teaching staff and five ancillary staff:* additional, auxiliary, supporting, extra, supplementary.

and conjunction together with, with, as well as, in addition to, also, too; besides, furthermore; informal plus.

anecdotal adjective *she had only anecdotal evidence on which to base her decision:* unscientific, unreliable, based on hearsay.
OPPOSITES: factual.

anecdote noun story, tale, narrative; informal yarn.

angel noun
1 *God sent an angel:* messenger of God, divine messenger; archangel, seraph, cherub.
2 *she's an absolute angel:* saint, paragon of virtue; gem, treasure, darling, dear; informal star.
OPPOSITES: devil.

angelic adjective
1 *angelic beings:* divine, heavenly, celestial, holy, seraphic.

2 *Sophie's angelic appearance:* innocent, pure, virtuous, good, saintly; beautiful, lovely.
OPPOSITES: demonic.

anger noun *his face was dark with anger:* annoyance, exasperation, irritation, vexation, indignation, displeasure; rage, fury, wrath, outrage; hostility, bitterness, resentment; literary ire.
OPPOSITES: pleasure.
▷ verb *she was angered by his terse reply:* annoy, irritate, exasperate, irk, vex, put out; enrage, incense, infuriate, madden; Brit. rub up the wrong way; informal make someone's blood boil, get someone's back up; aggravate, rile, hack off; Brit. informal wind up, nark.
OPPOSITES: pacify, placate.

angle¹ noun
1 *the wall is sloping at an angle of 33°:* gradient, slant, inclination.
2 *the angle of the roof:* corner, intersection, point, apex.
3 *consider the problem from a different angle:* perspective, point of view, viewpoint, standpoint, position, aspect, slant, direction.
▷ verb
1 *Anna angled her camera towards the tree:* tilt, slant, direct, turn.
2 *angle your answer so that it is relevant to the job for which you are applying:* present, tailor, adapt, adjust, orient.

angle² verb *he was angling for an invitation:* try to get, seek to obtain, fish for, hope for, be after.

angry adjective
1 *passengers are angry about the delays:* annoyed, irate, cross, vexed, irritated, indignant, irked; furious, enraged, infuriated, in a temper, incensed, raging, incandescent, fuming, seething, beside yourself, outraged; informal mad, wild, livid, apoplectic, up in arms, steamed up; Brit. informal shirty; N. Amer. informal sore.
2 *an angry debate:* heated, stormy, passionate; bad-tempered, ill-tempered, acrimonious, bitter.
3 *there was an angry wound on his cheek:* inflamed, infected, red, swollen, sore, painful.
OPPOSITES: pleased.

angst noun *teenage angst:* anxiety, anguish, worry, fear; malaise, disquiet, unease, uneasiness; stress.

anguish noun *she gave a cry of anguish:* agony, pain, suffering, torment, torture, distress, angst, misery, sorrow, grief, heartache, desolation, despair.
OPPOSITES: happiness.

anguished adjective agonized, tormented, tortured; grief-stricken, wretched, heartbroken, desolate, devastated.

a

angular adjective
1 *an angular shape:* sharp-cornered, pointed, V-shaped, Y-shaped.
2 *a tall, angular girl:* bony, raw-boned, lean, rangy, spare, thin, gaunt.
OPPOSITES: rounded, curving.

animal noun
1 *endangered animals:* creature, beast; (**animals**) wildlife, fauna.
2 *the man was an animal:* brute, beast, monster, devil, demon, fiend.
▷ **adjective**
1 *animal life:* zoological.
2 *a grunt of animal passion:* carnal, physical, bodily, animalistic; brutish, coarse, unrefined, uncultured.

> WORD LINKS
> **zoology** the scientific study of animals

animate verb *a sense of excitement animated the whole school:* enliven, vitalize, breathe (new) life into, energize, invigorate, revive, vivify, liven up; inspire, exhilarate, thrill, excite, fire, arouse, rouse; informal buck up, pep up.
OPPOSITES: depress.
▷ **adjective** *an animate being:* living, alive, live, breathing, sentient.
OPPOSITES: inanimate.

animated adjective *an animated discussion was taking place:* lively, spirited, excited, enthusiastic, exuberant, ebullient, energetic, full of life, eager, alive, active, vigorous, vibrant, vivacious, high-spirited; passionate, impassioned.
OPPOSITES: lethargic, lifeless.

animosity noun *there was considerable animosity between him and his brother:* antipathy, hostility, friction, antagonism, enmity, animus, bitterness, rancour, resentment, dislike, ill feeling/will, bad blood, hatred, hate, loathing; malice, spite.
OPPOSITES: goodwill, friendship.

annals plural noun records, archives, chronicles, accounts, registers.

annex verb
1 *ten amendments were annexed to the constitution:* add, append, attach, tack on.
2 *Charlemagne annexed northern Italy:* take over, take possession of, appropriate, seize, conquer, occupy.
▷ **noun** (also **annexe**) extension, addition; wing.

annexation noun *Hitler's annexation of Austria:* seizure, occupation, invasion, conquest, takeover, appropriation.

annihilate verb *this was an attempt to annihilate a whole people:* destroy, wipe out, obliterate, wipe off the face of the earth; kill, slaughter, exterminate, eliminate, eradicate.
OPPOSITES: create.

annotate verb *the text was annotated with explanatory notes:* comment on, add notes/footnotes to, gloss.

annotation noun note, comment, gloss, footnote; commentary, explanation, interpretation.

announce verb
1 *the Chancellor announced plans to raise the tax on petrol:* make public, make known, report, declare, state, give out, notify, reveal; publicize, broadcast, publish, advertise, circulate, proclaim.
2 *Victor announced the guests:* introduce, present, name.
3 *strains of music announced her arrival:* signal, indicate, herald, proclaim.

announcement noun
1 *an announcement by the Minister is expected this afternoon:* statement, declaration, report, proclamation, pronouncement; bulletin, communiqué, dispatch.
2 *the announcement of the decision:* declaration, notification.

announcer noun anchor, anchorman, anchorwoman; newsreader, newscaster, broadcaster; Brit. presenter.

annoy verb *such remarks never failed to annoy him:* irritate, anger, make angry/cross, exasperate, vex, irk, gall, pique, put out, antagonize, get on someone's nerves, make someone's hackles rise, rankle with; Brit. rub up the wrong way; informal aggravate, rile, needle, nettle, get to, bug, hack off, get someone's back up, drive mad/crazy; Brit. informal wind up.
OPPOSITES: please.

annoyance noun
1 *much to his annoyance, she didn't even notice:* irritation, exasperation, vexation, indignation, anger, displeasure, chagrin.
2 *they found him an annoyance:* nuisance, pest, bother, irritant, inconvenience, thorn in your flesh; informal pain, pain in the neck, hassle, bind, bore.

annoyed adjective irritated, cross, angry, vexed, exasperated, irked, piqued, displeased, put out, disgruntled, in a bad mood, in a temper; informal aggravated, peeved, miffed, nettled, riled, hacked off, hot under the collar; Brit. informal narked, shirty; N. Amer. informal sore.

annoying adjective irritating, infuriating, exasperating, maddening, trying, tiresome, troublesome, bothersome, irksome, vexing, vexatious, galling; informal aggravating.

annual adjective *an annual report:* yearly, once-a-year.

annually adverb yearly, once a year, each year, per annum.

annul verb *the European Court annulled the decision:* nullify, declare null and void, declare invalid, invalidate, void; repeal, reverse, rescind, revoke.

anodyne adjective *the conversation was anodyne:* bland, inoffensive, innocuous, neutral, unobjectionable.

anomalous adjective *anomalous results:* abnormal, atypical, irregular, aberrant, exceptional, freak; odd, peculiar, unusual, out of the ordinary.
OPPOSITES: normal, typical.

anomaly noun *there are a number of anomalies in the present system:* oddity, peculiarity, abnormality, irregularity, inconsistency, aberration.

anonymous adjective
1 *an anonymous donor:* unnamed, nameless, unidentified, unknown; incognito.
2 *an anonymous letter:* unsigned, unattributed.
3 *an anonymous housing estate:* characterless, nondescript, impersonal, faceless, unremarkable.

another determiner
1 *have another drink:* one more, a further, an additional; an extra, a spare.
2 *she left him for another man:* a different, an alternative.

answer noun
1 *I was about to give a flippant answer:* reply, response, rejoinder, reaction; retort, riposte; informal comeback.
2 *the answer is 150:* solution, key.
3 *a new filter is the answer:* solution, remedy, way out.
OPPOSITES: question.
▷verb
1 *'Of course I can,' he answered:* reply, respond, make a rejoinder, rejoin; retort.
2 *he has yet to answer the charges:* rebut, refute, defend yourself against.
3 *a man answering this description was seen behaving suspiciously in the area:* match, fit, correspond to, be similar to.
4 *we're trying to answer the needs of our audience:* satisfy, meet, fulfil, fill, measure up to.
5 *I answer to the Commissioner:* report to, be accountable to, be responsible to, be answerable to, work for/under, be subordinate to.
□ **answer for**
1 *he will answer for his crime:* pay for, be punished for, suffer for; make amends for, make reparation for, atone for.
2 *the government has a lot to answer for:* be accountable for, be responsible for, be liable for, be to blame for.

answerable adjective
1 *the Attorney General is answerable only to Parliament:* accountable, responsible; subject.
2 *an employer is answerable for the negligence of his employees:* responsible, liable.

antagonism noun *the antagonism between them is personal rather than political:* hostility, friction, antipathy, animus, enmity, opposition, rivalry; acrimony, bitterness, rancour, resentment, dislike, ill/bad feeling, ill will; Brit. informal needle.
OPPOSITES: rapport, friendship.

antagonist noun adversary, opponent, enemy, rival; literary foe; (**antagonists**) opposition, competition.
OPPOSITES: ally.

antagonistic adjective
1 *he was antagonistic to the reforms:* hostile to, against, dead set against, opposed to, ill-disposed to, resistant to, in disagreement with, antipathetic to; informal anti.
2 *an antagonistic group of bystanders:* hostile, aggressive, belligerent, bellicose, pugnacious.

antagonize verb *he seemed to be deliberately trying to antagonize her:* anger, annoy, provoke, irritate, vex; alienate; Brit. rub up the wrong way; informal aggravate, rile, needle, rattle someone's cage, get someone's back up; Brit. informal nark.
OPPOSITES: pacify, placate.

antecedent noun
1 *her antecedents have been traced:* ancestor, forefather, forebear, progenitor, primogenitor; (**antecedents**) ancestry, family tree, lineage, genealogy, roots.
2 *the guitar's antecedent:* precursor, forerunner, predecessor.
OPPOSITES: descendant.

antedate verb *a civilization that antedated the Roman Empire:* precede, predate, come/go before.

antediluvian adjective *regrettably, this antediluvian attitude persists:* out of date, outdated, outmoded, old-fashioned, antiquated, behind the times, passé.

anthem noun hymn, song, chorale, psalm, paean.

anthology noun *an anthology of poetry:* collection, selection, compendium, treasury, miscellany.

anticipate verb
1 *the police did not anticipate trouble:* expect, foresee, predict, be prepared for, bargain on, reckon on.
2 *Elaine was eagerly anticipating her meeting with Will:* look forward to, await.
3 *warders can't always anticipate the actions of prisoners:* pre-empt, forestall, second-guess.

anticipation noun
1 *my anticipation is that we will see a rise in interest rates:* expectation, prediction, forecast.
2 *her eyes sparkled with anticipation:* expectancy, expectation, excitement, suspense.

a

□ **in anticipation of**
they manned the phones *in anticipation of a flood of calls:* in the expectation of, in preparation for, ready for.

anticlimax noun *the rest of the journey was an anticlimax by comparison:* let-down, disappointment, non-event; Brit. damp squib; informal comedown.

antidote noun
1 *the antidote to this poison:* antitoxin, antiserum, antivenin.
2 *laughter is a good antidote to stress:* remedy, cure; nostrum.

antipathetic adjective *it is human nature to be antipathetic to change:* hostile, against, opposed, antagonistic, unsympathetic, ill-disposed; informal anti.
OPPOSITES: pro.

antipathy noun *she made no secret of her growing antipathy to him:* hostility, antagonism, animosity, animus, enmity, aversion, dislike, distaste, hatred, hate, abhorrence, loathing.
OPPOSITES: liking, affinity.

antiquated adjective *he still had not mastered the antiquated central heating system | antiquated Victorian values:* old-fashioned, outdated, out of date, outmoded, outworn, antediluvian, archaic, behind the times, anachronistic, passé; informal out of the ark.
OPPOSITES: modern, up to date.

antique noun collector's item, period piece, antiquity, objet d'art.
▷ adjective *antique furniture:* old, antiquarian, collectable; vintage, heritage.
OPPOSITES: modern.

antiquity noun
1 *the civilizations of antiquity:* ancient times, the ancient past, classical times, the distant past.
2 *Islamic antiquities:* antique, period piece, collector's item.
3 *a church of great antiquity:* age.

antiseptic adjective
1 *an antiseptic substance:* disinfectant, germicidal, bactericidal.
2 *antiseptic bandages:* sterile, aseptic, germ-free, uncontaminated; disinfected, sterilized.
3 *their antiseptic surroundings:* characterless, colourless, soulless; clinical, institutional; hygienic.
OPPOSITES: contaminated.
▷ noun disinfectant, germicide, bactericide.

antisocial adjective
1 *antisocial behaviour:* objectionable, offensive, unacceptable, distasteful, disruptive; sociopathic.
2 *I'm feeling a bit antisocial:* unsociable, unfriendly, uncommunicative, reclusive, misanthropic.

antithesis noun *love is the antithesis of selfishness:* direct opposite, converse, reverse, inverse, obverse, the other side of the coin; informal the flip side.

antithetical adjective *people whose religious beliefs are antithetical to mine:* directly opposed, contrasting, contrary, contradictory, conflicting, incompatible, irreconcilable, inconsistent, poles apart, at variance/odds.

anxiety noun
1 *we viewed these developments with growing anxiety:* worry, concern, apprehension, apprehensiveness, unease, uneasiness, fearfulness, fear, disquiet, disquietude, perturbation, agitation, angst, nervousness, nerves, tension.
2 *her anxiety to please:* eagerness, keenness, desire.
OPPOSITES: serenity.

anxious adjective
1 *anxious relatives waited for news:* worried, concerned, apprehensive, fearful, uneasy, troubled, distressed, fretful, agitated, nervous, edgy, on edge, tense, overwrought, worked up, keyed up, jumpy, with your heart in your mouth; informal uptight, on tenterhooks, jittery.
2 *she was anxious for news:* eager, keen, impatient.
OPPOSITES: carefree, unconcerned.

any determiner
1 *is there any cake left?* some, a piece/bit of.
2 *it doesn't make any difference:* the slightest bit of, a scrap/shred of, an iota of.
3 *any job will do:* whichever, no matter which, never mind which.
▷ adverb *is your father any better?* at all, in the least, to any extent, in any degree.

anyhow adverb
1 *anyhow, it doesn't really matter:* anyway, in any case/event, at any rate; however, be that as it may.
2 *her clothes were strewn about anyhow:* haphazardly, carelessly, heedlessly, in a muddle; informal all over the place.

apart adverb
1 *the villages are two miles apart:* away from each other, distant from each other.
2 *Isabel stood apart:* to one side, aside, separately, alone, by yourself/itself.
3 *his parents are living apart:* separately, independently, on your own.
□ **apart from**
there was little traffic, apart from a few taxis: except for, but for, aside from, with the exception of, excepting, excluding, bar, barring, besides, other than; formal save.

apartment noun
1 *a rented apartment:* flat, penthouse.
2 *the royal apartments:* suite, rooms, living quarters, accommodation.

apathetic adjective *the workforce was described as apathetic and demoralized:* uninterested, indifferent, unconcerned, unenthusiastic, unmoved, uninvolved, unmotivated, dispassionate, lukewarm, bored; informal couldn't-care-less.

apathy noun *there was widespread apathy amongst the electorate:* indifference, lack of interest/enthusiasm/concern, unconcern, unresponsiveness, lethargy, inertia, boredom, ennui; literary accidie.
OPPOSITES: enthusiasm, passion.

ape noun primate, simian; monkey.
▷ verb *he aped her accent:* imitate, mimic, copy, do an impression of; informal take off; Brit. informal send up.

> WORD LINKS
> **primatology** the branch of zoology concerned with apes and monkeys

aperture noun opening, hole, gap, slit, slot, vent, chink, crack, crevice, interstice, orifice.

apex noun
1 *the apex of a pyramid:* tip, top, vertex, peak, summit, head, crest, crown.
2 *the apex of his career:* climax, culmination, apotheosis; peak, pinnacle, summit, zenith, acme, apogee, high/highest point.
OPPOSITES: bottom, nadir.

aphorism noun saying, maxim, axiom, adage, epigram, dictum, proverb, saw; rare apophthegm.

aplenty adjective *the town has museums and galleries aplenty:* in abundance, in profusion, galore, in large quantities/numbers, by the dozen; informal by the truckload.

aplomb noun *he handled the crisis with surprising aplomb:* poise, self-assurance, self-confidence, calmness, composure, level-headedness, sangfroid, equanimity, equilibrium.

apocryphal adjective *an apocryphal story:* fictitious, made-up, untrue, fabricated; unsubstantiated, unverified, unauthenticated.

apologetic adjective *she was very apologetic about the whole incident:* contrite, sorry, regretful, remorseful, penitent, repentant; conscience-stricken, shamefaced, ashamed.
OPPOSITES: unrepentant.

apologia noun *he offers a spirited apologia for his methodology:* defence, justification, vindication, explanation; argument, case.

apologist noun *he has a reputation as an apologist for capitalism:* defender, supporter, upholder, advocate, proponent, exponent, propagandist, champion, campaigner.
OPPOSITES: critic.

apologize verb *I must apologize for disturbing you like this:* say sorry, express regret, ask forgiveness, be apologetic, make an apology, ask for pardon; eat humble pie.

apology noun *please accept my apologies for the delay:* expression of regret, your regrets.

apostle noun
1 *the 12 apostles of Jesus:* disciple, follower.
2 *a man once known as the apostle of free-market economics:* advocate, apologist, proponent, exponent, promoter, supporter, upholder, champion.

appal verb *civil-rights activists were appalled by the police brutality:* horrify, shock, outrage, scandalize, dismay, distress; disgust, repel, revolt, sicken, nauseate, offend.

appalling adjective
1 *police say it was an appalling crime:* shocking, horrific, horrifying, horrible, terrible, awful, dreadful, ghastly, hideous, horrendous, atrocious, abominable, abhorrent, outrageous, monstrous, frightful, heinous, egregious; disgusting, sickening, nauseating.
2 *the house was in an appalling state:* dreadful, awful, terrible, atrocious, abysmal, disgraceful, deplorable, lamentable, woeful; informal dire.

apparatus noun
1 *laboratory apparatus:* equipment, rig, tackle; appliance, instrument, machine, mechanism, device, contraption; informal gear.
2 *the apparatus of government:* structure, system, framework, organization, network.

apparent adjective
1 *their relief was all too apparent:* evident, plain, obvious, clear, manifest, visible, discernible, perceptible; unmistakable, crystal clear, conspicuous, palpable, patent, blatant, writ large.
2 *his apparent lack of concern:* seeming, ostensible, outward, superficial; supposed, alleged, professed.
OPPOSITES: unclear.

apparently adverb *apparently, he had a mild heart attack:* it seems that, it appears that, seemingly, by all accounts; allegedly, reputedly; ostensibly, on the face of it.

apparition noun
1 *a headless apparition:* ghost, phantom, spectre, spirit, wraith; vision, hallucination; informal spook.
2 *an apparition of the Virgin Mary:* appearance, manifestation, materialization; visitation.

appeal verb
1 *police are appealing for information:* ask urgently, make an urgent request, call, make a plea, plead.

2 *Andrew appealed to me to help them:* implore, beg, entreat, call on, plead with, exhort, ask, request, petition.
3 *the thought of travelling appealed to me:* attract, be attractive to, interest, take someone's fancy; fascinate, tempt, entice, draw, whet someone's appetite.
▷**noun**
1 *an appeal for help:* plea, urgent request, entreaty, call, cry, petition, supplication, cri de cœur.
2 *the cultural appeal of the island:* attraction, attractiveness, allure, charm; fascination, magnetism, drawing power, pull.

appealing adjective *she's such an appealing girl:* attractive, engaging, charming, delightful, enchanting, captivating, fascinating, tempting, enticing, seductive, irresistible, winning.
OPPOSITES: disagreeable.

appear verb
1 *a cloud of dust appeared on the horizon:* become visible, come into view/sight, materialize; informal pop up.
2 *fundamental differences were beginning to appear:* be revealed, emerge, surface, manifest itself, become apparent/evident, come to light; arise, crop up.
3 *Bill still hadn't appeared:* arrive, turn up, put in an appearance, come; informal show up, pitch up, roll in.
4 *they appeared to be completely devoted:* seem, look, give the impression, come across as, strike someone as.
OPPOSITES: disappear, vanish.

appearance noun
1 *she was conscious of her dishevelled appearance:* look, air, aspect, mien.
2 *she read the letter with an appearance of interest:* impression, air, show, semblance; facade, veneer, guise, pretence.
3 *the sudden appearance of her daughter startled her:* arrival, advent, coming, emergence, materialization.

appease verb *amendments have been added to appease local pressure groups:* placate, pacify, mollify, conciliate, win over, propitiate; informal sweeten.
OPPOSITES: provoke.

appeasement noun *a policy of appeasement:* conciliation, pacification, reconciliation; peacemaking.
OPPOSITES: provocation.

append verb *the results of the survey are appended to this chapter:* add, attach, affix, tack on, tag on.

appendage noun
1 *they treated Scotland as a mere appendage of England:* addition, adjunct, attachment, accessory, add-on.
2 *oxygen is absorbed through a pair of feathery appendages:* protuberance, projection.

appendix noun *the list was published as an appendix to the report:* supplement, addendum, postscript, codicil; coda, epilogue, afterword.

appetite noun
1 *a walk sharpens the appetite:* hunger, desire for food.
2 *my appetite for learning was insatiable:* desire, hunger, thirst, passion, craving, longing, yearning, hankering; enthusiasm, keenness, eagerness, taste, yen.

appetizer noun starter, first course, hors d'oeuvre, antipasto.

appetizing adjective
1 *a large, appetizing meal | the appetizing aroma of sizzling bacon:* mouth-watering, inviting, tempting; tasty, delicious, flavoursome, toothsome, delectable; informal yummy, moreish, scrumptious.
2 *the fixture is not a particularly appetizing prospect for Welsh fans:* appealing, attractive, inviting.

applaud verb
1 *the audience applauded:* clap, put your hands together, give someone an ovation; show your appreciation; informal give someone a big hand.
2 *police have applauded the decision:* praise, commend, acclaim, salute, welcome, celebrate, express admiration for, express approval of, approve of, sing the praises of, pay tribute to, speak highly of, take your hat off to.
OPPOSITES: jeer, criticize.

applause noun
1 *they gave him a round of applause:* clapping; an ovation.
2 *the museum's design won general applause:* praise, acclaim, acclamation, admiration, commendation, approbation, approval; compliments, accolades, tributes, plaudits.

appliance noun
1 *domestic appliances:* device, machine, instrument, gadget, contraption, apparatus, mechanism; utensil, implement, tool.
2 *the appliance of science could increase crop yields:* application, use, exercise, employment, implementation, utilization, practice, operation.

applicable adjective *the same considerations are equally applicable to accident claims:* relevant, appropriate, pertinent, apposite, germane, material, significant, related, connected.
OPPOSITES: inapplicable, irrelevant.

applicant noun candidate, interviewee, competitor, contender, entrant; claimant, supplicant, petitioner; job-seeker, job-hunter.

application noun
1 *no work should be started until an*

application for a grant has been approved: request, petition; claim, demand.
2 *the application of anti-inflation policies:* implementation, use, exercise, employment, utilization, operation, enactment.
3 *the argument is clearest in its application to the theatre:* relevance to, bearing on, pertinence to, significance for.
4 *the job takes a great deal of application:* diligence, industriousness, industry, commitment, dedication, devotion, conscientiousness, perseverance, persistence, tenacity, doggedness; concentration, attention, patience; effort, hard work.
5 *a vector graphics application:* program, software, routine.
6 *an application to relieve muscle pain:* ointment, lotion, cream, rub, salve, balm, embrocation, liniment, unguent.

apply verb
1 *we applied for a grant:* put in an application for, make a request for, request, ask for, seek, try to obtain, register for, petition for, bid for.
2 *the Act did not apply to Scotland:* be applicable to, be relevant to, relate to, be pertinent to, pertain to, have a bearing on, concern, affect, involve, refer to, cover, deal with, touch; formal appertain to.
3 *she applied some ointment:* put on, rub in, work in, spread, smear.
4 *a steady pressure should be applied:* exert, administer, implement, use, exercise, employ, utilize, bring to bear.
▫ **apply yourself**
if he applied himself he could be the best in the world: concentrate, work hard, exert yourself, be diligent, be industrious, be assiduous, dedicate yourself, devote yourself, make an effort, do your best, buckle down, persevere, persist; informal put your back in it, knuckle down.

appoint verb
1 *he was appointed chairman:* nominate, name, designate, install as, commission, engage, co-opt; select, choose, elect, vote in.
2 *the arbitrator shall appoint a date for the meeting:* specify, determine, assign; designate, set, fix, arrange, choose, decide on, establish, settle; ordain, prescribe, decree.

appointed adjective
1 *I reported to HQ at the appointed time:* scheduled, arranged, prearranged, specified, agreed, designated, set.
2 *the rooms are beautifully appointed:* furnished, decorated, fitted out, equipped.

appointment noun
1 *I have an appointment at 11 o'clock:* meeting, engagement, interview, consultation, session; date, rendezvous, assignation; commitment, fixture.
2 *the appointment of directors:* nomination, naming, designation, installation, commissioning, engagement, co-option; selection, choosing, election.
3 *he held an appointment at the university:* job, post, position, situation, place, office.

apportion verb *in many households, domestic work is not apportioned equally between partners:* share, divide, allocate, distribute, assign, allot, give out; ration, measure out; split.

apposite adjective *each chapter is prefaced by an apposite quotation:* appropriate, suitable, fitting, apt; relevant, pertinent, to the point, applicable, germane, material, felicitous.
OPPOSITES: inapposite.

appraisal noun
1 *an objective appraisal of the book:* assessment, evaluation, estimation, review, consideration, judgement, rating.
2 *a free insurance appraisal:* valuation, estimate, estimation, quotation.

appraise verb
1 *the two men stepped back to appraise their handiwork:* assess, evaluate, review, consider, judge, gauge, rate; informal size up.
2 *his goods were appraised at £1,800:* value, price, estimate.

> **USAGE**
>
> Do not confuse **appraise** with **apprise**. **Appraise** means 'to assess someone or something', while **apprise** means 'to inform or tell someone' (*I apprised him of the situation*).

appreciable adjective *the decision could have an appreciable effect on interest rates:* considerable, significant, sizeable, marked; perceptible, noticeable, visible.
OPPOSITES: negligible.

appreciate verb
1 *let him know how much you appreciate his skills:* value, treasure, admire, respect, hold in high regard, think highly of.
2 *I'd appreciate your advice:* be grateful for, value, welcome, be thankful for, be appreciative of.
3 *we appreciate the problems:* recognize, acknowledge, realize, know, be aware of, be conscious of, be sensitive to, understand, comprehend.
4 *a home that will appreciate in value:* increase, gain, grow, rise, go up.
OPPOSITES: disparage, depreciate.

appreciation noun
1 *he expressed his appreciation for the work they had done:* gratitude, thanks, gratefulness, thankfulness, recognition.
2 *he has a genuine appreciation of her musical talent:* admiration for, respect for, regard for, high opinion of; enjoyment of.
3 *an appreciation of the value of teamwork:* acknowledgement, recognition, realization, awareness, consciousness,

a

understanding, comprehension.
4 *an appreciation of the professor's work:* review, critique, criticism, critical analysis, assessment, evaluation, judgement, rating.
5 *the appreciation of the dollar against the pound:* increase, gain, growth, rise; inflation.
OPPOSITES: ingratitude, depreciation.

appreciative adjective
1 *children may not seem terribly appreciative at the time:* grateful, thankful, pleased; indebted, in someone's debt.
2 *an appreciative audience egged him on:* pleased, enthusiastic, admiring, responsive.

apprehend verb *police apprehended the thieves not far from the crime scene:* arrest, catch, capture, seize; take into custody, detain, put behind bars; informal nab, pick up, pull in; Brit. informal nick.

apprehension noun
1 *he was filled with apprehension:* anxiety, worry, unease, nervousness, misgivings, disquiet, concern, tension, trepidation, dread, fear, foreboding.
2 *the apprehension of the perpetrator:* arrest, capture, seizure, detention.

apprehensive adjective *I'm a bit apprehensive about seeing her again:* anxious, worried, nervous, uneasy, concerned, agitated, tense, afraid, scared, frightened, fearful.
OPPOSITES: confident.

apprentice noun trainee, learner, probationer, novice, beginner, starter; pupil, student; informal rookie.
OPPOSITES: veteran.

apprise verb *I thought it right to apprise Chris of what had happened:* inform, tell, notify, advise, brief, make aware, enlighten, update; informal fill in, put in the picture.

USAGE

Do not confuse **apprise** with **appraise**. **Apprise** means 'to inform or tell someone' while **appraise** means 'to assess someone or something' (*two independent reviewers appraised the evidence*).

approach verb
1 *a tall, well-built man approached them:* move towards, come/go towards, advance on, draw nearer to, near; close in on, gain on; bear down on.
2 *the trade deficit is approaching £20 million:* border on, verge on, come close to, touch, nudge, near, get on for.
3 *she approached him about leaving his job:* speak to, talk to; make advances to, make overtures to, make a proposal to, sound out, proposition.
4 *we approached the problem in a different way:* tackle, set about, address yourself

to, undertake, embark on, go about, get to grips with.
▷noun
1 *other local councils have adopted a similar approach:* method, procedure, technique, strategy, tactic, course of action, system, means; modus operandi, style, way, manner.
2 *the landowner made an approach to the developer:* proposal, proposition, offer, overture; submission, application, request.
3 *despite the approach of autumn, the weather had been warm:* arrival, advent, coming, appearance; advance.
4 *we plan to improve the northern approach to the station:* access, road, path; way in, entry, entrance.

approachable adjective
1 *the staff are very approachable:* friendly, easy to talk to, accessible, pleasant, agreeable, congenial, affable, cordial, welcoming; communicative, helpful, obliging.
2 *the south landing is approachable by boat:* accessible, attainable, reachable.
OPPOSITES: aloof, inaccessible.

approbation noun *he yearned for popular approbation:* approval, acceptance, appreciation, respect, esteem, admiration, praise, acclaim, congratulations, applause, commendation.
OPPOSITES: criticism.

appropriate adjective *this is an appropriate time to pay tribute to him:* suitable, proper, fitting, apt, right, correct; relevant, pertinent, apposite.
OPPOSITES: inappropriate.
▷verb
1 *the barons appropriated church lands:* seize, commandeer, annex; expropriate, arrogate, sequestrate, sequester; steal, take.
2 *his images have been appropriated by advertisers:* plagiarize, copy; poach, steal; informal rip off.
3 *we are appropriating funds for legal expenses:* allocate, assign, allot, earmark, set aside, devote.

approval noun
1 *their proposals went to the ministry for approval:* acceptance, agreement, consent, assent, permission, leave, sanction, endorsement, ratification, authorization, validation; support, backing; informal the go-ahead, the green light, the OK, the thumbs up.
2 *Lily looked at him with approval | step-parents need to win a child's approval:* approbation, appreciation, favour, liking, admiration, regard, esteem, respect, praise.
OPPOSITES: refusal, disapproval.

approve verb
1 *I do not approve of his methods:* agree with, hold with, subscribe to, recommend, advocate, be in favour of, favour, think

well of, like, appreciate, take kindly to; be pleased with, admire, applaud, praise.
2 *the government approved the proposals:* accept, agree to, consent to, assent to, give your blessing to, rubber-stamp; ratify, sanction, endorse, authorize, validate, pass; support, back; informal give the go-ahead, give the green light, give the OK, give the thumbs-up.
OPPOSITES: disapprove, refuse.

approximate adjective *all measurements are approximate:* estimated, rough, imprecise, inexact, broad, loose; N. Amer. informal ballpark.
OPPOSITES: precise.
▷**verb** *this scenario probably approximates to the truth:* be/come close to, be/come near to, approach, border on, verge on; resemble, be similar to, be not unlike.

approximately adverb *the guided tours last approximately an hour:* roughly, about, around, circa, more or less, in the neighbourhood of, in the region of, of the order of; near to, close to, nearly, almost, approaching; Brit. getting on for.
OPPOSITES: precisely.

approximation noun
1 *the figure is only an approximation:* estimate, estimation, guess, rough calculation; informal guesstimate; N. Amer. informal ballpark figure.
2 *an approximation of reality:* semblance of, resemblance to, likeness to.

a priori adjective *a priori assumptions:* theoretical, deduced, deductive, inferred.
OPPOSITES: empirical.
▷**adverb** *the results cannot be predicted a priori:* theoretically, deductively.

apropos preposition *he was asked a question apropos his resignation:* with reference to, with regard to, with respect to, regarding, concerning, on the subject of, connected with, about, re.

apt adjective
1 *it was a very apt description of how I felt:* suitable, fitting, appropriate, apposite, applicable; Brit. informal spot on.
2 *he is apt to exaggerate:* inclined, given, likely, liable, disposed, predisposed, prone.
3 *she proved an apt pupil:* clever, quick, bright, sharp, intelligent, able, gifted, adept, astute; informal smart.

aptitude noun *he showed a natural aptitude for skiing:* talent, gift, flair, bent, skill, facility, knack, genius; ability, capability, potential, capacity, faculty.

aquatic adjective *aquatic plants:* marine, water, freshwater, saltwater, seawater, sea, oceanic, river.

aqueduct noun conduit, channel, watercourse; bridge.

aquiline adjective *his aquiline nose:* hooked, curved, bent; beak-like.

arbiter noun
1 *he believed Britain could play a major role as arbiter between Moscow and Washington.* See **ARBITRATOR**.
2 *the great arbiter of fashion:* authority, judge, controller; master, expert, pundit.

arbitrary adjective
1 *an arbitrary decision:* random, chance, unpredictable; casual, unmotivated, motiveless, irrational, illogical, groundless, unjustified; capricious.
2 *a country under arbitrary government:* autocratic, dictatorial, authoritarian, autarchic, undemocratic, despotic, tyrannical; absolute, unlimited, uncontrolled.
OPPOSITES: reasoned, democratic.

arbitrate verb *the board has the power to arbitrate in disputes:* adjudicate, pass judgement, judge, referee, umpire; mediate, conciliate, intervene, intercede, settle, decide, resolve.

arbitration noun *the district judge may refer the matter for arbitration:* adjudication, judgement; mediation, conciliation, intervention; settlement.

arbitrator noun *the facts of the case were put to an independent arbitrator:* adjudicator, arbiter, judge; mediator, conciliator, intercessor, go-between.

arc noun curve, arch, crescent, semicircle; curvature, convexity.

arcade noun *a classical arcade:* gallery, colonnade, loggia, portico, cloister.

arcane adjective *the arcane language of criminal law:* mysterious, secret, esoteric, abstruse, recondite, recherché, impenetrable, obscure, opaque; enigmatic.

arch[1] noun *the arch of his spine:* curve, bow, bend, arc, curvature, convexity.
▷**verb** *she arched her eyebrows:* curve, arc; raise.

arch[2] adjective *an arch grin:* mischievous, teasing, knowing, playful, roguish, impish, cheeky, tongue-in-cheek.

arch- combining form *his arch-enemy:* chief, principal, foremost, leading, main, major, prime, premier, greatest; informal number-one.

archaic adjective *the prisons are run on archaic methods:* obsolete, out of date, old-fashioned, outmoded, behind the times, anachronistic, antiquated, superannuated, antediluvian, bygone; ancient, old, extinct, defunct; informal out of the ark.
OPPOSITES: modern.

arched adjective *a great arched ceiling:* vaulted, domed, curved, bowed.

archetypal adjective *Blackpool is the archetypal British seaside resort:* quintessential, classic, prototypical, most typical, representative; model, exemplary,

a

textbook, copybook; stock, stereotypical.
OPPOSITES: atypical.

archetype noun quintessence, essence, representative, model, embodiment; prototype, original, pattern, standard, paradigm; stereotype.

architect noun
1 *the architect of Durham Cathedral:* designer, planner, draughtsman.
2 *the architect of the National Health Service:* originator, creator, founder, father, founding father, author; engineer, inventor, mastermind.

architecture noun
1 *modern architecture:* building design, building style, planning, building, construction.
2 *the architecture of a computer system:* structure, construction, organization, layout, design, build, anatomy, make-up; informal set-up.

> WORD LINKS
> **architectonics** the scientific study of architecture

archive noun
1 *she delved into the family archives:* records, annals, chronicles, accounts; papers, documents, files; history.
2 *the National Sound Archive:* record office, registry, repository; store, cache.
3 *a data archive:* store, cache.
▷ verb *the videos are archived for future use:* file, log, catalogue, document, record, register; store, cache.

arctic adjective *February brought arctic weather conditions:* freezing, wintry, bitterly cold, frozen, icy, glacial, sub-zero; literary gelid.
OPPOSITES: tropical.

ardent adjective *an ardent supporter of the conservative cause:* passionate, fervent, zealous, enthusiastic, keen, eager, avid, committed, dedicated, wholehearted, vehement, fierce.
OPPOSITES: apathetic.

ardour noun *the rebuff did little to dampen his ardour:* passion, fervour, zeal, enthusiasm, eagerness, keenness, vehemence, fire, emotion; dedication.
OPPOSITES: apathy.

arduous adjective *they made an arduous two-day trek across the mountains:* onerous, tiring, exhausting, gruelling, punishing, taxing, difficult, hard, heavy, strenuous, laborious, back-breaking; demanding, tough, challenging, formidable.
OPPOSITES: easy.

area noun
1 *an inner-city area:* district, region, zone, sector, quarter; locality, locale, neighbourhood, parish.

2 *a large area of agricultural land:* tract, belt, expanse, swathe, stretch, patch.
3 *specific areas of scientific knowledge:* field, sphere, discipline, realm, domain, sector, province, territory.
4 *the dining area:* section, space; place, room.
5 *the area of a circle:* expanse, extent, size, scope, compass; dimensions, proportions.

arena noun
1 *an ice-hockey arena:* stadium; ground, field, ring, rink, pitch, court; amphitheatre.
2 *the political arena:* scene, sphere, realm, province, domain, world, sector, forum, territory.

arguable adjective
1 *he had an arguable claim for asylum:* tenable, defensible, sustainable, able to hold water; reasonable, viable, acceptable.
2 *it is arguable whether these routes are worthwhile:* debatable, questionable, open to question, uncertain, moot, doubtful; controversial, contentious.

arguably adverb *she is arguably the greatest female tennis player of all time:* possibly, probably, maybe, perhaps, conceivably.

argue verb
1 *they argued about money:* quarrel, disagree, squabble, fall out, bicker, fight, wrangle, have words, cross swords, lock horns, be at each other's throats; Brit. row.
2 *they argued that the government was to blame:* contend, maintain, hold, claim, assert, make the case, insist, reason, submit, allege.

argument noun
1 *he had an argument with Tony:* quarrel, disagreement, squabble, fight, altercation, dispute, wrangle, clash, contretemps, disputation, falling-out; Brit. row; informal tiff, barney.
2 *he rejected the argument that keeping the facility would be costly:* reasoning, justification, explanation, rationalization; case, defence, vindication; evidence, reasons, grounds.

argumentative adjective *he was argumentative, opinionated, and outspoken:* quarrelsome, truculent, combative, antagonistic, disputatious, cantankerous; belligerent, bellicose, pugnacious; formal captious.

arid adjective
1 *an arid landscape:* dry, dried up, waterless, parched, scorched, baked, thirsty, drought-ridden, desert; barren, infertile.
2 *this town has an arid, empty feel:* dreary, dull, drab, dry, sterile, colourless, uninspiring, flat, boring, uninteresting, lifeless.
OPPOSITES: wet, fertile, vibrant.

arise verb
1 *new problems had arisen:* come to light, become apparent, appear, emerge, crop up, turn up, surface, spring up; occur.
2 *injuries arising from defective products:* result, proceed, follow, ensue, derive, stem, originate; be caused by.

aristocracy noun *members of the aristocracy:* nobility, peerage, gentry, upper class, ruling class, elite, high society; aristocrats, lords, ladies, peers, nobles, noblemen, noblewomen; informal upper crust.

aristocrat noun member of the nobility, member of the aristocracy, nobleman, noblewoman, lord, lady, peer, peeress, grandee; Brit. informal toff, nob.
OPPOSITES: commoner.

aristocratic adjective
1 *an aristocratic family:* noble, titled, upper-class, blue-blooded, high-born, elite; Brit. upmarket; informal upper-crust, top-drawer; Brit. informal posh.
2 *he had a stately, aristocratic manner:* refined, polished, courtly, dignified, decorous, gracious, fine, gentlemanly, ladylike; haughty, proud.

arm¹ noun
1 *an arm of the sea:* inlet, creek, cove, fjord, bay; estuary, firth, strait, sound, channel.
2 *the political arm of the group:* branch, section, department, division, wing, sector, detachment, offshoot, extension.

arm² verb
1 *he armed himself with a revolver:* equip, provide, supply, furnish, issue, fit out.
2 *you have to arm yourself against criticism:* prepare, forearm, make ready, brace, steel, fortify.

armada noun *an armada of forty-five warships:* fleet, flotilla, squadron.

armaments plural noun arms, weapons, weaponry, firearms, guns, ordnance, artillery, munitions, materiel.

armistice noun *an armistice was concluded between the warring countries:* truce, ceasefire, peace, suspension of hostilities.

armour noun protective covering, armour plate; historical chain mail.

armoured adjective *an armoured vehicle:* armour-plated, steel-plated, ironclad; bulletproof, bombproof; reinforced, toughened.

armoury noun arsenal, arms depot, arms cache, ordnance depot, magazine, ammunition dump.

arms plural noun
1 *the illegal export of arms:* weapons, weaponry, firearms, guns, ordnance, artillery, armaments, munitions, materiel.
2 *the family arms:* crest, emblem, coat of arms, heraldic device, insignia, escutcheon, shield.

army noun
1 *the invading army:* armed force, military force, land force, military, soldiery, infantry, militia; troops, soldiers.
2 *an army of tourists:* crowd, swarm, multitude, horde, mob, gang, throng, mass, flock, herd, pack.

> WORD LINKS
> **martial**, **military** relating to war or armed forces

aroma noun *the tantalizing aroma of fresh coffee:* smell, odour, fragrance, scent, perfume, bouquet, nose.

aromatic adjective *an aromatic herb:* fragrant, scented, sweet-smelling, perfumed, fragranced.

around adverb
1 *there were houses scattered around:* on every side, on all sides, throughout, everywhere, all over the place; about, here and there.
2 *he turned around:* in the opposite direction, to face the other way, backwards, to the rear.
3 *there was no one around:* nearby, near, about, close by, at hand, in the vicinity.
▷ preposition
1 *the palazzo is built around a courtyard:* on all sides of, about, encircling, surrounding.
2 *they drove around town:* about, all over, in/to all parts of.
3 *it's around three miles:* approximately, about, round about, circa, roughly, more or less, in the region of, in the neighbourhood of; nearly, close to, approaching; Brit. getting on for.

arouse verb
1 *something about him aroused the guard's suspicion:* rouse, awaken, prompt, cause, bring out, provoke, engender, trigger, stir up, kindle, fire, spark off.
2 *his ability to arouse the masses:* stir up, rouse, galvanize, excite, electrify, stimulate, inspire, move, fire up, whip up, get going, inflame, agitate, goad, incite.
OPPOSITES: allay, pacify.

arraign verb *he was arraigned for murder:* indict, prosecute, put on trial, bring to trial, take to court, lay/file/prefer charges against, summons, cite; accuse of, charge with; US impeach.
OPPOSITES: acquit.

arrange verb
1 *I've arranged a meeting with Howard:* organize, fix up, set up, plan, schedule, coordinate; pencil in; settle on, decide, determine, agree; contrive, engineer.
2 *the catalogue is arranged in alphabetical order:* order, set out, lay out, position,

present, display, exhibit, array; organize, group, sort.
3 *he arranged the piece for a full orchestra:* adapt, set, score, orchestrate.

arrangement noun
1 *how are the arrangements for your trip going?* preparations, plans, provisions; planning, groundwork.
2 *the arrangement of the furniture:* layout, positioning, disposition, order, presentation, display; grouping, organization, alignment.
3 *we had an arrangement:* agreement, deal, understanding, bargain, settlement, pact.
4 *an arrangement of Beethoven's symphonies:* adaptation, orchestration, instrumentation, setting.

array noun *a huge array of cars met our eyes:* range, collection, selection, assortment, diversity, variety; arrangement, line-up, assemblage, formation; display, exhibition, exposition.
▷**verb**
1 *a buffet was arrayed on the table:* arrange, lay out, set out, place, position, range, display; assemble, group, order.
2 *he was arrayed in grey flannel:* dress, clothe, garb, deck out, get up; formal attire.

arrears plural noun *rent arrears:* debts, money owing, outstanding payments, liabilities, dues.
OPPOSITES: credit.
▢in arrears
behind, late, behindhand, overdue, in the red, in debt.

arrest verb
1 *police arrested him for murder:* apprehend, take into custody, take prisoner, detain, put in jail; informal pick up, pull in; Brit. informal nick.
2 *the spread of the disease can be arrested:* stop, halt, check, restrict, limit, inhibit, impede, curb; prevent, obstruct, block, hinder.
OPPOSITES: release, start.
▷**noun**
1 *I have a warrant for your arrest:* detention, apprehension, seizure, capture.
2 *a cardiac arrest:* stoppage, halt.

arresting adjective *an arresting image:* striking, eye-catching, conspicuous, attractive, impressive, imposing, spectacular, dramatic, breathtaking, dazzling, stunning, awe-inspiring; remarkable, outstanding, distinctive.

arrival noun
1 *they awaited Ruth's arrival:* coming, appearance, entrance, entry, approach.
2 *the arrival of democracy:* emergence, appearance, advent, coming, dawn, onset, inauguration, origin, birth.
OPPOSITES: departure.

arrive verb
1 *they arrived just before lunch:* come, turn

up, get here/there, appear, enter, present yourself, make it, materialize; informal show up, roll in/up, show your face.
2 *we eventually arrived at our hotel:* reach, get to, come to, make, gain, end up at; informal wind up at.
3 *they arrived at an agreement:* reach, achieve, attain, gain, accomplish; work out, draw up, put together, strike, settle on; hammer out, thrash out; informal clinch.
4 *the forecast rain arrived around 4 p.m.:* happen, occur, take place, come about; present itself, crop up.
5 *microcomputers arrived at the start of the 1970s:* emerge, appear, be born, come into being, arise.
OPPOSITES: depart, leave.

arrogant adjective *he's arrogant and opinionated:* haughty, conceited, self-important, full of yourself, superior; overbearing, domineering, imperious, pompous, bumptious, overweening, high-handed; proud, immodest, egotistical; informal high and mighty, too big for your boots, big-headed, uppity.
OPPOSITES: modest.

arrow noun
1 *a bow and arrow:* shaft, bolt, dart.
2 *the arrow pointed right:* pointer, indicator, marker, needle.

arsenal noun
1 *Britain's nuclear arsenal:* weapons, weaponry, arms, armaments.
2 *mutineers broke into the arsenal:* armoury, arms depot, arms cache, ordnance depot, magazine, ammunition dump.

arsonist noun incendiary, pyromaniac; Brit. fire-raiser.

art noun *she has had to learn the art of public speaking:* skill, craft, technique, knack, facility, ability.

artful adjective *an artful political ruse:* clever, crafty, cunning, wily, canny, shrewd; scheming, devious, Machiavellian, sly, sneaky, conniving, calculating, designing.

article noun
1 *small household articles:* object, thing, item, artefact, commodity, product.
2 *an article in the local paper:* report, account, story, write-up, feature, item, piece, column, review, commentary.
3 *the crucial article of the treaty:* clause, section, subsection, point, item, paragraph, division, subdivision, part, portion.

articulate adjective *an articulate speaker:* eloquent, fluent, lucid, persuasive, effective, expressive, silver-tongued; coherent, intelligible, comprehensible, understandable.
OPPOSITES: inarticulate.
▷**verb**
1 *they were unable to articulate their emotions:* express, put into words,

communicate, voice, vocalize, state; air, ventilate.
2 *he articulated each word with precision:* pronounce, enunciate, utter, say, speak.

artifice noun *an industry dominated by artifice:* trickery, guile, cunning, artfulness, wiliness, craftiness; deceit, deception, duplicity, chicanery, fraud.

artificial adjective
1 *artificial flowers:* synthetic, fake, faux, imitation, simulated, mock, ersatz, substitute, replica, reproduction; man-made, manufactured; plastic.
2 *she gave an artificial smile:* insincere, feigned, false, unnatural, contrived, put-on, forced, laboured, strained, hollow; informal phoney.
OPPOSITES: natural, genuine.

artillery noun ordnance, big guns, cannons, cannonry.

artisan noun craftsman, craftswoman; skilled worker, journeyman.

artist noun
1 *a Belfast mural artist:* painter, designer; old master.
2 *the surgeon is an artist with the knife:* expert, master, maestro, past master, virtuoso, genius; informal pro, ace; Brit. informal dab hand.

artiste noun entertainer, performer, showman, artist; player, musician, singer, dancer, actor, actress; star.

artistic adjective
1 *he's very artistic:* creative, imaginative, inventive, expressive, sensitive.
2 *artistic designs:* aesthetic, aesthetically pleasing, beautiful, attractive, tasteful, stylish, elegant, exquisite; decorative, ornamental.

artistry noun *all four perform with innate artistry:* creative skill, art, creativity, skill, talent, genius, brilliance, flair, proficiency, virtuosity, finesse, style; craftsmanship, workmanship.

artless adjective *her artless sincerity:* ingenuous, guileless, innocent, naive, childlike; open, sincere, unaffected, natural.

as conjunction
1 *she caught sight of him as he reached the top step:* while, just as, even as, just when, at the time that, at the moment that.
2 *we all felt as Frank did:* in the same way that, the same way; informal like.
3 *do as you're told:* what, that which.
4 *they were free, as the case had not been proved:* because, since, seeing that/as, in view of the fact that, owing to the fact that; informal on account of the fact that.
5 *relatively short distances, as Paris to Lyons:* such as, like, for instance, for example, e.g.

6 *I'm away a lot, as you know:* which, a fact which.
▷ preposition
1 *he was dressed as a police officer:* like, in the guise of, so as to appear to be.
2 *I'm speaking to you as your friend:* in the role of, acting as.
☐ as for/to
concerning, with respect to, on the subject of, in the matter of, as regards, with regard to, regarding, with reference to, re, apropos, vis-à-vis.
☐ as yet
so far, yet, still, up till now, up to now; formal thus far.

ascend verb *she ascended the stairs:* climb, go/come up; mount, scale, conquer; rise, take to the air, take off.
OPPOSITES: descend.

ascendancy noun *the ascendancy of good over evil:* dominance, domination, supremacy, superiority, predominance, primacy, dominion, hegemony, authority, control, command, power, rule, sovereignty, lordship, leadership, influence.
OPPOSITES: subordination.

ascendant noun
☐ in the ascendant
the communist parties of the republics were in the ascendant: on the rise, on the way up, up-and-coming, flourishing, prospering, burgeoning.

ascent noun
1 *the first ascent of the Matterhorn:* climb, scaling, conquest.
2 *a balloon ascent:* rise, climb, launch, take-off, lift-off, blast-off.
3 *the ascent grew steeper:* slope, incline, rise, gradient, inclination.
OPPOSITES: descent, drop.

ascertain verb *we ascertained the exact location of the vehicle:* find out, establish, determine, identify, work out, deduce, discover, learn; verify, confirm; informal figure out.

ascetic adjective *he led an ascetic life of prayer, fasting, and manual labour:* austere, self-denying, abstemious, abstinent, self-disciplined, self-abnegating, puritanical; simple, monastic, celibate, chaste.
OPPOSITES: sybaritic.

ascribe verb *he ascribed Jane's short temper to her upset stomach:* attribute, assign, put down, accredit, impute; blame on, lay at the door of; connect with, associate with.

ash noun cinders, embers, ashes, burnt remains, clinker.

ashamed adjective
1 *she felt ashamed that she had hit him:* sorry, shamefaced, abashed, guilty, contrite, remorseful, repentant, penitent, regretful, rueful, apologetic; sheepish,

a

embarrassed, mortified.
2 *he was ashamed to admit it:* reluctant, loath, unwilling, afraid.
OPPOSITES: proud, pleased.

ashen adjective *his face was ashen:* pale, wan, grey, colourless, pallid, white, waxen, bloodless.

aside adverb
1 *they stood aside:* to one side, to the side, on one side; apart, away, separately.
2 *that aside, he seemed a nice man:* apart, notwithstanding.

asinine adjective *Lydia ignored his asinine remark:* foolish, stupid, idiotic, ridiculous, ludicrous, absurd, brainless, mindless, senseless, nonsensical, fatuous, silly, inane, witless, empty-headed, imbecilic; informal half-witted, dumb, moronic; Brit. informal daft.
OPPOSITES: intelligent, sensible.

ask verb
1 *he asked what time we opened:* enquire, query, want to know.
2 *I asked her about her plans:* question, interrogate, quiz.
3 *they want to ask a few questions:* put, put forward, pose, raise, submit; get an answer to.
4 *don't be afraid to ask for advice:* request, seek; apply, appeal, call, solicit, petition, sue.
5 *she asked him to fetch help:* beg, implore, entreat.
6 *let's ask them to dinner:* invite; summon.
OPPOSITES: answer.

askance adverb *they look askance at anything foreign:* suspiciously, sceptically, cynically, mistrustfully, distrustfully, doubtfully, dubiously; disapprovingly, contemptuously, scornfully, disdainfully.
OPPOSITES: approvingly.

askew adjective *her hat was slightly askew:* crooked, lopsided, tilted, at an angle, skewed, slanted, aslant, awry, out of true, to/on one side, uneven, off-centre, asymmetrical; informal cockeyed, wonky; Brit. informal skew-whiff.
OPPOSITES: straight.

asleep adjective *she was asleep in bed:* sleeping, in a deep sleep, napping, catnapping, dozing, drowsing, slumbering; informal snoozing, dead to the world; humorous in the land of Nod.
OPPOSITES: awake.

aspect noun
1 *the photos depict every aspect of life:* feature, facet, side, characteristic, particular, detail; angle, slant.
2 *his face had a sinister aspect:* appearance, look, air, cast, expression, mien, demeanour; atmosphere, mood, quality, ambience, feeling.
3 *a summer house with a southern aspect:* outlook, view, exposure; situation, position, location.

4 *the front aspect of the hotel:* face, elevation, facade, side.

aspersions plural noun
□ **cast aspersions on**
no one is casting aspersions on you or your officers: criticize, malign, disparage, denigrate, run down, vilify, impugn, belittle, condemn, decry, denounce, pillory; slander, libel, defame, discredit; informal knock, bad-mouth.

asphyxiate verb *they were asphyxiated by the carbon monoxide fumes:* suffocate, choke to death, smother, stifle; throttle, strangle.

aspiration noun *their policies are not sufficiently orientated to the needs and aspirations of the people:* desire, hope, dream, wish, longing, yearning; aim, ambition, goal, target.

aspire verb *other people will aspire to be like you:* aim, have ambitions, desire, wish, want, hope, dream, long, yearn, set your heart on, set your sights on, seek, strive.

aspiring adjective *the theatre is offering aspiring actors the chance to work with a professional cast:* would-be, aspirant, hopeful, budding; potential, prospective, future; ambitious, determined; informal wannabe.

assail verb
1 *the Scots assailed Edward's army from the rear:* attack, assault, set upon/about, fall on; charge, rush, storm.
2 *she was assailed by doubts:* beset, rack, torment, plague, bedevil, dog, trouble, disturb, worry.

assailant noun attacker, mugger, assaulter.

assassin noun murderer, killer, gunman; executioner; informal hit man, hired gun.

assassinate verb *John F. Kennedy was assassinated in 1963:* murder, kill.

assault verb *he pleaded guilty to assaulting a police officer:* attack, hit, strike, punch, beat up, thump, batter; molest; informal lay into, do over, rough up.
▷ noun
1 *the argument was sparked by an assault on a young woman:* attack, act of violence; sexual assault, rape; Brit. grievous bodily harm, GBH, actual bodily harm, ABH.
2 *troops began an assault on the city:* attack, strike, raid, onslaught, offensive, charge, push, thrust, invasion, bombardment, sortie, incursion, blitz, campaign.

assemble verb
1 *a crowd had assembled outside the gate:* gather, collect, get together, congregate, convene, meet, rally; converge on; formal foregather.
2 *he assembled the remaining members of the group:* bring/call together, gather,

collect, round up, marshal, summon, rally, muster, mobilize.
3 *the new machine is being assembled:* construct, build, manufacture, produce, make; put/piece together, set up, erect.
OPPOSITES: disperse, dismantle.

assembly noun
1 *an assembly of dockers and labourers:* gathering, meeting, congregation, convention, rally, convocation; group, body, crowd, throng, company, assemblage; informal get-together.
2 *the labour needed in car assembly:* construction, manufacture, building, fabrication, erection.

assent noun *the charter received the assent of all heads of state at the summit:* agreement, acceptance, approval, approbation, consent, concurrence, acquiescence, compliance; sanction, endorsement, confirmation; permission, leave, blessing.
OPPOSITES: refusal.
▷ verb *he assented to the change:* agree to, accept, approve, consent to, acquiesce in, concur in, give your blessing to; sanction, endorse; formal accede to; informal give the go-ahead to, give the green light to, OK, give the thumbs up to.
OPPOSITES: refuse.

assert verb
1 *the company asserted that the cuts would not affect development:* declare, state, maintain, affirm, insist, announce, proclaim, pronounce; claim, contend, argue, submit, allege.
2 *we find it difficult to assert our rights:* insist on, stand up for, uphold, defend.
□ **assert yourself**
behave confidently, be assertive, put yourself forward, make your presence felt; informal put your foot down.

assertion noun *I questioned his assertion:* declaration, contention, statement, claim, allegation.

assertive adjective *the job may call for assertive behaviour:* confident, self-confident, bold, decisive, assured, self-assured; firm, forceful, authoritative, strong-willed, feisty, determined, commanding, insistent; informal pushy.
OPPOSITES: submissive, timid.

assess verb
1 *the committee must assess the relative importance of the issues:* evaluate, judge, gauge, estimate, appraise, get the measure of, determine, weigh up, analyse, rate; informal size up.
2 *the damage was assessed at £5 billion:* value, calculate, work out, determine, fix, cost, price; estimate.

assessment noun
1 *a teacher's assessment of the pupil's abilities:* evaluation, judgement, estimation,

appraisal, analysis, opinion, rating.
2 *some assessments valued the estate at £2 million:* valuation, calculation, costing; estimate.

asset noun
1 *he sees his age as an asset:* benefit, advantage, good point, strong point, strength, virtue, recommendation, attraction, resource, blessing, boon, merit, bonus; informal plus.
2 *the seizure of all their assets:* property, resources, estate, holdings, capital, money; possessions, effects, valuables, belongings, goods and chattels.
OPPOSITES: liability.

assiduous adjective *there is no doubt that he has been assiduous in his research:* diligent, careful, meticulous, thorough, conscientious, punctilious, painstaking, sedulous, rigorous, particular; persevering.

assign verb
1 *a young doctor was assigned the task:* allocate, give, set; charge with, entrust with.
2 *she was assigned to a new post:* appoint, promote, delegate, commission, post, co-opt; select for, choose for, install in.
3 *we assign large sums of money to travel budgets:* earmark, designate, set aside, reserve, appropriate, allot, allocate, apportion.
4 *he may assign the money to a third party:* transfer, make over, give, pass, hand over/down, convey, consign.

assignation noun *he and Jane arranged a secret assignation in town:* rendezvous, date, appointment, meeting; literary tryst.

assignment noun *I have to finish this assignment tonight:* task, piece of work, project, exercise; undertaking, mission, job, duty.

assimilate verb
1 *patients need time to assimilate the facts:* absorb, take in, understand, grasp, comprehend, digest.
2 *smaller societies have been assimilated into national and global cultures:* subsume, incorporate, absorb, integrate, engulf; co-opt, adopt, embrace, admit.

assist verb
1 *a senior academic will assist him in his work:* help, aid, lend a hand; collaborate with, work with; support, back up; oblige, accommodate.
2 *the exchange rates assisted the firm's expansion:* facilitate, aid, expedite, spur on, promote, boost, benefit, foster, encourage, advance, further, forward.
OPPOSITES: hinder, impede.

assistance noun *they said that they could manage and did not need assistance:* help, aid, support, backing, cooperation, collaboration; a hand, a good turn.
OPPOSITES: hindrance.

a

assistant noun subordinate, second in command, number two, right-hand man/woman, aide, deputy, attendant; helper, auxiliary; junior, apprentice; informal sidekick.

associate verb
1 *I associated wealth with freedom:* link, connect, relate, identify, equate, bracket, set side by side.
2 *she began associating with Marxists:* mix, fraternize, keep company, socialize, go around, rub shoulders, consort, have dealings; informal hobnob, hang out/around.
3 *the firm is associated with a local charity:* affiliate, align, connect, join, attach, team up, be in league, ally.
▷ noun *a business associate:* partner, colleague, co-worker, workmate; comrade, ally, confederate; contact, connection, acquaintance; collaborator; informal, derogatory crony.

associated adjective
1 *salaries and associated costs:* related, connected, linked, correlated; attendant, accompanying, incidental.
2 *they share in the results and net assets of their associated company:* affiliated, connected, related, sister, parent, allied; integrated, amalgamated, syndicated.
OPPOSITES: unrelated.

association noun
1 *a trade association:* alliance, consortium, syndicate, union, league, guild, federation, confederation, conglomerate, cooperative, partnership, coalition.
2 *the association between air pollution and ill health:* relationship, relation, interrelation, connection, interconnection, link; bond, union, tie, attachment, interdependence, affiliation.

assorted adjective *assorted artefacts were recovered from the site:* various, miscellaneous, mixed, varied, varying, diverse, different, heterogeneous, eclectic, sundry, multifarious.

assortment noun *the room was filled with an assortment of clothes:* mixture, collection, variety, array, miscellany, selection, medley, mix, melange, potpourri, diversity, mixed bag; informal ragbag.

assuage verb
1 *the letter assuaged the fears of most members:* relieve, allay, ease, alleviate, soothe, mitigate, palliate; moderate, lessen, diminish, reduce.
2 *an opportunity occurred to assuage her desire for knowledge:* satisfy, appease, gratify, fulfil, indulge, relieve, slake, quench.
OPPOSITES: aggravate, intensify.

assume verb
1 *I assumed he wanted me to keep the book:* presume, suppose, take it, take for granted, take as read, conjecture, surmise, conclude, deduce, infer, reckon,

reason, think, believe, understand, gather.
2 *he assumed a Southern accent:* affect, adopt, impersonate, put on, simulate, feign, fake.
3 *the disease may assume epidemic proportions:* acquire, take on, come to have.
4 *they are to assume more responsibility:* accept, shoulder, bear, undertake, take on/up, manage, handle, deal with.
5 *he assumed control of their finances:* seize, take, take over, appropriate, commandeer, expropriate, hijack, wrest, usurp.

assumed adjective *he may have travelled under an assumed name:* false, fictitious, invented, made-up, fake, bogus, sham, spurious.

assumption noun
1 *we're working on the assumption that the time of death was after midnight:* supposition, presumption, belief, premise, hypothesis, expectation, conjecture, speculation, surmise, guess; conclusion, deduction, inference.
2 *the assumption of power by revolutionaries:* seizure, appropriation, expropriation, commandeering, hijacking.

assurance noun
1 *he went about his business with quiet assurance:* self-confidence, confidence, self-assurance, self-possession, poise, aplomb, level-headedness; calmness, composure, sangfroid, equanimity, nerve; informal cool.
2 *he gave an assurance that work would begin on Monday:* promise, guarantee, undertaking, commitment; word of honour, word, pledge, vow.
3 *life assurance:* insurance, indemnity, indemnification, protection, security, cover.

assure verb
1 *we must assure him of our loyal support:* reassure, convince, satisfy, persuade, tell; promise, pledge, swear, vow.
2 *they guarantee to assure your life:* insure, provide insurance, cover, indemnify.

assured adjective
1 *an extremely assured performance:* confident, self-confident, self-assured, self-possessed, poised, level-headed; calm, composed, imperturbable, unruffled; informal unflappable, together.
2 *an assured supply of weapons:* guaranteed, certain, sure, secure, reliable, dependable; infallible, unfailing; informal sure-fire.

astonish verb *his reply astonished me:* amaze, astound, stagger, surprise, startle, stun, stupefy, daze, take aback, leave open-mouthed, leave aghast, confound, dumbfound; informal flabbergast, bowl over; Brit. informal knock for six.

astonished adjective *Monique looked genuinely astonished:* amazed, astounded, staggered, surprised, startled, stunned, thunderstruck, aghast, taken aback, dumbfounded, dumbstruck, stupefied, dazed; informal flabbergasted; Brit. informal gobsmacked.

astonishing adjective *the film is an astonishing achievement for a new director:* amazing, astounding, staggering, stunning, surprising, breathtaking; remarkable, extraordinary, incredible, unbelievable, phenomenal; informal mind-boggling.

astonishment noun amazement, surprise, incredulity, disbelief, speechlessness, stupefaction.

astound verb *Kate was astounded by his arrogance:* amaze, astonish, stagger, surprise, startle, stun, dumbfound, stupefy, leave open-mouthed, leave aghast, shock; informal flabbergast, bowl over; Brit. informal knock for six.

astounding adjective *the snow-capped summit offers astounding views:* amazing, astonishing, staggering, stunning, surprising, breathtaking, remarkable, extraordinary, incredible, unbelievable, phenomenal; informal mind-boggling.

astray adverb
1 *the shots went astray:* off target, wide of the mark, off course, awry.
2 *the older boys lead him astray:* into wrongdoing, away from the straight and narrow.

astringent adjective *an astringent critique of celebrity culture:* severe, sharp, harsh, acerbic, caustic, mordant, trenchant; scathing, cutting, incisive.

astronomical adjective
1 *astronomical alignments:* planetary, stellar; celestial.
2 (informal) *a club like ours just can't afford the astronomical transfer fees:* huge, enormous, massive, colossal, mammoth, tremendous, vast; extortionate, exorbitant.

astute adjective *he had a reputation as an astute businessman:* shrewd, sharp, canny, acute, quick, clever, intelligent, intuitive, perceptive, insightful, incisive, sagacious, wise, wily; informal on the ball, quick on the uptake, savvy, smart.
OPPOSITES: stupid.

asylum noun
1 *he fled to the Dominican Republic, were he has been granted asylum:* refuge, sanctuary, shelter, safety, protection, security, immunity; a safe haven.
2 (dated) *his father was committed to an asylum:* psychiatric hospital, mental hospital.

asymmetrical adjective *an asymmetrical design:* uneven, unsymmetrical, lopsided; unequal, irregular.

atheism noun *Wordsworth swung from atheism to orthodox Christianity:* non-belief, unbelief, disbelief, lack of faith; scepticism, doubt.

atheist noun *although an atheist he takes an interest in religion:* non-believer, disbeliever, unbeliever, sceptic, doubter.

athlete noun sportsperson, sportsman, sportswoman; Olympian; runner.

athletic adjective
1 *his athletic physique:* muscular, well built, strong, powerful, sinewy, sturdy, strapping, robust, vigorous, brawny, burly; fit, in good shape, in trim; informal sporty, hunky, beefy.
2 *athletic events:* sporting, sports.

atmosphere noun
1 *the gases present in the atmosphere:* air.
2 *the hotel has a relaxed atmosphere:* ambience, air, mood, feel, feeling, character, tone, aura, quality, flavour, tenor; undercurrent; informal vibes.

> WORD LINKS
> **meteorology** the study of atmospheric processes and conditions

atom noun *there wasn't an atom of truth in the allegations:* shred, scrap, grain, ounce, iota, trace, bit, jot, whit, scintilla, fragment, particle; informal smidgen.

atone verb *she was desperate to atone for her actions:* make amends for, make reparation for, make up for, compensate for, pay for, expiate, make good; do penance for.

atrocious adjective
1 *atrocious acts of violence:* brutal, barbaric, barbarous, savage, vicious; wicked, cruel, heinous, monstrous, vile, inhuman, ghastly, horrible; abominable, outrageous, hateful, disgusting, despicable, contemptible, loathsome, odious, abhorrent, sickening, horrifying, unspeakable.
2 *the food was good, but the service was atrocious:* appalling, dreadful, terrible, abysmal, very bad, execrable; informal dire, rotten, lousy; Brit. informal shocking.
OPPOSITES: admirable, superb.

atrocity noun *press reports detailed a number of atrocities:* act of brutality, act of cruelty, abomination, enormity, outrage, horror, monstrosity, obscenity, crime, abuse.

atrophy verb *a muscle that is not used will atrophy:* waste away, become emaciated, wither, shrivel up; deteriorate, degenerate, weaken, decay, decline.
OPPOSITES: strengthen, grow.
▷noun *muscular atrophy:* wasting, emaciation, withering; deterioration, degeneration, weakening, debilitation, enfeeblement, decay, decline.

attach verb
1 *a lead weight is attached to the cord:* fasten, fix, secure, affix, join, connect, link, make fast, tie, bind, chain; stick, glue, fuse;

append.

2 *he attached himself to the Liberal Party:* affiliate, associate, align, ally, unite, integrate, join; be in league with, form an alliance with.

3 *they attached great importance to research:* ascribe, assign, attribute.

4 *the medical officer attached to HQ:* assign, appoint, allocate, second.

OPPOSITES: detach, separate.

attached adjective

1 *I'm not interested in you—I'm attached:* married, engaged, spoken for, involved.

2 *she was very attached to him:* fond of, close to, devoted to.

attachment noun

1 *he has a strong attachment to his mother:* bond with, closeness to, devotion to, loyalty to; fondness for, love for, affection for, feeling for; relationship with.

2 *the shower had a massage attachment:* accessory, fitting, extension, add-on, appendage; Brit. fitment.

3 *he was on attachment from another regiment:* assignment, secondment, transfer.

attack verb

1 *he was attacked by two youths:* assault, set upon, beat up; ambush, pounce on; mug; informal lay into, do over, rough up; Brit. informal duff up.

2 *in February the Germans attacked Verdun:* strike, descend on, storm, rush, charge; raid, bombard, shell, blitz, strafe, fire on; assail.

3 *he attacked the government's defence policy:* criticize, condemn, denounce, censure, pillory, inveigh against, savage, revile, vilify; informal slam, lay into.

4 *they have to attack the problem soon:* address, attend to, deal with, confront, apply yourself to, get to work on, undertake, embark on; informal get stuck into.

5 *the virus attacks the liver:* affect, have an effect on, strike; infect, damage, injure.

OPPOSITES: defend.

▷ **noun**

1 *Armenian troops launched a full-scale attack on hills surrounding the city:* assault, offensive, strike, raid, onslaught, blitz, bombardment, charge, sortie, foray, incursion, invasion.

2 *he delivered a stinging attack on the Prime Minister:* criticism of, condemnation of, denunciation of, censure of, vilification of; tirade against, diatribe against, outburst against.

3 *an asthmatic attack:* fit, seizure, spasm, convulsion, paroxysm, bout.

OPPOSITES: defence.

attacker noun assailant, aggressor; mugger.

attain verb *he had now attained the goals he had set himself in the 1980s:* achieve, accomplish, reach, obtain, gain, secure, get,

win, earn; realize, fulfil.

attainable adjective *a challenging but attainable target:* achievable, within reach, obtainable, accessible, realizable; practicable, workable, realistic, reasonable, viable, feasible, possible.

attainment noun

1 *the attainment of your ambitions:* achievement, accomplishment, realization, fulfilment.

2 *his educational attainments were impressive:* achievement, accomplishment, qualification, skill; success.

attempt verb *I will attempt to answer your question:* try, endeavour, seek, strive, make an effort, venture, undertake; have a go at, try your hand at; formal essay; informal have a crack at, have a shot at, have a stab at.

▷ **noun** *an attempt to put the economy to rights:* effort, endeavour, try, venture; formal essay; informal crack, go, shot, stab

attend verb

1 *they attended a carol service:* be present at, take part in, sit in on; go to, appear at, present yourself at, turn up at, visit; informal show up at, show your face at.

2 *he had important business to attend to:* deal with, take care of, sort out, see to, organize, handle, take charge of, take in hand, manage, tackle.

3 *the wounded were attended to nearby:* care for, look after, tend, treat, nurse, help, aid, assist, minister to, succour.

4 *she had not attended to a word of his sermon:* pay attention to, listen to, concentrate on, take note of, bear in mind, take into consideration, heed.

5 *the queen was attended by an usher:* escort, accompany, chaperone, guide, lead, conduct, usher; assist, help, serve, wait on.

attendance noun

1 *you requested the attendance of a doctor:* presence, appearance.

2 *their gig attendances grew:* audience, turnout, house, gate; crowd, congregation, gathering.

▢ **in attendance**
present, here, there, near, nearby, at hand, available.

attendant noun *a royal attendant:* escort, companion, retainer, aide, lady-in-waiting, equerry, chaperone; servant, bodyguard.

▷ **adjective** *new discoveries and the attendant excitement:* accompanying, associated, related, connected; resultant, resulting, consequent; formal concomitant.

attention noun

1 *the issue needs further attention:* consideration, contemplation, deliberation, thought, study, observation, scrutiny; investigation, action.

2 *he tried to attract the attention of a police officer:* awareness, notice, observation, scrutiny, heed, regard.

3 *he had failed to give the patient adequate medical attention:* care, treatment, aid, help, assistance.
4 *she felt flattered by his attentions:* overtures, approaches, suit; compliments, flattery.

attentive adjective
1 *an attentive audience:* alert, intent, focused, concentrating, heedful.
2 *the most attentive of husbands:* conscientious, considerate, thoughtful, kind, caring, solicitous, obliging, accommodating, gallant, chivalrous; dutiful, responsible.

attest verb *the prints attest to his interest in mythology and the workings of the unconscious:* bear witness to, demonstrate, show, be evidence of, prove, confirm; certify, corroborate, verify, substantiate.

attic noun loft, roof space; garret.

attire (formal) noun *the sober attire of security service personnel:* clothing, clothes, dress, garments, garb, wear, costume; formal apparel; informal gear.
▷**verb** *she was attired in an elaborate evening gown:* dress, clothe, garb, array, deck out, turn out; swathe; informal get up.

attitude noun
1 *you seem ambivalent in your attitude:* view, opinion, viewpoint, outlook, perspective, stance, standpoint, position, inclination, approach; ideas, convictions, feelings, thinking; mood, frame of mind.
2 *an attitude of prayer:* position, posture, pose, stance.

attract verb
1 *the exhibition attracted more than 21,000 visitors:* draw, bring in, win.
2 *the plan attracted widespread criticism:* give rise to, lead to, produce, generate, prompt, cause.
3 *people were attracted by her intoxicating combination of beauty, wit, and charm:* draw, entice, lure, tempt, charm, win over, enchant, captivate, beguile, bewitch, entrance, seduce.
OPPOSITES: repel.

attraction noun
1 *the idea of fame held little attraction for him:* appeal, attractiveness, desirability, seductiveness, allure, magnetism; charisma, charm.
2 *the fair offers sideshows and other attractions:* entertainment, activity, diversion, interest.

attractive adjective
1 *she knew that he found her attractive:* good-looking, beautiful, pretty, handsome, lovely, striking, gorgeous, captivating, beguiling, engaging, charming, enchanting, appealing, delightful, fetching; sexy, desirable, alluring; informal fanciable, tasty, hot; Brit. informal fit; N. Amer.

informal cute; old use comely.
2 *setting up my own business was a very attractive proposition:* appealing, inviting, tempting, interesting; agreeable, pleasing.
OPPOSITES: unattractive.

attribute verb *he attributed the firm's success to the efforts of the managing director:* ascribe to, assign to, accredit to, put down to; blame on, impute to, pin on; connect with, associate with.
▷**noun** *he has all the attributes of a top player:* quality, characteristic, trait, feature, element, aspect, property, sign, hallmark, mark, distinction.

attrition noun
1 *a gradual attrition of the market economy:* wearing down/away, weakening, debilitation, enfeebling, sapping, attenuation.
2 *the skull shows attrition of the edges of the teeth:* abrasion, friction, erosion, corrosion, wearing away; deterioration.

attuned adjective *a royal family more attuned to the feelings of the public:* receptive to, responsive to, aware of, conscious of, familiar with, alive to.

atypical adjective *this trend appears to be atypical:* unusual, abnormal, unrepresentative, exceptional, aberrant, uncommon; out of the ordinary, strange, odd, peculiar, freak.
OPPOSITES: typical.

auburn adjective *her thick auburn hair:* reddish-brown, tawny, chestnut, copper, coppery, Titian, russet.

audacious adjective
1 *an audacious business plan:* bold, daring, fearless, intrepid, brave, courageous, valiant, heroic, plucky; enterprising; daredevil, devil-may-care, reckless, madcap; informal gutsy.
2 *an audacious remark:* impudent, impertinent, insolent, presumptuous, cheeky, discourteous, disrespectful, ill-mannered, rude, brazen, shameless.

audacity noun
1 *he whistled at the sheer audacity of the plan:* boldness, daring, fearlessness, intrepidity, bravery, courage, enterprise; recklessness.
2 *he had the audacity to contradict me:* impudence, impertinence, insolence, cheek, effrontery, temerity, gall, presumption, presumptuousness; informal nerve, brass neck, chutzpah.

audible adjective *her voice was weak and barely audible:* perceptible, discernible, detectable, hearable; clear, distinct, loud.
OPPOSITES: inaudible.

audience noun
1 *the audience applauded:* spectators, listeners, viewers, onlookers, patrons;

a

crowd, throng, congregation, turnout; house, gallery, stalls; Brit. informal punters.
2 *the radio station has a teenage audience:* market, public, following, fans; listenership, viewership.
3 *an audience with the Pope:* meeting, consultation, conference, hearing, reception, interview.

audit noun *an audit of the party accounts:* inspection, examination, scrutiny, investigation, probe, assessment, appraisal, evaluation, review, analysis.
▷ verb *we audited their accounts:* inspect, examine, go through, scrutinize, check, investigate, probe, vet, enquire into, assess, appraise, evaluate, review, analyse, study, survey.

auditorium noun theatre, hall, assembly room; chamber, room.

au fait adjective *he was au fait with all the latest technology:* familiar with, acquainted with, conversant with, up to date with, at home with, in touch with; abreast of, apprised of, well informed about, knowledgeable about, well versed in; informal clued up on.

augment verb *he taught private pupils at home in order to augment his salary:* increase, add to, supplement, boost, build up, enlarge, expand, extend, raise, multiply, swell; improve; Brit. top up; informal up, jack up, bump up.
OPPOSITES: decrease.

augur verb *these successes augur well for the future | the events augur a change in the political landscape:* bode, portend, herald, be a sign of, warn of, foreshadow, be an omen of, presage, indicate, signal, promise, threaten, spell.

august adjective *she was in august company:* distinguished, respected, eminent, venerable, hallowed, illustrious, prestigious, renowned, celebrated, honoured, acclaimed, esteemed, exalted; great, important, lofty, noble; imposing, impressive, stately, grand, dignified.

aura noun *the ceremony retains an aura of mystery:* atmosphere, ambience, air, quality, character, mood, feeling, feel, flavour; emanation, vibration; informal vibe.

auspices plural noun *the talks were to be held under the auspices of the UN:* patronage, aegis, umbrella, protection, care; support, backing, guardianship, trusteeship, guidance, supervision.

auspicious adjective *it was not an auspicious moment to hold an election:* favourable, propitious, promising, good, encouraging; opportune, timely, lucky, fortunate, providential, felicitous, advantageous.
OPPOSITES: inauspicious, unfavourable.

austere adjective
1 *an outwardly austere man:* severe, stern, strict, harsh, steely, flinty, dour, grim, cold, frosty, unemotional, unfriendly; formal, stiff, reserved, aloof, forbidding; grave, solemn, serious, unsmiling, unsympathetic, unforgiving; hard, unyielding, unbending, illiberal.
2 *an austere life:* ascetic, self-denying, self-disciplined, frugal, spartan, puritanical, abstemious, abstinent, self-sacrificing, strict, temperate, sober, simple, restrained; celibate, chaste.
3 *the buildings were austere:* plain, simple, basic, functional, modest, unadorned, unembellished, unfussy, restrained; stark, bleak, bare, clinical.
OPPOSITES: genial, self-indulgent, ornate.

authentic adjective
1 *the letter is now accepted as an authentic document:* genuine, real, bona fide, true; legitimate, lawful, legal, valid; informal the real McCoy, the real thing, pukka, kosher.
2 *an authentic depiction of the situation:* reliable, dependable, trustworthy, authoritative, honest, faithful; accurate, factual, true, truthful; formal veracious.
OPPOSITES: fake, unreliable.

authenticate verb *the evidence will authenticate his claim:* verify, validate, certify, prove, substantiate, corroborate, confirm, support, back up, give credence to.

authenticity noun
1 *the authenticity of the painting:* genuineness, bona fides; legitimacy, legality, validity.
2 *the authenticity of this account:* reliability, dependability, trustworthiness, credibility; accuracy, truth, veracity, fidelity.

author noun
1 *modern Canadian authors:* writer, wordsmith; novelist, dramatist, playwright, poet, essayist, biographer.
2 *the author of the peace plan:* originator, creator, founder, father, architect, designer; instigator, cause, agent.

authoritarian adjective autocratic, dictatorial, despotic, tyrannical, oppressive, undemocratic; disciplinarian, domineering, overbearing, high-handed, peremptory, imperious, strict, rigid, inflexible; informal bossy.
OPPOSITES: democratic, liberal.
▷ noun autocrat, despot, dictator, tyrant; disciplinarian, martinet.

authoritative adjective
1 *they provide clear and authoritative information:* reliable, dependable, trustworthy, sound, authentic, valid, verifiable; accurate.
2 *this is the authoritative study of the subject:* definitive, most reliable, best,

classic; authorized, accredited, recognized, accepted, approved.
3 *his voice was authoritative:* assured, confident, assertive, firm; commanding, masterful, lordly.

authority noun
1 *he had absolute authority over his subordinates:* power, jurisdiction, command, control, charge, dominance, rule, sovereignty, supremacy; influence, sway.
2 *military forces have the legal authority to arrest drug traffickers:* right, power, authorization, mandate, prerogative, licence.
3 *the money was spent without parliamentary authority:* authorization, permission, consent, leave, sanction, licence, dispensation, assent, agreement, approval, endorsement, clearance; informal the go-ahead, the thumbs up, the OK, the green light.
4 *the incident was reported to the authorities:* officials, officialdom; government, administration, establishment; police; informal the powers that be.
5 *he was an authority on the stock market:* expert, specialist, pundit, guru, sage; doyen.

authorization noun *they will require authorization from the Law Society or another regulator:* permission, consent, leave, sanction, licence, dispensation, clearance; assent, agreement, approval, endorsement; authority, right, power, mandate.

authorize verb
1 *the government authorized further aircraft production:* sanction, permit, allow, approve, agree to, consent to, assent to; ratify, endorse; informal give the green light, give the go-ahead, OK, give the thumbs up.
2 *the troops were authorized to use force:* empower, mandate; entitle.
OPPOSITES: forbid.

authorized adjective *authorized financial institutions:* approved, recognized, sanctioned; accredited, licensed, certified; official, lawful, legal, legitimate.
OPPOSITES: unauthorized.

autobiography noun memoirs, life story, personal history.

autocracy noun absolutism, totalitarianism, dictatorship, despotism, tyranny, autarchy.
OPPOSITES: democracy.

autocrat noun absolute ruler, dictator, despot, tyrant.

autocratic adjective
1 *an autocratic government:* despotic, tyrannical, dictatorial, totalitarian, autarchic, oppressive; undemocratic,

one-party.
2 *a man with a reputation for an autocratic management style:* domineering, dictatorial, overbearing, high-handed, peremptory, imperious; harsh, rigid, inflexible.

automatic adjective
1 *automatic garage doors:* mechanized, mechanical, automated, computerized, electronic, robotic; self-activating.
2 *an automatic reaction:* instinctive, involuntary, unconscious, reflex, knee-jerk, instinctual, subconscious; spontaneous, impulsive, unthinking; mechanical; informal gut.
3 *he is the automatic choice for the team:* inevitable, unavoidable, inescapable; certain, definite, undoubted, assured.
OPPOSITES: manual.

autonomous adjective *an autonomous republic:* self-governing, self-ruling, self-determining, independent, sovereign, free.

autonomy noun self-government, self-rule, home rule, self-determination, independence, sovereignty, freedom.

autopsy noun post-mortem, PM, necropsy.

auxiliary adjective
1 *an auxiliary power source:* additional, supplementary, supplemental, extra, reserve, backup, emergency, fallback, other.
2 *auxiliary nursing staff:* ancillary, assistant, support.
▷ noun *a nursing auxiliary:* assistant, helper, ancillary.

avail verb
1 *guests can avail themselves of all the facilities:* use, take advantage of, utilize, employ.
2 (literary) *his arguments cannot avail him now:* help, aid, assist, benefit, profit, be of service.
□ **to no avail**
he begged her to reconsider, but to no avail: in vain, without success, unsuccessfully, fruitlessly, for nothing.

available adjective
1 *refreshments will be available all afternoon:* obtainable, to/at hand, at your disposal, to be had, accessible; on sale; informal on tap.
2 *I'll see if he's available:* free, unoccupied; present, in attendance.

avalanche noun *he received an avalanche of angry emails:* barrage, storm, volley, flood, torrent, deluge, stream.

avant-garde adjective *her tastes were too avant-garde for her contemporaries:* innovative, original, experimental, inventive, ahead of the times, new, modern, advanced, forward-looking, state-of-the-art, trendsetting, pioneering,

progressive, groundbreaking, trailblazing, revolutionary; unfamiliar, unorthodox, unconventional, offbeat; informal edgy, left-field, way-out.
OPPOSITES: conservative.

avarice noun *he had a reputation for ruthlessness and avarice:* greed, acquisitiveness, cupidity, covetousness, rapacity; materialism.
OPPOSITES: generosity.

avenge verb *he vowed to avenge their murders:* take revenge for, take vengeance for, exact retribution for, repay.

avenue noun
1 *tree-lined avenues:* road, street, drive, parade, thoroughfare, boulevard.
2 *three possible avenues of research are open to us:* line, route, path; method, approach.

average noun
1 *the proportion of over-60s is above the EU average of 19 per cent:* mean, median.
2 *underground water reserves are below average for this time of year:* the norm, the standard.
▷ adjective
1 *the average temperature in May:* mean, median.
2 *an average day's filming starts at 7 a.m. and extends beyond 7 p.m.:* ordinary, standard, usual, normal, typical, regular.
3 *a very average director making very average movies:* mediocre, undistinguished, ordinary, middle-of-the-road, unexceptional, unremarkable, unmemorable, indifferent, pedestrian, lacklustre, forgettable, amateurish, second-rate; informal so-so, fair-to-middling.
OPPOSITES: exceptional, outstanding.
□ on average
generally, usually, ordinarily, normally, as a rule, typically; overall, by and large, on the whole.

averse adjective
1 *he's not averse to change:* opposed to, against, resistant to, antipathetic to, hostile to, ill-disposed to/towards; informal anti.
2 *she is not averse to expressing her opinions:* disinclined to, reluctant to, unwilling to, loath to.
OPPOSITES: keen.

> **USAGE**
>
> Do not confuse **averse** with **adverse**. **Averse** is typically used with 'to' and means 'very unwilling to'. **Adverse** means 'harmful' or 'unfavourable' (*the adverse publicity caused tourists to stay away from the area*).

aversion noun *their deep-seated aversion to the use of force:* dislike of, antipathy to, distaste for, abhorrence of, hatred of, loathing of, detestation of, hostility towards; reluctance, disinclination.
OPPOSITES: liking.

avert verb
1 *she averted her head:* turn aside, turn away.
2 *talks failed to avert a rail strike:* prevent, avoid, stave off, ward off, forestall, preclude.

avid adjective *an avid reader of science fiction:* keen, eager, enthusiastic, ardent, passionate, zealous; devoted, dedicated, wholehearted, earnest.
OPPOSITES: apathetic.

avoid verb
1 *avoid crowded places with poor ventilation:* keep away from, stay away from, give a wide berth to, fight shy of.
2 *he is trying to avoid his responsibilities:* evade, shirk, dodge, sidestep, escape, run away from; informal duck, wriggle out of, get out of, cop out of.
3 *she swerved to avoid a head-on collision:* prevent, avert, circumvent.
4 *you've been avoiding me all evening:* evade, stay away from, keep your distance from, hide from; ignore.
5 *you should avoid alcohol:* refrain from, abstain from, desist from, eschew.
OPPOSITES: confront.

avowed adjective *she's an avowed Marxist:* self-confessed, self-declared, acknowledged, admitted; open, overt.

await verb
1 *Peter was awaiting news:* wait for, expect, anticipate.
2 *many dangers await them:* be in store for, lie ahead of, lie in wait for, be waiting for.

awake verb
1 *she awoke early the following morning:* wake, wake up, awaken, stir, come to, come round.
2 *the alarm awoke him at 7.30:* wake, wake up, awaken, rouse, arouse.
3 *they finally awoke to the extent of the problem:* realize, become aware of, become conscious of.
4 *the words of the song awoke memories of her childhood:* awaken, arouse, stir up, trigger, revive.
▷ adjective
1 *she was still awake:* wakeful, sleepless, restless, restive.
2 *too few are awake to the dangers:* aware of, conscious of, mindful of, alert to; formal cognizant of.
OPPOSITES: asleep.

awaken verb
1 *I awakened early | the jolt awakened her.* See AWAKE senses 1, 2.
2 *he had awakened strong emotions in her:* arouse, rouse, engender, evoke, trigger, stir up, stimulate, kindle.

award verb *the society awarded him a silver medal:* give, grant, accord, assign; confer on, bestow on, present to, endow with, decorate with.
▷ noun
1 *an award for high-quality service:* prize,

trophy, medal, decoration; reward; informal gong.
2 *a libel award:* payment, settlement, compensation.
3 *the Arts Council gave him an award of £1,500:* grant, scholarship, endowment; Brit. bursary.
4 *the award of an honorary doctorate:* conferral, conferment, bestowal, presentation.

aware adjective
1 *she is aware of the dangers:* conscious of, mindful of, informed about, acquainted with, familiar with, alive to, alert to; formal cognizant of; informal wise to.
2 *we need to be more environmentally aware:* knowledgeable, enlightened, well informed, au fait; informal clued up; Brit. informal switched-on.
OPPOSITES: ignorant.

awareness noun consciousness, recognition, realization; understanding, grasp, appreciation, knowledge, insight; familiarity; formal cognizance.

awash adjective
1 *the road was awash:* flooded, under water, submerged.
2 *the city was awash with journalists:* inundated, flooded, swamped, teeming, overflowing, overrun; informal knee-deep in.

awe noun *the sight filled me with awe:* wonder, wonderment; admiration, reverence, respect; dread, fear.

awe-inspiring adjective. See AWESOME.

awesome adjective *an awesome achievement:* breathtaking, awe-inspiring, magnificent, marvellous, amazing, stunning, stupendous, staggering, imposing, impressive; formidable, spectacular; informal mind-blowing.
OPPOSITES: unimpressive.

awestruck adjective *she was too awestruck by her surroundings to reply:* amazed, awed, lost for words, open-mouthed; reverential; terrified, afraid, fearful.

awful adjective
1 *the place smelled awful:* disgusting, nasty, terrible, dreadful, ghastly, horrible, vile, foul, revolting, repulsive, repugnant, odious, obnoxious, frightful, sickening, nauseating; informal gross.
2 *an awful book:* dreadful, terrible, atrocious, appalling, abysmal, execrable; inadequate, inferior, substandard, lamentable, woeful; informal rotten, lousy, dire, poxy; Brit. informal duff, rubbish.
3 *an awful accident:* serious, grave, bad, terrible, dreadful.
4 *you look awful—go and lie down:* ill, unwell, sick, queasy, nauseous; Brit. peaky, off colour, poorly; informal rough; Brit. informal grotty, ropy.
5 *I felt awful for getting so angry:*

remorseful, guilty, ashamed, contrite, sorry, regretful, repentant, self-reproachful.
OPPOSITES: wonderful.

awkward adjective
1 *the box was awkward to carry:* difficult, tricky; cumbersome, unwieldy; Brit. informal fiddly.
2 *I'm sorry to call at such an awkward time:* inconvenient, difficult, unsuitable, inappropriate, inopportune, unseasonable.
3 *he had put her in a very awkward position:* embarrassing, uncomfortable, unpleasant, unwelcome, delicate, difficult, tricky, problematic, problematical; humiliating, compromising.
4 *she felt awkward alone with him:* uncomfortable, uneasy, tense, nervous, edgy; self-conscious, embarrassed.
5 *she was tall, skinny, and awkward in her movements:* clumsy, ungainly, uncoordinated, graceless, inelegant, gauche, gawky, wooden, stiff; unskilful, maladroit, inept; Brit. informal all fingers and thumbs.
6 (Brit.) *you're being damned awkward:* unreasonable, uncooperative, unhelpful, disobliging, difficult, obstructive; contrary, perverse; stubborn, obstinate; formal refractory; Brit. informal bloody-minded, bolshie.
OPPOSITES: easy, convenient, graceful, cooperative.

awning noun canopy, shade, sunshade, shelter, cover; Brit. blind.

awry adjective
1 *something was awry:* amiss, wrong; informal up.
2 *his wig looked awry:* askew, crooked, lopsided, tilted, skewed, to one side, off-centre, uneven; informal cockeyed; Brit. informal skew-whiff, wonky.
OPPOSITES: straight.

axe noun hatchet, cleaver, tomahawk, adze; Brit. chopper; historical battleaxe.
▷ verb
1 *the show was axed:* cancel, withdraw, drop, discontinue, terminate, end, scrap; informal ditch, pull the plug on.
2 *500 staff were axed:* dismiss, make redundant, lay off, let go, discharge, get rid of; informal sack, fire, give someone the sack; Brit. informal give someone their cards.

axiom noun accepted truth, general truth, dictum, truism; maxim, adage, aphorism; rare apophthegm.

axis noun
1 *the earth revolves on its axis:* centre line, central line.
2 *the Anglo-American axis:* alliance, coalition, bloc, union, confederation, confederacy, league.

axle noun shaft, spindle, rod, pivot.

azure adjective sky-blue, bright blue, blue.

Bb

babble verb

1 *she babbled away, ignoring the look on his face:* prattle, chatter, jabber, rattle on, gabble, go on, run on, ramble, burble, twitter, blather; informal yak, yatter, yammer; Brit. informal witter, rabbit, chunter, natter, waffle.
2 *just out of sight, a brook babbled gently:* burble, murmur, gurgle, tinkle; literary purl.

▷**noun** *a stream of continuous and incomprehensible babble:* prattle, gabble, chatter, jabber; Brit. informal waffle.

babel noun *I stood, silent amid the babel of discordant voices:* clamour, din, racket, tumult, uproar, hubbub; babble, babbling, shouting, yelling, screaming; Brit. row; Brit. informal hullabaloo.

baby noun *the baby started to cry:* infant, child; Medicine neonate; Scottish & N. English bairn; literary babe, babe in arms.

▷**adjective** *baby carrots:* miniature, mini, little, small; small-scale, scaled-down, toy, pocket; Scottish wee; informal teeny; Brit. informal titchy, tiddly.
OPPOSITES: giant.

> **WORD LINKS**
> **infantile** relating to or affecting babies

babyish adjective *she's grown out of that babyish habit:* childish, immature, infantile; juvenile, puerile.
OPPOSITES: mature.

back noun

1 *she broke her back in three places:* spine, backbone, spinal column, vertebral column.
2 *the back of the house was in the shade:* rear; Nautical stern.
3 *get to the back of the queue:* end, tail end, rear end, tail.
4 *a few notes were written on the back of an envelope:* reverse, other side; informal flip side.
OPPOSITES: front, head, face.

▷**adverb**

1 *he pushed his chair back and got to his feet:* backwards, behind you, to your rear, rearwards; away.
2 *a few months back she visited Chicago:* ago, earlier, previously, before, in the past.
OPPOSITES: forward.

▷**verb**

1 *the scheme was backed by the English Tourist Board:* sponsor, finance, fund, subsidize, underwrite, support.
2 *most people backed the idea of reform:* support, endorse, sanction, approve of, give your blessing to, favour, advocate, promote, uphold, champion; vote for, ally yourself with, stand behind, side with, be on the side of, defend; second; informal throw your weight behind.
3 *he backed Helter Skelter at 33–1:* bet on, gamble on, put money on.
4 *he took a step towards her and she backed away:* draw back, step back, move backwards, reverse, back off, pull back, retreat, withdraw, give ground, backtrack.
OPPOSITES: oppose, advance.

▷**adjective**

1 *the back seats were all taken:* rear, rearmost, hind, hindmost; Anatomy posterior.
2 *I thumbed through some back copies of 'Homes and Gardens':* past, old, previous, earlier, former, out of date.
OPPOSITES: front.

▢ **back down**
after three days of strike action, the council was forced to back down: give in, concede defeat, surrender, yield, submit, climb down, concede, reconsider; backtrack, back-pedal.

▢ **back out of**
if he backs out of the deal they'll sue him: renege on, go back on, withdraw from, pull out of, fail to honour, abandon, default on, back-pedal on.

▢ **back something up**
he makes a startling claim, then he backs it up with some evidence: substantiate, corroborate, confirm, support, bear out, endorse, bolster, reinforce, lend weight to.

▢ **back someone up**
if you need anyone to back you up I will be only too happy: support, stand by, give your support to, side with, be on someone's side, take someone's side, take someone's part; vouch for.

> **WORD LINKS**
> **dorsal**, **lumbar** relating to the back
> **supine** lying on your back

backbiting noun *all the backbiting and prejudice have shattered her confidence:* malicious talk, slander, abuse, character assassination, disparagement, denigration; slurs, aspersions; informal bitching, mud-slinging, bad-mouthing.

backbone noun
1 *the rib-eye muscle lies on each side of the cow's backbone:* spine, spinal column, vertebral column, vertebrae; back; Anatomy dorsum, rachis.
2 *small businesses are the backbone of many rural communities:* mainstay, cornerstone, foundation, keystone, buttress.
3 *he has enough backbone to see us through this difficult period:* strength of character, firmness of purpose, resolution, resolve, grit, determination, fortitude, mettle, spirit, nerve, courage; informal guts.

back-breaking adjective *six months of back-breaking labour:* gruelling, arduous, strenuous, onerous, punishing, demanding, exacting, exhausting, taxing; informal killing.
OPPOSITES: easy.

backer noun *£3 million was provided by the project's backers:* sponsor, investor, underwriter, financier, patron, benefactor; informal angel.

backfire verb *Bernard's plan backfired on him:* rebound, boomerang, come back; fail, miscarry, go wrong; informal blow up in someone's face.

background noun
1 *the sculpture is set against a background of high buildings:* backdrop, backcloth, surroundings, setting, scene.
2 *a mix of students from many different backgrounds:* social circumstances, environment, milieu, class, culture, tradition; upbringing.
3 *her nursing background was an advantage:* experience, record, history, past, training, education, grounding, knowledge.
4 *an understanding of the political background of the dispute:* circumstances, context, conditions, situation, environment, milieu, scene, scenario.
OPPOSITES: foreground.
▫ **in the background** *this tactic allows him to remain in the background:* behind the scenes, out of the public eye, out of the spotlight, out of the limelight, backstage; inconspicuous, unobtrusive, unnoticed.

backhanded adjective *a backhanded compliment:* ambiguous, indirect, oblique, equivocal; double-edged, two-edged, barbed; tongue-in-cheek.

backing noun
1 *he has the backing of his colleagues:* support, approval, endorsement, sanction, blessing, help, assistance, aid.
2 *you can't always get that sort of financial backing:* sponsorship, funding, patronage; money, investment, funds, finance; grant, contribution, subsidy.
3 *uptempo classical music played against a disco backing:* accompaniment; harmony.

backlash noun *several large rallies indicated a growing backlash against right-wing violence:* adverse reaction, counterblast, comeback; retaliation.

backlog noun *they took on extra staff to clear the backlog of work:* accumulation, logjam, pile-up.

back-pedal verb *the government has back-pedalled on its plans:* change your mind, backtrack, back down, climb down, do an about-face, do a U-turn, renege, go back on, back out of, withdraw, take back, default on; Brit. do an about-turn.

backslide verb *many things can cause slimmers to backslide:* relapse, lapse, regress, retrogress, weaken, lose your resolve, give in to temptation, go astray.

backup noun *there is always backup available:* help, support, assistance, aid; reinforcements, reserves, additional resources.

backward adjective
1 *he left without a backward glance:* rearward, to/towards the rear, to/towards the back, behind one; reverse.
2 *the court decision was a backward step for the UK:* retrograde, retrogressive, regressive, for the worse, in the wrong direction, downhill, negative.
3 *a war-torn, backward country:* underdeveloped, undeveloped.
OPPOSITES: forward, advanced.
▷ **adverb** *the car rolled slowly backward.* See **BACKWARDS**.

backwards adverb
1 *he walked backwards off the stage:* towards the rear, rearwards, backward.
2 *count backwards from twenty to ten:* in reverse, in reverse order.
OPPOSITES: forwards.

backwash noun
1 *there was a lot of backwash and the sea was hard to get out of:* wake, wash, slipstream, backflow.
2 *the backwash from the Cuban Missile Crisis:* repercussions, reverberations, after-effects, aftermath, fallout.

bacteria plural noun microorganisms, microbes, germs, bacilli, pathogens; informal bugs.

WORD LINKS
bacteriology the study of bacteria

bad adjective
1 *bad workmanship | a bad film:* substandard, poor, inferior, second-rate, second-class, unsatisfactory, inadequate,

unacceptable, not up to scratch, deficient, defective, imperfect, faulty, shoddy; informal lousy; Brit. informal duff.
2 *pesticides are bad for the environment | the bad effects of alcohol and tobacco:* harmful, damaging, detrimental, destructive, injurious, hurtful, inimical, ruinous, pernicious; adverse, unfavourable, disadvantageous, negative; unhealthy, unwholesome.
3 *I'm such a bad cook:* incompetent, poor, inept, unskilful, unskilled, inexpert; informal useless.
4 *I'm afraid I've got some bad news | I've had a bad day:* unpleasant, disagreeable, unwelcome, unfortunate; terrible, dreadful, awful, grim, distressing, upsetting, traumatic.
5 *a bad accident had closed both lanes of the A74:* severe, serious, grave, critical, acute; formal grievous.
6 *it was a bad time to arrive:* inopportune, inauspicious, unfortunate, inappropriate, unsuitable, untoward; awkward, inconvenient, embarrassing.
7 *we debated whether human nature is good or bad | he will suffer for his bad deeds:* wicked, sinful, immoral, evil, corrupt; criminal, villainous, nefarious, iniquitous, dishonest, dishonourable, unscrupulous, unprincipled
8 *you bad girl!* naughty, badly behaved, disobedient, wayward, wilful, self-willed, defiant, unruly, insubordinate, undisciplined.
9 *if you feel bad, stay in bed:* unwell, sick, poorly, indisposed; out of sorts, not yourself, under/below par; queasy, nauseous, nauseated; Brit. peaky, off colour; informal under the weather, lousy, rough; Brit. informal ropy.
10 *a bad knee:* injured, wounded, diseased, damaged, stiff, sore; Brit. informal gammy, knackered.
11 *I felt bad about leaving them:* guilty, conscience-stricken, remorseful, guilt-ridden, ashamed, uncomfortable.
12 *sex, violence, and bad language:* offensive, vulgar, crude, foul, obscene, rude, coarse, dirty, filthy, indecent; blasphemous, profane.
13 *the meat's gone bad:* rotten, off, decayed, decomposed, decomposing, putrid, mouldy; sour, rancid, rank, unfit for human consumption.
14 *all these bad cheques cost us money:* invalid, worthless; counterfeit, fake, false, bogus, fraudulent; informal phoney, dud.
OPPOSITES: good, beneficial.
□ **not bad**
500 points is not bad for a beginner: all right, adequate, good enough, fine, reasonable, fair, decent, average, tolerable, acceptable, passable, middling, moderate; informal OK, so-so.

badge noun
1 *a red plastic name badge:* pin, brooch.
2 *for some consultants, a waiting list was seen as a badge of status:* sign, symbol, indication, signal, mark; hallmark, trademark.

badger verb *his family were badgering an airport employee for news of his flight:* pester, harass, bother, plague, torment, hound, nag, chivvy, keep on at, go on at; informal hassle, bug.

badly adverb
1 *a series of badly written, boring articles:* poorly, incompetently, ineptly, inexpertly, inefficiently, unsatisfactorily, inadequately, shoddily.
2 *try not to think badly of me:* unfavourably, ill, critically, disapprovingly.
3 *the mosque was badly damaged in an earthquake:* severely, seriously, gravely; formal grievously.
4 *I was missing him badly and couldn't wait to get home:* desperately, sorely, intensely, very much, greatly, exceedingly.
OPPOSITES: well.

bad-tempered adjective irritable, irascible, tetchy, testy, grumpy, grouchy, crotchety, in a bad mood, cantankerous, curmudgeonly, ill-tempered, peevish, having got out of bed on the wrong side, cross, fractious, pettish, crabby; informal snappish; Brit. informal shirty, stroppy, ratty.
OPPOSITES: good-tempered, affable.

baffle verb *his recent team selections and tactical changes have baffled fans:* perplex, puzzle, bewilder, mystify, bemuse, confuse, confound; informal flummox, faze, stump, fox.

baffled adjective *she saw his baffled expression and smiled:* puzzled, bewildered, confused, perplexed, mystified, bemused; informal flummoxed, fazed.

baffling adjective *I found his explanation baffling:* puzzling, bewildering, perplexing, mystifying, confusing, bemusing, unclear; mysterious, inexplicable, incomprehensible, unfathomable, insoluble, impenetrable, cryptic.
OPPOSITES: clear, comprehensible.

bag noun
1 *I searched in my bag for my lipstick:* handbag, shoulder bag, clutch bag; N. Amer. pocketbook, purse.
2 *she began to unpack her bags:* suitcase, case, valise, portmanteau, holdall, grip; backpack, rucksack, knapsack, haversack, kitbag, duffel bag; satchel; (**bags**) luggage, baggage.

baggage noun luggage, suitcases, cases, bags.

baggy adjective *she wore scruffy jeans and a baggy T-shirt:* loose-fitting, loose, roomy, generously cut, full, ample, voluminous,

billowing; oversized, shapeless, ill-fitting, tent-like, sack-like.
OPPOSITES: tight.

bail verb
◻ **bail out**
1 *the pilot bailed out:* eject, parachute to safety.
2 *if you don't bail out now, it could well be the sack:* leave, quit, get out, withdraw, move on, make a move.
◻ **bail someone/something out**
the state will not bail out loss-making enterprises: rescue, save, relieve; finance, help, assist, aid; informal save someone's bacon/neck/skin.

bait noun
1 *the fish are ready to bite as soon as they see the bait:* lure, fly, worm.
2 *she was the bait to lure him into a trap:* enticement, lure, snare, trap, attraction, draw, magnet, incentive, temptation, inducement, carrot.
▷**verb** *Joe enjoyed baiting his brothers and Adam was easy prey:* taunt, tease, goad, pick on, torment, persecute, plague, harass, hound; informal needle; Brit. informal wind up.

bake verb
1 *bake the fish for 15–20 minutes:* cook, oven-bake, roast.
2 *the earth was baked by the burning sun:* scorch, burn, sear, parch, dry up, desiccate.

balance noun
1 *I tripped and lost my balance:* stability, equilibrium; footing.
2 *the importance of political balance in broadcasting:* fairness, justice, impartiality; parity, equity, equilibrium, evenness, even-handedness, equality, equivalence; correspondence, symmetry.
3 *we need to maintain the proper balance of nutrients in the soil:* proportion, ratio, combination, mix, mixture; interaction, relationship.
4 *I will pay you the balance on Thursday:* remainder, outstanding amount, rest, difference.
OPPOSITES: instability.
▷**verb**
1 *she balanced the vase on a pile of books:* steady, stabilize, level; support, rest, position, perch.
2 *we manage forests in a way that balances profitability and environmental sustainability:* combine, bring together, offset, even out/up; juggle.
3 *romantic music that will balance the harshness of the story:* counterbalance, offset, even out/up, counteract, compensate for, make up for.
4 *you need to balance the costs against the benefits:* weigh, weigh up, compare, evaluate, consider, assess, appraise, judge.
◻ **hang in the balance**
the fate of the firm hung in the balance: be uncertain, be undetermined, be unsettled, be unresolved, be unsure, be in limbo, be

up in the air, be at a turning point, be at a critical stage, be at a crisis point.
◻ **on balance**
on balance, people still perform better than machines: overall, all in all, all things considered, taking everything into consideration/account, by and large, on average.

balanced adjective
1 *a balanced point of view:* fair, unbiased, unprejudiced, objective, impartial, even-handed, dispassionate, equitable, just.
2 *you need to eat a balanced diet:* mixed, varied; healthy, sensible.

balcony noun
1 *the balcony of the villa faced south:* veranda, loggia; terrace, patio.
2 *the applause from the balcony was deafening:* gallery, upper circle; informal the gods.

bald adjective
1 *his bald head glistened with sweat:* hairless, smooth; shaven, shaved.
2 *a bald patch on the front tyre:* bare, worn, smooth.
3 *a bald statement of intent:* plain, simple, unadorned, unvarnished, stark, brutal, harsh, uncompromising; blunt, direct, forthright, straight, straightforward, frank, upfront.
OPPOSITES: hairy, vague.

baldness noun hair loss, hairlessness; Medicine alopecia.

bale[1] noun *a bale of hay:* bundle, pack, package, parcel.

bale[2] verb
◻ **bale out.** See BAIL.

baleful adjective
1 *Bill shot a baleful glance in her direction:* menacing, threatening, unfriendly, hostile, antagonistic, vindictive, malevolent, malicious, malign, sinister, evil.
2 *the baleful effects of global warming:* harmful, damaging, destructive, dangerous, injurious, detrimental, deleterious, pernicious, deadly.

balk verb. See BAULK.

ball[1] noun *a ball of clay:* sphere, globe, orb, spheroid.

ball[2] noun *a fancy-dress ball:* dance, party, dinner dance, masked ball; N. Amer. prom.

ballad noun song, folk song, shanty; poem, tale.

balloon noun hot-air balloon, barrage balloon; airship, dirigible, Zeppelin; informal blimp.
▷**verb**
1 *her long skirt ballooned in the wind:* billow, swell, puff out/up, bulge out, fill out.
2 *the company's debts have ballooned:* increase rapidly, soar, rocket, shoot up,

b

b

escalate, mount, surge, spiral; informal go through the roof, skyrocket.

ballot noun *the results of the ballot will be known on Thursday:* vote, poll, election, referendum, plebiscite, show of hands.

ballyhoo noun (informal) *after all the ballyhoo, the film was a flop:* publicity, build-up, advertising, promotion, marketing, puffery; fuss, excitement; informal hype.

balm noun
1 *a skin balm for use after shaving:* lotion, cream, moisturizer, salve, emollient, unguent; ointment, liniment, embrocation, rub, gel.
2 *the music is a balm for tired minds and troubled souls:* relief, comfort, ease; consolation, solace.

balmy adjective *the balmy days of late summer | a balmy breeze:* warm, summery, mild, fine, pleasant, clement; gentle, calm, tranquil, soft.

ban verb
1 *smoking has been banned in public places:* prohibit, forbid, veto, proscribe, disallow, bar, outlaw, make illegal, embargo, block, stop.
2 *he was banned from international athletics:* exclude, bar, debar; banish.
OPPOSITES: permit.
▷noun *a ban on smoking:* prohibition, veto, embargo, bar, moratorium, proscription, interdict, interdiction; injunction.

banal adjective *it's a simple tune with banal lyrics:* trite, hackneyed, clichéd, platitudinous, stock, conventional, stereotyped, overused, overdone, overworked, stale, worn out, tired, threadbare, hoary, unimaginative, unoriginal, uninteresting, dull, boring, vapid, commonplace; informal old hat, corny.
OPPOSITES: original.

band¹ noun *a long, narrow band of cloud:* strip, stripe, streak, line, bar, belt, swathe; technical striation.

band² noun
1 *the band played a few old favourite numbers:* group, ensemble, orchestra; informal outfit, combo.
2 *a band of volunteer drivers provides transport:* group, company, party, crew, body, team, troop, gang; association, society, club, circle, fellowship, league; clique, set, coterie.
▷verb *local people banded together and bought the mill:* join together, team up, join forces, pool resources, club together, get together; unite.

bandage noun *she had a bandage on her foot:* dressing, covering, compress, tourniquet; Brit. plaster.
▷verb *she bandaged my knee:* bind, bind up, dress, cover, wrap, strap up.

bandit noun *I'm a target for every bandit and assassin out there:* robber, thief, raider, mugger; outlaw, looter, marauder; literary brigand; dated desperado.

bandy¹ adjective *he had buck teeth and bandy legs:* bowed, curved, bent; bow-legged, bandy-legged.

bandy² verb
1 *a lot of facts and figures were bandied about:* spread about/around, pass on, discuss, mention, repeat, rumour; Brit. put about.
2 *I'm not here to bandy words with you:* exchange, swap, trade.

bane noun *critics are seen as the bane of writers' lives:* curse, plague, scourge, blight, thorn in your flesh/side.

bang noun
1 *the door slammed with a loud bang:* crash, clang, crack, clunk, thud, thump; boom, blast, report, explosion, detonation.
2 *he got a nasty bang on the head:* blow, knock, thump, bump, hit, smack, crack; informal bash, whack, thwack.
▷verb *he banged the table with his fist:* hit, strike, beat, thump, hammer, knock, rap, pound, thud, punch, smack, crack, slap; informal bash, whack, thwack.

bangle noun bracelet, wristlet, anklet, armlet.

banish verb
1 *Weber was eventually banished on a trumped-up charge:* exile, expel, deport, send away, eject; cast out, evict, throw out, exclude, shut out, ban; historical transport.
2 *I banished all thought of illness from my mind:* dispel, dismiss, drive away, chase away, shut out, get rid of.

banister noun handrail, railing, rail; baluster; balustrade.

bank¹ noun
1 *the banks of Lake Michigan:* edge, side; embankment, levee, border, verge, margin.
2 *we lay on a grassy bank | a bank of snow:* mound, ridge, hillock, hummock, knoll; slope, rise, incline; mass, accumulation, pile, heap, drift.
3 *he gestured towards a bank of switches:* panel, row, line, array, tier, group, series, set.
▷verb *Mike's aircraft banked sharply to the left:* tilt, lean, tip, slant, incline, angle, slope, pitch, dip, cant.

> WORD LINKS
> **riparian** relating to a river bank

bank² noun
1 *banks have raised their interest rates:* financial institution, merchant bank, savings bank, finance company.
2 *the dip in donations is hitting blood banks | a bank of knowledge:* store, reserve, stockpile, pool, cache, fund;

archive, storehouse, reservoir, repository, depository.
▷**verb** *I banked the money straight away:* deposit, pay in.
□**bank on**
investors are banking on a stock market recovery: rely on, depend on, count on, plan on, reckon on; anticipate, expect; be confident of, be sure of, pin your hopes/faith on.

bankrupt adjective

1 *the company was declared bankrupt:* insolvent, failed, ruined; in debt, in the red, in arrears; Brit. in administration, in receivership; informal bust, gone to the wall, broke.
2 *the government was bankrupt of ideas:* bereft, devoid, empty; completely lacking, without.
OPPOSITES: solvent.
▷**verb** *the strike nearly bankrupted the union:* ruin, bring someone to their knees, wipe out, break, finish, destroy.

bankruptcy noun

insolvency, liquidation, failure, financial ruin; Brit. administration, receivership.
OPPOSITES: solvency.

banner noun

1 *students waved banners:* placard, sign, poster, notice.
2 *the Star Spangled Banner:* flag, standard, ensign.

banquet noun

feast, dinner; informal spread, blowout; Brit. informal slap-up meal.

banter noun

a brief exchange of harmless banter: repartee, conversation, wordplay; teasing, badinage, raillery; chat.
▷**verb** *sightseers were bantering with the guards:* joke; chat; informal josh, wisecrack.

baptism noun

1 (Christianity) *the baptism ceremony:* christening, naming.
2 *this event constituted his baptism as a politician:* initiation, debut, introduction, inauguration, launch; rite of passage.

bar noun

1 *an iron bar:* rod, pole, stick, stake, shaft, rail, spar, strut, crosspiece, beam, girder, batten.
2 *a bar of chocolate:* block, slab, cake, tablet, brick, wedge; ingot.
3 *the EU may view the licence fee as a bar to free competition:* barrier, obstacle, obstruction, hurdle, impediment, hindrance.
▷**verb**
1 *they've barred the door:* bolt, lock, fasten, secure, block, barricade.
2 *he was barred from seeking re-election:* prohibit, debar, preclude, forbid, ban; exclude, keep out; obstruct, hinder, block.
▷**preposition** *everyone bar me.* See EXCEPT preposition.

barb noun

1 *the hook has a nasty barb:* spike, prong, thorn, needle, prickle, spine, spur, quill.
2 *celebrity interviews full of barbs and innuendo:* insult, jibe, cutting remark, slight, sneer, taunt; informal dig, put-down.

barbarian noun

these people are barbarians: savage, animal, brute, beast; boor, thug, lout, vandal, hoodlum, hooligan; Brit. informal yobbo, yob.

barbaric adjective

twenty innocent people were killed in the barbaric attack: brutal, barbarous, savage, vicious, cruel, wicked, ruthless, merciless, villainous, murderous, heinous, monstrous, vile, inhuman.

barbarity noun

words are insufficient to describe the barbarity of this act: brutality, cruelty, barbarism, barbarousness, savagery, viciousness, wickedness, inhumanity.

barbarous adjective. See BARBARIC.

barbed adjective

his scripts were littered with barbed jokes: hurtful, wounding, cutting, stinging, scathing, bitter, acid, caustic, vitriolic, pointed, sharp, mean, spiteful, malicious, nasty, cruel, vicious, unkind, snide; informal bitchy, catty.

bare adjective

1 *the dust clung to her bare legs:* naked, exposed, unclothed, uncovered, stripped, nude.
2 *the room was as bare as a prison cell:* empty, unfurnished; unadorned, unembellished, undecorated, plain, austere, spartan.
3 *a little hill, bare of shrubbery but covered with grass:* empty, devoid, bereft; without, lacking, free from/of.
4 *paint was applied to the bare metal:* uncovered, exposed, stripped; naked.
5 *the report limited itself to stating the bare facts:* basic, essential, fundamental, plain, straightforward, simple, pure, stark, bald, cold, hard, brutal, harsh.
OPPOSITES: dressed.
▷**verb** *I opened my shirt and bared my chest:* uncover, strip, lay bare, expose, reveal.
OPPOSITES: cover.

USAGE

Do not confuse **bare** with **bear**. **Bare** is an adjective meaning 'naked' or a verb meaning 'to uncover'. The main meaning of the verb **bear** is 'to carry', as in *he was bearing a tray of champagne glasses*.

barefaced adjective

that's a barefaced lie and you know it: flagrant, blatant, glaring, obvious, undisguised, naked; shameless, unabashed, unashamed, brazen.

barely adverb

we can barely afford this month's rent: hardly, scarcely, just, only just; narrowly, by the skin of your teeth, by a hair's breadth; informal by a whisker.

b

bargain noun
1 *how can I be certain that you'll keep your side of the bargain?* agreement, arrangement, understanding, deal; contract, pact; pledge, promise.
2 *the coat was a real bargain at £20:* good buy, cheap buy; informal snip, steal, giveaway.
▷ **verb** *sellers bargained with foreign visitors in fluent English:* haggle, negotiate, discuss terms, hold talks, deal; barter.
▷ **adjective** *most of the stuff is available at bargain prices:* low, reduced, cheap; informal rock-bottom.
□ **bargain for**
the hot-headed Frenchman got more than he bargained for: expect, anticipate, be prepared for, allow for, plan for, reckon with, take into account/consideration, contemplate, imagine, envisage, foresee, predict.
□ **into the bargain**
you pay no charges and earn extra interest into the bargain: also, as well, in addition, additionally, besides, on top of that, over and above that, to boot, for good measure.

barge noun canal boat, lighter; Brit. narrowboat, wherry.
▷ **verb** *he barged his way through the crowd:* push, shove, thrust, elbow, shoulder.
□ **barge in**
I'm sorry to barge in on your conversation: burst in, break in, butt in, cut in, interrupt; intrude, encroach; informal horn in.

bark verb
1 *the dogs barked at her:* woof, yap, yelp; howl, bay.
2 *'Okay, everyone outside!' he barked:* shout, yell, roar, bellow, thunder; snap; informal holler.

barn noun outbuilding, shed, outhouse, shelter; stable, stall; Brit. byre; old use grange.

baron noun *a right-wing British media baron:* magnate, tycoon, mogul, captain of industry.

baroque adjective *a complex world of fantasy and baroque imagery:* ornate, fancy, elaborate, extravagant, fussy, busy, ostentatious, showy.

barrack verb (Brit. & Austral./NZ) *the prime minister was barracked by angry firefighters:* jeer, heckle, shout at/down; interrupt, boo, hiss.

barracks plural noun garrison, camp, depot, billet, quarters, fort.

barrage noun
1 *an overnight artillery barrage killed at least four people:* bombardment; shelling; salvo, volley.
2 *Drummond faces a barrage of criticism following his appointment:* torrent, stream, storm, deluge, flood, tide, avalanche, hail, blaze.

barrel noun *red wine may be matured in oak barrels:* cask, keg, butt, vat, drum.

> WORD LINKS
> **cooper** a person who makes barrels

barren adjective *the land was rocky and barren:* unproductive, infertile, unfruitful, sterile, arid, dry, desert, waterless; empty, bleak, featureless, deserted, lifeless, dead.
OPPOSITES: fertile.

barricade noun *barricades went up and the riot police moved in:* barrier, roadblock, blockade; obstacle, obstruction.
▷ **verb** *I barricaded the door, but they broke it down:* seal up, close up, block off, shut off/up.

barrier noun
1 *barriers will be erected to prevent them moving on to the land:* fence, railing, barricade, blockade, roadblock.
2 *a barrier to international trade:* obstacle, obstruction, hurdle, stumbling block, bar, block, impediment, hindrance.

barring preposition *barring St John's, they have beaten everyone:* except for, with the exception of, bar, discounting, apart from, but for, other than, aside from, excluding, save for.

barrister noun counsel, Queen's Counsel, QC, lawyer; Scottish advocate; N. Amer. attorney; informal brief; (**barristers**) Brit. the Bar.

barter verb
1 *T-shirts were bartered for bread:* trade, swap, exchange.
2 *she bartered tirelessly with the carpet sellers:* haggle, bargain, negotiate.

base noun
1 *the base of the tower:* foundations, bottom, foot; support, stand, pedestal, plinth.
2 *she used existing data as the base for her study:* basis, foundation, starting point, point of departure.
3 *the Kharkov base had become a hive of activity:* headquarters, camp, site, station, settlement, post, centre.
▷ **verb**
1 *he based his argument on government statistics | the film is based on a novel by Pat Conroy:* construct, build, found, form, ground; use as a basis; (**be based on**) derive from, spring from, stem from, originate in, have its origin in.
2 *the company was based in London:* locate, situate, position, station, site, establish.

baseless adjective *she's already said that those rumours are baseless:* groundless, unfounded, ill-founded, without foundation; unsubstantiated, unproven, unsupported, uncorroborated, unconfirmed, unverified, unattested; unjustified, unwarranted; speculative, conjectural; unsound, unreliable, spurious, specious, trumped up, fabricated, untrue.

basement noun cellar; vault, crypt, undercroft; Brit. lower ground floor.

bashful adjective *many men are bashful about discussing their feelings:* shy, self-conscious, embarrassed, diffident, inhibited, insecure, unconfident; reticent, reluctant, hesitant, apprehensive, nervous.
OPPOSITES: bold, confident.

basic adjective
1 *certain basic rules must be obeyed | the basic principles of structuralism:* fundamental, essential, primary, elementary, principal, cardinal, quintessential, intrinsic, central, pivotal, critical, key, focal; vital, necessary, indispensable.
2 *although a bit basic, the apartments are all spotlessly clean:* plain, simple, unsophisticated, modest; unadorned, undecorated, without frills; spartan, stark, severe, austere, limited, rudimentary, minimal; rough and ready, crude, makeshift.
OPPOSITES: secondary, elaborate.

basically adverb *their conclusions were basically very similar:* fundamentally, essentially, in essence; at heart, at bottom; on the whole, by and large, substantially.

basics plural noun *the basics of computer programming:* fundamentals, essentials, rudiments, principles, first principles, foundations, preliminaries; essence, basis, core; informal nitty-gritty, brass tacks, nuts and bolts.

basin noun bowl, dish, pan.

basis noun
1 *trust is the basis for a good working relationship | the basis of a new trade agreement:* foundation, support, base; starting point, point of departure, beginning, premise, fundamental point/principle, principal constituent, main ingredient, cornerstone, core, heart, essence.
2 *the information used as the basis for her decision:* rationale, reasoning; reason, grounds, justification.
3 *he was employed on a part-time basis:* footing, status, position; arrangement, system, method.

bask verb
1 *cats basked on the stone window sills:* laze, lie, lounge, relax, sprawl, loll; sunbathe, sun yourself.
2 *he basked in the glory of his Olympic victory:* revel, delight, luxuriate, wallow, rejoice, glory; enjoy, relish, savour, lap up.

basket noun hamper, pannier, creel, punnet, trug.

bass adjective low, deep, low-pitched; resonant, sonorous, rumbling, booming, resounding; baritone.
OPPOSITES: high.

bastion noun *Augusta has always been a bastion of Republicanism:* stronghold, bulwark, defender, supporter, guard, protection, protector, defence, prop, mainstay.

batch noun group, quantity, lot, bunch, set, collection; bundle, pack; consignment, shipment.

bath noun
1 *he lay in the bath:* bathtub, hot tub, whirlpool, sauna, steam bath; trademark jacuzzi; informal tub.
2 *she had a bath, then got ready:* wash, soak, dip; shower.

bathe verb
1 *she bathed and dressed:* wash, bath, shower.
2 *they bathed his wounds in warm water:* clean, wash, rinse, wipe, soak.
3 *it is not safe for children to bathe here:* swim, go swimming, take a dip.

baton noun
1 *the conductor raised his baton:* stick, rod.
2 *he was hit by a police baton:* truncheon, club, cosh, cudgel, bludgeon, stick, mace.

battalion noun force, contingent, regiment, brigade, division, squadron, squad, company, section, detachment, corps.

batter verb *her attackers battered her about the head with baseball bats:* beat, hit, strike, pound, belabour, thrash, thump; informal lay into.

battered adjective *a battered old van:* shabby, worn out, falling to pieces, falling apart, dilapidated, rickety, ramshackle, the worse for wear, on its last legs.

battery noun
1 *you need to recharge the battery:* cell, accumulator.
2 *the cabinet housed a battery of fluorescent tubes:* array, set, bank, group, row, line, line-up, collection.
3 *I was subjected to a battery of medical tests:* series, sequence, string, succession, range.

battle noun
1 *the battle lasted for several hours:* fight, conflict, clash, struggle, skirmish, engagement, fray; fighting, warfare, combat, action, hostilities.
2 *a political battle over the future shape of Europe | a takeover battle:* conflict, clash, contest, struggle, dispute; war, campaign, crusade.
▷verb
1 *conservation groups battled to save the house from demolition:* fight, struggle, strive, work, campaign, lobby; war, feud.
2 *the company was battling lawsuits alleging copyright infringement:* contest, combat, contend with, resist, withstand, stand up to, confront.

battle cry noun *the battle cry of the feminist movement:* slogan, motto, watchword, catchphrase, rallying cry; mantra.

battlement noun parapet, rampart, wall; crenellations.

bauble noun trinket, knick-knack, ornament, gewgaw, bibelot.

baulk verb *he baulked at such a drastic solution:* be unwilling to accept, draw the line at, jib at, be reluctant to accept; resist, refuse to accept, shrink from, recoil from, demur from.

bawdy adjective *they dance and sing and make bawdy jokes:* ribald, risqué, racy, rude, spicy, earthy, suggestive, titillating, naughty, indecent, indelicate; euphemistic adult; informal blue, raunchy.

bawl verb
1 *'Come on!' he bawled:* shout, yell, roar, bellow, screech, scream, shriek, howl, bark, trumpet, thunder; informal holler.
2 *the children continued to bawl:* cry, sob, weep, wail, whine, howl; Scottish informal greet.
▷noun *he addressed every class in a terrifying bawl:* shout, yell, roar, bellow, screech, scream.
OPPOSITES: whisper.

bay[1] noun *we had a beautiful view across the bay:* cove, inlet, gulf, bight, firth, basin.

bay[2] noun *the satellite was finally released from the shuttle's cargo bay:* compartment, area; space, cavity, recess; hold, room; deck.

bay[3] verb
1 *we ran for the car, dogs baying at our heels:* howl, bark, yelp, cry, roar.
2 *the crowd bayed for an encore:* clamour, shout, call, yell, scream, shriek, roar; demand.
□ **at bay**
troops kept the horrified onlookers at bay: at a distance, away, off, at arm's length.

bayonet noun *he was stabbed by a man armed with a bayonet:* sword, knife; blade.
▷verb *some prisoners were bayoneted by the guards:* stab, knife, run through, spear.

bazaar noun
1 *the bazaars and cafes of Cairo:* market, market place, souk.
2 *we all helped with the bazaars and fund-raising:* fete, fair, jumble sale, bring-and-buy sale, car boot sale; fund-raiser.

beach noun *a sandy beach lapped by the warm ocean:* shore, seashore, seaside, coast, coastline, seaboard, water's edge; sands, lido; technical littoral; literary strand.
▷verb
1 *they beached the boat and walked up to the house:* land, ground, run aground, run ashore.
2 *65 dolphins have been beached on Cornish shores so far this year:* ground, strand, maroon, wash up/ashore.

beached adjective
1 *rows of beached fishing boats lay along the shore:* grounded; aground, ashore.
2 *she lay sprawled on the bed like a beached whale:* stranded, marooned, high and dry, stuck.

beacon noun
1 *the blue flare of a navigation beacon shone out:* signal, light, flare, fire; marker, sign.
2 *a satellite beacon:* transmitter, aerial, mast.

bead noun *a bead of sweat ran down the side of his face:* droplet, drop, blob, globule.

beaker noun cup, tumbler, glass, mug.

beam noun
1 *the two bells hung from a stout oak beam:* joist, lintel, rafter; spar, girder, timber, plank; support, strut; transom.
2 *a beam of light from the window lit up the path:* ray, shaft, stream, streak, pencil, finger; flash, gleam, glow, glimmer, glint, flare.
▷verb
1 *the message is beamed worldwide by satellite:* broadcast, transmit, relay, send/put out, disseminate; direct, aim.
2 *the sun's rays beamed down:* shine, burn, glare; gleam.
3 *he beamed broadly and shook my hand:* grin, smile; informal be all smiles.

bear[1] verb
1 *Bill arrived, bearing a large picnic hamper:* carry, bring, convey, take; informal tote.
2 *the bag clearly bore his name:* display, exhibit, be marked with, show, carry, have.
3 *the bridge was unable to bear the weight:* support, carry, hold, sustain, take.
4 *the company will bear most of the cost:* take responsibility for, assume, accept, shoulder, absorb.
5 *such a solution does not bear close scrutiny:* withstand, stand up to, stand, take, sustain.
6 *she had borne a grudge against him for years:* harbour, nurse, foster, entertain, cherish.
7 *she bore the pain stoically | I can't bear smoky pubs:* endure, tolerate, put up with, stand, cope with, abide, stomach, support; informal hack.
8 *the antelope bears one calf each year:* give birth to, deliver, be delivered of, have, produce.
9 *a shrub that bears waxy yellow berries:* produce, yield, grow, provide, supply, have.
10 *bear left at the junction:* veer, turn, fork.
□ **bear down on**
a large woman, obviously angry, was bearing down on us: approach, advance on, close in on, move in on, converge on.

□ **bear fruit**
it would be many years before the scheme would bear fruit: **yield results**, succeed, pay dividends, be successful, be effective, be profitable, work; informal pay off.

□ **bear something in mind**
please bear in mind that these plans may be revised: **take into account**, take into consideration, remember, consider, allow for, make allowances for.

□ **bear on**
points of view which bear on the issue of taxation: **be relevant to**, be pertinent to, pertain to, relate to, have a bearing on, have relevance to, apply to; formal appertain to.

□ **bear something out**
this assumption is not borne out by any evidence: **confirm**, corroborate, substantiate, support, justify, warrant, vindicate, uphold, endorse, prove, verify.

□ **bear up**
they were trying to bear up, but it was hard: **remain cheerful**, grin and bear it; cope, manage, get by, muddle through.

□ **bear with**
please bear with me while I explain the details: **be patient with**, show forbearance towards, make allowances for, put up with.

□ **bear witness/testimony to**
these ruined churches bear witness to the island's turbulent past: **testify to**, be evidence of, be proof of, attest to, evidence, prove; demonstrate, show, establish, indicate, reveal; formal bespeak.

USAGE

Do not confuse **bear** with **bare**. The chief meaning of the verb **bear** is 'to carry', while **bare** is both an adjective meaning 'naked' (*her bare legs*), and a verb meaning 'to uncover' (*he bared his chest*).

bear² noun

WORD LINKS
ursine relating to or resembling bears

bearable adjective *the physical pain was just about bearable:* **tolerable**, endurable, supportable.

bearer noun
1 *all regiments include a standard bearer:* **carrier**, porter.
2 *I'm sorry to be the bearer of bad news:* **messenger**, agent, conveyor, carrier, bringer.
3 *the cheque should be crossed and made payable to the bearer:* **holder**, possessor, owner.

bearing noun
1 *he was a man with a rather military bearing:* **posture**, stance; carriage, gait; Brit. deportment; formal comportment.
2 *there was something majestic about his bearing:* **demeanour**, manner, air, aspect, attitude, behaviour, mien, presence, style.
3 *the case has no bearing on the matter in hand:* **relevance to**, relation to, pertinence

to, relationship with, connection with, application to; influence on.
4 *continue on a bearing of 190 degrees for another 50m:* **direction**, orientation, course, trajectory, heading, tack, path, line.
5 (**bearings**) *I lost my bearings in the forest:* **orientation**, sense of direction, whereabouts, location, position.

beast noun
1 *this beast was believed to be the offspring of a panther and a camel:* **animal**, creature; N. Amer. informal critter.
2 *you filthy beast:* **brute**, monster, devil, fiend; ogre, savage.

beat verb
1 *he ran away from home after his father beat him:* **hit**, strike, punch, batter, thump, club, hammer, thrash, pound, pummel, slap; assault, attack, abuse; informal wallop, belt, bash, whack, clout, clobber, give someone a hiding.
2 *the waves beat against the cliffs:* **break on/against**, dash against, lash, strike; lap, wash against, splash against.
3 *South Korea beat Italy:* **defeat**, conquer, win against, get the better of, vanquish, trounce, rout, overpower, overcome, subdue; informal thrash.
4 *he beat the previous record by over five seconds:* **surpass**, exceed, better, improve on, go one better than, eclipse, top, trump, cap.
5 *her heart was beating furiously:* **pulsate**, pulse, palpitate, vibrate, throb; pump, pound, thump, thud, hammer, drum; pitter-patter.
6 *the bird beat its wings against the bars:* **flap**, flutter, thresh, thrash.
7 *beat the cream into the rest of the mixture:* **whisk**, mix, blend, whip.
8 *the metal is beaten into a narrow strip:* **hammer**, forge, form, shape, mould, work, stamp, fashion, model.

▷ **noun**
1 *music with a strong beat:* **rhythm**, pulse, cadence; stress, accent.
2 *he felt the beat of her heart against his chest:* **pulse**, pulsation, vibration, throb, palpitation; pounding, thump, thud, hammering, drumming; pit-a-pat.
3 *a community policeman on his inner-city beat:* **circuit**, round, route, way.

□ **beat someone/something off**
he managed to beat off his attackers | the company has beaten off competition from all over the UK: **repel**, fight off, fend off, stave off, repulse, drive away/back, force back, beat back, push back, put to flight.

□ **beat someone up**
four youths beat him up and stole his watch: **assault**, attack, mug; informal rough up, lay into; Brit. informal duff up.

beatific adjective *Adam looked up, a beatific smile on his face:* **rapturous**, joyful, ecstatic, blissful, seraphic, serene, happy, beaming.

b

beautiful adjective attractive, pretty, good-looking, lovely, delightful, gorgeous, stunning, striking, ravishing, glamorous; desirable, alluring, sexy; charming, appealing, enchanting, bewitching, captivating, beguiling; graceful, elegant, exquisite, magnificent; aesthetic, artistic; Scottish & N. English bonny; informal easy on the eye, tasty, hot; Brit. informal fit; old use comely, fair.
OPPOSITES: ugly.

beautify verb *considerable effort has been made to beautify the exterior of the building:* adorn, embellish, decorate, ornament, enhance, improve, smarten, prettify, glamorize, spruce up, deck out; informal do up, tart up.

beauty noun
1 *I was struck by her beauty | the beauty of the surroundings:* attractiveness, prettiness, good looks, loveliness; charm, appeal, allure; grace, elegance, exquisiteness, splendour, magnificence.
2 *the 21-year-old beauty already has a string of achievements to her name:* beautiful woman, belle, vision, Venus, goddess, English rose; informal looker, stunner, bombshell.
3 *the beauty of this plan is its simplicity:* advantage, attraction, strength, virtue, merit, selling point, good thing, strong point, benefit; boon, blessing.
OPPOSITES: ugliness, drawback.

beaver verb
□ **beaver away** (informal) *other members of the team beavered away at the report:* work hard, toil; persevere with, press on with, plough on with; informal slave away, slog away, plod away/on, keep your nose to the grindstone, stick at, soldier on with.

becalmed adjective motionless, still, at a standstill, at a halt, unmoving, stuck.

because conjunction *it's hard to get hold of her because she's always on the move:* since, as, in view of the fact that, owing to the fact that, seeing that.
□ **because of**
he was forced to pull out of the championship because of an injury: on account of, as a result of, as a consequence of, owing to, due to; thanks to, by/in virtue of; formal by reason of.

beckon verb
1 *the guard beckoned to him:* gesture, signal, wave, gesticulate, motion.
2 *rows of sunbeds beckon you to unwind beside the pool:* invite, tempt, coax, lure, charm, attract, draw, call.

become verb
1 *she became depressed and started drinking:* grow, get, turn, come to be.
2 *the child will become an adult:* grow into, turn into, develop into, change into.
3 *he became Foreign Secretary:* be

appointed, be nominated, be elected, be made.
4 *she wears a violet robe which becomes her well:* suit, flatter, look good on; set off, show to advantage; informal do something for.
□ **become of**
what has become of her? happen to, be the fate of; literary befall, betide.

becoming adjective *the dress looked very becoming:* flattering, fetching; attractive, lovely, pretty; stylish, elegant, chic.

bed noun
1 *I lay on the bed, staring at the ceiling:* couch, bunk; Brit. divan.
2 *a bed of tulips:* patch, plot, border, strip.
3 *before the mould is made, the figures are laid on a bed of clay:* base, foundation, substructure, substratum; layer.
4 *the bed of the stream:* bottom, floor.
□ **go to bed**
after supper I went to bed: retire, call it a day; informal hit the sack, turn in.

bedeck verb *the town was bedecked with flags:* decorate, adorn, ornament, embellish, trim, deck, dress up, trick out; swathe, wreathe, festoon.

bedevil verb *the system has been bedevilled by technical problems:* beset, plague, dog, curse, afflict, assail, beleaguer, rack, oppress.

bedlam noun *as he was led in, there was bedlam in the courtroom:* uproar, pandemonium, commotion, mayhem, confusion, disorder, chaos, anarchy, lawlessness; furore, upheaval, hubbub, hurly-burly, turmoil, riot, ruckus, rumpus, tumult; informal ructions; Brit. informal hullabaloo.
OPPOSITES: calm.

bedraggled adjective *he looked rather bedraggled | I ran a comb through my bedraggled hair:* dishevelled, untidy, unkempt, scruffy; wet, sodden; tousled, disarranged, messy, tangled.
OPPOSITES: neat.

bedridden adjective *she was bedridden for two months:* confined to bed, immobilized; informal laid up, flat on your back.

bedrock noun *in all civilized countries, the bedrock of democracy is the justice system:* core, basis, base, foundation, cornerstone, roots, heart, backbone, principle, essence.

beef (informal) noun *I have no beef about people earning an honest living:* complaint, criticism, objection, cavil, quibble, grievance, grumble, grouse; informal gripe, moan, whinge.
▷ verb *the security budget includes money to beef up airport security:* toughen up, strengthen, build up, reinforce, consolidate, improve.

beefy adjective (informal) *a big, beefy man in a Harley Davidson T-shirt:* muscular,

strapping, well built, brawny, burly, sturdy, hulking, robust, solid, strong, powerful, husky, heavy, hefty.
OPPOSITES: puny.

befall verb (literary) *this is the latest tragedy to befall young people travelling in Australia:* happen to, overtake, come upon, be visited on.

befitting adjective *he couldn't have chosen a more befitting slogan:* appropriate, apt, fit, suitable, suited, proper, right.

before preposition
1 *he'd had a quick drink before going out:* prior to, previous to, earlier than, preparatory to, in preparation for, preliminary to, in anticipation of, in expectation of; in advance of, ahead of, leading up to, on the eve of.
2 *he appeared before the magistrate on Tuesday morning:* in front of, in the presence of, in the sight of.
3 *these men are loyal to God before anything else:* in preference to, rather than, sooner than.
OPPOSITES: after.
▷adverb
1 *he had lied under oath before and would do so again:* previously, before now/then, until now/then, up to now/then; earlier, formerly, hitherto, in the past, in days gone by.
2 *a small party went on before to set up camp:* ahead, in front, in advance.
OPPOSITES: behind.

> WORD LINKS
> **pre-**, **ante-** forming words meaning 'before in time, place, order, etc.', such as *prearranged* ('arranged in advance') and *antenatal* ('before birth')

beforehand adverb *rooms must be booked beforehand:* in advance, in readiness, ahead of time; before, before now/then, earlier, previously, already.
OPPOSITES: afterwards.

befriend verb *I only made things worse for myself by befriending him:* make friends with, get to know, take someone under your wing.

befuddled adjective *Nathan's words finally penetrated her befuddled mind:* confused, muddled, addled, bewildered, disorientated, all at sea, fazed, perplexed; dazed, stupefied, groggy, muzzy, foggy, fuzzy; informal woozy.
OPPOSITES: clear.

beg verb
1 *we begged for more time:* ask for, plead for, appeal for, call for, sue for, seek, press for.
2 *he begged her not to go:* implore, entreat, plead with, appeal to, pray to, importune; ask, call on, petition; literary beseech.
3 *he was reduced to begging on the streets:*

ask for money; informal sponge, cadge, scrounge.

beget verb *violence begets violence:* cause, give rise to, lead to, result in, bring about, create, produce, generate, engender, spawn, occasion, bring on, precipitate, prompt, provoke, kindle, trigger, spark off, stir up, whip up, induce, inspire.

beggar noun *if you stop on the street for a moment, the beggars tug at your arms:* tramp, vagrant; informal scrounger, sponger, freeloader; Brit. informal dosser.

begin verb
1 *we began work first thing in the morning:* start, commence, set about, go about, embark on, launch into, get down to, take up; initiate, set in motion, institute, inaugurate, get ahead with; informal get cracking on, get going on.
2 *he began the meeting by asking the participants to introduce themselves:* open, lead off, get under way, get going, get off the ground, start, start off, commence; informal start the ball rolling, kick off, get the show on the road.
3 *when did the illness actually begin?* appear, arise, become apparent, spring up, come into existence, come into being, originate, start, commence, develop; literary come to pass.
OPPOSITES: finish, end, disappear.

> WORD LINKS
> **incipient**, **embryonic** beginning to happen or develop
> **initial** existing or occurring at the beginning

beginner noun novice, starter, new recruit, newcomer; trainee, apprentice, learner, probationer; tyro, neophyte, initiate; informal rookie.
OPPOSITES: expert, veteran.

beginning noun
1 *this change in attitude signified the beginning of socialism:* dawn, birth, inception, origination, genesis, emergence, rise, start, commencement, starting point, launch, onset; outset, day one; informal kick-off.
2 *I've read the beginning of the article:* opening, start, first part, introduction, preamble.
3 *the therapy has its beginnings in China:* origin, source, roots, starting point, birthplace.
OPPOSITES: end, conclusion.

begrudge verb
1 *it was obvious she begrudged Brian his affluence:* envy, grudge; resent, be jealous of, be envious of.
2 *nobody begrudges a single penny of the money spent:* resent, feel aggrieved about, feel bitter about, be annoyed about, be resentful of, grudge, mind, object to, take exception to, regret.

b

b

beguile verb
1 *she was beguiled by his charming manner:* charm, attract, enchant, entrance, win over, woo, captivate, bewitch, dazzle, hypnotize, mesmerize, seduce.
2 *they were beguiled into signing the treaty:* trick, dupe, deceive, hoodwink; informal con.
OPPOSITES: repel.

beguiling adjective *he spoke to her in that soft, beguiling voice:* charming, enchanting, entrancing, captivating, bewitching, hypnotizing, mesmerizing, magnetic, alluring, enticing, tempting, inviting, seductive, irresistible.

behalf noun
□ on behalf of/on someone's behalf
1 *I am writing to you on behalf of my client:* for, in the name of, in place of, on the authority of; literary at the behest of.
2 *he campaigned tirelessly on behalf of cyclists:* in the interests of, in support of, for, for the benefit of, for the good of, for the sake of.

behave verb
1 *he always behaved like a gentleman:* conduct yourself, act, acquit yourself.
2 *for once, the children behaved and we had a lovely afternoon:* act correctly, act properly, be well behaved, be good, be on your best behaviour; be polite, mind your manners, mind your Ps and Qs.
OPPOSITES: misbehave.

behaviour noun
1 *his behaviour yesterday was inexcusable:* conduct, actions, deportment, bearing; manners; formal comportment.
2 *we examined the structure and behaviour of these organisms:* functioning, action, performance, operation, working, reactions, responses.

> WORD LINKS
> **ethology** the biological study of behaviour

behead verb decapitate, cut someone's head off, guillotine.

behind preposition
1 *he hid behind a tree and waited:* at the back/rear of, beyond, on the far/other side of.
2 *a policeman walked behind him all the way to the office:* after, following, at the back/rear of, hard on the heels of, in the wake of.
3 *the group was behind the bombings in the capital:* responsible for, at the bottom of; to blame for, guilty of.
4 *they know they have the team behind them:* supporting, backing, on the side of, in agreement with; informal rooting for.
▷ adverb
1 *we're a bit behind, so don't stop:* late, running late, behind schedule, behindhand, not on time, behind time.
2 *he was behind with his rent:* in arrears,

overdue; late, behindhand.
OPPOSITES: ahead.
□ put something behind one
the team have to put last night's result behind them: put down to experience, forget about, regard as water under the bridge, consign to the past, ignore.

beige adjective fawn, pale brown, buff, sandy, oatmeal, biscuit-coloured, coffee-coloured, café au lait, camel, ecru.

being noun
1 *the single market came into being in 1993 | the people are exploring a new way of being:* existence, life, reality, actuality; living.
2 *we are all spiritual beings at heart:* creature, living entity, living thing, living soul, individual, person, human being.

belabour verb
1 *he belaboured the driver with his fists:* beat, hit, strike, smack, batter, pummel, pound, thrash; informal wallop, whack, clout, clobber.
2 *there is no need to belabour the point:* overemphasize, labour, overdo, overstress, overplay, make too much of, dwell on, harp on about.

belated adjective *Gilman makes her belated New York debut this summer:* late, overdue, behindhand, behind time, behind schedule, delayed, tardy.
OPPOSITES: early.

belch verb
1 *onions make me belch:* bring up wind; informal burp.
2 *the furnace belched smoke and flames:* emit, give off, give out, pour out, discharge, disgorge, spew out, spit out.
▷ noun *a loud belch:* informal burp; formal eructation.

beleaguered adjective *an effort by a beleaguered Congress to answer criticisms of the legal system:* hard-pressed, in difficulties, under pressure, troubled, with your back to the wall, in a tight corner, in a tight spot; informal up against it.

belie verb
1 *the quality of the music seems to belie the criticism:* contradict, be at odds with, call into question, give the lie to, disprove, discredit; formal confute.
2 *this light-hearted speech belies his deep disappointment:* conceal, cover, disguise.

belief noun
1 *it's my belief that party politics is becoming increasingly irrelevant:* opinion, view, conviction, judgement, thinking, way of thinking, idea, theory, conclusion, notion.
2 *my belief in God has been a tremendous source of comfort:* faith, trust, reliance, confidence, credence.
3 *he spoke out against traditional religious beliefs:* ideology, principle, ethic, tenet,

canon; doctrine, teaching, dogma, creed, credo.
OPPOSITES: disbelief, doubt.

believable adjective credible, plausible, tenable, able to hold water, conceivable, likely, probable, possible, feasible, reasonable, with a ring of truth.
OPPOSITES: unbelievable, implausible.

believe verb
1 *I'm afraid I don't believe you any more:* be convinced by, trust, have confidence in.
2 *the superintendent believed his story:* accept, be convinced by, give credence to, credit, trust; informal swallow, buy, go for.
3 *we believe that education is key to making poverty history:* be of the opinion, consider, think, hold the view; regard as, see as, hold to be, reckon to be
4 *I believe they've met before:* think, understand, be given to understand, gather.
OPPOSITES: doubt.
□ believe in
1 *they believed in his ability:* have faith in, pin your faith on, trust in, have every confidence in, cling to, set great store by, value; informal swear by.
2 *I don't believe in censorship of the arts:* approve of, subscribe to; be convinced by, be persuaded by.

belittle verb *the opposition constantly belittled the government's achievements:* disparage, denigrate, run down, deprecate, play down, trivialize, minimize, make light of, treat lightly; informal do down, pooh-pooh.
OPPOSITES: praise.

bell noun

> WORD LINKS
> **campanology** the art of bell-ringing

bellicose adjective *the extreme right adopted a bellicose attitude to Europe:* belligerent, aggressive, hostile, antagonistic, pugnacious, confrontational, militant, combative, warlike.
OPPOSITES: peaceable.

belligerent adjective *she stared round in a belligerent manner:* hostile, aggressive, confrontational, antagonistic, combative, threatening, pugnacious, bellicose; argumentative, quarrelsome, truculent; informal spoiling for a fight.
OPPOSITES: peaceable.

bellow verb *he cringed as she bellowed in his ear:* roar, shout, bawl, thunder, trumpet, boom, bark, yell, shriek, howl, scream; informal holler.
OPPOSITES: whisper.

belly noun stomach, abdomen, midriff, girth; paunch; informal tummy, gut, middle, pot belly.
▷ verb *her skirt bellied out in the wind:* billow out, bulge out, balloon out, fill out; become distended.

belong verb
1 *the house belongs to his mother:* be owned by, be the property of, be the possession of, be held by, be in the hands of.
2 *I no longer belong to a trade union:* be a member of, be in, be affiliated to, be allied to, be associated with.
3 *the garden belongs to the basement flat:* be part of, be attached to, go with.
4 *these creatures belong with the insects:* be classed, be classified, be categorized, be included, have a place, be located, be situated, be found, lie.
5 *she feels she doesn't belong here:* fit in, be welcome, be suited to, have a rightful place, have a home; informal go, click.

belonging noun *the club helps give people a sense of belonging:* affiliation, acceptance, association, attachment, integration; closeness, rapport, fellow feeling, fellowship.
OPPOSITES: alienation.

belongings plural noun *she carried a canvas bag containing all her belongings:* possessions, effects, worldly goods, property, goods and chattels; paraphernalia; informal gear, tackle, kit, things, stuff.

beloved adjective *he struggled to recover from the loss of his beloved wife:* darling, dear, dearest, precious, adored, much loved, cherished, treasured.

below preposition
1 *the water rushed below them:* beneath, under, underneath, further down than, lower than.
2 *their income is below the national average:* less than, lower than, under, not as much as, smaller than.
3 *a captain is below a major in rank:* lower than, under, inferior to, subordinate to, subservient to.
OPPOSITES: above, over.

> WORD LINKS
> **hypo-, sub-** forming words meaning 'under' or 'below normal', such as *hypothermia* ('the condition of having an abnormally low body temperature') and *subcutaneous* ('situated or applied under the skin')

belt noun
1 *she tied the belt around her waist:* girdle, sash, strap, band, cummerbund.
2 *farmers in the cotton belt are doing very well:* region, area, district, zone, sector, territory; tract, strip, stretch.
▷ verb (informal) *he belted down the hill.* See **RUSH** verb sense 1.
□ below the belt
she thinks what they have done is a bit below the belt: unfair, unjust, unjustified, unreasonable, uncalled for, unacceptable, unsporting; Brit. informal out of order.

bemoan verb *they were bemoaning the recent decline in moral standards:* lament,

b

bewail, deplore, complain about.
OPPOSITES: applaud.

bemused adjective *they wandered about with bemused expressions:* bewildered, confused, puzzled, perplexed, baffled, mystified, muddled, befuddled, at sea, at a loss, taken aback, disoriented, disconcerted, nonplussed; informal flummoxed, bamboozled, clueless, fazed.

bemusement noun bewilderment, confusion, puzzlement, perplexity, bafflement, befuddlement, mystification, disorientation.

bench noun
1 *he sat on a bench at the front of the hall:* pew, settle; Brit. form.
2 *in the centre of the lab was a huge bench:* workbench, work table, worktop, work surface, counter.
3 *the bench has now heard the evidence and must make a decision:* judges, magistrates, judiciary; court.

benchmark noun *the pay settlement will be a benchmark for other employers and workers:* standard, point of reference, gauge, yardstick, criterion; guide, guideline, touchstone, barometer, indicator, measure, model, pattern.

bend verb
1 *he bent down to tie his shoe:* stoop, bow, crouch, hunch, lean down/over.
2 *extend your left leg and bend your right:* flex, curve, curl, crook, angle, arch.
3 *bend the wire back with pliers | the aluminium structure had been bent out of shape:* twist, curve; buckle, warp, contort, distort.
4 *the road bent to the left:* turn, curve, incline, swing, veer, deviate, fork, loop.
OPPOSITES: straighten.
▷noun *he came to a bend in the road:* turn, curve, corner, hairpin bend, angle, arc, twist, loop, kink; dog-leg, zigzag.
OPPOSITES: straight.
▫bend over backwards (informal) *they have bent over backwards to ensure a fair trial:* try hard, do your best, do your utmost, do all you can, give your all, make every effort; informal go all out, pull out all the stops, bust a gut, move heaven and earth.

beneath preposition
1 *we sat in the shade beneath the trees:* under, underneath, below, at the foot of, at the bottom of; lower than.
2 *the rank beneath his is that of major:* below, lower in status than, subordinate to, inferior to.
3 *she thought such an attitude was beneath her:* unworthy of, unbecoming to, degrading to, below.
OPPOSITES: above.

benediction noun *the priest said a benediction:* blessing, prayer; grace.

benefactor noun *the work was paid for by a local benefactor:* patron, supporter, backer, sponsor; donor, contributor; philanthropist; informal angel.

beneficent adjective *in beneficent mood, the chancellor produced a '£4 billion giveaway':* benevolent, charitable, altruistic, humanitarian, public-spirited, philanthropic; generous, magnanimous, munificent, unselfish, open-handed, liberal, lavish, bountiful; literary bounteous.
OPPOSITES: unkind, mean.

beneficial adjective *the process was beneficial to both supplier and customer | the beneficial effects of regular exercise:* advantageous, favourable, helpful, useful, of use, of benefit, of assistance, valuable, of value, profitable, rewarding, gainful; salutary.
OPPOSITES: disadvantageous.

beneficiary noun *she was the major beneficiary of her uncle's will:* heir, heiress, inheritor, legatee; recipient.

benefit noun
1 *a life lived for the benefit of others:* good, sake, welfare, well-being, advantage, comfort, ease, convenience; help, aid, assistance, service.
2 *the numerous benefits of working for a large firm:* advantage, good point, reward, virtue, asset; informal perk.
3 *there is new hope for those who are dependent on benefit:* social security, welfare; income support, financial assistance; informal the dole.
OPPOSITES: detriment, disadvantage.
▷verb
1 *the deal benefited them both:* be advantageous to, be beneficial to, be of advantage to, profit, do good to, be of service to, serve, be useful to, be of use to, be helpful to, be of help to, help, aid, assist, be of assistance to; better, improve, strengthen, boost, advance, further.
2 *they may benefit from grants that are now available:* profit, gain, reap benefits, reap rewards; make the most of, exploit, turn to your advantage, put to good use, do well out of.
OPPOSITES: damage, suffer.

benevolence noun kindness, kind-heartedness, goodwill, charity, altruism, compassion; generosity, magnanimity, munificence, unselfishness, open-handedness, beneficence; literary bounty, bounteousness.

benevolent adjective *they thought him a benevolent and conscientious guardian:* kind, kindly, kind-hearted, well meaning, good-natured, good, benign, compassionate, caring, altruistic, humanitarian, philanthropic; generous, magnanimous, munificent, unselfish, open-handed, beneficent; literary bounteous.
OPPOSITES: unkind, mean.

benighted adjective *they saw themselves as bringing culture to poor benighted peoples:* ignorant, unenlightened, uneducated, backward, simple; primitive, uncivilized, unsophisticated, philistine.
OPPOSITES: enlightened.

benign adjective
1 *he adopted a benign, grandfatherly role:* kindly, kind, warm-hearted, good-natured, friendly, warm, affectionate, agreeable, genial, congenial, cordial, approachable, tender-hearted, gentle, sympathetic, compassionate, caring, well disposed, benevolent.
2 *the climate becomes more benign nearer the Black Sea:* temperate, mild, gentle, balmy, pleasant; healthy, wholesome; formal salubrious.
3 *a benign tumour:* harmless, non-malignant, non-cancerous; Medicine benignant.
OPPOSITES: unfriendly, unfavourable, malignant.

bent adjective
1 *a car with a bent mudguard:* twisted, crooked, warped, contorted, misshapen, out of shape; arched, curved, hooked.
2 *a small man with a bent back:* bowed, hunched, arched, curved.
3 (Brit. informal) *a bent cop.* See CORRUPT adjective sense 1.
OPPOSITES: straight.
▷ noun *she has an artistic bent:* inclination, leaning, tendency; talent, gift, flair, aptitude, facility, skill, capability, capacity; predisposition, disposition, instinct, orientation, predilection, proclivity, propensity.
☐ bent on
she's bent on going and nothing will stop her: intent on, set on, hell-bent on; determined to, resolved to, committed to.

benumbed adjective *a hoarse shout cut through his benumbed senses:* numb, unfeeling, insensible, stupefied, dazed, befuddled.

bequeath verb *he bequeathed his artworks to the city of Philadelphia:* leave, will, make over, pass on, hand on/down, entrust, grant, transfer; donate, give; bestow on, confer on, endow with; Law devise.

bequest noun *they received a bequest of over £300,000:* legacy, inheritance, endowment, settlement; estate.

berate verb *he was soon prowling the touchline, berating his players, the linesmen, and the referee:* scold, rebuke, reprimand, reproach, reprove, admonish, chide, criticize, upbraid, take to task, read someone the Riot Act; informal haul over the coals, tell off, give someone a talking-to, give someone a dressing-down, give someone a roasting, bawl out; Brit. informal tick off, have a go at, give someone

a rocket, give someone a rollicking, tear someone off a strip.
OPPOSITES: praise.

bereaved adjective grieving, mourning; orphaned, widowed.

bereft adjective
☐ bereft of
they are bereft of new ideas: lacking, without, devoid of, in need of, wanting, deprived of; informal minus.

berry noun fruit, currant.

berserk adjective
☐ go berserk
she went berserk, calling him names, screaming and crying: go mad, go crazy, go wild, become hysterical, become out of control, run amok, go on the rampage; informal freak out.

berth noun
1 *the vessel has now left its berth:* mooring, dock.
2 *a cabin with four berths:* bunk, bed; couchette.
▷ verb *the ship berthed in London Docks:* dock, moor, anchor, drop anchor, put in.
☐ give someone/something a wide berth
the public was outraged and gave the film a wide berth: avoid, shun, keep away from, stay away from, keep at arm's length, have nothing to do with; dodge, sidestep, circumvent, skirt round.

beseech verb (literary) *they beseeched him to stay:* implore, beg, entreat, plead with, appeal to, call on, pray to, ask, request, petition.

beset verb *he is beset by fears of failure:* plague, bedevil, dog, assail, beleaguer, afflict, torment, rack, oppress, trouble, worry.

beside preposition
1 *I walked beside him:* alongside, by/at the side of, next to, parallel to, abreast of, at someone's elbow; adjacent to, next door to, cheek by jowl with; bordering, abutting, neighbouring.
2 *beside Paula, she felt clumsy and useless:* compared with/to, in comparison with/to, by comparison with, next to, against, contrasted with, in contrast to/with.
☐ beside yourself
she was beside herself with worry: distraught, out of your mind, frantic, desperate, distracted, at your wits' end, frenzied, wound up, worked up, overcome; hysterical, unhinged, mad, crazed, demented.
☐ beside the point. See POINT.

besides preposition *who did you ask besides Mary?* in addition to, as well as, on top of; apart from, other than, aside from, but for, save for, not counting, excluding, not including, except, with the exception of, excepting, leaving aside.

b

▷**adverb**
1 *there's the stuff in the attic and a lot more besides:* in addition, as well, too, also, into the bargain, on top of that, to boot.
2 *besides, he's a man, so he wouldn't understand:* furthermore, moreover, further; anyway, in any case, be that as it may.

besiege verb
1 *the army unit which besieged the Croatian city of Vukovar:* lay siege to, blockade, surround.
2 *he was besieged by journalists and photographers:* surround, mob, crowd round, swarm round, throng round, encircle.
3 *local helplines were besieged with appeals for help:* overwhelm, inundate, deluge, flood, swamp, snow under; bombard.

besotted adjective *she won't listen—she's besotted with him:* infatuated, smitten, in love, head over heels in love, obsessed; informal crazy about, mad about, struck on.

bespeak verb (formal) *this literal-mindedness bespeaks a lack of imagination on his part:* indicate, be evidence of, be a sign of, denote, point to, testify to, evidence, reflect, demonstrate, show, manifest, signify; reveal, betray.

best adjective
1 *it's the best hotel in Paris:* finest, top, foremost, leading, greatest, pre-eminent, premier, prime, first, chief, principal, supreme, superlative, par excellence, second to none, without equal, unsurpassed, peerless, matchless, unparalleled, unbeaten, unbeatable, optimum, ultimate, incomparable, ideal, perfect; highest, record-breaking; informal star, number-one.
2 *do whatever you think best:* most advantageous, most useful, most suitable, most fitting, most appropriate; most prudent, most sensible, most advisable.
OPPOSITES: worst.
▷**noun** *only the best will do:* finest, top, cream, elite, crème de la crème, flower, jewel in the crown.
□**at your best**
Lily was not at her best yesterday evening: on top form, at your peak, in your prime, in the pink, in the best of health.
□**do your best**
they had done their best to help him: do your utmost, try your hardest, make every effort, do all you can, give your all; informal bend over backwards, go all out, pull out all the stops, move heaven and earth.

bestial adjective
1 *a war criminal of the most bestial kind:* savage, brutish, brutal, barbarous, barbaric, cruel, vicious, violent, inhuman, subhuman; depraved, degenerate, perverted, immoral, warped.

2 *bestial grunting noises:* animal, beast-like.
OPPOSITES: civilized, humane.

bestir verb
□**bestir yourself**
his friends urged him to bestir himself: exert yourself, make an effort, rouse yourself, get going, get moving, get on with it.

bestow verb *many favours were bestowed on him by the new king:* confer on, grant, accord, afford, endow someone with, vest in, present, award, give, donate, entrust with, vouchsafe.

bestride verb
1 *the oilfield bestrides the border between the two countries:* extend across, lie on both sides of, straddle, span, bridge.
2 *he bestrode his horse with an easy grace:* straddle, sit/stand astride.

best-seller noun great success, brand leader; informal hit, blockbuster, chart-topper, chartbuster.
OPPOSITES: failure, flop.

best-selling adjective very successful, very popular; informal number-one, chart-topping, hit.

bet verb
1 *he bet £10 on Liverpool to win the championship:* wager, gamble, stake, risk, venture; put/lay money; Brit. informal have a flutter, punt.
2 (informal) *I bet it was your idea:* be certain, be sure, be convinced, be confident; expect, predict, forecast, guess.
▷**noun**
1 *a £20 bet:* wager, gamble, stake, ante; Brit. informal flutter, punt.
2 (informal) *your best bet is to go early and avoid the traffic:* option, choice, alternative, course of action, plan.

betray verb
1 *I loved him and he betrayed me:* be disloyal to, be unfaithful to, play someone false, stab someone in the back.
2 *he betrayed some 400 British and French agents to the Germans:* inform on, denounce, give away, sell out; informal rat on, do the dirty on, sell down the river; Brit. informal grass on, shop.
3 *a spy who had betrayed American secrets to Moscow:* reveal, disclose, divulge, tell, give away, leak; expose.

betrayal noun disloyalty, treachery, faithlessness; duplicity, deception, double-dealing; breach of faith, breach of trust, stab in the back; sell-out; literary perfidy.
OPPOSITES: loyalty.

better adjective
1 *he is clearly a better player than Thompson:* superior, finer, of higher quality; preferable; informal a cut above, streets ahead, head and shoulders above.
2 *there couldn't be a better time to invest:*

more advantageous, more suitable, more fitting, more appropriate, more useful, more valuable, more desirable.
3 *I'm feeling better than I was | are you better?:* healthier, fitter, stronger; well, cured, healed, recovered; recovering, on the road to recovery, making progress, improving; informal on the mend.
OPPOSITES: worse, inferior.
▷verb *he bettered his previous time by ten minutes:* surpass, improve on, beat, exceed, top, cap, trump, eclipse.

betterment noun *his selfless devotion to the betterment of his country:* improvement, amelioration, advancement, development, upgrading, enhancement.

between preposition
1 *Philip stood between his parents:* in the middle of.
2 *the bond between her and her mother:* connecting, linking, joining; uniting, allying.

WORD LINKS
inter- forming words meaning 'between; among', such as *international* ('existing or occurring between nations') and *interbreed* ('to breed with an animal of a different species')

beverage noun drink, liquid refreshment; humorous libation.

bevy noun *he was always surrounded by a bevy of Hollywood starlets:* group, crowd, flock, horde, army, gathering, band, body, pack, herd; knot, cluster; informal bunch, gaggle, posse.

bewail verb *many experts bewail the decline of standards:* lament, bemoan, mourn, deplore, complain about.

beware verb *shoppers were warned to beware of cut-price fakes:* be on your guard, watch out, look out, mind out, be alert, be on the lookout, keep your eyes open/peeled, keep an eye out, keep a sharp lookout; take care, be careful, be cautious, have a care, watch your step.

bewilder verb *his sudden change of mood bewildered her:* baffle, mystify, bemuse, perplex, puzzle, confuse, confound, disconcert, nonplus; informal flummox, faze, stump, fox, floor.
OPPOSITES: enlighten.

bewildered adjective *Mark looked completely bewildered:* baffled, mystified, bemused, perplexed, puzzled, confused, disconcerted, nonplussed, at sea, at a loss, disorientated, taken aback; informal flummoxed, fazed.

bewildering adjective *the bewildering complexity of local politics:* baffling, perplexing, puzzling, mystifying, mysterious, confusing; complex, labyrinthine, convoluted, Byzantine.

bewitch verb
1 *his relatives were convinced he had been bewitched:* cast/put a spell on, enchant; possess; curse; N. Amer. hex.
2 *she was bewitched by her surroundings:* captivate, enchant, entrance, enrapture, charm, delight, fascinate, enthral.

beyond preposition
1 *the farm buildings were visible beyond the trees:* on the other side of, behind, past, after.
2 *nobody ever worked beyond six o'clock:* later than, past, after.
3 *inflation was running at way beyond 10 per cent:* greater than, more than, exceeding, in excess of, above, over and above, above and beyond, upwards of.
4 *there was little vegetation beyond a few stunted bushes:* apart from, except, other than, besides; formal save.

WORD LINKS
extra-, hyper-, para- forming words meaning 'beyond; outside', such as *extra-curricular* ('relating to activities done in addition to the normal curriculum'), *hypersonic* ('relating to speeds more than five times the speed of sound'), and *paranormal* ('beyond the scope of normal scientific understanding')

bias noun
1 *the chairman accused the media of bias | a team consisting of experts without any political bias:* prejudice, partiality, partisanship, favouritism, unfairness, one-sidedness; bigotry, intolerance, discrimination; leaning, tendency, inclination, predilection.
2 *his work showed a discernible bias towards philosophy:* concentration on, interest in, focus on
3 *a dress cut on the bias:* diagonal, cross, slant, angle.
OPPOSITES: impartiality.
▷verb *their recollections may be biased by discussions with other people:* prejudice, influence, colour, sway, weight; distort, skew, slant.

biased adjective *that's a very biased view, I must say:* prejudiced, partisan, one-sided, partial, blinkered; bigoted, intolerant, discriminatory.
OPPOSITES: impartial.

bicker verb *the kids were bickering about which movie they wanted to see:* squabble, argue, quarrel, wrangle, fight, spar, have words; Brit. row.

bid¹ verb
1 *United bid £1 million for the striker:* offer, make an offer of, put in a bid of, put up, tender, proffer, propose.
2 *she is bidding for a place in the England team:* try, make a pitch, make a bid; go.

b

▷**noun**
  1 *a bid of £3,000 was accepted:* offer, tender, proposal.
  2 *a frantic bid to cut crime before the election:* attempt, effort, endeavour, try; formal essay; informal crack, go, shot, stab.

bid² verb
  1 *she turned to bid him farewell:* wish.
  2 (old use) *I did as he bade me:* order, command, tell, instruct, direct, charge; formal enjoin.

biddable adjective *she was a pretty, biddable child, with none of her brother's temper:* obedient, acquiescent, compliant, tractable, amenable, cooperative, dutiful, submissive, complaisant.
  OPPOSITES: disobedient.

bidding noun *after dinner, at his bidding, we went into his study:* command, order, instruction, demand, summons, call; wish, desire; request.

big adjective
  1 *a big Victorian building:* large, sizeable, substantial, great, huge, immense, enormous, extensive, colossal, massive, mammoth, vast, tremendous, gigantic, giant, king-sized, monumental, mighty, gargantuan, elephantine, titanic, mountainous; towering, tall, high, lofty; outsize, oversized; capacious, voluminous, spacious; literary Brobdingnagian; informal jumbo, whopping, bumper, mega, humongous, monster, astronomical, almighty; Brit. informal whacking, ginormous.
  2 *a big man with a red face:* well built, sturdy, brawny, burly, broad-shouldered, muscular, muscly, rugged, hulking, strapping, thickset, stocky, solid, hefty, bulky; tall, huge; fat, stout, portly, plump, fleshy, paunchy, corpulent, obese; informal beefy.
  3 *it's a big decision, so don't rush it:* important, significant, major, momentous, weighty, consequential, far-reaching, key, vital, critical, crucial.
  4 (informal) *a big man in the government:* powerful, important, prominent, influential, high-powered, leading.
  5 *she's got a big heart:* generous, kind, caring, compassionate, loving.
  6 (informal) *African bands are big in Britain right now:* popular, successful, in demand, sought-after, all the rage; informal hot, in, cool, trendy, hip.
  7 *I fell out with my big brother:* elder, older; grown-up, adult, mature.
  OPPOSITES: small, minor, modest.

big-headed adjective (informal) *all you get is a bunch of big-headed movie stars trying to out-act each other:* conceited, full of yourself, cocky, arrogant, cocksure, above yourself, self-important; vain, self-satisfied, pleased with yourself, smug, complacent; informal swollen-headed, too

big for your boots.
  OPPOSITES: modest.

bigoted adjective *I was shocked at the bigoted attitudes I encountered:* prejudiced, biased, partial, one-sided; opinionated, dogmatic, intolerant, narrow-minded, blinkered, illiberal; racist, sexist, chauvinistic, jingoistic, xenophobic, homophobic, misogynistic.
  OPPOSITES: open-minded.

bigotry noun prejudice, bias, partiality, partisanship, discrimination; dogmatism, intolerance, narrow-mindedness; racism, sexism, chauvinism, jingoism.

bigwig noun (informal) *he arrived at the town hall with all the local politicians and bigwigs in attendance:* VIP, important person, notable, dignitary, grandee; celebrity; informal somebody, big shot, big noise.
  OPPOSITES: nonentity.

bilious adjective
  1 *I woke up feeling bilious:* nauseous, sick, queasy, nauseated.
  2 *his bilious disposition made him few friends:* bad-tempered, irritable, irascible, tetchy, testy, crotchety, ill-tempered, peevish, fractious, crabby, waspish, prickly, crusty, shrewish, quick-tempered.
  3 *a bilious green and pink colour scheme:* lurid, garish, loud, violent; sickly, nauseating.

bill¹ noun
  1 *have you paid the bill?* invoice, account, statement, list of charges; N. Amer. check; N. Amer. informal tab.
  2 *a bill to ban smoking would receive a lot of support:* draft law, proposal, measure.
  3 (N. Amer.) *a $10 bill:* banknote, note.
  ▷**verb**
  1 *please bill me for the work:* invoice, charge, debit.
  2 *the concert went ahead as billed:* advertise, announce; schedule, programme, timetable.
  3 *he was billed as 'the new Sean Connery':* describe, call, style, label, dub; promote, publicize, talk up; informal hype.

bill² noun *one of the swans had a fishing hook caught in its bill:* beak; technical mandibles.

billet noun *the troops returned to their billets:* quarters, rooms; accommodation, lodging, housing; barracks.
  ▷**verb** *most of the army was billeted in the town:* accommodate, quarter, put up, lodge, house; station, garrison.

billow noun *a huge billow of steam rose up:* cloud, mass.
  ▷**verb**
  1 *her dress billowed out around her:* puff up/out, balloon out, swell, fill out, belly out, ripple out.
  2 *smoke billowed from the chimney:* swirl,

spiral, roll, undulate, eddy; pour, flow, issue.

billowing adjective *billowing clouds of smoke:* rolling, swirling, undulating, surging, heaving, billowy, swelling, rippling.

bin noun *the beans are stored in round metal bins:* container, receptacle, holder; drum, canister, can, tin.

bind verb
1 *they bound her hands and feet:* tie up, fasten together, secure, make fast, attach; rope, strap, lash, truss, tether.
2 *Shelley bound up the wound with a clean dressing:* bandage, dress, cover, wrap; strap up, tape up.
3 *the experience had bound them together:* unite, join, bond, knit together, draw together.
4 *the edges are bound in a contrasting colour:* trim, hem, edge, border, fringe; finish.
5 *they are bound by the terms of the agreement:* constrain, restrict, restrain, tie, tie down, limit, shackle, trammel; hamper, hinder, inhibit.
OPPOSITES: untie, separate.
▷ noun (informal)
1 *having to start so early is a bind:* nuisance, annoyance, inconvenience, bore, bother, irritant, trial; informal pain, hassle, drag, pain in the neck, headache.
2 *these simple precautions may help you avoid getting into a bind:* predicament, difficult/awkward situation, mess, quandary; informal fix, hole.

binding adjective *they had entered into a binding legal agreement:* irrevocable, inescapable, unbreakable, contractual; compulsory, obligatory, mandatory.

binge verb (informal) *when you feel down you're more likely to binge on high-carbohydrate foods:* overindulge in, eat/drink too much of, eat/drink to excess, gorge yourself on; informal stuff yourself with, pig out on.

biography noun life story, life history, life, memoir; informal bio, biog.

bird noun fowl; chick, fledgling, nestling.

birth noun
1 *the birth of a child:* childbirth, delivery, nativity; technical parturition.
2 *the birth of Socialist Realism:* beginning, beginnings, emergence, genesis, dawn, dawning, advent, rise, start.
3 *he claims he is of noble birth:* ancestry, lineage, blood, descent, parentage, family, extraction, origin, heritage, stock, pedigree.
OPPOSITES: death, demise.

birthright noun *freedom is the birthright of every human being:* right, due, prerogative, privilege; inheritance, heritage.

biscuit noun (Brit.) cracker, wafer; N. Amer. cookie.

bisect verb *Kenya, a nation which is bisected by the Equator:* cut in half, halve, divide/cut/split in two, split down the middle; cross, intersect.

bishop noun diocesan, metropolitan, suffragan; formal prelate.

bit noun
1 *a bit of bread | add a bit of salt:* piece, portion, segment, section; chunk, lump, hunk, slice; fragment, scrap, shred, crumb, grain, speck; spot, drop, pinch, dash, soupçon, modicum; morsel, mouthful, bite, sample; iota, jot, whit, atom, particle, trace, touch, suggestion, hint, tinge; snippet, snatch; informal smidgen, tad.
2 *wait a bit:* moment, minute, second, while; informal sec, jiffy; Brit. informal mo, tick.
OPPOSITES: lot.
□ **a bit**
he looked a bit annoyed: rather, fairly, slightly, somewhat, quite, moderately; informal pretty.
□ **bit by bit**
bit by bit the truth emerged: gradually, little by little, in stages, step by step, piecemeal, slowly.

bitch verb (informal) *he's always bitching about colleagues:* criticize, run down, speak ill of, slander, malign; informal knock, pull to pieces, bad-mouth; Brit. informal slag off.

bitchy adjective (informal) *bitchy comments:* spiteful, malicious, mean, nasty, offensive, hurtful, wounding, cruel, unkind, vindictive; informal catty.

bite verb
1 *the dog bit his arm | she bit off a chunk of bread:* sink your teeth into, nip, tear at, gnaw on; crunch, munch, chew, champ.
2 *my wheels couldn't bite on the snow:* grip, hold, get a purchase/grip.
3 *the free-market measures are beginning to bite:* take effect, have an effect, be effective, work, act, have results.
▷ noun
1 *he had a nasty bite on his arm:* wound, injury; nip.
2 *she took a bite out of her sandwich:* mouthful, piece, bit.
3 (informal) *the menu has a selection of light bites:* snack; refreshments, something to eat.

b

b

4 *pepper cress gives a hot, sharp bite to salads:* piquancy, pungency, spiciness, tang, zest, sharpness, tartness; informal kick, punch.

biting adjective
1 *a biting satire on suburban life:* harsh, cruel, savage, cutting, sharp, bitter, scathing, caustic, acid, acerbic, stinging, vitriolic; incisive, penetrating.
2 *a biting east wind:* freezing, icy, arctic, glacial; bitter, piercing, penetrating, raw, wintry.
OPPOSITES: mild.

bitter adjective
1 *the raw berries have a very bitter flavour:* sharp, acid, acidic, tart, sour, biting, acrid, unsweetened, vinegary.
2 *Carla is a frustrated, bitter woman:* resentful, embittered, aggrieved, disgruntled, jaundiced, sour, with a chip on your shoulder.
3 *today's decision has come as a bitter blow:* painful, unpleasant, cruel, distressing, upsetting, heartbreaking, heart-rending, agonizing, traumatic, tragic, chilling; formal grievous.
4 *a bitter row broke out:* acrimonious, angry, rancorous, spiteful, vicious, vitriolic, savage, hate-filled, nasty, ill-natured.
5 *we were chilled by a bitter north wind:* freezing, icy, arctic, glacial; biting, piercing, penetrating, raw, wintry.
OPPOSITES: sweet, mild, gentle.

bitterness noun
1 *she grimaced at the bitterness of the drink:* sharpness, acidity, sourness, tartness, harshness.
2 *his bitterness against his parents grew:* resentment, rancour, grudge.
3 *there was no bitterness between them:* acrimony, hostility, antipathy, antagonism, enmity, animus, friction, rancour, hatred, ill feeling, ill will, bad blood.
OPPOSITES: sweetness, goodwill.

bitty adjective (Brit. informal) *the first 25 minutes of the show are too bitty:* disjointed, scrappy, incoherent, fragmented, jumbled; inconsistent, uneven, erratic, patchy.

bizarre adjective *his behaviour became more and more bizarre:* strange, peculiar, odd, funny, curious, outlandish, outré, eccentric, offbeat, unconventional, unorthodox, queer, extraordinary; informal weird, wacky, oddball, way out, freaky, off the wall.
OPPOSITES: normal, ordinary.

black adjective
1 *her long black hair:* dark, jet-black, coal-black, inky; Heraldry sable.
2 *the black night sky:* dark, pitch-dark, pitch-black, starless, moonless.
3 *it's a black day for this city:* tragic, disastrous, catastrophic, calamitous,

cataclysmic, wretched, dreadful, awful, terrible, grim.
4 *Mary was in a black mood:* miserable, melancholy, morose, gloomy, glum, mournful, doleful, bleak, wretched, desolate, despairing, disconsolate, downcast, dejected, dismal, forlorn, woeful.
5 *black humour:* cynical, macabre, ghoulish, morbid; informal sick.
6 *a black look.* See DIRTY sense 4.
OPPOSITES: white, bright, joyful.
□ **black out**
he tightened his grip and she felt herself begin to black out: faint, lose consciousness, pass out; literary swoon.
□ **in the black**
all bar one of its factories are in the black: in credit, debt-free, out of debt, solvent, financially sound, able to pay your debts, creditworthy.
□ **black and white**
1 *on the wall hung a framed black and white print:* monochrome.
2 *I wish to see the proposals in black and white:* in print, printed, written down, set down, on paper, recorded, on record, documented.
3 *he saw the world in black-and-white terms:* unambiguous, clear, clear-cut, clearly defined; polarized.

blackball verb *two committee members intended to blackball me in the ballot:* reject, debar, bar, ban, vote against, blacklist, exclude, shut out.

blacken verb
1 *the pollutants blackening the air over Mexico City:* darken; dirty, stain, pollute, soil.
2 *we stood watching the sky blacken in the west:* grow/become black, darken, dim, grow dim, cloud over.
3 *the whole incident had been contrived to blacken my name:* tarnish, drag through the mud, stain, taint, smear, disgrace, dishonour, bring discredit to, damage, ruin; literary besmirch, sully.

blacklist verb *200 suspected Communists were blacklisted by the major studios:* boycott, ostracize, exclude, avoid, embargo.

black magic noun sorcery, witchcraft, necromancy, the black arts.

blackout noun
1 *a generator would power the computer in the event of a blackout:* power cut, power failure; outage.
2 *she was suffering from blackouts:* fainting fit, faint, loss of consciousness, collapse; Medicine syncope; literary swoon.

blame verb
1 *the inquiry blamed the driver of the train:* hold responsible, hold accountable, find/consider guilty, assign fault/liability/guilt to, condemn, accuse.

2 *they blame youth crime on unemployment:* ascribe to, attribute to, impute to, lay at the door of, put down to; informal pin.
OPPOSITES: absolve.

▷**noun** *he was cleared of all blame for the incident:* responsibility, accountability, liability, guilt, culpability, fault.

blameless adjective *he led a blameless life:* innocent, guiltless, above reproach, irreproachable, unimpeachable, exemplary, perfect, virtuous, pure.

blameworthy adjective *in what way do you consider him blameworthy?* culpable, guilty, to blame, at fault, accountable, responsible, answerable; in the wrong.

blanch verb
1 *the cold light blanched her face:* turn pale, whiten, fade, bleach.
2 *he blanched as he looked at the bloodstained uniform:* grow pale, pale, whiten.
3 *blanch the spinach leaves in boiling water for about 30 seconds:* scald, boil briefly.

> **USAGE**
>
> Do not confuse **blanch** with **blench**. **Blanch** means 'to make or become white or pale', while **blench** means 'to flinch suddenly as a result of fear, pain, or disgust' (*she blenched at the smell of his breath*).

bland adjective
1 *the channel specializes in bland dramas:* uninteresting, unimaginative, uninspiring, uninspired, vapid, dull, boring, tedious, monotonous, dreary, unexciting, lacklustre, trite, vacuous.
2 *the food was bland but plentiful:* tasteless, flavourless, insipid, unseasoned; dull, uninteresting.
3 *when he turned round, his face was as bland as ever:* impassive, unemotional, emotionless, expressionless, blank.
OPPOSITES: interesting, tasty.

blandishments plural noun *he soon learned that such blandishments would not help his case:* flattery, compliments, honeyed words, smooth talk; cajolery, coaxing, wheedling, persuasion; informal sweet talk, soft soap.

blank adjective
1 *a blank sheet of paper | high blank walls:* empty, unmarked, unused, clear, bare, clean, plain.
2 *Jack continued to gaze down at Ken's blank face:* expressionless, impassive, unresponsive, inscrutable, deadpan; wooden, stony, poker-faced; glazed, fixed; vacuous, empty.
3 *Gina looked blank, then understanding dawned:* baffled, uncomprehending, mystified, puzzled, perplexed, bewildered, nonplussed, bemused, confused.
OPPOSITES: used, expressive.

▷**noun** space, gap; lacuna.

blanket noun *a thick blanket of snow:* covering, layer, carpet, coating; cloak, mantle, veil, shroud.

▷**adjective** *a blanket ban on tobacco advertising:* complete, total, comprehensive, overall, general, umbrella, inclusive, all-inclusive, all-round, wholesale, outright, across the board, sweeping, indiscriminate; universal, global, worldwide, international.
OPPOSITES: partial.

▷**verb** *a heavy fall of snow blanketed the mountains:* cover, coat, carpet, overlay; cloak, shroud, swathe, envelop.

blare verb *sirens blared all around:* blast, sound, trumpet, screech, shriek, roar, thunder, boom, bellow, resound.

▷**noun** *the blare of the siren made him jump:* blast, trumpeting, screech, shriek, roar, thunder, boom, bellow.

blasé adjective *she was becoming quite blasé about the dangers:* nonchalant, casual, offhand, indifferent, unconcerned, uncaring; uninterested, unimpressed, apathetic, unmoved, unresponsive; informal laid-back.

blaspheme verb swear, curse, take the Lord's name in vain.

blasphemous adjective *a blasphemous book that should be banned:* sacrilegious, profane, irreligious, impious, ungodly.

blasphemy noun *he has been accused of blasphemy:* profanity, sacrilege, irreligion; taking the Lord's name in vain.

blast noun
1 *they were thrown backwards by the blast:* shock wave; aftershock, impact.
2 *the blast killed two people | a shotgun blast:* explosion, detonation, discharge.
3 *a sudden blast of cold air:* gust, rush, gale, wind, draught, squall.
4 *the shrill blast of the trumpets:* blare, wail, roar, screech, shriek, hoot, honk, beep.

▷**verb**
1 *bombers were blasting enemy airfields:* blow up, bomb, blow to pieces, dynamite, explode; shell, strafe, bombard.
2 *the big guns were blasting away:* fire, shoot, blaze, let fly, discharge.
3 *he blasted his horn in frustration:* honk, beep, toot, sound.
4 *loud rock music blasted from massive speakers:* blare, boom, roar, thunder, bellow, pump, shriek, screech.

□ **blast off**
a rocket blasted off to rendezvous with the space station: take off, lift off, leave the ground, become airborne, take to the air.

blast-off noun launch, lift-off, take-off, ascent.
OPPOSITES: touchdown.

blatant adjective *that is a blatant lie:* flagrant, barefaced, glaring, obvious, undisguised, unconcealed, open; shameless, unashamed, brazen, unabashed.

blaze noun
1 *firemen fought the blaze all night:* fire, flames, conflagration, inferno.
2 *a blaze of light:* glare, gleam, flash, burst, flare, streak, beam; radiance, brilliance.
▷**verb**
1 *the fire blazed merrily in the hearth:* burn, flame; be on fire, be in flames.
2 *headlights blazed:* shine, flash, flare, glare, gleam, glint, dazzle, glitter.

blazon verb
1 *the sponsor's name is blazoned across the sails:* display, exhibit, spread, emblazon, plaster.
2 *accounts of their ordeal were blazoned to the entire nation:* report, make known, make public, announce, communicate, spread, circulate, publish, broadcast, trumpet.

bleach verb *her hair had been bleached by the sun:* turn white, whiten, turn pale, blanch, lighten, fade.
OPPOSITES: darken.

bleak adjective
1 *a bleak, rocky landscape lay before them:* bare, exposed, desolate, stark, empty, open, windswept, inhospitable; treeless, featureless, without vegetation, denuded, desert, barren.
2 *the future looks pretty bleak:* depressing, discouraging, disheartening, gloomy, black, dark, grim, hopeless; unpromising, unfavourable, inauspicious.
3 *a bleak room in a grimy hotel:* cheerless, unwelcoming, uninviting, dreary, dismal, dingy; stark, spartan, austere.
OPPOSITES: lush, promising.

bleary adjective *his bleary eyes filled with tears:* blurred, blurry, unfocused; fogged, clouded, dull, misty, watery, rheumy.
OPPOSITES: clear.

bleed verb
1 *his arm was bleeding badly:* lose blood, haemorrhage.
2 *one colour bled into another:* flow, run, seep, filter, percolate, leach.

blemish noun *not a single blemish marred her skin:* imperfection, flaw, defect, fault, deformity, discoloration, disfigurement; bruise, scar, pit, pock, scratch, cut, gash; mark, streak, spot, smear, speck, blotch, smudge.
▷**verb** *his reputation has been blemished by the controversy:* tarnish, blacken, taint; spoil, mar, ruin, disgrace, damage, undermine; literary besmirch, sully.
OPPOSITES: enhance.

blench verb *she blenched as he held out a glistening spoonful:* flinch, shy away, recoil, shrink, pull back, cringe, wince, quail, cower.

USAGE
Do not confuse **blench** with **blanch**. **Blench** means 'to flinch suddenly through fear, pain, or disgust', while **blanch** means 'to make or become white or pale' (*the cold light blanched her face*).

blend verb
1 *blend the ingredients until smooth:* mix, combine, stir, whisk, fold in.
2 *they play acoustic music which blends soulful blues, bluegrass, and jazz:* combine, merge, meld, fuse, coalesce, mix, intermix, mingle, synthesize; literary commingle.
3 *the new buildings blend well with the older ones:* harmonize, go well, fit in, be in tune, be compatible; coordinate, match, complement.
▷**noun** *a blend of bananas, raisins, and ginger:* mixture, mix, combination, amalgamation, amalgam, union, marriage, fusion, meld, synthesis; technical admixture.

bless verb
1 *the Cardinal blessed the memorial plaque:* consecrate, sanctify, dedicate to God; formal hallow.
2 *God has blessed us with free will:* endow, favour, grace; bestow on.
OPPOSITES: curse.

blessing noun
1 *may God give us his blessing:* protection, favour.
2 *a special blessing from the priest:* benediction, prayer, intercession; grace.
3 *she gave the plan her blessing:* sanction, endorsement, approval, approbation, favour, consent, assent, agreement; backing, support; informal the thumbs up.
4 *the stone floors kept the house cool in summer, which was a blessing:* boon, godsend, advantage, benefit, help, bonus; stroke of luck; informal plus.

blight verb *the scandal blighted the careers of several politicians:* ruin, wreck, harm, spoil, mar, disrupt, destroy, shatter, devastate; informal mess up, foul up, put paid to; Brit. informal scupper.
▷**noun**
1 *the derelict buildings are a blight on the city's landscape:* eyesore, blot, monstrosity
2 *the scandal was a blight on his fine reputation:* stain, blemish, taint; discredit.

blind adjective
1 *he has been blind since birth:* sightless, unsighted, visually impaired, unseeing; partially sighted.
2 *like most men, he's blind to her faults:* unaware of, oblivious to, unconscious of, ignorant of, impervious to.
3 *the blind acceptance of conventional opinion:* uncritical, unthinking, unreasoning, unconsidered, mindless.
4 *a blind rage:* wild, uncontrolled,

uncontrollable, unrestrained, furious, towering.
OPPOSITES: sighted, aware.

▷ **verb**
1 *he was blinded in a car crash:* make blind, deprive of sight, render sightless; put someone's eyes out.
2 *they try to blind you with statistics:* overawe, intimidate, confuse, bewilder, confound, perplex, overwhelm; informal faze, psych out.

▷ **noun** *I pulled the blind down:* screen, shade, sunshade, curtain, awning, canopy; louvre, shutter.

blink verb
1 *his eyes did not blink:* flutter, flicker, wink; bat.
2 *several red lights began to blink:* flash, flicker, wink.
3 *no one even blinks at the 'waitresses' in drag:* be surprised, look twice, bat an eyelid, turn a hair.

blinkered adjective *we should not be quite so blinkered in our outlook:* narrow-minded, inward-looking, parochial, provincial, insular, small-minded, short-sighted; hidebound, inflexible, entrenched.
OPPOSITES: broad-minded.

bliss noun *she gave a sigh of bliss:* joy, happiness, pleasure, delight, ecstasy, elation, rapture, euphoria.
OPPOSITES: misery.

blissful adjective *he turned to her with a blissful smile:* ecstatic, euphoric, joyful, elated, rapturous, on cloud nine, in seventh heaven; delighted, thrilled, overjoyed; literary joyous; informal over the moon, on top of the world.

blistering adjective
1 *we sweated in the blistering heat:* intense, extreme, ferocious, fierce; scorching, searing, blazing, burning, sweltering; informal boiling, baking, roasting.
2 *a blistering attack on the government:* savage, vicious, fierce, bitter, harsh, scathing, devastating, caustic, searing, vehement.
OPPOSITES: mild.

blithe adjective *he shows a blithe disregard for the rules:* casual, indifferent, unconcerned, unworried, untroubled, uncaring, careless, heedless, thoughtless; nonchalant, blasé.

blitz noun *election year heralds an ad blitz by the main parties:* campaign, onslaught, attack.
▷ **verb** *I had some posters made, and I blitzed the town with them:* fill, bombard, cover, saturate, hit.

blizzard noun snowstorm, white-out.

bloated adjective *a bloated stomach:* swollen, distended, bulging, enlarged, expanded, dilated, inflated.

blob noun
1 *a blob of gravy:* drop, droplet, globule.
2 *blobs of paint:* spot, dab, blotch, blot, dot, smudge; informal splotch; Brit. informal splodge.

bloc noun *all five parties moved towards forming a political bloc:* alliance, coalition, federation, confederation, league, union, partnership, body, association, group.

block noun
1 *a block of cheese:* chunk, hunk, lump, wedge, cube, brick, slab, piece; Brit. informal wodge.
2 *an apartment block:* building, complex, structure, development.
3 *a block of shares:* batch, group, set, quantity, tranche.
4 *a sketch block:* pad, notepad, sketch pad, jotter, tablet.
5 *a block to Third World development:* obstacle, bar, barrier, impediment, hindrance, check, hurdle, stumbling block, handicap, deterrent.

▷ **verb**
1 *weeds can block the drainage ditches:* clog, clog up, stop up, choke, plug, obstruct, gum up, dam up, congest, jam, close; technical occlude; informal bung up; Brit. informal gunge up.
2 *he stood up, blocking her escape | the antibodies block the development of infection:* obstruct, get in the way of; halt, stop, bar, check, prevent, impede, hinder, hamper, restrict, limit.
3 *he blocked a shot on the goal line:* stop, deflect, parry, fend off, hold off, repel, repulse.
□ **block something off**
one van was enough to block off a street: close up, shut off, seal off, barricade, bar, obstruct.
□ **block something out**
the trees blocked out the light: conceal, keep out, blot out, exclude, obliterate, blank out.

blockade noun
1 *a naval blockade of the island:* siege.
2 *rioters erected blockades in the streets:* barricade, barrier, roadblock; obstacle, obstruction.
▷ **verb** *rebels blockaded the capital:* barricade, block off, shut off, seal; besiege, surround.

blockage noun *there's a blockage in the main drain:* obstruction, stoppage, block; bottleneck, congestion.

bloke noun (Brit. informal). See **MAN** sense 1.

blonde, blond adjective *her blonde hair tumbled about her face:* fair, light, yellow, tow-coloured, golden, platinum, ash blonde, strawberry blonde; bleached; literary flaxen.
OPPOSITES: dark.

blood noun *a woman of noble blood:* ancestry, lineage, bloodline, descent,

b

parentage, family, birth, extraction, origin, genealogy, heritage, stock, pedigree.

blood-curdling adjective *he let out a blood-curdling scream:* terrifying, frightening, spine-chilling, chilling, hair-raising, horrifying, alarming; eerie, sinister, horrible.

bloodless adjective
1 *a bloodless revolution:* non-violent, peaceful.
2 *his face was bloodless:* ashen, colourless, chalky, waxen, white, deathly, pale, wan, pallid, anaemic, grey, pasty, drained, drawn.
3 *a shrewd and bloodless Hollywood mogul:* heartless, unfeeling, cruel, ruthless, merciless, pitiless; cold, hard, stony-hearted, cold-blooded, callous.
OPPOSITES: bloody, flushed.

bloodshed noun *the recent bloodshed has cost more than 1500 lives:* slaughter, massacre, killing; carnage, butchery, bloodletting; violence, fighting, warfare, battle.

bloodthirsty adjective *the most bloodthirsty of the Celtic warriors:* murderous, violent, vicious, barbarous, barbaric, savage, brutal, cut-throat, homicidal; fierce, ferocious, inhuman.

bloody adjective
1 *his hands were bloody:* bleeding.
2 *a pile of bloody bandages:* bloodstained, blood-soaked, gory.
3 *a bloody civil war threatened to erupt:* vicious, ferocious, savage, fierce, brutal, violent, gory.

bloody-minded adjective (Brit. informal) *he can be very bloody-minded when he wants to:* uncooperative, awkward, recalcitrant, disobliging, inflexible, uncompromising, contrary, perverse, obstinate, stubborn; difficult; informal pig-headed; Brit. informal bolshie.
OPPOSITES: compliant.

bloom noun
1 *a display of gorgeous orchid blooms:* flower, blossom, floweret, floret.
2 *her skin had lost its usual bloom:* radiance, glow, lustre, freshness; rosiness, pinkness, colour.
▷verb
1 *the roses had bloomed:* flower, blossom, open.
2 *the children bloomed in the Devonshire air:* flourish, thrive, prosper, blossom.
OPPOSITES: wither, decline.

blossom noun *pink blossom covered the branches:* flowers, blooms.
▷verb
1 *the apple trees began to blossom in March:* bloom, flower.
2 *the whole region had blossomed:* develop, grow, mature, progress, evolve; flourish, thrive, prosper, bloom.
OPPOSITES: fade, decline.

□ in blossom
the cherry trees are all in blossom: in flower, flowering, blossoming, blooming, in bloom; open, out.

blot noun
1 *a large blot of ink:* spot, dot, mark, blotch, smudge, patch, dab; informal splotch; Brit. informal splodge.
2 *the one blot on their record was their treatment of ethnic minorities:* blemish, taint, stain, blight, flaw, fault; disgrace, dishonour.
▷verb *blot any excess water with a paper towel:* soak up, absorb, sponge up, mop up; dry up/out; dab, pat.
□ blot something out
1 *clouds were starting to blot out the stars:* conceal, hide, obscure, exclude, obliterate; shadow, eclipse.
2 *he closed his eyes, trying to blot out the memory:* erase, efface, eradicate, expunge, wipe out.

blotch noun *his clothes were covered in blotches of paint:* patch, mark, smudge, dot, spot, blot, dab, daub; informal splotch; Brit. informal splodge.

blotchy adjective *her skin was pale and blotchy:* mottled, blotched, spotty, spotted, smudged; marked; informal splotchy; Brit. informal splodgy.

blow¹ verb
1 *outside an icy wind was blowing:* gust, roar, bluster, rush, storm.
2 *his ship was blown on to the rocks:* sweep, carry, toss, drive, push, force.
3 *leaves blew across the road:* drift, flutter, waft, float, glide, whirl, move.
4 *he blew cigar smoke in her face:* exhale, puff, expel, discharge.
5 *Albert was soon puffing and blowing:* wheeze, puff, pant, gasp.
6 *he blew his trumpet and everyone went quiet:* sound, blast, toot; play.
7 *a rear tyre had blown:* burst, explode, blow out, split, rupture, puncture.
8 *the bulb had blown again:* fuse, short-circuit, burn out, go.
9 (informal) *he blew a lot of his money on gambling:* squander, waste, spend, fritter away, go through, lose, dissipate, use up.
10 (informal) *if you blow this opportunity you might never get another chance:* spoil, ruin, bungle; waste, lose, squander; informal mess up.
□ blow over
the furore will soon blow over: calm down, fade away, disappear, recede, dwindle, peter out, die down, fizzle out.
□ blow up
1 *a lorryload of shells blew up in the mountains:* explode, detonate, go off, ignite, erupt.
2 *he blows up at whoever's in his way:* lose your temper, get angry, rant and rave, go berserk, flare up, erupt; informal go mad,

go crazy, go wild, hit the roof, fly off the handle.
3 *in 1967, a crisis blew up between the two countries:* break out, erupt, flare up, boil over.
▫ **blow something up**
1 *the hijackers had threatened to blow up the aircraft:* bomb, blast, destroy; explode, detonate.
2 *use a pump to blow up the balloons:* inflate, pump up, fill up, puff up, swell, expand.
3 *it was a domestic tiff which had been blown up out of all proportion:* exaggerate, overstate, overstress, overestimate, magnify, amplify; aggrandize.
4 *I blew the picture up on a photocopier:* enlarge, magnify, expand, increase.

blow² noun
1 *death was due to a blow on the head:* knock, bang, hit, punch, thump, smack, crack; informal whack, bash, clout, wallop.
2 *the news came as a crushing blow to the cast:* shock, surprise, thunderbolt, jolt; calamity, catastrophe, disaster, upset, setback; informal bombshell.

blowsy adjective *a loud, blowsy woman in a dress two sizes too small:* untidy, scruffy, messy, unkempt, dishevelled, frowzy; red-faced, florid.

blowy adjective *a blowy day:* windy, windswept, blustery, gusty, breezy; stormy, squally.
OPPOSITES: still.

bludgeon verb
1 *he was bludgeoned to death by his captors:* batter, club, beat, thrash, cudgel.
2 *she was determined not to be bludgeoned into submission:* coerce, force, pressurize, pressure, bully, browbeat, hector, dragoon, steamroller; informal strong-arm, railroad.

blue adjective
1 *the clear blue sky | a blue shirt:* azure, sky-blue, indigo, cobalt, sapphire, navy, Oxford blue, Cambridge blue, ultramarine, aquamarine, turquoise, cyan; literary cerulean.
2 (informal) *she was feeling a bit blue:* depressed, down, sad, unhappy, melancholy, miserable, gloomy, dejected, downhearted, downcast, despondent, low, glum; informal down in the dumps, down in the mouth, fed up.
3 (informal) *a blue movie:* pornographic, indecent, obscene, dirty, smutty, filthy; euphemistic adult.

blueprint noun
1 *he produced blueprints of the aircraft:* plan, design, diagram, drawing, sketch, map, layout, representation.
2 *this is a blueprint for similar measures in other countries:* model, plan, template, framework, pattern, example, guide, prototype, pilot.

blues plural noun (informal) *many people suffer from winter blues:* depression, sadness, unhappiness, melancholy, misery, sorrow, gloom, dejection, despondency, despair.

bluff¹ verb
1 *they are bluffing to hide their guilt:* pretend, put on an act, sham; lie, dissemble.
2 *I managed to bluff the board into believing me:* deceive, trick, fool, dupe, mislead, delude, hoodwink.
▷ noun *the announcement that he will leave is only a bluff:* pretence, deception, fraud, charade; trick, ruse, subterfuge.

bluff² adjective *Thomas had been a bluff hearty man with no finesse:* plain-spoken, straightforward, blunt, direct, no-nonsense, frank, open, candid, forthright, unequivocal; genial, good-natured; informal upfront.

bluff³ noun *he was standing on the edge of a bluff about fifty feet high:* cliff, promontory, headland, crag, bank, escarpment, scarp.

blunder noun *she stopped, finally aware of the terrible blunder she had made:* mistake, error, gaffe, slip, oversight, faux pas; informal slip-up, boo-boo; Brit. informal clanger, boob.
▷ verb
1 *the government admitted it had blundered:* make a mistake, miscalculate, bungle, be wrong, err; informal slip up, screw up; Brit. informal boob.
2 *she blundered down the steps to the cellar:* stumble, lurch, stagger, flounder, struggle, fumble, grope.

blunt adjective
1 *a blunt knife:* unsharpened, dull, worn.
2 *the leaf is broad with a blunt tip:* rounded, flat, stubby; technical obtuse.
3 *he delivered a blunt message to home owners:* forthright, direct, frank, straightforward, plain-spoken, candid, no-nonsense, stark, bald, undisguised, unvarnished, brutal, harsh; informal upfront.
OPPOSITES: sharp, pointed, subtle.
▷ verb
1 *ebony blunts tools very rapidly:* wear, take the edge off.
2 *age hasn't blunted my passion for life:* weaken, dull, deaden, dampen, sap, cool, temper; diminish, reduce, decrease, lessen, deplete.
OPPOSITES: sharpen, intensify.

blur verb *tears blurred her vision:* cloud, fog, obscure, dim, make hazy, make unclear.
OPPOSITES: sharpen, focus.
▷ noun *I could make out a blur on the horizon:* shape, smudge; form, outline.

blurred adjective *all he saw was a blurred grey oval:* indistinct, blurry, fuzzy, hazy, misty, foggy, shadowy, faint; unclear, vague, indefinite, unfocused, obscure, nebulous.

blurt verb
□ blurt something out
she blurted out the truth: burst out with, come out with; reveal, let slip, divulge, disclose, betray, give away; informal blab.

blush verb *Joan blushed at the compliment:* redden, turn/go pink, turn/go red, flush, colour, burn up; feel shy, feel embarrassed.
▷ **noun** *the darkness hid her fiery blush:* flush, rosiness, pinkness, bloom, high colour.

bluster verb
1 *he started blustering about the general election:* rant, hold forth, shout, bellow, roar, yell; be overbearing; informal throw your weight about/around, sound off.
2 *a winter gale blustered against the sides of the house:* blow, beat, gust, storm, roar, rush.

blustery adjective windy, blowy, gusty, stormy, squally, wild, tempestuous; howling, roaring.
OPPOSITES: calm.

board noun
1 *a wooden board:* plank, beam, panel, slat, timber, lath.
2 *the board of directors:* committee, council, panel, directorate, commission, group.
3 *your room and board will be free:* food, meals.
▷ **verb**
1 *he turned and boarded the aircraft:* get on, go aboard, enter, mount, ascend; embark; catch.
2 *a number of students boarded with them:* lodge, live, reside, be housed; informal put up, have digs.
3 *the dogs may have to be boarded at kennels:* accommodate, lodge, take in, put up, house; feed.
□ board something up/over
the windows had been boarded up: cover up/over, seal up, close up, shut up.

boast verb
1 *she boasted about her many conquests:* brag, show off, crow, gloat; Brit. blow your own trumpet; informal talk big, lay it on thick, swank.
2 *the hotel boasts two fine restaurants:* possess, have, own, enjoy, pride yourself/itself on, offer.
▷ **noun** *I said I would win and it wasn't an idle boast:* claim, assertion.

boastful adjective *I'm not being boastful, but everything I did was a cut above the rest:* bragging, full of yourself, cocky, conceited, arrogant, egotistical; literary vainglorious; informal big-headed, swollen-headed.
OPPOSITES: modest.

boat noun *a rowing boat:* vessel, craft, ship; literary barque.

bob verb
1 *their yacht bobbed about on the waves:* move up and down, bounce, toss, skip, dance, jounce; wobble, jiggle, joggle.
2 *she bobbed her head:* nod, incline, dip.
▷ **noun** *he agreed with a bob of his head:* nod, inclination, dip.

bode verb *their argument did not bode well for the future | the 12 per cent interest rate bodes dark days ahead for retailers:* augur, portend, herald, be a sign of, warn of, foreshadow, be an omen of, presage, indicate, signify, promise, threaten, spell, denote.

bodily adjective *bodily sensations:* physical, corporeal, corporal, fleshly; concrete, real, actual, tangible; technical somatic.
OPPOSITES: spiritual, mental.
▷ **adverb** *he hauled her bodily from the van:* forcefully, forcibly, violently.

body noun
1 *drawings of the human body:* figure, frame, form, physique, anatomy, skeleton; technical soma.
2 *he was hit by shrapnel in the head and body:* torso, trunk.
3 *the bodies were dumped in a hole in the ground:* corpse, carcass, skeleton, remains; Medicine cadaver; informal stiff.
4 *the body of the article:* main part, central part, core, heart.
5 *the body of the aircraft:* bodywork, hull; fuselage.
6 *a body of water:* expanse, mass, area, stretch, tract, sweep, extent.
7 *a growing body of evidence:* quantity, amount, volume, collection, mass, corpus, accumulation.
8 *the representative body of the employers:* association, organization, group, party, company, society, circle, syndicate, guild, corporation; delegation, contingent.
9 *a heavenly body:* object, entity.
10 *this lotion adds body to your hair:* fullness, thickness, substance, bounce, lift, shape.

bodyguard noun minder, guard, protector, guardian, defender; informal heavy.

boffin noun (Brit. informal) *a computer boffin:* expert, specialist, authority, genius, mastermind; scientist, technician, inventor.

bog noun marsh, swamp, mire, quagmire, morass, slough; fen, wetland.
□ bogged down
they do not want to get bogged down in expensive litigation: stuck, mired, embroiled, entangled; delayed, impeded, hindered, hampered; swamped, overwhelmed.

bogey noun
1 *he thinks if no one mentions the bogey of*

recession, it will go away: gremlin, spectre, demon, monster.
2 *this tax is the bogey of all wine producers:* bugbear, pet hate, bane, anathema, nightmare, curse.

boggy adjective *the plant grows in boggy areas:* marshy, swampy, muddy, miry, waterlogged, wet, soggy, sodden, squelchy; spongy, heavy.

bogus adjective *fraudsters face up to 10 years in prison for making bogus insurance claims:* fake, false, fraudulent, spurious; counterfeit, forged; informal phoney.
OPPOSITES: genuine.

bohemian adjective *she revelled in the bohemian life of Montparnasse:* unconventional, nonconformist, unorthodox, offbeat, avant-garde, alternative; artistic.
OPPOSITES: conventional.

boil¹ verb
1 *boil and mash the potatoes:* cook, simmer, braise; bring to the boil.
2 *the soup is boiling, so let's eat:* simmer, bubble.
3 *a huge cliff with the sea boiling below:* churn, seethe, froth, foam.
□ **boil down to**
the issues boil down to questions about corporate finance: come down to, amount to, add up to, be in essence.

boil² noun *a piece of plaster covered a boil on his neck:* swelling, spot, pimple, pustule, eruption, carbuncle, wen, abscess, ulcer.

boiling adjective
1 *a pan of boiling water:* at boiling point, scalding; very hot, piping hot; bubbling.
2 (informal) *it was absolutely boiling in the afternoon:* very hot, scorching, blistering, sweltering, sultry, torrid; informal roasting, baking.
OPPOSITES: freezing.

boisterous adjective *the children were very boisterous | a boisterous game:* lively, exuberant, spirited; unruly, rowdy, wild, unrestrained, undisciplined, rough-and-tumble, uninhibited, uncontrolled, disorderly, riotous; noisy, loud, clamorous; Brit. informal rumbustious.
OPPOSITES: restrained.

bold adjective
1 *this is a bold and innovative move:* daring, brave, courageous, audacious, fearless, valiant; adventurous, heroic, plucky, spirited, feisty, daredevil; enterprising, confident; informal gutsy, spunky.
2 *the design was characterized by bold colours and fantastic shapes:* striking, vivid, bright, strong, eye-catching, prominent.
3 *the departure times are in bold:* heavy type, thick type, black type.
OPPOSITES: timid, pale.

bolster verb *the fall in interest rates is starting to bolster confidence:* strengthen, boost, fortify, reinforce; support, buoy up, shore up, maintain, aid, help; augment, increase.
OPPOSITES: undermine.

bolt noun
1 *the bolt on the shed door had been forced:* bar, lock, catch, latch, fastener.
2 *tins of nuts and bolts:* rivet, pin, peg, screw.
3 *a bolt of lightning:* flash, shaft, streak, burst, flare.
4 *Mark made a bolt for the door:* dash, dart, run, sprint, leap, bound.
▷verb
1 *he bolted the door:* lock, bar, latch, fasten, secure.
2 *the lid was bolted down:* rivet, pin, peg, screw; fasten, fix.
3 *Anna bolted from the room:* dash, dart, run, sprint, hurtle, rush, fly, shoot, bound; escape, flee; informal tear.
4 *he bolted down his breakfast:* gobble, wolf, gulp, guzzle, devour; informal demolish, polish off, scoff, shovel down; N. Amer. informal scarf.
□ **a bolt from/out of the blue**
the job offer came like a bolt from the blue: shock, surprise, thunderbolt, revelation; informal turn-up for the books, bombshell.

bomb noun
1 *the house was destroyed by a bomb:* explosive, incendiary device; missile, projectile.
2 *the world has to live with the bomb:* nuclear weapons, the nuclear bomb, the atom bomb; weapons of mass destruction, WMD.
3 (Brit. informal) *that must have cost a bomb.* See FORTUNE sense 5.
▷verb
1 *their headquarters were bombed by separatists:* bombard, blast, shell, blitz, strafe, pound; attack, assault; blow up, destroy, demolish, flatten, devastate.
2 (Brit. informal) *they were bombing down the motorway.* See SPEED verb sense 1.
3 (informal) *the film bombed at the box office.* See FAIL sense 1.

bombard verb
1 *gun batteries bombarded the islands:* shell, pound, blitz, strafe, bomb; attack, assail, assault, batter, blast, pelt.
2 *we were bombarded with information:* inundate, swamp, flood, deluge, snow under; besiege, overwhelm.

bombastic adjective *he launched into a lengthy, bombastic speech:* pompous, blustering, turgid, verbose, orotund, high-flown, overblown, overwrought, florid, pretentious, grandiloquent; informal highfalutin.

bona fide adjective *it is questionable whether or not all such bodies were bona*

b

fide trade unions: authentic, genuine, real, true, actual; legal, legitimate, lawful, valid, proper; informal legit, pukka, the real McCoy.
OPPOSITES: bogus.

bonanza noun *workers stand to share in a massive £1 million cash bonanza:* windfall, bonus, stroke of luck; informal jackpot.

bond noun
1 *the women forged a close bond:* friendship, relationship, fellowship, partnership, association, affiliation, alliance, attachment.
2 *the prisoner struggled in vain with his bonds:* chains, fetters, shackles, manacles, restraints.
3 *a gentleman's word is his bond:* promise, pledge, vow, oath, word of honour, guarantee, assurance; agreement, contract, pact, bargain, deal.
▷verb *press the material to bond the layers together:* join, fasten, fix, affix, attach, secure, bind, stick, fuse.

bondage noun *the deliverance of the Israelites from Egypt's bondage:* slavery, enslavement, servitude, subjugation, subjection, oppression, domination.
OPPOSITES: liberty.

bonhomie noun *he exuded an aura of cheerful bonhomie:* geniality, affability, conviviality, cordiality, amiability, sociability, friendliness, warmth, joviality.
OPPOSITES: coldness.

bonus noun
1 *the work's fun, and coming back to Ireland is a real bonus:* benefit, advantage, boon, blessing, asset, attraction, extra; informal plus, perk.
2 *workers were rewarded with the promise of a 3% Christmas bonus:* extra payment, handout, gift, present, reward; informal perk.
OPPOSITES: disadvantage.

bony adjective *his bony frame was clothed in a grey lightweight suit:* angular, thin, skinny, lean, spare, spindly; gaunt, skeletal, emaciated, underweight.
OPPOSITES: plump.

book noun
1 *he published his first book in 1610:* volume, publication, title; novel, treatise, manual; paperback, hardback, softback; humorous tome.
2 *the council had to balance its books:* accounts, records; account book, record book, ledger, balance sheet.
▷verb
1 *I've booked four tickets:* reserve, prearrange, order.
2 *we've booked a jazz band for the evening do:* engage, organize, arrange, line up, lay on.
□ book in
he booked in at the St Francis Hotel: register, check in, sign in.

booking noun *we made a provisional booking for Friday afternoon:* reservation; arrangement, appointment, date.

bookish adjective *he is a bookish man and a confirmed bachelor:* studious, scholarly, academic, intellectual, highbrow, erudite, learned, educated, knowledgeable; cerebral, serious.

booklet noun pamphlet, brochure, leaflet, handbill, flyer; tract.

boom noun
1 *Mary could hear the boom of the waves below:* reverberation, thunder, echoing, crashing, drumming, pounding, roar, rumble.
2 *retailers are cashing in on an unprecedented boom in sales:* upturn, upsurge, upswing, increase, growth, boost, escalation, improvement, advance.
OPPOSITES: slump.
▷verb
1 *thunder boomed in the sky overhead:* reverberate, resound, resonate; rumble, thunder, blare, echo; crash, roll, clap, explode, bang.
2 *a voice boomed at her from a small doorway:* bellow, roar, thunder, shout, yell, bawl; informal holler.
3 *the property market continued to boom:* flourish, thrive, burgeon, prosper, grow, improve, expand.
OPPOSITES: whisper, slump.

booming adjective
1 *he had a booming voice that contradicted his diminutive stature:* resonant, sonorous, ringing, resounding, reverberating, carrying, thunderous; strident, stentorian, strong, powerful.
2 *the city's booming economy has cut unemployment by 20 per cent:* flourishing, burgeoning, thriving, successful, strong, buoyant; profitable, lucrative; expanding.

boon noun *his offer of rent-free accommodation was such a boon:* blessing, godsend, bonus, benefit, advantage, help, aid, asset; stroke of luck; informal plus.
OPPOSITES: curse.

boorish adjective *he should be held to account for his boorish behaviour:* coarse, uncouth, rude, loutish, ill-bred, ill-mannered, uncivilized, rough, thuggish; vulgar, gross, brutish, Neanderthal; Brit. informal yobbish.
OPPOSITES: refined.

boost verb *they used radio advertising to boost sales:* increase, raise, improve, grow, strengthen, inflate, push up, promote, advance, foster, stimulate; facilitate, help, assist, aid, encourage; informal bump up.

▷ **noun**
1 *the economy will benefit from a boost in sales:* increase, expansion, upturn, upsurge, upswing, rise, escalation, improvement, advance, growth, boom.
2 *the Prince's visit will give a welcome boost to local morale:* lift, uplift, encouragement, help, inspiration, stimulus, fillip, spur; informal shot in the arm.
OPPOSITES: decrease.

boot[1] **noun** *don't come in here in those muddy boots:* gumboot, wellington, wader; informal welly.
▷ **verb**
1 *his shot was booted away by the goalkeeper:* kick; propel, drive; Sport punt.
2 *the menu is ready as soon as you boot up your computer:* start up, fire up, activate.
□ **boot someone out** (informal). See DISMISS sense 1.

boot[2] **noun**
□ **to boot**
she was a woman of uninspiring appearance and a dreadful bore to boot: as well, also, too, besides, in addition, additionally, on top, moreover, furthermore, into the bargain.

booth noun *the market place was covered in booths for different traders:* stall, stand, kiosk.

bootleg adjective *he had a stall selling bootleg CDs:* illegal, unlawful, unauthorized, unlicensed, pirated; contraband, black-market.

booty noun *among the vast quantities of booty are treasures plundered from Buddhist monasteries:* loot, plunder, haul, spoils, stolen goods, ill-gotten gains, pickings; informal swag.

border noun
1 *the road runs from Kabul to the border:* frontier, boundary, borderline, perimeter; marches, bounds.
2 *the border of a medieval manuscript:* edge, margin; sides; rim, fringe, verge, perimeter.
▷ **verb**
1 *the fields were bordered by hedges and trees:* surround, enclose, encircle, circle, edge, fringe, bound, flank.
2 *years ago, the forest bordered on Broadmoor:* adjoin, abut, be next to, be adjacent to, be contiguous with, touch, join, meet, reach.
□ **border on**
he looked at her with something that bordered on contempt: verge on, approach, come close to, be comparable to, approximate to, be tantamount to, be similar to, resemble.

borderline noun *students whose work falls on the borderline between one degree class and another:* dividing line, divide, division, demarcation line, line; threshold,

margin, border, boundary.
▷ **adjective** *references may be required in borderline cases:* uncertain, undecided, doubtful, unclassifiable; questionable, debatable, controversial.

bore[1] **verb** *bore a hole in the ceiling to pass the cable through:* drill, punch, cut; tunnel, burrow, mine, dig, gouge, sink.
▷ **noun** *the anti-tank cannon has a bore of 88 millimetres:* calibre, diameter, gauge.

bore[2] **verb** *his career as a professional activist began to bore him:* pall on, weary, tire, leave cold; informal turn off.
OPPOSITES: interest.
▷ **noun** *it's such a bore cooking when you're alone:* tedious thing/person, bother, nuisance, pest, annoyance, trial; informal drag, pain, pain in the neck, headache, hassle.

boredom noun *I thought I was going to die of boredom:* weariness, ennui, apathy; frustration, dissatisfaction, restlessness, restiveness; tedium, dullness, monotony, repetitiveness, dreariness; literary accidie.

boring adjective *the work had been incredibly boring | a long, boring film:* tedious, dull, monotonous, repetitive, unrelieved, unvaried, unimaginative, uneventful; characterless, featureless, colourless, lifeless, insipid, uninteresting, unexciting, uninspiring, unstimulating, flat, bland, dry, stale, tired, banal, lacklustre, stodgy, dreary, humdrum, mundane; mind-numbing, soul-destroying, wearisome, tiring, tiresome, irksome, trying, frustrating; informal deadly; Brit. informal samey.
OPPOSITES: interesting, stimulating.

borrow verb
1 *I borrowed the money from my mother:* informal cadge.
2 *adventurous chefs often borrow foreign techniques where appropriate:* adopt, take on, acquire, embrace, use.
OPPOSITES: lend.

> **USAGE**
>
> Do not confuse **borrow** with **lend**. **Borrow** means 'to take and use something belonging to someone else with the intention of returning it', while the correct standard use of **lend** is 'to allow someone to use something on the understanding that it will be returned' (*Stuart asked me to lend him my car*). Interestingly there are no very good synonyms for either verb.

boss (informal) **noun** *he is the boss of a large trading company:* head, chief, principal, director, president, chief executive, chair, manager; supervisor, foreman, overseer, controller; employer, owner, proprietor, patron; Brit. informal gaffer, governor.
▷ **verb** *you have no right to boss me about:* order about/around, dictate to, lord it

b

over, bully, domineer, dominate, browbeat; call the shots, lay down the law; informal push around/about, bulldoze, walk all over, railroad.

bossy adjective (informal) *she was inclined to be bossy:* domineering, overbearing, imperious, officious, high-handed, authoritarian, dictatorial, controlling; peremptory; informal high and mighty.
OPPOSITES: submissive.

botch verb (informal) *the police botched the kidnap negotiations:* bungle, mismanage, mishandle, make a mess of; informal mess up, make a hash of, muff, fluff, foul up, screw up; Brit. informal bodge.

bother verb
1 *she had her own life, and no one bothered her:* disturb, trouble, inconvenience; pester, badger, harass, plague, nag, hound; annoy, upset, irritate; informal hassle, bug.
2 *the incident with the waiter was too small to bother about:* mind, care, concern yourself, trouble yourself, worry yourself.
3 *there was something in her voice that bothered him:* worry, trouble, concern, perturb, disturb, disquiet, disconcert, unnerve; upset, distress, agitate, prey on your mind, nag, niggle.
▷ noun
1 *I don't want to put you to any bother:* trouble, effort, exertion, inconvenience, fuss, pains; informal hassle.
2 *the food was such a bother to cook:* nuisance, rigmarole, trial, bore, inconvenience, trouble, problem; informal hassle, palaver, headache, pain in the neck, drag, pest.
3 *he went to sort out a spot of bother in the public bar:* disorder, trouble, ado, disturbance, agitation, commotion, uproar; informal kerfuffle.

bothersome adjective *now I can get rid of those bothersome cold callers:* annoying, irritating, maddening, exasperating, vexatious; tedious, wearisome, tiresome; troublesome, trying, taxing; informal aggravating.

bottle noun *a bottle of wine:* carafe, flask, decanter, pitcher, flagon, demijohn.
□ **bottle something up**
you've been bottling up your feelings for too long: suppress, repress, restrain, withhold, hold in, rein in, inhibit, smother, stifle, contain, conceal, hide; informal keep a lid on.

bottleneck noun traffic jam, jam, congestion, hold-up, gridlock, tailback; constriction, narrowing, restriction, obstruction, blockage; Brit. informal snarl-up.

bottom noun
1 *she paused at the bottom of the stairs:* foot, lowest part, lowest point, base; foundation.
2 *police examined the bottom of the car:* underside, underneath, undersurface, undercarriage.

3 *the boat sank to the bottom of Lake Ontario:* floor, bed, depths.
4 *there's a log cabin at the bottom of his garden:* farthest point, far end, extremity.
5 (Brit.) *she landed on her bottom:* rear end, rump, seat; buttocks; informal backside, behind, derrière; Brit. informal bum; humorous posterior.
▷ **adjective** *she sat on the bottom step holding a glass of champagne:* lowest, last, bottommost.
OPPOSITES: top.

bottomless adjective *a bottomless pit:* deep, unfathomable, immeasurable; inexhaustible, infinite, limitless, unlimited; literary fathomless.

bough noun branch, limb, arm, offshoot.

boulder noun rock, stone.

boulevard noun avenue, street, road, drive, lane, parade, thoroughfare.

bounce verb
1 *the ball hit the ground and bounced:* rebound, spring back, ricochet.
2 *he bounced down the stairs grinning:* bound, leap, jump, spring, bob, hop, skip, trip, prance.
3 *the car bounced down the narrow track:* jolt, bump, judder, jounce, lurch.
▷ noun
1 *the pitch's uneven bounce deceived many less experienced batsmen:* springiness, resilience, elasticity, give.
2 *she had lost a good deal of her bounce:* vitality, vigour, energy, vivacity, liveliness, animation, sparkle, verve, spirit, enthusiasm, dynamism; cheerfulness, happiness, buoyancy, optimism; informal get-up-and-go, pep, zing.
□ **bounce back**
Kramer bounced back after this early setback: recover, revive, rally, pick up, be on the mend; cheer up, brighten up, liven up; informal perk up, buck up.

bouncing adjective *a bouncing baby boy:* healthy, strong, robust, vigorous, thriving, flourishing, blooming.

bouncy adjective
1 *a soft perm will add waves or bouncy curls:* springy.
2 *she was always bouncy, and rarely lost for words:* lively, energetic, perky, jaunty, animated, spirited, buoyant, bubbly, sparkling, vivacious, vibrant, dynamic; enthusiastic, cheerful, upbeat; informal chirpy.

bound[1] adjective
1 *he raised his bound ankles and kicked the door:* tied, chained, fettered, shackled.
2 *she was so far ahead that she seemed bound to win:* certain, sure, destined.
3 *you're bound by the Official Secrets Act to keep this to yourselves:* obligated, obliged, compelled, required, constrained.
4 *religion and morality are bound up with*

one another: connected, linked, tied, united, allied, intertwined.

bound² verb *hares bound and skip in the warm sunshine:* leap, jump, spring, bounce, hop; skip, bob, dance, prance, gambol.
▷ noun *he crossed the room with a single bound:* leap, jump, spring, bounce, hop.

bound³ verb
1 *corporate freedom of action is bounded by law:* limit, restrict, confine, circumscribe, demarcate, delimit.
2 *the heath is bounded by a hedge of conifers:* enclose, surround, encircle, circle, border; close in/off, hem in.
3 *the garden was bounded to the east by Mill Lane:* border, adjoin, abut; be next to, be adjacent to.

boundary noun
1 *the river marks the boundary between the two countries:* border, frontier, borderline.
2 *guards patrolled the boundary of his estate:* border, periphery, perimeter, margins, edges, fringes, bounds, extremities.
3 *a community without class or political boundaries | jazz influences were softening the boundaries of rock:* dividing line, divide, division, borderline, demarcation line; parameters, limits, confines.

boundless adjective *children have boundless curiosity and enthusiasm:* limitless, unlimited, unbounded, untold, immeasurable, abundant; inexhaustible, unflagging, endless, infinite, unfailing, everlasting.
OPPOSITES: limited.

bounds plural noun
1 *landlords are managing to keep rents within reasonable bounds:* limits, confines, proportions.
2 *they owned land within the forest bounds:* borders, boundaries, confines, limits.
□ out of bounds
the lab was out of bounds to visitors: off limits, restricted; forbidden, banned; informal no go.

bountiful adjective
1 *the ocean provided a bountiful supply of fresh food:* abundant, plentiful, ample, copious, superabundant, inexhaustible, prolific, profuse; lavish, generous, handsome, rich; literary plenteous.
2 *he was exceedingly bountiful to people in distress:* generous, magnanimous, munificent, open-handed, unselfish, unstinting, lavish; benevolent, beneficent, charitable.
OPPOSITES: meagre, mean.

bounty noun (literary) *thanks to Robert's bounty I shall have a roof over my head:* generosity, magnanimity, munificence, bountifulness, largesse; benevolence, beneficence, charity, goodwill; blessings, favours.

bouquet noun
1 *she wanted orchids for her bridal bouquet:* bunch of flowers, posy, nosegay, spray, corsage.
2 *the Chardonnay has a fine bouquet:* aroma, nose, smell, fragrance, perfume, scent.

bourgeois adjective
1 *she came from a bourgeois family:* middle-class, conventional, conservative, traditional, conformist; provincial, suburban, small-town.
2 *foreign ideas were denounced as bourgeois decadence:* capitalistic, materialistic, money-oriented.

bout noun
1 *a short bout of exercise can ease insomnia:* period, spell, time, stretch, stint, session; burst, spurt, flurry.
2 *her breathlessness sparked off a coughing bout:* attack, fit, spasm, paroxysm, convulsion, burst, outburst.
3 *he is fighting only his fifth professional bout:* contest, match, competition, event, fixture; fight, encounter.

bow¹ verb
1 *she knelt and bowed her head:* bend, incline, nod, dip.
2 *the government reluctantly bowed to foreign pressure:* yield, submit, give in, give way, surrender, succumb, capitulate, defer; comply with, accept.
▷ noun *a perfunctory bow:* obeisance, salaam, bob, curtsy, nod.
□ bow out
he bowed out of the sport at the end of last season: withdraw, resign, retire, step down, pull out, back out; give up, quit, leave; informal pack in, chuck in; Brit. informal jack in.

bow² noun *the bow of the tanker swept by them:* prow, front, nose, head.

bow³ noun
1 *tie the ribbon in a bow:* loop, knot.
2 *a bow and arrow:* longbow, crossbow.

bowdlerized adjective *Plato was made available only in bowdlerized and misleading translations:* expurgated, censored, edited, cut, sanitized, watered down.

bowel noun
1 *chronic inflammation of the bowel:* intestines, small intestine, large intestine, colon; informal guts, insides, innards.
2 *the skipper emerged from the bowels of the ship:* interior, inside, core, belly; depths, recesses; informal innards.

bowl¹ verb
1 *he bowled a hundred or so balls:* pitch, throw, propel, hurl, toss, lob, fling, launch, deliver.
2 *the car bowled along the country roads:* speed, sweep, glide, shoot, whizz.

□ **bowl someone over**
1 *he was almost bowling people over in his haste:* knock down/over, fell, floor, prostrate.
2 (informal) *I was bowled over by the quality of the music:* overwhelm, greatly impress, astound, astonish, amaze, overawe, dazzle; informal blow away.

bowl² noun
1 *she cracked two eggs into a bowl:* dish, basin; container, vessel, receptacle.
2 *the town lay in a shallow bowl:* valley, hollow, dip, depression, trough, crater.
3 *the Hollywood Bowl:* stadium, arena, amphitheatre.

box noun *the Christmas decorations were kept in a box in the garage:* container, receptacle; case, crate, chest, coffer, casket; carton, pack, packet.
▷ **verb** *Muriel boxed up all his clothes:* package, pack, parcel, wrap, bundle, bale.
□ **box something/someone in**
he got boxed in by members of the press: hem in, shut in, fence in; trap, confine; surround, enclose, encircle.

boxer noun fighter, prizefighter; humorous pugilist.

boy noun male child, schoolboy; young man, youth; informal lad; humorous stripling.

boycott verb *the main opposition parties boycotted the elections:* stay away from, avoid, spurn, shun, abstain from, turn your back on, reject.
▷ **noun** *they called for a boycott on the use of tropical timbers:* ban, veto, embargo, moratorium, prohibition, sanction, restriction; avoidance, rejection, refusal.

boyfriend noun partner, lover, young man, man, significant other; dated beau.

boyish adjective *his tousled hair gave him an appealingly boyish appearance:* youthful, young, childlike.

brace verb
1 *the plane's wing is braced by a system of rods:* support, shore up, prop up, hold up, buttress, underpin; strengthen, reinforce.
2 *I braced my feet against the wall:* press, steady, secure, stabilize, fix.
3 *you'd better brace yourself for disappointment:* prepare, get ready, gear up, nerve, steel, strengthen, fortify; informal psych yourself up.

bracelet noun bangle, band, circlet, armlet, wristlet.

bracing adjective *we took a bracing walk along the coast* | *the bracing sea air:* invigorating, refreshing, energizing, exhilarating, reviving, restorative, rejuvenating, revitalizing, stimulating, fortifying, strengthening; fresh, brisk.

bracket noun *I'm now in a higher tax bracket:* group, category, grade, band, stratum, set, division; range.
▷ **verb** *women were bracketed with children for the purposes of wage assessment:* group, classify, categorize, class, grade, list, sort, place; couple, pair; liken, compare.

brag verb *she listened to him brag about his business connections:* boast, show off, crow, gloat, sing your own praises; Brit. blow your own trumpet; informal talk big, swank.

braggart noun *he was a braggart and a liar:* boaster, bragger; informal big-head, loudmouth, show-off.

braid noun
1 *the shoulder straps were bordered with gold braid:* cord, thread, tape, binding, ribbon.
2 *his long hair was worn in braids and tied at the back of his neck:* plait, pigtail, twist; cornrows, dreadlocks.
▷ **verb**
1 *they braided her hair with fancy ribbons:* plait, intertwine, interweave, weave, twist, twine.
2 *the sleeves are braided in scarlet and lined with ermine:* trim, edge, border, pipe, fringe.

brain noun
1 *the disease attacks certain cells in the brain:* cerebrum; Anatomy encephalon.
2 *success requires brains as well as brawn:* intelligence, intellect, brainpower, cleverness, wits, acumen, discernment, judgement, understanding, sense; informal nous, grey matter.

brainless adjective *her husband treats her like a brainless twit:* stupid, foolish, witless, unintelligent, ignorant, idiotic, simple-minded, empty-headed; informal dumb, half-witted, half-baked, moronic, cretinous, thick, dopey, dozy, birdbrained.

brainwash verb *women have been brainwashed into thinking they should go out to work:* indoctrinate, condition, programme, persuade, pressurize.

brainy adjective (informal) *he's incredibly brainy and speaks seven languages:* clever, intelligent, bright, brilliant, gifted; intellectual, erudite, academic, scholarly, studious, bookish; informal smart.
OPPOSITES: stupid.

brake verb *she braked at the traffic lights:* slow down, decelerate, reduce speed.
OPPOSITES: accelerate.

> **USAGE**
>
> Do not confuse **brake** with **break**. As a verb **brake** means 'to slow or stop a vehicle', while the main meanings of **break** are 'to separate into pieces' (*be careful not to break the glass*), or 'a pause or interruption' (*let's take a break for lunch*).

branch noun

1 *the branches of the tree creaked in the wind:* bough, limb, arm, offshoot.
2 *a branch of the river flows through Jonestown:* tributary, feeder, side stream.
3 *the judicial branch of government is completely independent:* division, subdivision, section, subsection, department, sector, part, side, wing.
4 *the corporation's New York branch was doing well:* office, bureau, agency; subsidiary, offshoot, satellite.

▷**verb**

1 *turn right where the road branches:* fork, bifurcate, divide, subdivide, split.
2 *several narrow paths branched off the road:* diverge from, deviate from, split off from; fan out from, radiate from.

□ **branch out**
the company is branching out into Europe: expand, open up, extend; diversify, broaden your horizons.

brand noun

1 *a new brand of low-fat spread:* make, line, label; type, kind, sort, variety; trade name, trademark, proprietary name; (only of cars) marque.
2 *I don't care for her particular brand of humour:* type, kind, sort, variety, class, category, genre, style.

▷**verb**

1 *the letter M was branded on each animal:* mark, stamp, burn, sear.
2 *the media branded us as communists:* stigmatize, mark out, label; denounce, discredit, vilify.

brandish verb *an old man approached me, brandishing a stick:* wave, flourish, shake, wield; swing.

brash adjective

1 *he was a brash, noisy little man:* self-assertive, cocksure, cocky, self-confident, arrogant, bold, brazen; forward, impudent, insolent, rude; informal pushy.
2 *it's a resort full of bustle and a brash sort of charm:* garish, gaudy, loud, flamboyant, showy, tasteless; informal flashy, tacky.
OPPOSITES: meek, muted.

bravado noun *despite all his bravado, he was actually very sensitive:* boldness, swagger, bluster; machismo; boasting, bragging; literary braggadocio.

brave adjective *they are the last of a generation of brave young men who risked their lives for their country:* courageous, plucky, valiant, valorous, intrepid, heroic, lionhearted, bold, fearless, daring; unflinching, unshrinking, unafraid, dauntless, doughty, mettlesome, stout-hearted, spirited; informal game, gutsy, spunky.
OPPOSITES: cowardly.

▷**verb** *around 400 fans braved freezing temperatures to see them play:* endure, put up with, bear, withstand, weather, suffer,

go through; face, confront, defy.

bravery noun courage, pluck, valour, intrepidity, nerve, daring, fearlessness, boldness, dauntlessness, stout-heartedness, heroism; backbone, grit, spine, spirit, mettle; informal guts, spunk; Brit. informal bottle.

bravura noun *Zelensky danced with technical bravura:* skill, brilliance, virtuosity, expertise, artistry, flair, talent, ability.

▷**adjective** *it was a bravura performance:* virtuoso, masterly, outstanding, excellent, superb, brilliant, first-class; informal ace.

brawl noun *three footballers have been accused of assault after a brawl in a nightclub:* fight, skirmish, scuffle, tussle, melee, fracas, free-for-all, scrum; fisticuffs; informal scrap, dust-up, set-to; Brit. informal punch-up; Law, dated affray.

▷**verb** *he ended up brawling with photographers at the airport:* fight, scuffle, tussle, exchange blows, grapple, wrestle, skirmish; informal scrap.

brawn noun *commando work required as much brain as brawn:* physical strength, strength, muscle; burliness, power, might, toughness.

brawny adjective *a tall brawny man with a crew cut:* strong, muscular, muscly, well built, powerful, mighty, strapping, burly, sturdy, rugged; bulky, hefty, meaty, solid; informal beefy.
OPPOSITES: puny, weak.

brazen adjective *he was unprepared for her brazen admission that she was cheating:* bold, shameless, unashamed, unabashed, unembarrassed, defiant; barefaced, blatant, flagrant.
OPPOSITES: timid.

□ **brazen it out**
David tried to brazen it out last night, as the list of his misdemeanours grew: put on a bold front, stand your ground, be defiant, be unrepentant, be unabashed.

breach noun

1 *this is a clear breach of the terms of the contract:* contravention, violation, infringement, infraction, transgression.
2 *there is a widening breach between government and Church:* rift, schism, division, gulf, chasm; estrangement, discord, dissension, disagreement; split, break, rupture.
3 *there were a number of breaches in the sea wall:* break, split, crack; gap, hole, opening.

▷**verb**

1 *on Tuesday the river breached its banks:* break, break through, burst, rupture; informal bust.
2 *he was sentenced to five months in prison for breaching the restraining order:* break, contravene, violate, infringe; defy, disobey, flout, fly in the face of.

breadth noun

1 *the breadth of the lake was about 500 metres:* width, broadness; span; diameter.
2 *nowhere else can you get the same breadth of experience in a single place:* range, extent, scope, depth, degree, reach, compass.

break verb

1 *the mirror fell to the floor and broke:* shatter, smash, crack, snap, fracture, fragment, splinter; informal bust.
2 *she had broken her leg in two places:* fracture, crack; sever.
3 *the bite had barely broken the skin:* pierce, puncture, penetrate, perforate; cut.
4 *the coffee machine has broken again:* stop working, break down, go wrong, malfunction, crash; informal go kaput, conk out, be on the blink, give up the ghost; Brit. informal pack up.
5 *traders who break the law will be prosecuted:* contravene, breach, infringe; defy, violate, flout, disobey, fly in the face of.
6 *at mid-morning they broke for coffee:* stop, pause, have a rest; informal knock off.
7 *the second film broke all box-office records:* beat, surpass, exceed, better, cap, top, outdo, outstrip, eclipse.
8 *fortunately, a pile of carpets broke his fall:* cushion, soften, take the edge off.
9 *the strategies used to break the union:* destroy, crush, quash, defeat, vanquish, overcome, overpower, overwhelm, suppress; weaken, undermine, wear/grind down; bankrupt, bring to its knees.
10 *he tried to break the news gently:* reveal, disclose, divulge, impart, tell; announce, release.
11 *Krycek managed to break the encryption code:* decipher, decode, decrypt, work out; informal crack.
OPPOSITES: repair, keep, abide by.

▷ **noun**
1 *the magazine has been published without a break since 1950 | there was no break in the traffic pouring into the streets:* interruption, gap, pause, interval, intermission, hiatus, discontinuation, suspension, disruption, stop, stoppage, cessation; breathing space, respite.
2 *let's have a break and get something to eat:* rest, pause; time out; informal breather.
3 *a break in the clouds | a break in the wall:* gap, hole, opening, space, slit, aperture, chink, interstice, crack, crevice, fissure, breach.
4 *a weekend break in Amsterdam:* holiday; N. Amer. vacation.
5 (informal) *the actress got her first break in 1951:* opportunity, chance, opening.
□ **break away**
1 *she attempted to break away from his grip:* escape, get away, break free, break loose, get out of someone's clutches.
2 *a small group broke away from the main party:* leave, split off from, part company with, separate from, secede from; defect from; form a splinter group.
□ **break down**
1 *his van broke down on the M6:* stop working, go wrong, malfunction; informal go kaput, conk out, give up the ghost; Brit. informal pack up.
2 *pay negotiations with the management broke down:* fail, collapse, founder, fall through, disintegrate; informal fizzle out.
3 *Vicky broke down, sobbing loudly:* burst into tears; lose control, be overcome, go to pieces; informal crack up, lose it.
□ **break something down**
1 *police broke the door down:* knock down, kick down, smash in, pull down, tear down, demolish.
2 *break big tasks down into smaller parts:* divide, separate.
3 *graphs show how the information can be broken down:* analyse, categorize, classify, itemize, organize; dissect.
□ **break in**
1 *thieves broke in and took her credit cards:* force your way in.
2 *'I don't want to interfere,' Mrs Hendry broke in:* interrupt, interject, interpose, chime in; butt in, cut in; informal chip in.
□ **break off**
the fuselage had broken off just behind the cockpit: snap off, come off, detach, separate.
□ **break something off**
1 *I broke off a branch from the tree:* snap off, pull off, sever, detach.
2 *they threatened to break off diplomatic relations:* end, terminate, stop, cease, call a halt to, finish, dissolve; suspend, discontinue; informal pull the plug on.
□ **break out**
1 *two suspected terrorists broke out of the detention centre:* escape from, abscond from, flee from; get free.
2 *fighting broke out between rival army units:* flare up, start suddenly, erupt, burst out.
□ **break up**
1 *after about an hour, the meeting broke up:* end, finish, stop, terminate; adjourn; N. Amer. recess.
2 *gradually the crowd began to break up:* disperse, scatter, disband, go their separate ways.
3 *Danny and I broke up last year:* split up, separate, part, part company.
□ **break something up**
1 *police tried to break up the demonstration:* disperse, scatter, disband.
2 *I'm not going to let you break up my marriage:* wreck, ruin, destroy.

USAGE

Do not confuse **break** with **brake**. The primary meanings of **break** are 'to separate into pieces', or 'a pause or interruption'. The verb **brake** means 'to slow or stop a vehicle' (*she braked sharply to avoid the car in front*).

breakable adjective *move any breakable objects from the children's reach:* fragile, delicate, flimsy; technical frangible.

breakaway adjective *a breakaway nationalist group had claimed responsibility:* separatist, splinter, secessionist, schismatic; rebel, renegade.

breakdown noun
1 *the breakdown of the negotiations was inevitable:* failure, collapse, disintegration.
2 *we need a detailed breakdown of the figures:* analysis, classification, examination, investigation, dissection.
3 *on the death of her father she suffered a breakdown:* collapse, nervous breakdown; informal crack-up.

break-in noun burglary, robbery, theft, raid; informal smash-and-grab.

breakneck adjective *the breakneck pace of technological change:* extremely fast, rapid, speedy, high-speed, lightning, whirlwind.
□ **at breakneck speed**
he drove at breakneck speed: extremely fast, at full tilt, flat out; informal hell for leather; Brit. informal like the clappers.

breakthrough noun *a major breakthrough in the fight against Aids:* advance, development, step forward, quantum leap, success, improvement; discovery, innovation, revolution.
OPPOSITES: setback.

break-up noun
1 *the break-up of the peace negotiations:* end, breakdown, failure, collapse, disintegration.
2 *getting her life back on keel after their break-up was difficult:* separation, split, parting, divorce; estrangement, rift; Brit. informal bust-up.
3 *the break-up of the former Soviet Union:* division, partition.

breakwater noun sea wall, jetty, mole, groyne, pier.

breath noun
1 *I took a deep breath:* inhalation, gulp; exhalation, expiration; Medicine respiration.
2 *the night was still, with barely a breath of wind:* puff, waft, faint breeze, whisper.
□ **take someone's breath away**
the scenery will take your breath away: astonish, astound, amaze, stun, stagger; awe, overawe, thrill; informal knock sideways, blow away, bowl over; Brit. informal knock for six.

breathe verb
1 *she was breathing deeply:* inhale and exhale, respire, draw breath; puff, pant, blow, gasp, wheeze.
2 *'Together at last,' she breathed:* whisper, murmur, sigh; say.

WORD LINKS
respiratory relating to breathing

breathless adjective
1 *Will ran back, arriving flushed and breathless:* out of breath, panting, puffing, gasping; winded, puffed out, short of breath; exhausted.
2 *the crowd waited, breathless with anticipation:* agog, open-mouthed, on the edge of your seat, on tenterhooks, in suspense; excited, impatient.

breathtaking adjective *visually, the movie is nothing short of breathtaking:* spectacular, magnificent, wonderful, awe-inspiring, awesome, astounding, astonishing, amazing, stunning, incredible; thrilling, exciting; literary wondrous; informal sensational, out of this world.

breed verb
1 *Asian elephants breed readily in captivity:* reproduce, multiply; mate; formal procreate.
2 *he breeds horses and cattle:* rear, raise; propagate
3 *she was born and bred in the village:* bring up, rear, raise, nurture.
4 *the political system bred massive discontent:* cause, bring about, give rise to, lead to, produce, generate, engender, foster, result in; literary beget.
▷ noun
1 *a rare breed of cow:* type, kind, sort; genus, species, variety, strain.
2 *he is one of a new breed of journalists:* type, kind, sort, class, generation.

breeding noun
1 *individual birds pair late in the season for breeding:* reproduction, procreation; mating.
2 *the breeding of rats for scientific experiments:* rearing, raising.
3 *her aristocratic breeding was never far from the surface:* upbringing, background; parentage, family, pedigree, blood, birth.

breeding ground noun *the school is a breeding ground for progressive ideas:* nursery, cradle; nest, den, hotbed.

breeze noun *a slight breeze ruffled the leaves:* wind, puff of air, gust; literary zephyr.
▷ verb (informal) *Roger breezed into her office:* saunter, stroll, sail, sweep.

breezy adjective
1 *it was a bright, breezy day:* windy, blowy, blustery, gusty; fresh, brisk.
2 *her breezy confidence impressed him:* jaunty, cheerful, cheery, upbeat, brisk, carefree, easy, casual, relaxed, informal, light-hearted.

brevity noun
1 *the report is notable for its clarity and brevity:* conciseness, concision, succinctness, economy of language, pithiness, incisiveness, compactness, shortness.
2 *the brevity of human life is all too apparent here:* shortness, briefness, transience, ephemerality, impermanence.
OPPOSITES: verbosity.

b

brew verb

1 *this beer is brewed in Frankfurt:* ferment, make.

2 *I'll go and brew some tea:* make, prepare; infuse.

3 *there's trouble brewing:* develop, loom, be imminent, be on the horizon, be in the offing, be just around the corner.

▷ **noun**

1 *she took a sip of the hot, reviving brew:* drink, beverage.

2 *a dangerous brew of political turmoil and violent conflict:* mixture, mix, blend, combination, amalgam.

bribe verb *he was accused of bribing government officials:* buy off, pay off; formal suborn; informal grease someone's palm; Brit. informal nobble.

▷ **noun** *a politician who had accepted bribes from lobbyists:* inducement, incentive; informal backhander, pay-off, kickback, sweetener; Brit. informal bung.

> WORD LINKS
> **venal** susceptible to bribery

bribery noun *the company faces charges of bribery:* corruption; informal palm-greasing, graft.

bric-a-brac noun *the Victorians crammed their homes with furniture and bric-a-brac:* ornaments, knick-knacks, trinkets; paraphernalia; informal bits and pieces; Brit. informal odds and ends.

brick noun *a brick of ice cream:* block, bar, cube, cake.

bridal adjective *her bridal gown | the bridal party emerged from the church:* wedding, marriage; nuptial, matrimonial, marital, conjugal.

bridge noun *the Romans built a bridge over the river:* viaduct, flyover, overpass, aqueduct.

▷ **verb** *an attempt to bridge the gap between the two cultures:* reduce, lessen, narrow; overcome, reconcile, straddle; join, link, connect, unite.

bridle verb *she bridled at his autocratic tone:* bristle, take offence, take umbrage, be affronted, be offended, get angry.

brief adjective

1 *he gave a brief account of what had happened:* concise, succinct, short, pithy, incisive; abridged, condensed, compressed, abbreviated, summary; compact, thumbnail, potted; formal compendious.

2 *a brief visit | a brief respite from the rain:* short, fleeting, flying, hasty, hurried, quick, short-lived; passing, temporary, momentary, transient; cursory, perfunctory.

3 *a pair of extremely brief black shorts:* skimpy, scanty, short; revealing.

OPPOSITES: long, lengthy.

▷ **noun** (Brit.) *the brief given to Ford's designers was to take a Fiesta and make it chic:*

instructions, directions, guidelines, outline; plan, job description.

▷ **verb** *council employees were briefed about the decision:* inform, tell, update, notify, advise, apprise; prepare, prime, instruct; informal fill in, put in the picture.

briefing noun *the daily press briefings at the White House:* conference, meeting, interview, session.

briefly adverb

1 *Henry paused briefly to catch his breath:* momentarily, temporarily, for a moment, fleetingly.

2 *briefly, the plot is as follows:* in short, in brief, to cut a long story short, in a word, in sum, in a nutshell, in essence.

brigade noun

1 *there were two regiments per brigade, each with a strength of around 4,000:* unit, battalion, regiment, division, squadron, company, platoon, section, corps, troop.

2 *the volunteer ambulance brigade:* squad, team, group, band, party, crew, force, outfit.

3 (informal) *the 'it's all in the mind' brigade have ridiculed sufferers of chronic fatigue syndrome for years:* group, contingent; school; informal crowd, lot, gang, squad, bunch, crew.

bright adjective

1 *she stood blinking in the bright sunlight | the bright surface of the metal:* shining, brilliant, dazzling, blinding, glaring; sparkling, glittering, gleaming, glowing, luminous, radiant; shiny, lustrous, glossy.

2 *it was a cold, bright morning:* sunny, cloudless, clear, fair, fine.

3 *she loved bright colours:* vivid, vibrant, brilliant, rich, strong, bold, fluorescent; gaudy, lurid, garish.

4 *he felt bright and full of youthful energy:* cheerful, happy, cheery, jolly, sunny, lively, exuberant, bubbly, perky; informal chirpy.

5 *he's a bright young man who should go far | a bright idea:* clever, intelligent, quick-witted, sharp, canny, astute, perceptive; ingenious, resourceful; gifted, brilliant; informal smart, brainy.

6 *the future looks bright for this company:* promising, encouraging, rosy, hopeful, optimistic; good, favourable, propitious, auspicious, golden.

OPPOSITES: dull, dark, stupid.

brighten verb

1 *the morning sunshine brightened the room:* illuminate, light up, make bright, make brighter, lighten, cast its light on.

2 *this colourful pottery will brighten up your shelves and dinner table:* enhance, enrich, prettify, beautify; informal jazz up.

3 *Sarah brightened up as she thought of Emily's words:* cheer up, rally; be enlivened, feel heartened, be uplifted, be encouraged, take heart; informal perk up, buck up.

brilliance noun

1 *he was a philosopher of great brilliance:* genius, talent, ability, prowess, skill, expertise, aptitude, flair, finesse, panache; greatness, distinction; intelligence, wisdom, sagacity, intellect.
2 *I was blinded by the brilliance of the sunshine:* brightness, vividness, intensity; sparkle, glitter, glittering, glow, blaze, luminosity, radiance.

brilliant adjective

1 *Marshall was a brilliant student:* gifted, talented, able, adept, skilful; bright, intelligent, clever, astute; elite, superior, first-class, first-rate, excellent; informal smart, brainy.
2 *this film was the high point of his brilliant career:* glorious, illustrious, impressive, remarkable, exceptional; glittering, stellar.
3 *brilliant sunshine illuminated the scene:* bright, shining, blazing, dazzling, gleaming, glaring, luminous, radiant.
4 *brilliant pink bougainvillea covered the old stone walls of the cottage:* vivid, intense, bright, bold, dazzling.
OPPOSITES: stupid, bad, dark.

brim noun

1 *he fingered the brim of his hat:* visor, shield, shade; Brit. peak.
2 *the cup was filled to the brim with cocoa:* rim, lip, edge, top.
▷ **verb**
1 *the pan was brimming with water:* be full, be filled; overflow, run over.
2 *her eyes were brimming with tears:* fill, fill up; overflow.

brimful adjective *the team are brimful of confidence:* full of, brimming with, filled with, bursting with, radiating.
OPPOSITES: empty.

bring verb

1 *Liz brought her a glass of water:* carry, fetch, bear, take; convey, transport, deliver.
2 *he brought them into the kitchen:* escort, conduct, guide, lead, usher, show, shepherd.
3 *continuing economic decline brought pressure for change:* cause, produce, create, generate, precipitate, lead to, give rise to, result in.
4 *the police contemplated bringing charges of assault:* prefer, initiate, institute.
5 *two important Chippendale lots brought £10,000 each:* earn, make, bring in, yield, net, gross, return, produce.
□ **bring something about**
the war brought about a large increase in government debt: cause, produce, give rise to, result in, lead to, occasion, effect; provoke, generate, engender, precipitate.
□ **bring something back**
1 *the smell brought back memories of her misspent youth:* remind someone of, put someone in mind of, bring/call to mind,

conjure up, evoke, summon up; take someone back.
2 *the conference voted to bring back capital punishment:* reintroduce, reinstate, re-establish, revive, resurrect.
□ **bring something down**
1 *a reduction in fraud will bring down the cost of motor insurance:* decrease, reduce, lower, cut, drop; informal slash.
2 *the unrest eventually brought down the government:* unseat, overturn, topple, overthrow, depose, oust.
□ **bring something forward**
we intend to bring forward proposals for new Sunday trading legislation: propose, suggest, advance, raise, table, present, move, submit, lodge.
□ **bring someone in**
it was nice of him to bring me in on the deal so early: involve, include, count in.
□ **bring something in**
the government brought in new laws tightening up the sale of fireworks: introduce, institute, put in place, launch, inaugurate, initiate.
□ **bring something off**
they knew he could bring off brilliant business coups: achieve, accomplish, bring about, pull off, manage, realize, complete; execute, perform, discharge.
□ **bring something on**
the case dragged on for years and the stress of it brought on a stroke: cause, give rise to, result in, lead to, produce, occasion, generate, engender, induce; trigger, provoke, precipitate.
□ **bring something out**
1 *the band are bringing out a new album later this month:* launch, release, produce, issue; publish, print.
2 *the scarf brings out the colour of your eyes:* accentuate, highlight, emphasize, accent, set off.
□ **bring someone round**
she's not keen, but I think I can bring her round: persuade, convince, talk round, win over, sway, influence.
□ **bring yourself to**
she could not bring herself to pull the trigger: force yourself to, make yourself, bear to.
□ **bring someone up**
she was brought up by her grandmother: rear, raise, care for, look after, nurture, provide for.
□ **bring something up**
later that evening he casually brought up the subject of money: mention, raise, broach, introduce, allude to, touch on; voice, air, suggest, propose, submit, put forward, bring forward, table.

brink noun *the two countries were on the brink of war:* verge, threshold, point, edge.

brisk adjective

1 *he set off at a brisk pace:* quick, rapid, fast, swift, speedy, hurried; energetic, lively, vigorous.

b

2 *the bar was already doing a brisk trade:* busy, lively, hectic; good.
3 *his tone was brisk:* no-nonsense, decisive, businesslike; brusque, abrupt, short, peremptory.
4 *there was a brisk breeze blowing in from the sea:* bracing, fresh, crisp, invigorating, refreshing, stimulating, energizing; biting, keen, chilly, cold; informal nippy.
OPPOSITES: slow, quiet.

bristle noun *he rubbed at the bristles on his face:* hair, whisker; (**bristles**) stubble.
▷**verb**
1 *Corbett sensed the danger, and the hair on the back of his neck bristled:* rise, stand up, stand on end.
2 *she swivelled round, bristling at his tone:* bridle, take offence, take umbrage, be affronted, be offended; get angry, be irritated.
3 *the roof of the outhouse bristled with antennae:* be covered with, be crowded with, be full of, abound with, teem with; informal be thick with.

bristly adjective
1 *the dunes were dotted with bristly little bushes:* prickly, spiky, thorny, scratchy, brambly.
2 *she rubbed the bristly skin of his cheek with the back of her hand:* stubbly, hairy, fuzzy, unshaven, whiskered, whiskery; scratchy, rough, coarse, prickly.
OPPOSITES: smooth.

Britain noun the United Kingdom, the UK, Great Britain, the British Isles; literary Albion; Brit. informal Blighty.

brittle adjective
1 *old shellac records were very brittle:* breakable, fragile; splintery; technical frangible.
2 *she began to speak in a brittle, staccato voice:* harsh, hard, sharp.
3 *a super-thin, brittle woman:* edgy, nervy, highly strung, tense; neurotic, unstable.
OPPOSITES: flexible, resilient.

broach verb *I made up my mind to broach the issue over lunch:* bring up, raise, introduce, talk about, mention, touch on, air.

broad adjective
1 *they descended a broad flight of steps:* wide.
2 *the leaves are six inches long and two inches broad:* wide, across, from side to side, in breadth, in width.
3 *the area consisted of broad open meadows, which frequently flooded:* extensive, sweeping, rolling, vast, immense, great, spacious, expansive, sizeable.
4 *we offer a broad range of opportunities for young entrepreneurs:* comprehensive, inclusive, extensive, wide, wide-ranging, all-embracing, eclectic, unlimited.
5 *this report gives a broad outline of our environmental performance:* general, non-

specific, unspecific, rough, approximate, basic; loose, vague.
6 *he dropped a broad hint about the likely outcome of the negotiations:* obvious, unmistakable, explicit, direct, plain, clear, transparent, undisguised, overt, straightforward, bald.
7 *he spoke in a broad Somerset accent:* pronounced, noticeable, marked, strong, thick.
OPPOSITES: narrow, limited, detailed.

broadcast verb
1 *the concert will be broadcast live:* transmit, relay, air, show, televise, telecast, screen.
2 *he has donated substantial amounts of money to charity but has never wanted to broadcast that fact:* report, publicize; spread, circulate, air, blazon, trumpet.
▷**noun** *nearly 18 million people watched the broadcast on CBS:* programme, show, production, transmission, telecast, screening.

broaden verb
1 *he let his expression broaden into a smile:* widen, expand, stretch out, draw out, spread; deepen.
2 *he is to assess how the party can broaden its appeal at the next election:* expand, enlarge, extend, widen; increase, augment, add to, amplify; develop, enrich, improve, build on.

broadly adverb
1 *the pattern of illness is broadly similar for men and women:* in general, on the whole, as a rule, in the main; loosely, roughly, approximately.
2 *he smiled broadly, shaking his head:* widely, openly.

broad-minded adjective *in Europe, music fans are usually more broad-minded:* liberal, tolerant, open-minded, freethinking, progressive, permissive, unshockable.
OPPOSITES: intolerant.

broadside noun *the 37-year-old all-rounder launched a broadside at the England selectors and captain last night:* attack, onslaught, diatribe, tirade; criticism, condemnation, censure.

brochure noun booklet, catalogue, prospectus; pamphlet, leaflet.

broke adjective (informal). See **PENNILESS**.

broken adjective
1 *the streets were covered in broken glass:* smashed, shattered, fragmented, splintered, crushed; in bits, in pieces; cracked, split; informal in smithereens.
2 *she suffered a broken arm in the attack:* fractured.
3 *the TV's broken:* out of order, not working, malfunctioning, inoperative; damaged, faulty, defective; down; informal

on the blink, kaput, bust; Brit. informal knackered.

4 *after three broken marriages, he's found stability with his fourth wife:* failed, unsuccessful.

5 *it was an enormous humiliation and he was left a broken man:* defeated, beaten, subdued; despairing, demoralized, dispirited, crushed.

6 *we endured a long night of broken sleep:* interrupted, disturbed, fitful, disrupted, discontinuous, intermittent, unsettled, troubled.

7 *he pressed on gingerly over the broken ground:* uneven, rough, irregular, bumpy; rutted, pitted.

8 *they expressed themselves in broken English with much arm waving:* halting, hesitating, disjointed, faltering, imperfect.

broken-down adjective *a broken-down Land Rover was parked by the roadside:* dilapidated, battered, ramshackle, in disrepair; broken, not working, malfunctioning, inoperative; informal clapped out; Brit. informal knackered.

broken-hearted adjective *the woman he left behind was broken-hearted:* heartbroken, grief-stricken, inconsolable, desolate, devastated, shattered, wretched, heavy-hearted; miserable, depressed, melancholy, sorrowful, forlorn.
OPPOSITES: overjoyed.

broker noun *the centralized lenders operate through brokers:* dealer, agent; middleman, intermediary.
▷ **verb** *the UN brokered a ceasefire:* arrange, negotiate, organize, orchestrate, work out, bring about.

bronzed adjective *with their youthful good looks and bronzed faces they were an attractive couple:* tanned, suntanned, tan, brown.

brood verb *it's useless to brood over the past:* dwell on, worry about, fret about, agonize about, mope about; think about, ponder, contemplate, meditate on, muse about, ruminate on.
▷ **noun** *the male then returns to his mate and helps her raise the brood:* offspring, young, progeny; family, hatch, clutch.

brook[1] noun *a small brook gurgled through the trees:* stream, rill, runnel; N. English beck; Scottish & N. English burn.

brook[2] verb (formal) *he was not, one gathers, a man to brook opposition:* tolerate, allow, stand, put up with, bear; accept, permit, countenance; informal stomach, stand for; old use suffer.

brotherhood noun
1 *the ideals of justice and brotherhood:* fellowship, friendship, camaraderie, solidarity, comradeship, understanding.
2 *he'd be a loss to the brotherhood if we expelled him:* society, fraternity, association, alliance, union, league, guild, order, body, community, club, circle.

brotherly adjective
1 *brotherly rivalry:* fraternal, sibling.
2 *he gave her a brotherly kiss:* affectionate, fond, loving, caring, friendly.

brow noun
1 *the doctor wiped his brow with a large handkerchief:* forehead, temple.
2 *the driver lost control as the car came over the brow of the hill:* top, crest, summit, peak, crown, apex.

browbeat verb *he had browbeaten his colleagues into agreeing:* bully, intimidate, force, coerce, compel, dragoon, bludgeon, pressure, pressurize, terrorize; hound; informal bulldoze, railroad.

brown adjective
1 *her thick brown hair:* brunette, chestnut, tawny.
2 *a brown coat | brown paint:* fawn, beige, buff, tan, camel, café au lait; hazel; sepia, mahogany, umber, burnt sienna.
3 *his face was thin and brown:* tanned, suntanned, bronzed; dark, swarthy, nut-brown.

browse verb
1 *you can browse and compare price and quality, without pressure to buy:* look around/round, window-shop.
2 *Stella browsed through the newspaper:* scan, skim, glance, look; thumb, leaf, flick; dip into.

bruise noun *she had a nasty bruise across her forehead:* contusion, mark, injury; swelling, lump, bump, welt.
▷ **verb** *she grabbed his arm, hard enough to bruise it:* mark, discolour, injure; rare contuse.

brunette adjective brown-haired, dark, dark-haired.

brunt noun *front-line staff bore the brunt of the abuse:* full force, chief impact, burden, shock; effect, repercussions, consequences.

brush[1] noun
1 *use a brush to sweep up the leaves:* broom, besom.
2 *his unfortunate and ill-timed brush with the law:* encounter, clash, confrontation, conflict, altercation; informal run-in.
▷ **verb**
1 *he spent most of his day brushing the floors:* sweep, clean, buff.
2 *she began to brush her hair:* groom, comb, neaten, tidy, smooth, arrange.
3 *she brushed a wisp of hair away from her face:* push, move, sweep.
☐ **brush something aside** *O'Neill brushed the criticisms aside:* disregard, ignore, dismiss, shrug off, wave aside; overlook, pay no attention to, take no notice of, turn a blind eye to; reject;

b

laugh off, make light of, trivialize; informal pooh-pooh.
□ **brush someone off**
he tried to start a conversation but she brushed him off: rebuff, spurn, reject, dismiss; ignore, disregard, snub, cut, turn your back on, give someone the cold shoulder; informal freeze out.
□ **brush something up, brush up on something**
I've been brushing up my Italian: revise, read up, go over, relearn, study; improve, sharpen up, polish up; hone, refine, perfect; informal bone up; Brit. informal swot up.

brush² noun *the area was covered in dense brush:* undergrowth, scrub, brushwood, shrubs, bushes.

brusque adjective *he was disliked because of his brusque manner:* curt, abrupt, blunt, short, sharp, terse, brisk, peremptory, gruff; offhand, discourteous, impolite, rude; informal snappy.
OPPOSITES: polite.

brutal adjective
1 *a brutal attack on an elderly man:* savage, violent, vicious, cruel, fierce, ferocious, barbaric, barbarous, murderous, bloodthirsty, cold-blooded, callous, heartless, merciless, sadistic; heinous, monstrous, abominable, atrocious.
2 *he replied with brutal honesty:* unsparing, uncompromising, blunt, direct, stark, frank, outspoken, forthright.
OPPOSITES: gentle.

brutalize verb
1 *the men were brutalized by their experiences in the trenches:* desensitize, dehumanize, harden, toughen, inure.
2 *the prison staff brutalized and tortured those in their custody:* attack, assault, beat, batter; abuse.

brute noun *he was a cold-blooded brute:* savage, beast, monster, animal, barbarian, fiend, ogre; sadist; thug.
▷ adjective *most break-ins are committed by people who rely on brute force to gain entry:* physical, bodily; sheer; crude, violent.

bubble noun (bubbles) effervescence, fizz, sparkle, froth; foam, suds.
▷ verb
1 *this wine bubbles nicely on the tongue:* sparkle, fizz, effervesce, foam, froth.
2 *the milk was bubbling above the flame:* boil, simmer, seethe, gurgle.
3 *I was bubbling with ideas, desperate to make things happen:* overflow, brim over, be filled, burst.

bubbly adjective
1 *a clear bubbly liquid:* effervescent, fizzy, gassy; bubbling, foaming, frothy, foamy; carbonated.
2 *Mary was a petite young woman with a bubbly personality:* vivacious, animated, exuberant, ebullient, lively, upbeat,

high-spirited; sparkling, bouncy, buoyant, carefree; happy, cheerful, perky, sunny, bright; informal chirpy.
OPPOSITES: still, dull.

buccaneering adjective *a buccaneering entrepreneur:* adventurous, risk-taking, bold, daring, daredevil; high-risk.
OPPOSITES: cautious.

buck verb *the £10 billion investment has bucked the trend and returned over 50 per cent to investors:* resist, oppose, defy, fight, kick against.

bucket noun *a bucket of water:* pail, can, tub.

buckle noun *a broad leather belt with a brass buckle:* clasp, clip, catch, hasp, fastener.
▷ verb
1 *he buckled the seat belt round his waist:* fasten, do up, hook, strap, secure, clasp, clip.
2 *his knees buckled and he fell to the pavement:* give way, crumple; collapse.
3 *the pillars were put in to stop the walls buckling:* bend, twist, curve, become distorted; bulge, arc, arch.
□ **buckle down**
it is time to stop making promises and buckle down to building a 21st-century health service: get down to work, set to work, get down to business; work hard, apply yourself, make an effort, focus; Brit. informal get stuck in.

bucolic adjective *the church is lovely, both in itself and for its bucolic setting:* rustic, rural, pastoral, country, countryside; literary Arcadian.

bud noun *the first green buds of spring:* sprout, shoot.

budding adjective *at least one scholarship is reserved for budding musicians:* promising, up-and-coming, rising, in the making, aspiring, future, prospective, potential, fledgling, developing; informal would-be.

budge verb
1 *the horse wouldn't budge:* move, shift, stir, go.
2 *even with my back against the door I couldn't budge it:* dislodge, shift, move; open.
3 *I tried to persuade him but he wouldn't budge:* give way, give in, yield, change your mind, acquiesce, compromise.

budget noun *this year's marketing budget of £500,000 will be spent primarily on direct mailing:* allowance, allocation, quota; grant, award, funds, resources, capital.
▷ verb
1 *the company budgeted $88m for World Cup promotions:* allocate, allot, allow, earmark, designate, set aside.
2 *it was initially budgeted at $100m, but that had doubled by the time filming had ended:* cost, price; estimate, schedule.

3 *in this business you should budget for periods of unemployment:* allow, plan, be ready/prepared, make allowances.
▷**adjective** *there are plenty of budget hotels:* cheap, inexpensive, low-cost, low-price; economy, cut-price, discount, bargain.
OPPOSITES: expensive.

buff[1] **verb** *he buffed the glass until it gleamed:* polish, rub, burnish, shine, clean.
▷**adjective** *a buff envelope lay on the table:* brown, fawn, light brown, beige.

buff[2] **noun** (informal) *Mr Woodward was something of a railway buff:* enthusiast, fan, devotee, lover, admirer; expert, aficionado, authority, pundit; informal nut, fanatic, addict.

buffer noun *family, friends, and colleagues can provide a buffer against the stressful effects of change:* cushion, bulwark, shield, barrier, guard, safeguard.
▷**verb**
1 *positive relationships helped to buffer the effects of living in high-risk urban settings:* lessen, reduce, diminish, moderate, soften, allay
2 *corals provide homes for sea creatures and buffer coastal areas from storms:* protect, shield, defend, cushion.

buffet[1] **noun**
1 *the occasion concluded with a buffet in the parish hall:* cold table, self-service meal; smorgasbord.
2 *he was waiting in the station buffet:* cafe, cafeteria, snack bar, canteen, restaurant.

buffet[2] **verb** *rough seas and wild winds buffeted the coast:* batter, pound, lash, dash against, strike, hit.

bug noun
1 (informal) *he's got some sort of stomach bug:* illness, disorder, infection, disease, sickness, complaint; bacterium, germ, virus; Brit. informal lurgy.
2 (informal) *the travel bug had truly taken a firm hold on him:* obsession, enthusiasm, craze, mania, passion, fixation.
3 *install the program in a separate subdirectory in case it has a hidden bug:* fault, error, defect, flaw; virus; informal glitch, gremlin.
4 *bugs and spiders conceal themselves in the bark:* insect; informal creepy-crawly.
5 *the bug must have been put in my case before I left Helsinki:* listening device, microphone; wire, wiretap, tap.
▷**verb**
1 *Wilson's offices had been bugged:* wire up, tap; informal mike up.
2 *she began to suspect her husband was bugging her telephone calls:* record, listen in on, eavesdrop on; tap, monitor; intercept.
3 (informal) *she really bugs me.* See ANNOY.

bugbear noun *the Commission tackles that big taxation bugbear of most*

homebuyers—stamp duty: pet hate, bête noire, bogey; bane, irritation, vexation, anathema, thorn in your flesh/side; nightmare, horror.

build verb
1 *a supermarket had been built on Gallowhill Road:* construct, erect, put up, set up, assemble.
2 *the kids were building a snowman:* make, construct, form, create, fashion, model, shape.
3 *they are building a business strategy for the next decade:* establish, develop, form, create, set up, initiate.
▷**noun** *police are looking for a man of slim build:* physique, frame, body, figure, form, shape, stature, proportions; informal vital statistics.
▢build something in/into
the new generation of processors will build in a new security capability: incorporate, include, contain.
▢build on
a new study will be undertaken to build on existing research: expand on, enlarge on, develop, elaborate, flesh out, amplify; refine, improve, perfect.
▢build up
the traffic is steadily building up: increase, grow, mount up, intensify, escalate; strengthen.
▢build something up
1 *he built up a huge export business:* establish, set up, found, institute, start, create; develop, expand, enlarge.
2 *he built up his stamina by playing football:* boost, strengthen, increase, improve, augment, raise, enhance; informal beef up.
3 *I have built up a collection of around 1,700 prints:* accumulate, amass, collect, gather; stockpile, hoard.

building noun
1 *the church is a plain red brick building:* structure, construction, erection, pile; property, premises, establishment; formal edifice.
2 *they are calling for a moratorium on the building of power stations:* construction, erection, fabrication, assembly.

WORD LINKS
architectural relating to building

build-up noun
1 *this build-up of military strength is worrying many experts:* increase, growth, expansion, escalation, development, proliferation.
2 *the build-up of carbon dioxide in the atmosphere:* accumulation, accretion.
3 *the build-up for her next movie has already begun:* publicity, promotion, advertising, marketing; informal hype, ballyhoo.

built-in adjective
1 *the cooker hood has a built-in fan for*

ventilation: fitted, integral, integrated.
2 *the system has a built-in resistance to change:* inherent, intrinsic, inbuilt; essential, implicit, basic, fundamental, deep-rooted.

bulb noun tuber, corm, rhizome.

bulbous adjective *he had a large red bulbous nose:* bulging, protuberant, round, fat; swollen, tumid, distended, bloated.

bulge noun
1 *the money made a fat bulge in his pocket:* swelling, bump, lump, protuberance, protrusion, prominence.
2 (informal) *a bulge in the prison population:* surge, upsurge, rise, increase, escalation.
▷ verb *the veins in his neck bulged:* swell, stick out, puff out, balloon out, fill out, belly, be distended; project, protrude, stand out.

bulging adjective *he clenched his fist, displaying his bulging biceps:* protuberant, protruding, huge, distended; swollen, bulbous, fat.

bulk noun
1 *arriving at the dockside, you are reminded of the sheer bulk of the ship:* size, volume, dimensions, proportions, mass, scale, magnitude, immensity.
2 *not surprisingly, the bulk of entrants were British:* majority, main part, major part, lion's share, preponderance; most, almost all.
OPPOSITES: minority.

bulky adjective
1 *bulky items of household refuse:* large, big, sizeable; outsize, oversized; cumbersome, unwieldy, unmanageable, heavy, weighty.
2 *he was a bulky man, not good at climbing:* heavily built, stocky, thickset, sturdy, well built, burly, strapping, solid, heavy, hefty, meaty; stout, fat, plump, chubby, portly, rotund, round, chunky; informal tubby, roly-poly, beefy; Brit. informal podgy.
OPPOSITES: small, slight.

bulldoze verb
1 *contractors moved in to bulldoze the Victorian building despite hundreds of objections:* demolish, knock down, tear down, pull down, flatten, level, raze, clear.
2 *Williams bulldozed his way through to score the equalizer:* force, push, shove, barge, elbow, shoulder, jostle.
3 (informal) *she tends to bulldoze everyone, operating by overpowering others:* bully, browbeat, intimidate, steamroller, bludgeon, coerce, pressurize, strong-arm; informal railroad, lean on.

bulletin noun
1 *our next bulletin is at 10.30 p.m.:* report, broadcast, newscast, dispatch; press release; statement, announcement.
2 *the Society produces a monthly bulletin:* newsletter, news-sheet, proceedings;

newspaper, magazine, digest, gazette, review.

bullish adjective *Gough was in bullish mood at a press conference last night:* confident, positive, optimistic, upbeat, buoyant, sanguine; assertive, self-assertive, bold, determined, feisty.

bully noun *one of the school bullies used to make my life very unpleasant:* persecutor, oppressor, tormentor; bully boy, thug.
▷ verb
1 *Alice bullied her into making all sorts of concessions:* coerce, pressure, pressurize, press, push; force, compel; browbeat, bludgeon, strong-arm; informal bulldoze, railroad.
2 *he was bullied by the neighbourhood gangs:* persecute, oppress, tyrannize, browbeat, intimidate, dominate; informal push around/about.

bulwark noun *the security forces remain the ultimate bulwark against the breakdown of society:* defence, protection, guard, buttress; mainstay, bastion, stronghold.

bum (informal) **verb**
1 *he bummed around Florida for a few months:* travel aimlessly, wander, drift, meander; informal mooch.
2 *they tried to bum money off him:* beg; informal scrounge, cadge, sponge.
▷ adjective *the album kicks off on such a bum note it's hard to imagine how the band will get things back on track:* bad, poor, second-rate, unsatisfactory, inadequate, unacceptable; dreadful, awful, terrible; informal rotten, lousy; Brit. informal duff.

bumbling adjective *officials became increasingly irritated by his bumbling interventions:* clumsy, inept, unskilful, incompetent, inefficient, inexpert, maladroit, bungling; informal ham-fisted, cack-handed.
OPPOSITES: efficient.

bump noun
1 *I was woken from my daydream by a loud bump:* thud, thump, blow, bang, crack, boom, clang, knock, clunk, crash; jolt, collision.
2 *the front wheel hit a bump in the road:* hump, lump, ridge, bulge, knob, protuberance.
3 *the police wanted to know how he got the bump on his head:* swelling, lump, bulge, injury, contusion.
▷ verb
1 *I almost bumped into him:* collide with, hit; crash, smash, slam, bang, knock, run, plough, ram; strike.
2 *we swerved round a cart bumping along the road:* bounce, jolt, jerk, rattle, shake.
□ **bump into** (informal) *he returned to his workshop, hoping to bump into her on the way:* meet, encounter, run into/across, come across, chance on, happen on.

bumper adjective *Jacques was prophesying a bumper harvest:* abundant, plentiful, copious, bountiful, good, fine, large, big, huge; successful; literary plenteous, bounteous; informal whopping.
OPPOSITES: meagre.

bumpkin noun *feeling rather like a country bumpkin, I attempted to check into the five-star hotel:* yokel, provincial, rustic, country cousin; N. Amer. informal hillbilly, hick.

bumptious adjective *an impossibly bumptious man who took any opportunity to further his own interests:* self-important, full of yourself, conceited, arrogant, self-assertive, pompous, overbearing, officious, opinionated.
OPPOSITES: modest.

bumpy adjective
1 *the main street was a narrow, bumpy lane piled up with rubble:* uneven, rough, rutted, pitted, potholed; lumpy, rocky.
2 *after a very bumpy ride they arrived at the top of Thorpe Street:* bouncy, rough, uncomfortable, jolting, lurching, jerky, jarring, bone-shaking.
3 *the season got off to a bumpy start:* inconsistent, erratic, patchy; rocky, turbulent, full of ups and downs.
OPPOSITES: smooth.

bunch noun
1 *a bunch of flowers:* bouquet, posy, nosegay, spray.
2 *a bunch of keys | a bunch of bananas:* bundle, cluster, clump; group.
3 (informal) *what a great bunch of people:* group, set, circle, company, collection, band; informal gang, crowd.
▷ verb
1 *he bunched the reins in his hands:* bundle, clump, group, gather; pack, fasten.
2 *the runners bunched up behind him:* cluster, gather, congregate, collect, mass, group, crowd, huddle.

bundle noun *a thick bundle of envelopes:* bunch, roll, clump, wad, parcel, sheaf, bale; pile, stack, heap, mass; informal wodge.
▷ verb
1 *she bundled up her things:* tie, roll, pack, parcel, wrap, fold.
2 (informal) *he was bundled into a van:* hustle, manhandle, frogmarch, hurry, rush; shove, push, thrust.

bung noun stopper, plug, cork, spigot, seal.

bungle verb *the four prisoners bungled their escape bid:* mishandle, mismanage, spoil, ruin; informal mess up, botch, muff, fluff, make a hash of, screw up; Brit. informal make a pig's ear of.

bungling adjective *the bungling burglar dropped a concrete block on his finger as he attempted to break into the house:* incompetent, amateurish, inept, unskilful, clumsy, awkward, bumbling; informal ham-fisted, cack-handed.

bunk[1] noun berth, bed; couchette.

bunk[2] verb (Brit. informal) *he bunked off school every Thursday afternoon:* truant from, skip, avoid, shirk; Brit. informal play truant from, skive off; N. Amer. informal play hookey, cut.

buoy noun *the channel is marked by red and green buoys:* float, marker, beacon.
▷ verb *the party was buoyed by an election victory:* cheer up, cheer, hearten, rally, invigorate, uplift, lift, encourage, stimulate; informal pep up, perk up, buck up.
OPPOSITES: depress.

buoyancy noun
1 *her natural buoyancy helped her cope:* cheerfulness, optimism; happiness, ebullience, high spirits, vivacity.
2 *greater buoyancy in overseas markets has boosted UK exports:* vigour, strength, growth, improvement, expansion.

buoyant adjective
1 *a buoyant substance:* light, floating.
2 *the players are in a buoyant mood after their 2–0 win over Real Madrid:* cheerful, ebullient, optimistic, upbeat, confident, positive; happy, bright, joyful, carefree, light-hearted, sunny, jolly; lively, jaunty, high-spirited, perky.
3 *in the US, demand has been buoyant:* booming, strong, vigorous, thriving; improving, expanding.

burble verb
1 *a stream burbled through the woods:* gurgle, bubble, murmur.
2 *he burbled on about annuities:* prattle, blather, babble, gabble, prate, ramble, maunder, go on; informal jabber, blabber, yatter; Brit. informal rabbit, witter, waffle, chunter.

burden noun
1 *the porters shouldered their burdens and we set off:* load, cargo, weight; pack, bundle.
2 *he took on a huge financial burden:* responsibility, onus, charge, duty, obligation, liability; trouble, problem, worry, difficulty, strain, encumbrance.
3 *the burden of his speech was as follows:* gist, substance, drift, thrust, meaning, significance, essence, import, message.
▷ verb
1 *he was burdened with a heavy pack:* load, weigh down, encumber, hamper; overload, overburden.
2 *I'm sorry to burden you with my problems | many families are already burdened by severe poverty:* trouble, worry, upset, distress, oppress; afflict, strain, stress, tax, overwhelm.

burdensome adjective *a burdensome task | burdensome responsibilities:* onerous, oppressive, weighty, stressful; hard, difficult, demanding, arduous, strenuous, laborious, exhausting, tiring, taxing, uphill, punishing, gruelling.

bureau noun
1 *a beautiful oak bureau:* desk, writing table, secretaire, escritoire; Brit. davenport.
2 *reservations can be made through the accommodation bureau's free room-finding service:* agency, service, office, business, company, firm.
3 *the Bureau is in close touch with key people in Brussels:* department, division, branch, section.

bureaucracy noun *his goal was to eliminate unnecessary bureaucracy in local government:* red tape, rules and regulations, protocol, paperwork; administration, officialdom.

bureaucrat noun official, administrator, civil servant, minister, functionary, mandarin; derogatory apparatchik.

bureaucratic adjective *current procedures are far too bureaucratic:* rule-bound, rigid, inflexible, complicated.

burgeon verb *the industry has burgeoned since the 1960s:* flourish, thrive, prosper; expand, escalate, grow, boom, mushroom, snowball, rocket, go from strength to strength.

burgeoning adjective *there is a burgeoning market for this type of entertainment:* flourishing, thriving, growing, expanding, booming.

burglar noun housebreaker, robber, thief; intruder.

burglary noun
1 *he received a two-year sentence for burglary:* housebreaking, breaking and entering, theft, stealing, robbery.
2 *a series of burglaries has made residents very nervous:* break-in, theft, robbery, raid.

burgle verb *her house was burgled last night:* rob, steal from; break into.

burial noun *the body was flown home for burial:* burying, interment, entombment; funeral, funeral rites, obsequies.
OPPOSITES: exhumation.

burial ground noun cemetery, graveyard, churchyard, necropolis, garden of remembrance; Scottish kirkyard.

burlesque noun *his novel is a burlesque of the literary life:* parody, caricature, satire, lampoon, skit; informal take-off, send-up, spoof.

burly adjective *two burly bodyguards stood beside him:* strapping, well built, sturdy, brawny, strong, muscular, muscly, thickset, big, hefty, bulky, stocky; informal beefy, hulking.
OPPOSITES: puny.

burn verb
1 *by nightfall, the whole city was burning:* be on fire, be alight, be ablaze, blaze, go up in smoke, be in flames, be aflame; smoulder, glow.
2 *he burned all her letters:* set fire to, set on fire, set alight, set light to, light, ignite; incinerate; informal torch.
3 *I left the iron on and burned my shirt:* scorch, singe, sear, char, blacken; scald, blister; brand.
4 *her forehead was burning and her throat ached:* be hot, be warm, be feverish, be on fire; blush, redden, go red, flush, colour.
5 *by this time, Martha was burning with curiosity:* be consumed, be eaten up, be obsessed, be tormented, be beside yourself.
6 *people differ considerably in the energy they burn up:* consume, use up, expend.

burning adjective
1 *a burning building:* blazing, flaming, on fire, ablaze, aflame, smouldering; raging, roaring.
2 *the burning midday sun:* hot, red-hot, blistering, scorching, searing, sweltering, torrid; informal baking, boiling, roasting, sizzling.
3 *a burning desire to win:* intense, passionate, ardent, fervent, urgent, fierce, consuming, deep-seated, profound, wholehearted, strong, eager.
4 *the burning issues of the day:* vital, crucial, significant, important, high-priority; urgent, pressing.

burnish verb *marks can be removed by scraping and burnishing the metal:* polish, shine, buff, buff up, rub.

burp (informal) verb *he burped surreptitiously:* belch, bring up wind.
▷ noun *Cranston let out a loud burp:* belch; formal eructation.

burrow noun *a rabbit's burrow:* warren, tunnel, hole; lair, set, den, earth.
▷ verb *the termites burrow downwards and start laying eggs:* tunnel, dig, excavate, make a hole.

burst verb
1 *one balloon burst:* split, rupture, break, tear.
2 *a shell burst a short distance away:* explode, blow up, detonate, go off.
3 *smoke and heat burst through the hole:* break, erupt, surge, gush, rush, stream, flow, pour, spill; spout, spurt, jet, spew.
4 *he burst into the room without knocking:* charge, barge, plough, hurtle, career, rush, dash, plunge; informal tear.
▷ noun
1 *the mortar bursts were further away than before:* explosion, detonation, blast, eruption, discharge, bang, report.
2 *a burst of gunfire shattered the stillness:* volley, salvo, fusillade, barrage, discharge; hail, rain.
3 *a sudden burst of activity | a burst of anger:* outbreak, eruption, flare-up, blaze,

attack, fit, rush, storm, surge, upsurge, spurt.
□ **burst out**
'I don't care!' she burst out angrily: exclaim, blurt out, cry, shout, yell.

bury verb
1 *the crew were buried at Stonefall cemetery:* inter, lay to rest, entomb.
2 *the countryside was buried under several feet of snow:* hide, conceal, cover, blanket, engulf.
3 *he buried himself in his work:* absorb, engross, immerse, occupy, engage, busy, involve.
OPPOSITES: exhume.

bush noun shrub; (**bushes**) undergrowth, shrubbery.

bushy adjective *his bushy black eyebrows almost met in the middle:* thick, shaggy, fuzzy, bristly, hairy; luxuriant.
OPPOSITES: sleek, wispy.

busily adverb *his assistant was busily typing away at the computer:* energetically, vigorously, enthusiastically; industriously, purposefully, diligently.

business noun
1 *she has to smile a lot in her business:* work, line of work, occupation, profession, career, trade, employment, job, position; vocation, calling; field, sphere; informal racket, game.
2 *who do you do business with in Manila?* trade, trading, commerce, dealing, merchandising; dealings, transactions, negotiations.
3 *she was running her own business:* firm, company, concern, enterprise, venture, organization, operation, undertaking; office, agency, franchise, practice; informal outfit, set-up.
4 *that's none of your business:* concern, affair, responsibility; problem, worry; Brit. informal lookout.
5 *the odd business with the keys remained unexplained:* affair, matter, case, circumstance, situation, event, incident, happening, occurrence; episode.

businesslike adjective *investors have been heartened by this new businesslike approach:* professional, efficient, practical, pragmatic, no-nonsense, slick, methodical, disciplined, systematic, orderly, organized, structured, competent.

businessman, businesswoman
noun entrepreneur, business person, industrialist, executive, manufacturer, tycoon, magnate; employer; dealer, trader, broker, merchant, buyer, seller, marketeer, merchandiser, vendor, tradesman, retailer, supplier.

bust[1] noun *a marble bust of Julius Caesar:* sculpture, carving, effigy, statue.

bust[2] (informal) verb
1 *the lock has bust | he bust the clip that held*

the lid down: break, crack, snap, smash, fracture, shatter; split, burst.
2 *they are clearly trying to bust the union:* overthrow, destroy, topple, bring down, ruin, break, overcome, defeat, get rid of.
□ **go bust**
his haulage business went bust in 1996: fail, collapse, fold, go under, founder; go bankrupt, go into receivership, go into liquidation, be wound up; informal crash, go broke, go to the wall, go belly up.

bustle verb *people clutching clipboards bustled about:* rush, dash, hurry, scurry, scuttle, scamper; informal scoot, beetle.
▷ noun *I loved the bustle of the market:* activity, action, liveliness, hustle and bustle, excitement; tumult, hubbub, whirl; informal toing and froing, comings and goings.

bustling adjective *the bustling streets of Kowloon:* busy, crowded, swarming, teeming, thronged; buzzing, hectic, lively; informal buzzy.
OPPOSITES: deserted.

busy adjective
1 *he's always busy with some scheme or other:* engaged in, occupied with, involved in, employed in, working at, hard at work on; rushed off your feet, hard-pressed; absorbed, engrossed, immersed; informal on the go, hard at it.
2 *I'm afraid he's busy at the moment:* unavailable, engaged, occupied; working, in a meeting, on duty; informal tied up.
3 *I've had a busy day:* hectic, active, lively, full, eventful; energetic, tiring, demanding.
4 *the town centre was unusually busy:* crowded, bustling, hectic, swarming, teeming, full, thronged; informal buzzy.
5 *the lavish designs are a little too busy:* ornate, over-elaborate, overblown, overwrought, overdone, fussy, cluttered, overworked.
OPPOSITES: idle, free, quiet.
▷ verb *he busied himself with paperwork:* occupy, involve, engage, concern, absorb, engross, immerse, preoccupy; distract.

busybody noun *others considered him an interfering busybody:* meddler, interferer, mischief-maker, troublemaker; gossip, scandalmonger; informal nosy parker, snoop.

butch adjective (informal) *a big, butch rapper:* masculine, manly, macho.
OPPOSITES: effeminate, feminine.

butcher verb
1 *they butchered 150 people:* massacre, murder, slaughter, kill, destroy, exterminate; literary slay.
2 *the film was butchered by the studio that released it:* ruin, wreck, spoil, mess up; informal make a hash of, screw up.

butchery noun *futile uprisings ending in butchery and defeat for the rebels:*

slaughter, massacre, mass murder,
bloodletting; genocide; literary slaying.

butt[1] verb *she butted him in the chest:* ram,
headbutt; push, shove, bump.
□ **butt in**
David butted in and asked about payment:
interrupt, break in, cut in, chime in,
interject; intervene, interfere; informal chip
in, poke your nose in, put your oar in.

butt[2] noun *she had been made the butt of
their jokes:* target, victim, object, subject;
laughing stock.

butt[3] noun
1 *he prodded me with the butt of the gun:*
stock, end, handle, hilt, haft.
2 *a cigarette butt:* stub, end, stump,
remnant; informal dog-end.

butt[4] noun *a water butt:* barrel, cask, keg,
vat; tub, bin, drum, canister.

butter verb
□ **butter someone up** (informal) *he's a PR man,
adept at buttering people up:* flatter, make
up to, play up to, ingratiate yourself with,
rub up the right way, curry favour with,
court; informal suck up to, keep someone
sweet, sweet-talk.

butterfly noun

> WORD LINKS
> **lepidopterist** a person who studies or
> collects butterflies and moths

buttocks plural noun rear, rump, seat; Brit.
bottom; informal backside, behind, derrière;
Brit. informal bum; humorous posterior.

button noun
1 *he did up his shirt buttons:* fastener, stud,
toggle; hook, catch, clasp.
2 *press the start button:* switch, knob,
control; lever, handle.

buttonhole verb (informal) *I was tired of
being buttonholed in the street by worried
investors.* See ACCOST.

buttress noun
1 *the wall was supported by stone
buttresses:* prop, support, abutment, pier,
stanchion.
2 *a buttress against social collapse:*
safeguard, defence, protection, guard;
support, prop; bulwark.
▷ verb *at that time, authority was buttressed
by religious belief:* strengthen, reinforce,
fortify, support, bolster, shore up,
underpin, cement, uphold, defend, back up.

buxom adjective *a buxom young woman
in a tight dress:* shapely, full-figured,
voluptuous, curvaceous, Rubenesque;
plump; informal well endowed, curvy.

buy verb
1 *they bought a new car:* purchase, acquire,

obtain, get, pick up, snap up; procure,
pay for; invest in; informal get hold of,
score.
2 *he was a man who could not be bought:*
bribe, buy off, suborn, corrupt; informal get
at; Brit. informal nobble.
OPPOSITES: sell.
▷ noun (informal) *the Merlot is a good buy at
£4.49:* purchase, investment; deal, bargain.

buyer noun *the advertising is aimed at
upmarket buyers:* purchaser, customer,
consumer, shopper, investor; (**buyers**)
market, clientele, patronage.

buzz noun
1 *the buzz of the bees filled the air:* hum,
humming, buzzing, murmur, drone.
2 *there was an insistent buzz from her
control panel:* noise, purr, ring, note, tone,
beep, bleep, warble.
3 (informal) *I got such a buzz out of this
competition:* thrill, feeling of excitement,
feeling of euphoria; informal kick, lift, high;
N. Amer. informal charge.
▷ verb
1 *bees buzzed in the clover:* hum, drone,
murmur.
2 *the intercom on her desk buzzed:* sound,
go off, purr, ring, beep, bleep, warble.
3 *the club is buzzing with excitement:* hum,
throb, pulse, vibrate.

bygone adjective *those are the values of a
bygone age:* past, former, earlier, previous,
one-time, long-ago, of old, olden, ancient;
departed, dead, extinct, defunct, out of
date, outmoded; literary of yore.
OPPOSITES: present, recent.

bypass noun *traffic will get heavier
when the new bypass opens:* ring road,
alternative route; Brit. relief road.
▷ verb
1 *bypass the farm and continue to the main
road:* go round, go past, make a detour
round; avoid.
2 *a manager may bypass formal channels of
communication:* avoid, circumvent, find a
way round, sidestep, evade; ignore.

by-product noun *he saw poverty as the by-
product of colonial prosperity:* side effect,
consequence, corollary; ramification,
repercussion, spin-off, fallout; fruits; Brit.
knock-on effect.

bystander noun *water cannons were
turned on marchers and innocent
bystanders alike:* onlooker, looker-on,
passer-by, non-participant, observer,
spectator, eyewitness, witness.

byword noun *the Court had become a
byword for administrative delay:* perfect
example, classic case, model, embodiment,
epitome, incarnation, personification.

Cc

cab noun
1 *she hailed a cab:* taxi, taxi cab; Brit. minicab; formal hackney carriage.
2 *a truck driver's cab:* driver's compartment, cabin.

cabal noun *government whips dismissed talk of a cabal of dissidents meeting privately:* clique, faction, coterie, cell; group, camp, caucus.

cabaret noun *the evening's cabaret drew to a close:* entertainment, show, performance; revue.

cabin noun
1 *a first-class cabin:* berth, stateroom, room, compartment.
2 *a cabin by the lake:* hut, log cabin, lodge, shack; chalet; shelter; Scottish bothy.
3 *the driver's cabin:* cab, compartment.

cabinet noun
1 *a walnut cabinet:* cupboard, bureau, chest of drawers, dresser.
2 *the cabinet met again on 15 January:* senior ministers, ministry, council, executive.

cable noun
1 *a thick cable moored the ship:* rope, cord, line, guy; Nautical hawser, stay.
2 *electric cables:* wire, lead, power line; Brit. flex.

cache noun *a cache of weapons:* hoard, store, stockpile, stock, supply, reserve; informal stash.

cachet noun *no other shipping company had quite the cachet of Cunard:* prestige, prestigiousness, status, standing, kudos, stature, pre-eminence, eminence; credibility.

cackle verb
1 *the geese cackled at him:* squawk, cluck.
2 *she cackled with glee:* laugh, crow, hoot, bray.

cacophonous adjective *cacophonous rock music blared from the speakers:* loud, noisy, ear-splitting, deafening, raucous; discordant, dissonant, tuneless, inharmonious, unmelodious, unmusical.

cacophony noun *a cacophony of deafening alarm bells:* din, racket, noise; discord, dissonance, discordance.

cadaverous adjective *his face was cadaverous:* deathly pale, pallid, ashen, grey; thin, bony, skeletal, emaciated, haggard, gaunt, drawn, pinched, hollow-cheeked, hollow-eyed.
OPPOSITES: ruddy, plump.

cadence noun *there is a biblical cadence in the last words he utters:* rhythm, tempo, metre, beat, pulse; intonation, modulation, lilt.

cadge verb (informal) *she cadged a cigarette from him:* scrounge; informal bum, touch someone for.

cadre noun *a cadre of professional managers:* corps, body, team, group.

cafe noun snack bar, cafeteria, buffet; coffee bar/shop, tea room/shop; bistro, brasserie; N. Amer. diner; informal eatery.

cafeteria noun canteen, self-service restaurant, cafe, buffet.

cage noun *an animal's cage:* enclosure, pen; coop, hutch; birdcage, aviary.
▷ verb *the dogs were caged in kennels:* confine, shut in/up, pen, coop up; formal immure.

cagey adjective (informal) *he was rather cagey about his plans:* secretive, guarded, non-committal, tight-lipped, reticent, evasive; informal playing your cards close to your chest.
OPPOSITES: open, frank.

cahoots plural noun
□ **in cahoots** (informal) *it was alleged that some of the unit's members were in cahoots with known criminals:* in league, colluding, in collusion, conspiring, collaborating, hand in glove.

cajole verb *he had been cajoled into escorting Nadia to a concert:* persuade, wheedle, coax, inveigle, talk into, prevail on; informal sweet-talk, soft-soap, twist someone's arm.

cajolery noun persuasion, wheedling, coaxing, inveiglement, cajolement; blandishments, blarney; informal sweet talk, soft soap, arm-twisting.

cake noun
1 *cream cakes:* bun, pastry, gateau.

C

2 *a cake of soap:* bar, tablet, block, slab, lump.
▷verb
1 *his boots were caked with mud:* coat, encrust, plaster, cover.
2 *the blood was beginning to cake:* clot, congeal, coagulate, solidify, set; technical inspissate.

calamitous adjective *the consequences of his decision were calamitous:* disastrous, catastrophic, cataclysmic, devastating, dire, tragic.

calamity noun *the fire was only the latest calamity to strike the area:* disaster, catastrophe, tragedy, cataclysm; blow, misfortune, mishap; adversity, tribulation, affliction.

calculate verb
1 *the interest is calculated on a daily basis:* compute, work out, reckon, assess; add up/together, count up, tally, total; Brit. tot up.
2 *his words were calculated to wound her:* intend, mean, design.

calculated adjective *the attack can only be seen as a calculated attempt to intimidate other groups of workers:* deliberate, premeditated, planned, pre-planned, preconceived, intentional, intended, purposive, conscious.
OPPOSITES: unintentional.

calculating adjective *he was a coolly calculating, ruthless man:* cunning, crafty, wily, shrewd, scheming, devious, designing, Machiavellian.
OPPOSITES: ingenuous.

calculation noun
1 *the calculation of the overall cost:* computation, reckoning, adding up, counting up, working out; Brit. totting up.
2 *the government's political calculations:* assessment, judgement; forecast, projection, prediction.

calendar noun
1 *a large wall calendar:* almanac.
2 *my social calendar is pretty full:* schedule, programme, diary.

calibre noun
1 *they could ill afford to lose a man of his calibre:* quality, merit, distinction, stature, excellence, pre-eminence; ability, expertise, talent, capability, capacity, proficiency.
2 *if only they could play rugby of this calibre every week:* standard, level, quality.
3 *the calibre of a gun:* bore, diameter, gauge.

call verb
1 *'Wait for me!' she called:* cry, shout, yell, bellow, roar, bawl, scream, vociferate; informal holler.
2 *I'll call you tomorrow:* phone, telephone; Brit. ring, give someone a ring; informal call up, give someone a buzz; Brit. informal give someone a bell.

3 *Rose called a taxi:* summon, send for, order.
4 *the prime minister called a meeting:* convene, summon, assemble; arrange, organize; formal convoke.
5 *he called at her house that afternoon:* pay a visit to, visit, pay a call on, call/drop/look in on, drop/stop by; informal pop into.
6 *they called their daughter Hannah:* name, christen, baptize; designate, style, term, dub.
7 *he's the only one I would call a friend:* describe as, regard as, look on as, consider to be, deem.
▷noun
1 *I heard calls from the auditorium:* cry, shout, yell, roar, scream, exclamation; informal holler.
2 *I'll give you a call tomorrow:* phone call, telephone call; Brit. ring; informal buzz; Brit. informal bell.
3 *he paid a call on Harold:* visit, social call.
4 *a call for party unity:* appeal, request, plea, entreaty.
5 *this is the last call for passengers on flight BA701:* summons, request.
6 *there's no call for that kind of language:* need, necessity, reason, occasion, justification, excuse.
7 *there's no call for expensive wine here:* demand, desire, market.
8 *walkers can't resist the call of the Cairngorms:* attraction, appeal, lure, allure, spell, pull, draw.
9 *a blackbird's call:* cry, song, sound.
□ call for
1 *desperate times call for desperate measures:* require, need, necessitate, make necessary, demand; justify, warrant.
2 *I'll call for you around seven:* pick up, collect, fetch.
□ call something off
the proposed tour of Australia was called off: cancel, abandon, scrap, drop, axe; informal scrub.
□ call on
1 *I might call on her later:* visit, pay a call on, go and see, look/drop in on; informal look up, pop in on.
2 *he called on the government to hold a plebiscite:* appeal to, ask, request, petition, urge.
3 *we are able to call on qualified staff:* have recourse to, avail yourself of, draw on, make use of.
□ call someone up
1 *they called up more than 20,000 reservists:* enlist, recruit, conscript; US draft.
2 *he was called up for the England team:* select, pick, choose; Brit. cap.
□ on call
on duty, on standby, available.

calling noun *he considered engineering one of the highest possible callings:* profession, occupation, vocation, career, work, employment, job, business, trade, craft, line of work.

callous adjective *his callous disregard for the feelings and wishes of others:* heartless, unfeeling, uncaring, cold, cold-hearted, hard, as hard as nails, hard-hearted, stony-hearted, insensitive, lacking compassion, hardbitten, unsympathetic; ruthless, cruel. OPPOSITES: kind, compassionate.

callow adjective *a callow youth:* immature, inexperienced, naive, green, untried, unworldly, unsophisticated; informal wet behind the ears. OPPOSITES: mature.

calm adjective
1 *she seemed very calm:* serene, tranquil, relaxed, unruffled, unperturbed, unflustered, untroubled; composed, {cool, calm, and collected}, cool-headed, self-possessed; equable, even-tempered, placid, unexcitable, unemotional, phlegmatic; informal unflappable, unfazed.
2 *the night was calm:* windless, still, tranquil, quiet.
3 *the calm waters of the lake:* tranquil, still, smooth, glassy, like a millpond. OPPOSITES: excited, nervous, stormy.
▷noun
1 *his usual calm deserted him:* composure, self-possession, sangfroid, coolness, calmness; serenity, tranquillity, equanimity, equability, placidness, placidity; informal cool, unflappability.
2 *the calm of the night was broken by a scream | we are hoping for a period of calm:* tranquillity, stillness, calmness, quiet, quietness, quietude, peace, peacefulness.
▷verb
1 *I tried to calm him down:* soothe, pacify, placate, mollify, appease, conciliate; Brit. quieten down.
2 *she forced herself to calm down:* compose yourself, recover/regain your composure, control yourself, pull yourself together, simmer down, cool down/off, take it easy; Brit. quieten down; informal get a grip, wind down, chill out; N. Amer. informal hang/stay loose, decompress. OPPOSITES: excite, upset.

calumny noun (formal) *a bitter struggle marked by calumny and litigation:* slander, defamation of character, character assassination, libel; vilification; informal mud-slinging.

camaraderie noun *he enjoyed the camaraderie of army life:* friendship, comradeship, fellowship, companionship; mutual support, team spirit, esprit de corps.

camouflage noun
1 *on the trenches were pieces of turf which served for camouflage:* disguise, concealment.
2 *much of her apparent indifference was merely camouflage:* a facade, a front, a smokescreen, a cover-up, a mask, a blind, a screen, a masquerade; pretence, dissimulation.

▷verb *the caravan was camouflaged with branches:* disguise, hide, conceal, keep hidden, mask, screen, cover.

camp[1] noun
1 *an army camp:* bivouac, encampment; campsite, camping ground.
2 *the liberal and conservative camps:* faction, wing, group, lobby, caucus, bloc; coterie, clique, cabal.
▷verb *they camped in a field:* pitch tents, set up camp, bivouac, encamp.

camp[2] (informal) adjective
1 *a heavily made-up and highly camp actor:* effeminate, effete.
2 *he gave a fabulously camp performance:* exaggerated, theatrical, affected; informal over the top, OTT, camped up.
□ camp it up
they camped it up for the cameras: posture, behave theatrically/affectedly, overact; informal ham it up.

campaign noun
1 *Napoleon's Russian campaign:* military operation, manoeuvres; war, battle, offensive, attack.
2 *the campaign to reduce vehicle emissions:* crusade, drive, push, struggle, fight; movement.
▷verb
1 *they are campaigning for political reform:* crusade, fight, battle, push, press, lobby, strive, struggle.
2 *she campaigned as a political outsider:* run/stand for office, canvass, electioneer.

campaigner noun crusader, fighter, activist; champion, advocate, promoter.

can noun tin, canister; jerrycan.

canal noun
1 *barges chugged up the canal:* inland waterway.
2 *the ear canal:* duct, tube, passage.

cancel verb
1 *the match was cancelled:* call off, abandon, scrap, drop, axe; informal scrub.
2 *his visa has been cancelled:* annul, invalidate, declare null and void, void, nullify; revoke, rescind, retract, countermand, withdraw.
3 *rising unemployment cancelled out earlier economic gains:* neutralize, counterbalance, counteract, balance out, countervail; negate, nullify, wipe out.

cancer noun
1 *most skin cancers are curable:* malignant growth, cancerous growth, tumour, malignancy.
2 *violence is a cancer in this part of the world:* evil, blight, scourge, poison, plague, canker.

> WORD LINKS
> **carcinogenic** causing cancer
> **oncology** the study and treatment of cancer

c

candid adjective

1 *his responses were remarkably candid:* frank, open, honest, direct, outspoken, forthright, blunt, plain-spoken; truthful, sincere; informal upfront, on the level.
2 *it's better to let the photographer mingle and take candid shots:* unposed, impromptu, informal, uncontrived, natural.
OPPOSITES: guarded.

candidate noun

1 *candidates should be computer-literate:* applicant, job-seeker, interviewee; contender, nominee, possible.
2 *A-level candidates:* examinee, entrant.

candour noun *a man of refreshing candour:* frankness, openness, honesty, candidness, forthrightness, directness, plain-spokenness, bluntness, outspokenness; truthfulness, sincerity; informal telling it like it is.

cane noun

1 *a silver-topped cane:* walking stick, staff; crook.
2 *tie the shoot to a cane:* stick, stake, upright, pole.
3 *he was being beaten with a cane:* stick, rod, birch.
▷ verb *he was caned for bullying:* beat, strike, hit, flog; informal give someone a hiding.

cannon noun mounted gun, field gun, piece of artillery; mortar, howitzer.
▷ verb *the couple behind almost cannoned into us:* collide with, hit, run into, crash into, plough into.

canny adjective *canny investors will switch banks if they think they are getting a raw deal:* shrewd, astute, sharp, sharp-witted, discerning, discriminating, perceptive, perspicacious, wise, sagacious; cunning, crafty, wily; informal savvy, smart.
OPPOSITES: foolish.

canoe noun kayak, dugout, outrigger.

canon noun

1 *the appointment violated the canons of fair play and equal opportunity:* principle, rule, law, tenet, precept; standard, convention, criterion.
2 *the Shakespeare canon:* works, writings, oeuvre.
3 *a set of ecclesiastical canons:* law, decree, edict, statute.

canonical adjective *the canonical form of the text:* recognized, authoritative, authorized, accepted, established, sanctioned, approved, orthodox.

canopy noun awning, shade, sunshade; cover, covering; (over an altar or throne) baldachin; (over a four-poster bed) tester.

cant¹ noun

1 *Smith challenged political, social, and religious cant:* hypocrisy,
sanctimoniousness, sanctimony, humbug, pietism.
2 *thieves' cant:* slang, jargon, idiom, argot, patois, speech, terminology, language; informal lingo.

cant² verb *the deck canted some twenty degrees:* tilt, lean, slant, slope, incline; tip, list, bank, heel.

cantankerous adjective *he's a cantankerous old man, set in his ways and prone to sulking to get what he wants:* bad-tempered, irascible, irritable, grumpy, grouchy, crotchety, tetchy, testy, crusty, curmudgeonly, ill-tempered, peevish, cross, fractious, pettish, crabby, prickly, touchy; informal snappy; Brit. informal stroppy, narky, ratty.
OPPOSITES: affable.

canteen noun

1 *the staff canteen:* restaurant, cafeteria, refectory; Military mess.
2 *a canteen of water:* container, flask, bottle.

canvass verb

1 *he's canvassing for the Green Party:* campaign, electioneer, seek votes.
2 *they promised to canvass all members:* poll, question, ask, survey, interview.
3 *they're canvassing support:* seek, try to obtain.
4 *early retirement was canvassed as a solution:* propose, suggest, discuss, debate, consider.

canyon noun ravine, gorge, gully, defile; chasm, abyss, gulf; N. Amer. gulch.

cap noun

1 *a small bottle with a white plastic cap:* lid, top, stopper, cork, bung, spigot.
2 *he raised the cap on local authority spending:* upper limit, ceiling; curb, check.
▷ verb
1 *mountains capped with snow:* top, crown, cover, coat.
2 *winning the cup would cap a memorable season:* round off, crown, be a fitting climax to.
3 *council budgets will be capped:* set a limit on, limit, restrict; curb, control, peg.
4 *they tried to cap each other's stories:* beat, better, improve on, surpass, outdo, outshine, upstage.
5 (Brit.) *he was capped for England:* choose, select, pick; informal give someone the nod.

capability noun *he's a man with great capability and great foresight:* ability, capacity, power, potential; competence, proficiency, aptitude, experience, skill, skilfulness, talent; informal know-how.

capable adjective *a very capable young woman:* competent, able, efficient, effective, proficient, accomplished, experienced, skilful, skilled, talented.
OPPOSITES: incompetent.
□ **be capable of**
1 *I'm quite capable of looking after myself:*

have the ability to, be equal to, be up to; informal have what it takes to.
2 *the strange events are capable of rational explanation:* be open/susceptible to, admit of, allow of.

capacious adjective *she rummaged in her capacious handbag:* roomy, spacious, ample, big, large, sizeable, generous.
OPPOSITES: small.

capacity noun
1 *the capacity of the freezer:* volume, size, magnitude, dimensions, measurements, proportions.
2 *his capacity to inspire trust.* See CAPABILITY.
3 *in his capacity as Commander-in-Chief:* position, post, job, office; role, function.

cape[1] noun *a woollen cape:* cloak, mantle, poncho; wrap, pashmina, shawl, stole, tippet.

cape[2] noun *the ship rounded the cape:* headland, promontory, point, head, foreland; bill, ness, mull.

caper verb *children were capering about the room:* skip, dance, gambol, prance, romp, frisk, cavort, frolic, leap, hop, jump.
▷ noun
1 *she did a little caper:* dance, skip, hop, leap, jump, curvet.
2 (informal) *I'm too old for this kind of caper:* escapade, stunt, prank, trick, antics, high jinks; informal lark, shenanigans.

capital noun
1 *Warsaw is the capital of Poland:* first city, seat of government; metropolis.
2 *he had enough capital to pull off the deal:* money, finances, funds, the wherewithal, the means, assets, wealth, resources, savings, investment capital.
3 *he wrote the name in capitals:* capital letter, upper-case letter, block capital.

capitalism noun private enterprise, free enterprise, the free market.
OPPOSITES: communism.

capitalize verb *the capacity to capitalize new ventures:* finance, fund, underwrite, provide capital for, back; informal bankroll.
▢ **capitalize on**
the sequel attempted to capitalize on the earlier film's success: take advantage of, profit from, make the most of, exploit; informal cash in on.

capitulate verb *the patriots had to capitulate to the enemy forces:* surrender, give in, yield, concede defeat, give up the struggle, submit; lay down your arms, raise/show the white flag, throw in the towel.
OPPOSITES: resist, hold out.

caprice noun
1 *his wife's caprices and demands made his life impossible:* whim, vagary, fancy, fad, quirk, eccentricity, foible.

2 *the staff tired of his caprice:* capriciousness, unpredictability, volatility; fickleness.

capricious adjective *a dark, enigmatic woman whose capricious behaviour drove him mad:* unpredictable, changeable, erratic, mercurial, volatile, temperamental, fickle, wayward, inconstant, variable; whimsical, fanciful.
OPPOSITES: predictable.

capsize verb *the boat capsized in heavy seas:* overturn, turn over, turn upside down, upend, flip/tip/keel over, turn turtle.

capsule noun
1 *vitamin E capsules:* pill, tablet; lozenge, pastille, drop.
2 *a space capsule:* module, craft, probe, pod.

captain noun
1 *the ship's captain:* commander, master; informal skipper.
2 *the team's captain:* leader, head; informal boss, skipper.
3 *a captain of industry:* magnate, tycoon, mogul, baron, industrialist; chief, head, leader, principal; informal boss, number one, bigwig, big shot, top dog.
▷ verb *the ship was captained by my father:* command, run, be in charge of, control, manage, govern; informal skipper.

caption noun title, heading, wording, head, legend, rubric.

captious adjective (formal) critical, fault-finding; hypercritical, pedantic, hair-splitting; informal nit-picking; Brit. informal pernickety.

captivate verb *he was captivated by her beauty:* enthral, charm, enchant, delight, bewitch, fascinate, beguile, entrance, enrapture, mesmerize; attract.
OPPOSITES: repel, bore.

captive noun *the captives were released:* prisoner, detainee; convict, inmate; prisoner of war, POW, internee, hostage.
▷ adjective *captive wild animals | they were kidnapped and held captive for nine months:* confined, caged, incarcerated, locked up; jailed, imprisoned, in prison, interned, detained, in captivity, under lock and key, behind bars.

captivity noun *the third month of their captivity passed:* imprisonment, confinement, internment, incarceration, detention; custody.
OPPOSITES: freedom.

captor noun jailer, guard; keeper.

capture verb
1 *the spy was captured in Moscow:* catch, apprehend, seize, arrest; take prisoner/captive, imprison, detain, put/throw in jail, put behind bars, put under lock and key, incarcerate; informal nab, pick up; Brit. informal nick.

c

2 *guerrillas captured a strategic district:* take possession of, take, seize, secure; occupy, invade, conquer.
3 *she did a series of sketches, trying to capture all his moods:* express, represent, record, reproduce, encapsulate.
4 *the story captured my imagination:* engage, attract, catch, seize, hold.
OPPOSITES: free, release.
▷ noun *he was killed while trying to evade capture:* arrest, apprehension, seizure, being taken prisoner/captive, imprisonment.

car noun
1 *he's got a new car:* motor car, automobile, vehicle; informal wheels.
2 *the train's dining car:* carriage, coach.

carafe noun flask, jug, pitcher, decanter, flagon.

caravan noun
1 *a holiday in a caravan:* mobile home, camper van, caravanette; N. Amer. trailer.
2 *a caravan of cars and trucks wound its way towards the edge of town:* convoy, cavalcade, procession, column, train.

carcass noun corpse, dead body, remains; Medicine cadaver; informal stiff.

card noun
1 *a piece of stiff card:* cardboard, pasteboard, board.
2 *I'll send her a card:* greetings card, postcard.
3 *she produced her card:* identification, ID, credentials; business card.
4 *she paid with her card:* credit card, debit card, cash card; informal plastic.

cardinal adjective *one of the cardinal rules of the sea was to stay by your boat:* fundamental, basic, main, chief, primary, prime, principal, paramount, pre-eminent, most important, key, essential.
OPPOSITES: unimportant.

care noun
1 *the number of fathers solely responsible for the care of their children is growing rapidly:* safe keeping, charge, supervision, custody, protection, control, responsibility; guardianship, wardship.
2 *great care is required when choosing the organization in which to invest your savings:* caution, circumspection, vigilance, heedfulness, heed, attention, attentiveness, thought, forethought; discretion, judiciousness.
3 *a place where you can escape from the cares of the day:* worry, anxiety, trouble, trial, concern, stress, pressure, strain, burden, hardship; sorrow, woe.
4 *a life of unblemished virtue and constant care for others:* concern, consideration, thought, regard, solicitude.
OPPOSITES: neglect, carelessness.
▷ verb *I don't care what she thinks:* be concerned, trouble/concern yourself,

bother, mind, be interested; informal give a damn/hoot/rap.
▢ care for
1 *he obviously cares for his children:* love, be fond of, be devoted to, treasure, adore, dote on, think the world of, worship, idolize.
2 *would you care for a cup of coffee?* like, want, desire, feel like; Brit. informal fancy.
3 *the hospice cares for the terminally ill:* look after, take care of, tend, attend to, minister to, nurse; be responsible for, keep safe, keep an eye on.

career noun
1 *he's still not sure what career he should pursue:* profession, occupation, vocation, calling, employment, line of work, walk of life, métier.
2 *the committee has had a chequered career:* history, existence, life.
▷ adjective *a career politician:* professional, permanent, full-time.
▷ verb *they careered down the hill:* rush, charge, race, hurtle, speed, shoot, dash, run, whizz, zoom, flash, streak, hare, fly, pelt; informal belt, scoot, tear; Brit. informal bomb.

carefree adjective *we were young and carefree:* unworried, untroubled, without a care in the world, relaxed, happy-go-lucky, free and easy, light-hearted, cheerful; blithe, airy, nonchalant, insouciant; informal laid-back.
OPPOSITES: careworn.

careful adjective
1 *you have to be careful when buying software online:* cautious, circumspect, vigilant, wary, heedful, alert, attentive, watchful.
2 *his mother had always been careful with money:* prudent, thrifty, economical, sparing, frugal.
3 *careful consideration of the facts:* attentive, conscientious, painstaking, meticulous, diligent, assiduous, scrupulous, punctilious, methodical, thorough, detailed.
OPPOSITES: careless, extravagant.

careless adjective
1 *careless motorists:* inattentive, negligent, remiss; heedless, irresponsible, impetuous, reckless.
2 *careless work:* shoddy, slapdash, slipshod, scrappy, negligent, lax, slack, disorganized, hasty, hurried, sloppy; informal slap-happy.
3 *a careless remark:* thoughtless, unthinking, insensitive, indiscreet, unguarded, incautious, ill-judged, inadvertent.
4 *she gave a careless shrug:* casual, nonchalant, insouciant, offhand, languid.
OPPOSITES: careful, meticulous.

caress verb *he caressed her tenderly:* stroke, touch, fondle; embrace, hug.

caretaker noun janitor, attendant, porter, custodian, concierge.

▷ **adjective** *the club's caretaker manager:* temporary, acting, interim, short-term, provisional, pro tem, stand-in, fill-in, stopgap, substitute.
OPPOSITES: permanent.

careworn adjective *a careworn expression:* worried, anxious, harassed, strained, stressed; drained, drawn, gaunt, haggard; informal hassled.
OPPOSITES: carefree.

cargo noun freight, load, consignment, delivery, shipment, haul; goods, merchandise.

caricature noun *a caricature of the Prime Minister:* cartoon, parody, satire, lampoon, burlesque; informal send-up, take-off.

▷ **verb** *she has turned to caricaturing her fellow actors:* parody, satirize, lampoon, make fun of, burlesque; Brit. informal send up; informal take off.

caring adjective *his father is such a caring person:* kind, kind-hearted, warm-hearted, tender; concerned, attentive, thoughtful, solicitous, considerate; affectionate, loving, doting, fond; sympathetic, understanding, compassionate, feeling.
OPPOSITES: cruel.

carnage noun *the carnage of the First World War:* slaughter, massacre, mass murder, butchery, bloodshed, bloodbath, bloodletting.

carnal adjective *carnal desire | carnal pleasures:* sexual, physical, bodily, fleshly, corporeal; sensual, erotic, libidinous.
OPPOSITES: spiritual.

carnival noun *the city's annual carnival:* festival, fiesta, fair, fete, jamboree, gala, celebration.

carnivorous adjective *a carnivorous lizard:* meat-eating, predatory.
OPPOSITES: herbivorous.

carouse verb *they danced and caroused until the drink ran out:* celebrate, revel, make merry, roister; informal paint the town red, party.

carp verb *investors are carping about the terms of the deal:* complain, moan, grumble, grouse, whine, bleat, cavil; informal bellyache, whinge, grouch.

carpenter noun woodworker, joiner, cabinetmaker.

carpet noun
1 *a Turkish carpet:* rug, mat, floor covering.
2 *a carpet of wild flowers:* covering, blanket, layer, cover, cloak, mantle.

▷ **verb** *the gravel was carpeted in moss:* cover, coat, overlay, overspread, blanket.

carriage noun
1 *a railway carriage:* coach, car.
2 *the carriage of bikes on trains:* transport, transportation, conveyance, carrying, shipment.

carrier noun bearer, conveyor, transporter; porter, courier; Brit. haulier.

carry verb
1 *she carried the box into the kitchen:* convey, transfer, move, take, bring, bear; fetch; informal cart, lug; Brit. informal hump.
2 *a coach operator carrying 12 million passengers a year:* transport, convey, move, handle.
3 *satellites carry the signal over the Atlantic:* transmit, conduct, relay, communicate, convey, dispatch, beam.
4 *the bridge is capable of carrying even the heaviest loads:* support, sustain, stand; prop up, shore up, bolster.
5 *the manager must carry most of the responsibility:* accept, bear, assume, shoulder, take on, undertake.
6 *she was carrying his baby:* be pregnant with, bear, expect.
7 *she carried herself with assurance:* conduct, bear, hold; act, behave, acquit; formal comport.
8 *a resolution was carried:* approve, vote for, accept, endorse, ratify; agree to, assent to, rubber-stamp; informal OK, give the thumbs up to.
9 *I carried the whole audience:* win over, sway, convince, persuade, influence; motivate, stimulate.
10 *the paper carried a detailed account of the current crisis:* publish, print; broadcast, transmit.
□ **be/get carried away**
lose your self-control, be/get overexcited, go too far; informal lose it.
□ **carry something off**
1 *she carried off four awards:* win, secure, gain, achieve, collect; informal land, net, bag, scoop.
2 *he has carried it off:* succeed, triumph, be victorious, be successful.
□ **carry on**
they carried on with their work: continue, keep on, go on; persist in, persevere with; informal stick with/at.
□ **carry something on**
their father carried on a number of businesses: engage in, conduct, be involved in, carry out, perform.
□ **carry something out**
1 *we carried out a market research survey:* conduct, perform, undertake.
2 *I carried out my promise to her | we have carried out your orders:* fulfil, carry through, honour, make good; keep, observe, abide by, adhere to, stick to, keep faith with; comply with, obey, discharge, implement, execute.

cart noun
1 *a horse-drawn cart:* wagon, carriage, dray.

2 *a man with a cart took their luggage:* handcart, trolley, barrow.

carton noun box, pack, packet, package; container, case.

cartoon noun
1 *a cartoon of the Prime Minister:* caricature, parody, lampoon; informal take-off, send-up.
2 *he was reading cartoons:* comic strip, comic, graphic novel.
3 *they watched cartoons on TV:* animated film, animation.

cartridge noun
1 *a toner cartridge:* cassette, canister, container.
2 *a rifle cartridge:* bullet, round, shell, charge, shot.

carve verb
1 *the altar was carved from a block of solid jade:* sculpt, sculpture; cut, hew, whittle; form, shape, fashion.
2 *I carved my initials on the tree:* engrave, etch, incise, score.
3 *he carved the chicken:* slice, cut up.
□ **carve something up**
after the First World War, the European powers carved up the old Ottoman Empire: divide, partition, subdivide, split up, break up; share out; informal divvy up.

carving noun sculpture, model, statue, statuette, figure, figurine.

cascade noun waterfall, cataract, falls; rapids, white water.
▷ verb *rain cascaded from the roof:* pour, gush, stream, spill, flow; surge, spurt, jet.

case[1] noun
1 *a classic case of overreaction:* instance, occurrence, manifestation, demonstration; example, illustration, specimen, sample, exemplification.
2 *if that is the case I will have to find somebody else:* situation, position, state of affairs, the lie of the land; circumstances, conditions, facts, how things stand; Brit. state of play; informal score.
3 *officers involved in the case raided nine London homes:* investigation, enquiry, examination, probe, inquest.
4 *urgent cases were turned away from the hospital:* patient, sick person, invalid, sufferer, victim.
5 *he lost his case and was ordered to pay £1.5 million in damages:* lawsuit, action, legal action, legal dispute, suit, trial, legal/judicial proceedings, litigation.
6 *he concluded that the case for reducing income tax was compelling:* argument, contention, defence, justification, vindication; thesis, reasoning, logic.

case[2] noun
1 *a cigarette case:* container, box, canister, receptacle, holder.
2 *a seed case:* casing, cover, covering,

sheath; envelope, sleeve, jacket; technical integument.
3 *she threw some clothes into a case:* suitcase, bag, valise, portmanteau; (**cases**) luggage, baggage.
4 *a case of wine:* crate, box; twelve bottles.
5 *a glass display case:* cabinet, cupboard.
▷ **verb**
1 *the towers are of steel cased in granite:* cover, surround, encase.
2 (informal) *a thief casing the joint:* reconnoitre, inspect, examine, survey; informal recce, check out.

cash noun
1 *a small amount of cash was taken from the till | how much cash do you have on you?* money, hard cash; -notes, coins, change; informal dough, bread, loot, the readies; Brit. informal dosh, brass, lolly.
2 *thousands of hospital beds are closing because of a lack of cash:* finance, money, resources, funds, assets, the means, the wherewithal.
OPPOSITES: cheque, credit.
▷ **verb** *the bank cashed her cheque:* exchange, change, convert into cash/money; honour, pay, accept; Brit. encash.
□ **cash in on**
landlords should take a long-term view rather than just cashing in on the rise in house prices: take advantage of, exploit, milk; make money from, profit from; informal make a killing out of.

cashier noun clerk, bank clerk, teller; treasurer, bursar, purser.

casing noun cover, case, shell, envelope, sheath, sheathing, sleeve, jacket, housing.

cask noun barrel, keg, butt, tun, vat, drum, hogshead; historical firkin.

casket noun
1 *a small wooden casket full of jewels:* box, chest, case, container, receptacle.
2 *his body lies in a silver casket:* coffin.

cast verb
1 *he cast the stone into the stream:* throw, toss, fling, pitch, hurl, lob; informal chuck, sling; Brit. informal bung.
2 *she cast a fearful glance over her shoulder:* direct, shoot, throw, send.
3 *thousands of people turned up to cast their votes:* register, record, enter, file; vote.
4 *the moon cast a pale light:* emit, give off, send out, radiate.
5 *the fire cast shadows over the room:* form, create, produce; project, throw.
6 *they were cast as extras:* choose, select, pick, name.
7 *a figure cast by hand:* mould, fashion, form, shape, model; sculpt, sculpture, forge.
▷ **noun** *the whole cast's acting was superb:* actors, performers, players, company; dramatis personae, characters.
□ **cast something aside**
the kids have cast aside their roller skates

and taken up skiing: discard, reject, throw away/out, get rid of, dispose of, abandon.
□ **cast down**
she was cast down by the criticism: depressed, downcast, unhappy, sad, miserable, gloomy, down, low; dejected, dispirited, discouraged, disheartened, downhearted, demoralized, disconsolate, crestfallen, despondent.

castigate verb *he was castigated for not setting a good example:* reprimand, rebuke, admonish, chastise, chide, upbraid, reprove, reproach, scold, berate, take to task, lambaste, censure; informal haul over the coals, tell off, rap someone on the knuckles, bawl out, lay into; Brit. informal tick off, have a go at.
OPPOSITES: praise, commend.

castle noun fortress, fort, stronghold, fortification, keep, citadel.

casual adjective
1 *a casual attitude to life:* relaxed, unconcerned, carefree, easy-going, free and easy, devil-may-care; blasé, nonchalant, insouciant, blithe, offhand, flippant; indifferent, uncaring, lackadaisical; informal laid-back.
2 *a casual remark:* offhand, spontaneous, unpremeditated, unthinking, unconsidered, impromptu, throwaway, unguarded; informal off-the-cuff.
3 *a casual glance:* cursory, perfunctory, superficial, passing, fleeting; hasty, brief, quick.
4 *a casual acquaintance:* slight, superficial.
5 *casual work:* temporary, part-time, freelance, impermanent, irregular, occasional.
6 *a casual meeting changed his life:* chance, accidental, unplanned, unintended, unexpected, unforeseen, unanticipated, fortuitous, serendipitous, adventitious; random.
7 *the hotel's casual atmosphere:* relaxed, friendly, informal, easy-going, free and easy; informal laid-back.
8 *a casual shirt:* informal, comfortable, leisure, everyday; informal sporty.
OPPOSITES: careful, planned, formal.

casualty noun victim, fatality, loss, death; dead and injured.

casuistry noun *the minister is engaging in casuistry:* sophistry, specious reasoning.

cat noun feline, tomcat, tom, kitten; informal pussy cat, puss; Brit. informal moggie.

cataclysm noun *the cataclysm of the First World War:* disaster, catastrophe, calamity, tragedy, devastation, upheaval, convulsion.

cataclysmic adjective *a cataclysmic earthquake:* disastrous, catastrophic, calamitous, tragic, devastating, ruinous; violent, destructive, awful., terrible, dreadful

catacombs plural noun underground cemetery, crypt, vault, tomb, ossuary.

catalogue noun
1 *a library catalogue:* directory, register, index, list, listing, record, archive, inventory, log.
2 *a mail-order catalogue:* brochure.
3 *the accident is the latest in a catalogue of disasters:* series, succession, string, sequence, list.
▷ verb *the collection is fully catalogued:* classify, categorize, index, list, archive, make an inventory of, inventory, record, log, itemize.

catapult verb *the explosion catapulted the car 30 yards along the road:* propel, launch, hurl, fling, send flying, fire, blast, shoot.

cataract noun waterfall, cascade, falls; rapids, white water.

catastrophe noun *climate scientists claimed that greenhouse gas emissions must be cut by 50% to avoid an environmental catastrophe:* disaster, calamity, cataclysm, tragedy; apocalypse.

catastrophic adjective *the catastrophic consequences of a major oil spill in Arctic seas:* disastrous, calamitous, cataclysmic, devastating, ruinous, tragic, fatal; awful, terrible, dreadful.

catcall noun whistle, boo, hiss, jeer, hoot, taunt; (**catcalls**) abuse, taunting, derision.

catch verb
1 *I managed to catch the glass before it fell to the ground | he caught her arm as she tried to push past him:* seize, grab, snatch, seize/grab/take hold of, grasp, grip, clutch, clench; receive, get, intercept.
2 *he held up eleven shops before the police caught him:* capture, seize; apprehend, arrest, take prisoner/captive, take into custody; trap, snare, ensnare; net, hook, land; informal nab, pick up,; Brit. informal nick.
3 *they were caught siphoning petrol from a car in Darlington:* discover, find, come upon/across, stumble on, chance on; surprise, catch red-handed, catch in the act.
4 *she caught the 7.45 bus:* be in time for, make, get; board, get on.
5 *her heel caught in a hole:* become trapped, become entangled, snag.
6 *the scheme caught his imagination:* engage, capture, attract, draw, grab, grip, seize; hold, absorb, engross.
7 *out of the corner of his eye he caught a movement in the back garden:* perceive, glimpse, catch a glimpse of, catch sight of, notice, spot, detect, make out.
8 *I couldn't catch what she was saying:* hear, perceive, discern, make out; understand, comprehend, grasp; formal apprehend.
9 *the film caught the flavour of the sixties:* evoke, conjure up, call to mind, recall,

c

capture, encapsulate.
10 *she fell and caught her head on the corner of the fireplace:* hit, strike, bang, smack.
11 *he caught malaria:* contract, become infected with, get, be taken ill with, develop, come down with, be struck down with; Brit. go down with.
OPPOSITES: drop, release, miss.
▷**noun**
1 *the fishermen were inspecting their catch:* haul, net, bag, yield.
2 *there must be a catch:* snag, disadvantage, drawback, problem, difficulty, fly in the ointment; trick, trap.
3 *the catch on the window was rusty:* latch, lock, fastener, clasp, hasp.
▢**catch on**
1 *version two of the game never really caught on:* become popular/fashionable, take off; boom, flourish, thrive.
2 *I caught on fast:* understand, comprehend, see the light; informal cotton on, get the picture/message.
▢**catch someone up**
draw level with, reach; gain on.

catching adjective *the disease isn't catching:* infectious, contagious, communicable, transmissible; infective.

catchphrase noun saying, slogan, quotation, quote.

catchy adjective *a catchy tune:* memorable, unforgettable; appealing, popular; melodious, tuneful, singable.

categorical adjective *a categorical assurance that the government will not raise VAT:* unqualified, unconditional, unequivocal, absolute, explicit, unambiguous, definite, direct, outright, emphatic, positive, point-blank, conclusive, without reservations.
OPPOSITES: qualified, equivocal.

categorize verb *silk is categorized as a luxury import:* classify, class, group, grade, rate, designate; order, arrange, sort, rank; file, catalogue, list, index.

category noun *the films were divided into several categories | there are four main categories of holiday insurance:* class, group, grouping, bracket, classification, division, heading, set; type, sort, kind, variety; grade, order, rank.

cater verb
▢**cater for**
1 *a seaside resort catering for older holidaymakers:* serve, provide for, meet the needs/wants of, accommodate.
2 *he seemed to cater for all tastes:* take into account/consideration, allow for, consider, bear in mind, make provision for, have regard for.
▢**cater to**
he catered to her every whim: satisfy, indulge, pander to, gratify, accommodate, give in to, fulfil.

caterwaul verb *it wasn't until afterwards I realized it was cats caterwauling:* howl, wail, cry, yell, scream, screech, yowl.

catharsis noun *this process of catharsis can bring improvements in both physical and mental health:* emotional release, relief; cleansing, purification, purging.

catholic adjective *her tastes are pretty catholic:* diverse, wide, broad, broad-based, eclectic; comprehensive, all-encompassing, all-embracing, all-inclusive.
OPPOSITES: narrow.

cattle plural noun cows, oxen, bulls; stock, livestock.

WORD LINKS
bovine relating to cattle

caucus noun
1 *22 people attended the Green Party caucus:* meeting, assembly, gathering, conference, rally.
2 *the right-wing caucus in the cabinet:* faction, camp, bloc, group, set, band, ring, cabal, coterie, pressure group.

cause noun
1 *the cause of the fire is not known | 35% of couples said financial issues were the major cause of rows:* source, origin, root, starting point, beginning; base, basis, foundation; agent, originator, author, creator, producer, instigator.
2 *there is no cause for alarm:* reason, grounds, justification, call, need, necessity, occasion; excuse, pretext.
3 *the cause of human rights | a good cause:* principle, ideal, belief; object, end, aim, objective, purpose; charity, movement.
4 *he went to plead his cause:* case, suit, lawsuit, action.
OPPOSITES: effect, result.
▷**verb** *this disease can cause blindness:* bring about, give rise to, lead to, result in, create, produce, engender, spawn, bring on, precipitate, prompt, provoke, trigger, make happen, induce, foster.

caustic adjective
1 *a caustic substance:* corrosive, corroding, acid.
2 *a caustic comment:* sarcastic, scathing, cutting, biting, mordant, sharp, sardonic, ironic, trenchant, acerbic, acid, bitter, scornful.

caution noun
1 *anyone receiving a suspect package should exercise extreme caution:* care, circumspection, wariness, carefulness, heedfulness, heed, attention, attentiveness, alertness, watchfulness, vigilance; discretion, prudence.
2 *a first offender may receive a caution:* warning, admonishment, reprimand.
▷**verb**
1 *advisers cautioned against tax increases:* advise, warn, counsel, urge.

2 *he was cautioned by the police:* warn, admonish; reprimand.

cautious adjective *a cautious driver:* careful, circumspect, wary, heedful, attentive, alert, watchful, vigilant, prudent, guarded.
OPPOSITES: reckless.

cavalcade noun *a royal cavalcade proceeded through the city:* procession, parade, motorcade, cortège; Brit. march past.

cavalier adjective *Anne was irritated by his cavalier attitude:* offhand, casual, dismissive, insouciant, unconcerned, indifferent, careless.

cave noun cavern, grotto, pothole, underground chamber.
▢ **cave in**
1 *the roof caved in:* collapse, fall in/down, give way, crumble, subside.
2 *the manager caved in to their demands:* yield, surrender, capitulate, give in, back down, make concessions, throw in the towel; comply with, accede to, acquiesce in, go along with.

> WORD LINKS
> **speleology** the study or exploration of caves

caveat noun *he added the caveat that the results still had to be corroborated:* warning, caution; proviso, condition, stipulation, provision, clause, rider, qualification.

cavern noun large cave, underground chamber, grotto.

cavernous adjective *he led them into a cavernous hall:* vast, huge, immense; deep, hollow, echoing, gaping, yawning, empty.

cavil verb *they cavilled at the cost:* complain, moan, carp, grumble, grouse; quibble; informal gripe, grouch, beef, bellyache, whinge.

cavity noun *customs officers found a secret cavity in the car:* space, chamber, hollow, hole, pocket, aperture; gap, crater, pit.

cavort verb *the children were cavorting in the snow:* skip, dance, romp, jig, caper, frisk, gambol, prance, frolic; leap, jump, bound, spring, hop.

cease verb
1 *hostilities had ceased:* end, come to an end, halt, come to a halt, stop, conclude, terminate, finish, draw to a close, be over.
2 *they ceased all military activity:* bring to an end, bring to a halt, end, halt, stop, conclude, terminate, finish, wind up, discontinue, suspend, break off.
OPPOSITES: start, continue.

ceaseless adjective *the fort was subjected to ceaseless bombardment:* continuous, constant, continual; incessant, unceasing, unending, endless, never-ending,

interminable, non-stop, uninterrupted, unremitting, relentless, unrelenting, unrelieved, sustained, persistent, perpetual.
OPPOSITES: intermittent.

cede verb *the island was ceded to the United Kingdom in 1842:* surrender, relinquish, yield, part with, give up, concede; hand over, deliver up, give over, make over, transfer.

ceiling noun *the government imposed a wage ceiling of 3 per cent:* upper limit, maximum, limitation.

celebrate verb
1 *they were celebrating their wedding anniversary:* commemorate, observe, mark, keep, honour, remember.
2 *let's celebrate!* enjoy yourself, have fun, have a good time, have a party, make merry; informal party, paint the town red, live it up, have a ball.
3 *he was celebrated for his achievements:* praise, honour, pay tribute to, extol, glorify, eulogize.
4 *the priest celebrated mass:* perform, observe, officiate at.

celebrated adjective *a celebrated photographer:* acclaimed, admired, highly rated, lionized, revered, honoured, esteemed, exalted, well thought of, vaunted; eminent, great, distinguished, prestigious, illustrious, pre-eminent, estimable, notable, of note, of repute.
OPPOSITES: unknown.

celebration noun
1 *the celebration of his 50th birthday:* commemoration, observance, marking, keeping.
2 *a cause for celebration:* jollification, merrymaking, enjoying yourself, revelry, revels, festivities; informal partying.
3 *a birthday celebration:* party, function, gathering, festivities; festival, fete, carnival, jamboree; informal do, bash.

celebrity noun
1 *a sporting celebrity:* famous person, VIP, very important person, personality, name, big name, household name, star, superstar, idol, luminary; informal celeb, megastar.
2 *she had achieved international celebrity:* fame, prominence, renown, eminence, pre-eminence, distinction, note, notability, prestige, stature, repute, reputation; stardom, popularity.
OPPOSITES: obscurity.

celestial adjective
1 *a celestial body:* in space, heavenly, astronomical, extraterrestrial, stellar, planetary.
2 *celestial beings:* heavenly, holy, saintly, divine, godly, ethereal; immortal.
OPPOSITES: earthly.

celibate adjective *many of the dons were still bachelors, for whom the celibate life* *was the norm:* unmarried, single; chaste, abstinent, self-denying.

cell noun
1 *a prison cell:* room, cubicle, chamber; lock-up; dungeon, oubliette.
2 *the cells of the honeycomb:* compartment, cavity, hole, hollow, section.
3 *terrorist cells:* unit, faction, group.

cellar noun basement, vault, underground room, lower ground floor; crypt, undercroft.

cemetery noun graveyard, churchyard, burial ground, necropolis.

censor verb *the original version of the film was censored for American audiences:* cut, edit, expurgate; bowdlerize, sanitize, blue-pencil; informal clean up.

censorious adjective *she used not to be so censorious of others' behaviour:* hypercritical, overcritical, judgemental, disapproving, condemnatory, disparaging, deprecatory, negative.
OPPOSITES: complimentary.

censure verb *the company was censured by inspectors from the Department of Trade:* criticize, condemn, denounce, attack, reprimand, chastise, take to task, rebuke, reprove; formal castigate.
▷ noun *two MPs were singled out for censure:* criticism, condemnation, disapproval, rebuke, reproof, reproach.
OPPOSITES: approval.

> **USAGE**
>
> Do not confuse **censure** and **censor**. **Censure** means 'to criticize severely' or 'strong disapproval', while **censor** means 'to officially suppress unacceptable parts of a book, film, or similar work' (*the original version of the film was censored for American audiences*), or 'an official who censors books etc.' (*four minutes of the scene were removed by the censors*).

central adjective
1 *a Roman basilica always occupied a central position:* middle, centre, halfway, midway, mid, focal; median, medial, mean.
2 *central London:* inner, innermost, middle, mid.
3 *the central issue facing the party was how to regain power:* main, chief, principal, primary, leading, foremost, first, most important, predominant, dominant, key, crucial, vital, essential, basic, fundamental, core, prime, premier, paramount, major, overriding; informal number-one.
OPPOSITES: outer, peripheral.

centralize verb *the minister announced a series of measures to centralize tax collection:* concentrate, consolidate, amalgamate, unify, streamline, focus; Brit. rationalize.
OPPOSITES: devolve.

centre noun *the centre of the town:* middle, nucleus, heart, core, hub; middle point, midpoint, halfway point, mean, median.
OPPOSITES: edge.
▷ verb *the film centres around an 18-year-old aspiring actor:* focus, concentrate, pivot, revolve, be based.

centrepiece noun *a masterwork by Titian forms the centrepiece of this glittering display of 80 paintings:* highlight, main feature, high point/spot, best part, climax; focus of attention, focal point, centre of attention/interest.

ceramics plural noun pottery, china.

ceremonial adjective *a ceremonial occasion:* formal, official, state, public; stately, courtly, solemn; ritual, ritualistic.
OPPOSITES: informal.
▷ noun *the procedure was conducted with all due ceremonial:* ritual, ceremony, formality, protocol; pomp and circumstance.

ceremonious dignified, majestic, imposing, impressive, solemn, stately, formal, courtly; regal, imperial, grand, glorious, splendid, magnificent, resplendent.

ceremony noun
1 *a wedding ceremony:* rite, ritual, ceremonial, observance; service, sacrament, liturgy, celebration.
2 *the new Queen was proclaimed with due ceremony:* pomp and circumstance, protocol, formalities, ritual, solemnity; decorum, etiquette.

certain adjective
1 *I'm certain he's guilty:* sure, confident, positive, convinced, in no doubt, satisfied, assured, persuaded.
2 *it is certain that more changes are in the offing:* unquestionable, beyond question, not in doubt, indubitable, undeniable, irrefutable, indisputable, definite; plain, clear, obvious, evident, recognized, confirmed, accepted, acknowledged, undisputed, undoubted, unquestioned; inevitable, unavoidable.
3 *they are certain to win:* sure, very likely, bound, destined.
4 *there is no certain cure for this:* reliable, dependable, trustworthy, foolproof, tried and tested, effective, guaranteed, sure, unfailing, infallible.
5 *he raised certain personal problems with me:* particular, specific, individual.
OPPOSITES: doubtful, possible, unlikely.

certainly adverb *this is certainly a late work:* unquestionably, definitely, beyond/without question, without doubt, indubitably, undeniably, irrefutably, indisputably, assuredly; obviously, patently, evidently, plainly, clearly, unmistakably, undisputedly, undoubtedly.
OPPOSITES: possibly.

certainty noun
1 *she knew with certainty that he was telling the truth:* confidence, conviction, certitude, assurance.
2 *he accepted defeat as a certainty:* inevitability, foregone conclusion; informal sure thing; Brit. informal cert.
OPPOSITES: doubt, possibility.

certificate noun guarantee, certification, document, authorization, authentication, credentials, accreditation, licence, diploma.

certify verb
1 *profits for the year had been certified by the auditors:* verify, guarantee, attest, validate, confirm, substantiate, endorse, vouch for, testify to; provide evidence, give proof, prove, demonstrate.
2 *For a farm to be certified as organic, all its products must be grown in accordance with organic standards:* accredit, recognize, license, authorize, approve.

certitude noun *the question may never be answered with certitude:* certainty, confidence, conviction, assurance.
OPPOSITES: doubt.

cessation noun *the cessation of hostilities:* end, ending, termination, stopping, halting, ceasing, finishing, stoppage, conclusion, winding up, discontinuation, abandonment, suspension, breaking off.
OPPOSITES: start, resumption.

chafe verb
1 *the collar chafed his neck:* rub against, graze, abrade, gall, scrape, scratch.
2 *the grommet stops the cable chafing on the metal:* wear away/down, erode, abrade, scrape away.
3 *the bank chafed at the restrictions:* be angry, be annoyed, be irritated, fume, be exasperated, be frustrated.

chaff verb *rival supporters chaffed one another good-humouredly:* tease, make fun of, poke fun at, rag; informal take the mickey out of, pull someone's leg.

chagrin noun *McLeish was enjoying Davidson's obvious chagrin:* annoyance, irritation, vexation, exasperation, displeasure, dissatisfaction, discontent, indignation, resentment; embarrassment, mortification, humiliation, shame.
OPPOSITES: delight.

chain noun
1 *he was held in chains:* fetters, shackles, irons, leg irons, manacles, handcuffs.
2 *a chain of events:* series, succession, string, sequence, train, course.
3 *a chain of shops:* group, multiple shop/store, multiple.
▷verb *she chained her bike to the railings | he had been chained up:* secure, fasten, tie, hitch, tether; restrain, shackle, fetter, manacle, handcuff.

chair noun
1 *he sat down on a nearby chair:* seat.
2 *the chair of the committee.* See CHAIRMAN.
3 *a university chair:* professorship.
▷verb *she chairs the economic committee:* preside over, take the chair of; lead, direct, run, manage, control, be in charge of.

chairman, chairwoman noun
chair, chairperson, president, leader; spokesperson, spokesman, spokeswoman.

chalk verb
□ **chalk something up**
1 *he chalked up his 50th Grand Prix win:* achieve, attain, accomplish, gain, earn, win, succeed in making, make, get, obtain, notch up, rack up.
2 *I forgot completely—chalk it up to age:* attribute, ascribe, put down, assign; blame on, pin on, lay at the door of.

chalky adjective *her skin was chalky and her hands were shaking:* pale, bloodless, colourless, ashen, white, wan, pallid, pasty.

challenge noun
1 *running the station is a challenge for a volunteer staff with other full-time jobs:* problem, difficult task, test, trial.
2 *he accepted the challenge:* dare, provocation; summons.
▷verb
1 *we challenged their statistics:* question, disagree with, dispute, take issue with, protest against, call into question, object to.
2 *the new coalition will challenge the government at the polls in next week's election:* compete against, stand against, oppose, go head to head with, pit yourself against.
3 *the job will challenge you and make you think:* make demands on, test, tax, strain; stretch, stimulate, inspire.
4 *he challenged one of my men to a duel:* dare, invite, summons.

challenging adjective *it's a brief but challenging book:* demanding, testing, taxing, exacting; stimulating, inspiring; difficult, tough, hard.
OPPOSITES: easy, uninspiring.

chamber noun
1 *a debating chamber:* room, hall, assembly room, auditorium.
2 *the left chamber of the heart:* compartment, cavity; Anatomy auricle, ventricle.

champion noun
1 *the world champion:* winner, title-holder, defending champion, gold medallist; prizewinner, victor; informal number one.
2 *he became a determined champion of a free press:* advocate, proponent, promoter, supporter, defender, upholder, backer, exponent; campaigner, lobbyist, crusader, apologist.
▷verb *they championed the rights of tribal peoples:* advocate, promote, defend,

uphold, support, back, stand up for, take someone's part; campaign for, lobby for, fight for, crusade for, stick up for.
OPPOSITES: oppose.

chance noun
1 *there was a chance he might be released | is there any chance of getting an agreement today?* possibility, prospect, probability, likelihood, expectation, anticipation; risk, threat, danger.
2 *I gave her a chance to answer my query:* opportunity, opening, occasion, turn, time, window of opportunity.
3 *he took an awful chance:* risk, gamble, speculation, long shot, leap in the dark.
4 *it was pure chance that made me notice the writing:* accident, coincidence, serendipity, fate, destiny, fortuity, providence, happenstance; good fortune, good luck, fluke.
▷**adjective** *a chance discovery:* accidental, fortuitous, fluky, coincidental, serendipitous, adventitious; unintentional, unintended, inadvertent, unplanned.
OPPOSITES: intentional.

▷**verb**
1 *I chanced to meet him:* happen.
2 (informal) *she chanced another look:* risk, hazard, venture, try.
□ **by chance**
fortuitously, by accident, accidentally, coincidentally, serendipitously; unintentionally, inadvertently.
□ **chance on**
come across/upon, run across/into, happen on, light on, stumble on, find by chance, meet by chance; informal bump into.

chancy adjective (informal) *intelligence-gathering is a chancy business:* risky, unpredictable, uncertain, precarious; unsafe, insecure, tricky, high-risk, hazardous, perilous; informal dicey, hairy.

change verb
1 *this could change the face of Britain | things have changed:* alter, make/become different, adjust, adapt, amend, modify, revise, refine, reshape, refashion, redesign, restyle, revamp, rework, remodel, reorganize, reorder; vary, transform, transfigure, transmute, metamorphose, evolve.
2 *he's changed his car:* exchange, swap, switch, replace, substitute; alternate, interchange.
OPPOSITES: preserve, keep.

▷**noun**
1 *a change of plan | there have been important changes to the pension scheme:* alteration, modification, variation, revision, amendment, adjustment, adaptation; remodelling, reshaping, rearrangement, restyling, reworking; metamorphosis, transformation, evolution; humorous transmogrification.
2 *a change of government:* exchange, substitution, swap, switch, replacement;

alternation, interchange.
3 *I've no change:* coins, loose/small change, cash, silver, coppers; technical specie.

changeable adjective *the weather will be changeable | He was very changeable in his moods, elated one moment and downhearted the next:* variable, unpredictable, inconstant, varying, changing, fluctuating, irregular; erratic, inconsistent, unstable, unsettled, turbulent; fickle, capricious, temperamental, volatile, mercurial; informal up and down.

changeless adjective *these stories tell changeless truths about the human psyche:* unchanging, unvarying, time-less, permanent, constant, unchanged, consistent, uniform, undeviating; stable, steady, unchangeable, unalterable, invariable, immutable; static, fixed.
OPPOSITES: variable.

channel noun
1 *the English Channel:* straits, sound, sea passage.
2 *the water ran down a channel:* conduit, trough, culvert, gutter, drain, sluice, spillway, race; duct.
3 *a channel of communication:* means, medium, instrument, mechanism, agency, vehicle, route, avenue.
▷**verb** *many countries channel their aid through charities:* convey, direct, send, pass on, transfer.

chant noun
1 *the protesters' chants:* shout, cry, rallying call, slogan.
2 *the melodious chant of the monks:* incantation, intonation, singing, song, recitative.
▷**verb**
1 *protesters were chanting slogans:* shout, chorus, repeat.
2 *the choir chanted Psalm 118:* sing, intone.

chaos noun *snow caused chaos in the region:* disorder, confusion, mayhem, havoc, bedlam, pandemonium, turmoil, tumult, commotion, disruption, disarray, disorganization, upheaval; a muddle, a mess; anarchy, lawlessness; informal a shambles.
OPPOSITES: order.

chaotic adjective *the political situation was chaotic:* disorderly, in disorder, in chaos, in disarray, confused, disorganized, topsy-turvy, in pandemonium, in turmoil; in a muddle, in a mess; anarchic, lawless; Brit. informal shambolic.

chap verb *his skin is very dry and chaps easily:* become raw, become sore, become inflamed, chafe, crack.

chaperone noun *I'm 26 years old: I don't need a chaperone:* companion, escort, protector, minder.
▷**verb** *she was chaperoned by her mother:* accompany, escort, attend, watch over, keep an eye on, protect.

chapter noun
1 *the first chapter of the book:* section, division, part, portion.
2 *a new chapter in our history:* period, phase, page, stage, epoch, era.

char verb *the large wooden beams had been charred by the fire:* scorch, burn, singe, sear, blacken.

character noun
1 *Jenny had a forceful character:* personality, nature, disposition, temperament, temper, mentality, make-up; features, qualities, properties, traits.
2 *we want to preserve the character of our town:* distinctiveness, individuality, identity, essence, spirit, ethos, complexion, tone, feel, feeling.
3 *a woman of character:* integrity, honour, moral strength/fibre, rectitude, uprightness; fortitude, strength, backbone, resolve, grit, will power.
4 *to what do I owe this attack on my character?* reputation, name, good name, standing, stature, position, status.
5 *he was a boorish character:* person, man, woman, soul, creature, individual; informal customer, sort.
6 *the characters develop throughout the play:* persona, role, part; (**characters**) dramatis personae.
7 *the file name must not exceed thirty characters:* letter, figure, symbol, sign, mark.

characteristic noun *these men have some interesting characteristics:* attribute, feature, quality, property, trait, aspect, element, facet; mannerism, habit, custom, idiosyncrasy, peculiarity, quirk, oddity, foible.
▷ **adjective** *his characteristic eloquence:* typical, usual, habitual, normal, predictable; distinctive, particular, special, especial, peculiar, idiosyncratic, singular, unique.

characterize verb
1 *the period was characterized by scientific advancement:* distinguish, make distinctive, mark, typify, set apart.
2 *the women are characterized as prophets of doom:* portray, depict, present, represent, describe, delineate; categorize, class, style, brand.

charade noun *the trial was a charade organized to guarantee a guilty verdict:* farce, pantomime, travesty, mockery, parody; pretence, act, masquerade.

charge verb
1 *most solicitors will only charge a few pounds for this service:* ask, make you pay, demand, levy; bill, invoice.
2 *the subscription will be charged to your account:* bill, debit from, take from.
3 *he was charged with the murder of his ex-wife:* accuse of, indict for, arraign for; prosecute for, try for, put on trial for; N. Amer. impeach.
4 *the committee was charged with reshaping the educational system:* entrust, task; burden, encumber, saddle.
5 *the cavalry charged the tanks:* attack, storm, assail, fall on, swoop on, descend on.
6 *we charged into the crowd:* rush, storm, stampede, push, plough, launch yourself, go headlong; informal steam.
7 *the songs are charged with emotional intensity:* suffuse, pervade, permeate, infuse, imbue, fill.
▷ **noun**
1 *all customers pay a charge:* fee, payment, price, tariff, amount, sum, fare, levy.
2 *he pleaded guilty to the charge:* accusation, allegation, indictment, arraignment; N. Amer. impeachment.
3 *an infantry charge:* attack, assault, offensive, onslaught, drive, push, thrust.
4 *the child was in her charge:* care, protection, safe keeping, control; custody, guardianship, wardship; hands.
5 *I am concerned for the safety of my charge:* ward, protégé, dependant.
□ **in charge of**
his daughter has been in charge of the company since 1992: responsible for, in control of, at the helm/wheel of; managing, running, administering, directing, supervising, overseeing, controlling; informal running the show.

charisma noun *he had enormous personal charisma:* charm, presence, force of personality, strength of character; magnetism, attractiveness, appeal.

charismatic adjective *he was a charismatic figure with great appeal to the public:* charming, fascinating; magnetic, captivating, beguiling, attractive, appealing, irresistible.

charitable adjective
1 *she became involved in many local charitable activities:* philanthropic, humanitarian, altruistic, benevolent, public-spirited; non-profit-making.
2 *he was charitable in his judgements:* magnanimous, generous, liberal, tolerant, easy-going, broad-minded, sympathetic, lenient, indulgent, forgiving, forbearing, kind, considerate.

charity noun
1 *an Aids charity:* fund, trust, foundation; non-profit-making organization, voluntary organization, charitable institution.
2 *we don't need charity:* financial assistance, aid, welfare, financial relief; handouts, gifts, presents, largesse; historical alms.
3 *his actions are motivated by charity:* philanthropy, humanitarianism, humanity, altruism, public-spiritedness, social conscience, beneficence.
4 *show a bit of charity:* goodwill,

compassion, consideration, concern, kindness, kind-heartedness, sympathy, indulgence, tolerance, leniency, forbearance.

charlatan noun *they denounced him as a charlatan:* **mountebank**, quack, fake, impostor, cheat, double-dealer, confidence trickster, swindler, fraudster; informal con man/artist.

charm noun
1 *she was a woman of great charm and style:* **attractiveness**, beauty, glamour; charisma, appeal, allure, magnetism.
2 *these traditions retain a lot of charm:* **appeal**, drawing power, attraction, allure, fascination.
3 *a lucky charm:* **talisman**, fetish, amulet, mascot.
▷verb
1 *I was charmed by the beautiful folk melodies:* **delight**, please, win over, attract; captivate, allure, fascinate, enchant, enthral, enrapture, seduce.
2 *he charmed his mother into agreeing:* **coax**, cajole, wheedle; informal sweet-talk, soft-soap.

charming adjective *he stayed with a French family and their charming daughter:* **delightful**, pleasing, pleasant, agreeable, likeable, endearing, lovely, lovable, adorable, appealing, attractive; fetching, captivating, enchanting.

chart noun *check your ideal weight on the chart:* **graph**, table, diagram; bar chart, pie chart, flow chart; Computing graphic.
▷verb *the book charts his progress through Chicago, New York, and finally Los Angeles:* **follow**, trace, describe, detail, record, document, chronicle, log.

charter noun
1 *a Royal charter:* **authority**, authorization, sanction, dispensation, consent, permission; permit, licence, warrant, franchise, right, privilege.
2 *the UN Charter:* **constitution**, code; fundamental principles, rules, laws.
▷verb *he chartered a plane to take him to Paris:* **hire**, lease, rent; engage.

chary adjective *she had been chary of telling the whole truth:* **wary**, cautious, reluctant, unwilling; distrustful, mistrustful, sceptical, suspicious, doubtful, hesitant, guarded; informal cagey, leery.

chase¹ verb
1 *the dog was chasing a hare:* **pursue**, run after, give chase to, follow; hunt, track, trail.
2 *she chased him out of the house:* **drive**, send, scare; informal send packing.
3 *photographers chased on to the runway:* **rush**, dash, race, charge, speed, streak, shoot, hurry, scurry, fly, pelt; informal belt, tear.
▷noun *they gave up the chase:* **pursuit**, hunt, trail.

chase² verb *the figures are chased on the dish:* **engrave**, etch, carve, inscribe, cut, chisel.

chasm noun
1 *a deep chasm:* **gorge**, canyon, ravine, gully, gulf, defile, crevasse, fissure; abyss, void.
2 *the growing chasm between rich and poor:* **gulf**, rift; difference, separation, division, schism.

chassis noun **framework**, frame, structure, substructure, shell, casing; bodywork, body.

chaste adjective
1 *I have led a chaste life:* **celibate**, abstinent, self-denying; pure, virtuous, innocent, sinless; virginal.
2 *a chaste kiss on the cheek:* **non-sexual**, platonic, innocent.
3 *a small, chaste bedroom:* **plain**, simple, bare, unadorned, undecorated, unembellished; functional, austere.

chasten verb *she looked away, chastened by his sharp reply:* **subdue**, deflate, squash, crush; take someone down a peg or two, put someone in their place.

chastise verb *he chastised them for their laziness:* **scold**, upbraid, berate, reprimand, reprove, rebuke, admonish, chide, censure, lambaste, take to task, read someone the Riot Act; formal castigate; informal tell off, bawl out, haul over the coals; Brit. informal tick off.
OPPOSITES: praise.

chastity noun *she devoted herself to a life of chastity:* **celibacy**, abstinence, self-denial; purity, virtue, innocence; virginity.

chat noun *I just popped in for a chat:* **talk**, conversation, gossip, heart-to-heart, tête-à-tête; informal confab; Brit. informal natter, chinwag.
▷verb *they chatted with their guests:* **talk**, speak, converse, engage in conversation, gossip, chatter; informal gas, jaw, chew the rag/fat; Brit. informal natter.
□ **chat someone up** (informal) **flirt with**, make advances to; informal come on to.

chatter verb *they spent the evening chattering about nothing in particular:* **talk**, gossip, prattle, jabber, rattle on, babble, blather; informal yak, gas, jaw; Brit. informal natter, witter, rabbit
▷noun *he was full of inconsequential but amusing chatter:* **chat**, talk, gossip, chit-chat, patter, jabber, prattle, blather.

chatty adjective
1 *he's very chatty:* **talkative**, communicative, effusive, expansive, garrulous, loquacious, voluble; friendly.
2 *a chatty letter:* **conversational**, gossipy, informal, friendly; informal newsy.
OPPOSITES: taciturn.

chauvinist adjective *pamphlets expressing chauvinist sentiments had been distributed illegally:* jingoistic, chauvinistic, excessively patriotic, excessively nationalistic, flag-waving, xenophobic.
▷ **noun** *she wrote off all the local males as hopeless chauvinists:* sexist, misogynist, woman-hater.

cheap adjective
1 *the tickets were very cheap | consumers were lured by the cheap prices:* inexpensive, low-priced, low-cost, economical, competitive, affordable, reasonable, reasonably priced, budget, economy, bargain, cut-price, reduced, discounted, discount, rock-bottom, giveaway.
2 *the dashboard is plain without looking cheap:* poor-quality, inferior, shoddy, second-rate, substandard; vulgar, tawdry, meretricious; informal tacky.
3 *that was a cheap joke:* despicable, contemptible, mean, distasteful, tasteless.
OPPOSITES: expensive.

cheapen verb
1 *she wouldn't cheapen herself by sleeping around:* demean, debase, degrade, lower, devalue, abase, disgrace, dishonour, shame.
2 *the depreciation of the dollar would cheapen US exports:* reduce the price of, lower the price of, mark down, discount; informal slash the price of.

cheat verb
1 *they are making an effort to repay customers who have been cheated:* swindle, defraud, deceive, trick, dupe, hoodwink, double-cross; short-change informal rip off, diddle, con, shaft, put one over on, pull a fast one on.
2 *she cheated Ryan out of his fortune:* deprive of, deny; informal do out of.
3 *the boy cheated death:* avoid, escape, evade, elude; foil, frustrate, thwart.
4 (informal) *his wife was cheating on him:* be unfaithful, commit adultery; informal two-time, play about/around.
▷ **noun** *he called the principal witness a liar and a cheat:* swindler, fraudster, confidence trickster, double-dealer, double-crosser; fraud, fake, charlatan; informal con man/artist.

check verb
1 *troops checked all vehicles | I checked her background:* examine, inspect, look at/over, scrutinize, survey; study, investigate, research, probe, look into, enquire into; informal check out, give something a/the once-over.
2 *he checked that the gun was loaded:* make sure, confirm, verify.
3 *two defeats checked their progress:* halt, stop, arrest, cut short; bar, obstruct, hamper, impede, inhibit, frustrate, foil, thwart, curb, block, stall, hold up, retard, delay, slow down.

4 *her tears could not be checked:* suppress, repress, restrain, control, curb, rein in, stifle, hold back, choke back.
▷ **noun**
1 *a careful check of the records has been made:* examination, inspection, scrutiny, perusal, study, investigation, probe, analysis; test, trial; check-up; informal once-over.
2 *a check on the abuse of authority:* control, restraint, constraint, curb, limitation.
3 (N. Amer.) *the waitress arrived with the check:* bill, account, invoice, statement; N. Amer. informal tab.
☐ **check in**
report your arrival, book in, register.
☐ **check out**
leave, depart; pay the bill, settle up.
☐ **keep something in check**
curb, restrain, hold back, keep a tight rein on, rein in/back; control, govern, master, suppress, stifle; informal keep a lid on.

check-up noun *you should go to the hospital for a check-up:* examination, inspection, test; check, health check, medical; informal once-over.

cheek noun *that's enough of your cheek!* impudence, impertinence, insolence, cheekiness, presumption, effrontery, gall, disrespect, bad manners, overfamiliarity; informal lip; Brit. informal backchat.
▷ **verb** *he always got away with cheeking his elders:* answer back, talk back to, be cheeky to, be impertinent to.

cheeky adjective *don't be so cheeky:* impudent, impertinent, insolent, forward, pert, disrespectful, impolite, discourteous, rude, bad-mannered; informal lippy; N. Amer. informal sassy.
OPPOSITES: respectful.

cheer verb
1 *MPs rose to cheer the Chancellor:* acclaim, hail, salute, shout for; applaud, clap; informal give someone a big hand.
2 *my arrival seemed to cheer him:* raise someone's spirits, make happier, please, brighten, buoy up, enliven, hearten, gladden, uplift, encourage; comfort, console; informal perk up, buck up.
▷ **noun**
1 *the cheers of the crowd:* hurrah, hurray, whoop, shout; hosanna, alleluia; (**cheers**) applause, ovation, acclaim, acclamation.
2 *it was an attempt to inject a little cheer into this gloomy season:* happiness, joy, cheerfulness, merriment, gaiety, jollity, high spirits, joviality, light-heartedness; hope, optimism; literary joyousness.
☐ **cheer someone on**
the cyclists were cheered on by the crowds: encourage, urge on, spur on, drive on, motivate, inspire, fire up.
☐ **cheer up**
he cheered up at the sight of food: brighten, brighten up, become more cheerful, liven up, rally, revive, bounce back, take heart; informal perk up, buck up.

C

□ **cheer someone up**
I asked her to dinner to try to cheer her up.
See **CHEER** verb sense 2.

cheerful adjective
1 *he arrived looking cheerful:* happy, jolly, in good/high spirits, glad, merry, joyful, light-hearted, full of the joys of spring, buoyant, upbeat, exuberant, ebullient, cock-a-hoop, elated, gleeful, bright, breezy, cheery, jaunty, radiant, smiling, sunny; jovial, genial, good-humoured; carefree, unworried, untroubled, without a care in the world; literary joyous; informal chirpy, bright-eyed and bushy-tailed, full of beans.
2 *a cheerful room:* pleasant, attractive, agreeable, cheering, bright, sunny, welcoming, inviting.
OPPOSITES: sad.

cheerless adjective *the rooms were ill-lit and cheerless:* gloomy, dreary, dull, dismal, bleak, drab, sombre, dark, dim, dingy, funereal; austere, stark, bare, comfortless, unwelcoming, uninviting; miserable, wretched, joyless, depressing, dispiriting.

cheery adjective. See **CHEERFUL** sense 1.

chef-d'œuvre noun *his chef-d'œuvre was his biography of George Washington:* masterpiece, masterwork, finest work, magnum opus, pièce de résistance, tour de force.

chequered adjective
1 *he has had a rather chequered career:* mixed, full of ups and downs, erratic; informal up and down.
2 *a chequered tablecloth:* checked, multicoloured.

cherish verb
1 *he needed a woman he could cherish:* adore, love, dote on, be devoted to, think the world of; care for, look after, protect, keep safe.
2 *I cherish her letters:* treasure, prize, value highly, hold dear.
3 *he had long cherished a secret fantasy about his future:* harbour, entertain, possess, hold, cling to, keep in your mind, nurse, nurture.

cherubic adjective *his round, cherubic face:* angelic, sweet, cute, adorable, appealing, lovable, innocent, seraphic.

chest noun
1 *he had several bullet wounds in his chest:* breast, upper body, torso, trunk.
2 *an oak chest:* box, case, casket, crate, trunk, coffer, strongbox.

WORD LINKS
pectoral, **thoracic** relating to the chest

chew verb *she chewed a mouthful of toast:* masticate, munch, champ, crunch, nibble, gnaw; eat, consume.
□ **chew something over**
Bernie was chewing over the pros and cons: consider, think about/over/through, mull over, ruminate on, meditate on, weigh up, ponder on, deliberate on, reflect on, muse on, dwell on, turn over in your mind; discuss, talk over.

chic adjective *she looked every inch the chic Frenchwoman:* stylish, smart, elegant, sophisticated, dressy; fashionable, high-fashion, in vogue, up to date, up to the minute, contemporary, à la mode.
OPPOSITES: scruffy, unfashionable.

chicanery noun *political chicanery of all sorts goes on behind closed doors:* trickery, deception, deceit, duplicity, dishonesty, deviousness, unscrupulousness, underhandedness, subterfuge, fraud, sharp practice, skulduggery; informal shenanigans; Brit. informal jiggery-pokery.

chide verb *she chided him for not replying to her letters:* scold, chastise, upbraid, berate, reprimand, reprove, rebuke, admonish, take to task; formal castigate; informal tell off; Brit. informal tick off, have a go at.
OPPOSITES: praise.

chief noun
1 *a Highland chief:* leader, chieftain, head, headman, ruler, overlord, master, commander; historical seigneur, liege.
2 *the chief of the central bank:* head, principal, chief executive, president, chairman, chairwoman, governor, director, manager; informal boss.
▷ **adjective**
1 *their chief aim is to eliminate fraud:* main, principal, most important, primary, prime, first, cardinal, central, key, crucial, essential, predominant, pre-eminent, paramount, overriding; informal number-one.
2 *the chief rabbi:* head, leading, principal, premier, highest, foremost, supreme; arch. most.
OPPOSITES: minor, subordinate.

chiefly adverb *he is remembered chiefly for his organ sonatas:* mainly, in the main, primarily, principally, predominantly, mostly, for the most part; usually, generally, on the whole, largely, by and large, as a rule, almost always.

child noun youngster, girl, boy; baby, infant, toddler; schoolboy, schoolgirl, minor, junior; son, daughter; (**children**) offspring, progeny; Scottish & N. English bairn; informal kid, nipper; Brit. informal, humorous sprog.

WORD LINKS
paediatrics the branch of medicine concerned with children

childbirth noun labour, delivery, giving birth; technical parturition.

WORD LINKS
obstetrics the branch of medicine concerned with childbirth

childhood noun youth, early years/life, infancy, babyhood, boyhood, girlhood.
OPPOSITES: adulthood.

childish adjective
1 *childish behaviour:* immature, juvenile, puerile, babyish, infantile; silly, foolish, irresponsible.
2 *a round childish face:* childlike, youthful, young, young-looking, girlish, boyish.
OPPOSITES: mature, adult.

childlike adjective *she spoke with a childlike directness:* innocent, artless, guileless, unworldly, unsophisticated, naive, ingenuous, trusting, unsuspicious; unaffected, without airs, uninhibited, natural, spontaneous.

chill noun
1 *there was a chill in the air:* coldness, chilliness, coolness, iciness, rawness, bitterness, nip.
2 *he caught a chill:* cold, dose of flu.
3 *business leaders fear a long-term chill in relations could hurt commerce:* unfriendliness, lack of warmth/ understanding, chilliness, coldness, coolness.
OPPOSITES: warmth.
▷verb
1 *the dessert is best chilled:* make cold, make colder, cool; refrigerate, ice.
2 *his quiet tone chilled Ruth:* scare, frighten, terrify, alarm, horrify; make someone's blood run cold, chill to the bone/marrow.
OPPOSITES: warm.
▷adjective *a chill wind:* cold, chilly, cool; wintry, frosty, icy, glacial, arctic, raw, bitter, bitterly cold, biting, freezing, frigid; literary gelid.

chilly adjective
1 *the weather had turned chilly | a chilly breeze:* cold, cool, crisp, wintry, frosty, icy, chill, glacial, arctic, raw, bitter, bitterly cold, freezing, frigid; literary gelid; informal nippy; Brit. informal parky.
2 *I woke up feeling chilly:* cold, chilled, shivery.
3 *he got a chilly reception:* unfriendly, unwelcoming, cold, cool, frosty, frigid.
OPPOSITES: warm.

chime verb
1 *the bells began to chime:* ring, peal, toll, sound; clang.
2 *the clock chimed eight o'clock:* strike, sound.
▷noun *the chimes of the bells:* peal, pealing, ringing, carillon, toll, tolling; ding-dong, tintinnabulation.
□ chime in
1 *'Yes, you do that,' Doreen chimed in:* interject, interpose, interrupt, butt in, cut in; informal chip in.
2 *his remarks chimed in with the ideas of Adam Smith:* accord, correspond, be consistent, be compatible, agree, be in

agreement, fit in, be in tune, be consonant; informal square.

chimera noun *the economic sovereignty she claims to defend is a chimera:* illusion, fantasy, delusion, dream.

china noun *a table laid with the best china:* dishes, plates, cups and saucers, crockery, porcelain, tableware.

chink¹ noun *a chink in the curtains:* opening, gap, space, hole, aperture, crack, fissure, crevice, cranny, cleft, split, slit, slot.

chink² verb *the glasses chinked:* jingle, jangle, clink, tinkle.

chip noun
1 *wood chips:* fragment, sliver, splinter, shaving, paring, flake.
2 *a chip in the glass:* nick, crack, scratch; flaw, fault.
3 *fish and chips:* fries, potato chips; Brit. French fried potatoes; N. Amer. French fries.
4 *gambling chips:* counter, token.
▷verb
1 *the teacup was chipped:* nick, crack, scratch; damage.
2 *the plaster had chipped:* break off, break, crack, crumble.
□ chip in
1 (informal) *'He's right,' Gloria chipped in:* interrupt, interject, interpose, cut in, chime in, butt in.
2 *parents and staff chipped in to raise the cash | we all chipped in about £20:* contribute, make a contribution/donation, club together; pay; informal fork out, shell out, cough up; Brit. informal stump up.

chirp verb *a canary chirped from a cage on the veranda:* tweet, twitter, chirrup, cheep, peep, chitter, chirr; sing, warble, trill.

chirpy adjective (informal) *he was in a chirpy mood.* See CHEERFUL sense 1.

chivalrous adjective
1 *his chivalrous treatment of women:* gallant, gentlemanly, honourable, respectful, considerate, thoughtful; courteous, polite, gracious, well mannered, mannerly.
2 (historical) *chivalrous pursuits:* knightly, noble, chivalric; brave, courageous, bold, valiant, valorous, heroic, daring, intrepid.
OPPOSITES: rude, cowardly.

chivalry noun
1 *acts of chivalry:* gallantry, gentlemanliness; courtesy, courteousness, politeness, graciousness, good manners.
2 (historical) *tales of chivalry and knightly deeds:* knight errantry, courtliness; bravery, courage, boldness, valour, heroism, daring.

chivvy verb *if you are owed money by people following the event, keep chivvying them to ensure they pay up:* badger, nag, harass, pester, keep on at, go on at; informal hassle.

C

choice noun

1 *their choice of candidate | freedom of choice:* selection, election, choosing, nomination; decision, say, vote.
2 *you have no other choice:* option, alternative, possible course of action.
3 *an extensive choice of wines:* range, variety, selection, assortment.

▷ **adjective**

1 *choice plums:* superior, first-class, first-rate, prime, premier, grade A, best, finest, excellent, select, quality, high-quality, top, top-quality, high-grade, prize, fine, special; hand-picked, carefully chosen; informal tip-top, top-notch.
2 *a few choice words:* rude, abusive, insulting, offensive.

choir noun singers, chorus, choristers, choral group.

> WORD LINKS
> **choral** relating to a choir

choke verb

1 *he started to choke:* gag, retch, cough, fight for breath.
2 *thick dust choked her:* suffocate, asphyxiate, smother, stifle.
3 *she had been choked to death:* strangle, throttle; asphyxiate, suffocate.
4 *the guttering was choked with leaves:* clog, clog up, bung up, stop up, block, obstruct, plug.

□ **choke something back**
she choked back her anger: suppress, hold back, fight back, bite back, swallow, check, restrain, control, repress, smother, stifle.

choose verb

1 *we chose a quiet country hotel:* select, pick, pick out, opt for, plump for, settle on, decide on, fix on; appoint, name, nominate, vote for.
2 *I'll stay as long as I choose:* wish, want, desire, feel/be inclined, please, like, see fit.

choosy adjective (informal) *she's become very choosy about the food she'll eat:* fussy, finicky, fastidious, over-particular, difficult/hard to please, exacting, demanding; informal picky; Brit. informal pernickety.

chop verb

1 *chop the potatoes into pieces:* cut up, cut into pieces, chop up, cube, dice.
2 *Jack was chopping wood outside the cabin:* chop up, cut up, cut into pieces, hew, split.
3 *four fingers were chopped off:* sever, cut off, hack off, slice off, lop off, saw off, shear off.
4 *they chopped down large areas of rainforest:* cut down, fell, hack down.

choppy adjective *the sea was very choppy:* rough, turbulent, heavy, heaving, stormy, tempestuous, squally.
OPPOSITES: calm.

chore noun *daily household chores like shopping and cleaning:* task, job, duty, errand; work, domestic work.

chortle verb *pleased with his joke, Robert chortled and slapped his thigh:* chuckle, laugh, giggle, titter, snigger.

chorus noun

1 *they all sang the chorus:* refrain.
2 *the chorus sang powerfully:* choir, ensemble, choral group, choristers, singers.

□ **in chorus**
in unison, together, simultaneously, as one; in concert, in harmony.

christen verb

1 *she was christened Sara:* baptize, name, give the name of, call.
2 *a group who were christened 'The Magic Circle':* call, name, dub, style, term, designate, label, nickname; formal denominate.

chronic adjective

1 *a chronic illness:* persistent, long-standing, long-term; incurable.
2 *chronic economic problems:* constant, continuing, ceaseless, unabating, unending, persistent, long-lasting; severe, serious, acute, grave, dire.
3 *a chronic liar:* inveterate, hardened, dyed-in-the-wool, incorrigible; compulsive; informal pathological.
4 (Brit. informal) *the film was chronic.* See **ABYSMAL**.
OPPOSITES: acute, temporary.

chronicle noun *a chronicle of the region's past:* record, written account, history, annals, archives; log, diary, journal.

▷ **verb** *his work chronicles the birth of modern India:* record, put on record, write down, set down, document, register, report; tell.

chronicler noun annalist, historian, archivist, diarist, recorder, reporter.

chronological adjective *the entries are in chronological order:* sequential, consecutive, in sequence, in order of time.

chubby adjective *a chubby five-year-old boy with a cheeky grin:* plump, tubby, fat, rotund, chunky, well covered; informal roly-poly, pudgy; Brit. informal podgy.
OPPOSITES: skinny.

chuck verb (informal)

1 *he chucked the letter on to the table:* throw, toss, fling, hurl, pitch, cast, lob; informal sling; Brit. informal bung.
2 *she kept the personal bits and pieces and chucked the rest:* throw away/out, discard, dispose of, get rid of, dump, scrap, jettison; informal ditch, junk, bin.
3 *I've chucked my job:* give up, leave, resign from; informal quit, pack in; Brit. informal jack in.
4 *Mary chucked him for another guy:* leave, throw over, break off with; jilt; Brit. finish with; informal dump; Brit. informal give someone the push.

chuckle verb *Adam chuckled to himself as he drove away:* chortle, laugh, giggle, titter; snicker, snigger.

chunk noun *huge chunks of masonry littered the street | cut the meat into chunks:* lump, hunk, block, slab, square, brick, cube, bar, wedge; informal wodge.

chunky adjective
1 *a chunky young man:* stocky, sturdy, thickset, heavily built, well built, burly, bulky, brawny, solid, heavy.
2 *a chunky sweater:* thick, bulky, heavy-knit.
OPPOSITES: slight, light.

church noun
1 *a village church:* place of worship, house of God; cathedral, minster, abbey, chapel, basilica.
2 *the Methodist Church:* denomination, creed, faith.

> WORD LINKS
> **ecclesiastical** relating to the Christian church or its clergy

churlish adjective *it seems churlish to complain:* rude, ungracious, ill-mannered, ill-bred, discourteous, impolite; inconsiderate, uncharitable; informal ignorant.
OPPOSITES: polite.

churn verb
1 *propellers churned up the water:* stir, agitate, disturb.
2 *the sea churned:* heave, boil, toss.
□ **churn something out**
the smaller studios churned out dozens of low-budget films: produce, make, turn out; informal crank out.

chute noun
1 *a refuse chute:* channel, slide, shaft, funnel, conduit.
2 *water chutes:* slide, flume.

cinch noun (informal) *installing the program is a cinch:* easy task, child's play; informal doddle, piece of cake, breeze, pushover; Brit. informal doss.
OPPOSITES: challenge.

cinders plural noun ashes, ash, embers.

cipher noun
1 *Polish mathematicians managed to crack the cipher:* code, cryptogram.
2 *he has become a cipher:* nobody, nonentity, unimportant person.

circa preposition *a survey by questionnaire of circa 100 companies:* approximately, about, around, in the region of, roughly.

circle noun
1 *a circle of gold stars:* ring, band, hoop, circlet; halo, disc.
2 *her circle of friends:* group, set, company, coterie, clique; band; informal gang, crowd, bunch, crew.

3 *I'm afraid I don't move in such illustrious circles:* sphere, world, milieu; society.
▷ verb
1 *seagulls circled above:* wheel, move round, revolve, rotate, whirl, spiral.
2 *satellites circling the earth:* orbit, revolve round; go round, travel round, circumnavigate.
3 *the abbey was circled by a huge wall:* surround, encircle, ring, enclose.

circuit noun
1 *a few circuits of the playing field:* lap, turn, round, circle.
2 (Brit.) *a racing circuit:* track, racetrack, running track, course.

circuitous adjective *we took a rather circuitous route:* roundabout, indirect, winding, meandering, serpentine; tortuous.
OPPOSITES: direct.

circular adjective *a circular window:* round, disc-shaped, ring-shaped; technical annular.
▷ noun *we sent a circular out to all members:* leaflet, pamphlet, flyer; letter, notice.

circulate verb
1 *the news was widely circulated:* spread about/around, communicate, disseminate, make known, make public, broadcast, publicize, advertise; distribute, give out, pass around.
2 *fresh air circulates freely:* flow, course, move round.
3 *they circulated among their guests:* socialize, mingle.

circumference noun *the circumference of the pit:* perimeter, border, boundary; edge, rim, verge, margin.

circumscribe verb *the power of the organization has until recently been severely circumscribed:* restrict, limit, keep within bounds, curb, confine, restrain; regulate, control.

circumspect adjective *she would have to be very circumspect in her dealings with Catherine:* cautious, wary, careful, chary, guarded, on your guard; informal cagey, playing your cards close to your chest.
OPPOSITES: unguarded.

circumstances plural noun
1 *the political and economic circumstances seemed favourable:* situation, conditions, state of affairs, position; factors, context, background, environment, events, incidents, occurrences.
2 *Jane explained the circumstances to him:* the facts, the details, the particulars, how things stand, the lie of the land; Brit. the state of play; informal the score.

circumvent verb *it was always possible to circumvent the regulations:* avoid, get round/past, evade, bypass, sidestep, dodge; informal duck.

C

C

cistern noun tank, reservoir, container.

citadel noun fortress, fort, stronghold, fortification, castle.

citation noun
1 *a citation from an eighteenth-century text:* quotation, quote, extract, excerpt, passage, line; reference, allusion.
2 *a citation for gallantry:* commendation, honourable mention.

cite verb
1 *cite the passage in full:* quote, reproduce.
2 *he cited the case of Leigh v. Gladstone:* refer to, mention, adduce, instance, name.
3 *he has been cited for bravery many times:* commend, pay tribute to, praise.

citizen noun
1 *a British citizen:* subject, national, passport holder.
2 *the citizens of Edinburgh:* inhabitant, resident, native, townsman, townswoman; old use burgher.

city noun town, municipality, metropolis; conurbation, urban area, metropolitan area; Scottish burgh.

WORD LINKS
urban, **civic**, **metropolitan** relating to cities and towns

civic adjective *civic buildings:* municipal, city, town, urban, metropolitan; public, civil, community.

civil adjective
1 *a civil marriage:* secular, non-religious.
2 *civil aviation:* non-military, civilian.
3 *a civil war:* internal, domestic, interior, national.
4 *he behaved in a civil manner:* polite, courteous, well mannered, well bred, gentlemanly, chivalrous, gallant, ladylike, mannerly; cordial, genial, pleasant, affable, civilized.
OPPOSITES: religious, military, international, rude.

civilian noun *the slaughter of unarmed civilians:* non-military person, non-combatant, ordinary/private citizen.

civility noun
1 *he treated me with civility:* courtesy, courteousness, politeness, good manners, graciousness, consideration, respect, politesse; formal comity.
2 *she didn't waste time on civilities:* polite remark, politeness, courtesy; formality.
OPPOSITES: rudeness.

civilization noun
1 *a higher stage of civilization:* human development, human achievement, advancement, progress, enlightenment, culture, refinement, sophistication.
2 *ancient civilizations:* culture, society, nation, people.

civilize verb *he built roads and attempted to civilize the people:* enlighten, edify, improve, educate, instruct, refine, cultivate, socialize, humanize.

civilized adjective *such an affront to civilized behaviour will no longer be tolerated:* polite, courteous, well mannered, civil, gentlemanly, ladylike, mannerly; cultured, cultivated, refined, sophisticated; enlightened, educated, advanced, developed.
OPPOSITES: rude, uncivilized.

civil servant noun public servant, government official; bureaucrat, mandarin, official, administrator, functionary.

clad adjective *they were clad in T-shirts and shorts:* dressed, clothed, garbed, rigged out, costumed; wearing, sporting; formal attired.

claim verb
1 *Davies claimed that she was lying:* assert, declare, maintain, state, hold, insist, protest, affirm, avow; argue, contend, allege, profess.
2 *no one claimed the items:* lay claim to, assert ownership of.
3 *you can claim compensation:* request, ask for, apply for; demand.
4 *the fire claimed four lives:* take, cause the loss of.
▷ noun
1 *his appeal is based on his claim that he was tricked into carrying the drugs through customs:* assertion, declaration, insistence, avowal, protestation; contention, allegation.
2 *a claim for damages:* request, application; demand, petition.
3 *we have first claim on their assets:* entitlement to, title to, right to.

claimant noun applicant, candidate; Law petitioner, plaintiff, litigant, appellant.

clairvoyance noun second sight, psychic powers, ESP, extrasensory perception, sixth sense; telepathy.

clairvoyant noun psychic, fortune-teller; medium, spiritualist; telepathist, mind-reader.
▷ adjective *he didn't tell me about it and I'm not clairvoyant:* psychic, having second sight, having a sixth sense; telepathic.

clamber verb *I clambered out of the trench:* scramble, climb, scrabble, claw your way.

clammy adjective
1 *his skin felt clammy:* moist, damp, sweaty, sticky; slimy, slippery.
2 *the clammy atmosphere of the cave:* damp, dank, wet; humid, close, muggy, heavy.
OPPOSITES: dry.

clamorous adjective *a jostling, clamorous mob | the clamorous radical wing of the party:* noisy, loud, vocal, vociferous,

raucous, rowdy; importunate, demanding, insistent, vehement.
OPPOSITES: quiet.

clamour noun

1 *her voice rose above the clamour:* din, racket, rumpus, loud noise, uproar, tumult, shouting, yelling, screaming, roaring; commotion, brouhaha, hue and cry, hubbub; Brit. row; Brit. informal hullabaloo.
2 *there is growing clamour from environmental lobby groups to ban the use of these crops:* demands, calls; protests, complaints, outcry.

▷**verb**
1 *the surging crowds clamoured for attention:* yell, shout loudly, bay, scream, roar.
2 *scientists are clamouring for a ban:* demand, call, press, push, lobby.

clamp noun

1 *a clamp was holding the wood:* brace, vice, press.
2 *clamps had been fitted to the car:* immobilizer, wheel clamp.

▷**verb**
1 *the sander is clamped on to the workbench:* fasten, secure, fix, attach; screw, bolt.
2 *a pipe was clamped between his teeth:* clench, grip, hold, press, clasp.
3 *his car was clamped:* immobilize, wheel-clamp.

□ **clamp down on**
a new initiative to clamp down on software piracy: suppress, prevent, stop, put a stop/end to, stamp out, limit, restrict, control, keep in check; informal crack down on.

clampdown noun (informal) *there's to be a clampdown on tax avoidance schemes:* suppression, prevention; crackdown, restriction, curb, check.

clan noun

1 *the Macleod clan:* family, house, dynasty, tribe.
2 *New York's clan of art collectors:* group, set, circle, clique, coterie; informal gang, crowd, bunch.

clandestine adjective *soon they were involved in a passionate affair, carried on in clandestine meetings and whispered telephone calls:* secret, covert, furtive, surreptitious, stealthy, cloak-and-dagger, hole-and-corner, closet, backstairs; informal hush-hush.

clang noun *the clang of the church bells:* reverberation, ringing, ring, ding-dong, peal, chime, toll.
▷**verb** *the huge bells clanged:* reverberate, resound, ring, peal, chime, toll.

clank noun *the clank of rusty chains:* jangling, clanging, rattling, clinking, jingling; clang, jangle, rattle, clangour, clink, jingle.

▷**verb** *I could hear the chain clanking:* jangle, rattle, clink, clang, jingle.

clannish adjective *he was regarded as an outsider in the clannish community:* cliquey, cliquish, insular, exclusive; unfriendly, unwelcoming.

clap verb

1 *the audience clapped enthusiastically:* applaud, clap your hands, give someone a round of applause, put your hands together; informal give someone a big hand; N. Amer. informal give it up.
2 *he clapped Owen on the back:* slap, strike, hit, smack, thump; pat.

▷**noun**
1 *everybody gave him a clap:* round of applause; informal hand.
2 *a clap on the shoulder:* slap, smack, thump; pat.
3 *a clap of thunder:* crack, crash, bang, boom; thunderclap.

clarify verb *their report clarified the situation:* make clear, shed/throw light on, elucidate, illuminate; explain, define, spell out, clear up.
OPPOSITES: confuse.

clarity noun

1 *the clarity of his account:* lucidity, clearness, coherence.
2 *the clarity of the image:* sharpness, clearness, crispness, definition.
3 *the crystal clarity of the water:* limpidity, clearness, transparency, translucency.
OPPOSITES: vagueness, opacity.

clash noun

1 *there were violent clashes between protesters and police:* confrontation, skirmish, fight, battle, engagement, encounter, conflict.
2 *the minister is preparing for a head-on clash with his opposite number tomorrow:* argument, altercation, confrontation, shouting match; contretemps, quarrel, disagreement, dispute; informal run-in; Brit. informal slanging match.
3 *a clash of tweeds and a striped shirt:* mismatch, discordance, discord, lack of harmony.
4 *the clash of dates is unfortunate:* coincidence, concurrence; conflict.
5 *the clash of cymbals:* striking, bang, clang, crash.

▷**verb**
1 *in a number of cities, demonstrators clashed with security forces:* fight, skirmish, come to blows, come into conflict; do battle.
2 *the prime minister clashed with union leaders:* disagree, wrangle, dispute, cross swords, lock horns, be at loggerheads.
3 *her red coat clashed with her hair:* be incompatible, not match, not go, be discordant.
4 *the dates clash:* conflict, coincide.
5 *she clashed the cymbals together:* bang, strike, clang, crash.

clasp verb

1 *Ruth clasped his hand:* grasp, grip, clutch, hold tightly; take hold of, seize, grab.
2 *he clasped her in his arms:* embrace, hug, enfold, fold, envelop; hold, squeeze.

▷ **noun**

1 *a gold clasp:* fastener, fastening, catch, clip, pin; buckle, hasp.
2 *his tight clasp:* embrace, hug, cuddle; grip, grasp.

class noun

1 *it has good accommodation for a hotel of this class:* category, grade, rating, classification, group, grouping.
2 *a new class of heart drug:* kind, sort, type, variety, genre, brand, breed, species.
3 *the middle class:* social division, social stratum, level, echelon, group, grouping; social status, social position.
4 *there are 30 pupils in the class:* form, study group, set, stream.
5 *a maths class:* lesson, period; seminar, tutorial, workshop.
6 *she's got class—she looks like a princess:* style, stylishness, elegance, chic, sophistication; taste, refinement.

▷ **verb** *the 12-seater is classed as a commercial vehicle:* classify, categorize, group, grade; bracket, designate, label, pigeonhole.

classic adjective

1 *the classic work on the subject:* definitive, authoritative; outstanding, best, finest, excellent, superior, masterly, first-rate, first-class.
2 *a classic example of Norman design:* typical, archetypal, quintessential, vintage; model, representative, perfect, prime, textbook.
3 *a classic style which never dates:* simple, elegant, understated; traditional, timeless, ageless.

▷ **noun** *a classic of the genre:* definitive example, model, epitome, paradigm, exemplar; great work, masterpiece.

classical adjective

1 *classical mythology:* ancient Greek, Hellenic, Attic; Latin, ancient Roman.
2 *classical music:* traditional; serious, highbrow.
3 *a classical style:* simple, pure, restrained, plain, austere; well proportioned, harmonious, balanced, symmetrical, elegant.
OPPOSITES: modern.

classification noun

1 *the classification of disease according to symptoms:* categorization, categorizing, classifying, grouping, grading, ranking, organization, sorting, codification, systematization.
2 *a series of new classifications:* category, class, group, grouping, grade, grading, ranking, bracket.

classify verb *the subjects were classified into three groups:* categorize, class, group,

grade, rank, order, organize, sort, codify, bracket, systematize; catalogue, list, file, index.

classy adjective (informal) *a classy hotel:* stylish, high-class, superior, exclusive, chic, elegant, smart, sophisticated; Brit. upmarket; informal posh, ritzy, swanky; Brit. informal swish.

clatter verb *the cups clattered on the tray:* rattle, clank, clink.

clause noun *a new clause had been added to the treaty:* section, paragraph, article, subsection; stipulation, condition, proviso, rider.

claw noun

1 *a bird's claw:* talon.
2 *a crab's claw:* pincer.

▷ **verb** *her fingers clawed his shoulders:* scratch, lacerate, tear, rip, scrape, graze, dig into.

clean adjective

1 *a clean shirt:* washed, laundered, scrubbed; spotless, immaculate, pristine.
2 *keep the wound clean:* disinfected, sterile, sterilized, decontaminated, hygienic.
3 *a clean sheet of paper:* blank, empty, clear, plain; unused, new, pristine, fresh, unmarked.
4 *the clean air of the mountains:* pure, clear, fresh; unpolluted, uncontaminated, untainted.
5 *a clean life:* virtuous, good, upright, upstanding; honourable, respectable, decent, righteous, moral, exemplary, blameless; innocent, pure, chaste.
6 *a good clean fight:* fair, honest, sporting, sportsmanlike, honourable, according to the rules.
7 *he is making a clean break with the past:* complete, thorough, total, absolute, conclusive, decisive, final, irrevocable.
8 *the clean lines of a good design:* simple, elegant, graceful, streamlined, smooth.
OPPOSITES: dirty, polluted.

▷ **verb** *I've cleaned the floor:* wash, cleanse, wipe, sponge, scrub, mop, rinse, scour, swab, hose down, sluice down, disinfect; launder.

cleanse verb

1 *the wound was cleansed:* clean, wash, bathe, rinse, disinfect.
2 *a plan to cleanse the environment of traces of lead:* rid, clear, free, purify, purge.
3 *only God can cleanse us from sin:* purify, absolve, free; deliver.

clear adjective

1 *clear instructions are essential:* understandable, comprehensible, intelligible, plain, uncomplicated, explicit, lucid, coherent, simple, straightforward, unambiguous, clear-cut, crystal clear; formal perspicuous.
2 *a clear case of harassment | it was clear*

that he was not telling the truth: obvious, plain, evident, definite, unmistakable, manifest, indisputable, patent, incontrovertible, irrefutable, beyond doubt, beyond question; palpable, visible, discernible, conspicuous, overt, blatant, glaring; as plain as a pikestaff, as plain as day; informal as plain as the nose on your face.
3 *the water was cold and clear:* transparent, limpid, translucent, crystal clear; unclouded; literary pellucid, crystalline.
4 *the sun was radiant in the clear blue sky:* bright, cloudless, without a cloud in the sky.
5 *the road was clear | I had a clear view in both directions:* unobstructed, unblocked, passable, open; unrestricted, unhindered.
6 *the algae were clear of toxins:* free, devoid, without, unaffected by; rid, relieved.
7 *her conscience was clear:* untroubled, undisturbed, free of guilt; peaceful, at peace, tranquil, serene, calm.
8 *you must give two clear days' notice:* whole, full, entire, complete.
OPPOSITES: vague, opaque, cloudy.

▷ **adverb**
1 *stand clear of the doors:* away from, at a safe distance from.
2 *Tommy's voice came loud and clear:* distinctly, clearly, as clear as a bell, plainly, audibly.

▷ **verb**
1 *the sky cleared briefly:* brighten, brighten up, lighten, clear up, become bright/brighter/, become sunny.
2 *the mist had cleared | the fever clears in two to four weeks:* disappear, go away, fade away, lift; peter out, decrease, lessen, diminish, wear off.
3 *Karen cleared away the dirty plates:* remove, take away, carry away, tidy away/up.
4 *staff were instructed to clear the building:* evacuate, empty; leave.
5 *I'm gradually clearing my debts:* pay off, pay, repay, settle, discharge.
6 *he was cleared by an appeal court:* acquit, declare innocent, find not guilty; absolve, exonerate.
7 *I was cleared to work on the atomic project:* authorize, give permission, permit, allow, pass, license, sanction; informal OK.
8 *I cleared the bar at my first attempt:* go over, pass over, sail over; jump over, vault over, leap over, hurdle.
▢ **clear something out**
1 *we cleared out the attic:* empty, empty out; tidy, tidy up, clear up.
2 *clear out the rubbish:* get rid of, throw out/away, discard, dispose of, scrap, jettison; informal chuck out/away, bin.
▢ **clear something up**
1 *I need to clear up the garden:* tidy, tidy up, put in order, straighten up, clean up, spruce up.
2 *we've cleared up the problem:* resolve,

straighten out; get to the bottom of, explain, solve; informal crack, figure out, suss out.

clearance noun
1 *slum clearance accelerated during the 1960s:* removal, clearing, demolition.
2 *you must have Home Office clearance:* authorization, permission, consent, approval, sanction, licence, dispensation, assent, agreement, endorsement; informal the OK.
3 *always give cyclists plenty of clearance:* space, room, margin, leeway.

clear-cut adjective *we now had a clear-cut objective:* definite, distinct, clear, well defined, precise, specific, explicit, unambiguous, unequivocal, black and white, cut and dried.
OPPOSITES: vague.

clearing noun *a small clearing in the forest:* glade, space, gap, opening; literary dell.

clearly adverb
1 *her ability to write clearly:* intelligibly, plainly, distinctly, comprehensibly, with clarity; legibly, audibly.
2 *clearly, substantial changes are needed:* obviously, evidently, patently, unquestionably, undoubtedly, without doubt, indubitably, plainly, undeniably, incontrovertibly, irrefutably, doubtless, needless to say.

cleft noun
1 *a deep cleft in the rocks:* split, slit, crack, fissure, crevice, rift, break, fracture, breach.
2 *the cleft in his chin:* dimple.
▷ **adjective** *a cleft tail:* split, divided; cloven.

clemency noun *they appealed for clemency:* mercy, mercifulness, leniency; compassion, humanity, pity, sympathy.
OPPOSITES: ruthlessness.

clench verb
1 *he clenched his hands into fists:* squeeze together, clamp together, close/shut tightly.
2 *he clenched the back of the chair:* grip, grasp, grab, clutch, clasp, hold tightly, seize, press, squeeze.

clergy noun clergymen, clergywomen, churchmen, churchwomen, clerics, priests, ecclesiastics, men/women of God; ministry, priesthood, holy orders, the church, the cloth.
OPPOSITES: laity.

clergyman, clergywoman noun priest, churchman, churchwoman, man/woman of the cloth, man/woman of God; cleric, minister, preacher, chaplain, father, ecclesiastic, bishop, pastor, vicar, rector, parson, curate, deacon, deaconess; informal reverend, padre.

clerical adjective
1 *clerical jobs:* office, desk, back-room;

administrative, secretarial; white-collar.
2 *he was still in his clerical clothes:*
ecclesiastical, church, priestly.
OPPOSITES: secular.

clerk noun office worker, clerical worker,
administrator; bookkeeper; cashier, teller;
informal pen-pusher.

clever adjective
1 *a clever young woman:* intelligent,
bright, astute, quick-witted, shrewd,
canny; talented, gifted, brilliant, capable,
able, competent, apt; educated, learned,
knowledgeable, wise; informal brainy, smart,
savvy.
2 *a clever scheme:* ingenious, inspired;
cunning, crafty, artful, slick; neat.
3 *she was clever with her hands:* skilful,
dexterous, adroit, adept, deft, nimble,
handy; skilled, talented.
4 *a clever remark:* witty, amusing, droll,
humorous, funny.
OPPOSITES: stupid.

cliché noun *it's a cliché that a trouble
shared is a trouble halved:* platitude,
hackneyed phrase, commonplace, truism,
stock phrase, trite phrase, banality; informal
old chestnut.

click verb
1 *cameras started clicking:* clack, snap.
2 (informal) *at first I was confused then
suddenly it clicked:* become clear, fall
into place, make sense, sink in, dawn on
someone, register with someone.
3 (informal) *we just clicked:* take to each
other, get along, be compatible, be like-
minded, feel a rapport, see eye to eye;
informal hit it off, get on like a house on fire,
be on the same wavelength.

client noun customer, buyer, purchaser,
shopper, consumer, user; patient; patron,
regular; Brit. informal punter; (**clients**)
clientele, patronage, public, market.

cliff noun precipice, rock face, crag, bluff,
ridge, escarpment, scarp, overhang.

climactic adjective *the movie's climactic
scene:* final, concluding, closing, ultimate;
exciting, thrilling, gripping, riveting,
dramatic, hair-raising; crucial, decisive,
critical.

> USAGE
>
> Do not confuse **climactic** with **climatic**
> which means 'relating to climate' (*climatic and
> environmental change affects us all*).

climate noun
1 *a mild climate:* weather conditions,
weather; atmospheric conditions.
2 *they come from colder climates:* region,
area, zone, country, place.
3 *the current political climate:*
atmosphere, mood, feeling, spirit, tenor;
tendency, ethos, attitude; environment,
milieu.

climax noun *the climax of his career:* peak,
pinnacle, height, high(est) point, top;
acme, zenith; culmination, crowning point,
crown; highlight, high spot, high water
mark.
OPPOSITES: nadir.
> **verb** *the event will climax with a gala
concert:* culminate, peak, reach a pinnacle,
come to a crescendo, come to a head.

climb verb
1 *we climbed the hill:* ascend, mount, scale,
scramble up, clamber up, shin up; go up,
walk up; conquer, gain.
2 *the plane climbed to 6,000 feet:* rise,
ascend, go up, gain altitude.
3 *the road climbs steeply:* slope upwards,
rise, go uphill, incline upwards.
4 *the shares climbed to 550 pence:* increase,
rise, go up; shoot up, soar, rocket.
5 *he climbed through the ranks:* advance,
rise, move up, progress, work your way.
6 *he climbed out of his car:* clamber,
scramble; step.
OPPOSITES: descend, drop, fall.
> **noun** *a steep climb:* ascent.
OPPOSITES: descent.
□ **climb down**
*the council was forced to climb down over
the planned rent increase:* back down,
admit defeat, surrender, capitulate,
yield, give in, give way, submit; retreat,
backtrack; do a U-turn; Brit. do an about-
turn.

clinch verb
1 *he clinched the deal:* secure, settle,
conclude, close, pull off, bring off,
complete, confirm, seal, finalize; informal
sew up, wrap up.
2 *these findings clinched the matter:* settle,
decide, determine; resolve.
3 *they clinched the title with a memorable
5–0 win:* win, secure; be victorious, come
first, triumph, prevail.
OPPOSITES: lose.
> **noun** *a passionate clinch:* embrace, hug,
cuddle, squeeze, hold, clasp.

cling verb *rice grains tend to cling together:*
stick, adhere, hold, cohere, bond, bind.
□ **cling (on) to**
1 *she clung to him:* hold on, clutch, grip,
grasp, clasp, attach yourself to, hang on;
embrace, hug.
2 *they clung on to their beliefs:* adhere
to, hold to, stick to, stand by, abide by,
cherish, remain true to, have faith in.

clinic noun medical centre, health centre,
surgery.

clinical adjective
1 *he seemed so clinical:* detached,
impersonal, dispassionate, objective,
unemotional, uninvolved, distant,
remote, aloof, removed; cold, indifferent,
unsympathetic, unfeeling.
2 *the room was clinical:* plain, simple,
unadorned, unembellished, stark, austere,

C

spartan, bleak, bare; clean; functional, basic, institutional, impersonal, characterless.
OPPOSITES: emotional, luxurious.

clip¹ noun *he undid the clip on his case:* fastener, clasp, hasp, catch, hook, lock, buckle.
▷ **verb** *she clipped the pages together:* fasten, attach, fix, join; pin, staple.

clip² verb
1 *I clipped the hedge:* trim, prune, cut, snip, crop, shear, pare; lop; neaten, shape.
2 *clip the coupon below:* remove, cut out, snip out, tear out, detach.
3 *his shot clipped the post:* hit, strike, touch, graze, glance off, run into.
▷ **noun** *a film clip:* extract, excerpt, snippet, cutting, fragment; trailer.

clipping noun *friends are sending us newspaper clippings from the British press:* cutting, snippet, extract, excerpt.

clique noun *his flat became a haven for a clique of young men of similar tastes:* coterie, set, circle, ring, in-crowd, group; informal gang.

cloak noun
1 *a woollen cloak:* cape, mantle, shawl, wrap; poncho.
2 *a cloak of secrecy:* cover, veil, screen, mask, shield.
▷ **verb** *a peak cloaked in mist:* conceal, hide, cover, veil, shroud, mask, obscure, cloud; envelop, swathe, surround.

clod noun *clods of earth:* lump, clump, chunk, hunk.

clog verb *the gutters were clogged up with leaves:* block, obstruct, choke, bung up, plug, stop up, fill up; congest, jam.

cloistered adjective *his cloistered life was devoted to writing:* secluded, sequestered, sheltered, protected, insulated; shut off, isolated, confined; solitary, monastic, reclusive.

close¹ adjective
1 *the town is close to Leeds:* near, adjacent; in the vicinity of, in the neighbourhood of, within reach of, not far from; neighbouring, adjoining, abutting, alongside, a stone's throw away; nearby, at hand, at close quarters; informal within spitting distance.
2 *the planes were flying in close formation:* dense, compact, tight, close-packed.
3 *I was close to tears:* near, on the verge of, on the brink of, on the point of.
4 *the race will be a close contest:* evenly matched, even, neck and neck.
5 *they became close friends:* intimate, dear, bosom; inseparable, devoted, faithful; special, good.
6 *there is a close resemblance between them:* strong, marked, distinct, pronounced.
7 *their work deserves close examination:* careful, detailed, thorough, minute, searching, painstaking, meticulous, rigorous, scrupulous.
8 *the weather was uncomfortably close:* humid, muggy, stuffy, airless, heavy, sticky, sultry, oppressive, stifling.
OPPOSITES: far, distant.

close² verb
1 *she closed the door:* shut, pull to, push to, slam; fasten, secure, lock.
2 *close the hole with a plug of cotton wool:* block up, stop up, plug, seal, cork, stopper; bung up, clog, clog up, choke, obstruct.
3 *we have failed to close the gap between the richest and poorest in society:* narrow, reduce, shrink, lessen, make smaller, diminish.
4 *the factory closed with the loss of 150 jobs:* shut down, close down, cease production, cease trading, be wound up, go out of business, go bankrupt, go into receivership, go into liquidation; informal fold, go to the wall, go bust.
5 *the members were thanked for attending and the meeting was closed:* end, conclude, finish, terminate, wind up.
6 *he expects to close the deal by the end of the month:* clinch, settle, secure, seal, confirm; complete, conclude, fix, agree, finalize; informal wrap up.
7 *the enemy were closing fast:* catch up, creep up, near, approach, gain on someone.
OPPOSITES: open, begin.
▷ **noun** *the close of the talks:* end, finish, conclusion, termination, cessation, completion, resolution; climax, denouement.
OPPOSITES: beginning.
□ **close down**. See CLOSE² verb sense 4.

closeness noun *the cuisine of Malta is influenced by the island's physical closeness to Italy:* proximity, propinquity, nearness.

closet noun *a clothes closet:* cupboard, wardrobe, cabinet, locker.
▷ **adjective** *a closet socialist:* secret, covert, private.
▷ **verb** *David was closeted in his den:* shut away, sequester, seclude, cloister, confine, isolate.

closure noun *the closure of rural schools:* closing down, shutting down, winding up.

clot noun
1 *a blood clot:* lump, mass; thrombosis, embolus.
2 (Brit. informal) *watch where you're going, you clot!* See FOOL noun sense 1.
▷ **verb** *the blood is likely to clot:* coagulate, congeal, thicken, curdle, set, solidify.

cloth noun *a piece of woollen cloth:* fabric, material; textiles.

clothe verb *she was clothed in a long white gown:* dress, robe, garb, array, costume, swathe, deck out, turn out, fit out, rig out; formal attire; informal get up.

clothes plural noun clothing, garments, garb, dress, wear, costume; formal attire; informal gear, togs, get-up; Brit. informal clobber.

> WORD LINKS
> **sartorial** relating to clothes

cloud noun *a cloud of exhaust smoke:* mass, billow, haze; pall, mantle, blanket.
▷ **verb**
1 *the sky clouded:* become overcast, cloud over, become cloudy, blacken, darken, lour.
2 *the sand was churned up, clouding the water:* make cloudy, make murky, dirty, darken, blacken.
3 *anger clouded my judgement:* confuse, muddle, obscure, fog.

cloudy adjective
1 *a cloudy sky:* overcast, clouded; leaden, dark, grey, black, murky; sombre, heavy, gloomy; sunless, starless, hazy, misty, foggy.
2 *the pond water is rather cloudy:* murky, muddy, milky, dirty, opaque, turbid.
3 *his eyes grew cloudy:* tearful, teary, weepy, lachrymose; moist, watery; misty, blurred.
OPPOSITES: clear.

cloven adjective *cloven hooves:* split, divided, cleft.

clown noun *Matt was the class clown:* joker, comedian, comic, wag, wit, prankster, jester; buffoon
▷ **verb** *he's always clowning around:* fool about/around, play the fool, play about; informal mess about/around, horse about/around; Brit. informal muck about/around.

cloy verb *the first sip gives a malty taste that never cloys:* pall, become sickening, become nauseating, become unpleasant.

cloying adjective *a romantic, rather cloying story:* sickly, syrupy, saccharine; sickening, nauseating; mawkish, sentimental; Brit. twee; informal schmaltzy.

club[1] noun
1 *a canoeing club:* society, association, organization, institution, group, ring; alliance, league, union.
2 *the city has great clubs:* nightclub, disco, discotheque, bar.
3 *the top club in the league:* team, squad, side, line-up.
□ **club together**
friends and colleagues clubbed together to buy him a suitable present: pool resources, join forces, team up, get together, pull together; informal have a whip-round.

club[2] noun *a wooden club:* cudgel, truncheon, cosh, bludgeon, baton, stick, bat.
▷ **verb** *he was clubbed with an iron bar:* beat, bludgeon, cudgel, hit, strike, batter, bash, cosh; informal clout, clobber.

clue noun
1 *archaeological evidence can provide clues about the past:* indication, sign, pointer; evidence, information; hint, inkling.
2 *police are still searching for clues:* lead, piece of evidence, piece of information.

clump noun
1 *a clump of trees:* cluster, thicket, group, bunch.
2 *a clump of earth:* lump, clod, mass.
▷ **verb**
1 *the particles tend to clump together:* cluster, group, collect, gather, mass.
2 *they were clumping around upstairs:* stamp, stomp, clomp, tramp, lumber; thump, thud, bang.

clumsy adjective
1 *she was terribly clumsy:* awkward, ungainly, uncoordinated, graceless, inelegant, gauche; inept, maladroit, accident-prone, like a bull in a china shop, all fingers and thumbs; informal cack-handed, ham-fisted.
2 *a clumsy contraption:* unwieldy, cumbersome, bulky, awkward.
3 *a clumsy remark:* tactless, insensitive, thoughtless, undiplomatic, ill-judged.
OPPOSITES: graceful, elegant.

cluster noun
1 *clusters of berries:* bunch, clump, mass, knot, group.
2 *a cluster of women had gathered around Jack:* crowd, group, knot, huddle, bunch, flock, pack, gang, band; informal gaggle.
▷ **verb** *they clustered around the television:* congregate, gather, collect, group, assemble; huddle, crowd, flock.

clutch[1] verb *she clutched his arm:* grip, grasp, clasp, cling to, hang on to, clench, hold.
□ **clutch at**
reach for, snatch at, make a grab for, catch at, claw at.

clutch[2] noun
1 *a clutch of eggs:* group, batch.
2 *the film won a clutch of awards:* group, collection; raft, armful; informal load, bunch.

clutches plural noun *at last she was free from his clutches:* power, control, domination, command, rule; hands, hold, grip, grasp.

clutter verb *the desk was cluttered with papers and notebooks:* cover, litter, fill, mess up; be strewn, be scattered.
▷ **noun** *a clutter of perfume bottles, cosmetics, and clothes were strewn across a room:* jumble, litter, muddle, hotchpotch; mess, disorder, disarray, confusion.

coach[1] noun
1 *a journey by coach:* bus, minibus.
2 *a railway coach:* carriage, wagon, compartment; N. Amer. car.
3 *a coach and horses:* horse-drawn carriage, trap, hackney, hansom, gig.

coach² noun *a football coach:* instructor, trainer; teacher, tutor.
▷**verb** *he coached Richard in maths:* instruct, teach, tutor, school, educate; drill; train.

coagulate verb *the heat causes the blood to coagulate:* congeal, clot, thicken, gel; solidify, harden, set, dry.

coal noun

> WORD LINKS
> **colliery** a coal mine
> **collier** a coal miner

coalesce verb *some of the puddles had coalesced into shallow streams:* merge, unite, join together, combine, fuse, mingle, blend; amalgamate, consolidate, integrate.

coalition noun *a coalition between Conservatives and Liberals:* alliance, union, partnership; federation, league, association, confederation, consortium, syndicate; amalgamation, merger.

coarse adjective
1 *coarse woollen blankets:* rough, scratchy, prickly, wiry.
2 *his coarse features:* large, rough, rough-hewn, heavy; ugly.
3 *a coarse boy:* oafish, loutish, boorish, uncouth, rude, impolite, ill-mannered; vulgar, crass.
4 *a coarse innuendo:* vulgar, crude, rude, indelicate, unseemly, crass, tasteless, offensive.
OPPOSITES: soft, delicate, refined.

coarsen verb
1 *her hands were coarsened by manual work:* roughen, toughen, harden.
2 *her experience had not coarsened her or made her cynical:* desensitize, dehumanize; brutalize.

coast noun *the west coast:* seaboard, coastal region, coastline, seashore, shore, shoreline, seaside, waterfront; technical littoral.
▷**verb** *the car coasted down a hill:* freewheel, cruise, taxi, drift, glide, sail.

coat noun
1 *a winter coat:* overcoat, jacket.
2 *an animal's coat:* fur, hair, wool, fleece; hide, pelt, skin.
3 *a coat of paint:* layer, covering, coating, skin, film, wash; glaze, varnish, veneer, patina; deposit.
▷**verb** *the tube was coated with wax:* cover, paint, glaze, varnish; surface, veneer, laminate, plate, face; daub, smear, cake, plaster.

coax verb *trainees were coaxed into doing the boring work:* persuade, wheedle, cajole, talk into, prevail on, get round; inveigle, manoeuvre; informal sweet-talk, soft-soap, twist someone's arm.

cobble verb
□ **cobble something together** *you can cobble together an emergency meal from whatever happens to be in the kitchen:* prepare hastily, throw together, put together; improvise, contrive, whip up; informal rustle up; Brit. informal knock up.

cock verb
1 *he cocked his head slightly to one side:* tilt, tip, angle, incline.
2 *she cocked her little finger:* bend, flex, crook, curve.
3 *the dog cocked its leg:* lift, raise, hold up.

cocksure adjective *he made a change from the cocksure men she usually met:* arrogant, conceited, overconfident, cocky, proud, vain, self-important, swollen-headed, egotistical; smug, pleased with yourself.
OPPOSITES: modest.

cocky adjective *I thought she was far too cocky:* arrogant, conceited, overconfident, cocksure, swollen-headed, self-important, boastful, self-assertive; forward, insolent, cheeky.
OPPOSITES: modest.

cocoon verb
1 *we felt cold even though we were cocooned in our sleeping bags:* wrap, swathe, swaddle, cloak, enfold, envelop, cover, fold.
2 *I grew up cocooned from the real world:* protect, shield, shelter, screen, insulate, isolate.

coddle verb *we never wanted to be one of those couples who coddle their pets like children:* pamper, cosset, mollycoddle; spoil, indulge, overindulge, pander to; wrap in cotton wool; baby, wait on hand and foot.
OPPOSITES: neglect.

code noun
1 *a secret code:* cipher, key; cryptogram.
2 *a strict social code:* set of conventions, set of principles; etiquette, protocol, morality.
3 *the penal code:* law, laws, rules, regulations; constitution, system.

> WORD LINKS
> **cryptography** the art of writing or solving codes
> **cryptology** the study of codes

codify verb *the bill codified these standards for the first time:* systematize, organize, arrange, order, structure; classify, categorize, catalogue, sort.

coerce verb *he was coerced into giving evidence:* pressure, pressurize, press, push, constrain, oblige; force, compel, browbeat, bludgeon, bully, threaten, intimidate, dragoon, twist someone's arm, harass; informal railroad, lean on.

C

coercion noun force, compulsion, constraint, duress, oppression, enforcement, harassment, intimidation, threats, arm-twisting, pressure.

coffer noun
1 *every church had a coffer:* strongbox, money box, treasure chest, safe; casket, box.
2 *the ensuing legal battle soon drained the company's dwindling coffers:* funds, reserves, resources, money, finances, wealth, cash, capital.

coffin noun sarcophagus; casket.

cogent adjective *they put forward some cogent arguments:* convincing, compelling, strong, forceful, powerful, potent, weighty, effective; impressive, persuasive, eloquent, credible, influential, telling; logical, reasoned, lucid, coherent, clear; valid, sound, plausible.

cognition noun *a theory of human cognition:* perception, understanding, learning, comprehension, apprehension; reasoning, thinking, thought.

coherent adjective *he has failed to provide a coherent account of his whereabouts:* logical, reasoned, rational, sound, cogent, consistent; clear, lucid, articulate; intelligible, comprehensible.
OPPOSITES: incoherent.

cohesion noun *rewarding individuals breaks the cohesion in the group:* unity, togetherness, solidarity, bond, coherence; connection, linkage.

cohort noun
1 *at the hotel, a cohort of officials was waiting for me:* group, party, contingent, body, band, company.
2 *the 1940–44 birth cohort of women:* grouping, group, category, class, set, division, batch; age group, generation.
3 *Jack arrived with three of his cohorts:* supporter, follower, companion; derogatory henchman; informal, derogatory crony.

coil noun *coils of rope:* loop, twist, turn, curl, convolution; spiral, helix, corkscrew.
▷ **verb** *he coiled her hair around his finger:* wind, loop, twist, curl, curve, bend, twine, entwine; spiral, corkscrew.

coin noun *he had stolen £128 in notes and coins from her handbag:* change, small change, silver, copper, coppers; coinage; technical specie.
▷ **verb**
1 *guineas and half-guineas were coined:* mint, stamp, strike, cast; make.
2 *he coined the term 'desktop publishing':* invent, create, make up, originate, think up, dream up, devise.

> WORD LINKS
> **numismatics** the study or collection of coins

coincide verb
1 *the events coincided:* occur simultaneously, happen together, be concurrent; clash.
2 *their interests do not always coincide:* tally, correspond, agree, accord, concur, match, fit, be consistent, harmonize, be compatible, dovetail, correlate; informal square.

coincidence noun
1 *the resemblances are too close to be mere coincidence:* accident, chance, serendipity, fortuity, providence, happenstance, fate; a fluke.
2 *the coincidence of inflation and unemployment:* co-occurrence, coexistence, conjunction.

coincident adjective *in two thirds of the patients, depression was coincident with the onset of panic disorder:* concurrent, coinciding; simultaneous, contemporaneous, coexistent; formal concomitant.

coincidental adjective *any resemblance between their reports is purely coincidental:* accidental, chance, fluky, random; fortuitous, serendipitous, adventitious; unexpected, unforeseen, unintentional, inadvertent, unplanned.

cold adjective
1 *a cold day:* chilly, chill, cool, freezing, icy, snowy, wintry, frosty, frigid; bitter, biting, raw, arctic; literary gelid; informal nippy; Brit. informal parky.
2 *I'm very cold:* chilly, chilled, freezing, frozen, shivery, numb.
3 *they met with a cold reception:* unfriendly, unwelcoming, forbidding, cool, frigid, frosty, glacial.
OPPOSITES: hot, warm.

cold-blooded adjective *a cold-blooded killer:* cruel, callous, sadistic, inhuman, inhumane, pitiless, merciless, ruthless, heartless; savage, brutal, barbaric, barbarous; cold, cold-hearted.

cold-hearted adjective *I don't want to appear cold-hearted:* unfeeling, unloving, uncaring, unsympathetic, unemotional, unfriendly, uncharitable, unkind, insensitive; hard-hearted, stony-hearted, heartless, hard, cold.

collaborate verb
1 *they collaborated on the project:* cooperate, join forces, team up, work together, combine, ally; pool resources, club together.
2 *they collaborated with the enemy:* fraternize, conspire, collude, cooperate.

collaborator noun
1 *his collaborator on the book:* co-worker, partner, associate, colleague, confederate; assistant.
2 *a wartime collaborator:* quisling, enemy sympathizer; traitor, fifth columnist.

collapse verb
1 *the roof collapsed on top of them:* cave in, fall in, fall down, give way, subside, crumple, disintegrate.
2 *he collapsed last night:* faint, pass out, black out, lose consciousness, keel over.
3 *peace talks have collapsed:* break down, fail, fall through, founder, miscarry, come to grief, be unsuccessful; end, disintegrate; informal fizzle out.
▷ **noun**
1 *the collapse of the roof:* caving in, subsidence.
2 *her collapse on stage:* blackout, faint, loss of consciousness.
3 *the collapse of the talks:* breakdown, failure, disintegration; end.
4 *he suffered a collapse:* breakdown, personal crisis; informal crack-up.

collate verb *all the relevant data is being collated:* collect, gather, accumulate, assemble; combine, aggregate, put together; arrange, organize.

collateral noun *she put up her house as collateral for the bank loan:* security, surety, guarantee, insurance, indemnity, indemnification.

colleague noun co-worker, fellow worker, workmate, teammate, associate, partner.

collect verb
1 *we are trying to collect as much information as possible:* gather, accumulate, assemble, amass; accrue.
2 *a small crowd soon collected:* gather, assemble, congregate, meet, muster, convene, converge, flock together.
3 *I must collect the children:* fetch, go to get, call for, meet.
4 *they're collecting money for charity:* raise, appeal for, ask for, seek.
5 *he paused to collect himself:* recover, regain your composure, pull yourself together, steady yourself; informal get a grip.
6 *she collected her thoughts:* muster, summon, gather, get together, marshal.
OPPOSITES: disperse, distribute.

collected adjective *outwardly they are cool, calm, and collected:* calm, cool, self-possessed, self-controlled, composed, poised; serene, tranquil, relaxed, unruffled, unperturbed, untroubled; informal unfazed, together, laid-back.
OPPOSITES: excited, hysterical.

collection noun
1 *a collection of stolen items:* hoard, pile, heap, stack, stock, store, stockpile; accumulation, reserve, supply, bank, pool, fund.
2 *a collection of people had gathered in the lobby:* group, crowd, body, gathering, throng, assemblage; knot, cluster, party, band, horde, bevy, pack, gang, flock, swarm; informal gaggle.
3 *a collection of Victorian dolls:* set, series; array, assortment.

4 *a collection of short stories:* anthology, selection, compendium, treasury, compilation, miscellany, potpourri.
5 *a collection for the poor:* donations, contributions, gifts, subscriptions; informal whip-round.
6 *a church collection:* offering, offertory.

collective adjective *collective ownership of the means of production:* joint, shared, combined, mutual, common, communal; united, allied, cooperative, collaborative.
OPPOSITES: individual.

college noun *a college of technology:* school, academy, university, institute; (for priests or rabbis) seminary; (for the study of classical music) conservatoire.

collide verb
1 *the trains collided with each other:* crash, impact; hit, strike, run into, bump into, meet head-on, cannon into, plough into.
2 *in his work, politics and metaphysics collide:* conflict, clash, be opposed; differ, diverge, disagree, be at odds, be incompatible.

collision noun
1 *a collision on the ring road | a head-on collision:* crash, accident, pile-up, smash; impact; Brit. RTA (road traffic accident); Brit. informal prang, shunt.
2 *a collision between two mutually inconsistent ideas:* conflict, clash, opposition; disagreement, incompatibility, contradiction.

colloquial adjective *she had a good grasp of colloquial Italian:* informal, conversational, everyday, non-literary; idiomatic, vernacular, popular, demotic.
OPPOSITES: formal.

collude verb *corrupt border officials colluded with the importers of dubious goods:* conspire, connive, collaborate, plot, scheme; informal be in cahoots.

colonist noun *European colonists of North America:* settler, colonizer; immigrant, incomer, newcomer.

colonize verb *the Germans colonized Tanganyika in 1885:* settle in, move into, establish a colony in; occupy, take over, seize.

colony noun
1 *a French colony:* territory, dependency, protectorate, satellite, settlement, outpost, province.
2 *the British colony in New York:* population, community.
3 *an artists' colony:* community; quarter, district; ghetto.

colossal adjective *a colossal building | a colossal amount of money:* huge, massive, enormous, gigantic, very big, giant, mammoth, vast, immense, monumental, prodigious, titanic, towering, king-sized;

informal **whopping, mega**; Brit. informal
ginormous.
OPPOSITES: tiny.

colour noun

1 *a rich brown colour | a range of bright
colours:* **hue, shade, tint, tone, coloration.**
2 *eight tubes of oil colour:* **paint, pigment,
colourant, dye, stain, tint.**
3 *she's got some colour back in her cheeks:*
**rosiness, pinkness, redness, ruddiness,
blush, flush; bloom.**
4 *anecdotes add colour to the text:*
**vividness, life, liveliness, vitality,
excitement, interest, richness, zest, spice,
piquancy.**
5 *the regimental colours.* See **FLAG**[1] noun.
▷ **verb**
1 *the wood was coloured blue:* **tint, dye,
stain, paint.**
2 *she coloured under his scrutiny:* **blush,
redden, go pink, go red, flush.**
3 *the experiences had coloured her outlook:*
**influence, affect; skew, distort, bias,
prejudice.**

WORD LINKS
chromatic relating to colour

colourful adjective

1 *a colourful painting | he loved
colourful clothes:* **brightly coloured,
vivid, vibrant, brilliant, radiant, rich;
multicoloured, multicolour, rainbow,
varicoloured, harlequin, polychromatic,
psychedelic, iridescent; gaudy, garish;**
informal **jazzy.**
2 *he regaled her with a colourful account
of that afternoon's meeting:* **vivid, graphic,
lively, animated, dramatic; fascinating,
interesting, stimulating, scintillating;
picturesque, evocative.**

colourless adjective

1 *her colourless face:* **pale, pallid, wan,
anaemic, bloodless, ashen, white, waxen,
pasty, sickly, drained, drawn;** Brit. **peaky.**
2 *a colourless personality:* **uninteresting,
dull, boring, tedious, dry, dreary; bland,
insipid, vapid, wishy-washy, lame, lifeless,
spiritless, anaemic, bloodless; nondescript,
characterless.**
OPPOSITES: rosy, colourful.

column noun

1 *the arches are supported by massive
columns:* **pillar, post, support, upright,
baluster, pier, pile, pilaster, stanchion;
obelisk, monolith.**
2 *I read your column in this Sunday's paper:*
**article, piece, item, feature, story, report,
write-up, review.**
3 *a column of tanks moved north-west:*
**line, file, row, procession, train, cavalcade,
convoy.**

columnist noun *a columnist for
the Irish Times:* **writer, contributor,
journalist, correspondent; critic, reviewer,
commentator;** informal **hack.**

coma noun **state of unconsciousness;**
Medicine **persistent vegetative state.**

comatose adjective

1 *he has been comatose for seven months:*
unconscious, in a coma, insensible.
2 (informal) *she lay comatose in the sun:*
**inert, inactive, lethargic, sluggish, torpid,
languid; somnolent, sleeping.**

comb verb

1 *she combed her hair:* **groom, brush,
untangle, smooth, straighten, neaten, tidy,
arrange.**
2 *police combed the area:* **search, scour,
hunt through, go over, go over with a fine-
tooth comb, explore, sweep, probe; leave
no stone unturned.**

combat noun *he was killed in combat:*
**battle, fighting, action, hostilities, conflict,
war, warfare.**
▷ **verb** *scientists are proposing a new method
to combat the spread of the disease:* **fight,
tackle, attack, resist, withstand, counter;
impede, block, thwart, inhibit; stop, halt,
prevent, check, curb.**

combatant noun *the war affected
civilians as well as combatants:* **fighter,
soldier, serviceman/woman; warrior.**
▷ **adjective** *combatant armies:* **warring,
at war, opposing, belligerent, fighting,
battling.**

combative adjective *he made some
enemies with his combative style:*
**pugnacious, aggressive, antagonistic,
belligerent, bellicose, militant,
argumentative, truculent, quarrelsome.**
OPPOSITES: conciliatory.

combination noun

1 *a combination of ancient and modern:*
**amalgamation, amalgam, blend,
mixture, mix, fusion, marriage, coalition,
integration, incorporation, synthesis,
composite.**
2 *he acted in combination with his brother:*
**cooperation, collaboration, association,
union, partnership, league.**

combine verb

1 *it's an album that combines the old
with the new:* **amalgamate, integrate,
incorporate, merge, mix, fuse, blend; bind,
join, marry, unify.**
2 *teachers combined to tackle the problem:*
**cooperate, collaborate, join forces, unite,
team up, link up, get together, club
together, pool your resources.**

combustible adjective *a combustible gas:*
inflammable, flammable.

combustion noun **burning; ignition.**

come verb

1 *come and look at this:* **move nearer, move
closer, approach, advance, draw close/
closer, draw near/nearer; proceed.**
2 *they came last night:* **arrive, get here/**

there, make it, appear, turn up, come along, materialize; informal show up, roll in/up.

3 *they came to a stream:* reach, arrive at, get to, make it to, make, gain; come across, run across, happen on, chance on, come upon, stumble on; end up at; informal wind up at.

4 *she comes from Belgium:* be from, be a native of, hail from; live in, reside in; originate in.

5 *the attacks came without warning | a chance like this doesn't come every day:* happen, occur, take place, come about, transpire, fall, present itself, crop up, materialize, arise, arrive, appear.

6 *the dress comes to her ankles:* extend, stretch, reach, come as far as.

OPPOSITES: go, leave.

□ **come about**
the story of how this film came about is fascinating: happen, occur, take place, transpire; literary come to pass.

□ **come across**
1 *they came across some of his friends at a party:* meet/find by chance, meet, run into, run across, come upon, chance on, stumble on, happen on; discover, encounter, find, locate; informal bump into.
2 *she came across as sincere:* seem, appear, look, sound, look to be; Brit. come over.

□ **come apart**
break up, fall to bits, fall to pieces, disintegrate, come unstuck, separate, split, tear.

□ **come between**
nothing should come between brothers: alienate, estrange, separate, divide, split up, break up, disunite, set at odds.

□ **come by**
accurate information was hard to come by: obtain, get, find, acquire, gain, secure; informal get your hands on, get hold of.

□ **come down to**
it came down to her word against Guy's: amount to, add up to, constitute, boil down to, be equivalent to.

□ **come down with**
I came down with flu: fall ill with, be taken ill with, become infected with, get, catch, develop, contract, fall victim to; Brit. go down with.

□ **come forward**
a local trader came forward to pay the fines: volunteer, offer your services, make yourself available.

□ **come in**
enter, gain admission, cross the threshold.

□ **come into**
he came into some money and set up his own business: inherit, be left, be bequeathed, be willed.

□ **come in for**
she has come in for a lot of criticism: receive, experience, be subjected to, encounter, face, suffer, be the object of.

□ **come off**
1 *this soufflé rarely comes off:* succeed, work, turn out well, work out, go as planned, produce the desired result, get results.
2 *she always came off worse:* end up, finish up.

□ **come on**
the project is coming on well: progress, develop, shape up, take shape, come along, turn out; improve.

□ **come out**
1 *it came out that he'd been to Rome:* become known, become apparent, come to light, emerge, transpire; get out, be discovered, be revealed, leak out, be disclosed.
2 *my book is coming out this spring:* be published, be issued, be released, be brought out, be printed, go on sale.
3 *the flowers have come out:* bloom, flower, open.
4 *I'm sure it will come out all right:* end, finish, conclude, work out, turn out; informal pan out.

□ **come out with**
she was puzzled that he should come out with this remark: utter, say, let out, blurt out, burst out with.

□ **come round**
1 *he's just come round from the anaesthetic:* regain consciousness, come to, recover, revive, awake, wake up.
2 *I came round to her view:* be converted, be won over, agree with, change your mind, be persuaded by; give way, yield, relent.
3 *Friday the 13th comes round every few months:* recur, reoccur, return, reappear; occur, take place, happen, come up; be imminent, be looming.
4 *she came round for a drink:* call in/round, look in, stop by, drop by/in/round, come over; visit; informal pop in/round/over.

□ **come through**
she's come through the operation and is now recuperating: survive, get through, ride out, weather, live through, pull through; withstand, endure.

□ **come to**
1 *the bill came to £17.50:* amount to, add up to, run to, total, equal; Brit. tot up to.
2 *I came to in the hospital:* regain consciousness, come round, recover, revive, awake, wake up.

□ **come up**
when the opportunity came up again we didn't hesitate: arise, occur, happen, come about, crop up.

□ **come up to**
1 *she came up to his shoulder:* reach, come to, be as tall as, extend to.
2 *he never came up to her expectations:* measure up to, match up to, live up to, fulfil, satisfy, meet, equal, compare with; be good enough.

□ **come up with**
after much deliberation they came up with a solution: devise, produce, think up, work out; hit on.

comeback noun *Wales produced a stunning second-half comeback to secure a dramatic victory over France:* resurgence, recovery, revival, return, rally, upturn; Brit. fightback.

comedian noun *a famous comedian:* comic, comedienne, funny man/woman, humorist, entertainer, wit, wag.

comedown noun (informal)
1 *patrol duty was a bit of a comedown for a sergeant:* loss of status, demotion, loss of face, humiliation, belittlement.
2 *it's such a comedown after Christmas:* anticlimax, let-down, disappointment.

comedy noun *they enjoyed the comedy of the film:* humour, fun, funny side, comical aspect, absurdity, drollness, farce, slapstick, buffoonery; satire.
OPPOSITES: tragedy.

comeuppance noun (informal) *in those films the villain always got his comeuppance:* just deserts, just punishment, due, retribution.

comfort noun
1 *he was born into a rich family who lived in comfort in New York State:* ease, relaxation, repose, serenity, tranquillity, contentment, cosiness; luxury, prosperity; bed of roses.
2 *it was difficult to offer any words of comfort:* consolation, solace; support, reassurance, cheer.
▷ **verb** *she tried to comfort her sister:* console, solace, support; reassure, soothe, calm; cheer, hearten.

comfortable adjective
1 *a comfortable lifestyle:* pleasant, free from hardship; affluent, prosperous, well-to-do, luxurious, opulent.
2 *a comfortable room:* cosy, snug, warm, pleasant, welcoming; restful; Brit. homely; informal comfy.
3 *comfortable clothes:* loose, loose-fitting, casual; informal comfy.
4 *a comfortable pace:* leisurely, unhurried, relaxed, easy, gentle, sedate, undemanding, slow; informal laid-back.
5 *they feel comfortable with each other:* at ease, relaxed, secure, safe, unworried, contented, happy.
OPPOSITES: hard, spartan, tense.

comforting adjective *I was grateful for his comforting words:* consoling, sympathetic, compassionate, solicitous, tender, warm, caring; supportive, reassuring, soothing, calming; cheering, heartening.

comfortless adjective *it was a cold, comfortless place:* gloomy, dreary, dismal, bleak, grim; joyless, cheerless, depressing, dispiriting, unwelcoming, uninviting; austere, spartan, institutional.
OPPOSITES: cosy.

comic adjective *a comic play:* humorous, funny, amusing, hilarious, uproarious; comical, farcical, silly, slapstick, zany; droll, witty, jocular.
OPPOSITES: serious.
▷ **noun**
1 *a stand-up comic:* comedian, comedienne, funny man/woman, humorist, wit.
2 *children's comics:* cartoon paper, comic paper, comic book, graphic novel.

comical adjective
1 *he could be quite comical:* funny, humorous, droll, witty, jocular, amusing, diverting, entertaining; informal waggish.
2 *they look comical in those suits:* silly, absurd, ridiculous, hilarious, laughable, risible, ludicrous, preposterous, foolish.
OPPOSITES: sensible.

coming adjective *the coming election:* forthcoming, imminent, impending, approaching; future, expected, anticipated; close, at hand, in store, in the offing, in the pipeline, on the horizon, on the way; informal on the cards.
▷ **noun** *a festival which celebrates the coming of spring:* approach, advance, advent, arrival, appearance, emergence, onset.

command verb
1 *he commanded his men to retreat:* order, tell, direct, instruct, call on, require; old use bid.
2 *Jones commanded a tank squadron:* be in charge of, be in command of, be the leader of; head, lead, control, direct, manage, supervise, oversee; informal head up.
3 *they command great respect:* receive, get, gain, secure.
▷ **noun**
1 *he obeyed her commands without question:* order, instruction, directive, direction, injunction, demand, requirement, bidding.
2 *he had 160 men under his command:* authority, control, charge, power, direction, dominion; leadership, rule, government, management, supervision, jurisdiction.
3 *she had a brilliant command of English:* knowledge, mastery, grasp, comprehension, understanding.

commandeer verb *everything surrounding the base was commandeered by the army:* seize, take, requisition, appropriate, expropriate, sequestrate, sequester, confiscate, annex, take over, claim; hijack, arrogate, help yourself to.

commander noun leader, head, chief, overseer, controller; commander-in-chief, commanding officer; informal boss, skipper, number one.

commanding adjective
1 *the world champion was in a commanding position:* dominant, dominating,

controlling, superior, powerful; advantageous, favourable.
2 *he was a tall, lean man with a commanding voice | an actor with a commanding screen presence:* authoritative, masterful, assertive, firm; imposing, impressive.

commemorate verb *the event commemorated the courage of the villagers:* celebrate, pay tribute to, pay homage to, honour, salute, toast; remember, recognize, acknowledge, observe, mark.

commence verb *the headmaster commenced his tour of inspection:* begin, start, embark on; get going, get under way, get off the ground, set about, launch into, lead off, get the ball rolling; open, initiate, inaugurate.
OPPOSITES: conclude.

commencement noun beginning, start, opening, outset, onset, inception, launch, initiation, inauguration.

commend verb
1 *we should commend him for his courageous actions:* praise, compliment, congratulate, applaud, salute, honour; sing the praises of, pay tribute to, take your hat off to, pat on the back.
2 *I commend her to you without reservation:* recommend, suggest, propose; endorse, advocate, vouch for, speak for, support, back.
OPPOSITES: criticize.

commendable adjective *he tackled the tasks with commendable zeal | the young actor gave a very commendable performance:* admirable, praiseworthy, creditable, laudable, meritorious, exemplary; noteworthy, worthy, respectable.

commendation noun
1 *they have received letters of commendation:* praise, congratulation, appreciation; acclaim, credit, recognition, respect, esteem, admiration, homage, tribute.
2 *a commendation for bravery:* award, accolade, prize, honour, honourable mention, citation.

commensurate adjective
1 *the salary will be commensurate with your experience and qualifications:* appropriate to, in keeping with, in line with, consistent with, corresponding to, according to, relative to; dependent on, based on.
2 *such heavy responsibility must receive commensurate reward:* corresponding, proportionate, proportional, comparable; equivalent, equal.

comment noun
1 *she was upset by their comments:* remark, observation, statement, utterance; pronouncement, judgement, reflection,

opinion, view; criticism.
2 *the story excited a great deal of comment:* discussion, debate; interest.
3 *a comment had been inserted in the register:* note, annotation, footnote, gloss, commentary, explanation.
▷**verb**
1 *I'm not in a position to comment on this issue:* speak about, talk about, discuss; mention, refer to.
2 *'It will soon be dark,' he commented:* remark, observe, reflect, say, state, declare, announce; interpose, interject.

commentary noun
1 *there will be a live commentary on Radio Four:* description, account, report.
2 *textual commentary:* explanation, interpretation, exegesis, analysis; assessment, appraisal, criticism, critique; notes, comments.

commentator noun
1 *a television commentator:* announcer, reporter, journalist; newscaster, sportscaster; Brit. presenter.
2 *a political commentator:* analyst, pundit, observer; blogger; writer, speaker.

commerce noun *the rapid increase in international commerce:* trade, trading, buying and selling, business, dealing; transactions, dealings.

commercial adjective
1 *a vessel built for commercial purposes:* trade, trading, business, mercantile.
2 *we turn good ideas into commercial products:* lucrative, moneymaking, profitable, money-spinning, remunerative, fruitful, gainful; viable, successful.
▷**noun** *a TV commercial:* advertisement, promotion; informal ad, advert, plug.

commercialized adjective *the art world became increasingly commercialized:* profit-orientated, money-orientated, commercial, materialistic, mercenary.

commiserate verb *he commiserated with them for their sufferings:* offer sympathy to, be sympathetic to, offer condolences to, condole with, sympathize with, empathize with, feel/express pity for, feel sorry for, feel for.

commiseration noun condolences, sympathy, pity; compassion, understanding.

commission noun
1 *the plan requires approval by an independent commission:* committee, board, council, panel, directorate.
2 *one of his first commissions was to redesign the building:* task, assignment, project, mission, undertaking, employment, job; duty, charge, responsibility.
3 *wholesalers give the farmers a price, take a commission, and then sell the produce on:* percentage, share, portion, fee,

C

consideration; informal cut.
▷ **verb**
1 *he commissioned an architect to manage the project:* engage, contract, employ, hire, recruit, retain, appoint, enlist, book, sign up.
2 *the portrait was commissioned by his widow:* order; authorize.
□ **in commission**
in service, in use, serviceable; working, functional, operative, up and running, in operation, in working order.
□ **out of commission**
not in service, not in use, unserviceable; not working, inoperative, out of order; down.

commit verb
1 *he committed a terrible crime:* carry out, perpetrate, do, execute, effect; be responsible for, be guilty of.
2 *the EU has committed to support the government's efforts to eradicate poverty in the country:* pledge, guarantee, promise, contract, undertake; vow.
3 *manufacturers will have to commit substantial funds to developing new engines:* set aside, allocate, give, earmark; pledge, devote, dedicate; spend
4 *she was committed to their care:* entrust, consign, assign, deliver, give, hand over, relinquish.
5 *the judge committed him to prison:* consign, send.

commitment noun
1 *he resigned because of the pressure of other commitments:* responsibility, obligation, duty, tie, liability; task; engagement, arrangement.
2 *her commitment to her students continued undiminished:* dedication, devotion, allegiance, loyalty, faithfulness, fidelity.
3 *you made a commitment:* vow, promise, pledge, oath; contract, undertaking.

committed adjective *we have a very committed team of volunteers | he's a committed socialist:* dedicated, loyal, faithful, staunch, firm, steadfast, unwavering, wholehearted, keen, enthusiastic, passionate, ardent, fervent, sworn; devout, devoted.
OPPOSITES: apathetic.

commodity noun *improving productivity will lower the cost of a commodity:* item, material, product, article, object; import, export.

common adjective
1 *stingrays and dolphins are a common sight in the bay:* familiar, ordinary, usual, routine, frequent, recurrent, regular, everyday, customary; standard, typical, conventional, commonplace, run-of-the-mill.
2 *it is a common belief that elephants have long memories:* widespread, general,
universal, popular, prevalent, prevailing, established, conventional, traditional, orthodox, accepted.
3 *they work together for the common good:* collective, communal, community, public, general; shared, combined, joint.
4 *they're so common:* uncouth, vulgar, coarse, ill-bred, uncivilized, rough, boorish, unladylike, ungentlemanly.
OPPOSITES: unusual, rare, uncommon.

commonly adverb *shift workers commonly complain of not being able to sleep:* often, frequently, regularly, repeatedly, routinely, habitually, customarily.

commonplace adjective
1 *a commonplace occurrence:* common, normal, usual, ordinary, familiar, routine, standard, everyday, customary, regular, frequent, habitual, typical, unremarkable.
2 *every paragraph is full of commonplace observations:* ordinary, unremarkable, unexceptional, prosaic, bland, uninteresting, unoriginal, banal, predictable, run-of-the-mill.
OPPOSITES: original, unusual.
▷ **noun** *it is a commonplace to talk of the young being alienated:* platitude, cliché, truism, hackneyed phrase, trite phrase, old chestnut, banality.

common sense noun *he is quick to praise her professionalism and common sense:* good sense, good judgement, level-headedness, astuteness, shrewdness, insight, wit; practicality, pragmatism, resourcefulness, enterprise; informal gumption, nous, savvy.

commotion noun *a commotion broke out in the street behind us:* disturbance, uproar, tumult, rumpus, ruckus, brouhaha, furore, hue and cry, fuss, storm; turmoil, disorder, confusion, chaos, mayhem, havoc, pandemonium; unrest, fracas, riot, breach of the peace; informal ructions, ballyhoo, kerfuffle; Brit. informal hullabaloo.

communal adjective
1 *the kitchen was communal:* shared, joint, for common use, public.
2 *they farm on a communal basis:* collective, cooperative, community.
OPPOSITES: private, individual.

commune¹ noun *she lives in a commune:* collective, cooperative, communal settlement; kibbutz.

commune² verb *the purpose of praying is to commune with God:* communicate, speak, talk, converse.

communicable adjective *the spread of communicable diseases:* contagious, infectious, catching, transmissible; infective.

communicate verb
1 *he communicated the news to his boss:*

convey, tell, impart, relay, transmit, pass on, announce, report, recount, relate, present; divulge, disclose, mention; spread, disseminate, broadcast.
2 *they communicate daily:* be in touch, be in contact, talk, speak, converse; liaise, have dealings, interface, meet.
3 *a politician must have the ability to communicate:* get your message across, explain yourself, be understood, get through to someone.
4 *the disease is communicated easily:* transmit, spread, pass on.
5 *each bedroom communicates with a bathroom:* adjoin, connect with, open on to, lead into.

communication noun
1 *the communication of information through the media is a vital part of a democratic society:* transmission, conveying; dissemination.
2 *I've had no communication with him for weeks:* contact, dealings, relations, connection, association; correspondence, dialogue, talk, conversation, discussion.
3 *an official communication:* message, statement, announcement, report, dispatch, communiqué, letter, bulletin.
4 *road and rail communications:* links, connections; services, routes.

communicative adjective *she is always very pleasant and communicative:* forthcoming, informative, expansive, unreserved, uninhibited, vocal, outgoing, open; talkative, chatty, loquacious.

communion noun *a sense of communion with others:* affinity, fellowship, kinship, friendship, fellow feeling, togetherness, closeness, harmony, understanding, rapport, connection, communication, empathy, accord, unity.

communiqué noun *the foreign ministry issued a communiqué:* statement, press release, bulletin, memo, dispatch, report, announcement, declaration.

community noun
1 *the views of certain individuals should not be mistaken for the views of the community as a whole* | *a representative cross section of the community:* population, populace, people, citizenry, public, general public, society; residents, inhabitants, citizens; district, region, area, neighbourhood.
2 *New York City is home to a community of musicians, artists, and producers:* group, body, set, colony.
3 *he joined a monastic community:* brotherhood, sisterhood, fraternity; order.
4 *the law presupposes a community of interest between employer and employees:* similarity, likeness, comparability, correspondence, agreement, closeness, affinity.

commute verb
1 *he commutes from Corby to Kentish Town:*

travel to and fro, travel back and forth; shuttle.
2 *his sentence was commuted:* reduce, lessen, lighten, shorten, cut, moderate.

compact[1] adjective
1 *a compact cluster of houses:* dense, close-packed, tightly packed.
2 *a compact camera:* small, little; portable; Scottish wee; Brit. informal dinky.
OPPOSITES: loose, large.
▷**verb** *the snow has been compacted:* compress, pack down, press down, tamp down, flatten.

compact[2] noun *the warring states signed a compact:* treaty, pact, accord, agreement, settlement, concordat; contract.

companion noun
1 *his circle of drinking companions* | *her travelling companion:* friend, associate; partner, escort; comrade; informal pal, chum; Brit. informal mate; N. Amer. informal buddy.
2 *the CD is a companion to the book:* complement, accompaniment, supplement.

companionable adjective *the most generous and companionable of men:* friendly, affable, cordial, genial, congenial, amiable, easy-going, good-natured, easy to get on with, pleasant, agreeable; sociable, convivial, outgoing, gregarious.

companionship noun *she needed the companionship of like-minded people:* friendship, fellowship, closeness, togetherness, camaraderie; company, society, social contact.

company noun
1 *an oil company:* firm, business, corporation, establishment, agency, office, bureau, institution, organization, concern, enterprise; conglomerate, consortium, syndicate, multinational; informal outfit.
2 *I enjoy his company:* companionship, friendship, fellowship; society.
3 *I'm expecting company:* guests, visitors, callers.
4 *the mayor addressed the assembled company* | *he had a company of friends with him:* group, crowd, party, assembly, gathering, band, gang, flock, herd, troupe, throng, congregation; informal bunch.

| WORD LINKS |
| **corporate** relating to a company |

comparable adjective
1 *families with comparable incomes:* similar, equivalent, commensurate, proportional, proportionate; like, matching.
2 *nobody is comparable with this athlete:* equal to, as good as, in the same league as, on a par with, on a level with, able to hold a candle to; a match for.

comparative adjective *they left the city for the comparative cool of the country:* relative; in/by comparison.

C

compare verb

1 *the survey compares prices in the UK with prices in other European countries:* set side by side, set against; contrast, juxtapose, weigh against; correlate.
2 *he was compared to Wagner:* liken, equate; class with, bracket with, draw a parallel between.
3 *sales were modest and do not compare with the glory days of the 1990s:* be as good as, be comparable to, bear comparison with, be the equal of, match up to, be on a par with, be in the same league as; match, resemble, emulate, rival.
□ **beyond compare** without equal, second to none, in a class of its own; peerless, matchless, unmatched, incomparable, inimitable, supreme, outstanding, consummate, unique, singular, perfect.

comparison noun

1 *a comparison of the results:* juxtaposition, correlation.
2 *there's no comparison between them:* resemblance, likeness, similarity, correspondence, correlation, parallel, parity, comparability.

compartment noun *a secret compartment:* section, part, recess, chamber, cavity; pocket.

compartmentalize verb *he developed an ability to compartmentalize his life—his family, his relationship with Meriel, and his work were all kept separate:* divide, separate, split, partition; categorize.

compass noun *the event had political repercussions which are beyond the compass of this book:* scope, range, extent, reach, span, breadth, ambit, limits, parameters, bounds.

compassion noun *the victims should be treated with compassion:* pity, sympathy, care, concern, solicitude, sensitivity, warmth, love, tenderness, mercy, leniency, tolerance, kindness, humanity, charity, empathy, fellow feeling.
OPPOSITES: indifference, cruelty.

compassionate adjective *he was a compassionate man who will be missed by all who knew him:* sympathetic, understanding, caring, warm, warm-hearted, empathetic; tolerant, considerate, kind, humane, charitable, big-hearted.

compatibility noun *they felt the bond of true compatibility:* like-mindedness, affinity, fellow feeling, harmony, rapport, empathy, sympathy.

compatible adjective

1 *the careers structure is not compatible with having a family:* reconcilable.
2 *they were never compatible:* well suited, well matched, like-minded, in tune, in harmony.
3 *the symptoms were compatible with gastritis or a peptic ulcer:* consistent, consonant; in keeping.

compatriot noun fellow citizen, fellow countryman.

compel verb *humanitarian agencies have been compelled to withdraw from the south of the country:* force, constrain, oblige, require, make; coerce into, pressure into, pressurize into.

compelling adjective

1 *it was a compelling performance:* enthralling, captivating, gripping, riveting, spellbinding, mesmerizing, absorbing, irresistible.
2 *he put forward a compelling argument:* convincing, persuasive, cogent, irresistible, forceful, powerful, strong, telling, conclusive, irrefutable, unanswerable; credible, sound, valid.
OPPOSITES: boring, weak.

compendium noun *a compendium of useful information about language:* collection, compilation, anthology, treasury, digest.

compensate verb

1 *we agreed to compensate him for his loss:* recompense, repay, pay back, reimburse, remunerate, indemnify.
2 *his flair compensated for his faults:* balance out, counterbalance, counteract, offset, make up for, cancel out, neutralize.

compensation noun *he is seeking compensation for injuries suffered at work:* recompense, repayment, reimbursement, remuneration, indemnification, indemnity, redress; damages.

compère noun host, anchor, anchorman/woman, master of ceremonies, MC, announcer; Brit. presenter.

compete verb

1 *they competed in a tennis tournament:* take part, participate, play, be a competitor, be involved; enter, go in for.
2 *they had to compete with other firms:* contend, vie, battle, go head to head, jockey for position; strive against, pit yourself against; challenge, take on.
3 *in this sort of form, no one can compete with him:* rival, challenge, keep up with, keep pace with, compare with, match, be in the same league as, come near to, come close to, touch; informal hold a candle to.

competence noun

1 *the players displayed varying degrees of competence:* capability, ability, competency, proficiency, accomplishment, expertise, skill, prowess, mastery, talent; informal know-how.
2 *doubts arose over the competence of the system:* adequacy, appropriateness, suitability, fitness; effectiveness; formal efficacy.
3 *matters within the competence of*

the courts: authority, power, control, jurisdiction, scope, remit, ambit.

competent adjective

1 *a highly competent surgeon:* capable, able, proficient, adept, adroit, accomplished, skilful, skilled, talented, expert; good, excellent; efficient.
2 *she spoke quite competent French:* adequate, reasonable, fair, decent, acceptable, satisfactory.
3 *the court was not competent to hear the case:* qualified, empowered, authorized.
OPPOSITES: incompetent.

competition noun

1 *fierce competition between the banks pushed down borrowing costs:* rivalry, competitiveness; opposition.
2 *he won the competition by one point:* contest, tournament, championship, match, game, race, heat, fixture, event.
3 *we must stay ahead of the competition:* opposition, other side, field; challengers, opponents, rivals.

competitive adjective

1 *the highly competitive world of journalism:* ruthless, fierce; informal dog-eat-dog, cut-throat.
2 *she has a strong competitive streak:* ambitious, combative, aggressive.
3 *we offer prompt service at competitive prices:* reasonable, affordable, moderate, keen; low, inexpensive, economical.

competitor noun

1 *the competitors in the race:* contestant, contender, challenger, participant, entrant; runner, player.
2 *our European competitors:* rival, challenger, opponent, adversary; competition, opposition.

compilation noun *there are thirty-three stories in this compilation:* collection, selection, anthology, treasury, compendium; album.

compile verb *he compiled a dossier of patients with tropical diseases:* assemble, put together, make, collate, compose, organize, arrange; gather, collect.

complacency noun *success brings with it the danger of complacency:* smugness, self-satisfaction, self-congratulation, self-regard; gloating, triumph, pride; satisfaction, contentment.

complacent adjective *no one in the industry can afford to stand still and be complacent:* smug, self-satisfied, pleased with yourself, self-congratulatory, self-regarding; gloating, triumphant, proud; satisfied, content, contented.

USAGE

Do not confuse **complacent** with **complaisant**. **Complacent** means 'smugly self-satisfied', while **complaisant** means 'willing to please other people or accept what

they do or say without protest' (*a complaisant husband willing to turn a blind eye to the antics of his wife*).

complain verb *we all complained bitterly about the food:* protest, grumble, moan, carp, cavil, grouse, make a fuss, whine, bleat; object to, speak out against, criticize, find fault with; informal whinge, kick up a fuss, bellyache, beef, sound off, gripe.

complaint noun

1 *their main complaint is about the price of petrol:* protest, objection, grievance, grouse, cavil, grumble; charge, accusation, criticism; informal beef, gripe, bellyache.
2 *there appears to be little cause for complaint:* dissatisfaction, grievance, grumbling, criticism, condemnation, disapproval.
3 *a kidney complaint:* disorder, disease, infection, illness, ailment, sickness; condition, problem, upset, trouble, affliction; informal bug, virus.

complaisant adjective willing, acquiescent, agreeable, amenable, cooperative, accommodating, obliging; biddable, compliant, docile, obedient.

USAGE

Do not confuse **complaisant** with **complacent**: see the note at COMPLACENT.

complement noun

1 *local ales provide the perfect complement to the fine food:* accompaniment, companion, addition, supplement, accessory, trimming.
2 *a full complement of lifeboats:* amount, total, contingent, quota, allowance.
▷**verb** *an extensive wine list complements the imaginative menu:* accompany, go with, round off, set off; enhance, complete; suit, harmonize with.

USAGE

The words **complement** and **compliment** are often confused. As a verb, **complement** means 'to add extra features to someone or something in a way that improves', while **compliment** means 'to congratulate or praise someone or something' (*he complimented Kate on her appearance*).

complementary adjective *neutral tones allow the widest choice of complementary furnishings and decoration:* harmonious, compatible, corresponding, matching.

USAGE

Do not confuse **complementary** with **complimentary**. **Complementary** means 'combining to form a whole or to improve each other', while **complimentary** means 'praising' (*there were some very complimentary reviews in the papers*), or 'given free of charge' (*a complimentary bottle of wine*).

C

complete adjective
1 *the complete interview will appear in next week's issue:* entire, whole, full, total; uncut, unabridged, unexpurgated.
2 *their research was complete:* finished, ended, concluded, completed, finalized; accomplished, achieved, done.
3 *you're acting like a complete fool:* absolute, utter, total, real, downright, thoroughgoing, veritable, prize, perfect, out-and-out, unqualified, unmitigated.
OPPOSITES: partial, unfinished, incomplete.
▷**verb**
1 *the first phase of the development has now been completed | the two clubs completed the deal this weekend:* finish, end, conclude; finalize, clinch, close; carry out, achieve; informal wrap up, sew up.
2 *a pair of cool sunglasses may be all you need to complete any outfit:* finish off, round off, top off, crown, cap; complement.
3 *please complete the attached form:* fill out, answer; Brit. fill in.

completely adverb *he had always been completely honest with her:* totally, entirely, utterly, absolutely, perfectly, quite, altogether, downright; thoroughly, fully, wholly, in every way, in every respect, one hundred per cent, every inch, to the hilt.

completion noun *the completion of all outstanding work:* finishing, finish, end, conclusion, close; accomplishment, achievement, finalization, resolution.

complex adjective
1 *the problem is complex and the solutions are even more complex:* complicated, involved, intricate, convoluted; difficult, knotty, tricky, thorny.
2 *a complex structure:* compound, composite, multiplex.
OPPOSITES: simple.
▷**noun**
1 *a complex of roads:* network, system, nexus, web; combination, aggregation.
2 *(informal) he had a complex about losing his hair:* obsession, fixation, preoccupation; neurosis; informal hang-up, thing, bee in your bonnet.

complexion noun
1 *a pale complexion:* skin, skin colour, skin tone.
2 *this puts an entirely new complexion on things:* perspective, angle, slant, interpretation; aspect, appearance, light, look.
3 *successive governments of all complexions:* type, kind, sort; nature, character.

complexity noun *an issue of great complexity | the complexities of the plot:* complication, problem, difficulty; intricacy; twist, turn, convolution.

compliance noun
1 *compliance with international law:* obedience to, observance of, adherence to, conformity to, respect for.
2 *he mistook her silence for compliance:* acquiescence, agreement, assent, consent, acceptance; complaisance, docility, submission.
OPPOSITES: violation, defiance.

compliant adjective *a compliant labour force:* acquiescent, amenable, biddable, tractable, complaisant, accommodating, cooperative; obedient, docile, malleable, pliable, submissive, tame, yielding, controllable, unresisting, persuadable.
OPPOSITES: recalcitrant.

complicate verb *more choice will complicate matters for the consumer:* make (more) difficult, make complicated, mix up, confuse, muddle.
OPPOSITES: simplify.

complicated adjective *a long and complicated saga:* complex, intricate, involved, convoluted, tangled, impenetrable, confusing, bewildering, perplexing, labyrinthine, tortuous; knotty, tricky, thorny.
OPPOSITES: straightforward.

complication noun
1 *there is a complication concerning ownership of the site:* difficulty, problem, obstacle, stumbling block, hurdle; drawback, snag, catch, hitch; informal fly in the ointment.
2 *the ever increasing complication of technology and of life:* complexity, intricacy.

complicity noun *they were accused of complicity in the attempt to overthrow the government:* collusion, involvement, collaboration, connivance; conspiracy; informal being in cahoots with someone.

compliment noun
1 *an unexpected compliment:* flattering remark, tribute, accolade, commendation, pat on the back; (**compliments**) praise, acclaim, admiration, flattery, blandishments, honeyed words.
2 *my compliments on your cooking:* congratulations, commendations, praise.
3 *Margaret sends her compliments:* greetings, regards, respects, good wishes, best wishes, salutations; formal felicitations.
OPPOSITES: insult.
▷**verb** *they complimented his performance:* praise, pay tribute to, speak highly/well of, flatter, wax lyrical about, make much of, commend, acclaim, applaud, salute, honour; congratulate.
OPPOSITES: criticize.

USAGE
Do not confuse **compliment** with **complement**; see the note at **COMPLEMENT**.

complimentary adjective
1 *complimentary remarks:* flattering,

appreciative, congratulatory, admiring, approving, commendatory, favourable, glowing; fulsome.
2 *complimentary tickets:* free, free of charge, gratis, for nothing; courtesy; informal on the house.
OPPOSITES: derogatory.

> **USAGE**
>
> Do not confuse **complimentary** with **complementary**; see the note at **COMPLEMENTARY**.

comply verb
1 *she complied with his wishes:* abide by, observe, obey, adhere to, conform to, follow, respect; agree to, assent to, go along with, yield to, submit to, defer to.
2 *second-hand furniture must comply with all the new regulations:* meet, satisfy, fulfil.
OPPOSITES: ignore, disobey.

component noun *the components of electronic devices:* part, piece, bit, element, constituent; ingredient; unit, module, section.
▷ **adjective** *the molecule's component elements:* constituent.

compose verb
1 *a poem composed by Shelley:* write, create, devise, produce; pen, author, draft.
2 *compose and draw a still life:* organize, arrange, set out.
3 *foreign workers composed more than six per cent of the labour force:* make up, constitute, form, comprise.
□ **compose yourself**
after taking a moment to compose herself, she entered the room quietly: calm down, control yourself, regain your composure, pull yourself together, collect yourself, steady yourself, keep your head; informal get a grip, keep your cool.

composed adjective *a very talented and composed young player:* calm, self-possessed, collected, cool, self-controlled; serene, tranquil, relaxed, at ease, unruffled, unperturbed, untroubled; equable, even-tempered, imperturbable; informal unflappable, together, laid-back.

composite adjective *a composite structure:* compound, complex.
▷ **noun** *a composite of plastic and metal:* amalgamation, amalgam, combination, compound, fusion, synthesis, mixture, blend.

composition noun
1 *the composition of the council:* make-up, constitution, configuration, structure, formation, form, framework, fabric, anatomy, organization; informal set-up.
2 *a literary composition:* work of art, work, creation, opus, oeuvre, piece, arrangement.
3 *the composition of a poem:* writing, creation.

4 *a school composition:* essay, paper, study, piece of writing.
5 *the composition of the painting:* arrangement, disposition, layout; proportions, balance, symmetry.

composure noun *she was struggling to regain her composure:* self-control, self-possession, calm, equanimity, equilibrium, serenity, tranquillity; aplomb, poise, sangfroid; informal cool.

compound noun *a compound of energy and idealism:* amalgamation, combination, composite, amalgam, blend, mixture, mix, fusion, synthesis.
▷ **adjective** *a compound substance:* composite, complex.
▷ **verb**
1 *a dialect compounded of Spanish and Dutch:* be composed of, be made up of, be formed from.
2 *his illness compounds their problems:* aggravate, exacerbate, worsen, add to, augment, intensify, heighten, increase, magnify; complicate.
OPPOSITES: alleviate.

comprehend verb *I couldn't comprehend what had happened:* understand, grasp, take in, see, follow, make sense of, fathom, get to the bottom of; formal apprehend; informal work out, figure out, make head or tail of, get your head around, take on board.

comprehensible adjective *clear and comprehensible English:* intelligible, understandable, accessible; lucid, coherent, clear, plain, explicit, unambiguous, straightforward.
OPPOSITES: incomprehensible.

comprehension noun *you clearly have no comprehension of the technical and practical difficulties involved:* understanding, grasp, conception, apprehension, awareness; cognition, knowledge, perception; interpretation.

comprehensive adjective *a comprehensive review of UK defence policy:* inclusive, complete; thorough, full, extensive, all-embracing, exhaustive, detailed, in-depth, encyclopedic, universal, catholic; far-reaching, radical, sweeping, across the board, wholesale; broad, wide, wide-ranging; informal wall-to-wall.
OPPOSITES: limited.

compress verb
1 *the skirt can be folded and compressed into a small bag:* squeeze, press, squash, stuff; tamp, pack, compact; constrict.
2 *Polly compressed her lips:* purse, press together, pucker.
3 *the text was compressed:* abridge, cut, condense, shorten, abbreviate, truncate; summarize, precis.
OPPOSITES: expand.

C

comprise verb

1 *the country comprises twenty states:* **consist of**, be made up of, be composed of, contain, encompass, incorporate; include; formal comprehend.
2 *this breed comprises half the herd:* **make up**, constitute, form, compose; account for.

> **USAGE**
>
> When using **comprise** with **of**, it is acceptable to use the passive form (e.g. *the country is comprised of twenty states*). However, in formal English you should avoid the active form **comprise of** (e.g. *the country comprises of twenty states*).

compromise noun

1 *eventually they reached a compromise:* **agreement**, understanding, settlement, accommodation; terms, deal, trade-off, bargain; middle ground, happy medium, balance.
2 *a happy marriage needs compromise:* **give and take**, concession, cooperation.
▷**verb**
1 *in the end we compromised:* **meet each other halfway**, come to an understanding, make a deal, make concessions, find a happy medium, strike a balance; give and take.
2 *his actions could compromise his reputation:* **undermine**, weaken, damage, harm; jeopardize, prejudice; discredit, dishonour.

compulsion noun

1 *he is under no compulsion to go:* **obligation**, constraint; coercion, duress, pressure, intimidation.
2 *he felt a great compulsion to tell her the truth:* **urge**, impulse, need, desire, drive; temptation.

compulsive adjective

1 *a compulsive desire:* **irresistible**, uncontrollable, compelling, overwhelming, urgent; obsessive.
2 *a compulsive liar | a compulsive gambler:* **inveterate**, chronic, incorrigible, incurable, hardened, hopeless, persistent; obsessive, addicted, habitual; informal pathological.
3 *the film is compulsive viewing:* **fascinating**, compelling, gripping, riveting, engrossing, enthralling, captivating.

compulsory adjective *the legislation made the wearing of seat belts compulsory | compulsory military service:* **obligatory**, mandatory, required, requisite, necessary, essential; imperative, unavoidable, enforced, demanded, prescribed.
OPPOSITES: optional.

compunction noun *she had no compunction about deceiving them:* **scruples**, misgivings, qualms, worries, unease, uneasiness, doubts, reservations; guilt, regret, contrition, self-reproach.

compute verb *the hire charge is computed on a daily basis:* **calculate**, work out, reckon, determine, quantify; add up, count up, tally, total; Brit. tot up.

comrade noun **companion**, friend; colleague, associate, partner, co-worker, workmate.

concatenation noun *a concatenation of events which had finally led to the murder:* **series**, sequence, succession, chain.

concave adjective **inward-curving**, hollow, depressed, sunken; indented, recessed.
OPPOSITES: convex.

conceal verb

1 *clouds concealed the sun:* **hide**, screen, cover, obscure, block out, blot out, mask, shroud, cloak, camouflage; secrete.
2 *he concealed his true feelings:* **hide**, cover up, disguise, mask, veil; keep secret, keep dark, draw a veil over; suppress, repress, bottle up; informal keep a/the lid on, keep under your hat.
OPPOSITES: reveal.

concealed adjective **hidden**, not visible, out of sight, invisible, covered, disguised, camouflaged, obscured; private, secret.

concealment noun

1 *he darted forwards from the concealment of the bushes:* **cover**, shelter, protection, screen; privacy, seclusion; secrecy.
2 *the deliberate concealment of facts:* **suppression**, hiding, cover-up; whitewash.

concede verb

1 *I had to concede that I'd overreacted:* **admit**, acknowledge, accept, allow, grant, recognize, own, confess; agree.
2 *he conceded the Auvergne to the king:* **surrender**, yield, give up, relinquish, cede, hand over.
OPPOSITES: deny.
□ **concede defeat**
capitulate, give in, surrender, yield, give up, submit, raise the white flag; back down, climb down, throw in the towel.

conceit noun

1 *Polly's eyes widened at his extraordinary conceit:* **vanity**, pride, arrogance, boastfulness, self-importance; narcissism, conceitedness, egotism, self-admiration, self-regard; self-satisfaction, smugness; informal big-headedness.
2 *the conceits of Shakespeare's verse:* **image**, imagery, metaphor, simile, trope.
OPPOSITES: modesty.

conceited adjective *he's so conceited he'd never believe anyone would turn him down:* **vain**, proud, arrogant, boastful, immodest, full of yourself, self-important, narcissistic, self-centred, egotistic, egotistical, egocentric; self-satisfied, smug; informal big-headed, too big for your boots,

swollen-headed, stuck-up.
OPPOSITES: modest.

conceivable adjective *the body was photographed from every conceivable angle | there is no conceivable reason for an attack:* imaginable, possible; plausible, feasible, tenable, credible, believable, thinkable.

conceive verb
1 *she was unable to conceive:* become pregnant.
2 *he conceived the idea for the project in 1977:* think up, think of, dream up, devise, formulate, design, originate, create, develop; hatch.
3 *I could hardly conceive what his life must be like:* imagine, envisage, visualize, picture, think, envision; grasp, appreciate; formal apprehend.

concentrate verb
1 *she was concentrating on the film:* focus on, pay attention to, keep your mind on, devote yourself to, apply yourself to; be absorbed in, be engrossed in, be immersed in.
2 *I'm going to concentrate my efforts on my career:* focus, direct, centre, centralize.
3 *troops were concentrating at the western front:* collect, gather, congregate, converge, mass, rally.
4 *the liquid is filtered and concentrated:* condense, boil down, reduce, thicken.
OPPOSITES: disperse, dilute.
▷**noun** *a fruit concentrate:* extract; decoction, distillation.

concentrated adjective
1 *a concentrated effort:* strenuous, vigorous, concerted, intensive, intense; informal all-out.
2 *a concentrated solution:* condensed, reduced, evaporated, thickened; undiluted, strong.
OPPOSITES: half-hearted, diluted.

concentration noun
1 *this is a work that requires concentration in order to be appreciated:* close attention, attentiveness, application, single-mindedness, absorption.
2 *the island is famous for its concentrations of barnacle geese:* gathering, cluster, mass, flock, congregation, assemblage.

concept noun *structuralism is a difficult concept | the concept of justice:* idea, notion, conception, abstraction; theory, hypothesis.

conception noun
1 *the product's conception:* inception, genesis, origination, creation, invention; beginning, origin.
2 *the original conception involved a shopping complex run by local people:* plan, scheme, project, proposal; intention, aim, idea.
3 *my conception of democracy:* idea,

concept, notion, understanding; theory, hypothesis; perception, image, impression.
4 *they had no real conception of our problems:* understanding, comprehension, appreciation, grasp, knowledge; idea, inkling; informal clue.

concern verb
1 *the book is primarily concerned with the eighteenth century:* be about, deal with, cover; discuss, go into, examine, study, review, analyse; relate to, pertain to.
2 *that doesn't concern you:* affect, involve, be relevant to, apply to, have a bearing on; be important to, interest.
3 *I won't concern myself with your affairs:* involve yourself in, take an interest in, busy yourself with, devote your time to, bother yourself with.
4 *one thing still concerns me:* worry, disturb, trouble, bother, perturb, unsettle, make anxious.
▷**noun**
1 *her voice was full of concern:* anxiety, worry, disquiet, apprehensiveness, unease, consternation.
2 *his concern for others:* solicitude, solicitousness, consideration, care, sympathy, regard, thought.
3 *housing is the concern of the council:* responsibility, business, affair, charge, duty, job; province, preserve; problem, worry.
4 *issues that are of concern to women:* interest, importance, relevance, significance.
5 *a publishing concern:* company, business, firm, organization, operation, corporation, establishment, house, office, agency; informal outfit, set-up.
OPPOSITES: indifference.

concerned adjective
1 *her mother looked concerned:* worried, anxious, upset, perturbed, troubled, distressed, uneasy, apprehensive, agitated.
2 *they are working closely with all the concerned parties:* interested, involved, affected; connected, related.

concerning preposition *there were further revelations concerning his role in the affair:* about, regarding, relating to, with reference to, referring to, with regard to, as regards, with respect to, respecting, dealing with, on the subject of, in connection with, re, apropos of.

concert noun musical performance, show, production, presentation; recital; informal gig.
□ **in concert**
together, jointly, in combination, in collaboration, in cooperation, in league, side by side; in unison.

concerted adjective
1 *you must make a concerted effort to curb this:* strenuous, vigorous, intensive, intense, concentrated; informal all-out.

2 *there were calls for concerted action:* joint, united, collaborative, collective, combined, cooperative.
OPPOSITES: half-hearted.

concession noun
1 *the government made several concessions:* compromise, allowance.
2 *tax concessions:* reduction, cut, discount, deduction, decrease; rebate; informal break.
3 *a logging concession:* right, privilege; licence, permit, franchise, warrant, authorization.

conciliate verb
1 *he tried to conciliate the peasantry:* appease, placate, pacify, mollify, soothe, humour, reconcile, win over, make peace with, assuage.
2 *he conciliated in the dispute:* mediate, act as peacemaker, arbitrate.
OPPOSITES: provoke.

conciliation noun *he held his hands up in a gesture of conciliation:* appeasement, pacification, peacemaking, placation, propitiation, mollification, reconciliation.
OPPOSITES: provocation.

conciliator noun peacemaker, mediator, go-between, middleman, intermediary, intercessor; dove.
OPPOSITES: troublemaker.

conciliatory adjective *a conciliatory gesture:* placatory, propitiatory, appeasing, pacifying, pacific, peacemaking.

concise adjective *a concise account of his career:* succinct, incisive, brief, pithy, short and to the point, short and sweet; abridged, condensed, compressed, abbreviated, compact, potted.
OPPOSITES: lengthy, wordy.

conclave noun *a conclave of American, European, and Japanese business leaders:* meeting, gathering, assembly, conference, council, summit.

conclude verb
1 *the meeting concluded at ten:* finish, end, draw to a close, be over, stop, cease.
2 *he concluded the press conference:* bring to an end, close, wind up, terminate, dissolve; round off; informal wrap up.
3 *the two countries have concluded a free trade agreement:* negotiate, broker, agree, come to terms on, settle, clinch, finalize, tie up; bring about, arrange, effect, engineer; informal sew up.
4 *I concluded that she was making the whole thing up:* deduce, infer, gather, judge, decide, conjecture, surmise.
OPPOSITES: commence.

conclusion noun
1 *the conclusion of his speech:* end, ending, finish, close, termination, cessation; culmination, denouement, coda.
2 *the conclusion of a trade agreement:* negotiation, brokering, settlement,

completion, arrangement, resolution.
3 *his conclusions have been verified:* deduction, inference, interpretation, reasoning; opinion, judgement, verdict; assumption, presumption, supposition.
OPPOSITES: beginning.
□ **in conclusion**
finally, in closing, to conclude; to sum up, in short.

conclusive adjective
1 *conclusive proof:* incontrovertible, undeniable, indisputable, irrefutable, unquestionable, unassailable, convincing, certain, decisive, definitive, definite, positive, categorical, unequivocal; airtight, watertight.
2 *a conclusive win:* emphatic, resounding, convincing.
OPPOSITES: inconclusive, unconvincing.

concoct verb
1 *she began to concoct a meal likely to appeal to him:* prepare, make, assemble; informal fix, rustle up; Brit. informal knock up.
2 *his cronies concocted a plan:* devise, create, dream up, make; formulate, hatch; informal cook up.

concoction noun
1 *a concoction containing gin and vodka:* mixture, brew, preparation, potion.
2 *a strange concoction of styles:* blend, mixture, mix, combination, hybrid.

concourse noun *the station concourse:* entrance, foyer, lobby, hall.

concrete adjective
1 *concrete objects:* solid, material, real, physical, tangible, palpable, substantial, visible, existing.
2 *I haven't got any concrete proof:* definite, firm, positive, conclusive, definitive; real, genuine, actual, solid.
OPPOSITES: abstract, imaginary.

concur verb
1 *we concur with this view:* agree, be in agreement, go along, be in sympathy; see eye to eye, be of the same mind, be of the same opinion.
2 *the two events concurred:* coincide, be simultaneous, be concurrent, coexist.
OPPOSITES: disagree.

concurrent adjective
1 *he was given nine concurrent life sentences:* simultaneous, coincident, contemporaneous, parallel.
2 *concurrent lines:* convergent, converging, meeting, intersecting.

condemn verb
1 *the club has repeatedly condemned bad behaviour by fans:* censure, criticize, deplore, denounce, revile; formal castigate.
2 *he was condemned to death:* sentence; convict, find guilty.
3 *his illness condemned him to a lonely childhood:* doom, destine, damn; consign.

4 *the house has been condemned:* declare unfit, declare unsafe.
OPPOSITES: praise.

condemnation noun *his comment provoked widespread condemnation:* censure, criticism, strictures, denunciation, vilification; formal castigation.

condemnatory adjective censorious, critical, damning.

condensation noun
1 *windows misty with condensation:* moisture, water droplets, steam.
2 *a readable condensation of the recent literature:* abridgement, summary, synopsis, precis, digest.

condense verb
1 *the moisture vapour in the air condenses into droplets of water:* precipitate, liquefy; technical deliquesce.
2 *he tried to condense the story into a few paragraphs:* abridge, shorten, cut, abbreviate; summarize, synopsize, precis.
OPPOSITES: vaporize, expand.

condensed adjective
1 *a condensed text:* abridged, shortened, cut, compressed, abbreviated, reduced, concise; thumbnail; informal potted.
2 *condensed milk:* concentrated, evaporated, reduced.

condescend verb
1 *take care not to condescend to your reader:* patronize, talk down to, look down your nose at, look down on, put down.
2 *he condescended to see me at his hotel:* deign, stoop, descend, lower yourself, demean yourself; vouchsafe, see fit, consent.

condescending adjective *she looked us up and down in a condescending manner:* patronizing, supercilious, superior, snobbish, disdainful, lofty, haughty; informal snooty, stuck-up; Brit. informal toffee-nosed.

condition noun
1 *always check the condition of the room upon arrival | the car is in very good condition:* state, shape, order; Brit. informal nick.
2 *they lived in appalling conditions:* circumstances, surroundings, environment, situation, set-up, setting; habitat.
3 *she was in tip-top condition:* state of health, form, shape, trim, fettle.
4 *a heart condition:* disorder, problem, complaint, illness, disease, sickness, infection, ailment, affliction.
5 *it is a condition of employment that employees should be paid through a bank:* stipulation, requirement, rule, term, specification, constraint; proviso, prerequisite, precondition, provision.
▷verb
1 *their choices are conditioned by the economy:* constrain, control, govern, determine, decide; affect, touch; form, shape, guide.
2 *our minds are conditioned by habit:* train, teach; accustom, adapt, habituate.
3 *a product to condition your skin:* improve, nourish, tone, moisturize.

conditional adjective
1 *further aid was conditional on reform:* subject to, dependent on, contingent on, based on, determined by, controlled by, tied to.
2 *the consortium have made a conditional offer:* provisional, provisory.

condolences plural noun *we offer our sincere condolences to his widow:* sympathy, commiseration; compassion.

condone verb *we cannot condone such behaviour:* accept, tolerate, allow, disregard, let pass, turn a blind eye to, overlook, ignore; forgive, pardon, excuse, let go.
OPPOSITES: condemn.

conducive adjective *an environment which is conducive to effective learning:* favourable, beneficial, advantageous, encouraging, promising, convenient, good, helpful, instrumental, productive, useful.
OPPOSITES: unfavourable.

conduct noun
1 *they complained about her conduct:* behaviour, actions, activities, deeds, exploits; habits, manners, demeanour.
2 *the conduct of the elections:* management, organization, running, direction, control, supervision, regulation, administration, coordination, orchestration, handling.
▷verb
1 *the election was conducted lawfully:* manage, direct, run, administer, organize, coordinate, orchestrate, handle, control, oversee, supervise, regulate, carry out.
2 *he was conducted through the corridors:* escort, guide, lead, usher, show; shepherd, see, bring, take, help.
3 *aluminium conducts heat:* transmit, convey, carry, transfer, channel, relay; diffuse, radiate.
□ conduct yourself
behave, act, acquit yourself.

conduit noun channel, duct, pipe, tube, gutter, trench, culvert, sluice.

confederacy noun *the Empire was a loosely organized confederacy of allies:* federation, confederation, alliance, league, association, coalition, consortium, syndicate, group, circle; bloc, axis.

confederate adjective *confederate councils:* federal, confederated, federated, allied, associated, united.
OPPOSITES: split.
▷noun *he met his confederate in the street:* associate, partner, accomplice, helper,

assistant, ally, collaborator.

confederation noun *a confederation of trade unions:* alliance, league, federation, association, confederacy, coalition, consortium, conglomerate, cooperative, syndicate, group, circle; society, union.

confer verb
1 *she conferred a knighthood on him:* bestow on; award, grant, give, accord; present with, decorate with, honour with, invest with.
2 *she went to confer with her colleagues:* consult, talk, speak, converse, have a chat, have a tête-à-tête.

conference noun
1 *an international conference:* congress, meeting, convention, colloquium, symposium, forum, summit.
2 *he gathered them round the table for a conference:* discussion, consultation, debate, talk.

confess verb
1 *he confessed that he had been having an affair:* admit, acknowledge, reveal, disclose, divulge; own up.
2 *they could not make him confess:* own up, admit your guilt, tell the truth, make a clean breast of it; informal come clean, get something off your chest.
3 *I must confess I believed you:* acknowledge, admit, concede, grant.
OPPOSITES: deny.

confession noun admission, acknowledgement; revelation, disclosure.

confidant, confidante noun *a close confidante of the princess:* close friend, bosom friend, intimate; mentor; informal, derogatory crony.

confide verb
1 *he confided his fears to his mother:* reveal, tell, disclose, divulge, lay bare, uncover; confess, admit.
2 *we were very close—he always confided in me:* open your heart to, unburden yourself to, confess to, tell all to.

confidence noun
1 *I have little confidence in these figures:* trust, belief, faith, reliance; credence.
2 *I can say with confidence that I have never been here before:* certainty, conviction, assurance.
3 *he's gained confidence and begun to stand up for himself a bit more:* self-assurance, self-confidence, belief in yourself, self-possession, assertiveness; poise, aplomb; courage, nerve.
4 *the girls exchanged confidences:* secret, private matter.
OPPOSITES: scepticism, doubt.

confident adjective
1 *a confident girl:* self-assured, assured, self-confident, positive, assertive, self-possessed, poised; fearless, unafraid.
2 *we are confident that business will improve:* optimistic, hopeful, sanguine; sure, certain, positive, convinced, in no doubt, satisfied, assured, persuaded.
OPPOSITES: diffident, insecure.

confidential adjective
1 *this information is confidential:* secret, classified, restricted; informal hush-hush.
2 *can we have a confidential chat?* private, quiet, unofficial, off the record.

confidentially adverb privately, in private, in confidence, between ourselves, off the record, quietly, secretly, in secret, behind closed doors; formal sub rosa.

configuration noun *the configuration of the stars at the moment of your birth:* arrangement, layout, geography, design, organization, order, grouping, positioning, disposition, alignment; shape, form, appearance, formation, structure, format.

confine verb
1 *they were confined in the house:* shut in/up, keep, lock in/up, coop up, trap; enclose, incarcerate, imprison, hold captive.
2 *he confined his remarks to the weather:* restrict, limit, keep.

confined adjective *the confined space of an aircraft cabin:* cramped, restricted, limited, small, narrow, tight, poky, uncomfortable.
OPPOSITES: roomy.

confinement noun *a long period of confinement:* imprisonment, incarceration, captivity, detention, custody.

confines plural noun *he became involved in artistic pursuits that took him beyond the confines of the Lower East Side:* limits, borders, boundaries, margins, edges, fringes; periphery, perimeter.

confirm verb
1 *records confirm the latest evidence:* corroborate, verify, prove, validate, authenticate, substantiate, justify, vindicate; support, uphold, back up, bear out, give credence to.
2 *he confirmed that help was on the way:* assure someone, give an assurance, affirm, reaffirm, repeat; promise, guarantee.
3 *his appointment was confirmed by the President:* ratify, validate, sanction, endorse, formalize, authorize, approve.
OPPOSITES: contradict, deny.

confirmation noun
1 *there was no independent confirmation of the reported deaths:* corroboration, verification, proof, substantiation, evidence, testimony.
2 *confirmation of your appointment is dependent upon satisfactory performance:* ratification, approval, authorization, validation, endorsement, formalization, acceptance.

confirmed adjective *he's a confirmed Marxist:* established, long-standing, committed, dyed-in-the-wool, through and through; staunch, loyal, faithful, devoted, steadfast; unapologetic, unashamed, inveterate, chronic, incurable; habitual, compulsive, persistent.

confiscate verb *the guards confiscated his camera:* take, take away, take possession of, seize, impound, commandeer, requisition, appropriate, expropriate, sequester, sequestrate.

confiscation noun seizure, requisition, appropriation, expropriation, sequestration.

conflict noun
1 *industrial conflicts:* dispute, quarrel, argument, disagreement, disputation, clash; discord, dissension, friction, strife, antagonism, hostility, contention, schism; feud.
2 *the Vietnam conflict:* war, campaign, battle, fighting, armed confrontation, engagement, struggle, hostilities; warfare, combat.
3 *a conflict between his business and domestic life:* clash, incompatibility, friction; mismatch, variance, difference, divergence, contradiction, inconsistency.
OPPOSITES: agreement, peace, harmony.
▷ verb *their interests sometimes conflict:* clash, be incompatible, vary, be at odds, be in conflict, differ, diverge, disagree, contrast, collide.

conflicting adjective *there are conflicting accounts of what occurred:* contradictory, incompatible, inconsistent, irreconcilable, contrary, opposite, opposing, antithetical, clashing, discordant, divergent; at odds.

confluence noun *the confluence of the Rhine and the Mosel:* convergence, meeting, junction.

conform verb
1 *visitors have to conform to our rules:* comply with, abide by, obey, observe, follow, keep to, stick to, adhere to, uphold, accept, go along with, fall in with, respect, defer to, heed; satisfy, meet, fulfil.
2 *they refuse to conform:* follow convention, be conventional, fit in, adapt, adjust, follow the crowd; comply, acquiesce, toe the line, follow the rules; submit, yield; informal play it by the book, play by the rules.
3 *goods must conform to their description:* match, fit, suit, answer, agree with, be like, correspond to, be consistent with, measure up to, tally with, square with.
OPPOSITES: flout, rebel.

confound verb
1 *the inflation figure confounded economic analysts:* amaze, astonish, dumbfound, take aback, surprise, startle, stun, stagger; throw, shake, bewilder, baffle, mystify, bemuse, perplex, puzzle, disconcert, confuse.

2 *these data have confounded his theory:* contradict, go against, disprove, prove wrong, invalidate, negate, drive a coach and horses through.

confront verb
1 *Jones confronted the thief | he was confronted by two men who held a knife to his throat:* challenge, face up to, come face to face with, square up to, meet; stand up to, take on, brave, tackle; accost, waylay.
2 *the economic problems confronting the government could hardly have been worse:* face, beset; burden, plague, blight, curse.
3 *the education authorities must confront the issue:* tackle, address, face, get to grips with, grapple with, take on, attend to, see to, deal with, take care of.
4 *she confronted him with the evidence:* present with; make someone face, make someone deal with.
OPPOSITES: avoid.

confrontation noun *a peaceful protest turned into a violent confrontation | many people refuse to discuss politics to avoid unnecessary confrontation:* conflict, clash, fight, head-to-head, face-off, skirmish, disagreement, dispute; antagonism, friction, strife, hostilities; informal set-to, run-in, showdown.

confuse verb
1 *his answer confused her:* bewilder, baffle, mystify, bemuse, perplex, puzzle, confound, nonplus; informal flummox, faze, stump.
2 *the points made by the authors confuse rather than clarify the issue:* complicate, muddle, blur, obscure, cloud, obfuscate.
3 *a lot of people confuse a stroke with a heart attack:* mix up, muddle up; mistake for.
OPPOSITES: enlighten, simplify.

confused adjective
1 *she was utterly confused about what had happened:* bewildered, bemused, puzzled, perplexed, baffled, mystified, nonplussed, dumbfounded, muddled, at sea, at a loss, taken aback, disoriented, disconcerted; informal flummoxed, bamboozled, fazed.
2 *a confused recollection:* unclear, muddled, indistinct, imprecise, hazy, shadowy, dim; imperfect, sketchy.
3 *a confused mass of papers lay on the desk:* disorderly, disordered, disorganized, disarranged, untidy, muddled, jumbled, mixed up, chaotic, topsy-turvy; informal higgledy-piggledy.
OPPOSITES: clear, precise, neat.

confusing adjective *the instructions are confusing:* bewildering, baffling, unclear, perplexing, puzzling, mystifying; ambiguous, misleading, inconsistent, contradictory; complex, complicated.

confusion noun
1 *there seems to be some confusion about which system does what:* uncertainty,

incertitude, doubt; misunderstanding, ignorance; formal dubiety.

2 *she stared about her in confusion:* bewilderment, bafflement, perplexity, puzzlement, mystification, befuddlement; shock, wonder, wonderment, astonishment; informal bamboozlement.

3 *the room was in a state of confusion:* disorder, disarray, disorganization, chaos, mayhem; turmoil, disruption, upheaval, uproar, muddle, mess; informal shambles.

4 *a confusion of boxes:* jumble, muddle, mess, heap, tangle.

congeal verb *the blood had congealed around the cut:* clot, coagulate, thicken, solidify, set, cake, curdle; technical inspissate.

congenial adjective
1 *I was working with a bunch of very congenial people:* like-minded, compatible; companionable, sociable, convivial, hospitable, genial, personable, agreeable, friendly, pleasant, likeable, amiable, nice.
2 *a congenial environment:* pleasant, pleasing, agreeable, enjoyable, appealing, satisfying, gratifying; suitable, favourable, well suited.
OPPOSITES: unpleasant, uncongenial.

congenital adjective
1 *a congenital defect:* inborn.
2 *a congenital liar:* inveterate, compulsive, persistent, chronic, regular, habitual, obsessive, confirmed; incurable, incorrigible, irredeemable, hopeless; unashamed, shameless; informal pathological.

congested adjective *the congested streets of the West End:* crowded, overcrowded, full, overflowing, packed, jammed, thronged, teeming, swarming; obstructed, blocked, clogged, choked; informal snarled up, gridlocked, jam-packed.
OPPOSITES: clear.

congestion noun overcrowding; obstruction, blockage; traffic jam, bottleneck; informal gridlock; Brit. informal snarl-up.

conglomerate noun
1 *the media conglomerate was broken up:* corporation, group, consortium, partnership, combine; firm, company, business, multinational.
2 *a conglomerate of disparate peoples:* mixture, mix, combination, composite; miscellany, hotchpotch.
▷ verb *the debris conglomerated into planets:* coalesce, unite, join, combine, merge, fuse, amalgamate.

congratulate verb
1 *she congratulated him on his marriage:* send your best wishes to, wish someone good luck, wish someone joy; drink someone's health, toast.
2 *they are to be congratulated:* praise, commend, applaud, salute, honour; pay

tribute to, pat on the back, take your hat off to.
OPPOSITES: criticize.
□ congratulate yourself
he congratulated himself on his performance: take pride, feel proud, flatter yourself, preen yourself, pat yourself on the back; feel satisfaction, take pleasure, glory, delight.

congratulations plural noun
1 *my mother sends her congratulations:* good wishes, best wishes, compliments formal felicitations.
2 *you all deserve congratulations:* praise, commendation, compliments, applause; a pat on the back.

congregate verb *some 4000 demonstrators had congregated at a border point:* assemble, gather, collect, come together, convene, rally, rendezvous, muster, meet, cluster, group.
OPPOSITES: disperse.

congregation noun
1 *the chapel congregation:* parishioners, parish, churchgoers, flock, faithful, brethren.
2 *large congregations of birds:* gathering, assembly, flock, swarm, pack, group, body, crowd, mass, multitude, horde, host, mob, throng.

congress noun
1 *an international congress on applied psychology:* conference, convention, symposium, forum, meeting, seminar, colloquium; assembly, gathering, rally, summit.
2 *elections for the new Congress:* legislature, legislative assembly; parliament.

congruence noun *he took care that there should be congruence of meaning and sound in his music:* compatibility, consistency, balance, congruity; agreement, accord, harmony, unity.
OPPOSITES: conflict.

conjectural adjective *the evidence was deemed too conjectural:* speculative, theoretical, hypothetical.

conjecture noun *conjectures about the newcomer were many and varied | his conjecture had proved to be true:* speculation, supposition, theory, surmise, assumption, postulation; inference, extrapolation; guesswork.
OPPOSITES: fact.
▷ verb *many people conjectured that she had a second husband in mind:* guess, speculate, surmise, infer, imagine, believe, think, suspect, presume, assume, hypothesize, suppose.

conjunction noun *a conjunction of favourable political and economic circumstances:* co-occurrence, concurrence, coincidence; coexistence, simultaneity, synchronicity.

conjure verb
1 *he appeared to conjure a cigarette out of the air:* produce, make something appear, magic.
2 *a special tune that conjures up a particular time and place:* bring to mind, call to mind, evoke, summon up, recall.

conjuror noun magician, illusionist; formal prestidigitator.

connect verb
1 *electrodes were connected to the device:* attach, join, fasten, fix, affix, couple, link, secure, hitch; stick, adhere, fuse; pin, screw, bolt, clamp, clip, hook up; add, append.
2 *he claimed that the majority of gun crime is connected to illegal drugs:* link, relate, tie; associate with, correlate with.
OPPOSITES: disconnect.

connection noun
1 *the connection between commerce and art:* link, relationship, relation, interconnection, interdependence, association, correlation; bond, tie, tie-in, correspondence, parallel, analogy.
2 *a poor connection in the plug:* attachment, fastening, coupling.
3 *he has the right connections:* contact, friend, acquaintance, colleague, associate; relation, relative.
□ **in connection with**
regarding, concerning, with reference to, with regard to, with respect to, respecting, relating to, in relation to, on, connected with, on the subject of, in the matter of, apropos, re.

connivance noun *this infringement of the law had taken place with the connivance of officials:* collusion, complicity, collaboration, involvement, assistance; tacit consent, conspiracy, intrigue.

connive verb
1 *wardens connived at offences:* deliberately ignore, overlook, disregard, pass over, take no notice of, make allowances for, turn a blind eye to, wink at, excuse, condone, let go; look the other way, let something ride.
2 *the government connived with security forces:* conspire, collude, collaborate, intrigue, be hand in glove, plot, scheme; informal be in cahoots.

conniving adjective scheming, calculating, devious, sly; manipulative, Machiavellian, cunning, crafty; deceitful, underhand, treacherous.

connoisseur noun *a connoisseur of fine wines:* expert, authority, good judge, specialist, pundit, arbiter of taste; gourmet, gastronome, epicure; informal buff.

connotation noun *the word 'discipline' has unhappy connotations of punishment and repression:* overtone, undertone, undercurrent, implication, nuance, hint, echo, resonance, association, intimation, suggestion.

connote verb *the word 'steel' connotes strength and permanence:* imply, suggest, indicate, signify, hint at, give the impression of, be associated with.

USAGE

Do not confuse **connote** with **denote**. **Denote** refers to the literal, main meaning of something, while **connote** refers to other characteristics suggested or implied by that thing. For example, the word **mother** *denotes* 'a woman who is a parent' but could be said to *connote* qualities such as protectiveness and affection.

conquer verb
1 *the Franks conquered the Visigoths:* defeat, beat, vanquish, triumph over, be victorious over, trounce, get the better of, worst; overcome, overwhelm, overpower, overthrow, subdue, subjugate, quell, quash, crush, rout.
2 *Peru was conquered by Spain:* seize, take, appropriate, subjugate, capture, occupy, invade, annex, overrun.
3 *the first men to conquer Mount Everest:* climb, ascend, mount, scale, top, crest.
4 *the only way to conquer fear is to face it:* overcome, get the better of, control, master, get a grip on, deal with, cope with, surmount, rise above, get over; quell, quash, beat, triumph over; informal lick.

conqueror noun victor, winner, champion, conquering hero.

conquest noun
1 *the conquest of the Aztecs:* defeat, overthrow, subjugation, subjection; victory over, triumph over.
2 *their conquest of the valley:* seizure, capture, occupation, invasion, annexation, acquisition, appropriation, takeover.
3 *the conquest of Everest:* ascent.
OPPOSITES: surrender.

conscience noun *her conscience wouldn't allow her to keep silent any longer:* sense of right and wrong, moral sense, inner voice; morals, standards, values, principles, ethics, beliefs; compunction, scruples, qualms.

conscience-stricken adjective *she was still conscience-stricken over her outburst:* guilt-ridden, remorseful, ashamed, shamefaced, apologetic, sorry, contrite, guilty, regretful, rueful, repentant, penitent, self-reproachful, abashed, sheepish.
OPPOSITES: unrepentant.

conscientious adjective *a conscientious man, he took his duties very seriously:* diligent, hard-working, industrious, meticulous, punctilious, painstaking, sedulous, assiduous, dedicated, careful, thorough, attentive.

conscious adjective
1 *the patient was still conscious:* aware, awake, alert, responsive, sentient.
2 *we are conscious of the extent of the problem:* aware of, alive to, alert to, mindful of; formal cognizant of.
3 *it was a conscious attempt to conceal the truth:* deliberate, intentional, intended, purposeful, knowing, considered, planned; calculated, wilful, premeditated.
OPPOSITES: unconscious, unintentional.

conscript verb *they were conscripted into the army:* call up, enlist, recruit; US draft.
▷ **noun** *an army conscript:* recruit; US draftee.
OPPOSITES: volunteer.

consecrate verb *the present Holy Trinity Church was consecrated in 1845:* sanctify, bless, make holy, make sacred; dedicate to God.

consecutive adjective *share prices fell for three consecutive days | they're aiming for their fifth consecutive win this summer:* successive, succeeding, in succession, running, in a row, one after the other, back-to-back, continuous, straight, uninterrupted; informal on the trot.

consensus noun
1 *there seems to be a consensus among professionals from widely different backgrounds:* agreement, unanimity; harmony, unity.
2 *the consensus was that they should act:* general opinion, majority opinion, common view.
OPPOSITES: disagreement.

consent noun *a change in the rules requires the consent of all members:* agreement, assent, acceptance, approval; permission, authorization, sanction, leave; backing, endorsement, support; informal go-ahead.
▷ **verb** *she consented to surgery:* agree to, allow, permit, give permission for, sanction, accept, approve, go along with, assent; yield, give in, submit.
OPPOSITES: refuse, decline.

consequence noun
1 *inflation is a consequence of a rapid growth in the money supply:* result, effect, upshot, outcome, repercussion, ramification, corollary, aftermath; fruits, product, by-product, end result; formal concomitant.
2 *the past is of no consequence:* importance, significance, account, import, substance, note, value, concern, interest.
OPPOSITES: cause.

consequent adjective *if accurate measurements are not taken, there will be consequent errors in construction:* resulting, resultant, ensuing, consequential, subsequent; attendant,

accompanying; collateral, associated, related; formal concomitant.

consequential adjective
1 *a fire and the consequential smoke damage:* resulting, resultant, ensuing, consequent; subsequent; attendant, accompanying; collateral, associated, related; formal concomitant.
2 *one of his more consequential initiatives:* important, significant, of importance.

consequently adverb *many of the subjects available are not taught in school, and consequently may be unfamiliar:* as a result, as a consequence, so, therefore, accordingly, hence, for this/that reason, because of this/that, on this/that account; inevitably, necessarily; formal thus.

conservation noun *the conservation of tropical forests:* preservation, protection, safeguarding, safe keeping; care, guardianship; upkeep, maintenance, repair, restoration; ecology, environmentalism.

conservative adjective
1 *they were very conservative in their outlook:* traditionalist, traditional, conventional, orthodox; moderate, middle-of-the-road; old-fashioned, dyed-in-the-wool, hidebound, unadventurous, set in your ways.
2 *the conservative wing of the party:* right-wing, right-of-centre, traditionalist; reactionary; Brit. Tory.
3 *a conservative suit:* conventional, sober, modest, plain, unobtrusive, restrained, subtle, low-key, understated, demure; informal square.
4 *a conservative estimate:* low, cautious, moderate.
OPPOSITES: socialist, radical, ostentatious.
▷ **noun** *liberals and conservatives have found common ground:* right-winger, traditionalist; reactionary, diehard; Brit. Tory.

conserve verb
1 *the funds raised will help conserve endangered meadowlands:* preserve, protect, save, safeguard, keep, look after; sustain, prolong, perpetuate.
2 *we need to conserve diminishing fossil fuels:* use sparingly, use economically, be economical with, husband.
OPPOSITES: squander.
▷ **noun** *cherry conserve:* jam, preserve, marmalade.

consider verb
1 *Isabel considered her choices:* think about, contemplate, reflect on, examine, review; mull over, ponder, deliberate on, chew over, meditate on, ruminate on; assess, evaluate, weigh up, appraise; informal size up.
2 *I consider him irresponsible | I've always considered her one of my best friends:* regard as, hold to be, believe to be, deem, think, judge to be; count, view as, see as.

3 *one service area is not enough when you consider the number of cars using this motorway:* take into consideration, take account of, allow for, bear in mind, be mindful of, remember.
4 *he considered the ceiling:* look at, contemplate, observe, regard, survey, view, scrutinize, scan, examine, inspect; informal check out.

considerable adjective
1 *he escaped with a considerable amount of money:* sizeable, substantial, appreciable, significant; hefty, handsome, decent, worthwhile; ample, plentiful, abundant, great, large, generous, goodly; informal tidy.
2 *he turned professional and met with considerable success:* much, great, a lot of, a great deal of, plenty of, a fair amount of; informal lots of.
3 *a considerable cricketer:* distinguished, noteworthy, important, significant, prominent, eminent, influential, illustrious; renowned, celebrated, acclaimed.
OPPOSITES: negligible, minor.

considerably adverb *alcoholic drinks vary considerably in strength:* greatly, very much, a great deal; significantly, substantially, appreciably, markedly, noticeably; informal a lot.

considerate adjective *she was unfailingly kind and considerate:* attentive, thoughtful, solicitous; obliging, accommodating, helpful, cooperative, patient; kind, unselfish, compassionate, sympathetic, caring, charitable, altruistic, generous; polite, sensitive, tactful.
OPPOSITES: inconsiderate.

consideration noun
1 *your case needs careful consideration:* thought, deliberation, reflection, contemplation; rumination, meditation; attention, examination, inspection, scrutiny, analysis.
2 *his health is the prime consideration:* factor, issue, matter, concern, detail, aspect, feature.
3 *she should show more consideration:* attentiveness, concern, care, thoughtfulness, solicitude; kindness, understanding, respect, sensitivity, tact, discretion; compassion, charity.
□ take something into consideration consider, give thought to, take into account, allow for, provide for, plan for, make provision for, accommodate; bargain for, reckon with, foresee, anticipate.

considering preposition *considering the circumstances, he was remarkably calm:* bearing in mind, taking into consideration, taking into account, keeping in mind, in view of, in the light of.

consign verb
1 *he was consigned to prison:* send, deliver, hand over, turn over, commit; sentence.
2 *I consigned her picture to the bin:* put in, deposit in; informal dump in.

consignment noun *a consignment of goods:* delivery, shipment, load, shipload, boatload, truckload, lorryload, cargo; batch.

consist verb
1 *the exhibition consists of 180 drawings:* be composed, be made up, be formed; comprise, contain, include, incorporate.
2 *he maintained that true freedom consists in the realization of one's true potential:* lie, reside, be present; be expressed by.

consistency noun
1 *the trend shows a degree of consistency:* uniformity, regularity, evenness, steadiness, stability, equilibrium; dependability, reliability.
2 *cream of pouring consistency:* thickness, density, viscosity, texture; firmness, solidity.

consistent adjective
1 *a consistent pattern of behaviour emerged | there has been consistent growth in our overall revenues:* regular, uniform, steady, stable, even, constant, unchanging, undeviating; dependable, reliable, predictable.
2 *the results are consistent with earlier research:* compatible, in accordance, in agreement, consonant, in harmony, in line, reconcilable; corresponding to, conforming to.
OPPOSITES: inconsistent, incompatible.

consolation noun *I murmured some words of consolation:* comfort, solace; sympathy, commiseration; encouragement, reassurance, support.

console[1] verb *she tried to console him:* comfort, solace; help, support, cheer up, cheer, hearten, encourage, reassure.

console[2] noun *a digital console:* control panel, instrument panel, keypad, keyboard, dashboard.

consolidate verb
1 *the company consolidated its position in the international market:* strengthen, secure, stabilize, reinforce, fortify; enhance, improve.
2 *all manufacturing activities have been consolidated in new premises:* combine, unite, integrate, bring together, amalgamate, merge, unify.

consonance noun *a constitution in consonance with the customs of the people:* agreement, accord, harmony; compatibility, congruence; formal concord.

consonant adjective
□ consonant with
these findings are consonant with recent research: in agreement with, consistent with, in accordance with, in harmony with, compatible with, in line with, in tune with.

C

consort noun *the queen and her consort:* partner, companion; spouse, husband, wife.
▷ **verb** *he had been consorting with known criminals:* associate, fraternize, keep company, mix, spend time, socialize, have dealings; informal run around, hang around, hang out.

conspicuous adjective *the male can be easily identified by the conspicuous white patch at the back of the head:* prominent, easily seen, striking, eye-catching, obvious, distinct, unmistakable, clear, visible, noticeable; informal standing out like a sore thumb, standing out a mile.

conspiracy noun *they were involved in a conspiracy to defraud the government:* plot, scheme, plan, machination, subterfuge, intrigue.

conspire verb
1 *the defendants denied conspiring to import cocaine and heroin:* plot, scheme, plan, intrigue, collude, collaborate, work hand in glove; informal be in cahoots.
2 *circumstances conspired against them:* act together, work together, combine, unite.

constancy noun
1 *she didn't think much of marriage, but she approved of constancy:* fidelity, faithfulness, loyalty, commitment, dedication, devotion; dependability, reliability, trustworthiness.
2 *the constancy of the tradition:* continuity, permanence, persistence, endurance, immutability.

constant adjective
1 *the constant background noise:* continual, continuous, persistent, sustained; ceaseless, unceasing, perpetual, incessant, never-ending, endless, unabating, non-stop, round-the-clock, unrelieved; interminable, unremitting, relentless; eternal, immutable.
2 *the disc revolves at a constant speed:* consistent, regular, steady, uniform, even, invariable, unvarying, unchanging, undeviating.
3 *a constant friend:* faithful, loyal, devoted, true, fast, firm, unswerving; steadfast, staunch, dependable, trustworthy, trusty, reliable, dedicated, committed.
OPPOSITES: fitful, variable, fickle.

constantly adverb *she was constantly in the media spotlight | it's been raining constantly since Friday evening:* always, all the time, continually, continuously; round-the-clock, night and day; endlessly, non-stop, incessantly, unceasingly, perpetually, eternally, forever; interminably, unremittingly, relentlessly; informal 24-7.
OPPOSITES: occasionally.

consternation noun *his proposals caused consternation among fellow cabinet members:* dismay, anxiety, disquiet, perturbation, distress; surprise, amazement, astonishment, alarm.
OPPOSITES: satisfaction.

constituent adjective *the constituent parts of the empire:* component.
▷ **noun**
1 *MPs must listen to their constituents:* voter, elector, member of a constituency.
2 *the essential constituents of the human diet:* component, ingredient, element; part, unit, piece, bit.

constitute verb
1 *farmers constituted 10 per cent of the population:* amount to, add up to, account for, form, make up, compose, comprise.
2 *this constitutes a breach of copyright:* be equivalent to, amount to, be.
3 *the courts were constituted in 1875:* establish, set up, create, found, inaugurate.

constitution noun
1 *the chemical constitution of the dye:* composition, make-up, structure, construction, configuration, formation, anatomy.
2 *she has the constitution of an ox:* health, physical condition.

constrain verb
1 *he felt constrained to explain:* compel, force, drive, impel, oblige.
2 *prices were constrained by state controls:* restrict, limit, curb, check, restrain, contain, rein in, hold back, hamper, hinder, impede.

constrained adjective *his constrained manner:* unnatural, awkward, self-conscious, forced, stilted, strained; controlled, restrained, reserved, guarded.
OPPOSITES: relaxed.

constraint noun
1 *many companies do not provide adequate training for their staff because of financial constraints:* restriction, limitation, restraint, control, curb, check; hindrance, impediment, obstruction, handicap.
2 *they were able to talk without constraint:* inhibition, uneasiness, embarrassment; restraint, guardedness, formality; self-consciousness, stiffness, awkwardness.

constrict verb
1 *a drug that constricts the blood vessels:* narrow, make narrower, compress, shrink, contract, squeeze.
2 *fear of crime constricts many people's lives:* restrict, impede, limit, inhibit, obstruct, interfere with.
OPPOSITES: expand, dilate.

constriction noun *the constriction in her throat:* tightness, pressure, compression; obstruction.

construct verb
1 *a new motorway was being constructed:*

build, erect, put up, set up, raise, establish, assemble, manufacture, fabricate, create, make.
2 *he constructed a faultless argument:* formulate, form, put together, create, devise, design, compose, work out; fashion, mould, shape, frame.
OPPOSITES: demolish.

construction noun
1 *the construction of a new airport:* building, erection, setting up, establishment; assembly, manufacture, fabrication, creation.
2 *the station was a spectacular construction:* structure, building; formal edifice.
3 *you could put an honest construction on their conduct:* interpretation, reading, meaning, explanation, construal; informal take.

constructive adjective *he described the talks as fruitful and constructive:* useful, helpful, productive, positive, encouraging; practical, valuable, profitable, worthwhile.

construe verb *his actions could be construed as an admission of guilt:* interpret, understand, read, see, take, take to mean, regard.

consult verb
1 *you need to consult a solicitor:* seek advice from, speak to, ask, call on, turn to, have recourse to; informal pick someone's brains.
2 *the government must consult with interested parties:* confer with, have discussions with, speak to, talk to, deliberate with.
3 *she consulted her diary:* refer to, turn to, look at.

consultant noun
1 *an engineering consultant:* adviser, expert, specialist, authority, pundit.
2 *a consultant at Guy's hospital:* senior doctor, specialist.

consultation noun
1 *the need for further consultation with industry:* discussion, dialogue, discourse, debate, negotiation, deliberation.
2 *a 30-minute consultation:* meeting, talk, discussion, interview; appointment, session.

consume verb
1 *vast amounts of food and drink were consumed:* eat, devour, ingest, swallow; drink; formal imbibe; informal put away.
2 *natural resources are being consumed at an alarming rate:* use, use up, utilize, expend; deplete, exhaust, drain.
3 *the fire consumed fifty houses:* destroy, demolish, lay waste, wipe out, annihilate, devastate, gut, ruin, wreck.
4 *Carolyn was consumed with guilt:* eat up, devour, obsess, grip, overwhelm; absorb, preoccupy.

consumer noun *the industry is not providing consumers with enough information to make informed choices:* purchaser, buyer, customer, shopper; user, end-user; client; (**consumers** or **the consumer**) the public, the market.

consuming adjective *his lifetime's consuming interest:* absorbing, compelling, compulsive, besetting, obsessive, overwhelming; intense, ardent, strong, powerful, burning, raging, fervid, profound, deep-seated.

consummate adjective *his consummate skill | a consummate politician:* supreme, superb, superlative, superior, accomplished, expert, proficient, skilful, skilled, masterly, master, first-class, talented, gifted, polished, practised.

consumption noun
1 *food unfit for human consumption:* eating, drinking, ingestion.
2 *the consumption of fossil fuels:* use, utilization, expending, depletion.

contact noun
1 *a disease transmitted through direct contact with rats:* touch, touching; proximity, exposure.
2 *foreign diplomats were asked to avoid all contact with him:* communication, correspondence; association, connection, relations, dealings.
3 *he had many contacts in Germany:* connection, acquaintance, associate, friend.
▷**verb** *anyone with information should contact the police:* get in touch with, communicate with, make contact with, approach, notify; telephone, phone, call, ring, speak to, talk to, write to; informal get hold of.

contagious adjective *a contagious disease:* infectious, communicable, catching, transmissible.

contain verb
1 *the archive contains much unpublished material:* include, incorporate, comprise, take in, involve, encompass, embrace; consist of, be made up of, be composed of.
2 *the boat contained four people:* hold, carry, accommodate, seat.
3 *he must contain his anger:* restrain, curb, rein in, suppress, repress, stifle, subdue, quell, swallow, bottle up, hold in, keep in check; control, master.

container noun receptacle, vessel, holder, repository.

contaminate verb *chemicals from a nearby industrial property had contaminated drinking water in the area:* pollute, taint, defile, poison; infect, foul, spoil, adulterate.
OPPOSITES: purify.

contemplate verb
1 *she contemplated her image in the mirror:* look at, view, regard, examine, inspect, observe, survey, study, scrutinize, scan, stare at, gaze at, eye.
2 *he contemplated his fate:* think about, ponder, reflect on, consider, mull over, muse on, deliberate over, meditate on, ruminate on, chew over, brood on/about, turn over in your mind.
3 *he was contemplating action for damages:* consider, think about, have in mind, intend, plan, propose; envisage, foresee.

contemplation noun
1 *the road is too busy for leisurely contemplation of the scenery:* viewing, inspection, observation, survey, study, scrutiny, examination.
2 *the monks sat in quiet contemplation:* thought, reflection, meditation, consideration, rumination, deliberation, reverie, introspection.

contemplative adjective *a peaceful, contemplative mood:* thoughtful, pensive, reflective, meditative, ruminative, introspective, brooding, deep/lost in thought, in a brown study.

contemporary adjective
1 *contemporary accounts of life in Elizabethan England:* of the time, of the day, contemporaneous.
2 *these paintings are contemporary with other works in an early style:* contemporaneous, concurrent, coeval, coexistent.
3 *contemporary society:* modern, present-day, present, current.
4 *a very contemporary design:* modern, up to date, up to the minute, fashionable; modish, latest, recent; informal trendy, funky.
OPPOSITES: old-fashioned, out of date.
▷ noun *Chaucer's contemporaries:* peer, fellow; formal compeer.

contempt noun *she regarded him with contempt:* scorn, disdain, disrespect, scornfulness, contemptuousness, derision; dislike, disgust, loathing, hatred, abhorrence.
OPPOSITES: respect.

contemptible adjective *a display of contemptible cowardice:* despicable, reprehensible, deplorable, disgraceful, shameful, ignominious, abject, low, mean, cowardly, discreditable, shabby, cheap, beyond contempt, unspeakable.
OPPOSITES: admirable.

contemptuous adjective *he spoke in a coldly contemptuous tone:* scornful, disdainful, disrespectful, insulting, insolent, derisive, mocking, sneering, withering, scathing, snide; condescending, supercilious, haughty, proud, superior, arrogant, dismissive, aloof; informal high and mighty.
OPPOSITES: respectful.

contend verb
1 *the pilot had to contend with torrential rain:* cope with, face, grapple with, deal with, take on, pit yourself against.
2 *three main groups were contending for power:* compete, vie, contest, fight, battle, tussle, go head to head; strive, struggle.
3 *he contends that the judge was wrong:* assert, maintain, hold, claim, argue, insist, state, declare, profess; allege; formal aver.

content[1] adjective *she seemed content:* contented, satisfied, pleased, gratified, glad; fulfilled, happy, cheerful; unworried, untroubled, at ease, at peace, tranquil, serene.
OPPOSITES: discontented, dissatisfied.
▷ verb *her reply seemed to content him:* satisfy, please; soothe, pacify, placate, appease, mollify.
▷ noun *a time of content.* See **CONTENTMENT**.

content[2] noun
1 *foods with a high fibre content:* amount, proportion, quantity.
2 (**contents**) *the contents of a vegetarian sausage:* constituents, ingredients, components, elements.
3 (**contents**) *the book's list of contents:* chapters, sections, divisions.
4 *the content of the essay:* subject matter, subject, theme, topic, argument, thesis, message, thrust, substance, matter, material, text, ideas.

contented adjective *a contented man.* See **CONTENT**[1] adjective.

contention noun
1 *the captured territory was the main area of contention between the two countries:* disagreement, dispute, disputation, argument, discord, conflict, friction, strife, dissension.
2 *the Marxist contention that capitalism equals exploitation:* argument, claim, submission, assertion, declaration; opinion, stand, position, view, belief, thesis, case.
OPPOSITES: agreement.
□ in contention
in competition, competing, contesting, contending, vying; striving, struggling.

contentious adjective
1 *a contentious issue:* controversial, disputable, debatable, disputed, open to debate, moot, vexed.
2 *the plan had been the subject of contentious debate:* heated, vehement, fierce, violent, intense, impassioned.

contentment noun *he found contentment in living a simple life in the country:* happiness, satisfaction, contentedness, content, fulfilment, gratification, pleasure; peace of mind, peace, ease, comfort, serenity, tranquillity.

contest noun
1 *a boxing contest:* competition, match,

tournament, game, meet, event, trial, bout, heat, fixture, tie, race.
2 *the contest for the party leadership:* fight, battle, tussle, struggle, competition, race.
▷**verb**
1 *he intended to contest the seat:* compete for, contend for, vie for, fight for, try to win, go for.
2 *three political groups contested the elections:* take part in, participate in, compete in, enter, fight; throw your hat in the ring.
3 *we contested the decision:* oppose, object to, challenge, argue against, take a stand against, take issue with, question, call into question.
4 *the issues have been hotly contested:* debate, argue about, dispute, quarrel over.

contestant noun competitor, participant, player, contender, candidate, entrant, aspirant; rival, opponent, adversary, antagonist.

context noun *the wider historical context:* circumstances, conditions, factors, state of affairs, situation, background, scene, setting, frame of reference.

contiguous adjective *the contiguous states of New Mexico, Arizona, Texas, and California:* adjacent, neighbouring, adjoining, bordering.

contingency noun *a detailed contract which attempts to provide for all possible contingencies:* eventuality, event, incident, happening, occurrence, juncture, possibility, accident, chance, emergency.

contingent adjective
1 *the merger is contingent on government approval:* dependent on, conditional on, subject to, determined by, hingeing on, resting on.
2 *contingent events:* chance, accidental, fortuitous, possible; unforeseeable, unpredictable, random.
▷**noun**
1 *a contingent of Japanese businessmen:* group, party, body, band, company, cohort, deputation, delegation; informal bunch, gang.
2 *a contingent of marines:* detachment, unit, group.

continual adjective
1 *a service disrupted by continual breakdowns:* frequent, repeated, constant, recurrent, recurring, regular.
2 *she was in continual pain | continual heavy rain ruined the harvests:* constant, continuous, unending, never-ending, unremitting, ceaseless, incessant, perpetual, persistent, unabating, relentless, unrelenting, unrelieved, uninterrupted, unbroken, round-the-clock.
OPPOSITES: occasional, temporary.

USAGE

On the distinction between **continual** and **continuous**, see the note at **CONTINUOUS**.

continuation noun *the continuation of discussions:* carrying on, continuance, extension, prolongation, protraction; resumption.
OPPOSITES: end.

continue verb
1 *he decided to continue with the investigation:* carry on, proceed, pursue, go on, keep on, persist, press on, persevere, keep at; informal stick at, soldier on.
2 *discussions continued throughout the year:* go on, carry on, last, extend, be prolonged, run on; drag on.
3 *we are keen to continue this relationship:* maintain, keep up, sustain, keep going, keep alive, preserve.
4 *his willingness to continue in office:* remain, stay, carry on, keep going.
5 *we continued our conversation after supper:* resume, pick up, take up, carry on with, return to, recommence.
OPPOSITES: stop, break off.

continuing adjective *a background of continuing civil war:* ongoing, continuous, sustained; persistent, relentless, uninterrupted, unabating, unremitting, unrelieved, unceasing.
OPPOSITES: sporadic.

continuity noun *a breakdown in the continuity of care:* continuousness, uninterruptedness, flow, progression.

continuous adjective *for the past few days there had been continuous rain:* continual, uninterrupted, unbroken, constant, ceaseless, incessant, steady, sustained, solid, continuing, ongoing, unceasing, without a break, non-stop, round-the-clock, persistent, unremitting, relentless, unrelenting, unabating, unrelieved, without respite, endless, unending, never-ending, perpetual, everlasting, eternal, interminable; consecutive, running.
OPPOSITES: intermittent.

USAGE

Continuous and **continual** can both mean 'constant, unending' (*years of continuous/continual warfare*), but only **continual** can be used to mean 'happening frequently' (*the continual arguments at home*).

contort verb *a spasm of pain contorted his face | chunks of contorted metal:* twist, distort, bend out of shape; warp, buckle, deform.

contour noun *the perfect contours of her body:* outline, shape, form; lines, curves, figure; silhouette, profile.

contraband adjective *she'd been selling contraband goods:* smuggled, black-market, bootleg, under the counter, illegal, illicit, unlawful; prohibited, banned, proscribed, forbidden; informal hot.

contract noun *a legally binding contract:* agreement, commitment, arrangement, settlement, understanding, compact, covenant, bond; deal, pact.

▷**verb**
1 *the market for such goods began to contract:* **shrink,** get smaller, decrease, diminish, reduce, dwindle, decline.
2 *her stomach muscles contracted:* **tighten,** tense, flex, constrict, draw in, narrow.
3 *she contracted her brow:* **wrinkle,** knit, crease, purse, pucker.
4 *his name was soon contracted to 'Jack':* **shorten,** abbreviate, cut, reduce; technical elide.
5 *the company contracted to rebuild the stadium:* **undertake,** pledge, promise, commit yourself, engage, covenant, agree, enter an agreement, make a deal.
6 *she contracted German measles:* **develop,** catch, get, pick up, come down with, be struck down by, be stricken with, succumb to; Brit. go down with.
7 *he contracted a debt of £3,300:* **incur,** run up.
OPPOSITES: expand, relax, lengthen.
□ **contract something out** subcontract, outsource, farm out.

contraction noun
1 *the contraction of the industry:* **shrinking,** shrinkage, decline, decrease, diminution, dwindling.
2 *the contraction of muscles:* **tightening,** tensing, flexing.
3 *my contractions started at midnight:* **labour pains,** labour; cramps.
4 *'goodbye' is a contraction of 'God be with you':* **abbreviation,** short form, shortened form.

contradict verb
1 *he contradicted the government's account of the affair:* **deny,** refute, rebut, dispute, challenge, counter; formal controvert, gainsay.
2 *nobody dared to contradict him:* **argue against,** go against, challenge, oppose.
3 *this research contradicts previous computer models:* **conflict with,** be at odds with, be at variance with, be inconsistent with, run counter to, disagree with.
OPPOSITES: confirm, agree with.

contradiction noun
1 *the contradiction between his faith and his lifestyle:* **conflict,** clash, disagreement, opposition, inconsistency, mismatch, variance.
2 *the second sentence appears to be a flat contradiction of the first:* **denial,** refutation, rebuttal, countering, counterstatement.
OPPOSITES: confirmation, agreement.

contradictory adjective *the two attitudes are contradictory:* **opposed,** in opposition, opposite, antithetical, contrary, contrasting, conflicting, at variance, at odds, opposing, clashing, divergent, discrepant, different; inconsistent, incompatible, irreconcilable.

contraption noun *a newfangled contraption for making coffee:* **device,** gadget, apparatus, machine, appliance, mechanism, invention, contrivance; informal gizmo, widget.

contrary adjective
1 *contrary views:* **opposite,** opposing, opposed, contradictory, clashing, conflicting, antithetical, incompatible, irreconcilable.
2 *she was sulky and contrary:* **perverse,** awkward, difficult, uncooperative, unhelpful, obstructive, disobliging, recalcitrant, wilful, self-willed, stubborn, obstinate, mulish, pig-headed, intractable; Brit. informal bloody-minded, bolshie.
OPPOSITES: compatible, accommodating.
▷**noun** *in fact, the contrary is true:* **opposite,** reverse, converse, antithesis.
□ **contrary to**
in conflict with, against, at variance with, at odds with, in opposition to, counter to, incompatible with.

contrast noun
1 *the contrast between rural and urban trends:* **difference,** dissimilarity, disparity, distinction, contradistinction, divergence, variance, variation, differentiation; contradiction, incongruity, opposition, polarity.
2 *Jane was a complete contrast to Sarah:* **opposite,** antithesis; foil, complement.
OPPOSITES: similarity.
▷**verb**
1 *this is a view which contrasts with his earlier opinion:* **differ from,** be at variance with, be contrary to, conflict with, go against, be at odds with, be in opposition to, disagree with, clash with.
2 *people contrasted her with her sister:* **compare,** set side by side, juxtapose; measure against; distinguish from, differentiate from.
OPPOSITES: resemble, liken.

contravene verb
1 *he contravened the Official Secrets Act:* **break,** breach, violate, infringe; defy, disobey, flout.
2 *the prosecution contravened the rights of the individual:* **conflict with,** be in conflict with, be at odds with, be at variance with, run counter to.
OPPOSITES: comply with.

contravention noun *a contravention of EC regulations:* **breach,** violation, infringement.

contretemps noun *before the game could even restart, he got himself involved in another contretemps with the referee:* **argument,** quarrel, squabble, disagreement, difference of opinion, dispute; Brit. row; informal tiff, set-to, run-in, spat; Brit. informal barney.

contribute verb

1 *the government contributed a million pounds:* give, donate, put up, subscribe, hand out, grant, provide, supply; bestow, present; informal chip in, fork out, shell out, cough up; Brit. informal stump up.
2 *an article contributed by Dr Clouson:* supply, provide, submit.
3 *numerous factors contribute to job satisfaction:* play a part in, be instrumental in, be a factor in, have a hand in, be conducive to, make for, lead to, cause.

contribution noun

1 *financial contributions:* donation, gift, offering, present, handout, grant, allowance, subscription; formal benefaction.
2 *contributions from local authors:* article, piece, story, item, chapter, paper, essay.

contributor noun

1 *the magazine's regular contributors:* writer, columnist, correspondent.
2 *campaign contributors:* donor, benefactor, subscriber, supporter, backer, patron, sponsor.

contrite adjective *he looked so contrite that she relented:* remorseful, repentant, penitent, regretful, sorry, apologetic, rueful, sheepish, hangdog, ashamed, chastened, shamefaced, conscience-stricken, guilt-ridden, in sackcloth and ashes.

contrition noun remorse, remorsefulness, repentance, penitence, sorrow, regret, ruefulness, pangs of conscience; shame, guilt, compunction.

contrivance noun

1 *a mechanical contrivance:* device, gadget, machine, appliance, contraption, apparatus, mechanism, implement, tool, invention; informal gizmo, widget.
2 *her matchmaking contrivances:* scheme, stratagem, tactic, manoeuvre, move, plan, ploy, gambit, trick, ruse, plot, machination.

contrive verb *his opponents contrived a cabinet crisis:* bring about, engineer, manufacture, orchestrate, stage-manage, create, devise, concoct, construct, plan, fabricate, plot, hatch; informal wangle, set up.

contrived adjective *David replied with contrived joviality:* forced, strained, studied, artificial, affected, false, feigned, manufactured, unnatural; laboured, overdone, elaborate.

control noun

1 *China retained control over the region:* jurisdiction, sway, power, authority, command, dominance, government, mastery, leadership, rule, sovereignty, supremacy, ascendancy; charge, management, direction, supervision, superintendence.
2 *the livestock industry is not alone in wanting tighter import controls:* restraint, constraint, limitation, restriction, check, curb, brake; regulation.
3 *her control deserted her:* self-control, self-restraint, self-possession, composure, calmness; informal cool.
4 *easy-to-use controls:* switch, knob, button, dial, handle, lever, pedal.
5 *mission control:* headquarters, HQ, base, centre of operations, command post.
▷verb
1 *one family had controlled the company since its formation:* be in charge of, run, manage, direct, administer, head, preside over, supervise, superintend, steer; command, rule, govern, lead, dominate, hold sway over, be at the helm of; informal head up, be in the driving seat, run the show.
2 *she struggled to control her temper:* restrain, keep in check, curb, check, contain, hold back, bridle, rein in, suppress, repress, master.
3 *public spending was controlled:* limit, restrict, curb, cap, constrain; informal put the brakes on.

controversial adjective *the death penalty is a very controversial issue:* contentious, disputed, at issue, disputable, debatable, vexed, tendentious.

controversy noun *he refused to be drawn into the political controversy:* disagreement, dispute, argument, debate, altercation, wrangle, quarrel, war of words, storm, contention, dissension; cause célèbre; Brit. row.

contusion noun bruise, discoloration, injury.

conundrum noun

1 *the conundrums facing policymakers in the 1980s:* problem, difficult question, vexed question, difficulty, quandary, dilemma; informal poser.
2 *he enjoyed conundrums and crosswords:* riddle, puzzle, word game; informal brain-teaser.

convalesce verb *he went abroad to convalesce:* recuperate, get better, recover, get well, get back on your feet, regain your strength.

convalescence noun recuperation, recovery, return to health, rehabilitation.

convalescent adjective *convalescent patients:* recuperating, recovering, getting better, on the road to recovery, improving; informal on the mend.

convene verb

1 *he convened a secret meeting:* summon, call, call together, order; formal convoke.
2 *the committee convened for its final session:* assemble, gather, meet, come together, congregate.

C

convenience noun
1 *for convenience, the handset is wall-mounted:* **ease of use**, usefulness, utility, serviceability, practicality, expedience.
2 *the kitchen has all the modern conveniences:* **appliance**, labour-saving device, gadget; amenity, facility; informal mod con.

convenient adjective
1 *try to agree on a mutually convenient time:* **suitable**, appropriate, fitting, fit, suited, opportune, timely, well timed, favourable, advantageous, expedient.
2 *a hotel that's convenient for the beach:* **near**, close to, within easy reach of, well situated for, handy for, not far from, just round the corner from; informal a stone's throw from, within spitting distance of.
OPPOSITES: inconvenient, awkward.

convent noun **nunnery**, priory, abbey, religious community.

convention noun
1 *a social convention:* **custom**, usage, practice, tradition, way, habit, norm, formality; rule, code, canon; propriety, etiquette, protocol; formal praxis; (**conventions**) mores.
2 *a convention signed by 74 countries:* **agreement**, accord, protocol, compact, pact, treaty, concordat, entente; contract, deal.
3 *the party's biennial convention:* **conference**, meeting, congress, assembly, gathering, summit, conclave.

conventional adjective
1 *the conventional wisdom of the day:* **orthodox**, traditional, established, accepted, received, prevailing, prevalent, accustomed, customary; popular, mainstream.
2 *a cross between a monorail and a conventional railway:* **normal**, standard, regular, ordinary, usual, traditional, typical, common.
3 *Karen was a very conventional woman:* **conservative**, traditional, traditionalist, conformist, old-fashioned, of the old school, bourgeois, small-town, suburban; informal straight, square, stick-in-the-mud.
4 *an unexciting and rather conventional compilation:* **unoriginal**, formulaic, predictable, stock, unadventurous, unremarkable.
OPPOSITES: unconventional, unorthodox.

converge verb
1 *Oxford Circus, a station where three lines converge:* **meet**, intersect, cross, connect, link up, coincide, join, unite, merge.
2 *90,000 fans converged on the Millennium Stadium:* **close in on**, bear down on, approach, move towards.
OPPOSITES: diverge, leave.

conversant adjective *he was fully conversant with the technology:* **familiar**, acquainted, au fait, well versed, well informed, knowledgeable, informed, abreast, up to date, at home; formal au courant; informal up to speed, clued up.

conversation noun *he must have overheard her conversation with Victoria:* **discussion**, talk, chat, tête-à-tête, heart-to-heart, head-to-head, exchange, dialogue; informal confab.

conversational adjective *she spoke fluent, conversational English:* **informal**, colloquial, idiomatic.

converse[1] verb *they conversed in low voices:* **talk**, speak, chat, have a conversation.

converse[2] noun *the converse is also true:* **opposite**, reverse, obverse, contrary, antithesis, other side of the coin; informal flip side.

conversion noun
1 *the conversion of waste into energy:* **change**, changing, transformation, transfiguration, transmutation; humorous transmogrification.
2 *the conversion of the building:* **adaptation**, alteration, modification, reconstruction, rebuilding, redevelopment, redesign, renovation, rehabilitation.

convert verb
1 *plants convert the sun's energy into chemical energy:* **change**, turn, transform, transfigure, transmute; humorous transmogrify.
2 *the factory was converted into flats:* **adapt**, turn, change, alter, modify, rebuild, reconstruct, redevelop, refashion, redesign, restyle, revamp, renovate, rehabilitate.
3 *they sought to convert sinners:* **proselytize**, evangelize.
▷noun *Christian converts:* **proselyte**, neophyte.

convey verb
1 *taxis conveyed guests to the station:* **transport**, carry, bring, take, fetch, bear, move, ferry, shuttle, shift, transfer.
2 *he conveyed the information to me:* **communicate**, pass on, make known, impart, relay, transmit, send, hand on, relate, tell, reveal, disclose.
3 *it's impossible to convey how I felt:* **express**, communicate, get across/over, put across/over, indicate, say.
4 *he conveys an air of competence:* **project**, exude, give off, emit, emanate.

conveyance noun *the conveyance of agricultural produce:* **transportation**, transport, carriage, transfer, movement, delivery, shipment; Brit. haulage.

convict verb *he was convicted of indecent assault:* **find guilty**, declare guilty; sentence.
OPPOSITES: acquit.

▷**noun** *two escaped convicts:* prisoner, inmate; criminal, felon; informal jailbird, old lag.

conviction noun
1 *his political convictions:* belief, opinion, view, thought, persuasion, idea, position, stance, article of faith; creed, credo.
2 *she spoke with conviction:* certainty, certitude, assurance, confidence, sureness, no shadow of a doubt.
OPPOSITES: acquittal, uncertainty.

convince verb
1 *he convinced me that I was wrong:* make someone certain, persuade, satisfy, prove to; assure, put/set someone's mind at rest.
2 *I convinced her to marry me:* persuade, induce, prevail on, get, talk into, cajole into, coax into.

convincing adjective
1 *a convincing argument:* cogent, persuasive, plausible, powerful, potent, strong, forceful, compelling, irresistible, telling, conclusive.
2 *a convincing 5–0 win:* resounding, emphatic, decisive, conclusive.

convivial adjective *he was always a convivial host:* friendly, genial, affable, amiable, congenial, agreeable, good-humoured, cordial, warm, sociable, outgoing, gregarious, companionable, cheerful, jolly, jovial, lively; enjoyable, festive.

conviviality noun friendliness, geniality, affability, amiability, bonhomie, congeniality, cordiality, warmth, good nature, sociability, gregariousness, cheerfulness, good cheer, joviality, jollity, liveliness.

convocation noun assembly, gathering, meeting, conference, convention, congress, council, symposium, colloquium.

convoluted adjective *an extraordinarily convoluted narrative:* complicated, complex, involved, elaborate, serpentine, labyrinthine, tortuous, tangled, Byzantine; confused, confusing, bewildering, baffling.
OPPOSITES: straightforward.

convolution noun
1 *the convolutions of the plot:* complexity, intricacy, complication, twist, turn, entanglement.
2 *crosses adorned with elaborate convolutions:* twist, turn, coil, spiral, twirl, curl, helix, whorl, loop, curlicue.

convoy noun *a convoy of vehicles:* group, fleet, procession, cavalcade, motorcade, line.

convulse verb *his whole body convulsed:* shake uncontrollably, go into spasms, shudder, jerk, thrash about, fit.

convulsion noun
1 *when the convulsions stop, put the person in the recovery position:* fit, seizure, paroxysm, spasm, attack.
2 (**convulsions**) *the audience collapsed in convulsions:* fits of laughter, paroxysms of laughter, uncontrollable laughter; informal hysterics.
3 *the political convulsions of the period:* upheaval, eruption, cataclysm, turmoil, turbulence, tumult, disruption, agitation, disturbance, unrest, disorder.

convulsive adjective *convulsive movements:* spasmodic, jerky, violent, uncontrollable; Medicine paroxysmal.

cook verb
1 *he'd cooked a meal of barbecued chicken and fried potatoes:* prepare, make, put together; informal fix, rustle up; Brit. informal knock up.
2 (informal) *he'd been cooking the books:* falsify, alter, doctor, tamper with, interfere with, massage, manipulate; Brit. informal fiddle.

cooking noun *authentic Italian cooking:* cuisine, cookery, baking; food.

WORD LINKS
culinary relating to cooking

cool adjective
1 *a cool breeze:* chilly, chill, cold, bracing, brisk, crisp, fresh, refreshing, invigorating; draughty; informal nippy; Brit. informal parky.
2 *a cool response:* unenthusiastic, lukewarm, tepid, indifferent, uninterested, apathetic, half-hearted; unfriendly, distant, remote, aloof, cold, chilly, frosty, unwelcoming, offhand; informal stand-offish.
3 *his ability to keep cool in a crisis:* calm, {cool, calm, and collected}, composed, as cool as a cucumber, collected, cool-headed, level-headed, self-possessed, controlled, self-controlled, poised, serene, tranquil, unruffled, unperturbed, unmoved, untroubled, imperturbable; informal unflappable, together, laid-back.
4 (informal) *she thinks she's so cool:* fashionable, attractive, sophisticated; informal trendy, funky, hip.
5 (informal) *a cool song.* See EXCELLENT.
OPPOSITES: warm, enthusiastic, agitated.

▷**noun**
1 *the cool of the evening:* chill, chilliness, coldness, coolness.
2 (informal) *Ken lost his cool:* self-control, control, composure, self-possession, calmness, equilibrium, calm; aplomb, poise, sangfroid, presence of mind.
OPPOSITES: warmth.

▷**verb**
1 *cool the sauce in the fridge:* chill, refrigerate.
2 *her reluctance did nothing to cool his interest:* lessen, moderate, diminish, reduce, dampen.
3 *Simpson's ardour had cooled:* subside, lessen, diminish, decrease, abate, moderate, die down, fade, dwindle, wane.

C

4 *after a while, she cooled off:* calm down, recover/regain your composure, compose yourself, control yourself, pull yourself together, simmer down.
OPPOSITES: heat, inflame, intensify.

coop noun *a hen coop:* pen, run, cage, hutch, enclosure.
▷ **verb** *he hates being cooped up at home:* confine, shut in/up, cage in, pen up/in, keep, detain, trap, incarcerate, imprison; formal immure.

cooperate verb
1 *police and social services cooperated in the operation:* collaborate, work together, liaise, work side by side, pull together, band together, join forces, team up, unite, combine, pool resources.
2 *he was happy to cooperate:* be of assistance, assist, help, lend a hand, be of service, do your bit; informal play ball.

cooperation noun
1 *cooperation between management and workers:* collaboration, joint action, combined effort, teamwork, partnership, coordination, liaison, association, synergy, give and take, compromise.
2 *thank you for your cooperation:* assistance, help, helpfulness, helping hand, support.

cooperative adjective
1 *a cooperative effort:* collaborative, collective, combined, common, joint, shared, mutual, united, concerted, coordinated.
2 *pleasant and cooperative staff:* helpful, eager to help, eager to be of assistance, obliging, accommodating, willing, amenable; adaptable.

coordinate verb
1 *the Justice Department appointed a task force to coordinate the various federal investigations:* organize, arrange, systematize, harmonize, synchronize, bring together, fit together, dovetail.
2 *care workers coordinate at a local level:* cooperate, liaise, collaborate, work together, negotiate, communicate, be in contact.
3 *floral designs coordinate with the decor:* match, complement, set off; harmonize, blend, fit in, go.

cope verb
1 *she couldn't cope on her own:* manage, survive, look after yourself, fend for yourself, shift for yourself, carry on, get by/through, bear up, hold your own, keep your end up, keep your head above water, subsist; informal make it, hack it.
2 *his inability to cope with the situation:* deal with, handle, manage, address, face up to, confront, tackle, get to grips with, get through, weather, come to terms with.

copious adjective *she took copious notes* | *dinner was washed down by copious*

amounts of red wine: plenty of, a lot of, a great many, a great deal of; abundant, plentiful, ample, profuse, full, extensive, generous, lavish, liberal, in abundance, numerous; informal galore.
OPPOSITES: sparse.

copse noun thicket, grove, wood, coppice, stand, clump, brake; Brit. spinney.

copy noun
1 *copies of the report had been sent to the tribunal:* duplicate, facsimile, photocopy, carbon copy; transcript; reprint.
2 *a copy of a sketch by Leonardo da Vinci:* replica, reproduction, print; imitation, likeness; forgery, fake.
▷ **verb**
1 *each form had to be copied and sent to a different department:* duplicate, reproduce; photocopy, xerox.
2 *portraits copied from original paintings by Reynolds:* reproduce, replicate; forge, fake, counterfeit.
3 *their sound was copied by a lot of jazz players:* imitate, reproduce, emulate, follow, echo, mirror, ape; plagiarize, steal; informal rip off.

coquettish adjective *she gave him a coquettish glance from beneath her eyelashes:* flirtatious, provocative, seductive, inviting, kittenish, coy, arch, teasing, playful; informal come-hither.

cord noun string, thread, thong, lace, ribbon, strap, tape, tie, line, rope, cable, wire, ligature; twine, yarn.

USAGE

Do not confuse **cord** with **chord**. **Cord** means 'thin string or rope', or 'a part of the body resembling string or rope' (*the spinal cord*). A **chord** is a group of musical notes (*an E major chord*).

---

cordial adjective *a cordial welcome* | *a cordial atmosphere:* friendly, warm, genial, affable, amiable, pleasant, warm-hearted, good-natured, gracious, hospitable, welcoming.

cordon noun *a cordon of police officers blocked the road:* barrier, line, row, chain, ring, circle.
▷ **verb** *troops cordoned off the area:* close off, shut off, seal off, fence off, separate off, isolate, enclose, surround.

core noun
1 *the earth's core:* centre, interior, middle, nucleus.
2 *the core of the argument:* heart, centre, nucleus, nub, kernel; essence, quintessence, crux, substance, basis, fundamentals.
▷ **adjective** *the core issue:* central, key, basic, fundamental, principal, primary, main, chief, crucial, vital, essential; informal number-one.
OPPOSITES: peripheral.

cork noun stopper, stop, plug, bung.

corn noun *a field of corn:* grain, cereal crop; maize, wheat, barley, oats, rye.

corner noun
1 *the cart lurched round the corner:* bend, curve, crook, dog-leg, hairpin bend; turn, turning, junction, fork, intersection.
2 *a charming corner of Italy:* area, region, district, part.
3 *he thought it was a crazy idea, but he was in a corner:* predicament, plight, tight spot, mess, muddle, difficulty, problem, dilemma, quandary; informal fix, hole.
▷verb
1 *he was eventually cornered by police dogs:* trap, run to earth, bring to bay, cut off, block off, hem in, pen in, surround; capture, catch.
2 *crime syndicates have cornered the stolen car market:* gain control of, take over, control, dominate, monopolize; capture; informal sew up.

cornerstone noun *the theory of natural selection is a cornerstone of biological thought:* foundation, basis, keystone, mainstay, linchpin, bedrock, base, backbone, key, centrepiece, core, heart, centre, crux.

corny adjective (informal) *there is a lot of corny dialogue and several pointless subplots:* trite, banal, hackneyed, clichéd, predictable, stereotyped, platitudinous, tired, stale, overworked, overused, well worn; mawkish, sentimental, cloying, syrupy, saccharine; Brit. informal cheesy, schmaltzy, slushy; Brit. informal soppy.

corollary noun *the corollary of increased car ownership has been a decline in public transport:* consequence, result, upshot, effect, repercussion, product, by-product; Brit. knock-on effect.

coronet noun. See **CROWN** noun sense 1.

corporation noun
1 *the chairman of the corporation:* company, firm, business, concern, operation, house, organization, agency, trust, partnership; conglomerate, group, chain, multinational; informal outfit, set-up.
2 (Brit.) *the corporation refused two planning applications:* council, town council, municipal authority.

corporeal adjective bodily, fleshly, carnal, human, mortal, earthly, physical, corporal; material, tangible, concrete, actual.

corps noun
1 *an army corps:* unit, division, detachment, section, company, contingent, squad, squadron, regiment, battalion, brigade, platoon.
2 *a corps of trained engineers:* group, body, band, team, crew, squad, party, cohort, gang.

corpse noun dead body, body, carcass, skeleton, remains; Medicine cadaver; informal stiff.

corpulent adjective *a short, corpulent man:* fat, obese, overweight, plump, portly, stout, chubby, heavy, bulky, chunky, meaty, fleshy, rotund, well upholstered, well padded, well covered; informal tubby, pudgy, beefy, porky; Brit. informal podgy.
OPPOSITES: thin.

correct adjective
1 *that's the correct answer | are you sure this information is correct?* right, accurate, true, exact, precise, unerring, faultless, flawless, error-free, perfect, word-perfect; informal on the mark, on the beam, on the nail; Brit. informal spot on, bang on.
2 *correct behaviour:* proper, seemly, decorous, decent, respectable, suitable, fit, fitting, befitting, appropriate, acceptable; apt; conventional, customary, traditional, orthodox, comme il faut.
OPPOSITES: wrong, incorrect.
▷verb
1 *no attempt has been made to correct these errors:* rectify, put right, set right, right, emend, remedy, repair.
2 *an attempt to correct the trade imbalance:* counteract, offset, counterbalance, compensate for, make up for, neutralize.
3 *the brakes need correcting:* adjust, regulate, standardize, calibrate.

correction noun rectification, rectifying, righting, emendation, repair.

corrective adjective remedial, restorative, curative, reparative, rehabilitative.

correlate verb
1 *socio-economic status often correlates with educational achievement:* correspond, parallel, relate, tally, tie in, be consistent.
2 *consumption of such foods was correlated with a decreased risk for certain cancers:* connect, establish a connection between, establish a relationship between, associate, relate.
OPPOSITES: contrast.

correlation noun *the correlation between smoking and lung cancer is well known:* connection, association, link, tie-in, tie-up, relation, relationship, interrelationship, interdependence, interconnection, interaction; correspondence, parallel.

correspond verb
1 *their policies do not correspond with their statements:* be consistent, agree, be in agreement, correlate, be compatible, be consonant, accord, be in harmony, be in tune, concur, coincide, tally, tie in, dovetail, fit in; match, parallel; informal square.
2 *a rank corresponding to the British rank of sergeant:* be equivalent, be analogous, be comparable, equate.
3 *Debbie and I corresponded for years:*

exchange letters, write, communicate, keep in touch/contact.

correspondence noun
1 *there is some correspondence between the two variables:* correlation, agreement, consistency, compatibility, consonance, conformity, similarity, resemblance, parallel, coincidence.
2 *his private correspondence:* letters, messages, mail, post; communication.

correspondent noun *the paper's foreign correspondent:* reporter, journalist, columnist, writer, contributor, commentator.

corresponding adjective *a change in money supply brings a corresponding change in expenditure:* matching, equivalent, parallel, correlated, proportional, proportionate, commensurate, analogous, comparable.

corridor noun passage, passageway, aisle, gangway, hall, hallway, gallery, arcade.

corroborate verb *the witness had corroborated the boy's account of the attack:* confirm, verify, validate; support, back up, bear out, bear witness to, substantiate.
OPPOSITES: contradict.

corrode verb
1 *the iron had corroded:* rust, become rusty, tarnish; wear away, disintegrate, crumble, perish; oxidize.
2 *acid rain corrodes buildings:* wear away, eat away at, gnaw away at, erode, abrade, destroy.

corrosive adjective *the workers are exposed to corrosive chemicals:* caustic, corroding, abrasive; harmful, harsh.

corrugated adjective *corrugated plastic sheeting:* ridged, ribbed, grooved, fluted, furrowed, crinkled.

corrupt adjective
1 *a corrupt official | corrupt practices:* dishonest, unscrupulous, dishonourable, unprincipled, unethical, untrustworthy, venal, underhand, double-dealing, fraudulent; criminal, illegal, unlawful, nefarious; informal crooked, shady, dirty; Brit. informal bent, dodgy.
2 *the earth was corrupt in God's sight:* immoral, depraved, degenerate, reprobate, vice-ridden, debauched, dissolute, dissipated, bad, wicked, evil, base, sinful, perverted.
3 *a corrupt text:* unreliable, debased, bastardized.
OPPOSITES: honest, ethical.
▷ verb
1 *the fear of firms corrupting politicians in the search for contracts:* bribe, suborn, buy off, pay off; informal grease someone's palm, give someone a backhander/sweetener; Brit. informal nobble.
2 *a book that might corrupt the minds of*

its readers: deprave, pervert, lead astray, warp; defile, contaminate, pollute.
3 *the apostolic writings had been corrupted:* alter, tamper with, interfere with, debase, bastardize.

corruption noun
1 *political corruption:* dishonesty, unscrupulousness, double-dealing, fraud, fraudulence, misconduct, crime, criminality, wrongdoing; bribery, venality; informal graft, sleaze.
2 *his fall into corruption:* immorality, depravity, vice, degeneracy, perversion, pervertedness, debauchery, decadence, wickedness, evil, sin, sinfulness.
OPPOSITES: honesty, morality.

cortège noun *a funeral cortège:* procession, parade, cavalcade, motorcade, convoy, train, column, file, line.

cosmetic adjective *most of the changes were merely cosmetic:* superficial, surface, skin-deep, outward, external, exterior; decorative.
OPPOSITES: fundamental.
▷ noun (**cosmetics**) *a new range of cosmetics:* make-up, beauty products.

cosmopolitan adjective
1 *the student body has a cosmopolitan character:* multicultural, international, global.
2 *a cosmopolitan audience | a cosmopolitan lifestyle:* worldly, well travelled, experienced, sophisticated, urbane; glamorous, exciting; informal jet-setting.

cosset verb *all her life she'd been cosseted by her family:* pamper, spoil, indulge, overindulge, mollycoddle, baby, pet, mother, pander to; wrap in cotton wool, wait on someone hand and foot.

cost verb
1 *the jacket costs £186:* be priced at, sell for, be valued at, come to; informal set someone back, go for.
2 *the proposal has not yet been costed:* put a price on, price, put a figure on, value, put a value on.
▷ noun
1 *the total cost for this treatment will be about £1,100:* price, asking price, market price, selling price, fee, tariff, charge; expense, expenditure, outlay.
2 *the human cost of the conflict:* sacrifice, loss, toll, penalty, expense, price.
3 (**costs**) *we need to make £10,000 to cover our costs:* expenses, outgoings, overheads, running costs, operating costs, fixed costs; expenditure, spending, outlay.

costly adjective
1 *there are several precautions homeowners can take to prevent costly repairs:* expensive, high-cost, highly priced, overpriced; Brit. dear; informal pricey, costing the earth.
2 *a costly mistake:* catastrophic, fatal,

disastrous, awful, terrible, dreadful; expensive.
OPPOSITES: cheap.

costume noun *they wore Elizabethan costumes:* clothes, garments, dress, clothing, garb; outfit, ensemble; uniform, livery; formal attire; informal get-up, gear; Brit. informal clobber.

cosy adjective
1 *a cosy country cottage:* snug, comfortable, warm, welcoming; safe, sheltered, secure; Brit. homely; informal comfy.
2 *a cosy chat:* intimate, relaxed, informal, friendly.

coterie noun *she had a small coterie of friends and advisers:* clique, set, circle, inner circle, crowd, gang, band, community; in-crowd.

cottage noun small house, lodge, chalet, cabin; shack, shanty; Scottish bothy.

couch noun *she seated herself on the couch:* sofa, divan, chaise longue, chesterfield, ottoman; Brit. settee.
▷ **verb** *his reply was couched in deferential terms:* express, phrase, word, frame, put.

cough verb
□ **cough something up** (informal) *the company coughed up $40 m in settlement of the legal claims:* pay, come up with, hand over, part with; informal fork out, shell out, lay out; Brit. informal stump up.

council noun
1 *the town council:* local authority, local government, municipal authority, administration, executive, assembly; Brit. corporation.
2 *the Schools Council:* advisory body, board, committee, commission, assembly, panel; synod, convocation.
3 *that evening, she held a family council:* meeting, gathering, conference, conclave.

> **USAGE**
>
> Do not confuse **council** with **counsel**. A **council** is a group of people who manage an area or advise on something, whereas **counsel** means 'advice' (*they disregarded her wise counsel*), or 'to advise someone' (*he counselled the team to withdraw from the deal*).

counsel noun
1 *her wise counsel helped tremendously in improving the quality of our programme:* advice, guidance, direction; recommendations, suggestions.
2 *the counsel for the defence:* barrister, lawyer; Scottish advocate; N. Amer. attorney; informal brief.
▷ **verb** *he counselled the team to withdraw from the deal:* advise, recommend, direct, encourage, urge, warn, caution; guide, give guidance.

counsellor noun adviser, mentor, guide.

count verb
1 *she counted the money again:* add up, add together, reckon up, total, tally, calculate, compute; Brit. tot up.
2 *the staff has shrunk to four, or five if you count the European director:* include, take into account, take account of, take into consideration, allow for.
3 *I count it a privilege to be asked:* consider, think, regard as, look on as, view as, hold to be, judge, deem, account.
4 *it doesn't matter what the critics think— it's the audience that counts:* matter, be of consequence, be significant, signify, be important, be of account, carry weight; informal cut any ice.
▷ **noun**
1 *at the last count, the committee had 579 members:* calculation, computation, reckoning, tally.
2 *her white blood cell count:* amount, number, total.
□ **count on**
1 *you can count on me:* rely on, depend on, bank on, trust, be sure of, have confidence in, believe in, put your faith in, take for granted.
2 *they hadn't counted on Rangers' indomitable spirit:* expect, reckon on, anticipate, envisage, allow for, be prepared for, bargain for/on.

countenance noun *his strikingly handsome countenance:* face, features, physiognomy; expression, look, appearance.
▷ **verb** *his mother would never countenance such a marriage:* tolerate, permit, allow, agree to, consent to, give your blessing to, go along with; informal stand for.

counter[1] noun *the idea of the game is to collect the most counters:* token, chip, disc; piece, man, marker.

counter[2] verb
1 *workers countered accusations of dishonesty with claims of oppression:* respond to, parry, hit back at, answer, retort to.
2 *the second argument is more difficult to counter:* oppose, argue against/with, contradict, counteract; dispute, challenge, contest; formal controvert.
OPPOSITES: support.
▷ **adjective** *a counter bid:* opposing, opposed, opposite.
□ **counter to**
his writing ran counter to the dominant trends of the decade: against, in opposition to, contrary to, at variance with, in defiance of, in contravention of, in conflict with, at odds with.

counteract verb
1 *new measures to counteract drug trafficking:* prevent, thwart, frustrate, foil, curb, check, put a stop/end to, defeat.
2 *a drug to counteract the possible effect on*

C

her heart: offset, counterbalance, balance out, cancel out, even out, counterpoise, compensate for, make up for, remedy; neutralize.
OPPOSITES: encourage, exacerbate.

counterbalance verb *the risk of failure tends to be counterbalanced by high rewards:* compensate for, make up for, offset, balance out, even out, counterpoise, counteract, equalize, neutralize; nullify, negate, undo.

counterfeit adjective *counterfeit £20 notes:* fake, forged, faked, bogus, imitation; informal phoney.
OPPOSITES: genuine.
▷noun *the notes were counterfeits:* fake, forgery, copy, reproduction; informal phoney.
OPPOSITES: original.
▷verb *his signature was hard to counterfeit:* fake, forge, copy, reproduce, imitate.

countermand verb *an order to arrest the strike leaders had been countermanded:* revoke, rescind, reverse, retract, withdraw, quash, overturn, overrule, cancel, undo.

counterpart noun *the minister held talks with his French counterpart:* equivalent, opposite number, peer, equal, parallel.

countless adjective *we have received countless numbers of calls and emails:* very many, innumerable, numerous; untold, without number, myriad, multitudinous, incalculable, limitless, infinite; informal umpteen, no end of, loads of, stacks of, heaps of.

countrified adjective *the countrified ambience was spoilt by the express trains:* rural, rustic, pastoral, bucolic, country; idyllic, unspoilt.
OPPOSITES: urban.

country noun
1 *foreign countries:* nation, state, sovereign state, kingdom, realm, territory, province, principality.
2 *he risked his life for his country:* homeland, native land, fatherland, motherland, the land of your fathers.
3 *the whole country took to the streets:* people, public, population, populace, citizenry, nation, body politic; electors, voters, taxpayers, grass roots.
4 *thickly forested country:* terrain, land, territory; landscape, scenery, setting, surroundings, environment.
5 *she hated living in the country:* the countryside, the provinces, rural areas, the great outdoors; informal, derogatory the sticks, the middle of nowhere.
▷adjective *country pursuits:* rural, countryside, outdoor, rustic, pastoral, bucolic.
OPPOSITES: urban.

countryman, countrywoman noun
1 *the traditions of his countrymen:* compatriot, fellow citizen.

2 *a countryman takes great interest in the weather:* country dweller, son/daughter of the soil, provincial; farmer.

countryside noun
1 *the mountainous countryside of Snowdonia:* landscape, scenery, surroundings, setting, environment; country, terrain, land.
2 *I was brought up in the countryside.* See COUNTRY noun sense 5.

county noun *the northern counties:* administrative unit, district; region, area; Brit. shire.
▷adjective (Brit.) *a county lady:* upper-class, aristocratic, landed, landowning.

coup noun
1 *a violent military coup:* seizure of power, coup d'état, putsch; revolution, rebellion, revolt, insurrection, insurgence, uprising.
2 *a major publishing coup:* success, triumph, feat, accomplishment, achievement, scoop, master stroke, stroke of genius.

coup d'état noun. See COUP sense 1.

couple noun
1 *a couple of girls were sitting on the sofa:* pair, duo, twosome, two; brace.
2 (informal) *he'll be okay in a couple of days:* few, one or two, two or three.
▷verb
1 *a sense of hope is coupled with a sense of loss:* combine, accompany, link, ally, associate, connect; add to, join to.
2 *a cable is coupled to one of the wheels:* connect, attach, join, fasten, fix, link, secure, tie, hitch, yoke, chain, hook up.

coupon noun
1 *money-off coupons:* voucher, token, ticket.
2 *fill in the coupon below:* form, tear-off slip, slip.

courage noun *the officers all showed great courage in trying to protect members of the public:* bravery, courageousness, pluck, pluckiness, fearlessness, nerve, boldness; daring, valour, intrepidity, heroism, gallantry; informal guts, spunk; Brit. informal bottle.
OPPOSITES: cowardice.

courageous adjective *his courageous actions helped to defeat the enemy attack:* brave, plucky, fearless, valiant, valorous, bold, undaunted, unflinching, unshrinking, unafraid, dauntless, indomitable; intrepid, heroic, lionhearted, daring, doughty, mettlesome, stout-hearted, gallant; informal game, gutsy, spunky.
OPPOSITES: cowardly.

courier noun
1 *the documents were sent by courier:* messenger, dispatch rider, runner.
2 *a courier for a package holiday company:* representative, tour guide.

course noun

1 *the island was not far off our course:* route, way, track, direction, tack, path, line, trajectory, bearing, orbit.
2 *an event which changed the course of history:* progression, development, progress, advance, evolution, flow, passage; sequence, order, succession.
3 *by adopting this sensible course, time and money will be saved:* procedure, plan, plan of action, course of action, approach, policy, strategy, programme, method, technique, way.
4 *a French course:* programme/course of study, curriculum, syllabus; classes, lectures, studies.
5 *a course of antibiotics:* programme, schedule, regimen.
6 *a waterlogged course:* racecourse, racetrack, track, ground.
▷**verb** *tears coursed down her cheeks:* flow, pour, stream, run, roll, rush, gush, cascade, flood.
□ **in due course**
I will explain everything in due course: at the appropriate time, in time, at a later date, by and by, sooner or later, in the end, eventually.
□ **of course**
there are, of course, exceptions to the rule: naturally, as might be expected, as you would expect, needless to say, certainly, obviously.

court noun

1 *the court found him guilty:* court of law, law court, tribunal; bench, judicature.
2 *he put on plays for the King's court:* royal household, royal establishment, retinue, entourage, courtiers, attendants.
▷**verb**
1 *it's Oscar season, and in Hollywood the movie studios are courting the media:* cultivate, curry favour with, try to win over, make up to, ingratiate yourself with; informal suck up to, butter up.
2 *he was busily courting public attention:* seek, pursue, go after, strive for, solicit.
3 *he's often courted controversy:* risk, invite, attract, bring on yourself.

courteous adjective *a cheerful and courteous young man:* polite, well mannered, civil, respectful, well bred, gracious, obliging, considerate, pleasant, cordial, urbane, polished, refined, civilized, mannerly; gentlemanly, chivalrous, gallant. OPPOSITES: rude.

courtesy noun *he treated the players with courtesy and good humour:* politeness, courteousness, good manners, civility, respect, respectfulness; consideration, graciousness, thought, thoughtfulness, cordiality, urbanity; chivalry, gallantry.

courtly adjective *a lawyer known for his courtly manner and diplomatic skills:* refined, polished, suave, cultivated, civilized, urbane, debonair; polite, civil, courteous, gracious, well mannered, chivalrous, gallant, dignified, decorous.

courtyard noun quadrangle, cloister; square, enclosure, yard.

cove noun *a small sandy cove:* bay, inlet.

covenant noun *a breach of the covenant:* contract, agreement, commitment, guarantee, pledge, promise, bond, undertaking.
▷**verb** *the landlord covenants to repair the property:* undertake, contract, guarantee, pledge, promise, agree, engage, commit yourself, bind yourself.

cover verb

1 *she covered her face with a towel:* protect, shield; hide, conceal, veil.
2 *his car was covered in mud:* cake, encrust, coat, plaster, smother, daub.
3 *snow covered the fields:* blanket, overlay, carpet, coat.
4 *a course covering all aspects of the business:* deal with, consider, take in, include, involve, comprise, incorporate, treat, embrace.
5 *the trial was covered by a range of newspapers:* report on, write about, describe, commentate on, publish/broadcast details of.
6 *he turned on the radio to cover their conversation:* mask, disguise, hide, camouflage, muffle, stifle, smother.
7 *I'm covering for Jill:* stand in for, fill in for, deputize for, take over from, relieve, take the place of, sit in for, understudy, hold the fort for; informal sub for.
8 *can you make enough to cover your costs?* pay, be enough for, fund, finance; pay back, make up for, offset.
9 *your home is covered against damage and loss:* insure, protect, secure, indemnify.
10 *we covered ten miles each day:* travel, journey, go, do, traverse.
OPPOSITES: expose.
▷**noun**
1 *a protective cover:* case, covering, sleeve, wrapping, wrapper, envelope, sheath, housing, jacket, casing, cowling; awning, canopy, tarpaulin.
2 *a manhole cover:* lid, top, cap.
3 *a book cover:* binding, jacket, dust jacket, dust cover, wrapper.
4 *a thick cover of snow:* coating, coat, covering, layer, carpet, blanket, overlay, dusting, film, sheet, veneer, crust, skin, cloak, mantle, veil, pall, shroud.
5 *panicking onlookers ran for cover:* shelter, protection, refuge, sanctuary, a haven, a hiding place.
6 *the company was a cover for an international swindle:* front, facade, smokescreen, camouflage, screen, disguise.
7 (Brit.) *your policy provides cover against damage by subsidence:* insurance, protection, security, indemnification, indemnity, compensation.

c

□ **cover something up**
officials tried to cover up the scandal:
conceal, hide, keep secret/dark,
whitewash, hush up, draw a veil over,
suppress, sweep under the carpet, gloss
over; informal keep a/the lid on.

coverage noun *they praised the
newspaper's coverage of the issue:*
reportage, reporting, treatment, handling,
presentation, investigation, commentary;
reports, articles, pieces, stories.

covering noun
1 *a canvas covering:* awning, canopy,
tarpaulin, cowling, casing, housing;
wrapping, wrapper, cover, case, envelope,
sheath, sleeve, jacket, lid, top, cap.
2 *a covering of snow:* layer, coating, coat,
carpet, blanket, overlay, topping, dusting,
film, sheet, veneer, crust, skin; cloak,
mantle, veil.
▷ **adjective** *a covering letter:* accompanying,
explanatory, introductory, prefatory.

covert adjective *covert surveillance |
covert military operations:* secret, furtive,
clandestine, surreptitious, stealthy,
hidden, concealed, private, undercover,
underground; cloak-and-dagger, under-
the-table, backstairs; informal hush-hush.
OPPOSITES: overt.

cover-up noun *a senior official claimed
that there had been a deliberate cover-up
of the facts:* whitewash, concealment,
camouflage, disguise, deception.
OPPOSITES: exposé.

covet verb *you have to remember that he
had coveted the job for years:* desire, yearn
for, crave, have your heart set on, want,
wish for, long for, hanker after/for, hunger
after/for, thirst for.

covetous adjective grasping, greedy,
acquisitive; envious, jealous.

cow verb *they had been cowed into silence:*
intimidate, browbeat, bully, tyrannize,
scare, terrorize, frighten, subdue; daunt,
dishearten.

coward noun weakling, milksop; informal
chicken, wimp, sissy.
OPPOSITES: hero.

cowardly adjective *a weak, cowardly
man:* spineless, craven, lily-livered,
faint-hearted, timid, timorous, fearful,
pusillanimous; informal yellow, chicken,
gutless, wimpish; Brit. informal wet.
OPPOSITES: brave.

cowboy noun cattleman, cowhand,
cowman, cowherd, herder, herdsman,
drover, stockman, rancher; (in South America)
gaucho.

cower verb *children cowered in terror
as the shoot-out erupted:* cringe, shrink,
crouch, recoil, flinch, pull back, draw
back, tremble, shake, quake, blench, quail,
grovel.

coy adjective *she treated him to a coy smile:*
arch, coquettish, flirtatious, kittenish,
simpering; demure, shy, modest, bashful,
reticent, diffident, self-effacing, timid.

crabby adjective *she was regarded
as crabby and reclusive:* irritable,
cantankerous, irascible, bad-tempered,
grumpy, grouchy, crotchety, tetchy, testy,
crusty, curmudgeonly, ill-tempered,
peevish, cross, fractious, prickly, waspish;
informal snappy; Brit. informal stroppy.
OPPOSITES: affable.

crack noun
1 *a crack in the glass:* split, break, chip,
fracture, rupture.
2 *a crack between two rocks:* space, gap,
crevice, fissure, cleft, breach, rift, cranny,
chink, interstice.
3 *the crack of a rifle:* bang, report,
explosion, detonation, pop; clap, crash.
4 *a crack on the head:* blow, bang, hit,
knock, rap, punch, thump, bump, smack,
slap; informal bash, whack, thwack, clout,
wallop, clip, biff.
▷ **verb**
1 *the glass cracked in the heat:* break, split,
fracture, rupture, snap.
2 *she cracked him across the forehead:* hit,
strike, smack, slap, beat, thump, knock,
rap, punch; informal bash, whack, thwack,
clobber, clout, clip, wallop, belt.
3 (informal) *you've got 48 hours to crack
the code:* decipher, decrypt, decode,
break; work out, solve, interpret; informal
figure out.
▷ **adjective** *he's a crack shot:* expert, skilled,
skilful, formidable, excellent, first-
rate, first-class, marvellous, wonderful,
magnificent, outstanding, superb,
superlative; deadly; informal great, fantastic,
ace, mean; Brit. informal brilliant.
□ **crack down on** (informal) *new plans have
been announced to crack down on benefit
fraud:* suppress, prevent, put a stop
to, stop, put an end to, end, stamp out,
eliminate, eradicate; clamp down on,
get tough on, come down hard on, limit,
restrain, restrict, check, keep in check,
control, keep under control.

cracked adjective *a cracked cup:* chipped,
broken, fractured, splintered, split;
damaged, defective, flawed, imperfect.

crackle verb *I could hear the sound of
bacon and eggs crackling in the frying pan:*
sizzle, hiss, fizz, snap, sputter.

cradle noun
1 *the baby's cradle:* crib, bassinet, Moses
basket; cot, carrycot.
2 *ancient Greece was the cradle
of democracy:* birthplace, fount,
fountainhead, source, spring, fountain,
origin, place of origin, seat.
▷ **verb** *she cradled his head in her arms:* hold,
support, pillow, cushion, shelter, protect;
rest, prop.

craft noun

1 *museum visitors can watch professional artists demonstrate their craft:* skill, art, talent, expertise, proficiency, ability, capability.
2 *the historian's craft:* activity, occupation, profession, work, line of work, pursuit.
3 *she used craft and diplomacy:* cunning, guile, craftiness, wiliness, artfulness, deviousness, slyness, trickery, subterfuge; wiles, ploys, ruses, schemes, stratagems, tricks.
4 *a sailing craft:* vessel, ship, boat.

craftsman, **craftswoman** noun
artisan, artist, skilled worker; expert, master.

craftsmanship noun *one of the finest examples of early twentieth-century Russian craftsmanship:* workmanship, artistry, craft, art, handiwork, work; skill, expertise, technique.

crafty adjective *a crafty smile crept across his face:* cunning, wily, guileful, artful, devious, sly, tricky, scheming, calculating, designing, sharp, shrewd, astute, canny; duplicitous, dishonest, deceitful.
OPPOSITES: honest.

crag noun cliff, ridge, precipice, height, peak, tor, escarpment, scarp, bluff.

craggy adjective
1 *the craggy cliffs:* steep, precipitous, sheer, perpendicular; rocky, rugged.
2 *his craggy face:* rugged, rough-hewn, strong, manly; weather-beaten, weathered.

cram verb
1 *the wardrobe was crammed with clothes:* fill, stuff, pack, jam, fill to overflowing, fill to the brim, overload; crowd, throng, overcrowd.
2 *he crammed his clothes into a suitcase:* thrust, push, shove, force, ram, jam, stuff, pack, pile, squash, compress, squeeze, wedge.
3 *they all crammed into the car:* crowd, pack, pile, squash, wedge yourself, force your way.
4 *most of the students are cramming for exams:* revise; informal swot, mug up, bone up.

cramp noun *stomach cramps:* spasm, pain, shooting pain.
▷verb *tighter rules will cramp economic growth:* hinder, impede, inhibit, hamper, constrain, hamstring, interfere with, restrict, limit; slow down, check, curb, retard.

cramped adjective
1 *cramped living quarters:* poky, uncomfortable, confined, restricted, small, tiny, narrow.
2 *cramped handwriting:* small, crabbed, illegible, unreadable, indecipherable.
OPPOSITES: spacious.

crank noun *when he first started to air his views, they labelled him a crank:* eccentric, madman/madwoman, lunatic; informal oddball, freak, nut, nutcase, head case; Brit. informal nutter.

cranky adjective (informal) *a cranky diet:* eccentric, bizarre, peculiar, odd, strange, unconventional, outlandish; silly, stupid, mad, crazy, idiotic; informal weird, wacky, crackpot, nutty; Brit. informal daft.

cranny noun *every little cranny was filled with drifted snow:* chink, crack, crevice, slit, split, fissure, rift, cleft, opening, gap, aperture, cavity, hole, hollow, niche, corner, nook, interstice.

crash verb
1 *the car crashed into a tree:* smash into, collide with, be in collision with, hit, strike, ram, cannon into, plough into, meet head-on, run into.
2 *he crashed his car:* smash, wreck; Brit. write off; Brit. informal prang; N. Amer. informal total.
3 *waves crashed against the shore:* dash, batter, pound, lash, slam, be hurled.
4 *thunder crashed overhead:* boom, crack, roll, bang, blast, blare, resound, reverberate, rumble, thunder, echo.
▷noun
1 *a crash on the motorway:* accident, collision, pile-up, smash, road traffic accident, RTA; derailment; N. Amer. wreck; Brit. informal prang, shunt.
2 *a loud crash:* bang, smash, smack, crack, bump, thud, clatter, clunk, clonk, clang; report, detonation, explosion; noise, racket, clangour, din.
▷adjective *a crash course:* intensive, concentrated, rapid, short; accelerated-learning, total-immersion.

crass adjective *a crass remark | a crass attempt at humour:* stupid, foolish, insensitive, mindless, thoughtless, witless, asinine; boorish, coarse, graceless, tasteless, tactless, clumsy, heavy-handed, blundering; informal ignorant.
OPPOSITES: intelligent.

crate noun case, packing case, box, chest, tea chest; container, receptacle.

crater noun hollow, bowl, basin, hole, cavity, pit, depression.

crave verb *he craved professional recognition:* long for, yearn for, desire, want, wish for, hunger for, thirst for, hanker after, covet, lust after, ache for, set your heart on, dream of, be bent on; informal itch for, be dying for.

craven adjective *a craven surrender:* cowardly, spineless, lily-livered, pusillanimous, weak, feeble; contemptible, abject, ignominious; informal gutless.
OPPOSITES: brave.

craving noun *her desperate craving for affection:* longing, yearning, desire, want,

crawl verb

1 *they crawled under the table:* creep, worm your way, go on all fours, go on hands and knees, wriggle, slither, squirm, scrabble.

2 *the place was crawling with soldiers:* be full of, be packed with, be crowded with, be overrun with, swarm with, overflow with, teem with, be alive with, be bristling with, be infested with; informal be stuffed with, be jam-packed with, be chock-a-block with, be chock-full of.

3 (informal) *I'm not going to go crawling to him:* grovel to, ingratiate yourself with, be obsequious to, kowtow to, pander to, toady to, bow and scrape to, curry favour with, make up to, fawn on/over; Brit. dance attendance on; informal suck up to.

craze noun *the latest fitness craze to sweep the country:* fad, fashion, trend, vogue, enthusiasm, mania, passion, rage, obsession, fixation, fascination, fetish.

crazed adjective *a crazed murderer:* mad, insane, out of your mind, deranged, demented, certifiable, lunatic; wild, raving, berserk, manic, frenzied; informal crazy, mental, raving mad; Brit. informal off your head, out of your head. See also **CRAZY** sense 1.
OPPOSITES: sane.

crazy adjective (informal)

1 *a crazy old man:* mad, insane, deranged, demented, out of your mind, not in your right mind, crazed, lunatic, disturbed; informal mental, nutty, off your rocker, off your trolley, round the bend, raving mad, batty, bonkers, loopy, loony, touched, gaga, doolally, not all there, out to lunch, away with the fairies; Brit. informal barmy, crackers, barking, potty, off your head, round the twist.

2 *a crazy idea:* stupid, foolish, idiotic, silly, asinine, absurd, ridiculous, ludicrous, preposterous, farcical, nonsensical, imbecilic; impracticable, unworkable, ill-conceived, senseless; informal hare-brained, cockeyed; Brit. informal daft.

3 *he's crazy about her:* passionate about, very keen on, enamoured of, infatuated with, smitten with, devoted to; very enthusiastic about; informal wild/mad/nuts about; fanatical about.
OPPOSITES: sane, sensible.

creak verb *the floorboards creaked:* squeak, grate, rasp; groan, complain.

cream noun

1 *skin creams:* lotion, moisturizer, emollient, unguent, cosmetic; salve, rub, embrocation, ointment, balm, liniment.

2 *the cream of the world's photographers:* best, finest, pick, flower, crème de la crème, elite.

▷ adjective *a cream linen jacket:* off-white, cream-coloured, ivory, yellowish-white, whitish.

creamy adjective *mix the flour and milk into a creamy paste:* smooth, thick, velvety; rich, buttery.

crease noun

1 *trousers with knife-edge creases:* fold, line, ridge; pleat, tuck.

2 *the creases at the corners of her eyes:* wrinkle, line, furrow, crinkle, pucker; (**creases**) crow's feet.

▷ verb *her skirt was creased and stained:* crumple, wrinkle, crinkle, line, scrunch up, rumple, ruck up.

create verb

1 *she has created a work of stunning originality:* produce, make, generate, fashion, bring into being, build, construct, fabricate; design, devise, originate, develop, shape, form, frame.

2 *regular socializing creates a good team spirit:* bring about, give rise to, lead to, result in, generate, engender, produce, make for, promote, contribute to, foster, cause, breed, sow the seeds of.

3 *the governments planned to create a free-trade zone:* establish, found, initiate, institute, inaugurate, launch, set up, form, organize, develop.

4 *she was created a life peer in 1990:* appoint, make; invest as, install as.
OPPOSITES: destroy.

creation noun

1 *the creation of a coalition government:* establishment, formation, foundation, initiation, institution, inauguration, constitution; production, generation, fabrication, fashioning, building, construction, origination, development.

2 *Dickens's literary creations:* work, work of art, production, opus, oeuvre; achievement.
OPPOSITES: destruction.

creative adjective *pupils are encouraged to be creative | some creative thinking provided the solution:* inventive, imaginative, innovative, innovatory, experimental, original; artistic, inspired, visionary; enterprising, resourceful; informal blue-sky.

creativity noun inventiveness, imagination, imaginativeness, innovation, innovativeness, originality; artistry, inspiration, vision; enterprise, initiative, resourcefulness.

creator noun *the creator of the series:* author, writer, designer, deviser, maker, producer; originator, inventor, architect, mastermind, prime mover.

creature noun

1 *the earth and its creatures:* animal, beast; living thing, living being.

2 *she was denounced as a creature of the*

liberals: lackey, minion, hireling, servant, puppet, tool, pawn, cat's paw; informal stooge, yes-man; Brit. informal poodle.

credence noun
1 *the government placed little credence in the scheme:* belief, faith, trust, confidence, reliance.
2 *later reports lent credence to this view:* credibility, plausibility.

credentials plural noun
1 *the police went to check the driver's credentials:* documents, documentation, papers, identity papers, ID, proof of identity, bona fides.
2 *recruitment is based mainly on academic credentials:* qualifications, certification, accreditation.

credibility noun
1 *the whole tale lacks credibility:* plausibility, probability, feasibility, credence.
2 *the party lacked moral credibility:* trustworthiness, reliability, dependability, integrity.

credible adjective *very few people found his story credible:* believable, plausible, tenable, able to hold water, conceivable, likely, probable, possible, feasible, reasonable, with a ring of truth, persuasive.
OPPOSITES: incredible.

credit noun *he never got much credit for the show's success:* acknowledgement, recognition, praise, acclaim, commendation, glory, esteem, respect, admiration, tributes, thanks, gratitude, appreciation.
▷ verb
1 *the wise will seldom credit all they hear:* believe, accept, give credence to, trust, have faith in; informal buy, swallow, fall for, take something as gospel.
2 *the scheme's success can be credited to the team's frugality:* ascribe, attribute, assign, accredit, chalk up, put down.

creditable adjective *the team worked hard and produced a creditable performance:* commendable, praiseworthy, laudable, admirable, estimable, meritorious, worthy, deserving, respectable.
OPPOSITES: deplorable.

credulous adjective *he sold 'miracle' cures to desperate and credulous clients:* gullible, naive, over-trusting, over-trustful, easily taken in, impressionable, unsuspecting, unsuspicious, unwary, unquestioning; innocent, ingenuous, inexperienced, unsophisticated, unworldly, wide-eyed.
OPPOSITES: suspicious.

creed noun
1 *people of many creeds and cultures:* faith, religion, religious belief, religious persuasion, faith community, Church, denomination, sect.

2 *his political creed:* system of belief, beliefs, principles, articles of faith, ideology, credo, doctrine, teaching, dogma, tenets, canons.

creek noun inlet, arm of the sea, bay, estuary, bight, fjord, sound; Scottish firth, frith.

creep verb *Tim crept out of the house:* tiptoe, steal, sneak, slip, slink, sidle, pad, edge, inch; skulk, prowl.

creepy adjective (informal) *that house is really creepy:* frightening, eerie, disturbing, sinister, weird, hair-raising; informal spooky, scary.

crest noun
1 *the bird's crest:* comb, plume, tuft of feathers.
2 *we reached the crest of the hill:* top, brow, crown, tip, peak, summit, pinnacle, apex.
3 *the Duke of Wellington's crest:* insignia, regalia, badge, emblem, coat of arms, arms, heraldic device.

crestfallen adjective *he came back empty-handed and crestfallen:* downhearted, downcast, despondent, disappointed, disconsolate, disheartened, discouraged, dispirited, dejected, depressed, desolate, sad, glum, gloomy, dismayed, doleful, miserable, unhappy, woebegone, forlorn; informal down in the mouth, down in the dumps.
OPPOSITES: cheerful.

crevasse noun *the sled slipped sideways into the crevasse:* chasm, abyss, fissure, cleft, crack, split, breach, rift, hole, cavity.

crevice noun *birds nested in every crevice of the cliff:* crack, fissure, cleft, chink, interstice, cranny, nook, slit, split, rift, fracture, breach; opening, gap, hole.

crew noun
1 *the ship's crew:* sailors, mariners, hands, ship's company, ship's complement.
2 *a crew of cameramen and sound engineers:* team, group, company, unit, corps, party, gang, squad.

crib noun
1 *the baby's crib:* cot, cradle, bassinet, Moses basket, carrycot.
2 *the oxen's cribs:* manger, stall, feeding trough.

crick verb *he cricked his neck during practice:* strain, twist, rick, sprain, pull, wrench; injure, hurt.

crime noun
1 *kidnapping is a very serious crime:* offence, unlawful act, illegal act, felony, misdemeanour, misdeed, wrong.
2 *the increase in crime:* lawbreaking, lawlessness, delinquency, wrongdoing, criminality, misconduct, illegality, villainy.
3 *a crime against humanity:* sin, evil, immoral act, wrong, atrocity, abomination, disgrace, outrage.

C

C

criminal noun *a convicted criminal:*
lawbreaker, offender, felon; villain,
wrongdoer, culprit, miscreant; convict;
formal malefactor; informal crook; N. Amer.
informal hood.
▷**adjective**
1 *criminal conduct:* unlawful, illegal,
illicit, lawless, felonious, actionable;
villainous, nefarious, corrupt, wrong, bad,
evil, wicked, iniquitous; informal crooked;
Brit. informal bent.
2 (informal) *a criminal waste of taxpayer's
money:* deplorable, shameful,
reprehensible, disgraceful, inexcusable,
unforgivable, unpardonable, outrageous,
monstrous, shocking, scandalous, wicked.
OPPOSITES: lawful.

cringe verb
1 *she cringed as he bellowed in her ear:*
cower, shrink, recoil, shy away, flinch,
blench, draw back, quail, tremble.
2 *it makes me cringe when I think of it:*
wince, shudder, squirm, feel embarrassed.

crinkle verb *Rose's face crinkled in
bewilderment:* wrinkle, crease, pucker,
furrow; rumple, scrunch up.

crinkly adjective wrinkled, crinkled,
wrinkly, creased, crumpled, rumpled,
corrugated, puckered, furrowed; wavy,
crimped.

cripple verb
1 *the accident crippled her:* disable,
paralyse, immobilize, incapacitate.
2 *the company had been crippled by the
recession:* devastate, severely damage;
paralyse, bring to a standstill, put out of
action, bring someone to their knees.

crisis noun
1 *the situation had reached a crisis:* critical
point, turning point, crossroads, head,
moment of truth, zero hour, point of no
return, climax, climacteric; informal crunch.
2 *the current economic crisis:* emergency,
disaster, catastrophe, calamity;
predicament, plight, mess, trouble,
difficulty, dire straits, extremity.

crisp adjective
1 *crisp bacon:* crunchy, crispy, brittle;
crumbly, friable, breakable; firm, dry.
2 *a crisp autumn day:* invigorating,
bracing, brisk, fresh, refreshing,
exhilarating, energizing; cool, chill, chilly,
cold.
3 *her answer was crisp:* brisk, decisive,
businesslike, no-nonsense, incisive, to the
point, matter-of-fact, brusque; succinct,
concise, brief, short, short and sweet,
laconic.
4 *crisp white bedlinen:* smooth, ironed;
starched.
OPPOSITES: soft, sultry.

criterion noun *In sport, there is only one
real criterion of success: the result* | *they
award a green label to products that meet

certain environmental criteria:* standard,
principle, benchmark, yardstick, measure,
gauge, test, touchstone, point of reference.

critic noun
1 *a literary critic:* reviewer, commentator,
evaluator, analyst, judge; expert, authority,
pundit.
2 *critics of the government:* detractor,
attacker.

critical adjective
1 *a highly critical report:* censorious,
unfavourable, condemnatory, disparaging,
disapproving, scathing, negative,
uncomplimentary; judgemental.
2 *a critical essay:* evaluative, analytical.
3 *the situation remains critical:* grave,
serious, dangerous, risky, perilous,
hazardous, precarious, touch-and-go, in the
balance, uncertain, desperate, dire, acute,
life-and-death; old use parlous.
4 *the choice of materials is critical for
product safety:* crucial, vital, essential, of
the essence, all-important, paramount,
fundamental, key, pivotal, decisive.
OPPOSITES: complimentary, favourable.

criticism noun
1 *she was stung by his criticism:*
censure, condemnation, denunciation,
disapproval, disparagement; attack,
broadside, strictures, recriminations; formal
opprobrium; informal flak, a bad press; Brit.
informal stick.
2 *literary criticism:* evaluation,
assessment, appraisal, analysis, judgement;
commentary, interpretation.

criticize verb *they criticized the
government for failing to meet its human
rights obligations:* find fault with, censure,
denounce, condemn, attack, lambaste,
pillory, rail against, inveigh against, cast
aspersions on, pour scorn on, disparage,
denigrate, give a bad press to, run down;
formal castigate; informal knock, pan, slam,
hammer, lay into, pull to pieces; Brit. informal
slate.
OPPOSITES: praise.

critique noun *the article is a critique of
recent scholarship in Roman art:* analysis,
evaluation, assessment, appraisal,
appreciation, criticism, review, study,
commentary, exposition, exegesis.

crook noun (informal) *the man's a crook:*
criminal, lawbreaker, villain, felon,
wrongdoer; cheat, swindler, racketeer;
thief, robber; formal malefactor.
▷**verb** *he crooked his finger and called the
waiter:* bend, flex, cock, curve, curl.

crooked adjective
1 *narrow, crooked streets:* winding,
twisting, zigzag, meandering, serpentine;
tortuous.
2 *a crooked spine:* bent, twisted,
misshapen, deformed, contorted, out of
shape, distorted.

3 *the picture over the bed looked crooked:* lopsided, askew, awry, off-centre, uneven, out of true, out of line, asymmetrical, tilted, at an angle; informal cockeyed; Brit. informal skew-whiff, wonky.
4 (informal) *crooked business deals:* dishonest, illegal, unlawful, fraudulent, corrupt, criminal.
OPPOSITES: straight.

crop noun
1 *some farmers lost their entire crop:* harvest, year's growth, yield; fruits, produce.
2 *the current crop of politicians:* batch, lot, assortment, selection, collection; supply, intake.
3 *a rider's crop:* whip, switch, cane, stick.
▷ verb
1 *she's had her hair cropped:* cut short, cut, clip, shear, shave, lop off, chop off, hack off; dock.
2 *a flock of sheep were cropping the turf:* graze on, browse on, feed on, nibble, eat.
□ **crop up**
some urgent business has cropped up: happen, occur, arise, turn up, emerge, materialize, surface, appear, come to light, present itself.

WORD LINKS
agronomy the science of crop production

cross noun
1 *a bronze cross:* crucifix, rood.
2 *we all have our crosses to bear:* burden, trouble, worry, trial, tribulation, affliction, misfortune, adversity, hardship, vicissitude; millstone, albatross, thorn in your flesh/side; misery, woe, pain, sorrow, suffering; curse, bane; informal hassle, headache.
3 *a cross between a yak and a cow:* hybrid, hybridization, cross-breed, mongrel; mixture, amalgam, blend, combination.
▷ verb
1 *they crossed the hills on foot:* travel across, traverse, range over; negotiate, navigate.
2 *a lake crossed by a fine stone bridge:* span, bridge; extend/stretch across, pass over.
3 *the point where the two roads cross:* intersect, meet, join, connect, criss-cross.
4 *no one dared cross him:* oppose, resist, defy; contradict, argue with, quarrel with, stand up to, take a stand against, take issue with.
5 *the breed was crossed with the similarly coloured Friesian:* hybridize, cross-breed, interbreed, cross-fertilize, cross-pollinate.
▷ **adjective** *he seemed to be very cross:* angry, annoyed, irate, irritated, in a bad mood, vexed, irked, put out, displeased; irritable, short-tempered, bad-tempered, crotchety, grouchy, grumpy, fractious, testy, tetchy, crabby; informal mad, hot under the collar, peeved, riled, up in arms, steamed up; Brit. informal aerated, shirty, stroppy, ratty; N. Amer. informal sore.
OPPOSITES: pleased.

□ **cross something out**
he crossed out several sentences: delete, strike out, ink out, score out, edit out, blue-pencil, cancel, obliterate.

cross-examine verb *the witness did not wish to be cross-examined by the police:* interrogate, question, cross-question, quiz, give someone the third degree; informal grill, pump.

crossing noun
1 *a busy road crossing:* junction, crossroads, intersection, interchange; level crossing.
2 *a short ferry crossing:* journey, passage, voyage.

crosswise, crossways adverb *there was just about room to lie crosswise in the bed:* diagonally, obliquely, aslant, at an angle; on the bias.

crotchety adjective *he was tired and crotchety:* bad-tempered, irascible, irritable, grumpy, grouchy, cantankerous, short-tempered, tetchy, testy, curmudgeonly, ill-tempered, peevish, cross, fractious, waspish, crabby, crusty, prickly, touchy; informal snappish, snappy; Brit. informal shirty, stroppy, ratty.
OPPOSITES: good-humoured.

crouch verb *we all crouched behind the wall:* squat, bend down, hunker down, hunch over, stoop, kneel down; duck, cower.

crow verb
1 *a cock crowed:* cry, squawk, screech, caw.
2 *try to avoid crowing about your success:* boast, brag, gloat, show off, preen yourself, sing your own praises; Brit. blow your own trumpet; informal talk big.

crowd noun
1 *a crowd of people gathered in the street outside:* throng, horde, mass, army, herd, flock, drove, swarm, sea, multitude, host, troupe, pack, press, crush, mob; collection, company, gathering, assembly, assemblage, congregation.
2 *the final attracted a capacity crowd:* audience, spectators, listeners, viewers; house, turnout, attendance, gate.
3 *she wanted to stand out from the crowd:* majority, multitude, common people, populace, general public, masses, rank and file; Brit. informal Joe Public.
4 (informal) *he's been hanging round with Hurley's crowd:* set, group, circle, clique, coterie; camp; informal gang, crew, lot.
▷ verb
1 *reporters crowded round her:* cluster, flock, swarm, mill, throng, huddle, gather, assemble, congregate, converge.
2 *the guests all crowded into the dining room:* surge, push your way, jostle, elbow your way; squeeze, pile, cram.
3 *the quayside was crowded with holidaymakers:* throng, pack, jam, cram, fill.

crowded adjective *the crowded city streets:* packed, full, filled to capacity, congested, overcrowded, overflowing, teeming, swarming, thronged, populous, overpopulated; busy; informal jam-packed, chock-a-block, chock-full, bursting at the seams.
OPPOSITES: deserted.

crown noun
1 *a jewelled crown:* coronet, diadem, circlet.
2 *his family were loyal servants of the Crown:* monarch, sovereign, king, queen, emperor, empress; monarchy, royalty.
3 *the world heavyweight crown:* title, award, accolade, distinction, prize; laurels.
▷verb
1 *Queen Elizabeth was crowned in 1953:* enthrone, install; anoint.
2 *a teaching post at Harvard crowned his career:* round off, cap, be the climax of, be the culmination of; complete, put the finishing touch to.
3 *a steeple crowned by a gilded weathercock:* top, cap, tip, head, surmount.

crucial adjective
1 *negotiations were at a crucial stage:* pivotal, critical, key, decisive, deciding; life-and-death.
2 *confidentiality is crucial in this case:* all-important, of the utmost importance, of the essence, critical, pre-eminent, paramount, essential, vital, indispensable.
OPPOSITES: unimportant.

crude adjective
1 *crude oil:* unrefined, unprocessed, untreated; coarse, raw, natural.
2 *a crude barricade:* simple, basic, rudimentary, primitive, rough, rough and ready, make-do, makeshift, improvised, unfinished.
3 *crude jokes:* vulgar, rude, naughty, suggestive, bawdy, off colour, indecent, obscene, offensive, lewd, salacious, licentious, ribald, coarse, indelicate, tasteless, crass, smutty, dirty, filthy, scatological; informal blue.
OPPOSITES: refined, sophisticated.

cruel adjective
1 *a cruel man:* brutal, savage, inhuman, barbaric, barbarous, brutish, bloodthirsty, murderous, vicious, violent, sadistic, wicked, evil, fiendish, diabolical, monstrous, abominable; callous, ruthless, merciless, pitiless, remorseless, heartless, stony-hearted, hard-hearted, cold-blooded, cold-hearted, unfeeling, unkind, inhumane.
2 *her death was a cruel blow:* harsh, severe, bitter, harrowing, heartbreaking, heart-rending, painful, agonizing, traumatic; formal grievous.
OPPOSITES: compassionate.

cruelty noun *he treated her with extreme cruelty:* brutality, savagery, inhumanity, barbarity, barbarousness, viciousness, sadism; callousness, ruthlessness, lack of compassion.

cruise noun *a cruise down the Nile:* voyage, trip, journey.
▷verb
1 *she cruised across the Atlantic:* sail, voyage, journey.
2 *a taxi cruised past:* drive slowly, travel slowly; informal mosey.

crumb noun *there was only one crumb of comfort:* fragment, bit, scrap, shred, grain, particle, speck, morsel.

crumble verb *his empire began to crumble around him:* disintegrate, fall apart, fall to pieces, fall down, break up, collapse, fragment; decay, fall into decay, deteriorate, degenerate, go to rack and ruin.

crumbly adjective *a crumbly pastry crust:* crisp, crispy, brittle, breakable, friable, powdery, granular.

crumple verb
1 *she crumpled the note in her fist:* crush, scrunch up, screw up, squash, squeeze; Brit. scrumple.
2 *his trousers were dirty and crumpled:* crease, wrinkle, crinkle, rumple, ruck up.
3 *her resistance crumpled:* collapse, give way, cave in, break down, crumble, be overcome.

crunch verb *she crunched the biscuit with relish:* munch, chomp, champ, scrunch, bite into.
▷noun (informal) *when the crunch comes, she'll be forced to choose:* moment of truth, critical point, crux, crisis, decision time, zero hour, point of no return; showdown.

crusade noun *they have vowed to continue their crusade against crime:* campaign, drive, push, movement, effort, struggle; battle, war, offensive.
▷verb *she likes crusading for the cause of the underdog:* campaign, fight, do battle, battle, take up arms, take up the cudgels, work, strive, struggle, agitate, lobby; champion, promote.

crusader noun campaigner, fighter, champion, advocate; reformer.

crush verb
1 *essential oils are released when the herbs are crushed:* squash, squeeze, press, compress; pulp, mash, macerate, mangle; flatten, trample on, tread on.
2 *your dress will get crushed:* crease, crumple, rumple, wrinkle, crinkle, scrunch up, ruck up; Brit. scrumple up.
3 *crush the biscuits with a rolling pin:* pulverize, pound, grind, break up, smash, crumble; mill.
4 *the new regime crushed all popular uprisings:* suppress, put down, quell, quash, stamp out, put an end to, overcome,

overpower, defeat, break, subdue, extinguish.
5 *Alan was crushed by her words:* mortify, humiliate, abash, chagrin, deflate, demoralize, flatten, put someone in their place; devastate, shatter.
▷ **noun**
1 *he elbowed his way through the crush of people in the hall:* crowd, throng, horde, swarm, sea, mass, pack.
2 (informal) *a teenage crush:* infatuation, obsession, love, passion.

crust noun *a crust of ice had formed on the pond:* covering, layer, coating, cover, coat, sheet, thickness, deposit; encrustation, scab.

crusty adjective
1 *crusty French bread:* crisp, crispy; crumbly, brittle.
2 *a crusty old man:* irritable, cantankerous, irascible, bad-tempered, grumpy, grouchy, crotchety, short-tempered, tetchy, testy, crabby, curmudgeonly, peevish, cross, fractious, prickly, waspish; informal snappish, snappy.
OPPOSITES: soft, good-natured.

crux noun *the crux of the matter is that attitudes have changed:* nub, heart, essence, central point, main point, core, centre, nucleus, kernel; informal bottom line.

cry verb
1 *Mandy started to cry:* weep, sob, shed tears, wail, cry your eyes out, bawl, howl; snivel, whimper; Scottish greet; informal, blub, blubber, turn on the waterworks.
2 *'Wait!' he cried:* call, shout, exclaim, yell, shriek, scream, screech, bawl, bellow, roar, squeal, yelp; informal holler.
▷ **noun**
1 *a cry of despair:* shout, exclamation, call, yell, shriek, scream, screech, bellow, roar, howl, squeal, yelp; informal holler.
2 *fund-raisers have issued a cry for help:* appeal, plea, entreaty, cry from the heart, cri de cœur.

crypt noun tomb, vault, mausoleum, burial chamber, sepulchre, catacomb, undercroft, ossuary.

cryptic adjective *his cryptic comments taxed her powers of comprehension:* enigmatic, mysterious, mystifying, perplexing, puzzling, unclear, confusing, obscure, arcane, ambiguous, elliptical, oblique, veiled; oracular, Delphic; informal as clear as mud.
OPPOSITES: clear.

cuddle verb
1 *she picked up the baby and cuddled it:* hug, embrace, clasp, hold tight, hold/fold in your arms.
2 *the pair were kissing and cuddling:* embrace, hug, caress; pet, fondle; informal canoodle, smooch.

3 *I cuddled up to him:* snuggle, nestle, curl, nuzzle, burrow against.

cudgel noun *a thick wooden cudgel:* club, stick, truncheon, baton, bludgeon, cosh.
▷ **verb** *she was cudgelled to death:* bludgeon, club, beat, batter, bash, cosh.

cue noun *he looked at his watch and Sylvie knew it was a cue for her to leave:* signal, sign, indication, prompt, reminder; nod, word, gesture.

cuff verb *Cullam cuffed him on the ear:* hit, strike, slap, smack, box, thump, punch; informal clout, wallop, belt, whack, bash, clobber, biff.
□ **off the cuff** (informal)
1 *an off-the-cuff remark:* impromptu, extempore, ad lib; unrehearsed, unscripted, unprepared, improvised, spontaneous, unplanned.
2 *I spoke off the cuff:* without preparation, without rehearsal, impromptu, ad lib; informal off the top of your head.

cuisine noun *the restaurant specializes in French cuisine:* cooking, cookery; food, dishes.

cul-de-sac noun no through road, blind alley, dead end.

cull verb
1 *these lists have been culled from a variety of critical essays and reviews:* select, choose, pick, take, obtain, glean.
2 *he sees culling deer as a necessity:* slaughter, kill, destroy.

culminate verb *the festival culminated in a dramatic fire-walking ceremony:* come to a climax, come to a head, peak, climax, reach a pinnacle; build up to, lead up to; end with, finish with, conclude with.

culmination noun *the appointment was the culmination of his distinguished medical career:* climax, pinnacle, peak, high point, highest point, height, high water mark, top, summit, crest, zenith, crowning moment, apotheosis, apex, apogee; consummation, completion, finish, conclusion.
OPPOSITES: nadir.

culpable adjective *I hold you personally culpable:* to blame, guilty, at fault, in the wrong, answerable, accountable, responsible, blameworthy.
OPPOSITES: innocent.

culprit noun *the police are doing all they can to catch the culprit:* guilty party, offender, wrongdoer, miscreant; criminal, lawbreaker, felon; formal malefactor; informal crook.

cult noun
1 *a religious cult:* sect, group, movement.
2 *the cult of youth in Hollywood:* obsession with, fixation on, mania for, passion for, idolization of, devotion to, worship of, veneration of.

cultivate verb
1 *the peasants who cultivated the land became its owners:* till, plough, dig, hoe, farm, work.
2 *they were encouraged to cultivate basic food crops:* grow, raise, rear, plant, sow.
3 *she explained that the focus was on cultivating the students' creative skills:* develop, foster, nurture, promote, encourage.
4 *it helps if you go out of your way to cultivate the local people:* win someone's friendship, woo, pay court to, keep sweet, curry favour with, ingratiate yourself with; informal get in someone's good books.

cultivated adjective *a remarkably cultivated man:* cultured, educated, well read, civilized, enlightened, discerning, discriminating, refined, polished; sophisticated, urbane, cosmopolitan.

cultural adjective
1 *cultural achievements:* aesthetic, artistic, intellectual; educational.
2 *cultural differences:* social, societal; lifestyle.

culture noun
1 *20th-century popular culture:* the arts, the humanities, intellectual achievement; literature, music, painting, philosophy.
2 *Afro-Caribbean culture:* customs, traditions, heritage, ideas, mores, values; civilization, society, way of life, lifestyle.
3 *a man of culture:* intellectual awareness, artistic awareness, education, enlightenment, discernment, discrimination, good taste, taste, refinement, sophistication.

cultured adjective *a sensitive, cultured man:* cultivated, intellectually/artistically aware, artistic, enlightened, civilized, educated, well educated, well read, well informed, knowledgeable, discerning, discriminating, refined, sophisticated.
OPPOSITES: ignorant.

cumbersome adjective
1 *she struggled with the cumbersome suitcase:* unwieldy, unmanageable, awkward, clumsy; bulky, large, heavy, hefty, weighty, burdensome; formal incommodious.
2 *cumbersome administrative procedures:* complicated, complex, involved, inefficient, unwieldy, slow.

cumulative adjective *the cumulative effect of two years of drought:* increasing, accumulative, growing, mounting; collective, aggregate; Brit. knock-on.

cunning adjective *a cunning scheme:* crafty, wily, artful, guileful, devious, sly, scheming, designing, calculating, Machiavellian; shrewd, astute, clever, canny, ingenious; deceitful, deceptive, duplicitous.
OPPOSITES: honest.

▷ noun *his political cunning:* guile, craftiness, deviousness; shrewdness, astuteness; trickery, duplicity.

cup noun
1 *a cup and saucer:* teacup, coffee cup, demitasse; mug, beaker; old use chalice.
2 *the winner was presented with a silver cup:* trophy, award, prize.

cupboard noun cabinet, sideboard, dresser, armoire, credenza.

cupidity noun *he was anxious to defend himself from charges of cupidity:* greed, avarice, avariciousness, acquisitiveness, covetousness, rapacity, materialism.
OPPOSITES: generosity.

curable adjective *most skin cancers are curable:* remediable, treatable, operable.

curative adjective *the curative properties of herbs:* healing, therapeutic, medicinal, remedial, corrective, restorative, tonic, health-giving.

curator noun custodian, keeper, guardian, caretaker, steward.

curb verb *he tried to curb his temper:* restrain, hold back/in, keep back, repress, suppress, fight back, bite back, keep in check, check, control, rein in, contain, bridle, subdue; informal keep a/the lid on.
▷ noun *a curb on public spending:* restraint, restriction, check, brake, control, limitation, limit, constraint; informal crackdown.

> **USAGE**
>
> Do not confuse **curb** with **kerb**. In British English **kerb** means 'the stone edging of a pavement'.

cure verb
1 *doctors had told him that he was cured:* restore to health, make well/better; heal.
2 *economic equality cannot cure all social ills:* rectify, remedy, put/set right, right, fix, mend, repair, heal, make better; solve, sort out, be the answer/solution to; eliminate, end, put an end to.
3 *some farmers cured their own bacon:* preserve, smoke, salt, dry, pickle.
▷ noun
1 *at present there is no known cure for the disease:* remedy; antidote, antiserum; treatment.
2 *interest rate cuts are not the cure for the problem:* solution, answer, antidote, nostrum, panacea, cure-all; informal magic bullet.

cure-all noun *the antibiotic was supposed to be the great cure-all:* panacea, cure for all ills, sovereign remedy, nostrum; informal magic bullet.

curio noun trinket, knick-knack, ornament, bauble, bibelot; objet d'art, collector's item, rarity, curiosity.

curiosity noun
1 *his evasiveness aroused my curiosity:*
interest, spirit of inquiry, inquisitiveness.
2 *the drawing room was full of curiosities:*
oddity, curio.

curious adjective
1 *she was curious to know what had
happened:* intrigued, interested, eager/
dying to know, agog; inquisitive.
2 *her curious behaviour:* strange, odd,
peculiar, funny, unusual, bizarre, eccentric,
unexpected, unfamiliar, extraordinary,
abnormal, out of the ordinary, surprising,
incongruous; informal weird.
OPPOSITES: uninterested, ordinary.

curl verb
1 *smoke curled up from his cigarette:* spiral,
coil, wreathe, twirl, swirl; wind, curve,
bend, twist and turn, loop, meander, snake,
corkscrew, zigzag.
2 *Ruth curled her arms around his neck:*
wind, twine, entwine, wrap.
3 *they curled up together on the sofa:*
nestle, snuggle, cuddle.
▷ noun
1 *the tangled curls of her hair:* ringlet,
corkscrew, kink; wave, kiss-curl.
2 *a curl of smoke:* spiral, coil, twirl, swirl,
twist, corkscrew, curlicue, helix.

curly adjective *she had thick, curly hair:*
wavy, curling, curled, crimped, permed;
frizzy, kinky.
OPPOSITES: straight.

currency noun
1 *foreign currency:* money, legal tender,
cash, banknotes, notes, coins, coinage.
2 *a term which has gained new currency:*
prevalence, circulation, exposure;
acceptance, popularity.

current adjective
1 *you should try to keep abreast of current
events:* contemporary, present-day,
modern, present; topical, in the news.
2 *the idea is still current:* prevalent,
prevailing, common, accepted, in
circulation, popular, widespread.
3 *a current driving licence:* valid, up to
date.
4 *the current prime minister:* incumbent,
present, in office, in power; reigning.
OPPOSITES: past, former.
▷ noun
1 *a current of air:* flow, stream,
backdraught, slipstream; airstream,
thermal, updraught, draught;
undercurrent, undertow, tide.
2 *the book reflects a new current of opinion
among American intellectuals:* trend,
direction, tendency, movement.

> **USAGE**
>
> Do not confuse **current** with **currant**.
> **Current** means 'happening now', or 'a flow
> of water, air, or electricity'. A **currant** is a
> dried grape.

curriculum noun syllabus, course of
study, programme of study, subjects,
modules.

curse noun
1 *she put a curse on him:* malediction; the
evil eye; N. Amer. hex.
2 *footballers should be involved in the
campaign to stamp out the curse of racism:*
evil, blight, scourge, plague, cancer,
canker, poison.
3 *the curse of unemployment:* affliction,
burden, cross to bear, bane.
4 *the driver let out a stream of curses:*
swear word, expletive, oath, profanity,
four-letter word, obscenity, blasphemy;
formal imprecation; informal cuss.
▷ verb
1 *it seemed as if the family had been cursed:*
put a curse on, put the evil eye on, jinx;
N. Amer. hex.
2 *she was cursed with feelings of
inadequacy:* afflict, trouble, plague,
bedevil.
3 *drivers cursed and sounded their horns:*
swear, blaspheme, take the Lord's name
in vain; informal cuss, turn the air blue, eff
and blind.

cursed adjective *a cursed city:* ill-fated,
ill-starred, damned, doomed; jinxed.

cursory adjective *he gave the figures a
cursory glance:* perfunctory, desultory,
casual, superficial, token; hasty, quick,
hurried, rapid, brief, passing, fleeting.
OPPOSITES: thorough.

curt adjective *his reply was curt:* terse,
brusque, abrupt, sharp, clipped, blunt,
short, monosyllabic, summary; gruff,
offhand, unceremonious, ungracious,
rude, impolite, discourteous; informal
snappy.
OPPOSITES: expansive, polite.

curtail verb
1 *economic policies designed to curtail
spending:* reduce, cut, cut down, decrease,
lessen, pare down, trim, retrench; restrict,
limit, curb, rein in/back; informal slash.
2 *his visit was curtailed:* shorten, cut short,
truncate.
OPPOSITES: increase, lengthen.

curtain noun *he drew the curtains:*
hanging, blind; N. Amer. drape.
▷ verb *the bed was curtained off from the rest
of the room:* conceal, hide, screen, shield;
separate, isolate.

curtsy verb *she curtsied to the king:* bend
your knee, bow, drop/bob a curtsy; genuflect.

curvaceous adjective *a curvaceous young
woman:* shapely, voluptuous, full-figured,
buxom, Junoesque; cuddly; informal curvy,
well endowed.
OPPOSITES: skinny.

curve noun *the serpentine curves of
the river:* bend, turn, loop, curl, twist;

arc, arch, bow, half-moon, undulation, curvature.

▷**verb** *the road curved back on itself:* bend, turn, loop, wind, meander, undulate, snake, spiral, twist, coil, curl; arc, arch.

curved adjective arched, bowed, crescent, curving, bent; wavy, sinuous, serpentine, meandering, undulating, curvilinear, curvy.
OPPOSITES: straight.

cushion noun *the bank may have less of a cushion against inflation than it thinks:* protection, buffer, shield, defence, bulwark.

▷**verb**
1 *she cushioned her head on her arms:* support, cradle, prop, rest.
2 *to cushion the blow, wages and pensions were increased:* soften, lessen, diminish, decrease, mitigate, temper, allay, alleviate, take the edge off, dull, deaden.
3 *residents are cushioned from the outside world:* protect, shield, shelter, cocoon.

custodian noun keeper, guardian, protector, curator, overseer, superintendent; caretaker, steward.

custody noun *the property was placed in the custody of a trustee:* care, charge, keeping, safe keeping, protection; guardianship, responsibility, tutelage; custodianship, trusteeship.
□ **in custody**
he is currently in custody awaiting trial on corruption charges: in prison, in jail, imprisoned, incarcerated, locked up, under lock and key, detained; on remand; informal behind bars; Brit. informal banged up.

custom noun
1 *he was unfamiliar with the local customs:* tradition, practice, usage, observance, way, convention, institution; ceremony, ritual, procedure; mores.
2 *it is our custom to visit the Lake District in October:* habit, practice, routine, way; policy, rule; formal wont.
3 (Brit.) *if you keep me waiting I will take my custom elsewhere:* business, patronage, trade.

customarily adverb *these discussions customarily take place in the evening:* usually, traditionally, normally, as a rule, generally, ordinarily, commonly; habitually, routinely.
OPPOSITES: occasionally.

customary adjective
1 *it's customary to mark such an occasion with a toast | customary social behaviour:* usual, traditional, normal, conventional; familiar, accepted, routine, established, time-honoured, regular, prevailing.
2 *her customary good sense:* usual, accustomed, habitual; literary wonted.
OPPOSITES: unusual.

customer noun consumer, buyer, purchaser, patron, client; shopper; Brit. informal punter.

customs plural noun. See TAX noun.

cut verb
1 *the knife slipped and cut his finger:* gash, lacerate, slash, slit, pierce, penetrate, wound, injure; sever; scratch, graze, nick, snick, score; lance.
2 *cut the onion into small pieces:* chop, cut up, slice, dice, cube, mince; carve.
3 *cut back the new growth to about half its length:* trim, snip, clip, crop, shear, shave; pare; prune, pollard, poll, lop, dock; mow.
4 *lettering had been cut into the stonework:* carve, engrave, incise, etch, score; chisel, whittle.
5 *we need to cut costs:* reduce, cut back/down on, decrease, lessen, trim, slim down, downsize, retrench; mark down, discount, lower; Brit. rationalize; informal slash.
6 *the text has been substantially cut:* shorten, abridge, condense, abbreviate, truncate; edit; bowdlerize, expurgate.
7 *oil supplies to the area had been cut:* discontinue, break off, suspend, interrupt; stop, end, put an end to.
8 *the point where the line cuts the vertical axis:* cross, intersect, bisect; meet, join.

▷**noun**
1 *he had a nasty cut on his jaw:* gash, slash, laceration, incision, wound, injury; scratch, graze, nick, snick.
2 *a cut in interest rates:* reduction, cutback, decrease.
3 *the elegant cut of his jacket:* style, design; tailoring, lines, fit.
4 *he followed this remark with the unkindest cut of all:* insult, slight, affront, slap in the face, jibe, barb; informal put-down, dig.
5 *a cut of beef:* joint, piece, section.
6 (informal) *the directors are demanding their cut:* share, percentage, portion; informal slice; Brit. informal whack.
□ **cut back**
companies cut back on foreign investment: reduce, cut, cut down on, decrease, lessen, economize on, trim, slim down, scale down, downsize, pull/draw in your horns, tighten your belt, retrench; Brit. rationalize; informal slash.
□ **cut someone/something down**
1 *24 hectares of trees were cut down:* fell, chop down, hack down, saw down, hew.
2 *he was cut down in his prime:* kill, slaughter, shoot down, mow down, gun down.
□ **cut and dried**
definite, decided, settled; explicit, specific, precise, unambiguous, clear-cut, unequivocal, black and white, hard and fast.
□ **cut in**
interrupt, butt in, break in, interject, interpose, chime in; informal chip in.

□ **cut someone/something off**
1 *they cut off his finger:* sever, chop off, hack off; amputate.
2 *oil and gas supplies were cut off:* discontinue, disconnect, suspend, break off; stop, end, bring to an end.
3 *a community cut off from the mainland by the flood waters | she's cut herself off from the world:* isolate, separate, keep apart; seclude, sequester, closet, cloister.
□ **cut out**
both the engines cut out: stop working, stop, fail, give out, break down; informal die, give up the ghost, conk out; Brit. informal pack up.
□ **cut something out**
1 *cut out all the diseased wood:* remove, take out, excise.
2 *it's best to cut out alcohol altogether:* give up, refrain from, abstain from, go without; exclude, leave out; informal quit, leave off, pack in, lay off, knock off.
□ **cut something short**
they decided to cut short their holiday: break off, truncate, curtail; terminate, end, stop, bring to an untimely end.

cutback noun *there have been cutbacks in defence spending:* reduction, cut, decrease, retrenchment; economy, saving.
OPPOSITES: increase.

cute adjective *a cute little blonde girl with white ribbons in her hair:* endearing, adorable, lovable, sweet, lovely, appealing, engaging, delightful, dear, darling, winning, winsome, attractive, pretty; informal twee.

cut-price adjective *cut-price footwear:* cheap, marked down, reduced, on (special) offer, discount.

cut-throat adjective *there is cut-throat competition between rival firms:* fierce, intense, aggressive, ruthless, dog-eat-dog.

cutting noun
1 *a newspaper cutting:* clipping, clip, snippet; article, piece, column, paragraph.

2 *plant cuttings:* scion, slip; graft.
3 *fabric cuttings:* piece, bit, fragment; sample, swatch.
▷ **adjective**
1 *a cutting remark:* hurtful, wounding, barbed, pointed, scathing, acerbic, mordant, caustic, acid, sarcastic, sardonic, snide, spiteful, malicious, mean, nasty, cruel, unkind; informal bitchy, catty.
2 *cutting winter winds:* icy, icy-cold, freezing, arctic, glacial, bitter, chilly, chill; biting, piercing, penetrating, raw, keen, sharp.
OPPOSITES: friendly, warm.

cycle noun
1 *the recurrent cycle of harvest failure, food shortages, and price increases:* round, pattern, sequence; rhythm.
2 *the painting is one of a cycle of seven:* series, set, sequence, succession.

cyclical adjective *the cyclical fluctuations in demand:* recurrent, recurring, regular, repeated; periodic, seasonal, circular.

cyclone noun hurricane, typhoon, tropical storm, storm, tornado, whirlwind.

cynic noun *some cynics thought the controversy was all a publicity stunt:* sceptic, doubter; pessimist, prophet of doom, Cassandra; informal doom and gloom merchant.

cynical adjective *she was cynical about men:* sceptical, doubtful, distrustful, suspicious; pessimistic, negative, world-weary, disillusioned, disenchanted, jaundiced.
OPPOSITES: idealistic.

cynicism noun scepticism, doubt, distrust, mistrust, suspicion; pessimism, negativity, world-weariness, disenchantment.
OPPOSITES: idealism.

cyst noun growth, lump; abscess, boil, carbuncle.

C

Dd

dab verb

1 *she dabbed her mouth with her napkin:*
pat, press, touch, blot.
2 *dab some disinfectant on the cut:* put,
daub; apply to.
▷**noun** *a dab of glue:* drop, spot, smear,
splash, speck, trace, touch, bit; informal
smidgen.

dabble verb

1 *they dabbled their feet in rock pools:*
splash, dip, paddle; immerse.
2 *he dabbled in left-wing politics:* toy with,
flirt with, dip into, tinker with, play with.

daft adjective (Brit. informal)

1 *that's a daft idea:* absurd, preposterous,
ridiculous, ludicrous, farcical, laughable;
mad, idiotic, stupid, foolish, silly, inane,
fatuous; informal crazy, potty, hare-brained,
half-baked; Brit. informal barmy.
2 *she's not as daft as she looks:* stupid,
idiotic, empty-headed, simple-minded,
vacuous; informal thick, dim, dopey, dumb,
dim-witted, half-witted, slow on the
uptake, soft in the head.
OPPOSITES: sensible.

daily adjective *a daily event:* everyday, day-
to-day; formal quotidian, diurnal.

dainty adjective

1 *a dainty china cup:* delicate, fine, small,
pretty, exquisite, elegant.
2 *a dainty morsel:* tasty, delicious, choice,
luscious, mouth-watering, delectable;
appetizing, tempting, toothsome; informal
scrumptious, yummy, scrummy, moreish.
3 *a dainty eater:* fastidious, fussy, finicky,
faddish; particular; informal choosy, picky;
Brit. informal pernickety, faddy.

dais noun platform, stage, podium,
rostrum, stand.

dale noun valley, vale; hollow; Brit. dene,
combe; Scottish glen.

dally verb

1 *latecomers who dallied in the pub
almost missed the opening goal:* dawdle,
linger, take your time, waste time, idle;
delay; literary tarry; informal dilly-dally, hang
about.
2 *the company was dallying with the idea
of opening a new office:* toy, flirt, think

about, consider, wonder about; informal kick
around.
OPPOSITES: hurry.

dam noun *the dam burst:* barrage, barrier,
wall, embankment, dyke, barricade,
obstruction.
▷**verb** *the river was dammed to form Lake
Powell:* block, obstruct, hold back.

damage noun

1 *bombing caused extensive damage
to the area:* harm, destruction; havoc,
devastation.
2 *the damage to his reputation was
considerable:* harm, injury, detriment,
impairment.
3 *she won £4,300 damages:* compensation,
recompense, restitution, redress,
reparation; indemnification, indemnity.
▷**verb**
1 *the painting had been damaged by
vandals:* harm, spoil, disfigure, deface,
mutilate.
2 *the scandal could seriously damage his
career:* harm, injure, hurt, impair.
OPPOSITES: repair.

damaging adjective *new cars are less
damaging to the environment* | *the episode
is likely to have a damaging effect on the
economy:* harmful, detrimental, injurious,
hurtful, dangerous, destructive, inimical,
deleterious; bad, adverse, undesirable,
unfavourable; corrosive, unhealthy,
unwholesome.
OPPOSITES: beneficial.

damn verb *the council report damned the
club's proposal for a new £30m stadium
on green-belt land:* condemn, censure,
criticize, attack, denounce, revile; find
fault with, give something a bad press;
informal slam, lay into, blast; Brit. informal
slate.
OPPOSITES: praise.

damnation noun perdition, eternal
punishment, condemnation to hell.

damning adjective

1 *in the face of such damning evidence
he had little defence:* incriminating,
condemnatory, damaging; conclusive,
strong.
2 *a damning indictment of the government's*

record: highly critical, fierce, savage, scathing, devastating, searing, blistering.

damp adjective

1 *her palms were damp:* slightly wet, moist, sweaty.
2 *a damp evening:* humid, steamy, muggy, clammy, sticky; dank, wet, rainy, drizzly, showery, misty, foggy.
OPPOSITES: dry.

▷ **noun** *the damp in the air:* moisture, dampness, humidity, wetness, wet, water, condensation, steam, vapour; clamminess, dankness.

▷ **verb**
1 *sweat damped his hair.* See DAMPEN sense 1.
2 *nothing damped my enthusiasm.* See DAMPEN sense 2.

dampen verb

1 *the fine rain dampened her face:* moisten, damp, wet.
2 *nothing could dampen her enthusiasm:* lessen, decrease, diminish, reduce, moderate, damp, put a damper on, throw cold water on, cool; suppress, extinguish, quench, stifle, curb, limit, check, restrain, inhibit.

dampness noun. See DAMP noun.

dance verb

1 *little girls danced round me:* caper, frolic, skip, prance, gambol, jig, cavort, frisk; leap, jump.
2 *flames danced in the fireplace:* flicker, leap, dart, play, flit, quiver; twinkle, shimmer.
3 *they danced till dawn:* gyrate; informal bop, boogie, jive, trip the light fantastic.

▷ **noun** *she met her husband at a dance:* ball, disco, discotheque; N. Amer. prom; informal hop.

danger noun

1 *there's an element of danger in the job:* peril, hazard, risk, jeopardy; perilousness, riskiness, precariousness, uncertainty, instability, insecurity.
2 *he is a danger to society:* menace, hazard, threat, risk.
3 *a serious danger of fire:* risk, chance, possibility, probability, likelihood, prospect.
OPPOSITES: safety.

dangerous adjective

1 *ice was making the roads dangerous:* hazardous, perilous, treacherous, fraught with danger, risky, high-risk, unsafe, precarious, insecure, unpredictable, touch-and-go; informal dicey, chancy, hairy; Brit. informal dodgy.
2 *a dangerous criminal* | *dangerous animals:* ruthless, vicious, violent, desperate, savage, wild; menacing, threatening.
OPPOSITES: safe, harmless.

dangle verb

1 *a chain dangled from his belt:* hang, be suspended, swing, sway, flap; droop, trail.
2 *he dangled the keys:* wave, swing, jiggle, brandish, flourish.
3 *he dangled money in front of the locals:* offer, hold out; entice someone with, tempt someone with.

dangling adjective hanging, dangly; drooping, pendulous, trailing; literary pendent.

dank adjective *he shivered as he entered the dank cellar:* damp, cold, chilly, clammy, musty, unaired.

dapper adjective *he looked very dapper in a dark silk suit:* smart, spruce, trim, neat, well dressed, well groomed, well turned out, elegant, chic, dashing, debonair; informal snazzy, sharp.
OPPOSITES: scruffy.

dapple verb *rays of sunlight dappled the surface of the lake:* dot, fleck, streak, speck, speckle, mottle, marble.

dappled adjective *the animals have dappled coats that match the broken light of a woodland floor:* speckled, spotted, mottled, marbled, flecked; piebald, pied, brindle; patchy, variegated.

dare verb

1 *nobody dared to say a word:* be brave enough, have the courage; venture, have the temerity, have the audacity; risk, take the liberty of; informal have the nerve, stick your neck out, go out on a limb.
2 *she dared him to go:* challenge, defy, invite; provoke, goad; throw down the gauntlet.

▷ **noun** *she accepted the dare:* challenge, invitation; provocation, goad.

daredevil adjective *a daredevil skydiver:* daring, bold, fearless, intrepid; impulsive, impetuous, madcap, death-or-glory, reckless, rash, foolhardy, incautious, harum-scarum.
OPPOSITES: cowardly, cautious.

daring adjective *a daring attack:* bold, brave, courageous, plucky, intrepid, fearless, unafraid, undaunted, dauntless, valiant, valorous, heroic, adventurous, venturesome; madcap, rash, reckless; informal gutsy, spunky.

▷ **noun** *his sheer daring:* boldness, bravery, courage, fearlessness, intrepidity, valour, heroism, pluck; informal nerve, guts; Brit. informal bottle.

dark adjective

1 *a dark night:* black, pitch-black, inky; unlit, unilluminated; starless, moonless; dim, gloomy, shadowy, shady.
2 *dark hair:* brunette, dark brown, chestnut, sable, black, jet-black, ebony.
3 *the dark days of the war:* tragic, disastrous, calamitous, catastrophic, cataclysmic; dire, awful, terrible, dreadful, horrible, harrowing; wretched, unhappy.
4 *my mind is full of dark thoughts:* gloomy,

d

dismal, pessimistic, negative, bleak, grim, fatalistic, black, sombre; despairing, despondent, melancholy, glum, morose, mournful, doleful.
5 *a dark secret:* mysterious, secret, hidden, concealed, veiled; enigmatic, obscure, impenetrable, incomprehensible, cryptic.
6 *a dark look crossed his features:* angry, forbidding, sinister, threatening, ominous; moody, brooding.
OPPOSITES: bright, light, fair.

▷**noun**
1 *I opened the door and stood blinking in the dark of the cellar:* darkness, blackness, gloom, murkiness, shadow, shade.
2 *she went out after dark:* night, night-time, darkness; nightfall, evening, twilight, sunset.
OPPOSITES: light, day.

darken verb
1 *the sky darkened:* grow dark, grow dim, become overcast, cloud over, lour.
2 *the abuse darkened the rest of their lives:* cast a shadow over, overshadow, blight, cloud; spoil, ruin.

darkness noun
1 *lights shone in the darkness:* dark, blackness, gloom, dimness, murkiness, shadow, shade; dusk, twilight; literary gloaming.
2 *darkness fell:* night, night-time, dark.

darling noun *she's the darling of the media:* favourite, pet, idol; informal blue-eyed boy/girl.

▷**adjective**
1 *his darling wife:* dear, dearest, precious, adored, beloved, cherished, treasured.
2 *a darling little hat:* adorable, cute, sweet, charming, endearing, dear, delightful, lovely, beautiful, attractive, gorgeous, fetching, appealing.

darn verb *I don't expect you to darn my socks:* mend, repair, sew up, stitch up, patch.

dart noun
1 *a poisoned dart:* arrow, bolt; missile, projectile.
2 *she made a dart for the door:* dash, rush, run, bolt, break, sprint, bound, leap, dive.

▷**verb**
1 *Karl darted across the road:* dash, rush, hurry, run, bolt, fly, shoot, charge, race, sprint, bound, leap, dive; scurry, scamper; informal tear, scoot.
2 *he darted a glance at her:* direct, cast, throw, shoot, send, flash.

dash verb
1 *we dashed back to the car:* rush, hurry, hasten, race, run, sprint, bolt, dart, charge, fly, speed, zoom, shoot, hurtle, career, scurry, scuttle, scamper; Brit. hare; informal tear, belt, pelt, scoot, zip, hotfoot it, leg it; Brit. informal bomb.
2 *he dashed the glass to the ground:* hurl,

throw, toss, fling, cast; smash, crash, slam; informal chuck, sling.
3 *rain dashed against the walls:* be hurled, crash, smash; batter, strike, beat, pound, lash.
4 *the budget dashed hopes of an increase in funding:* shatter, destroy, wreck, ruin, thwart; informal put paid to; Brit. informal scupper.
OPPOSITES: dawdle, raise.

▷**noun**
1 *they made a dash for the door:* rush, race, run, sprint, bolt, dart, leap, charge, bound, break.
2 *the soup needs a dash of salt:* pinch, touch, sprinkle, taste, spot, drop, dab, speck, smattering, sprinkling, splash, bit, modicum, little; informal smidgen, tad.

dashing adjective
1 *a dashing young pilot:* handsome, confident, debonair; bold, intrepid, daring, adventurous, devil-may-care.
2 *he looked exceptionally dashing:* stylish, smart, elegant, debonair; fashionable.

data noun *there is a lack of data on the drug's effect on humans:* facts, figures, statistics, details, particulars, specifics; information, intelligence, material; informal info.

date noun
1 *I can never remember the date of the wedding:* day, day of the month, time; year; anniversary.
2 *a later date is suggested for this bridge:* age, time, period, era, epoch; century, decade, year.
3 *I have a lunch date:* appointment, meeting, engagement, rendezvous, assignation; commitment.
4 (informal) *have you got a date for tonight?* partner, escort, girlfriend, boyfriend.

▷**verb**
1 *the sculpture can be dated accurately:* assign a date to, ascertain the date of, put a date on.
2 *the building dates from the 16th century:* be made in, be built in, originate in, come from, belong to, go back to.
3 *the best films don't date:* become old-fashioned, become outmoded, become dated, show its age.
4 (informal) *he's been dating her for a few months now:* go out with, be involved with, see.

◻**to date**
so far, yet, as yet, up to now, till now, until now, up to the present, hitherto; formal thus far.

┌─────────────────────────────┐
│ WORD LINKS
│ **chronological** relating to dates
└─────────────────────────────┘

dated adjective *the graphics are looking a bit dated:* old-fashioned, outdated, outmoded, passé, behind the times, archaic, antiquated; unfashionable; informal old hat.
OPPOSITES: modern.

daub verb *the walls were daubed with paint:* smear, bedaub, plaster, splash, spatter, splatter; cover, smother, cake, coat.
▷ noun *daubs of paint:* smear, smudge, splash, blot, spot, patch, blotch; informal splotch; Brit. informal splodge.

daunt verb *it will take more than December sleet and gales to daunt the crews:* discourage, deter, demoralize, put off, dishearten, dispirit; intimidate, alarm, overawe, frighten, scare, dismay, unsettle, unnerve; throw off balance; informal rattle, faze, shake up.
OPPOSITES: encourage.

dauntless adjective *his dauntless comrades:* fearless, determined, resolute, indomitable, intrepid, doughty, plucky, spirited, feisty; undaunted, undismayed, unflinching, unshrinking, bold, audacious, valiant, brave, courageous, daring; informal gutsy, spunky.

dawdle verb
1 *they dawdled over breakfast:* linger, dally, take your time, be slow, waste time, idle; delay, procrastinate, stall; informal dilly-dally.
2 *Ruth dawdled home:* amble, stroll, trail, walk slowly, move at a snail's pace; informal mosey; Brit. informal mooch.
OPPOSITES: hurry.

dawn noun
1 *we got up at dawn:* daybreak, sunrise, first light, daylight; first thing in the morning; literary cockcrow.
2 *the dawn of civilization:* beginning, start, birth, inception, origination, genesis, emergence, advent, appearance, arrival, dawning, rise, origin, onset; unfolding, development, infancy.
OPPOSITES: dusk, end.
▷ verb
1 *Thursday dawned crisp and sunny:* begin, break, arrive, emerge.
2 *a bright new future has dawned:* begin, start, commence, be born, appear, arrive, emerge; arise, rise, break; unfold, develop.
3 *the reality dawned on him:* occur to, come to, strike, hit, register with; enter someone's mind, enter someone's consciousness, cross someone's mind, suggest itself.

day noun
1 *I stayed for a day:* twenty-four-hour period, twenty-four hours.
2 *the animals hunt during the day:* daytime, daylight; waking hours.
3 *the leading architect of the day:* period, time, era, age, generation.
4 *in his day he had great influence:* heyday, prime, time.
OPPOSITES: night.
□ **day after day**
repeatedly, again and again, over and over again, time and time again, frequently, often, time after time; {day in, day out},

night and day, all the time; persistently, recurrently, constantly, continuously, continually, relentlessly, regularly, habitually, unfailingly, always; informal 24-7.
□ **day by day**
1 *day by day they were forced to retreat:* gradually, slowly, progressively; bit by bit, inch by inch, little by little, inchmeal.
2 *they follow the news day by day:* daily, every day, day after day.

> WORD LINKS
> **diurnal** relating to the day

daybreak noun *they rested for the night and journeyed on at daybreak:* dawn, crack of dawn, sunrise, first light, first thing in the morning; daylight; literary cockcrow.
OPPOSITES: nightfall.

daydream noun
1 *she was lost in a daydream:* reverie, fantasy, dream; inattentiveness, wool-gathering, preoccupation, absent-mindedness, abstraction.
2 *a big house was one of her daydreams:* dream, pipe dream, fantasy, fond hope; wishful thinking; informal pie in the sky.
▷ verb *stop daydreaming and get on with something useful!* dream, fantasize, be lost in thought, be in cloud cuckoo land, build castles in the air, build castles in Spain.

daydreamer noun dreamer, fantasist, romantic, wishful thinker, idealist, Walter Mitty.

daylight noun
1 *do the test in daylight:* natural light, sunlight.
2 *she only went there in daylight:* daytime, day; broad daylight.
3 *police moved in at daylight:* dawn, daybreak, break of day, crack of dawn, sunrise, first light, first thing in the morning, early morning; literary cockcrow.
OPPOSITES: darkness, night-time, nightfall.

day-to-day adjective *day-to-day expenditure such as food, household goods, and petrol:* regular, everyday, daily, routine, habitual, frequent, normal, standard, usual, typical.

daze verb
1 *he was dazed by the fall:* stun, stupefy; knock unconscious, knock out.
2 *she was dazed by the revelations:* astound, amaze, astonish, startle, dumbfound, stupefy, overwhelm, stagger, shock, confound, bewilder, take aback, nonplus, shake up; informal flabbergast, knock sideways; Brit. informal knock for six.
▷ noun *she's in a daze:* stupor, trance, haze; spin, whirl, muddle, jumble.

dazzle verb
1 *she was dazzled by the headlights:* blind temporarily, deprive of sight.
2 *I was dazzled by the exhibition:* overwhelm, overcome, impress, move,

stir, affect, touch, awe, overawe, leave speechless, take someone's breath away; hypnotize; informal bowl over, blow away, knock out.

dazzling adjective

1 *the sunlight was dazzling:* bright, blinding, glaring, brilliant.
2 *a dazzling performance:* impressive, remarkable, extraordinary, outstanding, exceptional; incredible, amazing, astonishing, phenomenal, breathtaking, thrilling; excellent, wonderful, magnificent, marvellous, superb, first-rate, superlative, matchless; informal mind-blowing, out of this world, fabulous, sensational, ace, awesome.

dead adjective

1 *my parents are dead:* passed on/away, departed, gone, no more; late, lost, lamented; fallen, slaughtered, killed, murdered; lifeless, extinct; formal deceased; literary slain; informal six feet under.
2 *a dead language:* obsolete, extinct, defunct, disused, vanished, forgotten; archaic, antiquated, ancient.
3 *the phone's dead:* not working, out of order, inoperative, inactive, broken, malfunctioning; informal kaput, on the blink; Brit. informal knackered.
4 *a dead leg:* numb, numbed, deadened, desensitized; frozen.
5 *a cold, dead voice:* emotionless, unemotional, unfeeling, impassive, unresponsive, indifferent, dispassionate, inexpressive, wooden, stony, cold; deadpan, flat; blank, vacant.
6 *the place is dead tonight:* dull, boring, lifeless, uninteresting, unexciting, uninspiring, flat, quiet, sleepy, slow.
OPPOSITES: alive, lively.
▷ adverb
1 *he was dead serious:* completely, absolutely, totally, deadly, perfectly, entirely, quite, thoroughly; in every way, one hundred per cent.
2 *flares were seen dead ahead:* directly, exactly, precisely, immediately, right, straight, due, squarely; informal bang, slap bang.

deaden verb

1 *surgeons tried to deaden the pain:* numb, dull, blunt, suppress; alleviate, mitigate, diminish, reduce, lessen, ease, soothe, relieve, assuage.
2 *the wood panelling deadened any noise:* muffle, mute, smother, stifle, dull, damp down; silence, quieten, soften; cushion, buffer, absorb.
3 *laughing might deaden us to the moral issue:* desensitize, numb, anaesthetize; harden your heart, toughen.
OPPOSITES: intensify, amplify, sensitize.

deadline noun

the deadline for submissions is Friday 5th February: time limit, limit, finishing date, latest time, cut-off point.

deadlock noun

the strike reached a deadlock: stalemate, impasse, stand-off; standstill, halt, full stop, dead end.

deadly adjective

1 *these drugs can be deadly | a deadly disease:* fatal, lethal, life-threatening, death-dealing, mortal, extremely dangerous; noxious, toxic, poisonous.
2 *the two men became deadly enemies:* mortal, irreconcilable, implacable, unforgiving, remorseless, merciless, pitiless; bitter.
3 *his aim is deadly:* unerring, unfailing, perfect.
OPPOSITES: harmless, mild.
▷ adverb *her voice was deadly calm:* completely, absolutely, totally, utterly, perfectly, entirely, wholly, quite, dead, thoroughly; in every way, one hundred per cent, to the hilt.

deadpan adjective

she delivered the speech in a deadpan voice: blank, expressionless, unexpressive, impassive, inscrutable, poker-faced, straight-faced.
OPPOSITES: expressive.

deaf adjective

1 *she's a bit deaf:* hard of hearing, with impaired hearing.
2 *she was deaf to their pleading:* unmoved by, untouched by, unaffected by, indifferent to, unresponsive to, unconcerned by; unaware of, oblivious to, impervious to.

deafening adjective

the guns started up with a deafening roar: very loud, very noisy, ear-splitting, overwhelming, almighty, mighty, tremendous; booming, thunderous, roaring, resounding, resonant, reverberating.
OPPOSITES: quiet.

deal noun

the deal was completed last night: agreement, contract, arrangement, transaction, sale; settlement, understanding, pact, bargain; treaty; terms.
▷ verb
1 *they got advice on how to deal with difficult patients:* cope with, handle, manage, treat, take care of, take charge of, take in hand, sort out, tackle, take on; control; act towards, behave towards.
2 *the article deals with advances in chemistry:* concern, be about, have to do with, discuss, consider, cover, pertain to; tackle, study, explore, investigate, examine, review, analyse.
3 *the company deals in high-tech goods:* trade in, buy and sell; sell, supply, stock, market, merchandise; traffic, smuggle; formal purvey; Brit. informal flog.
4 *the cards were dealt:* distribute, give out, hand out, pass out, dole out, dispense; share out, allocate.
5 *the court dealt a blow to government reforms:* deliver, administer, inflict, give, impose; aim.

□ **a great deal/a good deal**
a lot, a large amount, a fair amount, much, plenty; informal lots, loads, heaps, masses, tons, bags; Brit. informal a shedload.

dealer noun *an antique dealer:* trader, tradesman, tradesperson, merchant, broker, agent; salesman/woman, seller, vendor; buyer, merchandiser, distributor, supplier, shopkeeper, retailer, wholesaler; Brit. stockist; formal purveyor.

dealing noun
1 *share dealings | drug dealing:* trading, transactions, buying and selling; business, commerce; traffic, trafficking.
2 *his aristocratic stiffness handicapped his dealings with middle-class politicians:* relations, relationship, association, contact; negotiations.

dear adjective
1 *a dear friend:* beloved, cherished; close, intimate, bosom, special.
2 *her pictures were too dear to part with:* precious, treasured, valued, prized, cherished, special.
3 (Brit.) *twenty pounds—that's a bit dear!* expensive, costly, overpriced, exorbitant, extortionate; Brit. over the odds; informal pricey, steep.

dearly adverb
1 *I love my son dearly:* very much, a great deal, greatly, deeply, profoundly; fondly, tenderly.
2 *our freedom has been bought dearly:* at great cost, at a high price, with much suffering, with much sacrifice.

dearth noun *given the dearth of empirical data, their study is very important:* lack, scarcity, shortage, want, insufficiency, inadequacy, paucity, sparseness; absence. OPPOSITES: surfeit.

death noun
1 *she broke down when she learnt of their death:* demise, dying, end, passing, loss of life; murder, assassination, execution, slaughter, massacre; formal decease; literary quietus.
2 *the resulting fires caused many deaths:* fatality, casualty.
3 *the death of their dream:* end, finish, termination, extinction, extinguishing, collapse, ruin, destruction, eradication, obliteration.
OPPOSITES: life, birth.
□ **put someone to death**
execute, hang, behead, electrocute, shoot, gas; kill, murder, assassinate, eliminate, destroy.

WORD LINKS
thanatology the scientific study of death

debacle noun *the president resigned after a string of economic debacles:* fiasco, failure, catastrophe, disaster, mess; collapse, defeat; Brit. informal cock-up.

debar verb
1 *women were debarred from the club:* exclude, ban, bar, disqualify, declare ineligible, keep out, blackball.
2 *the unions were debarred from striking:* prevent, prohibit, proscribe, disallow, ban, stop; forbid to.
OPPOSITES: admit, allow.

debase verb *the moral code has been debased:* degrade, devalue, demean, cheapen, drag down, tarnish, defile; disgrace, dishonour, shame; damage, harm, undermine, corrupt; vulgarize, lower the tone of.

debatable adjective *the extent to which personality is inherited is debatable:* arguable, disputable, questionable, open to question, controversial, contentious; doubtful, dubious, uncertain, unsure, unclear; borderline, inconclusive, moot, unsettled, unresolved, unconfirmed, undetermined, undecided, up in the air.

debate noun *a debate on the proposed reforms | there has been much debate about prices:* discussion, exchange of views, dialogue, deliberation; argument, dispute, wrangle, war of words; argumentation, dissension, disagreement, conflict; negotiations, talks.
▷ **verb**
1 *MPs will debate our future:* discuss, consider, talk over/through, talk about, thrash out; argue, dispute.
2 *he debated whether to call her:* consider, think over/about, chew over, mull over, weigh up, ponder, deliberate, contemplate.

debauched adjective *a debauched lifestyle:* dissolute, dissipated, degenerate, unprincipled, immoral, corrupt, depraved; lascivious, lecherous, lewd, lustful, libidinous, licentious, promiscuous; decadent, profligate, intemperate, sybaritic.

debauchery noun dissipation, degeneracy, corruption, depravity, immorality, decadence; lasciviousness, lechery, lewdness, lust, promiscuity; profligacy, intemperance.

debilitate verb *she was severely debilitated by a stomach upset | subsequent urbanization has debilitated the farming sector:* weaken, enfeeble, enervate, sap, drain, exhaust, weary, fatigue, prostrate, incapacitate, lay low; undermine, impair. OPPOSITES: invigorate.

debility noun *his chronic debility made it hard to do even the basic things:* weakness, frailty, enfeeblement, enervation, exhaustion, weariness, fatigue; incapacity, indisposition, infirmity.

debonair adjective *a debonair young man:* suave, urbane, sophisticated, self-possessed, self-assured, confident, charming, courteous, gallant, chivalrous,

d

d

gentlemanly; well groomed, elegant, stylish, smart, dashing; informal smooth.

debrief verb *Soviet scientists were debriefed by the KGB:* question, quiz, interview, examine, interrogate; informal grill.

debris noun *the irrigation channels were blocked with debris:* detritus, refuse, rubbish, waste, litter; rubble, wreckage; remains; informal junk.

debt noun
1 *he couldn't pay his debts:* bill, account, dues, arrears, charges; financial obligation, outstanding payment, money owing; informal tab.
2 *I must acknowledge my debt to the author of this article:* indebtedness, sense of obligation; gratitude, appreciation, thanks.
□ **in debt** owing money, in arrears, behind with payments, overdrawn; insolvent, bankrupt; informal in the red, on the rocks.
□ **in someone's debt** indebted to, beholden to, obliged to, obligated to; grateful, thankful.

debtor noun borrower, mortgagor; bankrupt, insolvent, defaulter.
OPPOSITES: creditor.

debunk verb *during the programme leading art historians debunk the myths surrounding his extraordinary life:* explode, discredit, disprove, drive a coach and horses through, contradict, negate; challenge, call into question; informal shoot full of holes, blow sky-high.
OPPOSITES: confirm.

debut noun *the new car made its debut at the German Grand Prix:* first appearance, first performance, launch, coming out, entrance, premiere, introduction, inception, inauguration; informal kick-off.

decadence noun *the decadence of modern society:* dissipation, degeneracy, debauchery, moral decay, immorality; licentiousness, self-indulgence, hedonism; corruption, depravity, vice, sin.
OPPOSITES: morality.

decadent adjective *he turned his back on decadent city life:* dissolute, dissipated, degenerate, unprincipled, immoral; licentious, abandoned, profligate, sybaritic, hedonistic, pleasure-seeking, self-indulgent; corrupt, depraved, sinful.

decamp verb *he decamped with the profits:* abscond, make off, run off/away, flee, take flight, disappear, vanish, steal away, sneak away, escape, make a run for it, leave, depart; informal cut and run, do a disappearing act; Brit. informal do a bunk, do a runner, scarper.

decant verb *the wine was decanted into a clean flask:* pour out/off, draw off, siphon off, drain; transfer.

decapitate verb *he was found guilty of high treason and decapitated:* behead, guillotine, send to the guillotine.

decay verb
1 *organic material decays rapidly, especially in hot climates:* decompose, rot, putrefy, go bad, spoil, fester, perish, deteriorate; degrade, break down, moulder.
2 *facilities decay when money is not spent on refurbishment:* deteriorate, degenerate, decline, go downhill, slump, slide, go to rack and ruin, go to seed; disintegrate, fall to pieces, fall into disrepair; crumble, collapse; informal go to pot, go to the dogs.
▷ noun
1 *the fish showed no signs of decay:* decomposition, putrefaction, festering; rot, mould.
2 *the decay of moral and family values:* deterioration, decline, degeneration, weakening; disintegration, collapse.

decayed adjective decomposed, decomposing, rotten, putrescent, putrid, bad, off, spoiled, perished; mouldy, festering, fetid, rancid, rank.

decaying adjective
1 *the smell of decaying fish:* decomposing, rotting, rotten, putrescent, putrid, bad, off, perished; mouldy, festering, fetid, rancid, rank.
2 *the city's decaying infrastructure:* decrepit, run-down, in a state of disrepair, gone to rack and ruin, crumbling; in decline, in ruins.

deceit noun *she became enmeshed in a complicated web of deceit:* deception, deceitfulness, duplicity, double-dealing, misrepresentation, fraud, cheating, trickery, subterfuge, chicanery, deviousness, guile, lying, pretence, treachery.
OPPOSITES: honesty.

deceitful adjective *she was a deceitful and manipulative woman:* dishonest, untruthful, insincere, false, lying, mendacious; untrustworthy, unscrupulous, unprincipled, two-faced, duplicitous, double-dealing, underhand, crafty, cunning, sly, scheming, calculating, treacherous, Machiavellian; informal sneaky.
OPPOSITES: honest.

deceive verb
1 *phishing is a scam that deceives consumers into disclosing their personal information:* trick, cheat, hoodwink, hoax, dupe, take in, mislead, delude, fool, double-cross; swindle, defraud; informal con, rip off, shaft, pull a fast one on, take for a ride, pull the wool over someone's eyes.
2 *he deceived her with another woman:* be unfaithful to, betray, play someone false; informal cheat on, two-time.

decelerate verb *there is a whine from the*

gearbox every time I decelerate: slow down/ up, ease up, reduce speed, brake.

decency noun

1 *TV companies need to maintain standards of taste and decency:* propriety, decorum, good taste, respectability, correctness, good form; morality, virtue, modesty, delicacy.
2 *he had the decency to tell me first:* courtesy, politeness, good manners, civility, respect; consideration, thoughtfulness.

decent adjective

1 *he was a decent clean-living man:* respectable, upright, virtuous, good, honest, trustworthy, dependable, honourable
2 *after a decent interval, he married his late brother's fiancée:* proper, correct, appropriate, fitting, suitable; respectable, seemly; conventional, accepted, standard, traditional, orthodox.
3 *a job with decent pay:* satisfactory, reasonable, fair, acceptable, adequate, sufficient; tolerable, passable.
4 (Brit. informal) *that's very decent of you:* kind, obliging, helpful, accommodating, unselfish, generous, thoughtful, considerate; neighbourly, hospitable.
OPPOSITES: dishonest, indecent, unsatisfactory.

deception noun

1 *I'm not very good at deception:* deceit, deceitfulness, duplicity, double-dealing, fraud, cheating, misrepresentation, trickery, chicanery, subterfuge, deviousness, guile, lying, pretence, treachery.
2 *it was all a deception:* trick, deceit, sham, fraud, pretence, hoax, fake; ruse; cheat, swindle; informal con, set-up, scam.

deceptive adjective

1 *appearances can be deceptive:* misleading, illusory, unreliable, false.
2 *deceptive business practices:* deceitful, duplicitous, fraudulent, underhand; disingenuous, untrustworthy, unscrupulous, unprincipled, dishonest, insincere; informal sharp, shady, sneaky.

decide verb

1 *she decided to become a writer:* resolve, determine, make up your mind, make a decision; elect, choose, opt; plan, aim, have the intention, have in mind, set your sights on.
2 *the court is to decide the case:* adjudicate, arbitrate, adjudge, judge; hear, try, examine; sit in judgement on, pronounce on, give a verdict on, rule on.
3 *an exciting game was decided by a 90th-minute goal:* settle, determine, resolve.

decided adjective

1 *there has been a decided improvement:* distinct, clear, marked, pronounced, obvious, striking, noticeable, unmistakable, patent, manifest; definite, certain, undeniable, indisputable, unquestionable.
2 *he was very decided:* determined, resolute, firm, strong-minded, strong-willed, emphatic, dead set, unwavering, unyielding, unbending, inflexible, unshakeable, unrelenting; obstinate, stubborn.
3 *our future is decided:* settled, established, resolved, determined, agreed; set, fixed.

decidedly adverb *he looked decidedly uncomfortable:* distinctly, noticeably, unmistakably, positively, downright, undeniably, unquestionably; extremely, very, exceedingly, exceptionally, particularly, especially.

deciding adjective *taxes could be the deciding factor for millions of floating voters:* determining, decisive, conclusive; key, pivotal, crucial, critical, most significant, major, chief, principal, prime.

decipher verb

1 *he deciphered the code:* decode, decrypt, break, work out, solve, interpret, translate; unscramble, unravel; informal crack, figure out; Brit. informal suss out.
2 *visual signals help us to decipher what is being communicated:* make out, make sense of, interpret, understand, comprehend, grasp, fathom, discern, perceive, read, follow.
OPPOSITES: encode.

decision noun

1 *they came to a decision | the final decision must be yours:* resolution, conclusion, settlement, resolve; choice, selection.
2 *they're delighted with the judge's decision:* verdict, finding, ruling, recommendation, judgement, pronouncement, adjudication; order, rule.
3 *she was a woman of decision:* decisiveness, determination, resolution, resolve, firmness; strong-mindedness, purpose, purposefulness.

decisive adjective

1 *price remains the decisive factor for most consumers:* deciding, conclusive, determining; key, pivotal, critical, crucial, most significant, most influential, major, chief, principal, prime.
2 *he provided strong and decisive leadership:* resolute, firm, strong-minded, strong-willed, determined, unhesitating; purposeful, forceful.

deck verb

1 *the street was decked with bunting:* decorate, bedeck, adorn, ornament, trim, cover, hang, festoon, garland, swathe, wreathe, drape, trick out.
2 *Ingrid was decked out in blue:* dress, clothe, garb, robe, rig out; formal attire; informal get up.

declaim verb

1 *a preacher was declaiming from the pulpit:* make a speech, give an address; speak, hold forth, orate, preach, lecture, sermonize, moralize; informal sound off, speechify.
2 *they loved to hear him declaim poetry:* recite, read aloud/out; informal spout.

declamation noun *he delivered a passionate declamation:* speech, address, lecture, discourse, oration; monologue; recitation; formal disquisition.

declaration noun

1 *they issued a declaration:* announcement, statement, pronouncement, proclamation, promulgation.
2 *a declaration of love:* statement, affirmation, assertion, protestation; pledge.

declare verb

1 *the EU has declared its intention to make the European economy the most competitive in the world:* proclaim, announce, state, voice, express, set forth, publicize, broadcast, promulgate; informal come out with.
2 *he claims that he never revises his work:* state, say, assert, affirm, insist, maintain, hold, claim; formal aver.
3 *his speech declared him a gentleman:* show to be, reveal as, confirm as, prove to be, attest to someone's being.

decline verb

1 *she declined all invitations:* turn down, reject, refuse, dismiss; forgo, deny yourself, pass up; brush aside, rebuff, spurn; informal give something a miss.
2 *the number of traders has declined:* decrease, lessen, diminish, be reduced, dwindle, contract, shrink, fall off, tail off; drop, fall, go down, slump, plummet; informal nosedive, crash.
3 *standards steadily declined:* deteriorate, degenerate, decay, crumble, collapse, slump, slip, slide, go downhill, worsen; weaken, wane, ebb; informal go to pot, go to the dogs.
OPPOSITES: accept, increase, rise.

▷ **noun**
1 *a decline in profits:* reduction, decrease, downturn, downswing, devaluation, depreciation, diminution, ebb, drop, slump, plunge; informal nosedive, crash.
2 *forest decline:* deterioration, degeneration, degradation, shrinkage; death, decay.
▢ **in decline**
declining, decaying, crumbling, collapsing, failing; disappearing, dying, moribund; informal on its last legs, on the way out.

decode verb *battle plans sent out on Germany's Enigma machine were quickly decoded:* decipher, decrypt, work out, solve, interpret, translate; make sense of, unscramble, unravel, find the key to; informal crack, figure out; Brit. informal suss out.
OPPOSITES: encode.

decompose verb *as landfill waste decomposes, methane gas is released:* decay, rot, putrefy, go bad, perish, deteriorate; degrade, break down.

decomposition noun *the body is in an advanced state of decomposition:* decay, putrefaction.

decontaminate verb *chlorine tablets were used to decontaminate the water:* disinfect, cleanse, clean, purify; fumigate; sanitize, sterilize.

decor noun *inside, the decor is elegant and traditional:* decoration, furnishing, ornamentation; colour scheme.

decorate verb

1 *the door was decorated with a wreath:* ornament, adorn, trim, embellish, garnish, enhance, grace; festoon, garland, bedeck.
2 *he started to decorate his home:* refurbish, redecorate, renovate, spruce up, smarten up; informal do up, fix up, give something a facelift.
3 *he was decorated for courage:* give a medal to, honour, reward.

decoration noun

1 *inside the house there was little decoration:* ornamentation, adornment, trimming, embellishment; beautification, prettification; enhancements, frills, accessories, trimmings, finery, frippery.
2 *internal decoration.* See DECOR.
3 *a Christmas tree decoration:* ornament, bauble, trinket, knick-knack, spangle; trimming, tinsel.
4 *a decoration won on the battlefield:* medal, award, star, ribbon; Brit. informal gong.

decorative adjective *Art Nouveau is characterized by its highly decorative style:* ornamental, ornamented; fancy, ornate, elaborate; attractive.
OPPOSITES: functional.

decorous adjective *he always behaves towards her in a decorous way:* proper, seemly, decent, becoming, tasteful; correct, appropriate, suitable, fitting; polite, well mannered, genteel, respectable; formal, restrained, modest, gentlemanly, ladylike.
OPPOSITES: indecorous.

decorum noun

1 *he had acted with the utmost decorum:* propriety, seemliness, decency, good taste, correctness; politeness, courtesy, good manners; dignity, respectability, modesty.
2 *a breach of decorum:* etiquette, protocol, good form, custom, convention; formalities, niceties.
OPPOSITES: impropriety.

decoy noun *a decoy to distract their attention:* lure, bait, red herring; enticement, inducement, temptation, attraction, carrot; snare, trap.

▷**verb** *he was decoyed to the mainland:* lure, entice, tempt; entrap, snare, trap.

decrease verb
1 *pollution levels decreased:* lessen, drop, diminish, decline, dwindle, fall off, subside, tail off; plummet, plunge.
2 *you should decrease the amount of fat in your diet:* reduce, lessen, lower, cut, minimize; informal slash.
OPPOSITES: increase.
▷**noun** *a decrease in consumer spending:* reduction, drop, lessening, decline, falling off, downturn, cut, cutback.
OPPOSITES: increase.

decree noun
1 *a presidential decree:* order, edict, command, commandment, mandate, dictum, fiat.
2 *a court decree:* judgement, verdict, adjudication, ruling, resolution, decision.
▷**verb** *Henry Ford decreed that all Model Ts should be painted black:* order, command, rule, dictate, pronounce, ordain.

decrepit adjective
1 *a decrepit old man:* feeble, infirm, weak, frail, incapacitated, doddering; old, ancient; informal past it, over the hill.
2 *a decrepit house:* dilapidated, rickety, run-down, tumbledown, ramshackle, derelict, ruined, in disrepair, gone to rack and ruin; battered, decaying, crumbling, deteriorating.
OPPOSITES: strong, sound.

decry verb *they decried human rights abuses:* denounce, condemn, criticize, censure, attack, rail against, inveigh against, lambaste, deplore; informal slam, blast.
OPPOSITES: praise.

dedicate verb
1 *she dedicated her life to the sick | you will need to dedicate 10 to 12 hours a month to the committee:* devote, commit, pledge, give, surrender, sacrifice; set aside, allocate.
2 *the book is dedicated to his mother:* inscribe, address.
3 *the chapel was dedicated to the Virgin Mary:* devote, assign; bless, consecrate, sanctify.

dedicated adjective
1 *a dedicated socialist:* committed, devoted, staunch, firm, steadfast, resolute, unwavering, loyal, faithful, true, dyed-in-the-wool; wholehearted, single-minded, enthusiastic, keen, earnest, zealous, ardent, passionate, fervent; informal deep-dyed.
2 *data is accessed by a dedicated machine:* exclusive; custom built, customized.

dedication noun
1 *sport requires dedication:* commitment, application, diligence, industry, resolve, enthusiasm, zeal, conscientiousness, perseverance, persistence, tenacity, staying power, single-mindedness; hard work, effort.
2 *her dedication to this organization:* devotion, commitment, loyalty.
3 *the book has a dedication to his wife:* inscription, address, message.
4 *the dedication of the church:* blessing, consecration, sanctification, benediction.
OPPOSITES: apathy.

deduce verb *they deduced that the fish died from water pollution:* conclude, come to the conclusion, infer, reason, work out, judge; surmise, gather; informal figure out.

deduct verb *any tax due will be deducted from the pension:* subtract, take away, take off, debit, dock, discount; informal knock off.
OPPOSITES: add.

deduction noun
1 *the deduction of tax:* subtraction, removal.
2 *she was right in her deduction:* conclusion, inference, reasoning; supposition, hypothesis.

deed noun
1 *the heroic deeds of their forefathers:* act, action; feat, exploit, achievement, accomplishment, endeavour, undertaking, enterprise.
2 *the mortgage deeds are kept at the bank:* legal document, contract, instrument.

deem verb *the event was deemed a great success:* consider, regard as, judge, adjudge, hold to be, view as, see as, class as, count, find, suppose, reckon; think to be, believe to be, feel to be.

deep adjective
1 *a deep ravine:* cavernous, yawning, gaping, huge, extensive; bottomless; literary fathomless.
2 *a puddle about two inches deep:* in depth.
3 *their deep love for one another:* intense, profound, heartfelt, fervent, wholehearted, deep-seated, deep-rooted; sincere, genuine, earnest; great, extreme.
4 *Laura drifted into a deep sleep:* sound, heavy, intense.
5 *a deep analysis:* profound, serious, intelligent, discerning, penetrating, perceptive, insightful, learned, wise, scholarly; complex, weighty.
6 *deep philosophical questions:* obscure, abstruse, recondite, esoteric, arcane; puzzling, baffling, mystifying, unfathomable.
7 *he was deep in his own thoughts:* absorbed, engrossed, involved, immersed, rapt, preoccupied, lost.
8 *his deep voice:* low-pitched, low, bass, rich, powerful, resonant, booming, sonorous.
9 *a deep red:* dark, intense, rich, strong, bold, warm.
OPPOSITES: shallow, superficial.

deepen verb
1 *his love for her had deepened:* grow,

increase, intensify, strengthen, grow stronger.
2 *our programme appeals to people wishing to deepen their existing knowledge of the subject:* **improve**, broaden, augment; build on.
3 *they deepened the hole:* **dig out**, dig deeper, excavate.

deeply adverb *she was deeply affected by the tragedy:* **profoundly**, greatly, enormously, extremely, very much; strongly, powerfully, intensely, keenly, acutely.

deep-rooted adjective *her deep-rooted fears and anxieties:* **deep-seated**, deep, profound, fundamental, basic; established, ingrained, embedded, entrenched, unshakeable; persistent, abiding, lingering.
OPPOSITES: superficial.

deface verb *scores of monuments have been defaced with graffiti:* **vandalize**, spoil, disfigure, mar, ruin.

de facto adverb *the republic is de facto two states:* **in practice**, in effect, in fact, in reality, really, actually.
▷ adjective *they took de facto control of the land:* **effective**, actual, real.

defamation noun *he sued the newspaper for defamation:* **libel**, slander, character assassination; formal calumny.

defamatory adjective *there were defamatory statements in the book:* **libellous**, slanderous, malicious, vicious; derogatory, disparaging, insulting, abusive, scurrilous.

defame verb *he claimed that the article defamed his family:* **libel**, slander, malign, cast aspersions on, traduce, give someone a bad name, smear, discredit; literary besmirch; informal drag through the mud.
OPPOSITES: compliment.

default noun *the company will have to restructure its debts to avoid default:* **non-payment**, failure to pay.
▷ verb
1 *the dealer can repossess the goods if the customer defaults:* **fail to pay**, not pay, renege, back out.
2 *the program will default to its own style:* **revert to**, select automatically.

defeat verb
1 *Charles invaded Saxony and defeated the army that was sent against him:* **beat**, conquer, win against, triumph over, get the better of, vanquish, subjugate; overcome, overpower, crush; rout, trounce; informal thrash, wipe the floor with, make mincemeat of, slaughter, demolish.
2 *prisons can make people and crime worse, thus defeating the purpose of imprisonment:* **thwart**, frustrate, derail; obstruct, hinder, hamper; informal put paid to.
3 *the motion was defeated:* **reject**, overthrow, throw out, dismiss, outvote, turn down.
4 *this line of reasoning defeats me:* **baffle**, perplex, bewilder, mystify, bemuse, confuse, confound, throw; informal beat, faze, stump.
▷ noun
1 *the defeat of Napoleon in 1815 | an embarrassing 7–1 defeat:* **conquest**, subjugation; rout, trouncing; failure, downfall; informal thrashing, drubbing, pasting.
2 *the defeat of the bill:* **rejection**, dismissal.
OPPOSITES: victory, success.

defeatist adjective *a defeatist attitude:* **pessimistic**, fatalistic, negative, despondent, despairing, hopeless, bleak, gloomy; cynical.
OPPOSITES: optimistic.
▷ noun **pessimist**, fatalist, prophet of doom; misery, killjoy; cynic; informal quitter.
OPPOSITES: optimist.

defect[1] noun *he spotted a defect in the work:* **fault**, flaw, imperfection, deficiency, weakness, weak spot, inadequacy, shortcoming, limitation, failing; blemish; mistake, error; Computing bug; informal glitch, gremlin.

defect[2] verb *his chief intelligence officer defected:* **desert**, change sides, turn traitor; (in the British Parliament) cross the floor.

defective adjective
1 *they admitted the goods were defective:* **faulty**, imperfect, inoperative, malfunctioning, out of order; damaged, broken; flawed; informal on the blink.
2 *these methods are defective:* **lacking**, wanting, deficient, inadequate, insufficient.
OPPOSITES: perfect.

defector noun **deserter**, turncoat, traitor, renegade.

defence noun
1 *they relied on missiles for the country's defence:* **protection**, guarding, security; resistance, deterrent.
2 *he spoke in defence of his boss:* **vindication**, justification, support; apology, explanation.
3 *the enemy's defences:* **barricade**, fortification; fortress, rampart, bulwark, bastion.
4 *more spending on defence is necessary:* **armaments**, weapons, weaponry, arms; the military, the armed forces.

defenceless adjective
1 *defenceless animals:* **vulnerable**, helpless, powerless.
2 *the country is wholly defenceless:* **undefended**, unprotected, unguarded, unarmed; vulnerable, exposed, insecure.
OPPOSITES: resilient, impregnable.

defend verb
1 *35,000 troops were posted to defend the*

capital city: protect, guard, safeguard, secure, shield; fortify, garrison, barricade.
2 *Vicky defended her husband and his actions:* justify, make a case for, argue in favour of; support, back, stand by, stick up for, stand up for; excuse, explain; informal throw your weight behind.
OPPOSITES: attack, criticize.

defendant noun *the defendant was charged with murder:* accused, prisoner at the bar; suspect.
OPPOSITES: plaintiff.

defender noun
1 *defenders of the environment:* protector, guard, guardian; custodian, watchdog, keeper, overseer, superintendent, caretaker.
2 *a passionate defender of free speech:* supporter, backer, champion, advocate, apologist, proponent, exponent; adherent, believer.

defensible adjective *these arguments are all perfectly defensible:* justifiable, tenable; sound, sensible, reasonable, rational, logical; plausible, acceptable, valid, legitimate.
OPPOSITES: indefensible.

defensive adjective
1 *troops in defensive positions:* defending, protective.
2 *he was very defensive about that area of his life:* self-justifying, oversensitive; informal uptight, twitchy.
OPPOSITES: offensive.

defer[1] verb *the committee deferred their decision until February | the project has been deferred:* postpone, put off, delay, hold over/off, put back; shelve, suspend; informal put on ice, put on the back burner, put in cold storage.

defer[2] verb *they deferred to his judgement:* yield, submit, give way, give in, surrender, capitulate, acquiesce in; respect, honour.

deference noun *he addressed her with the deference due to age:* respect, respectfulness, dutifulness; submissiveness, submission, obedience, acquiescence.
OPPOSITES: disrespect.

deferential adjective *a deferential attitude:* respectful, dutiful, obedient, submissive, subservient, yielding, acquiescent, complaisant, compliant, tractable, biddable, docile; humble, obsequious.

deferment noun postponement, deferral, suspension, delay; respite, stay, reprieve.

defiance noun *he wasn't used to such outspoken defiance:* resistance, opposition, non-compliance, disobedience, insubordination, dissent, recalcitrance, truculence, rebellion; contempt, disregard.
OPPOSITES: obedience.

defiant adjective *the mood of the meeting was angry and defiant | his defiant refusal to resign:* intransigent, obstinate, uncooperative, non-compliant, recalcitrant; dissenting, disobedient, insubordinate; obstreperous, truculent, rebellious, mutinous; confrontational; Brit. informal stroppy, bolshie.
OPPOSITES: cooperative.

deficiency noun
1 *a vitamin deficiency | deficiencies in material resources:* lack, shortage, want, insufficiency, inadequacy, deficit, shortfall; scarcity, paucity, absence, undersupply.
2 *for all its deficiencies, the play is extremely powerful:* defect, fault, flaw, imperfection, weakness, weak point, inadequacy, shortcoming, limitation, failing.
OPPOSITES: surplus, strength.

deficient adjective
1 *their diet is deficient in vitamin A:* lacking, wanting, short of/on, low on, poor in; having an inadequate/insufficient amount of.
2 *deficient workmanship:* defective, faulty, inadequate, imperfect, substandard, second-rate, poor.

deficit noun *there was a large, continuing deficit in the federal budget:* shortfall, deficiency, shortage, undersupply; debt, arrears; loss.
OPPOSITES: surplus.

defile verb
1 *her capacity for love had been defiled:* spoil, mar, impair, debase, degrade; contaminate, taint, tarnish; destroy, ruin; literary sully.
2 *the tomb had been defiled:* desecrate, violate, profane, dishonour.

definable adjective *she wasn't ill, or at least she had no definable complaint:* determinable, ascertainable, known, definite, clear-cut, precise, exact, specific.

define verb
1 *the contract will seek to define the client's obligations:* determine, establish, fix, specify, designate, decide, stipulate, set out; demarcate, delineate.
2 *the dictionary defines it succinctly:* explain, give the meaning of, describe.

definite adjective
1 *I need a definite answer | we had no definite plans:* explicit, specific, precise, exact, clear-cut, direct, plain; fixed, established, confirmed, concrete, set.
2 *there was definite evidence of brain disease:* certain, conclusive, decisive, firm, concrete, unambiguous, unequivocal, clear, proven, sure, positive; guaranteed, assured, cut and dried.
3 *the styles show a definite '60s influence:* unmistakable, undeniable, decided, marked, distinct, clear.

d

d

4 *a definite geographical area:* fixed, marked, demarcated, delimited, stipulated, particular.
OPPOSITES: vague, indefinite, indeterminate.

definitely adverb *I shall definitely be at the airport to meet you | something is definitely wrong:* **certainly**, for sure, unquestionably, without doubt, without question, assuredly, undoubtedly, indubitably, undeniably, unmistakably, plainly, clearly, obviously, patently.

definition noun
1 *there is no agreed definition of 'intelligence':* **meaning**, denotation, sense; interpretation, explanation, elucidation, description.
2 *the definition of the picture can be aided by using computer graphics:* **clarity**, visibility, sharpness, crispness; resolution, focus, contrast.

definitive adjective
1 *a definitive decision:* **conclusive**, final, ultimate; categorical, positive, definite, decisive.
2 *the definitive guide to the movies:* **authoritative**, ultimate, best, finest; classic, standard, recognized, accepted, official.

deflate verb
1 *he deflated the tyres:* **let down**, let the air out of.
2 *the news had deflated him:* **subdue**, discourage, dishearten, dismay, dispirit; crush, bring down, take the wind out of someone's sails, chasten; informal knock the stuffing out of.
OPPOSITES: inflate, encourage.

deflect verb
1 *he raised his arm to deflect the blow | she sought to deflect criticism of the government's policy:* **turn aside/away**, divert, avert; head off, ward off, fend off, stave off, block, parry.
2 *the ball deflected off the wall:* **bounce**, glance, ricochet; veer, swerve.

deform verb disfigure, bend out of shape, contort, buckle, warp; damage, spoil.

deformed adjective misshapen, distorted, malformed, contorted, out of shape; twisted, crooked, bent, warped, buckled, gnarled; disfigured, injured.

deformity noun malformation, misshapenness, crookedness; imperfection, abnormality, irregularity; disfigurement; defect, flaw.

defraud verb *the men were alleged to have defrauded thousands of investors:* **swindle**, cheat, rob; deceive, dupe, hoodwink, double-cross, trick; informal con, do, diddle, rip off, shaft, fleece, pull a fast one on, put one over on.

defray verb *the rest of the money was used to defray the costs of restoring the house:* **pay for**, cover, meet, settle, clear, discharge.

deft adjective *a deft piece of footwork:* **skilful**, adept, adroit, dexterous, agile, nimble, handy; skilled, proficient, accomplished, expert, polished, slick, professional, masterly; clever, shrewd, astute, canny, sharp; informal nifty, nippy.
OPPOSITES: clumsy.

defunct adjective *the now defunct local paper mill:* **disused**, unused, inoperative, non-functioning, obsolete; no longer existing, discontinued; extinct.
OPPOSITES: working, extant.

defuse verb
1 *officers are taught how to defuse potentially explosive situations:* **ease**, calm, cool, smooth over, take the heat out of, restore order in/to; settle, resolve, sort out, iron out, put to rights, remedy, rectify; get control of.
2 *he tried to defuse the grenade:* **deactivate**, disarm, disable, make safe.
OPPOSITES: inflame, activate.

USAGE

Do not confuse **defuse** and **diffuse**. **Defuse** means 'to make a situation less tense or dangerous', while as a verb **diffuse** means 'to spread over a wide area' (*such ideas were diffused widely in the 1970s*).

---

defy verb
1 *smokers who defy the ban could be fined up to £1,000:* **disobey**, go against, flout, fly in the face of, disregard, ignore; break, violate, contravene, breach, infringe; informal cock a snook at.
2 *many of the scenes in the film defy any attempts at rational explanation:* **elude**, escape, defeat; frustrate, thwart.
3 *he glowered, defying her to mock him:* **challenge**, dare.
OPPOSITES: obey.

degeneracy noun *the fall of the city was blamed on the degeneracy of its people:* **decadence**, corruption, moral decay, dissipation, dissolution, profligacy, vice, immorality; debauchery.

degenerate adjective
1 *a degenerate form of classicism:* **debased**, degraded, corrupt, impure; formal vitiated.
2 *her degenerate brother:* **decadent**, dissolute, dissipated, debauched, reprobate, profligate; corrupt, immoral, unprincipled, dishonourable, disreputable, unsavoury.
OPPOSITES: pure, moral.
▷ **noun** *a group of degenerates:* **reprobate**, debauchee, profligate, libertine, roué.
▷ **verb**
1 *their quality of life had degenerated:* **deteriorate**, decline, slip, slide, worsen, go downhill, regress, retrogress; go to rack

and ruin; informal go to pot, go to the dogs, hit the skids, go down the toilet.
2 *the muscles started to degenerate:* waste away, waste, atrophy, weaken.
OPPOSITES: improve.

degradation noun
1 *many people are condemned to lives of extreme poverty and degradation:* humiliation, shame, loss of self-respect, indignity.
2 *the degradation of women:* demeaning, debasement, devaluing.
3 *the degradation of the tissues:* deterioration, degeneration, atrophy, decay; breakdown.

degrade verb
1 *she believed that many supposedly erotic pictures degraded women:* demean, debase, cheapen, devalue; shame, humiliate, dishonour.
2 *the polymer will not degrade:* break down, deteriorate, degenerate, decay.
OPPOSITES: dignify.

degrading adjective *claiming benefit can be a degrading experience:* humiliating, demeaning, undignified, ignominious, shameful.

degree noun *the job requires a high degree of skill:* level, standard, order; amount, extent, measure; magnitude, intensity, strength.
▫ **by degrees**
gradually, little by little, bit by bit, inch by inch, step by step, slowly; piecemeal.
▫ **to a degree**
to some extent, to a certain extent, up to a point.

dehydrate verb *alcohol dehydrates the skin:* dry out, dry, desiccate; dehumidify.
OPPOSITES: hydrate.

deify verb
1 *she was deified by the early Romans as a fertility goddess:* worship, revere, venerate, hold sacred; immortalize.
2 *he was deified by the press:* idolize, lionize, hero-worship; idealize, glorify, aggrandize; informal put on a pedestal.
OPPOSITES: demonize.

deign verb *Brown finally deigned to speak to me:* condescend, stoop, lower yourself, demean yourself, humble yourself; consent, vouchsafe; informal come down from your high horse.

deity noun god, goddess, divine being, supreme being, divinity, immortal.

dejected adjective *he stood in the street looking dejected:* downcast, downhearted, despondent, disconsolate, dispirited, crestfallen, disheartened; depressed, desolate, in the doldrums, sad, unhappy, doleful, melancholy, miserable, woebegone, forlorn, wretched, glum, gloomy; informal blue, fed up, down in the mouth, down in the dumps; Brit. informal

brassed off, cheesed off.
OPPOSITES: cheerful.

delay verb
1 *we were delayed by the traffic:* detain, hold up, make late, slow up/down, bog down; hinder, hamper, impede, obstruct.
2 *they delayed no longer:* linger, dally, drag your feet, be slow, hold back, dawdle, waste time; procrastinate, stall, hang fire, temporize, hesitate, dither; informal dilly-dally, shilly-shally.
3 *he may delay the cut in interest rates:* postpone, put off, defer, hold over, shelve, stay; reschedule; informal put on ice, put on the back burner.
OPPOSITES: hurry, advance.
▷ **noun**
1 *drivers will face lengthy delays:* hold-up, wait, stoppage.
2 *the delay of his trial:* postponement, deferral, deferment, stay.
3 *I set off without delay:* procrastination, hesitation, dithering, dallying, dawdling.

delectable adjective
1 *a delectable chocolate cake:* delicious, mouth-watering, appetizing, flavoursome, flavourful, toothsome; succulent, luscious, tasty; informal scrumptious, scrummy, yummy; Brit. informal moreish.
2 (humorous) *the delectable Ms Davis:* delightful, lovely, captivating, charming, enchanting, appealing, beguiling; beautiful, attractive, ravishing, gorgeous, stunning, alluring, sexy, seductive, desirable; informal divine, heavenly; Brit. informal tasty.
OPPOSITES: unpalatable, unattractive.

delectation noun (humorous) *they had all manner of goodies for our delectation:* enjoyment, gratification, delight, pleasure, satisfaction, relish; entertainment, amusement, titillation.

delegate noun *delegates from 28 countries attended the meeting:* representative, agent, envoy, deputy; spokesperson, spokesman/woman.
▷ **verb**
1 *she must delegate routine tasks to other team members:* assign, entrust, pass on, hand on/over, turn over, devolve, transfer.
2 *they were delegated to negotiate with the States:* authorize, commission, depute, appoint, nominate, mandate, empower, charge; choose, designate, elect.

delegation noun *he was a member of Sweden's delegation to the United Nations General Assembly:* deputation, delegacy, diplomatic mission, commission; delegates, representatives, envoys; contingent.

delete verb *the offending paragraph was deleted from the letter:* remove, cut out, take out, edit out, excise, eradicate, expunge, cancel; cross out, strike out, ink out, obliterate; rub out, erase.
OPPOSITES: add.

d

deleterious adjective
these policies are having a deleterious effect on British industry: harmful, damaging, detrimental, injurious; bad, adverse, disadvantageous, unfavourable, unfortunate, undesirable.
OPPOSITES: beneficial.

deliberate adjective
1 *a deliberate attempt to provoke him:* intentional, calculated, conscious, intended, planned, studied, knowing, wilful, wanton, purposeful, purposive, premeditated, pre-planned.
2 *he took slow, deliberate steps towards her:* careful, cautious; measured, regular, even, steady.
3 *a conscientious and deliberate worker:* methodical, systematic, careful, painstaking, meticulous, thorough.
OPPOSITES: accidental, hasty, careless.
▷ **verb** *she deliberated on his words:* think about/over, ponder, consider, contemplate, reflect on, muse on, meditate on, ruminate on, mull over, give thought to, weigh up; brood over, dwell on.

deliberately adverb
1 *he deliberately hurt me:* intentionally, on purpose, by design, knowingly, wittingly, consciously, purposely; wilfully, wantonly.
2 *he walked deliberately down the aisle:* carefully, cautiously, slowly, steadily, evenly.

deliberation noun
1 *after much deliberation, I accepted:* thought, consideration, reflection, contemplation, meditation, rumination.
2 *he replaced the glass with deliberation:* care, carefulness, caution.

delicacy noun
1 *the delicacy of the fabric:* fineness, exquisiteness, daintiness; flimsiness, fragility.
2 *I have to treat this matter with the utmost delicacy:* care, sensitivity, tact, discretion, diplomacy, subtlety.
3 *the crabs are an Australian delicacy:* choice food, gourmet food, dainty, treat, luxury, bonne bouche; speciality.

delicate adjective
1 *delicate embroidery | a delicate lace shawl:* fine, exquisite, intricate, dainty; flimsy, gauzy, filmy, floaty, diaphanous, wispy, insubstantial.
2 *a delicate shade of blue:* subtle, soft, muted; pastel, pale, light.
3 *delicate china cups:* fragile, breakable; technical frangible.
4 *his wife is rather delicate:* sickly, unhealthy, frail, feeble, weak.
5 *a delicate issue:* difficult, tricky, sensitive, ticklish, awkward, problematical, touchy; embarrassing; informal sticky.
6 *the matter required delicate handling:* careful, sensitive, tactful, diplomatic, discreet, kid-glove.
7 *his delicate palate:* discriminating, discerning; fastidious, fussy, finicky, dainty; informal picky, choosy; Brit. informal pernickety.
8 *a delicate mechanism:* sensitive, precision, precise.
OPPOSITES: coarse, lurid, strong, robust.

delicious adjective
1 *a delicious meal | delicious strawberry cheesecake:* tasty, appetizing, mouth-watering, delectable, flavoursome, flavourful, toothsome, succulent, luscious; informal scrumptious, scrummy, yummy; Brit. informal moreish.
2 *a delicious languor stole over her:* delightful, exquisite, lovely, pleasurable, pleasant; informal heavenly, divine.
OPPOSITES: unpalatable, unpleasant.

delight verb
1 *it's a film which is guaranteed to delight both young and old:* please greatly, charm, enchant, captivate, entrance, thrill; gladden, gratify, appeal to; entertain, amuse, divert.
2 *she delighted in his touch:* take pleasure, revel, luxuriate, wallow, glory; adore, love, relish, savour, lap up; informal get a kick out of, get a buzz out of, get a thrill out of.
OPPOSITES: dismay, disgust, dislike.
▷ **noun** *she squealed with delight:* pleasure, happiness, joy, glee; excitement, amusement; elation, euphoria, bliss, rapture.
OPPOSITES: displeasure.

delighted adjective
we're delighted to have him back: pleased, glad, happy, thrilled, overjoyed, ecstatic, elated; on cloud nine, walking on air, in seventh heaven, jumping for joy; enchanted, charmed; gleeful, cock-a-hoop; informal over the moon, tickled pink, as pleased as Punch, on top of the world; Brit. informal chuffed, as happy as Larry; N. English informal made up.

delightful adjective
1 *a delightful evening:* pleasant, lovely, pleasurable, enjoyable; amusing, entertaining, diverting; gratifying, satisfying; marvellous, wonderful, splendid, sublime; informal great, super, fabulous, terrific, heavenly, divine; Brit. informal brilliant.
2 *she's a delightful girl:* charming, enchanting, captivating, bewitching, appealing; sweet, endearing, cute, lovely, adorable, delectable, gorgeous.

delimit verb
their responsibilities will be more strictly delimited: determine, establish, set, fix, demarcate, define, delineate.

delineate verb
1 *the committee's aim is to delineate what is science and what is not science:* describe, set forth/out, define, specify, identify, map out, outline; present, portray, depict.
2 *a section delineated in red marker pen:* outline, trace, block in, mark, delimit.

delinquency noun *they agreed that failed parenting is often the cause of delinquency among young people:* crime, criminality, wrongdoing, lawlessness, misconduct, misbehaviour; misdemeanours, offences, misdeeds.

delinquent adjective *delinquent teenagers:* lawless, badly behaved, troublesome, difficult, unruly, disobedient, uncontrollable, errant.
OPPOSITES: dutiful.
▷ noun *teenage delinquents:* offender, wrongdoer, miscreant, criminal; hooligan, vandal, ruffian; young offender; Brit. tearaway.

delirious adjective
1 *she was delirious but had lucid intervals:* incoherent, raving, irrational, hysterical, wild; feverish, frenzied; deranged, demented.
2 *there was a great roar from the delirious home crowd:* ecstatic, euphoric, exultant, elated, thrilled, overjoyed, beside yourself, walking on air, on cloud nine, in seventh heaven, carried away, transported, rapturous; wild, excited; informal over the moon, on a high.

deliver verb
1 *the parcel was delivered to his house:* bring, take, convey, carry, transport; send, dispatch, remit.
2 *the money was delivered up to the official:* hand over, turn over, make over, sign over; surrender, give up, yield, cede; consign, commit, entrust, trust.
3 *the court delivered its verdict:* utter, give, make, read; pronounce, announce, declare, proclaim; return.
4 *she delivered a blow to his head:* administer, deal, inflict, give; informal land.
5 *he delivered the first ball:* bowl, launch, pitch, hurl, throw, cast, lob.
6 *he was delivered from his enemies:* save, rescue, free, liberate, release; redeem.

deliverance noun *death would have been a deliverance for her:* liberation, release, rescue; salvation.

delivery noun
1 *the delivery of the goods:* conveyance, carriage, transportation, transport, distribution; dispatch, remittance.
2 *we get several deliveries a day:* consignment, load, shipment.
3 *her delivery was stilted:* speech, pronunciation, enunciation, articulation, elocution; utterance.

delude verb *you're lying—why do you persist in trying to delude me?* mislead, deceive, fool, take in, trick, dupe, hoodwink, lead on; informal con, pull the wool over someone's eyes, lead someone up the garden path, take someone for a ride.

deluge noun
1 *homes were swept away by the deluge:* flood, torrent.
2 *the deluge turned the pitch into a swamp:* downpour, torrential rain; thunderstorm, cloudburst.
3 *they received a deluge of complaints:* barrage, volley; flood, torrent, avalanche, stream, spate, rush, outpouring.
▷ verb
1 *we have been deluged with calls:* inundate, overwhelm, flood, swamp, snow under, bombard.
2 *homes were deluged by the rains:* flood, inundate, submerge, swamp.

delusion noun *it's a popular delusion that the government wastes vast amounts of money through inefficiency:* misconception, misapprehension, mistake, error; fallacy, illusion, fantasy.

de luxe adjective *a de luxe hotel:* luxurious, luxury, sumptuous, palatial, opulent, lavish; grand, high-class, quality, exclusive, choice, fancy; expensive, costly; Brit. upmarket; informal plush, posh, classy, ritzy, swanky, pricey; Brit. informal swish.
OPPOSITES: basic, cheap.

delve verb
1 *she delved in her pocket:* rummage, search, hunt, scrabble about/around, root about/around, ferret, fish about/around in, dig; go through, rifle through; Brit. informal rootle around.
2 *we must delve deeper into the matter:* investigate, enquire, probe, explore, research, look into, go into.

demand noun
1 *I gave in to her demands | escalating prices led to demands for higher pay:* request, call, ultimatum, stipulation; claim.
2 *the demands of a young family | he's got enough demands on his time already:* requirement, need, desire, wish; claim, imposition.
3 *there's a big demand for such toys:* market, call, appetite, desire; run on, rush on.
▷ verb
1 *workers demanded wage increases:* call for, ask for, request, push for, hold out for; insist on, stipulate, claim.
2 *Harvey demanded that I tell him the truth:* order, command, urge; formal enjoin.
3 *'Where is she?' he demanded:* ask, inquire, question, interrogate; challenge.
4 *an activity demanding detailed knowledge:* require, need, necessitate, call for, involve, entail.
□ in demand
sought-after, desired, coveted, wanted, requested; desirable, popular, all the rage, at a premium, like gold dust; informal big, trendy, hot.

demanding adjective
1 *a demanding task:* difficult, challenging,

d

taxing, exacting, tough, hard, onerous, formidable, burdensome; arduous, uphill, rigorous, gruelling, back-breaking, punishing.
2 *she could be very demanding at times:* hard to please, trying, tiresome, wearing; importunate, clamorous, nagging, insistent; informal high-maintenance.
OPPOSITES: easy.

demarcate verb *plots of land demarcated by barbed wire:* separate, divide, mark out/off, delimit, delineate; bound.

demarcation noun
1 *maintaining a clear demarcation between the personal and the professional is essential:* separation, distinction, differentiation, division, delimitation, definition.
2 *territorial demarcations:* boundary, border, borderline, frontier; dividing line, divide.

demean verb *his actions only served to demean him in the eyes of the public:* discredit, lower, degrade, debase, devalue; cheapen, humiliate, disgrace, dishonour.
OPPOSITES: dignify.

demeaning adjective *a demeaning and badly paid job:* degrading, humiliating, shameful, ignominious, undignified, inglorious.

demeanour noun *his normally calm demeanour:* manner, air, attitude, appearance, look; bearing, carriage; behaviour, conduct.

demented adjective *the ravings of a demented old man:* mad, insane, deranged, out of your mind, not in your right mind, crazed, lunatic, unhinged; informal crazy, mental, nutty, off your rocker, off your trolley, round the bend, raving mad, batty, bonkers, loopy, loony, away with the fairies; Brit. informal barmy, crackers, barking, potty, off your head, round the twist.
OPPOSITES: sane.

demise noun
1 *her tragic demise:* death, dying, passing, loss of life, end; literary quietus.
2 *the demise of the Ottoman Empire:* end, break-up, disintegration, fall, downfall, collapse.
OPPOSITES: birth.

demobilize verb *the militia were demobilized:* disband, decommission, discharge; Brit. informal demob.

democracy noun *a system of parliamentary democracy:* representative government, elective government, constitutional government; self-government, autonomy; republic, commonwealth.
OPPOSITES: dictatorship.

democratic adjective *a democratic government:* elected, representative,

parliamentary, popular; egalitarian, classless; self-governing, autonomous, republican.

demolish verb
1 *the house was demolished to make way for a shopping centre:* knock down, pull down, tear down, bring down, destroy, flatten, raze to the ground, level, bulldoze; blow up; dismantle, disassemble.
2 *the article reports findings that comprehensively demolish the existing theory:* refute, disprove, discredit, overturn, explode, destroy, drive a coach and horses through; informal shoot full of holes.
OPPOSITES: construct, support.

demolition noun *the building is scheduled for demolition:* destruction, levelling, bulldozing, clearance.

demon noun
1 *the demons from hell:* devil, fiend, evil spirit; incubus, succubus; hellhound.
2 *this time the singer seems to have put her demons behind her:* problem, trouble, difficulty; fixation, obsession, compulsion; neurosis, complex, phobia; informal hang-up.
OPPOSITES: angel, saint.

demonic adjective
1 *demonic powers:* devilish, fiendish, diabolical, satanic; evil, wicked.
2 *the demonic intensity of his playing:* frenzied, wild, feverish, frenetic, frantic, furious, manic, like one possessed.

demonstrable adjective *a demonstrable improvement in the quality of services:* clear, apparent, evident, obvious, clear-cut, manifest, patent, distinct, noticeable; unmistakable, undeniable; verifiable, provable; verified, proven, confirmed.

demonstrate verb
1 *his findings demonstrate that diet, exercise, and not smoking can head off most heart attacks:* show, indicate, establish, prove, confirm, verify, corroborate, substantiate.
2 *he demonstrated how he was surfing the Web via WiFi provided by the coffee shop:* give a demonstration of, show how something is done; display, show.
3 *his work demonstrated a keen analytical ability:* reveal, indicate, signify, signal, denote, show, display, exhibit; bear witness to, testify to; formal bespeak.
4 *parents and children demonstrated against the closure of the school:* protest, rally, march; stage a sit-in.

demonstration noun
1 *acts of faith are not capable of mathematical demonstration:* proof, substantiation, confirmation, corroboration, verification, validation.
2 *is a prenuptial agreement a demonstration of a lack of commitment?* manifestation, indication, evidence, sign,

mark, token, testament; expression.
3 *a demonstration of woodcarving:* **exhibition**, presentation, display; informal demo.
4 *an anti-racism demonstration:* **protest**, march, rally, lobby, sit-in; vigil; informal demo.

demonstrative adjective
1 *a very demonstrative family:* **expressive**, open, forthcoming, communicative, unreserved, emotional, effusive, gushing; affectionate, loving, warm; informal touchy-feely, lovey-dovey.
2 *the successes are demonstrative of their skill:* **indicative**, suggestive, illustrative.
OPPOSITES: reserved.

demoralize verb *they kept wages low, which demoralized the staff:* **dishearten**, discourage, dispirit, depress, cast down, get someone down; cow, subdue.

demoralized adjective **dispirited**, discouraged, disheartened, downhearted, dejected, downcast, low, depressed, despairing; disconsolate, crestfallen, disappointed; crushed, cowed, subdued.

demote verb *the head of the army was demoted to deputy defence secretary:* **downgrade**, relegate; lower the rank of.
OPPOSITES: promote.

demur verb *Steed demurred when the suggestion was made:* **object**, take exception, take issue, protest, cavil; express reservations, be unwilling, be reluctant, baulk, think twice; drag your heels, refuse.
▷ **noun** *they accepted without demur:* **objection**, protest, protestation, complaint, dispute, dissent, opposition, resistance; reservation, hesitation, reluctance; doubts, qualms, misgivings, second thoughts; a murmur, a word.

demure adjective *a demure young woman in a plain white dress:* **modest**, unassuming, meek, mild, reserved, quiet, shy, bashful, diffident, reticent, timid, shrinking, coy; decorous, decent, seemly, ladylike, respectable, proper, virtuous, pure, innocent, chaste; sober, sedate, staid, prim, strait-laced.
OPPOSITES: brazen.

den noun
1 *the mink left its den:* **lair**, sett, earth, burrow, hole, shelter, hiding place, hideout.
2 *police described the place as a den of violent crime:* **hotbed**, breeding ground, nest.
3 *the poet scribbled in his den:* **study**, private place, sanctum, retreat, sanctuary, hideaway; informal hidey-hole.

denial noun
1 *he issued a furious denial of her claims at the employment tribunal:* **contradiction**, rebuttal, repudiation; disclaimer.

2 *the denial of insurance to certain people:* **refusal**, withholding, declining.

denigrate verb *doom and gloom merchants who denigrate their own country:* **disparage**, belittle, deprecate, decry, cast aspersions on, criticize, attack; speak ill of, give someone a bad name, defame, slander, libel; run down, abuse, insult, revile, malign, vilify; informal bad-mouth, pull to pieces; Brit. informal rubbish, slate, slag off.
OPPOSITES: extol.

denomination noun
1 *a Christian denomination:* **religious group**, faith community, sect, movement, body, branch, persuasion, order; Church.
2 *banknotes in a number of denominations:* **value**, unit, size.

denote verb *a strange word used to denote a complex mathematical procedure:* **designate**, represent, mean, be a sign of, signify, signal, be a symbol of, symbolize.

> **USAGE**
>
> Do not confuse **denote** with **connote**. **Denote** refers to the literal, main meaning of something, while **connote** refers to other characteristics suggested or implied by that thing. For example, the word **mother** *denotes* 'a woman who is a parent' but could be said to *connote* qualities such as protectiveness and affection.

denouement noun *the film's denouement:* **final scene**, end, ending, finish, close; culmination, climax, conclusion, resolution.

denounce verb
1 *the Assembly denounced the use of violence:* **condemn**, criticize, attack, censure, decry, revile, rail against; formal castigate.
2 *priests denounced him to the King for heresy:* **expose**, betray, inform against/on; incriminate, implicate, name, accuse.
OPPOSITES: praise.

dense adjective
1 *a dense forest:* **thick**, close-packed, tightly packed, crowded, compact, solid, tight; overgrown, impenetrable, impassable.
2 *dense smoke:* **thick**, heavy, opaque; concentrated, condensed.
3 (informal) *they were dense enough to believe me:* **stupid**, unintelligent, ignorant, brainless, mindless, foolish, slow, witless, simple-minded, empty-headed, idiotic; informal thick, dim, moronic, dumb, dopey, dozy; Brit. informal daft.
OPPOSITES: sparse, thin, clever.

density noun *vitamin D deficiency causes a lack of bone density:* **solidity**, thickness, substance, mass; compactness, tightness, hardness.

dent noun
1 *there's a dent in the passenger door:* **indentation**, dint, hollow.

d

2 *lawyer's fees will make a nasty dent in their finances:* **reduction**, depletion, deduction, cut.
OPPOSITES: increase.
▷ **verb** *the experience has dented her confidence:* **diminish**, reduce, lessen, weaken, erode, undermine, sap, shake, damage, impair, affect.

denude verb *the island had been denuded of trees:* **strip**, clear, deprive, rob, dispossess.

deny verb
1 *the report was denied by witnesses:* **contradict**, repudiate, challenge, contest, oppose, reject, rebut.
2 *he denied the request | access was denied:* **refuse**, turn down, reject, decline, veto; forbid, withhold; informal give the thumbs down to.
OPPOSITES: confirm.

depart verb
1 *James departed after lunch:* **leave**, go, withdraw, take your leave, absent yourself, exit, decamp, retreat, retire; set off/out, get under way, be on your way; informal make tracks, take off.
2 *this year's budget departed from the norm:* **deviate**, diverge; differ, vary; contrast with.
OPPOSITES: arrive.

department noun
1 *the council's finance department:* **division**, section, sector, unit, branch, arm, wing; office, bureau, agency, ministry.
2 (informal) *the cooking is not my department:* **domain**, territory, province, area; responsibility, duty, function, job, business, affair, charge, task, concern.

departure noun
1 *he tried to delay her departure:* **leaving**, going, leave-taking, withdrawal, exit, retreat; formal egress.
2 *the album doesn't represent a radical departure from the band's previous work:* **deviation**, divergence; variation, change, change of direction.

depend verb
1 *her career depends on a good reference:* **be contingent on**, be conditional on, be dependent on, hinge on, hang on, rest on, rely on; be decided by.
2 *my family is depending on me:* **rely on**, lean on; count on, bank on, trust in, have faith in, believe in; pin your hopes on.

dependable adjective *he was a solid and dependable person:* **reliable**, trustworthy, faithful, loyal, unfailing, steadfast, constant, unswerving; honourable, sensible, responsible.

dependant noun **child**, minor; ward, charge; (**dependants**) family, offspring.

dependency noun
1 *her dependency on her husband:*

dependence, reliance; need for.
2 *drug dependency:* **addiction**, dependence, reliance; craving, compulsion; abuse.
3 *a British dependency:* **colony**, protectorate, satellite state.
OPPOSITES: independence.

dependent adjective
1 *your placement is dependent on her decision:* **conditional**, contingent, based; subject to, determined by, influenced by.
2 *the economy is heavily dependent on oil exports:* **reliant on**; sustained by, supported by.
3 *she is dependent on drugs:* **addicted to**, unable to do without; informal hooked on.
OPPOSITES: independent.

depict verb
1 *the painting depicts the Last Supper:* **portray**, show, represent, picture, illustrate, delineate, reproduce, render; draw, paint.
2 *the novel depicts his midlife crisis:* **describe**, present, set forth, set out, outline, delineate, detail; represent, portray, characterize.

depiction noun
1 *a depiction of Aphrodite:* **picture**, painting, portrait, drawing, sketch, study, illustration; image, likeness.
2 *the film's depiction of women:* **portrayal**, representation, presentation, characterization.

deplete verb *clan warfare has severely depleted the food supply:* **exhaust**, use up, consume, expend, drain, empty; reduce, decrease, diminish, cut.
OPPOSITES: augment.

depletion noun **exhaustion**, use, consumption; reduction, decrease, diminution; impoverishment.

deplorable adjective
1 *your conduct was deplorable:* **disgraceful**, shameful, unacceptable, inexcusable, unpardonable, unforgivable; reprehensible, despicable, abominable, contemptible, execrable, beyond the pale.
2 *the garden is in a deplorable state:* **lamentable**, regrettable, wretched, atrocious, appalling, awful, terrible, dreadful, abysmal, diabolical; informal dire, lousy.
OPPOSITES: admirable.

deplore verb
1 *we deplore all violence:* **abhor**, find unacceptable, frown on, disapprove of, take a dim view of, take exception to, criticize; detest, despise; condemn, denounce.
2 *he deplored their lack of flair:* **lament**, regret, rue, bemoan, complain about.
OPPOSITES: applaud.

deploy verb
1 *forces were deployed at strategic locations:* **position**, station, post, place,

install, locate, situate, site, establish; base.
2 *she deployed all her skills:* use, utilize, employ, take advantage of, exploit; bring into service, call on, turn to, resort to.

deport verb *they were fined and deported:* expel, banish, exile, extradite, repatriate; evict, throw out; historical transport.

deportment noun (Brit.) *poise is concerned with good deportment:* posture, carriage, bearing, stance, gait.

depose verb *the president was deposed:* overthrow, unseat, oust, dethrone, topple, remove, supplant, displace, drive out, throw out, eject, get rid of.

deposit noun
1 *a thick deposit of ash:* accumulation, mass, layer, covering, coating; sediment, lees, precipitate.
2 *a copper deposit:* seam, vein, lode, layer, stratum, bed.
3 *they paid a deposit:* down payment, advance payment, prepayment, instalment.
▷**verb**
1 *she deposited her books on the table:* put, place, set, unload, rest; drop; informal dump, park; Brit. informal plonk.
2 *silt is deposited by flood water:* leave, precipitate; wash up, cast up.
3 *guests may deposit valuable property in the vault:* place, store, stow, put away, lodge; bank, pay in; informal stash.

deposition noun
1 *a commissioner is to take depositions from witnesses:* statement, sworn statement, affidavit, submission, declaration; testimony, evidence.
2 *the barons plotted the King's deposition:* overthrow, downfall, removal, dethronement, displacement, dismissal, expulsion, ejection.

depository noun *the department was a depository of a vast array of source materials:* repository, storehouse, store; cache, treasury, treasure house.

depot noun
1 *the bus depot:* terminal, terminus, station, garage; headquarters, base.
2 *an arms depot:* storehouse, warehouse, store, repository, depository, cache, dump; arsenal, magazine, armoury.

deprave verb *they have been depraved by pornography:* corrupt, lead astray, warp, pervert, debase, degrade.

depraved adjective corrupt, perverted, warped, twisted, deviant, degenerate, debased, immoral, unprincipled; debauched, dissolute, licentious, lecherous, indecent, sordid; wicked, sinful, vile; informal sick.

depravity noun corruption, vice, perversion, deviance, degeneracy, immorality, debauchery, dissipation, licentiousness, lechery, obscenity, indecency; wickedness, sin.

deprecate verb *the school deprecates such behaviour:* deplore, abhor, disapprove of, frown on, take a dim view of, take exception to; criticize, censure.
OPPOSITES: praise.

deprecatory adjective
1 *deprecatory remarks:* disapproving, censorious, critical, scathing, damning, condemnatory, disparaging, denigratory, derogatory, negative, unflattering.
2 *a deprecatory smile:* apologetic, rueful, regretful, sorry, remorseful, contrite, penitent, repentant; shamefaced, sheepish.

depreciate verb
1 *new cars depreciate quickly:* decrease in value, lose value, fall in price.
2 *the tendency in modern art to depreciate traditional materials and methods:* belittle, disparage, denigrate, decry, underrate, undervalue, underestimate, diminish, trivialize.
OPPOSITES: appreciate.

depredation noun *few survived the depredation of the barbarian invasion:* plundering, plunder, looting, pillaging, robbery; devastation, destruction, damage, rape; ravages, raids.

depress verb
1 *the news depressed him:* sadden, dispirit, cast down, dishearten, demoralize, weigh down, oppress, upset, distress; informal give someone the blues.
2 *new economic policies depressed sales:* slow down, reduce, lower, weaken, impair; limit, check, inhibit, restrict.
3 *imports will depress farm prices:* reduce, lower, cut, keep down, push down, deflate, devalue, diminish; informal slash.
4 *depress each key in turn:* press, push, hold down.
OPPOSITES: cheer, boost.

depressed adjective
1 *he felt lonely and depressed:* despondent, dejected, despairing, desolate, sad, unhappy, miserable, gloomy, glum, melancholy, disconsolate, downhearted, downcast, down, dispirited, low, heavy-hearted, morose; tearful, upset; informal blue, down in the dumps, down in the mouth, fed up.
2 *a depressed economy:* weak, enervated, devitalized; inactive, flat, slow, slack, sluggish, stagnant.
3 *depressed inner-city areas:* poverty-stricken, poor, disadvantaged, deprived.
OPPOSITES: cheerful, strong, prosperous.

depressing adjective
1 *depressing thoughts:* upsetting, distressing, painful; dispiriting, dismal, bleak, black, sombre, gloomy, grave, unhappy, melancholy, sad, doleful; informal morbid, blue.

d

2 *a depressing room:* gloomy, bleak, dreary, grim, drab, sombre, dark, dingy, funereal, cheerless, joyless, comfortless, uninviting.

depression noun
1 *shorter days and longer nights can induce feelings of depression:* despondency, dejection, despair, desolation, unhappiness, sadness, melancholy, misery, sorrow, gloom, low spirits, heavy heart; informal the blues.
2 *an economic depression:* recession, slump, decline, downturn, slowdown, standstill; stagnation.
3 *a depression in the ground:* hollow, indentation, dent, dint, cavity, concavity, dip, pit, hole, crater; basin, trough.

deprivation noun *unemployment and deprivation:* poverty, impoverishment, penury, privation, hardship, destitution; need, want, distress, indigence, ruin; straitened circumstances.
OPPOSITES: wealth.

deprive verb *she was deprived of her royal privileges:* dispossess of, strip of, divest of, relieve of, rob of, deny, prevent from having; cheat out of; informal do out of.

deprived adjective *the most deprived members of society:* disadvantaged, underprivileged, poverty-stricken, impoverished, poor, destitute, needy, unable to make ends meet; Brit. on the bread line.

depth noun
1 *the depth of the well:* deepness, distance downwards; drop, vertical extent.
2 *the depth of his knowledge | the depth of the problems:* extent, range, scope, breadth, width; magnitude, scale, degree.
3 *a work of great depth:* complexity, intricacy; profundity, gravity, weight, insight, wisdom.
4 *depth of colour:* intensity, richness, deepness, vividness, strength, brilliance.
OPPOSITES: shallowness, triviality.
□ **in depth** thoroughly, in detail, exhaustively, extensively, completely, fully; meticulously, scrupulously, rigorously, painstakingly.

deputation noun *the prime minister agreed to receive a deputation of bankers:* delegation, delegacy, commission; contingent, group, party.

depute verb
1 *he was deputed to handle the negotiations:* appoint, designate, nominate, assign, commission, charge, choose, select, elect; empower, authorize.
2 *the judge deputed smaller cases to others:* delegate, transfer, hand over, pass on, consign, assign, entrust, give.

deputize verb *the assistant's task is to deputize for the account executive:* stand in for, sit in for, fill in for, cover for, be

a substitute for, replace, take someone's place, relieve, take over from; act for, act on behalf of; hold the fort, step into the breach.

deputy noun *he handed over to his deputy:* second in command, number two, subordinate, assistant, aide; substitute, stand-in, fill-in, understudy; representative, proxy, agent, spokesperson.
▷ adjective *her deputy editor:* assistant, substitute, stand-in, acting, reserve, fill-in, caretaker, temporary, provisional, stopgap, surrogate; informal second-string.

deranged adjective *five schoolchildren were shot by a deranged gunman:* insane, mad, disturbed, unbalanced, unhinged; crazed, demented, berserk, frenzied, lunatic; informal crazy.

derelict adjective *a derelict building:* dilapidated, ramshackle, run-down, tumbledown, in ruins, falling apart; rickety, deteriorating, crumbling; neglected, untended, gone to rack and ruin, decrepit; disused, abandoned, deserted.

dereliction noun
1 *buildings were reclaimed from dereliction:* dilapidation, disrepair, deterioration, ruin, rack and ruin; abandonment, neglect, disuse.
2 *he was accused of dereliction of duty:* negligence, neglect; carelessness, laxity, sloppiness, slackness, irresponsibility.

deride verb *his poems have generally been derided as childish:* ridicule, mock, make fun of, poke fun at, laugh at, scoff at, pillory, disparage, denigrate, dismiss, sneer at, scorn.
OPPOSITES: praise.

derision noun *his stories were greeted with disbelief and derision:* mockery, ridicule, sneers; disdain, disparagement, denigration, disrespect, insults; scorn, contempt.

derisive adjective *he gave a harsh, derisive laugh:* mocking, scornful, contemptuous, disdainful; jeering, scoffing, snide, sneering, scathing, sarcastic.

derisory adjective *they were given a derisory pay rise:* inadequate, insufficient, tiny, small; trifling, paltry, pitiful, miserly, miserable; negligible, token, nominal; ridiculous, laughable; informal measly, stingy, lousy, pathetic.

derivation noun
1 *the derivation of theories from empirical observation:* deriving, deduction, inference; extraction.
2 *the derivation of a word:* origin, etymology, root, etymon, provenance, source; development, evolution.

derivative adjective *her work is very derivative:* imitative, unoriginal; copied,

plagiarized, second-hand; trite, hackneyed, clichéd, stale.
OPPOSITES: original.
▷**noun** *a derivative of opium:* by-product, subsidiary product.

derive verb
1 *he derives consolation from his poetry:* obtain, get, take, gain, acquire, draw, extract.
2 *'coffee' derives from the Turkish word 'kahveh':* originate in, stem from, descend from, come from, be taken from.
3 *his fortune derives from property:* originate in, be rooted in; stem from, come from, spring from, proceed from, issue from.

derogatory adjective *a derogatory remark:* disparaging, uncomplimentary, critical, pejorative, negative, disrespectful, insulting, offensive, abusive, rude, personal, unflattering; denigratory, deprecatory, defamatory, slanderous, libellous; informal bitchy, catty.
OPPOSITES: complimentary.

descend verb
1 *the plane started to descend:* go down, come down; drop, fall, sink, dive, plummet, plunge, nosedive.
2 *she descended the stairs:* climb down, go down, come down.
3 *the road descends to a village:* slope, dip, slant, go down, fall away.
4 *she saw Leo descend from the bus:* alight, disembark, get down, get off, dismount.
5 *they would not descend to such mean tricks:* stoop, lower yourself, demean yourself, debase yourself; resort, be reduced, go as far as.
6 *the militia descended on Rye:* attack, assail, assault, storm, invade, swoop on, charge.
7 *he is descended from a Flemish family:* be a descendant of, come from, originate from, spring from, derive from.
OPPOSITES: ascend, climb.

descendant noun *a descendant of Charles Darwin:* scion, heir; (**descendants**) offspring, progeny, family, lineage, line.
OPPOSITES: ancestor.

descent noun
1 *a steep descent:* slope, incline, dip, drop, gradient, declivity, slant; hill.
2 *his descent into alcoholism:* decline, slide, fall, degeneration, deterioration.
3 *she is of Italian descent:* ancestry, parentage, ancestors, family, antecedents; extraction, origin, derivation, birth; lineage, line, genealogy, heredity, stock, pedigree, blood, bloodline; roots, origins.

describe verb
1 *in the book, he describes his experiences as a doctor in the First World War:* give an account of, recount, report, relate, tell of, set out, narrate, chronicle; detail, catalogue, give a rundown of; explain.

2 *she described him as a pathetic figure:* characterize, portray, depict, present, represent, paint; call, refer to, speak of; categorize, class.
3 *the pen described a circle:* mark out, outline, trace, draw, delineate.

description noun
1 *a description of my travels:* account, report, explanation; narrative, story, chronicle; portrayal, portrait.
2 *vehicles of every description:* sort, variety, kind, type, category, order, class, designation, specification, genre, genus, brand, make, character.

descriptive adjective *her early work uses colourful, descriptive language:* illustrative, expressive, graphic, detailed; lively, vivid, striking; explanatory.

desecrate verb *invaders desecrated the temple:* violate, profane, defile, debase, dishonour; vandalize, damage, destroy, deface.

desert¹ verb
1 *his wife deserted him:* abandon, leave, turn your back on; throw over, jilt, break up with; leave high and dry, leave in the lurch, leave behind, strand, maroon; literary forsake; informal walk out on, run out on, dump, ditch.
2 *soldiers deserted in droves:* abscond, defect, run away, make off, decamp, flee, turn tail, take French leave, quit; Military go AWOL.

desert² noun *the African desert:* wasteland, wastes, wilderness, wilds, barren land; dust bowl.
▷**adjective** *desert conditions:* arid, dry, parched, waterless, scorched, hot; barren, bare, stark, infertile, sterile.
OPPOSITES: fertile.

deserted adjective
1 *a deserted wife:* abandoned, jilted, cast aside; literary forsaken.
2 *a deserted village:* empty, uninhabited, unoccupied, abandoned, evacuated; desolate, lonely.
OPPOSITES: populous.

deserter noun *a deserter from the Foreign Legion:* absconder, runaway, fugitive, escapee; renegade, defector, turncoat, traitor.

deserve verb *everyone involved with the book deserves the greatest praise:* be worthy of, be entitled to, have earned, have a right to; merit, warrant, rate, justify.

deserved adjective well earned, merited, warranted, justified, justifiable; rightful, due, right, just, fair, fitting, appropriate, suitable, proper, apt.

deserving adjective
1 *he was a very deserving winner:* worthy, commendable, praiseworthy, admirable, meritorious, estimable.

2 *a project deserving of our attention:* meriting, warranting, justifying, suitable for, worthy of.

desiccated adjective *desiccated coconut:* dried, dry, dehydrated; powdered.

design noun
1 *a design for the new offices:* plan, blueprint, drawing, sketch, outline, diagram, representation, scheme, model, prototype; map.
2 *tableware with a gold design:* pattern, motif, device; style, configuration, arrangement, composition, layout, shape, form.
3 *his design was to reach the top:* intention, aim, purpose, plan, intent, objective, object, goal, end, target; hope, desire, wish, dream, aspiration, ambition.
▷ **verb**
1 *he has designed an excellent marketing campaign | the artwork was designed by her brother:* plan, outline, map out, draft, draw.
2 *they designed a new engine:* invent, originate, create, think up, come up with, devise, formulate, conceive; make, produce, develop, fashion; informal dream up.
3 *this paper is designed to provoke discussion:* intend, aim, mean; tailor, adapt, gear; plan, devise.
▢ **by design**
deliberately, intentionally, on purpose, purposefully; knowingly, wittingly, consciously, calculatedly.

designate verb
1 *some firms designate a press officer:* appoint, nominate; select, choose, pick, elect, name.
2 *the rivers are designated 'Sites of Special Scientific Interest':* classify as, class as; label, name, call, entitle, term.

designation noun
1 *the designation of a leader:* appointment, nomination, naming, selection, election.
2 *the designation 'Generalissimo':* title, name, epithet, tag; description.

designer noun
1 *he was soon greatly in demand as a designer of gardens and houses:* creator, planner, deviser, inventor, originator; maker; architect.
2 *a young French designer made the dress:* couturier, tailor, costumier, dressmaker.

desirable adjective
1 *a desirable location:* attractive, sought-after, in demand, popular, desired, coveted, enviable; appealing, agreeable, pleasant; valuable, good, excellent; informal to die for.
2 *such a pact was desirable for both countries:* advantageous, advisable, wise, sensible; helpful, useful, beneficial, worthwhile, profitable, preferable.
3 *a very desirable woman:* sexually

attractive, beautiful, pretty, appealing; seductive, alluring, enchanting, beguiling, captivating, bewitching, irresistible; informal sexy.
OPPOSITES: undesirable, unattractive.

desire noun
1 *a desire to see the world:* wish, want, aspiration, fancy, inclination, impulse; yearning, longing, craving, yen, hankering, hunger; eagerness, enthusiasm, determination; informal itch.
2 *his eyes glittered with desire:* lust, sexual attraction, passion, sensuality, sexuality; lasciviousness.
▷ **verb**
1 *he never achieved the status he desired:* want, wish for, long for, yearn for, crave, hanker after, be desperate for, be bent on, covet, aspire to; have a yen for; Brit. informal fancy.
2 *there had been a time, years ago, when he had desired her:* be attracted to, lust after, burn for, be infatuated by; informal have the hots for; Brit. informal fancy.

desired adjective
1 *cut the cloth to the desired length:* required, necessary, proper, right, correct; appropriate, suitable; preferred, chosen, selected.
2 *the desired results:* wished for, wanted; sought-after, longed for, yearned for.

desist verb *we must desist from any industrial action that may disturb national unity:* abstain, refrain, forbear, hold back, keep; stop, cease, discontinue, suspend, give up, break off, drop, dispense with, eschew; informal lay off, quit, pack in.
OPPOSITES: continue.

desk noun writing table, bureau, escritoire; Brit. davenport.

desolate adjective
1 *desolate moorlands:* bleak, stark, bare, dismal, grim; wild, inhospitable; deserted, uninhabited, godforsaken, abandoned, empty, unfrequented, isolated, remote.
2 *I woke in the early hours feeling desolate:* miserable, despondent, depressed, disconsolate, devastated, despairing, inconsolable, broken-hearted, grief-stricken, crushed; sad, unhappy, downcast, down, dejected, forlorn, upset, distressed; lonely, bereft; informal blue, cut up.
OPPOSITES: populous, joyful.

desolation noun
1 *the stony desolation of the desert:* bleakness, starkness, barrenness, sterility; wildness; isolation, loneliness, remoteness.
2 *a feeling of utter desolation:* misery, sadness, unhappiness, despondency, sorrow, depression, grief, woe; broken-heartedness, wretchedness, dejection, devastation, despair, anguish, distress.

despair noun *her voice was full of self-hatred and despair:* hopelessness,

despondency, desperation; distress, anguish, unhappiness, depression, melancholy, misery, wretchedness, dejection; defeatism, pessimism.
OPPOSITES: hope, joy.
▷**verb** *we should not despair | she despaired of ever seeing him again:* lose hope, abandon hope, give up, lose heart, be discouraged, be despondent, be demoralized, resign yourself; be pessimistic, look on the black side.

despairing adjective *he was even more despairing when I next spoke to him:* hopeless, despondent, in despair, dejected, depressed, disconsolate, gloomy, miserable, wretched, desolate; disheartened, discouraged, demoralized; defeatist, pessimistic.
OPPOSITES: optimistic.

despatch verb & noun. See DISPATCH.

desperate adjective
1 *he gave me a desperate look | her parents were growing desperate:* despairing, hopeless, despondent; anguished, distressed, wretched, distraught, fraught; out of your mind, at your wits' end, beside yourself, at the end of your tether.
2 *a desperate attempt to escape:* last-ditch, last-gasp, eleventh-hour, do-or-die, final; frantic, frenzied, wild; futile, hopeless, doomed.
3 *there's a desperate shortage of teachers:* grave, serious, critical, acute; dire, awful, terrible, dreadful; urgent, pressing, drastic, extreme; informal chronic.
4 *they were desperate for food:* in great need of, urgently requiring, in want of; eager, longing, yearning, hungry, crying out; informal dying.
5 *a desperate act:* violent, dangerous, lawless; reckless, rash, hasty, impetuous, foolhardy, incautious, hazardous, risky; death-or-glory, do-or-die.

desperately adverb
1 *he screamed desperately for help:* in desperation, in despair, despairingly, in distress.
2 *they are desperately ill:* seriously, critically, gravely, severely, acutely, dangerously; very, extremely.

desperation noun *there was a note of desperation in her voice:* hopelessness, despondency, despair; distress, anguish, misery, wretchedness.

despicable adjective *these were particularly despicable crimes:* contemptible, loathsome, hateful, detestable, reprehensible, abhorrent, abominable, awful, heinous; odious, vile, low, mean, abject, shameful, ignominious, shabby, ignoble, disreputable, discreditable, unworthy; informal low-down.
OPPOSITES: admirable.

despise verb *he despised weakness in any*

form: detest, hate, loathe, abhor, deplore, dislike; scorn, disdain, be contemptuous of, look down on, deride, sneer at, revile; formal abominate, execrate.
OPPOSITES: adore.

despite preposition *he remains a great leader despite age and infirmity:* in spite of, notwithstanding, regardless of, in the face of, for all, even with.

despondency noun *the mood became one of gloom and despondency:* hopelessness, despair, low spirits, wretchedness; melancholy, gloom, misery, desolation, disappointment, dejection, sadness, unhappiness; informal the blues.

despondent adjective *as the days passed she grew more and more despondent:* disheartened, discouraged, dispirited, downhearted, downcast, crestfallen, down, low, disconsolate, despairing, wretched; melancholy, gloomy, morose, lugubrious, woebegone, miserable, depressed, dejected, sad; informal blue, down in the mouth, down in the dumps.
OPPOSITES: hopeful, cheerful.

despot noun *a cruel and merciless despot:* tyrant, oppressor, dictator, absolute ruler, autocrat.

despotic adjective *a despotic regime:* autocratic, dictatorial, totalitarian, absolutist, undemocratic, authoritarian; one-party, autarchic; tyrannical, tyrannous, oppressive, repressive, draconian.
OPPOSITES: democratic.

despotism noun tyranny, dictatorship, totalitarianism, absolute rule, absolutism; oppression, repression; autocracy, autarchy.

destabilize verb *the tsar's isolation helped to destabilize the regime:* undermine, weaken, damage, subvert, sabotage, unsettle, upset, disrupt.
OPPOSITES: strengthen.

destination noun *at around 1 p.m. we arrived at our destination:* journey's end, end of the line; terminus, stop, stopping place, port of call; goal, target, end.

destined adjective
1 *he was destined to lead a troubled life:* fated, ordained, predestined, meant; certain, sure, bound, assured, likely; doomed.
2 *computers destined for Pakistan:* heading, bound, en route, scheduled; intended, meant, designed, designated, allotted, reserved.

destiny noun
1 *man is master of his own destiny:* future, fate, fortune, doom; lot.
2 *he believed in destiny:* fate, providence; predestination; divine decree, God's will, kismet, the stars; luck, fortune, chance; karma.

d

d

destitute adjective

1 *she was left destitute:* penniless, poor, impoverished, poverty-stricken, impecunious, without a penny to your name; needy, in straitened circumstances, indigent; Brit. on the breadline; informal hard up, broke, cash-strapped, without a brass farthing, without two pennies to rub together, without a bean; Brit. informal stony broke, skint.
2 *he was jobless and destitute of funds:* devoid, bereft, deprived, in need; lacking, without, deficient in, wanting.
OPPOSITES: rich.

destitution noun
poverty, impoverishment, penury, pennilessness, privation; hardship, need, want, straitened circumstances, dire straits, deprivation, financial distress.

destroy verb

1 *many buildings had been destroyed during the war:* demolish, knock down, level, raze to the ground, obliterate, wipe out; wreck, ruin, devastate, wreak havoc on; blast, blow up, dynamite, explode, bomb.
2 *illness destroyed his career chances:* wreck, ruin, shatter, spoil, disrupt, undo, upset, put an end to, put a stop to, terminate, frustrate, blight, crush, quash, dash, scotch, sabotage; informal mess up, muck up, foul up, put paid to, put the kibosh on, do for; Brit. informal scupper, throw a spanner in the works of.
3 *the horse had to be destroyed:* kill, put down, put to sleep, slaughter.
4 *we had to destroy the enemy:* annihilate, wipe out, obliterate, wipe off the face of the earth, eliminate, eradicate; kill, slaughter, exterminate.
OPPOSITES: build.

destruction noun

1 *the destruction of the rainforest | the hurricane left a trail of destruction:* devastation, spoliation, ruination; damage, havoc, wreckage, ruins.
2 *the destruction of the enemies' forces:* annihilation, obliteration, elimination, eradication; killing, slaughter.

destructive adjective
the destructive effects of the war | one of the most destructive storms in Florida's history: devastating, ruinous, disastrous, catastrophic, crippling; harmful, damaging, detrimental, deleterious, injurious; violent, savage, fierce, brutal, deadly, lethal.

desultory adjective
he made desultory attempts to engage them in conversation: casual, half-hearted, perfunctory, cursory, aimless, unmethodical, unsystematic, irregular, intermittent, sporadic, fitful; superficial, token.

detach verb

1 *he detached the lamp from its bracket:* unfasten, disconnect, disengage, separate, uncouple, remove, loosen, unhitch, unhook, free; pull off, cut off, break off.
2 *he detached himself from the crowd:* free, separate; move away, split off; leave.
3 *he has detached himself from his family:* dissociate, divorce, alienate, separate, isolate, cut off; break away, disaffiliate; leave, quit, withdraw from, break with.
OPPOSITES: attach, join.

detached adjective

1 *a detached house:* free-standing, separate, unconnected.
2 *a detached observer:* dispassionate, objective, uninvolved, disinterested, neutral, unbiased, unprejudiced, impartial, non-partisan; indifferent, aloof, remote, distant, impersonal.

detachment noun

1 *she looked on everything with detachment:* objectivity, dispassion, disinterest, open-mindedness, neutrality, impartiality; indifference, aloofness.
2 *a detachment of soldiers:* unit, squad, troop, contingent, outfit, task force, patrol, crew; platoon, company, corps, regiment, brigade, battalion.

detail noun

1 *the information is correct in every detail:* particular, respect, feature, aspect, characteristic, specific, facet, part, component, constituent; fact, piece of information, point, item, element, circumstance, consideration.
2 *I don't want to get involved in all the details:* technicality, nicety, fine point; (**details**) minutiae.
3 *records with a considerable degree of detail:* precision, exactness, accuracy, thoroughness, carefulness, scrupulousness, particularity.
4 *a guard detail:* unit, detachment, squad, troop, contingent, outfit, task force, patrol.
▷ **verb**
1 *the report details our objections:* describe, explain, catalogue, list, spell out, itemize, identify, specify; state, declare, present, set out, frame; cite, quote, instance, mention, name.
2 *troops were detailed to prevent the escape:* assign, appoint, commission, charge, co-opt, delegate; send, post.
□ **in detail**
we will have to examine the proposals in detail: thoroughly, in depth, exhaustively, minutely, closely, meticulously, rigorously, scrupulously, painstakingly, carefully, point by point; completely, comprehensively, fully, extensively.

detailed adjective
he was able to give the police a detailed description of his attacker: comprehensive, full, complete, thorough, exhaustive, all-inclusive; elaborate, minute, intricate; explicit, specific, precise, exact, accurate, meticulous, painstaking; itemized, blow-by-blow.
OPPOSITES: general.

detain verb
1 *they were detained for questioning:*
hold, take into custody, take in, confine,
imprison, lock up, put in jail, intern; arrest,
apprehend, seize; informal pick up, run in,
haul in.
2 *don't let me detain you:* delay, hold up,
make late, keep, slow up/down; hinder,
hamper, impede, obstruct.
OPPOSITES: release.

detect verb
1 *no one detected a smell of gas | it's harder
to detect the early symptoms in elderly
patients:* notice, perceive, discern, be
aware of, note, recognize, distinguish,
remark, identify, diagnose; catch, sense.
2 *the public can help the police to detect
crime:* solve, clear up, get to the bottom of,
find the person behind; discover, uncover,
find, root out, expose, reveal; informal crack.
3 *the hackers were detected:* catch, hunt
down, track down, find, expose, reveal,
unmask.

detection noun *the early detection of fetal
abnormalities:* identification, discovery,
recognition, diagnosis, perception,
awareness.

detention noun *she was released after
spending over a year in police detention:*
custody, imprisonment, confinement,
incarceration, internment, detainment,
captivity; arrest, house arrest.

deter verb
1 *the high cost deterred many:* discourage,
dissuade, put off, scare off; dishearten,
demoralize, daunt, intimidate.
2 *the presence of a caretaker deters crime:*
prevent, stop, put a stop to, avert; hinder,
impede, hamper, obstruct, foil, forestall,
inhibit, curb.
OPPOSITES: encourage.

deteriorate verb
1 *their living conditions continued to
deteriorate:* worsen, get worse, decline,
degenerate; slump, slip, go downhill;
informal go to pot.
2 *these materials deteriorate if stored
wrongly:* decay, degrade, degenerate,
break down, decompose, rot, go off, spoil,
perish; break up, disintegrate, crumble.
OPPOSITES: improve.

deterioration noun *a deterioration in
living standards:* decline, drop, downturn,
slump, slip, degeneration, worsening.

determinate adjective *a determinate
hierarchy of authority:* fixed, specified,
established, defined, explicit, known,
determined, precise, definite.

determination noun *it took great
determination to win:* resolve, resolution,
will power, strength of character, single-
mindedness, commitment, dedication,
purposefulness; tenacity, perseverance,
persistence, staying power, strong-

mindedness, backbone; stubbornness,
doggedness, obstinacy.

determine verb
1 *chromosomes determine the sex of the
embryo:* control, decide, regulate, direct,
dictate, govern; affect, influence, mould.
2 *he determined to sell up:* resolve, decide,
make up your mind, choose, elect, opt.
3 *the hospital has been unable to determine
the cause of the problem:* ascertain, find
out, discover, establish, work out, deduce,
diagnose, discern, learn; calculate; informal
figure out.
4 *the rent shall be determined by an
accountant:* specify, set, fix, decide on,
settle, establish.

determined adjective
1 *he was determined to have his way:*
intent on, bent on, set on, insistent on,
resolved to.
2 *a very determined man:* resolute,
purposeful, firm, adamant, unswerving,
unwavering, undaunted, intent, insistent,
single-minded; steadfast, staunch,
stalwart; persevering, persistent,
indefatigable, tenacious; strong-minded,
strong-willed, unshakeable, steely,
dedicated, committed; stubborn, dogged,
obstinate, inflexible, intransigent,
unyielding, immovable.

determining adjective *the size of your
house may be the determining factor:*
deciding, decisive, key, pivotal, crucial,
critical, major, chief, prime.

deterrent noun *a 24-hour police presence
would be the most effective deterrent to
crime:* disincentive, discouragement,
brake, damper, curb; obstacle, hindrance,
impediment, obstruction, block, barrier.
OPPOSITES: incentive.

detest verb *I really detest the smell of stale
smoke:* abhor, hate, loathe, despise, shrink
from, recoil from, be unable to bear, find
intolerable, dislike, have an aversion to.
OPPOSITES: love.

detestable adjective *all violent crime is
detestable:* abhorrent, hateful, loathsome,
despicable, odious, abominable,
repellent, repugnant, repulsive, revolting,
disgusting, distasteful, horrible; heinous,
reprehensible, offensive, contemptible.

dethrone verb *he had hoped to dethrone
the king:* depose, unseat, oust, topple,
overthrow, bring down, dislodge, displace,
supplant, usurp, eject.

detonate verb
1 *the charge detonated under the engine:*
explode, go off, blow up; ignite.
2 *they detonated the bomb:* set off, explode,
let off, touch off, trigger; ignite.

detonation noun explosion, blowing up,
ignition; blast, bang, report.

detour noun *visiting Bagley meant a*

d

d

detour of only a mile or so: diversion, roundabout route, indirect route; digression, deviation.

detract verb *such an observation is not intended to detract from her achievement:* belittle, diminish, reduce, lessen, minimize, take away from, play down, trivialize, decry, depreciate, devalue, deprecate.

detriment noun *we have to find ways of housing a growing population without detriment to the countryside:* harm, damage, injury, hurt, impairment, loss, disadvantage, disservice.
OPPOSITES: benefit.

detrimental adjective *the erosion will have a detrimental effect on water quality:* harmful, damaging, injurious, hurtful, inimical, deleterious, destructive, bad, adverse, undesirable, unfavourable, unfortunate; unhealthy, unwholesome.
OPPOSITES: benign.

detritus noun *large areas of land are now littered with military detritus:* debris, waste, refuse, rubbish, litter, scrap, flotsam and jetsam, lumber, rubble; remains, remnants, fragments, scraps, dregs; N. Amer. trash, garbage.

devalue verb *I resent the way people have devalued my achievement:* undervalue, underestimate, underrate, diminish, reduce, trivialize, minimize, belittle, downgrade, depreciate, sell short; informal do down.

devastate verb
1 *the city was devastated by a huge earthquake:* destroy, ruin, wreck, lay waste, ravage, demolish, raze to the ground, level, flatten.
2 *he was devastated by the news:* shatter, shock, stun, daze, dumbfound, traumatize, crush, overwhelm, overcome; informal knock sideways; Brit. informal knock for six.

devastating adjective
1 *the storm will have a devastating effect on the area's economy:* destructive, ruinous, disastrous, catastrophic, calamitous, cataclysmic; harmful, dangerous, fatal, deadly, lethal.
2 *the news came as a devastating blow:* shattering, shocking, traumatic, overwhelming, crushing, dreadful, terrible.

devastation noun *the hurricane left a trail of devastation:* destruction, ruin, havoc, wreckage; ruins, ravages.

develop verb
1 *the industry developed rapidly:* grow, expand, spread; advance, progress, move on, evolve, mature; prosper, thrive, flourish.
2 *I tried to develop my knowledge of their culture and beliefs:* expand, extend, build up, broaden, increase, augment,

supplement; enhance, improve.
3 *a row developed:* start, begin, emerge; erupt, break out, blow up.

development noun
1 *the development of the firm:* growth, expansion, enlargement, spread, progress, evolution; success.
2 *keep me abreast of the latest developments:* event, occurrence, happening, circumstance, incident, situation, issue.
3 *a housing development:* estate, complex, site.

deviant adjective *deviant behaviour:* aberrant, abnormal, irregular, unorthodox; strange, odd, peculiar, bizarre, eccentric, unusual; warped, perverted.
OPPOSITES: normal.

deviate verb *you must not deviate from the agreed route:* diverge, depart, turn aside, drift, stray, veer; get sidetracked, digress.

deviation noun divergence, departure; difference, variation; aberration, abnormality, irregularity, anomaly.

device noun
1 *a labour-saving device:* implement, gadget, tool, utensil, appliance, apparatus, instrument, machine, mechanism; contraption; informal gizmo.
2 *an ingenious legal device:* ploy, tactic, move, stratagem, scheme, manoeuvre, expedient; plot, trick, ruse, contrivance, dodge; Brit. informal wheeze.
3 *their shields bear his device:* emblem, badge, crest, insignia, coat of arms; symbol, logo, mark, design, motif, monogram, hallmark, trademark.

devil noun
1 *God and the Devil:* Satan, Beelzebub, Lucifer, the Lord of the Flies, the Prince of Darkness; informal Old Nick.
2 *they drove out the devils from their bodies:* evil spirit, demon, fiend.

> **WORD LINKS**
> **diabolical** relating to the Devil

devil-may-care adjective *a devil-may-care young pilot:* reckless, rash, incautious, heedless, impetuous, impulsive, daredevil, hot-headed; nonchalant, casual, breezy, insouciant, happy-go-lucky, cheerful, unworried, untroubled, unconcerned.

devilry noun
1 *some devilry was afoot:* wickedness, evil, wrongdoing, villainy.
2 *a perverse sense of devilry urged her to lead him on:* mischief, mischievousness, devilment, naughtiness.

devious adjective
1 *the devious ways in which they bent the rules:* underhand, crafty, cunning, calculating, artful, conniving, scheming, sly, wily, sneaky; deceitful, dishonest,

dishonourable, unethical, unprincipled, unscrupulous, unfair.
2 *they arrived at the town by a rather devious route:* circuitous, roundabout, indirect, meandering, tortuous.

devise verb *scientists have devised a method of recycling oil contaminated with PCBs:* think up, work out, formulate, conceive, dream up; design, invent, construct, create, produce, develop; discover, hit on; hatch, concoct, contrive; informal cook up.

devoid adjective (**devoid of**) *her voice was devoid of emotion:* lacking, without, free from, wanting; informal minus.

devolve verb *the move would devolve responsibility to local units:* pass, hand down/over/on, delegate, transfer, assign, convey, entrust, turn over, give, cede, surrender, relinquish, deliver; decentralize.

devote verb *they need to devote considerable time to career planning:* allocate, assign, allot, commit, give, apportion; dedicate, set aside, earmark, reserve, designate.

devoted adjective *his devoted followers:* loyal, faithful, true, staunch, steadfast, constant, committed, dedicated, devout; fond, loving, affectionate, caring.

devotee noun
1 *a devotee of rock music:* enthusiast, fan, lover, aficionado, admirer; informal buff, freak, nut, fiend, fanatic, addict.
2 *devotees thronged the temple:* follower, adherent, believer, disciple.

devotion noun
1 *her devotion to her husband:* loyalty, faithfulness, fidelity, constancy, commitment, dedication; fondness, love, affection, care.
2 *a life of devotion:* devoutness, piety, spirituality, worship, religious observance.

devotional adjective *the devotional paintings of the period:* religious, sacred, spiritual, divine, church, ecclesiastical.
OPPOSITES: secular.

devour verb
1 *he devoured his meal in a matter of minutes:* eat hungrily, eat greedily, gobble, guzzle, gulp down, bolt down, wolf down, feast on, consume; informal scoff, demolish, polish off, shovel down, stuff yourself with, pig yourself on, put away.
2 *flames devoured the house:* consume, engulf, envelop; destroy, demolish, lay waste, devastate; gut, ravage, ruin, wreck.

devout adjective
1 *a devout Christian:* pious, religious, devoted, dedicated, God-fearing; holy, godly, saintly, faithful, dutiful, righteous, churchgoing.
2 *he's a devout fan and tries to make*

every match, home and away: dedicated, devoted, committed, loyal, faithful, staunch, firm, steadfast, unwavering, sincere, wholehearted, keen, enthusiastic, zealous, passionate, ardent, fervent, sworn; informal true blue, deep-dyed.

dexterity noun
1 *throughout the game he displayed awesome dexterity with the ball:* deftness, adeptness, adroitness, ability, talent, skill, proficiency, expertise, delicacy, artistry, finesse; agility.
2 *his political dexterity:* shrewdness, astuteness, sharp-wittedness, acumen, acuity, intelligence; ingenuity, inventiveness, cleverness; sense, insight, understanding, penetration, perception, perspicacity, discrimination; informal nous.

dexterous, dextrous adjective *a dexterous performer:* deft, adept, adroit, agile, handy, able, capable, skilful, skilled, proficient, expert, practised, polished; efficient, effortless, slick, professional, masterly; informal nifty.
OPPOSITES: clumsy.

diabolical adjective
1 *his diabolical cunning:* fiendish, demonic, evil, wicked, ungodly, unholy.
2 (informal) *a diabolical performance:* very bad, dreadful, awful, terrible, disgraceful, abysmal, shameful, lamentable, deplorable, appalling, atrocious; substandard, unsatisfactory, second-rate; informal dire, dismal, rotten, pathetic, pitiful, lousy; Brit. informal duff, rubbish.

diagnose verb *this is a procedure that is undertaken to help diagnose the causes of back ache:* identify, detect, determine, distinguish, recognize, find, discover, pinpoint, isolate.

diagnosis noun
1 *the diagnosis of coeliac disease:* identification, detection, recognition, determination, discovery.
2 *the results confirmed his diagnosis:* opinion, judgement, verdict, conclusion.

diagonal adjective *a diagonal line:* crosswise, crossways, slanting, slanted, aslant, oblique, angled, at an angle.

diagram noun drawing, line drawing, sketch, representation, illustration, picture, plan, outline, delineation, figure.

diagrammatic adjective *the information is presented in diagrammatic form:* graphic, graphical, representational, schematic, simplified.

dial verb *she dialled her parents:* phone, telephone, call, ring.

dialect noun *I found it hard to understand the unfamiliar dialect:* regional language, local language, local speech, vernacular, idiom; patois.

dialogue noun
1 *the book consists of a series of dialogues:* conversation, talk, discussion, interchange; chat, tête-à-tête; informal confab.
2 *they called for a serious political dialogue:* discussion, exchange, debate, discourse, exchange of views, talk, head-to-head, consultation, conference; talks, negotiations.

diameter noun *the pipe has a diameter of 14mm:* breadth, width, thickness; calibre, bore, gauge.

diametrical, diametric adjective *they set themselves in diametrical opposition to their society:* direct, absolute, complete, exact, extreme, polar.

diaphanous adjective *she wore a diaphanous dress of pale gold:* sheer, fine, delicate, light, thin, insubstantial, floaty, flimsy, filmy, silken, gossamer, gossamer-thin, gauzy; translucent, transparent, see-through.
OPPOSITES: thick, opaque.

diary noun
1 *he put the date in his diary:* appointment book, engagement book, personal organizer; trademark Filofax.
2 *her World War II diaries:* journal, memoir, chronicle, log, history, annal, record; blog, weblog.

diatribe noun *he launched into a diatribe against the government's foreign policy:* tirade, harangue, onslaught, attack, polemic, denunciation, broadside, fulmination, condemnation, criticism.

dicey adjective (informal) *refuelling at sea is a bit dicey in bad weather:* risky, uncertain, unpredictable, touch-and-go, precarious, unsafe, dangerous, fraught with danger, hazardous, perilous, high-risk, difficult; informal hairy; Brit. informal dodgy.
OPPOSITES: safe.

dichotomy noun *there is a great dichotomy between social theory and practice:* contrast, difference, polarity, conflict; gulf, chasm, division, separation, split.

dictate verb
1 *the tsar's attempts to dictate policy:* prescribe, lay down, impose, set down, order, command, decree, ordain, direct, determine, decide, control, govern.
2 *you are in no position to dictate to me:* give orders to, order about/around, lord it over; lay down the law; informal boss about/around, push around/about, throw your weight about/around.
3 *choice is often dictated by availability:* determine, control, govern, decide, influence, affect.
▷ noun *he is merely following the dictates of his leader:* order, command, commandment, decree, edict, ruling, dictum, diktat, directive, direction, instruction, mandate, requirement, stipulation, injunction, demand.

dictator noun autocrat, absolute ruler; despot, tyrant.

dictatorial adjective
1 *a dictatorial regime:* autocratic, undemocratic, totalitarian, authoritarian, autarchic, despotic, tyrannical, tyrannous, oppressive, repressive.
2 *his dictatorial manner:* domineering, autocratic, authoritarian, imperious, officious, overweening, overbearing, peremptory, dogmatic, high and mighty; severe, strict; informal bossy, high-handed.
OPPOSITES: democratic, meek.

dictatorship noun *an entire generation grew up in the shadow of dictatorship:* absolute rule, undemocratic rule, despotism, tyranny, autocracy, autarchy, authoritarianism, totalitarianism; oppression, repression.
OPPOSITES: democracy.

diction noun *she began to imitate his careful diction:* enunciation, articulation, elocution, pronunciation, speech, intonation, inflection; delivery; formal locution.

dictionary noun lexicon, word list; glossary.

WORD LINKS
lexicography the practice of writing dictionaries

dictum noun
1 *he received the head's dictum with evident reluctance:* pronouncement, proclamation, direction, injunction, dictate, command, commandment, order, decree, edict, mandate, diktat.
2 *the old dictum 'might is right':* saying, maxim, axiom, proverb, adage, aphorism, saw, precept, epigram, motto, truism, commonplace; expression, phrase.

didactic adjective *a didactic novel that set out to expose social injustice:* instructive, instructional, educational, educative, informative, edifying, improving, pedagogic, moralistic.

die verb
1 *her father died last year:* pass away, pass on, lose your life, expire, breathe your last, meet your death, lay down your life, go the way of all flesh, go to your last resting place, go to meet your maker, cross the great divide; literary perish; informal give up the ghost, kick the bucket, shuffle off this mortal coil; Brit. informal snuff it, pop your clogs.
2 *the wind had died down:* abate, subside, drop, lessen, ease off, let up, moderate, fade, dwindle, peter out, wane, ebb, relent, weaken; melt away, dissolve, vanish, disappear.
OPPOSITES: live, intensify.

diehard adjective *the committee was full of diehard Stalinists:* hard-line, reactionary, ultra-conservative, conservative, traditionalist, dyed-in-the-wool, intransigent, inflexible, uncompromising, rigid, entrenched, set in your ways; committed, staunch, steadfast.

diet noun *a vegetarian diet | make sure that your diet includes enough protein:* selection of food, food, foodstuffs.
▷ **verb** *she dieted for most of her life:* be on a diet, eat sparingly; slim, lose weight, watch your weight; informal weight-watch.

differ verb
1 *the second set of data differed from the first:* contrast with, be different from, be dissimilar to, be unlike, vary from, diverge from, deviate from, conflict with, run counter to, be incompatible with, be at odds with, go against, contradict.
2 *the two sides differed over this issue:* disagree, conflict, be at variance/odds, be in dispute, not see eye to eye.
OPPOSITES: resemble, agree.

difference noun
1 *the difference between the two sets of data:* dissimilarity, contrast, distinction, differentiation, disparity, discrepancy, inconsistency, variance, variation, divergence, deviation, imbalance, contradiction; gap, gulf, polarity.
2 *we've had our differences in the past:* disagreement, difference of opinion, dispute, argument, quarrel, wrangle, contretemps, altercation; Brit. row; informal tiff, set-to, run-in, spat.
3 *I am willing to pay the difference:* balance, remainder, rest, remaining amount, residue.
OPPOSITES: similarity.

different adjective
1 *people with different lifestyles | these methods produced different results:* dissimilar, unalike, unlike, contrasting, contrastive, divergent, differing, varying, disparate; poles apart, incompatible, mismatched, conflicting, clashing, inconsistent, contradictory; informal like chalk and cheese.
2 *suddenly everything in her life was different:* changed, altered, transformed, new, unfamiliar, unknown, strange.
3 *he visited the site on two different occasions:* distinct, separate, individual, discrete, independent.
4 *he wanted to try something different:* unusual, out of the ordinary, unfamiliar, novel, new, fresh, original, unconventional, exotic.
OPPOSITES: similar, related, ordinary.

differentiate verb
1 *he was unable to differentiate between fantasy and reality:* distinguish, discriminate, make/draw a distinction, tell the difference, tell apart.

2 *this differentiates their business from all other booksellers:* make different, distinguish, set apart, single out, separate, mark off.

differentiation noun distinction, difference; separation, demarcation, delimitation.

difficult adjective
1 *a very difficult job:* hard, strenuous, arduous, laborious, tough, onerous, demanding, punishing, gruelling, back-breaking, exhausting, tiring, fatiguing, wearisome, burdensome; informal hellish, killing.
2 *she found maths difficult | we are faced with a difficult problem:* hard, complicated, complex, involved, intractable; impenetrable, unfathomable, over/above your head, puzzling, baffling, perplexing, confusing, mystifying; problematic, intricate, knotty, thorny.
3 *you've come at a difficult time:* inconvenient, awkward, inopportune, unfavourable, unfortunate, inappropriate, unsuitable, untimely, ill-timed.
4 *a difficult child:* troublesome, tiresome, trying, exasperating, awkward, demanding, perverse, contrary, recalcitrant, unmanageable, obstreperous, unaccommodating, unhelpful, uncooperative, disobliging; hard to please, fussy, finicky.
OPPOSITES: easy, simple, accommodating.

difficulty noun
1 *the difficulty of balancing motherhood with a career:* strain, stress, trouble, problems, struggle; informal hassle.
2 *there are practical difficulties:* problem, complication, snag, hitch, pitfall, impediment, hindrance, obstacle, hurdle, stumbling block, obstruction, barrier; informal fly in the ointment, headache, hiccup.
3 *Charles got into difficulties:* trouble, predicament, plight, mess, hard times, dire straits; informal deep water, a fix, a jam, a hole.
OPPOSITES: ease.

diffidence noun *he regretted his diffidence and awkwardness in larger groups:* shyness, modesty, self-effacement, meekness, unassertiveness, timidity, humility, hesitancy, reticence, insecurity, self-doubt, uncertainty, self-consciousness, bashfulness.

diffident adjective *he was a rather diffident young man:* shy, modest, self-effacing, unassuming, meek, unconfident, unassertive, timid, timorous, humble, shrinking, reticent, hesitant, insecure, self-doubting, doubtful, uncertain, unsure, self-conscious, bashful.
OPPOSITES: confident.

diffuse verb *such ideas were diffused widely in the 1970s:* spread, spread

d

around, disseminate, distribute, circulate, communicate, propagate, transmit, broadcast, promulgate; Brit. put about.

▷**adjective**
1 *a diffuse community centred on the church*: spread out, scattered.
2 *a diffuse narrative*: verbose, wordy, prolix, long-winded, long-drawn-out, discursive, rambling, wandering, meandering, maundering, digressive, circuitous, roundabout, circumlocutory, periphrastic; Brit. informal waffly.

> **USAGE**
>
> Do not confuse **diffuse** and **defuse**. As a verb **diffuse** means 'to spread over a wide area', while **defuse** means 'to make a situation less tense or dangerous' (*officers are taught how to defuse potentially explosive situations*).

diffusion noun *the diffusion of Marxist ideas*: spread, dissemination, distribution, circulation, propagation, transmission, broadcasting, promulgation.

dig verb
1 *she began to dig the heavy clay soil*: turn over, work, break up; till, harrow, plough.
2 *they dug a large hole in the road*: excavate, dig out, quarry, hollow out, scoop out, gouge out; cut, bore, tunnel, burrow, mine.
3 *the bodies were hastily dug up*: exhume, disinter, unearth.
4 *Winnie dug her elbow into his ribs*: poke, prod, jab, stab, shove, ram, push, thrust, drive.
5 *he'd been digging into my past*: delve, probe, search, inquire, look, investigate, research, examine, scrutinize, check up on; informal check out.
6 *I dug up some disturbing information*: uncover, discover, find out, unearth, dredge up, root out, ferret out, turn up, reveal, bring to light, expose.

▷**noun**
1 *a dig in the ribs*: poke, prod, jab, stab, shove, push.
2 (informal) *they're always making digs at each other*: snide remark, cutting remark, jibe, jeer, taunt, sneer, insult, barb, insinuation; informal wisecrack, crack, put-down.

digest verb *she nodded slowly, digesting this information*: assimilate, absorb, take in, process; understand, comprehend, grasp; consider, think about, reflect on, ponder, contemplate, mull over.
▷**noun** *a digest of their findings*: summary, synopsis, outline, abstract, precis, résumé, summation; compilation.

digit noun *the door code has ten digits*: numeral, number, figure, integer.

dignified adjective *his dignified manner gained their respect*: stately, solemn, proud, composed, serious, grave, formal,

proper, ceremonious, decorous, reserved: imposing, impressive, grand, noble, courtly, majestic, distinguished, august.

dignify verb *the opening ceremony was dignified by the presence of the President of the Privy Council*: ennoble, distinguish, add distinction to, honour, grace, elevate, enhance.

dignitary noun *there are many foreign dignitaries attending today's ceremony*: worthy, personage, VIP, grandee, notable, pillar of society, luminary, leading light, big name; informal heavyweight, bigwig; dated notability.

dignity noun
1 *he bore himself with quiet dignity*: composure, solemnity, gravity, gravitas, pride, formality, decorum, propriety; stateliness, majesty.
2 *he had lost his dignity*: self-respect, pride, self-esteem, self-worth, amour propre.

digress verb *I have digressed a little from my original subject*: deviate, go off at a tangent, get off the subject, get sidetracked, lose the thread, diverge, turn aside/away, depart, drift, stray, wander.

digression noun deviation, departure; aside, incidental remark.

dilapidated adjective *a terrace of dilapidated Victorian houses*: run-down, tumbledown, ramshackle, broken-down, in disrepair, shabby, battered, rickety, shaky, crumbling, in ruins, ruined, decayed, decaying, decrepit; neglected, uncared-for, untended, the worse for wear, falling to pieces, falling apart, gone to rack and ruin, gone to seed.

dilate verb *her nostrils dilated*: enlarge, widen, expand, distend.
OPPOSITES: contract.

dilatory adjective
1 *he had been dilatory in appointing a solicitor*: slow, slow to act, tardy; lazy, sluggish.
2 *they resorted to dilatory tactics*: delaying, time-wasting.
OPPOSITES: fast.

dilemma noun *she was in a dilemma: she ought to refuse but she really wanted to go*: quandary, predicament, catch-22; awkward situation, plight, mess, difficulty, problem, trouble; informal no-win situation, fix, tight spot/corner.

dilettante noun *there is no room for the dilettante in this business*: dabbler, amateur, non-professional, non-specialist, layman, layperson.
OPPOSITES: professional.

diligence noun *through the diligence of our research assistants, the bibliography has grown to contain 293,859 records*: conscientiousness, assiduousness, assiduity, hard work, application, concentration, effort, care, industriousness, meticulousness, thoroughness; perseverance, persistence, tenacity, dedication, commitment, tirelessness, indefatigability, doggedness.

diligent adjective *he was a fast and diligent worker:* industrious, hard-working, assiduous, conscientious, particular, punctilious, meticulous, painstaking, rigorous, careful, thorough, sedulous, earnest; persevering, persistent, tenacious, zealous, dedicated, committed, unflagging, untiring, tireless, indefatigable, dogged. OPPOSITES: lazy.

dilly-dally verb (informal) *the board can't afford to dilly-dally over this issue:* waste time, dally, take your time, delay, temporize, stall, procrastinate, drag your feet; dither, hesitate, vacillate, waver; dawdle, loiter, linger; Brit. haver, hum and haw; informal shilly-shally, pussyfoot around, let the grass grow under your feet. OPPOSITES: hurry.

dilute verb
1 *strong bleach can be diluted with water:* make weaker, weaken, water down; thin out, thin; doctor, adulterate; informal cut.
2 *the original plans have been diluted:* weaken, moderate, tone down, water down; modify.

diluted adjective *wash the brushes in diluted bleach:* weak, dilute, thin, watered down, watery; adulterated. OPPOSITES: concentrated.

dim adjective
1 *the dim light:* faint, weak, feeble, pale, dull, wishy-washy; soft, subdued, muted.
2 *long dim corridors:* dark, badly lit, ill-lit, dingy, dismal, gloomy, murky; literary tenebrous.
3 *a dim figure:* indistinct, ill-defined, unclear, vague, shadowy, nebulous, obscured, blurred, blurry, fuzzy.
4 *dim memories:* vague, imprecise, imperfect, unclear, indistinct, sketchy, hazy, blurred, shadowy.
5 *their prospects for the future looked dim:* gloomy, unfavourable, discouraging, disheartening, depressing, dispiriting, hopeless, unpromising.
6 (informal) *he's a bit dim.* See STUPID sense 1. OPPOSITES: bright, distinct, encouraging.
▷ verb
1 *the lights were dimmed:* turn down, lower, dip, soften, subdue, mute.
2 *my memories have not dimmed with time:* fade, become vague, dwindle, blur.
3 *the fighting dimmed hopes of peace:* diminish, reduce, lessen, weaken, undermine. OPPOSITES: brighten, sharpen, intensify.

dimension noun
1 *the dimensions of the room:* size, measurements, proportions, extent; length, width, breadth, depth, area, volume, capacity; footage, acreage.
2 *the dimension of the problem:* size, scale, extent, scope, magnitude; importance, significance.
3 *the cultural dimensions of depression:* aspect, feature, element, facet, side.

diminish verb
1 *the pain will gradually diminish:* decrease, lessen, decline, subside, die down, abate, dwindle, fade, slacken off, moderate, let up, ebb, wane, recede, die away/out, peter out.
2 *new legislation diminished the courts' authority:* reduce, decrease, lessen, curtail, cut, cut down/back, restrict, limit, curb, check; weaken, blunt, erode, undermine, sap. OPPOSITES: increase.

diminution noun *a gradual diminution in mental faculties:* reduction, decrease, lessening, decline, dwindling, moderation, fading, weakening, ebb.

diminutive adjective *a diminutive figure dressed in black:* tiny, small, little, petite, elfin, minute, miniature, minuscule; Scottish wee; informal teeny, teeny-weeny, pint-sized; Brit. informal titchy, tiddly. OPPOSITES: enormous.

dimple noun indentation, hollow, cleft, dint.

dim-witted adjective (informal). See STUPID senses 1, 2.

din noun *he shouted above the din:* noise, racket, rumpus, cacophony, babel, hubbub, tumult, uproar, commotion, clangour, clatter; shouting, yelling, screaming, caterwauling, clamour, outcry; Brit. row; Brit. informal hullabaloo. OPPOSITES: silence.
▷ verb
1 *she had had the evils of drink dinned into her:* instil, inculcate, drive, drum, hammer, drill, ingrain; indoctrinate, brainwash.
2 *the sound dinned irritatingly into her head:* blare, blast, clang, clatter, crash, clamour.

dine verb
1 *we dined at a local restaurant:* have dinner, have supper, eat.
2 *they dined on lobster:* eat, feed on, feast on, banquet on; formal partake of; informal tuck into.

dingy adjective *a dingy basement flat:* gloomy, dark, badly/poorly lit, murky, dim, dismal, dreary, drab, sombre, grim, cheerless; dirty, grimy, shabby, run-down. OPPOSITES: bright.

dint noun *the dints and holes were the work of arrows:* dent, indentation, hollow, depression, dip, dimple, cleft, pit.
□ **by dint of**
by means of, using, utilizing, employing, through, with the help of, by virtue of,

d

by way of, on the strength of, taking advantage of, due to, thanks to, by; formal by reason of.

diocese noun bishopric, see.

dip verb
1 *he dipped a rag in the water:* immerse, submerge, plunge, duck, dunk, lower, sink.
2 *the sun dipped below the horizon:* sink, set, drop, go/drop down, fall, descend; disappear, vanish.
3 *the president's popularity has dipped:* decrease, fall, drop, fall off, decline, diminish, dwindle, slump, plummet, plunge; informal hit the floor.
4 *the road dipped:* slope down, descend, go down; drop away, fall, sink.
5 *he dipped his headlights:* dim, lower, turn down.
OPPOSITES: rise, increase.

▷**noun**
1 *give the fish a ten-minute dip in a salt bath:* immersion, plunge, ducking, dunking.
2 *chicken satay with peanut dip:* sauce, relish, salsa, dressing.
3 *a relaxing dip in the pool:* swim, bathe; paddle.
4 *the hedge at the bottom of the dip:* slope, incline, descent, hollow, depression, basin, indentation.
5 *a dip in sales:* decrease, fall, drop, drop-off, downturn, decline, fall-off, falling-off, slump, reduction, diminution, ebb.

diplomacy noun
1 *diplomacy failed to win them independence:* international relations, foreign affairs, statesmanship, statecraft, negotiation; discussions, talks, dialogue.
2 *Jack's quiet diplomacy:* tact, tactfulness, sensitivity, discretion, subtlety, finesse, delicacy, savoir faire, politeness, thoughtfulness, care, prudence.

diplomat noun ambassador, attaché, consul, chargé d'affaires, envoy, emissary, plenipotentiary.

diplomatic adjective *he tried to be diplomatic:* tactful, sensitive, subtle, delicate, polite, discreet, thoughtful, careful, judicious, prudent, politic, clever, skilful.
OPPOSITES: tactless, undiplomatic.

dire adjective
1 *the dire economic situation:* terrible, dreadful, appalling, frightful, awful, atrocious, grim, alarming; grave, serious, disastrous, ruinous, irretrievable, wretched, desperate; formal grievous; Brit. informal hopeless; old use parlous.
2 *he was in dire need of help:* urgent, desperate, pressing, crying, sore, grave, serious, extreme, acute, drastic.
3 *dire warnings of fuel shortages:* ominous, gloomy, grim, dismal, inauspicious, unfavourable, pessimistic.

4 (informal) *the concert was dire.* See **AWFUL** sense 2.
OPPOSITES: excellent, slight, auspicious.

direct adjective
1 *they had taken a direct route through the undergrowth to avoid detection:* straight, undeviating, unswerving; shortest, quickest.
2 *a direct flight:* non-stop, unbroken, uninterrupted, through.
3 *he is always very direct:* frank, candid, straightforward, honest, open, blunt, plain-spoken, outspoken, forthright, no-nonsense, matter-of-fact, not afraid to call a spade a spade; informal upfront.
4 *direct contact with the president:* face-to-face, personal, head-on, unmediated, immediate, first-hand.
5 *the direct opposite:* exact, absolute, complete, diametrical.
OPPOSITES: indirect.

▷**verb**
1 *was that remark directed at me?* aim at, target at, address to, intend for, mean for, design for.
2 *an economic elite directed the nation's affairs:* manage, govern, run, administer, control, conduct, handle, be in charge of, preside over, lead, head, rule, be at the helm of; supervise, superintend, oversee, regulate, orchestrate, coordinate.
3 *a man in uniform directed them to the hall:* give directions, show the way, guide, lead, conduct, accompany, usher, escort.
4 *the judge directed the jury to return a not guilty verdict:* instruct, tell, command, order, require, call on; old use bid.

direction noun
1 *a northerly direction:* way, route, course, line, run, bearing, orientation.
2 *the newspaper's political direction:* orientation, inclination, leaning, tendency, bent, bias, preference; drift, tack, attitude, tone, tenor, mood, current, trend.
3 *his direction of the project:* management, running, administration, conduct, handling, supervision, superintendence, regulation, orchestration; control, command, rule, leadership, guidance.
4 *explicit directions about nursing care:* instruction, order, command, prescription, rule, regulation, requirement.

directive noun *an EU directive on drinking water:* instruction, direction, command, order, charge, injunction, prescription, rule, ruling, regulation, law, dictate, decree, dictum, edict, mandate, fiat.

directly adverb
1 *they flew directly to New York:* straight, as the crow flies, right, non-stop.
2 *she spoke simply and directly:* frankly, candidly, honestly, openly, bluntly, outspokenly, forthrightly, without beating about the bush.
3 *the houses directly opposite:* exactly,

right, immediately, diametrically; informal bang.

4 *I went directly after breakfast:* immediately, at once, instantly, right away, straight away, post-haste, without delay, without hesitation, forthwith; quickly, promptly.

director noun *the director of a major British museum:* administrator, manager, chairman, chairwoman, chairperson, chair, head, chief, principal, leader, governor, president; managing director, MD, chief executive, chief executive officer, CEO; supervisor, controller, overseer; informal boss.

directory noun index, list, listing, register, catalogue, record, archive, inventory.

dirge noun *he wrote dirges for funerals:* elegy, lament, threnody, requiem, dead march.

dirt noun

1 *his face was streaked with dirt:* grime, filth; dust, soot, smut; muck, mud, mire, sludge, slime; smudges, stains.
2 *the packed dirt of the road:* earth, soil, ground.

dirty adjective

1 *a dirty sweatshirt | dirty water:* filthy, grimy, grubby, mucky, soiled, stained, unwashed, greasy, smeared, smeary, smutty, spotted, bespattered, cloudy, muddy, dusty, sooty; unclean, impure, polluted, contaminated, foul, unhygienic, insanitary, unsanitary.
2 *a dirty joke:* indecent, obscene, rude, naughty, vulgar, smutty, coarse, crude, filthy, bawdy, suggestive, ribald, racy, salacious, risqué, offensive, off colour, lewd, pornographic, explicit, X-rated; informal blue.
3 *dirty tricks:* dishonest, deceitful, unscrupulous, dishonourable, unsporting, ungentlemanly, below the belt, unfair, unethical, unprincipled; crooked, double-dealing, underhand, sly, crafty, devious, sneaky; Brit. informal dodgy.
4 *a dirty look:* malevolent, resentful, hostile, black, dark; angry, cross, indignant, annoyed, disapproving.
OPPOSITES: clean, honourable, friendly.
▷ **verb** *the dog had dirtied her dress:* soil, stain, muddy, blacken, mess up, mark, spatter, bespatter, smudge, smear, splatter, pollute, foul.
OPPOSITES: clean.

disability noun. See the note at **DISABLED**.

disable verb

1 *the bomb squad disabled the device:* deactivate, defuse, disarm, make safe, make inoperative, immobilize.
2 *the submarine was disabled by a fire:* incapacitate, immobilize, paralyse, put out of action.

disabled adjective

USAGE

Disabled is the standard term for people who have physical or mental disabilities. In the past, it was acceptable to use terms such as **handicapped** or **crippled** but these may now cause offence and should be avoided. More recently, expressions such as **physically challenged** or **differently abled** have been coined as synonyms for **disabled** in a conscious attempt to eradicate any negative perception or stigma that may be felt to be attached to the older terms: these may be appropriate in certain situations but they are best avoided in formal writing.
Similarly, **disability** should be used rather than words such as **handicap**, **incapacity**, or **impairment**. In the case of mental disability, the phrase **learning difficulties** is also used. This is seen to emphasize the difficulties experienced rather than any perceived 'deficiency' and so is seen as a more positive term.
It is also preferable to refer to **disabled people** rather than **the disabled**, as the latter expression can be regarded as dehumanizing or patronizing.

disabuse verb *he thought he was good enough to become a professional, but Dinah had disabused him:* disillusion, set straight, open someone's eyes, correct, enlighten, disenchant, shatter someone's illusions.

disadvantage noun *the disadvantage of copper printing plates was the limited number of impressions:* drawback, snag, downside, stumbling block, fly in the ointment, catch, hindrance, obstacle, impediment; flaw, defect, weakness, fault, handicap, con, trouble, difficulty, problem, complication, nuisance; Brit. disbenefit; informal minus.
OPPOSITES: advantage, benefit.

disadvantaged adjective *a disadvantaged rural area:* deprived, underprivileged, depressed, in need, needy, poor, impoverished, indigent.

disadvantageous adjective *prior to 1959, divorce settlements were generally disadvantageous to women:* unfavourable, detrimental, prejudicial, deleterious, harmful, damaging, injurious, hurtful; adverse, unfortunate, inconvenient, inopportune, ill-timed, untimely.

disaffected adjective *a plot by disaffected elements in the army:* dissatisfied, disgruntled, discontented, frustrated, alienated; disloyal, rebellious, mutinous, seditious, dissident, up in arms; hostile, antagonistic, unfriendly.
OPPOSITES: contented.

disagree verb

1 *no one was willing to disagree with him:* take issue, challenge, contradict, oppose; be at variance/odds, not see eye to eye,

differ, dissent, be in dispute, debate, argue, quarrel, wrangle, clash, be at loggerheads, cross swords, lock horns.
2 *their accounts disagree on details:* differ, be dissimilar, be different, vary, diverge; contradict each other, conflict, clash, contrast.
▫ **disagree with**
the spicy food disagreed with her: make ill, make unwell, nauseate, sicken, upset.

disagreeable adjective

1 *a disagreeable smell:* unpleasant, nasty, offensive, off-putting, obnoxious, objectionable, horrible, horrid, dreadful, frightful, abominable, odious, repugnant, repulsive, repellent, revolting, disgusting, foul, vile, nauseating, sickening, unpalatable.
2 *a disagreeable man:* bad-tempered, irritable, ill-tempered, curmudgeonly, cross, grumpy, peevish, sullen, prickly; unfriendly, unpleasant, nasty, mean, mean-spirited, rude, surly, discourteous, impolite, brusque, abrupt, churlish, disobliging.
OPPOSITES: agreeable.

disagreement noun

1 *there was some disagreement over possible solutions:* dispute, dissent, difference of opinion, controversy, variance, discord, contention, division.
2 *a heated disagreement:* argument, debate, quarrel, wrangle, squabble, falling-out, altercation, dispute, disputation, war of words, contretemps; Brit. row; informal tiff, spat.
3 *the disagreement between the results of the two assessments:* difference, variation, variance, discrepancy, dissimilarity, disparity, divergence, deviation; incompatibility, contradiction, conflict, clash, contrast.
OPPOSITES: agreement.

disallow verb *if the registration officer disallows your application he will let you know:* reject, refuse, dismiss, say no to; ban, bar, block, debar, forbid, prohibit; cancel, invalidate, overrule, quash, overturn, countermand, reverse, throw out, set aside.

disappear verb

1 *by 4 o'clock the mist had completely disappeared:* vanish, fade away, melt away, clear, dissolve, disperse, evaporate, dematerialize; literary evanesce.
2 *this way of life has disappeared:* die out, die, cease to exist, come to an end, end, pass away, pass into oblivion, vanish; literary perish.
OPPOSITES: materialize, appear, arise.

disappoint verb *I'm sorry to have disappointed you:* let down, fail, dissatisfy, dash someone's hopes; upset, dismay, sadden, disenchant, disillusion, shatter someone's illusions, disabuse.

disappointed adjective *thousands of disappointed customers were kept waiting:* upset, let down, cast down, saddened, disheartened, downhearted, downcast, depressed, dispirited, discouraged, despondent, dismayed, crestfallen, distressed, chagrined; disenchanted, disillusioned; displeased, discontented, dissatisfied, frustrated, disgruntled.
OPPOSITES: pleased.

disappointing adjective *it was disappointing that there were relatively few possibilities:* regrettable, unfortunate, discouraging, disheartening, dispiriting, depressing, upsetting, saddening; unsatisfactory.
OPPOSITES: pleasing.

disappointment noun

1 *she tried to hide her disappointment:* sadness, regret, dismay, sorrow; despondency, distress, chagrin; disenchantment, disillusionment; displeasure, dissatisfaction, disgruntlement.
2 *the trip was a bit of a disappointment:* let-down, non-event, anticlimax; Brit. damp squib.
OPPOSITES: pleasure, delight.

disapproval noun *they expressed their strong disapproval of the law:* unfavourable opinion, exception, objection, dislike; dissatisfaction, disfavour, displeasure, distaste; criticism, censure, condemnation, denunciation.

disapprove verb

1 *he disapproved of gambling:* object to, have a poor opinion of, take exception to, dislike, take a dim view of, look askance at, frown on, be against, not believe in; deplore, criticize, censure, condemn, denounce, decry, deprecate.
2 *the board disapproved the plan:* reject, veto, refuse, turn down, disallow, throw out, dismiss, rule against.
OPPOSITES: approve.

disapproving adjective *he cast a disapproving glance at Bridget:* reproachful, reproving, critical, censorious, condemnatory, disparaging, deprecatory, unfavourable; dissatisfied, displeased, hostile.

disarm verb

1 *the UN must disarm the country:* demilitarize, demobilize.
2 *police disarmed the bomb:* defuse, disable, deactivate, put out of action, make safe, make harmless.
3 *the warmth in his voice disarmed her:* win over, charm, persuade, thaw; mollify, appease, placate, pacify, conciliate, propitiate.

disarmament noun demilitarization, demobilization, decommissioning; arms reduction, arms limitation, arms control.

disarming adjective *a disarming smile:* winning, charming, irresistible, persuasive, beguiling; conciliatory, placatory, mollifying.

disarray noun *the room was in disarray:* disorder, confusion, chaos, untidiness, disorganization, dishevelment, mess, muddle, clutter, jumble, tangle, hotchpotch; informal shambles.
OPPOSITES: order.

disassemble verb *the furniture was disassembled for transport:* dismantle, take apart, take to pieces, take to bits, strip down, break up.

disaster noun
1 *a railway disaster:* catastrophe, calamity, cataclysm, tragedy, act of God, holocaust; accident.
2 *a string of personal disasters:* misfortune, mishap, misadventure, mischance, setback, reversal, stroke of bad luck, blow.
3 (informal) *the film was a disaster:* failure, fiasco, catastrophe, debacle; informal flop.
OPPOSITES: success.

disastrous adjective *a disastrous fire:* catastrophic, calamitous, cataclysmic, tragic; devastating, ruinous, harmful, dire, terrible, awful, shocking, appalling, dreadful; black, dark, unfortunate, unlucky, ill-fated, ill-starred, inauspicious.

disavow verb *the chairman publicly disavowed the press release:* deny, disclaim, disown, wash your hands of, repudiate, reject, renounce.
OPPOSITES: approve, agree with.

disavowal noun denial, rejection, repudiation, renunciation, disowning, disclaimer.
OPPOSITES: approval, agreement.

disband verb *the unit was scheduled to disband:* break up, disperse, part company, scatter, separate, go their separate ways, dissolve, demobilize.
OPPOSITES: band together, form.

disbelief noun *she stared at him in disbelief:* incredulity, scepticism, doubt; cynicism, suspicion, distrust, mistrust.

disbelieve verb *he totally disbelieved her statement:* doubt, distrust, mistrust, be unconvinced by, give no credence to, discredit, discount; reject, repudiate, question, challenge; be incredulous.
OPPOSITES: believe.

disbeliever noun *as a disbeliever I can still read the Bible for the beauty of its prose:* unbeliever, non-believer, atheist, nihilist; sceptic, doubter, agnostic, doubting Thomas, cynic.

disbelieving adjective *he gave a disbelieving laugh:* incredulous, doubtful, dubious, unconvinced; distrustful, mistrustful, suspicious, cynical, sceptical.

disc noun. See DISK.

discard verb *his old suit had been discarded:* throw away, dispose of, get rid of, toss out, throw out, jettison, scrap, dispense with, cast aside/off, throw on the scrapheap; reject, repudiate, abandon, drop, have done with, shed; informal chuck away/out, dump, ditch, bin, junk.
OPPOSITES: keep.

discern verb *in the dim light he could discern a handful of ghostly figures:* perceive, make out, pick out, detect, recognize, notice, observe, see, spot; identify, determine, distinguish.

discernible adjective *the figure was scarcely discernible in the pale moonlight:* visible, detectable, noticeable, perceptible, observable, distinguishable, recognizable, identifiable; apparent, evident, distinct, appreciable, clear, obvious, manifest, conspicuous.
OPPOSITES: indiscernible.

discerning adjective *we have some real treasures for the discerning collector:* discriminating, tasteful, sophisticated, sensitive, selective, shrewd, astute, intelligent, clever, sharp, perceptive, percipient, perspicacious, judicious, wise, aware, knowing.
OPPOSITES: undiscriminating.

discharge verb
1 *he was discharged from the RAF:* dismiss, eject, expel, throw out, give someone their notice, make redundant; release, let go; Military cashier; informal sack, fire.
2 *he was discharged from prison:* release, free, set free, let go, liberate, let out.
3 *oil is routinely discharged from ships:* release, pour out, let out, give off, send out, eject, void, vent, emit, exude, leak.
4 *he accidentally discharged a pistol:* fire, shoot, let off; set off, loose off, trigger, explode, detonate.
5 *they discharged their duties efficiently:* carry out, perform, execute, conduct, do; fulfil, accomplish, achieve, complete.
OPPOSITES: recruit, imprison, take in.
▷ noun
1 *his discharge from the service:* dismissal, release, ejection, expulsion; Military cashiering; informal the sack.
2 *her discharge from prison:* release, freeing, liberation.
3 *a discharge of diesel oil into the river:* release, emission, flow, leak, leakage.

disciple noun
1 *the disciples of Jesus:* apostle, follower.
2 *a disciple of Rousseau:* follower, adherent, believer, admirer, devotee, acolyte, votary; pupil, student.

disciplinarian noun *she was a strict disciplinarian:* martinet, hard taskmaster, authoritarian, stickler for discipline; tyrant, despot.

d

d

discipline noun

1 *a lack of proper parental discipline:* control, training, teaching, instruction, regulation, direction, authority, rule, strictness, a firm hand; routine, regimen, drilling.
2 *he was able to maintain discipline among his men:* good behaviour, order, control, obedience; self-control, self-discipline, self-restraint.
3 *sociology is a fairly new discipline:* field of study, branch of knowledge, subject, area; speciality, specialism; N. Amer. or Medicine specialty.

▷**verb**
1 *she had disciplined herself to ignore the pain:* train, drill, teach, school, coach; regiment.
2 *she learned to discipline her emotions:* control, restrain, regulate, govern, keep in check, check, curb, keep a tight rein on, rein in, bridle, tame, bring into line.
3 *he was disciplined by the management:* punish, penalize, bring to book; reprimand, rebuke, reprove, chastise, upbraid; informal dress down; Brit. informal carpet.

disclaim verb *the school disclaimed responsibility for his death:* deny, refuse to accept, reject.
OPPOSITES: accept.

disclose verb

1 *the information must not be disclosed to anyone:* reveal, make known, divulge, tell, impart, communicate, pass on, vouchsafe; release, make public, broadcast, publish, report, unveil; leak, betray, let slip, let drop, give away.
2 *exploratory surgery disclosed an aneurysm:* uncover, reveal, show, betray, bring to light.
OPPOSITES: conceal.

disclosure noun

1 *she was embarrassed by this unexpected disclosure:* revelation, declaration, announcement, news, report; exposé, leak.
2 *the disclosure of official information:* publication, broadcasting; revelation, communication, release, unveiling, exposure; leaking.

discoloration noun *a brown discoloration on the skin:* mark, stain, patch, soiling, streak, spot, blotch, tarnishing; blemish, flaw, defect, bruise, contusion, birthmark, naevus; liver spot, age spot; informal splotch; Brit. informal splodge.

discolour verb *smoke from the coal fire had discoloured the original paintwork:* stain, mark, soil, dirty, streak, smear, spot, tarnish; blacken, char; bleach, fade, yellow.

discoloured adjective stained, marked, spotted, dirty, soiled, tarnished, blackened, charred; bleached, faded, yellowed.

discomfit verb *she kissed Sir John on the cheek, which discomfited him even more:* embarrass, abash, disconcert, nonplus, discompose, discomfort, take aback, unsettle, unnerve, put someone off their stroke, ruffle, confuse, fluster, agitate, disorientate, upset, disturb, perturb, distress; mortify; informal faze, rattle.

discomfiture noun embarrassment, unease, awkwardness, discomfort, discomposure, abashment, confusion, agitation, nervousness, disorientation, perturbation, distress; mortification, shame, humiliation.

discomfort noun

1 *abdominal discomfort:* pain, aches and pains, soreness, tenderness, irritation, stiffness; ache, twinge, pang, throb, cramp; Brit. informal gyp.
2 *the various discomforts of life at sea:* inconvenience, difficulty, hardship, trial, tribulation, trouble, problem, bother, nuisance, vexation, drawback, disadvantage; informal hassle.
3 *Ruth flushed and Thomas noticed her discomfort:* embarrassment, discomfiture, unease, awkwardness, discomposure, confusion, nervousness, perturbation, distress, anxiety; mortification, shame, humiliation.

▷**verb** *his purpose was to discomfort the Prime Minister.* See DISCOMFIT.

discomposure noun *she laughed to cover her discomposure:* agitation, discomfiture, discomfort, unease, nervousness; anxiety, worry, consternation, disquiet; embarrassment.

disconcert verb *the abrupt change of subject disconcerted her:* unsettle, nonplus, discomfit, throw off balance, take aback, unnerve, disorient, perturb, disturb, perplex, confuse, bewilder, baffle, fluster, ruffle, shake, upset, agitate, worry, dismay, discountenance; surprise, take by surprise, startle, distract; informal throw, faze, rattle.

disconcerting adjective *the silence was even more disconcerting than the noise that preceded it:* unsettling, unnerving, disturbing, perturbing, troubling, upsetting, worrying, alarming, distracting, off-putting.

disconnect verb

1 *the trucks were disconnected from the train:* detach, disengage, uncouple, decouple, unhook, unhitch, undo, unfasten, unyoke.
2 *she felt as if she had been disconnected from the real world:* separate, cut off, divorce, sever, isolate, delink, divide, part, disengage, dissociate, remove.
3 *an engineer disconnected the appliance:* turn off, switch off, shut off, deactivate, unplug, cut.
OPPOSITES: connect.

disconnected adjective

1 *a world that seemed disconnected from*

reality: **detached,** divorced, cut off, isolated, separate, separated, dissociated, disengaged; apart.

2 *a disconnected narrative:* disjointed, incoherent, garbled, confused, jumbled, mixed up, rambling, wandering, disorganized, uncoordinated, ill-thought-out.

disconsolate adjective *Gita was looking increasingly disconsolate:* **unhappy,** sad, inconsolable, woebegone, dejected, downcast, downhearted, despondent, doleful, dispirited, crestfallen, cast down, depressed, down, disappointed, disheartened, discouraged, demoralized, low-spirited, forlorn, in the doldrums, melancholy, miserable, long-faced, glum, gloomy; informal fed up, blue.
OPPOSITES: cheerful.

discontent noun *there were reports of growing discontent among the military:* **dissatisfaction,** disaffection, discontentment, disgruntlement, grievances, unhappiness, displeasure, bad feelings, resentment, unrest, unease, frustration, irritation, annoyance.
OPPOSITES: contentment.

discontented adjective **dissatisfied,** disgruntled, disaffected, discontent, unhappy, aggrieved, displeased, resentful, envious; restless, frustrated, irritated, annoyed; informal fed up.
OPPOSITES: content.

discontinue verb *the ferry service was discontinued:* **stop,** end, terminate, put an end to, put a stop to, wind up, finish, call a halt to, cancel, drop, abandon, dispense with, do away with, get rid of, axe, scrap, cut, abolish, break off, withdraw; suspend, interrupt.

discontinuous adjective *a person with a discontinuous employment record:* **intermittent,** sporadic, broken, fitful, interrupted, on and off, disrupted, erratic, disconnected.

discord noun
1 *stress resulting from family discord:* **strife,** conflict, friction, hostility, antagonism, antipathy, enmity, bad feeling, ill feeling, bad blood, argument, quarrelling, squabbling, bickering, wrangling, feuding, contention, disagreement, dissension, dispute, difference of opinion, disunity, division, opposition.
2 *at times, the music is shattered by painful, pounding discords:* **dissonance,** disharmony, cacophony, jangling.
OPPOSITES: accord, harmony.

discordant adjective
1 *it is Burton's genius that enables him to synthesize these discordant elements:* **incongruous,** clashing, incompatible, inconsistent, irreconcilable, in disagreement, at variance, at odds, divergent, discrepant, different, contradictory, contrary, in conflict, conflicting, opposite, opposed, opposing.
2 *discordant sounds:* **inharmonious,** tuneless, off-key, dissonant, harsh, jarring, grating, strident, shrill, screeching, cacophonous; sharp, flat.
OPPOSITES: harmonious.

discount noun *students get a 10 per cent discount:* **reduction,** deduction, markdown, price cut, cut, concession, rebate.
OPPOSITES: supplement.
▷**verb**
1 *the recommended price is discounted in many stores:* **reduce,** mark down, cut, lower.
2 *I'd heard rumours, but discounted them:* **disregard,** pay no attention to, take no notice of, take no account of, not take seriously, dismiss, ignore, overlook, disbelieve, reject; informal take with a pinch of salt, pooh-pooh.
OPPOSITES: increase, believe.

discourage verb
1 *she was discouraged by his hostile tone:* **dishearten,** dispirit, demoralize, cast down, depress, disappoint, dash someone's hopes; put off, unnerve, crush.
2 *we want to discourage children from smoking:* **dissuade,** deter, disincline, put off, talk out of; advise against, urge against.
3 *he sought to discourage further conversation:* **prevent,** stop, put a stop to, avert, fend off, stave off, ward off; inhibit, hinder, check, curb, throw/pour cold water on; informal put a damper on.
OPPOSITES: encourage.

discouraged adjective *Doug must be feeling pretty discouraged:* **disheartened,** dispirited, demoralized, deflated, disappointed, let down, disconsolate, despondent, dejected, cast down, downcast, depressed, crestfallen, dismayed, gloomy, glum, pessimistic, unenthusiastic; put off, daunted, intimidated, cowed, crushed; informal fed up.

discouraging adjective **depressing,** demoralizing, disheartening, dispiriting, disappointing, gloomy, off-putting; unfavourable, unpromising, inauspicious.
OPPOSITES: encouraging.

discourse noun
1 *humour is surpassing political discourse as the vehicle for challenging the status quo:* **discussion,** dialogue, conversation, talk, consultation, deliberation, debate, disputation, exchange.
2 *a discourse on critical theory:* **essay,** treatise, dissertation, paper, study, critique, monograph, tract; lecture, address, speech, oration; sermon, homily; formal disquisition.
▷**verb** *he discoursed at length on his favourite*

topic: hold forth, expatiate, pontificate; talk, give a talk, give a speech, lecture, sermonize, preach.

discourteous adjective *it would be discourteous to ignore her:* rude, impolite, ill-mannered, bad-mannered, disrespectful, uncivil, unmannerly, unchivalrous, ungentlemanly, unladylike, ill-bred, churlish, boorish, crass, ungracious, graceless, uncouth; insolent, impudent, cheeky, presumptuous; curt, brusque, blunt, offhand, unceremonious, short, sharp; informal ignorant.
OPPOSITES: courteous.

discourtesy noun rudeness, impoliteness, ill manners, bad manners, incivility, disrespect, lack of respect, churlishness, boorishness, ill breeding; insolence, impudence, impertinence; curtness, brusqueness, abruptness.

discover verb
1 *firemen discovered a body in the debris:* find, locate, come across/upon, stumble on, chance on, light on, bring to light, uncover, unearth, turn up, track down.
2 *eventually, I discovered the truth:* find out, learn, realize, recognize, see, ascertain, work out, fathom out, dig up/out, ferret out, root out; informal figure out, tumble to.
3 *scientists discovered a new way of dating fossil crustaceans:* hit on, come up with, invent, originate, devise, design, contrive; pioneer, develop.

discoverer noun finder; originator, inventor, creator, deviser, designer; pioneer.

discovery noun
1 *the discovery of the body:* finding, location, uncovering, unearthing.
2 *the discovery that she was pregnant:* realization, recognition; revelation, disclosure.
3 *the discovery of new drugs:* invention, origination, creation, devising; pioneering.
4 *he failed to take out a patent on his discoveries:* find, finding; invention, creation, breakthrough, innovation; contraption, gadget; informal brainchild.

discredit verb
1 *an attempt to discredit him and his company:* bring into disrepute, disgrace, dishonour, damage the reputation of, blacken the name of, put/show in a bad light, reflect badly on, compromise, stigmatize, smear, tarnish, taint.
2 *that theory has been discredited:* disprove, prove wrong, invalidate, explode, refute; informal debunk.
OPPOSITES: honour, confirm.
▷ noun
1 *they committed crimes which brought discredit on the administration:* dishonour, disgrace, disrepute, ignominy, infamy, notoriety; censure, blame, reproach;

shame, humiliation; stigma; formal opprobrium.
2 *the ships were a discredit to the country:* disgrace, source of shame, reproach, blot on the escutcheon.
OPPOSITES: honour, glory.

discreditable adjective *his discreditable conduct:* dishonourable, reprehensible, shameful, deplorable, disgraceful, disreputable, blameworthy, ignoble, shabby, regrettable, unacceptable, unworthy.
OPPOSITES: creditable.

discreet adjective
1 *we made discreet enquiries in the area | you can rely on him to be discreet:* careful, circumspect, cautious, prudent, wary, guarded, tactful, diplomatic, judicious; low-profile, unobtrusive, inconspicuous; strategic, politic, delicate, sensitive.
2 *discreet lighting shows off the fine furnishings:* unobtrusive, inconspicuous, subtle, low-key, understated, subdued, muted, soft, restrained.
OPPOSITES: open, garish.

USAGE

Do not confuse **discreet** and **discrete**. **Discreet** means 'careful to keep something secret or to avoid attention', while **discrete** means 'separate' (*products are organized in discrete batches*).

discrepancy noun *the discrepancy between the two sets of figures:* difference, disparity, variance, variation, deviation, divergence, disagreement, inconsistency, dissimilarity, mismatch, incompatibility, conflict.
OPPOSITES: correspondence.

discrete adjective *speech sounds are produced as a continuous signal rather than discrete units:* separate, distinct, individual, detached, unattached, disconnected, discontinuous, disjunct, disjoined.
OPPOSITES: connected.

discretion noun
1 *you can rely on his discretion:* circumspection, carefulness, caution, wariness, guardedness; tact, tactfulness, diplomacy, delicacy, sensitivity, prudence.
2 *honorary fellowships are awarded at the discretion of the council:* choice, option, preference, disposition, volition; pleasure, liking, wish, will, inclination, desire.

discretionary adjective *a 12.5 per cent discretionary service charge:* optional, voluntary, elective.
OPPOSITES: compulsory.

discriminate verb
1 *he cannot discriminate between fact and opinion:* differentiate, distinguish, draw a distinction, tell the difference, tell apart, separate in your mind.

2 *existing employment policies discriminate against women:* be biased, be prejudiced; treat differently, treat unfairly, disadvantage; victimize.

discriminating adjective *he was a discriminating collector and patron of the arts:* discerning, selective, tasteful, refined, sensitive, cultivated, cultured, artistic, aesthetic, perceptive, astute, shrewd, judicious, perspicacious, insightful, keen.
OPPOSITES: undiscriminating.

discrimination noun
1 *racial discrimination:* prejudice, bias, bigotry, intolerance, narrow-mindedness, unfairness, inequity, favouritism, one-sidedness, partisanship.
2 *a man with no discrimination:* discernment, judgement, perception, perceptiveness, perspicacity, acumen, astuteness, shrewdness, judiciousness, insight; selectivity, taste, good taste, refinement, sensitivity, cultivation, culture.
OPPOSITES: impartiality.

discriminatory adjective *discriminatory employment practices:* prejudicial, biased, prejudiced, preferential, unfair, unjust, invidious, inequitable, weighted, one-sided, partisan.
OPPOSITES: impartial.

discursive adjective
1 *dull, discursive prose:* rambling, digressive, meandering, wandering, diffuse, long, lengthy, wordy, verbose, long-winded, prolix; circuitous, roundabout, circumlocutory; Brit. informal waffly.
2 *an elegant discursive style:* fluent, flowing, fluid, eloquent, expansive.
OPPOSITES: concise, terse.

discuss verb
1 *I discussed the matter with my wife:* talk over, talk about, talk through, converse about, debate, confer about, chew over, consider, thrash out.
2 *chapter three discusses this topic in detail:* examine, explore, study, analyse, go into, deal with, treat, consider, concern itself with, tackle.

discussion noun
1 *after a long discussion with her husband, she came to a decision:* conversation, talk, debate, exchange of views, dialogue, conference, consultation, deliberation, discourse, negotiations; chat, tête-à-tête, heart-to-heart; informal confab.
2 *the book's candid discussion of sexual matters:* examination, exploration, analysis, study; treatment, consideration.

disdain noun *she looked at him with disdain:* contempt, scorn, derision, disrespect; disparagement, condescension, superciliousness, hauteur, haughtiness, arrogance, snobbishness, indifference,

dismissiveness; distaste, dislike, disgust.
OPPOSITES: respect.
▷**verb** *she disdained such vulgar exhibitionism:* scorn, deride, pour scorn on, regard with contempt, sneer at, sniff at, look down your nose at, look down on; despise; informal turn your nose up at, pooh-pooh.

disdainful adjective *she gave him a disdainful look:* contemptuous, scornful, derisive, sneering, withering, slighting, disparaging, disrespectful, condescending, patronizing, supercilious, haughty, superior, arrogant, proud, snobbish, aloof, dismissive; informal high and mighty.
OPPOSITES: respectful.

disease noun illness, sickness, ill health; infection, virus, ailment, problem, trouble, disorder, complaint, affliction, condition, indisposition, upset, infirmity, plague, blight; literary malady; informal bug; old use pestilence.

> WORD LINKS
> **pathological** relating to disease
> **epidemiology** the study of the spread and control of diseases
> **pathology** the branch of medicine concerned with the causes and effects of diseases

diseased adjective *the dogs were painfully thin and many were diseased:* sick, ill, unhealthy, unwell, ailing, sickly, unsound; infected, septic, contaminated, blighted, rotten, bad.
OPPOSITES: healthy.

disembark verb *the passengers began to disembark:* get off, step off, leave, go ashore, land; formal alight.

disenchanted adjective *disenchanted with politics, he retired from the foreign service:* disillusioned, disappointed, let down, dissatisfied, discontented; cynical, soured, jaundiced; informal fed up.
OPPOSITES: happy.

disenchantment noun disillusionment, disappointment, dissatisfaction, discontent, rude awakening; cynicism.
OPPOSITES: happiness.

disengage verb
1 *I disengaged my hand from his:* remove, separate, release, extricate, disentangle, detach, free, loosen, loose, unclasp.
2 *American forces disengaged from the country:* withdraw, leave, pull out of, quit, retreat from.
OPPOSITES: engage, enter.

disentangle verb
1 *Allen was disentangling a coil of rope:* untangle, unravel, untwist, unwind, undo, untie, straighten out, smooth out; comb, card.
2 *he disentangled his fingers from her hair:* extricate, extract, free, remove, disengage,

d

untwine, release, loosen, detach, unfasten, unclasp, disconnect.
OPPOSITES: entangle.

disfavour noun *illegitimate children were not necessarily viewed with disfavour:* disapproval; dislike, displeasure, distaste, dissatisfaction, low opinion; formal disapprobation.
OPPOSITES: favour.

disfigure verb *litter disfigures the countryside:* mar, spoil, deface, scar, blemish, uglify; damage, injure, impair, blight, mutilate, deform, maim, ruin; vandalize.
OPPOSITES: adorn.

disfigurement noun
1 *the disfigurement of Victorian buildings:* defacement, spoiling, uglification, mutilation, damage, vandalizing, ruin.
2 *a permanent facial disfigurement:* blemish, flaw, defect, imperfection, discoloration, blotch; scar, pockmark; deformity, malformation, abnormality, injury, wound.

disgorge verb *the combine harvester disgorged a stream of grain:* pour out, discharge, eject, throw out, emit, expel, spit out, spew out, belch out, spout; vomit, regurgitate.

disgrace noun
1 *he brought disgrace on the family:* dishonour, shame, discredit, ignominy, degradation, disrepute, infamy, scandal, stigma, condemnation, vilification, contempt, disrespect; humiliation, embarrassment, loss of face; formal opprobrium.
2 *the unemployment figures are a disgrace:* outrage, scandal; discredit, reproach, affront, insult; stain, blemish, blot, blot on the escutcheon, black mark; informal crime, sin.
OPPOSITES: honour, pride.
▷verb
1 *you have disgraced the family name:* bring shame on, shame, dishonour, discredit, bring into disrepute, degrade, debase, defame, stigmatize, taint, tarnish, stain, blacken, drag through the mud/mire; literary besmirch, sully.
2 *he was publicly disgraced:* discredit, dishonour, stigmatize; humiliate, cause to lose face, chasten, humble.
OPPOSITES: honour.
□ in disgrace
out of favour, unpopular, in bad odour, under a cloud, disgraced; informal in someone's bad/black books, in the doghouse.

disgraceful adjective *a disgraceful waste of money:* shameful, shocking, scandalous, deplorable, reprehensible, despicable, contemptible, discreditable, base, mean, low, blameworthy, unworthy, ignoble, shabby, inglorious, outrageous, atrocious, disgusting, shameless, heinous, iniquitous, unspeakable.
OPPOSITES: admirable.

disgruntled adjective *judges receive many letters from disgruntled members of the public:* dissatisfied, discontented, aggrieved, resentful, displeased, unhappy, disaffected; angry, irate, annoyed, cross, exasperated, indignant; informal fed up.
OPPOSITES: content.

disguise verb *his controlled voice disguised his true feelings:* hide, conceal, cover up, mask, camouflage, screen, shroud, veil, cloak; paper over, gloss over; dissemble, put up a smokescreen.
OPPOSITES: reveal.
□ disguise yourself as
dress up as, pretend to be, pass yourself off as, impersonate, pose as.

disguised adjective *a disguised police officer:* in disguise, incognito, undercover, covert, camouflaged, in plain clothes.

disgust noun *a look of disgust:* revulsion, repugnance, aversion, distaste, nausea, abhorrence, loathing, detestation, odium, horror; contempt, outrage.
OPPOSITES: delight.
▷verb
1 *the smell disgusted me:* revolt, repel, repulse, sicken, nauseate, turn someone's stomach, make someone's gorge rise; informal turn off; N. Amer. informal gross out.
2 *Toby's behaviour disgusted her:* outrage, shock, horrify, appal, scandalize, offend.
OPPOSITES: please.

disgusting adjective
1 *the food was disgusting:* revolting, repellent, repulsive, sickening, nauseating, stomach-turning, off-putting, unpalatable, distasteful, foul, nasty; informal gross.
2 *I find racism disgusting:* abhorrent, loathsome, offensive, appalling, outrageous, objectionable, shocking, horrifying, scandalous, monstrous, unspeakable, shameful, vile, odious, obnoxious, detestable, hateful, sickening, contemptible, despicable, deplorable, abominable, beyond the pale.
OPPOSITES: delicious, appealing.

dish noun
1 *a china dish:* bowl, plate, platter, salver; container, receptacle.
2 *vegetarian dishes:* recipe, meal, course; (**dishes**) food, fare, cuisine, cooking.
□ dish something out
the waitress was dishing out free glasses of wine: distribute, dispense, hand out/round, give out, pass out/round, issue; deal out, dole out, share out, allocate, allot, apportion.
□ dish something up
Mrs Mackay dished up the porridge: serve, spoon out, ladle out, scoop out.

dishearten verb discourage, dispirit, demoralize, cast down, depress, disappoint, dismay, dash someone's hopes; put off, deter, unnerve, daunt, intimidate, cow.
OPPOSITES: encourage.

disheartened adjective *the weather got worse and he felt cold and disheartened:* discouraged, dispirited, demoralized, deflated, disappointed, disconsolate, despondent, dejected, cast down, downcast, depressed, crestfallen, dismayed, low-spirited, gloomy, glum, pessimistic; daunted, intimidated, cowed; informal fed up.

dishevelled adjective *a man with long dishevelled hair:* untidy, unkempt, scruffy, messy, in a mess, disordered, rumpled, bedraggled; uncombed, tousled, tangled, knotted, shaggy, straggly, windswept, wild.
OPPOSITES: tidy.

dishonest adjective *he is accused of dishonest business practices:* fraudulent, corrupt, cheating, double-dealing; underhand, crafty, cunning, devious, treacherous, unfair, unjust, dirty, unethical, immoral, dishonourable, untrustworthy, unscrupulous, unprincipled, amoral; criminal, illegal, unlawful; false, untruthful, deceitful, deceiving, lying, mendacious; informal crooked, shady; Brit. informal bent, dodgy.
OPPOSITES: honest.

dishonesty noun *he lost money as a result of his solicitor's dishonesty:* fraud, fraudulence, sharp practice, corruption, cheating, chicanery, double-dealing, deceit, deception, duplicity, lying, falseness, untruthfulness; cunning, trickery, artifice, underhandedness, subterfuge, skulduggery, treachery, untrustworthiness, unscrupulousness, criminality, misconduct; informal crookedness.
OPPOSITES: honesty.

dishonour noun *the incident brought dishonour upon the police profession:* disgrace, shame, discredit, humiliation, degradation, ignominy, scandal, infamy, disrepute, ill repute, loss of face, disfavour, ill favour, debasement; stigma; formal opprobrium.
▷ verb *his family name has been dishonoured:* disgrace, shame, discredit, bring into disrepute, humiliate, degrade, debase, lower, cheapen, drag down, drag through the mud, blacken the name of, give a bad name to; stain, taint, smear, stigmatize; literary besmirch, sully.

dishonourable adjective *he is accused of dishonourable conduct:* shameful, disgraceful, disreputable, discreditable, degrading, ignominious, ignoble, blameworthy, reprehensible, contemptible, despicable, shabby, shoddy, sordid, sorry, base, low, improper, unseemly, unworthy; unprincipled, unscrupulous, corrupt, untrustworthy, treacherous, traitorous; formal opprobrious.
OPPOSITES: honourable.

disillusion verb disabuse, enlighten, set straight, open someone's eyes; disenchant, shatter someone's illusions, disappoint, make sadder and wiser.
OPPOSITES: deceive.

disillusioned adjective *his experience at the club left him disillusioned:* disenchanted, disabused, disappointed, let down, discouraged; cynical, sour, negative, world-weary.

disincentive noun *high interest rates are a disincentive to investment:* deterrent, discouragement, damper, brake, curb, check, restraint, inhibitor; obstacle, impediment, hindrance, obstruction, block, barrier.
OPPOSITES: incentive.

disinclination noun *they show a disinclination to face up to these issues:* reluctance, unwillingness, lack of enthusiasm, indisposition, hesitancy; aversion, dislike, distaste; objection, resistance, opposition.
OPPOSITES: enthusiasm.

disinclined adjective reluctant, unwilling, unenthusiastic, unprepared, indisposed, ill-disposed, not in the mood, hesitant; loath, averse, antipathetic, resistant, opposed.
OPPOSITES: willing, inclined.

disinfect verb *use bleach to disinfect your kitchen surfaces:* sterilize, sanitize, clean, cleanse, purify, decontaminate; fumigate.
OPPOSITES: contaminate.

disinfectant noun antiseptic, bactericide, germicide, sterilizer, cleanser, decontaminant; fumigant.

disingenuous adjective *this journalist was being somewhat disingenuous as well as cynical:* insincere, dishonest, untruthful, false, deceitful, duplicitous, lying, mendacious; hypocritical.

disinherit verb *the Duke is seeking to disinherit his eldest son:* cut someone out of your will, cut off, dispossess; disown, repudiate, reject, cast off/aside, wash your hands of, have nothing more to do with, turn your back on.

disintegrate verb *the plane caught fire and disintegrated in the air:* break up, break apart, fall apart, fall to pieces, fragment, fracture, shatter, splinter; explode, blow up, blow apart, fly apart; crumble, deteriorate, decay, decompose, rot, moulder, dissolve, collapse; literary perish.

disinter verb *his corpse was disinterred and reburied in another grave:* exhume, unearth, dig up.
OPPOSITES: inter.

d

disinterest noun

1 *scholarly disinterest:* impartiality, neutrality, objectivity, detachment, lack of bias, lack of prejudice; open-mindedness, fairness, fair-mindedness, equity, balance, even-handedness.

2 *he looked at us with complete disinterest:* indifference, lack of interest, unconcern, impassivity; boredom, apathy.

OPPOSITES: bias.

disinterested adjective

1 *tax inspectors should give disinterested advice:* unbiased, unprejudiced, impartial, neutral, non-partisan, detached, uninvolved, objective, dispassionate, impersonal, clinical; open-minded, fair, just, equitable, balanced, even-handed, without fear or favour.

2 *he looked at her with disinterested eyes:* uninterested, indifferent, unconcerned, unmoved, unresponsive, impassive, passive, detached, incurious, unenthusiastic, lukewarm, bored, apathetic.

OPPOSITES: biased, interested.

USAGE

Strictly speaking, **disinterested** should only be used to mean 'impartial' (*the judgements of disinterested outsiders are likely to be more useful*) and should not be used to mean 'not interested' (in other words, the same as **uninterested**). The second meaning is very common, but is better avoided in formal writing as it is not accepted by everyone.

disjointed adjective *a disjointed series of impressions in her mind:* unconnected, disconnected, disunited, discontinuous, fragmented, disorganized, disordered, muddled, mixed up, jumbled, garbled, incoherent, confused; rambling, wandering.

OPPOSITES: coherent.

disk noun *download the files to disk:* diskette, floppy disk, floppy; hard disk, hard drive; CD, CD-ROM, DVD.

dislike verb *a man she had always disliked:* find distasteful, be averse to, have an aversion to, have no liking/taste for, disapprove of, object to, take exception to; hate, detest, loathe, abhor, despise, be unable to bear/stand, shrink from, shudder at, find repellent.

OPPOSITES: like.

▷ noun *she viewed the other woman with dislike:* distaste, aversion, disfavour, disapproval, enmity, animosity, hostility, antipathy, antagonism; hate, hatred, detestation, loathing, disgust, repugnance, abhorrence, disdain, contempt; formal disapprobation.

OPPOSITES: liking.

dislocate verb *trade was dislocated by the strike:* disrupt, disturb, throw into disarray, throw into confusion, play havoc with, interfere with, disorganize, upset.

dislodge verb

1 *replace any stones you dislodge:* displace, knock out of place/position, move, shift; knock over, upset.

2 *economic sanctions failed to dislodge the dictator:* remove, force out, drive out, oust, eject, get rid of, evict, unseat, depose, topple, drum out; informal kick out.

OPPOSITES: install.

disloyal adjective *many of her colleagues judged her disloyal:* faithless, unfaithful, untrustworthy, unreliable, undependable, fickle; treacherous, traitorous, subversive, seditious, unpatriotic, two-faced, double-dealing, double-crossing, deceitful; dissident, renegade; adulterous; literary false, false-hearted; informal back-stabbing.

OPPOSITES: loyal.

disloyalty noun faithlessness, unfaithfulness, fickleness, unreliability, untrustworthiness, betrayal; duplicity, double-dealing, treachery, treason, subversion, sedition, dissidence; adultery, infidelity; informal back-stabbing.

OPPOSITES: loyalty.

dismal adjective

1 *he had a dismal look in his eyes:* gloomy, glum, melancholy, morose, doleful, woebegone, forlorn, dejected, depressed, dispirited, downcast, despondent, disconsolate, miserable, sad, unhappy, sorrowful, desolate, wretched; informal blue, fed up.

2 *they were living in a dismal tower block:* dingy, dim, dark, gloomy, dreary, drab, dull, bleak, cheerless, depressing, uninviting, unwelcoming.

3 (informal) *a dismal performance.* See POOR sense 2.

OPPOSITES: cheerful, bright.

dismantle verb *he began to dismantle the revolver:* take apart, take to pieces/bits, pull apart, pull to pieces, disassemble, break up, strip; pull down, demolish.

OPPOSITES: assemble, build.

dismay verb *he was dismayed by the change in his friend:* appal, horrify, shock, shake; disconcert, take aback, alarm, unnerve, unsettle, throw off balance, discompose; disturb, upset, distress; informal rattle, faze.

OPPOSITES: encourage, please.

▷ noun *they greeted his decision with dismay:* alarm, shock, surprise, consternation, concern, distress, perturbation, disquiet, discomposure.

OPPOSITES: pleasure, relief.

dismember verb *a stag carcass was in the process of being dismembered:* disjoint, joint; pull apart, cut up, chop up, butcher.

dismiss verb

1 *the president dismissed five ministers:* give someone their notice, get rid of, discharge; lay off, make redundant; informal sack, fire.

2 *the servants were dismissed:* send away, let go, stand down, discharge, disband.
3 *he dismissed all morbid thoughts:* banish, set aside, disregard, brush off, shrug off, put out of your mind; reject, deny.
OPPOSITES: engage.

dismissal noun
1 *the threat of dismissal:* notice, discharge; redundancy, laying off; informal the sack.
2 *a condescending dismissal of ancient systems of thought:* rejection, repudiation, non-acceptance.
OPPOSITES: recruitment, acceptance.

dismissive adjective *she often talked of him in dismissive terms:* contemptuous, disdainful, scornful, sneering, snide, disparaging, negative.
OPPOSITES: admiring.

disobedient adjective *he was stern with disobedient employees:* insubordinate, rebellious, defiant, mutinous, recalcitrant, uncooperative, wilful, intractable, obstreperous, wayward, unruly, badly behaved, naughty, delinquent, disruptive, troublesome; Brit. informal bolshie.
OPPOSITES: obedient.

disobey verb *the king severely chastised those who disobeyed his orders:* defy, go against, flout, contravene, infringe, transgress, violate; disregard, ignore, pay no heed to.
OPPOSITES: obey.

disobliging adjective *we have such disobliging neighbours:* unhelpful, uncooperative, unaccommodating, unamenable, unreasonable, awkward, difficult.
OPPOSITES: obliging.

disorder noun
1 *he hates disorder:* untidiness, mess, disarray, chaos, confusion; clutter, jumble, a muddle; informal a shambles.
2 *incidents of public disorder:* unrest, disturbance, disruption, upheaval, turmoil, mayhem, pandemonium; violence, fighting, rioting, lawlessness, anarchy; breach of the peace, fracas.
3 *a blood disorder:* disease, infection, complaint, condition, affliction, sickness, illness, ailment, infirmity, irregularity; literary malady.
OPPOSITES: order.

disordered adjective
1 *her grey hair was disordered:* untidy, unkempt, messy, in a mess; disorganized, chaotic, confused, jumbled, muddled.
2 *a disordered digestive system:* dysfunctional, disturbed, unsettled, unbalanced, upset.
OPPOSITES: tidy, ordered.

disorderly adjective
1 *a disorderly desk:* untidy, disorganized, messy, cluttered; in disarray, in a mess, in a jumble, in a muddle; informal higgledy-

piggledy; Brit. informal shambolic.
2 *disorderly behaviour:* unruly, boisterous, rough, rowdy, wild, riotous; disruptive, troublesome, undisciplined, lawless, unmanageable, uncontrollable, out of hand, out of control.
OPPOSITES: tidy, orderly.

disorganized adjective
1 *a disorganized tool box:* disorderly, disordered, jumbled, muddled, untidy, messy, chaotic, topsy-turvy, haphazard; in disorder, in disarray, in a mess, in a muddle; informal higgledy-piggledy, in a shambles; Brit. informal shambolic.
2 *the main problem with being financially disorganized is that bills don't get paid:* unmethodical, unsystematic, undisciplined, badly organized, inefficient; haphazard, careless, slapdash.
OPPOSITES: organized.

disorientated, **disoriented** adjective *when he emerged into the street he was completely disorientated:* confused, bewildered, at sea; lost, adrift, off course, having lost your bearings; informal not knowing whether you are coming or going.

disown verb *he has been disowned by his parents:* reject, cast off/aside, abandon, renounce, deny; turn your back on, wash your hands of, have nothing more to do with; old use repudiate.

disparage verb *it has become fashionable to disparage Lawrence and his achievements:* belittle, denigrate, deprecate, play down, trivialize, make light of, undervalue, underrate; ridicule, deride, mock, scorn, scoff at, sneer at; run down, defame, discredit, speak badly of, cast aspersions on, impugn, vilify, traduce, criticize; informal knock, pooh-pooh; Brit. informal rubbish.
OPPOSITES: praise.

disparaging adjective *disparaging comments just antagonize him:* derogatory, deprecatory, belittling; critical, scathing, negative, unfavourable, uncomplimentary, uncharitable; contemptuous, scornful, snide, disdainful; informal bitchy.
OPPOSITES: complimentary.

disparate adjective *the document is made up from several disparate chunks:* contrasting, different, differing, dissimilar, unalike, poles apart; varying, various, diverse, diversified, heterogeneous, distinct, separate, divergent.
OPPOSITES: similar, homogeneous.

disparity noun *there was a disparity between the two sets of figures:* discrepancy, inconsistency, imbalance; variance, variation, divergence, gap, gulf; difference, dissimilarity, contrast.
OPPOSITES: agreement.

dispassionate adjective
1 *he dealt with life's disasters in a calm, dispassionate way:* unemotional, impassive, cool, calm, {cool, calm, and collected}, unruffled, unperturbed, composed, self-possessed, self-controlled, unexcitable; informal laid-back.
2 *a dispassionate analysis:* objective, detached, neutral, disinterested, impartial, non-partisan, unbiased, unprejudiced; scientific, analytical, rational.
OPPOSITES: emotional, biased.

dispatch verb
1 *all the messages were dispatched:* send, post, mail, forward, transmit, deliver, ship.
2 *the business was dispatched in the morning:* deal with, finish, conclude, settle, discharge, perform; expedite, push through.
3 *the good guy dispatched a host of villains:* kill, put to death, take/end the life of; slaughter, butcher, massacre, wipe out, exterminate, eliminate; murder, assassinate, execute; informal bump off; N. Amer. informal waste.
▷**noun**
1 *goods ready for dispatch:* sending, posting, mailing, forwarding, delivery, shipping.
2 *he carries out his duties with efficiency and dispatch:* promptness, speed, alacrity, swiftness, rapidity, briskness, haste.
3 *she read out the latest dispatch from the front:* communication, communiqué, bulletin, report, statement, letter, message, memo; news, intelligence.
4 *the capture and dispatch of the victims:* killing, slaughter, massacre, extermination, elimination; murder, assassination, execution.

dispel verb *the sunshine did nothing to dispel her feelings of dejection:* banish, eliminate, drive away/off, get rid of; relieve, allay, ease, quell.

dispensable adjective *he regards all of his lieutenants as highly dispensable:* expendable, disposable, replaceable, inessential, non-essential; unnecessary, redundant, superfluous, surplus to requirements.
OPPOSITES: indispensable.

dispensation noun
1 *the dispensation of justice:* administration, administering, delivery, discharge, dealing out, meting out.
2 *dispensation from National Insurance contributions:* exemption, immunity, exception, exoneration, reprieve, remission.

dispense verb
1 *staff dispensed cooling drinks and snacks to the passengers:* distribute, pass round, hand out, dole out, dish out, share out; allocate, supply, allot, apportion.
2 *the soldiers dispensed summary justice:* administer, deliver, issue, discharge, deal out, mete out.
3 *this product cannot be dispensed without a prescription:* prepare, make up; supply, issue, provide, sell.
□ **dispense with**
1 *let's dispense with the formalities:* forgo, omit, drop, leave out, do without.
2 *he dispensed with his crutches:* get rid of, throw away/out, dispose of, discard; manage without, cope without; informal ditch.

disperse verb
1 *the crowd began to disperse* | *police dispersed the demonstrators:* break up, split up, disband, scatter, leave, go their separate ways; drive away/off, chase away.
2 *the fog finally dispersed:* dissipate, dissolve, melt away, fade away, clear, lift.
3 *the seeds get dispersed by birds:* scatter, distribute, spread, broadcast, disseminate.
OPPOSITES: assemble, gather.

dispirited adjective *she was tired and dispirited after her long journey:* disheartened, discouraged, demoralized, downcast, low, dejected, downhearted, depressed, disconsolate; informal fed up.

dispiriting adjective disheartening, depressing, discouraging, daunting, demoralizing.

displace verb
1 *several roof tiles had been displaced by the gales:* dislodge, dislocate, move, shift, reposition.
2 *the minister was displaced:* depose, dislodge, unseat, remove from office, dismiss, eject, oust, expel, force out, drive out; overthrow, topple, bring down.
3 *English displaced the local language:* replace, take the place of, supplant, supersede.

display noun
1 *a display of dolls and puppets* | *a motorcycle display:* exhibition, exposition, array, arrangement, presentation, demonstration; spectacle, show, parade, pageant.
2 *they vied to outdo each other in display:* ostentation, showiness, extravagance, flamboyance, lavishness, splendour.
3 *his display of concern:* show, expression, manifestation.
▷**verb**
1 *the Crown jewels are displayed in London:* exhibit, show, put on show/view; arrange, array, present, lay out, set out.
2 *he displayed his fighting skills:* show off, parade, flaunt, reveal; publicize, make known, call/draw attention to.
3 *she displayed a vein of sharp humour:* manifest, show evidence of, reveal; demonstrate, show.
OPPOSITES: conceal.

displease verb *he was plainly displeased by Jenny's decision:* annoy, irritate, anger,

irk, vex, pique, gall; put out, upset; informal aggravate, rile, nettle.
OPPOSITES: please.

displeasure noun annoyance, irritation, crossness, anger, vexation, pique, rancour; dissatisfaction, discontent, disgruntlement, disapproval.
OPPOSITES: pleasure.

disposable adjective *a disposable razor:* throwaway, expendable, one-use; biodegradable.

disposal noun *rubbish ready for disposal:* throwing away, discarding, jettisoning, scrapping; informal dumping, ditching, chucking out/away.

dispose verb
1 *he disposed his attendants in a circle:* arrange, place, put, position, array, set up, form; marshal, gather, group.
2 *the experience disposed him to be kind:* incline, encourage, persuade, predispose, make willing, prompt, lead, motivate; sway, influence.
☐ dispose of
1 *the waste was disposed of:* throw away/out, get rid of, discard, jettison, scrap; informal dump, ditch.
2 *he had disposed of all his assets:* part with, give away, hand over, deliver up, transfer; sell, auction.

disposed adjective
1 *they are philanthropically disposed:* inclined, predisposed, minded.
2 *we are not disposed to argue:* willing, inclined, prepared, ready, minded, in the mood.
3 *he was disposed to be cruel:* liable, apt, inclined, likely, predisposed, prone, tending; capable of.

disposition noun
1 *the book is not recommended to readers of a nervous disposition:* temperament, nature, character, constitution, make-up, mentality.
2 *his disposition to clemency:* inclination, tendency, proneness, propensity, proclivity.
3 *the disposition of the armed forces:* arrangement, positioning, placement, configuration; set-up, line-up, layout, array; marshalling, mustering, grouping.

dispossess verb *the peasants have been dispossessed of their land:* deprive, strip, rob, cheat out of, divest.

disproportionate adjective *the sentences are disproportionate to the offences committed:* out of proportion to, not appropriate to, not commensurate with, relatively too large/small for; inordinate, unreasonable, excessive, undue.

disprove verb *new forensic evidence disproved the allegations:* refute, prove false, rebut, falsify, debunk, negate,

invalidate, contradict, confound, discredit; formal controvert.
OPPOSITES: prove.

disputable adjective *some of these figures are disputable:* debatable, open to debate/question, arguable, contestable, moot, questionable, doubtful; formal controvertible.
OPPOSITES: indisputable.

disputation noun *religious disputation:* debate, discussion, dispute, argument, arguing, altercation, dissension, disagreement, controversy.

dispute noun
1 *the extent of the king's powers was the subject of constant dispute:* debate, discussion, disputation, argument, controversy, disagreement, quarrelling, dissension, conflict, friction, strife, discord.
2 *they have settled their dispute:* quarrel, argument, altercation, squabble, falling-out, disagreement, difference of opinion, clash, wrangle; Brit. row.
OPPOSITES: agreement.
▷ verb
1 *he disputed with local writers:* debate, exchange views; quarrel, argue, disagree, clash, fall out, wrangle, bicker, squabble.
2 *they disputed his proposals:* challenge, contest, question, call into question, contradict, argue with, disagree with, take issue with; formal controvert.
OPPOSITES: agree, accept.

disqualified adjective *he admitted driving while disqualified:* banned, barred, debarred; ineligible.
OPPOSITES: allowed.

disquiet noun *there has been grave disquiet about the state of the prisons:* unease, worry, anxiety, concern; consternation, upset, malaise, angst; agitation, restlessness, fretfulness.
OPPOSITES: calm.
▷ verb *I was disquieted by the news:* worry, make uneasy, make anxious; perturb, agitate, upset, disturb, unnerve, unsettle, discompose, disconcert; trouble, concern.
OPPOSITES: reassure.

disregard verb *Annie disregarded the remark:* ignore, take no notice of, pay no attention/heed to; overlook, turn a blind eye to, turn a deaf ear to, shut your eyes to, gloss over.
OPPOSITES: heed.
▷ noun *he drove with blithe disregard for the rules of the road:* indifference, non-observance, inattention, heedlessness, neglect.
OPPOSITES: attention.

disrepair noun *a building in a state of disrepair:* dilapidation, decrepitude, collapse, ruin; abandonment, neglect, disuse.

disreputable adjective

1 *disreputable mortgage companies may target the elderly because they have built up so much equity:* dishonest, dishonourable, untrustworthy, unscrupulous, unprincipled, discreditable, unsavoury; dubious, questionable, suspect; informal shady; Brit. informal dodgy.

2 *his disreputable appearance:* scruffy, shabby, seedy, sleazy, unkempt; louche, rakish, raffish.

OPPOSITES: reputable, respectable.

disrepute noun *Beth had shamed herself and brought the family name into disrepute:* disgrace, shame, dishonour, discredit, ill repute, low esteem, ignominy, humiliation, infamy, notoriety; formal opprobrium.

OPPOSITES: honour.

disrespect noun

1 *there is a growing disrespect for authority:* contempt, scorn, disregard, disdain.

2 *he meant no disrespect to anybody:* discourtesy, rudeness, impoliteness, incivility, ill/bad manners; insolence, impudence, impertinence.

OPPOSITES: respect.

disrespectful adjective discourteous, rude, impolite, uncivil, ill-mannered, bad-mannered; insolent, impudent, impertinent, cheeky, flippant, insubordinate.

OPPOSITES: respectful.

disrupt verb *the strike disrupted public transport:* throw into confusion/disorder/disarray/chaos, play havoc with; disturb, interfere with, upset, unsettle; obstruct, impede, hold up, delay, interrupt, suspend.

disruptive adjective *a very disruptive child:* troublesome, unruly, badly behaved, rowdy, disorderly, undisciplined, wild; unmanageable, uncontrollable, uncooperative, out of control/hand.

OPPOSITES: well behaved.

dissatisfaction noun *polls revealed widespread dissatisfaction with the new law:* discontent, disaffection, disquiet, unhappiness, disgruntlement, vexation, annoyance, irritation, anger; disapproval, disfavour, displeasure; formal disapprobation.

OPPOSITES: satisfaction.

dissatisfied adjective *a dissatisfied customer:* discontented, disappointed, disaffected, unhappy, displeased; disgruntled, aggrieved.

OPPOSITES: satisfied.

dissect verb *the text of the gospels was dissected:* analyse, examine, study, scrutinize, pore over, investigate, evaluate, assess.

dissection noun *a thorough dissection of their policies:* analysis, examination, study, scrutiny, investigation; evaluation, assessment.

dissemble verb *she is an honest, sincere person who has no need to dissemble:* pretend, feign, act, masquerade, sham, fake, bluff, posture, dissimulate, hide your feelings, put on a false front.

dissembler noun liar, dissimulator, humbug, bluffer, actor.

disseminate verb *health authorities should foster good practice by disseminating information:* spread, circulate, distribute, promulgate, propagate, publicize, communicate, pass on, make known; Brit. put about.

dissension noun *there was dissension within the cabinet over these policies:* disagreement, difference of opinion, dispute, dissent, conflict, discord; argument, debate, controversy, disputation, contention.

OPPOSITES: agreement.

dissent verb *two members dissented:* differ, disagree, demur, fail to agree, be at variance/odds, take issue, protest, object, dispute, challenge, quibble.

OPPOSITES: agree.

▷ noun *murmurs of dissent:* disagreement, difference of opinion, argument, dispute; disapproval, objection, protest, opposition, defiance, conflict.

OPPOSITES: agreement.

dissenter noun dissident, objector, protester; rebel, renegade, maverick, independent, heretic.

dissertation noun essay, thesis, treatise, paper, study, discourse, tract, monograph; formal disquisition.

disservice noun *to call it a cartoon would be a disservice to its animators:* injustice, wrong, disfavour, unkindness; injury, harm, hurt, damage, bad turn.

OPPOSITES: favour.

dissidence noun *the chairman was faced by dissidence within his own party:* disagreement, dissent, discord, discontent; opposition, resistance, protest, sedition.

OPPOSITES: conformity.

dissident noun *a jailed dissident:* dissenter, objector, protester; rebel, revolutionary, recusant, subversive, agitator, insurgent, insurrectionist, refusenik.

OPPOSITES: conformist.

▷ adjective *dissident intellectuals:* dissenting, rebellious, revolutionary, recusant, nonconformist.

OPPOSITES: conformist.

dissimilar adjective *contact between dissimilar cultures:* different, differing, unalike, variant, diverse, divergent, heterogeneous, disparate, unrelated, distinct, contrasting.

OPPOSITES: similar.

dissimilarity noun difference, variance, diversity, heterogeneity, disparity, distinction, contrast, divergence.
OPPOSITES: similarity.

dissimulation noun *the government has used tactics ranging from dissimulation to outright deception:* pretence, dishonesty, guile, subterfuge; half-truths, hypocrisy, posturing.

dissipate verb
1 *his anger seemed to dissipate:* disappear, vanish, evaporate, dissolve, melt away, melt into thin air, be dispelled; disperse, scatter.
2 *he dissipated his fortune:* squander, fritter away, misspend, waste, be prodigal with, spend recklessly/freely, spend like water, run through, go through; informal blow.

dissipated adjective *the new heir was a dissipated youth:* dissolute, debauched, decadent, intemperate, profligate, self-indulgent, wild, depraved; licentious, promiscuous; drunken.
OPPOSITES: ascetic.

dissipation noun
1 *drunken dissipation:* debauchery, decadence, intemperance, excess, profligacy, self-indulgence, wildness; depravity, degeneracy; licentiousness, promiscuity; drunkenness.
2 *the dissipation of our mineral wealth:* squandering, frittering away, waste, misspending; expenditure, draining, depletion.
OPPOSITES: asceticism.

dissociate verb *the word 'spiritual' has become dissociated from religion:* separate, detach, disconnect, sever, cut off, divorce; isolate, alienate.
OPPOSITES: associate.
□ **dissociate yourself from**
1 *he dissociated himself from the Church of England:* break away from, end relations with, sever connections with; withdraw from, quit, leave, disaffiliate from, resign from, pull out of, drop out of, defect from.
2 *he dissociated himself from the statement:* disown, reject, disagree with, distance yourself from.

dissociation noun separation, detachment, disconnection, severance, divorce, split; segregation, division, isolation, alienation.
OPPOSITES: union.

dissolute adjective *a dissolute, alcoholic playboy:* dissipated, debauched, decadent, profligate, self-indulgent, wild, depraved; licentious, promiscuous; drunken.
OPPOSITES: ascetic.

dissolution noun
1 *the dissolution of parliament:* cessation, end, termination, winding up, abolition, discontinuation, suspension, disbanding; prorogation, recess.

2 *the dissolution of the empire:* disintegration, breaking up; decay, collapse, demise, extinction.
3 *a life of dissolution.* See DISSIPATION sense 1.
OPPOSITES: founding, formation.

dissolve verb
1 *his hopes dissolved:* disappear, vanish, melt away, evaporate, disperse, dissipate, disintegrate; dwindle, fade, wither.
2 *the crowd dissolved:* disperse, disband, break up, scatter.
3 *the assembly was dissolved:* disband, close down, break up, wind up, bring to an end, end, terminate, discontinue, abolish.
4 *their marriage was dissolved:* annul, nullify, void, invalidate.
OPPOSITES: appear, gather, found.
□ **dissolve into/in**
both boys dissolved in laughter: burst into, break into, be overcome with.

dissonant adjective *dissonant guitar chords:* discordant, clashing, inharmonious, atonal, off-key, cacophonous.
OPPOSITES: harmonious.

dissuade verb *I tried to dissuade him from telling that story:* discourage, deter, prevent, divert, stop; talk out of, persuade against, advise against, argue out of.
OPPOSITES: encourage.

distance noun
1 *they measured the distance:* interval, space, span, gap, extent; length, width, breadth, depth; range, reach.
2 *a mix of warmth and distance:* aloofness, remoteness, detachment, unfriendliness, coolness; reserve, reticence, restraint, formality; informal stand-offishness.
□ **distance yourself from**
he distanced himself from Hollywood, preferring to make his films elsewhere: dissociate yourself from, reject, withdraw from, turn your back on, have nothing more to do with, keep your distance from, sever connections with, disown.
□ **in the distance**
far away/off, just in view, on the horizon; literary afar.

WORD LINKS
tele- forming words meaning 'to or at a distance', such as *telecommunication* ('long-distance communication by means of cable, telephone, satellite, etc.')

distant adjective
1 *distant parts of the world:* faraway, far-off, far-flung, remote, outlying.
2 *a distant memory:* vague, faint, dim, indistinct, indefinite, sketchy, hazy.
3 *a distant family connection:* remote, indirect, slight.
4 *my father was always distant:* aloof, reserved, remote, detached, unapproachable; withdrawn, reticent, taciturn, uncommunicative,

undemonstrative, unforthcoming,
unresponsive, cool, unfriendly; informal
stand-offish.
5 *he had a distant look in his eyes:*
distracted, absent-minded, faraway,
detached, vague.
OPPOSITES: near, close.

distaste noun *Harry nurtured a distaste
for all things athletic:* dislike, aversion,
disinclination, disdain, repugnance,
disapproval.
OPPOSITES: taste.

distasteful adjective *distasteful
behaviour:* unpleasant, disagreeable,
undesirable; objectionable, offensive,
unsavoury, unpalatable, obnoxious;
disgusting, repellent.
OPPOSITES: pleasant.

distended adjective *a grossly distended
belly:* swollen, bloated, dilated, engorged,
enlarged, inflated, expanded, extended,
bulging, protuberant.

distil verb *he helped me to distil the key
information into a succinct format to
present to potential backers:* condense,
boil down, refine, encapsulate; abridge,
shorten, compress, summarize, digest.

distinct adjective
1 *the gallery is divided into five distinct
spaces:* discrete, separate, different,
unconnected, individual; precise, specific,
distinctive, contrasting.
2 *the haddock has a distinct black spot
above and behind the pectoral fin:* clear,
well defined, unmistakable, easily
distinguishable; recognizable, visible,
obvious.
OPPOSITES: overlapping, ill-defined.

distinction noun
1 *there is a sharp distinction between
domestic politics and international politics:*
difference, contrast, dissimilarity,
variance, variation, divergence; division,
differentiation, dividing line, gulf, gap.
2 *a painter of distinction:* importance,
significance, note, consequence; account,
renown, fame, celebrity, prominence,
eminence, pre-eminence, repute,
reputation.
3 *he had served with distinction:* honour,
credit, excellence, merit.
OPPOSITES: similarity, mediocrity.

distinctive adjective *each subculture
developed a distinctive dress style:*
distinguishing, characteristic, typical,
individual, particular, peculiar, unique,
exclusive, special.
OPPOSITES: common.

distinctly adverb
1 *there's something distinctly odd about
him:* decidedly, markedly, definitely;
clearly, noticeably, obviously, plainly,
unmistakably, manifestly, patently.
2 *Laura spoke quite distinctly:*

clearly, plainly, intelligibly, audibly,
unambiguously.

distinguish verb
1 *the child is perfectly capable of
distinguishing reality from fantasy:*
differentiate, tell apart, pick out,
discriminate, decide, tell the difference
between.
2 *he could distinguish shapes in the dark:*
discern, see, perceive, make out; detect,
recognize, identify.
3 *this is what distinguishes history from
other disciplines:* separate, set apart; single
out, mark off, characterize.

distinguishable adjective discernible,
recognizable, identifiable, detectable,
noticeable, marked, observable,
conspicuous, unmistakable; separable,
distinct.

distinguished adjective *a distinguished
physicist:* eminent, famous, renowned,
prominent, well known; esteemed,
respected, illustrious, acclaimed,
celebrated; notable, important, influential.
OPPOSITES: unknown, obscure.

distinguishing adjective *a distinguishing
feature of British society:* distinctive,
differentiating, identifying, characteristic,
typical, peculiar, unique.

distorted adjective
1 *his face was distorted with rage:*
contorted, twisted, misshapen, disfigured,
crooked.
2 *his report gives a distorted view of the
meeting:* misleading, inaccurate, false,
incorrect; biased, prejudiced, slanted.
OPPOSITES: natural, accurate.

distract verb *don't let me distract you from
what you were saying:* divert, sidetrack,
deflect, disturb, put off.

distracted adjective *he glanced at me
with a distracted smile:* preoccupied,
inattentive, vague, abstracted, absent-
minded, faraway, in a world of your own;
troubled, worried, harassed; informal miles
away.
OPPOSITES: attentive.

distracting adjective *some people
find even the slightest noise distracting:*
disturbing, intrusive, disconcerting, off-
putting, unsettling, upsetting, unnerving.

distraction noun
1 *a distraction from the real issues:*
diversion, interruption, disturbance,
interference.
2 *frivolous distractions:* amusement,
entertainment, diversion, recreation,
leisure pursuit, pastime.
3 *her uncharacteristic air of distraction:*
agitation, anxiety, worry, distress; frenzy,
hysteria.

distraught adjective *the poor woman was
distraught:* upset, worried, distressed,

fraught; overcome, overwrought, beside yourself, out of your mind, desperate, hysterical, worked up, at your wits' end; informal in a state.

distress noun
1 *she tried to conceal her distress:* anguish, suffering, pain, agony, torment, heartache, heartbreak; misery, wretchedness, sorrow, grief, woe, sadness, unhappiness, desolation, despair.
2 *a ship in distress:* danger, peril, difficulty, trouble, jeopardy, risk.
3 *a company experiencing financial distress:* difficulty, trouble, hardship, adversity, dire straits.
OPPOSITES: happiness, safety, prosperity.
▷ verb *he was distressed to find that Anna would not speak to him:* upset, sadden, pain, trouble, worry, bother, perturb, disturb, disquiet, agitate.
OPPOSITES: calm, please.

distressing adjective *it was distressing to hear her talking like that:* upsetting, agonizing, harrowing, worrying, disturbing, disquieting, painful, traumatic; sad, saddening, heartbreaking, heart-rending.
OPPOSITES: comforting.

distribute verb
1 *the proceeds were distributed among his creditors:* give out, deal out, dole out, dish out, hand out/round; allocate, allot, apportion, share out, divide out/up, parcel out.
2 *the newsletter is distributed free:* circulate, issue, publish, hand out, deliver.
3 *a hundred and thirty different species are distributed worldwide:* disperse, scatter, spread.
OPPOSITES: collect.

distribution noun
1 *the funds will help with the distribution of emergency food aid:* giving out, doling out, handing out/round, issuing; allocation, allotment, apportioning, sharing out, dividing up/out, parcelling out.
2 *the geographical distribution of the disease | factors determining the health and distribution of wildlife:* frequency, incidence, prevalence; position, location; spread, dissemination.

district noun *the business district of Manila:* area, region, locality, community, quarter, neighbourhood, sector, zone.

distrust noun *the general distrust of authority:* mistrust, suspicion, wariness, scepticism, doubt, cynicism, misgivings, qualms, disbelief; informal leeriness.
OPPOSITES: trust.
▷ verb *Louise distrusted him:* mistrust, be suspicious of, be wary of, suspect; be sceptical of, have doubts about, doubt, be unsure of/about, have misgivings about, wonder about, disbelieve; informal be leery of.
OPPOSITES: trust.

disturb verb
1 *we chose a table in the far corner of the restaurant, hoping nobody would disturb us:* interrupt, intrude on, butt in on, barge in on; distract, disrupt, bother, trouble, pester, harass; informal hassle.
2 *don't disturb his papers:* rearrange, interfere with, muddle, mix up, disorganize, disorder, disarrange.
3 *he wasn't disturbed by the allegations:* perturb, trouble, concern, worry, upset; agitate, fluster, discomfit, disconcert, dismay, distress, discompose, unsettle, ruffle.

disturbance noun
1 *we are concerned about the disturbance to local residents:* disruption, distraction, interference, interruption, intrusion, inconvenience, upset, bother, trouble, annoyance, irritation, harassment; informal hassle.
2 *police were called to a disturbance outside a city pub:* commotion, disruption, mayhem; fight, fracas, brawl, melee, free-for-all, riot; unrest, disorder; Brit. informal punch-up.
3 *emotional disturbance:* distress, trouble, worry, upset, agitation, neurosis, illness, sickness, disorder, complaint.

disturbed adjective
1 *disturbed sleep:* disrupted, interrupted, fitful, intermittent, broken.
2 *a secure care unit for disturbed children:* troubled, distressed; unbalanced, unstable, dysfunctional, maladjusted; informal mixed up.

disturbing adjective *this is disturbing news:* worrying, perturbing, troubling, upsetting, disconcerting, disquieting, unsettling, distressing, dismaying, alarming, frightening.
OPPOSITES: comforting.

disunite verb *these nations are never to be disunited:* break up, separate, divide, split up, partition.
OPPOSITES: unite.

disunity noun *there was disunity within the administration:* disagreement, dissent, dissension, argument, quarrelling, feuding; conflict, strife, friction, discord.
OPPOSITES: unity.

disused adjective *a disused building:* abandoned, neglected, deserted, vacated, unoccupied, uninhabited, unused, unemployed, idle.
OPPOSITES: in use.

ditch noun *a deep, muddy ditch:* trench, trough, channel, dyke, drain, gutter, gully, watercourse, conduit.
▷ verb (informal) *she decided to ditch her old curtains:* throw out, throw away, discard, get rid of, dispose of, do away with, shed; abandon, drop, shelve, scrap, axe, jettison; informal dump, junk, scrub, chuck away/out; Brit. informal get shot of.

d

dither verb *they wasted several minutes while she dithered:* hesitate, falter, waver, vacillate, be in two minds, be indecisive, be undecided, change your mind; informal shilly-shally.

dive verb
1 *the plane was diving towards the ground:* plunge, nosedive, fall, drop, swoop, pitch, plummet.
2 *they dived for cover:* leap, jump, lunge, plunge, duck, spring, dart, bound, launch yourself, throw yourself.
▷noun *the plane went into a steep dive:* plunge, nosedive, fall, drop, swoop, pitch.

diverge verb
1 *the two roads diverged:* separate, part, fork, divide, split, bifurcate.
2 *areas where our views diverge:* differ, disagree, be at variance/odds, conflict, clash.
3 *he diverged from his text:* deviate, digress, depart, stray.
OPPOSITES: converge, agree, adhere.

divergence noun
1 *there is a significant divergence of views among some of the opposition parties:* difference, dissimilarity, variance, disparity; disagreement, incompatibility, mismatch.
2 *divergence from standard behaviour:* deviation, digression, departure, straying, shift; variation, change, alteration.
OPPOSITES: agreement.

divergent adjective *they adopted divergent approaches to almost every issue:* differing, varying, different, dissimilar, unalike, disparate, contrasting, contrastive; conflicting, incompatible, contradictory, at odds, at variance.
OPPOSITES: similar.

diverse adjective *the company has to manage data from diverse databases:* varied, various, varying, miscellaneous, assorted, mixed, diversified, divergent, heterogeneous, disparate, different, differing, distinct, dissimilar.
OPPOSITES: uniform.

diversify verb
1 *a plan aimed at diversifying the local economy:* vary, bring variety to; expand, enlarge, grow.
2 *farmers looking for ways to diversify:* branch out, expand, extend operations.
OPPOSITES: contract, specialize.

diversion noun
1 *the diversion of resources from defence to civil research:* re-routing, redirection, deflection.
2 *traffic diversions:* detour, deviation, alternative route.
3 *the noise created a diversion:* distraction, disturbance, smokescreen.
4 *a city full of diversions:* entertainment, amusement, pastime, delight; fun, recreation.

diversity noun *ethnic diversity is increasing:* variety, variation, variance, diverseness, diversification, divergence, heterogeneity, difference, contrast.
OPPOSITES: uniformity.

divert verb
1 *a plan to divert Siberia's rivers:* re-route, redirect, change the course of, deflect, channel.
2 *he diverted her from her studies:* distract, sidetrack, disturb, draw away, put off.
3 *the story diverted them:* amuse, entertain, distract; delight, enchant, interest, fascinate, absorb, engross, rivet, grip, hold the attention of.

diverting adjective *a diverting comedy about two New York kids:* entertaining, enjoyable, pleasing, agreeable, delightful, appealing; interesting, fascinating, intriguing, absorbing, riveting, compelling; amusing, humorous, funny, witty, comical.
OPPOSITES: boring.

divest verb *he intends to divest you of all your power:* deprive, strip, dispossess, rob, cheat/trick out of; rid, free, clear, empty.

divide verb
1 *the mountains have divided the country into distinct regions with different lifestyles, foods, and dialects:* split, cut up, carve up, partition; dissect, bisect, halve, quarter.
2 *a curtain divided her cabin from the rest of the boat:* separate, segregate, partition, screen off, section off, split off.
3 *the stairs divide at the mezzanine:* diverge, separate, part, fork, split in two, bifurcate.
4 *Jack divided up the cash:* share out, ration out, parcel out, deal out, dole out, portion out, dish out, allocate, allot, apportion, distribute, dispense; informal divvy up.
5 *he aimed to divide his opponents:* disunite, drive apart, break up, split up, set at variance/odds; separate, isolate, estrange, alienate.
6 *living things are divided into three categories:* classify, sort, categorize, order, group, grade, rank.
OPPOSITES: unify, join, converge.
▷noun *the sectarian divide:* breach, gulf, gap, split; borderline, boundary, dividing line.

dividend noun
1 *an annual dividend:* share, payout, portion, premium, return, gain, profit; informal cut, rake-off.
2 *the research will produce dividends in the future:* benefit, advantage, gain; bonus, extra; informal plus.

d

divine¹ adjective

1 *a divine being:* godly, angelic, seraphic, saintly, beatific; holy, heavenly, celestial.
2 *divine worship:* religious, holy, sacred, sanctified, consecrated, blessed, devotional.
OPPOSITES: mortal, secular.

divine² verb

1 *Fergus had divined that she was afraid:* guess, surmise, conjecture, deduce, infer; discern, perceive, recognize, see, realize, appreciate, understand, grasp, comprehend; informal figure out; Brit. informal twig.
2 *they divined that this was an auspicious day:* foretell, predict, prophesy, forecast, foresee, prognosticate.

divinity noun

1 *they denied Christ's divinity:* divine nature, godliness, deity, godhead, holiness.
2 *the University's Faculty of Divinity:* theology, religious studies, religious education, religion, scripture.
3 *a female divinity:* deity, god, goddess, divine/supreme being.

division noun

1 *the division of the island | cell division:* dividing up, breaking up, break-up, carving up, splitting, dissection, bisection; partitioning, separation.
2 *the division of his estates:* sharing out, dividing up, parcelling out, dishing out, allocation, allotment, apportionment; splitting up, carving up; informal divvying up.
3 *the division between nomadic and urban cultures:* dividing line, divide, boundary, borderline, border, demarcation line.
4 *the main divisions of the book:* section, subsection, subdivision, category, class, group, grouping, set.
5 *an independent division of the executive:* department, branch, arm, wing, sector, section, subsection, subdivision, subsidiary.
6 *the causes of social division | the divisions in society:* disunity, split, schism, conflict, discord, disagreement, dissension, alienation, isolation, segregation.

divisive adjective *the divisive effects of government policy:* alienating, isolating; disruptive.
OPPOSITES: unifying.

divorce noun

1 *even the most amicable divorce can be a difficult experience:* annulment, official/judicial separation; English Law decree nisi, decree absolute.
2 *a growing divorce between the church and people:* separation, division, split, disunity, alienation; schism, gulf, chasm.
OPPOSITES: unity.
▷ verb
1 *her parents have divorced:* dissolve your

marriage, end your marriage; separate, break up, split up.
2 *religion cannot be divorced from morality:* separate, disconnect, divide, dissociate, detach, isolate, alienate, set apart, cut off.

divulge verb *he refused to divulge Father O'Neill's whereabouts:* disclose, reveal, tell, communicate, pass on, publish, broadcast, proclaim; expose, uncover, make public, give away, let slip.
OPPOSITES: conceal.

dizzy adjective *she still felt dizzy:* giddy, light-headed, faint, unsteady, shaky, muzzy, wobbly; informal woozy.

do verb

1 *she does most of the manual work:* carry out, perform, undertake, execute, discharge, accomplish, achieve.
2 *they can do as they please:* act, behave, conduct yourself.
3 *regular coffee will do:* suffice, be adequate, be satisfactory, fill/fit the bill, serve, meet your needs.
4 *the boys will do the dinner:* prepare, make, get ready, see to, arrange, organize, be responsible for, be in charge of; informal fix.
5 *her maid did her hair:* style, arrange, adjust; brush, comb, wash, dry, cut; informal fix.
6 *she's doing archaeology:* study, read, learn, take a course in.
7 *he is doing well at college:* get on/along, progress, fare, manage, cope; succeed, prosper.
□ **do away with**
they want to do away with the old customs: abolish, get rid of, discard, remove, eliminate, discontinue, stop, end, terminate, put an end/stop to, dispense with, drop, abandon, give up; informal scrap.
□ **do something up**
1 *she did her bootlace up:* fasten, tie, lace, knot; make fast, secure.
2 (informal) *he's had his house done up:* renovate, refurbish, refit, decorate, revamp, make over, modernize, improve, spruce up, smarten up.
□ **do without**
forgo, give up, abstain from, refrain from, eschew, cut out, renounce, dispense with, manage without.

docile adjective *a cheap and docile workforce:* compliant, obedient, pliant, dutiful, submissive, deferential, cooperative, amenable, accommodating, biddable, malleable.
OPPOSITES: disobedient, wilful.

dock¹ noun *his boat was moored at the dock:* harbour, marina, port, dockyard, wharf, quay, pier, jetty, landing stage.
▷ verb *the ship docked:* moor, berth, put in, tie up.

dock² verb

1 *they docked the money from his salary:*

deduct, subtract, remove, take off/away.
2 *workers had their pay docked:* reduce, cut, lower.
3 *the dog's tail was docked:* cut off, cut short, shorten, crop, lop, amputate, sever, chop off.

doctor noun *Tim went to see a doctor:* physician, medical practitioner, clinician; general practitioner, GP, consultant, registrar; informal doc, medic.
▷ *the reports have been doctored:* falsify, tamper with, interfere with, alter, change; forge, fake; informal cook.

doctrinaire adjective *democratic socialism was feared by doctrinaire Marxists:* strict, rigid, inflexible, uncompromising, dogmatic, intolerant, fanatical, extreme.
OPPOSITES: liberal.

doctrine noun *they rejected the doctrine of the Trinity:* creed, credo, dogma, belief, teaching, ideology; tenet, maxim, canon, principle, precept.

document noun *their solicitor drew up a document:* legal agreement, certificate, deed, record, contract; Law instrument; (**documents**) paperwork.
▷verb *many aspects of school life have been documented:* record, register, report, log, chronicle, archive, put on record, write down; detail, note, describe.

documentary adjective *documentary evidence:* recorded, documented, registered, written, chronicled, archived, on record/paper, in writing.

doddery adjective *coachloads of doddery pensioners:* tottering, staggering, shuffling, shambling, faltering, shaky, unsteady, wobbly; feeble, frail, weak.

dodge verb
1 *he dodged between the cars:* dart, dive, duck, leap, spring.
2 *he could easily dodge the two police officers:* elude, evade, avoid, escape, run away from, lose, shake off; informal give someone the slip.
3 *the minister tried to dodge the debate:* avoid, evade, get out of, sidestep; informal duck.
▷noun *a clever dodge:* ruse, ploy, scheme, tactic, stratagem, subterfuge, trick, cheat, deception; swindle, fraud; informal scam; Brit. informal wheeze.

dodgy adjective (Brit. informal)
1 *a dodgy second-hand car salesman.* See DISHONEST.
2 *the hotel was a bit dodgy:* second-rate, substandard, poor-quality, low-quality; Brit. informal ropy, grotty.

dog noun hound, canine; mongrel.
▷verb
1 *they dogged him the length of the country:* pursue, follow, track, trail, shadow, hound; informal tail.

2 *the scheme was dogged by bad weather:* beset, plague, curse, afflict, bedevil, beleaguer, blight.

WORD LINKS
canine relating to dogs

dogged adjective *success required dogged determination:* tenacious, determined, resolute, resolved, purposeful, persistent, persevering, single-minded, tireless; strong-willed, steadfast, staunch.
OPPOSITES: half-hearted.

dogma noun *a dogma of the Sikh religion:* teaching, belief, tenet, principle, precept, maxim, article of faith, canon; creed, credo, set of beliefs, doctrine, ideology.

dogmatic adjective *he criticized the Minister's strident, dogmatic style:* opinionated, doctrinaire, authoritarian, imperious, dictatorial, uncompromising, unyielding, inflexible, rigid.
OPPOSITES: flexible.

dole noun (Brit. informal) *he was on the dole:* unemployment benefit, social security, welfare; Brit. jobseeker's allowance.
▯dole something out
Dad began to dole out the sweets: share out, deal out, divide up, allocate, allot, distribute, dispense, hand out, give out, dish out/up; informal divvy up.

doleful adjective *she regarded him with doleful eyes:* mournful, woeful, sorrowful, sad, unhappy, depressed, gloomy, morose, melancholy, miserable, forlorn, wretched, woebegone, despondent, dejected, disconsolate, downcast, crestfallen, downhearted; informal blue.
OPPOSITES: cheerful.

domain noun
1 *they extended their domain:* realm, kingdom, empire, dominion, province, territory, land.
2 *the domain of art:* field, area, sphere, discipline, province, world.

domestic adjective
1 *a freak domestic accident left him with an injured leg:* household, home, family.
2 *she was not at all domestic:* domesticated, houseproud, housewifely; Brit. homely.
3 *small domestic animals:* domesticated, tame, pet, household.
4 *the domestic car industry:* national, state, home, internal, home-grown.

domesticated adjective
1 *domesticated animals:* tame, pet, domestic, trained, house-trained.
2 *I'm quite domesticated really:* home-loving, houseproud; Brit. homely.
OPPOSITES: wild.

dominance noun supremacy, superiority, ascendancy, pre-eminence, predominance, domination, dominion, mastery, power, authority, rule, command, control, sway.

dominant adjective

1 *the dominant classes:* ruling, governing, controlling, commanding, ascendant, supreme, leading, influential, powerful.
2 *he has a dominant personality:* assertive, authoritative, forceful; domineering, commanding, controlling; informal pushy.
3 *the dominant issues in psychology:* main, principal, prime, premier, chief, leading, foremost, primary, predominant, paramount, prominent; central, key, crucial, core; informal number-one.
OPPOSITES: subservient.

dominate verb

1 *the company dominates the market for operating systems software:* control, monopolize, command, be in charge of, rule, govern, direct, influence.
2 *the village is dominated by the viaduct:* overlook, command, tower above/over, loom over.

domination noun *they believed that Communists were aiming for world domination:* rule, government, sovereignty, control, command, power, dominion, dominance, mastery, supremacy, superiority, monopoly, ascendancy, sway.

domineering adjective *he was brought up by a cold, domineering father:* overbearing, authoritarian, imperious, high-handed, autocratic; dictatorial, despotic, oppressive, strict, harsh; informal bossy.

dominion noun

1 *France had dominion over Laos:* supremacy, authority, mastery, control, command, power, sway, rule, government, jurisdiction, sovereignty, suzerainty, ascendancy, dominance, domination, superiority, predominance, pre-eminence, hegemony.
2 *a British dominion:* dependency, colony, protectorate, territory, province, possession.

don[1] noun *an Oxford don:* lecturer, fellow, professor, reader, academic, scholar.

don[2] verb *he donned an overcoat:* put on, get dressed in, dress yourself in, get into, slip into/on.

donate verb *local people have donated thousands of pounds to the disaster fund:* give, contribute, gift, subscribe, grant, bestow; Brit. informal stump up.

donation noun *his employer also made a donation to the fund:* gift, contribution, subscription, present, handout, grant, offering; charity.

donkey noun ass.

donnish adjective *you can never talk with these quiet, donnish types:* scholarly, studious, academic, bookish, intellectual, learned, highbrow.

donor noun *the cost has been met by a generous donor:* contributor, giver, benefactor, benefactress, subscriber; supporter, backer, patron, sponsor.

doom noun *his impending doom:* destruction, downfall, ruin, ruination; extinction, annihilation, death.
▷verb *we were doomed to fail:* destine, fate, predestine, preordain, mean; condemn, sentence.

doomed adjective *a doomed friendship:* ill-fated, ill-starred, cursed, jinxed, damned.
OPPOSITES: blessed.

doorkeeper noun doorman, concierge, commissionaire.

dope verb *the horse was doped before the race:* drug, tamper with, interfere with; sedate; Brit. informal nobble.

dopey adjective (informal) *he became dopey and fell into a deep sleep:* groggy, dazed, sleepy, drowsy, stupefied, confused, muddled, befuddled, disorientated, muzzy; informal woozy.
OPPOSITES: alert.

dormant adjective *the parasite can lie dormant in your body for up to two years:* inactive, inert, quiescent, passive, latent.
OPPOSITES: active.

dose noun *a dose of cough mixture:* measure, portion, dosage.

dossier noun *we have a dossier on him:* file, report, case history; account, notes, documents, documentation, data, information, evidence.

dot noun *a pattern of tiny dots:* spot, speck, fleck, speckle; full stop, decimal point.
▷verb
1 *spots of rain dotted his shirt:* spot, fleck, mark, stipple, freckle, sprinkle, punctuate, pepper.
2 *restaurants are dotted around the site:* scatter, pepper, sprinkle, strew; spread, disperse, distribute.

dotage noun *Uncle Henry was in his dotage:* old age, winter/autumn/evening of your life, advanced years, declining years.

dote verb
□ dote on
she doted on the boy: adore, love, be devoted to, idolize, treasure, cherish, worship, hold dear; indulge, spoil, pamper.

doting adjective adoring, loving, besotted, infatuated; affectionate, fond, devoted, caring.

double adjective

1 *a double garage | double doors:* dual, duplex, twin, binary, duplicate, in pairs, coupled, twofold.
2 *a double helping:* twofold, doubled.
3 *a double meaning:* ambiguous,

d

equivocal, dual, two-edged, double-edged; ambivalent, cryptic, enigmatic.
OPPOSITES: single, unambiguous.

▷ **noun**
1 *if it's not her, it's her double:* lookalike, twin, clone, duplicate, exact likeness, replica, copy, facsimile, doppelgänger; informal spitting image, dead ringer.
2 *she used a double for the stunts:* stand-in, substitute.

▷ **verb**
1 *they doubled his salary:* multiply by two, increase twofold.
2 *the bottom sheet had been doubled up:* fold back, turn back, tuck under.
3 *the kitchen doubles as a dining room:* function, do, also serve.

> **WORD LINKS**
> **bi-, di-** forming words meaning 'having two' or 'double', such as *biped* ('an animal that walks on two feet') and *dioxide* ('an oxide with two atoms of oxygen to one of a metal or other element')

double-cross verb *he was blackmailed into double-crossing his own government:* betray, cheat, defraud, trick, hoodwink, mislead, deceive, swindle, play false; informal two-time.

double-dealing noun *one day his double-dealing would be discovered:* duplicity, treachery, betrayal, double-crossing, infidelity, bad faith, disloyalty, breach of trust, fraud, cheating, dishonesty, deceit, deception.
OPPOSITES: honesty.

double entendre noun *he was unable to resist a smutty double entendre:* ambiguity, double meaning, innuendo, play on words.

doubt noun
1 *there was some doubt as to the document's authenticity:* uncertainty, suspicion, scepticism, distrust, mistrust, doubtfulness, cynicism; formal dubiety.
2 *a weak leader racked by doubt:* indecision, hesitation, uncertainty, insecurity, lack of confidence; hesitancy, vacillation, irresolution; reservations, misgivings.
OPPOSITES: certainty, conviction.

▷ **verb**
1 *they doubted my story:* disbelieve, distrust, mistrust, suspect, have doubts about, be suspicious of, have misgivings about, feel uneasy about, query, question, challenge.
2 *I doubt whether he will come:* think something unlikely, have your doubts about, question, query, be dubious.
OPPOSITES: trust.

□ **in doubt**
1 *the outcome was in doubt:* doubtful, uncertain, open to question, unconfirmed, unknown, undecided, unresolved, in the balance.

2 *if you are in doubt, ask for advice:* uncertain, in two minds, undecided, in a quandary/dilemma, doubtful, unsure; irresolute, hesitant, vacillating, dithering, wavering, ambivalent.

□ **no doubt**
doubtless, undoubtedly, indubitably, without a doubt; unquestionably, undeniably, incontrovertibly, irrefutably; unequivocally, clearly, plainly, obviously, patently.

doubter noun *this is his chance to confound the doubters:* sceptic, doubting Thomas, non-believer, unbeliever, disbeliever, cynic, challenger, dissenter.
OPPOSITES: believer.

doubtful adjective
1 *I was doubtful about going:* unsure, uncertain, hesitant, irresolute, vacillating, dithering, wavering, in two minds, undecided, in a quandary/dilemma, blowing hot and cold; informal shilly-shallying.
2 *it is doubtful whether he will come:* in doubt, uncertain, open to question, unsure, unconfirmed, not definite, unknown, undecided, unresolved, in the balance, up in the air.
3 *the whole trip is looking rather doubtful:* unlikely, improbable, dubious, impossible.
4 *they are doubtful of the methods used:* distrustful, mistrustful, suspicious, wary, chary, apprehensive; sceptical, unsure, ambivalent, dubious, cynical.
5 *this decision is of doubtful validity:* questionable, arguable, debatable.
OPPOSITES: confident, certain, probable.

doubtless adverb *Henry was doubtless glad of the opportunity:* very probably, in all likelihood, surely, no doubt, undoubtedly, indubitably.

doughty adjective *a doughty fighter:* fearless, dauntless, determined, resolute, indomitable, intrepid, plucky, spirited, bold, valiant, brave, stout-hearted, courageous; informal gutsy.
OPPOSITES: cowardly, timid.

dour adjective *they were barely acknowledged by the dour receptionist:* stern, unsmiling, unfriendly, severe, forbidding, gruff, surly, grim, sullen, solemn, austere, stony.
OPPOSITES: cheerful, friendly.

douse verb
1 *a mob doused the thieves with petrol:* drench, soak, saturate, wet, splash, slosh.
2 *a guard doused the flames:* extinguish, put out, quench, smother, dampen down.

dovetail verb *this will dovetail well with the division's existing activities:* fit in, go together, be consistent, match, conform, harmonize, be in tune, correspond; informal square.

dowdy adjective *she had serviceable but dowdy clothes:* **unfashionable**, frumpy, old-fashioned, inelegant, shabby, scruffy, dull.
OPPOSITES: fashionable.

down adjective
1 *I'm feeling a bit down:* **depressed**, sad, unhappy, melancholy, miserable, wretched, sorrowful, gloomy, dejected, downhearted, despondent, dispirited, low; informal blue, fed up.
2 *the computer is down:* **not working**, inoperative, malfunctioning, out of order, broken; not in service, out of action, out of commission; informal bust, kaput.
OPPOSITES: elated, working.

down and out adjective *a novel about being down and out on the streets of London:* **destitute**, poverty-stricken, impoverished, penniless, in straitened circumstances, badly off; homeless, on the streets, vagrant, sleeping rough; informal hard up, broke.
OPPOSITES: prosperous.
▷ noun (**down-and-out**) *he gave his packed lunch to a down-and-out:* **homeless person**, destitute person, pauper, indigent; beggar, vagrant, tramp, drifter; N. Amer. hobo; informal dosser; N. Amer. informal bum.

downbeat adjective
1 *the mood is decidedly downbeat:* **pessimistic**, gloomy, negative, defeatist, cynical, bleak, dark, black; despairing, despondent, depressed, dejected, demoralized, hopeless, melancholy, glum.
2 *his downbeat joviality:* **relaxed**, easy-going, easy, casual, informal, understated; low-key, subtle, unostentatious, cool; informal laid-back.
OPPOSITES: upbeat.

downcast adjective *Morgan was understandably downcast following Scotland's defeat:* **despondent**, disheartened, discouraged, dispirited, crestfallen, down, low, disconsolate, despairing; sad, melancholy, gloomy, glum, morose, doleful, dismal, woebegone, miserable, depressed, dejected; informal blue.
OPPOSITES: elated.

downfall noun *the crisis led to the downfall of the government:* **ruin**, ruination, undoing; defeat, conquest, deposition, overthrow; nemesis, destruction, annihilation, elimination; end, collapse, fall, crash, failure.
OPPOSITES: rise.

downgrade verb *plans to downgrade three workers:* **demote**, lower, reduce/lower in rank; relegate.
OPPOSITES: upgrade, promote.

downhearted adjective *fans must not be downhearted even though we lost:* **despondent**, disheartened, discouraged, dispirited, downcast, crestfallen, down, low, disconsolate, wretched; melancholy, gloomy, glum, morose, doleful, dismal, woebegone, miserable, depressed, dejected, sorrowful, sad; informal blue.
OPPOSITES: elated.

downmarket adjective (Brit.) *the quality papers and the downmarket tabloids:* **cheap**, mass-market, popular, lowbrow, unsophisticated.
OPPOSITES: upmarket.

downpour noun *the drizzle was becoming a downpour:* **rainstorm**, cloudburst, deluge, torrent; thunderstorm.

downright adjective *it's a downright disgrace:* **complete**, total, absolute, utter, thorough, out-and-out, outright, sheer, arrant, positive, categorical, unmitigated.
▷ adverb *that's downright dangerous:* **thoroughly**, utterly, positively, profoundly, really, completely, totally, entirely, through and through; informal plain.

downside noun *the downside is that getting a patent costs big money:* **drawback**, disadvantage, snag, stumbling block, catch, pitfall; trouble, difficulty, problem; informal minus.
OPPOSITES: advantage.

down-to-earth adjective *she seemed a good down-to-earth type:* **practical**, sensible, realistic, matter-of-fact, responsible, reasonable, rational, logical, balanced, sober, pragmatic, level-headed, commonsensical, sane.
OPPOSITES: idealistic.

downtrodden adjective *she is into forming unions and standing up for the downtrodden worker:* **oppressed**, exploited, victimized, enslaved, ground down, crushed, subjugated, persecuted, repressed, tyrannized, bullied, henpecked; disadvantaged, underprivileged, powerless, helpless; abused, mistreated.
OPPOSITES: fortunate, thriving.

downward adjective *the downward flow of water:* **falling**, downhill, descending, sinking, dipping, sloping; earthbound, earthward.
OPPOSITES: upward.

downy adjective *I stroked the downy hair on my tiny son's head:* **soft**, fluffy, fuzzy, feathery, furry, silky, woolly, fleecy, velvety, smooth.
OPPOSITES: rough, shaggy.

doze verb *he dozed but woke with a start:* **nap**, catnap, drowse, sleep lightly, rest; informal snooze; Brit. informal kip.
▷ noun *she had a short doze before work:* **nap**, catnap, siesta, drowse, rest; informal snooze; Brit. informal kip.
□ **doze off**
fall asleep, go to sleep, drop off; informal nod off.

dozy adjective *he grew dozy at the end of a long day:* drowsy, sleepy, half asleep, heavy-eyed, somnolent; lethargic, listless, enervated, inactive, languid, weary, tired; informal dopey.
OPPOSITES: alert, fresh.

drab adjective
1 *the drab kitchen of their small apartment:* dingy, dreary, dismal, cheerless, gloomy, dowdy, sombre, grey, colourless.
2 *they settled into a drab suburban existence:* uninteresting, dull, boring, tedious, monotonous, dreary; unexciting, unimaginative, uninspiring, insipid, lacklustre, flat, stale, run-of-the-mill, mediocre, nondescript, characterless, mundane, unremarkable, humdrum.
OPPOSITES: bright, cheerful, interesting.

draconian adjective *collaborators suffered draconian reprisals:* harsh, severe, strict, extreme, drastic, stringent, tough, cruel, oppressive, ruthless, punitive, repressive; Brit. swingeing.
OPPOSITES: lenient, permissive.

draft noun
1 *the first draft of his speech:* first version, rough version, outline, plan, skeleton, abstract; main points, bare bones.
2 *a banker's draft:* cheque, banker's order, money order, bill of exchange, postal order.
▷ **verb** *he drafted a letter of resignation:* compose, write, prepare, frame, draw up, put together; outline, sketch out, rough out.

USAGE

Do not confuse **draft** with **draught**. **Draft** means 'a first version of a piece of writing' or 'to prepare the first version of a piece of writing', while in British English **draught** chiefly means 'a current of air' (*a cold draught from the hole in the roof*). **Draft** is the American spelling for both senses.

drag verb
1 *she dragged the chair backwards:* haul, pull, tug, heave, draw; trail, tow; informal lug, yank.
2 *the day dragged:* become tedious, pass slowly, creep along, hang heavy, wear on, go on too long, go on and on.
▷ **noun**
1 (informal) *working nine to five can be a drag:* bore, bother, nuisance, inconvenience, pest, trial; informal pain, pain in the neck, headache, hassle.
2 *the drag of the air brakes:* pull, resistance, tug, reaction.
□ **drag on**
the dispute between the two families dragged on for some years: continue, go on, carry on, extend, run on, be protracted, endure.
□ **drag something out**
the procedure was bound to drag out the

negotiations: prolong, protract, draw out, spin out, string out, extend, lengthen, carry on, keep going, continue.

dragoon verb *he dragooned his friends into participating:* coerce, pressure, pressurize, press, push; force, compel; hound, harass; browbeat, bludgeon, bully, twist someone's arm, strong-arm; informal railroad.

drain verb
1 *a valve for draining the tank:* empty, void, clear out, evacuate, unload.
2 *drain off any surplus liquid:* draw off, extract, withdraw, remove, siphon off, pour out, pour off; bleed, tap, void, discharge.
3 *the water drained away to the sea:* flow, pour, trickle, stream, run, rush, gush, flood; leak, ooze, seep, dribble, filter, bleed.
4 *more people would just drain our resources:* use up, exhaust, deplete, consume, expend, get through, sap; strain, tax.
5 *he drained his drink:* drink up/down, gulp down, guzzle, quaff, down, swallow, finish off; formal imbibe; informal sink, swig, swill down, toss off, slug.
OPPOSITES: fill.
▷ **noun**
1 *the drain filled with water:* sewer, channel, conduit, ditch, culvert, duct, pipe, gutter, trough, sluice.
2 *a drain on the battery:* strain, load, demand, pressure, burden.

dram noun *Menzies offered the man a dram from his flask:* drink, nip, tot, sip, drop, finger, splash, taste.

drama noun
1 *a television drama:* play, show, piece, theatrical work, dramatization.
2 *he is studying drama:* acting, the theatre, the stage, the performing arts, dramatic art, dramatics, stagecraft.
3 *I watched from the window as the drama continued to unfold:* incident, scene, spectacle, crisis; disturbance, commotion; excitement, thrills.

dramatic adjective
1 *dramatic art:* theatrical, thespian, stage.
2 *a dramatic increase in recorded crime:* considerable, substantial, sizeable, marked; sudden, unexpected, striking, remarkable, extraordinary, exceptional, phenomenal.
3 *there were dramatic scenes at Leeds Crown Court yesterday:* sensational, spectacular, exciting, stirring, action-packed; startling, unexpected, tense, gripping, riveting, fascinating, thrilling; rousing, lively, electrifying.
4 *dramatic mountain peaks:* striking, impressive, imposing, spectacular, breathtaking, sensational, awe-inspiring, remarkable.

5 *a dramatic gesture:* exaggerated, theatrical, ostentatious, actressy, stagy, showy, melodramatic, overdone, histrionic, affected.
OPPOSITES: insignificant, boring, unremarkable.

dramatist noun playwright, writer, scriptwriter, screenwriter, dramaturge.

dramatize verb *she had a tendency to dramatize things:* exaggerate, sensationalize, embellish, embroider, overdo, overstate, inflate, elaborate; informal blow up out of all proportion.
OPPOSITES: downplay.

drape verb
1 *she draped a shawl round her shoulders:* wrap, wind, swathe, fold, sling, hang, drop.
2 *the chair was draped with blankets:* cover, envelop, swathe, shroud, deck, festoon, overlay, cloak, wind, enfold, sheathe.

drastic adjective *drastic measures were necessary:* extreme, desperate, radical, far-reaching, momentous, serious, substantial; heavy, severe, harsh, rigorous; oppressive, draconian.
OPPOSITES: moderate.

draught noun
1 *the draught made me shiver:* breeze, wind, gust of air, current of air, rush of air.
2 *he took a deep draught of his beer:* gulp, drink, swallow, mouthful; informal swig, slug.

USAGE

Do not confuse **draught** and **draft**. The chief meaning of **draught** is 'a current of air', while **draft** means 'a first version of a piece of writing' (*the first draft of his speech*), or 'to prepare the first version of a piece of writing' (*he drafted a letter of resignation*).

---

draw verb
1 *I drew him lying on the bed:* sketch, make a drawing of, render, represent, portray, depict, outline, illustrate.
2 *she drew her chair in to the table:* pull, haul, drag, tug, heave, trail, tow; informal lug, yank.
3 *the train drew into the station:* move, go, come, proceed, progress, travel, advance, pass, drive; inch, roll, glide, cruise; forge, sweep.
4 *she drew the curtains:* close, shut, pull to; open, part, pull back, fling open.
5 *he drew some fluid off the knee joint:* drain, extract, withdraw, remove, suck, pump, siphon, bleed, tap.
6 *he drew his gun:* pull out, take out, produce, fish out, extract, withdraw; unsheathe.
7 *I drew £50 out of the bank:* withdraw, take out.
8 *she was drawing huge audiences:* attract, interest, win, capture, catch, engage; lure, entice.

9 *what conclusion can we draw?* deduce, infer, conclude, reach, derive, gather, glean.
▷noun
1 *she won the Christmas draw:* raffle, lottery, sweepstake, sweep, tombola, ballot.
2 *the match ended in a draw:* tie, dead heat, stalemate.
3 *the draw of central London:* attraction, lure, allure, pull, appeal, glamour, enticement, temptation, charm, seduction, fascination, magnetism.
□draw on
we can draw on centuries of experience: call on, have recourse to, avail yourself of, turn to, look to, fall back on, rely on, exploit, use, employ, utilize, bring into play.
□draw something out
1 *he drew out a gun.* See **DRAW** verb sense 6.
2 *they always drew their parting out:* prolong, protract, drag out, spin out, string out, extend.
□draw up
a car drew up beside us: stop, pull up, halt, come to a standstill, brake, park.
□draw something up
we drew up a list: compose, formulate, frame, write down, draft, prepare, devise, work out; create, invent, design.

drawback noun *the major drawback to this method is that it can be very time-consuming:* disadvantage, snag, downside, stumbling block, catch, hitch, pitfall, fly in the ointment; weak spot/point, weakness, limitation, trouble, difficulty, problem, complication; informal minus.
OPPOSITES: benefit, advantage.

drawing noun *he did a pencil drawing of the house:* sketch, picture, illustration, representation, portrayal, depiction, composition, study; diagram, outline, design, plan.

drawn adjective *she looked pale and drawn:* pinched, haggard, drained, wan, hollow-cheeked; stressed, strained, tense, worried, anxious, harassed, fraught; tired, fatigued, exhausted.
OPPOSITES: fresh.

dread verb *I used to dread going to school:* fear, be afraid of, worry about, be anxious about; be terrified of, shudder at, shrink from, flinch from; informal get cold feet about.
OPPOSITES: look forward to.
▷noun *she was filled with dread:* fear, apprehension, trepidation, anxiety, worry, concern, foreboding, disquiet, unease, angst; fright, panic, alarm; terror, horror; informal the jitters.
OPPOSITES: confidence.
▷adjective *he was stricken with the dread disease:* awful, terrible, horrible, dreadful; feared, frightening, alarming, terrifying, dire, dreaded.

dreadful adjective
1 *a dreadful accident*: **terrible**, frightful, horrible, grim, awful, dire; horrifying, alarming, shocking, distressing, appalling, harrowing; ghastly, fearful, horrendous; tragic, calamitous; formal grievous.
2 *a dreadful meal*: **very bad**, poor, inadequate, inferior, unsatisfactory; frightful, awful, abysmal, atrocious, disgraceful, deplorable, woeful; disagreeable, nasty, unpleasant, repugnant; informal rotten, sorry, lousy, ropy; Brit. informal shocking, rubbish.
OPPOSITES: pleasant, excellent.

dreadfully adverb
1 (Brit.) *I'm dreadfully hungry*: **extremely**, very, really, exceedingly, terribly, exceptionally, extraordinarily; decidedly, most, particularly; informal terrifically, desperately, awfully; Brit. informal jolly, dead, well.
2 (Brit.) *she missed James dreadfully*: **very much**, a great deal, intensely, desperately; informal a lot.
3 *the company performed dreadfully*: **very badly**, awfully, terribly, atrociously, abominably, appallingly, abysmally, poorly; informal diabolically.

dream noun
1 *I awoke from my dreams*: **vision**, fantasy, reverie, hallucination; nightmare.
2 *she went around in a dream*: **daydream**, reverie, trance, daze, stupor.
3 *he realized his childhood dream*: **ambition**, aspiration, hope, desire, wish, yearning; daydream, fantasy, pipe dream.
▷ verb
1 *I dreamt of making the Olympic team*: **fantasize about**, daydream about; wish for, hope for, long for, yearn for, hanker after, set your heart on.
2 *she's always dreaming*: **daydream**, be in a trance, be lost in thought, be preoccupied, stare into space, muse.
▷ adjective *his dream home*: **ideal**, perfect, fantasy.
□ dream something up
Leroy dreamed up an ingenious solution to the problem: **think up**, invent, concoct, devise, hatch, contrive, create, work out, come up with; informal cook up.

dreamer noun *you're just a bunch of naive dreamers*: **romantic**, sentimentalist, idealist, wishful thinker, fantasist, daydreamer.
OPPOSITES: realist.

dreamlike adjective *the fields were swathed in mist, giving them a strange dreamlike quality*: **unreal**, illusory, imaginary, insubstantial; ethereal, phantasmagorical; surreal; hazy, shadowy, indistinct, unclear.

dreamy adjective
1 *a dreamy recollection*: **dreamlike**, vague,

dim, hazy, shadowy, faint, indistinct, unclear.
2 *he gazed out of the window with a dreamy expression on his face*: **daydreaming**, dreaming; lost in thought, preoccupied, distracted, inattentive, wool-gathering, vague, absorbed, absent-minded, in a world of your own; informal miles away.
OPPOSITES: alert, clear.

dreary adjective
1 *a dreary round of working, eating, and trying to sleep*: **dull**, drab, uninteresting, flat, tedious, wearisome, boring, unexciting, uninspiring, soul-destroying; humdrum, monotonous, uneventful.
2 *a dreary day*: **gloomy**, dismal, dull, dark, dingy, murky, overcast; depressing, sombre.
OPPOSITES: exciting, bright.

dregs plural noun *the dregs from a bottle of wine*: **sediment**, deposit, residue, sludge, lees, grounds, remains.

drench verb *rain was falling fast, drenching the countryside*: **soak**, saturate, wet through, permeate, douse, souse; drown, swamp, inundate, flood; steep, bathe.

dress verb
1 *she was dressed in a navy blue suit*: **clothe**, garb, deck out, turn out, array, robe; formal attire; informal get up.
2 *they dressed his wounds*: **bandage**, cover, bind, wrap.
▷ noun
1 *a long blue dress*: **gown**, robe, shift; Brit. frock.
2 *full evening dress*: **clothes**, clothing, garments; costume, outfit, ensemble, garb, turnout; formal attire; informal gear, get-up.
□ dress something up
the tourist authority has to be very careful how it dresses up the reality of the situation: **present**, represent, portray; embellish, enhance, embroider.

WORD LINKS
sartorial relating to clothes or a person's style of dress

dressing noun
1 *salad dressing*: **sauce**, relish, condiment, dip.
2 *they put fresh dressings on her burns*: **bandage**, covering, compress; Brit. plaster.

dressmaker noun **tailor**, seamstress, needlewoman; outfitter, costumier, clothier; couturier, designer.

dribble verb
1 *his mouth was open and he was dribbling*: **drool**, slaver, slobber, salivate.
2 *rainwater dribbled down her face*: **trickle**, drip, drizzle; ooze, seep, run.

dried adjective **dry**, dehydrated, desiccated.

drift verb
1 *his raft drifted down the river:* **float**, bob, waft, meander, be carried, be borne.
2 *the guests drifted away:* **wander**, meander, stray, potter, stroll, amble.
3 *we seem to be drifting off the subject:* **stray**, deviate, diverge, veer, get side-tracked, digress.
4 *snow drifted over the path:* **pile up**, bank up, heap up, accumulate, gather, amass.
▷noun
1 *a drift from the country to urban areas:* **movement**, shift, flow, transfer, relocation.
2 *he caught the drift of her thoughts:* **gist**, essence, meaning, sense, substance, significance; thrust, direction, import, tenor; implication, intention.
3 *a drift of deep snow:* **pile**, heap, bank, mound, mass, accumulation.

drill noun
1 *parade-ground drill:* **training**, instruction, discipline, practice, exercise, coaching, teaching.
2 *Estelle knew the drill by now:* **procedure**, routine, practice, programme, schedule; method, system.
▷verb
1 *drill the piece of wood:* **bore**, pierce, puncture, penetrate, perforate.
2 *a sergeant was drilling new recruits:* **train**, discipline, exercise, put someone through their paces, instruct, coach, teach.
3 *his mother had drilled politeness into him:* **instil**, hammer, drive, drum, din, implant, ingrain; teach, indoctrinate, brainwash.

drink verb
1 *she drank her coffee:* **swallow**, gulp down, quaff, guzzle, sip, consume; drain; formal imbibe; informal swig, down, sink, toss off, slug.
2 *he never drank:* **drink alcohol**, tipple, indulge; carouse; informal hit the bottle, booze.
▷noun
1 *a selection of hot and cold drinks are available:* **beverage**; humorous libation.
2 *she took a drink of her wine:* **swallow**, gulp, sip, draught; informal swig, slug.
3 *he turned to drink:* **alcohol**, liquor; informal booze.
□**drink something in**
we stood at the window, drinking in the spectacular views: **absorb**, be absorbed in, take in, be rapt in, be lost in, be fascinated by, pay close attention to.

drinker noun *he was a notorious drinker and womanizer:* **drunkard**, drunk, inebriate, tippler, sot; alcoholic, dipsomaniac; informal boozer.
OPPOSITES: teetotaller.

drip verb
1 *a tap was dripping:* **dribble**, leak.
2 *sweat dripped from his chin:* **drop**, dribble, trickle, drizzle, run, splash, plop.

drive verb
1 *I've never driven a van:* **operate**, handle, manage; pilot, steer.
2 *I'll drive you to the airport:* **chauffeur**, run, give someone a lift, take, ferry, transport, convey, carry.
3 *the engine drives the front wheels:* **power**, propel, move, push.
4 *he drove a nail into the boot:* **hammer**, screw, ram, sink, plunge, thrust, propel, knock.
5 *the scandal almost drove him to resign:* **force**, compel, impel, make, prompt, spur.
6 *he drove his staff extremely hard:* **work**, push, tax.
▷noun
1 *an afternoon drive:* **excursion**, outing, trip, jaunt, tour; ride, run, journey; informal spin.
2 *the house has a long drive:* **driveway**, approach, access road.
3 *sexual drive:* **urge**, appetite, desire, need, impulse, instinct.
4 *she lacked the drive to succeed:* **motivation**, ambition, single-mindedness, willpower, dedication, doggedness, tenacity; enthusiasm, zeal, commitment, aggression, spirit; energy, vigour; informal get-up-and-go.
5 *an anti-corruption drive:* **effort**, push, initiative, movement, appeal, campaign, crusade.
□**drive at**
I can see what you're driving at but you're quite wrong: **suggest**, imply, hint at, allude to, intimate, insinuate, indicate; refer to, mean, intend, assert, claim; informal get at.

drivel noun *he was talking complete drivel:* **nonsense**, claptrap, balderdash, rubbish; N. Amer. garbage; informal poppycock, twaddle, piffle, tripe, baloney; Brit. informal rot, codswallop, tosh.
▷verb *you always drivel on:* **talk nonsense**, babble, ramble, gibber, blather, prattle; Brit. informal waffle, witter.

driver noun **motorist**, chauffeur; pilot, operator.

drizzle noun *Scotland will be cloudy with patchy drizzle:* **fine rain**, light showers.
▷verb
1 *it's beginning to drizzle:* **rain lightly**, spot; Brit. spit.
2 *drizzle the cream over the jelly:* **trickle**, drip, dribble, pour, splash, sprinkle.

droll adjective *a droll comment:* **funny**, humorous, amusing, comical; zany, quirky; jocular, witty, whimsical, wry, tongue-in-cheek; informal wacky.
OPPOSITES: serious.

drone verb
1 *a plane droned overhead:* **hum**, buzz, whirr, vibrate, murmur, rumble, purr.
2 *he droned on about right and wrong:*

talk at length, go on and on; intone, pontificate; informal spout, sound off.
▷ noun *the drone of aircraft taking off:* hum, buzz, whirr, vibration, murmur, rumble, purr.

drool verb *stay away from animals that appear to be drooling:* salivate, dribble, slaver, slobber.
▷ noun *a fine trickle of drool:* saliva, spit, spittle, dribble, slaver, slobber.

droop verb *his shaggy hair drooped over his eyes | the hydrangeas were beginning to droop in the heat:* hang, hang down, dangle, sag, flop, fall; bend down, wilt, sink, slump, become limp.

droopy adjective dangling, falling, dropping, draped; bent, bowed, stooping; sagging, flopping, wilting.

drop verb
1 *Eric dropped the box:* let fall, let go of, lose your grip on, release.
2 *a plane dropped out of the sky:* fall, descend, plunge, plummet, dive, nosedive, tumble, pitch.
3 *she dropped to her knees:* fall, sink, collapse, slump, tumble.
4 *the track dropped from the ridge:* slope downwards, descend, go down, fall away, sink, dip.
5 *the exchange rate dropped:* reduce, lessen, decrease, diminish; fall, decline, dwindle, sink, slump, plunge, plummet.
6 *pupils can drop history if they wish:* give up, withdraw from, abandon; discontinue, end, stop; Brit. finish with.
7 *the charity has decided to drop the word 'Royal' from its official title:* exclude, leave out, discard, omit, miss out.
8 *he dropped his unsuitable friends:* abandon, desert, throw over, renounce, disown, turn your back on, shun, reject, give up, neglect.
OPPOSITES: lift, rise, increase.
▷ noun
1 *a drop of water:* droplet, blob, globule, bead, bubble, tear, dot.
2 *it needs a drop of oil:* small amount, little, bit, dash, spot; dribble, sprinkle, trickle, splash; dab, speck, smattering, sprinkling.
3 *a small drop in profits:* reduction, decrease, decline, fall-off, downturn, slump; cut, cutback, curtailment.
OPPOSITES: increase.
□ drop back/behind
Alonso dropped behind his team-mate after the first lap:
fall back/behind, get left behind, lag behind; straggle, linger, dawdle, dally, hang back, loiter, bring up the rear; informal dilly-dally.

droppings plural noun excrement, excreta, faeces, stools, dung, ordure, manure.

dross noun *there are bargains if you have the patience to sift through the dross:*
rubbish, junk, bric-a-brac; debris, chaff, detritus; N. Amer. garbage, trash; informal bits and pieces; Brit. informal odds and ends.

drove noun
1 *a drove of cattle:* herd, flock.
2 *droves of tourists descend on the national park every year:* crowd, swarm, horde, multitude, mob, throng, host, mass, army, herd.

drown verb
1 *when the ice melted the valleys were drowned:* flood, submerge, immerse, inundate, deluge, swamp, engulf.
2 *his voice was drowned out by the engine noise:* make inaudible, smother, mask, muffle, stifle, extinguish, silence.

drowse verb *they like to drowse in the sun:* doze, nap, catnap, sleep lightly, rest; informal snooze; Brit. informal kip.
▷ noun *she had been woken from her drowse:* doze, nap, catnap, light sleep, rest; informal snooze; Brit. informal kip.

drowsy adjective
1 *the tablet made her drowsy:* sleepy, dozy, heavy-eyed, groggy, somnolent.
2 *a drowsy afternoon:* sleepy, soporific, sleep-inducing.
OPPOSITES: alert, invigorating.

drubbing noun *I gave him a good drubbing:* beating, thrashing, walloping, thumping, battering, pounding, pummelling, slapping, punching; informal belting, bashing, pasting, kicking.

drudge noun *a household drudge:* menial, slave, servant, labourer, lackey, minion, underling, galley slave; Brit. informal dogsbody, skivvy.

drudgery noun *a life of domestic drudgery:* hard work, menial work, toil, labour; chores; Brit. informal graft, skivvying, donkey work.

drug noun
1 *drugs prescribed by doctors:* medicine, medication, medicament; remedy, cure, antidote.
2 *she was under the influence of drugs:* narcotic, stimulant, hallucinogen; informal dope, gear.
▷ verb
1 *they were drugged to keep them quiet:* anaesthetize; knock out; informal dope.
2 *she drugged his coffee:* lace, doctor, poison, adulterate, contaminate, tamper with; informal dope, spike.

WORD LINKS
pharmacology the branch of medicine concerned with drugs
pharmaceutical relating to medicinal drugs

drum noun
1 *the steady drum of raindrops:* beat, rhythm, patter, tap, pounding, tattoo,

thump, thud, rattle, pitter-patter.
2 *a drum of radioactive waste:* canister, barrel, cylinder, tank, bin, can.
▷**verb**
1 *she drummed her fingers on the desk:* tap, beat, rap, thud, thump.
2 *the rules were drummed into us at school:* instil, drive, din, hammer, drill, ingrain, inculcate.
□**drum something up**
organizers are hoping to drum up support from local businesses: generate, attract, gather, canvass; get, obtain, win.

drunk adjective *they went to a pub and got drunk:* intoxicated, inebriated, drunken, incapable, tipsy, under the influence, the worse for drink; euphemistic tired and emotional; informal tight, merry, three sheets to the wind, plastered, wrecked, hammered, sloshed, sozzled; Brit. informal legless, paralytic.
OPPOSITES: sober.
▷**noun** *we staggered up the path like a couple of drunks:* drunkard, inebriate, drinker, tippler; heavy drinker, problem drinker, alcoholic, dipsomaniac; informal boozer, soak.
OPPOSITES: teetotaller.

drunkenness noun inebriation, intoxication, tipsiness; insobriety, intemperance, overindulgence; heavy drinking, alcoholism, alcohol abuse, dipsomania.

dry adjective
1 *much of the land is dry and rocky, making it unsuitable for growing crops:* arid, parched, scorched, baked; drought-affected, waterless; dehydrated.
2 *they heard the crunching of dry leaves:* dried, withered, shrivelled, wilted; brittle; dehydrated, desiccated.
3 *the dry scientific facts:* bare, simple, basic, fundamental, stark, bald.
4 *a dry debate over technicalities that the average film fan has never heard of:* dull, uninteresting, boring, unexciting, tedious, tiresome, wearisome, dreary, monotonous; unimaginative, sterile, flat, bland, lacklustre, stodgy, prosaic, humdrum, mundane; informal deadly.
5 *a dry sense of humour:* wry, subtle, laconic, sharp; ironic, sardonic, sarcastic, cynical; satirical, mocking, droll; informal waggish.
OPPOSITES: wet, moist, lively.
▷**verb** *chlorine, salt water, sun, and humidity can dry out skin and hair:* dehydrate, desiccate; parch, scorch, bake; dehumidify.
OPPOSITES: wet, moisten.

dual adjective *their dual role at work and home:* double, twin, twofold, binary; duplicate, matching, paired, coupled.
OPPOSITES: single.

dub verb *he was dubbed 'the world's sexiest man':* call, name, nickname, label, christen,

term, tag, entitle, style; designate, characterize as, nominate.

dubious adjective
1 *I was rather dubious about the idea:* doubtful, uncertain, unsure, hesitant, undecided, indefinite, unresolved, up in the air, vacillating, irresolute; sceptical, suspicious.
2 *dubious business practices:* suspicious, suspect, questionable, irregular, disreputable, untrustworthy, unreliable; informal shady, fishy; Brit. informal dodgy.
OPPOSITES: certain, trustworthy.

duck verb
1 *he ducked behind the wall:* bob down, bend down, crouch down, squat, hunker down.
2 *they ducked her in the river:* dip, dunk, plunge, immerse, submerge, lower, sink.

duct noun *a ventilation duct:* tube, channel, canal, vessel, conduit, culvert, pipe, pipeline, outlet, inlet, flue, shaft, vent.

due adjective
1 *their fees were due:* owing, owed, payable; outstanding, overdue, unpaid, unsettled, undischarged.
2 *the chancellor's statement is due today:* expected, anticipated, scheduled, awaited; required.
3 *the respect due to a great artist:* deserved by, merited by, warranted by; appropriate to, fit for, fitting for, right for, proper to.
4 *he drove without due care:* proper, correct, suitable, appropriate, apt, rightful; adequate, sufficient, enough, satisfactory, requisite.
▷**noun**
1 *he died in Venice having failed to receive the recognition he believed was his due:* right, entitlement, rightful treatment, reward.
2 *members have paid their dues in full:* fee, subscription, charge; payment, contribution.
□**due to**
1 *her death was due to an infection:* caused by, because of, attributable to, ascribed to, put down to.
2 *the train was cancelled due to staff shortages:* because of, owing to, on account of, as a consequence of, as a result of, thanks to, in view of.

duel noun
1 *he was killed in a duel:* single combat, head-to-head; informal face-off, shoot-out.
2 *a snooker duel:* contest, match, game, meet, encounter, struggle, tussle; Brit. derby.

dulcet adjective (often ironic) *the Grand Duchess Anna spoke in dulcet tones:* sweet, soothing, mellow, honeyed, mellifluous, euphonious, pleasant; melodious, melodic, lilting, lyrical, silvery, golden.
OPPOSITES: harsh.

d

dull adjective
1 *a dull novel:* uninteresting, boring, tedious, monotonous, unrelieved, unvaried, unimaginative, uneventful; characterless, featureless, colourless, lifeless, insipid, unexciting, uninspiring, unstimulating, flat, bland, dry, stale, tired, banal, lacklustre, stodgy, dreary, humdrum, mundane; mind-numbing, soul-destroying, wearisome, tiring, tiresome, irksome; informal deadly; Brit. informal samey.
2 *it was a miserably dull Saturday morning:* overcast, cloudy, gloomy, dark, dismal, grey, murky, sunless.
3 *dull colours:* drab, dreary, sombre, dark, subdued, muted, lacklustre, faded, washed out, muddy.
4 *a dull sound:* muffled, muted, quiet, soft, faint, indistinct; stifled, suppressed.
5 *the chisel became dull:* blunt, worn.
OPPOSITES: interesting, bright, resonant, sharp.

▷ verb
1 *the pain was dulled by drugs:* lessen, reduce, blunt, deaden, allay, ease, soothe, assuage, alleviate, decrease, diminish.
2 *sleep dulled her mind:* numb, benumb, deaden, desensitize, stupefy, daze.
OPPOSITES: intensify, enliven.

duly adverb *the document was duly signed:* properly, correctly, as required, appropriately, suitably, fittingly, as expected, as predicted.

dumb adjective *she stood dumb while he shouted:* mute, speechless, tongue-tied, silent, at a loss for words; taciturn, uncommunicative, tight-lipped; informal mum.

dumbfounded adjective *when you told me I had won I was dumbfounded:* astonished, astounded, amazed, staggered, surprised, startled, stunned, confounded, nonplussed, taken aback, dumbstruck, open-mouthed, speechless, thunderstruck; informal flabbergasted, knocked sideways; Brit. informal gobsmacked.

dummy noun
1 *a shop-window dummy:* mannequin, model, figure, doll; Art manikin.
2 *the book is just a dummy:* mock-up, imitation, likeness, lookalike, representation; substitute, sample, copy, model, toy, replica, reproduction; counterfeit, sham, fake, forgery.
▷ adjective *a dummy attack on the airfield:* simulated, feigned, pretended, practice, trial, mock, make-believe; informal pretend, phoney.
OPPOSITES: real.

dump noun
1 *take the rubbish to the dump:* tip, rubbish dump, rubbish heap, dumping ground, landfill, recycling centre.

2 (informal) *the house is a dump:* hovel, shack, slum; mess; informal hole, pigsty.
▷ verb
1 *he dumped his bag on the table:* put down, set down, deposit, place, shove, unload; drop, throw down; informal stick; Brit. informal plonk, bung.
2 *they will dump asbestos at the site:* dispose of, get rid of, throw away/out, discard, jettison; informal ditch.

dumpy adjective *that skirt makes you look dumpy and middle-aged:* short, squat; plump, stout, chubby, chunky, portly, fat; informal tubby; Brit. informal podgy.
OPPOSITES: tall, slender.

dunce noun *they all called him a dunce at school:* fool, idiot, dolt, ignoramus, simpleton; informal dope, ninny, nincompoop, dimwit, halfwit, dummy, blockhead, airhead, moron, imbecile; Brit. informal nit, nitwit, twit, clot.
OPPOSITES: genius.

dune noun *sand dunes:* bank, mound, hillock, hummock, knoll, ridge, heap, drift.

dung noun *manure,* muck; excrement, excreta, faeces, droppings, stools, ordure.

dungeon noun prison, oubliette; cell, jail, lock-up.

dupe verb *they were duped by a con man:* deceive, trick, hoodwink, hoax, swindle, defraud, cheat, double-cross; mislead, take in, fool; informal con, do, rip off, diddle.
▷ noun *an unwitting dupe in her game:* victim, fool, innocent; informal sucker; Brit. informal mug, muggins.

duplicate noun *a duplicate of the invoice:* copy, carbon copy, photocopy, facsimile, reprint; replica, reproduction, clone; trademark Xerox, photostat.
▷ adjective *a duplicate key:* identical, matching, twin, second, corresponding, equivalent.
▷ verb
1 *she will duplicate the newsletter:* copy, photocopy, photostat, xerox, reproduce, replicate, reprint.
2 *a feat difficult to duplicate:* repeat, redo, replicate.

duplicity noun *he made frequent observations about the duplicity of publicists:* dishonesty, deceit, deception, double-dealing, underhandedness, fraud, fraudulence, sharp practice, chicanery, trickery, subterfuge, skulduggery, treachery; informal crookedness, dirty tricks.
OPPOSITES: honesty.

durability noun toughness, robustness, sturdiness, solidity, strength, resilience, permanence, integrity, imperishability, longevity.
OPPOSITES: fragility.

durable adjective
1 *durable carpets:* hard-wearing, heavy-duty, tough, robust, sturdy, stout, solid, strong, indestructible, long-lasting, imperishable.
2 *a durable peace:* lasting, long-lasting, long-term, enduring, persistent, abiding; stable, secure, firm, permanent.
OPPOSITES: delicate, short-lived.

duration noun *the students' fees will be paid for the duration of their course:* length, time, period, term, span, extent; continuation.

duress noun *their confessions were extracted under duress:* coercion, compulsion, force, pressure, intimidation, constraint; threats; informal arm-twisting.

during preposition *the exhibit attracted 5,000 visitors during January:* throughout, through, in, during the course of, for the duration of, in the course of.

dusk noun twilight, nightfall, sunset, sundown, evening, close of day; gloom; literary gloaming.
OPPOSITES: dawn.

dusky adjective *the men prowled menacingly round a dusky stage:* shadowy, twilit, dark, dim, gloomy, murky, shady, unlit, unilluminated; sunless, moonless.
OPPOSITES: bright.

dust noun *the desk was covered in dust:* dirt, grime, grit, powder.
▷verb *dust the cake with icing sugar:* sprinkle, scatter, powder, dredge, sift, cover, strew.

dusty adjective
1 *the floor was very dusty:* dirty, grimy, grubby, mucky.
2 *dusty sandstone:* powdery, crumbly, chalky, friable; granular, gritty, sandy.

dutiful adjective *she helped out, as a dutiful daughter should:* conscientious, responsible, dedicated, devoted, faithful, attentive, respectful, good, obedient, compliant.
OPPOSITES: remiss.

duty noun
1 *it is my duty to uphold the law:* responsibility, obligation, commitment.
2 *he seems to have no sense of duty:* loyalty, allegiance, faith, fidelity.
3 *your duties will include operating the switchboard:* job, task, assignment, function, charge, role, responsibility, accountability.
4 *the duty was raised on alcohol:* tax, levy, tariff, excise, toll, rate; dues.
□ off duty
not working, at leisure, on holiday, on leave, off work, free.
□ on duty
working, at work, busy, occupied, engaged.

dwarf adjective *dwarf conifers:* miniature, small, tiny, toy, pocket, diminutive, baby, pygmy, stunted, undersized; Scottish wee; informal mini, micro, teeny, teeny-weeny; Brit. informal titchy.
OPPOSITES: giant.
▷verb
1 *the buildings dwarf the trees:* dominate, tower over, loom over, overshadow.
2 *her progress was dwarfed by her sister's success:* overshadow, outshine, surpass, exceed, outclass, outstrip, outdo, top, trump, transcend.

USAGE
The use of **dwarf** to mean 'an unusually small person' is normally considered to be offensive, as are **midget** or **pygmy**. However, no term has been established as a generally acceptable alternative: **person of restricted growth** has not gained wide currency. Words such as **homunculus** or **manikin** are sometimes found in literary or old-fashioned writing.

dwell verb (formal) *they currently dwell in the village of Petersburgh in New York State:* reside, live, be settled, be housed, lodge, stay; formal abide, be domiciled.
□ dwell on
Katherine had no time to dwell on her disappointment: linger over, mull over, muse on, brood about/over, think about; be preoccupied by, be obsessed by, eat your heart out over; harp on about, discuss at length.

dwindle verb *the population dwindled:* diminish, decrease, decline, reduce, lessen, shrink, contract; fall off, drop, slump; disappear, vanish, die out.
OPPOSITES: increase.

dye noun *a blue dye:* colouring, colourant, colour, dyestuff, pigment, tint, stain, wash.
▷verb *the gloves were dyed:* colour, tint, pigment, stain, wash.

dying adjective
1 *his dying aunt:* terminally ill, at death's door, on your deathbed, near death, fading fast, expiring, moribund, not long for this world, in extremis; informal on your last legs, with one foot in the grave.
2 *a dying art form:* declining, vanishing, fading, ebbing, waning; informal on the way out.
3 *her dying words:* final, last; deathbed.

dynamic adjective *he was eclipsed by his more dynamic colleagues:* energetic, vigorous, forceful, powerful, positive, spirited, active, lively, vital; high-powered, aggressive, bold, enterprising; magnetic, passionate, fiery, high-octane; informal go-getting, go-ahead.
OPPOSITES: half-hearted.

dynamism noun energy, vigour, forcefulness, power, spirit, liveliness, vitality; aggression, drive, ambition,

d

enterprise; magnetism, passion, fire; informal get-up-and-go.

dynasty noun *he was the fourth king of the Shang dynasty:* family, house, line, ancestral line, bloodline, lineage, ancestry, descent, succession, reign.

dyspeptic adjective *a rather dyspeptic senator put the blame on his European counterpart:* bad-tempered, irritable, testy, tetchy, touchy, crabby, crotchety, grouchy, cantankerous, peevish, cross; informal snappish.

d

Ee

each pronoun *there are 5000 books and each must be cleaned:* every one, each one, each and every one, all, the whole lot.
▷**determiner** *he visited each month:* every, each and every, every single.
▷**adverb** *it costs £20 each:* apiece, per person, per capita, individually, respectively.

eager adjective
1 *she was eager to talk to him:* keen, anxious, impatient, longing, determined; informal itching, dying.
2 *the grandstands were filled with thousands of eager fans:* expectant, hopeful, enthusiastic, avid; on the edge of your seat, on tenterhooks, on pins and needles.
OPPOSITES: apathetic.

eagerness noun keenness, enthusiasm, avidity; impatience, desire, longing, hunger, appetite, ambition.

ear noun *he still had the ear of the president:* attention, notice, heed, regard, consideration.
□ **play it by ear** improvise, extemporize, ad lib; make it up as you go along, think on your feet; informal busk it, wing it.

> WORD LINKS
> **aural**, **auditory** relating to the ears or to the sense of hearing

early adjective
1 *early copies of the book:* advance, forward; initial, preliminary, first; pilot, trial.
2 *an early death:* untimely, premature, unseasonable, before time.
3 *the study of early man:* primitive, ancient, prehistoric, primeval.
OPPOSITES: late, overdue.
▷**adverb**
1 *I've got to get up early:* in the early morning, in the small hours; at dawn, at daybreak, with the lark.
2 *we arrived two hours early:* before the usual time; prematurely, too soon, ahead of time, ahead of schedule, in advance.
OPPOSITES: late.

earmark verb *the cash had been earmarked for a big expansion programme:* set aside, keep back, reserve; designate, assign,

mark; allocate, allot, devote, pledge.

earn verb
1 *they earned £30,000:* be paid, take home, gross; receive, get, make, bring in, obtain, collect; informal pocket, bank, rake in, net.
2 *he has earned their trust:* gain, win, secure, obtain, get; deserve, merit, warrant, justify, be worthy of.
OPPOSITES: lose, forfeit.

earnest adjective
1 *an earnest young philosophy student:* serious, solemn, grave, sober, humourless, staid; intense; committed, dedicated, keen, diligent, zealous; thoughtful, cerebral, deep, profound.
2 *an earnest plea for tolerance and understanding:* heartfelt, wholehearted, sincere, impassioned, fervent, ardent, urgent.
OPPOSITES: frivolous, half-hearted.

earnings plural noun *they lived off his wife's earnings:* income, wages, salary, pay, payment, fees, remuneration, stipend; revenue, yield, profit, takings, proceeds, dividends, return.

earth noun
1 *the moon orbits the earth:* world, globe, planet.
2 *the pilot brought the plane gently back to earth:* land, ground, terra firma.
3 *a layer of earth:* soil, clay, loam; dirt.

> WORD LINKS
> **terrestrial** relating to the earth

earthly adjective
1 *the earthly environment:* terrestrial.
2 *the promise of earthly delights:* worldly, temporal, mortal, human; material; carnal, fleshly, bodily, physical, corporeal, sensual.
3 (informal) *there is no earthly explanation for this:* feasible, possible, likely, conceivable, imaginable.
OPPOSITES: extraterrestrial, heavenly.

earthquake noun tremor, shock; aftershock, convulsion; informal quake.

> WORD LINKS
> **seismic** relating to earthquakes
> **seismology** the branch of science concerned with earthquakes

earthy adjective *her earthy sensuality is intoxicating | an earthy sense of humour:* direct, uninhibited, unselfconscious, down-to-earth; bawdy, ribald, racy.

ease noun
1 *he defeated them all with ease:* effortlessness, no trouble, no problem; facility.
2 *a life of ease:* affluence, wealth, prosperity, luxury, plenty; comfort, contentment, enjoyment, well-being.
OPPOSITES: difficulty, trouble, hardship.
▷verb
1 *the alcohol eased his pain:* relieve, alleviate, mitigate, soothe, palliate, moderate, dull, deaden, numb; reduce, lighten, diminish.
2 *the rain eased off:* abate, subside, die down, let up, slacken off, diminish, lessen, peter out, relent, come to an end.
3 *work helped to ease her mind:* calm, quieten, pacify, soothe, comfort.
4 *we want to ease their adjustment to a new life:* facilitate, expedite, assist, help, aid, make easier, simplify.
5 *he eased out the cork:* guide, manoeuvre, inch, edge; slide, slip, squeeze.
6 *he eased his grip on my shoulder:* relax, slacken, loosen.
OPPOSITES: aggravate, worsen, hinder.
□ **at ease/at your ease**
relaxed, calm, serene, tranquil, unworried, contented, content, happy; comfortable.

easily adverb
1 *I overcame this problem easily:* effortlessly, comfortably, with ease, without difficulty, without a hitch, smoothly.
2 *he's easily the best:* undoubtedly, without doubt, without question, indisputably, undeniably, definitely, certainly, clearly, obviously; by far, far and away, by a mile.

eastern adjective east, easterly.

> **USAGE**
> See the note at **ORIENTAL**.

easy adjective
1 *downloading the software is very easy:* simple, straightforward, elementary, uncomplicated, undemanding, painless; effortless, trouble-free, plain sailing; informal easy as pie, a piece of cake, child's play, kids' stuff, a cinch, a doddle, a breeze; Brit. informal easy-peasy.
2 *he's such an easy baby:* docile, manageable, amenable, tractable, compliant, pliant, acquiescent, obliging, cooperative, easy-going.
3 *an easy target:* vulnerable, susceptible, defenceless; naive, gullible, trusting.
4 *Vic's easy manner made everyone feel at home:* natural, easy-going, amiable, affable, genial, good-humoured, friendly, casual, informal, unaffected, unreserved, uninhibited; carefree, nonchalant,

unconcerned; informal laid-back.
5 *an easy life:* calm, tranquil, serene, quiet, peaceful, untroubled, contented, relaxed, comfortable, secure, safe; informal cushy.
6 *the walkers set off at an easy pace:* leisurely, unhurried, comfortable, undemanding, easy-going, gentle, sedate, moderate, steady.
OPPOSITES: difficult, demanding, formal.

easy-going adjective *Fred was easy-going and a pleasure to work with:* relaxed, even-tempered, placid, mellow, mild, happy-go-lucky, carefree, free and easy, nonchalant, imperturbable; undemanding, accommodating, patient, tolerant, lenient, broad-minded, understanding; amiable, affable, friendly, good-natured, pleasant, agreeable; informal laid-back, unflappable.
OPPOSITES: intolerant.

eat verb
1 *we ate a hearty breakfast | he was eating a hamburger:* consume, devour; gobble up/down, bolt down, wolf down; swallow, chew, munch; feast on; formal partake of; informal tuck into, polish off, guzzle, scoff, put away, demolish, pig out on, get stuck into; N. Amer. informal scarf.
2 *they ate at a local restaurant:* have a meal, dine.
3 *acidic water can eat away at pipes:* erode, corrode, wear away, burn through, consume, dissolve; damage, destroy.

eatable adjective *the toast's a bit burnt but it's eatable:* edible, palatable, digestible; fit to eat, fit for human consumption.

eavesdrop verb *we tried to eavesdrop on his conversation:* listen in on, overhear; monitor, tap, record; informal bug.

ebb verb
1 *the tide ebbed:* recede, go out, retreat, flow back, fall back/away, subside.
2 *her strength was ebbing away:* diminish, dwindle, wane, fade away, peter out, decline, flag, decrease, weaken, subside.
OPPOSITES: increase.

ebony adjective *she tossed her thick ebony hair:* black, jet black, pitch black, coal black, inky, sooty, raven, dark; literary sable.

ebullience noun *the director's ebullience was a fantastic morale booster for the cast:* exuberance, buoyancy, cheerfulness, cheeriness, merriment, jollity, light-heartedness, high spirits; vivacity, enthusiasm, animation.

ebullient adjective *she was in a typically ebullient mood:* exuberant, buoyant, upbeat, cheerful, joyful, cheery, merry, jolly, sunny, jaunty, light-hearted, elated; animated, sparkling, vivacious, irrepressible, bubbly, bouncy; informal chirpy, full of beans.
OPPOSITES: depressed.

eccentric adjective *eccentric behaviour:* unconventional, abnormal, irregular, aberrant, anomalous, odd, queer, strange, peculiar, bizarre, outlandish, extraordinary; idiosyncratic, quirky, offbeat, nonconformist, outré; informal weird; Brit. informal rum.
OPPOSITES: conventional.
▷ noun *he was something of an eccentric:* oddity, individualist, nonconformist, free spirit; misfit; informal oddball.

eccentricity noun unconventionality, oddness, strangeness, quirkiness; peculiarity, foible, idiosyncrasy, quirk.

ecclesiastical adjective *his ecclesiastical duties:* priestly, ministerial, clerical, canonical, sacerdotal; church, religious, spiritual, holy, divine.

echelon noun *he reached the upper echelons of government:* level, rank, grade, step, rung, tier, position, order.

echo noun
1 *the hills sent back a faint echo of my shout:* reverberation, reflection, repetition, repeat.
2 *he saw an echo of his own childhood experience in Smith's troubled family life:* suggestion, reminder; parallel, similarity, repetition, repeat.
▷ verb
1 *his laughter echoed round the room:* reverberate, resonate, resound, reflect, ring.
2 *Bill echoed Rex's words:* repeat, restate, reiterate; quote, reproduce.

eclectic adjective *her musical tastes are eclectic | the college offers an eclectic mix of courses:* wide-ranging, broad-based, extensive, comprehensive, encyclopedic; varied, diverse, catholic, all-embracing, multifaceted, multifarious, heterogeneous, miscellaneous, assorted.

eclipse verb
1 *the sun was eclipsed by the moon:* blot out, block, cover, obscure, hide, conceal, obliterate, darken; shade.
2 *the success of this opera was eclipsed by the triumph of his next work:* outshine, overshadow, put into the shade, surpass, exceed, outclass, outstrip, outdo, top, trump, transcend, upstage.

economic adjective
1 *the government's economic policy:* financial, monetary, budgetary, fiscal.
2 *the firm cannot remain economic:* profitable, moneymaking; solvent, viable, cost-effective.
OPPOSITES: unprofitable.

economical adjective
1 *an economical car | economical prices:* cheap, inexpensive, low-cost, budget, economy, economic; cut-price, discount, bargain.

2 *a very economical shopper:* thrifty, provident, prudent, sensible, careful, frugal, sparing.
OPPOSITES: expensive, spendthrift.

economize verb *they economized by growing their own vegetables:* save money, cut costs; cut back, make cutbacks, retrench, budget, make economies, be thrifty, be frugal, scrimp, tighten your belt, draw in your horns, watch the/your pennies.

economy noun
1 *the nation's economy:* wealth, financial resources; financial system, financial management.
2 *one can combine good living with economy:* thrift, thriftiness, providence, prudence, careful budgeting, economizing, saving, restraint, frugality.
OPPOSITES: extravagance.

ecstasy noun *there was a look of ecstasy on his face | they went into ecstasies over the view:* rapture, bliss, elation, euphoria, joy, jubilation, exultation; transports, rhapsodies.
OPPOSITES: misery.

ecstatic adjective *ecstatic fans filled the stadium:* euphoric, elated, in raptures, rapturous, joyful, overjoyed, blissful; on cloud nine, in seventh heaven, beside yourself with joy, jumping for joy, delighted, thrilled, exultant; informal over the moon, on top of the world, blissed out.

eddy noun *the current was forming eddies along the bank:* swirl of water; whirlpool, vortex.
▷ verb *cold air eddied around her:* swirl, whirl, spiral, twist; flow, ripple.

edge noun
1 *the edge of the lake:* border, boundary, fringe, margin, side; lip, rim, brim, brink, verge; perimeter, circumference, periphery, limits, bounds, extremity.
2 *she had an edge in her voice:* sharpness, pointedness, severity, bite, sting.
3 *they have an edge over their rivals:* advantage, lead, head start, the whip hand, the upper hand; superiority, dominance, ascendancy, supremacy.
OPPOSITES: middle, disadvantage.
▷ verb
1 *poplars edged the orchard:* border, fringe; surround, enclose, encircle, circle, bound, encompass.
2 *a shawl edged with lace:* trim, pipe, decorate, finish; border, fringe; bind, hem.
3 *he edged closer to the fire:* creep, inch, work your way, pick your way, ease yourself; sidle, steal, slink.
□ **on edge**
the crowd was on edge: tense, nervous, edgy, anxious, apprehensive, uneasy, unsettled; twitchy, jumpy, nervy, keyed up, restive, skittish; informal uptight, wired.

edgy adjective

1 *she seemed edgy and paced to and fro:* tense, nervous, on edge, anxious, apprehensive, uneasy, unsettled; twitchy, jumpy, nervy, keyed up, restive, skittish; irritable, touchy, tetchy, prickly; informal uptight, wired.
2 (informal) *the track confirms that the band has lost none of its edgy style:* unconventional, original, innovative, cutting-edge, contemporary, sharp; avant-garde, experimental; informal left-field.
OPPOSITES: calm.

edible adjective *are these mushrooms edible?* safe to eat, fit for human consumption, eatable; digestible, palatable.
OPPOSITES: inedible.

edict noun *in 1762 a royal edict compelled the clergy to contribute a fifth of their income to charitable purposes:* decree, order, command, commandment, mandate, dictate, fiat; ruling, injunction, law, statute, act.

edifice noun (formal) **building**, structure, construction, erection, pile; property, development, premises.

edit verb

1 *parts of the text still need to be edited:* correct, check, copy-edit, emend; modify, adapt, revise, rewrite, reword, rework, redraft; shorten, condense, cut, abridge; informal clean up.
2 *he is currently editing a collection of essays on the poet Ronald Johnson:* select, choose, assemble, organize, put together.
3 *he edited The Times for many years:* be the editor of, direct, run, manage, head, lead, preside over.

edition noun *the early editions of tomorrow's papers:* issue, number, impression, publication; version, revision; volume.

educate verb *they decided to educate their children at home | a plan to educate young people on the dangers of drugs:* teach, school, tutor, instruct, train; guide, inform.

educated adjective *he was an educated and articulate man:* informed, well read, learned, knowledgeable, enlightened, cultivated, cultured, erudite; literate.

education noun *the education of young children:* teaching, schooling, tuition, tutoring, instruction, coaching, training, tutelage, guidance.

WORD LINKS
pedagogic relating to education

educational adjective

1 *an educational establishment:* academic, scholastic, teaching, pedagogic; instructional.
2 *an educational experience:* instructive, educative, informative, illuminating, enlightening.

eerie adjective *an eerie silence descended over the house:* uncanny, sinister, ghostly, unnatural, unearthly, weird, other-worldly; strange, abnormal, odd; frightening, spine-chilling, hair-raising, blood-curdling, terrifying; informal creepy, scary, spooky.

efface verb

1 *the words were effaced by the rain:* erase, eradicate, expunge, blot out, rub out, wipe out, remove, eliminate, obliterate.
2 *he attempted to efface himself:* make yourself inconspicuous, keep out of sight, keep out of the limelight, lie low, keep a low profile.

effect noun

1 *the effect of rapid social change:* result, consequence, upshot, outcome, repercussions, ramifications; end result, corollary, aftermath; fruits, product, by-product; formal concomitant; informal pay-off.
2 *the effect of the drug was wearing off:* impact, action, effectiveness; power, potency, strength; formal efficacy.
3 *the experience had a profound effect on all three men:* impact, influence; impression.
4 *they went through the dead man's effects:* belongings, possessions, worldly goods, chattels; property, paraphernalia; informal gear, things, stuff.
OPPOSITES: cause.
▷**verb** *they effected many changes:* bring about, carry out, implement, put into effect, achieve, accomplish, execute, engineer, perform; cause, create, produce, make, initiate.
□**in effect**
1 *the ban has been in effect since last June:* in force, effective, in operation, operational.
2 *in effect, he called the president a liar:* really, in reality, in truth, in fact, effectively, essentially, in essence, basically.
□**take effect**
1 *these measures will take effect in May:* come into force, come into operation, be implemented, begin, become valid, become law, apply, be applied.
2 *the drug started to take effect:* work, act, be effective, produce results.

USAGE

Do not confuse **effect** and **affect**. **Effect** is used both as a noun meaning 'a change which is the result of something' and as a verb meaning 'to bring something about'. **Affect** is a verb whose chief meaning is 'to make a difference to' (*climate change will affect the lives of millions*).

effective adjective

1 *an effective treatment for a wide range of psychological conditions:* successful, effectual, potent, powerful; helpful, beneficial, advantageous, valuable, useful; formal efficacious.
2 *a more effective argument:* convincing,

compelling, strong, forceful, potent, weighty, sound, valid, logical, coherent, cogent; impressive, persuasive, plausible, credible.
3 *the new law will be effective next week:* operative, in force, in effect; valid, official, lawful, legal, binding.
4 *the companies were under effective Soviet control:* virtual, practical, actual; implicit, tacit.
OPPOSITES: ineffective, weak, invalid.

effectiveness noun *it can be difficult to assess the effectiveness of advertising:* success, productiveness, potency, power; benefit, advantage, value, usefulness.

effectual adjective *tobacco smoke is the most effectual protection against midges:* effective, successful, productive; worthwhile, helpful, beneficial, advantageous, valuable, useful.
OPPOSITES: ineffectual.

effeminate adjective *as his manicured fingers played with the gold medallion around his neck, he looked very effeminate:* womanish, effete, unmanly, foppish, mincing; informal camp, limp-wristed.
OPPOSITES: manly.

effervesce verb *heat the mixture until it effervesces:* fizz, sparkle, bubble; froth, foam.

effervescence noun
1 *this wine is bone dry with a little effervescence:* fizz, fizziness, sparkle, bubbliness.
2 *his cheeky effervescence:* vivacity, liveliness, animation, high spirits, ebullience, exuberance, buoyancy, sparkle, gaiety, jollity, cheerfulness, enthusiasm, irrepressibility, vitality, energy, zest.

effervescent adjective
1 *an effervescent drink:* fizzy, sparkling, carbonated, aerated, gassy, bubbly; (of wine) mousseux, pétillant, spumante.
2 *effervescent young people:* vivacious, lively, animated, high-spirited, bubbly, upbeat, ebullient, buoyant, sparkling, light-hearted, jaunty, happy, jolly, cheery, cheerful, perky, sunny, enthusiastic, irrepressible, energetic, bouncy; informal chirpy, full of beans.
OPPOSITES: still, depressed.

effete adjective
1 *if you like French films about effete members of the bourgeoisie performing Pirandello you'll be disappointed:* affected, pretentious, precious, mannered, over-refined; informal pseud; Brit. informal poncey.
2 *an effete young man:* effeminate, feminine, girlish, unmanly, weak; informal wimpish, wimpy.
OPPOSITES: manly.

efficiency noun
1 *we need reforms to improve efficiency:* productivity, effectiveness, cost-effectiveness.
2 *I compliment you on your efficiency:* competence, capability, powers of organization, proficiency.

efficient adjective
1 *an efficient method of storing and retrieving information:* streamlined, effective, cost-effective, productive; organized, systematic; slick, smooth-running, well oiled.
2 *an efficient secretary:* competent, capable, able, organized, well organized, methodical, businesslike, proficient.
OPPOSITES: inefficient, incompetent.

effigy noun *they venerate an effigy of the saint:* statue, statuette, sculpture, model, figurine; likeness, image.

effluent noun waste, sewage, effluvium.

effort noun
1 *they made an effort to fix the problem:* attempt, try, endeavour; informal crack, shot, stab, bash.
2 *achieving good results will require considerable time and effort:* exertion, energy, work, endeavour, application, labour, toil, strain; informal sweat, elbow grease; Brit. informal graft.
3 *his score was a fine effort:* achievement, accomplishment, attainment, result; undertaking, enterprise, performance.

effortless adjective *he made his elaborate dance routines look so effortless:* easy, undemanding, unchallenging, simple, straightforward, elementary, uncomplicated, painless; fluent, natural; informal child's play, kids' stuff, a cinch, no sweat, a doddle, a breeze; Brit. informal easy-peasy.
OPPOSITES: difficult.

effrontery noun *one of the jurors had the effrontery to challenge the coroner's authority:* impudence, impertinence, cheek, insolence, audacity, temerity, presumption, gall, impoliteness, disrespect, bad manners; informal brass neck, nerve, face.

effusion noun
1 *an effusion of poisonous gas:* outflow, outpouring, emission, discharge, rush, current, flow.
2 *reporters' flamboyant effusions:* outburst, outpouring, flight of fancy.

effusive adjective *Salma was effusive in her praise of everyone who had worked on the project:* gushing, unrestrained, extravagant, fulsome, lavish, enthusiastic, lyrical; expansive, demonstrative; informal over the top, OTT.
OPPOSITES: restrained.

egg noun ovum; gamete; (**eggs**) roe, spawn.
□ **egg someone on**
both men were being egged on by the crowd:

urge, encourage, spur on, prompt, push, drive; incite, provoke, prod, goad.

WORD LINKS
oval, **ovate**, **ovoid** egg-shaped

ego noun *the criticism was a blow to his ego:* self-esteem, self-importance, self-worth, self-respect, self-image, self-confidence.

egocentric adjective *he's probably another egocentric rich boy who's used to getting everything he wants:* self-centred, egotistic, self-interested, selfish, self-seeking, self-absorbed, self-obsessed; narcissistic, vain, self-important.
OPPOSITES: altruistic.

egotism, **egoism** noun *in his arrogance and egotism, he underestimated Gill:* self-centredness, egomania, egocentricity, self-interest, selfishness, self-regard, self-obsession; self-love, narcissism, self-admiration, vanity, conceit, self-importance.

egotist, **egoist** noun *it's a sport that breeds egotists and exhibitionists:* narcissist, egomaniac, egocentric, self-seeker; informal big-head.

egotistic, **egoistic** adjective self-centred, selfish, egocentric, self-interested, self-seeking, self-absorbed, self-obsessed; narcissistic, vain, conceited, self-important.

egregious adjective *an egregious error of judgement:* shocking, appalling, terrible, awful, dreadful, horrendous, unforgivable; atrocious, abominable, outrageous, monstrous, heinous, unspeakable, shameful, intolerable.

egress noun
1 *the egress from the gallery was blocked:* exit, way out, escape route.
2 *a means of egress:* departure, exit, withdrawal, retreat; escape.
OPPOSITES: entrance.

eight cardinal number octet.

WORD LINKS
octagon an eight-sided figure

eject verb
1 *the volcano ejected lumps of lava:* emit, spew out, discharge, give off, send out, belch out; expel, release, disgorge.
2 *they were ejected from the hall:* throw out, turn out, remove, expel, evict; informal chuck out, kick out, turf out, boot out.
3 *the pilot had time to eject:* bail out, escape, get out.

ejection noun
1 *the ejection of electrons:* emission, discharge, release.
2 *their ejection from the ground:* expulsion, removal; eviction.

eke verb *I had to eke out my remaining funds:* use sparingly, be frugal with, be

sparing with, use economically, husband, be thrifty with; informal go easy on.
OPPOSITES: squander.
□ **eke out a living**
some farmers eke out a living by growing rice on small patches of land: subsist, survive, get by, scrape by, make ends meet, keep body and soul together, keep the wolf from the door, keep your head above water.

elaborate adjective
1 *an elaborate plan:* complicated, complex, intricate, involved; detailed, painstaking, careful; tortuous, convoluted, Byzantine.
2 *an elaborate plasterwork ceiling:* ornate, decorated, embellished, ornamented, fancy, fussy, busy, ostentatious, extravagant, showy, baroque, rococo, florid.
OPPOSITES: simple, plain.
▷ **verb** *both sides refused to elaborate on their reasons:* expand on, enlarge on, add to, flesh out, put flesh on the bones of, add detail to, expatiate on; develop, fill out, amplify.

elan noun *they played with great elan:* flair, style, panache, confidence, éclat; energy, vigour, vitality, liveliness, brio, esprit, animation, vivacity, zest, verve, spirit, enthusiasm, gusto, eagerness, feeling; informal pizzazz, oomph.

elapse verb *a month elapsed before the appeal hearing began:* pass, go by/past, wear on, slip by/away/past, roll by/past, slide by/past, tick by/past.

elastic adjective
1 *elastic material:* stretchy, elasticated, springy, flexible, pliant, pliable, supple, yielding, resilient.
2 *an elastic concept of nationality:* adaptable, flexible, adjustable, variable, fluid, accommodating, versatile.
OPPOSITES: rigid.

elasticity noun
1 *the skin's natural elasticity:* stretchiness, flexibility, pliancy, suppleness, resilience, springiness, give.
2 *the elasticity of the term:* adaptability, flexibility, adjustability, fluidity, versatility.

elated adjective *she's in the early stages of pregnancy and is said to be elated:* thrilled, delighted, overjoyed, ecstatic, euphoric, very happy, gleeful, jubilant, beside yourself, exultant, rapturous, in raptures, walking on air, on cloud nine, in seventh heaven, jumping for joy, in transports of delight; literary joyous; informal on top of the world, over the moon, on a high.
OPPOSITES: miserable.

elation noun euphoria, ecstasy, happiness, delight, transports of delight, joy, glee, jubilation, exultation, bliss, rapture; literary joyousness.

elbow verb *he elbowed his way through the crowd:* push, shove, force, shoulder, jostle, barge, muscle, bulldoze.

elbow room noun *selling these players for about £35m would give him some elbow room in the transfer market:* room to manoeuvre, room, space, breathing space, scope, freedom, play, free rein, licence, latitude, leeway; informal wiggle room.

elder adjective *his elder brother:* older, senior; big.
▷noun *the church elders:* leader, senior figure, patriarch, father.

elderly adjective *her elderly mother:* aged, old, advanced in years, ageing, long in the tooth, past your prime; grey-haired, grizzled, hoary; in your dotage, decrepit, doddering, doddery, senescent; informal getting on, past it, over the hill, no spring chicken.
OPPOSITES: youthful.
▷noun (**the elderly**) old people, senior citizens, pensioners, OAPs, retired people.

elect verb
1 *the country has elected a new president:* vote in, vote for, return, cast your vote for; choose, pick, select.
2 *she elected to stay behind:* choose, decide, opt, vote.
▷adjective *the president elect:* future, -to-be, designate, chosen, elected, coming, next, appointed, presumptive.
▷noun (**the elect**) the chosen, the elite, the favoured; the crème de la crème.

election noun *he was defeated in the 1992 election:* ballot, vote, popular vote; poll; Brit. by-election; US primary.

> WORD LINKS
> **psephology** the statistical study of elections

electioneering noun *the election will not be lost or won as a result of a few weeks of electioneering:* campaigning, canvassing, going on the hustings.

elector noun *each elector has one vote:* voter, member of the electorate, constituent.

electric adjective *the atmosphere was electric:* exciting, charged, electrifying, thrilling, heady, intoxicating, stirring, dramatic; tense, knife-edge, explosive, volatile.

electrify verb *his masterpiece was a revolutionary work that electrified cinema audiences around the world:* excite, thrill, stimulate, arouse, rouse, inspire, stir, stir up, exhilarate, intoxicate, galvanize, move, fire, fire someone's imagination; startle, jolt, shock; informal give someone a buzz, give someone a kick.

elegance noun
1 *he was attracted by her elegance:* style,

stylishness, grace, gracefulness, taste, tastefulness, sophistication, chic.
2 *the elegance of the idea:* neatness, simplicity; ingenuity.

elegant adjective
1 *an elegant black outfit:* stylish, graceful, tasteful, sophisticated, classic, chic, smart, fashionable; attractive, artistic, aesthetic, well designed.
2 *an elegant solution:* neat, simple, effective; ingenious, clever, deft, intelligent, inventive.
OPPOSITES: inelegant, clumsy.

elegy noun *he wrote an elegy for his father:* lament, requiem, funeral poem/song, dirge, threnody.

element noun
1 *an essential element of the local community | the affair had all the elements of a great tabloid story:* component, constituent, part, section, piece, bit; aspect, factor, feature, facet, ingredient, strand, detail, point; member, unit, module, item.
2 *there is an element of truth in this stereotype:* trace, touch, hint, smattering, soupçon.
3 (**elements**) *the elements of political science:* basics, essentials, principles, first principles; foundations, fundamentals, rudiments; informal nuts and bolts, ABC.
4 *I braved the elements:* the weather, the climate; the wind, the rain.

elemental adjective
1 *an elemental truth:* basic, primary, fundamental, essential, root, underlying.
2 *elemental forces:* natural, atmospheric, meteorological, environmental.

elementary adjective
1 *an elementary astronomy course:* basic, rudimentary; introductory, beginners', entry-level.
2 *a lot of the work is elementary:* easy, simple, straightforward, uncomplicated, undemanding, child's play, plain sailing; informal a piece of cake, no sweat, kids' stuff; Brit. informal easy-peasy.
OPPOSITES: advanced, difficult.

elevate verb
1 *a conveyor belt is used to elevate the grain into storage bins:* raise, lift, upraise; hoist, haul up, hike up.
2 *he was elevated to Secretary of State:* promote, upgrade, advance, move up, raise, prefer; ennoble, exalt, aggrandize.
OPPOSITES: lower, demote.

elevated adjective
1 *an elevated motorway:* raised, upraised, high up; overhead.
2 *elevated language:* lofty, grand, exalted, fine, noble; inflated, pompous, bombastic, orotund.
3 *the gentry were conscious of their elevated status:* high, higher, high-ranking, of high

e

standing, lofty, superior, exalted, eminent, grand.
OPPOSITES: lowly.

elevation noun
1 *his recent elevation to the peerage:* promotion, upgrading, advancement, advance, preferment, aggrandizement, ennoblement; informal step up the ladder.
2 *elevations in excess of 3000 metres:* height, altitude, hill, mountain, mount.

elfin adjective *her short hair accentuated her elfin face:* small, dainty, delicate, petite, little, tiny, slight, diminutive.

elicit verb *the appeal has already elicited a fantastic response from the public:* obtain, draw out, evoke, extract, bring out, prompt, generate, trigger, provoke; formal or literary call forth.

eligible adjective
1 *those people eligible to vote:* entitled, permitted, allowed, qualified, able.
2 *an eligible bachelor:* desirable, suitable; available, single, unmarried, unattached, unwed.
OPPOSITES: ineligible.

eliminate verb
1 *a policy that would eliminate inflation:* remove, get rid of, put an end to, do away with, end, stop, terminate, eradicate, destroy, annihilate, stamp out, wipe out, extinguish; informal knock something on the head.
2 *he was eliminated from the race:* knock out, beat; exclude, rule out, disqualify.

elite noun *the party attracted the elite of London society:* best, pick, cream, crème de la crème, flower, nonpareil; high society, jet set, beautiful people, beau monde, haut monde; aristocracy, nobility, upper class.
OPPOSITES: dregs.

elixir noun *an elixir guaranteed to induce love:* potion, concoction, brew, philtre, decoction, mixture; medicine, tincture; extract, essence, concentrate, distillate, distillation.

elliptical adjective *elliptical phraseology:* cryptic, ambiguous, obscure, oblique, Delphic; terse, concise, succinct, compact, economic, laconic, sparing.

elocution noun *she had lessons in singing and elocution:* pronunciation, enunciation, articulation, diction, speech, vocalization.

elongate verb
1 *an exercise that elongates the muscles:* lengthen, extend, stretch.
2 *the high notes were elongated:* prolong, protract, draw out, sustain.
OPPOSITES: shorten.

eloquence noun *he was known for the eloquence of his sermons:* fluency, articulacy, articulateness, expressiveness, persuasiveness, power; oratory, rhetoric.

eloquent adjective
1 *an eloquent speaker | an eloquent speech:* fluent, articulate, expressive, silver-tongued; persuasive, strong, forceful, powerful, potent, well expressed, effective, lucid, vivid, graphic; smooth-tongued, glib.
2 *her glance was more eloquent than words:* expressive, meaningful, suggestive, revealing, telling, significant, indicative.
OPPOSITES: inarticulate.

elsewhere adverb *the negatives are stored in one place, and the prints are kept elsewhere:* somewhere else, in/at/to another place, in/at/to a different place; not here, not present, absent, away, out.
OPPOSITES: here.

elucidate verb *collections of letters can elucidate what was uppermost in an artist's mind:* explain, make clear, illuminate, throw/shed light on, clarify, clear up, sort out, unravel; spell out; interpret.
OPPOSITES: confuse.

elucidation noun explanation, clarification, illumination; interpretation.

elude verb *he tried to elude the security guard by sneaking through a back door:* evade, avoid, get away from, dodge, escape from; lose, shake off, give the slip to, slip away from, throw off the scent; informal slip through someone's fingers, slip through the net.

elusive adjective
1 *her elusive husband:* difficult to find; evasive, slippery; informal always on the move.
2 *an elusive quality:* indefinable, intangible, impalpable; ambiguous.

emaciated adjective *the captives were sick and emaciated:* thin, skeletal, bony, gaunt, wasted, thin as a rake; scrawny, skinny, scraggy, skin-and-bones, raw-boned; starved, underfed, undernourished, underweight, half-starved; cadaverous, shrivelled, shrunken, withered; informal like a bag of bones.
OPPOSITES: fat.

emanate verb
1 *warmth emanated from the fireplace:* issue, spread, radiate, be sent out.
2 *they have no evidence that the leaks emanated from the administration itself:* originate, stem, be produced, proceed, issue, emerge, come.
3 *he emanated an air of power:* exude, emit, radiate, give off/out, send out/forth.

emanation noun
1 *she saw the insults as emanations of his own tortured personality:* product, consequence, result, fruit.
2 *the risk of radon gas emanation:* discharge, emission, radiation, effusion, outflow, outpouring, flow, leak.

emancipate verb *the serfs privately owned by members of the nobility were*

emancipated: free, liberate, set free, release, deliver; unchain, unfetter, unshackle, unyoke.
OPPOSITES: enslave.

emancipated adjective liberated, independent, unconstrained, uninhibited; free.

emasculate verb *an Act which emasculated the House of Lords:* weaken, enfeeble, debilitate, undermine; remove the sting from, pull the teeth of; informal water down.

embankment noun bank, mound, ridge, earthwork, causeway, barrier, levee, dam, dyke.

embargo noun *an embargo on oil sales:* ban, bar, prohibition, veto, moratorium, stoppage, interdict, proscription; restriction, block, barrier; boycott.
▷verb *arms sales were embargoed:* ban, bar, prohibit, stop, interdict, debar, proscribe, outlaw; restrict, block, obstruct; boycott.
OPPOSITES: allow.

embark verb
1 *he embarked at Dover:* board ship, go on board, go aboard.
2 *he embarked on a new career:* begin, start, commence, undertake, set about, take up, turn your hand to, get down to; enter into, venture into, launch into, plunge into, engage in, settle down to; informal get going on.

embarrass verb *I kept quiet because I didn't want to embarrass him:* humiliate, make uncomfortable, make self-conscious, mortify, shame, put someone to shame, discomfit; informal show up.

embarrassed adjective *I felt embarrassed when I talked to her:* mortified, ashamed, shamefaced, humiliated, chagrined, awkward, self-conscious, uncomfortable, not knowing where to look, sheepish, red-faced, blushing, abashed, discomfited; informal with egg on your face.

embarrassing adjective *an embarrassing mistake:* humiliating, shaming, shameful, mortifying, ignominious; awkward, uncomfortable, compromising; informal blush-making, cringeworthy, cringe-making, toe-curling.

embarrassment noun
1 *he was scarlet with embarrassment:* mortification, humiliation, shame, shamefacedness, chagrin, self-consciousness, sheepishness, discomfort, discomfiture; ignominy.
2 *his current financial embarrassment:* difficulty, predicament, plight, problem, mess; informal fix.

embassy noun *the Italian embassy:* consulate, legation, ministry.

embed, **imbed** verb *two bullets had embedded themselves in his torso:* implant,
fix, lodge, root, insert; sink, drive.

embellish verb
1 *he wore a crimson satin jacket richly embellished with gold chains and buttons:* decorate, adorn, ornament; beautify, enhance, grace; trim, garnish, gild; deck, bedeck, festoon, emblazon.
2 *the legend was embellished by an American academic:* elaborate, embroider, expand on, exaggerate.

embellishment noun
1 *architectural embellishments:* decoration, ornamentation, adornment; beautification, enhancement, trimming, trim, garnishing, gilding.
2 *we wanted the truth, not romantic embellishments:* elaboration, exaggeration, addition.

ember noun *the fire's dying embers:* glowing coal, live coal; cinder; (**embers**) ashes.

embezzle verb *she had embezzled £50,000 of company funds:* misappropriate, steal, thieve, pilfer, appropriate, defraud someone of, siphon off, pocket, help yourself to; put your hand in the till; formal purloin; informal pinch, rob, rip off, skim; Brit. informal nick.

embezzlement noun *an investigation into the alleged embezzlement of union funds:* misappropriation, theft, stealing, robbery, thieving, pilfering, appropriation; fraud; N. Amer. larceny.

embittered adjective *he died a lonely and embittered man:* bitter, resentful, rancorous, jaundiced, aggrieved, sour, frustrated, dissatisfied, disaffected, disillusioned.

emblazon verb
1 *shirts emblazoned with the company name:* adorn, decorate, ornament, embellish; inscribe.
2 *a flag with a hammer and sickle emblazoned on it:* display, depict, show.

emblem noun *the white rose was the emblem of the Yorkist side:* symbol, representation, sign, token, image, mark; insignia, crest, badge, device, stamp, seal, coat of arms, shield; logo, trademark.

emblematic adjective
1 *a situation that was emblematic of the industrialized twentieth century:* symbolic, representative, demonstrative, indicative; typical.
2 *emblematic works of art:* allegorical, symbolic, metaphorical, figurative.

embodiment noun *she was the living embodiment of '80s values:* personification, incarnation, realization, manifestation, expression, representation, actualization, symbol; paradigm, epitome, paragon, soul, model; type, essence, quintessence, exemplification, example, exemplar, ideal.

embody verb

1 *Gradgrind embodies the spirit of industrial capitalism:* personify, realize, manifest, symbolize, represent, express, concretize, be the incarnation of, epitomize, stand for, typify, exemplify.
2 *the changes in law embodied in the Children Act:* incorporate, include, contain, encompass; combine.

embolden verb *emboldened by the brandy, he walked over to her table:* fortify, make brave/braver, encourage, hearten, strengthen, brace, stiffen the resolve of, lift the morale of; rouse, stir, stimulate, cheer, rally, fire, animate, invigorate; informal buck up.
OPPOSITES: dishearten.

embrace verb

1 *he embraced her warmly:* hug, take/hold in your arms, hold, cuddle, clasp to your bosom, clasp, squeeze, clutch; caress; enfold, enclasp, encircle, envelop, entwine yourself around.
2 *most western European countries have embraced the concept:* welcome, accept, take up, take to your heart, adopt; espouse, support, back, champion.
3 *the faculty embraces a wide range of departments:* include, take in, comprise, contain, incorporate, encompass, cover, involve.
▷ noun *a fond embrace:* hug, cuddle, squeeze, clinch, caress; bear hug.

embrocation noun ointment, lotion, cream, rub, salve, liniment, balm.

embroider verb

1 *a cushion embroidered with a pattern of golden keys:* sew, stitch; decorate, adorn, ornament, embellish.
2 *she embroidered her stories with colourful detail:* elaborate, embellish, enlarge on, exaggerate, touch up, dress up, gild, colour; informal jazz up.

embroidery noun

1 *the girls were taught embroidery:* needlework, needlepoint, needlecraft, sewing, tapestry.
2 *fanciful embroidery of the facts:* elaboration, embellishment, adornment, ornamentation, colouring, enhancement; exaggeration, overstatement, hyperbole.

embroil verb *she became embroiled in a dispute between the two women:* involve, entangle, ensnare, enmesh, catch up, mix up, bog down, mire.

embryo noun

1 *a human embryo:* fetus, fertilized egg, unborn child/baby.
2 *the embryo of a capitalist economy:* germ, nucleus, seed; rudimentary version, rudiments, basics, beginning, start.

embryonic adjective

1 *an embryonic chick:* fetal, unborn, unhatched.
2 *an embryonic pro-democracy movement:* rudimentary, undeveloped, unformed, immature, incomplete, inchoate; fledgling, budding, nascent, emerging, developing, early, incipient, germinal.
OPPOSITES: mature.

emend verb *the journalistic practice of emending quotations in the areas of grammar and syntax:* correct, rectify, repair, fix, amend; edit, rewrite, revise, copy-edit, subedit, redraft, recast, rephrase, reword, rework, alter, change.

emerge verb

1 *a police officer emerged from the alley:* come out, appear, come into view, become visible, materialize, manifest yourself, issue, come forth.
2 *several unexpected facts emerged | it emerged that the two men were still at loggerheads:* become known, become apparent, be revealed, come to light, come out, transpire, unfold, turn out, prove to be the case.

emergence noun *the emergence of the environmental movement:* appearance, arrival, coming; advent, inception, dawn, birth, origination, start, beginning, development, rise.

emergency noun *a military emergency:* crisis, urgent situation, extremity; accident, disaster, catastrophe, calamity; difficulty, plight, predicament; formal exigency; informal panic stations.
▷ adjective
1 *an emergency meeting:* urgent, crisis; impromptu, extraordinary.
2 *emergency supplies:* reserve, standby, backup, fallback, in reserve.

emergent adjective *an emergent capitalist economy:* emerging, developing, rising, dawning, budding, embryonic, infant, fledgling, nascent, incipient.

emigrate verb *her parents emigrated to Australia:* move abroad, move overseas, leave your country, migrate; relocate, resettle; defect.
OPPOSITES: immigrate.

emigration noun moving abroad, moving overseas, expatriation, migration; exodus, diaspora; relocation, resettling; defection.

eminence noun *his eminence as a scientist:* renown, pre-eminence, fame, illustriousness, distinction, notability, greatness, prestige, importance, reputation, repute, note; prominence, superiority, stature, standing.

eminent adjective

1 *one of the world's most eminent statisticians:* illustrious, distinguished,

renowned, esteemed, pre-eminent, notable, noteworthy, great, prestigious, important, influential, outstanding, noted, of note; famous, celebrated, prominent, well known, lionized, acclaimed, exalted, revered, august, venerable.
2 *the eminent reasonableness of their claims:* obvious, clear, conspicuous, marked, singular; total, complete, utter, absolute, thorough, perfect, downright, sheer.
OPPOSITES: unknown.

eminently adverb *he was an eminently successful businessman:* very, highly, exceedingly, extremely, particularly, exceptionally, supremely, uniquely; obviously, clearly, conspicuously, markedly, singularly, outstandingly, strikingly, notably; totally, completely, utterly, absolutely, thoroughly, perfectly.

emissary noun *he sent an emissary to Constantinople for bilateral talks:* envoy, ambassador, delegate, attaché, consul; agent, representative, deputy; messenger, courier.

emission noun *targets for reducing carbon dioxide emissions:* discharge, release, outpouring, outflow, leak; emanation, effusion.

emit verb
1 *the hydrocarbons emitted from vehicle exhausts:* discharge, release, give out/off, pour out, throw out, void, vent, issue; leak, ooze, excrete, disgorge, secrete, eject; spout, belch, spew out; emanate, radiate, exude.
2 *he emitted a loud cry:* utter, voice, let out, produce, come out with, vocalize.
OPPOSITES: absorb.

emotion noun
1 *she was good at hiding her emotions:* feeling, sentiment; reaction, response.
2 *overcome by emotion, she turned away:* passion, strength of feeling, warmth of feeling.
3 *responses have to be based on historical insight, not simply on emotion:* instinct, intuition, gut feeling; sentiment, the heart.

emotional adjective
1 *he paid an emotional tribute to his wife:* poignant, moving, touching, affecting, powerful, heart-rending, impassioned; haunting.
2 *an emotional young man:* passionate, excitable, highly strung, temperamental, tempestuous, melodramatic; demonstrative, responsive, tender, loving, sentimental, sensitive.
OPPOSITES: cold, unfeeling.

emotionless adjective *a flat, emotionless voice:* unemotional, unfeeling, dispassionate, passionless, cool, cold, cold-blooded, impassive, indifferent, detached, remote, aloof; toneless, flat, dead, expressionless, blank, wooden, stony, deadpan, vacant.

emotive adjective *fox-hunting is an emotive issue:* controversial, contentious, inflammatory; sensitive, delicate, difficult, problematic, touchy, awkward, prickly.

empathize verb *counsellors need to be able to empathize with people:* identify with, understand, share someone's feelings, be in tune with; be on the same wavelength as, talk the same language as; relate to, feel for, sympathize with, have insight into; informal put yourself in someone else's shoes.

emperor noun ruler, sovereign, king, monarch, potentate.

> WORD LINKS
> **imperial** relating to an emperor

emphasis noun
1 *the curriculum gave more emphasis to reading and writing:* prominence, importance, significance, value; stress, weight, accent, attention, priority, pre-eminence.
2 *the emphasis is on the word 'little':* stress, accent, accentuation, weight; beat.

emphasize verb *the prime minister emphasized his commitment to reform:* stress, underline, highlight, focus attention on, point up, lay stress on, draw attention to, spotlight, foreground, play up, make a point of; bring to the fore, insist on; accent, accentuate, underscore; informal press home, rub it in.
OPPOSITES: understate.

emphatic adjective
1 *he issued an emphatic denial:* vehement, firm, wholehearted, forceful, forcible, vigorous, direct, insistent; certain, definite, out-and-out; decided, determined, categorical, unqualified, unconditional, unequivocal, unambiguous, absolute, explicit, downright, outright, clear.
2 *an emphatic victory:* conclusive, decisive, decided, unmistakable; resounding.
OPPOSITES: hesitant, narrow.

empire noun
1 *the Ottoman Empire:* kingdom, realm, dominion, territory; power, world power, superpower.
2 *the president of a worldwide shipping empire:* organization, corporation, multinational, conglomerate, consortium, company, business, firm, operation.

> WORD LINKS
> **imperial** relating to an empire

empirical adjective *they provided empirical evidence to support their argument:* experiential, practical, first-hand, hands-on; observed, seen; formal heuristic.
OPPOSITES: theoretical.

employ verb
1 *she employed a chauffeur:* hire, engage,

recruit, take on, secure the services of, sign up, sign, put on the payroll, enrol, appoint; retain.
2 *Sam was employed in carving a stone figure:* occupy, engage, involve, keep busy, tie up; absorb, engross, immerse.
3 *the team employed subtle psychological tactics:* use, utilize, make use of, avail yourself of; apply, exercise, practise, put into practice, exert, bring into play, bring to bear; draw on, resort to, turn to, have recourse to.
OPPOSITES: dismiss.

employed adjective *employed married women tend to delay their childbearing:* working, in work, in employment, holding down a job; earning, waged.

employee noun *the firm supports employees who show ambition:* worker, member of staff, member of the workforce; (**employees**) personnel, staff, workforce; informal liveware.

employer noun *the largest private sector employer in Sheffield:* firm, company, business, organization, manufacturer.

employment noun
1 *if you're not computer-literate it can often be it difficult to find employment:* work, a job, a post, a position, a situation; occupation, profession, trade, business, line of work.
2 *the employment of children:* hiring, hire, engagement, taking on; apprenticing.

emporium noun shop, store, outlet, retail outlet; department store, supermarket, superstore, megastore; establishment; Brit. hypermarket.

empower verb
1 *the Act empowered Henry to punish heretics:* authorize, entitle, permit, allow, license, mandate; qualify, enable, equip.
2 *movements to empower the poor:* emancipate, unshackle, set free, liberate.
OPPOSITES: forbid.

empress noun ruler, sovereign, queen, monarch, potentate.

emptiness noun *she had filled an emptiness in his life:* void, vacuum, empty space, gap, hole, vacancy.

empty adjective
1 *an empty house | the streets were empty of traffic:* vacant, unoccupied, uninhabited, untenanted; bare, desolate, deserted, abandoned; clear, free.
2 *an empty threat | his empty promises:* meaningless, hollow, idle, vain, futile, worthless, useless, insubstantial, ineffective, ineffectual.
3 *without her my life is empty:* futile, pointless, purposeless, worthless, meaningless, valueless, of no value, useless, of no use, aimless, senseless, hollow.
OPPOSITES: full, worthwhile.

▷**verb**
1 *I emptied the dishwasher:* unload, unpack; clear.
2 *he emptied out the contents of the case:* remove, take out, extract, tip out, pour out.
OPPOSITES: fill.

empty-headed adjective *certain types of men treat me like some empty-headed bimbo:* stupid, foolish, silly, unintelligent, idiotic, brainless, witless, vacuous, vapid, feather-brained, scatterbrained, thoughtless; informal half-witted, dumb, dim, dippy, dizzy, dopey, dozy, soft in the head; Brit. informal daft, scatty; N. Amer. informal ditzy.
OPPOSITES: intelligent.

emulate verb *she tried to emulate Lucy's glowing performance:* imitate, copy, mirror, echo, follow, model yourself on, take a leaf out of someone's book; match, equal, parallel, be on a par with, be in the same league as, come close to; compete with, contend with, rival, surpass.

enable verb *the Act enabled ordinary citizens to operate radio stations:* allow, permit, let, give the means to, equip, empower, make able, fit; authorize, entitle, qualify.
OPPOSITES: prevent.

enact verb
1 *the Bill was enacted in 1963:* pass, make law; approve, ratify, sanction, authorize; impose, lay down.
2 *members of the church enacted a nativity play:* act out, act, perform, appear in, stage, mount, put on, present.
OPPOSITES: repeal.

enactment noun
1 *the enactment of a Bill of Rights:* passing; ratification, sanction, approval, authorization; imposition.
2 *parliamentary enactments:* act, law, by-law, ruling, rule, regulation, statute, measure; (**enactments**) legislation.
3 *the enactment of the play:* acting, performing, performance, staging, presentation.

enamoured adjective *she was secretly enamoured of the prince:* in love with, infatuated with, besotted with, smitten with, captivated by, enchanted by, fascinated by, bewitched by, beguiled by; keen on, taken with; informal mad about, crazy about, wild about, bowled over by, struck on, sweet on, carrying a torch for.

encampment noun *they planned an attack on the enemy's encampment:* camp, military camp, bivouac, cantonment; campsite, camping ground; tents.

encapsulate verb
1 *their conclusions are encapsulated in one sentence:* summarize, sum up, give the gist of, put in a nutshell; capture, express.
2 *seeds encapsulated in resin:* enclose,

encase, contain, envelop, enfold, sheathe, cocoon, surround.

enchant verb *the play continued to enchant all who watched it:* captivate, charm, delight, enrapture, entrance, enthral, beguile, bewitch, fascinate, hypnotize, mesmerize, rivet, grip, transfix; informal bowl someone over.
OPPOSITES: bore.

enchanter noun wizard, witch, sorcerer, warlock, magician, necromancer, magus.

enchanting adjective captivating, charming, delightful, bewitching, beguiling, adorable, lovely, attractive, appealing, engaging, winning, fetching, winsome, alluring, irresistible, fascinating.

enchantment noun
1 *a race of giants skilled in enchantment:* magic, witchcraft, sorcery, wizardry, necromancy; charms, spells, incantations.
2 *the enchantment of the garden by moonlight:* allure, delight, charm, beauty, attractiveness, appeal, fascination, irresistibility, magnetism, pull, draw, lure.
3 *being with him was sheer enchantment:* bliss, ecstasy, heaven, rapture, joy.

encircle verb *medieval walls encircle the town:* surround, enclose, circle, girdle, ring, encompass; close in, shut in, fence in, wall in, hem in, confine.

enclose verb
1 *tall trees enclosed the garden:* surround, circle, encircle, ring, girdle, encompass; confine, close in, shut in, fence in, wall in, hedge in, hem in.
2 *please enclose a stamped addressed envelope:* include, insert, put in; send.

> WORD LINKS
> **claustrophobia** fear of enclosed spaces

enclosure noun *they drove the animals into the enclosure:* paddock, fold, pen, compound, stockade, ring, yard; sty, coop; N. Amer. corral.

encompass verb
1 *debates encompassing a vast range of subjects:* cover, embrace, include, incorporate, take in, contain, comprise, involve, deal with.
2 *soon the fog moved in, encompassing the entire landscape:* surround, cover; contain.

encounter verb
1 *we encountered a slight problem:* experience, run into, come up against, face, be faced with, confront.
2 *on the plane back to Boston he encountered one of his old Harvard professors:* meet, meet by chance, run into, come across/upon, stumble across/on, chance on, happen on; informal bump into.
▷ noun
1 *an unexpected encounter:* meeting, chance meeting.

2 *a violent encounter between police and demonstrators:* battle, fight, clash, confrontation, conflict, struggle, skirmish; informal run-in, set-to.

encourage verb
1 *the players were encouraged by the crowd's response:* hearten, cheer, reassure, buoy up, uplift, inspire, motivate, spur on, stir, stir up, fire up, stimulate, invigorate, vitalize, revitalize, embolden, fortify, rally; informal buck up, pep up, give someone a shot in the arm.
2 *she had encouraged him to go:* persuade, urge, press, coax, push, egg on; pressure, pressurize.
3 *the Government was keen to encourage local businesses:* support, promote, foster, nurture, cultivate, strengthen, stimulate; help, assist, aid, boost, fuel.
OPPOSITES: discourage, dissuade, hinder.

encouragement noun
1 *she needed a bit of encouragement:* reassurance, support, cheering up, inspiration; morale-boosting; informal a shot in the arm.
2 *they required no encouragement to get back to work:* persuasion, coaxing, urging; spur, inducement, incentive, bait; informal carrot.
3 *the encouragement of foreign investment:* support, promotion, fostering, nurture, cultivation, stimulation; help, assistance.

encouraging adjective
1 *an encouraging start:* promising, hopeful, auspicious, propitious, favourable, bright, rosy; heartening, reassuring, cheering, comforting, welcome, pleasing, gratifying.
2 *my parents were very encouraging:* supportive, understanding, helpful; positive, responsive, enthusiastic.

encroach verb *she didn't want to encroach on his privacy:* intrude, trespass, impinge, obtrude, impose yourself, invade, infringe, violate, interfere with, disturb; tread/step on someone's toes; informal horn in on, muscle in on.

encroachment noun intrusion, trespass, invasion, incursion, infringement, impingement.

encumber verb
1 *her movements were encumbered by her heavy skirts:* hamper, hinder, obstruct, impede, cramp, inhibit, restrict, limit, constrain, restrain, slow down; inconvenience, disadvantage, handicap.
2 *they are encumbered with debt:* burden, load, weigh down, saddle; overwhelm, overload, overburden; Brit. informal lumber.

encumbrance noun
1 *he soon found the old equipment a great encumbrance:* hindrance, obstruction, obstacle, impediment, constraint,

handicap, inconvenience, nuisance, disadvantage, drawback.
2 *she knew she was an encumbrance to him*: burden, responsibility, obligation, liability, weight, load, stress, strain, pressure, trouble, worry; millstone, albatross, cross to bear.

encyclopedic adjective *he has an encyclopedic knowledge of classical music*: comprehensive, complete, thorough, full, exhaustive, in-depth, wide-ranging, all-inclusive, all-embracing, all-encompassing, vast.

end noun
1 *the end of the novel*: conclusion, ending, finish, close; termination; resolution, climax, finale, culmination, denouement; epilogue, coda.
2 *the edge of the forest | a length of wire with a hook at the end*: extremity, furthermost part, limit; margin, edge, border, boundary, periphery; point, tip, tail end.
3 *a cigarette end*: butt, stub, stump, remnant; informal dog-end.
4 *wealth is a means and not an end in itself*: aim, goal, purpose, objective, object, holy grail, target, aspiration, wish, desire, ambition; intention, intent, design, motive.
5 *his end might come at any time*: death, demise, passing; formal decease.
OPPOSITES: beginning.
▷**verb**
1 *the show ended with a wedding scene*: finish, conclude, terminate, come to an end, draw to a close, close, stop, cease; culminate, climax; build up to, lead up to, come to a head.
2 *she ended their relationship*: break off, call off, bring to an end, put an end to, stop, finish, terminate, discontinue; dissolve, cancel, annul.
OPPOSITES: begin.

endanger verb *river pollution is likely to endanger fish*: put at risk, put in danger, imperil, jeopardize, risk; threaten, pose a threat to, be a danger to, be detrimental to, damage, injure, harm.

endearing adjective *hedgehogs are endearing creatures*: lovable, adorable, cute, sweet, dear, delightful, lovely, charming, appealing, attractive, engaging, winning, captivating, enchanting, beguiling, winsome.

endearment noun
1 *he murmured endearments*: term of affection, term of endearment, pet name; (**endearments**) sweet nothings, sweet talk.
2 *he spoke to her without endearment*: affection, fondness, tenderness, feeling, sentiment, warmth, love, liking.

endeavour verb *we will endeavour to solve these crimes as quickly as possible*: try, attempt, seek, set out, undertake, aspire, aim; strive, struggle, work, exert yourself,

apply yourself, do your best, do your utmost, give your all, be at pains; informal give something your best shot, go all out.
▷**noun**
1 *an endeavour to build a more buoyant economy*: attempt, try, bid, effort, venture.
2 *the team's tireless endeavour paid off in the end*: effort, exertion, struggle, labour, hard work, application, industry; pains; informal sweat, {blood, sweat, and tears}, elbow grease; Brit. informal graft.
3 *an extremely unwise endeavour*: undertaking, enterprise, venture, exercise, activity, exploit, deed, act, move; scheme, plan, project.

ending noun *the ending of the cold war | the story has a happy ending*: end, finish, close, conclusion; denouement, finale; cessation, stopping, termination, discontinuation.
OPPOSITES: beginning.

endless adjective
1 *a woman with endless energy*: unlimited, limitless, infinite, inexhaustible, boundless, unbounded, untold, immeasurable, incalculable; abundant, great; ceaseless, unceasing, unending, without end, everlasting, constant, continuous, continual, interminable, unfading, unfailing, perpetual, eternal, enduring, lasting.
2 *as children we played endless games*: countless, innumerable, numerous, very many; a great number of, infinite numbers of, a multitude of; informal umpteen, no end of, loads of, stacks of, heaps of, masses of.
OPPOSITES: limited, few.

endorse verb *they fully endorse a trade agreement*: support, back, agree with, approve of, favour, subscribe to, recommend, champion, stick up for, uphold, affirm, sanction; informal throw your weight behind.
OPPOSITES: oppose.

endorsement noun support, backing, approval, seal of approval, agreement, recommendation.

endow verb
1 *Henry II endowed a hospital for poor pilgrims*: finance, fund, pay for, subsidize, support financially, settle money on; establish, found, set up, institute.
2 *nature endowed the human race with intelligence*: provide, supply, furnish, equip, invest, favour, bless, grace, gift; give, bestow.

endowment noun
1 *the endowment of a Chair of Botany*: funding, financing, subsidizing; establishment, foundation, institution.
2 *a generous endowment*: bequest, legacy, inheritance; gift, present, grant, award, donation, contribution, subsidy, settlement.
3 *his natural endowments*: quality,

characteristic, feature, attribute, facility, faculty, ability, talent, gift, strength, aptitude, capability, capacity.

endurance noun
1 *she pushed him beyond the limit of his endurance:* **toleration**, tolerance, sufferance, forbearance, patience.
2 *the race is a test of endurance:* **stamina**, staying power, fortitude, perseverance, persistence, tenacity, doggedness, grit, indefatigability, resolution, determination; informal stickability.

endure verb
1 *he endured years of pain:* **undergo**, go through, live through, experience, meet, encounter; cope with, deal with, face, suffer, tolerate, put up with, brave, bear, withstand, sustain, weather.
2 *God's love will endure for ever:* **last**, live, live on, go on, survive, abide, continue, persist, remain, stay.

enduring adjective *an enduring commitment to democracy and human rights:* **lasting**, long-lasting, abiding, continuing, persisting, eternal, permanent, unending, everlasting, perennial; constant, stable, steady, steadfast, fixed, firm, unwavering, unfaltering, unchanging.
OPPOSITES: short-lived.

enemy noun **opponent**, adversary, rival, antagonist, combatant, challenger, competitor, opposer, opposition, competition, other side; literary foe.
OPPOSITES: ally.

energetic adjective
1 *an energetic woman:* **active**, lively, dynamic, spirited, animated, vital, vibrant, bouncy, bubbly, exuberant, perky, frisky, sprightly, tireless, indefatigable, enthusiastic, zestful, feisty; informal full of beans, bright-eyed and bushy-tailed.
2 *energetic exercises:* **vigorous**, strenuous, brisk; hard, arduous, demanding, taxing, tough, rigorous.
3 *an energetic advertising campaign:* **forceful**, vigorous, high-powered, all-out, determined, bold, powerful, high-octane; aggressive, hard-hitting; informal punchy, in-your-face.
OPPOSITES: lethargic, gentle, half-hearted.

energize verb
1 *people are energized by his ideas:* **enliven**, animate, vitalize, invigorate, excite, electrify, stimulate, stir up, fire up, rouse, motivate, move, drive, spur on, encourage, galvanize; informal pep up, buck up.
2 *floor sensors energized by standing passengers:* **activate**, trigger, trip, operate, actuate, switch on, turn on, start, power.

energy noun *she set out feeling full of energy:* **vitality**, vigour, life, liveliness, animation, vivacity, spirit, verve, enthusiasm, zest, vibrancy, spark, sparkle, effervescence, exuberance, buoyancy,

sprightliness; strength, stamina, forcefulness, power, dynamism, drive; fire, passion, ardour, zeal; informal zip, zing, pep, pizzazz, bounce, get-up-and-go, vim and vigour.

enervate verb *the scorching sun enervated her:* **exhaust**, tire, fatigue, weary, wear out, drain, sap, weaken, enfeeble, debilitate, incapacitate,; informal knock out.
OPPOSITES: invigorate.

enervation noun **fatigue**, exhaustion, tiredness, weariness, lack of energy, lassitude, weakness, feebleness, debilitation.

enfeeble verb *the animal was enfeebled by lack of nutrition:* **weaken**, debilitate, incapacitate, indispose, lay low; drain, sap, exhaust, tire, fatigue.
OPPOSITES: strengthen.

enfold verb
1 *the summit was enfolded in white cloud:* **envelop**, engulf, sheathe, swathe, swaddle, cocoon, shroud, veil, cloak, drape, cover; surround, enclose, encase, encircle.
2 *he enfolded her in his arms:* **clasp**, hold, fold, wrap, squeeze, clutch, gather; embrace, hug, cuddle.

enforce verb
1 *the role of the police is to enforce the law:* **impose**, apply, administer, implement, put into effect, bring to bear, discharge, execute, prosecute.
2 *they cannot enforce cooperation between the parties:* **force**, compel, coerce, exact.

enforced adjective *an enforced break from work:* **involuntary**, forced, imposed, obligatory, compulsory, required, requisite, stipulated, prescribed, contractual, necessary, unavoidable, inescapable.
OPPOSITES: voluntary.

enfranchise verb *women over thirty were enfranchised in 1918:* **give the vote to**, give/grant suffrage to.

engage verb
1 *kids need films that will engage their minds and their imaginations:* **attract**, draw, catch, grab, capture, gain, win, hold, grip, captivate, occupy, absorb.
2 *he engaged a new assistant:* **employ**, hire, recruit, take on, secure the services of, put on the payroll, enrol, appoint.
3 *government workers were prohibited from engaging in political activities:* **participate in**, take part in, join in, become involved in, go in for, share in, play a part/role in; have a hand in, be a party to, enter into; formal partake in.
4 *infantry units engaged the enemy:* **fight**, do battle with, wage war on/against, attack, take on, set upon, clash with, skirmish with; encounter, meet.

engaged adjective
1 *he's otherwise engaged:* **busy**, occupied,

unavailable; informal tied up.
2 *Travis and I are engaged:* engaged to be married; literary betrothed, affianced.
OPPOSITES: free, unattached.

engagement noun
1 *they broke off their engagement:* literary betrothal.
2 *a business engagement:* appointment, meeting, arrangement, commitment; date, assignation, rendezvous.
3 *Britain's continued engagement in open trading:* participation, involvement, association.
4 *the first engagement of the war:* battle, fight, clash, confrontation, encounter, conflict, skirmish; action, combat, hostilities.

engaging adjective *she had such an engaging smile:* charming, appealing, attractive, pretty, delightful, lovely, pleasing, pleasant, agreeable, likeable, lovable, sweet, winning, winsome, fetching, captivating, enchanting.
OPPOSITES: unappealing.

engender verb *his works engendered considerable controversy:* cause, be the cause of, give rise to, occasion, lead to, result in, produce, create, generate, bring about, arouse, inspire, provoke, kindle, trigger, spark, stir up.

engine noun
1 *a car engine:* motor, machine, mechanism.
2 *the main engine of change:* cause, agent, instrument, originator, initiator, generator.

engineer verb *he engineered a takeover deal:* bring about, arrange, pull off, bring off, negotiate, organize, orchestrate, choreograph, mastermind, manage, stage-manage, coordinate; contrive, manoeuvre; informal wangle.

engrained adjective. See INGRAINED.

engrave verb
1 *my name was engraved on the ring:* carve, inscribe, cut, incise, chisel, chase, score, notch, etch, imprint, impress.
2 *the image was engraved in his memory:* fix, set, imprint, stamp, brand, impress, embed, etch.

engraving noun *an engraving of a Georgian coffee house:* etching, print, impression, lithograph; plate, woodcut, linocut.

engross verb *the books are full of adventure and intrigue that will doubtless engross young readers:* absorb, engage, rivet, grip, hold, interest, involve, occupy; fascinate, captivate, enthral, intrigue.

engrossed adjective *he was totally engrossed in his book:* absorbed, involved, interested, occupied, immersed, caught up, riveted, gripped, rapt, fascinated, intent, captivated, enthralled, intrigued.

engrossing adjective absorbing, riveting, gripping, captivating, compelling, compulsive, fascinating, intriguing, enthralling; informal unputdownable.

engulf verb *their new home was engulfed by stinking brown flood water:* inundate, flood, deluge, immerse, swamp, swallow up, submerge; bury, envelop, overwhelm.

enhance verb *his dramatic appearance enhanced his reputation:* increase, add to, intensify, heighten, magnify, amplify, strengthen, build up, supplement, augment, boost, raise, lift, elevate, exalt; improve, enrich, complement.
OPPOSITES: diminish.

enigma noun *their way of conducting business was an enigma to me:* mystery, puzzle, riddle, conundrum, paradox, problem; a closed book; informal poser.

enigmatic adjective *she smiled that enigmatic smile again:* mysterious, inscrutable, puzzling, mystifying, baffling, perplexing, impenetrable, unfathomable, sphinx-like, Delphic, oracular; cryptic, ambiguous, obscure.

enjoin verb (formal) *the Code enjoined members to trade fairly and responsibly:* urge, encourage; instruct, direct, require, order, command, tell, call on, demand, charge.

enjoy verb
1 *he enjoys playing the piano | she sat on the balcony, enjoying the sun on her skin:* like, love, be fond of, be entertained by, take pleasure in, be keen on, delight in, appreciate, relish, revel in, adore, lap up, savour, luxuriate in, bask in; informal get a kick out of, get a thrill out of, get a buzz out of.
2 *she had always enjoyed good health:* benefit from, have the benefit of; be blessed with, be favoured with, be endowed with, be possessed of, possess, own, boast.
OPPOSITES: dislike, lack.
□ **enjoy yourself**
have fun, have a good time, have the time of your life; make merry, celebrate, revel; informal party, have a ball, have a whale of a time, let your hair down.

enjoyable adjective *a most enjoyable evening:* entertaining, amusing, diverting, delightful, to your liking, pleasant, congenial, convivial, lovely, fine, good, great, agreeable, pleasurable, satisfying, gratifying; marvellous, wonderful, magnificent, splendid; informal fantastic, fabulous, terrific, magic; Brit. informal brilliant.

enjoyment noun *all the songs have been carefully selected for your enjoyment | she devoured her sandwich with enjoyment:* pleasure, fun, entertainment, amusement, diversion, recreation, relaxation; delight, happiness; satisfaction, gratification, liking, relish, gusto; humorous delectation.

enlarge verb
1 *they enlarged the scope of their research:* extend, expand, add to, amplify, augment; widen, broaden, stretch.
2 *the lymph glands had enlarged:* swell, distend, dilate, blow up, puff up, balloon.
3 *he enlarged on this subject:* elaborate on, expand on, add to, develop, build on, flesh out, put flesh on the bones of, add detail to, expatiate on; fill out, embellish, embroider.
OPPOSITES: reduce, shrink.

enlargement noun *the modernization and enlargement of the factory:* expansion, extension, growth, amplification, augmentation; broadening.

enlighten verb *would you care to enlighten me as to the nature of their relationship?* inform, tell, make aware, open someone's eyes, apprise, brief, update, bring up to date, notify; disabuse, set straight; informal put in the picture, clue in, fill in, bring up to speed.

enlightened adjective informed, well informed, aware, sophisticated, advanced, developed, liberal, open-minded, broad-minded, educated, knowledgeable, wise; civilized, refined, cultured, cultivated.
OPPOSITES: benighted.

enlightenment noun *the reader will be hoping for enlightenment from the text:* insight, illumination, understanding, awareness, knowledge.

enlist verb
1 *he enlisted in the Royal Engineers:* join up, join, enrol in, sign up for, volunteer for.
2 *he was enlisted in the army:* recruit, call up, enrol, sign up; conscript; US draft.
3 *he enlisted the help of an independent consultant:* obtain, engage, secure, get, procure.

enliven verb
1 *a meeting enlivened by her wit and vivacity:* liven up, spice up, add spice to, make more interesting, ginger up, vitalize, leaven; informal perk up, pep up.
2 *the visit had enlivened my mother:* cheer up, brighten up, liven up, raise someone's spirits, uplift, gladden, buoy up, animate, vivify, vitalize, invigorate, restore, revive, refresh, stimulate, rouse; informal perk up, buck up, pep up.

en masse adverb *the Cabinet resigned en masse:* together, all together, as a group, as one, en bloc, as a whole, wholesale.

enmesh verb *they became increasingly enmeshed in political intrigue:* embroil, entangle, ensnare, snare, trap, ensnarl, involve, catch up, mix up, bog down, mire.

enmity noun *a world free from enmity between nations and races:* hostility, animosity, antagonism, opposition, friction, antipathy, animus, acrimony, bitterness, rancour, resentment, ill feeling, bad feeling, ill will, bad blood, hatred, hate, loathing, odium.
OPPOSITES: friendship.

enormity noun
1 *a thorough search disclosed the full enormity of the crime:* extent, magnitude, size; horror, atrocity, cruelty, inhumanity, brutality, savagery, viciousness.
2 *the enormity of the task:* immensity, hugeness; size, magnitude.
3 *the enormities of the regime:* outrage, horror, evil, atrocity, barbarity, iniquity; crime, sin, wrong, offence, injustice, abuse.

enormous adjective *enormous sums of money are involved* | *an enormous Victorian house:* huge, vast, immense, gigantic, very big, great, giant, massive, colossal, mammoth, tremendous, mighty, monumental, epic, prodigious, mountainous, king-sized, titanic, towering, gargantuan; informal mega, monster, whopping, humongous, jumbo, astronomical; Brit. informal whacking great, ginormous.
OPPOSITES: tiny.

enormously adverb
1 *an enormously important factor:* very, extremely, really, exceedingly, exceptionally, tremendously, immensely, hugely; singularly, particularly, eminently, terribly; informal terrifically, awfully.
2 *prices vary enormously:* considerably, greatly, very much, a great deal; informal a lot.
OPPOSITES: slightly.

enough determiner *they had enough food for the journey:* sufficient, adequate, ample, the necessary; informal plenty of.
OPPOSITES: insufficient.
▷ pronoun *there's enough for everyone:* sufficient, plenty, a sufficient amount, an adequate amount, as much as necessary; a sufficiency, an ample supply; your fill.

enquire verb
1 *I enquired about a job but was told there were no vacancies:* ask, make enquiries, question someone, request information.
2 *a committee was set up to enquire into the truth of the report:* investigate, conduct an enquiry, probe, look into; research, examine, explore; informal check out.

enquiring adjective *youngsters with enquiring minds:* inquisitive, curious, interested, questioning, probing, searching; investigative.

enquiry noun
1 *telephone enquiries:* question, query.
2 *an enquiry into alleged security leaks:* investigation, probe, examination, exploration; inquest, hearing.

e

enrage verb *the scheme is bound to enrage farmers:* anger, infuriate, incense, madden, inflame; antagonize, provoke, exasperate; informal drive mad/crazy, drive up the wall, make someone see red, make someone's blood boil, make someone's hackles rise, get someone's back up.
OPPOSITES: placate.

enraged adjective furious, infuriated, very angry, irate, incensed, raging, incandescent, fuming, seething, beside yourself; informal mad, hopping mad, wild, livid, boiling, apoplectic, hot under the collar, on the warpath, foaming at the mouth, steamed up, in a paddy.
OPPOSITES: calm.

enrapture verb *all of us were enraptured by the music:* delight, enchant, captivate, charm, enthral, entrance, bewitch, beguile, transport, thrill, excite, exhilarate, intoxicate, take someone's breath away; informal bowl someone over, blow someone's mind.

enrich verb *his communication techniques can be applied to enrich our relationships and our quality of life:* enhance, improve, better, add to; elevate, raise, lift.
OPPOSITES: spoil.

enrol verb
1 *they both enrolled for the course:* register, sign on/up, put your name down, apply, volunteer; matriculate; enter, join.
2 *280 new members were enrolled:* accept, admit, take on, register, sign on/up, recruit, engage.

en route adverb *he was en route from Paris to Bordeaux:* on the way, in transit, along/on the road, on the move; coming, going, proceeding, travelling; during the journey.

ensconce verb *Agnes ensconced herself in their bedroom:* settle, install, plant, position, seat, sit down; establish; informal park; Brit. informal plonk.

ensemble noun
1 *a Bulgarian folk ensemble:* group, band; company, troupe, cast; informal combo.
2 *the buildings present a charming provincial ensemble:* whole, entity, unit, body, set, combination, composite, package; sum, total, totality, entirety, aggregate.
3 *a pink and black ensemble:* outfit, costume, suit; separates, coordinates; informal get-up.

enshrine verb *the following rights should be enshrined in the treaty:* set down, set out, spell out, lay down, set in stone, embody, incorporate, contain, include; preserve, immortalize.

ensign noun *the ship flew a British ensign:* flag, standard, colours, banner, pennant, pennon, streamer.

enslavement noun *the enslavement of Africans continued for most of the nineteenth century:* slavery, servitude, bondage, forced labour; exploitation, oppression.
OPPOSITES: liberation.

ensnare verb *he becomes ensnared in a criminal conspiracy involving stolen works of art:* capture, catch, trap, entrap, snare, net; entangle, embroil, enmesh.

ensue verb *the fragile alliance crumbled and fierce fighting ensued:* result, follow, be consequent, develop; occur, happen, take place, come next/after, arise; literary supervene.

ensure verb
1 *ensure that the surface is completely clean:* make sure, make certain, see to it; check, confirm, establish, verify.
2 *legislation to ensure equal opportunities for all:* secure, guarantee, assure.

entail verb *this proposal will entail additional expenditure:* involve, necessitate, require, need, demand, call for; mean, imply; cause, produce, result in, lead to, give rise to, occasion.

entangle verb
1 *their parachutes became entangled:* twist, intertwine, entwine, tangle, snarl, knot, coil, mat.
2 *the fish are easily entangled in fine nets:* catch, capture, trap, snare, ensnare, entrap, enmesh.
3 *he was entangled in a lawsuit:* involve, embroil, mix up, implicate, catch up, bog down, mire.

entanglement noun
1 *their entanglement in the war:* involvement, embroilment.
2 *romantic entanglements:* affair, love affair, relationship, romance, amour, fling, dalliance, liaison, involvement, intrigue; complication.

entente noun *the Foreign Office was reluctant to upset the entente with France:* understanding, agreement, arrangement, entente cordiale, settlement, deal; alliance, treaty, pact, accord, concordat.

enter verb
1 *police entered the house:* go in/into, come in/into, get in/into, set foot in, cross the threshold of, gain access to.
2 *a bullet entered his chest:* penetrate, pierce, puncture, perforate.
3 *he entered politics in 2001:* get involved in, join, throw yourself into, engage in, embark on, take up; participate in, take part in, play a part/role in, contribute to.
4 *the planning entered a new phase:* reach, move into, get to, begin, start, commence.
5 *they entered the Army at eighteen:* join, become a member of, enrol in/for, enlist in, volunteer for, sign up for; take up.
6 *she entered a cookery competition:* go in

for, put your name down for, register for, enrol for, sign on/up for; compete in, take part in, participate in.

7 *the cashier entered the details in a ledger:* record, write, set down, put down, take down, note, jot down; put on record, minute, register, log.

8 *please enter your password:* key in, type in, tap in.
OPPOSITES: leave.

enterprise noun
1 *a joint enterprise between French and Japanese countries:* undertaking, endeavour, venture, exercise, activity, operation, task, business, proceeding, project, scheme, plan, programme, campaign.
2 *success came quickly, thanks to a mixture of talent, enterprise, and luck:* initiative, resourcefulness, entrepreneurialism, imagination, ingenuity, inventiveness, originality, creativity; quick-wittedness, native wit; enthusiasm, dynamism, drive, ambition, energy; informal gumption, get-up-and-go.
3 *a profit-making enterprise:* business, company, firm, venture, organization, operation, concern, corporation, establishment, partnership; informal outfit, set-up.

enterprising adjective *an enterprising young travel agent realized that this was a golden opportunity:* resourceful, entrepreneurial, imaginative, ingenious, inventive, creative; quick-witted, clever, bright, sharp, sharp-witted; enthusiastic, dynamic, ambitious, energetic, adventurous; informal go-ahead.

entertain verb
1 *Ron entertained us with stories about his own childhood:* amuse, divert, delight, please, charm; engage, interest, occupy, absorb, engross.
2 *he entertained many foreign visitors:* receive, play host/hostess to, invite round/over, throw a party for; wine and dine, cater for, treat, welcome, fete.
3 *we don't entertain much:* receive guests, have people round/over, have company, hold/throw a party.
4 *I would never entertain such a foolish idea:* consider, give consideration to, contemplate, think about, give thought to; countenance, tolerate, support.
OPPOSITES: bore.

entertainer noun performer, artiste, artist.

entertaining adjective *it's a well-crafted and very entertaining movie:* enjoyable, engaging, interesting, fascinating, absorbing, compelling; diverting, amusing, humorous, funny, comical.
OPPOSITES: boring.

entertainment noun
1 *he reads for entertainment:* amusement,

pleasure, leisure, recreation, relaxation, fun, enjoyment, interest, diversion.
2 *a theatrical entertainment:* show, performance, presentation, production, extravaganza, spectacle.

enthral verb *last night he enthralled fans from six to sixty:* captivate, fascinate, entrance, enchant, bewitch, beguile, absorb, engross, rivet, grip, transfix, hypnotize, mesmerize.
OPPOSITES: bore.

enthralling adjective fascinating, captivating, absorbing, engrossing, compelling, riveting, gripping, exciting, spellbinding, entrancing, enchanting; informal unputdownable.

enthuse verb
1 *Joe enthused about the music:* rave, be enthusiastic, gush, wax lyrical, be effusive, rhapsodize; praise to the skies; informal go wild/mad/crazy.
2 *he enthuses people and they get good results:* motivate, inspire, stimulate, encourage, spur on, galvanize, rouse, excite, stir up, fire.

enthusiasm noun
1 *she worked with enthusiasm:* eagerness, keenness, gusto, relish, ardour, fervour, passion, zeal, zest, energy, verve, vigour, vehemence, fire, spirit, avidity; wholeheartedness, commitment, willingness; informal get-up-and-go.
2 *the three enthusiasms of his life were politics, religion, and books:* interest, passion, obsession; pastime, hobby, recreation, pursuit.
OPPOSITES: apathy.

enthusiast noun *the perfect present for a railway enthusiast:* fan, devotee, aficionado, lover; expert, connoisseur, authority, pundit; informal buff, freak, fanatic, nut, fiend, addict, maniac.

enthusiastic adjective *an enthusiastic supporter of Scottish rugby:* eager, keen, avid, ardent, fervent, passionate, zealous, vehement; wholehearted, committed, devoted; excited; informal fanatical.
OPPOSITES: unenthusiastic, apathetic.

entice verb *the show should entice a new audience into the theatre:* tempt, lure, attract, appeal to; persuade, convince, beguile, coax; seduce.

enticement noun *the enticement of power:* lure, temptation, allure, attraction, appeal, draw, pull, bait; charm, seduction, fascination.

enticing adjective *we caught enticing glimpses of tables laden with food:* tempting, alluring, attractive, inviting, seductive, beguiling; irresistible.

entire adjective
1 *I devoted my entire life to him:* whole, complete, total, full; undivided.

2 *only one of the gates is entire:* intact, unbroken, undamaged, unscathed, unspoiled, perfect, in one piece.
3 *they are in entire agreement:* absolute, total, utter, thorough, wholehearted; unqualified, unreserved, outright.
OPPOSITES: partial.

entirely adverb
1 *that's entirely out of the question:* absolutely, completely, totally, wholly, utterly, quite; altogether, in every respect, thoroughly, downright, one hundred per cent.
2 *eight coaches solely for passenger transport:* solely, only, exclusively, just, purely, merely.

entirety noun *in the 1920s, cheap production constituted almost the entirety of British film-making:* whole, total, aggregate, totality, sum total.
OPPOSITES: part.
□ in its entirety
the poem is too long to quote in its entirety: completely, entirely, totally, fully, as a whole.

entitle verb
1 *this pass entitles you to visit the museum:* qualify, make eligible, authorize, allow, permit; enable, empower.
2 *a chapter entitled 'Comedy and Tragedy':* title, name, call, designate, label.

entitlement noun
1 *their entitlement to benefits:* right, claim; permission, dispensation, privilege, prerogative.
2 *your holiday entitlement:* allowance, allocation, quota, ration.

entity noun *a single entity:* being, creature, individual, organism, life form; person; body, object, article, thing.

entomb verb *mummified bodies were entombed in the Pyramids:* inter, lay to rest, bury.

entourage noun *the president and his entourage:* retinue, escort, train; staff, attendants, companions, retainers; bodyguard.

entrails plural noun intestines, bowels, guts, viscera, internal organs, vital organs; offal; informal insides, innards.

entrance[1] noun
1 *the main entrance:* entry, way in, access, ingress, approach; door, portal, gate; entrance hall, foyer, lobby, porch; opening, mouth.
2 *the entrance of Mrs Knight:* appearance, arrival, entry.
3 *he was refused entrance:* admission, admittance, entry, access, ingress.
OPPOSITES: exit, departure.

entrance[2] verb *I was entranced by her beauty:* enchant, bewitch, beguile, captivate, fascinate, mesmerize, enthral;

stun, overpower; charm, delight; informal bowl over, knock out.

entrant noun
1 *university entrants:* new member, new arrival, beginner, newcomer, recruit; fresher, freshman; novice, neophyte.
2 *a prize will be awarded to the best entrant:* competitor, contestant, contender, participant; candidate, applicant.

entrap verb
1 *fishing lines can entrap wildlife:* trap, snare, ensnare, enmesh; catch, capture.
2 *he was entrapped by an undercover police officer:* trick, deceive, dupe; trap; informal set up.

entreat verb *his friends entreated him not to go:* implore, beg, plead with, ask, request; appeal to, call on, petition, solicit; formal enjoin; old use bid.

entreaty noun *he ignored her entreaties:* plea, appeal, request, petition, solicitation, supplication; application, claim; prayer.

entrenched, intrenched adjective *an entrenched resistance to change:* ingrained, established, confirmed, fixed, firm, deep-seated, deep-rooted; unshakeable, indelible, ineradicable.

entrepreneur noun businessman, businesswoman, speculator, tycoon, magnate, mogul; dealer, trader; promoter, impresario; informal wheeler-dealer, whizz-kid, mover and shaker, go-getter, high-flyer.

entrust verb
1 *she entrusted him with the task of preparing her late husband's works for publication:* charge, make responsible for, trust.
2 *the powers entrusted to the Home Secretary:* assign, confer on, bestow on, vest in, consign; delegate, depute, devolve; give, grant, vouchsafe.
3 *she entrusted them to the hospital:* hand over, give custody of, turn over, commit, consign, deliver.

entry noun
1 *both men stood up at Becca's entry:* appearance, arrival, entrance.
2 *the entry to the flats:* entrance, way in, access, ingress, approach; door, portal, gate; entrance hall, foyer, lobby.
3 *he was refused entry into the country:* admission, admittance, entrance, access, ingress.
4 *entries in the cash book:* item, record, note, listing; memo, memorandum; account.
5 *twelve lucky winners were chosen from the hundreds of entries we received:* contestant, competitor, contender, entrant, participant; candidate, applicant; submission, entry form, application.
OPPOSITES: departure, exit.

entwine verb *her hair was entwined with ropes of pearls:* **wind**, twist, weave, intertwine, interlace, interweave; twine, braid, plait; entangle, tangle.

enumerate verb *he enumerated four objectives:* **list**, itemize, set out, give; name, specify, identify, spell out, cite, detail; formal particularize.

enunciate verb
1 *she enunciated each word slowly:* **pronounce**, articulate; say, speak, utter, voice, vocalize, sound, mouth.
2 *a document enunciating the policy:* **express**, state, put into words, declare, set forth.

envelop verb *a thick blanket of fog enveloped the countryside:* **surround**, cover, enfold, engulf, cocoon, swathe, enclose; cloak, wrap, veil, shroud.

envelope noun **wrapper**, wrapping, sleeve, cover, covering, casing.

enviable adjective *this hotel has an enviable position in the main square:* **desirable**, desired, sought-after, covetable, attractive; fortunate, lucky; informal to die for.

envious adjective *she felt envious of their happiness:* **jealous**, covetous, green with envy; grudging, begrudging, resentful; bitter.

environment noun
1 *birds and mammals from a wide range of environments:* **habitat**, territory; surroundings, conditions.
2 *proper research is impracticable in the hospital environment:* **situation**, setting, milieu, background, scene, location; context, framework; sphere, world, realm; ambience, atmosphere.
3 *the impact of pesticides on the environment:* **the natural world**, nature, the earth, the ecosystem, the biosphere; wildlife, flora and fauna.

environmentalist noun *environmentalists are pressing for a ban on logging:* **conservationist**, preservationist, ecologist; nature-lover.

environs plural noun *the environs of London:* **surroundings**, surrounding area, vicinity; locality, neighbourhood, district, region; precincts.

envisage verb
1 *we envisage that this development could lead to an enormous increase in production:* **anticipate**, expect, think likely; predict, forecast.
2 *I cannot envisage what the future holds:* **imagine**, contemplate, visualize, envision, picture; conceive of, think of.

envoy noun *he served as an envoy to France:* **ambassador**, emissary, diplomat, consul, attaché, chargé d'affaires; representative, delegate, proxy, spokesperson; agent, intermediary, mediator, go-between.

envy noun *she felt a pang of envy:* **jealousy**, covetousness; resentment, bitterness, discontent; the green-eyed monster.
▷verb
1 *I both admired and envied her:* **be envious of**, be jealous of; resent, be resentful of.
2 *I don't envy you your success:* **begrudge**, grudge.
3 *we envied her lifestyle:* **covet**, desire, aspire to, wish for, want, long for, yearn for, hanker after, crave.

ephemeral adjective *fashions are ephemeral:* **transitory**, transient, fleeting, passing, short-lived, momentary, brief, short; temporary, impermanent, short-term.
OPPOSITES: permanent.

epic noun
1 *the epics of Homer:* **heroic poem**; story, saga, legend, chronicle, romance, myth, fable, tale.
2 *a Hollywood epic:* informal **blockbuster**.
▷adjective *an epic 1200 mile journey across Western Australia | an epic task:* **ambitious**, heroic, grand, great, monumental; difficult, demanding, arduous, gruelling, Herculean.

epicure noun *as an epicure, he is entranced by their new range of speciality foods:* **gourmet**, gastronome, gourmand, connoisseur; informal foodie.

epicurean noun *he admits to being a shameless epicurean:* **hedonist**, sensualist, pleasure-seeker, sybarite, bon viveur; epicure, gourmet, gastronome, gourmand.
▷adjective *her family's epicurean lifestyle:* **hedonistic**, sensualist, pleasure-seeking, self-indulgent, sybaritic.

epidemic noun
1 *an epidemic of typhoid:* **outbreak**, pandemic; plague.
2 *an epidemic of violent crime:* **spate**, rash, wave, eruption, outbreak; upsurge, upturn, increase, growth, rise.
▷adjective *investigative reporting seems epidemic in an election year:* **rife**, rampant, widespread, extensive, pervasive; global, universal, ubiquitous; endemic, pandemic.

epigram noun *a witty epigram:* **witticism**, quip, jest, pun, bon mot; saying, maxim, adage, aphorism, epigraph; informal old chestnut.

epigrammatic adjective *her short, epigrammatic verses:* **concise**, succinct, pithy, aphoristic; incisive, short and sweet; witty, clever, piquant, sharp; informal snappy.
OPPOSITES: expansive.

epilogue noun *the body of the book is summarized in the epilogue:* **afterword**, postscript, coda, codicil, appendix, supplement, addendum; conclusion.
OPPOSITES: prologue.

episode noun
1 *the whole episode has been a major embarrassment:* incident, event, occurrence, happening; occasion, interlude, chapter, experience, adventure, exploit; matter, affair, thing.
2 *the final episode of the series:* instalment; part, portion, section, component; programme, show, chapter, passage.
3 *he had recurrent episodes of pancreatitis:* period, spell, bout, attack, phase; informal dose.

episodic adjective
1 *volcanic activity is highly episodic in nature:* intermittent, sporadic, periodic, fitful, irregular, spasmodic, occasional.
2 *an episodic account of the war:* in episodes, in instalments, in sections, in parts.
OPPOSITES: continuous.

epistle noun (formal) letter, communication, dispatch, note, line; correspondence, news; formal missive.

epithet noun *these works earned him the epithet 'the Spanish Heretic':* name, label, tag, description, designation.

epitome noun *he was the epitome of respectability:* personification, embodiment, incarnation, paragon; essence, quintessence, archetype, paradigm, typification; exemplar, model, soul, perfect example; height.

epitomize verb *the company epitomized the problems faced by British industry:* embody, typify, exemplify, represent, symbolize, illustrate, encapsulate; personify; formal reify.

epoch noun *the Tudor epoch:* era, age, period, time.

equable adjective
1 *an equable man:* even-tempered, calm, composed, collected, self-possessed, relaxed, easy-going; mellow, mild, tranquil, placid, stable, level-headed; imperturbable, unexcitable, untroubled, well balanced; informal unflappable, together, laid-back.
2 *an equable climate:* stable, constant, uniform, unvarying; moderate, temperate.
OPPOSITES: temperamental, extreme.

equal adjective
1 *lines of equal length:* the same, identical, uniform, alike, like, equivalent, matching, corresponding.
2 *the prices are equal to a fortnight's wages:* equivalent to, amounting to; proportionate to, commensurate with, on a par with.
3 *the right to equal treatment before the law:* unbiased, impartial, non-partisan, fair, just, equitable; unprejudiced, non-discriminatory, egalitarian; neutral, objective, disinterested.
4 *an equal contest:* evenly matched, even, balanced, level; on a par, on an equal footing; informal fifty-fifty, level pegging, neck and neck.
OPPOSITES: different, discriminatory.
▷ noun *they did not treat him as their equal:* equivalent, peer, fellow, coequal, like; counterpart, match, parallel.
▷ verb
1 *two plus two equals four:* be equal to, be equivalent to, be the same as; come to, amount to, make, total, add up to.
2 *he equalled the world record:* match, reach, parallel, be level with.
3 *the fable equals that of any other poet:* be as good as, be a match for, measure up to, equate with; be in the same league as, rival, compete with.
□ equal to
she was more than equal to the challenge of the new job: capable of, fit for, up to, good/strong enough for; suitable for, suited to, appropriate for; informal having what it takes.

equality noun
1 *the organization promotes equality for women:* fairness, equal rights, equal opportunities, egalitarianism; impartiality, even-handedness; justice.
2 *equality between supply and demand:* parity, correspondence; uniformity, evenness, balance, equilibrium; symmetry.

equalize verb
1 *the purpose is to equalize the workload:* make equal, make even, even out/up, level, regularize, standardize, balance, square, match; bring into line.
2 *Villa equalized in the second half:* level the score, draw level.

equanimity noun *she was able to confront the daily crises with equanimity:* composure, calm, level-headedness, self-possession, cool-headedness, presence of mind; serenity, tranquillity, imperturbability, equilibrium; poise, assurance, self-confidence, aplomb, sangfroid; informal cool.
OPPOSITES: anxiety.

equate verb
1 *people tend to equate success with money:* identify; associate, connect, link, relate.
2 *that sum equates to half a million pounds today:* correspond to, be equivalent to, amount to; equal.
3 *moves to equate supply and demand:* equalize, balance, even out/up, level, square, match; make equal, make even, make equivalent.

equatorial adjective *the equatorial regions:* tropical; hot, humid.
OPPOSITES: polar.

equilibrium noun
1 *the task is the maintenance of social equilibrium:* balance, equipoise, parity, equality; stability.
2 *his equilibrium was never shaken:*

composure, calm, equanimity, sangfroid; level-headedness, cool-headedness, imperturbability, poise, presence of mind; self-possession, self-command; tranquillity, serenity; informal cool.
OPPOSITES: imbalance, agitation.

equip verb
1 *the new houses are all equipped with solar panels | we equipped the rescue workers with satellite phones:* provide, supply, furnish; issue, kit out, stock, provision, arm.
2 *the course will equip them for the workplace:* prepare, qualify, suit.

equipment noun *the museum has a collection of early sound-recording equipment:* apparatus, appliances; tools, implements, utensils, instruments, hardware, gadgets, gadgetry; resources, supplies; paraphernalia, impedimenta, trappings, accoutrements; formal appurtenances; informal kit, gear.

equitable adjective *Parliament is to distribute the burden of tax in an equitable way:* fair, just, egalitarian, impartial, even-handed, unbiased, unprejudiced; disinterested, objective, neutral, non-partisan, open-minded.
OPPOSITES: inequitable.

equity noun
1 *standards were not perfect, but there was a degree of equity in the treatment:* fairness, justness, impartiality, egalitarianism; objectivity, balance.
2 *he owns 25% of the equity in the property:* value, worth; ownership, rights.

equivalence noun *equivalence of birth and death rates is rare in human populations:* equality, sameness, correspondence; similarity, likeness.

equivalent adjective *a degree or equivalent qualification is required | one unit of alcohol is roughly equivalent to half a pint of beer:* corresponding, similar, parallel, analogous, comparable, commensurate; equal, identical.

equivocal adjective *an equivocal statement:* ambiguous, indefinite, non-committal, vague, imprecise, inexact, inexplicit; unclear, cryptic, enigmatic; ambivalent, uncertain, unsure.
OPPOSITES: definite.

equivocate verb *the government have equivocated too often in the past:* prevaricate, be evasive, be non-committal, be vague, be ambiguous, dodge the issue, hedge your bets; informal sit on the fence, duck the issue, pussyfoot around; rare tergiversate.

era noun *leading photographers of the Victorian era:* epoch, age, period, time; generation.

eradicate verb *the Home Office promised even more measures and laws to eradicate racism:* eliminate, get rid of, remove; destroy, wipe out, stamp out, quash; erase, excise, expunge.

erase verb
1 *they erased his name from all the lists:* delete, rub out, wipe off; efface, expunge, excise, remove, obliterate, eliminate.
2 *the last vestiges of a rural economy were erased | the magic of the landscape erased all else from her mind:* destroy, wipe out, obliterate, eradicate, remove all the traces of, blot out.

erect adjective
1 *she held her body erect:* upright, straight, vertical, perpendicular, rigid, stiff; standing.
2 *the dog's fur was erect:* bristling, standing on end, upright.
▷ verb
1 *the bridge was erected in 1973:* build, construct, put up; assemble, put together, fabricate.
2 *the party that erected the welfare state:* establish, form, set up, found, institute, create.
OPPOSITES: demolish, dismantle.

erection noun
1 *the erection of a house:* construction, building, assembly, fabrication.
2 *a bleak concrete erection:* building, structure, construction; formal edifice.

erode verb
1 *the cliffs on this coast have been eroded by the sea:* wear away, wear down, eat away, abrade, grind down, weather; dissolve, corrode.
2 *this humiliation eroded what little confidence she had:* destroy, eat away at, undermine, weaken.

erosion noun *the erosion of the cliffs:* wearing away, abrasion, attrition; weathering; corrosion, destruction.

erotic adjective *erotic literature:* sexually arousing, sexually stimulating, suggestive, titillating; sexual, sexy, sensual; seductive, alluring, tantalizing; pornographic, sexually explicit.

err verb *the judge had erred in ruling that the evidence was inadmissible:* make a mistake, be wrong, be in error, be mistaken, be incorrect, miscalculate, get it wrong, blunder; informal slip up.

errand noun *she sent my father off to run some errands round town:* task, job, chore, assignment.

errant adjective *Scottish forces have already begun to levy fines on errant motorists:* offending, erring, guilty, culpable, delinquent, lawbreaking, misbehaving.

erratic adjective *there's no accounting for his erratic behaviour | her breathing*

was erratic: unpredictable, inconsistent, changeable, variable, inconstant, irregular, fitful, unstable, unsettled, changing, varying, fluctuating.
OPPOSITES: consistent.

erring adjective *the court case resulted in a heavy fine for the erring player:* offending, errant, misbehaving, guilty, culpable.

erroneous adjective *the report was based on an erroneous assumption:* wrong, incorrect, mistaken, in error, inaccurate, untrue, false, fallacious; specious, faulty, flawed; informal off beam, full of holes.
OPPOSITES: correct.

error noun *spelling errors* | *an error of judgement:* mistake, inaccuracy, slip; miscalculation, blunder, oversight; fallacy, misconception, delusion; misprint, erratum; informal slip-up, boo-boo; Brit. informal boob.
□ **in error**
the goods were dispatched to you in error: wrongly, by mistake, mistakenly, incorrectly; accidentally, by accident, inadvertently, unintentionally, by chance.

ersatz adjective *ersatz coffee* | *ersatz emotion:* artificial, substitute, imitation, synthetic, fake, false, mock, simulated; sham, bogus, spurious, counterfeit; informal phoney, pseudo.
OPPOSITES: genuine.

erstwhile adjective *a piece written in memory of the composer's erstwhile teacher:* former, old, past, one-time, ex-, late; previous.
OPPOSITES: present.

erudite adjective *he was so erudite that only people who were his equals in scholarship could understand him:* learned, scholarly, educated, knowledgeable, well read, well informed, intellectual; intelligent, clever, academic, literary; bookish, highbrow, cerebral; informal brainy.
OPPOSITES: ignorant.

erupt verb
1 *hot lava erupted from the fissure:* be ejected, be disgorged, spew, gush, issue, pour, shoot; explode.
2 *fierce fighting erupted between the army and guerrillas:* break out, flare up, start suddenly.

eruption noun
1 *an eruption of violence:* outbreak, flare-up, upsurge, outburst, breakout, explosion; wave, spate.
2 *a skin eruption:* rash, outbreak, inflammation.

escalate verb
1 *prices have escalated:* increase rapidly, soar, rocket, shoot up, mount, spiral, climb, go up; informal go through the roof, skyrocket.
2 *the dispute escalated* | *making a stand will only escalate the problem:* grow, develop,

build up, increase, heighten, intensify, accelerate; aggravate, exacerbate.
OPPOSITES: plunge, shrink.

escalation noun
1 *an escalation in oil prices:* increase, rise, hike, growth, leap, upsurge, upturn, climb.
2 *the need to avoid an escalation of the conflict:* intensification, aggravation, exacerbation; expansion, build-up.

escapade noun *he is a paragliding fanatic famous for his flying escapades:* exploit, deed, feat, adventure, venture, mission; stunt, caper, antics.

escape verb
1 *he escaped from prison:* run away/off, get out, break out, break free, make a break for it, bolt, flee, take flight, make off, take off, abscond, take to your heels, make your getaway, make a run for it; disappear, vanish, slip away, sneak away; informal cut and run, skedaddle, scarper, vamoose, do a vanishing act, fly the coop, leg it; Brit. informal do a bunk, do a runner.
2 *he escaped his pursuers:* get away from, elude, avoid, dodge, shake off; informal give someone the slip.
3 *she narrowly escaped serious injury after her car was hit by a speeding motorist:* avoid, evade, dodge, miss, circumvent.
4 *lethal gas escaped:* leak out, seep out, be discharged, issue, flow out, pour out, run out.
▷ **noun**
1 *his escape from prison:* getaway, breakout, bolt, flight; disappearance, vanishing act; Brit. informal flit.
2 *a narrow escape from death:* avoidance of, evasion of, circumvention of.
3 *a gas escape:* leak, leakage, spill, seepage, discharge, outflow, outpouring.
4 *romantic novels present an escape from the dreary realities of life:* distraction, diversion.

escapee noun runaway, absconder, fugitive; truant; deserter.

escapism noun *musicals always do well in a recession because people want escapism:* fantasy, unreality, distraction; daydreaming, daydreams, imagination, flight of fancy, pipe dreams, wishful thinking.
OPPOSITES: realism.

eschew verb *he firmly eschewed political involvement:* abstain from, refrain from, keep away from, forgo, shun, have nothing to do with, fight shy of; reject, renounce.

escort noun
1 *a police escort:* guard, bodyguard, protector, minder; attendant, chaperone; entourage, retinue, convoy.
2 *her escort for the evening:* companion, partner; informal date.

▷ **verb** *police officers escorted her to the car:* accompany, take, lead, conduct, guide, usher, shepherd.

esoteric adjective *esoteric philosophical debate:* abstruse, obscure, arcane, recherché, rarefied, recondite; complex, complicated, incomprehensible, opaque, impenetrable, mysterious.

especial adjective
1 *especial care is required:* particular, special, exceptional.
2 *her especial brand of charm:* distinctive, individual, special, particular, distinct, personal, unique.

especially adverb
1 *I used to enjoy walking along the lanes, especially in summer:* particularly, in particular, above all; mainly, chiefly, mostly, primarily, principally.
2 *a committee especially formed for the purpose:* expressly, specially, specifically, exclusively, just, particularly, explicitly.
3 *he is especially talented:* exceptionally, particularly, very, extremely, singularly, really.

espionage noun *the shadowy world of espionage:* spying, surveillance, intelligence.

espousal noun *his espousal of Western ideas:* adoption, embracing, acceptance; support, encouragement, promotion, endorsement, advocacy.

espouse verb *he espoused basic principles of economic liberalism:* adopt, embrace, take up, accept, welcome; support, back, champion, encourage, promote, endorse, advocate.
OPPOSITES: reject.

essay noun article, composition, study, paper, dissertation, thesis, discourse, treatise, monograph; commentary, critique; formal disquisition.

essence noun
1 *he has captured the very essence of the book:* quintessence, soul, spirit, intrinsic nature; core, heart, crux, nucleus, substance; principle, fundamental quality, sum and substance, reality, actuality.
2 *essence of ginger:* extract, concentrate, distillate.
□ **in essence**
an establishment that is, in essence, a single political party: essentially, basically, fundamentally; effectively, virtually; intrinsically, inherently.

essential adjective
1 *it is essential to keep up-to-date records | protein is an essential ingredient of our diet:* crucial, indispensable, vital, necessary, key, important, all-important, of the essence, critical, imperative.
2 *the essential simplicity of his style:* basic, fundamental, inherent, intrinsic, underlying; central, pivotal.

3 *the essential English gentleman:* ideal, absolute, complete, perfect, quintessential.
OPPOSITES: unimportant, inessential.

▷ **noun**
1 *this eyelash-curler is an essential for most make-up artists:* necessity, prerequisite, requisite, requirement; sine qua non; informal must.
2 *he was quick to grasp the essentials of his opponent's argument:* fundamentals, basics, first principles, foundations; essence, basis, core, kernel, crux; informal nitty-gritty.

establish verb
1 *the scheme was established in 1995:* set up, start, initiate, institute, form, found, create, inaugurate.
2 *police established that the passports were forgeries:* ascertain, discover, find, determine; confirm, verify, prove; demonstrate, show.
OPPOSITES: dissolve.

established adjective
1 *this is established practice:* accepted, traditional, orthodox, official; usual, customary, common, normal, general, prevailing, accustomed, familiar, habitual, expected, routine, typical, conventional, standard.
2 *an established composer:* well known, recognized, esteemed, respected, famous, prominent, noted, renowned.

establishment noun
1 *the establishment of a democracy:* foundation, founding, institution, formation, creation, inauguration, start, initiation.
2 *a dressmaking establishment:* business, firm, company, concern, enterprise, venture, organization, operation; factory, plant, shop, office, practice; informal outfit, set-up.
3 *educational establishments:* institution, place, premises, foundation, institute.
4 *they poked fun at the Establishment:* the authorities, the powers that be, the system, the ruling class; informal Big Brother.

estate noun
1 *the Balmoral estate:* property, grounds, gardens, park, parkland, land, lands.
2 *a housing estate:* area, site, development, complex.
3 *he left an estate worth £610,000:* assets, capital, wealth, riches, holdings, fortune; property, effects, possessions, belongings.

esteem noun *please accept this small gift as a mark of our esteem | he enjoyed immense public esteem during his lifetime:* respect, admiration, high regard, good opinion, appreciation, favour, recognition, honour.

▷ **verb** *such qualities are highly esteemed:* respect, admire, value, regard, appreciate, like, favour; prize, treasure.

estimate verb *they estimated the property to be worth £150,000:* calculate, assess, evaluate, judge, gauge, reckon, determine; consider, believe, deem; informal guesstimate.
▷**noun**
1 *an estimate of the cost:* calculation, approximation; costing, quotation, valuation, evaluation; informal guesstimate.
2 *his estimate of Paul's integrity:* evaluation, estimation, judgement, rating, appraisal, opinion, view.

estimation noun
1 *an estimation of economic growth:* estimate, approximation, rough calculation, rough guess, evaluation; informal guesstimate.
2 *he rated highly in Carl's estimation:* assessment, evaluation, judgement; esteem, opinion, view.

estrange verb *the retailer has estranged many of its core customers:* alienate, antagonize, turn away, drive away, distance; set at odds with, drive a wedge between.

estrangement noun *there seemed to be no obvious reason for their estrangement:* alienation, antagonism, antipathy, disaffection, hostility, unfriendliness; separation, parting, break-up, split.

estuary noun river mouth, firth; delta.

et cetera adverb *you need wellingtons, raincoat, umbrella, et cetera:* and so on, and so forth, and the like, and suchlike, among others, et al., etc.

etch verb
1 *intricate designs were etched into the stone and wood:* engrave, cut, carve, inscribe, incise, chase, score, print, mark.
2 *the incident was etched indelibly in her mind:* fix, imprint, stamp, impress.

etching noun engraving, print, impression, plate; woodcut, linocut.

eternal adjective
1 *the secret of eternal youth | eternal damnation:* everlasting, never-ending, endless, perpetual, undying, immortal, abiding, permanent, enduring, timeless.
2 *we've learned the importance of eternal vigilance:* constant, continual, continuous, perpetual, persistent, sustained, unremitting, relentless, unrelieved, unbroken, never-ending, non-stop, round-the-clock, endless, ceaseless.
OPPOSITES: transient, intermittent.

eternally adverb *I shall be eternally grateful:* forever, permanently, perpetually, for evermore, for ever and ever, for eternity, in perpetuity, enduringly.

eternity noun
1 *the memory will remain for eternity:* all time, time without end; perpetuity.

2 *souls destined for eternity:* the afterlife, everlasting life, life after death, the hereafter, the afterworld, the next world; heaven, paradise, immortality.
3 (informal) *I waited an eternity for you:* a long time, an age, ages, hours; forever.

ethereal adjective *her ethereal beauty:* delicate, exquisite, other-worldly, numinous, spiritual; fragile, light, insubstantial.

ethical adjective
1 *an ethical dilemma:* moral.
2 *ethical conduct:* morally correct, proper, right, principled, irreproachable, virtuous, good, moral; just, honourable, honest.
OPPOSITES: unethical.

ethics plural noun *the ethics of journalism:* moral code, morals, morality, values, rights and wrongs, principles, ideals, standards of behaviour.

ethnic adjective *a wide spectrum of ethnic groups:* racial, ethnological; cultural, national, tribal; traditional.

ethos noun *these two students effectively represent the aims and the ethos of the school:* spirit, character, ideals, values, attitudes, beliefs, creed; morality, moral code, principles, standards, ethics.

etiquette noun *the club's brochure includes advice on etiquette | the etiquette of golf:* protocol, manners, correct behaviour, rules of conduct, decorum, good form; courtesy, propriety, formalities, niceties, punctilios; custom, convention; informal the done thing.

eulogize verb *police eulogized the positive effect of speed cameras:* extol, acclaim, sing the praises of, praise to the skies, wax lyrical about, rhapsodize about, rave about, enthuse about.
OPPOSITES: criticize.

eulogy noun *an emotive eulogy was read by one of his closest friends:* accolade, tribute, commendation; praise, acclaim; literary panegyric, paean.

euphemistic adjective *euphemistic expressions for sacking someone, such as 'letting them go':* polite, indirect, evasive; diplomatic, inoffensive, neutral.

euphoria noun *they were swept up in the euphoria of victory:* elation, happiness, joy, delight, glee; excitement, exhilaration, jubilation, exultation; ecstasy, bliss, rapture.
OPPOSITES: misery.

euphoric adjective *more than 8,000 euphoric fans mobbed the team on their return from Europe:* elated, happy, joyful, delighted, gleeful; excited, exhilarated, jubilant, exultant; ecstatic, blissful, rapturous, on cloud nine, in seventh heaven; informal on the top of the world, over the moon, on a high.

euthanasia noun mercy killing, assisted suicide.

evacuate verb
1 *local residents were evacuated:* remove, clear, move out, take away.
2 *they evacuated the bombed town:* leave, vacate, abandon, desert, move out of, quit, pull out of, withdraw from, retreat from, decamp from, flee, depart from, escape from.

evacuation noun
1 *the evacuation of civilians:* removal, clearance.
2 *the evacuation of military bases:* vacation, abandonment, desertion; departure from, withdrawal from.

evade verb
1 *they managed to evade the guards:* elude, avoid, dodge, escape from, keep at arm's length, sidestep; lose, leave behind, shake off; informal give someone the slip.
2 *he evaded the question | I never sought to evade responsibility for my actions:* avoid, dodge, sidestep, bypass, hedge, skirt round, fudge, be evasive about; informal duck, cop out of.
OPPOSITES: confront.

evaluate verb *the study will evaluate the impact of the recent changes:* assess, judge, gauge, estimate, appraise, analyse, consider, weigh up, get the measure of; informal size up, check out.

evaluation noun assessment, appraisal, judgement, estimation, consideration, analysis.

evaporate verb
1 *the water evaporated:* vaporize, become vapour; dry up.
2 *the rock salt is washed and evaporated:* dry out, dehydrate, desiccate, dehumidify.
3 *his hopes of victory have evaporated:* disappear, vanish, fade, melt away, dissolve, dematerialize, fizzle out, peter out, cease to exist.
OPPOSITES: condense.

evasion noun
1 *the evasion of immigration control:* avoidance, dodging, sidestepping.
2 *she grew tired of all the evasion:* prevarication, evasiveness, beating about the bush, hedging, equivocation; Brit. humming and hawing.

evasive adjective *she was undeterred by his evasive replies:* equivocal, equivocating, prevaricating, ambiguous, non-committal, vague, unclear; roundabout, indirect; informal cagey.

eve noun *the eve of the election:* day before, evening before, night before; run-up to.

even adjective
1 *an even surface:* flat, smooth; level, plane.
2 *an even temperature | an even pace:* uniform, constant, steady, stable, consistent, unvarying, unchanging, regular.
3 *I'd say the two of them were pretty even:* equal, the same, like, alike, similar, comparable.
4 *the score was even:* level, drawn, tied, all square; neck and neck; Brit. level pegging.
5 *an even disposition:* even-tempered, balanced, stable, equable, placid, calm, composed, poised, cool, relaxed, easy, imperturbable, unruffled, untroubled; informal together, laid-back, unflappable.
OPPOSITES: uneven, irregular, unequal.
▷ verb
1 *the canal bottom was evened out:* flatten, level off/out, smooth off/out, plane; make uniform, make regular.
2 *the Lions evened the scores midway though the third quarter:* equalize, make equal, level up, balance.
▷ adverb *it got even colder:* still, yet, more, all the more.
□ even as
even as he spoke their baggage was being unloaded: while, whilst, as, just as, at the very time that, during the time that.
□ even so
it wasn't the most exciting of places but even so I was having a good time: nevertheless, nonetheless, all the same, just the same, anyway, still, yet, however, notwithstanding, despite that, in spite of that, for all that, be that as it may.
□ get even
have your revenge, avenge yourself, take vengeance, even the score, settle the score, hit back, give as good as you get, pay someone back, repay someone, reciprocate, retaliate, take reprisals, exact retribution; give someone their just deserts; informal get your own back, give someone a taste of their own medicine.

even-handed adjective *teachers must have an even-handed approach:* fair, just, equitable, impartial, unbiased, unprejudiced, non-partisan, non-discriminatory; disinterested, detached, objective, neutral.
OPPOSITES: biased.

evening noun night, close of day; twilight, dusk, nightfall, sunset, sundown.

event noun
1 *the tragic events of the past few weeks left us shocked and numb:* occurrence, happening, development, proceeding, incident, affair, circumstance, occasion, phenomenon.
2 *staff have been holding a number of events to raise money for charity:* function, gathering, occasion; informal bash, do.
3 *televised sporting events:* competition, contest, tournament, match, fixture; race, game, bout.

□ **in any event/at all events**
in any event I suspect the hearing will last more than one day: whatever happens, come what may, no matter what, at any rate, in any case, anyway, even so, still, nevertheless, nonetheless.

□ **in the event**
he was sent on a dangerous and, in the event, quite fruitless mission: as it turned out, as it happened, in the end, in fact.

even-tempered adjective *Richard was a gentle and even-tempered man:* calm, imperturbable, placid, equable, stable, level-headed, composed, relaxed, easy-going, tranquil, mellow, serene, unworried, untroubled, unruffled; informal unflappable, together, laid-back.
OPPOSITES: excitable.

eventful adjective *it had been a long and eventful day:* busy, action-packed, full, lively, active, hectic, strenuous; momentous, significant, important, historic, consequential, fateful.
OPPOSITES: dull.

eventual adjective *the eventual outcome of the competition:* final, ultimate, concluding, end; consequent, subsequent.

eventuality noun *it is impossible to anticipate every eventuality:* event, incident, occurrence, happening, development, phenomenon, situation, circumstance, case, contingency, chance, likelihood, possibility, probability; outcome, result.

eventually adverb *eventually I arrived at the hotel | they'll find out the truth eventually:* in the end, in due course, by and by, in time, after some time, after a while, finally, at last; ultimately, in the long run, one day, some day, sometime, sooner or later.

ever adverb
1 *do you ever regret leaving?* at any time, at any point, on any occasion.
2 *he was ever the optimist:* always, forever, eternally, at all times.
3 *an ever increasing rate of crime:* continually, constantly, always, perpetually, incessantly, unremittingly.

everlasting adjective *a symbol of everlasting love:* eternal, endless, never-ending, perpetual, undying, abiding, enduring; timeless.
OPPOSITES: transient.

every determiner
1 *he exercised every day:* each, each and every, every single.
2 *we make every effort to satisfy our clients:* all possible, the utmost.

everybody pronoun *everybody agrees with him:* everyone, every person, each person, all, one and all, all and sundry, the whole world, the public; informal {every Tom, Dick, and Harry}.

everyday adjective *traffic jams are an everyday occurrence in the city | everyday household tasks:* daily, day-to-day, regular, frequent; ordinary, common, commonplace, familiar, run-of-the-mill, standard, stock; Brit. common or garden; formal quotidian.
OPPOSITES: unusual.

everyone pronoun *she didn't want everyone to know her business:* everybody, every person, each person, all, one and all, all and sundry, the whole world, the public; informal {every Tom, Dick, and Harry}.

everywhere adverb *I've looked everywhere:* all over, all around, in every place, far and wide, high and low, {here, there, and everywhere}; the world over, worldwide; informal all over the place.

evict verb *the police moved in and evicted the squatters:* eject, remove, turn out, throw out, drive out, expel; informal chuck out, kick out, boot out, throw someone out on their ear; Brit. informal turf out.

eviction noun *his family are facing eviction from their home:* ejection, removal, expulsion.

evidence noun
1 *in the cases where we have evidence of racism, we take strong action to deal with it:* proof, confirmation, verification, substantiation, corroboration.
2 *the court accepted her evidence:* testimony, statement, submission.
3 *there was no obvious evidence of a break-in:* sign, indication; suggestion.
▷ verb *more and more ageing baby boomers are becoming entrepreneurs, as evidenced by the latest government data:* indicate, show, reveal, display, manifest; testify to, confirm, prove, substantiate, endorse, bear out.
□ **in evidence**
the city's medieval street plan is still in evidence today: noticeable, conspicuous, obvious, perceptible, visible, on view.

evident adjective *he regarded her with evident interest:* obvious, apparent, noticeable, conspicuous, perceptible, visible, discernible, clear, plain, manifest, patent; palpable, distinct, pronounced, marked, striking, glaring, blatant, unmistakable.

evidently adverb
1 *he was evidently dismayed:* obviously, clearly, plainly, visibly, manifestly, patently; unmistakably, undeniably, undoubtedly.
2 *evidently, she believed herself superior:* seemingly, apparently, from all appearances, on the face of it; it seems that, it appears that.

evil adjective
1 *an evil deed:* wicked, bad, wrong,

immoral, sinful, vile, dishonourable, corrupt, iniquitous, depraved, villainous, nefarious, malevolent, sinister, diabolical; monstrous, shocking, despicable, atrocious, heinous, odious, contemptible; informal low-down, dirty.
2 *an evil influence:* **harmful**, hurtful, injurious, detrimental, deleterious, inimical, bad, pernicious, malignant, malign; destructive.
OPPOSITES: good, beneficial.
▷ **noun**
1 *the evil in our midst:* **wickedness**, sin, immorality, vice, iniquity, degeneracy, corruption, depravity, villainy.
2 *nothing but evil would ensue:* **harm**, pain, misery, sorrow, suffering, trouble, disaster, misfortune, catastrophe, affliction, woe, hardship.
3 *the evils of war:* **abomination**, atrocity, obscenity, outrage, enormity, crime, monstrosity, barbarity.

evocative adjective *the book is powerfully evocative of life in Britain during the 1960s | his music is characterized by simple but evocative lyrics:* **suggestive**, reminiscent, redolent; expressive, vivid, graphic, powerful, haunting, moving, poignant.

evoke verb *the poems evoke a sense of desolate emptiness:* **bring to mind**, conjure up, summon up, invoke, elicit, stir up, awaken, arouse, induce, kindle, stimulate; recall, echo, capture.

evolution noun
1 *the evolution of Bolshevism:* **development**, emergence, growth, progress.
2 *his interest in evolution:* **Darwinism**, natural selection.

evolve verb *the economies of all four nations evolved in different ways:* **develop**, grow, progress, advance; mature, expand, spread; alter, change.

exacerbate verb *political changes have exacerbated the conflict:* **aggravate**, worsen, inflame, compound; intensify, increase, heighten, magnify, add to, amplify, augment; informal add fuel to the fire/flames.
OPPOSITES: ease.

exact adjective
1 *an exact description | an exact replica:* **precise**, accurate, correct, faithful, close, true; literal, strict, faultless, perfect; explicit, detailed, minute; informal on the nail, on the mark; Brit. informal spot on, bang on.
2 *an exact manager:* **careful**, meticulous, painstaking, punctilious, conscientious, scrupulous,; methodical, organized, orderly.
OPPOSITES: inexact, inaccurate, careless.
▷ **verb**
1 *she exacted high standards from them:* **demand**, require, insist on, request, expect.

2 *they exacted a terrible vengeance on him:* **inflict**, impose, administer.

exacting adjective
1 *an exacting training routine:* **demanding**, stringent, challenging, onerous, arduous, testing, taxing, gruelling, punishing, hard, tough.
2 *an exacting boss:* **strict**, stern, firm, demanding, tough, harsh.
OPPOSITES: easy, easy-going.

exactly adverb *it's exactly as I expected it to be:* **precisely**, entirely, absolutely, completely, totally, just, quite, in every way, in every respect, every inch.

exaggerate verb *they have exaggerated the extent of the problems:* **overstate**, overemphasize, overstress, play up, overplay, make too much of, magnify, amplify, inflate; embellish, embroider, elaborate, dramatize; stretch the truth; informal lay it on thick, make a mountain out of a molehill, blow something out of all proportion, make a big thing of.
OPPOSITES: understate.

exaggerated adjective *an exaggerated account of his exploits:* **overstated**, inflated, amplified; hyperbolic, elaborate, overdone, overplayed, overdramatized, highly coloured, melodramatic, sensational; informal over the top, OTT.

exaggeration noun **overstatement**, overemphasis, amplification; dramatization, elaboration, embellishment, embroidery, hyperbole, overkill.

exalt verb
1 *the party will continue to exalt their hero:* **extol**, praise, acclaim; pay homage to, revere, venerate, worship, lionize, idolize; informal put on a pedestal.
2 *this power exalts the peasant:* **elevate**, promote, raise, advance, aggrandize.
3 *his works exalt the emotions:* **ennoble**, dignify, elevate.

exalted adjective
1 *his exalted office:* **high**, high-ranking, elevated, superior, lofty, eminent, prestigious, illustrious, distinguished.
2 *his exalted aims:* **noble**, lofty, high-minded, elevated.
3 *she felt spiritually exalted:* **elated**, exultant, jubilant, joyful, rapturous, ecstatic, blissful, happy, exhilarated; informal high.

exam noun **test**, examination, assessment; paper, oral, practical; Brit. viva.

examination noun
1 *artefacts spread out for examination:* **scrutiny**, inspection, study, investigation, consideration, analysis, appraisal, evaluation; formal perusal.
2 *a medical examination:* **inspection**, check-up, assessment, review; probe, test, scan; informal once-over, overhaul.

3 *end-of-term examinations:* test, exam, assessment; paper, oral, practical; Brit. viva.

examine verb

1 *they examined the bank records:* inspect, scrutinize, investigate, look at, study, probe, analyse, review, consider; informal check out.
2 *students were examined each year:* test, question; assess, appraise.

example noun

1 *a fine example of Chinese porcelain:* specimen, sample, exemplification, exemplar; instance, case, illustration.
2 *we must follow their example:* precedent, lead, model, pattern, exemplar, ideal, standard; role model.
3 *he was hanged as an example to others:* warning, caution, lesson, deterrent.
□ **for example**
his collection included, for example, great works by Cézanne, Gauguin, Monet, and Renoir: for instance, e.g., by way of illustration, such as, like.

exasperate verb *Smith's erratic behaviour exasperated him:* infuriate, anger, annoy, irritate, madden, enrage, incense; antagonize, provoke, irk, vex, get on someone's nerves; informal aggravate, rile, bug, hack off, get someone's back up; Brit. informal nark.
OPPOSITES: please.

exasperating adjective infuriating, annoying, irritating, maddening, provoking, irksome, vexatious, frustrating; informal aggravating.

exasperation noun irritation, annoyance, vexation, anger, fury, frustration; informal aggravation.

excavate verb

1 *they excavated a narrow tunnel:* dig, bore, hollow out, scoop out; burrow, tunnel, sink, gouge.
2 *numerous artefacts have been excavated:* unearth, dig up, uncover, reveal; disinter, exhume.

exceed verb

1 *the cost will exceed £4000:* be more than, be greater than, be over, go beyond, top.
2 *economic growth exceeded expectations this year:* surpass, outdo, outstrip, transcend, top, beat, better.

exceedingly adverb *the team played exceedingly well:* extremely, exceptionally, tremendously, very, really, remarkably, extraordinarily, terribly, singularly; informal awfully, seriously.

excel verb

1 *he excelled at football:* be outstanding, be excellent, shine; stand out, be the best, be unparalleled, be unequalled, be second to none, be unsurpassed.
2 *he has excelled all his contemporaries:* surpass, outdo, outshine, outclass, outstrip, beat, top, transcend, better, pass, eclipse, overshadow; informal best, be head and shoulders above, be a cut above.

excellence noun *the children's hospital is a centre of medical excellence:* distinction, quality, superiority, brilliance, greatness, merit, calibre, eminence, pre-eminence, supremacy, peerlessness; skill, talent, virtuosity, accomplishment, mastery.

excellent adjective *their results are excellent:* very good, superb, outstanding, exceptional, marvellous, wonderful; pre-eminent, perfect, matchless, peerless, supreme, first-rate, first-class, superlative, splendid, fine; informal ace, great, terrific, tremendous, fantastic, fabulous, awesome, wicked, cool, out of this world, top-notch; Brit. informal brilliant.
OPPOSITES: inferior.

except preposition *they're open every day except Monday:* excluding, with the exception of, but, besides, apart from, aside from, barring, bar, other than, saving; not counting, not including, excepting, omitting.
OPPOSITES: including.
▷ **verb** *only three men were excepted from the general amnesty:* exclude, omit, leave out, disregard.
OPPOSITES: include.

> **USAGE**
>
> Do not confuse **except** with **accept**. **Except** means 'not including; apart from', while **accept** means 'to agree to receive or do something' (*she accepted the job*).

exception noun *this case is an exception:* anomaly, irregularity, special case, peculiarity, abnormality, oddity; informal freak.
□ **take exception**
McGregor took exception to these remarks: object, take offence, take umbrage, demur; resent, argue against, protest against, oppose, complain about; informal kick up a fuss.
□ **with the exception of.** See EXCEPT preposition.

exceptionable adjective (formal). See OBJECTIONABLE.

exceptional adjective

1 *price increases of this magnitude are not exceptional:* unusual, uncommon, abnormal, atypical, extraordinary, out of the ordinary, unexpected, surprising, unprecedented; strange, odd, freakish, anomalous.
2 *her exceptional ability:* outstanding, extraordinary, remarkable, special, excellent, phenomenal, prodigious; unequalled, unparalleled, unsurpassed, peerless, matchless, first-rate, first-class; informal top-notch.
OPPOSITES: normal, average.

exceptionally adverb
1 *it was exceptionally cold:* **unusually**, uncommonly, abnormally, atypically, extraordinarily, unexpectedly, surprisingly; strangely, oddly.
2 *an exceptionally acute mind:* **exceedingly**, outstandingly, extraordinarily, remarkably, especially, phenomenally, prodigiously.

excerpt noun *an excerpt from his latest novel:* **extract**, part, section, piece, portion, snippet, clip, bit; reading, quotation, quote, citation, line, passage.

excess noun
1 *PMS symptoms can be due to an excess of oestrogen:* **surplus**, surfeit, overabundance, superabundance, superfluity, glut; too much.
2 *the excess is turned into fat:* **remainder**, rest, residue; surplus, extra, difference.
3 *a life of excess:* **overindulgence**, intemperance, immoderation, profligacy, extravagance, decadence, self-indulgence.
OPPOSITES: lack, deficit.
▷ adjective *excess skin oils:* **surplus**, superfluous, redundant, unwanted, unneeded, excessive; extra.
□ **in excess of**
a top speed in excess of 20 knots: **more than**, over, above, upwards of, beyond.

excessive adjective
1 *he was drinking excessive amounts of alcohol:* **immoderate**, intemperate, inordinate; overindulgent, unrestrained, uncontrolled, extravagant; superfluous.
2 *the cost is excessive:* **exorbitant**, extortionate, unreasonable, outrageous, undue, uncalled for, extreme, unwarranted, disproportionate, too much; informal over the top.

excessively adverb *her father had excessively high standards:* **inordinately**, unduly, unnecessarily, unreasonably, ridiculously, overly; very, extremely, exceedingly, exceptionally, impossibly; immoderately, intemperately, too much.

exchange noun
1 *the exchange of ideas:* **interchange**, trade, trading, swapping.
2 *an acrimonious exchange:* **conversation**, dialogue, talk, discussion; debate, argument, altercation; Brit. row.
▷ verb *we exchanged shirts* | *he exchanged cigarettes for food:* **swap**, trade, switch, change, interchange.
□ **exchange blows**
fight, brawl, scuffle, tussle; informal scrap, have a set-to; Brit. informal have a punch-up.
□ **exchange words**
argue, quarrel, squabble, have an argument/disagreement; Brit. row; Brit. informal have a slanging match.

excise[1] noun *the excise on spirits:* **duty**, tax, levy, tariff.

excise[2] verb
1 *the tumours were excised:* **cut out/off**, take out, extract, remove.
2 *all unnecessary detail should be excised:* **remove**, take out, delete, cancel.

excitable adjective *she seems rather excitable:* **temperamental**, volatile, emotional, sensitive, highly strung; nervous, tense, edgy, jumpy, twitchy; neurotic; unstable; informal uptight, wired.
OPPOSITES: placid.

excite verb
1 *flying still excites me:* **thrill**, exhilarate, stimulate, animate, rouse, stir, galvanize, electrify; informal give someone a buzz/kick; N. Amer. informal give someone a charge.
2 *his partying and lavish lifestyle had excited much envy:* **give rise to**, engender, occasion, provoke, stir up, rouse, arouse, kindle, cause.
OPPOSITES: bore, depress.

excited adjective *the air was electric as the sell-out crowd waited in excited anticipation:* **thrilled**, exhilarated, electrified, animated; enthusiastic, intoxicated, feverish, delirious; expectant, agog; elated, ecstatic, euphoric, rapturous; informal high, fired up.

excitement noun
1 *the excitement of seeing a leopard in the wild:* **thrill**, pleasure, delight, joy; informal kick, buzz; N. Amer. informal charge.
2 *her cheeks were flushed with excitement:* **exhilaration**, elation, animation, enthusiasm, eagerness, anticipation.

exciting adjective *it was one of the most exciting matches I've ever seen:* **thrilling**, exhilarating, stirring, rousing, stimulating, intoxicating, electrifying; enthralling, gripping, compelling, powerful, dramatic.

exclaim verb *'That hurt!' she exclaimed angrily:* **cry**, declare, blurt out; call out, shout, yell.

exclamation noun **cry**, call, shout, yell, interjection.

exclude verb
1 *women were excluded from many scientific societies:* **keep out**, deny access to, shut out, debar, bar, ban, prohibit.
2 *the clause excluded any judicial review:* **eliminate**, rule out, preclude.
3 *the price excludes postage:* **be exclusive of**, not include.
4 *he excluded her name from the list:* **leave out**, omit, miss out, fail to include.
OPPOSITES: admit, include.

exclusive adjective
1 *one of the country's most exclusive club:* **select**, high-class, elite, chic, fashionable, stylish, elegant, premier; expensive; Brit. upmarket; informal posh, ritzy, classy; Brit. informal swish.
2 *the room is for your exclusive use:* **sole**, unshared, unique, only, individual, personal, private.
3 *prices were exclusive of VAT:* **not**

e

including, excluding, omitting, excepting.
4 *these are mutually exclusive alternatives:*
incompatible, irreconcilable.
OPPOSITES: inclusive.
▷**noun** *a six-page exclusive:* scoop, exposé.

excrescence noun
1 *an excrescence on his leg:* growth, lump,
swelling, nodule, outgrowth.
2 *the building is a sixties excrescence foisted
on an otherwise attractive street:* eyesore,
blot on the landscape, monstrosity.

excrete verb *the process by which waste
products are excreted from the body:* expel,
pass, void, discharge, eject, evacuate.
OPPOSITES: ingest.

excruciating adjective *an excruciating
pain:* agonizing, severe, acute, intense,
violent, racking, searing, piercing,
stabbing, raging; unbearable, unendurable.

excursion noun *an excursion to Blackpool:*
trip, outing, jaunt, expedition, journey,
tour; day trip, day out, drive; informal junket,
spin.

excusable adjective *an excusable mistake
under the circumstances:* forgivable,
pardonable, defensible, justifiable; venial.
OPPOSITES: inexcusable.

excuse verb
1 *such conduct can never be excused:*
justify, defend, condone, vindicate;
forgive, overlook, disregard, ignore,
tolerate, sanction.
2 *please excuse me for my behaviour last
night:* forgive, pardon.
3 *she has been excused from her duties:* let
off, release, relieve, exempt, free.
OPPOSITES: punish, blame, condemn.
▷**noun**
1 *that's no excuse for stealing:* justification,
defence, reason, explanation, mitigating
circumstances, mitigation, vindication.
2 *I needed an excuse to get away:* pretext,
ostensible reason, pretence; Brit. get-out.
3 (informal) *that pathetic excuse for a man!*
travesty of, poor specimen of; informal
apology for.

execrable adjective *an execrable piece of
work:* appalling, awful, dreadful, terrible,
atrocious, abysmal, lamentable, egregious;
unpleasant, disgusting, vile; informal
diabolical, lousy; Brit. informal shocking.
OPPOSITES: admirable.

execute verb
1 *the corporation executed a series of
financial deals:* carry out, put into effect,
effect, implement, accomplish, bring
off/about, achieve, complete, engineer;
perform; formal effectuate; informal pull off.
2 *he was convicted of treason and executed:*
put to death, kill; hang, shoot, behead,
electrocute.

execution noun
1 *the successful execution of the plan:*

implementation, carrying out,
accomplishment, bringing off/about,
engineering; performance.
2 *thousands were sentenced to execution:*
capital punishment, the death penalty;
hanging, the gallows, the guillotine, the
firing squad, a lethal injection; N. Amer. the
electric chair.

executive adjective *executive powers:*
administrative, decision-making,
managerial; law-making.
▷**noun**
1 *top-level bank executives:* chief, head,
director, senior official, senior manager,
CEO, chief executive officer; informal boss,
suit.
2 *the executive has increased in number:*
administration, management, directorate;
government, legislative body.

exemplar noun *he was regarded as an
exemplar of rationality and decorum:*
epitome, perfect example, model, paragon,
ideal, exemplification, textbook example,
embodiment, essence, quintessence.

exemplary adjective
1 *her exemplary behaviour:* perfect,
model, faultless, flawless, impeccable,
irreproachable; excellent, outstanding,
admirable, commendable, laudable, above/
beyond reproach.
2 *exemplary jail sentences:* cautionary,
warning, admonitory.
3 *her works are exemplary of certain
feminist arguments:* typical, characteristic,
representative, illustrative.
OPPOSITES: deplorable.

exemplify verb
1 *this case study exemplifies current trends:*
typify, epitomize, be a typical example of,
be representative of.
2 *he exemplified his point with an
anecdote:* illustrate, give an example of,
demonstrate.

exempt adjective *these patients are exempt
from all charges:* free, not liable, not
subject, exempted, excepted, excused.
OPPOSITES: subject to.
▷**verb** *he had been exempted from military
service:* excuse, free, release, give/grant
immunity, spare; informal let off.

exercise noun
1 *exercise improves your heart and lung
power:* physical activity, a workout,
working out; sports, games, training.
2 *translation exercises:* task, piece of work,
problem, assignment.
3 *the exercise of professional skill:* use,
utilization, employment; practice,
application.
4 *military exercises:* manoeuvres,
operations; war games.
▷**verb**
1 *he must learn to exercise patience | I intend
to exercise my right to vote:* use, employ,
make use of, utilize; practise, apply.

2 *she exercised every day:* work out, train; informal pump iron.
3 *the problem continued to exercise him:* worry, trouble, concern, make anxious, bother, disturb, perturb, distress, preoccupy, prey on someone's mind, make uneasy; informal bug.

exert verb
1 *he exerted considerable pressure on me:* bring to bear, apply, exercise, employ, use, utilize, deploy.
2 *soldiers and police officers exerted themselves to help alleviate the appalling situation:* make an/every effort, try hard, strive, endeavour, do your best/utmost, give your all, push yourself, drive yourself, work hard; informal go all out, pull out all the stops, bend over backwards, do your damnedest, move heaven and earth.

exertion noun
1 *she was panting with the exertion:* effort, strain, struggle, toil, endeavour, hard work, labour; Brit. informal graft.
2 *the exertion of pressure:* use, application, exercise, employment, utilization.

exhale verb *she exhaled her cigarette smoke:* breathe out, blow out, puff out.
OPPOSITES: inhale.

exhaust verb
1 *the effort had exhausted him:* tire out, wear out, overtire, fatigue, weary, drain, run someone into the ground; informal do in, take it out of someone, wipe out, knock out, shatter; Brit. informal knacker.
2 *the country has exhausted its reserves:* use up, run through, go through, consume, finish, deplete, spend, empty, drain; informal blow.
3 *I think we've exhausted the subject:* treat thoroughly, do to death, study in great detail.
OPPOSITES: invigorate, replenish.

exhausted adjective
1 *I'm exhausted:* tired out, worn out, weary, drained, fatigued, enervated; informal done in, all in, dead beat, ready to drop, dog-tired, shattered, bushed, knocked out, wiped out; Brit. informal knackered, whacked; N. Amer. informal pooped, tuckered out.
2 *the personal wealth he accumulated is nearly exhausted:* used up, consumed, finished, spent, depleted; empty, drained.

exhausting adjective *a long and exhausting journey:* tiring, wearying, taxing, fatiguing, wearing, enervating, draining; arduous, laborious, strenuous, onerous, demanding, gruelling, punishing; informal killing, murderous; Brit. informal knackering.

exhaustion noun
1 *sheer exhaustion forced Paul to give up:* extreme tiredness, overtiredness, fatigue, weariness.
2 *the exhaustion of fuel reserves:* consumption, depletion, using up, expenditure; draining, emptying.

exhaustive adjective *an exhaustive study of the subject:* comprehensive, all-inclusive, complete, full, encyclopedic, thorough, in-depth; detailed, meticulous, painstaking.
OPPOSITES: perfunctory.

exhibit verb
1 *the paintings were exhibited at Sotheby's:* put on display, put on show, display, show, put on public view, showcase; set out, lay out, array, arrange.
2 *Luke exhibited signs of jealousy:* show, reveal, display, manifest; express, indicate, demonstrate, present; formal evince.
▷ noun *an exhibit at the British Museum:* object on display, item, piece.

exhibition noun
1 *an exhibition of French sculpture:* display, show, showing, presentation, demonstration, exposition, showcase; N. Amer. exhibit.
2 *a convincing exhibition of concern:* demonstration, show, display, manifestation, expression.

exhibitionist noun posturer, self-publicist; extrovert; informal show-off, poser.

exhilarate verb *he was exhilarated by the speed:* thrill, excite, intoxicate, elate, delight, enliven, invigorate, energize, stimulate; informal give someone a thrill/buzz; N. Amer. informal give someone a charge.

exhilaration noun elation, euphoria, exultation, joy, happiness, delight, jubilation, rapture, ecstasy.

exhort verb *he exhorted delegates to fight corruption:* urge, encourage, call on, charge, press; appeal to, entreat, implore; formal enjoin; old use bid.

exhortation noun
1 *no amount of exhortation had any effect:* urging, encouragement, persuasion, pressure.
2 *consumers ignored exhortations to 'buy British':* entreaty, appeal, call.

exhume verb *four years later his body was exhumed:* disinter, dig up.
OPPOSITES: bury.

exigency noun (formal)
1 *the exigencies of the continuing war:* need, demand, requirement, necessity.
2 *financial exigency:* urgency, crisis, difficulty, pressure.

exile noun
1 *his exile from the land of his birth:* banishment, expulsion, deportation.
2 *political exiles:* émigré, expatriate; displaced person, DP, refugee, deportee; informal expat.
▷ verb *he was exiled from his country in 1972:*

e

expel, banish, deport, drive out, throw out, eject.

exist verb

1 *this is the most endangered large whale in the world—only 300 to 350 of the animals still exist:* live, be alive, be living; be, have being, have existence.
2 *the liberal climate that existed during his presidency:* prevail, occur, be found, be in existence; be the case.
3 *she had to exist on a low income:* survive, subsist, live, support yourself; manage, make do, get by, scrape by, make ends meet.

existence noun

1 *she kept the company alive when its very existence was threatened:* actuality, being, reality; survival, continuation.
2 *her suburban existence:* way of life, life, lifestyle.
□ **in existence**
1 *there are several million unidentified species in existence:* alive, existing, extant, existent.
2 *the only copy still in existence:* surviving, remaining, undestroyed, in circulation.

existent adjective *species that are no longer existent:* in existence, alive, existing, living, extant; surviving, remaining, undestroyed.

existing adjective *the existing social security system:* current, present, in existence, in force, in operation, in place; prevailing, extant, existent.

exit noun

1 *a fire exit:* way out, door, egress, escape route; doorway, gate, gateway.
2 *take the second exit:* turning, turn-off, turn.
3 *his sudden exit:* departure, leaving, withdrawal, retreat; flight, escape, exodus.
OPPOSITES: entrance, arrival.
▷ **verb** *the doctor had just exited:* leave, go out, depart, withdraw, retreat.
OPPOSITES: enter.

exodus noun *civil war began, leading to a massive exodus of refugees:* mass departure, withdrawal, evacuation, leaving; migration, emigration; flight, escape.

exonerate verb *the report completely exonerated the junior doctors:* absolve, clear, acquit, find innocent, discharge.

exorbitant adjective *the fees charged by the consultants were exorbitant:* extortionate, excessively high, excessive, prohibitive, outrageous, unreasonable, inflated, huge, enormous; Brit. over the odds; informal steep, stiff, over the top, a rip-off; Brit. informal daylight robbery.
OPPOSITES: reasonable.

exotic adjective

1 *exotic birds:* foreign, non-native; tropical.

2 *exotic places:* foreign, faraway, far-off, far-flung, distant, remote, unfamiliar, strange.
3 *Linda's exotic appearance:* striking, colourful, eye-catching; unusual, unconventional, offbeat, out of the ordinary; outlandish; informal off the wall.
OPPOSITES: native, nearby, conventional.

expand verb

1 *the company is expanding* | *he borrowed money to expand the business:* grow, become/make larger, become/make bigger, increase in size/scope; extend, augment, broaden, widen, develop, diversify, build up; branch out, spread, proliferate.
2 *metals expand when heated:* increase in size, become larger, enlarge; swell, dilate, inflate; lengthen, stretch, thicken, fill out.
3 *the minister expanded on the proposals:* elaborate on, enlarge on, go into detail about, flesh out, develop, expatiate on.
OPPOSITES: shrink, contract.

expanse noun *the wide expanse of grass:* area, stretch, sweep, tract, swathe, belt, region; sea, carpet, blanket, sheet.

expansion noun

1 *the expansion of the company:* growth, increase in size, enlargement, extension, development, buildout; spread, proliferation.
2 *expansion and contraction:* enlargement, increase in size, swelling, dilation; lengthening, elongation, stretching, thickening.
OPPOSITES: contraction.

expansive adjective

1 *the expansive moorlands:* extensive, sweeping, rolling.
2 *the paper was applauded for its expansive coverage of the events:* wide-ranging, extensive, broad, wide, comprehensive, thorough.
3 *Cara became engagingly expansive:* communicative, forthcoming, sociable, friendly, outgoing, chatty, talkative, garrulous, loquacious, voluble.

expatiate verb *he expatiated on his ideas at some length:* speak/write at length about, go into detail about, expound on, expand on, enlarge on, elaborate on; dwell on.

expect verb

1 *a 10 per cent rise was expected:* anticipate, await, look for, hope for, look forward to; predict, forecast, envisage, envision; contemplate, bargain for/on, bank on.
2 *I expect she'll be late:* suppose, presume, think, believe, imagine, assume, surmise; informal guess, reckon; N. Amer. informal figure.
3 *we expect total loyalty:* require, ask for, call for, want, insist on, demand.

expectancy noun *an atmosphere of feverish expectancy:* anticipation,

expectation, eagerness, excitement.

expectant adjective

1 *expectant fans arrived early:* eager, excited, agog, waiting with bated breath, hopeful; in suspense, on tenterhooks.
2 *an expectant mother:* pregnant; informal expecting.

expectation noun

1 *the expectation is that profits overall will rise:* belief, opinion, view; assumption, calculation, prediction.
2 *his body grew tense with expectation:* anticipation, expectancy, eagerness, excitement, suspense.

expedient adjective *a politically expedient strategy:* convenient, advantageous, in your own interests, useful, of use, beneficial, of benefit, helpful; practical, pragmatic, politic, prudent, wise, judicious, sensible.
▷ noun *a temporary expedient:* measure, means, method, stratagem, scheme, plan, move, tactic, manoeuvre, device, contrivance, ploy, machination, dodge.

expedite verb *he promised to expedite economic reforms:* speed up, accelerate, hurry, hasten, step up, quicken; advance, facilitate, ease, make easier, further, promote, aid, push through, urge on, boost, stimulate, spur on, help along.
OPPOSITES: delay.

expedition noun

1 *an expedition to the South Pole:* journey, voyage, trip, tour; exploration, safari, trek; mission, quest.
2 *a shopping expedition:* trip, excursion, outing, jaunt.

expeditious adjective *an expeditious system for examining claims for refugee status:* speedy, swift, quick, rapid, fast, efficient; prompt, immediate, instant.
OPPOSITES: slow.

expel verb

1 *he was expelled from the national party after publicly criticizing his colleagues:* throw out, eject, bar, ban, debar, drum out, oust, remove, get rid of, dismiss, exclude; Military cashier; informal chuck out, sling out, kick/boot out; Brit. informal turf out.
2 *he was expelled from the country:* banish, exile, deport, evict, drive out, throw out.
3 *she expelled a shuddering breath:* let out, discharge, eject, issue.
OPPOSITES: admit.

expend verb

1 *huge sums of money were expended on parachute training:* spend, pay out, disburse, dole out; waste, fritter away, dissipate; informal fork out, shell out, lay out, cough up; Brit. informal stump up.
2 *children expend a lot of energy:* use, use up, utilize, consume, get through, deplete.
OPPOSITES: save, conserve.

expendable adjective

1 *an accountant decided he was expendable:* dispensable, non-essential, inessential, unnecessary, not required, superfluous, disposable.
2 *an expendable satellite launcher:* disposable, throwaway, one-use, single-use.
OPPOSITES: indispensable.

expenditure noun

1 *the expenditure of funds:* spending, paying out, outlay, disbursement.
2 *reducing public expenditure:* outgoings, costs, payments, expenses, overheads, spending.
OPPOSITES: saving, income.

expense noun

1 *the extra features are well worth the expense:* cost, price, charge, outlay, fee, tariff, levy, payment; humorous damage.
2 *keep a note of your regular expenses:* outgoing, outlay, expenditure, payment, charge, bill, overhead.

expensive adjective *an expensive restaurant:* costly, high-priced; overpriced, exorbitant, extortionate; Brit. dear; informal pricey, costing an arm and a leg, costing the earth, costing a bomb.
OPPOSITES: cheap, economical.

experience noun

1 *her business experience was invaluable:* skill, knowledge, practical knowledge, understanding; background, record, history; informal know-how.
2 *his first experience of business:* involvement in, participation in, contact with, acquaintance with, exposure to, observation of, awareness of, insight into.
3 *an unforgettable experience:* event, occurrence, incident, happening, episode; adventure, exploit, escapade.
▷ verb *the company has experienced some difficulties:* encounter, undergo, come up against, meet, run into, come across, face, be faced with, come into contact with.

> WORD LINKS
> **empirical** based on experience and observation rather than theory or logic

experienced adjective

1 *an experienced pilot:* skilled, expert, accomplished, adept, adroit, proficient, trained, competent, capable, well trained, well versed; seasoned, practised, mature, veteran; qualified, professional.
2 *a well-travelled and experienced man:* worldly, worldly wise, sophisticated, suave, urbane, mature, knowing; informal streetwise.
OPPOSITES: inexperienced, naive.

experiment noun

1 *he carried out a series of experiments:* test, investigation, trial, examination, piece of research, observation; assessment, evaluation, appraisal, analysis, study.

e

2 *these results have been established by experiment:* research, experimentation, observation, analysis, testing.
▷**verb** *they experimented with various materials and techniques:* conduct experiments, carry out trials/tests, conduct research; test, trial, do tests on, try out, assess, appraise, evaluate.

experimental adjective
1 *the new drug is still in the experimental stage:* exploratory, investigational, trial, test, pilot; speculative, tentative, preliminary, untested, untried.
2 *experimental music:* innovative, new, original, avant-garde, alternative, unorthodox, unconventional; informal left-field, way-out.

expert noun *a financial expert | an expert in Italian Renaissance art:* specialist, authority, pundit; adept, maestro, virtuoso, past master, wizard; connoisseur, aficionado; informal ace, buff, pro, whizz, hotshot; Brit. informal dab hand.
OPPOSITES: novice.
▷**adjective** *an expert chess player:* skilful, skilled, adept, accomplished, talented, fine; master, masterly, brilliant, virtuoso, magnificent, outstanding, great, exceptional, excellent, first-class, first-rate, superb; proficient, good, able, capable, experienced, practised, knowledgeable; informal wizard, ace, crack, mean.
OPPOSITES: incompetent, inexpert.

expertise noun *technical expertise:* skill, skilfulness, prowess, proficiency, competence; knowledge, mastery, ability, aptitude, facility, capability; informal know-how.

expiate verb *he attempts to expiate his sins by becoming a minister:* atone for, make amends for, make up for, do penance for, pay for, redress, redeem, make good.

expire verb
1 *the lease has expired:* run out, become invalid, become void, lapse; end, finish, stop, come to an end, terminate.
2 *he expired ten days later of a second heart attack:* die, pass away/on, breathe your last.

explain verb
1 *he explained the situation:* describe, clarify, give an explanation of, make clear, spell out, put into words; shed light on, elucidate, expound, explicate; gloss, interpret.
2 *staff tried to explain away the bad service by claiming that the chef was ill:* account for, give an explanation for, give a reason for; justify, give a justification for, excuse, give an excuse for, legitimize.

explanation noun
1 *the guide offers a detailed explanation of how the tax system works:* clarification,

simplification; account, description; elucidation, exposition, explication; interpretation, commentary, exegesis.
2 *Freud tried to make sex the explanation for everything:* reason; justification, excuse, defence, vindication.

explanatory adjective *he added a number of explanatory notes to the second edition:* illuminating, helpful, expository; descriptive, illustrative.

expletive noun *she let out an expletive and slammed the phone down:* swear word, oath, curse, obscenity, profanity, four-letter word, dirty word; (**expletives**) bad language, foul language, strong language, swearing.

explicable adjective *differences in schools were not explicable in terms of differences in intake:* explainable, understandable, comprehensible, accountable, intelligible, interpretable.

explicate verb *scholars who have been devoted to explicating these stories:* explain, make explicit, clarify, spell out; interpret, elucidate, expound, illuminate, throw light on.

explicit adjective
1 *all participants were given explicit instructions about when and how to use these treatments:* clear, plain, straightforward, crystal clear, easily understandable; precise, exact, specific, unequivocal, unambiguous, definite, categorical; detailed, comprehensive, exhaustive.
2 *sexually explicit material:* uncensored, graphic, candid, full-frontal.
OPPOSITES: vague.

explode verb
1 *three people were killed when the bomb exploded last night:* blow up, detonate, go off.
2 *Britain had not yet exploded her first atomic device:* detonate, set off, let off, discharge.
3 *he exploded with rage:* lose your temper, blow up, get angry, become enraged; informal fly off the handle, hit the roof, go wild, see red, go off the deep end; Brit. informal go spare.
4 *between 1984 and 2000, the country's population exploded:* increase suddenly/rapidly, mushroom, snowball, escalate, multiply, burgeon, rocket.
5 *a team at the University of Queensland has exploded many myths about schizophrenia:* disprove, refute, rebut, invalidate, discredit, debunk, belie, give the lie to; informal shoot full of holes, blow out of the water.
OPPOSITES: defuse.

exploit verb
1 *500 companies sprang up to exploit this new technology:* utilize, use, make use of,

turn/put to good use, make the most of, capitalize on, benefit from; informal cash in on.

2 *a ruling class which exploited the workers:* take advantage of, abuse, impose on, treat unfairly, misuse, ill-treat; informal walk all over, take for a ride, rip off.

▷**noun** *his exploits brought him notoriety:* feat, deed, act, action, adventure, stunt, escapade; achievement, accomplishment.

exploitation noun
1 *the exploitation of mineral resources:* utilization, use.
2 *the exploitation of the poor:* misuse, abuse, ill-treatment, unfair treatment, oppression.

exploration noun
1 *an exploration of feminine identity and sexual politics:* investigation, study, survey, research, examination, scrutiny, observation; consideration, analysis, review, inspection.
2 *explorations into the mountains:* expedition, trip, journey, voyage; (**explorations**) travels.

exploratory adjective *surgeons performed an exploratory operation | the exploratory phase of the project:* investigative, investigational, fact-finding; preliminary, experimental, trial, provisional.

explore verb
1 *they explored all the possibilities:* investigate, look into, consider, inquire into; examine, evaluate, research, survey, scrutinize, study, review; informal check out.
2 *he explored uncharted forests in Korea:* travel over, tour, range over; survey, inspect, investigate, reconnoitre.

explorer noun traveller, voyager, adventurer; surveyor, scout, prospector.

explosion noun
1 *we heard the explosion and the building started to shake:* detonation; bang, blast, boom.
2 *an explosion of anger:* outburst, flare-up, outbreak, eruption, storm, rush, surge; fit, paroxysm, attack.
3 *the explosion of the urban population:* sudden/rapid increase, mushrooming, snowballing, escalation, multiplication, burgeoning.

explosive adjective
1 *explosive gases | an explosive device:* volatile, inflammable, flammable, combustible; incendiary.
2 *Marco's explosive temper:* fiery, stormy, violent, volatile, angry, passionate, tempestuous, turbulent, touchy, irascible, hot-headed, short-tempered.
3 *an explosive situation:* tense, highly charged, fraught, unstable, volatile, sensitive; dangerous, perilous, hazardous.
4 *explosive economic growth:* sudden, dramatic, rapid; escalating, rocketing.

▷**noun** *stocks of explosives:* bomb, incendiary device.

exponent noun
1 *an exponent of free-trade policies:* advocate, supporter, proponent, upholder, backer, defender, champion; promoter, propagandist, campaigner, fighter, crusader, enthusiast, apologist.
2 *the world's leading exponent of country rock guitar:* performer, player, practitioner.
OPPOSITES: critic, opponent.

export verb
1 *the country exports oil to the United States:* sell overseas/abroad, send overseas/abroad, trade internationally.
2 *the group have been trying to export their ideas to the rest of the western world:* transmit, spread, disseminate, circulate, communicate, pass on.
OPPOSITES: import.

expose verb
1 *he has been exposed as a liar | the situation exposed a conflict within the government:* uncover, reveal, unveil, unmask; discover, bring to light, disclose, bring into the open, make known, lay bare.
2 *many newcomers are exposing themselves to injury:* put at risk of, subject to, lay open to, make vulnerable to.
3 *they were exposed to liberal ideas:* introduce to, bring into contact with, make aware of, familiarize with, acquaint with.
4 *at low tide the sands are exposed:* reveal, uncover, lay bare.
OPPOSITES: cover.

exposé noun *a shocking exposé of a medical cover-up:* revelation, disclosure, exposure; report, feature, piece; informal scoop.
OPPOSITES: cover-up.

exposed adjective *the farm is on an exposed hillside:* unprotected, unsheltered, open to the elements/weather; vulnerable, defenceless, undefended.
OPPOSITES: sheltered.

exposition noun
1 *a lucid exposition of evolutionary theory:* explanation, description, elucidation, explication, interpretation; account, commentary, appraisal, assessment, discussion, exegesis.
2 *the exposition will feature 200 exhibits:* exhibition, trade fair, display, show, presentation, demonstration; N. Amer. exhibit.

expostulate verb *one of the prisoners expostulated with him:* remonstrate, take issue, argue, protest, disagree, express disagreement, raise objections.

exposure noun
1 *the exposure of the scandal blighted the careers of several leading politician:* uncovering, revelation, disclosure,

unveiling, unmasking, discovery, laying
bare.
2 *we're getting a lot of exposure:* publicity,
public interest/attention, media interest/
attention; informal hype.
3 *his literary sensibility and style were
shaped by his exposure to Bengali literature:*
introduction to, experience of, contact
with, familiarity with, acquaintance with,
awareness of.

expound verb
1 *he expounded his theories:* present, put
forward, set forth, propose, propound;
explain, give an explanation of, detail, spell
out, describe.
2 *a treatise expounding Paul's teachings:*
explain, interpret, explicate, elucidate;
comment on, give a commentary on.
□ **expound on**
he declined to expound on his decision:
elaborate on, expand on, expatiate on,
discuss at length.

express¹ verb
1 *community leaders expressed their anger:*
communicate, convey, indicate, show,
demonstrate, reveal, put across/over, get
across/over; articulate, put into words,
utter, voice, give voice to; state, assert,
proclaim, profess, air, make public, give
vent to.
2 *all the juice is expressed:* squeeze out,
press out, extract.
□ **express yourself**
communicate your thoughts, put your
thoughts into words, speak your mind, say
what's on your mind.

express² adjective *an express train:* rapid,
fast, high-speed, quick, speedy, swift; non-
stop, direct.
OPPOSITES: slow.

express³ adjective
1 *the solicitor was acting on express
instructions from his client:* explicit, clear,
direct, plain, distinct, unambiguous,
unequivocal, definite; specific, precise,
crystal clear, certain, categorical.
2 *the money was raised for the express
purpose of carrying out research:*
sole, specific, particular, exclusive,
specified.
OPPOSITES: implied.

expression noun
1 *the free expression of opposing points
of view:* utterance, uttering, voicing,
declaration, articulation.
2 *his expression was troubled:* look,
appearance, air, manner, countenance,
mien.
3 *an old-fashioned expression:* idiom,
phrase, idiomatic expression; proverb,
saying, adage, maxim, axiom, aphorism,
saw, motto, platitude, cliché.

expressionless adjective
1 *his face was expressionless:* inscrutable,
deadpan, poker-faced; blank, vacant,

without emotion; stony, wooden, impassive.
2 *a flat, expressionless tone:* dull, toneless,
monotonous, flat, unmodulated.
OPPOSITES: expressive, lively.

expressive adjective
1 *an expressive shrug:* eloquent,
meaningful, telling, revealing, suggestive.
2 *an expressive song:* emotional, full of
emotion/feeling, passionate, poignant,
moving, stirring, evocative, powerful,
emotionally charged.
3 *the film is expressive of larger social
trends:* indicative, demonstrative,
suggestive.
OPPOSITES: expressionless, unemotional.

expressly adverb
1 *he was expressly forbidden to discuss the
matter:* explicitly, clearly, directly, plainly,
distinctly, unambiguously, unequivocally;
absolutely; specifically, categorically.
2 *a machine expressly built for spraying
paint:* solely, specifically, particularly,
specially, exclusively, just, only.

expropriate verb *legislation to
expropriate land from absentee landlords:*
seize, take, appropriate, take possession
of, requisition, commandeer, claim,
sequestrate, confiscate.

expulsion noun *his expulsion from the
party:* removal, debarment, dismissal,
exclusion, ejection.
OPPOSITES: admission.

expunge verb *that moment can never be
expunged from his memory:* erase, remove,
delete, rub out, wipe out, efface; cross out,
strike out, blot out, blank out; destroy,
obliterate, eradicate, eliminate.

expurgate verb *the book had been
expurgated for use in schools:* censor,
bowdlerize, cut, edit; clean up, sanitize,
make more palatable, water down.

exquisite adjective
1 *exquisite antique glass:* beautiful, lovely,
elegant, fine; delicate, dainty, fragile;
magnificent, superb, excellent, wonderful,
well crafted, well made, perfect.
2 *she has exquisite taste:* discriminating,
discerning, sensitive, fastidious;
impeccable, refined, cultivated, cultured,
educated.
3 *Drake felt the blade pierce his stomach—
the pain was exquisite:* intense, acute,
keen, piercing, sharp.

extant adjective *only one copy of
Cavendish's book is extant:* still existing, in
existence, existent, surviving, remaining,
undestroyed.

extempore adjective *an extempore
speech:* impromptu, spontaneous,
unscripted, ad lib, extemporary,
extemporaneous; improvised,
unrehearsed, unplanned, unprepared, off
the top of your head; informal off-the-cuff.
OPPOSITES: rehearsed.

▷**adverb** *he was speaking extempore:* **without preparation**, extemporaneously, ad lib, spontaneously, without rehearsal, off the top of your head; informal off the cuff.

extemporize verb *he put the speech to one side and began to extemporize:* **improvise**, ad lib, play it by ear, think on your feet, do something off the top of your head; informal busk it, wing it, do something off the cuff.

extend verb
1 *he attempted to extend his dominions:* **expand**, enlarge, increase, make larger/bigger; lengthen, widen, broaden.
2 *the garden extends down to the road:* **continue**, carry on, run, stretch, reach, lead.
3 *we have extended our range of services:* **widen**, expand, broaden; augment, supplement, increase, add to, enhance, develop.
4 *this bill will extend the period of paid parental leave from 12 weeks to 14 weeks:* **prolong**, lengthen, increase, stretch; protract, spin out, string out.
5 *extend your arms and legs:* **stretch out**, spread out, reach out, straighten out.
6 *he extended a hand in greeting:* **hold out**, reach out, hold forth; offer, give, outstretch, proffer.
7 *we wish to extend our thanks to Mr Bayes:* **offer**, proffer, give, grant, bestow, accord.
OPPOSITES: reduce, narrow, shorten.
▢ **extend to**
UK consumer protection law did not extend to overseas traders: **include**, take in, incorporate, encompass.

extended adjective *an extended legal battle:* **prolonged**, protracted, long-lasting, long-drawn-out, lengthy, long.

extension noun
1 *they are planning an extension to their ground floor:* **addition**, add-on, adjunct, annexe, wing, supplementary building.
2 *the extension of government power:* **expansion**, increase, enlargement, widening, broadening; augmentation, enhancement, development, growth.
3 *if you can't complete your tax return by the deadline, request an extension:* **postponement**, deferral, delay, more/extra time.

extensive adjective
1 *a mansion with extensive grounds:* **large**, sizeable, substantial, considerable, ample, expansive, great, vast.
2 *his extensive knowledge of jazz:* **comprehensive**, thorough, exhaustive; broad, wide, wide-ranging, catholic.

extent noun
1 *the garden was about two acres in extent:* **area**, size, expanse, length; proportions, dimensions.
2 *she does not appreciate the extent of the* problem | *the extent of their knowledge varied greatly:* **degree**, scale, level, magnitude, scope; size, breadth, reach, range.

extenuating adjective *there were extenuating circumstances:* **mitigating**, acting in mitigation.

exterior adjective *the exterior walls:* **outer**, outside, outermost, outward, external.
▷**noun** *the exterior of the building:* **outside**, outer surface, external surface, outward appearance, facade.
OPPOSITES: interior.

exterminate verb *colonizers exterminated the native population:* **destroy**, wipe out, eliminate, eradicate, annihilate; kill, put to death, dispatch; slaughter, massacre, murder; informal do away with.

extermination noun **destruction**, elimination, eradication, annihilation; killing, murder, slaughter, massacre.

external adjective
1 *an external wall:* **outer**, outside, outermost, exterior; .
2 *an external examiner:* **outside**, independent, non-resident, from elsewhere.
OPPOSITES: internal.

extinct adjective
1 *an extinct species:* **vanished**, lost, died out, no longer existing, no longer extant; wiped out, destroyed.
2 *an extinct volcano:* **inactive**.
OPPOSITES: extant.

extinction noun **dying out**, disappearance, vanishing; extermination, destruction, elimination, eradication, annihilation.

extinguish verb
1 *the fire was extinguished:* **douse**, put out, stamp out, smother, beat out, dampen down.
2 *the bombings extinguished hopes that the economy was on the verge of recovery:* **destroy**, end, put an end to, bring to an end, wipe out, erase, eliminate, eradicate, obliterate.
OPPOSITES: light.

extol verb *for two years, I extolled the virtues of this diet to anyone who would listen:* **praise enthusiastically**, go into raptures about/over, wax lyrical about, sing the praises of, praise to the skies, acclaim, eulogize, rhapsodize over, rave about, enthuse about/over; formal laud; informal go wild about.
OPPOSITES: criticize.

extort verb *he was convicted of extorting money from local residents:* **obtain by force**, obtain by threats, blackmail someone for, extract, exact, wring, wrest, screw, squeeze.

e

extortion noun demanding money with menaces, blackmail.

extortionate adjective *the prices are extortionate:* exorbitant, excessively high, excessive, outrageous, unreasonable, inordinate, inflated, prohibitive, punitive; informal over the top, OTT.

extra adjective *some pensioners do have extra income from savings | we've taken on extra staff:* additional, more, added, supplementary, further, auxiliary, ancillary, subsidiary, secondary.

▷ adverb
1 *everyone is working extra hard:* exceptionally, particularly, especially, very, extremely; unusually, extraordinarily, uncommonly, remarkably, outstandingly, amazingly, incredibly, really, terribly; informal seriously, awfully.
2 *installation will cost about £60 extra:* in addition, additionally, as well, besides, on top.

▷ noun *an optional extra:* addition, supplement, adjunct, addendum, add-on; bonus.

extract verb
1 *he extracted the disk:* take out, draw out, pull out, remove, withdraw; free, release, extricate.
2 *a promise was unfairly extracted from me:* wrest, exact, wring, screw, squeeze, obtain by force, obtain by threats, extort.
3 *the roots are crushed to extract the juice:* squeeze out, express, press out, obtain.
4 *the text appears to have been extracted from an article in the 'Evening Advertiser':* excerpt, select, reproduce, copy, take.
OPPOSITES: insert.

▷ noun
1 *an extract from his article:* excerpt, passage, citation, quotation.
2 *natural plant extracts:* essence, distillation, concentrate, decoction; preparation.

extraction noun
1 *the extraction of minerals from the ground | the extraction of wisdom teeth:* removal, taking out, drawing out, pulling out, withdrawal.
2 *a man of Irish extraction:* descent, ancestry, parentage, ancestors, family, antecedents; lineage, line, origin, derivation, birth; genealogy, heredity, stock, pedigree, blood, bloodline; roots, origins.
OPPOSITES: insertion.

extradite verb *the government extradited him to Germany:* deport, send back, send home, repatriate.

extradition noun deportation, repatriation, expulsion.

extraneous adjective
1 *extraneous considerations:* irrelevant, immaterial, beside the point, unrelated, unconnected, inapposite, inapplicable.
2 *extraneous noise:* external, outside, exterior.

extraordinary adjective *an extraordinary coincidence | an extraordinary achievement:* remarkable, amazing, astonishing, astounding, sensational, stupendous, stunning, incredible, unbelievable, phenomenal; very great, exceptional, tremendous, enormous, immense, prodigious, monumental; striking, outstanding, momentous, impressive, singular, memorable, unforgettable, unique, noteworthy; out of the ordinary, unusual, uncommon, rare, surprising; informal fantastic, terrific, awesome.
OPPOSITES: ordinary, unremarkable.

extravagance noun
1 *he always avoided extravagance:* profligacy, improvidence, wastefulness, prodigality, lavishness, excess.
2 *the costliest brands are an extravagance:* luxury, indulgence, self-indulgence, treat, extra, non-essential.
3 *the extravagance of the decor:* ornateness, elaborateness, embellishment, ornamentation; ostentation, over-elaborateness, excess.

extravagant adjective
1 *an extravagant lifestyle:* lavish, indulgent; profligate, spendthrift, improvident, wasteful, prodigal.
2 *extravagant gifts:* expensive, costly, high-priced; valuable.
3 *extravagant praise:* excessive, immoderate, exaggerated, gushing, unrestrained, effusive, fulsome.
4 *an extravagant architectural style:* ornate, elaborate, decorated, ornamented, fancy; over-elaborate, ostentatious, exaggerated, baroque, rococo.
OPPOSITES: thrifty, cheap, plain.

extravaganza noun *a live extravaganza featuring a host of stars:* spectacular, display, spectacle, show, pageant.

extreme adjective
1 *they are in extreme danger | long periods of extreme cold:* the utmost, very great, greatest possible, maximum, highest, supreme, great, acute, enormous, severe, high, exceptional, extraordinary.
2 *extreme measures are necessary:* drastic, serious, desperate, radical, far-reaching; severe, harsh, tough, strict, rigorous, oppressive, draconian; Brit. swingeing.
3 *a person of very extreme views:* radical, extremist, immoderate, fanatical, revolutionary, subversive, militant.
4 *extreme sports:* dangerous, hazardous, risky, high-risk.
5 *the extreme north-west:* furthest, farthest, furthermost, farthermost, very, utmost.
OPPOSITES: slight, moderate.

▷**noun**
1 *the two extremes:* opposite, antithesis, side of the coin, pole.
2 *this attitude is taken to its extreme in the following quote:* limit, extremity, highest/greatest degree, maximum, height, top, zenith, peak.
□ **in the extreme.** See **EXTREMELY**.

> **WORD LINKS**
> **ultra-** forming words meaning 'to an extreme degree; very', such as *ultralight* ('extremely lightweight')

extremely adverb *we are all extremely worried* | *it was an extremely difficult job:* very, exceedingly, exceptionally, especially, extraordinarily, in the extreme, tremendously, immensely, vastly, intensely, acutely, singularly, uncommonly, unusually, decidedly, particularly, supremely, highly, remarkably, really, truly, terribly; informal terrifically, awfully, seriously, mega, ultra; Brit. informal well, dead, jolly.
OPPOSITES: slightly.

extremist noun *the attack was carried out by a group of right-wing extremists:* fanatic, zealot, fundamentalist, hardliner, militant, activist, radical.
OPPOSITES: moderate.

extremity noun
1 *the peninsula's eastern extremity:* limit, end, edge, side, farthest point, boundary, border, frontier; perimeter, periphery, margin.
2 *she lost all feeling in her extremities:* hands and feet, fingers and toes, limbs.
3 *the extremity of the violence:* intensity, magnitude, acuteness, ferocity, vehemence, fierceness, violence, severity, strength, power, powerfulness, force, forcefulness.

extricate verb
1 (**extricate yourself**) *he was trying to extricate himself from official duties:* escape, get out of, avoid; informal get someone/yourself off the hook.
2 *rescue workers managed to extricate the driver through a small hole in the wreckage:* free, extract, release, disentangle, get out, remove, withdraw, disengage.

extrinsic adjective *the animal population is influenced by extrinsic factors like food supply and predation:* external, exterior, outside, outward; extraneous.
OPPOSITES: intrinsic.

extrovert noun *like most extroverts he was a good dancer:* outgoing person, sociable person, socializer; informal life and soul of the party.
OPPOSITES: introvert.
▷**adjective** *his extrovert personality:* outgoing, extroverted, sociable, gregarious, genial, affable, friendly, unreserved.
OPPOSITES: introverted.

extrude verb *lava was extruded from the volcano:* force out, thrust out, express, eject, expel, release.

exuberant adjective
1 *his youthfully exuberant mood* | *the exuberant post-match celebrations:* ebullient, buoyant, cheerful, jaunty, light-hearted, high-spirited, excited, vivacious, enthusiastic, irrepressible, bubbly, bouncy, energetic, animated, full of life, lively, vigorous; elated, euphoric, joyful, jubilant; informal chirpy, full of beans.
2 *an exuberant welcome:* effusive, extravagant, fulsome, expansive, gushing, demonstrative.
3 (literary) *the exuberant foliage:* luxuriant, lush, rich, dense, thick, abundant, profuse, plentiful, prolific.
OPPOSITES: gloomy, restrained.

exude verb
1 *the plant exudes a milky sap:* give off/out, emit, discharge, release; ooze, weep, secrete, excrete.
2 *slime exudes from the fungus:* ooze, seep, issue, escape, be discharged, leak.
3 *he exuded self-confidence:* emanate, radiate, ooze; display, show, exhibit, manifest; embody.

exult verb
1 *her opponents exulted when she left:* rejoice, be joyful, be delighted, be elated, be ecstatic, be overjoyed, be cock-a-hoop, be jubilant, be rapturous, be in raptures, be thrilled, jump for joy, be on cloud nine, be in seventh heaven; celebrate, cheer; informal be over the moon, be on top of the world.
2 *he exulted in his triumph:* rejoice at/in, take great delight in, take great pleasure in, revel in, glory in, delight in, relish, savour; be/feel proud of, congratulate yourself on.
OPPOSITES: sorrow.

exultant adjective *the exultant winners waved to the crowd:* jubilant, thrilled, triumphant, delighted, happy, overjoyed, joyful, gleeful, cock-a-hoop, excited, ecstatic, euphoric, elated, rapturous, on cloud nine, in seventh heaven, exhilarated; literary joyous; informal over the moon.

exultation noun jubilation, rejoicing, happiness, joy, delight, glee, elation, euphoria, exhilaration, delirium, ecstasy, rapture, exuberance.

eye noun
1 *his sharp eyes had missed nothing:* eyesight, vision, sight, powers of observation, visual perception.
2 *to European eyes, it may seem that the city is overcrowded:* opinion, view, viewpoint, way of thinking, judgement
▷**verb** *he eyed the stranger suspiciously:* look at, regard, contemplate, observe, view, gaze at, stare at, survey, scrutinize,

consider, glance at; watch, keep an eye on; informal check out, size up; N. Amer. informal eyeball.

◻ **see eye to eye** *we see eye to eye on a large number of issues:* agree, concur, be in agreement, be of the same mind/opinion, be in accord, think as one; be on the same wavelength, get on/along.

> **WORD LINKS**
>
> **ocular, optic, ophthalmic** relating to the eyes, or to vision
>
> **ophthalmology** the study and treatment of eye diseases and disorders

eye-catching adjective *an eye-catching design:* striking, bold, arresting, noticeable, distinctive, dramatic, vivid, colourful; unusual, out of the ordinary.

eyesight noun *his eyesight is poor:* sight, vision, faculty of sight, ability to see, visual perception.

eyesore noun *the rubbish tip is a real eyesore:* ugly sight, blot on the landscape, monstrosity; informal sight.

eyewitness noun *eyewitnesses stated that one plane crashed in the harbour:* observer, onlooker, witness, bystander, spectator, watcher, viewer, passer-by.

Ff

fable noun
1 *the fable of the hare and the tortoise:* story, tale, parable, moral tale, allegory.
2 *the fables of ancient Greece:* myth, legend, saga, epic, folk tale, folk story, fairy tale; folklore, mythology.

fabled adjective
1 *the fabled god-giant of Irish myth:* legendary, mythical, mythological, fabulous, fairy-tale; fictitious, imaginary, made up.
2 *the fabled quality of French wine:* celebrated, renowned, famed, famous, well known, prized, acclaimed, noted, notable, legendary.
OPPOSITES: real-life, obscure.

fabric noun
1 *they weave the finest silk fabrics in the world:* cloth, material, textile.
2 *the fabric of the building has deteriorated:* structure, construction, framework, frame, form, substance, composition.

fabricate verb *he was found to have fabricated the research data:* invent, make up, concoct, trump up, fake, falsify.

fabrication noun *the story was a complete fabrication:* invention, concoction, piece of fiction, falsification, lie, untruth, falsehood, fib, myth, made-up story, fairy story/tale; informal cock and bull story.

fabulous adjective
1 *they are paid fabulous salaries:* huge, vast, enormous, tremendous, stupendous, prodigious, phenomenal, remarkable, exceptional; astounding, amazing, fantastic, breathtaking, staggering, unthinkable, unimaginable; informal mind-boggling, mind-blowing.
2 (informal) *we had a fabulous time.* See **EXCELLENT.**
3 *a fabulous horse-like beast with a human head:* legendary, mythical, mythological, fabled, fairy-tale; fictitious, imaginary, imagined, made up.

facade noun
1 *the house has a half-timbered facade:* front, frontage, face, elevation, exterior, outside.
2 *what lay behind their facade of bonhomie?* show, front, appearance, pretence, simulation, act, affectation, semblance, illusion, masquerade, charade, veneer.

face noun
1 *she has a beautiful face:* features, countenance, physiognomy; literary visage.
2 *her face grew sad again:* expression, look, appearance, countenance, mien.
3 *a cube has six faces:* side, surface, plane, facet, wall, elevation, aspect, flank.
4 *he put on a brave face for his audience:* front, show, display, act, appearance, facade, exterior, mask, masquerade, pretence, pose, veneer.
▷verb
1 *the hotel faces the sea:* look out on, front on to, look towards, be facing, look over/across, overlook, give on to, be opposite.
2 *you'll just have to face facts:* accept, become reconciled to, become resigned to, come to terms with, get used to, become accustomed to, adjust to, acclimatize yourself to, learn to live with, cope with, deal with.
3 *he faced a hostile reception from union delegates:* be confronted by, be faced with, encounter, experience, come into contact with, come up against.
4 *the difficulties facing small rural communities:* confront, trouble, bother, beset, worry, distress, torment, plague, blight, bedevil, curse.
5 *he faced this challenge boldly:* brave, face up to, meet head-on, confront; oppose, resist, withstand.
6 *a low wall faced with flint:* cover, clad, surface, veneer, overlay, dress, laminate, coat, line.
□ loss of face
he could step aside now without any loss of face: humiliation, embarrassment, indignity, ignominy, dishonour, discredit, loss of respect, shame, disgrace.
□ on the face of it
on the face of it, this decision is the height of folly: apparently, seemingly, outwardly, it seems that, it appears that, by all accounts, to all appearances, at first glance, on the surface, superficially.

facelift noun
1 *she's planning to have a facelift:* cosmetic surgery, plastic surgery.
2 (informal) *the theatre is reopening after a*

$20,000 facelift: **renovation,** redecoration, refurbishment, revamp, makeover, overhaul, modernization, restoration, redevelopment, refit.

facet noun
1 *the large number of facets preserves the size of the gem:* **surface,** face, side; technical plane.
2 *she'd also seen other facets of his character:* **aspect,** feature, side, dimension, characteristic, detail, point, ingredient, strand; component, constituent, element.

facetious adjective *the crew greeted my arrival on board with facetious comments:* **flippant,** frivolous, glib, tongue-in-cheek, joking, jokey, jocular, playful, teasing, mischievous; informal flip.
OPPOSITES: serious, respectful.

facile adjective *it is easy to fall into facile and unproductive stereotypes:* **simplistic,** superficial, oversimplified; shallow, glib, jejune, naive.
OPPOSITES: subtle, intelligent.

facilitate verb *working in pairs appears to facilitate learning:* **make easier,** ease, enable, assist, help, aid, oil the wheels of, expedite, speed up, accelerate, forward, advance, promote, further, encourage.
OPPOSITES: impede.

facility noun
1 *there are ample car-parking facilities:* **provision,** amenities, resources, services, equipment, space, room, means.
2 *the camera has a zoom facility:* **feature,** option, setting, mode.
3 *they set up a medical facility deep in the jungle:* **centre,** establishment, station, location, premises, site, post, base; informal outfit, set-up.
4 *his undoubted facility for drawing:* **aptitude,** talent, gift, flair, bent, skill, knack, genius; ability, proficiency, competence, capability, capacity, faculty.

facing noun
1 *a tartan jacket with green velvet facings:* **covering,** trimming, lining.
2 *the bricks were used as a facing on a concrete core:* **cladding,** skin, surface, facade, front, coating, covering, dressing, veneer, overlay, lamination, plating.
OPPOSITES: backing.

facsimile noun *here's an extremely rare facsimile of the score for Beethoven's Fifth:* **copy,** reproduction, duplicate, replica, likeness; print, reprint.
OPPOSITES: original.

fact noun
1 *it is a fact that the water supply is polluted:* **reality,** actuality, certainty; truth, gospel.
2 *one of the most remarkable facts about the universe:* **detail,** piece of information, particular, item, specific, element, point, factor, feature, characteristic, ingredient,
circumstance, aspect; (**facts**) information, data, evidence.
OPPOSITES: lie, fiction.
▫ **in fact**
actually, really, in reality, as a matter of fact, in truth, to tell the truth.

faction noun
1 *he was supported by a faction of the Liberal Party:* **clique,** coterie, caucus, cabal, bloc, camp, group, grouping, sector, section, wing, arm, branch, set; ginger group, pressure group.
2 *the council was increasingly split by faction:* **infighting,** dissent, dispute, strife, conflict, friction, argument, disagreement, controversy, discord, disunity, schism.
OPPOSITES: agreement.

factious adjective *he had transformed a fragmented, factious movement into a united one:* **divided,** split, schismatic, discordant, quarrelling, warring, at loggerheads, at odds.
OPPOSITES: harmonious.

factor noun *this had been a key factor in his decision to stand down:* **element,** component, ingredient, consideration, influence, circumstance, strand, constituent, point, detail, item, feature.

factory noun **works,** plant, yard, mill, industrial unit, workshop, shop.

factual adjective *balanced, factual information about consumer products is very useful:* **truthful,** true, accurate, authentic, historical, genuine, fact-based; true-to-life, correct, exact, honest, faithful, objective.
OPPOSITES: fictitious.

faculty noun
1 *he had quite lost the faculty of speech:* **power,** capability, capacity, facility, means.
2 *he had a faculty for unearthing new contributors to the fund:* **ability,** proficiency, competence, capability, potential, capacity, facility; aptitude, talent, gift, flair, bent, skill, knack, genius.
3 *the arts faculty of the university:* **department,** school, division, section.

fad noun *there is a general fad for see-through products:* **craze,** vogue, trend, fashion, mode, enthusiasm, passion, obsession, mania, rage, compulsion, fixation, fetish, fancy, whim, fascination.

fade verb
1 *the paintwork has faded and peeled:* **pale,** bleach, lose colour, discolour; dull, dim.
2 *sunlight had faded the picture:* **bleach,** wash out, blanch, whiten, dim, dull.
3 *remove the flower heads as they fade:* **wither,** wilt, droop, shrivel, die.
4 *the afternoon light began to fade:* **grow dim,** grow faint, fail, dwindle, die away, wane, disappear, vanish, decline, melt away.
5 *the economic boom is beginning to fade*

away: decline, die out, diminish, dwindle, come to an end, peter out, taper off, tail off.

fail verb

1 *they could not explain why the enterprise had failed:* be unsuccessful, not succeed, fall through, fall flat, collapse, founder, backfire, meet with disaster, come to nothing; informal flop, bomb.
2 *he failed all his exams:* not pass, not make the grade in; informal flunk.
3 *he felt his friends had failed him:* let down, disappoint; desert, abandon, betray, be disloyal to; literary forsake.
4 *the ventilation system failed:* break, break down, stop working, cut out, crash; malfunction, go wrong, develop a fault; informal conk out, go on the blink; Brit. informal pack up.
5 *900 businesses are failing each week:* collapse, crash, go under, go bankrupt, go into receivership, go into liquidation, cease trading, be wound up; informal fold, go bust, go to the wall.
OPPOSITES: succeed, pass.
□ **without fail**
she went to Mass every Sunday without fail: without exception, unfailingly, regularly, invariably, predictably, conscientiously, religiously, come what may.

failing noun *Jeanne accepted him despite his failings:* fault, shortcoming, weakness, imperfection, defect, flaw, frailty; foible, idiosyncrasy, vice.
OPPOSITES: strength.
▷**adjective** *the dry climate would be good for his failing health:* declining, weakened, weak, fragile, damaged.
OPPOSITES: robust, improving.

failure noun

1 *the failure of the assassination attempt improved police morale:* lack of success, non-fulfilment, defeat, collapse, foundering.
2 *every one of his schemes had been a failure:* fiasco, debacle, catastrophe, disaster; informal flop.
3 *he felt guilty for what seemed like a failure on his part:* negligence, dereliction of duty; omission, oversight.
4 *the failure of the camera:* breakdown, malfunction, fault; crash.
5 *the failure of several state-owned companies:* collapse, crash, bankruptcy, insolvency, liquidation, closure.
OPPOSITES: success.

faint adjective

1 *her skirt still had a faint mark on it:* indistinct, vague, unclear, indefinite, ill-defined, unobtrusive; pale, light, faded.
2 *the baby gave a faint cry:* quiet, muted, muffled, stifled; feeble, weak, whispered, murmured, indistinct; low, soft, gentle.
3 *the faint possibility of his returning to office:* slight, slender, slim, small, tiny,

negligible, remote, vague, unlikely, improbable.
4 *I suddenly felt hot and faint:* dizzy, giddy, light-headed, unsteady; informal woozy.
OPPOSITES: clear, loud, strong.
▷**verb** *he was so pale she thought he would faint:* pass out, lose consciousness, black out, keel over; literary swoon; informal flake out.
▷**noun** *she collapsed to the floor in a dead faint:* blackout, fainting fit, loss of consciousness; literary swoon.

> **USAGE**
>
> Do not confuse **faint** with **feint**. **Faint** means 'not clearly seen, heard, or smelt' or 'to lose consciousness'. **Feint** means 'a deceptive movement intended to make someone think that you are going to do something' (*the operation was originally conceived as a feint to draw away enemy troops*).

faint-hearted adjective *the more faint-hearted tenants left after the raid:* timid, timorous, nervous, nervy, easily scared, fearful, afraid; cowardly, craven, spineless, pusillanimous; informal yellow-bellied, gutless, wimpish.
OPPOSITES: brave.

faintly adverb

1 *Maria called his name faintly:* indistinctly, softly, gently, weakly, quietly, in a low voice.
2 *the new officer looked faintly bewildered:* slightly, vaguely, somewhat, quite, fairly, rather, a little, a bit, a touch, a shade; informal sort of, kind of.

fair¹ adjective

1 *the courts were generally regarded as fair* | *this is a fair decision:* just, equitable, impartial, unbiased, unprejudiced, non-partisan, neutral, even-handed, reasonable, honourable.
2 *I am hoping for fair weather next week:* fine, dry, bright, clear, good, sunny, cloudless, warm, pleasant, clement.
3 *she had long fair hair:* blonde, yellowish, golden, light; literary flaxen.
4 *Belinda's skin was very fair:* pale, light, white, creamy.
5 *scoring twenty points was a fair achievement:* reasonable, passable, tolerable, satisfactory, acceptable, respectable, decent, all right, good enough, pretty good, not bad, average, middling; informal OK, so-so.
OPPOSITES: unfair, inclement, dark.

fair² noun

1 *we visited the county fair:* fete, gala, festival, carnival.
2 *a local antiques fair:* market, bazaar, mart, exchange, sale.
3 *Manchester is to host a new British art fair:* exhibition, display, show, presentation, exposition.

fairly adverb

1 *all pupils were treated fairly:* justly,

equitably, honourably, impartially, without bias, without prejudice, neutrally, even-handedly, equally, the same.
2 *the pipes are in fairly good condition:* reasonably, passably, tolerably, adequately, moderately, quite, relatively, comparatively; informal pretty.
OPPOSITES: unfairly.

fair-minded adjective *he was respected as a fair-minded judge:* fair, just, even-handed, equitable, impartial, non-partisan, unbiased, unprejudiced, detached, neutral, independent.
OPPOSITES: biased.

fairy noun sprite, pixie, elf, imp, brownie, puck, leprechaun.

fairy tale, **fairy story** noun folk tale, folk story, traditional story, fable, myth, legend, saga, epic, fantasy.

faith noun
1 *he justified his boss's faith in him:* trust, belief, confidence, credence, conviction; optimism, hope.
2 *she gave her life for her faith:* religion, belief, creed, persuasion, ideology, teaching, doctrine; church, denomination, sect.
OPPOSITES: mistrust.

faithful adjective
1 *she stayed faithful all her married life* | *his faithful assistant:* loyal, devoted, constant, true, unswerving, staunch, steadfast, dedicated, committed; trusty, trustworthy, dependable, reliable.
2 *a faithful copy of a famous painting:* accurate, precise, exact, true, strict; realistic, authentic.
OPPOSITES: unfaithful, inaccurate.

faithless adjective
1 *the doomed Giselle and her faithless lover, Albrecht:* unfaithful, disloyal, inconstant, untrue, adulterous, treacherous; fickle, flighty, untrustworthy, unreliable; deceitful, two-faced, double-crossing; literary perfidious, false; informal cheating, two-timing.
2 *they live undisciplined, faithless lives:* unbelieving, godless, irreligious; agnostic, atheistic.
OPPOSITES: faithful.

fake noun
1 *the sculpture was found to be a fake:* forgery, counterfeit, copy, pirate copy, sham, fraud, hoax, imitation, dummy, reproduction; informal phoney.
2 *that so-called Doctor Dawes is a fake:* charlatan, impostor, hoaxer, quack, mountebank, sham, fraud, humbug, cheat, confidence trickster, fraudster; informal phoney, con man, con artist.
▷ adjective
1 *he gave his wife fake banknotes:* counterfeit, forged, imitation, false, bogus, pirated; invalid; informal phoney, dud.

2 *they covered themselves in fake diamonds:* imitation, artificial, synthetic, simulated, reproduction, replica, ersatz, man-made, dummy, false, faux, mock, bogus; informal pretend, phoney.
3 *she adopted a fake Liverpool accent:* feigned, faked, put-on, assumed, invented, affected; unconvincing, artificial, mock; informal phoney, pseudo.
OPPOSITES: genuine, authentic.
▷ verb
1 *the death certificate was faked:* forge, counterfeit, falsify, copy, pirate; doctor, alter, tamper with.
2 *he faked a yawn and left:* feign, pretend, simulate, put on, affect.

fall verb
1 *bombs could be seen falling from the plane* | *her hand slipped on the rope and she fell another three metres:* drop, descend, come down, go down; plummet, plunge, sink, dive, tumble; cascade, rain.
2 *he tripped and fell:* topple over, tumble over, keel over, fall down/over, go head over heels, go headlong, collapse, take a spill, pitch forward; trip up, stumble, slip.
3 *little by little, the water level began to fall:* subside, recede, fall away, go down, sink, drop.
4 *profits fell by 12 per cent:* decrease, decline, diminish, fall off, drop off, lessen, dwindle; plummet, plunge, slump, sink; depreciate, devalue; informal crash.
5 *we are worried that standards are falling:* decline, deteriorate, degenerate, go downhill, go to rack and ruin; decay, wither, fade, fail.
6 *a monument to those who fell in the war:* die, lose your life, be killed, be lost, meet your death; literary perish, be slain.
7 *the town fell to the Germans:* be taken by, be defeated by, be conquered by, be overwhelmed by, succumb; surrender, yield, submit, give in, capitulate.
OPPOSITES: rise, increase.
▷ noun
1 *he had a fall and broke his hip:* tumble, trip, spill, slip; collapse.
2 *September's figures showed a fall in sales:* decline, fall-off, drop, decrease, cut, dip, reduction, downswing; plunge, slump; informal nosedive, crash.
3 *the fall of the Roman Empire:* downfall, decline, collapse, failure, deterioration, degeneration; destruction, overthrow, demise.
4 *the fall of Saigon:* surrender, capitulation, submission; defeat.
OPPOSITES: increase, rise.
□ **fall apart**
my boots fell apart within weeks: fall/come to pieces, fall/come to bits, come apart; disintegrate, fragment, break up, break apart, crumble, decay, perish.
□ **fall asleep**
Claire tried hard not to fall asleep: doze

off, drop off, go to sleep; informal nod off, flake out.

□ **fall away**
the ground fell away abruptly: slope down, slant down, go down, drop away, descend, dip, sink, plunge.

□ **fall back on**
you can always fall back on the support of your family: resort to, turn to, look to, call on, have recourse to; rely on, depend on, lean on.

□ **fall behind**
the other walkers soon fell behind: lag behind, trail behind, be left behind, drop back, bring up the rear; straggle, dawdle, hang back.

□ **fall for**
1 *she fell for a younger man:* fall in love with, become infatuated with, lose your heart to, take a fancy to, be smitten by, be attracted to; Brit. informal fancy.
2 *she is far too astute to fall for that trick:* be deceived by, be duped by, be fooled by, be taken in by, believe, trust, be convinced by; informal go for, buy, swallow.

□ **fall in**
the roof of our house fell in during the earthquake: collapse, cave in, crash in, fall down; give way, crumble, disintegrate.

□ **fall out**
let's not fall out over silly things: quarrel, argue, fight, squabble, bicker, have words, disagree, be at odds, clash, wrangle, cross swords, lock horns, be at loggerheads, be at each other's throats; Brit. row; informal scrap.

□ **fall through**
unfortunately, the sale fell through at the last minute: fail, be unsuccessful, come to nothing, miscarry, go awry, collapse, founder, come to grief; informal flop, fold.

fallacious adjective *the fallacious assumption underlying this reasoning:* erroneous, false, untrue, wrong, incorrect, flawed, inaccurate, mistaken, misinformed, misguided; groundless, unfounded, unproven, unsupported, uncorroborated.
OPPOSITES: correct.

fallacy noun *the fallacy that we all work from nine to five:* misconception, misbelief, delusion, mistaken impression, misapprehension, error, mistake; untruth, myth.
OPPOSITES: fact.

fallible adjective *all human beings are fallible, including Mr Darley:* prone to error, imperfect, flawed, weak, frail, human.
OPPOSITES: infallible.

fallow adjective
1 *this mix is used to improve the soil in fallow areas before planting:* uncultivated, unploughed, unplanted, unsown; unused, dormant, resting.
2 *trading is set to emerge from a fallow period:* inactive, dormant, quiet, slack,

slow, stagnant; barren, unproductive.
OPPOSITES: cultivated, busy.

false adjective
1 *he gave a false account of his movements:* incorrect, untrue, wrong, erroneous, fallacious, flawed, distorted, inaccurate, imprecise; untruthful, fictitious, concocted, fabricated, invented, made up, trumped up, unfounded, spurious; counterfeit, forged, fraudulent.
2 *she would never wear false pearls:* fake, artificial, imitation, synthetic, faux, simulated, reproduction, replica, ersatz, man-made, dummy, mock; informal pretend.
OPPOSITES: correct, truthful, genuine.

falsehood noun *this is an exaggeration, if not a downright falsehood:* lie, untruth, fib, falsification, fabrication, invention, fiction, story, flight of fancy; humorous terminological inexactitude; informal tall story, cock and bull story.
OPPOSITES: truth.

falsify verb *she falsified the accounts in an attempt to cover her tracks:* forge, fake, counterfeit, fabricate; alter, change, doctor, tamper with.

falsity noun *he was compelled to reveal the falsity of these assertions:* untruthfulness, untruth, falsehood, inaccuracy; mendacity, dishonesty.
OPPOSITES: truth.

falter verb
1 *when war seemed imminent the government faltered:* hesitate, delay, stall; waver, vacillate, blow hot and cold.
2 *only in the death scene did she falter:* stumble, flounder, hesitate, lose your way; informal lose it.

fame noun *the stunning actress shot to fame as a teenage star:* celebrity, stardom, renown, popularity, prominence, greatness, eminence, note, prestige, status, glory, stature, repute; notoriety, infamy.
OPPOSITES: obscurity.

famed adjective *he is famed for his grace and artistry:* famous, celebrated, well known, prominent, noted, notable, renowned, respected, esteemed, acclaimed; notorious, infamous.
OPPOSITES: unknown.

familiar adjective
1 *I saw a lot of familiar faces | head lice are a familiar problem to most doctors:* well known, recognized, accustomed; common, commonplace, everyday, day-to-day, ordinary, habitual, usual, customary, routine, standard, stock, run-of-the-mill.
2 *are you familiar with this subject?* acquainted with, conversant with, versed in, knowledgeable about, well informed about; skilled in, proficient in; at home with, no stranger to, au fait with; informal well up on.
3 *he is too familiar with the teachers:*

f

overfamiliar, presumptuous, disrespectful, forward, bold, impudent, impertinent.
OPPOSITES: unfamiliar, formal.

familiarity noun
1 *he wants to gain greater familiarity with politics:* acquaintance, awareness, experience, insight; knowledge, understanding, comprehension, grasp.
2 *she was affronted by his familiarity:* overfamiliarity, presumption, boldness, audacity, cheek, impudence, impertinence, disrespect.
OPPOSITES: unfamiliarity, formality.

familiarize verb *I aim to familiarize students with a range of modern poets:* acquaint, make familiar; accustom, habituate, instruct, educate, school, prime, introduce.

family noun
1 *a family of four living in a three-bedroom house:* household, family unit.
2 *I finally met his family:* relatives, relations, kin, next of kin, kinsfolk, kindred, your flesh and blood, nearest and dearest, connections; extended family; clan, tribe; N. Amer. informal folks; dated people.
3 *her family have all grown up:* children, youngsters; offspring, progeny, brood; descendants, scions, heirs; Law issue; informal kids.

famine noun
1 *the nation is threatened by famine:* food shortages; starvation, malnutrition; hunger.
2 *the cotton famine of the 1860s:* shortage, scarcity, lack, want, dearth, deficiency, insufficiency, shortfall, paucity.
OPPOSITES: plenty.

famished adjective (informal) *the troops were exhausted and famished:* ravenous, hungry, starving, starved, empty, unfed.
OPPOSITES: full.

famous adjective *there were several famous artists in the exhibition:* well known, prominent, famed; renowned, noted, eminent, distinguished, esteemed, celebrated, respected, popular; of distinction, of repute; illustrious, acclaimed, great, legendary; notorious, infamous.
OPPOSITES: unknown.

fan[1] verb
1 *the article fanned public fears regarding nuclear power:* intensify, increase, agitate, inflame, exacerbate; stir up, whip up, fuel, kindle, spark, stimulate, arouse.
2 *the police squad fanned out, weapons at the ready:* spread, branch; divide, split.
OPPOSITES: allay, gather.

fan[2] noun *a basketball fan:* enthusiast, devotee, admirer, lover; supporter, follower, disciple, adherent, aficionado; informal buff, nut, addict, fanatic.

fanatic noun
1 *a religious fanatic:* zealot, extremist, militant, dogmatist, devotee; sectarian, partisan, radical, diehard; informal maniac, ultra.
2 (informal) *a keep-fit fanatic.* See FAN[2].

fanatical adjective
1 *a fanatical religious sect:* zealous, extreme, extremist, militant, dogmatic, radical, diehard; single-minded, inflexible, uncompromising.
2 (informal) *he was fanatical about cleanliness:* enthusiastic, eager, keen, fervent, ardent, passionate; obsessive, obsessed, fixated, compulsive; informal wild, crazy; Brit. informal potty.

fanciful adjective
1 *some of these stories were pretty fanciful:* fantastic, far-fetched, unbelievable, extravagant; ridiculous, absurd, preposterous; imaginary, made-up, make-believe, mythical, fabulous; informal tall.
2 *Maria is a fanciful girl:* over-imaginative, whimsical, impractical, dreamy, quixotic, in a world of your own.
3 *the fanciful cornices and turrets of the imperial palace:* ornate, ornamental, exotic, fancy, imaginative, extravagant, fantastic, curious, bizarre, eccentric, unusual.
OPPOSITES: literal, practical, plain.

fancy verb
1 (Brit. informal) *I fancied a change of scene:* wish for, want, desire, have a yen for, dream of, long for, yearn for, crave, thirst for, hanker after, covet; informal itch for.
2 (Brit. informal) *she'd fancied him for ages:* be attracted to, find attractive, be infatuated with, be taken with, desire; lust after; informal have a crush on, have the hots for.
3 (Brit.) *I fancied that I could see lights to the south:* think, imagine, believe, be of the opinion, be under the impression; informal reckon.
▷ adjective
1 *the design was very fancy:* elaborate, ornate, ornamental, decorated, decorative, intricate, embellished, fussy, busy.
2 *a fancy Italian restaurant:* sophisticated, stylish, chic, fashionable, elegant, luxurious, lavish, extravagant, expensive, ostentatious, showy, flamboyant; informal flash, ritzy, posh, classy; Brit. informal swish.
OPPOSITES: plain, ordinary, cheap.
▷ noun
1 *he was able to indulge his fancy to own a farm:* desire, urge, wish; inclination, whim, impulse, notion, whimsy; yearning, yen, longing, hankering, craving; informal itch.
2 *she had a vague fancy that it was cruel to leave the dolls in the dark:* idea, notion, thought, supposition, opinion, belief, impression, understanding; feeling, suspicion, hunch, inkling.

fanfare noun *the project was greeted with a great fanfare:* **fuss**, commotion, show, display; informal ballyhoo, hype.

fantasize verb *I fantasized about London and what I'd do when I lived there:* **daydream**, dream, muse, think, wonder, imagine.

fantastic adjective
1 *it's a fantastic notion, but it would explain a lot:* **fanciful**, extravagant, extraordinary, irrational, wild, absurd, far-fetched, incredible, unbelievable, implausible, improbable, unlikely, doubtful, dubious; informal crazy.
2 *Brooks Robinson made one of his famous diving catches:* **remarkable**, great, impressive, outstanding, phenomenal, tremendous, terrific.
3 *the mountains assumed fantastic shapes:* **strange**, weird, bizarre, outlandish, queer, peculiar, grotesque, freakish, surreal, exotic.
4 (informal) *he's got this fantastic new car:* **marvellous**, wonderful, sensational, outstanding, superb, excellent, first-rate, first-class, dazzling, out of this world, breathtaking; informal great, terrific, fabulous, super, magic, cool, wicked, awesome; Brit. informal brilliant; Austral./NZ informal bonzer.
OPPOSITES: rational, ordinary, poor.

fantasy noun
1 *the movie is an ambitious mix of fantasy and realism:* **imagination**, fancy, invention, make-believe; creativity, vision; daydreaming, reverie.
2 *his fantasy about appearing on television:* **dream**, daydream, pipe dream, wish; fond hope, chimera, delusion, illusion; informal pie in the sky.
OPPOSITES: realism.

far adverb
1 *we are not far from the palace:* **a long way**, a great distance, a good way; literary afar.
2 *the liveliness of the production far outweighs any flaws:* **greatly**, much, considerably, markedly, significantly, substantially, appreciably, noticeably; to a great extent, by a long way, by far, by a mile, easily.
▷ adjective *the department was on the far side of the campus:* **further**, more distant; other, opposite.
OPPOSITES: near.
□ **by far**
a compromise would be by far the best solution: **easily**, by a long way, by a mile, far and away; undoubtedly, without doubt, without question, positively, absolutely; much; Brit. by a long chalk.
□ **far and wide**
the influence of the Chinese economy is being felt far and wide: **everywhere**, {here, there, and everywhere}, all over the world, throughout the land, worldwide; informal all

over the place; Brit. informal all over the shop.
□ **far from**
the staff were far from happy with this outcome: **not**, not at all, not in the least, not the slightest bit, nowhere near; the opposite of.
□ **go far**
she was the type of girl who would go far: **be successful**, succeed, achieve a good deal, prosper, flourish, thrive, get on, set the world on fire; informal make a name for yourself, make your mark.
□ **go too far**
in the end they sacked him because he went too far: go to extremes; informal go overboard; Brit. informal go over the top.
□ **so far**
1 *nobody has taken any notice of me so far:* **until now**, up to now, up to this point, as yet, hitherto, up to the present, to date; formal thus far.
2 *his liberalism only extends so far:* **to a certain extent**, up to a point, to a degree, within reason, within limits.

faraway adjective
1 *they spent their time jetting off to faraway places:* **distant**, far off, far, remote, far-flung, exotic; obscure, out of the way, off the beaten track.
2 *she had that faraway look in her eyes again:* **dreamy**, abstracted, absent-minded, distracted, preoccupied, vague, in a world of your own; informal miles away.
OPPOSITES: nearby, attentive.

farce noun *the trial was a complete farce:* **mockery**, travesty, sham, pretence, masquerade, charade, joke, waste of time; informal shambles.

farcical adjective *the whole idea is farcical:* **ridiculous**, preposterous, ludicrous, absurd, laughable, risible, nonsensical; senseless, pointless, useless; silly, foolish, idiotic, stupid; informal crazy, hare-brained; Brit. informal barmy, daft.

fare noun
1 *we can't afford the air fare:* **ticket price**, cost, charge, fee, toll, tariff.
2 *when at home, they eat simple fare:* **food**, meals, sustenance, nourishment, nutriment, foodstuffs; cooking, cuisine; diet.
▷ verb *they went to see how their old friend was faring:* **get on**, get along, cope, manage, do; informal make out.

farewell exclamation *farewell, Patrick!* **goodbye**, adieu, au revoir; informal cheerio, so long, see you later, ciao; Brit. informal ta-ta, cheers.
▷ noun *it was an emotional farewell:* **goodbye**, adieu; leave-taking, parting, departure; send-off.

far-fetched adjective *the storyline was a bit far-fetched, to say the least:* **improbable**, unlikely, implausible, unconvincing,

dubious, doubtful, incredible, unbelievable, unthinkable; contrived, fanciful, unrealistic, ridiculous, absurd, preposterous.
OPPOSITES: likely.

farm noun *he owned a small farm in Cumbria:* smallholding, farmstead, plantation, estate; Brit. croft; N. Amer. ranch.
▷verb
1 *the marshes are being drained so that the land can be farmed:* cultivate, till, work, plough, dig, plant.
2 *the family farms sheep:* breed, rear, keep, raise, tend; grow.
□ **farm something out**
the job of building the models was farmed out to the Shawcroft division: contract out, outsource, subcontract, delegate, give.

farming noun agriculture, cultivation, land management, farm management, husbandry, agronomy; Brit. crofting.

far-reaching adjective *this is a far-reaching change in consumer law:* extensive, wide-ranging; comprehensive, widespread, all-embracing, overarching, sweeping, blanket, wholesale.
OPPOSITES: limited.

far-sighted adjective *his far-sighted approach to resource management:* visionary, prescient, percipient, shrewd, discerning, judicious, canny, prudent.
OPPOSITES: short-sighted.

farther adverb & adjective. See FURTHER.

farthest adjective. See FURTHEST.

fascinate verb *he was fascinated by Laura's stories about Alaska:* captivate, interest, engross, absorb, enchant, enthral, spellbind, entrance, transfix, rivet, mesmerize, engage, compel, intrigue, divert, entertain.
OPPOSITES: bore.

fascinating adjective *it's a fascinating tale of fame, fortune, and human frailty:* captivating, interesting, engrossing, absorbing, enchanting, enthralling, spellbinding, riveting, engaging, compelling, gripping, thrilling, intriguing, diverting, entertaining.
OPPOSITES: boring.

fascination noun *crime is a topic of endless fascination to most people:* interest, preoccupation, passion, obsession, compulsion; allure, lure, charm, attraction, intrigue, appeal, pull, draw.

fashion noun
1 *the latest Italian fashions | the current fashion among teenage boys for baggy clothes:* vogue, trend, craze, rage, mania, fad; style, look; tendency, convention, custom, practice.
2 *the work was carried out in a a sensible and organized fashion:* manner, way, method, mode, style; system, approach.

▷verb *the figure was fashioned from a tree trunk:* construct, produce, build, make, fabricate; cast, shape, form, mould, sculpt; forge, hew, carve.
□ **after a fashion**
the arrangement with the police worked after a fashion: to a certain extent, in a way, in a manner of speaking, in its way, to some degree.
□ **in fashion**
the Seventies look is very much in fashion right now: fashionable, in vogue, up to date, up to the minute, all the rage, chic, à la mode; informal trendy, cool, in, hot, big.
□ **out of fashion**
such gallantry towards the opposite sex is now out of fashion: unfashionable, dated, old-fashioned, out of date, outdated, outmoded, behind the times; unstylish, unpopular, passé; informal old hat, out.

fashionable adjective *she always wore fashionable, expensive clothes:* chic, in fashion, all the rage, voguish, modish, à la mode, trendsetting; stylish; popular; informal trendy, cool, in, hot, big.
OPPOSITES: unfashionable.

fast¹ adjective
1 *it's a very fast car | the game is played at a fast pace:* speedy, quick, swift, rapid; fast-moving, high-speed; accelerated, express, blistering, breakneck; hasty, hurried; literary fleet; informal nippy, supersonic; Brit. informal cracking.
2 *he slammed the door and held it fast:* secure, tight, firm; closed, shut, to.
3 *the dyes are boiled to produce a fast colour:* indelible, lasting, permanent, stable.
4 *they remained fast friends for years:* loyal, devoted, faithful, firm, steadfast, staunch, true, bosom, inseparable; constant, enduring, unswerving.
OPPOSITES: slow, loose.
▷adverb
1 *she drove fast down the drive towards the gates:* quickly, rapidly, swiftly, speedily, briskly, at speed, at full tilt; hastily, hurriedly, in a hurry, post-haste; informal like lightning, hell for leather, like the wind, like a bat out of hell.
2 *his front wheels were stuck fast:* securely, firmly; well and truly.
3 *he's fast asleep:* deeply, sound, completely.
OPPOSITES: slowly.

fast² verb *we must fast and pray for forgiveness:* eat nothing, abstain, go without food, go hungry, starve yourself; go on hunger strike.
OPPOSITES: eat.
▷noun *a five-day fast:* period of fasting; hunger strike; diet.
OPPOSITES: feast.

fasten verb
1 *he fastened the door behind him:* bolt, lock, secure, make fast, chain, seal.

2 *they fastened splints to his leg:* attach, fix, affix, clip, pin, tack; stick, bond, join.
3 *he fastened his horse to a tree:* tie, tether, bind, truss, fetter, lash, hitch, anchor, strap, rope.
4 *the dress fastens at the front:* button, zip up, do up, close.
OPPOSITES: open, untie, undo.

fastidious adjective *she dressed with fastidious care | he was fastidious about personal hygiene:* **scrupulous,** punctilious, painstaking, meticulous, fussy, finicky, over-particular; informal nit-picking, choosy; Brit. informal pernickety.

fat adjective
1 *a fat man in a Black Sabbath T-shirt:* **obese,** overweight, plump, stout, chubby, portly, flabby, paunchy, pot-bellied, beer-bellied, corpulent, gross, fleshy; informal tubby; Brit. informal podgy.
2 *he produced a fat book from the shelf:* **thick,** big, chunky, substantial.
3 (informal) *a fat salary:* **large,** substantial, sizeable, considerable; generous, lucrative.
OPPOSITES: thin, lean, small.
▷noun
1 *whales are insulated by layers of fat:* **blubber,** fatty tissue, adipose tissue; Brit. puppy fat; informal podge.
2 *fried bread swimming in fat:* **oil,** grease; lard, dripping, suet, butter, margarine.

fatal adjective
1 *a fatal disease:* **deadly,** lethal, mortal, death-dealing; terminal, incurable, untreatable, inoperable, malignant; literary deathly.
2 *he made a fatal mistake:* **disastrous,** devastating, ruinous, catastrophic, calamitous, dire; costly; formal grievous.

fatalism noun *a sense of fatalism prevented him from feeling any responsibility:* **acceptance,** resignation, stoicism; passivity.

fatality noun *there were hundreds of fatalities following the leak:* **death,** casualty, mortality, victim; fatal accident.

fate noun
1 *I was ready for whatever fate had in store for me:* **destiny,** providence, the stars, chance, luck, serendipity, fortune, karma.
2 *my fate was in their hands:* **future,** destiny, outcome, end, lot.
▷verb *his daughter was fated to face the same dilemma:* **predestine,** preordain, destine, mean, doom.

fateful adjective *that fateful day when she met him:* **decisive,** critical, crucial, pivotal, momentous, important, key, significant, historic, portentous.
OPPOSITES: unimportant.

father noun
1 *his father was Irish:* **male parent;** patriarch, paterfamilias; informal dad, daddy, pa, old man.

2 (literary) *the religion of my fathers:* **ancestors,** forefathers, forebears, predecessors, antecedents.
3 *one of the fathers of modern psychoanalysis:* **founder,** originator, prime mover, architect; pioneer.
▷verb *he fathered six children in as many years:* **sire,** bring into the world, spawn, breed; literary beget.

WORD LINKS
paternal relating to or like a father
patricide the killing of a father by his child
---

fatherland noun *they are traitors to the fatherland:* **native land,** native country, homeland, mother country, motherland, land of your birth.

fatherly adjective *all he needs is some fatherly advice:* **paternal;** protective, supportive, encouraging, affectionate, caring, sympathetic, indulgent.

fathom verb *after 15 minutes trying to fathom out what she was talking about I went to see her:* **understand,** comprehend, work out, make sense of, grasp, divine, puzzle out, get to the bottom of; informal make head or tail of, crack; Brit. informal suss, suss out.

fatigue noun *his face was pale with fatigue:* **tiredness,** weariness, exhaustion, enervation, prostration.
OPPOSITES: energy.
▷verb *the troops were fatigued:* **tire out,** exhaust, wear out, drain, weary, overtire, prostrate; informal whack, shatter; Brit. informal knacker, fag out.
OPPOSITES: invigorate.

fatty adjective *avoid fatty foods:* **greasy,** oily, oleaginous.
OPPOSITES: lean.

fatuous adjective *she was irritated by this fatuous remark:* **silly,** foolish, stupid, inane, idiotic, vacuous, asinine; pointless, senseless, ridiculous, ludicrous, absurd; Brit. informal gormless, daft.
OPPOSITES: sensible.

fault noun
1 *he has his faults, but he's a good man:* **defect,** failing, imperfection, flaw, blemish, shortcoming, weakness, frailty, foible, vice.
2 *engineers have still not located the fault:* **defect,** flaw, imperfection, bug; error, mistake, inaccuracy; informal glitch, gremlin.
3 *it was my fault that we were late:* **responsibility,** liability, culpability, guilt.
OPPOSITES: merit, strength.
▷verb *you couldn't fault any of the players:* **find fault with,** criticize, attack, censure, condemn, reproach; complain about; informal knock, gripe about.
□**at fault**
the police say the driver of the car was not at fault: **to blame,** blameworthy, culpable; responsible, guilty, in the wrong.

□ **to a fault**
Barry's generous to a fault: excessively, unduly, immoderately, overly, needlessly.

faultless adjective *Professor Ruiperez had sent me a letter of invitation in faultless English:* perfect, flawless, error-free, impeccable, accurate, precise, exact, correct, exemplary.
OPPOSITES: flawed.

faulty adjective
1 *the fire was caused by a faulty electric blanket:* malfunctioning, broken, damaged, defective, out of order; informal on the blink, acting up.
2 *her logic is faulty at the best of times:* defective, flawed, unsound, inaccurate, incorrect, erroneous, fallacious, wrong.
OPPOSITES: working, faultless.

faux pas noun *I committed a faux pas that they never let me forget:* gaffe, blunder, mistake, indiscretion, impropriety, solecism; informal boo-boo; Brit. informal boob.

favour noun
1 *will you do me a favour?* good turn, service, good deed, act of kindness, courtesy, indulgence.
2 *she looked on him with favour:* approval, approbation, goodwill, kindness, benevolence.
3 *they accused the referee of showing favour to the home team:* favouritism, bias, partiality, partisanship.
OPPOSITES: disservice, disfavour, neutrality.
▷ verb
1 *the party favours electoral reform:* advocate, recommend, approve of, be in favour of, support, back, champion, promote; campaign for, stand up for, press for, push for, lobby for.
2 *Robyn favours loose dark clothes:* prefer, go for, choose, opt for, select, pick, plump for, be partial to, like.
3 *the conditions favoured the other team:* benefit, be to the advantage of, help, assist, aid, be of service to, do someone a favour.
OPPOSITES: oppose, dislike, hinder.
□ **in favour of**
two thirds of the staff were in favour of strike action: on the side of, pro, for, giving support to, approving of, sympathetic to.

favourable adjective
1 *we received a favourable assessment of his ability:* approving, complimentary, commendatory, flattering, glowing, enthusiastic; encouraging, reassuring; informal rave.
2 *favourable conditions for economic growth:* advantageous, beneficial, in your favour, suitable, appropriate; propitious, auspicious, promising, encouraging.
3 *he hoped for a favourable reply to this request:* positive, affirmative.
OPPOSITES: unfavourable, critical, disadvantageous, negative.

favourably adverb positively, approvingly, sympathetically, enthusiastically, appreciatively.
OPPOSITES: unfavourably.

favoured adjective *he is the president's favoured candidate:* preferred, favourite, recommended, chosen, choice.

favourite adjective *Laura was his favourite aunt:* best-loved, most-liked, favoured, dearest; preferred, chosen, choice; informal best.
▷ noun *Brutus was always Caesar's favourite:* first choice, pick, preference, pet, darling; informal blue-eyed boy, golden boy/girl.

favouritism noun *we want one rule for everyone and no favouritism:* partiality, partisanship, preferential treatment, favour, prejudice, bias, inequality, unfairness, discrimination.
OPPOSITES: impartiality.

fawn[1] adjective *a hideous fawn carpet:* beige, yellowish-brown, pale brown, buff, sand, oatmeal, café au lait, camel, ecru, taupe, stone, mushroom.

fawn[2] verb *they were fawning over the President's wife:* be obsequious to, be sycophantic to, curry favour with, pay court to, play up to, crawl to, ingratiate yourself with; Brit. dance attendance on; informal suck up to, creep, grovel.

fawning adjective *he was surrounded by a circle of fawning civil servants:* obsequious, servile, sycophantic, flattering, ingratiating, unctuous, oleaginous, grovelling, crawling; informal bootlicking; Brit. informal smarmy.
OPPOSITES: proud.

fear noun
1 *she felt fear at entering the house:* terror, fright, horror, alarm, panic, agitation, trepidation, dread, anxiety, worry, unease, apprehension, nervousness, nerves, foreboding; informal the creeps, the willies, the heebie-jeebies.
2 *she overcame her fears and made it to the top:* phobia, aversion, antipathy, dread, bugbear, bogey, nightmare, horror, terror; anxiety, neurosis; informal hang-up.
▷ verb
1 *she feared her ex-husband:* be afraid of, be fearful of, be scared of, be apprehensive of, dread, live in fear of, be terrified of; be anxious about, worry about, feel apprehensive about.
2 *he feared to tell them what had happened:* be too afraid, be too scared, hesitate, dare not.
3 *doctors feared for his health:* worry about, be anxious about, be concerned about, have anxieties about.
4 *I fear that you may be right:* suspect, have a sneaking suspicion, be inclined to think, be afraid, have a hunch, think it likely.

fearful adjective

1 *the guards were ill-trained and fearful:* afraid, frightened, scared, apprehensive, terrified, petrified, nervous, trembling, quaking, cowed, daunted; timid, timorous, faint-hearted; informal jittery, jumpy, twitchy.
2 (informal) *there has been a fearful accident:* terrible, dreadful, awful, appalling, frightful, ghastly, horrific, horrible, horrifying, horrendous, terribly bad, shocking, atrocious, abominable, hideous, monstrous, gruesome.
OPPOSITES: unafraid, brave, minor.

fearfully adverb *she opened the door fearfully:* apprehensively, uneasily, nervously, timidly, timorously, hesitantly, with your heart in your mouth.

fearless adjective *he was cool and fearless in battle, and an excellent leader:* unafraid, brave, courageous, intrepid, valiant, valorous, gallant, plucky, heroic, daring, audacious, doughty; bold, undaunted, unflinching.
OPPOSITES: fearful.

fearsome adjective *the crocodile's teeth are a fearsome sight:* frightening, horrifying, terrifying, menacing, chilling, spine-chilling, hair-raising, alarming, unnerving, daunting, formidable, forbidding, disturbing; informal scary.

feasible adjective *there is only one feasible solution:* practicable, practical, workable, achievable, attainable, viable, realistic, sensible, reasonable; suitable, possible, expedient, constructive; informal doable.
OPPOSITES: impracticable.

feast noun

1 *the occasion was celebrated with a great feast:* banquet, meal, dinner; treat, entertainment; revels, festivities; informal spread.
2 *the feast of St Stephen:* festival, feast day, saint's day, holy day, holiday.
▷**verb** *they feasted on lobster:* dine on, gorge on, eat, devour, consume; formal partake of; informal stuff yourself with.

feat noun *the bridge is an extraordinary feat of engineering:* achievement, accomplishment, attainment, coup, triumph; undertaking, enterprise, venture, operation, exercise, endeavour, effort, performance, exploit.

feature noun

1 *this is a typical feature of French music:* characteristic, attribute, quality, property, trait, hallmark, trademark; aspect, facet, factor, ingredient, component, element, theme; peculiarity, idiosyncrasy, quirk.
2 (**features**) *his eyes swept over her delicate features:* face, countenance, physiognomy; literary visage; informal mug.
3 *her sculptures are a real feature of the garden:* centrepiece, special attraction, highlight, focal point, focus of attention, conversation piece.
4 *a series of short features on the Vikings:* article, piece, item, report, story, column, review, commentary, write-up.
▷**verb**
1 *Radio Ulster is featuring a week of live concerts:* present, promote, focus on, spotlight, highlight.
2 *she is to feature in a major advertising campaign:* appear, star, participate.

febrile adjective *the patient was febrile, with severe abdominal pains:* feverish, hot, burning, flushed, sweating.

feckless adjective *a runaway mother and a feckless, alcoholic father:* irresponsible, good-for-nothing, worthless, incompetent, inept, useless, ne'er-do-well; lazy, idle, slothful, indolent, shiftless; improvident; informal no-good, no-account.
OPPOSITES: responsible.

federal adjective *in 1967 a federal Europe was hardly on the agenda:* confederate, federated; combined, allied, united, amalgamated, integrated.
OPPOSITES: devolved, divided.

federation noun *Switzerland is a federation of cantons:* confederation, confederacy, league; combination, alliance, coalition, union, syndicate, guild, consortium, partnership, cooperative, association, amalgamation.

fee noun *for a small fee, you can have your mail redirected | an annual membership fee of £700:* payment; price, cost, charge, tariff, rate; subscription; (**fees**) dues.

feeble adjective

1 *he was old and feeble:* weak, weakened, frail, infirm, delicate, sickly, ailing, unwell, poorly, enfeebled, enervated, debilitated, incapacitated, decrepit.
2 *this a pretty feeble argument:* ineffective, ineffectual, inadequate, unconvincing, implausible, unsatisfactory, poor, weak, flimsy.
3 *he's too feeble to stand up to his boss:* cowardly, craven, faint-hearted, spineless, spiritless, lily-livered; timid, timorous, fearful, unassertive, weak, ineffectual; informal wimpy, chicken; Brit. informal wet.
4 *the lamp shed a feeble light:* faint, dim, weak, pale, soft, subdued, muted.
OPPOSITES: robust, strong, brave.

feeble-minded adjective *she must be very tired to give consideration to such feeble-minded notions:* stupid, idiotic, imbecilic, foolish, witless, doltish, empty-headed, vacuous; informal half-witted; Brit. informal daft.

feed verb

1 *she has a large family to feed:* provide for, cater for, cook for; nourish, sustain; suckle, breastfeed, bottle-feed.
2 *the birds feed on a diet of fish:* live on/off, exist on, subsist on, eat, consume.
3 *she fed secrets to the Russians for years:* supply, provide, give, deliver, furnish, issue.

feel verb

1 *she encourages her customers to feel the fabrics:* touch, stroke, caress, fondle, finger, thumb, handle.
2 *she felt a breeze on her back:* perceive, sense, detect, discern, notice, be aware of, be conscious of.
3 *the patient does not feel any pain during the procedure:* experience, undergo, go through, endure, suffer, bear.
4 *he felt his way towards the door:* grope, fumble, scrabble, pick.
5 *feel the temperature of the water:* test, try, assess, gauge; establish, ascertain.
6 *he feels that he should go to the meeting:* believe, think, consider, be of the opinion, hold, maintain, judge; informal reckon, figure.
7 *I feel that he is biding his time:* sense, have a feeling, get the impression, have a hunch.
8 *the air feels damp:* seem, appear, strike you as.

▷ **noun**
1 *I liked the feel of the embossed wallpaper:* texture, surface, finish; weight, thickness, consistency, quality.
2 *a change in lighting can alter the feel of a room:* atmosphere, ambience, aura, mood, feeling, air, impression, character, tenor, spirit, flavour; informal vibrations, vibes.
3 *he has a feel for languages:* aptitude, knack, flair, bent, talent, gift, faculty, ability.

□ **feel for**
the press persecuted John, and I felt for him: sympathize with, be sorry for, pity, feel sympathy for, feel compassion for, be moved by; commiserate with, condole with.

□ **feel like**
I feel like an ice cream: want, would like, wish for, desire, feel in need of, long for, have a yen for; informal be dying for; Brit. informal fancy.

feeling noun

1 *he laughed to conceal his true feelings:* emotion, sentiment.
2 *she was overcome by a feeling of nausea:* sensation, sense, consciousness.
3 *I had a feeling that I would win:* suspicion, notion, inkling, hunch, sneaking suspicion, feeling in your bones, fancy, idea; presentiment, premonition; informal gut feeling.
4 *the government is hopelessly out of touch with public feeling:* sentiment, emotion; opinion, attitude, belief, ideas, views.

5 *my feeling is that this claim is true:* opinion, belief, view, impression, intuition, instinct, hunch, estimation, guess.
6 *he hadn't meant to hurt her feelings:* sensibilities, sensitivities, self-esteem, pride.
7 *he was amazed at the strength of her feeling for him:* love, affection, fondness, tenderness, warmth, emotion, sentiment; passion, ardour, desire.
8 *a feeling of peace prevailed in the garden:* atmosphere, ambience, aura, sense, air, feel, mood, impression, spirit, quality, flavour.
9 *he has a remarkable feeling for language:* aptitude, knack, flair, bent, talent, gift, faculty, ability.

feign verb *she lay still and feigned sleep:* simulate, fake, sham, affect.

feigned adjective *he accepted the invitation with feigned enthusiasm:* pretended, simulated, affected, artificial, insincere, put-on, fake, false, sham; informal pretend, phoney.
OPPOSITES: sincere.

feint noun *the operation was conceived as a feint to draw off German troops during the Normandy landings:* bluff, blind, ruse, deception, subterfuge, hoax, trick, ploy, device, dodge, sham, pretence, cover, smokescreen, distraction, contrivance; informal red herring.

USAGE

Do not confuse **feint** with **faint**. A **feint** is a deceptive movement intended to make someone think that you are going to do something. **Faint** means 'not clearly seen, heard, or smelt' (*the faint murmur of voices*) or 'to lose consciousness' (*two women fainted and had to be carried out*).

---

felicitous adjective *the endings of his films may be happy, but they're seldom felicitous:* apt, well chosen, fitting, suitable, appropriate.
OPPOSITES: infelicitous.

felicity noun

1 *these feelings are but shadows of our endless felicity in heaven:* happiness, joy, joyfulness, bliss, delight, cheerfulness; contentedness, satisfaction, pleasure; literary joyousness.
2 *David expressed his feelings with his customary felicity:* eloquence, aptness, appropriateness, suitability.
OPPOSITES: unhappiness, infelicity.

fell verb

1 *all the dead sycamores had to be felled:* cut down, chop down, hack down, saw down, clear.
2 *she felled him with one well-aimed punch:* knock down/over, knock to the ground, strike down, bring down, bring to the ground, prostrate; knock out, knock unconscious; informal deck, floor, lay out.

fellow noun

1 *he seems like a decent sort of fellow:* **man**, boy; person, individual, soul; informal guy, lad, character; Brit. informal chap, bloke.

2 *he exchanged glances with his fellows:* **companion**, friend, comrade, partner, associate, co-worker, colleague; informal chum, pal, buddy; Brit. informal mate.

□ **fellow feeling** *she felt a rush of fellow feeling for the unfortunate woman:* **sympathy**, empathy, feeling, compassion, care, concern, solicitude, warmth, tenderness, brotherly love; pity, sorrow, commiseration.

fellowship noun

1 *a community of brothers bound together in fellowship:* **companionship**, comradeship, camaraderie, friendship, mutual support; togetherness, solidarity.

2 *a new member of the church fellowship:* **association**, society, club, league, union, guild, alliance, fraternity, brotherhood, sorority.

female adjective *these are typical female attributes:* **feminine**, womanly, ladylike. OPPOSITES: male.

feminine adjective

1 *men who have some feminine tact and sensitivity:* **female**, woman's, women's, womanly.

2 *his face was smooth, almost feminine:* **womanly**, girlish, womanish, effeminate OPPOSITES: masculine, manly.

fen noun **marsh**, marshland, fenland, wetland, bog, swamp, swampland.

fence noun *she crept through a gap in the fence:* **barrier**, paling, railing, enclosure, barricade, stockade, palisade.

▷ verb

1 *they intended to fence off many acres of prairie:* **enclose**, surround, encircle, separate off, isolate; circle, wall in; encompass.

2 *he fenced in his chickens:* **confine**, pen in, coop up, shut in/up; enclose, surround; N. Amer. corral.

fend verb

□ **fend off** *they were unable to fend off a Viking invasion:* **ward off**, head off, stave off, hold off, repel, repulse, resist, fight off, defend yourself against, prevent, stop, block, intercept, hold back.

□ **fend for yourself** *how could any mother leave a child to fend for itself?* **take care of yourself**, look after yourself, provide for yourself, shift for yourself, manage by yourself, cope by yourself, stand on your own two feet.

feral adjective

1 *a pack of feral dogs:* **wild**, untamed, undomesticated, untrained.

2 *a feral snarl:* **savage**, ferocious, vicious, fierce, predatory, menacing, bloodthirsty; animal, bestial. OPPOSITES: tame, pet.

ferment verb *the politicians and warlords who are fermenting this chaos:* **cause**, bring about, give rise to, generate, engender, instigate, provoke, incite, excite, stir up, whip up, foment; literary beget.

▷ noun *the country was in a state of religious ferment:* **excitement**, agitation, fever, frenzy, tumult; turmoil, upheaval, unrest, disquiet, uproar, turbulence, disruption, confusion, disorder, chaos, mayhem.

ferocious adjective

1 *bears are ferocious animals:* **fierce**, savage, wild, aggressive, dangerous.

2 *a ferocious attack on a police officer:* **brutal**, vicious, violent, bloody, barbaric, savage, sadistic, ruthless, cruel, merciless, heartless, bloodthirsty, murderous. OPPOSITES: gentle, mild.

ferocity noun *detectives were shocked by the ferocity of the attack:* **savagery**, brutality, cruelty, barbarity, viciousness, fierceness, violence. OPPOSITES: mildness.

ferret verb

1 *she ferreted in her handbag:* **rummage**, feel, grope, fish, poke about; search through, hunt through, rifle through.

2 *professionals in the Justice Department will be involved in ferreting out the truth:* **unearth**, uncover, discover, detect, search out, bring to light, track down, dig up, root out, nose out.

ferry verb *we got the air force to ferry spare parts from Phnom Penh to Bangkok:* **transport**, convey, carry, ship, fly, airlift, run, take, bring, shuttle.

fertile adjective

1 *the soil is moist and fertile:* **productive**, fruitful, rich, lush.

2 *von Schlieffen had applied his fertile brain to this problem:* **imaginative**, inventive, innovative, creative, visionary, original, ingenious; productive, prolific.

fertilize verb

1 *the field was ploughed up and fertilized:* **feed**, mulch, compost, manure, dress, top-dress.

2 *these orchids are fertilized by insects:* **pollinate**, cross-pollinate, cross-fertilize.

fertilizer noun **manure**, plant food, compost, dressing, top dressing, dung.

fervent adjective *William is a fervent rugby supporter:* **passionate**, avid, enthusiastic, keen, committed, dedicated, devout, intense, vehement, eager, ardent, sincere, fervid, heartfelt, zealous, wholehearted; informal fanatical. OPPOSITES: apathetic.

fervour noun *he preached with*

f

tremendous fervour to a packed hall:
passion, ardour, warmth, intensity,
zeal, vehemence, emotion, earnestness,
eagerness, enthusiasm, excitement,
animation, vigour, energy, fire, spirit.
OPPOSITES: apathy.

fester verb

1 the deep wound in his neck had begun to
fester: suppurate, turn septic, ulcerate,
weep, gather; Medicine maturate, be
purulent.
2 rubbish festered in the streets: rot,
moulder, decay, decompose, putrefy.
3 they must not allow their resentment
to fester: rankle, eat/gnaw away at your
mind, brew, smoulder.

festival noun

1 the annual garlic festival in July: fete,
fair, gala, carnival, fiesta, jamboree,
celebration, festivities; programme,
season.
2 forty days of fasting precede the festival:
holy day, feast day, saint's day.

festive adjective everyone was in a
festive mood despite the recession: happy,
merry, joyful, jolly, jovial, light-hearted,
cheerful, jubilant, convivial, high-spirited;
celebratory, holiday, carnival; literary joyous.
OPPOSITES: gloomy.

festivity noun

1 food plays an important part in
the festivities: celebration, festival,
entertainment, party, jamboree;
merrymaking, gaiety, feasting, revelry,
jollification, revels; informal bash, fun and
games.
2 we joined in the festivity of the Last Night
of the Proms: jollity, merriment, gaiety,
cheerfulness, cheer, joy, high spirits,
revelry.

festoon verb the room was festooned with
streamers: decorate, adorn, ornament,
trim, deck, deck out, hang, loop, drape,
swathe, garland, wreathe, bedeck, trick out.

fetch verb

1 he went to fetch a doctor from the nearby
village: get, go for, go to get, call for,
summon, pick up, collect, bring; carry,
convey, transport.
2 the estate in Caithness could fetch a
million pounds: sell for, bring in, raise,
realize, yield, make, command, be priced
at; cost; informal go for, set you back.

fetching adjective she looked rather
fetching in her uniform: attractive,
appealing, sweet, pretty, lovely, delightful,
charming, prepossessing, enchanting,
irresistible; Scottish & N. English bonny; old use
comely.
OPPOSITES: unattractive.

fete noun (Brit.) gala, bazaar, fair, festival,
fiesta, jubilee, carnival, garden party,
pageant, fund-raiser, charity event.

fetid adjective the fetid odour of damp

refuse filled the air: stinking, smelly, foul-
smelling, malodorous, reeking, pungent,
acrid, high, rank, foul, noxious.
OPPOSITES: fragrant.

fetish noun

1 he had a fetish for fast cars: fixation,
obsession, compulsion, mania; weakness,
fancy, fascination, fad; informal thing,
hang-up.
2 the thing is treated like a voodoo fetish:
idol, talisman, charm, amulet, totem, juju,
image, effigy.

fetter verb

1 the captive was branded and fettered:
shackle, manacle, handcuff, clap in irons,
put in chains, chain up.
2 these obligations do not fetter the
company's powers: restrict, restrain,
constrain, limit; hinder, hamper, impede,
obstruct, hamstring, inhibit, check, curb,
trammel.

fetters plural noun shackles, manacles,
handcuffs, irons, chains, restraints; informal
cuffs, bracelets.

fettle noun his best players were in fine
fettle: shape, trim, condition, form, fitness,
health; repair, order; Brit. informal nick.

feud noun the region was riven by tribal
feuds: vendetta, conflict; rivalry, hostility,
enmity, strife, discord; quarrel.
▷ verb he feuded constantly with his
teammates: quarrel, fight, argue, bicker,
squabble, fall out, dispute, clash, cross
swords; informal scrap.

fever noun

1 he developed a fever and was admitted
to hospital: high temperature; Medicine
pyrexia.
2 Terry was in a fever of excitement:
ferment, frenzy, ecstasy.
3 the nation has been gripped by World
Cup fever: excitement, frenzy, agitation,
passion, furore.

WORD LINKS
febrile having a fever
febrifuge a medicine used to reduce fever

fevered adjective

1 Fernando soothed her fevered brow:
feverish, febrile, hot, burning.
2 she wanted to see if the reality matched
her fevered imagination: excited, agitated,
frenzied, overwrought, fervid.
OPPOSITES: cool, calm.

feverish adjective

1 she's still sick and feverish: running
a temperature, fevered, febrile, hot,
burning.
2 he was thrown into a state of feverish
excitement: frenzied, frenetic, hectic,
agitated, excited, restless, nervous,
worked up, overwrought, frantic,
furious, hysterical, wild, uncontrolled,
unrestrained.

few determiner *police are revealing few details about the victim:* **not many**, hardly any, scarcely any; a small number of, one or two, a handful of.
OPPOSITES: many.

▷**adjective** *though the car parks are few, they are well placed:* **scarce**, insufficient, in short supply; infrequent, uncommon, rare.
OPPOSITES: plentiful.

□**a few**
for a few, overcoming their fear of flying becomes a challenge: **a small number**, a handful, one or two, a couple, two or three; not many, hardly any.

> **USAGE**
>
> On the difference between **fewer** and **less**, see the note at **LESS**.

fiancée, fiancé noun wife-to-be, husband-to-be, bride-to-be, future wife/ husband; literary betrothed; informal intended.

fiasco noun *the whole evening was a total fiasco:* **failure**, disaster, catastrophe, debacle, farce, wreck; informal shambles, flop, mess.
OPPOSITES: success.

fib noun *you're making it up—I know that's a fib:* **lie**, untruth, falsehood, invention, fabrication, deception, piece of fiction; white lie, half-truth; informal tall story/tale, whopper.
OPPOSITES: truth.

fibre noun
1 *fibres from his jumper were found on the body:* **thread**, strand, filament.
2 *designer clothing in natural fibres:* **material**, cloth, fabric.
3 *a lack of fibre in his diet:* **roughage**, bulk.

fickle adjective *today's fickle fans demand instant success from their heroes:* **capricious**, disloyal, unreliable, inconstant, changeable, volatile, mercurial, unpredictable; unfaithful, faithless, flighty, giddy; literary mutable.
OPPOSITES: constant.

fiction noun
1 *the traditions of British detective fiction:* **novels**, stories, writing, literature.
2 *the president dismissed the allegation as absolute fiction:* **lies**, nonsense, invention, fabrication, fibs, untruth, falsehood, fantasy.
OPPOSITES: fact.

fictional adjective *a fictional character from a bad Victorian novel:* **invented**, fictitious, imaginary, made up, make-believe, unreal, fabricated, mythical.
OPPOSITES: real.

fictitious adjective
1 *he used a fictitious name:* **false**, fake, fabricated, sham; bogus, spurious, assumed, affected, adopted, feigned,

invented, made up; informal pretend, phoney.
2 *a fictitious character.* See **FICTIONAL**.
OPPOSITES: genuine.

fiddle noun (Brit. informal) *the men were involved in a major VAT fiddle:* **fraud**, swindle, confidence trick; informal racket, scam, con trick.

▷**verb**
1 *he fiddled nervously with a beer mat:* **fidget**, play, toy, twiddle, fuss, fool about/ around; finger, thumb, handle.
2 *he fiddled with some dials and knobs:* **adjust**, tinker; tweak, play about/around, meddle, interfere.
3 (Brit. informal) *the government is fiddling the figures:* **falsify**, manipulate, massage, rig, distort, misrepresent, doctor, alter, tamper with, interfere with; informal fix, cook the books.

fidelity noun
1 *she was never tempted to stray from absolute fidelity to her husband:* **faithfulness**, loyalty, constancy, obedience, allegiance.
2 *the fidelity of the reproduction:* **accuracy**, precision, authenticity.
OPPOSITES: infidelity, inaccuracy.

fidget verb
1 *during the second act, the audience began to fidget:* **be/get restless**, wriggle, squirm, twitch, jiggle about, shuffle.
2 *she fidgeted with her scarf:* **play**, fiddle, fuss, toy, twiddle; informal mess about/ around.

fidgety adjective *she was fidgety and avoided eye contact:* **restless**, restive, on edge, uneasy, nervous, nervy, keyed up, anxious, agitated; informal jittery, twitchy.

field noun
1 *we crossed a large field full of cows:* **meadow**, pasture, paddock, grassland, pastureland; literary sward, lea, mead.
2 *a football field:* **pitch**, ground, sports field, playing field, recreation ground.
3 *the field of biotechnology:* **area**, sphere, discipline, province, department, domain, sector, branch, subject.
4 *the screen fills your field of vision:* **range**, scope, sweep, reach, extent.
5 *she is well ahead of the field:* **competitors**, entrants, competition; applicants, candidates.

▷**verb**
1 *she could field a ball with the best of the boys:* **catch**, stop, retrieve; return, throw back.
2 *they should have been disqualified for fielding an ineligible player:* **put in**, send out, play, put up.
3 *he fielded some rather awkward questions:* **deal with**, handle, cope with, answer, reply to, respond to.

fiend noun
1 *a fiend bent on global domination:* **brute**,

beast, villain, barbarian, monster, ogre, sadist.
2 (informal) *I'm a bit of a curry fiend:* **enthusiast,** maniac; fan, lover, devotee; informal fanatic, addict, buff, freak, nut.
OPPOSITES: saint.

fiendish adjective
1 *the fiendish atrocities which have been perpetrated in this country:* **wicked,** cruel, vicious, evil, villainous; brutal, savage, barbaric, barbarous, inhuman, murderous, ruthless, merciless.
2 *a fiendish plot by manufacturers to relieve the customers of their hard-earned cash:* **cunning,** clever, ingenious, crafty, canny, wily, devious, shrewd; informal sneaky.
3 (informal) *a fiendish puzzle that took hours to complete:* **difficult,** complex, challenging, complicated, intricate, involved, knotty, thorny.

fierce adjective
1 *a fierce black mastiff barred the way:* **ferocious,** savage, vicious, aggressive.
2 *they are facing fierce competition from the Americans:* **aggressive,** cut-throat, competitive; keen, intense, strong, relentless.
3 *a fierce jealousy filled his whole being:* **intense,** powerful, passionate, impassioned, vehement, fervent.
4 *a fierce wind was coming in off the sea:* **powerful,** strong, violent, forceful; stormy, blustery, gusty, tempestuous.
5 *a fierce pain shot up his leg:* **severe,** extreme, intense, acute, excruciating, agonizing, piercing.
OPPOSITES: gentle, mild.

fiery adjective
1 *the fiery breath of the volcano:* **burning,** blazing, flaming; on fire, ablaze.
2 *she had blushed a fiery red:* **bright,** brilliant, vivid, intense, deep, rich.
3 *her fiery spirit:* **passionate,** impassioned, ardent, fervent, fervid, spirited; quick-tempered, hot-headed, volatile, explosive; aggressive.
OPPOSITES: cool, pale, lifeless.

fiesta noun festival, carnival, holiday, celebration, party.

fight verb
1 *two men were fighting in the bar:* **brawl,** exchange blows, struggle, grapple, wrestle, tussle; informal scrap, have a set-to; Brit. informal have a punch-up.
2 *he fought in the First World War:* **do battle,** go to war, take up arms, see active service, serve, join up; engage, meet, clash, skirmish.
3 *a war fought for freedom:* **engage in,** wage, conduct, prosecute, undertake.
4 *she and her sister are always fighting:* **quarrel,** argue, bicker, squabble, fall out, wrangle, have words; Brit. row; informal scrap.
5 *textile workers are fighting for better*

working conditions: **campaign,** strive, battle, struggle, crusade, agitate, lobby, push, press.
6 *they will fight the decision tooth and nail:* **oppose,** contest, confront, challenge, combat, dispute, quarrel with, argue against/with, strive against, struggle against.
▷**noun**
1 *he'd got into a fight outside a club:* **brawl,** fracas, melee, skirmish, struggle, scuffle, scrum, clash, disturbance; fisticuffs; informal scrap, set-to; Brit. informal punch-up; N. Amer. informal rough house.
2 *a heavyweight championship fight:* **boxing match,** bout, contest.
3 *the Soviet Union's fight against the Germans:* **battle,** struggle, engagement, clash, conflict; war, campaign, crusade, action, hostilities.
4 *I'd just had a fight with my girlfriend:* **argument,** quarrel, squabble, wrangle, disagreement, contretemps, altercation, dispute; Brit. row; informal tiff, spat, scrap.
5 *their long fight for control of the company:* **struggle,** battle, campaign, push, effort.
6 *she had no fight left in her:* **will,** resistance, spirit, courage, pluck, pluckiness, grit, strength, backbone, determination, resolve; informal guts; Brit. informal bottle.
□**fight someone/something off**
he fought off a pit bull terrier that attacked him in the park: **repel,** repulse, beat off/back, ward off, fend off, keep/hold at bay, drive away/back, force back.

fighter noun *a guerrilla fighter:* **soldier,** warrior, combatant, serviceman, servicewoman, trooper; Brit. informal squaddie; old use man-at-arms.

fighting noun *200 were injured in the fighting:* **violence,** hostilities, conflict, action, combat; warfare, war, battles, skirmishing, rioting.
OPPOSITES: peace.

figment noun *all this nonsense about ghosts is just a figment of her imagination:* **invention,** creation, fabrication; hallucination, illusion, delusion, fancy, vision.

figurative adjective
1 *the role of figurative language in communication:* **metaphorical,** non-literal, symbolic, allegorical, representative, emblematic.
2 *Adam's early sculpture was figurative:* **representational,** pictorial; mimetic.
OPPOSITES: literal, abstract.

figure noun
1 *the production figures are down this month:* **statistic,** number, quantity, amount, level, total, sum; (**figures**) data, information.
2 *the second figure was 9:* **digit,** numeral, numerical symbol.
3 *her petite, curvaceous figure:* **physique,**

build, frame, body, proportions, shape, form, outline, silhouette.
4 *film stars, sports heroes, and other public figures have achieved a godlike status in the public consciousness:* **person**, personage, individual, man, woman, character, personality.
5 *geometrical figures:* **shape**, pattern, design, motif.
6 *the results are shown in figure 4:* **diagram**, drawing, picture, plate.
▷**verb** *the issue of nuclear policy figured prominently in the talks:* **feature**, appear, be featured, be mentioned, be referred to, be prominent.
▯**figure something out** (informal) *he tried to figure out what the message meant:* **work out**, make out, fathom, puzzle out, ascertain, make sense of, think through, get to the bottom of; understand, comprehend, see, grasp; informal get the hang of; Brit. informal suss out.

filament noun fibre, thread, strand; technical fibril.

file¹ noun
1 *he opened the file and began to read:* **folder**, portfolio, binder, document case.
2 *we have files on all the major companies:* **dossier**, document, record, report; data, information, documentation, annals, archives.
3 *the computer file was searched:* **document**, text; data bank, database.
▷**verb**
1 *make sure you file the documents correctly:* **put in place/order**, order, arrange, organize, categorize, classify, catalogue, record, store, archive.
2 *his wife has filed for divorce:* **apply**, register, ask.
3 *two women have filed a civil suit against him:* **bring**, press, lodge, place; formal prefer.

file² noun *a file of boys in football kit crossed the field:* **line**, column, row, string, chain, procession; Brit. informal crocodile.
▷**verb** *we filed out into the car park:* **walk**, march, parade, troop, process.

file³ verb *she has nothing to do but file her nails:* **smooth**, buff, rub, polish, shape; scrape, abrade, rasp, sandpaper, sand.

filial adjective *a display of filial affection:* **a son's, a daughter's**, dutiful, devoted, compliant, respectful, affectionate, loving.

filibuster verb *the opposition are filibustering:* **waste time**, stall, play for time, stonewall, procrastinate, buy time, use delaying tactics; Brit. talk something out.

filigree noun *a bench decorated with gold filigree:* **tracery**, fretwork, latticework, scrollwork, lacework.

fill verb
1 *she filled a suitcase with clothes:* **pack**, load, fill up, fill to the brim.
2 *journalists and photographers filled the room:* **crowd into**, throng, pack into, occupy, squeeze into, cram into; overcrowd, overfill.
3 *he began filling his shelves:* **stock**, pack, load, supply, replenish, restock, refill.
4 *fill all the holes with a wood-repair compound:* **block up**, stop up, plug, seal, pack, caulk.
5 *her perfume filled the room:* **pervade**, permeate, suffuse, penetrate, infuse.
6 *he had filled the post in an acting capacity for some time:* **hold**, occupy; informal hold down.
7 *community land trusts are a way to fill the pressing need for housing:* **satisfy**, meet, fulfil, answer.
OPPOSITES: empty.
▯**fill in**
I'm going to be filling in for Kim: **substitute**, deputize, stand in, cover, take over, act as stand-in, take the place of; informal sub, step into someone's shoes/boots.
▯**fill someone in**
Ian's filled me in on what's been happening: **inform**, advise, tell, brief, update; acquaint with, apprise of; informal put in the picture, bring up to speed.
▯**fill something in** (Brit.) *he filled in all the forms:* **complete**, answer, fill up; N. Amer. fill out.
▯**fill out**
she had filled out since we last saw her: **grow fatter**, grow plumper, flesh out, put on weight, get heavier.
▯**fill something out**
this account needs to be filled out by detailed evidence: **expand**, enlarge, add to, elaborate on, flesh out; supplement, extend, develop, amplify.

filling noun *filling for cushions:* **stuffing**, padding, wadding, filler; contents, inside.
▷**adjective** *a cheap but filling meal:* **substantial**, hearty, ample, satisfying, square; heavy, stodgy.
OPPOSITES: light.

fillip noun *this reduction in rates is a fillip to the housing market:* **stimulus**, boost, incentive, impetus; tonic, spur, aid, help; informal shot in the arm.

film noun
1 *a film of sweat covered his face:* **layer**, coat, coating, covering, cover, sheet, patina, overlay.
2 *he's in the UK to promote his latest film:* **movie**, picture, feature film, motion picture; informal flick.
3 *she would like to work in film:* **cinema**, movies; the silver screen, celluloid.
▷**verb**
1 *he immediately filmed the next scene:* **record**, shoot, capture, video.
2 *his eyes had filmed over:* **cloud**, mist, haze, blur.

WORD LINKS
cinematographic relating to film-making

filmy adjective *she wore a filmy black blouse:* **sheer**, translucent, diaphanous, transparent, see-through; delicate, fine, light, thin, gossamer.
OPPOSITES: thick, opaque.

filter noun *the water passes through a carbon filter:* **strainer**, sieve, riddle, gauze, netting.
▷**verb**
1 *the farmers filter the water:* **strain**, sieve, sift, filtrate, clarify, purify, refine, treat.
2 *the rain had filtered through her jacket:* **seep**, percolate, leak, trickle, ooze.

filth noun *stagnant pools of filth:* **dirt**, muck, grime, mud, mire, sludge, slime, ooze; pollution, contamination; Brit. informal gunge.

filthy adjective
1 *the room was filthy* | *a pile of filthy clothes:* **dirty**, mucky, grimy, muddy, unclean, unwashed; foul, squalid, sordid, soiled, black, blackened, stained; polluted, contaminated, unhygienic, insanitary.
2 *she told a series of filthy jokes:* **obscene**, indecent, dirty, smutty, rude, improper, coarse, bawdy, vulgar, lewd, racy, off colour, earthy, ribald, risqué, pornographic, explicit; euphemistic **adult**; informal blue, X-rated.
3 (informal) *he was in a filthy mood:* **bad**, foul, bad-tempered, ill-tempered, irritable, grumpy, grouchy, cross, fractious, peevish; informal snappy; Brit. informal shirty, stroppy.
OPPOSITES: clean, good.

final adjective
1 *the final year of study:* **last**, closing, concluding, finishing, end, terminating, ultimate.
2 *the referee's decisions are final:* **irrevocable**, unalterable, absolute, conclusive, irrefutable, incontrovertible, indisputable, unchallengeable, binding.
OPPOSITES: first, provisional.

finale noun *a firework display provided a fitting finale to the weekend:* **climax**, culmination; end, ending, finish, close, conclusion, termination; denouement, last act, final scene, last movement, coda.
OPPOSITES: beginning.

finalize verb *the two countries have yet to finalize a deal:* **conclude**, complete, clinch, settle, work out, secure, wrap up, wind up, put the finishing touches to; reach agreement on, agree on, come to terms on; informal sew up.

finally adverb
1 *she finally got her man to the altar:* **eventually**, ultimately, in the end, after a long time, at last; in the long run.
2 *finally, wrap the ribbon round the edge:* **lastly**, last, in conclusion, to conclude, to end.
3 *this should finally dispel that common misconception:* **conclusively**, irrevocably,

decisively, definitively, for ever, for good, once and for all.
OPPOSITES: initially.

finance noun
1 *he knows all about finance:* **financial affairs**, money, economics, commerce, business, investment.
2 *companies seeking short-term finance:* **funds**, assets, money, capital, resources, cash, reserves, revenue, income; funding, backing, sponsorship.
▷**verb** *the film-makers were constrained by the Internet company that financed the project:* **fund**, pay for, back, capitalize, subsidize, invest in; underwrite, guarantee, sponsor, support; informal bankroll.

financial adjective *a major financial institution:* **monetary**, money, economic, fiscal, banking, commercial, business, investment; formal pecuniary.

financier noun **investor**, venture capitalist, speculator, banker, capitalist, industrialist, businessman, businesswoman.

find verb
1 *I finally found the book I wanted* | *a group of schoolchildren found her in the street:* **discover**, locate, track down, unearth, pinpoint; search out, nose out, root out; come across, chance on, light on, happen on, stumble on, encounter; spot, notice.
2 *he's still struggling to find enough money for the trip:* **obtain**, get, come up with, raise, secure, earn, achieve, gain.
3 *caffeine is found in both coffee and tea:* be present, occur, exist, be existent, appear.
4 *you'll soon find that it's a lively area:* **discover**, become aware, realize, learn, observe, notice, perceive.
5 *I find their decision strange:* **consider**, think, believe to be, feel to be, look on as, view as, see as, judge, regard as.
6 *I'm still trying to find the courage to speak to her:* **summon**, summon up, gather, muster, muster up, screw up, call up.
7 *he was found guilty:* **judge**, adjudge, deem, rule, declare, pronounce.
OPPOSITES: lose.
▷**noun**
1 *this exciting find dates from the second century:* **discovery**, acquisition.
2 *this table is a real find for anyone who's short of space:* **good buy**, bargain; godsend, boon.
☐**find something out**
I found out that my husband was having an affair | *he found out the truth:* **discover**, become aware, learn, ascertain, detect, discern, perceive, get/come to know, realize; informal figure out; Brit. informal twig.

finding noun
1 *the finding of the leak:* **discovery**, location, detection, uncovering.
2 *he was appalled at the tribunal's findings:* **conclusion**, decision, verdict,

pronouncement, judgement, ruling, decree, order, recommendation; Law determination.

fine¹ adjective

1 *a fine collection of Regency furniture:* **excellent**, first-class, first-rate, great, exceptional, outstanding, superior, splendid, magnificent, exquisite, supreme, superb, wonderful, superlative, second to none.
2 *fine wines:* **select**, choice, prime, superior, of distinction, quality, premium.
3 *the food was fine, but the service was terrible:* **all right**, acceptable, good enough, passable, satisfactory, adequate, reasonable; informal OK.
4 *I feel fine:* **in good health**, well, healthy, all right, fighting fit, as fit as a fiddle, blooming, thriving, in good shape/condition, in fine fettle; informal OK, in the pink.
5 *it was a fine day:* **fair**, dry, bright, clear, sunny, warm, balmy, summery.
6 *she dressed him in fine clothes:* **elegant**, stylish, expensive, smart, chic, fashionable; fancy, sumptuous, lavish, opulent.
7 *her fine golden hair:* **thin**, light, delicate, wispy, flyaway.
8 *she sharpened her pencil to a fine point:* **sharp**, keen, acute.
9 *the fine material of her dress:* **sheer**, light, lightweight, thin, flimsy; diaphanous, filmy, gossamer, silky, transparent, translucent, see-through.
10 *a beautiful beach of fine, golden sand:* **fine-grained**, powdery; powdered, ground, crushed.
11 *for fine detailed work, you need a smaller brush:* **intricate**, delicate, detailed, elaborate, dainty, meticulous.
12 *a fine distinction:* **subtle**, nice, hair-splitting.
OPPOSITES: poor, unsatisfactory, ill, inclement, thick, coarse.

fine² noun *if convicted they face heavy fines:* **financial penalty**, sanction, fee, charge.
▷**verb** *they were fined for breaking environmental laws:* **penalize**, charge.

finery noun *she appeared, dressed in all her finery:* **regalia**, best clothes, Sunday best; informal glad rags.

finesse noun

1 *the comedy routine is performed with masterly finesse:* **skill**, expertise, subtlety, flair, panache, elan, polish, artistry, virtuosity, mastery.
2 *these situations call for a modicum of finesse:* **tact**, discretion, diplomacy, delicacy, sensitivity, savoir faire.
OPPOSITES: incompetence, indiscretion.

finger noun **digit**, thumb, index finger, forefinger; informal pinkie.
▷**verb** *she fingered her brooch uneasily:* **touch**, feel, handle, stroke, rub, caress, fondle, toy with, play with, fiddle with.

finicky adjective *quality service is often the deciding factor for finicky customers:* **fussy**, fastidious, punctilious, over-particular, difficult, exacting, demanding; informal picky, choosy; Brit. informal pernickety.
OPPOSITES: easy-going.

finish verb

1 *they'd finished the job by 6.30 | what time do you finish work?* **complete**, conclude, end, stop, bring to a conclusion, wind up, finalize; crown, cap, round off, put the finishing touches to; accomplish, discharge, carry out, do, get done, fulfil; informal wrap up, sew up.
2 *he finished off the last of his soup and stood up:* **consume**, eat up, devour, drink, gulp down, empty, drain; informal polish off, down.
3 *just as the music finished, Frederick appeared at her side:* **end**, come to an end, stop, come to a close, cease, terminate.
4 *some items were finished in a black lacquer:* **coat**, cover, laminate, face, veneer, paint, glaze.
OPPOSITES: start, begin.
▷**noun**
1 *the suffering did not end with the finish of the war:* **end**, ending, completion, conclusion, close, cessation, termination.
2 *the furniture has a mellow painted finish:* **veneer**, lacquer, lamination, glaze, coating, covering; surface, texture.
OPPOSITES: start, beginning.

finished adjective

1 *a finished performance:* **accomplished**, polished, flawless, faultless, perfect; expert, proficient, masterly, impeccable, virtuoso, skilful, skilled, professional.
2 *he knew he was finished:* **ruined**, defeated, beaten, wrecked, doomed, bankrupt, broken; informal washed up, through.

finite adjective *there is a finite amount of money available:* **limited**, restricted, determined, determinate, fixed, known, measurable.
OPPOSITES: infinite.

fire noun

1 *a fire broke out in the kitchen:* **blaze**, conflagration, inferno; flames, burning, combustion.
2 *he turned on an electric fire:* **heater**, radiator, convector.
3 *he lacked fire and animation:* **dynamism**, energy, vigour, animation, vitality, exuberance, zest, elan; passion, ardour, zeal, spirit, verve, vivacity; enthusiasm, eagerness, gusto, fervour; informal get-up-and-go.
▷**verb**
1 *howitzers were firing shells from beyond the river:* **launch**, shoot, discharge, let fly with.
2 *someone fired a gun at me:* **shoot**, discharge, let off, set off.
3 (informal) *he was fired:* **dismiss**, discharge,

give someone their notice, lay off, let go, get rid of, axe; Military cashier; informal sack; Brit. informal give someone their cards.

4 *the stories fired my imagination:* stimulate, stir up, excite, awaken, arouse, rouse, inflame, animate, inspire, motivate.

□ **catch fire**
the driver managed to get out before the car caught fire: ignite, catch light, burst into flames, go up in flames.

□ **on fire**
the restaurant was on fire: burning, alight, ablaze, blazing, in flames, aflame.

> **WORD LINKS**
> **pyromania** an obsessive desire to set fire to things

firebrand noun *a political firebrand who loved to antagonize:* radical, revolutionary, agitator, rabble-rouser, subversive, troublemaker.

fireproof adjective *he wore fireproof overalls:* non-flammable, incombustible, fire-resistant, fire-retardant, flame-resistant, heatproof.
OPPOSITES: inflammable.

firm¹ adjective
1 *the ground is fairly firm:* hard, solid, unyielding, resistant, compacted, compressed, dense, stiff, rigid, frozen, set.
2 *firm foundations:* secure, stable, steady, strong, sturdy, fixed, fast, set, taut, tight; immovable, stationary, motionless.
3 *a firm handshake:* strong, vigorous, forceful.
4 *I was very firm about what I wanted:* resolute, determined, decided, resolved, steadfast; adamant, emphatic, insistent, single-minded; sure, certain, definite.
5 *he's always been a firm Labour supporter:* wholehearted unfaltering, unwavering, unflinching, unswerving, unbending; hard-line, committed, dyed-in-the-wool.
6 *they became firm friends:* close, good, intimate, inseparable, dear, special; devoted, loving, faithful, long-standing, steady, steadfast.
7 *she had no firm plans:* definite, fixed, settled, decided, established, confirmed, agreed; unalterable, irreversible, set in stone.
OPPOSITES: soft, unstable, irresolute, indefinite.

firm² noun *an accountancy firm:* company, business, concern, enterprise, organization, corporation, conglomerate, office, bureau, agency, consortium; informal outfit.

first adjective
1 *the first chapter of Genesis:* earliest, initial, opening, introductory.
2 *we decided to start from first principles:* fundamental, basic, rudimentary, primary; key, cardinal, central, chief, vital, essential.
3 *our first priority is law and order:* foremost, principal, highest, greatest,

paramount, top, uppermost, prime, chief, leading, main, major; overriding, predominant, prevailing, central, core, dominant; informal number-one.
4 *he is hoping to win first prize:* top, best, prime, premier, winning.
OPPOSITES: last, closing.

▷ adverb
1 *the room they had first entered:* at first, to begin with, first of all, at the outset, initially.
2 *she wouldn't go—she'd die first!* sooner, rather, for preference.

first-class adjective *this is a first-class hotel:* superior, first-rate, top-quality, five-star, high-grade, high-quality, premier, premium, grade A, best, select, exclusive, excellent, superb, outstanding, exceptional, marvellous, magnificent, splendid.
OPPOSITES: poor.

first-hand adjective *they have first-hand experience of bringing up children:* direct, immediate, personal, hands-on, experiential, empirical.
OPPOSITES: vicarious.

first-rate adjective *they have done a first-rate job:* top-quality, high-quality, top-grade, first-class, second to none, fine; superlative, excellent, superb, outstanding, exceptional, exemplary, marvellous, magnificent, splendid; informal super, great, tremendous, terrific, fantastic.
OPPOSITES: second-rate.

fiscal adjective *the government's fiscal policies:* tax, budgetary; financial, economic, monetary, money.

fish verb
1 *she opened her bag and fished for her purse:* search, delve, look, hunt; grope, fumble, ferret about/around, root about/around, rummage.
2 *I'm not fishing for compliments:* look, solicit, angle, aim, hope, cast about/around, be after.
□ **fish someone/something out**
they eventually fished him out of the water: pull out, haul out, remove, extract, retrieve; rescue from, save from.

> **WORD LINKS**
> **ichthyology** the branch of zoology concerned with fish
> **pisciculture** the controlled breeding and rearing of fish

fishy adjective (informal) *there was something fishy going on.* See SUSPICIOUS.

fissure noun *fissures in the ocean floor:* opening, crevice, crack, cleft, breach, crevasse, chasm; break, fracture, fault, rift, rupture, split.

fit¹ adjective
1 *the house is not fit for human habitation | he is a fit subject for such a book:* suitable,

good enough; relevant, pertinent, apt, appropriate, suited, apposite, fitting.
2 *is he fit to look after a child?* competent, able, capable; ready, prepared, qualified, trained, equipped.
3 *he looked tanned and fit:* healthy, well, in good health, in good shape, in trim, in good condition, fighting fit; athletic, muscular, strong, robust, hale and hearty.
OPPOSITES: unsuitable, incompetent, unfit.

▷**verb**
1 *have your carpets fitted professionally:* lay, put in place/position, position, place, fix.
2 *the camera is fitted with a backlight button:* equip, provide, supply, furnish, kit out, rig out.
3 *concrete slabs were fitted together:* join, connect, put together, piece together, attach, link.
4 *a sentence that fits his crimes:* suit, be appropriate to, match, correspond to, tally with, go with, accord with, be commensurate with, correlate to, be congruent with, be consonant with.
5 *an MSc fits you for a professional career:* qualify, prepare, make ready, train, groom.

▷**noun** *the degree of fit between a school's philosophy and practice:* correlation, correspondence, agreement, consistency, equivalence, match, similarity, compatibility, concurrence.

◻**fit in**
he made a big effort to fit in: conform, adjust, blend in, be in harmony, be in line, be assimilated.

fit² noun
1 *an epileptic fit:* convulsion, spasm, paroxysm, seizure, attack; Medicine ictus.
2 *a fit of the giggles:* outbreak, outburst, explosion, attack, bout, spell.
3 *my mother would have a fit if she knew:* tantrum, fit of temper, outburst of anger/rage, frenzy; informal paddy.

fitful adjective *I drifted off into a brief and fitful sleep:* intermittent, sporadic, spasmodic, broken, disturbed, disrupted, patchy, irregular, uneven, unsettled.
OPPOSITES: continuous, restful.

fitness noun
1 *polo requires tremendous fitness:* good health, strength, robustness, vigour, athleticism, toughness, physical fitness, muscularity; good condition, good shape, well-being.
2 *he was examined to assess his fitness for active service:* suitability, capability, competence, ability, aptitude; readiness, preparedness, eligibility.
OPPOSITES: unfitness.

fitted adjective
1 *fitted cupboards:* built-in, integral, integrated, fixed, custom-made, shaped, made to measure.
2 *he wasn't fitted for the job:* well suited,

right, suitable; equipped, fit; informal cut out.

fitting noun
1 *the sprinkler is made of plastic with stainless steel fittings:* attachment, connection, piece, component, accessory.
2 (Brit.) *a manufacturer of bathroom fittings:* furnishings, furniture, fixtures, equipment, appointments; Brit. fitments.

▷**adjective** *this is a fitting conclusion to the book:* apt, appropriate, suitable, apposite; fit, proper, right, seemly, correct.
OPPOSITES: inappropriate, unsuitable.

five cardinal number quintet.

> WORD LINKS
> **pentagon** a five-sided figure
> **pentagram**, **pentangle** a five-pointed star drawn using a continuous line

fix verb
1 *new road signs were fixed to the lamp posts:* fasten, attach, affix, secure; join, connect, couple, link; install, implant, embed; stick, glue, pin, nail, screw, bolt, clamp, clip.
2 *let's fix a date for the meeting:* decide on, select, choose; determine, settle, set, arrange, establish, allot; designate, name, appoint, specify.
3 *his words are fixed in my memory:* stick, lodge, embed.
4 *he fixed my washing machine:* repair, mend, put right, get working, restore to working order; overhaul, service, renovate, recondition.
5 *James fixed it for his parents to watch the show from the wings:* arrange, organize, contrive, manage, engineer; informal swing, wangle.
OPPOSITES: remove.

▷**noun** (informal)
1 *they are in a bit of a fix:* predicament, plight, difficulty, corner, tight spot, dire straits; informal pickle, jam, hole.
2 *there is no quick fix for the industry's problems:* solution, answer, resolution, way out, remedy, cure; informal magic bullet.

fixated adjective *the family was fixated on cameras and home movies:* obsessed with, preoccupied with, obsessive about; focused on, keen on, immersed in, wrapped up in, engrossed in, enthusiastic about; informal fanatical about, hooked on.

fixation noun *the modern fixation with diet and fitness:* obsession with, preoccupation with, mania for, interest in, compulsion for, addiction to; informal craze for.

fixed adjective *a fixed period of time:* predetermined, set, established, arranged, specified, decided, agreed, determined, confirmed, prescribed, definite, defined, explicit, precise.
OPPOSITES: indeterminate.

fixture noun
1 *the hotel retains many of the original fixtures and fittings:* appliance, unit, installation; equipment, facility; Brit. fitment.
2 (Brit.) *their first fixture of the season:* match, race, game, competition, contest, event.

fizz verb *the lemonade was still fizzing at the top of his glass:* effervesce, sparkle, bubble, froth, fizzle.
▷**noun**
1 *the process that puts the fizz in champagne:* effervescence, sparkle, bubbles, gas, carbonation, froth.
2 (informal) *she saw that I had lost some of my fizz:* ebullience, exuberance, life, vivacity, animation, vigour, energy, verve, dash, spirit, sparkle, zest; informal pizzazz.

fizzle verb
◻fizzle out
their romance just fizzled out: peter out, die off, fade away, cool off, evaporate, melt away; tail off, wither away.

fizzy adjective *a fizzy drink:* effervescent, sparkling, carbonated, gassy, bubbly, frothy.
OPPOSITES: still, flat.

flabbergasted adjective (informal). See ASTONISHED.

flabby adjective
1 *his flabby stomach:* soft, loose, flaccid, slack, untoned, drooping, sagging.
2 *a flabby, balding man:* fat, obese, overweight, fleshy, plump, chubby, portly, rotund, corpulent; informal tubby; Brit. informal podgy.
3 *flabby, colourless prose:* weak, feeble, uninspiring, lacklustre, ineffectual, ineffective, loose.
OPPOSITES: firm, thin.

flaccid adjective
1 *his muscles were flaccid:* soft, loose, limp, slack, lax; drooping, sagging.
2 *his play seemed flaccid:* lacklustre, lifeless, listless, uninspiring, tame.
OPPOSITES: firm, spirited.

flag[1] noun *the Irish flag:* banner, standard, ensign, pennant, streamer, jack; colours.
▷**verb** *a spelling checker can flag the misspelt words:* indicate, identify, point out, mark, label, tag, highlight.
◻flag someone/something down
she flagged down a police car: hail, wave down, signal to stop, stop, halt.

flag[2] verb
1 *they were flagging towards the finish:* tire, weaken, wilt, droop.
2 *my energy flags in the afternoon:* fade, decline, wane, ebb, diminish, decrease, lessen, dwindle; wither, melt away, peter out, die away/down.
OPPOSITES: revive.

flagon noun jug, flask, carafe, decanter, ewer, pitcher, bottle, tankard.

flagrant adjective *the regime has shown a flagrant disregard for human rights:* blatant, glaring, obvious, overt, conspicuous, barefaced, shameless, brazen, undisguised, unconcealed.
OPPOSITES: secret, sheepish.

flail verb
1 *he fell headlong, his arms flailing:* wave, swing, thrash about, flap about.
2 *I was flailing about in the water:* flounder, struggle, thrash, writhe, splash.

flair noun
1 *he had a genuine flair for comedy:* aptitude, talent, gift, instinct, natural ability, facility, skill, bent, feel.
2 *though not conventionally pretty, she always dressed with flair:* style, panache, elan, poise, elegance; taste, good taste; informal class.

> **USAGE**
>
> Do not confuse **flair** with **flare**. **Flair** means 'a natural ability or talent', whereas **flare** means 'to burn or shine with sudden intensity' (*behind him, lightning flared*) or 'to become wider' (*her dress flared out from the hips*).

flak noun (informal) *he has come in for a lot of flak:* criticism, censure, disapproval, hostility, complaints; obloquy, vilification, abuse, brickbats; formal castigation, opprobrium, excoriation, disapprobation; Brit. informal stick.

flake noun *flakes of pastry:* sliver, wafer, shaving, paring; chip, scale; technical lamina.
▷**verb** *the paint was flaking:* peel, peel off, blister.

flaky adjective *her skin had healed, though it was very flaky:* flaking, peeling, scaly, blistering, scabrous; dry, brittle.

flamboyant adjective
1 *her flamboyant personality:* exuberant, confident, lively, animated, vibrant, vivacious; larger than life.
2 *he sported a flamboyant cravat:* colourful, brightly coloured, bright, vibrant, vivid; dazzling, eye-catching, bold; ostentatious, showy, gaudy, garish, lurid, loud; informal jazzy.
3 *a flamboyant architectural style:* elaborate, ornate, fancy; baroque, rococo.
OPPOSITES: restrained.

flame noun *a sheet of flames engulfed the house:* fire; blaze, conflagration, inferno.
▷**verb**
1 *the logs crackled and flamed:* burn, blaze, be ablaze, be alight, be on fire, be in flames; flare.
2 *Erica's cheeks flamed:* go red, blush, flush, redden, grow pink/crimson/scarlet, colour, glow.
◻in flames
two ships are in flames, drifting towards the harbour: on fire, burning, alight, flaming, blazing, ignited.

flaming adjective

1 *a flaming bonfire:* blazing, burning, ablaze, on fire, in flames, aflame.
2 *a flaming row:* furious, violent, vehement, frenzied, angry, passionate.
3 *in a flaming temper:* furious, enraged, fuming, seething, incensed, infuriated, angry, raging; informal livid.

flammable adjective *flammable liquids:* inflammable, combustible; unstable, volatile.
OPPOSITES: non-flammable.

> **USAGE**
>
> The words **flammable** and **inflammable** both mean 'easily set on fire'. To avoid confusion, it is safer to use **flammable**, because the *in-* part of **inflammable** can give the impression that the word means 'not flammable'.

flank noun

1 *he touched the horse's flanks:* side, haunch, quarter, thigh.
2 *the southern flank of the Eighth Army:* side, wing; face, aspect.
▷**verb** *the garden is flanked by two rivers:* edge, bound, line, border, neighbour, fringe.

flap verb

1 *the mallards flapped their wings angrily:* beat, flutter, agitate, wave, wag, swing.
2 *his shirt tails flapped in the breeze:* flutter, fly, blow, swing, sway, ripple, stir.
▷**noun**
1 *pockets with buttoned flaps:* fold, overlap, covering; lappet.
2 *the surviving bird made a few desperate flaps:* flutter; stroke, beat.

flare noun

1 *the flare of the match lit up his face:* blaze, flash, burst, glow, flicker.
2 *Kelly felt a flare of anger within her:* burst, rush, eruption, explosion, spasm; literary access.
▷**verb**
1 *the match flared as he lit a cigarette:* blaze, flash, flare up, flame, burn; glow, flicker.
2 *her nostrils flared:* spread, broaden, widen; dilate.
□ **flare up**
1 *the wooden houses flared up like matchsticks:* burn, blaze, go up in flames.
2 *violence flared up again at the end of the year:* recur, reoccur, reappear; break out, start suddenly, erupt, explode, blow up, escalate, boil over; develop.
3 *she flared up and yelled at him:* lose your temper, become enraged, fly into a temper, go berserk; informal blow your top, fly off the handle, go mad, hit the roof, go up the wall, have a fit; Brit. informal go spare, lose your rag.

> **USAGE**
>
> Do not confuse **flare** with **flair**: **flare** means 'to burn or shine with sudden intensity' or 'to become wider', whereas **flair** means 'a natural ability or talent' (*he had a real flair for design*).

flash verb

1 *a torch flashed:* light up, shine, flare, blaze, gleam, glint, sparkle, burn; blink, wink, flicker, shimmer, twinkle, glimmer, glisten, scintillate.
2 (informal) *he was always flashing his money about:* wave, flaunt, flourish, display, parade.
3 *racing cars flashed past:* race, speed, rush, hurtle, career, streak, shoot, dash, dart, fly, whistle, bolt, zoom, whizz, buzz; informal tear; Brit. informal bomb.
▷**noun**
1 *a flash of light:* flare, blaze, burst; gleam, glint, sparkle, flicker, shimmer, twinkle, glimmer.
2 *a sudden flash of inspiration:* burst, outburst, wave, rush, surge, flush.

flashy adjective (informal) *a big flashy car:* ostentatious, flamboyant, showy, conspicuous, extravagant, expensive; vulgar, tasteless, brash, lurid, garish, loud, gaudy; informal glitzy, bling.
OPPOSITES: discreet.

flat¹ adjective

1 *a flat surface:* level, horizontal; smooth, even, uniform, regular, plane.
2 *his voice was flat and without expression:* monotonous, droning, boring, dull, tedious, uninteresting, unexciting, soporific; bland, dreary, colourless, featureless, emotionless, expressionless, lifeless, spiritless, lacklustre.
3 *the UK housing market was still flat:* slow, inactive, sluggish, slack, quiet, static, depressed.
4 (Brit.) *the battery's flat battery:* dead, finished, used up, run out.
5 *I charge a £30 flat fee:* fixed, set, regular, unchanging, unvarying, invariable.
6 *a flat denial of any impropriety:* outright, absolute, definite, positive, straight, direct, plain, explicit; firm, resolute, adamant, assertive, emphatic, categorical, unconditional, unqualified, unequivocal.
OPPOSITES: vertical, uneven, lively, variable.
▷**adverb**
1 *she lay down flat on the floor:* stretched out, outstretched, spreadeagled, sprawled, prone, supine, prostrate, recumbent.
2 (informal) *she turned me down flat:* outright, absolutely, firmly, resolutely, adamantly, emphatically, insistently, categorically, unconditionally, unequivocally.

flat² noun *a two-bedroom flat in the city:* apartment, rooms, flatlet, penthouse, maisonette.

flatten verb

1 *Tom flattened the crumpled paper:* smooth, press, even out, level out/off.
2 *the cows flattened the grass:* compress, press down, crush, squash, compact, trample.
3 *tornadoes can flatten buildings in seconds:* demolish, raze to the ground, tear down, knock down, destroy, wreck, devastate, obliterate; N. Amer. informal total.
4 (informal) *Flynn flattened him with a single punch:* knock down/over, knock to the ground, fell, prostrate; informal floor, deck, lay out.
OPPOSITES: crumple, raise, build.

flatter verb

1 *it amused him to flatter her:* compliment, praise, express admiration for, say nice things about, pay court to, fawn on; cajole, humour; informal sweet-talk, soft-soap.
2 *I was flattered to be asked:* honour, gratify, please, delight, touch; informal tickle pink.
3 *a hairstyle that flattered her:* suit, become, look good on, go well with; informal do something for.
OPPOSITES: insult, offend.

flatterer noun *the prince is surrounded by flatterers:* sycophant, lickspittle; informal crawler, creep, toady, bootlicker.

flattering adjective

1 *the restaurant received an impressive amount of flattering reviews in the press:* complimentary, favourable, commendatory, admiring, appreciative, good.
2 *it was very flattering to be nominated:* pleasing, gratifying, satisfying, cheering, heart-warming, touching, welcome.
3 *she wore her most flattering dress:* becoming, fetching, attractive, pretty, stylish, elegant, chic.
OPPOSITES: unflattering.

flattery noun *the old man sounded convinced by their flattery:* praise, compliments, blandishments, adulation, honeyed words; fawning, blarney, cajolery; informal sweet talk, soft soap.

flaunt verb *he hated the way they flaunted their wealth:* show off, display ostentatiously, make a show of, put on show/display, parade; brag about, crow about, vaunt; informal flash.
OPPOSITES: hide.

USAGE

Be careful not to confuse **flaunt** with **flout**. **Flaunt** means 'to display something in a way intended to attract attention', while **flout** means 'to show that you have no respect for a rule or convention by openly failing to follow it' (*retailers have been flouting the law for years*).

flavour noun

1 *salami can give extra flavour:* taste, savour, seasoning, tastiness, flavouring, tang, relish, bite, piquancy, pungency, spice, zest; informal zing, zip.
2 *the tournament had a strong international flavour:* character, quality, feel, ambience, atmosphere, aura, air, mood, tone; spirit, essence, nature; informal vibes.
3 *this excerpt will give a flavour of the report:* impression, suggestion, hint, taste, smack.
▷ verb *spices for flavouring food:* season, spice up, add piquancy to, ginger up, make palatable; informal pep up.

flavouring noun

1 *this cheese is often combined with other flavourings:* seasoning, spice, herb, additive; condiment, dressing.
2 *vanilla flavouring:* essence, extract, concentrate.

flaw noun *Williams' car had a serious design flaw:* defect, fault, weakness, weak spot/point, imperfection, deficiency, inadequacy, shortcoming, limitation, failing, Achilles heel; Computing bug; informal glitch.
OPPOSITES: strength.

flawed adjective *the findings were fundamentally flawed:* unsound, defective, faulty, distorted, inaccurate, incorrect, erroneous, imprecise, fallacious, misleading.
OPPOSITES: sound.

flawless adjective

1 *her smooth, flawless skin | a flawless china plate:* perfect, unblemished, unmarked, unimpaired; whole, intact, sound, unbroken, undamaged, mint, pristine.
2 *a dazzling display of flawless virtuosity:* consummate, impeccable, immaculate, accurate, correct, faultless, error-free, unerring; exemplary, model, ideal, copybook
OPPOSITES: flawed.

fleck noun *a grey colour interspersed with flecks of pale blue:* spot, mark, dot, speck, speckle, freckle, patch, smudge, streak, blotch, dab; Brit. informal splodge.
▷ verb *the deer's flanks were flecked with white:* spot, mark, dot, speckle, bespeckle, freckle, stipple, stud, blotch, mottle, streak, splash, spatter, bespatter, scatter, sprinkle; informal splotch; Brit. informal splodge.

fledgling adjective *fledgling industries in the developing world:* emerging, emergent, sunrise, dawning, embryonic, infant, nascent; developing, in the making, budding, up-and-coming, rising.
OPPOSITES: mature, declining.

flee verb

1 *she fled to her room:* run, run away/off, run for it, make a run for it, escape, take flight, be gone, make off, take off, take to your heels, make a break for it, bolt, beat a retreat; informal beat it, clear off/out,

vamoose, skedaddle; Brit. informal scarper.
2 *they fled the country:* leave, escape from; informal skip, quit; old use fly.

fleecy adjective *he had on a fleecy green tracksuit:* fluffy, woolly, downy, soft, fuzzy, furry, velvety, shaggy.
OPPOSITES: smooth, coarse.

fleet noun navy, armada, flotilla, squadron, convoy, column.

fleeting adjective *we caught a fleeting glimpse of him through the trees:* brief, short, short-lived, quick, momentary, transient, ephemeral, fugitive, passing, transitory.
OPPOSITES: lasting.

flesh noun
1 *you need more flesh on your bones:* meat, muscle, brawn, tissue; informal beef.
2 *a fruit with juicy flesh:* pulp, marrow, meat.
3 *the pleasures of the flesh:* the body, human nature, physicality, carnality, animality; sensuality, sexuality.
□ **flesh something out**
soon all three were back at Harvard to flesh out Yavlinsky's plan: expand on, enlarge on, elaborate on, add to, add detail to, build on, augment, supplement, reinforce, fill out, add flesh to, put flesh on the bones of.
□ **in the flesh**
he's just as charming in the flesh as he is on TV: in person, in real life, before your very eyes, in front of you, live, physically, bodily, in bodily/human form, incarnate.

> WORD LINKS
> **carnivorous** (of an animal) flesh-eating

fleshly adjective *his laziness had made him prefer fleshly pleasures to work:* bodily, physical, of the flesh, animal, carnal, sexual, sensual, erotic.
OPPOSITES: spiritual.

fleshy adjective *Rufus had curiously sharp features for so fleshy a man:* plump, chubby, portly, fat, obese, overweight, stout, corpulent, paunchy, rotund; informal tubby; Brit. informal podgy.
OPPOSITES: thin.

flex[1] verb
1 *you must flex your elbow:* bend, crook, hook, cock, angle, double up.
2 *bodybuilders flexed their muscles:* tense, tauten, tighten, contract.
OPPOSITES: straighten, relax.

flex[2] noun (Brit.) *an electric flex:* cable, wire, lead; N. Amer. cord.

flexibility noun
1 *the timbers give the boat flexibility:* pliability, suppleness, pliancy, plasticity; elasticity, stretchiness, give, springiness, spring, resilience, bounce.
2 *he prefers the flexibility of an endowment loan:* adaptability, adjustability,

variability, versatility, open-endedness, freedom, latitude.
3 *the flexibility shown by the local authority regarding deadlines:* willingness to compromise, accommodation, adjustment, amenability, cooperation, tolerance.
OPPOSITES: rigidity, inflexibility, intransigence.

flexible adjective
1 *a flexible material:* pliable, supple, bendable, pliant, plastic; elastic, stretchy, whippy, springy, resilient; informal bendy.
2 *a flexible arrangement:* adaptable, adjustable, variable, open-ended, fluid.
3 *a flexible workforce:* accommodating, amenable, adaptable, willing to compromise, cooperative.
OPPOSITES: rigid, inflexible, intransigent.

flick noun *a flick of the wrist:* jerk, snap, flip, whisk.
▷ **verb**
1 *he flicked the switch:* click, snap, flip, jerk.
2 *the horse flicked its tail:* swish, twitch, wave, wag, waggle, shake.
□ **flick through**
Christina flicked through her diary: thumb through, leaf through, flip through, skim through, scan, look through, browse through, dip into, glance at/through, run your eye over, cast your eye over.

flicker verb
1 *the lights flickered:* glint, twinkle, sparkle, blink, wink, flash, flare, dance, gutter, glimmer; literary coruscate.
2 *her eyelids flickered in her sleep:* flutter, quiver, twitch, tremble, shiver, shudder, jerk.

flight noun
1 *the amazing history of flight:* aviation, flying, air transport, aerial navigation, aeronautics.
2 *Newton's theories allow us to predict the flight of a cricket ball:* trajectory, track, path, flight path, glide path, orbit.
3 *a flight of birds:* flock, skein, covey, swarm, cloud.
4 *his flight from England after the king's death:* escape, getaway, hasty departure, exit, exodus, breakout, bolt, disappearance; Brit. informal flit.

flighty adjective *she was regarded as too flighty for such responsibility:* irresponsible, giddy, erratic, reckless, wild, careless, thoughtless, empty-headed, untrustworthy, unreliable, fickle.
OPPOSITES: steady, responsible.

flimsy adjective
1 *flimsy wooden buildings were swept away:* fragile, weak, breakable, frail, shaky, unstable, wobbly, tottery, rickety, ramshackle, insubstantial, makeshift; jerry-built, shoddy, gimcrack.
2 *the flimsy material of her dress:* thin, light, fine, filmy, floaty, diaphanous, sheer,

delicate, insubstantial, wispy, gossamer, gauzy.
3 *this is very flimsy evidence on which to base an accusation:* weak, feeble, poor, inadequate, insufficient, thin, unsubstantial, unconvincing, implausible, unsatisfactory.
OPPOSITES: sturdy, thick, sound.

flinch verb
1 *he flinched at the noise:* wince, start, shudder, quiver, jerk, shy.
2 *he never flinched from his duty:* shrink from, recoil from, shy away from, swerve from, demur from, baulk at, jib at, quail at, fight shy of, dodge, evade, avoid; informal duck.

fling verb *he flung the axe into the river:* throw, toss, sling, hurl, cast, pitch, lob; informal chuck, heave; Brit. informal bung.
▷noun
1 *a birthday fling:* good time, bit of fun, spree, night out; revels; informal fun and games, binge.
2 *she had a brief fling with him years ago:* affair, love affair, relationship, romance, affaire de cœur, flirtation, dalliance, liaison, involvement, attachment.

flip verb
1 *the wave flipped the dinghy over | the plane flipped on to its back:* overturn, turn over, tip over, roll over, topple over, upturn, capsize; upend, invert, knock over; keel over, turn turtle.
2 *he flipped a few coins on to the bar:* throw, flick, toss, fling, sling, pitch, cast, spin, lob; informal chuck; Brit. informal bung.
3 *I flipped the transmitter switch:* flick, click, snap.
□ **flip through**
he flipped through his address book: thumb through, leaf through, flick through, skim through, scan, look through, browse through, dip into, glance at/through, run your eye over, cast your eye over.

flippancy noun *I was upset by her flippancy on such a solemn occasion:* frivolity, levity, facetiousness; disrespect, irreverence, cheek, impudence, impertinence.
OPPOSITES: seriousness, respect.

flippant adjective *a flippant remark:* frivolous, facetious, tongue-in-cheek; disrespectful, irreverent, cheeky, impudent, impertinent; informal flip, waggish.
OPPOSITES: serious, respectful.

flirt verb
1 *it amused him to flirt with her:* trifle with, toy with, tease, lead on; informal chat up.
2 *a painter who had flirted briefly with Cubism:* dabble in, toy with, trifle with, amuse yourself with, play with, tinker with, dip into, scratch the surface of.

▷noun *Anna was quite a flirt:* tease, coquette, heartbreaker.

flirtatious adjective coquettish, flirty, kittenish, teasing.

flit verb *butterflies flitted amongst the tall grasses:* dart, dance, skip, play, dash, trip, flutter, bob, bounce.

float verb
1 *the balloon floated in the air:* hover, be suspended, hang, levitate.
2 *a cloud floated across the moon:* drift, glide, sail, slip, slide, waft.
3 *they have just floated a number of new ideas:* suggest, put forward, come up with, submit, moot, propose, advance.
4 *the company was floated on the Stock Exchange:* launch, get going, get off the ground, offer, sell, introduce.

floating adjective
1 *floating masses of seaweed:* buoyant, on the surface, afloat, drifting.
2 *floating gas balloons:* hovering, suspended, hanging, defying gravity.
3 *floating voters:* uncommitted, undecided, in two minds, torn, split, uncertain, unsure, wavering, vacillating, indecisive, blowing hot and cold, undeclared; informal sitting on the fence.
4 *a floating population:* unsettled, transient; migrant, wandering, nomadic, on the move, migratory, travelling, itinerant.
5 *a floating exchange rate:* variable, changeable, changing, fluid, fluctuating.

flock noun
1 *a flock of sheep:* herd, drove.
2 *a flock of birds:* flight, congregation, covey, clutch, skein.
3 *flocks of people descended on the restaurant:* crowd, throng, horde, mass, multitude, host, army, pack, swarm, sea; informal gaggle.
▷verb
1 *people flocked around Jesus:* gather, collect, congregate, assemble, converge, mass, crowd, throng, cluster, swarm; formal foregather.
2 *tourists flock to the tiny village:* stream, go in large numbers, swarm, crowd, troop.

flog verb *the teenager was publicly flogged by a soldier:* whip, cane, thrash, beat, flagellate, lash, birch, tan/whip someone's hide.

flood noun
1 *several villages were cut off by the flood:* waters, deluge; torrent, overflow, inundation; Brit. spate.
2 *a flood of complaints:* succession, series, string, chain; barrage, volley, battery; avalanche, torrent, stream, tide, spate, storm, shower, cascade.
OPPOSITES: trickle.
▷verb
1 *the whole town was flooded:* inundate,

swamp, deluge, immerse, submerge, drown, engulf.
2 *the river could flood at any time:* overflow, burst its banks, brim over, run over.
3 *imports are flooding the domestic market:* glut, swamp, saturate, oversupply.
4 *refugees flooded in:* pour, stream, flow, surge, swarm, pile, crowd.
OPPOSITES: trickle.

floor noun *they live on the second floor:* storey, level, deck, tier.
▷**verb**
1 *he floored his attacker with a single punch:* knock down, knock over, bring down, fell, prostrate; informal lay out, deck.
2 (informal) *the question floored him:* baffle, defeat, confound, perplex, puzzle, nonplus, mystify; informal beat, flummox, stump, fox.

flop verb
1 *he flopped into a chair:* collapse, slump, crumple, subside, sink, drop.
2 *his hair flopped over his eyes:* hang, dangle, droop, sag, loll.
3 (informal) *the play flopped:* be unsuccessful, fail, not work, fall flat, founder, misfire, backfire, be a disappointment, do badly, lose money, be a disaster, be a fiasco; informal bomb, go to the wall, come a cropper.
OPPOSITES: succeed.
▷**noun** (informal) *the play was a flop:* failure, disaster, fiasco, debacle, catastrophe, loser; Brit. damp squib; informal washout.
OPPOSITES: success.

floppy adjective limp, flaccid, slack; drooping, droopy, loose, flowing.
OPPOSITES: erect, stiff.

florid adjective
1 *a florid complexion:* ruddy, red, red-faced, rosy, rosy-cheeked, pink; flushed, blushing, high-coloured; literary rubicund; old use sanguine.
2 *the florid plasterwork that graces every ceiling:* ornate, fancy, elaborate, embellished, extravagant, flamboyant, baroque, rococo, fussy, busy.
3 *a series of compliments expressed in florid English:* flowery, flamboyant, high-flown, high-sounding, grandiloquent, ornate, fancy, elaborate; bombastic, turgid; formal magniloquent; informal highfalutin.
OPPOSITES: pale, plain.

flounce[1] verb *she flounced off to her room:* storm, stride, sweep, stomp, stamp, march, strut, stalk, mince.

flounce[2] noun *a black suit with a little white flounce at the neckline:* frill, ruffle, ruff, peplum, jabot, furbelow, ruche.

flounder verb
1 *she floundered, not knowing quite what to say:* struggle, be out of your depth, have

difficulty, be confused; informal scratch your head, be flummoxed, be clueless, be foxed, be fazed, be floored.
2 *people were floundering about in the water:* struggle, thrash, flail, twist and turn, splash, stagger, stumble, reel, wallow, lurch, blunder, squirm, writhe.

> **USAGE**
>
> The words **flounder** and **founder** are often confused. **Flounder** chiefly means 'to have trouble doing or understanding something', while **founder** means 'to fail' (*a proposed merger between the two airlines foundered last year*).

flourish verb
1 *ferns flourish in the shade:* grow, thrive, prosper, do well, burgeon, increase, multiply, proliferate; spring up, shoot up, bloom, blossom, bear fruit, burst out, run riot.
2 *the arts flourished in this period:* thrive, prosper, bloom, burgeon, be vigorous, be in its heyday; progress, make progress, advance, make headway, develop, improve; evolve, make strides, expand.
3 *he flourished the sword at them:* brandish, wave, shake, wield; swing, twirl, swish; display, exhibit, flaunt, show off.
OPPOSITES: die, wither, decline.

flout verb *retailers have been flouting the law for years:* defy, disobey, break, violate, contravene, infringe, breach, transgress against; ignore, disregard; informal cock a snook at.
OPPOSITES: observe.

> **USAGE**
>
> Do not confuse **flout** with **flaunt**. **Flout** means 'to show that you have no respect for a rule or convention by openly failing to follow it', whereas **flaunt** means 'to display something in a way intended to attract attention' (*they flaunted their wealth*).

flow verb
1 *the water flowed down the channel she had dug:* run, course, glide, drift, circulate; trickle, seep, ooze, dribble, drip, drizzle; spill; stream, swirl, surge, sweep, gush, cascade, pour, roll, rush.
2 *many questions flow from today's announcement:* result, proceed, arise, follow, ensue, derive, stem; originate, emanate, spring, emerge.
▷**noun** *the pump produces a good flow of water:* current, motion, movement, flux, circulation; trickle, ooze, percolation, drip; stream, swirl, surge, gush, rush, spate, tide.

flowery adjective
1 *flowery fabrics:* floral, flower-patterned.
2 *his flowery language made no impression:* florid, flamboyant, ornate, fancy, convoluted; high-flown, high-sounding, grandiloquent, baroque, orotund,

overblown; formal magniloquent; informal
highfalutin, purple.
OPPOSITES: plain.

flowing adjective
1 *long flowing hair:* loose, free, unconfined,
draping.
2 *the new model will have soft, flowing
lines:* sleek, streamlined, aerodynamic,
smooth, clean; elegant, graceful.
3 *he writes in an easy, flowing style:* fluent,
fluid, free-flowing, effortless, easy,
natural, smooth.

fluctuate verb *the level of profit fluctuates
from year to year:* vary, change, differ,
shift, alter, waver, be unstable, swing,
oscillate, alternate, rise and fall, go up and
down, see-saw, yo-yo.

fluctuation noun *a series of fluctuations
in the earth's temperature:* variation,
change, shift, alteration, swing, movement,
oscillation, alternation, rise and fall;
instability, unsteadiness.
OPPOSITES: stability.

flue noun duct, tube, shaft, vent, pipe,
passage, channel, conduit; funnel,
chimney, smokestack.

fluent adjective
1 *he was a fluent speaker and broadcaster:*
articulate, eloquent, expressive, silver-
tongued; lucid, coherent, cogent.
2 *he has a very fluent running style:* fluid,
smooth, effortless, easy, natural; graceful,
elegant; regular, rhythmic.
OPPOSITES: inarticulate, jerky.

fluff noun *there was fluff on her sleeve:*
fuzz, lint, dust.
▷ **verb** (informal) *the extra fluffed his only
line:* bungle, make a mess of, fumble,
deliver badly, muddle up, miss, forget;
informal mess up, make a hash of, botch,
screw up; Brit. informal make a pig's ear of,
cock up.

fluffy adjective *a fluffy toy rabbit:* fleecy,
woolly, fuzzy, downy, furry; soft.
OPPOSITES: rough.

fluid noun *the fluid seeps up the tube:*
liquid solution; gas, vapour.
OPPOSITES: solid.
▷ **adjective**
1 *a fluid substance that allows the gas
bubbles to expand:* free-flowing; liquid,
liquefied, melted, molten, runny, running;
gaseous.
2 *at this early stage his plans were still
fluid:* adaptable, flexible, adjustable, open-
ended, open, changeable, variable.
3 *the fluid state of affairs in the Middle
East:* fluctuating, changeable, subject/
likely to change, shifting, inconstant;
unstable, unsettled, turbulent, volatile.
4 *he stood up in one fluid movement:*
smooth, fluent, flowing, effortless, easy,
continuous; graceful, elegant.
OPPOSITES: solid, firm, static, jerky.

fluke noun *by a fluke, there was a
cancellation:* chance, coincidence,
accident, twist of fate; piece of luck,
stroke of good luck/fortune.

fluky adjective *remember that fluky goal in
the last minute of the European Cup final?*
lucky, fortunate, providential, timely,
opportune, serendipitous, expedient,
heaven-sent; chance, fortuitous; Brit. informal
jammy.

flummox verb (informal) *I was completely
flummoxed by the whole thing:* baffle,
perplex, puzzle, bewilder, mystify, bemuse,
confuse, confound, nonplus; informal stump,
beat, fox, floor.

flurry noun
1 *a flurry of snow:* swirl, whirl, eddy,
billow, shower, gust.
2 *there was a brief flurry of activity in the
hall:* burst, outbreak, spurt, fit, spell, bout.
3 *the announcement led to a flurry of
phone calls and emails:* spate, wave, flood,
stream, tide; series, succession, string,
outbreak, rash, run.

flush¹ verb
1 *she flushed in embarrassment:* blush,
redden, go pink, go red, go crimson, go
scarlet, colour.
2 *fruit helps to flush toxins from the body:*
rinse, wash, sluice, swill, cleanse, clean.
3 *one of the beaters was flushing the birds
from their hiding place:* drive, chase, force,
dislodge, expel; frighten, scare.
OPPOSITES: pale.
▷ **noun**
1 *a flush crept over her face:* blush,
redness, high colour, colour, rosiness,
pinkness, ruddiness, bloom.
2 *the first flush of manhood:* bloom, glow,
freshness, radiance, vigour, rush.

flush² adjective (informal)
1 *the company was flush with cash:* well
supplied, well provided, well stocked,
overflowing; informal awash.
2 *soaring housing and equities markets
left consumers feeling flush:* well off, rich,
prosperous, wealthy; informal loaded, made
of money.
3 *the years when cash was flush:* plentiful,
abundant, in abundance.

flushed adjective
1 *I looked at the children's flushed faces:*
red, pink, ruddy, glowing, reddish,
pinkish, rosy, healthy-looking; florid, high-
coloured; burning, feverish; blushing,
red-faced, embarrassed.
2 *flushed with success, he was getting
into his stride:* elated, excited, thrilled,
exhilarated, happy, delighted, overjoyed,
gleeful, jubilant, exultant, ecstatic,
euphoric, rapturous; literary joyous; informal
over the moon.
OPPOSITES: pale.

fluster verb *she was flustered by his*

presence: unsettle, make nervous, unnerve, agitate, ruffle, upset, bother, put on edge, disquiet, disturb, worry, perturb, disconcert, confuse, throw off balance, confound, nonplus; informal rattle, faze.
OPPOSITES: calm.

▷ noun *the main thing is not to get in a fluster:* panic, frenzy, fret; informal flap, tizz, tizzy, state.

fluted adjective *the roof is supported by fluted columns:* grooved, channelled, furrowed, ribbed, corrugated, ridged.
OPPOSITES: smooth, plain.

flutter verb
1 *butterflies fluttered around:* flit, hover, dance, flap, dart, bob.
2 *a tern was fluttering its wings:* beat, move up and down, flap, quiver, agitate, vibrate.
3 *she fluttered her eyelashes:* flicker, bat.
4 *flags fluttered in the gentle breeze:* flap, wave, ripple, undulate, quiver; fly.

▷ noun
1 *the flutter of wings:* beating, flapping, quivering, agitation, vibrating.
2 *the flutter of the flags:* flapping, waving, rippling.
3 *a flutter of nervousness:* tremor, wave, rush, surge, flash, stab, flush, tremble, quiver, shiver, frisson, chill, thrill, tingle, shudder, ripple, flicker.
4 (Brit. informal) *he enjoys a flutter on the horses:* bet, wager, gamble; Brit. informal punt.

flux noun *things are in a state of flux:* change, variability, fluidity, instability, fluctuation, variation, shift, movement, oscillation, alternation, rise and fall, see-sawing, yo-yoing.
OPPOSITES: stability.

fly verb
1 *a bird flew overhead:* pass, soar, travel, wing its way, glide, flit, flutter, wheel; hover, hang; take to the air.
2 *military planes flew in food supplies:* transport, airlift, lift, jet, drop.
3 *he pretended he couldn't fly the plane:* pilot, operate, control, manoeuvre, steer.
4 *flags flew in the town:* flutter, flap, wave.
□ **fly at**
Robbie flew at him, fists clenched: attack, pounce on, set upon, set about, weigh into, let fly at, turn on, round on, lash out at, hit out at, belabour, fall on; informal lay into, pitch into, wade into, let someone have it; Brit. informal have a go at.

flyer, **flier** noun
1 *the memorial was for flyers killed in the war:* pilot, airman, airwoman; dated aviator.
2 *flyers promoting a new sandwich bar:* leaflet, handout, bill, handbill, circular, advertisement.

flying adjective
1 *a flying beetle:* winged; airborne, in the air, in flight.
2 *a flying visit:* brief, short, lightning,

fleeting, hasty, rushed, hurried, quick, whistle-stop, cursory, perfunctory.
OPPOSITES: long.

foam noun *the foam on the waves:* froth, spume, surf; fizz, effervescence, bubbles, head; lather, suds.

▷ verb *the water foamed:* froth, spume; fizz, effervesce, bubble; lather; ferment, rise; boil, seethe, simmer.

foamy adjective *leave the yeast mixture until it is foamy:* frothy, foaming, spumy, bubbly, aerated, bubbling; sudsy.

fob verb
□ **fob someone off**
I wasn't going to be fobbed off with excuses: put off, stall; placate, appease, deceive; informal give someone the runaround.
□ **fob something off on**
he fobbed off the chairmanship on Clifford: foist, impose, dump, get rid of, offload; saddle someone with something, lumber someone with something; informal unload, palm someone off with something, land someone with something.

focus noun
1 *schools are a focus of community life:* centre, focal point, central point, centre of attention, hub, pivot, nucleus, heart, cornerstone, linchpin; cynosure.
2 *the focus is on helping people find solutions:* emphasis, accent, priority, attention, concentration.
3 *the main focus of this chapter is local government:* subject, theme, concern, subject matter, topic, issue, thesis, point, thread; substance, essence, gist, matter.

▷ verb *the investigation will focus on areas of social need:* concentrate, centre, zero in, zoom in; address itself to, pay attention to, pinpoint, revolve around, have as its starting point.
□ **in focus**
any photos will do as long as they're in focus: sharp, crisp, distinct, clear, well defined.
□ **out of focus**
why are some of these shots out of focus? blurred, unfocused, indistinct, blurry, fuzzy, hazy, misty, cloudy, lacking definition.

foe noun (literary) *he was convinced the room had been bugged by his political foes:* enemy, adversary, opponent, rival, antagonist, combatant, challenger; competitor, opposition, competition.
OPPOSITES: friend, ally.

fog noun *he lost his way in the fog:* mist, smog, murk, haze.

▷ verb
1 *the windscreen fogged up:* steam up, mist over, cloud over, film over, make/become misty.
2 *his brain was fogged with sleep:* muddle, daze, stupefy, fuddle, befuddle, bewilder, confuse, befog.

foggy adjective misty, smoggy, hazy, murky.
OPPOSITES: clear.

foible noun *we have to tolerate each other's little foibles:* weakness, failing, shortcoming, flaw, imperfection, fault, defect, limitation; quirk, kink, idiosyncrasy, eccentricity, peculiarity.
OPPOSITES: strength.

foil[1] verb *their escape attempts were constantly foiled:* thwart, frustrate, counter, baulk, impede, obstruct, hamper, hinder, scotch, derail; stop, block, prevent, defeat; informal put paid to, stymie; Brit. informal scupper, snooker.
OPPOSITES: assist.

foil[2] noun *the black dress was a perfect foil for her complexion:* contrast, complement, antithesis, relief.

foist verb *poor-quality lagers are constantly being foisted on the public:* impose, force, thrust, offload, dump, fob off; pass off, get rid of; saddle someone with; informal land someone with, unload; Brit. informal palm off, lumber someone with.

fold[1] verb
1 *I folded the cloth and put it away:* double over/up, turn under/up/over; tuck, gather, pleat.
2 *fold the cream into the chocolate mixture:* mix, blend, stir gently.
3 *he folded her in his arms:* enfold, wrap, envelop; take, gather, clasp, squeeze, clutch; embrace, hug, cuddle, cradle.
4 *the firm folded last year:* fail, collapse, founder; go bankrupt, become insolvent, cease trading, go into receivership, go into liquidation, be wound up, be closed down, be shut down; informal crash, go bust, go under, go to the wall.
OPPOSITES: unfold.
▷ noun *there was a fold in the paper:* crease; wrinkle, crinkle, pucker, furrow; tuck, pleat, gather.

fold[2] noun *the sheep were safely in their fold:* enclosure, pen, paddock, pound, compound, ring; N. Amer. corral.

folder noun file, sleeve, wallet, portfolio, document case, envelope, binder, ring binder.

foliage noun *a garden bursting with green and gold foliage:* leaves; greenery, vegetation; literary verdure.

folk noun (informal)
1 *the folk of East Lancashire:* people, individuals, {men, women, and children}, souls, mortals; inhabitants, residents, population; formal denizens.
2 *my folks come from Scotland:* relatives, relations, blood relations, family, nearest and dearest, kinsfolk, kinsmen, kinswomen, kin, kith and kin, kindred, flesh and blood; dated people.

folklore noun *there is a lot of folklore about wolves:* mythology, lore, tradition, beliefs, customs, oral history, legends, fables, myths, folk tales, folk stories, old wives' tales.

follow verb
1 *I'll go with you and we'll let the others follow:* come behind, go after, go behind, go after, walk behind.
2 *he was expected to follow his father as laird:* take the place of, replace, succeed, take over from; informal step into someone's shoes.
3 *loads of people used to follow the band around:* accompany, go along with, go around with, travel with, escort, attend, trail around with, string along with; informal tag along with.
4 *the secret police followed her everywhere:* shadow, trail, stalk, track, dog, hound; informal tail.
5 *always follow the manufacturer's instructions:* obey, comply with, conform to, adhere to, stick to, keep to, act in accordance with, abide by, observe, heed, pay attention to.
6 *severe penalties may follow from such behaviour:* result, arise, be a consequence of, be caused by, be brought about by, be the result of, come after, develop, ensue, emanate, issue, proceed, spring, flow, originate, stem.
7 *I couldn't follow what he was saying:* understand, comprehend, take in, grasp, fathom, appreciate, see; formal apprehend; informal make head or tail of, get, figure out, savvy, get your head around, get the drift of; Brit. informal suss out.
8 *he follows Manchester United:* support, be a supporter of, be a fan of, be a follower of, be an admirer of, be a devotee of, be devoted to.
OPPOSITES: lead.
▢ **follow something through** *they lack the resources to follow the project through to the end:* complete, see something through; continue with, carry on with, keep on with, keep going with, stay with; informal stick something out.
▢ **follow something up** *I've got a hunch and I'm going to follow it up:* investigate, research, look into, dig into, delve into, make enquiries into, enquire about, ask questions about, pursue, chase up; informal check out.

follower noun
1 *a follower of Christ:* disciple, apostle, supporter, defender, champion; believer, worshipper.
2 *followers of Scottish football will be disappointed:* fan, enthusiast, admirer, devotee, lover, supporter, adherent.
OPPOSITES: opponent.

following noun *Flinders will not disappoint his devoted following:* admirers, supporters, backers, fans, adherents,

devotees, advocates, patrons, public, audience, circle; retinue, train.
OPPOSITES: opposition.

▷ **adjective**
1 *he sent a reply the following day:* next, ensuing, succeeding, subsequent.
2 *please answer the following questions:* below, further on, underneath; formal hereunder, hereinafter.
OPPOSITES: preceding, aforementioned.

folly noun *he cursed himself for his folly:* foolishness, foolhardiness, stupidity, idiocy, lunacy, madness, rashness, recklessness, imprudence, irresponsibility, thoughtlessness, indiscretion.
OPPOSITES: wisdom.

foment verb *the men were accused of fomenting civil unrest:* stir up, incite, provoke, agitate, excite, whip up, encourage, instigate, urge, fan the flames of.
OPPOSITES: quell.

fond adjective
1 *she was fond of dancing | I'm very fond of Chris:* keen on, partial to, addicted to, enthusiastic about, passionate about; attached to, attracted to, enamoured of, in love with, with a soft spot for; informal into, hooked on, struck on.
2 *his fond mother plied him with cakes:* adoring, devoted, doting, loving, caring, affectionate, warm, tender, kind, attentive.
3 *the fond hope that things might get better between them:* unrealistic, naive, foolish, over-optimistic, deluded, absurd, vain.
OPPOSITES: indifferent, uncaring, realistic.

fondle verb *he fondled the Labrador's ears:* caress, stroke, finger, pet, play with, tickle, pat.

fondness noun
1 *they look at each other with such fondness:* affection, love, liking, warmth, tenderness, kindness, devotion, endearment, attachment, friendliness.
2 *he has a fondness for spicy food:* liking, love, taste, partiality, keenness, inclination, penchant, predilection, relish, passion, appetite; weakness, soft spot; informal thing.
OPPOSITES: hatred.

food noun
1 *he went three days without food:* nourishment, sustenance, nutriment; refreshment, meals; old use meat.
2 *I love Italian food:* cooking, cuisine, fare.
3 *we stopped at the local supermarket to stock up on food:* foodstuffs, provisions, rations; formal comestibles; informal grub; dated victuals.
4 *food for the cattle and horses:* fodder, feed, provender.

> WORD LINKS
> **alimentary** relating to food or nutrition

fool noun
1 *you've acted like a complete fool:* idiot, dolt, ignoramus, simpleton, dunce; informal dope, ninny, nincompoop, chump, dimwit, halfwit, dummy, ass, blockhead, airhead, cretin, moron, imbecile, jerk; Brit. informal nit, nitwit, twit, clot, berk, prat, pillock, wally.
2 *she made a fool of me again:* laughing stock, figure of fun, dupe; informal sucker; Brit. informal mug.

▷ **verb**
1 *he found he'd been fooled by a schoolboy:* deceive, trick, hoax, dupe, take in, mislead, delude, hoodwink; swindle, defraud, cheat, double-cross; literary cozen; informal con, bamboozle, pull a fast one on, take for a ride, pull the wool over someone's eyes.
2 *I'm not fooling, I promise you:* pretend, feign, put on an act, act, sham, fake; joke, jest; informal kid, pull someone's leg, have someone on.

□ **fool around**
someone's been fooling around with the controls: fiddle, play about/around, toy, trifle, meddle, tamper, interfere, monkey about/around; informal mess about/around; Brit. informal muck about/around.

foolhardy adjective *this is a bold and possibly foolhardy move:* reckless, rash, irresponsible, impulsive, hot-headed, impetuous, precipitate, hasty; informal hare-brained.
OPPOSITES: prudent.

foolish adjective *it horrified her to think how foolish she had been | that's a very foolish idea:* stupid, silly, idiotic, brainless, mindless, thoughtless, unintelligent, witless; unwise, ill-advised, ill-considered, imprudent, foolhardy; absurd, senseless, pointless, nonsensical, inane, fatuous, ridiculous; informal dumb, dim, dim-witted, half-witted, dopey, half-baked, hare-brained; Brit. informal barmy, daft, gormless.
OPPOSITES: sensible, wise.

foolishness noun *I looked away, aware of the foolishness of my question:* folly, stupidity, idiocy, thoughtlessness, senselessness, imprudence, foolhardiness.
OPPOSITES: sense, wisdom.

foolproof adjective *a foolproof security system:* infallible, dependable, reliable, trustworthy, certain, sure, guaranteed, safe, sound, tried and tested; watertight, airtight, flawless, perfect; informal sure-fire.
OPPOSITES: flawed.

foot noun
1 *the animal's foot:* paw, hoof, trotter, pad.
2 *the foot of the hill:* bottom, base; foundation.

footing noun
1 *Jenny lost her footing and plunged into the river:* foothold, toehold, grip, purchase.
2 *the business was put on a solid financial footing:* basis, base, foundation, standing, support.

footling adjective *she insisted on a few footling changes to the text:* trivial, trifling, petty, insignificant, inconsequential, unimportant, minor, small; informal piffling.
OPPOSITES: important, large.

footnote noun note, annotation, comment, gloss; aside, incidental remark, digression, afterthought, postscript.

footprint noun footmark, impression, print, trace; (**footprints**) track, spoor.

footstep noun *he heard footsteps in the hall:* footfall, step, tread, stamp.

foppish adjective *he had an aristocratic, almost foppish look about him:* dandyish, dandified; affected, vain; effeminate, niminy-piminy, mincing, effete; informal camp.

forage verb *I foraged in the cupboard for something to eat:* hunt, search, look, scavenge, rummage, ferret about/around, root about/around, scratch about/around, nose around/about/; Brit. informal rootle around.
▷ noun *a nightly forage for food:* hunt, search, look, quest.

foray noun
1 *my first foray into journalism:* venture; experience of, encounter with, brush with.
2 *a brief foray into town:* trip, visit, outing, expedition, sortie, sally.

forbearance noun *through it all, the forbearance and good humour of the Peruvians was impressive:* patience, tolerance, flexibility, amenability; leniency, clemency, indulgence, forgiveness, compassion, kindness, understanding.
OPPOSITES: impatience, intolerance.

forbearing adjective *he was tactful and forbearing when I got angry:* patient, tolerant, easy-going, flexible, amenable; lenient, clement, indulgent, forgiving, long-suffering, understanding, accommodating.
OPPOSITES: impatient, intolerant.

forbid verb *the act forbids discrimination on the grounds of sex:* prohibit, ban, outlaw, make illegal, veto, proscribe, disallow, embargo, bar, debar; N. Amer. interdict.
OPPOSITES: permit.

forbidding adjective
1 *he had a rather forbidding manner:* hostile, unwelcoming, unfriendly, off-putting, unsympathetic, unapproachable, grim, stern, hard, tough, frosty.
2 *in the dark everything looked unfamiliar and forbidding:* threatening, ominous, menacing, sinister, brooding, daunting, fearsome, frightening, chilling, disturbing, disquieting.
OPPOSITES: friendly, inviting.

force noun
1 *the force of the explosion:* power, strength, energy, might, effort, exertion; impact, pressure, weight, impetus.
2 *they used force to achieve their aims:* coercion, compulsion, constraint, duress, oppression, harassment, intimidation, threats; informal arm-twisting.
3 *they couldn't deny the force of the argument:* cogency, weight, effectiveness, soundness, validity, strength, power, significance, influence, authority.
4 *the government sent in a peacekeeping force:* unit, detachment, team, squad, group, party, body; informal outfit, bunch.
5 *the Bureau is undeniably a force for good:* agency, power, influence, instrument, vehicle, means.
OPPOSITES: weakness.
▷ verb
1 *he was forced to pay the full amount | Howard forced her to agree:* compel, coerce, make, constrain, oblige, impel, drive, pressurize, pressure, press, push, press-gang, bully, dragoon, bludgeon; informal lean on, twist someone's arm, railroad, bulldoze.
2 *the door had to be forced:* break open, prise open, wrench open, burst open, knock down, smash down, kick in.
3 *I forced my way through the crowd:* push, thrust, shove, drive, press.
4 *no one was keen on the new arrangements but they were forced on us:* impose, inflict, foist, thrust.
□ **in force**
1 *the state of emergency is now in force:* effective, in operation, operative, operational, in action, valid.
2 *her fans were out in force:* in great numbers, in hordes, in full strength; Brit. informal mob-handed.

forced adjective
1 *a programme of forced repatriation:* enforced, coerced, forcible, compulsory, obligatory, mandatory, involuntary.
2 *Clara managed a forced smile:* strained, unnatural, artificial, false, feigned, simulated, contrived, laboured, stilted, studied, mannered, affected, unconvincing, insincere, hollow; informal phoney.
OPPOSITES: voluntary, natural.

forceful adjective
1 *he had a forceful personality:* assertive, authoritative, commanding, dominant, determined, insistent, domineering, energetic, driving, dynamic, vigorous, powerful, strong; informal bossy, pushy.
2 *the board was persuaded by his forceful argument:* convincing, compelling, cogent, coherent, strong, powerful, potent, weighty, effective, well founded, telling, persuasive, irresistible, eloquent.
OPPOSITES: weak, submissive, unconvincing.

forcible adjective
1 *forcible entry:* forced, violent.
2 *forcible repatriation.* See **FORCED** sense 1.

forebear noun *she speaks the language*

of her forebears: ancestor, forefather, antecedent, progenitor.
OPPOSITES: descendant.

foreboding noun

1 *she was seized with a sense of foreboding:* apprehension, anxiety, trepidation, disquiet, unease, uneasiness, misgiving, suspicion, worry, fear, fearfulness, dread, alarm.
2 *in the end their forebodings proved justified:* premonition, presentiment, bad feeling, sneaking suspicion, funny feeling, intuition; old use presage.
OPPOSITES: calm.

forecast verb *they forecast record profits:* predict, prophesy, prognosticate, foretell, foresee; forewarn of, warn of; project.
▷ **noun** *a gloomy forecast of the impact of global warming:* prediction, prophecy, forewarning, warning, prognostication; prognosis, projection, outlook.

forefather noun *they abandoned the customs of their forefathers:* forebear, ancestor, antecedent, progenitor.
OPPOSITES: descendant.

forefront noun *a Cabinet post thrust him to the forefront of British politics:* front, spearhead, front line, cutting edge, head, lead, fore, vanguard, van.
OPPOSITES: rear, background.

forego verb. See FORGO.

foregoing adjective *despite the foregoing criticisms, we welcome the changes:* preceding, aforesaid, aforementioned, previously mentioned, earlier, above; previous, prior, antecedent.
OPPOSITES: following.

foregone adjective
□ **a foregone conclusion** *they accepted the interest rate rise as a foregone conclusion:* certainty, inevitability, matter of course, predictable result; informal sure thing; Brit. informal cert.

foreign adjective

1 *foreign branches of UK banks:* overseas, international.
2 *foreign animal and plant species:* alien, non-native, non-indigenous.
3 *travellers from foreign lands:* faraway, distant, remote, far-flung; exotic.
4 *the concept is very foreign to people in the West:* unfamiliar, unknown, unheard of, strange, alien.
OPPOSITES: domestic, native, familiar.

foreigner noun foreign national, alien, non-native, stranger, outsider; immigrant, settler, newcomer, incomer.
OPPOSITES: native.

> WORD LINKS
> **xenophobia** an intense or irrational dislike or fear of foreigners

foreman, forewoman noun
supervisor, overseer, superintendent, team leader; foreperson; Brit. chargehand, captain, ganger, gangmaster.

foremost adjective *one of the foremost Spanish Renaissance artists:* leading, principal, premier, prime, top, top-level, greatest, best, supreme, pre-eminent, outstanding, most important, most prominent, most influential, most illustrious, most notable; N. Amer. ranking; informal number-one.
OPPOSITES: minor.

forerunner noun

1 *archosaurs were the forerunners of dinosaurs:* predecessor, precursor, ancestor, forebear, antecedent; prototype.
2 *a headache may be the forerunner of other complaints:* prelude, herald, harbinger, precursor, sign, signal, indication, warning.
OPPOSITES: descendant.

foresee verb *Henry foresaw further problems for them:* anticipate, predict, forecast, expect, envisage, envision, see; foretell, prophesy.

foreshadow verb *to what extent does the change in ministers foreshadow a change in policy?* signal, indicate, signify, spell, mean, be a sign of, suggest, herald; be a harbinger of, warn of, portend; prefigure, presage, promise, point to, anticipate; literary foretoken, betoken.

foresight noun *a little foresight might have saved them a lot of money:* forethought, planning, far-sightedness, vision, anticipation, prudence, care, caution, precaution, readiness, preparedness.
OPPOSITES: hindsight.

forest noun wood, woods, woodland, trees, plantation; jungle, rainforest; old use greenwood.

> WORD LINKS
> **sylvan** relating to forests
> **silviculture**, **arboriculture** the growing and cultivation of trees

forestall verb *the council resigned to forestall a vote of no confidence:* pre-empt, get in before, steal a march on; anticipate, second-guess; nip in the bud, thwart, frustrate, foil, stave off, ward off, fend off, avert, preclude, obviate, prevent.

foretaste noun *the opening parade gives a foretaste of the spectacle to come:* sample, taste, preview, specimen, example; indication, suggestion, hint, whiff; warning, forewarning; Brit. taster.

foretell verb

1 *the locals can foretell a storm:* predict, forecast, prophesy, prognosticate; foresee, anticipate, envisage, see.
2 *dreams really can foretell the future:* indicate, foreshadow, prefigure,

f

anticipate, warn of, point to, signal, portend, augur, presage, be an omen of.

forethought noun *forethought is needed before you embark on such a project:* anticipation, planning, forward planning, provision, precaution, premeditation, prudence, care, caution; foresight, far-sightedness, vision.
OPPOSITES: impulse, recklessness.

forever adverb
1 *their love would last forever:* for always, evermore, for ever and ever, for good, for all time, until the end of time, eternally; Brit. for evermore.
2 *he was forever banging into things:* always, continually, constantly, perpetually, incessantly, endlessly, persistently, repeatedly, regularly; non-stop, day and night, {morning, noon, and night}; all the time, the entire time; informal 24-7.
OPPOSITES: never, occasionally.

forewarn verb *he had been forewarned of a coup plot:* warn, warn in advance, give advance warning, give fair warning, give notice, apprise, inform; alert, put someone on their guard; informal tip off.

forewarning noun *government officials confirmed that there had been some forewarning of the rebel attack:* warning, advance warning, sign, indication.

foreword noun *he wrote the foreword to one of her books:* preface, introduction, prologue, preamble; informal intro.
OPPOSITES: epilogue.

forfeit verb *many women feel they have to forfeit a higher salary because they know they may need greater workplace flexibility:* lose, be deprived of, surrender, relinquish, sacrifice, give up, yield, renounce, forgo; informal pass up, lose out on.
OPPOSITES: retain.
▷**noun** *if they fail to obey they are liable to a forfeit:* penalty, sanction, punishment, penance; fine; confiscation, loss, forfeiture, surrender.

forfeiture noun *non-compliance may lead to forfeiture of the lease:* confiscation, loss; relinquishment, giving up, surrender, sacrifice; Law sequestration.

forge¹ verb
1 *the smith forged swords and knives:* fashion, beat, hammer, work, make.
2 *they forged a lifelong partnership:* build, construct, form, create, establish, set up.
3 *he forged her signature on the will:* fake, falsify, counterfeit, copy, imitate, reproduce.

forge² verb *they forged through the busy side streets:* advance, press on, push on, soldier on, march on, push forward, make progress, make headway.
□**forge ahead**
Jack's horse forged ahead and took the lead: advance, make rapid progress, accelerate, put a spurt on.

forged adjective *he was charged with passing forged banknotes:* fake, false, counterfeit, imitation, bogus; informal phoney, dud.
OPPOSITES: genuine.

forgery noun *the painting was discovered to be a forgery:* fake, counterfeit, fraud, sham, imitation, replica, copy; informal phoney.

forget verb
1 *he forgot where he had parked his car:* fail to remember, fail to recall.
2 *I never forget my briefcase:* leave behind, fail to take/bring.
3 *I forgot to close the door:* neglect, fail, omit.
4 *you must try to forget him:* stop thinking about, put out of your mind, dismiss from your mind, shut out, blank out.
OPPOSITES: remember.

forgetful adjective *I'm so forgetful these days:* absent-minded, vague, disorganized, dreamy, abstracted; informal scatterbrained; Brit. informal scatty.

forgetfulness noun *his excuse was forgetfulness:* absent-mindedness, poor memory, a lapse of memory, vagueness, abstraction; informal scattiness.

forgivable adjective *the odd lapse is forgivable:* pardonable, excusable, understandable, tolerable, permissible, allowable, justifiable.

forgive verb
1 *she cheated on him repeatedly, yet he forgave her:* pardon, excuse, exonerate, absolve; make allowances for, feel no resentment/malice towards, harbour no grudge against; bury the hatchet, let bygones be bygones; formal exculpate.
2 *please forgive his rude conduct:* excuse, overlook, disregard, ignore, pass over, make allowances for, allow, indulge, tolerate; turn a blind eye to, turn a deaf ear to, wink at.

forgiveness noun *we beg your forgiveness:* pardon, absolution, exoneration, remission, dispensation, indulgence, clemency, mercy; reprieve, amnesty.
OPPOSITES: mercilessness, punishment.

forgiving adjective *Cromwell was not renowned for his forgiving nature:* merciful, lenient, compassionate, magnanimous, humane, soft-hearted, forbearing, tolerant, indulgent, understanding.
OPPOSITES: merciless, vindictive.

forgo, forego verb *Simon was prepared to forgo his lunch hour to help them:* do without, go without, give up, waive, renounce, surrender, relinquish, part with,

drop, sacrifice, abstain from, refrain from, eschew, cut out; formal forswear, abjure.
OPPOSITES: keep.

forgotten adjective *Vivaldi's operas are largely forgotten:* **unremembered**, out of mind, consigned to oblivion; neglected, overlooked, ignored, disregarded, unrecognized.
OPPOSITES: remembered.

fork verb *where the road forks, bear left:* **split**, branch off, divide, subdivide, separate, part, diverge, bifurcate.

forked adjective *the red kite has a forked tail:* **split**, branching, branched, bifurcated, Y-shaped, V-shaped, pronged, divided.

forlorn adjective
1 *he sounded so forlorn:* **unhappy**, sad, miserable, sorrowful, dejected, despondent, disconsolate, wretched, abject, down, downcast, dispirited, downhearted, crestfallen, depressed, melancholy, gloomy, glum, mournful, despairing, doleful, woebegone; informal blue, fed up.
2 *the house had a forlorn air:* **desolate**, deserted, abandoned, forgotten, neglected; literary forsaken.
3 *his voice rose in a forlorn attempt to drown the racket:* **hopeless**, useless, futile, pointless, purposeless, vain, unavailing; formal nugatory; old use bootless.
OPPOSITES: happy.

form noun
1 *the general form of the landscape was established before the glaciers:* **shape**, configuration, formation, structure, construction, arrangement, appearance, exterior, outline, format, layout, design.
2 *the human form:* **body**, shape, figure, stature, build, frame, physique, anatomy; informal vital statistics.
3 *a common belief was that witches could change shape and appear in the form of an animal:* **manifestation**, appearance, embodiment, incarnation, semblance, shape, guise, outward form.
4 *sponsorship is a form of advertising:* **kind**, sort, type, class, classification, category, variety, genre, brand, style.
5 *you have to fill in an application form:* **questionnaire**, document, coupon, tear-off slip, paper.
6 *what form is your daughter in?* **class**, year; N. Amer. grade.
7 *he is in top form for the Olympics:* **physical fitness**, condition, fettle, shape, trim, health.
8 *he had been there before and he knew the form:* **etiquette**, protocol, procedure, rules, practice, custom, usage, convention, tradition; formal praxis.
OPPOSITES: content.

▷ **verb**
1 *the pads are formed from mild steel:* **make**, construct, build, manufacture,

fabricate, assemble, put together; create, produce, contrive, frame, fashion, shape.
2 *he formed a plan:* **formulate**, devise, conceive, work out, think up, lay, draw up, put together, prepare, produce, fashion, concoct, forge, hatch, develop; informal dream up.
3 *they plan to form a company:* **set up**, establish, found, launch, float, create, bring into being, institute, start, get going, initiate, bring about, inaugurate.
4 *a mist was forming in the valley | an idea began to form in his mind:* **develop**, come into being/existence, crystallize, emerge; take shape, appear, materialize.
5 *the parts of society form an integrated whole:* **comprise**, make, make up, constitute, compose, add up to.
OPPOSITES: dissolve, disappear.

formal adjective
1 *a formal dinner:* **ceremonial**, ceremonious, traditional, conventional, ritualistic, ritual; stately, courtly, solemn, dignified; elaborate.
2 *a very formal manner:* **aloof**, reserved, remote, detached, unapproachable; stiff, prim, stuffy, staid, ceremonious, correct, proper, decorous, conventional, precise, exact, punctilious, unbending, inflexible, strait-laced; informal stand-offish.
3 *the board will need to get formal permission from the Department of Health | I made a formal complaint:* **official**, legal, authorized, certified, documented, sanctioned.
4 *she had received no formal education:* **conventional**, mainstream; school, institutional.
OPPOSITES: informal, casual, unofficial.

formality noun
1 *he disliked the formality of the occasion:* **ceremony**, conventionality, ritual, decorum, solemnity; protocol, red tape.
2 *his formality was off-putting:* **aloofness**, reserve, remoteness, detachment, unapproachability; stiffness, primness, stuffiness, staidness, correctness, decorum, punctiliousness, inflexibility; informal stand-offishness.
3 *we keep the formalities to a minimum:* **official procedure**, bureaucracy, red tape, paperwork.
OPPOSITES: informality.

format noun *the journal has been well received in its new format:* **design**, style, presentation, appearance, look; form, shape, size; layout, arrangement, plan, structure, scheme, composition, configuration.

formation noun
1 *the formation of a new government:* **establishment**, setting up, start, initiation, institution, foundation, inception, creation, inauguration, launch, flotation.
2 *the aircraft were flying in tight formation:* **configuration**, arrangement, pattern,

array, alignment, positioning, disposition, order.
OPPOSITES: abolition, dissolution.

formative adjective
1 *a formative stage in the child's development:* developmental, developing, growing; malleable, impressionable, susceptible.
2 *the Fabians had a formative influence on British politics:* determining, controlling, influential, guiding, decisive, forming, shaping.

former adjective
1 *the former Bishop of London:* one-time, erstwhile, sometime, ex-, late; previous, foregoing, preceding, earlier, prior, past, last.
2 *in former times:* earlier, old, past, bygone, olden, long-ago, gone by, long past, of old.
3 *those who take the former view are mistaken:* first-mentioned, first.
OPPOSITES: future, next, latter.

formerly adverb *he was formerly the head of a large comprehensive school:* previously, earlier, before, until now/then, hitherto, once, once upon a time, at one time, in the past.

formidable adjective
1 *they face a formidable task:* onerous, arduous, taxing, difficult, hard, heavy, laborious, burdensome, strenuous, back-breaking, uphill, Herculean, monumental, colossal; demanding, tough, challenging, exacting.
2 *Jackson is a formidable opponent:* intimidating, forbidding, daunting, awesome, fearsome, awe-inspiring; strong, powerful, redoubtable, indomitable.
3 *a formidable pianist:* impressive, skilled, proficient, adept, accomplished, skilful, gifted, talented, masterly, virtuoso, expert.

formula noun
1 *a legal formula:* form of words, set expression, phrase, saying, aphorism.
2 *a peace formula:* recipe, prescription, blueprint, plan, road map, method, procedure, technique, system.
3 *a formula for removing grease:* preparation, concoction, mixture, compound, substance.

formulate verb
1 *the miners formulated a plan to keep the mines open:* devise, conceive, work out, think up, lay, draw up, put together, form, produce, fashion, concoct, contrive, forge, hatch, prepare, develop; informal dream up.
2 *this is how Marx formulated his question:* express, phrase, word, put into words, frame, couch, put, articulate, convey, say, state, utter.

forsake verb (literary)
1 *he forsook his wife:* abandon, desert, leave, leave high and dry, turn your back

on, cast aside; jilt, leave in the lurch, throw over, strand, leave stranded; informal walk out on, dump.
2 *I won't forsake my principles:* renounce, abandon, relinquish, dispense with, disclaim, disown, disavow, discard, wash your hands of; give up, drop, jettison, do away with; formal forswear; informal ditch.

fort noun fortress, castle, citadel, blockhouse, burg, stronghold, redoubt, fortification, bastion, fastness.

forte noun *acting had always been her forte:* strength, strong point, speciality, strong suit, talent, special ability, skill, bent, gift, métier.
OPPOSITES: weakness.

forth adverb (formal or literary)
1 *smoke billowed forth:* out, outside, away, off, ahead, forward, into view; into existence.
2 *from that day forth:* onwards, onward, on, forward; for ever, into eternity; until now.

forthcoming adjective
1 *forthcoming events:* imminent, impending, coming, upcoming, approaching, future; close, close at hand, in store, in the wind, in the air, in the offing, in the pipeline, on the horizon, on the way.
2 *no reply was forthcoming:* available, ready, at hand, accessible, obtainable, at someone's disposal, on offer; obtained, given, vouchsafed to someone.
3 *he was not very forthcoming about himself:* communicative, talkative, chatty, loquacious, vocal; expansive, expressive, uninhibited, outgoing, frank, open, candid.
OPPOSITES: past, current, unforthcoming.

forthright adjective *he was fearless and forthright in speaking out:* frank, direct, straightforward, honest, candid, open, sincere, outspoken, straight, blunt, plain-spoken, no-nonsense, bluff, matter-of-fact, to the point; informal upfront.
OPPOSITES: secretive, evasive.

forthwith adverb *the government insisted that all hostages be released forthwith:* immediately, at once, instantly, directly, right away, straight away, without delay, with immediate effect; quickly, speedily, promptly; informal pronto.

fortification noun rampart, wall, defence, bulwark, palisade, stockade, redoubt, earthwork, bastion, parapet, barricade.

fortify verb
1 *he rode in haste to fortify his castles and towns:* secure, strengthen, reinforce, defend, protect.
2 *the timber enclosure had been fortified by a stone wall:* strengthen, reinforce, toughen, consolidate, bolster, shore up, brace, buttress.

3 *he ordered a pot of coffee to fortify himself:* **invigorate**, strengthen, energize, enliven, liven up, animate, vitalize, revitalize, restore, revive, refresh; informal buck up, pick up.
OPPOSITES: weaken.

fortitude noun *he accepted his illness with fortitude:* **courage**, bravery, endurance, resilience, mettle, moral fibre, strength of mind, strength of character, strong-mindedness, backbone, spirit, grit, steadfastness.
OPPOSITES: weakness, resignation.

fortress noun fort, castle, citadel, blockhouse, burg, stronghold, redoubt, fortification, bastion; fastness.

fortuitous adjective
1 *his success depended on entirely fortuitous events:* **chance**, unexpected, unanticipated, unpredictable, unforeseen, unlooked-for, serendipitous, adventitious, casual, incidental, coincidental, random, accidental, inadvertent, unintentional, unintended, unplanned, unpremeditated.
2 *United were saved by a fortuitous penalty:* **lucky**, fluky, fortunate, providential, advantageous, timely, opportune, serendipitous, heaven-sent.
OPPOSITES: predictable, unlucky.

fortunate adjective
1 *he was fortunate to escape injury:* **lucky**, in luck, favoured, blessed with good luck, having a charmed life.
2 *we find ourselves in a fortunate position:* **favourable**, advantageous, providential, auspicious, welcome, heaven-sent, beneficial, propitious, fortuitous, opportune, happy, felicitous.
OPPOSITES: unfortunate.

fortunately adverb *fortunately, no one was injured:* **luckily**, by good luck, by good fortune, as luck would have it; mercifully, thankfully; thank goodness, thank God, thank heavens, thank the stars.
OPPOSITES: unfortunately.

fortune noun
1 *fortune favoured him:* **chance**, accident, coincidence, serendipity, destiny, fortuity, providence; N. Amer. happenstance.
2 *a change of fortune:* **luck**, fate, destiny, predestination, the stars, karma, kismet, lot.
3 (**fortunes**) *there should be an upswing in Sheffield's fortunes:* **circumstances**, state of affairs, condition, position, situation; plight, predicament.
4 *he made his fortune in steel:* **wealth**, riches, assets, means, substance, property, resources, estate.
5 (informal) *this dress cost a fortune:* **huge/vast amount**, king's ransom, millions, billions; informal packet, mint, bundle, pile; Brit. informal bomb; N. Amer. informal big bucks.
OPPOSITES: pittance.

fortune-teller noun clairvoyant, crystal-gazer, psychic, prophet, seer, soothsayer; palmist, palm-reader; (in ancient Greece and Rome) oracle, sibyl.

forum noun
1 *forums were held for staff to air grievances:* **meeting**, assembly, gathering, rally, conference, seminar, convention, symposium, colloquium; formal colloquy.
2 *the UN could provide a forum for discussion:* **setting**, place, scene, context, stage, framework, backdrop; medium, means, apparatus.

forward adverb *the traffic moved slowly forward:* **ahead**, forwards, onwards, onward, on, further.
OPPOSITES: backwards.
▷ **adjective**
1 *forward planning:* **advance**, future, forward-looking, for the future.
2 *the girls seemed very forward:* **bold**, brazen, brash, shameless, immodest, presumptuous, familiar, overfamiliar, pert; informal fresh.
OPPOSITES: retrospective, late, shy.
▷ **verb**
1 *my mother forwarded me your letter:* **send on**, post on, redirect, readdress, pass on.
2 *the goods were forwarded by sea:* **send**, dispatch, transmit, carry, convey, deliver, ship.

forward-looking adjective *meanwhile, the forward-looking countries of Europe forged ahead:* **progressive**, enlightened, dynamic, bold, enterprising, ambitious, pioneering, innovative, modern, avant-garde, positive, reforming, radical; informal go-ahead, go-getting.
OPPOSITES: backward-looking.

forwards adverb. See **FORWARD** adverb.

foster verb
1 *he was known for fostering the arts:* **encourage**, promote, further, stimulate, advance, cultivate, nurture, strengthen, enrich; help, aid, assist, contribute to, support, back.
2 *they have fostered a succession of children:* **bring up**, rear, raise, care for, take care of, look after, nurture, provide for; mother, parent.

foul adjective
1 *skunks produce a foul stench:* **disgusting**, revolting, repulsive, repugnant, abhorrent, loathsome, offensive, sickening, nauseating, nauseous, stomach-churning, stomach-turning, distasteful, obnoxious, objectionable, odious, noxious; literary miasmic, noisome; informal ghastly, gruesome, gross.
2 *he had been foul to her:* **unkind**, mean, nasty, horrible, horrid, unpleasant, unfriendly, malicious, spiteful, cruel, vicious, base, malevolent, despicable, contemptible; informal rotten; Brit. informal beastly.

f

3 *the weather was foul:* unpleasant, disagreeable, bad; cold, freezing, arctic; rough, stormy, squally, gusty, windy, blustery, wild, blowy, rainy, wet; Brit. informal filthy.
4 *foul drinking water was blamed for the outbreak:* contaminated, polluted, infected, tainted, impure, filthy, dirty, unclean.
5 *a foul tackle:* unfair, illegal, unsporting, unsportsmanlike, below the belt, dirty.
OPPOSITES: pleasant, kind, pure, clean.
▷**verb**
1 *the river had been fouled with chemical waste:* dirty, infect, pollute, contaminate, poison, taint, soil, stain, blacken, muddy, splash, spatter, smear, blight; literary sully.
2 *the vessel had fouled her nets:* tangle up, entangle, snarl, catch, entwine, enmesh, twist.

found verb
1 *he founded his company in 1989:* establish, set up, start, begin, get going, institute, inaugurate, launch, float, form, create, bring into being, originate, develop.
2 *they abandoned Attica and founded a new city:* build, construct, erect, put up; plan, lay plans for.
3 *their relationship was founded on trust:* base, build, construct, rest, hinge, depend; ground in, root in.
OPPOSITES: dissolve, liquidate, abandon, demolish.

foundation noun
1 *the weight of the wall is transmitted to the foundations:* foot, base, substructure, underpinning; bottom, bedrock, substratum.
2 *good records are the foundation of any personnel system:* basis, base, starting point, point of departure, beginning, premise; principles, fundamentals, rudiments; cornerstone, core, heart, essence, kernel.
3 *there was no foundation for the claim:* justification, grounds, defence, reason, rationale, cause, basis, motive, excuse, call, pretext, provocation.
4 *in his will he set up an educational foundation:* institution, agency, charity.

founder[1] noun *the founder of modern physics:* originator, creator, father, founding father, prime mover, architect, engineer, designer, developer, pioneer, author, planner, inventor, mastermind; informal godfather.

founder[2] verb
1 *the scheme foundered due to lack of funds:* fail, be unsuccessful, not succeed, fall flat, fall through, collapse, backfire, meet with disaster, come to nothing/naught; informal flop, bomb.
2 *the ship foundered on a voyage to Holland:* sink, go to the bottom, go down, be lost at sea.
OPPOSITES: succeed.

USAGE

The words **founder** and **flounder** are often confused. **Founder** chiefly means 'to fail', while **flounder** means 'to have trouble doing or understanding something' (*the school was floundering in confusion about its role in the world*).

fountain noun *a fountain of cold water:* jet, spray, spout, well, fount, cascade.

four cardinal number quartet, foursome.

WORD LINKS
quadrilateral a four-sided plane figure
tetrahedron a four-sided solid figure

foyer noun entrance hall, hall, hallway, entrance, entry, porch, reception area, atrium, concourse, lobby.

fracas noun *officers were kicked and punched in a fracas earlier this week:* disturbance, brawl, melee, rumpus, skirmish, struggle, scuffle, scrum, clash, fisticuffs; informal scrap; Brit. informal punch-up, bust-up; N. Amer. informal rough house; Law, dated affray.

fraction noun
1 *a fraction of the population:* part, subdivision, division, portion, segment, slice, section, sector; proportion, percentage, ratio, measure.
2 *this is only a fraction of the collection:* tiny part, fragment, snippet, snatch, smattering, selection.
3 *he moved a fraction closer:* little, bit, touch, soupçon, trifle, mite, shade, jot; informal tad.
OPPOSITES: whole.

fractious adjective *they squabble like fractious children:* grumpy, bad-tempered, irascible, irritable, crotchety, grouchy, cantankerous, short-tempered, tetchy, testy, curmudgeonly, ill-tempered, ill-humoured, peevish, cross; informal snappy; Brit. informal shirty, stroppy, ratty.
OPPOSITES: contented, affable.

fracture noun *tiny fractures in the rock:* crack, split, fissure, crevice, break, rupture, breach, rift, cleft, chink.
▷**verb** *she fell and fractured her skull:* break, crack, shatter, splinter, split, rupture; informal bust.

fragile adjective
1 *she was anxious about her fragile porcelain:* breakable, easily broken; delicate, dainty, fine, flimsy, eggshell; technical frangible.
2 *a fragile political alliance:* precarious, insecure, shaky, unreliable, vulnerable, weak.
3 *she is still very fragile after her ordeal:* weak, delicate, frail, debilitated; ill, unwell, ailing, poorly, sickly, infirm, enfeebled.
OPPOSITES: strong, durable, robust.

fragment noun

1 *small fragments of pottery:* piece, bit, particle, speck; chip, shard, sliver, splinter; shaving, paring, scrap, flake, shred, morsel.
2 *a fragment of conversation:* snatch, snippet, scrap.
▷ **verb** *explosions caused the chalk to fragment:* break up, break, break into pieces, crack open/apart, shatter, splinter, fracture; disintegrate, fall to pieces, fall apart.

fragmentary adjective *a few fragmentary descriptions are all we have:* incomplete, fragmented, disconnected, disjointed, broken, discontinuous, piecemeal, scrappy, sketchy, uneven, patchy; Brit. informal bitty.

fragrance noun

1 *the fragrance of spring flowers:* sweet smell, scent, perfume, bouquet; aroma, nose; old use redolence.
2 *a bottle of fragrance:* perfume, scent, eau de toilette, toilet water; eau de cologne, cologne; aftershave.

fragrant adjective *various fragrant herbs are used in aromatherapy:* sweet-scented, sweet-smelling, scented, perfumed, aromatic.
OPPOSITES: foul-smelling.

frail adjective

1 *a frail old lady:* weak, delicate, feeble, enfeebled, debilitated; infirm, ill, ailing, unwell, sickly, poorly, in poor health.
2 *a frail structure of cardboard and plywood:* fragile, breakable, easily damaged, delicate, flimsy, insubstantial, unsteady, unstable, rickety; technical frangible.
OPPOSITES: strong, robust.

frailty noun

1 *the frailty of old age:* infirmity, weakness, enfeeblement, debility; fragility, delicacy; ill health, sickliness.
2 *his many frailties:* weakness, fallibility; weak point, flaw, imperfection, defect, failing, fault, shortcoming, deficiency, inadequacy, limitation.
OPPOSITES: strength.

frame noun

1 *a tubular metal frame:* framework, structure, substructure, skeleton, chassis, shell, casing, body, bodywork; support, scaffolding, foundation.
2 *his clothes clung to his tall, slender frame:* body, figure, form, shape, physique, build, size, proportions.
3 *the photograph hung in a polished frame:* setting, mount, mounting.
▷ **verb**
1 *he had the picture framed:* mount, set, encase.
2 *the legislators who frame the regulations:* formulate, draw up, draft, plan, shape, compose, put together, form, devise, create, establish, conceive, think up, originate; informal dream up.

□ **frame of mind**
she was in a receptive frame of mind: mood, state of mind, humour, temper, disposition.

framework noun

1 *a metal framework:* frame, structure, skeleton, chassis, shell, body, bodywork; support, scaffolding, foundation.
2 *the changing framework of society:* structure, shape, fabric, order, scheme, system, organization, construction, configuration, composition; informal make-up.

franchise noun

1 *the extension of the franchise to women:* suffrage, the vote, the right to vote, voting rights, enfranchisement.
2 *the company lost its TV franchise:* licence, permit, charter, warrant; authorization, permission.

frank adjective

1 *he was quite frank with me:* candid, direct, forthright, plain, plain-spoken, straight, straightforward, straight from the shoulder, explicit, to the point, matter-of-fact; open, honest, truthful, sincere; outspoken, bluff, blunt, unsparing; informal upfront.
2 *she looked at Sam with frank admiration:* open, undisguised, unconcealed, naked, unmistakable, clear, obvious, transparent, patent, manifest, evident, perceptible, palpable; blatant, barefaced, flagrant.
OPPOSITES: evasive, disguised.

frankly adverb *he stated the case quite frankly:* candidly, directly, plainly, straightforwardly, straight from the shoulder, forthrightly, openly, honestly, without beating about the bush, without mincing your words, without prevarication, point-blank; bluntly, outspokenly.

frantic adjective *Mary was frantic with worry:* panic-stricken, beside yourself, at your wits' end, distraught, overwrought, worked up, agitated, distressed; frenzied, wild, frenetic, fraught, feverish, hysterical, desperate; informal in a state.
OPPOSITES: calm.

fraternity noun

1 *the meeting engendered a spirit of fraternity:* brotherhood, fellowship, kinship, friendship, mutual support, solidarity, community, union, togetherness; sisterhood.
2 *enthusiasts among the teaching fraternity:* profession, body; band, group, set, circle.

fraternize verb *she forbade her musicians to fraternize with the dancers:* associate, mix, consort, socialize, keep company, rub shoulders; informal hang out, hobnob.

fraud noun

1 *his business partner was arrested*

for fraud: cheating, sharp practice, fraudulence, swindling, embezzlement, deceit, deception, double-dealing, chicanery.
2 *social security frauds:* swindle, racket, deception, trick, cheat, hoax; informal scam, con, rip-off; Brit. informal fiddle.
3 *they exposed him as a fraud:* impostor, fake, sham, charlatan, quack, mountebank; swindler, fraudster, cheat, confidence trickster, liar; informal phoney, con man.

fraudulent adjective *he was convicted of fraudulent share dealing:* dishonest, corrupt, criminal, illegal, unlawful, illicit; deceitful, double-dealing, duplicitous, cheating, unscrupulous, unprincipled; informal crooked; Brit. informal bent.
OPPOSITES: honest.

fraught adjective *she sounded a bit fraught:* anxious, worried, stressed, upset, distraught, overwrought, worked up, agitated, distressed, distracted, desperate, frantic, panic-stricken, panicky; beside yourself, at your wits' end, at the end of your tether; informal wound up, in a state.

fray noun *he launched himself into the fray:* battle, fight, engagement, conflict, clash, skirmish, tussle, struggle, disturbance, scuffle, melee, brawl; informal scrap; Brit. informal punch-up; Law, dated affray.

frayed adjective
1 *a frayed shirt collar:* worn, well worn, threadbare, tattered, ragged, shabby; informal tatty.
2 *his frayed nerves couldn't take much more:* strained, fraught, tense, edgy, stressed.

freak noun
1 *the mouse was a genetically engineered freak:* aberration, abnormality, oddity; mutant.
2 *the accident was a complete freak:* anomaly, aberration, fluke; Brit. informal one-off.
3 (informal) *they were dismissed as a bunch of freaks:* oddity, eccentric, misfit; crank, lunatic; informal weirdo, nutcase; Brit. informal nutter.
4 (informal) *a freak occurrence:* enthusiast, fan, devotee, lover, aficionado; informal fiend, nut, fanatic, addict, buff.
▷**adjective** *a freak occurrence that is unlikely to happen again:* unusual, anomalous, aberrant, atypical, unrepresentative, irregular, fluky, exceptional, unaccountable, bizarre, queer, peculiar, odd, freakish; unpredictable, unforeseeable, unexpected, surprising.
OPPOSITES: normal.
▷**verb** (informal) *he freaked and started smashing the place up:* go crazy, go mad, go out of your mind, go to pieces, crack, snap, lose control; panic, become hysterical; informal crack up.

freakish adjective *freakish weather.* See FREAK adjective.

freaky adjective (informal). See ODD sense 2.

free adjective
1 *admission is free:* without charge, free of charge, for nothing; complimentary, gratis; informal for free, on the house.
2 *she was free of any pressures:* unencumbered by, unaffected by, clear of, without, rid of; exempt from, safe from, immune to.
3 *I'm free this afternoon:* unoccupied, not busy, available, between appointments; off duty, off work, off, on holiday, on leave; at leisure, with time on your hands, with time to spare.
4 *the bathroom's free now:* vacant, empty, available, unoccupied, not taken, not in use.
5 *a citizen of a proud, free nation:* independent, self-governing, self-governed, self-ruling, self-determining, non-aligned, sovereign, autonomous; democratic.
6 *the killer is still free:* on the loose, at liberty, at large, on the run; loose, around, about, in circulation.
7 *after a few minutes of squirming, he was free:* loose, unconfined, unbound, untied, unchained, untethered, unshackled, unfettered, unrestrained.
8 *you are free to leave:* able to, in a position to; allowed, permitted, entitled.
9 *the free flow of water:* unimpeded, unobstructed, unrestricted, unhampered, clear, open, unblocked.
10 *she was always very free with her money:* generous, liberal, open-handed, unstinting, bountiful; lavish, extravagant, prodigal.
OPPOSITES: busy, occupied, captive.
▷**verb**
1 *three of the hostages were freed:* release, set free, let go, liberate, rescue, extricate, discharge, deliver, pull free; set loose, let loose, turn loose, untie, unchain, unfetter, unshackle.
2 *they wish to be freed from all legal ties:* release, discharge, relieve.
OPPOSITES: confine, trap.
□**free and easy**
the restaurant has a free and easy atmosphere: easy-going, relaxed, casual, informal, natural, open, spontaneous, uninhibited, friendly; tolerant, liberal; informal laid-back.

freedom noun
1 *the prisoners made a desperate bid for freedom:* liberty, liberation, release, deliverance, discharge.
2 *national revolution was the only path to freedom:* independence, self-government, self-determination, self-rule, home rule, sovereignty, non-alignment, autonomy; democracy.
3 *they want freedom from political accountability:* exemption, immunity, dispensation; impunity.
4 *patients have more freedom to choose who*

treats them: right, entitlement, privilege, prerogative; scope, latitude, leeway, flexibility, space, breathing space, room, elbow room; licence, leave, free rein, a free hand, carte blanche.
OPPOSITES: captivity, subjection, liability.

freely adverb
1 *may I speak freely?* openly, candidly, frankly, directly; truthfully, honestly.
2 *these workers gave their time and labour freely:* voluntarily, willingly, readily; of your own volition, of your own accord, of your own free will.

freethinker noun *intellectuals, freethinkers, and radicals flourished in England:* nonconformist, individualist, independent, maverick; agnostic, atheist, non-believer, unbeliever.
OPPOSITES: conformist.

free will noun *enslaved by advertising, we were robbed of our free will:* freedom of choice, freedom, self-determination, autonomy, liberty, independence.
□ of your own free will
when he takes the drug, he takes it of his own free will: voluntarily, willingly, readily, freely, of your own accord, of your own volition.

freeze verb
1 *the stream had frozen overnight:* ice over, ice up, solidify.
2 *the campers stifled in summer and froze in winter:* be cold, be numb with cold, shiver, be chilled to the bone/marrow.
3 *she froze in horror:* stop dead, stop in your tracks, stop, stand stock still, go rigid.
4 *the prices of basic foodstuffs were frozen:* fix, hold, peg, set; limit, restrict, cap, confine, regulate; hold/keep down.
OPPOSITES: thaw.

freezing adjective *a freezing wind:* bitterly cold, bitter, icy, chill, frosty, glacial, wintry, sub-zero, arctic; raw, biting, piercing, penetrating, cutting, numbing.
OPPOSITES: balmy, hot.

freight noun
1 *freight is generally carried by rail:* goods, cargo; load, consignment, delivery, shipment; merchandise.
2 *do not underestimate the importance of air freight:* transportation, transport, conveyance, carriage, shipping, shipment; Brit. haulage.

frenetic adjective *Baker rushed from capital to capital at a frenetic pace:* frantic, wild, frenzied, hectic, fraught, feverish, fevered, mad, manic, hyperactive, energetic, intense, fast and furious.
OPPOSITES: calm.

frenzied adjective *there were scenes of frenzied activity:* frantic, wild, frenetic, hectic, fraught, feverish, fevered, mad, crazed, manic, intense, furious,

uncontrolled, out of control.
OPPOSITES: calm.

frenzy noun
1 *the crowd worked themselves into a state of frenzy:* hysteria, madness, mania, delirium, fever, agitation, turmoil, tumult; wild excitement, euphoria, elation, ecstasy.
2 *a frenzy of anger:* fit, paroxysm, spasm; literary access.

frequency noun *we saw an increase in the frequency of accidents due to increased overtime:* rate of occurrence, incidence, amount, prevalence; Statistics distribution.

frequent adjective
1 *he has frequent bouts of chest infection:* recurrent, recurring, repeated, periodic, continual, one after another, successive; many, numerous, several.
2 *she's a frequent business traveller:* habitual, regular.
OPPOSITES: infrequent.
▷ verb *many other well-known celebrities frequented the pub on a regular basis:* visit, patronize, spend time in, haunt; informal hang out at.

frequently adverb *she frequently questioned his actions:* often, regularly, habitually, customarily, routinely; many times, many a time, again and again, time and again, over and over again, repeatedly, all the time, continually; N. Amer. oftentimes.
OPPOSITES: infrequently.

fresh adjective
1 *fresh fruit:* raw, natural, unprocessed.
2 *a fresh sheet of paper:* clean, blank, empty, clear; unused, new, pristine, unmarked, untouched.
3 *a fresh approach:* new, recent, latest, up-to-date, modern, ultra-modern; original, novel, different, innovative, radical, revolutionary.
4 *fresh recruits:* young, youthful; new, inexperienced, naive, untrained, unqualified, untried, raw.
5 *her fresh complexion:* healthy, healthy-looking, clear, bright, youthful, blooming, glowing, unblemished; fair, rosy, rosy-cheeked, pink, ruddy.
6 *the night air was clear and fresh:* cool, crisp, refreshing, invigorating; pure, clean, clear, uncontaminated, untainted.
7 *a fresh wind had sprung up from the east:* chilly, chill, cool, cold, brisk, bracing, invigorating; strong.
OPPOSITES: stale, old, tired, warm.

freshen verb
1 *the cold water chilled his face and freshened him:* refresh, revitalize, restore, revive, wake up, rouse, enliven, liven up, energize, brace, invigorate; informal buck up.
2 *he opened a window to freshen the room:* ventilate, air; deodorize, purify, cleanse; refresh, cool.

f

freshman, freshwoman noun first-year student; newcomer, new recruit, starter, probationer; beginner, learner, novice; Brit. informal fresher.

fret verb *she was fretting about Jonathan:* worry, be anxious, feel uneasy, be distressed, be upset, fuss, upset yourself, concern yourself, agonize, brood.

fretful adjective *the heat was making the child fretful:* anxious, distressed, upset, unsettled, uneasy, ill at ease, uncomfortable, agitated, restless, worked up, tense, nervous, stressed; informal het up, uptight.
OPPOSITES: relaxed.

friable adjective *the soil was dark and friable:* crumbly, powdery, dusty, chalky, soft; dry, crisp, brittle.
OPPOSITES: hard, lumpy.

friction noun
1 *a lubrication system which reduces friction:* rubbing, chafing, grating, rasping, scraping, abrasion; resistance, drag.
2 *there was considerable friction between father and son:* discord, conflict, strife, disagreement, dissension, dissent, opposition, contention, dispute, argument, quarrelling, bickering, squabbling, wrangling, fighting, feuding, rivalry; hostility, animosity, antipathy, enmity, antagonism, resentment, acrimony, bitterness, bad feeling, ill feeling, bad blood.
OPPOSITES: harmony.

friend noun
1 *a close friend of mine:* companion, intimate, confidante, confidant, familiar, playmate, playfellow, classmate, schoolmate, workmate; ally, associate; sister, brother; informal pal, chum; Brit. informal mate; N. Amer. informal buddy, amigo.
2 *friends of the Royal Botanic Garden:* patron, backer, supporter, benefactor, benefactress, sponsor; well-wisher, champion.
OPPOSITES: enemy.

friendless adjective *she cared for those who were poor and friendless:* alone, solitary, lonely, unpopular, unwanted, unloved, abandoned, rejected, shunned, spurned, forlorn; N. Amer. lonesome.
OPPOSITES: popular.

friendliness noun *she appreciated her host's friendliness:* affability, amiability, geniality, bonhomie, cordiality, good nature, good humour, warmth, affection, conviviality, joviality, companionability, sociability, gregariousness, camaraderie, neighbourliness, hospitality, approachability, openness, kindness, kindliness, sympathy.
OPPOSITES: unfriendliness.

friendly adjective
1 *she's very friendly and approachable:* affable, amiable, genial, cordial, warm, affectionate, demonstrative, convivial, companionable, sociable, gregarious, outgoing, clubbable, neighbourly, hospitable, approachable, good-natured, kindly, benign, amenable, agreeable, obliging, sympathetic, well disposed, benevolent; informal chummy, pally; Brit. informal matey.
2 *she drew him into a friendly conversation:* amicable, congenial, cordial, pleasant, easy, relaxed, casual, informal; close, intimate, familiar.
OPPOSITES: unfriendly.

friendship noun
1 *lasting friendships are all too rare:* relationship, attachment, association, bond, tie, link, union.
2 *old ties of love and friendship:* camaraderie, friendliness, comradeship, companionship, fellowship, fellow feeling, closeness, affinity, rapport, understanding, harmony, unity; intimacy, mutual affection; formal amity.
OPPOSITES: hostility.

fright noun
1 *she was paralysed with fright:* fear, terror, horror, alarm, panic, dread, trepidation, dismay, anxiety, nervousness, agitation, apprehension, foreboding, disquiet, the shivers; informal the jitters, the willies, the creeps.
2 *the experience gave everyone a fright:* shock, scare, surprise, turn, jolt, start.

frighten verb *the incident had frightened her so much that she moved out of the area | the horse was frightened by a dog:* scare, startle, alarm, terrify, petrify, shock, chill, panic, shake, disturb, dismay, unnerve, intimidate, terrorize, daunt; informal spook; Brit. informal put the wind up; old use affright.

frightening adjective *it was a frightening ordeal:* terrifying, horrifying, alarming, chilling, spine-chilling, hair-raising, blood-curdling, disturbing, unnerving, intimidating, daunting, upsetting, harrowing, traumatic; eerie, sinister, fearsome, nightmarish, macabre, menacing; informal scary, spooky, creepy, hairy.

frightful adjective
1 *there's been a frightful accident:* horrible, horrific, ghastly, horrendous, serious, awful, dreadful, terrible, nasty; shocking, harrowing, appalling; hideous, gruesome, grisly.
2 (informal) *her hair was a frightful mess:* terrible, awful, dreadful.

frigid adjective
1 *the frigid climate of the north:* cold, freezing, frozen, frosty, icy, chilly, chill, wintry, bleak, sub-zero, arctic, glacial; literary gelid.
2 *she addressed him with frigid politeness:*

frosty, glacial, cold, icy, cool, unsmiling, forbidding, unfriendly, unwelcoming; stiff, formal, stony, unemotional, austere, distant, aloof, remote, reserved, unapproachable.
OPPOSITES: hot, friendly.

frill noun

1 *she wore a full skirt with a wide frill:* ruffle, flounce, ruff, furbelow, jabot, peplum, ruche, ruching, fringe.
2 *a comfortable flat with no frills:* ostentation, ornamentation, decoration, embellishment; trimming, extra, addition, non-essential, luxury, extravagance, superfluity.

frilly adjective *she wore a white frilly apron:* ruffled, flounced, frilled, ruched, trimmed, lacy, frothy; fancy, ornate.
OPPOSITES: plain.

fringe noun

1 *the eastern fringe of the county:* edge, margin, border, periphery, perimeter, extremity, limit, outer limit, bound; outskirts.
2 *blue curtains with a yellow fringe:* edging, edge, border, trimming, hem, frill, flounce, ruffle; tassels.
▷**adjective** *fringe theatre:* alternative, avant-garde, experimental, radical; informal left-field.
OPPOSITES: mainstream.
▷**verb**
1 *a robe of gold, fringed with black velvet:* trim, edge, hem, border, bind, braid; decorate, adorn, ornament, embellish, finish.
2 *the lake is fringed by a belt of trees:* border, edge, bound, skirt, line, surround, enclose, encircle, circle, girdle, encompass, ring.

frippery noun *a functional building with not a hint of frippery:* ostentation, showiness, embellishment, adornment, ornamentation, ornament, decoration, trimming, gilding.

frisk verb

1 *the spaniels frisked around my ankles:* frolic, gambol, cavort, caper, scamper, skip, dance, romp, trip, prance, leap, spring, hop, jump, bounce.
2 *the officer frisked him:* search, body-search, check.

frisky adjective *the donkey was quite frisky and pranced around the field:* lively, bouncy, bubbly, perky, active, energetic, animated, zestful; playful, coltish, skittish, spirited, high-spirited, in high spirits, exuberant.
OPPOSITES: passive, lethargic.

fritter verb *he frittered away the money his father left him:* squander, waste, dissipate; spend like water, be prodigal with, run through, get through; informal blow, pour something down the drain.
OPPOSITES: save.

frivolity noun *in such cases too much frivolity would be all wrong:* light-heartedness, levity, joking, jocularity, gaiety, fun, silliness, foolishness, flightiness, skittishness; superficiality, shallowness, vacuity, empty-headedness.
OPPOSITES: seriousness.

frivolous adjective

1 *all of the girls were idle and frivolous:* skittish, flighty, giddy, silly, foolish, superficial, shallow, irresponsible, thoughtless, empty-headed, vacuous; informal dizzy, dippy.
2 *frivolous remarks:* flippant, facetious, joking, jokey, light-hearted; fatuous, glib, inane, senseless, thoughtless; informal flip.
3 *new rules to stop frivolous lawsuits:* time-wasting, pointless, trivial, trifling, minor, petty, insignificant, unimportant; Law vexatious.
OPPOSITES: sensible, serious.

frizzy adjective *she had frizzy blonde hair:* curly, curled, corkscrew, ringlety, crimped, crinkly, kinky, frizzed; permed.
OPPOSITES: straight.

frock noun dress, gown, robe, shift; garment, costume.

frolic verb *children frolicked on the sand:* play, amuse yourself, romp, disport yourself, frisk, gambol, cavort, caper, scamper, skip, dance, prance, leap about, jump about; dated sport.
▷**noun** *the youngsters enjoyed their frolic:* play, caper, game, romp, escapade; (**frolics**) fun and games, antics, high jinks, merrymaking, amusement, skylarking.

front noun

1 *he pushed to the front of the crowd | at the front of the boat:* fore, foremost part, forepart, anterior part, forefront; foreground, nose, head; bow, prow.
2 *the car swerved and crashed into a shop front:* frontage, face, facade, elevation.
3 *the fighting at the front went badly over the summer:* front line, combat zone, theatre of war, firing line, trenches.
4 *she pushed her way to the front of the queue:* head, top, start, beginning, lead.
5 *she kept up a brave front for most of the week:* appearance, air, face, manner, demeanour, bearing, pose, exterior, veneer, outward show, act, pretence, affectation.
6 *the shop was a front for dealing in stolen goods:* cover, cover-up, false front, blind, disguise, facade, mask, cloak, screen, smokescreen, camouflage.
OPPOSITES: rear, back.
▷**adjective** *the front runners had already finished:* leading, lead, first, foremost; in first place.
OPPOSITES: last.
▷**verb** *the houses fronted on a reservoir:* overlook, look out on/over, face, lie opposite; have a view of, command a view of.

□ **in front**
he finished three lengths in front of me:
ahead, to/at the fore, at the head, up
ahead, in the lead, leading, first; at the
head of the queue.

frontier noun border, boundary,
borderline, dividing line, demarcation
line; perimeter, limit, edge, rim; marches,
bounds.
OPPOSITES: interior.

frost noun *the hedges were covered with
frost:* ice crystals, ice, verglas; hoar frost,
ground frost, black frost; literary rime.

frosty adjective
1 *a cold and frosty morning:* freezing, cold,
icy-cold, bitter, bitterly cold, chill, wintry,
frigid, glacial, arctic; frozen, icy.
2 *Mary fixed her frosty gaze on him:* cold,
frigid, icy, glacial, unfriendly, inhospitable,
unwelcoming, forbidding, hostile, stony,
stern, hard.
OPPOSITES: warm.

froth noun *the froth on top of the beer:*
foam, head; bubbles, frothiness, fizz,
effervescence; lather, suds; scum; literary
spume.
▷ **verb** *the liquid frothed up:* bubble, fizz,
effervesce, foam, lather; churn, seethe.

frothy adjective *a frothy liquid:* foaming,
foamy, bubbling, bubbly, fizzy, sparkling,
effervescent, gassy, carbonated; sudsy.
OPPOSITES: still, flat.

frown verb
1 *she frowned at him:* scowl, glower,
glare, lour, make a face, look daggers;
give someone a black look; knit/furrow
your brows; informal give someone a
dirty look.
2 *public displays of affection were frowned
on:* disapprove of, view with disfavour,
dislike, look askance at, not take kindly
to, take a dim view of, take exception to,
object to, have a low opinion of.
OPPOSITES: smile.

frozen adjective
1 *I've been digging in the frozen ground:*
icy, ice-bound, iced over, iced up, frosty,
frosted; frozen solid, hard.
2 *his hands were frozen:* freezing, icy, very
cold, chilled to the bone/marrow, numb,
numbed, frozen stiff.
OPPOSITES: boiling, hot.

frugal adjective
1 *a hard-working, frugal man:* thrifty,
economical, careful, cautious, prudent,
provident, sparing, parsimonious;
abstemious, abstinent, austere, self-
denying, ascetic, monkish, spartan.
2 *the boys finished their frugal breakfast:*
meagre, scanty, scant, paltry, skimpy;
plain, simple, spartan, inexpensive, cheap,
economical.
OPPOSITES: extravagant, lavish.

fruit noun *the fruits of their labours:*
reward, benefit, profit, product, return,
yield, legacy, issue; result, outcome,
upshot, consequence, effect.

fruitful adjective
1 *a fruitful tree:* fertile, fecund, prolific,
high-yielding; fruit-bearing, fruiting.
2 *the two days of talks had been fruitful:*
productive, constructive, useful, of use,
worthwhile, helpful, beneficial, valuable,
rewarding, profitable, advantageous,
gainful, successful, effective, well spent.
OPPOSITES: barren, futile.

fruition noun *scientific projects need
time to come to fruition:* fulfilment,
realization, actualization, materialization,
accomplishment, resolution; success,
completion, consummation, conclusion,
close, finish, perfection, maturity,
maturation, ripening, ripeness.

fruitless adjective *the search proved
fruitless:* futile, vain, in vain, to no avail,
to no effect, idle; pointless, useless,
worthless, wasted, hollow; ineffectual,
ineffective, inefficacious; unproductive,
unrewarding, profitless, unsuccessful,
unavailing, barren, abortive; old use for
naught.
OPPOSITES: productive.

fruity adjective *he had a wonderfully fruity
voice:* deep, rich, resonant, full, mellow,
clear, strong, vibrant.

frumpy adjective *her mother's frumpy
brown and grey clothes:* dowdy, frumpish,
unfashionable, old-fashioned; drab, dull,
shabby, scruffy.
OPPOSITES: fashionable.

frustrate verb
1 *his plans were frustrated by the weather:*
thwart, defeat, foil, block, stop, put a stop
to, counter, spoil, check, baulk, forestall,
dash, scotch, derail; obstruct, impede,
hamper, hinder, hamstring; informal stymie;
Brit. informal scupper.
2 *the delays frustrated him:* exasperate,
infuriate, annoy, anger, vex, irritate,
irk, try someone's patience; disappoint,
discontent, dissatisfy, discourage,
dishearten, dispirit.
OPPOSITES: help, please.

frustrating adjective *it is obviously
very frustrating when something
like this happens:* exasperating,
infuriating, annoying, irritating, trying,
irksome; disappointing, discouraging,
disheartening, dispiriting; informal
aggravating.
OPPOSITES: pleasing, satisfying.

frustration noun
1 *he clenched his fists in frustration:*
exasperation, annoyance, anger, vexation,
irritation; disappointment, dissatisfaction,
discontentment, discontent; informal
aggravation.

2 *the frustration of his attempts to introduce changes:* thwarting, defeat, prevention, foiling, blocking, circumvention, forestalling, derailment; obstruction, hampering, hindering; failure, collapse.
OPPOSITES: satisfaction, success.

fuddled adjective *she forced her weary, fuddled brain to work:* stupefied, addled, befuddled, confused, muddled, bewildered, dazed, stunned, muzzy, groggy, vague, disorientated; informal dopey, woozy, not with it.

fuddy-duddy noun (informal) *he is a bit younger, and probably thinks I'm an old fuddy-duddy:* fogey, conservative, traditionalist, conformist; fossil, dinosaur; Brit. museum piece; informal stick-in-the-mud, square, stuffed shirt.

fudge verb *the minister tried to fudge the issue:* evade, avoid, dodge, skirt, gloss over; hedge, prevaricate, vacillate, be non-committal, stall, beat about the bush, equivocate; Brit. hum and haw; informal duck, cop out, sit on the fence.

fuel verb
1 *power stations fuelled by low-grade coal:* power, fire, run.
2 *the rumours fuelled anxiety among opposition backbenchers:* intensify, feed, stoke up, inflame, fan; stimulate, encourage, provoke, incite, whip up; sustain, keep alive.
OPPOSITES: allay.

fugitive noun *the capture of a Mafia fugitive:* escapee, runaway, deserter, absconder; refugee.
▷**adjective**
1 *the FBI proposed to kidnap the fugitive US financier from the Bahamas:* runaway, on the run, escaped, on the loose, at large; wanted; informal AWOL.
2 *the fugitive nature of life:* fleeting, transient, transitory, ephemeral, fading, momentary, short-lived, short, brief, passing, impermanent; literary evanescent.
OPPOSITES: captive, permanent.

fulfil verb
1 *he fulfilled a lifelong ambition to visit Israel:* achieve, attain, realize, make happen, actualize, succeed in, bring to completion, bring to fruition, satisfy.
2 *she failed to fulfil her duties:* carry out, perform, accomplish, execute, do, discharge, conduct; complete, finish, conclude.
3 *they fulfilled the criteria:* meet, satisfy, comply with, conform to, fill, answer.

fulfilled adjective *he's happier and more fulfilled than I've ever seen him before:* satisfied, content, contented, happy, pleased; serene, placid, untroubled, at ease, at peace.
OPPOSITES: unfulfilled.

fulfilling adjective *the way to a prosperous and fulfilling career:* satisfying, rewarding, pleasing, gratifying, enjoyable, full, enriching; happy, pleasant, stimulating, interesting.
OPPOSITES: unfulfilling.

full adjective
1 *her glass was full:* filled, filled up, filled to capacity, filled to the brim, brimming, brimful.
2 *streets full of people:* crowded, packed, crammed, congested; teeming, swarming, thick, thronged, overcrowded, overrun; abounding, bursting, overflowing; informal jam-packed, wall-to-wall, stuffed, awash.
3 *all the seats were full:* occupied, taken, in use, unavailable.
4 *he was too full to manage a dessert:* replete, full up, satisfied, well fed, sated, satiated, surfeited; gorged, glutted; informal stuffed.
5 *she'd had a full life:* eventful, interesting, exciting, lively, fulfilled, action-packed, busy, energetic, active.
6 *a full list of available facilities:* comprehensive, thorough, exhaustive, all-inclusive, all-encompassing, all-embracing, in depth; complete, entire, whole, uncut, unabridged.
7 *a fire engine driven at full speed:* maximum, top, greatest, highest.
8 *she had a full figure:* plump, rounded, buxom, shapely, ample, curvaceous, voluptuous, womanly; informal busty, curvy.
9 *the dress had a very full skirt:* loose-fitting, loose, baggy, voluminous, roomy, capacious, billowing.
10 *his full baritone voice:* resonant, rich, sonorous, deep, vibrant, full-bodied, strong, fruity, clear.
11 *the full flavour of a Bordeaux:* rich, intense, full-bodied, strong, deep.
OPPOSITES: empty, hungry, selective, thin, tight.
▷**adverb** *she looked full into his face:* directly, right, straight, squarely, square, dead, point-blank; informal bang, plumb.
◻in full
my letter was published in full: in its entirety, in toto, unabridged, uncut.

full-blooded adjective *the full-blooded aggression of ice hockey:* uncompromising, all-out, out-and-out, committed, vigorous, strenuous, intense; unrestrained, uncontrolled, unbridled, hard-hitting, pulling no punches, no-holds-barred; informal full-on.
OPPOSITES: half-hearted.

full-blown adjective *this problem could flare up into a full-blown crisis:* fully developed, full-scale, full-blooded, fully fledged, out-and-out, complete, total, thorough, entire; advanced.
OPPOSITES: partial, undeveloped.

full-bodied adjective *a rich, full-bodied claret:* full-flavoured, full, flavourful,

flavoursome, full of flavour, rich, mellow, fruity, robust, strong, mature.
OPPOSITES: tasteless.

full-grown adjective *she was now a full-grown woman:* adult, mature, grown-up, of age; fully grown, fully developed, fully fledged, in your prime, in full bloom, ripe.

fullness noun
1 *the honesty and fullness of the information they provide:* comprehensiveness, completeness, thoroughness, exhaustiveness, all-inclusiveness.
2 *the fullness of her body:* plumpness, roundedness, shapeliness, curvaceousness, voluptuousness, womanliness; informal curviness.
3 *the recording has a fullness and warmth:* resonance, richness, intensity, depth, vibrancy, strength, clarity.

full-scale adjective
1 *a full-scale model:* full-size, life-size.
2 *a full-scale public inquiry:* thorough, comprehensive, extensive, exhaustive, complete, all-out, all-encompassing, all-inclusive, all-embracing, thoroughgoing, wide-ranging, sweeping, in-depth, far-reaching.
OPPOSITES: small-scale.

fully adverb *I fully agree with him:* completely, entirely, wholly, totally, quite, utterly, perfectly, altogether, thoroughly, in all respects, in every respect, without reservation, without exception, to the hilt.
OPPOSITES: partly.

fully fledged adjective *her ambition was to become a fully fledged teacher:* proper, real, trained, qualified, proficient, experienced.
OPPOSITES: novice.

fulminate verb *ministers fulminated against the new curriculum:* protest, rail, rage, rant, thunder, storm, declaim, inveigh, speak out, make/take a stand; denounce, decry, condemn, criticize, censure, attack.
OPPOSITES: praise.

fulmination noun *the fulminations of the media moralists:* protest, objection, complaint, rant, tirade, diatribe, harangue, invective, railing, obloquy; denunciation, condemnation, criticism, censure, attack, broadside, brickbats.
OPPOSITES: praise.

fulsome adjective *he paid fulsome tributes to his former secretary:* enthusiastic, effusive, rapturous, glowing, gushing, profuse, generous, lavish; flattering, complimentary; excessive, extravagant, overdone, immoderate, unctuous; informal over the top.

USAGE

The earliest meaning of **fulsome** was 'plentiful' (*the discussion is much enhanced by the fulsome details*), but this meaning was replaced by the negative sense 'excessively flattering', and is now generally thought to be incorrect. The word is often in heard in phrases such as *fulsome praise* or *fulsome tributes,* however, where the speaker just means that the praise is generous or enthusiastic rather than excessively flattering.

fumble verb
1 *he fumbled for his keys:* grope, fish, search, feel, scrabble.
2 *he fumbled about in the dark:* stumble, blunder, flounder, lumber, stagger, totter, lurch; feel your way, grope your way.
3 *the keeper fumbled the ball in the second half:* miss, drop, mishandle; misfield.

fume noun
1 *a fire giving off toxic fumes:* smoke, vapour, gas, effluvium; pollution.
2 *stale wine fumes:* smell, odour, stink, reek, stench.
▷ verb *Ella was still fuming at his arrogance:* be furious, be enraged, be very angry, seethe, be incensed, boil, be beside yourself; rage, rant and rave; informal be livid, foam at the mouth, see red.

fun noun
1 *I joined in with the fun:* enjoyment, entertainment, amusement, pleasure; jollification, merrymaking; recreation, diversion, leisure, relaxation; good time, great time.
2 *she's young, lively, and full of fun:* high spirits, cheerfulness, cheeriness, merriment, jollity, joviality, jocularity, gaiety, mirth, laughter, hilarity, glee, gladness, light-heartedness, levity.
3 *he became a figure of fun in the music press:* ridicule, derision, mockery, laughter, scorn, contempt.
OPPOSITES: boredom, misery.
□ in fun
some of the girls did go to extremes, but it was really all in fun: playful, in jest, as a joke, tongue in cheek, light-hearted; informal for a laugh.
□ make fun of
they made fun of his accent: mock, poke fun at, ridicule, tease, laugh at, taunt, jeer at, scoff at, deride; parody, lampoon, caricature, satirize; informal take the mickey out of; Brit. informal send up.

function noun
1 *the main function of the machine:* purpose, task, use, role.
2 *my function was to select and train the recruits:* responsibility, duty, assignment, obligation, charge, task, job, mission, undertaking, commission, role, concern, province, activity, capacity, post, situation, office, occupation, employment, business.
3 *he was obliged to attend political functions:* social event, party, occasion, affair, gathering, reception, soirée, jamboree, gala; informal do.

▷**verb**
1 *the electrical system had ceased to function:* work, go, run, be in working/ running order, operate, be operative.
2 *the museum functions as an educational and study centre:* act, serve, operate; perform, work, play the role of, do duty as.

functional adjective
1 *a small but functional kitchen:* practical, useful, utilitarian, utility, workaday, serviceable; minimalist, plain, simple, basic, modest, unadorned, unostentatious, no-frills; impersonal, characterless, soulless, institutional, clinical.
2 *the machine is now fully functional:* working, in working order, functioning, in service, in use; going, running, operative, operating, in operation, in commission, in action; informal up and running.
OPPOSITES: elaborate, fancy, out of action.

functionary noun *Flores had been a leading party functionary in the province:* official, office-holder, public servant, civil servant, bureaucrat, administrator; derogatory apparatchik.

fund noun
1 *the trustees would like to thank all who have contributed to the memorial fund:* collection, kitty, reserve, pool, purse; endowment, foundation, trust, investment; savings, nest egg.
2 *I was very short of funds:* money, cash, ready money; wealth, means, assets, resources, savings, capital, reserves.
3 *his inexhaustible fund of stories:* supply, store, stock, accumulation, collection, bank, pool, mine, reservoir, hoard.
▷**verb** *the agency was funded by the Treasury:* finance, pay for, back, sponsor, subsidize, underwrite, endow, support, maintain; informal bankroll.

fundamental adjective *fundamental political assumptions about the rights of the individual:* basic, underlying, core, rudimentary, elemental, primary, prime, cardinal, first, principal, chief, key, central, vital, essential, important, indispensable, necessary, crucial, pivotal, critical; structural, organic, constitutional, inherent, intrinsic.
OPPOSITES: secondary, unimportant.

fundamentally adverb *she was, fundamentally, a good person:* essentially, in essence, basically, at heart, at bottom, deep down, au fond; primarily, above all, first and foremost, first of all.

fundamentals plural noun *I learned the fundamentals of financial accounting:* basics, essentials, rudiments, foundations, basic principles, first principles, preliminaries, essence, core, heart, base, bedrock; informal nuts and bolts, nitty-gritty.

funeral noun burial, interment, entombment, committal, laying to rest; cremation; obsequies, last offices.

funereal adjective *the funereal atmosphere of the place depressed him:* sombre, gloomy, mournful, melancholy, lugubrious, sepulchral, miserable, doleful, sad, sorrowful, cheerless, joyless, bleak, dismal, depressing, dreary; literary dolorous.
OPPOSITES: cheerful.

funnel verb *the money was funnelled back into Europe:* channel, feed, direct, convey, move, pass; pour, filter.

funny adjective
1 *it is certainly a very funny film:* amusing, humorous, witty, comic, comical, droll, jocular, jokey; hilarious, riotous, uproarious; silly, farcical, slapstick; informal hysterical, rib-tickling, priceless.
2 *a funny coincidence:* strange, peculiar, odd, queer, bizarre, curious, freakish, freak, quirky; mysterious, mystifying, puzzling, perplexing; unusual, uncommon, anomalous, irregular, abnormal, exceptional, singular, extraordinary; informal weird.
3 *there's something funny about the whole business:* suspicious, odd, strange, peculiar, unsettling; suspect, dubious, untrustworthy, questionable; informal fishy; Brit. informal dodgy.
OPPOSITES: serious, unsurprising, trustworthy.

furious adjective
1 *he was furious when he found out what I was doing:* incensed, very angry, enraged, infuriated, irate, raging, incandescent, fuming, raving, seething, beside yourself, outraged; informal mad, hopping mad, wild, livid, apoplectic.
2 *a furious debate about the rights and wrongs of fox hunting:* heated, hot, passionate, fiery; fierce, vehement, violent, wild, unrestrained, turbulent, tempestuous, stormy.
OPPOSITES: calm.

furnish verb *grooms furnished us with horses for our journey:* supply, provide, equip, provision, issue, kit out, present, give, offer, afford, bestow; informal fix up.

furore noun *the letter caused a furore in Britain:* outcry, uproar, fuss, commotion, upset, storm, pandemonium, disturbance, rumpus, turmoil, brouhaha; stir, excitement; informal to-do, ballyhoo, kerfuffle, stink; Brit. informal hoo-ha, hullabaloo.

furrow noun
1 *the long, neat furrows in a ploughed field:* groove, trench, rut, trough, channel, hollow.
2 *the furrows on either side of her mouth:* wrinkle, line, crease, crinkle, crow's foot, corrugation.
▷**verb** *he furrowed his brow in concentration:* wrinkle, crease, crinkle, pucker, screw up, scrunch up, corrugate.

furry adjective **hairy**, downy, fleecy, soft, fluffy, fuzzy, woolly.

further adverb *further, it gave him an excellent excuse not to attend:* **furthermore**, moreover, what's more, also, additionally, in addition, besides, as well, too, to boot, on top of that, over and above that, into the bargain.
▷ **adjective**
1 *the further side of the field:* **more distant**, more remote, farther; far, other, opposite.
2 *for further information, phone our customer helpline:* **additional**, more, extra, supplementary, supplemental, other; new, fresh.
OPPOSITES: nearer.
▷ **verb** *an attempt to further his career:* **promote**, advance, forward, develop, facilitate, aid, assist, help, help along, lend a hand to; expedite, hasten, speed up, accelerate, step up, spur on, boost, encourage, cultivate, nurture, foster.
OPPOSITES: hinder, impede.

furtherance noun *he was acting in the furtherance of his business interests:* **promotion**, furthering, advancement, forwarding, development, facilitation, aiding, assisting, helping; hastening, acceleration, boosting, encouragement, cultivation, nurturing, fostering.
OPPOSITES: hindrance.

furthermore adverb *This program is simple to use. Furthermore, it can be used as a powerful document transmission system:* **moreover**, further, what's more, also, additionally, in addition, besides, as well, too, to boot, on top of that, over and above that, into the bargain.

furthest adjective *the furthest limits of the universe:* **most distant**, most remote, remotest, farthest, furthermost, farthermost; outlying, outer, outermost, extreme, uttermost, ultimate; old use outmost.
OPPOSITES: nearest.

furtive adjective *they cast furtive glances at one another:* **secretive**, secret, surreptitious, clandestine, hidden, covert, conspiratorial, cloak-and-dagger; sly, sneaky, under-the-table; sidelong, sideways, oblique, indirect; informal hush-hush, shifty.
OPPOSITES: open.

fury noun
1 *she exploded with fury:* **rage**, anger, wrath, outrage, spleen, temper; indignation, umbrage, annoyance, exasperation; literary ire.
2 *the fury of the storm finally abated:* **ferocity**, violence, turbulence, savagery; severity, intensity, vehemence, force, power, strength.

fuse verb
1 *a band which fuses rap with rock:* **combine**, amalgamate, put together, join, unite, marry, blend, merge, meld,
mingle, integrate, intermix, intermingle, synthesize; coalesce, compound, alloy.
2 *metal fused to a base of coloured glass:* **bond**, stick, bind, weld, melt, solder.
OPPOSITES: separate.

fusion noun *his novels are a disturbing fusion of metaphysics and politics:* **blend**, blending, combination, amalgamation, joining, union, marrying, bonding, merging, melding, mingling, integration, intermixture, intermingling, synthesis.

fuss noun
1 *what's all the fuss about?* **excitement**, agitation, bother, stir, commotion, confusion, disturbance, brouhaha, uproar, furore; informal to-do, ballyhoo, palaver, performance, kerfuffle; Brit. informal song and dance, hoo-ha, carry-on.
2 *they settled in with very little fuss:* **bother**, trouble, inconvenience, effort, exertion; informal hassle.
3 *he didn't put up a fuss:* **protest**, complaint, objection, grumble, grouse; informal gripe.
▷ **verb** *he was still fussing about his clothes:* **worry**, fret, be anxious, be agitated, agonize, upset yourself.

fussy adjective
1 *he's very fussy about what he eats:* **finicky**, particular, over-particular, fastidious, discriminating, selective, dainty; hard to please, difficult, exacting, demanding; faddish; informal choosy, picky; Brit. informal pernickety, faddy.
2 *a fussy, frilly bridal gown:* **over-elaborate**, over-decorated, ornate, fancy, overdone; busy, cluttered.
OPPOSITES: undemanding, simple.

fusty adjective *fusty clothes | a fusty atmosphere:* **stale**, musty, dusty; stuffy, airless, unaired; damp, mildewed; Brit. frowsty.
OPPOSITES: fresh.

futile adjective *a futile attempt to keep the company afloat:* **pointless**, useless, vain, fruitless, ineffectual, ineffective, inefficacious, to no effect, in vain, to no avail, unavailing; unsuccessful, failed, thwarted; unproductive, barren, unprofitable, abortive; impotent, hollow, empty, forlorn, idle, hopeless; old use bootless.
OPPOSITES: useful.

futility noun *he could see the futility of his actions:* **pointlessness**, uselessness, fruitlessness, ineffectiveness, inefficacy, hollowness, emptiness, forlornness, hopelessness; old use bootlessness.
OPPOSITES: point, usefulness.

future noun
1 *his plans for the future:* **time to come**, time ahead; what lies ahead.
2 *she knew her future lay in acting:* **destiny**, fate, fortune; prospects, expectations, chances.
OPPOSITES: past.

▷ **adjective**
1 *we arranged for repayment at a future date:* later, to come, following, ensuing, succeeding, subsequent, coming.
2 *his future wife:* to be, destined; intended, planned, prospective.
□ **in future**
their spending will be tighter in future: from now on, after this, in the future, from this day forward, hence, subsequently, in time to come; formal henceforward, hereafter.

fuzz noun *the soft fuzz on his cheeks:* hair, down; fur, fluff, fleeciness.

fuzzy adjective
1 *the baby had a mass of fuzzy blonde hair:* frizzy, fluffy, woolly, downy, soft.
2 *a fuzzy picture of Mum at Blackpool:* blurred, out of focus, indistinct, unclear, bleary, misty, lacking definition, low-resolution.
3 *that fuzzy line between right and wrong:* ill-defined, indefinite, vague, hazy, imprecise, inexact, loose, woolly.
4 *my mind was still fuzzy and unfocused:* confused, muddled, addled, fuddled, befuddled, groggy, disorientated, mixed up, foggy, dizzy, stupefied, benumbed.

f

Gg

gabble verb *he gabbled on in a panicky way:* **jabber,** babble, prattle, rattle, blabber, gibber, twitter; Brit. informal waffle, chunter, witter.

gad verb (informal) *she's been gadding about in Italy:* **travel,** have a good time, flit; wander, roam; informal gallivant; Brit. informal swan.

gadget noun *the kitchen had every kind of modern gadget:* **appliance,** device, machine, tool, implement, utensil, apparatus, instrument, mechanism, labour-saving device, invention, contraption; informal gizmo.

gaffe noun *I made some real gaffes at work:* **blunder,** mistake, error, slip, faux pas, miscalculation, indiscretion, impropriety, solecism; informal slip-up.

gag verb
1 *the government is trying to gag its critics:* **silence,** keep quiet, muzzle, muffle, suppress, stifle; curb, check, restrain, fetter, shackle, restrict.
2 *the stench made her gag:* **retch,** heave, dry-heave.

gaiety noun
1 *I was struck by her gaiety:* **cheerfulness,** light-heartedness, happiness, merriment, glee, joy, joie de vivre, joyfulness, delight, high spirits, good spirits, good humour, cheeriness, jollity, joviality, exuberance, elation; liveliness, vivacity, animation, effervescence, sprightliness, zest, zestfulness.
2 *the hotel restaurant was a scene of gaiety:* **festivity,** fun, celebration, merrymaking, frolics, revelry, jollification, pleasure; informal partying, fun and games.
OPPOSITES: misery.

gaily adverb
1 *she skipped gaily along the path:* **merrily,** cheerfully, cheerily, happily, joyfully, light-heartedly, jauntily, gleefully.
2 *gaily painted boats:* **brightly,** colourfully, brilliantly.
3 *she plunged gaily into speculation on the stock market:* **heedlessly,** without thinking, unthinkingly, thoughtlessly, carelessly; casually, nonchalantly, airily, breezily, blithely.

gain verb
1 *he has gained numerous honours and awards | the party gained 44 per cent of the vote:* **obtain,** get, secure, attain, achieve, win, earn; capture, clinch, pick up, reap; acquire, come by, procure; informal land, net, bag, scoop, walk away/off with.
2 *they stood to gain from the deal:* **profit,** make money, reap benefits, benefit, do well out of; informal make a killing.
3 *she had gained weight:* **put on,** increase in.
4 *the others were gaining on us:* **catch up with/on,** catch someone up, catch, close in on, near.
5 *we gained the ridge:* **reach,** arrive at, get to, come to, make, attain; informal hit.
OPPOSITES: lose.
▷**noun**
1 *his gain from the deal was negligible:* **profit,** advantage, benefit, reward; percentage, takings, yield, return, winnings, proceeds, dividend.
2 *shares showed gains of up to 21 per cent:* **increase,** rise, increment, augmentation; advance.
OPPOSITES: loss, decrease.

gainful adjective *they see no prospect of finding gainful employment:* **profitable,** paid, well paid, remunerative, lucrative, moneymaking; rewarding, fruitful, worthwhile, useful, productive, constructive, beneficial, advantageous, valuable.

gait noun *he had the gait of a professional soldier:* **walk,** way of walking, step, stride, pace, tread; bearing, carriage; Brit. deportment.

gala noun *the annual summer gala:* **festival,** party, jamboree, celebration, fair, fete, carnival, pageant; festivities.
▷**adjective** *a gala occasion:* **festive,** celebratory, merry, joyful; entertaining, enjoyable; spectacular; literary joyous.

galaxy noun
1 *a distant galaxy:* **star system,** solar system, constellation; stars, heavens.
2 *a galaxy of the rock world's biggest stars:* **host,** multitude, array, gathering, assemblage, assembly, throng, crowd, group, company.

gale noun
1 *a howling gale:* strong wind, high wind, hurricane, tornado, cyclone; storm, squall.
2 *everyone erupted into gales of laughter:* peal, howl, hoot, shriek, scream, roar; outburst, burst, fit, paroxysm.

gall¹ noun
1 *she had the gall to ask for money:* effrontery, audacity, cheek, temerity, impudence, impertinence, insolence; informal nerve, brass neck.
2 *scholarly gall was poured on this work:* bitterness, resentment, rancour, bile, spleen, spite, malice, venom, vitriol, poison.

gall² verb *it galled him to have to sit in silence:* irritate, annoy, anger, infuriate, exasperate, irk, vex, pique, put out, displease, antagonize, get on someone's nerves, make someone's hackles rise, rankle with; Brit. rub up the wrong way; informal aggravate, rile, nettle, bug, hack off, get/put someone's back up.

gallant adjective
1 *his gallant countrymen:* brave, courageous, valiant, bold, plucky, daring, fearless, intrepid, heroic, stout-hearted, doughty, valorous, mettlesome, dauntless, undaunted, unflinching, unafraid, lion-hearted; informal gutsy, spunky.
2 *her gallant companion:* chivalrous, attentive, gentlemanly, courteous, polite, considerate, thoughtful, respectful, gracious.

gallantry noun
1 *he received medals for gallantry:* bravery, courage, courageousness, valour, heroism, pluck, pluckiness, nerve, daring, boldness, fearlessness, dauntlessness, intrepidity, stout-heartedness.
2 *she acknowledged his selfless gallantry:* chivalry, chivalrousness, gentlemanliness, attentiveness, courtesy, courteousness, politeness, good manners, graciousness, respectfulness, respect.

gallery noun
1 *they sat up in the gallery:* balcony, circle, upper circle; informal gods.
2 *a long gallery with doors along each side:* passage, passageway, corridor, walkway, arcade.

galling adjective *his display of hypocrisy was galling:* annoying, irritating, exasperating, infuriating, maddening, vexing, vexatious, irksome, trying, tiresome, displeasing; informal aggravating.

gallivant verb (informal) *she quit her job to go gallivanting around the world:* travel, flit; roam, wander, rove; informal gad; Brit. informal swan.

gallop verb *Paul galloped across the clearing:* rush, race, run, sprint, bolt, dart, dash, career, charge, shoot, hurtle, fly, speed, zoom; informal tear, belt, pelt, leg it; Brit. informal bomb.
OPPOSITES: stroll.

gallows plural noun
1 *a wooden gallows:* gibbet, scaffold.
2 *he was saved from the gallows by a last-minute reprieve:* hanging, being hanged, execution, the noose, the rope, the gibbet, the scaffold.

galore adjective *the shop contained fine furniture and paintings galore:* aplenty, in abundance, in profusion, in great quantities, in large numbers, by the dozen; to spare.

galvanize verb *the letter galvanized him into action* | *delegates were galvanized by an electrifying performance from the former prime minister:* stir, spur, jolt, shock, startle, prod, stimulate, rouse, urge, impel; motivate, excite, arouse, awaken, invigorate, fire, animate, vitalize, energize, inspire, electrify.

gambit noun *if the American gambit fails, the next move would be for the UN to impose sanctions:* stratagem, scheme, plan, tactic, manoeuvre, move, course/line of action, device; machination, ruse, trick, ploy; Brit. informal wheeze.

gamble verb
1 *he started to gamble more often:* bet, place/lay a bet on something, stake money on something; Brit. informal punt, have a flutter.
2 *investors are gambling that the pound will fall:* take a chance, take a risk; informal stick your neck out, go out on a limb; Brit. informal chance your arm.
▷ noun
1 *his grandfather enjoyed a gamble:* bet, wager, speculation; Brit. informal flutter, punt.
2 *I took a gamble and it paid off:* risk, chance, leap in the dark; pot luck.

gambol verb *the foal gambolled beside its mother:* frolic, caper, frisk, skip, dance, prance, leap, hop, jump, spring, bound; play.

game noun
1 *team games such as football or rugby:* sport, activity, entertainment, pastime, recreation, amusement.
2 *the club haven't lost a game all season:* match, fixture, tie, meeting, contest; cup tie, final, cup final, play-off.
3 (informal) *they're both new to the game of politics:* business, profession, occupation, trade, line, line of work/business, activity; informal racket.
4 (informal) *I spoiled his little game:* scheme, plot, stratagem, ploy, gambit, tactics, plan; trick, manoeuvre, ruse, dodge, machination, subterfuge; Brit. informal wheeze.
5 *he hunted game in Africa:* wild animals, wild fowl, big game.

g

▷ **adjective**
1 *they weren't game enough to join in:* brave, plucky, bold, daring, intrepid, courageous; informal gutsy, spunky.
2 *I need a bit of help—are you game?* willing, prepared, ready; eager, keen, enthusiastic.
▷ **verb** *they were drinking and gaming all evening:* gamble, bet, place/lay bets.

gamut noun *the complete gamut of human emotion:* range, spectrum, span, scope, sweep, compass, breadth, reach, extent, scale, catalogue; variety.

gang noun
1 *a gang of teenagers:* group, crowd, band, pack, horde, throng, mob, herd, swarm, troop, cluster; company, gathering; informal bunch, posse, gaggle.
2 (informal) *John was one of our gang:* circle, social circle, social set, group, clique, in-crowd, coterie, ring; informal crew.
3 *a gang of workmen:* crew, team, group, squad, detachment, unit; shift.
▷ **verb** *they all ganged up to put me down:* conspire, cooperate, work together, act together, combine, join forces, team up, get together, unite, ally.

gangling, gangly adjective *a gangling teenager:* lanky, tall, thin, skinny, spindly, bony, angular, scrawny, spare; gawky, awkward, uncoordinated, ungainly, graceless, ungraceful.

gangster noun *they were held up at gunpoint by gangsters:* hoodlum, gang member, robber, thug, villain, criminal, ruffian; gunman; informal mobster, crook, hit man, hood.

gaol noun (Brit.) See **JAIL**.

gap noun
1 *a gap in the shutters:* opening, aperture, space, chink, slit, slot, crack, crevice, cranny, hole, cavity, interstice, perforation, break, breach, fracture, rift, rent, fissure, cleft, divide.
2 *he returned to the team after a gap of nearly two months:* interval, interlude, break, breathing space, pause; respite, hiatus.
3 *a gap in our records:* omission, blank, lacuna, void.
4 *the gap between rich and poor:* chasm, gulf, rift, split, separation, breach; contrast, difference, disparity, imbalance.

gape verb
1 *she gaped at him in astonishment:* stare, stare open-mouthed, stare in wonder, gaze; informal gawk, goggle, rubberneck; Brit. informal gawp.
2 *her bathrobe gaped as she stooped to light the fire:* open wide, open up, yawn; part.

gaping adjective *a gaping hole:* cavernous, yawning, wide, broad; vast, huge, enormous, immense, extensive.

garb noun *men and women in riding garb:* clothes, clothing, garments, dress, wear, costume; uniform, livery, regalia; formal attire; informal gear, get-up, togs, duds; Brit. informal clobber.
▷ **verb** *both men were garbed in black:* dress, clothe, kit out, costume, robe; formal attire; informal get up.

garbage noun
1 *the garbage is taken to landfill sites:* rubbish, refuse, waste, detritus, litter, junk, scrap; scraps, leftovers, remains; N. Amer. trash.
2 *most of what he says is garbage:* rubbish, nonsense, balderdash, claptrap; dross; informal rot, drivel, twaddle, hogwash, baloney, tripe, bilge, poppycock; Brit. informal tosh, codswallop.

garble verb *the message was garbled in transmission:* mix up, muddle, jumble, confuse, distort, obscure; misquote, misreport, misrepresent, mistranslate, misstate, misinterpret, misconstrue, twist.

gargantuan adjective *a gargantuan marble statue:* huge, enormous, gigantic, very big, giant, massive, colossal, mammoth, immense, vast, mighty, monumental, mountainous, titanic, towering, tremendous, king-sized, prodigious; informal mega, monster, whopping, humongous, jumbo; Brit. informal whacking, ginormous.
OPPOSITES: tiny.

garish adjective *they wore silly hats in garish colours:* gaudy, lurid, loud, fluorescent, harsh, glaring, showy, brassy, brash; tasteless, in bad taste, vulgar.
OPPOSITES: drab.

garland noun *a garland of flowers:* wreath, festoon, ring, swag; coronet, crown, chaplet; (in Polynesia) lei.
▷ **verb** *gardens garlanded with coloured lights:* festoon, hang, wreathe, swathe; adorn, decorate, deck, bedeck, ornament, embellish, array.

garment noun *she wore a shapeless black garment:* item of clothing, article of clothing; (**garments**) clothes, clothing, dress, garb, outfit, costume; formal attire; informal get-up, gear, togs, duds.

garner verb *he garnered as much information as possible before filing his report:* gather, collect, accumulate, amass, get together, assemble.

garnish verb *garnish the dish with chopped parsley:* decorate, adorn, ornament, trim, dress, embellish; add the finishing touch to.
▷ **noun** *keep a few sprigs for a garnish:* decoration, adornment, ornament, ornamentation, embellishment, finishing touch.

garrison noun *the English garrison had*

been burned alive: troops, militia, soldiers, forces; armed force, unit.
▷**verb**
1 *French infantry garrisoned the town:* defend, guard, protect, secure, barricade; man, occupy.
2 *troops were garrisoned in various regions:* station, post, deploy, put on duty, install; base, site, place, position.

garrulous adjective
1 *a garrulous old man:* talkative, loquacious, voluble, chatty; effusive, expansive, forthcoming, communicative.
2 *his garrulous reminiscences:* long-winded, wordy, verbose, prolix, long, lengthy, rambling, wandering, maundering; gossipy, chatty.
OPPOSITES: taciturn, concise.

gash noun *a gash on his forehead:* laceration, cut, slash, wound, injury; scratch, abrasion, lesion.
▷**verb** *he gashed his hand on some broken glass:* lacerate, cut, wound, injure, hurt, slash, tear, slit, split; scratch.

gasp verb
1 *I gasped in surprise:* catch your breath, draw in your breath, gulp; exclaim, cry out.
2 *he collapsed on the ground, gasping:* pant, puff, puff and pant, puff and blow, wheeze, breathe hard, choke, fight for breath.

gastric adjective *gastric pain:* stomach, abdominal.

gate noun *she went out through the gate:* gateway, doorway, door, opening, portal; entrance, entry, exit.

gather verb
1 *we gathered in the hotel lobby:* congregate, assemble, meet, come/get together, convene, rally, converge, mass; cluster together, crowd, flock.
2 *he gathered his family together:* summon, call together, bring together, assemble, convene, rally, round up, marshal, muster.
3 *knick-knacks she had gathered over the years:* collect, accumulate, amass, garner, accrue.
4 *the show soon gathered a fanatical following:* attract, draw, pull, pull in, collect, pick up.
5 *I gather he's a keen footballer:* understand, be given to understand, believe, be led to believe, deduce, infer, assume, take it, surmise, think, conclude; hear, hear tell, learn, discover.
6 *he gathered her in his arms:* clasp, clutch, pull, embrace, enfold, hold, hug, cuddle, squeeze.
OPPOSITES: disperse.

gathering noun *she rose to address the gathering:* assembly, meeting, convention, rally, forum; congregation, audience, crowd, group, throng, mass, multitude; informal get-together.

gauche adjective *she grew from a gauche teenager into a poised young woman:* awkward, ungraceful, gawky, inelegant, graceless, ungainly; unsophisticated, lacking in social grace, inexperienced, callow.
OPPOSITES: elegant, sophisticated.

gaudy adjective *cheap, gaudy clothes:* bright, garish, lurid, loud, showy, brassy; tasteless, in bad taste, vulgar.
OPPOSITES: drab, tasteful.

gauge noun
1 *the temperature gauge:* measuring device, measuring instrument, meter, measure; indicator, dial, scale, display.
2 *exports are an important gauge of economic activity:* measure, indicator, barometer, point of reference, guide, guideline, touchstone, yardstick, test, litmus test.
3 *guitar strings of a different gauge:* size, diameter, thickness, width, breadth; measure, capacity, magnitude; bore, calibre.
▷**verb**
1 *astronomers can gauge the star's intrinsic brightness:* measure, calculate, compute, work out, determine, ascertain; count, weigh, quantify, put a figure on.
2 *it is difficult to gauge how effective the ban was:* assess, evaluate, judge, estimate, form an opinion of, appraise, weigh up, get the measure of, guess; informal size up.

gaunt adjective
1 *a tall, gaunt man:* haggard, drawn, thin, lean, skinny, spindly, spare, bony, angular, raw-boned, pinched, hollow-cheeked, scrawny, scraggy, as thin as a rake, cadaverous, skeletal, emaciated; wasted, withered; informal like a bag of bones.
2 *the gaunt ruin of Pendragon Castle:* bleak, stark, desolate, bare, gloomy, dismal, sombre, grim, stern, harsh, forbidding, uninviting, cheerless.
OPPOSITES: plump.

gauzy adjective *she wore a loose gauzy dress:* thin, sheer, diaphanous, filmy, translucent, transparent, see-through, fine, delicate, flimsy, gossamer-like, wispy, light, floaty.
OPPOSITES: opaque, thick.

gawky adjective *she had been a thin, gawky adolescent:* awkward, ungainly, gangling, clumsy, maladroit, uncoordinated, graceless, ungraceful, inelegant; gauche, unsophisticated.
OPPOSITES: graceful.

gaze verb *he gazed at her in astonishment:* stare, gape, look fixedly, take a good look; eye, study, scrutinize; informal gawk, goggle; Brit. informal gawp.
▷**noun** *his piercing gaze:* stare, fixed look; regard, inspection, scrutiny.

g

gazette noun newspaper, paper, journal, periodical, organ, newsletter, bulletin; informal **rag**.

gear noun (informal)
1 *his fishing gear | camping gear:* equipment, apparatus, paraphernalia, articles, accoutrements, impedimenta; tools, utensils, implements, instruments, gadgets; things; rig, tackle; formal appurtenances; informal **stuff, kit**.
2 *I'll go back to my hotel and pick up my gear:* belongings, possessions, effects, personal effects, property; bags, baggage.
3 *the best designer gear:* clothes, clothing, garments, outfits, garb; dress, wear; formal attire; informal **togs, duds, get-up**; Brit. informal **clobber**.

gel verb
1 *leave the mixture to gel:* set, solidify, thicken, stiffen, harden; congeal, coagulate, cake, clot.
2 *things started to gel very quickly:* take shape, fall into place, come together, work out; crystallize.

gelatinous adjective *the grain is cooked until it becomes gelatinous:* glutinous, viscous, viscid, sticky, mucilaginous; informal **gooey**.

gem noun
1 *rubies and other gems:* jewel, precious stone, semi-precious stone, stone, gemstone.
2 *this recording contains some real gems:* masterpiece, tour de force, pièce de résistance; pearl, treasure, wonder.

genealogy noun *a lengthy genealogy of the kings of France:* lineage, line of descent, family tree, bloodline; pedigree, ancestry, heritage, parentage, birth, family, dynasty, house.

general adjective
1 *the general opinion was that prices would fall:* widespread, common, prevailing, popular, public, mainstream, extensive, universal, wide.
2 *a general pay increase:* comprehensive, overall, across the board, blanket, umbrella, mass, wholesale, sweeping, broad-ranging, inclusive; universal, global, worldwide, nationwide.
3 *it is not our general practice to confirm or deny such reports:* usual, customary, established, habitual, traditional, normal, conventional, typical, standard, regular, orthodox, accepted.
4 *a general description:* broad, imprecise, inexact, rough, loose, approximate, unspecific, vague.
OPPOSITES: restricted, exceptional, specific.

generality noun
1 *the debate has moved on from generalities:* generalization, general statement, general principle, sweeping statement; abstraction.
2 *the generality of the population:* majority, greater part/number, best/better part; bulk, mass, preponderance; most.
3 *the generality of the findings can only be established by further analysis:* universality, comprehensiveness, all-inclusiveness, broadness.
OPPOSITES: specific, minority.

generally adverb
1 *summers were generally hot:* normally, in general, as a rule, by and large, more often than not, almost always, mainly, mostly, for the most part, predominantly, on the whole; usually, habitually, customarily, typically, ordinarily, commonly.
2 *France was moving generally to the left:* overall, in general terms, generally speaking, broadly, on average, basically, effectively.
3 *the method was generally accepted:* widely, commonly, extensively, universally, popularly.

generate verb
1 *moves to generate extra business | the changes are likely to generate controversy:* produce, create, give rise to, lead to, result in, bring about, make; cause, engender, spawn, precipitate, prompt, provoke, trigger, spark off, stir up.
2 *the male most likely to generate offspring:* procreate, breed, father, sire, produce, have.

generation noun
1 *people of the same generation:* age, age group, peer group.
2 *the generation of wealth:* creation, production, origination, genesis.
3 *the next generation of computers:* crop, wave, range.

generic adjective
1 *chèvre is a generic term for all goats' milk cheese:* general, common, non-specific, inclusive, all-encompassing, broad, comprehensive, blanket, umbrella.
2 *generic drugs are cheaper than branded ones:* unbranded, non-proprietary.
OPPOSITES: specific.

generosity noun
1 *the generosity of our host:* kindness, largesse, munificence, magnanimity, open-handedness, liberality, unselfishness; benevolence, altruism, philanthropy, charity; literary **bounty**.
2 *diners certainly cannot complain about the generosity of portions:* abundance, plentifulness, copiousness, lavishness, liberality, largeness.

generous adjective
1 *a generous benefactor | she is generous with money:* bountiful, liberal, magnanimous, munificent, giving, open-handed, free-handed, unselfish, free; indulgent.
2 *it was generous of them to offer:* magnanimous, kind, benevolent, charitable, philanthropic, noble,

big-hearted, good, beneficent; altruistic, unselfish, self-sacrificing.
3 *a generous supply of food:* lavish, plentiful, copious, ample, liberal, large, abundant, profuse.
OPPOSITES: mean, selfish, meagre.

genesis noun
1 *the stock-market crash had its genesis in a decline of the dollar:* origin, source, root, beginning, start.
2 *the genesis of neurosis:* formation, development, evolution, emergence, inception, origination, creation.

genial adjective *Fred is genial and well liked:* friendly, affable, cordial, amiable, pleasant, easy-going, approachable, sympathetic, agreeable, congenial; good-natured, good-humoured, cheerful; neighbourly, hospitable, companionable, sociable, convivial, outgoing, gregarious.
OPPOSITES: unfriendly.

genius noun
1 *the world knew of his genius:* brilliance, intelligence, intellect, ability, brains, erudition, wisdom, fine mind; artistry, flair, skill.
2 *he has a genius for organization:* talent, gift, flair, aptitude, facility, knack, bent, ability, expertise, capacity, faculty; strength, forte.
3 *he is a genius:* brilliant person, gifted person, mastermind, Einstein, great intellect, brain; prodigy.
OPPOSITES: stupidity, dunce.

genocide noun mass murder, massacre; annihilation, extermination, eradication; ethnic cleansing, pogrom, holocaust.

genre noun *a whole new genre of novels:* category, class, group, set, classification; type, sort, kind, variety, style, model, school.

genteel adjective *an extremely genteel couple who have fallen on hard times:* refined, respectable, decorous, well mannered, courteous, polite, proper, correct, seemly; ladylike, gentlemanly, dignified, gracious.

gentility noun *middle-class gentility:* respectability, refinement, decorum, good manners, politeness, civility, courtesy, correctness, graciousness.

gentle adjective
1 *a gentle, sensitive man:* kind, kind-hearted, tender, tender-hearted, sympathetic, considerate, understanding, compassionate, warm-hearted, benevolent, good-natured; mild, placid, serene, sweet-tempered.
2 *a gentle breeze:* light, soft.
3 *a gentle slope:* gradual, slight, easy.
OPPOSITES: brutal, strong, steep.

gentlemanly adjective *the girls declined his gentlemanly offer to allow them to go first:* chivalrous, gallant, courteous, polite, gracious, civil, mannerly, thoughtful, considerate; honourable, noble, well bred, suave, urbane.
OPPOSITES: rude.

genuine adjective
1 *a genuine Picasso:* authentic, real, actual, original, bona fide, true, veritable; attested, authenticated, undisputed; informal pukka, kosher, the real McCoy, the real thing.
2 *a very genuine person:* sincere, honest, truthful, straightforward, direct, frank, candid, open; artless, natural, unaffected; informal straight, upfront, on the level.
OPPOSITES: fake, insincere.

genus noun (Biology) *a large genus of plants:* subdivision, division, group, grouping, subfamily.

germ noun
1 *this detergent kills germs:* microbe, microorganism, bacillus, bacterium, virus; informal bug.
2 *the germ of an idea:* start, beginning, origin, seed, embryo, root; rudiments.

WORD LINKS
germicide a substance that destroys germs

germane adjective *those factors are not germane to the present discussion:* relevant, pertinent, applicable, apposite, material, connected, related; apropos, to the point; appropriate, apt, fitting, suitable.
OPPOSITES: irrelevant.

germinate verb
1 *the grain is allowed to germinate:* sprout, shoot, bud; develop, grow.
2 *the idea began to germinate:* develop, take root, grow, evolve, mature, expand, advance, progress.

gestation noun
1 *a gestation of thirty days:* pregnancy, incubation.
2 *the gestation of a musical can take months:* development, evolution, formation, emergence, origination.

gesticulate verb *they were gesticulating wildly and pointing at the tyres:* gesture, signal, motion, wave, sign.

gesticulation noun gesture, gesturing, signal, sign, wave.

gesture noun
1 *a gesture of surrender:* signal, sign, motion, movement, indication, gesticulation.
2 *the decision to publish was a symbolic gesture in support of free speech:* action, act, deed, move.
▷ **verb** *she gestured that we should leave:* signal, motion, gesticulate, wave, indicate, give a sign.

get verb
1 *I got tickets for the first game of the season:* obtain, acquire, come by, gain,

earn, win, come into, take possession of, receive, be given; buy, purchase, procure, secure; gather, collect, pick up, hook, net, land; achieve, attain; informal get your hands on, get hold of.

2 *I got your letter:* **receive**, be sent, be in receipt of, be given.

3 *your tea's getting cold:* **become**, grow, turn, go.

4 *she's gone to get the children from school:* **fetch**, collect, pick up, bring, deliver, convey, ferry, transport.

5 *the chairman gets £650,000 a year:* **earn**, be paid, take home, bring in, make, receive, collect, gross; informal pocket, rake in, net, bag.

6 *I got a taxi:* **travel by/on/in**; take, catch, use.

7 *she got flu:* **catch**, contract, fall ill with, be taken ill with, develop, go/come down with, succumb to, sicken for, fall victim to, be struck down with, become infected with; Brit. go down with.

8 *I got a sudden pain in my chest:* **experience**, suffer, be afflicted with, sustain, feel, have.

9 *I'll get supper:* **prepare**, get ready, cook, make; informal fix, rustle up.

10 *you can get me at home if you need me:* **contact**, get in touch with, communicate with, make contact with, reach; phone, call; speak to, talk to; informal get hold of.

11 *they got her to sign the consent form:* **persuade**, induce, prevail on, influence; wheedle into, talk into, cajole into.

12 *we got to the reception at 4 o'clock:* **arrive**, reach, come, make it, turn up, appear, enter, present yourself, come along; informal show up, roll in.

13 *have the police got their man?* **apprehend**, catch, arrest, capture, seize; take prisoner, take into custody, detain, put in jail, put behind bars, imprison; informal nab, run in, pick up, pull in; Brit. informal nick.

14 *I'd like to get to meet him:* **contrive**, arrange, find a way, manage; succeed in; informal work it, fix it.

15 *he didn't get the joke:* **understand**, comprehend, grasp, see, follow; informal figure out; Brit. informal suss.

16 (informal) *I'll get him for that:* **take revenge on**, exact/wreak revenge on, get your revenge on, avenge yourself on, take vengeance on, get even with, pay back, get back at; Brit. informal get your own back on.

17 *He scratched his head. 'You've got me there.':* **baffle**, perplex, puzzle, bewilder, mystify, bemuse, confuse, confound; informal flummox, faze, stump, beat, fox.

18 *what gets me is how neurotic she is:* **annoy**, irritate, exasperate, anger, irk, vex, provoke, incense, infuriate, madden, try someone's patience; informal aggravate, rile, needle, hack off, get someone's back up, get on someone's nerves, drive mad; Brit. informal wind up, nark.

□ **get something across**
a photo will help get the message across: **communicate**, get over, impart, convey, transmit, make clear, express.

□ **get ahead**
people with ideas and the desire to get ahead: **succeed**, make it, advance, get on in the world, go up in the world, make good; prosper, flourish, thrive, do well; informal go places, get somewhere, make the big time.

□ **get along**
1 *does he get along with his family?* **be friendly**, be compatible, get on; agree, see eye to eye; informal hit it off, be on the same wavelength.

2 *he was getting along well at school:* **fare**, manage, progress, do, advance, get on, get by, cope.

□ **get at**
1 *it's difficult to get at the pipes:* **access**, get to, reach, touch.

2 *he had been got at by enemy agents:* **corrupt**, suborn, influence, bribe, buy off, pay off; informal fix; Brit. informal nobble.

□ **get away**
the prisoners got away: **escape**, run away/off, break out, break free, break loose, bolt, flee, take flight, make off, take off, decamp, abscond, make a run for it; slip away, sneak away; informal cut and run, do a disappearing act, scarper, leg it; Brit. informal do a bunk, do a runner.

□ **get back**
they should get back at dawn: **return**, come home, come back.

□ **get something back**
she got her gloves back from the lost property office: **retrieve**, regain, recover, reclaim, repossess, recapture, redeem; find, trace.

□ **get back at**
his one goal was to get back at the people responsible for his downfall: **take revenge on**, exact/wreak revenge on, avenge yourself on, take vengeance on, get even with, pay back, retaliate against, give someone their just deserts; Brit. informal get your own back on.

□ **get by**
he had just enough money to get by: **manage**, cope, survive, exist, subsist, muddle through/along, scrape by, make ends meet, make do, keep the wolf from the door.

□ **get someone down**
sometimes I can laugh it off but inside it gets me down: **depress**, sadden, make unhappy, dishearten, demoralize, discourage, crush, weigh down, oppress; upset, distress; informal give someone the blues, make someone fed up.

□ **get off**
1 *I got off the bus at the next stop:* **alight from**, step off, dismount from, descend from, disembark from, leave, exit.

2 (informal) *he was arrested but got off:* **escape punishment**, be acquitted, be absolved, be cleared, be exonerated.

□**get on**
1 *we got on the train:* **board**, enter, step aboard, climb on, mount, ascend, catch; informal hop on, jump on.
2 *how are you getting on?* **fare**, manage, progress, get along, do; cope, get by, survive, muddle through/along; informal make out.
3 *he got on with his job:* **continue**, proceed, go ahead, carry on, go on, press on, persist, persevere; keep at; informal stick with/at.
4 *we don't get on.* See **GET ALONG** sense 1.
□**get out**
1 *the prisoners got out.* See **GET AWAY**.
2 *the news got out:* **become known**, become common knowledge, come to light, emerge, transpire; come out, be uncovered, be revealed, be divulged, be disclosed, be reported, be released, leak out.
□**get out of**
he tried to get out of paying: **avoid**, evade, dodge, escape, sidestep; informal wriggle out of.
□**get over**
1 *I've just got over flu:* **recover from**, recuperate from, get better after; survive.
2 *we tried to get over this problem:* **overcome**, surmount, get round, find an/the answer to, deal with, cope with, sort out, take care of, get the better of, master, get a grip on, rise above; informal crack, lick.
□**get something over**. See **GET SOMETHING ACROSS**.
□**get round someone**
he got round his mother and she bought it for him: **cajole**, coax, persuade, wheedle, prevail on, win over, bring round, beguile, charm, inveigle; informal sweet-talk, soft-soap, butter up, twist someone's arm.
□**get someone/thing together**
I get the players together so they can start to focus on the match: **collect**, gather, assemble, bring together, rally, muster, marshal, amass.
□**get together**
we must get together soon: **meet up**, rendezvous, see each other, socialize.
□**get up**
I have to get up early: **get out of bed**, rise, stir, rouse yourself; informal surface.

getaway noun *guards spotted the gunman as he tried to make his getaway:* **escape**, breakout, bolt for freedom; disappearance, vanishing act.

get-together noun *we're having a get-together after work:* **party**, gathering, social event; meeting; informal do, bash.

ghastly adjective
1 *one of the most ghastly crimes ever committed:* **terrible**, dreadful, awful, horrible, horrific, horrifying, horrendous, grim, shocking, appalling, atrocious, monstrous, gruesome, grisly.
2 (informal) *that ghastly building ought to be pulled down:* **unpleasant**, objectionable, disagreeable, distasteful, awful, terrible, dreadful, horrible, nasty, horrid, revolting, hideous, vile.
3 *she felt ghastly:* **ill**, unwell, poorly, awful, terrible, dreadful; sick, queasy, nauseous; informal rough, lousy, rotten.
4 *his face had a ghastly pallor:* **pale**, white, pallid, bloodless, ashen, grey, waxy, wan, sickly.
OPPOSITES: pleasant, lovely, fine.

ghost noun *a ghost haunts the crypt:* **phantom**, spectre, wraith, spirit, presence; apparition; informal spook.

ghostly adjective *a ghostly figure | the ghostly, mist-shrouded waters of the lake:* **unearthly**, spectral, eerie, unnatural, weird, uncanny, sinister, frightening, terrifying, chilling, spine-chilling, hair-raising, blood-curdling; shadowy, insubstantial; informal creepy, scary, spooky.

ghoulish adjective *a ghoulish fascination with death:* **macabre**, morbid, gruesome, grisly, unhealthy, unwholesome; informal sick.

giant noun *he was a giant of a man, nearly seven feet tall:* **colossus**, titan, man mountain, behemoth.
▷adjective *a giant meteorite:* **huge**, colossal, massive, enormous, gigantic, mighty, mammoth, vast, immense, mountainous, titanic, towering, king-sized, gargantuan; substantial, hefty; literary Brobdingnagian; informal mega, monster, whopping, humongous, jumbo, hulking; Brit. informal ginormous.
OPPOSITES: miniature.

gibber verb *what are you gibbering about?* **jabber**, babble, gabble, prattle, twitter; informal yammer; Brit. informal witter.

gibberish noun *he just stared at her as if she was talking gibberish:* **nonsense**, rubbish, garbage, balderdash; informal drivel, gobbledegook, mumbo-jumbo, tripe, hogwash, baloney; Brit. informal codswallop, double Dutch.

gibe noun & verb. See **JIBE**.

giddiness noun **dizziness**, light-headedness; faintness, unsteadiness, shakiness, wobbliness.

giddy adjective
1 *she felt giddy:* **dizzy**, light-headed, faint, weak; unsteady, shaky, wobbly, reeling; vertiginous; informal woozy.
2 *her giddy young sister-in-law:* **flighty**, silly, frivolous, skittish, excitable; feather-brained; informal dippy; Brit. informal scatty; N. Amer. informal ditzy.
OPPOSITES: steady, sensible.

gift noun
1 *a generous gift:* **present**; donation, offering, contribution; bequest, endowment; handout.
2 *he had a unique gift for melody:* **talent**, flair, aptitude, facility, knack, bent, ability,

g

capacity, capability, faculty; expertise, genius, brilliance, skill, artistry.
▷**verb** *the company gifted 2,999 shares to the charity:* **present to**, give to, bestow on, confer on, donate to, award to, grant to; hand over, make over.

gifted adjective *a gifted pianist | gifted pupils:* **talented**, skilful, skilled, accomplished, expert, consummate, masterly, first-rate, able, adept, proficient; intelligent, clever, brilliant; precocious.

gigantic adjective *a gigantic red-brick building:* **huge**, enormous, vast, extensive, very big, very large, giant, massive, colossal, mammoth, immense, monumental, mountainous, titanic, towering, elephantine, gargantuan; informal mega, monster, whopping, humongous, jumbo, hulking; Brit. informal ginormous.
OPPOSITES: tiny.

giggle verb *she giggled at the look on his face:* **chuckle**, chortle, laugh, titter, snigger, snicker.

gilded adjective
1 *a gilded altar:* **gold**, golden.
2 *the city's gilded youth:* **wealthy**, rich, affluent, privileged, elite, upper class.

gimmick noun *the proposal was dismissed as a pre-election gimmick:* **publicity stunt**, trick, device, ploy, scheme, stratagem.

gingerly adverb *he stepped gingerly on to the ice:* **cautiously**, carefully, with care, warily, tentatively, hesitantly, nervously.

girl noun
1 *a five-year-old girl:* **female child**; schoolgirl; Scottish & N. English lass, lassie.
2 *a tall dark girl:* **young woman**, young lady, miss; Scottish lass, lassie; Irish colleen.

girlfriend noun *he's still living with his girlfriend:* **partner**, lover, significant other; girl, woman, fiancée.

girth noun *a tree ten feet in girth:* **circumference**; width, breadth.

gist noun *the gist of his speech:* **essence**, substance, central theme, central idea, nub, heart of the matter, burden; thrust, drift, sense, meaning, significance.

give verb
1 *he gave them £2000 | we gave the money to a local charity:* **present with**, let someone have, provide with, supply with, furnish with; hand over, offer, proffer; award, grant, bestow on, confer on, make over to; donate, contribute, put up.
2 *can I give him a message?* **convey**, pass on, communicate, transmit; send, deliver, relay; tell.
3 *a baby given into their care:* **entrust**, commit, consign, assign.
4 *sun-dried tomatoes give a wonderfully rich flavour to the casserole:* **lend**, afford, impart.
5 *he gave his life for them:* **sacrifice**, give

up, relinquish; devote, dedicate.
6 *he gave her time to think:* **allow**, permit, grant, accord; offer.
7 *we gave a party for her:* **organize**, arrange, lay on, throw, host, hold, have, provide.
8 *Dominic gave a bow:* **perform**, execute, make, do.
9 *she gave a shout:* **utter**, let out, emit, produce, make.
10 *the magistrate should have given her a stiffer punishment:* **administer**, impose, inflict; deliver, issue.
11 *the door gave:* **give way**, cave in, collapse, break, fall apart; bend, buckle.
OPPOSITES: receive, take.
▷**noun** *these fabrics have more give:* **elasticity**, flexibility, stretch, stretchiness; slack, play.
□**give someone away**
Luke would never forgive her if she gave him away: **betray**, inform on, incriminate; informal split on, rat on, do the dirty on, blow the whistle on, sell down the river; Brit. informal grass on, shop; N. Amer. informal finger.
□**give something away**
his face gave little away: **reveal**, disclose, divulge, let slip, leak, let out.
□**give in**
in the end, he was forced to give in: **capitulate**, concede defeat, admit defeat, give up, surrender, yield, submit, back down, give way, relent, throw in the towel.
□**give something off/out**
a small fire burned, giving off more smoke than heat: **emit**, produce, send out, throw out; discharge, release, exude, vent.
□**give out**
his strength was giving out: **run out**, be used up, be consumed, be exhausted, be depleted; fail, flag; dry up.
□**give something out**
thousands of leaflets were given out: **distribute**, issue, hand out, pass round, dispense; dole out, dish out, mete out; allocate, allot, share out.
□**give up. See GIVE IN.**
□**give something up**
I gave up smoking five years ago: **stop**, cease, discontinue, desist from, abstain from, cut out, renounce, forgo; resign from, stand down from; informal quit, pack in, lay off; Brit. informal jack in.

give and take noun *there has to be some give and take on both sides:* **compromise**, concession; cooperation, reciprocity, teamwork, interplay.

given adjective
1 *a given number of years:* **specified**, stated, designated, set, particular, specific; prescribed, agreed, appointed, prearranged, predetermined.
2 *she was given to fits of temper:* **prone**, liable, inclined, disposed, predisposed; apt, likely.
OPPOSITES: unspecified.
▷**preposition** *given the issue's complexity,*

g

a summary is difficult: considering, in view of, bearing in mind, in the light of; assuming.
▷**noun** *his aggression is taken as a given:* established fact, reality, certainty.

giver noun donor, contributor, donator, benefactor, provider; supporter, backer, patron, sponsor, subscriber.

glacial adjective
1 *glacial conditions:* freezing, very cold, icy, sub-zero, arctic, frozen, wintry; bitter, biting, raw, chill, frigid; literary gelid.
2 *Polly's tone was glacial:* unfriendly, hostile; frosty, icy, cold, chilly.

glad adjective
1 *I'm glad you're coming with us:* pleased, happy, delighted, thrilled, overjoyed; gratified, grateful, thankful; Brit. informal chuffed; N. English informal made up.
2 *I'd be glad to help:* willing, eager, happy, pleased, delighted; ready, prepared.
3 *glad tidings:* pleasing, welcome, happy, joyful, cheering, heartening, gratifying.

gladden verb *it gladdened him to see her again:* please, delight, make happy; cheer, cheer up, hearten, buoy up, give someone a lift; gratify.

gladly adverb *I would gladly have given him the money:* with pleasure, happily, cheerfully; willingly, readily, freely.

glamorous adjective
1 *a glamorous woman:* beautiful, attractive, elegant, chic, stylish, fashionable, smart; charismatic, captivating, appealing, alluring; informal classy.
2 *a glamorous lifestyle:* exciting, glittering, dazzling, colourful; cosmopolitan; informal ritzy, glitzy, jet-setting.
OPPOSITES: dowdy, dull.

glamour noun
1 *she had undeniable glamour:* beauty, elegance, chic, style; charisma, charm.
2 *the glamour of show business:* allure, appeal, attraction, fascination, charm, magic, romance, mystique; excitement, glitter, the bright lights.

glance verb
1 *Rachel glanced at him:* look briefly, look quickly, take a look, peek, peep.
2 *I glanced through the report:* read quickly, scan, skim, run your eye over; browse through, dip into.
3 *a bullet glanced off the ice:* ricochet, rebound, be deflected, bounce.
4 *sunlight glanced off her hair:* reflect, gleam, glint, glitter, glisten, glimmer, shimmer.
▷**noun** *he took a glance at his watch:* peek, peep, brief look, quick look.
□ **at first glance**
on the face of it, on the surface, at first sight, to the casual eye, to all appearances;

apparently, seemingly, outwardly, superficially, it would seem, it appears.

glare verb *she glared at him:* scowl, glower, stare angrily, frown, give someone a black look, look threateningly, look daggers, lour; informal give someone a dirty look.
▷**noun**
1 *a cold glare:* scowl, glower, angry stare, frown, black look.
2 *he narrowed his eyes against the glare of the sun:* bright light, dazzle, blaze, shine, beam; radiance, brilliance.

glaring adjective
1 *glaring lights:* dazzling, blinding, blazing, strong, bright, harsh.
2 *there is a glaring omission in the data:* obvious, conspicuous, unmistakable, inescapable, striking, blatant, flagrant; patent, overt, transparent, manifest.

glass noun
1 *a glass of water:* tumbler; flute, schooner, balloon, goblet; beaker; old use chalice.
2 *we sell china and glass:* glassware, crystal, crystalware.

> WORD LINKS
> **vitreous** resembling glass in appearance or (of a substance) containing glass

glassy adjective
1 *the glassy surface of the lake:* smooth, gleaming, shiny, glossy; calm, still, flat.
2 *a glassy stare:* expressionless, glazed, blank, vacant, fixed; emotionless, impassive, lifeless, wooden.

glaze verb
1 *the pots are glazed when dry:* varnish, enamel, lacquer; paint.
2 *his eyes glazed over:* become glassy, go blank; mist over, film over.
▷**noun** *pottery with a blue glaze:* varnish, enamel, lacquer, finish, coating; lustre, shine, gloss.

gleam verb *her eyes gleamed with satisfaction:* shine, glimmer, glint, glitter, shimmer, glisten, sparkle, twinkle, flicker, wink, flash.
▷**noun**
1 *a gleam of light:* glimmer, glint, shimmer, twinkle, flicker, flash, sparkle; beam, ray, shaft.
2 *the gleam of silver:* shine, lustre, gloss, sheen; glint, glitter, glimmer, sparkle; brilliance, radiance, glow.
3 *a gleam of hope:* glimmer, flicker, ray, spark, trace, suggestion, hint, sign.

glean verb *the information is gleaned from press cuttings:* obtain, get, take, draw, derive, extract, garner, gather, cull; learn, find out.

glee noun *she clapped her hands with glee:* delight, pleasure, happiness, joy, elation, euphoria, excitement; triumph, jubilation, relish, satisfaction, gratification.
OPPOSITES: disappointment.

g

gleeful adjective *a gleeful chuckle:* delighted, pleased, joyful, happy, glad, overjoyed, elated; triumphant, jubilant, exultant, cock-a-hoop.

glib adjective *the glib explanations rolled off his tongue | glib politicians:* slick, smooth, pat, plausible; fluent, smooth-talking, silver-tongued; disingenuous, insincere, facile, shallow, superficial.
OPPOSITES: sincere.

glide verb
1 *a gondola glided past:* slide, slip, sail, float, drift, flow; coast, freewheel, roll; skim, skate.
2 *seagulls gliding over the waves:* soar, wheel, plane; fly.

glimmer verb *moonlight glimmered on the lawn:* gleam, shine, glint, shimmer, glisten, glitter, glow, twinkle, sparkle, flicker, wink, flash.
▷noun
1 *a glimmer of light:* gleam, glint, flicker, shimmer, glow, twinkle, sparkle, flash, ray.
2 *a glimmer of hope:* gleam, flicker, ray, trace, sign, suggestion, hint.

glimpse noun *a glimpse of her face:* brief view/sight, sighting; quick look, glance, peek, peep.
▷verb *he glimpsed a figure standing in the shadows:* catch sight of, notice, discern, spot, spy, sight, pick out, make out.

glint verb *her ring glinted in the sunlight:* shine, gleam, catch the light, glitter, sparkle, twinkle, wink, glimmer, shimmer, glisten, flash.
▷noun *the glint of moonlight on steel:* glitter, gleam, sparkle, twinkle, glimmer, flash.

glisten verb *the sea glistened in the early morning light:* shine, sparkle, twinkle, glint, glitter, glimmer, shimmer.

glitter verb *crystal glittered in the candlelight:* shine, sparkle, twinkle, glint, gleam, shimmer, glimmer, wink, flash, catch the light.
▷noun
1 *the glitter of light on the water:* sparkle, twinkle, glint, gleam, shimmer, glimmer, flicker, flash; brilliance, luminescence.
2 *the glitter of show business:* glamour, excitement, thrills, attraction, appeal; dazzle; informal razzmatazz, glitz, razzle-dazzle.

gloat verb *she gloated over his recent humiliation:* delight, relish, take great pleasure, revel, rejoice, glory, exult, triumph, crow; boast, brag, be smug, congratulate yourself, preen yourself, pat yourself on the back.

global adjective
1 *the global economy:* worldwide, international, world, intercontinental.
2 *a global view of the problem:* comprehensive, overall, general, all-inclusive, all-encompassing, universal; broad, wide-ranging, far-reaching, extensive, sweeping, blanket.

globe noun
1 *people from every corner of the globe:* world, earth, planet.
2 *the sun is a globe:* sphere, ball, spheroid, orb, round.

globular adjective *the plant has globular pinkish-green blooms:* spherical, round, globe-shaped, ball-shaped, orb-shaped; rounded, bulbous.

globule noun *globules of sweat:* droplet, drop, bead, bubble, ball; informal blob.

gloom noun
1 *she peered into the gloom:* darkness, dark, dimness, blackness, shadows, shade; dusk, twilight; literary gloaming.
2 *his gloom deepened:* despondency, depression, dejection, low spirits, downheartedness, melancholy, unhappiness, sadness, glumness, gloominess, misery, sorrow, woe, wretchedness; despair, pessimism, hopelessness.

gloomy adjective
1 *a gloomy room:* dark, dim, shadowy, dingy, dreary, dismal, sombre, unwelcoming, cheerless, comfortless, funereal.
2 *Joanna looked gloomy:* despondent, downcast, downhearted, dejected, dispirited, disheartened, discouraged, demoralized, crestfallen; depressed, desolate, low, sad, unhappy, glum, sombre, melancholy, miserable, woebegone, mournful, forlorn, morose; informal fed up, blue, down in the mouth, down in the dumps.
3 *gloomy forecasts about the economy:* pessimistic, depressing, downbeat, disheartening, disappointing; unfavourable, bleak, bad, black, grim.
OPPOSITES: bright, cheerful, optimistic.

glorify verb
1 *the film does not glorify war nor present its characters as heroes:* celebrate, glamorize, romanticize, idealize, ennoble, dignify; promote, elevate; praise, honour, hail, extol, applaud.
2 *they gather to glorify God:* praise, worship, pay homage to, honour, give thanks to, extol, exalt, revere, venerate.

glorious adjective
1 *a glorious victory:* illustrious, celebrated, famous, acclaimed, distinguished, honoured; outstanding, great, magnificent, noble, triumphant.
2 *there are glorious views across the valley:* wonderful, marvellous, magnificent, superb, sublime, spectacular, lovely, fine, delightful; informal great, stunning, fantastic, terrific, tremendous, sensational, heavenly, divine, gorgeous,

fabulous, awesome, ace.
OPPOSITES: undistinguished.

glory noun

1 *a sport that won him glory:* renown, fame, prestige, honour, distinction, kudos, acclaim, praise; celebrity, recognition, reputation; informal bouquets.
2 *the house has been restored to its former glory:* magnificence, splendour, grandeur, nobility, majesty, resplendence; opulence, beauty, elegance.
3 *the glories of Paris:* wonder, beauty, delight, marvel, phenomenon; sight, spectacle.
4 *glory be to God:* praise, worship, homage, thanksgiving, thanks, adoration, veneration, honour, reverence.
OPPOSITES: shame, obscurity.
▷**verb** *we gloried in our independence:* take pleasure in, revel in, rejoice in, delight in; relish, savour; congratulate yourself on, be proud of; boast about; informal get a kick out of.

gloss¹ noun *hair with a healthy gloss:*
shine, sheen, lustre, gleam, patina, burnish, brilliance, shimmer.
▷**verb** *he tried to gloss over his problems:* conceal, cover up, hide, disguise, mask, veil; shrug off, brush aside, play down, minimize, understate, make light of; informal brush under the carpet.

gloss² noun *specialized terms have glosses in the margin:* explanation, interpretation, exegesis; annotation, note, footnote, commentary, comment; translation.
▷**verb** *difficult words are glossed in a footnote:* explain, interpret; annotate; translate, paraphrase.

glossy adjective *thick, glossy hair:* shiny, gleaming, lustrous, brilliant, shimmering, glistening, satiny, smooth; polished, burnished, lacquered, glazed.
OPPOSITES: dull.

glove noun mitten, mitt, gauntlet.

glow verb

1 *lights glowed from the windows:* shine, gleam, glimmer, flicker, radiate, flare.
2 *a fire glowed in the hearth:* radiate heat, smoulder, burn.
3 *her face glowed with embarrassment:* flush, blush, redden, colour; burn.
4 *she glowed with pride:* tingle, thrill; beam.
▷**noun**
1 *the glow of the fire:* radiance, light, shine, gleam, glimmer, incandescence; warmth, heat.
2 *a glow spread over her face:* flush, blush, rosiness, pinkness, redness, high colour; bloom, radiance.
3 *a warm glow deep inside her:* happiness, contentment, pleasure, satisfaction.

glower verb *she glowered at him:* scowl, glare, frown, give someone a black look, look daggers, lour; informal give someone a dirty look.
▷**noun** *the glower on his face:* scowl, glare, frown, black look.

glowing adjective

1 *a glowing light | glowing embers:* bright, shining, radiant, glimmering, flickering, twinkling, incandescent, luminous; lit up, lighted, illuminated, ablaze; aglow, smouldering.
2 *his glowing cheeks:* rosy, pink, red, flushed; radiant, ruddy, florid; hot, burning.
3 *glowing colours:* vivid, vibrant, bright, brilliant, rich, intense, strong, radiant, warm.
4 *his work received a glowing report:* complimentary, very favourable, enthusiastic, commendatory, rapturous, rhapsodic, ecstatic; fulsome.

glue noun *a tube of glue:* adhesive, fixative, gum, paste, cement; epoxy resin, size.
▷**verb**
1 *the planks were glued together:* stick, gum, paste; affix, fix, cement.
2 (informal) *she was glued to the television:* be riveted by, be mesmerized by, be transfixed by, be gripped by.

glum adjective *Ken looked glum and resentful:* gloomy, downcast, downhearted, dejected, despondent, crestfallen, disheartened; depressed, unhappy, doleful, melancholy, miserable, woebegone, mournful, forlorn, in the doldrums, morose; informal fed up, blue, down in the mouth, down in the dumps.
OPPOSITES: cheerful.

glut noun *there is a glut of cars on the market:* surplus, excess, surfeit, superfluity, overabundance, superabundance, oversupply; plethora.
OPPOSITES: dearth.
▷**verb** *factories for recycling paper are glutted:* cram full, overfill, overload, oversupply, saturate, flood, inundate, deluge, swamp; informal stuff.

glutinous adjective *a glutinous liquid:* sticky, viscous, viscid, treacly, tacky; adhesive; informal gooey.

glutton noun gourmand, big eater; informal pig, gannet.

gluttonous adjective *a gluttonous appetite:* greedy, voracious, insatiable, wolfish.

gluttony noun greed, greediness, overeating, gourmandizing, voracity, insatiability.

gnarled adjective

1 *a gnarled tree trunk:* knobbly, knotty, rough, lumpy, nodular; twisted, bent, crooked.
2 *gnarled hands:* twisted, bent, misshapen; arthritic; rough, wrinkled, wizened.

g

gnaw verb

1 *the dog gnawed at a bone:* chew, champ, chomp, chomp, bite, munch, crunch; nibble, worry.
2 *the pressures are gnawing away their independence:* erode, wear away, wear down, eat away.
3 *the doubts still gnawed at her:* nag, plague, torment, torture, trouble, worry, haunt, oppress, burden, hang over; bother, niggle.

go verb

1 *they started to go towards the main entrance:* move, proceed, make your way, advance, progress; walk, travel, journey.
2 *it's time to go:* leave, depart, take yourself off, go away, withdraw, absent yourself; set off, start out, get under way, be on your way; Brit. make a move; informal make tracks.
3 *the road goes to London:* extend, stretch, reach; lead.
4 *three years went by:* pass, elapse, slip by/past, roll by/past, tick away.
5 *a golden age that has gone for good:* disappear, vanish, be no more, be over, run its course, fade away; finish, end, cease.
6 *all our money had gone:* be used up, be spent, be exhausted, be consumed, be drained, be depleted.
7 *everything went well:* turn out, work out, develop, come out; result, end up; informal pan out.
8 *his hair had gone grey:* become, get, turn, grow.
9 *those colours don't go:* match, harmonize, be harmonious, blend, be complementary, be suited, coordinate, be compatible.
10 *my car won't go:* function, work, run, operate.
OPPOSITES: arrive, come.

▷ **noun**

1 *have another go:* attempt, try, effort, bid, endeavour; informal shot, stab, crack, bash.
2 *he has plenty of go in him:* energy, vigour, vitality, life, liveliness, spirit, verve, enthusiasm, animation, zest; stamina, dynamism, drive, push, determination; informal get-up-and-go.

□ **go about**
Ruth went about her tasks enthusiastically: set about, begin, embark on, undertake, address yourself to, get down to, start, commence, get to work on, get going on; approach, tackle, attack; informal get cracking on.

□ **go along with**
he seemed happy enough to go along with your plans: agree to/with, fall in with, comply with, cooperate with, acquiesce in, assent to, follow; submit to, yield to, defer to.

□ **go away.** See **go** verb sense 3.

□ **go back on**
she went back on her promise: renege on, break, fail to honour, default on, retract; do an about-face.

□ **go by**
we have to go by his decision: obey, abide by, comply with, keep to, conform to, follow, heed, defer to, respect.

□ **go down**
1 *the ship went down:* sink, founder, go under.
2 *interest rates are going down:* decrease, get lower, fall, drop, decline; plummet, plunge, slump.
3 *his name will go down in history:* be remembered, be recorded, be commemorated, be immortalized.

□ **go down with** (Brit.) *she's gone down with flu:* fall ill with, get, develop, contract, pick up, succumb to, fall victim to, be struck down with, become infected with.

□ **go for**
1 *I went for the tuna:* choose, pick, opt for, select, plump for, decide on.
2 *the man went for her:* attack, assault, hit, strike, beat up, set upon, rush at, lash out at; informal lay into, rough up; Brit. informal duff up.
3 *he goes for older women:* be attracted to, like; prefer, favour; informal have a thing about; Brit. informal fancy.

□ **go in for**
we don't normally go in for this sort of thing: take part in, participate in, get involved in, join in, enter into, engage in, undertake; practise, pursue; espouse, adopt, embrace.

□ **go into**
you'll need to go into the subject in greater detail: investigate, examine, enquire into, look into, research, probe, explore, delve into; consider, review, analyse.

□ **go off**
1 *the bomb went off:* explode, detonate, blow up.
2 (Brit.) *the milk's gone off:* go bad, go stale, go sour, turn, spoil, go rancid; decompose, go mouldy.

□ **go on**
1 *the lecture went on for hours:* last, continue, carry on, run on; endure, persist; take.
2 *I'm not sure what went on:* happen, take place, occur, transpire; N. Amer. informal go down.

□ **go out**
1 *the lights went out:* be turned off, be extinguished.
2 *he's going out with Kate:* see, take out, be involved with; informal date.

□ **go over**
1 *you'd better go over the figures:* examine, study, scrutinize, inspect, look at/over, check; analyse, review.
2 *we are going over our lines:* rehearse, practise, read through, run through.

□ **go round**
1 *the wheels were still going round:* spin, revolve, turn, rotate, whirl.
2 *a nasty rumour went round:* be spread, be circulated, be put about, circulate, pass round.

□ **go through**
1 *they've gone through a dreadful ordeal:* undergo, experience, face, suffer, be

subjected to, live through, endure, brave, bear, tolerate, withstand, put up with, cope with, weather.
2 *he went through hundreds of pounds:* spend, use up, run through, get through, expend, deplete; waste, squander, fritter away.
3 *he went through Susie's bag:* search, look, hunt, rummage, rifle.
4 *I have to go through the report:* examine, study, scrutinize, inspect, look over, check; analyse, review.
5 *the deal has gone through:* be completed, be concluded, be brought off; be approved, be signed, be rubber-stamped.
□ **go under**
go bankrupt, cease trading, go into receivership, go into liquidation, become insolvent, be liquidated, be wound up, be shut down; fail; informal go to the wall, fold.
□ **go without**
the children did not go without: be deprived, be in want, go short, go hungry, be in need.

goad verb *we were goaded into action:* provoke, spur, rouse, stir, stimulate, move, prompt, encourage, motivate, prod, egg on, incite, urge.
▷**noun** *a goad to political change:* stimulus, incentive, encouragement, inducement, spur, prod, prompt; motive, motivation.

goal noun *our long-term goal is a nuclear-free world:* objective, aim, end, target, design, intention, intent, plan, purpose; ambition, aspiration, wish, dream, desire, hope; holy grail.

gobble verb *he paused only to gobble down his lunch:* guzzle, devour, wolf, bolt, cram, gorge on; informal scoff, tuck into, put away, demolish, polish off, shovel down, stuff your face with, pig yourself on; N. Amer. informal scarf down/up.

go-between noun *an American firm acted as a go-between in the transaction:* intermediary, middleman, agent, broker, liaison, contact; negotiator, mediator, intercessor.

goblet noun wine glass, glass; old use chalice.

god noun *the gods and goddesses of Greek mythology:* deity, divine being, divinity, immortal.

> WORD LINKS
> **divine** relating to God or a god
> **theology** the study of God and religious belief

godforsaken adjective *what are you doing in this godforsaken place?* wretched, miserable, dreary, dismal, depressing, grim, cheerless, bleak, desolate, gloomy; deserted, neglected, isolated, remote.

godless adjective *a godless society:* unbelieving, irreligious, ungodly, faithless; non-religious, agnostic, atheistic, profane, secular.

godly adjective *how to live the godly life:* religious, devout, pious, reverent, believing, God-fearing, saintly, holy, prayerful, churchgoing.

godsend noun *the growing popularity of organic foods has been a godsend for these farmers:* boon, blessing, bonus, benefit, advantage, help, aid, asset; stroke of luck.

goggle verb *he goggled at her in disbelief:* stare, gape, gaze; informal gawk; Brit. informal gawp.

goings-on plural noun *neighbours complained to the police about the goings-on at the house:* events, happenings, affairs, business; misbehaviour, misconduct, funny business; informal monkey business, hanky-panky, shenanigans.

golden adjective
1 *her golden hair:* blonde, yellow, fair, tow-coloured; literary flaxen.
2 *a golden opportunity:* excellent, fine, superb, splendid; special, unique; favourable, opportune, promising; advantageous, profitable, valuable, providential.

gone adjective
1 *I wasn't gone long:* away, absent, off, out; missing, unavailable.
2 *those days are gone:* past, over, no more, done, finished, ended; forgotten, dead and buried.
3 *the milk's all gone:* used up, consumed, finished; at an end.

good adjective
1 *a good product:* fine, superior, impressive, quality; excellent, superb, outstanding, magnificent, exceptional, marvellous, wonderful, first-rate, first-class, sterling; satisfactory, acceptable, up to scratch, up to standard; informal great, ace, terrific, fantastic.
2 *she's a good driver:* capable, proficient, accomplished, skilful, skilled, able, adept, adroit, talented, masterly, expert; informal great, mean, wicked, ace.
3 *the dogs are in good condition:* healthy, fine, sound, tip-top, hale and hearty, fit, robust, sturdy, strong, vigorous.
4 *we've had some good news:* pleasing, pleasant, welcome, gratifying, encouraging.
5 *the play had good reviews:* favourable, complimentary, approving, positive, enthusiastic; rapturous, glowing.
6 *a good person:* virtuous, upright, upstanding, moral, ethical, high-minded, principled, reputable, decent, respectable, trustworthy, honourable, noble; exemplary, law-abiding, irreproachable, blameless, guiltless, unimpeachable; meritorious, praiseworthy, admirable.
7 *it was good of you to come:* kind, kind-

g

hearted, considerate, generous, charitable, magnanimous, gracious; altruistic, unselfish, selfless.
8 *the children were always good at school:* **well behaved**, obedient, dutiful, polite, well mannered, courteous, respectful.
9 *he's a good friend:* **close**, intimate, dear, bosom, valued, treasured; loyal, faithful, constant, reliable, dependable, trustworthy, trusty, true, unfailing, staunch.
10 *a good time was had by all:* **enjoyable**, pleasant, agreeable, pleasurable, delightful, nice, lovely; entertaining, amusing, diverting, jolly; informal great, fantastic, fabulous, terrific; Brit. informal brilliant.
11 *tomorrow would be a good time to call:* **convenient**, suitable, appropriate, fitting, fit; opportune, timely, favourable, advantageous, expedient, felicitous, happy, providential.
12 *milk is good for you:* **wholesome**, healthy, healthful, nourishing, nutritious, beneficial.
13 *give me one good reason why I should go:* **valid**, genuine, legitimate, sound, bona fide; convincing, persuasive, telling, potent, cogent, compelling.
14 *did you have good weather?* **fine**, fair, dry; bright, clear, sunny, cloudless; calm, windless; warm, mild, balmy, clement, pleasant, nice.
15 *he gave me some good advice:* **useful**, helpful, valuable, constructive, worthwhile
OPPOSITES: bad, poor, wicked.
▷**noun**
1 *issues of good and evil:* **virtue**, righteousness, morality, integrity, rectitude; honesty, truth, honour, probity; propriety; blamelessness, purity.
2 *it's all for your good:* **benefit**, advantage, profit, gain, interest, welfare, well-being; enjoyment, comfort, ease, convenience; help, aid, assistance, service; behalf.
OPPOSITES: wickedness, disadvantage.
□**make something good**
1 *he promised to make good any damage:* **repair**, mend, fix, put right, set right, see to; restore, remedy, rectify.
2 *he will make good his promise:* **fulfil**, carry out, discharge, honour; keep, observe, abide by, stick to, follow, be bound by, live up to, stand by, adhere to.

goodbye exclamation **farewell**, au revoir; literary adieu; informal bye, so long, see you, ciao; Brit. informal cheers, cheerio.

good-for-nothing adjective *a good-for-nothing layabout:* **feckless**, lazy, idle, shiftless, indolent, slothful; useless, worthless, incompetent, ne'er-do-well; informal no-good.
▷**noun** *lazy good-for-nothings:* **ne'er-do-well**, layabout, idler, sluggard, shirker; informal waster, slacker; Brit. informal skiver.

good-humoured adjective *he was too good-humoured to be offended:* **genial**, affable, friendly, amiable, pleasant, easy-going, approachable, good-natured, cheerful, cheery, cordial; companionable, sociable, convivial, gregarious.
OPPOSITES: grumpy.

good-looking adjective *a good-looking woman:* **attractive**, beautiful, pretty, handsome, lovely, fetching, stunning, striking, gorgeous, desirable; Scottish & N. English bonny; informal tasty, easy on the eye; Brit. informal fit; N. Amer. informal cute; old use comely, fair.
OPPOSITES: ugly.

good-natured adjective *his father was a plump, good-natured man:* **amiable**, affable, friendly, warm-hearted, easy-going, generous, benevolent, understanding, sympathetic; kind, kind-hearted, unselfish, considerate, thoughtful, obliging, helpful, accommodating, neighbourly; Brit. informal decent.

goodness noun
1 *he had some goodness in him:* **virtue**, good, righteousness, morality, integrity, rectitude; honesty, truth, truthfulness, honour, probity; propriety, decency, respectability, nobility, worth, merit; blamelessness, purity.
2 *slow cooking retains the food's goodness:* **nutritional value**, nutrients, wholesomeness, nourishment.

goods plural noun
1 *he dispatched the goods:* **merchandise**, wares, stock, commodities, produce, products, articles; imports, exports.
2 *I packed the car with all my worldly goods:* **property**, possessions, effects, chattels, valuables; informal things, stuff.
3 (Brit.) *most goods went by train:* **freight**, cargo; load, consignment, delivery, shipment.

good-tempered adjective *he was optimistic and remarkably good-tempered:* **equable**, even-tempered, easy-going, mellow, mild, mild-mannered, calm, relaxed, tranquil, placid; well balanced, stable, level-headed, imperturbable, unruffled, unflustered, untroubled, cheerful; informal laid-back.
OPPOSITES: bad-tempered.

goodwill noun *we made the offer as a gesture of goodwill:* **friendliness**, kindness, consideration, compassion, benevolence; cooperation, collaboration; decency, sympathy, understanding, neighbourliness; formal amity.
OPPOSITES: hostility.

gorge noun *the river runs through a gorge:* **ravine**, canyon, gully, defile; chasm, gulf.
▷**verb** *I gorged on fresh squid, giant prawns, and delicious French fries:* **feast on**, devour, wolf down, guzzle, gobble; informal stuff yourself with, pig out on, scoff, demolish, polish off; N. Amer. informal scarf down.

gorgeous adjective
1 *a gorgeous girl:* **good-looking**, attractive, beautiful, pretty, handsome, lovely, stunning, striking, fetching; delightful, charming, enchanting, captivating, appealing; irresistible, ravishing, desirable, sexy; Scottish & N. English bonny; informal tasty, hot, easy on the eye; Brit. informal fit; N. Amer. informal cute.
2 *a gorgeous view:* **spectacular**, splendid, magnificent, superb, wonderful, grand, impressive, awe-inspiring, awesome, amazing, stunning, breathtaking, incredible; informal sensational, fabulous, fantastic.
3 (informal) *the weather was gorgeous:* **excellent**, marvellous, superb, very good, first-rate, first-class, wonderful, glorious, magnificent, splendid; informal great, terrific, fantastic, fabulous, ace; Brit. informal brilliant.

gory adjective *a series of gory murders:* **grisly**, gruesome, ghastly, horrible, hideous, macabre, horrific, shocking, appalling; violent, bloody, brutal, savage.

gospel noun
1 *the Gospel was spread by missionaries:* **Christian teaching**, Christian doctrine, Christ's teaching; the word of God, the New Testament.
2 *articles in blogs shouldn't be treated as gospel:* **the truth**; fact, actual fact, reality, actuality, a certainty.
3 *his gospel of non-violence:* **doctrine**, dogma, teaching, principle, ethic, creed, credo, ideology, ideal; belief, tenet, canon.

gossamer adjective *a gossamer veil:* **gauzy**, fine, diaphanous, delicate, filmy, floaty, wispy, thin, light, insubstantial, flimsy; translucent, transparent, see-through, sheer.

gossip noun
1 *he became the subject of much local gossip:* **tittle-tattle**, tattle, rumours, whispers, hearsay, idle talk, canards; scandal; informal dirt.
2 *she's such a gossip:* **scandalmonger**, gossipmonger, tattler, busybody.
▷**verb** *it wasn't long before everyone was gossiping about their relationship:* **spread rumours**, spread gossip, tittle-tattle, tattle, talk, whisper, tell tales; informal dish the dirt.

gouge verb *a tunnel had been gouged out of the mountain:* **dig**, hollow, excavate, cut, scoop, scrape, scratch.

gourmand noun *gourmands who care more for quantity than quality:* **glutton**, big eater; informal pig, gannet.

gourmet noun *even the most demanding gourmets adore the restaurants on Lake Como:* **gastronome**, epicure, epicurean; connoisseur; informal foodie.

govern verb
1 *he had governed the country for the past 21 years:* **rule**, preside over, reign over, control, be in charge of, command, lead; run, head, administer, manage, regulate, oversee, supervise.
2 *the rules governing social behaviour:* **determine**, decide, control, regulate, direct, rule, dictate, shape; affect, influence, sway, act on, mould, modify.

government noun
1 *the government announced cuts in public services:* **administration**, executive, regime, authority, leadership, powers that be, directorate, council; cabinet, ministry.
2 *they help him in the government of the country:* **rule**, running, leadership, control, administration, regulation, management, supervision.

governor noun *the governor of Mississippi | the governor of Parkhurst prison:* **leader**, ruler, chief, head; premier, president, viceroy; administrator, principal, director, chairman/woman, chair, superintendent, commissioner, controller.

gown noun **dress**, robe; Brit. frock.

grab verb *I grabbed his arm:* **seize**, take hold of, grasp, snatch, grip, clasp, clutch; take.
▷**noun** *she made a grab for his gun:* **lunge**, snatch.

grace noun
1 *the grace of a ballerina:* **elegance**, poise, gracefulness; suppleness, agility, nimbleness, light-footedness.
2 *he had the grace to look sheepish:* **decency**, courtesy, good manners, politeness, decorum, respect, tact.
3 *he fell from grace:* **favour**, approval, approbation, acceptance, esteem, regard, respect; goodwill.
4 *he lived there by grace of the king:* **favour**, goodwill, generosity, kindness, indulgence.
5 *they have five days' grace to decide:* **deferment**, deferral, postponement, suspension, delay, pause; respite, stay, moratorium, reprieve.
OPPOSITES: inelegance, effrontery, disfavour.
▷**verb**
1 *the proceedings were graced by the presence of the Nobel Prize winner:* **dignify**, distinguish, honour, ennoble.
2 *magnificent oil paintings graced the walls:* **adorn**, decorate, ornament, embellish; enhance, beautify, prettify, enrich, bedeck.

graceful adjective *she walked towards him, her movements swift and graceful:* **elegant**, smooth, flowing, fluid, fluent, clean; agile, supple, nimble, light-footed.

graceless adjective *a sullen, graceless teenager:* **gauche**, awkward, maladroit, clumsy, ungainly, ungraceful, inelegant, uncoordinated, gawky, gangling;

g

insensitive, tactless, thoughtless, inconsiderate; informal ham-fisted.

gracious adjective

1 *a gracious host:* **courteous**, polite, civil, chivalrous, well mannered; tactful, diplomatic; kind, considerate, thoughtful, obliging, accommodating, generous, indulgent, magnanimous, benevolent; friendly, amiable, cordial, hospitable.
2 *gracious colonial buildings:* **elegant**, stylish, tasteful, graceful; luxurious, sumptuous, opulent, grand, high-class; informal swanky, plush.
OPPOSITES: rude.

gradation noun

1 *a gradation of ability:* **range**, scale; series, progression, hierarchy, ladder, pecking order.
2 *each pay band has a number of gradations:* **level**, grade, rank, position, stage, standard, echelon, rung, step, notch; class, stratum, group, grouping, set.

grade noun

1 *hotels within the same grade:* **category**, set, class, classification, grouping, group, bracket.
2 *his job is of the lowest grade:* **rank**, level, echelon, standing, position, class, status, order; step, rung, stratum, tier.
3 *the best grades in the school:* **mark**, score; assessment, evaluation, appraisal.
4 (N. Amer.) *they're all in the fifth grade:* **year**, form, class.
▷verb
1 *eggs are graded by size:* **classify**, class, categorize, bracket, sort, group, arrange, pigeonhole; rank, evaluate, rate, value.
2 *the colours grade into one another:* **pass**, shade, merge, blend.
□ **make the grade** (informal) succeed, qualify, pass; measure up, come up to scratch, pass muster; informal cut it.

gradient noun

1 *a steep gradient:* **slope**, incline, hill, rise, ramp, bank; acclivity, declivity.
2 *the gradient of the line:* **steepness**, angle, slant, slope, inclination.

gradual adjective

1 *a gradual transition:* **slow**, steady, progressive, continuous, systematic; step-by-step, little-by-little, bit-by-bit, piecemeal; measured, unhurried, cautious.
2 *a gradual slope:* **gentle**, moderate, slight, easy.
OPPOSITES: abrupt, steep.

gradually adverb *you can begin to introduce new ideas gradually:* **slowly**, slowly but surely, little by little, bit by bit, by degrees, piecemeal, cautiously, gently, gingerly; steadily, progressively, systematically.

graduate verb

1 *he graduated last summer:* **qualify**, pass

your exams, get your degree, complete your studies.
2 *she wants to graduate to serious drama:* **progress**, advance, move up.
3 *a thermometer graduated in Fahrenheit:* **calibrate**, mark off, measure out, grade.

graft noun

1 *grafts may die from lack of water:* **scion**, cutting, shoot.
2 *a skin graft:* **transplant**, implant.
▷verb
1 *graft a bud on to the stem:* **affix**, join, insert, splice.
2 *tissue is grafted on to the cornea:* **transplant**, implant.
3 *plate glass windows had been grafted on to the eighteenth century building:* **attach**, add, join; incorporate, combine.

grain noun

1 *the local farmers grow grain:* **cereal**, cereal crops; Brit. corn.
2 *a grain of corn:* **kernel**, seed, grist.
3 *grains of sand:* **granule**, particle, speck; bit, piece, crumb, fragment, morsel.
4 *a grain of truth:* **trace**, hint, tinge, suggestion, shadow; bit, soupçon; scrap, shred, ounce, iota, jot, whit; informal smidgen, tad.
5 *the grain of the timber:* **texture**, surface, finish; weave, pattern.

grammatical adjective

1 *the grammatical structure of a sentence:* **syntactic**, morphological.
2 *a grammatical sentence:* **well formed**, correct, proper; acceptable.

grand adjective

1 *a grand hotel:* **magnificent**, imposing, impressive, splendid, resplendent, majestic, monumental; palatial, stately, large; luxurious, sumptuous, lavish, opulent; Brit. upmarket; informal fancy, posh, plush, classy, swanky; Brit. informal swish.
2 *a grand scheme:* **ambitious**, bold, epic, big, extravagant.
3 *a grand old lady:* **dignified**, stately, proud, august, distinguished; aristocratic, noble, regal, blue-blooded, high-born, patrician; informal upper-crust; Brit. informal posh.
4 *a grand total of £2,000:* **complete**, comprehensive, all-inclusive, inclusive; final.
5 *the grand staircase:* **main**, principal, central; biggest, largest.
6 (informal) *you're doing a grand job:* **excellent**, very good, marvellous, splendid, first-class, first-rate, wonderful, outstanding, fine; informal terrific, great, ace; Brit. informal brilliant.
OPPOSITES: humble.

grandeur noun *the grandeur of formal royal occasions:* **splendour**, magnificence, impressiveness, glory, resplendence, majesty; stateliness, pomp, ceremony.

grandiloquent adjective *their grandiloquent phrases failed to convince*

me: **pompous**, bombastic, extravagant, ostentatious, high-flown, orotund, florid, flowery; pretentious, overwrought, overblown, overdone; formal magniloquent.

grandiose adjective

1 *the court's grandiose facade:* **grand**, palatial, luxurious, opulent; showy, ostentatious, elaborate, ornate, flamboyant; informal swanky, flash.
2 *his grandiose plans to transform the nation:* **ambitious**, grand, bold, overambitious, extravagant, inflated.
OPPOSITES: humble, modest.

grant verb

1 *he granted them leave of absence | she granted my request:* **allow**, permit, accord, vouchsafe; consent to, agree to, accede to.
2 *he granted them £20,000:* **give**, award, bestow on, confer on, present with, provide with, endow with, supply with.
3 *I grant that the difference is not absolute:* **admit**, accept, concede, allow, appreciate, acknowledge, confess; recognize, agree.
OPPOSITES: refuse, deny.
▷**noun** *a grant from the council:* **award**, allowance, subsidy, subvention, endowment, contribution, donation, handout, allocation, gift; scholarship; Brit. bursary.

granular adjective *plant food in a new granular form:* **powdered**, powder, powdery, grainy, granulated; gritty.

granule noun *minute granules of gold:* **grain**, particle, fragment, bit, crumb, speck.

graph noun **chart**, table, diagram; histogram, bar chart, pie chart.

graphic adjective

1 *his mature graphic work:* **visual**, pictorial, illustrative, diagrammatic.
2 *a graphic account:* **vivid**, detailed, explicit, expressive; colourful, striking, dramatic, powerful, effective; lurid, shocking.
OPPOSITES: vague.
▷**noun** *this printer's good enough for graphics:* **picture**, illustration, image; diagram, graph, chart.

grapple verb

1 *police officers grappled with him:* **wrestle**, struggle, tussle; brawl, fight, scuffle, battle.
2 *he grappled the young man around the throat:* **seize**, grab, catch hold of, take hold of, grasp.
3 *the museum's IT consultants are grappling with the problem:* **tackle**, confront, face, deal with, cope with, get to grips with; apply yourself to, devote yourself to.

grasp verb

1 *she grasped his hands:* **grip**, clutch, clasp, hold, clench; seize, grab, catch, snatch, latch on to.

2 *everybody grasped the important points:* **understand**, comprehend, follow, take in, see, perceive, assimilate, absorb; formal apprehend; informal get, get your head around, take on board.
3 *many companies grasped the opportunity to expand:* **take advantage of**, act on; seize, leap at, snatch, jump at, pounce on.
OPPOSITES: release.
▷**noun**
1 *the paper slipped from his grasp:* **grip**, hold, clasp.
2 *he broke free from his domineering mother's grasp:* **control**, power, clutches, command, domination, rule, tyranny.
3 *success lay within their grasp:* **reach**, scope, power, limits, range; sights.
4 *your grasp of history leaves a lot to be desired:* **understanding**, comprehension, perception, apprehension, awareness, grip, knowledge; mastery, command.

grasping adjective *a grasping corporate executive:* **avaricious**, greedy, rapacious, mercenary, materialistic, acquisitive; informal money-grubbing.

grass noun *he sat down on the grass:* **turf**, sod; lawn, green.

grate verb

1 *grate the cheese into the pasta sauce:* **shred**, grind, crumble.
2 *there was a sound of metal grating against metal:* **grind**, rub, rasp, scrape, jar, creak.
3 *the tune grates slightly:* **irritate someone**, set someone's teeth on edge, jar, be irritating/annoying/irksome; informal aggravate someone, get on someone's nerves.

grateful adjective *I was most grateful for your hospitality:* **thankful**, appreciative; indebted, obliged, obligated, in someone's debt, beholden.

gratification noun *ours is the civilization of instant gratification:* **satisfaction**, fulfilment, indulgence, relief; pleasure, enjoyment.

gratify verb

1 *it gratified him to be seen with her:* **please**, gladden, make happy, delight, make someone feel good, satisfy; informal give someone a kick.
2 *in reality, they are acting to gratify their own desires:* **satisfy**, fulfil, indulge, comply with, pander to, cater to, give in to, feed, accommodate.
OPPOSITES: displease, frustrate.

grating¹ adjective

1 *he pushed his chair away from the table with a grating noise:* **harsh**, jarring, rasping, scraping, scratching, grinding.
2 *his continual praise of 'the good old days' can be grating:* **irritating**, annoying, infuriating, irksome, maddening, tiresome; jarring, discordant; informal aggravating.

g

grating[2] noun *a strong iron grating:* grille, grate, mesh, grid, lattice.

gratis adverb *most places have endless coffee available gratis:* free, free of charge, without charge, for nothing, at no cost; informal on the house, for free.

gratitude noun *she expressed her gratitude for their support:* gratefulness, thankfulness, thanks, appreciation, indebtedness; recognition, acknowledgement, credit.

gratuitous adjective *an act of gratuitous violence:* unjustified, uncalled for, unwarranted, unprovoked, undue; indefensible, unjustifiable; needless, unnecessary, unmerited, groundless, senseless, wanton, indiscriminate; excessive, immoderate, inordinate, inappropriate.
OPPOSITES: necessary.

gratuity noun (formal) *gratuities are at the discretion of customers:* tip, gift, present, donation; (in India and some eastern countries) baksheesh.

grave[1] noun *she left flowers at his grave:* burial place, last resting place; tomb, sepulchre, vault, mausoleum, crypt.

grave[2] adjective
1 *this decision may have grave consequences | the country faces a grave economic crisis:* serious, important, profound, significant; critical, severe, acute, urgent, pressing; alarming, terrible, awful, dreadful, dire.
2 *he looked grave:* solemn, serious, sober, unsmiling, sombre; grim, severe, stern, dour.
OPPOSITES: trivial, cheerful.

gravel noun shingle, grit, pebbles, stones.

gravelly adjective
1 *a gravelly beach:* shingly, pebbly, stony, gritty.
2 *his gravelly voice:* husky, gruff, throaty, deep, croaky, rasping, harsh, rough.

gravestone noun headstone, tombstone, stone, monument, memorial.

graveyard noun cemetery, churchyard, burial ground, necropolis.

gravitas noun *a man of gravitas:* dignity, seriousness, solemnity, gravity.

gravitate verb *young people naturally gravitate to the big cities:* move, head, drift, be drawn, be attracted.

gravity noun
1 *the gravity of the situation:* seriousness, importance, significance, consequence, magnitude; severity, acuteness, urgency.
2 *the gravity of his demeanour:* solemnity, seriousness, sombreness, soberness; severity, grimness, sternness, dourness.

graze verb
1 *he grazed his knuckles on the box:* scrape, abrade, skin, scratch, chafe, bark, scuff, rasp; cut, nick.
2 *his shot grazed the far post:* touch, brush, shave, skim, kiss, scrape, clip, glance off.
▷noun *grazes on the skin:* scratch, scrape, abrasion, cut.

grease noun
1 *axle grease:* oil, lubricant, lubricator, lubrication.
2 *the cooker was covered with grease:* fat, oil, cooking oil; lard, suet.
▷verb *first grease the baking dish:* lubricate, oil, smear with oil.

greasy adjective
1 *greasy food:* fatty, oily, buttery, oleaginous.
2 *the pitch was very greasy:* slippery, slick, slimy; informal slippy.
3 *a greasy little man:* ingratiating, obsequious, sycophantic, fawning, unctuous, oily; informal slimy; Brit. informal smarmy.

great adjective
1 *they showed great interest | he was a man of great courage:* considerable, substantial, significant, exceptional, extraordinary, extreme.
2 *a great expanse of water:* large, big, extensive, expansive, broad, wide, sizeable; vast, immense, huge, enormous, massive, colossal.
3 *great writers | one of the greatest scientists of the 20th century:* prominent, eminent, important, distinguished, illustrious, celebrated, honoured, acclaimed, admired, esteemed, revered, renowned, notable, famous, famed, well known; leading, top, major, principal, matchless, peerless.
4 *the great nations of the world:* powerful, dominant, influential, strong, potent, formidable, redoubtable; leading, important, foremost, major, chief, principal.
5 *most discount airlines are smaller and this gives them a great advantage:* big, important, significant, crucial, critical, vital.
6 *the great castle of Montellana-Coronil:* magnificent, imposing, impressive, awe-inspiring, grand, splendid, majestic, sumptuous.
7 (informal) *she's a great cook:* expert, skilful, skilled, adept, accomplished, talented, fine, masterly, master, brilliant, virtuoso, marvellous, outstanding, first class, superb; informal crack, ace.
8 (informal) *we had a great time:* enjoyable, delightful, lovely, pleasant; entertaining, exciting, thrilling; excellent, marvellous, wonderful, fine, splendid, very good; informal terrific, fantastic, fabulous, cool; Brit. informal brilliant.
OPPOSITES: small, minor, poor.

greatly adverb *a frantic training programme greatly increases the risk of injury | she was greatly admired:* very

much, considerably, substantially, appreciably, significantly, markedly, sizeably, seriously, materially, profoundly; enormously, vastly, immensely, tremendously, extremely.
OPPOSITES: slightly.

greatness noun
1 *a woman destined for greatness:* eminence, distinction, illustriousness, repute, high standing; celebrity, fame, prominence, renown.
2 *his greatness as a writer:* brilliance, genius, prowess, talent, expertise, mastery, artistry, virtuosity, skill, proficiency; flair, finesse; calibre, distinction.

greed noun
1 *they are motivated only by greed:* avarice, cupidity, acquisitiveness, covetousness, rapacity; materialism.
2 *their greed for power:* desire, appetite, hunger, thirst, craving, longing, yearning, hankering, eagerness.
3 *her mouth began to water with unashamed greed:* gluttony, voracity, self-indulgence.

greedy adjective
1 *I made two bowls because I know how greedy you are:* gluttonous, ravenous, voracious, insatiable; informal piggish.
2 *greedy property developers, whose prime motive is profit:* avaricious, acquisitive, covetous, grasping, materialistic, mercenary; informal money-grubbing.
3 *he was greedy for success:* eager, avid, hungry, longing, yearning, hankering; impatient, anxious; informal dying.

green adjective
1 *a green scarf:* emerald green, bottle green, lime green, olive green, pea green, Lincoln green, sea green, eau de Nil.
2 *the green slopes of the Wye valley:* verdant, grassy, leafy.
3 *he promotes Green issues:* environmental, ecological, conservation, eco-.
4 *a green alternative to diesel:* environmentally friendly, non-polluting; carbon-neutral.
5 *green recruits, fresh from college:* inexperienced, new, raw, unseasoned, untried, untrained; naive, innocent, ingenuous, credulous, gullible, callow, immature; informal wet behind the ears.
▷noun
1 *a canopy of green over the road:* foliage, greenery, plants, leaves, leafage, vegetation.
2 *a village green:* lawn, common, grassy area; literary sward.

greenery noun *the hotel is surrounded by lush greenery:* foliage, vegetation, plants, leaves, leafage, undergrowth, plant life; technical flora; literary verdure.

greenhouse noun hothouse, glasshouse, conservatory.

greet verb
1 *she greeted Hank cheerily:* say hello to, address, salute, hail, acknowledge; welcome, meet, receive.
2 *members greeted the decision with dismay:* receive, respond to, react to, take.

greeting noun
1 *he shouted a greeting:* hello, salute, salutation, address; welcome; acknowledgement.
2 *birthday greetings:* best wishes, good wishes, congratulations; compliments, regards, respects; formal felicitations.
OPPOSITES: farewell.

gregarious adjective *he was fun-loving and gregarious:* sociable, companionable, outgoing, friendly, affable, amiable, genial, warm, convivial, clubbable.
OPPOSITES: unsociable.

grey adjective
1 *a grey suit:* slate grey, charcoal grey, iron grey, steel grey.
2 *grey hair:* white, silver, silvery; grizzled, hoary.
3 *a cold grey November day:* cloudy, overcast, dull, sunless, gloomy, dreary, dismal, sombre, bleak, murky.
4 *her face looked grey:* ashen, wan, pale, pallid, colourless, bloodless, white, waxen; sickly, pasty, drained, drawn, deathly; Brit. peaky.
5 *life seemed grey and quiet:* characterless, colourless, nondescript, unremarkable, dull, uninteresting, boring, tedious, monotonous.
6 *a grey area:* ambiguous, doubtful, unclear, uncertain, indefinite, open to question, debatable.
7 *the grey economy:* unofficial, informal, irregular, back-door.

grid noun
1 *a metal grid:* grating, grille, mesh, lattice.
2 *the grid of streets:* network, matrix, reticulation.

grief noun
1 *she was overcome with grief:* sorrow, misery, sadness, anguish, pain, heartache, heartbreak, agony, torment, suffering, woe, desolation, dejection, despair; mourning.
2 (informal) *the police gave me loads of grief:* trouble, annoyance, bother, irritation, vexation, harassment; informal aggravation, hassle.
OPPOSITES: joy.
□ **come to grief**
the whole project came to grief: fail, meet with disaster, miscarry, go wrong, go awry, fall through, fall flat, founder, come to nothing; informal come unstuck; Brit. informal go pear-shaped.

grief-stricken adjective *his grief-stricken widow:* heartbroken, broken-hearted, inconsolable, beside yourself with

g

grief, sorrowful, sorrowing, miserable, sad, anguished, desolate, devastated, despairing, tormented, suffering, wretched; mourning, grieving.

grievance noun *the website enabled staff to air their grievances:* complaint, criticism, objection, grumble; grudge, ill feeling, bad feeling, resentment, bitterness; informal gripe, moan, bone to pick.

grieve verb
1 *she grieved for her father:* mourn, lament, sorrow; cry, weep, shed tears, sob, keen, weep and wail.
2 *it grieved me to leave her:* sadden, upset, distress, pain, hurt, wound, break someone's heart, make someone's heart bleed.

grievous adjective (formal) *his death was a grievous blow:* serious, severe, grave, bad, dreadful, terrible, awful, crushing, calamitous; painful, agonizing, traumatic; sharp, acute.

grim adjective
1 *his expression was grim:* serious, unsmiling, stern, severe, forbidding, dour, harsh, stony; morose, gloomy, sombre.
2 *the asylum holds some grim secrets:* dreadful, ghastly, horrible, horrendous, terrible, awful, appalling, frightful, shocking, unspeakable, grisly, gruesome, hideous, macabre; depressing, distressing, upsetting, worrying, unpleasant.
3 *grim humour:* black, dark, mirthless, bleak, cynical.
4 *a grim little hovel:* bleak, dreary, dismal, dingy, wretched, miserable, depressing, cheerless, comfortless, joyless, gloomy, uninviting.
OPPOSITES: cheerful, pleasant.

grimace verb *Nina grimaced at him:* scowl, frown, glower, lour; pull a face.

grime noun *her skirt was smeared with grime:* dirt, filth, muck, mud, soot, dust.

grimy adjective *his shirt and trousers were grimy:* dirty, filthy, grubby, mucky, soiled, stained, smeared, muddy, smutty, sooty, dusty; Brit. informal manky.
OPPOSITES: clean.

grin verb *he grinned at her:* smile, smile broadly, beam, smile from ear to ear, grin like a Cheshire cat; smirk; informal be all smiles.
▷noun *a silly grin:* smile, broad smile; smirk.
OPPOSITES: frown, scowl.

grind verb
1 *the sandstone is ground into powder:* crush, pound, pulverize, mill, granulate, crumble, smash, press.
2 *the sound of a knife being ground on a wheel:* sharpen, whet, hone, file, strop; smooth, polish, sand.
3 *one tectonic plate grinds against another:* rub, grate, scrape, rasp.

▷noun *the daily grind:* drudgery, toil, hard work, labour, exertion, chores; informal slog, sweat; Brit. informal donkey work, fag.
□grind someone down
oppress, crush, persecute, tyrannize, ill-treat, maltreat.

grip verb
1 *she gripped the edge of the table:* grasp, clutch, hold, clasp, take hold of, clench, grab, seize, cling to; squeeze, press.
2 *we were gripped by the drama:* engross, enthral, absorb, rivet, fascinate, hold spellbound, mesmerize, bewitch, enrapture; interest.
OPPOSITES: release.
▷noun
1 *a tight grip:* grasp, hold.
2 *the wheels lost their grip on the road:* traction, purchase, friction, adhesion, resistance.
3 *he was in the grip of an obsession:* control, power, hold, stranglehold, clutches, command, mastery, influence.
4 *I had a pretty good grip on the situation:* understanding, comprehension, grasp, perception, awareness, apprehension, conception.
□come/get to grips with
the committee is trying to get to grips with this issue: deal with, cope with, handle, tackle, undertake, take on, grapple with, face, face up to, confront, grasp the nettle of.

gripping adjective *a gripping thriller:* enthralling, absorbing, riveting, captivating, fascinating, engrossing, compulsive, compelling, mesmerizing, spellbinding; thrilling, exciting, action-packed, dramatic, stimulating; informal unputdownable, page-turning.
OPPOSITES: boring.

grisly adjective *the town was shaken by a series of grisly crimes:* gruesome, ghastly, horrifying, hideous, macabre, horrible, horrendous, grim, awful, dreadful, terrible, horrific, shocking, appalling, abominable, monstrous, unspeakable, disgusting, sickening, repulsive, repugnant, revolting, repellent; brutal, violent, gory, bloody.

gristly adjective *a gristly piece of meat:* stringy, sinewy, fibrous; tough, leathery, chewy.

grit noun
1 *the grit from the paths:* gravel, pebbles, stones, shingle, sand; dust, dirt.
2 *the true grit of a seasoned campaigner:* courage, bravery, backbone, spirit, strength of character, strength of will, moral fibre, steel, nerve, resolve, resolution, determination, tenacity, perseverance, endurance, fortitude, toughness.
▷verb *Gina gritted her teeth:* clench, clamp together, shut tightly; grind, gnash.

gritty adjective
1 *it was a typically gritty performance by the British player:* courageous, brave, plucky, valiant, bold, spirited, intrepid, tough, determined, resolute, purposeful, dogged, tenacious; informal gutsy, spunky.*a gritty floor:* sandy, gravelly, pebbly, stony; powdery, dusty.
2 *a gritty look at urban life today:* uncompromising, hard-hitting, pulling no punches, unsparing, forthright, realistic, honest.

grizzled adjective *he tugged at his grizzled beard:* grey, greying, silver, silvery, snowy, white; grey-haired, hoary.

groan verb *she groaned and rubbed her stomach:* moan, whimper, cry, call out.
▷noun
1 *a groan of anguish:* moan, cry, whimper.
2 *despite moans and groans, they obeyed the orders:* complaint, grumble, grouse, objection, protest.

groggy adjective *she is still feeling groggy from the anaesthetic:* dazed, muzzy, befuddled, fuddled, disoriented, disorientated, dizzy, shaky, unsteady, wobbly, weak, faint; informal dopey, woozy, not with it.

groom verb
1 *his dark hair was carefully groomed:* brush, comb, arrange, do, tidy.
2 *they were groomed for stardom:* prepare, prime, ready; coach, train, drill, teach, school.

groove noun *water had worn a groove in the surface of the rock:* furrow, channel, trench, trough, hollow, rut, indentation, cut, fissure.

grooved adjective furrowed, fluted, corrugated, ribbed, ridged.

grope verb
1 *she groped for her glasses:* fumble, scrabble, rummage, feel, search, hunt, fish.
2 (informal) *one of the men started groping her:* fondle, touch; informal paw, feel up, touch up.

gross adjective
1 *a gross distortion of the truth:* flagrant, blatant, glaring, obvious, overt, naked, barefaced, shameless, brazen, undisguised, unconcealed, patent, transparent, manifest, palpable; out and out, utter, complete.
2 *their gross income:* total, whole, entire, complete, full, overall; before deductions, before tax.
3 (informal) *the place smelled gross:* disgusting, revolting, repellent, repulsive, vile, horrible, dreadful, awful, terrible, foul, nasty, sickening, nauseating.
4 *he rubbed his gross stomach:* fat, flabby, fleshy, corpulent, obese, portly, bloated; informal porky, pudgy, tubby.

▷verb *he grosses over a million dollars a month:* earn, make, bring in, take, get, receive; informal rake in.

grotesque adjective
1 *a grotesque creature:* misshapen, deformed, malformed, distorted, twisted, gnarled; ugly, unsightly, monstrous, hideous, freakish, unnatural, abnormal, strange, odd, peculiar.
2 *grotesque mismanagement of funds:* outrageous, monstrous, shocking, appalling, preposterous, unacceptable; ridiculous, ludicrous, farcical, unbelievable, incredible.
OPPOSITES: normal.

grouchy adjective *a grouchy old man:* grumpy, cross, irritable, bad-tempered, crotchety, crabby, cantankerous, curmudgeonly, testy, tetchy, waspish, prickly; informal snappy; Brit. informal ratty, like a bear with a sore head.

ground noun
1 *the ground was wet and covered with leaves:* earth, soil, turf; land, terrain.
2 *the team's home ground:* stadium, pitch, field, arena, track; Brit. informal park.
3 *he built a huge swimming pool in the grounds of his mansion:* estate, gardens, park, parkland, land, acres, property.
4 *he has good grounds for his complaint:* reason, basis, base, foundation, justification, rationale.
5 *coffee grounds:* sediment, dregs, lees, settlings, deposit, residue.
▷verb
1 *an assertion grounded on results of several studies:* base, found, establish, root, build, construct, form.
2 *they were grounded in classics and history:* instruct, coach, teach, tutor, educate, school, train, drill, prime, prepare; familiarize with, acquaint with.

groundless adjective *she dismissed their fears as groundless:* unfounded, without basis, without foundation, ill-founded, baseless, unsupported, uncorroborated, unproven, unsubstantiated, unwarranted, unjustified, unjustifiable, without cause, without reason, without justification, unreasonable, irrational, illogical, misguided.

groundwork noun *I had to do the groundwork for a revolutionary new project:* preliminary work, preliminaries, preparations, spadework, homework; planning, arrangements, organization; basics, essentials, fundamentals, underpinning, foundation.

group noun
1 *the exhibits were divided into three distinct groups:* category, class, classification, grouping, set, lot, batch, bracket, type, sort, kind, variety, family; grade, grading, rank, status.
2 *a group of tourists:* crowd, party, body,

band, company, gathering, congregation, assembly, collection, cluster, flock, pack, troop, gang; informal bunch.
3 *a coup attempt by a group within the parliament:* faction, division, section, clique, coterie, circle, set, ring, camp, bloc, caucus, cabal, fringe movement, splinter group.
4 *the women's group:* association, club, society, league, guild, circle, union.
5 *a small group of trees:* cluster, knot, collection, mass, clump.
6 *a local folk group:* band, ensemble, act; informal line-up, combo, outfit.
▷**verb**
1 *patients were grouped according to their symptoms:* categorize, classify, class, catalogue, sort, bracket, grade, rate, rank.
2 *wooden chairs were grouped round the table:* place, arrange, assemble, organize, range, line up, dispose.
3 *the two parties grouped together:* unite, join together/up, team up, join forces, get together, ally, form an alliance, affiliate, combine; collaborate, work together, pull together, cooperate.

grouse verb *she groused about the food:* grumble, complain, moan, carp, protest, make a fuss; informal bellyache, gripe, beef, grouch, whinge, sound off.
▷**noun** *our biggest grouse was about the noise:* grumble, complaint, grievance, objection; informal moan, beef, gripe, grouch.

grove noun *a villa sited in an olive grove:* copse, wood, thicket; orchard, plantation; Brit. spinney.

grovel verb
1 *George grovelled at his feet:* prostrate yourself, lie, kneel, cringe.
2 *she was not going to grovel to him:* be obsequious, kowtow, bow and scrape, toady, abase yourself, humble yourself; fawn on, flatter, make up to, play up to, ingratiate yourself with, curry favour with; Brit. dance attendance on; literary truckle; informal crawl, suck up to.

grow verb
1 *the boys had grown:* get bigger, get taller, increase in size, fill out.
2 *her debts continued to grow:* increase, swell, multiply, proliferate, snowball, mushroom, balloon, build up, mount up, pile up; rise, soar, escalate, shoot up; informal skyrocket.
3 *the family business grew:* expand, extend, develop, progress, make progress; flourish, thrive, burgeon, prosper, succeed, boom.
4 *flowers grew among the rocks:* sprout, germinate, shoot up, spring up, develop, bud, bloom, flourish, thrive, run riot.
5 *she grew vegetables:* cultivate, produce, propagate, raise, rear, nurture, tend; farm.
6 *the fable grew from an ancient Indian source:* originate, stem, spring, arise, emerge, issue; develop, evolve.

7 *Leonora grew bored:* become, get, turn, begin to feel.
OPPOSITES: shrink, decline.

growl verb *the dog growled at him:* snarl, bark, yap, bay.

grown-up adjective *she has two grown-up daughters:* adult, mature, of age; fully grown, full-grown, fully developed.

growth noun
1 *population growth | the growth in consumer credit:* increase, expansion, proliferation, multiplication, enlargement, mushrooming, snowballing, rise, escalation, build-up.
2 *the marked growth of local enterprises:* expansion, extension, development, progress, advance, advancement, headway, spread, buildout; rise, success, boom, upturn, upswing.
3 *the growth of plants:* development, maturation, growing, germination, sprouting; blooming.
4 *a growth on his jaw:* tumour, lump, malignancy, cancer; cyst, nodule, polyp; excrescence, outgrowth, swelling.
OPPOSITES: decrease, decline.

grub noun *a small black grub:* larva; maggot; caterpillar.
▷**verb**
1 *kids grubbed around in the dirt:* dig, poke, scratch.
2 *they grubbed up the old trees:* dig up, unearth, uproot, root up/out, pull up/out, tear out.
3 *he began grubbing about in the waste-paper basket:* rummage, search, hunt, delve, dig, scrabble, ferret, root, rifle, fish, poke; Brit. informal rootle.

grubby adjective *he pulled out a grubby handkerchief:* dirty, grimy, filthy, mucky, unwashed, stained, soiled, smeared, spotted, muddy, dusty, sooty; unhygienic, insanitary; Brit. informal manky.
OPPOSITES: clean.

grudge noun *a former employee with a grudge:* grievance; resentment, bitterness, disgruntlement, bad feelings, hard feelings, ill feelings, ill will, rancour, animosity, antipathy, antagonism, enmity, animus; informal a chip on your shoulder.
▷**verb**
1 *he grudged the time that the meetings involved:* begrudge, resent, feel aggrieved about, be resentful of, mind, object to, take exception to.
2 *I don't grudge you your success:* envy, begrudge, resent, be jealous of, be envious of, be resentful of.

grudging adjective *she offered a grudging apology:* reluctant, unwilling, forced, half-hearted, unenthusiastic, hesitant; begrudging, resentful.
OPPOSITES: eager.

gruelling adjective *he undertook a gruelling ten-mile run:* exhausting, extremely tiring, arduous, strenuous, back-breaking, punishing, laborious, taxing, debilitating; demanding, exacting, difficult, hard, harsh, severe, stiff; informal killing.

gruesome adjective *the gruesome evidence of a recent massacre:* grisly, ghastly, horrific, shocking, horrifying, hideous, horrible, horrendous, grim, awful, dreadful, terrible, appalling, disgusting, repulsive, repugnant, revolting, repellent, sickening; loathsome, abhorrent, odious, monstrous, unspeakable; gory, bloody.

gruff adjective
1 *a gruff reply:* abrupt, brusque, curt, short, blunt, no-nonsense; laconic, taciturn; grumpy, crotchety, crabby, cross, bad-tempered, short-tempered, crusty, tetchy, ungracious, unceremonious; informal grouchy.
2 *a gruff voice:* rough, guttural, throaty, gravelly, husky, croaking, rasping, raspy, hoarse, harsh; low, thick.
OPPOSITES: friendly, soft.

grumble verb *they grumbled about the disruption:* complain, moan, grouse, whine, mutter, bleat, carp, cavil, protest, make a fuss; informal bellyache, beef, grouch, whinge, sound off, gripe.
▷ noun *his customers' grumbles:* complaint, grouse, grievance, protest, cavil, quibble, criticism; informal grouch, moan, beef, gripe.

grumpy adjective *the bus was full and the driver grumpy:* bad-tempered, short-tempered, crabby, crotchety, tetchy, testy, waspish, prickly, touchy, irritable, irascible, crusty, cantankerous, curmudgeonly, surly, peevish, cross, fractious, disagreeable, pettish; informal grouchy, snappy; Brit. informal shirty, stroppy, ratty, like a bear with a sore head.
OPPOSITES: good-humoured.

guarantee noun
1 *all repairs have a one-year guarantee:* warranty.
2 *you have my guarantee that we will spare no effort to ensure their safety:* promise, assurance, word, word of honour, commitment, undertaking, pledge, vow, oath, bond, covenant.
3 *banks usually demand a personal guarantee for loans:* collateral, security, surety.
▷ verb
1 *we cannot guarantee that there will be no redundancies:* promise, give your word, give an assurance, give an undertaking, swear, swear to the fact, pledge, vow, take an oath.
2 *ring early to guarantee a place:* secure, be/make sure of, ensure.
3 *he agreed to guarantee the loan:* underwrite, put up collateral for.

guard verb
1 *infantry guarded the barricaded bridge:* protect, stand guard over, watch over, keep an eye on; cover, patrol, police, defend, shield, safeguard, keep safe, secure.
2 *the prisoners were guarded by armed men:* keep under surveillance, keep under guard, keep watch over, mind.
3 *forest wardens must guard against poachers:* beware of, keep watch for, be alert to, keep an eye out for, be on the alert/lookout for.
▷ noun
1 *border guards:* sentry, sentinel, security guard, nightwatchman; protector, defender, guardian; lookout, watch; garrison.
2 *her prison guard:* warder, warden, keeper; jailer.
3 *he let his guard slip and they escaped:* vigilance, vigil, watch, surveillance, watchfulness, caution, heed, attention, care, wariness.
4 *a metal guard keeps fingers out of the mechanism:* safety guard, safety device, protective device, shield, screen, fender; bumper, buffer.
□ off guard
unprepared, unsuspecting, with your defences down, unwary, unready; informal asleep at the wheel.
□ on your guard
vigilant, on the lookout, alert, on the alert, wary, watchful, cautious, careful, heedful, chary, circumspect, on your toes, prepared, ready, wide awake, attentive, observant, keeping your eyes peeled; informal keeping a weather eye out.

guarded adjective *he has given a guarded welcome to the idea:* cautious, careful, circumspect, wary, chary, on your guard; reluctant, unenthusiastic, restrained, reserved; informal cagey.

guardian noun *an indefatigable guardian of public morality:* protector, defender, preserver, custodian, warden, guard, keeper; curator, caretaker, steward, trustee.

> WORD LINKS
> **tutelary** acting as or relating to a guardian

guerrilla noun *there was fierce fighting between guerrillas and government troops:* freedom fighter, irregular, member of the resistance, partisan; rebel, radical, revolutionary.

guess verb
1 *he guessed she was about 40:* estimate, hazard a guess, reckon, gauge, judge, calculate; hypothesize, postulate, predict, speculate, conjecture, surmise; informal guesstimate.
2 (informal) *I guess I owe you an apology:* suppose, think, imagine, expect, suspect, dare say; informal reckon, figure.
▷ noun *my guess was right:* hypothesis,

theory, prediction, postulation, conjecture, surmise, estimate, belief, opinion, reckoning, judgement, supposition, speculation, suspicion, impression, feeling; informal guesstimate.

guesswork noun *their estimates were based largely on guesswork:* guessing, conjecture, surmise, supposition, assumptions, speculation, hypothesizing, theorizing, prediction; approximations, rough calculations; informal guesstimates.

guest noun
1 *I have two guests coming to dinner:* visitor, caller; company.
2 *hotel guests have free use of the swimming pool:* resident, patron, client; boarder, lodger.
OPPOSITES: host.

guffaw verb *he guffawed at his own punchline:* roar with laughter, laugh heartily/loudly, roar, bellow, cackle.

guidance noun
1 *she looked to her father for guidance:* advice, counsel, direction, instruction, enlightenment, information; recommendations, suggestions, tips, hints, pointers, guidelines.
2 *work continued under the guidance of a project supervisor:* direction, supervision, control, leadership, management, charge.

guide noun
1 *our guide took us back to the hotel:* escort, courier, attendant; usher; chaperone.
2 *he is my inspiration and my guide:* adviser, mentor, counsellor; guru.
3 *the light acted as a guide for shipping:* marker, indicator, pointer, signpost, mark, landmark; guiding light, sign, signal, beacon.
4 *the literature of the time is a guide to popular values and opinions:* pointer, indication, measure, yardstick, gauge, benchmark; model, pattern, template, example.
5 *a pocket guide of Paris:* guidebook, travelogue, vade mecum; companion, handbook, directory, A to Z.
▷**verb**
1 *he guided her to her seat:* lead, lead the way, conduct, show, show someone the way, usher, shepherd, direct, steer, pilot, escort, accompany, attend; see, take, help, assist.
2 *the chairman must guide the meeting:* direct, steer, control, manage, command, lead, conduct, run, be in charge of, have control of, govern, preside over, superintend, supervise, oversee; handle, regulate.
3 *he was always there to guide me:* advise, counsel, give advice to, direct, give direction to.

guidebook noun *they followed the tour in the museum guidebook:* guide, travel guide, travelogue, vade mecum; companion, handbook, directory.

guideline noun *the planning authorities have fairly strict guidelines:* recommendation, direction, suggestion, advice; regulation, rule, principle, guiding principle; standard, criterion, measure, gauge, yardstick; procedure, parameter.

guild noun *a member of the Women's Cooperative Guild:* association, society, union, league, organization, company, cooperative, fellowship, club, order.

guile noun *he maintained his position by a mixture of force and guile:* cunning, craftiness, craft, artfulness, art, wiliness, slyness, deviousness; wiles, ploys, schemes, stratagems, manoeuvres, subterfuges, tricks, ruses.

guileless adjective *Paul's questioning had the guileless innocence of a child:* artless, ingenuous, naive, open, genuine, natural, simple, childlike, innocent, unsophisticated, unworldly, unsuspicious, trustful, trusting; honest, truthful, sincere, straightforward.
OPPOSITES: scheming.

guilt noun
1 *the proof of his guilt:* culpability, guiltiness; wrongdoing, wrong, criminality, misconduct, sin.
2 *a terrible feeling of guilt:* self-reproach, self-condemnation, shame, a guilty conscience, pangs of conscience; remorse, remorsefulness, regret, contrition, compunction.
OPPOSITES: innocence.

guiltless adjective *I am entirely guiltless in this matter:* innocent, blameless, not to blame, without fault, above reproach, above suspicion, in the clear, unimpeachable, irreproachable, faultless; informal squeaky clean, whiter than white.

guilty adjective
1 *the guilty party must make restitution:* culpable, to blame, at fault, in the wrong, blameworthy, responsible; erring, errant, offending.
2 *I still feel guilty about the way I treated him:* ashamed, guilt-ridden, conscience-stricken, remorseful, sorry, contrite, repentant, penitent, regretful, rueful, abashed, shamefaced, sheepish, hangdog; in sackcloth and ashes.
OPPOSITES: innocent, unrepentant.

guise noun
1 *the god appeared in the guise of a swan:* likeness, outward appearance, appearance, semblance, form, shape, image; disguise.
2 *additional sums paid under the guise of consultancy fees:* pretence, disguise, front, facade, cover, blind, screen, smokescreen.

gulf noun
1 *our ship sailed into the gulf:* inlet, bay, creek, fjord, estuary, sound, arm of the sea; Scottish firth.
2 *the ice gave way and the gulf widened*

slowly: hole, cavity, fissure, crevasse, cleft, split, rift, chasm, abyss, void; ravine, gorge, canyon, gully.
3 *a growing gulf between rich and poor:* divide, division, separation, gap, breach, rift, split, chasm, abyss; difference, contrast, polarity.

gull verb *he had been gulled into believing that the documents were authentic:* hoodwink, trick, fool, dupe, deceive, delude, hoax; swindle, cheat, double-cross; informal con, bamboozle, pull a fast one on, put one over on.

gullible adjective *the swindler preyed on gullible old women:* credulous, naive, over-trusting, over-trustful, easily deceived, easily taken in, impressionable, suggestible, unsuspecting, unsuspicious, unwary, ingenuous, innocent, inexperienced, unworldly; informal born yesterday.
OPPOSITES: suspicious.

gully noun
1 *a steep icy gully:* ravine, canyon, gorge, pass, defile.
2 *water runs from the drainpipe into a gully:* channel, drain, conduit, gutter, trench, ditch, culvert.

gulp verb
1 *she gulped her juice:* swallow, quaff, swill down, down; informal swig, knock back.
2 *he gulped down the rest of his meal:* gobble, guzzle, devour, bolt, wolf, cram; informal demolish, scoff, polish off, shovel down.
3 *Jenny gulped back her tears:* choke back, fight back, hold back/in, suppress, stifle, smother.
OPPOSITES: sip.
▷ **noun** *a gulp of cold beer:* mouthful, swallow, draught; informal swig.

gum noun *photographs stuck down with gum:* glue, adhesive, fixative, paste, epoxy resin.
▷ **verb** *the receipts were gummed into a book:* stick, glue, paste; fix, affix, attach, fasten.
▢ **gum something up**
open and close the valves to make sure they don't get gummed up: clog, clog up, choke up, stop up, plug; obstruct; informal bung up

gumption noun (informal) *a journalist with the gumption to ask the right questions and demand proper answers:* initiative, resourcefulness, enterprise, determination, courage, backbone, nerve, spirit, pluck; astuteness, shrewdness, acumen, sense, common sense, wit; informal get-up-and-go, nous, savvy.

gun noun firearm, pistol, revolver, rifle, shotgun, automatic, handgun, machine gun; weapon.

gunfire noun *they heard the distant sounds of gunfire:* gunshots, shots, shooting,

firing, sniping; artillery fire, strafing, shelling.

gunman noun *gunmen broke into the bank through the roof:* armed robber, gangster; sniper, gunfighter; assassin, murderer, killer; informal hit man, hired gun.

gurgle verb *the water swirled and gurgled:* babble, burble, tinkle, bubble, ripple, murmur, splash; literary purl.
▷ **noun** *the gurgle of a small brook:* babbling, tinkling, bubbling, rippling, murmur, murmuring, splashing; literary purling.

guru noun
1 *a Hindu guru and mystic:* spiritual teacher, teacher, sage, mentor, spiritual leader, leader, master; Hinduism swami, Maharishi.
2 *a management guru:* expert, authority, pundit, leading light, master, specialist.

gush verb
1 *water gushed through the weir:* surge, stream, pour, rush, spill, well out, cascade, flood, burst, spout, spurt, squirt; flow, run, issue.
2 *everyone gushed about the script:* enthuse, rave, be enthusiastic, be effusive, rhapsodize, go into raptures, wax lyrical, praise to the skies; informal go mad/wild; Brit. informal go over the top.
▷ **noun** *a gush of water:* surge, stream, spurt, jet, spout, outpouring, outflow, burst, rush, cascade, flood, torrent.

gushing adjective *the gushing praise of the New York critics:* effusive, enthusiastic, overenthusiastic, unrestrained, extravagant, fulsome, lavish, rhapsodic, lyrical; informal over the top.
OPPOSITES: restrained.

gust noun
1 *a sudden gust of wind:* flurry, blast, puff, blow, rush; squall.
2 *gusts of laughter:* outburst, burst, eruption, fit, paroxysm; gale, peal, howl, hoot, shriek, roar.
▷ **verb** *wind gusted around the chimneys:* blow, bluster, flurry, roar.

gusto noun *he was attacking his breakfast with gusto:* enthusiasm, relish, appetite, enjoyment, delight, glee, pleasure, satisfaction, appreciation, liking; zest, zeal, fervour, keenness, avidity.
OPPOSITES: apathy.

gusty adjective *a gusty autumnal night:* blustery, windy, breezy, blowy; squally, stormy, tempestuous, wild, turbulent.

gut noun
1 *he had an ache in his gut:* stomach, belly, abdomen; intestines, bowels; informal tummy, insides, innards.
2 *fish heads and guts:* entrails; intestines, viscera; offal; informal insides, innards.
3 (**guts**) (informal) *he didn't have the guts*

g

to tell the truth: courage, bravery, nerve, pluck; Brit. informal bottle.

▷ **adjective** (informal) *I had a gut feeling that something was wrong:* instinctive, instinctual, intuitive, deep-seated.

▷ **verb** *the church was gutted by fire:* ravage, lay waste, ruin, wreck, destroy, devastate, demolish, wipe out.

> WORD LINKS
> **visceral**, **enteric** relating to the body's internal organs

gutter noun drain, sluice, culvert; channel, conduit, pipe; trough, trench, ditch, furrow, cut.

guttural adjective *he heard guttural shouts in a foreign language:* throaty, husky, gruff, gravelly, croaky, harsh, rough, rasping; deep, low, thick.

guy noun (informal) *he's a handsome guy:* man, fellow, gentleman; youth, boy; informal lad, geezer; Brit. informal chap, bloke.

▷ **verb** *she never stopped guying him about his weight:* make fun of, poke fun at, laugh at, mock, ridicule, jeer at, taunt.

guzzle verb
1 *he guzzled his burger:* gobble, bolt, wolf, devour; informal scoff, tuck into, demolish, polish off, stuff yourself with, pig out on, shovel down; N. Amer. informal scarf.
2 *she guzzled down the orange juice:* gulp, swallow, quaff, down; informal knock back, swig, swill, slug.

gyrate verb
1 *a crowd of girls were gyrating on the dance floor:* dance, sway; spin, whirl, twirl, revolve.
2 *he held his arms above his head, gyrating his hips to the music:* rotate, swivel.

Hh

habit noun

1 *it was his habit to go for a run every morning:* **custom**, practice, routine, pattern, convention, way, norm, tradition, rule, usage; formal wont.
2 *he failed to notice her many irritating habits:* **mannerism**, way, quirk, foible, trait, idiosyncrasy, peculiarity, oddity, eccentricity.
3 *the DJ had a bad habit of talking over the intros:* **tendency**, inclination, predisposition, propensity, proclivity.
4 *his cocaine habit:* **addiction**, dependence, dependency, craving, fixation, compulsion, obsession.

habitat noun *the thrill of spotting wildlife in its natural habitat:* **environment**, surroundings, home, domain, haunt.

habitation noun *a house fit for human habitation:* **occupation**, occupancy, residence, residency, tenancy.

habitual adjective

1 *they get into shoplifting and drug-taking, becoming habitual criminals:* **hardened**, confirmed, inveterate, incorrigible, ingrained, dyed-in-the-wool, chronic, regular, obsessive, compulsive, addicted; informal pathological.
2 *the commuters assembled in their habitual positions on the platform:* **customary**, accustomed, regular, usual, normal, set, fixed, established, routine, common, ordinary, familiar, traditional, typical, general, characteristic, standard, time-honoured; literary wonted.
OPPOSITES: occasional, unaccustomed.

habituate verb *it can take years for the animals to become habituated to humans:* **accustom**, make used, condition, attune, acclimatize, familiarize, adapt, adjust, inure, harden, acculturate.

habitué noun *the book should appeal to Vegas visitors and habitués alike:* **regular**, regular visitor/customer/client, familiar face, patron.

hack verb *I hacked the padlock off:* **cut**, chop, hew, lop, saw, slash.

hackneyed adjective *to use a hackneyed phrase, 'tomorrow is another day':* **overused**, overdone, overworked, worn out, time-worn, platitudinous, vapid, stale, tired, threadbare; trite, banal, hack, clichéd, hoary, commonplace, common, ordinary, stock, conventional, stereotyped, predictable; unimaginative, unoriginal, uninspired, prosaic, dull, boring, pedestrian, run-of-the-mill, routine; informal old hat, corny, played out.
OPPOSITES: original.

haggard adjective *he looked terrible, all grey and haggard:* **drawn**, tired, exhausted, drained, careworn, unwell, unhealthy, spent, washed out, run-down; gaunt, pinched, hollow-cheeked, hollow-eyed, thin, emaciated, wasted, cadaverous; pale, wan, grey, ashen; Brit. peaky.
OPPOSITES: healthy, fresh.

haggle verb *Italian tourists haggled enthusiastically over exotic handicrafts:* **bargain**, negotiate, beat someone down, barter, quibble, wrangle.

hail¹ verb

1 *a friend hailed him from the upper deck:* **call out to**, shout to, halloo, address; greet, say hello to.
2 *he stuck up his arm and hailed a cab:* **flag down**, wave down, signal to.
3 *critics hailed the film as a masterpiece:* **acclaim**, praise, applaud, rave about, extol, eulogize, hymn, lionize, sing the praises of, make much of, glorify, cheer, salute, toast; formal laud.
4 *Rick hails from Australia:* **come from**, be from, be a native of, have your/its roots in, be produced in.

hail² noun *he died in a hail of bullets:* **barrage**, volley, shower, rain, torrent, burst, stream, storm, avalanche, onslaught; bombardment, cannonade, battery, blast, salvo.
▷ verb *tons of gravel hailed down on us:* **beat**, shower, rain, fall, pour; pelt, pepper, batter, bombard.

hair noun

1 *her thick curly black hair:* **head of hair**, shock of hair, mane, mop; locks, tresses, curls.
2 *I like your hair:* **hairstyle**, haircut, cut, coiffure; informal hairdo.

3 *a dog with short, blue-grey hair:* fur, wool; coat, fleece, pelt; mane.

□ **split hairs** quibble, cavil, carp, niggle; informal nit-pick.

> **WORD LINKS**
> **trichology** the branch of medicine concerned with hair

hairdresser noun hairstylist, stylist, coiffeur, coiffeuse; barber.

hairpiece noun wig, toupee; informal rug.

hair-raising adjective *I thought skiing was pretty hair-raising, but rafting beats it:* terrifying, frightening, petrifying, alarming; chilling, horrifying, shocking, spine-chilling, blood-curdling, fearsome, nightmarish; informal hairy, scary.

hair-splitting adjective *legal experts have a particularly hair-splitting mentality:* pedantic, pettifogging; quibbling, niggling, cavilling, carping, critical, overcritical, hypercritical; informal nit-picking, picky; Brit. informal pernickety.

hairstyle noun haircut, cut, style, hair, coiffure; informal hairdo.

hairy adjective
1 *animals with hairy coats and huge horns:* shaggy, bushy, long-haired; woolly, furry, fleecy, fuzzy.
2 *a grin appeared on his hairy face:* bearded, bewhiskered, mustachioed; unshaven, stubbly, bristly; formal hirsute.
3 (informal) *it got very hairy when we tried to cross the border:* risky, dangerous, perilous, hazardous, touch-and-go; tricky, ticklish, difficult, awkward; informal dicey, sticky, scary; Brit. informal dodgy.

half adverb
1 *half-cooked chicken:* partially, partly; incompletely, inadequately, insufficiently; in part, part, slightly.
2 *I'm half inclined to believe you:* almost, to some extent/degree, up to a point.
OPPOSITES: fully.

> **WORD LINKS**
> **demi-, hemi-, semi-** forming words meaning 'half of something', such as *demisemiquaver* ('a musical note having half the time value of a semiquaver'), *hemisphere* ('a half of the earth'), and *semicircle* ('one half of a circle')

half-baked adjective (informal) *he wasted millions on this half-baked scheme:* ill-conceived, ill-judged, ill-considered, badly planned, impractical, unrealistic, unworkable, ridiculous, absurd; informal crazy, crackpot, hare-brained, cockeyed.
OPPOSITES: considered, well planned.

half-hearted adjective *the plan received a half-hearted welcome from the committee members:* unenthusiastic, cool, lukewarm, tepid, apathetic, indifferent, uninterested,

unconcerned, languid, listless; perfunctory, cursory, superficial, desultory, feeble, lacklustre.
OPPOSITES: enthusiastic, wholehearted.

halfway adjective *we have reached the halfway point:* midway, middle, mid, central, centre, medial, intermediate.
▷ adverb
1 *he stopped halfway down the passage:* midway, in the middle, in the centre; part of the way, part-way.
2 *he seemed halfway friendly:* to some extent/degree, in some measure, relatively, comparatively, moderately, somewhat, up to a point; just about, almost, nearly.

hall noun
1 *hang your coat in the hall:* entrance hall, hallway, entry, entrance, lobby, foyer, vestibule; atrium, concourse; passageway, passage, corridor.
2 *we met in the village hall:* assembly room, meeting room, chamber; auditorium, concert hall, theatre.

hallmark noun *the tiny bubbles are the hallmark of fine champagnes:* mark, distinctive feature, characteristic, sign, sure sign, telltale sign, badge, stamp, trademark, indication, indicator.

hallowed adjective *they have sworn to bury the bones in hallowed ground:* sacred, holy, consecrated, sanctified, blessed; venerated, honoured, sacrosanct.

hallucinate verb *the tablets were making me hallucinate:* see things, be delirious; informal trip.

hallucination noun *don't worry, it's only a hallucination:* delusion, illusion, figment of the imagination, vision, apparition, mirage, chimera, fantasy; (**hallucinations**) delirium; informal trip.

halt verb
1 *Len halted and turned round:* stop, come to a halt, come to a stop, come to a standstill; pull up, draw up.
2 *a further strike has halted production:* stop, bring to a stop, put a stop to, bring to an end, put an end to, terminate, end, wind up; suspend, break off, arrest; impede, check, curb, stem, staunch, block, stall, hold back.
OPPOSITES: start.
▷ noun
1 *the car drew to a halt:* stop, standstill.
2 *a halt in production:* stoppage, break, suspension, pause, interval, interruption, hiatus; cessation, termination, close, end.
OPPOSITES: start.

halting adjective *he spoke to us in halting English:* hesitant, faltering, hesitating, stumbling, stammering, stuttering; broken, imperfect.
OPPOSITES: fluent.

ham-fisted adjective (informal) *his ham-fisted handling of the situation attracted much criticism:* clumsy, bungling, incompetent, amateurish, inept, unskilful, inexpert, maladroit, gauche, awkward, bumbling; informal cack-handed, ham-handed.
OPPOSITES: expert.

hammer noun *a hammer and chisel:* mallet, beetle, gavel, sledgehammer.
▷ **verb**
1 *Sol hammered at the door:* batter, pummel, beat, bang, pound; strike, hit, knock on, thump on; cudgel, bludgeon, club; informal bash, wallop, clobber.
2 (informal) *we've hammered them twice this season.* See **TROUNCE**.
□ **hammer away**
they hammered away at their non-smoking campaign: work away, labour; persist with, persevere with, press on with; informal slog away, plod away/on, slave away, keep your nose to the grindstone, beaver away, stick at, soldier on with; Brit. informal graft away.
□ **hammer something in/into**
anti-racism had been hammered into her: drum, instil, inculcate, knock, drive, din; drive home to, impress upon; ingrain.
□ **hammer something out** *the area committees have hammered out a national plan:* work out, agree on, sort out, decide on, bring about, effect, produce, broker, negotiate, thrash out, reach an agreement on.

hamper[1] noun *the chef will pack you a picnic hamper:* basket, pannier; box, container, holder.

hamper[2] verb *the search was hampered by fog:* hinder, obstruct, impede, inhibit, baulk, thwart, foil, curb, delay, set back, slow down, hold up, interfere with; restrict, constrain, block, check, curtail, frustrate; informal stymie.
OPPOSITES: help.

hamstring verb *manufacturing companies were hamstrung by the economic chaos:* handicap, constrain, restrict, cripple, shackle, fetter, encumber, block, frustrate; hamper, hinder, obstruct, impede, inhibit, baulk, thwart; informal stymie.
OPPOSITES: help.

hand noun
1 *the clock's second hand had stopped:* pointer, indicator, needle, arrow, marker.
2 *a document written in his own hand:* handwriting, writing, script, calligraphy.
3 *the frontier posts remained in the hands of the government:* control, power, charge, authority; command, responsibility, management, care, supervision, jurisdiction; possession, keeping.
4 *he found work as a farm hand:* worker, factory worker, manual worker, unskilled worker, blue-collar worker, workman, labourer, operative, hired hand, crew member.
▷ **verb** *he handed each man a glass:* give, pass, reach, let someone have; present something to somebody, present somebody with something.
□ **at hand**
1 *check the online forums to make sure that plenty of help is at hand if you get stuck:* readily available, available, handy, to hand, within reach, accessible, close by, near, nearby, at the ready, at your fingertips, at your disposal, convenient.
2 *the time for action is at hand:* imminent, approaching, coming, about to happen, on the horizon; impending.
□ **hand something down**
a secret recipe handed down from generation to generation: pass on, pass down; bequeath, will, leave, make over, give, gift, transfer; Law devise.
□ **hand something on**
he handed on the family farm to his son: give, pass, hand, transfer, grant, cede, surrender, relinquish, yield; part with, let go of; bequeath, will, leave.
□ **hand something out**
the attendant handed out prayer books: distribute, hand round, give out/round, pass out/round, share out, dole out, dish out, deal out, issue, dispense; allocate, allot, apportion, disburse.
□ **hand something over**
it was suggested he might hand over power to his son: give up, give, yield, pass, grant, entrust, surrender, relinquish, cede, turn over, deliver up, forfeit, sacrifice.
□ **to hand**
have a pen and paper to hand: readily available, handy, at hand, within reach, accessible, ready, close by, near, nearby, at the ready, at your fingertips, at your disposal, convenient; informal get-at-able.

┌─────────────────────────────┐
│ WORD LINKS   │
│ **manual** relating to the hands │
└─────────────────────────────┘

handbag noun bag; N. Amer. purse, pocketbook.

handbill noun flyer, leaflet, circular, handout, pamphlet, brochure, advertisement, notice; informal ad, advert.

handbook noun manual, instructions, instruction book/manual, ABC, A to Z; almanac, companion, directory, compendium; guide, guidebook, vade mecum.

handcuff noun (handcuffs) manacles, shackles, irons, fetters, bonds, restraints; informal cuffs, bracelets.
▷ **verb** *he was handcuffed and led away:* manacle, shackle, fetter; restrain, clap/put someone in irons; informal cuff.

handful noun
1 *we've received only a handful of letters on the subject:* few, small number, scattering, trickle, one or two, some, not many.

h

2 (informal) (**a handful**) *she's a handful at the best of times:* uncontrollable, unmanageable, wild; difficult, awkward, disruptive, obstreperous, troublesome, trying, exasperating, naughty.

handicap noun

1 *he was born with a significant visual handicap:* disability.
2 *the legislation is a handicap to the competitiveness of the industry:* obstacle, hindrance, impediment, barrier, bar, obstruction, encumbrance, constraint, restriction, check, block, curb; disadvantage, drawback, stumbling block, difficulty, limitation; ball and chain, albatross, millstone round someone's neck.
OPPOSITES: benefit, advantage.
▷**verb** *chronic lack of funding handicapped the research:* hamper, impede, hinder, impair, hamstring; restrict, check, obstruct, block, curb, hold back, constrain, trammel, limit, encumber; informal stymie.
OPPOSITES: help.

handicapped adjective disabled, with learning difficulties.

> **USAGE**
>
> Until quite recently, **handicapped** was the standard term used in British English to refer to people with physical and mental disabilities. However, it has been superseded by terms such as **disabled** or, in reference to mental disability, **with learning difficulties**, and is now best avoided.

handicraft noun *workshops were set up to revive interest in traditional handicraft:* craft, handiwork, craftwork.

handiwork noun *jewellery which is the handiwork of Chinese goldsmiths:* creation, product, work, achievement; handicraft, craft, craftwork.

handkerchief noun tissue; trademark Kleenex; literary kerchief; informal hanky.

handle verb

1 *the measuring equipment must be handled with care:* hold, pick up, grasp, grip, lift; feel, touch, finger.
2 *a car which is fast and easy to handle:* control, drive, steer, operate, manoeuvre, manipulate.
3 *I think she handled the situation very well:* deal with, manage, tackle, take care of, take charge of, attend to, see to, sort out, apply yourself to, take in hand.
4 *the advertising company that is handling the account:* administer, manage, control, conduct, direct, guide, supervise, oversee, be in charge of, take care of, look after.
5 *the traders handled goods manufactured in the Rhineland:* trade in, deal in, buy, sell, supply, market; peddle, traffic in, hawk, tout.

▷**noun** *the knife's handle was damaged:* grip, handgrip, hilt, shank, stock, shaft, haft, butt, knob.

handout noun

1 *she existed on state handouts:* benefit, allowance, welfare payment, aid, charity, donation, subsidy.
2 *he produced a badly photocopied handout:* leaflet, pamphlet, brochure; handbill, flyer, notice, circular, mailshot.

handsome adjective

1 *a handsome man:* good-looking, attractive, gorgeous; informal dishy, tasty, hunky, fanciable; Brit. informal fit; N. Amer. informal cute.
2 *we made a handsome profit:* substantial, considerable, sizeable, princely, large, big, ample, bumper; informal tidy, whopping; Brit. informal whacking, ginormous.
OPPOSITES: ugly, meagre.

handwriting noun writing, script, hand, pen; penmanship, calligraphy; informal scrawl, scribble.

> WORD LINKS
> **graphology** the study of handwriting

handy adjective

1 *it's a handy reference book to have on your shelf:* useful, convenient, practical, easy-to-use, well designed, user-friendly, user-oriented, helpful, functional, serviceable.
2 *keep your credit card handy:* readily available, to hand, at hand, within reach, accessible, ready, close by, near, nearby, at your fingertips.
3 *he's very handy with a needle:* skilful, skilled, good with your hands, dexterous, deft, nimble-fingered, adroit, able, adept, proficient, capable, accomplished.
OPPOSITES: inept.

handyman noun odd-jobber, factotum, jack of all trades; Brit. odd-job man.

hang verb

1 *fairy lights hung from the trees:* be suspended, hang down, swing, sway, dangle, trail, tumble.
2 *a pall of smoke hung over the city:* hover, float, drift, be suspended.
3 *hang your pictures at eye level:* put up, fix, affix, attach, fasten, post, display, suspend, pin up, nail up.
4 *he was hanged for stealing a sheep:* execute, send to the gallows; informal string up.
▫**hang around** (informal)
1 *they spent their time hanging around in bars:* loiter, linger, wait around, waste time, kill time, mark time, while away the/ your time, kick/cool your heels, twiddle your thumbs; frequent, haunt; informal hang out in.
2 *she's hanging around with a bunch of hippies:* associate, mix, keep company, socialize, fraternize, consort, rub shoulders; informal hang out, run around, knock about/around.

□ **hang on**
1 *he hung on to her coat as they pushed through the crowd:* hold on, hold fast, grip, clutch, grasp, hold tightly, cling.
2 *her future hung on this decision:* depend on, be dependent on, turn on, hinge on, rest on, be contingent on, be determined by, be decided by.
3 *I'll hang on as long as I possibly can:* persevere, hold out, hold on, go on, carry on, keep on, keep going, keep at it, continue, persist, stay with it, struggle on, plough on; informal soldier on, stick at it, stick it out.
4 (informal) *hang on, let me think about this:* wait, wait a minute, hold on, stop.

hanger-on noun *he was surrounded by members of the press and a variety of hangers-on:* follower, camp follower, supporter, admirer, fan, disciple, acolyte; informal groupie.

hanging noun *Chinese silk wall hangings:* drape, curtain; drapery.

hang-out noun (informal) *the place became a student hang-out:* haunt, stamping ground, favourite spot, meeting place, territory, den, refuge, retreat; watering hole.

hang-up noun (informal) *the poor woman has a massive hang-up about her height:* neurosis, phobia, preoccupation, fixation, obsession, idée fixe; inhibition, mental block, psychological block, difficulty; informal complex, thing.

hank noun coil, roll, length, loop, twist, skein; lock, ringlet, curl.

hanker verb *they hankered for the bright lights of the capital:* yearn, long, crave, desire, wish, hunger, thirst, lust, ache, pant, have a yen, be eager, be desperate, pine; want, have your heart set on; informal be dying.

hankering noun *he often confessed to a certain hankering for normal family life:* longing, yearning, craving, desire, wish, yen, hunger, thirst, urge, ache, lust, appetite, fancy; informal itch.
OPPOSITES: aversion.

haphazard adjective *things were strewn around the room in a haphazard fashion:* random, unplanned, unsystematic, unmethodical, disorganized, disorderly, irregular, indiscriminate, chaotic, hit-and-miss, arbitrary, aimless, careless, casual, slapdash, slipshod; chance, accidental; informal higgledy-piggledy.
OPPOSITES: methodical.

hapless adjective *the hapless victims of exploitation:* unfortunate, unlucky, ill-starred, ill-fated, cursed, doomed; unhappy, forlorn, wretched, miserable, woebegone; literary star-crossed.
OPPOSITES: lucky.

happen verb
1 *remember what happened last time he was here:* occur, take place, come about, transpire, materialize, arise, crop up, come up, present itself, ensue, result; formal eventuate; literary come to pass, betide, supervene; N. Amer. informal go down.
2 *I wonder what happened to Susie?* become of; literary befall, betide.
3 *they just happened to be in London:* chance, have the good/bad luck.

happening noun *he was a witness to these bizarre happenings:* event, occurrence, incident, proceeding, affair, circumstance, phenomenon, episode, experience, occasion, development, eventuality.

happily adverb
1 *the children played happily for hours:* contentedly, cheerfully, cheerily, merrily, joyfully, gaily, gleefully.
2 *I will happily do as you ask:* gladly, willingly, readily, freely, cheerfully, ungrudgingly, with pleasure; old use fain.
3 *happily, we are now living in more enlightened times:* fortunately, luckily, thankfully, mercifully, by good luck, by good fortune, as luck would have it; thank goodness, thank heavens, thank the stars.
OPPOSITES: sadly, unwillingly.

happiness noun *people derive most of their happiness away from work:* pleasure, contentment, satisfaction, cheerfulness, merriment, gaiety, joy, joviality, jollity, glee, delight, good spirits, light-heartedness, well-being, enjoyment; exuberance, exhilaration, elation, ecstasy, jubilation, rapture, bliss, euphoria, transports of delight.
OPPOSITES: unhappiness, sadness.

happy adjective
1 *Melissa looked so happy and excited:* cheerful, cheery, merry, joyful, jovial, jolly, jocular, gleeful, carefree, untroubled, delighted, smiling, beaming, grinning, in good spirits, in a good mood, light-hearted, pleased, contented, content, satisfied, gratified, buoyant, radiant, sunny, beatific; thrilled, elated, exhilarated, ecstatic, blissful, euphoric, overjoyed, exultant, rapturous, in seventh heaven, on cloud nine, walking on air, jumping for joy, cock-a-hoop, jubilant; literary blithe, joyous; informal chirpy, over the moon, on top of the world, as pleased as Punch, on a high; Brit. informal chuffed, as happy as Larry; N. English informal made up.
2 *we will be happy to advise you on your finances:* glad, pleased, delighted; willing, ready, disposed.
3 *by a happy coincidence, it was also Richard's birthday:* fortunate, lucky, favourable, advantageous, opportune, timely, well timed, convenient.
OPPOSITES: unhappy, sad, unwilling, unfortunate.

h

happy-go-lucky adjective *their casual, happy-go-lucky manner did not exactly inspire confidence:* easy-going, carefree, casual, free and easy, devil-may-care, blithe, nonchalant, insouciant, blasé, unconcerned, untroubled, unworried, light-hearted; informal laid-back.
OPPOSITES: anxious.

harangue verb *he harangued his erstwhile colleagues for their complacency:* rant at, hold forth to, lecture, shout at; berate, criticize, attack, admonish; informal sound off at, mouth off at, blast.
▷noun *we were subjected to a ten-minute harangue about immigration:* tirade, rant, diatribe, lecture, polemic, fulmination, broadside, attack, onslaught; criticism, condemnation, censure, admonition, speech.

harass verb *council tenants who harass their neighbours:* persecute, intimidate, hound, plague, torment, bedevil, pressurize; pester, bother, worry, disturb, trouble, provoke, stress; informal hassle, bug, give someone a hard time.

harassed adjective *this scheme is a godsend for harassed parents:* stressed, pressurized, strained, hard-pressed, beleaguered, under pressure, at the end of your tether; worried, troubled; informal hassled.
OPPOSITES: carefree.

harassment noun *he knows how to make a noise and claim police harassment:* persecution, intimidation, provocation, trouble, victimization, hounding, pressure; informal hassle, grief, aggravation.

harbinger noun *these flowers are a true harbinger of spring:* herald, sign, indication, signal, portent, omen, augury, forewarning, presage; forerunner, precursor.

harbour noun *a picturesque harbour on the east coast:* port, dock, haven, marina; mooring, anchorage; waterfront.
▷verb
1 *he is harbouring a dangerous criminal:* shelter, conceal, hide, shield, protect, give sanctuary to.
2 *Rose had harboured a grudge against him for years:* bear, nurse, nurture, cherish, entertain, foster, hold on to, cling to.

hard adjective
1 *the ground was cold and hard:* firm, solid, rigid, stiff, resistant, unbreakable, inflexible, impenetrable, unyielding, solidified, frozen, hardened, set, dried, compact, compacted, dense, close-packed, compressed; steely, tough, strong, stony, flinty, as hard as iron, as hard as stone.
2 *I'm not afraid of hard physical work:* strenuous, tiring, exhausting, heavy, back-breaking, wearying, fatiguing, arduous, gruelling, laborious; difficult, taxing, exacting, testing, challenging,

demanding, punishing, tough, formidable, onerous, rigorous, uphill, Herculean; informal murderous, killing; Brit. informal knackering.
3 *a hard problem to deal with at such short notice:* difficult, puzzling, perplexing, baffling, bewildering, mystifying, knotty, thorny, problematic, complicated, complex, intricate, involved; insoluble, unfathomable, impenetrable, incomprehensible, unanswerable.
4 *they're hard workers and expect to be well paid:* industrious, hard-working, diligent, assiduous, conscientious, sedulous, energetic, keen, enthusiastic, zealous, earnest, persevering, persistent, dogged, unflagging, untiring, indefatigable; studious.
5 *times are hard and we have to make some tough decisions:* harsh, grim, difficult, bad, bleak, dire, tough, austere, unpleasant, uncomfortable, straitened; dark, distressing, painful, awful.
6 *Mr Gwilliam was a hard taskmaster:* strict, harsh, firm, severe, stern, tough, rigorous, demanding, exacting; callous, unkind, unsympathetic, cold, heartless, hard-hearted, unfeeling; intransigent, unbending, uncompromising, inflexible, implacable, unrelenting, unsparing; grim, ruthless, merciless, pitiless, cruel; standing no nonsense, ruling with a rod of iron.
7 *it was a long, hard winter:* cold, bitter, harsh, severe, bleak, freezing, icy, icy-cold, arctic.
8 *he received a hard blow to the head:* forceful, heavy, strong, sharp, smart, violent, powerful, vigorous, mighty, hefty, tremendous.
9 *you can't get many hard facts from an image alone:* reliable, definite, true, confirmed, substantiated, established, undeniable, indisputable, unquestionable, verifiable.
10 *he got into hard drugs:* addictive, habit-forming; strong, harmful.
OPPOSITES: soft, easy, lazy, gentle.
▷adverb
1 *George pushed her hard, making her stumble:* forcefully, forcibly, roughly, powerfully, strongly, heavily, sharply, vigorously, energetically, with all your might, with might and main.
2 *they had worked hard all day:* industriously, diligently, assiduously, conscientiously, sedulously, busily, enthusiastically, energetically, doggedly, steadily; informal like mad, like crazy.
3 *this prosperity has been hard won:* with difficulty, with effort, after a struggle, painfully, laboriously.
4 *it was raining hard:* heavily, strongly, in torrents, in sheets, steadily; informal cats and dogs.
5 *my mother looked hard at me:* closely, attentively, intently, carefully, keenly, searchingly, earnestly, sharply.

h

□ **hard and fast**
there are no hard and fast rules about personal taste: definite, fixed, set, strict, rigid, binding, clear-cut, cast-iron; inflexible, immutable, incontestable.

□ **hard feelings**
I had no hard feelings about being made redundant: resentment, animosity, ill feeling, ill will, bitterness, bad blood, resentfulness, rancour, malice, acrimony, antagonism, antipathy, animus, friction, anger, hostility, hate, hatred.

hardbitten adjective *even a hardbitten war reporter like him was shocked:* hardened, tough, cynical, unsentimental, hard-headed, case-hardened, as hard as nails; informal hard-nosed, hard-boiled.
OPPOSITES: sentimental.

hard-core adjective *he had a hard-core following on the football terraces:* diehard, staunch, dedicated, committed, steadfast, dyed-in-the-wool, long-standing; hard-line, extreme, entrenched, radical, intransigent, uncompromising, rigid.

harden verb
1 *this glue will harden in a matter of minutes:* set, solidify, congeal, clot, coagulate, stiffen, thicken, cake; freeze, crystallize.
2 *their years of suffering had hardened them:* toughen, desensitize, inure, case-harden, harden someone's heart; deaden, numb, benumb, anaesthetize; brutalize.
OPPOSITES: liquefy, soften.

hardened adjective
1 *we're dealing here with a hardened criminal:* habitual, seasoned, inveterate, compulsive, confirmed, dyed-in-the-wool, chronic; incorrigible, incurable, irredeemable, unregenerate.
2 *he was hardened to the violence he witnessed:* inured, desensitized, deadened; accustomed, habituated, acclimatized, used.

hard-headed adjective *he was a hard-headed businessman:* unsentimental, practical, pragmatic, businesslike, realistic, sensible, rational, clear-thinking, cool-headed, down-to-earth, matter-of-fact, no-nonsense, with both feet on the ground; tough, hardbitten; shrewd, astute, sharp, sharp-witted; informal hard-nosed, hard-boiled.
OPPOSITES: sentimental.

hard-hearted adjective *only the most hard-hearted man would have turned her away:* unfeeling, heartless, cold, hard, callous, unsympathetic, uncaring, unloving, unconcerned, indifferent, unmoved, unkind, cruel, uncharitable, unemotional, cold-hearted, cold-blooded, mean-spirited, stony-hearted, having a heart of stone, as hard as nails.
OPPOSITES: compassionate.

hard-hitting adjective *a hard-hitting TV campaign about drinking and driving:* uncompromising, blunt, forthright, frank, honest, direct, tough; critical, unsparing, strongly worded, straight-talking, pulling no punches, not mincing your words, not beating about the bush.

hardiness noun *the breed is renowned for its hardiness:* robustness, strength, toughness, ruggedness, sturdiness, resilience, stamina, vigour; healthiness, good health.
OPPOSITES: frailty.

hard-line adjective *he is a hard-line nationalist:* uncompromising, strict, extreme, tough, diehard, inflexible, intransigent, intractable, unyielding.
OPPOSITES: moderate.

hardly adverb *we hardly know each other:* scarcely, barely, only just.

hard-nosed adjective (informal) *you'll need to convince a panel of hard-nosed financiers:* tough-minded, unsentimental, no-nonsense, hard-headed, hardbitten, pragmatic, realistic, down-to-earth, practical, rational, shrewd, astute, businesslike; informal hard-boiled.
OPPOSITES: sentimental.

hard-pressed adjective *a package to help the hard-pressed construction industry:* in difficulties, under pressure, troubled, beleaguered, harassed, with your back to/against the wall, in a tight corner, in a tight spot, between a rock and a hard place; overburdened, overworked, overloaded, rushed off your feet; informal pushed, up against it.

hardship noun *the cuts caused severe hardship in some areas:* suffering, difficulty, distress, trouble, pain, misery, wretchedness, tribulation, adversity, trials, trials and tribulations, dire straits; poverty, deprivation, destitution, privation, austerity, want, need.
OPPOSITES: welfare, prosperity.

hardware noun *a shortage of military hardware:* equipment, apparatus, tackle, machinery, tools, paraphernalia, implements, instruments, appliances; informal gear, kit.

hard-wearing adjective *a hard-wearing fabric that looks great:* durable, strong, tough, resilient, long-lasting, made to last, stout, well made, rugged, heavy-duty.
OPPOSITES: flimsy.

hard-working adjective *unlike Tom, Bobby was loyal and hard-working:* industrious, diligent, conscientious, assiduous, sedulous, painstaking, persevering, unflagging, untiring, tireless, indefatigable, studious; keen, enthusiastic, zealous, busy, with your shoulder to the wheel; informal with your nose to the grindstone.
OPPOSITES: lazy.

h

hardy adjective *they were a couple of hardy outdoor types:* robust, healthy, fit, strong, sturdy, tough, rugged, hearty, lusty, vigorous.
OPPOSITES: delicate.

hare-brained (informal) adjective
1 *a hare-brained scheme to recycle industrial waste:* ill-judged, rash, foolish, foolhardy, reckless, madcap, wild, silly, stupid, ridiculous, absurd, idiotic, asinine, imprudent, impracticable, unworkable, unrealistic, unconsidered, ill-thought-out, ill-advised, ill-conceived; informal crackpot, crackbrained, cockeyed, half-baked, crazy; Brit. informal daft, barmy.
2 *a hare-brained young girl with no experience:* foolish, silly, idiotic, empty-headed, unintelligent, scatterbrained, feather-brained, brainless, giddy; informal dippy, dizzy, dopey, birdbrained.
OPPOSITES: sensible, intelligent.

hark verb (literary) listen, lend an ear, pay attention, attend, mark; old use hearken.
□ hark back to
paintings that hark back to Constable and Turner: recall, remind someone of, call/bring to mind, evoke, put someone in mind of.

harm noun
1 *the voltage is not sufficient to cause harm:* injury, hurt, pain, trauma; damage, impairment.
2 *I can't see any harm in it, can you?* wrong, ill, wickedness, mischief, sin.
OPPOSITES: help, benefit.
▷ verb
1 *he's never harmed anybody in his life:* injure, hurt, wound, lay a finger on, maltreat, mistreat, misuse, ill-treat, ill-use, abuse, molest.
2 *this ban could harm his World Cup prospects:* damage, spoil, mar, impair, have a bad effect on.
OPPOSITES: help, benefit.

harmful adjective *the harmful effects of smoking are well known:* damaging, injurious, detrimental, dangerous, deleterious, unfavourable, negative, disadvantageous, unhealthy, unwholesome, hurtful, destructive; noxious, hazardous, poisonous, toxic, deadly, lethal; bad, evil, malign, malignant, malevolent, corrupting, pernicious.
OPPOSITES: harmless, beneficial.

harmless adjective *it is a harmless substance if taken in moderation:* safe, innocuous, benign, gentle, mild, wholesome, non-toxic; non-addictive.
OPPOSITES: harmful.

harmonious adjective
1 *their debut album is released today and keeps up the harmonious accordion tradition:* tuneful, melodious, melodic, sweet-sounding, mellifluous, lyrical; informal easy on the ear; often ironic dulcet.
2 *the harmonious relationship between the two countries:* friendly, amicable, cordial, amiable, congenial, easy, peaceful, peaceable, cooperative; compatible, sympathetic, united.
3 *dishes providing a harmonious blend of colour, texture, flavour, and aroma:* balanced, well balanced, coordinated, in proportion, compatible, well matched, congruous.
OPPOSITES: discordant, hostile, incongruous.

harmonize verb
1 *colours which harmonize in a pleasing way:* coordinate, go together, match, blend, mix, balance, tone in; be compatible, be harmonious, suit each other, set each other off.
2 *the need to harmonize tax laws across states:* coordinate, correlate, integrate, synchronize, systematize, make consistent, bring in line.
OPPOSITES: clash, differentiate.

harmony noun
1 *the simplicity of the individual parts focused attention on the harmony of the whole structure:* balance, symmetry, congruity, consonance, coordination, compatibility, synthesis.
2 *the villagers live together in harmony:* agreement, accord, peace, peaceful existence, friendship, fellowship, cooperation, understanding, consensus, unity, sympathy, rapport, like-mindedness; unison, union, concert, oneness; formal amity, concord.
OPPOSITES: dissonance, disagreement.

harness verb *attempts to harness solar energy:* control, exploit, utilize, use, employ, make use of, put to use; channel, mobilize, apply, capitalize on.

harpoon noun spear, trident, dart, barb, gaff.

harried adjective *he seemed like a different person, much older, worn and harried:* harassed, bothered, flustered, agitated, distressed, beset; informal hassled, up against it.
OPPOSITES: calm.

harrowing adjective *he gave a harrowing account of how he disposed of the bodies:* distressing, upsetting, disturbing, shocking, painful, traumatic, appalling, horrifying; informal gut-wrenching.

harry verb
1 *the raiders spent three months harrying the area:* attack, assault, assail; charge, rush, strike, set upon.
2 *the government is being mercilessly harried by a new lobby group:* harass, hound, torment, pester, bother, worry, badger, plague, bedevil, nag, pressurize; informal hassle, bug, give someone a hard time.

h

harsh adjective

1 *her harsh voice:* **grating**, jarring, rasping, strident, raucous, brassy, discordant; screeching, shrill; rough, coarse, hoarse, gruff, croaky.
2 *the garden was drenched by a harsh white light | harsh colours:* **glaring**, bright, dazzling; loud, garish, gaudy, lurid, bold.
3 *during his harsh rule, thousands were exiled:* **cruel**, savage, barbarous, despotic, dictatorial, tyrannical; ruthless, merciless, pitiless, relentless; severe, strict, intolerant, illiberal; hard-hearted, heartless, unkind, inhuman, inhumane.
4 *politicians are taking harsh measures to end the crisis:* **severe**, stringent, firm, stiff, hard, stern, rigorous, grim, uncompromising; punitive, cruel, brutal.
5 *harsh words were exchanged and tempers got frayed:* **rude**, discourteous, uncivil, impolite; unfriendly, sharp, bitter, abusive, unkind, disparaging; abrupt, brusque, curt.
6 *the harsh conditions in the refugee camps:* **austere**, grim, spartan, tough, hard, inhospitable, stark, severe, bleak.
7 *harsh cream cleaners can scratch stains away:* **abrasive**, strong, caustic; coarse, rough.
OPPOSITES: soft, subdued, kind, friendly, mild.

harvest noun *a poor harvest:* **yield**, crop, vintage; fruits, produce.
▷ **verb** *once he's harvested the wheat crop, there are still the beans:* **gather in**, bring in, reap, pick, collect.

hassle (informal) noun *parking is such a hassle:* **nuisance**, bother, inconvenience, problem, trouble, struggle, difficulty, annoyance, irritation, thorn in your flesh/side, fuss; informal aggravation, pain, pain in the neck.
▷ **verb** *they were hassling him to pay what he owed them:* **harass**, pester, nag, keep on at, badger, hound, chivvy, bother, torment, plague; informal bug, give someone a hard time, get on someone's back.

hassled adjective (informal) *Gerry cast the hassled tour manager a sympathetic look:* **harassed**, agitated, stressed, flustered; beleaguered, hounded, bothered, beset, tormented; under pressure, hot and bothered; informal up against it.
OPPOSITES: calm.

haste noun *we worked with feverish haste:* **speed**, urgency, hurry, swiftness, rapidity, quickness, eagerness, alacrity, briskness, dispatch.
OPPOSITES: delay.
□ **in haste**
she went in haste along the landing towards her son's room: **quickly**, rapidly, fast, speedily, with urgency, in a rush, in a hurry.

hasten verb

1 *we hastened back to the house:* **hurry**, rush, dash, race, fly, shoot; scurry, scramble, dart, bolt, sprint, run, zoom; Brit. hare; informal tear, pelt, scoot, zip, belt, go hell for leather, hotfoot it, leg it; Brit. informal bomb; N. Amer. informal hightail; dated make haste.
2 *these chemicals can hasten the ageing process:* **speed up**, accelerate, quicken, precipitate, advance, hurry on, step up.
OPPOSITES: dawdle, delay.

hastily adverb

1 *Meg retreated hastily as the blades began to rotate:* **quickly**, hurriedly, fast, swiftly, rapidly, speedily, briskly, without delay, post-haste; as fast as possible, at breakneck speed, at a run, hotfoot, at the double; dated with all speed.
2 *the paintings looked as if they had been hastily completed to meet the exhibition's deadline:* **too quickly**, in too much of a hurry, too soon, prematurely, precipitately.
OPPOSITES: slowly, carefully.

hasty adjective

1 *Fran took several hasty steps backwards:* **quick**, hurried, fast, swift, rapid, speedy, brisk.
2 *we don't want to be trapped by hasty decisions:* **rash**, impetuous, impulsive, reckless, precipitate, overhasty, spur-of-the-moment, premature, unconsidered, unthinking.
OPPOSITES: slow, considered.

hatch verb

1 *the duck hatched a clutch of eggs:* **incubate**, brood, sit on.
2 *the little plot that you and Sylvia hatched last night:* **devise**, conceive, concoct, think up, dream up, brew, invent, plan, design, formulate; informal cook up.

hatchet noun axe, cleaver, mattock, tomahawk; Brit. chopper.

hate verb

1 *the boys hate each other:* **loathe**, detest, despise, dislike, abhor; be repelled by, be unable to bear/stand, recoil from, shrink from; formal abominate, execrate.
2 *I hate to bother you:* **be sorry**, be reluctant, be loath, be unwilling, be disinclined; regret.
OPPOSITES: love.
▷ **noun**
1 *I was eaten up by feelings of hate and revenge:* **hatred**, loathing, detestation, dislike, distaste, abhorrence, aversion; hostility, enmity, animosity, antipathy, revulsion, disgust, contempt, odium.
2 *his pet hate is filling in forms:* **bugbear**, bane, bête noire, bogey, aversion, thorn in your flesh/side.
OPPOSITES: love.

hateful adjective *that hateful, arrogant old woman:* **detestable**, horrible, horrid, unpleasant, awful, nasty, disagreeable, despicable, objectionable, insufferable; revolting, loathsome, abhorrent, abominable, execrable, odious, disgusting, distasteful, obnoxious, offensive, vile, heinous; informal ghastly; Brit. informal beastly. OPPOSITES: delightful.

hatred noun *she was full of hatred and bitterness:* loathing, hate, detestation, dislike, distaste, abhorrence, revulsion, disgust; aversion, hostility, ill will, ill feeling, enmity, animosity, antipathy, contempt, odium; formal abomination.

haughtiness noun arrogance, pride, superiority, self-importance, hauteur, pomposity, conceit, vanity, condescension, disdain, contempt; snobbishness, snobbery, superciliousness; informal snootiness. OPPOSITES: modesty.

haughty adjective *he tended to treat his critics with haughty disdain:* arrogant, proud, superior, self-important, pompous, supercilious, condescending, patronizing, vain, conceited, snobbish; scornful, contemptuous, disdainful; full of yourself, above yourself; informal stuck-up, snooty, hoity-toity, uppity, big-headed, high and mighty, la-di-da; Brit. informal toffee-nosed. OPPOSITES: humble.

haul verb *she hauled the basket up the slope:* drag, pull, tug, heave, draw, tow; informal yank, lug; Brit. informal hump.
▷ noun *the thieves were forced to abandon their haul:* booty, loot, plunder; spoils, stolen goods, ill-gotten gains; informal swag, boodle.

haunches plural noun
□ sit on your haunches
sit on your heels, squat, crouch down, hunker down.

haunt verb
1 *a ghost haunts this eighteenth-century house:* wander, frequent, visit, patrol, pervade.
2 *he haunts street markets and bazaars:* frequent, patronize, visit regularly; loiter in, linger in; informal hang out in.
3 *the sight haunted me for years:* torment, disturb, trouble, worry, plague, burden, beset, beleaguer; prey on, weigh on, gnaw at, nag at, weigh heavily on, obsess; informal bug.
▷ noun *the inn was a favourite haunt of artists of the time:* meeting place, stamping ground, territory, domain, resort, retreat, spot; informal hang-out; Brit. informal patch.

haunted adjective
1 *a haunted house:* possessed, cursed; ghostly, eerie; informal spooky, scary.
2 *his haunted eyes still stared at her:* tormented, anguished, troubled, tortured, worried, disturbed.

haunting adjective *the sweet and haunting sound of pan pipes:* evocative, emotive, affecting, moving, touching, stirring, powerful; poignant, nostalgic, wistful; memorable, unforgettable, indelible.

have verb
1 *he had a new car and a boat:* possess, own, be in possession of, be the owner of; be blessed with, boast, enjoy; keep, retain, hold, occupy.
2 *the flat has five rooms:* consist of, comprise, contain, include, incorporate, be composed of, be made up of, boast, encompass.
3 *I've had my tea:* eat, consume, devour, take; drink, quaff; formal partake of, imbibe; informal demolish, dispose of, put away, get outside of, scoff.
4 *we've decided to have a party:* hold, give, arrange, organize, host, throw, put on, lay on, set up, fix up.
5 *she's going to have a baby:* give birth to, bear, be delivered of, bring into the world; informal drop; old use beget.
6 *the taxi driver had trouble finding the restaurant:* experience, encounter, face, meet, find, run into, go through, undergo.
7 *I often have headaches:* suffer from, be affected by, be troubled with, be afflicted by.
8 *many of them have doubts about the new computer system:* harbour, entertain, feel, nurse, nurture; sustain, maintain.
9 *he had little patience with instruction manuals:* manifest, show, display, exhibit, demonstrate.
10 (**have to**) *I have to get up at six o'clock tomorrow morning:* must, be obliged to, be required to, be compelled to, be forced to, be bound to.
11 *he had his bodyguards throw Chris out:* ask to, get to, prevail on someone to; tell to, order to, command to.

haven noun *a safe haven in times of trouble:* refuge, retreat, shelter, sanctuary, asylum; port in a storm, oasis, sanctum.

havoc noun
1 *the hurricane ripped through Florida, causing havoc:* devastation, destruction, damage, desolation, ruin; disaster, catastrophe.
2 *her four young children create havoc wherever they go:* disorder, chaos, disruption, mayhem, bedlam, pandemonium, turmoil, tumult, uproar; commotion, furore; Brit. informal hullabaloo.

hawk verb *street traders were hawking bad costume jewellery:* peddle, sell, tout, vend, trade in, traffic in; informal push; Brit. informal flog.

hawk-eyed adjective *a hawk-eyed policeman saved the lives of dozens of shoppers:* vigilant, observant, alert, attentive, sharp-eyed, keen-eyed, eagle-eyed. OPPOSITES: inattentive.

haywire adjective (informal) *the radiation caused his communicator to go haywire:* out of control, erratic, faulty, malfunctioning, out of order; chaotic, confused, disorganized, disordered, topsy-turvy; informal on the blink.

hazard noun *the hazards of radiation:* danger, risk, peril, threat, menace; problem, pitfall.
▷ **verb**
1 *he hazarded a guess:* venture, advance, put forward, volunteer; conjecture, speculate, surmise; formal opine.
2 *the shipping business is too risky to hazard money on:* risk, jeopardize, gamble, stake, wager, bet, chance.

hazardous adjective *we work in extremely hazardous conditions:* dangerous, risky, unsafe, perilous, fraught with danger; unpredictable, uncertain, high-risk, insecure, precarious, touch-and-go; informal dicey, hairy, chancy; Brit. informal dodgy.
OPPOSITES: safe.

haze noun
1 *a thick haze lay on the sea:* mist, fog, cloud; smoke, vapour, steam.
2 *she walked around in a haze of confusion:* blur, daze, fuddle, fog.

hazy adjective
1 *a hot, hazy morning:* misty, foggy, cloudy, overcast; smoggy, murky.
2 *hazy memories of early childhood:* vague, indistinct, unclear, faint, dim, nebulous, shadowy, blurred, fuzzy, confused.

head noun
1 *her head hit the ground:* skull, crown, scalp; technical cranium; informal nut; Brit. informal bonce.
2 *this new job meant he had to use his head:* brains, brainpower, intellect, intelligence; wits, wisdom, mind, sense, reasoning, common sense; informal savvy, grey matter; Brit. informal loaf, nous.
3 *the head of an international organization:* leader, chief, controller, governor; commander, captain; director, manager; principal, president, premier; Brit. head teacher, headmaster, headmistress; informal boss, skipper; Brit. informal gaffer.
4 *the head of the queue:* front, beginning, start, fore, forefront, top.
▷ **adjective** *the head waiter was very unfriendly:* chief, principal; leading, main, first, prime, premier, top, highest, supreme, top-ranking; N. Amer. ranking.
▷ **verb**
1 *he heads a department which has accumulated a formidable bank of knowledge:* lead, run, manage, direct, supervise, be in charge of, superintend, oversee, preside over, rule, govern, control, command, captain, be at the helm of; informal be the boss of.
2 *last time I saw him, he was heading for the exit:* move towards, make for, aim for, go in the direction of, be bound for, make a beeline for; set out for, start out for.

☐ **come to a head**
the violence came to a head following the deaths of six youths: reach a crisis, come to a climax, reach a critical point, reach a crossroads.
☐ **head someone/something off**
1 *he ran up the road to head off the cars:* intercept, divert, deflect, redirect, reroute, draw away, turn away.
2 *they headed off a crisis by ordering a second investigation:* prevent, avoid, stop, avert, ward off, fend off, stave off, hold off, nip in the bud, forestall, keep at bay.
☐ **lose your head**
I lost my head and started a big argument about the bill: lose control, lose your composure, go to pieces; panic, get flustered, get confused, get hysterical; informal lose your cool, freak out; Brit. informal throw a wobbly.

WORD LINKS
cephalic relating to the head

heading noun
1 *the chapter headings are clearly laid out:* title, caption, legend, subtitle, subheading, rubric, headline.
2 *this topic falls under four main headings:* category, division, classification, class, section, group, grouping, subject, topic, area.

headland noun cape, promontory, point, head, foreland, peninsula, ness, bluff; Scottish mull.

headlong adverb
1 *he fell headlong into the tent:* head first.
2 *those who rush headlong to join the latest craze:* without thinking, precipitately, precipitously, impetuously, rashly, recklessly, carelessly, heedlessly, hastily, mindlessly, on a whim.
OPPOSITES: cautiously.
▷ **adjective** *a headlong dash through the city:* breakneck, whirlwind; reckless, precipitate, precipitous, rushed, hasty, careless, heedless.
OPPOSITES: cautious.

headquarters plural noun base, HQ, head office, main office, nerve centre, mission control, command post.

headstone noun gravestone, tombstone, stone, monument, memorial.

headstrong adjective *this headstrong girl is not going to play by the family's rules:* wilful, contrary, perverse, wayward, unruly, strong-willed, stubborn, obstinate, unyielding, obdurate; formal refractory.
OPPOSITES: compliant.

headway noun
☐ **make headway**
they appear to be making headway in bringing the rebels under control: make progress, progress, make strides, gain ground, advance, proceed, move, get ahead, come along, take shape.

h

heady adjective

1 *the heady days of my youth:* exhilarating, exciting, thrilling, stimulating, stirring, invigorating, electrifying, rousing; informal mind-blowing.
2 *several bottles of heady local wine:* intoxicating, potent, strong, powerful, hard, stiff, alcoholic; old use spirituous.
OPPOSITES: boring, weak.

heal verb

1 *his concern is to heal sick people:* cure, restore to health, make well, make better, treat.
2 *he had to wait until his knee had healed:* get better, get well, be cured, recover, mend, improve.
3 *time will eventually heal the pain of grief:* alleviate, ease, assuage, relieve, help, lessen, mitigate, allay; end, put an end to, bring to an end.
4 *we've been trying to heal the rift between them:* repair, set right, put right, remedy, resolve, correct, settle; conciliate, reconcile; informal patch up.
OPPOSITES: aggravate, worsen.

healing adjective
this flower is said to have healing properties: medicinal, therapeutic, curative, remedial, corrective, restorative, tonic, health-giving, healthy, beneficial.
OPPOSITES: harmful.

health noun

1 *he was restored to health:* well-being, healthiness, fitness, good condition, good shape, fine fettle; strength, vigour.
2 *bad health forced him to retire:* physical/mental condition, physical/mental state, physical/mental shape, constitution.
OPPOSITES: illness.

healthy adjective

1 *we're all fit and healthy:* well, in good health, fit, in good trim, in good shape, in fine fettle, in tip-top condition; blooming, thriving, hardy, robust, strong, vigorous, fighting fit, fit as a fiddle; Brit. in rude health; informal OK.
2 *a healthy balanced diet:* health-giving, healthful, good for you; wholesome, nutritious, nourishing; beneficial; formal salubrious.
OPPOSITES: unhealthy.

heap noun

1 *a disordered heap of boxes lay in the middle of the floor:* pile, stack, mound, mountain, mass, quantity, load, lot, jumble; collection, accumulation, assemblage, store, hoard.
2 (informal) *I took heaps of pictures | there's heaps of room:* a large amount, a fair amount, a good deal, a great deal, a lot, much, plenty, an abundance, a wealth, a profusion; a great many, a large number, numerous, scores; informal hundreds, thousands, millions, a load, loads, stacks, lots, masses, tons; Brit. informal a shedload.

▷ **verb** *her dirty clothes were heaped in a corner:* pile, stack; assemble, collect.
□ **heap something on**
they heaped praise on her: shower on, lavish on, load on; bestow on, confer on, give, grant, vouchsafe, favour with.

hear verb

1 *behind her she could hear men's voices:* perceive, make out, discern, catch, get; overhear.
2 *I heard that she had moved:* learn, discover, gather, be informed, be told, get word, find out, glean, ascertain; informal get wind.
3 *judges cannot hear cases in which they have previously been involved:* try, judge, adjudge; adjudicate, pass judgement on.

hearing noun

1 *she moved out of hearing:* earshot, hearing distance, range.
2 *I think I had a fair hearing:* chance to speak, opportunity to be heard; interview, audience.
3 *he gave evidence at the hearing:* trial, court case, inquiry, inquest, tribunal; investigation, inquisition.

> WORD LINKS
> **auditory**, **aural**, **acoustic** relating to hearing
> **audiology** the branch of medicine concerned with hearing

hearsay noun
a story based entirely on hearsay: rumour, gossip, tittle-tattle, tattle, idle talk; stories, tales; informal the grapevine.

heart noun

1 *his heart had stopped beating:* informal ticker.
2 *he poured out his heart to me | she captured my heart that afternoon:* emotions, feelings, sentiments; soul, mind, bosom, breast; love, affection, passion.
3 *he has no heart:* compassion, sympathy, humanity, feelings, fellow feeling, brotherly love, tenderness, empathy, understanding; kindness, goodwill.
4 *they may lose heart as the work mounts up:* enthusiasm, keenness, eagerness, spirit, determination, resolve, purpose, courage, nerve, will power, fortitude; informal guts, spunk; Brit. informal bottle.
5 *right in the heart of the city:* centre, middle, hub, core, nucleus, eye, bosom.
6 *now we're getting to the heart of the matter:* essence, crux, core, nub, root, gist, meat, marrow, pith, substance, kernel; informal nitty-gritty.
OPPOSITES: edge.
□ **at heart**
he's a good lad at heart: deep down, basically, fundamentally, essentially, in essence, intrinsically; really, actually, truly, in fact.

◻ **by heart**
I know the entire poem by heart: from memory, off pat, by rote, word for word, verbatim, word-perfect; Brit. parrot-fashion.

◻ **from the heart**
she spoke from the heart: sincerely, earnestly, fervently, passionately, truly, genuinely, heartily, with all sincerity.

◻ **have a change of heart**
you can get your money back if you have a change of heart: change your mind, change your tune, have second thoughts, have a rethink, think again, think twice; informal get cold feet.

◻ **heart and soul**
they had committed themselves heart and soul to the project: wholeheartedly, enthusiastically, eagerly, zealously; absolutely, completely, entirely, fully, utterly, to the hilt; informal one hundred per cent.

◻ **take heart**
Mary took heart from the encouragement that was offered: be encouraged, be heartened, be comforted; cheer up, brighten up, liven up, revive; informal perk up, buck up.

◻ **with your heart in your mouth**
she watched with her heart in her mouth as the plane lost height: in alarm, in fear, fearfully, apprehensively, on edge, with trepidation, in suspense, in a cold sweat, with bated breath, on tenterhooks; informal with butterflies in your stomach, in a state, in a sweat.

> WORD LINKS
> **cardiac** relating to the heart
> **cardiology** the branch of medicine concerned with the heart
> **coronary** relating to the arteries of the heart

heartache noun *some times of her life were filled with heartache and pain:* anguish, grief, suffering, distress, unhappiness, misery, sorrow, sadness, heartbreak, pain, hurt, agony, angst, despondency, despair, woe, desolation.
OPPOSITES: happiness.

heartbreak noun. See HEARTACHE.

heartbreaking adjective *it would be heartbreaking to see it all fall apart at this stage:* tragic, upsetting, disturbing, heart-rending, sad, painful, traumatic, agonizing, harrowing; pitiful, poignant, plaintive, moving; informal tear-jerking.
OPPOSITES: comforting.

heartbroken adjective *he was heartbroken when his wife left him:* devastated, broken-hearted, heavy-hearted, grieving, grief-stricken, inconsolable, crushed, shattered, desolate, despairing, anguished; upset, distressed, miserable, sorrowful, sad, downcast, disconsolate, crestfallen, despondent.
OPPOSITES: ecstatic.

heartburn noun indigestion, dyspepsia; Medicine pyrosis.

hearten verb *their success greatly heartened him:* cheer, cheer up, encourage, raise someone's spirits, boost, buoy up, uplift, elate; comfort, reassure; informal perk up, buck up, pep up.
OPPOSITES: depress.

heartfelt adjective *our heartfelt thanks for all you have done:* sincere, genuine, from the heart; earnest, profound, deep, wholehearted, ardent, fervent, passionate, enthusiastic, eager; honest, bona fide.
OPPOSITES: insincere.

heartily adverb
1 *we heartily welcome the changes:* wholeheartedly, sincerely, genuinely, warmly, profoundly, with all your heart; eagerly, enthusiastically, earnestly, ardently.
2 *they were heartily sick of her:* thoroughly, completely, absolutely, really, exceedingly, immensely, most, downright, utterly, quite.

heartless adjective *the heartless thieves stole the pushchair of a two-year old boy:* unfeeling, unsympathetic, unkind, uncaring, unconcerned, insensitive, inconsiderate, hard-hearted, stony-hearted, cold-hearted, mean-spirited; cold, callous, cruel, merciless, pitiless, inhuman.
OPPOSITES: compassionate.

heart-rending adjective *I heard a single heart-rending cry:* distressing, upsetting, disturbing, heartbreaking, sad, tragic, painful, traumatic, harrowing; pitiful, poignant, plaintive, moving; informal tear-jerking.

heart-throb noun (informal) idol, pin-up, star, superstar, hero; informal dreamboat.

heart-to-heart adjective *we had a heart-to-heart chat about things:* intimate, personal, man-to-man, woman-to-woman; candid, honest, truthful, sincere.
▷ noun *they had a long heart-to-heart:* conversation, tête-à-tête, one-to-one, head-to-head; chat, talk, word; informal confab; Brit. informal natter, chinwag.

heart-warming adjective *the conductor told me this heart-warming little story:* touching, moving, heartening, stirring, uplifting, encouraging, gratifying, pleasing, cheering, gladdening.
OPPOSITES: distressing.

hearty adjective
1 *there was hearty cheering from some 8,000 home fans:* exuberant, high-spirited, lively, enthusiastic, jovial, ebullient, cheerful, uninhibited, animated, vivacious, energetic, eager, effusive, loud, noisy.
2 *he expressed his hearty agreement | hearty congratulations:* wholehearted, heartfelt, sincere, genuine, real, true; earnest,

h

fervent, ardent, enthusiastic.
3 *a formidably hearty woman of sixty-five:* robust, healthy, hardy, fit, flourishing, blooming; vigorous, sturdy, strong; Brit. in rude health.
4 *they end each day with a hearty meal:* substantial, filling, large, ample, sizeable, generous, square, solid; healthy.
OPPOSITES: subdued, half-hearted, frail, light.

heat noun
1 *forecasters are predicting that the heat will continue:* warmth, high temperature; heatwave, hot spell.
2 *he took some of the heat out of the dispute:* passion, intensity, vehemence, warmth, fervour, ardour; enthusiasm, excitement, agitation; anger, fury.
OPPOSITES: cold.
▷**verb** *the room faces north and is difficult to heat | rice heats up quickly in the microwave:* warm, warm up, make/become warm.
OPPOSITES: cool.

> WORD LINKS
> **thermal**, **caloric** relating to heat

heated adjective *she had a heated argument with one of the officials:* passionate, spirited, impassioned, animated, lively, intense, excited, vehement, fiery, inflamed; angry, bitter, furious, fierce, stormy, tempestuous.

heath noun (Brit.) moor, heathland, moorland, scrub; common land.

heathen noun *he preached the common humanity of Christians and heathens:* pagan; infidel, idolater; unbeliever, non-believer, disbeliever, atheist, agnostic, sceptic; heretic.
OPPOSITES: believer.
▷**adjective** *a reformist agenda determined to stamp out heathen practices:* pagan; infidel, idolatrous; unbelieving, non-believing, atheistic, agnostic, heretical, faithless, godless, irreligious, ungodly, unholy; barbarian, barbarous, primitive.
OPPOSITES: devout.

heave verb
1 *she heaved the sofa back into place:* haul, pull, drag, draw, tug, heft; informal lug, yank; Brit. informal hump.
2 *he heaved a sigh of relief:* let out, breathe, give; emit, utter.
3 *the sea heaved beneath her:* rise and fall, roll, swell, surge, churn, seethe, swirl.

heaven noun
1 *the good will have a place in heaven:* paradise, Zion; the hereafter, the next world, the next life, the afterworld; literary Elysium, the Elysian Fields, Valhalla.
2 *lying by the sea with a good book is my idea of heaven:* bliss, ecstasy, rapture, contentment, happiness, delight, joy, seventh heaven; paradise, Utopia, nirvana.

3 *Galileo used a telescope to observe the heavens:* the sky, the skies, the upper atmosphere, the stratosphere; literary the firmament, the welkin.
OPPOSITES: hell, misery.
▫ **move heaven and earth**
if members tell us they are in dire straits, then we will move heaven and earth to help them: try your hardest, do your best, do your utmost, do all you can, give your all, spare no effort, put yourself out; strive, exert yourself, work hard; informal bend over backwards, go all out, bust a gut.

> WORD LINKS
> **celestial** relating to heaven

heavenly adjective *they saw visions of angels and heavenly choirs:* celestial, ethereal, holy, divine; angelic, seraphic, cherubic.

heaven-sent adjective *she was so afraid of losing this heaven-sent opportunity:* fortunate, lucky, happy, auspicious, providential, propitious, God-given, felicitous, opportune, golden, favourable, advantageous, serendipitous.
OPPOSITES: inopportune.

heavily adverb
1 *Dad walked heavily towards the door:* laboriously, slowly, ponderously, woodenly, stiffly; with difficulty, painfully, awkwardly, clumsily.
2 *we were heavily defeated in the by-election:* decisively, conclusively, roundly, soundly; utterly, completely, thoroughly.
3 *he started drinking heavily:* excessively, to excess, immoderately, copiously, inordinately, intemperately, a great deal, too much, overmuch.
4 *I became heavily involved in politics:* deeply, very, extremely.

heavy adjective
1 *the box was too heavy for me to carry:* weighty, hefty, substantial, ponderous; solid, dense.
2 *he was a heavy man of about sixty:* overweight, fat, obese, corpulent, large, bulky, stout, stocky, portly, plump, paunchy, fleshy; informal hulking, tubby; Brit. informal podgy.
3 *a heavy blow to the head:* forceful, hard, strong, violent, powerful, vigorous, mighty, hefty, sharp, smart, severe.
4 *a gardener comes in to do all the heavy work for me:* hard, arduous, physical, laborious, difficult, strenuous, demanding, tough, onerous, back-breaking, gruelling.
5 *the helicopter flew into heavy fog:* dense, thick, murky, impenetrable.
6 *we had heavy rain overnight:* torrential, relentless, copious, teeming, severe.
7 *we suffered heavy losses | a heavy fine:* big, hefty, sizeable, colossal, substantial, considerable, stiff; informal tidy, whopping, steep, astronomical.

8 *the boat encountered heavy seas:* rough, wild, stormy, choppy, turbulent, tempestuous, squally.
9 *the battalion has been involved in heavy fighting:* fierce, intense, vigorous, relentless, all-out, severe, serious.
10 *he's a heavy drinker:* immoderate, excessive, intemperate, overindulgent, unrestrained, uncontrolled.
OPPOSITES: light, thin, gentle.

heavy-handed adjective
1 *they tend to be a bit heavy-handed with the equipment:* clumsy, careless, awkward, maladroit, inept, unskilful; informal ham-fisted, cack-handed; Brit. informal all fingers and thumbs.
2 *heavy-handed policing did nothing to improve the atmosphere:* insensitive, oppressive, overbearing, harsh, stern, severe, hard-hitting, uncompromising, tyrannical, despotic, ruthless, merciless; tactless, undiplomatic, inept.
OPPOSITES: dexterous, sensitive.

heckle verb *he was booed and heckled when he tried to address the crowd:* jeer, taunt, jibe at, shout down, boo, hiss; Brit. & Austral./NZ barrack; informal give someone a hard time.
OPPOSITES: cheer.

hectic adjective *his hectic business schedule has taken its toll:* frantic, frenetic, frenzied, feverish, manic, busy, active, fast and furious; lively, brisk, bustling, buzzing.
OPPOSITES: leisurely.

hector verb *she's constantly hectoring her husband:* bully, browbeat, harass, torment, plague, intimidate; coerce, pressurize, strong-arm; informal bulldoze.

hedge noun
1 *he sees the fund as an excellent hedge against a fall in sterling:* safeguard, protection, shield, screen, guard, buffer, cushion; insurance, security.
2 *his analysis is full of hedges like 'probably' and 'perhaps':* equivocation, evasion, fudge, quibble, qualification; temporizing, uncertainty, prevarication, vagueness.
▷verb
1 *the fields were hedged with hawthorn:* surround, enclose, encircle, ring, border, edge, bound.
2 *the company hedged its position on the futures market:* safeguard, protect, shield, guard, cushion; cover, insure.
3 *he hedged at every new question:* prevaricate, equivocate, vacillate, quibble, hesitate, stall, dodge the issue, be non-committal, be evasive, be vague, beat about the bush, mince your words; Brit. hum and haw; informal sit on the fence, duck the question, pussyfoot.

hedonism noun *she runs away to lead a life of hedonism in Spain:* pleasure, pleasure-seeking, self-indulgence, self-gratification, lotus-eating; intemperance, immoderation, extravagance, luxury, high living.
OPPOSITES: self-restraint, asceticism.

hedonist noun pleasure-seeker, lotus-eater, sybarite, sensualist, voluptuary; bon viveur, bon vivant; epicure, gastronome.
OPPOSITES: ascetic.

hedonistic adjective *a shift towards a more casual, private, and hedonistic style of life:* pleasure-seeking, self-indulgent, sybaritic, lotus-eating, epicurean; unrestrained, intemperate, immoderate, extravagant, decadent.

heed verb *he should have heeded the warnings:* pay attention to, take notice of, take note of, pay heed to, attend to, listen to; bear in mind, be mindful of, mind, mark, consider, take into account, follow, obey, adhere to, abide by, observe, take to heart, be alert to.
OPPOSITES: disregard.
▷noun *if he heard what I said, he paid no heed:* attention, notice, note, regard; consideration, thought, care.

heedful adjective *on every side they cast a heedful eye:* attentive, careful, mindful, cautious, prudent, circumspect; alert, aware, wary, chary, watchful, vigilant, on guard, on the alert.
OPPOSITES: heedless.

heedless adjective *someone had stayed behind, heedless of the warnings:* unmindful, taking no notice, paying no heed, unheeding, neglectful, oblivious, inattentive, blind, deaf; incautious, imprudent, rash, reckless, foolhardy, improvident, unwary.
OPPOSITES: heedful.

heel verb *the ship heeled to starboard:* lean over, list, tilt, tip, incline, keel over; careen.

heft verb *Donald hefted a stone jar of whisky into position:* lift, raise, heave, hoist, haul; carry; informal lug, cart, tote; Brit. informal hump.

hefty adjective
1 *the horses hauled hefty loads of timber:* heavy, weighty, bulky, big, large, substantial, massive, ponderous; unwieldy, cumbersome; informal hulking.
2 *a hefty young man:* burly, heavy, sturdy, strapping, bulky, brawny, husky, strong, muscular, large, big, solid, well built; portly, stout; informal hulking, hunky, beefy.
3 *they face a hefty fine:* substantial, sizeable, considerable, stiff, extortionate, large, excessive; Brit. swingeing; informal steep, astronomical.
4 *he aimed a hefty kick at the door:* powerful, violent, hard, forceful, heavy, mighty.
OPPOSITES: light, slight, small.

h

height noun

1 *her height marked her out from other women:* stature.
2 *at a height of 5,000 metres above sea level:* altitude, elevation.
3 *they were at the height of their fame when they split up:* highest point, crowning moment, peak, acme, zenith, apogee, pinnacle, climax, high water mark.
4 *he is terrified of heights:* high places, high ground; precipices, cliffs.
OPPOSITES: depth, nadir.

> WORD LINKS
> **acrophobia** extreme fear of heights

heighten verb *her pleasure was heightened by a sense of guilt:* intensify, increase, enhance, add to, augment, boost, strengthen, deepen, magnify, amplify, reinforce.
OPPOSITES: lower, reduce.

heinous adjective *child abuse is a heinous offence:* wicked, evil, monstrous, abominable, detestable, contemptible, reprehensible, odious, despicable, egregious, horrific, terrible, atrocious, awful, abhorrent, loathsome, hideous, unspeakable, execrable, iniquitous, villainous.
OPPOSITES: admirable.

heir, heiress noun successor, next in line, inheritor, beneficiary, legatee; descendant, scion.

> WORD LINKS
> **hereditary** relating to an heir

helix noun spiral, coil, corkscrew, curl, twist, gyre, whorl, convolution.

hell noun

1 *they feared they would go to hell:* the underworld, the netherworld, the Inferno, the infernal regions, the abyss, eternal damnation, perdition; literary Hades, Gehenna.
2 *he put his son through years of hell:* misery, torture, agony, torment, anguish, wretchedness, woe; a nightmare, an ordeal.
OPPOSITES: heaven, paradise.

> WORD LINKS
> **infernal** relating to hell

hell-bent adjective *why are you hell-bent on leaving?* intent, bent, determined, set, dead set, insistent, fixed, resolved; single-minded, fixated.

hellish adjective

1 *I saw the hellish face of Death:* infernal, diabolical, fiendish, satanic, demonic; evil, wicked.
2 (informal) *it's been a hellish week:* horrible, awful, terrible, dreadful, appalling, horrid, vile, foul, atrocious, horrendous, frightful; difficult, unpleasant, nasty, disagreeable; stressful, taxing, tough, hard, frustrating, fraught, traumatic, gruelling; informal

ghastly, rotten, lousy, murderous; Brit. informal beastly.
OPPOSITES: heavenly, wonderful.

helm noun *the second mate took the helm:* tiller, wheel; rudder.
□ at the helm
a family-run business whose founder remains at the helm: in charge, in command, in control, responsible, in authority, at the wheel, in the driving seat, holding the reins, in the saddle; informal running the show, calling the shots.

help verb

1 *they helped her with the washing up:* assist, aid, lend a hand to, give assistance to, come to the aid of; be of service to, be of use to; do someone a favour, do someone a service, do someone a good turn, bail someone out, come to the rescue of; rally round, pitch in; informal get someone out of a tight spot, save someone's bacon, save someone's skin.
2 *using this credit card helps cancer research:* support, contribute to, give money to, donate to; promote, boost, back; further the interests of; informal bankroll.
3 *sore throats are helped by lozenges:* relieve, soothe, ease, alleviate, make better, improve, assuage, lessen; remedy, cure, heal.
4 *when he saw her, he could not help laughing:* resist, refrain from, keep from, forbear from, stop yourself, avoid.
OPPOSITES: hinder, impede, worsen.
▷ noun
1 *I asked for help from my neighbours | this could be of help to you:* assistance, aid, a helping hand, support, succour, advice, guidance; benefit, use, advantage, service, comfort; informal a shot in the arm.
2 *he sought help for his eczema:* relief, alleviation, improvement, healing; a remedy, a cure.
OPPOSITES: hindrance.
□ help yourself to
he helped himself to the contents of her purse: steal, take, appropriate, pocket, commandeer; formal purloin; informal swipe, pinch, filch, walk off with, run off with; Brit. informal nick, snaffle, whip, knock off.

helper noun *there was no shortage of helpers to relieve us:* assistant, aide, deputy, auxiliary, second, right-hand man/woman, attendant, acolyte; co-worker, workmate, teammate, associate, colleague, partner; literary helpmate, helpmeet; informal sidekick.

helpful adjective

1 *the staff are friendly and helpful:* obliging, eager to please, kind, accommodating, supportive, cooperative; sympathetic, neighbourly, charitable.
2 *we found it helpful to receive your comments:* useful, of use, beneficial, valuable, profitable, fruitful, advantageous, worthwhile, constructive;

informative, instructive.
3 *we recommend this helpful new power tool:* handy, useful, convenient, practical, easy-to-use, functional, serviceable; informal neat, nifty.
OPPOSITES: unhelpful, useless.

helping noun *there will be enough for six to eight helpings:* portion, serving, piece, slice, share, ration, allocation; informal dollop.

helpless adjective *the cubs are born blind and helpless:* defenceless, vulnerable, exposed, unprotected, open to attack; dependent, incapable, powerless, impotent, weak.
OPPOSITES: independent, powerful.

hem verb
□ hem someone/something in
1 *the bay was hemmed in by pine trees:* surround, border, edge, encircle, circle, ring, enclose, skirt, fringe, encompass.
2 *he was hemmed in by parked cars | we were hemmed in by the rules:* restrict, confine, trap, fence in; constrain, restrain, limit, curb, check.

hence adverb *many vehicle journeys (and hence a lot of pollution) would be saved:* consequently, as a consequence, as a result, because of that, that being so, for that reason, therefore, so, accordingly; formal thus, ergo.

henceforth, henceforward adverb (formal) *henceforth the director will be responsible for the whole establishment:* from now on, as of now, in future, hence, subsequently, from this day on/forth; formal hereafter.

henchman noun *the local warlord arrived with a group of henchmen:* aide, assistant, right-hand man, helper; underling, minion, lackey, flunkey; informal sidekick, stooge, crony, heavy, minder.

henpecked adjective *a henpecked husband who was at the end of his tether:* downtrodden, bullied, browbeaten; meek, timid, cringing; informal under someone's thumb, led by the nose.
OPPOSITES: domineering.

herald verb
1 *screams and shouts heralded their approach:* announce, proclaim, broadcast, publicize, declare, trumpet, blazon, advertise.
2 *the speech heralded a major policy change:* signal, indicate, announce, spell, presage, augur, portend, promise, foretell; usher in, pave the way for, be a harbinger of; literary foretoken, betoken.

Herculean adjective
1 *this is a Herculean task that he has undertaken:* difficult, hard, tough, gruelling, laborious, uphill, back-breaking, onerous, strenuous, arduous, demanding, exhausting, taxing, formidable, huge, massive.

2 *he was a man of Herculean build:* strong, muscular, muscly, powerful, robust, solid, strapping, brawny, burly; informal hunky, beefy, hulking.
OPPOSITES: easy, puny.

herd noun
1 *a herd of cows blocked the road:* drove, flock, pack; group, collection.
2 *I ran into a herd of movie actors:* crowd, group, bunch, horde, mob, host, pack, multitude, throng, swarm, company.
3 *they consider themselves above the herd:* common people, masses, rank and file, crowd, plebeians; hoi polloi, mob, proletariat, rabble; informal riff-raff, great unwashed, proles, plebs.
▷ verb
1 *we herded the sheep back into the pen:* drive, shepherd, guide; round up, gather, collect.
2 *we all herded into the waiting room:* crowd, pack, flock; cluster, huddle.
3 *they live by herding reindeer:* tend, look after, keep, mind, guard.

herdsman, herdswoman noun stockman, herder, drover, cattleman, cowherd, cowhand, cowman, cowboy, rancher, gaucho, shepherd; N. Amer. ranchero.

hereafter adverb (formal) *nothing I say hereafter is intended to offend:* from now on, after this, as of now, from this moment on, from this day forward, subsequently, in future; formal hence, henceforth, henceforward.
▷ noun *our preparation for the hereafter:* life after death, the afterlife, the afterworld, the next world; eternity, heaven, paradise.

hereditary adjective
1 *their hereditary right to hunt on this land:* inherited; ancestral, family.
2 *cystic fibrosis is a fatal hereditary disease:* genetic, congenital, inherited; in the family, in the blood, in the genes.
OPPOSITES: acquired.

heredity noun *the effects of heredity and environment:* genes, genetic make-up; ancestry, descent, extraction, parentage.

heresy noun *an old man called Walter Myln was burned for heresy at St Andrews:* dissent, nonconformity, heterodoxy, unorthodoxy, apostasy, blasphemy, freethinking; atheism, paganism, heathenism; idolatry; iconoclasm.
OPPOSITES: conformity, belief.

heretic noun dissenter, nonconformist, apostate, freethinker, iconoclast; atheist, non-believer, unbeliever, idolater, pagan, heathen.
OPPOSITES: conformist, believer.

heretical adjective *his opinion was denounced as heretical at Oxford in 1367:* dissenting, nonconformist, freethinking, heterodox, unorthodox; idolatrous, godless, pagan, blasphemous; iconoclastic.

heritage noun
1 *Europe's varied cultural heritage:* tradition, history, past, background; culture, customs.
2 *he is proud of his Greek heritage:* ancestry, lineage, descent, extraction, parentage, roots, background, heredity.

hermetic adjective airtight, tight, sealed; watertight, waterproof.

hermit noun *the tale of the English monk and hermit St Godric of Finchale:* recluse, solitary, loner, ascetic; historical anchorite, anchoress.

WORD LINKS
eremitic relating to a hermit

hermitage noun retreat, refuge, hideaway, hideout, shelter.

hero noun
1 *the heroes of the civil rights movements:* brave man/woman; man/woman of the hour.
2 *a football hero:* star, superstar, megastar, idol, celebrity, luminary; paragon; favourite, darling; informal celeb.
3 *the hero of the film is a young pianist:* leading man, male lead, lead actor, male protagonist, principal male character/role, starring role.
OPPOSITES: coward, villain.

heroic adjective
1 *their heroic deeds | heroic rescuers:* brave, courageous, valiant, valorous, intrepid, bold, fearless, daring, audacious; unafraid, undaunted, dauntless, doughty, plucky, stout-hearted, chivalrous, noble; informal gutsy, spunky.
2 *black granite obelisks on a heroic scale:* grand, enormous, huge, massive, titanic, colossal, monumental, prodigious, epic.

heroine noun
1 *she's a heroine—she saved my baby:* brave woman, hero, woman of the hour.
2 *the literary heroine of Moscow:* star, superstar, megastar, idol, celebrity, luminary, paragon; favourite, darling; informal celeb.
3 *the film's heroine makes a stand against the crooks:* leading lady, female lead, female protagonist, principal female character/role, starring role; prima donna, diva.

heroism noun *many of the women distinguished themselves by great acts of heroism:* bravery, courage, valour, boldness, daring, audacity, fearlessness, pluck, stout-heartedness; backbone, spine, grit, spirit, mettle; gallantry, chivalry; informal guts; Brit. informal bottle.

hero-worship noun idolization, adulation, admiration, lionization, worship, adoration, veneration.
OPPOSITES: contempt.

hesitancy noun. See HESITATION.

hesitant adjective
1 *clients are hesitant about buying:* uncertain, undecided, unsure, doubtful, dubious, sceptical; tentative, nervous, reluctant; indecisive, irresolute, hesitating, dithering, vacillating, blowing hot and cold; ambivalent, in two minds; Brit. havering, humming and hawing; informal iffy.
2 *the oldest of the children spoke in a hesitant voice:* timid, diffident, shy, bashful, insecure, lacking confidence; faltering.
OPPOSITES: certain, decisive, confident.

hesitate verb
1 *she hesitated, unsure of what to say:* pause, delay, wait; be in two minds, be uncertain, be unsure, be doubtful, be indecisive, dither, stall, temporize, equivocate, vacillate, waver, blow hot and cold, have second thoughts; Brit. haver, hum and haw; informal dilly-dally, shilly-shally.
2 *please don't hesitate to contact me:* be reluctant, be unwilling, be disinclined; scruple, have misgivings about, have qualms about, shrink from, demur from, think twice about, baulk at.

hesitation noun
1 *after a moment's hesitation, Mark followed:* pause, wait, delay; irresolution, indecision, indecisiveness, hesitancy; equivocation, vacillation, second thoughts; uncertainty, doubt, doubtfulness, dubiousness; dithering, stalling.
2 *I have no hesitation in recommending him:* reluctance, disinclination, hesitancy, unease, qualms, ambivalence, second thoughts.

heterodox adjective unorthodox, nonconformist, dissenting, dissident, rebellious, renegade, maverick; heretical, blasphemous, apostate.
OPPOSITES: orthodox.

heterogeneous adjective *the collection of heterogeneous tasks that make up housework:* diverse, varied, varying, different, differing, miscellaneous, assorted, mixed, sundry, disparate, unrelated; motley.
OPPOSITES: homogeneous.

hew verb *master carpenters hewed the logs with axes:* chop, hack, cut, lop, axe, cleave; fell; carve, shape, fashion, sculpt, model.

heyday noun *the paper has lost millions of readers since its heyday in 1964:* height, peak, pinnacle, zenith, acme; prime, bloom; prime of life, salad days.

hiatus noun *there has been a brief hiatus in the fighting:* pause, break, gap, interval, intermission, interlude, interruption, suspension, lull, respite; informal breather, let-up.

hidden adjective

1 *they watched the action via a hidden camera:* concealed, secret, invisible, unseen, out of sight; camouflaged, disguised, masked.
2 *people look for hidden meanings instead of what is already there:* obscure, cryptic, coded, mysterious, secret, covert, abstruse, arcane, unclear, concealed, indistinct, indefinite, vague, unfathomable, inexplicable, ulterior, deep, subliminal.
OPPOSITES: visible, obvious.

hide¹ verb

1 *he hid the money under the floor:* conceal, secrete, put out of sight; camouflage; stow away, cache; informal stash.
2 *they escaped after hiding in an air vent:* conceal yourself, secrete yourself, hide out, take cover, keep out of sight; lie low, go to ground, go to earth; informal hole up.
3 *clouds rolled across the sky and hid the moon:* obscure, block out, blot out, obstruct, cloud, shroud, veil, blanket, envelop, eclipse.
4 *he could not hide his dislike of this process:* conceal, keep secret, cover up, keep dark, keep quiet about, hush up, bottle up, suppress; disguise, mask, camouflage; informal keep under your hat, keep a/the lid on.
OPPOSITES: uncover, reveal, flaunt.

hide² noun *a cow hide:* skin, pelt, coat; leather.

hideaway noun *he started making plans to find a retirement hideaway in the Bahamas:* retreat, refuge, hiding place, hideout, den, bolt-hole, shelter, sanctuary, sanctum; informal hidey-hole.

hidebound adjective *hidebound traditionalists who refuse to accept change:* conservative, reactionary, conventional, orthodox; fundamentalist, diehard, hard-line, dyed-in-the-wool, set in your ways; narrow-minded, small-minded, intolerant, uncompromising, rigid; prejudiced, bigoted.
OPPOSITES: liberal.

hideous adjective

1 *his smile made him look more hideous than ever:* ugly, repulsive, repellent, unsightly, revolting, gruesome, grotesque, monstrous, ghastly, reptilian; informal as ugly as sin.
2 *hideous cases of torture have been reported:* horrific, terrible, appalling, awful, dreadful, frightful, horrible, horrendous, horrifying, shocking, sickening, gruesome, ghastly, unspeakable, abhorrent, monstrous, heinous, abominable, foul, vile, odious, execrable.
OPPOSITES: beautiful, pleasant.

hideout noun *the kidnappers did not want their hideout discovered:* hiding place, hideaway, retreat, refuge, shelter, bolt-hole, safe house, sanctuary, sanctum; informal hidey-hole.

hiding noun
□ **in hiding**
the fugitive priest is currently in hiding: hidden, concealed, lying low, gone to ground, gone to earth, in a safe house.

hierarchy noun *the initiative was with those lower down in the hierarchy:* pecking order, ranking, grading, ladder, scale, progression, chain of command, structure.

higgledy-piggledy (informal) adjective
it's a higgledy-piggledy mess of badly designed streets and clashing styles: jumbled, muddled, chaotic, disorganized, disordered, disorderly, untidy, messy, confused, unsystematic, irregular, out of order, in disarray, in a mess, in a muddle, haphazard, random; informal all over the place; Brit. informal shambolic.
OPPOSITES: tidy.
▷ adverb *the cars were parked higgledy-piggledy:* in a jumble, in a muddle, in disarray, in disorder, untidily, haphazardly, randomly, anyhow; informal all over the place, topsy-turvy, every which way; Brit. informal all over the shop.
OPPOSITES: tidily.

high adjective

1 *the top of a high mountain:* tall, lofty, towering, elevated, giant, big; multi-storey, high-rise.
2 *he rose to a high position in the government:* high-ranking, high-level, leading, top, top-level, prominent, pre-eminent, foremost, senior; influential, powerful, important, elevated, prime, premier, exalted; N. Amer. ranking.
3 *shop around to avoid high prices:* expensive, excessive, unreasonable, inflated, dear, costly, exorbitant, extortionate, prohibitive; Brit. over the odds; informal steep, stiff, pricey.
4 *their work was of a high standard:* excellent, outstanding, exemplary, exceptional, admirable, fine, good, first-class, first-rate, superior, superlative, superb; impeccable, irreproachable, unimpeachable, perfect, flawless.
5 *the voices rose to hit a high note:* high-pitched, high-frequency; soprano, treble, falsetto, shrill, sharp, piercing, penetrating.
6 (informal) *they are high on a cocktail of drugs:* intoxicated, inebriated, drugged, stupefied, befuddled, delirious, hallucinating; informal stoned, tripping.
OPPOSITES: short, lowly, cheap, low, deep.
▷ noun *commodity prices were at a rare high:* high level, high point, peak, maximum, high water mark; pinnacle, zenith, acme, height.
OPPOSITES: low.
□ **high and dry**
the company went bankrupt, leaving hundreds of employees high and dry: in

difficulties, in the lurch, in dire straits, destitute; bereft, helpless, abandoned, stranded, marooned; informal on the rocks.

□ **high and low** *we searched for her high and low:* everywhere, all over, all around, far and wide, {here, there, and everywhere}, extensively, thoroughly, widely, in every nook and cranny; informal all over the place; Brit. informal all over the shop.

□ **high and mighty** (informal) *her family were very high and mighty and ignored me whenever they could:* self-important, condescending, patronizing, disdainful, supercilious, superior, snobbish, snobby, haughty, conceited, above yourself; informal stuck-up, snooty; Brit. informal toffee-nosed.

□ **on a high** (informal) *he was on a high following the team's triumph:* ecstatic, euphoric, delirious, elated, thrilled, overjoyed, beside yourself, walking on air, on cloud nine, in seventh heaven, jumping for joy, in raptures, exultant, jubilant; informal over the moon, on top of the world.

> **WORD LINKS**
> **acrophobia** extreme fear of high places

highbrow adjective *his art has a small, mostly highbrow following:* intellectual, scholarly, bookish, well read, academic, educated, donnish, bluestocking; sophisticated, erudite, learned, enlightened, cultured; informal brainy.
OPPOSITES: lowbrow.

▷ **noun** *all those highbrows who squirm when they hear pop music:* intellectual, scholar, academic, bluestocking, thinker; informal egghead, bookworm; Brit. informal boffin.

high-class adjective *the pub where they gathered was a high-class establishment:* superior, first-rate; select, elite, choice, premier, top, top-flight, upper-class; luxurious, de luxe, high-quality, top-quality, excellent; Brit. upmarket; informal top-notch, classy, posh.

highfalutin adjective (informal). See PRETENTIOUS.

high-flown adjective *his speeches brimmed with high-flown rhetoric:* grand, extravagant, elaborate, flowery, ornate, overblown, overdone, overwrought, grandiloquent, grandiose, inflated, affected, pretentious, turgid; formal magniloquent; informal purple, highfalutin.
OPPOSITES: plain.

high-handed adjective *people are disenchanted by the government's high-handed approach:* imperious, arbitrary, domineering, peremptory, overbearing, heavy-handed, lordly, arrogant, haughty, inflexible, rigid, autocratic, authoritarian, dictatorial, tyrannical; informal pushy, bossy, high and mighty.
OPPOSITES: liberal.

highland noun upland, highlands, uplands, mountains, hills, heights, moors; tableland, plateau; Brit. wolds.

highlight noun *he views this as the highlight of his career:* climax, peak, pinnacle, height, high spot, high point, acme, zenith, summit, crowning moment, high water mark, best part.
OPPOSITES: nadir.

▷ **verb** *he has highlighted numerous shortcomings in the plan:* draw attention to, mention, identify, specify, name, refer to, indicate, spotlight, focus on, underline, feature, bring out, accentuate, accent, zero in on, stress, emphasize.

highly adverb
1 *a highly dangerous substance:* very, extremely, exceedingly, particularly, most, really, thoroughly, decidedly, distinctly, exceptionally, immensely, terribly, inordinately, singularly, extraordinarily; informal terrifically, awfully; Brit. informal dead, jolly.
2 *he was highly regarded by everyone who knew him:* favourably, well, appreciatively, admiringly, approvingly, positively, glowingly, enthusiastically.
OPPOSITES: slightly, unfavourably.

highly strung adjective *a young Russian artist who was rather highly strung:* nervous, nervy, excitable, temperamental, sensitive, unstable; brittle, on edge, edgy, jumpy, restless, anxious, tense; neurotic; informal uptight, twitchy.
OPPOSITES: relaxed.

high-powered adjective *the women were all very high-powered and impressive:* dynamic, ambitious, energetic, assertive, enterprising, vigorous, forceful, aggressive; informal go-ahead, go-getting, pushy.

high-pressure adjective *unscrupulous salesmen who use high-pressure tactics:* forceful, insistent, persistent; intensive, high-powered, aggressive, not taking no for an answer; informal pushy.

high-spirited adjective *he is just an ordinary high-spirited little boy:* exuberant, ebullient, lively, spirited, full of fun, full of joie de vivre, fun-loving, animated, bouncy, bubbly, sparkling, vivacious, buoyant, cheerful, joyful, jaunty, irrepressible; literary frolicsome; informal chirpy, full of beans.

high spirits plural noun *they were young, strong, and bursting with high spirits:* exuberance, ebullience, joie de vivre, liveliness, vivacity, vitality, spirit, sparkle, joy, cheerfulness, good humour, zest, energy, bounce.

hijack verb *three armed men hijacked a white van:* seize, seize control of, take over, commandeer.

hike noun *a five-mile hike on the Yorkshire*

moors: walk, trek, ramble, tramp, trudge, march; informal slog.
▷**verb**
1 *they hiked across the moors for miles:* walk, trek, ramble, tramp, trudge, march; informal slog, hoof it.
2 *the government hiked petrol prices by about 70 per cent:* increase, raise, up, put up, mark up, push up, inflate; informal jack up, bump up.

hilarious adjective *she told us a hilarious story about her friends:* funny, uproarious, riotous, farcical, rib-tickling; humorous, comic, amusing, entertaining; informal hysterical, side-splitting, priceless.
OPPOSITES: sad, serious.

hilarity noun *his bemused expression was the cause of much hilarity:* amusement, mirth, laughter, merriment, levity, fun, humour, jocularity, jollity, delight, glee, comedy.

hill noun high ground, prominence, hillock, foothill, hillside, rise, mound, mount, mountain, knoll, hummock, tor, fell, pike, mesa; bank, ridge, slope, incline, gradient; (**hills**) heights, downs; Scottish brae; formal eminence.

hillock noun mound, small hill, prominence, elevation, rise, knoll, hummock, hump, dune; bank, ridge; formal eminence.

hilt noun *the sword's hilt was beautifully crafted:* handle, haft, handgrip, grip, shaft, shank, stock.
□ **to the hilt**
we will support our elected leaders to the hilt: completely, fully, wholly, totally, entirely, utterly, unreservedly, unconditionally, in every respect, one hundred per cent, every inch, to the full, all the way, body and soul, heart and soul.

hinder verb *various technical problems have hindered our progress:* hamper, obstruct, impede, inhibit, baulk, thwart, foil, curb, delay, arrest, interfere with, set back, slow down, hold back, hold up, stop, halt; restrict, restrain, constrain, block, check, curtail, frustrate, handicap, hamstring; informal stymie.
OPPOSITES: facilitate.

hindrance noun *the bad weather was a major hindrance to the relief effort:* obstacle, impediment, barrier, bar, obstruction, handicap, block, hurdle, restraint, restriction, limitation, encumbrance; drawback, setback, difficulty, inconvenience, snag, catch, hitch, stumbling block; informal hiccup.
OPPOSITES: help.

hinge verb
□ **hinge on**
our future hinges on the outcome of next month's election: depend on, be dependent on, be determined by, be decided by, hang on, rest on, turn on, be contingent on, be conditional on, revolve around.

hint noun
1 *he had given no hint that he would leave:* clue, inkling, suggestion, indication, indicator, sign, signal, pointer, intimation, insinuation, innuendo, mention, whisper.
2 *a series of hints on how to promote your website:* tip, suggestion, pointer, clue, guideline, recommendation; advice, help; informal dos and don'ts.
3 *a very pleasant wine with just a hint of oak:* trace, touch, suspicion, suggestion, dash, soupçon, tinge, whiff, taste, undertone; informal smidgen, tad.
▷**verb** *he has hinted that his loyalties lie elsewhere:* imply, insinuate, intimate, suggest, indicate, signal; allude to, refer to, mean; informal get at.

hip noun

┌─────────────────────────────────┐
│ WORD LINKS   │
│ **sciatic** relating to the hips │
└─────────────────────────────────┘

hire verb
1 *we hired a car and drove to Wales:* rent, lease, charter.
2 *they hire and fire labour in line with demand:* employ, engage, recruit, appoint, take on, sign up, enrol, commission, enlist.
OPPOSITES: dismiss.
▷**noun** *a car hire company:* rental, rent, hiring, lease, leasing, charter.

historian noun chronicler, annalist, archivist, recorder; historiographer, antiquarian, chronologer.

historic adjective *it's a historic moment that will bring an end to 100 years of bloodshed:* significant, notable, important, momentous, consequential, of great consequence, memorable, unforgettable, remarkable; famous, famed, celebrated, renowned; landmark, groundbreaking, epoch-making, red-letter.
OPPOSITES: insignificant.

┌───┐
│ USAGE   │
│   │
│ **Historic** and **historical** do not   │
│ have the same meaning. **Historic**   │
│ means 'famous or important in history', │
│ while **historical** chiefly means   │
│ 'relating to history' (*there is   │
│ historical evidence to support this   │
│ theory*).   │
└───┘

historical adjective
1 *historical evidence is sparse, to say the least:* documented, recorded, chronicled, archival; authentic, factual, actual, true.
2 *famous historical figures:* past, bygone, ancient, old, former; traditional, time-honoured, established, customary; literary of yore.
OPPOSITES: contemporary.

history noun
1 *my interest in history gave me a new perspective on events:* the past, former

times, historical events, the olden days, the old days, bygone days, yesterday, antiquity; literary days of yore, yesteryear.
2 *I was reading a history of the Civil War:* account, record, narrative, tale, story, chronicle, archive, report, study; memoir.
3 *Kirsty calmly related the details of her history:* background, past, life story, experiences; antecedents.

histrionic adjective *the film's soaring score and histrionic performances don't help:* melodramatic, theatrical, dramatic, exaggerated, actressy, stagy, showy, affected, artificial, overacted, overdone; informal hammy, camp.

histrionics plural noun *Anna was accustomed to her mother's histrionics:* dramatics, theatrics, tantrums, overreaction, melodrama; affectation, staginess, artificiality.

hit verb
1 *he drew back his hand to hit her:* strike, slap, smack, cuff, punch, thump, swat; beat, thrash, batter, belabour, pound, pummel, box someone's ears; literary smite; informal whack, wallop, bash, biff, clout, clobber, sock, belt.
2 *a car hit the barrier and burst into flames:* crash into, run into, smash into, knock into, bump into, cannon into, plough into, collide with, meet head-on; informal smack into.
3 *the tragedy has hit her hard:* devastate, affect badly, hurt, harm, leave a mark on; upset, shatter, crush, shock, overwhelm, traumatize; informal knock sideways, knock the stuffing out of; Brit. informal knock for six.
4 (informal) *spending for this year will hit £1,800 million:* reach, touch, rise to, climb to.
5 *it hit me that I had forgotten to get the information I needed:* occur to, strike, dawn on, come to; enter your head, cross your mind, come to mind, spring to mind.
OPPOSITES: miss.
▷ noun
1 *he received a hit from behind:* blow, thump, punch, knock, bang, slap, smack, tap, crack, stroke; impact, collision, bump, crash; informal whack, thwack, wallop, bash, belt, biff, clout, sock.
2 *he directed many Broadway hits:* success, triumph, sensation, winner; sell-out; best-seller; informal smash.
OPPOSITES: failure.
□ **hit back**
prison officers have hit back at the critical report: retaliate, respond, reply, react, counter, defend yourself.
□ **hit home**
she could see that her remark had hit home: have the desired effect, strike home, hit the mark, register, be understood, get through, sink in.
□ **hit it off** (informal) *they're an unlikely pair, but they hit it off:* get on well, get along, be friends, be friendly, be compatible, feel a

rapport, see eye to eye, take to each other, warm to each other; informal click, get on like a house on fire.
□ **hit on**
Hannah hit on a novel idea for fund-raising: discover, come up with, think of, conceive of, dream up, work out, invent, create, devise, design, pioneer; uncover, stumble on, chance on, light on, come upon.
□ **hit out at**
he hit out at the government's lack of action: criticize, attack, censure, denounce, condemn, lambaste, pillory, rail against, inveigh against; informal knock, slam; Brit. informal slate, rubbish.

hitch verb
1 *she hitched up her skirt and climbed aboard:* pull, jerk, tug, heave; hike, lift, raise; informal yank.
2 *Tom hitched the pony to his cart:* harness, yoke, couple, fasten, connect, attach, tether.
▷ noun *it all went without a hitch:* problem, difficulty, snag, setback, hindrance, obstacle, obstruction, complication, impediment, stumbling block, barrier; hold-up, interruption, delay; informal headache, glitch, hiccup.

hitherto adverb *a further selection of hitherto unpublished poems:* previously, before, beforehand, earlier, formerly; so far, to date, as yet, until now, until then, up to now, up to then; formal thus far, heretofore.

hit-or-miss, **hit-and-miss** adjective *her work can be rather hit-or-miss at times:* erratic, haphazard, disorganized, undisciplined, unmethodical, uneven; careless, slapdash, sloppy, slipshod, casual, cursory, lackadaisical, perfunctory, random, aimless, undirected, indiscriminate; informal slap-happy.
OPPOSITES: meticulous.

hoard noun *a hoard of Roman gold and silver coins found in Sussex:* cache, stockpile, stock, store, collection, supply, reserve, reservoir, fund, accumulation; treasure house, treasure trove; informal stash.
▷ verb *many of them had hoarded their rations for weeks:* store up, stockpile, stock up on, put aside, put by, lay by, lay up, set aside, stow away, buy up; cache, amass, collect, save, gather, garner, accumulate, put aside for a rainy day; informal stash away, squirrel away, salt away.
OPPOSITES: squander.

USAGE

Do not confuse **hoard** and **horde**. A **hoard** is 'a secret store', while a **horde** is 'a large group of people' (*hordes of adoring fans flocked to the stadium*).

hoarse adjective *their voices were hoarse from shouting:* rough, harsh, croaky,

throaty, gruff, husky, guttural, growly, gravelly, grating, rasping.
OPPOSITES: mellow, clear.

hoary adjective *a hoary old adage favoured by Fleet Street editors:* trite, hackneyed, clichéd, banal, commonplace, predictable, overused, stale, time-worn, tired, unimaginative, unoriginal, uninspired; informal corny.
OPPOSITES: original.

hoax noun *the call was a hoax:* practical joke, joke, prank, trick; ruse, deception, fraud, bluff, confidence trick; informal con, spoof, scam.
▷verb *on April 1, the radio station hoaxed its listeners:* play a practical joke on, trick, fool; deceive, hoodwink, delude, dupe, take in, lead on; informal con, kid, have on.

hoaxer noun practical joker, prankster, trickster, fraud, fraudster, charlatan; informal con man.

hobble verb *he was still hobbling around on crutches:* limp, shamble, shuffle, totter, dodder, stagger, stumble.

hobby noun pastime, leisure activity, leisure pursuit, recreation, entertainment, amusement, enthusiasm; sideline, diversion; formal avocation.

hobnob verb (informal) *he was in his element, hobnobbing with the rich and famous:* socialize, mix, associate, keep company, spend time, go around, rub shoulders, mingle, consort, fraternize; informal hang around/out.

hog verb (informal) *he always hogged the limelight:* monopolize, keep for yourself, dominate, control; take over, corner.
OPPOSITES: share.

hoi polloi noun *royalty seem reluctant to let the hoi polloi into their homes:* ordinary people, the masses, the common people, the populace, the public, the multitude, the rank and file, the lower orders, the third estate, the plebeians, the proletariat; the mob, the herd, the rabble; informal riff-raff, the great unwashed, the plebs, the proles.

hoist verb *they refused to allow Ross to hoist the Dutch flag:* raise, haul up, lift, heave up, jack up, hike up, winch up, pull up, elevate, erect.
OPPOSITES: lower.
▷noun *a mechanical hoist used for fire-fighting purposes:* lifting gear, crane, winch, block and tackle, pulley, windlass, derrick.

hold verb
1 *she was holding a brown leather suitcase:* clasp, clutch, grasp, grip, clench, cling to, hold on to; carry, bear.
2 *I wanted to hold her in my arms:* embrace, hug, clasp, grasp, cradle, enfold, squeeze, fold in your arms.

3 *he holds a United Kingdom passport:* possess, have, own, bear, carry, have to your name.
4 *the branch seemed likely to hold my weight:* support, bear, carry, take, keep up, sustain, prop up, shore up.
5 *the police were holding him on a murder charge:* detain, hold in custody; imprison, lock up, put behind bars, put in prison, put in jail, incarcerate, keep under lock and key, confine, intern; informal put away, put inside.
6 *the story is certainly compelling enough to hold your attention:* keep, occupy, absorb, engross, captivate, fascinate, enthral, grip, rivet; engage, catch, capture, arrest.
7 *he held a senior post in the Foreign Office:* occupy, have, fill, fulfil; informal hold down.
8 *the tank held 250 gallons | the church is big enough to hold 400 people:* take, contain, accommodate, fit; have a capacity of, have room for.
9 *the court held that there was no evidence to support this assertion:* think, consider, take the view, believe, feel, deem, be of the opinion, maintain; judge, rule, decide; formal opine; informal reckon.
10 *let's hope the good weather holds for the rest of the week:* continue, persist, carry on, go on, hold out, keep up, last, endure, stay, remain.
11 *I'll have that coffee now, if the offer still holds:* be valid, hold good, stand, apply, remain, be available, exist, be the case, be in force, be in effect.
12 *the president held a meeting with party leaders:* convene, call, summon; conduct, have, organize, run; formal convoke.
OPPOSITES: release.
▷noun
1 *she kept a firm hold on my hand:* grip, grasp, clasp, clutch.
2 *Tom had some kind of hold over his father:* influence, power, control, dominance, authority, leverage, sway, mastery.
3 *the military tightened their hold on the capital:* control, grip, power, stranglehold, authority, dominion.
□ **get hold of**
1 *I managed to get hold of a ticket:* obtain, acquire, get, find, come by, pick up, procure; buy, purchase; informal get your hands on.
2 *I'll try to get hold of her solicitor:* contact, get in touch with, communicate with, make contact with, reach, notify; phone, call, speak to, talk to; Brit. ring; Brit. informal get on to.
□ **hold back**
he held back, remembering the mistake he had made before: hesitate, pause, delay, stop yourself, desist, forbear, demur.
□ **hold someone back**
I felt that my lack of experience held me back: hinder, hamper, impede, obstruct, check, curb, block, thwart, baulk, hamstring, restrain, frustrate, stand in someone's way.

□ **hold something back**
1 *Jane struggled to hold back the tears:* suppress, fight back, choke back, stifle, smother, subdue, rein in, repress, curb, control, keep a tight rein on; informal keep a/the lid on.
2 *don't hold anything back from me:* withhold, hide, conceal, keep secret, keep hidden, keep quiet about, hush up; informal sit on.

□ **hold forth**
Richard was holding forth about the qualities of good wine: speak at length, talk at length, go on; declaim, pontificate, orate, preach, sermonize; informal spout, speechify, preachify, drone on, sound off.

□ **hold off**
fortunately, the rain held off until evening: stay away, keep off, not come.

□ **hold something off**
he held off a late challenge by Vose to win by 13 seconds: resist, repel, repulse, rebuff, parry, deflect, fend off, stave off, ward off, keep at bay.

□ **hold on**
1 *hold on a minute, I'll be right back:* wait a minute, just a moment, just a second; stay here, stay put; hold the line; informal hang on, sit tight; Brit. informal hang about.
2 *if they can hold on a little longer, help might reach them in time:* keep going, persevere, survive, last, continue, struggle on, carry on, go on, hold out, see it through, stay the course; informal soldier on, stick at it.

□ **hold on to**
1 *he held on to the back of the chair:* clutch, hold, hang on to, clasp, grasp, grip, cling to.
2 *the company can't hold on to their most experienced staff:* retain, keep; informal hang on to.

□ **hold your own.** See **OWN.**

□ **hold out**
1 *I'm sure they can hold out until we come up with more evidence:* survive, manage, cope, get along/by, make do; continue, carry on, remain, persist, endure, persevere.
2 *we can stay here for as long as our supplies hold out:* last, remain, continue.

□ **hold out against**
British troops held out against constant attacks: resist, withstand, hold off, fight off, fend off, keep off, keep at bay, stand up to, stand firm against.

□ **hold something out**
Celia held out her hand: extend, proffer, offer, present; outstretch, reach out, stretch out, put out.

□ **hold something over**
the usual family gathering was held over until January: postpone, put off, put back, delay, defer, suspend, shelve, hold in abeyance; N. Amer. put over, table, take a rain check on; informal put on ice, put on the back burner.

□ **hold up**
their argument just doesn't hold up: be convincing, be logical, hold water, bear examination, be sound.

□ **hold something up**
1 *they held up the trophy for all to see:* display, hold aloft, exhibit, show, show off, flourish, brandish; informal flash.
2 *eight concrete pillars hold up the bridge:* support, hold, bear, carry, take, keep up, prop up, shore up, buttress.
3 *our flight was held up for three hours:* delay, detain, make late, set back, keep back, retard, slow up.
4 *a lack of cash has held up progress:* obstruct, impede, hinder, hamper, inhibit, baulk, thwart, curb, hamstring, frustrate, foil, interfere with, stop; informal stymie.

□ **hold water.** See **WATER.**

□ **hold with**
I don't hold with all this violence: approve of, agree with, be in favour of, endorse, accept, countenance, support, subscribe to, give your blessing to, take kindly to; informal stand for.

holder noun
1 *an overhead holder for sunglasses:* container, receptacle, bin, case, casing, cover, covering, housing, sheath; stand, rest, rack.
2 *he is a British passport holder:* bearer, owner, possessor, keeper; custodian.

holdings plural noun *they have holdings in various offshore funds:* assets, funds, capital, resources, savings, investments, securities, equities, bonds, stocks and shares, reserves; property, possessions.

hold-up noun
1 *I ran into a series of hold-ups and nearly didn't get here:* delay, setback, hitch, snag, difficulty, problem, trouble; traffic jam, tailback, gridlock; informal glitch, hiccup.
2 *there has been another bank hold-up:* robbery, armed robbery, raid; theft, burglary, mugging; informal stick-up; N. Amer. informal heist.

hole noun
1 *there was a huge hole in the roof:* opening, aperture, gap, space, orifice, vent, chink, breach; crack, leak, rift, rupture; puncture, perforation, cut, split, gash, slit, crevice, fissure.
2 *they were digging a hole in the ground:* pit, ditch, trench, cavity, crater, depression, hollow; well, borehole, excavation, dugout; cave, cavern, pothole.
3 *the rabbits were staying down their holes:* burrow, lair, den, earth, sett; retreat, shelter.
▷ **verb** *a fuel tank was holed in the attack:* puncture, perforate, pierce, penetrate, rupture, split, rent, lacerate, gash.

□ **hole up** (informal) *the snipers holed up in a nearby farmhouse:* hide, hide out, conceal yourself, secrete yourself, shelter, take cover, lie low, go to ground, go to earth.

holiday noun
1 *a ten-day holiday in Europe:* break,
rest; time off, leave, sabbatical; trip,
tour, journey, voyage; time out; recess;
N. Amer. vacation; Military furlough; formal
sojourn.
2 *the 25th of December is an official holiday:*
public holiday, bank holiday, festival,
feast day; saint's day, holy day.

hollow adjective
1 *each fibre has a hollow core that traps air:*
empty, void, unfilled, vacant.
2 *her hollow cheeks and bony face:* sunken,
deep-set, concave, depressed, indented.
3 *a hollow victory:* meaningless, empty,
valueless, worthless, useless, pyrrhic,
futile, fruitless, profitless, pointless.
4 *the women believed it was nothing but a
hollow promise:* insincere, hypocritical,
feigned, false, sham, deceitful, cynical,
spurious, untrue, two-faced; informal
phoney, pretend.
OPPOSITES: solid, full, worthwhile, sincere.
▷ noun
1 *we found a hollow at the base of a large
tree:* hole, pit, cavity, crater, trough, cave,
cavern; depression, indentation, dip; niche,
nook, cranny, recess.
2 *the village nestled in a hollow in the
Cotswolds:* valley, vale, dale; Scottish glen;
literary dell.
▷ verb *cut the top off the pumpkin and hollow
it out:* gouge, scoop, dig, cut; excavate,
channel.

holocaust noun *fears of a nuclear
holocaust:* cataclysm, disaster, catastrophe;
mass destruction, devastation,
annihilation; massacre, slaughter, mass
murder, carnage, butchery; genocide,
ethnic cleansing.

holy adjective
1 *holy men who are revered by pilgrims:*
religious, devout, God-fearing, godly,
pious, saintly, saintlike; righteous,
good, virtuous, sinless, pure; canonized,
beatified, ordained.
2 *a Jewish holy place:* sacred, consecrated,
hallowed, sanctified, venerated, revered,
divine.

homage noun
1 *the book was intended as an act of
homage:* respect, honour, reverence,
worship, admiration, esteem, adulation,
acclaim.
2 *the building is clearly a homage to the
Guggenheim Museum in Manhattan:*
tribute, acknowledgement, recognition;
accolade, salute; literary panegyric, paean.
OPPOSITES: disrespect, criticism.
□ pay homage to
*they paid homage to the local boy who
became president:* honour, acclaim,
applaud, salute, praise, commend, pay
tribute to, eulogize, take your hat off to;
formal laud.

home noun
1 *the floods forced people to flee their
homes:* house, residence; flat, apartment,
bungalow, cottage; accommodation,
property, quarters, lodgings, rooms; a
roof over your head; address; formal place
of residence, domicile, abode, dwelling,
habitation; informal pad, place.
2 *I am stuck here, far from my home:*
homeland, native land, home town,
birthplace, roots, fatherland, motherland,
mother country, country of origin, the old
country.
3 *a private home for the elderly:*
institution, nursing home, retirement
home, rest home; hospice, shelter, refuge,
retreat, hostel; dated asylum.
4 *the home of fine wines:* realm, domain,
origin, source, cradle, fount, fountainhead.
▷ adjective *we need to stimulate demand
within the UK home market:* domestic,
internal, local, national, interior.
OPPOSITES: foreign, international.
□ at home
1 *she felt at home in Milan:* comfortable, at
ease, relaxed, content; in your element.
2 *he is not particularly at home with
mathematics:* confident with, conversant
with, proficient in; used to, familiar with,
au fait with, skilled in, experienced in, well
versed in; formal au courant with; informal
well up on.
□ bring something home to someone
*Arthur's illness brought home to them the
gravity of the situation:* make someone
realize, make someone understand, make
something clear to someone; drive home,
press home, impress upon someone,
draw attention to, focus attention on,
underline, highlight, spotlight, emphasize,
stress.
□ hit home. See HIT.
□ home in on
her argument homes in on the real danger:
focus on, concentrate on, zero in on, centre
on, fix on; highlight, spotlight, underline,
pinpoint.

homeland noun *he left his homeland to
settle in London:* native land, country of
origin, home, fatherland, motherland,
mother country, land of your fathers, the
old country.

homeless adjective *the plight of young
homeless people:* without a roof over your
head, on the streets, vagrant, sleeping
rough; destitute, down and out.
▷ noun *charities for the homeless:* homeless
people, vagrants, down-and-outs, tramps,
vagabonds, itinerants, derelicts, drifters.

homely adjective
1 (Brit.) *a modern hotel with a homely
atmosphere:* cosy, homelike, comfortable,
snug, welcoming, friendly, congenial,
intimate, warm, hospitable, informal,
relaxed, pleasant, cheerful; N. Amer. homey;
informal comfy.

2 (Brit.) *a meal for those who enjoy the more homely delights of the table:* unsophisticated, everyday, ordinary, domestic, simple, modest, unpretentious, unassuming; homespun, folksy.
3 (N. Amer.) *she's rather homely and she needs a date:* unattractive, plain, unprepossessing, unlovely, ill-favoured, ugly; Brit. informal no oil painting.
OPPOSITES: uncomfortable, formal, sophisticated.

homespun adjective *he was a constant source of rural homespun philosophy:* unsophisticated, plain, simple, unpolished, unrefined, rustic, folksy; rough, crude, rudimentary; Brit. homely.
OPPOSITES: sophisticated.

homey adjective (N. Amer.)
1 *the house is homey yet elegant:* cosy, homelike, comfortable, snug, welcoming, informal, relaxed, intimate, warm, pleasant, cheerful; Brit. homely; informal comfy.
2 *an idealized version of peasant life as simple and homey:* unsophisticated, unrefined, unpretentious, plain, simple, modest; Brit. homely.

homicidal adjective *a homicidal attack:* murderous, violent, brutal, savage, ferocious, vicious, bloody, bloodthirsty, barbarous, barbaric; deadly, lethal, mortal, death-dealing.

homicide noun (N. Amer.) killing; murder, assassination, execution; patricide, matricide, infanticide; literary slaying.

homily noun *she delivered her homily about the need for patience:* sermon, lecture, address, lesson, talk, speech, discourse, oration.

homogeneous adjective
1 *a homogeneous group:* uniform; alike, similar, much the same, all of a piece; informal much of a muchness.
2 *if all jobs and workers were homogeneous, then it is reasonable to suppose that all wages would be equal:* similar, comparable, equivalent, like, analogous, corresponding, parallel; formal cognate.
OPPOSITES: heterogeneous, different.

homogenize verb *they wanted to wipe out differences and homogenize society:* standardize, unite, integrate, fuse, merge, blend, meld, coalesce, amalgamate, combine.
OPPOSITES: diversify.

hone verb
1 *he was carefully honing the long curved blade:* sharpen, whet, strop, grind, file.
2 *this gave me a great opportunity to hone my skills as a singer:* improve, develop, enhance, sharpen, polish up; upgrade.

honest adjective
1 *he is an honest man:* upright, moral, ethical, principled, honourable,
righteous, right-minded, respectable; virtuous, good, decent, law-abiding, high-minded, upstanding, incorruptible, truthful, trustworthy, trusty, reliable, conscientious, scrupulous, reputable.
2 *I haven't been completely honest with you:* truthful, sincere, candid, frank, open, forthright, straight; straightforward, plain-speaking, matter-of-fact; informal upfront, on the level.
3 *he'd made an honest mistake:* genuine, real, authentic, actual, true, bona fide, forgivable, legitimate, fair and square.
OPPOSITES: dishonest, insincere.

honestly adverb
1 *he earned the money honestly:* fairly, lawfully, legally, legitimately, honourably, decently, ethically, in good faith, by the book; informal on the level.
2 *we honestly believe this is for the best:* sincerely, genuinely, truthfully, truly, wholeheartedly; really, actually, in all honesty, in all sincerity.
OPPOSITES: dishonestly.

honesty noun
1 *his honesty is not in question:* integrity, uprightness, honour, morality, morals, ethics, high principles, righteousness; virtue, goodness, probity, high-mindedness, fairness, incorruptibility, truthfulness, trustworthiness, reliability, dependability.
2 *they spoke with honesty about their fears:* sincerity, candour, frankness, directness, truthfulness, truth, openness, straightforwardness.
OPPOSITES: dishonesty.

honeyed adjective *he woos her with honeyed words:* sweet, soothing, soft, sugary, saccharine, pleasant, flattering, adulatory, unctuous; mellow, mellifluous; often ironic dulcet.
OPPOSITES: harsh.

honour noun
1 *the general was a man of honour:* integrity, honesty, uprightness, high principles, morality, righteousness, high-mindedness; virtue, decency, probity.
2 *he earned the honour of having the building named after him:* distinction, privilege, glory, kudos, cachet, prestige; respect, esteem.
3 *our national honour is at stake:* reputation, good name, character, repute, image, standing, stature, status.
4 *she had the honour of meeting the Queen:* privilege, pleasure, pride, joy; compliment, favour.
5 *the highest military honours:* award, accolade, reward, prize, decoration, distinction, medal.
OPPOSITES: unscrupulousness, dishonour.

▷ **verb**
1 *we should love and honour our parents:* esteem, respect, admire, defer to, look up to; appreciate, value, cherish; reverence,

revere, venerate, worship.
2 *they were honoured at a special ceremony:* **applaud,** acclaim, praise, salute, recognize, celebrate, commemorate, commend, pay homage to, pay tribute to, sing the praises of; formal laud.
3 *he made sure we honoured the contract in every respect:* **fulfil,** observe, keep, obey, heed, follow, carry out, discharge, implement, execute, effect; keep to, abide by, adhere to, comply with, conform to, be true to, live up to.
4 *the bank informed us that the cheque would not be honoured:* **accept,** take, clear, pass, cash; Brit. encash.
OPPOSITES: dishonour, disobey, break.

honourable adjective
1 *a thoroughly decent and honourable man:* **honest,** moral, ethical, principled, righteous, right-minded; decent, respectable, virtuous, good, upstanding, upright, worthy, noble, fair, just, truthful, trustworthy, law-abiding, reliable, reputable, dependable.
2 *a long and honourable career:* **illustrious,** distinguished, eminent, great, glorious, prestigious, noble, creditable.
OPPOSITES: dishonourable, deplorable.

hoodwink verb *he kept an eye out for the young man who had hoodwinked him:* deceive, trick, dupe, outwit, fool, delude, cheat, take in, hoax, mislead, lead on, defraud, double-cross, swindle; literary cozen; informal con, diddle, rip off, take for a ride.

hook verb
1 *the truck had a red lamp hooked to its tailgate:* **attach,** hitch, fasten, fix, secure, clasp.
2 *he hooked his thumbs in his belt:* **curl,** bend, crook, loop, curve.
3 *he hooked a 24 lb pike:* **catch,** land, net, take, bag, snare, trap.
□ **off the hook** (informal) *I admit I lied to get him off the hook:* **out of trouble,** in the clear, free; acquitted, cleared, reprieved, exonerated, absolved; informal let off.

hooked adjective
1 *he had a long hooked nose:* **curved,** hook-shaped, hook-like, aquiline, angular, bent.
2 (informal) *they are hooked on cocaine:* **addicted to,** dependent on.
3 (informal) *he has been hooked on crosswords since his teens:* **keen on,** enthusiastic about, addicted to, obsessed with, fixated on; informal mad about, crazy about, fanatical about.
OPPOSITES: straight.

hooligan noun thug, lout, delinquent, vandal, ruffian, troublemaker; Brit. tearaway, rough; Brit. informal yob, lager lout; Scottish informal ned.

hoop noun ring, band, circle, circlet, loop; technical annulus.

hoot noun
1 *I heard the hoot of an owl:* **screech,** shriek, call, cry; tu-whit tu-whoo.
2 *the hoot of a horn was followed by the roar of an engine:* **beep,** honk, toot, blast, blare.
3 *there were hoots of derision from the audience:* **shout,** yell, cry, howl, shriek, whoop, whistle; boo, hiss, jeer, catcall.
▷ **verb**
1 *in the stillness of the night an owl hooted:* **screech,** shriek, call, cry; tu-whit tu-whoo.
2 *a car horn hooted, frightening her:* **beep,** honk, toot, blare, blast, sound.
3 *the delegates hooted in disgust:* **shout,** yell, cry, howl, shriek, whoop, whistle; boo, hiss, jeer, catcall.

hop verb *he hopped along the road:* jump, bound, spring, bounce, skip, jig, leap; prance, dance, frolic, gambol.

hope noun
1 *I had high hopes of making the Olympic team:* **aspiration,** desire, wish, expectation, ambition, aim, plan; dream, daydream.
2 *most of us begin married life filled with hope:* **optimism,** expectation, expectancy; confidence, faith, trust, belief, conviction, assurance; promise.
OPPOSITES: pessimism.
▷ **verb**
1 *he's hoping for a medal in the high jump:* **expect,** anticipate, look for, be hopeful of, pin your hopes on; want, wish for, dream of.
2 *we're hoping to address this issue as soon as possible:* **aim,** intend, be looking, have the intention, have in mind, plan, aspire.

hopeful adjective
1 *he remained hopeful that something could be worked out:* **optimistic,** full of hope, confident, positive, buoyant, sanguine, bullish, cheerful, upbeat.
2 *there are some hopeful signs of recovery in the US market:* **promising,** encouraging, heartening, reassuring, auspicious, favourable, optimistic, propitious, bright, rosy.

hopefully adverb
1 *he rode on hopefully:* **optimistically,** full of hope, confidently, buoyantly; expectantly.
2 *hopefully the road should be finished by next year:* **it is hoped that,** all being well, if all goes well, with luck; most likely, probably.

> **USAGE**
>
> The traditional meaning of **hopefully** is 'in a hopeful way'. Although the newer use, meaning 'it is to be hoped that', is now much more common some people still think that it is incorrect. It is advisable to avoid this use in formal writing.

hopeless adjective
1 *Jess looked at him, making a hopeless appeal:* **despairing,** desperate, wretched,

h

forlorn, pessimistic, defeatist, resigned; dejected, downhearted, despondent, demoralized.
2 *the situation is hopeless:* **beyond hope**, lost, beyond repair, irreparable, irreversible, irremediable; past cure, incurable; impossible, no-win, futile, unworkable, impracticable.
3 (Brit. informal) *Joseph was hopeless at maths:* **bad**, poor, awful, appalling, terrible, dreadful, atrocious; incompetent, unskilled; informal useless, lousy, rotten, pathetic; Brit. informal rubbish.

horde noun *hordes of people would make a pilgrimage there to visit the oracle:* **crowd**, mob, pack, gang, troop, army, swarm, mass; throng, multitude, host, band, flock; informal crew, tribe, load.

> **USAGE**
>
> Do not confuse **horde** and **hoard**. A **horde** is 'a large group of people' while a **hoard** is 'a secret store' (*two men with metal detectors stumbled across a hoard of treasure*).

horizon noun *she wanted to leave home and broaden her horizons:* **outlook**, perspective, perception; scope, range of experience, orbit.
□ **on the horizon**
trouble could be on the horizon: **imminent**, impending, close, near, approaching, coming, forthcoming, in prospect, at hand, on the way, about to happen, upon us, in the offing, in the pipeline, in the air, just around the corner; brewing, looming, threatening, menacing; informal on the cards.

horizontal adjective
1 *draw a horizontal line near the top of the wall:* **level**, flat, plane, smooth, even; straight, parallel.
2 *she was stretched horizontal on a sunbed:* **flat**, supine, prone, prostrate.
OPPOSITES: vertical.

horrendous adjective. See HORRIBLE.

horrible adjective
1 *there was a horrible murder here last year:* **dreadful**, awful, terrible, shocking, appalling, horrifying, horrific, horrendous, grisly, ghastly, gruesome, heinous, vile, unspeakable, loathsome, monstrous, abhorrent, hateful, abominable, atrocious, sickening; nightmarish, macabre.
2 *the tea tasted horrible* | *a horrible little man:* **nasty**, horrid, disagreeable, unpleasant, awful, dreadful, terrible, appalling, foul, repulsive, repellent, ghastly; obnoxious, hateful, odious, objectionable, insufferable, vile, loathsome, abhorrent, execrable; informal frightful; Brit. informal beastly.
OPPOSITES: pleasant.

horrid adjective. See HORRIBLE.

horrific adjective *a horrific car accident:* **dreadful**, horrendous, horrible, awful,

terrible, atrocious; horrifying, shocking, appalling, gruesome, hideous, grisly, ghastly, unspeakable, monstrous, nightmarish, sickening.

horrify verb *he was horrified at the sight that met his eyes:* **shock**, appal, fill with fear, frighten, scare, terrify, alarm; disgust, revolt, nauseate, sicken; outrage, scandalize.

horror noun
1 *children screamed in horror:* **terror**, fear, fright, alarm, panic; dread, trepidation.
2 *to her horror she found herself alone:* **dismay**, consternation, perturbation, alarm, distress; disgust, outrage, shock.
3 *photographs revealed the full horror of the tragedy:* **awfulness**, savagery, barbarity, hideousness, atrocity, enormity, magnitude.
4 (informal) *he's a little horror:* **rascal**, devil, imp, monkey; informal terror.
OPPOSITES: delight, satisfaction.

horse noun **mount**, charger, cob, nag, hack; N. Amer. bronco; literary steed.
□ **horse around/about** (informal) *they were shouting and horsing around in the garden:* **fool around/about**, play the fool, clown about/around, monkey about/around; informal mess about/around, lark about/around; Brit. informal muck about/around.

> **WORD LINKS**
> **equine** relating to horses
> **equestrian** relating to riding horses

horseman, horsewoman noun **rider**, equestrian, jockey; cavalryman, trooper; historical hussar, dragoon.

horseplay noun **boisterousness**, rough and tumble.

hose noun *a thirty-foot garden hose:* **pipe**, piping, tube, tubing, duct, outlet, pipeline, siphon.

hospitable adjective *everyone was very hospitable when we first moved in:* **welcoming**, friendly, congenial, genial, sociable, convivial, cordial; gracious, well disposed, amenable, helpful, obliging, accommodating, neighbourly, warm, kind, generous, bountiful.

hospital noun **infirmary**, sanatorium, hospice, clinic.

hospitality noun
1 *he is renowned for his hospitality:* **friendliness**, warm reception, helpfulness, neighbourliness, warmth, kindness, congeniality, geniality, cordiality, amenability, generosity.
2 *the delights of corporate hospitality:* **entertainment**; catering, food and drink.

host¹ noun *he was the host of a half-hour TV series:* **compère**, anchor, anchorman, anchorwoman, announcer; Brit. presenter.

▷ **verb**
1 *the Queen hosted a dinner for 600 guests:* give, hold, throw, put on, provide, arrange, organize.
2 *the show was hosted by some media celebrity:* present, introduce, compère, front, anchor.

host² noun
1 *a host of memories rushed into her mind:* multitude, lot, abundance, wealth, profusion; literary myriad; informal load, ton.
2 *a host of film stars:* crowd, throng, flock, herd, swarm, horde, mob, army, legion; assemblage, gathering.

hostage noun captive, prisoner, detainee, internee.

hostile adjective
1 *he wrote an extremely hostile review:* unfriendly, unkind, bitter, unsympathetic, malicious, vicious, rancorous, venomous; antagonistic, aggressive, confrontational, belligerent, truculent.
2 *hostile climatic conditions:* unfavourable, adverse, bad, harsh, grim, hard, tough, inhospitable, forbidding.
3 *people are very hostile to the idea:* opposed, averse, antagonistic, ill-disposed, unsympathetic, antipathetic; opposing, against; informal anti, down on.
OPPOSITES: friendly, favourable.

hostility noun
1 *on her arrival, she encountered open hostility from both colleagues and pupils:* antagonism, animosity, antipathy, opposition, unfriendliness, ill will, ill feeling, resentment, rancour; aggression, belligerence, enmity.
2 *we are hoping for a cessation of hostilities:* fighting, conflict, combat, warfare, war, bloodshed, violence.

hot adjective
1 *it was another hot day:* warm, balmy, summery; tropical, scorching, searing, blistering; sweltering, torrid, sultry, humid, muggy, close; informal boiling, baking, roasting.
2 *she felt very hot, and her throat was dry:* feverish, fevered, febrile; burning, flushed.
3 *they provided plenty of hot soup:* piping hot, steaming, boiling hot; scalding, red-hot.
4 *a hot chilli sauce:* spicy, spiced, highly seasoned, peppery, fiery; piquant.
5 (informal) *have I got some hot news for you!* new, fresh, up to date, up to the minute; just out, breaking.
6 (informal) *this band is seriously hot:* popular, in demand, sought-after, in favour; fashionable, in vogue, all the rage; informal big, cool.
7 (informal) *she's very hot on local history:* knowledgeable about, well informed about, au fait with, up on, well versed in; informal clued up about.
OPPOSITES: cold, chilly, mild.

hotbed noun *the place is a hotbed of political activity:* breeding ground, den, cradle, nest.

hot-blooded adjective *tips for hot-blooded lovers:* passionate, amorous, ardent, lustful, libidinous, sexy; informal horny, randy.

hotchpotch noun *the house was a hotchpotch of styles, ancient and modern:* mixture, mix, mixed bag, assortment, random collection, jumble, miscellany, medley, potpourri; melange, confusion; informal ragbag, mishmash.

hotel noun inn, motel, boarding house, guest house, bed and breakfast, B&B, hostel.

hotfoot adverb *he rushed hotfoot to the planning office to lodge an objection:* hastily, hurriedly, speedily, quickly, fast, rapidly, swiftly, without delay; at top speed, at full tilt, headlong, post-haste, helter-skelter; informal like the wind, like greased lightning; Brit. informal like the clappers.
OPPOSITES: slowly.
□ **hotfoot it** (informal) *we hotfooted it after him:* hurry, dash, run, race, sprint, bolt, dart, career, charge, shoot, hurtle, fly, speed, zoom, streak; Brit. hare; informal tear, belt, scoot; Brit. informal bomb; N. Amer. informal hightail it.

hot-headed adjective *a number of hot-headed youths started the trouble:* impetuous, impulsive, headstrong, reckless, rash, irresponsible, foolhardy, madcap; excitable, volatile, fiery, quick-tempered, unruly.

hotly adverb
1 *the rumours were hotly denied:* vigorously, vehemently, strenuously, fiercely, passionately, heatedly; angrily, indignantly.
2 *he rushed out, hotly pursued by Boris:* closely, swiftly, quickly.

hot-tempered adjective *he is arrogant, hot-tempered, and capable of violence:* irascible, quick-tempered, short-tempered, irritable, fiery, bad-tempered; touchy, volatile, testy, tetchy, fractious, prickly; informal snappy, on a short fuse; Brit. informal ratty.
OPPOSITES: easy-going.

hound verb
1 *she was hounded by the Italian press:* harass, persecute, badger, torment, bedevil, pester, bother; pursue, chase, follow, shadow, hunt down, stalk, track, trail; informal hassle.
2 *they hounded him out of office:* force, drive, pressure, pressurize, push, urge, coerce, dragoon, strong-arm; nag, bully, browbeat; informal bulldoze, railroad.

house noun
1 *an estate of 200 houses:* residence, home;

h

formal habitation, dwelling, abode, domicile.
2 *the house of Stewart:* family, clan, tribe;
dynasty, line, bloodline, lineage, ancestry,
family tree.
3 *the National Council is the country's
upper house:* legislative assembly,
legislative body, chamber, council,
parliament, congress, senate, diet.
▷**verb**
1 *most of the detainees were housed in large
overcrowded tents:* accommodate, put up,
lodge, quarter, board, billet, take in, give
someone a roof over their head; harbour,
shelter.
2 *this panel houses the main switch:*
contain, hold, store; cover, protect,
enclose.
◻ **on the house** (informal) *this round is on the
house:* free, free of charge, for nothing,
gratis, at no cost; courtesy, complimentary;
informal for free.

household noun *the whole household was
asleep:* family, house, residents, occupants,
tenants.
▷**adjective** *we sell all kinds of household
goods:* domestic, family; everyday,
workaday.

householder noun homeowner, owner,
occupant, resident; tenant, leaseholder;
proprietor, landlady, landlord; Brit. occupier,
owner-occupier, freeholder.

house-trained adjective domesticated,
trained; N. Amer. housebroken.

housing noun
1 *they invested heavily in housing:*
houses, homes, residences, buildings;
accommodation, living quarters; formal
dwellings, habitations.
2 *the protective housing for the radio
antennae:* casing, case, covering, cover,
holder, sheath, jacket, shell, capsule.

hovel noun shack, slum, shanty, hut.

hover verb
1 *army helicopters hovered overhead:* hang,
be poised, be suspended, levitate; fly.
2 *she hovered anxiously nearby:* linger,
loiter, dally, wait about, stay; informal hang
around; Brit. informal hang about.

however adverb
1 *people tend to put on weight in middle
age; however, this is not inevitable:*
nevertheless, nonetheless, but, still, yet,
though, although, even so, for all that,
despite that, in spite of that; anyway,
anyhow, be that as it may, having said that,
notwithstanding.
2 *however you look at it, it's a bit of a
disaster:* in whatever way, regardless of
how, no matter how.

howl noun
1 *she heard the howl of a wolf:* baying, cry,
yowl.
2 *he let out a howl of anguish:* wail, cry,
yell, yelp, yowl; bellow, roar, shout,
shriek, scream, screech.
▷**verb**
1 *dogs howled in the distance:* bay, cry,
yowl.
2 *somewhere nearby, a baby started to howl:*
wail, cry, yell, yowl, bawl, bellow, roar,
shriek, scream, screech, caterwaul.

hub noun
1 *spokes radiate from the hub of the wheel:*
centre, axis, axle, fulcrum, pivot.
2 *the kitchen was the hub of family life:*
centre, core, heart, focus, focal point,
nucleus, kernel, nerve centre.
OPPOSITES: edge.

hubbub noun *her voice was lost in the
hubbub:* noise, din, racket, commotion,
rumpus, clamour, cacophony, babel;
Brit. row.

hubris noun *their downfall was caused by
a mixture of hubris and muddled thinking:*
arrogance, conceit, hauteur, pride,
self-importance, superiority; informal big-
headedness.
OPPOSITES: humility.

huddle verb
1 *they huddled together for warmth:* crowd,
cluster, gather, bunch, throng, flock, herd,
collect, group, congregate; press, pack,
squeeze.
2 *he huddled beneath the sheets:* curl up,
snuggle, nestle, hunch up.
OPPOSITES: disperse, stretch out.
▷**noun** *a huddle of passengers gathered round
the information desk:* crowd, cluster,
bunch, knot, group, throng, flock, press,
pack; collection, assemblage; informal gaggle.

hue noun
1 *seaweeds are found in a variety of hues:*
colour, shade, tone, tint.
2 *men of all political hues soon forgot their
feuding:* complexion, type, kind, sort,
cast, stamp, character, nature, inclination,
persuasion, aspect.

hue and cry noun *her relatives raised a
hue and cry after the accident:* commotion,
outcry, uproar, fuss, clamour, storm, stir,
furore, ruckus, brouhaha, rumpus; Brit. row;
Brit. informal hullabaloo, song and dance.

huff noun (informal) *she walked off in a huff:*
bad mood, sulk, fit of pique, pet; temper,
tantrum, rage; Brit. informal paddy.

hug verb
1 *they kissed and hugged each other:*
embrace, cuddle, squeeze, clasp, clutch,
cling to, hold close, hold tight, take
someone in your arms, clasp someone to
your bosom.
2 *I headed north, hugging the coastline:*
follow closely, keep close to, stay near to,
follow the course of.
▷**noun** *there were tears and hugs as we left:*
embrace, cuddle, squeeze, clinch.

huge adjective *the house was absolutely*

huge | *there's a huge backlog of work:* **enormous**, vast, immense, large, very big, great, massive, tremendous, colossal, prodigious, gigantic, gargantuan, mammoth, monumental; giant, towering, mountainous, titanic; literary Brobdingnagian; informal mega, monster, whopping, humongous, astronomical; Brit. informal ginormous.
OPPOSITES: tiny.

hugely adverb *they are fighting a hugely expensive legal battle:* **very**, extremely, exceedingly, most, really, particularly, tremendously, greatly, decidedly, exceptionally, immensely, terribly, inordinately, extraordinarily, vastly; very much, to a great extent; informal terrifically, awfully.

hulk noun
1 *the rusting hulks of ships:* **wreck**, shipwreck, ruin; shell, skeleton, hull.
2 *a great clumsy hulk of a man:* **giant**, colossus, lump; oaf; informal gorilla; N. Amer. informal lummox.

hull[1] noun *the ship's hull was damaged:* **framework**, body, shell, frame, skeleton, structure.

hull[2] noun *seed hulls:* **shell**, husk, pod, case, covering; Botany integument, pericarp.
▷**verb** *the bird uses its beak to hull seeds:* **shell**, husk, peel, pare, skin; technical decorticate.

hullabaloo noun (Brit. informal) *there was a terrific hullabaloo over the by-election:* **fuss**, commotion, hue and cry, uproar, outcry, clamour, storm, furore, hubbub, ruckus, brouhaha; pandemonium, mayhem; Brit. row; Brit. informal song and dance.

hum verb
1 *the engine was humming and ready to go:* **murmur**, drone, purr, buzz, thrum, whirr, throb, vibrate.
2 *the workshops are humming as the men set about their various tasks:* **be busy**, be active, be lively, buzz, bustle, be a hive of activity, throb.
▷**noun** *a low hum of conversation:* **murmur**, drone, purr, buzz.

human adjective
1 *they're only human, so mistakes do occur | human frailty:* **mortal**, flesh and blood; fallible; physical, bodily, fleshly.
2 *the episode reveals the human side of politics:* **compassionate**, humane, kind, considerate, understanding, sympathetic, tolerant; approachable, accessible.
▷**noun** *I just want to be treated like a human and not some caged animal:* **person**, human being, mortal, member of the human race; man, woman; individual, living soul, being; Homo sapiens; (in Science Fiction) earthling.

WORD LINKS
anthropology the study of humankind
anthropophagy, **cannibalism** the eating of human flesh by other humans

humane adjective *regulations concerning the humane treatment of animals:* **compassionate**, kind, considerate, understanding, sympathetic, tolerant, humanitarian, benevolent, charitable.
OPPOSITES: inhumane.

humanitarian adjective
1 *they sought his release on humanitarian grounds | a humanitarian act:* **compassionate**, humane; unselfish, altruistic, generous, magnanimous, benevolent, merciful, kind, sympathetic.
2 *a humanitarian organization:* **charitable**, philanthropic, public-spirited, socially concerned, welfare.
OPPOSITES: selfish.
▷**noun** **philanthropist**, altruist, benefactor, social reformer, good Samaritan; derogatory do-gooder.

h

USAGE
Sentences such as *this is the worst humanitarian disaster this country has ever seen* represent a loose use of the word **humanitarian** to mean 'human' or 'relating to human beings'. This use is common in journalism but it should be avoided in careful writing.

humanities plural noun **arts**, liberal arts, literature; classics, classical studies, classical literature.

humanity noun
1 *humanity evolved from the higher apes:* **humankind**, mankind, man, people, the human race; Homo sapiens.
2 *the humanity of Christ:* **human nature**, mortality; physicality, corporeality; incarnation.
3 *he praised them for their humanity:* **compassion**, brotherly love, fellow feeling, kindness, consideration, understanding, sympathy, tolerance; leniency, mercy, pity, tenderness; benevolence, charity.

humanize verb *Dr Santiago has been fighting to humanize the hospital environment and improve the quality of patient care:* **civilize**, improve, better; develop, refine, polish.

humankind noun **the human race**, the human species, humanity, human beings, mankind, man, people, mortals; Homo sapiens.

humble adjective
1 *her bearing was very humble and apologetic:* **meek**, deferential, respectful, submissive, self-effacing, unassertive; unpresuming, modest, unassuming, self-deprecating.

2 *she came from a humble background:* lowly, poor, undistinguished, ignoble, low-born; common, ordinary, simple, inferior, unremarkable, insignificant, inconsequential; dated mean.
OPPOSITES: proud, noble, grand.
▷**verb**
1 *he had humbled himself to ask for my help:* humiliate, abase, demean, lower, debase; mortify, shame, make someone eat humble pie; take someone down a peg or two; informal cut someone down to size.
2 *Wales were humbled at Cardiff Arms Park by Romania:* defeat, beat, trounce, rout, overwhelm, bring someone to their knees; informal slaughter.

humbug noun
1 *to dress it up as concern for the environment is sheer humbug:* hypocrisy, sanctimoniousness, posturing, cant, empty talk; insincerity, dishonesty, falseness, deceit, deception, fraud.
2 *you are a coward as well as a humbug:* hypocrite, fraud, fake; charlatan, cheat, deceiver; informal phoney.

humdrum adjective *the humdrum routine of work stretched out before him:* mundane, dull, dreary, boring, tedious, monotonous, prosaic; unexciting, uninteresting, uneventful, unvaried, unremarkable; routine, ordinary, everyday, day-to-day, run-of-the-mill, commonplace, workaday, pedestrian; formal quotidian.
OPPOSITES: remarkable, exciting.

humid adjective *a hot and humid afternoon in July:* muggy, close, sultry, sticky, steamy, oppressive, airless, stifling, suffocating, stuffy, clammy, heavy.
OPPOSITES: fresh.

humiliate verb *you humiliated me in front of my colleagues:* embarrass, mortify, humble, shame, put to shame, disgrace; discomfit, chasten, abash, deflate, crush, squash; abase, debase, demean, degrade; cause to feel small, cause to lose face, take down a peg or two; informal show up, put down.

humiliating adjective *a humiliating election defeat:* embarrassing, mortifying, humbling, ignominious, inglorious, shameful; discreditable, undignified, chastening, demeaning, degrading.

humiliation noun *only a few tenants have the humiliation of finding the bailiffs at the door:* embarrassment, mortification, shame, indignity, ignominy, disgrace, dishonour, degradation, discredit; loss of pride, loss of face; blow to your pride, slap in the face, kick in the teeth; formal opprobrium.
OPPOSITES: honour.

humility noun *he lacks the humility to admit that he's wrong:* modesty, meekness, diffidence, self-effacement.
OPPOSITES: pride.

hummock noun hillock, hump, mound, knoll, prominence, elevation, rise, rising ground, dune; formal eminence.

humorist noun comic writer, wit, wag; comic, funny man/woman, comedian, comedienne, stand-up, joker; clown.

humorous adjective *the novel is a humorous account of hospital life:* amusing, funny, comic, comical, entertaining, witty, jocular, light-hearted, tongue-in-cheek, wry; hilarious, uproarious, riotous, zany, farcical, droll.
OPPOSITES: serious.

humour noun
1 *I can see the humour of the situation:* comedy, funny side, hilarity; absurdity, ludicrousness; satire, irony.
2 *the familiar stories are spiced up with humour:* jokes, jests, jesting, quips, witticisms, funny remarks, puns; wit, comedy, drollery; informal gags, wisecracks, one-liners.
3 *his good humour was infectious:* mood, temper, disposition, temperament, state of mind; spirits.
▷**verb** *she was always humouring him to prevent trouble:* indulge, accommodate, pander to, yield to, give way to, give in to, go along with; pamper, spoil, overindulge, mollify, placate, gratify, satisfy.

humourless adjective *she was thought of as a hard-working, humourless academic:* serious, solemn, sober, sombre, grave, grim, dour, unsmiling, stony-faced; gloomy, glum, sad, melancholy, dismal, joyless, cheerless, lugubrious.
OPPOSITES: jovial.

hump noun *the camel has a single hump:* lump, bump, bulge, swelling, ridge, prominence, protuberance, knob, protrusion, projection, hunch; growth, outgrowth.
▷**verb** (Brit. informal) *he humped the boxes up the stairs:* heave, carry, lift, hoist, heft; informal lug, tote; N. Amer. informal schlep.

hunch verb
1 *he thrust his hands in his pockets and hunched his shoulders:* arch, curve, hump, bow.
2 *I hunched up as small as I could:* crouch, huddle, curl; hunker down, bend, stoop, squat.
OPPOSITES: straighten.
▷**noun** *I have a hunch that his death was no accident:* feeling, feeling in your bones, suspicion, impression, inkling, idea, notion, fancy, intuition, guess; informal gut feeling.

hundred cardinal number century; informal ton.

hunger noun

1 *the serious issue of hunger in developing countries:* lack of food, starvation, malnutrition, malnourishment, undernourishment.
2 *there is a global hunger for news:* desire, craving, longing, yearning, hankering, appetite, thirst; want, need.
□ **hunger after/for**
all actors hunger for such a role: desire, crave; long for, yearn for, pine for, ache for, hanker after, have a yen for, thirst for, lust for; want, need; informal itch for.

hungry adjective

1 *I was feeling really hungry:* ravenous, empty; starving, starved; malnourished, undernourished, underfed; informal famished, peckish.
2 *the new team are hungry for success:* eager, keen, avid, longing, yearning, aching, greedy; hankering after; informal itching, dying.

hunk noun *soup was served with a hunk of bread:* chunk, wedge, block, slab, lump, square.

hunt verb

1 *in the autumn they hunted deer:* chase, stalk, pursue, course; track, trail, follow, shadow, tail.
2 *police are still hunting for her attacker:* search, look, scour the area; seek, try to find; cast about/around/round.
▷ **noun**
1 *the thrill of the hunt:* chase, pursuit.
2 *police have stepped up their hunt:* search, look, quest, campaign.

hunted adjective *his eyes had a hunted look:* harassed, persecuted, harried, hounded, beleaguered, troubled, stressed, tormented, careworn, haggard; distraught, desperate; informal hassled.
OPPOSITES: carefree.

hurdle noun

1 *his leg hit a hurdle as he jumped:* fence, jump, barrier, barricade, bar, railing, rail.
2 *this was the final hurdle for the college to overcome:* obstacle, difficulty, problem, barrier, bar, snag, stumbling block, impediment, obstruction, complication, hindrance.

hurl verb *rioters hurled bricks at the police:* throw, toss, fling, pitch, cast, lob, launch, catapult; project, propel, let fly; informal chuck, sling; Brit. informal bung.

hurly-burly noun *they wanted to escape the hurly-burly of city life:* bustle, hustle and bustle, confusion, disorder, tumult, pandemonium, mayhem, uproar, rumpus, hubbub.
OPPOSITES: calm, order.

hurricane noun cyclone, typhoon, tornado, whirlwind, storm, tempest, gale.

hurried adjective *Miss Barret took a hurried look around her office:* quick, fast, swift, rapid, speedy, brisk, hasty; cursory, perfunctory, rushed, brief, short, fleeting, passing, superficial.
OPPOSITES: slow, considered.

hurriedly adverb *a hurriedly assembled training film:* quickly, hastily, speedily, fast, rapidly, swiftly, briskly; cursorily, perfunctorily, superficially; impetuously, impulsively, precipitately, precipitously, rashly, incautiously, imprudently.

hurry verb

1 *you'd better hurry or you'll be late:* be quick, hurry up, hasten, speed up, press on, push on; run, dash, rush, race, fly; scurry, scramble, scuttle, sprint; informal get a move on; Brit. informal shift; dated make haste.
2 *she hurried him across the landing:* hustle, push, urge, drive, spur, goad, prod, usher; informal gee up.
OPPOSITES: dawdle, delay.
▷ **noun** *in all the hurry, we forgot the picnic:* rush, haste, flurry, hustle and bustle, confusion, commotion, hubbub, turmoil; race, scramble, scurry.

hurt verb

1 *my back hurts:* be painful, ache, be sore, be tender, cause pain, cause discomfort; smart, sting, burn, throb.
2 *Dad hurt his leg:* injure, wound, damage; bruise, cut, gash, graze, scrape, scratch, lacerate.
3 *his cruel words hurt her deeply:* distress, pain, wound, sting, upset, sadden, devastate, grieve, mortify; cut to the quick.
4 *high interest rates are hurting the local economy:* harm, damage, be detrimental to, weaken, blight, impede, jeopardize, undermine, ruin, wreck, sabotage, cripple.
OPPOSITES: comfort, benefit.
▷ **noun**
1 *knowing how to fall properly minimizes hurt:* pain, ache, suffering, discomfort, soreness, harm, injury, damage.
2 *she loved him, in spite of all the hurt he had caused:* distress, pain, suffering, grief, misery, anguish, trauma, woe, upset, sadness, sorrow; harm, damage, trouble.
OPPOSITES: joy.
▷ **adjective** *Anne's hurt expression spoke volumes:* pained, distressed, anguished, upset, sad, mortified, offended.
OPPOSITES: pleased.

hurtful adjective

1 *no more hurtful comments about people's looks:* upsetting, distressing, wounding, painful; unkind, cruel, nasty, mean, malicious, spiteful, insulting, cutting, barbed; informal bitchy.
2 *the law ought to prohibit only actions that are hurtful to society:* detrimental,

harmful, damaging, injurious, inimical, disadvantageous, unfavourable, prejudicial, deleterious.

hurtle verb *a speeding car hurtled towards them:* speed, rush, run, race, bolt, dash, career, whizz, zoom, charge, shoot, streak, gallop, fly, scurry, go like the wind; Brit. hare; informal belt, tear, scoot; Brit. informal bomb.

husband noun spouse, partner, mate, consort, man; groom, bridegroom; literary helpmate, helpmeet; informal hubby, old man.
▷**verb** *oil and gas reserves should be husbanded:* conserve, preserve, save, safeguard, put aside, put by, lay in, reserve, stockpile, hoard; use economically, use sparingly, be frugal with.
OPPOSITES: squander.

husbandry noun
1 *farmers have no money to invest in new methods of husbandry:* farm management, land management, farming, agriculture, agronomy; cultivation.
2 *the careful husbandry of their slender resources:* conservation, management; economy, thrift, frugality.

hush verb
1 *he placed a finger over his lips to hush her:* silence, quieten, shush; gag, muzzle; informal shut up.
2 *the lights dimmed and the crowd hushed:* fall silent, stop talking, quieten down, go quiet; informal pipe down, shut up.
▷**exclamation** *Hush! Someone will hear you:* be quiet, keep quiet, quieten down, be silent, stop talking, hold your tongue; informal shut up.
▷**noun** *a hush descended over the crowd:* silence, quiet, quietness; stillness, peace, peacefulness, calm, tranquillity.
OPPOSITES: noise.
▢**hush something up**
management took steps to hush up the dangers: keep secret, conceal, hide, suppress, cover up, keep quiet about; obscure, veil, sweep under the carpet.

husk noun shell, hull, pod, case, covering; Botany integument, pericarp.

husky adjective
1 *his voice deepened to a husky growl:* throaty, gruff, gravelly, hoarse, croaky, rough, guttural, harsh, rasping, raspy.
2 *Paddy was a husky guy:* strong, muscular, muscly, muscle-bound, brawny, hefty, burly, hulking, chunky, strapping, thickset, solid, powerful, heavy, robust, sturdy, well built; informal beefy, hunky.
OPPOSITES: shrill, soft, puny.

hustle verb
1 *they were hissed and hustled as they went out:* jostle, shove, push, bump, knock, nudge, elbow, shoulder.
2 *I was hustled away to a cold cell:*

manhandle, push, shove, thrust, frogmarch; rush, hurry, whisk; informal bundle.
▷**noun** *we were tired of the hustle and bustle of city life:* hurly-burly, bustle, tumult, hubbub, activity, action, life, excitement, agitation, flurry, whirl.
OPPOSITES: calm.

hut noun shack, shanty, cabin, log cabin, shelter, shed, lean-to; hovel.

hybrid noun *a hybrid between a brown and an albino mouse:* cross, cross-breed; mixture, blend, amalgam, amalgamation, combination, composite, fusion.
▷**adjective** *hybrid varieties of rose:* composite, cross-bred, crossed, interbred, mongrel; mixed, blended, compound.

hybridize verb *a wild relative of the potato was hybridized with the standard crop plant:* cross-breed, cross, interbreed, cross-fertilize, cross-pollinate; mix, blend, combine, amalgamate.

hygiene noun *poor standards of food hygiene:* cleanliness, sanitation, purity, sterility, disinfection; public health, environmental health.

hygienic adjective *this product will leave the kitchen area clean and hygienic:* sanitary, clean, germ-free, disinfected, sterilized, sterile, antiseptic, aseptic, uncontaminated; healthy, wholesome; formal salubrious.
OPPOSITES: unhygienic.

hymn noun song, anthem, canticle, chorale, psalm, carol, spiritual.

hype (informal) **noun** *her work relies on hype and headlines:* publicity, advertising, promotion, marketing, propaganda, exposure; informal plug, puff.
▷**verb** *a publicity stunt to hype a new product:* publicize, advertise, promote, push, boost, merchandise, build up, bang the drum for; informal plug, puff.

hyperbole noun *the usual media hyperbole that accompanied the final:* exaggeration, overstatement, embroidery, embellishment, excess, overkill; informal purple prose.
OPPOSITES: understatement.

hypercritical adjective *he was a sarcastic, hypercritical man:* overcritical, fault-finding, carping, cavilling, quibbling, hair-splitting, pedantic, fussy, finicky; formal captious; informal nit-picking; Brit. informal pernickety.
OPPOSITES: tolerant, easy-going.

hypnotic adjective *her voice had a hypnotic quality:* mesmerizing, mesmeric, spellbinding, entrancing, bewitching, irresistible, compelling; soporific, sedative, numbing.

hypnotize verb *they were hypnotized by*

the dancers: **entrance**, spellbind, enthral, transfix, captivate, bewitch, enrapture, grip, rivet, absorb.

hypochondriac noun *she is a hypochondriac who depends on pills for everything:* **valetudinarian**.
▷ **adjective** *her hypochondriac husband:* **valetudinarian**, health-obsessed, neurotic; malingering.

hypocrisy noun *plain speaking was important to him: he hated hypocrisy:* **sanctimoniousness**, sanctimony, pietism, piousness, false virtue, cant.
OPPOSITES: humility, sincerity.

hypocritical adjective *the hypocritical morality regarding sexual behaviour:* **sanctimonious**, pious, self-righteous, holier-than-thou, superior.
OPPOSITES: humble, sincere.

hypothesis noun *many people recognize that the hypothesis is not merely unprovable, but false:* **theory**, theorem, thesis, conjecture, supposition, postulation, postulate, proposition, premise, assumption, surmise.

hypothetical adjective *a hypothetical case | the hypothetical tenth planet:* **theoretical**, speculative, conjectured, conjectural, supposed, postulated, assumed, notional, academic.
OPPOSITES: actual.

hysteria noun *his voice had an edge of hysteria to it:* **frenzy**, feverishness, hysterics, derangement, mania, delirium; panic, alarm, distress, consternation; euphoria, ecstasy, elation.
OPPOSITES: calm.

hysterical adjective *Janet became hysterical and began screaming:* **overwrought**, overemotional, out of control, frenzied, frantic, wild, feverish; beside yourself, driven to distraction, agitated, berserk, manic, delirious, incoherent.

hysterics plural noun
1 *many actors scream their lines as if they're on the verge of hysterics:* **hysteria**, frenzy, irrationality, loss of control, delirium, derangement, mania, madness.
2 (informal) *the girls collapsed in hysterics:* **uncontrollable laughter**, fits of laughter, gales of laughter, convulsions; informal stitches.

h

Ii

ice noun

1 *the lake is covered with ice:* **frozen water**; black ice, verglas, frost; literary rime.
2 *a vanilla ice:* **ice cream**, water ice, sorbet.
▷**verb** *the lake iced over:* **freeze**, turn into ice, harden, solidify.
OPPOSITES: thaw.

> WORD LINKS
> **glacial** relating to ice

icon noun *an icon of the Madonna hangs on the wall:* **image**, portrait, representation, symbol; figure, statue; idol.

iconoclast noun **critic**, sceptic; heretic, dissident, dissenter, nonconformist, rebel, maverick, individualist.

icy adjective

1 *take care on the icy roads tonight:* **frosty**, frozen, ice-covered; slippery.
2 *an icy wind blew up:* **freezing**, chill, chilly, biting, bitter, raw, arctic, glacial; literary gelid.
3 *her voice was icy:* **unfriendly**, cold, cool, chilly, frigid, frosty, glacial, stern, hard, hostile.

idea noun

1 *the idea of death scares her:* **concept**, notion, conception, thought; hypothesis, postulation.
2 *our idea is to open a new shop:* **plan**, scheme, design, proposal, proposition, suggestion; aim, intention, objective, object, goal, target.
3 *Liz had other ideas on the subject:* **thought,** theory, view, opinion, feeling, belief, conclusion.
4 *I had an idea that this might happen:* **sense**, feeling, suspicion, inkling, hunch, theory, notion, impression.
5 *could you give me some idea of the cost?* **estimate**, estimation, approximation, guess, rough calculation; informal guesstimate.

ideal adjective

1 *it's ideal flying weather:* **perfect**, optimum, the best possible, excellent, exemplary, classic, model.
2 *the film-makers portray an ideal world:* **unattainable**, unachievable, impracticable; idealized, utopian, visionary, fairy-tale,

unreal, hypothetical, theoretical, ivory-towered, imaginary, fictitious.
OPPOSITES: real.
▷**noun**
1 *you're my ideal of how a man should be:* **perfection**, paragon, epitome, ne plus ultra, nonpareil; informal one in a million.
2 *tolerance and freedom are the liberal ideals:* **principle**, standard, value, belief, conviction; (**ideals**) morals, morality, ethics, ideology, creed.

idealist noun *he came to power with a reputation as a left-wing idealist:* **utopian**, visionary; fantasist, romantic, dreamer, daydreamer; Walter Mitty, Don Quixote.
OPPOSITES: realist.

idealistic adjective **utopian**, visionary, quixotic, romantic, unrealistic, starry-eyed, over-optimistic, impractical.
OPPOSITES: realistic.

idealize verb *they tend to idealize the post-war years:* **romanticize**, be unrealistic about, look at something through rose-tinted spectacles, paint a rosy picture of, glamorize.

ideally adverb *ideally, I would like to work part-time:* **in a perfect world**; preferably, if possible, for preference, by choice, as a matter of choice; all things being equal, theoretically, hypothetically, in theory, in principle, on paper.

identical adjective

1 *the guides wore identical badges:* **exactly the same**, indistinguishable, twin, interchangeable, undifferentiated, uniform, homogeneous, of a piece, cut from the same cloth; similar, alike, like, matching, like two peas in a pod; informal much of a muchness.
2 *I used the identical technique:* **the same**, the selfsame, the very same, one and the same; aforementioned, aforesaid; foregoing, preceding.
OPPOSITES: different.

identifiable adjective *there are no easily identifiable features on the shoreline:* **distinguishable**, recognizable, known; noticeable, perceptible, discernible, appreciable, detectable, visible; distinct,

marked, conspicuous, unmistakable, clear.
OPPOSITES: unrecognizable.

identification noun
1 *police have made some progress with the identification of the suspect:* recognition, naming, singling out, pinpointing.
2 *early identification of problems should save time later on:* determination, diagnosis, establishment, ascertainment, discovery; verification, confirmation.
3 *may I see your identification?* ID, identity papers, documents, credentials, bona fides; ID card, identity card, pass, warrant, licence, permit, passport.

identify verb
1 *Gail was able to identify her attacker:* recognize, single out, pick out, put a name to, name, know; informal finger.
2 *I identified four main problem areas:* determine, establish, ascertain, diagnose, pinpoint, discern, distinguish.
3 *we often identify sport with glamour:* associate, link, connect, relate, bracket, couple; mention in the same breath as, set side by side with.
4 *Peter identifies with the hero:* empathize, relate to, be in tune, have a rapport, feel at one, sympathize; be on the same wavelength as, speak the same language as, understand, feel for.

identity noun
1 *the identity of the owner remained a mystery:* name, identification, ID.
2 *she was afraid of losing her identity:* individuality, self, selfhood; personality, character, originality, distinctiveness, singularity, uniqueness.
3 *there is an identity between the company's own interests and those of the community:* affinity, similarity, closeness, likeness, accordance, uniformity, congruity, congruence.

ideology noun *the New Left challenged capitalist ideology:* beliefs, ideas, ideals, principles, ethics, morals; doctrine, creed, credo, teaching, theory; tenets, canon; convictions.

idiocy noun stupidity, folly, foolishness, foolhardiness; madness, insanity, lunacy; thoughtlessness, senselessness, irresponsibility, imprudence; inanity, absurdity, ludicrousness, fatuousness.

idiom noun
1 *he uses rather dated idioms:* expression, phrase, turn of phrase; formal locution.
2 *the poet's idiom is terse:* mode of expression, style, language, speech, usage, phraseology, phrasing, vocabulary; formal locution.

idiomatic adjective *the texts have been translated from Italian into idiomatic English:* colloquial, vernacular, everyday, conversational, natural; grammatical, correct.

idiosyncrasy noun *his idiosyncrasies included the recycling of cigar butts:* peculiarity, oddity, eccentricity, quirk, foible, habit, whim, trait, mannerism, characteristic, feature.

idiosyncratic adjective *each researcher had his or her own idiosyncratic approach:* distinctive, individual, individualistic, characteristic, peculiar, typical, special, specific, unique, personal; eccentric, unconventional, quirky, irregular, anomalous, odd, strange.

idiot noun *I felt like a complete idiot:* fool, dolt, ignoramus, simpleton, dunce; informal dope, ninny, nincompoop, chump, dimwit, halfwit, dummy, ass, blockhead, airhead, cretin, moron, imbecile, jerk; Brit. informal nit, nitwit, twit, clot, plonker, berk, prat, pillock, wally.

idiotic adjective *I can see absolutely no justification for this idiotic behaviour:* stupid, silly, foolish, brainless, mindless, thoughtless, unintelligent, witless; unwise, ill-advised, ill-considered, imprudent, foolhardy; absurd, senseless, pointless, nonsensical, inane, fatuous, ridiculous; informal dumb, dim, dim-witted, half-witted, dopey, half-baked, hare-brained; Brit. informal barmy, daft, gormless.

idle adjective
1 *she was idle and sometimes rude:* lazy, indolent, slothful, work-shy, shiftless, inactive, lackadaisical; good-for-nothing; informal bone idle.
2 *10.3% of the workforce is now idle:* unemployed, jobless, out of work, redundant, between jobs, unwaged, workless, unoccupied; Brit. informal on the dole.
3 *they left the machine idle:* inactive, unused, disused; out of action, inoperative, out of service.
4 *my social life was intended to give me as few idle moments as possible:* unoccupied, spare, empty, vacant, unfilled, available.
5 *he didn't indulge in idle remarks:* frivolous, trivial, trifling, minor, petty, lightweight, shallow, superficial, insignificant, unimportant, worthless, inane, fatuous; unnecessary, time-wasting.
6 *she was not a woman to make idle threats:* empty, meaningless, pointless, worthless, vain, insubstantial, futile, ineffective, ineffectual; groundless, baseless, without foundation.
OPPOSITES: industrious, employed, busy.
▷**verb**
1 *Lily idled on the window seat:* do nothing, be inactive, vegetate, take it easy, mark time, kick your heels, twiddle your thumbs, kill time, languish, laze, lounge, loll, loaf, slouch; informal hang around, veg out; Brit. informal hang about.
2 *they idled along the pavement:* saunter, stroll, dawdle, drift, potter, amble, wander, straggle; informal mosey, tootle;

Brit. informal pootle, mooch.
3 *he let the engine idle:* tick over.

idler noun *you were not brought into this world to be an idler:* layabout, good-for-nothing, ne'er-do-well, shirker, loafer, sluggard; informal skiver, waster, slacker, slob, slowcoach, lazybones.

idol noun
1 *there was an idol in a shrine at the roadside:* icon, effigy, statue, figure, figurine, fetish, totem; graven image, false god, golden calf.
2 *the pop world's latest idol:* hero, heroine, star, superstar, icon, celebrity; favourite, darling; informal pin-up, heart throb, blue-eyed boy/girl, golden boy/girl.

idolatry noun
1 *he preached against idolatry:* idol worship, iconolatry, fetishism.
2 *the idolatry of television celebrities:* idolization, worship, adulation, adoration, reverence, glorification, lionization, hero-worshipping.

idolize verb *he idolized his father:* hero-worship, worship, adore, revere, venerate, lionize; stand in awe of, look up to, admire; informal put on a pedestal.

idyll noun
1 *the rural idyll remains strongly evocative in most industrialized societies:* perfect period, perfect situation, Utopia, paradise, heaven on earth, Shangri-La.
2 *the poem began as a two-part idyll:* pastoral, eclogue, georgic.

idyllic adjective *she had an idyllic childhood, brought up in rural Devon by doting parents:* perfect, wonderful, blissful, halcyon, happy; ideal, idealized, utopian, heavenly, Elysian; peaceful, picturesque, unspoiled.

if conjunction
1 *if the weather is fine, we can walk:* on condition that, provided, providing, presuming, supposing, assuming, as long as, given that.
2 *if I go out she gets nasty:* whenever, every time.
3 *I wonder if he noticed:* whether, whether or not.

ignite verb
1 *he got to safety moments before the petrol ignited:* catch fire, burst into flames; be set off, explode.
2 *a cigarette ignited the fumes:* light, set fire to, set on fire, set alight, kindle, touch off; informal set/put a match to.
3 *the campaign failed to ignite voter interest:* arouse, kindle, trigger, spark, stimulate, stir up, excite; provoke, whip up, incite, fuel, instigate.
OPPOSITES: extinguish.

ignoble adjective *the war is being fought over an ignoble cause:* dishonourable,

unworthy, base, shameful, contemptible, despicable, shabby, sordid; unprincipled, discreditable.

ignominious adjective *their military forces suffered an ignominious defeat:* humiliating, undignified, embarrassing, mortifying, ignoble, inglorious.
OPPOSITES: glorious.

ignominy noun *he faces the ignominy of a public trial:* shame, humiliation, embarrassment; disgrace, dishonour, discredit, degradation, scandal, infamy, indignity, loss of face.

ignoramus noun fool, dunce, simpleton, informal dope, dimwit, imbecile, halfwit, blockhead, moron, dumbo, dummy, airhead, birdbrain; Brit. informal nit, nitwit, twit, clot.

ignorance noun
1 *ignorance of the law is no excuse:* unawareness, unconsciousness, lack of knowledge, inexperience, unfamiliarity with; informal cluelessness about.
2 *their attitudes are based on ignorance:* lack of knowledge, lack of education; lack of intelligence, stupidity, foolishness; unenlightenment, benightedness.
OPPOSITES: knowledge, education.

ignorant adjective
1 *an ignorant country girl:* uneducated, untaught, unschooled, untutored, untrained, uninformed, illiterate, unlettered, unenlightened, benighted; inexperienced, unworldly, unsophisticated, naive, innocent.
2 *they were ignorant of working-class life:* without knowledge, unaware, unconscious, unfamiliar with, unacquainted with, uninformed about; informal in the dark about, clueless about.
OPPOSITES: educated, knowledgeable.

ignore verb
1 *he ignored the customers:* take no notice of, pay no attention to, pay no heed to; turn a blind eye to, turn a deaf ear to, disregard.
2 *he was ignored by the countess:* snub, slight, spurn, shun, look right through, cold-shoulder; Brit. send to Coventry; informal give someone the brush-off, cut dead, freeze out; Brit. informal blank.
3 *doctors ignored her husband's instructions:* set aside, pay no attention to, take no account of; break, contravene, fail to comply with, fail to observe, disregard, disobey, breach, defy, flout.
OPPOSITES: acknowledge.

ilk noun *fascists, racists, and others of that ilk:* type, sort, class, category, group, set, bracket, genre, vintage, brand, stamp, variety.

ill adjective
1 *she was feeling rather ill:* unwell, sick, not very well, ailing, poorly, sickly,

indisposed, infirm; out of sorts, not yourself, under/below par, in a bad way; queasy, nauseous, nauseated; Brit. peaky, off colour; informal under the weather, lousy, rough; Brit. informal ropy.
2 *the project is designed to address the ill effects of deforestation:* harmful, damaging, detrimental, adverse, injurious, deleterious, hurtful, destructive, pernicious, dangerous; unhealthy, unwholesome.
OPPOSITES: well, healthy.

▷**noun**
1 *television is often blamed for all kinds of social ills:* problems, troubles, difficulties, misfortunes, trials, tribulations; worries, anxieties, concerns.
2 *he wished them no ill:* harm, hurt, injury, damage, pain, trouble, misfortune, suffering, distress.

▷**adverb**
1 *he can ill afford the loss of income:* barely, scarcely, hardly.
2 *we are ill prepared:* inadequately, unsatisfactorily, insufficiently, imperfectly, poorly, badly.
□**ill at ease**
awkward, uneasy, uncomfortable, embarrassed, self-conscious, out of place, inhibited; restless, restive, fidgety, discomfited, worried, anxious, on edge, edgy, nervous, tense; informal twitchy, jittery.
□**speak ill of**
denigrate, disparage, criticize, malign, be critical of, speak badly of, be malicious about, run down, insult, abuse, attack, revile, vilify, blacken the name of; informal bad-mouth, bitch about, pull to pieces; Brit. informal rubbish, slate, slag off.

ill-advised adjective *an ill-advised business venture:* unwise, injudicious, misguided, imprudent, ill-considered, ill-judged; foolhardy, rash, reckless; informal crazy, crackpot, hare-brained.
OPPOSITES: judicious.

ill-assorted adjective *an ill-assorted travelling party:* mismatched, ill-matched, incompatible, incongruous; dissimilar, unalike, varied, disparate.

ill-bred adjective *she was unlikely to be amused by ill-bred behaviour:* ill-mannered, bad-mannered, rude, impolite, discourteous, uncivil; boorish, churlish, loutish, vulgar, coarse, crass, uncouth, uncivilized, ungentlemanly, indecorous, unseemly; informal ignorant; Brit. informal yobbish.

ill-considered adjective *the government may force through this ill-considered legislation:* ill-advised, ill-judged, injudicious, imprudent, unwise, hasty, rash; misjudged, ill-conceived, badly thought out; informal hare-brained.
OPPOSITES: judicious.

ill-defined adjective *the boundary between the two estates was rather ill-defined:* vague, indistinct, unclear, imprecise; blurred, fuzzy, hazy, woolly.

ill-disposed adjective *the court may be ill-disposed to foreign companies:* hostile, antagonistic, unfriendly, unsympathetic, antipathetic, inimical, unfavourable, averse; informal anti.

illegal adjective *a significant number of gangmasters were involved in illegal activity:* unlawful, illicit, illegitimate, criminal, felonious; unlicensed, unauthorized, unsanctioned; outlawed, banned, forbidden, prohibited, proscribed; contraband, black-market, bootleg; informal crooked, shady; Brit. informal bent, dodgy.
OPPOSITES: lawful, legitimate.

> **USAGE**
>
> Note that **illegal** and **unlawful** have overlapping but slightly different meanings. An **illegal** act is against the law of a particular country or community, but an **unlawful** one usually only goes against the rules that apply in a particular situation. For example, handball in football is **unlawful** but not **illegal** and therefore subject only to the penalties set out in the rules of football.

illegible adjective *his writing is illegible:* unreadable, indecipherable, unintelligible; scrawled, scribbled, crabbed.

illegitimate adjective
1 *illegitimate share trading:* illegal, unlawful, illicit, criminal, felonious; unlicensed, unauthorized, unsanctioned; prohibited, outlawed, banned, forbidden, proscribed; fraudulent, corrupt, dishonest; informal crooked, shady; Brit. informal bent, dodgy.
2 *an illegitimate child:* born out of wedlock; old use or derogatory bastard.
OPPOSITES: legal, lawful.

ill-fated adjective *an ill-fated rebellion:* doomed, ill-starred, jinxed, blighted, damned, cursed.

ill-favoured adjective *an ill-favoured old woman:* unattractive, plain, ugly; N. Amer. homely; informal not much to look at.

ill-founded adjective *your faith in his expertise was ill-founded:* baseless, groundless, without foundation, unjustified; questionable, misinformed, misguided.

ill humour noun *the downward tilt to her mouth betrayed her ill humour:* bad mood, bad temper, irritability, irascibility, petulance, peevishness, pique, testiness, tetchiness, fractiousness, moodiness, sullenness, sulkiness, surliness, annoyance, anger.

illiberal adjective *the government moved towards more illiberal policies:* intolerant, conservative, reactionary, undemocratic, authoritarian, repressive, oppressive, totalitarian, despotic, tyrannical.

illicit adjective
1 *illicit drugs:* illegal, unlawful, illegitimate, criminal; outlawed, banned, forbidden, prohibited, proscribed; unlicensed, unauthorized; contraband, black-market, bootleg.
2 *an illicit love affair:* clandestine, secret; forbidden, socially unacceptable, taboo.
OPPOSITES: lawful, legal.

illimitable adjective (literary) limitless, unlimited, unbounded; endless, unending, never-ending, infinite, immeasurable.

illiteracy noun
1 *illiteracy was widespread:* inability to read or write.
2 *businessmen complain about the public's economic illiteracy:* ignorance, unawareness, inexperience, unenlightenment, lack of knowledge/ education.

illiterate adjective
1 *an illiterate peasant:* unable to read or write, unlettered.
2 *80% of them are politically illiterate:* ignorant, uneducated, uninformed, unschooled, untutored, untrained.

ill-judged adjective *she flinched at his ill-judged choice of words:* ill-considered, ill-advised, unwise, ill-thought-out; imprudent, incautious, injudicious, misguided, impolitic, inexpedient; rash, hasty, thoughtless, careless, reckless.
OPPOSITES: judicious.

ill-mannered adjective *ill-mannered children may not have been shown how to behave:* bad-mannered, discourteous, rude, impolite, uncivil, abusive; insolent, impertinent, impudent, cheeky, presumptuous, disrespectful; badly behaved, loutish, oafish, uncouth, uncivilized, ill-bred; informal ignorant.
OPPOSITES: polite.

illness noun *he was making a steady recovery from his recent illness:* sickness, disease, ailment, complaint, affliction, infection, indisposition; ill health, poor health, infirmity; literary malady; informal bug, virus; Brit. informal lurgy.

illogical adjective *he drew a strange and illogical conclusion:* irrational, unreasonable, unsound, unjustifiable; incorrect, erroneous, invalid, spurious, faulty, flawed, fallacious, unscientific, specious; absurd, preposterous, untenable.

ill-starred adjective *an ill-starred venture:* ill-fated, doomed, ill-omened, jinxed, cursed, blighted, damned; unlucky, luckless, unfortunate, hapless.
OPPOSITES: blessed.

ill temper noun bad mood, irritation, vexation, exasperation, indignation, moodiness, pet, pique; anger, crossness, bad temper; irritability, irascibility, peevishness, tetchiness, testiness; informal huff, grump; Brit. informal paddy, strop.

ill-tempered adjective *an ill-tempered woman:* bad-tempered, short-tempered, moody; in a bad mood, cross, irritable, irascible, tetchy, testy, crotchety, touchy, cantankerous, curmudgeonly, peevish, fractious, waspish, prickly, pettish; grumpy, grouchy, crabby, splenetic, dyspeptic, choleric; informal snappish; Brit. informal stroppy, ratty.

ill-timed adjective *their ill-timed foray into overseas property markets:* untimely, mistimed, badly timed; premature, early, hasty, inopportune.
OPPOSITES: timely.

ill-treat verb *her mother had ill-treated her when she was young:* abuse, mistreat, maltreat, ill-use, misuse; manhandle, handle roughly; harm, injure, damage; informal knock about/around.

ill-treatment noun abuse, mistreatment, maltreatment, ill use, ill usage, misuse; manhandling, rough treatment.

illuminate verb
1 *floodlights illuminated the stadium:* light up, light, throw light on, brighten, shine on.
2 *the manuscripts were beautifully illuminated:* decorate, illustrate, embellish, adorn, ornament.
3 *documents often illuminate people's thought processes:* clarify, elucidate, explain, reveal, shed light on, give insight into.

illuminating adjective *an illuminating account of the cultural life of the period:* informative, enlightening, revealing, explanatory, instructive, helpful, educational.

illumination noun
1 *a floodlamp provided illumination:* light, lighting, radiance, gleam, glow, glare; shining, gleaming, glowing.
2 *the illumination of a manuscript:* decoration, illustration, embellishment, adornment, ornamentation.
3 *these books give illumination on the subject:* clarification, elucidation, explanation, revelation, explication, edification.
4 *there may be moments of real illumination and discovery:* enlightenment, insight, understanding, awareness; learning, education.

illusion noun
1 *he had destroyed her illusions:* delusion, misapprehension, misconception, false impression; fantasy, fancy, dream, chimera.
2 *the lighting increases the illusion of depth:*

appearance, impression, semblance.
3 *it's just an illusion:* mirage, hallucination, apparition, figment of the imagination, trick of the light.

illusory adjective *the comfort these theories give is illusory:* deceptive, misleading, delusive, delusory; illusionary, imagined, imaginary, unreal; false, fallacious, fake, bogus, sham, mistaken, erroneous, misguided, untrue.
OPPOSITES: genuine.

illustrate verb
1 *the guide is illustrated with full-colour photographs:* decorate, adorn, ornament, accompany.
2 *this can be illustrated through a brief example:* explain, elucidate, clarify, make plain, demonstrate, show, emphasize; informal get across/over.
3 *his wit was illustrated by his remark to Lucy:* exemplify, show, demonstrate, display, represent.

illustrated adjective *an illustrated weekly magazine:* with illustrations, with pictures, with drawings, pictorial.

illustration noun
1 *the illustrations in children's books:* picture, drawing, sketch, figure, plate, print.
2 *the accident is an illustration of the disaster waiting to happen:* example, instance, typical case, case in point, exemplification, demonstration.

illustrative adjective
□ **be illustrative of** *the case was illustrative of a greater public willingness to take legal action:* demonstrate, show, indicate, reveal, signify, denote, exemplify.

illustrious adjective *an illustrious general:* eminent, distinguished, acclaimed, notable, noteworthy, prominent, pre-eminent, foremost, leading, important, influential; renowned, famous, famed, well known, celebrated; esteemed, honoured, respected, venerable, august, highly regarded, well thought of, of distinction.
OPPOSITES: unknown.

ill will noun *he didn't bear his wife any ill will:* animosity, hostility, enmity, acrimony, animus, hatred, hate, loathing, antipathy; ill feeling, bad blood, antagonism, unfriendliness, dislike; spite, spitefulness, resentment, hard feelings, bitterness.
OPPOSITES: goodwill.

image noun
1 *an image of the Madonna:* likeness, depiction, portrayal, representation; statue, statuette, sculpture, bust, effigy; painting, picture, portrait, drawing, sketch; photograph; reflection.
2 *87% of respondents said the campaign had improved their image of the city:* impression, idea, perception, conception, notion, mental picture; profile, persona.

WORD LINKS
iconography the study of images

imaginable adjective *the most severe weather conditions imaginable:* thinkable, conceivable, possible; believable, credible.

imaginary adjective *the imaginary world of the novel:* unreal, non-existent, fictional, fictitious, pretend, make-believe, mythical, fabulous, fanciful, illusory; made-up, dreamed-up, invented.
OPPOSITES: real.

imagination noun
1 *she was set in her ways and lacked imagination:* creativity, imaginativeness, creativeness; vision, inspiration, inventiveness, invention, resourcefulness, ingenuity; originality, innovation, innovativeness.
2 *the album captured the public's imagination:* interest, fascination, attention, curiosity.

imaginative adjective *she came up with an imaginative solution:* creative, inspired, inventive, resourceful, ingenious, visionary; original, innovative, innovatory, unorthodox, unconventional; fanciful, whimsical; informal blue-sky.

imagine verb
1 *she smiled as she imagined the touching scene:* visualize, envisage, envision, picture, see in the mind's eye; dream up, think up/of, conceive.
2 *I imagine he was at home:* assume, presume, expect, take it, suppose, think, dare say, surmise, believe, be of the view; informal guess, reckon.

imbalance noun *the political imbalance between North and South:* disparity, variance, variation, polarity, contrast, lack of harmony; gulf, breach, gap.

imbed verb. See EMBED.

imbue verb *his writings are imbued with a passionate love of nature:* permeate suffuse, pervade, fill, infuse; inspire.

imitate verb
1 *other artists have imitated his style:* copy, emulate, model yourself on, follow, echo, parrot.
2 *he imitated Winston Churchill:* mimic, do an impression of, impersonate, ape; parody, caricature, burlesque; informal take off; Brit. informal send up.

imitation noun
1 *the traders sold cheap imitations of Cartier watches:* copy, reproduction, replica.
2 *they learned by imitation:* emulation, copying.
3 *he did a good imitation of Bill Clinton:* impersonation, impression, parody,

mockery, caricature, burlesque, lampoon, pastiche; mimicry; informal send-up, take-off, spoof.
▷**adjective** *imitation leather:* **artificial,** synthetic, simulated, man-made, manufactured, ersatz, substitute; mock, sham, fake, false, faux, bogus; informal pseudo, phoney.
OPPOSITES: real, genuine.

imitative adjective
1 *news reports can lead to imitative crime:* **similar,** like, mimicking; informal copycat.
2 *I found the film empty and imitative:* **derivative,** unoriginal, unimaginative, uninspired, plagiarized; clichéd, hackneyed, stale, trite, banal.

imitator noun
1 *the show's success has sparked off many imitators:* **copier,** emulator, follower; literary epigone; informal copycat.
2 *an Elvis imitator:* **impersonator,** impressionist, mimic; parodist, caricaturist.

immaculate adjective
1 *the house was immaculate:* **spotless,** pristine, clean, as clean as a whistle, unsullied; shining, shiny, gleaming; neat, tidy, spick and span; informal squeaky clean.
2 *the car is still in immaculate condition:* **perfect,** pristine, mint; flawless, faultless, unblemished, unspoiled, undamaged; excellent, impeccable; informal tip-top, A1.
3 *he is an experienced driver with an immaculate record:* **unblemished,** spotless, impeccable, exemplary, perfect, unsullied, undefiled, untarnished; informal squeaky clean.

immaterial adjective *the difference in our ages was immaterial:* **irrelevant,** unimportant, inconsequential, insignificant, of no matter/moment, of little account, beside the point, neither here nor there.
OPPOSITES: significant.

immature adjective childish, juvenile, puerile, infantile, babyish, callow, inexperienced, unsophisticated, unworldly, naive, green, jejune; informal wet behind the ears.

immeasurable adjective *he dreamed of possessing immeasurable riches:* **incalculable,** inestimable, innumerable, untold; limitless, boundless, unbounded, unlimited, infinite, inexhaustible; vast, immense, great, abundant; literary illimitable.

immediate adjective
1 *the UN called for immediate action:* **instant,** instantaneous, swift, prompt, speedy, rapid, quick, expeditious; sudden, hurried, hasty, precipitate; informal snappy.
2 *their immediate concern was how to avoid taxes:* **current,** present, existing, actual; urgent, pressing, top-priority.

3 *our immediate neighbours:* **nearest,** near, close, closest, next-door; adjacent, adjoining.
4 *coronary thrombosis was the immediate cause of death:* **direct,** primary.
OPPOSITES: delayed, distant.

immediately adverb
1 *it was necessary to make a decision immediately:* **straight away,** at once, right away, instantly, now, directly, promptly, forthwith, this/that minute, this/that instant, there and then, here and now, without delay, without further ado, posthaste; quickly, as fast/soon as possible, speedily; informal pronto.
2 *I sat immediately behind him:* **directly,** right, exactly, precisely, squarely, just; informal slap bang.

immense adjective *an immense brick church dominates the town:* **huge,** vast, massive, enormous, gigantic, colossal, great, very large/big, monumental, towering, tremendous; giant, elephantine, monstrous, mammoth, titanic, king-sized; informal mega, monster, whopping, humongous, jumbo; Brit. informal whacking great, ginormous.
OPPOSITES: tiny.

immensely adverb *I was faced with an immensely difficult decision:* **extremely,** very, exceptionally, extraordinarily, tremendously, hugely, singularly, exceedingly, distinctly, outstandingly, uncommonly, unusually, decidedly, particularly, eminently, supremely, highly, remarkably, terribly, really, truly, thoroughly, in the extreme; informal terrifically, awfully.
OPPOSITES: slightly.

immerse verb
1 *litmus paper turns red on being immersed in acid:* **submerge,** dip, dunk, duck, sink; soak, drench, saturate, wet.
2 *Elliot was immersed in his work:* **absorb,** engross, occupy, engage, involve, bury; employ, preoccupy.

immigrant noun newcomer, settler, incomer, migrant; non-native, foreigner, alien.
OPPOSITES: emigrant.

imminent adjective *there was speculation that a ceasefire was imminent:* **close at hand,** near, approaching, impending, coming, forthcoming, on the way, about to happen, on the horizon, expected, anticipated, brewing, looming; informal on the cards.

immobile adjective *she sat immobile for a long time:* **motionless,** without moving, still, stock-still, static, stationary; rooted to the spot, rigid, frozen, transfixed, like a statue, not moving a muscle.

immobilize verb *the officer wanted to immobilize the vehicle:* **put out of action,**

disable, make inoperative, inactivate, deactivate, paralyse, cripple; bring to a standstill, halt, stop; clamp, wheel-clamp.

immoderate adjective *they were concerned about his immoderate drinking:* excessive, heavy, intemperate, unrestrained, unrestricted, uncontrolled, unlimited, unbridled, overindulgent, imprudent, reckless; undue, inordinate, unreasonable, unjustified, unwarranted, uncalled for, outrageous; extravagant, lavish, prodigal, profligate.

immodest adjective *her clothes and manner were most immodest:* indecorous, improper, indecent, indelicate, immoral; forward, bold, brazen, impudent, shameless, loose, wanton.

immoral adjective *they deplored immoral behaviour:* unethical, bad, morally wrong, wrongful, wicked, evil, unprincipled, unscrupulous, dishonourable, dishonest, disreputable, corrupt, villainous, iniquitous, nefarious, base; sinful, depraved, degenerate, debauched, dissolute, reprobate, lewd, licentious, promiscuous, wanton.
OPPOSITES: ethical, chaste.

> **USAGE**
>
> **Immoral** and **amoral** do not mean the same thing. While **amoral** means 'without morality' (*a violent and amoral underclass*), **immoral** means 'not following accepted standards of morality'.

immorality noun wickedness, immoral behaviour, evil, corruption, dishonesty; sinfulness, sin, depravity, vice, degeneracy, debauchery, lewdness, promiscuity.

immortal adjective
1 *our souls are immortal:* undying, eternal, deathless, everlasting, imperishable, indestructible, immutable.
2 *an immortal children's classic:* timeless, ageless, perennial, classic, time-honoured, enduring; famous, famed, renowned, great, outstanding, acclaimed, celebrated.

immortality noun
1 *the immortality of the gods:* eternal life, everlasting life, deathlessness; indestructibility, imperishability.
2 *the book has achieved immortality:* timelessness, legendary status, lasting fame/renown.

immortalize verb *the battle was immortalized in prose by Pushkin:* commemorate, memorialize; celebrate, eulogize, pay tribute to, honour, salute, exalt, glorify.

immovable adjective
1 *lock your bike to something immovable:* fixed, secure, stable, set firm, set fast.
2 *he sat immovable:* motionless, unmoving, stationary, still, stock-still, not moving a muscle, rooted to the spot.

3 *she was immovable in her loyalties:* steadfast, unwavering, unswerving, resolute, determined, firm, unshakeable, unfailing, dogged, tenacious, inflexible, unyielding, unbending, uncompromising, iron-willed.

immune adjective *they are immune to hepatitis B:* resistant, not subject, not liable, not susceptible, not vulnerable; protected from, safe from, secure against, unaffected by, not in danger of.
OPPOSITES: susceptible.

immunity noun
1 *millions of people now lack immunity to malaria:* resistance, non-susceptibility; ability to fight off, protection against, defences against.
2 *the rebels were given immunity from prosecution:* exemption, protection, freedom, release, dispensation; informal a let-off.
3 *diplomatic immunity:* indemnity, privilege, prerogative, right, liberty, licence; legal exemption, impunity, protection.

> **WORD LINKS**
> **immunology** the branch of medicine to do with immunity to infection

immunize verb *he immunized the children against measles:* vaccinate, inoculate, inject; protect from, safeguard against; informal give someone a jab/shot.

immutable adjective *an immutable set of rules:* fixed, permanent, unchanging, unvarying, established, lasting, enduring, constant, static; set, rigid, inflexible.

imp noun
1 sprite, devil, hobgoblin, goblin, elf, puck.
2 *a cheeky young imp:* rascal, monkey, devil, troublemaker, wretch; informal scamp, tyke.

impact noun
1 *his ribs were broken by the force of the impact:* collision, crash, smash, bang, knock, bump.
2 *the job losses will have a major impact:* effect, influence; consequences, repercussions, ramifications, reverberations.
▷verb *high interest rates have impacted on retail spending:* affect, influence, have an impact, have an effect, make an impression, hit; change, alter, modify, transform.

> **USAGE**
>
> Many people dislike the use of **impact** as a verb, found in the construction **impact on**. This may be partly because it is a verb that has been formed from an existing noun and partly because it is associated with business jargon. It is best avoided in formal writing.

impair verb *even one drink can impair driving performance:* have a negative

effect on, damage, harm, diminish, reduce, weaken, lessen, decrease, impede, hinder; undermine, compromise.
OPPOSITES: enhance.

impale verb *his head was impaled on a pike:* stick, skewer, spear, spike, transfix; pierce, stab, run through.

impalpable adjective *a glimpse of an idea that remained as impalpable as a dream:* intangible, insubstantial, indefinable, elusive, indescribable.

impart verb
1 *she had news to impart:* communicate, pass on, convey, transmit, relay, relate, recount, tell, make known, make public, report, announce; disclose, reveal, divulge.
2 *the mushrooms impart a wonderfully woody flavour to salads:* give, bestow, confer, lend, afford, provide, supply.

impartial adjective *the referee is obliged to be impartial:* unbiased, unprejudiced, neutral, non-partisan, disinterested, dispassionate, objective, open-minded, equitable, even-handed, fair, just.
OPPOSITES: biased, partisan.

impassable adjective *many roads were impassable after the flood:* closed, blocked, unnavigable, unpassable.

impasse noun *the negotiations seemed to have reached an impasse:* deadlock, dead end, stalemate, stand-off; standstill, halt, full stop.

impassioned adjective *he made an impassioned speech against the war:* emotional, heartfelt, passionate, fervent, wholehearted, earnest, sincere, ardent, fervid.

impassive adjective *she smiled at him, but his features remained impassive:* expressionless, inexpressive, inscrutable, blank, deadpan, poker-faced, straight-faced; stony, wooden, unresponsive.
OPPOSITES: expressive.

impatience noun
1 *he was shifting in his seat with impatience:* restlessness, frustration, irritation, irritability, exasperation, annoyance.
2 *I understand your impatience to get back to work:* eagerness, keenness, anxiety.

impatient adjective
1 *impatient drivers hooted their horns:* restless, frustrated, agitated; irritated, exasperated, annoyed, angry, testy, tetchy, cross; informal snappy, keyed up; Brit. informal twitchy, uptight.
2 *they are impatient to get back home:* anxious, eager, keen, longing, aching; informal itching, dying.

impeach verb
1 *there were moves to impeach the president:* indict, charge, accuse, lay charges against, arraign, take to court,
put on trial, prosecute.
2 *the headlines impeached their clean image:* challenge, question, call into question, raise doubts about.

impeccable adjective *he is a man of impeccable character:* flawless, faultless, unblemished, spotless, untarnished, perfect, exemplary, model; irreproachable, blameless, guiltless, sinless; informal squeaky clean.

impecunious adjective *she came from a respectable but impecunious family:* penniless, poor, impoverished, indigent, insolvent, poverty-stricken, needy, destitute; in straitened circumstances, unable to make ends meet; Brit. on the breadline; formal penurious; informal hard up, broke, cash-strapped; Brit. informal skint.
OPPOSITES: wealthy.

impede verb *the programme had been impeded by several problems:* hinder, obstruct, hamper, hold back/up, delay, interfere with, disrupt, slow down, retard; block, check, stop, thwart, frustrate, baulk, foil, derail; informal stymie; Brit. informal scupper.
OPPOSITES: facilitate.

impediment noun
1 *the debt burden is a serious impediment to economic improvement:* hindrance, obstruction, obstacle, barrier, bar, block, check, curb, restriction, limitation; setback, difficulty, snag, hitch, stumbling block; informal fly in the ointment, hiccup; Brit. informal spanner in the works.
2 *a speech impediment:* defect; stammer, stutter, lisp.

impedimenta plural noun paraphernalia, equipment, accessories, accoutrements, trappings; formal appurtenances; informal stuff, gear, bits and pieces.

impel verb *financial difficulties impelled her to seek work:* force, compel, constrain, oblige, require, make, drive, push, spur, prod, goad, incite, prompt, persuade.

impending adjective *she had a strange feeling of impending danger:* imminent, approaching, close at hand, near, nearing, coming, forthcoming, upcoming, to come, on the way, about to happen, in store, in the offing, on the horizon, in the air/wind, brewing, looming, threatening.

impenetrable adjective
1 *impenetrable armour plating:* unbreakable, indestructible, solid, thick, unyielding; impregnable, inviolable, unassailable.
2 *a dark, impenetrable forest:* impassable, inaccessible; dense, thick, overgrown.
3 *impenetrable legal jargon:* incomprehensible, unintelligible, baffling, bewildering, puzzling, perplexing, confusing, abstruse, opaque, unclear,

unfathomable; complex, complicated, difficult.

impenitent adjective unrepentant, unrepenting, without remorse, unashamed, unapologetic, unabashed.

imperative adjective *it is imperative that you find him:* vitally important, of vital importance, vital, crucial, critical, essential, all-important, necessary, urgent.
OPPOSITES: unimportant.
▷ noun *free movement of labour was an economic imperative:* necessity, essential, urgent requirement.

imperceptible adjective *the change was slow and imperceptible:* unnoticeable, undetectable, indistinguishable, indiscernible, invisible, inaudible, impalpable, unobtrusive; slight, small, subtle, faint, fine, negligible, infinitesimal.
OPPOSITES: noticeable.

imperfect adjective
1 *the goods were returned as imperfect:* faulty, flawed, defective, shoddy, inferior, second-rate, below standard, substandard; damaged, broken, incomplete; informal not up to scratch.
2 *she spoke imperfect Arabic:* broken, faltering, halting, hesitant; rudimentary, limited.
OPPOSITES: flawless.

imperfection noun
1 *the glass is free from imperfections:* defect, fault, flaw, discoloration, deformity, disfigurement; crack, scratch, chip, dent, blemish, stain, mark.
2 *he was aware of his imperfections:* flaw, fault, failing, deficiency, weakness, weak point, shortcoming, inadequacy, limitation.
OPPOSITES: strength.

imperial adjective
1 *the imperial family:* royal.
2 *his imperial bearing:* majestic, grand, dignified, proud, stately, noble, aristocratic, regal; magnificent, imposing, impressive.

imperil verb *a radiation leak would imperil life and health:* endanger, jeopardize, risk, put in danger, put in jeopardy, expose to danger; threaten, pose a threat to.

imperious adjective *he spoke to her in a very imperious manner:* peremptory, high-handed, overbearing, lordly, commanding, overweening, domineering, authoritarian, dictatorial, authoritative, assertive, arrogant; informal bossy, high and mighty.

imperishable adjective *the fruits of his inspired leadership and labours are imperishable:* enduring, everlasting, undying, immortal, perennial, long-lasting; indestructible, inextinguishable, ineradicable, unfading, permanent.

impermanent adjective *life has value precisely because it is impermanent:* temporary, transient, transitory, passing, fleeting, momentary, ephemeral, fugitive; short-lived, brief, {here today, gone tomorrow}.

impermeable adjective *the product is packaged in impermeable containers:* watertight, waterproof, damp-proof, airtight, sealed, hermetically sealed.

impersonal adjective
1 *the hand of fate is impersonal:* neutral, unbiased, non-partisan, unprejudiced, objective, disinterested, dispassionate, without favouritism.
2 *he remained strangely impersonal:* dispassionate, detached, unemotional, cool, aloof, distant, remote, reserved, withdrawn, unfriendly, formal, stiff, businesslike; informal stand-offish.
OPPOSITES: biased.

impersonate verb
1 *it's a serious offence to impersonate a police officer:* pose as, masquerade as, pass yourself off as, pretend to be.
2 *Nick started impersonating Sean Connery:* imitate, mimic, do an impression of, ape; parody, caricature, burlesque, satirize, lampoon; informal take off; Brit. informal send up.

impertinence noun rudeness, insolence, impoliteness, bad manners, discourtesy, discourteousness, disrespect, incivility; impudence, cheek, cheekiness, audacity, temerity, effrontery, gall; informal nerve, brass neck.

impertinent adjective *she asked a lot of impertinent questions:* rude, insolent, impudent, cheeky, impolite, ill-mannered, bad-mannered, discourteous, disrespectful, uncivil.
OPPOSITES: polite.

imperturbable adjective *my father was a solid, imperturbable man:* self-possessed, calm, composed, self-controlled, {cool, calm, and collected}, serene, relaxed, even-tempered, placid, phlegmatic, stolid, unexcitable; unperturbed, unflustered, unruffled; informal unflappable, unfazed, laid-back.
OPPOSITES: excitable.

impervious adjective
1 *he seemed impervious to the chill wind:* unaffected by, untouched by, immune to, not susceptible to, indifferent to, heedless of, oblivious to, proof against, not vulnerable to.
2 *an impervious damp-proof course:* impermeable, impenetrable, impregnable, waterproof, watertight; sealed, hermetically sealed.
OPPOSITES: susceptible, permeable.

impetuous adjective *she might live to regret this impetuous decision:* impulsive, rash, hasty, overhasty, incautious, imprudent, injudicious, ill-considered, reckless, foolhardy; spontaneous, impromptu, spur-of-the-moment, precipitate, hurried, rushed.

impetus noun
1 *the flywheel lost all its impetus:* **momentum,** propulsion, motive force, driving force, drive, thrust, impulsion; energy, force, power, push, strength.
2 *the sales force were given fresh impetus:* **motivation,** stimulus, incentive, inducement, inspiration, encouragement, boost; informal a shot in the arm.

impinge verb *these issues impinge on all of us:* **affect,** have an effect, touch, influence, make an impact, leave a mark.

impious adjective *the church was shamefully plundered by impious villains:* **godless,** ungodly, unholy, irreligious, sinful, immoral, unrighteous, sacrilegious, profane, blasphemous, irreverent; apostate, atheistic, agnostic, pagan, heathen, faithless.

impish adjective *he takes an impish delight in shocking the press:* **mischievous,** naughty, wicked, roguish, playful, puckish, rascally.

implacable adjective *he was their most implacable critic:* **unforgiving,** unrelenting, relentless, intransigent, inflexible, unyielding, unbending, uncompromising, ruthless, remorseless, merciless, cruel, hard, harsh, stern, tough.

implant verb
1 *the collagen is implanted under the skin:* **insert,** embed, lodge, place; graft.
2 *he implanted the idea in my mind:* **instil,** inculcate, introduce, establish, plant, sow, root, lodge.

implausible adjective *they despaired of his adherence to implausible theories:* **unlikely,** improbable, questionable, doubtful, debatable; unrealistic, unconvincing, far-fetched, incredible, unbelievable, inconceivable, fantastic, fanciful, ridiculous, absurd, preposterous.
OPPOSITES: convincing.

implement noun *garden implements:* **tool,** utensil, instrument, device, apparatus, gadget, contraption, appliance, machine, contrivance; informal gizmo.
▷verb *the cost of implementing the strategy has not been estimated:* **put into effect,** apply, put into practice, carry out/through, execute, perform, enact; fulfil, accomplish, bring about, achieve, realize.

implicate verb
1 *they have found no concrete evidence that implicates him:* **incriminate,** compromise; involve, connect.
2 *viruses are implicated in the development of cancer:* **involve in,** associate with, connect with.

implication noun
1 *he was smarting at their implication:* suggestion, inference, insinuation, innuendo, hint, intimation, imputation.
2 *the decision had important political implications:* **consequence,** result, ramification, repercussion, effect.
3 *their implication in the bribery case will increase public distrust of politicians:* **involvement,** connection, association.

implicit adjective
1 *his comments were seen as implicit criticism of the policies:* **implied,** indirect, suggested; unspoken, unexpressed, unstated, tacit.
2 *our charter sets out the values implicit in a Catholic education:* **inherent in,** intrinsic to; underlying.
3 *he had an implicit trust in human nature:* **absolute,** complete, total, unqualified, unconditional, wholehearted, utter; unshakeable, unquestioning, firm, steadfast.
OPPOSITES: explicit.

implicitly adverb *he trusted Sarah implicitly:* **completely,** absolutely, totally, wholeheartedly, utterly, unconditionally, unreservedly, without reservation.

implied adjective *there was implied criticism of the king's choice of commanders:* **implicit,** indirect, suggested, insinuated; unspoken, unexpressed, unstated, tacit.
OPPOSITES: explicit.

implore verb *she implored him to change his mind:* **plead with,** beg, entreat, appeal to, ask, call on; exhort, urge, press, push, petition; formal enjoin; literary beseech.

imply verb
1 *are you implying he is mad?* **insinuate,** suggest, hint, intimate, say indirectly, indicate, give someone to understand, make out.
2 *the project implies massive investment in education and training:* **mean,** suggest, presuppose, point to, signify, indicate, signal; necessitate, require, involve, entail.

USAGE
Do not confuse **imply** with **infer**: see the note at **INFER**.

impolite adjective *it would have been impolite to leave in the middle:* **rude,** bad-mannered, ill-mannered, discourteous, disrespectful, inconsiderate, boorish, churlish, ill-bred, ungentlemanly, unladylike, ungracious, uncivil; insolent, impudent, impertinent, cheeky; informal ignorant.

impolitic adjective *it would be impolitic to refuse:* **imprudent,** unwise, injudicious; ill-judged, ill-advised, misguided, incautious, rash, reckless, foolhardy, foolish, short-sighted; undiplomatic, tactless.
OPPOSITES: prudent.

import verb *the UK imports iron ore:* buy from abroad, bring in, buy in, ship in.
OPPOSITES: export.
▷**noun**
1 *a tax on imports:* imported commodity, foreign commodity.
2 *the import of foreign books:* importation, importing, shipping in.
3 *a matter of great import:* importance, significance, consequence, magnitude, substance, weight, gravity, seriousness.
4 *the full import of her words:* meaning, implication, sense, purport, message, thrust.
OPPOSITES: export.

importance noun
1 *the ratification of the treaty was an event of immense importance:* significance, consequence, momentousness, import, note, substance; seriousness, gravity, weight, urgency.
2 *he was a man who had a strong sense of his own importance:* power, influence, authority, prominence, eminence, distinction, notability, worth, status.
OPPOSITES: insignificance.

important adjective
1 *an important meeting | an important decision:* significant, consequential, momentous, of great import, major, historic; critical, crucial, vital, pivotal, decisive, urgent; serious, grave, weighty.
2 *the important thing is to get medical advice as quickly as possible:* main, chief, principal, key, major, prime, foremost, paramount, overriding, crucial, vital, critical, essential; central, fundamental; informal number-one.
3 *the school was important to the community:* of value, valuable, beneficial, necessary, essential, indispensable, vital.
4 *he was an important man:* powerful, influential, of influence, well-connected, high-ranking; prominent, eminent, pre-eminent, notable, noteworthy, of note; distinguished, respected.
OPPOSITES: trivial, insignificant, unimportant.

importunate adjective persistent, insistent, tenacious, unrelenting, tireless, indefatigable; aggressive, high-pressure; informal pushy.

importune verb beg, entreat, implore, plead with, appeal to, call on; harass, pester, press, badger, bother, nag; literary beseech; informal hassle.

impose verb
1 *he imposed his ideas on the art director:* foist, force, inflict, press; informal saddle someone with, land someone with.
2 *new taxes will be imposed:* levy, charge, apply, enforce; set, establish, institute, introduce, bring into effect.
3 *she realized she had imposed on Mark's kindness:* take advantage of, exploit, take liberties with, treat unfairly.

imposing adjective *an imposing Georgian mansion:* impressive, magnificent, splendid, grand, majestic, striking, eye-catching, arresting, dramatic, spectacular, stunning, awesome, formidable.
OPPOSITES: modest.

imposition noun
1 *the imposition of an alien culture on the indigenous inhabitants:* imposing, foisting, forcing, inflicting.
2 *the imposition of VAT:* levying, charging, enforcement, application, introduction.
3 *I felt that my arrival would be a bit of an imposition:* burden, encumbrance, strain, bother, worry; informal hassle.

impossible adjective
1 *gale force winds made fishing impossible:* out of the question, unfeasible, impractical, impracticable, non-viable, unworkable; unthinkable, unimaginable, inconceivable.
2 *an impossible dream:* unattainable, unachievable, unobtainable, hopeless, unrealistic, impractical, impracticable, far-fetched, ludicrous, preposterous.
3 (informal) *an impossible woman:* unreasonable, objectionable, difficult, awkward; intolerable, unbearable; exasperating, maddening, infuriating.
OPPOSITES: possible.

impostor noun impersonator, hoaxer, trickster, fraudster; fake, fraud, sham; informal phoney.

impotent adjective *a politically impotent opposition party:* powerless, helpless, weak, ineffective, ineffectual, useless, feeble, incompetent, incapable.
OPPOSITES: powerful, effective.

impound verb *officials began impounding documents:* confiscate, appropriate, take possession of, seize, commandeer, expropriate, sequester, sequestrate.

impoverish verb
1 *the wars had impoverished him:* make poor, make penniless, reduce to penury, bankrupt, ruin, make insolvent, pauperize.
2 *the trees were impoverishing the soil:* weaken, sap, exhaust, deplete.

impoverished adjective
1 *an impoverished peasant farmer:* poor, poverty-stricken, penniless, destitute, indigent, impecunious, needy; bankrupt, ruined, insolvent; Brit. on the breadline; formal penurious; informal broke, hard up; Brit. informal skint.
2 *the soil is impoverished:* weakened, exhausted, depleted; barren, unproductive, unfertile.
OPPOSITES: rich.

impracticable adjective *my colleagues thought it an impracticable plan:* unworkable, unfeasible, non-viable, unachievable, unattainable, unrealizable; impractical.

impractical adjective

1 *an impractical suggestion:* unrealistic, unworkable, unfeasible, non-viable, impracticable; ill-thought-out, impossible, unreasonable, foolish, silly.
2 *totally impractical footwear:* unsuitable, not sensible, inappropriate, unserviceable.
OPPOSITES: practical, sensible.

imprecise adjective

1 *a rather imprecise definition:* vague, loose, inexact, inaccurate, non-specific, unspecific, sweeping, broad, general; fuzzy, woolly, nebulous, ambiguous.
2 *an imprecise estimate:* inexact, approximate, estimated, rough; N. Amer. informal ballpark.
OPPOSITES: exact.

impregnable adjective

1 *a vast and impregnable fortress:* invulnerable, impenetrable, unassailable, inviolable, secure, strong, well fortified, well defended; unconquerable.
2 *the party has an impregnable parliamentary majority:* unassailable, unbeatable, invincible, undefeatable, unshakeable, invulnerable.
OPPOSITES: vulnerable.

impregnate verb

1 *the vaporizer contains a pad impregnated with natural oils:* soak, saturate, drench, infuse, steep.
2 *he was obliged to marry the woman he had impregnated:* make pregnant, inseminate, fertilize; informal put in the family way.

impresario noun *a theatrical impresario:* producer, manager, organizer; promoter, publicist, showman; director, conductor, maestro.

impress verb

1 *she had impressed him very much:* make an impression on, have an impact on, influence, affect, move, stir, rouse, excite, inspire; dazzle, awe, overawe, take someone's breath away, amaze, astonish; informal grab, stick in someone's mind.
2 *goldsmiths impressed his likeness on medallions:* imprint, print, stamp, mark, emboss, punch.
3 *you must impress upon her the need to save:* emphasize to, stress to, bring home to, instil in, inculcate into, drum into, din into.

impression noun

1 *he got the impression that she was hiding something:* feeling, feeling in your bones, sense, sneaking suspicion, inkling, intuition, hunch, fancy, notion; informal gut feeling.
2 *she had formed a favourable impression of him:* opinion, view, image, picture, idea, perception, judgement, verdict, estimation.
3 *his autobiography had a profound*

impression on me: impact, effect, influence.
4 *the cap had left a circular impression:* indentation, dent, mark, outline, imprint.
5 *he did a good impression of Tony Blair:* impersonation, imitation; parody, caricature, burlesque, lampoon; informal take-off, send-up, spoof.
6 *an artist's impression of the gardens:* representation, portrayal, depiction, rendition, interpretation, picture, drawing.
7 *a revised impression of the 1981 edition:* print run, imprint, reprint, issue, edition.

impressionable adjective *an impressionable adolescent girl:* easily influenced, suggestible, susceptible, pliable, malleable, pliant; ingenuous, trusting, naive, gullible.

impressive adjective

1 *the impressive Victorian building has recently been refurbished:* magnificent, majestic, imposing, splendid, spectacular, grand, awe-inspiring, stunning, breathtaking; stately, palatial.
2 *they played some impressive football:* admirable, masterly, accomplished, expert, skilled, skilful, consummate; excellent, outstanding, first-class, first-rate, fine; informal great, mean, ace.
OPPOSITES: ordinary, mediocre.

imprint verb

1 *patterns can be imprinted in the clay:* stamp, print, impress, mark, emboss.
2 *the image was imprinted on his mind:* fix, establish, stick, lodge, implant, embed.
▷noun
1 *her feet left imprints on the floor:* impression, print, mark, indentation.
2 *colonialism has left its imprint:* impact, lasting effect, influence, impression.

imprison verb *he was arrested and imprisoned for drug-smuggling:* incarcerate, send to prison, jail, lock up, put away, intern, detain, hold prisoner, hold captive; informal send down, put behind bars, put inside; Brit. informal bang up.

imprisonment noun incarceration, internment, confinement, detention, captivity.

improbability noun unlikelihood; implausibility, doubtfulness.

improbable adjective

1 *this account of events was seen by the jury as most improbable:* unlikely, implausible, doubtful, dubious, questionable, debatable; unthinkable, inconceivable, unimaginable, incredible.
2 *the characters all have improbable names:* unconvincing, unbelievable, incredible, ridiculous, absurd, preposterous.

impromptu adjective *he gave an impromptu speech:* unrehearsed, unprepared, unscripted, extempore, extemporized, extemporaneous,

improvised, spontaneous, unplanned; informal off-the-cuff.
▷ **adverb** *they played the song impromptu:* extempore, spontaneously, without preparation, without rehearsal, extemporaneously; informal off the cuff, off the top of your head.

improper adjective
1 *it is improper for police officers to accept gifts:* inappropriate, unacceptable, wrong, unprofessional, irregular; unethical, immoral, corrupt, dishonest, dishonourable.
2 *it was improper for young ladies to drive a young man home:* unseemly, indecorous, unsuitable, unfitting, unladylike, ungentlemanly, indelicate, indecent, immodest.
OPPOSITES: acceptable, decent.

impropriety noun *there is no suggestion of impropriety on his part:* wrongdoing, misconduct, dishonesty, corruption, unscrupulousness, unprofessionalism, unprofessional behaviour; indelicacy, indecency, immorality.

improve verb
1 *we are looking for ways to improve computer security:* make better, ameliorate, upgrade, refine, enhance, boost, build on, raise; informal tweak.
2 *communications improved during the 18th century:* get better, advance, progress, develop; make headway, make progress, pick up, look up.
3 *the dose is not repeated if the patient improves:* recover, get better, recuperate, rally, revive, get back on your feet, get over something; be on the road to recovery, be on the mend, turn the corner, take a turn for the better.
4 *resources are needed to improve the offer:* increase, make larger, raise, augment, supplement; Brit. top up; informal up, bump up.
OPPOSITES: worsen, deteriorate.
▢ **improve on**
he's hoping to improve on last year's performance: surpass, better, do better than, outdo, exceed, beat, top, cap.

improvement noun *in some areas, privatization has delivered real improvements in efficiency:* advance, development, upgrade, refinement, enhancement, amelioration, progress; boost, rally, recovery, upswing, upturn, gain.

improvident adjective *a feckless and improvident lifestyle:* spendthrift, thriftless, wasteful, prodigal, profligate, extravagant, free-spending, lavish, excessive, immoderate; imprudent, irresponsible, careless, reckless.
OPPOSITES: thrifty.

improvise verb
1 *she was improvising in front of the cameras:* extemporize, ad-lib, speak impromptu; informal speak off the cuff, speak off the top of your head, wing it.
2 *I improvised a costume out of an old dress:* make, devise, throw together, cobble together, rig up, contrive.

improvised adjective
1 *an improvised speech:* impromptu, unrehearsed, unprepared, unscripted, extempore, extemporized, spontaneous, unplanned; informal off-the-cuff.
2 *an improvised shelter:* makeshift, thrown together, cobbled together, rough and ready, make-do.

imprudent adjective *it would be imprudent to spend the money now:* unwise, incautious, misguided, ill-advised, injudicious, improvident, irresponsible, short-sighted, foolish.
OPPOSITES: sensible.

impudence noun impertinence, insolence, cheek, disrespect, rudeness, impoliteness, bad manners, discourteousness, effrontery, gall; informal brass neck, nerve.

impudent adjective *these impudent youngsters need to be taught a lesson:* impertinent, insolent, cheeky, disrespectful, rude, impolite, bad-mannered, ill-mannered, discourteous.
OPPOSITES: polite.

impulse noun
1 *she had an impulse to run and hide:* urge, instinct, compulsion; desire, whim, fancy, notion.
2 *he was a man of impulse:* spontaneity, impetuosity, recklessness, rashness.
3 *impulses from the spinal cord to the muscles:* pulse, current, wave, signal.
▢ **on (an) impulse**
impulsively, spontaneously, on the spur of the moment, without forethought, without premeditation.

impulsive adjective
1 *it was an impulsive decision and one she later regretted:* spur-of-the-moment, snap, spontaneous, impromptu, unpremeditated; impetuous, precipitate, hasty, rash, sudden, ill-considered, ill-thought-out.
2 *he had an impulsive nature:* impetuous, spontaneous, passionate, emotional, uninhibited; rash, reckless, foolhardy, unwise, madcap, devil-may-care, daredevil.
OPPOSITES: premeditated, cautious.

impunity noun *the impunity enjoyed by military officers:* immunity, indemnity, exemption, non-liability, licence; privilege, special treatment.
OPPOSITES: liability.
▢ **with impunity**
without punishment, without suffering the consequences.

impure adjective
1 *an impure form of heroin:* adulterated,

debased, mixed, blended, alloyed.
2 *the water was impure:* contaminated, polluted, tainted, poisoned; dirty, filthy, foul; unhygienic, insanitary.
3 *he had harboured impure thoughts:* immoral, sinful, wrongful, wicked; improper, indecent, lustful, lecherous, lewd, lascivious, unchaste.
OPPOSITES: pure.

impurity noun
1 *the impurity of the air:* contamination, pollution; dirtiness, filthiness, uncleanliness.
2 *the water is cleansed of impurities:* contaminant, pollutant, foreign body; dirt, filth.
3 *a struggle to rid the soul of sin and impurity:* immorality, sin, sinfulness, wickedness.

impute verb *he shares some of the bad qualities he imputes to Douglas:* attribute, ascribe, assign; connect with, associate with.

inability noun *her parents' inability to control her wild behaviour:* lack of ability, incapability, incapacity, powerlessness, impotence, helplessness.

inaccessible adjective
1 *an inaccessible region:* unreachable, out of reach; cut-off, isolated, remote, unfrequented, in the back of beyond, out of the way; lonely, godforsaken.
2 *opera is seen as the most inaccessible of art forms:* esoteric, arcane, recondite; elitist, exclusive, highbrow.

inaccuracy noun
1 *the article contained a number of inaccuracies:* error, mistake, slip, oversight, fault, blunder; fallacy; erratum.
2 *the inaccuracy of recent opinion polls:* incorrectness, inexactness, imprecision.

inaccurate adjective *the maps were notoriously inaccurate:* inexact, imprecise, incorrect, unreliable, wrong, erroneous, faulty, imperfect, flawed, defective, unsound; fallacious, false, mistaken, untrue; informal off beam.

inaction noun *wildlife is threatened by government inaction:* failure to act, lack of action, non-intervention, inactivity, inertia, apathy; neglect, negligence.

inactive adjective
1 *obesity cannot simply be attributed to an inactive lifestyle:* sedentary, not active; idle, indolent, lazy, lethargic, inert, sluggish, torpid, unenergetic.
2 *the device remains inactive while the computer is started up:* inoperative, non-functioning, idle; not working, out of service, not in use.

inadequacy noun
1 *the inadequacy of available resources:* insufficiency, deficiency, scarcity,

scarceness, sparseness, dearth, paucity, shortage, want, lack, undersupply.
2 *her feelings of personal inadequacy:* incompetence, incapability, unfitness, ineffectiveness, inefficiency, inefficacy, inexpertness, ineptness, uselessness, impotence, powerlessness.
3 *the inadequacies of the present system:* shortcoming, defect, fault, failing, weakness, weak point, limitation, flaw, imperfection.

inadequate adjective
1 *water and food supplies are inadequate:* insufficient, deficient, poor, scant, scanty, scarce, sparse, in short supply; paltry, meagre, limited; informal measly.
2 *I felt totally inadequate:* incompetent, incapable, ineffective, ineffectual, unfit, inefficient, unskilful, inexpert, inept, amateurish, unsatisfactory, not up to scratch, substandard, poor.

inadmissible adjective *inadmissible evidence:* invalid, unacceptable, not allowable, impermissible, disallowed, precluded.

inadvertent adjective *we apologize for the inadvertent omission:* unintentional, unintended, accidental, unwitting, unpremeditated, unplanned, innocent, uncalculated, unconscious, unthinking.
OPPOSITES: deliberate.

inadvertently adverb unintentionally, by accident, accidentally, unwittingly.

inadvisable adjective *an economically inadvisable move:* unwise, ill-advised, imprudent, ill-judged, ill-considered, injudicious, impolitic, foolish, misguided.
OPPOSITES: shrewd.

inane adjective *he tried to ignore her inane comment:* silly, foolish, stupid, fatuous, idiotic, ridiculous, ludicrous, asinine, frivolous, vapid; childish, puerile; informal dumb, moronic.
OPPOSITES: sensible.

inanimate adjective *inanimate objects:* lifeless, insentient, inert, without life; dead.
OPPOSITES: animate, living.

inappropriate adjective *the content may be inappropriate for a younger audience:* unsuitable, unfitting, unseemly, unbecoming, improper; incongruous, out of place/keeping, inapposite, inapt; informal out of order.
OPPOSITES: appropriate, suitable.

inarticulate adjective
1 *an inarticulate young man:* unable to express yourself; lost for words, tongue-tied.
2 *an inarticulate reply:* unintelligible, incomprehensible, incoherent, unclear, indistinct, mumbled, muffled.
OPPOSITES: articulate, fluent.

inattention noun *moments of inattention could cost lives:* distraction, inattentiveness, preoccupation, absent-mindedness, abstraction, carelessness, thoughtlessness, heedlessness, disregard.
OPPOSITES: attention, concentration.

inattentive adjective
1 *an inattentive audience:* distracted, lacking concentration, preoccupied, absent-minded, daydreaming.
2 *I was disappointed by the food and the inattentive service:* negligent, neglectful, remiss, slack, sloppy, slapdash, lax; careless, thoughtless, heedless.
OPPOSITES: attentive, alert.

inaudible adjective *her response was inaudible:* indistinct, difficult to hear, faint, unclear, muffled, soft, low, quiet, muted; out of earshot.
OPPOSITES: audible.

inaugural adjective *the inaugural meeting of the Geographical Society:* first, opening, initial, introductory.
OPPOSITES: final.

inaugurate verb
1 *he inaugurated a new policy:* initiate, begin, start, institute, put in place, launch, start off, get going, get under way, establish, lay the foundations of; bring in, usher in; informal kick off.
2 *the new President will be inaugurated in January:* admit to office, install, swear in; invest, ordain, crown.
3 *the museum was inaugurated in September:* open, declare open, unveil; dedicate, consecrate.

inauspicious adjective *it was an inauspicious start to the new season:* unpromising, unpropitious, unfavourable, unfortunate, infelicitous, ominous; discouraging, disheartening.
OPPOSITES: auspicious, promising.

inborn adjective *a child's inborn linguistic ability:* innate, inherent, natural, existing from birth; inherited, hereditary, in your genes.

inbuilt adjective
1 *a personal computer with an inbuilt CD-ROM drive:* built-in, integral, incorporated, internal.
2 *our inbuilt survival instinct:* inherent, intrinsic, innate, natural.

incalculable adjective *the archaeological treasures are said to be of incalculable value:* inestimable, immeasurable, untold, indeterminable, infinite; enormous, immense, huge, vast.

incandescent adjective
1 *incandescent fragments of lava:* glowing, radiant, bright, luminous.
2 *the minister was incandescent at the accusation:* furious, enraged, raging, very angry, incensed, seething, infuriated,
fuming, irate, beside yourself; informal livid, mad, wild, apoplectic.

incantation noun *he muttered some weird incantations:* chant, invocation, magic spell/formula, rune, conjuration.

incapable adjective
1 *he was incapable of grasping the subtleties of the argument:* unable to, not able to.
2 *there is a tendency to treat older people as dependent and incapable:* incompetent, inept, inadequate, ineffectual, feeble, unfit; informal not up to it.
3 *he was slumped on the ground, drunk and incapable:* incapacitated, helpless, powerless.
OPPOSITES: capable, competent.

incapacity noun
1 *his apparent incapacity to handle complex investigations:* inability, incapability, lack of ability, powerlessness; inadequacy, ineffectiveness.
2 *the long period of incapacity that preceded his death:* illness, disability, debility, indisposition.
3 *they are not subject to any legal incapacity:* disqualification, lack of entitlement.
OPPOSITES: capacity, capability.

incarcerate verb *he was incarcerated for expressing counter-revolutionary opinions:* imprison, put in prison, send to prison, jail, lock up, put under lock and key, put away, intern, confine, detain, hold, hold prisoner, hold captive; Brit. detain at Her Majesty's pleasure; formal immure; informal send down, put behind bars, put inside; Brit. informal bang up.

incarceration noun imprisonment, internment, confinement, detention, custody, captivity, restraint.

incarnate adjective *she looked at me as though I were the devil incarnate:* in human form, in the flesh, in physical form, in bodily form, made flesh; corporeal, physical, fleshly, embodied.

incarnation noun
1 *it is easy to see him as the incarnation of evil:* embodiment, personification, exemplification, type, epitome; manifestation.
2 *a previous incarnation:* lifetime, life, existence.

incautious adjective *his anger made him incautious:* rash, unwise, careless, heedless, thoughtless, reckless, unthinking, imprudent, misguided, ill-advised, ill-judged, injudicious, impolitic, unguarded, foolhardy, foolish; unwary, off-guard, inattentive.
OPPOSITES: cautious, circumspect.

incendiary adjective
1 *an incendiary bomb:* combustible, flammable, inflammable.

2 *an incendiary speech:* inflammatory, provocative, rabble-rousing, seditious, subversive; contentious, controversial.

incense verb *the suggestion incensed local residents:* enrage, infuriate, anger, madden, outrage, exasperate; antagonize, provoke; informal make someone see red, make someone's blood boil.

incensed adjective *Leonora glared back at him, incensed:* enraged, very angry, furious, infuriated, irate, incandescent, fuming, seething, beside yourself, outraged; informal mad, wild, livid, apoplectic.

incentive noun *the laws give factories a financial incentive to reduce pollution:* inducement, motivation, motive, reason, stimulus, spur, impetus, encouragement, reward; informal carrot, sweetener.
OPPOSITES: deterrent.

inception noun *the organization has grown dramatically since its inception in 1979:* establishment, institution, foundation, founding, formation, initiation, setting up, origination, constitution, inauguration, opening, day one; beginning, commencement, start, birth, dawn, genesis, origin; informal kick-off.

incessant adjective *incessant rain fell for several days:* ceaseless, unceasing, constant, continual, interminable, endless, unending, never-ending, unabating, perpetual, continuous, non-stop, uninterrupted, unbroken, unremitting, persistent, relentless, unrelenting, unrelieved, sustained.
OPPOSITES: intermittent.

incessantly adverb *she talked incessantly about her problems:* constantly, continually, all the time, non-stop, without stopping, without a break, round the clock, {morning, noon, and night}, interminably, unremittingly, ceaselessly, endlessly; informal 24-7.
OPPOSITES: occasionally.

incidence noun *there was an increased incidence of heart disease in women in their thirties:* occurrence, prevalence; rate, frequency; amount, degree, extent.

incident noun
1 *he recalled two incidents from his youth:* event, occurrence, episode, experience, happening, occasion, proceeding, affair, business; adventure, exploit, escapade; matter, circumstance, fact, development.
2 *police are investigating the incident:* disturbance, fracas, melee, commotion, rumpus, scene; fight, brawl, confrontation, altercation.
3 *the journey was not without incident:* excitement, adventure, drama; danger, peril.

incidental adjective *these are just incidental details:* less important, secondary, subsidiary; minor, peripheral, background, by-the-way, by-the-by, non-essential, inessential, unimportant, insignificant, inconsequential, tangential, extrinsic, extraneous.
OPPOSITES: essential.

incidentally adverb
1 *incidentally, I haven't had a reply yet:* by the way, speaking of which, by the by, in passing, en passant; informal btw, as it happens.
2 *the infection was discovered incidentally at the post-mortem:* by chance, by accident, accidentally, fortuitously, by a fluke.

incinerate verb *household waste should be incinerated to generate electricity:* burn, reduce to ashes, carbonize; cremate.

incise verb *an inscription incised in Roman letters:* engrave, etch, carve, cut, chisel, inscribe.

incision noun *a surgical incision:* cut, opening.

incisive adjective *he was an incisive political commentator:* penetrating, acute, sharp, sharp-witted, razor-sharp, keen, astute, trenchant, shrewd, piercing, perceptive, insightful, percipient, perspicacious, discerning, analytical, clever, quick; concise, succinct, pithy, to the point, crisp, clear; informal smart.
OPPOSITES: rambling, vague.

incite verb
1 *he was arrested for inciting racial hatred:* stir up, whip up, encourage, fan the flames of, stoke up, fuel, kindle, ignite, inflame, stimulate, instigate, provoke, excite, arouse, awaken, trigger, spark off, ferment, foment.
2 *she incited him to commit murder:* egg on, encourage, urge, goad, provoke, spur on, drive, stimulate, push, prod, prompt, induce, impel; rouse, inflame, sting, prick; informal put up to.
OPPOSITES: discourage, deter.

incivility noun *incivility on the part of staff will not be tolerated:* rudeness, discourtesy, discourteousness, bad manners, impoliteness, disrespect, boorishness, ungraciousness; insolence, impertinence, impudence.
OPPOSITES: politeness.

inclement adjective *the work was delayed by the inclement weather:* cold, chilly, bleak, wintry, freezing, snowy, icy; wet, rainy, drizzly, damp; stormy, blustery, wild, rough, squally, windy; unpleasant, bad, foul, nasty, filthy, severe, extreme, harsh.
OPPOSITES: clement, fine.

inclination noun
1 *his political inclinations:* tendency, leaning, propensity, proclivity, predisposition, disposition, predilection, desire, wish, impulse; preference, liking, penchant, partiality, appetite, interest,

affinity; stomach, taste.
2 *an inclination of 80°:* slope, gradient, incline, angle, slant.
OPPOSITES: disinclination, aversion.

incline verb
1 *his prejudice inclines him to overlook obvious facts:* predispose, lead, make, dispose; prompt, induce, influence, sway, prejudice; persuade, convince.
2 *I incline to the opposite view:* prefer, favour, go for; tend, lean, swing, veer, gravitate, be drawn.
3 *he inclined his head:* bend, bow, nod, bob, lower, dip.
4 *the columns incline away from the vertical:* lean, tilt, slope, slant, angle, tip, bend, curve, bank, cant, bevel; list, heel.
▷ **noun** *a steep incline:* slope, gradient, pitch, ramp, bank, ascent, rise, acclivity, upslope, dip, descent, declivity, downslope; hill.

inclined adjective
1 *I'm inclined to believe her:* disposed, minded, of a mind, willing, ready, prepared; predisposed.
2 *she's inclined to gossip:* prone, given, in the habit of, liable, likely, apt; formal wont.

include verb
1 *the bulletin includes articles from other publications:* incorporate, comprise, encompass, cover, embrace, involve, take in, number, contain; consist of, be made up of, be composed of.
2 *don't forget to include the cost of repairs:* allow for, count, take into account, take into consideration, add.
OPPOSITES: exclude.

including preposition *there are a wide range of sports facilities, including squash, tennis, and badminton:* inclusive of, counting, embracing, covering.

inclusive adjective
1 *an inclusive price | an inclusive definition:* all-in, all-inclusive, comprehensive, in toto, overall, full, all-round, umbrella, catch-all, all-encompassing.
2 *prices are inclusive of VAT:* including, incorporating, taking in, counting; comprising, covering.

incognito adverb & adjective *he travelled incognito:* under an assumed name, under a false name, in disguise, disguised, under cover, in plain clothes, camouflaged; secretly, anonymously.

incoherent adjective
1 *he made a long, incoherent speech:* unclear, confused, muddled, unintelligible, incomprehensible, hard to follow, disjointed, disconnected, disordered, mixed up, garbled, jumbled, scrambled; rambling, wandering, disorganized, illogical; inarticulate, mumbling, slurred.
2 *she was incoherent and shivering*

violently: delirious, raving, babbling, hysterical, irrational.
OPPOSITES: lucid.

income noun earnings, salary, pay, wages, remuneration, stipend; revenue, receipts, takings, profits, gains, proceeds, turnover, yield, dividend, incomings; means.
OPPOSITES: expenditure, outgoings.

incoming adjective
1 *incoming flights are delayed:* arriving, inbound; approaching.
2 *the incoming president:* newly elected, newly appointed, succeeding, new, next, future; elect, to-be, designate.
OPPOSITES: outgoing.

incomparable adjective *the incomparable beauty of Venice:* without equal, beyond compare, unparalleled, matchless, peerless, unmatched, without parallel, beyond comparison, second to none, in a class of its own, unequalled, unrivalled, inimitable, nonpareil, par excellence; transcendent, superlative, surpassing, unsurpassed, unsurpassable, supreme, top, outstanding, consummate, singular, unique, rare, perfect; informal one-in-a-million.

incomparably adverb *this beach is incomparably superior to the others on the island:* far and away, by far, infinitely, immeasurably, easily.

incompatible adjective
1 *she and McBride are totally incompatible:* unsuited, mismatched, ill-matched, poles apart, worlds apart, like day and night; Brit. like chalk and cheese.
2 *these two objectives are incompatible:* irreconcilable, mutually exclusive, conflicting, opposed, opposite, contradictory, antagonistic, clashing, contrasting.
3 *this theory is incompatible with that of his predecessor:* inconsistent with, at odds with, out of keeping with, at variance with, not consonant with, different to, divergent from, contrary to, in conflict with, in opposition to, diametrically opposed to, counter to, irreconcilable with.
OPPOSITES: compatible, consistent.

incompetent adjective *he lost his job due to his incompetent performance:* inept, unskilful, unskilled, inexpert, amateurish, unprofessional, inefficient, bungling, blundering, clumsy, inadequate, substandard, inferior, ineffective, deficient, ineffectual, wanting, lacking, leaving much to be desired; incapable, unfit, unqualified; informal useless, not up to it, not up to scratch.

incomplete adjective
1 *the project is still incomplete:* unfinished, uncompleted, partial, half-finished, half-done, half-completed.
2 *the records are incomplete:* partial,

patchy, sketchy, fragmentary; imperfect, deficient, insufficient, defective.

incomprehensible adjective *the manual does occasionally lapse into incomprehensible jargon:* **unintelligible,** impossible to understand, impenetrable, unclear, indecipherable, beyond your comprehension, beyond one, beyond your grasp, complicated, complex, involved, baffling, bewildering, mystifying, puzzling, confusing, perplexing; abstruse, esoteric, recondite, arcane, mysterious; informal over your head.
OPPOSITES: comprehensible, clear.

inconceivable adjective *it seemed inconceivable that the president had been unaware of what was going on:* **unbelievable,** beyond belief, incredible, unthinkable, unimaginable, extremely unlikely; impossible, beyond the bounds of possibility, out of the question, preposterous, ridiculous, ludicrous, absurd, incomprehensible; informal hard to swallow.
OPPOSITES: conceivable, likely.

inconclusive adjective *their findings were inconclusive:* **indecisive,** proving nothing; indefinite, indeterminate, unresolved, unproved, unsettled, still open to question/doubt, debatable, unconfirmed; moot; vague, ambiguous; informal up in the air, left hanging.
OPPOSITES: conclusive.

incongruous adjective *the duffel coat looked incongruous with the black dress she wore underneath:* **out of place,** out of keeping, inappropriate, unsuitable, unsuited, ill-matched, mismatched, off-key, inharmonious, discordant, incompatible, inconsistent, different, dissimilar, contrasting, disparate; wrong, strange, odd, extraneous.
OPPOSITES: appropriate.

inconsequential adjective insignificant, unimportant, of little no/consequence, neither here nor there, incidental, inessential, non-essential, immaterial, irrelevant; negligible, inappreciable, inconsiderable, slight, minor, trivial, trifling, petty; informal piffling.
OPPOSITES: important.

inconsiderate adjective *his inconsiderate behaviour hurt her:* **thoughtless,** unthinking, insensitive, selfish, self-centred, unsympathetic, uncaring, unkind, uncharitable, ungracious, impolite, discourteous, rude, disrespectful; tactless, undiplomatic, indiscreet, indelicate; informal ignorant.
OPPOSITES: considerate.

inconsistent adjective
1 *his behaviour became increasingly inconsistent:* **unpredictable,** changeable, erratic, unreliable, variable, varying, changing, unstable, irregular, fluctuating, unsteady, unsettled, uneven, inconstant;

self-contradictory, contradictory, paradoxical, capricious.
2 *he had done nothing inconsistent with his morality:* **incompatible with,** conflicting with, in conflict with, at odds with, at variance with, contrary to, in opposition to, opposed to, irreconcilable with, out of keeping with, out of step with; antithetical to.
OPPOSITES: consistent, predictable.

inconsolable adjective *his widow, Jane, was inconsolable:* **heartbroken,** broken-hearted, grief-stricken, beside yourself with grief, devastated, sick at heart, desolate, despairing, distraught.

inconspicuous adjective unobtrusive, unremarkable, undistinguished, ordinary, modest, unassuming, discreet, hidden, concealed, camouflaged; unseen, in the background, low-profile.
OPPOSITES: conspicuous, noticeable.

incontrovertible adjective *they had incontrovertible proof of the suspect's guilt:* **indisputable,** incontestable, undeniable, irrefutable, unassailable, beyond dispute, unquestionable, beyond question, indubitable, beyond doubt, unarguable, undebatable; certain, sure, definite, definitive, proven, decisive, conclusive, demonstrable, emphatic, categorical, airtight, watertight.
OPPOSITES: questionable.

inconvenience noun
1 *we apologize for any inconvenience caused:* **trouble,** bother, problems, disruption, difficulty, disturbance; irritation, annoyance, vexation; informal aggravation, hassle.
2 *his early arrival was clearly an inconvenience:* **nuisance,** trouble, bother, problem, trial, bore; informal headache, pain, pain in the neck, drag, aggravation, hassle.
▷verb *I don't want to inconvenience you:* **trouble,** bother, put out, put to any trouble, disturb, impose on, burden; formal incommode; informal hassle.

inconvenient adjective *she rang frequently, usually at inconvenient times:* **awkward,** difficult, unsuitable, inappropriate, inopportune, untimely, ill-timed, unfortunate; tiresome, irritating, annoying, vexing; informal aggravating.
OPPOSITES: convenient.

incorporate verb
1 *the region was incorporated into Moldavian territory:* **absorb,** include, subsume, assimilate, integrate, take in, swallow up.
2 *the model incorporates some advanced features:* **include,** contain, comprise, embody, embrace, build in, encompass.
3 *a small amount of salt is incorporated with the butter:* **blend,** mix, mingle, meld, combine; fold in, stir in.

incorrect adjective

1 *an incorrect answer:* wrong, erroneous, in error, mistaken, inaccurate, wide of the mark, off target; untrue, false, fallacious; informal off beam, out.
2 *incorrect behaviour:* inappropriate, wrong, unsuitable, inapt, inapposite; ill-advised, ill-considered, ill-judged, injudicious, unacceptable, unfitting, out of keeping, improper, unseemly, unbecoming, indecorous; informal out of order.
OPPOSITES: correct, right.

incorrigible adjective *she's an incorrigible flirt:* inveterate, habitual, confirmed, hardened, incurable, irredeemable, hopeless, beyond hope, beyond redemption; impenitent, unrepentant, unapologetic, unashamed.

incorruptible adjective *an incorruptible man:* honest, honourable, trustworthy, principled, high-principled, moral, ethical, good, virtuous.
OPPOSITES: venal.

increase verb

1 *demand is likely to increase:* grow, get bigger, get larger, enlarge, expand, swell; rise, climb, escalate, soar, surge, rocket, shoot up, spiral; intensify, strengthen, extend, heighten, stretch, spread, widen; multiply, snowball, mushroom, proliferate, balloon, build up, mount up, pile up, accrue, accumulate.
2 *higher expectations will increase user demand:* add to, make larger, make bigger, augment, supplement, build up, extend, raise, swell, inflate; magnify, intensify, strengthen, heighten, amplify; Brit. top up; informal up, jack up, hike up, bump up.
OPPOSITES: decrease, reduce.
▷ **noun** *the increase in size | an increase in demand:* growth, rise, enlargement, expansion, extension, multiplication, elevation, inflation; increment, addition, augmentation; magnification, intensification, amplification, step up, climb, escalation, surge, upsurge, upswing, spiral, spurt; informal hike.

increasingly adverb *the regime became increasingly draconian:* more and more, progressively, to an increasing extent, ever more.

incredible adjective

1 *I find his story incredible:* unbelievable, beyond belief, hard to believe, unconvincing, far-fetched, implausible, improbable, highly unlikely, dubious, doubtful; inconceivable, unthinkable, unimaginable, impossible; informal hard to swallow.
2 *the bridge is an incredible feat of engineering:* magnificent, wonderful, marvellous, spectacular, remarkable, phenomenal, prodigious, breathtaking, extraordinary, stupendous, tremendous, unbelievable, amazing, stunning, astounding, astonishing, awe-inspiring, staggering, formidable, impressive, supreme, great, awesome, superhuman; informal fantastic, mind-boggling, mind-blowing, out of this world.

incredulity noun *reports of UFO sightings were met with incredulity:* disbelief, incredulousness, scepticism, distrust, mistrust, suspicion, doubt, doubtfulness, dubiousness, lack of conviction; cynicism.

incredulous adjective *he related the details to an incredulous audience:* disbelieving, unbelieving, sceptical, distrustful, mistrustful, suspicious, doubtful, dubious, unconvinced; cynical.

increment noun *an annual salary increment:* increase, addition, supplement, augmentation; informal hike.
OPPOSITES: reduction.

incriminate verb *Drury persuaded one witness to incriminate Cooper:* implicate, involve; accuse, denounce, inform against, point the finger at, blame.

inculcate verb

1 *I tried to inculcate an attitude of enquiry in my pupils:* instil, implant, fix, impress, imprint; hammer into, drum into, drill into, din into.
2 *they will try to inculcate you with a respect for culture:* teach, inspire, fill, imbue.

incumbent adjective

1 *it is incumbent on the government to give a clear lead:* necessary for, essential for, imperative for.
2 *the incumbent president:* current, present, in office, in power; reigning.
▷ **noun** *the first incumbent of the post:* holder, bearer, occupant.

incur verb *kicking one's opponent incurs a 25-point penalty:* bring on yourself, expose yourself to, lay yourself open to; attract, earn, cause, give rise to, be liable/subject to, meet with, sustain, experience; run up.

incurable adjective

1 *an incurable illness:* untreatable, inoperable, chronic; terminal, fatal, mortal.
2 *an incurable romantic:* inveterate, confirmed, established, long-established, long-standing, absolute, complete, utter, thorough, thoroughgoing, out-and-out, through and through; unashamed, unapologetic, unrepentant, incorrigible, hopeless, dyed-in-the-wool.

incursion noun *the first Ottoman incursion into Europe took place in 1345:* attack, assault, raid, invasion, foray, sortie, sally, advance, push, thrust.
OPPOSITES: retreat.

indebted adjective *I shall always be indebted to them for their help:* beholden, under an obligation, obliged, obligated,

grateful, thankful, in someone's debt, owing someone a debt of gratitude.

indecent adjective

1 *indecent photographs:* obscene, pornographic, vulgar, improper, dirty, filthy, lewd, salacious, offensive.
2 *indecent clothes:* revealing, short, brief, skimpy, scanty, low-cut, flimsy, thin, seethrough.
3 *indecent haste:* unseemly, unsuitable, inappropriate, improper, indecorous, unceremonious, indelicate, unbecoming, unfitting; in bad taste, tasteless, unacceptable, crass.

indecipherable adjective *he scribbled something indecipherable on the back of a cigarette packet:* illegible, unreadable, hard to read, unintelligible, unclear; scribbled, scrawled.

indecision noun *the government's indecision over the tax calls into question its ability to govern:* indecisiveness, irresolution, hesitancy, hesitation, tentativeness; ambivalence, doubt, doubtfulness, uncertainty, incertitude; vacillation, equivocation, second thoughts; dithering, temporizing; Brit. humming and hawing; informal dilly-dallying, shillyshallying, sitting on the fence.

indecisive adjective

1 *an indecisive result:* inconclusive, proving nothing, settling nothing; uncertain, indeterminate, borderline, indefinite, unclear, ambiguous; informal up in the air.
2 *an indecisive leader:* irresolute, hesitant, tentative, weak; vacillating, equivocating, dithering, wavering; ambivalent, divided, blowing hot and cold, in two minds, in a dilemma, in a quandary, torn; doubtful, unsure, uncertain; undecided, uncommitted; informal sitting on the fence, shilly-shallying.
OPPOSITES: decisive.

indeed adverb *there was, indeed, quite a furore:* as expected, to be sure; in fact, as a matter of fact, in truth, actually, as it happens, if truth be told.

indefatigable adjective *he is one of those indefatigable researchers who won't take no for an answer:* tireless, untiring, unflagging, unwearying, unwearied; determined, tenacious, dogged, singleminded, assiduous, industrious, unswerving, unfaltering, unshakeable, indomitable; persistent, relentless.

indefensible adjective

1 *an indefensible system of dual justice:* unjustifiable, unacceptable, unwarrantable, unsustainable, untenable, unjustified, inexcusable; wrong, flawed, misguided.
2 *the towns were indefensible:* defenceless, vulnerable, exposed, open to attack.
OPPOSITES: defensible.

indefinable adjective *the curious, indefinable quality which sets his sculptures apart:* hard to describe, hard to define, indescribable, inexpressible, impalpable, elusive, nameless; vague, obscure.

indefinite adjective

1 *the project has been shelved for an indefinite period:* indeterminate, unspecified, undecided, undetermined, undefined, unknown, uncertain; unlimited, unrestricted.
2 *an indefinite meaning:* vague, ill-defined, unclear, imprecise, inexact, ambiguous, equivocal.
OPPOSITES: definite, fixed.

indefinitely adverb *the trial has been postponed indefinitely:* for an unspecified period, for an unlimited period, without limit; formal sine die.

indelible adjective *the story made an indelible impression on me:* ineradicable, permanent, lasting, enduring, unfading, unforgettable, haunting, never to be forgotten.

indelicate adjective

1 *an indelicate question:* insensitive, tactless, undiplomatic, indiscreet.
2 *an indelicate sense of humour:* vulgar, rude, crude, bawdy, racy, risqué, ribald, earthy, indecent, improper, naughty, indecorous.

indemnify verb

1 *he should be indemnified for his losses:* reimburse, compensate, recompense, repay, pay back, remunerate.
2 *they are indemnified against breach of contract:* insure, guarantee, protect, secure, underwrite.

indemnity noun

1 *no indemnity will be given for loss of cash:* insurance, assurance, protection, security, indemnification, surety, guarantee, warranty, safeguard.
2 *he became a State witness in exchange for indemnity from prosecution:* immunity, exemption, dispensation, freedom.
3 *the company was paid $100,000 in indemnity:* compensation, reimbursement, recompense, repayment, restitution, payment, redress, reparation, damages.

indentation noun hollow, depression, dip, dent, dint, cavity, concavity, notch; dimple, cleft.

independence noun

1 *the struggle for American independence:* self-government, self-rule, home rule, self-determination, sovereignty, autonomy, freedom, liberty, non-alignment.
2 *he valued his independence:* selfsufficiency, self-reliance.
3 *her independence of spirit:* freedom, individualism, unconventionality, unorthodoxy.

independent adjective

1 *an independent country:* self-governing, self-ruling, self-determining, sovereign, autonomous, autarkic, free, non-aligned.
2 *two independent groups of biologists verified the results:* separate, different, unconnected, unrelated, dissociated, discrete.
3 *an independent school:* private, non-state-run, private-sector, fee-paying; privatized, denationalized.
4 *her grown-up, independent children:* self-sufficient, self-supporting, self-reliant, standing on your own two feet.
5 *you should take independent advice:* impartial, unbiased, unprejudiced, neutral, objective, non-partisan, disinterested, dispassionate, with no axe to grind.
6 *an independent spirit:* freethinking, free, individualistic, unconventional, maverick, unconstrained, unfettered, untrammelled.
OPPOSITES: dependent.

independently adverb *he prefers to work independently:* alone, on your own, separately, unaccompanied, solo; unaided, unassisted, without help, by your own efforts, under your own steam, single-handed, off your own bat, on your own initiative.

indescribable adjective *the feeling of anticipation was indescribable:* beyond words/description, inexpressible, ineffable; unutterable, unspeakable; intense, extreme, acute, strong, powerful, profound, incredible.

indestructible adjective

1 *indestructible plastic containers:* unbreakable, shatterproof, durable.
2 *the indestructible qualities of the human mind:* lasting, enduring, everlasting, imperishable, deathless, undying.
OPPOSITES: fragile.

indeterminate adjective

1 *the ban will last for an indeterminate period of time:* undetermined, unspecified, indefinite, unfixed, uncertain, unknown.
2 *some indeterminate background noise:* vague, unclear, indistinct, unidentifiable, undefinable; amorphous, shapeless, formless.

index noun

1 *the library's subject index:* list, listing, inventory, catalogue, directory, register.
2 *the Retail Price Index:* measure, indicator, guide.

indicate verb

1 *sales indicate a growing market for such art:* point to, be a sign of, be evidence of, evidence, demonstrate, show, testify to, be a symptom of, be symptomatic of, denote, mark, signal, signify, suggest, imply; manifest, display, reflect, represent, reveal, betray; formal evince, bespeak.
2 *the president indicated his willingness to use force:* state, declare, make known, communicate, announce, mention, put on record; reveal, divulge, disclose, admit.
3 *please indicate your choice of prize on the form:* specify, designate, stipulate; show.
4 *he indicated the room with a sweep of his arm:* point to, point out, gesture towards.

indicated adjective *in such cases surgery is indicated:* advisable, recommended, desirable, preferable, best, sensible, wise, in someone's interests, prudent, necessary; needed, required, called for.

indication noun *pain may be an indication of injury:* sign, signal, indicator, symptom, mark, manifestation, demonstration, evidence; pointer, guide, hint, clue; warning, forewarning, intimation, omen, portent.

indicative adjective *the President's visit was indicative of improving diplomatic arrangements:* symptomatic, expressive, suggestive, representative, emblematic, symbolic; typical, characteristic.

indicator noun

1 *these tests are a reliable indicator of performance:* measure, gauge, barometer, guide, index, mark, sign, signal; standard, touchstone, yardstick, benchmark, criterion, point of reference, test, litmus test.
2 *the depth indicator:* meter, measuring device, measure, gauge, dial.

indict verb *he was indicted for murder:* charge, accuse, arraign, take to court, put on trial, prosecute; summons, prefer charges against, cite; N. Amer. impeach.

indictment noun charge, accusation, arraignment; citation, summons; Law, Brit. plaint; N. Amer. impeachment.

indifference noun

1 *his apparent indifference infuriated her:* lack of concern, lack of interest, disinterest, nonchalance, lack of enthusiasm, unconcern, apathy; boredom, unresponsiveness, impassivity, dispassion, detachment.
2 *the indifference of the midfield players:* mediocrity, lack of distinction, amateurishness, lack of inspiration.

indifferent adjective

1 *he gave an indifferent shrug:* unconcerned, uninterested, uncaring, casual, nonchalant, offhand, uninvolved, unenthusiastic, apathetic, lukewarm; unimpressed, bored, unmoved, unresponsive, impassive, dispassionate, detached, cool.
2 *it was a very indifferent performance:* mediocre, ordinary, average, middling, uninspired, undistinguished, run-of-the-mill, unexceptional, unexciting, unremarkable, pedestrian, prosaic, lacklustre, forgettable, amateurish; informal OK, so-so, fair-to-middling, no great

i

shakes, not up to much.
OPPOSITES: enthusiastic, brilliant.

indigenous adjective *indigenous peoples are being slowly wiped out as prospectors invade their lands:* native, original, aboriginal; earliest, first; Anthropology autochthonous.

indigestion noun dyspepsia, heartburn, stomach ache; Medicine pyrosis.

indignant adjective *he was indignant at the way he was being treated:* aggrieved, resentful, affronted, put out, disgruntled, displeased, cross, angry, annoyed, exasperated, vexed, offended, irritated, irked, piqued, in high dudgeon; informal peeved, miffed, aggravated, nettled, riled, in a huff.

indignation noun *she was filled with indignation at having been blamed so unjustly:* resentment, umbrage, disgruntlement, displeasure, anger, annoyance, irritation, exasperation, vexation, pique.

indignity noun *Annie has suffered the indignity of being dumped by her husband:* shame, humiliation, loss of self-respect, loss of pride, loss of face, embarrassment, mortification; disgrace, dishonour, stigma, discredit; affront, insult, injury, offence, injustice, slight, snub, discourtesy, disrespect; informal slap in the face, kick in the teeth.

indirect adjective
1 *pay levels have an indirect effect on interest rates:* incidental, accidental, unintended, secondary; collateral, contingent; formal concomitant.
2 *we took an indirect route:* roundabout, circuitous, wandering, meandering, serpentine, winding, tortuous, zigzag.
3 *his speech was an indirect attack on the government:* oblique, implicit, implied, inexplicit.
OPPOSITES: direct.

indiscreet adjective *an indiscreet remark:* imprudent, unwise, injudicious, incautious, irresponsible, ill-judged, ill-advised, misguided, ill-considered, careless, rash, unwary, impulsive, foolish, short-sighted; undiplomatic, indelicate, tactless, insensitive, unseemly.
OPPOSITES: discreet.

indiscretion noun
1 *he's paid a heavy price for a moment of indiscretion:* imprudence, injudiciousness, incaution, irresponsibility, carelessness, rashness, impulsiveness, foolishness, folly; tactlessness.
2 *his youthful indiscretions:* mistake, faux pas, error, slip, gaffe, miscalculation, impropriety; misdemeanour, misdeed, transgression, peccadillo; informal slip-up.

indiscriminate adjective *indiscriminate firing from the troops caused twenty*

deaths: non-selective, unselective, undiscriminating, uncritical, hit-or-miss, haphazard, random, arbitrary, unsystematic; wholesale, general, sweeping, blanket; thoughtless, unthinking, unconsidered, casual, careless.
OPPOSITES: selective.

indispensable adjective *education is indispensable for the preservation of democracy:* essential, necessary, all-important, of the utmost importance, of the essence, vital, crucial, key, needed, required, requisite; invaluable.
OPPOSITES: unnecessary.

indisposed adjective
1 *my wife is indisposed:* ill, unwell, sick, poorly, ailing, not very well, out of sorts, under/below par; Brit. off colour; informal under the weather.
2 *she was indisposed to help him:* reluctant, unwilling, disinclined, loath, unprepared, not disposed, not minded, averse.
OPPOSITES: well, willing.

indisposition noun *her sister had a mild indisposition:* illness, ailment, disorder, sickness, disease, infection; condition, complaint, problem; literary malady; informal bug, virus; Brit. informal lurgy.

indisputable adjective *there is indisputable evidence that terrorists are to blame:* incontrovertible, incontestable, undeniable, irrefutable, beyond dispute, unquestionable, beyond question, indubitable, not in doubt, beyond doubt, beyond a shadow of a doubt, unarguable, undebatable, airtight, watertight, unassailable; unequivocal, unmistakable, certain, sure, definite, definitive, proven, decisive, conclusive, demonstrable, self-evident, clear, clear-cut, plain, obvious, manifest, patent, palpable.
OPPOSITES: questionable.

indistinct adjective
1 *the distant shoreline was indistinct:* blurred, out of focus, fuzzy, hazy, misty, foggy, cloudy, shadowy, dim, nebulous; unclear, obscure, vague, faint, indistinguishable, barely perceptible, hard to see, hard to make out.
2 *the last two digits are indistinct:* indecipherable, illegible, unreadable, hard to read.
3 *indistinct sounds emerged from the cellar:* muffled, muted, low, quiet, soft, faint, inaudible, hard to hear; muttered, mumbled.
OPPOSITES: distinct, clear.

indistinguishable adjective
1 *the two girls were indistinguishable:* identical, difficult to tell apart, like two peas in a pod, like Tweedledum and Tweedledee, very similar, two of a kind.
2 *his words were indistinguishable in the crowd:* unintelligible, incomprehensible,

hard to make out, indistinct, unclear; inaudible.
OPPOSITES: unalike.

individual adjective
1 *a series of exhibitions devoted to individual artists:* single, separate, discrete, independent.
2 *he had his own individual style of music:* characteristic, distinctive, distinct, typical, particular, idiosyncratic, peculiar, personal, personalized, special.
3 *it was a chic and highly individual apartment:* original, unique, singular, different, unusual, striking, unorthodox.
▷ **noun**
1 *Peter was a rather stuffy individual:* person, human being, mortal, soul, creature; man, boy, woman, girl; character, personage; informal type, sort.
2 *she was a real individual:* individualist, free spirit, nonconformist, original, eccentric, maverick, rare bird; Brit. informal one-off.

individualist noun *horn players tend to be individualists:* free spirit, individual, nonconformist, original, eccentric, maverick, rare bird; Brit. informal one-off.
OPPOSITES: conformist.

individualistic adjective
unconventional, unorthodox, atypical, singular, unique, original, nonconformist, independent, freethinking; eccentric, maverick, strange, odd, peculiar, idiosyncratic.

individuality noun *we are motivated by the need to assert our individuality:* distinctiveness, uniqueness, originality, singularity, particularity, differentness, separateness; personality, character, identity, self.

individually adverb *a panel will look at all the applications individually:* one at a time, one by one, singly, separately, severally, independently, apart.
OPPOSITES: together.

indoctrinate verb *their goal was to indoctrinate the students with their ideas:* brainwash, propagandize, proselytize, re-educate, persuade, convince, mould; instruct, teach, school, drill, inculcate.

indolence noun *my failure is probably due to my own indolence:* laziness, idleness, slothfulness, sloth, shiftlessness, inactivity, inaction, inertia, sluggishness, lethargy, languor, languidness, torpor.

indolent adjective *he's too indolent to achieve anything worthwhile:* lazy, idle, slothful, work-shy, do-nothing, shiftless, lackadaisical, languid, inactive, inert, sluggish, lethargic, torpid, sluggardly; slack, lax, remiss, negligent, good-for-nothing, feckless; informal bone idle.
OPPOSITES: industrious.

indomitable adjective *these indomitable warriors have never been subjugated:* invincible, unconquerable, unbeatable, unassailable, invulnerable; indefatigable, unyielding, unbending, stalwart, stout-hearted, lionhearted, strong-willed, strong-minded, steadfast, staunch, resolute, firm, determined, adamant; unflinching, courageous, brave, valiant, heroic, fearless, plucky, gritty, steely.
OPPOSITES: submissive.

indubitable adjective unquestionable, indisputable, unarguable, undebatable, incontestable, undeniable, irrefutable, incontrovertible, unmistakable, unequivocal, certain, sure, positive, definite, absolute, conclusive, watertight; undoubtable, beyond doubt, beyond the shadow of a doubt, beyond dispute, beyond question, not in question, not in doubt.
OPPOSITES: doubtful.

induce verb
1 *the pickets induced many workers to stay away:* persuade, convince, prevail on, get, make, prompt, move, inspire, influence, encourage, motivate; coax into, wheedle into, cajole into, talk into; informal twist someone's arm.
2 *these activities induce a feeling of togetherness:* bring about, produce, effect, create, give rise to, generate, engender, occasion, lead to, result in, foster, promote, encourage; cause, instigate, trigger off, spark off, whip up, stir up, kindle, arouse, rouse.
OPPOSITES: dissuade, prevent.

inducement noun *shopkeepers began offering free gifts as an inducement to trade:* incentive, encouragement, stimulus, attraction, temptation, bait, lure, pull, draw, spur, impetus, motive, motivation; bribe, reward; informal carrot, come-on, sweetener.
OPPOSITES: deterrent.

induct verb *the new ministers were inducted into the government:* admit to, allow into, introduce to, initiate into, install in, swear in; appoint to.

indulge verb
1 *she was able to indulge a growing passion for literature:* satisfy, gratify, fulfil, feed; yield to, give in to, give way to.
2 *Bolton were indulging in idle dreams about the Champions' League:* wallow in, give yourself up to, give way to, yield to, abandon yourself to, give free rein to; luxuriate in, revel in, lose yourself in.
3 *she did not like her children to be indulged:* pamper, spoil, overindulge, coddle, mollycoddle, cosset, baby, spoon-feed, wrap in cotton wool, pander to, wait on hand and foot, cater to someone's every whim.
OPPOSITES: frustrate.

i

□ **indulge yourself**
treat yourself, give yourself a treat; informal go to town, splurge; Brit. informal splash out.

indulgence noun
1 *excess indulgence contributed to his ill health:* self-gratification, self-indulgence, overindulgence, intemperance, immoderation, excess, lack of restraint, extravagance, decadence, pleasure-seeking.
2 *they viewed holidays as an indulgence:* extravagance, luxury, treat, non-essential, extra, frill.
3 *his parents view his lapses with indulgence:* tolerance, forbearance, understanding, kindness, compassion, sympathy, forgiveness.

indulgent adjective *she had a very indulgent father:* generous, liberal, permissive, easy-going, tolerant, forgiving, forbearing, lenient, kind, kindly, soft-hearted, compassionate, understanding, sympathetic; fond, doting; compliant, obliging, accommodating, patient.
OPPOSITES: strict.

industrial adjective *industrial areas of the city:* industrialized, manufacturing; commercial, business, trade.

industrialist noun *industrialists are on the lookout for takeover targets:* manufacturer, producer, factory owner; captain of industry, big businessman, magnate, tycoon, capitalist, financier; informal, derogatory fat cat.

industrious adjective *he was honest, sober, and industrious:* hard-working, diligent, assiduous, conscientious, painstaking, sedulous, persevering, unflagging, untiring, tireless, indefatigable, studious; busy, active, energetic, on the go, dynamic, productive.
OPPOSITES: indolent.

industry noun
1 *British industry:* manufacturing, production; construction.
2 *the publishing industry:* business, trade, field.
3 *we were impressed by their industry:* hard work industriousness, diligence, application, dedication; activity, energy, productiveness.

inedible adjective uneatable, indigestible, unpalatable; stale, rotten, off, bad.

ineffable adjective *the ineffable beauty of the Everglades:* indescribable, inexpressible, beyond words; undefinable, unutterable, unimaginable; overwhelming, breathtaking, awesome, staggering, amazing.

ineffective adjective
1 *an ineffective strategy:* unsuccessful, unproductive, useless, fruitless, unprofitable, abortive, futile; ineffectual, inefficient, inefficacious, inadequate.
2 *an ineffective president:* ineffectual,

inefficient, inept, unsuccessful, powerless, impotent, inadequate, incompetent, weak, incapable, unfit; informal useless; Brit. informal hopeless.
OPPOSITES: effective.

inefficient adjective
1 *an inefficient worker:* ineffective, incompetent, inept, incapable, unskilful, inexpert, amateurish; disorganized, unprepared; negligent, lax, sloppy, slack, careless.
2 *inefficient processes:* uneconomical, wasteful, unproductive, time-wasting, slow; disorganized, unsystematic.
OPPOSITES: efficient.

inelegant adjective
1 *he hit the water with an inelegant bellyflop:* graceless, ungraceful, ungainly, uncoordinated, awkward, clumsy, lumbering; inept, unskilful, inexpert.
2 *an inelegant bellow of laughter:* unrefined, uncouth, unsophisticated, uncultivated, ill-bred.
OPPOSITES: elegant, graceful.

ineligible adjective *they were ineligible to vote:* not entitled, not permitted, not allowed; disqualified, ruled out.
OPPOSITES: eligible.

inept adjective *my attempts at cooking were inept, but I fumbled on:* incompetent, unskilful, unskilled, inexpert, amateurish; clumsy, awkward, maladroit, bungling, blundering; unproductive, unsuccessful, inefficient, not up to scratch; informal cack-handed, ham-fisted.
OPPOSITES: competent.

inequality noun imbalance, inequity, inconsistency, variation, variability; divergence, polarity, disparity, discrepancy, dissimilarity, difference; bias, prejudice, discrimination, unfairness.
OPPOSITES: equality, consistency.

inequitable adjective *the present taxes are inequitable:* unfair, unjust, unequal, uneven, unbalanced, one-sided, discriminatory, preferential, biased, partisan, prejudiced.
OPPOSITES: equitable, fair.

inert adjective *she lay inert in her bed:* unmoving, motionless, immobile, inanimate, still, stationary, static; dormant, sleeping; unconscious, comatose, lifeless, insensible, insensate, insentient; idle, inactive, sluggish, lethargic, listless, torpid.
OPPOSITES: active.

inertia noun *he showed signs of lapsing into inertia:* inactivity, inaction, inertness; enervation, lethargy, sluggishness, listlessness, torpor, apathy, idleness, sloth; motionlessness, immobility, lifelessness; literary accidie.

inescapable adjective *they concluded that political reform was inescapable:* unavoidable, inevitable, inexorable,

ineluctable; assured, certain; necessary, required, compulsory, mandatory.
OPPOSITES: avoidable.

inessential adjective *cut out the inessential details:* unnecessary, non-essential, needless, redundant, superfluous, excessive, surplus, dispensable, expendable, unwanted; unimportant, peripheral, minor, secondary.
OPPOSITES: essential.

inevitable adjective *he feared that war was inevitable:* unavoidable, inescapable, inexorable, ineluctable; assured, certain.
OPPOSITES: uncertain.

inevitably adverb *the poor crop will inevitably affect the price of wine:* naturally, necessarily, automatically, as a matter of course, of necessity, inescapably, unavoidably, certainly, surely, definitely, undoubtedly; informal like it or not.

inexact adjective *the figures are inexact:* imprecise, inaccurate, approximate, rough, crude, general; wrong, incorrect, erroneous, false; off, out.

inexcusable adjective *his behaviour was inexcusable:* indefensible, unjustifiable, unwarranted, unpardonable, unforgivable; blameworthy, censurable, reprehensible, deplorable, unconscionable, unacceptable, unreasonable; uncalled-for, unprovoked, gratuitous.

inexhaustible adjective
1 *he has an apparently inexhaustible supply of energy:* unlimited, limitless, infinite, boundless, endless, never-ending, unfailing, everlasting; copious, abundant, plentiful; literary illimitable.
2 *the dancers were inexhaustible:* tireless, indefatigable, untiring, unfaltering, unflagging.
OPPOSITES: limited.

inexorable adjective
1 *the inexorable march of new technology:* relentless, unstoppable, inescapable, inevitable, unavoidable; continuous, non-stop, steady, interminable, incessant, unceasing, unremitting, unrelenting, persistent.
2 *he was inexorable—there was nothing to be done:* intransigent, unbending, unyielding, inflexible, adamant, obdurate, immovable, unshakeable; implacable, unforgiving, unsparing, uncompromising, relentless.

inexpensive adjective *a retail chain specializing in inexpensive furniture:* cheap, low-priced, low-cost, economical, competitive, affordable, reasonable, budget, economy, bargain, cut-price, reduced, discounted, discount, rock-bottom, giveaway, bargain-basement.
OPPOSITES: expensive.

inexperience noun ignorance, unworldliness, naivety, innocence, immaturity.

inexperienced adjective *low wages attract inexperienced staff:* inexpert, untrained, unqualified, unskilled, unpractised, amateur; naive, unsophisticated, callow, immature, green.
OPPOSITES: experienced.

inexpert adjective *the crane was manoeuvred by inexpert operators:* unskilled, unskilful, amateur, amateurish, unprofessional, inexperienced; inept, incompetent, clumsy, maladroit, bungling, blundering; informal cack-handed, ham-fisted.

inexplicable adjective *she had an inexplicable change of heart:* unaccountable, incomprehensible, unfathomable, mysterious, strange; baffling, puzzling, perplexing, mystifying, bewildering.
OPPOSITES: understandable.

inexpressive adjective *their faces were utterly inexpressive:* expressionless, impassive, emotionless; inscrutable, unreadable, blank, vacant, glazed, lifeless, deadpan, wooden, stony; poker-faced, straight-faced.

inextricable adjective *economic difficulty and political dissatisfaction were inextricable:* inseparable, indivisible, entangled, tangled, mixed up.

infallible adjective *there is no infallible way to distinguish the genuine cases from the fraudulent:* unfailing, unerring, perfect, faultless, flawless, guaranteed, dependable, trustworthy, reliable, sure, certain, safe, foolproof; informal sure-fire.
OPPOSITES: fallible.

infamous adjective *an infamous gangster:* notorious, of ill repute, disreputable; legendary, fabled.
OPPOSITES: reputable.

infamy noun notoriety, disrepute, ill fame, ill repute.

infancy noun
1 *she died in infancy:* babyhood, early childhood.
2 *broadcasting was in its infancy:* beginnings, early days, early stages; start, commencement, rise, emergence, dawn, birth, inception.
OPPOSITES: end.

infant noun *a fretful infant:* baby, newborn, young child; Medicine neonate; Scottish & N. English bairn.
▷ adjective *infant industries:* developing, emergent, emerging, embryonic, nascent, new, fledgling, budding, up-and-coming.

infantile adjective *he refused to play their infantile games:* childish, babyish, immature, puerile, juvenile, adolescent; silly, inane, fatuous.

infantry noun infantrymen, foot soldiers; the ranks; cannon fodder; US GIs; Brit. informal Tommies.

infatuated adjective *Sarah seemed to be infatuated with him:* besotted, in love, head over heels, obsessed, taken; enamoured of, attracted to, devoted to, captivated by, enchanted by, bewitched by, under the spell of; informal smitten with, mad about, carrying a torch for.

infatuation noun passion, love, adoration, desire, devotion; obsession, fixation; informal crush.

infect verb
1 *carriers can infect their families:* pass infection to, spread disease to, contaminate.
2 *nitrates were infecting rivers:* contaminate, pollute, taint, foul, dirty, blight; poison.
3 *his high spirits infected everyone:* affect, influence, touch; excite, inspire, stimulate, animate.

infection noun
1 *a kidney infection:* disease, virus; illness, disorder, condition, complaint, sickness, affliction, ailment; informal bug; Brit. informal lurgy.
2 *strict hygiene will limit the risk of infection:* contamination, contagion; septicaemia; germs, bacteria.

infectious adjective
1 *the virus is highly infectious:* contagious, communicable, catching, transmittable, transmissible; epidemic.
2 *her laughter is infectious:* irresistible, contagious, catching.

infer verb *the judge inferred that the deceased was murdered:* deduce, conclude, surmise, reason, work out; gather, understand, presume, assume, take it; extrapolate.

> **USAGE**
>
> Do not confuse **infer** with **imply**. If you **infer** something from what has been said, you come to the conclusion that this is what is meant (e.g. *we inferred from his words that the General was a traitor*). If a person **implies** something (*he implied that the General was a traitor*), they are suggesting something but not stating it directly.

inference noun deduction, conclusion, reasoning; assumption, presumption, supposition, reckoning, extrapolation.

inferior adjective
1 *she made me feel inferior:* second-class, lower-ranking, subordinate, junior, lowly, humble, menial.
2 *inferior accommodation:* second-rate, substandard, low-quality, low-grade,

unsatisfactory, shoddy, poor, bad; Brit. downmarket.
OPPOSITES: superior, luxury.
▷noun *how dare she treat him as an inferior?* subordinate, junior, underling, minion.

infernal adjective *the infernal regions:* of hell, hellish, lower, nether, subterranean, underworld; literary chthonic.

infertile adjective
1 *infertile soil:* barren, unproductive, unfruitful; sterile, impoverished, poor.
2 *she was infertile:* sterile, barren.

infested adjective *her house is infested with cockroaches:* overrun, swarming, teeming, crawling, alive.

infidel noun (derogatory) unbeliever, non-believer, disbeliever; heretic, heathen, pagan.

infidelity noun *her husband never knew of her infidelity:* unfaithfulness, adultery; faithlessness, disloyalty, treachery, duplicity, deceit.

infiltrate verb *government spies infiltrated the organization:* gain access to, insinuate yourself into, worm your way into, invade.

infiltrator noun *the constant vigilance needed to outwit enemy infiltrators:* spy, agent, plant, mole, entryist; informant, informer.

infinite adjective
1 *the universe is infinite:* boundless, unbounded, unlimited, limitless, never-ending; immeasurable; extensive, vast; literary fathomless.
2 *an infinite number of birds:* countless, innumerable, incalculable, uncountable, inestimable, immeasurable, untold; great, huge, enormous; literary numberless.
3 *she bathed him with infinite care:* great, immense, supreme.
OPPOSITES: finite, limited.

infinitesimal adjective *a tiny fish with infinitesimal white scales:* minute, tiny, minuscule, very small; microscopic, imperceptible, indiscernible; informal teeny; Brit. informal titchy.
OPPOSITES: huge.

infinity noun *the infinity of space:* endlessness, infinitude, infiniteness, boundlessness, limitlessness; vastness, immensity.

infirm adjective frail, weak, feeble, debilitated; ill, unwell, sick, sickly, poorly, ailing.
OPPOSITES: healthy, strong.

infirmity noun
1 *they were excused due to infirmity:* frailty, weakness, feebleness, debility, poor health.
2 *the infirmities of old age:* ailment, illness,

disease, disorder, sickness, affliction, complaint; literary malady.

inflame verb

1 *the play inflames anti-Semitism:* provoke, incite, arouse, rouse, stir up, whip up, kindle, ignite, foment.
2 *his opinions inflamed his rival:* enrage, incense, anger, madden, infuriate, exasperate, provoke, antagonize.
3 *these comments inflamed what was already a sensitive situation:* aggravate, exacerbate, intensify, worsen, compound.
OPPOSITES: calm, soothe.

inflamed adjective *the skin had become inflamed:* swollen, puffy, reddened, red, hot, burning, itchy; raw, sore, painful, tender; infected, septic.

inflammable adjective *inflammable gases:* flammable, combustible; volatile, unstable.
OPPOSITES: non-flammable.

> **USAGE**
>
> The words **inflammable** and **flammable** both mean 'easily set on fire'. To avoid confusion, it is safer to use **flammable**, because the *in-* part of **inflammable** can give the impression that the word means 'not flammable'.

inflammation noun swelling, puffiness, redness; rawness, soreness, tenderness; infection, septicity.

inflammatory adjective *inflammatory language:* provocative, incendiary, rabble-rousing, like a red rag to a bull; controversial, contentious.

inflate verb

1 *to inflate the life jacket, pull the red tags:* blow up, pump up, fill up, fill with air, puff up/out; dilate, distend, swell.
2 *the demand inflated prices:* increase, raise, boost, escalate, put up; informal hike up, jack up, bump up.
3 *the figures were inflated by the press:* exaggerate, magnify, overstate, overplay, enhance, embellish.
OPPOSITES: deflate, decrease.

inflated adjective

1 *inflated prices:* high, sky-high, excessive, unreasonable, prohibitive, outrageous, exorbitant, extortionate; informal steep.
2 *he has an inflated sense of his own importance:* exaggerated, overblown, excessive, overstated, aggrandized.

inflexible adjective

1 *his inflexible attitude:* stubborn, obstinate, obdurate, intractable, intransigent, uncompromising, unbending, unaccommodating, adamant, single-minded.
2 *inflexible rules:* unalterable, hard and fast, unchangeable, immutable, unvarying; firm, fixed, set, established, entrenched.
3 *an inflexible structure:* rigid, stiff,

unyielding, unbending; hard, firm, inelastic.
OPPOSITES: flexible, accommodating.

inflict verb

1 *severe penalties will be inflicted on drug suppliers:* impose, wreak; administer to, deal out to, mete out to, cause to, give to.
2 *she is wrong to inflict her beliefs on everyone else:* impose, force, thrust, foist; saddle someone with, burden someone with.

influence noun

1 *their father had considerable influence over them:* effect on, impact on; control, hold, power, authority, mastery; guidance, direction.
2 *Fiona was a good influence on her:* example to, role model for, guide for, inspiration to.
3 *big companies have too much political influence:* power, authority, sway, leverage, weight, pull; standing, prestige, stature; informal clout.
▷verb
1 *bosses can influence our careers:* affect, have an impact on, determine, guide, control, shape, govern, decide; change, alter, transform.
2 *an attempt to influence the jury:* sway, bias, prejudice, suborn; pressurize, coerce, intimidate; informal lean on.

influential adjective

1 *an influential leader:* powerful, dominant, controlling, strong, authoritative; important, prominent, distinguished.
2 *he was influential in shaping her career:* instrumental, significant, important, crucial, pivotal.

influx noun *an influx of tourists:* flood, rush, stream, inundation; incursion, invasion.

inform verb

1 *she informed him that she was ill:* tell, notify, let someone know, apprise, advise; impart to, communicate to; brief, prime; informal fill in, clue in.
2 *they informed on their former comrades:* denounce, betray, incriminate, report; sell out, stab in the back; informal stitch up, blow the whistle, sell down the river, snitch; Brit. informal grass, shop.
3 *religion informs every aspect of their lives:* suffuse, pervade, permeate, infuse, imbue; influence.

informal adjective

1 *an informal discussion | an informal atmosphere:* unofficial, casual, relaxed, friendly, easy-going; open, easy, natural; informal laid-back.
2 *informal language:* colloquial, vernacular, idiomatic, demotic; simple, everyday, unpretentious; informal chatty.
3 *informal clothes:* casual, comfortable,

everyday; informal comfy.
OPPOSITES: formal, official.

informality noun lack of formality, lack of ceremony, casualness; ease, naturalness.

information noun *for further information write to the address below:* details, particulars, facts, figures, statistics, data; instruction, advice, guidance, direction, enlightenment; knowledge, intelligence, news; informal info, gen, the low-down, the inside story.

informative adjective *the speech was informative and entertaining:* instructive, instructional, illuminating, enlightening, revealing; factual, educational, educative, edifying; informal newsy.

informed adjective *he was well informed on the issue:* knowledgeable about, au fait with, conversant with, up to date on, abreast of, in the picture about; informal up to speed on.
OPPOSITES: ill-informed, ignorant.

informer noun informant; spy, double agent, infiltrator, plant; derogatory traitor, collaborator, fifth columnist; informal stool pigeon, whistle-blower, snake in the grass, snitch; Brit. informal grass, supergrass, nark.

infrequent adjective *his infrequent trips abroad:* rare, uncommon, unusual, exceptional, few; unaccustomed, unwonted; isolated, scarce, sporadic, irregular, intermittent; informal once in a blue moon.
OPPOSITES: frequent.

infringe verb
1 *the bid infringed EU rules:* contravene, violate, break, breach, transgress; disobey, defy, flout, fly in the face of; disregard, ignore; go beyond, overstep, exceed.
2 *surveillance could infringe personal liberties:* undermine, compromise, erode, encroach on, limit, diminish, weaken, impair, damage.
OPPOSITES: obey, preserve.

infuriate verb *his arrogance infuriated her:* enrage, incense, anger, madden, exasperate; antagonize, provoke, annoy, irritate, irk, vex; informal aggravate, rile, make someone see red, get someone's back up, make someone's blood boil.
OPPOSITES: please.

infuriating adjective exasperating, maddening, annoying, irritating, irksome, vexatious; informal aggravating.

infuse verb
1 *she was infused with a sense of hope:* fill, suffuse, imbue, inspire, charge, pervade, permeate.
2 *he infused new life into the group:* instil, breathe, inject, impart, introduce, add.
3 *infuse the leaves in vinegar:* steep, soak.

ingenious adjective *an ingenious solution:* inventive, imaginative, original, clever, creative, innovative, resourceful, enterprising, inspired, brilliant; astute, sharp-witted, quick-witted, shrewd; informal smart.

ingenuous adjective *he looked at her with wide ingenuous eyes:* naive, innocent, simple, childlike, trusting, trustful, over-trusting, unwary, unsuspecting; artless, guileless, open, sincere, honest, genuine, unworldly, inexperienced.
OPPOSITES: disingenuous, artful.

inglorious adjective *an inglorious retreat:* ignominious, dishonourable, shameful, discreditable, disgraceful, humiliating, mortifying, demeaning, ignoble, undignified, wretched.

ingrained, engrained adjective
1 *ingrained attitudes:* entrenched, established, deep-rooted, deep-seated, fixed, firm, unshakeable, ineradicable.
2 *ingrained dirt:* ground-in, embedded, permanent, indelible, ineradicable.

ingratiate verb
□ ingratiate yourself
they attempted to ingratiate themselves with the local aristocracy: curry favour with, cultivate, win over; informal get in someone's good books.

ingratiating adjective *he sidled up to her with an ingratiating smile:* sycophantic, unctuous, obsequious, toadying, fawning; flattering, insincere; smooth-tongued, silver-tongued, slick.

ingratitude noun *Harry was fuming at her ingratitude:* ungratefulness, lack of appreciation, lack of gratitude.

ingredient noun *investment is an essential ingredient of corporate success:* constituent, component, element; part, piece, bit, strand, portion, unit, feature, aspect, attribute; (**ingredients**) contents, makings.

inhabit verb *the greater part of this area is inhabited by Kurds:* live in, occupy; settle in, people, populate, colonize; reside in, have your home in; formal dwell in.

inhabitant noun resident, occupant, occupier, settler; (**inhabitants**) population, populace, people, public, community, citizenry, townsfolk, townspeople; formal dweller.

inhale verb *he inhaled a lungful of sea air:* breathe in, draw in, suck in.
OPPOSITES: exhale.

inherent adjective *he believed in the inherent goodness of man:* intrinsic, essential, fundamental, basic, innate, natural, instinctive, instinctual; inborn, ingrained, deep-rooted; structural, organic; literary immanent.

inherit verb
1 *she inherited his farm:* be bequeathed,

come into, be left, be willed; Law be devised.
2 *Richard inherited the title:* succeed to, assume, take over, come into.

inheritance noun legacy, bequest, endowment; birthright, heritage, patrimony.

> **WORD LINKS**
> **hereditary** relating to inheritance

inheritor noun heir, heiress, legatee; successor, next in line; Law devisee.

inhibit verb *these practices will inhibit economic growth:* impede, hinder, hamper, prevent, hold back, discourage, interfere with, obstruct, slow down, retard; curb, check, restrict, fetter, frustrate, stifle, block, thwart, foil, stop, halt.
OPPOSITES: assist, encourage.

inhibited adjective *men are far less inhibited about their bodies than women:* shy, reticent, reserved, self-conscious, diffident, bashful; wary, reluctant, hesitant, insecure, unconfident, timid; withdrawn, repressed, undemonstrative; informal uptight.

inhibition noun *when people are drunk, they tend to lose their inhibitions:* shyness, reticence, self-consciousness, reserve, diffidence; wariness, hesitance, hesitancy, insecurity, timidity; psychological block; informal hang-up.

inhospitable adjective
1 *a journey through dangerous and inhospitable terrain:* uninviting, unwelcoming; bleak, forbidding, cheerless, hostile, harsh; uninhabitable, barren, bare, desolate, stark.
2 *forgive me if I seem inhospitable:* unwelcoming, unfriendly, unsociable, antisocial, unneighbourly; aloof, cool, cold, frosty, distant, remote, indifferent, offhand; discourteous, ungracious, unkind, unsympathetic; informal stand-offish.
OPPOSITES: welcoming.

inhuman adjective *the prisoners had been subjected to inhuman and degrading treatment:* cruel, harsh, inhumane, brutal, callous, sadistic, savage, vicious, barbaric, monstrous, heinous; merciless, ruthless, pitiless, remorseless, cold-blooded, heartless, hard-hearted; unkind, inconsiderate, unfeeling, uncaring.
OPPOSITES: humane.

inhumane adjective *it is inhumane to separate a mother from her children:* cruel, inhuman, callous, harsh, brutal, barbaric, sadistic.

inimical adjective
1 *the policy is inimical to the industry's long-term interests:* harmful, injurious, detrimental, deleterious, prejudicial, disadvantageous, damaging, hurtful,

destructive; antagonistic, contrary, antipathetic, unfavourable, opposed, hostile.
2 *he fixed her with an inimical gaze:* hostile, unfriendly, antagonistic.
OPPOSITES: advantageous.

inimitable adjective *in his own inimitable style he provides sound advice:* unique, exclusive, distinctive, individual, special, idiosyncratic; incomparable, unparalleled, unrivalled, peerless, matchless, unequalled, unsurpassable, superlative, supreme, beyond compare, second to none, in a class of your own.

iniquity noun *the iniquity of his conduct:* wickedness, sinfulness, immorality; vice, evil, sin, crime, wrong, wrongdoing, villainy, criminality.

initial adjective *the initial stages of the project:* first, early, earliest, preliminary, primary, preparatory; opening, introductory, inaugural; embryonic, fledgling.
OPPOSITES: final.
▷noun *what do the initials stand for?* acronym, abbreviation, initialism.
▷verb *he initialled the warrant:* put your initials on, sign, countersign, endorse, witness.

initially adverb *initially, the assignment seemed straightforward:* at first, at the start, at the outset, in/at the beginning, to begin with, to start with, originally.

initiate verb
1 *the government initiated the scheme:* institute, launch, inaugurate, establish, put in place, set up, begin, start, sow the seeds of, start the ball rolling; originate, pioneer; informal kick off.
2 *he was initiated into a cult:* admit, introduce, induct, enrol, recruit, enlist, swear in.
3 *they were initiated into the mysteries of mathematics:* introduce to, teach, instruct in, school in, ground in; familiarize with, acquaint with; informal show someone the ropes.
▷noun *an initiate on the team:* novice, newcomer, beginner, learner, student, pupil, trainee, apprentice; recruit, tyro, neophyte.

initiative noun
1 *employers are looking for initiative:* enterprise, resourcefulness, inventiveness, imagination, ingenuity, originality, creativity; drive, dynamism, ambition, motivation, spirit, energy, vision; informal get-up-and-go.
2 *he has lost the initiative:* advantage, upper hand, edge, lead, whip hand, trump card.
3 *a government initiative to reduce crime:* plan, scheme, strategy, stratagem, measure, proposal, step, action, approach.

inject verb
1 *the doctor injected a painkilling drug:*
administer.
2 *patients were injected with the vaccine:*
vaccinate, inoculate.
3 *a pump injects air into the valve:* insert,
introduce, feed, push, force, shoot.
4 *he injected new life into the team:*
introduce, instil, infuse, imbue, breathe.

injection noun *an anti-tetanus injection:*
inoculation, vaccination, vaccine,
immunization, booster; dose; *informal*
jab, shot.

injudicious adjective *he will probably
pay dearly for his injudicious comments:*
imprudent, unwise, ill-advised, misguided,
ill-considered, ill-judged, incautious, hasty,
rash, foolish, foolhardy; inappropriate,
impolitic, inexpedient.
OPPOSITES: judicious.

injunction noun *a High Court injunction
banned the media from publishing the
photos:* order, ruling, direction, directive,
command, instruction; decree, edict,
dictum, fiat.

injure verb
1 *the explosion injured several people:* hurt,
wound, harm; maim, mutilate, deform,
disfigure.
2 *his arm was injured in the struggle:* hurt,
wound, damage; break, fracture.
3 *a libel calculated to injure her reputation:*
damage, harm, mar, spoil, impair, ruin,
blemish, tarnish, blacken.

injured adjective
1 *he can't walk because of his injured leg:*
hurt, wounded, damaged, sore, bruised;
disfigured, maimed, mutilated; broken,
fractured; Brit. informal gammy.
2 *the injured party:* wronged, maltreated,
mistreated, ill-used.
3 *an injured tone:* upset, hurt, wounded,
offended, reproachful, pained, aggrieved,
unhappy, put out.

injurious adjective *the drug has injurious
effects on the kidneys:* harmful, bad,
damaging, detrimental, deleterious;
disadvantageous, undesirable, adverse,
pernicious.

injury noun
1 *she sustained minor injuries:* wound,
bruise, cut, gash, scratch, graze,
abrasion, contusion, lesion; break,
fracture.
2 *they escaped without injury:* harm, hurt,
damage, pain, suffering, impairment.

injustice noun
1 *the injustice of the world:* unfairness,
unjustness, inequity, inequality;
bias, prejudice, discrimination,
intolerance.
2 *he suffered a grave injustice:* wrong,
offence, crime, sin, misdeed; outrage,
scandal, disgrace, affront.

inkling noun *I had an inkling of what was
going on:* idea, notion, sense, impression,
suggestion, sneaking suspicion, fancy,
hunch; hint, clue, intimation, sign.

inlaid adjective *a plaque inlaid with
mother of pearl:* inset, set, studded, lined,
panelled; decorated, ornamented.

inland adjective
1 *inland areas:* interior, inshore, central,
internal, upcountry.
2 *inland trade:* domestic, internal, home,
local.
OPPOSITES: coastal, international.
▷ adverb *the goods were carried inland:*
upcountry, inshore, to the interior.

inlet noun
1 *coastal inlets:* cove, bay, bight, creek,
estuary, fjord, sound; Scottish firth.
2 *a fresh air inlet:* vent, flue, shaft, duct,
channel, pipe, pipeline.

inmate noun
1 *the inmates of the hospital:* patient,
inpatient; resident, inhabitant, occupant.
2 *inmates rioted and tried to escape:*
prisoner, convict, captive, detainee,
internee.

inmost adjective. See INNERMOST.

innate adjective *people differ in terms of
their innate abilities:* inborn, inherent,
natural, intrinsic, instinctive, intuitive,
unlearned; hereditary, inherited, in the
blood; inbuilt, deep-rooted, deep-seated.
OPPOSITES: acquired.

inner adjective
1 *inner London:* central, innermost, mid,
middle.
2 *the inner gates:* internal, interior, inside,
inmost, innermost; intramural.
3 *her inner feelings:* private, personal,
secret, intimate.
4 *one's inner life:* mental, intellectual,
psychological, spiritual, emotional.
5 *the inner meaning:* hidden, secret, deep,
underlying, unapparent, veiled.
OPPOSITES: external, apparent.

innermost adjective
1 *the innermost layer:* inmost, central,
middle, internal.
2 *her innermost feelings:* deepest,
deep-seated, inward, inner, underlying,
intimate, private, personal, secret, hidden,
unexpressed.

innocence noun
1 *he protested his innocence:* guiltlessness,
blamelessness, irreproachability.
2 *she took advantage of his innocence:*
naivety, ingenuousness, credulity,
inexperience, gullibility, unworldliness,
guilelessness.

innocent adjective
1 *he was entirely innocent:* guiltless,
blameless, in the clear, irreproachable,

above suspicion, unimpeachable, faultless; honourable, honest, upright, law-abiding.
2 *an innocent young girl:* **virtuous**, pure, chaste, virginal, sinless, uncorrupted, undefiled.
3 *innocent foreigners were exploited:* **naive**, ingenuous, trusting, credulous, unsuspicious, unwary; impressionable, gullible, easily led; inexperienced, unworldly, unsophisticated, green; artless, guileless.
4 *she is innocent of guile:* **free from**, without, lacking in; unaware of, untouched by.
5 *a bit of innocent fun:* **harmless**, innocuous, inoffensive.
OPPOSITES: guilty.

innocuous adjective
1 *an innocuous comment:* **inoffensive**, harmless, innocent, unobjectionable, unexceptionable, anodyne, unremarkable, commonplace.
2 *an innocuous substance:* **harmless**, safe, non-toxic.
OPPOSITES: offensive, harmful.

innovation noun *the pace of technological innovation does not seem to be slowing down:* **change**, revolution, transformation, new ideas, new methods, modernization, modernism; reorganization, restructuring, rearrangement, remodelling.

innovative adjective *the store's products are innovative and effective:* **original**, innovatory, new, novel, fresh, unusual, avant-garde, experimental, inventive, ingenious; advanced, modern, state-of-the-art, pioneering, groundbreaking, revolutionary, radical; informal edgy.

innovator noun *the 19th century's prolific scientific innovators:* **pioneer**, trailblazer, pathfinder, groundbreaker; developer, modernizer, progressive; inventor, creator.

innuendo noun *he became the butt for their smutty innuendoes:* **insinuation**, suggestion, intimation, implication, hint, overtone, undertone, allusion, reference.

innumerable adjective *there are innumerable books on the art of public speaking:* **countless**, numerous, very many; untold, infinite, incalculable; literary numberless; informal umpteen, no end of, loads of, stacks of, heaps of, masses of.
OPPOSITES: few.

inoculate verb *he inoculated his patients against smallpox:* **immunize**, vaccinate.

inoculation noun **immunization**, vaccination; injection, booster; informal jab, shot.

inoffensive adjective *the victim was an inoffensive law-abiding citizen:* **harmless**, innocuous, unobjectionable, unexceptionable; mild, peaceful, peaceable, gentle; innocent.

inoperable adjective
1 *the airfield was left inoperable:* **unusable**, out of action, out of service, non-active.
2 *the agreement is now inoperable:* **impractical**, unworkable, unfeasible, unrealistic, non-viable, impracticable, unsuitable.

inoperative adjective
1 *the lift is inoperative:* **out of order**, out of service, broken, out of commission, unserviceable, faulty, defective; down; informal bust, kaput, on the blink; Brit. informal knackered.
2 *the contract is inoperative:* **void**, null and void, invalid, ineffective, non-viable; cancelled, revoked, terminated.
OPPOSITES: working, valid.

inopportune adjective *she turned up at the most inopportune moment:* **inconvenient**, unsuitable, inappropriate, unfortunate, infelicitous, inexpedient, unfavourable; untimely, ill-timed, unseasonable; awkward, difficult.
OPPOSITES: opportune.

inordinate adjective *the job had taken an inordinate amount of time:* **excessive**, undue, unreasonable, unjustifiable, disproportionate, unwarranted, unwarrantable, unnecessary, needless, uncalled for, exorbitant, extreme; immoderate, extravagant.

inorganic adjective *the spontaneous generation of life from inorganic matter:* **inanimate**, inert; lifeless; mineral.

input noun *an error resulted from invalid input:* **data**, details, information, material; facts, figures, statistics.
▷ verb *she input data into the file:* **key in**, type in, put in, load, insert.

inquest noun *they held an inquest into her death:* **inquiry**, investigation; probe, examination, review, analysis; hearing.

inquire verb
1 *the commission is to inquire into alleged illegal payments by the club:* **investigate**, conduct an inquiry, probe, look into; research, examine, explore; informal check out.
2 *I inquired about part-time courses:* **ask**, make inquiries, question someone.

inquiring adjective *he may be old but he has an inquiring mind:* **inquisitive**, curious, interested, questioning, probing, searching.

inquiry noun
1 *he will carry out a formal inquiry into the cause of the accident:* **investigation**, probe, examination, exploration; inquest, hearing.
2 *we have received telephone inquiries:* **question**, query.

inquisition noun *she sat down opposite him and started on her inquisition:* **interrogation**, questioning, cross-examination; informal grilling.

inquisitive adjective *their inquisitive neighbours had gathered at the gate:* curious, interested, intrigued; prying, eavesdropping, busybody, meddlesome; inquiring, questioning, probing; informal nosy.
OPPOSITES: uninterested.

insalubrious adjective *he moved from one insalubrious dwelling to another:* seedy, unsavoury, sordid, sleazy, unpleasant, dismal, wretched; slummy, squalid, shabby, scruffy, ramshackle, tumbledown, dilapidated, neglected, crumbling, decaying; informal scuzzy; Brit. informal grotty.
OPPOSITES: smart.

insane adjective
1 *she was declared insane:* mentally ill, of unsound mind, certifiable; psychotic; mad, deranged, demented, out of your mind, non compos mentis, sick in the head, unhinged, disturbed, crazed; informal crazy, not all there, bonkers, cracked, loony, loopy, nuts, off your rocker, off your trolley, round the bend; Brit. informal crackers, barmy, off your head, round the twist, not the full shilling.
2 *an insane suggestion:* foolish, idiotic, stupid, silly, senseless, nonsensical, absurd, ridiculous, ludicrous, preposterous, fatuous, inane, asinine, irrational, illogical; informal crazy; Brit. informal daft, barmy.
OPPOSITES: sensible.

insanitary adjective *disease spreads quickly in crowded and insanitary conditions:* unhygienic, unhealthy, dirty, filthy, contaminated, polluted, foul; infected, infested, germ-ridden.
OPPOSITES: hygienic.

insanity noun
1 *insanity runs in her family:* mental illness, madness, dementia.
2 *it would be pure insanity to take this loan:* folly, foolishness, madness, idiocy, stupidity, lunacy.

insatiable adjective *journalists have an insatiable appetite for news of any kind:* unquenchable, uncontrollable, voracious, ravenous; avid, eager, keen.

inscribe verb
1 *his name was inscribed above the door:* carve, write, engrave, etch, cut; imprint, stamp, impress, mark.
2 *a book inscribed to him by the author:* dedicate, address.

inscription noun
1 *the inscription on the headstone:* engraving, wording, writing, lettering, legend, epitaph, epigraph.
2 *the book's inscription:* dedication, address.

inscrutable adjective
1 *his face was inscrutable:* enigmatic, unreadable, mysterious; expressionless, impassive, inexpressive, emotionless, unemotional, blank, deadpan; informal poker-faced.
2 *the inscrutable language of international political agreements:* mysterious, incomprehensible, impenetrable, opaque, abstruse, arcane.
OPPOSITES: expressive, transparent.

insect noun

> WORD LINKS
> **entomology** the study of insects
> **insectivorous** insect-eating

insecure adjective
1 *an insecure young man:* unconfident, uncertain, unsure, doubtful, hesitant, self-conscious, unassertive, diffident, unforthcoming, shy, timid, timorous, retiring, inhibited, introverted; anxious, fearful, worried.
2 *insecure windows:* unprotected, ill-protected, vulnerable, defenceless, exposed.
3 *an insecure footbridge:* unstable, rickety, rocky, wobbly, shaky, unsteady, precarious; weak, flimsy, unsound, unsafe.
OPPOSITES: confident, secure.

insecurity noun
1 *he hid his insecurity:* lack of confidence, self-doubt, diffidence, unassertiveness, timidity, uncertainty, nervousness; anxiety, worry, unease.
2 *the insecurity of our situation:* vulnerability, defencelessness, danger; instability, fragility, frailty, shakiness, unreliability.

insensible adjective
1 *she was insensible on the floor:* unconscious, inert, comatose, insensate; informal out cold.
2 *he was insensible to the risks:* unaware of, ignorant of, unconscious of, unmindful of, oblivious to; indifferent to, impervious to, deaf to, blind to, unaffected by.
OPPOSITES: conscious, aware.

insensitive adjective
1 *an insensitive bully:* heartless, unfeeling, inconsiderate, thoughtless, uncaring, unconcerned, unsympathetic, unkind, hard-hearted, cold-blooded, callous; thick-skinned.
2 *she was remarkably insensitive to pain:* impervious to, immune to, oblivious to, unaware of, unresponsive to, indifferent to, unaffected by, untouched by.
OPPOSITES: sensitive.

inseparable adjective *these policy objectives were regarded as inseparable:* indivisible, inextricable, inextricably linked, bound together.

insert verb
1 *he inserted a tape in the machine:* put, place, push, thrust, slide, slip, load, fit, slot, install; informal pop, stick, bung.
2 *she inserted a clause in the contract:*

enter, introduce, incorporate, interpolate, interpose, interject.
OPPOSITES: extract, remove.
▷noun *the newspaper carried an insert:* enclosure, insertion, supplement; circular, advertisement, pamphlet, leaflet.

inside noun *the inside of a volcano:* interior, inner part; centre, core, middle, heart.
OPPOSITES: exterior.
▷adjective
1 *his inside pocket:* inner, interior, internal.
2 *inside information:* confidential, classified, restricted, privileged, private, secret, exclusive; informal hush-hush.
OPPOSITES: outer.
▷adverb
1 *she ushered me inside:* indoors, within, in.
2 (informal) *he's back inside:* in prison, in jail, in custody; locked up, imprisoned, incarcerated; informal behind bars, doing time; Brit. informal banged up.

> WORD LINKS
> **intra-** forming words meaning 'inside; within', such as *intramural* ('situated or done within a building')

insider noun *a Home Office insider leaked the information:* member, worker, employee, representative; person in the know.

insidious adjective *the insidious erosion of rights and liberties:* gradual, subtle, creeping, bit-by-bit, progressive; stealthy, surreptitious, cunning, crafty, sly, indirect.

insight noun
1 *your insight has been invaluable:* intuition, discernment, perception, awareness, understanding, comprehension, appreciation, penetration, acumen, perspicacity, judgement, acuity; vision, prescience, imagination.
2 *an insight into the government:* understanding of, appreciation of, revelation about; introduction to; informal eye-opener.

insignia noun badge, crest, emblem, symbol, sign, device, mark, seal, colours.

insignificant adjective *too many articles are devoted to insignificant details:* unimportant, trivial, trifling, negligible, inconsequential, of no account, inconsiderable, small; paltry, petty, insubstantial, worthless, irrelevant, immaterial, peripheral; formal nugatory.

insincere adjective *she flashed him an insincere smile:* false, fake, artificial, feigned, pretended, put-on, hollow; disingenuous, hypocritical, cynical, deceitful, duplicitous, two-faced; informal phoney, pretend.

insinuate verb
1 *he insinuated that she'd lied:* imply, suggest, hint, intimate, let it be known,

give someone to understand; informal make out.
2 *he insinuated his hand under hers:* slide, slip, manoeuvre, insert, edge.
▢**insinuate yourself into**
he insinuated himself into her family: worm your way into, ingratiate yourself with, curry favour with; foist yourself on, introduce yourself into; infiltrate, invade, sneak into, intrude on, impinge on.

insinuation noun *he resented the insinuation that he was past it:* implication, inference, suggestion, hint, intimation, innuendo, reference, allusion, undertone, overtone; slur.

insipid adjective
1 *insipid coffee:* tasteless, flavourless, bland, weak, wishy-washy; unappetizing, unpalatable.
2 *many artists continue to churn out insipid works:* unimaginative, uninspired, uninspiring, characterless, flat, uninteresting, lacklustre, dull, boring, humdrum, run-of-the-mill, commonplace, pedestrian, trite, tired, hackneyed, stale, lame, tame, jejune.
OPPOSITES: tasty, inspiring.

insist verb
1 *be prepared to insist:* stand firm, stand your ground, be determined, hold out, not take no for an answer; persevere, persist; informal stick to your guns.
2 *he insisted that he knew nothing:* maintain, assert, hold, contend, argue, protest, claim, vow, swear, declare, stress, repeat, reiterate.
3 *she insisted that they pay up:* demand, command, require.

insistence noun
1 *she sat down at Anne's insistence:* demand, bidding, command, instruction, requirement, request, entreaty, exhortation, urging.
2 *his insistence that he loved her:* assertion, declaration, contention, claim, assurance, affirmation, avowal.

insistent adjective
1 *despite Jake's insistent questioning, he refused to explain:* persistent, determined, adamant, importunate, tenacious, unyielding, dogged, unrelenting, relentless, inexorable; forceful, demanding, assertive.
2 *an insistent buzzing:* incessant, constant, unremitting, repetitive; obtrusive, intrusive.

insolent adjective *she hated the insolent tone of his voice:* impertinent, impudent, rude, discourteous, disrespectful, cheeky, ill-mannered, bad mannered, impolite, uncivil; bold, cocky, brazen; contemptuous, insulting.
OPPOSITES: polite.

insoluble adjective *some problems are insoluble:* unsolvable, unanswerable, unresolvable; unfathomable, impenetrable, unexplainable, inexplicable.

insolvency noun *the firm is on the brink of insolvency:* **bankruptcy**, liquidation, failure, collapse, financial ruin; Brit. receivership.

insolvent adjective **bankrupt**, ruined; penniless, impoverished, impecunious; Brit. in receivership, without a penny to your name; informal bust, broke, belly-up, gone to the wall, on the rocks, in the red.

insouciance noun *his anxieties increased, despite Jen's insouciance:* **nonchalance**, unconcern, indifference, calm, equanimity, composure, airiness; informal cool.
OPPOSITES: anxiety.

insouciant adjective *he had an insouciant disregard for authority:* **nonchalant**, blasé, untroubled, unworried, unruffled, unconcerned, indifferent, heedless, airy; relaxed, calm, equable, serene, composed, easy, carefree, free and easy, happy-go-lucky; informal cool, laid back.

inspect verb *the safety equipment is inspected by officials each year:* **examine**, check, scrutinize, investigate, vet, test, monitor, survey, study, look over, scan, observe; assess, appraise, review, evaluate; informal check out, give something a/the once-over.

inspection noun *environmental health officers make regular inspections of the premises:* **examination**, check, check-up, investigation, scrutiny, survey, observation; assessment, appraisal, review, evaluation.

inspector noun *the machinery was not acceptable to the factory inspector:* **examiner**, checker, scrutineer, investigator, surveyor, assessor, appraiser, reviewer, analyst; observer, overseer, supervisor, monitor, watchdog, ombudsman; auditor.

inspiration noun
1 *his work lacks inspiration:* **creativity**, inventiveness, innovation, ingenuity, imagination, originality; artistry, insight, vision; finesse, flair.
2 *he continues to be the inspiration for countless musicians:* **stimulus**, stimulation, motivation, fillip, encouragement, influence, muse, spur, lift, boost, incentive, impulse, catalyst; example, model.
3 *she had a sudden inspiration:* **bright idea**, revelation; informal brainwave; N. Amer. informal brainstorm.

inspire verb
1 *the landscape inspired him to write:* **stimulate**, motivate, encourage, influence, rouse, move, stir, energize, galvanize, animate, fire, incentivize; incite.
2 *she inspired great loyalty in her colleagues:* **arouse**, awaken, induce, create, produce, engender, bring out.
3 *the film inspired a musical:* **give rise to**, lead to, prompt; spawn.

inspired adjective *they gave an inspired performance:* **outstanding**, wonderful, marvellous, excellent, superb, magnificent, fine, exceptional, first-class, first-rate, virtuoso, supreme, superlative; innovative, innovatory, ingenious, original; informal tremendous, ace, awesome, out of this world; Brit. informal brilliant.
OPPOSITES: poor.

inspiring adjective *he was an inspiring example to his pupils:* **inspirational**, encouraging, heartening, uplifting, stirring, rousing, stimulating, electrifying; moving, affecting, influential.

instability noun
1 *the instability of political life:* **unreliability**, uncertainty, unpredictability, insecurity, perilousness, riskiness; impermanence, fluctuation.
2 *emotional instability:* **volatility**, unpredictability, variability, changeability, capriciousness, vacillation.
3 *the instability of the foundations:* **unsteadiness**, unsoundness, shakiness, frailty, fragility.
OPPOSITES: stability.

install verb
1 *a photocopier was installed in the office:* **put**, position, place, locate, situate, station, site, lodge; insert.
2 *they installed a new president:* **swear in**, induct, inaugurate, invest, instate; appoint, take on; ordain, consecrate, anoint; enthrone, crown.
3 *she installed herself behind the table:* **ensconce**, establish, position, settle, seat, lodge, plant; sit down; informal park; Brit. informal plonk.
OPPOSITES: remove.

installation noun
1 *the installation of radiators:* **installing**, fitting, putting in; insertion.
2 *the installation of the chancellor:* **swearing in**, induction, inauguration, investiture, instatement; ordination, consecration; enthronement, coronation.
3 *a new computer installation:* **unit**, appliance, fixture; equipment, machinery.

instalment noun
1 *I pay by monthly instalments:* **part payment**; Brit. hire purchase; Brit. informal the never-never.
2 *a story published in instalments:* **part**, section, segment, portion, bit; chapter, episode, volume, issue.

instance noun *an instance of racism:* **example**, occurrence, case, occasion; illustration.
▷verb *as an example I would instance Jones's work:* **cite**, quote, refer to, mention, allude to, give; specify, name, identify, draw attention to, put forward, offer, advance.

☐ **in the first instance**
initially, at first, at the start, at the outset, in/at the beginning, to begin with, to start with, originally.

instant adjective
1 *users have instant access to the latest information | I took an instant dislike to him:* immediate, instantaneous, on-the-spot, prompt, swift, speedy, rapid, quick, express, lightning; sudden, precipitate, abrupt.
2 *instant meals tend not to be very nutritious:* pre-prepared, pre-cooked, ready mixed, fast; microwaveable.
OPPOSITES: delayed.
▷ **noun**
1 *at that instant, the sun came out:* moment, time, minute, second; juncture, point.
2 *it all happened in an instant:* second, split second, moment, minute, trice, twinkling of an eye, flash; informal sec, jiffy, the blink of an eye.

instantaneous adjective *such an instantaneous response was not likely to be considered authoritative:* immediate, instant, on-the-spot, prompt, swift, speedy, rapid, quick, express, lightning; sudden, hurried, precipitate.
OPPOSITES: delayed.

instantly adverb *she fell asleep almost instantly:* immediately, at once, straight away, right away, instantaneously; suddenly, abruptly, all of a sudden; forthwith, there and then, here and now, this/that minute, this/that instant; quickly, rapidly, speedily, promptly; in an instant, in a moment, in a split second, in a trice, in/like a flash, like a shot, in the twinkling of an eye; informal pronto, in no time.

instead adverb *if you get carsick, travel by train instead:* as an alternative, in lieu, alternatively, as a substitute; rather, by contrast, for preference, by/from choice.
☐ **instead of**
we served wine instead of beer: as an alternative to, as a substitute for, as a replacement for, in place of, in lieu of, in preference to; rather than, as opposed to, as against, as contrasted with.

instigate verb
1 *they instigated formal proceedings:* set in motion, get under way, get off the ground, start, commence, begin, initiate, launch, institute, set up, put in place, inaugurate, establish, organize; actuate, generate, bring about; start the ball rolling; informal kick off.
2 *outsiders may have instigated the violence:* incite, encourage, provoke, whip up, stir up, kindle, spark off, arouse.

instigation noun *they became involved at his instigation:* prompting, suggestion; request, entreaty, demand, insistence; wish, desire, persuasion.

instigator noun *the instigators of the revolt:* initiator, prime mover, motivator, architect, designer, planner, mastermind, creator, agent; ringleader, agitator, troublemaker.

instil verb
1 *it's his job to instil confidence in the players:* inspire, promote, foster, engender, produce, generate, induce; inculcate, implant, impress, imprint, introduce; drum into.
2 *he instilled Monet with a love of nature:* imbue, inspire, infuse.

instinct noun
1 *birds have an instinct to build nests:* natural tendency, innate tendency; urge, drive, compulsion.
2 *her instincts told her to run:* impulse, inclination, intuition, feeling, sixth sense, hunch, presentiment.
3 *his instinct for making the most of his chances:* talent, gift, ability, aptitude, skill, flair, feel, genius, knack, bent; nose.

instinctive adjective *this is an instinctive reaction to stress:* intuitive, natural, innate, instinctual; automatic, reflex, knee-jerk, mechanical, spontaneous, involuntary, impulsive; unconscious, subconscious; informal gut.
OPPOSITES: learned, conscious.

institute noun *a research institute:* organization, establishment, institution, foundation, centre; academy, school, college, university; society, association, federation, body, guild.
▷ **verb**
1 *the new system was instituted to promote efficiency:* introduce, establish, initiate, launch, set up, create; inaugurate, found, organize; set in motion, get under way, get off the ground, start, commence, begin.
2 *he will be instituted as vicar:* install, induct, invest, swear in, instate; ordain, consecrate, anoint; appoint.

institution noun
1 *an academic institution:* establishment, organization, institute, foundation, centre; academy, school, college, university; consortium, society, association, body, guild.
2 *they spent their lives in institutions:* residential home, hospital; dated asylum.
3 *the institution of marriage:* practice, custom, convention, tradition; system, policy.
4 *the institution of new training procedures:* introduction, establishment, launch, setting up, creation, initiation, inauguration, start.

institutional adjective
1 *an institutional framework for discussions:* organized, established, bureaucratic, conventional, procedural, prescribed, set, routine, formal, systematic, systematized, methodical,

i

businesslike, orderly, coherent, structured, regulated.
2 *the rooms are rather institutional:* impersonal, stark, spartan, bare, clinical, sterile, unappealing, uninviting, unattractive, unwelcoming, dreary.

instruct verb
1 *the union instructed them to strike:* order, direct, command, tell, require, call on, mandate, charge; formal enjoin.
2 *he instructed them in the use of firearms:* teach, school, coach, train, educate, tutor, guide, prepare, prime, enlighten, inform.
3 *she instructed a solicitor of her own choice:* employ, authorize, brief.
4 *the bank was instructed that money would be withdrawn:* inform, tell, notify, apprise, advise, brief; informal put in the picture, fill in.

instruction noun
1 *do not disobey their instructions:* order, command, directive, direction, decree, edict, injunction, mandate, dictate, commandment, bidding; requirement, stipulation; informal say-so.
2 *read the instructions before use:* directions, specification; handbook, manual, guide.
3 *he received instruction in musical technique:* tuition, teaching, coaching, schooling, tutelage; lessons, classes, lectures; training, drill, preparation, grounding, guidance.

instructive adjective *a recent study of cooperatives makes instructive reading:* informative, useful, illuminating, enlightening, helpful; edifying, educational, educative.

instructor noun *a flying instructor:* trainer, coach, teacher, tutor, guide.

instrument noun
1 *the wound was made with a sharp instrument:* implement, tool, utensil; device, apparatus, gadget.
2 *check all the cockpit instruments:* measuring device, gauge, meter; indicator, dial, display.
3 *education was seen as an instrument of social reform:* agent, agency, channel, medium, means, mechanism, vehicle, organ.

instrumental adjective *he was instrumental in developing new diagnostic procedures:* involved, active, influential, contributory; helpful, useful, of service; significant, important; (**be instrumental in**) play a part in, contribute to, be a factor in, have a hand in; add to, help, promote, advance, further; be conducive to, make for, lead to, cause.

insubordinate adjective *he soon found a means of dealing with his insubordinate son:* disobedient, unruly, wayward, errant, badly behaved, undisciplined, delinquent,

disorderly, troublesome, rebellious, defiant, recalcitrant, uncooperative, wilful, intractable, unmanageable, uncontrollable; awkward, difficult, perverse, contrary; Brit. informal bolshie.
OPPOSITES: obedient.

insubordination noun disobedience, unruliness, indiscipline, bad behaviour, misbehaviour, misconduct, delinquency; rebellion, defiance, mutiny, revolt; recalcitrance, wilfulness, perversity.

insubstantial adjective
1 *an insubstantial structure:* flimsy, fragile, breakable, unstable, shaky, wobbly, rickety, ramshackle, frail.
2 *insubstantial evidence:* weak, flimsy, poor, inadequate, insufficient, tenuous, insignificant, inconsequential, unconvincing, implausible, unsatisfactory.
OPPOSITES: sturdy, sound.

insufferable adjective
1 *the heat will be insufferable by July:* intolerable, unbearable, unendurable, insupportable, overwhelming, overpowering.
2 *his win made him insufferable:* conceited, arrogant, boastful, cocky, cocksure, full of yourself, self-important; vain, self-satisfied, self-congratulatory, smug; informal swollen-headed, big-headed, too big for your boots.

insufficient adjective *there was insufficient time available | we have insufficient financial resources:* inadequate, not enough, too little/few, deficient, scant, scanty; scarce, in short supply, lacking, wanting; paltry, meagre, niggardly; restricted, limited.

insular adjective
1 *such insular people are not going to be swayed overnight:* narrow-minded, small-minded, blinkered, inward-looking, parochial, provincial, small-town, short-sighted, hidebound, set in your ways.
2 *monks are often said to lead an insular existence:* isolated, inaccessible, cut off, segregated, detached, solitary, lonely.
OPPOSITES: broad-minded, cosmopolitan.

insulate verb
1 *pipes must be insulated to prevent heat loss:* wrap, cover, sheathe, encase, enclose, envelop; lag, heatproof, soundproof; pad, cushion.
2 *they were insulated from the impact of the war:* protect, shield, shelter, cushion, cocoon, screen; isolate, segregate, sequester, detach, cut off.

insulation noun
1 *most new hot-water tanks come with a layer of insulation:* lagging; blanket, jacket, wrap.
2 *insulation from the rigours of city life:* protection, defence, shelter, cocoon,

screen, shield; isolation, segregation, separation, detachment.

insult verb *he insulted my wife:* abuse, be rude to, call someone names, slight, disparage, discredit, libel, slander, malign, defame, denigrate, cast aspersions on; offend, affront, humiliate, hurt, wound; informal bad-mouth; Brit. informal slag off.
OPPOSITES: compliment.

▷**noun** *the two men exchanged insults | the lack of interest is an insult to British businesses:* abusive remark, jibe, barb, slur; affront, slight.

insulting adjective *I would not put up with such insulting comments:* abusive, rude, offensive, disparaging, belittling, derogatory, deprecatory, disrespectful, uncomplimentary, pejorative; disdainful, derisive, scornful, contemptuous; defamatory, slanderous, libellous, scurrilous.

insuperable adjective *insuperable financial problems:* insurmountable, overwhelming, hopeless, impossible.

insupportable adjective
1 *he had arrived at a wholly insupportable conclusion:* unjustifiable, indefensible, inexcusable, unwarrantable, unreasonable; baseless, groundless, unfounded, unsupported, unsubstantiated, unconfirmed, uncorroborated, invalid, untenable; implausible, weak, flawed, specious, defective.
2 *the heat was insupportable:* intolerable, insufferable, unbearable, unendurable; overwhelming, overpowering.

insurance noun
1 *he took out insurance for the car:* cover, financial protection, indemnity; indemnification, security; Brit. assurance.
2 *a marquee was hired as an insurance against the weather:* protection, defence, safeguard, security, precaution, provision.

insure verb *they had failed to insure the building against fire:* cover, indemnify, protect, underwrite; guarantee, warrant; Brit. assure.

insurgent noun *troops are fighting armed insurgents:* rebel, revolutionary, revolutionist, mutineer, insurrectionist, renegade; guerrilla, freedom fighter.
OPPOSITES: loyalist.

▷**adjective** *the regime was overthrown by insurgent forces:* rebellious, rebel, revolutionary, mutinous, insurrectionist; renegade, seditious, subversive.
OPPOSITES: loyal.

insurmountable adjective *an insurmountable problem:* insuperable, insoluble; overwhelming, hopeless, impossible.

insurrection noun *the leaders of the insurrection surrendered:* rebellion, revolt, uprising, mutiny, revolution, insurgence,

riot, sedition; civil disorder, unrest, anarchy; coup, coup d'état.

intact adjective *the church was almost in ruins but the tower remained intact:* whole, entire, complete, in one piece, undamaged, unscathed, unharmed, unspoiled, unimpaired, unbroken, flawless, untouched, unblemished, unmarked, perfect, pristine; inviolate.
OPPOSITES: damaged.

intangible adjective
1 *the moonlight made things seem intangible:* impalpable, ethereal, insubstantial, incorporeal, unreal, shadowy.
2 *the rose symbolized something intangible about their relationship:* indefinable, indescribable, inexpressible, nameless; abstract, vague, indefinite, subtle, elusive, fugitive.

integral adjective
1 *communication is an integral part of all human behaviour:* essential, fundamental, basic, intrinsic, inherent, constitutive, structural; vital, necessary, indispensable.
2 *the unit comes with an integral pump and heater:* built-in, inbuilt, integrated, incorporated, fitted.
3 *the first integral recording of the ten Mahler symphonies:* unified, integrated, comprehensive; complete, whole.
OPPOSITES: peripheral.

integrate verb *he proposes to integrate our reserve forces more closely with the regular forces:* combine, amalgamate, merge, unite, incorporate, unify, assimilate, consolidate, bring together; fuse, blend, mingle, coalesce, intermingle, mix, meld; desegregate.
OPPOSITES: separate.

integrated adjective
1 *an integrated school benefits pupils, staff, and the local community:* desegregated, non-segregated, unsegregated, mixed.
2 *an integrated package of services:* linked, coordinated, cohesive, coherent, unified, united, consolidated, amalgamated, combined, merged.

integrity noun
1 *I never doubted his integrity:* honesty, probity, rectitude, honour, good character, principles, ethics, morals, morality, virtue, decency, fairness, scrupulousness, sincerity, truthfulness, trustworthiness, incorruptibility.
2 *the integrity of the federation:* unity, unification, coherence, cohesion, solidarity.
3 *the structural integrity of the aircraft:* soundness, strength, sturdiness, solidity, durability, stability.
OPPOSITES: dishonesty, division.

intellect noun
1 *it's a film that appeals more to the*

i

intellect than to the emotions: mind, brain, intelligence, reason, understanding, thought, brainpower, judgement, wisdom, wits; informal grey matter.
2 *he is one of the finest intellects of our age:* thinker, intellectual, sage; mind, brain.

intellectual adjective
1 *his intellectual capacity:* mental, cerebral, cognitive; rational, abstract, conceptual, theoretical, analytical, logical; academic.
2 *an intellectual man:* intelligent, clever, academic, educated, well read, erudite, cerebral, learned, knowledgeable, literary, bookish, donnish, highbrow, scholarly, studious, enlightened, cultured; informal brainy.
OPPOSITES: physical, stupid.
▷**noun** *prominent intellectuals were highly critical of the policy:* academic, scholar, learned person, intelligent person, man/woman of letters, member of the intelligentsia, bluestocking; thinker, brain, sage; genius, Einstein, polymath; informal egghead.

intelligence noun
1 *a man of great intelligence:* intellectual capacity, mental capacity, intellect, mind, brains, brainpower, judgement, reasoning, understanding, comprehension; acumen, wit, sense, insight, perception, penetration, discernment, quick-wittedness, astuteness, acuity, intuition, cleverness, brilliance, ability, talent.
2 *intelligence from our agents indicates a military build-up:* information, facts, details, particulars, data, knowledge, reports.
3 *military intelligence:* information-gathering, surveillance, observation, reconnaissance, spying, espionage, infiltration.

intelligent adjective
1 *she is intelligent and hard-working:* clever, bright, brilliant, quick-witted, astute, canny, intuitive, insightful, perceptive, perspicacious, discerning; knowledgeable; able, gifted, talented; informal smart, brainy, quick on the uptake.
2 *an intelligent being from another world:* rational, higher-order, capable of thought.
3 *intelligent machines may take over the world:* self-regulating, capable of learning; informal smart.

intelligentsia plural noun *there is a distrust of the intelligentsia and of theoretical learning:* intellectuals, intelligent people, academics, scholars, the literati, thinkers; the intelligent; informal eggheads.

intelligible adjective *statutes were drafted so as to be intelligible only to lawyers:* comprehensible, understandable, accessible; lucid, clear, coherent, plain,

explicit, precise, unambiguous, self-explanatory, user-friendly.

intemperate adjective *his work was subjected to an intemperate attack by his former publisher:* immoderate, extreme, unrestrained, uncontrolled; self-indulgent, overindulgent, extravagant; imprudent, reckless, wild.
OPPOSITES: moderate.

intend verb *he intended to move abroad:* plan, have in mind, have the intention, aim, propose, mean; aspire, hope, expect, be resolved, be determined; want, wish; contemplate, think of, envisage; design, earmark, set aside.

intended adjective *the foul was not intended:* deliberate, intentional, calculated, conscious, planned, done on purpose, premeditated, pre-planned, preconceived, purposeful.
OPPOSITES: accidental.

intense adjective
1 *the pain was intense:* extreme, great, acute, fierce, severe, sharp; exceptional, extraordinary; strong, powerful, potent, profound.
2 *a very intense young man:* passionate, impassioned, ardent, fervent, zealous, vehement, fiery, emotional; earnest, eager, animated, spirited, energetic, fanatical, committed.
OPPOSITES: mild.

intensify verb *they had intensified their military campaign:* escalate, increase, step up, boost, raise, strengthen, augment, reinforce; build up, heighten, deepen, extend, expand, amplify, magnify; aggravate, exacerbate, worsen, inflame, compound.
OPPOSITES: abate.

intensity noun
1 *the pain grew in intensity:* strength, power, potency, force; severity, ferocity, fierceness, harshness, acuteness; extremity.
2 *his eyes had a glowing intensity:* passion, ardour, fervour, zeal, vehemence, fire, heat, emotion; eagerness, animation, spirit, vigour, strength, energy; fanaticism.

intensive adjective *an intensive search of the area:* thorough, thoroughgoing, in-depth, rigorous, exhaustive, comprehensive, complete, full; vigorous, strenuous, concentrated, detailed, minute, close, meticulous, scrupulous, painstaking, methodical, careful.
OPPOSITES: cursory.

intent adjective
1 *he was intent on proving his point:* determined to, resolved to, set on, bent on, keen to; committed to, obsessive about, fanatical about; anxious to, impatient to.
2 *an intent expression:* attentive, absorbed, engrossed, fascinated, enthralled, rapt;

focused, earnest, concentrating, intense, studious, preoccupied; alert, watchful.

▷ **noun** *with alarm, she realized his intent:* **aim,** intention, purpose, objective, object, goal, target; design, plan, scheme; wish, desire, ambition, idea, aspiration.

◻ **to all intents and purposes**
in effect, effectively, in essence, essentially, virtually, practically; more or less, just about, all but, as good as, in all but name; almost, nearly; informal pretty much, pretty well.

intention noun

1 *it is his intention to be leader:* **aim,** purpose, intent, objective, object, goal, target; design, plan, scheme; resolve, resolution, determination; wish, desire, ambition, idea, dream, aspiration.
2 *he managed, without intention, to upset me:* **intent,** intentionality, design, calculation; premeditation, forethought, pre-planning.

intentional adjective *victims of intentional discrimination can claim compensation:* **deliberate,** calculated, conscious, intended, planned, done on purpose, premeditated, pre-planned, preconceived, meant, knowing, wilful, purposeful, purposive; Law aforethought.

intently adverb *she listened intently to Harry's story:* **attentively,** closely, keenly, earnestly, hard, carefully; fixedly, steadily.

inter verb *his remains were interred in the new cemetery:* **bury,** lay to rest, entomb.
OPPOSITES: exhume.

intercede verb *several nations offered to intercede on the captives' behalf:* **intervene,** step in, act, interpose; mediate, arbitrate, conciliate, negotiate, moderate; plead, petition.

intercept verb *an Italian naval vessel intercepted the boat:* **stop,** head off, cut off; catch, obstruct, impede, interrupt, block, check, detain; ambush, challenge, waylay.

intercession noun *he made contact with the Austrians through the intercession of the Serbs:* **mediation,** arbitration, conciliation, negotiation; intervention, involvement, agency; pleading, petition, entreaty; diplomacy.

interchange verb

1 *they interchange ideas:* **exchange,** trade, swap, bandy; barter.
2 *the terms are often interchanged:* **substitute,** transpose, exchange, switch, swap round, change round, reverse, invert, replace with one another.

▷ **noun**

1 *the interchange of ideas:* **exchange,** trade, swap, give and take; traffic.
2 *a motorway interchange:* **junction,** intersection, crossing.

interchangeable adjective *up to this point, their albums were interchangeable:* **similar,** identical, indistinguishable, alike, the same, undifferentiated; corresponding, equivalent, comparable, equal; informal much of a muchness.

intercourse noun

1 *social intercourse:* **dealings,** relations, relationships, association, connections, contact; interchange, communication, correspondence; negotiations, transactions, trade, traffic.
2 *she did not consent to intercourse:* **sexual intercourse,** sex, lovemaking, sexual relations, copulation; technical coitus, coition.

interest noun

1 *we listened with interest:* **attentiveness,** attention, absorption; curiosity, inquisitiveness; heed, regard, notice; enjoyment, delight.
2 *the hotel is within reach of many places of interest:* **attraction,** appeal, fascination, charm, beauty.
3 *this will be of interest to those involved:* **concern,** consequence, importance, import, significance, note, relevance, value.
4 *her interests include reading:* **hobby,** pastime, leisure pursuit, recreation, diversion, amusement, relaxation; passion, enthusiasm.
5 *he has a financial interest in the firm:* **stake,** share, claim, investment, stock, equity; involvement, concern.
6 *her savings earned interest:* **dividends,** profits, returns; a percentage.
OPPOSITES: boredom.

▷ **verb**

1 *choose a topic that interests you:* **appeal to,** be of interest to, attract, intrigue, fascinate; absorb, engross, rivet, grip, captivate; amuse, divert, entertain; arouse your curiosity, whet your appetite.
2 *can I interest you in a drink?* **persuade to have;** sell.
OPPOSITES: bore.

◻ **in someone's interests**
of benefit to, to the advantage of; for the sake of, for the benefit of.

interested adjective

1 *he looked interested:* **attentive,** intent, absorbed, engrossed, fascinated, riveted, gripped, captivated, rapt, agog; intrigued, inquisitive, curious; keen, eager; informal all ears.
2 *a summary will be sent to all interested parties:* **concerned,** involved, affected, connected, related.

interesting adjective *it is one of the most interesting novels of its time:* **absorbing,** engrossing, fascinating, riveting, gripping, compelling, compulsive, captivating, engaging, enthralling; amusing, entertaining, stimulating, thought-provoking, intriguing; appealing, attractive; informal unputdownable.

interfere verb
1 *a holiday job might interfere with his studies:* **impede**, obstruct, get in the way of, hinder, hamper, inhibit, restrict, handicap, cramp, check; disturb, disrupt, influence, affect.
2 *she tried not to interfere in his life:* **intervene**, get involved, encroach on, impinge on; meddle in, pry into, nose into, intrude into, butt into; informal poke your nose into, muscle in on.

interference noun
1 *they resent state interference:* **intrusion**, intervention, intercession, involvement; meddling, prying.
2 *radio interference:* **disruption**, disturbance, static.

interfering adjective *others considered him to be an interfering busybody:* **meddlesome**, meddling, intrusive, prying, inquisitive, overcurious; informal nosy.

interim noun *in the interim they did more research:* **meantime**, meanwhile, intervening time.
▷**adjective** *an interim advisory body:* **provisional**, temporary, pro tem, stopgap, short-term, fill-in, caretaker, acting, intervening, transitional, makeshift, improvised, impromptu.
OPPOSITES: permanent.

interior adjective
1 *the house has interior panelling:* **inside**, inner, internal; intramural.
2 *the interior deserts of the US:* **inland**, inshore, upcountry, inner, innermost, central.
3 *the country's interior affairs:* **internal**, home, domestic, national, state, civil.
4 *an interior monologue:* **inner**, mental, spiritual, psychological; private, personal, intimate, secret.
OPPOSITES: exterior, outer, foreign.
▷**noun**
1 *the interior of the yacht:* **inside**, inner part, depths, recesses, bowels, belly; centre, core, heart.
2 *the country's interior:* **centre**, heartland, hinterland.
OPPOSITES: exterior, outside.

interject verb
1 *she interjected a comment:* **interpose**, introduce, throw in, interpolate, add.
2 *he interjected before there was a fight:* **interrupt**, intervene, cut in, break in, butt in, chime in; informal put your oar in, chip in.

interjection noun *there was an astonished interjection from one of the audience:* **exclamation**; cry, shout, utterance.

interlock verb *the fixed panel should interlock with the sliding section:* **interconnect**, interlink, engage, mesh, intermesh, join, unite, connect, couple.

interloper noun *they were a close community and could not abide interlopers:* **intruder**, outsider, stranger; trespasser, invader, uninvited guest; informal gatecrasher.

interlude noun *a peaceful interlude in her busy day:* **interval**, intermission, break, pause, lull, respite, rest, breathing space, halt, stop, hiatus; informal breather, let-up.

intermediary noun *they concluded the deal through an intermediary:* **mediator**, go-between, negotiator, intercessor, arbitrator, conciliator, peacemaker; middleman, broker; Brit. linkman.

intermediate adjective *an intermediate stage in the cell's development:* **transitional**, intermediary, midway, halfway, middle, mid, median, medial; intervening.

interment noun *his body was taken for interment:* **burial**, burying, entombment; Archaeology inhumation.

interminable adjective *Wednesday was a day of interminable meetings:* **endless**, never-ending, unending, everlasting, ceaseless, unceasing, incessant, non-stop, constant, continual, uninterrupted, sustained; monotonous, long-winded, overlong, rambling.

intermingle verb *fact and fiction were intermingled:* **mix**, intermix, mingle, blend, merge, combine, unite; associate, fraternize.

intermission noun *the daily work went on without intermission:* **interval**, break, pause, interlude, rest, respite, breathing space, lull, gap, stop, halt; cessation, suspension; informal let-up, breather.

intermittent adjective *they heard intermittent bursts of gunfire:* **sporadic**, irregular, fitful, spasmodic, occasional, periodic, discontinuous, isolated, random, patchy, scattered.
OPPOSITES: continuous.

intern verb *they were interned without trial:* **imprison**, incarcerate, jail, put behind bars, detain, hold, lock up, confine.

internal adjective
1 *an internal courtyard:* **inner**, interior, inside, intramural; central.
2 *the state's internal affairs:* **domestic**, home, interior, civil; national, state.
3 *she was waging an internal battle with herself:* **mental**, psychological, emotional; personal, private, secret, hidden.
OPPOSITES: external, foreign.

international adjective *an international business community:* **global**, globalized, multinational, worldwide, intercontinental, universal; cosmopolitan, multiracial.
OPPOSITES: national.

interplay noun *the interplay between military and civilian populations:* interaction, interchange; teamwork, cooperation, reciprocation, reciprocity, give and take.

interpolate verb *the illustrations were interpolated in the text:* insert, interpose, enter, add, incorporate, inset, put, introduce.

interpose verb
1 *he interposed himself between the girls:* insinuate, place, put, insert.
2 *I must interpose a note of caution:* introduce, interject, add.
3 *they interposed to suppress the custom:* intervene, intercede, step in, involve yourself.

interpret verb
1 *the rabbis interpreted the Jewish laws:* explain, elucidate, expound, explicate, clarify, shed light on, illuminate.
2 *the remark was interpreted as an invitation:* understand, construe, take, see, regard.
3 *the symbols are difficult to interpret:* decipher, decode, make intelligible; understand, comprehend, make sense of; analyse, evaluate.

interpretation noun
1 *the interpretation of the Bible's teachings:* explanation, exegesis, elucidation, exposition, explication, clarification.
2 *she did not care what interpretation he put on her haste:* meaning, understanding, construal, explanation, inference.
3 *the interpretation of experimental findings:* analysis, evaluation, review, study, examination.
4 *his interpretation of the sonata:* rendition, rendering, execution, presentation, performance.

interrogate verb *two police officers interrogated her:* question, cross-question, cross-examine, quiz; interview, examine, debrief, give someone the third degree; informal pump, grill.

interrogative adjective *he gazed at me with a hard interrogative stare:* questioning, probing, searching, inquiring; inquisitive, quizzical, curious.

interrupt verb
1 *she opened her mouth to interrupt:* cut in, break in, butt in, intervene; Brit. put your pennyworth in; informal chime in, put your oar in, chip in.
2 *the band had to interrupt their tour:* suspend, break off, discontinue, adjourn; stop, halt, end, bring to an end/close; disrupt.
3 *the coastal plain is interrupted by large lagoons:* break up, punctuate, divide.

interruption noun
1 *he was not pleased at her interruption:* intervention, intrusion.

2 *an interruption of the power supply:* discontinuation, disruption, break, breaking off, suspension, stoppage.
3 *an interruption in her career:* interval, interlude, break, pause, gap.

intersect verb
1 *the lines intersect at right angles:* cross, criss-cross.
2 *the cornfield is intersected by a track:* bisect, divide, cut in two/half, cut across/through; cross, traverse.

intersection noun
1 *the intersection of the two curves:* crossing, criss-crossing.
2 *the driver stopped at an intersection:* junction, T-junction, interchange, crossroads; Brit. roundabout.

intersperse verb
1 *plants were interspersed among the rocks:* scatter, spread, strew, disperse, dot, sprinkle.
2 *the debate was interspersed with angry exchanges:* punctuate, break up, interrupt.

intertwine verb *a wreath of laurel intertwined with daffodils:* entwine, interweave, interlace, twist, twine, coil.

interval noun
1 *a 15-minute interval:* intermission, interlude, break, pause, recess; half-time.
2 *polling day was a week away and Baldwin made two speeches in the interval:* interim, interlude, intervening time/period, meantime, meanwhile.

intervene verb
1 *she intervened in the dispute:* intercede, involve yourself, get involved, interpose yourself, step in; interfere, intrude.
2 *had the war not intervened, they might have married:* occur, happen, take place, arise, crop up, come about; follow, ensue, result.

intervention noun *they resented the government's intervention:* involvement, intercession, interceding; interference, intrusion.

interview noun *all applicants will be called for an interview:* meeting, discussion, conference, examination; audience, talk, dialogue, exchange; talks.
▷verb *we interviewed seventy people for the survey:* talk to, question, interrogate, cross-examine; poll, canvass, survey, sound out.

interviewer noun questioner, interrogator, examiner, assessor; journalist, reporter.

interweave verb
1 *the threads are interwoven:* intertwine, entwine, interlace, splice, braid, plait; twist together, weave together, wind together.
2 *their fates were interwoven:* interlink, intertwine, link, connect; intermix, mix, merge, blend, interlock.

intestines plural noun gut, guts, viscera, entrails; small intestine, large intestine; informal insides, innards.

> WORD LINKS
> **enteric**, **visceral** relating to the intestines
> **enteritis** inflammation of the intestines

intimacy noun *the sisters re-established their old intimacy:* closeness, togetherness, affinity, rapport, attachment, familiarity, friendliness, affection, warmth.

intimate[1] adjective
1 *they are on intimate terms:* close, loving, affectionate, friendly, familiar.
2 *it's a small hotel with an intimate atmosphere:* friendly, warm, welcoming, hospitable, relaxed, informal; cosy, comfortable, snug; informal comfy.
3 *he has an intimate knowledge of the industry:* detailed, thorough, exhaustive, deep, in-depth, profound.
4 *he shared his intimate thoughts and dreams with her:* personal, private, confidential, secret; innermost, inner, inward, unspoken, undisclosed.
OPPOSITES: distant, formal.
▷noun *his circle of intimates:* close friend, best friend, bosom friend, confidant, confidante; informal, derogatory crony.

intimate[2] verb *he had already intimated that he might not be able to continue:* announce, state, make known, disclose, reveal, divulge; imply, suggest, hint, indicate, signal, allude to, refer to.

intimation noun *the first intimation of discord:* suggestion, indication, hint, sign, signal, inkling, suspicion, impression; undertone, whisper.

intimidate verb *he paid them to intimidate his rivals:* threaten, browbeat, bully, pressure, pressurize; frighten, menace, terrorize, terrify, scare, cow; informal lean on, use strong-arm tactics on.

intolerable adjective *the noise had become intolerable:* unbearable, insufferable, insupportable, unendurable, beyond endurance, more than flesh and blood can stand, too much to bear.
OPPOSITES: tolerable.

intolerant adjective
1 *she had discovered that he was extremely intolerant:* narrow-minded, small-minded, parochial, provincial, illiberal, uncompromising, dogmatic; bigoted, prejudiced, biased.
2 *her son was intolerant to several foods:* allergic, sensitive, hypersensitive.

intonation noun
1 *she spoke English with a German intonation:* cadence, inflection, modulation, tone, timbre, lilt; speech pattern.
2 *the intonation of hymns:* chanting, incantation, recitation, singing.

intone verb *grace before the meal was intoned in Gaelic:* chant, sing, recite.

intoxicate verb *he was intoxicated by the cinema:* exhilarate, thrill, elate, delight, captivate, entrance, enrapture, excite, stir, rouse, inspire, fire with enthusiasm; informal give someone a buzz, give someone a kick.

intoxicated adjective *he was cautioned for being intoxicated while on duty:* drunk, inebriated, drunken, tipsy, under the influence; euphemistic tired and emotional; informal tight, the worse for wear, three sheets to the wind, plastered, smashed, wrecked, tanked up, off your face, out of your skull; Brit. informal paralytic, legless, tiddly.
OPPOSITES: sober.

intoxicating adjective
1 *intoxicating drink:* alcoholic, strong, hard, potent, intoxicant; informal stiff; old use spiritous.
2 *an intoxicating sense of freedom:* heady, exhilarating, thrilling, exciting, rousing, stirring, stimulating, invigorating, electrifying; strong, powerful, potent; informal mind-blowing.
OPPOSITES: non-alcoholic.

intoxication noun drunkenness, inebriation, insobriety.

intractable adjective
1 *intractable problems:* unmanageable, insoluble, difficult, awkward, troublesome, demanding, challenging.
2 *an intractable man:* stubborn, obstinate, obdurate, inflexible, unbending, unyielding, uncompromising, unaccommodating, uncooperative, difficult, awkward, perverse, contrary, pig-headed; informal stiff-necked.
OPPOSITES: tractable, compliant.

intransigent adjective *his intransigent attitude led to quarrels with his friends:* uncompromising, inflexible, unbending, unyielding, unshakeable, rigid, unaccommodating, uncooperative, stubborn, obstinate, obdurate, pig-headed, single-minded, iron-willed; informal stiff-necked.
OPPOSITES: compliant.

intrenched adjective. See ENTRENCHED.

intrepid adjective *an intrepid explorer:* fearless, bold, daring, adventurous, unafraid, undaunted, unflinching, unshrinking, audacious, heroic, dynamic, spirited, indomitable; brave, courageous, valiant, valorous, stout-hearted, stalwart, plucky, doughty; informal gutsy, spunky.
OPPOSITES: fearful.

intricate adjective *an intricate design:* complex, complicated, detailed, elaborate, ornate; convoluted, twisted; formal involute; Brit. informal fiddly.
OPPOSITES: simple.

intrigue verb

1 *her answer intrigued him:* interest, fascinate, arouse someone's curiosity, attract.
2 *the ministers intrigued to bring about a resignation:* plot, conspire, make secret plans, scheme, manoeuvre, connive, collude.

▷**noun**
1 *the intrigue that accompanied the selection of a new leader:* plotting, scheming, machinations, conspiracy, subterfuge, conniving, collusion.
2 *the king's intrigues with his nobles' wives:* affair, liaison, amour, fling, flirtation, dalliance.

intriguing adjective *a wealth of intriguing stories appear in this book:* interesting, fascinating, absorbing, compelling, gripping, riveting, captivating, engaging, enthralling.

intrinsic adjective *pride was an intrinsic component of his personal make-up:* inherent, innate, inborn, natural; deep-rooted, indelible, ineradicable; integral, basic, fundamental, essential.

introduce verb

1 *he introduced a new system for the settlement of disputes:* institute, initiate, launch, bring in, set up, put in place, inaugurate, establish, found, originate, pioneer; set in motion, start, get going, get under way.
2 *you can introduce new ideas:* propose, put forward, suggest; raise, broach, bring up, mention, air, float.
3 *she introduced Lindsey to the young man:* present, make known, acquaint with.
4 *a device which introduces chlorine into the pool:* insert, inject, put, force, shoot, feed.
5 *she introduced a note of severity into her voice:* instil, infuse, inject, add.
6 *the same presenter introduces the programme each week:* announce, present, give an introduction to; start off, begin, open.

introduction noun

1 *the introduction of democratic reforms:* institution, establishment, initiation, launch, inauguration, foundation, origination, pioneering; start.
2 *he wished for an introduction to the king:* presentation; meeting with, audience with.
3 *an illustrated catalogue with an introduction by Elizabeth Frank:* foreword, preface, preamble, prologue, prelude; opening statement, beginning; informal intro.
4 *the handbook will include an introduction to the history of the period:* basic explanation, basic account; the basics, the rudiments, the fundamentals.
OPPOSITES: afterword.

introductory adjective

1 *the introductory chapter:* opening, initial, first, initiatory; prefatory, preliminary.
2 *an introductory course:* elementary, basic, rudimentary; preparatory.
OPPOSITES: final, advanced.

introspection noun *a period of quiet introspection can be extremely valuable:* self-analysis, soul-searching; contemplation, meditation, reflection, thoughtfulness, pensiveness; informal navel-gazing.

introspective adjective *a shy and introspective man:* inward-looking, introverted, introvert; contemplative, thoughtful, pensive, meditative, reflective; informal navel-gazing.

introverted adjective *an introverted and thoughtful person:* shy, reserved, withdrawn, reticent, diffident, retiring, quiet; introspective, introvert, inward-looking, self-absorbed; contemplative, thoughtful, pensive, meditative, reflective.
OPPOSITES: extroverted.

intrude verb

1 *they are intruding on people's privacy:* encroach, impinge, trespass; infringe, invade, violate, disturb, disrupt; informal muscle in.
2 *he intruded his own personality into his work:* force, push, obtrude, impose, thrust.

intruder noun trespasser, interloper, invader; burglar, thief, housebreaker.

intrusion noun *she didn't want his constant intrusion into her life:* encroachment; invasion, incursion, intervention, disturbance, disruption, interruption.

intrusive adjective unwelcome, unwanted, obtrusive, uninvited, invasive; prying, inquisitive; informal nosy.

intuition noun

1 *he works according to intuition:* instinct, intuitiveness; sixth sense.
2 *this confirms an intuition I had:* hunch, feeling, inkling, suspicion; premonition, presentiment; informal gut feeling.

intuitive adjective *we have an intuitive sense of right and wrong:* instinctive, instinctual; innate, inborn, inherent, natural; unconscious, subconscious; informal gut.

inundate verb

1 *we have been inundated by complaints:* overwhelm, overload, deluge, swamp, besiege, snow under.
2 *many buildings were inundated:* flood, deluge, swamp, submerge, engulf.

inure verb *they became inured to poverty:* harden, accustom, habituate, familiarize with, acclimatize, adjust, adapt; toughen, condition.
OPPOSITES: sensitize.

invade verb
1 *Napoleon's armies invaded Moscow:*
occupy, capture, seize, take, annex, win,
gain, secure, conquer, take over; enter,
march into, overrun, overwhelm, storm.
2 *he felt his privacy was being invaded:*
intrude on, violate, encroach on,
infringe on, trespass on, obtrude on,
disturb, disrupt; informal muscle in on, horn
in on.
OPPOSITES: withdraw.

invader noun attacker, raider, marauder;
occupier, conqueror; intruder.

invalid¹ noun *my mother is an invalid:* sick
person, valetudinarian.
▷ **adjective** *her invalid husband:* sick, ailing,
unwell, ill, infirm, in poor health, sickly,
poorly; incapacitated, bedridden, frail,
feeble, weak, debilitated.
OPPOSITES: healthy.
▷ **verb** *an officer invalided by a chest wound:*
disable, incapacitate, hospitalize, put out
of action, lay up; injure, wound, hurt.

invalid² adjective
1 *the vote was declared invalid due
to a technicality:* void, null and void,
unenforceable, not binding.
2 *the whole theory is invalid:* false,
incorrect, untrue, fallacious, spurious,
unfounded, ill-founded, unsound, wrong,
untenable; informal full of holes.
OPPOSITES: valid.

invalidate verb
1 *a low turnout invalidated the ballot:*
render invalid, render null and void,
nullify, negate, cancel.
2 *this case invalidates the general
argument:* disprove, refute, contradict,
rebut; explode, discredit, debunk; weaken,
undermine, compromise, belie; informal
shoot full of holes.
OPPOSITES: validate.

invaluable adjective *he is an invaluable
member of the organization:* indispensable,
crucial, key, vital, irreplaceable, all-
important, critical.
OPPOSITES: dispensable.

invariable adjective *his routine was
invariable:* unvarying, unchanging,
unvaried; steady, predictable, regular,
consistent, constant, stable, set, fixed;
unchangeable, unalterable, immutable.
OPPOSITES: variable.

invariably adverb *he is invariably
described as 'down to earth':* always, on
every occasion, at all times, without fail,
without exception; everywhere, in all
cases/instances; regularly, consistently,
repeatedly, habitually, unfailingly.

invasion noun
1 *the invasion of the islands:* occupation,
capture, seizure, annexation, annexing,
takeover; incursion, overrunning,
storming.

2 *the annual invasion of festival-goers:*
influx, incursion, inundation, inrush,
flood, stream, spate.
3 *an invasion of my privacy:* violation,
infringement, interruption, intrusion,
encroachment, disturbance, disruption.
OPPOSITES: withdrawal.

invective noun *he let out a stream of
invective:* abuse, insults, expletives,
swear words, swearing, curses, bad/foul
language, vituperation.

inveigh verb
□ **inveigh against**
*he went on to inveigh against pornography
and violence in the cinema:* denounce,
condemn, censure, decry, criticize;
fulminate against, rail against, protest
about, rage against; informal sound off about.

inveigle verb *he inveigled her back to his
room:* persuade, coax, cajole, wheedle;
tempt, lure, entice, seduce; informal sweet-
talk.

invent verb
1 *Louis Braille invented an alphabet to help
blind people:* create, originate, pioneer,
design, devise, develop, contrive; conceive,
think up, come up with.
2 *they invented the story for a laugh:* make
up, fabricate, concoct, hatch, dream up;
informal cook up.

invention noun
1 *the invention of the telescope:* creation,
origination, development, design,
devising.
2 *medieval inventions included the spinning
wheel:* innovation, creation, design,
contraption, contrivance, device, gadget;
informal brainchild.
3 *a journalistic invention:* fabrication,
concoction, piece of fiction, story, tale;
lie, untruth, falsehood, fib; myth, fantasy;
informal tall story, cock and bull story.

inventive adjective
1 *the most inventive composer of his time:*
creative, original, innovative, imaginative,
ingenious, resourceful.
2 *a fresh, inventive comedy:* original,
innovative, unusual, fresh, novel,
new; experimental, avant-garde,
groundbreaking, unorthodox,
unconventional.
OPPOSITES: unimaginative, hackneyed.

inventor noun originator, creator,
innovator; designer, deviser, developer,
maker, producer; author, architect;
pioneer.

inventory noun *a complete inventory of
all their belongings:* list, listing, catalogue,
record, register, checklist, log, archive.
▷ **verb** *I inventoried his collection:* list,
catalogue, record, register, log.

inverse adjective *studies have shown an
inverse relationship between exercise and
the risk of heart disease:* reverse, reversed,

opposite, converse, contrary, antithetical.
▷**noun** *alkalinity is the inverse of acidity:*
opposite, converse, obverse, antithesis;
informal flip side.

inversion noun *an inversion of the truth:*
reversal, transposition, turning upside
down; reverse, contrary, antithesis,
converse.

invert verb *the crew inverted the yacht's
mast:* **turn upside down**, upturn, upend,
turn around/about, turn back to front,
reverse, flip over.

invest verb
1 *he invested in a cotton mill:* **put money
into**, fund, provide capital for, back, finance,
underwrite; buy into, buy shares in.
2 *they invested £18 million:* **spend**, expend,
put in, plough in; venture, speculate, risk;
informal lay out.
3 *we have invested a great deal of time
and energy in the project:* **devote**, spend,
commit; sacrifice.
4 *he was invested as Head of State on
1 October 1936:* **admit to office**, install,
induct, swear in, instate; ordain, crown.

investigate verb *police are investigating
possible links between a number of
robberies in the area:* **inquire into**, look
into, go into, conduct an investigation
into, make inquiries about, gather
evidence about, probe, explore; scrutinize,
inspect, analyse, study, examine, consider,
research; informal check out.

investigation noun *this claim requires
further investigation | an investigation into
allegations of malpractice:* **examination**,
inquiry, study, exploration, consideration,
analysis, appraisal; research, scrutiny;
probe, review, survey, inspection.

investigator noun *social security fraud
investigators were called in:* **inspector**,
examiner; researcher, factfinder,
scrutineer, scrutinizer; detective.

investment noun
1 *you can lose money by bad investment:*
investing, speculation; funding, backing,
financing, underwriting.
2 *it's a good investment:* **venture**,
speculation, risk, gamble; asset,
acquisition, holding, possession.
3 *the company folded, and his entire
investment went down the drain:* **stake**,
share, money/capital invested, outlay.

inveterate adjective
1 *an inveterate gambler:* **confirmed**,
hardened, incorrigible, addicted,
compulsive, obsessive; informal pathological.
2 *an inveterate supporter of capitalism:*
staunch, steadfast, committed, devoted,
dedicated, dyed-in-the-wool, out-and-out,
diehard.
3 *inveterate hostility:* **ingrained**,
deep-seated, deep-rooted, entrenched,
ineradicable, incurable.

invidious adjective
1 *he had put her in an invidious position:*
unpleasant, awkward, difficult;
undesirable, unenviable.
2 *it seems invidious to single out any
individual performance:* **unfair**, unjust,
unwarranted.

invigorate verb *we were invigorated by
the fresh air:* **revitalize**, energize, refresh,
revive, rejuvenate, enliven, liven up, vivify,
wake up, animate, galvanize, stimulate,
rouse, exhilarate; informal perk up, buck up,
pep up.
OPPOSITES: tire.

invigorating adjective *a brisk,
invigorating walk:* **refreshing**, bracing,
stimulating, energizing, exhilarating,
revitalizing, restorative.

invincible adjective *a seemingly invincible
enemy:* **unbeatable**, unconquerable,
invulnerable, indestructible, indomitable;
unassailable, impregnable, inviolable.
OPPOSITES: vulnerable.

inviolable adjective *the inviolable right
to life:* **inalienable**, absolute, unalterable,
unchallengeable; sacrosanct, holy, sacred.

inviolate adjective *his home remained
inviolate:* **untouched**, undamaged,
unhurt, unharmed, unscathed; unspoiled,
undefiled, perfect, pristine, pure; intact,
unbroken, whole, entire, complete.

invisible adjective **impossible to see**;
undetectable, indiscernible, imperceptible,
inconspicuous; unseen, unnoticed,
unobserved, hidden, obscured, out of
sight.

invitation noun
1 *an invitation to dinner:* **request to
attend**, call, summons; informal invite.
2 *an open door is an invitation to a thief:*
encouragement, temptation, lure, magnet,
bait, enticement, attraction, allure;
provocation; informal come-on.

invite verb
1 *they invited us to lunch:* **ask**, summon,
have someone over/round, request (the
pleasure of) someone's company at.
2 *the chairman invited questions, but none
were forthcoming:* **ask for**, request, call for,
appeal for, seek, solicit.
3 *airing such views invites trouble:*
cause, create, generate, engender, foster,
encourage, lead to; elicit, bring on
yourself, arouse; induce, provoke, incite.

inviting adjective *the sea looked very
inviting:* **tempting**, enticing, alluring,
seductive, beguiling, irresistible;
attractive, appealing, pleasant, agreeable,
delightful; appetizing, mouth-watering.
OPPOSITES: repellent.

invocation noun
1 *the invocation of new disciplines and
methodologies:* **citation**, mention; appeal

to, reference to, allusion to.
2 *the invocation of an evil spirit:*
summoning, calling up, conjuring up.
3 *an invocation to the Holy Ghost:* prayer,
supplication, entreaty, petition, appeal,
intercession.

invoice noun *an invoice for the goods:*
bill, account, statement; N. Amer. check;
informal **tab.**
▷ **verb** *we'll invoice you for the damage:* bill,
charge, send an invoice/bill to.

invoke verb
1 *he invoked his statutory rights:* cite,
refer to, adduce, instance; resort to, have
recourse to, turn to, appeal to.
2 *I invoked the Madonna:* pray to, call on,
appeal to, supplicate, entreat, beg, implore.
3 *they invoked the spirits of their ancestors:*
summon, call up, conjure up.
4 *how could she explain how the accident
happened without invoking his wrath?*
cause, give rise to, evoke, elicit.

involuntary adjective
1 *she gave an involuntary shudder:*
reflex, automatic; spontaneous,
instinctive, unconscious, unintentional,
uncontrollable.
2 *the involuntary repatriation of
immigrants:* compulsory, forced,
obligatory, mandatory, coerced, compelled;
unwilling, unconsenting, against your will.
OPPOSITES: deliberate, optional.

involve verb
1 *the job involves a lot of travelling | any
investment involves an element of risk:*
entail, include, incorporate; require,
necessitate, demand, call for; mean, imply,
presuppose.
2 *the three-year police investigation
involved the whole organization:* include,
bring in, take into account; affect, concern;
cover, encompass, embrace.
3 *he stressed the need for parents to involve
themselves in their child's education:*
participate, take part, play a part, have a
hand in, share, help; engage yourself,
occupy yourself.
OPPOSITES: preclude, exclude.

involved adjective
1 *social workers involved in the case:*
associated, connected, concerned.
2 *a long and involved story:* complicated,
complex, difficult to understand,
elaborate, convoluted, impenetrable.
3 *they were totally involved in their work:*
engrossed, occupied, absorbed, immersed,
caught up, busy, engaged, intent.
4 *she began to take drugs and got involved
in criminal activity:* embroiled, caught up,
mixed up, associated.

involvement noun
1 *his involvement in a plot to overthrow
the government:* participation, action,
hand; collaboration, collusion, complicity;
association, connection, entanglement.

2 *her emotional involvement with Adam:*
attachment, friendship, intimacy;
relationship, relations, bond.

invulnerable adjective *no state in the
region is invulnerable to attack:* safe from,
secure against, proof against; impervious,
immune; invincible, indestructible,
impenetrable, impregnable, unassailable,
inviolable.

inward adjective
1 *our inward flight was delayed:* incoming,
ingoing, inbound, return, homeward.
2 *she felt an inward sense of relief:* inner,
internal, interior, innermost; private,
hidden, secret, concealed, unexpressed.
OPPOSITES: outward.
▷ **adverb** *the door opened inward.* See
INWARDS.

inwardly adverb *inwardly seething, she
did as she was told:* privately, deep down,
in your heart of hearts, internally, within;
secretly.

inwards adverb *light spilled inwards from
the porch:* inside, into the interior, inward,
within.

iota noun *nothing she said seemed to make
an iota of difference:* bit, scrap, shred,
ounce, jot.

irascible adjective *an irascible old man:*
irritable, quick-tempered, short-tempered,
tetchy, testy, touchy, waspish, dyspeptic;
bad-tempered, grouchy, cantankerous,
curmudgeonly, crotchety, crusty; informal
prickly, snappy, snappish.

irate adjective *staff are still fielding
calls from irate customers:* angry,
furious, enraged, infuriated, incensed,
incandescent, fuming, seething, cross;
beside yourself, outraged, up in arms,
indignant, annoyed, irritated, irked; informal
hot under the collar.

iridescent adjective *an iridescent purple
sheen:* shimmering, opalescent, shining,
gleaming, lustrous, luminous.

irk verb *her reticence about certain things
irked him:* irritate, annoy, exasperate,
gall, pique, try someone's patience, get
on someone's nerves, rankle with; anger,
infuriate; Brit. rub up the wrong way; informal
put someone's back up, rile, aggravate,
needle, get to, bug, hack off; Brit. informal
wind up.

irksome adjective irritating, annoying,
exasperating, vexing, vexatious, galling,
infuriating; tiresome, wearisome, trying,
tedious, troublesome.

iron verb
□ **iron something out**
he had ironed out all the minor snags:
resolve, straighten out, sort out, clear up,
settle, put right, solve, remedy, rectify;
eliminate, eradicate, erase, get rid of;
informal fix.

ironic adjective
1 *Edward's tone was ironic:* **sarcastic,** sardonic, dry; wry, mocking, satirical, derisive; Brit. informal sarky.
2 *it's ironic that I've ended up writing for a living:* **paradoxical,** odd, strange, peculiar, unexpected, incongruous.
OPPOSITES: sincere.

irony noun
1 *there was a note of irony in her voice:* **sarcasm;** wryness, mockery, satire.
2 *the irony of the situation:* **paradox,** incongruity, incongruousness.

irrational adjective *she told herself that it was an irrational fear:*
unreasonable, illogical, groundless, baseless, unfounded, unjustifiable; absurd, ridiculous, ludicrous, silly, foolish, senseless.
OPPOSITES: rational.

irreconcilable adjective
1 *these two views of the economy are irreconcilable:* **incompatible,** at odds, at variance, conflicting, clashing, antagonistic, mutually exclusive, diametrically opposed; disparate, variant, dissimilar, poles apart.
2 *irreconcilable enemies:* **implacable,** uncompromising, inflexible; bitter, deadly, sworn, mortal.

irrefutable adjective *there is irrefutable evidence that there will be a shortfall:*
indisputable, undeniable, unquestionable, incontrovertible, incontestable, beyond question, beyond doubt; conclusive, definite, definitive, decisive, certain, positive.

irregular adjective
1 *he had irregular features:* **asymmetrical,** uneven, non-uniform, crooked, lopsided.
2 *the instrument does not read accurately on irregular surfaces:* **rough,** bumpy, uneven, pitted, rutted.
3 *her heartbeat was irregular:* **uneven,** unsteady, fluctuating, erratic, unstable, fitful, inconsistent, variable, varying, changeable, changing, unsettled, spasmodic, intermittent.
4 *irregular financial dealings:* **against the rules,** out of order, improper, illegitimate, unethical, unprofessional, unorthodox, unacceptable; informal shady.
5 *irregular forces launched an attack against the army:* **guerrilla;** paramilitary.
OPPOSITES: regular.

irregularity noun
1 *the irregularity of his features:* **asymmetry,** unevenness, crookedness, lopsidedness.
2 *the irregularity of the surface:* **roughness,** unevenness, bumpiness.
3 *the irregularity of his breathing:* **unevenness,** unsteadiness, fluctuation, fitfulness, inconsistency, instability, variability.

4 *financial irregularities:* **impropriety,** wrongdoing, misconduct, dishonesty, corruption, unprofessional conduct.
5 *staff noted any irregularity in operation:* **abnormality,** anomaly, deviation, aberration, peculiarity.

irrelevant adjective *from a historian's point of view, this question is irrelevant:*
beside the point, immaterial, not pertinent, not germane, off the subject, unconnected, unrelated, extraneous, peripheral, inappropriate; unimportant, inconsequential, insignificant, trivial.
OPPOSITES: relevant.

irreligious adjective **atheistic,** unbelieving, non-believing, agnostic; heretical, faithless, godless, ungodly, impious, profane.
OPPOSITES: religious.

irreparable adjective *if the pump runs dry, irreparable damage can be done:* **irreversible,** permanent, lasting, irretrievable, unrectifiable, irrevocable; beyond repair.

irreplaceable adjective *if you make a mistake you may ruin an irreplaceable recording:* **unique,** priceless, one of a kind; treasured, prized, cherished; informal one-off.

irrepressible adjective
1 *I was gripped by an irrepressible urge to giggle:* **uncontrollable,** overpowering, overwhelming, uncontainable, unstoppable.
2 *his irrepressible personality:* **ebullient,** exuberant, buoyant, high-spirited, vivacious, animated, full of life, lively, bubbly, extrovert, uninhibited.

irreproachable adjective *his private life was irreproachable:* **impeccable,** exemplary, model, above/beyond reproach, blameless, faultless, flawless, unblemished, untarnished, spotless, immaculate, outstanding, exceptional, perfect; informal squeaky clean, whiter than white.
OPPOSITES: reprehensible.

irresistible adjective
1 *her irresistible smile:* **tempting,** enticing, alluring, inviting, seductive; attractive, appealing, desirable, captivating, enchanting, beguiling.
2 *she felt an irresistible urge to laugh:* **uncontrollable,** overwhelming, overpowering, compelling, irrepressible, ungovernable.

irresolute adjective *she stood irresolute outside his door:* **indecisive,** uncertain, undecided, unsure, hesitant, vacillating, equivocating, dithering, wavering; ambivalent, blowing hot and cold, in two minds, in a dilemma, in a quandary, torn.
OPPOSITES: resolute.

irresolution noun indecisiveness, indecision, uncertainty, hesitancy, hesitation, vacillation, equivocation, wavering, dithering.

irrespective adjective *each member has one vote, irrespective of the number of shares held:* regardless of, notwithstanding, without regard to/for, whatever, no matter what; informal irregardless of.

irresponsible adjective
1 *their irresponsible behaviour has put lives at risk:* reckless, thoughtless, inconsiderate, rash, careless, unwise, imprudent, ill-advised, injudicious, misguided, hasty, precipitate, foolhardy, impetuous, impulsive, hot-headed.
2 *an irresponsible teenager:* immature, unreliable, undependable, untrustworthy, feckless.
OPPOSITES: responsible.

irretrievable adjective *the situation was now irretrievable:* irreversible, unrectifiable, irremediable, irrecoverable, irreparable, beyond repair.
OPPOSITES: reversible.

irreverent adjective disrespectful, flippant, facetious, cheeky.
OPPOSITES: respectful.

irreversible adjective *the virus can do irreversible damage to your computer:* permanent, lasting, irreparable, beyond repair, unrectifiable, irremediable, irrevocable; unalterable, unchangeable.

irrevocable adjective *an irrevocable decision:* irreversible, unalterable, unchangeable, immutable, final, binding, permanent.

irrigate verb *the scheme aims to divert water from the river to irrigate the land:* water, bring water to; soak, flood, inundate.

irritability noun *his irritability puts people off:* irascibility, tetchiness, testiness, touchiness, grumpiness, moodiness, cantankerousness, bad temper, short temper.

irritable adjective *being out of work made him irritable:* bad-tempered, short-tempered, irascible, tetchy, testy, touchy, grumpy, grouchy, moody, crotchety, in a bad mood, cantankerous, curmudgeonly, ill-tempered, peevish, cross, fractious, crabby, waspish, prickly, splenetic, dyspeptic, choleric; Brit. informal shirty, stroppy.
OPPOSITES: good-humoured.

irritant noun *the council had clearly been an irritant to the government:* annoyance, irritation, thorn in someone's side/flesh, nuisance, inconvenience, bother, trial; informal aggravation, pain in the neck, headache.

irritate verb
1 *the smallest things may irritate you:* annoy, make angry, make cross, anger, exasperate, irk, vex, gall, pique, put out, antagonize, get on someone's nerves, try someone's patience, make someone's hackles rise, rankle with; infuriate, provoke; Brit. rub up the wrong way; informal rile, aggravate, get to, bug, hack off, needle, put someone's back up.
2 *some sand irritated my eyes:* cause discomfort to, hurt, cause pain to.

irritated adjective *Chris was irritated at the delay:* annoyed, cross, angry, exasperated, vexed, irked, piqued, put out, disgruntled, in a bad mood, in a temper, testy; irate, infuriated; informal aggravated, fed up, peeved, nettled, miffed, hacked off.

irritating adjective *an irritating habit:* annoying, infuriating, exasperating, maddening, trying, tiresome, vexing, vexatious, irksome, galling; informal aggravating.

irritation noun
1 *she tried not to show her irritation:* annoyance, exasperation, indignation, vexation, displeasure, pique, anger.
2 *I realize my presence is an irritation for you:* irritant, annoyance, thorn in someone's side/flesh, nuisance, inconvenience, bother, trial; informal aggravation, pain in the neck, headache.

island noun isle, islet, atoll; (**islands**) archipelago.

> WORD LINKS
> **insular** relating to an island

isolate verb
1 *she isolated herself from her family | the contaminated area was isolated:* separate, set/keep apart, segregate, cut off, shut away, divorce, detach, alienate, distance; keep in solitude, cloister, seclude; cordon off, seal off, close off, fence off.
2 *the laser beam can isolate the offending vehicles:* identify, single out, pick out, point out, spot, recognize, distinguish, pinpoint, locate.

isolated adjective
1 *isolated communities:* remote, out of the way, outlying, secluded, off the beaten track, inaccessible, cut-off, lonely; informal in the back of beyond, in the middle of nowhere, in the sticks.
2 *he lived a very isolated existence:* solitary, lonely, companionless, friendless; secluded, cloistered, segregated; unsociable, reclusive, hermitic.
3 *an isolated incident:* unique, lone, solitary; unusual, uncommon, exceptional, anomalous, abnormal, untypical, freak; informal one-off.
OPPOSITES: accessible.

isolation noun

1 *patients who need isolation:* separation, segregation, seclusion, keeping apart.
2 *their feeling of isolation:* solitariness, loneliness, friendlessness.
3 *the isolation of some villages:* remoteness, seclusion, inaccessibility.

issue noun

1 *the committee discussed the issue yesterday:* matter, matter in question, question, point at issue, affair, case, subject, topic; problem, bone of contention.
2 *the issue of a special stamp:* issuing, publication, publishing; circulation, distribution.
3 *the latest issue of our magazine:* edition, number, instalment, copy.
4 (Law) *she died without issue:* offspring, descendants, heirs, successors, children, progeny, family.

▷ **verb**

1 *the minister issued a statement:* put out, release, deliver, publish, announce, broadcast, communicate, circulate, distribute, disseminate, send out.
2 *the captain issued the crew with guns:* supply, provide, arm, equip, furnish, fit out, rig out, kit out; informal fix up.
3 *savoury smells issued from the kitchen:* emanate, emerge, flow, pour; be emitted, exude.
4 *large profits might issue from the deal:* result, follow, ensue, stem, spring, arise, proceed; be the result of, be brought about by, be produced by.

□ **at issue**
the point at issue is the control and use of Ukraine's oil and gas pipelines: in question, in dispute, under discussion, under consideration, for debate.

□ **take issue**
the Home Secretary took issue with this view: disagree, be in dispute, be in contention, be at variance, be at odds, argue, quarrel; challenge, dispute, call into question, question.

item noun

1 *there were several items for sale:* thing, article, object, artefact, piece, product.
2 *the main item in a badger's diet:* element, constituent, component, ingredient.
3 *the next item on the agenda:* issue, matter, case, subject, topic, question, point.
4 *a news item:* report, story, account, article, piece, write-up, bulletin, feature.
5 *items in the profit and loss account:* entry, record, statement, listing.

itemize verb *Steinburg itemized thirty-two design faults:* list, catalogue, inventory, record, document, register, detail, specify, identify; enumerate, number.

iterate verb *the process is iterated until a convincing agreement is reached:* repeat, go over/through again; recapitulate, recap, restate, reiterate, say again.

itinerant adjective *itinerant traders:* travelling, peripatetic, wandering, roaming; nomadic, migrant; of no fixed address/abode.

itinerary noun *his itinerary included an official visit to Canada:* route, journey; travel plan, schedule, timetable, programme, tour.

i

Jj

jab verb *he jabbed the man with his finger:* poke, prod, dig, nudge, ram; thrust, stab, push.
▷**noun** *a jab in the ribs:* poke, prod, dig, nudge; thrust, stab, push.

jabber verb *she jabbered on about her wonderful husband:* chatter, gabble, rattle on/away, babble, prattle, twitter, prate, blather; informal yak; Brit. informal witter, rabbit, natter.

jack verb
□ **jack something up**
they jacked up the car: raise, hoist, lift up, winch up, lever up, elevate.

jacket noun *a jacket for your hot-water tank will save at least £15 a year:* casing, cover, covering, wrapping, wrapper, sleeve, sheath.

jackpot noun *this week's lottery jackpot:* top prize, first prize, bonanza.
□ **hit the jackpot** (informal)
win a fortune, be successful, strike it rich; informal clean up, hit the big time.

jaded adjective
1 *she felt really jaded:* tired, tired out, weary, worn out, exhausted, fatigued, wearied, sapped, drained, spent; informal all in, done in, dead on your feet, bushed; Brit. informal knackered, whacked.
2 *a jaded palate:* satiated, sated, surfeited, glutted; dulled, blunted, deadened.
OPPOSITES: fresh.

jagged adjective spiky, barbed, rough, uneven, irregular, broken, ragged; serrated, sawtooth, indented.
OPPOSITES: smooth.

jail noun *they spent 15 years in jail:* prison, penal institution, lock-up, detention centre; N. Amer. penitentiary, jailhouse; informal slammer, clink; Brit. informal nick.
▷**verb** *the driver was jailed for 2 years:* imprison, put in prison, send to prison, incarcerate, lock up, put away, intern, detain; informal send down, put behind bars, put inside; Brit. informal bang up.

jailer noun prison officer, warder, wardress, warden, guard; informal screw.

jam¹ verb
1 *she jammed her fists into her pockets:*

shove, force, ram, thrust, press, push, stick, stuff, squeeze, cram.
2 *four of us were jammed in one compartment:* squeeze, pack, cram, stuff.
3 *the streets were jammed with tourist coaches:* crowd, throng, mob, fill, overcrowd, obstruct, block, clog, congest.
4 *the rudder had jammed:* stick, become stuck, catch, seize up, become trapped.
5 *dust can jam the mechanism:* immobilize, paralyse, disable, cripple, put out of action, bring to a standstill.
▷**noun**
1 *a traffic jam:* tailback, hold-up, congestion, bottleneck; N. Amer. gridlock; Brit. informal snarl-up.
2 (informal) *we are in a real jam:* predicament, plight, tricky situation, difficulty, problem, quandary, dilemma, muddle, mess; informal pickle, fix, hole, bind, tight spot, tight corner, hot/deep water.

jam² noun *raspberry jam:* preserve, conserve, jelly, marmalade.

jamb noun post, doorpost, upright, frame.

jamboree noun festival, party, celebration, fiesta, gala, carnival, fete; informal bash, shindig, junket.

jangle verb
1 *a bell jangled loudly:* ring, jingle, clink, tinkle.
2 *the noise jangled her nerves:* grate on, jar on, irritate, disturb, fray, put/set on edge.
▷**noun** *the shrill jangle of the doorbell:* ringing, jangling, jingling, tinkling, tintinnabulation.

janitor noun caretaker, custodian, porter, concierge, doorkeeper, doorman, warden; cleaner, maintenance man.

jar¹ noun *a jar of honey:* pot, crock, container.

jar² verb
1 *each step jarred my whole body:* jolt, jerk, shake, vibrate.
2 *her shrill voice jarred on him:* grate, set someone's teeth on edge, irritate, annoy, irk; informal rile, aggravate, get on someone's nerves.
3 *the play's symbolism jarred with the realism of its setting:* clash, conflict,

contrast, be incompatible, be at variance, be at odds, be inconsistent, be discordant.

jargon noun *legal jargon:* specialized language, technical language, idiom, parlance, argot; informal gobbledegook, lingo, -speak, -ese.

jarring adjective clashing, conflicting, contrasting, incompatible, incongruous; discordant, dissonant, inharmonious, harsh, grating, strident, shrill, cacophonous.
OPPOSITES: harmonious.

jaundiced adjective *a jaundiced view of the world:* bitter, resentful, cynical, sour, disenchanted, disillusioned, pessimistic, sceptical, distrustful, suspicious, misanthropic.

jaunt noun *their weekend jaunts to the country:* trip, outing, excursion, day trip, day out, mini-break; tour, drive, ride, run; informal spin.

jaunty adjective *he wore a cap pushed to one side to give him a jaunty air:* cheerful, cheery, happy, merry, jolly; lively, perky, bright, buoyant, bouncy, breezy, full of the joys of spring, in good spirits, exuberant, ebullient; carefree, airy, light-hearted, nonchalant, insouciant, happy-go-lucky; informal bright-eyed and bushy-tailed, full of beans, chirpy.
OPPOSITES: depressed, serious.

jaw noun
1 *a broken jaw:* jawbone; Anatomy mandible, maxilla.
2 *the whale seized a seal pup in its jaws:* mouth, maw.

jazz verb
□ **jazz something up** (informal) *jazz up your documents with a few unusual typefaces:* enliven, liven up, brighten up, make more interesting/exciting, add (some) colour to, ginger up, spice up; informal perk up, pep up.

jazzy adjective *jazzy ties:* bright, colourful, brightly coloured, striking, eye-catching, vivid, lively, vibrant, bold, flamboyant, showy, gaudy; informal flashy.
OPPOSITES: dull.

jealous adjective
1 *he was jealous of his brother's popularity:* envious, resentful, grudging, begrudging, green with envy, covetous.
2 *a jealous lover:* suspicious, distrustful, mistrustful, doubting, insecure; possessive, proprietorial, overprotective.
3 *they are very jealous of their rights:* protective, vigilant, watchful, heedful, mindful, careful, solicitous.

jealousy noun
1 *he was consumed with jealousy:* envy, resentment, resentfulness, bitterness, covetousness; informal the green-eyed monster.
2 *her married life was ruined by his*

unnecessary jealousy: suspicion, suspiciousness, distrust, mistrust, insecurity; possessiveness, overprotectiveness.

jeer verb *demonstrators jeered at the police:* taunt, mock, scoff at, ridicule, sneer at, deride, insult, abuse, shout abuse at, jibe at; heckle, boo; Brit. barrack.
OPPOSITES: cheer.
▷noun *the jeers of the crowd:* taunt, sneer, insult, shout, jibe, boo, catcall; abuse, heckling, catcalling, derision; Brit. barracking.
OPPOSITES: applause.

jell verb see GEL.

jeopardize verb *devaluing the dollar would jeopardize New York's position as a financial centre:* threaten, endanger, imperil, risk, put at risk, put in danger/ jeopardy; leave vulnerable; compromise, prejudice, be prejudicial to; be a danger to, pose a threat to.
OPPOSITES: safeguard.

jeopardy noun
□ **in jeopardy**
the peace talks are in jeopardy: in danger, at risk, under threat, vulnerable, in peril.

jerk noun
1 *she gave the reins a jerk:* tug, yank, pull, wrench, tweak, twitch, jog.
2 *he let the clutch in with a jerk:* jolt, lurch, bump, start, bounce, shake, shock.
▷verb
1 *she jerked her arm free:* pull, tug, yank, wrench, wrest, drag, pluck, snatch, seize, rip, tear.
2 *the car jerked along:* jolt, lurch, bump, rattle, bounce, shake, jounce.

jerky adjective
1 *jerky movements:* convulsive, spasmodic, fitful, twitchy, shaky.
2 *the coach drew to a jerky halt:* jolting, lurching, bumpy, bouncy, jarring.
OPPOSITES: smooth.

jerry-built adjective *jerry-built shacks:* shoddy, badly built, flimsy, rickety, ramshackle, crude, makeshift; inferior, poor-quality, second-rate, third-rate.
OPPOSITES: sturdy.

jersey noun pullover, sweater; Brit. jumper; informal woolly.

jest noun joke, witticism, funny remark, gag, quip, sally, pun; informal crack, wise-crack, one-liner.
▷verb joke, tease; informal josh, kid, have someone on, pull someone's leg.
□ **in jest**
in fun, as a joke, tongue in cheek, playfully, jokingly, light-heartedly, facetiously, flippantly, for a laugh.

jester noun joker, comedian, comic, humorist, wag, wit, prankster, jokester, clown.

j

jet¹ noun

1 *a jet of water:* stream, spurt, spray, squirt, spout; gush, rush, surge, burst.
2 *carburettor jets:* nozzle, head, spout.
3 *an executive jet:* jet plane, jetliner; aircraft, plane; Brit. aeroplane.

▷verb

1 *they jetted out of Heathrow:* fly, travel/go by jet, travel/go by plane.
2 *puffs of gas jetted out:* squirt, spurt, shoot, spray; gush, pour, stream, rush, pump, surge, spew, burst.

jet² adjective *her glossy jet hair:* black, jet-black, pitch-black, ebony, raven, sable, sooty.

jettison verb

1 *six aircraft jettisoned their loads:* dump, drop, discharge, throw out, tip out, unload, throw overboard; informal ditch.
2 *he jettisoned his unwanted papers | the scheme was jettisoned:* discard, dispose of, throw away/out, get rid of; reject, scrap, abandon, drop, axe; informal chuck away/out, dump, ditch.
OPPOSITES: retain.

jetty noun pier, landing stage, quay, wharf, dock; breakwater, mole, groyne.

jewel noun

1 *priceless jewels:* gem, gemstone, precious stone, brilliant; informal sparkler, rock.
2 *the jewel of his collection:* finest example/specimen, showpiece, pride, cream, crème de la crème, jewel in the crown, nonpareil, glory, prize, boast, pick, ne plus ultra.
3 *the girl is a jewel:* treasure, angel, paragon, marvel, find, godsend; informal one in a million.

jewellery noun jewels, gems, gemstones, precious stones, costume jewellery.

jib verb

1 *some farmers jib at paying large veterinary bills:* baulk at, fight shy of, recoil from, shrink from; be unwilling, be reluctant, be loath, demur at.
2 *the horse jibbed at the final fence:* stop (short) at, baulk at, shy at; refuse.

jibe noun *a jibe at his old rivals:* snide remark, cutting remark, taunt, sneer, jeer, insult, barb; informal dig, put-down.
▷verb *some cynics in the media may jibe at him:* jeer, taunt, mock, scoff, sneer.

jig verb *Joe jigged about with excitement:* jump, bob, spring, skip, hop, prance, bounce.

jiggle verb

1 *he jiggled his foot:* shake, joggle, waggle, wiggle.
2 *Thomas jiggled excitedly:* fidget, wriggle, squirm.

jilt verb leave, walk out on, abandon, throw over, break up with; Brit. finish with; informal chuck, ditch, dump, run out on, give someone the push/elbow, give someone the big E.

jingle noun

1 *the jingle of money in the till:* clink, chink, jangle.
2 *the jingle of the bell:* tinkling, ringing, ding, ping, ting-a-ling, chime, tintinnabulation.
3 *advertising jingles:* slogan, catchphrase; ditty, song, rhyme, tune.

▷verb

1 *her bracelets jingled noisily:* jangle, clink, chink.
2 *the bell jingled:* tinkle, ring, ding, ping, chime.

jingoism noun militarism, hawkishness, belligerence, bellicosity; chauvinism, xenophobia; nationalism, patriotism.

jinx noun curse, spell, malediction, hoodoo; bad luck; N. Amer. hex.
▷verb *the family is jinxed:* curse, cast a spell on, put the evil eye on, hoodoo.

job noun

1 *my job involves a lot of travelling:* position, post, situation, appointment, employment; occupation, profession, trade, career, work, métier, craft; vocation, calling; vacancy, opening.
2 *this job will take three months:* task, piece of work, assignment, project, chore, errand; undertaking, venture, operation, enterprise, business.
3 *it's your job to protect her:* responsibility, duty, charge, role, function, mission.

jobless adjective unemployed, out of work, out of a job, unwaged, between jobs, redundant; Brit. informal signing on, on the dole.
OPPOSITES: employed.

jockey verb *ministers began jockeying for position:* compete, contend, vie, struggle, fight, scramble, jostle.

jocular adjective humorous, funny, witty, comic, comical, amusing, droll, jokey, hilarious, facetious, tongue-in-cheek, teasing, playful; light-hearted, jovial, cheerful, cheery, merry.
OPPOSITES: solemn.

jog verb

1 *he jogged along the road:* run slowly, trot, lope, jogtrot, dogtrot.
2 *things are jogging along quite nicely:* continue, proceed, go on, carry on.
3 *a hand jogged his elbow:* nudge, prod, poke, push, bump, jar.
4 *something jogged her memory:* stimulate, prompt, stir, activate, refresh.
5 *she jogged her foot up and down:* joggle, jiggle, bob, bounce, jolt, jerk.

joie de vivre noun gaiety, cheerfulness, cheeriness, light-heartedness, happiness, joy, joyfulness, high spirits, jollity, joviality, exuberance, ebullience, liveliness, vivacity, verve, effervescence, buoyancy, zest, zestfulness; informal pep, zing.
OPPOSITES: sobriety.

join verb

1 *the two parts of the mould are joined with clay:* connect, unite, couple, fix, affix, attach, fasten, stick, glue, fuse, weld, amalgamate, bond, append, link, merge, secure, make fast, tie, bind, chain.
2 *here the path joins a major road:* meet, touch, reach, abut, adjoin; border.
3 *I joined the demonstration:* take part in, participate in, help in, join in, get involved in, contribute to, have a hand in, play a part in.
4 *she joined the army last year:* become a member of, enlist in, volunteer for, enrol in, sign up for, affiliate yourself to; join up.
5 *they joined up with a group of local environmentalists:* join forces, unite, get together, ally, team up.
OPPOSITES: separate, leave.
▷**noun** see JOINT.

joint noun *a leaky joint in the guttering:*
join, junction, juncture, intersection, link, linkage, connection; weld, seam.
▷**adjective** *matters of joint interest | a joint effort to boost tourism:* common, shared, communal, collective; mutual, cooperative, collaborative, concerted, combined, united.
OPPOSITES: separate.

jointly adverb *a survey organized jointly by the WWF and the Forestry Commission:*
together, in partnership, in cooperation, cooperatively, in conjunction, in combination, mutually.

joke noun

1 *do you know any good jokes?* funny story, jest, witticism, quip; pun, play on words; informal gag, wisecrack, crack, funny, one-liner.
2 *the others were playing a joke on her:* trick, practical joke, prank, stunt, hoax, jape; informal leg-pull, spoof.
3 (informal) *he soon became a joke to us:* laughing stock, figure of fun, object of ridicule; Brit. Aunt Sally.
4 (informal) *the present system is a joke:* farce, travesty, waste of time.
▷**verb**
1 *she joked with the guests:* tell jokes, jest, banter, quip; informal wisecrack, josh.
2 *I'm only joking:* fool about/around, play a trick, play a joke, tease, hoax, mess about/around; informal kid, have someone on, pull someone's leg; Brit. informal wind someone up.

joker noun humorist, wit, comedian,
comedienne, comic, jester; prankster, practical joker, hoaxer, trickster, clown; informal card, wag.

jolly adjective cheerful, happy, cheery,
good-humoured, jovial, merry, sunny, joyful, light-hearted, in high spirits, lively, bubbly, exuberant, ebullient, cock-a-hoop, gleeful, genial, fun-loving; literary joyous; informal chirpy, perky, bright-eyed and bushy-tailed.
OPPOSITES: miserable.

▷**verb** (informal) *he tried to jolly her along:* encourage, urge, coax, cajole, persuade.

jolt verb

1 *the train jolted the passengers to one side:* push, thrust, jar, bump, knock, bang; shake, joggle, jog.
2 *the car jolted along:* bump, bounce, jerk, rattle, lurch, shudder, judder, jounce.
3 *she was jolted out of her reverie:* startle, surprise, shock, stun, shake, take aback; astonish, astound, amaze, stagger, stop someone in their tracks; informal rock, floor, knock sideways; Brit. informal knock for six.
▷**noun**
1 *a series of sickening jolts:* bump, bounce, shake, jerk, lurch.
2 *he woke up with a jolt:* start, jerk, jump.
3 *the sight of the dagger gave him a jolt:* fright, the fright of your life, shock, scare, surprise; informal turn.

jostle verb

1 *she was jostled by noisy students:* bump into/against, knock into/against, bang into, cannon into, plough into, jolt; push, shove, elbow; mob.
2 *I jostled my way to the exit:* push, thrust, barge, shove, force, elbow, shoulder, bulldoze.
3 *people jostled for the best position:* struggle, vie, jockey, scramble.

jot verb *I've jotted down a few details:* write,
note, make a note of, take down, put on paper; scribble, scrawl.
▷**noun** *there's not a jot of evidence:* iota, scrap, shred, whit, grain, crumb, ounce, bit, speck, atom, particle, scintilla, trace, hint; informal smidgen.

journal noun

1 *a medical journal:* periodical, magazine, gazette, digest, review, newsletter, news-sheet, bulletin; newspaper, paper; daily, weekly, monthly, quarterly.
2 *he keeps a journal:* diary, daily record, log, weblog, blog, logbook, chronicle.

journalism noun

1 *a career in journalism:* the newspaper business, the press, the fourth estate; Brit. Fleet Street.
2 *his incisive style of journalism:* reporting, writing, reportage, feature writing, news coverage; articles, reports, features, pieces, stories.

journalist noun reporter, correspondent,
newspaperman, newspaperwoman, newsman, newswoman, columnist, writer, commentator, reviewer; Brit. pressman; informal news hound, hack, hackette, stringer, journo.

journey noun *his journey round the world:* trip, expedition, tour, trek, voyage,
cruise, ride, drive; crossing, passage, flight; travels, wandering, globetrotting, odyssey, pilgrimage.
▷**verb** *they journeyed south:* travel, go, sail,

j

cruise, voyage, fly, ride, drive, make your way, hike, trek; go on a trip/expedition, tour.

jovial adjective *his jovial manner:* cheerful, jolly, happy, cheery, good-humoured, convivial, genial, good-natured, friendly, amiable, affable, sociable, outgoing; smiling, merry, sunny, joyful, high-spirited, exuberant; literary joyous; informal chirpy, perky, bright-eyed and bushy-tailed.
OPPOSITES: miserable.

joy noun
1 *whoops of joy:* delight, great pleasure, joyfulness, jubilation, triumph, exultation, rejoicing, happiness, gladness, glee, exhilaration, exuberance, elation, euphoria, bliss, ecstasy, rapture; enjoyment, joie de vivre.
2 *it was a joy to be with her:* pleasure, delight, treat, thrill; informal buzz, kick.
OPPOSITES: misery, trial.

joyful adjective
1 *his joyful mood:* cheerful, happy, jolly, merry, sunny, light-hearted, in good spirits, bubbly, exuberant, ebullient, cock-a-hoop, cheery, smiling, radiant; jubilant, overjoyed, thrilled, ecstatic, euphoric, blissful, on cloud nine, elated, delighted, gleeful; jovial, genial, good-humoured, full of the joys of spring; literary joyous; informal chirpy, over the moon, on top of the world.
2 *joyful news:* pleasing, happy, good, cheering, gladdening, welcome, heart-warming.
3 *a joyful occasion:* happy, cheerful, merry, jolly, festive; literary joyous.
OPPOSITES: sad, distressing.

joyless adjective
1 *a joyless man:* gloomy, melancholy, morose, lugubrious, glum, sombre, saturnine, sullen, dour, humourless.
2 *a joyless room:* depressing, cheerless, gloomy, dreary, bleak, dispiriting, drab, dismal, austere, sombre; unwelcoming, uninviting, inhospitable.
OPPOSITES: cheerful, welcoming.

joyous adjective (literary) see JOYFUL senses 1, 3.

jubilant adjective *crowds of jubilant fans ran on to the pitch:* overjoyed, exultant, triumphant, joyful, rejoicing, cock-a-hoop, exuberant, elated, thrilled, gleeful, euphoric, ecstatic, enraptured, in raptures, walking on air, in seventh heaven, on cloud nine; informal over the moon, on top of the world, on a high.
OPPOSITES: despondent.

jubilation noun exultation, joy, elation, euphoria, ecstasy, rapture, glee, gleefulness, exuberance; literary joyousness.

jubilee noun anniversary, commemoration; celebration, festival; festivities, revelry.

Judas noun traitor, betrayer, back-stabber, double-crosser.

judge noun
1 *the judge sentenced him to five years:* justice, magistrate, recorder; Scottish sheriff; Brit. informal beak.
2 *a panel of judges will select the winner:* adjudicator, arbiter, assessor, evaluator, appraiser, examiner, moderator.
▷**verb**
1 *I judged that she was simply exhausted:* form the opinion, conclude, decide, deduce, consider, believe, think, deem, gather, infer, gauge, estimate, guess, surmise, conjecture; regard as, look on as, take to be, rate as, class as; informal reckon, figure.
2 *the case was judged by a tribunal:* try, hear; adjudicate, decide, give a ruling/verdict on.
3 *she was judged innocent of murder:* adjudge, pronounce, decree, rule, find.
4 *the competition will be judged by Alan Amey:* adjudicate, arbitrate, moderate.
5 *entries were judged by a panel of experts:* assess, appraise, evaluate, examine, review.

judgement noun
1 *his temper could affect his judgement:* discernment, acumen, shrewdness, astuteness, common sense, perception, perspicacity, acuity, discrimination, wisdom, wit, judiciousness, prudence, sharpness, sharp-wittedness, powers of reasoning, reason, logic; informal nous, savvy, horse sense, gumption; Brit. informal common; N. Amer. informal smarts.
2 *a court judgement:* verdict, decision, adjudication, ruling, pronouncement, decree, finding; sentence.
3 *critical judgement:* assessment, evaluation, appraisal; review, analysis, criticism, critique.
▫**against your better judgement**
reluctantly, unwillingly, grudgingly.
▫**in my judgement**
in my opinion, in my estimation, to my mind, I believe, I think, as I see it, it seems to me.

judgemental adjective *I don't like to sound judgemental, but it really was a big mistake:* critical, censorious, condemnatory, disapproving, disparaging, negative, overcritical, hypercritical.

judicial adjective *a judicial inquiry:* legal, official; Law juridical.

judicious adjective *a judicious course of action:* wise, sensible, prudent, politic, shrewd, astute, canny, well advised, well judged, commonsensical, sound, expedient.
OPPOSITES: ill-advised.

USAGE

Do not confuse **judicious** and **judicial**. **Judicious** means 'having or done with good judgement', whereas **judicial** means 'relating to a law court or judge' (*there will be a judicial inquiry into the allegations*).

jug noun pitcher, ewer, crock, jar, urn; carafe, flask, flagon, decanter.

juggle verb *defence chiefs juggled the figures on bomb tests:* manipulate, alter, massage, tamper with, falsify, distort, rig, fudge; informal fix, doctor; Brit. informal fiddle.

juice noun
1 *the juice from two lemons:* liquid, fluid, sap; extract.
2 *cooking juices:* liquid, liquor.

juicy adjective
1 *a juicy peach:* succulent, tender, moist; ripe.
2 (informal) *juicy gossip:* very interesting, fascinating, sensational, lurid, colourful; scandalous, racy, risqué, spicy; informal hot.
OPPOSITES: dry, dull.

jumble noun
1 *the books were in a jumble:* untidy heap, clutter, muddle, mess, confusion, disarray, tangle; hotchpotch, miscellany, motley collection, mixed bag; informal mishmash.
2 (Brit.) *bags of jumble:* junk, bric-a-brac; Brit. lumber.
▷verb *the photographs are all jumbled up:* mix up, muddle up, mess up, disarrange, disorganize, disorder, throw into disarray.

jumbo adjective (informal) see HUGE.

jump verb
1 *the cat jumped off his lap | Flora began to jump about:* leap, spring, bound, hop; skip, caper, dance, prance, frolic, cavort.
2 *he jumped the fence:* vault over, leap over, clear, sail over, hop over, hurdle.
3 *pre-tax profits jumped:* rise, go up, shoot up, soar, surge, climb, increase; informal skyrocket.
4 *the noise made her jump:* start, jerk, jolt, flinch, recoil; informal jump out of your skin.
5 *Polly jumped at the chance:* accept eagerly, leap at, seize on, snap up, grab, pounce on.
▷noun
1 *the short jump across the gully:* leap, spring, vault, bound, hop.
2 *the horse cleared the last jump:* obstacle, barrier; fence, hurdle.
3 *a jump in profits:* rise, leap, increase, surge, upsurge, upswing; informal hike.
4 *I woke up with a jump:* start, jerk, involuntary movement, spasm.
▢ jump the gun (informal) act prematurely, act too soon, be overhasty, be precipitate; informal be ahead of yourself.

jumper noun (Brit.) sweater, pullover, jersey; informal woolly.

jumpy adjective (informal) *he was tired and jumpy:* nervous, on edge, edgy, tense, anxious, ill at ease, uneasy, restless, fidgety, keyed up, overwrought, on tenterhooks; Brit. nervy; informal a bundle of nerves, jittery, like a cat on a hot tin roof, uptight, het up; Brit. informal like a cat on hot bricks.
OPPOSITES: calm.

junction noun
1 *the junction between the roof and the wall:* join, joint, intersection, seam, connection, juncture.
2 *the junction of the two rivers:* confluence, convergence, meeting point, juncture.
3 *turn right at the next junction:* crossroads, intersection, interchange, T-junction; turn, turn-off, exit; Brit. roundabout.

juncture noun *at this juncture, I am unable to tell you:* point, time, moment; period, phase.

jungle noun tropical forest, rainforest.

junior adjective
1 *the junior members of the family:* younger, youngest.
2 *a junior minister:* low-ranking, lower-ranking, subordinate, lesser, lower, minor.
OPPOSITES: senior, older.

junk (informal) noun *an attic full of junk:* rubbish, clutter, bric-a-brac; refuse, litter, scrap, waste, debris, detritus; Brit. lumber; N. Amer. garbage, trash; informal bits and pieces; Brit. informal odds and ends.
▷verb *junk all the rubbish:* throw away/ out, get rid of, dispose of, discard, scrap, jettison; informal chuck away/out, dump, ditch, bin.

junta noun *the military junta took power in a coup last February:* faction, group, cabal, set, ring, gang, league, confederacy.

jurisdiction noun
1 *an area under French jurisdiction:* authority, control, power, dominion, rule, administration, command, sway, leadership, sovereignty, hegemony.
2 *foreign jurisdictions:* territory, region, province, district, area, domain, realm.

just adjective
1 *a just decision | a just and democratic society:* fair, right, equitable, fair-minded, even-handed, impartial, unbiased, objective, neutral, disinterested, unprejudiced, open-minded, non-partisan; honourable.
2 *a just reward:* well deserved, well earned, merited; rightful, due, fitting, appropriate, suitable.
3 *just criticism:* valid, sound, well founded, justified, justifiable, warranted, legitimate.
OPPOSITES: unfair, undeserved.
▷adverb
1 *I just saw him:* a moment/second ago, a short time ago, very recently, not long ago.
2 *she's just right for him:* exactly, precisely, absolutely, completely, totally, entirely,

j

perfectly, utterly, wholly, thoroughly, in all respects; informal down to the ground, to a T, dead.

3 *we just made it:* narrowly, only just, by a hair's breadth; barely, scarcely, hardly; informal by the skin of your teeth, by a whisker.

4 *she's just a child:* only, merely, simply, nothing but, no more than.

□ **just about** (informal)
nearly, almost, practically, all but, virtually, as good as, more or less; informal pretty much.

justice noun

1 *I appealed to his sense of justice:* fairness, justness, fair play, fair-mindedness, equity, even-handedness, impartiality, objectivity, neutrality, disinterestedness; morals, morality.

2 *we are convinced of the justice of his case:* validity, justification, soundness, well foundedness, legitimacy.

3 *an order made by the justices:* judge, magistrate, recorder; Scottish sheriff; Brit. informal beak.

> WORD LINKS
> **judicial** relating to a law court or a system of justice

justifiable adjective
valid, legitimate, warranted, well founded, justified, just, reasonable; defensible, tenable, supportable, acceptable.
OPPOSITES: indefensible.

justification noun
the justification for government action: grounds, reason, basis, rationale, premise, rationalization, vindication, explanation; defence, argument, apologia, apology, case.

justify verb

1 *directors must justify the expenditure:* give grounds for, give reasons for, give a justification for, explain, give an explanation for, account for; defend, answer for, vindicate.

2 *the situation justified further investigation:* warrant, be good reason for, be a justification for.

justly adverb

1 *he is justly proud of his achievement:* justifiably, with reason, legitimately, rightly, rightfully, deservedly.

2 *they were treated justly:* fairly, with fairness, equitably, even-handedly, impartially, without bias, objectively, without prejudice; informal fairly and squarely.
OPPOSITES: unjustifiably, unfairly.

jut verb *a rock jutted out from the side of the bank:* stick out, project, protrude, bulge out, extend, overhang.

juvenile adjective

1 *juvenile offenders:* young, teenage, adolescent.

2 *juvenile behaviour:* childish, immature, puerile, infantile, babyish, foolish, stupid, silly.
OPPOSITES: adult, mature.

▷ **noun** *many victims are juveniles:* young person, child, teenager, adolescent, minor, youngster; informal kid.
OPPOSITES: adult.

juxtapose verb *her work juxtaposes images from serious and popular art:* place side by side, set side by side, mix; compare, contrast.

Kk

kaleidoscopic adjective

1 *the branches refracted the light into kaleidoscopic shapes on the pavement:* multicoloured, many-coloured, multicolour, many-hued, variegated, particoloured, varicoloured, psychedelic, rainbow.
2 *the country's kaleidoscopic political landscape:* ever-changing, changeable, shifting, fluid, protean, variable, inconstant, fluctuating, unpredictable, impermanent.
3 *the kaleidoscopic world we are living in:* multifaceted, varied; complex, intricate, complicated.
OPPOSITES: monochrome, constant.

keel noun *the upturned keel of the boat:* base, bottom, underside.
□ **keel over**
collapse, faint, pass out, black out, lose consciousness; literary swoon.

keen adjective

1 *she's keen to get back to work:* eager, anxious, impatient, determined, intent on; informal raring, itching, dying.
2 *a keen birdwatcher:* enthusiastic, avid, eager, ardent, passionate, fervent, zealous, fervid; conscientious, committed, dedicated.
3 *he made it obvious that he was keen on her:* interested in, attracted to, fond of, taken with, smitten with, enamoured of, infatuated with, passionate about; informal struck on, mad about, crazy about.
4 *an able administrator with a keen mind:* acute, sharp, razor-sharp, penetrating, incisive, perceptive, astute, shrewd, discerning, clever, intelligent, canny, percipient, perspicacious, insightful.
5 *she felt a keen sense of loss:* intense, acute, strong, powerful, fierce, burning.
OPPOSITES: reluctant, unenthusiastic.

keenness noun

1 *his keenness to get his message across:* eagerness, readiness, impatience; enthusiasm, avidity, fervour, wholeheartedness, zest, zeal, ardour, passion.
2 *the keenness of his mind:* acuity, sharpness, perceptiveness, astuteness, incisiveness, perspicacity, shrewdness, insight, intelligence.

3 *the keenness of his sense of loss:* intensity, acuteness, strength.

keep¹ verb

1 *he kept the ticket stub as a souvenir | you should keep all the old forms:* retain, hold on to, keep hold of, not part with; save, store, put by/aside, set aside; informal hang on to, stash away.
2 *I tried to keep calm:* remain, continue to be, stay, carry on being, persist in being.
3 *he keeps going on about the murder:* persist in, keep on, carry on, continue.
4 *I shan't keep you long:* detain, keep waiting, delay, hold up, slow down.
5 *most people kept the rules | he had to keep his promise:* comply with, obey, observe, conform to, abide by, adhere to, stick to, heed, follow; fulfil, carry out, act on, make good, honour, keep to, stand by.
6 *I like to keep the old traditions:* preserve, keep alive/up, keep going, carry on, perpetuate, maintain, uphold.
7 *the stand where her umbrella was kept:* store, house, stow, put, place, deposit.
8 *he is forced to steal to keep his family:* provide for, support, feed, keep alive, maintain, sustain; take care of, look after.
9 *she keeps rabbits:* breed, rear, raise, farm; own.
10 *today's consumers do not keep the Sabbath:* observe, respect, honour, hold sacred; celebrate, mark, commemorate.
OPPOSITES: throw away, break, abandon.
▷ noun *he had no money to pay for his keep:* maintenance, upkeep, sustenance, board and lodging, food, livelihood.
□ **keep at**
start work early and keep at it until lunchtime: persevere with, persist with, keep going with, carry on with, press on with, work away at, continue with; informal stick at, peg away at, plug away at, hammer away at.
□ **keep something back**
1 *every week she kept back some of the money he gave her:* keep in reserve, put by/aside, set aside; retain, hold back, keep, hold on to, not part with; informal stash away.
2 *she kept back the gory details:* conceal, keep secret, keep hidden, withhold, suppress, keep quiet about.

k

3 *she could hardly keep back her tears:* suppress, stifle, choke back, fight back, hold back/in, repress, keep in check, contain, smother, swallow, bite back.
□ **keep from**
she bit her lip to keep from screaming: refrain from, stop yourself, restrain yourself from, prevent yourself from, avoid, forbear from.
□ **keep someone from something**
1 *he could hardly keep himself from laughing:* prevent, stop, restrain, hold back.
2 *keep them from harm:* preserve, protect, keep safe, guard, shield, shelter, safeguard, defend.
□ **keep something from someone**
now you know what your mother tried to keep from you: keep secret, keep hidden, hide, conceal, withhold; informal keep dark.
□ **keep off**
1 *keep off my land:* stay off, not enter, keep/stay away from, not trespass on.
2 *I tried to keep off political subjects:* avoid, steer clear of, stay away from, evade, sidestep.
3 *you should keep off alcohol:* abstain from, do without, refrain from, give up, forgo, not touch; formal forswear; informal swear off.
4 *I hope the rain keeps off:* stay away, hold off, not start.
□ **keep on**
1 *they preferred to keep on working:* continue, go on, carry on, persist in, persevere in; soldier on, struggle on, keep going.
2 *the commander kept on about the need for vigilance:* talk constantly, talk endlessly, keep talking, go on, rant on; informal harp on.
□ **keep someone on**
the boss decided to keep him on: continue to employ, retain in your service, not dismiss, not sack.
□ **keep on at**
they kept on at him to hurry up: nag, go on at, harp on at, badger, chivvy, harass, hound, pester; informal hassle.
□ **keep something up**
keep up the good work: continue, keep on with, keep going, carry on with, persist with, persevere with.
□ **keep up with**
1 *she walked fast to keep up with him:* keep pace with, keep abreast of; match, equal.
2 *even while travelling he kept up with events at home:* keep informed about, keep up to date with, keep abreast of; informal keep tabs on, keep up to speed about.

keep² noun *the king's forces stormed the keep:* fortress, fort, stronghold, tower, castle, citadel, bastion, donjon.

keeper noun
1 *he was made keeper of the archives:* curator, custodian, guardian, administrator, overseer, steward, caretaker.

2 *she's not a child and you're not her keeper:* guardian, protector, minder, chaperone; carer, nursemaid, nurse.

keeping noun *the document is in the keeping of the county archivist:* safe keeping, care, custody, charge, possession, trust, protection.
□ **in keeping with**
this trend was in keeping with the mood of the times: consistent with, in harmony with, in line with, in accord with, in agreement with, in character with, compatible with; appropriate to, befitting, suitable for.

keepsake noun memento, souvenir, reminder, remembrance, token.

keg noun barrel, cask, vat, butt, tun, hogshead; historical firkin.

ken noun *their talk hinted at mysteries beyond my ken:* knowledge, awareness, perception, understanding, grasp, comprehension, realization, appreciation, consciousness.

kernel noun *the kernel of the argument:* essence, core, heart, nub, essentials, quintessence, fundamentals, basics, gist, substance; informal nitty-gritty.

key noun
1 *the key to the mystery:* answer, clue, solution, explanation.
2 *customer satisfaction is the key to success:* route, way, path, means, basis, foundation, passport, secret, recipe, formula.
3 (Music) *a song in a minor key:* tone; pitch, timbre.
▷**adjective** *he was a key figure in the resistance movement:* crucial, central, essential, indispensable, pivotal, critical, dominant, vital, principal, prime, chief, major, leading, main, important, significant.
OPPOSITES: peripheral.

keynote noun *the keynote of the paper was 'positive planning':* theme, central idea, basis, essential feature/element, essence, heart, core, substance, thrust.

keystone noun *cooperation remains the keystone of the government's security policy:* foundation, basis, linchpin, cornerstone, base, principle, guiding principle, core, heart, centre, crux, fundament.

kick verb
1 *he kicked the ball wide of the net:* boot; Football punt.
2 (informal) *he was struggling to kick his drug habit:* give up, break, abandon, end, stop, cease, desist from, renounce; informal quit.
▷**noun**
1 *he received a kick on the knee:* blow; Football punt; informal boot.
2 (informal) *I get a kick out of driving that car:* thrill, tingle; informal buzz, high, rush; N. Amer. informal charge.
3 (informal) *a drink with a powerful kick:*

effect; tang, zest, bite, edge, pungency, piquancy; informal punch, hit.
4 (informal) *his parents were on a health kick:* craze, mania; fashion, vogue, trend; informal fad, trip.
□ **kick against**
young people are expected to kick against the establishment: resist, rebel against, oppose, struggle/fight against; defy, disobey, reject, spurn.
□ **kick someone/something around** (informal)
1 *we feel we are undervalued and get kicked around:* abuse, mistreat, maltreat, trample on, take for granted; informal boss about/around, push around/about, walk all over.
2 *they began to kick a few ideas around:* discuss, talk over, debate, thrash out, consider, toy with, play with.
□ **kick off** (informal) *the festival kicks off on Monday:* start, begin, commence, get going, get off the ground, get under way; open, start off, set in motion, launch, initiate, introduce, inaugurate, usher in.
□ **kick someone out** (informal) *he was kicked out of the regiment:* expel, eject, throw out, evict, get rid of, oust; dismiss, discharge; Military cashier; informal chuck out, send packing, boot out, give someone their marching orders, sack, fire; Brit. informal turf out.

kick-off noun (informal) beginning, start, commencement, outset, opening.

kid[1] noun (informal) child, youngster, baby, toddler, infant, boy/girl, young person, adolescent, teenager, youth, minor, juvenile; offspring, son/daughter; Scottish & N. English bairn; informal kiddie, nipper, tot; Brit. informal, humorous sprog; derogatory brat.

kid[2] verb (informal)
1 *the village is called Hell—I'm not kidding:* joke, tease, jest, chaff, fool about/around; informal pull someone's leg, have on, rib; Brit. informal wind up.
2 *why did I kid myself that I'd succeed?* delude, deceive, fool, trick, hoodwink, beguile, dupe; informal con, pull the wool over someone's eyes.

kidnap verb abduct, seize, snatch, take as hostage, carry off, capture.

kill verb
1 *they threatened to kill the hostages:* murder, put to death, take the life of, execute, assassinate, eliminate, terminate, dispatch, finish off; slaughter, massacre, butcher, wipe out, annihilate, exterminate, liquidate, mow down, shoot down, cut down, cut to pieces; literary or N. Amer. slay; informal bump off, do away with, do in, take out; N. Amer. informal waste.
2 *media hostility would kill all hopes of progress:* destroy, put an end to, end, extinguish, dash, quash, ruin, wreck, shatter, smash, crush, scotch; informal put paid to, put the kibosh on, stymie; Brit. informal scupper.
3 *we had to kill several hours at the airport:*

while away, fill, occupy, pass, spend, waste.
4 (informal) *it would kill me to walk four miles:* exhaust, wear out, tire out, fatigue, weary, sap, drain, enervate, prostrate; informal knock out, shatter; Brit. informal knacker.
5 (informal) *my feet were killing me:* hurt, torture, torment, cause discomfort to; be painful, be sore, be uncomfortable.
6 *a shot of morphine to kill the pain:* alleviate, assuage, soothe, allay, dull, blunt, deaden.
▷ **noun**
1 *the wolf was moving in for the kill:* death blow, coup de grâce, killing, dispatch, end.
2 *lions feeding on their kill:* prey, quarry, victim.

> **WORD LINKS**
> **-cide** forming words that refer to a person or substance that kills, such as *insecticide* ('a substance used for killing insects'), or to the killing of a person, such as *infanticide* ('the killing of a baby or very young child')

killer noun murderer, assassin, butcher, serial killer, gunman; literary or N. Amer. slayer; executioner; informal hit man.

killing noun *the world was shocked by the brutal killing:* murder, assassination, manslaughter, execution; slaughter, massacre, butchery, carnage, bloodshed, extermination, annihilation; N. Amer. homicide; literary or N. Amer. slaying.
▷ **adjective**
1 *a killing blow:* deadly, lethal, fatal, mortal, death-dealing; murderous, homicidal; literary deathly.
2 (informal) *the Minister has a killing schedule:* exhausting, gruelling, punishing, arduous, tough, demanding, onerous, strenuous, rigorous, taxing, draining, wearing, crushing, tiring, fatiguing, debilitating, enervating; informal murderous; Brit. informal knackering.
□ **make a killing** (informal) *investors are set to make a killing in the sell-off:* make a large profit, make a/your fortune, make money; informal rake it in, clean up, make a packet, make a pretty penny; Brit. informal make a bomb; N. Amer. informal make big bucks.

killjoy noun spoilsport, prophet of doom; informal wet blanket, party-pooper, misery.

kilter noun
□ **out of kilter**
air travel throws everyone's body clock out of kilter: awry, off balance, unbalanced, out of order, disordered, confused, out of tune, out of step.

kin noun relatives, relations, family, kith and kin, kinsfolk, kinsmen, kinswomen, kindred; N. Amer. informal folks; dated people.

kind[1] noun
1 *she brought all kinds of gifts:* sort, type, variety, style, form, class, category, brand, model.

2 *different kinds of bird:* species, genus, family, breed, strain.
3 *the tests were different in kind from any that preceded them:* character, quality, nature, essence, make-up, style, manner, description.
□ **kind of** (informal)
rather, quite, fairly, somewhat, a little, slightly, a shade; informal sort of, a bit, pretty, a touch, a tad.

kind² **adjective** considerate, helpful, thoughtful, kindly, unselfish, selfless, altruistic, good, good-natured, kindly, kind-hearted, warm-hearted, caring, affectionate, loving, warm; compassionate, sympathetic, understanding, big-hearted, benevolent, benign, friendly, neighbourly, hospitable, well meaning, public-spirited; generous, liberal, open-handed, bountiful, beneficent, munificent; Brit. informal decent.
OPPOSITES: unkind, inconsiderate.

kind-hearted adjective kind, caring, warm-hearted, kindly, benevolent, good-natured, tender, warm, compassionate, sympathetic, understanding; indulgent, altruistic, benign, beneficent.
OPPOSITES: nasty.

kindle verb
1 *he kindled a fire:* light, ignite, set alight, set light to, set fire to, put a match to.
2 *it was Elvis who kindled my interest in music:* rouse, arouse, wake, awaken; inspire, stimulate, stir, stir up, excite, evoke, fire, trigger, activate, spark off; literary waken.
OPPOSITES: extinguish.

kindliness noun kindness, kind-heartedness, warm-heartedness, warmth, benevolence, tenderness, care, humanity, sympathy, compassion, understanding; generosity, charity, thoughtfulness, solicitousness.
OPPOSITES: unkindness, cruelty.

kindly adjective *a kindly old lady:* kind, kind-hearted, warm-hearted, benevolent, good-natured, warm, compassionate, caring, loving, benign, well meaning; helpful, thoughtful, considerate, good-hearted, nice, friendly, neighbourly; Brit. informal decent.
OPPOSITES: unkind, cruel.

▷ **adverb** *kindly explain what you mean by that:* please, if you please, if you wouldn't mind, have the goodness to; formal pray; old use prithee.
□ **not take kindly to**
she does not take kindly to being criticized: resent, object to, take exception to, take offence at, be annoyed by, be irritated by, feel aggrieved about, take umbrage at, be upset by.

kindness noun
1 *they thanked her for her kindness:* kindliness, kind-heartedness, warm-heartedness, warmth, gentleness, concern, care; consideration, considerateness, helpfulness, thoughtfulness, unselfishness, selflessness, altruism, compassion, sympathy, understanding, big-heartedness, benevolence, friendliness, neighbourliness, hospitality, public-spiritedness; generosity, magnanimity, charitableness.
2 *she has done us many a kindness:* kind act, good deed, good turn, favour, service.

kindred adjective
1 *the centre collects work on industrial relations and kindred subjects:* related, allied, connected, comparable, similar, like, parallel, associated, analogous; formal cognate.
2 *she was glad to find a kindred spirit:* like-minded, in sympathy, in harmony, in tune, of one mind, akin, similar, like, compatible; informal on the same wavelength.
OPPOSITES: unrelated, alien.

king noun
1 *Edward wanted to be the king of France:* ruler, sovereign, monarch, crowned head, Crown, emperor, prince, potentate, lord.
2 (informal) *he has become the king of international football:* star, leading light, luminary, superstar, giant, master; informal supremo, megastar.

> WORD LINKS
> **regal** relating to a king

kingdom noun realm, domain, dominion, country, empire, land, nation, sovereign state, territory.

kingly adjective
1 *his kingly authority:* royal, regal, monarchical, sovereign, imperial, princely.
2 *he had a liking for rich and kingly robes | a kingly procession:* majestic, stately, noble, lordly, dignified, distinguished, courtly; splendid, magnificent, grand, glorious, rich, gorgeous, resplendent, princely, superb, sumptuous; informal splendiferous.

kink noun
1 *the fishing line should have no kinks in it:* curl, twist, twirl, loop; knot, tangle, entanglement.
2 *a kink in the road:* bend, corner, dog-leg, hairpin bend, twist, turn, curve.
3 *we're making headway, but there are still some kinks to iron out:* flaw, defect, imperfection, problem, complication, hitch, snag, shortcoming, weakness; informal hiccup, glitch.

kinky adjective
1 (informal) *he was involved in a kinky relationship with two older women:* perverted, abnormal, deviant, unnatural; odd, bizarre; informal weird, pervy.
2 (informal) *kinky underwear:* provocative, sexy, sexually arousing, erotic, titillating, naughty, saucy, indecent, immodest.
3 *long kinky hair:* curly, wavy, permed, crimped, curled, curling, frizzy, frizzed.

k

kinship noun

1 *ties of descent and kinship:* relationship, being related, family ties, blood ties, common ancestry; formal consanguinity.
2 *she felt kinship with the others:* affinity, sympathy, rapport, understanding, empathy, closeness, fellow feeling, bond, compatibility, harmony, similarity.

kiosk noun booth, stand, stall, counter, news-stand.

kiss verb

1 *he kissed her softly:* brush your lips against; informal peck on the cheek, smooch, canoodle, neck, pet; Brit. informal snog; N. Amer. informal buss; rare osculate.
2 *allow your foot just to kiss the floor:* brush, brush against, touch gently, skim over, graze.
▷ **noun** *a quick kiss on the cheek:* informal peck, smacker; Brit. informal snog; rare osculation.

kit noun

1 *a tool kit:* equipment, tools, implements, instruments, gadgets, utensils, appliances, tools of the trade, tackle, hardware, paraphernalia, accoutrements; informal gear.
2 (Brit. informal) *the boys' football kit:* clothes, clothing, outfit, garments, dress, costume, garb, rig; formal attire, apparel; informal gear, get-up, rig-out.
3 *a model aircraft kit:* set, self-assembly set, flat-pack.
4 (informal) *we packed up all our kit and set off:* belongings, luggage, baggage, paraphernalia, effects, impedimenta; informal things, stuff, gear; Brit. informal clobber.
□ **kit someone/something out**
the studio is kitted out with six cameras | we were all kitted out in life jackets: equip, fit out/up, furnish, supply, provide, issue; dress, clothe, rig out, deck out; formal attire; informal fix up.

kitchen noun cooking area, kitchenette, kitchen-diner, cookhouse; Nautical galley.

kittenish adjective flirtatious, coquettish, playful, lively, skittish; informal flirty.

knack noun

1 *he has a knack for making money:* gift, talent, flair, genius, instinct, faculty, ability, capability, capacity, aptitude, aptness, bent, forte, facility.
2 *it takes practice to acquire the knack:* technique, method, trick, skill, art, expertise; informal the hang of something.
3 *he has a knack of getting injured at the wrong time:* tendency, propensity, habit, proneness, liability, predisposition.

knead verb

1 *I knead the dough for five minutes:* pummel, work, pound, squeeze, shape, mould.
2 *she kneaded the base of his neck:* massage, press, manipulate, rub.

kneel verb fall to your knees, get down on your knees, be on your knees; Religion genuflect; historical kowtow.

knick-knack noun ornament, trinket, curio, novelty, bauble, gewgaw, bibelot, gimcrack; memento, souvenir.

knife verb stab, run through, lacerate, cut, hack, gash, slash, pierce, spike, impale, bayonet, spear.

knit verb

1 *these disparate regions began to knit together:* unite, unify, become closer, bond, fuse, merge, blend, coalesce, meld.
2 *we expect broken bones to knit:* heal, mend, join, fuse.
3 *Marcus knitted his brows:* furrow, tighten, contract, gather, wrinkle.

knob noun

1 *the drake has a black bill with a knob at the base:* lump, bump, protuberance, protrusion, bulge, swelling, knot, node, nodule, ball, boss.
2 *he fiddled with the knobs on the radio:* dial, button, control, switch.
3 *she turned the knob on the door:* doorknob, handle.
4 *add a few knobs of butter:* piece, pat, ball, dollop, lump.

knock verb

1 *he knocked on the door:* bang, tap, rap, thump, pound, hammer, strike, hit, beat.
2 *she knocked her knee painfully on the table:* bump, bang, hit, strike, crack; injure, hurt, bruise; informal bash, thwack.
3 *he knocked into an elderly man:* collide with, bump into, bang into, be in collision with, run into, crash into, smash into, plough into; N. Amer. impact.
4 (informal) *I'm not knocking the company* see CRITICIZE.
▷ **noun**
1 *there was a sharp knock at the door:* tap, rap, rat-tat, knocking, bang, banging, pounding, hammering, drumming, thump, thud.
2 *the casing is tough enough to withstand knocks:* bump, blow, bang, jolt, jar, shock; collision, crash, smash, impact.
3 *a nasty knock on the head:* blow, bang, hit, slap, smack, crack, punch, cuff, thump, box; informal clip, clout, wallop, thwack, bash.
4 *the ability to deal with life's hard knocks:* setback, misfortune, piece of bad luck, mishap, reversal, difficulty, blow, disaster, calamity, disappointment, sorrow, trouble, defeat, failure; informal kick in the teeth.
□ **knock about/around** (informal)
1 *for a couple of years we knocked around the Mediterranean:* wander around, travel around, drift around, roam around, rove around, range over, journey around, voyage around, potter around; informal gallivant around, gad about.
2 *she knocks around with a bunch of weird*

k

artists: **associate**, socialize, consort, keep company, go around, mix, be friends, be friendly; informal hobnob, hang out, run around.

▢ **knock someone/something about/around** beat, beat up, batter, hit, punch, thump, thrash, slap; maltreat, mistreat, abuse, ill-treat, assault, attack; informal rough up, do over, give someone a hiding, clobber, clout, bash, belt, whack, wallop.

▢ **knock something back** (informal) gulp down, drink up, quaff, guzzle; informal slug, down, swig, swill down, toss off; N. Amer. informal scarf down/up.

▢ **knock someone down** fell, floor, flatten, bring down, knock to the ground; knock over, run over/down.

▢ **knock something down**
1 _the building was knocked down in the late seventies:_ **demolish**, pull down, tear down, destroy; raze to the ground, level, flatten, bulldoze.
2 (informal) _the firm has knocked down the prices of its machines:_ **reduce**, lower, cut, decrease, drop, put down, mark down; informal slash.

▢ **knock off** (informal) _they knock off at 5 o'clock:_ **stop work**, finish work, clock off, leave work.

▢ **knock someone off** (informal) see **KILL** verb sense 1.

▢ **knock something off**
1 (Brit. informal) _someone knocked off the video_ see **STEAL** verb sense 1.
2 (informal) _knock off 10% from the bill:_ **deduct**, take off/away, subtract, dock.

▢ **knock someone out**
1 _I hit him in the face and knocked him out:_ **knock unconscious**, knock senseless; floor, prostrate; informal lay out, put out cold, KO, kayo.
2 _England was knocked out by Belgium:_ **eliminate**, beat, defeat, vanquish; trounce.
3 (informal) _walking that far in one go has knocked her out:_ **exhaust**, wear out, tire out, overtire, fatigue, weary, drain; informal do in, take it out of; Brit. informal knacker, fag out.
4 (informal) _the view really knocked me out:_ **overwhelm**, stun, amaze, astound, astonish, stagger, take someone's breath away, stupefy; impress, dazzle, enchant, entrance; informal bowl over, flabbergast, knock sideways, blow away; Brit. informal knock for six.

▢ **knock someone up** (Brit. informal) _we were knocked up at five in the morning:_ **wake up**, wake, call, rouse, arouse, get out of bed, get up; literary waken.

▢ **knock something up** (Brit. informal) _I could knock up some picture frames for you:_ **produce**, make, prepare, build, whip up, rig up, throw together, cobble together, improvise, contrive; informal rustle up.

knoll noun _a grassy knoll:_ **hillock**, hummock, hill, mound, rise, hump, tor, bank, ridge, elevation; Scottish brae; formal eminence.

knot noun
1 _a small knot in the yarn:_ **tie**, twist, loop, join, fastening; tangle, entanglement.
2 _a knot in the wood:_ **nodule**, node; lump, knob, swelling, protuberance, bump.
3 _a small knot of people:_ **cluster**, group, gathering, crowd, huddle, bunch, circle, ring, company, throng, band.
▷ verb _their scarves were knotted round their throats:_ **tie**, fasten, secure, bind, do up.

knotted adjective **tangled**, matted, tangly, knotty, entangled, snarled, unkempt, uncombed, tousled; N. Amer. informal mussed up.

knotty adjective
1 _a knotty legal problem:_ **complex**, complicated, involved, intricate, convoluted; difficult, hard, thorny, taxing, awkward, tricky, problematic, troublesome.
2 _knotty roots:_ **gnarled**, knotted, nodular, knobbly, lumpy, bumpy.
3 _a knotty piece of thread:_ **knotted**, tangled, tangly, twisted, entangled, snarled, matted.
OPPOSITES: straightforward.

know verb
1 _she doesn't know I'm here:_ **be aware**, realize, be conscious, be informed; notice, perceive, see, sense, recognize; informal savvy, latch on.
2 _I don't know his address:_ **have knowledge of**, be informed of, be apprised of; formal be cognizant of.
3 _do you know the rules? | he asked whether I knew any French:_ **be familiar with**, be conversant with, be acquainted with, have knowledge of, be versed in, have mastered, have a grasp of, understand, comprehend; have learned, have memorized; informal be clued up on.
4 _I don't know many people here:_ **be acquainted with**, have met, be familiar with; be friends with, be friendly with, be on good terms with, be close to, be intimate with; Scottish ken.
5 _a man who had known better times:_ **experience**, go through, live through, undergo, taste.
6 _my brothers don't know a saucepan from a frying pan:_ **distinguish**, tell, differentiate, discriminate; recognize, pick out, identify.

know-all noun (informal) **wiseacre**; informal smart alec, wise guy, smarty, smarty-pants; Brit. informal clever clogs, clever Dick.

know-how noun (informal) **knowledge**, expertise, skill, skilfulness, proficiency, understanding, mastery, technique; ability, capability, competence, capacity, adeptness, dexterity, deftness, aptitude, adroitness, ingenuity, faculty; informal savvy.

knowing adjective
1 _a knowing smile:_ **significant**, meaningful, eloquent, expressive, suggestive; arch, sly, teasing, playful.

2 *she's a very knowing child:* sophisticated, worldly, worldly-wise, experienced; knowledgeable, shrewd, astute, canny, sharp, wily, perceptive.
3 *a knowing infringement of the rules:* deliberate, intentional, conscious, calculated, wilful, done on purpose, premeditated, preconceived, planned.

knowingly adverb deliberately, intentionally, consciously, on purpose, wilfully, wittingly, by design.

knowledge noun
  1 *his knowledge of history was limited:* understanding, comprehension, insight, grasp, command, mastery; expertise, skill; informal know-how.
  2 *people anxious to display their knowledge:* learning, erudition, education, scholarship, schooling, wisdom.
  3 *he slipped away without my knowledge:* awareness, consciousness, realization, cognition, apprehension, perception; formal cognizance.
  4 *the staff develop an intimate knowledge of the countryside:* familiarity, acquaintance, intimacy.
  OPPOSITES: ignorance.

knowledgeable adjective *we need someone who is knowledgeable about modern art:* well informed about, acquainted with, familiar with, conversant with, au fait with, well read on, having a good knowledge of, up on, up to date with, abreast of; informal clued up on.
OPPOSITES: ill-informed.

known adjective
  1 *a known criminal | a known fact:* recognized, well known, widely known, noted, celebrated, notable, notorious; acknowledged, self-confessed, declared, overt.
  2 *the known world:* familiar, known about, well known; studied, investigated.

knuckle verb
  □ **knuckle under**
  surrender, submit, capitulate, give in/up, yield, give way, succumb, climb down, back down, admit defeat, lay down your arms, throw in the towel; informal quit, raise the white flag.

kowtow verb *she didn't have to kowtow to a boss any more:* grovel, be obsequious, be servile, be sycophantic, fawn on, bow and scrape, toady, abase yourself, humble yourself; curry favour with, make up to, ingratiate yourself with; Brit. dance attendance on; informal crawl, creep, suck up, lick someone's boots.

kudos noun *she was looking for kudos rather than profit | the kudos of hosting one of the great sporting events in our city:* prestige, cachet, glory, honour, status, standing, distinction, prestigiousness, fame, celebrity; admiration, respect, esteem, acclaim, praise, credit

Effective Writing for College and Career

Introduction

This section of the *Compact Oxford Thesaurus for University and College Students* has been specially written to help students make the best use of a thesaurus to improve their writing in a variety of situations. Whether you are writing a college assignment, a report, or a job application to a prospective employer, this section is designed to help you express yourself more fluently, more accurately, and with confidence. The separate topics it contains are listed below.

Contents

You can also access extra information about improving your writing skills in the *Compact Oxford English Dictionary for Students* (OUP, 2006), and at the following websites:

- the Online Resource Centre (www.oup.com/uk/dictionaries/cotfs)
- www.AskOxford.com

SECTION 1:
Thesaurus basics

Knowing how a thesaurus is organized, what it can offer, and how to use it effectively will ensure that you keep your writing fresh and interesting and always choose the most appropriate word for the situation in question, whether you are writing an essay, a letter to a bank, or a job application to a prospective employer.

1.1 TYPES OF THESAURUS

There are two main types of thesaurus:

- Roget (thematic)
- A–Z

Here is a brief explanation of the differences between each approach.

Roget-style thesauruses

Thesauruses which use the Roget or thematic approach are named after the first person to compile a thesaurus, Dr Peter Mark Roget. Published in 1852, *Roget's Thesaurus of English Words and Phrases Classified and Arranged so as to Facilitate the Expression of Ideas and Assist in Literary Composition* (to give it its full title), was intended to help you find the word that best expressed what you wanted to say by listing words together that have a common theme. Nowadays there is no single edition of Roget's Thesaurus—any thesaurus organized according to a similar scheme can have the title and is known as a 'Roget'.

Under the Roget-style thematic system, words are grouped according to the ideas underlying them. Any Roget consists of two main sections:

- the main text
- an A–Z index

In the main text, the words are classified into around eight overall 'classes', such as 'abstract relations' and 'matter'. These are in turn split into between three and nine 'sections', which are then divided into approximately 1000 subsections called 'heads'.

If you master this system, you can find alternative words for *peace* by looking up the class headed 'Volition', then the section 'Antagonism', then the head 'Peace', and the part of that containing nouns.

However, most people do not find it easy to use a Roget in this way and look up *peace* straight away in the A–Z index: there you will usually be given a set of options covering different meanings of the word, each with their own reference number and part of speech (word class), for example:

> **peace**
> *silence* 384 n.
> *inactivity* 603 n.
> *agreement* 631 n.
> *freedom from war* 639 n.

From these short 'prompts', you choose the meaning of *peace* for which you want to find synonyms. So if you are interested in alternatives for the word *peace* with the meaning 'inactivity', you can see that you would need to go to number 603 in the main text, where you will find a list of words with varying degrees of similarity to your initial choice of *peace*, typically on these lines:

> **603 Inactivity**
> *noun* inactivity, inertia, torpor; peace, quiet, calm, stillness; strike, lockout, walkout; unemployment, absenteeism; laziness, idleness; idler, lazybones, sluggard.

In addition, most Roget-style thesauruses give numbers after many synonyms which direct you to other sections of the text. Although it is comprehensive and offers a wide range of options, this system of sorting words into themed sections and lists has several disadvantages:

- it can be lengthy, confusing, or cumbersome to use
- you need a fairly extensive knowledge of English
- the words in any given list cannot all be used instead of the word you first looked up because they do not all have sufficiently similar meanings: in the example above, *idler*, *lazybones*, and *sluggard* all refer to lazy people and are not suitable replacements for 'peace'
- there is no guidance given as to which words are informal or slang, which means that you might inadvertently opt for an inappropriate one which appears out of place within the context of the rest of your work (for example, choosing the informal phrase *figure out* as an alternative to *understand* in a scientific report). For more about this see **Choosing the right synonym** on page 12.

As a result, many people find thematic thesauruses off-putting or do not make the best use of them.

The A–Z approach

The other main type of thesaurus uses a single A–Z arrangement, as in this thesaurus: the entries are presented in alphabetical order and you simply look them up, as in a dictionary. The benefits of this style of organization are:

- as soon as you look up a word in the A–Z text, you immediately find synonyms, conveniently grouped in one place
- there is no need to use an index first to find out where to go for further information
- the alphabetical format focuses on supplying fewer but more relevant synonyms, saving you the trouble of having to consider and select from the highly diverse and long lists of words offered in a thematic thesaurus.

Overall, most people find that for all types of writing the A–Z approach is not only faster and much more straightforward to use but also more practical.

1.2 DICTIONARY OR THESAURUS?

Dictionaries

A dictionary is a record of the words in a language: most dictionaries provide a full profile of each word, including different senses and its part of speech (word class), alternative spellings, and its inflections (forms) if it does not follow a standard pattern—such as **caught** as the past tense of **catch**, or **leaves** as the plural of **leaf**.

Other information typically found in dictionaries includes:

- pronunciations
- a selection of phrases and idioms (such as **a whale of a time**).
- word origins (etymologies)
- words derived from the main word (such as **habitually** from **habitual**)
- notes giving information on how to use the word, for instance on beginning a sentence with 'and' or when to use 'who' and 'whom'.

The companion dictionary to this thesaurus is the *Compact Oxford English Dictionary for Students* (OUP, 2006). By comparing an entry in each book for the same word, it is easy to see the differences between the information provided:

quality

Compact Oxford English Dictionary for Students

quality noun (pl. qualities) **1** the standard of how good something is as measured against other similar things: *an improvement in product quality.* **2** general excellence. **3** a distinctive feature or characteristic: *strong leadership qualities.* **4** old use high social standing. •adjective informal of good quality; excellent: *he's a quality player.*
– ORIGIN Latin *qualitas.*

Compact Oxford Thesaurus for Students

quality noun
1 *an improvement in the quality of the service | the quality of education may suffer as class sizes increase:* **standard**, class, calibre, condition, character, nature, form, value, level, grade, rank.
2 *work of such quality remains a rarity:* excellence, calibre, superiority, merit, worth, value, virtue, eminence, distinction; talent, skill, virtuosity, craftsmanship.
3 *she has many good qualities:* feature, trait, attribute, characteristic, point, aspect, facet, side, property.

The dictionary entry gives definitions and examples of usage to enable users to understand the meaning of the word.

Thesauruses

The purpose of a thesaurus is to provide you with words that have a similar meaning and can be substituted for one that you have in mind. The ability to use synonyms appropriately is invaluable when writing in all kinds of situations, from essays and reports to job application letters. A thesaurus can help you to avoid repeating the same word in the same sentence or paragraph, to expand your vocabulary, and to ensure that you communicate your message in the most effective way (there is more about choosing the right word in section 2).

For example, in the sentence below, the word 'quality' is used twice, to mean two different things:

Kate's greatest quality is the quality of her narrative.

To prevent the reader from having to consult a thesaurus in their head to 'translate' the sentence, it would be easier to grasp if one of the instances of 'quality' were replaced with a synonym from the list given in the entry above. You can find alternatives for the first use of 'quality' at sense 3, and for the second at sense 2, giving you some options for rewording the sentence:

Kate's greatest quality is the excellence of her narrative.
Kate's greatest attribute is the quality of her narrative.

As well as lists of synonyms, most modern thesauruses also include other features, which will provide you with all the word resources you need to help you to improve your writing. You will find more information on the special features provided in this thesaurus in section 2.

Here are the other main distinctions between a dictionary and a thesaurus:

- synonyms may give you an idea of the sense of the word, but they are not the same as the accurate definitions you will find in a dictionary.

- a thesaurus contains entries for only a selected number of words and does not set out to describe every word in the language systematically. As it contains only words for which there are genuine alternatives with similar meanings, you will not find entries for certain words— typically names for specific things—such as **giraffe**, **acidify**, or **computer**.

- similarly, you will also not find specialist or scientific senses of words in a thesaurus. For instance, the word **hamstring** has an entry, but this only covers its use as a verb: you would need to use a dictionary to find out the meaning of the noun (that is, one of the tendons at the back of the knee).

Making effective use of dictionaries and thesauruses

Given the different purposes for which they are intended as outlined above, it should not be a question of using either a dictionary OR a thesaurus. If you want to produce written material to a high standard and broaden your understanding of the language, you need both types of book for different parts of the activity of choosing vocabulary.

For instance, you might have written the following sentence in your first draft:

Eventually, thanks to the women's dedication, they persuaded cleaners to join the TGWU and persuaded the union to accept them.

On a second reading, you decide that it would be better to choose another word in place of the second 'persuade'. If you look up *persuade* in this thesaurus, you will find that *inveigle* is given as a synonym of it. It looks quite a fresh alternative at first sight, but it is not always directly substitutable with *persuade*: choosing such a synonym simply because it looks new and imaginative could lead to unfortunate results and create the wrong impression.

If you are unfamiliar with a word such as *inveigle*, check the definition. If you look it up in the *Compact Oxford English Dictionary for Students*, you will see that *inveigle* means 'persuade someone to do something by deception or flattery'. Additionally, the typical example in the dictionary also shows that you *inveigle* someone *into* doing something, whereas the thesaurus example shows that you *persuade* them *to* do it:

Dictionary: he can inveigle any woman into bed in minutes
Thesaurus: he tried to persuade her to come with him.

Such distinctions mean that you should consider both the connotations of a potential synonym (i.e. the ideas or feelings suggested by a word beyond its basic meaning) and the grammatical patterns in which it is used before choosing it as a substitute (you also need to understand the way in which synonyms are ordered in an entry, as described in Vocabulary solutions: how to use a thesaurus on page 8).

In the example given above, you would probably decide that *inveigle* is not a good synonym for *persuade* in this context (because you do not want to imply that deception or flattery were involved) and you would opt for a more appropriate word instead:

> Eventually, thanks to the women's dedication, they persuaded cleaners to join the TGWU and prevailed on the union to accept them.

The more familiar you become with each kind of book and the distinctions between the information that they provide, the more you will be able to use them to help to develop your writing skills and choose the right word in every situation.

SECTION 2:
Vocabulary solutions: how to use a thesaurus

This section of the thesaurus has been specially written to help you make the most of the information contained in the main part of the book. It provides detailed guidance about:

■ how the entries are structured

■ the different types of information they contain

■ how to use this information to make your writing clear, interesting, and effective.

2.1 PARTS OF SPEECH (OR WORD CLASSES)

Here is the thesaurus entry for **alternative**:

> **alternative** adjective
> **1** *an alternative route:* different, other, another, second, possible, substitute, replacement; standby, emergency, reserve, backup, auxiliary, fallback.
> **2** *an alternative lifestyle:* unorthodox, unconventional, bohemian, non-standard, unusual, uncommon, out of the ordinary; radical, revolutionary, nonconformist, avant-garde, offbeat.
> ▷**noun** *there are a number of alternatives available:* option, choice, other possibility; substitute, replacement.

The first piece of information given after the entry word is its part of speech (or word class). Notice that the parts of the entry are separated out to show that **alternative** can be both an adjective and a noun: make sure you are looking at the right section of the entry for the sense you have in mind. If you want another way of saying **alternative**, is it the adjective (as in *an alternative route for cyclists*) or the noun (as in *there are a number of alternatives available*) that you are interested in? You can also use the example sentences to guide you to the right place.

2.2 SENSES AND EXAMPLES

Many words have more than one meaning or sense, each with their own set of synonyms. In this thesaurus, where an entry has more than one sense, the synonyms for each of these senses are introduced by an example (or examples) of real English showing how the word is actually used. These examples of words 'in action' help you to identify the meaning you are looking for, and so guide you to the most appropriate selection of alternatives to choose from. Here is the entry for **pale**:

> **pale**[1] **adjective**
> **1** *he looked pale and his breathing was laboured:* pallid, white, pasty, wan, colourless, anaemic, bloodless, washed out, ashen, grey, whey-faced, drained, sickly, sallow, as white as a sheet, deathly pale; Brit. peaky; informal like death warmed up.
> **2** *the red velvet dress accentuated the pale skin of her neck:* creamy, milky, ivory, white, milk-white, alabaster
> **3** *pale colours:* light, light-coloured, pastel, muted, subtle, soft; faded, bleached, washed out.
> **4** *the pale light of morning:* dim, faint, weak, feeble.
> **5** *the film is a pale imitation of the original:* feeble, weak, insipid, bland, poor, inadequate, unimpressive, lacklustre.
> OPPOSITES: dark.
> ▷**verb**
> **1** *his face paled:* go/turn white, grow/turn pale, blanch, lose colour.
> **2** *everything else pales by comparison:* decrease in importance, lose significance, pale into insignificance.

Consider which of the example sentences is closest to the idea you want to express and then look at the selection of synonyms following it. Are you looking for a word to describe the complexion of a person who looks unwell (*he was pale and his breathing was laboured*), or to describe attractively light skin (*the red velvet dress accentuated the pale skin of her neck*). Do you want a word to describe light colours, or is it the meaning of 'inferior' that you are looking for (*the film is a pale imitation of the original*)?

❗ All the examples used in this thesaurus are genuine, typical uses of the entry words and you may find that some of them are quite similar to the sentence you are writing yourself. Remember that this does not mean that every synonym provided will be suitable for you to use: you must still make a careful selection according to the situation or context in question. If you are unsure about a synonym, look it up it in a dictionary. A dictionary will give you more information about the meaning of a word and the way it is used than is possible in a thesaurus.

KEY POINTS

- Different senses of an entry word are illustrated with real examples of the word to help you distinguish the meaning you are looking for.

- It is important to make sure you are looking at the right sense or part of speech for the meaning you have in mind.

2.3 SYNONYMS

i) Arrangement of the synonyms

- Some thesauruses present their synonyms in simple A to Z order. The synonyms in *this* thesaurus are arranged in order of their closeness in meaning to the main entry word, or to its different senses. So the first synonym given is the term that is closest in meaning and it therefore has a very good chance of being suited to your needs. In the entry for allege below, the first synonym given is claim.

> **allege** verb *he alleged that he had been assaulted:* claim, assert, declare, state, contend, argue, affirm, attest.

Its position at the front of the list indicates that you are highly likely to be able to substitute claim for allege in a sentence, for example:

He alleged/claimed that the council had been negligent.

It is alleged/claimed that he failed to disclose important information.

The rest of the synonyms are listed according to their decreasing closeness in meaning to the entry word or sense. So, in the entry above attest, coming as it does at the end of the list, is generally less likely to be suitable as an alternative for allege than claim or assert.

- Synonyms are usually separated by commas, as in the entry above, but there are one or two important exceptions to this.

> **slender** adjective
> **1** *her tall slender figure:* slim, lean, willowy, sylphlike, svelte, lissom, graceful, slight; thin, skinny.
> **2** *the theory is based on very slender evidence:* meagre, limited, slight, scanty, scant, sparse, paltry, insubstantial, insufficient, deficient, negligible.
> **3** *the chances of winning seemed slender:* faint, remote, flimsy, tenuous, fragile, slim; unlikely, improbable.
> OPPOSITES: plump, abundant.

In this entry, the first synonym given for sense 1 is slim: this is offered as the word which is closest in meaning to this sense of slender.

Slim is an adjective with positive associations, as are the six synonyms which follow it, all separated by commas. For example,

a tall, slim, well-dressed woman = 'a woman whose slenderness is attractive'.

But note the semi-colon after slight. A semi-colon signals that the synonyms which follow it have a different nuance of meaning from the preceding group. In this case thin and skinny have rather negative associations and so they would create a different impression in a reader's mind from slim, lean, willowy, sylphlike, svelte, lissom, graceful, or slight. For example,

a tall, skinny woman with greying hair = 'a woman whose slenderness is potentially unattractive'.

Take a look at the entry for prosperous:

> **prosperous** adjective *a prosperous shipping firm | prosperous middle-class professionals:* thriving, flourishing, successful, profitable, lucrative, expanding, booming, burgeoning; affluent, wealthy, rich, moneyed, well off; informal rolling in it, on the up and up, in the money. OPPOSITES: ailing, poor.

Here the first set of synonyms, from thriving to burgeoning, generally apply particularly well to non-human things, as in the first example (*a prosperous shipping firm*). The second set, affluent to well off, which follow the semicolon, are better suited to humans, as in the second example (*prosperous middle-class professionals*). Whenever you choose an alternative word from a list provided in a thesaurus, say the sentence in which you want to use it to yourself to make sure that it sounds right. Most of the time the choices we make about language are instinctive, but when you are using a thesaurus to select a word this process becomes a conscious one and it is important to be careful, especially if you choose a word which is not entirely familiar to you. Double-check in a dictionary if you are in any doubt, or ask a friend for their opinion.

▪ Semicolons are also used to divide groups of synonyms which are governed by particular descriptive markers called *labels*. Labels show that a word (or group of words) is only appropriate to particular varieties of English or is best suited to particular types of writing. In the entry for prosperous above, the second semicolon is followed by an informal label. This means that the synonyms after this label are only suitable in spoken English, or in informal everyday writing such as emails between friends. It would create the wrong impression if you used in the money, rolling in it, or on the up and up in formal writing. For more information see the section on **Different types of English** below.

KEY POINTS

- The synonyms are arranged in order of their closeness in meaning to the main entry word and the synonym that is closest in meaning is placed at the front of the list. This helps you to be sure that the first synonyms are likely to be good choices to replace the word you have looked up.

- A semi-colon within a list of synonyms signals a slight change of direction: the synonyms which follow it will either have slightly different nuances or implications or else they will be appropriate only in certain contexts or situations.

ii) Choosing the right synonym

This section will help you to:

- use words in appropriate contexts
- avoid using words which are too informal for coursework assignments or job applications
- be aware of regional differences, e.g. British English versus US English
- avoid opting for rarer or more formal words just because they sound impressive.

The thesaurus provides a variety of information to help you choose and use the synonyms it offers you to make your writing clearer and more effective. As we have just seen, the order in which the synonyms in each entry or sense are arranged is an important indication of which synonyms are likely to be most useful to you. There are other elements which will help you to find the best synonyms and to use them in the correct way.

Different types of English

Most of the words and phrases in this thesaurus are classed as standard English, which means that they are generally appropriate to most written and spoken situations, from a conversation with friends to a written college assignment. Standard English represents the most accepted and established use of the language. But some words have a more restricted use, and to help you gauge the suitability of a word or phrase, all those terms that are NOT standard English are preceded by descriptive markers called *labels* which explain how or where the terms should be used (or not used). Such words or phrases will be found at the end of the main list of synonyms.

This thesaurus uses three different types of descriptive label:

- **register labels** describe a particular level of use in the language. They indicate whether a term is formal, informal, old-fashioned, and so on. Everyone instinctively varies the type of language they use in different situations, whether they are writing a college assignment, composing a job application letter, or emailing a friend. No one type of language is inherently 'better' than any other, the important thing is to choose language that is appropriate to the particular occasion in which it is used and that conveys your intended meaning in the best way for your particular purpose and audience.

- **geographical labels** mark a word as belonging to a variety of English used in a particular part of the world. While most of the words used in standard British English will be the same as those used in other regional varieties, there are some words which are only found in one type of English. The main regional types of English found in this thesaurus are British and North American (North America = the US *and* Canada).

- **subject labels** show that a word or sense is associated with a particular subject field or specialist activity, such as Music, Law, or Football, and is therefore not usually appropriate in general contexts.

A full list and explanation of all the descriptive labels used in this thesaurus is set out at the front of the book. The main register labels are described below as it is choosing the right register that is most important when you are writing college or university assignments, or composing job applications and CVs. You are generally unlikely to select a word that is marked as belonging to a particular regional variety of English or as being associated with a specific subject field unless you have a definite reason for doing so.

Formal language

Formal language tends to be found in academic journals and in official reports and letters, where it brings an added seriousness to the subject. It is often tempting to choose formal vocabulary in written assignments, in the hope that it will add more weight to what you are saying, or simply sound more impressive or sophisticated. But you should beware of choosing a formal word for these reasons, especially one with which you are not very familiar. By doing so, you run the risk of making your writing sound pompous or, worse still, of conveying the wrong meaning altogether. For example, you may make your writing unintentionally amusing: many people deliberately use formal language to create a humorous or comic effect.

Suppose you are looking for a synonym for **hate** in the sentence:

He was hated by many trade union members.

The thesaurus offers the following synonyms for this sense:

hate verb

1 *the boys hate each other:* loathe, detest, despise, dislike, abhor; be repelled by, be unable to bear/stand, recoil from, shrink from; formal abominate, execrate.

It would be wise to avoid the formal terms **abominate** or **execrate** unless you are very confident that they are appropriate to the context of your writing. Standard English alternatives such as **loathe** or **detest** would convey your meaning in the clearest and most effective way. Formal alternatives in a thesaurus should always be treated with caution: if you are not completely sure that they are appropriate, check in your dictionary for further guidance or ask friends for their opinion. Formal words tend to be longer than their standard English equivalents: remember that a long word is not necessarily *better* than a shorter one: it is just longer.

Technical language

All subjects have their own technical terminology. For example, **parturition**, meaning 'birth' is found mainly in medicine or biology, e.g.:

The hormone oxytocin is essential for lactation but not for parturition.

It would not be appropriate to choose this word in a more general context such as:

Tom and Katie are celebrating the birth of a baby girl

unless you are aiming to amuse your audience. It is of course important to show an understanding of your subject and its vocabulary, but bear in mind that you should not try to sound learned or superior by using a great many obscure technical terms in contexts for which they are not appropriate.

Informal language

Informal language is used mainly in conversation, emails, and texting, by people who know each other well, by particular social groups, or by people in particular occupations. As a rule, you should avoid all informal vocabulary in written work and job applications. It will make your writing seem less serious or considered, and there is also the danger that you will fail to communicate your meaning effectively: your reader may not understand an informal term or may interpret it incorrectly, as this type of language is often exclusive to certain groups of people. This thesaurus includes a selection of well-established informal vocabulary, preceded by the descriptive marker informal. Take care to use this vocabulary only in appropriate contexts and situations.

Note that words or phrases which are not part of standard English are to be found at the end of the main list of synonyms. You should also be aware that some entries or senses themselves belong to this category: in these cases the descriptive marker is found at the beginning of the entry, or directly after the sense number, if it only applies to one sense, and is placed in brackets. For example, in the entry for **accede** below, the descriptive marker after the part of speech (or word class) indicates that **accede** is usually found in formal or official writing.

> **accede** verb (formal) *he acceded to the government's demands:* agree to, consent to, accept, assent to, acquiesce in, comply with, go along with, concur with, yield to, give in to, give way to, defer to, surrender to.

In the entry **aggravate**, the descriptive marker following sense 2 shows that this meaning is an informal one.

> **aggravate** verb
> **1** *the new law could aggravate the situation:* worsen, make worse, exacerbate, inflame, compound; add fuel to the fire/flames, add insult to injury, rub salt in the wound.
> **2** (informal) *you don't have to aggravate people to get what you want:* annoy, irritate, exasperate, put out, provoke, antagonize, get on someone's nerves, try someone's patience; Brit. rub up the wrong way; informal bug, hack off; Brit. informal wind up.
> OPPOSITES: alleviate, improve.

KEY POINTS

- Choose synonyms that are part of standard English wherever possible.
- Treat any unfamiliar synonyms with caution, even if they sound impressive or learned.
- Avoid informal and regional synonyms unless you are writing to friends, or preparing a written assignment in which this type of vocabulary is appropriate (for example, you may have to write advertising copy as part of a marketing course).
- Always be aware of your intended audience and the purpose of what you are writing, and tailor your choice of synonyms accordingly.

! More detailed information about register and tone can be found in the *Compact Oxford Dictionary for Students.*

iii) Grammar: making sure a synonym works properly

Words that have the same general meaning as each other do not always follow the same grammatical patterns. This means that it is not always possible to substitute one word for another without making a few other changes to your sentence at the same time. It is very important to be aware of this potential issue when you are writing assignments, reports, or job applications. If you choose a good synonym but use it incorrectly this is likely to convey the idea that you are not really familiar with the word you have chosen, having selected it only because it sounds impressive or sophisticated (or is different from a word you have used before). Many of the thesaurus entries give specific guidance by showing the patterns followed by the different synonyms it offers, or the other words with which they are usually associated. Your dictionary can provide further help if you are still unsure.

Here is the thesaurus entry for **knowledgeable**:

> **knowledgeable** adjective *we need someone who is knowledgeable about modern art:* well informed about, acquainted with, familiar with, conversant with, au fait with, well read on, having a good knowledge of, up on, up to date with, abreast of; informal clued up on.
> OPPOSITES: ill-informed.

You will see that it not only provides synonyms, but also shows you how to use them if you substitute them for **knowledgeable** in a sentence similar to the one in the entry. If you choose, say, **acquainted** or **familiar**, you would have to say:

We need someone who is acquainted/familiar **with** modern art.

rather than:

We need someone who is acquainted/familiar **about** modern art.

Take a look at the entry for **award**:

> **award** verb *the society awarded him a silver medal:* give, grant, accord, assign; confer on, bestow on, present to, endow with, decorate with.

In this case, you have to be more careful with your choice of synonym. If you select, for example, **confer on** or **bestow on** as an alternative to **award**, this example sentence would have to be reworded:

The society conferred/bestowed a silver medal on him.

If you choose **present with**, you would need to say:

The society presented him with a silver medal.

In this case, the thesaurus entry alerts you to different grammar patterns, where they exist, but if you are not familiar with the synonym and the way it is used, you should be wary and consult a dictionary for further guidance.

KEY POINTS

■ Replacing one word with another may mean that you have to make further changes to a sentence so that it is still good English.

■ A thesaurus can help you use synonyms correctly by providing information about their grammatical behaviour.

■ Use your thesaurus in conjunction with a good, up-to-date dictionary for extra guidance about the way words behave in a sentence.

2.4 OPPOSITES (OR ANTONYMS)

You may sometimes find that you can only think of a word that means the opposite of the one you actually want. But you can still search for the word you want by looking up that opposite word in the thesaurus. For example, suppose you are in search of a word that describes how an organization or institution came to an end but you can only think of a word for starting one, such as found.

On 25 May, the regional assembly was [the opposite of founded].

Look up found in the thesaurus:

> **found** verb
> 1 *he founded his company in 1989:*
> establish, set up, start, begin, get going, institute, inaugurate, launch, float, form, create, bring into being, originate, develop.
> 2 *they abandoned Attica and founded a new city:* build, construct, erect, put up; plan, lay plans for.
> 3 *their relationship was founded on trust:* base, build, construct, rest, hinge, depend; ground in, root in.
> OPPOSITES: dissolve, liquidate, abandon

At the end of the entry you will see the opposites dissolve, liquidate, and abandon. You would probably choose dissolve:

On 25 May, the regional assembly was dissolved.

Of course, if none of the opposite words exactly fits the context you have in mind, you could choose the one that is nearest to the meaning you want and then look that up in turn: most of the antonyms in this thesaurus have main entries of their own, where a wider selection of alternatives will be offered.

2.5 OTHER FEATURES

This section shows how the thesaurus can help you to:

■ avoid confusing one word with another that looks or sounds very similar

- avoid choosing vocabulary that may cause offence
- expand your vocabulary.

i) Usage notes

Confusable words

There are many words in English which look or sound alike but have very different meanings. These words are easy to confuse with each other and this can create problems when using a thesaurus. If you have confused, for example, **flaunt** with **flout** (a very common mistake!), you may look up **flaunt** in your thesaurus hoping to find a selection of other words meaning 'fail to follow a law or rule' and be taken aback to discover a very different set of synonyms. In this thesaurus you will find notes at this type of entry, alerting you to the possible confusion and helping you choose the right word for the context you have in mind.

> **flaunt** verb *he hated the way they flaunted their wealth:* **show off**, display ostentatiously, make a show of, put on show/display, parade; brag about, crow about, vaunt; informal flash.
> OPPOSITES: hide.
>
> **USAGE**
>
> Be careful not to confuse **flaunt** with **flout**. **Flaunt** means 'to display something in a way intended to attract attention', while **flout** means 'to show that you have no respect for a rule or convention by openly failing to follow it' (*retailers have been flouting the law for years*).

Sensitive vocabulary

With changing social attitudes, some long-established English words have become less acceptable, especially those to do with ethnicity and disability. This thesaurus offers information and practical advice to ensure that you do not create the wrong impression by inadvertently choosing an inappropriate or even offensive term. For example:

> **disabled** adjective
>
> **USAGE**
>
> **Disabled** is the standard term for people who have physical or mental disabilities. In the past, it was acceptable to use terms such as **handicapped** or **crippled** but these may now cause offence and should be avoided. More recently, expressions such as **physically challenged** or **differently abled** have been coined as synonyms for **disabled** in a conscious attempt to eradicate any negative perception or stigma that may be felt to be attached to the older terms: these may be appropriate in certain situations but they are best avoided in formal writing.

As you can see from this note, terms which were once regarded as acceptable may now be seen as offensive because they are viewed as reinforcing negative stereotypes. It is important to be aware of this when you are writing and to avoid using such language.

ii) Word links

Many of the entries in this thesaurus have 'Word link' features providing terms which are connected to the entry word in some way, but are not synonyms. See for example, the entry for **eye**:

> **eye noun**
> **1** *his sharp eyes had missed nothing:* eyesight, vision, sight, powers of observation, visual perception.
> **2** *to European eyes, it may seem that the city is overcrowded:* opinion, view, viewpoint, way of thinking, judgement
> ▷ **verb** *he eyed the stranger suspiciously:* look at, regard, contemplate, observe, view, gaze at, stare at, survey, scrutinize, consider, glance at; watch, keep an eye on; informal check out, size up; N. Amer. informal eyeball.
> □ **see eye to eye** *we see eye to eye on a large number of issues:* agree, concur, be in agreement, be of the same mind/opinion, be in accord, think as one; be on the same wavelength, get on/along.
>
> WORD LINKS
> **ocular**, **optic**, **ophthalmic** relating to the eyes, or to vision
> **ophthalmology** the study and treatment of eye diseases and disorders

or the entry for **half**:

> **half adverb**
> **1** *half-cooked chicken:* partially, partly; incompletely, inadequately, insufficiently; in part, part, slightly.
> **2** *I'm half inclined to believe you:* almost, to some extent/degree, up to a point.
> OPPOSITES: fully.
>
> WORD LINKS
> **demi-**, **hemi-**, **semi-** forming words meaning 'half of something', such as *demisemiquaver* ('a musical note having half the time value of a semiquaver'), *hemisphere* ('a half of the earth'), and *semicircle* ('one half of a circle')

This type of information is especially useful for students interested in the English language and curious to find out more about it, and it can also help to add variety to your written work or expand your vocabulary.

SECTION 3:
Brush up your style

3.1 CLICHÉS

This section will help you to:

- identify a cliché
- avoid clichés
- choose other language which is fresher and more effective instead

As explained in the **Choosing the right synonym** section on page 12, when speaking informally to other people we naturally use familiar vocabulary and patterns of expression without giving the individual words too much thought: the main purpose is to get the message across quickly and clearly.

Clichés are particular words or expressions that have been used so often that they are no longer interesting or effective. Although they reveal a lack of original thought, they are a normal part of our everyday speech, even if we often do not realize that we are using them. They can also be used as 'fillers', words or groups of words without real meaning, to give emphasis, maintain our flow of words, and prevent gaps in the conversation. Here is a real example, taken from a transcript of a television news programme, containing two clichés that the speaker is using to emphasize their point:

> **When it's all said and done at the end of the day,** I can say I made a difference in the world.

As well as being a characteristic feature of speech, clichéd expressions occur especially in certain types of writing (such as journalism) or areas of activity (such as sport, business, or politics).

When communication happens on a more formal level, however, as in a written academic assignment or a job application letter to a prospective employer, your choice of words becomes more important. In such situations every word matters and is noted: while you cannot avoid them completely, overuse of clichés is a barrier to clear expression and gives an impression of laziness and a lack of originality and careful thought.

How to identify a cliché

This is often quite straightforward to do: we can all spot sentences which use some of the more striking or familiar clichés:

> Siddique said: 'I'm sick as a parrot about this but there was no way I could have fought'.

As this real example shows, some of the more noticeable clichés may have begun life as a simile, metaphor, or similar colourful phrase or saying: *as sick as a parrot* originated in sports journalism, and rapidly spread into the wider language.

Because we encounter such expressions all the time in the media, people tend to pick them up very quickly with the result that they soon become tired and overused. Once people start to deploy them indiscriminately in any situation, these vivid phrases begin to lose their impact and become yet another stale and prefabricated chunk of language: they can hinder clear communication instead of contributing to it.

The following table gives some examples of clichéd sayings, metaphors, and similar expressions to look out for and avoid in academic contexts and other formal writing. Some have a long history (*avoid like the plague*) while others are relatively new jargon from the world of sport or business (*cover all the bases*, *think outside the box*). The table also shows the meaning of the terms (with key words highlighted in blue) and suggested actions, such as focusing on key words and finding synonyms for them.

EXPRESSION	MEANING AND KEY WORDS	SUGGESTIONS FOR ACTION
avoid something or someone like the plague	= avoid something or someone completely	say 'avoid completely' or find synonyms for these key words
a baptism of fire	= a difficult introduction to a new job or activity	find synonyms for the key words
bring something to the table	= contribute something useful to a discussion etc.	say 'contribute something useful' or find synonyms for the key words
come full circle	= return to a previous situation	reword along the lines of the meaning given, or find synonyms for the key words
cover all the bases	= deal with something thoroughly	find synonyms for the key words
explore all avenues, explore every avenue, etc.	= investigate all the options available	look up synonyms for the key words.
a level playing field	= a situation in which everyone has an equal chance of success	reword along the lines of the meaning given, using alternatives for the key words if necessary

EXPRESSION	MEANING AND KEY WORDS	SUGGESTIONS FOR ACTION
par for the course	= what is normal or expected in any given circumstances	look up synonyms for the key word
take the path of least resistance	= take the easiest course of action	reword along the lines of the meaning given, or look up synonyms for the key words
think outside the box	= think in an original way; have creative ideas	look up synonyms for the key words.

However, clichés are not always as inventive or easy to spot as the examples shown above. There are some outworn informal and idiomatic expressions which crop up all the time in speech and in the media and which can have a tendency to creep into your writing without your realizing it. They should be avoided in formal contexts because they are often quite wordy and will give the impression to a reader that your work is waffly and imprecise.

As the table below shows, it can be perfectly acceptable and result in a more effective piece of writing if such long-winded and overused expressions are just omitted or replaced with very short and simple alternatives.

EXPRESSION	MEANING AND KEY WORDS	SUGGESTIONS FOR ACTION
at the end of the day	= essentially, finally	use one of the key words or look up synonyms for them
at this moment in time	= now	use the key word or look up alternatives for it
due in large measure to	= mainly because	look up synonyms for the key words
few and far between	= scarce, not frequent	use the key word or look up alternatives for it
in any shape or form, in any way, shape, or form	= in any way or under any circumstances	mainly used for emphasis and can often be omitted, or use the key words shown
in the event that	= if	use the key word or look up alternatives for it
in this day and age	= nowadays	use the key word or look up alternatives for it
it goes without saying	= obviously, clearly	use one of the key words or look up alternatives for them

EXPRESSION	MEANING AND KEY WORDS	SUGGESTIONS FOR ACTION
last but not least	= last in order of being mentioned but not in terms of importance	mainly used for emphasis and so can often be omitted, or find alternatives for the key words
to all intents and purposes	= more or less, in all important respects	mainly used for emphasis and can often be omitted
when all is said and done	= ultimately, when everything is taken into account	use the key word or look up synonyms for it

Taking action: analysis and alternatives

If you know that your written work tends to contain too many clichés, here are some suggested action points to help you brush up your style:

- **Extend your reading.** If you read a wide range of different types of material, from newspapers and magazines to novels and blogs, you will begin to spot clichés more readily and gain a better awareness of the effect that the overuse of such expressions has on a piece of writing.

- **Keep your own list.** As most people have a stock of outworn expressions that they are prone to use you may find it helpful to start keeping your own list. As in the tables given above, your list could show whether these are replaceable with alternatives or whether they contribute nothing in terms of meaning and so can be deleted.

- **Think about what you want to say when you reach for a cliché.** Whether or not you keep a list of clichés, try to get used to analysing the meanings of such expressions. Using a dictionary and thesaurus will help you to do this. You will often find that a cliché can be reduced to one or two words which convey your message in a clearer or more original way.

- **Use appropriate words and phrases.** Remember that the alternatives you choose should suit the context in which they are to appear, so look up any unfamiliar synonyms in a dictionary if you are unsure of their meaning. Also, be careful not to replace one cliché for another.

- **Build a 'cliché alert' into your final checking stages.** When you complete a formal piece of writing such as an essay, a report, or a job application letter, make it a habit to look out for clichés (and alter or omit them if necessary) along with other standard tasks such as proofreading for spelling and grammatical errors.

Following these tips will help you to get accustomed to identifying clichés and to thinking about their underlying meanings. Although you will not be able to avoid clichés completely, you should be able to ensure that you eliminate the more informal, jargon-type, and wordy expressions which are not appropriate in the context of formal writing and which hinder effective communication.

3.2 REDUNDANT EXPRESSIONS

What do all the phrases in bold (heavy) type in the sentences below have in common?

Many **new innovations** were introduced for the viewer.

Take the **following** steps **below** to get on track with your health.

The **pair of twins** were separated at birth.

They are all typical examples of redundant expressions: groups of words in which at least one word is unnecessary because it just repeats the meaning that is already contained in the other word or words. For example, an innovation is defined in the *Compact Oxford English Dictionary for Students* as 'a new method, idea, or product', so there is no need to use *new* to describe it. In the case of *twins*, there can only be two of them, so the word *pair* is superfluous; *following* means 'coming after', so you should not use *below* with it as well.

Redundant expressions crop up all the time in both speech and writing, often without the speaker or writer realizing that they are using them: all of the examples at the start of this section were taken from published material. In speech, they are sometimes used intentionally to emphasize what the speaker is saying.

However, in formal contexts, such as academic assignments, every word matters and empty verbiage is not considered to be good written style: redundant expressions are unnecessarily repetitive, hinder effective communication, and give the impression either that you do not know the meaning of the terms you are using or that you are careless in your choice of words.

The key to a good writing style which avoids redundancy (also known as *tautology*) is to develop your knowledge of what words mean and the ability to analyse your own style so that you become aware of any redundant expressions in your work. Ultimately, you should find that you begin to eliminate them automatically from your writing.

This section outlines some of the different types of redundant expressions to watch out for and offers suggestions on how a thesaurus or dictionary can help you to avoid them.

Types of redundant expressions

There are several ways in which an unwary writer can fall into the tautology trap. Here are some of the main types of redundant expressions and how to deal with them.

- Groups of words in which an adjective (a word used to describe a noun) repeats the meaning contained in the word that it is being used to qualify:

    They're constantly working on **new innovations** in gaming.
                           [adj.] [noun]

    It was a strange place for both of us to be, given our **past histories**.
                           [adj.][noun]

    In a moment of **hopeful optimism**, she jutted her chin out.
          [adj.]   [noun]

ACTION: stop and think about what you are writing and, if you need to, check the meaning of the noun in a dictionary. For instance, *optimism* means 'hopefulness and confidence about the future of something', so you do not need to use *hopeful* as well. Simply omit the unnecessary adjective:

    They're constantly working on **innovations** in gaming.

    It was a strange place for both of us to be, given our **histories**.

    In a moment of **optimism**, she jutted her chin out.

- Expressions that consist of an adverb (a word that gives more information about an adjective, verb, or other adverb) that repeats the meaning contained in a word (especially a verb) that begins with a prefix such as re- (meaning 'again' or 'back') or pro- ('out' 'forwards', etc.):

    She often **reverts back** to childish ways.
           [verb]   [adverb]

    The sign above the door **protruded out** over the sidewalk.
                   [verb]   [adverb]

ACTION: look up the prefix-word in a dictionary to check its meaning. Once you have established that one or other of the words is superfluous, the easiest course of action is simply to leave out the adverb:

    She often **reverts** to childish ways.

    The sign above the door **protruded** over the sidewalk.

Alternatively, you could keep the adverb and use a thesaurus to find a suitable synonym for the verb:

    She often **goes** back to childish ways.

    The sign above the door **jutted** out over the sidewalk.

- Groups of different words in which one means exactly the same as another or others:

    The fertilizer had no direct fungicidal effect **but nevertheless** it completely arrested the spread of the fungus.

    The **reason for this is because** nobody cares.

ACTION: these sorts of errors can usually be spotted by reading through your work and thinking carefully about what you are writing.

A thesaurus can help here, too: if you look up *nevertheless* you will find that *but* is given as a synonym for it. You can therefore deduce that *but* has a similar meaning to *nevertheless* and one or the other can be omitted:

> The fertilizer had no direct fungicidal effect **but** it completely arrested the spread of the fungus.

KEY POINTS

- Develop your knowledge of what words mean and the ability to analyse your own style so that you become aware of any redundant expressions in your work.

- Use a dictionary and a thesaurus to check any words you are unsure of, to choose appropriate alternatives, or to find out if they have the same meaning.

SECTION 4:
Close synonyms:
choosing the best word

It is often hard to know when to choose one word rather than another when both have broadly similar meanings. This section explains the differences between many groups of close synonyms to enable you to make well-informed decisions about word choice, and so make your writing more accurate and effective. The distinctions made are based on careful analysis of thousands of examples of real English.

1. accurate, precise, exact

All these words apply to information or statements that are correct.

- **accurate** means that a statement, description, or information is factually correct or corresponds to reality:

  Buyers of herbal medicines must have accurate information about the contents.

  I believe this poll to be an accurate reflection of public opinion.

- **precise** contains an idea of minute attention to detail and implies that something can be measured or quantified (if you say that it is 4.04 and 3 seconds, you are being precise but not necessarily *accurate*—your watch may be wrong):

  These samples allow precise measurements of the abundance of elements and isotopes in the sun.

  It may also be used for emphasis:

  At that precise moment, his phone rang.

- **exact** emphasizes that something has been definitely identified, with no margin for vagueness or error:

  We may never know the exact number of deaths.

  Like **precise**, it may also be used for emphasis:

  Alissa was in the exact spot where he had left her.

2. agree, consent, assent, acquiesce

These verbs all relate to reaching agreement and all of them can be used for giving permission, but the contributions made by each person or group involved may be different.

- **agree** is the only word of the four that describes sharing the same opinion about something with other people:

They agreed payment terms.

We'll have to decide what compromise we can agree on.

The company and the shareholders agreed to a lock-out clause.

- Someone who **consents to** something proposed to them has the power or legal status to accept or reject it. **Agree to** can also be used in this way:

  The Attorney General has to consent to any prosecution under the Act.

  The county council's barrister agreed to the adjournment.

- People also typically **consent to** undergoing medical treatment or scientific tests, and to sex (the word often appears in legal contexts):

  Patients must consent to any treatment they receive.

  We agree with the view of the police that the applicant consented to intercourse.

- A person who **assents to** a proposal is generally one whose approval is required, although they may not feel very strongly about it or be involved in it—they simply accept what is presented to them:

  The inspector assented to the remark with a nod.

- To **acquiesce** implies that a person is accepting something by default; often what is accepted is not something that the person really wants, and their agreement is due to lack of bargaining power or the will to resist:

  The majority acquiesced to the wishes of a handful of zealots.

3. *appropriate, suitable, proper, fitting*

- Something that is **appropriate** matches the requirements of a particular situation:

  She searched for an appropriate word.

  We need care packages appropriate to people's needs.

  It is often used for something that is considered to be socially or morally acceptable:

  Women needn't define themselves by what society dictates to be appropriate behaviour.

  Some of the subject matter may not be appropriate for younger children.

- **suitable** is a more general word for things that are right for a particular purpose or occasion, and they need not be the only correct or possible ones:

  He may be able to find suitable alternative work.

  The site isn't suitable for residential use.

- A **proper** person or thing may well be the only correct person or thing for a purpose or a job:

  If you do not wear proper running shoes, you may develop an assortment of knee, hip, and heel injuries.

proper is also used to mean 'socially acceptable', especially in literary contexts:

In those days, it was not proper for a girl to travel on her own.

■ **fitting** is only used to describe things (never people); such things are regarded as particularly apt, and usually desirable, in the circumstances:

The film is a fitting tribute to Naipaul in the year of his Nobel Prize.

4. artificial, synthetic, man-made

These words all describe something that does not occur naturally.

■ Something that is **artificial** has been deliberately made by people. The word is particularly used to describe copies or replacements of natural objects, substances, and body parts, made from a synthetic material:

Choose a brand that's free of sugar and artificial sweeteners.

She will need to learn how to use artificial limbs.

artificial is also used in a disapproving way, especially to describe behaviour or people that are affected or insincere:

Some people sound horribly artificial on the phone.

■ **synthetic** materials and substances are produced by humans through chemical processes, rather than grown naturally:

Synthetic fabrics can imitate everything from silk to rubber.

It can also be used to show disapproval of emotion or artistic expression that seems contrived and manufactured:

All the overt sexual stuff in movies is synthetic, contrived, and mass-produced.

■ The term **man-made** is usually neutral, conveying no criticism or disapproval. It describes something that has been created or happens through human intervention, and is applied chiefly to objects and materials, but also to undesirable events or effects:

Most climatologists believe global warming is a man-made disaster.

Such a tower would be taller than the world's tallest man-made structure.

5. care, caution, prudence, wariness

These words all refer to attention or thought that a person gives to something so as to avoid an undesirable outcome.

■ **care** describes consideration or attention given to something so that it will be done well, without resulting in mistakes or harm:

This is a sensitive subject that must be treated with care.

■ **caution** is typically used to refer to taking special measures when dealing with situations or things that involve physical or financial risks:

All farmers should exercise caution in dealing with the disease.
I would advise caution with respect to investing in equities this year.

- **prudence** refers to being sensible and showing forethought when making decisions or dealing with financial or political matters:
  He built up a fortune through a lifetime of financial prudence.

- If someone shows **wariness** of someone or something, it means that they suspect that they might be dangerous, untrustworthy, or likely to cause problems:
  She was infamous for her wariness of strangers.

6. characteristic, typical, distinctive

- **characteristic** describes a feature or quality that is immediately recognizable as an essential part of the nature of someone or something:
  He has behaved with characteristic generosity.
  Pinnacles of rock are characteristic of this mountain range.

- Something that is a **typical** member of a class of things has all the central defining features of the members of that class:
  The house is a typical example of a property built around this time.
  The site was typical of farmland in the area.

- A **distinctive** feature or quality is not necessarily essential or typical but serves to distinguish one person or thing from all others:
  The development's most distinctive feature is a two-mile monorail.
  She is one of the most distinctive soul voices around.

7. complicated, complex, intricate, involved

- **complicated** and **complex** have very similar meanings, both words being used to describe things that consist of many connected parts or strands:
  The equation works very well with complicated chemical structures like pesticides.
  His files are protected by a complex system of firewalls.

  While **complicated** may be used to describe something that is annoyingly difficult to understand or deal with, **complex** is often used more approvingly, to suggest that complexity makes someone or something interesting or intriguing:
  Two in three people thought pensions were too complicated.
  She knew his character to be deep and complex.

- **intricate** is typically used to show approval when describing an elaborate relationship of small details that calls for very close attention if it is to be appreciated or understood:
  The roofs are decorated with intricate iron trelliswork.

■ If something is **involved** it often has a confusing number of details, making it difficult to grasp:

Simple sentences are more likely to be grammatically correct than long, involved ones.

8. continual, continuous, constant, ceaseless

These words describe processes or situations which do not stop, but with different emphases.

■ **continual** mainly describes an event or action that is repeated again and again:

Look at the website for continual updates on performances, venues, etc.

■ **continuous** and **continual** can both be used to refer to a process or situation that never stops, although **continuous** is much more frequent in this sense. Of the two words, **continual** is more likely to be used to describe undesirable things:

Education is a continuous process.
He was in continual pain.

■ **continuous** can also describe a physically unbroken object or line:

The area is outlined in a continuous black line.

■ if something is **constant** then it does not stop (it shares this meaning with **continuous**):

The gallery attracted a constant stream of visitors.

constant may also be used to describe something that continues over time and does not vary in level, rate, or degree:

Store samples at a controlled constant temperature.

■ **ceaseless** is a more literary word describing, typically, something undesirable that does not stop:

The most critical problem involves the ceaseless guerrilla attacks.

9. convince, persuade, induce

All these words refer to causing someone to do something that you wish them to do.

■ **convince** refers mainly to causing someone to have a firm belief that something is the truth:

He managed to convince the police that his story was true.

Although **convince** can also mean 'persuade someone to do something', it is best to avoid this use in careful writing as some people regard it as incorrect.

■ If you **persuade** someone, you use reasoning or argument to make them do or believe something, possibly against their better judgement or personal preference:

My wife persuaded me to go to the doctor.
He persuaded her that nothing was going on.

- **Induce** is used to imply that the person doing the inducing may be bringing pressure to bear on someone in order to make them do something, or that they may have to resort to bribes, deception, or threats to do this rather than argument:

He alleged that the organization made misrepresentations to induce him to enter the contract.

10. discourage, deter, dissuade

Someone who lacks the authority to order another person not to do something may have to adopt other means of preventing them.

- If a person or situation **discourages** someone from doing something, it makes them reluctant to do or continue with it by undermining their confidence or optimism about their chances of success:

Her father discouraged her from going into the legal profession.
The college fears that higher fees will discourage mature students.

- To **deter** someone from doing something involves creating, forming, or pointing out a serious obstacle that will confront them if they go ahead with their plans:

High fees deter some patients from visiting a consultant.

An action can be **discouraged** or **deterred**, as well as a person:

Inflation discourages investment.
The mere existence of nuclear weapons was sufficient to deter aggression.

- To **dissuade** someone is to use reasoning to make them see the difficulty or undesirable nature of what they propose to do:

He attempted to dissuade them from resigning.

It is always a person or group that is **dissuaded**, not an action or event.

11. examine, review, study, survey

- To **examine** something is to investigate or describe it in depth, either in order to understand it or to help other people to understand it:

Researchers examined data from previous studies of more than 1,900 couples.
The next chapter examines the different coming-of-age rituals of boys and girls.

- **review** chiefly means to assess or evaluate an existing situation, with a view to making changes if necessary:

Monthly meetings will provide an opportunity for the team to meet to review the overall situation.

- To **study** something is to research and analyse a situation, subject, or phenomenon in detail, in order to understand it or to increase your knowledge of it:

The researchers studied five sites in subarctic Alaska, each with a different kind of plant cover.

The council will carefully study the legislation to see what impact it would have on the town.

■ To **survey** something is to carry out a general investigation or overview of it:

Professor Hopcroft competently surveys the standard literature on the topic.

12. flout, contravene, violate, infringe, breach

All these words describe breaking a law, agreement, or order. They are all more formal than the basic verb **break** and are found particularly in official writing.

■ **flout** and **violate** suggest that a law, agreement, or treaty has been broken deliberately. The implication is that the person or organization committing the act is aware of what they are doing:

French ministers decided to flout EU law and retain the ban.

Both countries are flagrantly violating global trade agreements.

■ **contravene** is often used of breaking distinct parts of a law or set of rules:

The scheme contravenes the provisions of article 43.

It may also describe acts which are not actually against the law, but which nevertheless do not comply with a particular set of directions or instructions:

Refuse collection crews may leave a bin unemptied if it contravenes certain guidelines.

■ **infringe** is used especially in business or commercial contexts. The offence may have been committed deliberately or inadvertently:

Anyone who infringes copyright—even unwittingly—may have their assets seized.

The company claimed that the website infringed its trademark.

■ **breach** is often used of breaking an order imposed by a court or similar body, or of breaking the terms of a contract:

He was sent to prison for breaching his anti-social behaviour order.

The workers had breached their contracts of employment.

13. forbid, ban, prohibit

These words refer to the issuing of orders by people in authority, to prevent something from happening or to stop someone from doing something.

■ To **forbid** is to order someone not to do something or to say that something may not be done, typically in matters of custom, religion, or personal behaviour:

Eric's mother forbade them to hold band practices at their house.

It is forbidden to destroy anything associated with God's worship.

- **ban** typically refers to a law or other official order that abolishes an existing practice, activity, or item:

The President banned imports from that country, citing a repressive military regime.

He was banned from driving for a year.

- To **prohibit** someone or something is to prevent them officially from doing something or to stop something from happening, usually by means of a law or regulation:

US Federal law prohibits the sale of human organs.

The couple were prohibited from owning any animals for five years.

14. idea, concept, notion

- **idea** has the widest range of these words. It covers both ways of understanding something and plans or intentions. An idea may be a belief or opinion, or a mental impression of what someone or something is like:

A trip up the Eiffel tower will give you a good idea of the layout of Paris.

Obviously we needed to move away from the Victorian ideas of bringing up children.

It may also be a thought or a suggestion as to a possible course of action, or a possible solution to a problem:

The idea of linking pay to performance has caught on.

She had an idea. It would only buy her a bit of time but it was worth a try.

- A **concept** is an understanding of something abstract, usually quite a broad subject. It is more fully developed or worked out than an idea:

His theories rest on his concept of consciousness.

The problem is that there is not just one concept of democracy.

- A **notion** is a belief or an understanding of something. Notions are generally vaguer or more tentative than ideas and there may be a suggestion, not present in the other two words, that the belief or understanding in question is mistaken or misguided:

The scheme should help to dispel the notion that HIV is a death sentence.

I come from a farming background so I don't have any romantic notions about living in the country.

15. illegal, unlawful, illicit

- An **illegal** action, activity, or object is one that is specifically forbidden by the laws of a particular country or state:

The police raid uncovered large quantities of illegal drugs.

The illegal dumping of industrial waste is on the rise.

- **illegal** and **unlawful** have overlapping but slightly different meanings, with **unlawful** having a wider, more general application than **illegal**. An unlawful act may be against the law:

The defendant also admitted unlawful possession of a firearm.

In other cases, it may just break the rules that apply in a particular context or situation rather than those of a country or state. This means that an unlawful act is not necessarily a criminal one. For example:

The striker was penalized for unlawful use of the hands.

In this case, it is the rules of *football* that have been broken, and so the act is subject only to the penalties set out by that game.

- **illicit** is typically used to refer to actions that do not conform to a set of accepted moral standards, or to things which are generally disapproved of by society. It implies secrecy and often the excitement or attraction of something that is clandestine or forbidden:

  Rachel had been having an illicit affair with an older man.
  The bar is perfect for intimate chats during those illicit late-night liaisons.

16. *inherent, intrinsic, essential, innate, inborn*

These words are all applied to qualities or features that are a central element in a person or thing's nature.

- **inherent** is typically used to describe something regarded as negative, or as having unpleasant associations:

  He was aware of the inherent dangers in motorcycle racing.
  The tensions inherent in Russian society were multiplied by the strains of the First World War.

- **intrinsic** is a more general term for a feature or quality regarded as central to a person or thing's nature. If something is described as intrinsic, it is typically regarded in a positive or a neutral light:

  The intrinsic value of biological diversity.
  I thought freedom and justice were intrinsic to a democratic state.

- **essential** features are so important that a person or thing would not be the same without them:

  The group is at pains to ensure that the essential character of the area is not lost.
  Conflict is one of the essential features of the genre.

  essential may be used to suggest that a characteristic is fundamental to someone's nature, even if more superficial characteristics appear to conceal or contradict it:

  He believed in the essential goodness of human nature.

- An **innate** characteristic is one that a person is born with, rather than one they acquire at a later stage in life:

  Children are born with the innate ability to learn language.
  They seem to have an innate desire to help other people.

■ **inborn** also describes something that has existed since birth, but it is much less common than **innate**. Unlike **innate**, it is used of physical qualities:

Proper guidance is needed, but inborn artistic talent matters more than anything.

Almost all cases of the disease result from an inborn defect in the production of collagen.

17. native, indigenous, aboriginal

These three words all describe a person or thing associated with a particular place as a result of their birth or origin.

■ **native** refers to the place where a person was born, or to a quality or ability that someone has had or learned from birth:

He left his native Russia to live in Australia.

She speaks German as well as Bosnian, her native language.

It can also describe people or things that originated in the region or country being discussed:

A survey of Britain's native species of birds, butterflies, and plants was published last week.

The plant is native to SE Asia.

It is best to avoid using **native** if you are referring generally to the people who originally lived in a non-European or non-Western country (*native peoples/native cultures*) but it is usually acceptable if used to describe a person who was born in a specified country:

A native Russian, he now lives in New Zealand.

■ **indigenous** is a more technical word. It refers to the people, animals, or plants that are naturally found in a particular place, and to things associated with them:

New Zealand's indigenous flora and fauna must be protected.

These palm trees are indigenous to the south-eastern US.

indigenous is also a more neutral word than **native**, and it is perfectly acceptable to use it to refer to groups of people:

The indigenous peoples of the Amazon basin.

■ **aboriginal** refers to the earliest known inhabitants of a place, for example those living in a country before settlers arrived from abroad and established colonies in it:

The aboriginal peoples of North America.

aboriginal is not used to refer to plants or animals. If you are referring specifically to the earliest inhabitants of Australia, the word is usually written with a capital letter.

The area is the centre of Sydney's Aboriginal community.

18. necessary, requisite, essential, indispensable

- Something that is **necessary** must be accepted or done, whether you like it or not. The word refers to something without which a condition cannot be fulfilled or which is needed for a particular purpose:

  All counsellors had the necessary qualifications and experience to be accredited by the BAC.

  It's not necessary for you to attend this meeting.

  The owners were advised that planning permission was necessary.

- **requisite** is very similar in meaning to **necessary**, but it is more formal and often describes something which is required by specific regulations:

  Each event must be staffed by the requisite number of officials.

  The application will not be processed until the requisite fee is paid.

  Note that **requisite** is almost always used before its noun.

- **essential** is the strongest of the four words, referring to something of the utmost importance in a particular situation or context:

  It is essential that our pilots are given the best possible training.

  Protein is an essential part of our diet.

- **indispensable** is typically used of someone or something that is already present. It tends to suggest that the possibility of having to do without them has been suggested or contemplated:

  Groves is indispensable to the success of the project.

  Email is an indispensable tool for modern communication, even though there is so much spam these days.

19. new, novel, original, innovative

These four synonyms emphasize different aspects of being new.

- **new** itself is a neutral word, implying neither approval nor disapproval of the thing that has not existed before:

  Last night we went to a new bar in Shoreditch.

  The company is looking at new ways to raise revenue.

- Something that is **novel** is interestingly new or unusual. The word implies that the new thing is either surprising or slightly strange, and it tends to convey approval or gentle amusement:

  Computers can develop interesting and novel design solutions.

  He came up with a novel way of keeping in touch with his family while he's away: he uses homing pigeons to carry messages.

  However **novel** is often used ironically, to suggest that something should not be a new or unusual phenomenon at all:

  Here's a novel idea—why not do some work this afternoon?

- **original** is used for things that are ingenious and neither derived from anything that has existed before nor dependent on anyone else's ideas:

The brasserie offers a refreshingly original menu.

It's a taut, fast-moving detective story with strikingly original characters.

- **innovative** products, methods, or approaches are new and advanced, and often provide solutions to a problem or difficult situation:

  It's a design that incorporates innovative environmental technology.

  Innovative strategies to combat malaria are needed.

20. permission, agreement, authorization, consent

- **permission** is generally given by someone who is in a position of power or authority, and who will not be involved in the activity for which permission is sought:

  The court gave them permission to stay in the UK for the next three years.

  You can't expect just to wander over someone else's land without asking permission first.

- **agreement** may be used in the same way as **permission**:

  I'm an adult and quite able to get married without my parents' agreement.

- **authorization** is official permission for or approval of an undertaking or action, and is usually given by a person of superior rank within an institution or system:

  The plan was presented to President Kennedy for authorization.

  Action should not be taken without the explicit authorization of the UN Security Council.

- **consent** is typically used in situations in which the point at issue is whether someone is able or allowed to make a free choice that is informed by at least some understanding or awareness of the possible alternatives and consequences:

  Health-care providers must obtain patients' written consent before they disclose any information.

  No change may be made without the consent of all the partners.

21. replace, supersede, supplant

These verbs are used when one person or thing takes the place of another, but each of them has different implications, making them more appropriate for different contexts.

- **replace** is the most neutral term. One person or thing may replace another as part of a normal process or in an emergency:

  Diesels gradually replaced steam locomotives.

  Brad Williams replaces Jason Gillespie, who is injured.

- If one thing is **superseded** by another, its place has been taken by something more up-to-date or advanced. The replacement is generally considered to be better than, or preferable to, the original:

His theory was superseded by subsequent research.

Many consumers view i-mode as an interim technology that will soon be superseded by 3G.

- If one person or thing **supplants** another, however, the implication is often that they are regarded as a poor substitute for the previous person or thing:

In his opinion, e-books will never supplant printed texts.

Good old-fashioned home-baking is often supplanted by processed food full of dubious ingredients.

22. restriction, constraint, restraint, limitation

All these words refer to something that limits what can be done or what can happen.

- A **restriction** is a law or rule made by someone in authority. If a restriction is not heeded, there are likely to be legal penalties:

There are planning restrictions on commercial development.

The US authorities began to lift flight restrictions yesterday.

- A **constraint** is a limiting factor that exists as a result of a current situation, rather than something that is made or imposed. There is less scope for changing or removing a **constraint** than a **restriction**:

The availability of water is the main constraint on food production.

The project had to be put back because of time constraints and budget difficulties.

- **restraint** can be used interchangeably with **constraint**, to refer to a factor or condition that already exists:

Decisions are made within the financial restraints of the budget.

But a **restraint** may be internal rather than external: it may proceed from a fear of what other people may think, or from someone's own sense of what is acceptable:

The book's message is that social restraints and modern technology hamper our ability to connect with one another.

- **limitation** is the most general of these terms: a limitation can be a rule made by an authority or an existing fact or condition:

The new administration imposed sharp limitations on borrowing or investment.

Some parts of the book had to be left out due to limitations of time.

23. sarcastic, ironic, sardonic, caustic

- A **sarcastic** comment expresses the opposite of what the words actually mean. It is usually intended to make fun of the person on the receiving end, either from a desire to be unpleasant to them or to entertain other people. It is not always easy to judge whether a comment is sarcastic or meant literally:

That's nice,' Broomhead said, in his most sarcastic manner.

'You're the expert, after all.' I wondered if she was being sarcastic.

- **sardonic** implies a slightly stronger element of mockery than **sarcastic**. Sardonic observations may be wry or cynical and are still likely to entertain or amuse other people, but they are unlikely to be misinterpreted:

We all respected him, and feared his sardonic wit.

He casts a sardonic eye on the absurdities of pop stardom.

- **ironic** remarks convey the opposite of their literal meaning in a more subtle way than either **sarcastic** or **sardonic**. The suggestion is of wry amusement rather than mockery, and there is rarely any intention of being unpleasant:

Suddenly it's sexy to be a Canadian novelist, he says, with an ironic smile.

The title of the film, **American Splendor**, is ironic.

- **caustic** remarks are critical, bitter, and intended to be hurtful: the mockery they convey is not intended to entertain other people but to wound the person at whom they are directed:

People made caustic remarks that took months, or even years, to forget.

Her caustic comments on the other housemates were pretty bitchy, but always spot on.

24. subject, topic, theme

- **subject** is the most general term for something that is (or could be) written, talked, or thought about:

His mind was no longer on the subject of politics.

Please send in questions on any subjects you would like discussed.

The issue is likely to be a subject for debate in the forthcoming elections.

It is also, of course, a branch of knowledge studied at school, college, or university:

Her A-level subjects will include history, English literature, and psychology.

- When distinguished from **subject**, **topic** can refer to a smaller and more specific area that is dealt with in a piece of writing or in speech. It is also the most common word for something discussed in conversation:

From this very complex subject, two topics have been selected for detailed discussion.

Once again, the main topic of conversation was the weather.

- A **theme** is typically associated with a relatively long piece of writing or discussion, or with an event or work of art. It tends to be an underlying idea that recurs throughout something so as to unify it:

His first novel explores the theme of emotional and cultural displacement.

Travel is the theme of this year's exhibition.

The central theme of Hopper's paintings is the loneliness of city life.

25. sure, certain, convinced, positive, definite

These adjectives all describe someone who is confident that something is the case or that it will happen.

- **sure** and **certain** have very similar meanings, although **certain** implies a slightly stronger degree of conviction than **sure**:

  Are you absolutely sure/certain about this?

  I'm sure/certain that he'll handle the situation well.

- **convinced** suggests that a person is confident about something because the evidence seems to prove it, or because someone else has persuaded them:

  Everyone seems convinced of his guilt.

  I'm still not convinced that your idea will work.

- **positive** is slightly more informal than **sure**, **certain**, or **convinced** and is often found in spoken contexts:

  'Are you sure she won't want to pursue the issue?' 'I'm positive.'

- If someone is **definite** about something, they are not only confident that it is true but are also stating their belief very firmly:

  She was definite about what she'd seen: it was the same man.

SECTION 5:
The vocabulary gap: words with no synonyms

There are some English words that have an enormous number of synonyms and seem to inspire ever more new alternatives. It is perhaps not surprising that the words which produce the most synonyms tend to be those which refer to parts of the body, bodily functions, sexual activity, etc., or which convey a negative opinion of someone or something. Many of the synonyms for this type of word are informal, or else they are 'taboo', i.e. they are likely to offend or shock people. Taboo terms should never be used in formal writing, and so this thesaurus does not include them, although it does contain a selection of established and well-known informal vocabulary.

But there are certain very common words that have surprisingly few synonyms, or even none at all, and this can be frustrating when you are trying to make your writing fresh and interesting. Here are a few examples of basic English words that lack standard alternatives:

1. shallow: having a short distance between the top and the bottom:

Max paddled in the shallow pool.

■ POSSIBLE SYNONYMS: none, apart from 'not deep'

2. deep: extending far down or in from the top or surface:

Lifeguards had warned the children not to swim in deep water.

■ POSSIBLE SYNONYMS: bottomless

You could perhaps use *bottomless* if you were writing in a literary style:

He sat in the shadow of the trees, the rocks and caverns at his back, the bottomless waters of the lake before him.

However, it would sound out of place in most types of writing.

3. borrow: to take and use something belonging to someone with the intention of returning it:

Could I borrow your phone for a minute?

■ POSSIBLE SYNONYMS: cadge

cadge is an informal word and so is not suitable for formal contexts. It also implies that someone is asking for something to which they are not strictly entitled, or that they do not intend to return it:

She decided to try to cadge some money from her ex-best-friend Lavinia.

Note that *lend* is commonly used as a synonym for *borrow* in some British dialects (e.g. *can I lend your pen?*), but it should not be used in this sense in formal writing.

4. forget: to fail to remember something:

I've forgotten her name.

■ POSSIBLE SYNONYMS: none, apart from 'not remember'

5. kiss: to touch with the lips as a sign of affection or greeting

The 70 soldiers hugged and kissed their wives and children, who have been waiting anxiously back home since the war began.

■ POSSIBLE SYNONYMS: peck on the cheek, snog

peck on the cheek is informal, while *snog* is very informal, and refers only to passionate kissing between lovers. You would not be able to use either of them in the example above.

6. drown: to die as a result of submersion in water:

A motorist drowned yesterday when her car plunged off the edge of the quay.

■ POSSIBLE SYNONYMS: go to a watery grave

This expression has a humorous ring to it and is likely to sound inappropriately light-hearted if substituted for *drown* in most contexts.

7. dissolve: (of a solid) to disperse into a liquid so as to form a solution

The powdered form of the drug dissolves in water.

■ POSSIBLE SYNONYMS: none

You could potentially rewrite this sentence as:

The powdered form of the drug breaks down in water.
or:
The powdered form of the drug goes into solution in water.

But the first alternative is not as precise, and the second is not very elegant.

In these kinds of situations, where no standard English synonym exists for the word you have in mind, there is no option but to reword your sentence or even to repeat the word, if its meaning is so specific that rewording would sound strained or fail to convey the idea precisely.

Some people argue that there are no true synonyms at all, and that every one is subtly different from even its closest cousins, whether in nuance, context, or usage. However, on most occasions, it is possible to use a thesaurus to find a good substitute for the word you have in mind or have used before. The important thing is to understand how your thesaurus presents its information and use it judiciously, in conjunction with a good dictionary, making sure that you never use a word with which you are not familiar without looking it up first, and then only if you are confident that you can use it appropriately. This will ensure that you convey your intended message in the most clear and effective way, and make a good impression on your reader or audience.

label noun

1 *the price is clearly stated on the label:* **tag**, ticket, tab, sticker, marker, docket, chit, chitty.
2 *a designer label:* **brand**, brand name, trade name, trademark, make, logo.
3 *I always resented the label the media came up with for me:* **designation**, description, tag; name, epithet, nickname, title, sobriquet, pet name; formal denomination, appellation, cognomen; informal moniker, handle.

▷ **verb**
1 *label each jar with the date:* **tag**, ticket, mark, docket.
2 *school tests labelled the children as underachievers:* **categorize**, classify, class, describe, designate, identify; mark, stamp, brand, condemn, pigeonhole, stereotype, typecast; call, name, term, dub, nickname.

laborious adjective

1 *tunnelling was a dangerous and laborious job:* **arduous**, hard, heavy, difficult, strenuous, gruelling, punishing, exacting, tough, onerous, burdensome, backbreaking, trying, challenging; tiring, fatiguing, exhausting, wearying, wearing, taxing, demanding, wearisome; tedious, boring.
2 *Doug's slow, laborious style:* **laboured**, strained, forced, contrived, affected, stiff, stilted, unnatural, artificial, overwrought, heavy, ponderous, convoluted.
OPPOSITES: easy, effortless.

labour noun

1 *manual labour:* **work**, hard work, toil, exertion, industry, drudgery, effort, menial work; literary travail; informal slog, grind, sweat, elbow grease; Brit. informal graft, donkey work.
2 *the conflict between capital and labour:* **workers**, employees, workmen, workforce, staff, working people, blue-collar workers, labourers, labour force, the proletariat.
3 *the labours of Hercules:* **task**, job, chore, mission, assignment, challenge.
4 *she had a long and difficult labour:* **childbirth**, birth, delivery; contractions, labour pains; technical parturition; dated confinement.
OPPOSITES: rest.

▷ **verb**
1 *a project on which he had laboured for many years:* **work**, work hard, toil, grind away, struggle, strive, exert yourself, work your fingers to the bone, work like a Trojan/slave; informal slave away, slog away, plug away, peg away; Brit. informal graft.
2 *Newcastle laboured to break down the home team's defence:* **strive**, struggle, endeavour, work, try hard, make every effort, do your best, do your utmost, do all you can, give your all, go all out, fight, put yourself out, apply yourself, exert yourself; informal bend over backwards, pull out all the stops.
3 *there is no need to labour the point:* **overemphasize**, belabour, overstress, overdo, strain, overplay, make too much of, exaggerate, dwell on, harp on about.
4 *he was labouring under a misapprehension:* **suffer from**, be a victim of, be deceived by, be misled by.

laboured adjective

1 *his harsh, laboured breathing:* **strained**, difficult, forced, laborious.
2 *a rather laboured joke:* **contrived**, forced, strained, stilted, unnatural, artificial, overdone, ponderous, laborious, unconvincing.
OPPOSITES: easy, natural.

labourer noun workman, worker,

working man, manual worker, unskilled worker, blue-collar worker, hand; dated navvy.

labyrinth noun

1 *a labyrinth of little streets:* **maze**, warren, network, complex, web.
2 *the labyrinth of conflicting laws and regulations:* **tangle**, web, morass, jungle, confusion, entanglement; jumble; informal mishmash.

labyrinthine adjective

1 *the stadium's labyrinthine corridors:* **maze-like**, winding, twisting, serpentine, meandering, wandering, rambling.
2 *a labyrinthine criminal justice system:* **complicated**, intricate, complex, involved, tortuous, convoluted, tangled, elaborate; confusing, puzzling, mystifying, bewildering, baffling, Byzantine.
OPPOSITES: straight, straightforward.

lace noun shoelace, bootlace, shoestring, lacing, thong, tie.
▷**verb**
1 *he laced up his shoes:* fasten, do up, tie up, secure, knot.
2 *he laced his fingers with mine:* entwine, intertwine, twine, entangle, interweave, link; braid, plait.
3 *a mug of tea laced with rum:* flavour, mix, blend, fortify, strengthen, stiffen, season, spice, enrich, liven up; doctor, adulterate; informal spike.

lacerate verb *the glass had lacerated his cheek:* cut, gash, slash, tear, rip, shred, scratch, scrape, graze, score; wound, injure, hurt; literary rend.

laceration noun gash, cut, wound, injury, tear, slash, abrasion, scratch, scrape, graze.

lack noun *we were hampered by a lack of cash:* absence, shortage, deficiency, dearth, shortfall, deficit, scarcity, want, need, paucity, unavailability, scarceness, insufficiency.
OPPOSITES: abundance.
▷verb *she's immature and lacks judgement:* be without, be lacking, be in need of, need, require, want, be short of, be deficient in, be bereft of, be low on, be pressed for, have insufficient.

lackadaisical adjective careless, lazy, lax, unenthusiastic, apathetic, half-hearted, indifferent, unconcerned, casual, offhand, blasé; informal laid back, couldn't-care-less, easy-going.

lackey noun *the general was described as a US lackey:* toady, minion; tool, puppet, instrument, pawn; informal yes-man, stooge.

lacking adjective
1 *what was lacking was hard evidence:* absent, missing, non-existent, unavailable.
2 *workers were asked in what ways they found their managers lacking:* deficient, inadequate, wanting, defective, flawed, faulty, unacceptable, imperfect, inferior.
3 *the game was lacking in atmosphere:* without, devoid of, bereft of; deficient in, low on, short on, in need of.

lacklustre adjective *he delivered a limp and lacklustre speech:* uninspired, uninspiring, unimaginative, dull, humdrum, colourless, characterless, bland, insipid, vapid, flat, dry, lifeless, tame, prosaic, spiritless; boring, monotonous, dreary, tedious.
OPPOSITES: inspired.

laconic adjective
1 *a laconic reply:* brief, concise, succinct, pithy, terse, short, monosyllabic; epigrammatic, aphoristic.
2 *their laconic press officer was as unhelpful as ever:* taciturn, uncommunicative, reticent, quiet, unforthcoming.
OPPOSITES: verbose, loquacious.

lad noun (informal)
1 *a twelve-year-old lad:* boy, schoolboy, youth, youngster, juvenile; informal kid, nipper, whippersnapper; Scottish informal laddie; old use or humorous stripling.
2 *a hard-working lad:* man, young man, fellow; informal guy; Brit. informal chap, bloke, geezer; N. Amer. informal dude.

ladder noun *I had begun to edge my way up the academic ladder:* hierarchy, scale, grading, ranking, pecking order.

laden adjective *a tray laden with dinner plates:* loaded, weighed down, piled high, burdened, overloaded, full, filled.

ladle verb spoon, scoop, dish out, serve.

lady noun
1 *several ladies replied to his letter:* woman, female; literary maid, damsel, wench; N. Amer. informal dame, broad.
2 *lords and ladies were once entertained at this house:* noblewoman, duchess, countess, peeress, viscountess, baroness; old use gentlewoman.

ladylike adjective genteel, polite, refined, well bred, cultivated, polished, decorous, proper, respectable, seemly, well mannered, cultured, sophisticated, elegant.
OPPOSITES: coarse.

lag verb *Elizabeth had lagged behind:* fall behind, straggle, fall back, trail behind, drag your feet, hang back, not keep pace, bring up the rear.
OPPOSITES: keep up.

lagoon noun inland sea, bay, lake, bight, pool; Scottish loch; Anglo-Irish lough; N. Amer. bayou.

laid-back adjective (informal) relaxed, easy-going, calm, free and easy, casual, nonchalant, insouciant, unexcitable, imperturbable, unruffled, blasé, cool, {cool, calm, and collected}, unperturbed, unflustered, unworried, unconcerned, leisurely, unhurried; stoical, phlegmatic, tolerant; informal unflappable.
OPPOSITES: uptight.

lair noun
1 *the animal retreated to its lair:* den, burrow, hole, tunnel, cave.
2 *the boat finally reached his lair, deep in the jungle:* hideaway, hiding place, hideout, refuge, sanctuary, haven, shelter, retreat; informal hidey-hole.

laissez-faire noun free enterprise, free trade, non-intervention, free-market capitalism.

lake noun pond, pool, tarn, reservoir, lagoon, waterhole, inland sea; Scottish loch; Anglo-Irish lough; N. Amer. bayou; literary mere.

WORD LINKS
lacustrine relating to lakes

lambaste verb criticize, take to task, chastise, censure, harangue, rail at, rant at, fulminate against; upbraid, scold, reprimand, rebuke, berate, reprove, admonish, chide; formal castigate, excoriate; informal lay into, pitch into, tear into, give someone a dressing-down, carpet, tell off, bawl out; Brit. informal tick off, have a go at; N. Amer. informal chew out.

lame adjective
1 *the horse was lame:* limping, hobbling; incapacitated.
2 *that's a pretty lame excuse:* feeble, weak, thin, flimsy, poor; unconvincing, implausible, unlikely.
OPPOSITES: convincing.

lament noun
1 *the widow's laments filled the room:* wail, wailing, lamentation, moan, moaning, weeping, crying, sob, sobbing, keening.
2 *a lament for the dead:* dirge, requiem, elegy, threnody, monody; Irish keen.
▷ verb
1 *he lamented the modernization of the palace buildings:* bemoan, bewail, complain about, deplore; protest against, object to, oppose, fulminate against, inveigh against, denounce.
2 *the women lamented over his dead body:* mourn, grieve, sorrow, wail, weep, cry, sob, keen, beat your breast.

lamentable adjective *the industry is in a lamentable state:* deplorable, regrettable, terrible, awful, appalling, dreadful, wretched, woeful, dire, disastrous, desperate, shameful, unfortunate, disappointing.
OPPOSITES: commendable.

lamentation noun weeping, wailing, crying, sobbing, moaning, lament, keening, grieving, mourning.

lamp noun light, lantern.

lampoon verb *the actor was lampooned by the press:* satirize, mock, ridicule, make fun of, caricature, parody, burlesque, take off; Brit. informal send up.
▷ noun satire, parody, caricature, burlesque, skit, mockery; informal send-up, take-off, spoof.

lance noun spear, pike, javelin; harpoon.
▷ verb *the boil was lanced to drain the pus:* cut open, slit, puncture, prick, pierce.

land noun
1 *Lyme Park has 1323 acres of land | publicly owned land:* grounds, fields, open space; property, acres, acreage, estate, lands, real estate; country, countryside, rural area, green belt.
2 *Tunisia is a land of variety:* country, nation, state, nation state, realm, kingdom, province; region, area.
3 *the lookout sighted land to the east:* terra firma, dry land; coast, coastline, shore.

▷ verb
1 *Allied troops landed in France:* disembark, go ashore, debark, alight, get off.
2 *the ship landed at Le Havre:* berth, dock, moor, anchor, drop anchor, tie up, put in.
3 *their plane landed at Chicago:* touch down, make a landing, come in to land, come down.
4 *a bird landed on the end of the branch:* perch, settle, come to rest, alight.
5 (informal) *Nick landed the job of editor:* obtain, get, acquire, secure, be appointed to, gain, net, win, achieve, attain, bag, carry off; informal swing; Brit. informal blag.
6 (informal) *that habit soon landed her in trouble:* bring, lead, get.
7 (informal) *they landed her with the bill:* burden, saddle, encumber; informal dump something on someone; Brit. informal lumber.
□ **land up**
many of them land up in prison: finish up, find yourself, end up; informal wind up, fetch up.

> WORD LINKS
> **terrestrial** relating to the earth or dry land

landing noun
1 *we made a forced landing:* touchdown.
2 *I walked down to the ferry landing:* harbour, berth, dock, jetty, landing stage, pier, quay, wharf, slipway.
OPPOSITES: take-off.

landlady, landlord noun
1 publican, licensee, innkeeper, pub-owner, barkeeper; hotelier, restaurateur; manager, manageress.
2 owner, proprietor, proprietress, lessor, householder, landowner.
OPPOSITES: tenant.

landmark noun
1 *the spire was once a landmark for ships:* marker, mark, indicator, beacon.
2 *one of London's most famous landmarks:* monument, distinctive feature, prominent feature.
3 *the ruling was hailed as a landmark by human rights activists:* turning point, milestone, watershed, critical point.

landscape noun *the soft colours of the Northumbrian landscape:* scenery, countryside, topography, country, terrain; outlook, view, prospect, vista, panorama, perspective.

landslide noun
1 *floods and landslides killed several people:* landslip, mudslide; avalanche.
2 *the Labour landslide of 1997:* decisive victory, overwhelming majority, triumph.

lane noun
1 *quiet country lanes:* byroad, byway, track, road, street, thoroughfare; path, pathway, alley, alleyway.
2 *cycle lanes | a three-lane highway:* track, course, path.

language noun
1 *the grammatical structure of language:* speech, writing, communication, discourse.
2 *the English language:* tongue, mother tongue, native tongue; informal lingo.
3 *the booklet is written in simple, everyday language | legal language:* wording, phrasing, phraseology, style, vocabulary, terminology, words, expressions, turns of phrase, form/mode of expression, choice of words; parlance, speech, idioms, jargon, slang; Linguistics idiolect; informal lingo.

> WORD LINKS
> **linguistic** relating to language
> **linguistics** the scientific study of language

languid adjective
1 *a languid wave of the hand:* relaxed, unhurried, languorous, slow, lazy, indolent, lethargic; informal laid back.
2 *languid days in the Italian sun:* leisurely, languorous, relaxed, restful, lazy.
3 *a pale, languid individual:* sickly, weak, feeble, frail, delicate, faint; tired, weary, fatigued.
OPPOSITES: energetic.

languish verb
1 *the plants languished and died:* grow weak, weaken, decline, deteriorate; wither, droop, wilt, fade, waste away; informal go downhill.
2 *the general is now languishing in prison:* waste away, rot, be abandoned, be neglected, be forgotten, suffer.
OPPOSITES: thrive.

languor noun
1 *she fought the sultry languor that was stealing over her:* tiredness, drowsiness, sleepiness, laziness, lassitude, lethargy, torpor, sluggishness, fatigue, weariness; inactivity, inertia.
2 *the languor of a hot, breezeless day:* stillness, tranquillity, calm, calmness; oppressiveness, heaviness.

lank adjective *lank, greasy hair:* limp, lifeless, dull, lustreless; straggling, straight, long.

lanky adjective *a pale, lanky youth:* tall, thin, lean, skinny, scrawny, spindly, spare, gangling, gangly, gawky, rangy.
OPPOSITES: stocky.

lap[1] noun *sit on my lap:* knee, knees, thighs.

lap[2] noun
1 *a race of eight laps:* circuit, round.
2 *the last lap of their four-day tour:* stage, part, section, stretch, phase, leg
▷ verb *she easily lapped the other runners:* overtake, outstrip, leave behind, pass, go past; catch up with.

lap[3] verb
1 *waves lapped against the sea wall:* splash, break, wash, swish, slosh, beat, strike, dash, roll.

2 *the dog lapped water out of a puddle:* drink, lick up, sup, swallow, slurp, gulp.
□ **lap something up**
she's lapping up the attention: relish, revel in, savour, delight in, enjoy, love, wallow in.

lapse noun
1 *a momentary lapse of concentration:* failure, failing, slip, error, mistake, blunder, fault, omission; informal slip-up.
2 *his lapse into petty crime:* decline, fall, descent, slide, sinking, slipping, drop, deterioration, degeneration, backsliding, regression, retrogression.
3 *after this lapse of time I can look at it more calmly:* interval, gap, pause, interlude, lull, hiatus, break; passage, course, passing.
▷ verb
1 *the planning permission has lapsed:* expire, become void, become invalid, run out, come to an end, cease, stop, terminate.
2 *the country has lapsed into chaos:* degenerate, deteriorate, sink, decline, backslide, fall, drop, slump, worsen, regress, retrogress, get worse; informal go downhill, go to pot, go to the dogs.
3 *during dinner she lapsed into silence:* revert, relapse; drift, slide, slip, sink.

lapsed adjective *a lapsed Catholic:* non-practising; backsliding, apostate.

larceny noun (N. Amer.) theft, stealing, robbery, pilfering, thieving; burglary, housebreaking, breaking and entering.

larder noun pantry, food store, cooler; Brit. buttery.

large adjective
1 *a large house | large numbers of people:* big, great, huge, sizeable, substantial, immense, enormous, colossal, massive, mammoth, vast, prodigious, tremendous, gigantic, giant, monumental, stupendous, gargantuan, elephantine, titanic, mountainous, monstrous; towering, tall, high; mighty, voluminous, king-size, giant-size; informal jumbo, whopping, mega, humongous, monster, astronomical; Brit. informal whacking, ginormous.
2 *a large, red-faced man:* big, burly, heavy, tall, bulky, thickset, chunky, strapping, hulking, hefty, muscular, brawny, solid, powerful, sturdy, strong, rugged; fat, plump, overweight, chubby, stout, meaty, fleshy, portly, rotund, flabby, paunchy, obese, corpulent; informal hunky, beefy, tubby, pudgy; Brit. informal podgy.
3 *a large supply of wool:* abundant, copious, plentiful, ample, liberal, generous, lavish, bountiful, bumper, boundless, good, considerable, superabundant; literary plenteous.
4 *the measure has large economic implications:* wide-reaching, far-reaching, wide, sweeping, large-scale, broad, extensive, comprehensive, exhaustive.
OPPOSITES: small, meagre.

□ **at large**
1 *fourteen criminals are still at large:* **at liberty**, free, on the loose, on the run, fugitive.
2 *what are the implications for society at large?* **as a whole**, generally, in general.
□ **by and large**
the children, by and large, treated him well: **on the whole**, generally, in general, all things considered, all in all, for the most part, in the main, as a rule, overall, almost always, mainly, mostly; on average, on balance.

WORD LINKS

macro-, **mega-** forming words referring to large entities, structures, etc., such as *macromolecule* ('a molecule containing a very large number of atoms') and *megastore* ('a very large shop')

largely adverb *Jessop was largely responsible for this pioneering work:* **mostly**, mainly, to a large/great extent, chiefly, predominantly, primarily, principally, for the most part, in the main; usually, typically, commonly.

large-scale adjective
1 *a large-scale privatization programme:* **extensive**, wide-ranging, far-reaching, comprehensive, exhaustive; mass, nationwide, global.
2 *a large-scale map:* **enlarged**, blown-up, magnified.

largesse noun *he took advantage of his friend's largesse:* **generosity**, liberality, open-handedness, munificence, bounty, bountifulness, beneficence, altruism, charity, philanthropy, magnanimity, charitableness.
OPPOSITES: meanness.

lark (informal) noun
1 *we were just having a bit of a lark:* **laugh**, fun, giggle, joke; escapade, prank, trick, jape, practical joke; (**larks**) antics, high jinks, horseplay, mischief, tomfoolery.
2 *I've got this snowboarding lark sussed:* **affair**, matter; informal business, caper, thing; stuff, malarkey.
▷ **verb** *he's always larking about:* **fool about/around**, play tricks, make mischief, monkey about/around, clown about/ around, have fun, skylark; informal mess about/around; Brit. informal muck about/ around.

lascivious adjective **lecherous**, lewd, lustful, licentious, libidinous, salacious, prurient, naughty, suggestive, ribald, indecent, dirty, smutty, lubricious; informal horny, randy.

lash verb
1 *rain lashed the window panes:* **beat against**, dash against, pound, batter, strike, hit, knock.
2 *he lashed the prisoner repeatedly across his back:* **whip**, flog, beat, thrash,

horsewhip, belt, strap, cane, strike, hit; informal wallop, whack, give someone a hiding.
3 *the tiger lashed its tail:* **swish**, flick, twitch, whip.
4 *two boats were lashed together:* **fasten**, bind, tie, tether, hitch, knot, rope, make fast.
▷ **noun** *he received twenty lashes:* **stroke**, blow, strike.
□ **lash out**
1 *the president lashed out at the opposition for opposing the policy:* **criticize**, chastise, censure, attack, condemn, denounce, lambaste, harangue, pillory; berate, upbraid, rebuke, reproach; formal castigate; informal lay into.
2 *she lashed out at him in fear:* **hit**, strike, let fly, take a swing; set upon/about, turn on, round on, attack; informal lay into, tear into, pitch into.

lass noun (Scottish & N. English) **girl**, young woman, young lady; Scottish lassie; Irish colleen; literary maid, maiden, damsel, wench; informal chick; Brit. informal bird; N. Amer. informal dame, broad; Austral./NZ informal sheila.

lassitude noun *she was overcome by lassitude and took to her bed:* **lethargy**, listlessness, torpor, sluggishness, languor, weariness, tiredness, fatigue, lifelessness, apathy.
OPPOSITES: vigour.

last¹ adjective
1 *the last woman in the queue:* **rearmost**, at the end, at the back, hindmost, endmost, furthest back, final, ultimate.
2 *Rembrandt spent his last years in Amsterdam:* **closing**, concluding, final, ending, end, terminal; later, latter.
3 *I'd be the last person to say anything against him:* **least likely**, most unlikely; least suitable, least appropriate.
4 *we met last year in Berlin:* **previous**, preceding; prior, former.
5 *this was his last chance to prove himself:* **final**, only remaining.
OPPOSITES: first, early, next.
▷ **adverb** *the candidate coming last is eliminated:* **at the end**, at/in the rear.
▷ **noun** *the most important business was left to the last:* **end**, ending, finish, close, conclusion, finale, termination.
OPPOSITES: beginning.
□ **at last**
at last the storm died away: **finally**, in the end, eventually, ultimately, at long last, after a long time, in time.
□ **the last word**
the spa is the last word in luxury and efficiency: **the ultimate**, the height, the best, the finest, the crème de la crème, the peak, the acme, the epitome, the nonpareil.

last² verb
1 *the storm lasted for six hours:* **continue**,

go on, carry on, keep on/going, take; linger, remain, persist.

2 *how long will he last as manager?* survive, endure, hold on/out, keep going, persevere; informal stick it out, hang on, hack it.

3 *the car is built to last:* endure, wear well, stand up, bear up.

lasting adjective *a lasting peace:* enduring, long-lasting, long-lived, abiding, continuing, long-term, surviving, persisting, permanent; durable, constant, stable, established, secure, long-standing; unchanging, irreversible, eternal, undying, everlasting, unending, never-ending, unfading, changeless, immutable, indestructible, unceasing, unwavering, unfaltering.
OPPOSITES: ephemeral.

lastly adverb finally, in conclusion, to conclude, to sum up, to end, last, ultimately.
OPPOSITES: firstly.

latch noun fastening, catch, fastener, clasp.
▷ verb fasten, secure, make fast.

late adjective
1 *the train was late:* behind schedule, behind time, behindhand; overdue, tardy, running late, delayed.
2 *her late husband:* dead, departed, lamented, passed on/away; formal deceased.
OPPOSITES: punctual, early.

▷ adverb
1 *she had arrived late:* behind schedule, behind time, behindhand, belatedly, tardily, at the last minute.
2 *I was working late:* after hours, overtime, late at night; informal till all hours.
□ of late
she'd been drinking too much of late: recently, lately, latterly.

lately adverb *he's had a bad press lately:* recently, of late, latterly, in recent times.

lateness noun unpunctuality, tardiness, delay.

latent adjective *they have a huge reserve of latent talent:* dormant, untapped, undeveloped, unused, undiscovered, potential, hidden, concealed, invisible, unseen, unrealized, unfulfilled.

later adjective *this question will be dealt with in a later chapter:* subsequent, following, succeeding, future, upcoming, to come, ensuing.
OPPOSITES: earlier.

▷ adverb
1 *later, the film rights were sold:* subsequently, eventually, then, next, later on, after this/that, afterwards, at a later date, in the future, in due course, by and by, in a while, in time.
2 *two days later a letter arrived:* afterwards, later on, after this/that, subsequently, following; formal thereafter.

lateral adjective
1 *lateral movements:* sideways, sideward, edgeways, oblique.
2 *lateral thinking:* unorthodox, inventive, creative, imaginative, original, innovative.

latest adjective *the latest fashions:* most recent, newest, just out, just released, fresh, up to date, up to the minute, state-of-the-art, cutting-edge, current, modern, contemporary, fashionable, in fashion, in vogue; informal cool, in, with it, trendy, hip, hot, happening.
OPPOSITES: old.

lather noun foam, froth, suds, soapsuds, bubbles; literary spume.

latitude noun
1 *Toronto is on the same latitude as Nice:* parallel.
2 *he gave them a lot of latitude in their day-to-day operations:* freedom, freedom of action, scope, leeway, space, flexibility, liberty, independence, free rein, licence, room to manoeuvre.
OPPOSITES: longitude, restriction.

latter adjective
1 *things improved in the latter half of the season:* later, closing, end, concluding, final; latest, most recent.
2 *Russia chose the latter option:* last-mentioned, second, last, later.
OPPOSITES: former.

> **USAGE**
> Use **latter** to refer to the second of two items: if more than two items are mentioned you should use **last** instead.

latter-day adjective *he saw himself as a latter-day Robin Hood, stealing from the rich to give to the poor:* modern, present-day, current, contemporary.

latterly adverb
1 *latterly, she has been in considerable pain:* recently, lately, of late, in recent times.
2 *latterly he worked as a political editor:* ultimately, finally, towards the end.

lattice noun grid, mesh, latticework, fretwork, open framework, openwork, trellis, trelliswork, network, reticulation.

laud verb (formal) *the second single was lauded by the music press as a return to form:* praise, extol, hail, applaud, acclaim, commend, celebrate, sing the praises of, speak highly of, lionize, eulogize, rhapsodize over/about; informal rave about.

laudable adjective *a laudable attempt to get more women into parliament:* praiseworthy, commendable, admirable, creditable, meritorious, worthy, deserving, estimable.
OPPOSITES: shameful.

laugh verb
1 *the audience began to laugh:* chuckle,

chortle, guffaw, giggle, titter, snigger, snicker, burst out laughing, roar/hoot with laughter, dissolve into laughter, split your sides, be doubled up; informal be in stitches, be rolling in the aisles, crease up, fall about, crack up.
2 *people laughed at his theories:* ridicule, mock, deride, scoff at, jeer at, sneer at, make fun of, poke fun at, scorn; lampoon, satirize, parody; informal take the mickey out of, pooh-pooh; Brit. informal send up.
▷ **noun**
1 *she gave a short laugh:* chuckle, chortle, guffaw, giggle, titter, snigger, snicker, roar/hoot of laughter, shriek of laughter, belly laugh.
2 (informal) *he was a right laugh:* joker, wag, wit, clown, jester, prankster, character; informal card, case, caution, hoot, scream, riot.
3 (informal) *I entered the contest for a laugh:* joke, prank, piece of fun, jest, escapade, caper, practical joke; informal lark.
□ **laugh something off**
she laughed off any criticism with characteristic good humour: dismiss, make a joke of, make light of, shrug off, brush aside, scoff at; informal pooh-pooh.

laughable adjective
1 *the idea that nuclear power is safe is laughable:* ridiculous, ludicrous, absurd, risible, preposterous; foolish, silly, idiotic, stupid, nonsensical, crazy, insane, outrageous; informal cockeyed; Brit. informal daft.
2 *if it wasn't so tragic, it'd be laughable:* funny, amusing, humorous, hilarious, uproarious, comical, comic, farcical.

laughter noun laughing, mirth, merriment, hilarity, chuckling, chortling, guffawing, giggling, tittering, sniggering; informal hysterics.

launch verb
1 *the government launched a new campaign:* set in motion, get going, get under way, embark on, initiate, inaugurate, set up, put in place, organize, introduce, start, begin, commence, bring into being; informal kick off.
2 *the town's lifeboat was launched:* set afloat, put to sea.
3 *they've launched the shuttle:* send into orbit, blast off, take off, lift off; fire, shoot.
4 *a chair was launched at him:* throw, hurl, fling, pitch, lob, let fly; informal chuck, heave, sling.
5 *he launched into a tirade against the government:* start, began, burst into, come out with.

lavish adjective
1 *he held lavish parties at his new home:* sumptuous, luxurious, gorgeous, costly, expensive, opulent, grand, splendid, rich, fancy; informal posh.
2 *he was lavish with his hospitality:* generous, liberal, open-handed, unstinting, unsparing, free, bountiful, munificent, extravagant, prodigal.
3 *lavish amounts of champagne were on offer:* abundant, copious, plentiful, liberal, prolific, generous; literary plenteous.
OPPOSITES: meagre, frugal.
▷ **verb** *she lavished money on her children:* give freely, spend generously, heap, pour, shower.

law noun
1 *the law of the land:* rules and regulations, body of laws, constitution, legislation, legal code.
2 *a new law was passed to make divorce easier:* regulation, statute, act, bill, enactment, decree, edict, rule, ruling, directive, resolution, command, order, dictate, diktat, fiat; by-law; N. Amer. ordinance.
3 *the law offers many career opportunities:* the legal profession, the bar.
4 *the laws of the game:* rule, regulation, principle, convention, instruction; guidelines.

> **WORD LINKS**
> **legal, judicial, juridical** relating to laws
> **jurisprudence** the theory or philosophy of law

law-abiding adjective honest, lawful, honourable, upright, upstanding, good, decent, obedient, dutiful, virtuous, moral, righteous.
OPPOSITES: criminal.

lawbreaker noun criminal, offender, felon, wrongdoer, evil-doer, transgressor, miscreant; villain, rogue, ruffian; Law malfeasant; formal malefactor; informal crook, con, jailbird.

lawful adjective legitimate, legal, licit, permissible, permitted, allowable, allowed, rightful, sanctioned, authorized, warranted, within the law, just; informal legit.
OPPOSITES: illegal.

lawless adjective anarchic, disorderly, ungovernable, unruly, insurgent, rebellious, insubordinate, riotous, mutinous.
OPPOSITES: orderly.

lawlessness noun anarchy, disorder, chaos, mob rule; criminality, crime.

lawsuit noun legal action, action, suit, case, legal/judicial proceedings, litigation, trial.

lawyer noun solicitor, legal practitioner, legal adviser, member of the bar, barrister, advocate, counsel, Queen's Counsel, QC; N. Amer. attorney, counselor; informal brief.

lax adjective *lax discipline in schools has fostered a contempt for authority:* slack, slipshod, negligent, remiss, slapdash, sloppy, careless, casual, heedless, unmindful; easy-going,

lenient, permissive, liberal, indulgent, overindulgent.
OPPOSITES: strict.

lay¹ verb

1 *Curtis laid the newspaper on the table:*
put, put down, place, set, set down, deposit, rest, situate, position; informal stick, dump, park; Brit. informal plonk, bung.
2 *the act laid the foundation for the new system:* **establish,** set out/up, set in place.
3 *they are going to lay charges:* **bring,** press, prefer, lodge, register, place, file.
4 *we laid plans for the voyage:* **devise,** arrange, make, prepare, work out, hatch, design, plan, conceive, put together, draw up, produce, develop, formulate; informal cook up.
5 *they tried to lay the blame on others:* **place,** put; assign to, attribute to, attach to.
6 *I'll lay money that Michelle will be there:* **bet,** wager, gamble, stake, risk, venture.

□ **lay something aside**
1 *farmers are laying aside areas for conservation:* **put aside,** put to one side, keep, save.
2 *protesters led the government to lay the plans aside:* **defer,** shelve, suspend, put on ice, mothball, set aside, put off/aside; informal put on the back burner.

□ **lay something down**
1 *he laid down his glass:* **put down,** set down, place down, deposit, rest.
2 *they were forced to lay down their weapons:* **relinquish,** surrender, give up, yield, cede; disarm, give in, submit, capitulate.
3 *the ground rules have been laid down:* **formulate,** stipulate, set down, draw up, frame; prescribe, ordain, dictate, decree; enact, pass, decide, determine, impose, codify.

□ **lay into** (informal)
1 *police laid into protestors* see ASSAULT verb sense 1.
2 *he laid into her with a string of insults* see CRITICIZE.

□ **lay off** (informal) *you really should lay off smoking:* **give up,** stop, refrain from, abstain from, desist from, cut out; informal pack in, leave off, quit.

□ **lay someone off**
cutbacks have forced the museum to lay off 200 staff: **make redundant,** dismiss, let go, discharge, give notice to; informal sack, fire, give someone their marching orders, give someone the boot/push; Brit. informal give someone their cards.

□ **lay something on**
refreshments had been laid on: **provide,** supply, line up, organize, prepare, produce, make available, furnish; informal fix up.

□ **lay something out**
1 *she laid the plans out on the desk:* **spread out,** set out, arrange, display.
2 *we have issued a statement laying out our priorities:* **outline,** detail, explain, describe, spell out.

lay² adjective

1 *a lay preacher:* **non-clerical,** unordained, secular.
2 *I cannot explain this in detail to a lay audience:* **non-professional,** amateur, non-specialist, non-technical, untrained, unqualified.

layabout noun idler, good-for-nothing, shirker, loafer, sluggard, malingerer; literary wastrel; informal skiver, waster, slacker, lazybones.

layer noun

1 *everything was covered in a layer of dust:* **coating,** coat, sheet, film, covering, blanket, skin, thickness.
2 *layers of rock:* **stratum,** seam.

layman noun. See LAYPERSON.

layout noun

1 *I found the layout of the house confusing:* **arrangement,** geography, design, organization; plan, map.
2 *we changed the magazine's layout:* **design,** format, arrangement, presentation; structure, organization, composition, configuration.

layperson noun

1 *a prayer book for laypeople:* **unordained person,** member of the congregation, layman, laywoman.
2 *engineering sounds highly specialized to the layperson:* **non-expert,** layman, laywoman, non-professional, amateur, non-specialist.

laze verb *she spent the day at home, reading the papers and generally lazing around:* **relax,** unwind, idle, do nothing, loaf around/about, lounge around/about, loll around/about, lie around/about, take it easy; informal chill, chill out, hang around; N. Amer. informal bum around.

lazy adjective idle, indolent, slothful, work-shy, shiftless, inactive, sluggish, lethargic; slack, lax, lackadaisical; informal bone idle.
OPPOSITES: industrious.

leach verb *a slow-release fertilizer will not leach into the groundwater:* **drain,** filter, filtrate, percolate, strain.

lead verb

1 *she led them into the house:* **guide,** show, lead the way, usher, escort, conduct, steer, pilot, shepherd, head; accompany, see, take.
2 *fascination with art led him to start a collection of paintings:* **prompt,** induce, move, persuade, influence, drive, make,

cause; incline, dispose, predispose, condition.

3 *this reform might lead to job losses:* **result in**, cause, give rise to, be the cause of, make happen, create, produce, occasion, bring on/about, effect, generate, contribute to, promote; provoke, stir up, spark off, arouse, instigate; involve, necessitate, entail.

4 *she led a coalition of Republican radicals:* **be the leader of**, be the head of, preside over, head, command, govern, rule, be in charge of, be in command of, be in control of, run, control, be at the helm of, spearhead; administer, organize, manage; reign over, be in power over; informal **head up**.

5 *Rangers were leading at half-time:* **be ahead**, be winning, be in front, be in the lead, be first.

6 *the champion was leading the field:* **be at the front of**, be first in, be ahead of, head; outrun, outstrip, outpace, leave behind, draw away from; outdo, outclass, beat; informal **leave standing**.

7 *I just want to lead a normal life:* **live**, have, experience, spend, pass.

▷ **noun**
1 *I was in the lead early on:* **leading position**, first place, van, vanguard; (**in the lead**) ahead, in front, winning.
2 *they took the lead in the personal computer market:* **first position**, forefront, dominance, superiority, ascendancy; pre-eminence, supremacy, advantage, upper hand, whip hand.
3 *sixth-formers should give a lead to younger pupils:* **example**, role model, exemplar, paradigm.
4 *he's not accustomed to playing the lead:* **leading role**, star/starring role, title role, principal part; principal character.
5 *detectives were following up a new lead:* **clue**, pointer, hint, tip, tip-off, suggestion, indication, sign; (**leads**) evidence, information.
6 *fortunately, the dog was on a lead:* **leash**, tether, cord, rope, chain.

▷ **adjective** *the lead position was occupied by an American:* **leading**, first, front, head, top, foremost; chief, principal, premier.

▢ **lead someone on**
deceive, mislead, delude, hoodwink, dupe, trick, fool, pull the wool over someone's eyes; tease; informal string along, lead up the garden path, take for a ride.

▢ **lead the way**
Britain is leading the way in aerospace technology: **take the initiative**, break new ground, blaze a trail, prepare the way.

▢ **lead up to**
the events leading up to the Wall Street crash: **precede**, happen before, go/come before; pave/prepare the way for, herald, introduce, set the scene for; cause.

leaden adjective

1 *he moved on leaden feet back to the staircase:* **sluggish**, heavy, lumbering, slow.
2 *he avoids the leaden prose style of so many academics:* **boring**, dull, unimaginative, uninspired, monotonous, heavy, laboured, wooden, lifeless.
3 *a leaden sky:* **grey**, greyish, black, dark; cloudy, gloomy, overcast, dull, murky, sunless, louring, oppressive, threatening.

leader noun

1 *he was a natural leader:* **chief**, head, principal; commander, captain; chairman, chairwoman, chairperson, chair; director, managing director, MD, manager, superior, superintendent, supervisor, overseer, administrator, employer, master, mistress; president, premier, governor; ruler, monarch, king, queen, sovereign, emperor informal boss, skipper, gaffer, number one.
2 *a world leader in the use of video conferencing:* **pioneer**, front runner, innovator, trailblazer, groundbreaker, trendsetter, torch-bearer; originator, initiator, founder, architect.
OPPOSITES: follower, supporter.

leadership noun

1 *she won the leadership of the Conservative Party:* **premiership**, headship, directorship, governorship, governance, administration, captaincy, control, ascendancy, rule, command, power, dominion.
2 *we need firm and committed leadership:* **guidance**, direction, control, management, superintendence, supervision; organization, government.

leading adjective

1 *he played the leading role in his team's narrow victory:* **main**, chief, major, prime, most significant, principal, foremost, key, central, focal, paramount, dominant, essential.
2 *the leading industrialized countries:* **most powerful**, most important, greatest, chief, pre-eminent, principal, dominant.
3 *Bailey was last season's leading scorer:* **top**, highest, best, first; front, lead; unparalleled, star.
OPPOSITES: subordinate, minor.

leaf noun

1 *the leaves of the sycamore tree:* **frond**, leaflet; Botany cotyledon, bract; (**leaves**) foliage.
2 *a sheaf of loose leaves fell out of the book:* **page**, sheet, folio.

▷ **verb** *he leafed through the pile of documents:* **flick**, flip, thumb, skim, browse, glance, riffle; scan, run your eye over.

▢ **turn over a new leaf**
reform, improve, mend your ways, make a fresh start, change for the better; informal go straight.

> **WORD LINKS**
> **foliar** relating to leaves

leaflet noun **pamphlet,** booklet, brochure, circular, flyer, mailshot, handout, handbill.

league noun
1 *he tried to form a league of chieftains:* **alliance,** confederation, confederacy, federation, union, association, coalition, consortium, affiliation, guild, cooperative, partnership, fellowship, syndicate, cartel.
2 *the store is not in the same league as the major supermarkets:* **class,** group, category, level.
▫ **in league with**
rogue cops were in league with drug dealers: **collaborating with,** cooperating with, in alliance with, allied with, conspiring with, hand in glove with; informal in cahoots with.

leak verb
1 *oil was leaking from the tanker:* **seep,** escape, ooze, drip, dribble, drain, bleed, emanate, issue.
2 *the tanks are leaking gasoline into the river:* **discharge,** exude, emit, release, drip, dribble, ooze, secrete.
3 *a report was leaked to the press:* **disclose,** reveal, divulge, make public, tell, release, pass on, relate, communicate, impart, broadcast, publish, let slip, bring into the open, expose; informal spill the beans.
▷ **noun**
1 *check that there are no leaks in the bag:* **hole,** opening, puncture, perforation, slit, nick, crack, fissure.
2 *a gas leak was discovered:* **discharge,** leakage, seepage, drip, escape.
3 *a series of leaks to the media:* **disclosure,** revelation, exposé.

leaky adjective **leaking,** dripping; cracked, split, punctured, perforated.
OPPOSITES: watertight.

lean[1] verb
1 *he leaned against the door:* **rest,** recline, be supported.
2 *a line of palm trees leaning in the wind:* **slant,** incline, bend, tilt, be at an angle, slope, tip; list.
3 *he leans towards existentialist philosophy:* **tend,** incline, gravitate; have a preference for, have an affinity with.
▫ **lean on**
1 *they've learned to lean on each other for support:* **depend on,** be dependent on, rely on, count on, bank on, have faith in, trust.
2 (informal) *she was determined not to let them lean on her:* **intimidate,** pressurize, put pressure on, bully, threaten, coerce, browbeat; informal twist someone's arm, put the screws on.

lean[2] adjective
1 *a tall, lean aristocratic man:* **slim,** thin, slender, rangy, wiry, lanky.
2 *a lean harvest will mean less food and fewer jobs:* **meagre,** sparse, poor, inadequate, insufficient, paltry, deficient, insubstantial.

3 *in lean times it is the poor who suffer most:* **unproductive,** arid, barren; hard, bad, difficult, tough, impoverished, poverty-stricken.
OPPOSITES: fat, abundant, prosperous.

leaning noun *his early leanings towards socialism are apparent in these articles:* **inclination,** tendency, preference, bias, bent, proclivity, propensity, penchant, predisposition, predilection, partiality, attraction, liking, fondness, taste.

leap verb
1 *he leapt over the gate:* **jump over,** vault over, spring over, bound over, hop over, hurdle, clear.
2 *as soon as the phone rang, we leapt into action:* **rush,** hurry, hasten, jump, burst.
3 *she had leapt at the chance of a free holiday:* **grab,** eagerly accept, take advantage of, seize, jump at.
4 *profits leapt by 55%:* **increase rapidly,** soar, rocket, skyrocket, shoot up, escalate.
▷ **noun**
1 *he cleared the brook in one leap:* **jump,** bound, vault, spring, hop.
2 *a leap of 33%:* **rise,** surge, upsurge, upswing, upturn.
▫ **in/by leaps and bounds**
productivity improved in leaps and bounds: **rapidly,** swiftly, quickly, speedily, dramatically.

learn verb
1 *we encourage students to learn a foreign language:* **master,** become competent in, become proficient in, pick up, grasp, acquire, take in, absorb, assimilate, digest, familiarize yourself with; study, read up on, be taught, have lessons in; informal get the hang of.
2 *she learnt the poem by heart:* **memorize,** commit to memory, learn parrot-fashion, learn by rote, get off pat.
3 *he learnt that the school would shortly be closing:* **discover,** find out, become aware, be informed, hear; gather, understand, ascertain, establish; informal get wind of the fact; Brit. informal suss out.

learned adjective **scholarly,** erudite, well educated, knowledgeable, widely read, well informed, lettered, cultured, intellectual, academic, literary, bookish, highbrow, studious; informal brainy.
OPPOSITES: ignorant.

learner noun **student,** trainee, apprentice, pupil; novice, newcomer, starter, probationer, tyro, neophyte; N. Amer. informal tenderfoot, greenhorn.
OPPOSITES: veteran.

learning noun
1 *the importance of the library as a centre of learning:* **study,** studying, education, schooling, tuition, teaching, academic work; research, investigation.
2 *the astonishing range of his learning:* **scholarship,** knowledge, education,

erudition, intellect, understanding, wisdom.
OPPOSITES: ignorance.

lease noun *a 15-year lease:* rental agreement, charter; rental, tenancy, tenure, period of occupancy.
▷**verb**
1 *the film crew leased a large hangar:* rent, hire, charter.
2 *they leased the mill to a reputable family:* rent out, rent, let out, let, hire out, sublet, sublease.

leash noun lead, rope, chain, strap, tether, restraint.

least determiner *I have not the least idea what this means:* slightest, smallest, minutest, tiniest.
□ **at least**
you should arrive at least an hour before take-off: at the minimum, no/not less than, more than.

leather noun skin, hide.

leathery adjective
1 *leathery skin:* weather-beaten, rough, lined, wrinkled, wrinkly, furrowed, wizened, gnarled.
2 *leathery slices of beef:* tough, hard, gristly, chewy, stringy.

leave¹ verb
1 *we were the last to leave:* depart, go, withdraw, take your leave, take yourself off, retire, absent yourself, exit, pull out, decamp, quit, vacate, desert; say your farewells/goodbyes, make yourself scarce; informal push off, shove off, clear out/off, cut and run, split, vamoose, scoot, make tracks, up sticks; Brit. informal sling your hook.
2 *the next morning we left for Leicester:* set off, head, make; set sail.
3 *he's left his wife:* abandon, desert, cast aside/off, jilt, leave in the lurch, leave high and dry, throw over; literary forsake; informal dump, ditch, chuck, drop, walk/run out on.
4 *he left his job in November:* resign from, retire from, step down from, withdraw from, pull out of, give up; informal quit.
5 *she left her handbag on the bus:* leave behind, forget, lose, mislay.
6 *I thought I'd leave it to the experts:* entrust, hand over, pass on, refer; delegate.
7 *he left her £100,000 in his will:* bequeath, will, endow, hand down, make over.
OPPOSITES: arrive.
□ **leave someone/something out**
1 *Adam left out the address:* miss out, omit, fail to include, overlook, forget; skip, miss, jump.
2 *he was left out of the England squad:* exclude, omit, drop, pass over.

leave² noun
1 *he was on leave from the Royal Engineers:* holiday, break, time off, sabbatical, leave of absence; N. Amer. vacation; Military furlough; informal hols, vac.
2 *the judge granted leave to appeal:* permission, consent, authorization, dispensation, sanction, warrant, approval, clearance, blessing, licence, acquiescence; informal the go-ahead, the green light, the OK, the rubber stamp.
3 *I will now take my leave of you:* departure, leaving, leave-taking, parting, withdrawal, exit, farewell, goodbye.

leaven verb *the formal proceedings were leavened by a touch of humour:* enliven, liven up, season, spice.

leavings plural noun residue, remainder, remains, remnants, leftovers, scraps, scrapings, oddments, rejects, dregs, refuse, rubbish; Brit. informal odds and ends.

lecherous adjective lustful, licentious, lascivious, libidinous, lewd, salacious, wanton, lubricious, dirty, filthy; informal randy, horny, goatish.
OPPOSITES: chaste.

lecture noun
1 *she gave a lecture on contemporary art:* speech, talk, address, presentation, discourse, oration; formal disquisition.
2 *he received a lecture on his poor table manners:* scolding, reprimand, rebuke, reproof, reproach, upbraiding, admonishment; informal dressing-down, telling-off, talking-to, tongue-lashing.
▷**verb**
1 *he visited schools to lecture on the dangers of drugs:* give a lecture/talk, talk, make a speech, speak, give an address; discourse, hold forth, declaim, expatiate; informal spout, sound off.
2 *she lectures at Dublin University:* teach, tutor.
3 *his family lectured him about his drinking:* scold, reprimand, rebuke, reprove, reproach, upbraid, berate, chide, chastise, admonish, criticize, take to task; informal give someone a dressing-down, give someone a talking-to, haul over the coals, tell off, bawl out; Brit. informal tick off, carpet.

lecturer noun
1 *the lecturer is a well-known journalist:* speaker, orator.
2 *a lecturer in economics:* university/college teacher, tutor, reader, don, professor, fellow; academic, scholar.

ledge noun shelf, sill, mantel, mantelpiece, shelving; projection, protrusion, overhang, ridge, prominence.

ledger noun account book, record book, register, log; records, books; balance sheet, financial statement.

lee noun *they sat in the lee of the wall:* shelter, protection, cover, refuge, safety, security.

leer verb ogle, look lasciviously, look suggestively, eye; informal give someone a/the once-over, lech after/over.

leeway noun *this has left the police with some leeway in interpreting the law:* freedom, scope, latitude, space, room, flexibility, liberty, licence, free hand, free rein; informal wiggle room.

left adjective left-hand; Nautical port; Heraldry sinister.
OPPOSITES: right, starboard.

leftover noun *put the leftovers in the fridge:* leavings, remainder, scraps, remnants, remains, residue; excess, surplus.
▷ adjective *any leftover food went to the dog:* remaining, left, uneaten, unconsumed; excess, surplus, superfluous, unused, unwanted, spare.

left-wing adjective socialist, communist, leftist; informal Commie, lefty, red, pink.
OPPOSITES: right-wing.

leg noun
1 *he's broken his leg:* lower limb, shank; informal peg, pin.
2 *a table leg:* upright, support, prop.
3 *the first leg of a European tour:* part, stage, segment, section, portion, phase, stretch, lap.
□ **on its last legs**
1 *my car is on its last legs:* dilapidated, worn out, rickety, about to fall apart, giving up the ghost.
2 *he bought a foundry business that was on its last legs:* failing, about to go bankrupt, near to ruin, going to the wall; informal going bust.
□ **pull someone's leg**
it's okay, I was only pulling your leg: tease, joke, rag, make fun of, play a joke on, play a trick on, chaff; fool, lead on, deceive, hoodwink, dupe, gull; informal kid, have on, take for a ride, take the mickey out of; Brit. informal wind up; N. Amer. informal put on.

legacy noun
1 *a legacy from a great-aunt had paid for their house:* bequest, inheritance, endowment, gift, settlement, patrimony, birthright; formal benefaction.
2 *the tragic legacy of the Vietnam War:* consequences, repercussions, results, effects, aftermath, upshot; by-product, spin-off.

legal adjective
1 *all their actions were perfectly legal:* lawful, legitimate, licit, within the law, legalized, valid; permissible, permitted, allowable, allowed, above board, admissible, acceptable; authorized, sanctioned, licensed, constitutional; informal legit.
2 *the legal profession:* judicial, juridical.
OPPOSITES: criminal, illegal.

legality noun lawfulness, legitimacy, validity, admissibility, permissibility; justice.

legalize verb decriminalize, make legal, legitimize, legitimatize, permit, allow, authorize, sanction, license, legitimate.
OPPOSITES: prohibit.

legate noun envoy, emissary, agent, ambassador, representative, commissioner, delegate, proxy, deputy, plenipotentiary, messenger.

legend noun
1 *the Arthurian legends:* myth, saga, epic, folk tale, folk story, fairy tale, fable; folklore, lore, mythology, fantasy, oral history, folk tradition.
2 *pop legends like the Beatles:* celebrity, star, superstar, giant, icon, phenomenon, luminary; informal celeb, megastar.
3 *experimental conditions were described in the legend to figure 5:* explanation, key, guide.

legendary adjective
1 *the legendary warrior kings of Ireland:* fabled, mythical, mythological, traditional, fairy-tale, storybook.
2 *he was a legendary figure in the trade union movement:* famous, celebrated, famed, renowned, acclaimed, illustrious, esteemed, honoured, exalted, venerable, well known, popular, prominent, distinguished, great, eminent, pre-eminent.
OPPOSITES: historical.

legibility noun readability, clarity, clearness, neatness.

legible adjective readable, easy to read, easily deciphered, clear, plain, neat, intelligible.

legion noun
1 *the Roman legions:* brigade, regiment, battalion, company, troop, division, squadron, squad, platoon, unit.
2 *there were legions of photographers and TV cameras:* horde, throng, crowd, army, multitude, mass, gang, swarm, flock, herd, score.
▷ adjective *her fans, who are legion, will love this:* numerous, countless, innumerable, very many, abundant, plentiful; literary myriad.

legislate verb *the government is determined to legislate against this practice:* make laws, pass laws, enact laws, formulate laws.

legislation noun law, body of laws, rules, rulings, regulations, measures, acts, bills, statutes, enactments; N. Amer. ordinances.

legislative adjective *a legislative assembly:* law-making, judicial, juridical, parliamentary, governmental, policymaking.

legislator noun lawmaker, lawgiver, parliamentarian, Member of Parliament, MP; congressman, congresswoman, senator.

legitimate adjective
1 *these gaming halls are the only form of legitimate gambling in the area:* legal, lawful, licit, legalized, authorized, permitted, permissible, allowable, allowed, admissible, sanctioned, approved, licensed, statutory, constitutional; informal legit.
2 *I am the legitimate heir:* rightful, lawful, genuine, real, true, proper, bona fide, authentic, acknowledged, recognized.
3 *there are legitimate grounds for unease:* valid, sound, well founded, justifiable, reasonable, sensible, just, warranted.
OPPOSITES: illegal, invalid.

legitimize verb *joining a union legitimizes workers' employment rights:* validate, legitimate, sanction, permit, authorize, license, condone, justify, endorse, support; legalize.

leisure noun free time, spare time, time off; recreation, relaxation, inactivity, pleasure; informal R & R.
OPPOSITES: work.
▢ **at your leisure**
wander at your leisure through the stunning selection of shops: at your convenience, when it suits you, in your own (good) time, without haste, unhurriedly.

leisurely adjective unhurried, relaxed, easy, gentle, sedate, comfortable, restful, undemanding, slow, lazy.
OPPOSITES: hurried.

lend verb
1 *can you lend me £20?* loan, let someone have/use; advance; Brit. informal sub.
2 *these examples lend weight to his assertions:* add, impart, give, bestow, confer, provide, supply, furnish, contribute.
OPPOSITES: borrow.
▢ **lend itself to**
the landscape here does not lend itself to walking: be suitable for, be suited to, be appropriate for, present opportunities for.

> USAGE
>
> Do not confuse **lend** and **borrow**. Although uses such as *can I lend your pen?* (meaning 'borrow') are common in some regional varieties of English, the correct standard use is *can I borrow your pen?*

length noun
1 *a length of three or four metres:* extent, distance, linear measure, span, reach; stretch, range.
2 *a considerable length of time:* period, duration, stretch, span.
3 *a length of pale blue silk:* piece, swatch, measure.
4 *MPs criticized the length of the speech:* protractedness, lengthiness, long-windedness, wordiness, prolixity, verbosity, verboseness.

▢ **at length**
1 *these aspects have been discussed at length:* in detail, in depth, extensively, exhaustively, fully, thoroughly, completely; for a long time, for ages, for hours.
2 *his search led him, at length, to Seattle:* after a long time, eventually, in time, finally, at last, in the end, ultimately.

lengthen verb
1 *the mascara will lengthen your eyelashes:* elongate, make longer, extend.
2 *throughout spring, the days are lengthening:* grow/get longer, draw out.
OPPOSITES: shorten.

lengthy adjective long, long-lasting, prolonged, extended, protracted, overlong, long-drawn-out; long-winded, verbose, wordy, prolix; tedious, boring, interminable.
OPPOSITES: short.

leniency noun mercifulness, mercy, clemency, forgiveness; tolerance, forbearance, humanity, charity, indulgence, mildness; pity, sympathy, compassion, understanding.

lenient adjective *the courts may be more lenient with female offenders:* merciful, forgiving, forbearing, tolerant, charitable, humane, indulgent, easy-going, magnanimous, sympathetic, compassionate.
OPPOSITES: severe.

lesion noun wound, injury, bruise, abrasion, contusion; ulcer, ulceration, sore, abscess; Medicine trauma.

less pronoun *the fare is less than £1:* not so/as much as, under, below.
OPPOSITES: more.
▷ **adverb** *we must use the car less:* not so/as much, to a lesser degree, to a smaller extent.
▷ **preposition** *you pay the list price less 10 per cent:* minus, subtracting, discounted by, excepting, without.
▷ **determiner** *there was less noise now that Des had left:* not so much, reduced; fewer.

> USAGE
>
> Many people use the words **fewer** and **less** incorrectly. The rule is that **fewer** should be used with plural nouns, as in *we need to eat fewer cakes and biscuits* or *there were fewer cars on the road this morning*. Use **less** with nouns referring to things that cannot be counted, as in *a job with less money* or *she had less time to spend with her children*. It is wrong to use **less** with a plural noun (*less people, less cars*).

lessen verb
1 *deep tissue massage significantly lessens the pain:* reduce, make less, minimize, decrease; allay, assuage, alleviate, ease, dull, deaden, blunt, moderate, mitigate,

dampen, soften, tone down, dilute, weaken.
2 *the pain began to lessen:* grow less, decrease, diminish, decline, subside, abate; fade, die down/off, let up, ease off, tail off, drop off/away, fall, dwindle, ebb, wane, recede.
3 *his behaviour lessened him in their eyes:* diminish, degrade, discredit, devalue, belittle.
OPPOSITES: increase.

lesser adjective

1 *his was a lesser offence:* less important, secondary, subsidiary, minor, insignificant, unimportant, petty.
2 *you look down on us lesser mortals:* subordinate, inferior, second-class, subservient, lowly, humble.
OPPOSITES: greater, superior.

lesson noun

1 *a maths lesson:* class, session, seminar, tutorial, lecture, period.
2 *he read a lesson from St. John's gospel:* Bible reading, scripture, text.
3 *the developments at the company should be a salutary lesson for all investors:* warning, deterrent; example, exemplar, message, moral.

lest conjunction *he cut the remark out of his speech, lest it should offend people:* in case, for fear that, in order to avoid.

let verb

1 *security guards refused to let him enter the building:* allow, permit, give/grant permission, authorize, sanction, give/grant the right, license, empower, entitle, enable; assent to, consent to, agree to, acquiesce in, tolerate, countenance, give your blessing to; formal accede to; informal give the green light to, give the go-ahead to, give the thumbs up to, give someone/something the nod, OK.
2 *they've let their flat:* rent out, rent, let out, lease, hire out, sublet, sublease.
OPPOSITES: prevent, prohibit.
□ **let someone down**
it's the other players who have let the team down: fail, disappoint, disillusion; abandon, desert, leave stranded, leave in the lurch.
□ **let go**
apply the brakes before you let go of the trolley: release, loose/loosen your hold on, relinquish; old use unhand.
□ **let someone go**
I was sorry we had to let him go after such a short period: make redundant, dismiss, discharge, lay off, give notice to; informal sack, fire, give someone their cards, give someone their marching orders, send packing, give someone the boot/push.
□ **let someone in**
allow to enter, allow in, admit, open the door to; receive, welcome, greet.
□ **let someone in on something**
he asked to be let in on the joke: include, count in, admit, allow to share in, let participate in, inform about, tell about.

□ **let something off**
the kids let off some fireworks in the garden: detonate, discharge, explode, set off, light, fire off.
□ **let someone off**
1 (informal) *I'll let you off this time, but don't do it again:* pardon, forgive; acquit, absolve, exonerate, clear; informal let someone off the hook.
2 *he let me off work early:* excuse from, exempt from, spare from.
□ **let on** (informal)
1 *I never let on that I felt so anxious:* reveal, disclose, mention, divulge, make known, make public, tell, let slip, give away; blab; informal let the cat out of the bag, give the game away.
2 *they all let on they didn't hear me:* pretend, feign, affect, make out, make believe, simulate.
□ **let something out**
1 *I let out a cry of triumph:* utter, emit, give vent to, produce, express, voice, release.
2 *she let it out that he'd given her a lift home:* reveal, disclose, divulge, make known, tell, mention, let slip, give away, let it be known, blurt out.
□ **let someone out**
release, let go, allow to leave, discharge, free, set free, liberate; set/turn loose.
□ **let up** (informal)
1 *the rain had let up, so we went for a walk:* abate, lessen, decrease, diminish, subside, relent, slacken, die down/off, ease, tail off; ebb, wane, dwindle, fade; stop, cease, finish.
2 *you never let up, do you?* relax, ease up/off, slow down; pause, take a break, rest, stop; informal take a breather.

let-down noun *the show was a bit of a let-down:* disappointment, anticlimax, non-event, fiasco; Brit. damp squib; informal comedown.

lethal adjective deadly, fatal, mortal, death-dealing, life-threatening, murderous; poisonous, toxic, noxious; literary deathly.
OPPOSITES: harmless, safe.

lethargic adjective sluggish, listless, torpid, slow, inert, inactive, lifeless, weary, tired, fatigued; languid, lazy, indolent, idle, shiftless, slothful, apathetic.

lethargy noun sluggishness, inertia, listlessness, lassitude, torpor, inactivity, inaction, lifelessness, slowness, weariness, tiredness, fatigue; languor, languidness, laziness, indolence, idleness, shiftlessness, sloth, apathy, passivity.
OPPOSITES: vigour, energy.

letter noun

1 *her name was spelled out in half-inch letters on a gold chain:* character, sign, symbol, mark, figure, rune.
2 *she received a letter from him yesterday:* message, written communication, note,

line, dispatch; correspondence, news, information, intelligence, word; post, mail; formal missive, epistle.

3 *he is truly a man of letters:* learning, scholarship, erudition, education, knowledge; intellect, intelligence, enlightenment, wisdom, sagacity, culture.

□ **to the letter**
he followed her instructions to the letter: strictly, precisely, exactly, accurately, closely, faithfully, religiously, punctiliously, literally, verbatim, in every detail.

> WORD LINKS
> **epistolary** relating to letters (i.e. correspondence)

let-up noun (informal) *there was no let-up in the bombing raids yesterday:* lull, pause, break, respite, interval, hiatus, suspension, cessation, stop; reduction, lessening, abatement, decrease, diminishing, diminution, decline, relaxation, relenting, remission, slackening, weakening, dying down, easing off, tailing off, dropping away/off.

level adjective

1 *a level surface:* flat, smooth, even, uniform, plane, flush, plumb.
2 *he did his best to keep his voice level:* steady, even, unchanging, unvarying, uniform, regular, constant, invariable; calm, unemotional, composed, equable, unruffled, serene, tranquil.
3 *at half-time the scores were level:* equal, even, drawn, tied, all square, neck and neck, level pegging, nip and tuck, on a par, evenly matched.
4 *his eyes were level with hers:* aligned, on the same level as, on a level, at the same height as, in line.
OPPOSITES: uneven, unsteady, unequal.

▷ noun
1 *the post is at a senior level:* rank, standing, status, position; echelon, degree, grade, gradation, stage, standard, rung; class, stratum, group, grouping, set, classification.
2 *a high level of employment:* quantity, amount, extent, measure, degree, volume, size, magnitude, intensity, proportion.
3 *the level of the water is rising:* height; altitude, elevation.
4 *the museum tour ends on the sixth level:* floor, storey, deck.

▷ verb
1 *tilt the tin to level the mixture:* make level, level out/off, make even, even off/out, make flat, flatten, smooth out, make uniform.
2 *bulldozers levelled the building:* raze to the ground, demolish, flatten, topple, destroy; tear down, knock down, pull down, bulldoze.
3 *he levelled his opponent with a single blow:* knock down/out, knock to the

ground, lay out, prostrate, flatten, floor, fell; informal KO, kayo.
4 *Carl levelled the score with a superb goal:* equalize, make equal, equal, even, even up, make level.
5 *he levelled his pistol at me:* aim, point, direct, train, focus, turn.
6 (informal) *I knew you'd level with me:* be frank, be open, be honest, tell the truth, tell all, hide nothing, be straight; informal be upfront.

□ **on the level** (informal)
honest, truthful, genuine, straight, above board, true, sincere, straightforward; informal upfront; N. Amer. informal on the up and up.

level-headed adjective sensible, calm, composed, having your feet on the ground, steady, well balanced, practical, realistic, prudent, pragmatic, reasonable, rational, mature, judicious, sound, sober, businesslike, no-nonsense, {cool, calm, and collected}, confident, equable, cool-headed, self-possessed; informal unflappable, together.
OPPOSITES: excitable.

lever noun
1 *you can insert a lever and prise the rail off:* crowbar, bar, jemmy.
2 *he pulled the lever but nothing happened:* handle, grip, pull, switch.

▷ verb *he levered the door open:* prise, force, wrench, pull, wrest, heave; N. Amer. pry; informal jemmy.

leverage noun
1 *the long handles provide increased leverage:* grip, purchase, hold; support, anchorage, force, strength.
2 *high levels of unionization gave the dockers significant leverage in negotiations:* influence, power, authority, weight, sway, pull, control, say, advantage, pressure; informal clout, muscle, teeth.

levitate verb float, rise into the air, hover, be suspended, glide, hang, fly, soar up.

levity noun *he tried to inject a note of levity into the proceedings:* light-heartedness, humour, fun, frivolity, frivolousness, jocularity, liveliness, cheerfulness, cheeriness, gaiety, amusement, mirth, laughter, merriment, comedy, wit, wittiness, jollity, joviality.
OPPOSITES: seriousness.

levy verb *a proposal to levy VAT on fuel:* impose, charge, exact, raise, collect.
▷ noun *the levy on spirits has risen:* tax, tariff, toll, excise, duty.

lewd adjective
1 *a lewd old man:* lecherous, lustful, lascivious, libidinous, dirty, prurient, salacious, licentious, lubricious; debauched, depraved, degenerate, perverted; informal horny, randy.
2 *a lewd song:* vulgar, crude, smutty, dirty, filthy, obscene, pornographic, coarse, off

colour, unseemly, indecent, salacious; rude, bawdy, ribald, racy, risqué, naughty, earthy, spicy; euphemistic adult; informal blue, raunchy, X-rated.
OPPOSITES: chaste, clean.

lexicon noun dictionary, wordbook, vocabulary list, glossary, word-finder, thesaurus.

liability noun
1 *the health authority does not accept any liability for the error:* legal responsibility, accountability, answerability; blame, blameworthiness, culpability.
2 *they have huge assets and some equally big liabilities:* financial obligations, debts, arrears, dues.
3 *she had come to be seen as an electoral liability:* hindrance, handicap, nuisance, inconvenience, embarrassment, burden, encumbrance; disadvantage, obstacle, impediment; millstone round your neck, albatross.
OPPOSITES: immunity, asset.

liable adjective
1 *the defendants are liable for negligence:* legally responsible, accountable, answerable, at fault, culpable, guilty.
2 *patients were liable to faint if they stood up quickly:* likely, prone, inclined, tending, disposed, apt, predisposed, given.
3 *low-lying areas may well be liable to flooding:* in danger of, at risk of, vulnerable, exposed, prone, subject, susceptible.

liaise verb cooperate, work together, collaborate; communicate, network, interface, link up.

liaison noun
1 *the Bank of England works in close liaison with the Treasury:* cooperation, contact, association, connection, collaboration, communication, alliance, partnership.
2 *he is our liaison with a number of interested parties:* contact, link, middleman, intermediary, go-between, representative, agent.
3 *she became involved in a liaison with William:* affair, relationship, romance, fling, attachment, amour, affair of the heart, romantic entanglement.

liar noun fibber, deceiver; Law perjurer, false witness; informal storyteller.

libel noun *she sued two newspapers for libel:* defamation of character, character assassination, misrepresentation; denigration, vilification, disparagement; insult; lie, slur, smear, untruth, false report; formal calumny; informal mud-slinging.
▷ verb *she alleged the magazine had libelled her:* defame, malign, blacken someone's name, traduce, smear, cast aspersions on, drag someone's name through the mud, vilify, denigrate, disparage, stigmatize, discredit; literary sully someone's reputation.

libellous adjective defamatory, derogatory, disparaging, false, untrue, insulting, scurrilous.

liberal adjective
1 *the values that are characteristic of a liberal society:* tolerant, unprejudiced, broad-minded, open-minded, enlightened; permissive, free, free and easy, easy-going, libertarian, indulgent, lenient.
2 *the Prime Minister launched a liberal social agenda:* progressive, advanced, modern, forward-looking, forward-thinking, enlightened, reformist, radical; informal go-ahead.
3 *a liberal education:* wide-ranging, broad-based, general.
4 *this is a liberal interpretation of the divorce laws:* flexible, broad, loose, rough, free, general, non-literal, non-specific.
5 *liberal amounts of wine had been consumed:* copious, abundant, ample, plentiful, generous, lavish, profuse, considerable, prolific; literary plenteous.
6 *they were liberal with their cash:* generous, open-handed, unsparing, unstinting, lavish, free, munificent, bountiful; beneficent, benevolent, big-hearted, philanthropic, charitable.
OPPOSITES: reactionary, strict, miserly.

liberate verb free, set free, release, let out/go, set/let loose, save, rescue, deliver; emancipate.
OPPOSITES: imprison, enslave.

liberation noun
1 *the liberation of prisoners was a high priority:* freeing, release, rescue, setting free; freedom, liberty; emancipation; historical manumission.
2 *the battle for women's liberation:* freedom, equality, equal rights; emancipation, enfranchisement.
OPPOSITES: confinement, oppression.

liberator noun rescuer, saviour, deliverer, emancipator, redeemer.

liberty noun
1 *we enjoy the liberty to pursue our own interests:* freedom, independence, free rein, license, self-determination, free will, latitude.
2 *parliamentary government is the essence of British liberty:* independence, freedom, autonomy, sovereignty, self-government, self-rule, self-determination; civil liberties, human rights.
3 *one should have the liberty to go where one pleases:* right, prerogative, entitlement, privilege; permission,

sanction, authorization, authority, licence.
OPPOSITES: constraint, slavery.

□ **at liberty**
1 *he was at liberty for three months before being recaptured:* **free**, on the loose, at large, unconfined; escaped, out.
2 *he's not at liberty to discuss the matter:* **free**, able, entitled, permitted, allowed, authorized.

libidinous adjective **lustful**, lecherous, lascivious, lewd, licentious, carnal, salacious, libertine, wanton, promiscuous.

libido noun **sex drive**, sexual appetite; sexual desire, passion, lust, sexuality, sexiness, sensuality.

licence noun
1 *a driving licence:* **permit**, certificate, document, documentation, authorization, warrant; certification, credentials; pass, papers.
2 *the army was given too much licence:* **freedom**, liberty, free rein, latitude, independence, scope, impunity, a free hand, carte blanche.
3 *products made under licence from US companies:* **permission**, consent, sanction, warrant, warranty, charter; franchise.

license verb *he was licensed to sell spirits:* **permit**, allow, authorize, grant/give authority to, grant/give permission to, sanction, approve; certify, accredit; empower, entitle.
OPPOSITES: ban.

licentious adjective **dissolute**, dissipated, debauched, degenerate, immoral, wanton, promiscuous, decadent, depraved; lustful, lecherous, lascivious, libidinous, lewd, lubricious.
OPPOSITES: moral.

lick verb
1 *a ginger cat licked up the milk:* **lap**, tongue.
2 *flames licked round the wood:* **flicker**, flick, play, dart, dance.

lid noun **cover**, top, cap, covering; stopper.

lie¹ noun *loyalty had made him tell lies:* **untruth**, falsehood, fib, fabrication, deception, invention, piece of fiction, falsification; white lie, half-truth, exaggeration; informal tall story, whopper.
OPPOSITES: truth.
▷ verb *he had lied to the police:* **tell a lie**, fib; dissemble, dissimulate; Law perjure yourself, commit perjury; informal lie through your teeth.
□ **give the lie to**
the success of our exports gives the lie to claims about the state of manufacturing: **disprove**, contradict, negate, deny, refute, belie, invalidate, discredit, debunk; challenge, call into question; formal confute, gainsay; informal shoot full of holes, shoot down in flames.

WORD LINKS
mendacious telling lies; untruthful

lie² verb
1 *he was lying on the sofa:* **recline**, be recumbent, be prostrate, be supine, be prone, be stretched out, sprawl, rest, repose, lounge, loll.
2 *a tiny principality lying on the border of Switzerland and Austria:* **be situated**, be located, be placed, be positioned, be found, be sited, sit.
3 *his body lies in a crypt below the cathedral:* **be buried**, be interred, be laid to rest, rest, be entombed.
4 *the difficulty lies in building real quality into the products:* **consist**, be found, exist, be present, reside.
OPPOSITES: stand.
□ **lie low**
the mafia don was apparently lying low in Bangkok: **hide**, hide out, go into hiding, conceal yourself, keep out of sight, go to ground; informal hole up.

USAGE

Do not confuse **lie** and **lay**. **Lie** means 'to be in a horizontal position to rest' (*why don't you lie on the bed?*), while the chief meaning of **lay** is 'to put something down' (*lay the paper on a flat surface*).

lieutenant noun **deputy**, second in command, right-hand man/woman, number two, assistant, aide; informal sidekick.

life noun
1 *the origins of life:* **existence**, being, animation; sentience, creation.
2 *the numerous threats to life on this planet:* **living beings/creatures**, the living; human/animal/plant life, fauna, flora, the ecosystem, the biosphere, the environment, biodiversity; human beings, humanity, humankind, mankind, man.
3 *an easy life:* **way of life**, lifestyle, situation.
4 *the last nine months of his life:* **lifetime**, life span, days, time on earth.
5 *the life of a parliament is limited to five years:* **duration**, lifetime, existence.
6 *he is happy and full of life:* **energy**, vivacity, animation, liveliness, vitality, verve, high spirits, exuberance, zest, enthusiasm, vigour, spirit, dynamism, elan, gusto, brio, fire; hustle and bustle, movement; informal oomph, pizzazz, pep, zing, zip, vim.
7 *more than 1,500 lives were lost in the accident:* **person**, human being, individual, soul.
8 *a life of Chopin:* **biography**, autobiography, life story/history, profile, chronicle, account, portrait; informal biog, bio.
9 *I'll miss you, but that's life:* **the way of the world**, the way things go, the human condition; fate, destiny, providence,

karma, fortune, luck, chance; informal the way the cookie crumbles.
OPPOSITES: death.

□ **give your life**
1 *he would give his life for her:* **die,** lay down your life, sacrifice yourself, offer your life.
2 *he gave his life to the company:* **dedicate yourself,** devote yourself, give yourself, surrender yourself.

> **WORD LINKS**
> **bio-** forming words meaning 'relating to life or living beings', such as *biosphere* ('the parts of the earth inhabited by living things')
> **animate** alive; having life

life-and-death adjective *a life-and-death decision:* **of vital importance,** crucial, critical, urgent, serious, pivotal, important, key, grave.

lifeblood noun *information is the lifeblood of a successful economy:* **life,** life force, heart, soul, essence, essential constituent, core, driving force, vital spark, inspiration, stimulus.

lifeless adjective
1 *they dropped the lifeless body on the ground:* **dead,** stiff, cold, rigid, limp, inert, inanimate, insentient.
2 *a lifeless planet:* **barren,** sterile, bare, desolate, stark, bleak, arid, infertile, uncultivated, uninhabited.
3 *a lifeless performance:* **lacklustre,** dull, boring, tedious, dreary, monotonous, unexciting, spiritless, apathetic, torpid, lethargic; expressionless, characterless, soulless.
OPPOSITES: alive, lively.

lifelike adjective **realistic,** true to life, representational, faithful, exact, precise, detailed, vivid, graphic, natural, naturalistic.
OPPOSITES: unrealistic.

lifelong adjective **lasting,** long-lasting, long-term, lifetime, enduring, stable, established, steady, permanent, constant.
OPPOSITES: ephemeral.

lifestyle noun **way of life/living,** life, situation; conduct, behaviour, customs, habits, ways, mores.

lifetime noun
1 *he made an exceptional contribution to conservation during his lifetime:* **life,** lifespan, days, time, existence, career.
2 *the lifetime of workstations is between three and five years:* **duration,** life, life expectancy, period of effectiveness.
3 *five weeks was a lifetime, anything could have happened:* **a very long time,** an eternity, years, aeons; informal ages, an age.

lift verb
1 *try and lift the pack on to your back:* **raise,** hoist, heave, haul up, uplift, heft, elevate; pick up, grab, take up, scoop up, snatch

up; winch up, jack up, lever up; Brit. informal hump.
2 *the news lifted his flagging spirits:* **boost,** raise, buoy up, elevate, cheer up, uplift, brighten up, gladden, encourage, stimulate, revive, ginger up; informal perk up, buck up.
3 *by noon, the fog had lifted:* **clear,** rise, disperse, dissipate, disappear, vanish, dissolve.
4 *the ban has finally been lifted:* **remove,** cancel, withdraw, revoke, rescind, annul, void, discontinue, end, stop, terminate.
OPPOSITES: drop, put down.
▷ **noun**
1 *the lift is out of order:* N. Amer. **elevator.**
2 *he gave me a lift to the airport:* **ride.**
3 *the goal will give his confidence a lift:* **boost,** fillip, stimulus, impetus, encouragement, spur, push; informal shot in the arm.
4 *a 10% lift in profits:* **rise,** increase, leap, upswing, improvement.
□ **lift off**
take off, become airborne, take to the air, take wing; be launched, blast off.

light¹ noun
1 *light from the candles filled the room:* **illumination,** brightness, luminescence, luminosity, shining, gleaming, gleam, brilliance, radiance, lustre, glowing, glow, blaze, glare, dazzle; sunlight, moonlight, starlight, lamplight, firelight; ray of light, beam of light; literary effulgence.
2 *switch on the lights:* **lamp;** headlight, headlamp, sidelight; street light, floodlight; lantern; torch, flashlight.
3 *we'll be driving home in the light:* **daylight,** daytime, day; natural light, sunlight.
4 *after this he saw the problem in a different light:* **aspect,** angle, slant, approach, interpretation, viewpoint, standpoint, context, hue, complexion.
OPPOSITES: darkness.
▷ **verb** *Alan lit a fire in the hearth:* **set alight,** set light to, set burning, set on fire, set fire to, put/set a match to, ignite, kindle, spark off.
OPPOSITES: extinguish.
▷ **adjective**
1 *a very light room:* **bright,** full of light, well lit, sunny.
2 *lighter shades suit you better:* **pale,** pastel, light-toned.
3 *a young woman with light hair:* **fair,** blonde, golden, tow-coloured; literary flaxen.
OPPOSITES: dark, gloomy.
□ **bring something to light**
the irregularities were first brought to light by an internal audit: **reveal,** disclose, expose, uncover, show up, unearth, dig up/out, bring to notice, identify, hunt out, nose out.
□ **come to light**
the thefts came to light last year: **be discovered,** be uncovered, be unearthed,

come out, become known, become apparent, appear, materialize, emerge.
▢ **in the light of**
in the light of this report, I see no reason to continue: taking into consideration/ account, considering, bearing in mind, in view of, taking note of.
▢ **light something up**
1 *a flare lit up the night sky:* make bright, brighten, illuminate, lighten, throw/ cast light on, shine on, irradiate; literary illumine.
2 *her enthusiasm lit up her face:* animate, irradiate, brighten, cheer up, enliven.
▢ **throw/cast/shed light on**
no one could shed any light on the mysterious accident: explain, elucidate, clarify, clear up, interpret.

> **WORD LINKS**
> **optics** the branch of science concerned with the behaviour of light

light² adjective

1 *the lightest palmtop PC on the market:* easy to lift, not heavy, lightweight, portable, easy to carry.
2 *a light cotton dress:* lightweight, thin, summerweight, flimsy, insubstantial; delicate, floaty, gauzy, diaphanous.
3 *we had a light dinner:* small, modest, simple, frugal.
4 *he heard light footsteps:* gentle, delicate, soft, dainty.
5 *I was put on light duties:* easy, simple, undemanding, untaxing; informal cushy.
6 *light entertainment | light reading:* entertaining, lightweight, diverting, undemanding, middle-of-the-road, popular, lowbrow; frivolous, superficial, trivial.
7 *you need plenty of sun and a light soil:* crumbly, friable, sandy, workable, loose, porous.
8 *I pitched in with a light heart:* carefree, light-hearted, cheerful, cheery, happy, merry, jolly, bright, sunny; buoyant, bubbly, jaunty, bouncy, breezy, optimistic, positive, upbeat, ebullient; literary blithe.
▢ **light on your feet**
nimble, agile, lithe, graceful, lissom, limber; light-footed, fleet-footed, quick, quick-moving, spry, sprightly; informal twinkle-toed.
OPPOSITES: heavy.

light³ verb
▢ **light on**
he lit on a possible solution: come across, chance on, hit on, happen on, stumble on/across, find, discover, uncover, come up with.

lighten¹ verb

1 *the sky was beginning to lighten:* become/ grow lighter, brighten.
2 *the first touch of dawn lightened the sky:* light up, brighten, illuminate, irradiate; literary illumine.
3 *he used lemon juice to lighten his hair:* bleach, whiten, make paler, blanch, fade.
OPPOSITES: darken.

lighten² verb

1 *we are lightening the burden of taxation:* lessen, reduce, decrease, diminish, ease; alleviate, mitigate, allay, relieve, palliate, assuage.
2 *I made an attempt to lighten her spirits:* raise, lift; brighten, enliven, boost, buoy up, uplift, revive, restore, revitalize, ginger up, gladden, hearten; informal perk up.
OPPOSITES: increase, depress.

light-headed adjective
dizzy, giddy, faint, muzzy; formal vertiginous; informal woozy.

light-hearted adjective
carefree, cheerful, cheery, happy, merry, glad, playful, jolly, jovial, joyful, gleeful, ebullient, high-spirited, upbeat, lively, bright, sunny, buoyant, vivacious, bubbly, jaunty, breezy; entertaining, amusing, diverting; literary blithe; informal chirpy.
OPPOSITES: miserable.

lightly adverb

1 *she kissed him lightly on the cheek:* softly, gently, faintly, delicately.
2 *season the stock very lightly:* sparingly, slightly, sparsely, moderately, delicately.
OPPOSITES: hard, heavily.

lightweight adjective

1 *a lightweight jacket:* light, thin, flimsy, insubstantial; summerweight, summery.
2 *snobs will no doubt dismiss the show as lightweight:* trivial, superficial, shallow, unintellectual, undemanding, lowbrow, frivolous.
OPPOSITES: heavy.

like¹ verb

1 *I liked her a lot:* be fond of, be attached to, have a soft spot for, have a liking for, think well of, admire, respect, esteem; be attracted to, find attractive, be keen on, be taken with; informal rate; Brit. informal fancy.
2 *he likes Italian food:* enjoy, have a taste for, have a preference for, have a liking for, be partial to, take pleasure in, be keen on, have a penchant/passion for, find enjoyable; appreciate, love, adore, relish; informal have a thing about, be into, be mad about, be hooked on, go a bundle on.
3 *feel free to say what you like:* choose, please, wish, want, see/think fit, care to, feel inclined to, will.
OPPOSITES: hate.

like² preposition

1 *you're acting like a teacher:* similar to, the same as, identical to.
2 *the creature hissed like a cat:* in the same way as, in the manner of, in a similar way to.
3 *cities like Birmingham need our backing:* such as, for example, for instance; in particular, namely, viz.
4 *Richard sounded scared, which isn't*

I

like him: **characteristic of**, typical of, in character with.

▷ **noun** *we shan't see his like again:* **equal**, match, equivalent, counterpart, twin, parallel.

▷ **adjective** *I have found myself in a like situation:* **similar**, much the same, comparable, corresponding, resembling, alike, analogous, parallel, equivalent, related, kindred; identical, same, matching.
OPPOSITES: dissimilar.

likeable adjective **pleasant**, friendly, agreeable, affable, amiable, genial, personable, charming, popular, good-natured, engaging, appealing, endearing, convivial, congenial, winning, delightful, lovely, enchanting, lovable, adorable, sweet; informal darling.
OPPOSITES: unpleasant.

likelihood noun *the changes could increase the likelihood of a miscarriage of justice:* **probability**, chance, prospect, possibility, likeliness, odds, feasibility; risk, threat, danger; hope, promise.

likely adjective
1 *it seemed likely that a scandal of some sort would break:* **probable**, distinctly possible, to be expected, odds-on, imaginable; expected, anticipated, predictable, predicted, foreseeable; informal on the cards.
2 *a more likely explanation can be found elsewhere:* **plausible**, reasonable, feasible, acceptable, believable, credible, tenable, conceivable.
3 *it didn't take long to find a likely-looking place:* **suitable**, appropriate, apposite, fit, fitting, acceptable, right; promising, hopeful.
OPPOSITES: improbable, unbelievable.

▷ **adverb** *he was most likely dead:* **probably**, in all probability, presumably, no doubt, doubtlessly; informal as like as not.

liken verb **compare**, equate, draw an analogy between, draw a parallel between; link, associate, bracket together.
OPPOSITES: contrast.

likeness noun
1 *her likeness to Anne is quite uncanny:* **resemblance**, similarity, correspondence; formal similitude.
2 *the handle was carved in the likeness of a naked woman:* **semblance**, guise, appearance, form, shape, image.
3 *few coins now bear the likeness of the last president:* **image**, representation, depiction, portrayal; picture, drawing, sketch, painting, portrait, photograph, study; statue, sculpture.
OPPOSITES: dissimilarity.

likewise adverb
1 *an ambush was out of the question, likewise poison:* **also**, in addition, too, as well; besides, moreover, furthermore.
2 *encourage your family and friends*

to do likewise: **the same**, similarly, correspondingly, in the same way, in similar fashion.

liking noun *he had a liking for whisky:* **fondness**, love, affection, penchant, attachment; enjoyment, appreciation, taste, passion; preference, partiality, predilection; desire, fancy, inclination.

lilt noun *there was a faint but recognizable Irish lilt in her voice:* **cadence**, rise and fall, inflection, intonation, rhythm.

limb noun
1 *he rubbed his aching limbs:* **arm**, **leg**, appendage; old use member.
2 *the limbs of the tree creaked in the wind:* **branch**, bough.

limber verb
☐ **limber up**
players were limbering up before the kick-off: **warm up**, loosen up, practise, train, stretch.

limbo noun
☐ **in limbo**
unresolved, undecided, undetermined, up in the air, in a state of uncertainty; in abeyance, unattended to, unfinished; suspended, deferred, postponed, put off, pending, on hold, on ice, in cold storage; informal on the back burner.

limelight noun *the shock win has thrust him into the limelight:* **the centre of public attention**, the public eye, the glare of publicity, prominence, the spotlight.
OPPOSITES: obscurity.

limit noun
1 *the campus was outside the city limits:* **boundary**, border, bound, partition line, frontier, edge, demarcation line; perimeter, outline, confine, periphery, margin, rim.
2 *the police set a limit of 4,500 supporters for Saturday's match:* **maximum**, ceiling, limitation, upper limit; restriction, check, control, restraint.
3 *our resources are stretched to the limit:* **utmost**, breaking point, greatest extent.

▷ **verb** *the pressure to limit costs:* **restrict**, curb, cap, hold in check, check, restrain, put a brake on, freeze, peg; regulate, control, govern, delimit.

limitation noun
1 *there have been calls for a limitation on the number of newcomers:* **restriction**, curb, restraint, control, check, ceiling; obstacle, obstruction, impediment, bar, barrier, block, deterrent.
2 *he is aware of his own limitations:* **imperfection**, flaw, defect, failing, shortcoming, weak point, deficiency, failure, frailty, weakness, foible.
OPPOSITES: increase, strength.

limited adjective *the competition for limited resources:* **restricted**, finite, in short supply, tight, slight, little,

short; meagre, scanty, sparse, deficient, inadequate, insufficient, paltry, poor, minimal.
OPPOSITES: ample, boundless.

limitless adjective infinite, boundless, unbounded, unlimited, endless, never-ending, unending, everlasting, untold, immeasurable, bottomless; unceasing, interminable, inexhaustible, constant, perpetual; literary illimitable, fathomless.

limp¹ verb hobble, walk with a limp, walk haltingly, falter.
▷ noun lameness, hobble, uneven gait.

limp² adjective
1 *her muscles went limp:* soft, flaccid, slack, loose, lax; floppy, drooping, droopy, sagging.
2 *he felt too limp to argue:* weak, tired, exhausted, worn out, enervated, dead on your feet.
3 *a limp and lacklustre speech:* uninspired, uninspiring, insipid, flat, lifeless, vapid.
OPPOSITES: firm, energetic.

limpid adjective
1 *a limpid mountain stream:* clear, transparent, glassy, crystal clear, crystalline, translucent, unclouded.
2 *his limpid prose style is to be admired:* lucid, clear, plain, understandable, intelligible, comprehensible, coherent, simple, vivid, sharp, crystal clear.
OPPOSITES: opaque.

line¹ noun
1 *a thick black line:* dash, rule, bar, score; underline, underscore, stroke, slash, solidus; stripe, strip, band, belt; Brit. oblique.
2 *there were lines round her eyes:* wrinkle, furrow, crease, crinkle, crow's foot.
3 *the classic lines of the vehicle's exterior:* contour, outline, shape, configuration, figure, delineation, profile, silhouette.
4 *he headed the ball over the line:* boundary, limit, border, borderline, bounding line, frontier, demarcation line, dividing line, edge, margin, perimeter.
5 *a line of soldiers:* file, rank, column, string, train, procession; row, queue; Brit. informal crocodile.
6 *he was adding up a line of figures:* column, row.
7 *this is just the latest in a long line of crass decisions:* series, sequence, succession, chain, string, set, cycle.
8 *the government must take a firm line on terrorism:* course of action, policy, approach, plan, plan of action, programme, procedure, tactic, tack; practice, position, stance, philosophy.
9 *she was intent on pursuing her own line of thought:* course, direction, drift, tack, tendency, trend.
10 *the line of flight of some bees:* trajectory, route, track, path, course.
11 *the opening line of the poem:* sentence, phrase, clause, utterance; passage, extract, quotation, quote, citation.
12 *he couldn't remember his lines:* words, part, script, speech.
13 *he is from a noble line:* ancestry, family, parentage, birth, descent, lineage, extraction, genealogy, roots, origin, background; stock, bloodline, pedigree.
14 *the heavy snow brought power lines down:* cable, wire; cord, rope, string.
▷ verb
1 *her face was lined with age:* furrow, wrinkle, crease.
2 *the driveway was lined by poplar trees:* border, edge, fringe, bound, rim.
□ draw the line at
he'd take them to the ballet and the theatre, but not the opera—he drew the line at opera: stop short of, baulk at, refuse to accept; object to, take issue with, take exception to.
□ in line
1 *the poor stood in line for food:* in a queue, in a row.
2 *the adverts are in line with the editorial style:* in agreement, in accord, in accordance, in harmony, in step, in compliance.
3 *hold the front sight in line with the bullseye:* in alignment, aligned, level, at the same height; abreast, side by side.
4 *the referee certainly kept him in line:* under control, in order, in check.
□ in line for
he was now in line for promotion: a candidate for, in the running for, on the shortlist for, being considered for.
□ line up
form a queue/line, queue up; Military fall in; Brit. informal form a crocodile.
□ line something up
we've lined up an all-star cast: assemble, get together, organize, prepare, arrange, prearrange, fix up, lay on; book, schedule, timetable.
□ on the line
it's police officers whose lives are on the line: at risk, in danger, endangered, in jeopardy.

line² verb *a basket lined with polythene:* face, put a lining in, interline, cover, back, pad.

lineage noun ancestry, family, parentage, birth, descent, line, extraction, derivation, genealogy, roots, origin, background; stock, bloodline, breeding, pedigree.

lined adjective
1 *lined paper:* ruled, feint, striped, banded.
2 *his lined, weather-beaten face:* wrinkled, wrinkly, furrowed, wizened.
OPPOSITES: plain, smooth.

line-up noun
1 *a star-studded line-up:* list of performers, cast, bill, programme.
2 *United's line-up for the final:* list of players, team, side, squad.

linger verb
1 *the crowd lingered for a while:* wait, stay, remain; loiter, dawdle, dally, take your time; literary tarry; informal stick around, hang around.
2 *the infection can linger for many years:* persist, continue, remain, stay, endure, carry on, last, keep on/up.
OPPOSITES: vanish.

lingering adjective
1 *there were still a few lingering doubts:* remaining, surviving, persisting, abiding, nagging, niggling.
2 *he died a lingering death:* protracted, prolonged, long-drawn-out, slow.

linguistic adjective verbal, rhetorical, semantic.

lining noun backing, interlining, facing, padding, liner.

link noun
1 *the links between transport and the environment:* connection, relationship, association, linkage, tie-up.
2 *their links with the labour movement:* bond, tie, attachment, connection, relationship, association, affiliation.
3 *a chain of steel links:* loop, ring, connection, connector, coupling, joint.
▷ verb
1 *the video cameras are linked to a computer:* connect, join, fasten, attach; clamp, secure, fix, tie, couple, yoke.
2 *newspaper reports have linked him to paramilitaries:* associate, connect, relate, bracket with.

lion noun big cat, king of the beasts.

WORD LINKS
leonine relating to lions

lionize verb *the band's lead guitarist has been lionized by the music press:* celebrate, fete, acclaim, applaud, praise, extol, hail, glorify, eulogize, honour, exalt; formal laud.
OPPOSITES: vilify.

lip noun *the lip of the crater:* edge, rim, brim, brink, border, verge.

liquefy verb melt, condense, liquidize; technical deliquesce.

liquid noun fluid, moisture, wet, wetness; liquor, solution, juice.
▷ adjective
1 *liquid fertilizer:* fluid, liquefied; melted, molten, thawed, dissolved; Chemistry hydrous.
2 *her dark liquid eyes:* clear, limpid, crystal clear, unclouded; literary pellucid.
3 *the liquid song of the birds:* pure, clear, mellifluous, sweet, sweet-sounding, soft, melodious, harmonious; often ironic dulcet.
4 *liquid assets:* convertible, disposable, usable, spendable.
OPPOSITES: solid.

liquidate verb
1 *the company was liquidated:* close down, wind up, put into liquidation, dissolve, disband.
2 *he would normally have liquidated his share portfolio:* convert to cash, cash in, sell off/up.
3 *the fund was raided for purposes other than liquidating the public debt:* pay off, pay in full, settle, clear, discharge, square, honour.

liquidize verb purée, blend, liquefy, cream.

liquor noun alcohol, spirits, alcoholic drink; informal booze, the hard stuff, hooch.

list¹ noun *a list of the world's wealthiest people:* catalogue, inventory, record, register, roll, file, index, directory, listing, checklist.
▷ verb *the accounts are listed alphabetically:* record, register, make a list of, enter; itemize, enumerate, catalogue, file, log, minute, categorize, inventory; classify, group, sort, rank, alphabetize, index.

list² verb *the boat listed to starboard:* lean, tilt, tip, heel, cant, careen, pitch, incline, slant, slope, bank.

listen verb
1 *listen carefully:* pay attention, attend, concentrate; keep your ears open, prick up your ears; informal be all ears, pin back your ears; literary hark.
2 *policymakers should listen to popular opinion:* take heed of, pay attention to, heed, take notice of, take note of, mind, mark, bear in mind, take into consideration/account.

listless adjective lethargic, enervated, sluggish, torpid, inactive, inert, lifeless, spiritless; languid, languorous.
OPPOSITES: energetic.

litany noun
1 *her lips moved, repeating the litany:* prayer, invocation, supplication, devotion.
2 *a litany of complaints soon followed:* list, catalogue, enumeration, inventory; recital, recitation.

literacy noun ability to read and write, reading/writing skills; book learning, education, schooling.

literal adjective
1 *the literal meaning of the word 'dreadful':* strict, exact, factual, plain, simple, straightforward; unembellished, undistorted, objective, correct, true, truthful, accurate, genuine, authentic.
2 *a literal translation:* word-for-word, verbatim, letter-for-letter; exact, precise, faithful, close, strict, accurate.
3 *his literal, unrhetorical manner:* literal-minded, down-to-earth, matter-of-fact, no-nonsense, unsentimental; prosaic,

unimaginative, pedestrian, uninspired, uninspiring.
OPPOSITES: figurative, loose.

literally adverb *the name, translated literally, means 'river':* **verbatim**, word for word, letter for letter; exactly, precisely, faithfully, closely, strictly, accurately.

literary adjective
1 *a selection of literary works:* **written**, poetic, artistic, dramatic.
2 *her literary friends | a literary magazine:* **scholarly**, learned, intellectual, cultured, erudite, bookish, highbrow, lettered, academic, cultivated; well read, widely read, well educated.

literate adjective **educated**, well educated, well read, widely read, scholarly, learned, knowledgeable, lettered, cultured, cultivated, sophisticated, well informed.
OPPOSITES: ignorant.

literature noun
1 *he studied English literature:* **creative writing**, literary texts.
2 *I've looked at the literature on prototype theory:* **publications**, published writings, texts, reports, studies.
3 *the noticeboards are covered in election literature:* **leaflets**, pamphlets, brochures, circulars, flyers, handouts, handbills, mailshots, documentation, publicity, notices; informal bumf, propaganda.

lithe adjective **agile**, graceful, supple, loose-limbed, flexible, nimble, lissom, limber.
OPPOSITES: clumsy.

litigant noun **claimant**, plaintiff, complainant, petitioner, appellant, disputant.

litigation noun **legal/judicial proceedings**, legal action, lawsuit, legal dispute, case, suit, prosecution.

litter noun
1 *always clear up after a picnic and never drop litter:* **rubbish**, refuse, junk, waste, debris, scraps, leavings, detritus; N. Amer. trash, garbage.
2 *she looked at the litter of glasses around her:* **clutter**, jumble, muddle, mess, heap, disorder, untidiness, confusion, disarray; informal shambles.
3 *a litter of kittens:* **brood**, family; young, offspring, progeny.
▷ **verb** *clothes and newspapers littered the floor:* **cover**, mess up, clutter up, be strewn about, be scattered about.

little adjective
1 *a little house:* **small**, small-scale, compact, mini, miniature, tiny, minute, minuscule; toy, baby, pocket, undersized; Scottish wee; informal teeny; Brit. informal titchy, tiddly, dinky.
2 *a little woman:* **short**, small, slight, petite, diminutive, tiny; elfin, Lilliputian;

Scottish wee; informal teeny, pint-sized.
3 *stay for a little while:* **brief**, short; fleeting, momentary, transitory, transient; fast, quick, hasty, cursory.
4 *we have a little problem:* **minor**, unimportant, insignificant, trivial, trifling, petty, paltry, inconsequential; formal nugatory.
5 *my little sister:* **young**, younger, junior, small, baby, infant.
OPPOSITES: big, large, important, elder.
▷ **determiner** *they have low status and little political influence:* **hardly any**, not much, slight, scant, limited, restricted, modest, little or no, minimal, negligible.
OPPOSITES: considerable.
▷ **adverb**
1 *he is little known in this country:* **hardly**, barely, scarcely, not much, only slightly.
2 *this disease is little seen nowadays:* **rarely**, seldom, infrequently, hardly ever, scarcely ever, not much.
OPPOSITES: well, often.
□ **a little**
1 *if the mixture is too thick, add a little water:* **some**, a small amount of, a bit of, a touch of, a soupçon of, a dash of, a taste of, a spot of; a shade of, a suggestion of, a trace of, a hint of, a suspicion of; a dribble of, a splash of, a pinch of, a sprinkling of, a speck of; informal a smidgen of, a tad of.
2 *after a little, Oliver came in:* **a short time**, a little while, a bit, an interval, a short period; a minute, a moment, a second, an instant; informal a sec, a mo, a jiffy.
3 *this reminds me a little of the Adriatic:* **slightly**, faintly, vaguely; somewhat, a little bit, quite, to some degree.
□ **little by little**
gradually, slowly, by degrees, by stages, step by step, bit by bit, progressively; subtly, imperceptibly.

liturgy noun **ritual**, ceremony, form of worship, service, rite, observance, celebration, sacrament; tradition, custom, practice, rubric; formal ordinance.

live[1] verb
1 *the greatest mathematician who ever lived:* **exist**, be alive, be, have life; breathe, draw breath, walk the earth.
2 *I live in London:* **reside**, have your home/residence, be settled; be housed, lodge; inhabit, occupy, populate; Scottish stay; formal dwell, be domiciled.
3 *they lived quietly:* **pass/spend your life**, have a lifestyle; behave, conduct yourself.
4 *she had lived a difficult life:* **lead**, experience, spend, pass, have, go through, undergo.
5 *Fred lived by his wits:* **survive**, make/earn a living; subsist, support yourself, sustain yourself, make ends meet, keep body and soul together, eke out a living.
6 *you should live a little:* **enjoy yourself**, enjoy life, have fun, live life to the full.
OPPOSITES: die, be dead.

□ **live it up** (informal) *those two are now living it up in Hawaii:* **enjoy yourself,** live in the lap of luxury; carouse, revel, have a good time, roister; informal party, push the boat out, paint the town red, have a ball, make whoopee; N. Amer. informal live high on/off the hog.

□ **live off/on**
the seabirds live off discarded fish: **subsist on,** feed on/off, eat, consume.

live² adjective
1 *live animals:* **living,** alive, having life, breathing, animate, sentient.
2 *her first live performance in Britain:* **in the flesh,** personal, in person.
3 *a live rail:* **electrified,** charged, powered, active.
4 *a live grenade:* **unexploded,** active; unstable.
5 *a live issue:* **topical,** current, controversial; burning, pressing, important, hot.
OPPOSITES: dead, inanimate, recorded.

livelihood noun *people whose livelihood depends on the sea:* **income,** means of support, living, subsistence, maintenance, sustenance, daily bread, bread and butter; job, work, employment, occupation.

lively adjective
1 *an attractive, lively young woman:* **energetic,** vivacious, active, animated, dynamic, full of life, outgoing, spirited, sprightly, spry, high-spirited, boisterous, enthusiastic, vibrant, buoyant, exuberant, effervescent, bubbly, perky; Brit. Tiggerish; informal full of beans, chirpy, chipper, peppy.
2 *a lively West End bar:* **busy,** crowded, bustling, buzzing; informal hopping.
3 *a lively debate:* **heated,** vigorous, animated, spirited, forceful; stimulating, interesting.
4 *a lively portrait of the local community:* **vivid,** colourful, striking, graphic, bold, strong.
5 *he bowled at a lively pace:* **brisk,** quick, fast, rapid, swift, speedy, smart; informal nippy, snappy.
OPPOSITES: quiet, dull.

liven verb
□ **liven up**
at the mention of food, he livened up: **brighten up,** cheer up, revive, rally, pick up, bounce back; informal perk up, buck up.
□ **liven someone/something up**
he could do with a drink to liven him up: **brighten up,** cheer up, enliven, animate, raise someone's spirits, spice up, ginger up, make lively, wake up, invigorate, revive, refresh, vivify, galvanize, stimulate, stir up, get going; informal perk up, buck up, pep up.

liver noun

> WORD LINKS
> **hepatic** relating to the liver
> **hepatitis** inflammation of the liver

livery noun
1 *servants in blue and gold livery:* **uniform,** regalia, costume, dress, garb, clothes, clothing, outfit, suit, garments, ensemble; formal attire, apparel; informal get-up, gear.
2 *the locomotive has reverted to its original green livery:* **colours,** colour scheme, paintwork; design, format, specification, look.

livid adjective
1 (informal) *she was absolutely livid* see FURIOUS sense 1.
2 *a livid bruise:* **purplish,** bluish, dark, discoloured, purple, greyish-blue; bruised; angry.

living noun
1 *she cleaned floors for a living:* **livelihood,** income, means of support, subsistence, maintenance, sustenance, daily bread, bread and butter; job, work, employment, occupation.
2 *making informed choices about healthy living | urban living:* **way of life,** lifestyle, life; conduct, behaviour, activities, habits.
▷ **adjective**
1 *living organisms:* **alive,** live, animate, sentient; breathing, existing, existent; informal alive and kicking.
2 *a living language:* **current,** contemporary, present; in use, active, surviving, extant, persisting, remaining, existing, in existence.
OPPOSITES: dead, extinct.

living room noun **sitting room,** lounge, reception room, family room; dated parlour.

load noun
1 *a lorry had shed its load on the motorway:* **cargo,** freight, consignment, delivery, shipment, goods, merchandise; pack, bundle, parcel; lorryload, truckload, shipload, boatload, vanload.
2 (informal) *I bought a load of clothes:* **a lot,** a great deal, a large amount/quantity, an abundance, a wealth, a mountain; many, plenty; informal a heap, a mass, a pile, a stack, a ton, lots, heaps, masses, bucketloads, piles, stacks, tons.
3 *a heavy teaching load:* **commitment,** responsibility, duty, obligation, burden, charge; trouble, worry, strain, pressure.
▷ **verb**
1 *we quickly loaded the van:* **fill,** pack, charge, stock, stack.
2 *he loaded boxes into the jeep:* **pack,** stow, store, stack, bundle; put, place, deposit, cram.
3 *loading the committee with responsibilities means less gets done:* **burden,** weigh down, saddle, charge; overburden, overwhelm, encumber, tax, strain, trouble, worry.
4 *he had already loaded the gun:* **prime,** charge, prepare.
5 *load the cassette into the camcorder:* **insert,** put, place, slot, slide, slip, drop.

6 *the dice are loaded against him:* bias, rig, fix; weight.

loaded adjective
1 *a loaded freight train:* full, filled, laden, packed, stuffed, crammed, brimming, stacked; informal chock-full, chock-a-block.
2 *a loaded gun:* primed, charged; live.
3 (informal) *they are all loaded* see RICH sense 1.
4 *a politically loaded word:* charged, emotive, sensitive, delicate.

loaf verb *he was just loafing around:* laze, lounge, loll, idle, waste time; informal hang around; Brit. informal hang about, mooch about/around; N. Amer. informal bum around.

loan noun *a loan of £20,000:* advance, credit; mortgage, overdraft; Brit. informal sub.
▷**verb** *the painting was loaned to Bolton Art Gallery in 2001:* lend, advance; give on loan, lease, charter, hire; Brit. informal sub.
OPPOSITES: borrow.

loath adjective *he was loath to discuss the matter:* reluctant, unwilling, disinclined, ill-disposed; against, averse, opposed, resistant.
OPPOSITES: willing.

> **USAGE**
> Do not confuse with **loathe**, which means 'to feel hatred or disgust for'.

loathe verb *the staff at school loathed him:* hate, detest, despise, abhor, not be able to bear/stand, be repelled by; formal abominate, execrate.
OPPOSITES: love.

> **USAGE**
> Do not confuse with **loath**, which means 'reluctant or unwilling'.

loathing noun hatred, hate, detestation, abhorrence, odium; antipathy, dislike, hostility, animosity, ill feeling, bad feeling, malice, animus, enmity, aversion; disgust, repugnance; formal execration, abomination.

loathsome adjective hateful, abhorrent, repulsive, odious, detestable, repugnant, repellent, disgusting, revolting, sickening, abominable, despicable, contemptible, reprehensible, execrable, damnable; vile, horrible, horrid, nasty, obnoxious, gross, foul; literary noisome.

lob verb throw, toss, fling, pitch, hurl, sling, launch, propel; informal chuck, heave; Brit. informal bung.

lobby noun
1 *the hotel lobby was empty:* entrance hall, entrance, hallway, hall, vestibule, foyer, reception area.
2 *the anti-hunt lobby:* pressure group, interest group, movement, campaign, crusade, lobbyists, supporters; faction, camp; Brit. ginger group.
▷**verb**
1 *readers are urged to lobby their MPs:* approach, work on, bring pressure to bear on, try to influence; petition, appeal to, pressurize, importune.
2 *a group lobbying for better rail services:* campaign, crusade, press, push, ask, call, demand; promote, advocate, champion.

local adjective
1 *the local council:* district, community, neighbourhood, regional, city, town, municipal, provincial, village, parish.
2 *a local restaurant:* neighbourhood, nearby, near, at hand, close by; accessible, handy, convenient.
3 *a local infection:* confined, restricted, contained, localized.
OPPOSITES: national, widespread.
▷**noun** *angry locals claim city councillors have got it wrong:* resident, local person, parishioner, native, inhabitant; formal denizen.
OPPOSITES: outsider.

locale noun *her summers were spent in a variety of exotic locales:* place, site, spot, area; position, location, setting, scene, venue, background, backdrop, environment; neighbourhood, district, region, locality.

locality noun *other schools in the locality were unaffected:* vicinity, neighbourhood, area, district, region; informal neck of the woods.

localize verb *medical teams are working to localize the outbreak:* limit, contain, restrict, confine, circumscribe, concentrate, delimit.

locate verb
1 *spotter planes are used to locate the shoals:* find, discover, pinpoint, detect, track down, run to earth, unearth, sniff out, smoke out, search out, ferret out, uncover.
2 *a company located near Pittsburgh:* situate, site, position, place, base; put, build, establish, found, station, install, settle.

location noun position, place, situation, site, locality, locale, spot, whereabouts, point, venue, address; scene, setting, area, environment; bearings, orientation.

lock[1] noun catch, fastener, bolt, clasp, hasp, latch; padlock.
▷**verb**
1 *he locked the door:* fasten, secure, seal; padlock, latch, bolt.
2 *pins are inserted to lock the rods together:* join, interlock, link, mesh, engage, unite, connect, yoke, couple.
3 *the wheels locked:* jam, stick, seize, go rigid.
4 *he locked her in an embrace:* clasp, clench, grasp, embrace, hug, squeeze.
OPPOSITES: unlock, open, separate.
□ **lock someone out**
she locked him out of his own house: keep

out, shut out, refuse entrance to, deny admittance to; exclude, bar, debar, ban.

□ **lock someone up**
he was locked up for five years over a minor traffic offence: **imprison,** jail, incarcerate, intern, send to prison, put behind bars, put under lock and key, pen, coop up; informal send down, put away, put inside.

lock² noun *a lock of hair:* **tress,** hank, strand, tuft, curl, ringlet, wisp, snippet.

locker noun cupboard, compartment, cabinet, chest, safe, box, coffer.

lock-up noun
1 *drunks were put in the lock-up overnight:* **jail,** prison, cell, detention centre; N. Amer. jailhouse; informal can, nick, cooler, slammer.
2 *they stored spare furniture in a lock-up:* **storeroom,** store, warehouse, depository; garage.

locomotion noun *the muscles concerned with locomotion:* **movement,** motion, moving, mobility; travel, travelling; walking, running, making progress; formal ambulation, perambulation; informal getting/moving about/around.

lodge noun
1 *the porter's lodge:* **gatehouse,** cottage.
2 *a hunting lodge:* **house,** cottage, cabin, chalet; Brit. shooting box.
3 *a beaver's lodge:* **den,** lair, hole, sett, shelter.
4 *a Masonic lodge:* **branch,** section, wing; hall, meeting room; N. Amer. chapter.
▷ **verb**
1 *you have 28 days in which to lodge an appeal:* **submit,** register, file, enter, put forward, present, tender, put on record, record, table.
2 *the man who lodged in the room next door:* **reside,** have lodgings, have rooms, stay, live, be quartered; N. Amer. room; formal dwell; informal have digs.
3 *they were lodged at a draughty old inn:* **accommodate,** put up, take in, house, board, billet, quarter, shelter.
4 *the bullet lodged in his back:* **stick,** embed itself, become embedded, get/become stuck, catch, become/get caught, wedge.
5 *the money was lodged in a bank:* **deposit,** put, bank; stash, store, stow, put away, squirrel away.

lodger noun boarder, paying guest, PG, tenant; N. Amer. roomer.

lodging noun accommodation, rooms, living quarters, place to stay, residence, a roof over your head, housing, shelter; formal abode, dwelling; informal digs, pad.

lofty adjective
1 *lofty towers and spires:* **tall,** high, giant, towering, soaring.
2 *we failed to live up to his lofty ideals:* **noble,** exalted, high, high-minded, worthy, grand, fine, elevated.

3 *he regarded us with lofty disdain:* **haughty,** arrogant, disdainful, supercilious, condescending, patronizing, scornful, contemptuous, self-important, conceited, snobbish; informal stuck-up, snooty, snotty; Brit. informal toffee-nosed.
OPPOSITES: low, short, base, lowly, modest.

log noun
1 *she tripped over a fallen log:* **branch,** trunk, piece of wood; (**logs**) timber, firewood.
2 *keep a detailed log of your activities:* **record,** register, logbook, journal, diary, weblog, blog, account, chronicle, record book; ledger.
▷ **verb**
1 *all complaints are logged by staff:* **record,** register, make a note of, note down, write down, jot down, put in writing, enter, file, minute.
2 *the pilot had logged 95 hours:* **attain,** achieve, chalk up, make, do, go, cover.

logic noun
1 *this case appears to defy all logic:* **reason,** judgement, logical thought, rationality, wisdom, sense, good sense, common sense, sanity.
2 *the logic of their argument:* **reasoning,** line of reasoning, rationale, argument, argumentation.

logical adjective
1 *the information is displayed in a logical fashion:* **reasoned,** well reasoned, rational, sound, cogent, well thought out, valid; coherent, clear, well organized, systematic, orderly, methodical, analytical, consistent, objective; informal joined-up.
2 *further privatization seems to be the logical outcome:* **natural,** reasonable, sensible, understandable; predictable, unsurprising, only to be expected, most likely, likeliest, obvious.
OPPOSITES: illogical, irrational, unlikely.

logistics plural noun *the logistics of the open-air concert proved overwhelming:* **organization,** planning, plans, management, arrangement, administration, orchestration, coordination, execution, handling, running.

logo noun emblem, trademark, symbol, design, sign, mark; insignia, crest, seal, coat of arms, shield, device, badge, motif, monogram, colophon.

loiter verb
1 *five or six teenagers loitered in front of the newsagents:* **stand about/around,** wait, skulk; loaf, lounge, idle, laze, waste time, linger; informal hang around; Brit. informal hang about, mooch about/around.
2 *the weather had tempted them to loiter along the banks of the river:* **dawdle,** dally, take your time; stroll, amble, saunter, meander, drift, potter; informal dilly-dally; Brit. informal mooch.

loll verb
1 *Louis lolled in an armchair by the window:* lounge, sprawl, drape yourself, stretch yourself; slouch, slump; laze, luxuriate, put your feet up, lean back, recline, relax, take it easy.
2 *her head lolled to one side:* hang, droop, sag, drop, flop, dangle.

lone adjective
1 *a lone police officer stood on the corner:* solitary, single, solo, unaccompanied, unescorted, alone, by yourself/itself, sole, companionless, isolated; unique.
2 *the difficulties of being a lone parent:* single, unmarried, unattached; separated, divorced, widowed.

loneliness noun
1 *his loneliness was unbearable:* isolation, friendlessness, aloneness; N. Amer. lonesomeness.
2 *the enforced loneliness of a prison cell:* solitude, solitariness, lack of company.

lonely adjective
1 *she was feeling very lonely:* isolated, alone, friendless, with no one to turn to, rejected, unloved, unwanted, abandoned; literary forsaken; N. Amer. lonesome.
2 *the lonely life of a writer:* solitary, unaccompanied, lone, by yourself/itself, companionless.
3 *a lonely road:* deserted, unfrequented, remote, isolated, out of the way, off the beaten track, uninhabited, unpopulated, desolate, in the back of beyond, godforsaken; informal in the middle of nowhere.
OPPOSITES: popular, sociable, crowded.

loner noun recluse, introvert, lone wolf, hermit, solitary, misanthrope, outsider; historical anchorite.

long¹ adjective *there was a long silence:* lengthy, extended, prolonged, protracted, long-lasting, long-drawn-out, spun out, seemingly endless, sustained, lingering, interminable.
OPPOSITES: short, brief.
□ **before long**
soon, shortly, presently, in the near future, in a little while, by and by, in a minute, in a moment, in a second; informal anon, in a jiffy; Brit. informal in a tick, in two ticks, in a mo; dated directly.

long² verb *I longed for the holidays:* yearn, pine, ache, hanker for/after, hunger, thirst, itch, be eager, be desperate, have a yen; crave, dream of, set your heart on; informal be dying.

longing noun *many city dwellers have a longing for the countryside:* yearning, craving, yen, ache, hankering, hunger, thirst; informal itch.
▷ adjective *he gave her a longing look:* yearning, eager, hungry, covetous, wistful.

long-lasting adjective *their long-lasting friendship:* enduring, lasting, abiding, long-lived, long-running, long-established, long-standing, lifelong, deep-rooted, time-honoured, traditional, permanent.
OPPOSITES: short-lived, ephemeral.

long-lived adjective see LONG-LASTING.

long-standing adjective well established, long-established, time-honoured, traditional, age-old; abiding, enduring, long-lived, surviving, persistent, prevailing, perennial, deep-rooted, long-term, confirmed.
OPPOSITES: new, recent.

long-suffering adjective patient, uncomplaining, stoical, forbearing, tolerant, resigned; forgiving, charitable, indulgent, accommodating.
OPPOSITES: impatient, complaining.

long-winded adjective verbose, wordy, lengthy, long, overlong, prolix, long-drawn-out, prolonged, protracted, interminable, tedious, boring; discursive, diffuse, rambling, tortuous, meandering, repetitious; Brit. informal waffly.
OPPOSITES: concise, succinct, laconic.

look verb
1 *people were looking at him | I looked out of the window:* glance, gaze, stare, gape, peer; peep, peek, take a look; watch, observe, view, eye, regard, examine, inspect, scan, scrutinize, survey, study, contemplate, consider, take in, ogle; informal take a gander, rubberneck, give someone/something a/the once-over; Brit. informal take a dekko, take a butcher's, take a shufti, gawp; N. Amer. informal eyeball.
2 *her room looked out on Broadway:* command a view of, face, overlook, front.
3 *they looked shocked:* seem, appear, have the appearance/air of being, give the impression of being, give every appearance/indication of being.
4 *I can't find them—I've looked everywhere:* search, hunt, turn somewhere upside down, go over something with a fine-tooth comb.
OPPOSITES: ignore.
▷ noun
1 *I'll have a quick look at the paper:* glance, glimpse, peek, peep, gaze, stare; examination, study, inspection, observation, scan, survey; informal eyeful, gander, look-see, once-over, squint, recce; Brit. informal shufti, dekko, butcher's.
2 *the look on her face:* expression.
3 *little details that help to create that rustic look:* appearance, air, impression, effect, feel; aspect, bearing, cast, mien, demeanour; informal vibe.
4 *Italian designers unveiled their latest look:* fashion, style, vogue, mode.
□ **look after**
we took it in turns to look after the children: take care of, care for, attend to, minister to, tend, mind, keep an eye on, keep safe,

be responsible for, protect; nurse, babysit, childmind.

☐ **look back on**
some day we'll all look back on this and laugh: **reflect on,** think back to, remember, recall, reminisce about.

☐ **look down on**
her mother had social pretensions and looked down on most of our neighbours: **regard with contempt,** disdain, scorn, look down your nose at, sneer at, despise.

☐ **look for**
the police have been looking for her: **search for,** hunt for, try to find, seek, cast about/around for, try to track down, scout out; literary quest after.

☐ **look forward to**
I'm really looking forward to the trip: **await with pleasure,** eagerly anticipate, lick your lips over, be unable to wait for, count the days until.

☐ **look into**
scientists are looking into ways that plants use vitamin C to defend against ozone: **investigate,** enquire into, probe, explore, follow up, research, study, examine; informal check out.

☐ **look like**
he looks like my brother: **resemble,** bear a resemblance to, look similar to, take after, have the look of, have the appearance of, remind you of, make you think of; informal be the spitting image of, be a dead ringer for.

☐ **look on**
people he looked on as friends took advantage of him: **regard,** consider, think of, deem to be, judge, see, view, count, reckon.

☐ **look out**
look out for any early warning signals: **beware,** watch out, mind out, be on your guard, be alert, be wary, be vigilant, be careful, take care, be cautious, pay attention, take heed, keep your eyes open/peeled, keep an eye out; watch your step.

☐ **look something over**
I've looked over the original transcripts: **inspect,** examine, scan, cast an eye over, take stock of, vet, view; look through, run through, read through; informal give something a/the once-over.

☐ **look to**
1 *we must look to the future:* **consider,** think about, turn your thoughts to, focus on; pay attention to, take heed of, attend to, address, mind, heed.
2 *they looked to the government for help:* **turn to,** resort to, have recourse to, fall back on, rely on.

☐ **look up**
things seem to be looking up at last: **improve,** get better, pick up, come along/on, progress, make progress, make headway, rally, take a turn for the better; informal perk up.

☐ **look someone up** (informal)
visit, pay a visit to, call on, go to see, look in on; N. Amer. visit with; informal drop in on.

☐ **look up to**
I think every actor in the world looked up to him: **admire,** respect, have a high opinion of, think highly of, hold in high regard, regard highly, esteem, value.

lookalike noun double, twin, clone, doppelgänger, duplicate, exact likeness, replica, copy, facsimile; informal spitting image, dead ringer.

lookout noun
1 *the lookout sighted sails on the horizon:* **watchman,** watch, guard, sentry, sentinel.
2 (Brit. informal) *I doubt if she'll fit in, but that's her own lookout:* **problem,** concern, business, affair, responsibility, worry.

☐ **be on the lookout/keep a lookout**
keep watch, keep an eye out, keep your eyes peeled, keep a vigil, be alert.

loom verb
1 *ghostly shapes loomed out of the fog:* **emerge,** appear, come into view, take shape, materialize, reveal itself.
2 *the church loomed above him:* **soar,** tower, rise, rear up; overshadow, dominate.
3 *without reforms, disaster looms:* **be imminent,** be on the horizon, be impending, threaten, brew, be just around the corner.

loop noun coil, hoop, ring, circle, oval, spiral, curl, bend, curve, arc, twirl, whorl, twist, helix.
▷ **verb** coil, wind, twist, snake, wreathe, spiral, curve, bend, turn.

loophole noun *they took advantage of a loophole in the regulations:* **ambiguity,** omission, flaw, inconsistency, discrepancy, let-out.

loose adjective
1 *a loose floorboard:* **unsecured,** unattached, detached, unfastened; wobbly, unsteady, movable.
2 *she wore her hair loose:* **untied,** unpinned, unbound, hanging down, free, down, flowing.
3 *there's a wolf loose in the woods:* **free,** at large, at liberty, on the loose, escaped, wandering about, roaming about.
4 *a loose interpretation of the drug laws:* **vague,** inexact, imprecise, indefinite, approximate; broad, general, rough; liberal.
5 *a loose jacket:* **baggy,** generously cut, roomy; oversized, shapeless, sagging, sloppy.
OPPOSITES: secure, literal, narrow, tight.
▷ **verb**
1 *the hounds have been loosed:* **free,** set free, unloose, turn loose, set loose, let loose, let go, release; untie, unchain, unfasten, unleash.
2 *his fingers loosed their hold:* **relax,** slacken, loosen, disengage; weaken.
OPPOSITES: confine, tighten.

☐ **at a loose end**
with nothing to do, unoccupied,

unemployed, at leisure, idle, adrift, with time to kill; bored, twiddling your thumbs, kicking your heels.

□ **on the loose**
free, at liberty, at large, escaped; on the run, fugitive.

> **USAGE**
>
> Do not confuse **loose** with **lose**. **Loose** means 'not fixed in place or tied up', while **lose** means 'to have something taken away' (*she might lose her job*) or 'to become unable to find something' (*I've lost my watch*).

loose-limbed adjective supple, lithe, lissom, willowy, limber; agile, nimble.

loosen verb
1 *loosen two screws:* slacken, unfasten, detach, release, disconnect, undo, unclasp, unlatch, unbolt.
2 *Philip loosened his grip:* slacken, relax, weaken, loose, ease, lessen, let go.
OPPOSITES: tighten.
□ **loosen up**
relax, unwind, ease up/off; informal let up, hang loose, lighten up, go easy.

loot verb *troops looted the cathedral:* plunder, pillage, ransack, sack, raid, rifle, rob, burgle; strip, clear out; literary despoil.
▷ **noun** *a bag full of loot:* booty, spoils, plunder, stolen goods, contraband, ill-gotten gains; informal swag, boodle.

lop verb cut, chop, hack, saw, hew, slash; prune, sever, clip, trim, snip, dock, crop.

lope verb stride, run, bound; lollop.

lopsided adjective crooked, askew, off-centre, awry, uneven, out of true, out of line, asymmetrical, tilted, at an angle, aslant, slanting; Scottish agley; informal cockeyed; Brit. informal skew-whiff, wonky.
OPPOSITES: even, level, balanced.

loquacious adjective talkative, voluble, communicative, expansive, garrulous, unreserved, chatty, gossipy, gossiping; informal having the gift of the gab, gabby; Brit. informal able to talk the hind legs off a donkey.
OPPOSITES: reticent, taciturn.

loquacity noun talkativeness, volubility, expansiveness, garrulousness, garrulity, chattiness; informal the gift of the gab.
OPPOSITES: reticence, taciturnity.

lord noun
1 *lords and ladies were once entertained in this house:* noble, nobleman, peer, aristocrat, patrician, grandee.
2 *it was his duty to obey his lord's wishes:* master, ruler, leader, chief, superior, monarch, sovereign, king, emperor, prince, governor, commander.
OPPOSITES: commoner, servant, inferior.
□ **lord it over someone**
when we were at school, he used to love to lord it over us: order about/around, dictate to, ride roughshod over, pull rank

on, tyrannize, have under your thumb; be overbearing, put on airs, swagger; informal boss about/around, walk all over, push around, throw your weight about/around.

lore noun
1 *Arthurian legend and lore:* mythology, myths, legends, stories, traditions, folklore, oral tradition.
2 *farming lore:* knowledge, learning, wisdom; informal know-how.

lorry noun truck, wagon, van, juggernaut, trailer; articulated lorry, heavy-goods vehicle, HGV; N. Amer. tractor trailer; dated pantechnicon.

lose verb
1 *I've lost my watch:* mislay, misplace, be unable to find, lose track of, leave behind, fail to keep/retain, fail to keep sight of.
2 *he managed to lose his pursuers:* escape from, evade, elude, dodge, avoid, give someone the slip, shake off, throw off, throw off the scent; leave behind, outdistance, outstrip, outrun.
3 *he lost his chance of Olympic glory:* waste, fail to take advantage of, squander, forfeit, neglect, use up, dissipate.
4 *they lost 2–0:* be defeated, be beaten, suffer defeat, be the loser, be conquered, be vanquished, be trounced, be worsted; informal come a cropper, go down.
OPPOSITES: find, regain, win.
□ **lose out** be the loser, fail to benefit, be disadvantaged; informal miss out.

> **USAGE**
>
> Do not confuse **lose** with **loose**, which means 'not fixed in place or tied up' (*she usually wore her hair loose*).

loser noun
1 *the loser will still get a medal:* runner-up, also-ran.
2 (informal) *he's such a loser:* failure, non-achiever, underachiever, dead loss; informal non-starter, no-hoper.
OPPOSITES: winner, success.

loss noun
1 *the loss of the documents is highly embarrassing:* mislaying, misplacement.
2 *loss of earnings is covered by insurance:* deprivation, forfeiture, erosion, reduction, depletion, shrinkage.
3 *the loss of her husband:* death, dying, demise, passing away/on; bereavement; formal decease.
4 *British losses in the war:* casualty, fatality, victim; dead; missing; death toll, number killed/dead/wounded.
5 *a loss of £15,000:* deficit, debit, debt, deficiency.
OPPOSITES: recovery, profit.
□ **at a loss**
baffled, nonplussed, mystified, puzzled, perplexed, bemused, bewildered, at sixes and sevens, confused, dumbfounded, stumped, stuck, blank; informal clueless,

flummoxed, bamboozled, fazed, floored; N. Amer. informal discombobulated.

lost adjective
1 *we were searching for her lost keys:* missing, mislaid, misplaced, gone missing/astray, nowhere to be found, vanished, disappeared; absent, strayed; informal gone walkabout.
2 *I think we're lost:* off course, off track, having lost your bearings, going round in circles, disorientated, adrift, at sea, gone astray.
3 *a lost opportunity:* missed, wasted, forfeited, squandered, gone by the board, neglected; informal down the drain.
4 *lost species and habitats:* extinct, died out, defunct, vanished, gone; destroyed, wiped out, ruined, eradicated.
5 *a lost cause:* hopeless, beyond hope, futile, forlorn, failed, beyond remedy, beyond recovery.
6 *she was lost in thought:* engrossed, absorbed, rapt, immersed, deep, intent, preoccupied.
OPPOSITES: current, saved.

lot pronoun *a lot of money | lots of friends:* a large amount, a fair amount, a good/great deal, a great quantity, quantities, an abundance, a wealth, a profusion, plenty; many, a great many, a large number, a considerable number, numerous, scores; informal hundreds, thousands, millions, billions, loads, bucketloads, masses, heaps, a pile, piles, oodles, stacks, scads, reams, wads, pots, oceans, a mountain, mountains, miles, tons, zillions; Brit. informal a shedload, lashings; N. Amer. informal a bunch, gazillions.
OPPOSITES: not much, a few, not many.
▷ adverb *I work in pastels a lot:* a great deal, a good deal, to a great extent, much; often, frequently, regularly.
OPPOSITES: a little, not much.
▷ noun
1 (informal) *what do your lot think?* group, set, crowd, circle, crew; informal bunch, gang, posse.
2 *the books were auctioned as a number of separate lots:* item, article; batch, set, collection, group, bundle, quantity.
3 *he was discontented with his lot in life:* fate, destiny, fortune; situation, circumstances, state, condition, position, plight, predicament.
□ throw in your lot
he threw in his lot with the nationalists: join forces, join up, form an alliance, ally yourself, align yourself, link up, make common cause.

lotion noun cream, ointment, salve, balm, rub, emollient, moisturizer, lubricant, unguent, liniment, embrocation.

lottery noun
1 *a national lottery:* prize draw, lotto, raffle, sweepstake, tombola.
2 *the procedure is something of a lottery:* gamble, matter of luck, pot luck, lucky dip.

loud adjective
1 *loud music | a loud voice:* noisy, blaring, booming, deafening, thunderous, thundering, ear-splitting, ear-piercing, piercing, roaring; carrying, clearly audible; lusty, powerful, forceful, stentorian; Music forte, fortissimo.
2 *the congestion led to loud complaints:* vociferous, clamorous, insistent, vehement, emphatic, urgent.
3 *a man in a loud check suit:* garish, gaudy, lurid, flamboyant, showy, ostentatious; vulgar, tasteless; informal flash, flashy, naff, kitsch, tacky.
OPPOSITES: quiet, soft, sober, tasteful.

loudly adverb at high volume, at the top of your voice; noisily, deafeningly, thunderously, piercingly; stridently, lustily, powerfully, forcefully; Music forte, fortissimo; informal as if to wake the dead.
OPPOSITES: quietly, softly.

loudspeaker noun speaker, monitor, woofer, tweeter; loudhailer, megaphone; public address system, PA system.

lounge verb *several guests were lounging about on the sofas reading newspapers:* laze, lie, loll, lie back, lean back, recline, stretch yourself, drape yourself, relax, rest, repose, take it easy, put your feet up, unwind, luxuriate; sprawl, slump, slouch, flop; loaf, idle, do nothing.
▷ noun living room, sitting room, drawing room, reception room, salon, family room.

louring, lowering adjective *a louring sky:* overcast, dark, leaden, grey, cloudy, clouded, gloomy, threatening, menacing.
OPPOSITES: sunny, bright.

lousy (informal) adjective
1 *a lousy film* see AWFUL sense 2.
2 *the lousy, double-crossing snake!* see DESPICABLE.
3 *I felt lousy* see ILL adjective sense 1.

lout noun hooligan, oaf, ruffian, thug, boor, rowdy; informal tough, roughneck, bruiser, yahoo; Brit. informal yob, yobbo.

loutish adjective uncouth, coarse, thuggish, boorish, oafish, rough, rude, impolite, ill-mannered, ill-bred, uncivilized; Brit. informal yobbish.
OPPOSITES: polite, well behaved.

lovable adjective adorable, sweet, cute, appealing, charming, endearing, lovely, darling, dear, delightful, captivating, enchanting, engaging, bewitching, pleasing, winsome, winning, fetching.
OPPOSITES: hateful, loathsome.

love noun
1 *his friendship with Helen grew into love:* deep affection, fondness, tenderness, warmth, intimacy, attachment; devotion, adoration, idolization, worship; passion, ardour, desire, lust, yearning, infatuation, besottedness.

2 *her love of fashion:* liking, enjoyment, appreciation, taste, delight, relish, passion, zeal, appetite, zest, enthusiasm, keenness, fondness, soft spot, weakness, bent, leaning, proclivity, inclination, disposition, partiality, predilection, penchant.
3 *their love for their fellow human beings:* compassion, care, concern, caring, regard, solicitude, kindness, charity, goodwill, sympathy, kindliness, altruism, unselfishness, philanthropy, benevolence, fellow feeling, humanity.
4 *her true love:* beloved, loved one, love of your life, dear, dearest, dear one, darling, sweetheart, sweet, angel, honey; lover.
5 *their love will survive:* relationship, love affair, romance, liaison, affair of the heart.
6 *my mother sends her love:* best wishes, regards, good wishes, kind/kindest regards.
OPPOSITES: hatred.

▷**verb**
1 *she loves him dearly:* care for, feel deep affection for, hold dear, adore, think the world of, be devoted to, dote on, idolize, worship; be in love with, be infatuated with, be smitten with, be besotted with; informal be mad/crazy/wild about, carry a torch for.
2 *Laura loved painting:* like, delight in, enjoy greatly, have a passion for, take pleasure in, derive pleasure from, relish, savour; have a weakness for, be partial to, have a soft spot for, have a taste for, be taken with; informal get a kick out of, have a thing about, be mad/crazy/wild about, be hooked on, go a bundle on, get a buzz out of.
OPPOSITES: hate.
▢**fall in love with**
become infatuated with, lose your heart to; informal fall for, be bowled over by, be swept off your feet by, develop a crush on.
▢**in love with**
infatuated with, besotted with, enamoured of, smitten with; captivated by, bewitched by, enthralled by, entranced by; devoted to; informal mad/crazy/wild about.

WORD LINKS
amatory relating to love

love affair noun
1 *he was involved in a love affair with a married woman:* relationship, affair, liaison, fling, romance, romantic entanglement, involvement, affair of the heart, affaire de cœur, amour; flirtation, dalliance.
2 *our culture's love affair with the motor car:* enthusiasm for, mania for, devotion to, passion for, obsession with, worship of.

loveless adjective passionless, unloving, without love, cold, frigid.
OPPOSITES: loving, passionate.

lovelorn adjective lovesick, unrequited in love, crossed in love; spurned, jilted, rejected; pining, moping.

lovely adjective
1 *a lovely young woman:* beautiful, pretty, attractive, good-looking, handsome, personable, appealing, sweet, adorable, exquisite, charming, enchanting, engaging, winsome; gorgeous, stunning, seductive, alluring, ravishing, glamorous; Scottish & N. English bonny; literary beauteous; informal tasty, knockout, drop-dead gorgeous; Brit. informal fit; N. Amer. informal cute; old use comely, fair.
2 *a lovely view:* scenic, picturesque, pleasing, easy on the eye; magnificent, stunning, splendid.
3 *we had a lovely day:* delightful, pleasant, agreeable, marvellous, wonderful, sublime, glorious, superb, fine, magical; informal terrific, fabulous, heavenly, divine, amazing.
OPPOSITES: ugly, horrible.

lover noun
1 *apparently, she had a secret lover:* boyfriend, girlfriend, love, sweetheart; partner, significant other; mistress; informal bit on the side, toy boy, fancy man, fancy woman; dated beau; old use paramour.
2 *a great present for dog lovers everywhere:* devotee, fan, enthusiast, aficionado, admirer; informal buff, nut.

WORD LINKS
-phile forming words meaning 'a lover of ——', such as *bibliophile* ('a person who loves books') or *Francophile* ('a person who loves France')

lovesick adjective lovelorn, pining, languishing, longing, yearning, infatuated; frustrated.

loving adjective affectionate, fond, devoted, adoring, doting, solicitous, demonstrative; caring, tender, warm, warm-hearted, close; amorous, ardent, passionate, amatory.
OPPOSITES: cold, cruel.

low¹ adjective
1 *a low fence:* small, little, short, squat, stubby, stunted, dwarf; low-lying, shallow.
2 *a dress with a rather low neckline:* low-cut, revealing, plunging, décolleté, skimpy.
3 *duty-free goods at amazingly low prices:* cheap, economical, moderate, reasonable, modest, bargain, bargain-basement, rock-bottom.
4 *fuel supplies were perilously low:* scarce, scanty, scant, skimpy, sparse, few, little, meagre, paltry; reduced, depleted, diminished.
5 *cheap goods of low quality:* inferior, substandard, poor, bad, low-grade, below par, second-rate, unsatisfactory, deficient, defective.
6 *they have very low expectations of their children:* unambitious, modest.
7 *most Americans have a low opinion of New York:* unfavourable, negative, poor, bad, adverse.

8 *he spoke in a low voice:* quiet, soft, faint, gentle, muted, subdued, muffled, hushed, whispered, stifled.
9 *hitting those low notes is very hard:* bass, low-pitched, deep, rumbling, booming, sonorous.
10 *she was feeling very low over Christmas:* depressed, dejected, despondent, downhearted, downcast, low-spirited, down, morose, miserable, dismal, heavy-hearted, mournful, forlorn, woebegone, crestfallen, dispirited; without energy, enervated, flat, sapped, weary; informal down in the mouth, down in the dumps, fed up, blue.
11 *the show thrives on cheap remarks and low comedy:* uncouth, uncultured, unsophisticated, rough, unrefined, tasteless, crass, common, vulgar, coarse, crude.
12 *a woman of low birth:* humble, lowly, low-ranking, plebeian, proletarian, peasant, poor; common, ordinary.
OPPOSITES: high, expensive, plentiful, superior, loud, cheerful.
▷**noun** *the dollar fell to an all-time low:* nadir, low point, lowest point, lowest level, depth, rock bottom.
OPPOSITES: high.

low² verb *cattle were lowing:* moo, bellow.

lowbrow adjective mass-market, popular, intellectually undemanding, tabloid, lightweight, accessible, unpretentious; unsophisticated, uncultured, trashy, simplistic; Brit. downmarket; informal dumbed-down.
OPPOSITES: highbrow, intellectual.

low-down (informal) adjective *that was a low-down trick:* unfair, dishonest, mean, despicable, reprehensible, contemptible, disgusting, shameful, low, shabby, base, dishonourable, unprincipled, sordid, underhand; informal rotten, dirty; dated dastardly.
OPPOSITES: kind, honourable.
▷**noun** *we'll give you the low-down on where to go—and where to avoid:* facts, information, story, data, facts and figures, intelligence, news; informal info, the score, the gen, the latest, the word, the dope.

lower¹ adjective
1 *her lower lip quivered:* bottom, bottommost, nether, under; underneath, further down, beneath.
2 *the lower house of parliament:* subordinate, lower-level, subsidiary, inferior, lesser, junior, secondary.
OPPOSITES: upper, higher.

lower² verb
1 *she lowered the mask:* move down, let down, take down, haul down, drop, let fall.
2 *please lower your voice:* soften, quieten, hush, modulate, tone down, muffle, turn down, mute.
3 *they are lowering their prices this*

autumn: reduce, decrease, lessen, bring down, mark down, cut, slash, curtail, prune, pare down.
4 *the water level lowered:* subside, fall, recede, ebb, wane; abate, die down, let up, moderate, diminish, lessen.
5 *don't lower yourself to their level:* degrade, debase, demean, abase, humiliate, downgrade, discredit, shame, dishonour, disgrace; belittle, cheapen, devalue; (**lower yourself**) stoop, sink, descend.
OPPOSITES: raise, increase.

low-grade adjective poor-quality, inferior, substandard, second-rate; shoddy, cheap, reject, trashy, gimcrack; informal rubbishy; Brit. informal duff, ropy, twopenny-halfpenny.
OPPOSITES: top-quality, first-class.

low-key adjective restrained, modest, understated, muted, subtle, quiet, low-profile, discreet, toned-down, inconspicuous, unobtrusive, unostentatious.
OPPOSITES: ostentatious, obtrusive.

lowly adjective humble, low-born, low-ranking, plebeian, proletarian; ordinary, average, modest, simple; inferior, subordinate, obscure, ignoble.
OPPOSITES: aristocratic, exalted.

loyal adjective faithful, true, devoted, staunch, steadfast, constant, dependable, reliable, trusted, trustworthy, trusty, dedicated, dutiful, unchanging, unwavering, unswerving; patriotic.
OPPOSITES: treacherous.

loyalty noun allegiance, fidelity, faithfulness, obedience, adherence, devotion; staunchness, steadfastness, dependability, reliability, trustiness, trustworthiness, duty, dedication, commitment; patriotism.
OPPOSITES: treachery.

lozenge noun
1 *a cough lozenge:* pastille, cough drop, cough sweet; tablet.
2 *a pattern of overlapping lozenge shapes:* diamond, rhombus.

lubricant noun grease, oil, lubrication, lubricator; informal lube.

lubricate verb oil, grease, make slippery.

lucid adjective
1 *a lucid description of this complex subject:* clear, cogent, coherent, comprehensible, intelligible, understandable, articulate, crystal clear, transparent, plain, simple, straightforward.
2 *he was not sufficiently lucid to explain what had happened:* rational, sane, in your right mind, in possession of your faculties, compos mentis, able to think clearly, balanced, clear-headed, sober; informal all there.
OPPOSITES: confusing, confused.

luck noun
1 *with luck you'll make it to Sheffield by this afternoon:* good fortune, good luck; fluke, stroke of luck; informal lucky break.
2 *I wish you luck:* success, prosperity, good fortune, good luck.
3 *it is a matter of luck whether it hits or misses:* chance, fate, fortune, destiny, karma, kismet; serendipity, fortuity; accident, a twist of fate.
OPPOSITES: misfortune.
□ **in luck**
fortunate, lucky, blessed with good luck, born under a lucky star; successful, having a charmed life; Brit. informal jammy.
□ **out of luck**
unfortunate, unlucky, luckless, hapless, unsuccessful, cursed, jinxed, ill-fated; informal down on your luck.

luckily adverb fortunately, by good fortune, as luck would have it, happily, providentially, opportunely, propitiously; mercifully, thankfully.

luckless adjective unlucky, unfortunate, unsuccessful, hapless, out of luck, cursed, jinxed, doomed, ill-fated; literary star-crossed; informal down on your luck.
OPPOSITES: lucky.

lucky adjective
1 *I'm lucky to have such good friends:* fortunate, in luck, blessed, blessed with good luck, favoured, born under a lucky star, charmed, successful; Brit. informal jammy.
2 *a lucky escape | a lucky guess:* fortuitous, serendipitous, fluky, fortunate; providential, heaven-sent, timely, opportune, auspicious, propitious.
OPPOSITES: unfortunate.

lucrative adjective profitable, profit-making, gainful, remunerative, moneymaking, paying, high-income, well paid, bankable; rewarding, worthwhile; thriving, flourishing, successful, booming.
OPPOSITES: unprofitable.

ludicrous adjective *that is the most ludicrous idea I've ever heard:* absurd, ridiculous, farcical, laughable, risible, preposterous, foolish, mad, insane, idiotic, stupid, inane, silly, asinine, nonsensical; informal crazy.
OPPOSITES: sensible.

lug verb *they lugged the baskets of laundry upstairs:* carry, lift, bear, heave, hoist, shoulder, manhandle; haul, pull, drag, tug, tow, transport, move, convey, shift; informal tote, N. Amer. informal schlep; Brit. informal hump.

luggage noun baggage; bags, suitcases, cases, trunks. See also BAG noun sense 2.

lugubrious adjective *his lugubrious face lit up in a brief smile:* mournful, gloomy, sad, unhappy, doleful, glum, melancholy, woeful, miserable, woebegone, forlorn,

long-faced, sombre, solemn, serious, sorrowful, morose, dour, cheerless, joyless, dismal; funereal, sepulchral; literary dolorous; informal down in the mouth.
OPPOSITES: cheerful.

lukewarm adjective
1 *a cup of lukewarm coffee:* tepid, warm, warmish, at room temperature.
2 *we received a lukewarm response from the committee:* unenthusiastic, cool, indifferent, half-hearted, tepid, apathetic, offhand, non-committal; informal unenthused.
OPPOSITES: hot, enthusiastic.

lull verb
1 *the sound of the bells lulled us to sleep:* soothe, calm, hush; rock to sleep.
2 *his suspicions were soon lulled:* assuage, allay, ease, alleviate, soothe, quiet, quieten; reduce, diminish; quell, banish, dispel.
OPPOSITES: arouse, intensify.
▷ noun *there was a brief lull in the fighting:* pause, respite, interval, break, hiatus, suspension, interlude, intermission, breathing space; informal let-up, breather.

lumber[1] verb *a herd of elephants lumbered past:* trudge, plod, tramp, trundle, clump, stump, lurch, shamble, shuffle, waddle, stumble; informal galumph.

lumber[2] noun
1 *a spare room packed with lumber:* jumble, clutter, flotsam and jetsam, cast-offs; refuse, rubbish, litter; N. Amer. trash; informal junk, bits and pieces, odds and sods, clobber; Brit. informal odds and ends.
2 *he worked in the lumber trade:* timber, wood.
▷ verb (Brit. informal) *she was lumbered with a useless husband and a sick child:* burden, saddle, encumber, hamper; load, trouble, tax, oppress; informal land, dump something on someone.

lumbering adjective clumsy, awkward, heavy-footed, ungainly, ungraceful, slow, blundering, bumbling, inept, maladroit, uncoordinated, gauche, lumpish, hulking, ponderous; informal clodhopping.
OPPOSITES: nimble, agile.

luminary noun *the luminaries of the art world gathered to pay homage:* leading light, guiding light, inspiration, role model, hero, heroine, leader, expert, master; legend, great, giant.
OPPOSITES: nobody.

luminous adjective shining, bright, brilliant, radiant, dazzling, glowing, gleaming; luminescent, phosphorescent, fluorescent, incandescent.
OPPOSITES: dark.

lump noun
1 *a lump of coal:* chunk, hunk, piece, mass, block, wedge, slab, cake, nugget, ball, brick, cube, pat, knob, clod, gobbet, dollop, wad; informal glob; N. Amer. informal gob.

2 *he had a nasty lump on his head:* swelling, bump, bulge, protuberance, protrusion, growth, outgrowth, nodule, hump.
▷**verb** *the media tend to lump women singer-songwriters together:* group, put, combine, bunch, aggregate, unite, pool, merge, collect, throw.

lumpy adjective
1 *a lumpy mattress:* bumpy, knobbly, uneven, bulging, rough, gnarled.
2 *lumpy custard:* clotted, curdled, congealed, coagulated.

lunacy noun
1 *the survivors descended into despair and lunacy:* insanity, madness, dementia, mania, psychosis.
2 *such a policy would be sheer lunacy:* folly, foolishness, foolhardiness, stupidity, idiocy, madness, rashness, recklessness, imprudence, irresponsibility, injudiciousness; informal craziness; Brit. informal daftness.
OPPOSITES: sanity, sense, prudence.

lunatic noun maniac, madman, madwoman, imbecile, psychopath, psychotic; fool, idiot; informal loony, nut, nutcase, head case, psycho, moron; Brit. informal nutter, mentalist.

lung noun

WORD LINKS
pulmonary relating to the lungs

lunge noun *he made a lunge at his attacker:* thrust, dive, rush, charge, grab.
▷**verb** *he lunged at her with a knife:* thrust, dive, spring, launch yourself, rush, make a grab.

lurch verb
1 *he lurched into the kitchen:* stagger, reel, totter, stumble, wobble, sway, roll, weave, pitch, blunder.
2 *the ship lurched alarmingly to one side:* sway, list, reel, heel, rock, roll, pitch, swerve.

lure verb *consumers are frequently lured into debt:* tempt, entice, seduce, attract, draw, lead, persuade, inveigle, coax, cajole, beguile, bewitch, ensnare.
OPPOSITES: deter, put off.
▷**noun** *the lure of the stage:* temptation, enticement, attraction, pull, draw, appeal, allure, fascination.

lurid adjective
1 *party dresses in lurid colours:* bright, loud, gaudy, fluorescent, glaring, dazzling, brilliant, vivid.
2 *a lurid account of prostitution and addiction:* sensational, sensationalist, melodramatic, colourful, graphic, explicit, shocking, exaggerated, extravagant; salacious, prurient; gruesome, gory, grisly; informal tacky, shock-horror, juicy, full-frontal, full-on.
OPPOSITES: muted, restrained.

lurk verb skulk, loiter, lie in wait, hide.

luscious adjective delicious, succulent, lush, juicy, mouth-watering, sweet, tasty, appetizing; informal scrumptious, moreish, scrummy, yummy.
OPPOSITES: unappetizing.

lush adjective
1 *lush vegetation:* luxuriant, rich, abundant, profuse, riotous, prolific, vigorous; dense, thick, rampant.
2 *a lush apartment:* luxurious, de luxe, sumptuous, palatial, opulent, lavish, elaborate, extravagant, fancy; informal plush, ritzy, posh, swanky; Brit. informal swish.
OPPOSITES: sparse, austere.

lust noun
1 *he was watching her with undisguised lust:* desire, passion, ardour, longing; libido, sex drive, sexuality; lechery, lecherousness, lasciviousness; informal the hots.
2 *he was driven by a lust for power:* greed, desire, craving, hunger, thirst, appetite, longing, yearning, hankering, eagerness.
OPPOSITES: dread, aversion.
▷**verb**
1 *he lusted after his employer's wife:* desire, ache for, covet; informal have the hots for, lech after/over, have a thing about/for, drool over; Brit. informal fancy.
2 *she lusted after adventure:* crave, desire, covet, want, wish for, long for, yearn for, dream of, hanker for, hanker after, hunger for, thirst for, ache for.
OPPOSITES: dread, avoid.

lustful adjective lecherous, lascivious, libidinous, wanton, unchaste, impure, naughty, immodest, indecent, dirty, licentious, salacious, prurient; passionate, sexy, erotic; formal concupiscent; informal horny, randy, raunchy.
OPPOSITES: chaste, pure.

lustily adverb heartily, vigorously, loudly, at the top of your voice, powerfully, forcefully, strongly; informal like mad, like crazy.

lustre noun sheen, gloss, shine, patina, glow, gleam, shimmer, polish.
OPPOSITES: dullness.

lustreless adjective dull, lacklustre, matt, unpolished, tarnished, dingy, dim, dark.
OPPOSITES: lustrous, bright.

lustrous adjective shiny, shining, satiny, glossy, gleaming, burnished, polished; radiant, bright, brilliant, luminous; dazzling, sparkling, glistening, shimmering, twinkling.
OPPOSITES: dull, dark.

lusty adjective
1 *a throng of lusty young men:* healthy, strong, fit, vigorous, robust, hale and hearty, energetic; rugged, sturdy, muscular, muscly, strapping, hefty, husky, burly; informal beefy.

2 *he sang a few bars in a lusty baritone:* **loud,** vigorous, hearty, strong, powerful, forceful.
OPPOSITES: feeble, quiet.

luxuriant adjective *luxuriant vegetation:* **lush,** rich, abundant, profuse, riotous, prolific, vigorous; dense, thick, rank, rampant; literary exuberant.
OPPOSITES: sparse.

luxuriate verb *she luxuriated in the warmth of the sun against her skin:* **revel,** bask, wallow, delight, take pleasure; (**luxuriate in**) enjoy, relish, savour, appreciate; informal get a kick out of, get a thrill out of.
OPPOSITES: dislike.

luxurious adjective **opulent,** sumptuous, de luxe, grand, palatial, splendid, magnificent, well appointed, extravagant, fancy; Brit. upmarket; informal plush, posh, classy, ritzy, swanky, bling; Brit. informal swish.
OPPOSITES: plain, basic.

luxury noun
1 *we'll live in luxury for the rest of our lives:* **opulence,** luxuriousness, sumptuousness, grandeur, magnificence, splendour, lavishness, the lap of luxury, milk and honey; informal the life of Riley.

2 *a TV is his only luxury:* **indulgence,** extravagance, self-indulgence, non-essential, treat, extra, frill.
OPPOSITES: simplicity, necessity.

lying noun **untruthfulness,** fibbing, white lies, fabrication; dishonesty, mendacity, deceit, duplicity, falseness, misrepresentation; Law perjury; literary perfidy.
OPPOSITES: honesty, truthfulness.
▷ adjective **untruthful,** mendacious, dishonest, deceitful, deceiving, duplicitous, double-dealing, two-faced, false; literary perfidious.
OPPOSITES: truthful.

lyrical adjective
1 *lyrical poetry:* **expressive,** emotional, deeply felt, personal, subjective, passionate.
2 *she was lyrical about her success:* **enthusiastic,** rhapsodic, effusive, rapturous, ecstatic, euphoric, carried away, impassioned.
OPPOSITES: unenthusiastic.
□ **wax lyrical be enthusiastic,** enthuse, rave, gush, get carried away.

lyrics plural noun **words,** text, lines, libretto.

l

Mm

macabre adjective

1 *a macabre series of murders:* gruesome, grisly, grim, gory, ghastly, grotesque, hideous, horrific, shocking, sickening, dreadful, loathsome, repugnant, repulsive.
2 *a macabre sense of humour:* morbid, ghoulish, black; informal sick.

Machiavellian adjective *his Machiavellian schemes secured him the English throne:* devious, cunning, crafty, shrewd, artful, wily, sly, scheming, unscrupulous, underhand.

machinations plural noun *they attributed the unrest to the machinations of the communists:* scheming, plotting, conspiracies, intrigues, ruses, tricks, wiles, stratagems, tactics, manoeuvring.

machine noun

1 *machines have replaced human labour in many industries:* apparatus, appliance, device, mechanism, engine, gadget, tool, instrument, contraption.
2 *the party's fund-raising is helping it to build a formidable political machine:* organization, system, structure, arrangement, machinery; informal set-up.

> **WORD LINKS**
> **mechanical** relating to or operated by a machine or machinery

machinery noun

1 *road-making machinery:* equipment, machines, mechanisms, apparatus, plant, hardware, gear, tackle; instruments, tools; gadgetry, technology.
2 *the machinery of local government:* workings, organization, system, structure, administration, procedures; informal set-up.

machismo noun masculinity, toughness, male chauvinism, sexism; virility, manliness; informal laddishness.

macho adjective male, masculine, manly, virile, red-blooded; informal laddish.

mad adjective

1 *he was killed by his mad brother:* insane, mentally ill, deranged, demented, of unsound mind, out of your mind, not in your right mind, sick in the head, crazed, lunatic, unhinged, disturbed, certifiable;

psychotic; informal crazy, mental, nuts, nutty, off your rocker, off your trolley, round the bend, batty, bonkers, dotty, cracked, loopy, loony, doolally; Brit. informal barmy, crackers, barking, round the twist, off your head, not the full shilling, potty.
2 *he came up with one mad scheme after another:* foolish, stupid, lunatic, foolhardy, idiotic, ludicrous, preposterous, senseless, absurd, impractical, silly, inane, asinine, wild, unwise, imprudent; informal crazy, crackpot, crackbrained, hare-brained; Brit. informal daft.
3 (informal) *he's mad about jazz:* enthusiastic, passionate; ardent, fervent, avid; addicted to, devoted to, infatuated with, in love with; informal crazy, nuts, wild, hooked on, fanatical.
4 *it was a mad dash to get ready:* frenzied, frantic, frenetic, feverish, hysterical, wild, hectic, manic.
OPPOSITES: sane, sensible.

madcap adjective

1 *he wanted me to invest in some madcap scheme:* foolish, reckless, rash, wild, hasty, imprudent, ill-advised; informal crazy, crackpot, crackbrained, hare-brained.
2 *a madcap comedy:* zany, eccentric, unconventional.

madden verb

1 *he was maddened by her reaction:* infuriate, exasperate, irritate; incense, anger, enrage, provoke, vex, irk, make someone's hackles rise, make someone see red; informal aggravate, make someone's blood boil, get someone's back up.
2 *they were maddened with pain:* drive mad, drive insane, unhinge.

made-up adjective *a made-up story:* invented, fabricated, trumped up, concocted, fictitious, fictional, false, untrue, bogus, apocryphal, imaginary.

madhouse noun (informal) *the place was a total madhouse:* bedlam, mayhem, chaos, pandemonium, uproar, turmoil, disorder, madness, all hell broken loose.

madman, madwoman noun lunatic, maniac, psychopath; informal loony, nut, nutcase, head case, psycho; Brit. informal nutter, mentalist.

m

madness noun
1 *today madness is called mental illness:*
insanity, mental illness, dementia,
derangement, lunacy; mania, psychosis.
2 *it would be madness to do otherwise | in
a moment of madness she agreed to marry
him:* folly, foolishness, idiocy, stupidity,
insanity, lunacy, silliness.
3 *it's absolute madness in here:* bedlam,
mayhem, chaos, pandemonium, uproar,
turmoil, disorder, all hell broken loose.
OPPOSITES: sanity, common sense, calm.

maelstrom noun
1 *the maelstrom of war:* turmoil, chaos,
upheaval, turbulence, disorder, tumult,
confusion, pandemonium, bedlam.
2 *hurricanes created maelstroms in the sea:*
whirlpool, vortex, eddy.

maestro noun *the Italian piano maestro
will give a concert on March 15:* virtuoso,
master, expert, genius, wizard, prodigy;
informal ace, whizz, pro, hotshot.

magazine noun journal, periodical,
supplement, colour supplement; fanzine;
informal glossy.

maggot noun grub, larva.

magic noun
1 *do you believe in magic?* sorcery,
witchcraft, wizardry, necromancy,
enchantment, the supernatural, occultism,
the occult, black magic, the black arts,
voodoo, shamanism; charm, spell, jinx;
N. Amer. mojo, hex.
2 *he does magic at children's parties:*
conjuring tricks, sleight of hand,
legerdemain; formal prestidigitation.
3 *the magic of the Cannes Film Festival:*
allure, attraction, excitement, fascination,
charm, glamour.
▷**adjective** *a magic spell:* supernatural,
magical, miraculous.

magical adjective
1 *magical incantations:* supernatural,
magic, occult, shamanistic, mystical,
paranormal, other-worldly.
2 *the news had a magical effect:*
extraordinary, remarkable, exceptional,
outstanding, incredible, phenomenal,
unbelievable, amazing, astonishing,
astounding, stupendous, stunning,
staggering, marvellous, magnificent,
wonderful, sensational, breathtaking,
miraculous; informal fantastic, fabulous,
out of this world, terrific, tremendous,
brilliant, mind-boggling, mind-blowing,
awesome.
3 *this magical land in the heart of Europe:*
enchanting, entrancing, spellbinding,
bewitching, beguiling, fascinating,
captivating, alluring, enthralling, charming,
attractive, lovely, delightful, beautiful;
informal dreamy, heavenly, divine, gorgeous.

magician noun
1 sorcerer, sorceress, witch, wizard,

warlock, enchanter, enchantress,
necromancer, shaman.
2 conjuror, illusionist; formal
prestidigitator.

magisterial adjective
1 *a magisterial pronouncement:*
authoritative, masterful, assured, lordly,
commanding, assertive.
2 *his magisterial style of questioning:*
domineering, dictatorial, autocratic,
imperious, overbearing, peremptory,
high-handed, arrogant, supercilious,
patronizing; informal bossy.

magnanimity noun generosity,
charity, benevolence, altruism,
philanthropy, beneficence; humanity,
clemency, mercy, leniency, forgiveness,
indulgence.
OPPOSITES: meanness, selfishness.

magnanimous adjective *she was
magnanimous in victory:* generous,
charitable, benevolent, beneficent, big-
hearted, altruistic, selfless, philanthropic;
forgiving, merciful, lenient, indulgent,
clement.
OPPOSITES: mean-spirited, selfish.

magnate noun *the real power lay in
the hands of a few rich magnates and
landowners:* tycoon, mogul, captain of
industry, baron, lord, king; industrialist,
proprietor; informal big shot, honcho;
derogatory fat cat.

magnet noun
1 *the poles of a magnet:* lodestone;
electromagnet, solenoid.
2 *the village is a magnet for tourists:*
attraction, focus, draw, lure.

magnetic adjective *he had a magnetic
personality and made friends easily:*
charismatic, attractive, alluring,
fascinating, captivating, enchanting,
enthralling, appealing, charming,
engaging, entrancing, seductive, inviting,
irresistible.

magnetism noun *his personal magnetism
attracted men to the brotherhood:*
charisma, charm, attraction, fascination,
appeal, draw, drawing power, pull,
enchantment, allure, seductiveness,
magic, spell.

magnification noun *a magnification of
ten times the normal size:* enlargement,
increase, augmentation, enhancement.
OPPOSITES: reduction.

magnificence noun splendour,
grandeur, impressiveness, glory, majesty,
nobility, pomp, stateliness, elegance,
sumptuousness, opulence, luxury,
lavishness, richness; brilliance, skill,
virtuosity.

magnificent adjective
1 *a magnificent view of the mountains:*
splendid, spectacular, impressive, striking,

m

glorious, superb, majestic, awesome, awe-inspiring, breathtaking.
2 *a magnificent apartment overlooking the lake:* sumptuous, grand, impressive, imposing, monumental, palatial, stately, opulent, luxurious, lavish, rich, resplendent, beautiful, elegant; informal ritzy, posh.
3 *a magnificent performance:* masterly, skilful, virtuoso, brilliant.
OPPOSITES: uninspiring, modest, poor.

magnify verb *the lens magnifies the image:* enlarge, increase, augment, maximize, boost, enhance; informal blow up.
OPPOSITES: reduce, minimize.

magnitude noun
1 *the magnitude of the task:* immensity, vastness, hugeness, enormity; size, extent, expanse, greatness.
2 *events of tragic magnitude:* importance, import, significance, weight, consequence, mark, notability, note.
3 *the magnitudes of all the economic variables could be determined:* value, number, measure, figure, order, quantity, vector, index, indicator.
4 *a star of magnitude 4.2:* brightness, brilliance, radiance, luminosity.
OPPOSITES: smallness, triviality.

maiden adjective
1 *a maiden aunt:* unmarried, spinster, unwed, single.
2 *the ship's maiden voyage:* first, initial, inaugural, introductory.

maidenly adjective virginal, chaste, pure, virtuous; demure, decorous, seemly.

mail noun
1 *there isn't much mail:* post, letters, correspondence, email.
2 *we do most of our business by mail:* postal system, postal service, post office; informal snail mail
▷**verb** *we mailed the parcels on the 14th January:* send, post, dispatch, direct, forward, redirect, ship; email.

maim verb *they are prepared to kill and maim innocent people in pursuit of their cause:* injure, wound, mutilate, disfigure, incapacitate, lacerate, mangle.

main adjective *security is the main issue:* principal, chief, head, leading, foremost, most important, major, ruling, dominant, central, focal, key, prime, premier, primary, first, fundamental, supreme, predominant, most prominent, pre-eminent, paramount, overriding, cardinal, crucial, critical, pivotal, salient, essential; staple.
OPPOSITES: subsidiary, minor.

mainly adverb *recruitment is based mainly on academic credentials:* mostly, for the most part, in the main, on the whole, largely, by and large, to a large extent, predominantly, chiefly, principally, primarily; generally, usually, typically, commonly, on average, as a rule, almost always.

mainspring noun *self-interest is the mainspring of economic action:* motive, motivation, impetus, driving force, incentive, impulse, prime mover, reason, root.

mainstay noun *agriculture was the mainstay of the economy:* central component, central figure, centrepiece, prop, linchpin, cornerstone, pillar, bulwark, buttress, chief support, backbone, anchor, foundation, base, staple.

mainstream adjective *the author never strays far from mainstream physics:* normal, conventional, ordinary, orthodox, conformist, accepted, established, recognized, common, usual, prevailing, popular.
OPPOSITES: fringe.

maintain verb
1 *they wanted to maintain peace:* preserve, keep, conserve, retain, keep going, keep alive, keep up, prolong, perpetuate, sustain, carry on, continue.
2 *the council maintains the roads:* keep in good condition, keep in good repair, keep up, service, care for, take good care of, look after.
3 *the costs of maintaining a family:* support, provide for, keep, sustain; nurture, feed, nourish.
4 *he always maintained his innocence | he maintains that he is innocent:* insist, declare, assert, protest, affirm, avow, profess, claim, allege, contend, argue, swear, hold to.
OPPOSITES: break, discontinue, deny.

maintenance noun
1 *the maintenance of peace is the UN's priority:* preservation, conservation, keeping, prolongation, perpetuation, carrying on, continuation, continuance.
2 *I can do a bit of car maintenance:* upkeep, service, servicing, repair, care, aftercare.
3 *the maintenance of his children:* support, keeping, upkeep, sustenance; nurture, feeding, nourishment.
4 *absent fathers are forced to pay maintenance:* financial support, child support, alimony; keep, subsistence, living expenses.
OPPOSITES: breakdown, discontinuation, neglect.

majestic adjective *the majestic snow-capped mountains:* magnificent, grand, splendid, imposing, impressive, spectacular, awe-inspiring, sublime, superb, glorious, august, noble, monumental.

majesty noun
1 *the majesty of Ben Nevis:* grandeur, magnificence, splendour, glory, impressiveness, sublimity, augustness, nobility.

2 *the majesty invested in the monarch:* sovereignty, authority, power, dominion, supremacy.

major adjective

1 *the major English poets:* greatest, best, finest, most important, chief, main, prime, principal, leading, star, foremost, outstanding, first-rate, pre-eminent; capital, cardinal; informal big-time.

2 *an issue of major importance:* crucial, vital, great, considerable, paramount, utmost, prime.

3 *they are planning major changes to the state pension system:* important, big, significant, key, sweeping, substantial, weighty.

OPPOSITES: minor, little, trivial.

majority noun

1 *the majority of electorate opposed EC membership:* larger part/number, greater part/number, best/better part, most, more than half; bulk, mass, main body, preponderance; lion's share.

2 *Labour retained the seat by a large majority:* margin; landslide.

3 *my son has reached his majority:* coming of age, legal age, adulthood, manhood/womanhood, maturity; age of consent.

OPPOSITES: minority.

make verb

1 *he makes models:* construct, build, assemble, put together, manufacture, produce, fabricate, create, form, fashion, model.

2 *she made me drink it:* force, compel, coerce, press, drive, pressure, pressurize, oblige, require; prevail on, dragoon, bludgeon, strong-arm, impel, constrain; informal railroad.

3 *don't make such a noise:* cause, create, give rise to, produce, bring about, generate, engender, occasion, effect.

4 *she made a little bow:* perform, execute, give, do, accomplish, achieve, bring off, carry out, effect.

5 *they made him chairman:* appoint, designate, name, nominate, select, elect, vote in, install; induct, institute, invest, ordain.

6 *I've made a mistake:* commit, perpetrate, be responsible for, be guilty of, be to blame for.

7 *he's made a lot of money:* acquire, obtain, gain, get, realize, secure, win, earn; gross, net, clear; bring in, take.

8 *he made tea:* prepare, get ready, put together, concoct, cook, dish up, throw together, whip up, brew; informal fix.

9 *we've got to make a decision:* reach, come to, settle on, determine on, conclude.

10 *she made a short announcement:* give, deliver, utter, give voice to, enunciate, recite, pronounce.

11 *the sofa makes a good bed:* be, act

as, serve as, function as, constitute, do duty for.

▷ **noun** *what make is the car?* brand, marque, label.

□ **make believe**
pretend, fantasize, daydream, build castles in the air, build castles in Spain, dream, imagine, play-act.

□ **make do**
scrape by, get by/along, manage, cope, survive, muddle through/along, improvise, make ends meet, keep the wolf from the door, keep your head above water; (**make do with**) make the best of, get by on, put up with.

□ **make for**
1 *she made for the door:* go for/towards, head for/towards, aim for, make your way towards, move towards, direct your steps towards, steer a course towards, be bound for, make a beeline for.
2 *constant arguing doesn't make for a happy marriage:* contribute to, be conducive to, produce, promote, facilitate, foster; be the recipe for.

□ **make it**
1 *he never made it as a singer:* succeed, be a success, distinguish yourself, get ahead, make good; informal make the grade, arrive, crack it.
2 *she's very ill—is she going to make it?* survive, come through, pull through, get better, recover.

□ **make love** see HAVE SEX at SEX.

□ **make off**
on seeing the police they made off: run away/off, take to your heels, beat a hasty retreat, flee, make your getaway, make a quick exit, run for it, make a run for it, take off, take flight, bolt, make yourself scarce, decamp, do a disappearing act; informal clear off/out, beat it, leg it, cut and run, skedaddle, vamoose, hightail it, hotfoot it, split; Brit. informal scarper, do a runner.

□ **make off with**
he's made off with my handbag! take, steal, snatch, pilfer, abscond with, run away/off with, carry off; kidnap, abduct; formal purloin; informal walk away/off with, pinch, swipe, filch, nab, lift; Brit. informal nick, snaffle, whip.

□ **make something out**
1 *I could just make out a figure in the distance:* see, discern, distinguish, perceive, pick out, detect, observe, recognize.
2 *he couldn't make out what she was saying:* understand, comprehend, follow, grasp, fathom, work out, make sense of, interpret, decipher, get, get the drift of, catch; informal make head or tail of.
3 *she made out that he was violent:* allege, claim, assert, declare, maintain, affirm, suggest, imply, hint, insinuate, indicate, intimate, impute.
4 *he made out a receipt for $20:* write out, fill out, complete, draw up; Brit. fill in.

m

▢ **make something over to someone** transfer, sign over, turn over, hand over/on/down, give, leave, bequeath, bestow, pass on, assign, consign, entrust.

▢ **make up** *let's kiss and make up:* be friends again, bury the hatchet, declare a truce, make peace, forgive and forget, shake hands, become reconciled, settle your differences, mend fences, call it quits.

▢ **make something up** **1** *exports make up 42% of earnings:* comprise, form, compose, constitute, account for.
2 *he made up an excuse:* invent, fabricate, concoct, dream up, think up, hatch, trump up; devise, manufacture, formulate, coin; informal cook up.

▢ **make up for** **1** *she tried to make up for what she'd said:* make amends for, atone for, compensate for, make recompense for, make reparation for, make redress for, make restitution for, expiate.
2 *job satisfaction can make up for low pay:* offset, counterbalance, counteract, compensate for; balance, neutralize, cancel out, even up, redeem.

▢ **make up your mind** decide, come to a decision, make/reach a decision; settle on a plan of action, come to a conclusion, reach a conclusion; determine, resolve.

▢ **make up to** (informal) *she spent the whole evening making up to Adam:* curry favour with, cultivate, try to win over, court, ingratiate yourself with; informal suck up to, butter up.

make-believe noun *she's living in a world of make-believe:* fantasy, pretence, daydreams, dreams, imagination, invention, fancy, fabrication, play-acting; charade, masquerade.
OPPOSITES: reality.

▷ **adjective** *make-believe adventures | a make-believe gun:* imaginary, imagined, made-up, fantasy, dreamed-up, fanciful, fictitious, feigned; fake, mock, sham, simulated; informal pretend, phoney.
OPPOSITES: real, actual.

maker noun *the maker's name is stamped on the back:* manufacturer, creator, designer, constructor, builder, producer.

makeshift adjective *she had been sleeping on a makeshift bed of pillows and blankets:* temporary, rough and ready, improvised; stopgap, standby, ad hoc, provisional, extempore, thrown together, cobbled together.
OPPOSITES: permanent.

make-up noun **1** *she wears too much make-up:* cosmetics; greasepaint, face paint; informal warpaint.
2 *the cellular make-up of plants:* composition, constitution, structure, configuration, arrangement, formation, organization.

3 *jealousy isn't part of his make-up:* character, nature, temperament, personality, disposition, mentality, persona, psyche; informal what makes someone tick.

making noun **1** *the making of cars:* manufacture, mass production, building, construction, assembly, production, creation, putting together, fabrication, forming, moulding, forging.
2 *she has the makings of a champion:* qualities, characteristics, ingredients; potential, promise, capacity, capability; essentials, essence, beginnings, rudiments, basics, stuff.

▢ **in the making** *a hero in the making:* budding, up and coming, emergent, developing, nascent, potential, promising, incipient.

maladjusted adjective *a school for maladjusted pupils:* disturbed, dysfunctional, unstable, neurotic; informal mixed up, screwed up, messed up.
OPPOSITES: normal, stable.

maladroit adjective *both men are unhappy about the maladroit way the matter has been handled:* inept, incompetent, inefficient, clumsy, bungling, heavy-handed, awkward, gauche, tactless, inconsiderate, undiplomatic; informal ham-fisted, cack-handed.
OPPOSITES: adroit, skilful.

malady noun (literary) *sea sickness, a malady with no respect for rank or courage:* illness, sickness, disease, infection, ailment, disorder, complaint, affliction; informal bug, virus; Brit. informal lurgy.

malaise noun *a society affected by a deep cultural malaise:* unhappiness, unease, uneasiness, melancholy, depression, despondency, dejection, angst, world weariness, Weltschmerz; ennui, lassitude, listlessness, weariness, enervation; illness, sickness, disease.

malcontent noun *a group of malcontents started a protest:* troublemaker, mischief-maker, agitator, dissident, rebel; complainer, grumbler; informal moaner.

▷ **adjective** *a malcontent employee:* disaffected, discontented, dissatisfied, disgruntled, unhappy, annoyed, irritated, displeased, resentful; rebellious, dissident, dissentient; informal fed up, browned off, hacked off; Brit. informal cheesed off, brassed off.

male adjective masculine, virile, manly, macho, red-blooded.
OPPOSITES: female.

malefactor noun (formal) *most malefactors are the victims of their environment:* wrongdoer, offender, culprit, miscreant, criminal, villain, felon, delinquent; sinner, transgressor; informal crook.

malevolence noun *his eyes gleamed with malevolence:* malice, hostility, spite, hate, hatred, ill will, enmity, ill feeling, venom, rancour, malignity, vindictiveness, viciousness, vengefulness, balefulness.
OPPOSITES: benevolence.

malevolent adjective *she shot a malevolent glare at her companion:* malicious, hostile, spiteful, baleful, evil-intentioned, venomous, malign, rancorous, vicious, vindictive, vengeful.
OPPOSITES: benevolent.

malformation noun *a congenital malformation of the larynx:* abnormality, deformity, disfigurement, distortion, crookedness, misshapenness.

malformed adjective deformed, misshapen, ill-proportioned, disfigured, distorted, crooked, contorted, twisted, warped; abnormal, grotesque.
OPPOSITES: perfect, normal, healthy.

malfunction verb *the computer has malfunctioned:* crash, go wrong, break down, fail, stop working; informal conk out, go kaput, fall over, act up; Brit. informal play up, pack up.
▷ noun *a computer malfunction:* crash, breakdown, fault, failure, bug; informal glitch.

malice noun *there was a hint of malice in her voice:* spite, spitefulness, malevolence, ill will, vindictiveness, vengefulness, malignity, evil intentions, animosity, animus, enmity, rancour; informal bitchiness, cattiness.
OPPOSITES: benevolence.

malicious adjective *he bore their malicious insults with dignity:* spiteful, malevolent, vindictive, vengeful, hostile, malign, mean, nasty, offensive, hurtful, wounding, cruel, unkind; informal bitchy, catty.
OPPOSITES: benevolent, kind.

malign adjective *a malign influence:* harmful, evil, bad, baleful, destructive, malignant, inimical, injurious.
OPPOSITES: beneficial.
▷ verb *he maligned an innocent man:* defame, slander, libel, blacken someone's name/character, smear, vilify, speak ill of, cast aspersions on, run down, denigrate, disparage, slur, abuse, revile; formal traduce; informal bad-mouth, knock.
OPPOSITES: praise.

malignant adjective
1 *a malignant disease:* virulent, very infectious, invasive, dangerous, deadly, fatal, life-threatening.
2 *a malignant growth:* cancerous; technical metastatic.
3 *a malignant thought:* spiteful, malicious, malevolent, evil-intentioned, vindictive, vengeful, malign, mean, nasty, hurtful, wounding, cruel, unkind; informal bitchy, catty.
OPPOSITES: benign, benevolent.

malinger verb *the doctor alleged that the plaintiff was malingering:* pretend to be ill, feign/fake illness, sham; shirk; informal put it on; Brit. informal skive, swing the lead.

mall noun shopping precinct, shopping centre, shopping complex, arcade; N. Amer. plaza.

malleable adjective
1 *a malleable substance:* pliable, ductile, plastic, pliant, soft, workable.
2 *a malleable young woman:* easily influenced, suggestible, susceptible, impressionable, pliable, amenable, compliant, tractable; biddable, complaisant, manipulable, persuadable, like putty in someone's hands.
OPPOSITES: hard, intractable.

malnutrition noun *there is a real danger of hunger and even malnutrition:* undernourishment, malnourishment, poor diet, inadequate diet, unhealthy diet, lack of food.

malpractice noun *she defended herself against accusations of medical malpractice:* wrongdoing, professional misconduct, breach of ethics, unprofessionalism, unethical behaviour; negligence, carelessness, incompetence.

maltreat verb *Keith was a bully and occasionally maltreated his wife:* ill-treat, mistreat, abuse, ill-use, misuse; knock about/around, hit, beat, strike, harm, hurt; informal beat up, rough up, do over.

maltreatment noun ill-treatment, mistreatment, abuse, ill use, ill usage, misuse; violence, harm.

mammoth adjective *fans must begin the mammoth task of raising £75,000 to keep the club afloat:* huge, enormous, gigantic, giant, colossal, massive, vast, immense, mighty, stupendous, monumental, Herculean, epic, prodigious, mountainous, monstrous, titanic, towering, king-sized, gargantuan; literary Brobdingnagian; informal mega, monster, whopping, humongous, astronomical; Brit. informal whacking great, ginormous.
OPPOSITES: tiny.

man noun
1 *two men got out of the car:* male, adult male, gentleman, youth; informal guy, geezer, gent; Brit. informal bloke, chap, lad, cove; N. Amer. informal dude.
2 *all men are mortal:* human being, human, person, mortal, individual, soul.
3 *the evolution of man:* the human race, the human species, Homo sapiens, humankind, humanity, human beings, humans, people, mankind.
▷ verb
1 *the office is manned from 9 a.m. to 5 p.m.:* staff, crew, occupy, people.
2 *firemen manned the pumps:* operate, work, use, utilize.

m

□ **man to man**
frankly, openly, honestly, directly, candidly, plainly, forthrightly, without beating about the bush; woman to woman.

> **WORD LINKS**
> **male**, **masculine**, **virile** relating to men
> **androcentric** focused or centred on men

manacle verb shackle, fetter, chain, put/ clap in irons, handcuff, restrain; secure; informal **cuff**.

manacles plural noun handcuffs, shackles, chains, irons, fetters, restraints, bonds; informal cuffs, bracelets.

manage verb
1 *she manages a staff of 80 people:* be in charge of, run, be head of, head, direct, control, preside over, lead, govern, rule, command, superintend, supervise, oversee, administer, organize, handle, guide, be at the helm of; informal head up.
2 *how much work can you manage this week?* accomplish, achieve, do, carry out, perform, undertake, bring about/ off, effect, finish; succeed in, contrive, engineer.
3 *will you be able to manage without him?* cope, get along/on, make do, be/fare/do all right, carry on, survive, get by, muddle through/along, fend for yourself, shift for yourself, make ends meet, weather the storm; informal make out, hack it.
4 *she can't manage that horse:* control, handle, master; cope with, deal with.

manageable adjective
1 *a manageable amount of work:* achievable, doable, practicable, possible, feasible, reasonable, attainable.
2 *a manageable child:* compliant, tractable, pliant, pliable, malleable, biddable, docile, amenable, governable, controllable, accommodating, acquiescent, complaisant, yielding.
OPPOSITES: difficult, impossible.

management noun
1 *he's responsible for the management of the firm:* administration, running, managing, organization; charge, care, direction, leadership, control, governing, governance, ruling, command, superintendence, supervision, overseeing, conduct, handling, guidance, operation.
2 *workers are in dispute with the management:* managers, employers, directors, board of directors, board, directorate, executives, administrators, administration; owners, proprietors; informal bosses, top brass.

manager noun
1 *the works manager recommended her for promotion:* executive, head of department, line manager, supervisor, principal, administrator, head, director, managing director, employer, superintendent, foreman, forewoman, overseer; proprietor; informal boss, chief, head honcho, governor; Brit. informal gaffer.
2 *the band's manager:* organizer, controller; impresario.

mandate noun
1 *he called an election to seek a mandate for his policies:* authority, approval, acceptance, ratification, endorsement, sanction, authorization.
2 *a mandate from the UN:* instruction, directive, decree, command, order, injunction, edict, charge, commission, bidding, ruling, fiat.

mandatory adjective *wearing helmets was made mandatory for cyclists:* obligatory, compulsory, binding, required, requisite, necessary, essential, imperative.
OPPOSITES: optional.

manful adjective *a manful attempt to smile:* brave, courageous, plucky, gallant, manly, heroic, bold, stout-hearted, valiant, valorous, dauntless, doughty; resolute, with gritted teeth, determined; informal gutsy, spunky.
OPPOSITES: cowardly.

manfully adverb *he tried manfully to put a brave face on things:* bravely, courageously, gallantly, pluckily, heroically, valiantly; resolutely, determinedly, hard, strongly, vigorously, with might and main, like a Trojan; with all your strength, to the best of your abilities, as best one can, desperately.

mangle verb
1 *the bodies were mangled beyond recognition:* mutilate, maim, disfigure, maul, damage, injure, crush; hack, cut up, lacerate, tear apart, butcher.
2 *he's mangling the English language:* spoil, ruin, mar, mutilate, make a mess of, wreck; informal murder, make a hash of, butcher.

mangy adjective *a mangy old armchair:* scruffy, moth-eaten, shabby, worn, dirty; informal tatty, the worse for wear.

manhandle verb
1 *he was manhandled by a gang of youths:* push, shove, jostle, hustle; maltreat, ill-treat, mistreat, maul; informal rough up.
2 *we manhandled the piano down the stairs:* heave, haul, push, shove; pull, tug, drag, carry, lift, manoeuvre; informal lug; Brit. informal hump.

manhood noun
1 *the transition from boyhood to manhood:* maturity, sexual maturity, adulthood.
2 *an insult to his manhood:* virility, manliness, machismo, masculinity, maleness; spirit, strength, mettle, fortitude, determination, bravery, courage, valour, heroism, boldness, intrepidity.

mania noun
1 *he suffered from fits of mania:* madness, derangement, dementia, insanity, lunacy,

psychosis, mental illness; delirium, frenzy, hysteria, raving.
2 *he had a mania for gadgets:* obsession, compulsion, fixation, fetish, fascination, preoccupation, passion, enthusiasm, desire, urge, craving, yen; craze, fad, rage; informal thing.

maniac noun *a homicidal maniac:* lunatic, madman, madwoman, psychopath; informal loony, nutcase, nut, psycho, head case; Brit. informal nutter, mentalist.

manic adjective
1 *the scream was followed by manic laughter:* mad, insane, deranged, demented, maniacal, lunatic, wild, crazed, hysterical, raving, unhinged, unbalanced; informal crazy.
2 *the threatened inspection caused manic activity:* frenzied, feverish, frenetic, hectic, intense; informal hyper, mad.
OPPOSITES: sane, calm.

manifest verb
1 *she manifested signs of depression:* display, show, exhibit, demonstrate, betray, present, reveal.
2 *strikes often manifest bad industrial relations:* be evidence of, be a sign of, indicate, show, attest, reflect, prove, establish; formal bespeak, evince.
OPPOSITES: hide, mask.
▷adjective *his manifest lack of interest:* obvious, clear, plain, apparent, evident, patent, palpable, distinct, definite, blatant, overt, glaring, barefaced, explicit, transparent, conspicuous, undisguised, unmistakable, noticeable, perceptible, visible, recognizable.
OPPOSITES: secret.

manifestation noun
1 *the winds have been identified as the first obvious manifestations of global warming:* sign, indication, evidence, token, symptom, testimony, proof, substantiation, mark, reflection, example, instance.
2 *the manifestation of anxiety:* display, demonstration, show, exhibition, presentation.
3 *a supernatural manifestation:* apparition, appearance, materialization, visitation.

manifesto noun *the Labour Party manifesto:* policy statement, mission statement, platform, programme, declaration of policy.

manifold adjective *the implications of this decision were manifold:* many, numerous, multiple, multifarious, legion, diverse, various, several, varied, different, miscellaneous.

manipulate verb
1 *he manipulated some knobs and levers:* operate, work; turn, pull, fiddle with, twiddle.
2 *she manipulated the muscles of his back:* massage, rub, knead, feel, palpate.
3 *the government tried to manipulate the situation:* control, influence, use/turn to your advantage, exploit, manoeuvre, engineer, steer, direct; twist someone round your little finger.
4 *they accused him of manipulating the data:* falsify, rig, distort, alter, change, doctor, massage, juggle, tamper with, tinker with, interfere with, misrepresent; informal cook; Brit. informal fiddle.

manipulative adjective *she was a ruthlessly manipulative woman:* scheming, calculating, cunning, crafty, wily, devious, designing, conniving, Machiavellian, artful, guileful, slippery, sly, unscrupulous, disingenuous.

mankind noun the human race, man, humanity, human beings, humans, Homo sapiens, humankind, people, men and women.

manly adjective
1 *his manly physique:* virile, masculine, strong, muscular, muscly, strapping, well built, sturdy, robust, rugged, tough, powerful, brawny, red-blooded; informal hunky.
2 *their manly deeds:* brave, courageous, bold, valiant, valorous, fearless, plucky, macho, manful, intrepid, daring, heroic, lionhearted, gallant, chivalrous, swashbuckling, adventurous, stout-hearted, dauntless, doughty, resolute, determined, stalwart; informal gutsy, spunky.
OPPOSITES: effeminate, cowardly.

man-made adjective *a blend of 80% wool and 20% man-made fibres:* artificial, synthetic, manufactured; imitation, mock, fake, false, faux, simulated, ersatz.
OPPOSITES: natural, real.

mannequin noun
1 *mannequins in a shop window:* dummy, model, figure.
2 (dated) *mannequins on the catwalk:* model, fashion model, supermodel.

manner noun
1 *the problem was dealt with in a very efficient manner:* way, fashion, mode, means, method, system, style, approach, technique, procedure, process, methodology, modus operandi.
2 *she had a rather unfriendly manner:* demeanour, air, mien, attitude, bearing, behaviour.
3 *the life and manners of Victorian society:* customs, habits, ways, mores, practices, conventions.
4 *it's bad manners to stare:* behaviour, conduct, way of behaving; form.
5 *you ought to teach him some manners:* correct behaviour, etiquette, social graces, good form, protocol, politeness, decorum, propriety, gentility, civility, Ps and Qs, breeding; informal the done thing.

m

mannered adjective *his mannered literary style:* affected, pretentious, unnatural, artificial, contrived, stilted, stiff, forced, put-on, precious, stagy, camp.
OPPOSITES: natural.

mannerism noun *she had adopted certain American phrases and mannerisms:* idiosyncrasy, trait, peculiarity, habit, characteristic, foible, quirk, oddity.

mannish adjective unfeminine, unwomanly, masculine, unladylike, Amazonian; informal butch.
OPPOSITES: feminine, girlish.

manoeuvre verb
1 *I manoeuvred the car into the space:* steer, guide, drive, navigate, pilot, direct, manipulate, move, work.
2 *he manoeuvred things to suit himself:* manipulate, contrive, manage, engineer, devise, plan, fix, organize, arrange, set up, orchestrate, choreograph, stage-manage; informal wangle.
3 *he began manoeuvring for the party leadership:* intrigue, plot, scheme, plan, lay plans, conspire, pull strings.
▷ noun
1 *a tricky parking manoeuvre:* operation, move, movement, exercise, activity, action.
2 *diplomatic manoeuvres resulted in the trio's release:* stratagem, tactic, gambit, ploy, trick, dodge, ruse, plan, scheme, operation, device, plot, machination, subterfuge, intrigue.
3 *German officers participated in Soviet military manoeuvres:* training exercises, exercises, war games, operations.

manservant noun valet, attendant, retainer, equerry, gentleman's gentleman, man; steward, butler, footman, flunkey, page.

mansion noun stately home, hall, manor, manor house, country house; Brit. seat; informal palace, pile.

mantle noun
1 *a dark green velvet mantle:* cloak, cape, shawl, wrap, stole.
2 *the houses were covered in a thick mantle of snow:* covering, layer, blanket, sheet, veil, curtain, canopy, cover, cloak, pall, shroud.
3 *she had the mantle of leadership thrust upon her:* role, burden, onus, duty, responsibility.
▷ verb *heavy mists mantled the forest:* cover, envelop, veil, cloak, curtain, shroud, swathe, wrap, blanket, conceal, hide, disguise, mask, obscure, surround.

manual adjective
1 *manual work makes a change from reading:* done with your hands, labouring, physical, blue-collar.
2 *a manual typewriter:* hand-operated, hand, non-automatic.
▷ noun *a training manual:* handbook, instruction book, instructions, guide, companion, ABC, guidebook; informal bible.

manufacture verb
1 *the company manufactures laser printers:* make, produce, mass-produce, build, construct, assemble, put together, create, fabricate, prefabricate, turn out, process, engineer.
2 *the story was manufactured by the press:* make up, invent, fabricate, concoct, hatch, dream up, think up, trump up, devise, formulate, frame, contrive; informal cook up.
▷ noun *the manufacture of aircraft engines:* production, making, manufacturing, mass production, construction, building, assembly, creation, fabrication, prefabrication, processing.

manufacturer noun maker, producer, builder, constructor, creator; factory owner, industrialist, captain/baron of industry.

manure noun dung, muck, excrement, droppings, ordure, guano, cowpats; fertilizer.

manuscript noun document, text, script, paper, typescript; codex, palimpsest, scroll; autograph, holograph.

many determiner, pronoun, & adjective *many tourists visit the site each year | there are many books on the subject:* numerous, a great/good deal of, a lot of, plenty of, countless, innumerable, scores of, crowds of, droves of, an army of, a horde of, a multitude of, a multiplicity of, multitudinous, multiple, untold; several, various, multifarious; copious, abundant, profuse, an abundance of, a profusion of; frequent; informal lots of, umpteen, loads of, masses of, stacks of, heaps of, piles of, bags of, tons of, oodles of, dozens of, hundreds of, thousands of, millions of.
OPPOSITES: few.
▷ noun *sacrificing the individual for the sake of the many:* the people, most people, the public, the masses, the multitude, the populace, the rank and file; derogatory the great unwashed, the riff-raff, the hoi polloi, the common herd, the mob, the proletariat, the proles.
OPPOSITES: few.

> WORD LINKS
> **multi-**, **poly-** forming words meaning 'more than one' such as *multicultural* ('relating to several cultural or ethnic groups') and *polyphonic* ('having many sounds or voices')

map noun plan, chart; road map, A to Z, street plan, guide; atlas, globe; sketch map, relief map, contour map; Mercator projection, Peters projection; Statistics cartogram.
▷ verb *the region was mapped from the air:* chart, plot, delineate, draw, depict, portray.

m

□ **map something out**
he mapped out a plan of campaign: outline, set out, lay out, sketch out, trace out, rough out, delineate, detail, draw up, formulate, work out, frame, draft, plan, plot out, arrange, design, programme.

> **WORD LINKS**
> **cartographic** relating to maps
> **cartography** the science of drawing maps

mar verb
1 *an ugly scar marred his features:* spoil, impair, disfigure, detract from, blemish, scar; deface, deform.
2 *the celebrations were marred by violence:* spoil, ruin, impair, damage, wreck; harm, hurt, blight, taint, tarnish; literary sully.
OPPOSITES: enhance.

marauder noun *they placed chains across the river mouth to keep out marauders:* raider, looter, robber, pirate, freebooter, bandit, rustler.

marauding adjective *reservists are being called up to protect civilians from marauding gunmen:* predatory, rapacious, thieving, plundering, pillaging, looting.

march verb
1 *the men marched past:* stride, walk, troop, step, pace; tramp, hike, trudge; parade, file, process; Brit. informal yomp.
2 *she marched in without even knocking:* stalk, stride, strut, flounce, storm, stomp, sweep.
3 *time marches on:* advance, progress, move on, roll on.
▷ **noun**
1 *a 20-mile march:* hike, trek, tramp, walk; route march, forced march; informal slog; Brit. informal yomp.
2 *police sought to ban the march:* parade, procession, march past, cortège; demonstration; informal demo.
3 *the march of technology:* progress, advance, progression, development, evolution; passage.

margin noun
1 *the margin of the lake:* edge, side, verge, border, perimeter, brink, brim, rim, fringe, boundary, limits, periphery, bound, extremity.
2 *there's no margin for error:* leeway, latitude, scope, room, room for manoeuvre, space, allowance, extra, surplus.
3 *they won by a narrow margin:* gap, majority, amount, difference.

marginal adjective
1 *the difference is marginal:* slight, small, tiny, minute, insignificant, minimal, negligible.
2 *a very marginal case:* borderline, disputable, questionable, doubtful.

marinate verb *marinate the fruit in the rum for 30 minutes:* soak, souse, steep, immerse, marinade.

marine adjective
1 *marine plants:* seawater, sea, saltwater, oceanic; aquatic; technical pelagic, thalassic.
2 *a marine insurance company:* maritime, nautical, naval.

mariner noun sailor, seaman, seafarer; informal tar, sea dog, old salt; Brit. informal matelot.

marital adjective *they were divorced after only three years of so-called marital bliss:* matrimonial, married, wedded, conjugal, nuptial; marriage, wedding.

maritime adjective
1 *maritime law:* naval, marine, nautical, seafaring.
2 *maritime regions:* coastal, seaside; technical littoral.

mark noun
1 *a dirty mark:* blemish, stain, streak, spot, blot, smear, speck, speckle, blotch, smudge, smut, fingermark, fingerprint; bruise, discoloration; birthmark; informal splotch; Brit. informal splodge.
2 *a punctuation mark:* symbol, sign, character; Linguistics diacritic.
3 *books bearing the mark of a well-known bookseller:* logo, seal, stamp, imprint, symbol, emblem, device, insignia, badge, brand, trademark, monogram, hallmark, watermark.
4 *unemployment passed the three million mark:* point, level, stage, degree.
5 *the flag was at half mast as a mark of respect:* sign, token, symbol, indication, badge, emblem; symptom, evidence, proof.
6 *the war left its mark on him:* impression, imprint, traces; effect, impact, influence.
7 *it is the mark of a civilized society to treat its elderly members well:* characteristic, feature, trait, attribute, quality, hallmark, badge, stamp, property, indicator.
8 *he got good marks for maths:* grade, grading, rating, score, percentage.
9 *the bullet missed its mark:* target, goal, aim, bullseye; objective, object, end.
▷ **verb**
1 *be careful not to mark the paintwork:* discolour, stain, smear, smudge, streak, blotch, blemish; dirty, pockmark, bruise; informal splotch; Brit. informal splodge.
2 *her possessions were clearly marked:* put your name on, name, initial, label; hallmark, watermark, brand.
3 *I've marked the relevant passages:* indicate, label, flag, tick; show, identify, designate, delineate.
4 *a festival to mark the town's 200th anniversary:* celebrate, commemorate, observe, recognize, acknowledge, keep, honour, solemnize, pay tribute to, salute, remember, memorialize.
5 *his style is marked by simplicity and concision:* characterize, distinguish, identify, typify, stamp.
6 *I have a pile of essays to mark:* assess,

m

evaluate, appraise, correct; N. Amer. grade.
□ **make your mark**
be successful, distinguish yourself,
succeed, be a success, prosper, get ahead/
on, make good; informal make it, make the
grade.
□ **mark something down**
*prices have been marked down for quick
sale:* reduce, decrease, lower, cut, put
down, discount; informal slash.
□ **mark someone out**
1 *his honesty marked him out from the
rest:* set apart, separate, single out,
differentiate, distinguish.
2 *she is marked out for fame:* destine,
ordain, predestine, preordain.
□ **mark something up**
they marked up the price by 66%: increase,
raise, up, put up, hike up, escalate; informal
jack up.
□ **quick off the mark**
alert, quick, quick-witted, bright, clever,
perceptive, sharp, sharp-witted, observant,
wide awake, on your toes; informal on the
ball, quick on the uptake.
□ **wide of the mark**
inaccurate, incorrect, wrong, erroneous,
off target, off beam, out, mistaken,
misguided, misinformed.

marked adjective *there had been a marked
deterioration in her health:* noticeable,
pronounced, decided, distinct, striking,
clear, glaring, blatant, unmistakable,
obvious, plain, manifest, patent, palpable,
prominent, significant, conspicuous,
notable, recognizable, identifiable,
distinguishable, discernible, apparent,
evident.
OPPOSITES: imperceptible.

market noun
1 shopping centre, marketplace, mart, flea
market, fair; (in Middle Eastern countries) bazaar,
souk.
2 *there's no market for such goods:* demand,
call, want, desire, need, requirement.
3 *the market is sluggish:* trade, trading,
business, commerce, buying and selling,
dealing.
▷ **verb** *the product was marketed worldwide:*
sell, retail, merchandise, trade; advertise,
promote; Law vend; derogatory peddle, hawk.
□ **on the market**
on sale, for sale, up for sale, on offer,
available, obtainable.

marksman noun sniper, sharpshooter,
good shot; informal crack shot.

maroon verb *they were marooned on
a desert island:* strand, cast away, cast
ashore; abandon, leave behind, leave,
leave in the lurch, desert; informal leave
high and dry.

marriage noun
1 *a proposal of marriage:* matrimony,
wedlock.
2 *the marriage took place at St Margaret's:*

wedding, wedding ceremony, nuptials.
3 *a marriage of jazz, pop, and gospel:*
fusion, mixture, mix, blend, combination,
union, alliance, amalgamation.
OPPOSITES: divorce, separation.

> WORD LINKS
> **marital, matrimonial, nuptial,
> conjugal** relating to marriage

married adjective *40 years of married bliss:*
marital, matrimonial, wedded, conjugal,
nuptial; literary connubial.
OPPOSITES: single.

marry verb
1 *the couple married last year:* get/be
married, wed, be wed, become man and
wife, plight/pledge your troth; informal tie
the knot, walk down the aisle, get hitched;
Brit. informal get spliced.
2 *John wanted to marry her:* wed; informal
make an honest woman of.
3 *the show marries poetry with art:* fuse,
mix, blend, combine, join, unite, merge,
knit, amalgamate, link, connect, couple,
yoke.
OPPOSITES: divorce, separate.

marsh noun swamp, marshland, bog, peat
bog, morass, mire, quagmire, slough, fen,
fenland, wetland; N. Amer. bayou.

marshal verb
1 *the king marshalled an army:* assemble,
gather together, collect, muster, call
together, draw up, line up, align, array,
organize, group, arrange, deploy, position,
order, dispose; mobilize, rally, round up.
2 *guests were marshalled to their seats:*
usher, guide, escort, conduct, lead,
shepherd, steer, take.

marshy adjective boggy, swampy, muddy,
waterlogged, fenny.
OPPOSITES: dry, firm.

martial adjective *the king's martial
exploits:* military, soldierly, soldier-like,
army, naval; warlike, fighting, combative,
militaristic.

martinet noun *the general was known to
be a martinet to his men:* disciplinarian,
slave-driver, stickler for discipline, hard
taskmaster, authoritarian, tyrant.

martyr verb *she was martyred for her faith:*
put to death, kill; burn, burn at the stake,
stone to death, crucify.

martyrdom noun death, suffering,
torture, torment, agony, ordeal; killing,
sacrifice, crucifixion, burning, auto-da-fé;
Christianity Passion.

marvel verb *she marvelled at their courage:*
be amazed, be astonished, be surprised,
be awed, stand in awe, wonder, not believe
your eyes/ears, be dumbfounded; informal be
flabbergasted.
▷ **noun** *the marvels of technology:* wonder,
miracle, sensation, phenomenon, spectacle.

m

marvellous adjective
1 *his solo climb was marvellous:* amazing, astounding, astonishing, awesome, breathtaking, sensational, remarkable, spectacular, stupendous, staggering, stunning; phenomenal, prodigious, miraculous, extraordinary, incredible, unbelievable.
2 *marvellous weather:* excellent, splendid, wonderful, magnificent, superb, glorious, sublime, lovely, delightful, too good to be true; informal super, great, fantastic, terrific, tremendous, sensational, heavenly, divine, gorgeous, grand, fabulous, fab, awesome, to die for, magic, ace, wicked, mind-blowing, far out, out of this world; Brit. informal brilliant.
OPPOSITES: commonplace, awful.

masculine adjective
1 *a masculine trait:* male, man's, men's; male-oriented.
2 *a powerfully masculine man:* virile, macho, manly, muscular, muscly, strong, strapping, well built, rugged, robust, brawny, powerful, red-blooded; informal hunky.
3 *a rather masculine woman:* mannish, unfeminine, unwomanly, unladylike; Amazonian; informal butch.
OPPOSITES: feminine, effeminate.

masculinity noun *he exuded an air of raw masculinity:* virility, manliness, maleness, machismo, strength, muscularity, ruggedness.

mash verb *mash the potatoes:* pulp, crush, purée, cream, pound, beat, smash, squash.
▷ noun *first pound the garlic to a mash:* pulp, purée, paste.

mask noun *he dropped his mask of good humour:* pretence, semblance, veil, screen, front, false front, facade, veneer, false colours, disguise, guise, concealment, cover, cover-up, cloak, camouflage.
▷ verb *poplar trees masked the factory:* hide, conceal, disguise, cover up, obscure, screen, cloak, camouflage, veil.

masquerade noun *he couldn't keep up the masquerade much longer:* pretence, deception, pose, act, front, facade, disguise, dissimulation, cover-up, bluff, play-acting, make-believe.
▷ verb *a woman masquerading as a man:* pretend to be, pose as, pass yourself off as, impersonate, disguise yourself as.

Mass noun *a Roman Catholic Mass:* Eucharist, Holy Communion, Communion, the Lord's Supper.

mass noun
1 *a soggy mass of fallen leaves:* pile, heap, accumulation, aggregation, accretion, concretion, build-up.
2 *he struggled through the mass of people waiting to gain admission:* crowd, horde, large group, throng, host, troop, army,

herd, flock, drove, swarm, mob, pack, press, crush, flood, multitude.
3 *the mass of the population don't care about this at all:* majority, greater part/number, best/better part, major part, most, bulk, main body, lion's share.
4 *I am not interested in writing for the masses:* the common people, the populace, the public, the people, the rank and file, the crowd, the third estate; informal the great unwashed; derogatory the hoi polloi, the mob, the proletariat, the common herd.
5 (informal) *there's masses of food* see LOT
pronoun.
▷ adjective *mass hysteria:* widespread, general, wholesale, universal, large-scale, extensive, pandemic.
▷ verb *they began massing troops in the region:* assemble, marshal, gather together, muster, round up, mobilize, rally.

massacre noun *a cold-blooded massacre of innocent civilians:* slaughter, wholesale/mass slaughter, indiscriminate killing, mass murder, mass execution, annihilation, liquidation, decimation, extermination; carnage, butchery, bloodbath, bloodletting, pogrom, genocide, ethnic cleansing, holocaust.
▷ verb *thousands were brutally massacred:* slaughter, butcher, murder, kill, annihilate, execute, put to death, exterminate, liquidate, eliminate, wipe out, mow down, cut down, put to the sword.

massage noun *massage can ease tiredness:* rubbing, kneading, palpation; shiatsu, reflexology, acupressure.
▷ verb
1 *he massaged her tired muscles:* rub, knead, palpate, manipulate, pummel, work.
2 *the statistics have been massaged:* alter, tamper with, manipulate, doctor, falsify, fiddle with, tinker with, distort, change, rig, interfere with, misrepresent; informal fix, cook.

massive adjective *these burial chambers were massive structures:* huge, enormous, vast, immense, large, big, mighty, great, colossal, tremendous, prodigious, gigantic, gargantuan, mammoth, monumental, giant, towering, mountainous, titanic; epic, Herculean; informal monster, mega, whopping, humongous, hulking, astronomical; Brit. informal whacking, ginormous.
OPPOSITES: tiny.

mast noun flagpole, flagstaff, pole, post, rod, upright; aerial, transmitter, pylon.

master noun
1 *he acceded to his master's wishes:* lord, overlord, lord and master, ruler, sovereign, monarch, suzerain; historical liege.
2 *the dog's master:* owner, keeper.
3 *he was a master at depicting light and*

m

shade: **expert**, adept, genius, past master, maestro, virtuoso, professional; authority, doyen; informal ace, pro, wizard, hotshot; Brit. informal dab hand.
4 *the master of the ship:* **captain**, commander; informal skipper.
5 (Brit.) *the geography master:* **teacher**, schoolteacher, tutor, instructor, preceptor; Brit. schoolmaster.
6 *their spiritual master:* **guru**, teacher, leader, guide, mentor; Hinduism swami, Maharishi.
OPPOSITES: servant, amateur, pupil.

▷ **verb**
1 *I managed to master my fears:* **overcome**, conquer, beat, quell, quash, suppress, control, overpower, triumph over, subdue, vanquish, subjugate, prevail over, govern, curb, check, tame, defeat, get the better of, get a grip on, get over; informal lick.
2 *it took ages to master the technique:* **learn**, become proficient in, know inside out, know backwards; pick up, grasp, understand; informal get the hang of.

▷ **adjective**
1 *a master craftsman:* **expert**, adept, proficient, skilled, skilful, deft, dexterous, adroit, practised, experienced, masterly, accomplished, demon, brilliant; informal crack, ace, mean, wizard.
2 *the master bedroom:* **principal**, main, chief; biggest.

masterful adjective
1 *a masterful tone of voice:* **commanding**, powerful, imposing, magisterial, authoritative, lordly; dominating, domineering, overbearing, overweening, imperious.
2 *their masterful handling of the situation:* **expert**, adept, clever, masterly, skilful, skilled, adroit, proficient, deft, dexterous, accomplished, polished, consummate; informal crack, ace.
OPPOSITES: weak, inept.

mastermind verb *he masterminded the whole campaign:* **plan**, control, direct, be in charge of, run, conduct, organize, arrange, preside over, orchestrate, stage-manage, engineer, manage, coordinate; conceive, devise, originate, initiate, think up, frame, hatch, come up with; informal be the brains behind.

▷ **noun** *the mastermind behind the project:* **genius**, mind, intellect, author, architect, organizer, originator, prime mover, initiator, inventor; informal brains.

masterpiece noun *a great literary masterpiece:* **chef-d'œuvre**, pièce de résistance, masterwork, magnum opus, finest/best work, tour de force.

master stroke noun *the takeover was hailed as a master stroke:* **stroke of genius**, coup, triumph, tour de force.

mastery noun
1 *her mastery of the language:* **proficiency**

in, knowledge of, understanding of, comprehension of, familiarity with, command of, grasp of.
2 *they played with tactical mastery:* **skill**, skilfulness, expertise, dexterity, finesse, adroitness, virtuosity, prowess, deftness, proficiency; informal know-how.
3 *man's mastery over nature:* **control**, domination, command, ascendancy, supremacy, pre-eminence, superiority; triumph, victory, the upper hand, the whip hand, rule, government, power, sway, authority, jurisdiction, dominion, sovereignty.

masticate verb **chew**, munch, champ, chomp, crunch, eat; ruminate, chew the cud.

mat noun
1 *she shut the front door and stood dripping on the mat:* **rug**, runner, carpet, drugget, doormat, hearthrug.
2 *a beer mat:* **coaster**, doily.
3 *his chest was covered by a thick mat of fair hair:* **mass**, tangle, knot, mop, thatch, shock, mane.

▷ **verb** *his hair was matted with blood:* **tangle**, entangle, knot, snarl up.

match noun
1 *a football match | a boxing match:* **contest**, competition, game, tournament, tie, cup tie, event, fixture, trial, meet, bout, fight; friendly; play-off, replay, rematch; Brit. derby.
2 *he was no match for the champion:* **equal**, rival, equivalent, peer, counterpart.
3 *the vase was an exact match of the one she already owned:* **twin**, double, lookalike, duplicate, mate, fellow, companion, counterpart, pair; replica, copy; informal spitting image, dead ringer.
4 *a love match:* **marriage**, relationship, partnership, union; literary betrothal.

▷ **verb**
1 *the curtains matched the duvet cover:* **go with**, coordinate with, complement, suit; be the same as, be similar to.
2 *did their statements match?* **correspond**, be in agreement, tally, agree, match up, coincide, accord, conform, square.
3 *no one can match him at chess:* **equal**, be a match for, measure up to, compare with, parallel, be in the same league as, be on a par with, touch, keep pace with, keep up with, emulate, rival, vie with, compete with, contend with; informal hold a candle to.
□ **match up to**
the film didn't match up to my expectations: **measure up to**, come up to, meet with, be equal to, be as good as, satisfy, fulfil, answer to.

matching adjective *use matching fabric for the curtains and duvet cover:* **coordinating**, complementary, toning; corresponding, equivalent; paired, twin, identical, like, alike.
OPPOSITES: different, clashing.

matchless adjective *the Parthenon has a matchless beauty:* incomparable, unrivalled, inimitable, beyond compare/ comparison, unparalleled, unequalled, without equal, peerless, second to none, unsurpassed, unsurpassable, nonpareil, unique, consummate, perfect, rare, transcendent, surpassing.

mate noun
1 *she's finally found her ideal mate:* partner, husband, wife, spouse, lover, significant other, companion, consort; literary helpmate, helpmeet; informal better half; Brit. informal other half.
2 *a plumber's mate:* assistant, helper, apprentice.
▷ verb *pandas rarely mate in captivity:* breed, couple, copulate.

material noun
1 *the decomposition of organic material:* matter, substance, stuff.
2 *the materials for a new building:* constituent, raw material, element, component.
3 *curtain material:* fabric, cloth, textiles; Brit. dated stuff.
4 *they were gathering material for a magazine article:* information, data, facts, facts and figures, statistics, evidence, details, particulars, background, notes.
▷ adjective
1 *the material world:* physical, corporeal, tangible, non-spiritual, mundane, worldly, earthly, secular, temporal, concrete, real, solid, substantial.
2 *she was too fond of material pleasures:* sensual, physical, carnal, corporal, fleshly, bodily.
3 *information that could be material to the inquiry:* relevant, pertinent, applicable, germane; apropos, to the point; vital, essential, key.
4 *the insects did not do any material damage to the crops:* significant, important, major.
OPPOSITES: spiritual, aesthetic.

materialistic adjective *a materialistic society that worships consumer goods:* consumerist, acquisitive, money-oriented, greedy; capitalistic, bourgeois.

materialize verb
1 *the forecast investment boom did not materialize:* happen, occur, come about, take place, come into being, transpire; informal come off.
2 *Harry materialized at the door:* appear, turn up, arrive, make/put in an appearance, present yourself/itself, emerge, surface, reveal yourself/itself, show your face; informal show up, pop up.

materially adverb *this will materially affect our plans:* significantly, greatly, much, very much, to a great extent, considerably, substantially, a great deal, appreciably, markedly, fundamentally, seriously, gravely.

maternal adjective
1 *her maternal instincts:* motherly, protective, caring, nurturing, loving, devoted, affectionate, fond, warm, tender, gentle, kind, kindly, comforting.
2 *his maternal grandparents:* on your mother's side, on the distaff side; Anthropology matrilineal.

mathematical adjective
1 *mathematical symbols:* arithmetical, numerical; statistical, algebraic, geometric, trigonometric.
2 *mathematical precision:* rigorous, meticulous, scrupulous, punctilious, scientific, strict, precise, exact, accurate, pinpoint, correct, careful, unerring.

matrimonial adjective *the matrimonial home:* marital, conjugal, married, wedded; nuptial.

matrimony noun marriage, wedlock, union; nuptials.
OPPOSITES: divorce.

matted adjective *his greasy, matted hair:* tangled, knotted, tousled, dishevelled, uncombed, unkempt, ratty; black English natty.

matter noun
1 *decaying vegetable matter:* material, substance, stuff.
2 *a great deal of research was done on this matter | his mother reported the matter to the police:* subject, topic, issue, question, point, point at issue, case, concern; affair, business, proceeding, situation, circumstance, event, happening, occurrence, incident, episode.
3 *what's the matter?* problem, trouble, difficulty, complication.
▷ verb *it doesn't matter what you wear:* be important, make any/a difference, be of importance, be of consequence, signify, be relevant, count; informal cut any ice.
□ as a matter of fact
actually, in fact, as it happens, really, believe it or not, in reality, in truth, to tell the truth.

matter-of-fact adjective *she tried to keep her tone light and matter-of-fact:* unemotional, practical, down-to-earth, sensible, realistic, rational, sober, unsentimental, pragmatic, businesslike, commonsensical, level-headed, hard-headed, no-nonsense; factual, literal, straightforward, plain, unembellished, unvarnished, unadorned.

mature adjective
1 *a mature woman:* adult, grown-up, grown, fully grown, full-grown, of age, fully developed; in your prime.
2 *he's very mature for his age:* sensible, responsible, adult, level-headed, reliable, dependable; wise, discriminating, shrewd, sophisticated.

3 *mature cheese:* ripe, ripened, mellow; ready to eat/drink.
4 *on mature reflection, he decided not to go:* careful, thorough, deep, considered.
OPPOSITES: adolescent, childish.

▷ **verb**
1 *kittens mature when they are about a year old:* **be fully grown**, be full-grown; come of age, reach adulthood, reach maturity.
2 *he's matured since he left home:* **grow up**, become more sensible/adult; blossom.
3 *leave the cheese to mature:* **ripen**, mellow; age.
4 *their friendship didn't have time to mature:* **develop**, grow, evolve, bloom, blossom, flourish, thrive.

maturity noun
1 *her progress from childhood to maturity:* **adulthood**, majority, coming-of-age, manhood/womanhood.
2 *he displayed a maturity beyond his years:* **responsibility**, sense, level-headedness; wisdom, discrimination, shrewdness, sophistication.

maudlin adjective
1 *whatever has happened, don't succumb to maudlin self-pity:* **sentimental**, over-sentimental, emotional, overemotional, tearful, lachrymose; informal **weepy**.
2 *a maudlin ballad:* **mawkish**, sentimental, over-sentimental; informal **mushy**, slushy, schmaltzy, cheesy, corny; Brit. informal **soppy**.

maul verb
1 *he had been mauled by a lion:* **savage**, attack, tear to pieces, lacerate, claw, scratch.
2 *she hated being mauled by men:* **molest**, feel, fondle, manhandle; informal **grope**, paw, touch up.

maunder verb *he maundered on about his problems:* **ramble**, prattle, blather, rattle, chatter, jabber, babble; informal **yak**, yatter; Brit. informal **rabbit**, witter, waffle, natter, chunter.

mausoleum noun **tomb**, sepulchre, crypt, vault, burial chamber, catacomb, undercroft; historical **charnel house**.

maverick noun *he was too much of a maverick to fit into any formal organization:* **individualist**, nonconformist, free spirit, unorthodox person, original, eccentric; rebel, dissenter, dissident.
OPPOSITES: conformist.

maw noun *a gigantic wolfhound with a fearful, gaping maw:* **mouth**, jaws, muzzle; throat, gullet; informal **trap**, chops; Brit. informal **gob**.

mawkish adjective *a long and mawkish poem:* **sentimental**, over-sentimental, maudlin, cloying, sickly, saccharine, sugary, syrupy; Brit. **twee**; informal **schmaltzy**, weepy, cheesy; Brit. informal **soppy**.

maxim noun *'You are what you eat' is a* *favourite maxim:* **saying**, adage, aphorism, axiom, proverb, motto, saw; truism, cliché; dictum, precept, epigram; rare **apophthegm**.

maximum adjective *the maximum amount:* **greatest**, highest, biggest, largest, top, topmost, most, utmost, maximal.
OPPOSITES: minimum.

▷ **noun** *production levels are near their maximum:* **upper limit**, limit, utmost, uttermost, greatest, most, extremity, peak, height, ceiling, top.
OPPOSITES: minimum.

maybe adverb *maybe I won't go back:* **perhaps**, possibly, conceivably, it could be, it is possible, for all one knows.

mayhem noun *complete mayhem broke out:* **chaos**, disorder, havoc, bedlam, pandemonium, tumult, uproar, turmoil, commotion, maelstrom, trouble, disturbance, confusion, riot, anarchy, violence.

maze noun *a maze of corridors:* **labyrinth**, complex network, warren; web, tangle, jungle, snarl.

meadow noun **field**, paddock; pasture, pastureland; literary **lea**.

meagre adjective *the refugee camps are full of people living on meagre rations:* **inadequate**, scanty, scant, paltry, limited, restricted, modest, insufficient, deficient, negligible, skimpy, slender, poor, sparse, miserable, pitiful, miserly, niggardly, beggarly; informal **measly**.
OPPOSITES: plentiful.

meal noun **snack**; feast, banquet; formal **repast**; informal **bite to eat**, spread, blowout.

WORD LINKS
prandial during or relating to a meal

mean[1] **verb**
1 *flashing lights mean the road is blocked:* **indicate**, signify, convey, show, denote, designate, connote, express, spell out; stand for, represent, symbolize; imply, suggest, intimate, hint at, insinuate, refer to, allude to.
2 *she didn't mean to break it:* **intend**, aim, plan, design, have in mind, contemplate, propose, set out, aspire, desire, want, wish, expect.
3 *he was hit by a bullet meant for a soldier:* **intend**, design; destine, predestine.
4 *the closures will mean a rise in unemployment:* **entail**, involve, necessitate, lead to, result in, give rise to, bring about, cause, engender, produce.
5 *this means a lot to me:* **matter**, be important, be significant.
6 *a red sky in the morning usually means rain:* **presage**, portend, foretell, augur, promise, foreshadow, herald, signal, bode.

mean[2] **adjective**
1 *he's too mean to leave a tip:* **miserly**,

niggardly, close-fisted, parsimonious, penny-pinching, cheese-paring; informal tight-fisted, stingy, tight, money-grubbing.
2 *that was a mean trick:* **unkind**, nasty, horrid, unpleasant, spiteful, malicious, unfair, cruel, shabby, foul, despicable, horrible, contemptible, vile, odious, loathsome, base, low; informal hateful, rotten, low-down.
3 *the truth was obvious to even the meanest intelligence:* **inferior**, poor, limited, restricted.
4 (informal) *he's a mean cook.* See **EXCELLENT**.
OPPOSITES: generous, kind, noble.

mean³ noun *we all need to find a mean between saving and splashing out:* **middle course**, middle way, midpoint, happy medium, golden mean, compromise, balance; median, norm, average.
▷ **adjective** *the mean temperature:* **average**, median, middle, medial, medium, normal, standard.

meander verb
1 *the river meandered gently:* **zigzag**, wind, twist, turn, curve, curl, bend, snake.
2 *we meandered along the path:* **stroll**, saunter, amble, wander, ramble, drift; informal mosey.

meandering adjective
1 *a meandering stream:* **winding**, zigzag, twisting, turning, curving, serpentine, sinuous, twisty.
2 *a meandering narrative:* **rambling**, circuitous, roundabout, digressive, indirect, tortuous, convoluted, maundering.
OPPOSITES: straight, succinct.

meaning noun
1 *the meaning of his remark was not clear:* **significance**, sense, signification, import, gist, thrust, drift, implication, tenor, message, essence, substance, purport.
2 *the word has several different meanings:* **definition**, sense, explanation, denotation, connotation, interpretation.
3 *my life has no meaning:* **value**, validity, worth, consequence, account, use, usefulness, significance, point.
4 *his smile was full of meaning:* **expressiveness**, significance, eloquence; implications, insinuations.

> WORD LINKS
> **semantic** relating to the meaning of words and sentences
> **semantics** the branch of linguistics concerned with meaning

meaningful adjective
1 *a meaningful remark:* **significant**, relevant, important, consequential, telling, valid, worthwhile.
2 *a meaningful relationship:* **sincere**, deep, serious, in earnest, significant, important.
3 *a meaningful glance:* **expressive**, eloquent, pointed, significant, meaning;

pregnant, speaking, telltale, revealing, suggestive.
OPPOSITES: inconsequential.

meaningless adjective
1 *a jumble of meaningless words:* **unintelligible**, incomprehensible, incoherent.
2 *she felt her life was meaningless:* **futile**, pointless, aimless, empty, hollow, vain, purposeless, valueless, useless, of no use, worthless, senseless, trivial, trifling, unimportant, insignificant, inconsequential.
OPPOSITES: worthwhile.

means plural noun
1 *a means of solving disputes without recourse to courts of law:* **method**, way, manner, mode, process, procedure, measure, technique, expedient, agency, medium, instrument, channel, vehicle, avenue, course.
2 *she doesn't have the means to support herself:* **money**, resources, capital, income, finance, funds, cash, the wherewithal, assets; informal dough, bread; Brit. informal dosh.
3 *a man of means:* **wealth**, riches, affluence, substance, fortune, property, money, capital.
□ **by means of**
the load was raised by means of a crane: **using**, utilizing, employing, through, with the help of; by dint of, by way of, by virtue of.

meanwhile adverb
1 *meanwhile, I'll stay here:* **for now**, for the moment, for the present, for the time being, meantime, in the meantime, in the interim, in the interval.
2 *cook for a further half hour; meanwhile, make the stuffing:* **at the same time**, simultaneously, concurrently.

measurable adjective
1 *a measurable amount:* **quantifiable**, assessable.
2 *a measurable improvement:* **appreciable**, noticeable, significant, visible, perceptible, definite, obvious.

measure verb
1 *they measured the length of the room:* **calculate**, compute, count, meter, quantify, weigh, size, evaluate, assess, determine, gauge, plumb.
2 *she did not need to measure herself against some ideal:* **compare with**, pit against, set against, test against, judge by.
▷ **noun**
1 *the move is the latest in a series of cost-cutting measures:* **action**, act, course of action, proceeding, procedure, step, means, expedient; manoeuvre, initiative, programme, operation.
2 *the Senate passed the measure:* **statute**, act, bill, law, legislation.
3 *the original dimensions were in imperial*

measure: system, standard, units, scale.
4 *a measure of egg white:* quantity, amount, portion.
5 *the states retain a measure of independence:* certain amount, degree; some.
6 *sales are the measure of the company's success:* yardstick, test, standard, barometer, touchstone, litmus test, criterion, benchmark.
7 *poetic measure:* metre, cadence, rhythm; foot.
□ **get/have the measure of** evaluate, assess, gauge, judge, weigh up; understand, fathom, read, be wise to, see through; informal have someone's number.
□ **measure up**
he was sacked because he didn't measure up: pass muster, match up, come up to standard, fit/fill the bill, be acceptable; informal come up to scratch, make the grade, cut the mustard.
□ **measure someone up**
the two men shook hands and silently measured each other up: evaluate, assess, appraise, judge, weigh up, rate; informal size up.
□ **measure up to**
we didn't measure up to the standards they set: meet, come up to, equal, match, bear comparison with, be on a level with; achieve, satisfy, fulfil.

measured adjective
1 *he set off with a measured tread:* regular, steady, even, rhythmic, rhythmical, unfaltering; slow, dignified, stately, sedate, leisurely, unhurried.
2 *his measured tones belied the turmoil in his mind:* thoughtful, careful, carefully chosen, studied, calculated, planned, considered, deliberate, restrained.

measureless adjective *Otto turned out to have measureless charm:* boundless, limitless, unlimited, unbounded, untold, immense, vast, endless, inexhaustible, infinite, immeasurable, incalculable; literary illimitable.
OPPOSITES: limited.

measurement noun
1 *measurement of the effect is difficult:* quantification, computation, calculation, mensuration; evaluation, assessment, gauging.
2 *all measurements are given in metric form:* size, dimension, proportions, magnitude, amplitude; mass, bulk, volume, capacity, extent; value, amount, quantity, area, length, height, depth, weight, width, range.

meat noun
1 *she needs more meat on her bones:* flesh, muscle.
2 *the meat of the matter:* substance, pith, marrow, heart, kernel, core, nucleus, nub, essence, essentials, gist, fundamentals, basics; informal nitty-gritty.

WORD LINKS
carnivorous (of an animal) feeding on meat
carnivore an animal that feeds on meat

---

meaty adjective
1 *a tall, meaty young man:* burly, brawny, muscular, powerful, sturdy, strapping, well built, solidly built, thickset; fleshy, stout; informal beefy.
2 *a good, meaty story:* interesting, thought-provoking, three-dimensional, stimulating; substantial, satisfying, meaningful, deep, profound.

mechanical adjective
1 *a mechanical device:* mechanized, machine-driven, automated, automatic, robotic.
2 *a mechanical response:* automatic, unthinking, robotic, involuntary, reflex, knee-jerk, habitual, routine, unemotional, unfeeling, lifeless; perfunctory, cursory, careless, casual.
OPPOSITES: manual.

mechanism noun
1 *an electrical mechanism:* machine, piece of machinery, appliance, apparatus, device, instrument, contraption, gadget; informal gizmo.
2 *the train's safety mechanism:* machinery, workings, works, movement, action, gears, components.
3 *the PCP provides a formal mechanism for citizens to lodge complaints:* procedure, process, system, method, technique, means, medium, agency, channel.

mechanize verb *agriculture started to become mechanized:* automate, industrialize, motorize, computerize.

medal noun *he won his first gold medal in 1998:* decoration, ribbon, star, badge, award; honour; Brit. informal gong.

meddle verb
1 *don't meddle in my affairs:* interfere, intrude, intervene, butt in, pry; informal poke your nose in, snoop, muscle in on.
2 *someone had been meddling with her things:* fiddle, interfere, tamper, tinker, finger; Brit. informal muck about/around.

meddlesome adjective *the country has a long history of meddlesome civil servants:* interfering, meddling, intrusive, prying, busybody; informal nosy.

mediate verb
1 *Austria tried to mediate between the belligerent nations:* arbitrate, act as peacemaker, conciliate, make peace; intervene, step in, intercede, act as an intermediary, liaise.
2 *a tribunal was set up to mediate disputes:* resolve, settle, arbitrate in, umpire, reconcile, referee; mend, clear up; informal patch up.
3 *he attempted to mediate a solution to the*

conflict: negotiate, bring about, effect; formal effectuate.

mediation noun arbitration, conciliation, reconciliation, intervention, intercession, good offices; negotiation, shuttle diplomacy.

mediator noun arbitrator, arbiter, negotiator, peacemaker, conciliator, go-between, middleman, intermediary, moderator, intercessor, broker, honest broker; liaison officer; umpire, referee, adjudicator, judge.

medicinal adjective *the plant is known for its medicinal properties:* curative, healing, remedial, therapeutic, restorative, corrective, health-giving; medical.

medicine noun medication, medicament, drug, prescription, dose, treatment, remedy, cure; nostrum, panacea, cure-all.

> WORD LINKS
> **pharmaceutical** relating to medicines

medieval adjective *the medieval period:* of the Middle Ages, of the Dark Ages, Dark-Age; Gothic.

mediocre adjective *he is an enthusiastic if mediocre painter:* ordinary, average, middling, uninspired, undistinguished, indifferent, unexceptional, unexciting, unremarkable, run-of-the-mill, pedestrian, prosaic, lacklustre, forgettable, amateur, amateurish; informal OK, so-so, fair-to-middling, no great shakes, not up to much.
OPPOSITES: excellent.

meditate verb contemplate, think, consider, ponder, muse, reflect, deliberate, ruminate, chew the cud, brood, mull something over; be in a brown study, be deep/lost in thought, debate with yourself; pray.

meditation noun contemplation, thought, thinking, consideration, reflection, deliberation, rumination, concentration; prayer.

meditative adjective *I found him in a meditative mood:* pensive, thoughtful, contemplative, reflective, ruminative, introspective, brooding, deep/lost in thought, in a brown study.

medium noun
1 *using technology as a medium for job creation:* means, method, way, form, agency, avenue, channel, vehicle, organ, instrument, mechanism.
2 *organisms growing in their natural medium:* habitat, element, environment, surroundings, milieu, setting, conditions.
3 *she consulted a medium:* spiritualist, spiritist, necromancer.
4 *a happy medium:* middle way, middle course, middle ground, middle, mean, median, midpoint; compromise, golden mean.

> adjective *the suspect is of medium height:* average, middling, medium-sized, middle-sized, moderate, normal, standard.

medley noun *a medley of Beatles songs:* assortment, collection, selection, variety, miscellany, mixture, melange, mixed bag, mix, potpourri, patchwork; motley collection, hotchpotch, jumble; informal ragbag, mishmash.

meek adjective *she brought her meek little husband along:* submissive, yielding, obedient, compliant, tame, biddable, tractable, acquiescent, deferential, timid, unprotesting, unresisting, like a lamb to the slaughter; quiet, mild, gentle, docile, shy, diffident, unassuming, self-effacing.
OPPOSITES: assertive.

meet verb
1 *I met an old friend on the train:* encounter, come face to face with, run into, run across, come across/upon, chance on, happen on, light on, stumble across/on; informal bump into.
2 *she first met Paul at a party:* get to know, be introduced to, make the acquaintance of.
3 *the committee met on Saturday:* assemble, gather, come together, get together, congregate, convene; formal foregather.
4 *the place where three roads meet:* converge, connect, touch, link up, intersect, cross, join.
5 *he met death bravely:* face, encounter, undergo, experience, go through, suffer, endure, bear; cope with, handle.
6 *the announcement was met with widespread hostility:* greet, receive, answer, treat.
7 *he does not meet the job's requirements:* fulfil, satisfy, fill, measure up to, match up to, conform to, come up to, comply with, answer.
8 *shipowners would meet the cost of oil spills:* pay, settle, clear, honour, discharge, pay off, square.

> noun *an athletics meet.* See MEETING sense 5.
□ meet someone halfway. See HALFWAY.

meeting noun
1 *he stood up to address the meeting:* gathering, assembly, conference, congregation, convention, summit, forum, convocation, conclave, council of war, rally; N. Amer. caucus; informal get-together.
2 *she demanded a meeting with the minister:* consultation, audience, interview.
3 *he intrigued her on their first meeting:* encounter, contact; appointment, assignation, rendezvous; literary tryst.
4 *the meeting of land and sea:* convergence, coming together, confluence, conjunction, union, junction, abutment; intersection, T-junction, crossing.
5 *an athletics meeting:* event, tournament, meet, rally, competition, match, game, contest.

m

megalomania noun *demanding changes in the script was an example of the star's megalomania:* delusions of grandeur, folie de grandeur, thirst for power; self-importance, egotism, conceit.

melancholy adjective *she felt a little melancholy:* sad, sorrowful, unhappy, desolate, mournful, gloomy, despondent, dejected, depressed, downhearted, downcast, disconsolate, glum, miserable, lugubrious, morose, woeful, woebegone, doleful, joyless, heavy-hearted; informal down in the dumps, down in the mouth, blue.
OPPOSITES: cheerful.
▷ noun *he had an air of melancholy about him:* sadness, sorrow, unhappiness, desolation, dejection, depression, despondency, gloom, gloominess, misery, woe; informal the blues.

melange noun *the simple decor is a melange of bright colours:* mixture, assortment, blend, variety, mixed bag, mix, miscellany, selection, medley, potpourri, patchwork; motley collection, hotchpotch, jumble; informal ragbag, mishmash.

melee noun *a number of people were trampled to death during the subsequent melee:* fracas, disturbance, disorder, rumpus, tumult, commotion, fray; brawl, fight, scuffle, struggle, skirmish, free-for-all, tussle; informal scrap, set-to, ruction.

mellifluous adjective *his low, mellifluous voice was instantly recognizable:* sweet-sounding, honeyed, mellow, soft, liquid, silvery, rich, smooth, tuneful, musical, harmonious, euphonious; often ironic dulcet.
OPPOSITES: cacophonous.

mellow adjective
1 *the mellow tone of his voice:* sweet-sounding, tuneful, melodious, mellifluous; soft, smooth, warm, full, rich; often ironic dulcet.
2 *a mellow wine:* full-bodied, mature, well matured, full-flavoured, rich, smooth.
3 *a mellow mood:* genial, affable, amiable, good-humoured, good-natured, amicable, pleasant, relaxed, easy-going; jovial, jolly, cheerful, happy, merry.

melodious adjective *the melodious chant of the monks:* tuneful, melodic, musical, mellifluous, sweet-sounding, silvery, harmonious, euphonious, lyrical; informal easy on the ear; often ironic dulcet.
OPPOSITES: discordant.

melodramatic adjective *he flung the door open with a melodramatic flourish:* exaggerated, histrionic, extravagant, overdramatic, overdone, over-sensational, sensationalized, overemotional; theatrical, stagy, actressy; informal hammy.

melody noun
1 *the concert started with some familiar melodies:* tune, air, strain, theme, song, refrain, piece of music.
2 *his unique gift for melody:* melodiousness, tunefulness, lyricism, musicality, euphony.

melt verb
1 *the snow was beginning to melt:* liquefy, thaw, defrost, dissolve; technical deliquesce.
2 *his smile melted her heart:* soften, disarm, touch, affect, move.
3 *his anger melted away:* vanish, disappear, fade away, dissolve, evaporate.

member noun
1 *a member of the club:* subscriber, associate, fellow, life member, founder member, card-carrying member.
2 *a member of a mathematical set:* constituent, element, component, part, portion, piece, unit.

membrane noun layer, sheet, skin, film, tissue; technical integument.

memento noun *you can purchase a memento of your visit:* souvenir, keepsake, reminder, remembrance, token, memorial; trophy, relic.

memoir noun
1 *the book is a touching memoir of her childhood:* account, history, record, chronicle, narrative, story, portrayal, depiction, sketch, portrait, profile, biography, monograph.
2 *he published his memoirs in 1955:* autobiography, life story, life, memories, recollections, reminiscences; journal, diary.

memorable adjective
1 *the victory was one of the most memorable of his career:* unforgettable, indelible; momentous, significant, historic, notable, noteworthy, important, consequential, remarkable, special, signal, outstanding, extraordinary, striking, vivid, arresting, impressive, distinctive, distinguished, famous, celebrated, renowned, illustrious, glorious.
2 *the show has some memorable tunes:* haunting, catchy.

memorandum noun
1 *a memorandum from the managing director:* message, memo, communication, note, email, letter; formal missive.
2 *hasty memoranda and jottings-down:* record, minute, note, aide-memoire, reminder.

memorial noun
1 *the war memorial:* monument, cenotaph, mausoleum; statue, plaque, cairn; shrine; tombstone, gravestone, headstone.
2 *the collection is a memorial to his life's work:* tribute, testimonial; remembrance.
▷ adjective *a memorial service for those who died:* commemorative, remembrance, commemorating; monumental.

memorize verb *Paula listened, memorizing every detail:* commit to memory, remember, learn by heart, get off by heart, learn, learn by rote, become word-perfect in, get off pat.

memory noun
1 *she's losing her memory:* ability to remember, powers of recall.
2 *she had many happy memories of her young days:* recollection, remembrance, reminiscence; impression.
3 *the town built a statue in memory of him:* commemoration, remembrance; honour, tribute, recognition, respect.
4 *a computer's memory:* memory bank, store, cache, disk, RAM, ROM.

> WORD LINKS
> **mnemonic** a pattern of letters or words that help someone remember something

menace noun
1 *an atmosphere full of menace:* threat, ominousness, intimidation; ill omen.
2 *a menace to British society:* danger, threat, hazard, peril, risk.
▷ verb
1 *the elephants are still menaced by poaching:* threaten, be a danger to, put at risk, jeopardize, imperil.
2 *a gang of skinheads menaced local residents:* intimidate, threaten, terrorize, bully, frighten.

menacing adjective *she shot him a menacing look:* threatening, ominous, intimidating, baleful, warning, forbidding, black, thunderous, glowering, unfriendly, hostile, sinister.
OPPOSITES: friendly.

mend verb
1 *workmen were mending faulty cabling:* repair, fix, put back together, piece together, restore; sew up, stitch up, darn, patch, cobble; renew, renovate; informal patch up.
2 *'How's Walter?' 'He'll mend':* get better, get well, recover, recuperate, improve; be well, be cured, heal.
3 *quarrels could be mended by talking:* put/set right, set straight, straighten out, sort out, rectify, remedy, cure, right, resolve, settle, put to rights, retrieve, improve, make better.
OPPOSITES: break, worsen.

mendacious adjective *the President dismissed the reports as mendacious propaganda:* lying, untruthful, dishonest, deceitful, false, dissembling, insincere, disingenuous, hypocritical, duplicitous; untrue, fictitious, falsified, fabricated, fallacious, invented, made up; euphemistic economical with the truth.
OPPOSITES: truthful.

menial adjective *a menial job:* unskilled, lowly, humble, low-grade, low-status, inferior, degrading; routine, humdrum, boring, dull.
▷ noun *they were treated like menials:* servant, drudge, minion, factotum, lackey; informal wage slave; Brit. informal dogsbody, skivvy.

mental adjective
1 *mental faculties:* intellectual, cognitive, cerebral, rational.
2 *a mental disorder:* psychiatric, psychological, psychogenic.
OPPOSITES: physical.

mentality noun *I can't understand the mentality of these people:* way of thinking, mind set, cast of mind, frame of mind, turn of mind, mind, psychology, mental attitude, outlook, disposition, make-up.

mentally adverb in your mind, in your head, inwardly, intellectually, cognitively.

mention verb
1 *don't mention the war:* allude to, refer to, touch on; bring up, raise, broach, introduce, moot.
2 *Jim mentioned that he'd met them before:* state, say, indicate, let someone know, disclose, divulge, reveal.
3 *I'll gladly mention your work to my friends:* recommend, commend, put in a good word for, speak well of.
▷ noun
1 *he made no mention of your request:* reference to, allusion to; remark, statement, indication.
2 *a mention in dispatches:* tribute, citation, acknowledgement, recognition.
3 *my book got a mention on the show:* recommendation, commendation, a good word.
□ not to mention in addition to, as well as; not counting, not including, to say nothing of, aside from, besides.

mentor noun
1 *though she was his political mentor, they disagreed on some issues:* adviser, guide, guru, counsellor, consultant.
2 *regular meetings between mentor and trainee:* trainer, teacher, instructor.

mercantile adjective *the mercantile community of Bordeaux:* commercial, trade, trading, business, merchant.

mercenary adjective
1 *society today is often accused of being too mercenary:* money-oriented, materialistic, acquisitive; grasping, greedy, avaricious; informal money-grubbing.
2 *mercenary soldiers:* hired, paid, bought, professional.
▷ noun *a group of mercenaries:* soldier of fortune, professional soldier, hired soldier; informal hired gun.

merchandise noun *the store offers a wide range of merchandise:* goods, wares, stock, commodities, products, lines.

m

▷**verb** *a new product that can be easily merchandised:* promote, market, sell, retail; advertise, publicize.

merchant noun trader, dealer, wholesaler, broker, agent, seller, buyer, vendor, distributor.

merciful adjective
1 *he was a merciful man at heart:* forgiving, compassionate, forbearing, clement, lenient, humane, kind, tender-hearted, gracious, sympathetic, humanitarian, liberal, tolerant, indulgent, generous, magnanimous, benign, benevolent.
2 *a merciful silence fell:* welcome, blessed.
OPPOSITES: cruel.
□ **be merciful to**
have mercy on, have pity on, show mercy to, spare, pardon, forgive, be lenient on/to; informal go easy on, let off.

mercifully adverb *mercifully, the event passed off without incident:* luckily, fortunately, happily.

merciless adjective *Mithra was merciless to his enemies:* ruthless, remorseless, pitiless, unforgiving, unsparing, implacable, inexorable, relentless, inflexible, inhumane, inhuman, unsympathetic, unfeeling, intolerant, rigid, severe, cold-blooded, hard-hearted, stony-hearted, heartless, harsh, callous, cruel, brutal, barbarous.
OPPOSITES: compassionate.

mercy noun
1 *he showed no mercy to the others:* leniency, clemency, compassion, grace, pity, charity, forgiveness, forbearance, humanity, quarter; soft-heartedness, tender-heartedness, kindness, sympathy, indulgence, tolerance, generosity, magnanimity.
2 *we must be thankful for small mercies:* blessing, godsend, boon, favour, piece/stroke of luck.
OPPOSITES: ruthlessness, cruelty.
□ **at the mercy of**
1 *they found themselves at the mercy of the tyrant:* in the power of, under/in the control of, in the clutches of, under the heel of, subject to.
2 *he was at the mercy of the elements:* defenceless against, vulnerable to, exposed to, susceptible to, prey to, wide open to.

mere adjective *I was a mere boy at the time:* no more than, just, only, merely; no better than.

merely adverb *they were merely exercising their rights:* only, purely, solely, simply, just, but.

meretricious adjective worthless, spurious, superficial, misleading, tawdry, cheap, vulgar, trashy, tasteless; informal tacky.

merge verb
1 *the company merged with a European firm:* join together, join forces, amalgamate, unite, affiliate, team up, link up.
2 *the two organizations were merged:* amalgamate, bring together, join, consolidate, unite, unify, combine, conflate, incorporate, integrate, link up, knit, yoke.
3 *the two colours merged:* mingle, blend, fuse, mix, intermix, intermingle, coalesce.
OPPOSITES: separate.

merger noun *a merger between two supermarket chains:* amalgamation, combination, union, fusion, affiliation, unification, incorporation, consolidation, link-up, alliance, coalition.
OPPOSITES: split.

merit noun
1 *composers of outstanding merit:* excellence, quality, calibre, worth, credit, value, distinction, eminence.
2 *the merits of the scheme:* good point, strong point, advantage, benefit, value, asset; informal plus.
OPPOSITES: fault, disadvantage.
▷**verb** *the accusation did not merit a response:* deserve, earn, be deserving of, warrant, rate, justify, be worthy of, be worth, be entitled to, have a right to, have a claim to/on.

meritorious adjective *the captain was awarded a medal for meritorious conduct:* praiseworthy, laudable, commendable, admirable, estimable, creditable, worthy, deserving, excellent, exemplary, good.
OPPOSITES: discreditable.

merriment noun *her eyes were dancing with merriment:* high spirits, high-spiritedness, exuberance, cheerfulness, gaiety, fun, effervescence, liveliness, verve, joy, joyfulness, jollity, happiness, jocularity, conviviality, festivity, merrymaking, revelry, mirth, glee, gleefulness, laughter, hilarity, light-heartedness, amusement, pleasure, levity.
OPPOSITES: misery.

merry adjective *merry throngs of students:* cheerful, cheery, in high spirits, high-spirited, light-hearted, buoyant, lively, carefree, without a care in the world, joyful, jolly, convivial, festive, mirthful, gleeful, happy, glad, laughing, smiling; formal joyous, jocund; informal chirpy.
OPPOSITES: miserable.

mesh noun *wire mesh:* netting, net, network; web, webbing, lattice, latticework.
▷**verb**
1 *one gear meshes with the input gear:* engage, connect, lock, interlock.
2 *our ideas just do not mesh:* harmonize, fit together, match, dovetail.

m

mesmerize verb *they were mesmerized by his performance:* enthral, captivate, enchant, fascinate, transfix, entrance, dazzle, bewitch, charm, grip, spellbind, hypnotize.

mess noun
1 *'What a mess,' he said, glancing round the kitchen:* disarray, disorder, untidiness, clutter, jumble, muddle, chaos; informal shambles; Brit. informal tip.
2 *cat mess:* excrement, faeces, excreta.
3 *I've got to get out of this mess:* plight, predicament, tight spot/corner, difficulty, trouble, quandary, dilemma, problem, muddle; informal jam, fix, hole.
4 *the project is a complete mess:* muddle, bungle; informal botch, hash, foul-up; Brit. informal cock-up.
□ make a mess of
mismanage, mishandle, bungle, fluff, spoil, ruin, wreck; informal mess up, botch, make a hash of, muck up, foul up.
□ mess about/around
1 *he loves messing about in boats:* potter about, pass the time, fool about/around; Brit. informal muck about/around.
2 *has someone been messing around with the computer?* interfere, meddle, tamper, tinker, fiddle.
□ mess something up
1 *he messed up my kitchen:* dirty; clutter up, disarrange, jumble; dishevel, rumple.
2 (informal) *Eddie messed things up.* See MAKE A MESS OF.

message noun
1 *are there any messages for me?* communication, note, memo, memorandum, email, letter, report, communiqué, dispatch; formal missive.
2 *the message of his teaching:* meaning, sense, import, idea; point, thrust, gist, essence, content, subject, subject matter, substance, implication, drift, lesson.

messenger noun courier, runner, dispatch rider, envoy, emissary, agent, go-between; historical herald.

messy adjective
1 *messy oil spills | messy hair:* dirty, filthy, grubby, soiled, grimy; mucky, muddy, sticky, stained, smeared, smudged; dishevelled, scruffy, unkempt, rumpled, matted, tousled, bedraggled, tangled.
2 *a messy kitchen:* untidy, cluttered, in disarray, in a muddle, chaotic, disorganized, in a jumble; informal like a bomb's hit it.
3 *a messy legal battle:* complex, intricate, tangled, confused, convoluted; unpleasant, nasty, bitter, acrimonious.
OPPOSITES: clean, tidy.

metallic adjective *a metallic sound:* tinny, jangling, jingling; grating, harsh, jarring, dissonant.

metamorphose verb *formerly an Irish pub, it's metamorphosed into a hot spot*

for hip locals: change, be transformed, be transmuted, be converted, be remodelled, be recast, be reconstructed; humorous be transmogrified.

metamorphosis noun *his metamorphosis from presidential candidate to talk-show host:* transformation, transmutation, change, alteration; humorous transmogrification.

metaphor noun figure of speech, image, trope; analogy, comparison, symbol, word picture.

metaphorical adjective *there is no clear line between literal and metaphorical senses:* figurative, allegorical, symbolic; imaginative, extended.
OPPOSITES: literal.

metaphysical adjective
1 *metaphysical questions:* abstract, theoretical, conceptual, notional, philosophical, speculative, intellectual, academic.
2 *Good and Evil are inextricably linked in a metaphysical battle:* transcendental, spiritual, supernatural.

mete verb
□ mete something out
the judges were unwilling to mete out harsh punishment: dispense, hand out, give out, administer, allocate, allot, apportion, issue, assign, deal out, dole out, dish out.

meteor noun falling star, shooting star, meteorite, meteoroid; technical bolide.

meteoric adjective *her meteoric rise to fame:* rapid, lightning, swift, fast, quick, speedy, accelerated, instant, sudden, spectacular.
OPPOSITES: gradual.

method noun
1 *they use very old-fashioned methods:* procedure, technique, system, practice, routine, modus operandi, process; strategy, tactic, plan.
2 *there's method in his madness:* order, orderliness, organization, structure, form, system, logic, planning, design.
OPPOSITES: disorder.

methodical adjective *a methodical approach to the evaluation of computer systems:* orderly, well ordered, well organized, well planned, efficient, businesslike, systematic, structured, logical, analytic, disciplined; meticulous, punctilious.

meticulous adjective *his work shows meticulous attention to detail:* careful, conscientious, diligent, methodical, scrupulous, punctilious, painstaking, accurate; thorough, rigorous, detailed, perfectionist, studious.
OPPOSITES: careless.

métier noun
1 *he had another métier besides the*

m

priesthood: occupation, job, work, profession, business, employment, career, vocation, trade, craft, line of work; N. Amer. specialty.
2 *television is more my métier:* forte, strong point, strength, speciality, talent, bent; informal thing, cup of tea.

metropolis noun *their trip to London gave them nine days in the metropolis:* capital, capital city, chief town; conurbation, megalopolis.

mettle noun *the team showed their mettle in the second half:* spirit, fortitude, strength of character, moral fibre, steel, determination, resolve, resolution, backbone, grit, courage, courageousness, bravery, valour, fearlessness, daring; informal guts, spunk.

mew verb
1 *the cat mewed plaintively:* miaow, mewl, cry.
2 *above them, seagulls mewed:* cry, screech.

mewl verb *the baby fretted and mewled:* whimper, cry, whine; informal grizzle.

microbe noun *microbes which cause dangerous diseases:* microorganism, bacillus, bacterium, virus, germ; informal bug.

microscopic adjective *microscopic algae:* tiny, minute, minuscule; not visible to the naked eye.

midday noun noon, twelve noon, high noon, noontide, noonday.
OPPOSITES: midnight.

middle adjective *a small hole is drilled through the quill below its middle point:* central, mid, medium, medial, midway, halfway, intermediate; mean, median.
▷ noun
1 *a shallow dish with a spike in the middle:* centre, midpoint, halfway point, dead centre, focus, hub; eye, heart, core, kernel.
2 *he had a towel round his middle:* midriff, waist, belly, stomach, abdomen.
OPPOSITES: outside.

middleman noun *we give value for money by cutting out the middleman and selling direct:* intermediary, go-between; dealer, broker, agent, factor, wholesaler, distributor.

middling adjective *a spa town of the middling kind, neither rich nor poor:* average, standard, normal, middle-of-the-road; ordinary, commonplace, everyday, workaday, tolerable, passable, moderate; run-of-the-mill, fair, mediocre, undistinguished, unexceptional, unremarkable; informal OK, so-so, bog-standard, fair-to-middling.

midget noun

used to mean 'an unusually small person', there is no term that has been established as an acceptable alternative: **person of restricted growth** has not gained wide currency. The terms **homunculus** or **manikin** are found chiefly in literary or old-fashioned writing.

midnight noun the middle of the night, twelve midnight, twenty-four hundred hours, the witching hour.
OPPOSITES: midday.

midst noun
◻ **in the midst of**
1 *in the midst of the town stand the ruins of Swansea Castle:* at/in the middle of, at/in the centre of, at/in the heart of; in the depths of.
2 *a nation in the midst of an economic downturn:* in the course of, halfway through, going through
◻ **in our midst**
among us, amid us, in our group, with us.

midway adverb *Peter came to a halt midway down the street:* halfway, in the middle, at the midpoint, in the centre; part-way.

mien noun *he has a cautious, academic mien:* appearance, look, air, expression, countenance, demeanour, attitude, manner, bearing.

might noun *a convincing display of military might:* strength, force, power, powerfulness; vigour, energy.

mighty adjective
1 *a mighty blow:* powerful, forceful, violent, vigorous, hefty, thunderous.
2 *a mighty warrior:* strong, powerful, muscular, strapping, brawny, big, tough, robust.
3 *mighty industrial countries:* dominant, influential, strong, powerful, important.
4 *mighty oak trees:* huge, enormous, massive, gigantic, big, large, giant, colossal, mammoth, immense.
OPPOSITES: feeble, puny.

migrant noun immigrant, emigrant; nomad, itinerant, traveller, transient; displaced person.

migrate verb *rural populations migrated to urban areas:* relocate, resettle, move; emigrate, go abroad, go overseas.

migratory adjective *migratory birds:* migrant, migrating, moving, travelling.

mild adjective
1 *as I am a mild man, I'm alarmed by such outbursts:* gentle, placid, calm, tranquil, equable, peaceable, good-natured, affable.
2 *a mild criticism:* gentle, light; compassionate, merciful, humane.
3 *he was eyeing her with mild interest:* slight, faint, vague, minimal, nominal, token, feeble.

4 *mild weather:* warm, balmy, temperate, clement.
OPPOSITES: harsh, strong, severe.

milieu noun *the social, political, and artistic milieu in Britain:* environment, sphere, background, setting, context, atmosphere, backdrop; location, conditions, surroundings, environs.

militant adjective *with the growing economic crisis, the unions may become more militant:* aggressive, confrontational, violent, belligerent, bellicose, combative, pugnacious, forceful, active; radical, extremist, extreme, zealous, fanatical.
▷ noun *the demands of the militants:* activist, extremist, radical, zealot.

militaristic adjective *the militaristic image of the current leadership:* warmongering, warlike, martial, hawkish, pugnacious, combative, aggressive, belligerent, bellicose; informal gung-ho.
OPPOSITES: peaceable.

military adjective *the government suspended all military activity in the area:* fighting, army, armed, defence, martial.
OPPOSITES: civilian.
▷ noun *the military took power:* armed forces, services, militia; army, navy, air force, marines.

militate verb *anger may militate against success in the negotiations:* tend to prevent, work against, hinder, discourage, prejudice, be detrimental to.

> **USAGE**
>
> Do not confuse **militate** and **mitigate**. **Militate** is used with **against** to mean 'to be a strong factor in preventing something', while **mitigate** means 'to make something bad less severe' (*the drugs mitigate the symptoms of the disease*).

milk verb *phoney psychics can milk their rich clients for years:* exploit, take advantage of, cash in on, suck dry; informal bleed, squeeze, fleece.

> **WORD LINKS**
>
> **lactic** relating to or obtained from milk

milky adjective *not a blemish marred her milky skin:* pale, white, milk-white, off-white, cream, creamy, alabaster, ivory.

mill noun
1 *workers from the steel mill:* factory, processing plant, works, workshop, shop, foundry, industrial unit.
2 *a pepper mill:* grinder, quern.
▷ verb *the wheat is milled into flour:* grind, pulverize, powder, granulate, pound, crush, press.
□ **mill around/about**
people were milling about in the streets: throng, swarm, seethe, crowd.

millstone noun *she had become a*

millstone round his neck: burden, encumbrance, dead weight, cross to bear, albatross; duty, obligation, liability.

mime noun dumb show, pantomime.
▷ verb *she mimed picking up a phone:* act out, pantomime, gesture, simulate, represent, indicate by dumb show.

mimic verb
1 *she mimicked his accent:* imitate, copy, impersonate, do an impression of, ape, caricature, parody, lampoon, burlesque; informal take off, spoof; Brit. informal send up.
2 *most hoverflies mimic wasps:* resemble, look like, have the appearance of, simulate.
▷ noun *he was a superb mimic:* impersonator, impressionist, imitator, mimicker; parodist, caricaturist, lampooner, lampoonist; informal copycat.

mimicry noun *his mimicry of her Glaswegian accent:* imitation, imitating, impersonation, copying, aping.

mince verb
1 *mince the meat and onions:* grind, chop up, cut up, dice; N. Amer. hash.
2 *she minced out of the room:* walk affectedly, strut; informal sashay.
□ **not mince your words**
talk straight, not beat about the bush, call a spade a spade, speak straight from the shoulder, pull no punches; informal tell it like it is.

mincing adjective *he had a strange, mincing walk, his hips slightly swaying:* affected, effeminate, niminy-piminy, dainty; pretentious; informal camp; Brit. informal poncey.

mind noun
1 *she had a sharp, analytical mind:* brain, intelligence, intellect, intellectual capabilities, brains, brainpower, wits, understanding, reasoning, judgement, sense, head; informal grey matter; Brit. informal loaf.
2 *he kept his mind on the job:* attention, thoughts, concentration, attentiveness.
3 *the tragedy affected her mind:* sanity, mental faculties, senses, wits, reason, reasoning, judgement; informal marbles.
4 *his words stuck in her mind:* memory, recollection.
5 *he was one of the greatest minds of his generation:* intellect, thinker, brain, scholar, academic.
6 *they are of the same mind:* opinion, way of thinking, outlook, attitude, view, viewpoint, point of view.
▷ verb
1 *do you mind if I smoke?* care, object, be bothered, be annoyed, be upset, take offence, disapprove, dislike it, look askance; informal give/care a damn, give/care a toss.
2 *mind the step!* be careful of, watch out for, look out for, beware of, be on your guard for, be wary of.

m

3 *her husband was minding the baby:* look after, take care of, keep an eye on, attend to, care for, tend.
4 *mind you wipe your feet:* be/make sure that, see that; remember to.
□ **be in two minds**
be undecided, be uncertain, be unsure, hesitate, waver, vacillate, dither; Brit. haver, hum and haw; informal dilly-dally, shilly-shally.
□ **bear/keep something in mind**
remember, note, be mindful of, take note of.
□ **cross your mind**
occur to you, enter your mind/head, strike you, dawn on you.
□ **have something in mind**
think of, contemplate; intend, plan, propose, desire, want, wish.
□ **mind out**
take care, be careful, watch out, look out, beware, be on your guard, be wary.
□ **out of your mind**
1 *you must be out of your mind!* See **MAD** sense 1.
2 *I've been out of my mind with worry:* frantic, beside yourself, distraught, in a frenzy.
□ **to my mind**
in my opinion, in my view, as I see it, personally, in my estimation, it seems to me, in my book, if you ask me.

> **WORD LINKS**
> **mental**, **cognitive** relating to the mind
> **psychology** the study of the mind
> **psychiatry** the branch of medicine concerned with the mind

mindful adjective *he was mindful of the difficulties involved:* aware of, conscious of, sensible to/of, alive to, alert to, acquainted with, heedful of, wary of; informal wise to.
OPPOSITES: heedless.

mindless adjective
1 *a mindless idiot:* stupid, idiotic, brainless, imbecilic, imbecile, asinine, witless, foolish, empty-headed, slow-witted, obtuse, feather-brained; informal cretinous, moronic, thick, dopey, dim, half-witted.
2 *mindless acts of vandalism:* unthinking, thoughtless, senseless, gratuitous, wanton, indiscriminate.
3 *a mindless task:* mechanical, automatic, routine; tedious, boring, monotonous, brainless, mind-numbing.

mine noun
1 *a coal mine:* colliery, pit, excavation, quarry, workings, diggings.
2 *the book is a mine of information:* rich source, repository, store, storehouse, gold mine, treasure house, treasury, fund, wealth, stock.
3 *he was killed by a mine:* explosive, bomb, landmine.

▷ **verb**
1 *the iron ore was mined from shallow pits:* quarry, excavate, dig, extract, remove.
2 *medical data was mined for relevant statistics:* search, analyse, scrutinize, research, exploit, utilize.

miner noun collier, pitman.

mingle verb
1 *fact and fiction are skilfully mingled in his novels:* mix, blend, intermingle, intermix, interweave, interlace, combine, merge, fuse, unite, join, meld, mesh, amalgamate.
2 *wedding guests mingled in the marquee:* socialize, circulate, fraternize, get together, associate with others; informal hobnob.
OPPOSITES: separate.

miniature adjective *a miniature railway:* small-scale, mini, tiny, minute, minuscule, diminutive, little, small, baby, toy, pocket; Scottish wee; informal teeny; Brit. informal titchy, tiddly.
OPPOSITES: giant.

minimal adjective *the committee approved the report with minimal alteration:* very little, minimum, the least possible; nominal, token, negligible.
OPPOSITES: maximum.

minimize verb
1 *the aim is to minimize costs:* keep down, keep at/to a minimum, reduce, decrease, cut down, lessen, curtail, diminish; informal slash.
2 *we should not minimize his contribution:* belittle, make light of, play down, underestimate, underrate, downplay, undervalue, understate; informal pooh-pooh.
OPPOSITES: maximize, exaggerate.

minimum noun *costs will be kept to the minimum:* lowest level, lower limit, bottom level, rock bottom; least, lowest, slightest.
OPPOSITES: maximum.

▷ **adjective** *the minimum amount of effort:* minimal, least, smallest, least possible, slightest, lowest, minutest.

minion noun underling, henchman, flunkey, lackey, hanger-on, follower, servant, hireling; informal yes-man, stooge; Brit. informal poodle.

minister noun
1 *a government minister:* member of the government, cabinet minister, secretary of state, undersecretary.
2 *a minister of religion:* clergyman, clergywoman, cleric, ecclesiastic, pastor, vicar, rector, priest, parson, father, man/woman of the cloth, man/woman of God, churchman, churchwoman; curate, chaplain; informal reverend, padre.
3 *the British minister in Egypt:* ambassador, diplomat, consul,

representative, chargé d'affaires, plenipotentiary, envoy, emissary.

▷ **verb** *doctors were ministering to the injured:* tend, care for, take care of, look after, nurse, treat, attend to, see to, administer to, help, assist.

ministrations plural noun *it took the tender ministrations of his physiotherapist to ensure he made it to the tournament:* attention, treatment, help, assistance, aid, care, services.

ministry noun
1 *the ministry for foreign affairs:* government department, bureau, agency, office.
2 *he's training for the ministry:* holy orders, the priesthood, the cloth, the church.
3 *the ministry of Jesus:* teaching, preaching, evangelism.
4 *Gladstone's first ministry:* period of office, term of office, administration.

minor adjective
1 *a minor problem:* slight, small; unimportant, insignificant, inconsequential, inconsiderable, subsidiary, negligible, trivial, trifling, paltry, petty; informal piffling.
2 *a minor poet:* little known, unknown, lesser, unimportant, insignificant, obscure; informal small-time.
OPPOSITES: major, important.
▷ **noun** *the heir to the throne was a minor:* child, infant, youth, adolescent, teenager, boy, girl.
OPPOSITES: adult.

minstrel noun (historical) *minstrels accompanied the banquet:* musician, singer, balladeer; literary bard; historical troubadour, jongleur.

mint noun (informal) *the bank made a mint out of the deal:* a vast sum of money, a king's ransom, millions, billions; informal a fortune, a tidy sum, a bundle, a packet, a pile; Brit. informal a bomb, big money.
▷ **adjective** *the album is in mint condition:* brand new, pristine, perfect, immaculate, unblemished, undamaged, unmarked, unused, first-class, excellent.
▷ **verb**
1 *the shilling was minted in 1742:* coin, stamp, strike, cast, forge, manufacture.
2 *the slogan had been freshly minted:* create, invent, make up, think up, dream up.

minuscule adjective *the newsroom was minuscule, not much more than a cubbyhole:* tiny, minute, very small, little, diminutive, miniature; Scottish wee; informal teeny; Brit. informal titchy, tiddly.
OPPOSITES: huge.

minute[1] noun
1 *it'll only take a minute:* moment, short time, little while, second, bit, instant;

informal sec, jiffy; Brit. informal tick, mo, two ticks.
2 *at that minute, Tony walked in:* point, moment, instant, juncture.
3 *their objection was noted in the minutes:* records, proceedings, log, notes; transcript, summary.
□ **at the minute** (Brit. informal)
at present, at the moment, now, currently.
□ **this minute**
at once, immediately, directly, this second, instantly, straight away, right away/now, forthwith; informal pronto.
□ **up to the minute**
latest, newest, up to date, modern, fashionable, smart, chic, stylish, all the rage, in vogue; informal trendy, with it, in, funky.

minute[2] adjective
1 *minute particles of dust:* tiny, minuscule, microscopic, very small, little, diminutive, miniature, baby, toy, Lilliputian; Scottish wee; informal teeny; Brit. informal titchy, tiddly.
2 *the committees consider the proposal in minute detail:* exhaustive, painstaking, meticulous, rigorous, scrupulous, punctilious, detailed.
OPPOSITES: huge.

minutiae plural noun *the captain cannot be concerned with the minutiae of shipboard life:* details, niceties, finer points, particulars, trivia, trivialities.

miracle noun
1 *Christ's first miracle:* supernatural phenomenon, mystery, prodigy.
2 *Germany's economic miracle:* wonder, marvel, sensation, phenomenon.

miraculous adjective *passengers had a miraculous escape after a fire raged through the aircraft:* amazing, astounding, astonishing, remarkable, extraordinary, incredible, unbelievable, sensational, wonderful, inexplicable, unaccountable.

mirage noun optical illusion, hallucination, figment of the imagination, vision; apparition, fantasy, chimera.

mire noun
1 *acres of land had been reduced to a mire:* swamp, bog, morass, quagmire; swampland, wetland, marshland.
2 *her horse was spattered with mire:* mud, slime, dirt, filth, muck.
3 *he struggled to pull the country out of the mire caused by decades of hard-line Communist rule:* mess, difficulty, plight, predicament, trouble.
▷ **verb** *he has become mired in lawsuits:* entangle, tangle up, embroil, catch up, mix up, involve, bog down.

mirror noun *he took a quick look in the mirror:* looking glass; Brit. glass.
▷ **verb** *pop music mirrored the mood of desperation:* reflect, match, echo, parallel,

m

correspond to; reproduce, imitate, simulate, copy, mimic.

mirth noun *she giggled, making an effort to control her mirth:* amusement, laughter, merriment, glee, hilarity, fun, enjoyment.
OPPOSITES: misery.

mirthless adjective humourless, unamused, ironic, sardonic.
OPPOSITES: cheerful.

misadventure noun *a series of misadventures:* accident, problem, difficulty, misfortune, mishap; setback, reversal of fortune, stroke of bad luck, blow; failure, disaster, tragedy, calamity, woe, trial, tribulation, catastrophe.

misanthrope noun *Scrooge wasn't the mean-spirited misanthrope most of us believe him to be:* hater of mankind, cynic; recluse.

misanthropic adjective *the experience had made him misanthropic and he lived alone:* antisocial, unsociable, unfriendly, reclusive; cynical, jaundiced.

misapply verb *the idea of permissiveness has been overstated or misapplied:* misuse, mishandle, misemploy, abuse; misinterpret, misconstrue, misrepresent, distort.

misapprehension noun misunderstanding, misinterpretation, misreading, misjudgement, misconception, misbelief, false impression, the wrong idea, delusion.

misappropriate verb *he confessed to having misappropriated $2.2bn from his clients' portfolios:* embezzle, expropriate, steal, thieve, pilfer, pocket, help yourself to; informal pinch, filch, rip off; Brit. informal nick.

misappropriation noun embezzlement, expropriation, stealing, theft, thieving, pilfering.

misbegotten adjective *she was drawn into her brother's misbegotten schemes:* ill-conceived, ill-advised, badly planned, badly thought-out; informal hare-brained.

misbehave verb *parents are summoned to the school if their children misbehave:* behave badly, be naughty, be disobedient, get up to mischief, get up to no good; be bad-mannered, be rude; informal play up, act up.

misbehaviour noun bad behaviour, misconduct, naughtiness, disobedience, mischief, mischievousness; bad/poor manners, rudeness.

misbelief noun *the new project should dispel commonly held misbeliefs about the indigenous peoples:* false belief, delusion, illusion, fallacy, error, mistake, misconception, misapprehension.

miscalculate verb *he had grossly miscalculated the time the task would take:* misjudge, calculate wrongly, estimate wrongly, overestimate, underestimate, overvalue, undervalue; make a mistake, go wrong, err, be wide of the mark.

miscalculation noun error of judgement, misjudgement, mistake, overestimate, underestimate.

miscarry verb
1 *the shock caused her to miscarry:* lose your baby, have a miscarriage, abort.
2 *our plan miscarried:* go wrong, go awry, go amiss, be unsuccessful, fail, misfire, founder, come to nothing, fall through, fall flat; informal flop, go up in smoke.
OPPOSITES: succeed.

miscellaneous adjective *a variety of miscellaneous tasks:* various, varied, different, assorted, mixed, sundry, diverse, disparate, heterogeneous; motley, multifarious.

miscellany noun *a miscellany of poems by several hands:* assortment, collection, selection, assemblage, mixture, variety, mixed bag, mix, medley, potpourri, melange, blend; hotchpotch; informal ragbag, mishmash.

mischance noun *by pure mischance, the secret was revealed:* accident, bad luck, misfortune, mishap, misadventure.

mischief noun
1 *the boys are always getting up to mischief:* misbehaviour, bad behaviour, naughtiness, mischievousness, misconduct, disobedience; pranks, tricks, devilry; informal monkey business.
2 *there was mischief in her eyes:* playfulness, impishness, roguishness, devilment.
3 *she was bent on making mischief:* harm, trouble, damage.

mischievous adjective
1 *a mischievous child:* naughty, badly behaved, misbehaving, disobedient, troublesome, full of mischief.
2 *a mischievous smile:* playful, teasing, wicked, impish, roguish, arch.
3 *a mischievous allegation for which there is not a shred of evidence:* malicious, spiteful, vicious, mean, nasty, cruel, unkind, hurtful.
OPPOSITES: well behaved.

misconceive verb *many lawyers misconceive their own role:* misunderstand, misinterpret, misconstrue, misapprehend, mistake, misread; miscalculate, err, be mistaken, get the wrong idea.

misconception noun *it's a popular misconception that all stress is bad for you:* misunderstanding, misapprehension, mistake, error, misinterpretation, misconstruction, misjudgement, misreading, misbelief, miscalculation, false impression; illusion, fallacy, delusion.

misconduct noun
1 *she was found guilty of professional misconduct:* wrongdoing, malpractice, negligence, impropriety, unethical behaviour; crime, criminality.
2 *misconduct in the classroom:* misbehaviour, bad behaviour, misdeeds, misdemeanours, disorderly conduct, mischief, naughtiness.

misconstrue verb *his indifference can easily be misconstrued as arrogance:* misunderstand, misinterpret, mistake, misread, misapprehend, misconceive; be mistaken about, get the wrong idea about.

miscreant noun *police have guaranteed that the miscreants will be brought to justice:* criminal, culprit, wrongdoer, offender, villain, lawbreaker, delinquent, reprobate; formal malefactor.

misdeed noun *he repented of his misdeeds and vowed to change his ways:* wrongdoing, wrong, evil deed, crime, felony, misdemeanour, misconduct, offence, error, transgression, sin.

misdemeanour noun *he preferred to turn a blind eye to his son's misdemeanours:* wrongdoing, misdeed, offence, error, peccadillo, transgression, sin, crime.

miser noun *a typical miser, he hid his money in the house in various places:* penny-pincher, Scrooge; informal skinflint, cheapskate; N. Amer. informal tightwad.
OPPOSITES: spendthrift.

miserable adjective
1 *I'm too miserable to eat:* unhappy, sad, sorrowful, dejected, depressed, downcast, downhearted, down, despondent, disconsolate, wretched, glum, gloomy, dismal, melancholy, woebegone, doleful, forlorn, heartbroken; informal blue, down in the mouth/dumps.
2 *their miserable surroundings:* dreary, dismal, gloomy, drab, wretched, unpleasant, depressing, grim, cheerless, bleak, desolate; poor, shabby, squalid, seedy, dilapidated.
3 *a miserable old man:* morose, sullen, gloomy, bad-tempered, ill-tempered, dour, surly, sour, moody, saturnine, lugubrious.
4 *they worked long hours for miserable wages:* inadequate, meagre, paltry, small, poor, pitiful, niggardly; informal measly, stingy.
OPPOSITES: cheerful, lovely.

miserliness noun meanness, niggardliness, close-fistedness, parsimony, parsimoniousness; informal stinginess, tight-fistedness.

miserly adjective
1 *his miserly great-uncle proved to be worth nearly £1 million:* mean, niggardly, parsimonious, close-fisted, penny-pinching, cheese-paring, grasping; informal stingy, tight, tight-fisted.

2 *the prize is a miserly £300:* meagre, inadequate, paltry, negligible, miserable, pitiful; informal measly, stingy.
OPPOSITES: generous.

misery noun
1 *I went through periods of intense misery:* unhappiness, distress, wretchedness, suffering, anguish, anxiety, angst, torment, pain, grief, heartache, heartbreak, despair, despondency, dejection, depression, desolation, gloom, melancholy, woe, sadness, sorrow; informal the dumps, the blues.
2 *the miseries of war:* affliction, misfortune, difficulty, problem, ordeal, trouble, hardship, deprivation; pain, sorrow, trial, tribulation, woe.
3 (Brit. informal) *he's a real old misery:* killjoy, dog in the manger, spoilsport, pessimist; informal sourpuss.
OPPOSITES: contentment, pleasure.

misfire verb *his plan had misfired:* go wrong, go awry, be unsuccessful, fail, founder, fall through/flat; backfire; informal flop, go up in smoke.

misfit noun *he was something of a social misfit:* eccentric, nonconformist, maverick, individualist, square peg in a round hole, odd man out; informal oddball, freak.

misfortune noun *they endured many misfortunes:* problem, difficulty, setback, trouble, adversity, stroke of bad luck, reversal of fortune, misadventure, mishap, blow, failure, accident, disaster; sorrow, misery, woe, trial, tribulation.

misgiving noun *despite occasional misgivings, he was optimistic:* qualm, doubt, reservation; suspicion, distrust, mistrust, lack of confidence, second thoughts; trepidation, scepticism, anxiety, apprehension, unease, uneasiness, disquiet.

misguided adjective
1 *the policy is misguided | a misguided belief:* ill-conceived, misconceived, ill-advised, ill-considered, ill-judged, inappropriate, unwise, injudicious, imprudent; erroneous, misplaced, unfounded.
2 *you are quite misguided:* misinformed, misled, labouring under a misapprehension, wrong, mistaken, deluded.

mishandle verb
1 *the officer mishandled the situation:* mismanage, bungle, make a mess of, spoil, ruin, wreck; informal botch, make a hash of, mess up, muck up.
2 *the equipment could be dangerous if mishandled:* misuse, abuse, handle/treat roughly.

mishap noun *the event passed without mishap:* accident, trouble, problem, difficulty, setback, adversity, reversal

m

of fortune, misfortune, blow; failure, disaster, tragedy, catastrophe, calamity.

mishmash noun *a bizarre mishmash of colours and patterns:* jumble, hotchpotch, confusion, farrago, patchwork, assortment, medley, miscellany, mixture, melange, blend, mix, potpourri; informal ragbag.

misinform verb *I'm afraid you have been misinformed:* mislead, misguide, give someone wrong information, delude, take in, deceive, lie to, hoodwink; informal lead up the garden path, take for a ride.

misinformation noun *a lot of misinformation was received:* disinformation, false/misleading information; lie.

misinterpret verb *he explained that his proposal had been misinterpreted:* misunderstand, misconstrue, misread, mistake, misconceive, misapprehend; confuse, take amiss, be mistaken, get the wrong idea.

misjudge verb *I have misjudged her—she didn't tell anyone:* get the wrong idea about, get wrong, judge incorrectly, estimate wrongly, be wrong about, miscalculate, misread; overestimate, underestimate, overvalue, undervalue, underrate.

m **mislay** verb *I seem to have mislaid my driving licence:* lose, misplace, put in the wrong place, be unable to find.

mislead verb *it seemed that he had deliberately misled her:* deceive, delude, take in, lie to, fool, hoodwink, throw off the scent, pull the wool over someone's eyes, misguide, misinform, give someone wrong information; informal lead up the garden path, take for a ride.

misleading adjective *the leaflet was full of misleading statements:* deceptive, confusing, deceiving, equivocal, ambiguous, fallacious, specious, spurious, false.

mismanage verb *the campaign had been mismanaged:* bungle, mishandle, make a mess of, spoil, ruin, wreck; informal botch, make a hash of, mess up, muck up.

mismatch noun *there is still a mismatch between policy and practice:* discrepancy, inconsistency, contradiction, incongruity, conflict, discord, failure to correspond.

mismatched adjective *mismatched kitchen units:* ill-assorted, ill-matched, incongruous, clashing, dissimilar; unsuited, incompatible, inconsistent, at odds, unalike, different, out of keeping, at variance, disparate, unrelated, divergent, contrasting.
OPPOSITES: matching.

misogynist noun *a bachelor and renowned misogynist:* woman-hater, anti-feminist, male chauvinist, sexist; informal male chauvinist pig, MCP.

misplace verb *he had misplaced the tickets:* lose, mislay, put in the wrong place, be unable to find.
OPPOSITES: find.

misplaced adjective *his comments were misplaced:* misguided, unwise, ill-advised, ill-considered, ill-judged, inappropriate.

misprint noun *the book is full of misprints:* mistake, error, typographical mistake, erratum, corrigendum; Brit. literal; informal typo.

misquote verb *my original statement has been misquoted:* misreport, misrepresent, misstate, take/quote out of context, distort, twist, slant, bias, put a spin on, falsify.

misrepresent verb *you are misrepresenting the views of the government:* misstate, misreport, misquote, quote/take out of context, misinterpret, put a spin on, falsify, distort.

misrule noun
1 *thirty years of misrule by the one-party government:* bad government, misgovernment, mismanagement, malpractice, incompetence.
2 *there is sometimes complete misrule at football games:* lawlessness, anarchy, disorder, chaos, mayhem.
OPPOSITES: order.

miss verb
1 *the shot missed her by inches:* fail to hit, be/go wide of, fall short of.
2 *he missed the ball:* fail to catch, drop, fumble, fluff, mishandle, misfield, mishit.
3 *I've missed my bus:* be too late for, fail to catch/get.
4 *I missed what you said:* fail to hear, mishear.
5 *you can't miss the station:* fail to see/notice, overlook.
6 *she never missed a meeting:* fail to attend, be absent from, cut, skip; Brit. play truant from; informal skive off.
7 *don't miss this exciting opportunity!* let slip, fail to take advantage of, let go/pass, pass up.
8 *I left early to miss the rush-hour traffic:* avoid, beat, evade, escape, dodge, sidestep, elude, circumvent, steer clear of, find a way round, bypass.
9 *she missed him when he was away:* pine for, yearn for, ache for, long for, long to see.
OPPOSITES: hit, catch.
□ miss someone/something out leave out, exclude, miss (off), fail to mention, pass over, skip; Brit. informal give something a miss.

misshapen adjective deformed, malformed, distorted, crooked, twisted, warped, out of shape, bent, asymmetrical, irregular, ill-proportioned, disfigured, grotesque.

missing adjective
1 *his wallet is missing:* lost, mislaid, misplaced, absent, gone astray, unaccounted for.
2 *passion was missing from her life:* absent, not present, lacking, wanting.
OPPOSITES: present.

mission noun
1 *a two-week fact-finding mission:* assignment, commission, undertaking, task, job; expedition, journey, trip, operation.
2 *her mission in life:* vocation, calling, goal, aim, purpose, function.
3 *a trade mission:* delegation, deputation, commission, legation, delegacy.
4 *a bombing mission:* sortie, operation, raid.

missionary noun evangelist, apostle, proselytizer.

missive noun (formal) *a missive arrived from the Foreign Office:* letter, message, communication, note, memo, memorandum, communiqué, dispatch.

misspent adjective *he's trying to make up for his misspent youth:* wasted, dissipated, squandered, thrown away, frittered away, misused.

misstate verb *they were accused of misstating the underlying purpose of the transaction:* misreport, misrepresent, distort, twist, put a spin on, falsify.

mist noun *the mist was clearing:* haze, fog, smog, murk, cloud.
□ **mist over/up**
steam up, become misty, fog over/up, film over, cloud over.

mistake noun
1 *I assumed it had been a mistake:* error, slip, blunder, oversight, gaffe, faux pas; miscalculation, misunderstanding, misinterpretation; omission, inaccuracy, fault; Grammar solecism; informal slip-up, boo-boo, howler; Brit. informal boob, clanger.
2 *the book is full of spelling mistakes:* misprint, typographical error, erratum; Brit. literal; informal typo.
▷ **verb**
1 *men are apt to mistake their own feelings:* misunderstand, misinterpret, get wrong, misconstrue, misread.
2 *children often mistake vitamin pills for sweets:* confuse with, mix up with, take for, misinterpret as.
□ **be mistaken**
be wrong, be in error, be under a misapprehension, be misinformed, be misguided; informal be barking up the wrong tree, get the wrong end of the stick.
□ **make a mistake**
go wrong, err, make an error, blunder, miscalculate; informal slip up.

mistaken adjective wrong, incorrect, erroneous, inaccurate, off beam, false, fallacious, unfounded, misguided, misinformed.
OPPOSITES: correct.

mistakenly adverb
1 *we often mistakenly imagine that when a problem is diagnosed it is solved:* wrongly, in error, erroneously, incorrectly, falsely.
2 *Matt mistakenly opened the letter:* by accident, accidentally, inadvertently, unintentionally, unwittingly, unconsciously, by mistake.

mistimed adjective *the delegates did not laugh at his mistimed jokes:* ill-timed, badly timed, inappropriate, inopportune, untimely, unseasonable.

mistreat verb *foreign nationals held hostage in the country had been mistreated:* ill-treat, maltreat, abuse, knock about/around, hit, beat, strike, molest, injure, harm, hurt; misuse, mishandle; informal beat up, rough up.

mistreatment noun ill-treatment, maltreatment, abuse, beating, molestation, injury, harm; mishandling, manhandling.

mistress noun *his wife never found out about his mistress:* lover, girlfriend, kept woman; old use paramour, concubine.

mistrust verb *I mistrust his motives:* be suspicious of, distrust, be mistrustful of, be distrustful of, be sceptical of, be wary of, have doubts about, have misgivings about, have reservations about, suspect, question, doubt, have no confidence/faith in.
▷ **noun** *mistrust of Russia was widespread:* suspicion, distrust, doubt, misgivings, wariness.

mistrustful adjective *he wondered if he had been unduly mistrustful of her:* suspicious, distrustful, wary, chary, doubtful, dubious, uneasy, sceptical.

misty adjective
1 *the misty air:* hazy, foggy, cloudy, murky; smoggy.
2 *a misty figure:* blurry, blurred, dim, indistinct, unclear, vague.
3 *misty memories:* vague, unclear, hazy, indefinite, nebulous.
OPPOSITES: clear.

misunderstand verb *she misunderstood his motives:* misinterpret, misconstrue, mistake, misread, misapprehend, misconceive; be mistaken, get the wrong idea, get the false impression; informal be barking up the wrong tree, get (hold of) the wrong end of the stick.

misunderstanding noun
1 *a fundamental misunderstanding of juvenile crime:* misinterpretation, misconception, misreading,

m

misconstruction, misapprehension, the wrong idea, false impression.
2 *we have had some misunderstandings*: disagreement, difference of opinion, dispute, falling-out, quarrel, argument, altercation, squabble, wrangle, clash; Brit. row; informal spat, scrap, tiff.

misuse verb
1 *he was found guilty of misusing public funds*: put to wrong use, embezzle, use fraudulently; abuse, squander, waste.
2 *she had been misused by her husband*: ill-treat, maltreat, mistreat, abuse, knock about/around, hit, beat, injure, harm, hurt; mishandle, manhandle; informal beat up, rough up.
▷ **noun**
1 *a misuse of company assets*: wrong use, embezzlement, fraud; squandering, waste.
2 *the misuse of drugs*: illegal use, abuse.

mitigate verb *the drugs mitigate the symptoms of Parkinson's disease*: alleviate, reduce, diminish, lessen, weaken, lighten, take the edge off, allay, ease, assuage, palliate, relieve, tone down, attenuate.

> **USAGE**
>
> The words **mitigate** and **militate** are often confused. **Mitigate** means 'to make something bad less severe'. **Militate** is used with **against** and means 'to be a strong factor in preventing something' (*anger may militate against success in the negotiations*).

mitigating adjective *he would have faced a prison sentence but for mitigating circumstances*: extenuating, acting in mitigation.

mitigation noun
1 *the mitigation of the problems*: alleviation, reduction, lessening, easing, assuaging, relief.
2 *what did she say in mitigation?* extenuation, explanation, excuse.

mix verb
1 *mix all the ingredients together*: blend, combine, mingle, put together; amalgamate, incorporate, meld, marry, coalesce, homogenize, intermingle, intermix, join, fuse, unite, unify.
2 *she mixes with all sorts*: associate, socialize, fraternize, keep company, consort; mingle, circulate; informal hang out/around, hobnob.
3 *we just don't mix*: be compatible, get along/on, be in harmony, see eye to eye, agree; informal hit it off, click, be on the same wavelength.
OPPOSITES: separate.
▷ **noun** *a mix of ancient and modern*: mixture, blend, combination, compound, fusion, alloy, union, amalgamation; medley, melange, collection, selection, assortment, variety, mixed bag, miscellany, potpourri; jumble, hotchpotch, patchwork, farrago; informal ragbag.

□ **mix something up**
I mixed up the dates: confuse, get confused, muddle up, get muddled up, mistake.
□ **mixed up in**
I'm sure he was mixed up in this business: involved in, embroiled in, caught up in.

mixed adjective
1 *a mixed collection*: assorted, varied, miscellaneous, heterogeneous, diverse, disparate, sundry; motley, jumbled.
2 *chickens of mixed breeds*: hybrid, cross-bred, interbred.
3 *mixed reactions*: ambivalent, equivocal, contradictory, conflicting.
OPPOSITES: homogeneous.

mixture noun
1 *gunpowder is a mixture of charcoal, potassium nitrate, and sulphur*: blend, mix, combination, concoction; composition, compound, alloy, amalgam.
2 *a strange mixture of people*: assortment, collection, selection, variety, mixed bag, mix, miscellany, medley, melange, blend, diversity, potpourri; hotchpotch, patchwork, farrago; informal ragbag, mishmash.
3 *the animals were a mixture of genetic strands*: cross, cross-breed, mongrel, hybrid.

mix-up noun (informal) *there's been a mix-up over the tickets*: muddle, misunderstanding, mistake, error, confusion.

moan verb
1 *he moaned in agony*: groan, wail, cry, sob, whimper.
2 *the wind moaned in the trees*: sough, sigh, murmur.

mob noun
1 *troops dispersed the mob of protesters*: crowd, horde, rabble, mass, throng, group, gathering, assemblage, multitude.
2 (Brit. informal) *all the usual mob were there*: group, set, crowd, lot, circle, pack, band; informal gang, bunch.
3 *the mob were excluded from political life*: the common people, the masses, the rank and file, the commonalty, the third estate, the plebeians, the proletariat; the hoi polloi, the lower classes, the rabble; informal the riff-raff, the proles, the plebs.
▷ **verb**
1 *the Chancellor was mobbed when he visited Berlin*: surround, swarm around, besiege, jostle.
2 *reporters mobbed her hotel*: crowd into, fill, pack, throng, press into, squeeze into.

mobile adjective
1 *both patients are mobile*: able to move, moving, walking; Medicine ambulant; Zoology & Botany motile.
2 *her mobile features registered her shock and disappointment*: expressive, eloquent, animated.

3 *a mobile library:* travelling; itinerant, peripatetic.
4 *an increasingly mobile workforce:* adaptable, flexible.
OPPOSITES: static.

mobilize verb
1 *the government mobilized most of its trained troops:* marshal, deploy, muster, rally, call up, assemble, mass, organize, prepare.
2 *he used the press to mobilize support for his party:* rally, marshal, organize, galvanize, stimulate, stir up, whip up, encourage.

mock verb
1 *the local children mocked the old people:* ridicule, jeer at, sneer at, deride, scorn, make fun of, laugh at, scoff at, tease, taunt; informal take the mickey out of.
2 *they mocked the way he speaks:* parody, imitate, mimic, ape, take off, satirize, lampoon; Brit. informal send up.
▷adjective *he threw up his hands in mock horror:* simulated, feigned, fake, insincere, sham; informal pretend, put-on.
OPPOSITES: genuine.

mockery noun
1 *stung by her mockery, he hung his head:* ridicule, derision, jeering, sneering, contempt, scorn, teasing, taunting, sarcasm.
2 *the trial was decried as a mockery of justice:* travesty, charade, farce, parody.

mocking adjective *a mocking smile:* sneering, contemptuous, scornful, derisive, sardonic, ironic, sarcastic.

mode noun
1 *there is a trend towards more energy-efficient modes of transport:* method, means, way, manner, system; style, approach, technique, procedure, process, practice.
2 *set the camera to manual mode:* function, position, operation.
3 *in the Seventies, the mode for active wear took hold:* fashion, vogue, style, look, trend; craze, fad.

model noun
1 *a model of St Paul's Cathedral:* replica, copy, representation, mock-up, dummy, imitation, duplicate, reproduction, facsimile.
2 *the American model of airline deregulation:* prototype, stereotype, archetype, type, version; blueprint, pattern, design, template, framework, mould.
3 *she was a model as a teacher:* ideal, paragon, perfect example/specimen; perfection, acme, epitome, crème de la crème, nonpareil.
4 *the latest model of car:* version, type, design, variety, kind, sort.
5 *models strode down the catwalk:* fashion model, supermodel; dated mannequin.
6 *an artist's model:* sitter, poser, subject.

▷adjective
1 *model trains:* replica, toy, miniature, dummy, imitation, reproduction, facsimile, duplicate.
2 *a model teacher:* ideal, perfect, exemplary, flawless, faultless, classic.

moderate adjective
1 *the club enjoyed moderate success last season:* average, modest, limited, adequate, fair, mediocre, middling, passable, tolerable; informal fair-to-middling.
2 *moderate prices:* reasonable, acceptable, fair, low, inexpensive, modest.
3 *a man of moderate views:* middle-of-the-road, non-extreme, non-radical.
4 *moderate alcohol consumption may provide some health benefits:* restrained, sensible, controlled, modest.
OPPOSITES: great, extreme.
▷verb
1 *the wind has moderated:* die down, abate, let up, calm down, lessen, decrease, diminish; recede, weaken, subside.
2 *you can help to moderate her anger:* curb, control, check, temper, restrain, subdue; lessen, decrease, lower, reduce, diminish, alleviate, allay, appease, assuage, ease, soothe, calm, tone down.
3 *the Speaker moderates the assembly:* chair, take the chair of, preside over.
OPPOSITES: increase.

moderately adverb *the event was moderately successful:* somewhat, quite, fairly, reasonably, comparatively, relatively, to some extent, rather; tolerably, passably, adequately; informal pretty.

moderation noun
1 *he urged them to show moderation:* self-restraint, restraint, self-control, self-discipline, temperance.
2 *a moderation of their confrontational style:* relaxation, easing off, reduction, tempering, softening, lessening; modulation, modification; informal let-up.
▢ **in moderation**
in moderate quantities/amounts, within (sensible) limits; moderately.

modern adjective
1 *modern times:* present-day, contemporary, present, current, twenty-first-century, latter-day, recent.
2 *her clothes are very modern:* fashionable, stylish, chic, in fashion, in vogue, trendsetting, up to date, à la mode, voguish, modish; the latest, new, newest, modernistic, advanced; informal trendy, cool, in, hip, funky.
OPPOSITES: past, old-fashioned.

modernize verb
1 *they are modernizing their manufacturing facilities:* update, bring up to date, streamline, overhaul; renovate, remodel, revamp, refashion; Brit. rationalize.

m

2 *we must modernize to survive:* get up to date, move with the times, innovate.

modest adjective
1 *she was modest about her poetry:* self-effacing, self-deprecating, humble, unpretentious, unassuming; shy, bashful, self-conscious, diffident, reserved, reticent, coy.
2 *a period of modest success:* moderate, fair, limited, tolerable, passable, adequate, satisfactory, acceptable, unexceptional.
3 *a modest house:* small, ordinary, simple, plain, humble, inexpensive, unostentatious, unpretentious.
4 *her modest dress:* decorous, decent, seemly, demure, proper.
OPPOSITES: conceited.

modesty noun
1 *Hannah's modesty hides many talents:* self-effacement, humility, unpretentiousness; shyness, bashfulness, self-consciousness, reserve, reticence, timidity.
2 *the modesty of his political aspirations:* limited scope, moderation.
3 *modesty forbade her to undress in front of so many people:* decorum, decorousness, decency, seemliness, demureness.

modicum noun *people with only a modicum of scientific knowledge:* small amount, particle, speck, fragment, scrap, crumb, grain, morsel, shred, jot, iota, whit, atom, smattering, scintilla, hint, suggestion; informal smidgen, tad.

modification noun
1 *the design is undergoing modification:* alteration, adjustment, change, adaptation, refinement, revision.
2 *some minor modifications were made:* revision, refinement, improvement, amendment, adaptation, adjustment, change, alteration.
3 *the modification of his views:* softening, moderation, tempering, qualification.

modify verb
1 *their economic policy has been modified:* alter, change, adjust, adapt, amend, revise, reshape, refashion, restyle, revamp, rework, remodel, refine; informal tweak.
2 *he modified his more extreme views:* moderate, revise, temper, soften, tone down, qualify.

modish adjective *a modish new restaurant:* fashionable, stylish, chic, modern, contemporary, all the rage, in vogue, voguish, up to the minute, à la mode; informal trendy, cool, in, hip, happening.

modulate verb *the cells modulate the body's response:* regulate, control, adjust, set, modify, moderate.

modus operandi noun *every killer has his own modus operandi:* method of working, method, way, MO, manner,

technique, style, procedure, approach, methodology, strategy, plan, formula.

mogul noun *Hollywood movie moguls:* magnate, tycoon, captain of industry, baron, grandee, nabob; VIP, personage, notable; informal bigwig, big shot.

moist adjective
1 *the air was moist:* damp, steamy, humid, muggy, clammy, dank, wet, sweaty, sticky.
2 *a moist fruitcake:* succulent, juicy, soft.
3 *her eyes grew moist:* tearful, watery, misty.
OPPOSITES: dry.

moisten verb *the compost should be moistened before use:* dampen, wet, damp, water, humidify.

moisture noun *dehumidifiers will remove moisture from the air:* wetness, wet, water, liquid, condensation, steam, vapour, dampness, damp, humidity.

moisturizer noun lotion, cream, balm, salve, emollient, lubricant, unguent.

mole[1] noun *he was shopped by a KGB mole inside CIA's headquarters:* spy, agent, undercover agent, operative, plant, infiltrator; N. Amer. informal spook.

mole[2] noun *the mole protecting the harbour:* breakwater, groyne, pier, causeway, sea wall, dyke.

molest verb *he was charged with molesting a ten-year-old boy:* sexually abuse, sexually assault, interfere with, rape; literary violate.

mollify verb *nature reserves were set up round power stations to mollify local conservationists:* appease, placate, pacify, conciliate, soothe, calm, calm down.

mollycoddle verb *his parents mollycoddle him:* pamper, cosset, coddle, spoil, indulge, overindulge, baby, wait on hand and foot, wrap in cotton wool.

molten adjective *molten metal:* liquefied, liquid, fluid, melted, flowing.

moment noun
1 *I'll be back in a moment:* minute, short time, bit, instant, second; informal sec, jiffy; Brit. informal tick.
2 *she was waiting for the right moment to tell him:* point, juncture, time, opportunity.
□ **in a moment**
very soon, in a minute, in a second, shortly, any minute, in a trice; informal in a jiffy, in no time; Brit. informal in a tick, in two ticks.

momentarily adverb *he paused momentarily:* briefly, fleetingly, for a moment, for a second, for an instant.

momentary adjective *a momentary lapse of concentration may have led to the crash:* brief, short, short-lived, fleeting, passing, transient, ephemeral.
OPPOSITES: lengthy.

momentous adjective *it is a momentous decision that could influence US politics for decades:* important, significant, historic, portentous, critical, crucial, life-and-death, decisive, pivotal, consequential, of great consequence, far-reaching; informal earth-shattering.
OPPOSITES: insignificant.

momentum noun *the vehicle gained momentum as the road dipped:* impetus, speed, velocity, energy, force, power, strength, thrust.

monarch noun sovereign, ruler, Crown, crowned head, potentate; king, queen, emperor, empress, prince, princess.

monarchy noun
1 *the country is a constitutional monarchy:* kingdom, sovereign state, principality, empire.
2 *few questioned the justification for hereditary monarchy:* kingship, sovereignty, autocracy, monocracy, absolutism.

monastery noun religious community; friary, abbey, priory, cloister.

monastic adjective
1 *a monastic community:* cloistered.
2 *a monastic existence:* ascetic, austere, simple, solitary, monkish, celibate, quiet, cloistered, sequestered, secluded, reclusive, hermit-like.

monetary adjective *the documents have little or no monetary value:* financial, pecuniary, money, cash, economic, fiscal, budgetary.

money noun
1 *I haven't got enough money:* cash, ready money; the means, the wherewithal, funds, capital, finances; banknotes, notes, coins, change, silver, copper, currency; Brit. sterling; technical specie; informal dough, bread, loot, readies; Brit. informal dosh, brass, lolly.
2 *she married him for his money:* wealth, riches, fortune, affluence, assets, resources, means.
3 *the money here is better:* pay, salary, wages, remuneration; stipend; formal emolument.
□ **for my money**
in my opinion, to my mind, in my view, as I see it, it seems to me, personally, in my estimation, in my judgement, if you ask me.

WORD LINKS
pecuniary, monetary relating to money
numismatics the study or collection of coins and banknotes

moneyed adjective *the Industrial Revolution created a new moneyed class:* rich, wealthy, affluent, well-to-do, well off, prosperous, opulent, of means, of substance; informal in the money, rolling in

it, loaded, stinking/filthy rich, well heeled, made of money.
OPPOSITES: poor.

moneymaking adjective *the tournament was a public relations exercise rather than a moneymaking venture:* profitable, profit-making, remunerative, lucrative, successful, financially rewarding.
OPPOSITES: loss-making.

mongrel noun cross-breed, cross, mixed breed; mutt, tyke, cur.
▷adjective *a mongrel dog:* cross-bred, of mixed breed.
OPPOSITES: pedigree.

monitor noun
1 *monitors covered all entrances:* detector, scanner, recorder; security camera, CCTV.
2 *UN monitors declared the referendum had been fair:* observer, watchdog, overseer, supervisor.
3 *a computer monitor:* screen, visual display unit, VDU.
▷verb *his movements were closely monitored:* observe, watch, track, keep an eye on, keep under observation, keep watch on, keep under surveillance, record, note, oversee; informal keep tabs on.

monk noun brother, coenobite, contemplative, mendicant; friar; abbot, prior; novice, postulant.

WORD LINKS
monastic relating to a monk

monkey noun simian, primate, ape.
□ **monkey with**
don't monkey with that lock: tamper with, fiddle with, interfere with, meddle with, tinker with, play with; informal mess with; Brit. informal muck about with.

WORD LINKS
primatology the branch of zoology concerned with monkeys and apes

monolith noun standing stone, menhir, sarsen stone, megalith.

monolithic adjective
1 *a monolithic building:* massive, huge, vast, colossal, gigantic, immense, giant, enormous; featureless, characterless.
2 *the old monolithic Communist party had become an anachronism:* inflexible, rigid, unbending, unchanging, fossilized.

monologue noun *the skilfully varied tone and pace of her 40-minute monologue:* soliloquy, speech, address, lecture, sermon.

monomania noun *his profound interest in the subject verges on monomania:* obsession, fixation, consuming passion, mania, compulsion.

monopolize verb
1 *the company has monopolized the market:*

m

corner, control, take over, gain control/
dominance over.
2 *he monopolized the conversation:*
dominate, take over; informal hog.
3 *she monopolized the guest of honour:* take
up all the attention of, keep to yourself;
informal tie up.

monotonous adjective
1 *the purpose of this technology is to free
people from monotonous tasks:* tedious,
boring, dull, uninteresting, tiresome,
wearisome, repetitive, repetitious,
unvarying, unchanging, unvaried,
humdrum, routine, mechanical, mind-
numbing, soul-destroying; colourless,
featureless, dreary; informal deadly; Brit.
informal samey.
2 *she spoke in a low monotonous voice:*
toneless, flat, uninflected, soporific.
OPPOSITES: interesting.

monotony noun
1 *the monotony of everyday life:* tedium,
tediousness, lack of variety, dullness,
boredom, repetitiveness, repetitiousness,
uniformity of tone, lack of excitement,
uneventfulness, dreariness, colourlessness,
featurelessness.
2 *the monotony of her voice:* tonelessness,
flatness.

monster noun
1 *her husband is a monster:* brute, fiend,
beast, ogre, devil, barbarian, savage,
animal; informal swine, pig.
2 *he's a monster of a man:* giant, mammoth,
colossus, titan, leviathan.

monstrosity noun *the airport itself is a
concrete monstrosity:* eyesore, blot on the
landscape, excrescence, carbuncle.

monstrous adjective
1 *a monstrous creature emerged from the
blackness:* grotesque, hideous, misshapen,
ugly, ghastly, gruesome, horrible, horrific,
horrifying, grisly, disgusting, repulsive,
repellent, dreadful, frightening, terrifying.
2 *such monstrous acts of violence had
never been seen in the country:* appalling,
heinous, evil, wicked, abominable, terrible,
horrible, dreadful, vile, outrageous,
shocking, disgraceful, egregious;
unspeakable, despicable, vicious, savage,
barbaric, barbarous, inhuman.
3 *a monstrous tidal wave swamped the
surrounding countryside:* enormous,
huge, immense, gigantic, giant, massive,
colossal, mammoth, tremendous, mighty,
vast.

monument noun
1 *a stone monument:* memorial, statue,
pillar, column, obelisk, cross; cenotaph,
tomb, mausoleum, shrine.
2 *a monument was placed over the grave:*
gravestone, headstone, tombstone.
3 *the project is a monument to a past era
of aviation:* testament, record, reminder,
remembrance, memorial, commemoration.

monumental adjective
1 *they face a monumental task:* huge, great,
enormous, gigantic, massive, colossal,
mammoth, immense, tremendous, mighty,
stupendous.
2 *she had made a monumental error of
judgement:* terrible, dreadful, awful,
colossal, staggering, huge, enormous,
unforgivable, shocking, egregious.
3 *it is one of Beethoven's most monumental
piano works:* impressive, striking,
outstanding, remarkable, magnificent,
majestic, stupendous, ambitious, large-
scale, grand, awe-inspiring, important,
significant, distinguished, memorable,
immortal.

mood noun
1 *she's in a good mood:* frame/state of
mind, temper, humour; disposition, spirit,
tenor.
2 *he's obviously in a mood:* bad mood, bad
temper, sulk, fit of pique; low spirits, the
doldrums, the blues; informal the dumps,
grump; Brit. informal paddy.
3 *the mood of the film was one of hope:*
atmosphere, feeling, spirit, ambience,
aura, character, tenor, flavour, feel,
tone.
◻ **in the mood**
in the right frame of mind, feeling like,
wanting to, inclined to, disposed to,
minded to, eager to, willing to.

moody adjective *he became moody and
bad-tempered:* temperamental, emotional,
volatile, capricious, changeable, mercurial;
sullen, sulky, morose, glum, depressed,
dejected, despondent, doleful, dour,
sour, saturnine; informal blue, down in the
dumps/mouth.
OPPOSITES: cheerful.

moon noun satellite.
▷ **verb**
1 *stop mooning about:* waste time, loaf,
idle, mope; Brit. informal mooch.
2 *he's still mooning over her photograph:*
mope, pine, brood, daydream, fantasize.
◻ **over the moon** (informal). See ECSTATIC.

> WORD LINKS
> **lunar** relating to the moon

moor¹ verb *a boat was moored to the quay:*
tie up, secure, make fast, fix, anchor, berth,
dock.

moor² noun *a walk on the moor helped him
gather his thoughts:* upland, moorland; Brit.
heath, fell, wold.

moot adjective *whether the temperature
rise was due to the greenhouse effect was a
moot point:* debatable, open to discussion/
question, arguable, questionable, at issue,
open to doubt, disputable, controversial,
contentious, disputed, unresolved,
unsettled, up in the air.
▷ **verb** *the idea was first mooted in the 1930s:*
raise, bring up, broach, mention, put

forward, introduce, advance, propose, suggest.

mop noun *her tousled mop of hair:* shock, mane, tangle, mass.
□ **mop something up**
1 *I mopped up the spilt coffee:* wipe up, clean up, sponge up.
2 *troops mopped up the last pockets of resistance:* finish off, deal with, dispose of, take care of, clear up, eliminate.

mope verb
1 *it's no use moping:* brood, sulk, be miserable, be despondent, pine, eat your heart out, fret, grieve; informal be down in the dumps/mouth.
2 *she was moping about the house:* languish, moon, loaf; Brit. informal mooch.

moral adjective
1 *there are moral as well as political issues involved here:* ethical, social, to do with right and wrong.
2 *for all his faults, he was a very moral man:* virtuous, good, righteous, upright, upstanding, high-minded, principled, honourable, honest, just, noble, incorruptible, scrupulous, respectable, clean-living, law-abiding.
3 *we can at least give him our moral support:* psychological, emotional, mental. OPPOSITES: unethical.
▷ **noun**
1 *the moral of the story is: don't mix business with pleasure:* lesson, message, meaning, significance, signification, import, point, teaching.
2 *he has no morals:* moral code, code of ethics, moral standards/values, principles, standards, sense of morality, scruples.

morale noun *morale in the team was higher than it had been for a long time:* confidence, self-confidence, self-esteem, spirit, team spirit, esprit de corps.

moral fibre noun *an ineffectual man with no moral fibre:* strength of character, fortitude, resolve, backbone, spine, firmness of purpose, mettle.

morality noun
1 *the morality of the possession of nuclear weapons:* ethics, rights and wrongs, ethicality.
2 *standards of morality seem to be dropping:* moral standards, standards/principles of behaviour, morals, ethics, principles; honesty, rectitude, integrity, propriety, virtue, honour.

moralize verb *doctors should not moralize but simply deal with the patient's medical condition:* preach, pontificate, sermonize, lecture; informal preachify.

morass noun
1 *in winter the track beneath the bridge became a muddy morass:* bog, swamp, quagmire, marsh, mire, slough.
2 *they were bogged down in a morass of* bureaucracy: quagmire, labyrinth, maze, chaos, muddle, tangle, imbroglio.

moratorium noun *a temporary moratorium on all nuclear testing:* embargo, ban, prohibition, suspension, postponement, stay, stoppage, halt, freeze, standstill; respite.

morbid adjective *he had a morbid fascination with contemporary warfare:* ghoulish, macabre, unhealthy, gruesome, unwholesome; informal sick.

mordant adjective *a mordant sense of humour:* caustic, trenchant, biting, cutting, acerbic, sardonic, sarcastic, scathing, acid, sharp, keen; critical, virulent, vitriolic, bitter.

more determiner *we need more supplies:* additional, further, extra, added, increased, new, other, supplementary. OPPOSITES: less, fewer.
▷ **adverb** *he was able to concentrate more on his writing:* to a greater extent, further, for longer, better.
▷ **pronoun** *we're going to need more:* extra, an additional amount/number, an addition, an increase. OPPOSITES: less, fewer.
□ **more or less**
approximately, roughly, nearly, almost, close to, about, of the order of, in the region of.

moreover adverb *moreover, statistics show that competition for places is growing:* besides, furthermore, what's more, in addition, also, as well, too, to boot, additionally, on top of that, into the bargain, more.

mores plural noun *factors that shaped the social mores of the community:* customs, conventions, ways, way of life, traditions, practices, habits.

morgue noun mortuary, funeral parlour; Brit. chapel of rest.

moribund adjective *the moribund shipbuilding industry:* declining, in decline, waning, dying, stagnating, stagnant, crumbling, on its last legs. OPPOSITES: thriving.

morning noun
1 *I've got a meeting this morning:* before noon, before lunch, a.m.
2 *morning is on its way:* dawn, daybreak, sunrise, first light; literary cockcrow.

moron noun. See FOOL noun sense 1.

moronic adjective. See STUPID sense 1.

morose adjective *Louis sat alone at a table, looking morose:* sullen, sulky, gloomy, bad-tempered, ill-tempered, surly, sour, dour, glum, moody, melancholy, melancholic, doleful, miserable, depressed, dejected, despondent, downcast, unhappy, in low spirits, low, down, grumpy, irritable,

m

cantankerous, crotchety, cross, crabby, grouchy, testy, peevish; informal snappish, fed up, blue, down in the dumps/mouth.
OPPOSITES: cheerful.

morsel noun *she pushed a morsel of toast into her mouth:* mouthful, bite, bit, nibble, taste, spoonful, forkful, soupçon, sliver, dollop, spot; titbit.

mortal adjective
1 *the mortal remains of the victims | all men are mortal:* perishable, physical, bodily, corporeal, fleshly, earthly; human, impermanent.
2 *a mortal blow:* deadly, fatal, lethal, death-dealing, murderous; terminal.
3 *the men were mortal enemies:* irreconcilable, deadly, sworn, bitter, out-and-out, implacable.
4 *she had committed a mortal sin:* unpardonable, unforgivable.
5 *parents live in mortal fear of the disease:* extreme, great, terrible, awful, dreadful, intense.
OPPOSITES: immortal, venial.
▷noun *we are mere mortals:* human being, human, person, man/woman; (in Science Fiction) earthling.

mortality noun
1 *her death brought home a sense of his own mortality:* impermanence, transience, perishability.
2 *the disease is the leading cause of infant mortality in the developing world:* death, loss of life, dying.

mortification noun
1 *scarlet with mortification, she looked away:* embarrassment, humiliation, shame, chagrin, discomfiture, discomposure.
2 *mortification of the flesh has a long tradition in some branches of the religion:* subduing, suppression, subjugation, control, controlling; discipline, punishment.

mortify verb
1 *I'd be mortified if my friends found out:* embarrass, humiliate, chagrin, shame, crush, abash, horrify, appal, discomfit.
2 *he prayed from sunrise to sunset, mortifying the flesh:* subdue, suppress, subjugate, control; discipline, punish.

mortuary noun morgue, funeral parlour; Brit. chapel of rest.

most pronoun *most of the guests brought flowers:* nearly all, almost all, the greatest part/number, the majority, the bulk, the preponderance.
OPPOSITES: few, little.

mostly adverb
1 *the other passengers were mostly businessmen:* mainly, for the most part, on the whole, in the main, largely, by and large, to a large extent, chiefly, predominantly, principally, primarily.

2 *I mostly wear jeans:* usually, generally, in general, as a rule, ordinarily, normally, typically, most of the time, almost always.

moth-eaten adjective *a moth-eaten tweed jacket:* threadbare, worn, well worn, old, shabby, scruffy, tattered; informal tatty, the worse for wear.

mother noun
1 *their mother was Scottish:* female parent; materfamilias, matriarch informal ma, mam; Brit. informal mum, mummy.
2 *the foal's mother:* dam.
▷verb *she mothered her husband:* look after, care for, take care of, nurse, protect, tend; pamper, mollycoddle, cosset, fuss over.

WORD LINKS
maternal relating to or like a mother
matricide the killing of a mother by her child

motherly adjective *she held her arms wide in a gesture of motherly love:* maternal, maternalistic, protective, caring, loving, devoted, affectionate, fond, warm, tender, gentle, kind, kindly, understanding, compassionate.

motif noun
1 *a colourful tulip motif:* design, pattern, decoration, figure, shape, device, emblem.
2 *time is a recurring motif in his work:* theme, idea, concept, subject, topic, leitmotif, element.

motion noun
1 *the rocking motion of the boat | a planet's motion around the sun:* movement, moving, locomotion; progress, passage, passing, transit, course, travel.
2 *a motion of the hand:* gesture, movement, signal, sign, indication; wave, nod, gesticulation.
3 *the motion failed to obtain a majority:* proposal, proposition, recommendation, suggestion.
▷verb *he motioned her to sit down:* gesture, signal, direct, indicate; wave, beckon, nod, gesticulate.
□in motion
moving, on the move, going, travelling, running, functioning, operational.
□set something in motion
start, activate, get going, get off the ground; trigger off, set off, spark off, generate, cause.

WORD LINKS
kinetic relating to or resulting from motion

motionless adjective unmoving, still, stationary, stock-still, immobile, static, at a standstill; not moving a muscle, rooted to the spot, transfixed, paralysed, frozen.
OPPOSITES: moving.

motivate verb
1 *he was primarily motivated by the desire for profit:* prompt, drive, move, inspire,

stimulate, influence, activate, impel, push, propel, spur on.
2 *it's the teacher's job to motivate the child:* inspire, stimulate, encourage, spur on, excite, incentivize, fire with enthusiasm.

motivation noun
1 *escape can be a strong motivation for travel:* motive, motivating force, incentive, stimulus, stimulation, inspiration, inducement, spur, reason.
2 *keep staff up to date to maintain interest and motivation:* enthusiasm, drive, ambition, initiative, enterprise; informal get-up-and-go.

motive noun *police were unable to establish the motive for his murder:* reason, motivation, motivating force, rationale, grounds, cause, basis, object, purpose, intention; incentive, inducement, inspiration, stimulus, stimulation, spur.
▷ **adjective** *steam engines supplied the motive power:* kinetic, driving, propulsive, propelling, motor.

motley adjective *a motley collection of old clothes:* miscellaneous, disparate, diverse, assorted, heterogeneous, varied, diversified.
OPPOSITES: homogeneous.

mottled adjective spotted, speckled, streaked, streaky, blotchy, marbled, flecked, freckled, dappled, stippled; brindled, brindle.

motto noun *their school motto was 'Serve and Obey':* maxim, saying, proverb, aphorism, adage, saw, axiom, expression, phrase, dictum, precept; slogan, catchphrase; truism, cliché, platitude; rare apophthegm.

mould¹ noun
1 *the molten metal is poured into a mould:* cast, die, form, matrix, template, pattern, frame.
2 *she was an actress in the traditional Hollywood mould:* style, form, type, kind, pattern, model, format; archetype, prototype.
▷ **verb**
1 *the figure was moulded from clay:* shape, form, fashion, model, work, construct, make, create, manufacture, sculpt, sculpture; forge, cast.
2 *Moffat was one of the figures who were helping to mould US policy:* determine, direct, control, guide, lead, influence, shape, form, fashion.

mould² noun *the walls were stained with mould:* mildew, fungus, must, mouldiness.

mould³ noun *leaf mould:* earth, soil, dirt, loam, humus.

moulder verb *his body still lay mouldering in some forgotten field:* decay, decompose, rot, putrefy, go mouldy, spoil.

mouldy adjective *a lump of mouldy cheese:*

mildewed, musty, mouldering; decaying, rotting, rotten, bad, decomposing.

mound noun
1 *a mound of leaves:* heap, pile, stack, mountain; mass, accumulation.
2 *he built his castle high on the mound:* hillock, hill, knoll, rise, hummock, hump, embankment, bank, ridge, elevation; Scottish brae.
3 *a burial mound:* barrow, tumulus.

mount verb
1 *he mounted the stairs:* go up, ascend, climb, scale.
2 *the committee mounted the platform:* climb on to, get on to.
3 *the museum is mounting an exhibition:* put on display, exhibit, present, install; organize, put on, stage.
4 *the company mounted a takeover bid:* organize, stage, prepare, arrange, set up; launch, set in motion, initiate.
5 *their losses mounted rapidly:* increase, grow, rise, escalate, soar, spiral, shoot up, rocket, climb, accumulate, build up, multiply.
6 *cameras were mounted above the door:* install, place, fix, set, put up, put in position.
OPPOSITES: descend.
▷ **noun** *a decorated photograph mount:* setting, backing, support, mounting, frame.

mountain noun
1 *one of the world's highest mountains:* peak, height, mount, summit, pinnacle, alp; Scottish ben, Munro; (**mountains**) range, massif, sierra.
2 *there's a mountain of paperwork:* a great deal, a lot, a large quantity of; abundance; backlog; informal heap, pile, stack, lots, loads, heaps, piles, tons, masses.
3 *the EC's butter mountain:* surplus, surfeit, glut, oversupply.

mountainous adjective
1 *some communities survive in the mountainous regions of northern Greece:* hilly, craggy, rocky, alpine; upland, highland.
2 *middle-income earners are struggling under mountainous debts:* huge, enormous, gigantic, massive, giant, colossal, immense, tremendous, mighty; informal whopping, humongous; Brit. informal whacking, ginormous.
OPPOSITES: flat.

mourn verb
1 *Isobel mourned her husband:* grieve for, sorrow over, lament for, weep for, wail/keen over.
2 *he mourned the loss of the beautiful buildings:* deplore, bewail, bemoan, rue, regret.

mournful adjective *a mournful expression:* sad, sorrowful, doleful, melancholy, melancholic, woeful,

m

grief-stricken, miserable, unhappy, heartbroken, broken-hearted, gloomy, desolate, dejected, despondent, depressed, downcast, disconsolate, woebegone, forlorn, lugubrious, joyless, cheerless, dismal.
OPPOSITES: cheerful.

mourning noun
1 *a period of mourning:* grief, grieving; sorrowing, lamentation, keening, wailing, weeping.
2 *she was dressed in mourning:* black clothes, widow's weeds.

mousy adjective
1 *mousy hair:* lightish brown, brownish, brownish-grey, dun-coloured, dull.
2 *a small, mousy woman:* timid, quiet, shy, self-effacing, diffident, unassertive, unforthcoming, withdrawn, fearful, nervous, timorous.

mouth noun
1 *open your mouth:* lips, jaws; maw, muzzle; informal trap, chops; Brit. informal gob.
2 *the mouth of the cave:* entrance, opening, entry, way in, access, ingress.
3 *the mouth of the bottle:* opening, rim, lip.
4 *the mouth of the river:* outfall, outlet, debouchment; estuary, firth.
▷verb *he mouthed platitudes:* utter, speak, say, voice, express; say insincerely, say for form's sake.
▫ **mouth off** (informal) *he was mouthing off about school, teachers, and society in general:* rant, hold forth, fulminate, spout; informal sound off.

> WORD LINKS
> **oral**, **buccal** relating to the mouth

mouthful noun
1 *a mouthful of pizza:* bite, nibble, taste, bit, piece; spoonful, forkful.
2 *a mouthful of beer:* draught, sip, swallow, drop, gulp; informal swig, slug.

mouthpiece noun *he has no power—he's just a mouthpiece for the government:* spokesperson, spokesman, spokeswoman, agent, representative, propagandist, voice.

movable adjective *put away all movable objects:* portable, transportable, transferable, detachable; mobile.
OPPOSITES: fixed.

move verb
1 *she moved to the door | don't move!* go, walk, proceed, progress, advance; budge, stir, shift, change position.
2 *he moved the chair closer to the fire:* carry, transport, transfer, shift.
3 *things were moving too fast:* develop, make headway, advance, progress.
4 *he urged the council to move quickly:* take action, act, take steps, do something, take measures; informal get moving.
5 *she's moved to Cambridge:* relocate, move

house, change address, leave, go away, decamp; Brit. informal up sticks.
6 *I was deeply moved by the story:* affect, touch, impress, shake, upset; make an impression on.
7 *she was moved to find out more about it:* inspire, prompt, stimulate, motivate, provoke, influence, rouse, induce, incite.
8 *they are not prepared to move on this issue:* change, budge, shift your ground, change your tune, change your mind, have second thoughts; do a U-turn, do an about-face; Brit. do an about-turn.
9 *she moves in the art worlds:* circulate, mix, socialize, keep company, associate; informal hang out/around; Brit. informal hang about.
10 *I move that we adjourn:* propose, submit, suggest, advocate, recommend, urge.
▷noun
1 *his eyes followed her every move:* movement, motion, action; gesture, gesticulation.
2 *his recent move to London:* relocation, change of address, transfer, posting.
3 *the latest move in the war against drugs:* initiative, step, action, act, measure, manoeuvre, tactic, stratagem.
4 *it's your move:* turn, go; opportunity, chance.
▫ **make a move** *they're waiting for the other side to make a move:* act, take action, take the initiative; informal get moving, get the ball rolling.

movement noun
1 *there was almost no movement:* motion, action, activity.
2 *Rachel made a sudden movement:* move, motion, gesture, gesticulation, sign, signal.
3 *the movement of supplies:* transportation, conveyance, moving, transfer, shift, shifting.
4 *the labour movement:* political group, party, faction, wing, lobby, camp.
5 *a movement to declare war on poverty:* campaign, crusade, drive, push.
6 *there have been movements in the financial markets:* development, change, fluctuation, variation.
7 *the movement towards equality:* trend, tendency, drift, swing.
8 *some movement will be made by the end of the month:* progress, progression, advance.
9 *a symphony in three movements:* part, section, division.
10 *the clock's movement:* mechanism, machinery, works, workings.

> WORD LINKS
> **kinetic** relating to or resulting from movement

movie noun
1 *he's just finished work on his latest movie:* film, picture, motion picture, feature film; informal flick.
2 *she wanted to work in the movies:* cinema,

the film industry, the silver screen; informal the big screen.

moving adjective

1 *moving parts | a moving train:* in motion, operating, operational, working, going, on the move, active; movable, mobile.
2 *a moving book:* affecting, touching, poignant, heart-warming, heart-rending, emotional; inspiring, inspirational, stimulating, stirring.
3 *the party's moving force:* driving, motivating, dynamic, stimulating, inspirational.
OPPOSITES: fixed, stationary.

mow verb *she had mown the grass:* cut, trim.
□ **mow someone/something down** kill, gun down, shoot down, cut down, cut to pieces, butcher, slaughter, massacre, annihilate, wipe out.

much determiner *did you get much help?* a lot of, a great/good deal of, a great/large amount of, plenty of, ample, copious, abundant, plentiful, considerable; informal lots of, loads of, heaps of, masses of, tons of.
OPPOSITES: little.
▷**adverb**
1 *it didn't hurt much:* greatly, to a great extent/degree, a great deal, considerably, appreciably; informal a lot.
2 *does he come here much?* often, frequently, many times, repeatedly, regularly, habitually, routinely, usually, normally, commonly; informal a lot.
▷**pronoun** *he did so much for our team:* a lot, a great/good deal, plenty; informal lots, loads, heaps, masses.

muck noun

1 *I'll just clean the muck off the windscreen:* dirt, grime, filth, mud, slime, mess; informal gunk; Brit. informal gunge.
2 *farmers spread muck over their fields:* manure, dung, excrement, droppings.
□ **muck something up** (informal) make a mess of, mess up, bungle, spoil, ruin, wreck; informal botch, make a hash of, muff, fluff, foul up.
□ **muck about/around** (Brit. informal)
1 *he was mucking about with his mates:* fool about/around, play about/around, clown about/around; informal mess about/around, horse about/around, lark about/around.
2 *someone's been mucking about with the video:* interfere, fiddle, play about/around, tamper, meddle, tinker; informal mess about/around.

mucky adjective *a pair of mucky boots:* dirty, filthy, grimy, muddy, grubby, messy, soiled, stained, smeared, slimy, sticky, bespattered.
OPPOSITES: clean.

mud noun mire, sludge, ooze, silt, dirt, soil.

muddle verb

1 *the papers have got muddled up:* mix up, jumble up, disarrange, disorganize, disorder, disturb, mess up.
2 *it would only muddle you:* bewilder, confuse, bemuse, perplex, puzzle, baffle, nonplus, mystify.
▷**noun**
1 *the files are in a muddle:* mess, confusion, jumble, tangle, hotchpotch, chaos, disorder, disarray, disorganization; informal mishmash.
2 *a bureaucratic muddle:* bungle, misunderstanding; informal mix-up, foul-up.
□ **muddle along/through**
we're muddling along as best we can: cope, manage, get by/along, scrape by/along, make do.

muddled adjective

1 *she felt muddled—she couldn't keep track:* confused, bewildered, bemused, perplexed, disorientated, disoriented, in a muddle, befuddled.
2 *the statement betrayed muddled thinking on the refugee issue:* incoherent, confused, muddle-headed, woolly.
3 *a muddled pile of photographs:* jumbled, in a muddle, in a mess, chaotic, in disorder, in disarray, topsy-turvy, disorganized, disordered, disorderly, mixed up, at sixes and sevens; informal higgledy-piggledy.

muddy adjective

1 *muddy ground:* waterlogged, boggy, marshy, swampy, squelchy, mucky, spongy, wet, soft, heavy.
2 *muddy boots:* mud-caked, muddied, dirty, filthy, mucky, grimy, soiled.
3 *muddy water:* dirty, murky, cloudy, muddied, turbid.
OPPOSITES: clean, clear.
▷**verb**
1 *the linoleum floor was muddied:* make muddy, dirty, soil, spatter, bespatter.
2 *these results muddy the situation:* make unclear, obscure, confuse, obfuscate, cloud.
OPPOSITES: clarify.

muff verb (informal) *the administration muffed several of its biggest projects:* mishandle, mismanage, mess up, make a mess of, bungle; informal botch, make a hash of, fluff, foul up.

muffle verb

1 *everyone was muffled up in coats:* wrap, wrap up, swathe, enfold, envelop, cloak.
2 *the sound of their footsteps was muffled:* deaden, dull, damp down, mute, soften, quieten, tone down, mask, stifle, smother.

muffled adjective *I heard muffled shouts:* indistinct, faint, muted, dull, soft, stifled, smothered.
OPPOSITES: loud.

m

mug noun *a china mug:* beaker, cup; tankard, glass, stein, flagon.
▷ **verb** (informal) *he was mugged by three youths:* assault, attack, set upon, beat up, rob.

muggy adjective *it was a hog, muggy evening:* humid, close, sultry, sticky, oppressive, airless, stifling, suffocating, stuffy, clammy, damp, heavy.
OPPOSITES: fresh.

mulish adjective *George could sometimes be rather mulish:* obstinate, stubborn, pig-headed, recalcitrant, inflexible, stiff-necked, intransigent, unyielding; Brit. informal bloody-minded, bolshie.

mull verb
□ **mull something over** *she sat there for a while, mulling things over:* ponder, consider, think over/about, reflect on, contemplate, turn over in your mind, chew over, give some thought to; formal cogitate on.

multicoloured adjective *multicoloured lights stretched across the bar:* kaleidoscopic, colourful, multicolour, many-coloured, many-hued, psychedelic, rainbow, jazzy, harlequin, polychromatic, varicoloured, variegated.
OPPOSITES: monochrome.

multifarious adjective *the multifarious local and ethnic traditions that are found in the USA:* diverse, many, numerous, various, varied, multiple, manifold, multitudinous, multifaceted, different, heterogeneous, miscellaneous, assorted.
OPPOSITES: homogeneous.

multiple adjective *words with multiple meanings:* numerous, many, various, different, diverse, several, manifold, multifarious.
OPPOSITES: single.

multiplicity noun *the demand for higher education depends on a multiplicity of different factors:* variety, range; abundance, mass, host, array, profusion; diversity, heterogeneity, plurality.

multiply verb
1 *their difficulties seem to be multiplying:* increase, grow, become more numerous, accumulate, proliferate, mount up, mushroom, snowball.
2 *the rabbits have multiplied:* breed, reproduce, procreate.
OPPOSITES: decrease.

multitude noun
1 *the island is home to a multitude of birds:* a lot, a great/large number, a great/large quantity, host, horde, mass, swarm, abundance, profusion; scores, quantities, droves; informal lots, loads, masses, stacks, heaps, tons, dozens, hundreds, thousands, millions.
2 *Father Peter addressed the multitude:* crowd, gathering, assembly, congregation, flock, throng, horde, mob; formal concourse.

3 *political power was in the hands of the multitude:* the (common) people, the populace, the masses, the rank and file, the commonalty, the plebeians; derogatory the hoi polloi, the mob, the proletariat, the common herd, the rabble, the proles, the plebs.

multitudinous adjective *the multitudinous stars:* numerous, many, abundant, profuse, prolific, copious, multifarious, innumerable, countless, infinite; literary numberless.

mumble verb *the old man shuffled away, mumbling to himself:* mutter, murmur, speak indistinctly, talk under your breath, speak sotto voce.

mumbo-jumbo noun *we prefer straight talk to bureaucratic mumbo-jumbo:* nonsense, gibberish, claptrap, rubbish, hocus-pocus; informal gobbledegook, double Dutch.

munch verb *he munched his sandwich:* chew, champ, chomp, masticate, crunch, eat.

mundane adjective
1 *I want some adventure, a life beyond this mundane suburban existence:* humdrum, dull, boring, tedious, monotonous, tiresome, wearisome, unexciting, uninteresting, uneventful, unvarying, unremarkable, repetitive, routine, ordinary, everyday, day-to-day, run-of-the-mill, workaday.
2 *the mundane world:* earthly, worldly, terrestrial, material, temporal, secular.
OPPOSITES: extraordinary, spiritual.

municipal adjective *land use is controlled by the municipal authorities:* civic, civil, metropolitan, urban, city, town, borough.
OPPOSITES: rural.

municipality noun *each municipality has its own quota of subsidy:* borough, town, city, district; Scottish burgh.

munificence noun *the institution has benefited from the munificence of private donors:* generosity, largesse, bountifulness, open-handedness, magnanimity, liberality, philanthropy, charitableness, beneficence.

munificent adjective *his munificent bequest had depleted the family fortune:* generous, bountiful, open-handed, magnanimous, philanthropic, princely, handsome, lavish, liberal, charitable, big-hearted, beneficent.
OPPOSITES: mean.

murder noun
1 *a brutal murder:* killing, assassination, execution; slaughter, butchery, massacre; manslaughter; N. Amer. homicide.
2 (informal) *driving there was murder:* hell, a nightmare, an ordeal, a trial, misery, torture, agony.

▷**verb** *someone tried to murder him:* kill, assassinate, execute, put to death, eliminate; butcher, slaughter, massacre, wipe out; informal bump off, do in, do away with, take out.

murderer noun killer, assassin, serial killer, butcher; informal hit man, hired gun.

murderous adjective
1 *the guerrillas carried out a number of murderous attacks in the region:* homicidal, brutal, violent, savage, ferocious, fierce, vicious, bloodthirsty, barbarous, barbaric.
2 (informal) *the team had a murderous schedule of four games in ten days:* arduous, gruelling, strenuous, punishing, onerous, exhausting, taxing, difficult, rigorous; informal killing, hellish.

murky adjective
1 *a murky winter afternoon:* dark, gloomy, grey, leaden, dull, dim, overcast, cloudy, clouded, sunless, dismal, dreary, bleak.
2 *murky water:* dirty, muddy, cloudy, turbid.
3 *a government minister with a murky past:* questionable, suspicious, suspect, dubious, dark, mysterious, secret; informal shady.
OPPOSITES: bright, clear.

murmur noun
1 *his voice was a murmur:* whisper, undertone, mutter, mumble.
2 *there were murmurs in Tory ranks:* complaint, grumble, grouse; informal gripe, moan.
3 *the distant murmur of traffic:* noise, sound, hum, humming, buzz, buzzing, thrum, thrumming, drone.
▷**verb**
1 *he heard them murmuring in the hall:* mutter, mumble, whisper, talk under your breath, speak softly, speak sotto voce.
2 *no one murmured at the delay:* complain, mutter, grumble, moan, grouse; informal gripe.
3 *the wind was murmuring through the trees:* rustle, sigh.

muscle noun
1 *he had muscle but no brains:* strength, power, muscularity, brawn, burliness; informal beef, beefiness.
2 *the company has considerable financial muscle:* influence, power, strength, might, force, forcefulness, weight; informal clout.

USAGE
Do not confuse **muscle** with **mussel**. A **muscle** is a tissue that moves a body part (*I've pulled a muscle in my leg*) and is also used to mean 'power, influence, or strength'. A **mussel** is a type of shellfish.

muscular adjective
1 *muscular tissue:* fibrous, sinewy.
2 *he's very muscular:* strong, brawny, muscly, sinewy, powerfully built, well muscled, burly, strapping, sturdy, powerful, athletic; informal hunky, beefy.

muse[1] noun *the poet's muse:* inspiration, creative influence, stimulus.

muse[2] verb *I mused on Toby's story:* ponder, consider, think over/about, mull over, reflect on, contemplate, turn over in your mind, chew over, give some thought to; think, be lost in contemplation/thought, daydream; formal cogitate on.

mush noun
1 *the flowers had been flattened to a sodden pink mush:* pulp, mass; paste, purée, mash; informal goo.
2 *the film's not just romantic mush:* sentimentality, pap; informal schmaltz, slush.

mushroom noun fungus.
▷**verb** *ecotourism mushroomed in the 1980s:* proliferate, grow/develop rapidly, burgeon, spread, increase, expand, boom, explode, snowball, rocket, skyrocket; thrive, flourish.

mushy adjective *cook until the fruit is mushy:* soft, semi-liquid, pulpy, sloppy, spongy, squelchy; informal squishy, gooey; Brit. informal squidgy.
OPPOSITES: firm.

musical adjective *they burst out into rich, musical laughter:* tuneful, melodic, melodious, harmonious, sweet-sounding, sweet, mellifluous, euphonious; often ironic dulcet.
OPPOSITES: discordant.

musician noun player, performer, instrumentalist, accompanist, soloist, virtuoso, maestro.

musing noun *his musing was interrupted by the sound of footsteps:* meditation, thinking, contemplation, deliberation, pondering, reflection, rumination, introspection, daydreaming, reverie, dreaming, preoccupation, brooding.

must verb *I must go:* ought to, should, have (got) to, need to, be obliged to, be required to, be compelled to.
▷**noun** (informal) *this video is a must:* not to be missed, very good; necessity, essential, requirement, requisite.

muster verb
1 *they mustered 50,000 troops:* assemble, mobilize, rally, raise, summon, gather together, mass, collect, convene, call up, call to arms, recruit, conscript; US draft.
2 *reporters mustered outside her house:* congregate, assemble, gather, come together, collect together, convene, mass, rally.
3 *she mustered her courage:* summon, summon up, screw up, call up, rally.
□ **pass muster**
be good enough, come up to standard, come up to scratch, measure up, be

m

acceptable/adequate, fill/fit the bill; informal make the grade.

musty adjective *the room smelled musty:* stale, fusty, damp, dank, mouldy, stuffy, airless, unventilated.
OPPOSITES: fresh.

mutant noun freak of nature, monstrosity, monster, mutation.

mutate verb *rhythm and blues mutated into rock and roll:* change, metamorphose, evolve; be transmuted, be transformed, be converted.

mutation noun change, alteration, variation; modification, transformation, metamorphosis, transmutation.

mute adjective
1 *Yasmin remained mute:* silent, speechless, dumb, unspeaking, tight-lipped, taciturn; informal mum.
2 *she gazed at him in mute appeal:* wordless, silent, dumb, unspoken, unvoiced, unexpressed.
▷ **verb**
1 *the noise was muted by the heavy curtains:* deaden, muffle, dampen, soften, quieten; stifle, smother, suppress.
2 *Bruce muted his criticisms:* restrain, soften, tone down, moderate, temper.
OPPOSITES: intensify.

muted adjective
1 *she could hear the muted hum of traffic:* muffled, faint, indistinct, quiet, soft, low.
2 *the landscape is painted in muted tones:* subdued, pastel, delicate, subtle, understated, restrained.

mutilate verb
1 *the bodies had been mutilated:* maim, disfigure, dismember, cut up, butcher, mangle; cripple.
2 *the carved screen had been mutilated:* vandalize, damage, deface, ruin, destroy, wreck.

mutinous adjective *mutinous troops seized three military bases:* rebellious, insubordinate, insurgent, insurrectionary, subversive, seditious, rebel, riotous.

mutiny noun *a mutiny over pay arrears spread to several sections of the armed forces:* rebellion, revolt, riot, uprising, insurrection, insurgence, insubordination.
▷ **verb** *thousands of soldiers mutinied:* rise up, rebel, revolt, riot, disobey/defy authority.

mutter verb
1 *a group of men stood muttering:* talk under your breath, murmur, mumble, whisper, speak in an undertone, speak sotto voce.
2 *backbenchers muttered about the reshuffle:* grumble, complain, moan, grouse, carp; informal gripe, beef, whinge.

mutual adjective *their partnership is based on mutual respect and understanding:* reciprocal, reciprocated; joint, shared, common; returned, requited.

muzzle noun *the dog's velvety muzzle:* snout, nose, mouth, maw.
▷ **verb** *attempts to muzzle the media failed:* gag, silence, keep silent, censor, stifle, restrain, check.

muzzy adjective
1 *she felt muzzy:* groggy, light-headed, faint, dazed, confused, befuddled, muddled; informal dopey, woozy.
2 *a slightly muzzy picture:* blurred, blurry, fuzzy, unfocused, unclear, ill-defined, foggy, hazy.
OPPOSITES: clear.

myopic adjective *the government still has a myopic attitude to public spending:* short-sighted, without foresight, short-term; unimaginative, unadventurous, narrow-minded.
OPPOSITES: far-sighted.

myriad (literary) noun *myriads of stars invisible to the naked eye:* multitude, mass, host, horde, scores, quantities, droves; informal lots, loads, masses, stacks, tons, hundreds, thousands, millions.
▷ **adjective** *the myriad lights of the city:* innumerable, countless, infinite, untold, unnumbered, immeasurable, multitudinous, numerous; literary numberless.

mysterious adjective
1 *he vanished in mysterious circumstances:* puzzling, strange, peculiar, curious, funny, queer, odd, bizarre, mystifying, inexplicable, baffling, perplexing, incomprehensible, unexplainable, unfathomable; informal weird.
2 *he was being very mysterious:* enigmatic, inscrutable, secretive, reticent, evasive, furtive, surreptitious.

mystery noun
1 *his death remains a mystery:* puzzle, enigma, conundrum, riddle, secret, unsolved problem.
2 *her past is shrouded in mystery:* secrecy, obscurity, uncertainty, mystique.
3 *a murder mystery:* thriller, detective story/novel; informal whodunnit.

mystical, mystic adjective
1 *a mystical experience:* spiritual, religious, transcendental, other-worldly, supernatural, occult, metaphysical.
2 *mystical rites:* symbolic, symbolical.
3 *a figure of mystical significance:* arcane, esoteric, hidden, inexplicable, unfathomable, mysterious, secret.

mystify verb *I was completely mystified by his disappearance:* bewilder, puzzle, perplex, baffle, confuse, confound, bemuse, nonplus, throw; informal flummox, stump, bamboozle, faze, fox.

mystique noun *a certain mystique still*

surrounds the family: charisma, glamour, romance, mystery, magic, charm, appeal, allure.

myth noun
1 *ancient Greek myths:* folk tale, folk story, legend, fable, saga; lore, folklore; technical mythos.
2 *the campaign seeks to dispel the myths surrounding this disease:* misconception, fallacy, false notion, old wives' tale, fiction; informal story.

mythical adjective
1 *mythical beasts:* legendary, mythological, fabled, folkloric, fabulous, fairy-tale, storybook; fantastical, imaginary, imagined, fictitious.
2 *her mythical child:* imaginary, fictitious, make-believe, fantasy, invented, made-up, non-existent; informal pretend.

mythological adjective *the tree of life is one of the oldest of all mythological symbols:* mythical, mythic, fabled, folkloric, legendary, traditional.

mythology noun myths, legends, folklore, folk tales/stories, lore, tradition; technical mythos.

m

Nn

nabob noun very rich person, tycoon, magnate, millionaire, billionaire, multimillionaire; informal fat cat.

nadir noun *that awful speech is likely to be seen as his political nadir:* the lowest point, the all-time low, the low watermark, the bottom, rock bottom; informal the pits.
OPPOSITES: zenith.

nag verb
1 *she's constantly nagging me:* pester, harass, badger, chivvy, hound, criticize, find fault with, moan at, grumble at; henpeck; informal hassle, give someone a hard time.
2 *a question that had been nagging him for weeks:* trouble, worry, bother, plague, torment, niggle, prey on your mind; annoy, irritate; informal bug, aggravate.

nagging adjective
1 *a nagging pain:* persistent, continuous, niggling, gnawing, lingering, unrelenting, unremitting.
2 *his nagging wife:* shrewish, complaining, sharp-tongued, critical, fault-finding, carping.

nail noun
1 *the panel is fastened on with nails:* tack, spike, pin, rivet; hobnail.
2 *her nails are too long:* fingernail, thumbnail, toenail; claw, talon.
▷verb fasten, attach, fix, affix, secure, tack, hammer, pin.

naive adjective innocent, unsophisticated, unrealistic, artless, ingenuous, inexperienced, guileless, unworldly, trusting, gullible, credulous, immature, callow, raw, green; informal wet behind the ears.
OPPOSITES: worldly.

naivety noun innocence, inexperience, ingenuousness, guilelessness, unworldliness, trustfulness; gullibility, credulousness, credulity, immaturity, callowness.

naked adjective
1 *a naked woman:* nude, bare, in the nude, stark naked, having nothing on, stripped, undressed, unclothed, in a state of nature; informal without a stitch on, in your

birthday suit, in the raw, in the buff, in the altogether; Brit. informal starkers.
2 *the naked truth | naked hostility:* undisguised, plain, unadorned, unvarnished, unqualified, stark, bald; overt, obvious, open, patent, palpable, evident, apparent, manifest, unmistakable, blatant.

nakedness noun nudity, state of undress, déshabillé, bareness.

namby-pamby adjective weak, feeble, ineffectual, spineless, effeminate, effete; informal wet, limp-wristed, weedy, wimpy, sissy.

name noun
1 *I've forgotten his name:* designation, title, honorific, tag, epithet, label; formal denomination, appellation, cognomen; informal moniker, handle.
2 *the good name of the firm:* reputation, character, repute, standing, stature, prestige, cachet, kudos; renown, popularity, notability, distinction.
▷verb
1 *the child was named Edward:* call, dub; label, style, term, title, entitle; baptize, christen.
2 *fear of assault was named as the main reason:* identify, specify, cite, mention, single out.
3 *Wilkinson was named as England captain:* choose, select, pick, decide on, nominate, designate, appoint.

named adjective
1 *a girl named Jasmine:* called, by the name of, baptized, christened, known as; dubbed, entitled, styled, termed, labelled.
2 *the policy applies only to named individuals:* specified, designated, identified, cited.

nameless adjective
1 *a nameless photographer:* unnamed, unidentified, anonymous, incognito, unspecified, unacknowledged, uncredited; unknown, unsung, uncelebrated.
2 *they were prone to nameless fears:* unspeakable, inexpressible, indescribable, unutterable; indefinable, vague, unspecified, unspecifiable.

namely adverb *he has something rare to*

offer, namely charisma: that is, i.e., to be specific, specifically, viz., to wit.

nanny noun childminder, au pair; dated nursemaid, governess.
▷ **verb** mollycoddle, baby, cosset, coddle, wrap in cotton wool, feather-bed; spoil, pamper, indulge, overindulge.

nap[1] noun *he's taking a nap upstairs:* rest, lie-down, catnap, siesta, doze, sleep; informal snooze, forty winks; Brit. informal kip.
▷ **verb** *the cat was napping in a patch of warm sunlight:* doze, drowse, rest, sleep, take a nap, catnap; informal snooze, snatch forty winks, get some shut-eye; Brit. informal kip.
□ **catch someone napping** (informal) *his free kick caught the Leeds defence napping:* catch off guard, catch unawares, surprise, take by surprise, catch out, find unprepared; Brit. informal catch on the hop.

nap[2] noun *the nap of the velvet:* pile, fibres, threads, weave, surface, grain.

narcissism noun vanity, conceit, self-love, self-admiration, self-absorption, self-obsession, self-centredness, self-regard, egotism, egoism.

narcissistic adjective vain, conceited, self-admiring, self-absorbed, self-obsessed, self-centred, self-regarding, egotistic, egotistical, egoistic.

narcotic noun sedative, soporific, tranquillizer, opiate; painkiller, analgesic, anaesthetic; informal downer.

narrate verb tell, relate, recount, describe, chronicle, report, set forth; voice-over.

narrative noun account, story, description, chronicle, history, record, report.

narrator noun
1 *the narrator of the 'Arabian Nights':* storyteller, chronicler; raconteur, anecdotalist.
2 *the documentary's narrator:* voice-over, commentator.
OPPOSITES: listener, audience.

narrow adjective
1 *her narrow waist:* small, slender, slim, thin, attenuated.
2 *a pair of narrow-legged trousers:* tapered, tapering.
3 *a narrow space:* confined, cramped, tight, restricted, limited, constricted.
4 *a narrow range of foods:* limited, restricted, circumscribed, small, inadequate, insufficient, deficient.
5 *a narrow view of the world* see NARROW-MINDED.
6 *nationalism in the narrowest sense of the word:* strict, literal, exact, precise.
7 *a narrow escape:* by a very small margin, close, by a hair's breadth; informal by a whisker.
OPPOSITES: wide, broad.

▷ **verb**
1 *the path narrowed:* get narrower, taper, shrink, contract, constrict.
2 *narrowing the gap between rich and poor:* reduce, make narrower, diminish, decrease, limit, shrink.

narrowly adverb
1 *one bullet narrowly missed him:* just, barely, scarcely, hardly, by a hair's breadth; informal by a whisker.
2 *she looked at me narrowly:* closely, carefully, searchingly, attentively, intently.

narrow-minded adjective intolerant, illiberal, reactionary, conservative, parochial, provincial, insular, small-minded, petty, blinkered, inward-looking, narrow, hidebound, prejudiced, bigoted; Brit. parish-pump.
OPPOSITES: tolerant, broad-minded.

nascent adjective *the country's nascent film industry:* budding, just beginning, developing, growing, embryonic, incipient, young, fledgling, evolving, emergent, dawning, burgeoning.

nastiness noun
1 *the nastiness of the subject matter:* unpleasantness, disagreeableness, offensiveness, vileness, foulness.
2 *her uncharacteristic nastiness towards him:* unkindness, unpleasantness, unfriendliness, disagreeableness, rudeness, churlishness, spite, spitefulness, malice, meanness, ill temper, viciousness, malevolence; informal bitchiness, cattiness.

nasty adjective
1 *a nasty smell:* unpleasant, disagreeable, disgusting, distasteful, awful, dreadful, horrible, horrid, terrible, vile, foul, revolting, repulsive, repellent, repugnant, horrendous, appalling, sickening, nauseating, atrocious, abominable, offensive, objectionable, obnoxious, frightful, loathsome, odious, unsavoury, unappetizing, off-putting; noxious, stinking, rank, fetid, malodorous, mephitic; informal ghastly, filthy, gruesome, diabolical, gross; N. Amer. informal lousy.
2 *she can be really nasty to him:* unkind, unpleasant, unfriendly, disagreeable, rude, spiteful, catty, malicious, mean, churlish, ill-tempered, vicious, malevolent, obnoxious, hateful, hurtful; informal bitchy.
3 *a nasty accident | a nasty cut:* serious, severe, dangerous, bad, awful, dreadful, terrible, ugly.
4 *they wrote nasty things on the wall:* obscene, indecent, offensive, crude, rude, dirty, filthy, vulgar, foul, gross, disgusting, pornographic, smutty, lewd; informal sick.
OPPOSITES: nice.

nation noun country, state, land, realm, kingdom, republic; fatherland, motherland; people, race.

n

national adjective
1 *national politics:* **state**, public, federal; civic, civil, domestic, internal.
2 *a national strike:* **nationwide**, countrywide, state, general, widespread.
▷noun *a French national:* **citizen**, subject, native; voter.

nationalism noun *the resurgence of nationalism in Europe:* **patriotism**; derogatory xenophobia, chauvinism, jingoism.

nationalistic adjective **patriotic**, nationalist; derogatory xenophobic, chauvinistic, jingoistic.

nationality noun
1 *in 1938 he took British nationality:* **citizenship**.
2 *the main nationalities of Ethiopia:* **ethnic group**, race, nation, tribe, clan.

nationwide adjective **national**, countrywide, state, general, widespread, extensive, coast to coast.
OPPOSITES: local.

native adjective
1 *the native population:* **indigenous**, original, first, earliest, aboriginal; Anthropology autochthonous.
2 *native produce | native plants:* **domestic**, home-grown, home-made, local; indigenous.
3 *a native instinct for politics:* **innate**, inherent, inborn, instinctive, intuitive, natural; hereditary, inherited.
4 *her native tongue:* **mother**, vernacular.
▷noun *a native of Sweden:* **inhabitant**, resident, local; citizen, national.
OPPOSITES: foreigner.

nativity noun **birth**, childbirth.

natural adjective
1 *a natural occurrence:* **normal**, ordinary, everyday, usual, regular, common, commonplace, typical, routine, standard, established, customary, accustomed, habitual.
2 *natural produce:* **unprocessed**, organic, pure, wholesome, unrefined, pesticide-free, additive-free.
3 *Alex is a natural leader:* **born**, naturally gifted, untaught.
4 *his natural instincts:* **innate**, inborn, inherent, native, instinctive, intuitive, in your blood; hereditary, inherited, congenital.
5 *she seemed very natural:* **unaffected**, spontaneous, uninhibited, relaxed, unselfconscious, genuine, open, artless, guileless, ingenuous, unpretentious, without airs.
6 *it was quite natural to think she admired him:* **reasonable**, logical, understandable, only to be expected, predictable.
OPPOSITES: abnormal, artificial, affected.

naturalism noun **realism**, verisimilitude, authenticity.

naturalist noun **natural historian**, life scientist; biologist, botanist, zoologist, ornithologist, entomologist, ecologist, conservationist, environmentalist.

naturalistic adjective *a naturalistic drama:* **realistic**, real-life, true-to-life, authentic, lifelike, graphic, representational, photographic; kitchen-sink.

naturalize verb
1 *he was naturalized in 1950:* **grant citizenship to**, make a citizen, give a passport to, enfranchise.
2 *coriander has now been naturalized in southern Britain:* **establish**, introduce, acclimatize, domesticate.

naturally adverb
1 *he's naturally shy:* **by nature**, by character, inherently, innately, congenitally.
2 *try to act naturally:* **normally**, in a natural manner/way, unaffectedly, spontaneously, genuinely, unpretentiously.
3 *naturally, they wanted everything kept quiet:* **of course**, as might be expected, needless to say; obviously, clearly.

naturalness noun **unselfconsciousness**, spontaneity, spontaneousness, straightforwardness, genuineness, openness, ingenuousness, lack of sophistication, unpretentiousness.

nature noun
1 *the beauty of nature:* **the natural world**, the environment, Mother Nature, Mother Earth; wildlife, flora and fauna, the countryside.
2 *such crimes are, by their very nature, difficult to hide:* **essence**, inherent/basic/essential qualities, inherent/basic/essential features, character, complexion.
3 *it was not in Daisy's nature to be bitchy:* **character**, personality, disposition, temperament, make-up, psyche, constitution.
4 *experiments of a similar nature:* **kind**, sort, type, variety, category, class, species, genre, style, cast, order, ilk, kidney, mould, stamp; N. Amer. stripe.

naughty adjective
1 *a naughty boy:* **badly behaved**, disobedient, bad, misbehaved, wayward, wilful, defiant, unruly, insubordinate, undisciplined, uncontrollable, ungovernable, disorderly, disruptive, fractious, recalcitrant, wild, obstreperous, difficult, troublesome, awkward, contrary, perverse, incorrigible; mischievous, playful, impish, roguish, rascally.
2 *naughty jokes:* **indecent**, risqué, rude, racy, ribald, bawdy, suggestive, improper, indelicate, indecorous; vulgar, dirty, filthy, smutty, crude, coarse, lewd, pornographic; euphemistic adult; informal blue, raunchy, saucy.
OPPOSITES: well behaved, decent.

n

nausea noun sickness, queasiness, biliousness; vomiting, retching, gagging.

nauseate verb turn someone's stomach, make someone's gorge rise, sicken, disgust, revolt; N. Amer. informal gross out.

nauseating adjective sickening, disgusting, revolting, repellent, repulsive, offensive, loathsome, obnoxious, odious, foul; stomach-churning, nauseous, emetic; informal sick-making, gross.

nauseous adjective sick, nauseated, queasy, bilious, ill, unwell; informal green about the gills.

nautical adjective maritime, marine, naval, seafaring; boating, sailing, yachting.

navel noun informal belly button, tummy button; Medicine umbilicus.

> WORD LINKS
> **umbilical** relating to the navel

navigable adjective passable, negotiable; clear, open, unobstructed, unblocked.

navigate verb
1 *he navigated the yacht across the Atlantic:* steer, pilot, guide, direct, helm, captain; informal skipper.
2 *the upper reaches are dangerous to navigate:* sail across/over, cross, traverse, negotiate.

navigation noun
1 *the skills of navigation:* helmsmanship, steersmanship, seamanship, map-reading.
2 *the navigation of the ship:* steering, piloting, sailing, guiding, directing, guidance.

navigator noun helmsman, steersman, pilot, guide.

navy noun fleet, flotilla, armada; squadron.

near adverb
1 *her children all live near:* close by, nearby, close/near at hand, in the neighbourhood, in the vicinity, at hand, within reach, on the doorstep, a stone's throw away; informal within spitting distance.
2 *near perfect conditions:* almost, nearly, practically, virtually; informal just about.
▷ **preposition** *a hotel near the seafront:* close to, close by, a short distance from, in the vicinity of, in the neighbourhood of, within reach of, a stone's throw away from; informal within spitting distance of.
▷ **adjective**
1 *the nearest house:* close, nearby, close/near at hand, at hand, a stone's throw away, within reach, accessible, handy, convenient; informal within spitting distance.
2 *the final judgement is near:* imminent, in the offing, close/near at hand, at hand, impending, looming; literary nigh.
3 *a near escape:* narrow, close, by a hair's

breadth; informal by a whisker.
OPPOSITES: far, far-off, distant.
▷ **verb**
1 *by dawn we were nearing Moscow:* approach, draw nearer to, get closer to, advance towards, close in on.
2 *the death toll is nearing 3,000:* verge on, border on, approach.

nearby adjective *a nearby village:* not far away, close/near at hand, close by, near, within reach, at hand, neighbouring; accessible, handy, convenient.
OPPOSITES: faraway.
▷ **adverb** *she lives nearby:* close by, close/near at hand, near, a short distance away, in the neighbourhood, in the vicinity, at hand, within reach, on the doorstep.

nearly adverb almost, more or less, practically, virtually, about, all but, as good as, not far off, well-nigh; not quite; informal pretty much, pretty well.

nearness noun
1 *the town's nearness to Rome:* closeness, proximity, propinquity; accessibility, handiness.
2 *the nearness of death:* imminence, closeness, immediacy.

neat adjective
1 *the room was neat and clean:* tidy, orderly, well ordered, in good order, spick and span, uncluttered, shipshape, in apple-pie order, straight, trim.
2 *the suspect had a neat appearance:* smart, well groomed, well turned out, spruce, trim, immaculate, dapper; informal natty, snappy.
3 *her neat writing:* well formed, regular, elegant, well proportioned.
4 *a neat little gadget:* compact, well designed, handy; Brit. informal dinky.
5 *his neat footwork:* skilful, deft, dexterous, adroit, adept, expert; informal nifty.
6 *a neat solution:* clever, ingenious, inventive, elegant, apt.
7 *he was drinking neat gin:* undiluted, straight, unmixed, pure; N. Amer. informal straight up.
OPPOSITES: untidy.

neaten verb tidy, tidy up, straighten, straighten up, smarten up, spruce up, put in order; N. Amer. informal fix up.

neatly adverb
1 *neatly arranged papers:* tidily, methodically, systematically; smartly, sprucely.
2 *the point was neatly put:* cleverly, aptly, elegantly.
3 *a neatly executed header:* skilfully, deftly, adroitly, adeptly, expertly.

neatness noun
1 *the neatness of the cottage:* tidiness, orderliness, order, trimness, spruceness; smartness.

n

2 *the neatness of her movements:* grace, gracefulness, nimbleness, skill, skilfulness, deftness, dexterity, adroitness, agility.

nebulous adjective

1 *nebulous concepts:* **vague**, ill-defined, unclear, hazy, uncertain, indefinite, indeterminate, amorphous, imprecise, muddled, confused, ambiguous.
2 *a nebulous figure:* **indistinct**, unclear, vague, hazy, cloudy, fuzzy, misty, blurred, blurry, foggy; faint, shadowy, obscure, formless.
OPPOSITES: clear.

necessarily adverb *an increase in the supply of money will not necessarily have much effect on spending:* **as a consequence**, as a result, automatically, as a matter of course, of necessity, by definition, certainly, surely, definitely, incontrovertibly, undoubtedly, inevitably, unavoidably, inescapably, ineluctably.

necessary adjective

1 *planning permission is necessary:* **obligatory**, requisite, required, compulsory, mandatory, imperative, needed, de rigueur; essential, indispensable, vital, needful.
2 *a necessary consequence of their actions:* **inevitable**, unavoidable, inescapable, inexorable, ineluctable; predetermined, preordained.

necessitate verb *such a level of public spending would necessitate tax increases:* **make necessary**, entail, involve, mean, require, demand, call for, be grounds for, warrant, force.

necessity noun

1 *air conditioning is a necessity in this climate:* **essential**, indispensable item, requisite, basic, prerequisite, sine qua non, desideratum; informal must.
2 *political necessity forced him to resign:* **force of circumstance**, obligation, need; force majeure; formal exigency.
3 *the necessity of growing old:* **inevitability**, certainty, inescapability, inexorability, ineluctability.
4 *necessity made them steal:* **poverty**, need, neediness, want, deprivation, privation, penury, destitution, indigence.
□ **of necessity**
necessarily, inevitably, unavoidably, inescapably; as a matter of course, naturally, automatically, certainly, surely, definitely, incontrovertibly, undoubtedly.

neck noun

□ **neck and neck**
level, equal, tied, side by side, nip and tuck; Brit. level pegging.

necklace noun chain, choker, necklet; beads, pearls; pendant, locket.

necromancer noun sorcerer, sorceress, wizard, warlock, witch, black magician, occultist.

necromancy noun sorcery, black magic, witchcraft, witchery, wizardry, the occult, occultism.

need verb

1 *they need money:* **require**, be in need of, have need of, want; be crying out for, be desperate for; demand, call for, entail, involve; lack, be without, be short of, could do with.
2 *you need to bring sheets:* **have to**, be obliged to, be compelled to, must.
3 *she needed him so much:* **yearn for**, pine for, long for, desire, miss; depend on, rely on.
▷ **noun**
1 *there's no need to apologize:* **necessity**, obligation, requirement, call, demand.
2 *basic human needs:* **requirement**, essential, necessity, want, requisite, prerequisite, demand, desideratum; formal exigency.
3 *my hour of need:* **difficulty**, trouble, distress; crisis, emergency, urgency, extremity.
□ **in need**
needy, deprived, disadvantaged, underprivileged, poor, impoverished, poverty-stricken, destitute, impecunious, indigent; Brit. on the breadline; formal necessitous.

needed adjective necessary, required, essential, requisite, compulsory, obligatory, mandatory; wanted, desired, lacking.
OPPOSITES: optional.

needle noun

1 *the virus is transmitted via needles:* **hypodermic needle**.
2 *put the needle on the record:* **stylus**.
3 *the needle on the meter barely moved:* **indicator**, pointer, marker, arrow, hand.

needless adjective *the needless destruction of wildlife habitats:* **unnecessary**, pointless, gratuitous, unneeded, unwanted, uncalled for, inessential, non-essential; dispensable, expendable, superfluous, redundant.
OPPOSITES: necessary.
□ **needless to say**
of course, as you would expect, not unexpectedly, it goes without saying, obviously, naturally.

needlework noun sewing, stitching, embroidery, needlepoint, needlecraft, tapestry.

needy adjective *the food went to needy families in the area:* **poor**, deprived, disadvantaged, underprivileged, in need, in straitened circumstances, poverty-stricken, indigent, impoverished, destitute, impecunious, penniless, pauperized; Brit. on the breadline; formal necessitous; informal hard up, broke, strapped for cash, cash-strapped, without two pennies to rub together, on your

n

uppers; Brit. informal skint, in Queer Street.
OPPOSITES: wealthy.

ne'er-do-well noun good-for-nothing, layabout, loafer, idler, shirker, sluggard, drone; informal waster, lazybones; Brit. informal skiver; N. Amer. informal bum.

nefarious adjective *the nefarious activities of bodysnatchers:* wicked, evil, sinful, iniquitous, heinous, vile, foul, abominable, odious, depraved, monstrous, fiendish, diabolical, unspeakable, despicable; villainous, criminal, corrupt, illegal, unlawful.

negate verb
1 *alcohol negates the effect of the drug:* neutralize, cancel out, nullify, undo, reverse.
2 *the supreme court attempted to negate the decision:* invalidate, annul, nullify, void, revoke, rescind, repeal, retract, countermand, overrule, overturn
3 *negating the political nature of education:* deny, dispute, contradict, refute, rebut, reject, repudiate; formal controvert.
OPPOSITES: validate, confirm.

negation noun
1 *evil is not just the negation of goodness:* opposite, reverse, antithesis, contrary, inverse, converse; absence, want.
2 *negation of the findings:* denial, contradiction, repudiation, refutation, rebuttal; nullification, revocation, repeal, retraction.

negative adjective
1 *a negative reply:* opposing, opposed, contrary, anti-, dissenting, dissentient; saying 'no', in the negative.
2 *stop being so negative:* pessimistic, defeatist, gloomy, cynical, jaundiced, fatalistic, dismissive; unenthusiastic, uninterested, unresponsive.
3 *a negative effect on the economy:* harmful, bad, adverse, damaging, detrimental, unfavourable, disadvantageous.
OPPOSITES: positive, optimistic, favourable.
▷ noun *he murmured a negative:* 'no', refusal, rejection, veto; contradiction, dissension; denial.

negativity noun pessimism, defeatism, gloom, cynicism, hopelessness, despair, despondency; apathy, indifference.

neglect verb
1 *he neglected his studies:* pay no attention to, let slide, not attend to, be remiss about, be lax about, leave undone, shirk, abandon, turn your back on.
2 *don't neglect our advice:* disregard, ignore, pay no attention to, take no notice of, pay no heed to, overlook; disdain, scorn, spurn.
3 *I neglected to inform her:* fail, omit, forget.
OPPOSITES: attend to, heed, remember.

▷ noun
1 *the place had an air of neglect:* disrepair, dilapidation, deterioration, shabbiness, disuse, abandonment.
2 *her doctor was guilty of neglect:* negligence, dereliction of duty, remissness, carelessness, heedlessness, laxity, slackness, irresponsibility; formal delinquency.
3 *the relative neglect of women:* disregard, ignoring, overlooking; inattention to, indifference to.
OPPOSITES: care, attention.

neglected adjective
1 *neglected animals:* uncared for, abandoned; mistreated, maltreated.
2 *a neglected cottage:* derelict, dilapidated, tumbledown, ramshackle, untended; overgrown.
3 *a neglected masterpiece:* disregarded, forgotten, overlooked, ignored, unrecognized, unnoticed, unsung, underestimated, undervalued, unappreciated.

neglectful adjective see NEGLIGENT.

negligent adjective *the council had been negligent in its supervision of the children in care:* remiss, careless, lax, irresponsible, neglectful, inattentive, thoughtless, unmindful; slack, sloppy; N. Amer. derelict.
OPPOSITES: dutiful.

negligible adjective trivial, trifling, insignificant, unimportant, minor, inconsequential; minimal, small, slight, inappreciable, infinitesimal, petty; paltry, inadequate, insufficient, meagre, pitiful; formal nugatory.
OPPOSITES: significant.

negotiable adjective
1 *the salary will be negotiable:* open to discussion, flexible, open to modification; unsettled, undecided, not set in stone.
2 *the path was negotiable on foot:* passable, navigable, crossable, traversable; clear, unblocked, unobstructed.

negotiate verb
1 *he was unwilling to negotiate with the union:* discuss terms, talk, consult, parley, confer, debate; compromise; mediate, intercede, arbitrate, moderate, conciliate; bargain, haggle.
2 *they negotiated a new contract:* arrange, broker, work out, hammer out, thrash out, agree on; settle, clinch, conclude, pull off, bring off, transact; informal sort out, swing.
3 *I negotiated the obstacles:* get round, get past, get over, clear, cross; surmount, overcome, deal with, cope with.

negotiation noun
1 *the negotiations resume next week:* discussions, talks, deliberations; conference, debate, dialogue, consultation; mediation, arbitration, conciliation.

2 *the negotiation of the deal:* arrangement, brokering; settlement, conclusion, completion, transaction.

negotiator noun mediator, arbitrator, arbiter, moderator, go-between, middleman, intermediary, conciliator; representative, spokesperson, broker.

neigh verb whinny, bray, nicker, snicker, whicker.

neighbourhood noun
1 *a quiet neighbourhood:* district, area, locality, locale, quarter, community; part, region, zone; Brit. informal neck of the woods; N. Amer. informal hood.
2 *in the neighbourhood of Canterbury:* vicinity, environs, purlieus, precincts.
□ **in the neighbourhood of**
the cost was believed to be in the neighbourhood of £4.5 million: approximately, about, around, roughly, in the region of, of the order of, nearly, almost, close to, just about, practically, there or thereabouts, circa; Brit. getting on for.

neighbouring adjective *the owner of the neighbouring property:* adjacent, adjoining, bordering, connecting, abutting; near, close at hand, next-door, nearby, in the vicinity; formal proximate.
OPPOSITES: remote.

neighbourly adjective obliging, helpful, friendly, kind, amiable, amicable, affable, genial, agreeable, hospitable, companionable, well disposed, civil, cordial, good-natured, nice, pleasant, generous; considerate, thoughtful, unselfish; Brit. informal decent.
OPPOSITES: unfriendly.

nemesis noun
1 *this could be the bank's nemesis:* downfall, undoing, ruin, ruination, destruction, Waterloo.
2 *the nemesis that his crime deserved:* retribution, vengeance, punishment, just deserts; fate, destiny.

neophyte noun *four-day cooking classes are offered to neophytes and experts:* beginner, learner, novice, newcomer, tyro; trainee, apprentice, probationer; initiate; informal rookie; N. Amer. informal tenderfoot, greenhorn.

nepotism noun favouritism, preferential treatment, the old boy network, looking after your own, bias, partiality, partisanship; Brit. jobs for the boys, the old school tie.
OPPOSITES: impartiality.

nerd noun (informal) bore; informal dork, dweeb, geek; Brit. informal anorak, trainspotter, spod, propeller-head.

nerve noun
1 *the match will be a test of nerve:* courage, bravery, pluck, boldness, fearlessness,

daring, intrepidity; confidence, assurance, cool-headedness, self-possession; determination, will power, spirit, backbone, fortitude, mettle, grit, stout-heartedness; informal guts, spunk; Brit. informal bottle.
2 (informal) *he had the nerve to chat her up:* audacity, cheek, effrontery, gall, temerity, presumption, boldness, brazenness, impudence, impertinence, arrogance, cockiness; informal face, front, brass neck, chutzpah.
3 *pre-wedding nerves:* anxiety, tension, nervousness, stress, worry, cold feet, apprehensiveness; informal butterflies in your stomach, collywobbles, the jitters, the shakes.
□ **get on someone's nerves**
irritate, annoy, irk, provoke, exasperate, infuriate, displease, vex, gall, pique, needle, try someone's patience; jar on, grate on, rankle with; Brit. rub the wrong way; informal aggravate, get to, bug, rile, nettle, hack off; Brit. informal wind up.
□ **nerve yourself**
brace yourself, steel yourself, summon your courage, gear yourself up, prepare yourself; fortify yourself; informal psych yourself up.

WORD LINKS
neural relating to nerves in the body
neuralgia pain along a nerve in the body
neurosurgery surgery performed on the nervous system

---

nerveless adjective
1 *her nerveless fingers:* inert, lifeless; weak, feeble.
2 *the 21-year-old's nerveless performance:* confident, self-confident, self-assured, self-possessed, cool, calm, {cool, calm, and collected}, composed, relaxed.
OPPOSITES: nervous.

nerve-racking adjective stressful, tense, worrying, fraught, nail-biting, traumatic, anxious, difficult, worrisome, daunting, frightening; informal scary, hairy.

nervous adjective
1 *a thin, nervous girl:* highly strung, neurotic, tense, excitable, jumpy, skittish; Brit. nervy.
2 *he was so nervous he couldn't eat:* anxious, apprehensive, on edge, edgy, tense, stressed, agitated, uneasy, worried, restless, worked up, keyed up, overwrought, jumpy; fearful, frightened, scared, shaky, in a cold sweat; informal with butterflies in your stomach, jittery, twitchy, in a state, uptight, wired, in a flap, het up; Brit. informal strung up.
3 *a nervous disorder:* neurological, neural.
OPPOSITES: relaxed, calm.

nervous breakdown noun mental collapse, breakdown, crisis, trauma; informal crack-up.

nervousness noun anxiety, edginess,

tension, agitation, stress, worry, apprehension, uneasiness, disquiet, fear, trepidation, alarm; Brit. nerviness; informal butterflies in your stomach, collywobbles, the jitters, the willies, the heebie-jeebies, the shakes.

nervy adjective see **NERVOUS** sense 1.

nest noun
1 *the birds have built a nest in the eaves:* roost, eyrie.
2 *a squirrels' nest:* lair, den, burrow, set.
3 *a cosy love nest:* hideaway, hideout, retreat, shelter, refuge, snuggery, den; informal hidey-hole.
4 *a nest of intrigue:* hotbed, den, breeding ground.

nest egg noun savings, cache, funds, reserve, something for a rainy day.

nestle verb snuggle, cuddle, curl up, huddle, nuzzle, settle, burrow.

nestling noun chick, fledgling, baby bird.

net¹ noun
1 *a mosquito net:* trap, snare.
2 *a piece of green net:* netting, meshwork, webbing, tulle, fishnet, openwork, lace.
▷ verb *they netted several criminals:* catch, capture, trap, snare, ensnare, entrap, bag, hook, land; informal nab, collar.

net² adjective
1 *net earnings:* after tax, after deductions, take-home, final; informal bottom line.
2 *the net result:* final, end, ultimate; overall, actual, effective.
OPPOSITES: gross.
▷ verb *she netted £50,000 from the sale:* earn, make, get, gain, obtain, acquire, accumulate, take home, bring in, pocket, realize, be paid; informal rake in.

nether adjective *the nether regions of the building:* lower, low, bottom, bottommost, under; underground.
OPPOSITES: upper.

nettle verb (informal) irritate, annoy, irk, gall, exasperate, infuriate, provoke, vex, anger; upset, displease, offend, affront, pique, get on someone's nerves, try someone's patience, rankle with; Brit. rub up the wrong way; informal aggravate, rile, needle, get to, bug, hack off; Brit. informal wind up.

network noun
1 *a network of arteries:* web, lattice, net, matrix, mesh, criss-cross, grid; technical reticulation.
2 *a network of lanes:* maze, labyrinth, warren, tangle.
3 *a network of friends:* system, complex, nexus, web.

neurosis noun mental illness, psychological disorder; psychoneurosis, psychopathy; obsession, phobia, fixation, complex.

neurotic adjective
1 (Medicine) *neurotic patients:* mentally ill, mentally disturbed, unstable, unbalanced, maladjusted.
2 *a neurotic, self-obsessed woman:* highly strung, overanxious, oversensitive, nervous, tense, paranoid; obsessive, fixated, hysterical, overwrought, irrational; Brit. nervy.
OPPOSITES: stable, calm.

neuter adjective asexual, sexless, unsexed; androgynous, epicene.
▷ verb sterilize, castrate, spay, geld, cut, fix, desex; Brit. informal doctor.

neutral adjective
1 *he found it impossible to be politically neutral:* impartial, unbiased, unprejudiced, objective, open-minded, non-partisan, uncommitted, disinterested, dispassionate, detached, impersonal, unemotional, indifferent.
2 *Switzerland remained neutral during the war:* unaligned, non-aligned, unaffiliated, unallied, uninvolved; non-combatant.
3 *a neutral topic of conversation:* inoffensive, bland, unobjectionable, unexceptionable, anodyne, unremarkable, ordinary, commonplace; safe, harmless, innocuous.
4 *a neutral background:* pale, light; beige, cream, taupe, oatmeal, ecru, buff, fawn, grey; colourless, achromatic; nondescript, dull, drab.
OPPOSITES: biased, partisan, provocative.

neutralize verb counteract, offset, counterbalance, balance, counterpoise, compensate for, make up for; cancel out, nullify, negate; equalize.

never adverb
1 *his room is never tidy:* not ever, at no time, not at any time.
2 *she will never agree:* under no circumstances, on no account; informal no way, not on your life, not in a million years.
OPPOSITES: always.

never-ending adjective incessant, continuous, unceasing, ceaseless, constant, continual, perpetual, uninterrupted, unbroken, steady, unremitting, relentless, persistent, interminable, non-stop, endless, unending, everlasting, eternal.

nevertheless adverb nonetheless, even so, however, but, still, yet, though; in spite of that, despite that, be that as it may, for all that, that said, just the same, all the same; notwithstanding, regardless, anyway, anyhow.

new adjective
1 *new technology:* modern, current, contemporary, up to date, latest, recent, advanced, state-of-the-art, cutting-edge, innovative, experimental, modernist, unconventional, avant-garde, futuristic; derogatory newfangled; informal trendy.

n

2 *we need some new ideas:* novel, original, fresh, imaginative, creative.
3 *a new car:* unused, brand new, pristine, in mint condition, fresh.
4 *a new job with new responsibilities:* different, another, alternative; additional, extra, further, more, supplementary.
5 *he's new to this job:* inexperienced, unaccustomed, unfamiliar, untried, a stranger.
6 *she came back a new woman:* rejuvenated, revitalized, restored, revived, refreshed, reinvigorated, renewed, improved.
OPPOSITES: old, hackneyed, second-hand.

> WORD LINKS
> **neophobia** fear or dislike of anything new or unfamiliar

newborn noun young baby, infant; Medicine neonate.

newcomer noun
1 *a newcomer to the village:* new arrival, incomer, settler, immigrant; stranger, outsider, foreigner, alien; N. English offcomer; informal johnny-come-lately, new kid on the block.
2 *photography tips for the newcomer:* beginner, novice, learner, neophyte, tyro; trainee, apprentice, probationer; initiate; informal rookie; N. Amer. informal tenderfoot, greenhorn.

newfangled adjective new, the latest, modern, ultra-modern, state-of-the-art, advanced, contemporary; gimmicky; informal trendy.
OPPOSITES: old-fashioned.

newly adverb recently, just, lately, freshly; not long ago, a short time ago, only now, of late.

news noun report, announcement, story, account; article, news flash, newscast, headlines, press release, communication, communiqué, bulletin; message, dispatch, statement, intelligence; disclosure, revelation, word, talk, gossip; literary tidings; informal scoop.

newspaper noun paper, journal, news-sheet, gazette, periodical, organ; tabloid, broadsheet; Brit. red top; informal rag.

newsworthy adjective *a horde of reporters on the trail of a potentially newsworthy story:* interesting, topical, notable, noteworthy, important, significant, momentous, historic, remarkable, sensational.
OPPOSITES: unremarkable.

next adjective
1 *the next chapter:* following, succeeding, upcoming, to come.
2 *the next house:* neighbouring, adjacent, adjoining, next-door, bordering, connected, attached, contiguous; closest, nearest.
OPPOSITES: previous.

▷ **adverb** *what happened next?* then, after, afterwards, later, subsequently.
OPPOSITES: before.

□ **next to**
beside, by, alongside, by the side of, next door to, adjacent to, side by side with; close to, near, neighbouring, adjoining.

nibble verb
1 *he nibbled a biscuit:* eat, munch, pick at, snack on, chew, gnaw, peck at; toy with; taste, sample; informal graze on.
2 *the mouse nibbled his finger:* bite, nip.
▷ **noun** *drinks and nibbles available from 6 p.m.:* snack, titbit, canapé, hors d'oeuvre.

nice adjective
1 *have a nice time:* enjoyable, pleasant, agreeable, good, satisfying, gratifying, pleasurable, delightful, lovely, marvellous; entertaining, amusing, diverting; informal great, fun; N. Amer. informal neat.
2 *he's such a nice guy:* pleasant, likeable, agreeable, personable, congenial, amiable, affable, kind, good-natured, genial, friendly, charming, delightful, engaging; sympathetic, compassionate, good.
3 *nice manners:* polite, courteous, civil, refined, polished, genteel, elegant.
4 *it's a nice day:* fine, pleasant, clement, beautiful; dry, sunny, warm, mild.
5 *that's a rather nice distinction:* subtle, fine, delicate, minute, precise, strict, close; careful, meticulous, scrupulous.
OPPOSITES: unpleasant, nasty.

nicety noun *they will not be deterred by legal niceties:* subtlety, fine point, nuance, refinement, detail; (**niceties**) minutiae.

niche noun
1 *a niche in the wall:* recess, alcove, hollow, bay, cavity, cubbyhole, pigeonhole.
2 *I finally found my niche in life:* ideal position, place, role, function, vocation, calling, métier, job.

nick noun *a slight nick in the blade:* cut, scratch, incision, snick, notch, chip; dent, indentation.
▷ **verb** *I nicked my toe:* cut, scratch, snick, chip, dent.

nickname noun sobriquet, tag, label, epithet; pet name, diminutive; formal cognomen; informal moniker.

nifty adjective (informal)
1 *nifty camerawork:* skilful, deft, agile, capable, adroit, slick.
2 *a nifty little gadget:* useful, handy, practical.
3 *a nifty suit:* fashionable, stylish, smart.
OPPOSITES: clumsy.

niggardly adjective
1 *a niggardly person:* mean, miserly, parsimonious, close-fisted, penny-pinching, cheese-paring, grasping; informal stingy, tight, tight-fisted.
2 *niggardly rations:* meagre, inadequate,

scanty, scant, skimpy, paltry, sparse, insufficient, deficient, short, lean, small, slender, poor, miserable, pitiful, puny; informal measly, stingy.
OPPOSITES: generous.

niggle verb
1 *his behaviour does niggle me:* irritate, annoy, exasperate, gall, irk, rankle with, upset, bother; informal rile, get to, bug.
2 *they've been niggling at each other for weeks:* complain, criticize, moan, carp, grumble, grouse, cavil; informal nit-pick.
▷ noun *they had some niggles about the lack of equipment:* complaint, criticism, grumble, grouse, cavil, quibble; informal gripe, moan, beef, grouch.

niggling adjective *niggling doubts:* persistent, nagging, lingering, irritating, annoying.

night noun night-time; hours of darkness, dark.
OPPOSITES: day.
▢ night and day
all the time, around the clock, {morning, noon, and night}, {day in, day out}, ceaselessly, endlessly, incessantly, unceasingly, interminably, constantly, perpetually, continually, relentlessly; informal 24-7.

> WORD LINKS
> **nocturnal** relating to night or active at night

nightclub noun disco, discotheque, club, bar; informal nightspot, niterie.

nightfall noun sunset, sundown, dusk, twilight, evening, close of day, dark; literary the gloaming.
OPPOSITES: dawn.

nightmare noun
1 *she woke screaming from a nightmare:* bad dream, night terrors.
2 *the nightmare began when the two raiders forced their way into the house:* ordeal, trial, torture, torment, horror, hell, misery, agony; curse, bane of your life; informal murder.

nightmarish adjective horrific, terrifying, spine-chilling, hair-raising, macabre, surreal, hideous, unspeakable, gruesome, grisly, ghastly, harrowing, disturbing, dreadful, terrible; informal scary, creepy.

nihilistic adjective negative, bleak, black, pessimistic, cynical, sceptical, jaundiced.

nil noun nothing, none; nought, zero, o; Tennis love; Cricket a duck.

nimble adjective
1 *he was nimble on his feet:* agile, light, quick, graceful, lithe, lively, sprightly, spry; skilful, deft, dexterous, adroit; informal nippy, twinkle-toed.
2 *a nimble mind:* quick-witted, quick, alert, lively, wide awake, observant, astute, perceptive, penetrating, discerning,

shrewd, sharp; intelligent, bright, clever, brilliant; informal smart, brainy, quick on the uptake.
OPPOSITES: clumsy, dull.

nip verb
1 *one of the dogs nipped her leg:* bite, peck; pinch, tweak, squeeze, grip.
2 (Brit. informal) *I'm just nipping out:* go, run, rush, dash, hurry, scurry; informal pop, whip.
▢ nip something in the bud
stop, check, curb, thwart, frustrate, halt, arrest, stifle, obstruct, block, squash, quash, subdue, stamp out; informal crack down on, put the kibosh on.

nippy adjective (informal)
1 *a nippy hatchback:* fast, quick, speedy; informal zippy.
2 *a nippy scrum half:* agile, light-footed, nimble, light on your feet, fleet of foot; informal twinkle-toed.
3 *it's a bit nippy in here:* cold, chilly, icy, bitter, raw.
OPPOSITES: slow, warm.

nirvana noun paradise, heaven; bliss, ecstasy, joy, peace, serenity, tranquillity.
OPPOSITES: hell.

nit-picking adjective (informal) see PEDANTIC.

nitty-gritty noun (informal) basics, essentials, essence, fundamentals, substance, quintessence, heart of the matter; nub, crux, gist, meat; informal brass tacks, nuts and bolts.

no adverb absolutely not, of course not, under no circumstances, by no means, not at all, negative, never; informal no way, nope, not on your life.
OPPOSITES: yes.

nobility noun
1 *a member of the nobility:* aristocracy, aristocrats, peerage, peers of the realm, lords, nobles, noblemen, noblewomen, patricians.
2 *the nobility of his deed:* virtue, goodness, honour, decency, integrity; magnanimity, generosity, selflessness.

noble adjective
1 *a noble family:* aristocratic, patrician, blue-blooded, high-born, titled.
2 *a noble cause | noble deeds:* good, virtuous, righteous, honourable, upright, decent, worthy, moral, ethical, reputable; magnanimous, generous, unselfish, self-sacrificing.
3 *a noble pine forest:* magnificent, splendid, grand, stately, imposing, dignified, proud, striking, impressive, majestic, glorious, awesome, monumental, statuesque, regal, imperial.
OPPOSITES: humble, dishonourable, base.
▷ noun *the king imposed a tax on both nobles and peasants:* aristocrat, nobleman, noblewoman, lord, lady, peer, peeress, patrician.

n

nocturnal adjective active at night, happening at night, night, night-time, nightly.
OPPOSITES: diurnal.

nod verb
1 *she nodded her head:* incline, bob, bow, dip, wag.
2 *he nodded to me to start:* signal, gesture, gesticulate, motion, sign, indicate.
▷noun
1 *she gave a nod to the manager:* signal, indication, sign, cue; gesture.
2 *a quick nod of his head:* inclination, bob, bow, dip.
□**give someone/thing the nod** (informal)
1 *the Dutch winger was given the nod:* select, choose, pick, go for; Brit. cap.
2 *the Lords will give the treaty the nod:* approve, agree to, sanction, ratify, endorse, rubber-stamp; informal OK, give something the green light, give something the thumbs up.
□**nod off**
fall asleep, go to sleep, doze off, drop off; informal drift off, flake out, go out like a light.

node noun *the intersection of two or more such highways would become major traffic nodes:* junction, intersection, interchange, fork, confluence, convergence, crossing.

noise noun *I was woken by a terrible noise at around 1 a.m.:* sound, din, hubbub, clamour, racket, uproar, tumult, commotion, pandemonium, babel; Brit. row; Brit. informal hullabaloo.
OPPOSITES: silence.

noisy adjective
1 *the noisy revving of jet engines:* loud, blaring, booming, deafening, thunderous, tumultuous, ear-splitting, piercing, strident, cacophonous, raucous; Music fortissimo.
2 *a noisy group of children:* rowdy, clamorous, boisterous, rackety; chattering, talkative, vociferous.
OPPOSITES: quiet, soft.

nomad noun itinerant, traveller, migrant, wanderer, roamer, rover; transient, drifter, vagabond, vagrant, tramp.

nomadic adjective *nomadic tribes | a nomadic lifestyle:* itinerant, travelling, wandering, migrant, migratory, roaming, roving, peripatetic; vagrant.

nominal adjective
1 *the nominal head of the campaign:* in name only, titular, formal, official; theoretical, supposed, ostensible, so-called.
2 *we only pay a nominal rent:* token, symbolic; tiny, minute, minimal, small, insignificant, trifling; Brit. peppercorn.
OPPOSITES: real, considerable.

nominate verb
1 *you may nominate a candidate for leader:* propose, recommend, suggest, name, put forward, present, submit.
2 *the company nominated her as a delegate:* appoint, select, choose, elect, commission, designate, name.

non-believer noun unbeliever, sceptic, doubter, doubting Thomas, cynic, nihilist; atheist, agnostic, freethinker; infidel, pagan, heathen.

nonchalant adjective calm, composed, unconcerned, cool, {cool, calm, and collected}, cool as a cucumber; indifferent, blasé, dispassionate, apathetic, casual, insouciant; informal laid-back.
OPPOSITES: anxious.

non-combatant adjective non-fighting, non-participating, civilian; pacifist, neutral, non-aligned.

non-committal adjective evasive, equivocal, guarded, circumspect, reserved; vague, uncommunicative, tactful, discreet, diplomatic; informal cagey.
□**be non-committal**
prevaricate, give nothing away, dodge the issue, sidestep the issue, hedge, fence, beat about the bush, equivocate, temporize, vacillate, waver; Brit. hum and haw; informal pussyfoot around, sit on the fence, shilly-shally.

nonconformist noun dissenter, dissident, protester, rebel; freethinker, apostate, heretic, iconoclast, renegade; individualist, free spirit, maverick, eccentric.

nondescript adjective undistinguished, unremarkable, unexceptional, featureless, characterless, unmemorable; ordinary, commonplace, average, run-of-the-mill, mundane; uninteresting, uninspiring, colourless, bland; informal bog-standard; Brit. informal common or garden.
OPPOSITES: distinctive.

nonentity noun *he was widely regarded as a political nonentity:* nobody, unimportant person, cipher, non-person, nothing, small fry, lightweight, mediocrity; informal no-hoper, non-starter.
OPPOSITES: celebrity.

non-essential adjective unnecessary, inessential, unessential, needless, unneeded, superfluous, redundant, dispensable, expendable, unimportant, extraneous.

nonetheless adverb nevertheless, even so, however, but, still, yet, though; in spite of that, despite that, be that as it may, for all that, that said, just the same, all the same; notwithstanding, regardless, anyway, anyhow.

non-existent adjective imaginary, imagined, unreal, fictional, fictitious, made up, invented, fanciful, mythical; illusory, hallucinatory, chimerical, notional, shadowy, insubstantial; missing, absent.
OPPOSITES: real.

n

non-intervention noun laissez-faire, non-participation, non-interference, inaction, passivity, neutrality; live and let live.

non-observance noun infringement, breach, violation, contravention, transgression, non-compliance, infraction; dereliction, neglect.

nonplussed adjective surprised, taken aback, disconcerted, confused, thrown, at a loss, puzzled, bemused, perplexed, baffled, bewildered; informal fazed, flummoxed.

nonsense noun
1 *he was talking nonsense:* rubbish, garbage, balderdash, gibberish, claptrap, blather; informal rot, drivel, hogwash, guff, baloney, tripe, gobbledegook, bilge, hot air, poppycock, twaddle; Brit. informal codswallop, tosh, double Dutch.
2 *she stands no nonsense:* mischief, naughtiness, bad behaviour, misbehaviour, misconduct, misdemeanour; pranks, tricks, clowning, buffoonery, funny business; informal tomfoolery, monkey business, shenanigans.
3 *they dismissed the concept as a nonsense:* absurdity, folly, stupidity, inanity, foolishness, idiocy, insanity, madness.
OPPOSITES: sense, wisdom.

nonsensical adjective foolish, stupid, idiotic, illogical, irrational, senseless, absurd, silly, inane, ridiculous, ludicrous, preposterous, insane; informal crazy, crackpot, hare-brained, nutty; Brit. informal daft.
OPPOSITES: logical, sensible.

non-stop adjective *non-stop entertainment:* continuous, constant, continual, perpetual, incessant, unceasing, ceaseless, uninterrupted, round-the-clock; unremitting, relentless, persistent.
OPPOSITES: occasional.
▷ adverb *we worked non-stop:* continuously, continually, incessantly, unceasingly, ceaselessly, all the time, constantly, perpetually, round the clock, steadily, relentlessly, persistently; informal 24-7.
OPPOSITES: occasionally.

nook noun *a Tudor-style home, full of nooks and crannies:* quiet corner, recess, alcove, niche, bay, inglenook, cavity, cranny, cubbyhole, pigeonhole; opening, gap; hideaway, hiding place, hideout; informal hidey-hole.

noon noun midday, twelve o'clock, twelve hundred hours, twelve noon, high noon, noonday.

norm noun
1 (the norm) *long tailbacks on this stretch of road are now the norm:* standard, usual, the rule, normal, typical, average, unexceptional, expected.
2 *norms of diplomatic behaviour:* convention, standard; criterion, yardstick, benchmark, touchstone, rule, formula, pattern, guide, guideline, model, exemplar.

normal adjective
1 *you should apply in the normal way:* usual, standard, customary, ordinary, conventional, habitual, accustomed, expected; typical, stock, common, everyday, regular, routine, established, set, fixed, traditional; literary wonted.
2 *they're just a normal couple:* ordinary, average, typical, run-of-the-mill, middle-of-the-road, common, conventional, mainstream, unremarkable, unexceptional; N. Amer. garden-variety; informal bog-standard; Brit. informal common or garden.
3 *the man was not normal:* sane, in your right mind, right in the head, of sound mind, compos mentis, lucid, rational, coherent; informal all there.
OPPOSITES: unusual, insane.

normality noun *we are beginning to see some semblance of normality returning to the city:* routine, business as usual, the daily round, order, regularity.

normally adverb
1 *normally we'd keep quiet about this:* usually, ordinarily, as a rule, generally, in general, mostly, for the most part, by and large, mainly, most of the time, on the whole; typically, customarily, traditionally.
2 *she was behaving normally:* naturally, conventionally; as usual, as normal.

northern adjective *the northern coasts of Europe:* north, northerly; polar, Arctic; technical boreal.

nose noun
1 *a punch on the nose:* snout, muzzle, trunk, proboscis; informal conk, hooter, schnozzle.
2 *a journalist with a nose for a good story:* instinct, feeling, sixth sense, intuition, insight, perception.
3 *a dry wine with a fruity nose:* smell, bouquet, aroma, fragrance, perfume, scent, odour.
4 *the plane's nose dropped:* nose cone, bow, prow, front end.
▷ verb
1 *he nosed the car into the traffic:* ease, inch, edge, move, manoeuvre, steer, guide.
2 *she's always nosing into my business:* pry, inquire, poke about/around, interfere in, meddle in; be a busybody, stick/poke your nose in; informal snoop.
3 *the dog nosed the ball:* nuzzle, nudge, push.
▯ **nose around/about** investigate, explore, ferret about/around, rummage, search; delve into, peer into; prowl around; informal snoop about/around.

WORD LINKS
nasal, **rhinal** relating to the nose

nosedive noun *the company is experiencing a nosedive in sales and profits:*

n

fall, descent, decline, drop, plunge, plummet.
OPPOSITES: upturn, rise.
▷**verb** *prices nosedived after the market collapsed:* **plummet**, fall, plunge, decline, drop.
OPPOSITES: soar, rise.

nosegay noun **posy**, bouquet, bunch, spray, sprig, buttonhole, corsage.

nostalgia noun *I was overcome with nostalgia for my first days in Italy:* **longing**, yearning, wistfulness, homesickness; reminiscence, remembrance; sentimentality.

nostalgic adjective *nostalgic memories of childhood:* **wistful**, sentimental, dewy-eyed, romantic, longing, yearning; regretful, maudlin.

nostrum noun *right-wing nostrums such as cutting public spending:* **panacea**, cure-all, magic formula, recipe for success, remedy, prescription, answer; informal silver bullet.

nosy adjective (informal) **prying**, inquisitive, curious, busybody, spying, eavesdropping, intrusive; informal snooping.

notability noun **noteworthiness**, prominence, importance, significance, eminence; fame, renown, notoriety.

notable adjective
1 *a notable example of the neoclassical style:* **noteworthy**, remarkable, outstanding, important, significant, memorable; marked, striking, impressive; unusual, special, exceptional.
2 *a notable author:* **prominent**, important, well known, famous, famed, noted, distinguished, great, eminent, illustrious, respected, esteemed, renowned, celebrated, acclaimed, influential, prestigious, of note.
OPPOSITES: unremarkable, unknown.
▷**noun** *movie stars and other notables:* **celebrity**, public figure, VIP, personage, dignitary, worthy, luminary; star, superstar, big name; informal celeb, somebody, bigwig, big shot; dated notability.
OPPOSITES: nonentity.

notably adverb
1 *other countries, notably the USA:* **in particular**, particularly, especially, specially; primarily, principally.
2 *he has been a notably successful chairman:* **remarkably**, especially, specially, very, extremely, exceptionally, singularly, particularly, peculiarly, distinctly, significantly, unusually, extraordinarily, uncommonly, incredibly, really, decidedly, surprisingly, conspicuously.

notation noun
1 *the formula is written in algebraic notation:* **symbols**, alphabet, script; code, cipher, hieroglyphics.

2 *there were several notations in the margin:* **annotation**, jotting, comment, footnote, entry, memo, gloss, explanation.

notch noun
1 *a notch in the end of the arrow:* **nick**, cut, incision, score, scratch, slit, snick, slot, groove, cleft, indentation.
2 *her opinion of Nick dropped a notch:* **degree**, level, rung, point, mark, measure, grade.
▢**notch something up**
score, achieve, attain, gain, earn, make; rack up, chalk up; register, record.

note noun
1 *she made a note in her diary:* **record**, entry, reminder, memo, memorandum, aide-memoire; notation, jotting.
2 *he will take notes of the meeting:* **minutes**, record, details; report, account, commentary, transcript, proceedings; synopsis, summary, outline.
3 *see note iv below:* **annotation**, footnote, comment, gloss; marginalia, exegesis.
4 *he dropped me a note:* **message**, communication, letter, line, memo.
5 (Brit.) *a £20 note:* **banknote**; N. Amer. bill; US informal greenback.
6 *there was a note of hopelessness in her voice:* **tone**, intonation, inflection, sound; hint, indication, sign, element, suggestion.
▷**verb**
1 *please note the following amendments to the timetable:* **bear in mind**, be mindful of, consider; observe, heed, notice, take notice of, pay attention to, take in.
2 *the letter noted the ministers' concern:* **mention**, refer to, touch on, indicate, point out, make known, state.
3 *note the date in your diary:* **write down**, put down, jot down, take down, inscribe, enter, mark, record, register, pencil.
▢**of note**
a composer of note: **distinguished**, important, eminent, famous, well known, acclaimed, renowned, celebrated, prestigious, illustrious, great.

notebook noun **notepad**, exercise book; logbook, log, diary, daybook, journal, record; Brit. jotter, pocketbook.

noted adjective *a noted Australian painter:* **renowned**, well known, famous, famed, prominent, celebrated; notable, of note, important, eminent, distinguished, illustrious, acclaimed, esteemed, of distinction, of repute.
OPPOSITES: unknown.

noteworthy adjective **notable**, interesting, significant, important, worth mentioning; remarkable, impressive, striking, outstanding, memorable, unique, special; unusual, extraordinary, singular, rare.
OPPOSITES: unexceptional.

nothing pronoun
1 *there's nothing I can do:* **not a thing**, not

anything, nil, zero; informal zilch, sweet
Fanny Adams, sweet FA.
2 *the share value fell to nothing:* zero,
nought, o; Tennis love; Cricket a duck.
▫ **be nothing to do with**
1 *his departure has nothing to do with
money:* be unconnected with, be unrelated
to; be irrelevant to, be inapplicable to, be
inapposite to.
2 *I'll have nothing to do with him:* avoid,
have no truck with, have no contact with,
steer clear of, give a wide berth to.
▫ **for nothing**
1 *she hosted the show for nothing:* free of
charge, gratis, without charge, at no cost;
informal for free, on the house.
2 *all this trouble for nothing:* in vain, to
no avail, to no purpose, with no result,
needlessly, pointlessly.
▫ **nothing but**
he's nothing but trouble: merely, only, just,
solely, simply, purely, no more than.

notice noun
1 *nothing escaped his notice:* attention,
observation, awareness, consciousness,
perception; regard, consideration, scrutiny;
watchfulness, vigilance, attentiveness.
2 *a notice on the wall:* poster, bill, handbill,
advertisement, announcement, bulletin;
flyer, leaflet, pamphlet; sign, card; informal
ad, advert.
3 *times may change without notice:*
notification, advance warning,
announcement; information, news,
communication, word.
4 *I handed in my notice:* resignation.
5 *the film got bad notices:* review, write-up,
critique, criticism; Brit. informal crit.
▷ **verb** *I noticed that the youths were behaving
suspiciously:* observe, become aware, note,
see, perceive, discern, detect, spot, mark,
remark; Brit. informal clock.
OPPOSITES: overlook.
▫ **take no notice of**
he took no notice of her remarks: ignore,
pay no attention to, disregard, pay no heed
to, take no account of, brush aside, shrug
off, turn a blind eye to, pass over, let go,
overlook, look the other way.

noticeable adjective distinct, evident,
obvious, apparent, manifest, patent,
plain, clear, marked, conspicuous,
unmistakable, undeniable, pronounced,
prominent, striking, arresting; perceptible,
discernible, detectable, observable, visible,
appreciable.
OPPOSITES: imperceptible.

noticeboard noun pinboard, cork board,
bulletin board; hoarding.

notification noun
1 *she received notification that he was
on the way:* information, word, advice,
news, intelligence; communication,
message.
2 *the notification of the victim's wife:*
informing, telling, alerting.

notify verb
1 *we will notify you as soon as possible:*
inform, tell, advise, let someone know, put
someone in the picture, apprise of; alert,
warn.
2 *births should be notified to the registrar:*
report, make known, announce, declare,
communicate, disclose.

notion noun
1 *deep-rooted notions about gender:*
idea, belief, conviction, opinion, view,
thought, impression, perception;
hypothesis, theory; feeling, suspicion,
hunch.
2 *Claire had no notion of what he could
have meant:* understanding, idea,
awareness, knowledge, clue, inkling.
3 *he got a notion to return:* impulse,
inclination, whim, desire, wish, fancy.

notional adjective *the scenario is purely
notional:* hypothetical, theoretical,
speculative, conjectural, suppositional,
putative, conceptual; imaginary, fanciful,
unreal, illusory.
OPPOSITES: actual.

notoriety noun infamy, disrepute, ill
repute, bad name, dishonour, discredit.

notorious adjective infamous,
scandalous; well known, famous, famed,
legendary.

notwithstanding preposition
*notwithstanding his workload, he is a
dedicated father:* despite, in spite of,
regardless of, for all.
▷ **adverb** *she is bright—notwithstanding, she
is now jobless:* nevertheless, nonetheless,
even so, all the same, in spite of this,
despite this, however, still, yet, that said,
just the same, anyway, in any event, at
any rate.

nought noun nil, zero, o; Tennis love; Cricket
a duck.

nourish verb
1 *mammals produce milk to nourish their
young:* feed, sustain, maintain.
2 *it's important to nourish a child's talent:*
encourage, promote, foster, nurture,
cultivate, stimulate, boost, advance, assist,
help, aid, strengthen, enrich.
3 *the hopes Ursula had nourished:* cherish,
nurture, foster, harbour, nurse, entertain,
maintain, hold, have.

nourishing adjective nutritious,
nutritive, wholesome, good for you,
healthy, health-giving, healthful,
beneficial, sustaining.
OPPOSITES: unhealthy.

nourishment noun food, sustenance,
nutriment, nutrition, subsistence,
provisions, fare; informal grub, nosh, chow.

novel[1] noun book, paperback, hardback;
story, tale, narrative; best-seller; informal
blockbuster.

n

novel² adjective *a novel way of reducing pollution:* new, original, unusual, unfamiliar, unconventional, unorthodox; different, fresh, imaginative, innovative, innovatory, inventive, modern, avant-garde, pioneering, groundbreaking, revolutionary, cutting-edge; unique, singular, unprecedented, rare; experimental, untested, untried; strange, exotic; derogatory newfangled; informal left-field.
OPPOSITES: traditional.

novelty noun
1 *the novelty of our approach:* originality, newness, freshness, unconventionality, unfamiliarity; difference, imaginativeness, creativity, innovation, modernity.
2 *we sell seasonal novelties:* knick-knack, trinket, ornament, bauble, toy, trifle, gewgaw, gimcrack.

novice noun
1 *a five-day course for novices:* beginner, learner, newcomer, initiate, neophyte, tyro; apprentice, trainee, probationer, student, pupil; informal rookie; N. Amer. informal tenderfoot, greenhorn.
2 *novices in the convent do not wear the full nuns' habit:* postulant, neophyte, novitiate.
OPPOSITES: expert, veteran.

now adverb
1 *I'm extremely busy now:* at the moment, at present, at the present time, currently; N. Amer. presently; Brit. informal at the minute.
2 *television is now the main source of news:* nowadays, today, these days.
3 *you must leave now:* at once, straight away, right away, right now, this minute, this instant, immediately, instantly, directly, without further ado, promptly, without delay, as soon as possible; informal pronto, asap.
□ **as of now**
from this time on, from now on, from this day forward, in future; formal henceforth, henceforward, hereafter.
□ **for now**
for the time being, for the moment, for the present, for the meantime.
□ **now and again**
occasionally, now and then, from time to time, sometimes, every so often, every now and again, at times, on occasion, once in a while; periodically, once in a blue moon.

nowadays adverb *nowadays, all graduates are computer-literate:* these days, today, at the present time, now, currently, at the moment, at present; N. Amer. presently.

noxious adjective *a chemicals factory that emitted noxious fumes:* poisonous, toxic, deadly, harmful, dangerous, damaging, destructive, pernicious; unpleasant, nasty, horrid, disgusting, awful, dreadful, horrible, terrible; vile, revolting, foul, nauseating, appalling, offensive; malodorous, fetid, putrid; informal ghastly.
OPPOSITES: harmless, innocuous.

nuance noun *the pianist's nuances of tone and expression:* fine distinction, subtle difference; shade, shading, gradation, variation, degree; subtlety, nicety, overtone.

nub noun *the nub of his argument:* crux, central point, main point, core, heart of the matter, nucleus, essence, quintessence, kernel, marrow, meat, pith; gist, substance; informal nitty-gritty.

nubile adjective sexually mature, marriageable; sexually attractive, desirable, sexy, luscious; informal beddable.

nucleus noun
1 *the nucleus of the British film industry:* core, centre, central part, heart, nub, hub, middle, eye, focus, focal point, pivot, crux.
2 *a nucleus of union men supported him:* small group, caucus, cell, coterie, clique, faction.

nude adjective naked, stark naked, bare, undressed, with nothing on, stripped, in a state of nature, au naturel; informal without a stitch on, in your birthday suit, in the raw, in the altogether, in the buff; Brit. informal starkers.
OPPOSITES: dressed.

nudge verb
1 *he nudged Ben in the ribs:* poke, prod, elbow, dig, jog, jab.
2 *the canoe nudged a bank:* touch, bump against, push against, run into.
3 *we nudged them into action:* prompt, encourage, stimulate, prod, galvanize.
4 *unemployment was nudging 3,000,000:* approach, near, come close to, be verging on, border on.
▷ noun *I felt a nudge in my side:* poke, dig in the ribs, prod, jog, jab, push.

nudity noun nakedness, state of undress, déshabillé, bareness.

nugget noun lump, chunk, piece, hunk, nub, gobbet.

nuisance noun *spam is becoming a real nuisance—my spam filter catches more than 50 messages a day:* annoyance, inconvenience, bore, bother, irritation, problem, trouble, trial, burden; pest, plague, thorn in your side/flesh; informal pain, pain in the neck, hassle, bind, drag, aggravation, headache.
OPPOSITES: blessing.

null adjective invalid, null and void, void; annulled, nullified, cancelled, revoked.
OPPOSITES: valid.

nullify verb
1 *they nullified the legislation:* render null and void, invalidate, void, annul; cancel, reverse, repeal, rescind, revoke, countermand, abolish, terminate, quash; Law vacate.

2 *the costs would nullify any tax relief:* cancel out, negate, neutralize, negative, wipe out.
OPPOSITES: ratify.

numb **adjective**
1 *my feet were numb with cold:* without sensation, without feeling, numbed, desensitized, benumbed, insensible; anaesthetized; frozen.
2 *the tragic events left us numb:* dazed, stunned, stupefied, paralysed, immobilized.
OPPOSITES: sensitive.
▷ **verb**
1 *the cold had numbed her senses:* deaden, desensitize, dull, benumb; anaesthetize, freeze.
2 *she was numbed by grief:* daze, stun, stupefy, paralyse, immobilize.
OPPOSITES: sensitize.

number **noun**
1 *a whole number:* numeral, integer, figure, digit; character, symbol; decimal, unit; cardinal number, ordinal number.
2 *a large number of complaints:* amount, quantity; total, aggregate, tally; quota.
3 *the band performed another number:* song, piece of music, tune, track; routine, sketch, dance, act.
4 *the wedding of one of their number:* group, company, crowd, circle, party, band, crew, set; informal gang.
▷ **verb**
1 *visitors numbered more than two million:* add up to, amount to, total, come to, comprise.
2 *he numbers her among his closest friends:* include, count, reckon, deem.
3 *research studies on the subject can be numbered on the fingers of one hand:* count, calculate, compute, reckon, tally, total; assess; Brit. tot up.
4 *his days are numbered:* limit, restrict, fix.
□ **a number of**
several, various, quite a few, sundry.
□ **without number**
countless, innumerable, unlimited, endless, limitless, untold, uncountable, uncounted; numerous, many, multiple, manifold, legion; literary numberless.

> WORD LINKS
> **numerical** relating to numbers

numberless **adjective** *there are numberless questions to be answered:* innumerable, countless, unlimited, endless, limitless, untold, uncountable, uncounted; numerous, many, multiple, manifold, myriad, legion.

numbing **adjective**
1 *menthol has a numbing action:* desensitizing, deadening, anaesthetic, anaesthetizing; paralysing.
2 *numbing cold:* freezing, raw, bitter, biting, arctic.
3 *numbing boredom:* stupefying, mind-numbing, stultifying; soporific.

numeral **noun** number, integer, figure, digit; character, symbol, unit.

numerous **adjective** *Bradford Council received numerous complaints from residents upset by the noise:* many, a lot of, scores of, countless, innumerable; several, quite a few, various; plenty of, copious, a quantity of, an abundance of, a profusion of, a multitude of, myriad; frequent; literary numberless; informal umpteen, lots of, loads of, masses of, stacks of, heaps of, tons of, millions of.
OPPOSITES: few.

nun **noun** sister, abbess, prioress, Mother Superior, Reverend Mother; novice; bride of Christ.

nunnery **noun** convent, priory, abbey; the cloister.

nuptial **adjective** matrimonial, marital, marriage, wedding, conjugal, bridal; married, wedded; literary connubial.

nuptials **plural noun** wedding, marriage, union.

nurse **noun**
1 *there are over 540 qualified nurses at the hospital:* carer, caregiver; informal Florence Nightingale.
2 *she had been his nurse when he was a child:* nanny, nursery nurse, childminder, au pair; dated nursemaid, governess.
▷ **verb**
1 *they nursed smallpox patients:* care for, take care of, look after, tend, minister to.
2 *he nursed a secret desire to try and make amends:* harbour, have, bear, hold, cherish, nurture, entertain, cling to, retain, keep alive.
3 *Rosa was nursing her baby:* breastfeed, suckle, feed.

nursery **noun** crèche, playgroup, kindergarten.

nurture **verb**
1 *she nurtured her children into adulthood:* bring up, care for, take care of, look after, tend, rear, raise, support; parent, mother.
2 *we nurtured these plants:* cultivate, grow, keep, tend.
3 *he nurtured my love of art:* encourage, promote, stimulate, develop, foster, cultivate, boost, contribute to, strengthen, fuel.
OPPOSITES: neglect, hinder.
▷ **noun**
1 *we are what nature and nurture have made us:* upbringing, rearing, raising, childcare; training, education.
2 *the nurture of ideas:* encouragement, promotion, fostering, development, cultivation.
OPPOSITES: nature.

nut **noun**
1 *nuts in their shells:* kernel.

n

2 (informal) maniac, lunatic, madman, madwoman; eccentric; informal loony, nutcase, fruitcake, head case, crank, crackpot, weirdo; Brit. informal nutter, mentalist.

nutriment noun nourishment, nutrients, sustenance, goodness, nutrition, food.

nutrition noun nourishment, nutriment, nutrients, sustenance, food; informal grub, chow, nosh.

nutritious adjective nourishing, good for you, full of nutrients, nutritive; wholesome, healthy, healthful, beneficial, sustaining.

nuts and bolts plural noun practicalities, fundamentals, basics, practical details, essentials, mechanics; informal nitty-gritty, ins and outs, brass tacks.

nuzzle verb
1 *the horse nuzzled at her pocket:* nudge, nose, prod, push.
2 *she nuzzled up to her boyfriend:* snuggle, cuddle, nestle, burrow; embrace, hug.

n

Oo

oaf noun *the thoughtless actions of a few loud-mouthed oafs:* lout, boor, barbarian; fool, idiot, imbecile; informal cretin, goon, oik; Brit. informal yob, yobbo.

oafish adjective *her oafish idiot of a son:* stupid, foolish, idiotic; loutish, uncouth, uncultured, boorish, rough, coarse, ill-mannered, unrefined; awkward, clumsy, lumbering; informal clodhopping; Brit. informal yobbish.

oasis noun *the castle gardens were a cool oasis in the heart of the city:* refuge, haven, retreat, sanctuary, sanctum, harbour.

oath noun
1 *an oath of allegiance:* vow, pledge, promise, avowal, affirmation, word of honour, bond, guarantee.
2 *he uttered a stream of oaths:* swear word, profanity, expletive, four-letter word, dirty word, obscenity, vulgarity, curse.

obedient adjective *Lucinda had always been very obedient:* compliant, biddable, acquiescent, tractable, amenable, malleable, pliable, pliant; dutiful, good, law-abiding, deferential, respectful, duteous, well trained, well disciplined, manageable, governable, docile, tame, meek, passive, submissive, unresisting, yielding.
OPPOSITES: disobedient, rebellious.

obeisance noun *a gesture of obeisance:* respect, homage, worship, adoration, reverence, veneration, honour, submission, deference.

obelisk noun column, pillar, monolith, monument.

obese adjective *he ate excessively and became obese:* fat, overweight, corpulent, gross, stout, fleshy, heavy, portly, paunchy, bulky, bloated, flabby; informal porky; Brit. informal podgy.
OPPOSITES: thin.

obey verb
1 *I obeyed him without question:* do what someone says, carry out someone's orders; submit to, defer to, bow to, yield to.
2 *he refused to obey the order:* carry out, follow, perform, act on, execute, discharge, implement, fulfil.

3 *health and safety regulations have to be obeyed:* comply with, adhere to, observe, abide by, act in accordance with, conform to, respect, follow, keep to, stick to; play it by the book, toe the line.
OPPOSITES: disobey, defy, ignore.

obfuscate verb *the debate all too often obfuscates the issue:* obscure, confuse, blur, muddle, complicate, muddy, cloud, befog; muddy the waters.
OPPOSITES: clarify.

object noun
1 *small metal objects:* thing, article, item, device, gadget.
2 *he became the object of criticism:* target, butt, focus, recipient, victim.
3 *his object was to resolve the crisis:* objective, aim, goal, target, purpose, end, plan, object of the exercise, point; ambition, design, intent, intention, idea.
▷ verb *teachers objected to the scheme:* protest about, oppose, raise objections to, express disapproval of, take exception to, take issue with, take a stand against, argue against, quarrel with, condemn, draw the line at, demur at, complain about, cavil at, quibble about; beg to differ; informal kick up a fuss/stink about.
OPPOSITES: approve, accept.

objection noun *the search was carried out regardless of her objections:* protest, protestation, demur, demurral, complaint, expostulation, grievance, cavil, quibble; opposition, argument, disagreement, disapproval, dissent.

objectionable adjective *he was one of the most objectionable people I had ever met:* unpleasant, disagreeable, distasteful, obnoxious, offensive, off-putting, undesirable, nasty, horrible, disgusting, appalling, insufferable, odious, vile, foul, unsavoury, repulsive, repellent, repugnant, revolting, abhorrent, loathsome, hateful, reprehensible, deplorable; informal ghastly.
OPPOSITES: pleasant.

objective adjective
1 *an interviewer must try to be objective:* impartial, unbiased, unprejudiced, non-partisan, disinterested, neutral, uninvolved, even-handed, equitable,

o

fair, fair-minded, just, open-minded, dispassionate, detached.
2 *the world of objective knowledge:* factual, actual, real, empirical, verifiable.
OPPOSITES: biased, subjective.
▷ noun *our objective is to build a profitable business:* aim, intention, purpose, target, goal, intent, object, object of the exercise, point, end; idea, design, plan, ambition, aspiration, desire, hope.

objectively adverb *the bank will do all it can to investigate your complaint objectively:* impartially, without bias, without prejudice, even-handedly, dispassionately, fairly, justly, with an open mind, without fear or favour.

objectivity noun impartiality, lack of bias/prejudice, fairness, fair-mindedness, neutrality, even-handedness, open-mindedness, disinterest, detachment, dispassion, dispassionateness.
OPPOSITES: bias, subjectivity.

obligate verb *many companies have internal codes of conduct that obligate employees to report illegal activity to their managers:* oblige, require, constrain, compel, force, commit, bind.

obligation noun
1 *his professional obligations:* duty, commitment, responsibility; function, task, job, assignment, commission, burden, charge, liability, requirement.
2 *a sense of obligation:* duty, compulsion, indebtedness; duress, necessity, pressure, constraint.
□ **under an obligation**
she didn't want to be under an obligation to him: beholden, obliged, in someone's debt, indebted, obligated, owing someone a debt of gratitude; duty-bound, honour-bound.

obligatory adjective *the use of seat belts in cars is obligatory:* compulsory, mandatory, prescribed, required, statutory, enforced, binding, incumbent; requisite, necessary, imperative, unavoidable, inescapable, essential.
OPPOSITES: optional.

oblige verb
1 *both parties are obliged to accept the decision:* require, compel, bind, constrain, obligate, leave someone no option, force.
2 *I'll be happy to oblige you:* do someone a favour, accommodate, help, assist, serve; gratify someone's wishes, indulge, humour.

obliged adjective *if you hear from her, I'd be obliged if you'd let me know:* thankful, grateful, appreciative; beholden, indebted, in someone's debt.

obliging adjective *he was a cheerful, obliging sort of chap:* helpful, accommodating, cooperative, willing, considerate, agreeable, amenable, generous, kind, neighbourly, hospitable,

pleasant, good-natured, amiable, gracious, unselfish, civil, courteous, polite; Brit. informal decent.
OPPOSITES: unhelpful, disobliging.

oblique adjective
1 *he drew an oblique line on the graph:* slanting, slanted, sloping, at an angle, angled, diagonal.
2 *an oblique reference to what had gone before:* indirect, inexplicit, implicit, implied, elliptical, backhanded; roundabout, circuitous, circumlocutory, evasive.
OPPOSITES: straight, direct.
▷ noun slash, solidus, backslash, diagonal.

obliquely adverb
1 *the sun shone obliquely across the tower:* diagonally, at an angle, slantwise, sideways, sidelong, aslant.
2 *he referred obliquely to the war:* indirectly, in a roundabout way, not in so many words, circuitously, evasively.

obliterate verb
1 *a nuclear explosion that would obliterate a city:* destroy, wipe out, annihilate, demolish, liquidate, wipe off the face of the earth, wipe off the map; informal zap.
2 *he tried to obliterate the memory:* erase, eradicate, expunge, efface, wipe out, blot out, rub out, remove all traces of.
3 *the clouds were darkening, obliterating the sun:* hide, obscure, blot out, block, cover, screen.

oblivion noun *they rescued him from artistic oblivion:* obscurity, anonymity, neglect, disregard; limbo.
OPPOSITES: fame.

oblivious adjective *he seemed completely oblivious to his surroundings:* unaware of, unconscious of, heedless of, unmindful of, impervious to, unconcerned by, unaffected by, insensible of, ignorant of, blind to, deaf to; unsuspecting.
OPPOSITES: conscious.

obnoxious adjective *he's a thoroughly obnoxious man:* unpleasant, disagreeable, nasty, distasteful, offensive, objectionable, horrible, horrid, unsavoury, awful, terrible, dreadful, revolting, repulsive, repellent, repugnant, disgusting, odious, vile, foul, abhorrent, loathsome, nauseating, sickening, hateful, insufferable, intolerable; informal ghastly, gross.
OPPOSITES: delightful.

obscene adjective
1 *obscene literature* | *obscene jokes:* pornographic, indecent, smutty, dirty, filthy, X-rated, explicit, lewd, rude, vulgar, coarse, crude, immoral, scatological, profane; euphemistic adult; informal blue.
2 *an obscene crime:* shocking, scandalous, vile, foul, atrocious, outrageous, heinous, odious, abhorrent, abominable, monstrous,

disgusting, hideous, repugnant, repulsive, revolting, repellent, loathsome, nauseating, sickening, awful, dreadful, terrible.

obscenity noun
1 *the book was banned on the grounds of obscenity:* indecency, immorality, impropriety.
2 *the men scowled and muttered obscenities:* expletive, swear word, oath, profanity, curse, four-letter word, dirty word.

obscure adjective
1 *his origins and parentage remain obscure:* unclear, uncertain, unknown, in doubt, doubtful, dubious, mysterious, hazy, vague, indeterminate; concealed, hidden.
2 *obscure references to Proust:* mystifying, puzzling, perplexing, baffling, ambiguous, cryptic, enigmatic, oblique, opaque, elliptical, unintelligible, incomprehensible, impenetrable, unfathomable; abstruse, recondite, arcane, esoteric, Delphic, oracular; informal as clear as mud.
3 *an obscure Peruvian painter:* little known, unknown, unheard of, undistinguished, unimportant, nameless, minor; unsung, unrecognized, forgotten.
OPPOSITES: clear, plain, famous.
▷ verb
1 *grey clouds obscured the sun:* hide, conceal, cover, veil, shroud, screen, mask, cloak, cast a shadow over, shadow, block, obliterate, eclipse, darken.
2 *recent events have obscured the issue:* confuse, complicate, obfuscate, cloud, blur, muddy; muddy the waters.
OPPOSITES: reveal, clarify.

obscurity noun
1 *the discovery rescued him from relative obscurity:* insignificance, unimportance, anonymity; limbo, oblivion.
2 *poems of impenetrable obscurity:* incomprehensibility, impenetrability, unintelligibility, opacity.
OPPOSITES: fame, clarity.

obsequious adjective *an obsequious manservant welcomed them:* servile, ingratiating, sycophantic, fawning, unctuous, oily, oleaginous, grovelling, cringing, subservient, submissive.

observable adjective *temperature has an observable effect on wines containing carbon dioxide:* noticeable, visible, perceptible, detectable, distinguishable, discernible, recognizable, evident, apparent, clear, distinct, plain, unmistakable.

observance noun
1 *strict observance of the rules:* compliance with, adherence to, accordance with, respect for, observation of, obedience to; keeping, obeying.
2 *religious observances:* rite, ritual, ceremony, celebration, practice, service, office, festival, tradition, custom, usage, formality.

observant adjective *lifeguards should be observant and stop risky situations before they start:* alert, attentive, vigilant, sharp-eyed, having eyes like a hawk, keen-eyed, perceptive, watchful, heedful, aware; on the lookout, having your eyes open/peeled; informal beady-eyed, not missing a trick, on the ball.
OPPOSITES: inattentive.

observation noun
1 *detailed observation of the animal's behaviour:* monitoring, scrutiny, examination, inspection, survey, surveillance, attention, consideration, study.
2 *his observations were concise and to the point:* remark, comment, statement, utterance, pronouncement, declaration; opinion, impression, thought, reflection.

observe verb
1 *police officers observed a group of men at the bus shelter at about 2 a.m.:* notice, see, note, perceive, discern, spot.
2 *she was alarmed to discover he had been observing her:* watch, look at, eye, contemplate, regard, view, survey, keep an eye on, scrutinize, keep under observation, keep watch on, monitor, keep under surveillance; informal keep tabs on.
3 *'You look tired,' she observed:* remark, comment, say, mention, declare, announce, state, pronounce; formal opine.
4 *both countries agreed to observe the ceasefire:* comply with, abide by, keep, obey, adhere to, honour, fulfil, respect, follow, accept.
5 *townspeople observed the one-year anniversary of the flood:* commemorate, mark, keep, memorialize, remember, celebrate.

observer noun
1 *a casual observer might not have noticed:* spectator, onlooker, watcher, looker-on, fly on the wall, viewer, witness.
2 *industry observers expect the deal to be finalized today:* commentator, reporter; monitor.

obsess verb *the thought obsessed him:* preoccupy, be uppermost in someone's mind, prey on someone's mind, prey on, possess, haunt, consume, plague, torment, hound, bedevil, beset, take control of, take over, take/have a hold on, grip.

obsessed adjective *he's completely obsessed by her:* fixated on, possessed by, consumed with; infatuated with, besotted with; informal hung up on, smitten with.

obsession noun *the idea grew in his mind until it became an obsession:* fixation, ruling/consuming passion, mania, idée fixe, compulsion, infatuation, addiction, fetish, craze; hobby horse, preoccupation;

phobia, complex, neurosis; informal bee in your bonnet, hang-up, thing.

obsessive adjective *reckless and obsessive love:* **all-consuming,** consuming, compulsive, obsessional, fanatical, neurotic, excessive; informal pathological.

obsolescent adjective *the country has a large supply of aircraft but most of it is obsolescent | obsolescent industries:* ageing, moribund, on its last legs, out of date, outdated, old-fashioned, outmoded, past its prime; dying out, on the decline, declining, waning, on the wane, disappearing; informal on the way out, past it.

obsolete adjective *the disposal of old and obsolete machinery | the phrase was obsolete after 1625:* **out of date,** outdated, outmoded, old-fashioned; no longer in use, disused, fallen into disuse, superannuated, outworn, antiquated, antediluvian, anachronistic, discontinued, old, archaic, ancient, fossilized, extinct, defunct. OPPOSITES: current, modern.

obstacle noun *the major obstacle to achieving that goal is money:* **barrier,** hurdle, stumbling block, obstruction, bar, block, impediment, hindrance, snag, catch, drawback, hitch, handicap, deterrent, complication, difficulty, problem, disadvantage, curb, check; informal fly in the ointment; Brit. informal spanner in the works. OPPOSITES: advantage, aid.

obstinacy noun **stubbornness,** inflexibility, intransigence, intractability, obduracy, mulishness, pig-headedness, wilfulness, contrariness, perversity, recalcitrance, implacability; persistence, tenacity, tenaciousness, doggedness, single-mindedness, determination; Brit. informal bloody-mindedness.

obstinate adjective *her obstinate refusal to back down | he can be very obstinate when he wants to be:* **stubborn,** unyielding, inflexible, unbending, intransigent, intractable, obdurate, mulish, stubborn as a mule, pig-headed, self-willed, strong-willed, headstrong, wilful, contrary, perverse, recalcitrant, uncooperative, unmanageable, stiff-necked, uncompromising, implacable, unrelenting, immovable, unshakeable; persistent, tenacious, dogged, single-minded, adamant, determined; Brit. informal bloody-minded, bolshie. OPPOSITES: compliant.

obstreperous adjective *obstreperous customers who have had a drop too much to drink:* **unruly,** unmanageable, disorderly, undisciplined, uncontrollable, rowdy, disruptive, truculent, difficult, rebellious, mutinous, riotous, out of control, wild, uproarious, boisterous; noisy, loud, clamorous, raucous, vociferous; Brit. informal stroppy, bolshie, rumbustious. OPPOSITES: quiet, restrained.

obstruct verb
1 *ensure that air bricks and vents are not obstructed | she was obstructing the entrance:* **block,** clog up, get in the way of, cut off, shut off, bung up, choke; barricade, bar; technical occlude.
2 *he was charged with obstructing the traffic:* **hold up,** bring to a standstill, stop, halt, block.
3 *the nationalist army obstructed the distribution of food supplies:* **impede,** hinder, interfere with, hamper, block, interrupt, hold up, stand in the way of, frustrate, thwart, baulk, hamstring, sabotage; slow down, retard, delay, stonewall, stop, halt. OPPOSITES: clear, facilitate.

obstruction noun *the issue was the major obstruction to progress:* **obstacle,** barrier, stumbling block, hurdle, bar, block, impediment, hindrance, snag, difficulty, catch, drawback, hitch, hold-up; blockage, bottleneck.

obstructive adjective *you're being deliberately obstructive:* **unhelpful,** uncooperative, awkward, difficult, unaccommodating, disobliging, perverse, contrary; Brit. informal bloody-minded, bolshie. OPPOSITES: helpful.

obtain verb *the newspaper obtained a copy of the letter:* **get,** acquire, come by, secure, procure, come into the possession of, pick up, be given; gain, earn, achieve, attain; informal get hold of, get/lay your hands on, land. OPPOSITES: lose.

obtainable adjective *frozen food is acceptable if fresh vegetable or meat are not obtainable:* **available,** to be had, in circulation, on the market, on offer, in season, at your disposal, at hand, attainable, accessible; informal up for grabs, on tap, get-at-able.

obtrusive adjective *the new hotel is very obtrusive:* **conspicuous,** prominent, noticeable, obvious, unmistakable, intrusive, out of place; informal sticking out a mile, sticking out like a sore thumb. OPPOSITES: unobtrusive, inconspicuous.

obtuse adjective *she looked at me as if I was being deliberately obtuse:* **stupid,** foolish, slow-witted, slow, unintelligent, ignorant; insensitive, imperceptive, uncomprehending; informal dim, dim-witted, dense, dumb, slow on the uptake, half-witted, moronic, thick, dopey, dozy. OPPOSITES: clever.

obviate verb *the settlement obviated the need for the separate cases to be heard in court:* **preclude,** prevent, remove, get rid of, get round, eliminate, make unnecessary.

obvious adjective *it was obvious that he was lying | her obvious lack of interest:* clear, plain, evident, apparent, manifest, patent, conspicuous, pronounced, transparent, palpable, marked, decided, distinct, noticeable, perceptible, visible, discernible; unmistakable, indisputable, self-evident, incontrovertible, incontestable, undeniable, as plain as a pikestaff, crystal clear, as clear as day, staring someone in the face; overt, open, undisguised, unconcealed, frank, glaring, blatant, written all over someone; informal as plain as the nose on your face, sticking out like a sore thumb, sticking out a mile.
OPPOSITES: imperceptible.

obviously adverb *he was obviously in great pain:* clearly, evidently, plainly, patently, visibly, discernibly, manifestly; unmistakably, undeniably, incontrovertibly, demonstrably, unquestionably, undoubtedly, without doubt, doubtless; of course, naturally, needless to say.
OPPOSITES: perhaps.

occasion noun
1 *there are very few occasions when cancelling a cheque is justified:* time, instance, juncture, point; event, occurrence, incident; situation, case, circumstance.
2 *a family occasion:* social event, event, affair, function, celebration, party, get-together, gathering; informal do, bash.
3 *I doubt if the occasion will arise:* opportunity, right moment, chance, opening, window.
4 *it's the first time I've had occasion to complain:* reason, cause, call, grounds, justification, need, motive.
▷ **verb** *her situation occasioned a good deal of sympathy:* give rise to, cause, bring about, result in, lead to, elicit, produce, create, arouse, generate, engender, inspire, prompt, precipitate, provoke.

occasional adjective *his occasional visits and phone calls:* infrequent, intermittent, irregular, periodic, sporadic, odd, random, uncommon, few and far between, isolated, rare.
OPPOSITES: regular, frequent.

occasionally adverb *he's got a flat in London now, though he still comes home occasionally:* sometimes, from time to time, every now and then, every now and again, at times, every so often, once in a while, on occasion, periodically, at intervals, irregularly, sporadically, infrequently, intermittently, on and off, off and on.
OPPOSITES: often.

occult noun *he was interested in the occult:* the supernatural, supernaturalism, magic, black magic, witchcraft, sorcery, necromancy, wizardry, the black arts; mysticism.
▷ **adjective** *occult powers:* supernatural, magic, magical, mystical, mystic, psychic, preternatural, transcendental.

occupancy noun *rents paid by individuals are directly related to their occupancy of council houses:* occupation, tenancy, tenure, residence, residency, habitation.

occupant noun
1 *the occupants of the houses:* resident, inhabitant, owner, householder, tenant, leaseholder, lessee; Brit. occupier, owner-occupier.
2 *the first occupant of the post:* incumbent, holder.

occupation noun
1 *his father's occupation took him abroad a lot:* job, profession, work, trade, employment, position, post, situation, business, career, métier, vocation, calling, craft.
2 *her leisure occupations included horse-riding:* pastime, activity, hobby, pursuit, interest, entertainment, recreation, amusement.
3 *a property suitable for occupation by older people:* residence, residency, habitation, occupancy, tenancy, tenure, lease, living in.
4 *the Roman occupation of Britain:* conquest, capture, invasion, seizure, takeover, annexation, subjugation, subjection, appropriation; colonization, rule, control.

occupational adjective *long and irregular hours are an occupational hazard in medicine:* job-related, work-related, professional.

occupied adjective
1 *the tasks kept her occupied all day:* busy, engaged, working, at work, active; informal tied up, hard at it, on the go.
2 *all the tables were occupied:* in use, full, engaged, taken.
3 *only two of the flats are occupied:* inhabited, lived-in, tenanted.
OPPOSITES: free, vacant.

occupy verb
1 *Carol occupied the basement flat:* live in, inhabit, be the tenant of, lodge in; move into, take up residence in; people, populate, settle; Scottish stay in.
2 *two windows occupied almost the whole of the end wall:* take up, fill, fill up, cover, use up.
3 *he occupies a senior post at the Treasury:* hold, fill, have; informal hold down.
4 *I need something to occupy my mind:* engage, busy, employ, distract, absorb, engross, preoccupy, hold, interest, involve, entertain, amuse, divert.
5 *the region was occupied by Soviet troops:* capture, seize, take possession of, conquer,

O

invade, overrun, take over, colonize, garrison, annex, subjugate.

occur verb

1 *the accident occurred at about 3.30:* happen, take place, come about; arise, crop up; N. Amer. informal go down.
2 *the disease occurs chiefly in tropical climates:* be found, be present, exist, appear, prevail, present itself, manifest itself, turn up.
3 *an idea occurred to her:* enter your head/ mind, cross your mind, come to mind, spring to mind, strike you, dawn on you, suggest itself.

occurrence noun

1 *vandalism used to be a rare occurrence:* event, incident, happening, phenomenon, affair, matter, circumstance.
2 *the occurrence of cancer increases with age:* incidence, development; frequency, rate, prevalence; instance.

ocean noun. See **SEA**.

odd adjective

1 *an odd man:* strange, peculiar, queer, funny, eccentric, unusual, unconventional; informal weird.
2 *quite a few odd things had happened:* strange, unusual, peculiar, funny, curious, bizarre, uncanny, queer, outlandish, outré; unexpected, unfamiliar, abnormal, atypical, anomalous, different, out of the ordinary, extraordinary, puzzling, mystifying, mysterious, perplexing, baffling, unaccountable, uncommon, irregular, deviant, aberrant, freakish; informal weird.
3 *we have the odd drink together | he does odd jobs for friends:* occasional, casual, irregular, isolated, random, sporadic, periodic; miscellaneous, various, sundry.
4 *he's wearing odd shoes | an odd sock:* mismatched; single, lone, solitary, extra, surplus, leftover, remaining.
OPPOSITES: normal, ordinary, regular.
□ **odd man out**
outsider, exception, oddity, nonconformist, maverick, individualist, misfit, fish out of water, square peg in a round hole.

oddity noun

1 *she was regarded as a bit of an oddity:* eccentric, maverick, nonconformist; misfit, crank; informal oddball, crackpot, nut, freak; Brit. informal nutter.
2 *his work remains an oddity in some respects:* anomaly, aberration.
3 *the oddities of human nature:* peculiarity, idiosyncrasy, eccentricity, quirk, irregularity, twist.

oddment noun *oddments of material:* scrap, remnant, bit, piece, leftover, fragment, snippet, offcut, shred, tail end; Brit. informal fag end; (**oddments**) bits and bobs; informal bits and pieces; Brit. informal odds and ends.

odds plural noun *the odds are that he is no longer alive:* likelihood, probability, chances, chance.
□ **at odds**
1 *he was at odds with his colleagues:* in conflict, in disagreement, on bad terms, at cross purposes, at loggerheads, quarrelling, arguing, at daggers drawn, at each other's throats.
2 *behaviour at odds with the interests of the company:* at variance, out of keeping, out of line, in opposition, conflicting, contrary, incompatible, inconsistent, irreconcilable.
□ **odds and ends** (Brit. informal)
bits and bobs, paraphernalia, miscellanea, sundries; bric-a-brac, knick-knacks, oddments; informal bits and pieces.

odious adjective *the odious methods they had used to suppress dissent | an odious crime:* revolting, repulsive, repellent, repugnant, disgusting, horrible, vile, foul, abhorrent, loathsome, nauseating, sickening, hateful, detestable, execrable, abominable, monstrous, appalling, reprehensible, deplorable, insufferable, intolerable, despicable, contemptible, unspeakable, atrocious, awful, terrible, dreadful, frightful, obnoxious, offensive, objectionable, unsavoury, unpalatable, unpleasant, disagreeable, nasty, distasteful.

odorous adjective *odorous fumes:* smelly, malodorous, pungent, acrid, foul-smelling, evil-smelling, stinking, reeking, fetid, rank.

odour noun *an odour of sweat:* smell, stench, stink, reek; Brit. informal pong, whiff.

odyssey noun journey, voyage, trek, travels, quest, pilgrimage, wandering, journeying.

off adjective

1 *Surinder's off today:* away, absent, unavailable, not at work, off duty, on holiday, on leave; free, at leisure; N. Amer. on vacation.
2 *the game's off:* cancelled, postponed, called off.
3 *the fish was off:* rotten, bad, stale, mouldy, high, sour, rancid, turned, spoiled, putrid, putrescent.
4 (Brit. informal) *that remark was a bit off:* unfair, unjust, uncalled for, below the belt, unjustified, unjustifiable, unreasonable, unwarranted, unnecessary; informal a bit much; Brit. informal out of order.
5 (Brit. informal) *he was really off with me:* unfriendly, aloof, cool, cold, distant, frosty; informal stand-offish.
□ **off and on**
periodically, at intervals, on and off, once in a while, every so often, every now and then, from time to time, occasionally, sometimes, intermittently, irregularly.

offbeat adjective *the suggestion was a little*

offbeat: **unconventional**, unorthodox, unusual, eccentric, idiosyncratic, outré, outlandish, strange, bizarre, peculiar, odd, out of the ordinary; alternative, zany, quirky; informal weird, wacky, left-field, way-out, off the wall, oddball, kooky.
OPPOSITES: conventional.

off colour adjective

1 (Brit.) *I'm feeling a bit off colour:* **unwell**, ill, poorly, out of sorts, indisposed, not yourself, sick, queasy, nauseous, liverish, run-down, washed out, below par; Brit. peaky; informal under the weather, rough, green about the gills; Brit. informal ropy.
2 *off-colour jokes:* **rude**, dirty, smutty, crude, suggestive, indecent, indelicate, risqué, racy, bawdy, naughty, blue, vulgar, ribald, coarse; informal raunchy.
OPPOSITES: well.

offence noun

1 *he denied having committed any offence:* **crime**, illegal/unlawful act, misdemeanour, breach of the law, felony; wrongdoing, wrong, misdeed, peccadillo, sin, transgression.
2 *the outcome is an offence to basic justice:* **affront**, slap in the face, insult, outrage, violation.
3 *I do not want to cause offence:* **annoyance**, anger, resentment, indignation, irritation, exasperation, wrath, displeasure, bad feelings, disgruntlement, pique, vexation, animosity.
□ **take offence**
most of the guests laughed at the joke, but a small number took offence: **be offended**, take exception, take something personally, feel affronted, feel resentful, take something amiss, take umbrage, get upset, get annoyed, get angry; informal get into a huff.

offend verb

1 *I'm sorry if I offended him | she was offended by the question:* **hurt someone's feelings**, give offence to, affront, upset, distress, hurt, wound; annoy, anger, exasperate, irritate, vex, pique, gall, irk; Brit. rub up the wrong way; informal rile, put someone's back up.
2 *the smell of cigarette smoke offended him:* **displease**, be distasteful to, be disagreeable to, be offensive to, disgust, repel, revolt, sicken, nauseate.
3 *criminals who offend again and again:* **break the law**, commit a crime, do wrong, sin, transgress.

offended adjective *she was so offended that she asked him to leave at once:* **affronted**, insulted, displeased, upset, hurt, wounded, disgruntled, put out, annoyed, angry, cross, indignant, irritated, piqued, vexed, irked, aggrieved, resentful, in high dudgeon; informal riled, miffed, peeved, aggravated, in a huff; Brit. informal narked.
OPPOSITES: pleased.

offender noun *he claimed that prison should be reserved for persistent offenders:* **wrongdoer**, criminal, lawbreaker, miscreant, felon, delinquent; culprit, guilty party, sinner, transgressor; formal malefactor.

offensive adjective

1 *later, he apologized for his extremely offensive comments:* **insulting**, rude, disrespectful, derogatory, personal, hurtful, wounding, abusive; discourteous, uncivil, impolite, impertinent, insolent; annoying, irritating, galling, provocative.
2 *an offensive smell:* **unpleasant**, disagreeable, nasty, distasteful, displeasing, objectionable, off-putting, awful, terrible, dreadful, frightful, obnoxious, abominable, horrible, horrid, disgusting, repulsive, repellent, repugnant, revolting, abhorrent, loathsome, odious, vile, foul, sickening, nauseating; informal ghastly, gross.
3 *an offensive air action:* **hostile**, attacking, aggressive, combative, belligerent, on the attack.
OPPOSITES: complimentary, pleasant, defensive.
▷ **noun** *a military offensive:* **attack**, assault, onslaught, drive, invasion, push, thrust, charge, sortie, sally, foray, raid, incursion, blitz, campaign.

offer verb

1 *Frank offered another suggestion | our main aim is to offer practical advice to health-care professionals:* **put forward**, proffer, present, give, make available, come up with, suggest.
2 *she offered to help:* **volunteer**, volunteer your services, be at someone's disposal, be at someone's service, step/come forward, show willing.
3 *the product is offered at a competitive price:* **put up for sale**, put on the market, sell, market.
4 *he offered $200:* **bid**, tender, put in a bid of, put in an offer of.
5 *a job offering good career prospects:* **provide**, afford, supply, give, present, hold out.
6 *she offered no resistance:* **attempt**, try, give, show, express.
7 *birds were offered to the gods:* **sacrifice**, offer up, immolate.
OPPOSITES: withdraw, refuse.
▷ **noun**
1 *offers of help:* **proposal**, suggestion, approach, overture.
2 *the highest offer:* **bid**, tender, bidding price.
□ **on offer**
on sale, up for sale, on the market; available, obtainable, to be had.

offering noun

1 *you may place offerings in the charity box:* **contribution**, charitable donation, gift, present, handout.

2 *many offerings were made to the goddess:* sacrifice, burnt offering, immolation, libation, oblation.

offhand adjective *in a very offhand manner, she told me that the item I'd ordered had been discontinued:* casual, careless, uninterested, unconcerned, indifferent, cool, nonchalant, blasé, insouciant, cavalier, glib, perfunctory, cursory, unceremonious, ungracious, dismissive, discourteous, uncivil, impolite, terse, abrupt, curt; informal couldn't-care-less, take-it-or-leave-it.

▷ adverb *I can't think of a better answer offhand:* on the spur of the moment, without consideration, extempore, impromptu, ad lib; extemporaneously, spontaneously; informal off the cuff, off the top of your head, just like that.

office noun
1 *her office in Aldersgate Street:* place of work, place of business, workplace, workroom.
2 *the newspaper's Paris office:* branch, division, section, bureau, department; agency.
3 *he assumed the office of President:* post, position, appointment, job, occupation, role, situation, function, capacity.
4 (**offices**) *he was saved by the good offices of his uncle:* assistance, help, aid, services, intervention, intercession, mediation, agency.

officer noun *the officers of the society:* official, office-holder, committee member, board member; public servant, administrator, executive, functionary, bureaucrat; derogatory apparatchik.

official adjective
1 *an official inquiry* | *official non-governmental organizations:* authorized, approved, validated, certified, accredited, endorsed, sanctioned, licensed, recognized, accepted, legitimate, legal, lawful, valid, bona fide, proper, authenticated.
2 *an official college function:* formal, ceremonial.
OPPOSITES: unofficial, informal.
▷ noun *a union official:* officer, office-holder, administrator, executive, appointee, functionary; representative, agent; bureaucrat, mandarin; derogatory apparatchik.

officiate verb
1 *he officiated in the first two matches:* be in charge of, take charge of, preside over; oversee, superintend, supervise, conduct, run.
2 *Father Buckley officiated at the wedding service:* conduct, perform, celebrate, solemnize.

officious adjective *the security people in the foyer were even more officious:* self-important, bumptious, self-assertive, overbearing, overzealous, domineering; informal bossy.
OPPOSITES: self-effacing.

offing noun
▢ **in the offing** *important changes were in the offing:* on the way, coming, close at hand, near, imminent, in prospect, on the horizon, in the wings, just around the corner, in the air, in the wind, brewing, upcoming, forthcoming; informal on the cards.

off-key adjective
1 *an off-key rendition of 'Amazing Grace':* out of tune, flat, tuneless, discordant, unharmonious.
2 *the cinematic effects are distractingly off-key:* incongruous, inappropriate, unsuitable, out of place, out of keeping, jarring, dissonant, inharmonious.
OPPOSITES: harmonious.

offload verb
1 *the cargo was being offloaded:* unload, remove, empty out, tip out.
2 *this is not the best time to offload aviation stocks and shares:* dispose of, get rid of, dump, jettison, transfer, shift.

off-putting adjective
1 *an off-putting smell:* unpleasant, unappealing, uninviting, disagreeable, offensive, distasteful, unsavoury, unpalatable, unappetizing; objectionable, nasty, horrible, disgusting, revolting, repellent.
2 *her manner was off-putting:* discouraging, disheartening, demoralizing, dispiriting, daunting, disconcerting, unnerving, unsettling.

offset verb *profits and losses on each investment tend to offset each other:* counterbalance, balance out, cancel out, even out/up, counteract, neutralize; compensate for, make up for, make good.

offshoot noun
1 *the plant's offshoots:* side shoot, shoot, sucker, tendril, runner, scion; twig, branch, bough, limb.
2 *the organization was an offshoot of the San Francisco Art Association:* spin-off, development, product, by-product.
3 *the large-scale crime we read about is an offshoot of unemployment:* consequence, result, effect, upshot; product, by-product

offspring noun *anxious parents watched over their offspring:* children, sons and daughters, progeny, family, youngsters, babies, infants, brood; descendants, heirs, successors; informal kids.

often adverb *he often asks after you* | *she often works until eleven at night:* frequently, many times, many a time, on many/numerous occasions, as often as not, repeatedly, again and again; regularly, routinely, usually, habitually, commonly,

generally, in many cases/instances.
OPPOSITES: seldom.

ogle verb *he'd been ogling her ever since she entered the room:* leer at, stare at, eye, make eyes at; informal eye up, give someone the glad eye, lech after.

ogre noun
1 *an ogre with two heads:* monster, giant, troll.
2 *he is not the ogre he sometimes seems to be:* brute, monster, beast, barbarian, savage; tyrant, martinet, slave-driver.

oily adjective
1 *a plate of rich, oily brown stew:* greasy, fatty, oleaginous.
2 *an oily little man:* unctuous, ingratiating, smooth-talking, fulsome, flattering; obsequious, sycophantic, oleaginous; informal slimy; Brit. informal smarmy.

ointment noun lotion, cream, salve, liniment, embrocation, rub, gel; balm, emollient, unguent.

OK, okay (informal) adjective
1 *the film was OK:* satisfactory, all right, acceptable, competent; adequate, tolerable, passable, reasonable, fair, decent, not bad, average, middling, moderate, unremarkable, unexceptional; informal so-so, fair-to-middling.
2 *Jo's feeling OK now:* fine, all right, well, in good shape, in good health, fit, healthy.
3 *is it OK to wear jeans?* permissible, allowable, acceptable, all right, in order, permitted; fitting, suitable, appropriate.
OPPOSITES: unsatisfactory, ill.
▷ exclamation *OK, I'll go with him:* all right, very well, fine.
▷ noun *he's just given me his OK:* authorization, approval, seal of approval, agreement, consent, assent, permission, endorsement, ratification, sanction, approbation, confirmation, blessing, leave; informal the go-ahead, the green light, the thumbs up, say-so.
OPPOSITES: refusal.
▷ verb *the move must be okayed by the president:* authorize, approve, agree to, consent to, sanction, pass, ratify, endorse, allow, rubber-stamp.
OPPOSITES: refuse, veto.

old adjective
1 *an old man:* elderly, aged, venerable, senior, advanced in years; long in the tooth, grey-haired, grizzled, hoary; ancient, superannuated, doddering, doddery, senescent, senile; informal getting on, past it, over the hill.
2 *old agricultural machinery:* dilapidated, decrepit, broken-down, run-down, tumbledown, ramshackle, decaying, crumbling, disintegrating; ancient, superannuated, antiquated, antediluvian, obsolescent.
3 *piles of old clothes:* worn, worn out, shabby, threadbare, torn, frayed, patched,

tattered, moth-eaten, ragged; old-fashioned, out of date, outmoded; cast-off, hand-me-down; informal tatty.
4 *a beautiful old car:* vintage, veteran, antique.
5 *she's old for her years:* mature, wise, sensible, experienced, worldly-wise, knowledgeable.
6 *an old girlfriend:* former, previous, ex-, past, earlier, one-time, sometime, erstwhile.
7 *they come out with the same old phrases:* hackneyed, banal, trite, overused, tired, worn out, stale, clichéd, platitudinous, unimaginative, stock; out of date, outdated, old-fashioned, outmoded, hoary; informal old hat, corny, played out.
OPPOSITES: young, new, modern.
□ **old age**
declining years, advanced years, age, winter/autumn of your life; senescence, dotage.

┌───┐
│ WORD LINKS   │
│ **geriatric** relating to old people   │
│ **geriatrics** the branch of medicine   │
│   concerned with old people   │
│ **gerontology** the scientific study of old age │
│   and old people   │
└───┘

old-fashioned adjective
1 *an old-fashioned typewriter | old-fashioned clothes:* out of date, outdated, dated, outmoded, unfashionable, passé, démodé, frumpy; old, archaic, obsolescent, obsolete, ancient, antiquated, superannuated, antediluvian, quaint, anachronistic; informal square, out of the ark, clunky.
2 *her parents are very old-fashioned:* conservative, traditional; behind the times, backward-looking; informal square.
OPPOSITES: modern.

omen noun *perhaps her dream was an omen of things to come:* portent, sign, signal, token, forewarning, warning, foreshadowing, prediction, forecast, prophesy, harbinger, augury; writing on the wall.

ominous adjective *ominous black clouds gathered on the horizon | the profits warning is an ominous sign for the retail industry:* threatening, menacing, baleful, forbidding, sinister; inauspicious, unpropitious, unfavourable, unpromising; black, dark, gloomy, grim.
OPPOSITES: promising.

omission noun
1 *the omission of recent publications from his biography:* exclusion; deletion, cut, excision, elimination.
2 *the damage was not caused by any omission on behalf of the carrier:* negligence, neglect, dereliction, forgetfulness, oversight, lapse, failure.

omit verb
1 *they omitted his name from the list:* leave

out, miss out, miss; exclude, take out, drop, cut; delete, eliminate, cross out, strike out.
2 *I omitted to mention our guest lecturer:* forget, neglect, fail.
OPPOSITES: add, include, remember.

omnipotence noun all-powerfulness, supremacy, pre-eminence, supreme power, unlimited power; invincibility.

omnipotent adjective *an omnipotent deity:* all-powerful, almighty, supreme, pre-eminent; invincible, unconquerable.

omnipresent adjective *in fairy tales, evil is as omnipresent as virtue:* ubiquitous, all-pervasive, everywhere; rife, pervasive, prevalent.

omniscient adjective *the story is told by an omniscient fictional narrator:* all-knowing, all-wise, all-seeing.

on adjective *the washing machine's on:* in operation, in use, functioning, working, operating.
OPPOSITES: off.
□ **on and off**
it rained on and off for the rest of the afternoon: periodically, at intervals, off and on, once in a while, every so often, every now and then, from time to time, occasionally, sometimes, intermittently, irregularly.
□ **on and on**
she droned on and on about her boyfriend: for a long time, for ages, for hours, at length, incessantly, ceaselessly, constantly, continuously, continually, endlessly, unendingly, interminably, unremittingly, relentlessly, indefatigably, without let-up, without a pause/break, without cease.

once adverb
1 *I only met him once:* on one occasion, one time, one single time.
2 *he never once complained:* ever, at any time, on any occasion, at all.
3 *they were friends once:* formerly, previously, in the past, at one time, at one point, in days/times gone by, in times past, in the old days, long ago.
OPPOSITES: often, now.
▷ conjunction *he'll be all right once she's gone:* as soon as, when, after.
□ **at once**
1 *you must leave at once:* immediately, right away, right now, this moment/instant/second/minute, now, straight away, instantly, directly, forthwith, promptly, without delay/hesitation, without further ado; quickly, as fast as possible, as soon as possible; informal asap, like a shot, in a flash.
2 *all the guests arrived at once:* at the same time, at one and the same time, together, simultaneously; as a group.
□ **once and for all**
he hoped to settle the argument once and for all: conclusively, decisively, finally, positively, definitely, definitively,

irrevocably; for good, for always, forever, permanently.
□ **once in a while**
I still see her once in a while: occasionally, from time to time, every now and then, every so often, on occasion, at times, sometimes, off and on, at intervals, periodically, sporadically, intermittently.

oncoming adjective *he lost control on a bend and collided with an oncoming car | the air outside was chill, a sign of the oncoming winter:* approaching, advancing, forthcoming, on the way, imminent, impending, looming, gathering, close at hand, about to happen, to come.

one cardinal number
1 unit, item.
2 *only one person came:* a single, a solitary, a sole, a lone.
3 *her one concern was her daughter:* only, single, solitary, sole.
4 *they have now become one:* united, a unit, unitary, amalgamated, consolidated, integrated, combined, incorporated, allied, affiliated, linked, joined, unified, in league, in partnership; married, wedded.

onerous adjective *he found his duties increasingly onerous:* arduous, difficult, hard, taxing, demanding, exacting, strenuous, effortful, formidable, laborious, burdensome, Herculean, exhausting, tiring, punishing, gruelling, wearing, wearisome, fatiguing, uphill, back-breaking.
OPPOSITES: easy.

one-sided adjective
1 *we heard a rather one-sided account from the fans:* biased, prejudiced, partisan, partial, preferential, slanted; unfair, unjust, inequitable.
2 *it was a very one-sided game:* unequal, uneven, unevenly matched, unbalanced.
OPPOSITES: impartial.

one-time adjective *a one-time county cricketer:* former, ex-, old, previous, past, sometime, erstwhile; lapsed.

ongoing adjective *negotiations are ongoing | the ongoing political campaign:* in progress, under way, continuing, proceeding, progressing, developing; unfinished.

onlooker noun *an onlooker described the scene as one of utter devastation:* eyewitness, witness, bystander, observer, looker-on, spectator, watcher.

only adverb
1 *there was only enough for two:* at most, at best, just, no/not more than; barely, scarcely, hardly.
2 *he only works on one picture at a time:* exclusively, solely, to the exclusion of everything else.
3 *you're only saying that:* merely, simply, just.

o

▷ **adjective** *their only son:* sole, single, one and only, solitary, lone, unique; exclusive.

onset noun *treatment was administered soon after the onset of symptoms |
the onset of winter:* start, beginning, commencement, arrival, first appearance, day one; outbreak.
OPPOSITES: end.

onslaught noun *French soldiers held their trenches against German onslaughts at Verdun:* assault, attack, offensive, advance, charge, storming, sortie, sally, raid, descent, incursion, invasion, foray, push, thrust, drive, blitz, bombardment, barrage, salvo.

onus noun *the onus is on the plaintiff to obtain the police report:* burden, responsibility, liability, obligation, duty.

ooze verb
1 *blood oozed from the wound:* seep, trickle, drip, dribble, be discharged, escape, leak, drain, flow, issue.
2 *she was positively oozing charm:* exude, gush, drip, pour out, emanate, radiate.

opalescent adjective *a large opalescent shell:* iridescent, lustrous, shimmering, gleaming; pearly, nacreous.

opaque adjective
1 *through the opaque glass she could make out a large, burly shape:* non-transparent, frosted; cloudy, blurred, smeared, smeary, misty.
2 *the technical jargon was opaque to her:* obscure, unclear, unfathomable, incomprehensible, unintelligible, impenetrable, puzzling, perplexing, baffling, mystifying, confusing, mysterious; informal as clear as mud.
OPPOSITES: transparent, clear.

open adjective
1 *the door's open:* not shut, not closed, unlocked, unbolted, unlatched, off the latch, unfastened, unsecured; ajar.
2 *a blue silk shirt, open at the neck:* unfastened, not done up, undone, unbuttoned, loose.
3 *the main roads are open:* clear, passable, navigable, unblocked, unobstructed.
4 *open countryside | open spaces:* unenclosed, rolling, sweeping, extensive, wide open, unfenced, exposed; spacious, airy, uncrowded, uncluttered; undeveloped.
5 *a map was open beside him:* spread out, unfolded, unfurled, unrolled, extended, stretched out.
6 *the bank wasn't open:* trading, working, in operation.
7 *the position is still open:* available, vacant, free, unfilled; informal up for grabs.
8 *the system is open to abuse:* vulnerable, subject, susceptible, liable, exposed, an easy target for, at risk of.
9 *she was open about her feelings:* frank, candid, honest, forthcoming, communicative, forthright, direct, unreserved, plain-spoken, outspoken, free-spoken, not afraid to call a spade a spade; informal upfront.
10 *they stared at him with open hostility:* overt, obvious, patent, manifest, palpable, conspicuous, plain, undisguised, unconcealed, clear, apparent, evident; blatant, flagrant, barefaced, brazen.
11 *the case is still open:* unresolved, undecided, unsettled, up in the air; open to debate, open for discussion, arguable, debatable, moot.
12 *it's important to keep an open mind:* impartial, unbiased, unprejudiced, objective, disinterested, non-partisan, neutral, dispassionate, detached.
13 *I'm open to suggestions:* receptive, amenable, willing/ready to listen, responsive.
14 *what other options are open to us?* available, accessible, on hand, on offer; possible.
15 *an open meeting:* public, general, unrestricted, non-exclusive.
OPPOSITES: shut, closed.
▷ verb
1 *she opened the front door:* unfasten, unlatch, unlock, unbolt, unbar; throw wide.
2 *the children began to open their presents:* unwrap, undo, untie.
3 *Adam opened the map:* spread out, unfold, unfurl, unroll, straighten out.
4 *we're hoping to open next month:* start trading, open for business, set up shop.
5 *the prime minister opened the meeting:* begin, start, commence, set in motion, launch, get going, get under way, set the ball rolling, get off the ground; informal kick off, get the show on the road.
6 *the lounge opens on to a terrace:* lead, be connected.
7 *he opened his heart to her:* reveal, uncover, expose, lay bare, bare, pour out, disclose, divulge.
OPPOSITES: close, shut, end.

> WORD LINKS
> **agoraphobia** irrational fear of open or public places

open-air adjective *an open-air concert:* outdoor, out-of-doors, outside; alfresco.
OPPOSITES: indoor.

opening noun
1 *an opening in the centre of the roof:* hole, gap, space, aperture, orifice, vent, crack, slit, chink; crevice, fissure.
2 *the opening of the session:* beginning, start, commencement, outset; introduction; informal kick-off.
3 *the opening of a new art gallery:* opening ceremony, launch, inauguration; opening/first night, premiere.
4 *United created openings but were unable to score:* opportunity, chance, window of opportunity, possibility.

o

5 *we have openings for software developers of varying talents and experience:* vacancy, position, job.

openly adverb
1 *drugs were openly on sale:* publicly, blatantly, flagrantly, overtly.
2 *he spoke openly of his problems:* frankly, candidly, explicitly, honestly, forthrightly, bluntly, without constraint, without holding back, straight from the shoulder.
OPPOSITES: secretly.

open-minded adjective *he stressed that the government would adopt an open-minded attitude towards the proposals:* unbiased, unprejudiced, neutral, non-judgemental, objective, disinterested; receptive, open, open to suggestions, amenable, flexible; tolerant, liberal, broad-minded.
OPPOSITES: prejudiced, narrow-minded.

open-mouthed adjective *he stared at her open-mouthed:* astounded, amazed, in amazement, surprised, stunned, bowled over, staggered; aghast, stupefied, taken aback, shocked, speechless, dumbfounded, dumbstruck, thunderstruck; informal flabbergasted; Brit. informal gobsmacked.

operate verb
1 *there is a shortage of workers to operate the new machine:* work, run, use, utilize, handle, control, manage; drive, steer, manoeuvre.
2 *the machine ceased to operate:* function, work, go, run, be in working/running order, be operative.
3 *the committee will examine the way the law operates in practice:* take effect, act, apply, be applied, function.
4 *many foreign companies operate factories in the US:* control, be in control/charge of, manage, run, direct, administer, superintend, supervise, oversee.
5 *doctors decided to operate:* perform surgery, intervene, carry out an operation.

operation noun
1 *the smooth operation of the payment system:* functioning, working, running, performance, action.
2 *the operation of the factory:* management, running, administration, supervision.
3 *he's recovering from his recent bypass operation:* surgery.
4 *a military operation:* action, activity, exercise, undertaking, enterprise, manoeuvre, campaign; procedure.
5 *he reopened his operation under a different name:* business, enterprise, company, firm; informal outfit.

operational adjective *the new laboratory will be operational by the beginning of November:* up and running, working, functioning, operative, in operation, in use, in action; in working order, workable, serviceable, functional, usable.

operative adjective
1 *the act is not operative at the moment:* in force, in operation, in effect, valid.
2 *I went for a crash course in ballroom dancing—crash being the operative word:* key, significant, important, relevant, apposite, applicable, pertinent, germane; crucial, critical.
OPPOSITES: invalid.
▷ noun
1 *the operatives clean the machines at the end of every shift:* machinist, operator, mechanic, engineer, worker, workman, hand, blue-collar worker.
2 *an operative of the CIA:* secret agent, undercover agent, spy, mole, plant, double agent; N. Amer. informal spook.

opinion noun *she did not share her husband's opinion:* belief, judgement, thoughts, thinking, way of thinking, view, point of view, viewpoint, attitude, stance, position, standpoint.
□ a matter of opinion
the extent to which he succeeded is a matter of opinion: open to question, debatable, open to debate, a moot point.
□ be of the opinion
I am of the opinion that his critics are completely wrong: believe, think, consider, maintain, reckon, estimate, feel, be convinced; formal opine.
□ in my opinion
in my opinion this was an error of judgement: as I see it, it seems to me, to my mind, to my way of thinking, in my estimation, if you ask me.

opinionated adjective *an arrogant and opinionated man:* self-important, overbearing, dogmatic, of fixed views, doctrinaire; inflexible, uncompromising.

opponent noun *he beat his Republican opponent by a landslide:* rival, adversary, opposer, the opposition, fellow contestant, fellow competitor, enemy, antagonist, combatant, contender, challenger; literary foe.
OPPOSITES: ally, supporter.

opportune adjective *it's an opportune moment to review the current situation:* convenient, timely; suitable, appropriate, apt, fitting, good; auspicious, propitious, favourable, advantageous, golden, felicitous.
OPPOSITES: inopportune.

opportunism noun *many are saying that the early election was prompted by political opportunism:* expediency, pragmatism; striking while the iron is hot, making hay while the sun shines.

opportunity noun *a slowdown in the housing market would provide a good opportunity for first time buyers:* chance, occasion, moment, time, opening, window of opportunity, possibility; informal break.

oppose verb *residents, charity groups, and a number of councillors opposed the decision:* be against, object to, be hostile to, be in opposition to, disagree with, disapprove of; resist, take a stand against, put up a fight against, stand up to, fight, challenge; take issue with, dispute, argue with/against, quarrel with; informal be anti.
OPPOSITES: support.

opposed adjective
1 *the population is opposed to the nuclear power plants:* against, dead set against; averse, hostile, antagonistic, antipathetic, resistant; informal anti.
2 *their interests were opposed:* conflicting, contrasting, incompatible, irreconcilable, antithetical, contradictory, clashing, at variance, at odds, divergent, poles apart.
OPPOSITES: in favour of.
□ **as opposed to**
in contrast with, as against, as contrasted with, rather than, instead of.

opposing adjective
1 *the two opposing points of view:* conflicting, contrasting, opposite, incompatible, irreconcilable, contradictory, antithetical, clashing, at variance, at odds, divergent, opposed, poles apart.
2 *opposing sides in the war:* rival, opposite, enemy.

opposite adjective
1 *they sat opposite each other:* facing, face to face with, across from; informal eyeball to eyeball with.
2 *the opposite page:* facing, opposing.
3 *opposite views:* conflicting, contrasting, incompatible, irreconcilable, antithetical, contradictory, opposed, opposing, poles apart; clashing, at variance, at odds, different, differing, divergent, dissimilar, disagreeing.
4 *opposite sides in a war:* rival, opposing, enemy.
▷ noun *in fact the opposite was true:* reverse, converse, antithesis, contrary, inverse, obverse; the other side of the coin; informal flip side.

opposition noun
1 *the proposal met with opposition:* resistance, objection, hostility, antagonism, antipathy, dissent, disapproval; defiance, non-compliance, obstruction.
2 *they beat the opposition 5–0:* opponents, opposing side, other side/team, competition, opposers, rivals, adversaries.
3 *the opposition between the public and the private domains:* conflict, clash, disparity, antithesis, polarity.

oppress verb
1 *the government was accused of oppressing ethnic minorities:* persecute, tyrannize, crush, repress, suppress, subjugate, rule with a rod of iron, ride roughshod over; abuse, maltreat, ill-treat.

2 *the gloom oppressed her:* depress, make gloomy/despondent, weigh down, weigh heavily on, cast down, dampen someone's spirits, dispirit, dishearten, discourage, sadden, get down.

oppressed adjective persecuted, downtrodden, subjugated, tyrannized; abused, maltreated, ill-treated; disadvantaged, underprivileged.

oppression noun persecution, tyranny, repression, subjection, subjugation; abuse, maltreatment, ill-treatment, cruelty, brutality, injustice.

oppressive adjective
1 *an oppressive dictatorship:* harsh, cruel, brutal, ruthless, repressive, tyrannical, autocratic, dictatorial, despotic, undemocratic.
2 *an oppressive sense of despair:* overwhelming, overpowering, unbearable, unendurable, intolerable.
3 *the weather was overcast and oppressive:* muggy, close, heavy, hot, humid, sticky, steamy, airless, stuffy, stifling, sultry.

oppressor noun persecutor, tyrant, despot, autocrat, dictator, tormentor.

opprobrious adjective (formal) *a couple of students shouted opprobrious remarks at him:* critical, derogatory, disparaging, insulting, offensive; scornful, contemptuous, derisive.

opprobrium noun (formal)
1 *the government endured months of opprobrium:* vilification, abuse, vituperation, condemnation, criticism, censure, denunciation, obloquy, revilement.
2 *the opprobrium that once attached to informers in all walks of life no longer exists:* disgrace, shame, dishonour, stigma, humiliation, loss of face, ignominy, disrepute, infamy, notoriety.
OPPOSITES: praise, honour.

opt verb *she opted for a cream silk shirt:* choose, select, pick, pick out, decide on, go for, settle on, plump for.

optimism noun hopefulness, hope, confidence, buoyancy; a positive attitude.

optimistic adjective
1 *she felt optimistic about the future:* positive, confident, hopeful, upbeat, sanguine, bullish, buoyant.
2 *the forecast is optimistic:* encouraging, promising, hopeful, upbeat, favourable, auspicious, propitious.
OPPOSITES: pessimistic.

optimum adjective *the optimum pupil–teacher ratio:* best, most favourable, most advantageous, ideal, perfect, prime, optimal.

option noun *the way I see it, we have two options:* choice, alternative, possibility, course of action.

o

optional adjective *registration was obligatory but voting was optional:* voluntary, discretionary, non-compulsory, non-mandatory; elective.
OPPOSITES: compulsory.

opulence noun
1 *the opulence of the room:* luxuriousness, sumptuousness, lavishness, richness, luxury, splendour, magnificence, grandeur.
2 *a display of opulence:* wealth, affluence, riches, prosperity, prosperousness, money.
OPPOSITES: poverty.

opulent adjective
1 *an opulent New York hotel:* luxurious, sumptuous, palatial, lavishly appointed, rich, splendid, magnificent, grand, fancy; informal plush, swanky; Brit. informal swish.
2 *an opulent family:* wealthy, rich, affluent, well off, well-to-do, moneyed, prosperous; informal well heeled, rolling in money, loaded, made of money.
OPPOSITES: spartan, poor.

opus noun *his acclaimed opus 'In Search of Excellence':* composition, work, work of art, creation, piece, publication; oeuvre.

oral adjective *an oral agreement:* spoken, verbal, unwritten.
OPPOSITES: written.

oration noun *his voice gave out half an hour into his three-hour oration:* speech, address, talk, discourse, declamation; homily, sermon, lecture; informal spiel.

orator noun public speaker, speechmaker, rhetorician.

oratory noun *he whipped the meeting up into a frenzy with his oratory:* rhetoric, eloquence, grandiloquence; public speaking, speech-making, declamation; formal magniloquence.

orb noun *the red orb of the sun sank beneath the horizon:* sphere, globe, ball, circle.

orbit noun
1 *the earth's orbit around the sun | the satellite will complete one orbit every 12 hours:* course, path, circuit, track, trajectory, rotation, revolution, circle.
2 *the hope of drawing the administration within the orbit of the United Nations:* sphere, sphere of influence, area of activity, range, scope, ambit, compass, jurisdiction, authority, remit, domain, realm, province, territory; informal bailiwick.
▷ **verb** *Mercury orbits the sun:* revolve round, circle round, go round, travel round.

orchestrate verb
1 *the piece was orchestrated by Mozart:* arrange, adapt, score.
2 *he threatened to orchestrate a campaign of civil disobedience:* organize, arrange, plan, mobilize, mount, stage, stage-manage, mastermind, coordinate, direct, engineer, set up, bring about.

ordain verb
1 *the Church of England voted to ordain women as priests in 1992:* confer holy orders on, anoint, consecrate.
2 *the path ordained by God:* predetermine, predestine, preordain, determine, prescribe, designate.
3 *he ordained that anyone hunting in the forest was to pay a fine:* decree, rule, order, command, lay down, prescribe, pronounce.

ordeal noun *both women were understandably shaken by their ordeal | he was spared the ordeal of giving evidence in court:* unpleasant experience, painful experience, trial, tribulation, nightmare, trauma, hell, trouble, difficulty, suffering, torture, torment, agony.

order noun
1 *the names are in alphabetical order | you must install the files in the correct order:* sequence, arrangement, system, series, succession.
2 *his keen sense of order made him unhappy with anything that seemed vague or confused:* orderliness, organization, method, system; symmetry, uniformity, regularity; tidiness, neatness.
3 *the police were needed to keep order | the breakdown of law and order:* peace, control, discipline, calm, harmony.
4 *the equipment was in good order:* condition, state, repair, shape.
5 *I had to obey his orders:* command, instruction, directive, direction, decree, edict, injunction, mandate, dictate, commandment, diktat; law, rule, regulation; demand, bidding, requirement, stipulation; formal ordinance.
6 *the carrier has emerged from bankruptcy and put in an order for 75 planes:* commission, purchase order, request, requisition; booking, reservation.
7 *the established social order:* class system, hierarchy, pecking order, grading, ranking, scale.
8 *the lower orders of society:* class, level, rank, grade, degree, position, category.
9 *the higher orders of insects:* taxonomic group; class, family, species, breed.
10 *a religious order:* community, brotherhood, sisterhood.
11 *the ancient order of Knights Templar:* organization, association, society, fellowship, fraternity, guild, league, union.
12 *this is craftsmanship of a very high order:* type, kind, sort, nature, variety; quality, calibre, standard.
OPPOSITES: chaos.
▷ **verb**
1 *he ordered me to return:* instruct, command, direct, tell, require, charge; formal enjoin.
2 *he ordered that their assets be confiscated:* decree, ordain, rule, dictate, prescribe.
3 *you can order your tickets by phone:* request, apply for, place an order for; book, reserve.

4 *the messages are ordered chronologically:* organize, put in order, arrange, sort out, lay out; group, classify, categorize, catalogue, codify, systematize.
□ **in order**
1 *list the dates in order:* in sequence, in alphabetical order, in numerical order, in order of priority.
2 *he found everything in order:* tidy, neat, orderly, straight, trim, shipshape, in apple-pie order; in position, in place.
3 *I think it's in order for him to take the credit:* appropriate, fitting, suitable, acceptable, all right, permissible, permitted, allowable; informal okay.
□ **order someone about/around**
tell someone what to do, give orders to, dictate to; lay down the law; informal boss about/around, push about/around.
□ **out of order**
1 *the lift's out of order:* not working, not in working order, not functioning, broken, broken-down, out of service, out of commission, faulty, defective, inoperative; down; informal conked out, bust, kaput.
2 (Brit. informal) *that comment is totally out of order:* unacceptable, unfair, unjust, unjustified, uncalled for, below the belt, unreasonable, unwarranted, beyond the pale; informal not on, a bit much.

orderly adjective
1 *an orderly, peaceful room:* neat, tidy, well ordered, in order, trim, in apple-pie order, spick and span.
2 *the orderly presentation of information:* organized, well organized, efficient, methodical, systematic; coherent, structured, logical, well planned, well regulated, systematized.
3 *the crowd was orderly:* well behaved, law-abiding, disciplined, peaceful, peaceable, non-violent.
OPPOSITES: untidy, disorganized.

ordinarily adverb *he ordinarily worked outside the UK:* usually, normally, as a rule, generally, in general, for the most part, mainly, mostly, most of the time, typically, habitually, commonly, routinely.

ordinary adjective
1 *the ordinary course of events:* usual, normal, standard, typical, common, customary, habitual, everyday, regular, routine, day-to-day; formal quotidian.
2 *my life seemed very ordinary:* average, normal, run-of-the-mill, standard, typical, middle-of-the-road, conventional, unremarkable, unexceptional, workaday, undistinguished, nondescript, colourless, commonplace, humdrum, mundane, unmemorable, pedestrian, prosaic, uninteresting, uneventful, dull, boring, bland, suburban; informal nothing to write home about, no great shakes.
OPPOSITES: unusual.
□ **out of the ordinary**
nothing out of the ordinary happened: unusual, exceptional, remarkable,

extraordinary, unexpected, surprising, unaccustomed, unfamiliar, abnormal, atypical, different, special, exciting, memorable, noteworthy, unique, singular, outstanding; unconventional, unorthodox, offbeat, strange, peculiar, odd, queer, curious, bizarre, outlandish; informal weird.

ordnance noun guns, cannon, artillery, weapons, arms; munitions.

organ noun
1 *the internal organs:* body part.
2 *the official organ of the Communist Party:* newspaper, paper, journal, periodical, publication, mouthpiece.

organic adjective
1 *organic matter:* living, live, animate; biological, biotic.
2 *organic vegetables:* pesticide-free, additive-free, natural.
3 *the love scenes were an organic part of the drama:* essential, fundamental, integral, intrinsic, vital, indispensable, inherent.
4 *he described society as an organic whole:* coherent, cohesive, harmonious, integrated, coordinated, ordered, organized, structured.

organism noun
1 *fish and other organisms:* living thing, being, creature, animal, plant, life form.
2 *a complex political organism:* structure, system, organization, entity.

organization noun
1 *the organization of conferences:* planning, arrangement, coordination, administration, organizing, running, management.
2 *the overall organization of the book:* structure, arrangement, plan, pattern, order, form, format, framework, composition.
3 *his lack of organization:* efficiency, order, orderliness, planning.
4 *a large international organization:* company, firm, corporation, institution, group, consortium, conglomerate, agency, association, society; informal outfit, set-up.

organize verb
1 *much thought has gone into how we organize information on the Web:* arrange, order, structure, sort, sort out, assemble, marshal, group, classify, categorize, catalogue, codify, systematize.
2 *they organized a search party | I'll sort out the food and drink:* make arrangements for, arrange, plan, coordinate, assemble, put together, fix up, set up, orchestrate, take care of, see to, deal with, sort out, manage, administrate, mobilize; schedule, timetable, programme.

organized adjective *it was a very organized campaign | she used to be so organized:* well ordered, well run, well planned, structured, coordinated; orderly,

O

efficient, methodical, systematic; informal together.
OPPOSITES: disorganized, inefficient.

orgiastic adjective *an orgiastic celebration:* debauched, wild, riotous, wanton.

orgy noun
1 *a drunken orgy:* wild party, carousal, revel, revelry; informal binge, booze-up, bender.
2 *an orgy of conspicuous consumption:* bout, spree; excess, surfeit.

orient, orientate verb
1 *there were no street names to enable her to orient herself:* get/find your bearings, establish your location.
2 *you need to orientate yourself to your new way of life:* adapt, adjust, familiarize, acclimatize, accustom, attune.
3 *magazines oriented to the business community:* aim at, direct at, pitch at, design for, intend for.
4 *the fires are oriented in line with the sunset:* align, place, position.

oriental adjective *his priceless collection of oriental art:* eastern; Chinese, Japanese.

> **USAGE**
>
> The term **oriental** is now regarded as old-fashioned and potentially offensive as a term referring to people from eastern Asia. In US English, **Asian** is the standard accepted term in modern use. In British English, where **Asian** tends to refer to people from the Indian subcontinent, specific terms such as **Chinese** or **Japanese** are preferable, while **South-East Asian** has also emerged as a more general term. The word **Asiatic**, while standard in scientific and technical use, can be offensive when used of individual people and should be avoided in that context.

orientation noun
1 *the orientation of the radar station:* positioning, location, position, situation, placement, alignment.
2 *his orientation to his new way of life:* adaptation, adjustment, acclimatization.
3 *a movement that was broadly Marxist in orientation:* attitude, inclination; belief, view, outlook.
4 *a four-day orientation course for newly elected councillors:* induction, training, familiarization.

orifice noun opening, hole, aperture, interstice; slot, slit, cleft.

origin noun
1 *the origins of life:* beginning, start, commencement, origination, genesis, birth, dawning, dawn, emergence, creation, birthplace, cradle; source, basis, cause, roots.
2 *the Latin origin of the word:* source, derivation, root, provenance, etymology; N. Amer. provenience.
3 *his Scottish origins:* descent, ancestry,

parentage, pedigree, lineage, line of descent, heritage, birth, extraction, family, stock, blood, bloodline.

original adjective
1 *the original inhabitants of the country:* indigenous, native, aboriginal; first, earliest, early; Anthropology autochthonous.
2 *original Rembrandts:* authentic, genuine, actual, true, bona fide; informal pukka, kosher.
3 *the film is highly original | he's come up with some original ideas:* innovative, creative, imaginative, innovatory, inventive; new, novel, fresh, refreshing; unusual, unconventional, unorthodox, groundbreaking, pioneering, avant-garde, unique, distinctive; informal left-field, edgy.
▷ noun *the sculpture is thought to be a Roman copy of a Hellenistic original:* archetype, prototype, source, master.

> **WORD LINKS**
>
> **proto-, ur-** forming words meaning 'original; first', such as *prototype* ('the first version of something, from which other versions are developed') and *urtext* ('the original or earliest version of a text')

originality noun *the film suffers from a distinct lack of originality:* inventiveness, ingenuity, creativeness, creativity, innovation, freshness, imagination, imaginativeness, individuality, uniqueness, distinctiveness.

originally adverb *the conference was originally scheduled for November:* first, in/at the beginning, to begin with, initially, in the first place, at the outset.

originate verb
1 *the story apparently originated in the US:* arise, have its origin, begin, start, stem, spring, emerge, emanate.
2 *Bill Levy originated the idea:* invent, create, initiate, devise, think up, dream up, conceive, formulate, form, develop, produce, mastermind, pioneer.

originator noun inventor, creator, architect, author, initiator, innovator, founder, pioneer, mastermind.

ornament noun
1 *the desk was covered with little ornaments:* knick-knack, trinket, bauble, bibelot, gewgaw.
2 *these Gothic buildings are notable for their finely detailed ornament:* decoration, adornment, embellishment, ornamentation; trimming, accessories.
▷ verb *her robe was ornamented with precious jewels:* decorate, adorn, embellish, trim, bedeck, deck, deck out, festoon.

ornamental adjective *the ornamental plasterwork on the ceiling:* decorative, fancy, ornate.

ornamentation noun decoration,

adornment, embellishment, ornament; trimming, accessories.

ornate adjective

1 *an ornate gilt mirror:* decorated, elaborate, embellished, adorned, ornamented, fancy; fussy, ostentatious, showy; informal flash, flashy.
2 *ornate language:* elaborate, flowery, florid; grandiose, pompous, pretentious, high-flown, orotund, grandiloquent, rhetorical, oratorical, bombastic, overwrought, overblown, extravagant; formal magniloquent; informal highfalutin.
OPPOSITES: plain.

orthodox adjective *Burke's views were orthodox in his time:* conventional, mainstream, conformist, established, standard, traditional, traditionalist, conservative; prevalent, popular.
OPPOSITES: unorthodox, unconventional.

orthodoxy noun

1 *he challenged many of the established orthodoxies:* doctrine, belief, conviction, creed, dogma, credo, theory, tenet, teaching.
2 *a pillar of orthodoxy:* conventionality, conventionalism, conformism, conservatism, traditionalism, conformity.

oscillate verb

1 *the pendulum started to oscillate:* swing to and fro, swing back and forth, sway.
2 *he was oscillating between fear and bravery:* waver, swing, fluctuate, alternate, see-saw, yo-yo, sway, vacillate, hover.

ossify verb

1 *these cartilages may ossify:* turn into bone, become bony.
2 *the business sector has been allowed to ossify:* become inflexible, become rigid, become fossilized, rigidify, stagnate.

ostensible adjective *the ostensible cause of the conflict:* apparent, outward, superficial, professed, supposed, alleged, purported.
OPPOSITES: genuine.

ostensibly adverb *it is ostensibly a book about football:* apparently, seemingly, on the face of it, to all intents and purposes, outwardly, superficially, allegedly, supposedly, purportedly.

ostentation noun showiness, show, flamboyance, ostentatiousness, conspicuousness, pretentiousness, vulgarity, gaudiness, brashness, extravagance; informal flashiness.

ostentatious adjective *an ostentatious display of wealth:* showy, flamboyant, conspicuous, obtrusive, pretentious, brash, vulgar, loud, gaudy, extravagant, fancy, ornate; informal flash, flashy, over the top.
OPPOSITES: restrained.

ostracize verb *individuals who took such action risked being ostracized by their*

fellow workers: exclude, shun, spurn, cold-shoulder, reject, shut out, avoid, ignore, snub, cut dead, keep at arm's length, leave out in the cold; blackball, blacklist; Brit. send to Coventry; informal freeze out.
OPPOSITES: welcome.

other adjective

1 *these homes use other fuels:* alternative, different, distinct, contrasting.
2 *one other word of advice | are there any other questions?* more, further, additional, extra, added, supplementary.

otherwise adverb

1 *hurry up, otherwise we'll be late:* or, or else, if not.
2 *she's exhausted, but otherwise she's fine:* in other respects, apart from that.
3 *he could not have acted otherwise:* in any other way, differently.

other-worldly adjective *her face had a distant, other-worldly look:* ethereal, spiritual, mystic, mystical; unearthly, unworldly.

ounce noun *it took every ounce of courage she possessed to board the plane:* particle, scrap, bit, speck, trace, atom, shred, crumb, fragment, grain, drop, spot, iota, whit, jot.

oust verb *armed forces ousted the new coalition government:* drive out, expel, force out, throw out, remove from office/power, eject, get rid of, depose, topple, unseat, defeat, overthrow, bring down, overturn, dismiss, dislodge, displace; informal boot out, kick out; Brit. informal turf out.

out adjective & adverb

1 *she's out at the moment:* not here, not at home, not in, away, elsewhere, absent.
2 *the secret was out:* revealed, out in the open, common/public knowledge, known, disclosed, divulged.
3 *the roses are out:* in flower, flowering, in bloom, blooming, in blossom, blossoming, open.
4 *the book should be out soon:* available, obtainable, in the shops, published, in print.
5 *the fire was nearly out:* extinguished, no longer alight.
6 *smoking is out:* forbidden, not permitted, not allowed, proscribed, unacceptable; informal not on.
7 *he was slightly out in his calculations:* mistaken, inaccurate, incorrect, wrong, in error.
OPPOSITES: in.

out-and-out adjective *he really is an out-and-out chauvinist:* utter, downright, thoroughgoing, absolute, complete, thorough, total, unmitigated, outright, real, perfect, consummate; informal deep-dyed; Brit. informal right.

outbreak noun

1 *a fresh outbreak of violence:* eruption,

upsurge, outburst, epidemic, rash, wave, spate, flood, explosion, flare-up, burst, flurry.
2 *the outbreak of war:* start, beginning, commencement, onset, outset.

outburst noun *a sudden outburst of laughter | outbursts of fighting:* eruption, explosion, burst, outpouring, surge, upsurge, outbreak, flare-up.

outcast noun *a social outcast:* pariah, persona non grata, reject, outsider.

outclass verb *he completely outclassed his rivals:* surpass, outshine, be superior to, be better than, overshadow, eclipse, outdo, outplay, outmanoeuvre, outstrip, get the better of, upstage; top, cap, beat, defeat; informal be a cut above, be head and shoulders above, run rings round.

outcome noun *the outcome of the court case is far from certain:* result, consequence, effect, upshot; after-effect, aftermath, conclusion, issue, end result.

outcry noun *public outcry led to the closure of the bank:* protests, protestations, anger, complaints, objections, furore, fuss, commotion, uproar, opposition, dissent; informal ballyhoo, ructions, stink; Brit. informal hullabaloo.

outdated adjective *an outdated rail network | outdated social attitudes:* old-fashioned, out of date, outmoded, dated, old, behind the times, obsolete, antiquated; out of fashion, unfashionable, passé; informal old hat, square, out of the ark, clunky.
OPPOSITES: modern.

o

outdistance verb
1 *Gil was the fastest and swiftly outdistanced the other two:* outrun, outstrip, outpace, leave behind, get ahead of; overtake, pass.
2 *the company has outdistanced all its rivals:* surpass, outshine, outclass, outdo, exceed, transcend, top, cap, beat, better, leave behind; informal leave standing.

outdo verb *the men tried to outdo each other in their generosity:* surpass, outshine, eclipse, outclass, outmanoeuvre, get the better of, put in the shade, overshadow, upstage; exceed, transcend, top, cap, beat, better, leave behind, get ahead of; informal be a cut above, be head and shoulders above, run rings round.

outdoor adjective *a popular outdoor activity:* open air, out-of-doors, outside, al fresco.
OPPOSITES: indoor.

outer adjective
1 *the outer layer is a waterproof, breathable fabric:* outside, outermost, outward, exterior, external, surface.
2 *outer areas of the city:* outlying, distant, remote, faraway, furthest, peripheral; suburban.
OPPOSITES: inner.

outface verb *the king lacked political skill and determined ministers could always outface him:* stand up to, face down, overawe, intimidate, cow.

outfit noun
1 *her outfit accentuated her blue eyes:* clothes, clothing, dress; costume, suit, ensemble, garb; formal attire; informal get-up, gear, togs.
2 *a first-aid outfit:* kit, equipment, tools, implements, apparatus, paraphernalia.
3 (informal) *a local manufacturing outfit:* organization, set-up, enterprise, company, firm, business; group, band, body, team.
▷ verb
1 *the wardens were outfitted in special suits:* dress, clothe; formal attire.
2 *he outfitted them all with state-of-the-art computers:* equip, provide, supply, kit out, fit out/up, arm.

outflow noun *the seabed was forced apart by the outflow of lava:* discharge, outflowing, outpouring, outrush, rush, flood, deluge, issue, spurt, jet, cascade, stream, torrent, gush, outburst; flow, flux.

outgoing adjective
1 *she's always been very outgoing and she's got lots of friends:* sociable, gregarious, friendly, convivial, lively, extrovert, uninhibited, unreserved, demonstrative, affectionate, warm, genial, cordial, affable, easy-going; communicative, responsive, open.
2 *the outgoing president:* departing, retiring, leaving.
OPPOSITES: introverted, incoming.

outgoings plural noun *monthly outgoings exceeded income:* expenses, expenditure, spending, outlay, payments, costs, overheads.

outgrowth noun *the eye first appears as an outgrowth from the brain:* protuberance, swelling, excrescence, growth, lump, bump, bulge; development.

outing noun *family outings to the seaside:* trip, excursion, jaunt, expedition, day out, tour, drive, ride, run; informal junket, spin.

outlandish adjective *he had a mass of long unkempt blond hair and a penchant for outlandish outfits:* bizarre, odd, unconventional, unusual, extraordinary, strange, peculiar, funny, curious, far out, quirky, zany, eccentric, offbeat, idiosyncratic, unorthodox, unfamiliar; informal weird, off the wall, way-out, wacky, oddball.
OPPOSITES: ordinary.

outlast verb *the buildings outlasted generations of occupants:* outlive, survive; ride out, weather, withstand.

outlaw noun *bands of outlaws held up the trains:* fugitive, wanted criminal, desperado, outcast; bandit, robber.

▷**verb** *they voted to outlaw fox-hunting:* ban, bar, prohibit, forbid, veto, disallow, make illegal, proscribe, interdict.
OPPOSITES: permit.

outlay noun *the project involved comparatively little financial outlay:* expenditure, cost, expenses, spending, outgoings, price, payment, investment.
OPPOSITES: profit.

outlet noun
1 *a central-heating outlet:* vent, way out; outfall, opening, channel, conduit, duct.
2 *an outlet for farm produce:* market, retail outlet, marketplace, shop, store.
3 *an outlet for their energies:* means of expression, release, vent, avenue, channel.

outline noun
1 *the outline of the building:* silhouette, profile, shape, contours, form, line, delineation; diagram, sketch.
2 *an outline of the proposal:* summary, rundown, synopsis; framework, main points, essence, gist; rough idea, thumbnail sketch, bare bones, draft, sketch.
▷**verb**
1 *the plane was outlined against the sky:* silhouette, define, demarcate; sketch, delineate, trace.
2 *she outlined the plan briefly:* summarize, sketch out, draft, give a rough idea of, rough out.

outlive verb *she outlived her husband by nearly thirty years:* live on after, live longer than, outlast, survive.

outlook noun
1 *the two men were wholly different in outlook:* point of view, viewpoint, views, opinion, thinking, way of thinking, perspective, attitude, standpoint, stance, frame of mind.
2 *a lovely open outlook:* view, vista, prospect, panorama, scene, aspect.
3 *the outlook for the economy:* prospects, expectations, prognosis, hopes, future, lookout.

outlying adjective *an outlying village:* distant, remote, outer, off the beaten track, out of the way, far-flung, inaccessible.

outmanoeuvre verb *he outmanoeuvred his critics:* outwit, outsmart, out-think, outplay, outflank, steal a march on, trick, get the better of; informal outfox, put one over on.

outmoded adjective *inefficient and outmoded working practices:* out of date, old-fashioned, outdated, dated, behind the times, antiquated, obsolete, passé; informal old hat, out of the ark.

out of date adjective
1 *everything in her wardrobe was hopelessly out of date | they are working with out-of-date equipment:* old-fashioned, outmoded,

out of fashion, unfashionable, frumpish, frumpy, outdated, dated, old, passé, behind the times; obsolete, antiquated; informal square, not with it, out of the ark, clunky.
2 *my passport is out of date:* invalid, (null and) void; lapsed, expired.
OPPOSITES: fashionable, current.

out of the way adjective *he has lived in some very out-of-the-way places:* remote, distant, faraway, far-flung, isolated, lonely, godforsaken, inaccessible, off the beaten track.
OPPOSITES: accessible.

outpouring noun *his sudden death prompted outpourings of public grief | a tremendous outpouring of new ideas:* outburst, eruption, explosion, storm, torrent, upsurge, surge, flow, stream, flood.

output noun *industrial output fell by 2.8%:* production, amount/quantity produced, yield, gross domestic product; productivity.

outrage noun
1 *the original plan was shelved in the face of widespread public outrage:* indignation, fury, anger, rage, disapproval, wrath, resentment.
2 *it is an outrage that I have to put up with such treatment:* scandal, offence, insult, injustice, disgrace.
3 *one of the worst terrorist outrages of modern times:* atrocity, act of violence/wickedness, crime, wrong, barbarism, inhumane act.
▷**verb** *his remarks outraged his parishioners:* enrage, infuriate, incense, anger, scandalize, offend, give offence to, affront, shock, horrify, disgust, appal.

outrageous adjective
1 *the men engaged in outrageous acts of cruelty:* shocking, disgraceful, scandalous, atrocious, appalling, monstrous, heinous; evil, wicked, abominable, terrible, horrendous, dreadful, foul, nauseating, sickening, vile, nasty, odious, loathsome, unspeakable.
2 *I never thought anyone would believe such an outrageous story:* far-fetched, unlikely, doubtful, dubious, questionable, implausible, unconvincing, unbelievable, incredible, preposterous, extravagant.
3 *he was known for wearing rather outrageous clothes:* eye-catching, flamboyant, bold, unusual, showy, extravagant; shameless, shocking.

outré adjective *radio stations that mixed rock with more outré forms of music:* bizarre, outlandish, unconventional, unorthodox, funny, unusual, extraordinary, strange, unfamiliar, peculiar, odd, out of the way, quirky, eccentric; informal weird, way-out, wacky, off the wall, left-field.

outright adverb
1 *he rejected the proposal outright:* completely, entirely, wholly, fully, totally,

O

categorically, absolutely, utterly, flatly, unreservedly.

2 *I told her outright:* directly, openly, explicitly, frankly, candidly, honestly, sincerely, bluntly, plainly, in plain language, truthfully, to someone's face, straight from the shoulder; Brit. informal straight up.

3 *they were killed outright:* instantly, instantaneously, immediately, at once, straight away, then and there, on the spot.

▷ **adjective**
1 *an outright disaster:* out-and-out, absolute, complete, downright, utter, sheer, categorical, unmitigated, unqualified, unconditional.
2 *the outright winner:* definite, unequivocal, clear, unqualified, incontestable, unmistakable.

outrun verb *an antelope could easily outrun a lion:* run faster than, outstrip, outdistance, outpace, leave behind, lose; informal leave standing.

outset noun *the project was flawed from the outset:* start, starting point, beginning, commencement, inception, opening, launch, inauguration, dawn, birth, origin; informal the word go.
OPPOSITES: end.

outshine verb *she was outshone by her elder sister:* surpass, overshadow, eclipse, outclass, put in the shade, upstage, top, cap, beat, better; informal be a cut above, be head and shoulders above, run rings round.

outside noun *the outside of the building:* exterior, facade, outer/external surface, outer side/layer, case, skin, shell, covering.
▷ **adjective**
1 *outside lights:* exterior, external, outer, outdoor, out-of-doors.
2 *outside contractors:* independent, hired, temporary, freelance, casual, external, extramural.
3 *an outside chance:* slight, slender, slim, small, tiny, faint, negligible, remote, vague.
▷ **adverb** *they went outside | shall we eat outside?* outdoors, out of doors; alfresco.
OPPOSITES: inside.

> **WORD LINKS**
> **extra-** forming words meaning 'outside, beyond', such as *extramarital* ('occurring outside marriage')

outsider noun *to an outsider, the scene would have appeared normal:* stranger, visitor, non-member; incomer, newcomer; foreigner, alien.

outsize adjective *an outsize suitcase | their outsize pay package:* huge, oversized, enormous, gigantic, very big/large, great, giant, colossal, massive, mammoth, vast, immense, tremendous, monumental, prodigious, mountainous, king-sized;

informal mega, monster, whopping, humongous, jumbo; Brit. informal whacking great, ginormous.

outskirts plural noun *a house on the outskirts of the town:* outlying districts, edges, fringes, periphery, suburbs, suburbia; purlieus, borders, environs.

outsmart verb *buyers and sellers attempt to outsmart each other:* outwit, outmanoeuvre, outplay, steal a march on, trick, get the better of; informal outfox, pull a fast one on, put one over on.

outspoken adjective *an outspoken critic of the government:* forthright, direct, candid, frank, straightforward, honest, open, straight from the shoulder, plain-spoken; blunt, abrupt, bluff, brusque.

outspread adjective *the kestrels were soaring with outspread wings:* outstretched, extended, spread out, unfolded, unfurled, wide open.

outstanding adjective
1 *an outstanding performance:* excellent, marvellous, magnificent, superb, fine, wonderful, superlative, exceptional, first-class, first-rate, impressive; informal great, terrific, tremendous, amazing, fantastic, sensational, fabulous, ace, mean, awesome, out of this world; Brit. informal brilliant.
2 *her green eyes were her most outstanding feature:* remarkable, extraordinary, exceptional, striking, eye-catching, arresting, distinctive, unforgettable, memorable, special, notable, noteworthy.
3 *much of the work is still outstanding:* to be done, undone, unattended to, unfinished, incomplete, remaining, pending, ongoing.
4 *the firm's outstanding debts are mounting:* unpaid, unsettled, owing, owed, to be paid, payable, due, overdue, undischarged.
OPPOSITES: unexceptional.

outstrip verb
1 *he outstripped the police cars:* go faster than, outrun, outdistance, outpace, leave behind, get ahead of, lose; informal leave standing.
2 *demand far outstrips supply:* surpass, exceed, be more than, top, eclipse.

outward adjective *an outward display of friendliness:* external, outer, outside, exterior; surface, superficial, seeming, apparent, ostensible.
OPPOSITES: inward.

outwardly adverb *the house is outwardly no different from any of the others:* externally, on the surface, superficially, on the face of it, to all intents and purposes, apparently, ostensibly, seemingly.

outweigh verb *the advantages greatly outweigh the disadvantages:* be greater than, exceed, override, supersede, offset, cancel out; prevail over, have the edge on/over, more than make up for, compensate for.

outwit verb *constant vigilance is needed to outwit enemy infiltrators:* outsmart, outmanoeuvre, outplay, steal a march on, get the better of, trick, deceive, fool; informal outfox, pull a fast one on, put one over on.

outworn adjective *an outworn social ideal:* out of date, outdated, old-fashioned, outmoded, dated, behind the times, antiquated, obsolete, passé; informal old hat, out of the ark.
OPPOSITES: up to date.

oval adjective egg-shaped, ovoid, ovate, elliptic, elliptical.

ovation noun *the performance received a thundering ovation from the crowd:* round of applause, clapping, cheering, cheers, bravos, tribute, standing ovation; informal big hand.

over preposition
1 *there was an oxygen tent over the bed:* above, on top of, atop, covering.
2 *over 200,000 people live in the area:* more than, above, in excess of, upwards of.
3 *he has three people over him:* superior to, above, higher up than; in charge of, responsible for.
OPPOSITES: under.
▷ adverb
1 *a flock of geese flew over:* overhead, on high, above, past, by.
2 *the relationship is over:* at an end, finished, concluded, terminated, ended, no more, a thing of the past.
3 *he had some money over:* left, left over, remaining, unused, surplus, in excess, in addition.
□ over and above
he's earning a quarter of a million a year, over and above his parliamentary salary: in addition to, on top of, as well as, besides, along with; informal plus.
□ over and over
the song is little more than a chorus repeated over and over: repeatedly, again and again, over and over again, time and time again, many times over, frequently, constantly, continually, persistently, ad nauseam.

> WORD LINKS
> **super-**, **hyper-** forming words meaning 'over; above normal' such as *superstructure* ('a structure built on top of something else') and *hyperactive* ('abnormally or excessively active')

overact verb *she's a weepy actress with a strong tendency to overact:* exaggerate, overdo it, overplay it; informal ham it up, camp it up.

overall adjective *the overall cost | the overall effect is impressive:* all-inclusive, comprehensive, all-embracing, final, inclusive; general.
▷ adverb *overall, things have improved:* generally, in general, altogether, all in

all, on balance, for the most part, in the main, on the whole, by and large, to a large extent.

overawe verb *many of the players seemed overawed by the atmosphere and the occasion:* intimidate, daunt, unnerve, subdue, dismay, frighten, alarm, scare; informal psych out.

overbalance verb *she turned round so fast that she almost overbalanced:* fall over, topple over, lose your balance, keel over, tip over; push over, upend, upset.

overbearing adjective *her life was controlled by her overbearing mother:* domineering, imperious, overpowering, high-handed, bullying; authoritarian, dictatorial, autocratic, tyrannical; informal bossy.

overblown adjective *an overblown piece of writing | overblown rhetoric:* pretentious, grandiose, pompous, bombastic, exaggerated, over-elaborate, florid, flowery, overwrought, high-flown, turgid, grandiloquent, orotund; formal magniloquent; informal highfalutin.

overcast adjective *the sky was still overcast:* cloudy, clouded, sunless, dark, grey, black, leaden, heavy, dull, murky, dismal, dreary.
OPPOSITES: bright.

overcharge verb *clients are being overcharged:* swindle, charge too much, cheat, defraud, fleece, short-change; informal rip off, sting, diddle, do.

overcome verb
1 *an experienced England side overcame the home team:* defeat, beat, get the better of, triumph over, conquer, vanquish, overwhelm, overpower, prevail over, win over/against, outdo, outclass, trounce.
2 *they overcame their fear of flying:* get the better of, prevail over, control, get/bring under control, master, conquer, defeat, beat; get over, get a grip on, subdue; informal lick.
3 *her father was overcome with grief:* overwhelm, devastate, daze, stun; informal knock sideways; Brit. informal knock for six.

overconfident adjective *he's overconfident and incredibly arrogant:* cocksure, cocky, smug, conceited, presumptuous, brash, heading for a fall, riding for a fall; informal too big for your boots.

overcritical adjective *overcritical parents can do untold damage to their children's self esteem:* judgemental, censorious, negative, fault-finding, hypercritical, over-particular, pedantic, over-scrupulous; formal captious; informal nit-picking; Brit. informal pernickety.

overcrowded adjective *a new plan to tackle the country's overcrowded prisons:* packed, overfull, overflowing, full to

overflowing/bursting, crammed full, congested, overpopulated, crowded, teeming; informal bursting/bulging at the seams, full to the gunwales, jam-packed.
OPPOSITES: empty.

overdo verb
1 *she overdoes the cockney scenes:* exaggerate, overplay, overdramatize, overstate, overemphasize; informal go overboard with, ham up, camp up.
2 *they overdid the beef:* overcook, burn, ruin.
OPPOSITES: understate.
□ **overdo it**
work too hard, overwork, do too much, burn the candle at both ends, overtax yourself, drive/push yourself too hard, work/run yourself into the ground, wear yourself to a shadow, wear yourself out, bite off more than you can chew, strain yourself; informal kill yourself, knock yourself out.

overdone adjective *the flattery was overdone:* excessive, too much, undue, immoderate, inordinate, disproportionate, inflated, overstated, exaggerated, over-emphasized, overenthusiastic; informal a bit much, over the top, OTT.
OPPOSITES: understated.

overdue adjective
1 *the train was overdue:* late, behind schedule, behind time, delayed.
2 *overdue payments:* unpaid, unsettled, owing, owed, payable, due, outstanding, undischarged.
OPPOSITES: early, punctual.

overeat verb *most of us are inclined to overeat occasionally:* eat too much, be greedy, gorge yourself, overindulge, feast; informal binge, make a pig of yourself, pig out.
OPPOSITES: starve.

overemphasize verb *the importance of adequate preparation cannot be overemphasized:* place/lay too much emphasis on, overstress, place/lay too much stress on, exaggerate, make too much of, overplay, overdo; informal make a big thing about/of, blow up out of all proportion.
OPPOSITES: understate.

overflow verb *the river has overflowed its banks:* spill over, flow over, brim over, well over, pour over, stream over, flood.
▷ **noun**
1 *an overflow from the tank:* overspill, spill, spillage, flood.
2 *to accommodate the overflow, five more offices were built:* surplus, excess, additional people/things, extra people/things, remainder, overspill.

overflowing adjective *an overflowing rubbish bin:* overfull, full to overflowing/bursting, crammed full, overloaded, overcrowded; informal bursting/bulging at

the seams, jam-packed.
OPPOSITES: empty.

overhang verb *the shrubs overhang the lawn:* hang over, extend over, stick out over, project over, protrude over, jut out over, bulge out over.

overhaul noun *a comprehensive overhaul of the building is needed to bring the facilities up to date:* modernization, refit, redevelopment, revamp, improvement, upgrade, makeover, facelift.
▷ **verb** *I've been overhauling the gearbox:* check, examine, service, repair, mend, fix, recondition.

overhead adverb *a burst of thunder erupted overhead:* up above, high up, up in the sky, on high, above/over your head.
OPPOSITES: below.
▷ **adjective** *overhead lines:* aerial, elevated, raised.
OPPOSITES: underground.

overheads plural noun *businesses with high overheads:* running costs, operating costs, fixed costs, expenses.
OPPOSITES: profit.

overindulge verb
1 *we tend to overindulge at Christmas:* drink/eat too much, overeat, be greedy, overdo it, drink/eat to excess, gorge yourself, feast; informal binge, stuff yourself, go overboard, make a pig of yourself, pig yourself.
2 *his mother had overindulged him:* spoil, pander to, indulge, pamper, mollycoddle.
OPPOSITES: abstain.

overjoyed adjective *the girls were overjoyed at their success:* ecstatic, euphoric, thrilled, elated, delighted, on cloud nine, in seventh heaven, jubilant, rapturous, jumping for joy, delirious, blissful, in raptures, as pleased as Punch, cock-a-hoop; informal over the moon, on top of the world, tickled pink; Brit. informal as happy as Larry.
OPPOSITES: dejected.

overlay verb *the wooden statues are painted with black resin and overlaid with gold in parts:* cover, face, surface, veneer, inlay, laminate, plaster; coat, varnish, glaze.
▷ **noun** *an overlay of glass-fibre insulation:* covering, cover, layer, face, surface, veneer, lamination; coat, varnish, glaze, wash.

overload verb
1 *avoid overloading the boat:* overburden, put too much in, weigh down.
2 *the staff are overloaded with casework:* overwhelm, swamp, overburden, weigh down, overtax, overwork.
▷ **noun** *an overload of information:* excess, overabundance, superabundance, glut, surfeit, surplus, superfluity; avalanche, deluge, flood.

O

overlook verb

1 *he overlooked the mistake:* fail to notice, fail to spot, miss.
2 *she was willing to overlook his faults:* ignore, disregard, take no notice of, make allowances for, turn a blind eye to, excuse, pardon, forgive.
3 *his work has been overlooked:* pay no attention to, pass over, disregard, neglect, ignore, forget.
4 *the breakfast room overlooks the garden:* have a view of, look over/across, look on to, look out on/over, give on to, command a view of.

overly adverb *she was a jealous and overly possessive woman:* unduly, excessively, inordinately, too; wildly, absurdly, ridiculously, outrageously, unreasonably, impossibly.

overpower verb

1 *police officers finally overpowered the man:* gain control over, prevail over, get the better of, subdue, suppress, bring someone to their knees, defeat.
2 *a flood of emotions overpowered him:* overcome, overwhelm; stun, devastate, leave speechless; informal knock sideways; Brit. informal knock for six.

overpowering adjective

1 *overpowering grief:* overwhelming, unbearable, unendurable, intolerable.
2 *an overpowering smell:* strong, pungent; nauseating, offensive, acrid, fetid, mephitic.
3 *overpowering evidence:* irrefutable, undeniable, indisputable, incontestable, incontrovertible, compelling, conclusive.

overrate verb *it is easy to overrate what Frederick achieved:* overestimate, overvalue, attach too much importance to, exaggerate, think too much of, praise too highly, glorify.
OPPOSITES: underestimate.

overreach verb
□ overreach yourself
he waited for his opponents to overreach themselves: try to do too much, overestimate your ability, overdo it, overstretch yourself, wear/burn yourself out, bite off more than you can chew.

overreact verb *I had to admit that I'd overreacted:* lose your sense of proportion, blow something up out of all proportion, make a mountain out of a molehill; Brit. informal go over the top.

override verb

1 *the court could not override her decision:* reject, overrule, overturn, set aside, countermand, veto, quash; cancel, reverse, rescind, revoke, repeal, nullify, invalidate, negate.
2 *the government can override all opposition:* disregard, pay no heed to, take no account of, turn a deaf ear to, ignore, ride roughshod over.
3 *this commitment should override all other considerations:* outweigh, take precedence over, take priority over, supersede.

overriding adjective *safety was the overriding consideration:* most important, of greatest importance, principal, primary, paramount, chief, main, major, foremost, uppermost, top, first, first and foremost, highest, pre-eminent, predominant, central, key, pivotal; informal number-one.

overrule verb *this ban was overruled by a federal court:* overturn, override, countermand, cancel, reverse, rescind, repeal, revoke, veto, quash, annul, nullify, invalidate, negate.

overrun verb

1 *guerrillas overran the barracks:* invade, storm, occupy, swarm into, surge into, inundate, overwhelm.
2 *the talks overran the deadline:* exceed, go beyond/over, run over.

oversee verb *a manager was appointed to oversee the building work:* supervise, superintend, be in charge/control of, be responsible for, look after, keep an eye on, inspect, administer, organize, manage, direct, preside over.

overseer noun supervisor, foreman, forewoman, team leader, controller, manager, head of department, superintendent; Brit. gangmaster; informal boss, chief, governor; Brit. informal gaffer.

overshadow verb

1 *an enormous oak tree overshadows the cottage:* cast a shadow over, shade, screen; tower over, dwarf, dominate, overlook.
2 *it is easy to let this feeling of tragedy overshadow his story:* cast a pall over, cast gloom over, blight, take the edge off, mar, spoil, ruin.
3 *he was overshadowed by his brilliant elder brother:* outshine, eclipse, surpass, be superior to, outclass, outstrip, outdo, upstage, put in the shade; informal be head and shoulders above.

oversight noun

1 *a stupid oversight:* mistake, error, omission, lapse, slip, blunder; informal slip-up.
2 *this could well have been due to oversight:* carelessness, inattention, negligence, forgetfulness, laxity.
3 *the government's oversight of the health-care industry:* supervision, superintendence, surveillance, charge, care, administration, management.

overstate verb *he admitted that he had perhaps overstated his case:* exaggerate, overdo, overemphasize, overplay, dramatize, embroider, embellish; informal blow up out of all proportion.
OPPOSITES: understate.

overstatement noun exaggeration, overemphasis, dramatization, embroidery, embellishment, hyperbole.

overt adjective *it was an overt act of aggression:* undisguised, blatant, unconcealed, plain, clear, conspicuous, obvious, manifest, patent, open.
OPPOSITES: covert.

overtake verb
1 *a green car overtook the taxi:* pass, go past/by, get/pull ahead of, leave behind, outdistance, outstrip; Brit. overhaul.
2 *tourism overtook coffee as the main earner of foreign currency:* outstrip, surpass, overshadow, eclipse, outshine, outclass; dwarf, put in the shade, exceed, top, cap.
3 *the calamity which overtook us:* happen to, come upon, hit, strike, overwhelm, overcome, be visited on; literary befall.

overthrow verb
1 *the President was overthrown:* remove from office/power, bring down, topple, depose, oust, displace, supplant, unseat.
2 *an attempt to overthrow Soviet rule:* put an end to, defeat, conquer.
▷ **noun**
1 *the overthrow of the Shah:* removal from office/power, downfall, fall, toppling, deposition, ousting, displacement, supplanting, unseating.
2 *the overthrow of capitalism:* ending, defeat, fall, collapse, downfall, demise.

overtone noun *the media are treating it as a human interest story with political overtones:* implication, connotation, association, undercurrent, undertone, reverberation, resonance, suggestion, feeling, nuance.

overture noun
1 *the overture to Don Giovanni:* prelude, introduction, opening.
2 *the talks were no more than an overture to a long debate:* preliminary, prelude, introduction, lead-in, start, beginning.
3 *recently the government have made overtures towards union leaders:* opening move, approach, advances, feeler, proposal, proposition.

overturn verb
1 *the boat overturned:* capsize, turn turtle, keel over, tip over, topple over, turn over; Nautical pitchpole.
2 *I overturned the stool:* upset, tip over, turn over, knock over, upend.
3 *the Senate may overturn this ruling:* cancel, reverse, rescind, repeal, revoke, retract, countermand, override, overrule, veto, quash, overthrow, annul, nullify, invalidate.

overused adjective *an overused phrase:* hackneyed, overworked, worn out, time-worn, tired, played out, clichéd, stale, trite, banal, stock, unoriginal.

overweening adjective *his overweening ambition:* overconfident, arrogant, conceited, cocksure, cocky, proud, vain, self-important, imperious, overbearing; informal high and mighty.
OPPOSITES: unassuming.

overweight adjective *people who are overweight are more likely to have heart attacks:* fat, obese, stout, corpulent, fleshy, plump, portly, chubby, rotund, flabby, well upholstered, well padded, broad in the beam; informal porky, tubby; Brit. informal podgy.
OPPOSITES: skinny.

overwhelm verb
1 *flood waters overwhelmed hundreds of houses:* swamp, submerge, engulf, bury, deluge, flood, inundate.
2 *Spain overwhelmed Russia in the hockey:* defeat heavily, beat hollow, trounce, rout, conquer, vanquish, be victorious over, triumph over, worst, overcome, overthrow, crush; informal thrash, lick, wipe the floor with.
3 *she was overwhelmed by a sense of tragedy:* overcome, overpower, strike, shake, devastate, leave speechless; Brit. informal knock for six.

overwhelming adjective
1 *an overwhelming number of voters:* very large, enormous, immense, inordinate, massive, huge.
2 *she had an overwhelming desire to laugh:* very strong, forceful, uncontrollable, irrepressible, irresistible, overpowering, compelling.

overwork verb
1 *he's been overworking—he's taken on far too much:* work too hard, work/run yourself into the ground, wear yourself to a shadow, work your fingers to the bone, burn the candle at both ends, overtax yourself, burn yourself out, do too much, overdo it, strain yourself, overload yourself, drive/push yourself too hard; informal kill yourself, knock yourself out.
2 *my colleagues did not overwork me:* drive too hard, exploit, drive into the ground, tax, overtax, overburden, put upon, impose on.

overworked adjective
1 *overworked staff:* overtaxed, overburdened, overloaded, exhausted, worn out, stressed.
2 *an overworked phrase:* hackneyed, overused, worn out, tired, played out, clichéd, threadbare, stale, trite, banal, stock, unoriginal.
OPPOSITES: relaxed, original.

overwrought adjective
1 *she was too overwrought to listen:* tense, agitated, nervous, on edge, edgy, keyed up, worked up, highly strung, neurotic, overexcited, beside yourself, distracted, distraught, frantic, hysterical; informal in a

state, uptight, wound up, het up; Brit. informal
strung up.
2 *the painting is overwrought:* over-
elaborate, over-ornate, overblown,
overdone, contrived.
OPPOSITES: calm, understated.

owe verb *I still owe them a lot of money | I
owe you for saving Dana's life:* **be in debt,
be in arrears; be indebted to, be under an
obligation to.**

owing adjective *the rent was owing:*
unpaid, to be paid, payable, due, overdue,
undischarged, owed, outstanding, in
arrears.
OPPOSITES: paid.
□ **owing to**
*he has been forced to withdraw from the
competition owing to a family illness:*
because of, as a result of, due to, as a
consequence of, on account of, thanks to,
in view of.

own adjective *each family handed down
its own stories:* **personal,** individual,
particular, private, personalized, unique.
▷ **verb**
1 *I don't own anything very valuable:* **be
the owner of,** possess, be the possessor
of, have in your possession, have to your
name.

2 *she had to own that she agreed:* **admit,**
concede, grant, accept, acknowledge,
agree, confess.
□ **get your own back** (informal)
have/get your revenge, be revenged, hit
back, get even, pay someone back, give
someone their just deserts, retaliate, take
reprisals, exact retribution, give someone a
taste of their own medicine.
□ **on your own**
1 *I am all on my own:* **alone,** by yourself,
solitary, unaccompanied; informal by your
lonesome; Brit. informal on your tod.
2 *she works well on her own:* **unaided,**
unassisted, without help, without
assistance, by yourself, independently.
□ **own up**
he still couldn't own up to the lie: **confess
to,** admit to; plead guilty, accept blame/
responsibility, tell the truth, make a clean
breast of it, tell all; informal come clean.

owner noun **possessor,** holder, proprietor/
proprietress, homeowner, landlord,
landlady; Brit. freeholder.

WORD LINKS
proprietary relating to an owner
---

ownership noun *the ownership of land:*
possession, proprietorship, proprietary
rights, title; Brit. freehold.

O

Pp

pace noun
1 *he stepped back a pace:* step, stride.
2 *a slow, steady pace:* gait, stride, walk, march.
3 *he drove home at a furious pace:* speed, rate, velocity; informal clip, lick.
▷ verb *she paced up and down:* walk, stride, tread, march, pound, patrol.

pacific adjective
1 *a pacific community:* peace-loving, peaceable, pacifist, non-violent, non-aggressive, non-belligerent.
2 *their pacific intentions:* conciliatory, peacemaking, placatory, propitiatory, appeasing, mollifying.
3 *the pacific waters:* calm, still, smooth, tranquil, placid, like a millpond.
OPPOSITES: aggressive, stormy.

pacifism noun peacemaking, conscientious objection, passive resistance, peace-mongering, non-violence.

pacifist noun peace-lover, conscientious objector, passive resister, peacemaker, peace-monger, dove; Brit. informal conchie.
OPPOSITES: warmonger.

pacify verb *Gregory tried to think of a way of pacifying his wife:* placate, appease, mollify, calm, calm down, soothe, conciliate, propitiate.
OPPOSITES: enrage.

pack noun
1 *a pack of cigarettes:* packet, package, box, carton, container; parcel.
2 *a pack of American tourists:* crowd, group, band, party, gang, troop, herd, horde, throng, mass, assembly, gathering, mob; informal crew, bunch.
3 *we picked up our packs and trudged off:* backpack, rucksack, knapsack, kitbag, bag.
▷ verb
1 *she helped him pack the hamper:* fill, load.
2 *he had already packed his belongings into crates:* stow, put away, store, box up.
3 *the glasses were packed in straw:* wrap, package, parcel up, encase; store.
4 *Christmas shoppers packed the store:* throng, crowd into, fill, cram, jam, squeeze into.
5 *pack the cloth against the wall:* compress, press, squash, squeeze, tamp.

□ pack something up
put away, tidy up/away, clear up/away.

package noun
1 *a large cardboard package:* parcel, packet, box, container.
2 *a package of measures to stem antisocial behaviour:* collection, set, series, combination, bundle.
▷ verb *the goods are packaged in recyclable materials:* wrap; pack, parcel up, box, encase.

packaging noun wrapping, wrappers, packing, covering.

packed adjective *the train was completely packed with grumpy commuters | the packed city streets:* crowded, full, filled to capacity, crammed, jammed, solid, overcrowded, overfull, teeming; informal jam-packed, chock-full, chock-a-block, full to the gunwales, bursting/bulging at the seams.

packet noun *a packet of cigarettes:* pack, carton, box, container, case, package.

pact noun *the guerrilla group made a peace pact with the government:* agreement, treaty, entente, deal, settlement, protocol, concordat; armistice, truce.

pad[1] noun
1 *he had a pad over his eye:* piece of cotton wool, dressing, padding, wadding, wad.
2 *she nodded thoughtfully, making notes on the pad in front of her:* notebook, notepad, writing pad, memo pad, jotter, block, sketch pad, sketchbook; N. Amer. scratch pad.
▷ verb *a quilted jacket padded with duck feathers:* stuff, fill, pack, wad.
□ pad something out
don't pad out your answer in an attempt to make it seem impressive: expand, fill out, amplify, increase, lengthen, spin out, elaborate.

pad[2] verb *he padded along towards the bedroom:* walk quietly, tread warily, creep, tiptoe, steal.

padding noun
1 *the thick padding of his jacket lessened the impact:* wadding, cushioning, stuffing,

packing, filling, lining.
2 *a concise style with no padding:* verbiage, verbosity, wordiness, prolixity; Brit. informal waffle.

paddle¹ noun *use the paddles to row ashore:* oar, scull, blade.

paddle² verb *children were paddling in the water:* splash about, wade; dabble your feet.

paddock noun field, meadow, pasture; pen, enclosure; N. Amer. corral.

padlock verb *you should padlock ladders to something secure:* lock, fasten, secure.

pagan noun *pagans worshipped the sun:* heathen, infidel, idolater, idolatress.
▷**adjective** *pagan festivals:* heathen, idolatrous, irreligious, infidel.

page¹ noun *a page of A4 paper:* folio, sheet, side, leaf.

page² noun
1 *a page in a hotel:* errand boy, messenger boy; N. Amer. bellboy, bellhop.
2 *a page at a wedding:* attendant, pageboy, train-bearer.
▷**verb** *could you please page Mr Johnson?* call, summon, send for.

pageant noun *the Queen attended a 1,000-horse pageant:* parade, procession, cavalcade, tableau vivant; spectacle, extravaganza, show.

pageantry noun spectacle, display, ceremony, magnificence, pomp, splendour, grandeur, show; informal razzle-dazzle, razzmatazz.

pain noun
1 *she endured great pain:* suffering, agony, torture, torment, discomfort.
2 *a pain in the stomach:* ache, aching, soreness, throb, throbbing, sting, stinging, twinge, shooting pain, stab, pang; discomfort, irritation, tenderness.
3 *the pain of losing a loved one:* sorrow, grief, heartache, heartbreak, sadness, unhappiness, distress, desolation, misery, wretchedness, despair; agony, torment, torture, trauma.
4 *he took great pains to hide his feelings:* care, effort, bother, trouble.
▷**verb**
1 *Keira was pained by her mother's words:* sadden, grieve, distress, trouble, cause anguish to.
2 *her foot is still paining her:* hurt, be painful, be sore, be tender, ache, throb, sting; informal kill.
□ **be at pains**
the company was at pains to avoid any accusations that it was selling out: try hard, make a great effort, take great pains, put yourself out; strive, endeavour, try, do your best, do your utmost, go all out; informal bend over backwards.

USAGE

Do not confuse **pain** with **pane**. **Pain** means 'an unpleasant feeling caused by illness or injury', while **pane** means 'a sheet of glass' (*thieves had smashed the window panes*).

pained adjective *she stared at Hebden with a pained expression on her face:* upset, hurt, wounded, injured, insulted, offended, aggrieved, displeased, disgruntled, indignant, resentful.

painful adjective
1 *her arm was still painful:* sore, hurting, tender, aching, throbbing.
2 *a painful experience:* upsetting, unpleasant, distressing, traumatic, bitter, miserable, sad, heartbreaking, agonizing, harrowing.

painkiller noun analgesic, anaesthetic, anodyne; palliative.

painless adjective
1 *any killing of animals should be painless:* pain-free.
2 *if you do it overnight, the journey is relatively painless:* easy, trouble-free, effortless, undemanding, simple, plain sailing; informal as easy as pie, a piece of cake, child's play, a cinch.
OPPOSITES: painful, difficult.

painstaking adjective *the two books are the product of years of painstaking research:* careful, meticulous, assiduous, sedulous, attentive, diligent, industrious, conscientious, punctilious, scrupulous, thorough, rigorous, particular; pedantic, fussy.
OPPOSITES: slapdash.

paint noun colouring, colourant, pigment, colour, tint, dye, stain.
▷**verb**
1 *slogans had been painted on the wall:* daub, smear, spray-paint, airbrush.
2 *Vuillard painted his mother more than 500 times:* portray, picture, paint a picture of, depict, represent.
3 *the article paints him as a dangerous extremist:* describe, depict, portray, represent, present, delineate.

painting noun picture, illustration, portrayal, depiction, representation, image, artwork; oil, watercolour, canvas, fresco, mural.

pair noun *a pair of gloves:* set of two, couple, twosome, duo, brace, two, two of a kind, twins.
▷**verb** *a cardigan paired with a matching skirt:* match, put together, couple, twin.
□ **pair off/up**
get together, team up, form a couple, make a twosome.

palace noun castle, chateau, schloss, mansion, stately home.

p

palatable adjective

1 *an array of palatable dishes:* tasty, appetizing, flavourful, flavoursome, delicious, mouth-watering, toothsome, succulent; informal scrumptious, yummy, scrummy, moreish.
2 *the truth is not always palatable:* pleasant, acceptable, pleasing, agreeable, easy to take, to your liking.
OPPOSITES: disagreeable.

palate noun

1 *menus to suit the tourist palate:* taste, appetite, stomach.
2 *wine with a peachy palate:* flavour, savour, taste.

> **USAGE**
>
> Do not confuse **palate** with **palette** or **pallet**. **Palate** means 'the roof of the mouth' or 'a person's sense of taste', while a **palette** is 'an artist's board for mixing paints', and a **pallet** is 'a portable platform for moving goods' or 'a makeshift bed'.

palatial adjective *a palatial five-star hotel:* luxurious, de luxe, magnificent, sumptuous, splendid, grand, opulent, lavish; fancy; Brit. upmarket; informal plush, swanky, posh, ritzy, swish.
OPPOSITES: modest.

pale¹ adjective

1 *he looked pale and his breathing was laboured:* pallid, white, pasty, wan, colourless, anaemic, bloodless, washed out, ashen, grey, whey-faced, drained, sickly, sallow, as white as a sheet, deathly pale; Brit. peaky; informal like death warmed up.
2 *the red velvet dress accentuated the pale skin of her neck:* creamy, milky, ivory, white, milk-white, alabaster
3 *pale colours:* light, light-coloured, pastel, muted, subtle, soft; faded, bleached, washed out.
4 *the pale light of morning:* dim, faint, weak, feeble.
5 *the film is a pale imitation of the original:* feeble, weak, insipid, bland, poor, inadequate, unimpressive, lacklustre.
OPPOSITES: dark.

▷ **verb**
1 *his face paled:* go/turn white, grow/turn pale, blanch, lose colour.
2 *everything else pales by comparison:* decrease in importance, lose significance, pale into insignificance.

pale² noun *the pales of a fence:* stake, post, pole, upright.
□ **beyond the pale**
the language he used was beyond the pale: unacceptable, unseemly, intolerable, disgraceful, deplorable, outrageous, scandalous, shocking; informal not on, out of order, out of line.

palisade noun fence, paling, barricade, stockade.

pall¹ noun *a pall of black smoke hung over the city:* cloud, layer, blanket, covering, cloak, veil, shroud, mantle.
□ **cast a pall over**
the robbery cast a pall over the final stages of the tournament: spoil, cast a shadow over, overshadow, cloud, put a damper on.

pall² verb *the high life was beginning to pall:* become/grow tedious, become/grow boring, lose its/their interest, lose its/their attraction, cloy; weary someone, irritate someone, irk someone.

pallid adjective *his face was gaunt and pallid:* pale, white, pasty, wan, colourless, anaemic, washed out, whey-faced, ashen, grey, drained, sickly, sallow; Brit. peaky; informal like death warmed up.

pallor noun *her dark hair accentuated the pallor of her skin:* paleness, lack of colour, ashen hue, pastiness, peakiness, sallowness.

palm verb
□ **palm something off**
the opposition accused him of trying to palm off the blame on to lowly civil servants: foist, fob off, get rid of, dispose of; informal unload.

palpable adjective *his reluctance was palpable:* unmistakable, obvious, clear, plain, evident, apparent, manifest, staring someone in the face, written all over someone; perceptible, noticeable, discernible, tangible.
OPPOSITES: imperceptible.

palpitate verb *her heart began to palpitate:* beat rapidly, pound, throb, pulsate, pulse, thud, thump, hammer, race.

paltry adjective

1 *a paltry sum of money:* small, meagre, trifling, insignificant, negligible, inadequate, insufficient, derisory, pitiful, miserable, niggardly, beggarly; informal measly, pathetic.
2 *naval glory struck him as paltry:* worthless, petty, trivial, unimportant, insignificant, inconsequential, of little account.
OPPOSITES: considerable.

pamper verb *his elder sister pampered him:* spoil, indulge, overindulge, cosset, mollycoddle, coddle, baby, wait on someone hand and foot.

pamphlet noun brochure, leaflet, booklet, circular, flyer, handbill.

pan¹ noun

1 *a heavy pan:* saucepan, frying pan, wok, skillet.
2 *salt pans:* hollow, pit, depression, dip, crater, concavity.
□ **pan out**
1 *Harold's idea hadn't really panned out:* succeed, be successful, work, work out, turn out well.

2 *the deal panned out badly:* turn out, work out, end up, come out, fall out.

pan[2] verb *the camera panned across to the building:* swing, sweep, move, turn, circle.

panacea noun *a panacea for the country's economic problems:* universal cure, cure-all, cure for all ills, universal remedy, elixir, wonder drug; informal magic bullet.

panache noun *they played with panache and authority:* flamboyance, confidence, self-assurance, style, flair, elan, verve, zest, spirit, brio, éclat, vivacity, gusto, liveliness, vitality, energy.

pandemic adjective *the disease is pandemic in Africa:* widespread, prevalent, pervasive, rife, rampant.

pandemonium noun *we heard a massive bang and then there was complete pandemonium:* bedlam, chaos, mayhem, uproar, turmoil, tumult, commotion, confusion, anarchy, furore, hubbub, rumpus; Brit. informal hullabaloo.
OPPOSITES: peace.

pander verb
□ pander to
David was always there to pander to her every whim: indulge, gratify, satisfy, cater to, give in to, accommodate, comply with.

panel noun
1 *a control panel:* console, instrument panel; instruments, controls, dials, switches.
2 *a panel of judges:* group, team, body, committee, board.

pang noun
1 *hunger pangs:* pain, shooting pain, twinge, stab, spasm.
2 *a pang of remorse:* qualm, twinge, prick.

panic noun *a wave of panic swept over her | I ran home in a panic:* alarm, anxiety, nervousness, fear, fright, trepidation, dread, terror, agitation, hysteria, consternation, perturbation, dismay, apprehension; informal flap, fluster, cold sweat.
OPPOSITES: calm.
▷verb
1 *there's no need to panic:* be alarmed, be scared, be nervous, be afraid, take fright, be agitated, be hysterical, lose your head/nerve, get overwrought, get worked up, overreact; informal flap, get into a flap, lose your cool, freak out; Brit. informal get the wind up.
2 *talk of love panicked her:* frighten, alarm, scare, unnerve; informal freak out; Brit. informal put the wind up.

panic-stricken adjective *panic-stricken victims rushed out of their blazing homes:* alarmed, frightened, scared, terrified, terror-stricken, petrified, horrified, horror-stricken, fearful, afraid, panicky, frantic, in a frenzy, nervous, agitated,

hysterical, beside yourself, worked up, overwrought; informal in a cold sweat, in a flap, in a fluster.

panoply noun
1 *this exhibition gathers together a panoply of artistic subjects, techniques and media:* array, range, collection.
2 *the full panoply of state is revealed in the coronation ceremony:* trappings, regalia; splendour, spectacle, ceremony, ritual.

panorama noun
1 *the tower offers a wonderful panorama of the city:* view, vista, prospect.
2 *a panorama of 20th-century art:* overview, survey, review, presentation, appraisal.

panoramic adjective
1 *a panoramic view:* sweeping, wide, extensive, scenic, commanding.
2 *a panoramic survey of more than a century of the country's music:* wide-ranging, extensive, broad, far-reaching, comprehensive, all-embracing.

pant verb
1 *he was panting as they reached the top:* breathe heavily, breathe hard, puff, huff and puff, gasp, wheeze.
2 *the opening song makes you pant for more:* yearn for, long for, crave, hanker after/for, ache for, hunger for, thirst for, wish for, desire, want; informal itch for, be dying for.
▷noun *she was breathing in shallow pants:* gasp, puff, wheeze, breath.

panting adjective out of breath, breathless, short of breath, puffed out, puffing, huffing and puffing, gasping for breath, wheezing, wheezy.

paper noun
1 *the local paper ran the story:* newspaper, journal, gazette, periodical; tabloid, broadsheet; informal rag.
2 *he has just published a paper on the topic:* essay, article, monograph, thesis, work, dissertation, treatise, study, report, analysis, tract, critique, review.
3 *his personal papers:* documents, certificates, letters, files, deeds, records, archives, paperwork, documentation.
4 *they asked us for our papers:* identification papers/documents, identity card, ID, credentials.
□ paper something over
they tried to paper over their differences: cover up, hide, conceal, disguise, camouflage, gloss over.
□ on paper
1 *he put his thoughts down on paper:* in writing, in black and white, in print.
2 *the combatants were evenly matched on paper:* in theory, theoretically, supposedly.

papery adjective *the bulbs are covered with papery skin:* thin, paper-thin, flimsy, delicate, light, dry, brittle.

p

par noun
□ below par
1 *their performances have been below par this season:* substandard, inferior, not up to scratch, under par, below average, second-rate, mediocre, poor, undistinguished.
2 *I'm feeling below par:* slightly unwell, not yourself, out of sorts; ill, unwell, poorly, washed out, run-down; Brit. off colour, peaky; informal under the weather, lousy, rough; Brit. informal ropy; Austral./NZ informal crook.
□ on a par with
he's on a par with the likes of Al Pacino and a young Robert De Niro: as good as, comparable with, in the same class/league as, equivalent to, equal to, on a level with, of the same standard as.
□ par for the course
we had a lot of rain in October which is par for the course: normal, typical, standard, usual, what you would expect.

parable noun *the parable of the prodigal son:* allegory, moral story/tale, fable.

parade noun
1 *a St George's Day parade | a military parade:* procession, march, cavalcade, motorcade, spectacle, display, pageant; review, tattoo; Brit. march past.
2 *she walked along the parade:* promenade, walkway, esplanade, mall; N. Amer. boardwalk; Brit. informal prom.
▷ **verb**
1 *the teams paraded through the city:* march, process, file, troop, walk.
2 *20 glamorous models paraded up and down the catwalk:* strut, stride, swagger.
3 *he was keen to parade his knowledge:* display, exhibit, make a show of, flaunt, show off, demonstrate.

paradigm noun *the institutional arrangements of a particular society cannot serve as a paradigm for all others:* model, pattern, example, exemplar, standard, prototype, archetype.

paradise noun
1 *the souls in paradise:* heaven, the kingdom of heaven; literary Elysium, the Elysian Fields, Valhalla, Avalon.
2 *Adam and Eve's expulsion from Paradise:* the Garden of Eden, Eden.
3 *a tropical paradise:* Utopia, Shangri-La, heaven, idyll, nirvana.
4 *this is sheer paradise!* bliss, heaven, ecstasy, delight, joy, happiness, nirvana, heaven on earth.
OPPOSITES: hell.

paradox noun *the apparent paradox of simultaneous unemployment and skilled-labour shortages:* contradiction, self-contradiction, contradiction in terms, inconsistency, incongruity, conflict, anomaly; enigma, puzzle, mystery, conundrum.

paradoxical adjective contradictory, self-contradictory, inconsistent, incongruous, anomalous; illogical, puzzling, baffling, inexplicable.

paragon noun *she is a paragon of fortitude and cheerfulness:* perfect example, shining example, model, epitome, archetype, ideal, exemplar, nonpareil, embodiment, personification, quintessence, apotheosis.

paragraph noun
1 *the concluding paragraph:* section, subdivision, part, subsection, division, portion, segment, passage.
2 *a paragraph in the newspaper:* report, article, item, piece, write-up, mention.

parallel adjective
1 *parallel lines:* side by side, aligned, collateral, equidistant.
2 *parallel careers:* similar, analogous, corresponding, like, of a kind, akin, related, equivalent, matching.
3 *a parallel universe:* coexisting, coexistent, concurrent; contemporaneous, simultaneous, synchronous.
OPPOSITES: divergent.
▷ **noun**
1 *an exact parallel:* counterpart, analogue, equivalent, likeness, match, twin, duplicate, mirror.
2 *there is an interesting parallel between these figures:* similarity, likeness, resemblance, analogy, correspondence, equivalence, correlation, relation, symmetry, parity.
▷ **verb**
1 *his experiences parallel mine:* resemble, be similar to, be like, bear a resemblance to; correspond to, be analogous to, be comparable/equivalent to, equate with/to, correlate with, imitate, echo, duplicate, mirror, follow, match.
2 *her performance has never been paralleled:* equal, match, rival, emulate.

paralyse verb
1 *his leg was paralysed as a result of the accident:* disable, immobilize, incapacitate.
2 *Maisie was paralysed by the sight of him:* immobilize, transfix, stun, render motionless; be rooted to the spot.
3 *the capital was paralysed by a general strike:* bring to a standstill, immobilize, bring to a (grinding) halt, shut down, freeze, cripple, disable.

parameter noun *the parameters of the debate | the parameters within which the media work:* framework, limit, boundary, limitation, restriction, criterion, guideline.

paramount adjective *the safety of patients is the paramount concern:* most important, of greatest/prime importance; uppermost, supreme, chief, overriding, predominant, foremost, prime, primary, principal, highest, main, key, central, leading, major, top; informal number-one.

paraphernalia plural noun equipment, apparatus, implements, tools, utensils, materials, appliances, accoutrements, things; formal appurtenances; informal gear, kit, stuff, bits and pieces; Brit. informal odds and ends.

paraphrase verb *you can either quote or paraphrase literary texts:* reword, rephrase, put/express in other words.

parcel noun
1 *a parcel of clothes:* package, packet; pack, bundle, box, case, bale.
2 *a parcel of land:* plot, piece, patch, tract; N. Amer. lot.
▷ verb
1 *she parcelled up the papers:* pack, package, wrap up, tie up, bundle up.
2 *the remaining cash is likely to be parcelled out by autumn:* divide up, distribute, share out, apportion, allocate, allot, hand out, dole out, dish out; informal divvy up.

parched adjective *the parched earth:* dry, bone dry, dried up/out, arid, desiccated, dehydrated, baked, burned, scorched; withered, shrivelled.
OPPOSITES: soaking.

pardon noun
1 *he obtained pardon for his sins:* forgiveness, absolution.
2 *he offered the five convicted men a full pardon:* amnesty, reprieve, exoneration, release, discharge.
▷ verb
1 *I know she will pardon me | he pardoned their faults:* forgive, absolve, have mercy on; excuse.
2 *they were subsequently pardoned:* exonerate, acquit; reprieve, release, free; informal let off.
OPPOSITES: blame, punish.

pardonable adjective *a pardonable error:* excusable, forgivable, understandable; minor, venial, slight.
OPPOSITES: inexcusable.

pare verb
1 *pare the peel from the lemon:* cut, trim, peel, strip, skin.
2 *domestic operations have been pared down:* reduce, diminish, decrease, cut back/down, trim, slim down, prune, curtail.

parent noun *her parents have divorced:* mother, father, birth/biological parent; guardian; formal progenitor.

> WORD LINKS
> **parricide** the killing of a parent or other near relative

parentage noun *a young woman of African parentage:* origins, extraction, birth, family, ancestry, lineage, heritage, pedigree, descent, blood, stock, roots; ancestors, forebears.

pariah noun *they were treated as social pariahs:* outcast, persona non grata, leper, undesirable.

parish noun
1 *a large rural parish:* district.
2 *the vicar scandalized the parish:* parishioners, churchgoers, congregation, fold, flock, community.

> WORD LINKS
> **parochial** relating to a parish

parity noun *parity of incomes between rural workers and those in industrial occupations:* equality, equivalence, uniformity, consistency, correspondence, congruity, coequality.

park noun
1 *children were playing in the park:* public garden, recreation ground, playground, play area.
2 *the house is set in its own park:* parkland, woodland, gardens, lawns, grounds, estate.
▷ verb *he parked his car outside her house:* leave; stop, pull up.

parlance noun *in military parlance these bombs are known as Improvised Explosive Devices:* jargon, language, phraseology, vocabulary, terminology, talk, speech; argot, patois; informal lingo, -speak.

parley noun *a peace parley:* negotiation, talks, conference, summit, discussion, powwow.
▷ verb *the two parties were willing to parley:* talk, hold talks, negotiate, discuss terms.

parliament noun *the Russian parliament:* legislature, legislative assembly, congress, senate, upper/lower house, upper/lower chamber, diet, assembly.

parliamentary adjective *a parliamentary assembly:* legislative, law-making, governmental, congressional; democratic, elected, representative.

parlour noun *a beauty parlour:* salon, establishment, shop.

parochial adjective *parochial attitudes:* narrow-minded, small-minded, provincial, narrow, small-town, conservative, illiberal, intolerant; Brit. parish-pump.
OPPOSITES: broad-minded.

parody noun
1 *a parody of the gothic novel:* satire, burlesque, lampoon, pastiche, caricature; imitation, mockery; informal spoof, take-off, send-up.
2 *a parody of the truth:* distortion, travesty, caricature, misrepresentation, perversion, corruption, debasement.
▷ verb *his speciality was parodying schoolgirl fiction:* satirize, lampoon, caricature, mimic, imitate, ape, copy, make fun of, take off; Brit. informal send up.

paroxysm noun *a paroxysm of rage:*

spasm, attack, fit, burst, bout, outburst, eruption, explosion.

parrot verb *they parroted slogans without appreciating their significance:* repeat mindlessly, repeat mechanically, echo.

parrot-fashion adverb *she had just repeated the phrase parrot-fashion:* mechanically, by rote, automatically.

parry verb
1 *Sharpe parried the blow:* ward off, fend off; deflect, hold off, block, counter, repel, repulse.
2 *I parried her constant questions:* evade, sidestep, avoid, dodge, field, fend off.

parsimonious adjective *even the parsimonious Joe paid for drinks all round:* mean, miserly, close-fisted, penny-pinching, niggardly, Scrooge-like; informal tight-fisted, tight, stingy, mingy.
OPPOSITES: generous.

parsimony noun meanness, miserliness, parsimoniousness, close-fistedness, penny-pinching, niggardliness; informal stinginess, tight-fistedness.
OPPOSITES: generosity.

parson noun vicar, rector, clergyman, cleric, chaplain, pastor, curate, man of the cloth, ecclesiastic, minister, priest, preacher; informal reverend, padre.

part noun
1 *divide the circle into three equal parts | a large part of their life:* piece, portion, section, segment, bit; percentage, fraction.
2 *car parts:* component, bit, constituent, element, module, unit.
3 *the last part of the book:* section, division, chapter, act, scene, instalment.
4 *another part of the country:* district, neighbourhood, quarter, section, sector, area, region.
5 *she took the part of Juliet:* role, character, persona.
6 *he was jailed for his part in the affair:* involvement, role, contribution, hand.
OPPOSITES: whole.
▷verb *after a brief kiss, they parted from each other:* leave, take your leave, say goodbye/farewell, say your goodbyes/farewells, separate, go your separate ways, go away, depart.
OPPOSITES: join, meet.
☐in part
the cause of her illness is in part psychological: to a certain extent/degree, to some extent/degree, partly, partially, slightly, in some measure, up to a point.
☐on the part of
an error on the part of his solicitor: by, carried out by, caused by, from.
☐part with
she had no wish to part with any of her land: give up/away, relinquish, forgo, surrender, hand over, let go of, dispose of.

☐take part
millions of people took part in the demonstrations: participate, join in, get involved, enter, play a part/role, be a participant, contribute, have a hand, help, assist, lend a hand; informal get in on the act.
☐take someone's part
her sister was the one person who had always taken her part: support, give your support to, take the side of, side with, stand by, stick up for, be supportive of, back, back up, give your backing to, be loyal to, defend, come to the defence of, champion.

partial adjective
1 *this is a question to which we have only partial answers:* incomplete, limited, qualified, imperfect, fragmentary, unfinished.
2 *the paper gave a very partial view of the situation:* biased, prejudiced, partisan, one-sided, slanted, skewed, distorted, unbalanced.
OPPOSITES: complete, unbiased.
☐be partial to
you know I'm very partial to bacon and eggs: like, love, enjoy, have a liking for, be fond of, be keen on, have a soft spot for, have a taste for, have a penchant for; informal adore, be mad about/on, have a thing about.

partiality noun
1 *the government's perceived partiality towards their cause:* bias, prejudice, favouritism, favour, partisanship.
2 *her partiality for brandy:* liking, love, fondness, taste, soft spot, predilection, penchant, passion.

partially adverb *the plan was only partially successful:* to a limited extent/degree, to a certain extent/degree, partly, in part, not totally, not entirely, relatively, moderately, up to a point, somewhat, comparatively, slightly.

participant noun
1 *staff are to be active participants in the decision-making process:* contributor to, party to.
2 *there were over 500 participants in this year's race:* entrant, competitor, contestant.

participate verb *400,000 people participated in the peaceful demonstration:* take part, engage, join, get involved, share, play a part/role, be a participant, have a hand in, be associated with; help, assist, lend a hand.

participation noun involvement, part, contribution, association.

particle noun
1 *minute particles of rock:* bit, piece, speck, spot, fleck; fragment, sliver, splinter.
2 *he never showed a particle of sympathy:* iota, jot, whit, bit, scrap, shred, crumb, drop, hint, touch, trace, suggestion, whisper, suspicion, scintilla; informal smidgen.

p

particular adjective

1 *the action seems to discriminate against a particular group of companies | it is hard to pick out one particular song:* specific, certain, distinct, separate, discrete; single, individual.
2 *an issue of particular importance:* special, especial, exceptional, unusual, singular, uncommon, remarkable, unique.
3 *she was very particular about cleanliness:* fussy, fastidious, finicky, meticulous, punctilious, selective, painstaking, exacting, demanding; informal choosy, picky; Brit. informal pernickety, faddy.
OPPOSITES: general, careless.

▷ noun *he is wrong in every particular:* detail, item, point, specific, element, aspect, respect, regard, particularity, fact, feature.
□ in particular
1 *they chatted about nothing in particular:* specific, special.
2 *the poor, in particular, were hit by rising prices:* particularly, specifically, especially, specially.

particularity noun

1 *the central figures of his novels are stripped of their particularity:* individuality, distinctiveness, uniqueness, singularity.
2 *parties must present their case with a great degree of particularity:* detail, precision, accuracy, thoroughness, scrupulousness, meticulousness.

particularize verb (formal) *the indictment particularized several incidents:* specify, detail, itemize, list, enumerate, spell out, cite, stipulate, instance.

particularly adverb

1 *the acoustics are particularly good:* especially, very, extremely, exceptionally, singularly, unusually, extraordinarily, terribly, remarkably, outstandingly, amazingly, incredibly, really; informal seriously, awfully.
2 *he particularly asked that I should help you:* specifically, explicitly, expressly, in particular, especially.

parting noun

1 *it was an emotional parting:* farewell, leave-taking, goodbye, adieu, departure; valediction.
2 *the parting of the Red Sea:* division, dividing, separation, separating, splitting, breaking up/apart.
▷ adjective *a parting kiss:* farewell, goodbye, last, final, valedictory.

partisan noun

1 *Conservative partisans:* supporter, follower, adherent, devotee, champion; enthusiast, stalwart, zealot.
2 *the partisans opened fire from the woods:* guerrilla, freedom fighter, resistance fighter.
▷ adjective *newspapers had become increasingly partisan | a partisan point of view:* biased, prejudiced, one-sided, discriminatory, partial, blinkered.
OPPOSITES: unbiased, open-minded.

partisanship noun bias, prejudice, one-sidedness, discrimination, favour, favouritism, partiality.

partition noun

1 *the partition of the country:* dividing up, partitioning, separation, division, dividing, subdivision, splitting up, breaking up, break-up.
2 *a glass partition:* screen, room divider, dividing wall, barrier, panel.
▷ verb
1 *an agreement was reached to partition the territory:* divide up, subdivide, separate, split up, break up; share out, parcel out.
2 *the bedroom was partitioned off with tall wooden screens:* separate off, section off, screen off.

partly adverb *the book is partly autobiographical:* to a certain extent/degree, to some extent/degree, in part, partially, a little, somewhat, not totally, not entirely, relatively, moderately, up to a point, in some measure, slightly.
OPPOSITES: completely.

partner noun

1 *business partners:* colleague, associate, co-worker, fellow worker, collaborator, teammate.
2 *his partner in crime:* accomplice, accessory, collaborator, fellow conspirator; informal sidekick.
3 *your relationship with your partner:* spouse, husband, wife; lover, girlfriend, boyfriend, fiancé, fiancée, significant other; informal better half; Brit. informal other half.

partnership noun

1 *the close partnership between our two countries:* cooperation, association, collaboration, alliance, union, coalition, affiliation, relationship, connection.
2 *the partnership now owns twenty-two department stores:* company, firm, business, corporation, organization, association, consortium, syndicate.

party noun

1 *over 150 people attended the party:* gathering, function, get-together, celebration, reunion, festivity, jamboree, reception, at-home, soirée; dance, ball, ceilidh; informal bash, shindig, do.
2 *a party of British tourists | a search party:* group, band; team, crew, squad, company, contingent, gang.
3 *the left-wing parties:* political party, group, grouping, alliance.
4 *a contract between two parties:* person, individual.
□ be party to
he was party to some very shady deals: be involved in/with, be associated with, be a participant in.

p

parvenu noun (derogatory) **upstart**, social climber, arriviste.

pass[1] verb
1 *residents are fed up with the number of cars and lorries passing through the village:* **go**, proceed, move, progress, make your way, travel.
2 *a car passed him:* **overtake**, go past/by, pull ahead of, leave behind; Brit. overhaul.
3 *time seemed to pass very slowly:* **elapse**, go by/past, advance, wear on, roll by, tick by.
4 *he passed the time writing letters:* **occupy**, spend, fill, use, employ, while away.
5 *the storm passed:* **come to an end**, fade away, blow over, run its course, die out, finish, end, cease.
6 *pass me the salt:* **hand**, let someone have, give, reach.
7 *he passed the ball back:* **kick**, hit, throw, lob.
8 *her estate passed to her grandson:* **be transferred**, go, be left, be bequeathed, be handed down/on, be passed on; Law devolve.
9 *he passed the exam:* **be successful in**, succeed in, gain a pass in, get through.
10 *the Senate passed the bill:* **approve**, vote for, accept, ratify, adopt, agree to, authorize, endorse, legalize, enact.
11 *she could not let that comment pass:* **go unnoticed**, stand, go unremarked, go undisputed.
12 *his death passed almost unnoticed:* **happen**, occur, take place, come about.
OPPOSITES: stop, fail, reject.
▷noun
1 *you must show your pass:* **permit**, warrant, authorization, licence.
2 *a cross-field pass:* **kick**, hit, throw, shot.
□ **pass away/on.** See DIE sense 1.
□ **pass as/for**
she could easily pass for someone half her age: **be mistaken for**, be taken for, be accepted as.
□ **pass off**
1 *the rally passed off peacefully:* **take place**, go off, happen, occur, be completed, turn out.
2 *when the dizziness passed off he sat up:* **wear off**, fade away, pass, die down.
□ **pass out**
she banged her head when she passed out: **faint**, lose consciousness, black out.
□ **pass something over**
the court cannot possibly pass over these offences: **disregard**, overlook, ignore, pay no attention to, let pass, gloss over, take no notice of, pay no heed to, turn a blind eye to.
□ **pass something up**
I can't pass up a bargain like this: **turn down**, reject, refuse, decline, give up, forgo, let pass, miss, miss out on; informal give something a miss.

pass[2] noun *a pass through the mountains:* **route**, way, road, passage, defile, cut, gap.

passable adjective
1 *the beer was passable:* **adequate**, all right, fairly good, acceptable, satisfactory, moderately good, not bad, average, tolerable, fair; mediocre, middling, ordinary, indifferent, unremarkable, unexceptional; informal OK, so-so, nothing to write home about, no great shakes.
2 *the road is still passable:* **navigable**, traversable, negotiable, unobstructed, open, clear.

passage noun
1 *their passage through the country:* **transit**, progress, passing, movement, travelling.
2 *the passage of time:* **passing**, advance, progress, course, march.
3 *an overnight passage:* **voyage**, crossing, trip, journey.
4 *he cleared a passage to the front door:* **way**, route, path.
5 *a passage to the kitchen.* See PASSAGEWAY sense 1.
6 *a passage between the buildings.* See PASSAGEWAY sense 2.
7 *the nasal passages:* **duct**, orifice, opening, channel; inlet, outlet.
8 *the passage to democracy:* **transition**, development, progress, move, change, shift.
9 *a passage from 'Macbeth':* **extract**, excerpt, quotation, quote, citation, reading, piece, selection.

passageway noun
1 *the passageway led to another lift:* **corridor**, hall, passage, hallway, walkway, aisle.
2 *a narrow passageway off the main street:* **alley**, alleyway, passage, lane, path, pathway, footpath, track.

passé adjective. See OLD-FASHIONED.

passenger noun
1 *rail passengers:* **traveller**, commuter.
2 *we can't afford passengers:* **hanger-on**, parasite; informal freeloader.

passing adjective
1 *his death was of only passing interest:* **fleeting**, transient, transitory, ephemeral, brief, short-lived, temporary, momentary.
2 *a passing glance:* **hasty**, rapid, hurried, brief, quick; cursory, superficial, casual, perfunctory.
▷noun *the passing of time:* **passage**, course, progress, advance, march.
□ **in passing**
the research was mentioned only in passing: **incidentally**, by the by/way; briefly, casually.

passion noun
1 *Jerry spoke with passion and determination about his campaign:* **fervour**, ardour, emotion, enthusiasm, eagerness, zeal, zealousness, vigour, energy, intensity, fire, fervency, animation,

spirit, spiritedness; fanaticism.
2 *he worked himself up into a passion:* rage, fit of anger/temper, temper, towering rage, fury, frenzy; Brit. informal paddy.
3 *their all-consuming passion for each other:* love, desire, lust, ardour, infatuation.
4 *his passion for football:* enthusiasm, love, mania, fascination, obsession, fixation, compulsion, addiction; informal thing.
5 *English literature is a passion with me:* obsession, preoccupation, craze, mania, hobby horse.
6 *the Passion of Christ:* crucifixion, suffering, agony, martyrdom.
OPPOSITES: apathy.

passionate adjective
1 *a passionate debate | a passionate entreaty:* impassioned, ardent, fervent, intense, vehement, emotional, heartfelt, eager, animated, spirited, energetic.
2 *McGregor is passionate about sport:* very keen, very enthusiastic, addicted; informal mad, crazy.
3 *a passionate embrace:* amorous, ardent, loving; informal steamy.
4 *a passionate woman:* excitable, emotional, fiery, hot-blooded, volatile, mercurial, quick-tempered, highly strung, impulsive, temperamental.
OPPOSITES: apathetic.

passionless adjective *he was not as passionless as they made out:* unemotional, cold, cold-blooded, cool, unfeeling, unloving, unresponsive, undemonstrative.

passive adjective
1 *his passive acceptance of the situation:* submissive, acquiescent, unresisting, compliant, pliant, obedient, docile, tractable, malleable, pliable.
2 *they were used to playing a passive role on the European scene:* inactive, non-active, uninvolved.
OPPOSITES: proactive, active.

passport noun *good qualifications are the passport to success:* key; path, way, route, avenue.

past adjective
1 *those days are past | the philosophers of past centuries:* gone, over, no more, former, of old, bygone, olden, long-ago.
2 *the past few months:* last, recent, preceding.
3 *a past chairman:* previous, former, foregoing, erstwhile, one-time, sometime, ex-; formal quondam.
OPPOSITES: present, future.
▷ noun *I don't know much about her past:* history, background, life.
◻ in the past
formerly, previously, in days/years/times gone by, in former times, once, in the old days, in days of old, in olden times.

paste noun
1 *blend the ingredients to a paste:* purée, pulp.
2 *wallpaper paste:* adhesive, glue, gum, fixative.
3 *fish paste:* spread, pâté.
▷ verb *a notice was pasted on the door:* glue, stick, gum, fix, affix.

pastel adjective *pastel colours:* pale, soft, light, light-coloured, muted, subtle, subdued, soft-hued.
OPPOSITES: dark, bright.

pastiche noun *the operetta is a pastiche of 18th-century style:* imitation, parody; informal take-off.

pastille noun lozenge, sweet, drop; tablet, pill.

pastime noun hobby, leisure activity/pursuit, sport, game, recreation, amusement, diversion, entertainment, interest, sideline.

past master noun *the manager was a past master at recharging faltering spirits:* expert, master, wizard, genius, old hand, veteran, maestro; informal ace, pro, star, hotshot; Brit. informal dab hand.

pastor noun priest, minister, parson, clergyman, cleric, chaplain, ecclesiastic, man of the cloth, churchman, vicar, rector, curate, preacher; informal reverend, padre.

pastoral adjective
1 *a pastoral scene:* rural, country, countryside, rustic, bucolic.
2 *his pastoral duties:* priestly, clerical, ecclesiastical, ministerial.

pasture noun grazing land, grassland, grass, pastureland, pasturage, meadows, fields.

pasty adjective *a young man with a thin face and a pasty complexion:* pale, pallid, wan, colourless, anaemic, white, grey, pasty-faced, washed out, sallow, unhealthy.

pat[1] verb *he patted her shoulder gently:* tap, touch.
▷ noun
1 *a pat on the cheek:* tap, touch.
2 *a pat of butter:* piece, dab, lump, portion, knob, ball.
◻ pat someone on the back
congratulate, praise, take your hat off to; commend, compliment, applaud, acclaim.

pat[2] adjective *his answers sounded too pat:* glib, simplistic, facile, unconvincing.
◻ off pat
a film whose dialogue I can repeat off pat: by heart, by rote, by memory, parrot-fashion; word-perfect

patch noun
1 *she had a patch over one eye:* covering, pad.
2 *the bird has a bright red patch under its wing:* mark, spot, speckle, streak; informal

p

splotch; Brit. informal splodge.
3 *a patch of ground:* **plot**, area, piece, strip, tract, parcel; N. Amer. lot.
4 (Brit. informal) *they're going through a difficult patch:* **period**, time, spell, phase, stretch.
▷**verb** *her jeans were neatly patched:* **mend**, repair, sew up, darn.

patchwork noun *a patchwork of different styles:* **assortment**, mixture, melange, medley, blend, mixed bag, mix, collection, assemblage, combination, potpourri, jumble, hotchpotch; N. Amer. hodgepodge; informal ragbag, mishmash.

patchy adjective
1 *there will be patchy rain in the north and west:* **intermittent**, fitful, sporadic, erratic, irregular.
2 *his performance was patchy to say the least:* **uneven**, inconsistent, erratic, variable.
3 *my knowledge of the subject is patchy:* **limited**, sketchy, inadequate, insufficient; Brit. informal bitty.
OPPOSITES: uniform, comprehensive.

patent noun *there is a patent on the chemical:* **copyright**, licence, registered trademark.
▷**adjective**
1 *a patent violation of their democratic rights:* **obvious**, clear, plain, evident, manifest, self-evident, transparent, overt, conspicuous, blatant, downright, barefaced, flagrant, undisguised, unconcealed, unmistakable.
2 *patent medicines:* **proprietary**, patented, licensed, branded.

paternal adjective
1 *my elders in the newsroom kept a paternal eye on me:* **fatherly**, protective, solicitous, compassionate, sympathetic.
2 *his paternal grandfather:* **on your father's side**; Anthropology patrilineal.

paternity noun *he refused to admit paternity of the child:* **fatherhood**.

path noun
1 *a path down to the beach:* **footpath**, pathway, track, trail, trackway, bridleway, bridle path, lane, alley, alleyway, passage, passageway; cycle path/track.
2 *journalists blocked his path | the expected path of the missile:* **route**, way, course; direction, bearing, line; orbit, trajectory.
3 *the best path towards a peace settlement:* **course of action**, route, road, avenue, line, approach, tack, strategy, tactic.

pathetic adjective
1 *it was a truly pathetic sight:* **pitiful**, pitiable, piteous, moving, touching, poignant, distressing, upsetting, harrowing, forlorn.
2 (informal) *that's a pathetic excuse:* **feeble**, woeful, sorry, poor, pitiful, lamentable, deplorable, contemptible, inadequate.

pathological adjective (informal) *he's a pathological gambler:* **compulsive**, obsessive, inveterate, habitual, persistent, chronic, hardened, confirmed.

pathos noun *the pathos of her predicament:* **poignancy**, tragedy, sadness, pitifulness, piteousness.

patience noun *this is a job that requires a great deal of patience:* **forbearance**, tolerance, restraint, self-restraint, stoicism; calmness, composure, imperturbability; perseverance, persistence, staying power, doggedness.

patient adjective *I'm a patient man and I don't expect overnight miracles:* **forbearing**, uncomplaining, tolerant, stoical, resigned, long-suffering, philosophical; calm, composed, even-tempered, imperturbable, accommodating, understanding, indulgent; persevering, persistent, tenacious, dogged; informal unflappable, cool.
▷**noun** *a doctor's patient:* **sick person**, case; invalid, convalescent, outpatient, inpatient.

patio noun **terrace**, courtyard; N. Amer. sun deck.

patois noun *the nurse talked to me in a patois that even Italians would have had difficulty in understanding:* **vernacular**, local dialect, regional language; informal lingo.

patrician adjective *a patrician family:* **aristocratic**, noble, titled, blue-blooded, high-born, upper-class; informal upper-crust.

patrimony noun *constant wars and invasions have destroyed the country's cultural patrimony:* **heritage**, inheritance, birthright; legacy.

patriotic adjective **nationalist**, nationalistic, loyalist, loyal; derogatory chauvinistic, jingoistic, flag-waving.
OPPOSITES: traitorous.

patriotism noun **nationalism**, allegiance/loyalty to your country; derogatory chauvinism, jingoism, flag-waving.

patrol noun
1 *his nightly patrol of the premises | troops are on patrol in the city:* **surveillance**, reconnoitre, patrolling, monitoring, policing; guard, watch; informal recce.
2 *the patrol stopped a suspect:* **patrolman**, patrolwoman, sentinel, sentry; guard.
▷**verb** *security guards are patrolling the area:* **keep guard on**, guard, keep watch on; police, make the rounds of; stand guard over, keep a vigil on, defend, safeguard.

patron noun
1 *a celebrated patron of the arts:* **sponsor**, backer, benefactor, benefactress, contributor, subscriber, donor; philanthropist, promoter, friend, supporter; informal angel.

p

2 *the car park is reserved for patrons of the restaurant:* customer, client, frequenter, user, visitor, guest; informal regular.

patronage noun
1 *the arts could no longer depend on private patronage:* sponsorship, backing, funding, financing, promotion, assistance, support.
2 *recruits are selected on merit, not through political patronage:* power of appointment, favouritism, nepotism, preferential treatment.
3 *thank you for your patronage:* custom, trade, business.

patronize verb
1 *please don't patronize me:* condescend to, treat condescendingly, look down on, talk down to, put down, treat like a child, treat with disdain.
2 *they patronized local tradesmen:* do business with, buy from, shop at, be a customer of, be a client of, deal with, trade with, frequent, support.

patronizing adjective *'She's a good-hearted girl,' he said in a patronizing voice:* condescending, superior, supercilious, disdainful; informal high and mighty.

patter¹ verb
1 *raindrops pattered against the window:* pitter-patter, tap, drum, beat, rattle.
2 *she pattered across the floor:* scurry, scuttle, scamper.
▷ noun *the patter of rain against the glass:* pitter-patter, pit-a-pat, tapping, pattering, drumming, beating, rattle.

patter² noun *the salesmen's patter:* sales pitch, sales talk; informal line, spiel.

pattern noun
1 *the pattern on the wallpaper:* design, motif, device, decoration, marking, ornamentation.
2 *the change in working patterns | the overall pattern is consistent with earlier research:* system, order, arrangement, sequence, form, method, structure, scheme, plan, framework.
3 *this would set the pattern for future generations:* model, example, standard, point of reference, benchmark; blueprint, archetype, prototype.

patterned adjective decorated, fancy, ornamented.
OPPOSITES: plain.

paucity noun *the paucity of information is a major concern:* scarcity, shortage, lack, dearth, insufficiency, deficiency, want.
OPPOSITES: abundance.

pauper noun poor person, indigent, down-and-out.

pause verb *Hannah paused for a moment:* stop, halt, break off; rest, wait, hesitate, hang back, falter.
▷ noun *there was a brief pause in the rain:* break, interruption, lull, respite, breathing space, hiatus, gap, interlude; rest, wait, hesitation; informal let-up.

pave verb
□ pave the way for
the peace deal paved the way for the transitional government which took office in July 2003: prepare (the way) for, make preparations for, lay the foundations for, clear the way for, get ready for; herald, precede.

pavement noun footpath, walkway; N. Amer. sidewalk.

pawn noun *she was just a pawn in the battle for the throne:* puppet, dupe, tool, cat's paw, instrument.

pay verb
1 *he claims they never paid him for the work | I'll pay you for the damage:* remunerate, give money to; reimburse, recompense, pay back.
2 *the club paid £650,000 for the Danish striker:* spend, expend, pay out, disburse; informal lay out, shell out, fork out, cough up.
3 *he's paid his debts:* discharge, settle, pay off, clear, liquidate.
4 *hard work will pay dividends:* yield, return, produce.
5 *the developers have to make the business pay:* be profitable, make money, make a profit.
6 *it may pay you to be early:* be advantageous to, benefit, be of advantage to, be beneficial to.
7 *you should pay her more respect:* give, show, offer.
8 *he will pay for his mistakes:* suffer the consequences of, suffer for, be punished for, pay the penalty/price for; make amends for, atone for.
▷ noun *we should get equal pay for equal work:* salary, wages, payment; earnings, remuneration, income; revenue; formal emolument.
□ pay someone back
I'll pay you back for this: get your revenge on, be revenged on, avenge yourself on, get back at, get even with, settle accounts with, exact retribution on.
□ pay something back
they did eventually pay back the money: repay, give back, return, reimburse, refund.
□ pay for
her parents paid for the trip: finance, fund; treat someone to; informal foot the bill for.
□ pay something off
you use the proceeds to pay off your loan: pay in full, settle, discharge, clear, liquidate.
□ pay off (informal) *his hard work paid off:* meet with success, be successful, be effective, get results.
□ pay something out
she had to pay out £300 for treatment:

p

spend, expend, pay, put up, hand over; informal shell out, fork out/up, lay out, cough up.
□ **pay up**
he's been allowed a week to pay up: make payment, settle up, pay in full.

payable adjective *capital gains tax is payable if the shares are sold:* due, owed, owing.

payment noun
1 *there are discounts for early payment:* remittance, settlement.
2 *interest-free monthly payments:* instalment, premium, remittance.
3 *extra payment for good performance:* salary, wages, pay, earnings, fees, remuneration, income.

pay-off noun (informal)
1 *the lure of enormous pay-offs:* payment, payout, reward; bribe, inducement, incentive; informal kickback, sweetener, backhander.
2 *a pay-off of £160,000:* return, return on your investment, yield, payback, profit, gain, dividend.
3 *such research has already produced a dramatic pay-off:* outcome, result, effect; advantage, benefit.

peace noun
1 *I just want some peace—I need to relax:* tranquillity, calm, rest, peace and quiet, quiet; privacy, solitude.
2 *he has finally found peace of mind:* serenity, tranquillity, equanimity, calm, composure, ease, contentment.
3 *a lasting peace:* treaty, truce, ceasefire, armistice, cessation/suspension of hostilities.
OPPOSITES: noise, war.

peaceable adjective
1 *a peaceable man:* peace-loving, non-violent, non-aggressive, easy-going, placid, gentle, inoffensive, good-natured, even-tempered, amiable, amicable, friendly, affable, genial, pacific, dovelike.
2 *a peaceable society:* peaceful, free from strife, harmonious; law-abiding, disciplined, orderly, civilized.
OPPOSITES: aggressive.

peaceful adjective
1 *everything was quiet and peaceful:* tranquil, calm, restful, quiet, still, relaxing, soothing, undisturbed, untroubled.
2 *his peaceful mood:* serene, calm, tranquil, composed, placid, at ease, untroubled, unworried, content.
3 *peaceful relations:* harmonious, at peace, peaceable, on good terms, amicable, friendly, cordial, non-violent.
OPPOSITES: noisy, agitated, hostile.

peacemaker noun arbitrator, arbiter, mediator, negotiator, conciliator, go-

between, intermediary, pacifier, appeaser, peace-monger, pacifist, peace-lover, dove; informal peacenik.
OPPOSITES: warmonger.

peak noun
1 *the peaks of the mountains:* summit, top, crest, pinnacle, apex, crown, cap.
2 *they climbed all six peaks:* mountain, hill, height, mount, alp; Scottish ben, Munro.
3 (Brit.) *the peak of a cap:* brim, visor.
4 *the peak of his career:* height, high point, high spot, pinnacle, summit, top, climax, culmination, apex, zenith, crowning point, acme, apogee, prime, heyday.
OPPOSITES: nadir, trough.
▷**verb** *inflation has finally peaked:* reach its height, climax, reach a climax, come to a head.
OPPOSITES: bottom out.
▷**adjective** *storage capacity has to be adequate to meet peak loads:* maximum, top, greatest, highest; ultimate, best, optimum.
OPPOSITES: minimum.

peaky adjective (Brit.) *you're looking a bit peaky:* pale, pasty, wan, drained, washed out, drawn, pallid, anaemic, ashen, grey, pinched, sickly, sallow; ill, unwell, poorly, run-down.
OPPOSITES: healthy.

peal noun
1 *a peal of bells:* chime, carillon, ring, ringing, tintinnabulation.
2 *peals of laughter:* shriek, shout, scream, howl, gale, fit, roar, hoot.
3 *a peal of thunder:* rumble, roar, boom, crash, clap, crack.
▷**verb**
1 *the bell pealed:* ring, chime, clang, sound, ding, jingle.
2 *the thunder pealed:* rumble, roar, boom, crash, resound.

peasant noun *peasants working the land:* agricultural worker, small farmer, rustic, villein, serf.

peccadillo noun *the sexual peccadillos of celebrities aren't necessarily news:* misdemeanour, petty offence, indiscretion, lapse, misdeed.

peculiar adjective
1 *something peculiar began to happen:* strange, unusual, odd, funny, curious, bizarre, queer, unexpected, unfamiliar, abnormal, atypical, anomalous, out of the ordinary; informal weird.
2 *mannerisms peculiar to the islanders:* characteristic of, typical of, representative of, indicative of, suggestive of, exclusive to.
3 *their own peculiar contribution:* distinctive, characteristic, distinct, individual, special, unique, personal.
OPPOSITES: ordinary.

peculiarity noun
1 *a legal peculiarity:* oddity, anomaly,

abnormality, idiosyncrasy, quirk.
2 *one of the peculiarities of the city:*
characteristic, feature, quality, property,
trait, attribute, hallmark, trademark.
3 *the peculiarity of this notion:*
strangeness, oddness, abnormality,
unfamiliarity, incongruity, outlandishness,
unconventionality, idiosyncrasy,
eccentricity, quirkiness; informal weirdness.

pecuniary adjective (formal) *he was free
from all pecuniary anxieties:* financial,
monetary, money, fiscal, economic.

pedagogic, pedagogical adjective
they show great pedagogic skills:
educational, educative, teaching,
instructional, instructive, didactic;
academic, scholastic.

pedant noun *pedants insist that the
21st century started with 2001:* purist,
dogmatist, literalist, formalist, doctrinaire,
perfectionist; quibbler, hair-splitter; informal
nit-picker.

pedantic adjective *a pedantic
interpretation of the rules:* over-
scrupulous, scrupulous, precise, exact,
perfectionist, punctilious, meticulous,
fussy, fastidious, finicky; dogmatic, purist,
literalist, literalistic, formalist; hair-
splitting, quibbling; informal nit-picking; Brit.
informal pernickety.

pedantry noun over-scrupulousness,
scrupulousness, perfectionism,
fastidiousness, punctiliousness,
meticulousness; dogmatism, purism,
literalism, formalism; quibbling, hair-
splitting; informal nit-picking.

peddle verb
1 *manufacturers even set up roadside
stands to peddle their latest products:* sell,
hawk, tout, vend; trade, deal in, traffic in.
2 *the book peddles the same old
mythological view of Hollywood:* promote,
put forward, proclaim, propound,
advocate, champion, preach, spread,
disseminate.

USAGE

Do not confuse **peddle** with **pedal**. **Peddle**
is a verb meaning 'to sell goods' or 'to
promote an idea'. **Pedal** is a noun referring
to a foot-operated lever, as on a bicycle; as a
verb it means 'to work the pedals of a bicycle'
(*we pedalled along the road*).

pedestal noun *a bust on a pedestal:*
plinth, base, support, mounting, stand,
foundation, pillar, column, pier.
□ **put someone on a pedestal**
admire, revere, worship, idealize, lionize,
look up to, respect, hold in high regard,
think highly of, esteem.

pedestrian adjective *they lead such
pedestrian lives:* dull, boring, tedious,
monotonous, uneventful, unremarkable,
tiresome, wearisome, uninspired,

unimaginative, unexciting, uninteresting;
unvarying, unvaried, repetitive, routine,
commonplace, workaday; ordinary,
everyday, run-of-the-mill, mundane,
humdrum.
OPPOSITES: exciting, interesting.

pedigree noun *a long pedigree:* ancestry,
descent, lineage, line of descent, bloodline,
genealogy, family tree, parentage,
extraction, origins, heritage, background,
roots.
▷ **adjective** *a pedigree cat:* pure-bred,
thoroughbred, pure-blooded.

pedlar noun
1 *pedlars of watches:* travelling salesman,
door-to-door salesman, huckster; street
trader, hawker.
2 *a drug pedlar:* trafficker, dealer; informal
pusher.

peek verb
1 *they peeked from behind the curtains:*
peep, have a peek, have a peep, spy, sneak
a look; informal take a gander, have a squint;
Brit. informal have a dekko, have/take a
butcher's, take a shufti.
2 *the deer's antlers peeked out from the
trees:* stick out slightly, be just visible,
show; appear, come into view/sight,
emerge, peep out.
▷ **noun** *a peek at the map:* peep, glance,
glimpse, quick look; informal gander, squint;
Brit. informal dekko, butcher's, shufti.

peel verb
1 *peel and core the fruit:* pare, skin, take
the skin/rind off; hull, shell, husk, shuck.
2 *use a long knife to peel off the veneer:* trim
off, pare, strip off, shave off, remove.
3 *the wallpaper was peeling:* flake off, peel
off, come off in layers/strips.
▷ **noun** *orange peel:* rind, skin, zest; hull, pod,
covering; technical integument.

peep¹ verb
1 *I peeped through the keyhole:* look
quickly, take a quick look, sneak a look,
peek, glance; informal take a gander, have a
squint; Brit. informal have a dekko, have/take a
butcher's, take a shufti.
2 *the moon peeped through the clouds:*
appear, show, come into view/sight,
become visible, emerge, peek, peer out.
▷ **noun** *I'll just take a peep at it:* quick look,
brief look, sneaky look, peek, glance;
informal gander, squint; Brit. informal dekko,
butcher's, shufti.

peep² noun
1 *I heard a quiet peep:* cheep, chirp,
chirrup, tweet, twitter, chirr, warble.
2 *there's been not a peep out of the children:*
sound, noise, cry, word.
3 *the painting was sold without a peep:*
complaint, grumble, mutter, murmur,
grouse, objection, protest, protestation.
▷ **verb** *the fax peeped:* cheep, chirp, chirrup,
tweet, twitter, chirr, warble.

p

peephole noun opening, gap, cleft, spyhole, slit, crack, chink, keyhole, squint, judas hole.

peer[1] verb *he peered at the manuscript:* look closely, try to see, narrow your eyes, screw up your eyes, squint.

peer[2] noun
1 *hereditary peers:* noble, nobleman, noblewoman, peer of the realm, peeress, lord, lady, titled person, aristocrat, patrician.
2 *his academic peers:* equal, coequal, fellow, confrère; contemporary.

peerage noun nobility, peers and peeresses, lords and ladies, aristocracy, patriciate; the House of Lords, the Lords.

peerless adjective *a peerless performance:* incomparable, matchless, unrivalled, inimitable, beyond compare/comparison, unparalleled, unequalled, without equal, second to none, unsurpassed, unsurpassable, nonpareil; unique, consummate, perfect, rare, transcendent, surpassing.

peeved adjective (informal) *he sounded quite peeved at the result:* irritated, annoyed, cross, angry, vexed, displeased, disgruntled, indignant, exasperated, galled, irked, put out, aggrieved, offended, affronted, piqued; informal aggravated, miffed, riled, nettled, hacked off, browned off; Brit. informal narked; N. Amer. informal sore.
OPPOSITES: pleased.

peevish adjective *'You are causing me a lot of bother,' he added, in a peevish tone:* irritable, fractious, petulant, querulous, pettish, crabby, crotchety, cantankerous, curmudgeonly, bad-tempered, short-tempered, touchy, testy, tetchy, irascible, waspish, prickly, crusty, dyspeptic; Brit. informal ratty; N. Amer. informal cranky.
OPPOSITES: good-humoured.

peg noun pin, nail, dowel, skewer, spike, rivet, brad, screw, bolt, hook, spigot.
▷verb
1 *the flysheet is pegged to the ground:* fix, pin, attach, fasten, secure, make fast.
2 *the cost of adult season tickets has been pegged at last season's price:* freeze, hold, keep, fix, set.

pejorative adjective *'permissiveness' is used almost universally as a pejorative term:* disparaging, derogatory, deprecatory; defamatory, slanderous, libellous, abusive, insulting; informal bitchy.
OPPOSITES: complimentary.

pelt[1] verb
1 *they pelted him with snowballs:* bombard, shower, pepper, attack, assail.
2 *rain was pelting down:* pour down, teem down, stream down, rain hard; informal rain cats and dogs; Brit. informal tip down, bucket down, come down in stair rods.

pelt[2] noun *an animal's pelt:* skin, hide, fleece, coat, fur.

pen[1] verb *he penned a number of articles:* write, compose, draft, dash off; write down, jot down, set down, take down, scribble.

pen[2] noun *a sheep pen:* enclosure, fold, pound, compound, stockade; sty, coop; N. Amer. corral.
▷verb *the hostages had been penned up in a basement:* confine, coop up, cage, shut in, box up/in, lock up/in, trap, imprison, incarcerate; formal immure.

penal adjective
1 *a penal institution:* disciplinary, punitive, corrective; N. Amer. correctional.
2 *penal rates of interest:* exorbitant, extortionate, excessive, inflated, sky-high, punitive, punishing.
OPPOSITES: reasonable, generous.

penalize verb
1 *if you break the rules you will be penalized:* punish, discipline, inflict a penalty on.
2 *people with certain medical conditions would be penalized:* handicap, disadvantage, put at a disadvantage, cause to suffer, hurt.
OPPOSITES: reward, help.

penalty noun
1 *there are severe penalties for dumping oil at sea:* punishment, sanction, punitive action, retribution; fine, forfeit, sentence; penance.
2 *one of the financial penalties of staying single:* disadvantage, difficulty, drawback, handicap, downside, minus; trial, tribulation, bane, affliction, burden, trouble.
OPPOSITES: reward, advantage.

penance noun *self-awareness is the necessary ingredient for penance:* atonement, expiation, self-punishment, self-mortification, self-abasement, amends; punishment, penalty.

penchant noun *he has a penchant for champagne:* liking, fondness, taste, relish, appetite, partiality, soft spot, love, passion, desire, fancy, whim, weakness, inclination, bent, bias, preference, proclivity, predilection, predisposition.
OPPOSITES: aversion.

pencil noun *a pencil of light:* beam, ray, shaft, finger, gleam.
▷verb
1 *he pencilled his name inside the cover:* write, jot, scribble, note, take down.
2 *pencil a line along the top of the moulding:* draw, trace, sketch.

pending adjective
1 *nine cases were still pending:* unresolved, undecided, unsettled, undetermined, open, up in the air, awaiting a decision, awaiting

action, hanging fire, ongoing, outstanding, not done, unfinished, incomplete; informal on the back burner.

2 *with a general election pending:* imminent, impending, about to happen, forthcoming, upcoming, on the way, coming, approaching, looming, gathering, near, nearing, close, close at hand, in the offing, to come.

▷ **preposition** *they were released on bail pending an appeal:* awaiting, until, until there is/are.

pendulous adjective *this magnolia produces large, white, pendulous flowers:* drooping, dangling, trailing, droopy, sagging, saggy, floppy; hanging; literary pendent.
OPPOSITES: erect.

penetrate verb
1 *the knife penetrated his lungs:* pierce, puncture, make a hole in, perforate, stab, prick, gore, spike.
2 *the oil has penetrated into the stones:* seep, soak, percolate, filter, spread, diffuse; infiltrate, permeate, saturate, suffuse, drench.
3 *they penetrated enemy territory:* infiltrate, slip into, sneak into, insinuate yourself into.
4 *he seemed to have penetrated the mysteries of nature:* understand, comprehend, fathom, grasp, perceive, discern, get to the bottom of, solve, resolve, make sense of, interpret, puzzle out, work out, unravel, decipher; formal apprehend; informal crack, get, figure out, make head or tail of; Brit. informal suss, suss out.
5 *his words finally penetrated:* register, sink in, be understood, be comprehended, become clear, fall into place; informal click.

penetrating adjective
1 *a penetrating wind:* piercing, cutting, biting, stinging, keen, sharp, harsh, raw, freezing, chill, wintry, cold.
2 *a penetrating voice:* shrill, strident, piercing, carrying, loud, high, high-pitched, piping, ear-splitting, screechy, intrusive.
3 *her penetrating gaze:* observant, searching, intent, alert, shrewd, perceptive, probing, piercing, sharp, keen.
4 *a penetrating analysis:* perceptive, insightful, keen, sharp, sharp-witted, intelligent, clever, incisive, piercing, razor-edged, trenchant, astute, shrewd, clear, acute, percipient, perspicacious, discerning, sensitive, thoughtful, deep, profound; informal smart.
OPPOSITES: mild, soft.

penetration noun
1 *some of the rot is attributable to rain penetration:* infiltration, entry, inflow, percolation, filtering, seepage, soaking, saturation, drenching, diffusion.
2 *remarks of great penetration:* insight,

discernment, perception, perceptiveness, intelligence, cleverness, incisiveness, keenness, sharpness, trenchancy, astuteness, shrewdness, acuteness, clarity, acuity, perspicacity, discrimination, sensitivity, thoughtfulness, profundity.
OPPOSITES: stupidity.

peninsula noun headland, promontory, point, head, cape, foreland, ness, horn, bill, bluff, mull.

penitence noun *the writer prays to God in penitence:* repentance, contrition, regret, remorse, ruefulness, sorrow, pangs of conscience, self-reproach, shame, guilt, compunction.

penitent adjective repentant, contrite, remorseful, sorry, apologetic, regretful, conscience-stricken, rueful, ashamed, shamefaced, abject, in sackcloth and ashes.
OPPOSITES: unrepentant.

pen-name noun pseudonym, nom de plume, assumed name, alias, professional name.

pennant noun *pennants fly from the tower:* flag, standard, ensign, colours, banner, guidon.

penniless adjective destitute, poverty-stricken, impoverished, poor, indigent, impecunious, in penury, needy; bankrupt, insolvent; Brit. on the breadline; formal necessitous; informal broke, strapped for cash; Brit. informal skint.
OPPOSITES: wealthy.

penny-pincher noun miser, Scrooge, niggard; informal skinflint, cheapskate; N. Amer. informal tightwad.
OPPOSITES: spendthrift.

penny-pinching adjective *penny-pinching governments with a utilitarian approach to the arts:* mean, miserly, niggardly, parsimonious, close-fisted, cheese-paring, grasping, Scrooge-like; informal stingy, tight, tight-fisted.
OPPOSITES: generous.

pensioner noun retired person, old-age pensioner, OAP, senior citizen, senior; N. Amer. retiree.

pensive adjective *a pensive mood:* thoughtful, reflective, contemplative, musing, meditative, introspective, ruminative, absorbed, preoccupied, deep/lost in thought, brooding.

pent-up adjective *a release of pent-up emotion:* repressed, suppressed, stifled, smothered, restrained, confined, bottled up, held in/back, kept in check, curbed, bridled.

penury noun *he couldn't face another year of penury:* extreme poverty, destitution, impecuniousness, impoverishment, indigence, privation, beggary.

p

people noun

1 *crowds of people:* **human beings,** persons, individuals, humans, mortals, living souls, {men, women, and children}; informal folk.
2 *the British people:* **citizens,** subjects, electors, voters, taxpayers, residents, inhabitants, public, general public, citizenry, nation, population, populace.
3 *a man of the people:* **common people,** proletariat, masses, populace, rank and file, commonality, commonalty, third estate, plebeians; derogatory great unwashed, hoi polloi, common herd, proles, plebs.
4 (dated) *her people don't live far away:* **family,** parents, relatives, relations, folk, kinsmen, kin, kith and kin, kinsfolk, flesh and blood, nearest and dearest, loved ones; N. Amer. informal folks.
5 *the peoples of Africa:* **ethnic group,** race, tribe.
▷**verb** *the aborigines who first peopled the island:* **populate,** settle in, colonize; inhabit, live in, occupy.

> **WORD LINKS**
> **anthropology** the study of people, cultures, and human origins
> **ethnic** relating to a people who have a common national or cultural tradition
> **demotic** (of language) used by ordinary people

pep verb

☐ **pep someone/thing up** (informal) *new measures to pep up the economy:* **enliven,** animate, liven up, put some/new life into, invigorate, vitalize, revitalize, vivify, ginger up, energize, galvanize, put some spark into, stimulate; brighten up, cheer up; informal perk up, buck up.

pepper verb

1 *stars peppered the desert skies:* **sprinkle,** fleck, dot, spot, stipple; cover, fill.
2 *another burst of bullets peppered the tank:* **bombard,** pelt, shower, rain down on, attack, assail, batter, strafe, rake, blitz, hit.

perceive verb

1 *I immediately perceived the flaws in her story:* **discern,** recognize, become aware of, see, distinguish, realize, grasp, understand, take in, make out, find, identify, hit on, comprehend, appreciate, sense, divine; formal apprehend; informal figure out.
2 *he perceived a flush creeping up her neck:* **see,** notice, discern, detect, catch sight of, spot, observe.
3 *he was perceived as too negative:* **regard,** look on, view, consider, think of, judge.

perceptible adjective

a perceptible decline in public confidence: **noticeable,** perceivable, detectable, discernible, visible, observable, recognizable, appreciable; obvious, apparent, evident, manifest, patent, clear, distinct, plain, conspicuous.
OPPOSITES: imperceptible.

perception noun

1 *our perception of our own limitations:* **recognition,** awareness, consciousness, appreciation, realization, knowledge, grasp, understanding, comprehension, apprehension.
2 *popular perceptions of old age:* **impression,** idea, conception, notion, thought, belief, judgement, estimation.
3 *he talks with great perception:* **insight,** perspicacity, understanding, sharpness, intelligence, intuition, cleverness, incisiveness, trenchancy, astuteness, shrewdness, acuteness, discernment, sensitivity, penetration, thoughtfulness, profundity.
OPPOSITES: obtuseness.

perceptive adjective

an extraordinarily perceptive account of their relationship: **insightful,** discerning, sensitive, intuitive, observant; piercing, penetrating, percipient, perspicacious, clear-sighted, far-sighted, intelligent, clever, canny, keen, sharp, sharp-witted, astute, shrewd, quick, acute, discriminating; informal smart, on the ball.
OPPOSITES: obtuse.

perch verb

1 *three swallows perched on the telegraph wire:* **roost,** sit, rest; alight, settle, land, come to rest.
2 *she perched her glasses on her nose:* **put,** place, set, rest, balance.
3 *the church is perched on a hill:* **be located,** be situated, be positioned, be sited, stand; teeter.

percipient adjective. See PERCEPTIVE.

percolate verb

1 *water percolated through the soil:* **filter,** seep, ooze, trickle, drain, drip, dribble, leak, leach.
2 *these views began to percolate through society as a whole:* **spread,** be disseminated, filter, pass; permeate, pervade.

peremptory adjective

she had come to dread his peremptory orders: **brusque,** imperious, high-handed, brisk, abrupt, summary, commanding, dictatorial, autocratic, overbearing, dogmatic, arrogant, overweening, lordly, magisterial, authoritarian; emphatic, firm, insistent; informal bossy.

perennial adjective

the perennial fascination with crime: **abiding,** enduring, lasting, everlasting, perpetual, eternal, continuing, unending, unceasing, never-ending, endless, undying, ceaseless, persisting, permanent, constant, continual, unfailing, unchanging, never-changing.
OPPOSITES: ephemeral.

perfect adjective

1 *she strove to be the perfect wife:* **ideal,** model, exemplary, best, ultimate, copybook, without fault, faultless,

flawless, consummate, quintessential; unrivalled, unequalled, matchless, unparalleled, beyond compare, without equal, second to none, incomparable, nonpareil, peerless, inimitable, unsurpassed, unsurpassable.
2 *an E-type Jaguar in perfect condition:* flawless, mint, as good as new, pristine, impeccable, immaculate, superb, superlative, optimum, prime, optimal, peak, excellent, faultless, unspoiled, unblemished, undamaged, spotless; informal tip-top, A1.
3 *a perfect copy:* exact, precise, accurate, faithful, correct, unerring, true, strict.
4 *the perfect Christmas present for golfers everywhere:* ideal, just right, appropriate, fitting, suitable, apt, made to order, tailor-made; very.
5 *she felt a perfect idiot:* absolute, complete, total, real, out-and-out, thorough, thoroughgoing, downright, utter, sheer, arrant, unmitigated, unqualified, veritable, in every respect, unalloyed; Brit. informal right.
OPPOSITES: imperfect.

▷ verb *he's busy perfecting his bowling technique:* improve, polish up, hone, refine, put the finishing/final touches to, brush up, fine-tune.

perfectionist noun *he's a perfectionist in all that he does:* purist, stickler, idealist; pedant.

perfectly adverb
1 *a perfectly cooked meal:* superbly, superlatively, excellently, flawlessly, faultlessly, to perfection, without fault, inimitably, incomparably, impeccably, immaculately, exquisitely; informal like a dream, to a T.
2 *I think we understand each other perfectly:* absolutely, utterly, completely, altogether, entirely, wholly, totally, thoroughly, fully, in every respect.
3 *you know perfectly well that is not what I meant:* very, quite, full.
OPPOSITES: imperfectly.

perforate verb *fragments of a bullet perforated his intestines:* pierce, penetrate, enter, puncture, prick, bore through, riddle.

perform verb
1 *I have my duties to perform:* carry out, do, execute, discharge, bring about, bring off, accomplish, achieve, fulfil, complete, conduct, effect, dispatch, implement; informal pull off.
2 *a car which performs well at low speeds:* function, work, operate, run, go, respond, behave, act, acquit yourself/itself.
3 *the play has been performed in Britain:* stage, put on, present, mount, enact, act, produce.
4 *the band performed live in Hyde Park:* appear, play, be on stage.

performance noun
1 *the evening performance:* show, production, showing, presentation, staging; concert, recital; informal gig.
2 *their performance of Mozart's Concerto in E flat:* rendition, rendering, interpretation, playing, acting, representation.
3 *the continual performance of a single task:* carrying out, execution, discharge, accomplishment, completion, fulfilment, dispatch, implementation.
4 *the performance of the processor:* functioning, working, operation, running, behaviour, capabilities, capability, capacity, power, functionality, potential.

performer noun player, artist, artiste, interpreter, practitioner.

perfume noun
1 *a bottle of perfume:* scent, fragrance, eau de toilette, toilet water.
2 *the heady perfume of lilacs:* smell, scent, fragrance, aroma, bouquet; old use redolence.

perfumed adjective *perfumed soap:* scented, fragranced, sweet-smelling, fragrant, perfumy, aromatic.
OPPOSITES: fragrance-free.

perfunctory adjective *the guards gave a perfunctory look up and down the carriage:* cursory, desultory, quick, brief, hasty, hurried, rapid, fleeting, token, casual, superficial, careless, half-hearted, sketchy, mechanical, automatic, routine, offhand, inattentive.
OPPOSITES: careful, thorough.

perhaps adverb *perhaps he'll come home tomorrow:* maybe, possibly, it's possible, it could be, it may be, conceivably, for all you know; old use perchance.

peril noun *a situation fraught with peril:* danger, jeopardy, risk, hazard, insecurity, uncertainty, menace, threat; pitfall, problem.

perilous adjective *a perilous journey through the mountains | the company is in a perilous position:* dangerous, hazardous, risky, unsafe, treacherous, fraught with danger; precarious, vulnerable, uncertain, insecure, exposed, at risk, in jeopardy, in danger, touch-and-go; informal dicey.
OPPOSITES: safe.

perimeter noun
1 *the perimeter of a circle:* circumference, outside, outer edge.
2 *the perimeter of the vast estate:* boundary, border, limits, bounds, confines, edge, margin, fringes, periphery, verge.

period noun
1 *a six-week period:* time, spell, interval, stretch, term, span, phase, bout, run, duration; chapter, stage; while.
2 *the post-war period:* era, age, epoch, time, days, years.

p

3 *a double Maths period:* **lesson**, class, session.

periodic adjective *Michael had to make periodic visits to the hospital:* **regular**, periodical, at fixed intervals, recurrent, recurring, repeated, cyclical, cyclic, seasonal; occasional, infrequent, intermittent, sporadic, spasmodic, odd.

periodical noun *he wrote for two scientific periodicals:* **journal**, magazine, newspaper, paper, review, digest, gazette, newsletter, organ, quarterly; publication.

peripatetic adjective *his peripatetic way of life | a peripatetic music teacher:* **nomadic**, itinerant, travelling, visiting, wandering, roving, roaming, migrant, migratory, unsettled.
OPPOSITES: settled, resident.

peripheral adjective
1 *the city's peripheral housing estates:* **outlying**, outer, on the edge/outskirts, surrounding, suburban.
2 *mere peripheral issues:* **secondary**, subsidiary, incidental, tangential, marginal, minor, unimportant, lesser, non-essential, immaterial, ancillary.
OPPOSITES: inner, central.

periphery noun *rambling estates on the periphery of the city:* **edge**, outer edge, margin, fringe, boundary, border, perimeter, rim, verge; outskirts, suburbs, outer limits/reaches, bounds.
OPPOSITES: centre.

perish verb
1 (literary) *millions of soldiers perished:* **die**, lose your life, be killed, fall, expire, meet your death, be lost, lay down your life, breathe your last, pass away, give up the ghost, meet your maker; informal kick the bucket, turn up your toes, buy it; Brit. informal snuff it.
2 (literary) *must these hopes perish so soon?* **come to an end**, die, disappear, vanish, fade, dissolve, evaporate, melt away, wither.
3 *the rubber had perished:* **rot**, decay, decompose, putrefy.

perk¹ verb
□ **perk up** (informal)
1 *you seem to have perked up:* **cheer up**, brighten up, liven up, take heart; informal buck up.
2 *the economy has been slow to perk up:* **recover**, rally, improve, revive, take a turn for the better, look up, pick up, bounce back.
□ **perk someone/something up** *you could do with something to perk you up:* **cheer up**, liven up, brighten up, raise someone's spirits, give someone a boost/lift, vitalize, invigorate, energize, enliven, ginger up, put new life/heart into, put some spark into, rejuvenate, refresh, revitalize; informal buck up, pep up.

perk² noun (informal) *a job with a lot of perks:* **benefit**, additional benefit, fringe benefit, advantage, bonus, extra; formal perquisite; informal plus, freebie.

perky adjective *I felt much more perky after I put the phone down:* **cheerful**, lively, vivacious, animated, bubbly, effervescent, bouncy, spirited, high-spirited, in high spirits, cheery, merry, buoyant, ebullient, exuberant, jaunty, frisky, sprightly, spry, bright, sunny, jolly; informal full of beans, chirpy, chipper.
OPPOSITES: depressed.

permanence noun *our craving for some sense of permanence in a rapidly changing world:* **stability**, durability, fixity, continuity, fixedness, immutability, endurance, constancy, immortality, indestructibility, perpetuity, endlessness.
OPPOSITES: impermanence.

permanent adjective
1 *permanent brain damage:* **lasting**, enduring, indefinite, continuing, perpetual, everlasting, eternal, abiding, constant, irreparable, irreversible, lifelong, indissoluble, indelible, standing, perennial, unending, endless, never-ending, immutable, undying, imperishable, indestructible, ineradicable.
2 *a permanent job:* **long-term**, stable, secure, durable.
OPPOSITES: temporary.

permanently adverb
1 *the attack left her permanently disabled:* **forever**, for good, for evermore, in perpetuity.
2 *I was permanently hungry:* **continually**, constantly, perpetually, always.
OPPOSITES: temporarily.

permeate verb *the delicious smell permeated the entire flat:* **pervade**, spread through, fill, filter through, diffuse through, imbue, penetrate, pass through, percolate through, suffuse, steep, impregnate, saturate, inform; literary perfuse.

permissible adjective *permissible levels of atmospheric pollution:* **permitted**, allowable, allowed, acceptable, legal, lawful, legitimate, admissible, licit, authorized, sanctioned, tolerated.
OPPOSITES: forbidden.

permission noun *you must get permission from your manager for all absences:* **authorization**, consent, leave, authority, sanction, licence, dispensation, assent, acquiescence, agreement, approval, endorsement, blessing, imprimatur, clearance; informal go-ahead.

permissive adjective *the permissive society of the 1960s:* **liberal**, broad-minded, open-minded, free, free and easy, easy-going, live-and-let-live, laissez-faire, libertarian, tolerant, forbearing, indulgent,

lenient; overindulgent, lax, soft.
OPPOSITES: intolerant, strict.

permit verb *I cannot permit you to leave:*
allow, let, authorize, give permission,
sanction, grant, license, empower, enable,
entitle, qualify; consent to, assent to, give
your blessing to, acquiesce in, agree to;
legalize, legitimate; informal give the go-
ahead to.
OPPOSITES: forbid.
▷ **noun** *I need to see your permit:*
authorization, licence, pass, ticket,
warrant, document, certification; passport,
visa.

permutation noun *all the possible
permutations were explored:* arrangement,
order, grouping, disposition, presentation,
sorting, organization, variation, alteration,
combination.

pernicious adjective *a pernicious
influence on society:* harmful,
damaging, destructive, injurious,
hurtful, detrimental, deleterious,
dangerous, adverse, inimical, unhealthy,
unfavourable, bad, evil, baleful, wicked,
malign, malevolent, malignant, poisonous,
corrupting.
OPPOSITES: beneficial.

pernickety adjective (Brit. informal) *she's
very pernickety about her food:* fussy,
finicky, fastidious, over-fastidious, difficult
to please, particular, over-particular,
faddish, punctilious, hair-splitting, critical,
overcritical; informal nit-picking, choosy,
picky; Brit. informal faddy.
OPPOSITES: easy-going.

perpendicular adjective
1 *the perpendicular stones:* upright,
vertical, erect, plumb, straight, on end,
standing, upended.
2 *lines perpendicular to each other:* at right
angles, at 90 degrees.
3 *the perpendicular hillside:* steep, sheer,
precipitous, abrupt, bluff, vertiginous.
OPPOSITES: horizontal.

perpetrate verb *right-wing elements
perpetrated a series of attacks and assaults:*
commit, carry out, perform, execute, do,
effect, bring about, accomplish; be guilty
of, be to blame for, be responsible for,
inflict, wreak; informal pull off.

> **USAGE**
>
> Do not confuse **perpetrate** and
> **perpetuate**. Perpetrate means 'to
> carry out a bad or illegal act', whereas
> **perpetuate** means 'to make something
> continue for a considerable time' (e.g. *a
> monument to perpetuate the memory of
> those killed in the war*).

perpetual adjective *deep caves in
perpetual darkness:* permanent, eternal,
everlasting, never-ending, unending,
endless, without end, incessant,
interminable, uninterrupted, unbroken,
lasting, long-lasting, constant, continuous,
continual, abiding, enduring, persistent,
perennial, round-the-clock, timeless,
ageless, deathless, undying, immortal;
unfailing, unchanging, never-changing,
changeless, unfading, unremitting,
sustained.
OPPOSITES: temporary.

perpetuate verb *a monument to
perpetuate the memory of those killed in
the war:* preserve, continue, maintain,
keep going, keep alive, conserve, sustain,
extend, carry on, keep up, prolong.

perpetuity noun
□ **in perpetuity**
*the land was to remain in their possession in
perpetuity:* forever, permanently, for good,
perpetually, for evermore, for all time.

perplex verb *she was perplexed by her
husband's attitude:* puzzle, baffle, mystify,
bemuse, bewilder, confound, confuse,
nonplus, disconcert, dumbfound, throw;
informal flummox, stump, bamboozle,
floor, fox.

perplexing adjective puzzling, baffling,
mystifying, mysterious, bewildering,
confusing, disconcerting, unaccountable,
difficult to understand, beyond you,
paradoxical, peculiar, funny, strange, odd;
informal weird.

perplexity noun
1 *he scratched his head in perplexity:*
confusion, bewilderment, puzzlement,
bafflement, incomprehension,
mystification; informal bamboozlement.
2 *the perplexities of international relations:*
complexity, complication, intricacy,
problem, difficulty, mystery, puzzle,
enigma, paradox.

per se adverb *possessing a knife was not
per se an unlawful act:* in itself, of itself,
by itself, as such, intrinsically; by its
very nature, in essence, by definition,
essentially.

persecute verb
1 *they were persecuted for their religious
beliefs:* oppress, abuse, victimize, ill-treat,
mistreat, maltreat, tyrannize, torment,
torture; martyr.
2 *she was persecuted by the press:* harass,
hound, plague, intimidate, pick on, pester,
bother, bedevil, bully, victimize, terrorize;
informal hassle.

persecution noun
1 *victims of religious persecution:*
oppression, victimization, maltreatment,
ill-treatment, mistreatment, abuse, ill-
usage, discrimination, tyranny; informal
witch hunt.
2 *the persecution I endured at school:*
harassment, hounding, intimidation,
bullying, victimization.

perseverance noun *medicine is a*

p

field which requires dedication and perseverance: persistence, tenacity, determination, staying power, purpose; patience, endurance, application, diligence, dedication, commitment, doggedness, assiduity, tirelessness, stamina; intransigence, obstinacy; informal stickability.

persevere verb she persevered, in spite of these discouraging setbacks: persist, continue, carry on, go on, keep on, keep going, struggle on, hammer away, be persistent, be determined, see/follow something through, keep at it, press on/ahead, not take no for an answer, be tenacious, stand your ground, stand fast/firm, hold on, go the distance, stay the course, plough on, stop at nothing, leave no stone unturned; informal soldier on, plug away, peg away, stick to your guns, stick it out.
OPPOSITES: give up.

persist verb
1 Corbett persisted with his questioning. See **PERSEVERE**.
2 if dry weather persists, water the lawn thoroughly: continue, hold, carry on, last, keep on, keep up, remain, linger, stay, endure.

persistence noun. See **PERSEVERANCE**.

persistent adjective
1 a very persistent man: tenacious, persevering, determined, resolute, purposeful, dogged, single-minded, tireless, indefatigable, patient, unflagging, untiring, insistent, importunate, relentless, unrelenting; stubborn, intransigent, obstinate, obdurate.
2 persistent rain: constant, continuous, continuing, continual, non-stop, never-ending, steady, uninterrupted, unbroken, interminable, incessant, unceasing, endless, unending, perpetual, unremitting, unrelenting, relentless, unrelieved, sustained.
3 a persistent cough: chronic, permanent, nagging, frequent; habitual.
OPPOSITES: irresolute, intermittent.

person noun human being, individual, man/woman, human, being, living soul, mortal, creature; character, customer; informal type, sort.
▢in person
physically, in the flesh, in propria persona, personally; yourself; informal as large as life.

persona noun his brash public persona is a facade for a very vulnerable man: image, face, public face, character, personality, identity, self; front, facade, guise, exterior, role, part.

personable adjective a personable young man: pleasant, agreeable, likeable, nice, amiable, affable, charming, congenial, genial, engaging, pleasing; attractive, presentable, good-looking, nice-looking, pretty, appealing; Scottish & N. English bonny.
OPPOSITES: disagreeable, unattractive.

personage noun a succession of Hollywood personages: VIP, celebrity, personality, name, famous name, household name, public figure, star, leading light, luminary, dignitary, notable, worthy; informal celeb, somebody, big shot; dated notability.
OPPOSITES: nobody.

personal adjective
1 a highly personal style: distinctive, characteristic, unique, individual, your own, particular, peculiar, idiosyncratic, individualized, personalized.
2 a personal appearance: in person, in the flesh, actual, live, physical.
3 his personal life: private, intimate; confidential, secret.
4 a personal friend: intimate, close, dear, great, bosom.
5 I have personal knowledge of the family: direct, empirical, first-hand, immediate, experiential.
6 personal remarks: derogatory, disparaging, insulting, critical, rude, disrespectful, offensive, pejorative, belittling.
OPPOSITES: public.

personality noun
1 her cheerful personality: character, nature, disposition, temperament, make-up, persona, psyche.
2 she had loads of personality: charisma, magnetism, strength/force of personality, character, charm, presence.
3 a famous personality: celebrity, VIP, star, superstar, name, famous name, household name, big name, somebody, leading light, luminary, notable, personage; informal celeb.

personalize verb products which can be personalized to your requirements: customize, individualize.

personally adverb
1 I'd like to thank him personally: in person, yourself.
2 personally, I think it's a good idea: for my part, for myself, to my way of thinking, to my mind, in my estimation, as far as I am concerned, in my view/opinion, from my point of view, from where I stand, as I see it, if you ask me, for my money, in my book; privately.
▢take something personally
take offence, take something amiss, be

p

offended, be upset, be affronted, take umbrage, take exception, feel insulted, feel hurt.

personification noun *he was the very personification of British pluck and diplomacy:* embodiment, incarnation, epitome, essence, quintessence, soul, model, exemplification, exemplar, image, symbol, representation.

personify verb *you personify every foreigner's image of the perfect English gentleman:* epitomize, embody, be the incarnation of, typify, exemplify, represent, symbolize, stand for.

personnel noun *sales personnel must dress smartly:* staff, employees, workforce, workers, labour force, manpower, human resources.

perspective noun *her perspective on things had changed:* outlook, view, viewpoint, point of view, standpoint, position, stand, stance, angle, slant, attitude, frame of mind, frame of reference, approach, way of looking at something, interpretation.

perspicacious adjective *his more perspicacious advisers recommended caution:* discerning, shrewd, perceptive, astute, penetrating, observant, percipient, clear-sighted, far-sighted, sharp-witted, sharp, alert, acute, clever, canny, intelligent, insightful, wise, sage, sensitive, intuitive, understanding, aware, discriminating; informal smart, on the ball.
OPPOSITES: stupid.

persuadable adjective *he was very persuadable:* malleable, tractable, pliable, compliant, amenable, adaptable, accommodating, cooperative, flexible, acquiescent, yielding, biddable, complaisant, like putty in your hands, suggestible.

persuade verb
1 *he tried to persuade her to come with him:* prevail on, talk into, coax, convince, make, get, induce, win over, bring round, coerce, influence, sway, inveigle, entice, tempt, lure, cajole, wheedle; Law procure; informal sweet-talk, twist someone's arm.
2 *shortage of money persuaded them to abandon the scheme:* cause, lead, move, dispose, incline.
OPPOSITES: dissuade, deter.

persuasion noun
1 *Monica needed plenty of persuasion:* coaxing, persuading, coercion, inducement, convincing, blandishment, encouragement, urging, cajoling; informal sweet-talking, arm-twisting.
2 *various political and religious persuasions:* group, grouping, sect, denomination, party, camp, side, faction, affiliation, school of thought, belief, creed, credo, faith, philosophy.

persuasive adjective *a persuasive argument:* convincing, cogent, compelling, potent, forceful, powerful, eloquent, impressive, influential, sound, valid, strong, effective, winning, telling; plausible, credible.
OPPOSITES: unconvincing.

pert adjective
1 *a pert little hat:* jaunty, neat, trim, stylish, smart, perky, rakish.
2 *a young girl with a pert manner:* impudent, impertinent, cheeky, irreverent, forward, insolent, disrespectful, flippant, familiar, presumptuous, bold, brazen; informal fresh, lippy.
OPPOSITES: respectful.

pertain verb
1 *developments pertaining to the economy:* concern, relate to, be related to, be connected with, be relevant to, apply to, be pertinent to, refer to, have a bearing on, bear on, affect, involve, touch; formal appertain to.
2 (formal) *the economic situation which pertained in Britain at that time:* exist, be the order of the day, be the case, prevail.

pertinent adjective *she asked me a lot of very pertinent questions:* relevant, to the point, apposite, appropriate, suitable, fitting, fit, apt, applicable, material, germane, apropos.
OPPOSITES: irrelevant.

perturb verb *David's behaviour perturbed his parents:* worry, disturb, concern, trouble, disquiet; disconcert, discomfit, unsettle, unnerve, upset, alarm, bother, distress, dismay, agitate, fluster, ruffle, exercise; informal rattle.
OPPOSITES: reassure.

perturbed adjective upset, worried, unsettled, disturbed, concerned, troubled, anxious, ill at ease, uneasy, disquieted; disconcerted, distressed, unnerved, alarmed, bothered, dismayed, agitated, flustered, ruffled, shaken; informal rattled.
OPPOSITES: calm.

peruse verb (formal) *as he sipped his coffee, he perused his newspaper:* read, study, scrutinize, inspect, examine.

> **USAGE**
>
> The verb **peruse** means 'to read something thoroughly and carefully'. It is sometimes taken to mean 'to read through something quickly', but this is a mistake.

pervade verb *a strong smell of floor polish pervaded the house:* permeate, spread through, fill, suffuse, be diffused through, imbue, penetrate, filter through, percolate through, infuse, flow through; steep, saturate, impregnate, inform; literary perfuse.

pervasive adjective *a pervasive smell of staleness:* prevalent, pervading, permeating, extensive, ubiquitous, omnipresent, universal, rife, widespread, general.

perverse adjective

1 *he is being deliberately perverse:* awkward, contrary, difficult, unreasonable, uncooperative, unhelpful, obstructive, disobliging, recalcitrant, stubborn, obstinate, obdurate, mulish, pig-headed; informal cussed; Brit. informal bloody-minded, bolshie.
2 *a verdict that is manifestly perverse:* illogical, irrational, unreasonable, wrong, wrong-headed.
3 *an evil life dedicated to perverse pleasure:* perverted, depraved, unnatural, abnormal, deviant, degenerate, immoral, warped, twisted, corrupt; wicked, base, evil; informal kinky, sick.
OPPOSITES: accommodating, reasonable.

perversion noun

1 *a twisted perversion of the truth:* distortion, misrepresentation, falsification, travesty, misinterpretation, misconstruction, twisting, corruption, subversion, misuse, misapplication, debasement.
2 *sexual perversion:* deviance, abnormality; depravity, degeneracy, debauchery, corruption, vice, wickedness, immorality.

perversity noun

1 *out of sheer perversity, he refused:* contrariness, awkwardness, recalcitrance, stubbornness, obstinacy, obduracy, mulishness, pig-headedness; informal cussedness; Brit. informal bloody-mindedness.
2 *the perversity of the decision:* unreasonableness, irrationality, illogicality, wrong-headedness.

pervert verb

1 *people who attempt to pervert the rules:* distort, corrupt, subvert, twist, bend, abuse, misapply, misuse, misrepresent, misinterpret, falsify.
2 *men can be perverted by power:* corrupt, lead astray, warp; pollute, poison, debase, deprave.

perverted adjective *it's impossible to understand the perverted mentality of someone who could do such a thing:* unnatural, deviant, warped, corrupt, twisted, abnormal, unhealthy, depraved, immoral, evil, wicked, vile, wrong; informal sick.
OPPOSITES: decent.

pessimism noun defeatism, negativity, doom and gloom, cynicism, fatalism; hopelessness, depression, despair, despondency, angst.
OPPOSITES: optimism.

pessimist noun *pessimists attempted to paint a picture of a nation in decline:* defeatist, fatalist, prophet of doom, cynic, doomsayer, doomster, Cassandra; sceptic, doubter, doubting Thomas; misery, killjoy,

Job's comforter; informal doom and gloom merchant, wet blanket.
OPPOSITES: optimist.

pessimistic adjective *a pessimistic outlook on life:* gloomy, negative, defeatist, downbeat, cynical, bleak, fatalistic, dark, black, despairing, despondent, depressed, hopeless; suspicious, distrustful, doubting.
OPPOSITES: optimistic.

pest noun *that child is a real pest:* nuisance, annoyance, irritation, irritant, thorn in your flesh/side, trial, the bane of your life, menace, trouble, problem, worry, bother; informal pain, pain in the neck, headache.
OPPOSITES: help, joy.

pester verb *I've been pestered by reporters for days:* badger, hound, harass, plague, annoy, bother, trouble, keep after, persecute, torment, bedevil, worry, beleaguer; chivvy, nag; informal hassle, bug.

pet noun *the teacher's pet:* favourite, darling, the apple of your eye; Brit. informal blue-eyed boy/girl; N. Amer. informal fair-haired boy/girl.
▷ **adjective**
1 *a pet lamb:* tame, domesticated, domestic, house-trained; N. Amer. housebroken.
2 *his pet theory:* favourite, favoured, cherished, dear to your heart; particular, special, personal.
OPPOSITES: wild.
▷ **verb**
1 *the cats came to be petted:* stroke, caress, fondle, tickle, pat.
2 *couples were petting in their cars:* kiss, cuddle, embrace, caress; informal canoodle, neck, smooch; N. Amer. informal make out.
□ **pet name**
affectionate name, term of endearment, endearment, nickname, diminutive.

peter verb
□ **peter out**
the economic recovery is in danger of petering out: fizzle out, fade away, die away/out, dwindle, diminish, taper off, tail off, trail away/off, wane, ebb, melt away, evaporate, disappear, come to an end, subside.

petite adjective *she was dark, petite, and sophisticated:* small, dainty, diminutive, slight, little, tiny, elfin, delicate, trim, small-boned; Scottish wee; informal pint-sized.
OPPOSITES: burly.

petition noun

1 *over 1,000 people signed the petition:* appeal, round robin.
2 *a form of prayer consisting of petitions to God:* entreaty, supplication, plea, prayer, appeal, request, invocation.
▷ **verb** *they petitioned the king to revoke the decision:* appeal to, entreat, beg, implore, plead with, request, ask, call on, apply to, press, urge.

petrified adjective
1 *she looked petrified:* terrified, horrified, scared/frightened out of your wits, scared/frightened to death.
2 *the petrified remains of prehistoric animals:* ossified, fossilized, calcified.

petrify verb terrify, horrify, frighten, scare, scare/frighten to death, scare/frighten the living daylights out of, scare/frighten the life out of, strike terror into, put the fear of God into; paralyse, transfix.

petty adjective
1 *petty regulations:* trivial, trifling, minor, small, unimportant, insignificant, inconsequential, inconsiderable, negligible, paltry, footling, pettifogging; informal piffling, fiddling.
2 *a petty form of revenge:* small-minded, mean, ungenerous, shabby, spiteful.
OPPOSITES: important, magnanimous.

petulant adjective *he sounded as petulant as a small child:* sulky, sullen, moody, bad-tempered, querulous, fractious, pettish, piqued, disgruntled, ill-humoured, in a bad mood, put out, grumpy; informal grouchy; Brit. informal ratty.
OPPOSITES: good-humoured.

phantom noun
1 *a phantom who haunts lonely roads:* ghost, apparition, spirit, spectre, wraith; informal spook.
2 *the phantoms of an overactive imagination:* delusion, figment of the imagination, hallucination, illusion, vision, mirage.

phase noun
1 *the final phase of the campaign:* stage, period, chapter, episode, part, step, point, time, juncture.
2 *he's going through a difficult phase:* period, stage, time, spell; Brit. informal patch.
□ **phase something in**
the changes will be phased in over the next 12 months: introduce gradually, begin to use, ease in, roll out.
□ **phase something out**
the scheme is being phased out: withdraw gradually, discontinue, stop using, run down, wind down.

phenomenal adjective *sales growth has been nothing short of phenomenal:* remarkable, exceptional, extraordinary, amazing, astonishing, astounding, stupendous, sensational, stunning, incredible, unbelievable; marvellous, magnificent, wonderful, outstanding, unprecedented; informal fantastic, terrific, tremendous, stellar, out of this world.
OPPOSITES: ordinary.

phenomenon noun
1 *a rare phenomenon:* event, occurrence, happening, incident, episode; fact, situation, circumstance, experience, case.
2 *the band was a pop phenomenon:* marvel, sensation, wonder, prodigy, miracle, rarity.

philander verb womanize, have affairs, flirt; informal carry on, play the field, sleep around; N. Amer. informal fool around.

philanderer noun *everyone warned me he was a philanderer:* womanizer, Casanova, Don Juan, Lothario, flirt, ladies' man, playboy; informal skirt-chaser, ladykiller.

philanthropic adjective *a philanthropic millionaire:* charitable, generous, benevolent, humanitarian, altruistic, public-spirited, magnanimous, munificent, open-handed, bountiful, liberal, beneficent, caring, compassionate, unselfish.
OPPOSITES: selfish, mean.

philanthropist noun *the trust was founded by an American philanthropist:* benefactor, benefactress, patron, patroness, donor, contributor, sponsor, backer, helper, good Samaritan; derogatory do-gooder, Lady Bountiful.

philanthropy noun benevolence, generosity, humanitarianism, altruism, charity, public-spiritedness, social conscience, brotherly love, fellow feeling, magnanimity, munificence, liberality, largesse, open-handedness, bountifulness, beneficence, unselfishness, humanity, compassion.

philistine adjective *a philistine businessman:* uncultured, lowbrow, anti-intellectual, uncultivated, uncivilized, uneducated, unenlightened, commercial, materialist, bourgeois; ignorant, crass, boorish, barbarian.
OPPOSITES: cultured.

philosopher noun thinker, theorist, theorizer, theoretician, metaphysicist, metaphysician; scholar, intellectual, sage, wise man.

philosophical adjective
1 *a philosophical question:* theoretical, metaphysical.
2 *a philosophical mood:* thoughtful, reflective, pensive, meditative, contemplative, introspective, ruminative.
3 *he was philosophical about losing the contract:* calm, composed, cool, collected, {cool, calm, and collected}, self-possessed, serene, tranquil, stoical, impassive, dispassionate, phlegmatic, unperturbed, imperturbable, unruffled, patient, forbearing, long-suffering, resigned, rational, realistic.
OPPOSITES: angry, resentful.

philosophize verb *he paused for a while to philosophize on racial equality:* theorize, speculate; pontificate, preach, sermonize, moralize.

philosophy noun
1 *the philosophy of Aristotle:* thinking, thought, reasoning.

p

2 *her political philosophy:* beliefs, credo, convictions, ideology, ideas, thinking, notions, theories, doctrine, tenets, principles, views, school of thought.

phlegm noun *phlegm and determination carried them through many difficult situations:* calmness, coolness, composure, equanimity, tranquillity, placidity, impassivity, stolidity, imperturbability; informal cool, unflappability.

phlegmatic adjective *a phlegmatic attitude to every crisis:* calm, cool, composed, {cool, calm, and collected}, controlled, serene, tranquil, placid, impassive, stolid, imperturbable, unruffled, dispassionate, philosophical; informal unflappable.
OPPOSITES: excitable.

phobia noun abnormal fear, irrational fear, obsessive fear, dread, horror, terror; hatred, loathing, detestation, aversion, antipathy, revulsion; complex, neurosis; informal thing, hang-up.

phoney (informal) adjective *a phoney address | a phoney French accent:* bogus, false, fake, fraudulent, spurious; imitation, sham, mock, artificial; simulated, pretended, feigned, contrived, affected, insincere; informal pseudo, pretend.
OPPOSITES: authentic.
▷noun
1 *he's nothing but a phoney:* impostor, sham, fake, fraud, charlatan; informal con artist.
2 *the diamond's a phoney:* fake, imitation, counterfeit, forgery.

photograph noun *a photograph of her father:* picture, photo, snapshot, shot, print, slide, transparency, still, enlargement; informal snap.
▷verb *she was photographed leaving the castle:* take someone's picture/photo, shoot, film; informal snap.

phrase noun *familiar words and phrases:* expression, group of words, construction, turn of phrase; idiom, idiomatic expression; saying, tag; formal locution.
▷verb *how could I phrase the question?* express, put into words, put, word, style, formulate, couch, frame, articulate, verbalize.

phraseology noun *legal phraseology:* wording, phrasing, choice of words, way of speaking/writing, usage, idiom, diction, parlance, words, language, vocabulary, terminology; jargon; formal locution; informal lingo.

physical adjective
1 *physical pleasure:* bodily, corporeal, corporal, somatic; carnal, fleshly, non-spiritual.
2 *hard physical work:* manual, labouring, blue-collar.
3 *the physical universe:* material, concrete,

tangible, palpable, solid, substantial, real, actual, visible.
OPPOSITES: mental, spiritual.

physician noun doctor, medical doctor, doctor of medicine, MD, medical practitioner, general practitioner, GP, clinician; specialist, consultant; informal doc; Brit. informal quack, medic, medico.

physique noun *a sturdy, muscular physique:* body, build, figure, frame, anatomy, shape, form, proportions; muscles, musculature; informal vital statistics.

pick verb
1 *he was picked for the England squad | pick the time that suits you best:* choose, select, pick out, single out, opt for, plump for, elect, decide on, settle on, fix on, sort out; name, nominate, vote for.
2 *I got a job picking apples:* harvest, gather in, collect, pluck.
3 *he tried to pick a fight:* provoke, start, cause, incite, stir up, whip up, instigate, prompt, bring about.
▷noun
1 *take your pick | Lauren should have first pick:* choice, selection, option, decision; preference, favourite.
2 *the pick of the crop:* best, finest, top, choice, choicest, prime, cream, flower, prize, pearl, gem, jewel, jewel in the crown, crème de la crème, elite.
□pick on
why don't you pick on somebody else? bully, victimize, torment, persecute, tyrannize, criticize, harass, hound, taunt, tease; informal needle; Brit. informal get at.
□pick something out
1 *one painting was picked out for special mention:* choose, select, pick, single out, opt for, plump for, decide on, elect, settle on, fix on; name, nominate.
2 *she picked out Jessica in the crowd:* see, make out, distinguish, discern, spot, perceive, detect, notice, recognize, identify, catch sight of, glimpse.
□pick up
the economy will soon pick up again: improve, recover, be on the road to recovery, rally, make a comeback, bounce back, look up, take a turn for the better, turn the/a corner, be on the mend, make headway, make progress; informal perk up.
□pick someone/something up
she picked up the baby and carried him upstairs: lift, take up, raise, hoist, scoop up, gather up, snatch up.
□pick someone up
I'll pick you up after lunch: fetch, collect, call for.
□pick something up
1 *we picked it up at a flea market:* find, discover, come across, stumble across, happen on, chance on; acquire, obtain, come by, get, procure; purchase, buy; informal get hold of, get/lay your hands on, bag, land.

p

2 *he picked up the story in the 1950s:* resume, take up, start again, recommence, continue, carry on with, go on with.
3 *she picked up a virus:* catch, contract, get, go/come down with.
4 *he told us the bits of gossip he'd picked up:* hear, hear tell, be told, learn; glean, garner; informal get wind of.
5 *we're picking up a distress signal:* receive, detect, get, hear.

picket noun
1 *forty pickets were arrested:* striker, demonstrator, protester, picketer; flying picket.
2 *fences made of cedar pickets:* stake, post, paling; upright, stanchion, pier, piling.
▷ **verb** *over 200 people picketed the factory:* demonstrate at, form a picket at, man the picket line at; blockade, shut off.

pickup noun *a pickup in the housing market:* improvement, recovery, revival, upturn, upswing, rally, comeback, resurgence, turn for the better.
OPPOSITES: slump.

pictorial adjective *a pictorial history of Gateshead:* illustrated, in pictures, in picture form, in photographs, photographic, graphic, diagrammatic.

picture noun
1 *pictures in an art gallery:* painting, drawing, sketch, oil painting, watercolour, print, canvas, portrait, portrayal, illustration, artwork, depiction, likeness, representation, image, icon, miniature, old master; fresco, mural; informal oil.
2 *we were told not to take pictures:* photograph, photo, snapshot, shot, print, slide, transparency, exposure, still, enlargement; informal snap.
3 *a picture of the sort of person the child should be:* concept, idea, impression, view, mental image, vision, visualization, notion.
4 *a picture starring Robert De Niro:* film, movie, feature film, motion picture; informal flick.
▷ **verb**
1 *Andy and Julia are pictured above in a wedding photo:* show, portray, depict, illustrate, photograph, shoot, film, paint, draw, sketch; informal snap.
2 *Anne pictured Richard as he had been in his youth:* visualize, imagine, see in your mind's eye, conjure up a picture/image of, evoke.
□ **put someone in the picture**
he called me last night to put me in the picture about the deal: inform, fill in, explain the situation/circumstances to, bring up to date, update, brief, keep posted; informal bring up to speed.

picturesque adjective *a picturesque village:* attractive, pretty, beautiful, lovely, scenic, charming, quaint, pleasing, delightful.
OPPOSITES: ugly.

pie noun pastry, tart, tartlet, quiche, pasty, patty, turnover, strudel.

piebald adjective. See PIED.

piece noun
1 *a piece of cheese | a piece of wood:* bit, slice, chunk, segment, section, lump, hunk, wedge, slab, block, cake, bar, cube, stick, length; offcut, sample, fragment, sliver, splinter, wafer, chip, crumb, scrap, remnant, shred, shard, snippet; mouthful, morsel; Brit. informal wodge.
2 *the pieces of a clock:* component, part, bit, section, segment, constituent, element; unit, module.
3 *a piece of furniture:* item, article, specimen.
4 *a piece of the profit:* share, portion, slice, quota, percentage, amount, quantity, ration, fraction, division; informal cut, rake-off.
5 *the glass-blowers make one-off pieces that are really sculptures:* work of art, work, objet d'art, creation, production, opus.
6 *six pieces for piano:* composition, piece of music, work, opus.
7 *the reporter who wrote the piece:* article, item, story, report, essay, study, review, composition, column.
8 *the pieces on a chess board:* token, counter, man, disc, chip, marker.
□ **in one piece**
1 *the camera was still in one piece:* unbroken, intact, undamaged, unharmed, entire, whole.
2 *I'll bring her back in one piece:* unhurt, uninjured, unscathed, safe, safe and sound.
□ **in pieces**
broken, in bits, shattered, smashed; informal in smithereens, bust.

pièce de résistance noun *the pièce de résistance of the meal was ice cream flambé:* masterpiece, magnum opus, chef-d'œuvre, masterwork, tour de force, showpiece, prize, jewel in the crown.

piecemeal adverb *the reforms were implemented piecemeal:* a little at a time, piece by piece, bit by bit, little by little, gradually, slowly, in stages, in steps, step by step, by degrees, in/by fits and starts.
OPPOSITES: wholesale.

pied adjective multicoloured, piebald, skewbald, dappled, brindle, spotted, mottled, speckled, flecked; N. Amer. pinto.

pier noun
1 *a boat was tied to the pier:* jetty, landing stage, mole, quay, wharf, dock.
2 *the piers of the bridge:* support, cutwater, pile, piling, abutment, buttress, stanchion, prop, stay, upright, pillar, post, column.

pierce verb *the metal pierced his flesh:* puncture, prick, perforate, penetrate, lance; stab, spike, stick, impale, transfix, bore through, drill through.

p

piercing adjective
   1 *his piercing gaze:* searching, probing, penetrating, penetrative, shrewd, sharp, keen.
   2 *a piercing shriek:* shrill, ear-splitting, high-pitched, penetrating, strident, loud.
   3 *the piercing wind:* bitter, biting, cutting, penetrating, sharp, keen, stinging, raw; freezing, frigid, glacial, arctic, chill.

piety noun *the piety of a saint:* devotion, devoutness, piousness, religion, holiness, godliness, saintliness; veneration, reverence, faith, religious duty, spirituality, religious zeal, fervour; pietism, religiosity.

pig noun

> WORD LINKS
> **porcine** relating to pigs

pigeonhole noun *journalistic pigeonholes:* category, categorization, class, classification, group, grouping, designation, slot.
   ▷ **verb** *they were pigeonholed as an indie guitar band:* label, tag, characterize, classify, categorize, compartmentalize, designate, brand.

pig-headed adjective *he was an arrogant, pig-headed man:* obstinate, stubborn, mulish, obdurate, headstrong, self-willed, wilful, perverse, contrary, recalcitrant; uncooperative, inflexible, uncompromising, intractable, intransigent, unyielding; Brit. informal bloody-minded, bolshie.
   OPPOSITES: cooperative.

pigment noun colour, colouring, colourant, colouring matter, tint, dye, dyestuff.

pile[1] noun *a pile of stones:* heap, stack, mound, pyramid, mass, quantity; collection, accumulation, assemblage, store, stockpile, hoard.
   ▷ **verb**
   1 *he piled up the plates:* heap up, stack, put on top of each other.
   2 *he piled his plate with fried eggs:* load, heap, fill, stack, charge, stock.
   3 *we piled into the car:* crowd, climb, pack, squeeze, push, shove, tumble, spill.
   □ **pile up**
   his debts were piling up: increase, grow, mount up, escalate, soar, spiral, leap up, shoot up, rocket, climb, accumulate, accrue, build up, multiply.

pile[2] noun *a wall supported by timber piles:* post, stake, pillar, column, support, foundation, piling, abutment, pier, cutwater, buttress, stanchion, upright.

pile[3] noun *a carpet with a short pile:* nap, fibres, threads.

pile-up noun *a pile-up on the motorway:* crash, multiple crash, collision, multiple collision, smash, accident, road accident; Brit. RTA (road traffic accident); informal smash-up; Brit. informal shunt.

pilfer verb *the gun was part of a cache pilfered from the air force:* steal, thieve, take, snatch, loot, pillage; formal purloin; informal pinch, swipe, rip off, lift, filch; Brit. informal nick, snaffle, whip, knock off.

pill noun *a sleeping pill:* tablet, capsule, pellet, lozenge, pastille; informal tab.

pillage verb
   1 *the abbey was pillaged:* ransack, plunder, raid, rob, loot; sack, devastate, lay waste, ravage; literary despoil.
   2 *columns pillaged from an ancient town:* steal, thieve, take, snatch, loot, pilfer; formal purloin; informal pinch, swipe, rip off, lift, filch; Brit. informal nick, snaffle, whip, knock off.

pillar noun
   1 *stone pillars:* column, post, support, upright, baluster, pier, pile, pilaster, stanchion, prop, newel; obelisk, monolith, needle.
   2 *a pillar of the community:* stalwart, mainstay, bastion, rock; leading light, worthy, backbone, support, upholder, champion.

pillory verb
   1 *he was pilloried by the press:* attack, criticize, censure, condemn, denigrate, lambaste, savage, stigmatize, denounce; formal excoriate; informal knock, slam, pan, crucify; Brit. informal slate, rubbish.
   2 *they were pilloried at school:* ridicule, jeer at, sneer at, deride, mock, scorn, make fun of, poke fun at, laugh at, scoff at, tease, taunt, rag; Brit. informal take the mickey out of.

pillow verb *she pillowed her head on folded arms:* cushion, cradle, rest, lay, support.

pilot noun
   1 *a fighter pilot:* airman/airwoman, flyer, aviator; captain, co-pilot, wingman.
   2 *a harbour pilot:* navigator, helmsman, steersman, coxswain.
   ▷ **adjective** *a pilot project:* experimental, exploratory, trial, test, sample, speculative; preliminary.
   ▷ **verb**
   1 *he piloted the jet to safety:* steer, guide, manoeuvre, control, direct, navigate, captain; fly, drive, sail; informal skipper.
   2 *one-day workshops for part-time staff were piloted in June:* test, trial, try out; assess, appraise, evaluate.

pimple noun spot, pustule, boil, swelling, eruption, blackhead, carbuncle, bleb, blister; acne; informal zit.

pin noun
   1 *the rusted drawing pins had been hammered in:* tack, nail, staple, safety pin, fastener.
   2 *a broken pin in the machine:* peg, bolt, rivet, dowel, screw.

3 *they wore name pins:* badge, brooch.
▷ **verb**
1 *she pinned the brooch to her dress:* attach, fasten, affix, fix, tack, clip; join, secure.
2 *they pinned him to the ground:* hold, press, hold fast, hold down; restrain, pinion, immobilize.
□ **pin someone/something down**
1 *our troops can pin down the enemy:* confine, trap, hem in, corner, close in, shut in, hedge in, pen in, restrain, immobilize.
2 *she tried to pin him down to a plan:* make someone decide, make someone commit themselves, pressure, pressurize, constrain, tie down, nail down.
3 *it evoked a memory but he couldn't pin it down:* define, put your finger on, put into words, express, name, specify, identify, pinpoint, place.
□ **pin something on someone**
they pinned the crime on him: blame for, hold responsible for, attribute to, impute to, ascribe to; lay something at someone's door; informal stick on.

pinch verb
1 *he pinched my arm:* nip, tweak, squeeze, grasp.
2 *my new shoes pinch my toes:* hurt, squeeze, crush, cramp; be uncomfortable.
▷ **noun**
1 *he gave her arm a pinch:* nip, tweak, squeeze.
2 *a pinch of salt:* bit, touch, dash, spot, trace, soupçon, speck, taste; informal smidgen, tad.
□ **at a pinch**
if necessary, if need be, in an emergency, just possibly, with difficulty; Brit. informal at a push.

pinched adjective *their pinched faces:* strained, stressed, fraught, tense, taut; tired, worn, drained, sapped; wan, pale, grey, blanched; thin, drawn, haggard, gaunt; Brit. peaky.
OPPOSITES: relaxed, healthy.

pine verb *I am pining away from love:* languish, waste away, decline, weaken, wilt, wither, fade, sicken, droop; brood, mope, moon.
□ **pine for**
he was pining for his son: yearn for, long for, ache for, sigh for, hunger for, languish for; miss, mourn, lament, grieve over, shed tears for, bemoan, rue, eat your heart out over.

pinion verb *he was pinioned to the ground:* hold, pin, restrain, hold fast, immobilize; tie, bind, truss up, shackle, fetter, hobble, manacle, handcuff.

pink adjective rose, rosy, rosé, pale red, salmon, coral; flushed, blushing.

pinnacle noun
1 *the pinnacle of his career:* highest point, peak, height, high point, top, apex, zenith, apogee, acme.
2 *pinnacles of rock:* peak, needle, crag, tor; summit, crest, apex, tip.
3 *the pinnacles of the clock tower:* turret, minaret, spire, finial, mirador.
OPPOSITES: nadir.

pinpoint noun *a pinpoint of light:* point, spot, speck, dot, speckle.
▷ **adjective** *pinpoint bomb-aiming:* precise, accurate, exact, careful, strict, meticulous, scrupulous, punctilious.
▷ **verb** *we must pinpoint the cause of the trouble:* identify, determine, distinguish, discover, find, locate, detect, track down, spot, diagnose, recognize, pin down, home in on, put your finger on.

pioneer noun
1 *the pioneers of the Wild West:* settler, colonist, colonizer, frontiersman/woman, explorer, trailblazer.
2 *a pioneer of motoring:* developer, innovator, trailblazer, groundbreaker, spearhead; founder, founding father, architect, creator, inventor.
▷ **verb** *he pioneered the sale of insurance:* introduce, develop, evolve, launch, instigate, initiate, spearhead, institute, establish, found, be the father/mother of, originate, set in motion, create; lay the groundwork for, prepare the way for, blaze a trail for; break new ground.

pious adjective
1 *a pious family:* religious, devout, God-fearing, churchgoing, spiritual, prayerful, holy, godly, saintly, dedicated, reverent, dutiful, righteous.
2 *a pious platitude:* sanctimonious, hypocritical, insincere, self-righteous, holier-than-thou, churchy; informal goody-goody.
OPPOSITES: irreligious.

pip noun *an apple pip:* seed, stone, pit.

pipe noun
1 *a central-heating pipe:* tube, conduit, hose, main, duct, line, channel, pipeline, drain; tubing, piping; siphon.
2 *she was playing a pipe:* whistle, penny whistle, flute, recorder, fife; chanter.
▷ **verb**
1 *the beer is piped into barrels:* siphon, feed, channel, run, convey.
2 *programmes piped in from London:* transmit, feed, relay, patch.

pipe dream noun *the plans are likely to remain a pipe dream:* fantasy, false hope, illusion, delusion, daydream, chimera; castle in the air, castle in Spain; informal pie in the sky.

pipeline noun *a gas pipeline:* pipe, conduit, main, line, duct, tube.
□ **in the pipeline**
on the way, coming, forthcoming, upcoming, imminent, about to happen, near, close, brewing, in the offing, in the wind.

piquant adjective
1 *a piquant sauce:* spicy, tangy, peppery, hot; tasty, flavoursome, savoury; pungent, sharp, tart, zesty, strong, salty.
2 *a piquant story:* intriguing, stimulating, interesting, fascinating, colourful, exciting, lively; spicy, provocative, racy; informal juicy.
OPPOSITES: bland, dull.

pique noun *a fit of pique:* irritation, annoyance, resentment, anger, displeasure, indignation, petulance, ill humour, vexation, exasperation, disgruntlement, discontent; offence, umbrage.
▷ verb
1 *his curiosity was piqued:* stimulate, arouse, rouse, provoke, whet, awaken, excite, kindle, stir.
2 *she was piqued by his neglect:* irritate, annoy, bother, vex, displease, upset, offend, affront, anger, exasperate, gall, irk; informal peeve, miff, rile, nettle; Brit. informal nark.

piracy noun *software piracy:* illegal copying, copyright infringement, bootlegging, plagiarism.

pirate noun *pirates boarded the ship:* freebooter, marauder, raider; historical privateer.
▷ verb *designers may pirate good ideas:* copy illegally, reproduce illegally, plagiarize, poach, steal, appropriate, bootleg; informal crib, lift, rip off.

pirouette noun *she did a little pirouette:* spin, twirl, whirl, turn.
▷ verb *she pirouetted before the mirror:* spin round, twirl, whirl, turn round, revolve, pivot.

pit[1] noun
1 *a pit in the ground:* hole, hollow, excavation, cavity, crater, pothole, ditch, trench, trough; shaft, mineshaft.
2 *pit closures:* mine, colliery, quarry.
3 *the pits in her skin:* pockmark, pock, hollow, indentation, depression, dent, dint, dimple.
▷ verb *raindrops pitted the bare earth:* indent, dent, dint, make hollows in, make holes in.
□ pit someone/something against
a chance to pit your wits against the world champions: set against, match against, put in opposition to, put in competition with; compete with, contend with, vie with, wrestle with.

pit[2] noun *cherry pits:* stone, pip, seed.

pitch[1] noun
1 *the pitch was unfit for cricket:* field, playing field, ground, sports field; stadium, arena; Brit. park.
2 *her voice rose in pitch:* tone, timbre, key, modulation, frequency.
3 *the pitch of the roof:* gradient, slope, slant, angle, steepness, tilt, incline, inclination.

4 *her anger reached such a pitch that she screamed:* level, intensity, point, degree, height, extent.
5 *a pitch of the ball:* throw, fling, hurl, toss, lob; delivery; informal chuck, heave.
6 *his sales pitch:* patter, talk; informal spiel, line.
7 *street traders reserved their pitches:* site, place, spot, station; Brit. informal patch.
▷ verb
1 *he pitched the note into the fire:* throw, toss, fling, hurl, cast, lob, flip, propel, bowl; informal chuck, sling, heave; Brit. informal bung.
2 *he pitched overboard:* fall, tumble, topple, plunge, plummet.
3 *they pitched their tents by the lake:* put up, set up, erect, raise.
4 *the boat pitched in the heavy seas:* lurch, toss about, plunge, roll, reel, sway, rock, list, wallow.
□ pitch in
everyone pitched in to complete the task on time: help, assist, lend a hand, join in, participate, contribute, do your bit, chip in, cooperate, collaborate; Brit. informal muck in.
□ pitch into
he pitched into the youths with such fury that they ran off: attack, set upon, turn on, lash out at, assault, fly at, tear into, weigh into; informal lay into.

pitch[2] noun *cement coated with pitch:* bitumen, asphalt, tar.

pitch-black adjective *the sky was pitch-black:* black, dark, pitch-dark, inky, jet-black, coal-black, jet, ebony; starless, moonless.

pitcher noun jug, ewer, jar, crock, urn; carafe, flask, flagon, decanter.

piteous adjective *a piteous cry:* sad, pitiful, pitiable, pathetic, heart-rending, heartbreaking, moving, touching; plaintive, poignant, forlorn; poor, wretched, miserable.

pitfall noun *the pitfalls of setting up an office at home:* hazard, danger, risk, peril, difficulty, catch, snag, stumbling block, drawback.

pith noun
1 *the pith of the argument:* essence, main point, fundamentals, heart, substance, nub, core, quintessence, crux, gist, meat, kernel, marrow, burden; informal nitty-gritty.
2 *he writes with pith and exactitude:* succinctness, conciseness, concision, pithiness, brevity; cogency, weight, depth, force.

pithy adjective *his characteristically pithy comments:* succinct, concise, compact, short and sweet, brief, condensed, to the point, epigrammatic, crisp, terse, thumbnail; significant, meaningful, expressive, telling.
OPPOSITES: verbose.

p

pitiful adjective

1 *a child in a pitiful state:* distressing, sad, piteous, pitiable, pathetic, heart-rending, heartbreaking, moving, touching; plaintive, poignant, forlorn; poor, sorry, wretched, abject, miserable; informal tear-jerking.
2 *a pitiful £50 a month:* paltry, miserable, meagre, insufficient, trifling, negligible, derisory; informal pathetic, measly.
3 *his performance was pitiful:* dreadful, awful, terrible, abysmal, appalling, lamentable, poor, bad, feeble, pitiable, woeful, inadequate, below par, deplorable, laughable; informal pathetic, useless, dire; Brit. informal hopeless.

pitiless adjective *a pitiless executioner:* merciless, ruthless, cruel, heartless, remorseless, hard-hearted, cold-hearted, harsh, callous, severe, unsparing, unforgiving, unfeeling, uncaring, unsympathetic, uncharitable, brutal, inhuman, barbaric, sadistic.
OPPOSITES: merciful.

pity noun

1 *a voice full of pity:* compassion, commiseration, condolence, sympathy, fellow feeling, understanding; sorrow, regret, sadness.
2 *it's a pity he never had children:* shame, bad luck.
OPPOSITES: indifference, cruelty.
▷ **verb** *they pitied me:* feel sorry for, feel for, sympathize with, empathize with, commiserate with, take pity on, be moved by, condole with, grieve for.
□ **take pity on**
feel sorry for, be compassionate towards, be sympathetic towards, have mercy on, help, help out, put someone out of their misery; relent.

pivot noun

1 *the machine turns on a pivot:* swivel, axis, axle, fulcrum; pin, shaft, hub, spindle, hinge, kingpin, gudgeon.
2 *the pivot of government policy:* centre, focus, hub, heart, nucleus, crux, keystone, cornerstone, linchpin, kingpin.
▷ **verb**
1 *the panel pivots inwards:* swivel, turn, rotate, revolve, spin.
2 *it all pivoted on his response:* depend, hinge, turn, centre, hang, rely, rest; revolve around.

pivotal adjective *Japan's pivotal role in the world economy:* central, crucial, vital, critical, focal, essential, key, decisive.
OPPOSITES: peripheral, incidental.

pixie noun elf, fairy, sprite, imp, brownie, puck, leprechaun.

placard noun *placards with slogans that read 'Work not Charity':* notice, poster, sign, board, bill, advertisement; banner.

placate verb *John did his best to placate*
her: pacify, calm, appease, mollify, soothe, win over, conciliate, propitiate, make peace with, humour.
OPPOSITES: provoke.

place noun

1 *an ideal place for dinner:* location, site, spot, setting, position, situation, area, region, locale, venue.
2 *foreign places:* country, state, area, region, town, city; locality, district.
3 *at last she had a place of her own:* home, house, flat, apartment; accommodation, property, pied-à-terre; rooms, quarters; informal pad.
4 *if I were in your place, I'd agree:* situation, position, circumstances; informal shoes.
5 *a place was reserved for her:* seat, chair, space.
6 *I offered him a place in the company:* job, position, post, appointment, situation, office; employment.
7 *I know my place:* status, position, standing, rank, niche.
8 *it was not her place to sort it out:* responsibility, duty, job, task, role, function, concern, affair; right, privilege, prerogative.
▷ **verb**
1 *a jug of iced water had been placed beside my bed:* put, put down, set, set down, lay, deposit, position, plant, rest, stand, station, situate, leave; informal stick, dump, park, pop; Brit. informal bung, plonk.
2 *the trust you placed in me:* put, lay, set, invest.
3 *a survey placed the company sixth:* rank, order, grade, class, classify, categorize; put, set, assign.
4 *Joe couldn't quite place her:* identify, recognize, remember, put a name to, pin down; locate, pinpoint.
5 *we were placed with foster parents:* accommodate, house; allocate, assign, appoint.
□ **in place of**
instead of, rather than, as a substitute for, as a replacement for, in exchange for, in lieu of; in someone's stead.
□ **out of place**
1 *she never had a hair out of place:* out of position, out of order, in disarray, disarranged, in a mess, messy, topsy-turvy, muddled.
2 *he said something out of place:* inappropriate, unsuitable, unseemly, improper, untoward, out of keeping, unbecoming, wrong.
3 *she seemed out of place in a launderette:* incongruous, out of your element, like a fish out of water; uncomfortable, uneasy.
□ **take place**
happen, occur, come about, transpire, crop up.
□ **take the place of**
replace, stand in for, substitute for, act for, fill in for, cover for, relieve.

p

placement noun

1 *the placement of the chairs:* positioning, placing, arrangement, deployment, location, position, disposition.
2 (Brit.) *a teaching placement:* job, post, assignment, posting, position, appointment, engagement.

placid adjective

1 *she's normally very placid:* even-tempered, calm, tranquil, equable, unexcitable, serene, mild, {cool, calm, and collected}, composed, self-possessed, poised, easy-going, level-headed, steady, unruffled, unperturbed, phlegmatic; informal unflappable.
2 *their launch disturbed the placid waters:* calm, still, like a millpond, smooth, glassy, flat, motionless, peaceful, undisturbed, restful, sleepy, quiet.
OPPOSITES: excitable, rough.

plagiarism noun *there were accusations of plagiarism:* copying, infringement of copyright, piracy, theft, stealing; informal cribbing.

plagiarize verb copy, infringe the copyright of, pirate, steal, poach, appropriate, borrow; informal rip off, crib.

plague noun *a plague of cat fleas:* infestation, epidemic, pandemic, invasion, swarm.

▷ verb
1 *he was plagued by poor health:* afflict, bedevil, torment, trouble, beset, dog, curse.
2 *he plagued her with questions:* pester, harass, badger, bother, torment, persecute, bedevil, harry, hound, trouble, irritate, nag, annoy, molest; informal hassle, bug.

plain adjective

1 *it was plain that something was wrong:* obvious, clear, crystal clear, apparent, manifest, evident, patent; discernible, perceptible, noticeable, recognizable, unmistakable, transparent; pronounced, marked, striking, conspicuous, self-evident, indisputable.
2 *plain English:* intelligible, comprehensible, understandable, clear, coherent, uncomplicated, lucid, unambiguous, simple, straightforward, basic, user-friendly.
3 *plain speaking:* candid, frank, outspoken, forthright, direct, honest, truthful, blunt, bald, explicit, unequivocal; informal upfront.
4 *a plain dress:* simple, ordinary, unadorned, unembellished, unornamented, unostentatious, unfussy, basic, modest, unsophisticated, without frills; restrained, muted; everyday, workaday; Brit. homely.
5 *a plain girl:* unattractive, unprepossessing, ugly, ill-favoured, unlovely, ordinary; N. Amer. homely.
6 *it was plain bad luck:* sheer, pure, downright, out-and-out, unmitigated.
OPPOSITES: obscure, fancy, attractive, pretentious.

▷ adverb *this is just plain stupid:* downright, utterly, absolutely, completely, totally, really, thoroughly, positively, simply, unquestionably, undeniably.

▷ noun *the plains of North America:* grassland, flatland, lowland, pasture, meadowland, prairie, savannah, steppe; tableland, tundra, pampas, veld.

plain-spoken adjective *he was well known for being plain-spoken:* candid, frank, outspoken, forthright, direct, honest, truthful, open, blunt, straightforward, explicit, unequivocal, unambiguous, not afraid to call a spade a spade; informal upfront.
OPPOSITES: evasive.

plaintive adjective *a plaintive cry:* mournful, sad, wistful, doleful, pathetic, pitiful, piteous, melancholy, sorrowful, unhappy, wretched, woeful, forlorn, woebegone.

plan noun

1 *a plan for raising money:* scheme, idea, proposal, proposition, suggestion; project, programme, system, method, procedure, strategy, stratagem, formula, recipe; way, means, measure, tactic.
2 *her plan was to win a medal:* intention, aim, idea, intent, objective, object, goal, target, ambition.
3 *the plans for the clubhouse:* blueprint, drawing, diagram, sketch, chart, layout; illustration, representation.

▷ verb
1 *plan your route in advance:* organize, arrange, work out, design, outline, map out, prepare, schedule, formulate, frame, develop, devise, concoct; plot, scheme, hatch, brew.
2 *he plans to buy a house:* intend, aim, propose, mean, hope, want, wish, desire; envisage, be thinking of, contemplate.
3 *I'm planning a new garden:* design, lay out, map out, sketch out, draw up.

plane¹ noun

1 (technical) *a horizontal plane:* flat surface, level surface; the flat, horizontal.
2 *a higher plane of achievement:* level, degree, standard, stratum; position, rung, echelon.

▷ adjective *a plane surface:* flat, level, horizontal, even; smooth, regular, uniform.

▷ verb
1 *seagulls planed overhead:* soar, glide, float, drift, wheel.
2 *boats planed across the water:* skim, glide.

plane² noun *the plane took off:* aircraft, jet, airliner, warplane, flying machine; Brit. aeroplane; N. Amer. airplane, ship.

plank noun board, floorboard, timber, stave.

p

planning noun *the planning should be every bit as enjoyable as the event itself:* preparation, organization, arrangement, design; forethought, groundwork.

plant noun
1 *garden plants:* flower, vegetable, herb, shrub, weed; (**plants**) vegetation, greenery, flora; literary verdure.
2 *a CIA plant:* spy, informant, informer, secret agent, mole, infiltrator, operative; N. Amer. informal spook.
3 *the plant commenced production:* factory, works, facility, foundry, mill, workshop, yard.
▷ verb
1 *plant the seeds this autumn:* sow, scatter, seed; dig in, bed out, transplant.
2 *he planted his feet on the ground:* place, put, set, position, situate, settle.
3 *she planted the idea in his mind:* instil, implant, impress, imprint, put, place, introduce, fix, establish, lodge.
4 *police had smashed the drugs ring by planting a hidden microphone at their headquarters:* hide, conceal, secrete.

> WORD LINKS
> **botany** the scientific study of plants
> **herbivorous** plant-eating
> **herbicide** a substance used to kill plants

plaque noun *a commemorative plaque:* plate, tablet, panel, sign; Brit. brass.

plaster noun
1 *the plaster covering the bricks:* plasterwork, stucco, pargeting.
2 *a statuette made of plaster:* plaster of Paris, gypsum.
3 (Brit.) *waterproof plasters:* adhesive dressing; Brit. sticking plaster; trademark Elastoplast, Band-Aid.
▷ verb
1 *bread plastered with butter:* smother, smear, cake, spread thickly, coat thickly.
2 *his hair was plastered down with sweat:* stick down, slick down, smooth down, flatten down.

plastic adjective
1 *at high temperatures the rocks become plastic:* malleable, pliable, pliant, ductile, flexible, workable, soft.
2 *the plastic minds of children:* impressionable, malleable, receptive, pliable, pliant, flexible; compliant, tractable, biddable, persuadable, susceptible, manipulable.
3 *a plastic smile:* artificial, false, faux, fake, superficial, bogus, unnatural, insincere; informal phoney, pseudo, pretend.
OPPOSITES: rigid, genuine.

plate noun
1 *a dinner plate:* dish, platter, salver; old use trencher, charger.
2 *a plate of spaghetti:* plateful, helping, portion, serving.
3 *steel plates:* panel, sheet, layer, pane, slab.
4 *a brass plate on the door:* plaque, sign, tablet; Brit. brass.
5 *the book has colour plates:* picture, print, illustration, photograph, photo.
▷ verb *the roof was plated with steel:* cover, coat, overlay, laminate, veneer; electroplate, galvanize, gild.

plateau noun *a windswept plateau:* upland, tableland, high plain, mesa, highland.

platform noun
1 *he made a speech from the platform:* stage, dais, rostrum, podium, soapbox.
2 *the Democratic Party's platform:* policy, programme, party line, manifesto, plan, principles, objectives, aims.

platitude noun *a string of empty platitudes:* cliché, truism, commonplace, banality, old chestnut.

platitudinous adjective *much of the book consists of worthy but platitudinous generalities:* hackneyed, overworked, overused, clichéd, banal, trite, commonplace, well worn, stale, tired, unoriginal; informal corny, old hat.
OPPOSITES: original.

platonic adjective *our relationship is purely platonic:* non-sexual, non-physical, chaste; intellectual, friendly.
OPPOSITES: sexual.

platoon noun *a platoon of Royal Marines:* unit, patrol, troop, squad, squadron, team, company, corps, outfit, detachment, contingent.

platter noun *the meat was arranged on silver platters:* plate, dish, salver, tray; old use trencher, charger.

plaudits plural noun *the network has received plaudits for its sports coverage:* praise, acclaim, commendation, congratulations, accolades, compliments, cheers, applause, tributes, bouquets; a pat on the back.
OPPOSITES: criticism.

plausible adjective *a plausible explanation:* credible, reasonable, believable, likely, feasible, tenable, possible, conceivable, imaginable; convincing, persuasive, cogent, sound, rational, logical, thinkable.
OPPOSITES: implausible.

play verb
1 *the children played with toys:* amuse yourself, entertain yourself, enjoy yourself, have fun; relax, occupy yourself, divert yourself; frolic, frisk, romp, caper; informal mess about/around; Brit. informal lark about/around.
2 *I used to play football:* take part in, participate in, be involved in, join in, compete in, do.

p

3 *Liverpool play Oxford on Sunday:* compete against, play against, take on, challenge, vie with.
4 *he was to play Macbeth:* act the part of, take the role of, appear as, portray, perform, depict, impersonate, represent, render.
5 *he learned to play the flute:* perform on, make music on; blow, sound.
6 *the sunlight played on the water:* dance, flit, ripple, touch; sparkle, glint.

▷ **noun**
1 *a balance between work and play:* amusement, entertainment, relaxation, recreation, diversion, distraction, leisure; enjoyment, pleasure, fun, games; horseplay, merrymaking, revelry; informal fun and games.
2 *a Shakespeare play:* drama, theatrical work; comedy, tragedy; production, performance, show, sketch.
3 *there was a little play in the rope:* movement, slack, give; room to manoeuvre, scope, latitude.

□ **play something down**
ministers sought to play down the extent of the damage: understate, downplay, gloss over, make light of, make little of, soft-pedal, tone down, diminish, trivialize, underrate, underestimate, undervalue; disparage, belittle, scoff at, sneer at, shrug off; informal pooh-pooh.

□ **play for time**
he urged the developers to stop playing for time and submit their proposal: stall, temporize, delay, hold back, hang fire, procrastinate, drag your feet.

□ **play it by ear**
we'll just have to play it by ear until we can get something definite sorted out: improvise, extemporize, ad-lib; informal busk it, wing it.

□ **play on**
they play on our fears: exploit, take advantage of, use, turn to account, profit by, capitalize on, trade on, milk, abuse.

□ **play up** (Brit.)
1 (informal) *the boys really did play up:* misbehave, be bad, be naughty, get up to mischief, be disobedient, cause trouble.
2 *the boiler's playing up:* malfunction, not work properly, be defective, be faulty; informal act up.
3 *his leg was playing up:* hurt, ache, be painful, be sore, cause discomfort.

□ **play something up**
the press has played up the problems: emphasize, accentuate, call attention to, point up, underline, highlight, spotlight, foreground, feature, stress, accent.

playboy noun *Nigel isn't the marrying type—he's just a playboy:* socialite, pleasure-seeker, sybarite; ladies' man, womanizer, philanderer, libertine; informal skirt-chaser, ladykiller.

player noun
1 *a tournament for young players:* participant, contestant, competitor, contender; sportsman/woman, athlete.
2 *the players in the orchestra:* musician, performer, instrumentalist, soloist, virtuoso.
3 *the players of the Royal Shakespeare Company:* actor, actress, performer, thespian, entertainer, artiste, trouper.

playful adjective
1 *a playful mood:* frisky, jolly, lively, full of fun, sportive, high-spirited, exuberant, perky; mischievous, impish, rascally, tricksy; literary frolicsome.
2 *a playful remark:* light-hearted, in jest, joking, jokey, teasing, humorous, jocular, good-natured, tongue-in-cheek, facetious, frivolous, flippant, arch.
OPPOSITES: serious.

playmate noun friend, playfellow, companion; informal chum, pal; Brit. informal mate; N. Amer. informal buddy.

playwright noun dramatist, dramaturge, scriptwriter, screenwriter, writer; tragedian.

plea noun
1 *a plea for aid:* appeal, entreaty, supplication, petition, request, call, solicitation.
2 *her plea of a headache was unconvincing:* claim, explanation, defence, justification; excuse, pretext.

plead verb
1 *he pleaded with her to stay:* beg, implore, entreat, appeal to, supplicate, petition, request, ask, call on.
2 *she pleaded ignorance:* claim, use as an excuse, assert, allege, argue, state.

pleasant adjective
1 *a pleasant evening:* enjoyable, pleasurable, nice, agreeable, pleasing, satisfying, gratifying, good; entertaining, amusing, delightful, charming.
2 *the staff are pleasant:* friendly, agreeable, amiable, nice, genial, cordial, likeable, amicable, good-humoured, good-natured, personable; hospitable, approachable, gracious, courteous, polite, obliging, helpful, considerate; charming, lovely, delightful, sweet, sympathetic.
OPPOSITES: unpleasant.

pleasantry noun
1 *we exchanged pleasantries:* polite remark, conventional remark; (pleasantries) banter, badinage.
2 *he laughed at his own pleasantry:* joke, witticism, quip, jest, gag, bon mot; informal wisecrack, crack.

please verb
1 *he'd do anything to please her:* make happy, give pleasure to, make someone feel good; delight, charm, amuse, entertain; satisfy, gratify, humour, oblige, content, suit.
2 *do as you please:* like, want, wish, desire,

see fit, think fit, choose, will, prefer.
OPPOSITES: annoy.

pleased adjective *Ed seemed really pleased to see me:* happy, glad, delighted, gratified, grateful, thankful, content, contented, satisfied; thrilled, elated, overjoyed, cock-a-hoop; informal over the moon, tickled pink, on cloud nine; Brit. informal chuffed.
OPPOSITES: displeased.

pleasing adjective
1 *a pleasing day:* pleasant, pleasurable, agreeable, nice, lovely, satisfying, gratifying, good, enjoyable, entertaining, amusing, charming, delightful.
2 *her pleasing manner:* friendly, amiable, pleasant, agreeable, affable, nice, genial, likeable, good-humoured, charming, engaging, delightful, lovely.

pleasurable adjective *a pleasurable experience:* pleasant, enjoyable, delightful, nice, lovely, pleasing, agreeable, gratifying; fun, entertaining, amusing, diverting.

pleasure noun
1 *she smiled with pleasure:* happiness, delight, joy, gladness, glee, satisfaction, gratification, contentment, enjoyment, amusement.
2 *his greatest pleasures in life:* joy, amusement, diversion, recreation, pastime; treat, thrill.
3 *don't mix business and pleasure:* enjoyment, fun, entertainment; recreation, leisure, relaxation.
4 *a life of pleasure:* hedonism, indulgence, self-indulgence, self-gratification, lotus-eating.
□ **take pleasure in** enjoy, delight in, love, like, adore, appreciate, relish, savour, revel in, glory in; informal get a kick out of, get a thrill out of.
□ **with pleasure** gladly, willingly, happily, readily; by all means, of course.

pleat noun & verb *a curtain pleat | the dress is pleated at the front:* fold, crease, gather, tuck, crimp, crinkle, furrow, pucker.

plebeian noun *plebeians and gentry lived together:* proletarian, commoner, working-class person, worker; peasant; informal pleb, prole.
OPPOSITES: gentry, aristocrat.
▷ **adjective**
1 *people of plebeian descent:* lower-class, working-class, proletarian, common, peasant; humble, lowly.
2 *plebeian tastes:* uncultured, unsophisticated, uncultivated, unrefined, lowbrow, philistine, uneducated; coarse, uncouth, common, vulgar.
OPPOSITES: noble, refined.

plebiscite noun *a plebiscite for the approval of constitutional reforms:* referendum, vote, ballot, poll.

pledge noun
1 *his election pledge:* promise, undertaking, vow, word of honour, word, commitment, assurance, oath, guarantee.
2 *take this as a pledge of my sincerity:* token, symbol, sign, earnest, mark, testimony, proof, evidence.
3 *he had given the ring as a pledge to a creditor:* security, collateral, guarantee, deposit, bond, surety.
▷ **verb**
1 *he pledged to root out corruption | the Chancellor pledged that there would be no increase in VAT:* promise, vow, swear, take an oath, undertake, engage, commit yourself, declare, affirm, avow.
2 *they pledged £100 million:* promise to give, donate, contribute, give, put up; Brit. covenant.
3 *his home is pledged as security against the loan:* mortgage, put up as collateral, guarantee, pawn.

plenary adjective
1 *the council has plenary powers:* unlimited, unrestricted, unconditional, unqualified, absolute, sweeping, comprehensive, plenipotentiary.
2 *a plenary session of the parliament:* full, complete, entire.

plenipotentiary noun *a plenipotentiary in Paris:* diplomat, ambassador, minister, emissary, attaché, chargé d'affaires, envoy.
▷ **adjective** *plenipotentiary powers.* See PLENARY sense 1.

plentiful adjective *a plentiful supply of food:* abundant, copious, ample, profuse, rich, lavish, generous, bountiful, large, great, bumper, superabundant, inexhaustible, prolific; informal galore.
OPPOSITES: scarce.

plenty noun *times of plenty:* prosperity, affluence, wealth, opulence, comfort, luxury, abundance.
▷ **pronoun** *there are plenty of books:* a lot of, many, a great deal of, a plethora of, enough, enough and to spare, no lack of, sufficient, a wealth of; informal loads of, lots of, heaps of, stacks of, masses of, tons of.

plethora noun *a plethora of newspaper opinion polls:* excess, abundance, superabundance, surplus, glut, superfluity, surfeit, profusion, too many, too much, enough and to spare.
OPPOSITES: dearth.

pliable adjective
1 *leather is pliable:* flexible, pliant, bendable, elastic, supple, malleable, workable, plastic, springy, ductile; informal bendy.
2 *pliable teenage minds:* malleable, impressionable, pliant, amenable, susceptible, suggestible; flexible, adaptable, receptive.
OPPOSITES: rigid, obdurate.

p

pliant adjective. See **PLIABLE**.

plight noun *an attempt to highlight the plight of the homeless:* predicament, difficult situation, dire straits, trouble, difficulty, dilemma, extremity; informal tight corner, tight spot, hole, bind, jam, fix.

plod verb
1 *Mum plodded wearily upstairs:* trudge, walk heavily, clump, stomp, tramp, lumber; informal slog.
2 *I plodded slowly through a pile of paperwork:* wade, plough, trawl, toil, labour; informal slog.

plot noun
1 *a plot to overthrow the king:* conspiracy, intrigue, secret plan; machinations.
2 *the plot of her novel:* storyline, story, scenario, action, thread.
3 *a three-acre plot:* piece of ground, patch, area, tract, site.
▷ verb
1 *he plotted their downfall:* plan, scheme, arrange, organize, hatch, concoct, devise, dream up; informal cook up.
2 *his brother was plotting against him:* conspire, scheme, intrigue, collude, connive, machinate.
3 *the fifty-three sites were plotted:* mark, chart, map, represent, record.

plotter noun conspirator, schemer, intriguer, machinator.

plough verb
1 *the fields were ploughed:* till, furrow, harrow, cultivate, work, dig, break up.
2 *the car ploughed into a lamp post:* crash, smash, career, plunge, bulldoze, hurtle, cannon, run, drive.
3 *they ploughed through deep snow:* trudge, plod, toil, wade; informal slog.

ploy noun *perhaps this had been a ploy to revive her husband's fading interest:* ruse, tactic, move, device, stratagem, scheme, trick, gambit, plan, manoeuvre, dodge, subterfuge, wile.

pluck verb
1 *he plucked a thread from his lapel:* remove, pick, pull, extract, take.
2 *she plucked at his T-shirt:* pull at, tug at, clutch at, snatch at, grab, catch, tweak, jerk; informal yank.
3 *she plucked the guitar strings:* pick, twang, ping, strum, thrum.
▷ noun *the task took a lot of pluck:* courage, bravery, nerve, backbone, spine, daring, spirit, fearlessness, mettle, grit, determination, fortitude, resolve, stout-heartedness, valour, heroism; informal guts; Brit. informal bottle.

plucky adjective *plucky bank staff defeated armed raiders:* brave, courageous, bold, daring, fearless, intrepid, spirited, valiant, valorous, stout-hearted, dauntless, undaunted, resolute, determined, unflinching, unafraid, doughty,

mettlesome; informal gutsy.
OPPOSITES: timid.

plug noun
1 *she pulled out the plug:* stopper, bung, cork, seal, spigot; N. Amer. stopple.
2 (informal) *a plug for his new book:* advertisement, promotion, commercial, recommendation, mention, good word; informal hype, puff.
▷ verb
1 *trucks arrived with gravel to plug the hole and clear the road:* stop up, seal, close, cork, stopper, bung, block, fill; N. Amer. stopple.
2 (informal) *the band took the opportunity to plug their new album:* publicize, promote, advertise, mention, bang the drum for, draw attention to; informal hype, puff.

plumb¹ verb *an attempt to plumb her psyche:* explore, probe, delve into, search, examine, investigate, fathom, penetrate, understand.
▷ adjective *a plumb drop:* vertical, perpendicular, straight.

plumb² verb
□ plumb something in (Brit.) *he plumbed in the washing machine:* install, put in, connect, fit.

plummet verb *the plane plummeted to the ground:* plunge, dive, nosedive, drop, tumble, pitch, crash, fall.

plump¹ adjective *a plump child:* chubby, fat, stout, rotund, well padded, ample, round, chunky, portly, overweight; fleshy, paunchy, bulky, corpulent; informal tubby, pudgy; Brit. informal podgy.
OPPOSITES: thin.

plump² verb
1 *Jack plumped down on to a chair:* flop, collapse, sink, fall, drop, slump; Brit. informal plonk yourself.
2 *she plumped her bag on the table:* put, set, place, deposit, dump; informal stick; Brit. informal plonk.
□ plump for
I plumped for a cream cake: choose, decide on, go for, opt for, pick, settle on, select, take, elect.

plunder verb
1 *they plundered the countryside:* pillage, loot, rob, raid, ransack, strip, ravage, lay waste, devastate, sack; literary despoil.
2 *money plundered from pension funds:* steal, thieve, seize, pillage; embezzle; formal purloin.
▷ noun
1 *the plunder of the villages:* looting, pillaging, plundering, raiding, ransacking, ravaging, devastation, sacking.
2 *the army took huge quantities of plunder:* booty, loot, stolen goods, spoils, ill-gotten gains.

plunge verb
1 *Joy plunged into the sea:* dive, jump,

throw yourself, launch yourself.
2 *the aircraft plunged to the ground:* plummet, nosedive, drop, fall, pitch, tumble, descend.
3 *the car plunged down an alley:* charge, hurtle, career, plough, cannon; informal tear.
4 *oil prices plunged:* fall sharply, plummet, drop, go down, tumble, slump; informal crash, nosedive.
5 *he plunged the dagger into her back:* thrust, sink, drive, push, shove, force, ram, stab, stick, jab.
6 *plunge the pears into water:* immerse, submerge, dip, dunk.
7 *the room was plunged into darkness:* throw, cast, pitch.
▷**noun**
1 *a plunge into the deep end:* dive, jump, nosedive, fall, pitch, drop, plummet, tumble, descent.
2 *a plunge in profits:* fall, drop, slump, tumble; informal nosedive, crash.
▫ **take the plunge**
commit yourself, throw caution to the wind, risk it; informal go for it, jump in at the deep end, go for broke.

plurality noun *a plurality of theories:* wide variety, diversity, range, lot, multitude, multiplicity, galaxy, wealth, profusion, abundance, plethora, host; informal mass.

plus (informal) **preposition** *he wrote four novels plus various poems:* as well as, together with, along with, in addition to, and, not to mention, besides.
▷**noun** *one of the pluses of the job:* advantage, good point, asset, pro, benefit, bonus, extra, attraction; informal perk.
OPPOSITES: disadvantage.

plush adjective (informal) *a plush hotel:* luxurious, luxury, de luxe, sumptuous, palatial, lavish, opulent, magnificent, rich, expensive, fancy, grand; Brit. upmarket; informal posh, classy; Brit. informal swish.
OPPOSITES: austere.

plutocrat noun *champagne-swilling plutocrats:* tycoon, magnate, nabob, baron; millionaire, billionaire, multimillionaire; nouveau riche; informal fat cat, moneybags, affluential.

ply¹ verb
1 *the gondolier plied his oar:* use, wield, work, manipulate, handle, operate, utilize, employ.
2 *he plied a profitable trade:* engage in, carry on, pursue, conduct, practise.
3 *ferries ply between all lake resorts:* shuttle, run, travel, go back and forth.
4 *she plied me with scones:* provide, supply; lavish.
5 *he plied her with questions:* bombard, assail, beset, pester, plague.

ply² noun *a three-ply tissue:* layer, thickness, sheet, leaf, strand.

poach verb *workers were poached by*

other firms: headhunt, tempt away, give someone a golden hello.

pocket noun
1 *a bag with two pockets:* pouch, compartment.
2 *the jewellery was beyond her pocket:* means, budget, resources, finances, funds, money, wherewithal.
3 *there were pockets of disaffection in parts of the country:* isolated area, patch, region, island, enclave, cluster, centre.
▷**adjective** *a pocket dictionary:* small, little, miniature, mini, compact, concise, abridged, potted, portable.
▷**verb**
1 *he pocketed $900,000 of their money:* steal, take, appropriate, thieve, misappropriate, embezzle; formal purloin; informal pinch, filch, swipe; Brit. informal nick, snaffle, whip.
2 *the chief executive pockets a £10 million pay package:* be paid, take home, gross; earn, receive, get, make, bring in, bank, obtain, collect; informal rake in, net.

pockmark noun *his face was covered with pockmarks:* scar, pit, pock, mark, blemish.

pod noun *pea pods:* shell, husk, hull, case; N. Amer. shuck.

podgy adjective (Brit. informal) chubby, plump, fat, stout, rotund, well padded, ample, round, chunky, portly, overweight; fleshy, paunchy, bulky, corpulent; informal tubby, pudgy.
OPPOSITES: thin.

podium noun platform, stage, dais, rostrum, stand, soapbox.

poet noun versifier, rhymester, rhymer, sonneteer, lyricist; laureate; derogatory poetaster.

poetic, poetical adjective
1 *poetic compositions:* verse, metrical, lyrical, lyric, elegiac.
2 *poetic language:* expressive, figurative, symbolic, flowery, artistic, elegant, fine, beautiful; sensitive, imaginative, creative.

poetry noun poems, verse, versification, metrical composition, rhymes, balladry.

poignancy noun pathos, emotion, tenderness, pitifulness, piteousness, sadness, sorrow, mournfulness, wretchedness, misery, tragedy.

poignant adjective *the victim's father bade a poignant farewell to his son:* touching, moving, affecting, tender, emotional, pitiful, piteous, pathetic, sad, sorrowful, mournful, wretched, miserable, distressing, heart-rending, plaintive, tragic; Brit. tear-jerking.

point noun
1 *the point of a needle:* tip, end, extremity; prong, spike, tine, nib, barb.
2 *points of light:* pinpoint, dot, spot, speck, fleck.

p

3 *a meeting point:* place, position, location, site, spot, venue, area.
4 *this point in her life:* time, stage, juncture, period, phase.
5 *the tension had reached a high point:* level, degree, stage, pitch, extent.
6 *there are many important points to discuss:* factor, consideration, argument, element, detail, item, fact, thing; subject, issue, topic, question, matter.
7 *it took her a long time to get to the point:* heart of the matter, most important part, essence, nub, keynote, core, pith, crux; meaning, significance, gist, substance, thrust, burden; informal brass tacks, nitty-gritty.
8 *what's the point of this?* purpose, aim, object, objective, goal, intention; use, sense, value, advantage, profit.
9 *he had his good points:* attribute, characteristic, feature, trait, quality, property, aspect, side.
▷ **verb** *she pointed the gun at him:* aim, direct, level, train.
□ **beside the point**
Eliot's arguments are beside the point: irrelevant, immaterial, unimportant, neither here nor there, inconsequential, incidental, out of place, unconnected, peripheral, tangential, extraneous.
□ **point of view**
opinion, view, belief, attitude, feeling, sentiment, thoughts; position, perspective, stance, viewpoint, standpoint, outlook.
□ **point something out**
1 *I pointed out a small heap of stones:* indicate, draw attention to, point to, gesture towards, signal.
2 *she pointed out that he'd been in the office that morning:* observe, mention.
□ **point something up**
he did much to point up the plight of the refugees: emphasize, highlight, draw attention to, accentuate, underline, spotlight, foreground, put emphasis on, stress, play up, accent, bring to the fore.
□ **point to**
the evidence pointed to his guilt: indicate, suggest, evidence, signal, signify, denote, reveal, manifest; formal bespeak.
□ **to the point**
his evidence was brief and to the point: relevant, pertinent, apposite, germane, applicable, apropos, appropriate, apt, fitting, suitable, material.
□ **up to a point**
partly, to some extent, to a certain degree, in part, somewhat, partially.

point-blank adjective *a point-blank refusal:* blunt, direct, straight, straightforward, frank, candid, forthright, explicit, unequivocal, plain, clear, flat, decisive, unqualified, categorical, outright.
▷ **adverb**
1 *he fired the pistol point-blank:* at close range, close up, close to.
2 *she couldn't say it point-blank:* bluntly,

directly, straight, frankly, candidly, openly, explicitly, unequivocally, unambiguously, plainly, flatly, categorically, outright.

pointed adjective
1 *a pointed stick:* sharp, tapering; conical; informal pointy.
2 *a pointed remark:* cutting, trenchant, biting, incisive, acerbic, caustic, scathing, venomous, sarcastic.

pointer noun
1 *the pointer moved to 100rpm:* indicator, needle, arrow, hand.
2 *a pointer to the outcome of the election:* indication, indicator, clue, hint, sign, signal, evidence, intimation, inkling, suggestion.
3 *I can give you a few pointers:* tip, hint, suggestion, guideline, recommendation.

pointless adjective *speculating like this is a pointless exercise:* senseless, futile, hopeless, fruitless, useless, needless, in vain, unavailing, aimless, idle, worthless, valueless; absurd, insane, stupid, silly, foolish.
OPPOSITES: valuable.

poise noun
1 *poise and good deportment:* grace, elegance, balance, control.
2 *in spite of the setback she retained her poise:* composure, equanimity, self-possession, aplomb, presence of mind, self-assurance, self-control, nerve, calm, sangfroid, dignity; informal cool.
▷ **verb**
1 *she was poised on one foot:* balance, hold yourself steady, be suspended, remain motionless, hang, hover.
2 *he was poised for action:* prepare yourself, ready yourself, brace yourself, gear yourself up, stand by.

poison noun
1 *a deadly poison:* toxin, venom.
2 *Marianne was spreading her poison:* malice, ill will, hate, malevolence, bitterness, spite, venom, acrimony, rancour; bad influence, cancer, corruption, pollution.
▷ **verb**
1 *their food had been poisoned:* contaminate, put poison in, adulterate, lace, doctor; informal spike.
2 *the Amazon is being poisoned:* pollute, contaminate, taint, blight, spoil.
3 *they poisoned his mind:* prejudice, bias, jaundice, embitter, sour, warp, corrupt, subvert.

> WORD LINKS
> **toxicology** the branch of science concerned with poisons

poisonous adjective
1 *a poisonous snake:* venomous, deadly.
2 *a poisonous chemical:* toxic, noxious, deadly, fatal, lethal, mortal, death-dealing.
3 *her poisonous remarks:* malicious,

malevolent, hostile, vicious, spiteful, bitter, venomous, vindictive, vitriolic, rancorous, malign, pernicious, mean, nasty; informal bitchy.
OPPOSITES: harmless, non-toxic, benevolent.

poke verb
1 *she poked him in the ribs:* prod, jab, dig, nudge, butt, shove, jolt, stab.
2 *wisps of grey hair poked out from under her hat:* stick out, jut out, protrude, project, extend.
▷ noun *Carrie gave him a poke:* prod, jab, dig, elbow, nudge, shove, stab.
□ poke about/around
you've got no right to go poking about in that cupboard: search, hunt, rummage, forage, grub, root about/around, scavenge, nose around, ferret about/around; sift through, rifle through, scour, comb, probe; Brit. informal rootle around.
□ poke fun at
the other kids poked fun at her hair and her clothes: mock, make fun of, ridicule, laugh at, jeer at, sneer at, deride, scorn, scoff at, pillory, lampoon, tease, taunt, rag, chaff, jibe at; informal take the mickey out of.
□ poke your nose into
don't poke your nose into things which are none of your business: pry into, interfere in, intrude on, butt into, meddle with; informal snoop into.

poky adjective *a poky room:* cramped, tiny, confined, restricted, boxy; euphemistic compact, bijou.
OPPOSITES: spacious.

polar adjective
1 *the polar regions:* Arctic, Antarctic; cold, freezing, icy.
2 *depression and its polar opposite, mania:* diametrical, direct, complete, absolute.

polarity noun *the polarity between social and biological explanations:* difference, dichotomy, separation, opposition, contradiction, antithesis, antagonism.

pole[1] noun *the notice was pinned on a wooden pole:* post, stick, stake, paling, pillar, stanchion, support, prop, batten, bar, rail, rod, beam; staff, stave, cane, baton.

pole[2] noun *points of view at opposite poles:* extremity, extreme, limit.
□ poles apart
completely different, directly opposed, antithetical, incompatible, irreconcilable, worlds apart, at opposite extremes; Brit. like chalk and cheese.

polemic noun
1 *a polemic against injustice:* diatribe, invective, rant, tirade, broadside, attack, harangue, condemnation, criticism; informal blast.
2 (also **polemics**) *he is skilled in polemics:* argumentation, argument, debate, contention, disputation, discussion.

polemical adjective *the first of his*

polemical tracts against modernism: critical, hostile, bitter, polemic, virulent, vitriolic, venomous, caustic, trenchant, cutting, acerbic, sarcastic, scathing, sharp, incisive, devastating.

police noun the police force, the police service, the police officers, policemen, policewomen, officers of the law, the forces of law and order; Brit. constabulary; informal the cops; Brit. informal the force.
▷ verb
1 *a UN military force will police the no-fly zone:* guard, watch over, protect, defend, patrol; control.
2 *the regulations will be policed by the ministry:* enforce, regulate, oversee, supervise, monitor, check.

police officer noun policeman, policewoman; Brit. constable; informal cop; Brit. informal copper, bobby.

policy noun *government policy on education:* plans, strategy, stratagem, approach, code, system, guidelines, theory; line, position, stance, attitude.

polish verb
1 *he polished his shoes:* shine, buff, rub up/down; gloss, burnish; wax.
2 *I need time to polish up my essay:* perfect, refine, hone, enhance, improve; brush up, revise, edit, correct, rewrite, go over, touch up.
▷ noun
1 *furniture polish:* wax, oil.
2 *harder marble allows for a higher polish:* shine, gloss, lustre, sheen, sparkle, patina, finish.
3 *his polish made him stand out:* sophistication, refinement, urbanity, suaveness, elegance, style, grace, finesse, cultivation, civility, gentility, breeding, courtesy, good manners; informal class.

polished adjective
1 *a polished table:* shiny, glossy, gleaming, lustrous, glassy; waxed, buffed, burnished.
2 *a polished performance:* expert, accomplished, masterly, masterful, skilful, adept, adroit, dexterous; impeccable, flawless, perfect, consummate, exquisite, outstanding, excellent, superb, superlative, first-rate, fine; informal ace.
3 *polished manners:* refined, cultivated, civilized, well bred, polite, courteous, urbane, suave, sophisticated, elegant, gracious.
OPPOSITES: dull, inexpert, gauche.

polite adjective
1 *a very polite girl:* well mannered, civil, courteous, mannerly, respectful, deferential, well behaved, well bred, gentlemanly, ladylike, genteel, gracious, urbane; tactful, diplomatic.
2 *polite society:* civilized, refined, cultured, sophisticated, genteel, courtly.
OPPOSITES: rude, uncivilized.

p

politic adjective *I did not think it politic to express my reservations:* wise, prudent, sensible, judicious, canny, sagacious, shrewd, astute; recommended, advantageous, beneficial, profitable, desirable, advisable; appropriate, suitable, fitting, apt.
OPPOSITES: impolitic.

political adjective *the political affairs of the nation:* governmental, government, state, constitutional, ministerial, parliamentary, diplomatic, legislative, administrative, bureaucratic; public, civic.

politician noun legislator, Member of Parliament, MP, minister, statesman, stateswoman, public servant; senator, congressman/woman; informal politico.

politics noun
1 *a career in politics:* government, affairs of state, public affairs; diplomacy.
2 *he studies politics:* political science, civics, statecraft.
3 *what are his politics?* political views, political leanings, party politics.
4 *office politics:* power struggle, machinations, manoeuvring, opportunism, realpolitik.

poll noun
1 *the second-round poll for a new leader:* vote, ballot, show of hands, referendum, plebiscite; election.
2 *the poll was unduly low:* voting figures, vote, returns, count, tally.
3 *a poll to investigate holiday choices:* survey, opinion poll, straw poll, canvass, market research, census.
▷ **verb**
1 *most of those who were polled supported him:* canvass, survey, ask, question, interview, ballot.
2 *she polled 119 votes:* get, gain, register, record, return.

pollute verb
1 *oil spills have polluted the lakes and rivers:* contaminate, taint, poison, foul, dirty, soil, infect.
2 *a society polluted by racism:* corrupt, poison, defile, blight; literary sully.
OPPOSITES: purify.

pollution noun contamination, impurities, contaminants.

pomp noun *the pomp and popular jubilation accompanying his arrival:* ceremony, ceremonial, ritual, display, spectacle, pageantry; show, showiness, ostentation, splendour, grandeur, magnificence, majesty, stateliness, solemnity, glory, opulence, brilliance, drama, resplendence; informal razzmatazz.

pompous adjective *a pompous official who kept quoting the rules:* self-important, overbearing, domineering, magisterial, imperious, pontifical, sententious, grandiose, affected, pretentious, puffed

up, full of yourself.
OPPOSITES: modest.

pond noun pool, waterhole, lake, tarn, reservoir; literary mere.

ponder verb *she had plenty of time to ponder the incident:* think about, contemplate, consider, review, reflect on, mull over, meditate on, muse on, deliberate about, dwell on, brood on, ruminate on, chew over, puzzle over, turn over in your mind; formal cogitate on.

ponderous adjective
1 *a ponderous giant of a man:* clumsy, heavy, awkward, lumbering, slow, cumbersome, ungainly, graceless, uncoordinated, blundering; informal clodhopping, clunky.
2 *his ponderous sentences:* laboured, laborious, awkward, clumsy, forced, stilted; stodgy, lifeless, plodding, pedestrian, boring, dull, tedious, monotonous; over-elaborate, convoluted, turgid.
OPPOSITES: light, agile, lively.

pontificate verb *he began to pontificate about life and art:* hold forth, expound, declaim, preach, lay down the law, sermonize, moralize, lecture; informal mouth off, sound off.

pool¹ noun
1 *pools of water:* puddle, pond.
2 *the hotel has a pool:* swimming pool, baths; Brit. swimming baths, lido.

pool² noun
1 *a pool of skilled labour:* supply, reserve, reservoir, fund; store, stock, accumulation, cache.
2 *a pool of money for emergencies:* fund, reserve, kitty, pot, bank, purse, nest egg.
▷ **verb** *they pooled their skills:* combine, amalgamate, group, join, unite, merge, integrate, share.
OPPOSITES: split.

poor adjective
1 *a poor family:* poverty-stricken, penniless, impoverished, impecunious, indigent, needy, destitute, pauperized, on your beam-ends; insolvent, in debt; Brit. on the breadline; formal necessitous; informal broke, hard up, cleaned out, strapped, on your uppers; Brit. informal skint.
2 *poor workmanship:* substandard, inferior, below par, bad, imperfect, defective, faulty, deficient; appalling, abysmal, atrocious, awful, terrible, dreadful, unsatisfactory, second-rate, third-rate, shoddy, crude, lamentable, deplorable, inadequate, unacceptable; informal crummy, dire, dismal, rotten; Brit. informal ropy, rubbish, dodgy.
3 *a poor crop:* meagre, scanty, scant, paltry, disappointing, insufficient, inadequate, sparse, deficient, insubstantial, skimpy.
4 *poor soil:* unproductive, barren,

p

unyielding, unfruitful; arid, sterile.
5 *the waters are poor in nutrients:*
deficient, lacking, wanting; short of,
low on.
6 *you poor thing!* unfortunate, unlucky,
luckless, unhappy, hapless, ill-fated, ill-
starred, pitiable, pitiful, wretched.
OPPOSITES: rich, superior, good.

poorly adverb *the school has been
performing poorly:* badly, inadequately,
unsatisfactorily.
▷ **adjective** *she felt poorly:* ill, unwell, ailing,
indisposed, out of sorts, under/below
par; sick, queasy, nauseous; Brit. off colour,
peaky; informal under the weather, lousy,
rough; Brit. informal grotty.
OPPOSITES: well.

pop verb
1 *champagne corks popped:* go bang, go
off; crack, snap, burst, explode.
2 (informal) *I'm just popping home:* go;
drop in, stop by, visit; informal whip; Brit.
informal nip.
3 (informal) *pop a bag over the pot:* put, place,
slip, slide, stick, set, lay, position, arrange.
▷ **noun** *the balloons burst with a pop:* bang,
crack, snap; explosion, report.
□ **pop up** (informal) *many familiar faces pop
up during the twenty-six episodes:* appear,
turn up, materialize, arrive; happen,
emerge, occur, crop up, present itself;
informal show up.

pope noun pontiff, Bishop of Rome, Holy
Father, His Holiness.

> WORD LINKS
> **papal**, **pontifical** relating to the pope
> **papacy** the position or period of office of
> the pope

populace noun *the party misjudged the
mood of the populace:* people, population,
community, nation, country, public,
general public, inhabitants, residents;
common people, man/woman in the
street, masses, multitude, rank and file,
proletariat; Brit. informal Joe Public.

popular adjective
1 *the restaurant is very popular:* well
liked, fashionable, in vogue, all the rage,
hot, favoured, sought-after, in demand,
desired, wanted; commercial, marketable;
informal in, cool, big.
2 *popular science:* non-specialist, non-
technical, amateur, lay person's, general,
middle-of-the-road; accessible, simplified,
plain, simple, easy, straightforward,
understandable; mass-market,
middlebrow, lowbrow, pop.
3 *contrary to popular opinion, many adult
cats dislike milk:* widespread, general,
common, current, prevalent, prevailing,
standard, stock; ordinary, usual, accepted,
established, acknowledged, conventional,
orthodox.
4 *a popular movement for independence:*

mass, people's, general, communal,
collective, social, collaborative, group,
civil, public.
OPPOSITES: unpopular, highbrow, minority.

popularize verb
1 *tobacco was popularized by Sir Walter
Raleigh:* make popular, make fashionable;
market, publicize, spread, propagate;
informal hype.
2 *he set out to popularize the subject,
writing many books for the layman:*
simplify, make accessible, give mass-
market appeal to.

popularly adverb
1 *old age is popularly associated with
illness:* commonly, generally, universally,
widely, usually, customarily, habitually,
conventionally, traditionally, as a rule.
2 *the rock was popularly known as 'Arthur's
Seat':* informally, unofficially.
OPPOSITES: technically.

populate verb
1 *the state is populated by 40,000 people:*
inhabit, occupy, people; live in, reside in.
2 *an attempt to populate the island:* settle,
colonize, people, occupy, move into, make
your home in.
OPPOSITES: depopulate.

population noun *95% of the population
live in rural areas:* inhabitants, residents,
people, citizens, citizenry, public,
community, nation, populace, society,
natives, occupants.

populous adjective *the country's second
most populous city:* densely populated,
heavily populated, congested, crowded,
packed, teeming; informal jam-packed.
OPPOSITES: deserted.

porch noun entrance, lobby, foyer,
vestibule, entry, doorway, portico.

pore¹ noun *pores in the skin:* opening,
orifice, aperture, hole, outlet, inlet, vent.

pore² verb
□ **pore over/through**
they pored over the map: study, read intently,
scrutinize, be engrossed in, be absorbed in,
scan, examine, go over; formal peruse.

> USAGE
> Do not confuse **pore** and **pour**. **Pore** is used
> with **over** or **through** and means 'to study
> or read something closely', while **pour** means
> 'to flow in a steady stream' (*water poured off
> the roof*).

pornographic adjective obscene,
indecent, crude, lewd, dirty, vulgar,
smutty, filthy; erotic, suggestive, sexy,
risqué; off colour, X-rated, hard-core, soft-
core; euphemistic adult; informal blue.

porous adjective *porous rock:* permeable,
pervious, penetrable, cellular; absorbent,
absorptive, spongy.
OPPOSITES: impermeable.

p

port[1] noun *the liner will be putting into port again today:* harbour, docks, marina; anchorage, mooring, harbourage, roads.

port[2] noun *push the supply pipes into the ports:* aperture, opening, outlet, inlet, socket, vent.

portable adjective *a portable television:* transportable, movable, mobile, travel; lightweight, compact, handy, convenient.
OPPOSITES: fixed.

portal noun doorway, gateway, entrance, exit, opening; door, gate.

portend verb *the sound of the death-watch beetle was thought to portend the death of someone in the house:* warn of, be an omen of, indicate, herald, signal, bode, promise, threaten, signify, spell, denote, presage, augur, foreshadow, foretell, prophesy, be a sign of.

portent noun *a portent of things to come:* warning, omen, sign, signal, token, forewarning, foreshadowing, prediction, forecast, prophecy, harbinger, augury, auspice, presage, writing on the wall, indication, hint.

portentous adjective
1 *this portentous year in Canadian history:* momentous, important, significant, of great importance, of great significance; life-and-death, pivotal, critical.
2 *the author's portentous moralizing:* pompous, bombastic, self-important, pontifical, solemn, sonorous, grandiloquent.
3 *the earthquake that rocked the city on the day of his death was seen as a portentous omen:* ominous, warning; threatening, menacing, ill-omened, inauspicious, unfavourable.

portion noun
1 *the upper portion of the chimney:* part, piece, bit, section, segment.
2 *her portion of the allowance:* share, slice, quota, allocation, ration, part, percentage, amount, quantity, fraction, division, measure, quantum.
3 *a portion of cake:* helping, serving; slice, piece, chunk, wedge, slab, hunk; plateful, bowlful.
▷ verb *she portioned out the food:* share out, allocate, allot, apportion; distribute, hand out, deal out, dole out, give out, dispense.

portly adjective *a portly, florid-faced man:* stout, plump, fat, obese, overweight, heavy, corpulent, fleshy, paunchy, pot-bellied, well padded, rotund; informal tubby, pudgy; Brit. informal podgy.
OPPOSITES: slim.

portrait noun
1 *a portrait of the King:* painting, picture, drawing, sketch, likeness, image, study, miniature; informal oil.
2 *a vivid portrait of musical life in 19th-century Italy:* description, portrayal, representation, depiction, impression, account; sketch, vignette, profile.

portray verb
1 *he portrays Windermere in sunny weather:* depict, draw, sketch, picture, paint, represent, illustrate, render.
2 *the dons portrayed by Waugh:* describe, depict, characterize, represent, delineate, evoke.
3 *the actor portrays a spy:* play, act the part of, take the role of, represent, appear as.

portrayal noun
1 *the icon is considered to be a realistic portrayal of the saint:* picture, representation, illustration, depiction, study, rendering; painting, portrait, drawing, sketch.
2 *the portrayal of adolescence in her book:* description, representation, characterization, depiction, account, evocation.
3 *Brando's portrayal of Corleone:* performance, representation, interpretation, rendering, account.

pose verb
1 *pollution poses a threat to health:* constitute, present, create, cause, produce, be.
2 *the question posed earlier:* raise, ask, put, set, submit, advance, propose, suggest, moot.
3 *she posed for the artist:* model, sit, be a model.
4 *fashion victims were posing at the bar:* behave affectedly, strike a pose, posture, attitudinize, put on airs; informal show off.
▷ noun
1 *a sexy pose:* posture, position, stance, attitude, bearing.
2 *she dropped her pose of aggrieved innocence:* pretence, act, affectation, facade, show, front, display, masquerade, posture.
□ **pose as**
the gang posed as police officers in order to gain entry: pretend to be, impersonate, pass yourself off as, masquerade as, profess to be, represent yourself as.

poser[1] noun (informal) *he's such a poser:* exhibitionist, poseur, poseuse, posturer; informal show-off, pseud.

poser[2] noun (informal) *this situation's a bit of a poser:* difficult question, vexed question, awkward problem, puzzle, mystery, conundrum, enigma, riddle; informal facer.

poseur noun. See POSER[1].

posh adjective
1 (informal) *a posh hotel:* smart, elegant, stylish, fancy, high-class, fashionable, chic, luxurious, luxury, de luxe, exclusive, opulent, lavish, grand, showy; Brit. upmarket; informal classy, flash; Brit. informal swish.

p

2 (Brit. informal) *a posh accent:* upper-class, aristocratic; Brit. upmarket, Home Counties; informal upper-crust.
OPPOSITES: rough, common.

posit verb *there are those who posit a purely biological basis for this phenomenon:* put forward, propose, postulate, advance, propound, submit, hypothesize, suggest, assert, claim.

position noun
1 *the distress call had given the ship's position:* location, place, situation, spot, site, locality, setting, area; whereabouts, bearings, orientation.
2 *a standing position:* posture, stance, pose, attitude, bearing.
3 *our financial position is grim:* situation, state, condition, circumstances; predicament, plight, straits.
4 *their position in society:* status, place, level, rank, standing, class; stature, prestige, influence, reputation, importance, consequence.
5 *a secretarial position:* job, post, situation, appointment, role, occupation, employment; office, capacity, duty, function; opening, vacancy; Brit. placement.
6 *the government's position on the matter:* viewpoint, opinion, outlook, attitude, stand, standpoint, stance, perspective, approach, slant, thinking, policy, feelings.
▷**verb** *he positioned a chair between them:* put, place, locate, situate, set, site, stand, station; plant, stick, install; arrange, dispose; informal pop, park; Brit. informal plonk.

positive adjective
1 *a positive response:* affirmative, favourable, good, approving, enthusiastic, supportive, encouraging.
2 *a chance to do something positive:* constructive, practical, useful, productive, helpful, worthwhile, beneficial, effective.
3 *she seems a lot more positive these days:* optimistic, hopeful, confident, cheerful, sanguine, buoyant, upbeat.
4 *positive economic signs:* favourable, good, promising, encouraging, heartening, propitious, auspicious.
5 *positive proof:* definite, conclusive, certain, categorical, unequivocal, incontrovertible, indisputable, undeniable, unmistakable, irrefutable, definitive, reliable, concrete, tangible, clear-cut, explicit, firm, decisive, real, actual.
6 *I'm positive he's coming back:* certain, sure, convinced, confident, satisfied, assured.
OPPOSITES: negative, pessimistic, doubtful.

positively adverb
1 *I could not positively identify the voice:* confidently, definitely, emphatically, categorically, with certainty, conclusively, definitively.
2 *he was positively livid:* absolutely, really, downright, thoroughly, completely, utterly, totally, extremely; informal plain.

possess verb
1 *this was the only hat she possessed:* own, have, be in possession of, hold.
2 *he did not possess a sense of humour:* have, be blessed with, be endowed with; enjoy, boast.
3 *a supernatural force possessed him:* take control of, take over, control, dominate, influence; bewitch, enchant, enthral.
4 *she was possessed by a need to talk to him:* obsess, haunt, preoccupy, consume; eat someone up, prey on someone's mind.

possessed adjective *she screamed like a woman possessed:* mad, demented, insane, crazed, berserk, out of your mind; bewitched, enchanted, haunted, under a spell.

possession noun
1 *the estate came into their possession:* ownership, control, hands, keeping, care, custody, charge, hold, title, guardianship.
2 *she packed her possessions:* belongings, things, property, personal effects, assets, goods and chattels, worldly goods, movables, valuables; luggage, baggage; informal stuff, gear, junk, bits and pieces; Brit. informal clobber.
3 *Britain's former colonial possessions:* colony, dependency, territory, holding, protectorate.
□ **take possession of**
the state government took possession of the land: seize, appropriate, impound, expropriate, sequestrate, sequester, confiscate; take, get, acquire, obtain, procure, possess yourself of, get hold of, get your hands on; capture, commandeer, requisition.

possessive adjective *kids are possessive of their own property:* proprietorial, unwilling to share, selfish, controlling, dominating, overprotective, jealous.
OPPOSITES: easy, generous.

possibility noun
1 *there is a possibility that he might be alive:* chance, likelihood, probability, hope, prospect; risk, hazard, danger, fear.
2 *they discussed the possibility of launching a new project:* feasibility, practicability, chances, odds.
3 *buying a smaller house is one possibility:* option, alternative, choice, course of action, solution.
OPPOSITES: impossibility.

possible adjective
1 *it's not possible to check the figures:* feasible, practicable, viable, within the bounds/realms of possibility; attainable, achievable, workable; informal on, doable.
2 *a possible reason for his disappearance:* conceivable, plausible, potential, imaginable, believable, credible, likely, probable, prospective.
OPPOSITES: impossible, inconceivable.

p

possibly adverb

1 *possibly he took the boy with him:* perhaps, maybe, it is possible, for all you know, very likely.
2 *you can't possibly refuse:* conceivably, under any circumstances, by any means.
3 *could you possibly help me?* please, kindly, at all, be so good as to.

post¹ noun *wooden posts:* pole, stake, upright, shaft, prop, support, picket, strut, pillar, pale, paling, stanchion.

▷ verb
1 *the notice was posted on a wall:* affix, attach, fasten, display, pin, put up, stick.
2 *the group posted a net profit of £460,000:* announce, report, make known, publish.

post² noun (Brit.)

1 *the winners will be notified by post:* mail, the postal service; informal snail mail.
2 *did we get any post?* letters, correspondence, mail.

▷ verb
1 (Brit.) *post the order form today:* send, send off, mail, put in the post/mail.
2 *post the transaction in the second column:* record, write in, enter, register.

post³ noun

1 *there were seventy candidates for the post:* job, position, appointment, situation, place; vacancy, opening.
2 *back to your posts!* position, station.

▷ verb
1 *he'd been posted to Berlin:* send, dispatch, transfer, assign.
2 *armed guards were posted beside the exit:* put on duty, station, position, situate, locate.

poster noun *a poster advertising his latest film:* notice, placard, bill, sign, advertisement, playbill; Brit. fly-poster.

posterior adjective *the posterior part of the skull:* rear, hind, back, hinder.
OPPOSITES: anterior.

posterity noun *their names are recorded for posterity:* future generations, generations to come, the future.

post-mortem noun

1 *the hospital carried out a post-mortem:* autopsy, PM, necropsy.
2 *a post-mortem of her failed relationship:* analysis, evaluation, assessment, appraisal, examination, review.

postpone verb *he had to postpone his scheduled trip to South Africa:* put off, put back, delay, defer, reschedule, adjourn, shelve.
OPPOSITES: bring forward.

postponement noun deferral, deferment, delay, putting off/back, rescheduling, adjournment.

postulate verb *such hypotheses have been postulated by highly reputable geologists:* put forward, propose, suggest, advance, propound, submit, posit, hypothesize; assume, presuppose, presume, take for granted.

posture noun

1 *a kneeling posture:* position, pose, attitude, stance.
2 *good posture is very important:* bearing, carriage, stance, comportment; Brit. deportment.
3 *trade unions adopted a militant posture:* attitude, stance, stand, standpoint, point of view, viewpoint, outlook, opinion, position.

▷ verb *Keith postured, flexing his biceps:* pose, strike an attitude, strut.

posy noun *a posy of snowdrops and violets:* bouquet, bunch, spray, nosegay, corsage, buttonhole.

pot noun

1 *cooking pots:* pan, saucepan, casserole, stewpot, stockpot.
2 *earthenware pots:* jar, crock; jug, ewer; flowerpot, planter, jardinière.

potency noun *the potency of his words:* force, effectiveness, persuasiveness, cogency, influence, strength, authority, power.

potent adjective

1 *a potent political force:* powerful, strong, mighty, formidable, influential, dominant, forceful.
2 *a potent argument:* forceful, convincing, cogent, compelling, persuasive, powerful, strong.
3 *a potent drug:* powerful, effective.
OPPOSITES: impotent, weak.

potentate noun *diplomatic missions to foreign potentates:* ruler, monarch, head of state, prince, sovereign.

potential adjective *a potential source of conflict:* possible, likely, prospective, future; budding, promising, probable; latent, dormant, inherent, undeveloped.

▷ noun *the country has great economic potential:* possibilities, potentiality, prospects; promise, capability, capacity, scope.

potion noun *Dotty concocted strange potions from the herbs in her garden:* concoction, mixture, brew, elixir, philtre, drink, draught, decoction; medicine, tonic.

potpourri noun *the book is a potpourri of curious animal stories:* mixture, assortment, collection, selection, assemblage, medley, miscellany, mix, variety, mixed bag, patchwork; hotchpotch, jumble, farrago; informal ragbag.

potter verb *we pottered down to the library:* amble, wander, meander, stroll, saunter; informal mosey.
□ potter about/around
I'm quite happy to potter about by myself: do nothing much, fiddle about/around,

p

footle about/around; informal mess about/around; Brit. informal muck about/around.

pottery noun china, crockery, ceramics, porcelain, earthenware, stoneware.

potty adjective (Brit. informal)
1 *I'm going potty.* See **CRAZY** sense 1.
2 *she's potty about you.* See **CRAZY** sense 3.

pouch noun *he kept his money in a leather pouch:* bag, purse, sack, sac, pocket; Scottish sporran.

pounce verb *the two men pounced on him and knocked him to the ground:* attack, set on, jump on, leap on, spring at, lunge at, dive at.

pound¹ verb
1 *the two men pounded him with their fists:* beat, strike, hit, batter, thump, pummel, punch, rain blows on, belabour, hammer, thrash; informal bash, clobber, wallop.
2 *waves pounded the seafront:* beat against, crash against, batter, dash against, lash, buffet.
3 *gunships pounded the capital:* bombard, bomb, shell, fire on.
4 *pound the cloves with salt:* crush, grind, pulverize, mill, mash, pulp.
5 *I heard him pounding along the gangway:* stamp, thunder, stomp, thump, clomp, clump, tramp, trudge, lumber.
6 *her heart was pounding:* throb, thump, thud, hammer, pulse, race, go pit-a-pat.

pound² noun *a dog pound:* enclosure, compound, stockade, fold, pen, yard; N. Amer. corral.

pour verb
1 *blood was pouring from his nose:* stream, flow, run, gush, course, jet, spurt, surge, spill.
2 *Amy poured wine into his glass:* tip, let flow, splash, spill, decant.
3 *it was pouring with rain:* teem down, pelt down, come down in torrents/sheets, rain hard; informal rain cats and dogs; Brit. informal bucket down, tip down, come down in stair rods.
4 *thousands of people poured into the streets:* crowd, surge, swarm, stream, flood, spill.

> **USAGE**
>
> Do not confuse **pour** and **pore**. **Pour** means 'to flow in a steady stream', while **pore** is used with **over** or **through** and means 'to study or read something closely' (e.g. *I spent hours poring over the plans*).

pout verb *Crystal pouted sullenly:* look petulant, pull a face, look sulky.
▷ noun *a childish pout:* petulant expression, sulky expression, moue.

poverty noun
1 *they live in abject poverty:* penury, destitution, indigence, pennilessness, impoverishment, neediness, need, hardship.
2 *the poverty of choice:* scarcity, deficiency, dearth, shortage, paucity, insufficiency, absence, lack.
OPPOSITES: wealth, abundance.

poverty-stricken adjective *his family were poverty-stricken and starving:* extremely poor, impoverished, destitute, penniless, in penury, impecunious, indigent, needy; Brit. on the breadline, without a penny to your name; informal on your uppers; Brit. informal in Queer Street.

powdery adjective *a powdery residue:* dusty, fine, chalky, floury, sandy, crumbly, grainy, granular, pulverized, friable, loose, dry.

power noun
1 *the power of speech:* ability, capacity, capability, potential, faculty, competence.
2 *the unions wield enormous power:* control, authority, influence, dominance, mastery, domination, dominion, sway, weight, leverage; informal clout, teeth.
3 *police have the power to stop and search:* authority, right, authorization, warrant, licence.
4 *a major European power:* state, country, nation.
5 *the power of his arguments:* force, potency, strength, cogency, persuasiveness, effectiveness.
6 *the new engine has more power:* driving force, horsepower, hp, acceleration, torque.
7 *generating power from waste:* electricity, energy, potential.
OPPOSITES: inability, weakness.

powerful adjective
1 *his powerful shoulders:* strong, muscular, muscly, sturdy, strapping, robust, brawny, burly, athletic, manly, well built, solid.
2 *a powerful blow:* violent, forceful, hard, mighty.
3 *he felt a powerful desire to kiss her:* intense, keen, fierce, passionate, ardent, burning, strong, irresistible, overpowering, overwhelming.
4 *a powerful nation:* influential, strong, important, dominant, commanding, potent, forceful, formidable.
5 *a powerful critique of nationalism:* cogent, compelling, convincing, persuasive, forceful, effective; dramatic, graphic, vivid, moving.
OPPOSITES: weak, gentle.

powerless adjective *we felt intimidated and powerless:* impotent, helpless, ineffectual, ineffective, useless, defenceless, vulnerable.
OPPOSITES: empowered.

practicable adjective *it is important that all practicable steps be taken to prevent violence breaking out:* realistic, feasible, possible, within the bounds/realms of possibility, viable, reasonable, sensible, workable, achievable; informal doable.
OPPOSITES: impracticable.

p

practical adjective

1 *they have no practical experience:* actual, hands-on, active, applied, empirical, experiential; formal heuristic.
2 *there are no practical alternatives:* feasible, practicable, realistic, viable, workable, possible, reasonable, sensible; informal **doable**.
3 *a very practical piece of software:* useful, functional, helpful, convenient, handy, easy-to-use, well designed, user-friendly, user-oriented.
4 *please make sure you wear practical shoes and warm clothing:* functional, serviceable, sensible, utilitarian, workaday.
5 *try to be more practical:* realistic, sensible, down-to-earth, businesslike, commonsensical, pragmatic, hard-headed, no-nonsense; informal hard-nosed.
6 *it's a practical certainty:* virtual, effective, near.
OPPOSITES: theoretical, impractical.

practicality noun

1 *the practicality of the proposal:* feasibility, practicability, viability, workability.
2 *practicality of design:* usefulness, functionality, serviceability, ease of use, user-friendliness, utility, functionalism.
3 *his calm practicality:* common sense, realism, pragmatism.
4 *the practicalities of army life:* practical details, actual experience, realities, actualities, everyday demands; informal nitty gritty, nuts and bolts.
OPPOSITES: impracticality.

practical joke noun trick, joke, prank, jape, hoax; informal leg-pull.

practically adverb

1 *the cinema was practically empty:* almost, very nearly, virtually, just about, all but, more or less, as good as, to all intents and purposes, verging on, bordering on; informal pretty nearly, pretty well.
2 *'You can't afford it,' he pointed out practically:* realistically, sensibly, reasonably.
OPPOSITES: impractically.

practice noun

1 *product placement is a common practice in American movies:* custom, procedure, policy, convention, tradition.
2 *it takes lots of practice | the team's final practice:* training, rehearsal, repetition, preparation; practice session, run-through; Brit. dummy run; informal dry run.
3 *the practice of medicine:* profession, career, business, work.
4 *a small legal practice:* business, firm, partnership, company, office; informal outfit.
□ **in practice**
in theory, this method is ideal—in practice, it doesn't work: in reality, in real life, in actual experience, realistically, practically.
□ **put something into practice**
the recommendations proved too expensive
to put into practice: use, make use of, put to use, utilize, apply, carry out/through.

USAGE

Practice is the correct spelling for the noun in both British and American English (e.g. *putting policy into practice*). **Practice** is also the spelling for the verb in American English, but in British English, the verb should be spelled **practise** (*I need to practise my French*).

practise verb

1 *he practised the songs every day:* rehearse, run through, go over/through, work on/at; polish, perfect.
2 *the performers were practising:* train, rehearse, prepare, go through your paces.
3 *we still practise these rituals today:* carry out, perform, observe.
4 *she practises medicine:* work in/at, pursue a career in.

practised adjective *Sam was a practised judge of character:* expert, experienced, seasoned, skilled, skilful, accomplished, proficient, talented, able, adept, adroit, consummate, master, masterly; informal ace, mean.
OPPOSITES: incompetent.

pragmatic adjective

my father was entirely pragmatic in his response to difficult situations: practical, matter-of-fact, sensible, down-to-earth, commonsensical, businesslike, having both/your feet on the ground, hard-headed, no-nonsense; informal hard-nosed.
OPPOSITES: impractical.

praise verb

1 *the police praised Pauline for her courage:* commend, applaud, congratulate, compliment, express admiration for, give credit to, pay tribute to, speak highly of, pat on the back, take your hat off to, acclaim, eulogize, lionize.
2 *let us praise God:* worship, glorify, honour, exalt, adore, pay tribute to, give thanks to, venerate, reverence.
OPPOSITES: criticize.

▷ noun
1 *he was full of praise for the medical teams:* admiration, acclaim, plaudits, tributes, congratulations, accolades, compliments, commendations; approval, approbation; eulogy; literary panegyric, paean.
2 *give praise to God:* worship, glory, honour, thanks, devotion, adoration, reverence.

praiseworthy adjective

the government's praiseworthy efforts: commendable, admirable, laudable, worthy of admiration, deserving, creditable, meritorious, estimable.
OPPOSITES: blameworthy.

prance verb *he was prancing around in his underpants:* dance, cavort, jump, leap, spring, bound, skip, hop, frisk, romp, frolic, jig, trip, caper.

prank noun *a silly student prank:* practical joke, trick, piece of mischief, escapade, stunt, caper, jape, game, hoax, antic; informal lark.

prattle verb *he prattled on for ages.* See CHAT verb.
▷noun *childish prattle.* See CHATTER noun.

pray verb *she prayed God to forgive her:* invoke, call on, implore, appeal to, entreat, beg, petition, supplicate.

prayer noun
1 *the priest's murmured prayers:* invocation, intercession, devotion.
2 *it is our prayer that the progress on human rights will be sustained:* hope, wish, desire, dream, aspiration.

preach verb
1 *he preached to a large congregation:* give a sermon, deliver a homily, speak; address.
2 *preaching the good news of Jesus:* proclaim, teach, spread, propagate, expound.
3 *they preach toleration:* advocate, champion, recommend, advise, urge, teach, counsel.
4 *who are you to preach at me?* moralize, sermonize, pontificate; lecture, harangue; informal preachify.

preamble noun *they began to draft a preamble to the constitution:* introduction, preface, prologue, foreword, prelude; informal intro.

precarious adjective *the club's precarious financial position:* insecure, shaky, unsafe, risky, hazardous, dangerous, perilous, vulnerable; unsettled, uncertain, unpredictable, unstable; informal dicey; Brit. informal dodgy.
OPPOSITES: secure.

precaution noun *have your car serviced regularly as a precaution against mechanical breakdowns:* safeguard, preventative/preventive measure, safety measure, insurance, protection, defence; informal backstop.

precautionary adjective *keeping him in overnight was just a precautionary measure:* preventative, preventive, safety, protective, defensive.

precede verb
1 *adverts preceded the film:* go/come before, lead up to, pave/prepare the way for, herald, introduce, usher in.
2 *Catherine preceded him into the studio:* go ahead of, go in front of, go before; go first, lead the way.
3 *he preceded the book with a poem:* preface, introduce, begin, open.
OPPOSITES: follow.

precedence noun *quarrels over precedence:* priority, seniority, superiority, primacy, pre-eminence, rank, standing.

precedent noun *we hope to set a legal precedent:* model, exemplar, example, pattern, previous case, prior instance/ example; paradigm, criterion, yardstick, standard.

preceding adjective *this discussion amplifies many of the issues raised in the preceding chapters:* foregoing, previous, prior, former, earlier, above, aforementioned, precedent, antecedent.
OPPOSITES: following.

precept noun *science cannot prove religious precepts to be false:* principle, rule, tenet, canon, doctrine.

precinct noun
1 *within the precincts of the City:* bounds, boundaries, limits, confines, neighbourhood, environs, vicinity.
2 (Brit.) *a shopping precinct:* area, zone, sector, quarter, district; mall, arcade, galleria.
3 *the cathedral precinct:* enclosure, close, court.

precious adjective
1 *precious works of art:* valuable, costly, expensive; invaluable, priceless, beyond price.
2 *her most precious possession:* valued, cherished, treasured, prized, favourite, dear, dearest, beloved, darling, adored, loved, special.
3 *his precious manners:* affected, over-refined, pretentious; informal la-di-da.
OPPOSITES: worthless, unpretentious.

precipice noun cliff, rock face, crag, bluff, escarpment, scarp, sheer drop, height.

precipitate verb
1 *the incident precipitated a crisis:* bring about/on, cause, lead to, give rise to, instigate, trigger, spark, touch off, provoke, hasten, accelerate.
2 *they were precipitated down the mountain:* hurl, catapult, throw, plunge, launch, fling, propel.
▷adjective *their actions were precipitate:* hasty, overhasty, rash, hurried, rushed; impetuous, impulsive, spur-of-the-moment, precipitous, incautious, imprudent, injudicious, ill-advised, reckless, harum-scarum; informal previous.

precipitous adjective
1 *a precipitous drop:* steep, sheer, perpendicular, abrupt, sharp, vertical.
2 *his fall from power was precipitous:* sudden, rapid, swift, abrupt, headlong, speedy, quick, fast.
OPPOSITES: gentle.

precis noun *a precis of the report:* summary, synopsis, résumé, abstract, outline, summation; abridgement, digest, overview.
▷verb *he precised what was in the memo:* summarize, sum up, give a summary/ precis of, give the main points of; abridge,

p

condense, shorten, abstract, outline, abbreviate.

precise adjective

1 *I need to provide precise measurements:* exact, specific, detailed, explicit, unambiguous, definite; accurate, correct.
2 *the director was precise with his camera positions:* meticulous, careful, exact, scrupulous, punctilious, conscientious, particular, methodical, strict, rigorous.
3 *at that precise moment the car stopped:* exact, particular, very, specific.
OPPOSITES: imprecise.

> **USAGE**
>
> **Precise** does not mean exactly the same as **accurate**. **Accurate** means 'correct in all details', while **precise** contains the idea of trying to specify details exactly. If you say 'The time is 4.04 and 12 seconds' you are being *precise,* but not necessarily *accurate* (the clock you are looking at might be slow).

precisely adverb

1 *fertilization can be timed precisely:* accurately, exactly, correctly, right.
2 *make sure you are here at 2 o'clock precisely:* exactly, sharp, on the dot; promptly, prompt, dead on, on the stroke of —.
3 *he's precisely the kind of man I am looking for:* exactly, absolutely, just, in all respects.
OPPOSITES: imprecisely, approximately.

precision noun *the deal was planned and executed with great precision:* accuracy, exactitude, exactness, correctness; care, meticulousness, scrupulousness, punctiliousness, rigour.
OPPOSITES: imprecision.

p

preclude verb *his difficulties preclude him from leading a normal life:* prevent, stop, prohibit, hinder, impede, inhibit, exclude, make it impossible for, rule out, debar, bar.
OPPOSITES: enable, allow.

precocious adjective *some of the boys were extremely precocious:* advanced for your age, forward, mature, gifted, talented, clever, intelligent, quick; informal smart.
OPPOSITES: backward.

preconceived adjective *some people tend to have preconceived ideas about us:* predetermined, premature, prejudiced, prejudged, biased.

preconception noun *they had no preconceptions about his personality or his politics:* preconceived idea/notion, presupposition, assumption, presumption, prejudgement; prejudice.

precondition noun *political stability is a precondition for economic revival:* prerequisite, condition, necessary condition, requirement, necessity, essential, imperative, sine qua non; informal must.

precursor noun *a three-stringed precursor of the guitar:* forerunner, predecessor, forefather, father, antecedent, ancestor, forebear.
OPPOSITES: successor.

predatory adjective

1 *predatory birds:* predacious, carnivorous, hunting, raptorial; of prey.
2 *he personified the predatory ethics of the 1980s:* exploitative, rapacious, grasping, grabbing, acquisitive; informal on the make.

predecessor noun

1 *the Prime Minister's predecessor:* forerunner, precursor, antecedent.
2 *our Victorian predecessors:* ancestor, forefather, forebear, antecedent.
OPPOSITES: successor, descendant.

predestined adjective *some people claim that everything is predestined:* preordained, ordained, foreordained, predetermined, destined, fated.

predetermined adjective

1 *a predetermined budget:* prearranged, established in advance, preset, set, fixed, agreed.
2 *our predetermined fate:* predestined, preordained.

predicament noun *I cannot understand how you could have allowed yourself to get into such a predicament:* difficulty, plight, mess, difficult situation, dilemma, quandary, dire straits; informal deep water, hole, fix, jam.

predicate verb *all the social sciences are predicated on the notion that individuals are not isolated:* base, found, establish, rest, ground, premise.

predict verb *it's difficult to predict what the outcome will be:* forecast, foretell, foresee, prophesy, anticipate, tell in advance, envision, envisage.

predictable adjective *Guido's reaction was predictable:* foreseeable, to be expected, anticipated, foreseen, unsurprising, inevitable.

prediction noun *seven months later, his prediction came true:* forecast, prophecy, prognosis, prognostication; projection, conjecture, guess.

predilection noun *her predilection for married men:* liking, fondness, preference, partiality, taste, penchant, weakness, soft spot, fancy, inclination, leaning, bias, propensity, bent, proclivity, predisposition, appetite.
OPPOSITES: dislike.

predispose verb

1 *lack of exercise may predispose an individual to high blood pressure:* make susceptible, make liable, make prone, make vulnerable, put at risk of.
2 *attitudes which predispose people to*

behave badly: lead, influence, sway, induce, prompt, dispose; bias, prejudice.

predisposed adjective *the audience were young and predisposed to like the film:* inclined, prepared, ready, of a mind, disposed, minded, willing.
OPPOSITES: unwilling, unlikely.

predisposition noun
1 *a predisposition to heart disease:* susceptibility, proneness, tendency, liability, inclination, disposition, vulnerability.
2 *their political predispositions:* preference, predilection, inclination, leaning, tendency.

predominance noun
1 *the predominance of women carers:* prevalence, dominance, preponderance.
2 *Soviet military predominance:* supremacy, mastery, control, power, ascendancy, dominance, pre-eminence, superiority.
OPPOSITES: minority, subordination.

predominant adjective
1 *health care and the economy remain the predominant concerns of many voters:* main, chief, principal, most important, primary, prime, central, leading, foremost, key, paramount; informal number-one.
2 *the predominant political forces:* controlling, dominant, predominating, more/most powerful, pre-eminent, ascendant, superior, in the ascendancy.
OPPOSITES: subsidiary.

predominantly adverb *although predominantly a disease of older men, it is not unknown in people of his age:* mainly, mostly, for the most part, chiefly, principally, primarily, in the main, on the whole, largely, by and large, typically, generally, usually.
OPPOSITES: occasionally.

predominate verb
1 *small-scale producers predominate:* be in the majority, preponderate, be predominant, prevail, be most prominent.
2 *private interest predominates over the public good:* prevail, dominate, be dominant, carry most weight; override, outweigh.

pre-eminence noun superiority, supremacy, predominance, greatness, excellence, distinction, prominence, eminence, importance, prestige, stature, fame, renown, celebrity.

pre-eminent adjective *the country's pre-eminent environmentalist:* greatest, leading, foremost, best, finest, chief, outstanding, excellent, distinguished, prominent, eminent, important, top, famous, renowned, celebrated, illustrious, supreme.
OPPOSITES: undistinguished.

pre-eminently adverb *the novel is*

pre-eminently a realistic genre: primarily, principally, above all, chiefly, mostly, mainly, in particular.

pre-empt verb *his action may have pre-empted war:* forestall, prevent.

preen verb
1 *the robin preened its feathers:* clean, tidy, groom, smooth, arrange.
2 *she preened before the mirror:* admire yourself, primp yourself, prink yourself, groom yourself, spruce yourself up; informal titivate yourself.
□ **preen yourself** congratulate yourself, be pleased with yourself, be proud of yourself, pat yourself on the back, feel self-satisfied.

preface noun *the preface to the novel:* introduction, foreword, preamble, prologue, prelude; informal intro.
▷ **verb** *each chapter is prefaced by a poem:* precede, introduce, begin, open, start.
OPPOSITES: follow.

prefatory adjective *three further prefatory remarks are necessary:* introductory, preliminary, opening, initial, preparatory, initiatory, precursory.
OPPOSITES: closing.

prefer verb *I prefer white wine to red:* like better, would rather have, would sooner have, favour, be more partial to; choose, select, pick, opt for, go for, plump for.

preferable adjective *personal pension plans may be preferable if you change jobs frequently:* better, best, more desirable, more suitable, advantageous, superior, preferred, recommended.

preferably adverb *applicants should be graduates, preferably with some relevant experience:* ideally, if possible, for preference, from choice.

preference noun
1 *her preference for boys' games:* liking, partiality, predilection, fondness, taste, inclination, leaning, bias, bent, penchant, proclivity, predisposition.
2 *my musical preference is rock:* favourite, first choice, selection.
3 *preference will be given to applicants speaking Japanese:* priority, favour, precedence, preferential treatment.
□ **in preference to** rather than, sooner than, instead of, in place of.

preferential adjective *preferential interest rates may be offered to employees:* special, better, privileged, superior, favourable; partial, discriminatory, partisan, biased.
OPPOSITES: standard.

prefigure verb *his work prefigures that of the magic realists:* foreshadow, presage, anticipate, be a harbinger of, herald, signal, promise, threaten, spell.

p

pregnancy noun gestation.

pregnant adjective
1 *she is heavily pregnant:* expecting a baby, expectant, carrying a child; technical gravid; informal expecting, in the family way; old use with child.
2 *a ceremony pregnant with religious significance:* filled, charged, heavy; full of.
3 *a pregnant pause:* meaningful, significant, suggestive, expressive, charged.

prehistoric adjective *prehistoric times:* ancient, early, antediluvian, primeval, primordial, primal, primitive.
OPPOSITES: modern.

prejudice noun
1 *male prejudices about women:* preconceived idea, preconception, prejudgement.
2 *they are motivated by prejudice:* bias, partisanship, partiality, intolerance, bigotry, discrimination, unfairness, inequality.
3 *without prejudice to the interests of others:* detriment, harm, damage, injury, hurt, loss.
OPPOSITES: impartiality.
▷ verb
1 *the article could prejudice the jury:* bias, influence, sway, predispose, colour.
2 *this could prejudice his chances of victory:* damage, be detrimental to, be prejudicial to, injure, harm, hurt, spoil, impair, undermine, hinder, compromise.
OPPOSITES: improve.

prejudiced adjective *his prejudiced views:* biased, bigoted, discriminatory, partisan, intolerant, narrow-minded, unfair, unjust, inequitable, coloured.
OPPOSITES: impartial.

prejudicial adjective *disclosure of the information would be prejudicial to the interests of the company:* detrimental, damaging, injurious, harmful, disadvantageous, hurtful, deleterious.
OPPOSITES: beneficial.

preliminary adjective *the discussions are still at a preliminary stage:* preparatory, introductory, initial, early, opening, prefatory, precursory, exploratory.
OPPOSITES: final.
▷ noun
1 *he began without any preliminaries:* introduction, preamble, opening/prefatory remarks, formalities.
2 *a preliminary to the resumption of war:* prelude, preparation, preparatory measure.

prelude noun
1 *the ceasefire had been agreed as a prelude to peace negotiations:* preliminary, overture, introduction, lead-in, precursor, opening, preparation, start, commencement, beginning.

2 *the passage forms a prelude to Part III:* introduction, preface, prologue, foreword, preamble; informal intro.

premature adjective
1 *his premature death:* untimely, early, too soon, unseasonable, before time.
2 *such a step would be premature:* rash, overhasty, hasty, precipitate, impulsive, impetuous; informal previous.
OPPOSITES: overdue, opportune.

prematurely adverb *don't act prematurely:* rashly, overhastily, hastily, precipitately, precipitously, incautiously.
OPPOSITES: opportunely.

premeditated adjective *premeditated murder:* planned, pre-planned, prearranged, intentional, deliberate, calculated, cold-blooded, conscious.
OPPOSITES: unpremeditated.

premeditation noun advance planning, forethought, pre-planning, intent, criminal intent; Law malice aforethought.
OPPOSITES: impulse.

premier adjective *a premier chef:* leading, foremost, chief, principal, head, top-ranking, top, prime, primary, first, highest, pre-eminent, senior, outstanding, master.
▷ noun *the Italian premier:* head of government, prime minister, PM, president, chancellor.

premiere noun *the new musical is having its world premiere at the Haymarket Theatre tonight:* first performance, first night, opening night.

premise noun *the premise that human life consists of a series of choices:* proposition, hypothesis, thesis, postulation, surmise, supposition, presupposition, assumption, presumption, assertion, conjecture, speculation, belief.

premises plural noun *the company had moved to new premises in Gloucester:* buildings, property, site, office, headquarters.

premium noun *you must pay a premium for organic fruit:* surcharge, supplement, additional payment, extra amount.
▫ at a premium
scarce, in great demand, hard to come by, in short supply, thin on the ground.
▫ put/place a premium on
I place a high premium on our relationship: value greatly, attach great/special importance to, set great store by, put a high value on.

premonition noun *he had a premonition of imminent disaster:* foreboding, presentiment, intuition, hunch, feeling in your bones; misgiving, apprehension, fear.

preoccupation noun
1 *an air of preoccupation:* pensiveness, concentration, engrossment, absorption, self-absorption, musing, thinking, deep

p

thought, brooding; abstraction, absent-mindedness, distraction, forgetfulness, inattentiveness, wool-gathering, daydreaming.
2 *their main preoccupation was feeding their family:* obsession, concern; passion, enthusiasm, hobby horse.

preoccupied adjective
1 *officials who were preoccupied with their careers:* obsessed, concerned, absorbed, engrossed, intent, involved, wrapped up.
2 *she looked preoccupied:* lost/deep in thought, in a brown study, pensive, absent-minded, distracted, abstracted.

preoccupy verb engross, concern, absorb, take up someone's attention, distract, obsess, occupy, prey on someone's mind.

preordain verb *he believes that everything we do is preordained:* predestine, destine, foreordain, ordain, fate, predetermine, determine.

preparation noun
1 *the preparation of contingency plans:* devising, putting together, drawing up, construction, composition, production, getting ready, development.
2 *preparations for the party are almost complete:* arrangements, planning, plans, preparatory measures.
3 *preparation for exams:* instruction, teaching, coaching, training, tutoring.
4 *a preparation that kills off mites:* mixture, compound, concoction, solution, tincture, medicine, potion, cream, ointment, lotion.

preparatory adjective *preparatory work:* preliminary, initial, introductory, prefatory, opening, precursory, exploratory, experimental.
□ **preparatory to**
in preparation for, before, prior to, preliminary to.

prepare verb
1 *I want you to prepare a report:* make/get ready, put together, draw up, produce, arrange, assemble, construct, compose, formulate.
2 *the meal was easy to prepare:* cook, make, get, put together, concoct; informal fix, rustle up; Brit. informal knock up.
3 *the government was preparing for war:* get ready, make preparations, arrange things, make provision, make arrangements, get everything set.
4 *prepare yourself for a shock:* brace, make ready, tense, steel, steady.

prepared adjective
1 *he needs to be well prepared:* ready, all set, equipped, primed; waiting, on hand, poised, in position.
2 *I'm not prepared to cut the price:* willing, ready, disposed, predisposed, inclined, of a mind, minded.
OPPOSITES: unprepared.

preponderance noun
1 *the preponderance of women among older people:* prevalence, predominance, dominance.
2 *the preponderance of the evidence:* bulk, majority, greater quantity, larger part, best/better part, most; almost all.

preponderant adjective
1 *the preponderant numbers of women who enrol in our course:* greater, superior.
2 *the Western states remained militarily preponderant in the region:* dominant, predominant, pre-eminent, in control, more/most powerful, superior, supreme, ascendant, in the ascendancy.
OPPOSITES: lesser, subordinate.

prepossessing adjective *he was not a prepossessing sight:* attractive, beautiful, pretty, handsome, good-looking, fetching, charming, delightful, enchanting, captivating.
OPPOSITES: unprepossessing.

preposterous adjective *a preposterous suggestion:* absurd, ridiculous, foolish, stupid, ludicrous, farcical, laughable, comical, risible, nonsensical, senseless, insane; outrageous, monstrous; informal crazy.
OPPOSITES: sensible.

prerequisite noun *training is a prerequisite for competence:* condition, necessary condition, precondition, essential, requirement, requisite, necessity, sine qua non; informal must.
▷ adjective *the prerequisite qualifications:* necessary, required, called for, essential, requisite; obligatory, compulsory.
OPPOSITES: unnecessary.

prerogative noun *in some countries, higher education is predominantly the prerogative of the rich:* entitlement, right, privilege, advantage, benefit, due, birthright, province.

presage verb *the owl's hooting presages death:* portend, augur, foreshadow, foretell, prophesy, be an omen of, herald, be a sign of, be the harbinger of, warn of, signal, bode, promise, threaten, spell, indicate.
▷ noun *a sombre presage of his final illness:* omen, sign, indication, portent, warning, forewarning, harbinger, augury, prophecy; literary foretoken.

prescience noun *the article displays the uncanny prescience of much of her work:* far-sightedness, foresight, foreknowledge; psychic powers, clairvoyance; prediction, prognostication, divination, prophesy, augury; insight, intuition, perception.

prescient adjective prophetic, predictive, visionary; psychic, clairvoyant; far-sighted, prognostic, divinatory; insightful, intuitive, perceptive, percipient.

prescribe verb

1 *the doctor prescribed antibiotics:* write a prescription for, authorize; advise, recommend.

2 *these rules prescribe the grounds upon which an appeal may be made:* stipulate, lay down, dictate, specify, determine, establish, fix.

USAGE

Do not confuse the words **prescribe** and **proscribe**. **Prescribe** means either 'to issue a medical prescription' or 'to state authoritatively that something should be done', whereas **proscribe** means 'to forbid something officially' (*strikes remained proscribed in the armed forces*).

---

prescription noun

1 *the doctor wrote a prescription:* instruction, authorization, order, direction.

2 *he fetched the prescription from the chemist:* medicine, drug, medication.

3 *a painless prescription for improvement:* method, measure; recommendation, suggestion, recipe, formula.

prescriptive adjective *guidelines must avoid being too prescriptive:* dogmatic, rigid, narrow, arbitrary, authoritarian, repressive, dictatorial.
OPPOSITES: liberal.

presence noun

1 *the presence of chlorine in the atmosphere:* existence.

2 *I requested the presence of an adjudicator:* attendance, appearance; company, companionship.

3 *a woman of great presence:* aura, charisma, strength/force of personality; poise, self-assurance, self-confidence.

4 *she felt a presence in the castle:* ghost, spirit, spectre, phantom, apparition, supernatural being; informal spook.
OPPOSITES: absence.

□ presence of mind
composure, equanimity, self-possession, level-headedness, self-assurance, calmness, sangfroid, imperturbability; alertness, quick-wittedness; informal cool, unflappability.

present¹ adjective

1 *a doctor must be present at the ringside:* in attendance, here, there, near, nearby, at hand, available.

2 *organic compounds are present in the waste:* in existence, existing, extant.

3 *the present economic climate:* current, present-day, existing.
OPPOSITES: absent.

▷ noun (**the present**) *forget the past and think about the present:* now, today, the present time/moment, the here and now.
OPPOSITES: past, future.

□ at present
at the moment, currently, at the present time, just now, right now.

□ for the present
for the time being, for now, for the moment, for a while, temporarily, pro tem.

present² verb

1 *Eddy presented a cheque to the winner:* hand over/out, give, confer, bestow, award, grant, accord.

2 *the committee presented its report:* submit, set forth, put forward, proffer, offer, tender, table.

3 *may I present my wife?* introduce, acquaint someone with.

4 *I called to present my warmest compliments:* offer, give, express.

5 *they presented their new product last month:* demonstrate, show, put on show/display, exhibit, display, launch, unveil.

6 *they presented a series of Italian operas:* stage, put on, produce, perform.

7 *she presents a TV show:* host, introduce, compère; Brit. be the presenter of.

8 *the authorities present him as a common criminal:* represent, describe, portray, depict.

□ present yourself

1 *he presented himself at ten o'clock:* be present, make an appearance, appear, turn up, arrive.

2 *an opportunity that presented itself:* occur, arise, happen, come about/up, appear, crop up, turn up.

present³ noun *a birthday present:* gift, donation, offering, contribution.

presentable adjective

1 *I'm making the place look presentable:* tidy, neat, straight, clean, spick and span, in good order, shipshape.

2 *make yourself presentable:* smart, respectable, decent, tidy, well groomed, elegant, trim, spruce.

3 *he has directed some presentable videos:* fairly good, passable, all right, satisfactory, moderately good, not bad, average, fair; informal OK.

presentation noun

1 *the presentation of his certificate:* awarding, presenting, giving, handing over/out, bestowal, granting, award.

2 *the presentation of food is important:* appearance, arrangement, packaging, disposition, display, layout.

3 *the presentation of new proposals:* submission, proffering, offering, tendering, advancing, proposal, suggestion, mooting, tabling.

4 *a sales presentation:* demonstration, talk, lecture, address, speech, show, exhibition, display, introduction, launch, unveiling.

5 *a presentation of his latest play:* staging, production, performance, mounting, showing.

present-day adjective current, present, contemporary, latter-day, present-time, modern, twenty-first-century; up to

date, up to the minute, fashionable, trendsetting, the latest, new, newest.

presentiment noun *I understood that you had some sort of presentiment of disaster:* premonition, foreboding, intuition, hunch, feeling in your bones, sixth sense.

presently adverb
1 *I shall see you presently:* soon, shortly, directly, quite soon, in a short time, in a little while, at any moment/minute/ second, in next to no time, before long; N. Amer. momentarily; informal pretty soon, any moment/time now, in a jiffy.
2 *he is presently abroad:* at present, currently, at the/this moment, at the present moment/time, now, nowadays, these days; Brit. informal at the minute.

preservation noun
1 *the preservation of old buildings:* conservation, protection, maintenance, care, repair.
2 *the preservation of the status quo:* continuation, maintenance, upholding, sustaining, perpetuation.

preserve verb
1 *oil helps preserve wood:* conserve, protect, maintain, care for, look after.
2 *they wish to preserve the status quo:* continue, conserve, keep going, maintain, uphold, sustain, perpetuate.
3 *a place for preserving endangered species:* guard, protect, keep, defend, safeguard, shelter, shield.
▷noun
1 *strawberry preserve:* jam, jelly, marmalade, conserve.
2 *the civil service had become the preserve of an educated middle class:* domain, area, field, sphere, orbit, realm, province, territory; informal turf, bailiwick.
3 (N. Amer.) *a game preserve:* sanctuary, reserve, reservation.

preside verb *the prime minister will preside at an emergency cabinet meeting:* chair, officiate at, conduct, lead.
□ preside over
be in charge of, be responsible for, be at the head/helm of, head, be head of, manage, administer, be in control of, control, direct, lead, govern, rule, command, supervise, oversee; informal head up, be boss of.

president noun
1 *the president of the society:* head, chief, director, leader, governor, principal.
2 *the president of the company:* chairman; managing director, MD, chief executive, chief executive officer, CEO.

press verb
1 *press the paper down firmly:* push, force, hold, thrust, squeeze, compress.
2 *Winnie pressed his hand:* squeeze, grip, clutch.

3 *the crowd pressed round:* cluster, gather, converge, congregate, flock, swarm, throng, crowd.
4 *they pressed him to agree:* urge, put pressure on, pressurize, push, try to persuade, try to force.
5 *they pressed for a ban on the ivory trade:* call, campaign, demand, push.
6 *his shirt had been washed and pressed:* iron, smooth out.
▷noun *the freedom of the press:* the media, the newspapers, the papers, the news media, the fourth estate; journalists, reporters.
□ be pressed for
I'm very pressed for time: have too little, be short of, have insufficient, lack, be lacking.
□ press on
the team regrouped and pressed on: proceed, keep going, continue, carry on, make progress, make headway, press ahead, forge on/ahead, push on, keep on, struggle on, persevere, keep at it, stay with it, plough on; informal soldier on.

pressing adjective *pressing economic and political problems* | *he had pressing business in Scotland:* urgent, important, high-priority, top-priority; critical, crucial, acute, serious, grave.

pressure noun
1 *the gates were buckling under the pressure of the crowd outside:* force, load, stress, thrust; compression, weight.
2 *they put pressure on us to borrow more money:* coercion, force, compulsion, constraint, duress; pestering, harassment, intimidation, arm-twisting, persuasion.
3 *the pressures of city life:* strain, stress, tension, trouble, difficulty; informal hassle.
▷verb *they pressured him into resigning.* See **PRESSURIZE**.

pressurize verb *don't let anyone pressurize you into snap decisions:* coerce, pressure, put pressure on, press, push, persuade, force, badger, browbeat, bully, bludgeon, twist someone's arm; informal railroad.

prestige noun *he experienced a tremendous increase in prestige following his victory:* status, standing, stature, reputation, repute, regard, honour, esteem, celebrity, importance, prominence, influence, eminence; kudos, cachet.
OPPOSITES: disgrace.

prestigious adjective
1 *a prestigious scientific journal:* respected, distinguished, esteemed, eminent, august, highly regarded, well thought of, reputable, acclaimed, authoritative, celebrated, illustrious, leading, renowned.
2 *a prestigious job:* impressive, important, prominent, high-ranking, influential, powerful, glamorous; well paid, expensive; Brit. upmarket.
OPPOSITES: obscure, minor.

p

presumably adverb *presumably he'll get the job:* probably, in all probability, in all likelihood, as likely as not, doubtless, undoubtedly, no doubt, I presume, I expect, I assume, I take it, I suppose, I imagine, I dare say, I guess.

presume verb
1 *I presume that you're leaving today:* assume, suppose, dare say, imagine, take it, expect, believe, think, surmise, guess, judge, conjecture, speculate, postulate, presuppose.
2 *let me presume to give you some advice:* venture, dare, have the audacity/effrontery, be so bold as, take the liberty of.
□ presume on
he was wary of presuming on their friendship: take advantage of, exploit, take liberties with; count on, bank on, place reliance on.

presumption noun
1 *this presumption may be easily rebutted:* assumption, supposition, presupposition, belief, guess, judgement, surmise, conjecture, speculation, hypothesis, postulation, inference, deduction, conclusion.
2 *he apologized for his presumption:* arrogance, brazenness, boldness, temerity, audacity, forwardness; cockiness, insolence, impudence, bumptiousness, impertinence, effrontery, cheek; rudeness, impoliteness, disrespect, familiarity; informal nerve, chutzpah.

presumptive adjective *a presumptive diagnosis:* conjectural, speculative, tentative; theoretical, unproven, unconfirmed.

presumptuous adjective *it's rather presumptuous to judge my character on such short acquaintance:* arrogant, overconfident, brazen, bold, forward, familiar, impertinent, insolent, impudent, cocky; cheeky, rude, impolite, uncivil, bumptious.

presuppose verb
1 *this way of thinking about morality presupposes a religious conception of life:* require, imply, entail, mean; assume, presume.
2 *your argument presupposes that it doesn't matter who is in power:* presume, assume, take it for granted, take it as read, suppose.

presupposition noun presumption, assumption, preconception, supposition, hypothesis, surmise, thesis, theory, premise, belief, postulation.

pretence noun
1 *they have finally abandoned their secrecy and pretence:* make-believe, play-acting, putting on an act, acting, dissembling, simulation, dissimulation, posturing; deception, deceit, fraud, duplicity, subterfuge, trickery, dishonesty, hypocrisy, falsity, lying, mendacity.
2 *he made a pretence of being unconcerned:* show, semblance, affectation, false appearance, outward appearance, impression, false front, guise, facade, display.
3 *she had dropped any pretence to faith:* claim, profession.
OPPOSITES: honesty.

pretend verb
1 *pretend you're asleep | is she really ill or just pretending?* make as if, profess, affect; dissimulate, dissemble, put it on, put on a false front, go through the motions, sham, fake it.
2 *I'll pretend to be the dragon:* put on an act, make believe, play at, act, play-act, impersonate.
3 *it was useless to pretend innocence:* feign, fake, simulate, put on, affect.
□ pretend to
he cannot pretend to sophistication: claim, lay claim to, purport to have, profess to have.

pretended adjective *her eyes widened in pretended astonishment:* fake, faked, affected, assumed, professed, spurious, mock, imitation, simulated, make-believe, sham, false, bogus; informal pretend, pseudo, phoney.

pretender noun *a pretender to the throne:* claimant, aspirant.

pretension noun
1 *a low-budget film without artistic pretensions:* aspiration, claim, pretence, profession.
2 *she spoke without pretension:* affectation, affectedness, ostentation, artificiality, airs, posing, posturing, show, flashiness; pomposity, grandiloquence; formal magniloquence.

pretentious adjective *his pretentious philosophizing becomes increasingly hard to stomach:* affected, ostentatious, showy; overambitious, pompous, artificial, inflated, overblown, high-sounding, flowery, grandiose, elaborate, extravagant, flamboyant, ornate, grandiloquent; formal magniloquent; informal highfalutin, la-di-da, pseudo.

pretext noun *he called at her home on the pretext of enquiring after her father:* excuse, ostensible reason, alleged reason; guise, ploy, ruse.

prettify verb *nothing has been done to prettify the site:* beautify, make attractive, make pretty, titivate, adorn, ornament, decorate, smarten up; informal doll up, do up.
OPPOSITES: disfigure.

pretty adjective *a pretty child:* attractive, lovely, good-looking, nice-looking, fetching, prepossessing, appealing, charming, delightful, personable, cute, as pretty as a picture; Scottish & N. English bonny.
OPPOSITES: plain, ugly.

▷ **adverb** (informal) *a pretty large sum:* quite, rather, somewhat, fairly, reasonably, comparatively, relatively.

prevail verb
1 *common sense will prevail in the end:* triumph, win through, be victorious, carry the day, come out on top, succeed, prove superior.
2 *the conditions that prevailed in the 1950s:* exist, be in existence, be present, be the case, occur, be prevalent, be current, be the order of the day, be customary, be common, be widespread, be in force/effect; formal obtain, pertain.
□ **prevail on**
Jane had prevailed on Dorothy to come: persuade, induce, talk someone into, coax, convince, make, get, press someone into, argue someone into, urge, pressure someone into, pressurize someone into, coerce; informal sweet-talk.

prevailing adjective *a research project examined prevailing attitudes in the classroom:* current, existing, prevalent, usual, common, general, widespread.

prevalence noun *the prevalence of smoking among teenagers:* commonness, occurrence, incidence, currency, frequency, generality, pervasiveness, universality, extensiveness; popularity.
OPPOSITES: scarcity.

prevalent adjective widespread, prevailing, frequent, usual, common, current, popular, general, universal; endemic, rampant, rife.
OPPOSITES: rare.

prevaricate verb *he seemed to prevaricate when journalists asked pointed questions about his involvement:* be evasive, beat about the bush, hedge, fence, dodge the issue, sidestep the issue, equivocate; temporize, stall, play for time.

prevent verb *action must be taken to prevent further accidents:* stop, avert, nip in the bud, fend off, stave off, ward off; hinder, impede, hamper, obstruct, baulk, foil, thwart, forestall, counteract, inhibit, curb, restrain, preclude, pre-empt, save, help; disallow, prohibit, forbid, proscribe, exclude, debar, bar.
OPPOSITES: allow, assist.

preventive adjective *preventive measures can be taken to avoid risks:* pre-emptive, precautionary, protective, deterrent.

previous adjective
1 *the previous five years | her previous boyfriend:* preceding, foregoing, antecedent; old, earlier, prior, former, ex-, past, last, sometime, one-time, erstwhile.
2 (informal) *I was a bit previous:* overhasty, hasty, premature, precipitate, impetuous; informal ahead of yourself.
OPPOSITES: next.

□ **previous to**
before, prior to, until, leading up to, earlier than, preceding.

previously adverb *museums and art galleries which had previously been open to the public:* formerly, earlier, before, hitherto, once, at one time, in the past, in days/times gone by, in bygone days, in times past, in former times.

prey noun
1 *the lions killed their prey:* quarry, kill.
2 *she was easy prey:* victim, target, dupe, gull; informal sucker, soft touch, pushover.
OPPOSITES: predator.
□ **prey on**
1 *hoverfly larvae prey on aphids:* hunt, catch, predate; eat, feed on, live on/off.
2 *they prey on the elderly:* exploit, victimize, pick on, take advantage of; trick, swindle, cheat, hoodwink; informal con, fleece.
3 *the problem preyed on his mind:* oppress, weigh on, lie heavy on, gnaw at; trouble, worry, beset, disturb, distress, haunt, nag, torment, plague, obsess.

price noun
1 *the purchase price:* cost, asking price, charge, fee, fare, levy, amount, sum; outlay, expense, expenditure; valuation, quotation, estimate; humorous damage.
2 *she can't move around the city in peace any more—that's the price of fame:* consequence, result, cost, penalty, sacrifice; downside, snag, drawback, disadvantage, minus.
▷ **verb** *tickets are priced at £5.00:* fix/set the price of, cost, value, rate.

priceless adjective
1 *priceless works of art:* of incalculable value/worth, of immeasurable value/worth, invaluable, beyond price; irreplaceable, incomparable, unparalleled.
2 (informal) *that's priceless!* See HILARIOUS sense 1.
OPPOSITES: worthless, cheap.

pricey adjective (informal). See EXPENSIVE.

prick verb
1 *prick the potatoes with a fork:* pierce, puncture, make/put a hole in, stab, perforate, jab.
2 *his eyes began to prick:* sting, smart, burn, prickle.
3 *his conscience pricked him:* trouble, worry, distress, perturb, disturb, torment, plague, prey on, gnaw at.
4 *ambition pricked him on to greater effort:* goad, prod, incite, provoke, urge, spur, stimulate, encourage, inspire, motivate, push, propel, impel.
5 *the horse pricked up its ears:* raise, erect.

prickle noun
1 *the cactus is covered with prickles:* thorn, needle, barb, spike, point, spine.

p

2 *she felt a prickle of excitement:* tingle, tingling, prickling, chill, thrill.

prickly adjective
1 *a prickly shrub:* spiky, thorny, barbed, spiny; rough, scratchy.
2 *this is a prickly subject:* problematic, awkward, controversial, tricky, delicate, sensitive, difficult, knotty, thorny.
3 *she came across as prickly and difficult.* See IRRITABLE.

pride noun
1 *winning the tournament is a tremendous source of pride:* self-esteem, self-respect, self-worth, self-regard, pride in yourself, dignity, honour.
2 *take pride in a good job well done:* pleasure, delight, gratification, fulfilment, satisfaction, sense of achievement.
3 *he refused her offer out of pride | the worst sin in a ruler was pride:* arrogance, vanity, self-importance, hubris, conceit, self-love, self-admiration, narcissism, egotism.
4 *the ship was the pride of the German Navy:* source of satisfaction, pride and joy, treasured possession, joy, delight.
OPPOSITES: shame, humility.
□ **pride yourself on**
she prided herself on her sincerity: be proud of, be proud of yourself for, take pride in, take satisfaction in, congratulate yourself on, pat yourself on the back for.

priest noun clergyman, clergywoman, minister, cleric, ecclesiastic, pastor, vicar, rector, parson, churchman, churchwoman, man/woman of the cloth, man/woman of God, father, curate, chaplain, curé, evangelist, preacher.

WORD LINKS
clerical, hieratic, sacerdotal relating to priests

priestly adjective *their priestly duties:* clerical, pastoral, ecclesiastical, sacerdotal, hieratic.

priggish adjective *a priggish old woman:* self-righteous, holier-than-thou, sanctimonious, moralistic, prudish, puritanical, prim, strait-laced, stuffy, prissy, narrow-minded; informal goody-goody, starchy.
OPPOSITES: broad-minded.

prim adjective *a prim, fastidious woman:* demure, prim and proper, stuffy, strait-laced, prudish; prissy, priggish, puritanical; Brit. po-faced; informal starchy.

primacy noun *he maintained the primacy of art over everything else, including morality:* pre-eminence, superiority, supremacy, ascendancy, dominance, dominion; priority, precedence.

primarily adverb *such work is undertaken primarily for large institutions:* mostly, for the most part, chiefly, mainly, in the main, on the whole, largely, to a large extent, especially, generally, usually, typically, commonly, as a rule.

primary adjective
1 *our primary aim is to see significant reductions in unemployment:* main, chief, key, prime, central, principal, foremost, first, most important, predominant, paramount; informal number-one.
2 *the primary cause:* original, earliest, initial, first; essential, fundamental, basic.
OPPOSITES: secondary.

prime¹ adjective
1 *their prime concern is the well-being of the patients:* main, chief, key, primary, central, principal, foremost, first, most important, paramount, major; informal number-one.
2 *prime agricultural land:* top-quality, best, first-class, first-rate, grade A, superior, supreme, choice, select, finest; excellent, superb, fine; informal top-notch.
3 *the novel is a prime example of the genre:* archetypal, prototypical, typical, classic, excellent, characteristic, quintessential.
OPPOSITES: secondary.
▷ noun *he is in his prime:* heyday, best days/years, prime of your life; youth, salad days; peak, pinnacle, high point/spot, zenith.

prime² verb
1 *he primed the gun:* prepare, load, get ready.
2 *Lucy had primed him well in advance:* brief, fill in, prepare, put in the picture, inform, advise, coach, drill; informal clue in, give someone the low-down.

prime minister noun premier, first minister, head of the government.

primeval adjective
1 *primeval forest:* ancient, earliest, first, prehistoric; original.
2 *primeval fears:* instinctive, unreasoning, primitive, basic, primal, primordial, intuitive, inborn, innate, inherent.

primitive adjective
1 *primitive times:* ancient, earliest, first, prehistoric, primordial, primeval, primal.
2 *primitive cultures:* undeveloped, preliterate, non-industrialized; uncivilized, simple.
3 *primitive tools:* crude, simple, rough and ready, basic, rudimentary, unsophisticated.
OPPOSITES: modern, civilized.

primordial adjective
1 *the primordial oceans:* ancient, earliest, first, prehistoric, primeval.
2 *their primordial desires:* instinctive, basic, fundamental, primal, primeval, inborn, innate, inherent.

principal adjective *the principal cause of poor air quality | the principal reason for his departure:* main, chief, primary, leading, foremost, first, most important, predominant, most prominent; key, crucial, essential, basic, prime, central, focal;

paramount, major, overriding, cardinal, pre-eminent, uppermost, highest, top, topmost; informal number-one.
OPPOSITES: minor.
▷ noun
1 *the principal of the firm:* chief, chief executive, chief executive officer, CEO, chairman, chairwoman, managing director, MD, president, director, manager, head; informal boss; Brit. informal gaffer, governor.
2 *the school's principal:* director; Brit. head teacher, headmaster, headmistress, head.
3 *a principal in a soap opera:* leading actor/actress, leading player/performer, leading role, lead, star.
4 *creditors have agreed to forgo all repayments of the principal until March 2007:* capital; debt, loan.

principally adverb *the decline is principally due to overfishing:* mainly, mostly, chiefly, for the most part, in the main, on the whole, largely, to a large extent, predominantly, basically, primarily.

principle noun
1 *the basic principles of their faith:* tenet, proposition, concept, idea, belief, doctrine, creed, credo, code, dictum, rule, law; fundamentals, basics.
2 *a woman of principle | he's sticking to his principles:* morals, morality, code of ethics, beliefs, ideals, standards; integrity, uprightness, virtue, probity, honour, decency, conscience, scruples.
□ in principle
1 *there is no reason, in principle, why we couldn't work together:* in theory, theoretically, on paper.
2 *he has accepted the idea in principle:* in general, in essence, on the whole, in the main.

principled adjective *a brave and principled man:* moral, ethical, upright, upstanding, high-minded, honourable, honest, incorruptible, virtuous.

print verb
1 *they printed 30,000 copies of the book:* publish, issue, release, run off, reprint.
2 *patterns of birds and trees were printed on the cloth:* imprint, impress, stamp, mark.
3 *the incident is printed on her memory:* fix, imprint, engrave, etch, stamp.
▷ noun
1 *small print:* type, printing, letters, lettering, characters, type size, typeface, font.
2 *prints of his left hand:* impression, fingerprint, footprint.
3 *sporting prints:* picture, engraving, etching, lithograph, linocut, woodcut; reproduction, copy.
4 *prints and negatives:* photograph, photo, snapshot, picture, still; informal snap.
5 *soft floral prints:* printed cloth/fabric, patterned cloth/fabric, chintz.

prior adjective *a prior arrangement:*

earlier, previous, preceding; existing.
OPPOSITES: subsequent.
□ prior to
she visited me on the day prior to her death: before, preceding, leading up to.

priority noun
1 *safety is our priority:* prime concern, most important consideration, primary issue.
2 *giving priority to primary education:* precedence, greater importance, preference, pre-eminence, predominance, primacy, first place.
3 *traffic on the roundabout has priority:* right of way, precedence.

priory noun religious house, abbey; monastery, friary; convent, nunnery.

prise verb
1 *I prised the lid off:* lever, jemmy; wrench, wrest, twist.
2 *he had to prise information from them:* wring, wrest, worm out, winkle out, screw, squeeze, extract.

prison noun jail, penal institution, detention centre, lock-up; N. Amer. jailhouse, penitentiary, correctional facility; informal clink, slammer; Brit. informal nick; N. Amer. informal can, cooler; (**be in prison**) be in custody; informal be inside, be behind bars, do time; Brit. informal do bird, do porridge.

prisoner noun
1 *a prisoner serving a life sentence:* convict, detainee, inmate; informal jailbird; Brit. informal old lag; N. Amer. informal yardbird.
2 *the army took many prisoners:* prisoner of war, POW, internee, captive.

prissy adjective *he hated it when she swore, but he didn't like to sound prissy:* prudish, priggish, prim, prim and proper, strait-laced; Brit. po-faced; informal starchy.

pristine adjective *a pristine white handkerchief:* immaculate, perfect, in mint condition, as new, unspoilt, spotless, unmarked, unblemished, flawless, clean, fresh, new, virgin, pure, unused.
OPPOSITES: dirty, spoilt.

privacy noun *a walled garden ensures complete privacy:* seclusion, solitude, isolation, freedom from disturbance, freedom from interference.

private adjective
1 *his private plane:* personal, own, individual, special, exclusive, privately owned.
2 *private talks:* confidential, unofficial, off the record, closet, in camera; backstage, one-on-one, tête-à-tête; secret, classified, privileged.
3 *private thoughts:* intimate, personal, secret; innermost, undisclosed, unspoken, unvoiced.
4 *a very private man:* reserved, introvert, introverted, self-contained, reticent, discreet, uncommunicative,

p

unforthcoming, retiring, unsociable, withdrawn, solitary, reclusive.
5 *they found a private place in which to talk:* secluded, undisturbed, concealed, hidden, isolated, out of the way, sequestered.
6 *the Queen attended in a private capacity:* unofficial, personal.
7 *private industry:* independent, non-state; privatized, denationalized; commercial, private-enterprise.
OPPOSITES: public, open, official, state.
□ **in private** *I need to talk to you in private:* in secret, secretly, privately, behind closed doors, in camera; in confidence, confidentially, between ourselves, entre nous, off the record.

private detective noun private investigator; informal private eye, sleuth; N. Amer. informal gumshoe.

privately adverb
1 *we must talk privately:* in secret, secretly, in private, behind closed doors, in camera; in confidence, confidentially, between ourselves, entre nous, off the record.
2 *privately, I am glad:* secretly, inwardly, deep down, personally, unofficially.
3 *he lived very privately:* out of the public eye, out of public view, in seclusion, in solitude, alone.
OPPOSITES: publicly.

privation noun *years of rationing and privation:* deprivation, hardship, destitution, impoverishment, want, need, austerity.
OPPOSITES: plenty, luxury.

privilege noun
1 *senior pupils have certain privileges:* advantage, benefit; prerogative, entitlement, right; concession, freedom, liberty.
2 *it was a privilege to meet her:* honour, pleasure.

privileged adjective
1 *a privileged background:* wealthy, rich, affluent, prosperous; lucky, fortunate, elite, socially advantaged.
2 *privileged information:* confidential, private, secret, restricted, classified, not for publication, off the record, inside; informal hush-hush.
OPPOSITES: underprivileged, disadvantaged.

prize noun
1 *Britain's most prestigious prize for contemporary art:* award, reward; trophy, medal; honour, accolade, crown, laurels, palm.
2 *the prizes of war:* spoils, booty, plunder, loot, pickings.
▷adjective
1 *a prize bull:* champion, award-winning, prize-winning, winning, top, best.
2 *a prize example of how well organic farming can function:* outstanding,

excellent, superlative, superb, supreme, very good, prime, fine, magnificent, marvellous, wonderful; informal great, terrific, tremendous, fantastic.
3 *a prize idiot:* utter, complete, total, absolute, real, perfect, positive, veritable; Brit. informal right.
▷verb *many collectors prize his work:* value, set great store by, rate highly, attach great importance to, esteem, hold in high regard, think highly of, treasure, cherish.

prized adjective *his prized collection of soccer memorabilia:* treasured, precious, cherished, much loved, beloved, valued, esteemed, highly regarded.

probability noun
1 *the probability of winning:* likelihood, prospect, expectation, chance, chances, odds.
2 *relegation is a distinct probability:* probable event, prospect, possibility, good/fair/reasonable bet.

probable adjective *it is probable that the economic situation will deteriorate further:* likely, most likely, expected, anticipated, predictable, foreseeable, ten to one, odds-on; informal on the cards, a good/fair/reasonable bet.
OPPOSITES: unlikely.

probably adverb *I knew I would probably never see her again:* in all likelihood, in all probability, as likely as not, very likely, ten to one, the chances are, doubtless, no doubt.

probe noun *a probe into the alleged corruption:* investigation, enquiry, examination, inquest, exploration, study, analysis.
▷verb
1 *hands probed his body:* examine, feel, explore, check.
2 *police are probing the tragedy:* investigate, enquire into, look into, study, examine, scrutinize, analyse, go into, carry out an inquest into.

probity noun *the chancellor exuded confidence and fiscal probity:* integrity, honesty, uprightness, decency, morality, rectitude, virtue, right-mindedness, trustworthiness, truthfulness, honour.
OPPOSITES: untrustworthiness.

problem noun
1 *there was just one problem—the NHS would not pay for the treatment | he has some financial problems:* difficulty, trouble, worry, complication, difficult situation, dilemma, snag, hitch, drawback, stumbling block, obstacle, hurdle, hiccup, setback, catch; informal headache.
2 *I don't want to be a problem:* nuisance, bother, pest, irritant, thorn in your side/ flesh; informal drag, pain, pain in the neck.
3 *arithmetical problems:* puzzle, question, enigma, riddle, conundrum; informal brain-teaser, poser.

▷ **adjective** *a problem child:* troublesome, difficult, unmanageable, unruly, disobedient, uncontrollable, recalcitrant, delinquent.

problematic adjective *reducing subsidies for any goods or services is always a problematic political issue:* difficult, hard, taxing, tricky, awkward, controversial, ticklish, complicated, complex, knotty, thorny, prickly, vexed, troublesome; informal sticky.
OPPOSITES: easy, simple, straightforward.

procedure noun *the council agreed a procedure for dealing with future breaches of the law:* course of action, line of action, policy, series of steps, method, system, strategy, way, approach, formula, mechanism, methodology, MO (modus operandi), technique; routine, drill, practice.

proceed verb
1 *you need to sign these forms before we can proceed:* begin, make a start, get going, move, set something in motion; take action, act, go ahead, make progress, make headway.
2 *we should proceed with the talks:* go ahead, carry on, go on, continue, keep on, press on, push on; pursue.
3 *he proceeded down the road:* go, make your way, advance, move, progress, carry on.
4 *there is not enough evidence to proceed against him:* take someone to court, start/take proceedings against, prosecute, sue.
5 *all power proceeds from God:* originate, spring, stem, come, derive, arise, issue, flow, emanate.
OPPOSITES: stop.

proceedings plural noun
1 *the evening's proceedings got off to a good start:* events, activities, happenings, goings-on.
2 *criminal proceedings were brought against him:* legal action, court/judicial proceedings, litigation; lawsuit, case, prosecution.
3 *you should read the proceedings of the meeting:* report, record, minutes, transactions; annals, archives.

proceeds plural noun *all proceeds from the event will go to Animal Welfare:* profits, earnings, receipts, returns, takings, income, revenue.

process noun
1 *faxing a 70-page document is an expensive process:* procedure, operation, action, activity, exercise, affair, business, job, task, undertaking.
2 *a new manufacturing process:* method, system, technique, means, practice, way, approach, methodology.
▷ **verb** *applications are processed rapidly:* deal with, attend to, see to, sort out, handle, take care of, action.

□ **in the process of**
we are in the process of installing extra phone lines: in the middle of, in the midst of, busy with, occupied in/with, taken up with/by, involved in.

procession noun
1 *a procession through the town:* parade, march, cavalcade, motorcade, cortège; column, file, train.
2 *a procession of performances by different musicians:* series, succession, string, sequence.

proclaim verb
1 *messengers proclaimed the good news:* declare, announce, pronounce, state, make known, promulgate, trumpet, blazon.
2 *the men proclaimed their innocence:* assert, declare, profess, maintain, protest, avow, affirm.
3 *he proclaimed himself president:* declare, pronounce, announce, decree.

proclamation noun *the shooting resulted in the proclamation of a state of emergency:* declaration, announcement, pronouncement; decree, order, command, edict, ruling.

proclivity noun *his sexual proclivities are none of your business | she has a proclivity for hard work:* inclination, tendency, leaning, disposition, propensity, bent, bias, penchant, predisposition; predilection, partiality, liking, preference, taste, fondness, weakness.

procrastinate verb *fear of failure is often the reason why people procrastinate:* delay, put off doing something, postpone action, defer action, be dilatory, use delaying tactics, stall, temporize, drag your feet/heels, take your time, play for time, play a waiting game.

procreate verb *the biological imperative to procreate:* produce offspring, reproduce, multiply, propagate, breed.

procure verb *he managed to procure a ticket:* obtain, acquire, get, secure, pick up, find, come by; buy, purchase; informal get hold of, get your hands on.

prod verb
1 *Cassie prodded him in the chest:* poke, jab, dig, nudge, elbow, butt, stab.
2 *they hoped to prod the government into action:* spur, stimulate, stir, rouse, prompt, drive, galvanize; persuade, urge, chivvy, nudge; incite, goad, egg on, provoke.
▷ **noun**
1 *a prod in the ribs:* poke, jab, dig, nudge, butt.
2 *they need a prod to get them to act:* stimulus, push, prompt, reminder, spur; incitement, goad.

prodigal adjective
1 *prodigal habits die hard:* wasteful, extravagant, spendthrift, profligate, improvident, imprudent.

p

2 *a composer who is prodigal with his talents:* generous, lavish, liberal, unstinting, unsparing.
OPPOSITES: thrifty, mean.

prodigious adjective *his prodigious talent | a prodigious amount of work:* enormous, huge, colossal, immense, vast, great, massive, gigantic, mammoth, tremendous, stupendous, inordinate, monumental; amazing, astonishing, astounding, staggering, stunning, remarkable, phenomenal, terrific, impressive, striking, startling, sensational, spectacular, extraordinary, exceptional, breathtaking, incredible; informal fantastic, fabulous, awesome.
OPPOSITES: small, unexceptional.

prodigy noun
1 *a seven-year-old prodigy:* genius, mastermind, virtuoso, wunderkind; informal whizz-kid.
2 *Germany seemed a prodigy of industrial discipline:* model, classic example, paragon, paradigm, epitome, exemplar, archetype.

produce verb
1 *the firm was producing furniture of a very high standard:* manufacture, make, construct, build, fabricate, put together, assemble, turn out, create; mass-produce.
2 *the vineyards produce excellent wines:* yield, give, supply, provide, furnish.
3 *she produced ten puppies:* give birth to, bear, deliver.
4 *this decision produced a fierce reaction:* give rise to, bring about, cause, occasion, generate, engender, lead to, result in, effect, induce, set off; provoke, precipitate, breed, spark off, trigger.
5 *she produced an ID card:* pull out, extract, fish out; present, offer, proffer, show, display.
6 *no evidence was produced:* present, offer, provide, furnish, advance, put forward, bring forward, come up with.
7 *he produced and directed two of the plays:* stage, put on, mount, present.
▷ **noun** *the demand for organic produce is increasing:* food, foodstuffs, products; crops, fruit, vegetables.

producer noun
1 *a car producer:* manufacturer, maker, builder, constructor, fabricator.
2 *coffee producers:* grower, farmer.
3 *the producer of the show:* impresario, manager, administrator, promoter.

product noun
1 *a household product:* commodity, manufactured article; artefact, creation, invention; (**products**) goods, wares, merchandise, produce.
2 *his skill is a product of experience:* result, consequence, outcome, effect, upshot, fruit.

production noun
1 *the production of cars:* manufacture, making, construction, building,
fabrication, assembly; mass production.
2 *agricultural production:* output, yield; productivity.
3 *admission only on production of a valid ticket:* presentation, proffering, display.
4 *a theatre production:* performance, staging, presentation, show, piece, play.

productive adjective
1 *a productive artist:* prolific, inventive, creative.
2 *the discussions were very productive:* useful, constructive, profitable, fruitful, gainful, valuable, effective, worthwhile, helpful, beneficial.
3 *productive land:* fertile, fruitful, rich, fecund.

productivity noun
1 *workers have boosted productivity by 30 per cent:* efficiency, work rate; output, yield, production.
2 *the productivity of the soil:* fruitfulness, fertility, richness, fecundity.

profane adjective
1 *subjects both sacred and profane:* secular, lay, non-religious, temporal.
2 *profane language:* obscene, blasphemous, indecent, offensive, foul, vulgar, crude, filthy, dirty, smutty, coarse, rude, indecorous.
OPPOSITES: sacred, holy, decorous.
▷ **verb** *invaders profaned our temples:* desecrate, violate, defile.

profanity noun
1 *he hissed a profanity | an outburst of profanity:* oath, swear word, expletive, curse, obscenity, four-letter word; blasphemy, swearing, bad language, cursing; formal imprecation.
2 *some traditional festivals were tainted with profanity:* sacrilege, blasphemy, irreligion, ungodliness, impiety, disrespect.

profess verb
1 *he professed his love for her:* declare, announce, proclaim, assert, state, affirm, avow, maintain, protest.
2 *she professed to loathe publicity:* claim, purport, affect, pretend; make out.

professed adjective
1 *for all her professed populism, she was seen as remote from ordinary people:* supposed, purported, ostensible, self-styled; apparent.
2 *a professed Christian:* declared, self-acknowledged, self-confessed, confessed, sworn, avowed, confirmed.

profession noun
1 *his chosen profession of teaching:* career, occupation, calling, vocation, métier, line of work, job, business, employment, trade, craft.
2 *her professions of delight rang hollow:* declaration, assertion, avowal, claim, protestation.

professional adjective
1 *people in professional occupations:*
white-collar, non-manual.
2 *a professional cricketer:* paid, salaried.
3 *a thoroughly professional performance:*
expert, accomplished, skilful, masterly,
masterful, fine, polished, skilled,
proficient, competent, able, experienced,
practised, trained, seasoned, deft.
4 *he has not behaved in a very professional
way:* appropriate, fitting, proper,
honourable, ethical, correct.
OPPOSITES: manual, amateur,
unprofessional.

proffer verb *Coleman proffered his
resignation | I proffered my warrant card:*
offer, tender, submit, volunteer, suggest,
propose, put forward; extend, hold out.

proficiency noun skill, expertise,
experience, accomplishment, competence,
mastery, prowess, professionalism,
deftness, adroitness, dexterity, finesse,
ability, facility; informal know-how.
OPPOSITES: incompetence.

proficient adjective *a proficient
horsewoman:* skilled, skilful, expert,
experienced, accomplished, competent,
masterly, adept, adroit, deft, dexterous,
able, professional, consummate, master;
informal crack, ace, mean.
OPPOSITES: incompetent.

profile noun
1 *his handsome profile:* side view, outline,
silhouette, contour, shape, form.
2 *he opens his profile of Brando by
recounting a legendary scene from an early
film:* description, account, study, portrait,
portrayal, depiction, sketch, outline.
▷ **verb** *he was profiled in the Irish Times:*
describe, write about, give an account of,
portray, depict.
□ **keep a low profile**
lie low, keep quiet, keep out of the public
eye, avoid publicity, keep out of sight.

profit noun
1 *the company has registered record pre-tax
profits:* financial gains, returns, yield,
proceeds, earnings, surplus, excess; informal
bottom line.
2 *there was little profit in going on:*
advantage, benefit, value, use, good, avail;
informal mileage.
OPPOSITES: loss, disadvantage.
▷ **verb**
1 *the only people to profit from the episode
were the lawyers:* make money out of,
make a profit out of, gain from, benefit
from, derive benefit from, do well out of.
2 *it would profit us to change our plans:*
benefit, be beneficial, be of benefit to,
be advantageous to, be of advantage to, be
of use to, pay, be of value to.

profitable adjective
1 *a profitable company:* moneymaking,
profit-making, commercial, successful,

solvent, in the black, gainful,
remunerative, financially rewarding,
paying, lucrative, bankable.
2 *he'd had a very profitable day:* rewarding,
productive, valuable, fruitful, useful,
beneficial, worthwhile, well spent.
OPPOSITES: unprofitable, fruitless.

profiteer verb *seven shopkeepers were
charged with profiteering:* overcharge,
racketeer; cheat someone; informal rip
someone off, fleece someone, rob
someone.

profligate adjective
1 *profligate local authorities:* wasteful,
extravagant, spendthrift, improvident,
prodigal.
2 *a profligate lifestyle:* dissolute,
degenerate, dissipated, debauched,
corrupt; promiscuous, licentious, libertine,
decadent, loose-living.
OPPOSITES: thrifty, frugal.
▷ **noun** *he was an out-and-out profligate:*
libertine, debauchee, degenerate, roué,
rake.

profound adjective
1 *a feeling of profound relief | they
expressed their profound sympathy for
all the victims:* heartfelt, intense, keen,
great, extreme, acute; deep, deep-seated,
overpowering, overwhelming, fervent,
ardent, sincere, earnest.
2 *the profound silence was unnerving:*
complete, utter, total, absolute.
3 *the film evokes a society in the throes of
profound change:* far-reaching, radical,
extensive, sweeping, thoroughgoing.
4 *a profound analysis of modern global
capitalism:* learned, scholarly, sage,
erudite, intelligent, wise; discerning,
penetrating, perceptive, astute,
thoughtful, insightful, percipient.
5 *profound truths are expressed in simple
language:* complex, abstract, deep,
weighty.
OPPOSITES: superficial, mild, slight.

profuse adjective
1 *he offered profuse apologies | his
performances have won profuse media
accolades:* copious, prolific, abundant,
unstinting, fulsome, effusive, extravagant,
lavish, gushing; informal over the top.
2 *the recent heavy rains have encouraged
profuse growth:* luxuriant, plentiful,
abundant, lush, rich, riotous, teeming,
rampant.
OPPOSITES: meagre, sparse.

profusion noun *a rich profusion
of shrubs and flowers:* abundance,
mass, host, cornucopia, riot, plethora,
superabundance; informal wealth.

progenitor noun
1 *the progenitor of an illustrious family:*
ancestor, forefather, forebear, parent,
primogenitor.
2 *the progenitor of modern jazz:* originator,

p

creator, founder, architect, inventor, pioneer.

progeny noun *physical characteristics are passed on from parents to their progeny:* offspring, young, babies, children, sons and daughters, family, brood; descendants, heirs, scions.

prognosis noun
1 *his prognosis looks good though treatment will need to be long term:* outlook, future, prospects.
2 *my prognosis is that she will make a full recovery:* forecast, prediction; opinion, belief, view, judgement.

programme noun
1 *our programme for the day:* schedule, agenda, timetable, calendar; order of events, line-up.
2 *the government's reform programme:* scheme, plan of action, series of measures, strategy.
3 *a television programme:* broadcast, production, show, presentation, transmission, performance, telecast.
4 *a programme of study:* course, syllabus, curriculum.
▷verb *demolition of these properties is programmed for next year:* schedule, plan, timetable, line up; arrange, organize, map out.

progress noun
1 *the strong headwind made progress difficult:* forward movement, advance, progression, headway.
2 *scientific progress seems to accelerate all the time:* development, advance, advancement, headway, step forward; improvement, betterment, growth.
▷verb
1 *they progressed slowly down the road:* go, make your way, move, move forward, go forward, proceed, advance, go on, continue, make headway, work your way.
2 *the school has progressed rapidly:* develop, make progress, advance, make headway, take steps forward, move on, proceed; improve, get better, come on, make strides.
□in progress
work on the building is in progress: under way, going on, ongoing, happening, occurring, taking place, proceeding, continuing; unfinished.

progression noun *progression to the next stage depends on the test results:* progress, advancement, movement, passage; development, growth.

progressive adjective
1 *dementia is a progressive deterioration in the functioning of the brain:* continuing, continuous, increasing, growing, developing, ongoing; gradual, step-by-step, cumulative, steady.
2 *he has very progressive views:* modern, liberal, advanced, forward-thinking,

enlightened, innovative, pioneering, dynamic, bold, avant-garde, reforming, reformist, radical; informal go-ahead.
OPPOSITES: conservative, reactionary.

prohibit verb
1 *a city by-law prohibits the use of public parks for demonstrations:* forbid, ban, interdict, proscribe, make illegal, embargo, outlaw, disallow, veto, bar.
2 *a cash shortage prohibited the visit:* prevent, stop, rule out, preclude, make impossible.
OPPOSITES: allow.

prohibited adjective *smoking is prohibited in many public places:* forbidden, banned, not permitted; illegal, against the law.

prohibition noun
1 *the prohibition of performance-enhancing drugs including steroids and amphetamines:* banning, forbidding, prohibiting, debarment, vetoing, proscription, interdiction, outlawing.
2 *a prohibition was imposed:* ban, bar, veto, embargo, injunction, moratorium, interdict.

prohibitive adjective *the cost of the project was simply prohibitive:* excessively high, extortionate, unreasonable, exorbitant; out of the question, beyond your means; informal steep.

project noun
1 *an engineering project:* scheme, plan, programme, enterprise, undertaking, venture; proposal, idea, concept.
2 *I've got a history project to hand in next week:* assignment, piece of work, piece of research, task.
▷verb
1 *profits are projected to rise this year:* forecast, predict, expect, estimate, calculate, reckon; extrapolate.
2 *his projected book:* intend, plan, propose, devise, design, outline.
3 *balconies projected over the lake:* stick out, jut out, protrude, extend, stand out, bulge out, poke out, overhang.
4 *he tried to project an image of strength and resolution:* convey, put across, put over, communicate, present.
5 *the single light projected shadows on the wall:* cast, throw, send, shed, shine.
6 *seeds are projected from the tree:* propel, discharge, send, throw, cast, fling, hurl, shoot.

projectile noun missile.

projecting adjective *a series of projecting timber masts and struts:* sticking out, protuberant, protruding, prominent, jutting; overhanging.

projection noun
1 *a sales projection:* forecast, prediction, prognosis, expectation, estimate.
2 *tiny projections on the cliff face:* protuberance, protrusion, prominence,

eminence, outcrop, outgrowth, jut, jag, snag; overhang, ledge, shelf.

proletarian adjective *a proletarian background:* working-class, plebeian.
▷ noun *disaffected proletarians:* working-class person, worker, plebeian; derogatory prole.

proletariat noun the workers, working-class people, wage-earners, the labouring classes, the masses, the commonalty, the rank and file, the third estate, the plebeians; informal the great unwashed; derogatory the hoi polloi, the plebs, the proles.

proliferate verb *hackers, viruses, worms, spam, spyware, and phishing sites continue to proliferate:* multiply, increase in number, become more numerous, mushroom, snowball.
OPPOSITES: decrease, dwindle.

prolific adjective
1 *Haydn was a prolific composer:* productive, creative, inventive, fertile.
2 *an island with prolific bird life:* plentiful, abundant, bountiful, profuse, copious, rich.

prolix adjective *his prolix speeches could often be tiresome:* long-winded, verbose, wordy, discursive, rambling, long-drawn-out, lengthy, overlong, protracted, interminable; Brit. informal waffly.

prologue noun *the prologue to his book:* introduction, foreword, preface, preamble, prelude; informal intro.
OPPOSITES: epilogue.

prolong verb *unwilling to prolong the conversation, Kate said her goodbyes:* lengthen, extend, draw out, drag out, protract, spin out, stretch out, string out, elongate; carry on, continue, keep up.
OPPOSITES: shorten.

promenade noun
1 *the tree-lined promenade:* esplanade, front, seafront, parade, walk, boulevard, avenue; N. Amer. boardwalk; Brit. informal prom.
2 *our nightly promenade:* walk, stroll.
▷ verb *we promenaded along the waterfront:* walk, stroll, saunter, wander, amble, take a turn; stretch your legs.

prominence noun
1 *his growing prominence as one of the UK's finest leading actors:* fame, celebrity, eminence, pre-eminence, importance, distinction, renown, notability, prestige, stature, standing, position.
2 *the press gave prominence to the reports:* good coverage, importance, a high profile, top billing.
3 *a rocky prominence:* hillock, hill, mound; outcrop, crag, spur, rise, ridge; peak, pinnacle; promontory, cliff, headland.

prominent adjective
1 *a prominent surgeon:* important, well known, leading, eminent, distinguished, notable, noteworthy, noted, illustrious, celebrated, famous, renowned, acclaimed, famed.
2 *a prominent feature of the landscape:* conspicuous, noticeable, easily seen, obvious, unmistakable, eye-catching, pronounced, salient, striking, dominant; obtrusive.
3 *his large, red, prominent ears:* protuberant, protruding, projecting, jutting out, standing out, sticking out; bulging, bulbous.
OPPOSITES: unimportant, unknown, inconspicuous.

promiscuous adjective sexually indiscriminate, licentious, wanton, immoral, of easy virtue, fast; informal easy.
OPPOSITES: chaste, virtuous.

promise noun
1 *you broke your promise:* word, word of honour, assurance, pledge, vow, guarantee, oath, bond, undertaking, agreement, commitment, contract, covenant.
2 *he shows promise:* potential, ability, aptitude, capability, capacity.
3 *dawn came with a promise of fine weather:* indication, hint, suggestion, sign.
▷ verb
1 *she promised to go with me:* give your word, swear, pledge, vow, undertake, guarantee, contract, engage, give an assurance, commit yourself, bind yourself, swear/take an oath, covenant.
2 *the skies promised sunshine:* indicate, lead you to expect, point to, denote, signify, be a sign of, be evidence of, give hope of, presage, augur, herald, bode, portend; formal bespeak.

promising adjective
1 *it was a promising start to the season | he has a promising future ahead of him:* good, encouraging, favourable, hopeful, full of promise, auspicious, propitious, bright, rosy.
2 *a promising actor:* with potential, budding, up-and-coming, rising, coming, in the making; talented.
OPPOSITES: unfavourable, bad.

promontory noun headland, point, cape, head, foreland, spit, peninsula; Scottish mull.

promote verb
1 *policies designed to promote economic growth and stability in the developing countries:* encourage, further, advance, assist, aid, help, contribute to, support, foster, nurture, develop, boost, stimulate.
2 *she's been promoted at work:* upgrade, give promotion to, elevate, advance, move up.
3 *he's promoting his new film:* advertise, publicize, give publicity to, beat/bang the drum for, market; informal push, plug, hype.
OPPOSITES: obstruct, demote.

promoter noun *the president was a fierce promoter of European integration:* advocate, champion, supporter, backer, proponent, campaigner.

p

promotion noun
1 *her promotion means a big pay increase:*
upgrading, preferment, elevation,
advancement, step up.
2 *the fund was launched in April 1993 for
the promotion of science and technology in
the country:* encouragement, furtherance,
furthering, advancement, assistance,
contribution to, fostering, stimulation.
3 *the promotion of his latest album:*
advertising, publicizing, marketing;
publicity, campaign; informal hype.
OPPOSITES: demotion, obstruction.

prompt verb
1 *curiosity prompted him to look inside:*
induce, make, move, motivate, lead,
persuade, incline, encourage, stimulate,
prod, impel, spur on, inspire.
2 *the statement prompted an angry
response from local residents:* give rise to,
bring about, cause, occasion, result in, lead
to, elicit, produce, engender, precipitate,
trigger, spark off, provoke.
3 *'You were saying?' she prompted him,
when he looked lost in thought:* remind,
cue, help out; jog someone's memory.
OPPOSITES: deter.
▷**adjective** *a prompt reply:* quick, swift,
rapid, speedy, fast, direct, immediate,
instant, expeditious, early, punctual, in
good time, on time, timely.
OPPOSITES: slow, late.
▷**adverb** *he set off at 3.30 prompt:* exactly,
precisely, sharp, on the dot, punctually, on
the nail.

promptly adverb
1 *Will arrived promptly at 7.30:*
punctually, on time; informal on the dot,
bang on.
2 *I expect the matter to be dealt with
promptly:* without delay, straight away,
right away, at once, immediately, now, as
soon as possible; quickly, swiftly, rapidly,
speedily, fast, expeditiously; informal pronto,
asap.
OPPOSITES: late, slowly.

promulgate verb
1 *he continued to develop and promulgate
his right-wing views:* make known, make
public, publicize, spread, communicate,
propagate, disseminate, broadcast,
promote, preach.
2 *the law was promulgated in 1942:* put
into effect, enact, implement, enforce.

prone adjective
1 *farmed fish are prone to diseases:*
susceptible, vulnerable, subject, liable; at
risk of.
2 *she's prone to jump to conclusions:* given,
predisposed, likely, disposed, inclined, apt.
3 *she was lying prone on the mattress | his
prone body:* face down, face downwards,
on your stomach/front; lying flat,
horizontal, prostrate.
OPPOSITES: resistant, immune, upright.

prong noun tine, spike, point, tip,
projection.

pronounce verb
1 *his name is quite difficult to pronounce:*
say, enunciate, articulate, utter, voice,
vocalize, get your tongue round.
2 *the House of Lords pronounced that he
could be prosecuted for former crimes
against humanity:* announce, proclaim,
declare, affirm, assert; judge, rule, decree.

pronounced adjective *a deep voice with
a pronounced German accent | she had a
pronounced limp:* marked, strong, distinct,
definite, decided, conspicuous, striking,
noticeable, prominent, unmistakable,
obvious, recognizable, identifiable.
OPPOSITES: slight.

pronouncement noun *his public
pronouncements were brilliantly timed and
phrased:* announcement, proclamation,
declaration, assertion; judgement, ruling,
decree.

pronunciation noun *his English was
fluent and his pronunciation excellent:*
enunciation, articulation, vocalization;
accent, way of speaking, diction, elocution.

proof noun *proof of ownership may
be important for insurance purposes:*
evidence, verification, corroboration,
authentication, confirmation, certification,
documentation, validation, attestation,
substantiation.
▷**adjective** *armour could not be made proof
against bullets without being excessively
heavy:* resistant, immune, unaffected,
invulnerable, impenetrable, impervious,
repellent.

prop noun
1 *the roof is held up by props:* pole, post,
support, upright, brace, buttress, stay,
strut, stanchion, pier.
2 *for more than a decade, the organization
has acted as the main political prop of the
Italian social democrats:* mainstay, pillar,
anchor, backbone, support, foundation,
cornerstone.
▷**verb**
1 *he propped his bike against the wall:* lean,
rest, stand, balance, steady.
2 *this post is propping the wall up:* hold
up, shore up, bolster up, buttress, support,
brace, underpin.
3 *they prop up loss-making industries:*
subsidize, underwrite, fund, finance,
support.

propaganda noun *political propaganda:*
information, promotion, advertising,
publicity; agitprop, disinformation,
counter-information, brainwashing.

propagandist noun *an enthusiastic
propagandist for the government's
reforms:* promoter, champion, supporter,
proponent, advocate, campaigner,
crusader, publicist, evangelist, apostle.

p

propagate verb
1 *try propagating your own house plants from cuttings:* cultivate, grow, breed.
2 *these shrubs propagate easily:* reproduce, multiply, proliferate, spread, self-seed, self-sow.
3 *they propagated socialist ideas:* spread, disseminate, communicate, make known, promulgate, circulate, broadcast, publicize, proclaim, preach, promote.

propel verb
1 *a boat propelled by oars:* move, power, push, drive.
2 *confusion propelled her into action:* spur, drive, prompt, precipitate, catapult, motivate, force, impel.

propensity noun
a criminal record is objective evidence of a propensity to commit further offences: tendency, inclination, predisposition, proneness, proclivity, readiness, liability, disposition.

proper adjective
1 *he's not a proper scientist:* real, genuine, actual, true, bona fide; informal kosher.
2 *they had not followed the proper procedures:* right, correct, accepted, orthodox, conventional, established, official, formal, regular, appropriate, suitable.
3 *they were terribly proper:* respectable, decorous, seemly, refined, ladylike, gentlemanly, genteel; formal, conventional, correct, comme il faut, polite, punctilious.
OPPOSITES: fake, wrong.

property noun
1 *she wanted Oliver and his property out of the flat by the weekend:* possessions, belongings, things, effects, chattels, goods and chattels; informal gear, stuff.
2 *private property—keep off | plans for major renovation work on council properties in the area:* building/buildings, house/houses, premises; land, estates; N. Amer. real estate.
3 *garlic is known for its healing properties:* quality, attribute, characteristic, feature, power, trait, mark, hallmark.

prophecy noun
1 *her prophecy is coming true:* prediction, forecast, prognostication, prognosis.
2 *the gift of prophecy:* foretelling the future, fortune-telling, second sight, soothsaying.

prophesy verb
many commentators prophesied disaster: predict, foretell, forecast, foresee, forewarn of, prognosticate.

prophet, prophetess noun
seer, soothsayer; (in ancient Greece or Rome) oracle, sibyl.
□ **prophet of doom** pessimist, doom-monger, doomsayer, Cassandra, Jeremiah; informal doom and gloom merchant.

prophetic adjective
his words proved prophetic—in less than a week he was dead: prescient, far-seeing, prognostic, divinatory.

prophylactic adjective
prophylactic measures: preventive, preventative, precautionary, protective.
▷ **noun** *a prophylactic against malaria:* preventive measure, precaution, safeguard, safety measure; preventive medicine.

prophylaxis noun
the use of HRT as a prophylaxis against osteoporosis: preventive treatment, prevention, protection, precaution.

propitiate verb
George's attempts to propitiate his father did not work: appease, placate, mollify, pacify, make peace with, conciliate, make amends to, soothe, calm.
OPPOSITES: provoke.

propitious adjective
the timing for such a meeting seemed propitious: favourable, auspicious, promising, providential, advantageous, heaven-sent, hopeful; opportune, timely.
OPPOSITES: inauspicious.

proponent noun
a strong proponent of the free market and liberal trade policies: advocate, champion, supporter, backer, promoter, protagonist, campaigner.

proportion noun
1 *a small proportion of the population | a higher proportion of US citizens attend religious services than any other industrial nation:* part, amount, quantity, percentage, section, segment, share; number.
2 *the proportion of water to alcohol:* ratio, distribution, relative amount/number; relationship.
3 *this could lead to a humanitarian crisis of huge proportions:* size, dimensions, magnitude; measurements.

proportional, proportionate
adjective *an increase in working hours unaccompanied by a proportional increase in wages:* corresponding, proportionate, comparable, in proportion, pro rata, commensurate, equivalent, consistent, relative, analogous.
OPPOSITES: disproportionate.

proposal noun
the proposal was rejected: scheme, plan, idea, project, motion, proposition, suggestion, submission; bid, tender.

propose verb
1 *he proposed a solution:* put forward, suggest, submit, advance, offer, present, move, come up with, table; nominate.
2 *do you propose to go?* intend, mean, plan, have in mind/view, aim, want.
OPPOSITES: withdraw.

proposition noun
1 *the analysis derives from one proposition:*

p

theory, hypothesis, thesis, argument,
premise, theorem, concept, idea, statement.
2 *a business proposition:* proposal, scheme,
plan, project, suggestion, idea.
3 *United faced Arsenal in the semi-final, a
difficult proposition for any team:* task, job,
undertaking, venture, activity, affair.

propound verb *the theory of relativity
was first propounded by Albert Einstein:*
put forward, propose, advance, present,
set forth, submit, suggest, postulate, posit.

proprietor, **proprietress** noun
owner, possessor, holder; landowner,
landlord/landlady; innkeeper, hotel-
keeper, hotelier, restaurateur; Brit. publican.

propriety noun
1 *he behaved with the utmost propriety:*
decorum, respectability, decency,
correctness, protocol, appropriateness,
good manners, courtesy, politeness,
rectitude, morality, civility, modesty,
seemliness; sobriety, refinement,
discretion, delicacy.
2 *he was careful to preserve the proprieties
in public:* etiquette, conventions, social
graces, niceties, your Ps and Qs, protocol,
standards, civilities, formalities.
OPPOSITES: impropriety.

propulsion noun *these seabirds use their
wings for propulsion under water:* thrust,
motive force, impetus, impulse, drive,
driving force, push, pressure, power.

prosaic adjective *the prosaic nature of day-
to-day life | at times the writing is rather
prosaic:* ordinary, everyday, commonplace,
conventional, straightforward, routine,
run-of-the-mill, workaday; unimaginative,
uninspired, uninspiring, matter-of-
fact, dull, dry, dreary, tedious, boring,
humdrum, mundane, pedestrian,
lacklustre, plodding; bland, banal, trite.
OPPOSITES: interesting, imaginative,
inspired.

proscribe verb
1 *gambling was proscribed:* forbid,
prohibit, ban, bar, interdict, make illegal,
embargo, outlaw, disallow, veto.
2 *the practice was proscribed by the
Catholic Church:* condemn, denounce,
attack, criticize, censure.
OPPOSITES: allow, accept.

USAGE

Do not confuse **proscribe** and **prescribe**.
The main meaning of **proscribe** is 'to forbid
something officially'. **Prescribe** means
either 'to issue a medical prescription' (*her
GP prescribed a course of antibiotics*) or 'to
state authoritatively that something should be
done' (*the rules which prescribe five acts for a
play are purely arbitrary*).
---

proscription noun
1 *the proscription of alcohol:* banning,
forbidding, prohibition, prohibiting,

vetoing, interdiction, outlawing.
2 *a proscription was imposed:* ban,
prohibition, bar, interdict, veto, embargo,
moratorium.

prosecute verb
1 *we always prosecute shoplifters:* take to
court, bring/institute legal proceedings
against, bring an action against, take legal
action against, sue, try, bring to trial, put
on trial.
2 *this was a serious threat to the
government's ability to prosecute the war:*
pursue, carry on, conduct, engage in,
proceed with, continue.

prospect noun
1 *there is little prospect of a reconciliation:*
likelihood, hope, expectation, anticipation,
chance, odds, probability, possibility,
promise, lookout; danger.
2 *unemployed people who want to improve
their job prospects:* chances, opportunities;
possibilities, expectations, outlook, future.
3 *the daunting prospect of going it alone
kept stopping her:* idea, thought, vision.
4 *a viewpoint commanding a magnificent
prospect of the estuary:* view, vista,
outlook, panorama, aspect.
▷ verb *they are prospecting for oil:* search,
look, explore, survey, scout, hunt.
□ in prospect
*another period of economic instability was
in prospect:* expected, likely, on the way,
to come, at hand, near, imminent, in the
offing, in store, on the horizon, in the air,
in the wind, looming; informal on the cards.

prospective adjective *a prospective
buyer | prospective changes in government
legislation:* potential, possible, probable,
likely, future, eventual, -to-be, in the
making; intending, aspiring, would-be;
forthcoming.

prosper verb *the European personal
computer market continued to prosper:*
flourish, thrive, burgeon, boom, expand,
do well, bloom, blossom, progress, be
successful; informal go places.
OPPOSITES: fail.

prosperity noun *Britain's prosperity
depends on its exports:* success,
profitability, affluence, wealth; security,
well-being.

prosperous adjective *a prosperous
shipping firm | prosperous middle-class
professionals:* thriving, flourishing,
successful, profitable, lucrative,
expanding, booming, burgeoning; affluent,
wealthy, rich, moneyed, well off; informal
rolling in it, on the up and up, in the money.
OPPOSITES: ailing, poor.

prostitute noun sex worker, call girl; rent
boy; informal working girl, member of the
oldest profession; N. Amer. informal hooker;
derogatory whore.
▷ verb *artists who prostitute their talent for*

fame: betray, debase, degrade, demean, devalue, cheapen, misuse; abandon your principles, be untrue to yourself, sell out.

prostrate adjective
1 *the prostrate body of his victim:* prone, lying flat, lying down, stretched out, spreadeagled, horizontal; recumbent.
2 *his wife was prostrate with shock:* overwhelmed, overcome, overpowered, brought to your knees, stunned, dazed; speechless, helpless; informal knocked/hit for six.
OPPOSITES: upright, fresh.
▷ **verb** *she was prostrated by the tragedy:* overwhelm, overcome, overpower, bring someone to their knees, devastate; debilitate, weaken, enfeeble.
□ **prostrate yourself**
throw yourself on the ground, lie down, stretch yourself out, throw yourself at someone's feet.

protagonist noun
1 *the film's protagonist is an American intelligence officer:* central character, principal, hero/heroine, leading man/lady, title role, lead.
2 *a protagonist of deregulation:* champion, advocate, upholder, supporter, backer, promoter, proponent, exponent, campaigner, fighter, crusader; apostle, apologist.
OPPOSITES: opponent.

protect verb *he tried to protect Kelly from the attack | armed troops protect the convoys of vehicles transporting food and medical supplies:* keep safe, keep from harm, save, safeguard, preserve, defend, shield, cushion, insulate, shelter, screen; guard, watch over, look after, take care of.
OPPOSITES: expose, harm.

protection noun
1 *the protection of our natural habitat:* defence, preservation, conservation, safe keeping, safeguarding.
2 *he had sought the protection of the American Embassy:* safety, sanctuary, shelter, refuge, immunity.
3 *a strip of woodland provides good protection against noise:* barrier, buffer, shield, screen, cushion, bulwark.

protective adjective
1 *protective clothing should be worn at all times | last year's onslaught of computer viruses showed that some basic protective measures are still neglected:* defensive, safety, precautionary, preventive, preventative.
2 *he felt protective towards the girl:* solicitous, caring, paternal/maternal; overprotective, possessive, jealous.

protector noun
1 *he became her protector, adviser, and friend:* defender, guardian, champion, guardian angel, patron; chaperone, escort; bodyguard, minder; keeper, custodian; watchdog.

2 *ear protectors:* guard, shield.

protégé, protégée noun *Ruskin submitted his protégé's name for election:* pupil, student, trainee, apprentice; disciple, follower.

protest noun
1 *the programme of closures has prompted a wave of protests:* objection, complaint, cry of disapproval, remonstration, protestation, outcry.
2 *hundreds of employees staged a protest yesterday:* demonstration, march, rally; sit-in; work-to-rule, stoppage, strike, walkout; informal demo.
▷ **verb**
1 *residents protested at the plans:* express opposition, object, take issue, make/take a stand, put up a fight, complain, express disapproval, make a fuss, speak out; informal kick up a fuss.
2 *the workers have been protesting over unpaid wages:* demonstrate, march, hold a rally; work to rule, take industrial action, stop work, down tools, strike, go on strike, walk out.
3 *he protested that it had been an accident | she continued to protest her innocence:* insist, declare, maintain, assert, affirm, proclaim, profess, contend, argue, claim, vow, swear.
OPPOSITES: acquiesce, support, deny.

protestation noun
1 *his protestations of innocence were in vain:* declaration, profession, assertion, claim, assurance, vow.
2 *we helped him despite his protestations:* objection, protest, complaint; opposition, remonstration, outcry.

protocol noun
1 *a breach of protocol:* rules of conduct, procedure, accepted behaviour, conventions, formalities, customs, etiquette, propriety, proprieties, good form.
2 *the two countries signed a protocol:* agreement, treaty, entente, concordat, convention, deal, pact, contract, compact.

prototype noun
1 *our engineering team has completed a prototype of the new product:* original, first model, preliminary version; mock-up, sample; blueprint, template.
2 *the prototype of an ideal wife:* typical example, paradigm, archetype, exemplar.

protract verb *the Opposition will try to protract the discussion:* prolong, lengthen, extend, draw out, drag out, spin out, stretch out, string out, elongate; carry on, continue, keep up; filibuster.
OPPOSITES: curtail, shorten.

protracted adjective prolonged, long-lasting, extended, long-drawn-out, spun out, lengthy, long, overlong.
OPPOSITES: brief.

protrude verb *a handle protrudes from the*

p

motor housing: stick out, jut out, project, extend, stand out, bulge out, poke out, thrust out.

protruding adjective sticking out, protuberant, projecting, prominent, jutting, overhanging; bulging.

protrusion noun *the neck vertebrae have short vertical protrusions:* bump, lump, knob; protuberance, projection, prominence, outgrowth.

protuberance noun *on exhumation, his skull was found to have two horn-like protuberances:* bump, lump, knob, projection, protrusion, prominence, outgrowth; Biology & Anatomy process.

protuberant adjective sticking out, protruding, projecting, prominent, jutting, overhanging, proud, bulging; informal sticky-out.
OPPOSITES: sunken, flush.

proud adjective
1 *the proud parents beamed:* pleased, glad, happy, delighted, joyful, overjoyed, thrilled, satisfied, gratified, content.
2 *this is a proud day for the school:* pleasing, gratifying; happy, good, glorious, memorable, notable, red-letter.
3 *I'm not too proud to admit I'm wrong:* arrogant, self-important, full of yourself, conceited, vain, smug, complacent; informal big-headed, swollen-headed, too big for your boots, high and mighty, stuck-up.
4 *the family were poor but proud:* self-respecting, dignified.
OPPOSITES: ashamed, shameful, humble, modest.

prove verb
1 *that proves I'm right* | *the accusation is difficult to prove:* show, show to be true, demonstrate, demonstrate the truth of, show beyond doubt, produce proof/evidence; witness to, give substance to, substantiate, corroborate, verify, validate, authenticate, bear out, confirm, establish.
2 *the rumour proved to be correct:* turn out, be found, happen.
OPPOSITES: disprove.
□ **prove yourself**
he saw the race as an opportunity to prove himself to his father: demonstrate your abilities/qualities, show your mettle, show what you are made of.

provenance noun *the police were suspicious about the provenance of the paintings* | *words of French provenance:* origin, source, place of origin; pedigree, derivation, root; Linguistics etymology.

proverb noun saying, adage, saw, maxim, axiom, motto, aphorism, epigram; words of wisdom; rare apophthegm.

proverbial adjective *the pirate's greed was as proverbial as his cowardice:* well known, famous, famed, renowned, traditional,

time-honoured, legendary; notorious, infamous.

provide verb
1 *the International Development Research Centre provided the funds for the project:* supply, give, issue, furnish, come up with, bestow, donate, contribute, pledge, put up; informal fork out, lay out.
2 *he was provided with the necessary tools:* equip, issue, supply, outfit; fit out, rig out, kit out, arm, provision, furnish; informal fix up.
3 *this technology may provide a solution to housing shortages in developing nations:* present, produce, yield, offer, afford, give, bring.
4 *we have provided for further restructuring:* prepare, allow, make provision, be prepared, get ready, plan, cater.
5 *he had to provide for his family:* support, maintain, keep, sustain, provide sustenance for, feed; finance.
6 *the banks have to provide against bad debts:* take precautions, take steps/measures, guard, forearm yourself; make provision for.
7 *the Act provides that factories must be kept clean:* stipulate, lay down, make it a condition, require, order, ordain, demand, prescribe, state, specify.
OPPOSITES: refuse, deprive.

provided conjunction *the plant needs no special cultivation, provided it has well-drained soil:* if, on condition that, providing, presuming, assuming, on the assumption that, as long as, given that, with the provision/proviso that, with/on the understanding that, contingent on.

providence noun *a life mapped out by providence:* fate, destiny, God's will, divine intervention, the stars.

provident adjective *we have to be provident, but no real sacrifices are demanded:* prudent, far-sighted, careful, judicious, circumspect, sensible; thrifty, economical.
OPPOSITES: improvident.

providential adjective *the battle was won with the aid of a providential wind:* opportune, advantageous, favourable, auspicious, propitious, heaven-sent, welcome, lucky, fortunate, felicitous, timely, well timed, convenient, expedient.
OPPOSITES: inopportune.

provider noun *the state is still the main provider of welfare:* supplier, source, giver, contributor, donor.

providing conjunction. See **PROVIDED**.

province noun
1 *a province of the Ottoman Empire:* territory, region, state, department, canton, area, district, zone, division.
2 *people in the provinces:* non-metropolitan areas/counties, the rest of

the country, middle England, rural areas/ districts, the countryside, the backwoods; informal the sticks.
3 *she knew little about wine—that had been her father's province:* responsibility, area of activity, area of interest, area of knowledge, sphere, field, domain, territory, preserve; business, affair, concern; speciality, forte; jurisdiction, authority; informal bailiwick, department.

provincial adjective
1 *the provincial government | provincial elections:* regional, district, local; county.
2 *provincial areas:* non-metropolitan, rural, country, outlying, backwoods.
3 *they're so dull and provincial:* unsophisticated, narrow-minded, parochial, small-town, suburban, insular, parish-pump, inward-looking, conservative.
OPPOSITES: national, metropolitan, cosmopolitan.

provision noun
1 *the provision of food and drink:* supply, supplying, providing, giving, presentation, donation.
2 *there has been limited provision for gifted children:* facilities, services, amenities, resources, arrangements; means, funds, benefits, assistance, allowance.
3 *he made no provision for the future:* preparations, plans, arrangements, precautions, contingency plans.
4 *we stocked up on provisions for the trip:* supplies, food and drink, stores, groceries, foodstuffs, provender.
5 *the provisions of the Act:* term, clause; requirement, specification, stipulation; proviso, condition, qualification, restriction, limitation.

provisional adjective *the provisional government | a provisional booking:* interim, temporary, pro tem; transitional, changeover, stopgap, short-term, fill-in, acting, caretaker; to be confirmed, subject to confirmation, pencilled in, working, tentative.
OPPOSITES: permanent, definite.

provisionally adverb *the meeting was provisionally arranged for 9 October:* for the time being, pro tem, for the interim, for the present, for now; subject to confirmation, tentatively.

proviso noun *he let his house out for one year, with the proviso that his own staff should remain to run it:* condition, stipulation, provision, clause, rider, qualification, restriction, caveat.

provocation noun *he remained calm despite severe provocation:* goading, harassment, pressure; annoyance, irritation; informal hassle, aggravation.

provocative adjective
1 *provocative remarks:* annoying, irritating, exasperating, infuriating,
maddening, galling; insulting, offensive, inflammatory, incendiary, controversial, contentious.
2 *a provocative pose:* sexy, sexually arousing, sexually exciting, alluring, seductive, suggestive, inviting, tantalizing, titillating; coquettish, amorous, flirtatious; informal come-hither.

provoke verb
1 *the decision provoked a storm of protest from civil rights organizations:* arouse, cause, give rise to, engender, generate, result in, lead to, occasion, produce, bring on, precipitate, prompt, trigger, stimulate, spark off; elicit.
2 *he was provoked into replying:* goad, sting, rouse, stir, move, stimulate, spur, prod; egg on, incite.
3 *please try not to provoke him:* annoy, anger, incense, enrage, irritate, infuriate, exasperate, madden; tease, taunt, torment; informal aggravate, rile, needle, get someone's back up; Brit. informal wind up.
OPPOSITES: allay, deter, pacify.

prow noun *the prow of a ship:* bow, front, nose, head.

prowess noun
1 *his prowess as a winemaker | their culinary prowess:* skill, expertise, mastery, facility, ability, capability, capacity, talent, genius, adeptness, aptitude, dexterity, deftness, competence, accomplishment, proficiency, finesse; informal know-how.
2 *the knights' prowess in battle:* courage, bravery, gallantry, valour, heroism, intrepidity, nerve, pluck, pluckiness, boldness, daring, fearlessness.
OPPOSITES: inability, ineptitude, cowardice.

prowl verb *youths have been prowling around the back of the flats at night:* move stealthily, slink, skulk, steal, sneak, creep.

proximity noun *the development's proximity to local facilities and transport links:* closeness, nearness, propinquity; accessibility.

prude noun *he's very correct but no prude:* puritan, prig, killjoy, moralist; informal goody-goody.

prudence noun *his reputation for financial prudence:* caution, care, providence, far-sightedness, foresight, shrewdness, circumspection; wisdom, judgement, good judgement, common sense, sense, sagacity; thrift, economy.
OPPOSITES: folly, recklessness.

prudent adjective
1 *a prudent decision:* wise, well judged, sensible, politic, judicious, sage, shrewd, advisable, well advised.
2 *a prudent approach to borrowing:* cautious, careful, provident, far-sighted, judicious, shrewd, circumspect; thrifty, economical.
OPPOSITES: imprudent, reckless.

p

prudish adjective *his grandmother was a rather prudish woman:* prim, prim and proper, easily shocked/offended, priggish, puritanical, moralistic, sententious, censorious, strait-laced, stuffy; informal prissy.
OPPOSITES: permissive.

prune verb
1 *now is the time to prune your roses:* cut back, trim, thin out; pollard.
2 *prune any lateral shoots of wisteria:* cut off/away, lop off, chop off, clip, snip off, nip off, dock.
3 *staff numbers have been pruned:* reduce, cut, pare down, scale down, slim down, make reductions in, make cutbacks in, trim, decrease, downsize, shrink; informal slash.

prurient adjective *she'd been the subject of much prurient curiosity:* salacious, voyeuristic, lascivious.

pry verb *I'm sorry, I didn't mean to pry:* be inquisitive, interfere, intrude; informal stick/poke your nose in, be nosy, snoop.

pseudo adjective (informal) *she argued that many of the claims made by the diet were based on 'pseudo science' | a pseudo American accent:* bogus, sham, phoney, artificial, mock, ersatz, quasi-, fake, false, spurious; assumed, contrived, pretentious, affected, insincere; informal put-on.

pseudonym noun *Hanbury wrote a novel under the pseudonym of James Aston:* pen-name, nom de plume, assumed name, false name, alias, professional name, sobriquet, stage name, nom de guerre.

psych verb (informal)
□ **psych someone out**
guys try to lift heavy weights in a mistaken attempt to psych the others out: intimidate, daunt, cow, scare, frighten, dishearten, unnerve, subdue; browbeat, bully.
□ **psych yourself up**
we had to psych ourselves up for the race: nerve yourself, steel yourself, brace yourself, summon your courage, prepare yourself, gear yourself up, urge yourself on, gird (up) your loins.

psyche noun *Laura saw clearly the effect of beautiful surroundings on the psyche:* soul, spirit, inner self, inner man/woman, subconscious, mind.
OPPOSITES: body.

psychiatrist noun psychotherapist, psychoanalyst; informal shrink.

psychic adjective
1 *psychic powers | psychic experiences:* supernatural, paranormal, other-worldly, extrasensory.
2 *how would I know—I'm not psychic:* clairvoyant, telepathic, having second sight, having a sixth sense.
3 *the children's psychic development:* cognitive, psychological, intellectual, mental; emotional, spiritual, inner.
OPPOSITES: normal, physical.

▷ **noun** *she is a psychic:* clairvoyant, medium, spiritualist, telepathist, telepath, mind-reader.

psychological adjective
1 *his psychological state:* mental, emotional, intellectual, inner; cognitive.
2 *they believed that her pain was psychological:* psychosomatic, in the mind.
OPPOSITES: physical.

psychology noun *the psychology of the road user:* mindset, mind, mental processes, thought processes, way of thinking, cast of mind, mentality, persona, psyche, attitude, make-up.

pub noun (Brit.) bar, inn; Brit. public house; informal local, watering hole; old use hostelry, tavern.

puberty noun *the onset of puberty may occur as early as eleven or twelve:* adolescence, pubescence, sexual maturity.

public adjective
1 *public affairs | public services:* national, state; civic, civil, social, municipal, community, local; nationalized.
2 *the growing public concern over environmental issues | the company is simply responding to public demand:* popular, general, common, collective, shared, joint, universal, widespread.
3 *a public figure:* prominent, well known, important, influential, leading, noted; celebrated, household, famous.
4 *a public library | public amenities:* open to the public, communal, accessible to all, available, free, unrestricted, community.
5 *the news became public:* known, publicized, in circulation.
OPPOSITES: private, restricted.

▷ **noun**
1 *the British public:* people, citizens, subjects, general public, electors, electorate, voters, taxpayers, residents, inhabitants, citizenry, population, populace, community, society, country, nation, world; everyone.
2 *his adoring public:* audience, spectators, followers, following, fans, devotees, admirers; patrons, clientele, market, consumers, buyers, customers, readers.
□ **in public**
publicly, in open view, openly, in the open, for all to see; overtly, blatantly, flagrantly, brazenly.

WORD LINKS
agoraphobia a fear of open or public places

publication noun
1 *the author of this publication:* book, volume, title, work, opus; newspaper, paper, magazine, periodical, newsletter, organ, bulletin, journal, report; booklet, brochure, catalogue; humorous tome.
2 *the publication of her new book:* issuing, publishing, printing, appearance.

3 *the publication of the April trade figures:* announcement, notification, reporting, declaration, communication, proclamation, broadcasting, publicizing, distribution, dissemination.

publicity noun
1 *the case attracted wide publicity in the press:* public attention, public interest, public notice, media attention/interest, exposure; limelight.
2 *according to the advance publicity for the film, it is based on a number of different sources:* promotion, advertising; informal hype.

publicize verb
1 *I never publicize that fact:* make known, make public, publish, advertise, announce, report, communicate, broadcast, air; disclose, reveal, divulge.
2 *he just wants to publicize his book:* advertise, promote, talk up, push, beat the drum for; informal hype, plug.
OPPOSITES: conceal, suppress.

public-spirited adjective *the debris was left for public-spirited citizens to remove:* socially concerned, community-minded; philanthropic, charitable, humanitarian, altruistic, generous, unselfish.

publish verb
1 *we publish novels and reference books:* issue, bring out, produce, print.
2 *the findings of this inquiry were published in August 2001:* make known, make public, publicize, announce, report, post, broadcast, issue, put out, distribute, disseminate, circulate, communicate, air; disclose, reveal.

pucker verb *she puckered her forehead:* wrinkle, crinkle, crease, furrow, scrunch up, screw up; purse.

puckish adjective *he had a very puckish sense of humour:* mischievous, naughty, impish, roguish, playful; informal waggish.

pudding noun dessert, sweet, second course, last course; Brit. informal afters.

puddle noun *puddles of water:* pool; spill, splash.

puerile adjective *puerile behaviour | puerile jokes:* childish, juvenile, immature, infantile; silly, foolish, asinine, inane, fatuous, jejune.
OPPOSITES: mature, sensible.

puff noun
1 *a puff of wind:* gust, blast, flurry, rush, draught, waft, breeze, breath.
2 *he took a puff at his cigar:* pull; informal drag.
▷ verb
1 *he walked fast, puffing a little:* breathe heavily, pant, blow; gasp, fight for breath.
2 *she puffed at her cigarette:* smoke, draw on, drag on, suck at/on.
□ **puff out/up**
if she went for a walk her ankles puffed up: swell, become swollen, balloon up/out, become distended, become bloated; expand, inflate, enlarge.

puffy adjective *her face was red and puffy:* swollen, puffed up, bloated, distended, enlarged, inflated.

pugnacious adjective *the bouncer that night was a pugnacious 42-year-old from East London:* combative, aggressive, antagonistic, belligerent, bellicose, quarrelsome, argumentative, truculent, hostile, threatening, warlike; fiery, hot-tempered.
OPPOSITES: peaceable.

pull verb
1 *he pulled the box towards him:* tug, haul, drag, draw, tow, heave, jerk, wrench; informal yank, lug.
2 *he pulled a handkerchief out of his pocket:* extract, take out, remove.
3 *I've pulled a muscle:* strain, sprain, wrench, rick, tear; damage.
4 *in recent years, the Abba tribute band has pulled crowds of more than 30,000:* attract, draw, bring in, pull in; lure, seduce, entice, tempt, interest, fascinate.
OPPOSITES: push.
▷ noun
1 *give the chain another pull:* tug, jerk, heave; informal yank.
2 *she took a pull on her beer:* gulp, draught, drink, swallow, mouthful; informal swill, swig, slug.
3 *he took a long pull on a cigarette:* puff; informal drag.
4 *she felt the pull of the sea:* attraction, draw, lure, enticement, magnetism, temptation, fascination, appeal.
5 *he has a lot of pull in this city:* influence, sway, power, authority, say, prestige, standing, weight, leverage, muscle, teeth; informal clout.
□ **pull something apart**
dismantle, disassemble, take/pull to pieces, take/pull to bits, take apart, strip down; demolish, destroy, break up.
□ **pull back**
the army was forced to pull back: withdraw, retreat, fall back, back off; pull out, retire, disengage; flee, turn tail.
□ **pull something down**
several old buildings were pulled down: demolish, knock down, tear down, dismantle, raze to the ground, level, flatten, bulldoze, destroy.
□ **pull in**
a police car pulled in behind us: stop, draw up, halt, come to a halt, pull over, pull up, brake, park.
□ **pull someone/something in**
1 *they pulled in big audiences.* See PULL verb sense 4.
2 (informal) *the police pulled him in:* arrest, apprehend, detain, take into custody, seize, capture, catch; informal nab, nick, run in, bust.

p

□ **pull someone's leg**
tease, fool, play a trick on, pull the wool over someone's eyes; informal kid, have on, lead up the garden path, take for a ride; Brit. informal wind up.

□ **pull something off**
they pulled off a record sponsorship deal with the UK's second largest brewery: achieve, accomplish, bring off, carry off, perform, succeed in, complete, clinch, fix, effect, engineer.

□ **pull out**
one of their star players has pulled out with stomach trouble: withdraw, bow out, back out, give up; resign, leave, retire, step down; informal quit.

□ **pull through**
she has serious injuries, but we are all praying for her to pull through: get better, get well again, improve, recover, rally, come through, recuperate.

□ **pull something to pieces**
1 *don't pull my radio to pieces.* See PULL SOMETHING APART.
2 *they pulled the plan to pieces:* criticize, attack, find fault with, pillory, censure, condemn; informal knock, slam, pan, lay into; Brit. informal slate, rubbish.

□ **pull yourself together**
regain your composure, recover, get a grip on yourself, get over it; informal snap out of it, get your act together, buck up.

□ **pull up.** See PULL IN.

pulp noun
1 *boiling the vegetables for too long will reduce them to a pulp:* mush, mash, paste, purée, pap, slop.
2 *the fruit contains sweet, juicy pulp:* flesh.
▷ **verb** *pulp the gooseberries:* crush, mash, purée, press, squash, pound, macerate.
▷ **adjective** *pulp fiction:* trashy, cheap, sensational, lurid, tasteless; informal tacky.

pulsate verb
1 *a vein pulsated in his forehead:* palpitate, pulse, throb; flutter, quiver.
2 *loud music pulsated through the house:* vibrate, throb, pulse, beat, thump, drum, thrum

pulse noun
1 *she grabbed his wrist, and could feel a weak pulse:* heartbeat, pulsation, pulsing, throbbing, pounding.
2 *the pulse of the music:* rhythm, beat, tempo, cadence, pounding, thudding, drumming.
3 *pulses of ultrasound:* burst, blast, surge; vibration.
▷ **verb** *music pulsed through the building:* throb, pulsate, vibrate, pound, thud, thump, drum, thrum, reverberate.

pulverize verb *the seeds are pulverized into flour:* grind, crush, pound, powder, mill, press.

pummel verb *he felt like a boxer who had been pummelled mercilessly:* batter, pound, belabour, drub, beat; punch, strike, hit, thump, thrash; informal clobber, wallop, bash, whack, lay into.

pump verb
1 *an engine pumped air out of the tube:* force, drive, push; suck, draw, siphon, extract, drain.
2 *she pumped up the tyre:* inflate, blow up, fill up.
3 *blood was pumping from a wound on his leg:* spurt, spout, squirt, gush, stream, flow, pour, spill, run, course.

pun noun play on words, wordplay, double entendre, innuendo, witticism, quip, bon mot.

punch[1] **verb** *he punched her in the face and ran off:* hit, strike, thump, jab, smash, cuff, clip; batter, pound, pummel; informal sock, slug, biff, bop, wallop, clobber, bash, whack, thwack, clout; Brit. informal stick one on, slosh.
▷ **noun**
1 *a punch on the nose:* blow, hit, thump, jab, clip; uppercut, hook; informal slug, biff, bop, wallop, bash, whack, clout.
2 *this version of the song lacks much of the punch of the original:* vigour, vitality, strength, zest, verve, enthusiasm; impact, interest, excitement; informal oomph.

punch[2] **verb** *he punched her ticket:* make a hole in, perforate, puncture, pierce.

punchy adjective *he has a talent for comic timing and fast, punchy dialogue:* forceful, incisive, strong, powerful, vigorous, effective, impressive, compelling; dramatic, graphic, vivid; informal in-your-face.

punctilious adjective *his punctilious implementation of orders impressed the king:* meticulous, conscientious, diligent, scrupulous, careful, painstaking, rigorous, methodical, particular, strict; fussy, fastidious, finicky, pedantic; informal nit-picking; Brit. informal pernickety.

punctual adjective *she liked her guests to be punctual:* on time, prompt, on schedule, in (good) time.
OPPOSITES: late.

punctuate verb
1 *how to punctuate direct speech:* add punctuation to, put punctuation marks in, dot, apostrophize.
2 *slides punctuated the talk:* break up, interrupt, intersperse, pepper, sprinkle, scatter.

puncture noun
1 *surgeons operate through small punctures in the skin:* hole, perforation; cut, slit.
2 *my car has a puncture:* flat tyre; informal flat.
▷ **verb**
1 *the knife had punctured one of his lungs:* pierce, perforate, make a hole in, cut, slit, prick, spike.

2 *the earlier mood of optimism was punctured:* put an end to, cut short, deflate.

pundit noun *leading pundits predict a further interest-rate cut this year:* expert, authority, specialist, doyen, master, guru, sage, savant; informal buff.

pungent adjective
1 *the pungent smell of frying onions | a pungent taste:* strong, powerful, pervasive, penetrating; sharp, acid, sour, bitter, tart, vinegary; tangy, highly flavoured, aromatic, spicy, piquant, peppery, hot.
2 *he made some fairly pungent comments:* caustic, biting, trenchant, cutting, sardonic, acerbic, scathing, acrimonious, barbed, sharp, tart.
OPPOSITES: bland, mild.

punish verb
1 *I did wrong and I was punished for it:* discipline, bring someone to book, teach someone a lesson; Brit. informal give someone what for.
2 *higher charges would punish the poor:* penalize, unfairly disadvantage, hurt.
3 *the strikers punished the defence's mistakes:* exploit, take advantage of, turn to account, profit from, capitalize on, cash in on.

punishable adjective *money-laundering is a punishable offence:* illegal, unlawful, criminal, actionable, indictable, penal; outlawed, banned, forbidden, prohibited, proscribed.

punishing adjective *a punishing schedule:* arduous, demanding, taxing, onerous, burdensome, strenuous, rigorous, stressful, trying; hard, difficult, tough, exhausting, tiring, gruelling, crippling, relentless; informal killing.
OPPOSITES: easy.

punishment noun
1 *the punishment should fit the crime:* penalty, sanction; sentence; discipline.
2 *your machine can take a fair amount of punishment before falling to bits:* maltreatment, mistreatment, abuse, ill-use; damage.

WORD LINKS
penal, **punitive** relating to punishment

punitive adjective
1 *he called for punitive measures to tackle antisocial behaviour:* penal, disciplinary, corrective; N. Amer. correctional.
2 *the elderly could find themselves paying punitive taxes:* harsh, severe, stiff, crushing, crippling; high, sky-high, inflated, exorbitant, extortionate, excessive, inordinate, unreasonable; Brit. swingeing.

puny adjective
1 *he was rather a puny child:* undersized, undernourished, slight, small; weak, feeble, sickly, delicate, frail; informal weedy.

2 *profits were $1.5 million—a puny amount for a company as big as this:* pitiful, pitiable, inadequate, insufficient, derisory, miserable, sorry, meagre, paltry, trifling; informal pathetic, measly.
OPPOSITES: sturdy, substantial.

pupil noun
1 *former pupils of the school:* student, scholar; schoolchild, schoolboy, schoolgirl.
2 *the guru's pupils:* disciple, follower, student, protégé.

puppet noun
1 *a puppet show:* marionette.
2 *a puppet of the federal government:* pawn, tool, instrument, cat's paw, poodle, creature; mouthpiece, minion.

purchase verb *they purchased the film rights in 1983:* buy, pay for, acquire, obtain, pick up, procure; invest in; informal get hold of.
OPPOSITES: sell.
▷ noun
1 *he's very happy with his purchase:* acquisition, buy, investment; shopping, goods.
2 *he could get no purchase on the wall:* grip, grasp, hold, foothold, toehold, contact, attachment, support, leverage.
OPPOSITES: sale.

purchaser noun buyer, shopper, customer, consumer.

pure adjective
1 *pure gold | pure alcohol:* unadulterated, uncontaminated, unmixed, undiluted, unalloyed, unblended; sterling, solid, 100%; flawless, perfect, genuine, real.
2 *the air is so pure | the pure waters of the lake:* clean, clear, fresh, unpolluted, uncontaminated, untainted.
3 *she is pure in body and mind:* virtuous, moral, good, innocent, righteous, saintly, wholesome, clean, upright, exemplary, irreproachable; chaste, virginal, maidenly; spotless, unsullied, uncorrupted, undefiled; informal squeaky clean.
4 *pure maths:* theoretical, abstract, conceptual.
5 *a howl of pure rage:* sheer, utter, absolute, out-and-out, complete, total, perfect, unmitigated.
OPPOSITES: adulterated, polluted, immoral.

purely adverb *he seemed to regard the exchange purely as a joke:* entirely, completely, absolutely, wholly, exclusively, solely, only, just, merely.

purgatory noun *separation from Alex was purgatory:* torment, torture, misery, agony, hell, suffering, anguish; an ordeal, a nightmare.
OPPOSITES: paradise.

purge verb
1 *he helped to purge her of the guilt that had haunted her for so long:* cleanse, clear, purify.

p

2 *lawbreakers were purged from the army:* remove, get rid of, expel, eject, dismiss, oust, eradicate, weed out.
▷ **noun** *he carried out a widespread purge of dissident elements in trade unions:* removal, expulsion, ejection, eviction, dismissal, eradication.

purify verb *the filtration plant is able to purify 70 tons of water a day:* clean, cleanse, refine, decontaminate, filter; disinfect, sterilize.

purist noun *purists complain that the Germans have forgotten how to speak their own language correctly:* pedant, perfectionist, formalist, literalist, traditionalist, dogmatist.

puritanical adjective *his puritanical parents saw any kind of pleasure as the road to damnation:* moralistic, puritan, strait-laced, prudish, prim, priggish, stuffy, narrow-minded, sententious, censorious; austere, severe, ascetic, abstemious; informal goody-goody, starchy.
OPPOSITES: permissive.

purity noun
1 *the purity of the water:* cleanness, clearness, freshness.
2 *white is meant to represent purity:* virtue, morality, goodness, righteousness, saintliness, integrity; innocence, chastity.

purport verb *this work purports to be authoritative:* claim, profess, pretend; appear, seem, be ostensibly.
▷ **noun** *I did not understand the purport of his remarks:* meaning, sense, thrust, implication, intention, significance.

purpose noun
1 *what was the purpose of his visit?* motive, cause, occasion, reason, basis.
2 *their purpose was to subvert the economy:* intention, aim, object, objective, goal, end, plan, target; ambition, aspiration.
3 *I cannot see any purpose in this plan:* advantage, benefit, good, use, value, merit, worth, profit; informal mileage.
4 *the original purpose of the porch:* function, role, use.
5 *they started the game with real purpose:* determination, resolution, resolve, drive, enthusiasm, ambition, motivation, commitment, conviction, dedication, single-mindedness.
□ **on purpose**
I think he missed the train on purpose: deliberately, intentionally, purposely, by design, wilfully, knowingly, consciously, of your own volition.

purposeful adjective *he went about his business in a purposeful, dignified manner:* determined, resolute, single-minded, firm, deliberate, decisive; committed, dedicated, persistent, dogged, unfaltering, unwavering.
OPPOSITES: aimless.

purse noun
1 *the money fell out of her purse:* wallet; N. Amer. change purse, billfold.
2 (N. Amer.) *a woman's purse:* bag, handbag.
3 *the public purse:* funds, kitty, coffers, bank, treasury, exchequer; money, finances, wealth, reserves, cash, capital, assets.
4 *the fight will net him a £75,000 purse:* prize, reward, award; winnings, stakes.
▷ **verb** *he pursed his lips:* press together, compress, tighten, pucker, pout.

pursue verb
1 *I pursued him down the garden:* follow, run after, chase.
2 *the organization pledged to cease all armed activity, and pursue its aims through political channels:* strive for, work towards, seek, aim at/for, aspire to.
3 *he had been pursuing her for weeks:* woo, pay court to, chase, run after; informal make up to.
4 *she pursued a political career:* engage in, practise, follow, devote yourself to, take up, undertake, carry on.
5 *we will not pursue the matter any further:* investigate, inquire into, look into, examine, delve into, probe, research.
OPPOSITES: avoid, shun.

pursuit noun
1 *the pursuit of profit:* search for, quest after/for.
2 *a worthwhile pursuit:* activity, hobby, pastime, diversion, recreation; occupation, trade, vocation, business, work, job, employment.

purveyor noun (formal) *a local purveyor of gourmet sandwiches:* seller, vendor, retailer, supplier, stockist, trader.

pus noun suppuration, matter; discharge, secretion.

┌─────────────────────────────┐
WORD LINKS
purulent consisting of or containing pus
└─────────────────────────────┘

push verb
1 *a police officer tried to stop them, but they pushed him aside:* shove, thrust, propel, elbow; send, drive, force; sweep, bundle, hustle, manhandle.
2 *she pushed her way through the crowded streets:* force, shove, thrust, elbow, shoulder, bundle, work.
3 *he pushed the panic button:* press, depress, hold down, squeeze; operate, activate.
4 *a friend heard about the vacancy and pushed me into applying:* urge, press, pressure, pressurize, force, impel, coerce, nag; prevail on, browbeat into; informal lean on, twist someone's arm, bulldoze.
5 *all this controversy is just a clever way to push his new movie:* advertise, publicize, promote, bang the drum for; sell, market, merchandise; informal plug, hype.
OPPOSITES: pull.

p

▷ **noun**
1 *Sarah felt a push on the small of her back:* shove, thrust, prod, poke.
2 *the enemy's eastward push:* advance, drive, thrust, charge, attack, assault, onslaught, onrush, offensive, sortie, sally, incursion.
□ **push someone around**
I'm fed up with him pushing me around: bully, domineer, ride roughshod over, trample on, bulldoze, browbeat, intimidate, threaten, victimize, pick on; informal lean on, boss about/around.
□ **push for**
the trade unions will be likely to push for wage increases: demand, call for, request, press for, campaign for, lobby for, speak up for; urge, promote, advocate, champion, espouse.
□ **push on**
I decided to push on towards the coast: press on, continue your journey, carry on, advance, proceed, go on, progress.

pushover noun
1 *he was mild-mannered but no pushover:* weakling; informal soft touch, easy touch.
2 *thanks to the Internet, shopping around for consumer goods and financial products is a pushover:* easy task, child's play; informal doddle, piece of cake, cinch.

pushy adjective *the pushy salesman wouldn't take no for an answer:* assertive, self-assertive, overbearing, domineering, aggressive, forceful, officious; thrusting, ambitious; overconfident, cocky.
OPPOSITES: submissive.

pusillanimous adjective *their reaction to the revolt came across as ineffective and pusillanimous:* timid, timorous, cowardly, fearful, faint-hearted, lily-livered, spineless, craven; informal gutless, wimpy, wimpish.
OPPOSITES: brave.

pussyfoot verb (informal) *you can't pussyfoot around any longer:* equivocate, be evasive, be non-committal, sidestep the issue, prevaricate, hedge, beat about the bush; Brit. hum and haw; informal duck the question, sit on the fence, shilly-shally; rare tergiversate.

pustule noun pimple, spot, boil, swelling, eruption, carbuncle, blister, abscess; informal zit.

put verb
1 *she put the parcel on a chair:* place, set, set down, lay, lay down, deposit, position, settle; leave, plant; informal stick, dump, park, pop; Brit. informal plonk, bung.
2 *he didn't want to be put in a category:* assign to, consign to, allocate to, place in.
3 *don't put the blame on me:* lay, place; attribute to, impute to, ascribe to.
4 *the proposals were put to the committee:* submit, present, tender, offer, suggest, propose.

5 *we were, to put it mildly, shocked by his response:* express, word, phrase, frame, couch; state, say, utter.
6 *some reports put the cost at £ 80 million:* estimate, reckon, calculate, assess.
□ **put something about** (Brit.) *the rumour had been deliberately put about by the authorities:* spread, circulate, make public, disseminate, broadcast, publicize, pass on, propagate, bandy about.
□ **put something across/over**
the party needs to put across its message more effectively: communicate, convey, get across/over, explain, make clear, spell out; get through to someone.
□ **put something aside**
1 *we've got a bit put aside in the bank:* save, put by, set aside, deposit, store, stockpile, hoard, stow, cache; reserve; informal salt away, squirrel away, stash away.
2 *they put aside their differences:* disregard, set aside, ignore, forget, discount, bury.
□ **put something back**
1 *he put the books back:* replace, return, put away, tidy away.
2 *they put back the film's release date.* See PUT SOMETHING OFF.
□ **put someone down**
1 (informal) *he often puts me down in public:* criticize, belittle, disparage, denigrate, slight, humiliate; informal cut down to size.
2 *I put him down as shy:* consider to be, judge to be, reckon to be, take to be; regard as, have down as, take for.
□ **put something down**
1 *he put his ideas down on paper:* write down, note down, jot down, take down, set down; list, record, register, log.
2 *they put down the rebellion:* suppress, check, crush, quash, squash, quell, overthrow, stamp out, repress, subdue.
3 *the horse had to be put down:* destroy, put to sleep; kill.
4 *he found it almost impossible to get another job and he put this down to his age:* attribute, ascribe, chalk up, impute; blame on.
□ **put something forward.** See PUT sense 4.
□ **put in for**
some people put in for voluntary redundancy: apply for, put in an application for, try for; request, seek, ask for.
□ **put someone off**
the smell put Lisa off: deter, discourage, dissuade; daunt, unnerve, intimidate, scare off; repel, repulse; distract, disturb, sidetrack; informal turn off.
□ **put something off**
the preliminary hearing was put off until September: postpone, defer, delay, put back, hold over, reschedule, shelve; informal put on ice, put on the back burner.
□ **put it on**
he laughed but Olivia thought he was putting it on: pretend, play-act, make believe, fake it, go through the motions.

p

□ **put something on**
1 *she put on a pair of jeans and a tight black T-shirt:* dress in, don, pull on, throw on, slip into, change into; informal doll yourself up in.
2 *I put the light on:* switch on, turn on, activate.
3 *they put on an extra train:* provide, lay on, supply, make available.
4 *the museum put on an exhibition:* organize, stage, mount, present, produce.
5 *she put on an American accent:* feign, fake, simulate, affect, assume.

□ **put someone out**
1 *Maria was put out by the slur:* annoy, anger, irritate, offend, affront, displease, irk, vex, pique, gall, upset; informal nettle, rile, miff, peeve; Brit. informal nark.
2 *I don't want to put you out:* inconvenience, trouble, bother, impose on, disoblige; informal put someone on the spot.

□ **put something out**
1 *firemen put out the blaze:* extinguish, quench, douse, smother; blow out, snuff out.
2 *he wrote to the PR firm that had put out the press release:* issue, publish, release, bring out, circulate, publicize, post.

□ **put someone up**
1 *we can put him up for a few days:* accommodate, house, take in, lodge, quarter, billet; give someone a roof over their head.
2 *they put up a candidate in each constituency:* nominate, propose, put forward, recommend.

□ **put something up**
1 *the building was put up 100 years ago:* build, construct, erect, raise.
2 *she put up a sign in the local community centre:* display, pin up, stick up, hang up, post.
3 *local architects put up some alternative schemes:* propose, put forward, present, submit, suggest, tender.
4 *the chancellor put up taxes:* increase, raise; informal jack up, hike, bump up.
5 *he put up most of the funding:* provide, supply, furnish, give, contribute, donate, pledge, pay; informal fork out, cough up, shell out.

□ **put upon** (informal) *his eagerness to please ensured that he was put upon:* take advantage of, impose on, exploit, use, misuse; informal walk all over.

□ **put someone up to something** (informal) *Who else would play a trick like that on me?*

I expect Rose put him up to it: persuade to do, encourage to do, urge to do, egg on to, incite to, goad into.

□ **put up with**
Harriet told him she was not prepared to put up with such behaviour: tolerate, take, stand for, accept, stomach, swallow, endure, abide, bear, support, take something lying down; informal lump it; Brit. informal stick, be doing with.

putative adjective *the putative father of her child:* supposed, assumed, presumed; reputed, alleged, reported, rumoured.

put-down noun (informal) *he was still smarting from the put-down:* snub, slight, affront, rebuff, disparagement, humiliation, barb, jibe, criticism; informal dig.

putrefy verb *in these conditions anything organic is going to putrefy very rapidly:* decay, rot, decompose, go bad, go off, fester, spoil.

putrid adjective *putrid meat | a putrid smell:* decomposing, decaying, rotting, rotten, bad, off, putrefied, putrescent, rancid; foul, fetid, rank.

puzzle verb
1 *her decision puzzled me:* perplex, bemuse, confuse, baffle, mystify, confound, bewilder; informal flummox.
2 *she puzzled over the problem:* think hard about, mull over, muse over, ponder, contemplate, meditate on, consider, deliberate on, chew over, wonder about.
3 *she tried to puzzle out what he meant:* work out, understand, comprehend, sort out, make sense of, make head or tail of, get to the bottom of, solve, unravel, decipher; informal figure out, suss out.
▷ noun *the poem has always been a puzzle:* enigma, mystery, paradox, conundrum, riddle, problem; informal poser.

puzzled adjective *Fiona looked puzzled:* perplexed, bemused, confused, bewildered, baffled, mystified, confounded, nonplussed, at a loss, at sea; informal flummoxed.

puzzling adjective *his explanation was rather puzzling:* baffling, perplexing, bewildering, confusing, unclear, mysterious; enigmatic, ambiguous, obscure, unfathomable, incomprehensible, impenetrable, cryptic.
OPPOSITES: straightforward, clear.

p

Qq

quadrangle noun courtyard, quad, cloister; square, plaza, piazza.

quaff verb *he quaffed pint after pint of ale:* drink, swallow, gulp down, guzzle, down, drain; consume, sup; formal partake of, imbibe; informal sink, glug, swig, swill, slug, knock back; Brit. informal neck.

quagmire noun swamp, morass, bog, marsh, mire.

quail verb *she quailed at his tone:* cower, cringe, flinch, shrink, recoil, shy away, pull back; tremble, quake, blench, blanch.

quaint adjective
1 *quaint country cottages:* picturesque, charming, sweet, attractive, old-fashioned; Brit. twee.
2 *a quaint old custom:* unusual, curious, eccentric, quirky.

quake verb
1 *the ground quaked beneath their feet:* shake, tremble, quiver, shudder, rock, wobble, move, heave, convulse.
2 *she put on a brave face even though she was quaking with fear:* tremble, shake, quiver, shudder.

qualification noun
1 *I have a professional teaching qualification:* certificate, diploma, degree, licence; training.
2 *the manufacturer is liable, subject to the qualifications stated in the guarantee:* condition, proviso, caveat, restriction, exception, reservation; alteration, modification.

qualified adjective certified, chartered, licensed, professional; trained, fit, competent, accomplished, proficient, skilled, experienced, expert.

qualify verb
1 *the family qualifies for income support:* be eligible, meet the requirements; be entitled to, be allowed.
2 *many of the new arrivals qualify as refugees:* count, be classed, be categorized, be considered.
3 *she qualified as a solicitor last year:* be certified, be licensed; pass, graduate, make the grade, succeed.
4 *the course qualified them to teach young children:* authorize, allow, permit, license; equip, prepare, fit.
5 *the authors later qualified their findings:* modify, revise, limit, restrict; moderate, temper, mitigate.

quality noun
1 *an improvement in the quality of the service* | *the quality of education may suffer as class sizes increase:* standard, class, calibre, condition, character, nature, form, value, level, grade, rank.
2 *work of such quality remains a rarity:* excellence, calibre, superiority, merit, worth, value, virtue, eminence, distinction; talent, skill, virtuosity, craftsmanship.
3 *she has many good qualities:* feature, trait, attribute, characteristic, point, aspect, facet, side, property.

qualm noun *I have no qualms about going:* misgiving, doubt, reservation, second thought, worry, concern, anxiety; (**qualms**) hesitation, reluctance, apprehension, trepidation, unease; compunction, scruples.

quandary noun *I found myself in a quandary—should I disclose the truth or not:* dilemma, state of uncertainty, state of indecision, state of confusion; predicament, plight.

quantify verb *it's impossible to quantify the extent of the black economy:* measure, put a figure on, determine, gauge, assess.

quantity noun
1 *the quantity and quality of the fruit can be controlled:* amount, number, total, aggregate, sum, quota; mass, weight, volume, bulk.
2 *a quantity of ammunition was seized during the raid:* great deal, good deal, lot, abundance; informal tons, lots, loads, heaps, masses, stacks; Brit. informal shedloads.

quarrel noun *things came to a head after a quarrel between his father and his employer:* argument, disagreement, squabble, fight, altercation, contretemps, dispute, wrangle, clash, disputation, falling-out, shouting match; Brit. row; informal tiff, run-in; Brit. informal barney, bust-up, slanging match.
▷ **verb** *they quarrelled about money:* argue,

fight, disagree, fall out; bicker, squabble, cross swords, lock horns, be at each other's throats; differ, be at odds; Brit. row.
□ **quarrel with**
you can't quarrel with the verdict: disagree with, criticize, object to, oppose, take exception to, fault, attack, take issue with, impugn, contradict, dispute; formal controvert, gainsay; informal knock.

quarrelsome adjective *he was a quarrelsome man who made many enemies:* argumentative, confrontational, pugnacious, combative, antagonistic, bellicose, belligerent, cantankerous; formal captious; Brit. informal stroppy.
OPPOSITES: peaceable.

quarry noun prey, victim; object, goal, target.

quarter noun
1 *the Latin quarter of Paris:* district, area, region, part, neighbourhood, precinct, locality, sector, zone; ghetto, community.
2 *the servants' quarters:* accommodation, lodgings, rooms, chambers; home, residence; formal abode, domicile; informal pad, digs.
3 *the riot squads showed no quarter:* mercy, leniency, clemency, compassion, pity.
▷ **verb** *they were quartered in a huge villa:* accommodate, house, board, lodge, put up, take in, install, shelter; Military billet.

quash verb
1 *the appeal judge may quash the sentence:* cancel, reverse, rescind, repeal, revoke, retract, countermand, withdraw, overturn, overrule, annul, nullify.
2 *we want to quash these rumours once and for all:* put an end to, stamp out, crush, check, curb, nip in the bud, squash, quell, subdue, suppress, extinguish, stifle.

quasi- combining form
1 *a quasi-scientific method:* seemingly, apparently; supposedly, allegedly, ostensibly, outwardly, superficially, purportedly, nominally; pseudo-.
2 *a quasi-autonomous organization:* partly, partially, part, to a certain extent, to some extent, relatively, comparatively, up to a point; almost, nearly, virtually.

quaver verb *his voice quavered with emotion:* tremble, quiver, shake, waver, falter.

quay noun wharf, pier, jetty, landing stage, berth; marina, dock, harbour.

queasy adjective *he still felt queasy and was grateful for the fresh air:* nauseous, nauseated, bilious, sick; ill, unwell, poorly; Brit. off colour; informal green about the gills.

queen noun
1 *the Queen's coronation:* monarch, sovereign, ruler, head of state; Her Majesty.

2 (informal) *the queen of soul music:* doyenne, star, superstar, leading light, luminary.

WORD LINKS
regal relating to a king or queen

queer adjective *it seemed queer to see him here | she had a queer feeling that they were being watched:* odd, strange, unusual, funny, peculiar, curious, bizarre; abnormal, anomalous, atypical, untypical, out of the ordinary, incongruous; puzzling, perplexing, mysterious, unaccountable; informal weird.
OPPOSITES: normal.

quell verb
1 *troops were called in to quell the unrest:* put an end/stop to, end, crush, put down, check, curb, nip in the bud, squash, quash, suppress, overcome, stamp out; informal crack down on.
2 *she quelled an urge to race up the stairs:* suppress, restrain, stifle, smother, curb, contain, control, check.

quench verb *they quenched their thirst with spring water:* satisfy, slake, sate, satiate, gratify, relieve, assuage.

querulous adjective *the old man complained in a querulous voice:* petulant, peevish, pettish, fractious, fretful, irritable, testy, tetchy, cross, crabby, crotchety, grumpy, bad-tempered, sullen, sulky; informal grouchy; Brit. informal ratty, cranky; N. English informal mardy.

query noun *if you have any queries please telephone the number below:* question, enquiry.
▷ **verb**
1 *'Why not?' queried Isobel:* ask, enquire, question.
2 *folk may query his credentials:* question, doubt, have doubts about, have suspicions/reservations about; challenge, dispute.

quest noun *nothing will stop their quest for her killer:* search, hunt.
□ **in quest of**
his works reflect a mind constantly in quest of intellectual stimulus: in search of, in pursuit of, seeking, looking for, on the lookout for, after.

question noun
1 *senior staff will be on hand to answer questions from the public:* enquiry, query.
2 *there is no question that he is ill:* doubt, dispute, argument, debate, uncertainty.
3 *he wrote essays on the political questions of the day:* issue, matter, business, problem, concern, topic, theme, case; debate, argument, dispute, controversy.
OPPOSITES: answer, certainty.
▷ **verb**
1 *the magistrate may question the suspect:* interrogate, examine, cross-examine, cross-question, quiz; interview, debrief, give someone the third degree; informal grill, pump.

q

2 *she questioned his motives:* query, call into question, challenge, dispute, doubt, have doubts about, suspect, have suspicions/reservations about.

□ **beyond question**
1 *her loyalty is beyond question:* undoubted, beyond doubt, certain, indisputable, incontrovertible, unquestionable, undeniable, indubitable; clear, patent, manifest.
2 *the results demonstrated this beyond question:* indisputably, irrefutably, incontestably, incontrovertibly, unquestionably, undeniably, undoubtedly, beyond doubt, without doubt, clearly, patently, obviously.

□ **in question**
the aircraft in question were seen flying over Hamburg: at issue, under discussion, under consideration, on the agenda.

□ **out of the question**
going back to the station was clearly out of the question: impossible, impracticable, not feasible, unworkable, inconceivable, unimaginable; informal not on.

> WORD LINKS
> **interrogative** expressing a question

questionable adjective
1 *a scrutiny of the records reveals a number of questionable assumptions:* doubtful, dubious, contentious, uncertain, debatable, arguable; unverified, unproved, unconvincing, implausible, improbable; borderline, marginal, moot.
2 *some of his questionable financial dealings have been investigated:* suspicious, suspect, dubious, irregular; informal shady; Brit. informal dodgy.
OPPOSITES: indisputable, honest.

queue noun
1 *a queue of people were waiting for the bus:* line, row, column, file; chain, string; Brit. informal crocodile.
2 *he was in a taxi, stuck in a queue along Knightsbridge:* traffic jam, tailback, gridlock; Brit. informal snarl-up.
▷ **verb** *we queued for ice creams:* line up, form a queue, queue up, wait in line, form a line.

quibble noun *I have just one quibble:* criticism, objection, complaint, grumble, grouse; informal niggle, moan, gripe, beef.
▷ **verb** *some people quibbled about the price:* object to, complain about, question, query, cavil at; split hairs; criticize, find fault with; informal nit-pick.

quick adjective
1 *he's generally a quick worker | the pace was too quick for me:* fast, swift, rapid, speedy, expeditious, brisk, smart; literary fleet; informal nippy.
2 *she took a quick look round:* hasty, hurried, cursory, perfunctory, desultory, superficial, summary; brief, short, fleeting.
3 *children like to see quick results from*

their efforts: prompt, immediate, instant.
4 *she isn't as quick as the others:* intelligent, bright, clever, astute, quick-witted, sharp-witted; observant, alert, sharp, perceptive; informal smart, on the ball, quick on the uptake.
OPPOSITES: slow, long.

quicken verb
1 *she unconsciously quickened her pace:* speed up, accelerate, step up; informal gee up.
2 *the film quickened his interest in nature:* stimulate, excite, arouse, rouse, stir, activate, galvanize, whet, inspire, kindle.

quickly adverb
1 *he walked quickly down the road:* fast, swiftly, briskly, rapidly, speedily, at the double, post-haste,; informal double quick; N. Amer. informal lickety-split.
2 *you'd better leave quickly:* immediately, directly, at once, now, straight away, right away, instantly, forthwith, without delay, without further ado; promptly; informal asap, pronto.

quick-witted adjective intelligent, bright, clever, astute, quick, sharp-witted; observant, alert, sharp, perceptive; informal smart, on the ball, quick on the uptake.
OPPOSITES: slow.

quiet adjective
1 *the whole room was suddenly quiet:* silent, still, hushed.
2 *she spoke in a quiet voice:* soft, low, muted, hushed, whispered, faint, muffled, indistinct, inaudible.
3 *a quiet village outside Perth:* peaceful, sleepy, tranquil, calm, still, restful, undisturbed; secluded, unfrequented.
4 *can I have a quiet word?* private, confidential, secret, discreet, unofficial, off the record.
5 *you can't keep it quiet for long:* secret, confidential, classified, under wraps; informal hush-hush, mum.
OPPOSITES: loud, busy.

▷ **noun** *after London, we longed for the quiet of the countryside:* peacefulness, peace, restfulness, calm, tranquillity, serenity; silence, quietness, stillness, still, hush.

quieten verb
1 *her mother tried to quieten her:* silence, hush, shush, quiet; calm, calm down, pacify.
2 *her travelling companions had quietened:* fall silent, stop talking, hush; informal shut up.

quietly adverb
1 *she entered the room quietly:* silently, in silence, noiselessly, soundlessly, inaudibly.
2 *he spoke quietly so as not to disturb anyone:* softly, in a low voice, in a whisper, in a murmur, under your breath, sotto voce, gently; faintly, weakly, feebly.

quintessence noun *the family farm is the*

q

quintessence of old English society: **perfect example**, exemplar, epitome, embodiment, ideal; prototype, stereotype.

quintessential adjective *he was the quintessential tough guy—strong, silent, and self-contained:* **typical**, archetypal, classic, model, standard; ideal, consummate, exemplary, best, ultimate; prototypical, stereotypical.

quip noun *the quip failed to provoke a smile:* **joke**, remark, witticism, jest, pun, pleasantry, bon mot; informal one-liner, gag, crack, wisecrack.

quirk noun
1 *they accepted her attitude as one of her little quirks:* **idiosyncrasy**, peculiarity, oddity, eccentricity, foible, whim, vagary, habit, characteristic, trait.
2 *we met by a quirk of fate:* **chance**, fluke, twist.

quirky adjective *her sense of humour was decidedly quirky:* **eccentric**, idiosyncratic, unconventional, unorthodox, unusual, strange, bizarre, peculiar, odd, offbeat, outlandish, far out, zany; informal wacky, way-out, kooky.
OPPOSITES: conventional.

quit verb
1 *by 1818, the last foreign troops had quit the country:* **leave**, vacate, exit, depart from, withdraw from; abandon, desert.
2 (informal) *he's decided to quit his job:* **resign from**, leave, give up, stand down from, walk out of, retire from; informal chuck, pack in.

quite adverb
1 *this is a quite different problem* | *I quite agree:* **completely**, entirely, totally, wholly, absolutely, utterly, thoroughly, altogether.
2 *it's quite warm outside:* **fairly**, rather, somewhat, slightly, relatively, comparatively, moderately, reasonably,

to a certain extent; informal pretty, kind of, sort of.

quiver verb *I quivered with fear:* **tremble**, shake, shiver, quaver, quake, shudder.
▷ noun *there was a quiver in her voice:* **tremor**, tremble, shake, quaver, flutter, waver.

quixotic adjective *he has spent $200 million and many years of his life on this quixotic venture:* **idealistic**, romantic, visionary, utopian, starry-eyed, unrealistic, impracticable, unworkable, impossible.

quiz noun *a music quiz:* **competition**, test.
▷ verb *four men are being quizzed by police:* **question**, interrogate, cross-examine, cross-question, interview, give someone the third degree; informal grill, pump.

quizzical adjective *he gave me a quizzical look:* **enquiring**, questioning, curious, puzzled, perplexed.

quota noun *the minister promised that Spanish trawlers would not exceed their annual quota:* **allocation**, share, allowance, limit, ration, portion; percentage, proportion, amount, quantity.

quotation noun
1 *a quotation from 'King Lear':* **citation**, quote, excerpt, extract, passage, line, paragraph, verse, phrase; reference, allusion.
2 *we will send you a quotation for the building work:* **estimate**, quote, price, tender, bid, costing.

quote verb
1 *he quoted a passage from Shakespeare:* **recite**, repeat; take, extract, copy out.
2 *she quoted one case in which a woman had died:* **cite**, mention, refer to, name, instance, specify, identify; point to, present, put forward.
▷ noun. See QUOTATION.

q

Rr

rabble noun
1 *a rabble of noisy, angry youths:* mob, crowd, throng, gang, swarm, horde, pack, mass, group.
2 *the elite tried to dissociate themselves from the rabble:* common people, masses, populace, multitude, rank and file, mob, proletariat, peasantry, hoi polloi, lower classes; informal riff-raff, proles, plebs.

rabble-rouser noun *he was nothing more than a Communist rabble-rouser:* agitator, troublemaker, firebrand, demagogue.

rabid adjective *a rabid anti-royalist:* extreme, fanatical, passionate, fervent, diehard, uncompromising; informal gung-ho, raving.
OPPOSITES: moderate.

race[1] noun
1 *more than 200 competitors took part in the race:* contest, competition, event, fixture, heat, trial.
2 *the race for naval domination accelerated:* competition, rivalry, contention, scrabble; quest.
▷ **verb**
1 *both men will race in the final:* compete, contend; run, take part.
2 *I raced after him:* hurry, dash, rush, run, sprint, bolt, dart, gallop, career, charge, shoot, hurtle, fly, speed, scurry; Brit. hare; informal tear, belt, pelt, scoot; Brit. informal bomb.
3 *she tried to calm herself, but her heart was racing:* pound, beat, throb, thud, thump, hammer, palpitate, flutter, pitter-patter, quiver, pump.

race[2] noun ethnic group, ethnic origin, ethnic background; people, community.

racial adjective ethnic, ethnological, race-related; cultural, national, tribal.

racism noun racial discrimination, racial prejudice, racialism; xenophobia, chauvinism, bigotry.

racist noun *he was exposed as a racist:* racial bigot, racialist; xenophobe, chauvinist.
▷ **adjective** *a racist society:* racially discriminatory, racialist, prejudiced, racially bigoted.

rack noun *we put the cake on a wire rack to cool:* frame, framework, stand, holder, trestle, support, shelf.
▷ **verb** *she was racked with guilt:* torment, afflict, torture; plague, bedevil, persecute, trouble, worry.

racket noun *his voice was barely audible above the racket in the pub:* noise, din, hubbub, clamour, uproar, tumult, commotion, rumpus, pandemonium, babel; Brit. row.

raconteur noun storyteller, narrator, anecdotalist, conversationalist.

racy adjective *the show included a rather racy striptease revue:* risqué, suggestive, naughty, sexy, spicy, ribald; indecorous, indecent, immodest, off colour, dirty, rude, smutty, crude, salacious; euphemistic adult; informal saucy, raunchy.
OPPOSITES: prim.

radiance noun *the radiance of the sunset dwindled:* light, brightness, brilliance, luminosity, beams, rays, illumination, blaze, glow, gleam, glare; luminescence, incandescence.

radiant adjective
1 *we lay beneath the radiant moon:* shining, bright, brilliant, gleaming, glowing, ablaze, luminous, luminescent, incandescent, dazzling.
2 *she looked flushed and radiant:* joyful, elated, thrilled, overjoyed, jubilant, rapturous, ecstatic, euphoric, delighted.
OPPOSITES: dark, gloomy.

radiate verb
1 *the hot stars radiate energy:* emit, give off, give out, discharge, diffuse; shed, cast.
2 *a faint light radiated from the hall:* shine, beam, emanate, spread.
3 *four spokes radiate from the hub:* fan out, spread out, branch out/off, extend, issue.

radical adjective
1 *radical reform is long overdue:* thoroughgoing, thorough, complete, total, comprehensive, exhaustive, sweeping, far-reaching, wide-ranging, extensive, profound, major, stringent, rigorous.
2 *there are radical differences between the two theories:* fundamental, basic,

r

essential; structural, deep-seated, intrinsic, organic, profound.
3 *he became involved in a radical political movement:* revolutionary; extreme, extremist, fanatical, militant.
OPPOSITES: superficial, minor, conservative.
▷ **noun** *the arrested man was a left-wing radical:* revolutionary; militant, zealot, extremist, fanatic, diehard.
OPPOSITES: conservative.

raffle noun lottery, prize draw, sweepstake, sweep, tombola.

ragbag noun *a ragbag of products of all shapes and sizes:* jumble, hotchpotch; assortment, mixture, miscellany, medley, mixed bag, melange, variety, diversity, potpourri; informal mishmash.

rage noun
1 *his rage is due to frustration:* fury, anger, wrath, outrage, indignation, temper, spleen, resentment, pique, annoyance, vexation, displeasure; tantrum, frenzy; literary ire, choler.
2 *the current rage for DIY:* craze, passion, fashion, taste, trend, vogue, fad, enthusiasm, obsession, compulsion, fixation, fetish, mania, preoccupation.
▷ **verb**
1 *she raged silently all the way back to the cottage:* seethe, be beside yourself, rant and rave, storm, fume; informal have a fit.
2 *he raged against the reforms:* protest about, complain about, oppose, denounce; fulminate, storm, rail.
3 *a storm was raging outside:* blow, howl; thunder.

ragged adjective
1 *a pair of ragged jeans:* tattered, in tatters, torn, ripped, holey, moth-eaten, frayed, worn, worn out, falling to pieces, threadbare, scruffy, shabby; informal tatty.
2 *a ragged coastline stretched off into the distance:* jagged, craggy, rugged, uneven, rough, irregular; serrated, indented; technical crenulated.

raging adjective
1 *a raging mob howled for vengeance:* angry, furious, enraged, incensed, infuriated, irate, fuming, seething, ranting; literary wrathful; informal livid.
2 *a raging forest fire:* fierce, roaring, powerful, violent, wild, uncontrollable, turbulent, tempestuous, stormy, blustery, severe, huge.
OPPOSITES: calm, gentle.

raid noun
1 *the raid on Dieppe:* attack, assault, blitz, incursion, sortie; onslaught, charge, offensive, invasion, blitzkrieg.
2 *clothing was stolen during a raid on the shop:* robbery, burglary, hold-up, break-in, ram raid; informal smash-and-grab, stick-up; N. Amer. informal heist.
3 *police found stolen ammunition during a raid on the flat:* swoop, search; informal bust.

▷ **verb**
1 *they raided enemy ships in the harbour:* attack, assault, set upon, swoop on, blitz, assail, storm, rush.
2 *armed men raided the store:* rob, hold up, break into; plunder, steal from, pillage, loot, ransack, sack; informal stick up.
3 *their homes were raided by police:* search, swoop on; informal bust.

raider noun robber, burglar, thief, housebreaker; plunderer, pillager, looter, marauder; attacker, assailant, invader.

rail verb *he rails against injustice and oppression:* protest, fulminate, inveigh, rage, speak out, make a stand; (**rail against**) condemn, denounce, criticize, expostulate about.

railing noun fence, fencing, rails, paling, palisade, balustrade, banister, hurdle.

rain noun *the plants were washed away by unusually heavy rain:* rainfall, precipitation, raindrops, wet weather; drizzle, shower, cloudburst, torrent, downpour, deluge, storm.
▷ **verb**
1 *it rained heavily during the night:* pour, pour down, pelt down, teem down, beat down, lash down, sheet down; fall, drizzle, spit; informal rain cats and dogs; Brit. informal bucket down, tip down.
2 *bombs rained on the city:* fall, hail, drop, shower.

> WORD LINKS
> **pluvial** relating to rain

rainy adjective wet, showery, drizzly, damp, inclement.
OPPOSITES: dry.

raise verb
1 *he raised a hand in greeting:* lift, hold up, elevate, uplift, upraise; hoist, haul up, hitch up.
2 *there was no alternative but to raise prices:* increase, put up, push up, up, inflate; informal hike up, jack up, bump up.
3 *they were able to raise public awareness of the issues involved:* heighten, intensify, increase, boost, augment.
4 *how will you raise the money?* get, obtain, acquire; accumulate, amass, collect, fetch, net, make.
5 *the region raised an army to fight for the government:* recruit, enlist, sign up, conscript, call up, mobilize, rally, assemble, muster; US draft.
6 *you have raised a very interesting point:* bring up, air; present, table, propose, submit, advance, suggest, moot, put forward.
7 *most parents raise their children successfully:* bring up, rear, nurture, look after, care for, provide for, parent, tend; educate, train.
8 *he raised cattle in Nebraska:* breed, rear, keep, tend; grow, farm, cultivate, produce.
OPPOSITES: lower, reduce.

r

▷ **noun** (N. Amer.) *the workers wanted a raise:* rise, pay rise, pay increase, increment.

rake verb
1 *he raked the leaves into a pile:* scrape, collect, gather.
2 *she raked the gravel:* smooth out, level, even out, flatten.
3 *the cat raked his arm with its claws:* scratch, lacerate, scrape, rasp, graze.
4 *she raked a hand through her hair:* drag, pull, scrape, tug, comb.
5 *machine-gun fire raked the streets:* sweep, strafe, pepper; Military enfilade.

rakish adjective *his moustache gave him a slightly rakish look:* dashing, debonair, stylish, jaunty, devil-may-care; raffish, disreputable.

rally verb
1 *the French troops rallied and held their ground:* regroup, reassemble, re-form.
2 *ministers rallied to denounce the rumours:* come together, band together, assemble, join forces, unite, ally, collaborate, cooperate, pull together.
3 *share prices rallied in the afternoon:* recover, improve, get better, pick up, revive, bounce back, look up; informal perk up.
OPPOSITES: disperse, split, slump.
▷ **noun**
1 *there was a rally in support of the strike:* mass meeting, gathering, assembly; demonstration, protest march; informal demo.
2 *investors are hoping for a rally in oil prices:* recovery, upturn, improvement, comeback, resurgence.
OPPOSITES: slump.

ram verb
1 *he rammed his sword back into its sheath:* force, thrust, plunge, push, sink, dig, stick, cram, jam, stuff, pack.
2 *a stolen van rammed the police car:* hit, strike, crash into, collide with, impact, run into, smash into.

ramble verb
1 *we rambled around the Cornish countryside:* walk, hike, tramp, trek, backpack; wander, stroll, saunter, amble, roam, range, rove, traipse; formal perambulate.
2 *she does ramble on about environmental issues:* chatter, babble, prattle, prate, blather, gabble, jabber, twitter, rattle; Brit. informal natter, waffle, rabbit.
▷ **noun** *we were looking forward to a leisurely ramble in the hills:* walk, hike, trek; wander, stroll, saunter, amble, promenade.

rambler noun walker, hiker, backpacker, wanderer, rover; literary wayfarer.

rambling adjective
1 *a long, rambling speech:* long-winded, verbose, wordy, prolix, lengthy; digressive, roundabout, circuitous, circumlocutory; disconnected, disjointed, incoherent.

2 *an old, rambling house:* sprawling, spread out, extensive, labyrinthine, spacious, commodious, ample, vast, large, substantial.
OPPOSITES: concise, compact.

ramification noun *the political ramifications of closing the factory would be immense:* consequence, result, aftermath, outcome, effect, upshot; implication; by-product.

ramp noun slope, bank, incline, gradient, tilt; rise, ascent, acclivity; drop, descent, declivity.

rampage verb *angry mobs rampaged through the streets:* riot, run riot, go on the rampage, run amok, go berserk; storm, charge; informal tear.

rampant adjective
the rampant inflation of the mid 70s: uncontrolled, unrestrained, unchecked, unbridled, widespread; out of control, rife, endemic, spreading, flourishing.

rampart noun wall, embankment, earthwork, parapet, battlement, bulwark.

ramshackle adjective *he lived up the hill in a ramshackle old cottage:* tumbledown, dilapidated, derelict, decrepit, neglected, run-down, gone to rack and ruin, crumbling, decaying; rickety, shaky, unsound.
OPPOSITES: sound.

rancid adjective sour, stale, rank, putrid, foul, rotten, bad, off; fetid, stinking, malodorous, foul-smelling, high, gamy; literary noisome.
OPPOSITES: fresh.

rancorous adjective *a rancorous and protracted argument:* bitter, spiteful, ill-tempered, bad-tempered, resentful, acrimonious, hostile, venomous, vindictive, vitriolic, nasty; informal bitchy.

rancour noun *there was an atmosphere of rancour and distrust:* bitterness, spite, hate, hatred, resentment, malice, ill will, malevolence, animosity, antipathy, enmity, hostility, acrimony, venom, vitriol; informal bitchiness.
OPPOSITES: goodwill.

random adjective *a series of random attacks:* unsystematic, arbitrary, unplanned, undirected, unmethodical, casual, indiscriminate, non-specific, haphazard, stray, erratic; chance, accidental.
OPPOSITES: systematic.
□ **at random**
they picked out ten people at random: unsystematically, arbitrarily, randomly, unmethodically, haphazardly, erratically.

range noun
1 *the car's outside my price range:* bracket, limit.
2 *fantasy is capable of dealing with topics outside the range of the traditional novel:*

r

scope, parameters, compass, sweep, span, area, ambit.
3 *we have introduced a new range of quality foods:* assortment, variety, diversity, mixture, collection, array, selection, choice, spectrum.
4 *the T72 has the longest range and the most accurate cannons of any tank:* reach, limit, extent, scope, sweep, field, depth, distance, height, orbit.
5 *we flew over a range of mountains:* row, chain, sierra, ridge, massif; line, string, series.
▷ **verb**
1 *charges range from 1% to 5%:* vary, differ; extend, reach, go, run.
2 *on the stalls are ranged all sorts of fresh foods:* arrange, line up, order, position, dispose, set out, array.
3 *herdsmen ranged over the steppes:* roam, rove, traverse, travel, journey, wander, drift, ramble, meander, stroll, walk, hike, trek.

rangy adjective long-limbed, long-legged, leggy, tall; slender, slim, lean, thin, gangling, gangly, lanky, spindly, skinny, spare.
OPPOSITES: squat.

rank¹ noun
1 *he was elevated to ministerial rank:* position, level, grade; class, status, standing; dated station.
2 *the first rank of riflemen was instructed to fire:* row, line, tier, bank.
▷ **verb**
1 *the plant is ranked as endangered:* classify, class, categorize, rate, grade, bracket, group, pigeonhole, designate; catalogue, file, list.
2 *he ranked below the others:* be graded, have a status, be classed, be classified, be categorized; belong.

rank² adjective
1 *rank vegetation covered the clearing:* abundant, lush, luxuriant, dense, profuse, vigorous, overgrown.
2 *sheep were everywhere, and there was a rank smell from underfoot:* offensive, unpleasant, nasty, revolting, sickening, obnoxious; noxious, foul, fetid, smelly, stinking, reeking, high, off, rancid, putrid, malodorous; literary noisome.
3 *this failure was down to rank stupidity:* downright, utter, outright, out-and-out, absolute, complete, sheer, arrant, thoroughgoing, unqualified, unmitigated, positive, perfect, patent, pure, total.
OPPOSITES: sparse, pleasant.

rankle verb *it rankled my parents to have to pay for parking:* annoy, irritate, displease, irk, vex, pique, gall, upset, anger, offend, affront; informal rile, nettle; Brit. informal nark.

ransack verb plunder, pillage, raid, rob, loot, sack, strip; ravage, devastate; scour, rifle through, comb, search; literary despoil.

ransom noun *they demanded a huge ransom:* pay-off, price, payment.
▷ **verb** *the girl was ransomed for £4 million:* release, free, liberate.

rant verb *she ranted on about the unfairness of it all:* hold forth, go on, fulminate, spout, pontificate, bluster, declaim; shout, yell, bellow.
▷ **noun** *he went into a rant about the decline in morality:* tirade, diatribe, broadside, polemic.

rap verb
1 *I rapped on the door:* knock, tap, bang, hammer, pound.
2 *he rapped the boy's fingers with a ruler:* hit, strike, beat, crack, smack, thump; literary smite; informal whack, bash, wallop.
▷ **noun**
1 *there was a rap at the door:* knock, tap, rat-tat, bang, hammering, pounding.
2 *she received a rap on the knuckles:* blow, knock, bang, crack, smack, thump; informal whack, bash, wallop.

rapacious adjective *consumers must be protected against rapacious moneylenders:* grasping, greedy, avaricious, acquisitive, covetous; mercenary, materialistic; insatiable, predatory; informal money-grubbing.
OPPOSITES: charitable.

rape verb
1 *he raped her at knifepoint:* sexually assault, sexually abuse, violate, force yourself on; literary ravish.
2 *they have raped our country:* ravage, violate, desecrate, defile, plunder, pillage; lay waste, ransack, sack; literary despoil.
▷ **noun**
1 *he was charged with rape:* sexual assault, sexual abuse.
2 *the rape of the rainforests:* destruction, violation, ravaging, pillaging, plundering, desecration, defilement.

rapid adjective *we made a rapid exit | his rapid rise to stardom:* fast, quick, swift, speedy, expeditious, express, brisk; lightning, meteoric, whirlwind; sudden, instantaneous, instant, immediate; hurried, hasty, precipitate; literary fleet.
OPPOSITES: slow.

rapidly adverb fast, quickly, swiftly, speedily, post-haste, hotfoot, at full tilt, briskly; hurriedly, hastily, in haste, in a rush, precipitately; informal hell for leather, at the double, like a bat out of hell, like greased lightning, like the wind.
OPPOSITES: slowly.

rapport noun *he had a real rapport with his team:* affinity, close relationship, good relationship, good communications, mutual understanding, bond, empathy, sympathy, accord.
OPPOSITES: antipathy.

r

rapt adjective *they watched in rapt attention:* fascinated, enthralled, spellbound, captivated, riveted, gripped, mesmerized, enchanted, entranced, bewitched; transported, enraptured, thrilled, ecstatic.
OPPOSITES: inattentive.

rapture noun *she gazed at him in rapture:* ecstasy, bliss, euphoria, elation, joy, enchantment, exaltation, delight, happiness, pleasure.
OPPOSITES: misery.

rapturous adjective *he was given a rapturous reception by the flag-waving crowds:* ecstatic, joyful, elated, euphoric, enraptured, blissful, happy; enthusiastic, delighted, thrilled, overjoyed, rapt.
OPPOSITES: miserable.

rare adjective
1 *they treasured their rare moments of privacy:* infrequent, scarce, sparse, unusual, uncommon, few and far between, thin on the ground, in short supply; occasional, limited, odd, isolated, unaccustomed, unwonted; Brit. like gold dust.
2 *he is a man of rare talent:* exceptional, outstanding, unparalleled, unique, unrivalled, inimitable, beyond compare, without equal, second to none, unsurpassed, peerless, matchless; consummate, superior, superlative, first-class.
OPPOSITES: common, commonplace.

rarefied adjective *this rarefied musical world is closed to all but the most sensitive of artists:* esoteric, exclusive, select; elevated, lofty.
OPPOSITES: mundane.

rarely adverb *the couple are rarely seen in public these days:* seldom, infrequently, hardly ever, scarcely; once in a while, now and then, occasionally; informal once in a blue moon.
OPPOSITES: often.

raring adjective *the mission crew are raring to go:* eager, keen; impatient, longing, desperate, anxious; ready; informal dying, itching.
OPPOSITES: reluctant.

rarity noun
1 *the rarity of good historical records from these countries:* infrequency, unusual nature; scarcity, dearth, paucity, famine, inadequacy, insufficiency.
2 *this book is something of a rarity:* collector's item, rare bird; wonder, one of a kind; curiosity, oddity; anomaly, aberration, freak; Brit. informal one-off.
OPPOSITES: prevalence.

rascal noun rogue, scoundrel, wretch, imp, monkey, scallywag, mischief-maker; informal scamp, tyke, horror, monster; old use rapscallion.

rash[1] noun
1 *the next day, he broke out in a rash:* spots, breakout, eruption; hives; Medicine urticaria.
2 *the incident provoked a rash of articles in the press:* series, succession, rush, spate, wave, flood, deluge, torrent, flurry, outbreak, epidemic, explosion.

rash[2] adjective *this was a rash decision that he will live to regret:* reckless, impulsive, impetuous, hasty, foolhardy, incautious, precipitate; careless, heedless, thoughtless, imprudent, foolish.
OPPOSITES: prudent.

rasping adjective *she spoke in a quiet, rasping voice that made Kathryn shiver:* harsh, grating, jarring; raspy, scratchy, hoarse, rough, gravelly, croaky, gruff, husky, throaty, guttural.
OPPOSITES: mellow.

rate noun
1 *a fixed rate of interest:* percentage, ratio, proportion; scale, standard.
2 *an hourly rate of £30:* charge, price, cost, tariff, fare, levy, toll; fee, remuneration, payment, wage, allowance.
3 *the rate of change has increased:* speed, pace, tempo, velocity, momentum.
▷verb
1 *they were asked to rate their ability at various driving manoeuvres:* assess, evaluate, appraise, judge, weigh up, estimate, calculate, gauge, measure; grade, rank, classify, categorize.
2 *the scheme was rated as no more than moderately effective:* consider, judge, reckon, think, hold, deem, find; regard as, look on as, count as.
3 *he rated only a brief mention in the report:* merit, deserve, warrant, be worthy of.

rather adverb
1 *it's rather complicated, I'm afraid:* quite, a bit, a little, fairly, slightly, somewhat, relatively, comparatively, up to a point, to some extent; informal pretty, sort of, kind of.
2 *her true feelings—or rather, lack of feelings:* more precisely, to be precise, to be exact, strictly speaking.
3 *she seemed sad rather than angry:* more; as opposed to, instead of.
4 *it was not impulsive, but rather a carefully considered decision:* on the contrary, instead.

ratify verb confirm, approve, sanction, endorse, agree to, accept, uphold, authorize, formalize, validate, recognize; sign.
OPPOSITES: reject.

rating noun *the hotel's four-star rating is well deserved:* grading, grade, classification, ranking, rank, category, designation; assessment, evaluation, appraisal; mark, score.

r

ratio noun proportion, relationship, correspondence, correlation; percentage, fraction, quotient.

ration noun
1 *she allowed herself a daily ration of chocolate:* allowance, allocation, quota, share, portion, helping; amount, quantity, measure, proportion, percentage.
2 (**rations**) *the garrison ran out of rations:* supplies, provisions, food, foodstuffs; stores; formal comestibles; informal grub; dated victuals.
▷ **verb** *after the war, fuel supplies were still rationed:* control, limit, restrict; conserve.

rational adjective
1 *a rational approach to the problem:* logical, reasoned, sensible, reasonable, cogent, intelligent, judicious, shrewd, common-sense, sound, prudent; down-to-earth, practical, pragmatic.
2 *she was not rational at the time of signing the agreement:* sane, compos mentis, in your right mind, of sound mind; normal, balanced, lucid, coherent; informal all there.
3 *we like to think that humans are rational beings:* intelligent, thinking, reasoning; cerebral, logical, analytical.
OPPOSITES: illogical, insane, irrational.

rationale noun reason, reasons, reasoning, thinking, logic, grounds, sense; principle, theory, argument, case; motive, motivation, explanation, justification, excuse.

rationalize verb
1 *he tried to rationalize his behaviour:* justify, explain away, explain, account for, defend, vindicate, excuse.
2 (Brit.) *they embarked on an attempt to rationalize the industry:* streamline, reorganize, modernize, update; trim, hone, simplify, downsize, prune.

rattle verb
1 *hailstones rattled against the window:* clatter, patter; clink, clunk.
2 *he rattled some coins:* jingle, jangle, clink, tinkle.
3 *the bus rattled along:* jolt, bump, bounce, jounce, shake, judder.
4 (informal) *she turned round quickly, rattled by his presence:* unnerve, disconcert, disturb, fluster, shake, perturb, throw, discompose, discomfit, ruffle; informal faze.
▷ **noun** *he heard the rattle of chains behind him:* clatter, clank, clink, clang; jingle, jangle.
▢ **rattle something off** (informal) *she rattled off the names of the films he had directed:* reel off, recite, list, fire off, run through, enumerate.

raucous adjective
1 *outbursts of raucous laughter drifted across the fields:* harsh, strident, screeching, piercing, shrill, grating,
discordant, dissonant; noisy, loud, cacophonous.
2 *she found herself on a raucous hen night:* rowdy, noisy, boisterous, roisterous, wild.
OPPOSITES: soft, quiet.

raunchy adjective (informal). See SEXY sense 2.

ravage verb *their land had been ravaged by famine and plague:* lay waste, devastate, ruin, destroy, wreak havoc on, leave desolate; pillage, plunder, ransack, sack, loot; literary despoil.

rave verb
1 *the old man was still raving about Armageddon:* talk wildly, rant, babble, jabber, gibber, go on.
2 *he raved about her talent and predicted she'd win:* praise, go into raptures about/over, wax lyrical about, sing the praises of, rhapsodize over, enthuse about/over, acclaim, eulogize, extol; formal laud.
OPPOSITES: criticize.

ravenous adjective
1 *by dinner time I'm absolutely ravenous:* starving; informal famished.
2 *nothing would satisfy her ravenous appetite:* voracious, insatiable; greedy, gluttonous.

ravine noun gorge, canyon, gully, defile, couloir; chasm, abyss, gulf; N. Amer. gulch.

ravings plural noun *he dismissed her words as the ravings of a hysterical woman:* gibberish, rambling, babbling, incoherencies.

ravishing adjective beautiful, gorgeous, stunning, wonderful, lovely, striking, magnificent, dazzling, radiant; delightful, charming, enchanting.
OPPOSITES: hideous.

raw adjective
1 *a piece of raw carrot:* uncooked, fresh.
2 *the cost of raw materials is likely to rise:* unprocessed, untreated, unrefined, crude, natural.
3 *a bunch of raw recruits:* inexperienced, untrained, untried, untested; callow, immature, green, naive.
4 *his skin is raw in places:* sore, red, painful, tender; abraded, chafed; Medicine excoriated.
5 *it was a raw morning with a bitter east wind:* cold, chilly, freezing, icy, icy-cold, wintry, bitter; informal nippy.
6 *the raw emotions depicted in such stories are hard to deal with:* strong, intense, passionate, fervent, powerful, violent; undisguised, unconcealed, unrestrained, uninhibited, naked.
OPPOSITES: cooked, processed.

ray noun *rays of light shone through the trees:* beam, shaft, streak, stream, finger.

raze verb demolish, tear down, pull down, knock down, level, flatten, bulldoze, destroy, wipe out, lay waste.

r

re preposition *a discussion took place re the appointment of a new manager:* about, concerning, regarding, with regard to, relating to, apropos, on the subject of, in respect of, with reference to, in connection with.

reach verb

1 *Travis reached out his hand:* stretch out, hold out, extend, outstretch, thrust out, stick out.
2 *reach me that book:* pass, hand, give.
3 *soon she reached Helen's house:* arrive at, get to, come to; end up at.
4 *the temperature reached 50 degrees:* get to, attain, rise to, climb to; fall to, sink to, drop to; informal hit.
5 *the two leaders failed to reach an agreement:* achieve, work out, draw up, put together, negotiate, thrash out, hammer out.
6 *I have been trying to reach you all day:* contact, get in touch with, get through to, get, speak to; informal get hold of; Brit. informal get on to.
7 *our central concern is to reach more people:* influence, sway, get through to, make an impression on, have an impact on.
▷ **noun**
1 *Bobby moved out of her reach:* grasp, range.
2 *set yourself small goals that are within your reach:* capabilities, capacity.
3 *they may be beyond the reach of the law by now:* jurisdiction, authority, influence; scope, range, compass, ambit.

react verb *how would he react if she told him the truth?* respond, reply, answer; behave, act, take it, conduct yourself.

reaction noun

1 *his reaction had bewildered her:* response, answer, reply, rejoinder, retort, riposte, counterblast; informal comeback.
2 *a reaction against modernism is inevitable:* backlash, swing.
3 *the forces of reaction:* conservatism, the right wing.

reactionary adjective *government policy became increasingly reactionary:* right-wing, conservative, rightist, traditionalist, conventional, unprogressive, neoconservative.
OPPOSITES: progressive.
▷ **noun** *he was later to become an extreme reactionary:* right-winger, conservative, arch-conservative, rightist, traditionalist, neoconservative.
OPPOSITES: radical.

read verb

1 *he was reading the newspaper:* study, scrutinize, look through; pore over, be absorbed in; run your eye over, cast an eye over, leaf through, scan, flick through, skim through, thumb through; formal peruse.
2 *he read her a passage from the letter:* read out/aloud, recite, declaim.
3 *I can't read my own writing:* decipher, make out, make sense of, interpret, understand.
4 *how do you read the situation?* interpret, understand, explain, analyse, construe, take, see.
5 *he read modern history at university:* study, take; N. Amer. & Austral./NZ major in; informal do.
□ **read something into something** *officials cautioned against reading too much into the statistics:* infer from, extrapolate from, assume from, deduce from, conclude from, attribute to; read between the lines.

> **WORD LINKS**
> **legible** clear enough to read
> **illegible** not clear enough to read
> **literacy** the ability to read and write
> **illiteracy** the inability to read and write

readable adjective

1 *the inscription is still perfectly readable:* legible, easy to read, decipherable, clear, intelligible, comprehensible.
2 *her novels are immensely readable:* enjoyable, entertaining, interesting, absorbing, gripping, enthralling, engrossing, stimulating; informal unputdownable.
OPPOSITES: illegible, unreadable.

readily adverb

1 *Durkin readily offered to drive him to the station:* willingly, gladly, happily, cheerfully, with pleasure, without hesitation, ungrudgingly, unhesitatingly, eagerly, promptly.
2 *the island is readily accessible:* easily, with ease, effortlessly, comfortably, without difficulty.
OPPOSITES: reluctantly.

readiness noun

1 *he questioned their readiness to accept new technology:* willingness, inclination, enthusiasm, eagerness, keenness, wish, desire.
2 *we need to maintain our forces in a state of readiness:* preparedness, preparation.
3 *I was surprised at the readiness of his reply:* promptness, alacrity, rapidity, swiftness, speed.
OPPOSITES: unwillingness, unreadiness.

reading noun

1 *a cursory reading of the financial pages shows this to be the case:* study, scan, scanning; browse through, look through, glance through, leaf through, flick through, skim through, thumb through; formal perusal.
2 *a series of readings from the Bible:* passage, lesson; section, piece; recital, recitation.
3 *my reading of the situation is quite different:* interpretation, understanding, explanation, analysis, construal.
4 *the blood pressure reading was not*

r

particularly low: indication, measurement, figure, record.

ready adjective

1 *are you ready for the trip?* prepared, all set, organized, primed, in readiness, geared up; informal fit, psyched up.
2 *we'll have the paint job ready by the morning:* completed, finished, organized, done, arranged, fixed.
3 *he's always ready to help:* willing, prepared, pleased, happy, glad, inclined, disposed, predisposed; eager, keen; informal game.
4 *she looked ready to collapse:* about to, on the point of, on the verge of, close to, liable to, likely to.
5 *we always kept a ready supply of food:* easily available, accessible, handy, close/near at hand, to/on hand, convenient, within reach, at the ready, near, at your fingertips.
6 *he is blessed with great charm and a ready wit:* prompt, quick, swift, speedy, fast, immediate, unhesitating.
▷ **verb** *he needed time to ready himself:* prepare, get/make ready, organize, gear yourself up; informal psych yourself up.
▫ **at the ready**
a group of parents stood, camcorders at the ready: in position, poised, ready for use/action, waiting.
▫ **make ready**
the crew were busy making ready for our departure: prepare, make preparations, get everything ready, gear up.

ready-made adjective

1 *I dislike ready-made clothing:* ready-to-wear, off-the-shelf; Brit. off-the-peg.
2 *ready-made meals used to be stodgy and bland:* pre-cooked, oven-ready, convenience, ready.
OPPOSITES: tailor-made.

real adjective

1 *is she a fictional character or a real person?* actual, non-fictional, factual; historical; material, physical, tangible, concrete, palpable.
2 *do you think it's real gold?* genuine, authentic, true, proper, bona fide; informal pukka, kosher.
3 *there were tears of real grief in his eyes:* sincere, genuine, true, unfeigned, heartfelt, unaffected.
4 *he was a real man:* proper, true; informal regular.
5 *you're a real idiot:* complete, utter, thorough, absolute, total, prize, perfect; Brit. informal right, proper.
OPPOSITES: fictitious, imaginary, imitation, feigned.

realism noun

1 *his optimism was tinged with realism:* pragmatism, practicality, common sense, level-headedness.
2 *both stories portrayed frontier life with a degree of realism:* authenticity, fidelity,

verisimilitude, truthfulness, faithfulness, accuracy; naturalism.
OPPOSITES: idealism, fantasy.

realistic adjective

1 *you've got to be realistic and accept what has happened:* practical, pragmatic, matter-of-fact, down-to-earth, sensible, commonsensical; rational, reasonable, level-headed, clear-sighted, businesslike; informal keeping both feet on the ground, hard-nosed, no-nonsense.
2 *a regional settlement remains a realistic aim:* achievable, attainable, feasible, practicable, viable, reasonable, sensible, workable; informal doable.
3 *a realistic portrayal of war:* true to life, lifelike, truthful, faithful, real-life, naturalistic, graphic, authentic.
OPPOSITES: idealistic, unrealistic, fanciful.

reality noun

1 *he is incapable of distinguishing fantasy from reality:* the real world, real life, actuality; truth; physical existence.
2 *the harsh realities of life:* fact, actuality, truth.
3 *the reality of Marryat's account remains unquestioned:* verisimilitude, authenticity, realism, fidelity.
OPPOSITES: fantasy, unreality.
▫ **in reality**
she sounded sympathetic but in reality she was furious: in fact, as a matter of fact, actually, really, in truth; in practice.

realization noun

1 *there was a growing realization of the danger:* awareness, understanding, comprehension, consciousness, appreciation, recognition, discernment; formal cognizance.
2 *the realization of our dreams was a thrilling experience for all concerned:* fulfilment, achievement, accomplishment, attainment; fruition, embodiment, manifestation; conclusion, completion.

realize verb

1 *he suddenly realized what she had meant:* register, perceive, discern, be/become aware of, be/become conscious of, notice; understand, grasp, comprehend, see, recognize, work out, fathom; formal apprehend, be/become cognizant of; informal latch on to, cotton on to, tumble to, figure out; Brit. informal suss, suss out.
2 *they realized their dream by restoring the castle:* fulfil, achieve, accomplish, make a reality, make happen, bring to fruition, bring about/off, carry out/through; formal effectuate.
3 *when the goods were auctioned, they realized £3000:* be sold for, sell for, fetch, go for, make, net.

really adverb

1 *he is really very wealthy:* in fact, actually, in reality, as a matter of fact, in truth, to tell the truth.

2 *he really likes her:* genuinely, truly, honestly; undoubtedly, without a doubt, indubitably, certainly, assuredly, unquestionably.
3 *they were really kind to me:* very, extremely, thoroughly, decidedly, exceptionally, exceedingly, immensely, tremendously, uncommonly, remarkably, eminently, extraordinarily, most, downright; informal awfully, dreadfully, terribly, terrifically, ultra, seriously; Brit. informal dead, jolly; old use exceeding.

realm noun
1 *his prime concern was to promote peace in the realm:* kingdom, country, land, nation, dominion.
2 *the realm of academic research is new to me:* domain, world, field, sphere, area, province, territory, arena.

reap verb *the company is reaping the benefits of these investments:* receive, obtain, get, acquire, secure, realize, enjoy.

rear[1] noun
1 *the door at the rear of the building was unlocked:* back, hind part, back end; Nautical stern.
2 *get to the rear of the queue:* tail end, tail, end, rear end, back end.
OPPOSITES: front.
▷ **adjective** *the rear bumper was dented:* back, rearmost; hind, hindmost; Anatomy posterior; Nautical aft.

rear[2] verb
1 *I was born and reared in Newcastle:* bring up, raise, care for, look after, nurture, parent; educate.
2 *the need to rear the livestock and crops we depend on:* breed, raise, keep; grow, cultivate.
3 *he stiffened and reared his head:* raise, lift, hold up, uplift.
4 *Creagan Hill reared up before them:* rise, rise up, tower, soar, loom.

rearrange verb *the furniture has been rearranged to make more room:* reposition, move round, change round, arrange differently, reorganize, alter, adjust, reschedule; Brit. rejig.

reason noun
1 *the reasons for their visit are not entirely clear:* cause, grounds, basis, rationale; motive, motivation, purpose, point, aim, intention, objective, goal; explanation, justification, argument, defence, vindication, excuse, pretext.
2 *now voices are railing against reason and science:* rationality, logic, logical thought, reasoning, cognition; formal ratiocination.
3 *he felt he was losing his reason:* sanity, mind, mental faculties; senses, wits; informal marbles.
4 *Richard realized he couldn't make her see reason:* sense, good sense, good judgement, common sense, wisdom, sagacity.

▷ **verb**
1 *a young child is unable to reason:* think rationally, think logically, use your head/brain, think things through.
2 *Scott reasoned that Annabel might be ill:* conclude, come to the conclusion, reckon, think, judge, calculate, deduce, infer, surmise; informal figure.
□ **reason with someone**
her husband tried to reason with her: talk round, bring round, win round, persuade, prevail on, convince, make someone see the light.
□ **with reason**
he was anxious, with good reason, about his political survival: justifiably, justly, legitimately, rightly, not unreasonably.

> WORD LINKS
> **rational** relating to reason

reasonable adjective
1 *he's a reasonable man | it seemed a reasonable explanation:* sensible, rational, logical, fair, fair-minded, just, equitable; intelligent, wise, level-headed, practical, realistic; sound, well reasoned, valid, commonsensical, tenable, plausible, credible, believable.
2 *you must take all reasonable precautions to ensure his safety:* within reason, practicable, sensible; appropriate, suitable.
3 *most hire cars are in reasonable condition:* fairly good, acceptable, satisfactory, average, adequate, fair, all right, tolerable, passable; informal OK.
4 *good hot food at reasonable prices:* affordable, inexpensive, moderate, low, cheap, budget, bargain; competitive.
OPPOSITES: unreasonable.

reasoned adjective *we succeeded through reasoned argument:* logical, rational, well thought out, clear, lucid, coherent, cogent, well expressed, well presented, considered, sensible.
OPPOSITES: arbitrary, illogical.

reasoning noun *what was the reasoning behind the decision?* thinking, reason, train of thought, thought process, logic, analysis, interpretation, explanation, rationalization; reasons, rationale, arguments.

reassure verb put/set someone's mind at rest, put someone at ease; encourage, hearten, buoy up, cheer up; comfort, soothe.
OPPOSITES: alarm.

rebate noun partial refund, partial repayment; discount, deduction, reduction, concession, percentage, commission.
OPPOSITES: premium, surcharge.

rebel noun
1 *the rebels took control of the capital:* insurgent, revolutionary, insurrectionist, mutineer, terrorist, guerrilla, freedom fighter.

r

2 *the modern concept of the artist as a rebel:* nonconformist, dissenter, dissident, iconoclast, maverick, refusenik, individualist, independent, free spirit, freethinker, original.

▷ **verb**
1 *the citizens rebelled against this new law:* revolt, mutiny, riot, rise up, take up arms, stage a rebellion, be insubordinate.
2 (**rebel against**) *most teenagers rebel against their parents:* defy, disobey, refuse to obey, kick against, challenge, oppose, resist.
OPPOSITES: conform, obey.

▷ **adjective**
1 *rebel troops were executed on the spot:* insurgent, revolutionary, mutinous, rebellious, insurrectionary.
2 *the rebel MPs have given the government a rough ride:* rebellious, defiant, disobedient, insubordinate, subversive, recalcitrant; nonconformist, maverick, iconoclastic.
OPPOSITES: compliant.

rebellion noun
1 *troops were sent in to suppress the rebellion:* uprising, revolt, insurrection, mutiny, revolution, insurgence, insurgency; rioting, riot, disorder, unrest.
2 *he resigned as an act of rebellion:* defiance, disobedience, rebelliousness, insubordination, resistance, non-conformity, independence.
OPPOSITES: conformity.

rebellious adjective
1 *rebellious troops went on the rampage:* rebel, insurgent, mutinous, insurrectionary.
2 *a rebellious adolescent:* defiant, disobedient, insubordinate, unruly, mutinous, wayward, obstreperous, recalcitrant, intractable; maverick, independent, nonconformist, freethinking, individualistic; formal refractory; Brit. informal bolshie.
OPPOSITES: loyal, compliant.

rebirth noun *the rebirth of right-wing ideology:* revival, renaissance, resurrection, reawakening, renewal, regeneration; formal renascence.

rebound verb
1 *the ball rebounded off the wall:* bounce, ricochet, glance off, be deflected, spring back, recoil.
2 *later, sterling rebounded and closed half a cent higher:* recover, rally, pick up, make a recovery.
3 *Thomas's tactics rebounded on him:* backfire, boomerang, have unwelcome repercussions; old use redound on.

rebuff verb *his offer was immediately rebuffed:* reject, turn down, spurn, refuse, decline, snub, slight, repulse, repel, dismiss, brush off, give someone the cold

shoulder; informal give someone the brush-off.
OPPOSITES: welcome.

▷ **noun** *the rebuff did little to dampen his ardour:* rejection, snub, slight, repulse; refusal; informal brush-off, slap in the face.

rebuild verb reconstruct, renovate, restore, remodel, remake, reassemble, revamp.
OPPOSITES: demolish.

rebuke verb *she never rebuked him in front of others:* reprimand, reproach, scold, admonish, reprove, chastise, upbraid, berate, take to task, criticize, censure; formal castigate; informal tell off.
OPPOSITES: praise.

▷ **noun** *Damian was silenced by the rebuke:* reprimand, reproach, reproof, scolding, admonishment, admonition, upbraiding; formal castigation; informal telling-off.
OPPOSITES: praise.

rebut verb *Labour councillors rebutted the allegations:* refute, deny, disprove; invalidate, negate, contradict, counter, discredit, give the lie to, explode; formal confute, controvert.
OPPOSITES: confirm.

rebuttal noun refutation, denial, countering, invalidation, negation, contradiction.
OPPOSITES: confirmation.

recalcitrant adjective *she was faced with a class of 30 recalcitrant 15-year-olds:* uncooperative, intractable, insubordinate, defiant, rebellious, wilful, wayward, headstrong, self-willed, contrary, perverse, difficult, awkward; formal refractory; Brit. informal bloody-minded, bolshie.
OPPOSITES: cooperative, amenable.

recall verb *he recalled his student days with affection:* remember, recollect, call to mind; think back on/to, look back on, reminisce about.
OPPOSITES: forget.

▷ **noun** *with practice, people can improve their recall of dreams:* recollection, memory.

recant verb
1 *he was forced to recant his political beliefs:* renounce, disavow, deny, repudiate, renege on; formal forswear, abjure.
2 *charged with heresy, he refused to recant:* change your mind; backtrack.

recapitulate verb *allow me to recapitulate some of the main points of the argument:* summarize, sum up, recap; restate, repeat, reiterate, go over, review.

recede verb
1 *the flood waters receded:* retreat, go back/down, move back/away, withdraw, ebb, subside, abate.
2 *the lights receded into the distance:* disappear, fade, be lost to view.

r

3 *fears of widespread violence have receded:* diminish, lessen, decrease, dwindle, fade, abate, subside, ebb, wane.
OPPOSITES: advance, grow.

receipt noun
1 *the receipt of his letter threw Clara into ecstasy:* receiving, getting, obtaining; arrival, delivery.
2 *always make sure you get a receipt:* proof of purchase, sales voucher, till receipt, ticket.
3 (**receipts**) *receipts from council house sales:* proceeds, takings, money/payment received, income, revenue, earnings; profits, returns, return.

receive verb
1 *Tony received an award | they received £650 in damages:* be given, be presented with, be awarded, collect; get, obtain, gain, acquire; win, be paid, earn, gross, net.
2 *she received a letter from the council threatening court action:* be sent, be in receipt of, accept delivery of.
3 *his family received the news on Monday:* be told, hear, discover, find out, learn; informal get wind of.
4 *she received a serious injury:* sustain, meet with, suffer, get, experience, undergo.
5 *the couple looked radiant as they received their guests:* greet, welcome, meet, say hello to.
OPPOSITES: give, send.

recent adjective *recent research has failed to support this claim:* new, the latest, current, fresh, modern, contemporary, up to date, up to the minute.
OPPOSITES: old.

recently adverb not long ago, a short time ago, in the past few days/weeks/months, a little while back; lately, latterly, just now.

receptacle noun container, holder, repository, vessel; box, tin, bin, can, canister, case, basket, pot, bag.

reception noun
1 *the reception of foreign diplomats was his wife's responsibility:* greeting, welcoming, entertaining, meeting.
2 *they met with a chilly reception from my mother:* response, reaction, welcome, treatment.
3 *there was a small reception after the preview:* party, function, soirée; informal do, bash.

receptive adjective *a receptive audience | the institution was receptive to new ideas:* open-minded, responsive, amenable, welcoming, well disposed, sympathetic, flexible, approachable, accessible.
OPPOSITES: unreceptive.

recess noun
1 *the two recesses had been fitted with bookshelves:* alcove, bay, niche, nook, corner, hollow.

2 *the Christmas recess begins on Thursday:* break, adjournment, holiday, rest, interlude, interval; N. Amer. vacation.

recession noun economic decline, downturn, depression, slump, trough, slowdown.
OPPOSITES: boom.

recherché adjective *most of the titles are recherché and long out of stock:* obscure, rare, esoteric, abstruse, arcane, recondite, exotic, strange, unusual, unfamiliar.

recipe noun *low taxes are not always a recipe for success:* means, prescription, formula, blueprint, guarantee, key, passport, answer, solution.

recipient noun receiver, beneficiary, legatee, donee, payee, addressee.
OPPOSITES: donor, sender.

reciprocal adjective *reciprocal care between neighbours grows where trust is high:* mutual, common, shared, joint, corresponding, complementary, returned.
OPPOSITES: one-sided.

reciprocate verb
1 *I was happy to reciprocate:* do the same in return, return the favour, respond in kind.
2 *her love for him was not reciprocated:* requite, return, give back.

recital noun
1 *he gave his first piano recital at the age of 16:* concert, performance, solo; informal gig.
2 *her recital of Adam's failures:* listing, litany, catalogue, enumeration, detailing, recounting; account, list, report, description, recapitulation.
3 *a recital of the Lord's Prayer.* See RECITATION sense 1.

recitation noun
1 *the recitation of his poem was greeted with wild applause:* recital, reading, declamation, rendering, rendition, delivery, performance.
2 *do not respond to a question with a recitation of your life story:* account, description, narration, narrative.

recite verb
1 *he began to recite verses from the Koran:* say, repeat from memory, declaim, quote, deliver, render, perform.
2 *Sir John recited the facts they knew:* list, enumerate, detail, reel off; recount, relate, describe, narrate, give an account of, recapitulate, rehearse, repeat.

reckless adjective rash, careless, thoughtless, heedless, unheeding, hasty, overhasty, precipitate, precipitous, impetuous, impulsive, daredevil, devil-may-care; irresponsible, foolhardy, ill-advised, injudicious, madcap, imprudent, unwise, ill-considered.
OPPOSITES: cautious.

r

reckon verb

1 *the cost was reckoned at £6,000:* calculate, compute, work out, put a figure on, figure; count up, add up, total; Brit. tot up.

2 *category A prisoners are reckoned the most dangerous:* regard as, consider, judge, hold to be, think of as; deem, rate, gauge, count.

3 *Anselm reckoned Hugh among his friends:* include, count, consider to be, regard as, look on as.

4 (informal) *I reckon I can manage that:* believe, think, be of the opinion/view, be convinced, dare say, guess, suppose, consider; N. Amer. informal figure.

5 *they had reckoned on a day or two more of privacy:* expect, anticipate, hope for, be looking for; count on, rely on, depend on, bank on; N. Amer. informal figure on.

□ **reckon with**

1 *it's her mother you'll have to reckon with:* deal with, contend with, face.

2 *they hadn't reckoned with her burning ambition:* take into account, take into consideration, bargain for/on, allow for, anticipate, foresee, be prepared for, consider; formal take cognizance of.

□ **reckon without**

unfortunately, he had reckoned without the police sniffer dogs: overlook, fail to take account of, disregard, forget about.

reckoning noun *by my reckoning, this comes to £2 million:* calculation, estimation, computation, working out, summation, addition.

reclaim verb

1 *travelling expenses can be reclaimed:* get back, claim back, recover, regain, retrieve, recoup.

2 *the fuel rods are reprocessed to reclaim the uranium:* recover, save, rescue, recycle, reuse, reprocess.

recline verb *she was reclining on a sun lounger by the pool:* lie back, lie down, lean back; be recumbent; relax, repose, loll, lounge, sprawl, stretch out; literary couch.

reclusive adjective solitary, secluded, private, isolated, hermit-like, cloistered.
OPPOSITES: gregarious.

recognition noun

1 *there was no sign of recognition on his face:* identification, recollection, remembrance.

2 *his recognition of his lack of experience is very refreshing:* acknowledgement, acceptance, admission; realization, awareness, consciousness, knowledge, appreciation; formal cognizance.

3 *we have sought official recognition on several occasions:* approval, certification, accreditation, endorsement, validation.

4 *you deserve some recognition for the tremendous job you are doing:* appreciation, gratitude, thanks, credit, congratulations, commendation, acclaim, acknowledgement.

recognizable adjective identifiable, noticeable, perceptible, discernible, detectable, distinguishable, observable, perceivable; distinct, unmistakable, clear.
OPPOSITES: unrecognizable, imperceptible.

recognize verb

1 *Hannah recognized him at once:* identify, place, know, put a name to; remember, recall, recollect; know by sight.

2 *though they never liked him, they recognized Alan's ability:* acknowledge, accept, admit; realize, be aware of, be conscious of, perceive, discern, appreciate; formal be cognizant of.

3 *many therapists are recognized by the BPS:* approve, certify, accredit, endorse, sanction, validate.

4 *the Trust has finally recognized their hard work:* pay tribute to, show appreciation of, appreciate, be grateful for, acclaim, commend.

recoil verb

1 *as he leaned towards her, she instinctively recoiled:* draw back, jump back, pull back; flinch, shy away, shrink back, blench.

2 *he pictured them in his mind and recoiled from the thought:* feel revulsion at, feel disgust at, be unable to stomach, shrink from, baulk at.

3 *his rifle recoiled violently:* kick back, jump, jerk, spring back.

recollect verb remember, recall, call to mind, think of; think back to, look back on, reminisce about.
OPPOSITES: forget.

recollection noun memory, remembrance, impression, reminiscence.

recommend verb

1 *his former employer recommended him for the post:* suggest, put forward, propose, nominate, put up; speak well of, put in a good word for, vouch for, endorse, commend.

2 *the committee recommended a cautious approach:* advise, counsel, urge, exhort, argue for, back, support; suggest, advocate, propose; formal enjoin.

recommendation noun

1 *the government accepted the advisory group's recommendations:* advice, counsel, guidance, direction; suggestion, proposal.

2 *a personal recommendation is best when looking for an agent:* commendation, endorsement, good word, testimonial; suggestion, tip.

recompense verb compensate, repay, reimburse, indemnify, make reparation to, make amends to.

reconcile verb

1 *the news of his death reconciled us:* reunite, bring back together, restore friendly relations between, conciliate.

2 *he is trying to reconcile his religious beliefs with his career:* square, make congruent, make something fit in with, balance, harmonize, combine.
OPPOSITES: alienate.
☐ **reconcile yourself to**
they had to reconcile themselves to drastic losses: accept, come to accept, resign yourself to, come to terms with, learn to live with, get used to, make the best of.

reconciliation noun
1 *the reconciliation of the disputants was a long way off:* reuniting, bringing together, conciliation.
2 *there was little hope of reconciliation:* restoration of harmony, agreement, compromise, understanding, peace; formal concord.
3 *the reconciliation of theory with practice can be problematic:* squaring, balancing, harmonization.

recondite adjective *such recondite topics as Elizabethan Classicists, and early translations of Homer:* obscure, abstruse, arcane, esoteric, recherché; difficult, complex, complicated.

recondition verb *the ship is currently being reconditioned:* overhaul, rebuild, renovate, restore, repair, reconstruct, remodel, refurbish; informal do up, revamp.

reconnaissance noun survey, exploration, observation, investigation, examination, inspection; patrol, search; informal recce.

reconnoitre verb *a squadron was dispatched to reconnoitre the area:* survey, explore, scout out; investigate, examine, scrutinize, inspect, observe; patrol; informal recce.

reconsider verb rethink, review, revisit, revise, re-examine, re-evaluate, reassess, reappraise; change, alter, modify; have second thoughts, change your mind.

reconsideration noun rethink, review, re-examination, re-evaluation, reassessment, reappraisal.

reconstruct verb
1 *the building had to be substantially reconstructed:* rebuild, recreate, remake, reassemble, restore, renovate, remodel, refashion, revamp, recondition, refurbish.
2 *reconstructing the events of that day has proved hard:* recreate, build up a picture/impression of, piece together, re-enact.

record noun
1 *there are no written records of the investigation:* account, document, documentation, data, file, dossier, evidence, report; chronicle, annals, archives; minutes, transactions, proceedings, transcript; certificates, deeds; register, log, logbook.
2 *he would have gone to prison had it not been for his previous good record:* history,

track record, reputation, background.
3 *it was a great run, and a new British record:* best performance, personal best; fastest time.
4 *this will be a lasting record of what they have achieved:* reminder, memorial, souvenir, memento, remembrance, testament.
▷ **adjective** *the company has announced record profits:* record-breaking, unsurpassed, unparalleled, unequalled, second to none.
▷ **verb**
1 *the doctor recorded her blood pressure:* write down, take down, note, make a note of, jot down; document, put on record, enter, minute, register, log; list, catalogue.
2 *the team recorded their fourth away win:* achieve, accomplish, chalk up, notch up; informal clock up.
☐ **off the record**
his comments were strictly off the record: unofficial, confidential, private, in confidence, between ourselves, not for publication.

recount verb tell, relate, narrate, give an account of, describe, report, outline, delineate, relay, convey, communicate, impart.

recoup verb get back, recover, regain, win back, retrieve, redeem.

recourse noun
☐ **have recourse to**
all three countries had recourse to the IMF for loans: resort to, make use of, avail yourself of, turn to, call on, look to, fall back on.

recover verb
1 *it took time to recover from his heart attack:* recuperate, get better, convalesce, regain your strength, get stronger, get back on your feet; be on the mend, pick up, rally, respond to treatment, improve, heal, pull through, bounce back.
2 *the stolen material has been recovered:* retrieve, regain possession of, get back, recoup, reclaim, repossess, redeem, find, track down, rescue, salvage, save.
OPPOSITES: deteriorate, lose.

recovery noun
1 *her recovery may be slow, even with physiotherapy:* recuperation, convalescence, response to treatment, improvement, rally.
2 *the recovery of the stolen goods was a high priority:* retrieval, regaining, repossession, reclamation, recouping, redemption.
OPPOSITES: relapse, deterioration, loss.

recreation noun
1 *cycling is a popular form of recreation:* pleasure, leisure, relaxation, fun, enjoyment, entertainment, amusement; play, sport; informal R & R.
2 *his favourite recreations were skating and*

r

fishing: pastime, hobby, leisure activity.
OPPOSITES: work.

recrimination noun *de Gaulle did not spend much time in recriminations against those responsible for the defeat:* accusation, counter-accusation, countercharge, counter-attack, retaliation, reproach, denunciation.

recruit verb
1 *more soldiers were recruited:* enlist, call up, conscript; US draft.
2 *the company is currently recruiting staff:* hire, employ, take on, engage, appoint.
OPPOSITES: demobilize, dismiss.
▷ **noun**
1 *hundreds of new recruits were enlisted:* conscript; US draftee.
2 *the profession continues to attract top-quality recruits:* starter, newcomer, new entrant, initiate, beginner, novice, trainee, apprentice.

rectify verb *mistakes made now cannot be rectified later:* correct, put right, put to rights, sort out, deal with, amend, remedy, repair, fix, make good, resolve, settle; informal patch up.

rectitude noun *no one dared challenge the rectitude of the chief constable:* virtue, morality, integrity, probity, honesty, honour, righteousness, principle, trustworthiness, uprightness, decency, good character.
OPPOSITES: immorality.

recumbent adjective *he didn't move from his recumbent position on the sofa:* lying, flat, horizontal, stretched out, sprawled, reclining, prone, prostrate, supine; lying down.
OPPOSITES: upright.

recuperate verb *after the operation, he went to France to recuperate:* get better, recover, convalesce, get well, regain your strength/health, get over something.

recur verb *his symptoms recurred when the drug was reintroduced:* happen again, reoccur, repeat itself; come back, return, reappear, appear again.

recurrent adjective repeated, recurring, repetitive, periodic, continual, cyclical, seasonal, perennial, regular, frequent; intermittent, sporadic, spasmodic.
OPPOSITES: single, one-off.

recycle verb reuse, reprocess, reclaim, recover; salvage, save.

red adjective
1 *a red dress:* scarlet, vermilion, ruby, cherry-red, cerise, carmine, blood-red; coral, rose; brick-red, maroon.
2 *he was red in the face:* flushed, reddish, pink, florid; ruddy, rosy, glowing; burning, feverish; literary rubicund.
3 *she had long red hair:* ginger, auburn, Titian, chestnut; rufous.

□ **in the red**
overdrawn, in debt, in debit, in deficit, in arrears.

redden verb *she reddened at this description of herself:* blush, flush, colour, burn.

redeem verb
1 *in the second half, Cox redeemed his earlier mistake with a tremendous goal:* compensate for, make up for, cancel out.
2 *Billy finally redeemed his drums from the pawnbrokers:* retrieve, regain, recover, get back, reclaim, repossess; buy back.
3 *this voucher can be redeemed at any branch:* exchange, cash in, convert, trade in.

redeeming adjective *a terrible film with no redeeming features:* compensating, saving, compensatory, extenuating, mitigating.

redemption noun
1 *cash must be made available for the redemption of their possessions:* retrieval, recovery, reclamation, repossession, repurchase, return.
2 *the redemption of credit vouchers is optional:* exchange, cashing in, conversion.

redolent adjective *the old church is redolent of everything English:* evocative, reminiscent, suggestive, expressive.

redoubtable adjective *the redoubtable Miss Fortescue chaired as usual:* formidable, awe-inspiring, forbidding, fearsome, daunting; impressive, commanding, indomitable, doughty.
OPPOSITES: approachable.

redress verb *people no longer take to the streets to redress social wrongs:* rectify, correct, right, put right, amend, remedy, make good, resolve, settle, revenge.
▷ noun *your best hope of redress is through the courts:* compensation, reparation, restitution, recompense, repayment, indemnification; retribution, satisfaction, revenge; justice.

reduce verb
1 *the aim is to reduce pollution | an effort to reduce the gap between rich and poor:* cut, lessen, lower, bring down, decrease, diminish, minimize; narrow, contract, shorten.
2 *the workforce has been reduced to some 6,000:* cut, trim, prune, shrink, scale back, streamline, downsize; Brit. rationalize
3 *he reduced her to tears:* bring, drive, force.
OPPOSITES: increase.

reduction noun
1 *an overall reduction in pollution levels:* lessening, lowering, decrease; diminution, narrowing, contraction.
2 *the closure has led to a reduction in staff:* cut, cutback, scaling down,

r

pruning, streamlining, downsizing; Brit. rationalization.
3 *substantial price reductions:* discount, markdown, deduction, cut, concession.
OPPOSITES: increase.

redundancy noun lay-off, downsizing; dismissal, sacking, discharge; unemployment.

redundant adjective
1 *many country churches are sadly redundant:* unnecessary, unneeded, uncalled for, surplus to requirements, superfluous.
2 *2,000 workers were now redundant:* unemployed, jobless, out of work, out of a job.
OPPOSITES: necessary, employed.
▫ **make someone redundant**
lay off, let go, give notice to, dismiss, discharge, put out of a job; informal sack, fire, give someone their cards.

reek verb *the whole place reeked:* stink, smell.
▷ **noun** *the reek of cattle dung:* stink, smell, stench; literary miasma.

reel verb
1 *he reeled as the ship began to roll:* stagger, lurch, sway, rock, stumble, totter, wobble, falter.
2 *we were still reeling from the share crisis:* be shaken, be stunned, be in shock, be shocked, be taken aback, be staggered, be aghast, be upset.
▫ **reel something off**
the waitress proceeded to reel off the dishes of the day: recite, list, run through, enumerate, detail, itemize; informal rattle off.

refer verb *the matter has now been referred to my solicitor:* pass, hand on/over, send on, transfer, remit, entrust, assign.
▫ **refer to**
1 *he referred indirectly to various errors in the article:* mention, make reference to, allude to, touch on, speak of/about, talk of/about, write about, comment on, deal with, point out, call attention to.
2 *these figures refer only to 2001:* apply to, be relevant to, concern, relate to, be connected with, pertain to, be pertinent to, cover; formal appertain to.
3 *the name refers to a Saxon village:* denote, describe, indicate, mean, signify, designate.
4 *the constable referred to his notes:* consult, look at, glance at, read, check, turn to, have recourse to.

referee noun
1 *the referee blew his whistle again:* umpire, judge, adjudicator, linesman; informal ref.
2 *include the names of two referees with your application:* supporter, character witness, advocate.
▷ **verb** *he refereed the game for the last time:* umpire, judge, adjudicate.

reference noun
1 *his journal contains many references to railways:* mention of, allusion to, comment on, remark about.
2 *references are given in the bibliography:* source, citation, authority, credit.
3 *the case can only be resolved by reference to a higher court:* referral, transfer, remission.
4 *he received a glowing reference:* testimonial, recommendation.
▫ **with reference to**
apropos of, with regard to, as regards, regarding, with respect to, on the subject of, re; in relation to, relating to, in connection with.

referendum noun vote, plebiscite, ballot, poll.

refine verb
1 *we lose fibre by refining our cereal foods:* purify, process, treat, polish.
2 *this course helps students to refine their language skills:* improve, perfect, polish up, hone, fine-tune; touch up, revise, edit.

refined adjective
1 *we don't need highly refined sugar:* purified, processed, treated.
2 *she was very refined, a real lady:* cultivated, cultured; stylish, elegant, sophisticated, urbane; polite, gracious, well mannered, well bred, gentlemanly, ladylike, genteel.
3 *a person of refined taste such as yourself:* discriminating, discerning, fastidious, exquisite, impeccable, fine.
OPPOSITES: crude, coarse.

refinement noun
1 *he feels his writing needs endless refinement:* improvement, polishing, honing, fine-tuning; touching up, revision, editing.
2 *she was a woman of great refinement:* style, elegance, finesse, sophistication, urbanity; politeness, grace, good manners, good breeding, gentility; cultivation, taste, discrimination.

reflect verb
1 *the snow reflected the light:* send back, throw back.
2 *their expressions reflected their feelings:* indicate, show, display, demonstrate, manifest, be evidence of, register, reveal, betray, disclose; formal evince.
3 *he reflected on his responsibilities:* think about, give thought to, consider, review, mull over, contemplate, meditate on, muse on, brood on/over, turn over in your mind; formal cogitate about/on.
▫ **reflect badly on**
the incident reflected badly on the government: discredit, disgrace, shame, put in a bad light, damage, tarnish the reputation of, give a bad name to, bring into disrepute.

r

reflection noun

1 *healthy skin is a reflection of good health in general:* indication, display, demonstration, manifestation; expression, evidence.
2 *the results of the survey are no reflection on the business as a whole:* discredit to, reproach to, criticism of, slur on.
3 *after some reflection, he turned the offer down:* thought, consideration, contemplation, deliberation, pondering, meditation, musing, rumination; formal cogitation.
4 *write down your reflections on the subject:* opinion, thought, view, belief, feeling, idea, impression, conclusion, assessment; comment, observation, remark.

reflex adjective *sneezing is a reflex action:* instinctive, automatic, involuntary, impulsive, intuitive, spontaneous, unconscious.
OPPOSITES: conscious, learned.

reform verb

1 *a comprehensive plan to reform the health-care system:* improve, make better, ameliorate, refine, change, adjust, adapt, amend, reshape, refashion, redesign, revamp, remodel, reorganize.
2 *after his marriage he reformed completely:* mend your ways, turn over a new leaf.
▷ noun *reform of the prison system is a high priority:* improvement, amelioration, refinement; change, amendment, reshaping, refashioning, reorganization.

refrain verb *he should refrain from making comments on subjects he knows little about:* abstain, desist, hold back, stop yourself, forbear, avoid, eschew; renounce; formal forswear; informal swear off.

refresh verb

1 *I'm sure the cool air will refresh me:* reinvigorate, revitalize, revive, restore, fortify, enliven, stimulate, energize, wake up; informal perk up, buck up, pep up.
2 *let me refresh your memory:* jog, prompt, prod.

refreshing adjective

1 *enjoy a refreshing drink in our juice bar:* invigorating, revitalizing, reviving, restoring, restorative, bracing, fortifying, enlivening, stimulating, energizing.
2 *this is a refreshing change of direction:* welcome, stimulating, fresh, imaginative, innovative.

refreshment noun

1 *refreshments were available in the interval:* food and drink, sustenance; snacks, titbits; formal comestibles; informal nibbles; dated victuals.
2 *we are in need of spiritual refreshment:* invigoration, revival, renewal, stimulation, reanimation, rejuvenation, regeneration.

refuge noun

1 *homeless people are seeking refuge in subway stations:* shelter, protection, safety, security, asylum, sanctuary.
2 *she founded a refuge for mountain gorillas:* sanctuary, shelter, haven; retreat, bolt-hole, hiding place, hideaway, hideout.

refugee noun asylum seeker, fugitive, displaced person, stateless person, exile, outcast.

refund verb

1 *we will refund your money if you're not satisfied:* repay, give back, return, pay back.
2 *they refunded the subscribers:* reimburse, compensate, recompense, remunerate, indemnify.
▷ noun *I loudly demanded a full refund:* repayment, reimbursement.

refurbish verb *the premises have been completely refurbished:* renovate, recondition, rehabilitate, revamp, overhaul, restore, renew, refit, redevelop, redecorate, spruce up, upgrade; informal do up.

refusal noun

1 *we had one refusal to our invitation:* rejection, non-acceptance, no, demurral, turndown; regrets, apologies.
2 *the refusal of planning permission was a disappointment:* withholding, denial.

refuse¹ verb

1 *he refused their invitation:* decline, turn down, say no to; reject, spurn; send your regrets; informal pass up.
2 *the Council refused planning permission:* withhold, deny, turn down.
OPPOSITES: accept, grant.

refuse² noun *piles of refuse lay in the streets:* rubbish, waste, debris, litter, detritus, dross; N. Amer. garbage, trash.

refute verb

1 *there have been numerous attempts to refute Einstein's theory:* disprove, prove wrong/false, rebut, give the lie to, explode, debunk, discredit, invalidate; formal confute, controvert.
2 *she refuted the allegation:* deny, reject, repudiate, rebut; contradict; formal gainsay.
OPPOSITES: prove, admit.

regain verb recover, get back, win back, recoup, retrieve, reclaim, repossess; take back, retake, recapture, reconquer.

regal adjective *his regal forebears:* royal, kingly, queenly, princely.

regale verb

1 *he regaled her with colourful stories:* entertain, amuse, divert, delight, fascinate, captivate.
2 *they were regaled with refreshments wherever they went:* entertain, wine and dine, fete, feast, serve.

r

regard verb
1 *we regard these results as very encouraging:* consider, look on, view, see, think of, judge, deem, assess, reckon, adjudge, rate.
2 *he regarded her coldly:* look at, eye, contemplate, gaze at, stare at; watch, observe, view, study, scrutinize; literary behold.

▷**noun**
1 *he has no regard for human life:* consideration, concern, thought, notice, heed, care, attention.
2 *doctors are held in high regard:* esteem, respect, admiration, approval, estimation.
3 *Jamie sends his regards:* best wishes, greetings, kind/kindest regards, salutations, respects, compliments, best; formal felicitations.
4 *in this regard I'm afraid I disagree with you:* respect, aspect, point, item, particular, detail, specific; matter, issue, topic, question.

regarding preposition concerning, as regards, with/in regard to, with respect to, with reference to, relating to, respecting, re, about, apropos of, on the subject of, in connection with, vis-à-vis.

regardless adverb *he decided to go, regardless:* anyway, anyhow, in any case, nevertheless, nonetheless, despite everything, in spite of everything, even so, all the same, in any event, come what may; informal irregardless.

□ **regardless of**
the allowance is paid regardless of age or income: irrespective of, without regard to, without reference to, disregarding, ignoring, notwithstanding, no matter.

regenerate verb *the money will be used to regenerate the town centre:* revive, revitalize, renew, restore, breathe new life into, rejuvenate, reanimate, resuscitate; informal give a shot in the arm to.

regime noun
1 *the former Communist regime:* government, administration, leadership, authorities, rule, authority, command; system, establishment.
2 *there is a very favourable tax regime here:* system, arrangement, scheme, plan, programme.

regiment noun *the regiment was fighting in France:* unit, outfit, force, corps, division, brigade, battalion, squadron, company, platoon.

regimented adjective strictly regulated, organized, disciplined, controlled, ordered, systematic; rigid, inflexible.

region noun *a major wine-producing region of France:* area, zone, district, sector, belt, quarter, province, territory, division.

□ **in the region of**
annual sales were in the region of £30 million. See **APPROXIMATELY**.

regional adjective
1 *there is considerable regional variation:* geographical, territorial.
2 *a regional parliament:* local, provincial, district, parochial, devolved.
OPPOSITES: national.

register noun
1 *are you on the register of electors?* list, roll, roster, index, directory, catalogue, inventory.
2 *we checked the parish register:* record, chronicle, log, logbook, ledger, archive; annals, files.

▷**verb**
1 *I wish to register a complaint:* record, put on record, enter, file, lodge, submit, report, note, minute, log.
2 *it is not too late to register:* enrol, put your name down, enlist, sign on/up, apply.
3 *her face registered anger:* display, show, express, exhibit, betray, evidence, reveal, manifest, demonstrate; formal evince, bespeak.

regress verb *the patient has regressed to a dependent and helpless state:* revert, retrogress, relapse, lapse, backslide, slip back; deteriorate, decline, worsen, degenerate; informal go downhill.
OPPOSITES: progress.

regret verb
1 *they came to regret their decision:* be sorry about, rue, repent.
2 *this is a poem regretting the passing of his youth:* mourn, grieve for/over, lament, sorrow for, deplore.
OPPOSITES: welcome.

▷**noun**
1 *both players later expressed regret:* remorse, sorrow, contrition, repentance, penitence, guilt.
2 *they left the area with genuine regret:* sadness, sorrow, disappointment, unhappiness, grief.
OPPOSITES: satisfaction, joy.

regretful adjective sorry, remorseful, contrite, repentant, rueful, penitent, conscience-stricken, apologetic, guilt-ridden, ashamed, shamefaced.
OPPOSITES: unrepentant.

regrettable adjective unfortunate, undesirable, unwelcome, sorry, woeful, disappointing; deplorable, lamentable, shameful, disgraceful.

regular adjective
1 *plant them at regular intervals in a light soil:* uniform, even, constant, fixed, consistent.
2 *the proposal is the subject of regular protests:* frequent, repeated, continual, recurrent, periodic, constant, perpetual.
3 *these are regular methods of business:*

r

established, conventional, orthodox, proper, official, approved, bona fide, standard, usual, traditional, tried and tested.
4 *his regular route to work took him past the church:* usual, normal, customary, habitual, routine, typical, accustomed, established; literary wonted.
OPPOSITES: irregular, occasional.

regulate verb
1 *the flow of the river has been regulated:* control, adjust, manage.
2 *the organization was set up to regulate the activities of local housing associations:* control, administer, manage; oversee, monitor, supervise.

regulation noun
1 *we are hampered by EU regulations:* rule, ruling, order, directive, act, law, by-law, statute, edict, pronouncement, decree, command.
2 *the regulation of financial markets:* control, management; supervision, monitoring.

regurgitate verb
1 *a cow or other ruminant continually regurgitates food:* bring up, disgorge.
2 *we were required to regurgitate large amounts of information:* repeat, say again, restate, reiterate, recite, parrot; informal trot out.

rehabilitate verb
1 *efforts to rehabilitate patients have proved unsuccessful:* reintegrate, readapt, reaccustom.
2 *former dissidents were gradually rehabilitated:* reinstate, restore, bring back; pardon, absolve, exonerate, forgive; formal exculpate.
3 *we are committed to rehabilitating vacant housing:* refurbish, restore, renovate, recondition, revamp, overhaul, redevelop, refit; upgrade, modernize; informal do up.

rehearsal noun practice, trial, read-through, run-through; informal dry run.

rehearse verb
1 *I rehearsed the role ceaselessly:* prepare, practise, read through, run through/over, go over; train, drill.
2 *the document rehearsed all the arguments in favour of the award:* enumerate, list, itemize, detail, spell out, catalogue, recite; restate, repeat, reiterate, go over, run through.

reign verb
1 *Robert II reigned for nineteen years:* be king/queen, sit on the throne, wear the crown, rule.
2 *for a few moments, chaos reigned:* prevail, exist, be present, rule, occur, be rife, be rampant, be the order of the day, be in force, be in effect; formal obtain.
▷ **noun**
1 *the later years of Henry's reign were far*

from happy: rule, sovereignty, monarchy.
2 *his reign as manager was at an end:* time, period, incumbency, managership, leadership.

reigning adjective
1 *the reigning monarch:* ruling; on the throne.
2 *he is the reigning world champion:* incumbent, current, presiding.

reimburse verb
1 *they will reimburse your travel costs:* repay, refund, return, pay back.
2 *don't worry, we'll reimburse you in full:* compensate, recompense, repay.

rein verb *the government failed to rein in public spending:* keep under control, restrain, check, curb, hold back/in, regulate, restrict, control, limit, curtail.
□ **free rein**
you'd be given free rein to run the show how you wanted it: freedom, a free hand, leeway, latitude, flexibility, liberty, independence, licence, room to manoeuvre, carte blanche.

reinforce verb
1 *hundreds of volunteers reinforced the dam:* strengthen, bolster up, shore up, buttress, prop up, underpin, brace, support.
2 *we are reinforcing links between colleges and companies:* strengthen, support; cement, boost, promote, encourage, deepen, enhance, intensify, improve.
3 *the need to reinforce NATO troops on the ground:* supplement, increase, add to, augment, boost; Brit. top up.
OPPOSITES: weaken.

reinforcements plural noun *they returned later with reinforcements:* additional troops, reserves, auxiliaries; support, backup, help.

reinstate verb restore, re-establish, return to power, reappoint, recall, put back, bring back, reinstitute, reinstall.

reiterate verb repeat, say again, restate, recapitulate, go over, rehearse.

reject verb
1 *the miners rejected the government's offer:* turn down, refuse, decline, say no to, spurn.
2 *she had been in love with Jamie, but he had rejected her:* rebuff, spurn, shun, snub, repudiate, cast off/aside, discard, abandon, desert, turn your back on; literary forsake.
OPPOSITES: accept.
▷ **noun** *I got it cheap—it's only a reject:* discard, second.

rejection noun
1 *the chairman's rejection of the offer:* refusal, declining, turning down, spurning.
2 *it took him a while to get over Madeleine's*

rejection: repudiation, rebuff.
OPPOSITES: acceptance.

rejoice verb *fans rejoiced at the victory over their local rivals:* be delighted, be thrilled, be happy, be pleased, be glad, be elated, be ecstatic, be euphoric, be overjoyed; exult, revel, celebrate.
OPPOSITES: mourn.

rejoicing noun happiness, pleasure, joy, delight, elation, jubilation, euphoria, exultation; celebration, revelry, merrymaking.
OPPOSITES: misery.

rejoinder noun *a smart rejoinder usually occurs to me on the bus later:* answer, reply, response, retort, riposte, counter; informal comeback.

rejuvenate verb *the leadership change was an attempt to rejuvenate the party:* revive, revitalize, regenerate, breathe new life into, bring fresh blood into; informal give a shot in the arm to, pep up, buck up.

relapse verb
1 *most patients get well, but a few relapse:* get ill/worse again, deteriorate, degenerate, take a turn for the worse.
2 *she relapsed into silence:* revert, lapse; slip back.
OPPOSITES: improve.

relate verb
1 *high unemployment is related to high crime rates:* connect, associate, link, correlate; ally, couple.
2 *many versions of the story have been related by local people:* tell, recount, narrate, report, chronicle, outline, recite, repeat.
□ **relate to**
1 *recent changes to the legislation relating to pensions:* apply to, be relevant to, concern, pertain to, have a bearing on, involve; formal appertain to.
2 *kids related to him because he was so rebellious:* get on with, identify with, empathize with, understand, feel sympathy with, feel for; informal hit it off with.

related adjective *in agriculture and related activities, women make up only 18.2 per cent of the workforce:* connected, interconnected, associated, linked, allied, affiliated, corresponding, parallel, comparable, equivalent; formal concomitant.
OPPOSITES: unrelated.

relation noun
1 *the king understood the relation between church and state:* connection, relationship, association, link, correlation, correspondence, parallel, alliance, bond, interrelation, interconnection.
2 *this information had no relation to national security:* relevance, applicability, reference, pertinence; bearing on.

3 *are you a relation of his?* relative, member of someone's family, kinsman, kinswoman; (**relations**) family, kin, kith and kin, kindred.
4 (**relations**) *he sought to improve relations with India:* dealings, communication, relationship, connections, contact, interaction.

relationship noun
1 *the study assesses the relationship between unemployment and political attitudes:* connection, relation, association, link, correlation, correspondence, interrelation, interconnection.
2 *he reacted badly to the end of their relationship:* romance, affair, liaison.

relative adjective
1 *do not underestimate the relative importance of each factor:* comparative, respective, comparable, parallel, corresponding.
2 *the food required is relative to body weight:* proportionate, proportional, in proportion, commensurate, corresponding.
3 *Semtex could be smuggled with relative ease:* moderate, reasonable, a fair degree of, considerable, comparative.
▷ **noun** *he's a relative of mine:* relation, member of someone's family, kinsman, kinswoman; (**relatives**) family, kin, kith and kin, kindred, kinsfolk.

relatively adverb *the hotel was clean and relatively cheap:* comparatively, by comparison; quite, fairly, reasonably, rather, somewhat, to a certain extent/degree, tolerably; informal pretty.

relax verb
1 *yoga is helpful in learning to relax:* unwind, loosen up, ease up/off, slow down, unbend, rest.
2 *a walk will relax you:* calm, calm down, unwind, loosen up, soothe, pacify, compose.
3 *he relaxed his grip on the mug:* loosen, loose, slacken, unclench, weaken.
4 *she felt her muscles relax:* become less tense, loosen, slacken, unknot.
5 *the ministry relaxed some of the restrictions:* ease, ease up on, temper, moderate, loosen, lighten, dilute, weaken, reduce, decrease; informal let up on.
OPPOSITES: tense, tighten.

relaxation noun
1 *I just play for relaxation nowadays:* recreation, enjoyment, amusement, entertainment, fun, pleasure, leisure; informal R & R.
2 *relaxation of censorship rules:* easing, loosening, lightening, moderation; weakening, reduction.

relay noun *we heard a live relay of the performance:* broadcast, transmission, showing.
▷ **verb** *it is not helpful relaying messages through a third party:* pass on, hand on, transfer, patch through, repeat,

r

communicate, send, transmit, disseminate, spread, circulate.

release verb

1 *all political prisoners were released:* free, set free, liberate, set at liberty, let out, allow to leave, let go.
2 *she released Stephen from his promise:* excuse, exempt, discharge, deliver, absolve; informal let off.
3 *police released the news yesterday:* issue, make known, make public, break, announce, declare, report, reveal, divulge, disclose, publish, broadcast, circulate, communicate, disseminate.
4 *the film has been released on video:* launch, put out, put on sale, bring out, make available.
OPPOSITES: imprison, withdraw.

▷ noun

1 *the government ordered the release of 100 political prisoners:* freeing, liberation, deliverance; freedom, liberty.
2 *the release of the news is subject to approval:* issuing, announcement, reporting, revelation, disclosure, publication, communication, dissemination.
3 *the group's last release was a big seller:* CD, album, single, record, song; video, film.

relegate verb *we've been relegated to the Second Division:* downgrade, demote, lower in rank/status, move down.
OPPOSITES: promote.

relent verb *the Ministry of Defence relented and lifted the prohibition order:* change your mind, do a U-turn, back-pedal, back down, give way/in, yield, capitulate; Brit. do an about-turn.

relentless adjective

1 *their relentless pursuit of quality has paid dividends:* persistent, continuing, constant, continual, continuous, non-stop, never-ending, interminable, incessant, unceasing, endless, unending, unremitting, unrelenting, remorseless; unfaltering, unflagging, untiring, unwavering, dogged, single-minded, tireless, indefatigable.
2 *he proved to be a relentless taskmaster:* harsh, severe, strict, remorseless, uncompromising, inflexible.
OPPOSITES: sporadic, intermittent.

relevant adjective pertinent, applicable, apposite, appropriate, material, to the point, germane; connected, related, linked.
OPPOSITES: irrelevant.

reliable adjective

1 *there is an absence of reliable evidence:* dependable, sound, well founded, authentic, valid, genuine, true.
2 *Jay proved a reliable friend:* trustworthy, dependable, true, faithful, devoted, steadfast, staunch, constant, loyal, trusty, dedicated.
OPPOSITES: unreliable.

reliance noun

1 *a personal pension reduces reliance on the state:* dependence.
2 *he displayed a lack of reliance on his own judgement:* trust, confidence, faith, belief, conviction.
OPPOSITES: independence, distrust.

relic noun

1 *the farmer uncovered a Viking relic:* artefact, antiquity, antique.
2 *a new generation of Internet users will view emails as a relic of the past:* leftover, remnant, vestige, survival, throwback.

relief noun

1 *finding out that there were other people who felt the same was a huge relief:* reassurance, consolation, comfort, solace; a weight of your mind.
2 *I used opium for the relief of pain:* alleviation, lessening, reduction, soothing, easing, palliation, assuagement.
3 *all she needed was a little light relief:* respite, amusement, diversion, distraction, entertainment, recreation.
OPPOSITES: worry, intensification.

relieve verb

1 *this simple device helps relieve pain:* alleviate, lessen, reduce, ease, diminish, mitigate, assuage, dull, palliate.
2 *there was no shortage of helpers to relieve us:* replace, take over from, stand in for, fill in for, substitute for, deputize for, cover for.
3 *this relieves the teacher of a heavy load:* free, set free, release, exempt, excuse, absolve, let off, discharge.
4 *study was a way of relieving the boredom:* counteract, counter, alleviate, mitigate; interrupt, vary, stop, dispel, prevent.
OPPOSITES: aggravate.

relieved adjective *I'll be relieved when it's all over:* glad, thankful, grateful, pleased, happy, reassured, consoled, comforted.
OPPOSITES: worried.

religion noun faith, belief, creed; church, faith community, denomination, sect, cult.

> WORD LINKS
> **divinity**, **theology** the study of religion

religious adjective

1 *I am not a religious person:* devout, pious, reverent, godly, God-fearing, churchgoing.
2 *she would not compromise her religious beliefs:* spiritual, theological, scriptural, doctrinal, ecclesiastical, church, holy, divine, sacred.
3 *they paid religious attention to detail:* scrupulous, conscientious, meticulous, sedulous, punctilious, strict, rigorous, close.

relinquish verb

1 *he relinquished control of the company:* renounce, give up/away, hand over, let go of.

2 *he offered to relinquish his post:* leave, resign from, stand down from, bow out of, give up; informal quit.
OPPOSITES: keep.

relish noun
1 *he seizes the opportunity with relish:* enjoyment, gusto, delight, pleasure, glee, rapture, satisfaction, contentment, appreciation, enthusiasm, appetite.
2 *the sauce may be served as a hot relish:* condiment, sauce, dressing, flavouring, seasoning, dip.
OPPOSITES: dislike.
▷**verb** *he was relishing his moment of glory:* enjoy, delight in, love, adore, take pleasure in, rejoice in, appreciate, savour, revel in, luxuriate in, glory in.
OPPOSITES: hate.

reluctance noun unwillingness, disinclination, aversion, resistance; hesitation, wavering; doubts, second thoughts, misgivings.
OPPOSITES: willingness.

reluctant adjective *her parents were reluctant to buy her a cat:* unwilling, disinclined, unenthusiastic, resistant, opposed, loath, averse; hesitant.
OPPOSITES: willing.

rely verb
□ rely on
we can rely on his discretion: depend on, count on, bank on, reckon on, be confident of, be sure of, believe in, have faith in, trust in; informal swear by; N. Amer. informal figure on.

remain verb
1 *a cloister is all that remains of the monastery:* survive, exist, continue to exist, endure.
2 *her husband remained at the flat:* stay, wait, be left, hang on, linger; informal hang around; Brit. informal stop.
3 *union leaders remain sceptical:* continue to be, stay, persist in being, carry on being.
4 *a few tickets remain for the Valentine's Party Night:* be left; be available, be unused.

remainder noun residue, balance, remaining part/number, rest, others, remnant, surplus, extra, excess, overflow.

remaining adjective
1 *Scotland's few remaining native pine-woods:* residual, surviving.
2 *my only remaining memories of these years:* surviving, lasting, enduring, continuing, lingering, abiding.
3 *ladle the soup into a serving bowl and top it with any remaining chopped herbs:* surplus, left over, spare, unused, extra.

remains plural noun
1 *she downed the remains of her drink:* remainder, residue, remaining part/number, rest, remnant.
2 *the saint's remains are housed in the cathedral:* corpse, body, carcass; bones, skeleton, relics.

remark verb *'You're quiet,' he remarked:* comment, say, observe, mention, reflect, state.
▷noun *his remarks have been misinterpreted:* comment, statement, utterance, observation.
□ remark on
many critics remarked on the rapport between the two stars: comment on, mention, refer to, speak of, pass comment on.

remarkable adjective *a remarkable achievement* | *a truly remarkable performance:* extraordinary, exceptional, outstanding, out of the ordinary, unusual, uncommon, surprising, amazing, astonishing, astounding, sensational, stunning, stupendous, incredible, unbelievable, phenomenal, momentous, marvellous, wonderful, tremendous; literary wondrous; informal fantastic, terrific, awesome.
OPPOSITES: ordinary.

remedy noun
1 *we provide traditional herbal remedies:* treatment, cure, curative, relief, antidote, medicine, medication, medicament.
2 *marriage is seen as a remedy for all kinds of problems:* solution, answer, cure, antidote, corrective, nostrum, panacea, cure-all; informal magic bullet.
▷verb *little has been done to remedy the situation:* correct, rectify, right, put/set right, put/set to rights, redress, solve, sort out, straighten out, counteract, resolve, repair, mend, fix, make good.

remember verb
1 *I remembered happier times:* recall, call to mind, recollect, think of; reminisce about, look back on.
2 *can you remember all that, or shall I write it down?* memorize, commit to memory, retain; learn off by heart.
3 *you must remember she's only five:* bear/keep in mind, not forget; take into account, take into consideration.
4 *remember to feed the cat:* be sure, be certain; mind that you, make sure that you.
5 *the nation remembered those who gave their lives:* commemorate, pay tribute to, honour, salute, pay homage to.
OPPOSITES: forget.

remembrance noun
1 *Ali's face took on an expression of remembrance:* recollection, reminiscence, recall.
2 *we sold poppies in remembrance of those who died:* commemoration, memory, recognition.

remind verb
1 *I left a note to remind him:* jog someone's memory, help someone remember, prompt.

2 *the song reminded me of my sister:* make you think of, make you remember, put you in mind of, bring/call to mind, evoke.

reminder noun prompt, aide-memoire; mnemonic.

reminisce verb
□ reminisce about
remember, cast your mind back to, look back on, be nostalgic about, recall, recollect, reflect on, call to mind, hark back to.

reminiscences plural noun memories, recollections, reflections, remembrances.

reminiscent adjective
□ reminiscent of
a sophisticated style reminiscent of Italian art: similar to, comparable with, evocative of, suggestive of, recalling, redolent of.

remiss adjective *I can see that I have been very remiss:* negligent, neglectful, irresponsible, careless, thoughtless, heedless, lax, slack, slipshod, lackadaisical.
OPPOSITES: careful.

remission noun
1 *we demanded the remission of all parking fees:* cancellation, setting aside, suspension, revocation.
2 *the cancer is in remission:* respite, abeyance.
3 (formal) *the remission of sins:* forgiveness, pardoning, absolution, exoneration; formal exculpation.

remit noun *that decision is outside his remit:* area of responsibility, sphere, orbit, scope, ambit, province; brief, instructions, orders; informal bailiwick.
▷ verb
1 *they refused to remit the customs duties to the authorities:* send, dispatch, forward, hand over; pay.
2 *the fines imposed on him were remitted:* cancel, set aside, suspend, revoke.

remittance noun *send the form with your remittance:* payment, money, fee; cheque; formal monies.

remnant noun
1 *we cleared up the remnants of the picnic:* remains, remainder, residue, rest, leftover, leavings.
2 *she made a rag doll from remnants of cloth:* scrap, piece, bit, fragment, leftover, shred, offcut, oddment.

remonstrate verb *they remonstrated with the referee:* protest to, complain to, argue with, challenge, take issue with.

remorse noun contrition, regret, repentance, penitence, guilt, compunction, remorsefulness, ruefulness; pangs of conscience.

remorseful adjective sorry, full of regret, regretful, apologetic, ashamed, contrite, repentant, penitent.
OPPOSITES: unrepentant.

remorseless adjective
1 *the remorseless military build-up continued:* relentless, unrelenting, unremitting, unabating, inexorable, implacable, unstoppable.
2 *a remorseless killer:* heartless, pitiless, merciless, ruthless, callous, cruel, hard-hearted, stony-hearted, having a heart of stone, cold-hearted, inhumane.
OPPOSITES: faltering, remorseful.

remote adjective
1 *a remote mountain village:* isolated, out of the way, off the beaten track, secluded, lonely, in the back of beyond, godforsaken, inaccessible; informal in the sticks, in the middle of nowhere.
2 *it is still only a remote possibility:* unlikely, improbable, implausible, doubtful, dubious; faint, slight, slim, small, slender.
3 *she seems very remote:* aloof, distant, detached, withdrawn, reserved, uncommunicative, unforthcoming, unapproachable, unresponsive, unfriendly, unsociable; informal stand-offish.
OPPOSITES: central, strong, friendly.

removal noun
1 *the removal of customs barriers within the EU:* taking away, moving, withdrawal, elimination.
2 *opposition parties demanded his removal from office:* dismissal, ejection, expulsion, displacement; informal sacking, firing.
OPPOSITES: imposition, appointment.

remove verb
1 *switch off the power and remove the plug:* detach, unfasten; pull out, take out, disconnect, extract.
2 *she took the box and removed the lid:* take off, undo, unfasten, lift off.
3 *police removed several boxes of documents:* take away, carry away, move, transport; confiscate; informal cart off.
4 *in the bathroom Sheila removed the mud:* clean off, wash off/away, wipe off/away, rinse off.
5 *Henry removed his coat:* take off, pull off, slip out of.
6 *he was removed from his post as head of security:* dismiss, discharge, get rid of, dislodge, displace, expel, oust, depose; informal sack, fire, kick out, boot out; Brit. informal turf out.
7 *Gabriel removed two words from the title:* delete, erase, rub out, cross out, strike out, score out.
OPPOSITES: attach, insert, replace.

remuneration noun *it's a demanding job which deserves adequate remuneration:* payment, pay, salary, wages; earnings, fee, reward, recompense, reimbursement; formal emolument.

remunerative adjective lucrative, well paid, financially rewarding, gainful, profitable, profit-making, money-spinning, commercial.

renaissance noun *the renaissance of the British film production industry:* revival, renewal, resurrection, reawakening, re-emergence, rebirth, resurgence; formal renascence.

render verb
1 *her fury rendered her speechless:* make, turn, leave.
2 *I am in the process of rendering assistance:* give, provide, supply, furnish, contribute; offer, proffer.
3 *her paintings are rendered in wonderfully vivid colours:* paint, draw, depict, portray, represent, execute.
4 *the film's Jewish characters are vividly rendered:* act, perform, play, depict, interpret.
5 *the phrase was almost impossible to render into English:* translate, put, express, rephrase, reword.

rendezvous noun *Edward was late for their rendezvous:* meeting, appointment, assignation; literary tryst; informal date.
▷ **verb** *the bar where they had agreed to rendezvous:* meet, come together, gather, assemble.

rendition noun
1 *our stirring rendition of Beethoven's Fifth:* performance, rendering, interpretation, presentation, execution, delivery.
2 *the artist's rendition of Adam and Eve is revolutionary:* depiction, portrayal, representation.
3 *an interpreter's rendition of the message:* translation, interpretation, version.

renegade noun *he was denounced as a renegade:* traitor, defector, deserter, turncoat, rebel, mutineer.
▷ **adjective** *350 troops led by a renegade colonel:* traitorous, treacherous, disloyal, rebel, mutinous.
OPPOSITES: loyal.

renege verb
□ renege on
he has reneged on his promise to keep taxes down: default on, fail to honour, go back on, break, back out of, withdraw from, retreat from, backtrack on; break your word/promise.

renew verb
1 *I renewed my search:* resume, return to, take up again, start again, restart, recommence; continue, carry on with.
2 *they renewed their vows at a cathedral service:* reaffirm, reassert; repeat, reiterate, restate.
3 *they renewed Jackie's contract after three months:* extend, prolong.

renewal noun
1 *the renewal of our friendship has meant a lot to me:* resumption, recommencement, re-establishment; continuation.

2 *we need a source of spiritual renewal:* regeneration, revival, reinvigoration, revitalization.
3 *the comprehensive scheme of urban renewal:* renovation, restoration, modernization, reconditioning, overhauling, redevelopment, rebuilding, reconstruction, rehabilitation.

renounce verb
1 *Edward renounced his claim to the throne:* give up, relinquish, abandon, abdicate, surrender, waive, forgo; formal forswear.
2 *Hungary renounced the agreement on environmental grounds:* reject, refuse to abide by, repudiate.
3 *she renounced her entire family:* repudiate, deny, reject, abandon, wash your hands of, turn your back on, disown, spurn, shun; literary forsake.
OPPOSITES: assert, accept.

renovate verb *the hotel has been completely renovated:* modernize, refurbish, revamp, recondition, rehabilitate, overhaul, redevelop, restore; update, upgrade, refit; informal do up.

renown noun fame, distinction, eminence, pre-eminence, prominence, repute, reputation, prestige, acclaim, celebrity, notability.

renowned adjective *Satyajit Ray, the renowned Indian film-maker:* famous, celebrated, famed, eminent, distinguished, acclaimed, illustrious, pre-eminent, prominent, great, esteemed, of note, well known.
OPPOSITES: unknown.

rent verb
1 *she rented a car:* hire, lease, charter.
2 *if you don't want to sell the flat, why don't you rent it out?* let out, let, lease out, hire out.

renunciation noun *their renunciation of violence:* repudiation, rejection, denial, abandonment; formal forswearing.
OPPOSITES: promotion, espousal.

reorganize verb *we need to reorganize the business:* restructure, reshape, transform, change, alter, adjust, shake up, overhaul, rearrange; Brit. rationalize.

repair verb *the car was taken to a garage to be repaired:* mend, fix, put/set right, restore to working order, overhaul, service; informal patch up.
▷ **noun**
1 *the repair of war-damaged property:* mending, fixing, overhaul, restoration, renovation, refurbishment.
2 *all the tools are in good repair:* condition, working order, state, shape, fettle.

repair² verb (formal) *relax in the stylish bar before repairing to the dining room:* go to, head for, adjourn to, wend your way to, make your way to, move to, withdraw to; literary betake yourself to.

r

reparation noun *ways in which offenders may make reparation to their victims:* amends, restitution, redress, compensation, recompense, repayment, atonement.

repartee noun banter, badinage, bantering, raillery, witticisms, ripostes, quips, joking, jesting; formal persiflage.

repast noun (formal) meal, feast, banquet; informal spread; Brit. informal nosh-up.

repay verb
1 *I'm making an effort to repay customers who have been cheated:* reimburse, refund, pay back, recompense, compensate, indemnify.
2 *the grants have to be repaid in full:* pay back, return, refund, reimburse.
3 *Walsh intends to repay them for the gamble they took:* reward, recompense, pay back.

repayment noun *the repayment of tax:* refund, refunding, reimbursement, paying back.

repeal verb *the Act was repealed in 1990:* revoke, rescind, cancel, reverse, annul, nullify, declare null and void, quash, abolish.
OPPOSITES: enact.
▷noun *the repeal of the law has proved controversial:* revocation, rescinding, cancellation, reversal, annulment, nullification, quashing, abolition.

repeat verb
1 *she repeated her story in a flat voice:* say again, restate, reiterate, go/run through again, recapitulate, recap.
2 *children can remember and repeat large chunks of text:* recite, quote, parrot, regurgitate; informal trot out.
3 *Steele was invited to repeat his work in a laboratory:* do again, redo, replicate, duplicate.
4 *the episodes were repeated on Thursday nights:* show again, rerun, reshow, rebroadcast.
▷noun
1 *the final was a repeat of the previous year's fixture:* repetition, replication, duplicate.
2 *repeats of his TV show are shown constantly:* rerun.

repeated adjective *we have made repeated attempts to contact him:* frequent, numerous, many, persistent, continual, constant, ceaseless; regular, recurrent.
OPPOSITES: occasional.

repeatedly adverb *the men were repeatedly assaulted:* frequently, often, again and again, over and over again, time and time again, many times, many a time; persistently, constantly, continually, regularly.

repel verb
1 *the rebels were repelled by army units:* fight off, repulse, drive back/away, force back, beat back, push back; hold off, ward off, keep at bay; Brit. see off.
2 *the plastic coating will repel water:* be impervious to, be impermeable to, keep out, resist.
3 *the thought of kissing him repelled me:* revolt, disgust, repulse, sicken, nauseate, turn someone's stomach, be repulsive, be distasteful, be repugnant; informal turn off; N. Amer. informal gross out.

repellent adjective
1 *a frankly repellent show in which contestants have to eat raw animal body parts:* revolting, repulsive, disgusting, repugnant, sickening, nauseating, vile, nasty, foul, horrible, awful, dreadful, terrible, obnoxious, loathsome, offensive, objectionable; abhorrent, odious, hateful, execrable; informal ghastly, gross.
2 *a water-repellent coating:* impermeable, impervious; -proof, -resistant.
OPPOSITES: delightful.

repent verb *she came to repent her hasty judgement:* regret, feel remorse about, be sorry for, be ashamed of, rue.

repentance noun *he showed no repentance for his past crimes:* remorse, contrition, penitence, regret, ruefulness, remorsefulness, shame, guilt.

repentant adjective *he was truly repentant, but I was not ready to forgive:* penitent, contrite, remorseful, apologetic, chastened, ashamed, shamefaced, regretful, rueful.
OPPOSITES: unrepentant, impenitent.

repercussion noun *the decision would have grave repercussions for the entire region:* consequence, result, effect, outcome; reverberation, backlash, aftermath, fallout.

repetition noun
1 *the statistics have already been quoted and they bear repetition:* reiteration, repeating, restatement, retelling.
2 *the repetition of words you have just heard:* repeating, echoing, parroting.
3 *she didn't want a repetition of the scene in the kitchen:* recurrence, reoccurrence, rerun, repeat.
4 *there is some repetition, but not enough to detract from the book's message:* repetitiousness, repetitiveness, redundancy, tautology.

repetitious adjective *it's repetitious and tedious work.* See REPETITIVE.

repetitive adjective *they sit in front of machines and perform the same repetitive tasks all day:* monotonous, tedious, boring, dreary, tiresome, humdrum, routine, mechanical, mundane; unvaried, unchanging, unvarying; recurrent, recurring, repeated, repetitious.

r

rephrase verb *let me rephrase the question:* reword, put in other words, express differently, paraphrase.

replace verb
1 *I replaced the book in its proper place on the shelf:* put back, return, restore.
2 *a new chairman came in to replace him:* take the place of, succeed, take over from, supersede; stand in for, substitute for, deputize for, cover for, relieve; informal step into someone's shoes/boots.
3 *she replaced the spoon with a fork:* substitute, exchange, change, swap.
OPPOSITES: remove.

replacement noun
1 *the main speaker was ill and we had to find a replacement:* substitute, stand-in, locum, relief, cover; successor.
2 *the wiring was in need of replacement:* renewal, replacing.

replenish verb
1 *she replenished their glasses:* refill, fill up, recharge; Brit. top up; N. Amer. freshen.
2 *their supplies were replenished by a new airlift:* stock up, restock, restore, replace.
OPPOSITES: empty, exhaust.

replete adjective
1 *the guests, replete with this sumptuous dinner, lingered over coffee:* well fed, sated, satiated, full; glutted, gorged; informal stuffed.
2 *a sumptuous environment replete with priceless antiques:* filled, full, well stocked, well supplied, crammed, packed, jammed, teeming, overflowing, bursting; informal jam-packed, chock-a-block.

replica noun *a replica of the original painting:* copy, duplicate, reproduction; model, dummy, imitation, facsimile; clone.

replicate verb *there's a long-standing presumption that Roman art was a mishandled attempt to replicate Greek art:* copy, reproduce, duplicate, recreate, repeat; clone.

reply verb *'I'm fine—just leave me alone,' he replied | they didn't reply to my letter:* answer, respond, rejoin, retort, come back; acknowledge.
▷ noun *I received a swift reply:* answer, response, rejoinder, retort, riposte; acknowledgement; informal comeback.

report verb
1 *the government reported that the official unemployment rate had fallen to two per cent:* announce, declare, proclaim; disclose, reveal, make public, communicate; detail, outline.
2 *I reported him to the police:* inform on, make a complaint against; informal shop, tell on, squeal on, rat on; Brit. informal grass on.
3 *Juliet reported for duty:* present yourself, arrive, turn up, clock in, sign in; Brit. clock on; informal show up.
▷ noun
1 *a report on the use of biotechnology in agriculture | an official police report of the incident:* account, review, investigation, analysis; record, description, statement; transactions, proceedings, transcripts, minutes.
2 *the police received reports of drug dealing in the area:* news, information, word, intelligence.
3 *press reports suggested that the secret police were helping to maintain public order:* story, account, article, piece, item, column, feature, bulletin, dispatch.
4 (Brit.) *his last school report had been good:* assessment, evaluation, appraisal.
5 *reports of his imminent resignation circulated:* rumour, whisper.
6 *they heard the report of a gun:* bang, blast, crack, shot, gunshot, explosion; noise.

reporter noun journalist, correspondent, newspaperman, newspaperwoman, columnist, blogger; Brit. pressman; informal hack, stringer.

repose noun *in repose, her face still showed signs of strain:* rest, relaxation; sleep, slumber.
▷ verb
1 *the icon now reposes in a Russian Orthodox monastery:* lie, rest, be placed, be situated, be kept.
2 *the beds on which we reposed:* lie, recline, rest, sleep.

repository noun store, storehouse, depository; reservoir, bank, cache, treasury, fund, mine.

reprehensible adjective *we must take a hard line on such reprehensible behaviour:* deplorable, disgraceful, discreditable, shameful, despicable, blameworthy, culpable, wrong, bad, dishonourable, unworthy, objectionable, inexcusable, unforgivable, indefensible, unjustifiable; scandalous, iniquitous; formal exceptionable, opprobrious.
OPPOSITES: praiseworthy.

represent verb
1 *his solicitor represented him in court:* appear for, act for, speak for, speak on behalf of.
2 *this figure represents eleven per cent of total sales:* constitute, be, amount to.
3 *this group was picked to represent a cross-section of the community:* exemplify, typify, be a typical example of, be typical of, epitomize.
4 *the first painting represents the Last Judgement:* depict, portray, render, picture, delineate, show, illustrate, present.
5 *white lilies represent purity and innocence:* symbolize, be a symbol of, stand for, embody; designate, denote.

r

representation noun

1 *the representation of women in the Australian film industry:* portrayal, depiction, delineation, presentation.
2 *representations of the human form:* likeness, painting, drawing, picture, illustration, sketch, image, model, figure, figurine, statue, statuette.

representative adjective

1 *the exhibition is representative of the current trends in the art world:* typical, characteristic, illustrative.
2 *a system of representative government:* elected, elective, democratic, popular.
OPPOSITES: atypical, totalitarian.

▷ noun
1 *a representative of the Royal Society:* spokesperson, spokesman, spokeswoman, agent, official, mouthpiece.
2 *a sales representative:* salesperson, agent; informal rep.
3 *the Cambodian representative at the UN:* delegate, ambassador, attaché, envoy, emissary.
4 *he acted as his father's representative:* deputy, substitute, stand-in, proxy, agent.

repress verb

1 *the uprisings were successfully repressed:* suppress, quell, quash, subdue, put down, crush, extinguish, stamp out, defeat, conquer, rout.
2 *the ruling class repressed and exploited the workers:* oppress, subjugate, keep down, rule with a rod of iron, intimidate, tyrannize, crush.
3 *she tried to repress a cry of pain:* restrain, hold back/in, keep back, suppress, keep in check, curb, stifle, bottle up.

repressed adjective

1 *the repressed migrant community:* oppressed, subjugated, subdued, tyrannized.
2 *repressed feelings:* suppressed, kept in check, stifled, pent up, bottled up.
3 *he is a reclusive, emotionally repressed man:* inhibited, frustrated; informal uptight.

repression noun

1 *the brutal repression of peaceful protests:* suppression, quashing, subduing, crushing, stamping out.
2 *20 years of political repression:* oppression, subjugation, suppression, tyranny, despotism, authoritarianism, dictatorship, totalitarianism.
3 *the repression of sexual urges:* restraint, restraining, holding back, suppression, control, stifling, bottling up.

repressive adjective *a cruel and repressive regime:* oppressive, authoritarian, despotic, tyrannical, dictatorial, autocratic, totalitarian, undemocratic, illiberal.

reprieve verb

1 *she was sentenced to death, then reprieved:* pardon, spare, grant an amnesty to, amnesty; informal let off.
2 *the project has been reprieved:* save, rescue.

▷ noun *he was saved by a last-minute reprieve:* stay of execution, remission, pardon, amnesty; informal let-off.

reprimand verb *he was publicly reprimanded for his behaviour:* rebuke, admonish, chastise, chide, upbraid, reprove, reproach, scold, berate, take to task, lambaste, criticize, censure; formal castigate; informal tell off, give someone a talking-to, haul over the coals, bawl out, blast, give someone a roasting; Brit. informal tick off, carpet, tear someone off a strip, give someone a rocket, give someone a rollicking.
OPPOSITES: praise.

▷ noun *they received a severe reprimand:* rebuke, reproof, admonishment, admonition, reproach, scolding, upbraiding, censure; informal telling-off, dressing-down, roasting; Brit. informal ticking-off, carpeting.
OPPOSITES: commendation.

reprisal noun *he resolved to speak out despite fear of reprisal:* retaliation, counter-attack, comeback; revenge, vengeance, retribution.

reproach verb *her friends reproached her for not thinking about her family:* rebuke, admonish, chastise, chide, upbraid, reprove, reprimand, scold, berate, take to task; formal castigate; informal tell off; Brit. informal tick off.

▷ noun *he gave a her look of reproach | the reproaches of our wives:* disapproval, reproof, rebuke, admonishment, admonition, scolding, reprimand.
□ **beyond/above reproach** *her public image had to be beyond reproach:* perfect, blameless, above suspicion, without fault, faultless, flawless, irreproachable, exemplary, impeccable, immaculate, unblemished, spotless, untarnished, stainless, unsullied, whiter than white; informal squeaky clean.

reproachful adjective *she gave him a reproachful look:* disapproving, reproving, critical, censorious, disparaging, withering, accusatory.
OPPOSITES: approving.

reprobate noun *even a hardened reprobate like myself has standards:* rogue, rascal, scoundrel, miscreant, good-for-nothing, villain; rake, degenerate; dated cad; old use blackguard.

reproduce verb

1 *each artwork is reproduced in full colour:* copy, duplicate, replicate; photocopy, xerox, print.
2 *this work has not been reproduced in other laboratories:* repeat, replicate,

recreate, redo; simulate, imitate, emulate, mirror, mimic.
3 *some animals reproduce prolifically:* breed, produce offspring, procreate, propagate, multiply, spawn.

reproduction noun
1 *the reproduction of copyright material:* copying, duplication, duplicating; photocopying, reprinting.
2 *this is a reproduction of the original:* print, copy, reprint, duplicate, facsimile, carbon copy, photocopy; trademark Xerox.
3 *the means of reproduction varies from species to species:* breeding, procreation, multiplying, propagation.

reproductive adjective generative, procreative; sexual, genital.

reproof noun *he shook his finger in reproof | a stern reproof:* rebuke, reprimand, reproach, admonishment, admonition; disapproval, censure, criticism; informal telling-off; Brit. informal ticking-off.

repudiate verb
1 *he has repudiated policies associated with previous party leaders:* reject, renounce, abandon, give up, turn your back on, disown, cast off, lay aside; formal forswear.
2 *Cranham repudiated the allegations:* deny, refute, contradict, rebut, dispute, dismiss, brush aside; formal controvert, gainsay.
3 (Law) *breach of a condition gives the other party the right to repudiate a contract:* cancel, rescind, renege on, go back on, refuse to fulfil; formal abrogate.
OPPOSITES: embrace, confirm.

repudiation noun
1 *he sees repudiation of art as starving the soul of nourishment:* rejection, renunciation, abandonment, giving up.
2 *this was a direct repudiation of the Chancellor's statement:* denial, refutation, rebuttal, rejection.

repugnance noun *his touch made her skin crawl with repugnance:* revulsion, disgust, abhorrence, repulsion, loathing, hatred, detestation, aversion, distaste, antipathy.

repugnant adjective *cannibalism seems repugnant to us:* abhorrent, revolting, repulsive, repellent, horrible, disgusting, offensive, objectionable, vile, foul, nasty, horrid, loathsome, sickening, nauseating, hateful, detestable, execrable, abominable, monstrous, appalling, grotesque; informal ghastly, gross.
OPPOSITES: pleasant.

repulse verb
1 *the rebels were once again repulsed:* repel, drive back/away, fight back/off, put to flight, force back, beat off/back; ward off, hold off; Brit. see off.
2 *she tried to show him affection, but was*

repulsed: rebuff, reject, spurn, snub, cold-shoulder; informal give someone the brush-off, freeze out; Brit. informal knock back.
3 *his bid for the company was repulsed:* reject, turn down, refuse, decline.
4 *the brutality of the film repulsed her:* revolt, disgust, repel, sicken, nauseate, turn someone's stomach, be repugnant to; informal turn off; N. Amer. informal gross out.
▷**noun**
1 *the repulse of the attack afforded some breathing space:* repelling, driving back; warding off, holding off.
2 *he was mortified by this repulse:* rebuff, rejection, snub, slight; informal brush-off, knock-back.

repulsion noun *people talked about the case with a mixture of fascination and repulsion:* disgust, revulsion, abhorrence, repugnance, nausea, horror, aversion, distaste; formal abomination.

repulsive adjective *a repulsive smell emanated from the room:* revolting, disgusting, abhorrent, repellent, repugnant, offensive, objectionable, horrible, horrid, vile, foul, nasty, loathsome, sickening, nauseating, hateful, detestable, execrable, abominable, monstrous, awful, terrible, dreadful, frightful, obnoxious, unsavoury, unpleasant, disagreeable, distasteful; ugly, hideous, grotesque, noxious; ; literary noisome; informal ghastly, gross.
OPPOSITES: pleasant.

reputable adjective *make sure you buy from a reputable company:* well thought of, highly regarded, well respected, respectable, of good repute, prestigious, established; reliable, dependable, trustworthy.
OPPOSITES: disreputable.

reputation noun *his professional reputation was at stake:* good name, name, character, repute, standing, stature, status, position, renown, esteem, prestige.

repute noun
1 *a woman of ill repute:* reputation, name, character.
2 *a firm of international repute:* fame, renown, distinction, high standing, stature, prestige.

reputed adjective
1 *they are reputed to be very rich:* thought, said, reported, rumoured, believed, held, considered, regarded, deemed, reckoned.
2 *his reputed father died in obscurity:* supposed, putative.
3 *he rose to become a reputed naturalist:* well thought of, well respected, highly regarded.

reputedly adverb *the penthouse apartment reputedly sold for £2 million:* supposedly, by all accounts, allegedly, so people say.

r

request noun
1 *we received several requests for assistance:* appeal, entreaty, plea, petition, application, demand, call, supplication.
2 *Charlotte spoke to him at Ursula's request:* bidding, entreaty, demand, insistence.
3 *indicate your requests on the booking form:* requirement, wish, desire; choice.
▷ verb
1 *the government requested military aid:* ask for, appeal for, call for, seek, solicit, plead for, apply for, demand.
2 *I requested him to help:* call on, beg, entreat, implore; literary beseech.

require verb
1 *the child required hospital treatment:* need, be in need of.
2 *the project will require a great deal of time and effort:* necessitate, demand, call for, involve, entail.
3 *unquestioning obedience is required:* demand, insist on, call for, ask for, expect.
4 *she was required to pay costs:* order, instruct, command, oblige, compel, force.
5 *do you require anything else?* want, wish for, desire; lack, be short of.

required adjective
1 *this book is required reading:* essential, vital, indispensable, necessary, compulsory, obligatory, mandatory, prescribed.
2 *cut it to the required length:* desired, preferred, chosen; correct, proper, right.
OPPOSITES: optional.

requirement noun
1 *the four basic requirements of food, fuel, shelter, and clothing | a kitchen specifically designed to meet your requirements:* need, wish, demand, want; necessity, essential.
2 *applicants must satisfy the normal entry requirements:* condition, prerequisite, stipulation.

requisite adjective *he lacks the requisite skills:* necessary, required, prerequisite, essential, vital.
OPPOSITES: optional.
▷ noun
1 *toilet requisites will be supplied:* requirement, need, necessity, essential.
2 *she believed privacy to be a requisite for a peaceful life:* necessity, essential, requirement, prerequisite, precondition, sine qua non; informal must.

requisition noun
1 *the department has placed requisitions for extra staff:* order, request, call, application, claim, demand.
2 *the illegal requisition of cultural treasures:* appropriation, commandeering, seizure, confiscation, expropriation.
▷ verb *the house was requisitioned by the army:* commandeer, appropriate, take over, take possession of, occupy, seize, confiscate, expropriate.

rescind verb *the Ombudsman cannot rescind planning permission:* revoke, repeal, cancel, reverse, overturn, overrule, annul, nullify, void, invalidate, quash, abolish.
OPPOSITES: enforce.

rescue verb
1 *an attempt to rescue the hostages failed:* save, come to the aid of; free, set free, release, liberate.
2 *Boyd bent hastily to rescue his papers:* retrieve, recover, salvage, get back.
▷ noun *the rescue of ten crewmen:* saving, rescuing; release, freeing, liberation, deliverance.
□ come to someone's rescue
he came to our rescue with a loan of £1,000: help, assist, lend a helping hand to, bail out; informal save someone's bacon, save someone's neck, save someone's skin.

research noun
1 *further research is needed to establish the causes of asthma:* investigation, experimentation, testing, analysis, fact-finding, examination, scrutiny, exploration.
2 *he could no longer afford to continue his researches:* experiments, experimentation, tests, inquiries, studies.
▷ verb
1 *the phenomenon has been widely researched:* investigate, study, inquire into, look into, probe, explore, analyse, examine, scrutinize, review.
2 *I researched all the available material:* study, read up on, sift through; informal check out.

resemblance noun *the points of resemblance between animal and human psychology:* similarity, likeness, correspondence, congruity, congruence, coincidence, comparability, parallelism, sameness; formal similitude.
OPPOSITES: dissimilarity.

resemble verb *she resembles her grandmother:* look like, be similar to, be like, bear a resemblance to, remind someone of, take after, favour, have the look of, correspond to.

resent verb *she resented his accusations:* feel aggrieved at/about, feel bitter about, be annoyed at/about, be resentful of, dislike, take exception to, object to, take amiss, take offence at, take umbrage at; begrudge, grudge, bear/harbour a grudge about.
OPPOSITES: welcome.

resentful adjective *if you both help out, then one of you won't end up feeling resentful:* aggrieved, indignant, piqued, put out, disgruntled, discontented, offended, in high dudgeon, dissatisfied, bitter, jaundiced; envious, jealous; informal miffed, peeved; Brit. informal narked.

resentment noun *this lucrative contract caused resentment in some quarters:* bitterness, indignation, pique, disgruntlement, discontentment, discontent, resentfulness, dissatisfaction, bad feelings, hard feelings, ill will, acrimony, rancour, animosity, jaundice; envy, jealousy.

reservation noun
1 *the government expressed grave reservations about the proposals:* doubts, misgivings, scepticism, unease, hesitation; qualms, scruples; objection.
2 *groups should make reservations well in advance:* booking, advance booking.
3 *the Yanomami Indian reservation:* reserve, enclave, territory, homeland; sanctuary.
▫ **without reservation**
I can say without reservation that this film is as close to perfection as a movie can be: wholeheartedly, unreservedly, without qualification, fully, completely, totally, entirely, wholly, unconditionally.

reserve verb
1 *ask your newsagent to reserve you a copy:* put to one side, put aside, set aside, keep, save, hold back, keep in reserve, earmark.
2 *he reserved a table for three:* book, make a reservation for, order, secure.
3 *reserve your judgement until you know him better:* defer, postpone, put off, delay, withhold.
▷ **noun**
1 *they had to use some of their precious reserves of petrol for the journey:* stock, store, supply, stockpile, pool, hoard, cache.
2 *a nature reserve:* national park, sanctuary, conservation area; N. Amer. preserve.
3 *Carrie found it hard to penetrate his natural reserve:* reticence, detachment, remoteness, coolness, aloofness, constraint, formality; shyness, inhibition.
▷ **adjective** *a reserve goalkeeper:* substitute, stand-in, relief, replacement, fallback, spare, extra.
▫ **in reserve**
keep some cash in reserve, just in case: available, to/on hand, ready, in readiness, set aside, at your disposal.

reserved adjective
1 *he's rather reserved:* reticent, quiet, private, uncommunicative, unforthcoming, undemonstrative, unsociable, formal, constrained, cool, aloof, detached, distant, remote, unapproachable, unfriendly, withdrawn, secretive, silent, taciturn; shy, retiring, self-effacing, inhibited, introverted.
2 *the corner table is reserved, I'm afraid:* booked, taken, spoken for.
OPPOSITES: outgoing.

reshuffle verb *the prime minister reshuffled his cabinet:* reorganize, restructure, rearrange, change around, shake up, shuffle.
▷ **noun** *a management reshuffle:* reorganization, restructuring, change, rearrangement; informal shake-up.

reside verb
1 *Carol Ann resides in a house on Vancouver Street:* live in, occupy, inhabit, stay in, lodge in; formal dwell in.
2 *the paintings reside in an air-conditioned vault:* be kept, be situated, be found, be located, lie.
3 *executive power resides in the president:* be vested in, be bestowed on, be conferred on, be in the hands of.

residence noun *her private residence:* home, house, address; quarters, lodgings; formal dwelling place, place of residence, domicile, abode; informal pad, place.

resident noun
1 *the residents of New York City:* inhabitant, local, citizen, native; householder, homeowner, occupier, tenant; formal denizen; old use burgher.
2 (Brit.) *the bar is open to residents only:* guest.
▷ **adjective**
1 *he is currently resident in the UK:* living, residing; formal dwelling.
2 *we have a resident nanny:* live-in, living in.
3 *the resident registrar in obstetrics:* permanent, incumbent.

residual adjective
1 *residual income after tax and mortgage payments:* remaining, leftover, unused.
2 *she still feels some residual affection for her husband:* lingering, enduring, abiding, surviving.

residue noun *she left the residue of her estate to James and Jonathan Arthur:* remainder, remaining part, rest, remnant; surplus, extra, excess; remains, leftovers.

resign verb
1 *the senior manager resigned after the losses were announced:* leave, hand in your notice, give notice, stand down, step down; informal quit.
2 *19 MPs resigned their seats:* give up, leave, vacate, stand down from; informal quit.
3 *we resigned ourselves to a long wait:* reconcile yourself to, become resigned to, come to terms with.

resignation noun
1 *she handed in her resignation yesterday:* notice.
2 *he accepted his fate with resignation:* stoicism, fortitude, fatalism, acceptance, acquiescence, compliance, passivity; patience, forbearance.

resigned adjective *his mood was one of resigned acceptance:* stoical, long-suffering, uncomplaining, philosophical, fatalistic, acquiescent, compliant, passive; patient, forbearing.

r

resilient adjective

1 *he was still young and resilient:* strong, tough, hardy, robust, able to bounce back; adaptable.
2 *a resilient fabric:* durable, hard-wearing, robust, stout, strong, sturdy, tough; flexible, supple, springy.

resist verb

1 *the vine is able to resist cold winters:* withstand, combat, weather, endure, be resistant to, keep out, be proof against.
2 *they resisted his attempts to change things:* oppose, fight, object to, defy, set your face against; obstruct, impede, hinder, block, thwart, frustrate.
3 *I resisted the urge to say anything:* refrain from, forbear from, not give in to, restrain yourself from, stop yourself from.
4 *Hamilton bravely resisted his attacker:* struggle with/against, fight, stand up to, withstand, hold off, fend off, ward off.
OPPOSITES: succumb, submit.
□ cannot resist
he is a man who cannot resist a challenge: love, adore, relish, like, delight in, enjoy, take great pleasure in; have a weakness for, be very keen on; informal get a kick/thrill out of.

resistance noun

1 *his resistance to change:* opposition, hostility, refusal to accept.
2 *Jay put up a spirited resistance:* opposition, fight, stand, struggle.
3 *he joined the French resistance:* resistance movement, freedom fighters, underground, partisans.

resistant adjective

1 *the adhesive is resistant to water:* impervious to, proof against, unaffected by; immune to.
2 *she is very resistant to change:* opposed, averse, hostile, inimical, against; informal anti.
OPPOSITES: susceptible, receptive.

resolute adjective *his resolute defence of the principles of social justice:* determined, purposeful, adamant, single-minded, firm, unswerving, unwavering, steadfast, staunch, stalwart, resolved, unfaltering, unhesitating, persistent, indefatigable, tenacious, dogged, strong-willed, unshakeable, stubborn.
OPPOSITES: irresolute, half-hearted.

resolution noun

1 *despite her resolution not to drink, she felt tempted:* intention, resolve, decision, intent, aim, plan; commitment, pledge, promise.
2 *the committee passed the resolution unanimously:* motion, proposal, proposition.
3 *she handled the work with resolution:* determination, purpose, purposefulness, resolve, resoluteness, single-mindedness, firmness; steadfastness, staunchness,

perseverance, persistence, indefatigability, tenacity, tenaciousness, doggedness, staying power, dedication, commitment.
4 *a satisfactory resolution of the problem:* solution, answer, end, ending, settlement, conclusion.

resolve verb

1 *this matter cannot be resolved overnight:* settle, sort out, solve, find a solution to, fix, straighten out, hammer out, thrash out; deal with, put right, put to rights, rectify; informal figure out.
2 *I resolved not to wait any longer:* determine, decide, make up your mind, take a decision.
3 *the committee resolved that the project should proceed:* vote, pass a resolution, rule, decide formally, agree.
▷ noun *his threats will not weaken our resolve:* determination, purpose, purposefulness, resoluteness, resolution, single-mindedness, firmness of purpose; steadfastness, indefatigability, tenacity, tenaciousness, doggedness, dedication, commitment.

resolved adjective *he was resolved to speak to her:* determined; intent, set.

resonant adjective

1 *his resonant voice:* deep, low, sonorous, full, vibrant, rich, clear, ringing; loud, booming.
2 *valleys resonant with the sound of church bells:* reverberating, reverberant, resounding, echoing, filled.
3 *that most resonant of words—home:* evocative, suggestive, expressive, redolent.

resort noun

1 *they could settle the matter without resort to legal proceedings:* recourse to, turning to, the use of.
2 *strike action would be our last resort | his only resort was to take legal action:* expedient, measure, step, strategy, course of action, recourse, alternative, option, choice, possibility, hope.
□ in the last resort
that belief, in the last resort, is what separates modern from medieval man: ultimately, in the end, in the long run.
□ resort to
I don't have to resort to such underhand tricks in order to succeed: have recourse to, fall back on, turn to, make use of, use, employ, avail yourself of; stoop to, descend to, sink to.

resound verb

1 *the explosion resounded round the silent street:* echo, reverberate, ring out, boom, thunder, rumble.
2 *a large building resounding with the clang of hammers:* reverberate, echo, resonate, ring.

resounding adjective

1 *a resounding bass voice:* loud, booming,

ringing, sonorous, resonant, reverberating, reverberant.
2 *the show was a resounding success:* enormous, huge, great, tremendous, outstanding, remarkable, phenomenal; emphatic, decisive, conclusive; complete, total, thorough.

resource noun
1 *they made good use of their limited resources:* assets, funds, money, capital; supplies, materials, stores, stocks, reserves.
2 *the database could be used as a teaching resource:* facility, amenity, aid, help, support.

resourceful adjective *this is an industry filled with bright, resourceful people:* enterprising, inventive, creative, ingenious; clever, talented, able, capable.

respect noun
1 *I have great respect for him as a director:* admiration, regard, high opinion, esteem; reverence, deference.
2 *he spoke to her with respect:* due regard, politeness, courtesy, civility, deference.
3 *it was normal to pay one's respects to the local military leader:* regards, compliments, greetings, best/good wishes, salutations.
4 *the report was accurate in every respect:* aspect, particular, point, detail, regard, facet, feature, way, sense.
OPPOSITES: contempt.

▷ verb
1 *he is highly respected for his achievements:* admire, esteem, think highly of, have a high opinion of, hold in high regard, hold in high esteem, look up to, revere.
2 *they respected our privacy:* show consideration for, have regard for, observe, be mindful of, be heedful of.
3 *her father respected her wishes:* abide by, comply with, follow, adhere to, conform to, act in accordance with, defer to, obey, observe, keep.
OPPOSITES: despise, disobey.
□ with respect to/in respect of *the ministry should be more responsive to parents' wishes with respect to the curriculum:* concerning, regarding, in/with regard to, as regards, with reference to, respecting, re, about, apropos, on the subject of, in connection with, vis-à-vis.

respectable adjective
1 *a young man from a respectable family:* good, decent, reputable, upright, honest, honourable, trustworthy, well bred, clean-living.
2 *he earns a respectable salary:* fairly good, decent, fair, reasonable, acceptable, moderately good, adequate.
OPPOSITES: disreputable, paltry.

respectful adjective *we sat in respectful silence:* deferential, reverent, reverential,
dutiful; polite, well mannered, civil, courteous, gracious.
OPPOSITES: disrespectful, rude.

respective adjective *the girls had gone back to their respective schools:* separate, own, particular, individual, specific; different, various.

respite noun *the thought of a brief respite from their duties was tempting:* rest, break, breathing space, interval, intermission, interlude, lull, pause, time out; relief, relaxation; informal breather, let-up.

resplendent adjective *the bride looked resplendent in a gown of white lace and satin:* splendid, magnificent, brilliant, dazzling, gorgeous, impressive, spectacular, striking, stunning, majestic.

respond verb
1 *they do not respond to my letters:* answer, reply; acknowledge.
2 *'No, I don't,' she responded:* reply, answer, say, retort, counter.
3 *the police were slow to respond:* react, make a response; retaliate.

response noun
1 *there was laughter at his response to the question:* answer, reply, retort, riposte; informal comeback.
2 *the move drew an angry response from the opposition benches:* reaction, reply; retaliation; informal comeback.
OPPOSITES: question.

responsibility noun
1 *it was his responsibility to find witnesses:* duty, task, function, job, role, business.
2 *the organization denied responsibility for the bomb attack:* blame, fault, guilt, culpability, liability.
3 *individuals have a responsibility to control their behaviour:* obligation, moral obligation, duty.

responsible adjective
1 *the cabinet minister responsible for education:* in charge of, in control of, at the helm of; accountable for.
2 *every effort will be made to find the person responsible and bring them to justice:* to blame, guilty, culpable, blameworthy, at fault, in the wrong; liable.
3 *she had risen rapidly to a highly responsible post in the civil service:* important, powerful.
4 *he is responsible to the president:* answerable, accountable.
5 *small children should be supervised by a responsible adult:* trustworthy, sensible, mature, reliable, dependable.
OPPOSITES: irresponsible.

responsive adjective *we need a service that is responsive to changing social patterns | an enthusiastic and responsive student:* quick to react, reactive, receptive, open to suggestions, amenable, flexible, adaptable.

r

rest¹ verb

1 *you need to rest:* relax, take a rest, ease up/off, let up, slow down, take a break, unwind, recharge your batteries, take it easy, put your feet up; lie down, go to bed, sleep; informal take five, take a breather, chill out.
2 *his hands rested on the rail:* lie, be laid, repose, be placed, be positioned, be supported by.
3 *she rested her basket on the ground:* support, prop, lean, lay, set, stand, position, place, put.

▷**noun**
1 *go home and get some rest:* relaxation, sleep; time off/out.
2 *after two hours they stopped for a well-earned rest:* break, breathing space, pause; informal breather.
3 *she took the poker from its rest:* stand, base, holder, support, rack, frame, shelf.

rest² noun *take what you want and throw the rest away:* remainder, remaining number/quantity, others, those left, residue; remains; surplus, excess; balance.

restful adjective *the place has a wonderfully restful atmosphere:* relaxed, relaxing, quiet, calm, calming, tranquil, soothing, peaceful, leisurely, undisturbed, untroubled, placid.
OPPOSITES: exciting.

restitution noun

1 *claims for the restitution of the land seized by the occupying power:* return, restoration, handing back, surrender.
2 *he was ordered to pay $50,000 in restitution for the damage caused:* compensation, recompense, reparation, damages, indemnification, indemnity, reimbursement, repayment, redress.

restive adjective *the crowd was becoming increasingly restive:* restless, fidgety, impatient, agitated, keyed up, worked up; unruly, disorderly.

restless adjective

1 *as time went on, Maria grew more and more restless:* impatient, agitated, fidgety, restive, worked up, keyed up; uneasy, ill at ease, edgy, on edge, tense, nervous, anxious, on tenterhooks, fretful; Brit. nervy; informal jumpy, jittery, twitchy, uptight, like a cat on a hot tin roof; Brit. informal like a cat on hot bricks.
2 *he had spent a restless night:* sleepless, wakeful; fitful, broken, disturbed, troubled, unsettled.

restoration noun

1 *the restoration of the monarchy:* re-establishment, reinstitution, reinstatement, return.
2 *the restoration of derelict housing:* repair, refurbishment, reconditioning, rehabilitation, rebuilding, reconstruction, overhaul, redevelopment, renovation.

restore verb

1 *his aim was to restore democracy* | *order was eventually restored by riot police:* re-establish, bring back, reinstitute, reinstall, reinstate.
2 *the building has been carefully restored:* repair, refurbish, recondition, rehabilitate, rebuild, reconstruct, remodel, overhaul, redevelop, renovate.
3 *he restored the bicycle to its rightful owner:* return, give back, hand back.
OPPOSITES: abolish.

restrain verb

1 *Charles tried to restrain his impatience:* control, keep under control, check, hold/keep in check, curb, suppress, repress, contain, subdue, smother, choke back, stifle, bottle up, rein back/in; informal keep the lid on.
2 *she could barely restrain herself from swearing:* prevent, stop, keep, hold back.
3 *leg cuffs may be used for restraining and transporting violent criminals:* control, hold down, keep under control, secure.

restrained adjective

1 *Julie was very restrained:* self-controlled, unemotional, undemonstrative, dispassionate; quiet, reserved, subdued.
2 *the restrained elegance of the new floral wallpapers:* muted, discreet, subtle, quiet, unobtrusive, understated, tasteful.

restraint noun

1 *the initial spending restraints imposed by the chancellor proved politically unpopular:* constraint, check, control, restriction, limitation, brake.
2 *he urged the protesters to exercise restraint:* self-control, self-restraint, self-discipline, control, moderation.
3 *the room has been decorated with commendable restraint:* subtlety, understatedness, taste, tastefulness.
4 *a child restraint:* belt, harness, strap.

restrict verb

1 *some roads may have to be closed at peak times to restrict the number of visitors:* limit, regulate, control, moderate, cut down.
2 *the cuff supports the ankle without restricting movement:* hinder, interfere with, impede, hamper, obstruct, block, check, curb.
3 *he restricted himself to a 15-minute speech:* confine, limit.

restricted adjective

1 *Western scientists had only restricted access to the site:* limited, controlled, regulated; reduced.
2 *a restricted space:* cramped, confined, constricted, small, narrow, tight.
3 *she parked in a restricted zone:* out of bounds, off limits; private.
4 *restricted information:* secret, top secret, classified.
OPPOSITES: unlimited.

restriction noun
1 *there are planning restrictions on commercial development in the area:* limitation, limit, constraint, control, check, curb.
2 *the restriction of personal freedom:* reduction, limitation, curtailment; control.

result noun
1 *the ultimate result of that decision was the series of economic crises that began in the late 1960s:* consequence, outcome, upshot, effect, sequel, repercussion, ramification; product, end-product.
2 *the result of the trial:* verdict, decision, outcome, judgement.
3 *exam results:* mark, score, grade.
4 *the results were published in an American medical journal:* findings; information, data.
OPPOSITES: cause.
▷ verb
1 *a landslide resulting from the flood killed 23 people:* be caused by, be brought about by, be produced by, stem, spring, arise, derive; occur, happen, take place, come about; follow, ensue, develop.
2 *he claims that increased alcohol availability will result in more social problems:* end in, culminate in, lead to, prompt, precipitate, trigger; cause, bring about, occasion, give rise to, produce, engender, generate.

resume verb
1 *the government agreed to resume negotiations:* restart, recommence, begin again, start again, reopen; renew, return to, continue with, carry on with, proceed with.
2 *the priest resumed his kneeling posture:* return to, come back to, take up again, reoccupy.
OPPOSITES: suspend, abandon.

résumé noun *a quick résumé of our findings:* summary, synopsis, outline, precis, abstract, summarization, digest; overview, review.

resumption noun *the resumption of the peace talks:* restart, restarting, recommencement, reopening, renewal, return to, continuation of.

resurgence noun *there has been a resurgence of interest in the scheme:* renewal, revival, reawakening, resurrection, re-emergence; increase, growth; recovery, comeback.

resurrect verb *he's hoping the film will give him a chance to resurrect his career:* revive, restore, regenerate, revitalize, breathe new life into, reinvigorate, resuscitate, rejuvenate, stimulate, re-establish, relaunch.

resuscitate verb
1 *medical staff tried to resuscitate him:* bring round, revive; give artificial

respiration to, give the kiss of life to.
2 *measures to resuscitate the economy:* revive, resurrect, restore, regenerate, revitalize, breathe new life into, reinvigorate, rejuvenate, stimulate, boost.

retain verb
1 *the government retained a share in the privatized industries:* keep, keep possession of, keep hold of, hold on to; informal hang on to.
2 *existing footpaths are to be retained:* maintain, keep, preserve, conserve.
3 *he was not good at retaining information:* remember, absorb.
OPPOSITES: give up, abolish.

retaliate verb *the blow stung and she retaliated immediately:* hit back, fight back, respond, react, reply, reciprocate, counter-attack, give someone a taste of their own medicine; get even, pay someone back; informal get your own back.

retaliation noun *he did not want to give his name for fear of retaliation against his family:* revenge, vengeance, reprisal, retribution, repayment; response, reaction, reply, counter-attack.

retard verb *the worst thing governments can do is retard this process:* delay, slow down/up, hold back/up, set back, decelerate; hinder, hamper, obstruct, inhibit, impede, check, restrain, restrict.
OPPOSITES: accelerate.

reticent adjective *he was extremely reticent about his personal affairs:* uncommunicative, unforthcoming, tight-lipped, quiet, taciturn, silent, guarded, secretive; reserved, withdrawn, introverted; shy, inhibited.
OPPOSITES: expansive.

retinue noun *the visiting US President and his retinue:* entourage, escort, attendants, aides, assistants, bodyguard; staff, personnel, retainers; court, household, train; informal groupies.

retire verb
1 *he retired two years ago:* give up work, stop working, stop work.
2 *Gita retired to her office:* withdraw, go away, take yourself off, decamp, shut yourself away; formal repair.
3 *every effort was made to persuade his forces to retire:* retreat, withdraw, pull back, fall back, disengage, back off, give ground.
4 *everyone retired early that night:* go to bed, call it a day; informal turn in, hit the sack.

retired adjective *a retired schoolteacher:* former, ex-, past, in retirement.

retiring adjective *he was such a quiet, retiring man:* shy, diffident, self-effacing, unassuming, unassertive, reserved, reticent, quiet, timid, modest; private, withdrawn, introverted, unsociable.
OPPOSITES: outgoing.

r

retort verb *'There's no need to shout,' she retorted:* answer, reply, respond, say, return, counter, retaliate, snap back.

▷ noun *she opened her mouth to give a suitably cutting retort:* answer, reply, response, return, rejoinder, riposte, retaliation; informal comeback.

retract verb
1 *unlike a dog, a cat can retract its claws:* pull in/back, draw in.
2 *he retracted his allegation | the rebels retracted an earlier promise to release the hostages by Christmas:* take back, withdraw, go back on, backtrack on.

retreat verb
1 *the American army was forced to retreat:* withdraw, retire, draw back, pull back/out, fall back, give way, give ground.
2 *the government had to retreat over the plan:* change your mind, change your plans; back down, climb down, do a U-turn, backtrack, back-pedal, give in, concede defeat; Brit. do an about-turn.
OPPOSITES: advance.

▷ noun
1 *a counteroffensive caused the retreat of the imperial army:* withdrawal, pulling back.
2 *Democrats welcomed the President's retreat on the tax issue:* climbdown, about-face, U-turn; Brit. about-turn.
3 *she invited us to her retreat in rural Sweden:* refuge, haven, sanctuary; hideaway, hideout, hiding place.

retrench verb
1 *not all the directors wanted to retrench:* economize, cut back, make cutbacks, make savings, make economies, tighten your belt.
2 *welfare services will have to be retrenched:* reduce, cut, cut back/down, pare down, slim down, trim, prune, streamline; Brit. rationalize; informal slash.
OPPOSITES: expand.

retribution noun *he didn't want his name used because he feared retribution | the club is seeking retribution through the courts:* punishment; revenge, reprisal, retaliation, vengeance, an eye for an eye (and a tooth for a tooth), tit for tat; redress, reparation, restitution, recompense.

retrieve verb
1 *I was sent to retrieve the ball from their garden:* get back, bring back, recover; regain, reclaim, repossess.
2 *companies need to be able to retrieve archived data quickly and easily:* find, locate, get back, extract.
3 *they were working hard to retrieve the situation:* put/set right, rectify, remedy, restore, sort out, straighten out, resolve.

retrograde adjective
1 *the closure of the factory is a retrograde step:* for the worse, regressive, negative, unwelcome, backward.
2 *the retrograde motion of the planets:* backward, reverse, rearward.
OPPOSITES: positive.

retrospect noun
□ in retrospect
in retrospect, I probably shouldn't have agreed: looking back, on reflection, in/with hindsight.

retrospective adjective *the Government introduced retrospective legislation to change the rules:* backdated, retroactive; formal ex post facto.

return verb
1 *he returned to London:* go back, come back, arrive back, go home, come home.
2 *the symptoms returned after a few days:* recur, reoccur, repeat itself; reappear.
3 *he returned the money he had been given:* give back, pay back, repay.
4 *the stolen property was returned it to its rightful owner:* give back, send back, restore, hand back, take back; reunite with.
5 *Peter returned the book to the shelf:* restore, put back, replace.
6 *I hope I can return the favour:* reciprocate, give/do in return, repay.
7 *the jury returned a unanimous verdict:* deliver, bring in, hand down.
8 *the club returned a small profit last year:* yield, make, earn, realize, net, gross, clear.
9 *the Labour candidate was returned with a reduced majority:* elect, vote in, choose, select.
10 *'Later,' returned Isabel coldly:* answer, reply, respond, counter, retort.

▷ noun
1 *failing health forced his return to Paris:* return journey, return trip, journey home; homecoming.
2 *treatment was continued until the end of the week to ensure that there was no return of the problem:* recurrence, reoccurrence, repeat, repetition, reappearance.
3 *the company hoped for a quick return on its investments:* yield, profit, gain, revenue, interest, dividend.
□ in return for
he promised them a great deal in return for their loyalty and support: in exchange for, as a reward for, as compensation for, for.

revamp verb
1 *they revamped the offices at a cost of £125,000:* renovate, redecorate, refurbish, recondition; refit, re-equip; remodel, refashion, redesign; informal do up, give something a facelift.
2 *he hired an advertising agency to revamp the company's website:* make over, overhaul, upgrade; redesign, restyle; informal give something a facelift.

reveal verb
1 *the police can't reveal details of his*

whereabouts: divulge, disclose, release, give away/out, make known, make public, broadcast, publicize, circulate, disseminate; tell, let slip/drop, blurt out, leak; informal let on.
2 *he let the garage door slide up to reveal his new car:* show, display, exhibit, disclose, uncover.
3 *the data reveals a good deal of information about Norman household life:* bring to light, uncover, lay bare, unearth, unveil.
OPPOSITES: hide.

revel verb *Bill was revelling in his new-found fame:* enjoy, delight in, love, like, adore, take great pleasure in, appreciate, relish, lap up, savour; informal get a kick out of.
▷ **noun** *there are a few spots in town for late-night revels:* celebrations, festivities, jollifications, merrymaking, carousing, partying.

revelation noun
1 *the government has been rocked by further revelations about his personal life:* disclosure, announcement, report; discovery, exposé; admission, confession.
2 *the revelation of confidential information:* disclosure, disclosing, leaking, leak, exposure, uncovering.

revelry noun *they headed off to the bar for a night of drunken revelry:* celebration, revels, festivity, festivities, jollification, merrymaking, carousing; informal partying.

revenge noun *she is seeking revenge for the murder of her husband:* vengeance, retribution, retaliation, reprisal, requital, an eye for an eye (and a tooth for a tooth), redress, satisfaction.
▷ **verb**
1 *he was determined to revenge his brother's murder:* avenge, take/exact revenge for, exact retribution for, get/obtain redress for.
2 *I'll be revenged on the whole pack of you:* take revenge on, get your revenge on, avenge yourself on, take vengeance on, get even with, settle a/the score with, pay back, take reprisals against; informal get your own back on.

revenue noun *traders have lost £10,000 in revenue since the traffic scheme was implemented:* income, takings, receipts, proceeds, earnings; profits.
OPPOSITES: expenditure.

reverberate verb *the shot reverberated around the valley:* resound, echo, re-echo, resonate, ring, boom, rumble.

reverberation noun
1 *thunder rolled overhead and its reverberation filled the hall:* resonance, echo, echoing, resounding, ringing, booming, rumbling.
2 *the political reverberations of this event could be significant:* repercussions, effects, consequences, result,

ramifications, backlash, aftermath, fallout; legacy.

revere verb *he was revered by his contemporaries:* respect, admire, think highly of, have a high opinion of, esteem, hold in high esteem/regard, look up to; venerate, worship, pay homage to.
OPPOSITES: despise.

reverence noun *those who saw him on stage speak of him with reverence:* respect, regard, esteem, admiration, veneration; awe, deference.
OPPOSITES: scorn.

reverent adjective *everyone spoke in hushed, reverent tones:* respectful, reverential, admiring; awed, deferential.
OPPOSITES: irreverent.

reverie noun *a knock on the door disturbed her reverie:* daydream, daydreaming, trance, musing; wool-gathering, preoccupation, absorption, abstraction, lack of concentration.

reversal noun
1 *there was to be no reversal on this issue:* turnaround, turnabout, about-face, volte-face, change of heart, U-turn, backtracking; Brit. about-turn.
2 *a reversal of roles:* exchange, change, swapping, interchange; transposition.
3 *the reversal of the decision followed intense public criticism:* overturning, overthrow, overriding, overruling, revocation, rescinding, annulment, nullification, invalidation.
4 *the champions suffered an unexpected reversal this weekend:* setback, reverse, upset, misfortune, mishap, blow, disappointment, defeat; bad luck.

reverse verb
1 *the car reversed into a lamp post:* back, drive backwards, move backwards.
2 *the decision was reversed by the Court of Appeal:* overturn, overthrow, override, overrule, retract, revoke, rescind, annul, nullify, void, invalidate; change; Brit. do an about-turn on.
3 *it may be a good idea if you reverse your roles:* swap, change round, exchange, interchange, switch; transpose.
▷ **noun**
1 *years ago, you could get good deals at Christmas because no one wanted to be away, but these days the reverse is true:* opposite, contrary, converse; inverse, antithesis.
2 *the deadlines are listed on the reverse of the page:* other side, reverse side, back, underside, obverse.

revert verb
1 *he swore he would not let this happen again but he eventually reverted to his old ways:* return, go back, change back, default; fall back, regress, relapse.
2 *the property reverted to the landlord:* be returned.

r

review noun

1 *a comprehensive review of UK defence policy:* analysis, evaluation, assessment, appraisal, examination, study, investigation; inquiry, probe.
2 *the rent is due for review:* reconsideration, reassessment, re-evaluation.
3 *he began to write book reviews:* critique, criticism, assessment, evaluation, commentary; Brit. informal crit.
4 *their annual review of the local economy:* survey, report, study, analysis, account, description, overview.

▷ verb

1 *first, I reviewed the evidence:* survey, study, research, consider, analyse, examine, scrutinize, explore, look into, probe, investigate, assess, appraise, weigh up; informal size up.
2 *the referee reviewed his decision:* reconsider, re-examine, reassess, re-evaluate.
3 *she reviewed the play for a local paper:* comment on, evaluate, assess, appraise, critique.

revile verb *he was reviled as a traitor:* criticize, censure, condemn, attack, inveigh against, rail against, lambaste, denounce, vilify; formal excoriate.
OPPOSITES: praise.

revise verb

1 *she eventually revised her opinion:* reconsider, review, re-examine, reassess, re-evaluate, reappraise, rethink; change, alter, modify.
2 *the editor has completely revised the text:* amend, emend, correct, alter, change, edit, rewrite, redraft, rephrase, rework.
3 (Brit.) *you need to revise all your lecture notes:* go over, reread, memorize; informal bone up on; Brit. informal swot up.

revision noun *the report called for a major revision of the exam system:* reconsideration, review, re-examination, reassessment, re-evaluation, reappraisal, rethink; change, alteration, modification.

revitalize verb *a package of spending cuts intended to revitalize the economy:* reinvigorate, re-energize, boost, regenerate, revive, revivify, rejuvenate, resuscitate, refresh, stimulate, breathe new life into; informal give a shot in the arm to, pep up, buck up.

revival noun

1 *a revival in the party's fortunes:* improvement, rallying, change for the better, upturn, upswing, resurgence, recovery.
2 *there is widespread interest in the revival of traditional crafts | flamenco enjoyed a major international revival in the 1980s:* reintroduction, restoration, resurrection, regeneration; comeback, reappearance, renaissance, rebirth.
OPPOSITES: downturn.

revive verb

1 *attempts to revive her failed:* resuscitate, bring round.
2 *the man soon revived:* regain consciousness, come round, wake up.
3 *a cup of tea revived her:* reinvigorate, revitalize, refresh, energize, revivify, restore, rejuvenate, enliven.
4 *we are reviving many of the old traditions:* reintroduce, re-establish, restore, resurrect, bring back.
5 *an attempt to revive falling sales:* regenerate, resuscitate, restore, revivify; boost, stimulate, improve; informal give a shot in the arm to, buck up.

revoke verb *although the decree was never revoked, it was never effectively enforced:* cancel, repeal, rescind, reverse, annul, nullify, void, invalidate, countermand; formal abrogate.

revolt verb

1 *the people revolted against colonial rule:* rebel, rise up, take to the streets, riot, mutiny.
2 *the smell of the meat revolted him:* disgust, sicken, nauseate, make someone sick, turn someone's stomach, be repugnant to, be repulsive to, put off, be offensive to; informal turn off; N. Amer. informal gross out.

▷ noun *an armed revolt forced the president from office:* rebellion, revolution, insurrection, mutiny, uprising, riot; rioting, insurgence, coup, coup d'état.

revolting adjective *the revolting smell lingered in the air:* disgusting, sickening, nauseating, stomach-churning, repulsive, repellent, repugnant, appalling, abominable, hideous, horrible, horrid, awful, dreadful, terrible, obnoxious, vile, nasty, foul, loathsome, offensive, objectionable, off-putting, distasteful, disagreeable; literary noisome; informal ghastly, putrid, gross.
OPPOSITES: attractive, pleasant.

revolution noun

1 *the revolution brought down the communist regime:* rebellion, revolt, insurrection, uprising, insurgence, coup, coup d'état, mutiny.
2 *a revolution in printing techniques:* dramatic/profound change, sea change, metamorphosis, transformation; informal shake-up.
3 *one revolution of the wheel takes 15 seconds:* turn, rotation, circle, spin; circuit, lap.

revolutionary adjective

1 *a revolutionary new product:* new, pioneering, original, innovative, innovatory; unconventional, unorthodox.
2 *his son was deposed by revolutionary forces which took control of the country:* rebellious, rebel, insurgent, mutinous, renegade, insurrectionist, seditious, subversive; extremist.
3 *a period of revolutionary change:*

r

radical, sweeping, far-reaching, extensive, profound, thoroughgoing, thorough, comprehensive, complete, total.
▷ **noun** *the political revolutionaries hung on to power:* rebel, insurgent, insurrectionist, subversive.

revolutionize verb *his book revolutionized the economic theories of the day:* transform, alter dramatically, shake up, turn upside down, reshape.

revolve verb
1 *overhead, a fan revolved slowly:* go round, turn round, rotate, spin, whirl.
2 *the moon revolves around the earth:* circle, travel, orbit.
3 *his life revolves around cars:* be focus on, centre around, be preoccupied with, be concerned with.

revulsion noun *news of the attack was met with sorrow and revulsion:* disgust, repulsion, abhorrence, repugnance, nausea, horror, distaste.
OPPOSITES: delight.

reward noun *he deserves a reward for all the hard work he's put in:* recompense, prize, award, bonus, present, gift, payment; honour; formal perquisite; informal perk.
▷ **verb** *they were well rewarded for their efforts:* recompense, pay, make something worth someone's while; give an award to.
OPPOSITES: punish.

rewarding adjective *working with the community has been an immensely rewarding experience:* satisfying, gratifying, pleasing, fulfilling, enriching, life-affirming; edifying, illuminating, beneficial, worthwhile, valuable, productive, fruitful.

reword verb *this clause will need to be reworded:* rewrite, rephrase, recast, express differently, redraft, rework, revise; paraphrase.

rewrite verb *I put together a rough draft and then rewrote it:* revise, recast, reword, rephrase, rework, redraft.

rhetoric noun
1 *Churchill's rhetoric inspired the British people to fight on:* oratory, effective/persuasive speaking, eloquence, command of language, speech-making.
2 *all we have from the Opposition is empty rhetoric:* bombast, words, talk, grandiloquence; wordiness, verbosity; exaggeration, hyperbole; formal magniloquence; informal hot air.

rhetorical adjective *a series of expressions used for rhetorical effect:* stylistic, oratorical, linguistic, verbal.

rhyme noun poem, verse, ditty; (**rhymes**) poetry.

rhythm noun
1 *the rhythm of the music:* beat, cadence, tempo, time; pulse, throb.

2 *limericks have a characteristic rhythm and rhyme scheme:* metre, measure, pattern, cadence.
3 *the rhythm of daily life:* pattern, ebb and flow, tempo.

rhythmic adjective *the rhythmic beat of the drums:* rhythmical, steady, pulsating, regular, even, measured; throbbing, beating.

ribald adjective *the novel is part gothic mystery, part ribald comedy:* bawdy, rude, risqué, racy, earthy, irreverent; informal raunchy, blue, saucy.

rich adjective
1 *she comes from a rich family:* wealthy, affluent, moneyed, well off, well-to-do, prosperous; informal rolling in it, in the money, loaded, well heeled, made of money.
2 *there are 50 well-appointed rooms, all with rich period furnishings:* sumptuous, opulent, luxurious, de luxe, lavish, gorgeous, splendid, magnificent, costly, expensive, fancy; informal posh, plush, ritzy, swanky, classy; Brit. informal swish.
3 *the town offers a rich supply of restaurants:* plentiful, abundant, copious, ample, profuse, lavish, liberal, generous, bountiful.
4 *an area of the country which is rich in wildlife:* full of, abounding in, packed with, bursting with, well provided with, well stocked with, crammed with; informal jam-packed with.
5 *the island's rich cultural heritage:* full of variety, varied, multifarious; interesting, fascinating.
6 *the city is surrounded by rich agricultural land:* fertile, productive, fecund, fruitful.
7 *mussels do not need a rich sauce:* creamy, fatty, heavy.
8 *the rich colours of autumn:* strong, deep, full, intense, vibrant, vivid, warm.
9 *her rich contralto voice:* sonorous, full, resonant, deep, clear, mellow, mellifluous.
OPPOSITES: poor, light.

riches plural noun *a handful of these Russian businessmen have amassed vast riches:* money, wealth, funds, cash, wherewithal, means, assets, capital, resources, reserves; affluence, prosperity.

richly adverb
1 *he gazed round the richly furnished chamber:* sumptuously, opulently, luxuriously, lavishly, splendidly, magnificently.
2 *the joy she so richly deserves:* fully, thoroughly, well, completely, wholly, totally, entirely, absolutely, amply, utterly.

rickety adjective *we went carefully up the rickety old staircase:* shaky, unsteady, unsound, unsafe; tumbledown, broken-down, dilapidated, ramshackle.

rid verb *the same measures were used to*

r

rid the city of drug dealers: clear, cleanse, purge, free, empty.

□ **get rid of**
1 we must get rid of some stuff: dispose of, throw away/out, clear out, discard, scrap, dump, jettison; informal chuck away, ditch, bin, junk, get shut of; Brit. informal get shot of.
2 it was relatively easy for union officials to get rid of troublemakers: remove, eject, expel, throw out.

riddle¹ noun they still hope for an answer to this riddle: puzzle, conundrum, problem, question, enigma, mystery; informal poser.

riddle² verb
1 his car was riddled by sniper fire: perforate, hole, pierce, puncture, pepper.
2 the political system was riddled with corruption: fill, pervade, permeate, infest, overrun.

ride verb
1 he taught me to ride a bike when I was about six: manage, handle, control; use, operate, work.
2 they ride round the town on motor bikes: travel, drive, cycle, pedal; roar, speed, hurtle.
▷ **noun** he took us out for a ride: trip, journey, drive, run, excursion, outing, jaunt; informal spin.

ridicule noun he had to face the ridicule of the tabloid press: mockery, derision, laughter, scorn, scoffing, contempt, jeering, sneering, sneers, jibes, jibing, taunts, taunting, sarcasm, satire.
OPPOSITES: respect.
▷ **verb** his theory was ridiculed and dismissed: deride, mock, laugh at, heap scorn on, jeer at, jibe at, sneer at, treat with contempt, scorn, make fun of, poke fun at, scoff at; satirize, lampoon, caricature, parody; taunt; informal take the mickey out of.

ridiculous adjective that's a ridiculous suggestion | he's still wearing that ridiculous baseball cap: ludicrous, absurd, farcical, laughable, risible, preposterous, foolish, idiotic, stupid, inane, silly, asinine, fatuous, senseless, outrageous; informal crazy.
OPPOSITES: sensible.

rife adjective
1 violence is rife in our cities: widespread, pervasive, prevalent, common, universal, extensive, ubiquitous, omnipresent, rampant, endemic, inescapable, insidious.
2 the village was rife with gossip: full of, alive with.

rifle verb
1 she rifled through her wardrobe: rummage, search, hunt, forage.
2 he kept her talking while his accomplice rifled her home: burgle, rob, loot, raid, plunder, ransack.

rift noun
1 a deep rift in the Arctic ice: crack, fault,

flaw, split, break, breach, fissure, fracture, cleft, crevice, cavity, opening.
2 the deepening rift between Jeremy and his father: breach, divide, division, split, gap, gulf, chasm, schism; argument, dispute, conflict, feud; estrangement.

rig¹ verb
1 the boats were rigged with a single sail: equip, kit out, fit out, supply, provide, furnish, arm.
2 I rigged myself out in black: dress, clothe, robe, garb, array, deck out, drape, outfit, get up, trick out/up; formal attire; informal doll up.
3 he will rig up a shelter: set up, erect, assemble; throw together, cobble together, put together, get together, whip up, improvise, contrive; Brit. informal knock up.
▷ **noun** he used to own a CB radio rig: apparatus, appliance, machine, device, instrument, contraption, system; tackle, gear, kit, outfit.

rig² verb the results of the election had been rigged: manipulate, tamper with, interfere with; misrepresent, distort; informal fix; Brit. informal fiddle.

right adjective
1 it wouldn't be right to do that | you've done the right thing: just, fair, equitable, proper, moral, ethical, honourable, honest; acceptable, justifiable, justified.
2 that's the right answer: correct, accurate, exact, precise; true; Brit. informal spot on.
3 he's the right person for the job: suitable, appropriate, fitting, correct, proper, desirable, preferable, ideal, best.
4 I was waiting for the right moment to ask her: opportune, advantageous, favourable, propitious, good, providential, felicitous; timely, seasonable, convenient, expedient, suitable, appropriate.
5 (informal) I felt a right idiot: absolute, complete, total, real, thorough, utter, unmitigated, veritable.
OPPOSITES: wrong.
▷ **adverb**
1 I'm right out of ideas: completely, totally, absolutely, utterly, thoroughly, quite.
2 the hotel is right in the middle of the village: exactly, precisely, directly, immediately, just, squarely, dead; informal bang, slap bang, smack, plumb.
3 keep going right on till you come to the lights: straight, directly, all the way.
4 (informal) don't move—I'll be right back: straight, immediately, instantly, at once, straight away, now, right now, this minute, directly, forthwith, without further ado, promptly, quickly; informal asap.
5 he had guessed right: correctly, accurately, rightly.
6 nothing's going right for me this season: well, favourably, advantageously, profitably, providentially.
OPPOSITES: wrong, badly.

r

▷ **noun**

1 *the difference between right and wrong:* justice, fairness, equity, propriety, morality, honesty, honour, integrity, rectitude.

2 *you have the right to say no:* entitlement, prerogative; freedom, liberty, licence, permission, dispensation, leave, sanction, authority.
OPPOSITES: wrong.

▷ **verb** *we must do what we can to right the situation:* remedy, put right, rectify, retrieve, fix, resolve, sort out, straighten out, correct, repair, mend, redress, make amends for, make good.

▢ **right away**
she wants to see you right away: at once, straight away, now, right now, this minute, this instant, immediately, instantly, directly, forthwith, without further ado, promptly, quickly, without delay; informal pronto, asap.

▢ **within your rights**
you're quite within your rights to ask for your money back: entitled, permitted, allowed, at liberty.

righteous adjective

1 *rules for righteous living:* good, virtuous, upright, upstanding, decent; ethical, principled, moral, high-minded, law-abiding, honest, honourable, blameless, irreproachable, noble; saintly, godly, pure.

2 *a look of righteous anger came over his face:* justifiable, justified, legitimate, defensible; understandable, excusable.
OPPOSITES: sinful, unjustifiable.

rightful adjective

1 *I intend to return the car to its rightful owner | the rightful heir:* legal, lawful, real, true, proper, correct, recognized, genuine, valid, legitimate, bona fide; licensed.

2 *women have been denied their rightful place in society:* deserved, due, just, right, fair, proper, fitting, appropriate.

right-wing adjective
conservative, rightist, right-of-centre; reactionary, traditionalist, unprogressive; neoconservative.
OPPOSITES: left-wing.

rigid adjective

1 *a rigid material:* stiff, hard, inflexible, inelastic.

2 *rigid bureaucratic controls:* fixed, set, firm, inflexible, unalterable, unchangeable, immutable, unvarying, invariable, hard and fast, cast-iron.

3 *poorer nations warned against a rigid approach to funding:* strict, severe, stern, stringent, rigorous, inflexible, uncompromising, intransigent.
OPPOSITES: flexible, lenient.

rigmarole noun
there's no need to go through all the rigmarole of a further inquiry: fuss, bother, trouble, ado; informal palaver, performance, to-do, pantomime, hassle; Brit. informal carry-on, song and dance.

rigorous adjective

1 *his rigorous attention to detail:* meticulous, conscientious, punctilious, careful, diligent, attentive, scrupulous, painstaking, exact, precise, accurate, thorough, particular, fastidious, strict, demanding, exacting.

2 *a rigorous enforcement of the ban:* strict, severe, stern, stringent, tough, harsh, rigid, unsparing, inflexible, draconian, intransigent, uncompromising.
OPPOSITES: slapdash, lax.

rigour noun

1 *a speech noted for its intellectual rigour:* meticulousness, thoroughness, carefulness, diligence, scrupulousness, exactness, exactitude, precision, accuracy.

2 *the organization must comply with the full rigour of UK and European competition law:* strictness, severity, stringency, toughness, rigidity, inflexibility, intransigence.

3 *she could not face the rigours of the journey:* hardship, ordeal, misery, trial; discomfort, inconvenience, privation.

rim noun

1 *the rim of her cup:* brim, edge, lip.

2 *the rim of the crater:* edge, border, side, margin, brink, fringe, boundary, perimeter, limits, periphery.

rind noun
the rind of a lemon: skin, peel; zest.

ring[1] noun

1 *a ring of light surrounds the sun and the moon:* circle, band, halo, disc; loop.

2 *the crowd went wild as he stepped into the ring:* arena, enclosure, field, ground; amphitheatre, stadium.

3 *a spy ring existed right under their noses:* gang, syndicate, cartel, network; circle, organization, association, society, alliance, league.

▷ **verb** *police ringed the building:* surround, circle, encircle, enclose, form a ring around.

> **WORD LINKS**
> **annular** ring-shaped

ring[2] verb

1 *church bells rang all day:* toll, sound, peal, chime, clang, bong; ding, jingle, tinkle.

2 *the room rang with laughter:* resound, reverberate, resonate, echo.

3 *I'll ring you tomorrow:* telephone, phone, call; informal give someone a buzz; Brit. informal give someone a bell.

▷ **noun**

1 *there was the ring of a bell from the gate:* chime, toll, peal, clang, ding, jingle, tinkle, tintinnabulation; sound.

2 *I'll give Chris a ring tomorrow:* call, telephone call, phone call; informal buzz; Brit. informal bell.

r

rinse verb *she rinsed her face with cold water:* wash, clean, cleanse, bathe; swill, sluice.

riot noun
1 *riots broke out in the capital:* disturbance, violence, fighting, street fighting, mayhem, turmoil, lawlessness, anarchy; melee, fracas, fray, free-for-all.
2 *the film's sex scenes caused a riot in Cannes:* uproar, commotion, furore, tumult.
▷**verb** *miners rioted and attacked the local party HQ:* go on the rampage, rampage, run riot, fight in the streets, run amok, go berserk.
▢**run riot**
1 *the children can run riot in the family rooms:* rampage, go on the rampage, run riot, run amok, go berserk; informal raise hell.
2 *the vegetation has run riot:* grow profusely, proliferate, spread uncontrolled, grow rapidly, spread like wildfire; burgeon, multiply.

riotous adjective
1 *a riotous crowd:* unruly, rowdy, disorderly, uncontrollable, unmanageable, undisciplined; violent, wild, ugly, lawless, anarchic.
2 *a riotous party:* uproarious, lively, loud, noisy, unrestrained, unruly, boisterous, rollicking; Brit. informal rumbustious.
OPPOSITES: peaceable.

rip verb
1 *he ripped the posters down:* tear, wrench, pull, snatch, tug, drag, pluck, wrest; informal yank.
2 *she ripped Leo's note into pieces:* tear, slash, cut.
▷**noun** *there's a rip in my sleeve:* tear, slit, split, rent; laceration, cut, gash, slash.
▢**rip someone/thing off** (informal)
1 *I think the taxi driver ripped me off:* overcharge, cheat, swindle, short-change; defraud.
2 *his latest film is a shameless collection of ideas ripped off from other movies:* steal, plagiarize, poach; formal purloin; informal lift, nick, pinch.

ripe adjective
1 *a ripe peach:* ready to eat, ripened; luscious, juicy, tender, sweet, succulent; mature.
2 *the land is ripe for development:* ready, fit, suitable.
3 *we felt that the time was ripe for a new approach:* right, opportune, advantageous, favourable, auspicious, propitious, promising, good, providential, felicitous; convenient, suitable, appropriate, fitting.
OPPOSITES: unripe, unsuitable.

riposte noun *his mother forestalled his indignant riposte by replacing the receiver:* retort, rejoinder, answer, reply, response, sally, return; informal comeback.

rise verb
1 *the aircraft rose into the sky:* move up/upwards, make its way up, ascend, climb, mount, soar.
2 *he rose from his chair:* stand up, get to your feet, get up, jump up, leap up; formal arise.
3 *land prices continue to rise:* go up, increase, soar, shoot up, surge, leap, jump, rocket, escalate, spiral.
4 *living standards have risen:* improve, get better, go up, soar, shoot up.
5 *his voice rose in anger:* get louder, grow, increase, swell, intensify.
6 *in the east, the land rises to a range of forested hills:* slope upwards, go uphill, incline, climb.
7 *he rose through the ranks to become managing director:* progress, climb, advance, work your way, be promoted.
8 *the mountains rose above us:* loom, tower, soar, rise up, rear up.
9 *the court rose at midday:* adjourn, recess, be suspended.
OPPOSITES: fall, descend, drop.
▷**noun**
1 *a rise in interest rates:* increase, hike, leap, jump, upsurge, upswing, climb, escalation.
2 *he got a rise of 11%:* raise, pay increase, wage increase; increment.
3 *a rise in standards:* improvement, upturn, leap.
4 *his rise to power:* progress, climb, promotion, elevation.
5 *we walked slowly up the rise:* slope, incline, acclivity; hillock, hill; formal eminence.

risible adjective *the highly respected principal of the university dismissed the plans as risible:* laughable, ridiculous, absurd, farcical, preposterous, ludicrous, outrageous.

risk noun
1 *all surgery carries an element of risk:* chance, uncertainty, unpredictability, precariousness, instability, insecurity, hazardousness, perilousness, riskiness.
2 *avoid using candles—the risk of fire is too great:* possibility, chance, probability, likelihood, danger, hazard, threat, peril.
▷**verb**
1 *he risked his life to save them:* endanger, jeopardize, imperil, gamble with, chance; put at risk, put in jeopardy, put on the line, hazard.
2 *in a tweed coat you risk getting cold and wet:* be in danger of, run the risk of, stand a chance of.
▢**at risk**
hundreds of native species are at risk: in danger, in peril, in jeopardy, under threat.

risky adjective *you may not get insurance cover for such a risky undertaking:* dangerous, hazardous, perilous, fraught with danger, unsafe, insecure, precarious, touch-and-go, treacherous; uncertain, unpredictable; informal chancy, dicey, hairy. OPPOSITES: safe.

risqué adjective *a play laced with risqué double entendres:* ribald, rude, bawdy, racy, earthy, indecent, suggestive, naughty; crude, coarse, obscene; informal raunchy, saucy.

rite noun *the rites of the Anglican Church:* ceremony, ritual, ceremonial; service, sacrament, liturgy, office; act, practice, custom, tradition, convention, procedure.

ritual noun *the official thanksgiving was an elaborate civic ritual* | *religious rituals:* ceremony, rite, ceremonial; service, sacrament, liturgy; act, practice, custom, tradition, convention; procedure, protocol, observances.

rival noun
1 *his chief rival for the nomination:* opponent, challenger, competitor, contender; adversary, antagonist, enemy; literary foe.
2 *in terms of versatility, the tool has no rival:* equal, match, peer, equivalent, counterpart, like.
OPPOSITES: ally.
▷ **verb** *few countries can rival Slovakia for scenery:* match, emulate, compare with, compete with, vie with, equal, be in the same league as, be on a par with, touch, challenge; informal hold a candle to.
▷ **adjective** *there are only two serious rival candidates:* competing, opposing, contending.

rivalry noun competitiveness, competition; opposition, conflict, antagonism, friction.

riven adjective (literary) *a country riven by civil war:* torn apart, torn in two, split; literary cleft, torn asunder, rent.

river noun
1 *the river has burst its banks:* watercourse, waterway, tributary, stream, rivulet, brook, inlet, rill, runnel; Scottish & N. English burn; N. English beck; N. Amer. & Austral./ NZ creek; Austral. billabong.
2 *a river of molten lava:* stream, torrent, flood, deluge, cascade.

> WORD LINKS
> **fluvial** relating to or found in a river
> **riparian, riverine** relating to or situated on the banks of a river

riveted adjective
1 *she stood riveted to the spot:* fixed, rooted, frozen, glued.
2 *he was riveted by the newsreels:* fascinated, engrossed, gripped, captivated, enthralled, spellbound, mesmerized, transfixed.
OPPOSITES: bored.

riveting adjective *his book is a riveting read:* fascinating, gripping, engrossing,

interesting, intriguing, absorbing, captivating, enthralling, compelling, spellbinding, mesmerizing; informal unputdownable.
OPPOSITES: boring.

road noun
1 *the roads were crowded with traffic:* street, thoroughfare, roadway, carriageway, avenue; N. Amer. highway.
2 *the road to economic recovery:* way, path, route, course.

roam verb *we roamed about the city all day* | *a mysterious, large black cat has been witnessed roaming the local countryside:* wander, rove, ramble, drift, walk, traipse; range, travel, tramp, traverse, trek; formal perambulate; informal cruise.

roar noun
1 *the roars of the crowd increased in intensity:* shout, bellow, yell, cry, howl; clamour; informal holler.
2 *the roar of the sea:* boom, crash, rumble, thundering.
3 *his claims were greeted with roars of laughter:* guffaw, howl, hoot, shriek, gale, peal.
▷ **verb**
1 *'Get out!' roared Angus:* bellow, yell, shout, bawl, howl; informal holler.
2 *thunder roared overhead:* boom, rumble, crash, roll, thunder.
3 *the movie left them roaring with laughter:* guffaw, laugh, hoot; informal split your sides, be doubled up, crack up, be in stitches; Brit. informal crease up, fall about.
4 *a motorbike roared past:* speed, zoom, whizz, flash; informal belt, tear, zip; Brit. informal bomb.

roasting adjective (informal) *another roasting day in London:* hot, sweltering, scorching, blistering, searing, torrid; informal boiling, baking.

rob verb
1 *the gang robbed the local bank:* burgle, steal from, hold up, break into; raid, loot, plunder, pillage.
2 *the accused then robbed two men in the street:* steal from; informal mug.
3 *he was robbed of his savings:* cheat, swindle, defraud; informal do out of, con out of.
4 *defeat robbed him of the chance of regaining his title:* deprive, strip, divest, deny.

robber noun burglar, thief, housebreaker, mugger, shoplifter; raider, looter; bandit; literary brigand; informal crook.

robbery noun burglary, theft, stealing, breaking and entering, housebreaking, shoplifting; hold-up, break-in, raid; N. Amer. larceny; informal mugging, smash-and-grab, stick-up; N. Amer. informal heist.

robe noun *the queen was wearing her robes of state:* garb, regalia, costume, finery;

r

garments, clothes; formal apparel; old use raiment, vestments.

robot noun automaton; (in Science Fiction) android, cyborg.

robust adjective
1 *a large, robust man:* strong, vigorous, sturdy, tough, powerful, solid, muscular, rugged, hardy, strapping, brawny, burly, husky; healthy, fit, hale and hearty, in fine fettle; informal beefy, hunky.
2 *these knives are very robust:* durable, resilient, tough, hard-wearing, long-lasting, sturdy, strong.
3 *Libby took her usual robust view of things:* down-to-earth, practical, realistic, pragmatic, common-sense, commonsensical, matter-of-fact, businesslike, sensible, unromantic, unsentimental; informal no-nonsense.
OPPOSITES: frail, fragile, romantic.

rock¹ verb
1 *the ship rocked on the water:* move to and fro, move back and forth, sway, see-saw; roll, pitch, toss, lurch, reel, list; wobble, oscillate.
2 *the building began to rock:* shake, vibrate, quake, tremble.
3 *the local community was rocked by the news:* stun, shock, stagger, stupefy, devastate; informal knock sideways; Brit. informal knock for six.

rock² noun
1 *a gully strewn with rocks:* boulder, stone, pebble.
2 *a castle built on a rock:* crag, cliff, outcrop.
3 *he was the rock on which they all relied:* foundation, cornerstone, support, prop, mainstay; tower of strength, bulwark, anchor.
□ **on the rocks** (informal)
1 *her career is on the rocks:* in difficulty, in trouble, breaking up, over; in tatters, in ruins, ruined.
2 *a Scotch on the rocks:* with ice, on ice.

WORD LINKS
petrography, petrology the study of the composition and properties of rocks

rocket noun *guerrillas fired rockets at the capital:* missile, projectile.
▷ verb *prices have rocketed:* shoot up, soar, increase rapidly, rise rapidly, escalate, spiral; informal go through the roof.
OPPOSITES: plummet.

rocky adjective
1 *a rocky path:* stony, pebbly, shingly; rough, bumpy; craggy, mountainous.
2 *their marriage had been rocky from the start:* difficult, problematic, precarious, shaky, unstable, unreliable; informal up and down.

rod noun *an iron rod:* bar, stick, pole, staff; shaft, strut, rail, spoke.

rogue noun *he's a rogue without ethics or scruples:* scoundrel, villain, reprobate, good-for-nothing, ne'er-do-well, wretch.

roguish adjective
1 *a roguish and untrustworthy character:* unprincipled, dishonest, deceitful, unscrupulous, untrustworthy; villainous; informal shady, rascally.
2 *he gave me a roguish grin:* mischievous, playful, teasing, cheeky, naughty, wicked, impish, devilish, arch; informal waggish.

role noun
1 *I had a small role in the film:* part, character.
2 *the equipment will play a vital role in the fight against cancer:* function, part.
3 *Stevens took over the role of chief constable in July 1998:* position, job, post, office; capacity, duty, responsibility, mantle.

roll verb
1 *the ball rolled across the floor | the wheels began to roll:* bowl, spin, rotate, revolve, turn round.
2 *waiters rolled in the trolleys:* wheel, push, trundle.
3 *tears rolled down her cheeks:* flow, run, course, stream, pour, spill, trickle.
4 *the months rolled by:* pass, go, slip, fly; elapse, wear on, march on.
5 *mist rolled across the fields:* billow, undulate.
6 *he rolled his handkerchief into a ball:* wind, coil, fold, curl; twist.
7 *roll out the pastry:* flatten, level; even out.
8 *thunder rolled overhead:* rumble, reverberate, echo, resound, boom, roar, grumble.
9 *the ship began to roll:* lurch, toss, rock, pitch, sway, reel, list.
▷ noun
1 *a roll of paper:* cylinder, tube, scroll.
2 *a roll of film:* reel, spool.
3 *a roll of notes:* wad, bundle.
4 *a roll of the dice:* throw, toss, turn, spin.
5 *the parish has only 100 people on its electoral roll:* list, register, directory, record, file, index, catalogue, inventory; census.
□ **roll in** (informal)
1 *money has been rolling in:* pour in, flood in, flow in.
2 *he rolled in at nine o'clock:* arrive, turn up, appear, show your face; informal show up, roll up, blow in.
□ **roll something out**
the company have just rolled out a new desktop PC aimed at small and mid-sized businesses: introduce, unveil, reveal, bring in/out, release, issue.

rollicking adjective *a rollicking adventure story with lots of colourful characters:* lively, spirited, exuberant, boisterous; riotous, noisy, wild, roisterous; Brit. informal rumbustious.

romance noun
1 *despite the age gap, their romance blossomed:* love, passion, ardour, adoration, devotion; affection, fondness, attachment.
2 *a best-selling author of historical romances:* love story, novel; romantic fiction; informal tear-jerker, bodice ripper.
3 *he had been smitten by the romance of the sea:* mystery, mystique, glamour, excitement, exoticism; appeal, allure, charm.

romantic adjective
1 *he's very handsome, and so romantic:* loving, tender, affectionate, passionate; sentimental; informal lovey-dovey.
2 *the DJ kept all the romantic records for the end of the night:* sentimental.
3 *a beautiful cottage in a romantic setting:* idyllic, picturesque, fairy-tale; beautiful, lovely, charming, pretty.
4 *romantic notions of rural communities:* idealistic, idealized, sentimental, unrealistic, fanciful, impractical; head-in-the-clouds, starry-eyed, utopian, fairy-tale.
OPPOSITES: unsentimental, realistic.
▷ noun *he's an incurable romantic:* idealist, sentimentalist, romanticist; dreamer, utopian.
OPPOSITES: realist.

romp verb
1 *two fox cubs romped playfully on the bank:* play, frolic, frisk, gambol, skip, prance, caper, cavort.
2 *South Africa romped to a six-wicket win over India:* sail, coast, sweep; win hands down, run away with it; informal win by a mile, walk it.

room noun
1 *there isn't much room in here:* space, capacity; headroom, legroom; area, expanse; informal elbow room.
2 *there's always room for improvement:* scope, capacity, leeway, latitude, freedom; opportunity, chance.
▷ verb *he roomed there in September:* lodge, board, live, stay; be quartered, be housed; formal dwell, reside.

roomy adjective *The interior is astonishingly roomy for a car in this class:* spacious, capacious, sizeable, generous, big, large, extensive; voluminous, ample; formal commodious.
OPPOSITES: cramped.

root noun
1 *the fungus attacks the plant's roots:* rootstock, rhizome, tuber.
2 *the root of the problem was probably stress:* source, origin, cause, starting point, basis; beginning, seed, genesis.
3 *by going commercial, he has rejected his roots:* origins, beginnings, family, ancestors, predecessors, heritage; birthplace, homeland.
▷ verb *he rooted around in the cupboard:* rummage, hunt, search, rifle, delve, forage, dig, nose, poke; Brit. informal rootle.

□ **root and branch**
1 *the organization should be eradicated, root and branch:* completely, entirely, wholly, totally, thoroughly.
2 *a root-and-branch reform:* complete, total, thorough, radical.
□ **root something out**
we are determined to root out corruption: eradicate, eliminate, weed out, destroy, wipe out, stamp out, extirpate, abolish, end, put a stop to.
□ **take root**
Protestantism took root in nations living on the North Sea: become established, take hold; develop, thrive, flourish.

rooted adjective
1 *such views are rooted in our culture:* embedded, fixed, established, entrenched, ingrained.
2 *Neil was rooted to the spot:* frozen, riveted, paralysed, glued, fixed; stock-still, motionless, unmoving.

rootless adjective *a drab town populated by lost, rootless, and drug-dependent kids:* drifting, unsettled, uprooted, alienated; homeless, of no fixed abode.

rope noun cord, cable, line, hawser, halyard; string.
▷ verb *his feet were roped together:* tie, bind, lash, truss; secure, fasten, attach; hitch, tether, lasso.
□ **rope someone in/into**
Drew roped me into helping him: persuade to/into, talk into, inveigle into; enlist, engage.

roster noun schedule, list, listing, calendar, timetable; Brit. rota.

rostrum noun dais, platform, podium, stage.

rosy adjective
1 *a rosy complexion:* pink, pinkish, reddish; glowing, healthy, fresh, radiant, blooming; blushing, flushed; ruddy, high-coloured, florid.
2 *his future looks rosy:* promising, optimistic, auspicious, hopeful, upbeat, encouraging, favourable, bright, golden.
OPPOSITES: pale, bleak.

rot verb
1 *the floorboards rotted away:* decay, decompose, become rotten; disintegrate, crumble, perish.
2 *the meat began to rot:* go bad, go off, spoil; moulder, putrefy, fester.
3 *poor neighbourhoods have been left to rot:* deteriorate, degenerate, decline, decay, go to rack and ruin, go to seed, go downhill; informal go to pot, go to the dogs.
OPPOSITES: improve.
▷ noun
1 *the leaves turned black with rot:* decay, decomposition, mould, mildew, blight, canker; putrefaction, putrescence.
2 *traditionalists said the rot had set in:*

r

deterioration, decline; corruption, cancer, canker.

rota noun (Brit.) roster, schedule, list, listing, calendar, timetable.

rotary adjective *the rotary motion of the engine:* rotating, rotatory, rotational, revolving, turning, spinning, gyrating.

rotate verb
1 *the wheels rotate continuously to provide power:* revolve, go round, turn round, spin, gyrate, whirl, twirl, swivel, circle, pivot.
2 *many nurses rotate jobs:* alternate, take turns, change, switch, interchange, exchange, swap; move around.

rotation noun
1 *the rotation of the wheels:* revolving, turning, spinning, gyration, circling.
2 *a single rotation of the Earth around the sun:* turn, revolution, orbit.
3 *each member takes the chair for six months in rotation:* sequence, succession; alternation, cycle.

rotten adjective
1 *the smell of rotten meat:* decaying, decayed, rotting, bad, off, decomposing, putrid, putrescent, perished, mouldy, mouldering, rancid, festering, fetid; addled.
2 *he's rotten to the core:* corrupt, unprincipled, dishonest, dishonourable, unscrupulous, untrustworthy, immoral; villainous, bad, wicked, evil, iniquitous, venal, vile, contemptible, despicable; informal crooked, warped; Brit. informal bent.
3 (informal) *it was a rotten thing to do:* nasty, unkind, unpleasant, spiteful, mean, malicious, hateful, hurtful; unfair, uncalled for, shabby; informal low-down; Brit. informal out of order.
4 (informal) *she's a rotten cook:* bad, poor, dreadful, awful, terrible, appalling, abysmal, atrocious; informal pathetic, useless, lousy; Brit. informal hopeless, duff, rubbish.
OPPOSITES: fresh, honourable, pleasant, good.

rotund adjective
1 *a small, rotund man:* plump, chubby, fat, stout, portly, dumpy, round, chunky, overweight, heavy, ample; flabby, paunchy, fleshy, bulky, corpulent, obese; informal tubby, roly-poly, pudgy, beefy; Brit. informal podgy.
2 *huge stoves bearing rotund cauldrons blazed away:* round, bulbous, spherical.
OPPOSITES: thin.

rough adjective
1 *she stumbled on the rough ground:* uneven, irregular, bumpy, stony, rocky, rugged, craggy, rutted, pitted, lumpy, knobbly.
2 *the terrier's coat is rough and thick:* coarse, bristly, scratchy, prickly; shaggy, hairy, bushy.

3 *the cream brings relief to rough skin:* dry, chapped, calloused, scaly; leathery, weather-beaten.
4 *he can get pretty rough when he's drunk:* violent, brutal, vicious; aggressive, belligerent, pugnacious; rowdy, disorderly, unruly, riotous.
5 *we were tossed about for days on rough seas:* turbulent, stormy, tempestuous, wild, violent, heavy, heaving, choppy.
6 *she prepared a rough draft:* preliminary, hasty, quick, sketchy, basic, unpolished; incomplete, unfinished.
7 *a rough idea of the number of patients involved:* approximate, inexact, imprecise, estimated, vague; N. Amer. informal ballpark.
8 *the customers sat at rough wooden tables:* plain, basic, simple, rough and ready, rude, crude, primitive, spartan, rudimentary.
9 *his voice was rough and angry:* gruff, hoarse, harsh, rasping, husky, throaty, gravelly, guttural.
10 *a bottle of rough red wine:* sharp, sour, acidic, acid, vinegary.
11 *Sophie disliked his rough manners:* uncouth, coarse, crude, boorish, oafish, loutish, unrefined, unladylike, ungentlemanly.
12 (informal) *he's had a rough time recently:* difficult, hard, tough, bad, unpleasant; demanding, arduous.
13 (informal) *you were a bit rough on her:* harsh, hard, tough, stern, severe, unfair, unjust; insensitive, nasty, unkind, unsympathetic.
14 (informal) *I'm feeling really rough.* See **ILL** adjective sense 1.
OPPOSITES: smooth, sleek, soft, gentle, calm, exact.
□ **rough something out**
by the end of the morning he had roughed out a plan: draft, sketch out, outline, mock up.

rough and ready adjective *this is a somewhat rough-and-ready solution to the problem:* basic, simple, crude, unsophisticated; makeshift, provisional, stopgap, improvised, ad hoc.

roughly adverb
1 *he shoved her roughly away:* violently, forcefully, forcibly, abruptly, unceremoniously.
2 *a deal worth roughly £2.4 million:* approximately, about, around, circa, in the region of, something like, of the order of, or so, or thereabouts, more or less, give or take; nearly, close to, approaching; Brit. getting on for.

round adjective
1 *a small round object:* circular, disc-shaped; spherical, globular, globe-shaped; cylindrical; bulbous, rounded, rotund; technical annular.
2 *a short round man:* plump, chubby, fat, stout, rotund, portly, dumpy, chunky, overweight, pot-bellied, paunchy; corpulent, fleshy, bulky, obese; informal

tubby, roly-poly, pudgy, beefy, porky; Brit. informal podgy.

3 *a round dozen:* complete, entire, whole, full.

OPPOSITES: thin.

▷ **noun**
1 *the first round of the contest:* stage, level; heat, game, bout, contest.

2 *an endless round of late-night parties:* succession, sequence, series, cycle.

3 *the gun fires thirty rounds a second:* bullet, cartridge, shell, shot.

4 *the security guard continued his rounds:* circuit, beat, route, tour.

5 *shape the pastry into rounds:* ball, sphere, globe, circle, disc, ring.

▷ **preposition & adverb**
1 *the maze of alleys round the station:* around, about, encircling; near, in the vicinity of.

2 *casinos dotted round the south of France:* throughout, all over, here and there in.

▷ **verb** *the ship rounded the Cape of Good Hope:* go round, travel round, skirt.

□ **round about**
he earns round about £40,000 a year: approximately, about, around, circa, roughly, more or less, close to, practically; or so, or thereabouts, give or take a few; not far off, nearly, almost, approaching; Brit. getting on for.

□ **round the clock**
1 *I've got a team working round the clock:* day and night, night and day, all the time, {morning, noon, and night}, continuously, non-stop, steadily, unremittingly; informal 24-7.

2 *she needs round-the-clock supervision:* continuous, constant, non-stop, continual, uninterrupted.

□ **round something off**
the party rounded off a successful year: complete, finish off, crown, cap, top; conclude, close, end.

□ **round on someone**
Guido rounded on Rosie, as though she were to blame: turn on, attack, snap at, weigh into, let fly at, lash out at, hit out at; informal bite someone's head off, jump down someone's throat, lay into, tear into; Brit. informal have a go at; N. Amer. informal light into.

□ **round someone/something up**
Wilson rounded up the remaining men, women, and children: gather together, herd together, muster, marshal, rally, assemble, collect, group; N. Amer. corral.

roundabout adjective
1 *the bus took a very roundabout route:* circuitous, indirect, meandering, serpentine, tortuous.

2 *in a roundabout way, he was fishing for information:* indirect, oblique, circuitous, circumlocutory, long-winded; evasive.

OPPOSITES: direct.

roundly adverb
1 *the 3 per cent pay increase was roundly*

condemned: vehemently, emphatically, fiercely, forcefully, severely.

2 *she was roundly defeated:* utterly, completely, thoroughly, decisively, conclusively, heavily, soundly.

round-up noun *here's Geraldine with a round-up of the latest news:* summary, synopsis, overview, review, outline.

rouse verb
1 *he roused Ralph at dawn:* wake up, wake; formal waken; Brit. informal knock up.

2 *she roused herself and looked around:* wake up, wake, awaken, come to, bestir yourself.

3 *he roused the crowd with a stirring speech:* stir up, excite, galvanize, electrify, stimulate, inspire, move; inflame, agitate, goad, provoke; incite, spur on.

4 *he's got a nasty temper when he's roused:* provoke, annoy, anger, madden, incense, vex, irk; informal aggravate.

5 *his evasiveness roused my curiosity:* arouse, awaken, prompt, provoke, stimulate, pique, trigger, kindle.

OPPOSITES: calm, pacify, allay.

rousing adjective *he delivered a rousing speech to the packed auditorium:* stirring, inspiring, exciting, stimulating, moving, electrifying; enthusiastic, vigorous, spirited.

rout noun
1 *the army's offensive turned into an ignominious rout:* retreat, flight.

2 *Newcastle scored 13 tries in the 76-4 rout:* defeat, trouncing, annihilation; debacle, fiasco; informal drubbing, hammering, thrashing, pasting.

OPPOSITES: victory.

▷ **verb**
1 *his army was routed at the Battle of Milvian Bridge:* put to flight, drive off, scatter; defeat, beat, conquer, vanquish, crush, overpower.

2 *she went on to rout the defending champion 6-1, 6-0:* beat hollow, trounce, annihilate; informal drub, hammer, clobber, thrash, demolish, wipe the floor with, walk all over.

route noun *let's take the scenic route:* way, course, road, path, direction; passage, journey.

▷ **verb** *enquiries are routed to the relevant desk:* direct, send, convey, dispatch, forward, patch.

routine noun
1 *his morning routine never varied:* procedure, practice, pattern, drill, regime, regimen; programme, schedule, system; customs, habits.

2 *his stand-up routine is hilarious:* act, performance, number, turn, piece; informal spiel, patter.

▷ **adjective** *a routine health check | routine safety procedures:* standard, regular, customary, normal, usual, ordinary, typical,

everyday, day-to-day, run-of-the-mill.
OPPOSITES: unusual.

rove verb *gangs of children roved around:*
wander, roam, drift, meander; range,
travel.

row[1] noun
1 *rows of children stood in the corridor:*
line, column, file, queue; chain, string,
succession; informal crocodile.
2 *the middle row of seats was empty:* tier,
line, rank, bank.
□ **in a row**
it rained for three days in a row:
consecutively, in succession; running,
straight; informal on the trot.

row[2] (Brit.) noun
1 *have you two had a row?* argument,
quarrel, squabble, fight, contretemps,
falling-out, altercation, shouting match;
informal tiff, set-to, run-in, spat; Brit. informal
barney, bust-up, slanging match.
2 *the director is at the centre of a row over
policy decisions:* dispute, disagreement,
argument, clash.
3 *I could hardly hear over the row the crowd
was making:* din, noise, racket, clamour,
uproar, tumult, hubbub, commotion,
brouhaha, rumpus, pandemonium, babel;
Brit. informal hullabaloo.
▷ **verb** *they rowed about money quite a lot:*
argue, quarrel, squabble, bicker, fight,
fall out, disagree, have words, be at
loggerheads.

rowdy adjective *gangs of rowdy
youths often congregate in the area at
weekends:* unruly, disorderly, badly
behaved, undisciplined, uncontrollable,
ungovernable, disruptive, out of control,
riotous; boisterous, noisy, loud; Brit. informal
rumbustious.
OPPOSITES: peaceful.

royal adjective regal, kingly, queenly,
princely; sovereign, monarchical.

rub verb
1 *Polly rubbed her arm:* massage, knead.
2 *he rubbed sun lotion on her back:* apply,
smear, spread, work in, massage.
3 *my shoes began to rub painfully:* chafe,
pinch; hurt, be painful.
▷ **noun** *she gave his back a rub:* massage,
rub-down.
□ **rub it in** (informal) *there's no need to rub it
in:* emphasize, underline, highlight; go
on, harp on; informal rub someone's nose
in it.
□ **rub off on**
*when parents are having a hard time,
their tension can easily rub off on the
kids:* be transferred to, be passed on to,
be transmitted to, be communicated to;
affect, influence.
□ **rub something out**
he rubbed out the lines and started again:
erase, delete, remove, efface, obliterate,
expunge.

rubbish noun
1 *the storage containers were full to
overflowing with rubbish:* refuse, waste,
litter, debris, detritus, scrap; flotsam and
jetsam, lumber; N. Amer. garbage, trash;
informal junk.
2 *she's talking rubbish:* nonsense,
balderdash, gibberish, claptrap, garbage;
informal rot, hogwash, baloney, tripe,
drivel, bilge, bunk, poppycock, twaddle,
gobbledegook; Brit. informal codswallop, tosh.
▷ **adjective** (Brit. informal) *I'm rubbish at keeping
secrets.* See HOPELESS sense 3.

rubble noun debris, remains, ruins,
wreckage.

ruction noun (informal) *the ongoing political
ructions have exacerbated the situation:*
fuss, uproar, furore, hue and cry, rumpus,
trouble, fracas, disturbance, kerfuffle;
quarrel, argument, disagreement.

ruddy adjective *a ruddy complexion:* rosy,
red, pink, florid, high-coloured; healthy,
glowing, fresh; flushed, blushing; literary
rubicund.
OPPOSITES: pale.

rude adjective
1 *a rude, arrogant young man:* ill-
mannered, bad-mannered, impolite,
discourteous, uncivil; impertinent,
insolent, impudent, disrespectful,
cheeky; churlish, curt, brusque, brash,
offhand, short, sharp; offensive, insulting,
derogatory, disparaging, abusive; tactless,
undiplomatic, uncomplimentary.
2 *rude jokes:* vulgar, coarse, smutty, dirty,
filthy, crude, lewd, obscene, off colour,
offensive, indelicate, tasteless, risqué,
naughty, ribald, bawdy, racy; informal blue;
Brit. informal near the knuckle.
OPPOSITES: polite, well mannered, clean.

rudimentary adjective
1 *this can be done by anyone with
rudimentary carpentry skills:* basic,
elementary.
2 *the equipment in the workshop was
rudimentary:* primitive, crude, simple,
unsophisticated, rough and ready,
makeshift.
OPPOSITES: advanced, sophisticated.

rudiments plural noun *the rudiments
of music theory:* basics, fundamentals,
essentials, first principles, foundations;
informal nuts and bolts, ABC.

rue verb *she might live to rue this impetuous
decision:* regret, repent of; lament,
bemoan, bewail.

rueful adjective *she shook her head with a
rueful grin:* regretful, apologetic, sorry,
sheepish, hangdog, contrite, repentant,
penitent, conscience-stricken, self-
reproachful, remorseful, shamefaced;
sorrowful.

ruffian noun thug, lout, hooligan, vandal,

delinquent; scoundrel, villain, rogue; informal **tough**, bruiser, heavy, yahoo; Brit. informal **yob**, yobbo.

ruffle verb

1 *he ruffled her hair:* **disarrange**, tousle, dishevel, rumple, riffle, disorder, mess up; N. Amer. informal **muss up**.
2 *the wind ruffled the water:* **ripple**, riffle.
3 *he had been ruffled by her questions:* **disconcert**, unnerve, fluster, agitate, upset, disturb, discomfit, put off, perturb, unsettle, bother; informal **rattle**, faze, throw, get to.
OPPOSITES: smooth, soothe.
▷ **noun** *a shirt with ruffles:* **frill**, flounce, ruff, ruche.

rugged adjective

1 *the rugged coast path meanders among tall cliffs:* **rough**, uneven, bumpy, rocky, stony, pitted, jagged, craggy.
2 *a frown crossed his rugged features:* **strong**, craggy, rough-hewn; manly, masculine; weathered.
3 *rugged outdoor clothing:* **robust**, durable, sturdy, strong, tough, resilient.
OPPOSITES: smooth, delicate, flimsy.

ruin noun

1 *the buildings may now be saved from ruin:* **disintegration**, decay, disrepair, dilapidation, ruination; destruction, demolition, wreckage.
2 *the ruins of a church:* **remains**, remnants, fragments, relics; rubble, debris, wreckage.
3 *many shopkeepers are facing ruin:* **bankruptcy**, insolvency, penury, poverty, destitution, impoverishment; failure.
4 *in televised debates a single misstep could spell political ruin:* **downfall**, collapse, defeat, undoing, failure, ruination.
▷ **verb**
1 *heavy rain on 3 July ruined his plans:* **wreck**, destroy, spoil, blight, shatter, dash; sabotage, wreak havoc on; informal **screw up**, foul up, put the kibosh on; Brit. informal **scupper**.
2 *the bank's collapse ruined them all:* **bankrupt**, make insolvent, impoverish, pauperize, wipe out, cripple; bring someone to their knees.
3 *a country ruined by civil war:* **destroy**, devastate, lay waste, ravage.
OPPOSITES: save, rebuild.
□ **in ruins**
1 *the abbey is in ruins:* **derelict**, ruined, in disrepair, falling to pieces, dilapidated, tumbledown, ramshackle, decrepit, decaying, ruinous.
2 *his career is in ruins:* **destroyed**, ruined, in pieces, in ashes; over, finished; informal **in tatters**, on the rocks, done for.

ruined adjective *a ruined castle:* **derelict**,
in ruins, dilapidated, tumbledown, ramshackle, decrepit, falling to pieces, crumbling, decaying, disintegrating.

ruinous adjective

1 *the spectre of a ruinous trade war loomed:* **disastrous**, devastating, catastrophic, calamitous, crippling, crushing, damaging, destructive, harmful; costly.
2 *ruinous interest rates:* **extortionate**, exorbitant, excessive, sky-high, outrageous, inflated; Brit. over the odds; informal **criminal**, steep.

rule noun

1 *anybody who breaks the rules will be disqualified | new health and safety rules:* **regulation**, ruling, directive, order, law, statute, edict, canon, command, dictate, decree, injunction, stipulation, requirement; guideline, direction; formal **ordinance**.
2 *the general rule is that problems are referred to the committee:* **procedure**, practice, protocol, convention, norm, routine, custom, habit; formal **praxis**.
3 *the revolution brought an end to British rule:* **control**, jurisdiction, command, power, dominion; government, administration, sovereignty, leadership, supremacy, authority.
▷ **verb**
1 *the territory was ruled by the Ottoman Empire for centuries:* **govern**, control, lead, run, head, administer, preside over, manage.
2 *Mary ruled for six years:* **be in power**, be in control, be in command, be in charge, govern; reign, be monarch, be sovereign.
3 *an industrial tribunal ruled that he had been unfairly dismissed:* **decree**, order, pronounce, judge, adjudge, ordain; decide, find, determine, resolve, settle.
4 *on the streets, chaos ruled:* **prevail**, predominate, be the order of the day, reign supreme; formal **obtain**.
□ **as a rule**
I don't get hangovers as a rule, but when I do, they're really bad: **usually**, generally, in general, normally, ordinarily, customarily, for the most part, on the whole, by and large, in the main, mainly, mostly, commonly, typically.
□ **rule something out**
investigators have not ruled out the possibility that heroin supplies might have been contaminated deliberately | bad weather ruled out further play: **exclude**, eliminate, discount, disregard, dismiss; preclude, prohibit, prevent.

ruler noun **leader**, sovereign, monarch,
potentate, king, queen, emperor, empress, prince, princess; crowned head, head of state, president, premier, governor; overlord, chief, chieftain, lord; dictator, autocrat.
OPPOSITES: subject.

ruling noun *the judge's ruling was
severely criticized:* **judgement**, decision, adjudication, finding, verdict, pronouncement; decree, order.
▷ **adjective**
1 *Japan's ruling party:* **governing**, controlling, in power.

r

2 *football was their ruling passion:* main, chief, principal, major, prime, dominating, foremost; predominant, central; informal number-one.

rumble verb boom, thunder, roll, reverberate, echo.

ruminate verb *we sat ruminating on the meaning of life:* think about, contemplate, consider, meditate on, muse on, mull over, ponder on/over, deliberate about/on, chew over, puzzle over; formal cogitate about.

rummage verb *she rummaged in her bag for her keys:* search, hunt, root about, ferret about, poke about, dig, delve, go through, explore, sift through, rifle through.

rumour noun gossip, hearsay, talk, tittle-tattle, speculation, word; (**rumours**) reports, stories, whispers; informal the grapevine, the word on the street, the buzz.

rumple verb
1 *the sheet was rumpled:* crumple, crease, wrinkle, crinkle, ruck up, scrunch up.
2 *Ian rumpled her hair:* ruffle, disarrange, tousle, dishevel, riffle; mess up; N. Amer. informal muss up.
OPPOSITES: smooth.

rumpus noun (informal) *there was a bit of a rumpus in Bath Street late in the evening and police were called in:* disturbance, commotion, uproar, furore, brouhaha, hue and cry, ruckus; fracas, melee, tumult, noise, racket, din; Brit. row; informal to-do, kerfuffle; Brit. informal hullabaloo, carry-on.

run verb
1 *she ran across the road:* sprint, race, dart, rush, dash, hasten, hurry, scurry, scamper, bolt, fly, gallop, career, charge, shoot, hurtle, speed, zoom, go like lightning, go like the wind; jog, trot; Brit. hare; informal tear, pelt, scoot, hotfoot it, belt, zip; Brit. informal bomb; N. Amer. informal hightail it.
2 *her attacker turned and ran:* flee, run away, run off, run for it, take flight, make off, take off, take to your heels, make a break for it, bolt, make your getaway, escape; informal beat it, clear off/out, vamoose, skedaddle, split, leg it, scram; Brit. informal do a runner, scarper, do a bunk.
3 *he ran in the London marathon:* compete, take part, participate.
4 *she runs a large catering business:* be in charge of, manage, direct, control, head, govern, oversee, administer; operate, conduct, own.
5 *they decided to run some more tests:* carry out, do, perform, execute.
6 *a bus runs to Sorrento three times a day:* travel, shuttle, go.
7 *it's expensive to run a car:* maintain, keep, own, have.
8 *he left the engine running:* operate, function, work, go; tick over, idle.
9 *I'll run you home:* drive, take, bring,

ferry, chauffeur, give someone a lift.
10 *rainwater ran from the eaves:* flow, pour, stream, gush, flood, cascade, roll, course, spill, trickle, drip, dribble, leak.
11 *a shiver ran down my spine:* go, pass, slide, move, travel.
12 *he ran his eye down the list:* cast, pass, skim, flick.
13 *the road runs the length of the valley:* extend, stretch, reach, continue.
14 *the lease runs for twenty years:* be valid, last, be in effect, be operative, continue, be effective.
15 *the show ran for two years:* continue, be on; be performed, be screened, be shown.
16 *he ran for president in 1984:* stand for, be a candidate for, be a contender for.
17 *the paper ran the story on Friday:* publish, print, feature, carry, put out, release, issue.
▷ noun
1 *his early morning run along the river bank:* sprint, jog.
2 *I'll be back in time to do the school run:* route, journey; circuit, round.
3 *we went for a run in the car:* drive, ride, turn; trip, excursion, outing, jaunt, airing; informal spin.
4 *an unbeaten run of victories:* series, succession, sequence, string, chain, streak, spell, stretch, spate.
5 *against the run of play, he scored again:* trend, tendency, course, direction, movement, drift, tide.
6 *the wire mesh of a chicken run:* enclosure, pen, coop.
□ **in the long run**
in the long run this will save us money: eventually, in the end, ultimately.
□ **on the run**
other members of the gang are still on the run: on the loose, at large, loose; running away, fleeing; informal AWOL.
□ **run across**
we ran across David while we were in LA: meet, meet by chance, come across, run into, chance on, stumble on, happen on; informal bump into.
□ **run away.** See **RUN** verb sense 2.
□ **run someone down**
1 *he was run down by joyriders:* run over, knock down/over; hit, strike.
2 *she ran him down in front of other people:* criticize, denigrate, belittle, disparage, find fault with; informal put down, bad-mouth; Brit. informal slag off.
□ **run something down**
1 *she finally ran a copy of the book down:* find, discover, locate, track down, trace, unearth.
2 *employers ran down their workforces gradually:* reduce, cut back on, downsize, decrease, trim; phase out, wind down/up.
□ **run into**
1 *a car ran into his van:* collide with, hit, strike, crash into, smash into, plough into, ram, impact.
2 *I ran into Hugo the other day:* meet, meet

by chance, run across, chance on, stumble on, happen on; informal bump into.
3 *we ran into a problem:* experience, encounter, meet with, be faced with, be confronted with.
4 *his debts run into six figures:* reach, extend to, be as much as.
□ **run off**
1 *the youths ran off.* See **RUN** verb sense 2.
2 (informal) *he ran off with her money.* See **STEAL** verb sense 1.
□ **run on**
1 *the call ran on for hours:* continue, go on, carry on, last, keep going.
2 *your mother does run on:* talk incessantly, go on, chatter on, ramble on; Brit. informal rabbit on, witter on, talk the hind leg off a donkey.
□ **run out**
1 *food supplies were running out:* be used up, dry up, be exhausted, be finished, peter out.
2 *they soon ran out of cash:* be out of; use up, consume, eat up; informal be fresh out of, be cleaned out of.
3 *her contract ran out in June:* expire, end, terminate, finish; lapse.
□ **run out on someone** (informal). See **ABANDON** verb sense 3.
□ **run over**
1 *the bathwater's running over:* overflow, spill over.
2 *he quickly ran over the story | I need to run over my notes again:* recapitulate, recap on, repeat, run through, go over, reiterate, review; look over, read through.
□ **run someone over.** See **RUN SOMEONE DOWN** sense 1.
□ **run through**
1 *a sense of personal loss runs through many of his lyrics:* pervade, permeate, suffuse, imbue, inform.
2 *he ran through his notes.* See **RUN OVER** sense 2.
3 *let's run through scene three:* rehearse, practise, go over, recap on, repeat.
□ **run to**
1 *the bill ran to £22,000:* amount to, add up to, total, come to, equal, reach, be as much as.
2 *sorry, but we can't run to champagne:* afford, stretch to, manage.

runaway noun *a teenage runaway:* fugitive, escapee; refugee; truant; absconder, deserter.
▷ **adjective**
1 *a runaway horse:* out of control, escaped, loose, on the loose.
2 *a runaway victory:* easy, effortless; informal as easy as pie.
3 *runaway inflation:* rampant, out of control, unchecked, unbridled.

rundown noun *can you give me a quick rundown of the findings?* summary, synopsis, precis, run-through, review, overview, sketch, outline, recap.

run-down adjective
1 *a run-down inner-city area:* dilapidated,

tumbledown, ramshackle, derelict, in ruins, crumbling; neglected, uncared-for, depressed; seedy, shabby, squalid.
2 *she was feeling rather run-down:* unwell, ill, poorly; tired, drained, exhausted, fatigued, worn out, below par, washed out; Brit. off colour, peaky; informal under the weather.
OPPOSITES: well maintained, salubrious.

runner noun
1 *the runners were limbering up:* athlete, sprinter; jogger.
2 *a runner from the strawberry plant:* shoot, offshoot, sprout, tendril.

running noun
1 *the day-to-day running of the school:* administration, management, organization, coordination, orchestration, handling, direction, control, regulation, supervision.
2 *the smooth running of her department:* operation, working, functioning, performance.
▷ **adjective**
1 *the sound of running water:* flowing.
2 *a running argument:* ongoing, sustained, continuous; recurrent, recurring.
3 *she was late two days running:* in succession, in a row, in sequence, consecutively; informal on the trot.
□ **in the running**
he's in the running for a prize: likely to get, a candidate for, in line for, on the shortlist for, up for.

run-of-the-mill adjective *a pretty run-of-the-mill action movie:* ordinary, average, middle-of-the-road, commonplace, humdrum, mundane, standard, nondescript, characterless, conventional; unremarkable, unexceptional, uninteresting, dull, boring, routine, bland, lacklustre; informal nothing to write home about; Brit. informal common or garden.
OPPOSITES: exceptional.

rupture verb
1 *the reactor core might rupture:* break, fracture, crack, burst, split; tear; informal bust.
2 *the October 1962 war ruptured India's relations with China:* sever, break off, breach, disrupt.
▷ **noun**
1 *a recent series of pipeline ruptures:* break, fracture, crack, burst, split, fissure; tear.
2 *the rupture with his father could never be mended:* rift, estrangement, falling-out, break-up, breach, split, separation, parting, division; schism; informal bust-up.

rural adjective *rural communities | life on the farm was not the rural idyll she had hoped for:* country, countryside; rustic, bucolic, pastoral; agricultural, agrarian; literary sylvan.
OPPOSITES: urban.

r

ruse noun *she had thought of a ruse to get him out of the house:* ploy, stratagem, tactic, scheme, trick, gambit, dodge; Brit. informal wheeze.

rush verb
1 *she rushed after him:* hurry, dash, run, race, sprint, bolt, dart, career, charge, shoot, hurtle, fly, speed, zoom, scurry, scuttle, scamper, hasten; Brit. hare; informal tear, belt, pelt, scoot, zip, whip, hotfoot it, leg it; Brit. informal bomb; N. Amer. informal hightail it.
2 *water rushed along the gutters:* flow, pour, gush, surge, stream, cascade, run, course.
3 *the tax bill was rushed through parliament:* push, hurry, hasten, speed, hustle, press, force.
4 *demonstrators rushed the cordon of troops:* attack, charge, run at, assail, storm.
▷ **noun**
1 *the spectators made a rush for the the exit:* dash, run, sprint, bolt, charge, scramble; stampede.
2 *there was a last-minute rush for flights:* demand, clamour, call, request; run on.
3 *a rush of cold night air:* gust, draught, flurry.
4 *I'm not in a rush | she realized that in all the rush she'd forgotten her bag:* hurry, haste, urgency.
5 *he felt a sudden rush of anger:* surge, burst, flare.

rushed adjective
1 *a rushed divorce:* hasty, fast, speedy, quick, swift, rapid, hurried.
2 *he was too rushed to enjoy his stay:* pushed for time, pressed for time, busy, in a hurry, run off your feet.
OPPOSITES: leisurely.

rust verb *wrought iron garden furniture has to be specially coated to prevent it from rusting:* corrode, oxidize, become rusty, tarnish.

rustic adjective *a rustic setting:* rural, country, countryside, countrified, pastoral, bucolic; literary sylvan.
OPPOSITES: urban.

rustle verb *a light wind rustled through the trees:* swish, whisper, sigh.
▷ **noun** *the rustle of the leaves:* swish, whisper, rustling; literary susurration.
□ **rustle something up** (informal) *I'll rustle up something to eat:* prepare, throw/put together, make, assemble; informal fix; Brit. informal knock up.

rusty adjective
1 *a heap of rusty metal:* rusted, rust-covered, corroded, oxidized; tarnished, discoloured.
2 *my French is a little rusty:* out of practice, below par; unpractised.

rut noun furrow, groove, trough, hollow; pothole.

ruthless adjective *a ruthless killer:* merciless, pitiless, cruel, heartless, hard-hearted, cold-hearted, cold-blooded, harsh, callous, unfeeling, unmerciful, unforgiving, uncaring, unsympathetic, uncharitable; remorseless, unbending, inflexible, implacable; brutal, savage, sadistic, vicious.
OPPOSITES: merciful.

r

Ss

sable adjective (literary) *her long sable hair:* black, jet-black, pitch-black, ebony, raven, inky, coal-black.

sabotage verb *a guerrilla group sabotaged the national electricity grid | an attempt to sabotage the peace negotiations:* damage, wreck, destroy, cripple, incapacitate, vandalize; obstruct, hinder, disrupt, spoil, ruin, undermine, threaten, subvert.
▷ **noun** *a coordinated campaign of sabotage:* damage, destruction, vandalism; obstruction, disruption, subversion.

sac noun bag, pouch; Medicine cyst.

sack[1] noun
1 *a sack of flour:* bag, pouch, pack.
2 (informal) *he got the sack:* dismissal; informal the boot, your marching orders, the elbow, the push; Brit. informal your cards.
▷ **verb** (informal) *she was sacked for stealing:* dismiss, throw out, discharge; let go, lay off, make redundant; informal fire, kick out, boot out, give someone the sack, give someone their marching orders, show someone the door; Brit. informal give someone their cards.

sack[2] verb *raiders sacked the town:* ravage, lay waste, devastate, raid, ransack, strip, plunder, pillage, loot, rob; literary despoil.

sacred adjective
1 *the priest entered the sacred place:* holy, hallowed, blessed, consecrated, sanctified; venerated, revered.
2 *sacred music:* religious, spiritual, devotional, church, ecclesiastical.
3 *he has built his reputation on a body of work in which nothing is sacred:* sacrosanct, inviolable, inviolate.
OPPOSITES: secular, profane.

sacrifice noun
1 *the sacrifice of animals:* ritual slaughter, offering, immolation.
2 *the calf was a sacrifice to the gods:* offering, votive offering, burnt offering, gift, oblation.
3 *the sacrifice of sovereignty:* surrender, giving up, abandonment, renunciation; forfeiture, loss.
▷ **verb**
1 *two goats were sacrificed:* offer up, immolate, slaughter.
2 *he's sacrificed his principles for political gain:* give up, abandon, surrender, forgo, renounce, relinquish, forfeit; betray.

sacrilege noun *the sacrilege of committing a murder on holy ground:* desecration, profanity, profanation, blasphemy, impiety, irreligion, unholiness, irreverence, disrespect.
OPPOSITES: piety.

sacrilegious adjective *he condemned the book as a vicious, sacrilegious attack on their faith:* profane, blasphemous, impious, sinful, irreligious.

sacrosanct adjective *the individual's right to work has been upheld as sacrosanct:* sacred, inviolable, inviolate, hallowed, respected, invulnerable, untouchable, inalienable; protected, defended, secure, safe.

sad adjective
1 *she felt sad and lonely after they left:* unhappy, sorrowful, dejected, depressed, downcast, miserable, down, despondent, despairing, disconsolate, desolate, wretched, glum, gloomy, doleful, dismal, melancholy, mournful, woebegone, forlorn, crestfallen, heartbroken, inconsolable; informal blue, down in the mouth, down in the dumps.
2 *they knew her sad story:* tragic, unhappy, unfortunate, awful, miserable, wretched, sorry, pitiful, pathetic, traumatic, heartbreaking, heart-rending, harrowing; upsetting, distressing.
3 *it's a sad state of affairs:* unfortunate, regrettable, sorry, deplorable, lamentable, pitiful, shameful, disgraceful.
OPPOSITES: happy, cheerful, fortunate.

sadden verb *his untimely death has saddened us all:* upset, distress, grieve, break someone's heart; depress, dispirit, dishearten, bring down.

saddle verb *this decision saddled the company with £70 million in additional debts:* burden, encumber, lumber, hamper; land; impose something on, thrust something on, fob something off on to.

sadistic adjective *a sadistic killer:* callous, barbarous, vicious, brutal, cruel, fiendish, cold-blooded, inhuman, ruthless, heartless, merciless; perverted.

sadness noun *there will be great sadness at this news:* unhappiness, sorrow, dejection, depression, misery, despondency, despair, desolation, wretchedness, gloom, gloominess, dolefulness, melancholy, mournfulness, woe, heartache, grief.

safe adjective
1 *the jewels are safe in the bank | they were still not safe from the militia:* secure, protected, shielded, sheltered, guarded, out of harm's way; not at risk, not in danger.
2 *the children were found safe and well after a frantic two-hour search:* unharmed, unhurt, uninjured, unscathed, in one piece, out of danger.
3 *a safe place to hide:* secure, impregnable, unassailable, invulnerable.
4 *a safe driver:* cautious, circumspect, prudent.
5 *the drug is safe:* harmless, innocuous, benign, non-toxic, non-poisonous; wholesome.
OPPOSITES: at risk, dangerous, reckless.
▷ noun *I keep the ring in a safe:* strongbox, safety-deposit box, safe-deposit box; strongroom, vault.

safeguard noun *the enhanced security features offer further safeguards against viruses, data corruption, and unauthorized access:* protection, defence, guard, screen, buffer, preventive, precaution, provision, security; surety, cover, insurance, indemnity.
▷ verb *the contract will safeguard 1000 jobs:* protect, save, secure, preserve, conserve, shield, guard, keep safe.
OPPOSITES: jeopardize.

safety noun
1 *the safety of our residents is paramount:* welfare, well-being, protection, security.
2 *we reached the safety of the shore:* shelter, sanctuary, refuge, protection.

sag verb
1 *he sagged back in his chair:* sink, slump, loll, flop, crumple.
2 *the bed sags in the middle | tights which sag at the knees:* dip, droop, hang down; bag, bulge.
3 *exports are forging ahead while home sales have sagged:* decline, fall, drop, decrease, diminish, slump, plummet; informal nosedive.

saga noun
1 *medieval Icelandic sagas:* epic, chronicle, legend, tale, romance, history, narrative, adventure, myth.
2 *she launched into the saga of how they met:* story, tale, epic; rigmarole; informal spiel.

sagacious adjective *they were sagacious enough to avoid any outright confrontation:* wise, sensible, shrewd, astute, canny,

clever, intelligent, sage, discerning, judicious, perceptive, perspicacious.
OPPOSITES: foolish.

sage noun wise person, learned person, philosopher, thinker, scholar, savant; authority, expert, guru.
▷ adjective *they nodded in agreement at these sage remarks:* wise, sagacious, learned, knowledgeable, profound, deep; astute, shrewd, perceptive, insightful, perspicacious, percipient.

sail verb
1 *we sailed across the Atlantic:* voyage, travel, steam, cruise.
2 *the catamaran sails at 3.30:* set sail, put to sea, leave port, hoist sail, weigh anchor.
3 *sailed his yacht from the US to the UK in 12 days:* steer, pilot, navigate; captain; informal skipper.
4 *clouds were sailing past:* glide, drift, float, flow, sweep, skim, coast, flit.
□ **sail through**
she sailed through her exams: succeed easily at, pass easily, romp through, walk through.

sailor noun seaman, seafarer, mariner; boatman, yachtsman, yachtswoman; Brit. informal matelot.

saintly adjective *he was a saintly but somewhat ineffective archbishop:* holy, godly, pious, religious, devout, spiritual, prayerful; virtuous, righteous, good, God-fearing; sinless, guiltless, irreproachable, pure, innocent.
OPPOSITES: ungodly.

sake noun
□ **for the sake of**
1 *allow me to simplify for the sake of clarity | she gave up smoking for the sake of her health:* in the interest of, for the purpose of.
2 *she had to be brave for the sake of her family:* for the good of, for the benefit of, out of consideration for, in order to help.

salacious adjective *male members of the unit allegedly made up salacious stories about female personnel:* lewd, obscene, pornographic, indecent, crude, vulgar, rude, dirty, smutty; prurient.

salary noun *his annual salary was £35,000:* pay, income, earnings, wages, payment, remuneration, fee, stipend; formal emolument.

sale noun
1 *the sale of firearms:* selling, vending; trade.
2 *they make a sale every minute:* deal, transaction.
OPPOSITES: purchase.
□ **for sale**
the house is up for sale again: on the market, on sale, on offer, available.

salient adjective *the salient points stuck out clearly in her mind:* important, main,

principal, major, chief, primary; notable, noteworthy, outstanding, conspicuous, striking, noticeable, obvious, remarkable, prominent, predominant, dominant; key, crucial, vital, essential, pivotal, prime, central, paramount.
OPPOSITES: minor.

sallow adjective *his cheeks were sunken and sallow:* yellowish, jaundiced, pallid, wan, pale, anaemic, bloodless, pasty; unhealthy, sickly; Brit. peaky.

sally noun
1 *the garrison made a sally against us:* sortie, charge, foray, thrust, drive, offensive, attack, assault, raid, incursion, invasion, onset, onslaught.
2 *a fruitless sally into Wales:* expedition, excursion, trip, visit, outing, jaunt; foray.
3 *he was delighted with his sally:* witticism, smart remark, quip, barb, pleasantry; joke, pun, jest, bon mot; retort, riposte, rejoinder; informal gag, wisecrack, comeback.

salon noun
1 *a hairdressing salon:* shop, parlour, establishment, premises; boutique, store.
2 *the chateau's mirrored salon:* reception room, drawing room, sitting room.

salty adjective *salty water:* salt, salted, saline, briny, brackish.

salubrious adjective
1 (formal) *the natural beauty and salubrious climate of the islands:* healthy, health-giving, healthful, beneficial, wholesome.
2 *he found himself living in a freezing bedsit in one of the less salubrious parts of London:* pleasant, agreeable, well kept, select, high-class; clean, sanitary; Brit. upmarket; informal posh, classy.
OPPOSITES: insalubrious, unhealthy.

salutary adjective *these developments should be a salutary lesson for all investors:* beneficial, advantageous, profitable, helpful, useful, valuable, worthwhile; timely.

salutation noun *she turned around to acknowledge the salutation:* greeting, salute, address, welcome.

salute noun *he raised his arms in a triumphant salute:* greeting, salutation, gesture of respect, acknowledgement, welcome, address.
▷**verb**
1 *he saluted the ambassadors:* greet, hail, welcome, acknowledge, address; toast.
2 *we salute a truly great photographer:* pay tribute to, pay homage to, honour, celebrate, acknowledge, take your hat off to.

salvage verb
1 *all attempts to salvage the vessel were called off:* rescue, save, recover, retrieve, raise, reclaim.
2 *a desperate attempt to salvage his party's reputation:* save, rescue, retain, preserve, conserve; recover, retrieve, regain.
▷**noun** *the salvage of the Russian submarine:* rescue, recovery, reclamation.

salvation noun
1 *salvation by way of repentance:* redemption, deliverance.
2 *fitness training and going to the gym have been his salvation:* lifeline, way out, help.
OPPOSITES: damnation.

salve noun *wash the wound with water and apply a salve:* ointment, cream, lotion, balm, unguent, emollient; embrocation, liniment.
▷**verb** *he exploited his workforce and then gave away his money to salve his troubled conscience:* soothe, assuage, ease, allay, lighten, comfort, mollify.

salver noun *he offered her caviar from a silver salver:* platter, plate, dish, tray.

same adjective
1 *we stayed at the same hotel last year:* identical, selfsame, very same, one and the same.
2 *day in, day out they followed the same routine:* unchanging, unvarying, unvaried, identical, invariable, consistent, uniform.
3 *they had the same symptoms* | *all the protesters wore the same black T-shirts:* matching, identical, alike, duplicate, carbon-copy, twin; indistinguishable, interchangeable, corresponding, equivalent, parallel, like, comparable, similar.
4 *that same year I travelled to Boston:* selfsame; aforesaid, aforementioned.
OPPOSITES: another, different, dissimilar.
▢ **all the same**
1 *I was frightened all the same:* in spite of everything, despite that, nevertheless, nonetheless, even so, however, still, yet, be that as it may, notwithstanding, regardless, anyway.
2 *it's all the same to me:* immaterial, of no importance, of no consequence, inconsequential, unimportant, of little account, irrelevant, insignificant, trivial, petty.

WORD LINKS
homogeneous consisting of parts which are all of the same kind (*an area with a largely homogeneous population*)

sample noun
1 *a sample of the fabric* | *here's a sample of what's coming up in the channel's first week on air:* specimen, example, bit, snippet, representative piece, taste, tester; pilot, trial; swatch; Brit. taster.
2 *a sample of 10,000 people nationwide:* cross section, variety, sampling.
▷**verb** *we sampled the culinary offerings:* try, taste, test, put to the test, experiment with; appraise, evaluate; informal check out.

S

▷ **adjective** *the sample group is too small | a sample copy can be obtained:* representative, specimen, test, trial.

sanatorium noun infirmary, clinic, hospital, medical centre; sickbay, sickroom.

sanctify verb
1 *he came to sanctify the site:* consecrate, bless, make holy, hallow, make sacred, dedicate to God.
2 *may God sanctify his soul:* purify, cleanse, free from sin, absolve, redeem; rare lustrate.
3 *the intervention was not sanctified by the UN:* sanction, authorize, legitimize, endorse.

sanctimonious adjective *one tries to set a bit of an example, if that's not too sanctimonious:* self-righteous, holier-than-thou, pious, moralizing, smug, superior, priggish; hypocritical, insincere; informal goody-goody, pi.

sanction noun
1 *he advocates the use of trade sanctions to enforce environmental measures:* penalty, punishment, deterrent, punitive action, restriction; embargo, ban, prohibition, boycott.
2 *the scheme has the sanction of the court:* authorization, consent, permission, authority, dispensation, assent, acquiescence, agreement, approval, approbation, endorsement, blessing, imprimatur; warrant, accreditation, ratification, validation; informal the go-ahead, the thumbs up, the OK, the green light.
▷ **verb**
1 *the rally was sanctioned by the government:* authorize, permit, give permission for, allow, endorse, approve, accept, back, support; license, warrant, accredit; informal OK.
2 *the penalties available to sanction crime:* punish, discipline someone for.
OPPOSITES: prohibit.

sanctity noun
1 *the sanctity of St Francis:* holiness, godliness, blessedness, saintliness, spirituality, piety, piousness, devoutness, righteousness, virtue, purity, sacredness; formal sanctitude.
2 *the sanctity of human life:* inviolability, sacrosanctity; importance, paramountcy.

sanctuary noun
1 *he was given sanctuary in the embassy:* refuge, safety, protection, shelter, immunity, asylum.
2 *the flat is my sanctuary, the only place I have any privacy:* haven, refuge, sanctum, shelter, retreat, bolt-hole, hideaway.
3 *a bird sanctuary:* reserve, park, reservation; N. Amer. preserve.
4 *the sanctuary at Delphi:* holy place, temple; shrine, altar; sanctum, holy of holies.

sanctum noun
1 *the sanctum in the temple:* holy place, shrine, sanctuary, holy of holies.
2 *a private sanctum for the bar's regulars:* refuge, retreat, bolt-hole, hideout, hideaway, den.

sand noun *she ran across the sand:* beach, sands, shore, seashore; literary strand.

sane adjective
1 *the accused is presumed to be sane:* of sound mind, in your right mind, compos mentis, lucid, rational, balanced, stable; informal all there.
2 *I actually think this is a fairly sane way to resolve many disputes:* sensible, practical, advisable, realistic, prudent, wise, reasonable, rational, level-headed, commonsensical, judicious, politic.
OPPOSITES: mad, foolish.

sangfroid noun *he recovered his usual sangfroid:* composure, equanimity, self-possession, equilibrium, aplomb, poise, self-assurance, self-control, nerve, calm, presence of mind; informal cool, unflappability.

sanguine adjective *analysts are relatively sanguine about the company's prospects:* optimistic, bullish, hopeful, upbeat, buoyant, positive, confident, cheerful.
OPPOSITES: gloomy.

sanitary adjective *improvements in health are also the result of more sanitary conditions:* hygienic, clean, antiseptic, aseptic, sterile, disinfected, unpolluted, uncontaminated, healthy, wholesome; formal salubrious.

sanitize verb
1 *the chlorine used to sanitize pools breaks down the natural sebum found on your hair:* sterilize, disinfect, clean, cleanse, purify, decontaminate; fumigate.
2 *the diaries have not been sanitized:* make presentable, make acceptable, make palatable, clean up; expurgate, bowdlerize, censor.

sanity noun
1 *I began to doubt my own sanity:* mental health, faculties, reason, rationality, saneness, stability, lucidity; sense, wits, mind.
2 *sanity has prevailed:* common sense, wisdom, prudence, judiciousness, rationality.

sap verb *the severe climate and terrain is sapping the strength of ground combat units:* weaken, erode, wear away/down, deplete, reduce, lessen, attenuate, undermine, exhaust, drain, bleed.

sarcasm noun derision, mockery, ridicule, scorn; irony.

sarcastic adjective *I've had enough of your sarcastic comments:* sardonic, ironic, ironical; derisive, snide, scornful, contemptuous, mocking, sneering, jeering; caustic, scathing, trenchant, cutting, sharp, acerbic; Brit. informal sarky.

sardonic adjective *his sardonic wit:* mocking, satirical, sarcastic, ironic, ironical; cynical, scornful, contemptuous, derisive, sneering, jeering; scathing, caustic, trenchant, cutting, sharp, acerbic.

sash noun belt, cummerbund, waistband, girdle.

Satan noun. See DEVIL sense 1.

sate verb *the parents described the children's ravenous appetites, which no amount of food could sate.* See SATIATE.

satellite noun
1 *the European Space Agency's ERS-1 satellite:* space station, space capsule, spacecraft.
2 *the state was then a Russian satellite:* dependency, colony, protectorate, possession, holding.
▷ adjective *a satellite state:* dependent, subordinate, subsidiary; puppet.

satiate verb *he leaned back against the cushions, satiated by the Christmas fare:* satisfy, sate; slake, quench; gorge, stuff.

satiny adjective *the satiny, honey-coloured wood:* smooth, shiny, glossy, shining, gleaming, lustrous, sleek, silky.

satire noun
1 *a stinging satire on American politics:* parody, burlesque, caricature, lampoon, skit; informal spoof, take-off, send-up.
2 *he has become the subject of satire:* mockery, ridicule, derision, scorn, caricature; irony, sarcasm.

satirical adjective *a collection of satirical essays on English social life:* mocking, ironic, ironical, satiric, sarcastic, sardonic; caustic, trenchant, mordant, biting, cutting, stinging, acerbic; critical, irreverent, disparaging, disrespectful.

satirize verb *pseudo-intellectualism of the kind satirized by Woody Allen:* mock, ridicule, deride, make fun of, poke fun at, parody, lampoon, burlesque, caricature, take off; criticize; informal take the mickey out of; Brit. informal send up.

satisfaction noun
1 *he derived great satisfaction from his work:* contentment, content, pleasure, gratification, fulfilment, sense of achievement, enjoyment, happiness, pride; self-satisfaction, smugness, complacency.
2 *the satisfaction of consumer needs:* fulfilment, gratification; appeasement, assuaging.
3 *investors turned to the courts for satisfaction:* compensation, recompense, redress, reparation, restitution, repayment, payment, settlement, reimbursement, indemnification, indemnity.
OPPOSITES: dissatisfaction.

satisfactory adjective *overall, our performance was satisfactory but the results could have been much better:* adequate, all right, acceptable, good enough, sufficient, reasonable, quite good, competent, fair, decent, average, passable; fine, in order, up to scratch, up to the mark, up to standard, up to par; informal OK, so-so.
OPPOSITES: unsatisfactory, inadequate.

satisfied adjective
1 *a satisfied smile:* pleased, well pleased, content, contented, happy, proud, triumphant; smug, self-satisfied, pleased with yourself, complacent; Brit. informal like the cat that's got the cream.
2 *the pleasure of satisfied desire:* fulfilled, gratified.
3 *I am satisfied that she is happy with the decision:* convinced, certain, sure, positive, persuaded, easy in your mind.
OPPOSITES: dissatisfied, unhappy.

satisfy verb
1 *nothing about her job satisfied her any more:* content, please, make happy, fulfil.
2 *a last chance to satisfy his hunger for romance:* fulfil, gratify, meet, fill; indulge, cater to, pander to; appease, assuage; quench, slake, satiate, sate, take the edge off.
3 *products which satisfy the EU's criteria:* comply with, meet, fulfil, answer, conform to; measure up to, come up to; suffice, be good enough, fit/fill the bill.
4 *she satisfied herself that it had been an accident:* convince, persuade, assure; reassure, put someone's mind at rest.
5 *there was insufficient collateral to satisfy the loan:* repay, pay off, settle, make good, discharge, square, liquidate, clear.
OPPOSITES: dissatisfy, frustrate.

satisfying adjective *it's hard work but very satisfying:* fulfilling, rewarding, gratifying, pleasing, enjoyable, pleasurable, to your liking.

saturate verb
1 *heavy rain saturated the ground:* soak, drench, waterlog, wet through; souse, steep, douse.
2 *the air was saturated with the stench of joss sticks:* permeate, suffuse, pervade, charge, infuse, fill, imbue.
3 *the industry has saturated the world market:* flood, glut, oversupply, overfill, overload.

saturated adjective
1 *his clothes were saturated:* soaked, soaking, wet through, sopping wet, sodden, dripping, wringing wet, drenched; soaked to the skin.
2 *the saturated ground:* waterlogged, soggy, squelchy, heavy, muddy, boggy.
OPPOSITES: dry.

saturnine adjective
1 *a man with a somewhat saturnine*

temperament: **gloomy**, sombre, melancholy, moody, lugubrious, dour, glum, morose, unsmiling, humourless.
2 *his saturnine good looks:* **swarthy**, dark, dark-skinned, dark-complexioned; mysterious, mercurial, moody.
OPPOSITES: cheerful.

saucy adjective (informal)
1 *saucy postcards:* **suggestive**, titillating, risqué, rude, bawdy, racy, ribald; informal raunchy.
2 *you saucy little minx!* **cheeky**, impudent, impertinent, irreverent, forward, disrespectful, bold, as bold as brass, brazen.

saunter verb *they sauntered back to the car:* **stroll**, amble, wander, meander, drift, walk; stretch your legs, take the air; informal mosey, tootle; Brit. informal pootle.

savage adjective
1 *packs of savage dogs roamed the streets:* **ferocious**, fierce, vicious; wild, untamed, undomesticated, feral.
2 *he was the victim of a savage assault:* **vicious**, brutal, cruel, sadistic, ferocious, fierce, violent, bloody, bloodthirsty, murderous, homicidal.
3 *a savage attack on European free-trade policy:* **fierce**, blistering, scathing, searing, stinging, devastating, mordant, trenchant, caustic, cutting, biting, withering, virulent, vitriolic.
4 *the decision was a savage blow for the town:* **severe**, crushing, devastating, crippling, catastrophic, calamitous, ruinous, dreadful, terrible, awful.
5 *a savage landscape:* **rugged**, rough, wild, inhospitable, uninhabitable.
6 (in historical contexts) *a savage race:* **primitive**, uncivilized, non-literate.
OPPOSITES: tame, mild, civilized.
▷ noun *she described her son's assailants as savages:* **brute**, beast, monster, barbarian, sadist, animal.
▷ verb
1 *the child was savaged by a pit bull terrier:* **maul**, attack, tear to pieces, lacerate, claw, bite.
2 *critics savaged the film:* **criticize severely**, attack, lambaste, condemn, denounce, pillory, revile; informal pan, tear to pieces, hammer, slam, do a hatchet job on, crucify; Brit. informal slate, rubbish; N. Amer. informal trash.

savant noun *Sir Isaiah Berlin, the Oxford savant:* **intellectual**, scholar, sage, philosopher, thinker, wise/learned person; guru, master.

save verb
1 *the captain was saved by his crew:* **rescue**, come to someone's rescue, save someone's life; set free, free, liberate, extricate; bail out; informal save someone's bacon/neck/skin.
2 *the farmhouse has been saved from demolition:* **preserve**, keep safe, keep,

protect, safeguard; salvage, retrieve, reclaim, rescue.
3 *the scheme is aimed at educating consumers on how best to save electricity:* **economize on**, cut back on, use sparingly.
4 *start saving old newspapers for wrapping china:* **put aside**, set aside, put by, put to one side, save up, keep, retain, reserve, conserve, stockpile, store, hoard, save for a rainy day; informal salt away, squirrel away, stash away, hang on to.
5 *asking me first would have saved a lot of trouble:* **prevent**, obviate, forestall, spare; stop; avoid, avert.
OPPOSITES: waste, squander.

saving noun
1 *a considerable saving in development costs:* **reduction**, cut, decrease, economy.
2 *I'll have to use some of my savings:* **nest egg**, money put by for a rainy day, life savings; capital, assets, funds, resources, reserves.

saving grace noun *the bungalow's only saving grace was a room with spectacular views of the sea:* **redeeming feature**, good point, thing in its/your favour, advantage, asset, selling point.

saviour noun *he portrayed himself as his country's saviour:* **rescuer**, liberator, deliverer, emancipator; champion, knight in shining armour, friend in need, good Samaritan.

savoir faire noun *he had been faced with a situation that even his charm and savoir faire had been unable to resolve:* **social skill**, social graces, urbanity, suavity, finesse, sophistication, poise, aplomb, adroitness, polish, style, smoothness, tact, tactfulness, diplomacy, discretion, delicacy, sensitivity; informal savvy.

savour verb
1 *she wanted to savour every moment:* **relish**, enjoy, appreciate, delight in, revel in, luxuriate in, bask in.
2 *such a declaration savoured of immodesty:* **suggest**, smack of, have the hallmarks of, seem like, have the air of, show signs of.
▷ noun
1 *the fish was tender and tangy, with a savour of the sea:* **smell**, aroma, fragrance, scent, perfume, bouquet; taste, flavour, tang; trace, hint, suggestion, touch.
2 *her usual diversions had lost their savour:* **piquancy**, interest, attraction, flavour, spice, zest, excitement, enjoyment.

savoury adjective
1 *a selection of sweet and savoury dishes:* **salty**, spicy, piquant, tangy.
2 *one of the less savoury aspects of the affair:* **acceptable**, pleasant, respectable, wholesome, honourable, proper, seemly.
OPPOSITES: sweet, unsavoury.

say verb
1 *'I must go,' she said:* **declare**, announce,

state; remark, observe, mention, comment, note, add; reply, respond, answer, rejoin; informal come out with.
2 *she felt her stomach flutter as he said her name:* speak, utter, voice, pronounce, give voice to, vocalize.
3 *Newall says he's innocent:* claim, maintain, assert, hold, insist, contend; allege, profess; formal opine, aver.
4 *I can't conjure up the words to say how I feel:* express, put into words, articulate, communicate, put/get across, convey, phrase, verbalize; reveal, divulge, impart, disclose; imply, suggest.
5 *they sang hymns and said a prayer:* recite, repeat, utter; declaim, orate.
6 *the dial of her watch said 1.20:* indicate, show, read.
7 *I'd say it's about five miles:* estimate, judge, guess, hazard a guess, predict, speculate, surmise, conjecture, venture; informal reckon.
8 *let's say you'd just won a million pounds:* suppose, assume, imagine, presume, hypothesize, postulate, posit.
▷ **noun**
1 *everyone is entitled to their say:* chance to speak, turn to speak, opinion, view, voice.
2 *don't I have any say in the matter?* influence, sway, weight, voice, input.

saying noun *you know the old saying about all work and no play?* proverb, maxim, aphorism, axiom, adage, saw, tag, motto, epigram, dictum; expression, phrase, formula; slogan, catchphrase; platitude, cliché, commonplace, truism; rare apophthegm.
□ **it goes without saying**
it goes without saying that rivalry between these companies is intense: of course, naturally, needless to say, it's taken for granted, it's understood/assumed, it's taken as read, it's an accepted fact; obviously, self-evidently.

scalding adjective *a jet of scalding water:* extremely hot, burning, blistering, searing, red-hot; informal boiling, sizzling.

scale noun
1 *women were asked to rate their experience on a 5-point scale (0 = never, 5 = always):* gradation, progression, succession, sequence, series.
2 *opposite ends of the social scale:* hierarchy, ladder, ranking, spectrum, pecking order, order.
3 *the scale of the map:* ratio, proportion, relative size.
4 *no one foresaw the scale of the disaster:* extent, size, scope, magnitude, dimensions, range, breadth, compass, degree, reach.
▷ **verb** *thieves scaled the eight-foot fence:* climb, climb over, ascend, clamber up, shin up, scramble up, mount.
□ **scale something down**
manufacturing capacity has been scaled down: reduce, cut down, cut back, cut,

decrease, lessen, lower, trim, slim down, prune.
□ **scale something up**
the departments intend to scale up their activities: increase, develop, expand, augment, build up, grow, add to; step up, boost, escalate.

scaly adjective *scaly patches of dead skin:* dry, flaky, flaking, scurfy, rough, scabrous, mangy.

scamper verb *his dogs scampered around the yard | the children scampered off the bus and into the playground:* run, rush, race, gambol, frisk; scurry, scuttle, dash, dart, hurry, hasten; informal scoot.

scan verb
1 *Adam scanned the horizon:* scrutinize, examine, study, inspect, survey, search, scour, sweep, rake; look at, stare at, gaze at, eye, watch; informal check out; N. Amer. informal scope.
2 *I scanned the papers:* glance through, look through, have a look at, run/cast your eye over, skim through, flick through, flip through, leaf through, thumb through.
▷ **noun**
1 *a careful scan of the terrain:* inspection, scrutiny, examination, survey.
2 *a quick scan through the report:* glance, look, flick, browse.
3 *a brain scan:* examination, screening.

scandal noun
1 *revelation of the sex scandal forced him to resign:* wrongdoing, impropriety, misconduct, immoral behaviour, unethical behaviour; offence, transgression, crime, sin; skeleton in the closet.
2 *it's a scandal that the disease is not adequately treated:* disgrace, outrage, injustice; crying shame.
3 *there is no scandal attached to her name:* malicious gossip, malicious rumours, slander, libel, defamation; formal calumny; informal dirt.

scandalize verb *Henry is said to have been scandalized by William's conduct:* shock, appal, outrage, horrify, disgust; offend, affront, insult.
OPPOSITES: impress, please.

scandalous adjective
1 *a scandalous waste of taxpayers' money:* disgraceful, shocking, outrageous, monstrous, criminal, wicked, shameful, appalling, deplorable, reprehensible, inexcusable, insupportable, unforgivable, unpardonable.
2 *a series of scandalous liaisons:* discreditable, disreputable, dishonourable, improper, unseemly, sordid.

scant adjective *he paid scant attention to these wider issues:* little, little or no, minimal, limited, negligible, meagre; insufficient, inadequate, deficient.
OPPOSITES: abundant, ample.

s

scanty adjective

1 *their scanty wages:* meagre, scant, paltry, minimal, limited, modest, restricted, sparse; tiny, small, negligible, insufficient, inadequate, deficient; informal measly, pathetic.
2 *her scanty nightdress:* skimpy, revealing, short, brief; low, low-cut; indecent.
OPPOSITES: ample, plentiful.

scar noun

1 *the scar on his left cheek:* mark, blemish, disfigurement, cicatrix; pockmark.
2 *deep psychological scars:* trauma, damage, injury.
▷ verb
1 *he's likely to be scarred for life:* mark, blemish, disfigure; pockmark, pit.
2 *a landscape which has been scarred by strip-mining:* mar, spoil, deface, ruin, damage.
3 *she was profoundly scarred by the incident:* traumatize, damage; distress, disturb, upset.

scarce adjective

1 *food was scarce:* in short supply, scant, scanty, meagre, sparse, hard to find, hard to come by, insufficient, deficient, inadequate; at a premium; paltry.
2 *birds that prefer dense forest are becoming scarcer:* rare, few and far between, thin on the ground; uncommon, unusual.
OPPOSITES: plentiful.

scarcely adverb *she could scarcely hear what he was saying:* hardly, barely, only just.
OPPOSITES: easily.

scarcity noun *the scarcity of affordable housing:* shortage, dearth, lack, undersupply, insufficiency, paucity, deficiency, inadequacy.
OPPOSITES: glut.

scare verb *stop it, you're scaring me:* frighten, startle, alarm, terrify, petrify, unnerve, intimidate, terrorize, cow; informal spook; Brit. informal put the wind up.
▷ noun *you gave me a scare—how did you get here?* fright, shock; informal turn.

scared adjective *it was growing dark and she began to feel scared:* frightened, afraid, fearful, nervous, panicky; terrified, petrified, horrified; informal in a cold sweat; N. Amer. informal spooked.

scaremonger noun alarmist, prophet of doom, Cassandra, doom-monger; informal doom and gloom merchant.

scary adjective (informal) *a scary movie:* frightening, terrifying, horrifying, hair-raising, spine-chilling, blood-curdling, nerve-racking, unnerving; eerie, sinister; informal creepy, spooky.

scathing adjective *he launched a scathing attack on the government:* fierce, ferocious, savage, withering, blistering, searing, devastating, stinging, biting, cutting, virulent, caustic, vitriolic, scornful, sharp, bitter, harsh.
OPPOSITES: mild.

scatter verb

1 *scatter the seeds as evenly as possible:* spread, strew, sprinkle, sow, distribute, disseminate.
2 *the crowd scattered | onlookers were scattered in all directions:* disperse, break up, disband, separate, dissolve; drive, send, chase, put to flight.
3 *the sky was scattered with stars:* fleck, stud, dot, cover, sprinkle, stipple, spot, pepper.
OPPOSITES: gather, assemble.

scatterbrained adjective *a scatterbrained young woman:* absent-minded, forgetful, disorganized; dreamy, with your head in the clouds, feather-brained; informal with a mind/memory like a sieve, dippy; Brit. informal scatty.

scavenge verb *pigs and poultry scavenged for food around the farm:* search, hunt, look, forage, rummage, root about/around, grub about/around.

scenario noun

1 *every possible scenario must be explored:* sequence of events, course of events, chain of events.
2 *he wrote scenarios for a major Hollywood studio:* plot, outline, storyline; screenplay, script.

scene noun

1 *the scene of the accident:* location, site, place, position, point, spot; locale, whereabouts.
2 *the scene is London, in the late 1890s:* setting, background, context, milieu, backdrop, mise en scène.
3 *terrible scenes of violence:* incident, event, episode, happening.
4 *an impressive mountain scene:* view, vista, outlook, panorama, sight; landscape, scenery.
5 *she made an embarrassing scene:* fuss, exhibition of yourself, performance, tantrum, commotion, disturbance, upset, furore, brouhaha; Brit. row; informal to-do; Brit. informal carry-on.
6 *the political scene:* arena, stage, sphere, world, milieu, realm, domain, theatre; area of interest, field, province, preserve.

scenery noun

1 *the beautiful scenery of west Wales:* landscape, countryside, country, terrain, topography, setting, surroundings, environment; view, vista, panorama.
2 *everyone helped with the scenery and costumes:* stage set, set, mise en scène, backdrop; Brit. backcloth.

scenic adjective *the most scenic route from Florence to Siena:* picturesque, pretty,

pleasing, attractive, lovely, beautiful, charming, spectacular, breathtaking, panoramic.
OPPOSITES: ugly.

scent noun
1 *the scent of freshly cut hay:* smell, fragrance, aroma, perfume, odour, bouquet; old use redolence.
2 *a bottle of scent:* perfume, fragrance, toilet water, eau de toilette.
3 *the hounds picked up the scent of a hare:* spoor, trail, track.
▷verb *Rose looked at him, scenting a threat:* sense, become aware of, detect, discern, recognize.

scented adjective *scented soap:* perfumed, fragranced, sweet-smelling, fragrant, aromatic.
OPPOSITES: unscented.

sceptic noun
1 *sceptics questioned the wisdom of spending 800 million euros to build and upgrade stadiums:* cynic, doubter; pessimist, prophet of doom.
2 *sceptics who have found faith:* agnostic, atheist, unbeliever, non-believer, disbeliever, doubting Thomas.
OPPOSITES: believer.

> **USAGE**
>
> Do not confuse **sceptic** with **septic**. **Sceptic** means 'a person who tends to question or doubt accepted opinions', whereas **septic** means 'infected with bacteria' (*the wound had gone septic*).

sceptical adjective *they were sceptical about the Treasury's forecast of inflation dropping:* dubious, doubtful, doubting, cynical, distrustful, mistrustful, suspicious, disbelieving, unconvinced, incredulous.
OPPOSITES: certain, convinced.

scepticism noun
1 *his ideas were met with scepticism:* doubt, disbelief, cynicism, distrust, mistrust, suspicion, incredulity.
2 *he passed from scepticism to religious belief:* agnosticism, doubt, atheism, unbelief, non-belief.
OPPOSITES: trust, belief.

schedule noun
1 *we need to draw up a production schedule:* plan, programme, timetable, scheme.
2 *I have a very busy schedule:* timetable, agenda, diary, calendar; itinerary.
▷verb *another meeting was scheduled for 20th April:* arrange, organize, plan, programme, timetable, set up, line up.

scheme noun
1 *adventurous fund-raising schemes:* plan, project, programme, strategy, stratagem, tactic, course of action; system, procedure, design, formula, recipe; informal game plan.

2 *police uncovered a scheme to steal the paintings:* plot, plan, conspiracy, intrigue; ruse, ploy, stratagem, manoeuvre; subterfuge; machinations; informal game, racket.
3 *the sonnet's rhyme scheme:* arrangement, system, organization, configuration, design, pattern, layout, format.
▷verb *he schemed to bring about the collapse of the government:* plot, conspire, intrigue, connive, manoeuvre, plan.

scheming adjective *they had mean, scheming little minds:* cunning, crafty, calculating, devious, designing, conniving, wily, sly, tricky, artful, slippery, slick, manipulative, Machiavellian, unscrupulous, disingenuous.
OPPOSITES: honest, ingenuous.

schism noun *the widening schism between church leaders and politicians:* division, split, rift, breach, break, separation, severance; chasm, gulf, quarrel, disagreement.
OPPOSITES: unity.

schismatic adjective separatist, heterodox, dissident, dissenting, heretical; breakaway, splinter.
OPPOSITES: orthodox.

scholar noun *a leading biblical scholar:* academic, intellectual, man/woman of letters, mind, intellect, polymath, highbrow; authority, expert; informal egghead; Brit. informal boffin.

scholarly adjective *an earnest, scholarly man:* learned, erudite, academic, well read, intellectual, literary, lettered, educated, knowledgeable, highbrow; studious, bookish, donnish, cerebral.
OPPOSITES: uneducated, illiterate.

scholarship noun
1 *a centre of medieval scholarship:* learning, knowledge, erudition, education, letters, culture.
2 *a scholarship of £1000 a year:* grant, award, endowment, payment; Brit. bursary, exhibition.

scholastic adjective *her scholastic achievements:* academic, educational; scholarly.

school noun
1 *a large inner-city comprehensive school:* college, academy, institute.
2 *the university's School of English:* department, faculty, division.
3 *the great school of Dutch painters | the school of Rembrandt:* group, set, circle; followers, disciples, apostles, students, pupils, admirers, devotees, votaries.
4 *the school of linguistics associated with his ideas:* way of thinking, school of thought, approach, method, style, brand, persuasion, creed, credo, doctrine.
▷verb *he schooled her in horsemanship:* train, teach, tutor, coach, instruct, educate,

S

drill, discipline, direct, guide, prepare, groom; prime, verse.

schooling noun *his parents paid for his schooling:* education, tuition, teaching, coaching, training, instruction, tutoring, tutelage; lessons.

schoolteacher noun teacher, tutor; Brit. schoolmaster, schoolmistress, master, mistress; N. Amer. informal schoolmarm.

science noun *the science of criminology:* technology, field of study, discipline, branch of knowledge, art.

scientific adjective
1 *scientific research:* technological, technical; research-based, knowledge-based, empirical.
2 *you need to approach the task in a more scientific way:* systematic, methodical, organized, ordered, orderly, meticulous, rigorous; exact, precise, accurate, mathematical; analytical, rational.
OPPOSITES: unscientific.

scintillate verb sparkle, shine, gleam, glitter, flash, shimmer, twinkle, glint, glisten, wink.

scintillating adjective *a scintillating second-half performance:* brilliant, dazzling, exciting, exhilarating, stimulating; sparkling, lively, witty, clever.

scoff verb
□ scoff at
they scoffed at her article: mock, deride, ridicule, sneer at, jeer at, taunt, make fun of, poke fun at, laugh at, scorn, laugh to scorn, dismiss, belittle.

scold verb *her mother took her away, scolding her for her bad behaviour:* rebuke, reprimand, chastise, upbraid, berate, chide, reprove, admonish, take to task; formal castigate; informal tell off; Brit. informal tick off, have a go at.
OPPOSITES: praise.

scoop verb
□ scoop something out
1 *a hole was scooped out in the floor:* hollow out, gouge out, dig, excavate, cut out.
2 *cut the tomatoes in half and scoop out the flesh:* remove, take out, spoon out, scrape out.
□ scoop someone/something up
she scooped up armfuls of clothes: pick up, gather up, lift, take up; snatch up, grab.

scope noun
1 *the scope of the investigation:* extent, range, breadth, width, reach, sweep, span, horizon; area, sphere, field, realm, compass, orbit, ambit, terms/field of reference, jurisdiction, remit; confines, limits; formal purview.
2 *the scope for change is limited by political realities:* opportunity, possibility, freedom, latitude, leeway, capacity, liberty, room to manoeuvre, elbow room.

scorch verb
1 *the buildings were scorched by the fire:* singe, char, sear, burn, blacken, discolour.
2 *grass scorched by the sun:* dry up, desiccate, parch, wither, shrivel; burn, bake.

scorching adjective
1 *the scorching July sun:* extremely hot, blazing, flaming, fiery, burning, blistering, searing, sweltering, torrid; informal boiling, baking, sizzling.
2 *a scorching indictment of the government's immigration policy:* fierce, savage, scathing, withering, blistering, searing, devastating, severe, harsh, stinging, biting, caustic, vitriolic.
OPPOSITES: freezing, mild.

score noun
1 *the final score was 4–3:* result, outcome; total, sum total, tally, count.
2 *an IQ score of 161:* rating, grade, mark, percentage.
▷ verb
1 *he's already scored 13 goals this season:* achieve, get, gain, chalk up, make; record, rack up, notch up.
2 *the piece was scored for flute, violin, and continuo:* orchestrate, arrange, set, adapt; write, compose.
3 *score the wood in criss-cross patterns:* scratch, cut, notch, incise, scrape, nick, snick, chip, gouge; mark.
□ score something out/through
she scored out the last word: cross out, strike out, put a line through, ink out, scratch out; delete, obliterate.

scorn noun *he was unable to hide the scorn in his voice:* contempt, derision, disdain, mockery, sneering.
OPPOSITES: admiration, respect.
▷ verb *critics scorned the painting:* deride, hold in contempt, treat with contempt, pour scorn on, look down on, look down your nose at, disdain, mock, scoff at, sneer at, jeer at, laugh at, laugh out of court; disparage, slight; dismiss; informal turn your nose up at.
OPPOSITES: admire, respect.

scornful adjective *Isabel ignored his scornful remarks:* contemptuous, derisive, mocking, scoffing, sneering, jeering, withering, scathing, snide, disparaging, supercilious, disdainful, superior.
OPPOSITES: admiring, respectful.

scotch verb *their plans were scotched by the Pentagon:* end, put an end to, put a stop to; ruin, wreck, destroy, smash, shatter, demolish; frustrate, thwart; informal put paid to, put the lid on; Brit. informal scupper.

scot-free adverb *the real criminals behind the racket are getting away scot-free:* unpunished; unscathed, unhurt, unharmed, without a scratch.

scoundrel noun *the lying scoundrel admitted that he was married to another* *woman:* rogue, rascal, good-for-nothing, miscreant, reprobate; cheat, swindler, fraudster, trickster, charlatan; informal villain, wretch.

scour¹ verb *she scoured the cooker and cleaned out the cupboards:* scrub, rub, clean, wash, cleanse, wipe; polish, buff up, shine, burnish; abrade.

scour² verb *I scoured the shops for a suitable gift:* search, comb, hunt through, rummage through, go through with a fine-tooth comb, root through, rake through, look high and low in; ransack, turn upside-down.

scourge noun *inflation was the scourge of the mid-1970s:* affliction, bane, curse, plague, menace, evil, misfortune, burden, cross to bear; blight, cancer, canker.
OPPOSITES: blessing, godsend.

scout noun
1 *scouts reported that the enemy were massing ahead:* lookout, outrider, advance guard, vanguard; spy.
2 *a record company scout:* talent spotter, talent scout.
▷verb
1 *I scouted around for some logs:* search, look, hunt, ferret, root.
2 *a night patrol was sent to scout the area:* reconnoitre, explore, make a reconnaissance of, inspect, investigate, scout out, spy out, survey; examine, scan, study, observe; informal check out, case; Brit. informal recce.

scowl verb *she scowled at him defiantly:* glower, frown, glare, grimace, lour, look daggers, give someone a black look; make a face, pull a face, pout; informal give someone a dirty look.
OPPOSITES: smile, grin.

scramble verb
1 *we scrambled over the boulders:* clamber, climb, crawl, claw your way, scrabble, grope your way, struggle; N. Amer. shinny.
2 *small children scrambled for the scattered coins:* jostle, scuffle, tussle, struggle, strive, compete, contend, vie, jockey.
3 *maybe the alcohol has scrambled his brains:* mix up, jumble up, disorganize, disorder, muddle, confuse, disturb, mess up.
▷noun *I lost Tommy in the scramble for a seat:* tussle, jostle, scrimmage, scuffle, struggle, free-for-all, competition, contention, vying, jockeying; muddle, confusion, melee.

scrap noun
1 *a scrap of paper:* fragment, piece, bit, snippet, shred; offcut, oddment, remnant.
2 *there wasn't a scrap of evidence:* bit, speck, iota, particle, ounce, whit, jot, atom, shred, scintilla, tittle, jot or tittle; informal smidgen, tad.
3 *he slept rough and lived on scraps:*

leftovers, leavings, remains, remnants, residue; informal bits and pieces; Brit. informal odds and ends.
4 *the whole thing was made from bits of scrap:* waste, rubbish, refuse, litter, debris, detritus, recycled material; N. Amer. garbage, trash; informal junk.
▷verb
1 *old cars which are due to be scrapped:* throw away, throw out, dispose of, get rid of, toss out, throw on the scrapheap, discard; decommission, recycle, break up, demolish; informal chuck away/out, ditch, dump, bin, junk; Brit. informal get shot of.
2 *campaigners called for the plans to be scrapped:* abandon, drop, abolish, withdraw, throw out, do away with, put an end to, cancel, axe, jettison; informal ditch, dump, junk.
OPPOSITES: keep, preserve.

scrape verb
1 *he scraped all the paint off the windows:* scratch, scour, grate, rub, file, rasp, sand, sandpaper.
2 *Ellen had scraped her shins on the wall:* graze, scratch, scuff, rasp, skin, rub raw, lacerate, bark, chafe, abrade.
3 *their boots scraped along the floor:* grate, creak, rasp, grind, scratch.
4 *she scraped her hair back behind her ears:* rake, drag, pull, tug, draw.
▷noun *there was a long scrape on his shin:* graze, scratch, abrasion, cut, laceration, wound.
□ scrape by
students have to scrape by on an inadequate grant: manage, cope, survive, muddle through/along, make ends meet, get by/along, make do; informal make out.

scrappy adjective *the match was a scrappy affair:* disorganized, untidy, disjointed, unsystematic, uneven, sketchy; piecemeal; fragmentary, incomplete, unfinished; Brit. informal bitty.

scratch verb
1 *some yobs had scratched the side of her car with a key:* score, scrape, scuff, abrade.
2 *thorns scratched her arm:* graze, scrape, abrade, skin, rub raw, cut, lacerate, bark, chafe; wound.
3 *she was forced to scratch from the race:* withdraw, pull out of, back out of, bow out of, stand down.
▷noun
1 *a scratch on the paintwork:* score, mark, line, scrape, scuff, abrasion.
2 *he had two scratches on his cheek:* graze, scrape, abrasion, cut, laceration, wound.
□ scratch something out
many names had been scratched out: cross out, strike out, score out, delete, erase, remove, eliminate, expunge, obliterate.
□ up to scratch
is her work up to scratch? good enough, up to the mark, up to standard, up to

S

par, satisfactory, acceptable, adequate, passable, sufficient, all right; informal OK.

scrawl verb *he scrawled his name at the bottom of the page:* scribble, scratch, dash off, jot down, write carelessly/hurriedly.
▷ **noun** *pages of handwritten scrawl:* scribble, squiggles, jottings, careless/hurried writing; informal hieroglyphics.

scrawny adjective *he was small and scrawny:* skinny, thin, as thin as a rake, skin-and-bones, gaunt, bony, angular, gawky, scraggy.
OPPOSITES: fat.

scream verb *he screamed in pain:* shriek, cry out, howl, screech, yell, yelp, squeal, squawk, wail, bawl, shout, bellow, roar, call out; informal holler.
▷ **noun**
1 *a scream of pain:* shriek, cry, howl, screech, yell, yelp, squeal, squawk, wail, bawl, shout, bellow, roar; informal holler.
2 (informal) *the whole thing's a scream:* laugh, hoot; informal gas, giggle, riot, bundle of fun/laughs.

screech verb & noun. See SCREAM.

screen noun
1 *he dressed hurriedly behind the screen:* partition, room divider, curtain, blind; windbreak.
2 *a computer with a 19-inch screen:* display, monitor, visual display unit, VDU, viewscreen.
3 *every window has a screen because of mosquitoes:* mesh, net, netting.
▷ **verb**
1 *the end of the hall had been screened off:* partition, divide, separate, curtain.
2 *the cottage was screened by the trees:* conceal, hide, veil; shield, shelter, shade, protect, guard.
3 *the prospective candidates will have to be screened:* vet, check, check up on, investigate; clear, be given security clearance; informal check out.
4 *all donated blood is screened for the virus:* check, test, examine, investigate.
5 *the programme is screened on Thursday evenings:* show, broadcast, transmit, televise, put out, put on the air.

screw verb
1 *he screwed the lid back on the jar:* wind, tighten, twist, turn, wring.
2 *the bracket was screwed in place:* fasten, fix, attach, secure.
□ **screw something up**
1 *Christina screwed up her face in disgust:* wrinkle up, pucker, crumple, crease, furrow, contort, distort, twist, purse.
2 (informal) *they'll screw up the whole economy:* wreck, ruin, destroy, wreak havoc on, damage, spoil, mar; dash, shatter, scotch, make a mess of, mess up; informal foul up, do for; Brit. informal scupper.

scribble verb *he scribbled a few lines on a*

piece of paper: scrawl, scratch, dash off, jot down, write hurriedly/untidily; doodle.
▷ **noun** *a page of scribble:* scrawl, squiggles, jottings; doodle, doodlings; informal hieroglyphics.

scrimp verb *she scrimped for six months to buy those shoes:* economize, skimp, save, scrimp and save; be thrifty, be frugal, tighten your belt, cut back, husband your resources, count/watch the pennies.

script noun
1 *her neat, tidy script:* handwriting, writing, hand, pen, penmanship, calligraphy.
2 *the script of the play:* text, screenplay, lines, dialogue, words, libretto.

scrounge verb *they were always scrounging food from the tourists:* beg, borrow; informal sponge, bum, touch someone for, freeload; Brit. informal cadge.

scrounger noun beggar, borrower, parasite; informal sponger, freeloader; Brit. informal cadger.

scrub[1] verb *he scrubbed the kitchen floor:* scour, rub; clean, cleanse, wash, wipe.

scrub[2] noun *there the buildings ended and the scrub began:* brush, brushwood, scrubland, undergrowth.

scruffy adjective *he wore scruffy jeans:* shabby, worn, ragged, tattered, dirty; untidy, unkempt, bedraggled, messy, dishevelled; Brit. down at heel; informal tatty, the worse for wear.
OPPOSITES: smart, tidy.

scrunch verb *Flora scrunched the handkerchief into a ball:* crumple, crush, crunch, rumple, screw up, squash, squeeze, compress; informal squidge.

scruples plural noun *he had no scruples about eavesdropping:* qualms, compunction, conscience, hesitation, reservations, second thoughts, doubts, misgivings, uneasiness, reluctance.

scrupulous adjective
1 *scrupulous attention to detail:* meticulous, careful, painstaking, thorough, assiduous, sedulous, attentive, conscientious, punctilious, particular, strict, rigorous, searching, close, minute.
2 *a scrupulous man:* honest, honourable, upright, upstanding, high-minded, right-minded, moral, ethical, good, virtuous, principled, incorruptible.
OPPOSITES: careless, dishonest.

scrutinize verb *they scrutinized the painting:* examine, inspect, survey, study, scan, look at; investigate, explore, probe, inquire into, go into, check; formal peruse.

scrutiny noun *Frick continued his scrutiny of the room:* examination, inspection, survey, study, scan, look; investigation, exploration, probe, inquiry; formal perusal; informal going-over.

scuff verb *the girl scuffed the toe of her shoe in the gravel:* scrape, scratch, graze, grate, scour, rub, abrade; mark.

scuffle noun *there was a scuffle outside the pub:* fight, struggle, tussle, brawl, fracas, free-for-all, scrimmage, fisticuffs; informal scrap; Brit. informal punch-up, ding-dong; N. Amer. informal rough house.
▷ verb *demonstrators scuffled with police:* fight, struggle, tussle, exchange blows, come to blows, brawl, clash; informal scrap.

sculpt verb *the Minoans were adept at sculpting human figures from ivory:* carve, model, chisel, sculpture, fashion, form, shape, cast, cut, hew.

sculpture noun *a bronze sculpture:* model, carving, statue, statuette, figure, figurine, effigy, bust, head, likeness, cast.

scum noun *the water was covered with a thick green scum:* film, layer, covering, froth.

scupper verb (Brit.). See SCUTTLE².

scurrilous adjective *a scurrilous attack on her character:* defamatory, slanderous, libellous, scandalous, insulting, offensive, gross; abusive, vituperative, malicious; informal bitchy.

scurry verb *pedestrians scurried for cover:* hurry, hasten, run, rush, dash; scamper, scuttle, scramble; informal scoot, beetle.
OPPOSITES: amble.

scuttle¹ verb. See SCURRY.

scuttle² verb
1 *public safety groups scuttled the plan:* ruin, wreck, destroy, sabotage, torpedo, spoil, mess up; Brit. scupper; informal screw up, foul up, put the kibosh on, do for.
2 *the captain scuttles his own ship rather than face defeat:* sink, submerge, send to the bottom; Brit. scupper.

sea noun
1 *the sea sparkled in the sun:* ocean, waves; Brit. informal the briny.
2 *a sea of roofs and turrets:* expanse, stretch, area, tract, sweep, blanket, sheet, carpet, mass; multitude, host, profusion, abundance, plethora.
OPPOSITES: land.
▷ adjective *sea creatures | the golden age of sea travel:* marine, ocean, oceanic; saltwater, seawater; ocean-going, seagoing, seafaring; maritime, naval, nautical.
□ **at sea**
the council's smooth-talking spokesman was all at sea with the cross-referencing system: confused, perplexed, puzzled, baffled, mystified, bemused, bewildered, nonplussed, disconcerted, disoriented, dumbfounded, at a loss, at sixes and sevens; informal flummoxed, bamboozled, fazed.

> **WORD LINKS**
> **marine, maritime, nautical** relating to the sea
> **submarine** existing, happening, or used under the sea
> **hydrography** the science of surveying and charting the sea

seafaring adjective *an ancient seafaring people:* maritime, nautical, naval, seagoing, sea.

seal noun *the king put his seal on the letter:* emblem, symbol, insignia, device, badge, crest, coat of arms, mark, monogram, stamp.
▷ verb
1 *seal each bottle while it is hot:* stop up, seal up, make airtight/watertight, cork, stopper, plug.
2 *he held out his hand to seal the bargain:* clinch, secure, settle, conclude, complete, establish, set the seal on, confirm, guarantee; informal sew up.
□ **seal of approval**
the Minister gave his seal of approval to the project: ratification, approval, blessing, consent, agreement, permission, sanction, endorsement, clearance.
□ **seal something off**
police sealed off the High Street: close off, shut off, cordon off, fence off, isolate.

seam noun
1 *the seam on her sleeve was coming undone:* join, stitching.
2 *a seam of coal:* layer, stratum, vein, lode.

seaman noun sailor, seafarer, mariner, boatman, hand, crewman; informal old salt, sea dog; Brit. informal matelot.
OPPOSITES: landlubber.

seamy adjective *he seemed very knowledgeable about the seamy side of life:* sordid, disreputable, seedy, sleazy, squalid, insalubrious, unwholesome, unsavoury, rough, unpleasant.
OPPOSITES: salubrious.

sear verb
1 *the heat of the blast seared his face:* scorch, burn, singe, char.
2 *sear the meat before adding the other ingredients:* flash-fry, seal, brown.

search verb
1 *I searched for the key in my handbag:* hunt, look, seek, forage, fish about/around, look high and low, cast about/around, ferret about/around, root about/around, rummage about/around; Brit. informal rootle about/around.
2 *he searched the house thoroughly:* look through, hunt through, explore, scour, rifle through, go through, sift through, comb, go through with a fine-tooth comb; turn upside down, turn inside out, leave no stone unturned in.
3 *the guards searched him for weapons:* examine, inspect, check, frisk.

S

▷ **noun** *we continued our search for a hotel:* **hunt**, look, quest; pursuit.

◻ **in search of**
he worked for the Press Association, travelling the world in search of great pictures: **searching for**, hunting for, seeking, looking for, on the lookout for, in pursuit of.

searching adjective *searching questions:* **penetrating**, piercing, probing, keen, shrewd, sharp, intent.
OPPOSITES: casual, vague.

searing adjective
1 *the searing heat:* **scorching**, blistering, sweltering, blazing, burning, fiery, torrid; informal boiling, baking, sizzling, roasting.
2 *searing pain:* **intense**, excruciating, agonizing, sharp, stabbing, shooting, stinging, severe, extreme, racking.
3 *a searing attack:* **fierce**, savage, blistering, scathing, stinging, devastating, mordant, trenchant, caustic, cutting, biting, withering.
OPPOSITES: mild.

seaside noun *a day out at the seaside:* **coast**, shore, seashore, waterside; beach, sand, sands.

season noun *the rainy season:* **period**, time, time of year, spell.

▷ **verb**
1 *season the casserole to taste:* **flavour**, add salt/pepper to, spice.
2 *his albums include standard numbers seasoned with a few of his own tunes:* **enliven**, leaven, spice up, liven up; informal pep up.

◻ **in season**
available, obtainable, to be had, on offer, on the market; plentiful, abundant.

seasonable adjective *seasonable weather:* **usual**, expected, predictable, normal for the time of year.
OPPOSITES: unseasonable.

seasoned adjective *seasoned travellers:* **experienced**, practised, well versed, knowledgeable, established, veteran, hardened, battle-scarred.
OPPOSITES: unseasoned.

seasoning noun **flavouring**, salt and pepper, herbs, spices, condiments.

seat noun
1 *a wooden seat:* **chair**, bench, stool; Brit. informal pew.
2 *the seat of government:* **headquarters**, base, centre, nerve centre, hub, heart; location, site, whereabouts, place.
3 *the family's country seat:* **residence**, ancestral home, mansion, stately home.

▷ **verb**
1 *they seated themselves round the table:* **position**, put, place; ensconce, install, settle; informal park.
2 *the hall seats 500:* **accommodate**, have room for, take, sit, hold, contain.

seating noun *the theatre has seating for 600:* **seats**, room, places, chairs, accommodation.

secede verb *the Kingdom of Belgium seceded from the Netherlands in 1830:* **break away from**, break with, separate yourself from, leave, split with, split off from, disaffiliate from, resign from, withdraw from, pull out of; informal quit.
OPPOSITES: join.

secluded adjective *the house overlooks a quiet, secluded garden:* **isolated**, private, tucked away, sheltered, concealed, hidden, unfrequented, sequestered.
OPPOSITES: accessible, busy.

seclusion noun *he spends much of his time in seclusion at his mountain cottage:* **isolation**, solitude, retreat, privacy, retirement, withdrawal, purdah; concealment, hiding, secrecy.

second[1] adjective
1 *the second day of the trial:* **next**, following, subsequent, succeeding.
2 *he keeps a second pair of glasses in his office:* **additional**, extra, alternative, another, spare, backup, relief, fallback; N. Amer. alternate.
OPPOSITES: first.

▷ **noun** *Eva had been working as his second:* **assistant**, attendant, helper, aide, supporter, auxiliary, right-hand man/woman, second in command, number two, deputy, understudy, subordinate; informal sidekick.

▷ **verb** *George Beale seconded the motion:* **support**, endorse, back, approve, vote for.

second[2] noun *I'll only be gone for a second:* **moment**, bit, little while, short time, instant, split second; informal sec, jiffy; Brit. informal mo, tick, two ticks.

second[3] verb *he was seconded to their Welsh office:* **assign temporarily**, lend; transfer, move, shift, relocate, reassign, send.

secondary adjective
1 *a secondary issue:* **subordinate**, lesser, minor, peripheral, incidental, ancillary, subsidiary, non-essential, of little account, unimportant.
2 *secondary infections:* **accompanying**, attendant, consequential, resulting, resultant; formal concomitant.
OPPOSITES: primary, main.

second-class adjective *we were treated like second-class citizens:* **second-rate**, second-best, inferior, lesser, unimportant.

second-hand adjective
1 *second-hand clothes:* **used**, old, worn, pre-owned, handed-down, hand-me-down, cast-off; Brit. informal reach-me-down.
2 *second-hand information:* **indirect**, derivative; vicarious.
OPPOSITES: new, direct.

S

▷**adverb** *I was discounting anything I heard second-hand:* indirectly, at second hand, on the bush telegraph; informal on the grapevine.
OPPOSITES: directly.

secondly adverb *firstly it is wrong, and secondly it is difficult to implement:* furthermore, also, moreover; second, in the second place, next; secondarily.

second-rate adjective *he replied tetchily that he never made second-rate films:* inferior, substandard, low-quality, below par, bad, poor, deficient, defective, faulty, imperfect, shoddy, inadequate, insufficient, unacceptable; Brit. informal ropy, duff, rubbish.
OPPOSITES: first-rate, excellent.

secrecy noun
1 *the secrecy of the material:* confidentiality, classified nature.
2 *a government which thrived on secrecy:* secretiveness, furtiveness, stealth.

secret adjective
1 *a secret plan:* confidential, top secret, classified, undisclosed, unknown, private, under wraps; informal hush-hush.
2 *a secret drawer in the table:* hidden, concealed, disguised; invisible.
3 *a secret operation to infiltrate terrorist groups:* clandestine, covert, undercover, underground, surreptitious, stealthy, furtive, conspiratorial, cloak-and-dagger, hole-and-corner, closet; informal hush-hush.
4 *a secret message | a secret code:* cryptic, encoded, coded; mysterious, abstruse, recondite, arcane, esoteric, cabbalistic.
5 *a secret place:* secluded, private, concealed, hidden, unfrequented, out of the way, tucked away, isolated.
6 *a very secret person.* See **SECRETIVE**.
OPPOSITES: public, open.

▷**noun**
1 *her ex-husband has recently revealed more of her secrets:* confidence, private affair; skeleton in the cupboard.
2 *the secrets of the universe:* mystery, enigma, paradox, puzzle, conundrum, riddle; informal poser.
3 *the secret of their success:* recipe, magic formula, blueprint, key, answer, solution.
□**in secret**
they've been meeting in secret for months: secretly, in private, privately, behind closed doors, behind the scenes, in camera, under cover, discreetly, behind someone's back, furtively, stealthily, on the sly, on the quiet, conspiratorially, covertly, on the side.

secret agent noun spy, double agent, counterspy, undercover agent, operative, plant, mole; N. Amer. informal spook.

secretary noun assistant, personal assistant, PA, administrator; amanuensis.

secrete¹ verb *a substance secreted by the prostate gland:* produce, discharge, emit, excrete, release, send out.
OPPOSITES: absorb.

secrete² verb *we secreted ourselves in the bushes:* conceal, hide, cover up, shroud, screen, stow away; bury, cache; informal stash away.
OPPOSITES: reveal.

secretive adjective *a secretive person:* uncommunicative, secret, unforthcoming, playing your cards close to your chest, reticent, reserved, silent, quiet, tight-lipped, close-mouthed, taciturn.
OPPOSITES: open, communicative.

secretly adverb
1 *they met secretly for a year:* in secret, in private, privately, behind closed doors, behind the scenes, in camera, under cover, under the counter, behind someone's back, furtively, stealthily, on the sly, on the quiet, conspiratorially, covertly, on the side.
2 *he was secretly jealous of Bartholomew:* privately, in your heart of hearts, deep down.

sect noun *he joined a rather weird religious sect:* cult, religious group, faith community, denomination, persuasion, religious order; splinter group, faction.

sectarian adjective *the party should offer voters a real alternative to sectarian politics:* factional, separatist, partisan, parti pris; doctrinaire, dogmatic, extreme, fanatical, rigid, inflexible, bigoted, hidebound, narrow-minded.
OPPOSITES: integrated, tolerant.

section noun
1 *the separate sections of a train:* part, piece, bit, segment, component, division, portion, element, unit, constituent.
2 *the last section of the questionnaire:* subdivision, part, subsection, division, portion, bit, chapter, passage, clause.
3 *the reference section of the library:* department, area, part, division.

sector noun
1 *every sector of the industry is affected:* branch, arm, part, division, area, department, field, sphere.
2 *the north-eastern sector of the town:* district, quarter, part, section, zone, region, area, belt.

secular adjective *secular issues:* non-religious, lay, temporal, worldly, earthly, profane.
OPPOSITES: sacred, religious.

secure adjective
1 *check to ensure that all bolts are secure:* fastened, fixed, secured, done up; closed, shut, locked.
2 *an environment in which children can feel secure:* safe, protected from harm/danger, out of danger, sheltered, safe and sound,

S

out of harm's way, in a safe place, in safe hands, invulnerable.
3 *a secure future:* certain, assured, reliable, dependable, settled, fixed.
OPPOSITES: insecure.

▷ **verb**
1 *pins secure the handle to the main body:* fix, attach, fasten, affix, connect, couple.
2 *the doors had not been properly secured:* fasten, close, shut, lock, bolt, chain, seal.
3 *they sought to secure the country against attack:* protect, make safe, fortify, strengthen.
4 *a written constitution would secure the rights of the individual:* assure, ensure, guarantee, protect, confirm, establish.
5 *the division secured a major contract:* obtain, acquire, gain, win, get; informal get hold of, land.

security noun
1 *the security of the nation's citizens:* safety, freedom from danger, protection.
2 *he could give her the security she needed:* peace of mind, happiness, confidence, stability, certainty.
3 *security at the court was tight:* safety measures, safeguards, surveillance, defence, protection.
4 *additional security for your loan may be required:* guarantee, collateral, surety, pledge, bond.
OPPOSITES: insecurity.

sedate¹ verb *the patient had to be sedated:* tranquillize, put under, drug.
OPPOSITES: stimulate, revive.

sedate² adjective
1 *a sedate pace:* slow, steady, dignified, unhurried, relaxed, measured, leisurely, slow-moving, easy, easy-going, gentle.
2 *he had lived a sedate and straightforward life:* calm, placid, tranquil, quiet, uneventful; boring, dull.
OPPOSITES: fast, exciting.

sedative adjective *sedative drugs:* tranquillizing, calming, calmative, relaxing, soporific; depressant.
OPPOSITES: stimulant.

▷ **noun** *the doctor gave him a sedative:* tranquillizer, calmative, sleeping pill, narcotic, opiate; depressant; informal downer.
OPPOSITES: stimulant.

sedentary adjective *a sedentary job:* sitting, seated, desk-bound; inactive.
OPPOSITES: active.

sediment noun *there is a thick layer of sediment on the bottom:* deposit, settlings, residue, remains, dregs, grounds; lees; Chemistry precipitate; Geology silt, alluvium.

sedition noun rabble-rousing, subversion, troublemaking, provocation; rebellion, insurrection, mutiny, insurgence, civil disorder.

seditious adjective *a seditious speech:* rabble-rousing, provocative, inflammatory, subversive, troublemaking; rebellious, insurrectionist, mutinous, insurgent.

seduce verb
1 *he took her to his hotel room and tried to seduce her:* persuade to have sex; humorous have your wicked way with; dated take advantage of.
2 *a firm which had seduced customers into buying worthless products:* tempt, lure, entice, beguile, allure, attract, inveigle, manoeuvre.

seducer noun *the man was an accomplished seducer:* womanizer, philanderer, Don Juan, Casanova, playboy, ladies' man; informal ladykiller.

seductive adjective *she appears in the guise of a seductive temptress:* sexy, alluring, tempting, enticing, irresistible, provocative, exciting, sultry; coquettish, flirtatious; informal vampish.

seductress noun temptress, siren, femme fatale, Mata Hari; flirt, coquette; informal vamp.

see verb
1 *he saw her running across the road:* notice, spot, catch sight of, glimpse, catch/get a glimpse of, make out, pick out, spy, distinguish, detect, discern, perceive, note; literary espy; informal clap/lay/set eyes on, clock.
2 *I saw a documentary about it last week:* watch, look at, view; catch.
3 *would you like to see the house?* inspect, view, look round, tour, survey, examine, scrutinize.
4 *I finally saw what she meant:* understand, grasp, comprehend, follow, take in, realize, appreciate, recognize, work out, get the drift of, perceive, fathom, fathom out; informal get, latch on to, cotton on to, catch on to, tumble to, figure out; Brit. informal twig, suss, suss out.
5 *I must go and see what Vic is up to:* find out, discover, learn, ascertain, determine, establish.
6 *see that no harm comes to him:* ensure, make sure/certain, see to it, take care, mind.
7 *I see trouble ahead:* foresee, predict, forecast, prophesy, anticipate, envisage, picture, visualize.
8 *about a year later, I saw him in town:* encounter, meet, run into/across, come across, stumble on/across, happen on, chance on; informal bump into.
9 *they still see each other from time to time:* meet, meet up with, get together with, socialize with.
10 *you'd better see a doctor:* consult, confer with, talk to, speak to, have recourse to, call on, call in, turn to, ask.
11 *he's seeing someone else now:* go out

with, date, take out, be involved with; informal go steady with.
12 *he saw her to her car:* escort, accompany, show, walk, conduct, lead, take, usher, attend.
□ **see through**
I saw through him from the start: understand, get/have the measure of; informal be wise to, have someone's number, know someone's game, be able to read someone like a book.
□ **see something through**
I want to see the job through: persevere with, persist with, continue with, carry on with, keep at, follow through, stay with; finish, conclude, finalize, clinch, round off; informal stick at, wrap up, sew up.
□ **see to**
I'll see to Dad's tea: take care of, deal with, see about, attend to, look after, sort out, fix, organize, arrange.

seed noun
1 *mind the large seeds in these grapes:* pip, stone, pit.
2 *each war contains within it the seeds of a fresh war:* beginnings, starting point, potential for; cause, reason, motivation, motive, grounds; genesis, source, origin, germ, root.

seedy adjective
1 *the seedy world of prostitution:* sordid, disreputable, seamy, sleazy, squalid, unwholesome, unsavoury, insalubrious.
2 *a seedy block of flats:* dilapidated, tumbledown, ramshackle, falling to pieces, decrepit, gone to rack and ruin, run-down, down at heel, shabby, dingy, insalubrious, squalid; Brit. informal grotty.
OPPOSITES: salubrious, high-class.

seek verb
1 *they sought shelter from the winter snows:* search for, try to find, look for, be on the lookout for, be after, hunt for, be in quest of.
2 *the company is seeking a judicial review of the decision:* try to obtain, work towards, be intent on, aim at/for.
3 *he sought help from the police:* ask for, request, solicit, call for, entreat, beg for, petition for, appeal for, apply for, put in for.
4 *we constantly seek to improve the service:* try, attempt, endeavour, strive, work, do your best.

seem verb *she seemed annoyed at this:* appear to be, appear, look, have the appearance/air of being, give the impression of being, look as though you are, look like, show signs of, look to be; come across as, strike someone as, sound.

seeming adjective *there is a seeming contradiction here:* apparent, ostensible, supposed, outward, surface, superficial.
OPPOSITES: actual, genuine.

seemingly adverb apparently, ostensibly,

on the face of it, on the surface, to all appearances, outwardly, superficially, supposedly.
OPPOSITES: actually, genuinely.

seemly adjective *it was not thought seemly to look in a mirror in those days:* proper, decorous, decent, becoming, fitting, suitable, appropriate, apt, apposite, in good taste, genteel, polite, right, correct, acceptable, comme il faut; informal the done thing; old use meet.
OPPOSITES: unseemly.

seep verb *oil continued to seep out of the sunken vessel:* ooze, flow, leak, escape, trickle, exude, drip, dribble, issue, drain, bleed, filter, percolate, soak.

seer noun *a seer had foretold that the earl would assume the throne:* soothsayer, prophet, fortune-teller; (in ancient Greece and Rome) oracle, sibyl.

see-saw verb *the market see-sawed as rumours spread:* fluctuate, swing, rise and fall, go up and down, yo-yo, oscillate, alternate, vary.

seethe verb
1 *I seethed at the injustice of it all:* be angry, be furious, be enraged, be incensed, be beside yourself, simmer, fume, smoulder; informal be hot under the collar.
2 *the cellar was seething with spiders:* teem, swarm; be full of, be crowded with, be alive with.

see-through adjective *a dress with see-through sleeves:* transparent, translucent, thin, flimsy, sheer, diaphanous, filmy, gossamer, gauzy, lightweight; literary pellucid.
OPPOSITES: opaque.

segment noun
1 *orange segments:* piece, bit, section, part, chunk, portion, division, slice; fragment, wedge, lump, tranche.
2 *all segments of society:* part, section, sector, division, constituent, element, unit, compartment; branch, wing.
▷ **verb** *they plan to segment their market share:* divide up, subdivide, separate, split, cut up, carve up, slice up, break up; segregate, partition, section.
OPPOSITES: amalgamate.

segregate verb *he campaigns for routes which segregate cycles from motor vehicles:* separate, keep apart, isolate, partition, divide, detach, disconnect, sever, dissociate, quarantine, closet.
OPPOSITES: integrate.

seize verb
1 *she seized the microphone:* grab, grasp, snatch, take hold of, get your hands on; grip, clutch.
2 *rebels seized the area:* capture, take, overrun, occupy, conquer, take over, annex, invade.

S

3 *the drugs were seized by customs:* confiscate, impound, commandeer, requisition, appropriate, expropriate, take away, sequester.
4 *terrorists seized his wife:* kidnap, abduct, take captive, take prisoner, take hostage, hold to ransom; informal snatch.
OPPOSITES: relinquish, release.

seizure noun
1 *Napoleon's seizure of Spain:* capture, takeover, annexation, invasion, conquest, occupation.
2 *the seizure of defaulters' property:* confiscation, impounding, requisitioning, appropriation, expropriation, sequestration.
3 *the seizure of UN staff by rebels:* kidnapping, kidnap, abduction.
4 *the baby suffered a seizure:* convulsion, fit, spasm, paroxysm.

seldom adverb *he was seldom absent:* rarely, infrequently, hardly ever, scarcely ever, almost never; now and then, occasionally, sporadically, intermittently; informal once in a blue moon.
OPPOSITES: often.

select verb *they had selected Beattie as their spokesperson:* choose, pick, pick out, single out; opt for, decide on, settle on, determine, nominate, appoint, elect.
▷ **adjective**
1 *a select group of SAS members:* choice, hand-picked, prime, first-rate, first-class, superior, finest, best, top-class, supreme, superb, excellent; informal A1, top-notch.
2 *a select clientele:* exclusive, elite, favoured, privileged; wealthy; informal posh.
OPPOSITES: inferior.

selection noun
1 *when you have made your selection, press 'Enter':* choice, pick; option, preference.
2 *we offer a wide selection of dishes:* range, array, diversity, variety, assortment, mixture.
3 *a selection of his poems:* anthology, assortment, collection, assemblage; miscellany, medley, potpourri.

selective adjective *he is very selective in his reading:* discerning, discriminating, discriminatory, critical, exacting, demanding, particular; fussy, fastidious, faddish; informal choosy, picky; Brit. informal faddy, pernickety.
OPPOSITES: indiscriminate.

self noun *these whispers come from our inner self:* ego, yourself, persona, person, identity, character, personality, psyche, soul, spirit, mind, inner self.

> WORD LINKS
> **autobiography** an account of a person's life written by that person
> **egomania** obsessive self-centredness
> **suicide** the action of killing yourself deliberately

self-assurance noun self-confidence, confidence, assertiveness, self-reliance, self-possession, composure, presence of mind, aplomb.
OPPOSITES: diffidence.

self-assured adjective *a stubborn and self-assured lady:* self-confident, confident, assertive, assured, commanding, self-reliant, self-possessed, poised.
OPPOSITES: diffident.

self-centred adjective *your father's too self-centred to care what you do:* egocentric, egotistic, egotistical, egomaniacal, self-absorbed, self-obsessed, self-seeking, self-interested, self-serving; narcissistic, vain; inconsiderate, thoughtless.
OPPOSITES: altruistic, modest.

self-confidence noun *she took care to build up his self-confidence by involving him in the planning:* morale, confidence, self-assurance, assurance, assertiveness, self-reliance, self-possession, composure.
OPPOSITES: self-doubt, diffidence.

self-conscious adjective *he gave me a self-conscious grin:* embarrassed, uncomfortable, uneasy, nervous; unnatural, inhibited, gauche, awkward; modest, shy, diffident, bashful, retiring, shrinking.
OPPOSITES: confident.

self-contained adjective
1 *each train was a self-contained unit:* complete, independent, separate, free-standing, enclosed.
2 *a very self-contained child:* independent, self-sufficient, self-reliant; introverted, quiet, private, aloof, insular, reserved, reticent, secretive.

self-control noun *he had recovered his self-control:* self-discipline, restraint, self-possession, will power, composure, coolness; moderation, temperance, abstemiousness; informal cool.

self-denial noun *a farm built up over the years by hard work and self-denial:* self-sacrifice, selflessness, unselfishness; self-discipline, asceticism, self-deprivation, abstemiousness, abstinence; moderation, temperance.
OPPOSITES: self-indulgence.

self-discipline noun *his observance of his diet was a show of tremendous self-discipline:* self-control; restraint, self-restraint; will power, purpose, strong-mindedness, resolve, moral fibre; doggedness, persistence, determination, grit.

self-employed adjective *a self-employed painter and decorator:* freelance, independent; consultant, consulting; temporary, jobbing, casual, visiting, peripatetic, outside, external, extramural.
OPPOSITES: employed.

S

self-esteem noun *assertiveness training for those with low self-esteem:* self-respect, pride, dignity, self-regard, faith in yourself; morale, self-confidence, confidence, self-assurance.
OPPOSITES: self-doubt.

self-evident adjective *the reason for this is self-evident:* obvious, clear, plain, evident, apparent, manifest, patent, transparent, palpable.
OPPOSITES: unclear.

self-explanatory adjective *this paragraph is largely self-explanatory:* easily understood, comprehensible, intelligible, straightforward, unambiguous, accessible, crystal clear, user-friendly, simple, self-evident, obvious.
OPPOSITES: impenetrable.

self-governing adjective *Singapore became a self-governing state in 1959:* independent, sovereign, autonomous, self-determining, free.
OPPOSITES: dependent.

self-important adjective *he was given the nickname 'Colonel' because he was so self-important:* conceited, arrogant, bumptious, full of yourself, puffed up, swollen-headed, pompous, overbearing, opinionated, cocky, presumptuous, sententious, vain, overweening, proud, egotistic; informal snooty, uppity.
OPPOSITES: humble.

self-indulgent adjective *a self-indulgent lifestyle:* hedonistic, pleasure-seeking, sybaritic, indulgent, luxurious, lotus-eating, epicurean; intemperate, immoderate, overindulgent, excessive, extravagant, decadent.
OPPOSITES: abstemious.

self-interest noun *an economic system based on individualism and self-interest:* self-seeking, self-serving, self-obsession, self-absorption, self-regard, egocentrism, egotism, egomania, selfishness.
OPPOSITES: altruism.

self-interested adjective self-seeking, self-serving, self-obsessed, self-absorbed, wrapped up in yourself, egocentric, egotistic, egotistical, egomaniacal, selfish.
OPPOSITES: altruistic, modest.

selfish adjective *he is just selfish by nature:* egocentric, egotistic, egomaniacal, self-centred, self-absorbed, self-obsessed, self-seeking, self-serving, wrapped up in yourself; inconsiderate, thoughtless, unthinking, uncaring, uncharitable; mean, miserly, grasping, greedy, mercenary, acquisitive.
OPPOSITES: unselfish.

selfless adjective *an act of selfless devotion:* unselfish, altruistic, self-sacrificing, self-denying; considerate, compassionate, kind, noble, generous, magnanimous,

ungrudging, charitable, benevolent, open-handed.
OPPOSITES: selfish.

self-possessed adjective *a woman who has been shy or awkward can become quite self-possessed as she cares for her new baby:* assured, self-assured, confident, self-confident, poised, imperturbable, calm, cool, composed, at ease, unruffled; informal together, unfazed, unflappable.

self-possession noun assurance, self-assurance, confidence, self-confidence, poise, composure, imperturbability, self-control, impassivity, equanimity, nonchalance, aplomb, presence of mind, nerve, sangfroid; informal cool.
OPPOSITES: self-doubt.

self-reliant adjective *ineligible for social security, they have to be entirely self-reliant:* self-sufficient, self-supporting, self-sustaining, able to stand on your own two feet; independent, autarkic.
OPPOSITES: dependent.

self-respect noun *she lost her self-respect and begged him not to leave:* self-esteem, self-regard, amour propre, faith in yourself, pride, dignity, morale, self-confidence.

self-restraint noun *with great self-restraint, he did not grab the rod from his friend's hand:* self-control, restraint, self-discipline, self-possession, will power, forbearance; moderation, temperance, abstemiousness, abstention.
OPPOSITES: self-indulgence.

self-righteous adjective *you're too self-righteous to see your own frailties:* sanctimonious, holier-than-thou, self-satisfied, smug, priggish, complacent, pious, moralizing, superior, hypocritical.
OPPOSITES: humble.

self-sacrifice noun *self-sacrifice involved giving up her fine mansion and living in cheap lodgings:* self-denial, self-deprivation, selflessness, unselfishness, self-discipline, asceticism, abnegation, moderation, austerity, temperance, abstinence.
OPPOSITES: self-indulgence.

self-satisfied adjective *a self-satisfied smile:* complacent, self-congratulatory, smug, superior, puffed up, pleased with yourself.

self-seeking adjective *the self-seeking aggrandizement of Party bosses:* self-interested, self-serving, selfish; egocentric, egotistic, self-obsessed, self-absorbed; inconsiderate, thoughtless, unthinking; informal looking after number one.
OPPOSITES: altruistic.

self-styled adjective *self-styled experts:* soi-disant, self-titled, self-appointed,

S

so-called, would-be, professed, self-confessed.

self-sufficient adjective *the economy became nearly self-sufficient in many foodstuffs:* self-supporting, self-reliant, self-sustaining, able to stand on your own two feet; independent, autarkic.
OPPOSITES: dependent.

sell verb
1 *he decided to sell the car:* put up for sale, offer for sale, put on sale, put on the market; dispose of, vend, auction off; trade, barter.
2 *we sell a variety of electrical goods:* trade in, deal in, stock, carry, offer for sale, retail, market; derogatory peddle, hawk, traffic in.
OPPOSITES: buy.
□ **sell someone out**
you sold me out to the cops, didn't you?
betray, inform on; be disloyal to, be unfaithful to, double-cross, break faith with, stab in the back; informal tell on, squeal on, stitch up; Brit. informal grass on, shop; N. Amer. informal finger.
□ **sell someone short**
don't sell yourself short—you've got what it takes: undervalue, underrate, underestimate, disparage, deprecate, belittle.

seller noun *sellers of fruit and vegetables:* vendor, retailer, supplier, stockist, trader, merchant, dealer; shopkeeper, salesperson, salesman, saleswoman, sales assistant, shop assistant, travelling salesperson, pedlar, hawker; auctioneer.

semblance noun *there remained at least a semblance of discipline:* appearance, air, impression, show, facade, front, veneer, guise, pretence.

seminal adjective *her paper is still considered a seminal work on the subject:* influential, formative, major, important; groundbreaking, pioneering, original, innovative.

seminar noun
1 *a seminar for education officials:* conference, symposium, meeting, convention, forum, summit, discussion, consultation.
2 *teaching in the form of seminars:* study group, workshop, tutorial, class, lesson.

send verb
1 *they sent a message to HQ:* dispatch, post, mail, address, consign, direct, forward; transmit, convey, communicate; fax, email, text.
2 *the volcano sent clouds of ash up into the air:* propel, project, eject, discharge, spout, fire, shoot, release, launch, throw.
3 *it's enough to send you mad:* make, drive, turn.
OPPOSITES: receive.
□ **send for**
we sent for a doctor: call, summon, contact;

ask for, request, order.
□ **send someone off** (Sport) order off, dismiss; show someone the red card; informal red-card, send for an early bath, sin-bin.
□ **send someone/something up** (Brit. informal) *we used to send him up something rotten:* satirize, ridicule, make fun of, parody, lampoon, mock, caricature, imitate, ape; informal take off, take the mickey out of.

send-off noun *she was given a rousing send-off at her retirement party:* farewell, goodbye, adieu, leave-taking, valediction; funeral.
OPPOSITES: welcome.

send-up noun (informal) satire, burlesque, lampoon, pastiche, caricature, imitation, impression, impersonation; mockery, mimicry; informal spoof, take-off, mickey-take.

senior adjective
1 *senior school pupils:* older, elder.
2 *a senior officer:* superior, higher-ranking, more important; high-ranking, top, chief; N. Amer. ranking.
OPPOSITES: junior, subordinate.

seniority noun *the Chief Clerk was next in seniority:* rank, superiority, standing, primacy, precedence, priority; age.

sensation noun
1 *he burning sensation | she had the sensation that she was being watched:* feeling, sense, awareness, consciousness, perception, impression.
2 *he caused a sensation by donating £1m:* commotion, stir, uproar, furore, scandal, impact; interest, excitement; informal splash.
3 *the new cars were a sensation:* triumph, success, sell-out; talking point; informal smash, smash hit, hit, winner, crowd-puller.

sensational adjective
1 *a sensational murder trial:* shocking, scandalous; amazing, startling, astonishing; exciting, thrilling, electrifying, stirring; fascinating, interesting, noteworthy, remarkable, momentous, historic, newsworthy.
2 *sensational stories:* overdramatized, melodramatic, exaggerated; graphic, explicit, lurid.
3 (informal) *she looked sensational:* gorgeous, stunning, wonderful, exquisite, lovely, radiant, delightful, charming, enchanting, captivating; striking, spectacular, arresting, eye-catching, remarkable, outstanding; marvellous, superb; informal great, terrific, tremendous, super, fantastic, fabulous; Brit. informal smashing, brilliant.
OPPOSITES: dull, understated, unremarkable.

sense noun
1 *a sense of guilt:* feeling, awareness, sensation, consciousness, recognition.

S

2 *a sense of humour:* appreciation, awareness, understanding, comprehension.
3 *she had the sense to press the panic button:* common sense, presence of mind, wit, wisdom, sagacity, intelligence, shrewdness, judgement, reason, logic, brains; informal gumption, nous.
4 *I can't see the sense in this:* purpose, point, reason, object, motive; use, value, advantage, benefit.
5 *the different senses of 'well':* meaning, definition, signification, implication; drift, gist, thrust, tenor, message, purport.
▷ **verb** *she sensed their hostility:* detect, feel, observe, notice, recognize, pick up, be aware of, discern, distinguish, make out, identify, see, appreciate, realize, suspect, have a hunch; formal apprehend.

senseless adjective
1 *a senseless waste of time and money:* pointless, futile, useless, needless, unavailing, in vain, purposeless, meaningless, unprofitable; absurd, foolish, insane, stupid, idiotic, ridiculous, ludicrous.
2 *they found him senseless on the floor:* unconscious, stunned, insensible, comatose, knocked out, out cold, out for the count.
OPPOSITES: prudent, conscious.

sensibility noun *the wording might offend their sensibilities:* feelings, finer feelings, emotions, sensitivities, moral sense.

sensible adjective *isn't this the sensible thing to do?* practical, realistic, responsible, reasonable, commonsensical, rational, logical, sound, balanced, sober, no-nonsense, pragmatic, level-headed, thoughtful, down-to-earth, wise, prudent, judicious, sagacious, shrewd.
OPPOSITES: foolish.

sensitive adjective
1 *some babies are more sensitive to changes in their surroundings:* responsive to, reactive to, sensitized to; alive to, aware of, conscious of; susceptible to, affected by, vulnerable to.
2 *sensitive skin:* delicate, fragile.
3 *the matter needs sensitive handling:* tactful, careful, thoughtful, diplomatic, delicate, subtle, kid-glove; sympathetic, compassionate, understanding.
4 *he's sensitive about his bald patch:* touchy, oversensitive, hypersensitive, easily offended, easily upset, easily hurt, thin-skinned, defensive; paranoid, neurotic; informal uptight.
5 *a sensitive issue:* controversial, emotive; problematic, difficult, delicate, tricky, awkward, ticklish.
OPPOSITES: insensitive, tough, thick-skinned.

sensitivity noun
1 *the sensitivity of the skin to sunlight:*

responsiveness, sensitiveness, reactivity; susceptibility, vulnerability.
2 *the company showed a lack of sensitivity in their dealings with local people:* tact, care, thoughtfulness, consideration, diplomacy, delicacy, subtlety; understanding, empathy, sensibility, feeling, responsiveness.
3 *her sensitivity on the subject of boyfriends:* touchiness, oversensitivity, hypersensitivity, defensiveness; paranoia.

sensual adjective
1 *sensual pleasure:* physical, carnal, bodily, fleshly, animal; hedonistic, epicurean, sybaritic.
2 *a beautiful, sensual woman:* sexually attractive, sexy, voluptuous, sultry, seductive, passionate; sexually arousing, erotic, sexual.
OPPOSITES: spiritual.

sensuous adjective *the sensuous qualities of the painting:* aesthetically pleasing, gratifying, rich, sumptuous; sensory.

USAGE

Strictly speaking there is a difference between **sensuous** and **sensual**. **Sensual**, which means 'relating to the physical senses as a source of pleasure', traditionally has stronger sexual connotations than **sensuous**, with its more neutral meaning 'relating to the senses rather than the intellect'. In practice, this distinction is quite difficult to maintain. If you are trying to convey a neutral meaning it is advisable to word your sentence differently or choose another term.

---

sentence noun
1 *Jones showed no emotion as the judge passed sentence:* judgement, ruling, decision, verdict, punishment.
2 *her husband is serving a three-year sentence for fraud:* term; informal time, stretch, stint.
▷ **verb** *they were sentenced to death:* condemn, doom; convict, punish.

sententious adjective *his sententious remarks were unbearable:* moralistic, moralizing, sanctimonious, self-righteous, pious, priggish, judgemental; pompous, pontifical, self-important; informal preachy.

sentient adjective *sentient creatures:* feeling, living, live; conscious, aware, responsive, reactive.

sentiment noun
1 *the comments echo my own sentiments:* view, feeling, attitude, thought, opinion, belief.
2 *there's no room for sentiment in sport:* sentimentality, mawkishness, emotion; informal schmaltz; Brit. informal soppiness.

sentimental adjective
1 *she kept the vase for sentimental reasons:* nostalgic, emotional.
2 *the film is too sentimental:* mawkish,

S

overemotional, cloying, saccharine; romantic; informal slushy, mushy, weepy, schmaltzy, cheesy, corny; Brit. informal soppy. **3** *she is sentimental about animals:* softhearted, tender-hearted, soft; informal soppy.
OPPOSITES: practical, gritty.

sentry noun guard, sentinel, lookout, watchman, picket, patrol.

separable adjective *body and soul are not separable:* divisible, distinct, independent, distinguishable; detachable, removable.

separate adjective
1 *he tried to keep his private life and his work separate | this raises two separate issues:* unconnected, unrelated, different, distinct, discrete; detached, divorced, disconnected, independent, autonomous.
2 *the infirmary was separate from the school:* detached, set apart; cut off, segregated, isolated; free-standing, selfcontained.
OPPOSITES: linked, attached.
▷verb
1 *police were trying to separate two rioting mobs:* split up, break up, part, pull apart, divide.
2 *the connectors can be separated:* disconnect, detach, disengage, uncouple, unyoke, disunite, disjoin; split, divide, sever; disentangle.
3 *the wall that separated the two estates:* divide, partition, come between, keep apart; bisect, intersect.
4 *they separated at the airport:* part company, go your separate ways, split up; disperse, disband, scatter.
5 *the road separated:* fork, divide, branch, bifurcate, diverge.
6 *her parents separated last year:* split up, break up, part, become estranged, divorce.
7 *you must separate fact from fiction:* distinguish, differentiate, dissociate; isolate, set apart, segregate; sort out, sift out, filter out, remove, weed out.
OPPOSITES: unite, join, link, meet.

separately adverb *I'll have to interview you all separately:* individually, one by one, one at a time, singly, severally; apart, independently, alone, by yourself, on your own.
OPPOSITES: together.

separation noun
1 *the separation of the two companies:* splitting, division, disconnection, detachment, severance, dissociation, disaffiliation, segregation, partition.
2 *her parents' separation:* break-up, split, parting, estrangement, rift, rupture, breach; divorce; Brit. informal bust-up.
3 *the separation between art and life:* distinction, difference, differentiation, division, dividing line; gulf, gap, chasm.
OPPOSITES: merger.

septic adjective *a septic finger:* infected, poisoned, inflamed, diseased, festering, purulent, suppurating.
OPPOSITES: healthy.

sepulchral adjective *a speech delivered in sepulchral tones:* gloomy, lugubrious, sombre, melancholy, sorrowful, mournful, doleful, dismal.
OPPOSITES: cheerful.

sepulchre noun tomb, vault, burial chamber, mausoleum, crypt, undercroft, catacomb; grave.

sequence noun
1 *the sequence of events:* succession, order, course, series, chain, train, string, progression, chronology; pattern, flow.
2 *a sequence from his film:* clip, excerpt, extract, episode, section.

sequester verb
1 *he sequestered himself from the world:* isolate yourself, hide away, shut yourself away, seclude yourself, cut yourself off, segregate yourself; closet yourself, withdraw, retire.
2 *the government sequestered his property.* See SEQUESTRATE.

sequestrate verb *in November 1956 the property was sequestrated by the Egyptian authorities:* confiscate, seize, appropriate, expropriate, impound, commandeer, sequester.

seraphic adjective *he listened with an expression of seraphic contentment on his face:* blissful, beatific, sublime, rapturous, ecstatic, joyful, rapt; serene, ethereal; cherubic, saintly, angelic.

serendipitous adjective *their diligent efforts were coupled with the joys of serendipitous discovery:* chance, accidental, coincidental; lucky, fluky, fortuitous; unexpected, unforeseen.

serendipity noun chance, accident, fluke; luck, good luck, good fortune, providence; happy coincidence.

serene adjective
1 *on the surface she seemed serene:* calm, composed, tranquil, untroubled, relaxed, at ease, unperturbed, unruffled, unworried; placid, equable; informal together, unflappable.
2 *the lake serves as a serene campus focus:* peaceful, tranquil, quiet, still, restful, relaxing, undisturbed.
OPPOSITES: agitated, turbulent.

series noun *the explosion was the latest in a series of accidents:* succession, sequence, string, chain, run, round; spate, wave, rash; set, course, cycle; row, line; formal concatenation.

serious adjective

1 *a serious expression:* solemn, earnest, grave, sombre, sober, unsmiling, stern, grim, dour, humourless, stony-faced; thoughtful, preoccupied, pensive.
2 *serious decisions:* important, significant, consequential, momentous, weighty, far-reaching, major, grave; urgent, pressing, crucial, critical, vital, life-and-death, high-priority.
3 *this is a proposal that deserves serious consideration:* careful, detailed, in-depth, deep.
4 *a serious play:* intellectual, highbrow, heavyweight, deep, profound, literary, learned, scholarly; informal heavy.
5 *serious injuries:* severe, grave, bad, critical, acute, terrible, dire, dangerous, perilous; old use parlous.
6 *we're serious about equality:* in earnest, earnest, sincere, wholehearted, genuine; committed, resolute, determined.
OPPOSITES: light-hearted, trivial, superficial, lowbrow, minor.

seriously adverb

1 *Faye nodded seriously:* solemnly, earnestly, gravely, soberly, sombrely, sternly, grimly, dourly, humourlessly; pensively, thoughtfully.
2 *she was seriously injured:* severely, gravely, badly, critically, acutely, dangerously.
3 *do you seriously expect me to come?* really, actually, honestly.
4 *seriously, I'm very pleased:* joking aside, to be serious, honestly, truthfully, truly.

sermon noun homily, address, speech, talk, discourse, oration; lesson.

serried adjective *serried ranks of gravestones:* dense, tight, compact; close together, packed together.

servant noun attendant, retainer; lackey, flunkey, minion, drudge; Brit. informal skivvy.

serve verb

1 *they served their masters faithfully:* work for, attend, minister to, assist, be in the service of, be employed by; obey.
2 *she served another customer:* attend to, deal with, see to; assist, help, look after.
3 *this job serves the community:* be of service to, be of use to, help, assist, aid, make a contribution to, do your bit for, do something for, benefit.
4 *serve the soup hot:* dish up/out, give out, distribute, present.
□ serve as
a saucer serving as an ashtray: act as, function
as, do the work of, be a substitute for.
□ serve on
she served on the committee for years: be a member of, work on, be on, sit on, have a place on.

service noun

1 *your conditions of service:* work, employment, employ, labour.
2 *he has done us a service:* favour, kindness, good turn, helping hand; (**services**) assistance, help, aid, offices, ministrations.
3 *he took his car in for a service:* overhaul, routine maintenance.
4 *a marriage service:* ceremony, ritual, rite, observance; worship, liturgy, sacrament; formal ordinance.
5 *a range of local services:* amenity, facility, resource, utility.
▷ verb *the appliances are serviced regularly:* overhaul, maintain, check, go over; repair, mend, recondition.
□ be of service
please let us know if we can be of service in any way: help, assist, be of assistance, serve, be useful, be of use; do someone a good turn.
□ out of service
the lift is out of service: out of order, broken, broken-down, out of commission, unserviceable, faulty, defective, inoperative, down.

serviceable adjective

1 *a serviceable heating system:* working, in working order, functioning, functional, operational, operative; usable, workable, viable.
2 *serviceable lace-up shoes:* functional, utilitarian, sensible, practical; hard-wearing, durable, tough, robust.
OPPOSITES: unserviceable, impractical.

servile adjective *his attitude towards Mandeville can only be described as servile:* obsequious, sycophantic, deferential, subservient, fawning, ingratiating, unctuous, grovelling, toadying, slavish, self-abasing; informal bootlicking; Brit. informal smarmy.
OPPOSITES: assertive.

serving noun *a large serving of spaghetti:* portion, helping, plateful, plate, bowlful; amount, quantity, share, ration.

session noun

1 *a special session of the committee:* meeting, sitting, assembly, conclave, plenary; hearing; conference, discussion, forum, symposium.
2 *treatment by experienced physiotherapists is available at £50 a session:* period, time, spell, stretch.
3 *the next college session begins in August:* academic year, school year; term, semester.

set¹ verb

1 *Beth set the bag on the table:* put, put down, place, lay, deposit, position, settle, leave, stand, plant, posit; informal stick, dump, park, pop; Brit. informal plonk, bung.
2 *the fence is set in concrete:* fix, embed, insert; mount.
3 *I'll go and set the table:* lay, prepare, arrange.

S

4 *we set them some easy tasks:* assign, allocate, give, allot, prescribe.

5 *they set a date for the election:* decide on, select, choose, arrange, schedule; fix, settle on, determine, designate, name, appoint, specify, stipulate.

6 *his jump set a national record:* establish, create, institute.

7 *he set his watch:* adjust, regulate, synchronize; calibrate; put right, correct; programme, activate, turn on.

8 *the adhesive will set in an hour:* solidify, harden, stiffen, thicken, gel, cake, congeal, coagulate, clot, freeze, crystallize.

9 *the sun was setting:* go down, sink, dip; vanish, disappear.

□ **set about**
1 *Mike set about raising £5000:* begin, start, commence, go about, get to work on, get down to, embark on, tackle, address yourself to, undertake.
2 *the youths set about him:* attack, assail, assault, tear into, set upon, fall on; informal lay into, lace into, pitch into.

□ **set someone apart**
his ability and self-effacing modesty have set him apart: distinguish, differentiate, mark out, single out, separate, demarcate.

□ **set something apart**
one pew was set apart from the rest: isolate, separate, segregate, put to one side.

□ **set something aside**
1 *set aside some money each month:* save, put by, put aside, put away, lay by, keep, reserve; store, stockpile, hoard, stow away; informal salt away, squirrel away, stash away.
2 *they set aside their differences:* disregard, put aside, ignore, forget, discount, shrug off, bury.
3 *the Appeal Court set aside the decision:* overrule, overturn, reverse, revoke, countermand, nullify, annul, cancel, quash, dismiss, reject, repudiate.

□ **set someone back** (informal) *the new tyre set me back £125.* See **cost** verb sense 1.

□ **set someone/something back**
the growth of American trade unionism was set back by economic depression: hinder, impede, obstruct, hamper, inhibit, frustrate, thwart; delay, hold up, hold back, slow down/up, retard, check.

□ **set in**
bad weather set in: begin, start, arrive, come, develop.

□ **set off**
on the appointed day, we set off for Heathrow: set out, start out, sally forth, leave, depart, embark, set sail; informal hit the road.

□ **set something off**
1 *the bomb was set off:* detonate, explode, blow up, touch off, trigger; ignite.
2 *the incident set off a wave of violent attacks across the country:* give rise to, cause, lead to, set in motion, occasion, bring about, initiate, precipitate, prompt, trigger, spark off, touch off, provoke, incite.

3 *the blue dress set off her auburn hair:* enhance, bring out, emphasize, show off, throw into relief; complement.

□ **set on/upon**
he and his friends were set on by a gang. See **set about**.

□ **set out**
1 *he set out early.* See **set off**.
2 *you've done what you set out to achieve:* aim, intend, mean, seek; hope, aspire, want.

□ **set something out**
the gifts were set out on tables: arrange, lay out, put out, array, dispose, display, exhibit.

□ **set someone up**
1 *his father set him up in business:* establish, finance, fund, back, subsidize.
2 (informal) *she set him up for Newley's murder:* falsely incriminate, frame, entrap; Brit. informal fit up.

□ **set something up**
1 *a monument to her memory was set up:* erect, put up, construct, build, raise, elevate.
2 *she set up her own business:* establish, start, found, create, initiate, institute, put in place.
3 *they set up a meeting:* arrange, organize, fix up, schedule, timetable, line up.

set[2] **noun**
1 *a set of colour postcards:* group, collection, series; assortment, selection, compendium, batch, number; arrangement, array.
2 *she's got a good set of friends:* crowd, coterie, circle, clique, group, gang, crew, band, company; informal bunch.
3 *a stage set:* scenery, setting, backdrop; mise en scène.

set[3] **adjective**
1 *a set routine:* fixed, established, predetermined, hard and fast, prearranged, prescribed, specified, defined; unvarying, unchanging, invariable, unvaried, rigid, inflexible, cast-iron, strict, settled, predictable; routine, standard, customary, regular, usual, habitual, accustomed; literary wonted.
2 *she had set ideas:* inflexible, rigid, fixed, firm, deep-rooted, deep-seated, ingrained, entrenched.
3 *he had a set speech for such occasions:* stock, standard, routine, rehearsed, well worn, formulaic, conventional.
4 *I was all set for the evening:* ready, prepared, organized, equipped, primed; informal geared up, psyched up.
5 *he's set on marrying her:* determined to, intent on, bent on, hell-bent on, resolute about, insistent about.
6 *you were dead set against the idea:* opposed to, averse to, hostile to, resistant to, antipathetic to, unsympathetic to; informal anti.
OPPOSITES: variable, flexible, original, unprepared.

setback noun *Alexander was faced with one setback after another:* problem, difficulty, hitch, complication, upset, disappointment, misfortune, mishap, reversal; blow, stumbling block, hindrance, impediment, obstruction; delay, hold-up; informal glitch, hiccup.
OPPOSITES: breakthrough.

setting noun
1 *a rural setting:* surroundings, position, situation, environment, background, backdrop, milieu, environs, habitat; spot, place, location, locale, site, scene; area, region, district.
2 *a garnet in a gold setting:* mount, fixture, surround.

settle verb
1 *they settled the dispute:* resolve, sort out, clear up, end, fix, work out, iron out, straighten out, set right, rectify, remedy, reconcile; informal patch up.
2 *she settled their affairs:* put in order, sort out, tidy up, arrange, organize, order, clear up.
3 *she went down to the lobby to settle her bill:* pay, settle up, square, clear.
4 *he settled in London:* make your home, set up home, take up residence, put down roots, establish yourself; live, move to, emigrate to.
5 *immigrants settled much of Australia:* colonize, occupy, inhabit, people, populate.
6 *a brandy will settle your nerves:* calm, quieten, quiet, soothe, pacify, quell.
7 *he settled into an armchair:* sit down, seat yourself, install yourself, ensconce yourself, plant yourself; informal park yourself; Brit. informal plonk yourself.
8 *a butterfly settled on the flower:* land, come to rest, alight, descend, perch.
9 *sediment settles at the bottom:* sink, subside, fall, gravitate.
□ **settle down**
the class wouldn't settle down: calm down, quieten down, be quiet, be still; informal shut up.
□ **settle down to**
Catherine settled down to her work: apply yourself to, get down to, set about, attack; concentrate on, focus on, devote yourself to.
□ **settle for**
they settled for a 4.2% pay rise: accept, agree to, assent to, content yourself with.
□ **settle on**
they settled on a date for the wedding: decide on, set, fix, agree on, name, establish, arrange, appoint, designate, assign; choose, select, pick.

settlement noun
1 *a pay settlement:* agreement, deal, arrangement, resolution, bargain, understanding, pact.
2 *the settlement of the dispute:* resolution, settling, solution, reconciliation.
3 *a frontier settlement:* community, colony, outpost, encampment, post; village, commune.
4 *the settlement of the area:* colonization, settling, populating.
5 *the settlement of their debts:* payment, discharge, liquidation, clearance.

settler noun colonist, colonizer, frontiersman, frontierswoman, pioneer; immigrant, newcomer, incomer.
OPPOSITES: native.

set-up (informal) noun
1 *a telecommunications set-up:* system, structure, organization, arrangement, framework, layout, configuration.
2 *a set-up called Film International:* organization, group, body, agency, association, operation; company, firm; informal outfit.

seven cardinal number septet.

> WORD LINKS
> **heptagon** a seven-sided figure

sever verb
1 *the head was severed from the body:* cut off, chop off, detach, disconnect, separate, part; amputate, dock.
2 *a knife had severed the artery:* cut through, cut, rupture, split, pierce.
3 *they severed diplomatic relations:* break off, discontinue, suspend, end, terminate, cease, dissolve.
OPPOSITES: join, maintain.

several adjective
1 *several people disagreed with me:* some, many, a fair number of, a few.
2 *they sorted out their several responsibilities:* respective, individual, own, particular, specific; separate, different, disparate, distinct; various.

severe adjective
1 *severe injuries:* acute, very bad, serious, grave, critical, dreadful, terrible, awful; dangerous, life-threatening; formal grievous; old use parlous.
2 *severe storms:* fierce, violent, strong, powerful, intense; tempestuous, turbulent.
3 *a severe winter:* harsh, bitter, cold, bleak, freezing, icy, arctic, extreme.
4 *a severe test of their stamina:* difficult, demanding, tough, arduous, formidable, exacting, rigorous, punishing, onerous, gruelling.
5 *severe criticism:* harsh, scathing, sharp, strong, fierce, savage, devastating, caustic, biting, withering.
6 *his severe expression:* stern, dour, grim, forbidding, disapproving, unsmiling, unfriendly, sombre, grave, serious, stony, steely; cold, frosty.
7 *a severe style of architecture:* austere, simple, plain, unadorned, unembellished, unornamented, stark, spartan, ascetic; clinical, uncluttered.
OPPOSITES: minor, gentle, mild.

S

severely adverb

1 *he was severely injured:* badly, seriously, critically; formal grievously.
2 *she was severely criticized:* sharply, roundly, soundly, fiercely, savagely.
3 *murderers should be treated more severely:* harshly, strictly, sternly, rigorously.
4 *she looked severely at Harriet:* sternly, grimly, dourly, disapprovingly; coldly, frostily.
5 *she was dressed severely:* austerely, simply, plainly.

sew verb *she sewed the seams of the tunic:* stitch, tack, baste, hem; embroider; attach, fasten.

□ **sew something up**
the tear had been sewn up: darn, mend, stitch up, repair, patch.

sewing noun stitching, needlework, needlecraft, mending, fancy-work, embroidery.

sex noun

1 *she's always talking about sex:* sexual intercourse, lovemaking, making love, the sex act, sexual relations; mating, copulation; technical coitus; formal fornication.
2 *adults of both sexes:* gender.

□ **have sex**
have sexual intercourse, make love, sleep with someone, go to bed with someone; mate, copulate; formal fornicate.

sexual adjective

1 *the sexual organs:* reproductive, genital, sex, procreative.
2 *sexual activity:* carnal, erotic.

sexuality noun

1 *she had begun to understand the power of her sexuality:* sensuality, physicality, eroticism; sexual appetite, passion, desire, lust.
2 *I'm open about my sexuality:* sexual orientation, sexual preference, leaning, persuasion.

sexy adjective

1 *she's so sexy:* sexually attractive, seductive, desirable, alluring, sensual, sultry; nubile; informal fanciable; Brit. informal fit.
2 *sexy videos:* erotic, sexually explicit, arousing, exciting, stimulating, titillating, racy, naughty, risqué, X-rated; euphemistic adult; informal raunchy, steamy.

shabby adjective

1 *a shabby little bar:* run-down, down at heel, scruffy, dilapidated, ramshackle, tumbledown, seedy, insalubrious, squalid, sordid; Brit. informal grotty.
2 *a shabby grey coat:* scruffy, old, worn out, threadbare, frayed, tattered, battered, faded, moth-eaten, mangy; informal tatty, the worse for wear.
3 *he hasn't forgiven them for the shabby treatment he received:* mean, nasty, shameful, sorry, ignoble, unfair, unworthy, unkind, contemptible, despicable, dishonourable, discreditable; informal rotten, low-down.
OPPOSITES: smart, decent.

shack noun hut, shanty, cabin, lean-to, shed; hovel.

shackle verb *he was shackled to the wall:* chain, fetter, manacle, handcuff, clap in irons; secure, tie, bind, tether, hobble.

shackles plural noun

1 *the men filed through their shackles:* chains, fetters, irons, manacles, handcuffs.
2 *the shackles of bureaucracy:* restrictions, restraints, constraints, obstacles, barriers, obstructions.

shade noun

1 *they sat in the shade:* shadows, shelter, cover; cool.
2 *shades of blue:* tone, tint, tinge, hue, colour.
3 *shades of meaning:* nuance, gradation, degree, difference, variation, variety; nicety, subtlety; undertone, overtone.
4 *her skirt was a shade too short:* little, bit, trace, touch, modicum, tinge; slightly, rather, somewhat; informal tad, smidgen.
5 *the window shade:* blind, screen, awning, canopy, cover, covering.

▷ **verb**
1 *I shaded my eyes against the sun:* screen, shelter, cover.
2 *she shaded in the picture:* darken, colour in, pencil in, block in, fill in; cross-hatch.
3 *the sky shaded from turquoise to blue:* change, turn, go; merge, blend.

□ **put someone/something in the shade**
he put his rivals in the shade: surpass, outshine, outclass, overshadow, eclipse, transcend, cap, top, outstrip, outdo, put to shame, beat, outperform, upstage; informal run rings around, be a cut above, leave standing.

□ **shades of**
a terrifying thriller with shades of Alfred Hitchcock: echoes of, a reminder of, memories of, suggestions of, hints of.

shadow noun

1 *he saw her shadow in the doorway:* silhouette, outline, shape, contour, profile.
2 *he emerged from the shadows:* shade, darkness, twilight, gloom, murk.
3 *she knew without any shadow of doubt:* trace, scrap, shred, crumb, iota, scintilla, jot, whit, grain; informal smidgen, tad.
4 *a shadow of a smile:* trace, hint, suggestion, suspicion, ghost, glimmer.

▷ **verb** *he is shadowing a poacher:* follow, trail, track, stalk, pursue, hunt; informal tail, keep tabs on.

shadowy adjective

1 *a shadowy corridor:* dark, dim, shady, shaded, gloomy, murky, twilit, crepuscular.
2 *a shadowy figure:* indistinct, hazy, indefinite, vague, nebulous, ill-defined,

faint, blurred, unrecognizable; ghostly, spectral, wraithlike.
OPPOSITES: bright, clear.

shady adjective
1 *a shady garden:* shaded, shadowy, dim, dark; sheltered, screened, shrouded; leafy.
2 (informal) *shady financial deals:* suspicious, suspect, questionable, dubious, doubtful, disreputable, untrustworthy, dishonest, dishonourable, devious, underhand, unscrupulous, irregular, unethical; informal fishy, murky; Brit. informal dodgy.
OPPOSITES: bright, honest.

shaft noun
1 *the shaft of a golf club:* handle, stem, shank, hilt, pole, stick, rod, staff.
2 *shafts of sunlight:* ray, beam, gleam, streak, finger, pencil.
3 *a ventilation shaft:* passage, duct, flue, vent, hole, well, tunnel, pit, borehole, bore.

shaggy adjective *his shaggy beard:* bushy, thick, woolly, hairy, tangled, tousled, unkempt, dishevelled, untidy, matted.
OPPOSITES: sleek.

shake verb
1 *the whole building shook:* vibrate, tremble, quiver, quake, shiver, shudder, judder, jiggle, wobble, rock, sway; convulse.
2 *she shook the bottle of ketchup, but to no avail:* jiggle, joggle, agitate; informal waggle.
3 *he shook his stick at them:* brandish, wave, flourish, swing, wield.
4 *the look in his eyes really shook her:* upset, distress, disturb, unsettle, disconcert, unnerve, trouble, throw off balance, agitate, fluster; shock, alarm, frighten, scare, worry; informal rattle, faze.
5 *this will shake their confidence:* weaken, undermine, damage, impair, harm; reduce, diminish, decrease.
□ **shake someone off**
Manville thought he had shaken off his pursuer: get away from, escape, elude, dodge, lose, leave behind, get rid of, give someone the slip, throw off the scent.
□ **shake something off**
he has shaken off his back trouble: recover from, get over; get rid of, free yourself from; Brit. informal get shot of.
□ **shake someone/something up**
plans to shake up the legal profession: reorganize, restructure, revolutionize, alter, change, transform, reform, overhaul.

shaky adjective
1 *her legs were still shaky:* trembling, shaking, tremulous, quivering, quivery, unsteady, wobbly, weak; tottering, tottery, doddery; informal trembly.
2 *I felt a bit shaky for some time after the crash:* faint, dizzy, light-headed, giddy; weak, wobbly, quivery, groggy, muzzy; informal trembly, woozy.
3 *a shaky table:* unsteady, unstable, wobbly, precarious, rocky, rickety, ramshackle; Brit. informal wonky.

4 *the evidence is shaky:* unreliable, untrustworthy, questionable, dubious, doubtful, tenuous, suspect, flimsy, weak, unsound, unsupported, unsubstantiated, unfounded; informal iffy; Brit. informal dodgy.
OPPOSITES: steady, stable, sound.

shallow adjective *a shallow analysis of contemporary society:* superficial, facile, simplistic, oversimplified; flimsy, insubstantial, lightweight, empty, trivial, trifling; surface, skin-deep; frivolous, foolish, silly.
OPPOSITES: profound.

sham noun
1 *his tenderness had been a sham:* pretence, fake, act, fiction, simulation, fraud, feint, lie.
2 *the doctor was a sham:* fraud, impostor, fake, charlatan, pretender; quack, mountebank; informal phoney.
▷ adjective *he even agreed to a sham marriage to protect her immigration status:* fake, bogus, false; pretended, feigned, insincere, contrived; informal phoney.
OPPOSITES: genuine.
▷ verb
1 *she shams indifference:* feign, fake, pretend, put on, simulate, affect.
2 *was he ill or just shamming?* pretend, fake, dissemble; malinger; informal put it on.

shambles plural noun
1 *we have to sort out this shambles:* chaos, mess, muddle, confusion, disorder, havoc; Brit. informal dog's dinner/breakfast.
2 *the room was a shambles:* mess, pigsty; informal disaster area; Brit. informal tip.

shambolic adjective (Brit. informal). See CHAOTIC.

shame noun
1 *her face was scarlet with shame:* humiliation, mortification, chagrin, ignominy, embarrassment, indignity, abashment, discomfort.
2 *I felt shame at telling this lie:* guilt, remorse, contrition, compunction.
3 *he brought shame on the family:* disgrace, dishonour, discredit, ignominy, disrepute, infamy, scandal, contempt; formal opprobrium.
4 *it's a shame she never married:* pity, misfortune, sad thing; bad luck.
OPPOSITES: pride, honour, blessing.
▷ verb
1 *you shamed your family's name:* disgrace, dishonour, discredit, debase; stigmatize, taint, tarnish, blacken, drag through the mud; literary besmirch, sully.
2 *he was shamed in public:* humiliate, mortify, chagrin, embarrass, abash, chasten, humble, take down a peg or two; informal show up, cut down to size.
OPPOSITES: honour.
□ **put someone/something to shame**
a quality piece of cinema which puts many Hollywood blockbusters to shame: outshine,

S

outclass, eclipse, surpass, excel, outstrip, outdo, put in the shade, upstage; informal run rings around, leave standing.

shamefaced adjective *Giles looked shamefaced:* ashamed, abashed, sheepish, guilty, conscience-stricken, guilt-ridden, contrite, sorry, remorseful, repentant, penitent, regretful, rueful, apologetic; embarrassed, mortified, red-faced, chagrined, humiliated.
OPPOSITES: unrepentant.

shameful adjective
1 *their behaviour after the match was shameful:* disgraceful, deplorable, despicable, contemptible, dishonourable, discreditable, reprehensible, low, unworthy, ignoble, shabby.
2 *a shameful secret:* embarrassing, mortifying, humiliating, degrading, ignominious.
OPPOSITES: admirable.

shameless adjective *his shameless hypocrisy:* flagrant, blatant, barefaced, overt, brazen; unabashed, unashamed, unblushing, unrepentant; brash, audacious, outrageous, undisguised, unconcealed, transparent.
OPPOSITES: shamefaced.

shape noun
1 *the shape of the dining table:* form, appearance, configuration, formation, structure; contours, lines, outline, silhouette, profile; figure, build, physique, body.
2 *you're in pretty good shape:* condition, health, trim, fettle, order; Brit. informal nick.
▷ verb
1 *the metal is shaped into tools:* form, fashion, make, mould, model, cast; sculpt, carve, cut, whittle.
2 *attitudes were shaped by his report:* determine, form, fashion, mould, define, develop; influence, affect.
□ take shape
the past few months have seen their policies begin to take shape: become clear, become definite, become tangible, crystallize, come together, fall into place.

shapeless adjective
1 *a shapeless mass of metal:* formless, amorphous, nebulous, lumpy, unformed, indefinite, irregular.
2 *a shapeless dress:* baggy, saggy, ill-fitting, sack-like, oversized, unshapely.
OPPOSITES: well defined, shapely.

shapely adjective *her shapely figure was swathed in blue silk:* attractive, well proportioned, clean-limbed, sexy, curvaceous, voluptuous, full-figured; informal curvy.
OPPOSITES: shapeless.

shard noun *shards of glass:* fragment, sliver, splinter, chip, piece, bit.

share noun *her share of the profits:*
portion, part, division, quota, allowance, ration, allocation, measure, due, quantum; informal cut, slice.
▷ verb
1 *we share the bills:* split, divide, go halves on; informal go fifty-fifty, go Dutch.
2 *they shared out the food:* apportion, divide up, allocate, portion out, ration out, parcel out, measure out; carve up.
□ share in
we all share in the learning process: participate in, take part in, play a part in, be involved in, contribute to, have a hand in; formal partake in.

sharp adjective
1 *a sharp knife:* keen, razor-edged, honed.
2 *a sharp needle:* pointed, fine, spiked, spiky; informal pointy.
3 *a sharp pain:* excruciating, agonizing, intense, stabbing, shooting, severe, acute, keen, fierce, searing; exquisite.
4 *a sharp taste:* tangy, piquant, acidic, acid, sour, tart, pungent, acrid, bitter.
5 *a sharp cry of pain:* loud, piercing, shrill, high-pitched, penetrating, harsh, strident, ear-splitting, deafening.
6 *a sharp wind:* cold, chilly, chill, brisk, keen, penetrating, biting, icy, bitter, freezing, raw; informal nippy.
7 *sharp words were exchanged:* harsh, bitter, cutting, scathing, caustic, barbed, trenchant, acrimonious, acerbic, sarcastic, sardonic, spiteful, venomous, malicious, vitriolic, vicious, hurtful, nasty, cruel, abrasive; informal bitchy.
8 *your photos are quite sharp:* clear, crisp, distinct, focused, high-resolution.
9 *the edge of the gully had a very sharp drop:* steep, sudden, sheer, abrupt, precipitous, vertical.
10 *a sharp decline in sales:* sudden, steep, unexpected, unforeseen; marked, striking.
11 *his sharp eyes missed nothing:* keen, perceptive, observant, acute, beady, hawklike.
12 *she was sharp and witty:* perceptive, quick-witted, clever, astute, intelligent, bright, alert, quick off the mark, insightful, knowing, percipient, perspicacious, incisive, sensitive, keen, acute, shrewd, canny, intuitive; informal smart, on the ball, quick on the uptake.
OPPOSITES: blunt, mild, sweet, soft, kind.
▷ adverb *nine o'clock sharp:* precisely, exactly, on the dot; promptly, prompt, punctually, dead on.
OPPOSITES: roughly.

sharpen verb
1 *I sharpened the carving knife:* hone, whet, strop, grind, file.
2 *the players need to sharpen up their skills:* improve, brush up, polish up, better, enhance; hone, fine-tune, perfect.

sharp-eyed adjective *a sharp-eyed witness contacted the police with details of a car spotted nearby:* observant, perceptive,

eagle-eyed, hawk-eyed, keen-eyed;
watchful, vigilant, alert, on the lookout;
informal beady-eyed.

shatter verb
1 *the glasses shattered:* smash, break,
splinter, crack, fracture, fragment,
disintegrate; informal bust.
2 *the announcement shattered their
hopes:* destroy, wreck, ruin, dash, crush,
devastate, demolish, torpedo, scotch;
informal do for, put paid to; Brit. informal
scupper.
3 *we were shattered by the news:* devastate,
shock, stun, daze, traumatize, crush,
distress; informal knock sideways; Brit. informal
knock for six.

shave verb
1 *he shaved his beard:* cut off, snip off;
crop, trim, barber.
2 *shave off excess wood:* plane, pare,
whittle, scrape.
3 *shave Parmesan over the top:* grate,
shred.
4 *he shaved the MP's majority to 2,000:*
reduce, cut, lessen, decrease, pare down,
shrink, slim down.
5 *his shot shaved the post:* graze, brush,
touch, glance off, kiss.

sheaf noun *a sheaf of papers:* bundle,
bunch, stack, pile, heap, mass; Brit. informal
wodge.

sheath noun
1 *put the sword in its sheath:* scabbard,
case.
2 *the wire has a plastic sheath:* covering,
cover, case, casing, envelope, sleeve,
wrapper, capsule.

shed¹ noun *a small wooden shed:* hut,
shack, lean-to, outhouse, outbuilding,
woodshed, cabin.

shed² verb
1 *the trees shed their leaves:* drop, scatter,
spill, lose.
2 *the caterpillar shed its skin:* slough off,
cast off, moult.
3 *we shed our jackets:* take off, remove,
shrug off, discard, doff, climb out of, slip
out of, divest yourself of; Brit. informal peel
off.
4 *the firm is to shed ten workers:* make
redundant, dismiss, let go, discharge, get
rid of, discard; informal sack, fire; Brit. informal
give someone their cards.
5 *the moon shed a watery light:* cast,
radiate, diffuse, give out.
□ **shed tears**
weep, cry, sob; lament, grieve, mourn.

sheen noun *her hair, once so dark and
lustrous, had lost its sheen:* shine, lustre,
gloss, patina, burnish, polish, shimmer,
brilliance, radiance.

sheepish adjective *Sam looked
sheepish and apologetic:* embarrassed,
uncomfortable, hangdog, self-conscious;

shamefaced, ashamed, abashed, mortified,
chastened, remorseful, contrite, apologetic,
rueful, regretful, penitent, repentant.
OPPOSITES: brazen.

sheer¹ adjective
1 *the sheer audacity of the plan:*
utter, complete, absolute, total, pure,
downright, out-and-out, arrant, thorough,
thoroughgoing, veritable, unmitigated,
plain, nothing but.
2 *a sheer drop:* steep, vertical,
perpendicular, precipitous, abrupt, bluff,
sharp.
3 *a sheer dress:* diaphanous, gauzy,
filmy, floaty, gossamer, thin, translucent,
transparent, see-through, insubstantial,
flimsy.
OPPOSITES: gradual, thick.

> **USAGE**
>
> Do not confuse **sheer** and **shear**. As an
> adjective **sheer** chiefly means 'nothing but;
> complete or absolute'; **sheer** is also a verb
> meaning 'to change course quickly' (*the boat
> sheered off*). **Shear** is a verb meaning 'to cut
> the wool off a sheep'.

sheer² verb
1 *the boat sheered off along the coast:*
swerve, veer, slew, skew, swing.
2 *her mind sheered away from his image:*
turn away, flinch, recoil, shy away; avoid.

sheet noun
1 *a sheet of ice:* layer, stratum, covering,
blanket, coating, coat, film, skin.
2 *a sheet of glass:* pane, panel, piece, plate;
slab.
3 *she put a fresh sheet of paper in the
printer:* piece, leaf, page, folio.
4 *a sheet of water:* expanse, area, stretch,
sweep.

shelf noun ledge, sill, bracket, rack;
mantelpiece; shelving.

shell noun
1 *peanut shells:* pod, husk, hull, casing,
case, covering.
2 *shells passing overhead:* projectile, bomb,
explosive; grenade; bullet, cartridge.
3 *the metal shell of the car:* framework,
frame, chassis, skeleton, body, bodywork,
hull, fuselage, exterior.
▷ **verb** *rebel artillery shelled the city:*
bombard, fire on, shoot at, attack, bomb,
blitz, strafe.

shelter noun
1 *the trees provide shelter for animals:*
protection, cover, screening, shade; safety,
security, refuge, sanctuary, asylum.
2 *a shelter for abandoned cats:* sanctuary,
refuge, home, haven, safe house; harbour,
port in a storm.
OPPOSITES: exposure.
▷ **verb**
1 *the hut sheltered him from the wind:*
protect, shield, screen, cover, shade, save,

S

safeguard, preserve, defend, cushion, guard, insulate.
2 *the anchorage where the convoy sheltered:* take shelter, take refuge, seek sanctuary, take cover; informal hole up.
OPPOSITES: expose.

sheltered adjective
1 *a sheltered stretch of water:* protected, screened, shielded, covered; calm, shady, cosy.
2 *she led a sheltered life:* secluded, cloistered, isolated, protected, withdrawn, sequestered, reclusive; privileged, secure, safe, quiet, cosy.
OPPOSITES: exposed.

shelve verb *plans to reopen the school have been shelved:* postpone, put off, delay, defer, put back, reschedule, hold over/off, put to one side, suspend, stay, put in abeyance, mothball; abandon, drop, give up, stop, cancel, jettison, axe; informal put on ice, put on the back burner, ditch.

shepherd verb *we shepherded them away:* usher, steer, herd, lead, take, escort, guide, conduct, marshal, walk; show, see, chaperone.

shield verb *he shielded his eyes:* protect, cover, screen, shade; save, safeguard, preserve, defend, secure, guard; cushion, insulate.
OPPOSITES: expose.

shift verb
1 *a team from the power company shifted the cables away from the house:* move, carry, transfer, transport, convey, haul, fetch; relocate, reposition, rearrange; informal lug, cart.
2 *ministers are extremely unlikely to shift their stance:* change, alter, adjust, vary; modify, revise, reverse, retract; do a U-turn; Brit. do an about-turn.
3 *the cargo has shifted:* move, slide, slip, be displaced.
4 *the wind shifted:* veer, alter, change, turn, swing round, back.
5 (Brit. informal) *this brush really shifts the dirt:* get rid of, remove, get off, budge, lift, expunge.
▷**noun**
1 *the southward shift of people:* movement, move, transference, transport, transposition, relocation.
2 *a shift in public opinion:* change, alteration, adjustment, amendment, variation, modification, revision, reversal, retraction, U-turn; Brit. about-turn.
3 *they worked three shifts:* stint, stretch, spell, period.

shiftless adjective *he thought the whole family shiftless and dishonest:* lazy, idle, indolent, slothful, lethargic, lackadaisical; spiritless, apathetic, feckless, good-for-nothing, worthless; unambitious, unenterprising.
OPPOSITES: energetic.

shifty adjective (informal) *he had a shifty look about him:* devious, evasive, slippery, untrustworthy, dishonest, shady, underhand, duplicitous, false, deceitful, wily, crafty, tricky, sneaky, treacherous, artful, sly, scheming; Brit. informal dodgy.
OPPOSITES: honest.

shilly-shally verb (informal) *the government shilly-shallied about the matter:* dither, be indecisive, be irresolute, vacillate, waver, hesitate, blow hot and cold, falter, drag your feet; Brit. haver, hum and haw.

shimmer verb *the lake shimmered:* glint, glisten, twinkle, sparkle, flash, scintillate, gleam, glow, glimmer, glitter, wink.
▷**noun** *the shimmer of lights from the traffic:* glint, glisten, twinkle, sparkle, flash, scintillation, gleam, glow, glimmer, lustre, glitter.

shin verb *he shinned up a tree:* climb, clamber, scramble, swarm; mount, ascend, scale; descend.

shine verb
1 *rays of sun shone through the clouds | the lights of the town were shining in the darkness below:* beam, radiate, gleam, glow, glint, glimmer, sparkle, twinkle, glitter, glisten, shimmer, flash, fluoresce, luminesce.
2 *he shone his shoes:* polish, burnish, buff, wax, gloss, rub up.
3 *they shone at university:* excel, be outstanding, be brilliant, be successful, stand out.
▷**noun** *linseed oil restores the shine:* polish, burnish, gleam, gloss, lustre, sheen, patina.

shiny adjective *a shiny red mackintosh:* glossy, glassy, bright, polished, gleaming, satiny, sheeny, lustrous.
OPPOSITES: matt.

ship noun boat, vessel, craft.
▷**verb**
1 *the wine was shipped overseas:* transport, convey, carry, send, dispatch, deliver, post, mail.
2 *the company is preparing to ship its GPS-enabled hand-held games console:* supply, market, offer, sell, retail, make available, launch, promote, package, bundle.

> WORD LINKS
> **marine, maritime, nautical** relating to ships or the sea

shipment noun load, cargo, consignment, delivery, batch, payload; freight, goods, merchandise.

shirk verb *she did not try to shirk her duties:* evade, dodge, avoid, get out of, sidestep, shrink from, slide out of, skip, miss; neglect; informal duck out of; Brit. informal skive off.

shiver verb *she was shivering with fear:* tremble, quiver, shake, shudder, quaver, quake, vibrate.

S

▷ **noun** *she gave a shiver as the door opened:* tremble, quiver, shake, shudder, quaver, quake, tremor, twitch.

shivery adjective trembling, trembly, quivery, shaky, shuddering, shuddery, quavery, quaking; cold, chilly.

shock noun
1 *the news came as a shock:* blow, upset; surprise, revelation, bolt from the blue, thunderbolt, rude awakening, eye-opener; informal bombshell.
2 *you gave me a shock:* fright, scare, jolt, start; informal turn.
3 *the first shock of the earthquake:* impact, blow, shock wave, jolt, jar, shake, jerk, vibration, reverberation.
▷ **verb** *the revelations shocked the nation:* stun, rock, stagger, astound, astonish, amaze, startle, surprise, dumbfound, shake, take aback, throw, unnerve, traumatize, distress, upset, disturb, disquiet, unsettle; appal, horrify, outrage, revolt, disgust, nauseate, sicken.

shocking adjective *it was the next day before they heard the shocking news:* startling, surprising, astonishing, amazing, unexpected, unforeseen, staggering, stunning; extraordinary, remarkable, dramatic; disturbing, unsettling, perturbing, disconcerting, disquieting; frightening, alarming, scary; appalling, horrifying, horrific, dreadful, awful, frightful, terrible; scandalous, outrageous, disgraceful, vile, abominable, abhorrent, atrocious; odious, repugnant, disgusting, nauseating, sickening.

shoddy adjective
1 *shoddy goods:* poor-quality, inferior, second-rate, cheap, trashy, jerry-built; informal rubbishy; Brit. informal duff.
2 *shoddy workmanship:* careless, slapdash, sloppy, slipshod, scrappy, crude; negligent, cursory.

shoot verb
1 *they shot him in the street | he was shot in the leg:* gun down, mow down; hit, wound, injure; put a bullet in, pick off, kill; informal blast.
2 *they shot at the enemy:* fire, open fire, aim, snipe, let fly; bombard, shell, strafe.
3 *a car shot past:* race, speed, flash, dash, dart, rush, hurtle, streak, whizz, go like lightning, zoom, charge; career, sweep, fly, wing; informal belt, tear, zip, whip, go hell for leather; Brit. informal bomb, bucket, shift.
4 *these scenes were shot in Tunisia:* film, photograph, take, capture, record; televise, video; informal snap.

shop noun *a shop selling clothes:* store, outlet, retail outlet, retail unit, boutique, cash and carry, emporium, department store, supermarket, superstore, chain store, concession, market, mart, trading post; Brit. hypermarket.

shopper noun buyer, purchaser, customer, consumer, client, patron.

shore[1] noun *he swam out from the shore:* seashore, beach, foreshore, sands, shoreline, waterside, front, coast, seaboard.

> WORD LINKS
> **littoral** relating to the shore of the sea or a lake

shore[2] verb *we had to shore up the building:* prop up, hold up, bolster, support, brace, buttress, strengthen, fortify, reinforce, underpin.

short adjective
1 *a short red-haired woman emerged from behind the door:* small, little, petite, tiny, diminutive; Scottish wee; informal pint-sized.
2 *a short report:* concise, brief, succinct, compact, summary, economical, crisp, pithy, epigrammatic, laconic, thumbnail, abridged, abbreviated, condensed, summarized, truncated; formal synoptic.
3 *a short inspection of the new system:* brief, quick; cursory, fleeting, passing.
4 *money is a bit short:* scarce, in short supply, scant, insufficient, deficient, inadequate, lacking, wanting.
5 *he was rather short with her:* curt, sharp, abrupt, blunt, brusque, terse, offhand, gruff, surly, testy, rude, uncivil; informal snappy.
OPPOSITES: tall, long, plentiful.
▫ **in short**
in short, we don't have the players to beat them: briefly, in a word, in a nutshell, in essence, to come to the point; in conclusion, in summary, to sum up.
▫ **short of**
1 *I know you're short of cash right now:* deficient in, lacking, wanting, in need of, low on, short on, missing; informal strapped for, pushed for.
2 *short of searching everyone, there is nothing we can do:* apart from, other than, aside from, besides, except for, without.

shortage noun *the shortage of people with adequate training:* scarcity, dearth, paucity, poverty, insufficiency, deficiency, inadequacy, famine, lack, want, deficit, shortfall.
OPPOSITES: abundance.

shortcoming noun *he was fully aware of his own shortcomings:* defect, fault, flaw, imperfection, deficiency, limitation, failing, drawback, weakness, weak point, foible, frailty, vice.
OPPOSITES: strength.

shorten verb *you can shorten your essay without losing its balance:* cut, abridge, trim, crop, pare down, prune; curtail, truncate, contract; condense, abbreviate, precis, synopsize, compress; reduce, shrink, diminish, dock.
OPPOSITES: extend.

S

short-lived adjective
this was a short-lived setback: brief, short, momentary, temporary, impermanent, cursory, fleeting, passing, fugitive, lightning, transitory, transient, ephemeral, quick.
OPPOSITES: long-lasting.

shortly adverb
1 *she will be with you shortly:* soon, presently, in a little while, at any moment, in a minute, before long, by and by; N. Amer. momentarily; informal anon, any time now, pretty soon, in a jiffy.
2 *'I know,' he replied shortly:* curtly, sharply, abruptly, bluntly, brusquely, tersely, gruffly, testily, rudely; informal snappily.

short-sighted adjective
1 *I'm a little short-sighted:* myopic; N. Amer. nearsighted.
2 *the cost-cutting measure was criticized by union leaders as short-sighted:* ill-considered, ill-advised, misguided, lacking foresight, hasty, short-term; unimaginative, lacking imagination.
OPPOSITES: long-sighted, far-sighted.

short-tempered adjective
he was notoriously short-tempered: irritable, irascible, hot-tempered, quick-tempered, fiery, touchy, volatile, crabby, crotchety, cantankerous, prickly; informal snappish, snappy.
OPPOSITES: easy-going, placid.

shot noun
1 *a shot rang out:* report, crack, bang, blast, explosion; (shots) gunfire.
2 *a winning shot:* stroke, hit, strike; kick, throw, pitch, lob.
3 *a shot of us on holiday:* photograph, photo, snapshot, picture, print, slide, still; informal snap.

shoulder verb
1 *Britain shouldered the primary responsibility:* take on, undertake, accept, assume; bear, carry.
2 *another lad shouldered him aside:* push, shove, thrust, jostle, elbow, force, bulldoze, bundle.

shout verb
'Help,' he shouted: yell, cry, call, roar, howl, bellow, bawl, bark, clamour, shriek, scream; raise your voice; informal holler.
OPPOSITES: whisper.
▷noun *a shout of pain:* yell, cry, call, roar, howl, bellow, bawl, shriek, scream; informal holler.
OPPOSITES: whisper.

shove verb
1 *she shoved him back into the chair:* push, thrust, propel, drive, force, ram, knock, elbow, shoulder; jostle, bundle, hustle, manhandle.
2 *she shoved past him:* push, force your way, barge, elbow your way, shoulder your way.

▷noun *a hefty shove:* push, thrust, bump, jolt.

show verb
1 *the stitches do not show:* be visible, be seen, be in view, be obvious.
2 *he wouldn't show the picture:* display, exhibit, put on show/display, put on view, uncover, reveal.
3 *she was showing signs of mental instability:* manifest, exhibit, reveal, display; betray.
4 *I'll show you how the device works:* demonstrate, explain, describe, illustrate; teach, instruct.
5 *experts say this shows the benefit of regular inspections:* prove, demonstrate, confirm; substantiate, corroborate, verify, establish, attest, certify, testify, bear out.
6 *a young woman showed them to their seats:* direct, guide, take, escort, accompany, conduct, lead, usher, steer, shepherd.
OPPOSITES: conceal.
▷noun
1 *a spectacular show of bluebells:* display, array, exhibition, spectacle.
2 *the motor show:* exhibition, exposition, fair, extravaganza, spectacle; N. Amer. exhibit.
3 *the show starts at 7.30:* entertainment, performance, presentation, production, spectacle.
4 *she was wary of any show of affection:* appearance, display, manifestation, exhibition.
□ show off (informal) *he was showing off, trying to make a really big impression:* behave affectedly, put on airs, put on an act, swagger around, strut, strike an attitude, posture; draw attention to yourself; informal swank.
□ show something off
she showed off her gold medal to the crowd: display, show to advantage, exhibit, demonstrate, parade, draw attention to, flaunt.
□ show up
1 *cancers show up on X-rays:* be visible, be obvious, be seen, be revealed.
2 (informal) *they were billed to appear but didn't show up:* arrive, turn up, appear, come, get here/there, enter, present yourself, make it, materialize; informal show your face.
□ show someone/something up
1 *the sun showed up the shabbiness of the room:* expose, reveal, make obvious, highlight, draw attention to.
2 (informal) *they showed him up in front of his friends.* See HUMILIATE.

showdown noun
the team will have six days to prepare for their showdown with the champions: confrontation, clash, fight, battle, head-to-head, face-off.

shower noun
1 *a shower of rain:* light fall, drizzle, sprinkling, mizzle.

S

2 *a shower of arrows:* volley, hail, salvo, bombardment, barrage, fusillade, cannonade.
3 *a shower of awards:* avalanche, deluge, flood, spate, flurry; profusion, abundance, plethora.
▷ **verb**
1 *confetti showered down on us:* rain, fall, hail.
2 *she showered them with gifts:* deluge, flood, inundate, swamp, engulf; overwhelm, overload, snow under.
3 *he faced the accusation of showering honours on his cronies:* lavish, heap, bestow freely.

showing noun
1 *another showing of the series:* broadcast, airing, presentation.
2 *the party's present showing is not that impressive:* performance, record, track record, results, success, achievement.

show-off noun (informal) *he was a show-off with a big, flashy car:* exhibitionist, extrovert, swaggerer, self-publicist; informal poser, pseud.

showy adjective *she wore a great deal of showy costume jewellery:* ostentatious, flamboyant, extravagant, fancy, ornate, conspicuous; gaudy, garish, brash, vulgar, loud; informal flash, flashy, bling-bling.
OPPOSITES: restrained.

shred noun
1 *her dress was torn to shreds:* tatter, strip, ribbon, scrap, rag, fragment, sliver, tiny piece.
2 *there isn't a shred of evidence:* scrap, bit, speck, iota, particle, ounce, whit, jot, crumb, morsel, fragment, grain, drop, trace, scintilla; informal smidgen.
▷ **verb** *shred the cabbage finely:* chop, slice, cut, tear up.

shrewd adjective *a shrewd businessman:* astute, sharp-witted, sharp, acute, intelligent, clever, canny, perceptive, perspicacious, sagacious, wise; informal smart, on the ball.
OPPOSITES: stupid.

shriek verb *she shrieked with laughter:* scream, screech, squeal, squawk, roar, howl, shout, yelp; informal holler.
▷ **noun** *a shriek of laughter:* scream, screech, squeal, squawk, roar, howl, shout, yelp; informal holler.

shrill adjective *a shrill scream rent the air:* high-pitched, piercing, high, sharp, ear-piercing, ear-splitting, penetrating, screeching, shrieking, screechy.

shrine noun
1 *the shrine of St James:* holy place, temple, church, chapel, tabernacle, sanctuary, sanctum; tomb.
2 *a shrine to the Beatles:* memorial, monument.

shrink verb
1 *the workforce shrank to a thousand:* get smaller, contract, be diminished, reduce, decrease, dwindle, decline, fall off, drop off.
2 *he shrank back against the wall:* draw back, recoil, back away, retreat, withdraw, cringe, cower, quail.
3 *he doesn't shrink from naming names:* recoil, shy away, demur, flinch, have scruples, have misgivings, have qualms, be loath, be reluctant, be unwilling, be averse, fight shy of, be hesitant, be afraid, hesitate, baulk at.
OPPOSITES: expand, increase.

shrivel verb *full sun is likely to shrivel the leaves:* wither, shrink, wrinkle, wilt, dry up, desiccate, dehydrate, parch, frazzle.

shroud noun *a shroud of mist | a shroud of secrecy:* covering, cover, cloak, mantle, mask, blanket, layer, cloud, veil.
▷ **verb** *a mist shrouded the jetties:* cover, envelop, veil, cloak, blanket, screen, conceal, hide, mask, obscure.

shrug verb
□ **shrug something off**
he shrugged off suggestions that he was keen to quit politics: dismiss, play down, make light of, brush off; reject, deny; disregard, take no notice of, ignore, pay no heed to.

shudder verb *she shuddered at the thought:* shake, shiver, tremble, quiver, quake, vibrate, convulse, palpitate.
▷ **noun** *a shudder racked his body:* shake, shiver, tremor, tremble, trembling, quiver, quivering, quake, vibration, convulsion, palpitation.

shuffle verb
1 *they shuffled along the passage:* shamble, drag your feet, totter, stumble, dodder, hobble.
2 *she shuffled her feet:* scrape, drag, scuffle, scuff.
3 *he shuffled the cards:* mix up, mingle, rearrange, jumble.

shun verb *he was shunned in public by his former colleagues:* avoid, ignore, steer clear of, shy away from, keep your distance from, give a wide berth to, have nothing to do with; snub, give someone the cold shoulder, cold-shoulder, cut dead, look right through; reject, rebuff, spurn, ostracize; informal give someone the brush-off, freeze out; Brit. informal send to Coventry.
OPPOSITES: welcome.

shut verb *please shut the door:* close, pull/push to, slam, fasten; put the lid on, bar, lock, secure.
OPPOSITES: open, unlock.
□ **shut down**
the factory has shut down: cease trading, close, close down, cease operating, be shut down; informal fold.

S

□ **shut someone/something in**
they shut him in a small dark room:
confine, enclose, impound, shut up, pen
in/up, fence in, lock up/in, cage, imprison,
intern, incarcerate; N. Amer. corral; formal
immure.

□ **shut someone/something out**
1 *he shut me out of the house:* lock out,
keep out, refuse entrance to.
2 *she shut out the memories:* block,
suppress.
3 *clouds shut out the stars:* keep out, block
out, screen, veil.

□ **shut up** (informal) *just shut up and listen:* be
quiet, keep quiet, hold your tongue; stop
talking; informal belt up.

shuttle verb *minibuses shuttle between the
centre and the car park:* ply, run, commute,
go/travel back and forth, go/travel to and
fro; ferry.

shy adjective *I was painfully shy:* bashful,
diffident, timid, reserved, reticent,
introverted, retiring, self-effacing,
withdrawn, timorous, mousy, nervous,
insecure, inhibited, repressed, self-
conscious, embarrassed.
OPPOSITES: confident.

□ **shy away from**
*he's not one to shy away from speaking his
mind:* flinch from, demur at, recoil from,
hang back from, have scruples about, have
misgivings about, have qualms about,
be chary about, be diffident about, be
bashful about, be coy about; be loath to, be
reluctant to, be unwilling to, be disinclined
to, be hesitant about, hesitate to, baulk at.

sick adjective
1 *the children are still sick:* ill, unwell,
poorly, ailing, indisposed; Brit. off colour;
informal laid up, under the weather.
2 *he was starting to feel sick:* nauseous,
nauseated, queasy, bilious; informal green
about the gills.
3 *I'm sick of this music:* bored with, tired
of, weary of; informal fed up.
4 (informal) *a sick joke:* macabre, black,
ghoulish, morbid, perverted, gruesome,
sadistic, cruel.
OPPOSITES: well.

□ **be sick** (Brit.)
vomit; informal throw up, chuck up.

sicken verb
1 *the stench sickened him:* make someone
feel sick, make someone feel nauseous;
turn someone's stomach, revolt, disgust;
informal make someone want to throw up;
N. Amer. informal gross out.
2 *she sickened and died:* become ill, fall ill,
be taken ill.
3 *I'm sickening for something:* become ill
with, fall ill with, be taken ill with, show
symptoms of, develop, come down with;
Brit. go down with.

sickening adjective *a sickening stench | his
sickening crimes:* nauseating, repulsive,

revolting, disgusting, repellent, repugnant,
appalling, obnoxious, nauseous, vile, nasty,
foul, loathsome, offensive, objectionable,
off-putting, distasteful, gruesome; informal
gross.

sickly adjective
1 *a thin, sickly child:* unhealthy, in poor
health, delicate, frail, weak.
2 *a tall boy with a sickly complexion:* pale,
wan, pasty, sallow, pallid, ashen, anaemic.
3 *the walls were painted a sickly green:*
bilious, lurid, garish.
4 *sickly love songs:* sentimental, mawkish,
cloying, sugary, syrupy, saccharine; informal
mushy, slushy, schmaltzy, corny; Brit. informal
soppy.
OPPOSITES: healthy.

sickness noun
1 *she was absent through sickness | he
was prone to colds and sicknesses:* illness,
disease, ailment, complaint, infection,
infirmity, indisposition; literary malady;
informal bug, virus; Brit. informal lurgy.
2 *a wave of sickness:* nausea, biliousness,
queasiness, vomiting.
OPPOSITES: health.

side noun
1 *the side of the road:* edge, border, verge,
margin, fringes, flank, bank; boundary,
perimeter, periphery, extremity, outer
limit, limits, bounds.
2 *the wrong side of the road:* half, part;
carriageway, lane.
3 *the east side of the city:* district, quarter,
area, region, part, neighbourhood, sector,
section, zone.
4 *one side of the paper:* surface, face;
technical plane.
5 *his side of the argument:* point of view,
viewpoint, perspective, opinion, way of
thinking, standpoint, stance, position,
outlook, slant, angle, aspect.
6 *the losing side in the war:* faction, camp,
bloc, party, wing.
7 *the players in their side:* team, squad,
line-up.
OPPOSITES: centre, end.

▷ **adjective** *a side issue:* subordinate,
secondary, minor, lesser, peripheral,
incidental, ancillary, subsidiary, of little
account, extraneous.
OPPOSITES: central.

□ **side with**
the English love siding with the underdog.
See TAKE SOMEONE'S SIDE.

□ **take someone's side**
my mother always took his side: support,
side with, be on someone's side, stand by,
back, give someone your backing, be loyal
to, defend, champion, ally yourself with,
sympathize with, favour.

> WORD LINKS
> **lateral** relating to the side of something

sideline noun *he founded the company as
a sideline:* secondary occupation, second

job, second string to your bow; hobby, leisure activity/pursuit, recreation.
□ **on the sidelines**
without taking part, without getting involved.

sidelong adjective *a sidelong glance:* indirect, oblique, sideways, sideward; surreptitious, furtive, covert, sly.
OPPOSITES: straight, open.
▷ **adverb** *he looked sidelong at her:* indirectly, obliquely, sideways, out of the corner of your eye; surreptitiously, furtively, covertly, slyly.
OPPOSITES: straight, openly.

sidestep verb *he neatly sidestepped the questions about crime:* avoid, evade, dodge, circumvent, skirt round, bypass; informal duck.

sidetrack verb *he allows himself to be constantly sidetracked by minor problems:* distract, divert, deflect, draw away.

sideways adverb
1 *I slid off sideways:* to the side, laterally.
2 *the expansion slots are mounted sideways:* edgewise, sidewards, side first, edgeways, end on.
3 *he looked sideways at her.* See SIDELONG adverb.
▷ **adjective** *a sideways look.* See SIDELONG adjective.

sidle verb *she sidled into the room apologetically:* creep, sneak, slink, slip, slide, steal, edge, inch, move furtively.
OPPOSITES: stride.

siege noun blockade, encirclement.
OPPOSITES: relief.

sieve noun *use a sieve to strain the mixture:* strainer, filter, riddle, screen.
▷ **verb**
1 *sieve the mixture into a bowl:* strain, sift, screen, filter.
2 *the coins were sieved from the ash:* separate out, filter out, sift, sort out, divide, segregate, extract.

sift verb
1 *sift the flour into a large bowl:* sieve, strain, screen, filter.
2 *we sift out unsuitable applications:* separate out, filter out, sort out, put to one side, weed out, get rid of, remove.
3 *intelligence officers were sifting every scrap of information:* search through, look through, examine, inspect, scrutinize, pore over, investigate, analyse, dissect, review.

sigh verb
1 *she sighed with relief:* breathe out, exhale; groan, moan.
2 *the wind sighed in the trees:* rustle, whisper, murmur, sough.
3 *he sighed for days gone by:* yearn, long, pine, ache, grieve, cry for/over, weep for/over, rue, miss, mourn, lament, hanker for/after.

sight noun
1 *she has excellent sight:* eyesight, vision, eyes.
2 *her first sight of the house:* view, glimpse, glance, look.
3 *they were now within sight of the enemy:* range of vision, field of vision, view.
4 *the city's historic sights:* landmark, place of interest, monument, spectacle, view, marvel, wonder.
▷ **verb** *one of the helicopters sighted wreckage:* glimpse, catch/get a glimpse of, catch sight of, see, spot, spy, notice, observe, make out.
□ **catch sight of**
when she caught sight of him she smiled: glimpse, catch/get a glimpse of, see, spot, spy, make out, pick out; notice, observe, perceive, discern, sight; literary behold, espy.
□ **set your sights on**
Katya is setting her sights on a gold medal: aspire to, aim at/for, try for, strive for/towards, work towards.

WORD LINKS
optical, visual relating to sight

USAGE

Do not confuse **sight** and **site**. **Sight** chiefly means 'the ability to see'. As a noun, **site** means 'a place where something is located or has happened' (*the site of the battle*).

---

sightseer noun tourist, visitor, tripper; Brit. holidaymaker.

sign noun
1 *the shops are full, a sign that the recession is past its worst:* indication, signal, symptom, pointer, suggestion, intimation, mark, manifestation, demonstration, token, evidence.
2 *a sign of things to come:* portent, omen, warning, forewarning, augury, presage; promise, threat.
3 *at his sign the soldiers followed:* gesture, signal, wave, gesticulation, nod, cue, prompt.
4 *signs saying 'keep out':* notice, signpost, signboard.
5 *the dancers were daubed with signs:* symbol, mark, cipher, letter, character, figure, hieroglyph, ideogram, rune, emblem, device, logo.
▷ **verb**
1 *he signed the letter:* autograph, endorse, initial, countersign.
2 *the government signed the agreement:* endorse, validate, certify, authenticate, sanction, authorize; agree to, approve, ratify, adopt.
3 *we have signed a new player:* recruit, hire, engage, employ, take on, appoint, sign on/up, enlist.
4 *she signed to Susan to leave:* gesture, signal, give a sign to, motion; wave, beckon, nod.
□ **sign on/up**
he signed on for a career in the Air Force:

S

enlist, join up, take a job, enrol, register, volunteer.
□ **sign someone on/up**. See **SIGN** verb sense 3.

signal¹ noun
1 *he raised his hand as a signal to stop:* gesture, sign, wave, gesticulation, cue, prompt, indication, warning, motion.
2 *a clear signal that the company is in trouble:* indication, sign, symptom, hint, pointer, intimation, clue, demonstration, evidence, proof.
3 *the announcement was the signal for scores of journalists to gather at the stadium:* cue, prompt, impetus, stimulus; informal go-ahead.
▷ **verb**
1 *the driver signalled to her to cross:* gesture, sign, direct, motion; wave, beckon, nod.
2 *they signalled their displeasure by refusing to cooperate:* indicate, show, express, communicate, convey.
3 *his death signals the end of an era:* mark, signify, mean, be a sign of, be evidence of, herald.

signal² adjective
although a signal failure, the campaign produced one benefit: notable, noteworthy, remarkable, striking, glaring, significant, momentous, memorable, unforgettable, obvious, special, extraordinary, exceptional, conspicuous.

significance noun
1 *a matter of considerable significance:* importance, import, consequence, seriousness, gravity, weight, magnitude; formal moment.
2 *the significance of his remarks became clear:* meaning, sense, signification, import, thrust, drift, gist, implication, message, essence, substance, point.

significant adjective
1 *a significant increase in sales:* notable, noteworthy, worthy of attention, worthy of note, important, of importance, of consequence, appreciable; considerable, sizeable, marked, striking, remarkable, serious.
2 *a significant look:* meaningful, expressive, eloquent, suggestive, knowing, telling.
OPPOSITES: insignificant.

significantly adverb
1 *the results are significantly better this year:* notably, appreciably; markedly, considerably.
2 *he paused significantly:* meaningfully, suggestively, knowingly.

signify verb
1 *this signified a fundamental change:* be evidence of, be a sign of, mark, signal, mean, spell, be symptomatic of, herald, indicate.
2 *the egg signifies life:* mean, denote, designate, represent, symbolize, stand for.

3 *signify your agreement by signing below:* express, indicate, show, proclaim, declare.

silence noun
1 *the silence of the night:* quiet, quietness, still, stillness, hush, tranquillity, peace, quietude.
2 *she had withdrawn into sullen silence:* speechlessness, muteness; taciturnity, reticence.
OPPOSITES: noise, speech.
▷ **verb**
1 *he silenced her with a kiss:* quieten, hush, shut up.
2 *the government's attempts to silence the press:* keep quiet, gag, muzzle, censor.
3 *the screens silenced the traffic noise outside:* muffle, deaden, soften, mute, smother, dampen, damp down, mask, suppress, reduce.

silent adjective
1 *the streets were dark and silent:* completely quiet, still, hushed.
2 *they remained obstinately silent:* speechless, quiet, unspeaking, dumb, mute, taciturn, uncommunicative, tight-lipped; informal mum.
3 *the two women caught each other's eye in silent agreement:* unspoken, wordless, unsaid, unexpressed, unvoiced, tacit, implicit, understood.
OPPOSITES: audible, noisy.

silently adverb
1 *Nancy crept silently up the stairs:* quietly, inaudibly, noiselessly, soundlessly, in silence.
2 *they drove on silently:* without a word, saying nothing, in silence.
3 *I silently said goodbye:* without words, wordlessly, in your head.

silhouette noun
the silhouette of the dome: outline, contours, profile, form, shape, figure, shadow.
▷ **verb** *the castle was silhouetted against the sky:* outline, delineate, define; stand out.

silky adjective
she had long, silky hair: smooth, soft, sleek, fine, glossy, satiny, silken.

silly adjective
1 *don't be so silly | that was a really silly remark:* foolish, stupid, unintelligent, idiotic, brainless, mindless, witless, imbecilic, senseless; imprudent, thoughtless, rash, reckless, foolhardy, irresponsible, unwise, injudicious, misguided; mad, scatterbrained, feather-brained; frivolous, inane, immature, childish, puerile, empty-headed; informal crazy, thick, dim, dim-witted, half-witted, dippy; Brit. informal daft, scatty.
2 *he would brood about silly things:* trivial, trifling, frivolous, footling, petty, small, insignificant, unimportant; informal piffling.
OPPOSITES: sensible.

silt noun *the flooding brought more silt:* sediment, deposit, alluvium, mud.

similar adjective
1 *you two are very similar:* alike, much the same, indistinguishable, almost identical; informal much of a muchness.
2 *northern India and similar areas:* comparable, like, corresponding, equivalent, analogous.
OPPOSITES: different, unlike.
□ similar to
other parts were similar to Wales: like, much the same as, comparable to.
□ be similar to
resemble, be like, look like, have the appearance of, approach.

similarity noun *the similarity between him and his daughter was startling:* resemblance, likeness, comparability, correspondence, parallel, equivalence, uniformity; formal similitude.
OPPOSITES: difference.

similarly adverb *The diaries of politicians tend to be self-justificatory. Similarly, autobiographies may be idealized.:* likewise, in similar fashion, in like manner, comparably, correspondingly, uniformly, indistinguishably, analogously, equivalently, in the same way, the same, identically.
OPPOSITES: differently.

similitude noun (formal). See SIMILARITY.

simmer verb
1 *the soup was simmering on the stove:* boil gently, cook gently, bubble.
2 *she was simmering with resentment:* be furious, seethe, fume, smoulder, be enraged, be angry, be incensed, be infuriated; informal be steamed up, be hot under the collar.
□ simmer down
he stormed out of the theatre in a rage, but soon simmered down: calm down, cool off/down, be placated, control yourself, become calmer, become quieter, quieten down, become less angry.

simple adjective
1 *it's really pretty simple:* straightforward, easy, uncomplicated, effortless, painless, undemanding, elementary, child's play; informal as easy as pie, a piece of cake, a cinch, no sweat, a doddle, a pushover, kids' stuff, a breeze; Brit. informal easy-peasy.
2 *he set out to explain everything in simple, non-technical language:* clear, plain, straightforward, intelligible, comprehensible, uncomplicated, in words of one syllable, accessible; informal user-friendly.
3 *a simple whitewashed room with two chairs and a huge bed:* plain, unadorned, undecorated, unembellished, unornamented, unelaborate, basic, unsophisticated, no-frills; classic, understated, uncluttered, restrained.

4 *the simple truth is that Australia were a better team:* candid, frank, honest, sincere, plain, absolute, unqualified, bald, stark, unadorned, unvarnished, unembellished; basic, fundamental.
5 *simple country people:* unpretentious, unsophisticated, ordinary, unaffected, unassuming, modest, natural, honest-to-goodness.
OPPOSITES: difficult, complex, fancy, sophisticated.

simplicity noun
1 *the simplicity of the recipes:* straightforwardness, ease, effortlessness.
2 *the simplicity of the language:* clarity, clearness, plainness, intelligibility, comprehensibility, straightforwardness, accessibility.
3 *the building's simplicity:* plainness, lack/absence of adornment, lack/absence of decoration, clean lines, austerity, spareness.
4 *the simplicity of their lifestyle:* unpretentiousness, ordinariness, lack of sophistication, lack of affectation, naturalness.
OPPOSITES: complexity, elaborateness.

simplify verb *the government intends to simplify the existing legislation:* make simple/simpler, make less complex, make easy/easier to understand, make plainer, clarify, make more comprehensible/intelligible; paraphrase, put in words of one syllable.
OPPOSITES: complicate.

simplistic adjective *their simplistic view of the debate just sees the extremes:* facile, superficial, oversimple, oversimplified, schematic, black and white; shallow, jejune, naive.
OPPOSITES: profound.

simply adverb
1 *he spoke simply and forcefully:* straightforwardly, clearly, plainly, intelligibly, lucidly, unambiguously, in words of one syllable.
2 *she was dressed simply in dark jeans and a black T-shirt:* plainly, without adornment, without decoration, without ornament/ornamentation, soberly.
3 *they lived simply:* unpretentiously, modestly, quietly.
4 *they are welcomed simply because they have plenty of money:* merely, just, purely, solely, only.
5 *Mrs Marks was simply livid:* utterly, absolutely, completely, positively, really; informal plain.
6 *it's simply the best thing ever written:* without doubt, unquestionably, undeniably, incontrovertibly, certainly, categorically.

simulate verb
1 *they simulated pleasure:* feign, pretend, fake, sham, affect, put on, give the appearance of.

S

2 *a training exercise intended to simulate conditions created by a nuclear strike:* imitate, reproduce, replicate, duplicate, mimic.

simulated adjective
1 *she howled in simulated anguish:* feigned, fake, mock, affected, sham, insincere, false, bogus; informal pretend, put on, phoney.
2 *simulated leather:* artificial, imitation, fake, faux, mock, synthetic, man-made, ersatz.
OPPOSITES: real.

simultaneous adjective *officers carried out simultaneous raids on homes across the city:* concurrent, at the same time, contemporaneous, coinciding, coincident, synchronous, synchronized; formal concomitant.

simultaneously adverb *the changes did not occur simultaneously:* at the same time, at one and the same time, at the same instant/moment, at once, concurrently; together, in unison, in concert, in chorus; formal concomitantly.

sin noun
1 *a sin in the eyes of God:* immoral act, wrong, wrongdoing, act of evil/wickedness, transgression, crime, offence, misdeed, misdemeanour.
2 *the human capacity for sin:* wickedness, wrongdoing, wrong, evil, evil-doing, sinfulness, immorality, iniquity, vice, crime.
3 (informal) *wasting money—it's a sin:* scandal, crime, disgrace, outrage.
OPPOSITES: virtue.
▷ **verb** *I have sinned:* behave immorally, transgress, do wrong, go astray.

sincere adjective
1 *they offered their sincere thanks to Paul:* heartfelt, wholehearted, profound, deep; genuine, real, unfeigned, unaffected, true, honest.
2 *a sincere person:* honest, genuine, truthful, straightforward, direct, frank, candid; informal straight, upfront, on the level.
OPPOSITES: insincere.

sincerely adverb *I sincerely hope that this scheme will succeed:* genuinely, honestly, really, truly, truthfully, wholeheartedly, earnestly, fervently, profoundly.
OPPOSITES: insincerely.

sincerity noun genuineness, straightforwardness, openness, candour; honesty, truthfulness, integrity, probity, trustworthiness.
OPPOSITES: insincerity.

sinewy adjective *he was tall, dark, and sinewy:* muscular, muscly, brawny, powerfully built, burly, strapping, sturdy, rugged, strong, powerful, athletic, muscle-bound; informal hunky.
OPPOSITES: puny.

sinful adjective
1 *sinful conduct:* immoral, wicked, morally wrong, evil, unrighteous, ungodly, bad, iniquitous, corrupt, criminal, nefarious, depraved, degenerate.
2 *a sinful waste of money:* reprehensible, scandalous, disgraceful, deplorable, shameful, criminal.
OPPOSITES: virtuous.

sinfulness noun immorality, wickedness, sin, wrongdoing, evil, ungodliness, evil-doing, iniquity, corruption, depravity, degeneracy, vice.
OPPOSITES: virtue.

sing verb
1 *Miguel began to sing the words softly to himself:* chant, croon, carol, trill, intone.
2 *the birds were singing:* warble, trill, chirp, chirrup, cheep, peep.

singe verb *the fire singed my sleeve:* scorch, burn, sear, char.

singer noun vocalist, soloist, songster, songstress, cantor, chanteuse.

single adjective
1 *a single red rose:* one only, sole, lone, solitary, by itself/yourself, unaccompanied, alone.
2 *one, two, or three single wires are strung between the posts:* individual, separate, distinct, particular.
3 *is she single?* unmarried, unattached, free, a bachelor, a spinster.
OPPOSITES: multiple, married.
□ **single someone/something out** *the prime minister singled him out for promotion:* select, pick out, choose, decide on; target, earmark, mark out, separate out, set apart.

> **WORD LINKS**
> **monomania** obsession with a single thing

single-handed adverb *he's been running the place single-handed:* by yourself, alone, on your own, solo, unaided, unassisted, without help, independently.

single-minded adjective *I've never met anyone so ambitious and single-minded:* determined, committed, unswerving, unwavering, resolute, purposeful, devoted, dedicated, uncompromising, tireless, tenacious, persistent, indefatigable, dogged.
OPPOSITES: half-hearted.

singly adverb *we should interview people singly and discreetly:* one by one, one at a time, one after the other, individually, separately, by yourself, on your own.
OPPOSITES: together.

singular adjective
1 *the gallery's singular capacity to attract sponsors:* remarkable, extraordinary, exceptional, outstanding, signal, notable, noteworthy; rare, unique, unparalleled,

unprecedented, amazing, astonishing, phenomenal, astounding; informal fantastic, terrific.
2 *why was she behaving in so singular a fashion?* strange, unusual, odd, peculiar, funny, curious, extraordinary, bizarre, eccentric, queer, unexpected, unfamiliar, abnormal, atypical, unconventional, out of the ordinary, untypical, puzzling, mysterious, perplexing, baffling, unaccountable; informal weird.

singularity noun
1 *his singularity of purpose:* uniqueness, oneness, unity, consistency; distinctiveness, individuality.
2 *a nobleman more remarkable for his singularities than his rank:* idiosyncrasy, quirk, foible, peculiarity, individuality, oddity, eccentricity.

sinister adjective
1 *there was a sinister undertone in his words:* menacing, threatening, ominous, forbidding, baleful, frightening, alarming, disturbing, disquieting, dark, black.
2 *a sinister motive:* evil, wicked, criminal, corrupt, nefarious, villainous, base, vile, malevolent, malicious; informal shady.
OPPOSITES: benign, innocent.

sink verb
1 *the sun was sinking towards the horizon:* descend, fall, drop, go down/downwards, set.
2 *the cruise liner sank yesterday:* founder, go under, go to the bottom, submerge, become submerged, be engulfed.
3 *they sank their ships:* scuttle, send to the bottom; Brit. scupper.
4 *sink the posts into the ground:* embed, insert, drive, dig, plant.
5 *the announcement sank hopes of a recovery:* destroy, ruin, wreck, put an end to, demolish, smash, shatter, dash; informal put paid to; Brit. informal scupper.
6 *Loretta sank into an armchair:* lower yourself, flop, collapse, drop down, slump; Brit. informal plonk yourself.
7 *she would never sink to your level:* stoop, lower yourself, descend.
OPPOSITES: rise.
□ **sink in**
he had to read the letter twice before its meaning sank in: register, be understood, be comprehended, be grasped, get through.

sinner noun wrongdoer, evil-doer, transgressor, reprobate, miscreant, offender, criminal; formal malefactor.
OPPOSITES: saint.

sinuous adjective
1 *a sinuous river:* winding, windy, serpentine, curving, twisting, meandering, snaking, zigzag, curling, coiling.
2 *her sinuous grace:* lithe, supple, agile, graceful, loose-limbed, limber, lissom.
OPPOSITES: straight, stiff.

sip verb *Amanda sipped her coffee:* drink

slowly; taste, sample.
▷ **noun** *a sip of whisky:* mouthful, swallow, drop, dram, nip, taste; informal swig.
OPPOSITES: gulp.

sit verb
1 *I sat down next to him:* take a seat, seat yourself, be seated, perch, ensconce yourself, plump yourself, flop; informal take the load/weight off your feet; Brit. informal plonk yourself, take a pew.
2 *she sat the package on the table:* put, place, set, lay, deposit, rest, stand; informal stick, dump, park; Brit. informal plonk, bung.
3 *she sat for Picasso:* pose, model.
4 *the committee sits on Saturday:* meet, assemble, convene, be in session.
OPPOSITES: stand.

site noun *the site of the battle:* location, place, position, situation, locality, spot, whereabouts, setting, context, environment, surroundings, ground, plot, field, theatre.
▷ **verb** *the public can anonymously leave weapons in bins sited at police stations:* place, put, position, situate, locate, station, install.

USAGE

Do not confuse **site** and **sight**. As a noun, **site** means 'a place where something is located or has happened', while **sight** chiefly means 'the ability to see' (*he lost his sight as a baby*).

sitting noun *all-night sittings:* session, meeting, assembly, hearing, period, term.
▷ **adjective** *a sitting position:* sedentary, seated.
OPPOSITES: standing.

sitting room noun living room, lounge, drawing room, reception room, salon, family room, front room; dated parlour.

situate verb *hypermarkets are usually situated on the outskirts of towns:* locate, position, place, put, site, build, station, establish.

situation noun
1 *the club's dire financial situation:* circumstances, state of affairs, state, condition; plight, predicament.
2 *I'll fill you in on the situation:* the facts, how things stand, the lie of the land, what's going on; Brit. the state of play; informal the score.
3 *the hotel's pleasant situation:* location, position, spot, site, setting, environment.
4 (formal) *he was offered a situation in America:* job, post, position, appointment, opening; employment.

six cardinal number sextet.

WORD LINKS
hexagon a six-sided figure

size noun *the room was of medium size:* dimensions, measurements, proportions,

S

magnitude, area, expanse; breadth, width, length, height, depth; immensity, hugeness, vastness; scale, extent, scope.

sizeable adjective *sizeable sums of money:* large, substantial, considerable, significant, largish, biggish, goodly, respectable, decent, handsome.
OPPOSITES: small.

sizzle verb *slabs of bacon sizzled in the pan:* crackle, hiss, frizzle, sputter, spit.

skeletal adjective
1 *a skeletal man:* emaciated, very thin, as thin as a rake, cadaverous, skin-and-bones, skinny, bony, gaunt; informal anorexic.
2 *a skeletal knowledge of ancient Roman history:* limited, patchy, sketchy, incomplete, outline, fragmentary, thumbnail.
OPPOSITES: fat, detailed.

skeleton noun
1 *the concrete skeleton of an unfinished building:* framework, frame, structure, bones, chassis.
2 *a topic or scenario will give the children the skeleton of a story:* outline, rough draft, abstract, bare bones, plan, summary.
▷ adjective *a skeleton staff:* minimum, minimal, basic; essential.

sketch noun
1 *a sketch of the proposed design:* preliminary drawing, outline; diagram, design, plan; informal rough.
2 *she gave a rough sketch of what had happened:* outline, rundown, main points, thumbnail sketch, bare bones; summary, synopsis, precis, résumé.
3 *a biographical sketch:* description, portrait, profile, portrayal, depiction, cameo.
4 *a hilarious sketch:* skit, scene, routine, piece, item.
▷ verb
1 *he sketched the garden:* draw, portray, depict, rough out, outline.
2 *the company sketched out its plans:* describe, outline, give a brief idea of, rough out; summarize, precis.

sketchily adverb *the idea is only sketchily outlined in the prologue:* perfunctorily, cursorily, incompletely, patchily, vaguely, imprecisely; hastily, hurriedly.

sketchy adjective *he has only been able to provide the police with sketchy details of the youths:* incomplete, limited, patchy, fragmentary, cursory, perfunctory, scanty, vague, imprecise.
OPPOSITES: detailed.

skilful adjective *he was also a skilful diplomat:* expert, accomplished, skilled, proficient, masterly, virtuoso, consummate, brilliant, talented, gifted, adept, adroit, deft, dexterous, good; informal mean, wicked, crack, ace.
OPPOSITES: incompetent.

skill noun
1 *his skill as a politician:* expertise, expertness, adeptness, adroitness, deftness, dexterity, ability, prowess, brilliance, flair, mastery, competence, capability, aptitude, artistry, virtuosity, talent.
2 *practical skills such as cooking:* ability, facility, faculty, strength, gift, talent, technique, knack, accomplishment, attainment.
OPPOSITES: incompetence.

skilled adjective *a team of skilled engineers:* expert, accomplished, skilful, proficient, talented, gifted, adept, adroit, deft, dexterous, able, good, competent, capable, experienced, trained; informal crack.
OPPOSITES: unskilled.

skim verb
1 *you can skim off the fat before using the broth:* remove, cream off, scoop off.
2 *the boat skimmed over the water:* glide, sail, skate, slide, float, dance.
3 *he skimmed the pebble across the water:* throw, toss, cast, pitch; bounce.
4 *she skimmed through the newspaper:* glance, flick, flip, leaf, thumb, read quickly, scan, run your eye over.
5 *Hannah skimmed over this part of the story:* gloss over, skate over.

skimp verb *don't skimp on the quantity:* stint, scrimp, economize, cut back, be sparing, be frugal, be mean, be parsimonious, cut corners; informal be stingy, be mingy, be tight.

skimpy adjective *she was wearing a very skimpy outfit:* tiny, short, low, low-cut, revealing, indecent.
OPPOSITES: voluminous.

skin noun
1 *leopard skins:* hide, pelt, fleece.
2 *a banana skin:* peel, rind; Botany integument.
3 *milk with a skin on it:* film, layer, membrane.
4 *the plane's skin was damaged:* casing, exterior.
▷ verb
1 *first skin the tomatoes:* peel, pare.
2 *he skinned his knee:* graze, scrape, abrade, bark, rub something raw, chafe; Medicine excoriate.
□ **by the skin of your teeth** only just, just, narrowly, by a hair's breadth, by a very small margin; informal by a whisker.

WORD LINKS
cutaneous relating to or affecting the skin
subcutaneous situated or applied under the skin
dermatology the branch of medicine concerned with skin disorders

---

skinny adjective. See **THIN** adjective sense 3.

s

skip verb

1 *the girls skipped down the path:* prance, dance, caper, trip, gambol, frisk, romp, cavort.

2 *we skipped the boring stuff:* omit, leave out, miss out, dispense with, pass over, skim over, disregard; informal give something a miss.

3 *I skipped school:* miss; Brit. play truant from; Brit. informal skive off.

skirmish noun *the unit was caught up in several skirmishes:* fight, battle, clash, conflict, encounter, engagement, combat; informal scrap.

▷ **verb** *they skirmished with enemy soldiers:* fight, do battle with, engage with, close with, combat, clash with.

skirt verb

1 *he skirted the city:* go round, walk round, circle.

2 *the fields that skirt the highway:* border, edge, flank, line, lie alongside.

3 *he carefully skirted round the subject:* avoid, evade, sidestep, dodge, pass over, gloss over; informal duck.

skit noun *a skit on daytime chat shows:* comedy sketch, comedy act, parody, pastiche, burlesque, satire; informal spoof, take-off, send-up.

skittish adjective

1 *his horse was skittish:* restive, excitable, nervous, frisky, jumpy, highly strung.

2 *she grew increasingly skittish:* playful, lively, high-spirited, sportive, frisky, unpredictable.

OPPOSITES: relaxed, calm.

skulduggery noun *there is no evidence to support any allegations of skulduggery:* underhand activity, fraudulent activity, dishonesty, sharp practice, chicanery, cheating, trickery; informal shenanigans; Brit. informal jiggery-pokery.

skulk verb *he spent most of his time skulking about in the corridors:* lurk, loiter, hide; creep, sneak, slink, prowl.

skull noun cranium.

> WORD LINKS
> **cranial** relating to the skull

slab noun *slabs of concrete:* piece, block, hunk, chunk, lump, slice, cake, tablet, brick.

slack adjective

1 *the rope went slack:* loose, limp.

2 *slack skin:* flaccid, flabby, loose, sagging, saggy.

3 *business is rather slack:* sluggish, slow, quiet, slow-moving, flat, depressed, stagnant.

4 *slack accounting procedures:* lax, negligent, remiss, careless, slapdash, slipshod, sloppy, lackadaisical, inefficient, casual; informal slap-happy.

OPPOSITES: taut, brisk, punctilious.

▷ **noun**

1 *the rope had some slack in it:* looseness, play, give.

2 *foreign demand will help pick up the slack:* surplus, excess, residue, spare capacity.

3 *a little slack in the daily routine:* lull, pause, respite, break, hiatus, breathing space; informal let-up, breather.

▷ **verb** (Brit. informal) *she ticked the girls off if she caught them slacking:* idle, shirk, be lazy, be indolent, waste time, lounge about; Brit. informal skive.

slacken verb

1 *he slackened his grip:* loosen, release, relax, loose, lessen, weaken.

2 *the rain is slackening:* decrease, lessen, subside, ease up/off, let up, abate, slack off, diminish, die down, fall off.

OPPOSITES: tighten, increase.

slacker noun (informal). See LAYABOUT.

slake verb *slake your thirst with a citron pressé:* quench, satisfy, sate, satiate, relieve, assuage.

slam verb *he slammed the door behind him:* bang, throw shut, crash.

slander noun *he could sue us for slander:* defamation of character, character assassination; misrepresentation, scandalmongering, malicious gossip, disparagement, denigration; lie, slur, smear, false accusation; formal calumny; informal mud-slinging.

▷ **verb** *they were accused of slandering the minister:* defame, malign, blacken someone's name, speak ill of, smear, cast aspersions on, tarnish, taint; traduce, vilify, disparage, denigrate, run down; literary besmirch, sully someone's reputation.

> USAGE
>
> Note that **slander** is the crime of making a false and damaging statement about someone; with the crime of **libel** the damaging statements are made in print rather than spoken.

slanderous adjective *you have no right to make such slanderous accusations:* defamatory, disparaging, libellous, pejorative, false, misrepresentative, scurrilous, scandalous, malicious, abusive, insulting.

OPPOSITES: complimentary.

slang noun informal language, colloquialisms, patois, argot, cant.

slant verb

1 *the floor was slanting:* slope, tilt, incline, be at an angle, tip, cant, lean, dip, pitch, shelve, list, bank.

2 *their findings were slanted in our favour:* bias, distort, twist, skew, weight, give a bias to.

S

▷ **noun**
 1 *the slant of the roof:* slope, tilt, incline, gradient, pitch, angle, cant, rake, camber, inclination.
 2 *a feminist slant:* point of view, viewpoint, standpoint, stance, angle, perspective, approach, view, attitude, position; bias, leaning.

slanting adjective *the slanting angle of the deck:* sloping, angled, at an angle, on an incline, inclined, tilting, tilted, slanted, raked, aslant, diagonal, oblique, canted, cambered.
OPPOSITES: flat.

slap verb
 1 *he slapped her hard:* smack, cuff, spank, strike, hit, clout, thump, punch; informal whack, thwack, wallop, biff, bash.
 2 *he slapped down a £10 note:* slam, bang, fling, throw, toss; Brit. informal plonk.
 3 *slap on a coat of paint:* daub, plaster, spread.
▷ **noun** *a slap across the cheek:* smack, cuff, spank, blow, thump, clout, punch; informal whack, thwack, clip, biff, bash.
▢ **a slap in the face**
 rebuff, rejection, snub, insult, humiliation; informal put-down.
▢ **a slap on the back**
 congratulations, commendation, approval, accolade, compliment, tribute, pat on the back, praise, acclaim, acclamation.
▢ **a slap on the wrist**
 reprimand, rebuke, reproof, scolding, admonishment; informal telling-off, rap over the knuckles, dressing-down; Brit. informal ticking-off.

slapdash adjective *he gave a slapdash performance:* careless, slipshod, sloppy, hurried, haphazard, hit-or-miss, unsystematic, disorganized, untidy, messy, slovenly, negligent, lax; informal slap-happy; Brit. informal shambolic.
OPPOSITES: meticulous.

slash verb *her tyres had been slashed:* gash, cut open, slit, split, knife, incise, lacerate, rip, tear.
▷ **noun**
 1 *a slash across his temple:* gash, cut, slit, split, laceration, incision, rip, tear; wound.
 2 *sentence breaks are indicated by slashes:* oblique, diagonal, solidus; backslash.

slaughter verb *innocent civilians are being slaughtered:* massacre, murder, butcher, kill, annihilate, exterminate, liquidate, eliminate, destroy, decimate, wipe out, put to death.
▷ **noun**
 1 *the slaughter of 20 demonstrators:* massacre, murder, mass murder, mass killing, mass execution, annihilation, extermination, liquidation, decimation, butchery, genocide.
 2 *a scene of slaughter:* carnage, bloodshed, bloodletting, bloodbath.

slave noun
 1 *the work was done by slaves:* serf, vassal.
 2 *Anna was his willing slave:* servant, drudge, man/maid of all work, lackey; informal gofer; Brit. informal skivvy, dogsbody.
OPPOSITES: freeman, master.
▷ **verb** *I'm slaving away for a pittance:* toil, labour, grind, sweat, work your fingers to the bone, work like a Trojan/dog; informal work your socks off, sweat blood, slog away; Brit. informal graft.

slaver verb *the Labrador was slavering at the mouth:* drool, slobber, dribble, salivate.

slavery noun *thousands were sold into slavery:* bondage, enslavement, servitude, thraldom, thrall, serfdom.
OPPOSITES: freedom.

slavish adjective
 1 *slavish lackeys of the government:* servile, subservient, fawning, obsequious, sycophantic, toadying, unctuous; informal bootlicking.
 2 *a slavish imitation of current trends:* unoriginal, uninspired, unimaginative, imitative.
OPPOSITES: proud, inventive.

sleazy adjective
 1 *sleazy arms dealers:* corrupt, immoral, unsavoury, disreputable; informal shady.
 2 *a sleazy bar:* squalid, seedy, seamy, sordid, rough, insalubrious, mean, cheap, low-class, run-down, scruffy; Brit. informal grotty.
OPPOSITES: reputable, upmarket.

sledge noun (Brit.) toboggan, bobsleigh, sleigh; N. Amer. sled.

sleek adjective
 1 *his sleek dark hair:* smooth, glossy, shiny, shining, lustrous, silken, silky.
 2 *the car's sleek lines:* streamlined, clean, flowing, graceful, trim, elegant.
 3 *sleek young men in city suits:* well groomed, stylish, wealthy-looking.
OPPOSITES: rough, jagged.

sleep noun *go and have a sleep:* nap, doze, siesta, catnap; informal snooze, forty winks; Brit. informal kip.
▷ **verb** *she slept for about an hour:* be asleep, doze, take a siesta, take a nap, catnap; informal snooze, catch forty winks, get some shut-eye; Brit. informal kip, get your head down.
▢ **go to sleep**
 fall asleep, get to sleep; informal drop off, nod off, drift off, crash out, flake out.

┌─────────────────────────────┐
│ WORD LINKS │
│ **sedative, soporific** causing drowsiness │
│ or sleep │
└─────────────────────────────┘

sleepless adjective *she spent a sleepless night agonizing over what had happened:* wakeful, restless, disturbed, insomniac; wide awake, unsleeping, tossing and turning.
OPPOSITES: asleep.

sleeplessness noun insomnia, wakefulness.
OPPOSITES: sleep.

sleepy adjective
1 *she felt very sleepy:* drowsy, tired, somnolent, languid, languorous, heavy-eyed; lethargic, sluggish, enervated, torpid; informal dopey, dead on your feet.
2 *the sleepy heat of the afternoon:* soporific, sleep-inducing, somnolent.
3 *a sleepy little village:* quiet, peaceful, tranquil, placid, slow-moving; dull, boring.
OPPOSITES: awake, fresh, lively.

sleight of hand noun
1 *fans of magic will be impressed by his sleight of hand:* dexterity, adroitness, deftness, nimbleness, skill.
2 *this is financial sleight of hand of the worst kind:* deception, deceit, dissimulation, cunning, chicanery, trickery, sharp practice.

slender adjective
1 *her tall slender figure:* slim, lean, willowy, sylphlike, svelte, lissom, graceful, slight; thin, skinny.
2 *the theory is based on very slender evidence:* meagre, limited, slight, scanty, scant, sparse, paltry, insubstantial, insufficient, deficient, negligible.
3 *the chances of winning seemed slender:* faint, remote, flimsy, tenuous, fragile, slim; unlikely, improbable.
OPPOSITES: plump, abundant.

slice noun *a slice of cheese:* piece, portion, slab, sliver, wafer, rasher, shaving.
▷verb *slice the cheese thinly:* cut, carve, chop, shear, sever.

slick adjective
1 *a slick advertising campaign:* efficient, smooth, smooth-running, polished, well organized, well run, streamlined.
2 *a slick salesman:* suave, smooth, smooth-talking, glib, fluent, plausible, urbane, polished, assured, self-assured; Brit. informal smarmy.
3 *her slick brown hair:* shiny, glossy, shining, sleek, smooth.
▷verb *his hair was slicked down:* smooth, sleek, grease, oil, gel.

slide verb
1 *the glass slid across the table:* glide, slip, slither, skim, skate; skid, slew.
2 *four men slid out of the shadows:* creep, steal, slink, slip, tiptoe, sidle.
3 *share prices slid in late trading:* fall, sink, drop, descend, slump; decline, degenerate.
▷noun *the current slide in house prices:* fall, decline, drop, slump, downturn, downswing.
OPPOSITES: rise.

slight adjective
1 *the chance of success is slight:* small, modest, tiny, minute, minuscule,

negligible, insignificant, minimal, remote, slim, faint.
2 *the book is a slight work:* minor, inconsequential, trivial, unimportant, lightweight, superficial, shallow.
3 *Elizabeth's slight figure:* slim, slender, petite, diminutive, small, delicate, dainty.
OPPOSITES: considerable, major, full.
▷verb *he wanted to take revenge on the men who had slighted him:* insult, affront, snub, rebuff, repulse, spurn, treat disrespectfully, give someone the cold shoulder, cut dead, scorn; informal give someone the brush-off, put down, freeze out.
OPPOSITES: respect.
▷noun *an unintended slight:* insult, affront, snub, rebuff; informal put-down, dig.
OPPOSITES: compliment.

slightly adverb *she felt slightly ill at ease:* a little, a bit, somewhat, rather, moderately, to a certain extent, faintly, vaguely, a shade.
OPPOSITES: very.

slim adjective
1 *she was tall and slim:* slender, lean, thin, willowy, sylphlike, svelte, lissom, trim, slight, slightly built.
2 *a slim silver bracelet:* narrow, slender, slimline.
3 *a slim chance of escape:* slight, small, slender, faint, poor, remote, unlikely, improbable.
OPPOSITES: fat, broad, good.
▷verb (Brit.)
1 *I'm trying to slim:* lose weight; informal reduce, lose some pounds/inches, get into shape; N. Amer. slenderize.
2 *the number of staff had been slimmed down:* reduce, cut down/back, scale down, decrease, diminish, pare down.

slime noun *the steps were covered in green and black slime:* ooze, sludge, muck, mud, mire; informal goo, gunk; Brit. informal gunge.

slimy adjective
1 *the floor was slimy:* slippery, slithery, greasy, muddy, mucky, sludgy, wet, sticky; informal slippy.
2 (informal) *her slimy press agent.* See OBSEQUIOUS.

sling verb
1 (Brit. informal) *she took off her jacket and slung it on the sofa:* throw, toss, hurl, fling, pitch, cast, lob, bowl, launch, catapult; project, propel, let fly; informal chuck; Brit. informal bung.
2 *a hammock was slung between two trees:* hang, suspend, string, swing.

slink verb *she slunk past the open door of the living room:* creep, sneak, steal, slip, slide, sidle, tiptoe.

slinky adjective (informal)
1 *a slinky black dress:* tight-fitting, close-fitting, figure-hugging, sexy.

S

2 *Eleanor is played by a slinky Anjelica Huston:* sinuous, willowy, graceful, sleek, lithe, lissom.

slip¹ verb

1 *she slipped on the ice:* slide, skid, slither, glide; fall, fall over, lose your balance, tumble.
2 *we slipped out by a back door:* creep, steal, sneak, slide, sidle, slope, slink, tiptoe.
3 *standards have slipped:* decline, deteriorate, degenerate, worsen, fall, drop, go down; informal go downhill, go to the dogs, go to pot.
4 *she slipped the map into her pocket:* put, tuck, shove; informal pop, stick, stuff.
OPPOSITES: rise.

▷ **noun**
1 *a single slip could send them plummeting downwards:* false step, slide, skid, fall, tumble.
2 *a careless slip:* mistake, error, blunder, gaffe, slip of the tongue/pen; oversight, omission, lapse, inaccuracy; informal slip-up, boo-boo, howler; Brit. informal boob, clanger, bloomer.
▢ **let something slip**
they let slip that they had met him before: reveal, disclose, divulge, let out, give away, blurt out; informal let on, let the cat out of the bag, give the game away, spill the beans; Brit. informal blow the gaff.
▢ **slip away**
1 *they managed to slip away:* escape, get away, break free; Brit. informal do a bunk, do a runner.
2 *she slipped away in her sleep.* See DIE sense 1.
▢ **slip into**
Sarah slipped into a black skirt: put on, pull on, don, dress in; change into.
▢ **slip out of**
she slipped out of her clothes: take off, remove, pull off; Brit. informal peel off.
▢ **slip up** (informal) *we can't afford to slip up like that again:* make a mistake, make a blunder, get something wrong, make an error, err; informal make a boo-boo; Brit. informal boob, drop a clanger.

slip² noun *a slip of paper:* piece, scrap, sheet, note; chit.

slippery adjective

1 *the roads are slippery:* slithery, greasy, oily, icy, glassy, smooth, slimy, wet; informal slippy.
2 *a slippery customer:* evasive, unreliable, unpredictable; devious, crafty, cunning, wily, tricky, artful, slick, sly, sneaky, scheming, untrustworthy, deceitful, duplicitous, dishonest, treacherous, two-faced; informal shady, shifty; Brit. informal dodgy.

slipshod adjective *he'd caused many problems with his slipshod management:* careless, lackadaisical, slapdash, disorganized, haphazard, hit-or-miss, untidy, messy, unsystematic,

unmethodical, casual, negligent, remiss, lax, slack, sloppy; informal slap-happy.
OPPOSITES: meticulous.

slit noun

1 *three diagonal slits:* cut, incision, split, slash, gash, laceration.
2 *a slit in the curtains:* opening, gap, chink, crack, aperture, slot.
▷ **verb** *he threatened to slit her throat:* cut, slash, split open, slice open, gash, lacerate, make an incision in.

slither verb *a snake slithered silently across the grass:* slide, slip, glide, wriggle, twist, squirm, writhe, crawl; skid.

sliver noun *slivers of glass:* splinter, shard, shiver, chip, flake, shred, scrap, slither, shaving, paring, piece, fragment.

slobber verb drool, slaver, dribble, salivate.

slog (informal) verb

1 *they were all slogging away:* work hard, toil, labour, work your fingers to the bone, work like a Trojan/dog, exert yourself, grind, slave, grub, plough, plod, peg; informal beaver, plug, work your guts out, work your socks off, sweat blood; Brit. informal graft.
2 *they slogged around the streets:* trudge, tramp, traipse, toil, plod, trek, drag yourself.
OPPOSITES: relax.

▷ **noun**
1 *10 months' hard slog:* work, toil, labour, effort, exertion, grind, drudgery; informal sweat; Brit. informal graft.
2 *a steady uphill slog:* trudge, tramp, traipse, plod, trek.

slogan noun *well-known advertising slogans:* catchphrase, catchline, jingle, caption.

slop verb *water slopped over the edge:* spill, flow, overflow, run, slosh, splash.

slope noun

1 *the slope of the roof:* slant, tilt, incline, angle, gradient, inclination, pitch, cant, rake, lean, ascent, rise, decline, fall.
2 *a grassy slope:* hill, hillside, hillock, bank, escarpment, scarp.
3 *the ski slopes:* piste, run.
▷ **verb** *the garden sloped down to a stream:* slant, incline, tilt, shelve, lean, cant, list, bank; drop away, fall away, decline, descend; rise, ascend, climb.

sloping adjective *a sloping floor:* slanting, angled, at an angle, on an incline, inclined, tilting, tilted, slanted, raked, aslant, oblique, diagonal, canted, cambered.
OPPOSITES: flat.

sloppy adjective

1 *sloppy chicken curry:* runny, watery, thin, liquid, semi-liquid, mushy; informal gloopy.
2 *United's defending was sloppy:* careless, slapdash, slipshod, lackadaisical, haphazard, lax, slack, slovenly; informal

slap-happy; Brit. informal shambolic.
3 *sloppy T-shirts:* baggy, loose-fitting, loose, generously cut; shapeless, sack-like, oversized.
4 (informal) *he wrote really sloppy letters:* sentimental, mawkish, cloying, saccharine, sugary, syrupy; romantic, hearts-and-flowers; informal slushy, schmaltzy, lovey-dovey; Brit. informal soppy.

slosh verb
1 *beer sloshed over the side of the glass:* spill, slop, splash, flow, overflow, run.
2 *workers sloshed round in boots:* splash, swash, squelch; informal splosh.
3 *she sloshed more wine into her glass:* splash, slop, pour.

slot noun
1 *he slid a coin into the slot:* aperture, slit, crack, hole, opening.
2 *a mid-morning slot:* spot, time, period, niche, space; informal window.
▷ **verb** *he slotted a cassette into the machine:* insert, slide, slip, tuck, fit, put.

sloth noun
laziness, idleness, indolence, inactivity, inertia, sluggishness, shiftlessness, apathy, listlessness, lassitude, lethargy, languor, torpidity; literary accidie.
OPPOSITES: energy, industry.

slothful adjective
fatigue made him slothful: lazy, idle, indolent, work-shy, inactive, sluggish, apathetic, lethargic, listless, languid, torpid; informal bone idle.
OPPOSITES: energetic, industrious.

slouch verb
Nick slouched back in his chair: slump, hunch, sprawl, loll, flop, lounge, droop.

slovenly adjective
1 *his slovenly appearance:* scruffy, untidy, messy, unkempt, ill-groomed, slatternly, dishevelled, bedraggled, tousled, rumpled, frowzy.
2 *his work is slovenly:* careless, slapdash, slipshod, sloppy, haphazard, hit-or-miss, untidy, messy, negligent, lax, lackadaisical, slack; informal slap-happy.
OPPOSITES: tidy, careful.

slow adjective
1 *their slow pace:* unhurried, leisurely, steady, deliberate, sedate, slow-moving, plodding, heavy, laborious, dawdling, sluggish.
2 *a slow process:* lengthy, time-consuming, long-drawn-out, protracted, prolonged, gradual.
3 *he can be so slow:* stupid, idiotic, obtuse, brainless, insensitive, slow-witted, dull-witted, unintelligent, witless; informal dense, dim, dim-witted, thick, slow on the uptake, dumb, dopey; Brit. informal dozy.
4 *they were slow to voice their opinions:* reluctant, unwilling, disinclined, loath, hesitant, afraid, chary, shy.
OPPOSITES: quick, ready.

▷ **verb**
1 *the traffic forced him to slow down:* reduce speed, go slower, decelerate, brake.
2 *you need to slow down:* relax, take it easy, ease up/off, take a break, slacken off, let up; informal chill out, have a breather.
OPPOSITES: accelerate.

slowly adverb
1 *Rose walked off slowly:* at a slow pace, without hurrying, unhurriedly, steadily, at a leisurely pace, at a snail's pace, deliberately, heavily, laboriously.
2 *her health is improving slowly:* gradually, piecemeal, by degrees, bit by bit, little by little, slowly but surely, step by step.
OPPOSITES: quickly.

sludge noun
mud, muck, mire, ooze; Geology silt, alluvium; informal gunk; Brit. informal gunge.

sluggish adjective
1 *the game moves at a fairly sluggish pace:* slow, lumbering, ponderous, leaden, deliberate, laborious, laboured, sedate, measured, lethargic, languid, lazy, leisurely, unhurried.
2 *Alex felt tired and sluggish:* lethargic, listless, lacking in energy, inert, inactive, torpid, languid, apathetic, weary, tired, fatigued, sleepy, drowsy, enervated; lazy, idle, indolent, slothful; informal dozy, dopey.
3 *the economy is sluggish:* inactive, quiet, slow, slack, flat, depressed, stagnant.
OPPOSITES: fast, vigorous.

sluice verb
crews sluiced down the decks: rinse, flush, swill, wash, clean, cleanse; Brit. informal sloosh.

slum noun
hovel, shack; (**slums**) ghetto, shanty town.

slummy adjective
a slummy area of town: squalid, run-down, down at heel, shabby, scruffy, dilapidated, ramshackle, insalubrious, downmarket, seedy, wretched, mean; informal crummy; Brit. informal grotty.
OPPOSITES: smart.

slump verb
1 *he slumped into a chair:* flop, collapse, sink, fall; Brit. informal plonk yourself.
2 *house prices slumped:* fall steeply, plummet, tumble, drop, go down; informal crash, nosedive, go through the floor.
3 *reading standards have slumped:* decline, deteriorate, degenerate, worsen, slip; informal go downhill.
OPPOSITES: rise.

▷ **noun**
1 *a slump in profits:* steep fall, drop, tumble, downturn, downswing, slide, decline, decrease; informal nosedive.
2 *an economic slump:* recession, economic decline, depression, slowdown, stagnation.
OPPOSITES: rise, boom.

slur verb
she was slurring her words: mumble, blur, garble, mutter, stumble over.

S

▷ noun *he was fired from the department for making racial slurs:* insult, slight, affront, slander, aspersion, smear, allegation, insinuation, jibe, taunt.

sly adjective
1 *she's rather sly:* cunning, crafty, clever, wily, artful, guileful, tricky, scheming, devious, deceitful, duplicitous, dishonest, underhand, sneaky.
2 *a sly grin:* knowing, mischievous, impish, playful, wicked, arch, roguish.
3 *she took a sly sip of water:* surreptitious, furtive, stealthy, covert, discreet, secret, clandestine.
OPPOSITES: honest, open.
▫ **on the sly**
in secret, secretly, surreptitiously, furtively, covertly, discreetly, on the quiet, behind someone's back.

smack¹ noun
1 *she gave him a smack:* slap, cuff, spank, clout, thump, punch, blow, rap, crack; informal whack, thwack, clip, biff, wallop, swipe.
2 *the parcel landed with a smack:* crack, crash, bang, thud, thump.
▷ verb
1 *he tried to smack her:* slap, cuff, spank, hit, strike, clout, thump, punch; box someone's ears; informal whack, clip, wallop, biff, swipe.
2 *the waiter smacked a plate down:* bang, slam, crash, thump; sling, fling; Brit. informal plonk.

smack² verb
▫ **smack of**
1 *the tea smacked of tannin:* taste of, remind you of.
2 *the plan smacked of self-promotion:* suggest, hint at, have overtones of, give the impression of, have the stamp of, have all the hallmarks of; savour of, smell of, reek of.

small adjective
1 *a small flat:* little, tiny; compact, bijou, poky, cramped, boxy; Scottish wee; informal teeny, weeny; Brit. informal tiddly, titchy, dinky.
2 *a very small woman:* short, little, tiny, petite, diminutive, elfin, Lilliputian; Scottish wee; informal teeny, pint-sized.
3 *I've made a few small changes:* slight, minor, unimportant, trifling, trivial, insignificant, inconsequential, negligible; formal nugatory.
OPPOSITES: big, tall, major.

small-minded adjective *a bunch of small-minded bigots:* narrow-minded, petty, mean-spirited, uncharitable; short-sighted, myopic, blinkered, inward-looking, unimaginative, parochial, provincial, insular, small-town; intolerant, illiberal, conservative, hidebound, dyed-in-the-wool, set in your ways, inflexible; prejudiced, bigoted; Brit. parish-pump.
OPPOSITES: broad-minded.

small-time adjective (informal) *small-time crooks:* minor, petty, unimportant, insignificant, inconsequential, small-scale; informal piffling.
OPPOSITES: major.

smarmy adjective (Brit. informal) *she encounters the smarmy real-estate agent:* unctuous, ingratiating, slick, smooth-talking, glib, oily, greasy, obsequious, sycophantic, fawning; informal slimy.

smart adjective
1 *you look very smart:* well dressed, stylish, chic, fashionable, modish, elegant, neat, spruce, trim, dapper; informal cool, sharp, snappy, snazzy, natty.
2 *a smart restaurant:* fashionable, stylish, high-class, exclusive, chic, fancy; Brit. upmarket; informal trendy, posh, ritzy, plush, classy, swanky, glitzy; Brit. informal swish.
3 *a smart pace:* brisk, quick, fast, rapid, swift, lively, spanking, energetic, vigorous; informal snappy, cracking.
4 *a smart blow on the snout:* sharp, hard, severe, forceful, violent.
OPPOSITES: untidy, downmarket, slow, gentle.
▷ verb
1 *her eyes were smarting:* sting, burn, tingle, prickle; hurt, ache.
2 *she smarted at the accusations:* feel annoyed, feel upset, take offence, feel aggrieved, feel indignant, be put out, feel hurt.

smarten verb *you'd better smarten yourself up a bit before the inspection:* spruce up, tidy up, neaten, tidy, groom, freshen, preen, primp, beautify, clean up, redecorate, refurbish, modernize; informal do up, titivate, doll up; Brit. informal tart up, posh up.

smash verb
1 *he smashed a window:* break, shatter, splinter, crack; informal bust.
2 *she's smashed the car:* crash, wreck; Brit. write off; Brit. informal prang; N. Amer. informal total.
3 *Don smashed him over the head:* hit, strike, thump, punch, smack; informal whack, bash, biff, clout, wallop, crown; Brit. informal slosh.
▷ noun
1 *a motorway smash:* crash, collision, pile-up, accident, bump; Brit. RTA (road traffic accident); N. Amer. wreck; Brit. informal prang, shunt.
2 (informal) *a box-office smash:* success, sensation, sell-out, triumph; informal hit, winner, crowd-puller, knockout.
OPPOSITES: fiasco.
▫ **smash into**
they smashed into a wall: crash into, collide with, hit, strike, ram, plough into, run into, bump into; informal smack into, slam into.

smashing adjective (Brit. informal). See **MARVELLOUS** sense 2.

smattering noun *Edward had only a smattering of Welsh:* bit, little, modicum, touch, soupçon; nodding acquaintance; rudiments, basics; informal smidgen.

smear verb
1 *the table was smeared with grease:* streak, smudge, mark, soil, dirty; informal splotch; Brit. informal splodge.
2 *smear the meat with olive oil:* cover, coat, spread, rub, daub, dab, smother, plaster, slick.
3 *she smeared sunblock on her skin:* spread, rub, slap, daub, slather, plaster; apply.
4 *they are trying to smear our reputation:* tarnish, blacken, drag through the mud, taint, damage, defame, discredit, malign, slander, libel; literary besmirch, sully.
▷ noun
1 *smears of blood:* streak, smudge, daub, dab, spot, patch, blotch, mark; informal splotch; Brit. informal splodge.
2 *press smears about his closest aides:* lie, untruth, slur, false accusation, slander, libel, defamation; formal calumny.

smell noun *there was a very strong smell that lingered for several minutes:* odour, aroma, fragrance, scent, perfume; bouquet, nose; stench, stink, reek; Brit. informal pong, niff, whiff; old use redolence.
▷ verb
1 *he smelled her perfume:* detect, get a sniff of, scent.
2 *the dogs smelled each other:* sniff, nose.
3 *the cellar smells:* stink, reek; Brit. informal pong, hum, niff, whiff.
□ smell like
it smells like a hoax to me: smack of, have all the hallmarks of, seem like, have the air of, suggest.

> WORD LINKS
> **olfactory** relating to the sense of smell

smelly adjective *a large tank full of very smelly water:* foul-smelling, stinking, reeking, fetid, malodorous, pungent, rank, noxious; off, gamy, high; musty, fusty; informal stinky; Brit. informal pongy, whiffy, humming.
OPPOSITES: fragrant.

smile verb & noun beam, grin; smirk, simper, leer.
OPPOSITES: frown.

smitten adjective
1 *he was smitten with cholera:* struck down, laid low, suffering, stricken, affected, infected, afflicted, plagued.
2 *Jane's smitten with you:* infatuated, besotted, in love, obsessed, head over heels in love; enamoured of, attracted to, taken with; captivated, enchanted, under someone's spell; informal bowled over, swept off your feet, crazy about, mad about, keen on; informal, dated sweet on.

smoke verb *he smoked his cigarette:*
puff on, draw on, pull on; inhale; light; informal drag on.
▷ noun *the smoke from the bonfire:* fumes, exhaust, gas, vapour.

smoky adjective *her smoky eyes:* grey, sooty, dusky, dark.

smooth adjective
1 *the smooth, flat rocks | a sheet of smooth white fabric:* even, level, flat, plane, featureless; glossy, silky, silken, polished.
2 *a smooth sea:* calm, still, tranquil, undisturbed, unruffled, unwrinkled, even, flat, waveless, like a millpond; glassy.
3 *a smooth sauce:* creamy, lump-free, velvety, blended.
4 *the smooth running of the equipment:* steady, regular, uninterrupted, unbroken, fluid, fluent; straightforward, easy, effortless, trouble-free.
5 *a smooth wine:* mellow, mild, agreeable, pleasant.
6 *the smooth tone of the clarinet:* dulcet, soft, soothing, mellow, sweet, silvery, honeyed, mellifluous, melodious, lilting, lyrical, harmonious.
7 *a smooth, confident man:* suave, urbane, sophisticated, polished, debonair; courteous, gracious, glib, slick, ingratiating, unctuous; Brit. informal smarmy.
OPPOSITES: uneven, rough, irregular.
▷ verb
1 *she smoothed the soil:* flatten, level out/off, even out/off; press, roll, steamroll, iron; plane, sand, polish.
2 *I have managed to smooth his way from work to retirement:* ease, facilitate, expedite, assist, aid, help, oil the wheels of, lubricate, clear the way for, pave the way for.
OPPOSITES: roughen, hinder.

smoothly adverb
1 *her hair was combed smoothly back:* evenly, level, flat, flush.
2 *the door closed smoothly:* fluidly, fluently, steadily, easily; quietly.
3 *the plan had gone smoothly:* without a hitch, like clockwork, without difficulty, easily, effortlessly, according to plan, satisfactorily, very well; informal like a dream, swimmingly.

smother verb
1 *she tried to smother her baby:* suffocate, asphyxiate, stifle, choke.
2 *we smothered the flames:* extinguish, put out, snuff out, stamp out, dampen, douse, choke.
3 *we smothered ourselves with suncream:* smear, daub, plaster, spread, cover, coat.
4 *she smothered a sigh:* stifle, muffle, strangle, repress, suppress, hold back, fight back, bite back, swallow, contain, bottle up, conceal, hide; bite your lip; informal keep a/the lid on.

smoulder verb
1 *the bonfire was still smouldering:* smoke, glow, burn.

2 *she was smouldering with resentment:* seethe, boil, fume, burn, simmer, be beside yourself; informal be livid.

smudge noun *a smudge of blood:* streak, smear, daub, mark, stain, blotch, stripe, blob, dab; informal splotch; Brit. informal splodge.

▷**verb** *her face was smudged with dust:* streak, smear, mark, dirty, soil, blotch, blacken, blot, daub, stain; informal splotch; Brit. informal splodge.

smug adjective *he was feeling smug after his win:* self-satisfied, self-congratulatory, complacent, superior, conceited, priggish, pleased with yourself, self-approving.
OPPOSITES: humble.

smutty adjective *he told a series of smutty jokes:* vulgar, rude, crude, dirty, filthy, coarse, obscene, lewd, pornographic; risqué, racy, earthy, bawdy, suggestive, naughty, ribald, off colour; euphemistic adult; informal blue, saucy.
OPPOSITES: clean.

snack noun *she made herself a snack:* light meal, sandwich, treat, refreshments, nibbles; informal bite to eat; Brit. informal elevenses.

▷**verb** *don't snack on sugary foods:* eat between meals, nibble, munch; informal graze.

snag noun *the snag is that this might affect inflation:* complication, difficulty, catch, hitch, obstacle, stumbling block, pitfall, problem, impediment, hindrance, inconvenience, setback, disadvantage, downside, drawback.

▷**verb**
1 *she snagged her tights:* tear, rip, ladder.
2 *the zip snagged on the fabric:* catch, get caught, hook.

snake noun literary serpent.

▷**verb** *the road snakes inland:* twist, wind, meander, zigzag, curve.

> WORD LINKS
> **ophidian** resembling a snake or typical of a snake

snap verb
1 *the branch snapped:* break, fracture, come apart, split, crack, splinter; informal bust.
2 *a dog was snapping at his heels:* bite; gnash its teeth.
3 *she snapped after years of violence:* flare up, lose your self-control, go to pieces, get worked up; informal crack up, freak out, lose your cool.
4 *'Shut up!' Anna snapped:* snarl, bark, growl; say roughly, say brusquely, say abruptly, say angrily, retort, rejoin, retaliate; round on someone; informal jump down someone's throat.
5 (informal) *photographers snapped the royals:* photograph, picture, take, shoot, film, capture.

▷**noun**
1 *she closed her purse with a snap:* click, crack, pop.
2 *a cold snap:* period, spell, time, interval, stretch; Brit. informal patch.
□ **snap something up**
people are snapping up bargains all over the place: buy eagerly, accept eagerly, jump at, take advantage of, grab, seize, grasp/seize with both hands, pounce on.

snappy (informal) **adjective**
1 *why is he so snappy this morning?* irritable, irascible, short-tempered, hot-tempered, quick-tempered, fiery, touchy, volatile; cross, crabby, crotchety, cantankerous, grumpy, bad-tempered, testy, tetchy; informal grouchy; Brit. informal ratty.
2 *a snappy catchphrase:* concise, succinct, brief, memorable, catchy, neat, clever, crisp, pithy, witty, incisive.
3 *a snappy dresser:* smart, fashionable, stylish, chic, elegant, neat, spruce, trim, dapper; informal snazzy, natty, sharp, cool.
□ **make it snappy**
hurry up, be quick, speed up; informal get cracking, get a move on, look lively, step on it, move it, buck up, shake a leg; Brit. informal get your skates on.

snare noun *the hare was caught in a snare:* trap, gin, net, noose.

▷**verb**
1 *game birds were snared:* trap, catch, net, bag.
2 *five blackmailers were snared in the undercover operation:* ensnare, entrap, catch, get hold of, bag, hook, land.

snarl[1] verb *'Shut it!' he snarled:* growl, snap, bark, say roughly, say brusquely; informal jump down someone's throat.

snarl[2] verb
1 *the rope got snarled up in a bush:* tangle, entangle, entwine, enmesh, knot, foul.
2 *this case has snarled up the court process:* impede, hinder, obstruct, hamper, hold back/up, delay, slow down, interfere with, disrupt.
OPPOSITES: disentangle, facilitate.

snatch verb
1 *she snatched the sandwich:* grab, seize, take hold of, get your hands on, take, pluck, clutch at, wrest something from someone, wrench something out of someone's hands.
2 (informal) *someone snatched my bag.* See STEAL verb sense 1.
3 (informal) *she snatched the newborn baby from the hospital.* See ABDUCT.

▷**noun**
1 *brief snatches of sleep:* period, spell, time, interval, stretch, bout, fit.
2 *a snatch of conversation:* fragment, snippet, bit, scrap, part, extract, excerpt, portion.

sneak verb

1 *I sneaked out:* creep, slink, steal, slip, slide, sidle, edge, move furtively, tiptoe, pad, prowl.
2 *she sneaked a camera in:* bring/take surreptitiously, bring/take secretly, bring/take illicitly, smuggle, spirit, slip.
3 *he sneaked a doughnut:* take furtively, take surreptitiously; steal; informal snatch.
4 (Brit. informal) *it felt wrong, like sneaking to an adult:* inform, tell tales, report, give someone away; informal squeal, rat, blow the whistle, peach, snitch, put the finger on; Brit. informal grass, split, shop; N. Amer. informal finger.
▷**adjective** *a sneak preview:* furtive, secret, stealthy, sly, surreptitious, clandestine, covert; private, quick.

sneaking adjective

1 *she had a sneaking admiration for him:* secret, private, hidden, concealed, inward, unvoiced, undisclosed, undeclared, unexpressed.
2 *a sneaking feeling:* slight, funny, strange, vague; persistent, niggling, lingering.
OPPOSITES: open, definite.

sneaky adjective *it was a sneaky trick and I fell for it:* sly, crafty, cunning, devious, wily, artful, scheming, deceitful, dirty, duplicitous, underhand, unscrupulous; furtive, secretive, secret, stealthy, surreptitious, clandestine, covert.
OPPOSITES: open, honest.

sneer noun

1 *she had a sneer on her face:* smirk, curl of the lip, scornful smile, contemptuous smile.
2 *the sneers of others:* jibe, barb, jeer, taunt, insult, slight, affront, slur; informal dig.
▷**verb** *he looked at me and sneered:* smirk, curl your lip, smile scornfully, smile contemptuously.
□**sneer at**
it is easy to sneer at them: scoff at, scorn, disdain, mock, jeer at, hold in contempt, ridicule, deride, insult, slight.

snide adjective *I'm fed up with your snide remarks:* disparaging, derogatory, disrespectful, insulting, contemptuous, mocking, taunting, sneering, scornful, derisive, sarcastic, spiteful, nasty, mean; Brit. informal sarky.

sniff verb

1 *she sniffed and blew her nose:* snuffle, breathe in, inhale.
2 *Tom sniffed the fruit:* smell, get a whiff of.
▷**noun**
1 *she gave a loud sniff:* snuffle, breath in, inhalation.
2 *a sniff of fresh air:* smell, whiff; lungful.
□**sniff at**
scorn, disdain, hold in contempt, look down your nose at, treat as inferior, look down on, sneer at, scoff at; informal turn your nose up at.

snigger verb (Brit.) *they sniggered at him behind his back:* titter, giggle, chuckle, chortle, laugh scornfully; sneer, smirk.

snip verb *snip off the faded flowers:* trim, prune, cut, clip, chop, lop, dock, crop, sever, detach, remove.

snippet noun *snippets of information:* piece, bit, scrap, fragment, particle, shred; excerpt, extract.

snivel verb

1 *he slumped in a chair, snivelling:* sniffle, snuffle, whimper, whine, weep, cry; informal blub, blubber; Brit. informal grizzle.
2 *don't snivel about your punishment:* complain, protest, moan, grumble, grouse, groan, carp, bleat, whine; informal gripe, grouch, beef, bellyache, whinge, sound off.

snobbery noun *there was a complete lack of snobbery about staff mingling with guests:* affectation, pretension, arrogance, haughtiness, airs and graces, elitism; disdain, condescension, superciliousness; informal snootiness, uppitiness; Brit. informal side.
OPPOSITES: humility.

snobbish adjective *the writer takes a rather snobbish tone:* elitist, snobby, superior, supercilious; arrogant, haughty, disdainful, condescending; pretentious, affected; informal snooty, la-di-da, stuck-up, hoity-toity, snotty; Brit. informal toffee-nosed.
OPPOSITES: humble.

snoop (informal) verb

1 *don't snoop into our affairs:* pry, inquire, be inquisitive, be curious, poke about/around, be a busybody; interfere in, meddle in, intrude on; informal poke your nose into, be nosy.
2 *they snooped around the building:* investigate, explore, search, nose, have a good look; prowl.
▷**noun** *he went for a snoop around:* search, nose, look, prowl, ferret, poke, investigation.

snooper noun (informal) spy, eavesdropper; investigator, detective; busybody; informal private eye, sleuth; nosy parker.

snooty adjective (informal) *snooty neighbours:* arrogant, proud, haughty, conceited, aloof, superior, self-important, disdainful, supercilious, snobbish, snobby, patronizing, condescending; informal uppity, high and mighty, la-di-da, stuck-up, hoity-toity; Brit. informal toffee-nosed.
OPPOSITES: humble.

snooze (informal) noun *a good place for a snooze:* nap, doze, sleep, rest, siesta, catnap; informal forty winks; Brit. informal kip.
▷**verb** *she gently snoozed:* nap, doze, sleep, rest, take a siesta, catnap; informal catch forty winks, get some shut-eye; Brit. informal kip, get your head down.

S

snub verb *they snubbed their hosts:* rebuff, spurn, repulse, cold-shoulder, brush off, give the cold shoulder to, keep at arm's length; cut dead, ignore; insult, slight, affront, humiliate; informal freeze out.

▷ **noun** *a very public snub:* rebuff, repulse, slap in the face; humiliation, insult, slight, affront; informal brush-off, put-down, knock-back.

snuff verb *a breeze snuffed out the candle:* extinguish, put out, douse, smother, choke, blow out, quench, stub out.

snug adjective
1 *our tents were snug:* cosy, comfortable, warm, welcoming, restful, intimate, sheltered, secure; Brit. homely; informal comfy.
2 *a snug dress:* tight, skintight, close-fitting, figure-hugging, slinky.
OPPOSITES: bleak, loose.

snuggle verb *I snuggled down in my sleeping bag:* nestle, curl up, huddle up, cuddle up, nuzzle, settle.

soak verb
1 *soak the beans in water:* immerse, steep, submerge, submerse, dip, dunk, bathe, douse, marinate, souse.
2 *we got soaked outside:* drench, wet through, saturate, waterlog, deluge, inundate, submerge, drown, swamp.
3 *the sweat soaked his clothes:* permeate, penetrate, percolate, seep into, spread through, infuse, impregnate.
4 *use towels to soak up the water:* absorb, suck up, blot up, mop up, sponge up, sop up.

soaking adjective *get your jacket off, it's soaking:* drenched, wet through, soaked, sodden, soggy, waterlogged, saturated, sopping wet, wringing wet.
OPPOSITES: dry.

soar verb
1 *the bird soared into the air:* fly, wing, ascend, climb, rise; take off, take flight.
2 *the gulls soared on the winds:* glide, plane, float, drift, wheel, hover.
3 *the cost of living soared:* increase, escalate, shoot up, rise, spiral; informal go through the roof, skyrocket.
OPPOSITES: plummet.

sob verb *he broke down and sobbed like a child:* weep, cry, shed tears, snivel, whimper; howl, bawl; informal blub, blubber; Brit. informal grizzle.

sober adjective
1 *the driver was clearly sober:* clear-headed; teetotal, abstinent, abstemious, dry; informal on the wagon.
2 *a sober view of life:* serious, solemn, sensible, thoughtful, grave, sombre, staid, level-headed, businesslike, down-to-earth, commonsensical, pragmatic, conservative; unemotional, dispassionate, objective, matter-of-fact, no-nonsense, rational, logical, straightforward.
3 *a sober suit:* sombre, subdued, severe; conventional, traditional, quiet, drab, plain.
OPPOSITES: drunk, frivolous, flamboyant.

▷ **verb** *his expression sobered her:* calm down, subdue, quieten, steady; bring someone down to earth, make someone stop and think, give someone pause for thought.

sobriety noun *the mayor is a model of sobriety:* seriousness, solemnity, gravity, dignity, level-headedness, common sense, pragmatism, practicality, self-control, self-restraint, conservatism.

so-called adjective *she could trust him more than any of her so-called friends:* supposed, alleged, presumed, ostensible, reputed; nominal, titular, self-styled, professed, would-be, self-appointed, soi-disant.
OPPOSITES: genuine.

sociable adjective *being a sociable person, Eva loved entertaining:* friendly, affable, companionable, gregarious, convivial, clubbable, amicable, cordial, warm, genial, communicative, responsive, forthcoming, open, outgoing, extrovert, hail-fellow-well-met, approachable; informal chummy, clubby; Brit. informal matey.
OPPOSITES: unsociable.

social adjective
1 *a major social problem:* public, societal, civil, community; general, communal, collective, group; popular.
2 *a social club:* recreational, leisure, entertainment, amusement.
3 *a uniquely social animal:* gregarious; collaborative, organized,.
OPPOSITES: individual, solitary.

▷ **noun** *the club has a social once a month:* party, gathering, function, get-together, celebration, reunion; informal bash, do; Brit. informal jolly.

socialist adjective *the socialist movement:* left-wing, leftist, Labour, Labourite, Fabian, progressive, reform; radical, revolutionary, militant, red; communist; informal, derogatory lefty, Commie.
OPPOSITES: conservative.

▷ **noun** *a well-known socialist:* left-winger, leftist, Fabian, Labourite, progressive, progressivist, reformer; radical, revolutionary, militant, red; communist; informal, derogatory lefty, Commie.
OPPOSITES: conservative.

socialize verb *guests can socialize in a real holiday atmosphere:* mingle, mix, get together, meet, fraternize, join in, converse, talk, be sociable, interact, consort; entertain, go out; informal hobnob.

society noun
1 *a danger to society:* the community, the public, the general public, the people,

the population; civilization, humankind, mankind, humanity.
2 *an industrial society:* culture, community, civilization, nation, population.
3 *a local history society:* association, club, group, circle, fellowship, guild, lodge, league, union, alliance.
4 *she shunned the society of others:* company, companionship, fellowship, friendship, comradeship, camaraderie.
5 *Lady Angela will help you enter society:* high society, polite society, the upper classes, the elite, the A-list, the smart set, the beautiful people, the beau monde, the haut monde; informal the upper crust, the top drawer.

> WORD LINKS
> **sociology** the study of the structure and functioning of human society

sodden adjective
1 *his clothes were sodden:* soaking, soaked, wet through, saturated, drenched, sopping wet, wringing wet.
2 *sodden fields:* waterlogged, soggy, saturated, boggy, swampy, miry, marshy; heavy, squelchy, soft.
OPPOSITES: dry, arid.

soft adjective
1 *cook for two minutes until the fruit is soft:* mushy, squashy, pulpy, slushy; informal squishy, gooey; Brit. informal squidgy.
2 *the narrow wheels got stuck in the soft ground:* swampy, marshy, boggy, miry; heavy, squelchy.
3 *a soft cushion:* squashy, spongy, compressible, supple, springy, pliable, pliant, resilient, malleable.
4 *soft fabric:* velvety, smooth, fleecy, downy, furry, silky, silken, satiny.
5 *the soft light of the moon:* dim, low, faint, subdued, muted, mellow.
6 *a spacious lounge furnished in soft colours:* pale, pastel, muted, understated, restrained, subdued, subtle, neutral.
7 *they spoke in soft voices:* quiet, low, faint, muted, subdued, muffled, hushed, whispered, stifled, murmured, gentle; indistinct, inaudible; often ironic dulcet.
8 *she's too soft with her pupils:* lenient, easy-going, tolerant, forgiving, forbearing, indulgent, clement, permissive, liberal, lax.
OPPOSITES: hard, firm, rough, harsh, strict.

soften verb
he tried to soften the blow of new taxes: alleviate, cushion, ease, relieve, soothe, take the edge off, assuage, moderate, mitigate, palliate, diminish, blunt, deaden.

soft-hearted adjective
you ought to have turned her away, but you were always soft-hearted: kind, kindly, tender-hearted, tender, gentle, sympathetic, compassionate, humane; generous,

indulgent, lenient, merciful, benevolent; sentimental.
OPPOSITES: hard-hearted.

soggy adjective
the thick, soggy mass of fallen leaves: mushy, squashy, pulpy, slushy, squelchy; swampy, marshy, boggy, miry; soaking, soaked through, wet, saturated, drenched; informal squishy; Brit. informal squidgy.
OPPOSITES: dry, hard.

soil¹ noun
1 *acid soil:* earth, loam, topsoil, humus, dirt, clay, ground.
2 *British soil:* territory, land, domain, dominion, jurisdiction, space, region, country.

soil² verb
1 *he soiled his tie:* dirty, stain, splash, spot, spatter, splatter, smear, smudge, spoil, foul; literary sully.
2 *our reputation is being soiled:* dishonour, damage, stain, blacken, tarnish, taint, blemish, defile, blot, smear, drag through the mud; literary besmirch, sully.
OPPOSITES: clean, clear.

solace noun
they found solace in each other: comfort, consolation, cheer, support, relief.
OPPOSITES: despair.

soldier noun
fighter, trooper, serviceman, servicewoman, fighting man, fighting woman; warrior; US GI; Brit. informal squaddie.
□ **soldier on** (informal). See PERSEVERE.

sole adjective
my sole aim was to contribute to the national team: only, one and only, single, singular, solitary, lone, unique, exclusive.
OPPOSITES: multiple.

solely adverb
people are appointed solely on the basis of merit: only, simply, just, merely, uniquely, exclusively, entirely, wholly; alone.

solemn adjective
1 *a solemn occasion:* dignified, ceremonious, ceremonial, stately, formal, courtly, majestic; imposing, awe-inspiring, splendid, magnificent, grand.
2 *he looked very solemn:* serious, grave, sober, sombre, unsmiling, stern, grim, dour, humourless; pensive, meditative.
3 *a solemn promise:* sincere, earnest, honest, genuine, firm, heartfelt, wholehearted, sworn.
OPPOSITES: frivolous, light-hearted, insincere.

solicit verb
1 *he began to solicit funds for his campaign:* ask for, request, seek, apply for, put in for, call for, press for, beg, plead for.
2 *historians and critics are solicited for their opinions by the auction houses:* ask, appeal to, petition, importune, call on, press.

S

solicitous adjective *she was always solicitous about the welfare of her students:* concerned, caring, considerate, attentive, mindful, thoughtful, interested; anxious, worried.
OPPOSITES: uncaring.

solid adjective
1 *the ice cream was solid:* hard, rock-hard, rigid, firm, solidified, set, frozen.
2 *solid gold:* pure, 24-carat, unalloyed, unadulterated, genuine.
3 *a solid line:* continuous, uninterrupted, unbroken, non-stop, undivided.
4 *solid houses:* well built, sound, substantial, strong, sturdy, durable.
5 *a solid argument:* well founded, valid, sound, reasonable, logical, authoritative, convincing, cogent, plausible, credible, reliable.
6 *a solid friendship:* dependable, reliable, firm, unshakeable, trustworthy, stable, steadfast, staunch, constant.
OPPOSITES: liquid, broken, flimsy.

solidarity noun *there was a great feeling of solidarity between us all:* unanimity, unity, like-mindedness, agreement, accord, harmony, consensus, concurrence, cooperation, cohesion.
OPPOSITES: division.

solidify verb *these droplets of liquefied rock solidify rapidly:* harden, set, freeze, thicken, stiffen, congeal, cake, dry, bake; ossify, fossilize, petrify.
OPPOSITES: liquefy.

solitary adjective
1 *a solitary life:* lonely, companionless, unaccompanied, by yourself, on your own, alone, friendless; antisocial, unsociable, withdrawn, reclusive, cloistered.
2 *solitary farmsteads:* isolated, remote, lonely, out of the way, in the back of beyond, outlying, off the beaten track, godforsaken, obscure, inaccessible, cut off; secluded, private, sequestered, desolate; informal in the sticks, in the middle of nowhere.
3 *a solitary piece of evidence:* single, lone, sole, unique; only, one, individual; odd.
OPPOSITES: sociable, accessible, multiple.

solitude noun *she savoured her solitude:* isolation, seclusion, loneliness, solitariness, withdrawal, privacy, peace.

solo adjective *a solo flight:* unaccompanied, single-handed, companionless, unescorted, unattended, unchaperoned, independent, solitary; alone, on your own, by yourself.
OPPOSITES: accompanied.
▷ **adverb** *she sailed solo:* unaccompanied, alone, on your own, single-handed, by yourself, unescorted, unattended, unchaperoned, unaided, independently.
OPPOSITES: accompanied.

solution noun
1 *an easy solution to the problem:* answer, resolution, way out, panacea; key, formula, explanation.
2 *a solution of ammonia in water:* mixture, mix, blend, compound, suspension, tincture, infusion, emulsion.

solve verb *there's only one way to solve their problem:* resolve, remedy, sort out, deal with, put right, correct, fix, straighten out, clear up; answer, find a solution to, find the key to, work out, puzzle out, fathom, decipher, decode, get to the bottom of, unravel, piece together, explain; informal figure out, crack; Brit. informal suss out.

solvent adjective *interest rate rises have very severe effects on normally solvent companies:* financially sound, debt-free, in the black, in credit, creditworthy, solid, secure, profit-making.

sombre adjective
1 *sombre clothes:* dark, drab, dull, dingy; restrained, subdued, sober, funereal.
2 *a sombre expression:* solemn, earnest, serious, grave, sober, unsmiling, stern, grim, dour, humourless, reverential; gloomy, depressed, sad, glum, melancholy, dismal, doleful, mournful, lugubrious.
OPPOSITES: bright, cheerful.

somehow adverb *I knew that I had to be involved somehow:* by some means, by any means, in some way, one way or another, no matter how, by fair means or foul, by hook or by crook, come what may.

sometime adverb
1 *I'll visit sometime:* some day, one day, one of these days, at a future date, sooner or later, by and by, in due course, in the long run.
2 *it happened sometime on Sunday:* at some time, at some point; during, in the course of.
OPPOSITES: never.
▷ **adjective** *the sometime editor of the paper:* former, past, previous, prior, foregoing, late, erstwhile, one-time, ex-.

sometimes adverb *sometimes I want to do things on my own:* occasionally, from time to time, now and then, every so often, once in a while, on occasion, at times, off and on, at intervals, periodically, sporadically, spasmodically, intermittently.

somewhat adverb
1 *matters have improved somewhat:* a little, a bit, to some extent, up to a point, in some measure, rather, quite; informal kind of, sort of.
2 *a somewhat thicker book:* slightly, relatively, comparatively, moderately, fairly, rather, quite, marginally.
OPPOSITES: considerably.

somnolent adjective
1 *he felt somnolent after lunch:* sleepy, drowsy, tired, languid, dozy, groggy, lethargic, sluggish, enervated, torpid; literary slumberous; informal snoozy, dopey, yawny.

S

2 *a somnolent village:* quiet, restful, tranquil, calm, peaceful, relaxing, soothing, undisturbed, untroubled. OPPOSITES: lively.

song noun
1 *a beautiful song:* air, strain, ditty, melody, tune, number, track.
2 *the song of the birds:* call, chirping, cheeping, peeping, chirruping, warble, warbling, trilling, twittering; birdsong.

sonorous adjective
1 *a sonorous voice:* resonant, rich, full, round, booming, deep, clear, mellow, orotund, fruity, strong, resounding, reverberant.
2 *sonorous words of condemnation:* impressive, imposing, grandiloquent, high-flown, lofty, orotund, bombastic, grandiose, pompous, pretentious, overblown, turgid; oratorical, rhetorical; formal magniloquent; informal highfalutin. OPPOSITES: high, thin, plain.

soon adverb
1 *we'll be there soon:* shortly, presently, before long, in a little while, in a minute, in a moment, any minute, any day, by and by; informal in a jiffy, in no time, before you know it, before you can say Jack Robinson, anon; Brit. informal in a tick, in two ticks.
2 *how soon can you get here?* early, quickly, promptly, speedily, punctually.

sooner adverb
1 *he should have done it sooner:* earlier, before, beforehand, in advance, ahead of time; already.
2 *I would sooner stay:* rather, preferably, by preference, by choice, more willingly, more readily.

soothe verb
1 *Rachel tried to soothe him:* calm, calm down, pacify, comfort, hush, quiet, subdue, lull, tranquillize; appease, conciliate, mollify; Brit. quieten.
2 *an anaesthetic to soothe the pain:* alleviate, ease, relieve, lessen, reduce, take the edge off, assuage, allay, palliate, diminish, decrease, dull, blunt, deaden. OPPOSITES: agitate, aggravate.

soothing adjective
1 *soothing music:* relaxing, restful, calm, calming, tranquil, peaceful, gentle, soporific.
2 *soothing ointment:* healing, emollient, palliative, mild, calmative. OPPOSITES: invigorating, irritating.

sophisticated adjective
1 *sophisticated techniques:* advanced, modern, state-of-the-art, the latest, new, up to the minute, cutting-edge, innovatory, trailblazing, revolutionary, futuristic, avant-garde; highly developed, complex, complicated, intricate.
2 *a sophisticated woman:* worldly, worldly-wise, experienced, enlightened, cosmopolitan, knowledgeable; urbane, cultured, cultivated, civilized, polished, refined; elegant, stylish; informal cool. OPPOSITES: crude, naive.

sophistication noun worldliness, experience; urbanity, culture, civilization, polish, refinement; elegance, style, poise, finesse, savoir faire; informal cool. OPPOSITES: naivety.

sophistry noun *to claim this is pure sophistry:* specious reasoning, fallacy, sophism, casuistry.

soporific adjective *Valium is widely regarded as a soporific drug:* sleep-inducing, sedative, calmative, tranquillizing. OPPOSITES: invigorating.

sorcerer, sorceress noun wizard, witch, magician, warlock, enchanter, enchantress, magus; shaman, witch doctor.

sorcery noun magic, black magic, the black arts, wizardry, witchcraft, witching, witchery, enchantment, charms, spells, incantation, shamanism.

sordid adjective
1 *a sordid tale of bribery and corruption:* sleazy, seedy, seamy, unsavoury, tawdry, squalid, cheap, dishonourable, disreputable, discreditable, contemptible, ignominious, ignoble, shameful, wretched.
2 *a sordid little street:* squalid, slummy, dirty, filthy, mucky, grimy, shabby, scruffy, messy, run-down, down at heel, insalubrious, downmarket, seedy; informal crummy; Brit. informal grotty. OPPOSITES: respectable, smart.

sore adjective
1 *a sore leg:* painful, hurting, hurt, aching, throbbing, smarting, stinging, agonizing, excruciating; inflamed, sensitive, tender, raw, bruised, wounded, injured.
2 *we are in sore need of you:* dire, urgent, pressing, desperate, critical, acute, grave, serious, drastic, extreme, life-and-death, great, terrible; old use parlous.
▷noun *a sore on his leg:* inflammation, swelling, lesion; wound, scrape, abrasion, cut, laceration, graze, contusion, bruise; ulcer, boil, abscess, carbuncle.

sorrow noun
1 *he felt great sorrow at her death:* sadness, unhappiness, misery, despondency, regret, depression, despair, desolation, dejection, wretchedness, gloom, melancholy, woe, heartache, grief.
2 *the sorrows of life:* trouble, difficulty, problem, adversity, misery, woe, affliction, trial, tribulation, misfortune, setback, reverse, blow, failure, tragedy. OPPOSITES: joy.

sorrowful adjective
1 *she looked at him with sorrowful eyes:*

S

sad, unhappy, dejected, downcast, miserable, downhearted, despondent, despairing, disconsolate, desolate, glum, gloomy, doleful, dismal, melancholy, mournful, woeful, woebegone, forlorn, crestfallen, heartbroken; informal blue, down in the mouth, down in the dumps.
2 *the sorrowful news of his father's death:* tragic, sad, unhappy, awful, miserable, sorry, pitiful; traumatic, upsetting, depressing, distressing, dispiriting, heartbreaking, harrowing.
OPPOSITES: joyful, joyous.

sorry adjective
1 *I was sorry to hear about his accident:* sad, saddened, upset, unhappy, sorrowful, distressed, downcast, downhearted, disheartened, despondent; heartbroken, inconsolable, grief-stricken.
2 *he felt sorry for her:* full of pity, sympathetic, compassionate, moved, empathetic, concerned.
3 *I'm sorry if I was brusque:* apologetic, regretful, remorseful, contrite, repentant, rueful, penitent, abject, guilty, self-reproachful, ashamed, sheepish, shamefaced.
4 *he looks a sorry sight:* pitiful, pitiable, heart-rending, distressing; unfortunate, unhappy, wretched, unlucky, shameful, regrettable, awful.
OPPOSITES: glad, unsympathetic, unapologetic.

sort noun *what sort of book is it?* type, kind, nature, manner, variety, class, category, style; calibre, quality, form, group, set, bracket, genre, species, family, order, generation, vintage, make, model, brand, stamp, ilk, cast, grain, mould.
▷ verb *his written work can be sorted into three categories:* classify, class, categorize, catalogue, grade, group; organize, arrange, order, marshal, assemble, systematize, pigeonhole.
□ **sort of** (informal)
1 *you look sort of familiar:* slightly, faintly, remotely, vaguely; somewhat, moderately, quite, rather, fairly, reasonably, relatively; informal pretty, kind of.
2 *he sort of pirouetted:* as it were, kind of, somehow.
□ **sort something out**
1 *she sorted out the clothes: some to be kept, some to be thrown away.* See **SORT** verb sense 1.
2 *they must sort out their problems:* resolve, settle, solve, fix, work out, thrash out, hammer out, straighten out, deal with, put right, set right, rectify, iron out; answer, explain, fathom, unravel, clear up, patch up; informal sort, figure out.

sortie noun
1 *the garrison mounted a sortie against their besiegers:* foray, sally, charge, offensive, attack, assault, raid, onset, onslaught, thrust, drive.

2 *a bomber sortie:* mission, operation, flight.

soul noun
1 *in the depths of her soul, she knew | though their bodies are dead, their souls will live on:* spirit, psyche, inner self, inner being, life force, vital force; subconscious, anima.
2 *he is the soul of discretion:* embodiment, personification, incarnation, epitome, quintessence, essence; model, exemplification, exemplar, image, manifestation.
3 *there was not a soul in sight:* person, human being, individual, man, woman, mortal, creature.
4 *their music lacked soul:* inspiration, feeling, emotion, passion, animation, intensity, fervour, ardour, enthusiasm, warmth, energy, vitality, spirit.

soulful adjective *she gave him a soulful glance:* emotional, deep, profound, fervent, heartfelt, sincere, passionate; meaningful, significant, eloquent, expressive; moving, stirring; sad, mournful, doleful.
OPPOSITES: unfeeling.

soulless adjective
1 *a soulless room:* characterless, featureless, bland, dull, colourless, lacklustre, dreary, drab, uninspiring, undistinguished, anaemic, insipid.
2 *it was soulless work:* boring, dull, tedious, dreary, dry, humdrum, tiresome, wearisome, uninteresting, uninspiring, unexciting, soul-destroying, mind-numbing, monotonous, repetitive.
OPPOSITES: exciting.

sound[1] noun *she heard the sound of the car outside:* noise, note; din, racket, hubbub; resonance, reverberation; Brit. row.
OPPOSITES: silence.
▷ verb
1 *the buzzer sounded:* make a noise, resonate, resound, reverberate, go off, blare; ring, chime, peal.
2 *drivers must sound their horns:* blow, blast, toot, blare; operate, set off; ring.
3 *do you sound the 'h' in 'Delhi'?* pronounce, say, voice, enunciate, articulate, vocalize, verbalize.
4 *it sounds a crazy idea:* appear to be, look like, seem to, strike someone as, give every indication of being.

> WORD LINKS
> **acoustic, sonic, aural** relating to sound

sound[2] adjective
1 *your heart is pretty sound:* healthy, in good condition, in good shape, fit, hale and hearty, in fine fettle; undamaged, unimpaired.
2 *a sound building:* well built, solid, substantial, strong, sturdy, durable, stable, intact, unimpaired.

3 *this is sound advice:* well founded, valid, reasonable, logical, weighty, authoritative, reliable.
4 *a sound judge of character:* reliable, dependable, trustworthy, fair, competent; good, sensible, wise, judicious, sagacious, shrewd, perceptive.
5 *the company is financially sound:* solvent, debt-free, in the black, in credit, creditworthy, secure.
6 *a sound sleep:* deep, undisturbed, uninterrupted, untroubled, peaceful.
OPPOSITES: unhealthy, unsafe, unreliable.

sound³ verb *sound the depth of the river:* measure, gauge, determine, test, investigate, survey, plumb, fathom, probe.
□ **sound someone/something out** *officials arrived to sound out public opinion:* investigate, test, check, examine, probe, research, look into; canvass, survey, poll, question, interview, sample.

sour adjective
1 *sour wine:* acid, acidic, acidy, acidulated, tart, bitter, sharp, vinegary, pungent.
2 *sour milk:* bad, off, turned, curdled, rancid, high, rank, foul, fetid.
3 *a sour old man:* embittered, resentful, rancorous, jaundiced, bitter; nasty, spiteful, irritable, peevish, fractious, cross, crabby, crotchety, cantankerous, querulous, grumpy, bad-tempered, ill-humoured, sullen, surly, churlish; informal snappy, grouchy; Brit. informal ratty, stroppy, shirty.
OPPOSITES: sweet, fresh, amiable.
▷ verb
1 *the war had soured him:* embitter, disillusion, disenchant, poison, alienate; dissatisfy, frustrate.
2 *the dispute soured relations:* spoil, mar, damage, harm, impair, wreck, upset, poison, blight.
OPPOSITES: sweeten, improve.

source noun
1 *the source of the river:* spring, origin, head, headspring, headwaters.
2 *the source of the rumour:* origin, birthplace, spring, fountainhead, fount, starting point; history, provenance, derivation, root, beginning, genesis, start, rise; author, originator, initiator, inventor.
3 *a historian uses primary and secondary sources:* reference, authority, informant; document.

souse verb *a crunchy bruschetta soused in green olive oil:* drench, douse, soak, steep, saturate, plunge, immerse, submerge, dip, sink, dunk.

soused adjective *a soused herring:* pickled, marinated.

southern adjective *the southern coast of England:* south, southerly, meridional; technical austral.

souvenir noun *the recording provides a souvenir of a great production:* memento, keepsake, reminder, remembrance, token, memorial; trophy, relic.

sovereign noun ruler, monarch, crowned head, head of state, potentate, suzerain, overlord, dynast, leader; king, queen, emperor, empress, prince, princess, regent, emir, sheikh, sultan.
▷ adjective
1 *they have sovereign control of their territory:* supreme, absolute, unlimited, unrestricted, boundless, ultimate, total, unconditional, full; principal, chief, dominant, predominant, ruling; royal, regal, monarchical.
2 *a sovereign state:* independent, autonomous, self-governing, self-determining; non-aligned, free.

sovereignty noun
1 *their sovereignty over the islands:* jurisdiction, rule, supremacy, dominion, power, authority, control, influence, ascendancy, suzerainty, hegemony, domination.
2 *full sovereignty was achieved in 1955:* autonomy, independence, self-government, self-rule, home rule, self-determination, freedom.
OPPOSITES: subjection, dependence.

sow verb
1 *sow the seeds in rows:* plant, scatter, spread, broadcast, disperse, strew, disseminate, distribute, drill.
2 *the new policy has sown confusion and doubt:* cause, bring about, occasion, create, lead to, produce, engender, generate, introduce, spread.

space noun
1 *there was not enough space:* room, capacity, area, volume, expanse, extent, scope, latitude, margin, leeway, play, clearance.
2 *green spaces in London:* area, expanse, stretch, sweep, tract.
3 *the space between the timbers:* gap, interval, opening, aperture, cavity, cranny, fissure, crack.
▷ verb *the chairs were spaced widely:* position, arrange, range, array, dispose, lay out, locate, situate, set, stand.

spacious adjective *a spacious house:* roomy, capacious, palatial, airy, sizeable, generous, large, big, vast, immense, extensive, expansive, sweeping, rolling, rambling, open.
OPPOSITES: cramped.

spadework noun *the politicians coming along have benefited from the spadework done for them:* groundwork, preliminary work, preliminaries, preparatory measures, preparations, planning, foundations; hard work, labour, drudgery, toil; informal grind; Brit. informal donkey work, graft.

S

span noun

1 *a six-foot wing span:* extent, length, width, reach, stretch, spread, distance, range.
2 *the span of one working day:* period, space, time, duration, course, interval.
▷ verb
1 *an arch spanned the stream:* bridge, cross, straddle, traverse, pass over, arch over, reach across.
2 *his career spanned twenty years:* last, cover, extend, spread over, comprise.

spank verb *she was spanked for spilling ink on the carpet:* smack, slap, cuff; cane, birch, flog, whip; informal wallop, belt, whack, give someone a hiding.

spar verb *a lawyer who was not above sarcasm while sparring with the senator:* argue, dispute, wrangle, disagree, bandy words, cross swords, differ, be at odds, be at variance, lock horns, be at loggerheads, clash, squabble; humorous argufy.

spare adjective

1 *a spare set of keys:* extra, supplementary, additional, second, other, alternative; emergency, reserve, backup, relief, fallback, substitute; fresh; N. Amer. alternate.
2 *they sold off the spare land:* surplus, left over, remaining, superfluous, excessive; redundant, unnecessary, unneeded, uncalled for, dispensable, disposable, expendable, unwanted; informal going begging.
3 *your spare time:* free, leisure, own.
▷ verb
1 *he could not spare any money:* afford, do without, manage without, dispense with, part with, give, provide.
2 *they were spared by their captors:* pardon, forgive, reprieve, release, free; be merciful to, show mercy to, have mercy on, be lenient to, have pity on; informal let off.

sparing adjective *he was more sparing with his admiration than with his criticism:* economical, thrifty, frugal, canny, careful, prudent, cautious; mean, ungenerous, miserly, niggardly, parsimonious, close-fisted, penny-pinching, cheese-paring, close, grasping; informal stingy, tight-fisted, tight, mingy, money-grubbing.
OPPOSITES: lavish.

spark noun *a spark of light:* flash, glint, twinkle, flicker, flare, pinprick.
▷ verb *the trial sparked a furious row:* cause, give rise to, lead to, occasion, bring about, start, initiate, precipitate, prompt, trigger, provoke, stimulate, stir up.

sparkle verb

1 *her earrings sparkled in the candlelight:* glitter, glint, glisten, twinkle, flash, shimmer, glimmer, shine, gleam.
2 *she sparkled as the hostess:* be lively, be vivacious, be animated, be exuberant, be witty, be bubbly, be effervescent, be full of life.

sparkling adjective

1 *a sparkling diamond ring:* glittering, glinting, twinkling, flashing, shimmering, gleaming, flickering, glistening.
2 *sparkling wine:* effervescent, fizzy, carbonated, aerated, gassy, bubbly, frothy.
3 *a sparkling performance:* brilliant, dazzling, scintillating, exciting, exhilarating, stimulating, invigorating; vivacious, lively, vibrant, animated.
OPPOSITES: dull, still.

sparse adjective *areas of sparse population | details are sparse:* scant, scanty, scattered, scarce, infrequent, few and far between; meagre, paltry, limited, negligible, in short supply.
OPPOSITES: abundant, dense.

spartan adjective *a spartan life:* austere, harsh, hard, frugal, stringent, rigorous, strict, stern, severe, ascetic, abstemious; bleak, joyless, grim, bare, stark, plain.
OPPOSITES: luxurious.

spasm noun

1 *a muscle spasm:* contraction, convulsion, cramp; twitch, jerk, tic, shudder, shiver, tremor.
2 *a spasm of coughing:* fit, attack, burst, bout, seizure, paroxysm, outburst, outbreak; literary access.

spasmodic adjective *spasmodic fighting continued:* intermittent, fitful, irregular, sporadic, erratic, occasional, infrequent, scattered, patchy, isolated, periodic, periodical.
OPPOSITES: regular, frequent, continuous.

spate noun *a spate of burglaries:* series, succession, run, cluster, string, rash, epidemic, outbreak, wave, flurry, rush, flood, deluge, torrent.
OPPOSITES: lack, dearth.

spatter verb *specks of blood spattered his face:* splash, bespatter, splatter, spray, sprinkle, shower, speck, speckle, fleck, mottle, blotch, cover; informal splotch; Brit. informal splodge.

spawn verb *he wrote in a dry style that spawned hundreds of imitations:* give rise to, bring about, occasion, generate, engender, originate; lead to, result in, effect, induce, initiate, start, set off, precipitate, trigger; breed, bear.

speak verb

1 *she refused to speak about it:* talk, say anything/something.
2 *he spoke the truth:* utter, state, declare, express, voice, pronounce, articulate, enunciate, vocalize, verbalize.
3 *we spoke the other day:* converse, have a conversation, talk, communicate, chat, pass the time of day, have a word, gossip; informal have a confab, chew the fat; Brit. informal natter.

S

4 *the Minister spoke to a large audience:* give a speech, talk, lecture, hold forth, discourse, expound, expatiate, orate, sermonize, pontificate; informal spout.
□ **speak for**
1 *she speaks for the Liberal Democrats:* represent, act for, appear for, express the views of, be spokesperson for.
2 *I spoke for the motion:* advocate, champion, uphold, defend, support, promote, recommend, back, endorse, sponsor, espouse.
□ **speak of**
he was spoken of as a promising student: mention, talk about, discuss, refer to, remark on, allude to.
□ **speak out**
women have been speaking out on this issue for some time: speak publicly, speak openly, speak frankly, speak your mind, stand up and be counted; informal sound off.
□ **speak up**
you'll have to speak up to be heard: speak loudly, speak clearly, raise your voice; shout, yell, bellow; informal holler.

speaker noun speech-maker, lecturer, talker, speechifier, orator; spokesperson, spokesman/woman, mouthpiece; reader, lector, commentator, broadcaster, narrator.

spearhead noun *the spearhead of the struggle against Fascism:* leaders, driving force; forefront, front runners, front line, vanguard, van, cutting edge.
▷ **verb** *she spearheaded the campaign:* lead, head, front; be in the van, be in the vanguard.

special adjective
1 *he's a very special person:* exceptional, unusual, singular, uncommon, notable, noteworthy, remarkable, outstanding, unique.
2 *our town's special character:* distinctive, distinct, individual, particular, specific, peculiar.
3 *a special occasion:* momentous, significant, memorable, signal, important, historic, festive, gala, red-letter.
4 *a special tool for cutting tiles:* specific, particular, purpose-built, tailor-made, custom-built.
OPPOSITES: ordinary, general.

specialist noun *a specialist in electronics:* expert, authority, professional, pundit; connoisseur; master, maestro, adept, virtuoso; informal pro, buff, ace, whizz; Brit. informal dab hand.
OPPOSITES: amateur.

speciality noun
1 *his speciality was watercolours:* forte, strong point, strength, métier, strong suit, talent, skill, bent, gift; N. Amer. & Medicine specialty; informal thing.
2 *a speciality of the region:* delicacy, fine food/product, traditional food/product; N. Amer. specialty.

species noun *there are several species of spadefoot toad:* type, kind, sort, variety, strain, breed; class, classification, category, set, bracket; style, manner, form, genre.

specific adjective
1 *they can customize their software to suit a company's specific business needs:* particular, specified, fixed, set, distinct, definite; single, individual, peculiar, discrete, express, precise.
2 *I gave specific instructions:* detailed, explicit, express, clear-cut, unequivocal, precise, exact, meticulous, strict, definite.
OPPOSITES: general, vague.

specification noun
1 *a clear specification of objectives:* statement, identification, definition, description, setting out, framing, designation, detailing, enumeration; stipulation, prescription.
2 *a shelter built to their specifications:* instructions, orders, parameters, stipulations, requirements, conditions, provisions, restrictions.

specify verb *the manufacturer would not specify the sums involved:* state, name, identify, define, describe, set out, frame, itemize, detail, list, spell out, enumerate, cite, instance; stipulate, prescribe; formal particularize.

specimen noun *he was asked for a specimen of his handwriting:* sample, example, instance, illustration, demonstration, exemplification; bit, snippet; model, prototype, pattern, dummy, pilot, trial, tester; Brit. taster.

specious adjective *a specious argument:* misleading, deceptive, false, fallacious, unsound, casuistic, sophistic; plausible.
OPPOSITES: sound.

speck noun
1 *a mere speck in the distance:* dot, pinprick, spot, fleck, speckle.
2 *a speck of dust:* particle, grain, atom, molecule; bit, trace.

speckled adjective *a large speckled brown egg:* flecked, speckly, specked, freckled, freckly, spotted, spotty, dotted, mottled, dappled.
OPPOSITES: plain.

spectacle noun
1 *a spectacle fit for a monarch:* display, show, pageant, parade, performance, exhibition, extravaganza, spectacular.
2 *don't make a spectacle of yourself:* exhibition, laughing stock, fool.

spectacular adjective *a spectacular view:* impressive, striking, magnificent, glorious, splendid, dazzling, sensational, dramatic, picturesque, breathtaking, arresting, eye-catching, remarkable, outstanding, memorable, unforgettable; informal out of this world.
OPPOSITES: unimpressive.

S

spectator noun *the game attracted about 40,000 spectators:* viewer, observer, onlooker, watcher, bystander, witness, monitor, commentator, reporter, blogger.

spectral adjective ghostly, phantom, wraithlike, shadowy, incorporeal, insubstantial, disembodied, unearthly, other-worldly; informal spooky.

spectre noun
1 *the spectres in the crypt:* ghost, phantom, apparition, spirit, wraith, shadow, presence; informal spook.
2 *the looming spectre of war:* threat, menace, shadow, cloud; prospect; danger, peril, fear, dread.

spectrum noun *a broad spectrum of opinion:* range, gamut, sweep, scope, span; compass, orbit, ambit.

speculate verb
1 *they speculated about my private life:* conjecture, theorize, hypothesize, guess, surmise; think, wonder, muse.
2 *investors speculate on the stock market:* gamble, take a risk, wager; invest, play the market; Brit. informal have a flutter, punt.

speculative adjective
1 *any discussion is largely speculative:* conjectural, theoretical, hypothetical, putative, academic, notional, abstract; tentative, unproven, unfounded, groundless, unsubstantiated.
2 *a speculative investment:* risky, hazardous, unsafe, uncertain, unpredictable; informal chancy, dicey, iffy; Brit. informal dodgy.

speech noun
1 *the power of speech:* speaking, talking, verbal expression, verbal communication.
2 *her speech was slurred:* diction, pronunciation, articulation, enunciation, elocution; utterance, words.
3 *an after-dinner speech:* talk, address, lecture, discourse, oration, deliverance, presentation; sermon, homily; monologue, soliloquy; formal disquisition, peroration; informal spiel.

speechless adjective *she was momentarily speechless:* lost for words, dumbstruck, bereft of speech, tongue-tied, inarticulate, mute, dumb, silent.
OPPOSITES: talkative.

speed noun
1 *the speed of their progress:* rate, pace, tempo, velocity, momentum.
2 *the speed with which they responded:* rapidity, swiftness, promptness, dispatch, immediacy, briskness, sharpness; haste, hurry.
▷ verb
1 *I sped home:* hurry, rush, dash, run, race, sprint, bolt, dart, gallop, career, charge, shoot, hurtle, fly, zoom, scurry, scuttle, scamper, hasten; Brit. hare; informal tear, belt,

pelt, scoot, zip, whip, hotfoot it, leg it; Brit. informal bomb; N. Amer. informal hightail it.
2 *a holiday will speed his recovery:* hasten, expedite, speed up, accelerate, advance, further, promote, boost, stimulate, aid, assist, facilitate.
OPPOSITES: dawdle, slow, hinder.
□ speed up
Smith shouted at them to speed up: hurry up, accelerate, go faster, put a spurt on, pick up speed, gather speed; informal get cracking, get moving, get a move on, step on it.

WORD LINKS
tachometer an instrument used for measuring the working speed of an engine

speedily adverb *you should ensure that complaints are handled speedily:* rapidly, swiftly, quickly, fast, post-haste; promptly, immediately, without delay.
OPPOSITES: slowly.

speedy adjective *a speedy reply:* rapid, swift, quick, fast; prompt, immediate, expeditious, express, brisk, sharp; whirlwind, lightning, meteoric; hasty, hurried, precipitate, breakneck, rushed; informal snappy.
OPPOSITES: slow.

spell¹ verb *the drought spelled disaster for them:* signal, mean, signify, amount to, add up to, constitute; portend, augur, herald, bode, promise; involve.
□ spell something out
Chapman spelled out his aims for the club: explain, make clear, make plain, elucidate, clarify; specify, indicate, itemize, detail, enumerate, list, expound, catalogue; formal particularize.

spell² noun
1 *the witch recited a spell:* charm, incantation, formula; (**spells**) magic, sorcery, witchcraft.
2 *she surrendered to his spell:* influence, animal magnetism, charisma, allure, lure, charm, attraction, enticement; magic, romance, mystique.
□ cast a spell on
bewitch, enchant, entrance; curse, jinx.

spell³ noun
1 *a spell of dry weather:* period, time, interval, season, burst, stretch, run, course, streak; Brit. informal patch.
2 *a spell of dizziness:* bout, fit, episode, attack.

spellbinding adjective *a spellbinding tale of her life in India:* enthralling, fascinating, entrancing, bewitching, captivating, riveting, engrossing, gripping, absorbing, compelling, compulsive, mesmerizing, hypnotic.
OPPOSITES: boring.

spellbound adjective *the audience was spellbound:* enthralled, fascinated, rapt, riveted, transfixed, gripped, captivated, bewitched, enchanted, mesmerized, hypnotized; informal hooked.

spend verb
1 *she spent £185 on shoes:* pay out, expend, disburse; squander, waste, fritter away; lavish; informal fork out, lay out, shell out, cough up, blow, splurge; Brit. informal stump up, blue, splash out.
2 *the morning was spent gardening:* pass, occupy, fill, take up, while away.
3 *I've spent hours on this essay:* put in, devote; waste.

spendthrift noun *he is such a spendthrift:* profligate, prodigal, waster; literary wastrel; informal big spender.
OPPOSITES: miser.
▷**adjective** *his spendthrift father:* profligate, improvident, thriftless, wasteful, extravagant, prodigal.
OPPOSITES: frugal.

spew verb *factories spewed out yellow smoke:* emit, discharge, belch out, pour out, spout, gush, spurt, disgorge, eject, expel.

sphere noun
1 *a glass sphere:* globe, ball, orb, spheroid, globule; bubble.
2 *our sphere of influence:* area, field, orbit; range, scope, extent.
3 *the sphere of foreign affairs:* domain, realm, province, field, area, territory, arena, department.

spherical adjective *a spherical Japanese lantern:* round, spheroidal, globular, ball-shaped.

spice noun
1 *the spices in curry powder:* seasoning, flavouring, condiment.
2 *the risk added spice to their affair:* excitement, interest, colour, piquancy, zest; an edge; informal a kick.
▫ **spice something up**
spice up your life with this new seductive fragrance: enliven, liven up, make more exciting, vitalize, put some life into, ginger up, galvanize, electrify, boost, leaven; informal pep up, perk up, jazz up.

spicy adjective
1 *a spicy casserole:* piquant, tangy, peppery, hot, picante; spiced, seasoned; tasty, highly flavoured, flavoursome, zesty, strong, pungent.
2 *spicy stories:* risqué, suggestive, indecent, indelicate, improper, unseemly, provocative, sexual, sexy, off colour, ribald, titillating, bawdy, naughty, salacious, dirty, smutty; entertaining, colourful, racy, exciting, lively, spirited, scandalous, piquant, zesty; informal raunchy, saucy, juicy.
OPPOSITES: bland, boring.

spiel noun (informal) *he went into his long spiel about recycling:* speech, patter, sales pitch, talk; monologue; rigmarole, story, saga; informal line.

spike noun
1 *a metal spike:* prong, barb, point; skewer, stake, spit; tine, pin; spur.
2 *the spikes of a cactus:* thorn, spine, prickle, bristle; Zoology spicule.
▷**verb**
1 *she spiked an oyster:* impale, spear, skewer; pierce, penetrate, perforate, stab, stick, transfix.
2 (informal) *his drink was spiked with drugs:* adulterate, contaminate, drug, lace; informal dope, doctor, cut.

spill verb
1 *Kevin spilled his drink:* knock over, tip over, upset, overturn.
2 *the bath water spilled on to the floor:* overflow, flow, pour, run, slop, slosh, splash; leak, escape.
3 *students spilled out of the building:* stream, pour, surge, swarm, flood, throng, crowd.
▷**noun** *an oil spill:* spillage, leak, leakage, overflow, flood.

spin verb
1 *the bike's wheels are still spinning:* revolve, rotate, turn, go round, whirl, twirl, gyrate, circle.
2 *she spun round to face him:* whirl, wheel, twirl, turn, swing, twist, swivel, pirouette, pivot.
3 *her head was spinning:* reel, whirl, go round, swim.
▷**noun**
1 *a spin of the wheel:* revolution, rotation, turn, whirl, twirl, gyration.
2 *he tried to put a positive spin on the campaign:* slant, angle, interpretation.
3 *he took Lily for a spin in the car:* trip, jaunt, outing, excursion, journey; drive, ride, run, turn, airing.
▫ **spin something out**
the longer you can spin out the negotiations the better: prolong, protract, draw out, drag out, string out, extend, carry on, continue; fill out, pad out.

spindle noun pivot, pin, rod, shaft, axle, capstan; axis.

spindly adjective *he was pale and spindly:* lanky, thin, skinny, lean, spare, gangling, gangly, scrawny, bony, rangy, angular.
OPPOSITES: stocky.

spine noun
1 *he injured his spine:* backbone, spinal column, vertebral column; back.
2 *the spines of a hedgehog:* prickle, bristle, needle, spike, barb, quill; thorn.

spine-chilling adjective *a spine-chilling ghost story:* terrifying, blood-curdling, hair-raising, petrifying, frightening, chilling, horrifying, fearsome; eerie, sinister, ghostly; informal scary, creepy, spooky.

spineless adjective *a spineless coward:*

S

weak, weak-willed, feeble, soft,
ineffectual, irresolute, indecisive;
cowardly, timid, timorous, fearful, faint-
hearted, pusillanimous, craven, unmanly,
namby-pamby, lily-livered; informal wimpish,
wimpy, sissy, yellow-bellied, gutless; Brit.
informal wet.
OPPOSITES: bold, brave.

spiny adjective *spiny clumps of blackthorn:*
prickly, spiky, thorny, bristly, bristled,
spiked, barbed, scratchy, sharp.

spiral adjective *a spiral column of smoke:*
coiled, helical, corkscrew, curling,
winding, twisting, snaking, whorled.
▷ **noun** *a spiral of smoke:* coil, helix, corkscrew,
curl, twist, whorl, scroll; literary gyre.
▷ **verb**
1 *smoke spiralled up:* coil, wind, swirl,
twist, wreathe, snake, gyrate.
2 *prices spiralled:* soar, shoot up, rocket,
increase rapidly, rise rapidly, escalate,
climb; informal skyrocket, go through the
roof.
3 *the economy is spiralling downward:*
deteriorate, decline, degenerate, worsen,
get worse; informal go downhill, take a
nosedive, go to pot, go to the dogs, hit the
skids, go down the tube.
OPPOSITES: fall, improve.

spire noun steeple, flèche, pinnacle, spike.

spirit noun
1 *harmony between body and spirit:* soul,
psyche, inner self, inner being, inner man/
woman, mind, ego, id.
2 *a spirit haunts the island:* ghost,
phantom, spectre, apparition, wraith,
presence; informal spook.
3 *that's the spirit:* attitude, frame of mind,
way of thinking, point of view, outlook,
idea.
4 *she was in good spirits when I left:* mood,
frame of mind, state of mind, emotional
state, humour, temper, morale.
5 *the spirit of the age:* ethos, prevailing
tendency, motivating force, essence,
quintessence; atmosphere, mood, feeling,
climate; attitudes, beliefs, principles,
standards, ethics.
6 *his spirit never failed him:* courage,
bravery, pluck, valour, strength of
character, fortitude, backbone, mettle,
stout-heartedness, determination,
resolution, resolve, fight, grit; informal guts,
spunk; Brit. informal bottle.
7 *they played with great spirit:* energy,
vigour, dynamism, eagerness, keenness,
liveliness, vivacity, vivaciousness,
animation, enthusiasm, verve, zest, dash,
elan, panache, sparkle, exuberance, gusto,
brio, pep, fervour, zeal, fire, passion; informal
get-up-and-go.
8 *the spirit of the law:* real/true meaning,
true intention, essence, substance.
9 *he doesn't drink spirits:* strong liquor/
drink; informal hard stuff, firewater, hooch.
OPPOSITES: body, flesh.

□ **spirit someone/something away**
*the girl was spirited away before we got
anywhere near her:* whisk away/off,
vanish with, make off with, make
someone/something disappear, run
away with, abscond with, carry off, steal
someone/something away, abduct, kidnap,
snatch, seize.

spirited adjective *an attractive and
spirited young woman:* lively, vivacious,
vibrant, full of life, vital, animated,
high-spirited, sparkling, sprightly,
energetic, active, vigorous, dynamic,
dashing, enthusiastic, passionate; feisty,
determined, resolute, purposeful; informal
spunky, have-a-go, gutsy.
OPPOSITES: timid, apathetic, lifeless.

spiritual adjective
1 *your spiritual well-being:* inner,
mental, psychological; non-material,
incorporeal, intangible; transcendent,
ethereal, other-worldly, mystic, mystical,
metaphysical.
2 *spiritual writings:* religious, sacred,
divine, holy, church, ecclesiastical,
devotional.
OPPOSITES: physical, secular.

spit¹ verb
1 *Cranston coughed and spat:* expectorate,
hawk; Brit. informal gob.
2 (Brit.) *it began to spit:* drizzle, spot; N. English
mizzle.
▷ **noun** *spit dribbled from his mouth:* saliva,
spittle, sputum, slobber, dribble; Brit. informal
gob.

spit² noun *chicken cooked on a spit:* skewer,
brochette, kebab stick, rotisserie.

spite noun *she sabotaged his plans out of
spite:* malice, malevolence, ill will, animus,
enmity, revenge, vindictiveness, evil
intentions, vengefulness, malignity; informal
bitchiness, cattiness.
OPPOSITES: kindness.
▷ **verb** *he did it to spite me:* hurt, upset,
torment, distress, wound, make miserable,
grieve, pain, injure.
OPPOSITES: please.
□ **in spite of**
*they married in January, in spite of
her family's fierce opposition:* despite,
notwithstanding, regardless of, for all;
undeterred by, in defiance of, in the face
of; even though, although.

spiteful adjective *the other girls made
spiteful remarks about Paula:* malicious,
vindictive, mean, nasty, hurtful,
mischievous, wounding, cruel, unkind,
malevolent, vengeful, malign; informal
bitchy, catty.
OPPOSITES: kind.

splash verb
1 *splash cool water over your face:* sprinkle,
spray, shower, splatter, slosh, slop, squirt;
daub; wet.

S

2 *his boots were splashed with mud:* spatter, bespatter, splatter, speck, speckle, blotch, smear, stain, mark; informal splotch; Brit. informal splodge.

3 *waves splashed on the beach:* wash, break, lap, swash; dash, beat, lash, batter, crash, buffet.

4 *children splashed in the water:* paddle, wade, dabble, slosh, wallow; informal splosh.

5 *the story was splashed across the front pages:* blazon, display, spread, plaster, trumpet, publicize; informal splatter.

▷**noun**

1 *a splash of fat on his shirt:* spot, blob, dab, daub, smudge, smear, streak, speck, fleck, patch; mark, stain, burst; informal splotch; Brit. informal splodge.

2 *a splash of lemonade:* drop, dash, bit, spot, soupçon, dribble, driblet.

▫**make a splash** (informal)
cause a sensation, cause a stir, attract attention, draw attention to yourself/itself, get noticed, make an impression, make an impact.

▫**splash out** (Brit. informal)
she splashed out on a Mercedes: be extravagant, go on a spending spree, spare no expense, spend lavishly; informal lash out, splurge; Brit. informal push the boat out.

spleen noun *he vented his spleen on me:* bad temper, bad mood, ill temper, ill humour, anger, wrath, vexation, annoyance, irritation, displeasure, dissatisfaction, resentment, rancour; spite, ill feeling, malice, maliciousness, bitterness, animosity, antipathy, hostility, malevolence, venom, gall, acrimony, bile, hatred, hate.

splendid adjective

1 *their splendid costumes:* magnificent, sumptuous, grand, impressive, imposing, superb, spectacular, resplendent, opulent, luxurious, de luxe, rich, fine, costly, expensive, lavish, ornate, gorgeous, glorious, dazzling, elegant, handsome, beautiful; stately, majestic, princely, noble, proud, palatial; informal plush, posh, swanky, ritzy, splendiferous; Brit. informal swish.

2 *we had a splendid holiday:* excellent, wonderful, marvellous, superb, glorious, sublime, lovely, delightful, first-class, first-rate; informal super, great, amazing, fantastic, terrific, tremendous, phenomenal, sensational, heavenly, gorgeous, dreamy, grand, fabulous, fab, awesome, magic, ace, cool, out of this world; Brit. informal smashing, brilliant.
OPPOSITES: simple, modest, awful.

splendour noun *a wedding long remembered for its splendour:* magnificence, sumptuousness, grandeur, resplendence, opulence, luxury, richness, fineness, lavishness, ornateness, glory, beauty, elegance; majesty, stateliness. OPPOSITES: simplicity, modesty.

splice verb *the ropes are spliced together:* interweave, braid, plait, entwine, intertwine, interlace, knit, mesh; Nautical marry.

splinter noun *a splinter of wood:* sliver, shiver, chip, shard; fragment, piece, bit, shred; (**splinters**) matchwood, flinders.

▷**verb** *the windscreen splintered:* shatter, disintegrate, crumble, smash, fracture, split, crack; informal smash into smithereens.

split verb

1 *the axe split the wood:* chop, break, cut, hew, lop, cleave; snap, crack.

2 *the ice cracked and split:* break, fracture, rupture, fissure, snap, come apart, splinter.

3 *her dress was split:* tear, rip, slash, slit.

4 *the issue could split the Party:* divide, disunite, sever, cause a schism in; bisect, partition.

5 *they split the money between them:* share, divide, apportion, allocate, allot, distribute, dole out, parcel out, measure out; carve up, slice up; informal divvy up.

6 *the path split:* fork, divide, bifurcate, diverge, branch.
OPPOSITES: join, unite, pool, converge.

▷**noun**

1 *a split in the rock face:* crack, fissure, cleft, crevice, break, fracture, breach.

2 *a split in the curtain:* rip, tear, cut, rent, slash, slit.

3 *a split in the Party:* division, rift, breach, schism, rupture, partition, break-up.

4 *the acrimonious split with his wife:* break-up, split-up, separation, parting, estrangement, rift; divorce; Brit. informal bust-up.
OPPOSITES: unification, marriage.

▫**split up**
they split up last year: break up, separate, part, part company, become estranged; divorce, get divorced; Brit. informal bust up.

spoil verb

1 *too much sun spoils the complexion:* mar, damage, impair, blemish, disfigure, blight, flaw, deface, scar, injure, harm; ruin, destroy, wreck.

2 *rain spoiled my plans:* ruin, wreck, destroy, upset, undo, mess up, make a mess of, dash, sabotage, scotch, torpedo; informal foul up, louse up, muck up, screw up, do for; Brit. informal scupper, throw a spanner in the works of.

3 *his sisters spoil him:* pamper, overindulge, indulge, mollycoddle, cosset, coddle, baby, wait on hand and foot, kill with kindness; nanny.

4 *stockpiled food may spoil:* go bad, go off, go rancid, turn, go sour, go mouldy, go rotten, rot, perish.
OPPOSITES: improve, help.

spoils plural noun *the spoils of war:* booty, loot, stolen goods, plunder, ill-gotten gains, haul, pickings; informal swag, boodle.

spoilsport noun *don't be such a spoilsport!* killjoy, dog in the manger, misery, damper;

S

informal wet blanket, party-pooper.

spoken adjective *spoken communication:* verbal, oral, vocal, uttered, said, stated; unwritten; by word of mouth.
OPPOSITES: non-verbal, written.

spokesman, spokeswoman noun spokesperson, representative, agent, mouthpiece, voice, official; informal spin doctor.

sponge verb
1 *she sponged the blood away:* wash, clean, wipe, swab; mop, rinse, sluice, swill.
2 (informal) *he lived by sponging off others:* scrounge, be a parasite, beg; live off; informal freeload, bum; Brit. informal cadge.

spongy adjective *the material has a spongy texture:* soft, squashy, cushioned, resilient, elastic, compressible, yielding, springy; porous, absorbent, permeable; Brit. informal squidgy.
OPPOSITES: hard, solid.

sponsor noun *the production cost £50,000 with most of the money coming from local sponsors:* backer, patron, promoter, benefactor, benefactress, supporter, contributor, subscriber, friend, guarantor, underwriter; Theatre, informal angel.
▷verb *a bank sponsored the event:* finance, put up the money for, fund, subsidize, back, promote, support, contribute to, be a patron of, guarantee, underwrite; informal foot the bill for, pick up the tab for, bankroll.

sponsorship noun backing, support, promotion, patronage, subsidy, funding, financing, aid, financial assistance.

spontaneous adjective
1 *a spontaneous display of affection:* unplanned, unpremeditated, unrehearsed, impulsive, impetuous, unstudied, impromptu, spur-of-the-moment, extempore, extemporaneous; unforced, voluntary, unconstrained, unprompted, unbidden, unsolicited; informal off-the-cuff.
2 *a spontaneous reaction to danger:* reflex, automatic, mechanical, natural, knee-jerk, involuntary, unthinking, unconscious, instinctive, instinctual; informal gut.
3 *a spontaneous kind of person:* natural, uninhibited, relaxed, unselfconscious, unaffected, open, genuine, easy, free and easy; impulsive, impetuous.
OPPOSITES: planned, calculated, conscious, inhibited.

spontaneously adverb
1 *they applauded spontaneously:* of your own accord, on impulse, impulsively, on the spur of the moment, without being asked, voluntarily, extempore, extemporaneously; informal off the cuff.
2 *he reacted spontaneously:* automatically, mechanically, unthinkingly, involuntarily, instinctively, naturally, without thinking, by yourself/itself.

sporadic adjective *we braved the sporadic showers:* occasional, infrequent, irregular, periodic, scattered, patchy, isolated, odd; intermittent, spasmodic, fitful, desultory, erratic, unpredictable.
OPPOSITES: frequent, continual, steady.

sport noun *we did a lot of sport:* competitive games, physical recreation, physical activity, physical exercise; pastime.
▷verb *he sported a rather flamboyant tie:* wear, have on, dress in; display, exhibit, show off, flourish, parade, flaunt.

sporting adjective *it was sporting of you to let me have first go:* sportsmanlike, generous, gentlemanly, considerate; fair, just, honourable; Brit. informal decent.
OPPOSITES: dirty, unfair.

spot noun
1 *a grease spot on the wall:* mark, patch, dot, fleck, smudge, smear, stain, blotch, blot, splash; informal splotch; Brit. informal splodge.
2 *a spot on his nose:* pimple, pustule, blackhead, boil, swelling, eruption, wen; informal zit, whitehead; (**spots**) acne.
3 *a secluded spot:* place, location, site, position, point, situation, scene, venue, setting, locale, locality, area, neighbourhood, region.
▷verb
1 *she spotted him in his car:* notice, see, observe, note, discern, detect, perceive, make out, recognize, identify, locate; catch sight of, glimpse, spy; literary espy; Brit. informal clock.
2 *her clothes were spotted with grease:* mark, stain, fleck, speckle, smudge, streak, splash, spatter; informal splotch; Brit. informal splodge.

spotless adjective
1 *the kitchen was spotless:* perfectly clean, ultra-clean, pristine, immaculate, shining, shiny, gleaming, spick and span.
2 *a spotless reputation:* unblemished, unsullied, untarnished, untainted, unstained, pure, whiter than white, innocent, impeccable, blameless, irreproachable, above reproach; informal squeaky clean.
OPPOSITES: dirty, tarnished.

spotlight noun *she was constantly in the spotlight:* public eye, glare of publicity, limelight; focus of public/media attention.
▷verb *this article spotlights the problem:* focus attention on, highlight, point up, draw/call attention to, give prominence to, throw into relief, turn the spotlight on, bring to the fore.

spotted adjective
1 *the spotted leaves:* mottled, dappled, speckled, flecked, freckled, freckly, dotted, stippled; informal splotchy.

2 *a black-and-white spotted dress:* polka-dot, spotty, dotted.
OPPOSITES: plain.

spotty adjective
1 *a spotty dog:* spotted, mottled, speckled, speckly, flecked, specked, stippled; informal splotchy; Brit. informal splodgy.
2 *a spotty dress:* polka-dot, spotted, dotted.
3 (Brit.) *his spotty face:* pimply, pimpled, acned, pockmarked.
OPPOSITES: plain, smooth.

spouse noun partner, marriage partner, mate, consort; informal better half; Brit. informal other half. See also HUSBAND noun, WIFE.

spout verb
1 *blood was spouting from the cuts on his hands | the volcano spouted ash and lava:* spurt, gush, spew, erupt, shoot, squirt, spray; disgorge, discharge, emit, belch out.
2 *the woman spouted about her brilliant plan | he spouts worldly wisdom to his daughter:* hold forth, go on, talk at length, discourse, expatiate, drone on, pontificate; utter, speak, talk, express, voice; informal mouth off, sound off, speechify, spiel; trot out.
▷noun *a can with a spout:* nozzle, jet, mouth, lip, head, rose.

sprawl verb
1 *he sprawled on a sofa:* stretch out, lounge, loll, lie, recline, drape yourself, slump, flop, slouch.
2 *the town sprawled ahead of them:* spread, stretch, extend, be strung out, be scattered, straggle, spill.

spray¹ noun
1 *a spray of water:* shower, sprinkling, sprinkle, jet, mist, drizzle; spume, spindrift; foam, froth.
2 *a perfume spray:* aerosol, atomizer, vaporizer, nebulizer, sprinkler, shower.
▷verb
1 *water was sprayed around:* sprinkle, shower, spatter.
2 *water sprayed into the air:* spout, jet, gush, spurt, shoot, squirt.

spray² noun
1 *a spray of holly:* sprig, twig.
2 *a spray of flowers:* bouquet, bunch, posy, nosegay; corsage, buttonhole.

spread verb
1 *he spread the map out:* lay out, open out, unfurl, unroll, roll out; straighten out, fan out; stretch out, extend.
2 *the landscape spread out below:* extend, stretch, open out, be displayed, be exhibited, be on show; sprawl.
3 *papers were spread all over his desk:* scatter, strew, disperse, distribute.
4 *he's been spreading rumours:* disseminate, circulate, pass on, communicate, diffuse, make public, make known, broadcast, publicize, propagate, promulgate; repeat; Brit. put about.

5 *she spread cold cream on her face:* smear, daub, smooth, rub, plaster, slather, lather, apply.
6 *he spread the toast with butter:* cover, coat, layer, daub, smother.
OPPOSITES: fold up, suppress.
▷noun
1 *the spread of learning:* expansion, proliferation, extension, growth, buildout, roll-out; dissemination, diffusion, transmission, propagation.
2 *a spread of six feet:* span, width, extent, stretch, reach.
3 *a wide spread of subjects:* range, span, spectrum, sweep; variety.

spree noun
1 *a shopping spree:* bout, fling, orgy; informal binge, splurge.
2 *a drinking spree:* drinking bout, debauch; informal binge, bender, session, booze-up.

sprig noun *a sprig of lilac:* spray, twig.

sprightly adjective *she was quite sprightly for her age:* spry, lively, agile, nimble, energetic, active, full of energy, vigorous, spirited, animated, vivacious, frisky; informal full of vim and vigour.
OPPOSITES: doddery, lethargic.

spring verb
1 *the cat sprang off her lap:* leap, jump, bound, vault, hop.
2 *the branch sprang back:* fly, whip, flick, whisk, kick, bounce.
3 *all art springs from feelings:* originate, derive, arise, stem, emanate, proceed, issue, evolve, come, have its roots.
4 *fifty men sprang from nowhere:* appear suddenly, appear unexpectedly, materialize, shoot up, sprout, develop quickly; proliferate, mushroom; informal pop up.
▷noun
1 *with a sudden spring he leapt on to the table:* leap, jump, bound, vault, hop; pounce.
2 *the mattress has lost its spring:* springiness, bounce, resilience, elasticity, flexibility, stretch, stretchiness, give.
3 *there was a spring in his step:* confidence, bounce, energy, liveliness, jauntiness, sprightliness, buoyancy.
4 *a mineral spring:* source, well head, spa, geyser.
▢spring something on someone *he sprang the truth on me:* surprise someone with something, announce something unexpectedly to someone.

WORD LINKS
vernal relating to the season of spring

springy adjective *the turf was springy beneath her feet:* bouncy, resilient, spongy, elastic, stretchy, stretchable, tensile, flexible, pliant, pliable, whippy.
OPPOSITES: rigid, squashy.

S

sprinkle verb
1 *he sprinkled water over the towel:* spray, shower, drizzle, trickle, splash, spatter.
2 *sprinkle sesame seeds over the top:* scatter, strew, spread.
3 *sprinkle the cake with icing sugar:* dredge, dust.
4 *the sky was sprinkled with stars:* dot, stipple, stud, fleck, speckle, spot, pepper; scatter, cover.

sprinkling noun
1 *a sprinkling of nutmeg:* scattering, sprinkle, scatter, dusting; pinch, dash.
2 *the audience was mainly women, but there was a sprinkling of men:* few, one or two, couple, handful, small number, scattering.

sprint verb *she sprinted across the square:* run, race, dart, rush, dash, hasten, hurry, scurry, scamper, bolt, fly, gallop, career, charge, shoot, hurtle, speed, zoom, go like lightning, go like the wind; Brit. hare; informal tear, pelt, scoot, hotfoot it, leg it, belt, whip, go hell for leather; Brit. informal bomb; N. Amer. informal hightail it.

sprout verb *the weeds begin to sprout:* grow, spring up, shoot up, come up, appear, germinate, burgeon, develop, put/send out shoots, bud.

spruce adjective *the Captain looked very spruce in his dress uniform:* smart, neat, dapper, trim, elegant, chic, well groomed, well turned out, well dressed; informal natty, snazzy.
OPPOSITES: scruffy.
▷ **verb**
□ **spruce something up**
smarten, tidy, neaten, put in order, clean; informal do up; Brit. informal tart up, posh up.
□ **spruce yourself up**
groom, tidy, smarten, preen, primp, prink; informal titivate, doll up; Brit. informal tart up.

spry adjective *he's remarkably spry for a man of his age:* sprightly, lively, agile, nimble, energetic, active, full of energy, vigorous, spirited, animated, vivacious, frisky; informal full of vim and vigour.
OPPOSITES: doddery, lethargic.

spur noun
1 *competition can be a spur:* stimulus, incentive, encouragement, inducement, fillip, impetus, prod, motivation, inspiration; informal kick up the backside, shot in the arm.
2 *a spur of bone:* projection, spike, point, jag.
OPPOSITES: disincentive, discouragement.
▷ **verb** *the thought spurred him into action:* stimulate, encourage, prompt, propel, prod, induce, impel, motivate, move, galvanize, inspire, incentivize, urge, drive, egg on, stir; incite, goad, provoke, prick, sting.
OPPOSITES: discourage.

□ **on the spur of the moment**
impulsively, on impulse, impetuously, without thinking, without premeditation, unpremeditatedly, impromptu, extempore, spontaneously; informal off the cuff.

spurious adjective *it was possible to arrange retirements on spurious medical grounds:* bogus, fake, false, counterfeit, forged, fraudulent, sham, artificial, imitation, simulated, feigned, deceptive, misleading, dubious, questionable; informal phoney, pretend; Brit. informal cod.
OPPOSITES: genuine.

spurn verb *he spurned her offer:* reject, rebuff, scorn, turn down, treat with contempt, disdain, look down your nose at, despise; snub, slight, jilt, dismiss, brush off, turn your back on; give someone the cold shoulder, cold-shoulder; informal turn your nose up at, give someone the brush-off, kick in the teeth; Brit. informal knock back.
OPPOSITES: welcome, accept.

spurt verb *water spurted from the tap* | *the kettle boiled and spurted scalding water:* squirt, shoot, jet, erupt, gush, pour, stream, pump, surge, spew, course, well, spring, burst; disgorge, discharge, emit, belch out, expel, eject; Brit. informal sloosh.
▷ **noun**
1 *a spurt of water:* squirt, jet, spout, gush, stream, rush, surge, flood, cascade, torrent.
2 *Daisy put on a spurt:* burst of speed, turn of speed, sprint, rush, burst of energy.

spy noun *a foreign spy:* secret agent, intelligence agent, espionage officer, undercover agent, double agent, counterspy, mole, plant, scout; N. Amer. informal spook, operative.
▷ **verb**
1 *he spied for the West:* be a spy, gather intelligence, work for the secret service; informal snoop.
2 *she spied a coffee shop:* notice, observe, see, spot, sight, catch sight of, glimpse, make out, discern, detect; literary espy; informal clap/lay/set eyes on; Brit. informal clock.
□ **spy on**
the government spied on civil rights leaders: observe furtively, keep under surveillance/observation, watch, keep a watch on, keep an eye on, track, monitor; informal tail, keep tabs on.

spying noun espionage, intelligence gathering, surveillance, eavesdropping, infiltration, undercover work, cloak-and-dagger activities.

squabble noun *there was a squabble over which way they should go:* quarrel, disagreement, argument, contretemps, falling-out, dispute, clash, altercation, exchange; Brit. row; informal tiff, set-to, run-in, spat, scrap, dust-up; Brit. informal barney, ding-dong.

S

▷**verb** *the boys were squabbling over a ball:* quarrel, argue, bicker, fall out, disagree, have words, dispute, spar, cross swords, lock horns, be at loggerheads; Brit. row; informal scrap, argufy.

squad noun
1 *an assassination squad:* team, crew, gang, band, cell, body, mob, outfit, force.
2 *a firing squad:* detachment, detail, unit, platoon, battery, troop, patrol, squadron, cadre.

squalid adjective
1 *a squalid prison:* dirty, filthy, grubby, grimy, mucky, foul, vile, poor, sorry, wretched, miserable, mean, seedy, shabby, scruffy, sordid, insalubrious, neglected, uncared-for, broken-down, run-down, down at heel, depressed, dilapidated, ramshackle, tumbledown, gone to rack and ruin, crumbling, decaying; Brit. informal grotty.
2 *a squalid deal with the opposition:* improper, sordid, unseemly, unsavoury, sleazy, seedy, seamy, shoddy, cheap, corrupt, dishonest, dishonourable, disreputable, despicable, discreditable, disgraceful, contemptible, shameful.
OPPOSITES: clean, pleasant, honourable.

squalor noun *the squalor of their living conditions:* dirt, filth, grubbiness, grime, muck, vileness, poverty, wretchedness, meanness, seediness, shabbiness, sordidness, sleaziness; neglect, decay, dilapidation; informal scruffiness.

squander verb *£100 million of taxpayers' money has been squandered:* waste, misspend, misuse, throw away, fritter away, spend recklessly, lavish, spend unwisely, spend like water; informal blow, go through, splurge, pour down the drain, flush down the toilet; Brit. informal blue.
OPPOSITES: save.

square noun *a shop in the square:* market square, marketplace, plaza, piazza; arcade, mall; Brit. precinct.
▷**adjective**
1 *a square table:* quadrilateral, rectangular, oblong, right-angled, at right angles, perpendicular; straight, level, parallel, horizontal, upright, vertical, true, plane.
2 *the sides were square at half-time:* level, even, drawn, equal, tied; neck and neck, level pegging, nip and tuck, side by side, evenly matched.
OPPOSITES: crooked, uneven.
▷**verb**
1 *the theory does not square with the data:* agree, tally, be in agreement, be consistent, match up, correspond, fit, coincide, accord, conform, be compatible.
2 *his goal squared the match 1–1:* level, even, make equal.
3 *would you square the bill?* pay, settle, discharge, clear, meet.

4 (informal) *they tried to square the press:* bribe, buy off, buy, corrupt, suborn; informal grease someone's palm, give a backhander to.
5 *Tom squared things with his boss:* resolve, sort out, settle, clear up, work out, iron out, smooth over, straighten out, deal with, put right, set right, put to rights, rectify, remedy; informal patch up.

squash verb
1 *the fruit got squashed:* crush, squeeze, flatten, compress, press, smash, distort, pound, trample, stamp on; pulp, mash, cream, liquidize, beat, pulverize.
2 *she squashed her clothes into the bag:* force, ram, thrust, push, cram, jam, stuff, pack, compress, squeeze, wedge, press.
3 *the proposal was immediately squashed:* reject, block, cancel, scotch, frustrate, thwart, suppress, put a stop to, nip in the bud; informal put paid to, put the lid on, put the kibosh on, stymie; Brit. informal scupper.

squashy adjective
1 *a squashy pillow:* springy, resilient, spongy, soft, pliant, pliable, yielding, elastic, compressible.
2 *squashy pears:* mushy, pulpy, slushy, squelchy, oozy, doughy, soft; informal squishy; Brit. informal squidgy.
OPPOSITES: solid, hard.

squat verb *I was squatting on the floor:* crouch down, hunker down, sit on your haunches, sit on your heels.
▷**adjective** *he was muscular and squat:* stocky, thickset, dumpy, stubby, stumpy, short, small.
OPPOSITES: tall, lanky.

squawk verb & noun *a pheasant squawked | the gull gave a squawk:* screech, squeal, shriek, scream, croak, crow, caw, cackle, cry, call.

squeak noun & verb
1 *the vole's dying squeak | the rat squeaked:* peep, cheep, squeal, tweet, yelp, whimper.
2 *the squeak of the hinge | the hinges of the gate squeaked:* screech, creak, scrape, grate, rasp, jar, groan.

squeal noun & verb *the harsh squeal of a fox | the pig squealed in terror:* screech, scream, shriek, squawk.

squeamish adjective
1 *I'm too squeamish to gut fish:* easily nauseated, nervous; (be squeamish about) be put off by, cannot stand the sight of.
2 *less squeamish nations will sell them arms:* scrupulous, principled, fastidious, particular, punctilious, honourable, upright, upstanding, high-minded, righteous, right-minded, moral, ethical.

squeeze verb
1 *I squeezed the bottle:* compress, press, crush, squash, pinch, nip, grasp, grip, clutch, flatten.
2 *squeeze the juice from both oranges:* extract, press, force, express.

S

3 *Sally squeezed her feet into the sandals:* force, thrust, cram, ram, jam, stuff, pack, wedge, press, squash.
4 *we all squeezed into Sanjeev's van:* crowd, crush, cram, pack, jam, squash, wedge yourself, shove, push, force your way.
5 *councils will want to squeeze as much money out of the taxpayers as possible:* extract, force, wrest, wring, extort, milk; informal bleed someone of something.
▷ **noun**
1 *he gave her hand a squeeze:* press, pinch, nip; grasp, grip, clutch, hug, clasp; compression.
2 *it was a tight squeeze in the tiny hall:* crush, jam, squash, press, huddle; congestion.
3 *a squeeze of lemon juice:* dash, splash, few drops, dribble, trickle, spot, hint, touch.

squint verb
1 *the sun made them squint:* screw up your eyes, narrow your eyes, peer, blink.
2 *he has squinted from birth:* be cross-eyed, have a squint; Medicine suffer from strabismus; Brit. informal be boss-eyed.

squirm verb
1 *she squirmed in his grasp, trying to get away:* wriggle, wiggle, writhe, twist, slide, slither, turn, shift, jiggle, twitch, thresh, flounder, flail, toss and turn.
2 *he squirmed as everyone laughed:* wince, shudder, feel embarrassed, feel ashamed.

squirt verb
1 *a jet of ink squirted out of the tube:* spurt, shoot, spray, fountain, jet, erupt; gush, rush, pump, surge, stream, spew, well, spring, burst, issue, emanate; emit, belch out, expel, eject; Brit. informal sloosh.
2 *she squirted me with water:* splash, wet, spray, shower, spatter, splatter, sprinkle.
▷ **noun** *a squirt of water:* spurt, jet, spray, fountain, gush, stream, surge.

stab verb
1 *he stabbed the youth in the stomach:* knife, run through, skewer, spear, bayonet, gore, spike, stick, impale, transfix, pierce, prick, puncture.
2 *she stabbed at the earth with a fork:* lunge, thrust, jab, poke, prod, dig.
▷ **noun**
1 *a stab in the leg:* knife wound, puncture, incision, prick, cut, perforation.
2 *they made stabs into the air:* lunge, thrust, jab, poke, prod, dig, punch.
3 *a stab of pain:* twinge, pang, throb, spasm, cramp, dart, blaze, prick, flash, thrill.
□ **stab someone in the back** betray, be disloyal to, be unfaithful to, desert, break your promise to, double-cross, break faith with, sell out, play false, inform on/against; informal sell down the river, squeal on, stitch up, peach on, do the dirty on; Brit. informal grass on, shop.

stability noun
1 *the stability of play equipment:* steadiness, solidity, firmness, strength, security, safety.
2 *his mental stability:* mental health, balance of mind, sanity, normality, soundness, rationality, reason, sense.
3 *the stability of their relationship:* firmness, steadiness, solidity, strength, durability, lasting nature, enduring nature, permanence, changelessness, invariability, immutability, indestructibility, reliability, dependability.

stable adjective
1 *a stable structure:* steady, solid, firm, secure, fixed, fast, safe, moored, anchored, stuck down, immovable.
2 *a stable person:* well balanced, steady, reasonable, sensible, sober, down-to-earth, matter-of-fact, having both your feet on the ground; of sound mind, compos mentis, sane, normal, right in the head, rational; informal all there.
3 *a stable relationship:* secure, solid, strong, steady, firm, sure, steadfast, unwavering, unvarying, unfaltering; established, abiding, durable, enduring, lasting, permanent, reliable, dependable.
OPPOSITES: loose, wobbly, insecure.

stack noun *a stack of boxes:* pile, heap, mound, mountain, pyramid, tower.
▷ **verb**
1 *Leo was stacking plates:* pile up, heap up, make a pile/heap/stack of; assemble, put together.
2 *they stacked the shelves:* load, fill up, pack, charge, stuff, cram; stock.

stadium noun arena, field, ground, pitch; bowl, amphitheatre, coliseum, ring, dome, manège; track, course; (in ancient Rome) circus.

staff noun
1 *there is a reluctance to take on new staff:* employees, workers, workforce, personnel, human resources, manpower, labour; informal liveware.
2 *he carried a wooden staff:* stick, stave, pole, crook.
▷ **verb** *the legal advice centre is staffed by volunteers:* run, operate; man, people.

stage noun
1 *this stage of the development:* phase, period, juncture, step, point, time, moment, instant, level.
2 *the last stage of the race:* part, section, portion, stretch, leg, lap, circuit.
3 *a theatre stage:* platform, dais, podium, rostrum, apron, staging, stand, grandstand.
4 (**the stage**) the theatre, drama, dramatics, dramatic art, thespianism, theatrics; informal the boards.
5 *the political stage:* scene, setting; context, frame, sphere, field, realm, arena, backdrop; affairs.

▷**verb**
1 *they staged two plays:* put on, present, produce, mount, direct; perform, act, give.
2 *workers staged a protest:* organize, arrange, coordinate, lay on, put together, get together, set up; orchestrate, choreograph, mastermind, engineer; take part in, participate in, join in.

stagger verb
1 *he staggered to the door:* lurch, walk unsteadily, reel, sway, teeter, totter, stumble, wobble.
2 *I was absolutely staggered:* amaze, astound, astonish, surprise, startle, stun, confound, dumbfound, stupefy, daze, nonplus, take aback, leave open-mouthed, leave aghast; informal flabbergast, bowl over; Brit. informal knock for six.
3 *meetings are staggered throughout the day:* spread, space, time at intervals; overlap.
4 *stagger the screws at each joint:* alternate, step, arrange in a zigzag.

stagnant adjective
1 *stagnant water:* still, motionless, static, stationary, standing, dead; foul, stale, putrid, smelly.
2 *a stagnant economy:* inactive, sluggish, slow-moving, lethargic, static, flat, depressed, declining, moribund, dying, dead, dormant.
OPPOSITES: flowing, fresh, vibrant.

stagnate verb
1 *obstructions allow water to stagnate:* stop flowing, become stagnant, become trapped; stand; become foul, become stale; fester, putrefy.
2 *exports stagnated:* languish, decline, deteriorate, fall, become stagnant, stand still, be sluggish; informal do nothing.
OPPOSITES: flow, rise, boom.

staid adjective *staid old ladies:* sedate, respectable, quiet, serious, serious-minded, steady, conventional, traditional, unadventurous, unenterprising, set in your ways, sober, proper, decorous, formal, stuffy, stiff; informal starchy, stick-in-the-mud.
OPPOSITES: frivolous, daring, informal.

stain verb
1 *her clothing was stained with blood:* discolour, blemish, soil, mark, spot, spatter, splatter, smear, splash, smudge, blotch, blacken.
2 *the report stained his reputation:* damage, injure, harm, blacken, tarnish, taint, smear, bring discredit to, dishonour, drag through the mud; literary besmirch, sully.
3 *the wood was stained:* tint, colour, dye, tinge, pigment, colour-wash.
▷**noun**
1 *a mud stain:* mark, spot, spatter, splatter, blotch, smudge, smear, discoloration.
2 *a stain on his character:* blemish, injury,

taint, blot, smear, discredit, dishonour; damage.
3 *dark wood stain:* tint, colour, dye, tinge, pigment, colourant, colour wash.

stake¹ noun *a stake in the ground:* post, pole, stick, spike, upright, support, prop, strut, pale, paling, picket, pile, piling, cane.
▷**verb**
1 *the plants have to be staked:* prop up, tie up, tether, support, hold up, brace, truss.
2 *he staked his claim:* assert, declare, proclaim, state, make, lay, put in.
□**stake something out**
1 *builders staked out the plot:* mark off/out, demarcate, measure out, delimit, fence off, section off, close off, shut off, cordon off.
2 (informal) *the police staked out his flat:* observe, watch, keep an eye on, keep under observation, keep watch on, monitor, keep under surveillance; informal keep tabs on, case.

stake² noun
1 *playing dice for high stakes:* bet, wager, ante.
2 *they are racing for record stakes:* prize money, purse, pot, winnings.
3 *we'll keep you one step ahead in the fashion stakes:* competition, contest, challenge, rivalry, race, struggle.
4 *a 40% stake in the business:* share, interest, equity, ownership, involvement.
▷**verb** *he staked all his week's pay:* bet, wager, lay, put on, gamble, chance, venture, risk, hazard.

stale adjective
1 *stale food:* old, past its best, past its sell-by date; off, dry, hard, musty, rancid.
2 *stale air:* stuffy, close, musty, fusty, stagnant; Brit. frowsty, fuggy.
3 *stale beer:* flat, turned, spoiled, off, insipid, tasteless.
4 *stale jokes:* hackneyed, tired, worn out, overworked, threadbare, warmed-up, banal, trite, clichéd, platitudinous, unoriginal, unimaginative, uninspired, flat, out of date, outdated, outmoded, passé, obsolete; N. Amer. warmed-over; informal old hat, corny, out of the ark.
OPPOSITES: fresh, original.

stalemate noun *the talks had reached a stalemate:* deadlock, impasse, stand-off; draw, tie, dead heat.

stalk¹ noun *the stalk of a plant:* stem, shoot, trunk, stock, cane, bine, bent, haulm, straw, reed.

stalk² verb
1 *a stoat was stalking a rabbit:* creep up on, trail, follow, shadow, track down, go after, be after, course, hunt; informal tail.
2 *without saying a word she turned and stalked out:* strut, stride, march, flounce, storm, stomp, sweep.

S

stall noun

1 *a market stall:* stand, table, counter, booth, kiosk.
2 *stalls for larger animals:* pen, coop, sty, corral, enclosure, compartment.

▷ **verb**

1 *the Government has stalled the project:* obstruct, impede, interfere with, hinder, hamper, block, interrupt, hold up, hold back, thwart, baulk, sabotage, delay, stonewall, check, stop, halt, derail, put a brake on; informal stymie; Brit. informal scupper.
2 *she's stalling for time:* use delaying tactics, play for time, temporize, gain time, procrastinate, hedge, beat about the bush, drag your feet, delay, filibuster, stonewall.
3 *stall him for a bit:* delay, divert, distract; hold off, stave off, fend off, keep off, ward off, keep at bay.

stalwart adjective *a stalwart supporter of the cause:* staunch, loyal, faithful, committed, devoted, dedicated, dependable, reliable, steady, constant, trusty, hard-working, steadfast, redoubtable, unwavering.
OPPOSITES: disloyal, unreliable.

stamina noun *their secret is stamina rather than speed:* endurance, staying power, tirelessness, fortitude, strength, energy, toughness, determination, tenacity, perseverance, grit.

stammer verb *he began to stammer:* stutter, stumble over your words, hesitate, falter, pause, halt, splutter.
▷ **noun** *he had a stammer:* stutter, speech impediment, speech impairment, speech defect, speech difficulty.

stamp verb

1 *he stamped on my toe:* trample, step, tread, tramp; crush, squash, flatten.
2 *John stamped off, muttering:* stomp, stump, clomp, clump.
3 *the name is stamped on the cover:* imprint, print, impress, punch, inscribe, emboss, brand, frank.
4 *his face was stamped on her memory:* fix, inscribe, etch, carve, imprint, impress.
▷ **noun** *the stamp of authority:* mark, hallmark, indication, sign, seal, sure sign, telltale sign, quality, smack, smell, savour, air.
□ **stamp something out**
urgent action is required to stamp out corruption: end, stop, put an end/stop to, crush, put down, curb, nip in the bud, scotch, squash, quash, quell, subdue, suppress, extinguish, stifle, abolish, get rid of, eliminate, eradicate, beat, overcome, defeat, destroy, wipe out; informal crack down on.

stampede noun *the noise caused a stampede:* charge, panic, rush, flight, rout.
▷ **verb** *the sheep stampeded:* bolt, charge, flee, take flight; race, rush, career, sweep, run.

stance noun

1 *a natural golfer's stance:* posture, body position, pose, attitude.
2 *a liberal stance:* attitude, stand, point of view, viewpoint, opinion, way of thinking, outlook, standpoint, position, angle, perspective, approach, line, policy.

stand verb

1 *the two men stood up:* rise, get/rise to your feet, get up, straighten up, pick yourself up, be upstanding.
2 *today a house stands on the site | the hotel stands in three acres of gardens:* be, be situated, be located, be positioned, be sited.
3 *don't stand the plant in direct sunlight:* put, set, place, position, situate, locate; informal park.
4 *my decision stands:* remain in force, remain valid/effective/operative, remain in operation, hold, hold good, be unchanged, exist.
5 *his heart could not stand the strain:* withstand, endure, bear, put up with, take, cope with, handle, sustain, resist, stand up to.
6 (informal) *I won't stand cheek:* endure, tolerate, bear, put up with, take, abide, support, countenance; Scottish thole; informal swallow, stomach; Brit. informal stick, wear.
7 (informal) *I can't stand the smell:* bear, tolerate, endure, put up with, take, abide; informal stomach; Brit. informal stick.
OPPOSITES: sit, lie.

▷ **noun**

1 *the party's tough stand on immigration:* attitude, stance, point of view, viewpoint, opinion, way of thinking, outlook, standpoint, position, approach, thinking, policy, line.
2 *a large mirror on a stand:* base, support, mounting, platform, rest, plinth, bottom; tripod, rack, trivet.
3 *a beer stand:* stall, counter, booth, kiosk.
□ **make/take a stand against**
we have to take a stand against racism: oppose, fight, put up a fight against, combat, resist.
□ **stand by**
two battalions were on their way and a third was standing by: wait, be prepared, be in readiness, be ready for action, be on full alert, wait in the wings.
□ **stand by someone/something**
1 *she stood by her husband:* remain loyal to, stick with/by, remain true to, stand up for, support, back up, defend, stick up for.
2 *the government must stand by its pledges:* abide by, keep, adhere to, hold to, stick to, observe, comply with.
□ **stand for**
1 *V stands for volts:* mean, be an abbreviation of, represent, signify, denote, indicate, symbolize.
2 *we stand for animal welfare:* advocate,

champion, uphold, defend, stand up for, support, back, endorse, be in favour of, promote, recommend, urge.

□ **stand in**
the foreign affairs spokesman stood in for the party leader during his brief paternity leave: deputize, act, act as deputy, substitute, fill in, sit in, do duty, take over, be a proxy, cover, hold the fort, step into the breach; replace, relieve, take over from; informal fill someone's shoes, step into someone's shoes.

□ **stand out**
1 *the veins in his neck stood out:* project, stick out, bulge out, jut out.
2 *she stood out in the crowd:* be noticeable, be visible, be obvious, be conspicuous, stick out, be striking, be distinctive, be prominent, attract attention, catch the eye, leap out; informal stick/stand out a mile, stick/stand out like a sore thumb.

□ **stand up**
he has no proof that would stand up in court: remain/be valid, be sound, be plausible, hold water, hold up, stand questioning, bear examination, be verifiable.

□ **stand up for someone/something**
we should stand up for democracy: support, defend, back, stick up for, champion, promote, uphold, take someone's part, take the side of, side with.

□ **stand up to someone/something**
1 *the film will help children stand up to bullies:* defy, confront, challenge, resist, take on, put up a fight against, argue with, take a stand against.
2 *the old house has stood up to the war:* withstand, survive, come through unscathed, outlast, outlive, weather, ride out.

standard noun
1 *the standard of her work:* quality, level, grade, calibre, merit, level of excellence, level of attainment.
2 *the wages are low by today's standards:* norm, yardstick, benchmark, measure, criterion.
3 *a standard to live by:* principle, ideal; (**standards**) code of behaviour, code of honour, morals, scruples, ethics.
4 *the regiment's standard:* flag, banner, pennant, ensign, colours.

▷ **adjective**
1 *peer-review is standard procedure in the sciences:* normal, usual, typical, common, ordinary, customary, conventional, established, set, fixed, traditional, prevailing; literary wonted.
2 *the standard work on the subject:* definitive, established, classic, recognized, accepted, authoritative, most reliable.
OPPOSITES: unusual, special.

standardize verb
there had been some attempt to standardize the terminology in this field: systematize, make consistent, make uniform, regulate, normalize, bring

into line, make something conform to a standard.

stand-in noun
a stand-in for the minister: substitute, replacement, deputy, surrogate, proxy, understudy, locum, fill-in, cover, relief, reserve, stopgap; informal temp.

standing noun
1 *his standing in the community:* status, rank, ranking, position; reputation, estimation, stature.
2 *a person of some standing:* seniority, rank, eminence, prominence, prestige, repute, stature, esteem, importance, account, consequence, influence, distinction; informal clout.
3 *a squabble of long standing:* duration, existence, continuance, endurance, life.

▷ **adjective**
1 *standing stones:* upright, erect, vertical, plumb, upended, on end, perpendicular; on your feet; Heraldry rampant.
2 *standing water:* stagnant, still, motionless, static, stationary.
3 *a standing invitation:* permanent, remaining in force, continuing, indefinite, open-ended.
OPPOSITES: flat, seated, flowing.

stand-off noun
the 16-day-old stand-off was no closer to being resolved: deadlock, stalemate, impasse.

stand-offish adjective
(informal) *she is very stand-offish with strangers:* aloof, distant, remote, detached, withdrawn, reserved, uncommunicative, unforthcoming, unapproachable, unresponsive, unfriendly, unsociable.
OPPOSITES: friendly, approachable.

standpoint noun
she writes on religion from the standpoint of a believer: point of view, viewpoint, perspective, vantage point, attitude, stance, view, opinion, position, way of thinking, outlook.

standstill noun
the traffic came to a standstill: halt, stop, dead stop, stand.

staple adjective
rice was the staple crop grown in most villages: main, principal, chief, major, primary, leading, foremost, first, most important, basic, standard; informal number-one.

star noun
1 *the sky was full of stars:* celestial body, heavenly body; sun.
2 *the stars of the film:* principal, leading lady/man, lead, female/male lead, hero, heroine.
3 *he became an international football star:* celebrity, superstar, big name, famous name, household name, someone, somebody, leading light, VIP, personality, personage, luminary; informal celeb, big shot, big noise, megastar.

▷ **adjective**
1 *a star pupil:* brilliant, talented,

S

gifted, able, exceptional, outstanding, bright, clever, precocious, prodigious, consummate.
2 *the star attraction:* top, leading, best, greatest, foremost, major, pre-eminent.

> **WORD LINKS**
> **astral, sidereal, stellar** relating to stars
> **astronomy** the science of stars, planets, and the universe

stare verb *he stared at her in amazement:* gaze, look fixedly, gape, peer; glare; ogle; informal goggle, gawk; Brit. informal gawp.

stark adjective
1 *his position is in stark contrast to that of Curran:* sharp, sharply defined, distinct, clear, striking.
2 *a stark landscape:* desolate, bare, barren, arid, empty, godforsaken, bleak, sombre, depressing, cheerless, joyless.
3 *a stark room:* austere, severe, bleak, plain, simple, bare, unadorned, unembellished, undecorated.
4 *the stark facts speak for themselves:* blunt, bald, bare, simple, basic, plain, unvarnished, harsh, grim.
5 *he came running back in stark terror:* sheer, utter, complete, absolute, total, pure.

start verb
1 *the meeting started at 7.45:* begin, commence, get under way, get going; informal kick off.
2 *since his illness started, he has lost two stone | the trouble started in June:* come into being, begin, come into existence, appear, emerge, arise, originate, develop; erupt, burst out.
3 *the earthquake started a fire, which destroyed the central business district:* cause, make happen, precipitate, provoke, trigger.
4 *she started her own charity:* establish, set up, found, create, bring into being, institute, initiate, inaugurate, introduce, open, launch, float, get something off the ground, pioneer, organize, mastermind.
5 *we plan to start building in the autumn:* embark on, make a start on, begin, take the first step, make the first move, get going, set things moving, start/get/set the ball rolling, buckle to/down, turn to; informal get stuck in, get down to business, get the show on the road.
6 *he started across the field:* set off, set out, start out, begin your journey, get on the road, depart, leave, get under way, make a start, sally forth, embark, sail; informal hit the road.
7 *you can start the machine now:* activate, set in motion, switch on, start up, turn on, fire up, boot up.
8 *he turned the key and the engine started:* begin working, start up, get going, spring into life.
9 *she looked at herself in the mirror and*

started with surprise: flinch, jerk, jump, twitch, recoil, shrink, blench, wince.
OPPOSITES: finish, stop.

▷**noun**
1 *the start of the event:* beginning, commencement, inception.
2 *the start of her illness:* onset, emergence, appearance, eruption.
3 *they're anxious to give their child the best start in life:* opportunity, chance; advantage.
4 *the woman gave a nervous start:* jerk, jump, twitch, flinch, wince.
OPPOSITES: end, finish, culmination.

startle verb *a sudden sound in the doorway startled her:* surprise, frighten, scare, alarm, give someone a shock/fright, make someone jump, catch someone unawares; informal give someone a turn, make someone jump out of their skin.

startling adjective *startling news awaited him at Naples:* surprising, astonishing, amazing, unexpected, unforeseen, staggering, shocking, stunning; extraordinary, remarkable, dramatic; frightening, alarming.

starvation noun *the country's people face starvation as a result of the civil war:* famine, lack of food, undernourishment, malnourishment.

starving adjective
1 *a lot of these children are not only starving, they have tropical diseases like malaria:* dying of hunger, deprived of food, undernourished, malnourished.
2 (informal) *I don't know about you, but I'm starving:* very hungry, ravenous, empty; informal famished, starved.

stash (informal) verb *police found 100 kg of heroin stashed away in a rented warehouse in Barking:* store, stow, cache, hide, conceal, secrete; hoard, save, stockpile; informal salt away, squirrel away.
▷**noun** *a stash of money:* cache, hoard, stock, stockpile, store, supply, accumulation, collection, reserve.

state¹ noun
1 *the state of the company's finances:* condition, situation, circumstances, position, shape, health.
2 *an autonomous state:* country, nation, land, sovereign state, nation state, kingdom, realm, power, republic, confederation, federation; formal polity.
3 *the country is divided into thirty-two states:* province, federal state, region, territory, canton, department, county, district.
4 *the power of the state:* the government, parliament, the administration, the authorities.
5 (informal) *she got into a bit of a state:* fluster, fret, panic, state of agitation/anxiety; informal flap, tizzy.
▷**adjective** *a state visit to China:* ceremonial,

official, formal, governmental, national, public.
▫ **in a state**
she just rang me and she seemed in a bit of a state: upset, flustered, anxious, worried, agitated, nervous, jumpy, edgy, on edge, tense, keyed up, panicky; informal rattled, in a flap, uptight, jittery.
OPPOSITES: unofficial, private.

state² verb *I stated my views:* express, voice, utter, put into words, declare, announce, make known, put across/over, communicate, air; proclaim, present, expound; set out, set down; reveal, disclose, divulge; informal come out with.

stated adjective *routine health checks will be carried out at stated intervals:* specified, fixed, settled, set, agreed, declared, designated, laid down.

stately adjective *a stately procession:* dignified, majestic, ceremonious, imposing, impressive, solemn, awe-inspiring, regal, courtly, elegant, grand, glorious, splendid, magnificent, resplendent; slow-moving, measured, deliberate.

statement noun *ministers issued a joint statement* | *a clear statement of his views:* declaration, expression of views/facts, announcement, utterance, communication, proclamation, presentation; account, report, bulletin, communiqué; testimony, evidence

state-of-the-art adjective *the studio boasted state-of-the-art recording equipment:* modern, the latest, new, the newest, up to the minute, cutting-edge, pioneering; advanced, highly developed, innovatory, revolutionary; sophisticated.

statesman, stateswoman noun senior politician, respected political figure, elder statesman, political leader, national leader.

static adjective
1 *interest rates remained static:* unchanged, fixed, stable, steady, unchanging, unvarying, invariable, constant, consistent.
2 *a static display:* stationary, motionless, immobile, unmoving, still.
OPPOSITES: variable, mobile, active, dynamic.

station noun
1 *a railway station:* stop, halt; terminus, terminal, depot.
2 *a research station* | *coastal radar stations:* establishment, base, camp, post; site, facility, installation; office.
3 *a radio station:* channel, broadcasting organization; wavelength.
4 *the lookout resumed his station:* post, position, place.
▷ verb *the regiment was stationed at Woolwich:* put on duty, post, position,

place; establish, install; deploy, base, garrison.

stationary adjective
1 *a long queue of stationary traffic:* not moving, still, motionless, immobile, unmoving, stock-still, at a standstill, standing, static.
2 *a stationary population:* static, unchanging, unvarying, invariable, unchanged.
OPPOSITES: moving, shifting.

> **USAGE**
>
> Do not confuse **stationary** and **stationery**: **stationary** is an adjective meaning 'not moving or changing', while **stationery** is a noun meaning 'paper and other writing materials'.

statue noun sculpture, figure, effigy, statuette, figurine, idol; carving, bronze; (with reference to the Bible) graven image.

statuesque adjective *a statuesque woman:* tall and dignified, imposing, striking, stately, grand, impressive.

stature noun
1 *she was small in stature:* height; size, build.
2 *an architect of international stature:* reputation, repute, standing, status, position, prestige, distinction, eminence, pre-eminence, prominence, importance, influence, note, fame, celebrity, renown, acclaim.

status noun
1 *their status in American society:* standing, rank, ranking, position, social position, level, place, estimation.
2 *those who enjoy wealth and status:* high standing, high rank, prestige, stature, regard, fame, renown, esteem, importance, prominence, consequence, distinction, influence, authority, eminence.

statute noun law, regulation, enactment, act, decree, edict, rule, ruling.

staunch¹ adjective *a staunch supporter:* stalwart, loyal, faithful, committed, devoted, dedicated, dependable, reliable, steady, constant, trusty, hard-working, steadfast, unwavering, redoubtable.
OPPOSITES: disloyal, unreliable.

staunch² verb *she tried to staunch the flow of blood:* stem, stop, halt, check, hold back, restrain, restrict, control, contain, curb; slow, lessen, reduce, diminish.

stave verb
▫ **stave something in**
the door had been staved in: break in, smash in, put a hole in, push in, kick in, cave in.
▫ **stave something off**
the government is introducing emergency measures to stave off a crisis: avert, prevent, avoid, preclude, forestall, nip in

S

the bud; ward off, fend off, head off, keep off, keep at bay.

stay verb
1 *he stayed in the bar a bit longer:* remain, stay put; wait, linger, be left, hold on, hang on; informal hang around; Brit. informal hang about, stop.
2 *try to stay calm:* continue to be, remain, keep, persist in being, carry on being, go on being.
3 *the girls are staying with friends:* visit, spend time, put up, stop off/over; holiday; N. Amer. vacation.
4 *the family are still staying in bed and breakfast accommodation:* lodge, room, board, be housed, be accommodated.
OPPOSITES: leave.
▷noun
1 *a stay at a hotel:* visit, stop, stop-off, stopover, break, holiday; N. Amer. vacation.
2 *a stay of judgement:* postponement, putting off, delay, deferment, deferral.

steadfast adjective
1 *a steadfast friend:* loyal, faithful, committed, devoted, dedicated, dependable, reliable, steady, stalwart, true, constant, staunch, trusty.
2 *he remained steadfast in his commitment:* firm, determined, resolute, unwavering, unfaltering, unswerving, unflinching, unshakeable.
OPPOSITES: disloyal, irresolute.

steady adjective
1 *the ladder must be steady:* stable, firm, fixed, secure, fast, safe, immovable; anchored, braced.
2 *keep the camera steady:* motionless, still, static, stationary, unmoving.
3 *a steady gaze:* fixed, intent, unwavering, unfaltering.
4 *a steady decline in the national birth rate | a steady stream of visitors:* constant, unchanging, regular, consistent, invariable, even; continuous, unceasing, ceaseless, non-stop.
5 *a steady job:* regular, established, settled.
6 *a solid, steady young man:* sensible, level-headed, rational, settled, mature, down-to-earth, full of common sense, reliable, dependable, serious-minded, responsible.
OPPOSITES: unsteady, unstable, fluctuating, sporadic.
▷verb
1 *he steadied the rifle:* stabilize, hold steady; brace, support; balance, poise; secure, fix, make fast.
2 *she needed a moment to steady her nerves:* calm, soothe, quieten, compose, settle; subdue, quell, control, get a grip on.

steal verb
1 *the raiders stole computer equipment worth more than £500,000:* take, thieve, help yourself to, loot, carry off, shoplift, pilfer; embezzle, misappropriate; have your fingers/hand in the till; formal purloin;

informal walk off with, pinch, swipe, nab, rip off, lift, filch, snitch; Brit. informal nick, half-inch, snaffle, whip, knock off.
2 *copyright law protects individuals or groups from having their ideas stolen:* plagiarize, copy, pass off as your own, pirate, poach, borrow; informal rip off, lift, crib.
3 *he stole out of the room:* creep, sidle, tiptoe, slip, sneak, move stealthily.

WORD LINKS
kleptomania a recurrent urge to steal things

stealing noun *he was convicted of stealing:* theft, robbery, burglary, shoplifting, looting; embezzlement; N. Amer. larceny.

stealth noun furtiveness, secretiveness, secrecy, surreptitiousness.

stealthy adjective *her movements were slow and stealthy:* surreptitious, furtive, cautious, secretive, secret, clandestine, covert, conspiratorial, sly.
OPPOSITES: open.

steam noun water vapour, condensation, moisture, mist.

steamy adjective
1 *the steamy jungles of South-East Asia:* humid, muggy, sticky, sultry, sweaty, damp, clammy, steaming.
2 (informal) *they had a steamy affair:* passionate, torrid, amorous, ardent, lustful.

steel verb
□ **steel yourself**
his team were steeling themselves for disappointment: brace yourself, nerve yourself, summon your courage, screw up your courage, gear yourself up, prepare yourself, get in the right frame of mind; fortify yourself, harden yourself; informal psych yourself up.

steep[1] adjective
1 *steep cliffs:* precipitous, sheer, abrupt, sharp, perpendicular, vertical, bluff, vertiginous.
2 *a steep increase in the price of oil:* sharp, sudden, precipitate, precipitous, rapid.
OPPOSITES: gentle, gradual.

steep[2] verb
1 *the ham is then steeped in brine:* marinade, marinate, soak, souse, macerate; pickle.
2 *winding sheets were steeped in mercury sulphate:* soak, saturate, immerse, wet through, drench.
3 *a city steeped in history:* imbue with, fill with, permeate with, pervade with, suffuse with, infuse with, soak in.

steer verb
1 *he steered the boat towards the busy quay:* guide, direct, manoeuvre, drive, pilot, navigate.
2 *Luke steered them down the path:*

guide, conduct, direct, lead, take, usher, shepherd, marshal, herd.

□ **steer clear of**
tourists were warned to steer clear of the area: keep away from, keep your distance from, keep at arm's length, give a wide berth to, avoid, avoid dealing with, have nothing to do with, shun, eschew.

stem[1] noun *a plant stem:* stalk, shoot, trunk, stock, cane.

□ **stem from**
her depression stems from low self-esteem: have its origins in, arise from, originate in, spring from, derive from, come from, emanate from, flow from, proceed from; be caused by, be brought on/about by, be produced by.

stem[2] verb *he managed to stem the flow of blood:* staunch, stop, halt, check, hold back, restrict, control, contain, curb; slow, lessen, reduce, diminish.

stench noun *the stench of rotting fish:* stink, reek; Brit. informal niff, pong, whiff, hum.

step noun
1 *Frank took a step forward:* pace, stride.
2 *she heard a step on the stairs:* footstep, footfall, tread.
3 *she left the room with a springy step:* gait, walk, tread.
4 *the top step:* stair, tread, rung; (**steps**) stairs, staircase, stairway.
5 *handing in your notice would be a very serious step:* course of action, measure, move, act, action, initiative, decision.
6 *a significant step towards a ceasefire:* advance, development, move, movement; breakthrough.
7 *the first step on the managerial ladder:* stage, level, grade, rank, degree; notch.

▷ **verb**
1 *she stepped forward:* walk, move, tread, pace, stride.
2 *the bull had stepped on his hat:* tread, stamp, trample; squash, crush, flatten.

□ **in step**
he is in step with mainstream thinking: in accord, in harmony, in agreement, in tune, in line, in keeping, in conformity.

□ **mind/watch your step**
you'd better watch your step with him—he's not as innocent as he looks: be careful, take care, step/tread carefully, exercise care/caution, mind how you go, look out, watch out, be wary, be on your guard, be on the qui vive.

□ **out of step**
the paper was often out of step with public opinion: at odds, at variance, in disagreement, out of tune, out of line, not in keeping, out of harmony.

□ **step by step**
he took us through the process step by step: one step at a time, bit by bit, gradually, in stages, by degrees, slowly, steadily.

□ **step down**
he was forced to step down as party leader:

resign, stand down, give up your post/job, bow out, abdicate; informal quit.

□ **step in**
1 *officials have asked the government to step in:* intervene, intercede, involve yourself, become/get involved, take a hand.
2 *I stepped in for a sick colleague:* stand in, sit in, fill in, cover, substitute, take over; replace, take someone's place; informal sub.

□ **step something up**
1 *the army stepped up its offensive:* increase, intensify, strengthen, augment, escalate; informal up, crank up.
2 *I stepped up my pace:* speed up, increase, accelerate, quicken, hasten.

stereotype noun *the stereotype of the cowboy:* standard/conventional image, received idea, cliché, hackneyed idea, formula.

▷ **verb** *women are often stereotyped as scheming:* typecast, pigeonhole, conventionalize, categorize, label, tag.

stereotyped adjective *stereotyped images of village life:* stock, conventional, stereotypical, standard, formulaic, predictable; hackneyed, clichéd, cliché-ridden, banal, trite, unoriginal; typecast; informal corny, old hat.
OPPOSITES: unconventional, original.

sterile adjective
1 *as hybrids, mules are almost always sterile:* infertile, unable to reproduce/conceive, unable to have children/young.
2 *vast tracts of sterile desert land:* unproductive, infertile, unfruitful, barren, lifeless.
3 *a sterile political debate:* pointless, unproductive, unfruitful, unrewarding, useless, unprofitable, profitless, futile, vain, idle; unimaginative, uninspired, uninspiring, unoriginal, stale.
4 *sterile conditions:* aseptic, sterilized, germ-free, antiseptic, disinfected; uncontaminated, clean; sanitary, hygienic.
OPPOSITES: fertile, productive.

sterilize verb
1 *an autoclave is used to sterilize surgical instruments after each use:* disinfect, decontaminate, make sterile; sanitize, clean, cleanse, purify; fumigate.
2 *stray pets are usually sterilized:* neuter, castrate, geld, spay.
OPPOSITES: contaminate.

sterling adjective (Brit.) *the organization does sterling work for youngsters:* excellent, first-class, first-rate, exceptional, outstanding, splendid, superlative, praiseworthy, laudable, commendable, admirable, valuable, worthy, deserving.

stern[1] adjective
1 *David looked at her with a stern expression:* serious, unsmiling, frowning, severe, forbidding, unfriendly, austere,

S

dour, stony, flinty, steely, unrelenting, unforgiving, unbending, unsympathetic, disapproving.
2 *stern measures are needed to protect national security:* strict, severe, stringent, harsh, drastic, hard, tough, extreme, rigid, rigorous, exacting, demanding, uncompromising, inflexible, authoritarian, draconian.
OPPOSITES: genial, friendly, lenient, lax.

stern² noun *the stern of the ship:* rear, back, transom; poop deck.
OPPOSITES: bow.

stew noun *a beef stew:* casserole, hotpot, ragout, goulash, daube.
▷ verb *stew the meat for about an hour:* braise, casserole, simmer.

steward noun
1 *an air steward:* flight attendant, member of the cabin crew.
2 *the race stewards:* official, marshal, organizer.
3 *the steward of the estate:* manager, agent, overseer, custodian, caretaker; Brit. land agent, bailiff; Scottish factor.

stick¹ noun
1 *a fire made of sticks:* piece of wood, twig, small branch.
2 *he walked with a stick:* walking stick, cane, staff, crutch; alpenstock; crook.
3 *the plants need supporting on sticks:* cane, pole, post, stake, upright, rod.
☐ **the sticks** (informal, derogatory) *they live somewhere out in the sticks:* the country, the countryside, rural areas, the provinces; the backwoods, the back of beyond, the wilds, the hinterland, a backwater; informal the middle of nowhere; N. Amer. informal the boondocks.

stick² verb
1 *he stuck his fork into the sausage:* thrust, push, insert, jab, poke, dig, plunge.
2 *the bristles stuck into his skin:* pierce, penetrate, puncture, prick, stab.
3 *the cup stuck to its saucer:* adhere, cling, be fixed, be fused.
4 *stick the stamp there:* affix, attach, fasten, fix; paste, glue, gum, tape.
5 *the wheels stuck fast:* become trapped, become jammed, jam, catch, become wedged, become lodged, become fixed, become embedded.
6 *one particular incident stuck in his mind:* remain, stay, linger, dwell, persist, continue, last, endure.
7 (informal) *the charges won't stick:* be upheld, hold, be believed; informal hold water.
☐ **stick at**
if you want to learn a language, you must stick at it: persevere with, persist with, keep at, work at, continue with, carry on with, not give up with, hammer away at, stay with; go the distance, stay the course; informal soldier on with, hang in there.

☐ **stick by**
whatever happens I'll stick by him: be loyal to, be faithful to, be true to, stand by, keep faith with, keep your promise to.
☐ **stick it out**
I decided to stick it out for another couple of months: put up with it, grin and bear it, keep at it, keep going, stay with it, see it through; persevere, persist, carry on, struggle on; informal hang in there, soldier on, tough it out.
☐ **stick out**
1 *his front teeth stuck out:* protrude, jut out, project, stand out, extend, poke out; bulge, overhang.
2 *they stuck out in their strange clothes:* be noticeable, be visible, be obvious, be conspicuous, stand out, be obtrusive, be prominent, attract attention, catch the eye, leap out, show up; informal stick/stand out a mile, stick/stand out like a sore thumb.
☐ **stick to**
he stuck to his promise: abide by, keep, adhere to, hold to, comply with, fulfil, make good, stand by.
☐ **stick up for**
I don't know anyone else who would stick up for me the way you do: support, take someone's side, side with, be on the side of, stand by, stand up for, take someone's part, defend, come to the defence of, champion, speak up for, fight for.

stick-in-the-mud noun (informal) *he's just an old stick-in-the-mud:* conservative, traditionalist; fossil, troglodyte; Brit. museum piece; informal fuddy-duddy, square, stuffed shirt.

sticky adjective
1 *a sticky label:* adhesive, self-adhesive; gummed.
2 *sticky clay:* glutinous, viscous, viscid, ropy; gluey, tacky, treacly; Brit. claggy; informal gooey.
3 *another hot and sticky day:* humid, muggy, close, sultry, steamy, sweaty.
4 (informal) *a sticky situation:* awkward, difficult, tricky, ticklish, problematic, delicate, touch-and-go, embarrassing, sensitive, uncomfortable.
OPPOSITES: dry, fresh, cool.

stiff adjective
1 *stiff cardboard:* rigid, hard, firm, inelastic, inflexible.
2 *a stiff paste:* semi-solid, viscous, viscid, thick, stiffened, firm.
3 *I'm stiff all over:* aching, achy, painful; arthritic, rheumatic; informal creaky.
4 *she greeted him with stiff politeness:* formal, reserved, unfriendly, chilly, cold, frigid, icy, austere, wooden, forced, strained, stilted, constrained; informal starchy, stand-offish.
5 *they face stiff fines and a possible prison sentence:* harsh, severe, heavy, crippling, punishing, punitive, stringent, drastic, draconian; Brit. swingeing.

S

6 *the rebel forces put up a stiff resistance:* vigorous, strong, determined, full of determination, spirited, resolute, tenacious, steely, four-square, unflagging, unyielding, dogged.
7 *a long, stiff climb:* difficult, hard, arduous, tough, strenuous, laborious, uphill, exacting, tiring, demanding, formidable, challenging, punishing, gruelling.
8 *a stiff breeze:* strong, fresh, brisk.
9 (informal) *a stiff drink:* strong, potent, alcoholic.
OPPOSITES: flexible, supple, relaxed, gentle, weak.

stiffen verb
1 *stir until the mixture stiffens:* become stiff, thicken; set, become solid, solidify.
2 *she stiffened her muscles | without exercise, joints will stiffen:* make/become stiff, tense, tighten, tauten.
3 *intimidation only stiffened their resolve:* strengthen, harden, toughen, fortify, reinforce, give a boost to.
OPPOSITES: soften, relax, weaken.

stifle verb
1 *those who died in the streets suffered the same fate and were stifled by the fumes:* suffocate, choke, asphyxiate.
2 *Eleanor stifled a giggle:* suppress, smother, restrain, fight back, choke back, gulp back, check, swallow, curb, silence.
3 *high taxes were stifling private enterprise:* constrain, hinder, hamper, impede, hold back, curb, check, restrain, prevent, inhibit, suppress.
OPPOSITES: encourage.

stifling adjective *in summer, Venice is often stifling:* airless, suffocating, oppressive; very hot, sweltering; humid, close, muggy; informal boiling.
OPPOSITES: fresh.

stigma noun *the stigma of bankruptcy:* shame, disgrace, dishonour, ignominy, humiliation; formal opprobrium.
OPPOSITES: honour, credit.

stigmatize verb *the institution was stigmatized as a last resort for the destitute:* brand, label, mark out; condemn, denounce, disparage, vilify.

still adjective
1 *she lay very still, her eyes closed:* motionless, unmoving, not moving a muscle, stock-still, immobile, like a statue, as if turned to stone, rooted to the spot, transfixed, static, stationary.
2 *a still night:* quiet, silent, hushed, soundless, noiseless, undisturbed; calm, peaceful, serene, windless.
3 *the lake was still:* calm, flat, even, smooth, placid, tranquil, glassy, like a millpond, unruffled.
OPPOSITES: moving, noisy.
▷**noun** *the still of the night:* quietness, quiet, quietude, silence, stillness, hush, soundlessness; calm, tranquillity, peace, serenity.
OPPOSITES: noise.
▷**adverb**
1 *he still lives with his mother:* up to this time, up to the present time, until now, even now, yet.
2 *He's crazy. Still, he's harmless:* nevertheless, nonetheless, all the same, just the same, anyway, anyhow, even so, yet, but, however, notwithstanding, despite that, in spite of that, for all that, be that as it may, in any event, at any rate.
▷**verb**
1 *his words stilled the crowd:* quieten, quiet, silence, hush; calm, settle, soothe, pacify, subdue.
2 *the wind stilled:* abate, die down, lessen, subside, ease up/off, let up, moderate, slacken, weaken.

stilted adjective *the conversation was rather stilted:* strained, forced, contrived, constrained, laboured, stiff, self-conscious, awkward, unnatural, wooden.
OPPOSITES: natural, spontaneous.

stimulant noun *population growth is a major stimulant to industrial development:* stimulus, incentive, encouragement, impetus, inducement, fillip, boost, spur, prompt; informal shot in the arm.
OPPOSITES: deterrent.

stimulate verb *I want to stimulate their imaginations | the course stimulated her passion for learning:* encourage, act as a stimulus/incentive/impetus/fillip/spur to, prompt, prod, move, motivate, trigger, spark, spur on, galvanize, kindle, fire, fire with enthusiasm, fuel, whet, nourish; inspire, incentivize, rouse, excite, animate, electrify.
OPPOSITES: discourage.

stimulating adjective
1 *plant extracts which have a stimulating effect on the circulation:* restorative, tonic, invigorating, bracing, energizing, reviving, refreshing, revitalizing.
2 *a stimulating lecture:* thought-provoking, interesting, fascinating, inspiring, inspirational, lively, sparkling, exciting, stirring, rousing, intriguing, giving you food for thought, refreshing; provocative, challenging.
OPPOSITES: sedative, uninspiring.

stimulus noun *cheap energy provided a major stimulus to economic development in western Europe:* spur, stimulant, encouragement, impetus, boost, prompt, prod, incentive, inducement, inspiration, fillip; motivation, impulse; informal shot in the arm.
OPPOSITES: deterrent.

sting noun
1 *a bee sting:* prick, wound, injury, puncture.
2 *this cream will take the sting away:*

S

smart, pricking; pain, soreness, hurt, irritation.

3 *I recalled the sting of his betrayal:* pain, hurt, anguish.

4 *she smiled to take the sting out of her words:* sharpness, severity, bite, edge, pointedness, asperity.

▷ **verb**
1 *she was stung by a scorpion:* prick, wound; poison.
2 *the smoke made her eyes sting:* smart, burn, hurt, be irritated, be sore.
3 *the criticism stung her:* upset, wound, cut to the quick, hurt, pain, mortify.
4 *he was stung into action by an article in the paper:* provoke, goad, incite, spur, prick, prod, rouse, drive, galvanize.

stink verb
1 *his clothes stank of sweat:* reek, smell.
2 (informal) *he thinks the values of our society stink:* be very unpleasant, be despicable, be contemptible, be disgusting, be repellent; N. Amer. informal suck.

▷ **noun** *the stink of sweat:* stench, reek, smell; literary miasma; Brit. informal pong, niff, hum.

stinking adjective
1 *piles of stinking rubbish:* foul-smelling, smelly, reeking, fetid, malodorous, rank, putrid, noxious; literary noisome.
2 (informal) *a stinking cold:* dreadful, awful, terrible, ghastly, nasty, foul, vile; Brit. informal rotten, shocking.
OPPOSITES: fragrant.

stint verb *we saved by stinting on food:* skimp, scrimp, be economical, economize, be sparing, hold back, be frugal; be mean, be parsimonious; limit, restrict; informal be stingy, be mingy.

▷ **noun** *a two-week stint in the office:* spell, stretch, turn, session, term, shift, tour of duty.

stipulate verb *he stipulated certain conditions before their marriage:* specify, set down, set out, lay down; demand, require, insist on, make a condition of, impose.

stipulation noun *the only stipulation was that Edwards should retain his job as chairman for three years:* condition, precondition, proviso, provision, prerequisite, specification; demand, requirement; rider, caveat, qualification.

stir verb
1 *stir the mixture well:* mix, blend, agitate; beat, whip, whisk, fold in.
2 *Travis stirred in his sleep:* move slightly, change your position, shift.
3 *a breeze stirred the leaves:* disturb, rustle, shake, move, flutter, agitate.
4 *he finally stirred at ten o'clock:* get up, get out of bed, rouse yourself, rise; wake, wake up, awaken; informal rise and shine, surface.
5 *as he grew older he seldom stirred from*

the house: move, budge, make a move, shift, go away; leave.
6 *symbolism can stir the imagination:* arouse, rouse, fire, kindle, inspire, stimulate, excite, awaken, quicken.
7 *the war stirred him to action:* spur, drive, rouse, prompt, propel, prod, motivate, encourage; urge, impel; provoke, goad, prick, sting, incite.

▷ **noun** *the news caused a stir:* commotion, disturbance, fuss, excitement, turmoil, sensation; informal to-do; Brit. informal hoo-ha, hullabaloo.

□ **stir something up**
he accused me of trying to stir up trouble: cause, provoke, whip up, trigger, spark off, precipitate, incite.

stirring adjective *stirring accounts of our heroic history:* exciting, thrilling, rousing, stimulating, moving, inspiring, inspirational, passionate, impassioned, emotional, heady.

stitch verb *the seams are stitched by hand:* sew, baste, tack; hem; darn.

stock noun
1 *the shop has a fast turnover of stock:* merchandise, goods, wares, items/articles for sale.
2 *a stock of fuel:* store, supply, stockpile, reserve, bank, accumulation, quantity, collection; hoard, cache.
3 *farm stock:* animals, livestock, beasts; flocks, herds.
4 *blue-chip stocks:* shares, securities, equities, bonds.
5 *his mother was of French stock:* descent, ancestry, origin, parentage, pedigree, lineage, line of descent, heritage, birth, extraction, family, blood, bloodline.
6 *chicken stock:* bouillon, broth.
7 *the stock of a weapon:* handle, butt, haft, grip, shaft, shank.

▷ **adjective**
1 *a stock size:* standard, regular, normal, established, set; common, readily/widely available; staple.
2 *the stock response:* usual, routine, predictable, set, standard, customary, familiar, conventional, traditional, stereotyped, clichéd, hackneyed, unoriginal, formulaic.
OPPOSITES: unusual, unexpected.

▷ **verb**
1 *we do not stock GM food:* sell, carry, keep in stock, offer, retail, supply.
2 *the fridge was well stocked with milk:* supply, provide, furnish, provision, equip, fill, load.

□ **in stock**
for/on sale, available, on the shelf.

□ **stock up on/with**
you'd better stock up with fuel: amass supplies of, stockpile, lay in, buy up/in, put away/by, put/set aside, collect, accumulate, save, hoard, cache; informal squirrel away, salt away, stash away.

S

□ **take stock of**
we'll have to take stock of the situation and see what needs to be done: review, assess, weigh up, appraise, evaluate; informal size up.

stockpile noun *a stockpile of weapons:* stock, store, supply, accumulation, collection, reserve, hoard, cache; informal stash.

▷ **verb** *food had been stockpiled:* store up, amass, accumulate, stock up on, collect, lay in, put away, put/set aside, put by, stow away, save, hoard, cache; informal salt away, stash away.

stocky adjective *a short, stocky man:* thickset, sturdy, heavily built, chunky, burly, strapping, brawny, solid, heavy, hefty; informal beefy.
OPPOSITES: slender, skinny.

stodgy adjective
1 *a stodgy pudding:* solid, substantial, filling, heavy, starchy, indigestible.
2 *his stodgy prose never brings its subject to life:* boring, dull, uninteresting, dreary, turgid, tedious, dry, heavy going, unimaginative, uninspired, unexciting, unoriginal, monotonous, humdrum, prosaic, staid.
OPPOSITES: light, lively.

stoical adjective *my mother was more stoical and scorned such self-pity:* long-suffering, uncomplaining, patient, forbearing, accepting, tolerant, resigned, phlegmatic, philosophical.
OPPOSITES: complaining, intolerant.

stoicism noun patience, forbearance, resignation, fortitude, endurance, acceptance, tolerance, phlegm.
OPPOSITES: intolerance.

stolid adjective *Roger was a stolid chap who worked in the City:* impassive, imperturbable, phlegmatic, unemotional, cool, calm, placid, unexcitable, even-tempered; dependable; unimaginative, uninspiring, dull.
OPPOSITES: emotional, lively.

stomach noun
1 *I've got a pain in my stomach:* abdomen, belly, gut; informal tummy, insides.
2 *his fat stomach:* paunch, pot belly, beer belly; informal beer gut.
3 *he had no stomach for a fight:* desire, inclination, appetite, taste, hunger, thirst.
▷ **verb**
1 *if you can't stomach orange juice, try apple juice:* digest, keep down, manage to eat/consume, tolerate, take.
2 *I can't stomach his self-righteous attitude:* tolerate, put up with, take, stand, endure, bear, abide; informal hack; Brit. informal stick.

> WORD LINKS
> **gastric** relating to the stomach
> **gastroenterology** the branch of medicine which deals with disorders of the stomach and intestines

stomach ache noun indigestion, dyspepsia; colic, gripe.

stone noun
1 *demonstrators threw stones at police officers:* rock, pebble, boulder.
2 *a memorial stone:* tablet, monument, monolith, obelisk; gravestone, headstone, tombstone.
3 *paving stones:* slab, flagstone, flag.
4 *a precious stone:* gem, gemstone, jewel.
5 *a peach stone:* kernel, pit.

stony adjective
1 *a stony path:* rocky, pebbly, gravelly, shingly; rough, hard.
2 *a stony stare:* unfriendly, hostile, cold, chilly, frosty, icy; hard, flinty, steely, stern, severe, unfeeling, uncaring, unsympathetic, indifferent, cold-hearted, callous, heartless, hard-hearted.

stooge noun (informal) *a government stooge:* underling, minion, lackey, subordinate; henchman; puppet, pawn, cat's paw; informal sidekick; Brit. informal poodle.

stoop verb
1 *she stooped to pick up the pen:* bend down, lean down, crouch down.
2 *he stooped his head:* lower, bend, incline, bow, duck.
3 *he stoops when he walks:* hunch your shoulders, walk with a stoop, be round-shouldered.
4 *Davis would never stoop to crime:* lower yourself, sink, descend, resort; go as far as, sink as low as.

stop verb
1 *we need long-term solutions to stop the economic decline | the system has been very effective at stopping credit-card fraud:* put an end/stop/halt to, bring to an end/stop/halt, end, halt, cut short, nip in the bud.
2 *he stopped running | I'm trying to stop smoking:* cease, discontinue, desist from, break off; give up, abandon, abstain from, cut out; informal quit, leave off, knock off, pack in, lay off; Brit. informal jack in.
3 *the car stopped suddenly:* pull up, draw up, come to a stop/halt, come to rest, pull in, pull over; park.
4 *the music stopped:* come to an end/stop, cease, end, finish, draw to a close, be over, conclude, terminate; pause, break off; peter out, fade away.
5 *her parents tried to stop her leaving the house:* prevent, obstruct, impede, hinder; block, bar; dissuade from.
6 *divers stopped the flow of oil:* stem, staunch, hold back, check, curb; block, dam.
OPPOSITES: start, begin, continue, resume.
▷ **noun**
1 *all business came to a stop:* halt, end, finish, standstill; cessation, stoppage.
2 *a brief stop in the town:* break, stopover, stop-off, stay, visit.

S

3 *the next stop is Oxford Street:* stopping place, halt, station.
4 *type stops after each initial:* full point, point; Brit. full stop; N. Amer. period.

stopgap noun *he seems destined to be used as a stopgap, filling in whenever another player is injured or suspended:* temporary solution, expedient, makeshift; substitute, stand-in.
▷**adjective** *a stopgap measure:* temporary, provisional, interim, pro tem, short-term, working, makeshift, emergency; caretaker, acting, stand-in, fill-in.
OPPOSITES: permanent.

stopover noun *a brief stopover in the United Kingdom en route to the US:* break, stop, stop-off, visit, stay.

stoppage noun
1 *the stoppage of production | a power stoppage:* discontinuation, stopping, halting, cessation, end; interruption, suspension.
2 *an unofficial stoppage by workers over holiday entitlements:* strike, walkout.
3 *a stoppage of the blood supply:* obstruction, blockage, block.

stopper noun bung, plug, cork, spigot, seal.

store noun
1 *a store of food:* stock, supply, stockpile, hoard, cache, reserve, bank; fund, pool.
2 *a grain store:* storeroom, storehouse, repository, depository, stockroom, depot, warehouse; informal lock-up.
3 *ship's stores:* supplies, provisions, stocks, necessities; food, rations; materials, equipment, hardware.
4 *a DIY store:* shop, retail outlet, boutique, department store, emporium; supermarket, superstore, megastore; Brit. hypermarket.
▷**verb** *the country is able to feed itself by storing surplus food during bumper harvests:* keep, keep in reserve, stockpile, lay in, put/set aside, put away/by, save, collect, accumulate, hoard, cache; informal squirrel away, salt away, stash away, put away for a rainy day.
OPPOSITES: use, discard.
□ **set store by**
she sets great store by first impressions: value, attach great importance to, put a high value on, put a premium on; think highly of, hold in high regard, have a high opinion of; informal rate.

storehouse noun warehouse, depository, repository, store, storeroom, depot.

storey noun *a small flat on the second storey:* floor, level, deck.

USAGE

Do not confuse **storey** with **story**. In British English, **storey** means 'a floor of a building', while **story** means 'an account told for entertainment' (*an adventure story*).

storm noun
1 *severe storms battered Scotland and northern England last night:* tempest, squall; gale, hurricane, tornado, cyclone, typhoon; thunderstorm, rainstorm, hailstorm, snowstorm, blizzard.
2 *a storm of bullets:* volley, salvo, fusillade, barrage, cannonade; shower, spray, hail, rain.
3 *his remarks caused a storm in Germany:* uproar, outcry, fuss, furore, brouhaha, rumpus, trouble, hue and cry, controversy; Brit. row; informal to-do, ructions; Brit. informal hoo-ha, hullabaloo.
4 *when the scheme was introduced last year there was a storm of protest:* outburst, outbreak, explosion, eruption, outpouring, surge, blaze, flare-up, wave.
▷**verb**
1 *she stormed out:* stride angrily, march, stalk, flounce, stamp, stomp.
2 *'Don't patronize me!' she stormed:* rant, rave, shout, bellow, roar, thunder, rage.
3 *police stormed the building and arrested a 47-year-old man:* attack, charge, rush, descend on, swoop on.

stormy adjective
1 *stormy weather | stormy seas:* blustery, squally, windy, gusty, blowy; rainy, thundery; wild, tempestuous, turbulent, rough.
2 *a long and stormy debate:* angry, heated, fiery, fierce, furious, passionate, turbulent, violent, intense.
OPPOSITES: calm, peaceful.

story noun
1 *an adventure story:* tale, narrative, account, anecdote; informal yarn, spiel.
2 *the novel has a good story:* plot, storyline.
3 *the story appeared in all the papers:* news item, news report, article, feature, piece.
4 *there have been a lot of stories going round:* rumour, piece of gossip, whisper; speculation.
5 *Harper changed his story:* testimony, statement, report; account of events, version of events.

USAGE

Do not confuse **story** and **storey**. The chief meaning of **story** is 'an account told for entertainment', while **storey** means 'a floor of a building' (*a flat on the second storey*).

storyteller noun narrator, raconteur.

stout adjective
1 *a short, stout man:* fat, plump, portly, rotund, chubby, dumpy, chunky; stocky, burly, bulky, hefty, solidly built, thickset; informal tubby, pudgy; Brit. informal podgy.
2 *stout leather shoes:* strong, sturdy, solid, substantial, robust, tough, durable, hard-wearing.
3 *he put up a stout resistance:* determined, vigorous, forceful, spirited; staunch, steadfast, stalwart, firm, resolute,

S

unyielding, dogged; brave, bold, courageous, valiant, valorous, gallant; informal **gutsy, spunky.**
OPPOSITES: thin, flimsy, feeble.

stow verb *Barney stowed her luggage in the boot:* pack, load, place, put, deposit; store, stash.
□ **stow away**
he stowed away on a ship bound for South Africa: hide, conceal yourself, travel secretly.

straddle verb
1 *she straddled the motorbike:* sit/stand astride, bestride, mount, get on.
2 *a mountain range straddling the border:* lie on both sides of, extend across, span.

strafe verb *military aircraft strafed the village:* bomb, shell, bombard, fire on, machine-gun, rake with gunfire.

straggle verb *a few of the men were straggling the rest:* trail, lag, dawdle, walk slowly; fall behind, bring up the rear.

straggly adjective *a thin woman with straggly hair:* untidy, messy, unkempt, straggling, dishevelled.

straight adjective
1 *a straight line:* without a bend, without a curve, undeviating, linear.
2 *that picture isn't straight:* level, even, in line, aligned; vertical, perpendicular; horizontal.
3 *we must get the place straight:* in order, tidy, neat, shipshape, orderly, spick and span, organized, arranged, sorted out, straightened out.
4 *he gave me a straight answer:* honest, direct, frank, candid, truthful, sincere, forthright, straightforward, plain-spoken, blunt, straight from the shoulder, unequivocal, unambiguous; informal upfront.
5 *three straight wins:* successive, in succession, consecutive, in a row, running; informal on the trot.
6 *straight brandy:* undiluted, neat, pure.
OPPOSITES: winding, crooked, evasive.
▷ **adverb**
1 *he looked me straight in the eyes:* right, directly, squarely, full; informal smack, bang, slap bang.
2 *she drove straight home:* directly, right, by a direct route.
3 *I'll call you straight back:* right away, straight away, immediately, directly, at once.
4 *I told her straight:* frankly, directly, candidly, honestly, forthrightly, plainly, point-blank, bluntly, straight from the shoulder, without beating about the bush, without mincing your words, unequivocally, unambiguously, in plain English, to someone's face.
5 *he couldn't think straight:* logically, rationally, clearly, lucidly, coherently, cogently.

□ **go straight**
reform, mend your ways, turn over a new leaf, get back on the straight and narrow.
□ **straight away**
we must leave straight away: at once, right away, now, this/that minute, this/that instant, immediately, instantly, directly, forthwith, without further/more ado, promptly, quickly, without delay, then and there, here and now, as soon as possible, as quickly as possible; informal pronto.

> **USAGE**
>
> Do not confuse **straight** with **strait**. **Straight** means 'without a curve or bend', while **strait** means 'a narrow passage of water' (*the Straits of Gibraltar*) or 'trouble or difficulty' (*the economy is in dire straits*).

straighten verb
1 *she stood up and straightened her clothes:* tidy, neaten, adjust, arrange, rearrange, spruce up.
2 *we must straighten things out with Viola:* put/set right, sort out, clear up, settle, resolve, put in order, regularize, rectify; informal patch up.
3 *he straightened up:* stand up, stand upright.

straightforward adjective
1 *the process was remarkably straightforward:* uncomplicated, simple, easy, effortless, painless, undemanding, plain sailing, child's play; informal as easy as falling off a log, as easy as pie, a piece of cake, a cinch, a doddle, a breeze.
2 *a straightforward man:* honest, frank, candid, open, truthful, sincere, on the level; forthright, plain-speaking, direct, unambiguous; informal upfront.
OPPOSITES: complicated.

strain[1] verb
1 *take care that you don't strain yourself:* overtax, overwork, overextend, overreach, overdo it; exhaust, wear out; informal knacker, knock yourself out.
2 *you've strained a muscle:* injure, damage, pull, wrench, twist, sprain.
3 *we strained to haul the guns up the slope:* struggle, labour, toil, make every effort, try very hard, break your back, push/drive yourself to the limit; informal pull out all the stops, go all out, bust a gut.
4 *the flood of refugees is straining the relief services:* make excessive demands on, overtax, be too much for, test, tax, put a strain on.
5 *the bear strained at the chain:* pull, tug, heave, haul, jerk; informal yank.
6 *strain the mixture into a bowl:* filter; sift, sieve.
▷ **noun**
1 *the rope snapped under the strain:* tension, tightness, tautness.
2 *the strain of her job was beginning to tell:* pressure, demands, burdens, worry; stress; informal hassle.

S

3 *Melissa was showing signs of strain:* stress, tension; exhaustion, fatigue, pressure of work, overwork.
4 *the strains of Brahms's lullaby could be heard in the background:* sound, music; melody, tune.

strain² noun
1 *a different strain of flu:* variety, kind, type, sort; breed, genus.
2 *they have injected a strain of solemnity into the film:* element, strand, vein, note, trace, touch, suggestion, hint.
3 *there was a strain of insanity in the family:* tendency towards, susceptibility to, propensity for, proneness to.

strained adjective
1 *relations between them were strained:* awkward, tense, uneasy, uncomfortable, edgy, difficult, troubled.
2 *Jean's strained face:* drawn, careworn, worn, pinched, tired, exhausted, drained, haggard.
3 *a strained smile:* forced, constrained, unnatural; artificial, insincere, false, affected, put-on.
OPPOSITES: relaxed.

strait noun
1 *a strait about six miles wide:* channel, sound, inlet, stretch of water.
2 *the company is in desperate straits:* a difficult situation, a bad situation, difficulty, trouble, crisis, a mess, a predicament; informal hot/deep water, a jam, a hole, a bind, a fix.

> USAGE
>
> Do not confuse **strait** with **straight**. **Strait** means 'a narrow passage of water' or 'trouble or difficulty', while **straight** means 'without a curve or bend' (*a long, straight road*).

straitened adjective *he died in 1886, leaving the family in straitened circumstances:* impoverished, poverty-stricken, poor, destitute, impecunious; unable to make ends meet, in reduced circumstances; Brit. on the breadline; informal broke, strapped for cash, cash-strapped, on your uppers.

strait-laced adjective *his strait-laced parents were horrified:* prim and proper, prudish, puritanical, niminy-piminy; respectable, conservative, old-fashioned, stuffy, staid, narrow-minded; informal starchy, square, fuddy-duddy.
OPPOSITES: broad-minded.

strand noun
1 *strands of wool:* thread, filament, fibre; length.
2 *the various strands of the ecological movement:* element, component, factor, ingredient, aspect, feature, strain.

stranded adjective
1 *a stranded ship:* beached, grounded, run aground, high and dry; shipwrecked,
wrecked, marooned.
2 *she was stranded in a strange city:* helpless, without resources, in difficulties; in the lurch, abandoned, deserted, marooned.

strange adjective
1 *strange things have been happening:* unusual, odd, curious, peculiar, funny, bizarre, uncanny, queer, weird; unexpected, unfamiliar, atypical, anomalous, out of the ordinary, extraordinary, puzzling, mystifying, mysterious, perplexing, baffling, unaccountable, inexplicable, singular, freakish; suspicious, questionable.
2 *her strange clothes:* odd, eccentric, peculiar, funny, bizarre, unusual; unconventional, offbeat, outlandish.
3 *when children visit a strange house, they are often a little shy:* unfamiliar, unknown, new, alien.
OPPOSITES: ordinary, familiar.

stranger noun *he was a stranger in the town:* newcomer, new arrival, visitor, outsider; foreigner.
▫ **a stranger to** *he was a stranger to their customs and their language:* unaccustomed to, unfamiliar with, unused to, new to, inexperienced in.

strangle verb
1 *the victim was strangled with a scarf:* throttle, choke, garrotte; informal strangulate.
2 *she strangled a sob:* suppress, smother, stifle, repress, restrain, fight back, choke back.
3 *bureaucracy is strangling commercial activity:* hamper, hinder, impede, restrict, inhibit, curb, check, constrain, squash, crush, suppress, repress.

strap noun *thick leather straps:* thong, tie, band, belt.
▷ verb
1 *a bag was strapped to the bicycle:* fasten, secure, tie, bind, make fast, lash, truss.
2 *his knee was strapped up:* bandage, bind.

strapping adjective *they had three strapping sons:* big, strong, well built, brawny, burly, broad-shouldered, muscular, rugged; informal hunky, beefy.
OPPOSITES: weedy.

stratagem noun *he deployed various cunning stratagems:* plan, scheme, tactic, manoeuvre, ploy, device, trick, ruse, plot, machination, dodge; subterfuge, artifice; Brit. informal wheeze.

strategic adjective *strategic planning | a strategic decision:* long-term, forward-looking, looking to the future; politic, judicious, prudent, shrewd, far-sighted.

strategy noun *the government's economic strategy:* master plan, grand design, plan of action, policy, programme; tactics; informal game plan.

S

stratum noun
1 *a stratum of flint:* layer, vein, seam, lode.
2 *this stratum of society:* level, class, echelon, rank, group, set.

stray verb
1 *the gazelle had strayed from the herd:* wander off, go astray, get separated, get lost.
2 *we strayed from our original topic:* digress, deviate, wander, get sidetracked, go off at a tangent; get off the subject.
▷ adjective
1 *a stray dog:* homeless, lost, abandoned.
2 *she was killed by a stray bullet:* random, chance; isolated, lone, single.

streak noun
1 *a streak of orange light:* band, line, strip, stripe, ray; vein.
2 *streaks of oil:* mark, smear, smudge, blotch; informal splotch.
3 *a streak of self-destructiveness:* element, vein, touch, strain; trait, characteristic.
4 *a winning streak:* period, spell, stretch, run; Brit. informal patch.
▷ verb
1 *the sky was streaked with red:* stripe, band, fleck.
2 *overalls streaked with paint:* mark, daub, smear; informal splotch.

streaky adjective *a songbird with streaky brown plumage:* striped, stripy, streaked, brindled; banded, veined.

stream noun
1 *a mountain stream:* brook, rivulet, rill, runnel; tributary; Scottish & N. English burn; N. English beck; N. Amer. & Austral./NZ creek.
2 *a stream of boiling water:* jet, flow, rush, gush, surge, torrent, flood, cascade, outpouring, outflow.
3 *a steady stream of visitors:* succession, series, string.
▷ verb
1 *tears were streaming down her face:* flow, pour, course, run, gush, surge, flood, cascade, spill.
2 *children streamed out of the classrooms:* pour, surge, flood, swarm, pile, crowd.
3 *a flag streamed from the mast:* flutter, float, flap, fly, blow, waft, wave.

streamer noun pennant, flag, banner.

streamlined adjective
1 *a new generation of streamlined aluminium trams:* aerodynamic, smooth, sleek, elegant.
2 *a streamlined organization:* efficient, smooth-running, well run, well organized, well oiled, slick; time-saving, labour-saving.

street noun *Amsterdam's narrow cobbled streets:* road, thoroughfare, avenue, drive, boulevard, parade; lane; N. Amer. highway.
□ on the streets
homeless, sleeping rough, down and out.

strength noun
1 *a man of enormous physical strength:* power, brawn, muscle, muscularity, burliness, sturdiness, robustness, toughness, hardiness; vigour, force, might.
2 *Oliver began to regain his strength:* health, fitness, vigour, stamina.
3 *her great inner strength:* fortitude, resilience, spirit, backbone, strength of character; courage, bravery, pluck, pluckiness, courageousness, grit; informal guts, spunk.
4 *the strength of the retaining wall:* robustness, sturdiness, firmness, toughness, soundness, solidity, durability.
5 *Europe's military strength:* power, influence, dominance, ascendancy, supremacy; informal clout.
6 *the strength of feeling against the president:* intensity, vehemence, force, forcefulness, depth, ardour, fervour.
7 *the strength of their argument:* cogency, forcefulness, force, weight, power, potency, persuasiveness, soundness, validity.
8 *what do you regard as your strengths?* strong point, advantage, asset, forte, talent, skill; speciality.
OPPOSITES: weakness.
□ on the strength of
I went to see the film on the strength of your recommendation: because of, by virtue of, on the basis of.

strengthen verb
1 *calcium strengthens growing bones:* make strong/stronger, build up, give strength to.
2 *engineers strengthened the walls:* reinforce, make stronger, buttress, shore up, underpin.
3 *the wind had strengthened:* become strong/stronger, gain strength, intensify, pick up.
4 *his insistence strengthened her determination:* fortify, bolster, make stronger, boost, reinforce, harden, stiffen, toughen.
5 *they strengthened their efforts:* step up, increase, escalate; informal up, crank up, beef up.
6 *the argument is strengthened by this evidence:* reinforce, lend more weight to; support, back up, confirm, bear out, corroborate.
OPPOSITES: weaken.

strenuous adjective
1 *a strenuous climb:* arduous, difficult, hard, tough, taxing, demanding, exacting, exhausting, tiring, gruelling, back-breaking; informal killing; Brit. informal knackering.
2 *the council has made strenuous efforts to address the problem of antisocial behaviour:* vigorous, energetic, zealous, forceful, determined, tireless, indefatigable, dogged.
OPPOSITES: easy, half-hearted.

S

stress noun
1 *he's under a lot of stress:* strain, pressure, tension; worry, anxiety.
2 *the stresses and strains of public life:* worry, problem, difficulty, burden; pressure, demand; informal hassle.
3 *he started to lay greater stress on the government's role in industry:* emphasis, importance, weight.
4 *the stress falls on the first syllable:* emphasis, accent, accentuation; beat.
5 *the distribution of stress is uniform across the bar:* pressure, tension, strain.
▷ verb
1 *they stressed the need for reform:* emphasize, draw attention to, underline, underscore, point up, place emphasis on, lay stress on, highlight, accentuate, press home.
2 *the last syllable is stressed:* emphasize, place the accent on.
OPPOSITES: play down.

stressed adjective *all the staff are stressed:* overstretched, overtaxed, under pressure, pressurized; harassed, worried, anxious, fraught; informal hassled

stressful adjective *he had had a particularly stressful day:* demanding, trying, taxing, difficult, hard, tough; fraught, traumatic, pressured, tense, frustrating.
OPPOSITES: relaxing.

stretch verb
1 *squares of canvas were stretched over the bamboo frame:* pull, draw out.
2 *she stretched out on the sofa:* lie down, recline, lean back, be recumbent, sprawl, lounge, loll.
3 *she stretched out her hand to him:* reach out, hold out, extend, outstretch.
4 *he stretched his arms and yawned:* extend, straighten, straighten out.
5 *the beach stretches for over four miles:* extend, reach, spread, continue.
6 *why not stretch your weekend into a mini vacation?* prolong, lengthen, make longer, extend, spin out.
7 *the court case really stretched their finances:* put a strain on, overtax, over-extend, drain, sap.
8 *my budget won't stretch to a new car:* be sufficient for, be enough for, cover; afford, have the money for.
▷ noun
1 *magnificent stretches of forest:* expanse, area, tract, belt, sweep, extent.
2 *a four-hour stretch:* period, time, spell, run, stint, session, shift.

strew verb *his room was strewn with books and papers:* scatter, spread, litter, cover.

strict adjective
1 *her father was very strict:* stern, severe, uncompromising, authoritarian, austere, harsh.
2 *the government placed strict controls on public spending:* stringent, rigorous, severe, harsh, hard, rigid, tough.
3 *a strict interpretation of the law:* precise, exact, literal, rigorous, scrupulous.
4 *this will be treated in strict confidence:* absolute, utter, complete, total.
OPPOSITES: liberal, lenient, loose.

stricture noun
1 *ministers are to impose new strictures on police and social workers:* constraint, restriction, limitation, restraint, curb.
2 *the constant strictures of the nuns:* criticism, censure, condemnation, reproof, reproach, admonishment.

stride verb *she strode down the path:* march, sweep, stalk; informal sashay.

strident adjective *a strident voice interrupted the consultation:* harsh, raucous, rough, grating, rasping, jarring, loud, shrill, screeching, piercing, ear-piercing.
OPPOSITES: soft.

strife noun *the history of the Empire is full of strife:* conflict, friction, discord, disagreement, dissension, dispute, argument, quarrelling, wrangling, bickering, controversy; ill/bad feeling, bad blood, hostility, animosity.
OPPOSITES: peace.

strike verb
1 *he raised his hand as if to strike me:* hit, beat, slap, smack, thrash, spank, thump, punch, cuff; cane, whip, club; informal clout, wallop, belt, swipe, whack, thwack, bash, clobber, bop, biff.
2 *the car struck a tree:* crash into, collide with, hit, run into, bump into, smash into, bang into; N. Amer. impact.
3 *the disease tends to strike infants and young children:* affect, afflict, attack, hit.
4 *she was asleep when the killer struck:* attack, pounce.
5 *a thought struck me:* occur to, come to, dawn on you, hit, spring to mind, enter your head.
6 *you strike me as intelligent:* seem to be, appear to be, give the impression of being.
7 *we have struck a deal:* agree, agree on, reach, come to an agreement about, settle on; sign.
8 *train drivers are striking:* take industrial action, go on strike, down tools, walk out, withdraw your labour; work to rule.
9 *they have struck oil:* discover, find, come upon.
▷ noun
1 *a 48-hour strike:* industrial action, walkout, stoppage; work-to-rule.
2 *a military strike:* attack, assault, bombing.
□ strike something up
1 *the band struck up another tune:* begin to play, start playing.
2 *we struck up a friendship:* begin, start, embark on; establish.

S

striking adjective

1 *Lizzie bears a striking resemblance to her sister:* unmistakable, strong, marked, prominent, obvious, conspicuous, noticeable, notable; remarkable, extraordinary, incredible, amazing, astonishing.

2 *Kenya's striking landscape:* impressive, grand, splendid, magnificent, spectacular, breathtaking, superb, marvellous, wonderful, stunning, sensational, dramatic, memorable.

3 *a striking woman with a magnetic personality:* beautiful, attractive, good-looking, stunning, glamorous, gorgeous.
OPPOSITES: unremarkable.

string noun

1 *a ball of string:* twine, cord, yarn, thread.

2 *they lease their pubs to a string of brewers:* chain, group, firm, company.

3 *there'd been a string of burglaries in the area:* series, succession, chain, sequence, run.

4 *a string of pearls:* strand, rope, necklace.

5 (**strings**) (informal) *a guaranteed loan with no strings attached:* conditions, provisos, caveats, stipulations, riders, constraints, restrictions.

▷ **verb**

1 *lights were strung across the promenade:* hang, suspend, sling, stretch, run; thread, loop, festoon.

2 *beads strung on a silver chain:* thread, loop, link.

□ **string someone along** (informal) *she had no plans to marry him—she was just stringing him along:* mislead, deceive, take advantage of, dupe, make a fool of, play with, toy with, dally with, trifle with; informal lead up the garden path, take for a ride.

stringent adjective *the safety regulations are very stringent:* strict, firm, rigid, rigorous, precise, tight, exacting, demanding, inflexible, hard and fast.

strip¹ verb

1 *he stripped and got into bed:* undress, strip off, take your clothes off, disrobe, strip naked.

2 *strip off the existing paint:* remove, take off.

3 *they stripped him of his doctorate:* take away from, dispossess, deprive, divest, relieve; confiscate.

4 *the house had been stripped:* empty, clear, clean out, rob, burgle, loot, pillage, ransack; literary despoil.

5 *they stripped down my engine:* dismantle, disassemble, take to bits/pieces, take apart.
OPPOSITES: dress.

▷ **noun** *the team's new strip:* outfit, clothes, clothing, garments, dress, garb; Brit. kit; informal gear, get-up.

strip² noun *a strip of paper | a cat with light orange fur and darker strips of the same*

colour: narrow piece, slip, bit; band, stripe, belt, ribbon.

stripe noun *green tracksuit bottoms with a yellow stripe on the side:* line, band, strip, belt, bar, streak, vein, flash, blaze.

stripy adjective *a stripy T-shirt | the cat's stripy fur:* striped, banded; streaky, variegated.

strive verb

1 *I shall strive to keep costs low:* try, try hard, attempt, endeavour, aim, make an effort, exert yourself, do your best, do all you can, do your utmost, labour, work; informal go all out, give it your best shot, pull out all the stops.

2 *scholars must strive against bias:* struggle, fight, battle, combat; campaign, crusade.

stroke noun

1 *five strokes of the cane:* blow, hit, thump, punch, slap, smack.

2 *a wonderful ground stroke from Seamus Prendergast picked out Paul O'Brien:* shot, hit, strike.

3 *massage the cream into the skin using light upward strokes:* movement, action, motion.

4 *broad brush strokes:* mark, line.

5 *he suffered a stroke:* thrombosis, seizure.

▷ **verb** *she stroked the cat:* caress, fondle, pat, pet, touch; rub, massage.

stroll verb *they strolled along the river:* saunter, amble, wander, meander, ramble, promenade, walk, go for a walk, stretch your legs, get some air; informal mosey.

▷ **noun** *a stroll in the park:* saunter, amble, wander, walk, turn, promenade; informal mosey.

strong adjective

1 *a strong lad:* powerful, muscular, brawny, powerfully built, strapping, sturdy, burly, meaty, robust, athletic, tough, rugged, strong as an ox/horse; fit, healthy; informal beefy, hunky, husky.

2 *the current is very strong in this part of the river:* forceful, powerful, vigorous, fierce.

3 *a strong fortress:* secure, well built, indestructible, well fortified, well protected, impregnable, solid.

4 *strong cotton bags:* durable, hard-wearing, heavy-duty, tough, sturdy, well made, long-lasting.

5 *a strong leader:* powerful, forceful, determined, strong-minded, strong-willed, assertive, tough, formidable, redoubtable, uncompromising, resolute, unshakeable, unbending; dominant, controlling, influential, authoritative.

6 *she was a strong supporter of the women's movement:* keen, passionate, fervent, ardent, zealous, eager, enthusiastic, dedicated, staunch, loyal, steadfast.

7 *the minister put forward some strong arguments:* compelling, cogent, forceful,

S

powerful, potent, weighty, convincing, sound, valid, well founded, persuasive.
8 *she bore a very strong resemblance to Vera:* marked, noticeable, pronounced, distinct, definite, unmistakable, notable.
9 *his strong voice carried over the murmuring crowd:* loud, powerful, forceful, resonant, sonorous, deep, booming.
10 *a strong blue colour:* intense, deep, rich, bright, brilliant, vivid.
11 *strong lights:* bright, brilliant, dazzling, glaring.
12 *strong cheese:* highly flavoured, flavourful, flavoursome; piquant, tangy, spicy.
OPPOSITES: weak, gentle, mild.

strong-arm adjective *strong-arm tactics were deployed by both sides:* aggressive, forceful, bullying, coercive, threatening, intimidatory; informal bully-boy.

stronghold noun
1 *the enemy stronghold:* fortress, fort, castle, citadel, garrison.
2 *the north of the county remains a stronghold of Welsh culture and tradition:* bastion, bulwark, protector, defender; centre.

strong-minded adjective *a strong-minded, independent woman:* determined, firm, resolute, purposeful, strong-willed, uncompromising, unbending, forceful, persistent, tenacious; informal gutsy, spunky.

strong-willed adjective *he was strong-willed and independent:* determined, strong-minded, uncompromising; stubborn, obstinate, wilful, headstrong, self-willed, unbending, unyielding, intransigent, intractable, obdurate.

stroppy adjective (Brit. informal). See BAD-TEMPERED.

structure noun
1 *a vast Gothic structure:* building, construction, erection, pile; formal edifice.
2 *the structure of local government:* construction, form, formation, shape, composition, anatomy, make-up, constitution; organization, system, arrangement, design, framework, configuration.
▷ verb *the programme is structured around periods of residential study:* arrange, organize, design, shape, construct, build, put together.

struggle verb
1 *they struggled to do better:* strive, try hard, endeavour, make every effort, do your best/utmost, bend over backwards, put yourself out; informal go all out, give it your best shot; formal essay.
2 *James struggled with the raiders:* fight, grapple, wrestle, scuffle, brawl, spar; informal scrap.
3 *both teams were continuously struggling*

for the lead: compete, contend, vie, fight, battle, jockey.
4 *she struggled over the dunes:* scramble, flounder, stumble, fight/battle your way, labour.
▷ noun
1 *there were signs of a struggle and there was a lot of blood:* fight, scuffle, brawl, tussle, skirmish, fracas; informal scrap, dust-up; Brit. informal punch-up.
2 *the army suspended the armed struggle:* conflict, fight, battle, confrontation, clash, skirmish; hostilities, fighting.
3 *a power struggle for the party leadership:* contest, competition, fight; rivalry, friction, feuding, conflict.
4 *the community's long struggle to regain control of the land:* endeavours, efforts, exertions, labours; campaign, battle, crusade, drive, push.
5 *it was a struggle to make herself understood:* effort, trial, battle.

strut verb *he strutted around his vast office:* swagger, parade, stride, sweep; informal swank; N. Amer. informal sashay.

stub noun
1 *a cigarette stub:* butt, end; informal dog-end.
2 *a ticket stub:* counterfoil, tab.
3 *a stub of pencil:* stump, remnant, end.

stubble noun
1 *a field of stubble:* stalks, straw.
2 *a weather-beaten face covered in grey stubble:* bristles, whiskers; informal five o'clock shadow.

stubbly adjective *his stubbly chin:* bristly, unshaven, whiskered; prickly, rough, coarse, scratchy.

stubborn adjective *you're too stubborn to admit you were wrong:* obstinate, pig-headed, obdurate; headstrong, wilful, strong-willed, difficult, contrary, perverse, recalcitrant, inflexible, iron-willed, uncompromising, unbending; formal pertinacious, refractory; informal stiff-necked; Brit. informal bloody-minded.
OPPOSITES: compliant.

stuck adjective
1 *a message was stuck to his screen:* fixed, fastened, attached, glued, pinned.
2 *the gate was stuck:* immovable, stuck fast, jammed.
3 *I can't do any more, I'm stuck:* at a loss, beaten, defeated; baffled; informal stumped.
□ **get stuck into** (informal) *Walsh got stuck into the project:* get down to, make a start on, embark on, get to work at, tackle, launch yourself into, throw yourself into.
□ **stuck with** (informal) *he was stuck with her for two months:* lumbered with, made responsible for; informal landed with.

stuck-up adjective (informal). See SNOBBISH.

student noun
1 *a university student:* undergraduate, postgraduate; scholar.

2 *a former student of the school:* pupil, schoolchild, schoolboy, schoolgirl, scholar.
3 *a nursing student:* trainee, probationer, novice; informal rookie.

studied adjective *the words were said with studied politeness:* deliberate, careful, considered, conscious, calculated, intentional; affected, forced, strained, artificial.

studio noun workshop, workroom, atelier.

studious adjective
1 *he is quiet and studious:* scholarly, academic, intellectual, bookish; serious-minded, hard-working, conscientious.
2 *he gave studious attention to the question:* diligent, careful, thoughtful, attentive, assiduous, painstaking, thorough, meticulous.
3 *his studious absence from public view:* deliberate, conscious, intentional.

study noun
1 *two years of study:* learning, education, schooling, academic work, scholarship, tuition, research.
2 *a study of the causes of malnutrition:* investigation into, examination of, analysis of, enquiry into, review of, survey of; research into.
3 *a critical study of Jane Austen's novels:* essay, article, work, review, paper, dissertation; formal disquisition.
4 *the Dean was in his study:* office, work-room, studio.
▷ verb
1 *she's supposed to be studying for her exams:* work, revise; informal swot, cram, mug up.
2 *he studied electronics:* learn, read, be taught.
3 *scientists studying the effects of global climate change on crop yields:* investigate, inquire into, research, look into, examine, analyse, explore, review, survey.
4 *she studied her friend thoughtfully:* scrutinize, examine, inspect, consider, regard, look at, eye, observe, watch, survey; formal peruse.

stuff noun
1 *all the cleaning stuff is under the sink:* items, articles, objects, things, goods; informal bits and pieces; Brit. informal odds and ends.
2 *there was some sticky stuff on the floor:* matter, substance, material.
3 *he went upstairs and packed his stuff:* belongings, possessions, things, effects, goods and chattels, paraphernalia; informal gear, kit.
4 *he knows his stuff:* facts, information, data, subject.
▷ verb
1 *feathers were used to stuff the pillows:* fill, pack, pad.
2 *she stuffed her clothes into a bag:* shove, thrust, push, ram, cram, squeeze, force, jam, pack, pile, stick.

stuffy adjective
1 *a stuffy atmosphere:* airless, close, stifling, unventilated, oppressive; musty, stale; Brit. frowsty.
2 *a stuffy young man:* staid, sedate, sober, prim, priggish, pompous; conservative, old-fashioned, strait-laced, conformist, conventional, narrow-minded; informal square, straight, starchy, fuddy-duddy.
OPPOSITES: airy.

stultifying adjective *the heroine is dissatisfied with her stultifying life in the French provinces:* restrictive, stifling, oppressive, constrained; tedious, dull, dreary, soul-destroying.
OPPOSITES: stimulating.

stumble verb
1 *he stumbled and fell heavily:* trip, lose your balance, lose/miss your footing, slip.
2 *he stumbled back home:* stagger, totter, teeter, hobble, move clumsily.
3 *he stumbled through his speech:* stammer, stutter, hesitate, falter, speak haltingly; informal fluff your lines.
□ **stumble across/on** *scientists stumbled across the vaccine by chance:* come across/upon, chance on, happen on, light on; discover, find, unearth, uncover; informal dig up.

stumbling block noun *the language problem is a fundamental stumbling block:* obstacle, hurdle, barrier, bar, hindrance, impediment, handicap, disadvantage; snag, hitch, catch, drawback, difficulty, problem; informal fly in the ointment.

stump verb
1 (informal) *they were stumped by the question:* baffle, perplex, puzzle, confound, nonplus, defeat, put at a loss; informal flummox, fox, throw, floor.
2 *she stumped along the landing:* stomp, stamp, clomp, clump, lumber, thump, thud.

stun verb
1 *the man was stunned by a blow to the head:* daze, knock unconscious, knock out.
2 *she was stunned by the news:* astound, amaze, astonish, dumbfound, stupefy, stagger, shock, take aback; informal flabbergast, knock sideways, bowl over; Brit. informal knock for six.

stunning adjective
1 *a stunning victory:* remarkable, extraordinary, staggering, incredible, outstanding, amazing, astonishing, marvellous, phenomenal, splendid; informal fabulous, fantastic, tremendous.
2 *she looked stunning.* See **BEAUTIFUL**.
OPPOSITES: ordinary.

stunt[1] verb *a disease that stunts growth:* inhibit, impede, hamper, hinder, restrict, retard, slow, curb, check.
OPPOSITES: promote.

S

stunt[2] noun *acrobatic stunts:* feat, exploit, trick.

stupefaction noun
1 *a state of drug-induced stupefaction:* oblivion, obliviousness, unconsciousness, insensibility, stupor, daze.
2 *Don shook his head in stupefaction:* bewilderment, confusion, perplexity, wonder, amazement, astonishment.

stupefy verb
1 *the blow had stupefied her:* stun, daze, knock unconscious, knock out.
2 *the amount stupefied us:* shock, stun, astound, dumbfound, overwhelm, stagger, amaze, astonish, take aback, take someone's breath away; informal flabbergast, knock sideways, floor; Brit. informal knock for six.

stupendous adjective
1 *their stupendous achievements:* amazing, astounding, astonishing, extraordinary, remarkable, phenomenal, staggering, breathtaking; informal fantastic, mind-boggling, awesome.
2 *a building of stupendous size:* colossal, immense, vast, gigantic, massive, mammoth, huge, enormous, tremendous.
OPPOSITES: ordinary.

stupid adjective
1 *don't be so stupid | a stupid remark:* unintelligent, obtuse, ignorant, dense, foolish, silly, dim-witted, idiotic, imbecilic, inane, fatuous, absurd, ludicrous, ridiculous, laughable, risible, asinine, mindless, empty-headed, scatterbrained; ill-advised, ill-considered, unwise, injudicious; informal thick, dim, dumb, dopey, dozy, moronic, half-witted, soft in the head; Brit. informal daft, gormless, half-baked.
2 *he drank himself stupid:* into a stupor, into oblivion.
OPPOSITES: intelligent, sensible.

stupidity noun foolishness, folly, ignorance, idiocy, inaneness, inanity, absurdity, fatuousness.

stupor noun *they left him slumped in a drunken stupor:* daze, state of unconsciousness, torpor; insensibility, oblivion, stupefaction.

sturdy adjective
1 *his sturdy physique:* strapping, well built, muscular, athletic, strong, hefty, brawny, powerful, solid, burly, rugged, robust, tough, hardy; informal husky, beefy.
2 *a pair of sturdy boots:* robust, strong, strongly made, well built, solid, stout, tough, resilient, durable, long-lasting, hard-wearing.
3 *his team put up a sturdy resistance:* vigorous, strong, stalwart, firm, determined, resolute, staunch, steadfast.
OPPOSITES: weak.

stutter verb *he stuttered over the word:* stammer, stumble, falter.

style noun
1 *differing styles of management:* manner, way, technique, method, methodology, approach, system, mode, form, modus operandi; informal MO.
2 *a non-directive style of counselling:* type, kind, variety, sort, genre, school, brand, pattern, model.
3 *she always dresses with style and taste:* flair, stylishness, chic, elegance, grace, gracefulness, poise; polish, suaveness, sophistication, urbanity, panache; informal class.
4 *Laura travelled in style:* comfort, luxury, elegance, opulence, lavishness.
5 *the latest styles from the hottest designers:* fashion, trend, vogue, design, look.
▷verb
1 *a collection of dresses and skirts styled by Prada:* design, tailor.
2 *men who were styled 'knight':* call, name, title, entitle, dub, designate, term, label, tag, nickname.

stylish adjective *a stylish black outfit:* fashionable, chic, smart, sophisticated, elegant, modern, up to date, modish; informal trendy, classy.
OPPOSITES: unfashionable.

suave adjective *a suave middle-aged man:* charming, sophisticated, debonair, urbane, polished, refined, poised, self-possessed, dignified, civilized, gentlemanly, gallant; smooth, polite, well mannered, civil, courteous, tactful, diplomatic.
OPPOSITES: unsophisticated.

subconscious adjective *subconscious desires:* unconscious, latent, suppressed, repressed, subliminal, dormant, under-lying, unacknowledged.

subdue verb
1 *she could not subdue her longing:* curb, restrain, hold back, constrain, contain, repress, suppress, stifle, smother, keep in check, rein in, control, master, quell; informal keep a/the lid on.
2 *he subdued all his enemies:* conquer, defeat, vanquish, overcome, overwhelm, crush, quash, beat, subjugate, suppress, bring someone to their knees.

subdued adjective
1 *Lewis's subdued air:* sombre, low-spirited, downcast, dejected, depressed, gloomy, despondent, dispirited, disheartened, forlorn; reflective, preoccupied, withdrawn, quiet; informal down in the mouth, down in the dumps.
2 *they spoke in subdued tones:* hushed, muted, quiet, low, soft, faint, muffled, indistinct.
3 *her eyes adjusted to the subdued light:* dim, muted, softened, soft, lowered, subtle.
OPPOSITES: cheerful, bright.

S

subject noun

1 *the subject of this chapter* | *I've said all I have to say on this subject:* theme, subject matter, topic; issue, question, concern, point.
2 *popular university subjects:* branch of study, area of study, discipline, field.
3 *six subjects took part in the trials:* participant, volunteer; informal guinea pig.
4 *they are British subjects:* citizen, national, passport-holder; taxpayer, voter.
▷ **verb** *he subjected her to a terrifying ordeal:* put through, cause to undergo, cause to go through; expose to.
□ **subject to**
1 *the proposal is subject to budgetary approval:* conditional on, contingent on, dependent on.
2 *these fish are subject to a variety of diseases:* susceptible to, liable to, prone to, vulnerable to, predisposed to, at risk of.
3 *we are all subject to the law:* bound by, constrained by, accountable to.

subjection noun *the subjection of aboriginal peoples:* subjugation, domination, oppression, repression, suppression.

subjective adjective *standards can be judged on quantitative data rather than on subjective opinion:* personal, individual, emotional, instinctive, intuitive; biased, prejudiced.
OPPOSITES: objective.

subjugate verb *Norman leaders had subjugated most of Ireland's Gaelic population:* conquer, vanquish, defeat, crush, quash, bring someone to their knees, enslave, subdue, suppress.
OPPOSITES: liberate.

sublime adjective

1 *Mozart's most sublime sacred music:* exalted, elevated, noble, lofty, awe-inspiring, majestic, magnificent, glorious, superb, wonderful, marvellous.
2 *he has the sublime confidence of youth:* supreme, total, complete, utter.

subliminal adjective *subliminal messages:* subconscious; hidden, inexplicit.
OPPOSITES: explicit.

submerge verb

1 *the U-boat submerged:* go under water, dive, sink.
2 *submerge the bowl in water:* immerse, plunge, sink.
3 *the farmland was submerged:* flood, inundate, deluge, swamp.
4 *she was submerged in work:* overwhelm, inundate, deluge, swamp, bury, engulf, snow under.
OPPOSITES: surface.

submission noun

1 *Tim raised his hands in submission:* surrender, capitulation, resignation, defeat.
2 *reports should be prepared for submission to the Board:* presentation, presenting, tendering.
3 *the plan was put forward by Stirling in his original submission:* proposal, suggestion, proposition, recommendation.
4 *the judge rejected their submission:* argument, assertion, contention, statement, claim.
OPPOSITES: defiance, resistance.

submissive adjective *Mary was far from being a timid or submissive woman:* compliant, yielding, acquiescent, unassertive, passive, obedient, biddable, dutiful, docile, meek, subservient; informal under someone's thumb.

submit verb

1 *she submitted under duress:* give in/way, yield, back down, cave in, capitulate; surrender, knuckle under.
2 *he refused to submit to their authority:* be governed by, abide by, be regulated by, comply with, accept, adhere to, be subject to, agree to, consent to, conform to; formal accede to
3 *we submitted an unopposed bid:* put forward, present, offer, proffer, tender, propose, suggest; put in, send in, register.
4 *they submitted that the judgement was inappropriate:* contend, assert, argue, state, claim, posit, postulate.
OPPOSITES: resist.

subordinate adjective

1 *subordinate staff:* lower-ranking, junior, lower; supporting, ancillary.
2 *this issue played only a subordinate role in policymaking:* secondary, lesser, minor, subsidiary, ancillary, auxiliary.
OPPOSITES: senior.
▷ **noun** *the manager and his subordinates:* junior, assistant, second in command, number two, right-hand man/woman, deputy, aide; underling, minion; informal sidekick.
OPPOSITES: superior.

subscribe verb

1 *he subscribes to 'Private Eye':* pay a subscription, take, buy regularly.
2 *millions subscribe to the NSPCC:* donate, make a donation, make a subscription, give money, contribute to.
3 *I can't subscribe to that theory:* agree with, accept, believe in, endorse, back, support.

subscription noun

1 *the club's subscription:* membership fee, dues, annual payment, charge.
2 *the school was built by public subscription:* donation, contribution, gift, grant.

subsequent adjective *the subsequent months:* following, ensuing, succeeding, later, future, coming, to come, next.
OPPOSITES: previous.

□ **subsequent to**
he refers to a conversation I had with him subsequent to the meeting: following, after, at the close/end of.

subsequently adverb *he made a bid for the remaining shares and subsequently acquired them:* later, at a later date, afterwards, in due course, following this/that, eventually.

subservient adjective
1 *a subservient woman:* submissive, deferential, compliant, obedient, dutiful, biddable, docile, meek, passive, unassertive, subdued, downtrodden; informal under someone's thumb.
2 *individual rights are subservient to the interests of the state:* subordinate, secondary, subsidiary, ancillary, auxiliary, less important.
OPPOSITES: independent.

subside verb
1 *wait until the storm subsides:* abate, let up, quieten down, calm, slacken off, ease up, relent, die down, recede, lessen, diminish, decline, dwindle, weaken, fade, wane, ebb.
2 *the flood waters have subsided:* recede, ebb, fall, go down, get lower.
3 *the island is gradually subsiding:* sink, cave in, collapse.
OPPOSITES: intensify, rise.

subsidiary adjective *a subsidiary role:* subordinate, secondary, lesser, auxiliary, ancillary; subservient.
OPPOSITES: principal.
▷ noun *the company's Spanish subsidiary:* subordinate company, branch, division, subdivision, offshoot.

subsidize verb *they were unwilling to subsidize the poorer southern republics:* give money to, pay a subsidy to, fund, contribute to, invest in, sponsor, support, finance, underwrite; informal bankroll, shell out for, fork out for, cough up for.

subsidy noun *the theatre receives a subsidy of £1.7 million a year:* grant, allowance, endowment, contribution, donation, bursary, handout; backing, support, sponsorship, finance, funding.

subsist verb *he subsists on his pension:* survive, live, stay alive, exist, eke out an existence; support yourself, manage, get along/by, make ends meet.

subsistence noun *they depend on fish for their subsistence:* survival, existence, living, life, sustenance, nourishment.

substance noun
1 *an organic substance:* material, matter, stuff.
2 *ghostly figures with no substance:* solidity, body, corporeality, reality; density, mass, weight, shape, structure.
3 *none of the objections have any substance:* weight, validity, force, foundation, significance, importance.
4 *the substance of the tale is very thin:* content, subject matter, theme, message, essence.

substandard adjective *children were being educated in substandard buildings:* inferior, second-rate, low-quality, poor, below par, imperfect, faulty, defective, shoddy, shabby, unsound, unsatisfactory.
OPPOSITES: superior.

substantial adjective
1 *substantial progress has been made:* considerable, real, significant, important, valuable, useful.
2 *a substantial amount of cash:* sizeable, considerable, significant, large, appreciable.
3 *a row of substantial Victorian villas:* sturdy, solid, stout, strong, well built, durable, long-lasting, hard-wearing.
4 *there was substantial agreement on the need for reform:* fundamental, essential, basic.
5 *substantial beings:* real, actual; physical, solid, material, concrete, corporeal.
OPPOSITES: negligible, flimsy.

substantially adverb
1 *the cost has fallen substantially:* considerably, significantly, to a great/large extent, greatly, markedly, appreciably.
2 *things will remain substantially the same over the next ten years:* largely, for the most part, by and large, on the whole, in essence, basically, fundamentally, to all intents and purposes.
OPPOSITES: slightly.

substantiate verb *none of the allegations were ever substantiated:* prove, show to be true, give substance to, support, uphold, bear out, justify, vindicate, validate, corroborate, verify, authenticate, confirm, endorse, give credence to.
OPPOSITES: disprove.

substitute noun *computers must not be seen as a substitute for teachers or practical experience:* replacement, alternative, surrogate.
▷ adjective *a substitute teacher:* acting, replacement, relief, surrogate, stand-in, temporary.
▷ verb
1 *curd cheese can be substituted for yogurt:* exchange, replace with, use instead of, use as an alternative to, use in place of, swap.
2 *the Senate was empowered to substitute for the President:* deputize, act as deputy, act as a substitute, stand in, cover; replace, relieve, take over from.

substitution noun *the substitution of low-fat spreads for butter:* exchange, change; replacement, replacing, swapping, switching.

S

subterfuge noun

1 *you shouldn't resort to subterfuge to get a story unless it's in the public interest:* trickery, deviousness, deceit, deception, dishonesty, cheating, duplicity, guile, cunning, chicanery.
2 *I hated all the subterfuges:* lie, deception, pretence, ruse, ploy, stratagem, artifice.
OPPOSITES: honesty.

subtle adjective

1 *a subtle distinction:* fine, fine-drawn, precise, nice; nuanced.
2 *subtle colours | subtle lighting:* understated, muted, unobtrusive, discreet, subdued, restrained, low-key; delicate, faint, pale, soft.
3 *he tried a more subtle approach:* indirect, oblique, discreet, delicate, tactful, sensitive, low-key, softly-softly; ingenious, clever, cunning.
4 *a subtle mind:* astute, keen, quick, fine, acute, sharp, shrewd, perceptive, discerning, discriminating.
OPPOSITES: broad, garish.

subtlety noun

1 *the subtlety of his performance:* delicacy, sensitivity; understatedness, restraint.
2 *the subtleties of English grammar:* fine point, fine detail, nicety, nuance.

subtract verb *the value of their child benefit is subtracted from their total welfare payments:* take away/off, deduct, debit, dock; informal knock off.
OPPOSITES: add.

suburb noun *a densely populated suburb of Amsterdam:* residential area, dormitory area, commuter belt; suburbia.

suburban adjective

1 *a large suburban area:* residential.
2 *her drab suburban existence:* dull, boring, uninteresting, conventional, ordinary, commonplace, unremarkable, unexceptional; provincial, unsophisticated, parochial, bourgeois, middle-class.

subversive adjective *both men were imprisoned pending investigation of suspected subversive activities:* seditious, disruptive, troublemaking, inflammatory; insurrectionary, revolutionary, rebellious, rebel, dissident.

subvert verb *a plot to subvert the state:* destabilize, unsettle, overthrow, overturn; bring down, topple, depose, oust; disrupt, wreak havoc on, sabotage, ruin, undermine, weaken, damage.

subway noun

1 *he walked quickly through the subway:* underpass, pedestrian tunnel.
2 *Tokyo's subway:* underground, underground railway, metro; Brit. trademark tube.

succeed verb

1 *people who can demonstrate they have the ideas, skills, and determination to succeed:* triumph, achieve success, be successful, do well, flourish, thrive; informal make it, make the grade, make a name for yourself.
2 *the plan succeeded:* be successful, turn out well, work, work out, be effective; informal come off, pay off.
3 *Rosebery succeeded Gladstone as Prime Minister:* replace, take the place of, take over from, follow, supersede; informal step into someone's shoes.
4 *he succeeded to the throne:* inherit, assume, attain; formal accede to.
OPPOSITES: fail, precede.

succeeding adjective *strands of DNA are reproduced through succeeding generations:* subsequent, successive, following, ensuing, later, future, coming.

success noun

1 *all staff worked extremely hard to ensure the success of the project:* favourable outcome, successful result, triumph.
2 *the trappings of success:* prosperity, affluence, wealth, riches.
3 *a West End success:* triumph, best-seller, box-office success, sell-out; informal hit, winner.
4 *her performance made her an overnight success:* star, superstar, celebrity, big name, household name; informal megastar.
OPPOSITES: failure.

successful adjective

1 *a successful campaign:* victorious, triumphant, winning.
2 *a successful designer:* prosperous, affluent, wealthy, rich; famous, eminent, top; informal on the up and up.
3 *successful companies:* flourishing, thriving, booming, doing well, profitable, moneymaking, profit-making, lucrative; informal on the up and up.
OPPOSITES: unsuccessful.

succession noun

1 *a succession of exciting events:* sequence, series, progression, chain, cycle, round, string, train, line, run; flow, stream.
2 *his succession to the throne:* accession, elevation, assumption.
□ **in succession**
in a terrible start to the season, they lost seven games in succession: one after the other, in a row, consecutively, successively, in sequence; running; informal on the trot.

successive adjective *the team have made a great start with three successive wins:* consecutive, in a row, straight, sequential, in succession, running; informal on the trot.

successor noun *Mary was the rightful successor to the English throne:* heir, inheritor, next-in-line.
OPPOSITES: predecessor.

succinct adjective *use short, succinct sentences:* concise, short, brief, to the

S

point, pithy, compact, condensed, crisp, laconic.
OPPOSITES: verbose.

succour noun *the group provides succour to those in need:* aid, help, a helping hand, assistance; comfort, ease, relief, support.

succulent adjective *succulent tropical fruits:* juicy, moist, luscious, soft, tender; choice, mouth-watering, appetizing, tasty, delicious, flavoursome.
OPPOSITES: dry.

succumb verb
1 *she succumbed to temptation:* yield, give in/way, submit, surrender, capitulate, cave in.
2 *he succumbed to the disease:* die from/of; catch, develop, contract, fall ill with; informal come/go down with.
OPPOSITES: resist.

suck verb
1 *they sucked orange juice through straws:* sip, drink, slurp.
2 *Fran sucked in a deep breath:* draw, pull, breathe, gasp; inhale.
3 *they got sucked into petty crime:* involve in, draw into; informal mix up in.

sudden adjective *a sudden downpour took us by surprise | he made a sudden decision:* unexpected, unforeseen, unanticipated, unlooked-for; abrupt, rapid, swift, quick, impulsive; surprising, startling.

suddenly adverb *he died very suddenly from a heart attack:* unexpectedly, without warning, out of the blue; all of a sudden, all at once, quickly, abruptly, swiftly.

suds plural noun lather, foam, froth, bubbles, soap.

sue verb
1 *he sued his employers for negligence:* take legal action against, take to court, bring an action/suit against, proceed against.
2 *the rebels were forced to sue for peace:* appeal, petition, ask, solicit, request, seek.

suffer verb
1 *I hate to see him suffer:* be in pain, feel pain; be in distress, be upset, be miserable.
2 *he suffers from asthma:* be afflicted by, be affected by, be troubled with, have.
3 *England suffered a humiliating defeat:* undergo, experience, be subjected to, sustain, meet with, receive, endure, face.
4 *the school's reputation has suffered:* be impaired, be damaged, deteriorate, decline.

suffering noun *the war caused widespread civilian suffering:* hardship, distress, misery, wretchedness, adversity, tribulation; pain, agony, anguish, trauma, torment, torture, hurt, affliction, sadness, unhappiness, sorrow, grief, woe, angst, heartache, heartbreak, stress.

suffice verb *two examples should suffice:* be enough, be sufficient, be adequate, do,

answer/meet your needs, answer/serve the purpose.

sufficient adjective & determiner *they had secured sufficient evidence to justify a charge:* enough, adequate, plenty of, ample.
OPPOSITES: insufficient.

suffocate verb
1 *she suffocated her victim:* smother, asphyxiate, stifle; choke, strangle.
2 *she was suffocating in the heat:* be breathless, be short of air, struggle for air; be too hot, swelter; informal roast, bake, boil.

suffrage noun *the campaign for women's suffrage:* the franchise, the right to vote, the vote, enfranchisement.

suffuse verb *a feeling of relief suffused her:* permeate, spread over, spread through, cover, bathe, pervade, wash through, saturate, imbue.

suggest verb
1 *I suggest that we wait a day or two | they suggested Mumbai as an alternative venue:* propose, recommend, advocate, moot, put forward; advise.
2 *evidence suggests that teenagers are responsive to price increases:* indicate, lead someone to the belief, argue, demonstrate.
3 *sources are suggesting that the Prime Minister will change his Cabinet:* hint, imply, intimate, indicate.

suggestion noun
1 *here are some suggestions for tackling the problem:* proposal, proposition, submission, recommendation; advice, idea, tip, clue, hint.
2 *there is no suggestion that he was party to a conspiracy:* insinuation, hint, implication, intimation.
3 *there was a suggestion of a smirk on his lips:* hint, trace, touch, suspicion; ghost, semblance, shadow, glimmer, impression, whisper.

suggestive adjective
1 *suggestive remarks:* indecent, indelicate, improper, unseemly, sexual, smutty, ribald, bawdy, racy, risqué, lewd, vulgar, coarse.
2 *an odour that was strongly suggestive of a brewery:* redolent, evocative, reminiscent; characteristic, indicative, typical.

suit noun
1 *she wore a dark suit:* outfit, set of clothes, ensemble.
2 *a medical malpractice suit:* legal action, lawsuit, case, court case, action, legal/judicial proceedings, litigation.
▷ verb
1 *blue really suits you:* look good on, become, flatter, enhance the appearance of.
2 *savings schemes to suit all pockets | what time would suit you?* be suitable for, fit, meet the requirements of, accommodate, be acceptable to, be convenient for.

S

suitable adjective
1 *a suitable candidate for the job:* well suited, appropriate, good; informal cut out for.
2 *a drama suitable for all ages:* appropriate, suited, fitting, fit, acceptable, right.
3 *they treated him with suitable respect:* proper, appropriate, fitting, befitting, correct, due.
4 *would this be a suitable time to speak to him?* convenient, appropriate, fitting, timely.
OPPOSITES: unsuitable.

suitcase noun travelling bag, travel bag, case, valise, portmanteau; (**suitcases**) luggage, baggage.

suite noun
1 *a penthouse suite:* apartment, flat, set of rooms.
2 *the Queen and her suite:* retinue, entourage, train, escort, royal household, court; attendants, retainers, servants.

suited adjective *their courses are suited to anyone with an interest in interior design:* appropriate, suitable, right; tailored, adapted, designed, geared, oriented.

sulk verb *still sulking, she ate her breakfast in silence:* mope, brood, be sullen, have a long face, be in a bad mood, be grumpy, be moody; informal be in a huff.
▷ noun *he sank into a deep sulk:* bad mood, mood, fit of pique, pet, bad temper, temper, the sulks; informal huff, grump.

sulky adjective *disappointment was making her sulky:* sullen, moody, petulant, disgruntled, ill-humoured, in a bad mood, out of humour; bad-tempered, grumpy, glum, gloomy, morose, surly.
OPPOSITES: cheerful.

sullen adjective *he lapsed into sullen silence:* surly, sulky, sour, morose, resentful, moody, gloomy, grumpy, bad-tempered, ill-tempered; unresponsive, uncommunicative.
OPPOSITES: cheerful.

sully verb (literary) *they were outraged that anyone should sully their good name:* taint, defile, tarnish, stain, blemish, spoil, mar.

sultry adjective
1 *a sultry day:* humid, close, airless, stifling, oppressive, muggy, sticky, sweltering, tropical, heavy; hot; informal boiling, roasting.
2 *a sultry film star:* seductive, alluring, sexy.

sum noun
1 *a large sum of money:* amount, quantity, volume.
2 *you will have to pay a small sum:* amount of money, charge, fee; price, cost.
3 *the sum of two numbers:* total, grand total, sum total, tally, aggregate, summation.
4 *the sum of his wisdom:* entirety, totality, total, whole, aggregate, summation, beginning and end.
5 *do your sums first, then the shock will not be too great:* calculation, working out.
□ sum up
he was summing up on day two of a historic test case: summarize the evidence, review the evidence, give a summing-up.
□ sum someone/something up
1 *selfish—that summed her character up:* encapsulate, put in a nutshell, summarize; capture, describe, express.
2 *he summed up his reasons:* summarize, make/give a summary of, precis, outline, give an outline of, recapitulate, recap, review.

summarily adverb *he was accused of conspiracy and summarily executed:* immediately, instantly, right away, straight away, at once, on the spot, promptly; speedily, swiftly, rapidly, without delay; arbitrarily, without formality, peremptorily, without due process.

summarize verb *he summarized these ideas in a single phrase:* sum up, condense, encapsulate, outline, give an outline of, put in a nutshell; recapitulate, recap, give/make a summary of, give a synopsis of, precis, give a résumé of, give the gist of.

summary noun *a summary of the findings:* synopsis, precis, résumé, abstract, digest, encapsulation, abbreviated version; outline, sketch, rundown, review, summing-up, overview, recapitulation, recap, conspectus.
▷ adjective
1 *a summary financial statement:* brief, concise, succinct, short.
2 *summary execution:* immediate, instant, instantaneous, on-the-spot; speedy, swift, rapid, without delay, sudden; arbitrary, without formality, peremptory.

summit noun
1 *the summit of Mont Blanc:* top, peak, crest, crown, tip, cap.
2 *the summits of world literature:* acme, peak, height, pinnacle, zenith, apex, high point/spot, crowning glory, best, finest, nonpareil.
3 *the next superpower summit:* meeting, negotiations, conference, discussions, talks.
OPPOSITES: base, nadir.

summon verb
1 *he was summoned to the Embassy:* send for, call for, request the presence of; ask, invite.
2 *they were summoned as witnesses:* serve with a summons, summons, subpoena.
3 *the director summoned a meeting:* convene, assemble, order, call, announce.

S

4 *he summoned the courage to move closer:* muster, gather, collect, rally, screw up.
5 *names that summon up their memories of home:* call to mind, call up/forth, conjure up, evoke, recall, revive, arouse, kindle, awaken, spark.
6 *they summoned spirits of the dead:* conjure up, call up, invoke.

summons noun
1 *the court issued a summons:* writ, subpoena, warrant, court order.
2 *a summons to go to the boss's office:* order, directive, command, instruction, demand, call, request.
▷ **verb** *he was summonsed to appear in court:* subpoena, summon, cite.

sumptuous adjective *a sumptuous palace:* lavish, luxurious, opulent, magnificent, resplendent, gorgeous, splendid, grand, lavishly appointed, palatial, rich; informal plush, ritzy; Brit. informal swish.
OPPOSITES: plain.

sun noun *she could feel the sun on her face:* sunshine, sunlight, light, warmth; beams, rays.

> WORD LINKS
> **solar** relating to the sun or its rays

sunbathe verb *she lay sunbathing on the hot sand:* sun yourself, bask, get a tan, tan yourself; informal catch some rays.

sunburnt adjective burnt, sunburned, red, peeling.

sundry adjective *prawn and garlic vol-au-vents and sundry other delicacies:* various, varied, miscellaneous, assorted, mixed, diverse; several, numerous, many, multifarious.

sunken adjective *her face was white, with high cheekbones and sunken cheeks:* hollowed, hollow, deep-set, concave.

sunny adjective
1 *a sunny day:* bright, sunlit, clear, fine, cloudless, without a cloud in the sky.
2 *her sunny disposition:* cheerful, cheery, happy, light-hearted, bright, merry, joyful, bubbly, animated, buoyant, ebullient, upbeat, vivacious.
OPPOSITES: dull, miserable.

sunrise noun *the infantry advanced at sunrise:* dawn, daybreak, break of day, first light, early morning; literary cockcrow.

sunset noun *stroll along the beach at sunset:* nightfall, close of day, twilight, dusk, evening, sundown; literary gloaming.

super adjective (informal) *you could win a super holiday for two in San Francisco:* excellent, superb, superlative, first-class, outstanding, marvellous, magnificent, wonderful, splendid, glorious; informal great, fantastic, fabulous, terrific, ace,

divine, wicked, cool; Brit. informal smashing, brilliant.

superannuated adjective
1 *a superannuated civil servant:* retired, pensioned off.
2 *superannuated computing equipment:* old, old-fashioned, antiquated, outdated, out of date, outmoded, obsolete.

superb adjective
1 *he scored a superb goal:* excellent, superlative, first-rate, first-class, outstanding, remarkable, marvellous, magnificent, wonderful, splendid, admirable, impressive, fine, exquisite, exceptional, glorious; informal great, fantastic, fabulous, terrific, super, awesome, ace, cool; Brit. informal brilliant, smashing.
2 *a superb 14th-century castle:* magnificent, majestic, splendid, grand, impressive, imposing, awe-inspiring, breathtaking; gorgeous.
OPPOSITES: poor, inferior.

supercilious adjective *a supercilious young minister:* arrogant, haughty, conceited, disdainful, condescending, superior, patronizing, overbearing, pompous, imperious, proud, scornful; informal hoity-toity, high and mighty, snooty, stuck-up.

superficial adjective
1 *the building suffered only superficial damage:* surface, exterior, external, outer; slight, cosmetic.
2 *a superficial investigation:* cursory, perfunctory, casual, sketchy, desultory, token, slapdash, offhand, rushed, hasty, hurried.
3 *the creature's spines gave it a superficial resemblance to a hedgehog:* apparent, seeming, outward, ostensible.
4 *a superficial person:* facile, shallow, empty-headed, trivial, frivolous, silly, inane.
OPPOSITES: deep, thorough.

superficially adverb *some reptiles and amphibians are superficially very alike:* apparently, seemingly, ostensibly, outwardly, on the surface, on the face of it, to all intents and purposes, at first glance, to the casual eye.

superfluity noun *nowadays, there's a superfluity of news outlets rather than a scarcity:* surplus, excess, overabundance, glut, surfeit, profusion, plethora.
OPPOSITES: shortage.

superfluous adjective
1 *superfluous material:* surplus, redundant, unneeded, excess, extra, spare, remaining, unused, left over, in excess, waste.
2 *words seemed superfluous:* unnecessary, unneeded, redundant, uncalled for, unwarranted.
OPPOSITES: necessary.

superhuman adjective *his superhuman effort to win the fight against cancer:* extraordinary, phenomenal, prodigious, stupendous, exceptional, immense, heroic.

superintend verb *he superintended the land reclamation scheme:* supervise, oversee, be in charge of, be in control of, preside over, direct, administer, manage, run, be responsible for.

superintendent noun
1 *the superintendent of the museum:* manager, director, administrator, supervisor, overseer, controller, chief, head, governor; informal boss.
2 (N. Amer.) *the building's superintendent:* caretaker, janitor, warden, porter.

superior adjective
1 *a superior officer:* higher-ranking, higher-level, senior, higher, higher-up.
2 *the superior candidate:* better, better qualified, more accomplished, more skilful; worthier.
3 *a superior hotel:* high-quality, first-class, first-rate, top-quality; choice, select, exclusive, prime, fine, excellent.
4 *that girl is terribly superior:* condescending, supercilious, patronizing, haughty, disdainful; informal high and mighty, hoity-toity, snooty, stuck-up.
OPPOSITES: junior, inferior.
▷ noun *my immediate superior:* manager, chief, supervisor, senior, foreman; informal boss.
OPPOSITES: subordinate.

superiority noun *the military superiority of the government forces:* supremacy, advantage, lead, dominance, primacy, ascendancy, pre-eminence.
OPPOSITES: inferiority.

superlative adjective *he is without doubt a superlative photographer:* excellent, magnificent, wonderful, marvellous, supreme, consummate, outstanding, remarkable, fine, choice, first-rate, first-class, premier, prime, unsurpassed, unequalled, unparalleled, unrivalled, pre-eminent; informal crack, ace.
OPPOSITES: mediocre.

supernatural adjective
1 *supernatural powers:* paranormal, psychic, magic, magical, occult, mystic, mystical; superhuman, preternatural, miraculous, mysterious, unnatural.
2 *a supernatural being:* ghostly, phantom, spectral, other-worldly, unearthly.

supersede verb *I found myself superseded by much younger men:* replace, take the place of, take over from, succeed; supplant, displace, oust, overthrow, remove, unseat.

superstition noun *the old superstitions held by sailors:* myth, belief, unfounded belief, old wives' tale, fallacy; legend, story.

superstitious adjective *superstitious beliefs:* mythical, irrational, groundless, unfounded; traditional.

supervise verb
1 *he had to supervise the work of two committees:* superintend, oversee, be in charge of, preside over, direct, manage, run, look after, be responsible for, organize, handle, administer.
2 *nurses were supervised by a consultant psychiatrist:* watch, observe, monitor, keep an eye on.

supervision noun
1 *the supervision of the banking system:* administration, management, control, charge; superintendence, regulation, government, governance.
2 *we need extra people to assist with the supervision of the children:* observation, charge, safe keeping, care; control.

supervisor noun *she exchanged a few words with the shift supervisor:* manager, overseer, controller, superintendent, governor, chief, head; steward, foreman; Brit. gangmaster; informal boss; Brit. informal gaffer.

supine adjective
1 *she lay supine on the sand:* flat on your back, face upwards, flat, horizontal, recumbent, stretched out.
2 *the government was supine in the face of racial injustice:* weak, spineless, yielding, effete; docile, acquiescent, pliant, submissive, passive, inert, spiritless.
OPPOSITES: upright, strong.

supplant verb
1 *the technology was not intended to supplant human labour:* replace, supersede, displace, take over from, take the place of.
2 *the man he supplanted as Prime Minister:* oust, usurp, overthrow, remove, topple, unseat, depose, dethrone.

supple adjective
1 *her supple body:* lithe, limber, lissom, willowy, flexible, loose-limbed, agile, acrobatic, nimble.
2 *supple leather:* pliant, pliable, flexible, soft, bendable, workable, malleable, stretchy, elastic, springy, yielding.
OPPOSITES: stiff, rigid.

supplement noun
1 *a supplement to the article:* appendix, addendum, end matter, tailpiece, postscript, addition, coda, codicil.
2 *there's a single room supplement:* surcharge, addition, extra cost.
▷ verb *they supplemented their incomes by cash-in-hand work:* augment, increase, add to, boost, swell; Brit. top up.

supplementary adjective *do you have any supplementary income?* additional, supplemental, extra, more, further; add-on, subsidiary, auxiliary, ancillary.

S

supply verb

1 *most of the money was supplied by private donors | the cooperatives supply fuel directly to other industries:* give, contribute, provide, furnish, donate, bestow, grant; formal purvey; informal put up, fork out, shell out.
2 *they struggled to supply the besieged island with aircraft:* provide, furnish; equip, arm.
3 *windmills supply their power needs:* satisfy, meet, serve, fulfil, cater for.

▷ **noun**
1 *a limited supply of food:* stock, store, reserve, reservoir, stockpile, hoard, cache; fund, mine, bank.
2 *we are running out of supplies:* provisions, stores, stocks, rations, food, necessities; formal comestibles.

▷ **adjective** *a supply teacher:* substitute, stand-in, fill-in, locum, temporary, stopgap.

support verb

1 *a roof supported by pillars:* hold up, bear, carry, prop up, keep up, brace, shore up, underpin, buttress, reinforce.
2 *he struggled to support his family:* provide for, maintain, sustain, keep, take care of, look after.
3 *I'd like to thank my family and friends who have supported me during this difficult time:* comfort, sustain, fortify, encourage, buoy up, hearten, reassure, console, solace.
4 *the proposal was supported by most of the delegates:* back, champion, advocate, recommend, promote, favour, subscribe to, espouse; vote for, stand behind, sponsor, second, endorse, sanction; informal throw your weight behind.
5 *these studies support our findings:* substantiate, back up, bear out, corroborate, confirm, attest to, verify, prove, validate, authenticate, endorse, ratify.
6 *the money supports many charitable projects:* help, aid, assist; contribute to, back, subsidize, fund, finance; informal bankroll.
OPPOSITES: oppose.

▷ **noun**
1 *water was rushing frighteningly fast around the bridge supports:* pillar, post, prop, upright, crutch, plinth, brace, buttress; base, substructure, foundation, underpinning.
2 *the bank provided financial support:* help, assistance, aid; backing, funding, funds, finance, capital, subsidy, money; donations, contributions.
3 *backbenchers voiced their support for him:* backing, endorsement, approval.
4 *the organization offers support for those who are affected by problem drinking:* comfort, encouragement, strength, solace, succour, friendship.

supporter noun

1 *supporters of the legislation:* advocate, backer, adherent, promoter, champion, defender, upholder, crusader, proponent, campaigner, apologist.
2 *Labour supporters:* backer, helper, adherent, follower, ally, voter, disciple; member.
3 *the charity relies on its supporters:* contributor, donor, benefactor, sponsor, backer, patron, subscriber, well-wisher.
4 *the team's supporters:* fan, follower, enthusiast, devotee.

supportive adjective *my friends and colleagues have been very supportive:* encouraging, positive, helpful, sympathetic, reassuring, understanding, caring, concerned, kind, kindly.

suppose verb

1 *I suppose he's used to this:* assume, presume, expect, dare say, take it; believe, think, suspect, sense; guess, surmise, reckon, conjecture, deduce, infer, gather; Brit. fancy.
2 *suppose he had been murdered—what then?* assume, imagine, say; hypothesize, theorize, speculate.
3 *the procedure supposes that a will has already been proved:* presuppose, assume; require.

supposed adjective

1 *a team was sent to investigate the supposed accident | a supposed expert in this field:* apparent, ostensible, seeming; alleged, putative, reputed, purported; professed, declared.
2 *I'm supposed to meet him at 8.30:* meant, intended, expected; required, obliged.

supposition noun *there is a widespread supposition that there is nothing of any value in these techniques:* belief, surmise, idea, notion, theory, hypothesis, assumption, presumption, postulation, conjecture, speculation, inference, guess, suspicion, feeling, hunch.

suppress verb

1 *the rebellion was savagely suppressed:* subdue, crush, quell, quash, stamp out, repress; defeat, conquer, overpower, put down; end, put an end to, stop.
2 *she suppressed her irritation:* repress, restrain, stifle, smother, bottle up, hold back, control, check, curb, contain, bridle.
3 *the report was suppressed:* censor, keep secret, conceal, hide, hush up, withhold, cover up, stifle; sweep under the carpet.

supremacy noun *she sought supremacy over her rivals:* ascendancy, predominance, primacy, dominion, hegemony, authority, mastery, control, power, rule, sovereignty, influence; dominance, superiority, advantage, the upper hand, the whip hand, the edge.

supreme adjective

1 *the supreme commander:* highest ranking, chief, head, top, foremost,

principal, superior, premier, first, prime; greatest, dominant, predominant, pre-eminent.
2 *a supreme achievement:* extraordinary, remarkable, incredible, phenomenal, rare, exceptional, outstanding, great, incomparable, unparalleled, peerless.
3 *the supreme sacrifice:* ultimate, final, last; utmost, extreme, greatest, highest.
OPPOSITES: subordinate, insignificant.

sure adjective
1 *I am sure that they didn't think you were rude:* certain, positive, convinced, confident; satisfied, persuaded.
2 *someone was sure to be blamed:* bound, certain.
3 *in our part of London, the blackbird's song is a sure sign of spring:* reliable, definite, dependable, unfailing, infallible, certain, true, foolproof, established, guaranteed, unerring, proven; informal sure-fire.
4 *the sure hand of the soloist:* firm, steady, stable, assured, confident, unfaltering, unwavering, unhesitating.
OPPOSITES: uncertain, unsure.
□ **make sure**
go and make sure everything's okay: check, confirm, make certain, ensure, assure yourself; verify.

surface noun *the surface of the door:* outside, exterior; top, side; finish, veneer.
OPPOSITES: inside, interior.
▷ **verb**
1 *a submarine surfaced:* come to the surface, come up, rise.
2 *problems began to surface about two years ago:* emerge, appear, become apparent, come to light, materialize, crop up, spring up.
OPPOSITES: dive.
□ **on the surface**
on the surface, everything seemed fine: at first glance, to the casual eye, outwardly, to all appearances, apparently, ostensibly, superficially, externally.

surfeit noun *viewers have a surfeit of choices these days when it comes to TV:* excess, surplus, abundance, oversupply, superabundance, superfluity, glut; too much; informal bellyful.
OPPOSITES: lack.

surge noun
1 *a surge of water:* gush, rush, outpouring, stream, flow.
2 *a surge in oil production:* increase, rise, growth, upswing, upsurge, escalation, leap.
3 *a sudden surge of anger:* rush, storm, torrent, upsurge, blaze, outburst, eruption.
4 *the surge of sea:* swell, heaving, rolling, roll, swirling; tide.
▷ **verb**
1 *the water surged into people's homes:* gush, rush, stream, flow, burst, pour, cascade, spill, overflow, sweep, roll.
2 *crowds of fans surged forward:* charge, rush, sweep, push, stampede.

3 *the Dow Jones index surged 47.63 points:* increase, rise, escalate, leap.

surly adjective *a surly shop assistant:* sullen, sulky, moody, sour, unfriendly, unpleasant, scowling, unsmiling; bad-tempered, grumpy, crotchety, prickly, cantankerous, irascible, testy, short-tempered; abrupt, brusque, curt, gruff, churlish, ill-humoured, crabby; informal grouchy.
OPPOSITES: friendly.

surmise verb *she surmised that something must be wrong:* suppose, conjecture, deduce, infer, conclude; assume, presume, gather, feel, sense, think, believe, imagine, reckon, suspect, guess; theorize, speculate.

surmount verb
1 *surmounting these difficulties will take a very long time:* overcome, conquer, prevail over, get over, triumph over, beat, vanquish.
2 *the dome is surmounted by a statue:* cap, top, crown.

surpass verb *last year's festival surpassed all previous attendance figures:* exceed, improve on, top, trump, cap, beat, better, outperform; excel, outdo, outshine, outstrip, outclass, overshadow, eclipse.

surplus noun *a surplus of grain:* excess, surfeit, superabundance, superfluity, oversupply, glut, plethora; remainder, residue, remains, leftovers.
OPPOSITES: dearth.
▷ **adjective** *they are taxed so heavily that they rarely have any surplus cash to invest:* excess, leftover, unused, remaining, extra, additional, spare; superfluous, unneeded, dispensable, expendable, redundant, unwanted.

surprise noun
1 *my sister looked at me in surprise:* astonishment, amazement, wonder, incredulity, bewilderment, stupefaction, disbelief.
2 *the news came as a big surprise:* shock, bolt from the blue, bombshell, revelation, rude awakening, eye-opener; informal turn up for the books, shocker.
▷ **verb**
1 *I was so surprised that I dropped the phone:* astonish, amaze, startle, astound, stun, stagger, shock; leave open-mouthed, take someone's breath away, dumbfound, daze, take aback, shake up; informal bowl over, floor, flabbergast; Brit. informal knock for six.
2 *the couple surprised the intruder in an upstairs bedroom:* catch unawares, catch off guard, catch red-handed, catch in the act, catch out; Brit. informal catch on the hop.

surprised adjective *he was very surprised when he received the letter:* astonished, amazed, astounded, startled, stunned, staggered, nonplussed, shocked, taken aback, dumbfounded, dumbstruck,

S

speechless, thunderstruck; informal bowled over, flabbergasted.

surprising adjective *the researchers made a surprising discovery:* unexpected, unforeseen; astonishing, amazing, startling, astounding, staggering, incredible, extraordinary, breathtaking, remarkable; informal mind-blowing.

surrender verb
1 *the army surrendered:* capitulate, give in, give yourself up, yield, concede defeat, submit; give way, climb down, back down, cave in, crumble; lay down your arms, raise the white flag, throw in the towel.
2 *they surrendered power to the government:* give up, relinquish, renounce; cede, abdicate, sacrifice, waive, forfeit; hand over, turn over, yield.
OPPOSITES: resist, seize.
▷ **noun** *the surrender of the hijackers:* capitulation, submission, yielding; fall, defeat.

surreptitious adjective *I tried to sneak a surreptitious glance at my watch:* secret, furtive, covert, stealthy, sneaky, sly; secretive, clandestine, undercover, cloak-and-dagger.
OPPOSITES: blatant.

surrogate noun *wives of MPs are often looked on as surrogates for their husbands while the latter are at Westminster:* substitute, proxy, replacement; deputy, representative, stand-in, standby, stopgap, relief, understudy.

surround verb
1 *the hotel is surrounded by its own gardens:* encircle, enclose, ring, bound, encompass, girdle.
2 *we were surrounded by police:* hem in, fence in, confine, cut off; besiege, trap
▷ **noun** *a fireplace with a wood surround:* border, edging, edge, perimeter, boundary, margin, skirting, fringe.

surrounding adjective *the surrounding countryside:* neighbouring, nearby, local; adjoining, adjacent.

surroundings plural noun *a family-run hotel in exotic surroundings:* environment, setting, milieu, background, backdrop, conditions, circumstances, situation, context; vicinity, locality, habitat.

surveillance noun *leading members of the party were to be kept under surveillance:* observation, scrutiny, watch, view, inspection, supervision; spying, espionage, infiltration, reconnaissance; informal bugging, wiretapping.

survey verb
1 *he surveyed his work:* look at, look over, observe, view, contemplate, regard, gaze at, stare at, eye; scrutinize, examine, inspect, scan, study, consider, review, take stock of; informal size up.

2 *they surveyed 4000 drug users:* interview, question, canvass, poll, cross-examine, investigate, research, study, probe, sample.
3 *he was asked to survey the house:* appraise, assess; make a survey of, value.
▷ **noun**
1 *a survey of the current literature:* study, review, consideration, overview; scrutiny, examination, inspection, appraisal.
2 *a survey of sexual behaviour:* poll, review, investigation, inquiry, study, probe, questionnaire, census, research.
3 *a thorough survey of the property:* appraisal, assessment, valuation.

survive verb
1 *they survived by eating insects and berries:* remain alive, sustain yourself, keep going, pull through, get through, hold on/out, make it, keep body and soul together.
2 *he has survived several assassination attempts:* live through, come through, withstand, weather.
3 *he was survived by his wife and three children:* outlive.

susceptible adjective
1 *patients with liver disease are susceptible to infection:* at risk of, vulnerable to, liable to, prone to, subject to, open to.
2 *an inappropriate story for young, susceptible children:* impressionable, innocent, ingenuous, naive, easily led, gullible, credulous; sensitive, easily upset.
3 *the problem is not susceptible of a simple solution:* open to, capable of, admitting of.
OPPOSITES: immune, resistant.

suspect verb
1 *I suspected she'd made a mistake:* have a suspicion, have a feeling, feel, be inclined to think, think, reckon, guess, surmise, conjecture, conclude, have a hunch; suppose, presume, deduce, fear; Brit. fancy.
2 *he had no reason to suspect my honesty:* doubt, distrust, mistrust, have misgivings about, be sceptical about, have qualms about, be suspicious of, be wary of, harbour reservations about; informal smell a rat.
▷ **noun** *the murder suspect:* suspected person; accused, defendant.
▷ **adjective** *banks are obliged to monitor and report suspect transactions of this kind:* suspicious, dubious, doubtful, questionable; odd; informal fishy.

suspend verb
1 *production has been suspended until safety checks have been carried out:* discontinue, halt, stop, interrupt, break off
2 *the court case was suspended:* adjourn, postpone, delay, defer, put off; prorogue.
3 *he was suspended from his duties pending the outcome of the investigation:* exclude, debar, remove.

S

4 *lights were suspended from the ceiling:* hang, sling, string; swing, dangle.

suspense noun *I can't bear the suspense:* tension, uncertainty, anticipation, expectation, expectancy, excitement; anxiety, apprehension, strain.
◻ **in suspense**
the crowd waited in suspense: eagerly, agog, with bated breath, on tenterhooks.

suspension noun
1 *the suspension of military action:* discontinuation, interruption, halt, stoppage, cessation, end.
2 *the suspension of his trial:* adjournment, postponement, delay, deferral, deferment.

suspicion noun
1 *she had a suspicion that he didn't like her:* intuition, feeling, impression, inkling, hunch, fancy, notion, belief, idea, theory; presentiment, premonition; informal gut feeling, sixth sense.
2 *I confronted him with my suspicions:* misgiving, doubt, qualm, reservation, hesitation, question; scepticism, uncertainty, distrust, mistrust.
3 *wine with a suspicion of soda:* trace, touch, suggestion, hint, soupçon, tinge, shade, whiff, bit, drop, dash.

suspicious adjective
1 *she gave him a suspicious look:* doubtful, sceptical, distrustful, mistrustful, dubious, disbelieving, unconvinced, cynical, unsure, wary, chary.
2 *a highly suspicious character:* disreputable, unsavoury, dubious, suspect, untrustworthy; informal shifty, shady; Brit. informal dodgy.
3 *she disappeared in rather suspicious circumstances:* questionable, odd, strange, dubious, mysterious, murky; informal fishy.
OPPOSITES: trusting, credulous.

sustain verb
1 *her memories sustained her while they were apart:* comfort, help, encourage, succour, support, strengthen, fortify, give strength to, buoy up, carry through, cheer up, hearten, nurture; informal buck up.
2 *he ate a bit of bread and cheese to sustain him until he got home:* nourish, feed; fortify, keep your strength up, keep alive, keep going.
3 *they were unable to sustain the coalition:* continue, carry on, keep up, maintain, perpetuate.
4 *she sustained slight injuries:* undergo, experience, suffer, endure.
5 *the balcony might not be able to sustain the weight:* bear, support, carry, stand, keep up, prop up, shore up, underpin.
6 *the allegation was not sustained:* uphold, validate, confirm, endorse.

sustained adjective *several years of sustained economic growth | there has been sustained pressure on the government:* continuous, ongoing, steady, continual, constant, prolonged, persistent; nonstop, unremitting, unabating, relentless, unrelieved.
OPPOSITES: intermittent, sporadic.

sustenance noun
1 *his stomach rumbled, reminding him that a human body needed sustenance:* nourishment, food, nutriment, nutrition.
2 *the sustenance of his family:* support, maintenance, keep; subsistence.

swagger verb *they swaggered into the arena:* strut, parade, stride; walk confidently; N. Amer. informal sashay.

swallow verb
1 *she swallowed another mouthful:* eat, gulp down, guzzle, consume, devour; ingest; drink, quaff; formal imbibe; informal polish off, scoff, swig, swill, down.
2 *he seemed ready to swallow any insult:* tolerate, endure, stand, put up with, bear, stomach, take, accept; informal hack; Brit. informal stick.
3 *he swallowed my story:* believe, accept; informal fall for, buy, go for, {swallow something, hook, line, and sinker}.
4 *she swallowed her tears:* suppress, hold back, fight back, repress, stifle, smother, hide, bottle up; overcome, control, curb.
◻ **swallow someone/something up**
1 *the darkness swallowed them up:* engulf, envelop, enfold.
2 *the colleges were swallowed up by universities:* take over, engulf, absorb, assimilate, incorporate.

swamp noun *his horse got stuck in a swamp:* marsh, bog, quagmire, mire, morass, fen; quicksand.
▷ verb
1 *a huge wave swamped the canoes:* flood, inundate, deluge; soak, drench, saturate.
2 *the reporter who wrote the article was swamped with letters and phone calls:* overwhelm, inundate, flood, deluge, engulf, snow under, overload, weigh down, besiege, beset.

swampy adjective *the swampy ground:* marshy, boggy; soft, soggy, muddy, spongy, heavy, squelchy, waterlogged, sodden, wet.

swap verb
1 *she swapped her silver Alfa Romeo for a Honda Prelude:* exchange, switch, change, replace, substitute; trade, barter, interchange.
2 *we swapped jokes:* bandy, exchange, trade.
▷ noun *a job swap:* exchange, interchange, trade, switch.

swarm noun *swarms of screaming teenage fans:* crowd, horde, mob, throng, host, mass, army, herd, pack, gang.
▷ **verb** *protesters were swarming into the building:* flock, crowd, throng, surge, stream.

S

□ **be swarming with**
the city was swarming with sightseers:
be crowded with, be thronged with, be
overrun with, be full of, be teeming with,
bristle with, be alive with, be crawling
with, be infested with, overflow with;
informal be thick with.

swarthy adjective *he has long dark hair
and a swarthy complexion:* dark-skinned,
olive-skinned, tanned.
OPPOSITES: pale.

swathe verb *his hands were swathed in
bandages:* wrap, envelop, bind, swaddle,
bandage, cover, drape, wind, enfold,
shroud.

sway verb
1 *the curtains swayed in the breeze:* swing,
move to and fro, move back and forth,
undulate, shake, oscillate.
2 *she swayed on her feet:* stagger, wobble,
rock, lurch, reel.
3 *she's too easily swayed by other people:*
influence, control, manipulate, affect,
persuade, talk round, win over.
▷ **noun**
1 *the sway of her hips:* swing, roll,
undulation.
2 *a province under the sway of the
Franks:* jurisdiction, rule, government,
sovereignty, dominion, control, command,
power, authority, ascendancy, domination,
mastery.
□ **hold sway**
*warlords still hold sway in parts of the
country:* hold power, wield power, rule, be
in control, predominate; have the upper
hand, have the edge, have the whip hand.

swear verb
1 *she made me swear that I would never tell
anyone:* promise, vow, pledge, give your
word, take an oath, undertake, guarantee,
make a commitment.
2 *Kate spilled wine and swore under
her breath:* curse, blaspheme, utter
profanities, utter oaths, use bad language,
take the Lord's name in vain; informal eff
and blind.
□ **swear by** (informal) *Iris swears by their
products:* have great confidence in, have
faith in, trust, believe in; set great store by,
value greatly.

swearing noun *sixty per cent thought
there was too much swearing on TV:* bad
language, strong language, cursing,
blaspheming, blasphemy; profanities,
obscenities, curses, oaths, expletives,
swear words; formal imprecations; informal
effing and blinding, four-letter words.

sweat noun *beads of sweat broke out on his
forehead:* perspiration, moisture.
▷ **verb**
1 *she was sweating heavily:* perspire.
2 *I've sweated over project for six months:*
work, work hard, work like a Trojan,
labour, toil, slave, work your fingers to

the bone; informal graft, slog.

WORD LINKS
sudorific relating to or causing sweating

---

sweaty adjective *his hands were hot and
sweaty:* perspiring, sweating, clammy,
sticky; moist, damp.

sweep verb
1 *she swept the floor | I swept the crumbs
off the table:* brush, clean, wipe, clear, dust.
2 *he was swept out to sea:* carry, pull, drag.
3 *a limousine swept past:* glide, sail, breeze;
speed, fly, zoom, whizz.
4 *a wave of riots swept the country:* engulf,
overwhelm.
▷ **noun**
1 *an expansive sweep of his hand:* gesture,
stroke, wave, movement.
2 *a long sweep of golden sand:* expanse,
tract, stretch, extent.
□ **sweep something aside**
he swept aside the criticism: disregard,
ignore, take no notice of.
□ **sweep something under the carpet**
*the department cannot continue to sweep
its mistakes under the carpet:* hide, conceal,
suppress, hush up, cover up; ignore, take
no notice of, forget about.

sweeping adjective
1 *the president is planning sweeping changes
to the country's political system:* extensive,
wide-ranging, global, broad, comprehensive,
wholesale, thoroughgoing, thorough, far-
reaching, across the board; radical, root-and-
branch; informal wall-to-wall.
2 *there is no justification for such sweeping
statements:* generalized, general, broad;
oversimplified, simplistic.
OPPOSITES: limited, specific.

sweet adjective
1 *a cup of hot sweet tea:* sugary, sweetened,
sugared.
2 *the sweet scent of roses:* fragrant,
aromatic, perfumed.
3 *her sweet voice:* melodious, lyrical,
mellifluous, musical, tuneful, soft,
harmonious, silvery, honeyed, mellow,
rich, golden; often ironic dulcet.
4 *life was still sweet:* pleasant, pleasing,
agreeable, lovely, delightful, good,
satisfying, enjoyable; informal great.
5 *she has a sweet nature | it was sweet
of you to come:* engaging, appealing,
charming, delightful, lovely, likeable,
pleasant, agreeable, friendly, affectionate;
kind, thoughtful, considerate.
6 *a sweet little two-month-old kitten:* cute,
lovable, adorable, endearing, charming,
enchanting.
OPPOSITES: sour, savoury, disagreeable.
▷ **noun** (Brit.)
1 *a bag of sweets:* confectionery; chocolate,
bonbon, fondant, toffee; N. Amer. candy.
2 *I'm afraid there isn't any sweet:* dessert,
pudding, second course, last course; Brit.
informal afters.

sweeten verb
1 *they tried to sweeten the blow by saying job losses would be limited to 1,500:* soften, ease, mitigate, temper, cushion.
2 (informal) *a bigger dividend to sweeten up the shareholders:* mollify, placate, soothe, soften up, pacify, appease, win over.

sweetheart noun *she married her college sweetheart:* lover, love, boyfriend, girlfriend; suitor, admirer.

swell verb
1 *her ankle swelled up:* become distended, puff up, become swollen, become bloated, balloon, bulge, tumefy.
2 *she swelled with pride:* be filled, be bursting, brim, overflow.
3 *the population swelled:* grow, enlarge, increase, expand, multiply, proliferate, snowball, mushroom.
4 *the graduate scheme swelled entry numbers:* increase, enlarge, augment, boost; Brit. top up.
5 *the low murmur swelled to a roar:* grow loud, grow louder, be amplified, intensify, heighten, rise, escalate.
OPPOSITES: shrink, decrease.

swelling noun
1 *applying a cold compress will help to reduce the swelling:* puffiness, inflammation, distension.
2 *there was a huge swelling under his eye:* bump, lump, bulge, protuberance, excrescence; boil, blister.

sweltering adjective *a sweltering July afternoon:* hot, stifling, humid, sultry, sticky, muggy, close, stuffy, tropical, torrid, searing, blistering; informal boiling, baking, roasting, sizzling.
OPPOSITES: freezing.

swerve verb *she swerved to the left to avoid hitting the animal:* veer, deviate, skew, sheer, weave, zigzag, change direction.

swift adjective
1 *a swift response:* rapid, quick, fast, speedy, prompt, expeditious, immediate, instant, instantaneous, sudden; abrupt, hasty, hurried, precipitate.
2 *a swift pace:* fast, rapid, quick, speedy, brisk, lively.
OPPOSITES: slow, leisurely.

swill verb *he swilled out a glass:* wash, rinse, sluice, clean, flush.

swim verb
1 *they swam in the lake:* bathe, take a dip, splash around.
2 *his food was swimming in gravy:* be saturated in, be drenched in, be immersed in, be covered with, be full of.

swindle verb *she swindled investors out of millions of pounds:* defraud, cheat, trick, dupe, deceive, fool, hoodwink; informal fleece, do, con, diddle, rip off, bamboozle, take for a ride, pull a fast one on, put one over on.

▷noun *he was mixed up in a £10 million insurance swindle:* fraud, trick, deception, cheat, dodge, racket; sharp practice; informal con, rip-off; Brit. informal fiddle.

swindler noun fraudster, fraud, cheat, confidence trickster, rogue, mountebank, charlatan, impostor; informal con man, con artist, shark, crook.

swing verb
1 *the sign swung in the wind:* sway, oscillate, move back and forth, move to and fro, wave, wag, rock, flutter, flap, twirl.
2 *the road swings off to the north:* curve, bend, veer, turn, bear, wind.
3 *the balance swung from one party to the other:* change, fluctuate, shift, oscillate, see-saw, yo-yo, vary.
4 (informal) *I managed to swing a ticket for tonight's game:* get, obtain, acquire, secure, net, win; informal wangle, land.

▷noun
1 *a swing of the pendulum:* oscillation, sway, wave.
2 *a 3% swing to the Conservatives | a massive swing in public opinion:* change, move, movement, drift; turnaround, turnabout, change of heart, U-turn.
3 *his unpredictable mood swings:* fluctuation, change, shift, variation.

swingeing adjective (Brit.) *swingeing cuts in public expenditure:* severe, extreme, serious, substantial, drastic, harsh, stringent, heavy.
OPPOSITES: minor.

swirl verb *the snow swirled around them:* whirl, eddy, billow, spiral, circulate, revolve, spin, twist; flow, stream, surge, seethe.

switch noun
1 *the guard hit a switch and the gate swung open:* button, lever, control, dial.
2 *the switch from analogue television to digital:* change, move, shift, transition; changeover, transfer, conversion; substitution, exchange.

▷verb
1 *I studied architecture briefly, before switching to fashion:* change, move.
2 *he managed to switch the envelopes:* exchange, swap, interchange, substitute, replace.
□ **switch something on**
he switched the computer on: turn on, power up, put on, activate, start, set going, set in motion, boot up.
□ **switch something off**
have you switched the TV off? turn off, put off, shut off, deactivate, power down.

swivel verb *she swivelled round in her seat:* turn, rotate, revolve, pivot, swing; spin, twirl, whirl, wheel, gyrate, pirouette.

swollen adjective *his face was bruised and swollen:* distended, enlarged, bulging, bloated, puffed up, puffy, tumescent; inflamed.

S

swoop verb
1 *the aircraft swooped down over the rooftops:* dive, fly down, descend, sweep, plunge, plummet.
2 *armed police swooped on the flat:* raid, search; descend on, pounce on, attack, charge; informal bust.

sword noun *a ceremonial sword:* blade, rapier, sabre, scimitar, foil, épée, cutlass.
□ cross swords
she has crossed swords with several senior members of the organization: argue, quarrel, disagree, dispute, wrangle, be at odds, be at loggerheads, lock horns; fight.

sybaritic adjective *their sybaritic lifestyle:* luxurious, hedonistic, extravagant, lavish, self-indulgent, pleasure-seeking, epicurean.
OPPOSITES: ascetic.

sycophant noun *he was surrounded by flatterers and sycophants:* toady, flatterer, lickspittle; informal yes-man.

sycophantic adjective *he submitted a very sycophantic review of the band's latest offering:* obsequious, servile, unctuous, subservient, deferential, ingratiating, toadying, fawning, flattering, cringing, slavish; Brit. informal smarmy.

syllabus noun *the A-level chemistry syllabus:* curriculum, course, course of study, programme of study, course outline; timetable, schedule.

symbol noun
1 *the lotus is a symbol of purity:* emblem, token, sign, representation, figure, image; metaphor, allegory.
2 *the chemical symbol for helium:* sign, character, mark, letter, ideogram.
3 *the Red Cross symbol:* logo, emblem, badge, stamp, trademark, crest, insignia, coat of arms, seal, device, monogram, hallmark, flag, motif.

symbolic adjective
1 *the Colosseum is symbolic of the Roman Empire:* emblematic, representative; indicative, suggestive.
2 *the use of symbolic language:* figurative, representative, emblematic, metaphorical, allegorical, allusive.
OPPOSITES: literal.

symbolize verb *the wheel symbolizes the power of peaceful change:* represent, stand for, be a sign of, be a symbol of, exemplify; denote, signify, mean, indicate, convey, express, imply, suggest, allude to; embody, epitomize, encapsulate, personify, typify.

symmetrical adjective regular, uniform, consistent; evenly shaped, aligned, equal; mirror-image; balanced, proportional, even.
OPPOSITES: asymmetrical.

symmetry noun *the garden is neat, laid out with perfect symmetry:* regularity,

evenness, uniformity, consistency; balance, proportion.

sympathetic adjective
1 *a sympathetic listener:* compassionate, caring, concerned, solicitous, understanding, sensitive, supportive; considerate, kind, tender-hearted, comforting.
2 *the most sympathetic character in the book:* likeable, pleasant, agreeable, congenial, friendly, genial.
3 *I was sympathetic to his cause:* in favour of, in sympathy with, pro, on the side of; well disposed to, favourably disposed to, receptive to.
OPPOSITES: unsympathetic, opposed.

sympathize verb
1 *he sympathized with his wife:* pity, feel sorry for, be sympathetic towards, show compassion for, commiserate with, feel for; console, comfort, solace; empathize with, identify with, understand, relate to.
2 *they sympathize with the critiques of traditional theory:* agree with, support, look favourably on, favour, approve of.

sympathy noun
1 *he shows great sympathy for the victims of the flood:* compassion, pity, sorrow; concern, solicitude, care, support; consideration, kindness.
2 *the special sympathy between the two boys was obvious to all:* fellow feeling, affinity, empathy, harmony, understanding, compatibility.
3 *I have some sympathy for this view:* agreement with, support for, approval of.
OPPOSITES: indifference, hostility.

> **USAGE**
>
> The words **sympathy** and **empathy** have close but distinct meanings. The chief meaning of **sympathy** is 'the feeling of being sorry for someone who is unhappy or in difficulty'. **Empathy** means 'the ability to understand and share the feelings of another person' (*the artist developed a considerable empathy with his elderly subject*).

symptom noun
1 *the symptoms of the disease include fever and headaches:* manifestation, indication, indicator, sign, mark, feature.
2 *a symptom of the country's present turmoil:* expression, sign, indication, mark, token, manifestation; portent, warning, clue, hint; testimony, evidence, proof.

symptomatic adjective *such incidents were symptomatic of tensions within the socialist movement:* indicative, suggestive, characteristic, typical, representative.

synopsis noun *a basic synopsis of the play:* summary, summarization, precis, abstract, outline, digest, rundown, round-up, abridgement.

synthesis noun *the painting is a synthesis of elements from a variety of different types of art:* combination, union, amalgam, blend, fusion, composite, mixture, compound; unification, amalgamation, marriage.

synthetic adjective *a jacket made of synthetic fur:* artificial, fake, faux, imitation, mock, simulated, ersatz; man-made, manufactured, fabricated.
OPPOSITES: genuine.

system noun
1 *a grid-like system of canals:* structure, organization, arrangement, complex, network; informal set-up.
2 *a system for regulating sales:* method, methodology, technique, process, procedure, approach; means, way, mode, framework, modus operandi; scheme, plan, policy, programme, regimen, formula, routine.
3 *there was no system in his work:* order, method, orderliness, systematization, planning, logic, routine.
4 *youngsters have no faith in the system:* the establishment, the administration, the authorities, the powers that be; bureaucracy, officialdom; the status quo.

systematic adjective *these interviews were conducted in a systematic way:* structured, methodical, organized, orderly, planned, systematized, standardized, standard, regular, routine; logical, coherent, consistent; efficient, businesslike, practical.
OPPOSITES: unsystematic, disorganized.

S

Tt

tab noun tag, label, flap.

table noun *the report has numerous tables:* chart, diagram, figure, graph, plan.
▷**verb** *she tabled a question in parliament:* submit, lodge, file, introduce, put forward, propose, suggest, move, air, moot.

tableau noun *the girl fixed her eyes upon the central figure in the tableau before her:* scene, arrangement, group, grouping; picture, spectacle, image, vignette.

tablet noun
1 *the drug is available in tablet form:* pill, capsule, lozenge, pastille.
2 (Brit.) *a tablet of soap:* bar, cake, slab, brick, block, chunk, piece.
3 (Brit.) *a carved stone tablet:* slab, stone; panel, plaque, plate, sign.

taboo noun *the taboo against working on the sabbath:* prohibition, proscription, veto, ban, restriction, interdict.
▷**adjective** *gambling was taboo in our house:* forbidden, prohibited, banned, proscribed, outlawed, illegal, illicit, unlawful.
OPPOSITES: acceptable.

tabulate verb arrange, set out, chart, organize, order, systematize, catalogue, list, index, classify, class, codify; compile, group, log.

tacit adjective *the deal relies on this tacit agreement:* implicit, understood, implied, inferred, hinted, suggested; unspoken, unstated, unsaid, unexpressed, unvoiced; taken for granted, taken as read.
OPPOSITES: explicit.

taciturn adjective *Mark was a shy, taciturn man:* reticent, uncommunicative, unforthcoming, quiet, secretive, discreet, tight-lipped, close-mouthed; silent, inarticulate; reserved, withdrawn.
OPPOSITES: talkative.

tack noun
1 *tacks held the carpet down:* pin, drawing pin, nail, tin tack.
2 *he changed tack and tried a different approach:* approach, policy, tactic, plan, strategy, stratagem; path, line, angle, direction, course.

▷**verb**
1 *there was a photo tacked to the wall:* pin, nail.
2 *the dress was roughly tacked together:* stitch, sew.
□**tack something on**
some poems tacked are on at the end of the book: add, append, attach, join on, tag on.

tackle noun
1 *he's brought his fishing tackle:* equipment, gear, apparatus, kit, hardware; implements, instruments, accoutrements, paraphernalia, trappings; formal appurtenances; informal things, stuff, clobber.
2 *a hard tackle by the scrum half:* interception, challenge, block, attack.
▷**verb**
1 *we must tackle environmental problems now:* deal with, take care of, see to, try to sort out, attend to, take on, handle, manage, get to grips with, address, get to work on, set your hand to, approach.
2 *I tackled Nina about it and she admitted it:* confront, speak to, interview, question, cross-examine; accost, waylay; remonstrate with.
3 *he was stabbed as he tackled a masked intruder:* confront, face, face up to, take on, contend with, challenge; seize, grab, grapple with, intercept, stop; informal have a go at.
4 *the winger got tackled:* intercept, grab, bring down, floor, fell, block, stop.

tacky[1] adjective *the paint was still tacky:* sticky, wet, gluey, gummy, adhesive, viscous, treacly; informal gooey.
OPPOSITES: dry, set.

tacky[2] adjective (informal) *tacky red plastic roses:* tawdry, tasteless, kitsch, vulgar, crude, trashy, cheap, worthless; informal cheesy; Brit. informal naff.
OPPOSITES: tasteful.

tact noun diplomacy, sensitivity, delicacy, subtlety, discretion, prudence, judiciousness, savoir faire, understanding, thoughtfulness, consideration.
OPPOSITES: insensitivity.

tactful adjective diplomatic, sensitive, delicate, subtle, discreet, judicious, perceptive, courteous, polite, decorous,

respectful, understanding, thoughtful, considerate.
OPPOSITES: tactless.

tactic noun *they resorted to tactics such as returning reports for further clarification:* scheme, stratagem, plan, manoeuvre; method, expedient, gambit, move, approach, tack, strategy; device, trick, ploy, dodge, ruse, machination, contrivance.

tactical adjective calculated, planned, strategic, deliberate; prudent, politic, diplomatic, judicious, shrewd, astute, adroit, cunning.

tactless adjective undiplomatic, insensitive, indelicate, unsubtle, clumsy, heavy-handed, graceless, awkward, inept, gauche; thoughtless, inconsiderate; rude, impolite, discourteous, crass, tasteless.
OPPOSITES: tactful.

tag noun *I looked for a price tag:* label, ticket, sticker, badge, mark, marker, tab, docket, stub, counterfoil, flag.
▷ **verb** *bottles tagged with coloured stickers:* label, mark, ticket, identify, flag, indicate.
□ **tag along**
he was tagging along behind her: follow, trail; come after, go after, shadow, dog; accompany; informal tail.

tail noun *the tail of the queue:* back, rear, end, extremity; bottom.
OPPOSITES: front.
▷ **verb** (informal) *the paparazzi tailed them all over London:* follow, shadow, stalk, trail, track, hunt, hound, dog, pursue, chase.
□ **tail off/away**
the economic boom was beginning to tail off: fade, wane, ebb, dwindle, decrease, lessen, diminish, decline, subside, abate, drop off, peter out, taper off; let up, ease off, die away, die down, come to an end.

USAGE

Do not confuse **tail** with **tale**. **Tail** means 'the rear or end part of an animal or thing', while **tale** means 'a story' (a *fairy tale*).

---

tailback noun traffic jam, queue, line; congestion.

tailor verb *services can be tailored to customer requirements:* customize, adapt, adjust, modify, change, convert, alter, attune, mould, gear, fit, cut, shape, tune.

taint verb
1 *fraudulent firms taint the reputation of our business:* tarnish, blacken, stain, blot, blemish, stigmatize, mar, corrupt, defile, soil, muddy, damage, harm, hurt; drag through the mud; literary sully, besmirch.
2 *the wilderness is tainted by pollution:* contaminate, pollute, infect, blight, spoil, soil.
▷ **noun** *nowhere is free from the taint of corruption:* trace, touch, suggestion, hint, tinge; stain, blot, blemish, stigma.

take verb
1 *Anna smiled as she took his hand:* grasp, grip, clasp, clutch, grab, lay hold of, get hold of.
2 *he took an envelope from his pocket:* remove, pull, draw, withdraw, extract, fish, produce.
3 *the following passage is taken from my book:* extract, quote, cite, derive, copy, cull.
4 *many thousands of prisoners were taken:* capture, seize, catch, arrest, apprehend, take into custody; carry off, abduct.
5 *someone's taken my wallet:* steal, remove, appropriate, make off with, pilfer; formal purloin; informal pinch, filch, swipe; Brit. informal nick, snaffle.
6 *take four from the total:* subtract, deduct, remove; discount; informal knock off, minus.
7 *all the seats had been taken:* occupy, use, utilize, fill, hold; reserve, engage; informal bag.
8 *I took the equipment back to London:* bring, carry, bear, transport, convey, move, transfer, shift, ferry; informal cart, tote.
9 *the priest took her home:* escort, accompany, help, assist, show, lead, guide, see, usher, convey.
10 *I can't take much more of this:* endure, bear, tolerate, stand, put up with, abide, stomach, accept, allow, countenance, support; formal brook.
11 *the journey took six hours:* last, continue for, go on for, carry on for; require, call for, need, necessitate, entail, involve.
12 *Liz took the news badly:* receive, respond to, react to, meet, greet; deal with, cope with.
OPPOSITES: give, add.
▷ **noun** *her wry take on gender issues:* view, reading, version, interpretation, understanding, account, analysis; approach to, attitude to.
□ **take after**
Jenny takes after her mother: resemble, look like; remind you of, make you think of; informal be the spitting image of.
□ **take something apart**
we took the washing machine apart: dismantle, take to pieces, disassemble, strip down; tear/pull apart, demolish, destroy, wreck.
□ **take something back**
1 *I take back every word:* retract, withdraw, renounce, disclaim, unsay, disavow, recant.
2 *I must take the keys back to Marjorie:* return, bring back, give back, restore.
□ **take something down**
the police officer took down her particulars: write down, note down, jot down, set down, record, register, document, minute.
□ **take someone in**
1 *Mrs Smith took in paying guests:* accommodate, board, house, feed, put up, admit, receive; harbour.
2 *you were taken in by a cruel hoax:* deceive, delude, hoodwink, mislead, trick, dupe, fool, cheat, defraud, swindle, outwit, hoax; informal con, bamboozle, put one over on.

t

□ **take something in**
at first she could hardly take in the news: comprehend, understand, grasp, follow, absorb; informal get.

□ **take something in hand**
the time has come to take matters in hand: deal with, apply yourself to, get to grips with, set your hand to, grapple with, take on, attend to, see to, sort out, take care of, handle, manage; informal get stuck into.

□ **take off**
1 *he took off at great speed:* run away/off, flee, take flight, leave, go, depart, make off, bolt, take to your heels, escape; informal clear off, skedaddle, vamoose.
2 *the plane finally took off:* become airborne, take to the air, take wing; lift off, blast off.
3 *the newly launched magazine has really taken off:* succeed, do well, become popular, catch on, prosper, flourish, thrive, boom.

□ **take someone off**
when he took off the prime minister he made everyone laugh: mimic, impersonate, imitate, ape, parody, mock, caricature, satirize, burlesque, lampoon, ridicule; informal spoof; Brit. informal send up.

□ **take someone on**
1 *there was no real challenger to take him on:* compete against, oppose, challenge, confront, face, fight, vie with, contend with, stand up to.
2 *we took on extra staff for the summer:* engage, hire, employ, enrol, enlist, sign up.

□ **take something on**
1 *he has been forced to take on more responsibility:* undertake, accept, assume, shoulder, carry, bear.
2 *the study took on a political dimension:* acquire, assume, come to have.

□ **take something over**
she took over the paper in 1989: assume control of, take charge of, take command of.

□ **take something up**
1 *when he retired he took up painting:* start, begin, venture into, become interested in; informal get into.
2 *the meetings took up all her time:* consume, fill, absorb, use, occupy; waste.
3 *her cousin took up the story:* resume, recommence, restart, carry on, continue, pick up, return to.
4 *he took up their offer of a job:* accept, say yes to, agree to.

take-off noun
1 *the plane crashed on take-off:* departure, lift-off, launch, blast-off.
2 (informal) *a take-off of a talent show:* parody, pastiche, satire, caricature, lampoon, mimicry, imitation, impression, impersonation; informal send-up, spoof.
OPPOSITES: landing.

takeover noun buyout, merger, amalgamation; purchase, acquisition.

takings plural noun proceeds, receipts, earnings, returns, winnings, pickings, spoils; profit, gain, income, revenue; gate, purse.
OPPOSITES: outgoings.

tale noun *a grim tale of witches and black magic:* story, narrative, anecdote, report, account, history; legend, fable, myth, parable, allegory, saga; informal yarn.

> **USAGE**
>
> Do not confuse **tale** with **tail**. **Tale** means 'a story', while **tail** means 'the rear or end part of an animal or thing' (*the dog wagged its tail*).

talent noun *you don't often find someone with a talent for this sort of work:* flair, aptitude, facility, gift, knack, technique, touch, bent, ability, expertise, capacity, faculty; strength, forte, genius, brilliance; dexterity, skill, artistry.

talented adjective *a talented young musician:* gifted, skilful, skilled, brilliant, accomplished, expert, consummate, masterly, adroit, dexterous, able, competent, capable, apt, deft, adept, proficient; informal crack, ace.
OPPOSITES: inept.

talisman noun lucky charm, amulet, mascot.

talk verb
1 *we sat in the kitchen and talked for hours:* speak, converse, chat; chatter, gossip, prattle, babble, rattle on, blather; informal chew the fat/rag, yak, jaw; Brit. informal natter.
2 *I need to talk to my manager:* consult, confer with, speak to, communicate with, discuss the situation with; negotiate.
3 *nothing they did would make her talk:* confess, speak out/up, reveal all, tell tales, open your mouth; informal come clean, blab, squeal, let the cat out of the bag, give the game away, spill the beans, grass.
4 *we'd better go or people will talk:* gossip, pass comment, make remarks; criticize.
5 *he talked her into parting with her art collection:* persuade, argue, cajole, coax, bring round, inveigle, wheedle, sweet-talk, prevail on; informal hustle, fast-talk.

▷ **noun**
1 *he was bored with all this talk:* chatter, chat, chit-chat, gossip, prattle, jabber, babble, gabble; Brit. informal nattering.
2 *she needed to have a talk with Vivian:* conversation, chat, discussion, tête-à-tête, heart-to-heart, dialogue, consultation, meeting; formal colloquy; informal confab, powwow.
3 *the peace talks were held in Rome:* negotiations, discussions; conference, summit, meeting, consultation, dialogue, symposium, seminar, conclave; informal powwow.
4 *she gave a talk on her travels in Ghana:*

lecture, speech, presentation, address, discourse, oration, report, sermon; informal spiel.
5 *there was talk of a takeover:* gossip, rumour, hearsay, tittle-tattle; news, report.

□ **talk something down**
people constantly talk down the coal industry: denigrate, deprecate, disparage, belittle, diminish, criticize; informal knock, put down.

□ **talk down to**
he never talks down to his audiences: condescend to, patronize, look down your nose at, put down.

talkative adjective *the talkative driver hadn't shut up since Mark got into the cab:* chatty, loquacious, garrulous, voluble, communicative; gossipy, verbose.
OPPOSITES: taciturn.

tall adjective
1 *he was a very tall man:* big, large, huge, towering, colossal, gigantic, giant; leggy.
2 *we were hemmed in by tall buildings:* high, big, lofty, soaring, towering, elevated; multi-storey.
OPPOSITES: short, low.

tally noun *his tally of 1,816 wickets is still a county record:* total, running total, count, sum, score, record, reckoning.
▷ **verb**
1 *these statistics tally with government figures:* correspond, agree, accord, concur, coincide, match, fit, be consistent, conform, equate, harmonize, be in tune, dovetail, correlate, parallel; Brit. chime; informal square.
2 *the votes were tallied using an abacus:* count, calculate, add up, total, compute; figure out, work out, reckon, measure, quantify; Brit. tot up.
OPPOSITES: disagree.

tame adjective
1 *there are tame kangaroos in many wildlife parks:* domesticated, domestic, docile, tamed, trained; gentle, mild; pet, house-trained.
2 *the concert was a pretty tame affair:* unexciting, uninteresting, uninspiring, dull, bland, flat, insipid, spiritless, pedestrian, colourless, run-of-the-mill, mediocre, ordinary, humdrum, boring; harmless, safe, inoffensive.
OPPOSITES: wild, exciting.
▷ **verb** *wild parrots can be tamed:* domesticate, train.

tamper verb *the prosecution claimed that the detectives had tampered with the evidence:* interfere, meddle, tinker, fiddle, fool around, play around; doctor, alter, change, adjust, damage; informal mess about/around, monkey around; Brit. informal muck about/around.

tan adjective *he wore a tan waistcoat:* yellowish-brown, light brown, pale brown, tawny.
▷ **verb** *use a sunscreen to help you tan safely:* get a tan, get a suntan, become suntanned, go brown, become bronzed.

tang noun flavour, taste, savour; sharpness, zest, bite, edge, smack, piquancy, spice; smell, odour, aroma, fragrance, perfume.

tangible adjective
1 *we offer a tangible product rather than a service:* actual, palpable, material, physical, real, substantial, corporeal, solid, concrete.
2 *organizations will want to see some tangible benefit from the scheme:* visible, noticeable, actual, definite, clear, clear-cut, distinct, manifest, evident, unmistakable, perceptible, discernible.
OPPOSITES: intangible.

tangle verb
1 *her skirt got tangled up in the back wheel:* entangle, snarl, catch, entwine, twist, knot, enmesh, coil, mat.
2 *he tangled with his old rival:* come into conflict, dispute, argue, quarrel, fight, wrangle, squabble, contend, cross swords, lock horns.
OPPOSITES: untangle.
▷ **noun** *all I could see was a tangle of branches:* mass, network, knot, mesh; informal mishmash.

tangled adjective
1 *her tangled hair took hours to comb:* knotted, knotty, entangled, snarled up, twisted, matted, tangly, messy; tousled, unkempt, ratty; N. Amer. informal mussed up.
2 *a tangled bureaucratic mess:* confused, jumbled, mixed up, messy, chaotic, complicated, involved, complex, intricate, knotty, tortuous.
OPPOSITES: simple.

tangy adjective zesty, sharp, acid, acidic, tart, sour, bitter, piquant, spicy, tasty, flavoursome, pungent.
OPPOSITES: bland.

tank noun
1 *we have no hot water tank:* container, receptacle, vat, cistern, repository, reservoir, basin.
2 *a tank full of fish:* aquarium, bowl.
3 *the army's use of tanks:* armoured vehicle; armour.

tantalize verb tease, torment; tempt, entice, lure, allure, beguile; excite, fascinate, titillate, intrigue.

tantamount adjective
□ **tantamount to**
this behaviour is tantamount to mutiny: equivalent to, equal to, as good as, more or less, much the same as, comparable to, on a par with, commensurate with.

t

tantrum noun fit of temper, emotional outburst, pet, paroxysm of rage, frenzy; informal **paddy, wobbly**; N. Amer. informal hissy fit.

tap¹ noun

1 *she turned the tap on:* valve, stopcock; N. Amer. faucet, spigot.
2 *the Act gave the Home Secretary the power to authorize phone taps:* surveillance, monitoring, intercept; bug.

▷ verb

1 *their telephones were tapped:* bug, monitor, intercept.
2 *the resources were to be tapped for our benefit:* draw on, exploit, milk, mine, use, utilize, turn to account.

tap² verb

1 *she tapped on the door:* knock, rap, strike, beat, drum.
2 *Dad tapped me on the knee:* pat, hit, touch, nudge, strike, poke, dig.

▷ noun

1 *there was a sharp tap at the door:* knock, rap.
2 *Jack was startled by a tap on the shoulder:* pat, blow, touch, nudge, poke, dig.

tape noun

1 *she produced a package tied with tape:* binding, ribbon, string, braid.
2 *they listened to tapes:* cassette, audio cassette, recording, audio tape; video.

▷ verb

1 *a card was taped to the lid of the box:* bind, stick, fix, fasten, secure, attach.
2 *police taped his confession:* record, tape-record; video.

taper verb

1 *the leaves taper at the tip:* narrow, thin, come to a point, become attenuated.
2 *sales have also begun to taper off in France:* decrease, lessen, dwindle, diminish, decline, die down, peter out, wane, ebb, slacken off, fall off, let up, thin out.

OPPOSITES: thicken, increase.

target noun

1 *she was the target for a wave of abuse from the press:* victim, butt, recipient, focus, object, subject.
2 *eagles can spot their targets from half a mile away:* prey, quarry, kill.
3 *they exceeded their profit target last year:* objective, goal, aim, end; plan, intention, intent, design, aspiration, ambition, ideal, desire, wish.

▷ verb

1 *he was targeted by a gunman:* pick out, single out, earmark, fix on; attack, aim at.
2 *the product is targeted at a very specific market:* aim, direct, level; intend for, focus on.

□ **on target**
1 *the striker was bang on target:* accurate, precise, unerring, sure, on the mark; Brit. informal spot on.

2 *the project was on target:* on schedule, on track, on course, on time.

tariff noun

1 *the reduction of import tariffs:* tax, duty, toll, excise, levy, charge, rate, fee.
2 *phone companies all have such different tariffs:* price list, schedule, list of charges, rate.

tarnish verb

1 *gold does not tarnish easily:* discolour, stain, dull, oxidize, corrode, blacken, rust.
2 *he felt that this behaviour tarnished his reputation:* taint, blacken, stain, blemish, blot, soil, ruin, disgrace, mar, damage, harm, hurt, undermine; literary sully, besmirch.

OPPOSITES: enhance, clear.

▷ noun *this will not overcome the tarnish on his reputation:* smear, stain, blemish, blot, taint, stigma.

tart¹ noun *a jam tart:* pastry, flan, tartlet, quiche, pie.

tart² verb (informal)

□ **tart yourself up** (Brit.) *she tarted herself up for the evening:* dress up, make yourself up, smarten yourself up, preen yourself, beautify yourself, groom yourself; informal doll yourself up, titivate yourself.
□ **tart something up**
we must tart this place up a bit: decorate, renovate, refurbish, redecorate; smarten up; informal do up, fix up.

tart³ adjective

1 *choose an apple that is quite tart:* sour, sharp, acid, tangy, piquant.
2 *she regretted her rather tart reply:* acerbic, sharp, biting, cutting, astringent, caustic, trenchant, incisive, barbed, scathing, sarcastic.

OPPOSITES: sweet, gentle.

task noun *she has been set a daunting task:* job, duty, chore, charge, assignment, mission, engagement, occupation, undertaking, exercise, business, responsibility, burden, endeavour, enterprise, venture.

□ **take someone to task**
he took some experts to task for their optimistic predictions: rebuke, reprimand, reprove, reproach, remonstrate with, upbraid, scold, berate, lecture, censure, criticize, admonish, chide, chastise; formal castigate; informal tell off, bawl out; Brit. informal tick off.

taste noun

1 *a cheese with a distinctive sharp taste:* flavour, savour, relish, tang.
2 *honey is too sweet for my taste:* palate, taste buds, appetite, stomach.
3 *a millionaire with a taste for adventure:* liking, love, fondness, fancy, desire, preference, penchant, predilection, inclination, partiality; hankering, appetite, hunger, thirst, relish.

4 *this was my first taste of prison:* experience, impression; exposure to, contact with, involvement with.
5 *the house was furnished with immense taste:* judgement, discrimination, discernment, refinement, finesse, elegance, grace, style.
6 *the photo was rejected on grounds of taste:* decorum, propriety, etiquette, politeness, delicacy, sensitivity, discretion.
7 *would you care for a taste of brandy?* mouthful, drop, sip, nip, swallow; morsel, bite; touch, bit, soupçon, dash, modicum.
▷**verb**
1 *Adam tasted the wine:* sample, test, try; sip.
2 *he could taste blood:* detect, distinguish, discern, perceive, make out.
3 *a beer that tasted of cashews:* have a flavour, savour, smack, be reminiscent; suggest.
4 *it'll be good to taste real coffee again:* consume, drink, have, enjoy; eat; formal partake of.
5 *he tasted defeat for the first time:* experience, encounter, come face to face with, come up against, undergo; know.

> WORD LINKS
> **gustatory** relating to the sense of taste

tasteful adjective *the decor is simple and tasteful:* aesthetically pleasing, in good taste, refined, cultured, elegant, stylish, smart, chic, attractive, exquisite; restrained, well chosen, well judged, appropriate.
OPPOSITES: tasteless.

tasteless adjective
1 *the food was tasteless and not very warm:* flavourless, bland, insipid, unappetizing, watery, weak.
2 *there was tasteless burgundy leather panelling everywhere:* vulgar, tawdry, garish, gaudy, loud, showy, ostentatious, cheap, inelegant, kitsch; informal flash, flashy, tacky; Brit. informal naff.
3 *that was a tasteless remark:* crude, vulgar, coarse, indelicate, indecorous, indecent, unseemly, inappropriate, crass, tactless, undiplomatic, indiscreet, offensive.
OPPOSITES: tasty, tasteful.

tasty adjective delicious, palatable, luscious, mouth-watering, delectable, toothsome, flavoursome, flavourful; appetizing, tempting; informal yummy, scrummy, scrumptious, moreish.
OPPOSITES: tasteless.

tatters plural noun *the satin had frayed to tatters:* rags, scraps, shreds, bits, pieces, ribbons.
◻in tatters
1 *his clothes were in tatters:* ragged, tattered, torn, ripped, frayed, in pieces, worn out, moth-eaten, falling to pieces, threadbare.
2 *her marriage is in tatters:* in ruins, on the rocks, destroyed, finished, on its last legs.

taunt noun *he ignored the taunts of his classmates:* jeer, jibe, sneer, insult, barb, catcall; (**taunts**) teasing, provocation, goading, derision, mockery; informal dig, put-down.
▷**verb** *she taunted him about his job:* jeer at, sneer at, scoff at, poke fun at, make fun of, insult, tease, torment, goad, ridicule, deride, mock, heckle; informal rib, needle, rag; Brit. informal get at.

taut adjective
1 *the rope was pulled taut:* tight, rigid.
2 *his muscles remained taut:* flexed, tense, hard, solid, firm, rigid, stiff.
OPPOSITES: slack, relaxed.

tawdry adjective
1 *a tawdry affair:* sordid, unsavoury, distasteful, unpleasant, seamy, dishonourable, discreditable, contemptible, ignominious, shameful.
2 *tawdry jewellery:* showy, gaudy, garish, loud; tasteless, vulgar, trashy, cheap, worthless; informal tacky.
OPPOSITES: respectable, tasteful.

tax noun duty, excise, customs, dues; levy, tariff, toll, charge, fee.
▷**verb** *his constant whining taxed her patience:* strain, stretch, try; wear out, exhaust, sap, drain, weary, weaken.

> WORD LINKS
> **fiscal** relating to the income received by a government through taxes

taxing adjective *they found the work very taxing:* demanding, exacting, challenging, burdensome, arduous, onerous, difficult, hard, tough, laborious, back-breaking, strenuous, rigorous, punishing; tiring, exhausting, wearing, stressful; informal murderous.
OPPOSITES: easy.

teach verb
1 *she teaches small children:* educate, instruct, school, tutor, coach, train; drill.
2 *teach your teenager how to negotiate:* train, instruct, guide, show, demonstrate.

> WORD LINKS
> **didactic, pedagogic** relating to teaching or intended to teach

teacher noun schoolteacher, tutor, instructor; coach, trainer; lecturer, professor, don; guide, mentor, guru, counsellor; Brit. schoolmaster, schoolmistress; formal pedagogue.

team noun *the company's new sales team | the cricket team:* group, squad, company, party, crew, troupe, band, side, line-up; informal bunch, gang.
▷**verb** *team a T-shirt with matching shorts:* match, coordinate, complement, pair up.
◻team up
she teamed up with another artist for an

t

exhibition: join forces, collaborate, get together, work together; unite, combine, cooperate, link up, associate, club together.

> **USAGE**
>
> Do not confuse **team** with **teem**. **Team** means 'a group of people playing or working together' or 'to join with another person to achieve something'. **Teem** means 'to be full of something' (*every garden is teeming with wildlife*) or 'to pour down' (*rain teemed down all morning*).

tear¹ verb

1 *I tore the letter into pieces:* rip, shred.
2 *his flesh was torn:* lacerate, cut, cut open, gash, slash, scratch, hack, pierce, stab; injure, wound.
3 *the traumas tore her family apart:* split, break; divide, sever, disunite, rupture; literary rend, sunder.
4 *Gina tore the book from his hands:* snatch, grab, seize, rip, wrench, wrest, pull, pluck; informal yank.
5 (informal) *Jack tore down the street:* rush, race, run, dart, sprint, dash, hasten, hurry, bolt, fly, career, charge, shoot, hurtle, speed, whizz, zoom, go like lightning, go like the wind; Brit. informal pelt, scoot, hotfoot it, leg it, belt, zip, whip; Brit. informal go like the clappers, bomb; N. Amer. informal hightail it.
OPPOSITES: unite, saunter.

▷ **noun** *there was a tear in her dress:* rip, split, slash, slit, rent, hole; ladder, snag.

□ **tear something down**
the theatre was torn down to make way for a hotel: demolish, knock down, raze to the ground, flatten, level, bulldoze; dismantle, disassemble.

tear² noun *tears were falling from her eyes:* teardrop.

□ **in tears**
his kids were in tears, and his wife was terrified: crying, weeping, in floods of tears, sobbing, wailing, howling, bawling, whimpering; tearful, upset; informal weepy, blubbing, blubbering, in floods.

> **WORD LINKS**
>
> **lachrymal** relating to tears
> **lachrymose** tending to cry easily or causing tears

tearaway noun (Brit.) hooligan, ruffian, lout, rowdy, roughneck; Brit. informal yob, yobbo.

tearful adjective

1 *Georgina was tearful:* close to tears, emotional, upset, distressed, sad, unhappy; in tears, crying, weeping, sobbing, snivelling; formal lachrymose; informal weepy.
2 *it was a tearful farewell:* emotional, upsetting, distressing, sad, heartbreaking, sorrowful; poignant, moving, touching; informal tear-jerking.
OPPOSITES: cheerful.

tease verb *the girl teased me for being so vain:* make fun of, poke fun at, laugh at; taunt, bait, goad, pick on; deride, mock, ridicule; informal take the mickey out of, rib, josh, have on, pull someone's leg; Brit. informal wind up, send up.

technical adjective

1 *an important technical achievement:* practical, scientific, technological, high-tech.
2 *this might seem very technical, but it isn't:* specialist, specialized, scientific; complex, complicated, esoteric.
3 *a minor technical fault:* mechanical; operational.

technique noun

1 *there are different techniques for solving the problem:* method, approach, procedure, system, modus operandi, MO, way; means, strategy, tack, tactic, line; routine, practice.
2 *I was impressed with his technique:* skill, ability, proficiency, expertise, mastery, talent, genius, artistry, craftsmanship; aptitude, adroitness, deftness, dexterity, facility, competence; informal know-how.

tedious adjective *at first I found the subject very tedious:* boring, dull, dreary, wearisome, mind-numbing, soul-destroying, tiresome; monotonous, repetitive, unvaried, uneventful; uninteresting, unexciting, lifeless, uninspiring, flat, bland, characterless, colourless, dry, stale, tired, lacklustre, stodgy; informal deadly.
OPPOSITES: exciting, interesting.

tedium noun boredom, dreariness, dullness, monotony, ennui, uniformity, repetitiveness, routine, dryness, blandness, insipidity.
OPPOSITES: variety.

teem¹ verb

□ **teem with**
as usual, the old town was teeming with tourists: be full of, be brimming with, abound in, be swarming with, be alive with; be packed with, be crawling with, be overrun by, bristle with, seethe with, be thick with; informal be stuffed with, be jam-packed with, be chock-full of.

> **USAGE**
>
> Do not confuse **teem** with **team**. **Teem** means 'to be full of something' or 'to pour down'. **Team** means 'a group of people playing or working together' or 'to join with another person to achieve something' (*she teamed up with another artist for the exhibition*).

teem² verb *the rain was teeming down:* pour, pelt, beat, lash, sheet; come down in torrents/sheets; informal rain cats and dogs; Brit. informal bucket, tip, come down in stair rods.

teenager noun adolescent, youth, young

person, minor, juvenile; informal teen, tween, teeny-bopper.

teeter verb
1 *Daisy teetered towards them:* totter, wobble, toddle, sway, stagger, stumble, reel, lurch, pitch.
2 *the situation teetered between tragedy and farce:* see-saw, veer, fluctuate, oscillate, swing, alternate, waver.

teetotal adjective *he's teetotal—he stopped drinking nearly six years ago:* abstinent, sober, dry; informal on the wagon.

telepathy noun mind-reading, thought transference; extrasensory perception, ESP; clairvoyance, sixth sense.

telephone noun *Sophie picked up the telephone:* phone, handset, receiver.
▷ verb *he telephoned me last night:* phone, call, dial; Brit. ring, give someone a ring; informal give someone a buzz; Brit. informal give someone a bell; N. Amer. informal call up.

televise verb broadcast, screen, air, telecast; transmit, relay.

tell verb
1 *why didn't you tell me before?* inform, notify, let know, make aware, acquaint with, apprise, advise, put in the picture, brief, fill in; alert, warn; informal clue in/up, bring up to speed.
2 *she told the story slowly:* relate, recount, narrate, unfold, report, recite, describe, sketch, weave, spin; utter, voice, state, declare, communicate, impart; reveal, divulge.
3 *she told him to leave:* instruct, order, command, direct, call on, require; formal charge, enjoin; old use bid.
4 *I tell you, I did nothing wrong:* assure, promise, give your word, swear, guarantee.
5 *promise you won't tell?* talk, tell tales; informal spill the beans, give the game away, let the cat out of the bag, blab; Brit. informal blow the gaff.
6 *it was hard to tell which one he meant:* know, understand, comprehend, see, ascertain, determine, work out, make out, deduce, discern, perceive, identify, recognize, distinguish, differentiate, discriminate; informal figure out; Brit. informal suss out.
□ **tell someone off** (informal). See REPRIMAND verb.
□ **tell on**
she was bound to tell on him: inform on, tell tales on, give away, denounce, sell out; informal split on, blow the whistle on, rat on, peach on, squeal on; Brit. informal grass on, sneak on, shop; N. Amer. informal finger.

teller noun
1 (N. Amer.) *the cheque is handed to the teller, accompanied by a deposit slip:* cashier, clerk.
2 *such tales held more truth than their tellers realized:* narrator; raconteur, storyteller, anecdotalist.

telling adjective *this is a telling critique of*

the military mind: revealing, significant, weighty, important, meaningful, influential, striking, potent, powerful, compelling.
OPPOSITES: insignificant.

telling-off noun (Brit. informal). See REPRIMAND noun.

telltale adjective *I noticed the telltale blush on her face:* revealing, significant, meaningful, suggestive, enlightening, explanatory, revelatory; informal giveaway.
▷ noun (Brit.) *'Sue did it,' said Nigel the telltale:* informer, whistle-blower; informal snitch, squealer; Brit. informal sneak.

temerity noun *a customs officer had the temerity to stop her and search her baggage:* audacity, effrontery, impudence, impertinence, cheek, gall, presumption; informal nerve, face, front, brass neck, chutzpah.

temper noun
1 *he walked out in a temper:* rage, fury, fit of rage, fit of pique, tantrum, mood, bad mood, pet, sulk; informal huff; Brit. informal strop, paddy.
2 *this was an uncharacteristic display of temper:* anger, fury, rage, annoyance, vexation, irritation, ill humour, spleen, pique, petulance, testiness, tetchiness; literary ire; Brit. informal stroppiness.
3 *she struggled to keep her temper:* composure, equanimity, self-control, self-possession, sangfroid, calm, good humour; informal cool.
▷ verb *their idealism is tempered with realism:* balance, counterbalance, moderate, modify, modulate; lighten, soften, neutralize.
□ **lose your temper**
he lost his temper and started shouting and swearing at her: get angry, fly into a rage, erupt, lose control, go berserk, flare up, boil over; informal go mad, go crazy, go bananas, have a fit, see red, fly off the handle, blow your top, hit the roof, go off the deep end, go ape, flip, freak out; Brit. informal go spare, go crackers, throw a wobbly, do your nut, lose your rag.

temperament noun nature, character, personality, make-up, constitution, mind, spirit; stamp, mettle, mould; disposition, mood, frame of mind, attitude, outlook, humour.

temperamental adjective
1 *a temperamental chef:* volatile, excitable, emotional, capricious, erratic, unpredictable, changeable, mercurial, inconsistent; hot-headed, fiery, quick-tempered, irritable, irascible, impatient; touchy, moody, sensitive, oversensitive, highly strung, neurotic, melodramatic.
2 *he had a temperamental dislike of conflict:* inherent, innate, natural, inborn, constitutional, deep-rooted, ingrained, congenital.
OPPOSITES: placid.

t

temperate adjective

1 *I prefer more temperate climates:* mild, clement, benign, gentle, balmy.
2 *he was temperate in his consumption of alcohol:* restrained, moderate, self-controlled, disciplined; abstemious, self-denying, austere, ascetic.
OPPOSITES: extreme, intemperate.

tempest noun storm, gale, hurricane, tornado, whirlwind, cyclone, typhoon.

tempestuous adjective

1 *they embarked on a tempestuous affair:* turbulent, stormy, wild, passionate, torrid, explosive.
2 *the outspoken and tempestuous Galileo:* emotional, passionate, impassioned, fiery, intense; temperamental, volatile, excitable, mercurial, capricious, unpredictable, quick-tempered.
OPPOSITES: calm, placid.

temple noun house of God, shrine, sanctuary; Christianity church, cathedral; Islam mosque; Jewish synagogue; Sikhism gurdwara; Hinduism mandir; Hinduism or Buddhism pagoda.

tempo noun

1 *the tempo of the music quickened:* beat, pulse, rhythm, speed, cadence, time; measure, metre.
2 *the frantic tempo of life in Western society:* pace, rate, speed, velocity.

temporal adjective *the temporal power of the papacy:* secular, non-spiritual, worldly, profane, material, mundane, earthly, terrestrial; non-religious, lay.
OPPOSITES: spiritual.

temporarily adverb

1 *the girl was temporarily placed with a foster family:* for the time being, for now, for the moment, for the present, in the interim, in/for the meantime, in the meanwhile; provisionally, pro tem; informal for the minute.
2 *he was temporarily blinded by the light:* briefly, for a short time, momentarily, fleetingly.
OPPOSITES: permanently.

temporary adjective

1 *we were still living in temporary accommodation:* short-term, interim, makeshift, stopgap.
2 *the temporary captain:* acting, stand-in, provisional, caretaker.
3 *a temporary loss of self-control:* brief, short-lived, momentary, fleeting, passing.
OPPOSITES: permanent, lasting.

tempt verb

1 *the manager tried to tempt him to stay:* entice, persuade, convince, inveigle, induce, cajole, coax, woo; informal sweet-talk.
2 *more customers are being tempted by credit:* allure, attract, appeal to, whet the appetite of; lure, seduce, beguile, tantalize, draw.
OPPOSITES: discourage, deter.

temptation noun

1 *Mary resisted the temptation to answer back:* desire, urge, itch, impulse, inclination.
2 *the temptations of London:* attraction, lure, draw, pull, appeal, seduction, fascination, enticement; siren song.

tempting adjective enticing, alluring, attractive, appealing, inviting, captivating, seductive, beguiling, tantalizing; irresistible.
OPPOSITES: off-putting, uninviting.

ten cardinal number decade.

> WORD LINKS
> **decimal** relating to a system of numbers based on the number ten
> **decagon** a ten-sided figure

tenable adjective *ideas that, 150 years later, are no longer tenable:* defensible, justifiable, supportable, sustainable, arguable, able to hold water, reasonable, rational, sound, viable, plausible, credible.
OPPOSITES: untenable.

tenacious adjective *you're tenacious and you get at the truth:* persistent, persevering, determined, dogged, strong-willed, tireless, indefatigable, resolute, patient, purposeful, unflagging, staunch, steadfast, untiring, unwavering, unswerving, unshakeable, unyielding, insistent.
OPPOSITES: irresolute, half-hearted.

tenacity noun persistence, perseverance, determination, doggedness, strength of purpose, tirelessness, indefatigability, resolution, resolve, firmness, patience, purpose, staunchness, staying power, application.

tenancy noun occupancy, occupation, residence, holding, possession; tenure, lease, rental, leasehold.

tenant noun occupant, resident, inhabitant; leaseholder, lessee, renter; Brit. occupier, sitting tenant.
OPPOSITES: owner, freeholder.

tend¹ verb

1 *I tend to get very involved in my work:* be inclined, be apt, be disposed, be prone, be liable, have a tendency, have a propensity.
2 *younger voters tended towards the left:* incline, lean, gravitate, move; prefer, favour.

tend² verb *alone again, she tended her garden:* look after, take care of, care for, minister to, attend to, see to, wait on; watch over, keep an eye on, mind, protect, watch, guard; nurse, nurture, cherish.
OPPOSITES: neglect.

tendency noun

1 *his tendency to take the law into his own hands:* inclination, readiness, propensity, proclivity, proneness, aptness, disposition, predisposition, bent, habit, leaning,

penchant, preference, predilection.
2 *this tendency towards cohabitation:*
trend, movement, drift, swing, gravitation,
direction.

tender¹ adjective

1 *he is a gentle, tender man:* caring,
kind, kindly, kind-hearted, soft-hearted,
tender-hearted, compassionate,
sympathetic, gentle, mild, benevolent,
generous.
2 *he planted a tender kiss on her forehead:*
affectionate, fond, loving, emotional,
warm, gentle, soft; informal lovey-dovey.
3 *enjoy an album of tender love songs:*
romantic, sentimental, emotional,
emotive, touching, moving, poignant; Brit.
informal soppy.
4 *simmer until the meat is tender:* soft;
succulent, juicy.
5 *these tender young plants need lots of
care:* delicate, easily damaged, fragile.
6 *her ankle was swollen and tender:*
sore, painful, sensitive, inflamed, raw,
red, chafed, bruised; hurting, aching,
throbbing, smarting.
7 *the tender age of fifteen:* young, youthful;
impressionable, inexperienced, immature,
unsophisticated, unseasoned, juvenile,
callow, green, raw; informal wet behind the
ears.
OPPOSITES: hard-hearted, callous, tough.

tender² verb

1 *she tendered her resignation:* offer,
proffer, present, put forward, propose,
suggest, advance, submit, extend, give,
render; hand in.
2 *two firms of interior decorators tendered
for the work:* bid, quote, estimate.
▷ **noun** *six contractors were invited to submit
tenders:* bid, offer, quotation, quote,
estimate, price; proposal, submission.

tenderness noun

1 *I felt an enormous tenderness for her:*
affection, fondness, love, devotion,
emotion, sentiment.
2 *with unexpected tenderness, he told her
what had happened:* kindness, kindliness,
kind-heartedness, tender-heartedness,
compassion, care, concern, sympathy,
gentleness, benevolence, generosity.
3 *abdominal tenderness:* soreness, pain,
inflammation, bruising; ache, aching,
smarting, throbbing.

tenet noun *the basic tenets of their religion:*
principle, belief, doctrine, precept, creed,
credo, article of faith, dogma, canon;
theory, thesis, conviction, idea, view,
opinion, position, hypothesis, postulation;
(**tenets**) ideology, code of belief, teaching.

tenor noun *officials played down the
revolutionary tenor of the President's
comments:* sense, meaning, theme, drift,
thread, import, purport, intent, intention,
thrust, significance, message; gist,
essence, substance, spirit.

tense adjective

1 *she massaged the tense muscles of his
neck:* taut, tight, rigid, flexed, stretched,
strained, stiff.
2 *Loretta was feeling tense and irritable:*
anxious, nervous, on edge, edgy, strained,
stressed, under pressure, agitated, ill at
ease, uneasy, restless, worked up, keyed
up, overwrought, jumpy, on tenterhooks,
worried, apprehensive, panicky; informal a
bundle of nerves, jittery, twitchy, uptight,
stressed out.
3 *it was a tense moment for everyone:*
nerve-racking, stressful, anxious, fraught,
worrying, charged, strained, nail-biting,
difficult, uneasy, uncomfortable;
exciting.
OPPOSITES: slack, calm.
▷ **verb** *Hebden tensed his muscles:* tighten,
tauten, tense up, flex, contract, brace,
stiffen; screw up, knot, strain, stretch.
OPPOSITES: relax.

tension noun

1 *I adjusted the tension of the rope:*
tightness, tautness, rigidity, strain, pull,
load, traction.
2 *the tension was unbearable:* strain, stress,
anxiety, pressure; suspense, uncertainty,
anticipation, excitement.
3 *the coup followed months of tension
between the military and the government:*
strained relations, strain; ill feeling,
friction, antagonism, antipathy, hostility,
enmity.
OPPOSITES: slackness, calm, harmony

tentative adjective

1 *tentative arrangements | a tentative
conclusion:* provisional, unconfirmed,
pencilled in, preliminary, to be
confirmed, subject to confirmation;
speculative, conjectural, exploratory,
experimental.
2 *he took a few tentative steps:* hesitant,
uncertain, cautious, timid, hesitating,
faltering, shaky, unsteady, halting;
wavering, unsure.
OPPOSITES: definite, confident.

tenterhooks plural noun
□ **on tenterhooks**
*she had been on tenterhooks all night,
waiting for Joe to return:* in suspense,
waiting with bated breath; nervy,
apprehensive, anxious, worried, worried
sick, on edge, edgy, tense, strained,
stressed, agitated, restless, worked up,
keyed up, jumpy, with your heart in your
mouth, like a cat on a hot tin roof; informal
with butterflies in your stomach, jittery,
twitchy, in a state, uptight.

tenuous adjective *the tenuous link
between interest rates and investment:*
slight, insubstantial, flimsy, weak,
doubtful, dubious, questionable, suspect;
vague, nebulous, hazy.
OPPOSITES: convincing, strong.

t

tenure noun

1 *residents should at least have security of tenure:* tenancy, occupancy, occupation, residence; possession, ownership.

2 *his tenure as Secretary of State for Industry:* time in office, period in/of office, term of office, incumbency.

tepid adjective

1 *tepid water:* lukewarm, warmish, slightly warm; at room temperature.

2 *his speech received a tepid response:* unenthusiastic, apathetic, half-hearted, indifferent, cool, lukewarm, uninterested.

OPPOSITES: hot, enthusiastic.

term noun

1 *a dictionary of scientific and technical terms:* word, expression, phrase, turn of phrase, idiom; name, title, designation, label.

2 (**terms**) *a protest in the strongest possible terms:* language, phraseology, terminology; words, phrases, expressions.

3 *the terms of the contract:* condition, stipulation, specification, provision, proviso; restriction, qualification; detail, particular, point, clause.

4 (**terms**) *a policy offering more favourable terms:* rates, prices, charges, costs, fees; tariff.

5 *the President is elected for a four-year term:* period, time, spell, stint, duration; stretch, run; period of office, incumbency.

6 *the start of the summer term:* session; N. Amer. semester, trimester, quarter.

▷ **verb** *he has been termed the father of modern theology:* call, name, entitle, title, style, designate, describe as, dub, label, tag; nickname.

□ **come to terms with**

she eventually came to terms with her situation: accept, come to accept, reconcile yourself to, learn to live with, become resigned to, make the best of; face up to.

terminal adjective

1 *a terminal bonus may be payable when a policy matures:* final, last, concluding, closing, end.

2 *a terminal illness:* incurable, untreatable, inoperable; fatal, mortal, deadly.

▷ **noun** *a computer terminal:* workstation, VDU, visual display unit, monitor.

terminate verb *the bosses decided to terminate his contract on December 31:* end, bring to a close/conclusion, close, conclude, finish, stop, put an end to, wind up, discontinue, cease, abort, axe; informal pull the plug on.

OPPOSITES: start.

termination noun *the termination of a contract:* ending, end, closing, close, conclusion, finish, stopping, winding up, discontinuance, discontinuation; cancellation, dissolution.

OPPOSITES: start.

terminology noun language, terms, expressions, words, phraseology, parlance, vocabulary, nomenclature; usage, idiom; jargon, cant, argot; informal lingo.

terrain noun land, ground, territory; topography, landscape, countryside, country.

terrestrial adjective earthly, worldly, mundane, earthbound.

OPPOSITES: extraterrestrial, celestial.

terrible adjective

1 *a terrible crime | he sustained terrible injuries:* dreadful, awful, appalling, horrific, horrifying, horrible, horrendous, atrocious, abominable, abhorrent, frightful, shocking, hideous, ghastly, grim, dire, unspeakable, gruesome, monstrous, sickening, heinous, vile; serious, grave, acute; formal grievous.

2 *there was a terrible smell in the room:* nasty, disgusting, awful, dreadful, ghastly, horrid, horrible, vile, foul, abominable, frightful, loathsome, revolting, repulsive, odious, nauseating, repellent, horrendous, hideous, appalling; informal gruesome, putrid, sick-making, gross; Brit. informal beastly.

3 *he was in terrible pain:* severe, extreme, intense, excruciating, agonizing, unbearable, intolerable, unendurable.

4 *the film was terrible:* dreadful, awful, abysmal, appalling, frightful, atrocious, poor; informal pathetic, pitiful, useless, lousy, dire; Brit. informal hopeless, chronic, rubbish.

OPPOSITES: minor, slight, pleasant, wonderful.

terribly adverb

1 *she's terribly upset:* very, extremely, really, immensely, thoroughly, exceptionally, exceedingly; informal awfully, dreadfully, terrifically, seriously; Brit. informal jolly, dead.

2 *he played terribly:* very badly, dreadfully, atrociously, awfully, appallingly, abysmally, execrably; informal pitifully, diabolically.

3 *I shall miss you terribly:* very much, greatly, a great deal; informal a lot, lots, loads.

terrific adjective

1 *there was a terrific bang:* tremendous, huge, massive, gigantic, colossal, mighty, great, prodigious, formidable; intense, extreme, extraordinary; informal mega, whopping, humongous; Brit. informal whacking great, ginormous.

2 (informal) *a terrific game of top-quality football | you look terrific:* marvellous, wonderful, sensational, outstanding, superb, excellent, first-rate, first-class, dazzling, out of this world, breathtaking; informal great, fantastic, fabulous, fab, mega, super, ace, magic, cracking, cool, wicked, awesome; Brit. informal brilliant, smashing.

OPPOSITES: slight, poor.

terrified adjective petrified, frightened,

t

scared, scared/frightened to death, scared stiff, scared/frightened out of your wits, scared witless, horrified; with your heart in your mouth, shaking in your shoes.

terrify verb *she clung to the edge of her seat, terrified by the venom in his voice:* petrify, horrify, frighten, scare, scare/frighten to death, scare/frighten the living daylights out of, scare/frighten the life out of, scare/frighten someone out of their wits, scare witless, strike terror into, put the fear of God into; informal scare the pants off.

territory noun
1 *a tiny British territory on the outskirts of Polynesia:* dependency, colony, protectorate, dominion, possession, enclave, country, state, land, area, region.
2 *a dangerous journey through enemy territory:* land, ground, terrain, country, countryside.

terror noun *she screamed in terror:* horror, dread, fear, fright, alarm, panic, shock.

terrorist noun bomber, gunman, hijacker, paramilitary, revolutionary, insurgent, radical, guerrilla, freedom fighter.

terrorize verb persecute, victimize, torment, tyrannize, intimidate, menace, threaten, bully, browbeat; scare, frighten, terrify, petrify.

terse adjective *he issued a terse warning:* brusque, abrupt, curt, clipped, blunt; brief, short, to the point, concise, succinct, crisp, pithy, incisive, short and sweet, laconic, elliptical.
OPPOSITES: polite, long-winded.

test noun
1 *a series of scientific tests were carried out:* trial, experiment, pilot, try-out; check, examination, assessment, evaluation, appraisal, investigation, inspection, analysis, scrutiny, study, probe, exploration; screening.
2 *candidates may be required to take a test:* exam, examination; N. Amer. quiz.
▷ **verb**
1 *a small-scale prototype was tested:* try out, trial, put to the test, put through its paces, experiment on/with, pilot; check, examine, assess, evaluate, appraise, investigate, analyse, scrutinize, study, probe, explore; sample; screen.
2 *such behaviour would test any marriage:* put a strain on, strain, tax, try; stretch, challenge.

testament noun *an achievement which is a testament to his professionalism:* testimony, witness, evidence, proof, attestation; demonstration, indication, exemplification; monument, tribute.

testify verb
1 *you may be required to testify in court:* give evidence, be a witness, appear.

2 *he testified that he had been threatened by a fellow officer:* attest, swear, state on oath, state, declare, assert, affirm; allege, submit, claim.
3 *the exhibits testify to the talents of the local sculptors:* be evidence/proof of, attest to, confirm, prove, bear out; show, demonstrate, bear witness to, indicate, reveal; formal bespeak.

testimonial noun reference, character reference, recommendation, commendation.

testimony noun
1 *Smith was in court to hear her testimony:* evidence, sworn statement, attestation, affidavit; declaration, assertion, affirmation; allegation, submission, claim; Law deposition.
2 *the work is a testimony to his professional commitment:* testament, witness; evidence, proof, attestation; confirmation; demonstration, indication.

testing adjective *it was a testing time for the organization:* difficult, challenging, tough, hard, demanding, exacting, taxing, stressful.
OPPOSITES: easy.

testy adjective. See TETCHY.

tetchy adjective *he didn't get much affection from his testy, disapproving father:* irritable, cantankerous, irascible, bad-tempered, grumpy, grouchy, crotchety, crabby, testy, ill-tempered, ill-humoured, peevish, cross, fractious, pettish, prickly, waspish; informal snappish, snappy; Brit. informal shirty, stroppy, ratty.
OPPOSITES: good-humoured.

tête-à-tête noun conversation, chat, talk, heart-to-heart, one-on-one, one-to-one; informal confab; Brit. informal natter, chinwag.

tether verb *the horse had been tethered to a post:* tie, hitch, rope, chain; fasten, secure.
OPPOSITES: untie.

text noun
1 *the pictures are clear and relate well to the text:* words, wording, context, copy, content, body.
2 *a list of recommended texts:* book, textbook, publication, work; journal, periodical; piece of writing.
3 *a text from the First Book of Samuel:* passage, extract, quotation, verse, line; reading.

textile noun fabric, cloth, material.

texture noun feel, touch; appearance, finish, surface, grain; quality, consistency; weave, nap.

thank verb
1 *she thanked her family for all their support:* express your gratitude to, express/offer/extend your thanks to, say thank you to, show your appreciation to, acknowledge, recognize.

t

2 *you have only yourself to thank for the plight you are in:* blame, hold responsible.

thankful adjective grateful, appreciative, filled with gratitude, relieved, pleased, glad.

thankless adjective *a thankless task:* unenviable, difficult, unpleasant, disagreeable, unrewarding; unappreciated, unrecognized, unacknowledged.
OPPOSITES: rewarding.

thanks plural noun *they expressed their thanks and wished her well:* gratitude, appreciation; acknowledgement, recognition, credit.
□ **thanks to**
Scully survives, thanks to a bulletproof vest: as a result of, owing to, due to, because of, through, as a consequence of, on account of, by virtue of, by dint of.

thaw verb melt defrost, unfreeze, soften, liquefy, dissolve.
OPPOSITES: freeze.

theatre noun
1 *there's a good play on at the local theatre:* playhouse, auditorium, amphitheatre.
2 *what made you go into the theatre?* acting, the stage, drama, the dramatic arts, dramaturgy, theatricals, performing, show business; informal the boards, showbiz.
3 *the lecture theatre was packed:* hall, room, auditorium.

theatrical adjective
1 *a theatrical career:* dramatic, stage, thespian, dramaturgical; show-business; informal showbiz.
2 *Henry looked over his shoulder with theatrical caution:* exaggerated, ostentatious, stagy, showy, melodramatic, overacted, overdone, histrionic, affected, mannered; informal hammy, camp.

theft noun robbery, stealing, thieving, shoplifting, burglary, misappropriation, embezzlement; raid, hold-up; N. Amer. larceny; informal smash-and-grab; N. Amer. informal stick-up.

theme noun
1 *the theme of her speech:* subject, topic, subject matter, matter, thesis, argument, text, thrust; thread, motif, keynote.
2 *the first violin takes up the theme:* melody, tune, air; motif, leitmotif.

then adverb
1 *I was living in Cairo then:* at that time, in those days; at that point, at that moment, on that occasion.
2 *she won the first and then the second game:* next, after that, afterwards, subsequently.
3 *there's the money I'm owed, and then there's another problem:* in addition, also, besides, as well, additionally, on top of that, over and above that, moreover, furthermore, what's more, to boot; too.

theoretical adjective
1 *theoretical debate without supporting evidence is unscientific:* conceptual, intellectual, abstract, pure, academic; speculative.
2 *the purely theoretical risk that the disease could cross the species barrier:* hypothetical, notional, assumed, presumed, untested, unproven, unsubstantiated.
OPPOSITES: practical, real.

theorize verb *Einstein theorized that the speed of gravity was about the speed of light:* speculate, conjecture, hypothesize, postulate, propose, posit, suppose.

theory noun
1 *I reckon that confirms my theory:* hypothesis, thesis, conjecture, supposition, speculation, postulation, postulate, proposition, premise, assumption, presupposition; opinion, view, belief, contention.
2 *modern economic theory | the theory of relativity:* principles, ideas, concepts; philosophy, ideology, science.
□ **in theory**
in theory this method is ideal: in principle, on paper, in the abstract, all things being equal, in an ideal world; hypothetically.

therapeutic adjective
1 *the therapeutic effects of acupuncture:* healing, curative, medicinal, restorative, remedial, health-giving, corrective, beneficial, positive, good, salutary.
2 *he liked housework—it was therapeutic and helped relieve the stress:* calming, relaxing, restful, soothing; helpful, beneficial.
OPPOSITES: harmful, stressful.

therapist noun psychotherapist, analyst, psychoanalyst, psychiatrist; informal shrink.

therapy noun
1 *a wide range of complementary therapies:* treatment, remedy, cure.
2 *he's currently in therapy:* psychotherapy, psychoanalysis, analysis.

thereafter adverb after that, following that, afterwards, subsequently, then, next.
OPPOSITES: hitherto.

therefore adverb consequently, so, as a result, hence, accordingly, for that reason; formal thus, ergo.

thesis noun
1 *the central thesis of his lecture:* theory, contention, argument, line of argument, proposal, proposition, statement, premise, assumption, hypothesis, postulation, supposition.
2 *he's researching his thesis at the moment:* dissertation, essay, paper, treatise, composition, monograph, study; formal disquisition.

thick adjective

1 *the walls are five feet thick:* wide, across, broad, deep, in extent/diameter.

2 *his short, thick legs:* stocky, sturdy, chunky, hefty, thickset, meaty, solid; fat, stout, plump; informal beefy.

3 *a thick Aran sweater:* chunky, bulky, heavy, dense, solid.

4 *the thick summer vegetation:* plentiful, abundant, profuse, luxuriant, bushy, rich, riotous; rank, rampant; dense, close-packed, impenetrable, impassable.

5 *he smeared a thick paste over the wall:* firm, stiff, semi-solid, heavy; clotted, coagulated, viscous, gelatinous; concentrated.

6 *a motorway pile-up in thick fog:* dense, heavy, opaque, impenetrable, soupy, murky.

7 (informal) *he's a bit thick.* See **STUPID** sense 1.

OPPOSITES: thin, slender.

thicken verb stiffen, set, condense, reduce, solidify, gel, congeal, clot, coagulate, cake.

OPPOSITES: thin.

thicket noun *a thicket of young trees:* copse, coppice, grove, brake, covert, clump; wood; Brit. spinney.

thickness noun

1 *timing depends on the thickness of the steaks:* width, breadth, depth, diameter, bulk.

2 *several thicknesses of limestone:* layer, stratum, seam, vein; sheet, coat, coating.

thickset adjective *a thickset man with a florid complexion:* stocky, sturdy, heavily built, chunky, burly, strapping, brawny, solid, heavy, hefty, meaty; informal beefy.

OPPOSITES: slight.

thick-skinned adjective *I suppose you have to be pretty thick-skinned to be an MP:* insensitive, unfeeling, tough, impervious, hardened, case-hardened; informal hard-boiled.

OPPOSITES: sensitive.

thief noun robber, burglar, housebreaker, cat burglar, shoplifter, pickpocket, sneak thief, mugger, bandit; embezzler, swindler; kleptomaniac.

thieve verb steal, take, help yourself to, snatch, pilfer, loot; embezzle, misappropriate; have your fingers/hand in the till; formal purloin; informal pinch, rob, swipe, nab, rip off, lift, filch; Brit. informal nick, knock off.

thieving noun theft, stealing, robbery, pilfering; burglary, shoplifting, housebreaking, breaking and entering, embezzlement; N. Amer. larceny.

thin adjective

1 *a thin white line was painted on the wall:* narrow, fine, attenuated.

2 *a tall, thin woman dressed all in black:* slim, lean, slender, rangy, willowy, svelte, sylphlike, spare, slight; skinny, underweight, scrawny, scraggy, bony, angular, raw-boned, gaunt, as thin as a rake, stick-like, skin-and-bones, emaciated, skeletal, wasted, pinched, undernourished, underfed; lanky, spindly, gangly, gangling, weedy.

3 *she was wearing a thin cotton nightdress:* lightweight, light, fine, delicate, floaty, flimsy, diaphanous, gossamer, insubstantial; sheer, gauzy, filmy, transparent, see-through.

4 *he ran a hand over his thin grey hair:* sparse, wispy, thinning.

5 *I was offered a bowl of thin soup:* watery, weak, dilute, insipid; runny, sloppy.

6 *her thin voice trailed off:* weak, faint, feeble, small, soft; reedy, high-pitched.

7 *the plot of the movie is very thin:* insubstantial, flimsy, slight, feeble, lame, poor, weak, tenuous, inadequate.

OPPOSITES: thick, broad, fat.

▷ verb

1 *the paint must be thinned before use:* dilute, water down, weaken.

2 *the crowds were beginning to thin out:* disperse, dissipate, scatter; become less dense/numerous, decrease, diminish, dwindle.

thing noun

1 *the room was full of strange things:* object, article, item, artefact, commodity; device, gadget, instrument, utensil, tool, implement; entity, body.

2 (things) *I'll come back tomorrow to collect my things:* belongings, possessions, property, worldly goods, personal effects, paraphernalia, bits and bobs; luggage, baggage, bags; informal gear, stuff, junk, bits and pieces; Brit. informal clobber.

3 (things) *he went to get his gardening things:* equipment, apparatus, tackle; implements, tools, utensils, paraphernalia; accoutrements; informal gear, stuff, kit.

4 *I've got several things to do today:* task, job, chore; activity, act, action, deed, undertaking.

5 *I've got other things on my mind just now:* matter, affair, concern, thought, idea, worry, preoccupation.

6 *quite a few odd things have happened:* incident, episode, event, happening, occurrence, phenomenon.

7 (things) *how are things with you?* matters, affairs, circumstances, conditions, relations; state of affairs, situation, life.

8 *one of the things I like about you is your optimism:* characteristic, quality, attribute, property, trait, feature, point, aspect, facet.

9 *there's another thing you should know:* fact, piece of information, point, detail, particular, factor.

10 *Dora developed a thing about noise:*

t

phobia, fear, dislike, aversion; obsession, fixation; complex, neurosis; informal hang-up, bee in your bonnet.
11 *she had a thing about men who wore glasses:* penchant, preference, taste, inclination, partiality, predilection, soft spot, weakness, fancy, fondness, liking, love; fetish, obsession, fixation.

think verb
1 *I think he's gone home:* believe, be of the opinion, be of the view, be under the impression; expect, imagine, anticipate; surmise, suppose, guess; conclude, determine, reason; Brit. fancy; informal reckon, figure.
2 *his family was thought to be enormously rich:* consider, reckon, estimate, judge, hold, deem, presume; regard as, view as.
3 *Jack thought for a moment:* ponder, reflect, deliberate, consider, meditate, contemplate, muse, ruminate, be lost in thought, brood; concentrate, rack your brains; formal cogitate.
4 *she thought of all the visits she had made to her father:* recall, remember, recollect, call to mind, think back to.
5 *she forced herself to think of how he must be feeling:* imagine, picture, visualize, envisage; dream about, fantasize about.
□ **think something over**
she went home to think over his offer: consider, contemplate, deliberate about, weigh up, consider the pros and cons of, mull over, ponder, reflect on, muse on, ruminate on.
□ **think something up**
the idea was thought up by one of my students: devise, dream up, come up with, invent, create, concoct, make up; hit on.

thinker noun
theorist, philosopher, scholar, savant, sage, intellectual, intellect, brain.

thinking adjective
every thinking person acknowledges that we're in a mess: intelligent, sensible, reasonable, rational; logical, analytical; thoughtful, reflective, meditative, contemplative, pensive, philosophical.
OPPOSITES: stupid.
▷ **noun** *what was the thinking behind the campaign?* reasoning, ideas, theory, thoughts, line of thought, philosophy, beliefs; opinions, views, position, judgement, assessment, evaluation.

thirst noun
his thirst for knowledge: craving, desire, longing, yearning, yen, hunger, hankering, keenness, eagerness, lust, appetite; informal itch.
▷ **verb**
□ **thirst for**
she thirsted for power: crave, want, covet, desire, hunger for, lust after, hanker after, have your heart set on, wish for, long for.

thirsty adjective
longing for a drink, dry, dehydrated; informal parched, gasping.

thorny adjective
1 *dense thorny undergrowth:* prickly, spiky, barbed, spiny, sharp.
2 *the thorny subject of confidentiality:* problematic, tricky, ticklish, delicate, controversial, awkward, difficult, knotty, tough, trying, troublesome; complicated, complex, involved, intricate; vexed; informal sticky.
OPPOSITES: soft, easy, simple.

thorough adjective
1 *a thorough investigation was called for:* rigorous, in-depth, exhaustive, thoroughgoing, minute, detailed, close, meticulous, methodical, careful, complete, comprehensive, full, extensive, widespread, sweeping.
2 *he is slow but thorough:* meticulous, scrupulous, assiduous, conscientious, painstaking, punctilious, methodical, careful, diligent.
3 *the child is being a thorough nuisance:* utter, downright, thoroughgoing, absolute, complete, total, out-and-out, real, perfect, proper, sheer, unqualified, unmitigated.
OPPOSITES: superficial, careless.

thoroughly adverb
1 *we will investigate all complaints thoroughly:* rigorously, in depth, exhaustively, from top to bottom, minutely, closely, in detail, meticulously, scrupulously, assiduously, conscientiously, painstakingly, methodically, carefully, comprehensively, fully.
2 *she is thoroughly spoilt:* utterly, downright, absolutely, completely, totally, entirely, really, perfectly, positively, in every respect, through and through; informal plain.

though conjunction
though she smiled bravely, she looked pale and tired: although, even though/if, in spite of the fact that, notwithstanding the fact that, for all that.
▷ **adverb** *You can't always do that. You can try, though:* nevertheless, nonetheless, however, but, even so, be that as it may, for all that, despite that, having said that.

thought noun
1 *what are your thoughts on the matter?* idea, notion, opinion, view, impression, feeling, theory; judgement, assessment, conclusion.
2 *it only took a moment's thought:* thinking, contemplation, musing, pondering, consideration, reflection, introspection, deliberation, rumination, meditation, brooding, reverie, concentration.
3 *he gave up any thought of taking a degree:* hope, aspiration, ambition, dream; intention, idea.
4 *have you no thought for other people?* consideration, sympathy, understanding, concern, regard, care, sensitivity, compassion, solicitude, empathy.

t

thoughtful adjective
1 *Albert paused, looking thoughtful:* pensive, reflective, contemplative, meditative, introspective, philosophical, ruminative, absorbed, engrossed, rapt, preoccupied, deep/lost in thought.
2 *how very thoughtful of you!* considerate, understanding, concerned, caring, sensitive, attentive, sympathetic, solicitous, helpful, friendly, obliging, accommodating, kind, neighbourly, unselfish, compassionate, charitable.
OPPOSITES: blank, thoughtless.

thoughtless adjective *I'm so sorry—how thoughtless of me:* inconsiderate, uncaring, insensitive, inattentive, unkind, tactless, undiplomatic, indiscreet, careless, unhelpful.
OPPOSITES: thoughtful.

thousand cardinal number informal K, thou.

> **WORD LINKS**
> **kilo-** forming units of measurement meaning 'one thousand ——', such as *kilometre* (1,000 metres) or *kilowatt* (1,000 watts)
> **millennium**, **millenary** a period of a thousand years, or an anniversary of a thousand years

thrash verb
1 *she thrashed him across the head and shoulders:* hit, beat, strike, cane, cudgel, club, birch, whip, flog, tan/whip someone's hide; informal give someone a hiding, wallop, belt, bash, whack, thwack, clobber, tan.
2 (informal) *Newcastle were thrashed 8–1.* See **TROUNCE**.
3 *he was thrashing around in pain:* flail, writhe, thresh, jerk, toss, twist, twitch.
□ thrash something out
1 *it's better if we can thrash out our difficulties first:* discuss, talk through, debate, air, ventilate; resolve, settle, sort out, straighten out, iron out, clear up.
2 *they tried to thrash out an agreement:* work out, negotiate, agree on, bring about, hammer out, produce, effect.

thread noun *a needle and thread:* cotton, yarn, twine; strand, filament, fibre.
▷ verb
1 *he threaded the rope through a pulley:* pass, string, work, ease, push, poke.
2 *she threaded her way through the crowd:* weave your way, work your way, wind your way, squeeze your way, make your way.

threadbare adjective *we have just replaced that threadbare stair carpet:* worn, well worn, old, thin, worn out, holey, moth-eaten, mangy, ragged, frayed, tattered, battered; decrepit, shabby, scruffy; having seen better days, falling apart at the seams, falling to pieces; informal tatty, ratty.
OPPOSITES: smart, new.

threat noun
1 *Maggie ignored his threats:* threatening remark, warning, ultimatum; (**threats**) duress; Brit. menaces.
2 *the tower poses a possible threat to aircraft:* danger, peril, hazard, menace, risk.
3 *the company faces the threat of liquidation proceedings:* possibility, chance, probability, likelihood, risk.

threaten verb
1 *how dare you threaten me!* menace, intimidate, browbeat, bully, terrorize.
2 *these events could threaten the stability of Europe:* endanger, be a danger/threat to, jeopardize, imperil, put at risk, put in jeopardy.

threatening adjective
1 *a threatening letter:* menacing, intimidating, bullying, aggressive, hostile.
2 *banks of threatening clouds:* ominous, sinister, menacing, dark, black, thunderous.
OPPOSITES: benign.

three cardinal number trio, threesome, triple, trilogy.

> **WORD LINKS**
> **triangle** a three-sided figure
> **tercentenary** a three-hundredth anniversary

threesome noun trio, triumvirate, triad, trinity, troika; triplets.

threshold noun
1 *he paused on the threshold of the church:* doorstep, sill, doorway, entrance, entry.
2 *we are on the threshold of a new era:* start, beginning, brink, verge, dawn, opening.
3 *the human threshold of pain:* boundary, tolerance level, limit, minimum, maximum.

thrift noun economy, frugality, providence, prudence, good management/ husbandry, saving, scrimping and saving, abstemiousness, parsimony, penny-pinching.
OPPOSITES: extravagance.

thrifty adjective economical, frugal, sparing, careful, provident, prudent, abstemious, parsimonious, penny-pinching.
OPPOSITES: extravagant.

thrill noun
1 *the thrill of jumping out of an aeroplane:* excitement, adventure, stimulation, pleasure; fun, enjoyment, amusement, delight, joy; informal buzz, kick.
2 *a thrill of excitement ran through her:* sensation, feeling, wave, rush, surge, flash, blaze, stab, dart, throb, tremor, quiver, flutter, shudder, tingle.
▷ verb *the 1992 champion thrilled the watching millions with his glorious come-back:* excite, stimulate, arouse, inspire, delight, exhilarate, intoxicate, stir,

electrify, galvanize, move; informal give someone a buzz, give someone a kick.
OPPOSITES: bore.

thrilling adjective exciting, stirring, action-packed, rip-roaring, gripping, riveting, fascinating, dramatic, hair-raising; rousing, stimulating, moving, inspirational, inspiring, electrifying, heady, soul-stirring.
OPPOSITES: boring.

thrive verb *a plant that thrives in sandy soil:* flourish, prosper, burgeon, grow, bloom, blossom, do well, advance, progress in/by leaps and bounds, be vigorous, succeed, boom.
OPPOSITES: decline, wither.

thriving adjective *a thriving market town:* flourishing, prosperous, growing, vigorous, developing, burgeoning, blooming, healthy, successful, booming, profitable, expanding; informal going strong.
OPPOSITES: moribund.

throat noun gullet, oesophagus; windpipe, trachea; maw; old use gorge.

> WORD LINKS
> **jugular** relating to the neck or throat

throaty adjective gravelly, husky, rough, guttural, deep, thick, gruff, growly, hoarse, croaky, croaking; rasping.
OPPOSITES: high-pitched, smooth.

throb verb *a vein throbbed in his neck:* pulsate, beat, pulse, palpitate, pound, thud, thump, drum, thrum, vibrate, go pit-a-pat, quiver.
▷ noun *the throb of the ship's engines:* pulsation, beat, rhythm, pulse, palpitation, pounding, thudding, thumping, drumming, thrumming, pit-a-pat.

throes plural noun *the death throes of the stricken animal:* agony, pain, suffering.
□ in the throes of
we are in the throes of an anguished debate between the environmental unit and the energy department: in the middle of, in the midst of, busy with, occupied with, taken up with/by, involved in; struggling with, wrestling with, grappling with, dealing with.

thrombosis noun clot, blood clot, embolism, embolus; Medicine infarction.

throng noun *a throng of people blocked her way:* crowd, horde, mob, mass, multitude, host, army, herd, gang, flock, pack, drove, swarm, sea, crush; company, gathering, assembly, assemblage, congregation; informal gaggle, bunch.
▷ verb
1 *the pavements were thronged with tourists:* fill, crowd, pack, cram, jam.
2 *visitors thronged round him:* crowd, cluster, mill, swarm, congregate, gather; **(throng round)** mob, surround, jostle, besiege.

throttle verb choke, strangle, garrotte.

through preposition
1 *he worked through the night:* throughout, all through, for the duration of.
2 *he got the job through an advertisement:* by means of, by way of, by dint of, via, using, thanks to, by virtue of, as a result of, as a consequence of, on account of, owing to, because of.
□ through and through
he was obviously a city kid through and through: in every respect, to the core; thoroughly, utterly, absolutely, completely, totally, wholly, fully, entirely, unconditionally, unreservedly, altogether, out-and-out.

throughout preposition
1 *the dispute had repercussions throughout Europe:* all over, in every part of, everywhere in, all through, all round.
2 *Rose had generally been very fit throughout her life:* all through, all, for the duration of, for the whole of.

throw verb
1 *she threw the ball back:* toss, hurl, fling, pitch, cast, lob, launch, catapult, project, propel; bowl; informal chuck, heave, sling; Brit. informal bung.
2 *a chandelier threw its light over the walls:* cast, send, give off, emit, radiate, project.
3 *he threw another punch:* deliver, give, land.
4 *she threw a withering glance at him:* direct, cast, send, dart, shoot.
5 *his question threw me:* disconcert, unnerve, fluster, ruffle, agitate, discomfit, put off, throw off balance, discountenance, unsettle, confuse; informal rattle, faze.
6 *he threw a farewell party for them:* give, host, hold, have, provide, put on, lay on, arrange, organize.
▷ noun *we were allowed two throws each:* toss, lob, pitch; go; bowl, ball.
□ throw something away
1 *she hated throwing old clothes away:* discard, throw out, dispose of, get rid of, do away with, toss out, scrap, throw on the scrapheap, clear out, dump, jettison; informal chuck away/out, ditch, bin, junk; Brit. informal get shot of.
2 *Cambridge threw away a 15–0 lead:* squander, waste, fritter away, fail to exploit, lose, let slip; informal blow, throw something down the drain.
□ throw something off
the country was eager to throw off its colonial past: shake off, get away from, escape, get rid of, lose, leave behind.
□ throw someone out
1 *four Britons were also thrown out of the country:* eject, expel, evict, show someone the door; banish, deport, exile; informal boot out, kick out, give someone the boot; Brit. informal turf out.
2 *the government was thrown out after only eight months:* remove, get rid of, depose, topple, unseat, overthrow, bring

t

down, overturn, dislodge, displace, supplant; informal boot out, kick out; Brit. informal turf out.

▢ **throw something out**
1 *throw out food that's past its sell-by date.* See **THROW SOMETHING AWAY** sense 1.
2 *his case was thrown out by the magistrate:* reject, dismiss, turn down, refuse, disallow, veto.
3 *a light bulb throws out a lot of heat:* radiate, emit, give off, send out, diffuse.
▢ **throw up** (informal). See **VOMIT** verb sense 1.

throwaway adjective
1 *they serve meals on throwaway plates rather than have a dishwasher:* disposable, non-returnable; single-use.
2 *a series of throwaway remarks:* casual, passing, careless, unthinking, unconsidered, offhand.
OPPOSITES: reusable, considered.

thrust verb
1 *she thrust her hands into her pockets:* shove, push, force, plunge, stick, drive, propel, ram, poke.
2 *fame had been thrust on him:* force, foist, impose, inflict.
3 *he thrust his way past her:* push, shove, force, elbow, shoulder, barge.
▷ **noun**
1 *he gave the gate a hard thrust:* shove, push, poke.
2 *a sudden armoured thrust by the Third Army:* advance, push, drive, attack, assault, onslaught, offensive, charge, sortie, foray, raid, sally, invasion, incursion.
3 *only one engine is producing thrust:* force, propulsion, power, impetus, momentum.
4 *they failed to grasp the thrust of the speech:* gist, substance, drift, meaning, significance, signification, sense, theme, message, import, tenor.

thrusting adjective *a thrusting young politician:* ambitious, forceful, aggressive, assertive, self-assertive, full of yourself, determined, power-hungry; informal pushy.
OPPOSITES: meek.

thud noun & verb thump, bang, clunk, clonk, crash, smack; stomp, stamp, clump, clomp.

thug noun ruffian, lout, hooligan, bully boy, vandal, hoodlum, gangster, villain, criminal; informal tough, bruiser, heavy, hired gun; N. Amer. informal hood, goon.

thumb verb *he thumbed through his notebook:* leaf, flick, flip, riffle, skim, browse, look.

thumbnail adjective *a thumbnail sketch of the political climate at the time:* concise, short, brief, succinct, to the point, compact, crisp, short and sweet, quick, rapid; potted.
OPPOSITES: detailed.

thump verb
1 *the two men kicked and thumped him:* hit, strike, smack, cuff, punch, belabour,

pound, pummel, box someone's ears; informal whack, wallop, bash, biff, clout, clobber, sock, belt; Brit. informal stick one on, slosh.
2 *her heart thumped with fright:* throb, pound, thud, hammer, beat, pulsate, pulse, pump, palpitate, race.
▷ **noun**
1 *a well-aimed thump on the jaw:* blow, punch, cuff, smack; informal whack, thwack, wallop, bash, belt, biff, clout, sock.
2 *she put the box down with a thump:* thud, clunk, clonk, crash, smack, bang.

thunder noun *the ceaseless thunder of the traffic:* rumble, boom, roar, pounding, thud, crash, beat.
▷ **verb**
1 *the motorbike thundered into life:* rumble, boom, roar, pound, thud, thump, bang; resound, reverberate, beat.
2 *'Answer me!' he thundered:* roar, bellow, bark, yell, shout, bawl; informal holler.

thunderous adjective *the applause was thunderous:* deafening, tumultuous, booming, roaring, resounding, very loud, reverberant, ringing, ear-splitting, noisy.
OPPOSITES: quiet.

thunderstruck adjective *we were thunderstruck by this revelation:* astonished, amazed, astounded, staggered, surprised, startled, stunned, shocked, aghast, taken aback, dumbfounded, dumbstruck, stupefied, dazed, speechless; informal flabbergasted; Brit. informal gob-smacked.

thus adverb (formal) *the studio handled production, thus cutting its costs:* thereby, so, consequently, accordingly, hence, as a result; formal ergo.

thwart verb *a fund was set up to thwart the plans of their former manager:* foil, frustrate, stand in the way of, impede, obstruct, hinder, hamper, forestall, derail, dash, stop, check, block, prevent, defeat; informal put paid to, do for, stymie; Brit. informal scupper, snooker.
OPPOSITES: facilitate.

ticket noun
1 *can I see your ticket?* permit, pass, authorization, warrant, token, coupon, voucher.
2 *a price ticket:* label, tag, sticker, tab, marker, docket.

tickle verb *the idea tickled Lewis:* amuse, entertain, divert, please, delight.

ticklish adjective
1 *privacy is a ticklish business where close neighbours are concerned:* difficult, problematic, tricky, delicate, sensitive, awkward, prickly, thorny, tough; vexed; informal sticky.
2 *groom these ticklish areas with a tea cloth:* sensitive, delicate, soft, tender.

t

tide noun *the whole tide of history seemed to be quickening:* course, movement, direction, trend, current, drift, run, turn, tendency.
□ **tide someone over**
she needed a small loan to tide her over: sustain, keep someone going, keep someone's head above water, see someone through; keep the wolf from the door; help out.

tidy adjective
1 *a tidy room:* neat, orderly, uncluttered, well ordered, in good order, well kept, shipshape, in apple-pie order, immaculate, spick and span, straight, trim, spruce.
2 *he's a very tidy person:* neat, trim, spruce, dapper, well groomed, well turned out; well organized, meticulous; fastidious.
3 (informal) *a tidy sum:* large, sizeable, considerable, substantial, generous, significant, appreciable, handsome, respectable, decent, goodly; informal not to be sneezed at.
OPPOSITES: untidy, messy.
▷ verb
1 *I'd better tidy up the living room:* put in order, clear up, sort out, straighten up, clean up, spruce up.
2 *she tidied herself up in the bathroom:* groom yourself, spruce yourself up, freshen yourself up, smarten yourself up; informal titivate yourself.

tie verb
1 *his hands were tied behind his back* | *we tied the other end of the rope to the truck:* bind, tether, hitch, strap, truss, rope, chain; make fast, moor, lash, attach, fasten, fix, secure, join, connect, link, couple.
2 *he bent to tie his shoelaces:* do up, lace, fasten, knot.
3 *women can feel tied by their childcare responsibilities:* restrict, restrain, limit, tie down, constrain, trammel, confine, cramp, hamper, handicap, hamstring, encumber, shackle, inhibit.
4 *a pay deal tied to a productivity agreement:* link, connect, couple, relate, join, marry; make conditional on, bind up with.
5 *they tied for second place:* draw, be equal, be even, be neck and neck.
▷ noun
1 *he tightened the ties of his robe:* lace, string, cord, fastening, fastener.
2 *it is important that we maintain our family ties:* bond, connection, link, relationship, attachment, affiliation, allegiance, friendship.
3 *there was a tie for first place:* draw, dead heat, deadlock.
4 (Brit.) *Turkey's World Cup tie against Holland:* match, game, contest, fixture, event.
□ **tie someone down**
she was afraid of being tied down. See **TIE** verb sense 3.

□ **tie in**
1 *the venue has been selected to tie in with preparations for the British Open:* fit in, harmonize, dovetail; take advantage of.
2 *does it all tie in when you look at the original requirements?* be consistent, tally, agree, accord, concur, be in tune, correspond, match; informal square.
□ **tie someone/something up**
1 *we tied the boat up and went ashore:* moor, make fast, tether.
2 *robbers tied her up and ransacked her home:* bind, truss up, chain up, fetter.
3 *he is tied up in meetings all morning:* occupy, engage, keep busy.
4 *they were anxious to tie up the contract:* finalize, conclude, complete, finish off, seal, set the seal on, settle, secure, clinch; informal wrap up.

tie-in noun connection, link, association, correlation, tie-up, interrelation, relationship, relation, interconnection.

tier noun
1 *I saw two tiers of empty seats:* row, rank, bank, line; layer, level.
2 *the most senior tier of management:* grade, echelon, layer, level, stratum.

tight adjective
1 *he took a tight grip on her arm:* firm, fast, secure, fixed, clenched.
2 *the rope was pulled tight:* taut, rigid, stiff, tense, stretched, strained.
3 *tight jeans:* tight-fitting, close-fitting, narrow, figure-hugging, skintight.
4 *the stuffing is a tight mass of fibres:* compact, compacted, compressed, dense, solid.
5 *it was certainly a tight space:* small, tiny, narrow, limited, restricted, confined, cramped, constricted, uncomfortable.
6 *tight limits on the use of pesticides:* strict, rigorous, stringent, tough, rigid, firm, uncompromising.
7 *he's in a tight spot:* difficult, tricky, delicate, awkward, problematic, worrying, precarious; informal sticky; Brit. informal dodgy.
8 *a nice tight piece of writing:* succinct, concise, pithy, incisive, crisp, condensed, to the point.
9 *it's going to be a tight race:* close, even, evenly matched, well matched; hard-fought, neck and neck.
10 *money is a bit tight just now:* limited, restricted, in short supply, scarce, depleted, diminished, low, inadequate, insufficient.
OPPOSITES: slack, loose, spacious.

tighten verb
1 *I tightened the screws:* screw up, give another turn to, make fast.
2 *he tightened his grip:* strengthen, harden.
3 *she tightened the rope:* tauten, make/draw tight, stretch, strain, stiffen, tense.
4 *he tightened his lips:* narrow, constrict, contract, compress, screw up, pucker, purse.
5 *security in the area has been tightened:*

increase, make stricter, toughen up, heighten, scale up; informal beef up .
OPPOSITES: loosen, slacken, relax.

tight-fisted adjective (informal) mean, miserly, parsimonious, niggardly, close-fisted, penny-pinching, cheese-paring, Scrooge-like, close; informal stingy, tight; N. Amer. informal cheap.
OPPOSITES: generous.

tight-lipped adjective *her father remained tight-lipped during the drive home:* reticent, uncommunicative, unforthcoming, silent, taciturn; informal mum.
OPPOSITES: forthcoming.

tilt verb *the ground seemed to tilt:* slope, tip, lean, list, bank, slant, incline, pitch, cant, careen, angle.
▷ noun *a tilt of some 45°:* slope, list, camber, gradient, bank, slant, incline, pitch, cant, bevel, angle.
□ **at full tilt**
they charged full tilt down the side of the hill: at full speed, at full pelt, as fast as your legs can carry you, at a gallop, helter-skelter, headlong, at breakneck speed; literary apace; informal hell for leather, at the double, like the wind, like greased lightning; Brit. informal like the clappers, at a rate of knots.

timber noun
1 *the houses were built of timber:* wood; N. Amer. lumber.
2 *we burned the timbers of wrecked ships:* beam, spar, plank, batten, lath, board, joist, rafter.

timbre noun tone, sound, quality, voice, colour, tonality, resonance.

time noun
1 *late at night was the best time to leave:* moment, point, juncture, occasion; hour, minute, second.
2 *he worked there for a time:* while, spell, stretch, stint, span, season, interval, period, length of time, duration, run, space, phase, stage, term; Brit. informal patch.
3 *the time of the dinosaurs:* era, age, epoch, period, years, days; generation, date.
4 *tunes in waltz time:* rhythm, tempo, beat; metre, measure, cadence, pattern.
▷ verb *the meeting was timed for three o'clock:* schedule, set, set up, arrange, organize, fix, fix up, book, line up, slot in, prearrange, timetable, plan; N. Amer. slate.
□ **all the time**
he works all the time: constantly, the entire/whole time, around the clock, day and night, night and day, {morning, noon, and night}, {day in, day out}, at all times, always, without a break, ceaselessly, endlessly, incessantly, perpetually, permanently, interminably, continuously, continually, eternally, unremittingly, remorselessly, relentlessly; informal 24-7.

□ **at one time**
she was a nurse at one time: formerly, previously, once, in the past, at one point, once upon a time, in days/times gone by, in times past, in the old days, long ago.
□ **at the same time**
1 *they arrived at the same time:* simultaneously, at the same instant/ moment, together, as a group, at once, at one and the same time; in unison, in concert, en masse, as one.
2 *I can't really explain it, but at the same time I'm not convinced:* nonetheless, even so, however, but, still, yet, though; in spite of that, despite that, be that as it may, for all that, that said; notwithstanding, regardless, anyway, anyhow.
□ **at times**
at times she can be very cruel: occasionally, sometimes, from time to time, now and then, every so often, once in a while, on occasion, off and on, at intervals, periodically, sporadically.
□ **behind the times**
the book is years behind the times: old-fashioned, out of date, outmoded, outdated, dated, old, passé; informal out of the ark, clunky.
□ **for the time being**
the project has been put on the back burner for the time being: for now, for the moment, for the present, in the interim, in/for the meantime, for a short time, briefly; temporarily, provisionally, pro tem; informal for the minute.
□ **from time to time**
I still travel abroad from time to time: occasionally, sometimes, now and then, every so often, once in a while, on occasion, on and off, off and on, at intervals, periodically, sporadically.
□ **in time**
1 *I came back in time for the party:* early enough, in good time, punctually, on time, not too late, with time to spare, on schedule.
2 *in time, she will forget about him:* eventually, in the end, in due course, by and by, finally; one day, some day, sometime, sooner or later.
□ **many a time**
many a time they went to bed hungry: frequently, regularly, often, very often, all the time, habitually, customarily, routinely; again and again, time and again, over and over again, repeatedly, continually; N. Amer. oftentimes.
□ **on time**
the train arrived on time: punctually, in good time, to/on schedule, when expected; informal on the dot, bang on time.
□ **time after time.** See **MANY A TIME.**

> WORD LINKS
> **chronological, temporal** relating to time
> **horology** the study and measurement of time

time-honoured adjective *the barley is turned by hand in the time-honoured*

fashion: traditional, established, long-established, long-standing, long-lived, age-old, enduring, lasting, tried and tested.
OPPOSITES: modern.

timeless adjective *the timeless beauty of the music:* lasting, enduring, ageless, permanent, perennial, abiding, unfailing, unchanging, unvarying, never-changing, changeless, unfading, unending, undying, deathless, immortal, eternal, everlasting, immutable.
OPPOSITES: ephemeral.

timely adjective *a timely warning:* opportune, well timed, at the right time, convenient, appropriate, expedient, seasonable, felicitous.
OPPOSITES: ill-timed.

timetable noun *a bus timetable | I have a very full timetable:* schedule, programme, agenda, calendar, itinerary, roster, rota, list.
▷ verb *German lessons were timetabled for Wednesdays:* schedule, set, arrange, organize, fix, time, line up; N. Amer. slate.

time-worn adjective *a time-worn expression:* hackneyed, trite, banal, platitudinous, clichéd, stock, conventional, unoriginal, overused, overworked, tired, stale; informal old hat.
OPPOSITES: new, fresh.

timid adjective *a timid boy with little self-confidence:* fearful, afraid, faint-hearted, timorous, nervous, scared, frightened, cowardly, pusillanimous, lily-livered, spineless; shy, diffident, self-effacing; informal wimpish, gutless.
OPPOSITES: bold.

tinge verb
1 *a mass of white blossom tinged with pink:* tint, colour, stain, shade.
2 *his optimism is tinged with realism:* touch, colour, qualify, temper; imbue, permeate.
▷ noun
1 *the light had a blue tinge to it:* tint, colour, shade, tone, hue.
2 *a tinge of cynicism:* trace, note, touch, suggestion, hint, bit, scintilla, savour, flavour, element, streak, vein, suspicion, soupçon.

tingle verb *her flesh still tingled from the shock:* prickle, sting; tremble, quiver, shiver.
▷ noun *she felt a tingle of anticipation:* prickle, tingling, pricking, sting; tremor, thrill, quiver, shiver; goose pimples, gooseflesh; N. Amer. goosebumps.

tinker verb *a workman was tinkering with the engine:* fiddle with, adjust, play about with; Brit. informal muck about with.

tinkle verb & noun ring, jingle, jangle, chime, peal, ding, ping.

tinny adjective
1 *tinny music played in the background:* jangly, jingly, tinkly, thin.
2 *a tinny little car:* cheap, inferior, gimcrack, shoddy, jerry-built; informal tacky, tatty, rubbishy.

tint noun *the sky was taking on an apricot tint:* shade, colour, tone, hue, tinge, cast, tincture, flush, blush.

tiny adjective minute, minuscule, microscopic, very small; little, mini, diminutive, miniature, scaled down, baby, toy, Lilliputian; Scottish wee; informal teeny, teensy, itsy-bitsy, pint-sized; Brit. informal titchy, tiddly.
OPPOSITES: huge.

tip¹ noun
1 *the tip of the spear was still sharp:* point, end, extremity, head, spike, prong, tine, nib.
2 *the sticks have steel tips fitted to protect them:* cap, cover, ferrule.

tip² verb
1 *the boat tipped over:* overturn, turn over, topple over, fall over; keel over, capsize, turn turtle.
2 *a whale could tip over a small boat:* upset, overturn, topple over, turn over, knock over, push over, upend, capsize.
3 *the car tipped to one side:* lean, tilt, list, slope, bank, slant, incline, pitch.
4 *she tipped the water into the trough:* pour, empty, drain, unload, dump; decant.

tip³ noun
1 *he left the waiter a generous tip:* present, gift, reward, bonus; formal gratuity; (in India and some eastern countries) baksheesh.
2 *lots of useful tips to help you make the right choice:* piece of advice, suggestion, pointer, recommendation; clue, hint.

tip-off noun (informal) *the police were acting on an anonymous tip-off:* warning, lead, forewarning; hint, clue; advice, notification, information, intelligence.

tirade noun *TV bosses have scrapped a tribute to the footballer because of his drunken tirade:* diatribe, harangue, rant, onslaught, attack, polemic, denunciation, broadside, fulmination, condemnation, censure, criticism.

tire verb
1 *the ascent grew steeper and he began to tire:* get tired, weaken, flag, droop.
2 *the journey had tired him:* exhaust, tire out, wear out, fatigue, drain, weary, wash out, overtire, enervate; informal knock out, take it out of, do in; Brit. informal knacker.
3 *they soon tired of his difficult behaviour:* weary, get tired, get sick; informal get fed up.

tired adjective
1 *you're just tired from all the travelling:* exhausted, worn out, weary, fatigued,

t

drained, enervated; informal done in, all in, ready to drop, dead beat, dog-tired, shattered, bushed, knocked out, wiped out; Brit. informal knackered, whacked.
2 *are you tired of having him here yet?* bored with/by, weary of, sick of; informal fed up with.
3 *a series of tired clichés:* hackneyed, overused, overworked, worn out, stale, clichéd, hoary, stock, stereotyped, predictable, unimaginative, unoriginal, uninspired, dull, boring, routine; informal old hat, corny, played out.
OPPOSITES: energetic, lively, fresh.

tiredness noun fatigue, weariness, exhaustion, enervation, inertia; sleepiness, drowsiness, somnolence.
OPPOSITES: energy.

tireless adjective vigorous, energetic, industrious, determined, enthusiastic, keen, zealous, spirited, dynamic, dogged, tenacious, persevering, untiring, unwearying, indefatigable, unflagging.
OPPOSITES: lazy.

tiresome adjective *his lengthy speeches could be very tiresome:* boring, dull, tedious, wearisome, wearing, uninteresting; annoying, irritating, trying, irksome, vexatious, troublesome; informal aggravating.
OPPOSITES: interesting, enjoyable.

tiring adjective *a long and tiring journey:* exhausting, wearying, taxing, fatiguing, wearing, enervating, draining; hard, heavy, arduous, strenuous, onerous, uphill, demanding, gruelling; informal killing, murderous; Brit. informal knackering.
OPPOSITES: easy.

tissue noun *the X-rays were able to penetrate living tissue:* matter, material, substance, structure; flesh.

titbit noun
1 *a plate of tasty titbits:* delicacy, tasty morsel, dainty, treat; snack, nibble, savoury, appetizer; informal goody.
2 *a fascinating titbit:* piece of gossip, bit of scandal, piece of information.

titillate verb *the play shocked and titillated audiences around the world when it first hit the theatre:* excite, tantalize, stimulate, stir, thrill, arouse; interest, attract, fascinate; informal turn on.
OPPOSITES: bore.

> **USAGE**
>
> Do not confuse **titillate** with **titivate**. **Titillate** means 'to interest or excite someone, especially sexually', while **titivate** means 'to make smarter or more attractive' (*she titivated herself in front of the mirror*).

titillating adjective exciting, arousing, stimulating, sexy, thrilling, provocative, tantalizing, interesting, fascinating; suggestive, salacious, lurid; informal saucy.

titivate verb (informal) *she titivated herself in front of the hall mirror:* groom, smarten up, spruce up, freshen up, preen, primp, prink; tidy, arrange; informal doll up, tart up.

title noun
1 *can you read the title under the picture?* name, heading, caption, headline.
2 *the title 'Duke of Marlborough':* description, designation, name, form of address; epithet; rank, office, position.
3 *the company publishes 400 titles a year:* publication, work, book, newspaper, paper, magazine, periodical.
4 *an Olympic title:* championship, crown, first place; medal, gold.
5 *the occupiers gained title to the land two years later:* ownership, right, claim, entitlement, proprietorship, possession, tenure.
▷ verb *a policy paper titled 'Law and Order':* call, entitle, name, dub, designate, style, term.

titter verb & noun giggle, snigger, chuckle, laugh; informal chortle.

tittle-tattle noun *she would never listen to tittle-tattle:* gossip, rumours, idle talk, hearsay, whispers; scandal.

toast noun
1 *he raised his glass in a toast:* tribute, salute.
2 *he was the toast of the West End:* darling, favourite, pet, heroine, hero; talk; Brit. informal blue-eyed boy/girl.
▷ verb
1 *I toasted a piece of bread and buttered it:* grill, brown.
2 *we toasted the couple with champagne:* drink to the health of, drink to, salute, honour, pay tribute to.

today adverb *the complex tasks demanded of computers today:* nowadays, now, these days, in these times, currently, at the moment, at present.

toddle verb *the child toddled towards him:* totter, teeter, wobble, falter, stumble.

together adverb
1 *they are good friends and work together:* with each other, in conjunction, jointly, in cooperation, in collaboration, in partnership, in combination, in league, side by side, hand in hand, shoulder to shoulder; in collusion, hand in glove.
2 *they both spoke together:* simultaneously, at the same time, at once, all together, as a group, in unison, in concert, in chorus, as one, with one voice.
OPPOSITES: separately.

toil verb
1 *she rolled up her sleeves and toiled all night:* work hard, labour, slave, grind away, strive, work your fingers to the bone, work like a Trojan/slave; informal slog away, plug away, beaver away, keep your nose to

the grindstone, work your socks off, sweat blood; Brit. informal **graft**.
2 *she began to toil up the steep cliff path:* struggle, trudge, tramp, traipse, plod, trek, drag yourself; informal **slog**; N. Amer. informal **schlep**.
▷ **noun** *all he knew was a life of toil:* hard work, labour, exertion, slaving, drudgery, effort, industry, {blood, sweat, and tears}; informal **slog**, **elbow grease**; Brit. informal **graft**.

token noun
1 *please accept this as a token of our appreciation:* symbol, sign, emblem, badge, representation, indication, mark, manifestation, expression, pledge, demonstration, recognition; evidence, proof.
2 *a book token:* voucher, coupon, credit note.
3 *I need a car-wash token:* counter, disc, chip, piece, man.
▷ **adjective**
1 *a one-day token strike:* symbolic, emblematic, indicative, representative.
2 *the practice now meets only token resistance:* slight, nominal, minimal, minor, mild, superficial, inconsequential, perfunctory, half-hearted, desultory.

tolerable adjective
1 *we try to make life more tolerable for them:* bearable, endurable, supportable.
2 *he had a tolerable voice:* fairly good, passable, adequate, all right, acceptable, satisfactory, not bad, average, fair; informal OK, so-so.
OPPOSITES: intolerable.

tolerance noun
1 *an attitude of tolerance towards other people:* forbearance, toleration, acceptance, indulgence, understanding, open-mindedness, broad-mindedness, liberalism, patience, charity.
2 *the plant's tolerance of pollution:* resistance to, resilience to, endurance of.
3 *a 1% maximum tolerance in measurement:* deviation, variation, fluctuation, play, leeway; inaccuracy, imprecision.
OPPOSITES: intolerance.

tolerant adjective
forbearing, open-minded, broad-minded, liberal, unprejudiced, unbiased, patient, long-suffering, understanding, charitable, lenient, indulgent, permissive, free and easy, easy-going, lax.
OPPOSITES: intolerant.

tolerate verb
1 *a regime that is unwilling to tolerate dissent:* allow, permit, condone, accept, swallow, countenance; formal **brook**.
2 *he couldn't tolerate her moods any longer:* endure, put up with, bear, take, stand, abide, support, stomach; informal **hack**; Brit. informal **stick**, **be doing with**.

toleration noun
forbearance, tolerance,

acceptance, indulgence, understanding, open-mindedness, broad-mindedness, liberalism, patience, charity.

toll[1] noun
1 *a motorway toll:* charge, fee, payment, levy, tariff, duty, tax.
2 *the toll of dead and injured:* number, count, tally, reckoning, total, sum total, grand total, sum; record, list, listing.

toll[2] verb
I heard the bell toll: ring, chime, strike, peal; sound, clang, resound, reverberate.

tomb noun
burial chamber, sepulchre, mausoleum, vault, crypt, undercroft, catacomb, grave; historical **charnel house**.

tombstone noun
gravestone, headstone; memorial, monument.

tome noun
(humorous) *every 10 years he publishes a weighty tome about British social life:* book, volume, work, opus, publication, title.

tone noun
1 *the warm tone of the tuba:* timbre, sound, sound quality, voice, colour.
2 *his friendly tone:* intonation, tone of voice, way of speaking.
3 *the somewhat impatient tone of his letter:* mood, air, feel, flavour, note, attitude, character, temper.
4 *all I got was a dialling tone:* note, signal, beep, bleep.
5 *light tones of primrose, lavender, and rose:* shade, colour, hue, tint, tinge.
▷ **verb** *the caramel shirt toned well with her cream skirt:* harmonize, go, blend, coordinate, team; match, suit, complement.
□ **tone something down**
1 *the colour needs to be toned down a bit:* soften, lighten, mute, subdue.
2 *the papers refused to tone down their criticism:* moderate, modify, modulate, mitigate, temper, dampen, soften, subdue.

tongue noun
1 *he spoke in a foreign tongue:* language, vernacular; informal **lingo**.
2 *her sharp tongue:* way/manner of speaking, speech, expression, parlance.

WORD LINKS
lingual relating to the tongue or to speech or language

tongue-tied adjective
lost for words, speechless, inarticulate, struck dumb, dumbstruck; mute, dumb, silent.
OPPOSITES: talkative.

tonic noun
ginseng can be used as a natural tonic: stimulant, restorative, refreshment, booster; informal **pick-me-up**.

too adverb
1 *invasion would be too risky:* excessively, overly, over-, unduly, immoderately, inordinately, unreasonably.
2 *he was unhappy, too, you know:* also, as

well, in addition, additionally, into the bargain, besides, furthermore, moreover, on top of that, to boot.

tool noun *garden tools:* implement, utensil, instrument, device, apparatus, gadget, appliance, machine, contrivance, contraption; informal gizmo.
▷ **verb** *the red leather cover is tooled in gold:* ornament, embellish, decorate, work, cut, chase.

tooth noun fang, tusk; molar, incisor; informal gnasher.

> WORD LINKS
> **dental** relating to teeth
> **odontology** the scientific study of teeth

top noun
1 *we got to the top of the cliff:* summit, peak, crest, crown, brow, head, tip, apex, vertex.
2 *the top of the table:* surface, upper part, upper layer.
3 *the top of the coffee jar:* lid, cap, cover, stopper, cork.
4 *by 1981 he was at the top of his profession:* height, high point, peak, pinnacle, zenith, acme, culmination, climax, crowning point; prime.
OPPOSITES: bottom, base.
▷ **adjective**
1 *the top floor:* highest, topmost, uppermost, upmost.
2 *one of the top generals in the army just quit:* highest-ranking, most important, chief, foremost, leading, principal, pre-eminent, greatest, elite, premier.
3 *the top Paris hotels:* best, finest, superior, choice, prime, premier, superlative, second to none, select, superb, top-quality, top-grade, first-rate, first-class, grade A; informal top-notch.
4 *they are travelling at top speed:* maximum, maximal, greatest, utmost.
OPPOSITES: bottom, inferior, minimum.
▷ **verb**
1 *sales are expected to top £1.3 billion:* exceed, surpass, go beyond, better, beat, outstrip, outdo, outshine, eclipse, cap, go one better than.
2 *their debut CD is currently topping the charts:* lead, head, be at the top of.
3 *as they topped the next hill, the city came into view:* reach the top of, crest, conquer; climb, scale.
4 *chocolate mousse topped with cream:* cover, cap, coat, smother; finish, garnish.
□ **over the top** (informal)
her reaction was a bit over the top: excessive, immoderate, inordinate, extreme, exaggerated, extravagant, overblown, too much, unreasonable, disproportionate, undue, unwarranted, uncalled for, unnecessary, going too far; informal a bit much, OTT.
□ **top something up** (Brit.)
fill, refill, refresh, freshen, replenish, recharge; supplement, add to, augment.

topic noun subject, subject matter, theme, issue, matter, point, talking point, question, concern, argument, thesis, text, keynote.

topical adjective current, up to date, up to the minute, contemporary, recent, relevant; newsworthy, in the news.
OPPOSITES: passé.

topmost adjective *the tree's topmost branches:* highest, top, uppermost, upmost.

topple verb
1 *she toppled over:* fall, tumble, overbalance, overturn, tip, keel; lose your balance.
2 *protesters toppled a huge statue:* knock over, upset, push over, tip over, upend.
3 *a plot to topple the government:* overthrow, bring down, oust, unseat, depose, overturn, defeat, get rid of, dislodge, eject.

topsy-turvy adjective
1 *there is one constant in a topsy-turvy world:* upside-down, muddled, chaotic, mad, crazy; informal messed-up.
2 *everything in the flat was topsy-turvy:* in disarray, in a mess, in a muddle, in disorder, disordered, chaotic, disorganized, awry, upside down, at sixes and sevens; informal every which way, higgledy-piggledy.
OPPOSITES: ordered, neat.

torment noun *months of mental and emotional torment:* agony, suffering, torture, ordeal, pain, anguish, misery, distress, affliction, trauma; hell, purgatory.
▷ **verb**
1 *she was tormented by shame:* torture, afflict, rack, harrow, plague, haunt, distress, agonize.
2 *she began to torment the two younger boys:* tease, taunt, bait, harass, provoke, goad, plague, bother, trouble, persecute; informal needle.

torn adjective
1 *a torn shirt:* ripped, cut, slit; ragged, tattered, in tatters, in ribbons; literary rent.
2 *she was torn between the two options:* wavering, vacillating, irresolute, dithering, uncertain, unsure, undecided, in a dilemma, in two minds.

tornado noun hurricane, cyclone, typhoon, whirlwind, storm; N. Amer. twister.

torpor noun *my opportunity to escape from the torpor into which I had sunk:* lethargy, sluggishness, inertia, inactivity, listlessness, languor, lassitude, idleness, passivity, somnolence, weariness, sleepiness; literary accidie.

torrent noun
1 *a torrent of water:* flood, deluge, inundation, spate, cascade, rush, stream, current, flow, tide.

t

2 *a torrent of abuse:* outburst, outpouring, stream, flood, volley, barrage, tide, spate.
OPPOSITES: trickle.

torrential adjective *torrential rain caused the game to be stopped:* heavy, pouring, pelting, teeming, driving, lashing, drenching, pounding, persistent, relentless, copious, severe, violent.

torrid adjective
1 *I was panting like a dog in the torrid heat and thin air:* hot, dry, scorching, searing, blazing, blistering, sweltering, burning; informal boiling, baking, sizzling.
2 *a torrid affair:* passionate, ardent, lustful, amorous; informal steamy, sizzling, hot.
OPPOSITES: cold.

tortuous adjective
1 *a tortuous route up the mountain:* twisting, twisty, winding, windy, zigzag, sinuous, snaky, meandering, wandering, serpentine.
2 *a tortuous argument:* convoluted, complicated, complex, labyrinthine, lengthy, involved, confusing, hard to follow.
OPPOSITES: straight, straightforward.

torture noun
1 *the torture of political prisoners:* abuse, cruel treatment, ill-treatment, maltreatment, persecution.
2 *the sheer torture of waiting for the results:* torment, agony, suffering, anguish, misery, distress, trauma; hell, purgatory.
▷verb
1 *the security forces routinely tortured suspects:* abuse, hurt, inflict pain on, treat cruelly, ill-treat, mistreat, maltreat, persecute; informal work over.
2 *he was tortured by grief:* torment, rack, afflict, harrow, plague, agonize.

toss verb
1 *he tossed his tools into the boot:* throw, hurl, fling, cast, pitch, lob, propel, project, launch; Brit. informal bung; informal heave, chuck, sling.
2 *he tossed a coin and it landed heads up:* flip, spin, flick.
3 *I tossed and turned all night:* flail, thrash about, wriggle, writhe, squirm.
4 *the ship tossed about on the waves:* pitch, lurch, rock, roll, plunge, reel, sway, wallow, make heavy weather.
5 *toss the salad ingredients together:* shake, stir, turn, mix, combine.

tot[1] noun *a tot of rum:* drink, nip, drop; Scottish dram; informal shot, slug, finger; Brit. informal snifter.

tot[2] verb
□ tot something up (Brit.)
1 *he totted up some figures:* add, total, count, calculate, compute, reckon, tally.
2 *we've totted up 89 victories:* accumulate, build up, amass, accrue, notch up, achieve.

total adjective
1 *the total cost of the funeral:* entire, complete, whole, full, comprehensive, combined, aggregate, gross, overall.
2 *it was a total disaster:* complete, utter, absolute, thorough, perfect, downright, out-and-out, outright, thoroughgoing, all-out, sheer, positive, prize, rank, unmitigated, unqualified; Brit. informal right, proper.
▷noun *a total of £160,000:* sum, sum total, grand total, aggregate; whole, entirety, totality.
▷verb
1 *the prize money totalled £33,050:* add up to, amount to, come to, run to, make, work out as.
2 *he totalled up his score:* add up, count, reckon, compute, work out; Brit. tot up.

totalitarian adjective autocratic, undemocratic, one-party, dictatorial, tyrannical, despotic, fascistic, oppressive, repressive, illiberal; authoritarian, absolute, absolutist, fundamentalist.
OPPOSITES: democratic.

totality noun entirety, whole, total, aggregate, sum, sum total; all, everything.

totally adverb completely, entirely, wholly, fully, utterly, thoroughly, absolutely, perfectly, unreservedly, unconditionally, quite, altogether, downright; in every way, in every respect, one hundred per cent, every inch, to the hilt.
OPPOSITES: partly.

totter verb *he tottered off down the road:* teeter, stagger, wobble, stumble, shuffle, shamble, toddle; reel, sway, roll, lurch.

touch verb
1 *his shoes were touching the end of the bed:* be in contact with, come into contact with, meet, join, connect with, converge with, be against.
2 *he touched her cheek:* press, tap, pat, feel, stroke, fondle, caress, pet; brush, graze.
3 *sales touched twenty grand last year:* reach, come to, attain, make; rise to, soar to; sink to, drop to; informal hit.
4 *nobody can touch him when he's on form:* compare with, be on a par with, equal, match, be a match for, be in the same class/league as, rival, come/get close to, measure up to; better, beat; informal hold a candle to.
5 *you're not supposed to touch the things in the exhibition:* handle, hold, pick up, feel, move; meddle with, play with, fiddle with, interfere with, tamper with, disturb; use, make use of.
6 *state companies which have been touched by privatization:* affect, have an effect/impact on, make a difference to.
7 *Lisa felt touched by his kindness:* affect, move, stir, tug at someone's heartstrings; leave an impression on, have an effect on.

▷ **noun**
1 *her touch on his shoulder was hesitant:*
hand, fingers; caress, grip, embrace;
contact.
2 *he has lost none of his political touch:*
skill, skilfulness, expertise, dexterity,
deftness, adroitness, adeptness, ability,
talent, flair, facility, proficiency, knack,
technique, approach, style.
3 *there was a touch of bitterness in her
voice* | *add a touch of vinegar:* trace, bit,
suggestion, suspicion, hint, scintilla, tinge,
overtone, undertone; dash, taste, spot,
drop, dab, pinch, speck, soupçon.
4 *the gas lights are a nice touch:* detail,
feature, point; addition, accessory.
5 *have you been in touch with him?* contact,
communication, correspondence.
□ **touch and go**
*he's in recovery now, but the doctor said it
was touch and go for a while:* uncertain,
critical, hanging by a thread, close;
precarious, risky, hazardous, dangerous.
□ **touch down**
his plane touched down at Nice airport:
land, alight, come down, put down, arrive.
□ **touch something off**
*the proposal touched off a major political
storm:* cause, spark off, trigger, start, set in
motion, ignite, stir up, provoke, give rise
to, lead to, generate.
□ **touch on**
1 *many television programmes have
touched on the subject:* refer to, mention,
comment on, remark on, bring up, raise,
broach, allude to; cover, deal with.
2 *a self-confident manner touching on the
arrogant:* come close to, verge on, border
on, approach.
□ **touch something up**
*these paints are handy for touching up
small areas:* repaint, retouch, patch up,
fix up; renovate, refurbish, revamp; informal
do up.

┌─────────────────────────────────┐
│ **WORD LINKS**
│ **tactile** relating to the sense of touch
└─────────────────────────────────┘

touching adjective *there was a touching
reunion at the airport:* moving, affecting,
heart-warming, emotional, emotive,
tender, sentimental; poignant, sad; informal
tear-jerking.

touchstone noun *for nationalists, the
touchstone was their degree of independence
from the US:* criterion, standard, yardstick,
benchmark, barometer, litmus test;
measure, point of reference, norm, gauge,
test, guide, exemplar, model, pattern.

touchy adjective
1 *she can be so touchy:* sensitive, oversensitive, hypersensitive, easily offended,
thin-skinned; irritable, tetchy, testy,
crotchety, peevish, querulous, bad-
tempered, petulant; highly strung, tense;
informal snappy; Brit. informal ratty; N. Amer.
informal cranky.
2 *a touchy subject:* delicate, sensitive,

tricky, ticklish, embarrassing, awkward,
difficult; contentious, controversial.
OPPOSITES: affable.

tough adjective
1 *I donned a pair of tough leather gloves:*
durable, strong, resilient, sturdy, rugged,
solid, stout, hard-wearing, long-lasting,
heavy-duty, well built, made to last.
2 *the steak was rather tough:* chewy,
leathery, gristly, stringy, fibrous.
3 *he'll survive—he's pretty tough:* robust,
resilient, strong, hardy, rugged, fit; informal
hard.
4 *tough sentencing for persistent offenders:*
strict, stern, severe, stringent, rigorous,
hard, firm, hard-hitting, uncompromising;
unsentimental, unsympathetic.
5 *the training was pretty tough:* hard,
difficult, demanding, exacting, strenuous,
gruelling, arduous, heavy going, taxing,
tiring, exhausting, punishing, laborious,
stressful.
6 *these are tough questions for American
policymakers:* difficult, hard, knotty,
thorny, tricky.
OPPOSITES: flimsy, tender, soft, mild, easy.
▷ **noun** *a gang of toughs:* ruffian, thug,
hooligan, bully boy; informal roughneck,
heavy, bruiser; Brit. informal yob, yobbo.

toughen verb
1 *the process toughens the wood fibres:*
strengthen, reinforce, harden, fortify,
temper, anneal.
2 *measures to toughen prison discipline:*
stiffen, tighten up; increase, step up;
informal beef up.
OPPOSITES: weaken.

tour noun
1 *a three-day walking tour:* trip, excursion,
journey, expedition, jaunt, outing; trek,
safari.
2 *we had a tour of the factory:* visit,
inspection, guided tour, walkabout.
3 *his tour of duty in Ulster:* stint, stretch,
spell, turn, assignment, period.
▷ **verb**
1 *this hotel is well placed for touring
Somerset:* travel round, explore, visit;
holiday, sightsee; informal do.
2 *the prince toured a local factory:* visit, go
round, walk round, inspect.

tourist noun traveller, sightseer,
visitor, backpacker, globetrotter, day
tripper, tripper; Brit. holidaymaker; N. Amer.
vacationer.
OPPOSITES: local.

tournament noun competition, contest,
championship, meeting, meet, event,
match, fixture.

tousled adjective *she ran a hand through
her tousled hair:* untidy, unkempt,
dishevelled, wind-blown, messy, messed
up, rumpled, uncombed, ungroomed,
tangled, wild; N. Amer. informal mussed up.
OPPOSITES: tidy.

t

tout verb
1 *in the street, merchants were touting their wares:* peddle, sell, hawk, offer; Brit. informal flog.
2 *he's being touted as the next Scotland manager:* recommend, endorse, talk up, support, propose.
□ **tout for**
minicab drivers were touting for business: solicit, seek, drum up, canvas, look for, ask for, appeal for.

tow verb *the car was towed back to the garage:* pull, haul, drag, draw, tug; informal lug.

towards preposition
1 *they were driving towards her flat:* in the direction of, to; on the way to, on the road to, en route for.
2 *towards evening dark clouds gathered:* just before, shortly before, near, nearing, around, approaching, close to, coming to, getting on for.
3 *her attitude towards politics:* regarding, as regards, with regard to, in regard to, respecting, in relation to, concerning, about, apropos.
4 *a grant towards the cost of new buses:* as a contribution to, for, to help with.

tower noun platform, column, mast, turret, steeple, spire, belfry, campanile, minaret.
▷ verb *snow-capped peaks towered over the valley:* soar, rise, rear, loom; (**tower over**) overshadow, overhang, dominate.

towering adjective
1 *towering buildings of glass and steel:* high, tall, lofty, soaring, multi-storey; giant, gigantic, enormous, huge, massive; informal ginormous.
2 *he was a towering intellect:* outstanding, pre-eminent, leading, foremost, finest, top, surpassing, supreme, great, incomparable, unrivalled, unsurpassed, peerless.
3 *he was in a towering rage:* terrible, intense, overpowering, mighty, violent, vehement, passionate; incandescent, burning.

town noun urban area, built-up area, conurbation, municipality; city, metropolis, megalopolis; Brit. borough; Scottish burgh.
OPPOSITES: country.

WORD LINKS
municipal, **urban** relating to a town

toxic adjective poisonous, virulent, noxious, dangerous, harmful, injurious, pernicious.
OPPOSITES: harmless.

toy noun
1 *he always gets loads of toys for Christmas:* plaything, game.
2 *an executive toy:* gadget, device; trinket, knick-knack; informal gizmo.

▷ adjective *he brandished a toy gun:* model, imitation, replica; miniature.
□ **toy with**
1 *I was toying with the idea of writing a book:* think about, consider, flirt with, entertain the possibility of; informal kick around.
2 *Adam toyed with his glasses:* fiddle with, play with, fidget with, twiddle; finger.

trace verb
1 *police hope to trace the owner of the jewellery:* track down, find, discover, detect, unearth, turn up, hunt down, ferret out, run to ground.
2 *the analysis traces the history of such beliefs:* outline, map out, sketch out, delineate, depict, show, indicate.
▷ noun
1 *no trace had been found of the missing plane:* vestige, sign, mark, indication, evidence, clue; remains, remnant, relic, survival.
2 *a trace of bitterness crept into her voice:* bit, touch, hint, suggestion, suspicion, shadow, whiff; drop, dash, tinge, speck, shred; informal smidgen, tad.
3 *the ground was hard and they left no traces:* trail, tracks, marks, prints, footprints; spoor.

track noun
1 *we followed a gravel track:* path, pathway, footpath, lane, trail, route, way, course.
2 *the final lap of the track:* course, racecourse, racetrack; Brit. circuit.
3 *he found the tracks of a grey fox:* traces, marks, prints, footprints, trail, spoor.
4 *commuters had to walk along the track:* line, railway line, rails.
5 *the album's title track:* song, recording, number, piece.
▷ verb *he tracked a bear for 40 km:* follow, trail, trace, pursue, shadow, stalk, keep an eye on, keep in sight; informal tail.
□ **track someone/something down**
it took seven years to track down the wreck of the ship: discover, find, detect, hunt down/out, unearth, uncover, turn up, dig up, ferret out, bring to light, run to earth, run to ground.

tract noun *the chiefs owned large tracts of land:* area, region, expanse, sweep, stretch, extent, belt, swathe, zone.

tractable adjective *children are not as tractable as they used to be:* malleable, manageable, amenable, pliable, yielding, complaisant, compliant, persuadable, accommodating, docile, biddable, obedient, submissive, meek.
OPPOSITES: intractable, recalcitrant.

traction noun grip, purchase, friction, adhesion.

trade noun
1 *a move to ban all trade in ivory:* commerce, buying and selling, dealing, business, marketing, merchandising;

dealings, transactions; traffic, trafficking.
2 *the glazier's trade:* craft, occupation, job, career, profession, business, line of work, métier, vocation, calling, walk of life, field; work, employment.
▷ **verb**
1 *he made his fortune trading in beaver pelts:* deal, buy and sell, market, merchandise; peddle, hawk, traffic; Brit. informal flog.
2 *the business is trading at a loss:* operate, run, do business.
3 *I traded the old machine for a newer model:* swap, exchange, switch; barter.

> WORD LINKS
> **mercantile** relating to trade or commerce

trademark noun
1 *the company's trademark:* logo, emblem, sign, mark, stamp, symbol, device, badge, crest, monogram, colophon; trade name, brand name, proprietary name.
2 *it had all the trademarks of a Mafia hit:* characteristic, hallmark, telltale sign, sign, trait, quality, attribute, feature.

trader noun dealer, merchant, buyer, seller, distributor, vendor, supplier, shopkeeper, retailer, wholesaler, broker, agent; trafficker; formal purveyor.

tradesman, tradeswoman noun
1 *tradesmen standing nonchalantly outside their stores:* shopkeeper, retailer, vendor; N. Amer. storekeeper; formal purveyor.
2 *a qualified tradesman:* craftsman, workman, artisan, technician.

tradition noun *an age-old tradition in our society:* custom, practice, convention, ritual, observance, way, unwritten law, usage, habit, institution.

traditional adjective *traditional Christmas festivities:* established, customary, time-honoured, classic, accustomed, standard, regular, normal, conventional, usual, orthodox, habitual, set, fixed, routine, ritual; old, age-old; literary wonted.

traffic noun
1 *the bridge is not open to traffic:* vehicles, cars and lorries, transport, transportation, freight, shipping.
2 *the illegal traffic in stolen art:* trade, trafficking, dealing, commerce, business, buying and selling; smuggling, black market; dealings, transactions.
▷ **verb** *he confessed to trafficking in gold and ivory:* trade, deal, do business, buy and sell; smuggle; informal run.

tragedy noun disaster, calamity, catastrophe, cataclysm; misfortune, trial, tribulation, affliction, adversity.

tragic adjective
1 *a tragic accident:* disastrous, calamitous, catastrophic, cataclysmic, devastating, terrible, dreadful, awful, appalling, horrendous; fatal, deadly, mortal, lethal.

2 *a tragic tale:* sad, unhappy, pathetic, moving, distressing, painful, harrowing, heart-rending, wretched, sorry; melancholy, doleful, mournful; informal gut-wrenching.
3 *a tragic waste of talent:* dreadful, terrible, awful, deplorable, lamentable, regrettable; formal grievous.
OPPOSITES: fortunate, happy.

trail noun
1 *he left a trail of clues:* series, string, chain, succession, sequence.
2 *hungry wolves on the trail of their injured prey:* track, spoor, path, scent; traces, marks, signs, prints, footprints.
3 *a trail of ants:* line, column, train, file, procession, string, chain, convoy; queue.
4 *country parks with nature trails:* path, pathway, way, footpath, track, course, route.
▷ **verb**
1 *her robe trailed along the ground:* drag, sweep, be drawn.
2 *the roses grew wild, their stems trailing over the banks:* hang, droop, dangle, fall, spill, cascade.
3 *Sharpe suspected that they were trailing him:* follow, pursue, track, shadow, stalk; informal tail.
4 *the defending champions were trailing 10–5 at half time:* lose, be down, be behind, lag behind.
5 *I hate trailing round the shops:* trudge, plod, drag yourself, traipse, trek.
6 *her voice trailed off:* fade, tail off/away, grow faint, die away, dwindle, subside, peter out, fizzle out.

train verb
1 *the bank is training its staff to use the software:* instruct, teach, coach, tutor, school, educate, prime, drill, ground; inculcate, indoctrinate.
2 *she's training to be a hairdresser:* study, learn, prepare.
3 *with the Olympics in mind, athletes are training hard:* exercise, work out, get into shape, practise.
4 *she trained the gun on his chest:* aim, point, direct, level, focus; take aim, zero in on.
▷ **noun**
1 *we saw a train of elephants:* procession, line, file, column, convoy, cavalcade, caravan, queue, string.
2 *a minister and his train of attendants:* retinue, entourage, cortège, following, staff, household, court; attendants, retainers, followers, bodyguards informal groupies.
3 *a bizarre train of events:* chain, string, series, sequence, succession, set, course, cycle, concatenation.

trainer noun coach, instructor, teacher, tutor, mentor; handler.

training noun
1 *in-house training for staff:* instruction, teaching, coaching, tuition, tutoring,

schooling, education; indoctrination, inculcation.
2 *four months' hard training before the match:* exercise, exercises, working out; practice, preparation.

traipse verb *I haven't time to go traipsing round art galleries:* trudge, trek, tramp, trail, plod, drag yourself; informal slog.

trait noun characteristic, attribute, feature, quality, property; habit, custom, mannerism, idiosyncrasy, peculiarity, quirk, oddity, foible.

traitor noun *he was tried in a military court as a traitor:* betrayer, back-stabber, double-crosser, double-dealer, renegade, Judas, quisling, fifth columnist; turncoat, defector, deserter; collaborator, informer, double agent.

traitorous adjective treacherous, disloyal, treasonous, treasonable, back-stabbing; double-crossing, double-dealing, faithless, unfaithful, two-faced, duplicitous, deceitful; literary false, perfidious.
OPPOSITES: loyal.

trajectory noun course, path, route, track, line, orbit.

tramp verb
1 *men were tramping through the shrubbery:* trudge, plod, stamp, trample, lumber, clump, clomp, stump, stomp; informal galumph.
2 *he spent ten days tramping through the jungle:* trek, trudge, drag yourself, walk, hike, march, traipse; informal slog.
▷ noun
1 *a dirty old tramp:* vagrant, vagabond, homeless person, down-and-out; beggar, mendicant; N. Amer. hobo; N. Amer. informal bum.
2 *the regular tramp of the sentry's boots:* footstep, step, footfall, tread, stamp, stomp.
3 *we went for a tramp round Norwich:* trek, trudge, hike, march, walk, traipse; informal slog.

trample verb tread, tramp, stamp, stomp, walk over; squash, crush, flatten.

trance noun daze, stupor, dream, fugue.

tranquil adjective
1 *a wonderfully tranquil village:* peaceful, calm, restful, quiet, still, relaxing, undisturbed.
2 *Martha smiled, perfectly tranquil:* calm, serene, relaxed, unruffled, unperturbed, unflustered, untroubled, composed, {cool, calm, and collected}.
OPPOSITES: busy, excitable.

tranquillity noun *the tranquillity of the Norfolk countryside:* peace, restfulness, repose, calm, quiet, stillness.

tranquillize verb sedate, put under sedation, drug.
OPPOSITES: stimulate.

tranquillizer noun sedative, barbiturate, sleeping pill, narcotic, opiate; informal downer.
OPPOSITES: stimulant.

transact verb conduct, carry out, negotiate, do, perform, execute, take care of; settle, conclude, finish, clinch, accomplish.

transaction noun
1 *property transactions:* deal, undertaking, arrangement, bargain, negotiation, agreement, settlement; proceedings.
2 *the transactions of the Historical Society:* proceedings, report, records, minutes, account; archives.
3 *the transaction of government business:* conduct, carrying out, performance, execution.

transcend verb
1 *an issue that transcended party politics:* go beyond, rise above, cut across.
2 *his military exploits far transcended those of his predecessors:* surpass, exceed, beat, top, cap, outdo, outclass, outstrip, leave behind, outshine, eclipse, overshadow, put in the shade, upstage.

transcribe verb
1 *each interview was taped and transcribed:* write out/down, copy out, put on paper.
2 *a person who can take and transcribe shorthand:* transliterate, interpret, translate.

transcript noun text, transliteration, written/printed record.

transfer verb
1 *the hostages were transferred to a safe house:* move, convey, take, bring, shift, remove, carry, transport; transplant, relocate, resettle.
2 *the property was transferred to his wife:* hand over, pass on, make over, turn over, sign over, consign, devolve, assign, delegate.
▷ noun *he died shortly after his transfer to hospital:* move, conveyance, transferral, transference, relocation, removal, transplantation.

transfigure verb transform, transmute, change, alter, metamorphose; humorous transmogrify.

transfix verb
1 *he was transfixed by the images on the screen:* mesmerize, hypnotize, spellbind, bewitch, captivate, entrance, enthral, fascinate, enrapture, grip, rivet; root to the spot, paralyse.
2 *a field mouse is transfixed by the owl's curved talons:* impale, stab, spear, pierce, spike, skewer, gore, stick, run through.

transform verb *during his time there, he completely transformed the company:* change, alter, transfigure, transmute; revolutionize, overhaul; remodel, reshape, remould, reconstruct, rebuild, reorganize, rearrange, rework, renew, revamp, remake, convert; humorous transmogrify.

transformation noun *the radical transformation of British society:* change, alteration, metamorphosis, transfiguration, transmutation, sea change; revolution, overhaul; remodelling, reshaping, reconstruction, conversion, rebuilding, reorganization, rearrangement, reworking, renewal, revamp, remaking; humorous transmogrification.

transgress verb
1 *if they transgress, the punishment is harsh:* misbehave, behave badly, break the law, err, fall from grace, stray from the straight and narrow, sin, do wrong, go astray.
2 *she had transgressed an unwritten social law:* infringe, breach, contravene, disobey, defy, violate, break, flout.

transgression noun *this was a harsh punishment for past transgressions:* offence, crime, sin, wrong, wrongdoing, misdemeanour, misdeed, lawbreaking; error, lapse, fault.

transgressor noun wrongdoer, offender, miscreant, lawbreaker, criminal, villain, felon, guilty party, culprit; sinner, evil-doer; formal malefactor.

transient adjective *these transient joys will fade all too soon:* short-lived, temporary, transitory, short-term, ephemeral, impermanent, brief, short, momentary, fleeting, passing, fugitive, {here today, gone tomorrow}; literary evanescent.
OPPOSITES: permanent.

transit noun *the transit of goods between states:* transport, transportation, movement, conveyance, shipment, carriage, transfer; Brit. haulage.
□ in transit
the painting was damaged in transit: en route, on the journey, on the way, along/on the road, during transport.

transition noun change, passage, move, transformation, conversion, metamorphosis, alteration, changeover, shift, switch, jump, leap, progression, progress, development, evolution.

transitional adjective
1 *we are now in a transitional period:* intermediate, interim, changeover; changing, fluid, unsettled.
2 *the transitional government:* interim, temporary, provisional, pro tem, acting, caretaker.

transitory adjective *the transitory nature of fame and celebrity:* short-lived, transient, temporary, brief, short, short-term, impermanent, ephemeral, momentary, fleeting, passing, fugitive, {here today, gone tomorrow}; literary

evanescent.
OPPOSITES: permanent.

translate verb
1 *the German original had been translated into English:* render, put, express, convert, change; transcribe, transliterate; paraphrase, reword, rephrase; decipher, decode, gloss.
2 *interesting ideas cannot always be translated into effective movies:* convert, adapt, transform, alter, change, turn, transmute.

translation noun
1 *the translation of the Bible into English:* rendition, rendering, conversion; transcription, transliteration.
2 *the translation of these environmental policies into practice:* conversion, change, transformation, alteration, adaptation, transmutation.

translucent adjective semi-transparent, limpid, clear; diaphanous, gossamer, sheer; literary pellucid.
OPPOSITES: opaque.

transmission noun
1 *the transmission of knowledge and culture to the next generation:* transference, transferral, communication, conveyance; dissemination, spread, circulation.
2 *a live transmission from Washington:* broadcast, programme, show, relay, telecast.

transmit verb
1 *the use of computers to transmit information:* transfer, pass on, communicate, convey, impart, channel, carry, relay, dispatch; disseminate, spread, circulate.
2 *the programme will be transmitted on Sunday:* broadcast, relay, send out, air, televise.

transmute verb *the raw material of his experience was transmuted into stories:* change, alter, adapt, transform, convert, metamorphose, translate; humorous transmogrify.

transparency noun
1 *the transparency of the glass:* translucency, clarity, limpidity.
2 *colour transparencies:* slide, diapositive.

transparent adjective
1 *transparent blue water:* clear, crystal clear, see-through, translucent, limpid, glassy; literary pellucid.
2 *fine transparent fabrics:* see-through, sheer, filmy, gauzy, diaphanous.
3 *the symbolism of this myth is transparent:* obvious, unambiguous, unequivocal, clear, crystal clear, plain, apparent, unmistakable, manifest, conspicuous, patent, palpable, indisputable, evident, self-evident.
OPPOSITES: opaque, obscure.

t

transpire verb
1 *it transpired that her family had moved away:* become known, emerge, come to light, be revealed, turn out, come out, be discovered, become apparent, prove to be the case.
2 *I'm going to find out exactly what transpired:* happen, occur, take place, arise, come about, turn up, chance; literary befall.

transplant verb
1 *it was proposed to transplant the club to the vacant site:* transfer, move, remove, shift, relocate, reposition, take.
2 *the seedlings should be transplanted into larger pots:* replant, repot, uproot.
3 *kidneys must be transplanted within 48 hours of removal:* transfer, implant.

transport verb
1 *the concrete blocks were transported by lorry:* convey, carry, take, transfer, move, shift, send, deliver, truck, ship, ferry; informal cart.
2 *she was completely transported by the excitement:* thrill, delight, carry away, enrapture, entrance, enchant, enthral, electrify, captivate, bewitch, fascinate, spellbind, charm.
▷ noun
1 *alternative forms of transport:* conveyance, transportation; vehicle.
2 *the transport of crude oil:* transportation, conveyance, carriage, shipment, shipping; transit; Brit. haulage.

transpose verb
1 *the blue and black plates were transposed:* interchange, exchange, switch, swap, reverse, invert.
2 *the themes are transposed from the sphere of love to that of work:* transfer, shift, relocate, transplant, move, displace.

transverse adjective crosswise,
crossways, cross, horizontal, diagonal, oblique.
OPPOSITES: longitudinal.

trap noun
1 *an animal caught in a trap:* snare, net, gin.
2 *the question was set as a trap:* trick, ploy, ruse, deception, subterfuge; booby trap; informal set-up.
▷ verb
1 *police trapped the two men, who admitted blackmail:* snare, ensnare, lay a trap for, entrap; capture, catch, corner, catch up with.
2 *a rat was trapped in the barn:* confine, cut off, corner, shut in, pen in, hem in; imprison, hold captive.
3 *I hoped to trap him into an admission:* trick, dupe, deceive, lure, inveigle, beguile, fool, hoodwink; catch out, trip up.

trappings plural noun *the spectacular ritual and trappings of the monarchy:* regalia, panoply, finery, paraphernalia, apparatus, equipment, effects, features, accessories, accoutrements, ornamentation, adornment, decoration; formal appurtenances.

trash noun
1 (N. Amer.) *the subway entrance was blocked with trash:* rubbish, refuse, waste, litter, junk, detritus; N. Amer. garbage.
2 *if they read at all, they read this trash:* rubbish, nonsense, trivia, pulp fiction, pap; N. Amer. garbage; informal drivel, dreck.
▷ verb (N. Amer. informal) *the apartment had been totally trashed:* wreck, ruin, destroy, devastate; vandalize; damage; N. Amer. informal total.

trauma noun
1 *the trauma of divorce took its toll:* shock, upheaval, distress, stress, strain, pain, anguish, suffering, upset, agony, misery, sorrow, grief, heartache, heartbreak, torture; ordeal, trial, tribulation, trouble, worry, anxiety; nightmare.
2 *the gallstone can be extracted without severe trauma to the liver:* injury, damage, wounding; cut, laceration, lesion, abrasion, contusion.

traumatic adjective *witnessing the attack was a very traumatic experience for the children:* disturbing, distressing, upsetting, heartbreaking, painful, agonizing, hurtful, stressful, damaging, injurious, harmful, awful, terrible, shocking, devastating, harrowing; informal gut-wrenching.

travel verb
1 *he spent much of his time travelling abroad:* journey, tour, take a trip, voyage, go sightseeing, globetrot, trek, backpack; informal gallivant.
2 *we travelled the length and breadth of the island:* journey through, cross, traverse, cover; roam, rove, range.
3 *light travels faster than sound:* move, be transmitted.
▷ noun *he amassed great wealth during his travels:* journeys, expeditions, trips, tours, excursions, voyages, explorations, wanderings; travelling, touring, sightseeing, backpacking, globetrotting; informal gallivanting.

traveller noun *thousands of travellers were left stranded as a result of the strike:* tourist, tripper, sightseer, visitor, globetrotter, backpacker; pilgrim; passenger, commuter; Brit. holidaymaker; N. Amer. vacationer.

travelling adjective
1 *a travelling population:* nomadic, itinerant, peripatetic, wandering, roaming, roving, migrant, vagrant, of no fixed address/abode.

2 *a little travelling clock:* portable, lightweight, compact, miniature.

traverse verb
1 *he traversed the deserts of Persia:* travel over/across, cross, journey over/across, pass over; cover; ply; wander, roam, range.
2 *a ditch traversed by a wooden bridge:* cross, bridge, span, stretch across.

travesty noun *this is a travesty of justice:* misrepresentation, distortion, perversion, corruption, poor substitute, mockery, parody, caricature; farce, charade, pantomime, sham; informal apology for, excuse for.

treacherous adjective
1 *two treacherous Scottish lords betrayed Wallace's whereabouts:* traitorous, disloyal, faithless, unfaithful, duplicitous, deceitful, back-stabbing, double-crossing, double-dealing, two-faced, untrustworthy, unreliable; literary false, perfidious; informal two-timing.
2 *treacherous driving conditions:* dangerous, hazardous, perilous, unsafe, precarious, risky; informal dicey, hairy; Brit. informal dodgy.
OPPOSITES: loyal, safe.

treachery noun betrayal, disloyalty, unfaithfulness, infidelity, breach of trust, duplicity, deceit, deception, a stab in the back, back-stabbing, double-dealing, untrustworthiness; treason; literary perfidy; informal two-timing.
OPPOSITES: loyalty.

tread verb
1 *he trod purposefully down the hall:* walk, step, stride, pace, go; march, tramp, plod, stomp, trudge.
2 *the snow had been trodden down by the horses:* flatten, crush, press, squash; trample, tramp, stamp; compact.
▷ noun *we heard his heavy tread on the stairs:* step, footstep, footfall, tramp.

treason noun treachery; disloyalty, betrayal, unfaithfulness, sedition, subversion, mutiny, rebellion; literary perfidy.
OPPOSITES: loyalty.

treasonable adjective *there was no evidence of treasonable activity:* traitorous, treacherous, disloyal; seditious, subversive, mutinous, rebellious; literary perfidious.
OPPOSITES: loyal.

treasure noun
1 *they uncovered a casket of treasure:* valuables, riches, jewels, gems, gold, money, cash; wealth, fortune; Brit. treasure trove.
2 *the treasures of the ancient world:* valuable, work of art, masterpiece.
3 (informal) *she's a real treasure:* gem, angel; find, prize; informal star, one in a million.
▷ verb *I treasure the photographs I took*

of Jack: cherish, hold dear, prize, value; adore, dote on, love dearly, be devoted to, worship.

treasury noun
1 *she transferred billions from the national treasury to her own account:* exchequer, purse; bank, coffers.
2 *the area is a treasury of early fossils:* rich source, repository, storehouse, treasure house; fund, mine, bank.

treat verb
1 *Charlotte treated both him very badly:* behave towards, act towards, use; deal with, handle.
2 *police are treating both the fires as arson:* regard, consider, view, look on; put down as.
3 *the book treats its subject with great insight:* deal with, tackle, handle, discuss, explore, investigate; consider, study, analyse.
4 *she was treated at Addenbrooke's Hospital:* care for, nurse, tend, attend to.
5 *the plants may prove useful in treating cancer:* cure, heal, remedy; deal with, manage.
6 *he treated her to a slap-up lunch:* stand; take out for, buy, give; pay for; entertain, wine and dine; informal foot the bill for.
7 *delegates were treated to authentic Indonesian dance performances:* entertain with, regale with, fete with, amuse with, divert with.
▷ noun
1 *I bought you some chocolate as a treat:* present, gift, delicacy, luxury, indulgence, extravagance.
2 *it was a real treat to see them:* pleasure, delight, thrill, joy.

treatise noun *his famous treatise on medical ethics:* essay, paper, exposition, discourse, dissertation, thesis, monograph, study, work, critique; formal disquisition.

treatment noun
1 *the company's appalling treatment of its workers:* behaviour towards, conduct towards; handling of, dealings with.
2 *she's responding well to treatment:* medical care, therapy, nursing; medication, drugs.
3 *her treatment of the topic:* discussion, handling, investigation, exploration, consideration, study, analysis, critique.

treaty noun agreement, settlement, entente, concordat, accord, convention, pact, compact, protocol; deal, contract, covenant, bargain, pledge.

tree noun

WORD LINKS
arboreal living in trees or relating to trees
arboriculture, **silviculture** the growing and cultivation of trees

trek noun *a three-day trek across the desert:*

journey, trip, expedition, safari, odyssey; hike, march, footslog, tramp, walk; long haul; informal slog.
▷**verb** *we trekked through the jungle for weeks:* hike, tramp, march, trudge, traipse, walk; travel, journey; informal slog.

trellis noun lattice, framework; network, mesh, tracery; grille, grid; latticework, trelliswork; technical reticulation.

tremble verb
1 *Joe's hands were trembling:* shake, quiver, twitch; quaver, waver.
2 *the entire building trembled:* shake, shudder, judder, wobble, rock, vibrate, move, sway, totter, teeter.
3 *she trembled at the thought of what he had in store for her:* be afraid, be frightened, be apprehensive, worry; quail, shrink, blench.
▷**noun** *I noticed the slight tremble in her hands:* tremor, shake, shakiness, trembling, quiver, twitch.
OPPOSITES: steadiness.

tremendous adjective
1 *tremendous sums of money were involved:* huge, enormous, immense, colossal, massive, prodigious, stupendous, monumental, mammoth, vast, gigantic, giant, mighty, epic, titanic, towering, king-sized, gargantuan; substantial, considerable; informal whopping, thumping, astronomical, humongous; Brit. informal whacking, ginormous.
2 *there was a tremendous explosion:* loud, deafening, ear-splitting, booming, thundering, thunderous, resounding.
3 (informal) *I've seen him play and he's tremendous:* excellent, splendid, wonderful, marvellous, magnificent, superb, glorious, sublime; informal great, amazing, fantastic, terrific, sensational, fabulous, awesome, magic, ace, wicked; Brit. informal smashing, brilliant.
OPPOSITES: tiny, small, poor.

tremor noun
1 *the sudden tremor of her hands:* trembling, shaking, shakiness, tremble, shake, quivering, quiver, twitching, twitch, tic.
2 *a tremor of fear ran through her:* frisson, shiver, spasm, thrill, tingle, stab; wave, surge, rush, ripple.
3 *the epicentre of the tremor:* earthquake, earth tremor, shock; informal quake.

tremulous adjective
1 *he addressed the crowd in a tremulous voice:* shaky, trembling, shaking, unsteady, quavering, quivering, quaking, weak.
2 *Surinder gave a tremulous smile:* timid, diffident, shy, hesitant, uncertain, nervous, fearful, frightened, scared, anxious, apprehensive; informal trepidatious.
OPPOSITES: steady, confident.

trench noun ditch, channel, trough, excavation, furrow, rut, conduit, cut, drain, waterway, watercourse, moat.

trenchant adjective *he made trenchant criticisms of her leadership style:* incisive, penetrating, sharp, keen, acute, shrewd, piercing; vigorous, forceful, strong, telling, emphatic, forthright; cutting, biting.
OPPOSITES: vague.

trend noun
1 *an upward trend in unemployment:* tendency, movement, direction, drift, swing, shift, course, current; inclination, leaning.
2 *the latest trend in dance music:* fashion, vogue, style, mode, craze, mania, rage; informal thing.

trendy adjective (informal) *trendy clothes | a trendy bar:* fashionable, modern, contemporary, in vogue, popular, up to date, up to the minute, all the rage, modish, à la mode, trendsetting; stylish, chic; informal cool, funky, in, hot, big, hip.
OPPOSITES: unfashionable.

trepidation noun *her first impression of her new school filled her with trepidation:* fear, apprehension, dread, fearfulness, agitation, anxiety, worry, nervousness, tension, misgivings, unease, uneasiness, foreboding, disquiet, dismay, consternation, alarm, panic; informal butterflies, the jitters, a cold sweat.
OPPOSITES: equanimity, composure.

trespass verb *there is no excuse for trespassing on railway property:* enter without permission, encroach on, invade; squat in.
▷**noun** *his alleged trespass on council land:* unlawful entry, intrusion, encroachment, invasion.

trespasser noun intruder, interloper, unwelcome visitor; squatter.

tresses plural noun hair, head of hair, mane, mop of hair, shock of hair; locks, curls, ringlets.

trial noun
1 *the trial is expected to last several weeks:* case, court case, lawsuit, suit, hearing, inquiry, tribunal, litigation, legal/judicial proceedings, legal action; court martial; appeal, retrial.
2 *the drug is undergoing clinical trials:* test, try-out, experiment, pilot study; examination, check, assessment, evaluation, appraisal, trial/test run; Brit. dummy run; informal dry run.
3 *she could be a bit of a trial at times:* nuisance, pest, bother, irritant, problem, inconvenience, plague, thorn in your flesh, the bane of your life, your cross to bear; informal pain, pain in the neck, headache, drag, nightmare.
▷**adjective** *a three-month trial period:* test, experimental, pilot, exploratory, probationary, provisional.
▷**verb** *the scheme has been trialled by several local authorities:* test, try out, put

to the test, put through its paces; pilot.

tribe noun people, community, ethnic group; family, dynasty, house; clan.

> **USAGE**
>
> The word **tribe** can cause offence when used to refer to a community living within a traditional society today, and it is better in such cases to use alternative terms such as **community** or **people**. However, if you are talking about such communities in the past, it is perfectly acceptable to say **tribe**, for example *the area was once inhabited by Slavic tribes.*

tribulation noun
1 *the tribulations of her personal life:* trouble, difficulty, problem, worry, anxiety, burden, ordeal, trial, adversity, hardship, tragedy, trauma, affliction; setback, blow; informal hassle.
2 *his time of tribulation was just beginning:* suffering, distress, trouble, misery, wretchedness, unhappiness, sadness, heartache, woe, grief, pain, anguish, agony.

tribunal noun
1 *he was summoned to a rent tribunal:* board, panel, committee.
2 *an international war-crimes tribunal:* court, court of justice, court of law, law court; court of inquiry.

tribute noun
1 *tributes flooded in from his many friends and colleagues:* accolade, praise, commendation, salute, testimonial, homage, eulogy; congratulations, compliments, plaudits; formal encomium; literary panegyric, paean.
2 *it is a tribute to his determination that he ever played again:* testimony to, indication of, evidence of, proof of, demonstration of, manifestation of.
OPPOSITES: criticism, condemnation.
□ **pay tribute to**
Mr Robinson paid tribute to the firefighters: praise, sing the praises of, speak highly of, commend, acclaim, take your hat off to, applaud, salute, honour, show appreciation of, recognize, acknowledge, pay homage to, extol; formal laud.

trick noun
1 *he's capable of any mean trick:* stratagem, ploy, ruse, scheme, device, manoeuvre, contrivance, machination, artifice, wile, dodge; deceit, deception, trickery, subterfuge, chicanery, sharp practice; swindle, hoax, fraud, confidence trick; informal con, set-up, scam, sting; Brit. informal wheeze.
2 *I think he's playing a trick on us:* joke, prank, jape; informal leg-pull.
3 *he entertained the kids with conjuring tricks:* feat, stunt; (**tricks**) sleight of hand, legerdemain, prestidigitation; magic.
4 *it was probably a trick of the light:* illusion, optical illusion, figment of the imagination; mirage; hallucination.
5 *the tricks of the trade:* knack, art, skill, technique; secret.
▷ **verb** *many people have been tricked by villains with false identity cards:* deceive, delude, hoodwink, mislead, take in, dupe, fool, double-cross, cheat, defraud, swindle, catch out, hoax; informal con, bamboozle, diddle, put one over on, pull a fast one on, pull the wool over someone's eyes, take for a ride, lead up the garden path.
□ **trick someone/something out**
she was tricked out in a red sash and a necklace of silver dollars: dress, array, rig out, garb, get up; adorn, decorate, deck out, bedeck, festoon; formal attire.

trickery noun *the streetwise dealer resorted to trickery:* deception, deceit, dishonesty, cheating, duplicity, double-dealing, sleight of hand, guile, craftiness, deviousness, subterfuge, skulduggery, chicanery, fraud, fraudulence, swindling, sharp practice; informal jiggery-pokery.
OPPOSITES: honesty.

trickle verb *blood was trickling from two cuts in his lip:* drip, dribble, ooze, leak, seep, spill.
OPPOSITES: pour, gush.
▷ **noun** *trickles of water ran down his arm:* dribble, drip, thin stream, rivulet.

trickster noun swindler, cheat, fraud, fraudster; charlatan, impostor; rogue, villain, scoundrel; informal con man/artist.

tricky adjective
1 *this is a tricky situation for him:* difficult, awkward, problematic, delicate, ticklish, sensitive, embarrassing, touchy; risky, uncertain, precarious; thorny, knotty; informal sticky, dicey.
2 *he was a tricky and unscrupulous politician:* cunning, crafty, wily, guileful, artful, devious, sly, scheming, calculating, sharp, shrewd, astute, canny; duplicitous, dishonest, deceitful, unscrupulous.
OPPOSITES: straightforward, honest.

tried and tested adjective *tried-and-tested marketing techniques:* reliable, dependable, trustworthy, trusted, tried and trusted, certain, sure; proven, proved, tested, established, fail-safe; reputable.

trifle noun *we needn't bother the headmaster over such a trifle:* triviality, unimportant matter, inessential, nothing; technicality; (**trifles**) trivia, minutiae.
□ **a trifle**
he looked a trifle apprehensive: a little, a bit, somewhat, a touch; informal a tad.
□ **trifle with**
men who trifle with women's affections: play with, toy with, dally with, play fast and loose with; informal mess about with.

trifling adjective *chief executives should not be bothered by such trifling matters:* trivial, unimportant, insignificant,

t

inconsequential, petty, minor, of little/no account, of little/no consequence, footling, incidental; small, tiny, inconsiderable, nominal, negligible; informal piffling.
OPPOSITES: important.

trigger verb
1 *the incident triggered an acrimonious debate*: precipitate, prompt, set off, spark off, touch off, provoke, stir up; cause, give rise to, lead to, set in motion, occasion, bring about, generate, engender, start, initiate.
2 *burglars had triggered the alarm*: activate, set off, set going, trip.

trill verb warble, sing, chirp, chirrup, tweet, twitter, cheep, peep.

trim verb
1 *his hair had been washed and trimmed*: cut, shorten, clip, crop, barber; style, neaten, shape, tidy up.
2 *trim off the lower leaves using a sharp knife*: cut off, remove, take off, snip off, chop off, lop off; prune, pollard.
3 *production costs need to be trimmed*: reduce, decrease, cut down, cut back, scale down, prune, slim down, pare down, dock.
4 *the story was severely trimmed for the film version*: shorten, abridge, condense, abbreviate, telescope, truncate.
5 *a pair of black leather gloves trimmed with fake fur*: decorate, adorn, ornament, embellish; edge, pipe, border, hem, fringe.
▷noun *white curtains with a blue trim*: edging, trimming, ornamentation, adornment, embellishment; border, piping, hem, fringe, frill.
▷adjective
1 *a cropped, fitted jacket looks nice and trim with a long-line skirt*: smart, stylish, chic, spruce, dapper, elegant, crisp.
2 *he always kept his garden trim*: neat, tidy, neat and tidy, orderly, in good order, well kept, well maintained, shipshape, in apple-pie order, immaculate, spick and span.
3 *her trim figure appeared in the doorway*: slim, slender, lean, clean-limbed, sleek, willowy, lissom, sylphlike, svelte; streamlined.
OPPOSITES: untidy, messy.
□in trim *she keeps herself in trim with regular exercise*: fit, in good health; slim, in shape.

trimming noun
1 *a black dress with lace trimming*: decoration, trim, ornamentation, adornment, embroidery; border, edging, piping, fringes, frills.
2 *roast turkey with all the trimmings*: accompaniments, extras; frills, accessories.
3 *I've swept up all the hedge trimmings*: cuttings, clippings, parings, shavings.

trinket noun knick-knack, bauble,

ornament, curio, trifle, toy, novelty, gimcrack.

trio noun threesome, three, triumvirate; trilogy, triptych; triplets.

trip verb
1 *he tripped on the loose stones*: stumble, lose your footing, slip, lose your balance, fall, tumble, topple.
2 *the question was intended to trip him up*: catch out, trick, outwit, outsmart; throw off balance, disconcert, unsettle, discountenance, discomfit; informal throw, wrong-foot; Brit. informal catch on the hop.
3 *they tripped up the terrace steps*: skip, run, dance, prance, bound, spring, scamper.
4 *Hoffman had tripped the alarm*: set off, activate, trigger; turn on, switch on, throw.
▷noun
1 *we went on a trip to Paris*: excursion, outing, jaunt; holiday, visit, tour, journey, expedition, voyage; drive, run, day out, day trip; informal spin.
2 *trips and falls cause nearly half such accidents*: stumble, slip; fall, tumble, spill.

triple adjective
1 *a triple alliance*: three-way, tripartite; threefold.
2 *they paid him triple the going rate*: three times, treble.

trite adjective *this observation struck me as both trite and irrelevant*: banal, hackneyed, clichéd, platitudinous, vapid, commonplace, conventional, stereotyped, overused, overdone, overworked, stale, worn out, time-worn, tired, hoary, hack, unimaginative, unoriginal, uninteresting, dull; informal old hat, corny.
OPPOSITES: original, imaginative.

triumph noun
1 *the monument was built to celebrate Napoleon's many triumphs*: victory, win, conquest, success; achievement.
2 *his eyes shone with triumph*: jubilation, exultation, elation, delight, joy, happiness, glee, pride, satisfaction.
3 *the bridge is a triumph of Victorian engineering*: tour de force, masterpiece, coup, wonder, sensation.
OPPOSITES: defeat, disappointment.
▷verb
1 *he triumphed in the British Grand Prix*: win, succeed, come first, be victorious, carry the day, carry all before you, prevail, take the honours, come out on top.
2 *they had no chance of triumphing over the Nationalists*: defeat, beat, conquer, overcome, overpower, overwhelm, get the better of; prevail against, subdue, subjugate; informal lick, best.
OPPOSITES: lose.

triumphant adjective
1 *the triumphant British team*: victorious, successful, winning, conquering; unbeaten, undefeated.
2 *she looked up, a triumphant expression*

on her face: jubilant, exultant, elated, rejoicing, joyful, delighted, gleeful, proud; gloating; literary joyous.
OPPOSITES: unsuccessful, despondent.

trivia plural noun *the worst blogs are filled with daily trivia that only a mother could struggle through:* minor details, minutiae, niceties, technicalities, trivialities, trifles, non-essentials.

trivial adjective
1 *your problems are trivial in comparison with Peter's:* unimportant, insignificant, inconsequential, minor, of no account, of no consequence, of no importance; incidental, petty, trifling, footling, small, slight, little, inconsiderable, negligible, paltry, inessential, non-essential; informal piffling.
2 *I used to be quite a trivial person:* frivolous, superficial, shallow, unthinking, empty-headed, lightweight, foolish, silly.
OPPOSITES: important, significant, serious.

triviality noun
1 *the triviality of the subject matter annoyed me:* unimportance, insignificance, inconsequentiality, pettiness.
2 *he need not concern himself with such trivialities:* minor detail, trifle, non-essential, nothing; technicality; (**trivialities**) trivia, minutiae.

trivialize verb *the problem was either trivialized or ignored by teachers:* minimize, play down, underestimate, underplay, make light of, treat lightly, dismiss; informal pooh-pooh.

troop noun
1 *a troop of tourists tramped along behind a tiny guide:* group, party, band, bevy, body, company, troupe, crowd, throng, horde, pack, gang, drove, flock, swarm, multitude, host, army; informal bunch, gaggle, posse.
2 *British troops were stationed here:* soldiers, forces, servicemen/women; the services, the army, the military, soldiery.
▷ **verb**
1 *we trooped out of the hall:* walk, march, file; flock, crowd, throng, stream, swarm, surge, spill.
2 *Caroline and I trooped wearily home:* trudge, plod, traipse, trail, drag yourself, tramp.

trophy noun cup, medal; prize, award.

tropical adjective hot, sweltering, humid, sultry, steamy, sticky, oppressive, stifling, suffocating, heavy; informal boiling.
OPPOSITES: cold, arctic.

trot verb *Doyle trotted across the patio:* run, jog; scuttle, scurry, bustle, scamper.
□ **on the trot** (Brit. informal) *they lost seven matches on the trot:* in succession, one after the other, in a row, consecutively, successively; running, straight.
□ **trot something out** (informal) *he trotted out the official Downing Street line:* recite,

repeat, regurgitate, churn out; come out with, produce.

trouble noun
1 *you've caused quite enough trouble already:* problems, difficulty, bother, inconvenience, worry, anxiety, distress, stress, agitation, harassment, unpleasantness; informal hassle.
2 *she poured out all her troubles:* problem, misfortune, difficulty, trial, tribulation, trauma, burden, pain, woe, grief, heartache, misery, affliction, suffering.
3 *he's gone to a lot of trouble to help you:* bother, inconvenience, fuss, effort, exertion, work, labour; pains, care, attention, thought.
4 *I wouldn't want to be a trouble to you or your family:* nuisance, bother, inconvenience, irritation, irritant, problem, trial, pest, thorn in someone's flesh/side; informal headache, pain, pain in the neck, drag.
5 *you're too gullible, that's your trouble:* problem, difficulty; weakness, weak point, failing, fault, imperfection, defect, blemish.
6 *he had a history of heart trouble:* disease, illness, sickness, ailments, complaints, problems; disorder, disability.
7 *the crash was due to engine trouble:* malfunction, failure, breakdown.
8 *a match marred by serious crowd trouble:* disturbance, disorder, unrest, fighting, ructions, fracas.
▷ **verb**
1 *this matter had been troubling her for some time:* worry, bother, concern, disturb, upset, agitate, distress, perturb; annoy, irritate, vex, irk; nag, niggle, prey on someone's mind, weigh down, burden; informal bug.
2 *he was troubled by bouts of ill health:* afflict, burden; suffer from, be cursed with.
3 *I'm sorry to trouble you:* inconvenience, bother, impose on, disturb, put out, disoblige; informal hassle.
□ **in trouble**
suppliers cannot get payments from businesses that are in trouble: in difficulty, in difficulties, in a mess, in a bad way, in a predicament; informal in a tight corner/spot, in a fix, in a hole, in hot water, up against it.

troubled adjective
1 *Joanna looked troubled:* anxious, worried, concerned, perturbed, disturbed, bothered, ill at ease, uneasy, unsettled, agitated; distressed, upset, dismayed.
2 *we live in troubled times:* difficult, challenging, stressful, problematic, unsettled, hard, tough, dark.

troublemaker noun mischief-maker, rabble-rouser, firebrand, agitator, agent provocateur, ringleader; demagogue; scandalmonger, gossipmonger, meddler; informal stirrer.

t

troublesome adjective

1 *this is indeed a troublesome problem:* annoying, irritating, exasperating, maddening, infuriating, irksome, vexatious, vexing, bothersome, tiresome, worrying, worrisome, disturbing, upsetting, niggling, nagging; difficult, awkward, problematic, taxing; informal aggravating.

2 *she really is a troublesome child:* difficult, awkward, trying, demanding, uncooperative, rebellious, unmanageable, unruly, obstreperous, disruptive, badly behaved, disobedient, naughty, recalcitrant.
OPPOSITES: simple, cooperative.

trough noun

1 *a large feeding trough:* manger, feedbox, feeder, crib.

2 *we dug a thirty-yard trough:* channel, conduit, trench, ditch, gully, drain, culvert, gutter.

trounce verb

his team were trounced 5–0 away to Southampton in the third round of the FA Cup: defeat, beat, crush, overwhelm, rout; informal hammer, clobber, thrash, drub, pulverize, massacre, demolish, destroy, annihilate, wipe the floor with, make mincemeat of.

troupe noun

group, company, band, ensemble, set; cast.

truant noun

□ **play truant** (Brit.) *566,000 secondary school pupils played truant at least once in the school year:* stay away from school, truant; Brit. informal skive off, bunk off; N. Amer. informal play hookey.

truce noun

ceasefire, armistice, suspension of hostilities, peace; respite, lull; informal let-up.

truck[1] noun

a heavily laden truck: lorry, wagon, heavy goods vehicle, juggernaut; van, pickup truck; Brit. HGV; dated pantechnicon.

truck[2] noun

we are to have no truck with him: dealings, association, contact, communication, connection, relations; business, trade.

truculent adjective

the airline staff were quizzed by truculent passengers: defiant, aggressive, antagonistic, belligerent, pugnacious, confrontational, obstreperous, argumentative, quarrelsome, uncooperative; Brit. informal stroppy, bolshie.
OPPOSITES: cooperative, amiable.

trudge verb

plod, tramp, drag yourself, plough, toil, trek, traipse; informal slog.

true adjective

1 *you'll see that what I say is true | it's a true story:* correct, accurate, right, verifiable, in accordance with the facts, the case, so; faithful, literal, factual, unvarnished.

2 *people are still willing to pay for true craftsmanship:* genuine, authentic, real, actual, bona fide, proper; informal honest-to-goodness, kosher, pukka, legit, the real McCoy.

3 *who is the true owner of the goods?* rightful, legitimate, legal, lawful, authorized, bona fide.

4 *there is a need for true repentance:* sincere, genuine, real, unfeigned, heartfelt, from the heart.

5 *he is a true friend:* loyal, faithful, constant, devoted, staunch, steadfast, unswerving, unwavering; trustworthy, trusty, reliable, dependable.

6 *a true reflection of life in the 1950s:* accurate, true to life, faithful, telling it like it is, realistic, close, authentic, lifelike.
OPPOSITES: untrue, false, disloyal, inaccurate.

true-blue adjective

they are true-blue supporters of the club: staunch, loyal, faithful, stalwart, committed, card-carrying, confirmed, dyed-in-the-wool, devoted, dedicated, firm, steadfast, unswerving, unwavering, unfaltering.
OPPOSITES: fickle.

truism noun

platitude, commonplace, cliché, stock phrase, banality, old chestnut.

truly adverb

1 *tell me truly what you want:* truthfully, honestly, frankly, candidly, openly, to someone's face, laying your cards on the table; informal pulling no punches.

2 *I'm truly grateful to them:* sincerely, genuinely, really, indeed, from the bottom of your heart, heartily, profoundly; very, extremely, immensely, tremendously, incredibly, terribly, most; informal awfully, terrifically; Brit. informal jolly.

3 *a truly dreadful song:* really, absolutely, simply, utterly, totally, perfectly, thoroughly, positively, completely.

4 *this is truly a miracle:* without doubt, unquestionably, undoubtedly, certainly, surely, definitely, beyond doubt/question, indubitably, undeniably, beyond the shadow of a doubt; in truth, really, in reality, actually, in fact.

5 *the streaming system does not truly reflect children's ability:* accurately, correctly, exactly, precisely, faithfully.

trump verb

by wearing the simplest of dresses, she had trumped them all: outshine, outclass, upstage, put in the shade, eclipse, surpass, outdo, outperform; beat, better, top, cap; informal leave standing; Brit. informal knock spots off.

trumped up adjective

the men were arrested on trumped-up charges of espionage: bogus, spurious, specious, false, fabricated, invented, manufactured, contrived, made-up, fake; informal phoney.
OPPOSITES: genuine.

trumpet verb

1 *'Come on!' he trumpeted:* shout, bellow, roar, yell, cry out, call out; informal holler.
2 *companies trumpeted their enthusiasm for the multimedia revolution:* proclaim, announce, declare, shout something from the rooftops.
▫ **blow your own trumpet** (Brit.) boast, brag, sing your own praises, show off, congratulate yourself; informal swank.

truncate verb

his career was truncated by injury: shorten, cut, cut short, curtail, bring to an untimely end; abbreviate, condense, reduce.
OPPOSITES: lengthen, extend.

trunk noun

1 *she leaned against the trunk of a tree:* stem, bole, stock.
2 *he revealed his powerful trunk:* torso, body.
3 *an elephant's trunk:* proboscis, nose, snout.
4 *his belongings were kept in an enormous tin trunk:* chest, box, crate, coffer; case.
5 (N. Amer.) *the trunk of his car was open:* luggage compartment; Brit. boot.

truss noun

the bridge is supported by three steel trusses: support, buttress, joist, brace, prop, strut, stay, stanchion, pier.
▷ **verb** *they trussed us up with ropes and chains:* tie up, bind, chain up; pinion, tether, secure.

trust noun

1 *they have to be able to win the trust of other people:* confidence, belief, faith, certainty, assurance, conviction; reliance.
2 *as manager, you occupy a position of trust:* responsibility.
3 *the money is to be held in trust for his son:* safe keeping, keeping, protection, charge, care, custody; trusteeship, guardianship.
OPPOSITES: distrust, mistrust, doubt.
▷ **verb**
1 *I should never have trusted her:* put your trust in, have faith in, have confidence in, believe in, pin your hopes/faith on.
2 *he can be trusted to carry out an impartial investigation:* rely on, depend on, bank on, count on.
3 *I trust we shall meet again:* hope, expect, take it, assume, presume.
4 *they don't like to trust their money to anyone outside the family:* entrust, consign, commit, give, hand over, turn over, assign.
OPPOSITES: distrust, mistrust.

> WORD LINKS
> **fiduciary** relating to or involving trust

trustee noun

administrator, agent; custodian, keeper, steward, depositary; executor, executrix.

trusting adjective

I would have written up a formal contract—you're too trusting: trustful, unsuspecting, unquestioning, unguarded, unwary; naive, innocent, childlike, ingenuous, wide-eyed, credulous, gullible.
OPPOSITES: distrustful, suspicious.

trustworthy adjective

leave a spare key with a trustworthy neighbour: reliable, honest, able to be trusted, dependable, honourable, upright, principled, true, truthful, as good as your word, ethical, virtuous, incorruptible, unimpeachable, above suspicion; responsible; safe, sound, reputable; informal on the level.
OPPOSITES: untrustworthy, unreliable.

trusty adjective

fortunately, he had two trusty sidekicks to help him with his schemes: reliable, dependable, trustworthy, unfailing, trusted; loyal, faithful, true, staunch, steadfast, constant.
OPPOSITES: unreliable.

truth noun

1 *he doubted the truth of her statement:* veracity, truthfulness, verity, sincerity, candour, honesty; accuracy, correctness, validity, factuality, authenticity.
2 *it's the truth, I swear it:* what happened, the case, so; gospel truth, the honest truth.
3 *truth is stranger than fiction:* fact, reality, real life, actuality.
4 *these ideas are accepted as scientific truths:* fact, verity, certainty; law, principle.
OPPOSITES: lies, fiction, falsehood.
▫ **in truth**
in truth Gouzenko's knowledge was extremely limited, but no one appreciated that: in fact, in reality, really, actually, to tell the truth, if truth be told.

truthful adjective

1 *I consider her to be a very truthful person:* honest, sincere, genuine, trustworthy; candid, frank, open, forthright, straight; informal upfront, on the level; N. Amer. informal on the up and up.
2 *a truthful account of what happened:* true, accurate, correct, factual, faithful, reliable; unvarnished, unembellished; formal veracious.
OPPOSITES: untruthful, untrue.

try verb

1 *I will try to help him:* attempt, endeavour, make an effort, exert yourself, strive, do your best, do your utmost, move heaven and earth; informal have a go, give it your best shot, bend over backwards, do your damnedest, pull out all the stops, go all out.
2 *try it and see what you think:* test, put to the test, experiment with, sample, taste; inspect, investigate, examine, appraise, evaluate, assess; informal check out, give something a go/whirl.
3 *Mary tried everyone's patience:* tax, strain, test, stretch, sap, drain, exhaust, wear out.
4 *the case is to be tried by a jury:* adjudicate, consider, hear, examine.

▷ **noun** *I'll have one last try:* attempt, effort, endeavour; informal go, shot, crack, stab, bash, whack.

◻ **try something out**
I've been trying out the software and so far I've been pleased: test, trial, experiment with, pilot; put through its paces; assess, evaluate.

trying adjective
1 *it's been a very trying day:* stressful, taxing, demanding, difficult, tough, hard, pressured, frustrating, fraught; arduous, gruelling, tiring, exhausting; informal hellish.
2 *her sister was very trying at the best of times:* annoying, irritating, exasperating, maddening, infuriating; tiresome, irksome, troublesome, bothersome; informal aggravating.

tub noun
1 *a large wooden tub:* container, butt, barrel, cask, drum, keg.
2 *a tub of yogurt:* pot, carton.
3 (informal) *I was enjoying a soak in the tub:* bath, bathtub; hot tub.

tubby adjective (informal) *a small, tubby man appeared:* chubby, plump, stout, dumpy, chunky, portly, rotund, round, fat, overweight, fleshy, paunchy, pot-bellied, corpulent; informal pudgy, beefy, porky, roly-poly, blubbery; Brit. informal podgy.
OPPOSITES: skinny.

tuck verb
1 *Rayner tucked his letter back into the envelope:* push, insert, slip; thrust, stuff; informal pop.
2 *he tucked the knife behind his seat:* hide, conceal, secrete; store, stow; informal stash.
▷ **noun** *she wore a red dress with tucks all along the bodice:* pleat, gather, fold, ruffle.
◻ **tuck someone in/up**
he carried her back to bed and tucked her in: make comfortable, settle down, cover up; put to bed.
◻ **tuck in/into** (informal) *I tucked into the bacon and eggs:* eat heartily, devour, consume, gobble up, wolf down; informal get stuck into, dispose of, polish off, get outside of, put away, scoff; Brit. informal shift; N. Amer. informal scarf down.

tuft noun
1 *spiky tufts of grass grew on the forecourt:* clump, bunch, knot, cluster, tussock.
2 *she tugged at a tuft of hair:* lock, wisp; crest, topknot, plume.

tug verb
1 *Ben tugged at her sleeve:* pull, pluck, tweak, twitch, jerk, wrench; catch hold of; informal yank.
2 *she tugged him towards the door:* drag, pull, draw, haul, heave, tow, trail; informal lug.
▷ **noun** *one good tug would loosen all that earth:* pull, jerk, wrench, heave; informal yank.

tuition noun instruction, teaching, coaching, tutoring, tutelage, lessons, education, schooling; training, drill; preparation, guidance.

tumble verb
1 *he tumbled over:* fall over, topple over, lose your balance, keel over, go headlong, go head over heels, trip up, stumble; informal come a cropper.
2 *a brook tumbled over the rocks:* cascade, fall, flow, pour, spill, stream.
3 *oil prices tumbled:* plummet, plunge, fall, dive, nosedive, drop, slump, slide, decrease, decline; informal crash.
OPPOSITES: rise.
▷ **noun**
1 *I took a tumble in the nettles:* fall, trip, spill; informal nosedive, header.
2 *a tumble in share prices:* drop, fall, plunge, dive, nosedive, slump, decline, collapse; informal crash.
OPPOSITES: rise.

tumbledown adjective *a row of tumbledown cottages:* dilapidated, ramshackle, decrepit, neglected, run-down, gone to rack and ruin, falling to pieces, decaying, derelict, crumbling, rickety.

tumbler noun glass, beaker.

tummy noun (informal) stomach, abdomen, belly, gut; informal middle, insides.

tumour noun cancerous growth, malignant growth, cancer, malignancy; lump, growth; Medicine carcinoma, sarcoma.

tumult noun
1 *she added her voice to the tumult:* clamour, din, noise, racket, uproar, commotion, ruckus, rumpus, hubbub, pandemonium, babel, bedlam, brouhaha, furore, fracas, melee, frenzy; Brit. row; Brit. informal hullabaloo.
2 *we have endured years of political tumult:* turmoil, confusion, disorder, unrest, chaos, turbulence, mayhem, havoc, upheaval, ferment, agitation, trouble.
OPPOSITES: tranquillity, peace.

tumultuous adjective
1 *he arrived to tumultuous applause:* loud, deafening, thunderous, uproarious, noisy, clamorous, vociferous.
2 *a tumultuous crowd had gathered:* disorderly, unruly, rowdy, turbulent, boisterous, excited, agitated, restless, wild, riotous, frenzied; Brit. informal rumbustious.
OPPOSITES: restrained, orderly.

tune noun *she hummed a cheerful tune:* melody, air, strain, theme; song, jingle, ditty.
▷ **verb** *a body clock tuned to the tides:* attune, adapt, adjust; regulate, modulate.
◻ **change your tune**
by the following week, she had changed her tune: change your mind, do a U-turn, have a change of heart; Brit. do an about-turn.

tuneful adjective melodious, melodic, musical, mellifluous, euphonious, harmonious, lyrical, lilting, sweet; often often dulcet.
OPPOSITES: tuneless, discordant.

tuneless adjective discordant, dissonant, unmelodious, harsh, cacophonous.
OPPOSITES: tuneful, melodious.

tunnel noun *they built a tunnel under the hill:* passage, underpass, subway; shaft; burrow, hole.
▷ verb *he tunnelled under the fence:* dig, burrow, mine, bore, drill.

turbid adjective *the turbid waters of the Mississippi:* murky, opaque, cloudy, muddy, thick.
OPPOSITES: clear, limpid.

turbulent adjective
1 *the country's turbulent past has not been forgotten:* tempestuous, stormy, unstable, unsettled, tumultuous, chaotic, troubled; violent, anarchic, lawless.
2 *we found ourselves adrift on the turbulent southern seas:* rough, stormy, tempestuous, storm-tossed, heavy, violent, wild, choppy, agitated.
OPPOSITES: peaceful, calm.

turgid adjective *his turgid prose sent me to sleep:* bombastic, pompous, overblown, inflated, high-flown, affected, pretentious, grandiose, florid, ornate, grandiloquent, orotund; formal magniloquent; informal highfalutin.
OPPOSITES: simple.

turmoil noun *the country was in a state of turmoil:* confusion, upheaval, turbulence, tumult, disorder, disturbance, agitation, ferment, unrest, trouble, disruption, chaos, mayhem.
OPPOSITES: peace.

turn verb
1 *the wheels were still turning:* go round, revolve, rotate, spin, roll, circle, wheel, whirl, gyrate, swivel, pivot.
2 *I turned and headed back:* change direction, change course, make a U-turn, turn about/round, wheel round.
3 *the car turned the corner:* go round, round, negotiate, take.
4 *the path turned to right and left:* bend, curve, wind, twist, meander, snake, zigzag.
5 *he turned his pistol on Liam:* aim at, point at, level at, direct at, train on; focus on.
6 *their honeymoon turned into a nightmare:* become, develop into, turn out to be; be transformed into, metamorphose into.
7 *Emma turned red:* become, go, grow, get.
8 *he turned the house into flats:* convert, change, transform, make; adapt, modify, rebuild, reconstruct.
9 *in later life, he turned to politics:* take up, become/get involved in, go in for, enter, undertake; informal get into.

10 *we can now turn to another topic:* move on to, go on to, consider, attend to, address; take up.
▷ noun
1 *a turn of the wheel sent us skidding across the road:* rotation, revolution, spin, whirl, gyration, swivel.
2 *the vehicle slowed and made a turn to the left:* change of direction, move, lurch.
3 *we're approaching the turn:* bend, corner; turning, junction, crossroads.
4 *you'll get your turn in a minute:* opportunity, chance, say; stint, time; try; informal go, shot, stab, crack.
5 *a highly entertaining comic turn:* act, routine, performance, number, piece.
6 (informal) *you gave me quite a turn!* shock, start, surprise, jolt; fright, scare.
7 *she did me some good turns:* service, deed, act; favour, kindness; disservice, wrong.
□ **in turn**
let's deal with these points in turn: one after the other, one by one, one at a time, in succession, successively, sequentially.
□ **turn of events**
she was utterly unprepared for this turn of events: development, incident, occurrence, happening, circumstance.
□ **turn against someone**
people had turned against him after the court case: become hostile to, take a dislike to.
□ **turn someone away**
reporters were turned away from the house: send away, refuse/deny access to; informal send packing.
□ **turn back**
they turned back before reaching the church: retrace your steps, go back, return; retreat.
□ **turn someone/something down**
1 *she turned down his offer of marriage:* reject, spurn, rebuff, refuse, decline; Brit. informal knock back.
2 *Pete turned the sound down:* reduce, lower, decrease, lessen; muffle, mute.
□ **turn someone in**
she turned her husband in to the police: betray, inform on, denounce, sell out, stab someone in the back; informal blow the whistle on, rat on, peach on, squeal on; Brit. informal grass on, shop; N. Amer. informal finger.
□ **turn of mind**
the book is for those of a less scientific turn of mind: disposition, inclination, tendency, propensity, bias, bent.
□ **turn off**
they turned off the road and stopped: leave, branch off; informal take a left/right; N. Amer. informal hang a left/right.
□ **turn something off**
she turned off the light: switch off, shut off, power down, put off, extinguish, deactivate; informal kill, cut.
□ **turn on**
the decision turned on the meaning of the word 'reasonable': depend on, rest on, hinge on, be contingent on, be decided by.

t

□ **turn something on**
she turned on the TV: switch on, power up, put on, start up, boot up, activate, trip.

□ **turn on someone**
he turned on her with cold savagery: attack, set on, let fly at, lash out at, hit out at, round on; informal lay into, tear into, let someone have it, bite someone's head off, jump down someone's throat.

□ **turn out**
1 *a huge crowd turned out to meet us:* come, be present, attend, appear, turn up, arrive; assemble, gather; informal show up.
2 *it turned out that she had been abroad:* transpire, emerge, come to light, become apparent.
3 *things didn't turn out as I'd intended:* happen, occur, come about; develop, work out, come out, end up; formal eventuate; informal pan out.

□ **turn someone out**
his landlord turned him out: throw out, eject, evict, expel, drive out, banish; informal kick out, send packing, boot out, show someone the door, turf out.

□ **turn something out**
1 *turn out the light.* See TURN SOMETHING OFF.
2 *they turn out a million engines a year:* produce, make, manufacture, fabricate, put out, churn out.
3 *she turned out the cupboards:* clear out, clean out, empty.

□ **turn over**
the little dinghy turned over in the wind: overturn, upturn, capsize, keel over, turn turtle, be upended.

□ **turn something over**
1 *I turned over a few pages and then noticed the picture:* flip over, flick through, leaf through.
2 *she turned the proposal over in her mind:* think about/over, consider, weigh up, ponder, contemplate, reflect on, chew over, mull over, muse on, ruminate on.
3 *he turned over the business to his brother:* transfer, hand over, pass on, consign, commit.

□ **turn of phrase**
he is famed for his non-committal turns of phrase: expression, idiom, phrase, term, word.

□ **turn to someone/something**
1 *they turned to social services for advice:* seek help from, approach, have recourse to, apply to, appeal to.
2 *he turned to drink:* take to, resort to.

□ **turn up**
1 *the missing documents turned up:* be found, be discovered, be located, reappear.
2 *the police finally turned up:* arrive, appear, present yourself; informal show up, show your face.
3 *I'm sure something better will turn up:* present itself, occur, happen, crop up.

□ **turn something up**
1 *she turned up the volume:* increase, raise, amplify, intensify.
2 *they turned up lots of information:* discover, uncover, unearth, find, dig up, ferret out, root out, expose.
3 *I turned up the hem:* take up, raise; shorten.

turncoat noun traitor, renegade, defector, deserter, Judas; fifth columnist, quisling.

turning noun turn-off, turn, side road, exit.

turning point noun watershed, critical moment, decisive moment, moment of truth, crossroads, crisis.

turnout noun *the lecture attracted a good turnout:* attendance, audience, house; crowd, gathering, throng, assembly, assemblage, congregation.

turnover noun
1 *we have an annual turnover of £2.25 million:* revenue, income, yield; sales.
2 *DDI has a high turnover of staff:* change, movement, throughput; churn rate.

tussle noun *his glasses were smashed in the tussle:* scuffle, fight, struggle, skirmish, brawl, scrum, rough and tumble, free-for-all, fracas, fray, rumpus, melee; informal scrap, dust-up, spat, ruck; Brit. informal punch-up, ding-dong, bust-up.
▷ **verb** *demonstrators tussled with police:* scuffle, fight, struggle, brawl, grapple, wrestle, clash; informal scrap.

tutor noun *he's a history tutor at Cambridge:* teacher, instructor, educator, lecturer; trainer, mentor; formal pedagogue.
▷ **verb** *he was tutored at home:* teach, educate, instruct, school; coach, train, drill.

tutorial noun lesson, class, seminar.

tweak verb
1 *he tweaked the boy's ear:* pull, jerk, tug, twist, twitch, pinch, squeeze.
2 (informal) *the programme can be tweaked to suit your needs:* adjust, modify, alter, change, adapt; refine, fine-tune.
▷ **noun**
1 *he gave her hair a tweak:* pull, jerk, tug, twist, pinch, twitch, squeeze.
2 (informal) *a few minor tweaks were required:* adjustment, modification, alteration, change; refinement.

twee adjective (Brit.)
1 *I love all those twee little shops:* quaint, sweet, pretty; informal cute, cutesy.
2 *the lyrics are too twee in places:* sentimental, over-sentimental, mawkish; Brit. informal soppy.

twelve cardinal number dozen.

> WORD LINKS
> **duodecimal** relating to twelve
> **dodecagon** a twelve-sided figure

twenty cardinal number score.

twiddle verb *she twiddled the dials*

impatiently: turn, twist, swivel, twirl; adjust, move, jiggle; fiddle with, play with.
□ **twiddle your thumbs**
they're running late apparently so I'm sitting here twiddling my thumbs: be idle, kick your heels, kill time, waste time; informal hang around.

twig[1] noun *a bunch of leafy twigs:* stick, sprig, shoot, stem.

twig[2] verb (Brit. informal) *she finally twigged what I was on about:* realize, understand, grasp, comprehend, take in, fathom, see, recognize; informal latch on to, cotton on to, tumble to, get, get wise to, figure out; Brit. informal suss.

twilight noun
1 *we arrived at twilight:* dusk, sunset, sundown, nightfall, evening, close of day.
2 *the tower was scarcely visible in the twilight:* half-light, semi-darkness, gloom; literary gloaming.
OPPOSITES: dawn.
▷ **adjective** *he inhabited a sinister twilight world of treason and murder:* shadowy, dark, shady, obscure, hidden; sinister.

> WORD LINKS
> **crepuscular** resembling or relating to twilight

twin adjective
1 *the twin towers of the stadium:* matching, identical, matched, paired.
2 *the twin aims of conservation and recreation:* twofold, double, dual; related, linked, connected; corresponding, parallel, complementary, equivalent.

twine noun *a ball of twine:* string, cord, thread, yarn.
▷ **verb**
1 *she twined her arms around him:* wind, entwine, wrap, wreathe.
2 *convolvulus twined around the tree:* entwine itself, coil, loop, twist, spiral, curl.
3 *a flower was twined in her hair:* weave, interlace, intertwine, braid, twist.

twinge noun
1 *she experienced twinges in her stomach:* pain, spasm, ache, throb; cramp, stitch.
2 *I felt a twinge of guilt:* pang, prick; qualm, scruple.

twinkle verb *the lights of the city twinkled:* glitter, sparkle, shine, glimmer, shimmer, glint, gleam, glisten, flicker, flash, wink.
▷ **noun** *the twinkle of the lights:* glitter, sparkle, glimmer, shimmer, glint, gleam, flicker, flash, wink.

twinkling adjective *the twinkling lights of the city below:* glittering, sparkling, glimmering, glinting, gleaming, flickering, winking, shining, glistening.

twirl verb
1 *she twirled her parasol:* spin, whirl, turn, gyrate, pivot, swivel, twist, revolve, rotate.

2 *she twirled her hair round her fingers:* wind, twist, coil, curl, wrap.
▷ **noun** *she did a quick twirl:* pirouette, spin, whirl, turn, twist, rotation, revolution, gyration.

twist verb
1 *the impact twisted the chassis of the car:* crumple, crush, buckle, mangle, warp, deform, distort.
2 *her face twisted with rage:* contort, screw up.
3 *Mother anxiously twisted a handkerchief:* wring, squeeze.
4 *he twisted round in his seat:* turn round, swivel, spin round, pivot, rotate, revolve.
5 *she twisted out of his grasp:* wriggle, squirm, worm, wiggle.
6 *I've twisted my ankle:* sprain, wrench, turn, rick, crick.
7 *you are twisting my words:* distort, misrepresent, change, alter, skew, misinterpret, misconstrue, spin.
8 *he twisted the radio knob:* twiddle, adjust, turn, rotate, swivel, spin.
9 *she twisted her hair round her finger:* wind, twirl, coil, curl, wrap.
10 *the wires were twisted together:* intertwine, twine, interlace, weave, plait, braid, coil, wind.
11 *the road twisted and turned round the mountainside:* wind, bend, curve, turn, meander, weave, zigzag, swerve, snake.
▷ **noun**
1 *her voice faded with the twist of a dial:* turn, twirl, spin.
2 *long twists of black hair stuck out from under her hat:* ringlet, curl, corkscrew, coil; lock, hank.
3 *the twists in the road made me feel sick:* bend, curve, turn, zigzag, kink, dog-leg, hairpin bend.
4 *the twists of the plot are quite baffling:* convolution, complication, complexity, intricacy; surprise, revelation.
5 *a new twist on an old theme:* interpretation, slant, outlook, angle, approach, treatment; variation, take.
□ **twist someone's arm** (informal) *I didn't really want to come, but Sarah twisted my arm:* pressurize, persuade, talk into, prevail on, convince, make, coerce, force; informal lean on.

twisted adjective
1 *a mass of twisted metal:* crumpled, bent, crushed, buckled, warped, misshapen, distorted, deformed.
2 *he gave me a twisted smile:* crooked, lopsided; contorted, wry.
3 *his twisted mind:* perverted, warped, deviant, depraved, corrupt, abnormal, unhealthy, aberrant, distorted; informal sick.

twisty adjective winding, windy, twisting, bendy, zigzag, meandering, curving, sinuous.
OPPOSITES: straight.

t

twitch verb
1 *he twitched and then lay still:* jerk, convulse, have a spasm, quiver, tremble, shiver, shudder.
2 *he twitched the note out of my hand:* snatch, tweak, pluck, pull, tug; informal yank.
▷ **noun**
1 *a twitch of her lips was all I could make out:* spasm, convulsion, quiver, tremor, shiver, shudder; tic.
2 *he felt a twitch of annoyance:* pang, twinge, dart, stab, prick.

twitter verb *sparrows twittered under the eaves:* chirp, chirrup, cheep, tweet, peep, chatter, trill, warble, sing.
▷ **noun** *I heard a bird's twitter:* chirp, chirrup, cheep, tweet, peep, trill, warble, song.

two cardinal number pair, duo, duet, double.

> **WORD LINKS**
> **binary**, **dual** composed of or involving two things
> **biannual** occurring twice a year
> **biennial** occurring every two years
> **bicentenary** a two-hundredth anniversary

two-faced adjective deceitful, insincere, hypocritical, back-stabbing, false, untrustworthy, duplicitous, deceiving, dishonest, double-dealing; disloyal, treacherous, faithless; literary perfidious.
OPPOSITES: sincere.

twosome noun couple, pair, duo.

tycoon noun magnate, mogul, businessman, captain of industry, industrialist, financier, entrepreneur; millionaire, multimillionaire; informal big shot, bigwig; Brit. informal supremo; derogatory fat cat.

type noun
1 *we need a new type of politics for the 21st century:* kind, sort, variety, class, category, set, genre, species, order, breed; style, nature, manner, rank; generation, vintage, school; stamp, ilk, cast, grain, mould.
2 (informal) *I hate all these sporty types:* person, individual, character, sort.
3 *the headings are in italic type:* print, typeface, face, characters, lettering, letters; font; Brit. fount.

typhoon noun cyclone, tropical storm, storm, tornado, hurricane, whirlwind; N. Amer. twister.

typical adjective
1 *a typical example of Art Deco:* representative, classic, quintessential, archetypal, model, prototypical; stereotypical.
2 *it was a fairly typical day:* normal, average, ordinary, standard, regular, routine, run-of-the-mill, conventional, unremarkable, unexceptional; informal bog-standard.
3 *it's typical of him to forget the date:* characteristic, in keeping, usual, normal, predictable, true to form; customary, habitual.
OPPOSITES: unusual, exceptional, atypical.

typify verb *he typified a new breed of civil servant:* epitomize, exemplify, characterize, be representative of; personify, embody.

tyrannical adjective *a deranged and tyrannical leader:* dictatorial, despotic, autocratic, oppressive, repressive, totalitarian, undemocratic, illiberal; authoritarian, high-handed, imperious, harsh, strict, severe, cruel, brutal, ruthless.
OPPOSITES: liberal.

tyrannize verb *they have tyrannized the people for more than 20 years:* dominate, browbeat, intimidate, bully, lord it over; persecute, victimize, torment; oppress, rule with a rod of iron, repress, crush, subjugate.

tyranny noun despotism, absolute power, autocracy, dictatorship, totalitarianism; oppression, repression, subjugation, enslavement; authoritarianism, bullying, cruelty, brutality, ruthlessness.

tyrant noun *an evil tyrant who has imprisoned all who oppose his regime:* dictator, despot, autocrat, oppressor; slave-driver, martinet, bully.

tyro noun *he first entered parliament in 1977 as a 34-year-old political tyro:* novice, beginner, learner, neophyte, newcomer, initiate, fledgling; apprentice, trainee, probationer; informal rookie; N. Amer. informal tenderfoot, greenhorn.
OPPOSITES: veteran.

t

Uu

ubiquitous adjective *fibre-optic lamps and brown leather sofas became ubiquitous status symbols:* omnipresent, ever-present, everywhere, all over the place; universal, widespread, pervasive, rife, inescapable.
OPPOSITES: rare.

ugly adjective
1 *a fat, ugly man:* unattractive, ill-favoured, hideous, plain, unprepossessing, unsightly; N. Amer. homely; informal not much to look at; Brit. informal no oil painting.
2 *players, officials, and supporters became embroiled in ugly scenes following the match:* unpleasant, nasty, tense; angry, hostile, violent.
OPPOSITES: beautiful, pleasant.

ulcer noun sore, ulceration, abscess, boil, carbuncle, blister.

ulterior adjective *could there be an ulterior motive behind his request?* underlying, undisclosed, undivulged, concealed, hidden, covert, secret, personal, private, selfish.
OPPOSITES: overt.

ultimate adjective
1 *the decline and ultimate collapse of the Empire:* eventual, final, concluding; resulting, ensuing, consequent, subsequent.
2 *ultimate truths about civilization:* fundamental, basic, primary, elementary, elemental, absolute; central, key, crucial, essential.
3 *for some artists, the ultimate accolade is having a memorial created in your honour:* best, greatest, supreme, superlative, highest, utmost; ideal, optimum.
▷ noun *a studio apartment offering the ultimate in luxury living:* utmost, optimum, last word, height, peak, pinnacle, acme, zenith, nonpareil; informal the bee's knees.

ultimately adverb
1 *the cost will ultimately fall on us:* eventually, in the end, in the long run, finally, sooner or later, in time, one day, some day.
2 *two ultimately contradictory reasons:* fundamentally, basically, primarily, essentially, at heart, deep down.

ultra- combining form *an ultra-conservative view:* extremely, very, exceedingly, immensely, especially, exceptionally; excessively.

umbrage noun
□ **take umbrage**
she took umbrage at his remarks: take offence, be offended, take exception, be affronted, be annoyed, be angry, be indignant, be put out, be insulted, be hurt, be piqued, be aggrieved.

umpire noun *the umpire reversed his decision:* referee, linesman, adjudicator, judge; informal ref.
▷ verb *he umpired a boat race:* referee, adjudicate, judge; informal ref.

unabashed adjective *he remains an unabashed advocate of the use of military power to achieve political and economic objectives:* unashamed, unembarrassed, unrepentant, unconcerned; blatant, flagrant, brazen.

unable adjective *Steven nodded, unable to say anything:* powerless, at a loss, incapable.

unabridged adjective *each story is unabridged and wholly authentic:* complete, entire, whole, intact, uncut, unexpurgated.

unacceptable adjective *this development would create an unacceptable level of noise | his behaviour was totally unacceptable:* intolerable, inadmissible, inappropriate, unsuitable, unreasonable; informal out of order.
OPPOSITES: acceptable, satisfactory.

unaccompanied adjective *no unaccompanied children were allowed in:* alone, on your own, by yourself, solo, lone, solitary; unescorted, unchaperoned; Brit. informal on your tod.

unaccountable adjective
1 *for some unaccountable reason, the horse stopped short:* inexplicable, incomprehensible, unfathomable, puzzling, perplexing, baffling, bewildering, mystifying, mysterious, peculiar, strange, odd.
2 *the Council is unaccountable to*

u

anyone: not answerable, not liable, not responsible.

unaccustomed adjective

1 *the visitors were unaccustomed to the local culture:* unused, new; unfamiliar with, inexperienced in, unacquainted with.
2 *he showed unaccustomed emotion:* unusual, unfamiliar, uncommon, unwonted, exceptional, extraordinary, surprising, abnormal, atypical.
OPPOSITES: habitual.

unadorned adjective *simple whitewashed wooden structures with unadorned interiors:* unembellished, undecorated, plain, basic; bare, austere, stark, spartan, clinical.
OPPOSITES: ornate.

unadventurous adjective *some critics have labelled his works as unadventurous and middlebrow:* cautious, careful, circumspect; conservative, conventional, unexciting, unimaginative, boring, strait-laced, stuffy; informal square, stick-in-the-mud.

unaffected adjective

1 *his later work was largely unaffected by contemporary developments in French art:* unchanged, unaltered, uninfluenced; untouched, unresponsive to; proof against, impervious to, immune to.
2 *her effortless, unaffected charm:* genuine, real, sincere; unassuming, unpretentious, natural, easy, open.

unanimous adjective *doctors were unanimous in their diagnoses:* united, in agreement, in accord, of one mind, in harmony, undivided.

unanswered adjective *there were a number of unanswered questions:* unresolved, undecided, unsettled; pending, up in the air.

unappetizing adjective *unappetizing hospital food | one of the unappetizing features of politics:* unpalatable, uninviting, off-putting, disagreeable, distasteful, unpleasant, unsavoury.

unapproachable adjective *her boss appeared unapproachable:* aloof, distant, remote, detached, uncommunicative, unresponsive, unforthcoming, unfriendly, unsympathetic, unsociable; cool, cold, frosty, stiff, formal; informal stand-offish.
OPPOSITES: approachable, friendly.

unarmed adjective *troops fired into a crowd of unarmed civilians:* defenceless, unprotected, undefended, unguarded; vulnerable.

unassailable adjective

1 *an unassailable fortress:* impregnable, invulnerable, impenetrable, inviolable, invincible; secure, safe, strong, indestructible.
2 *his logic was unassailable:* indisputable,

undeniable, unquestionable, incontestable, incontrovertible, irrefutable, indubitable, watertight, sound.
OPPOSITES: defenceless.

unassuming adjective *a quiet, unassuming man:* modest, self-effacing, meek, humble, reserved, diffident; unobtrusive, unostentatious, unpretentious, unaffected, natural, artless, ingenuous.

unattached adjective

1 *they were both unattached:* single, unmarried, available, footloose and fancy free, on your own.
2 *we are unattached to any organization:* unaffiliated; autonomous, independent, non-aligned, self-governing, neutral, separate, unconnected.

unattended adjective

1 *his cries went unattended:* ignored, disregarded.
2 *it is not acceptable for parents to leave children unattended at that age:* unaccompanied, unsupervised, alone, on your own, by yourself.

unattractive adjective *an unattractive little town:* ugly, plain, ill-favoured, unsightly, unprepossessing, hideous; N. Amer. homely; informal not much to look at; Brit. informal no oil painting.
OPPOSITES: beautiful.

unauthorized adjective *unauthorized access to the computer system:* unofficial, unlicensed; prohibited, barred, forbidden, illegal, unlawful, proscribed.
OPPOSITES: authorized, official.

unavailing adjective *persistent calls for justice were unavailing:* ineffective, ineffectual, to no avail, inefficacious, vain, futile, useless, unsuccessful, fruitless, profitless, unprofitable, abortive.
OPPOSITES: effective.

unavoidable adjective *the unavoidable consequences of growing old | redundancies are unavoidable:* inescapable, inevitable, inexorable, ineluctable, certain, assured.

unaware adjective *the President was unaware of what was going on:* ignorant, unconscious, oblivious, unsuspecting, uninformed, unenlightened, unwitting, innocent; blind, deaf; informal in the dark.
OPPOSITES: aware, conscious.

unawares adverb *the photographer had caught her unawares:* by surprise, unexpectedly, without warning, suddenly, unprepared, off-guard; Brit. informal on the hop.

unbalanced adjective

1 *he is unbalanced and dangerous:* unstable, mentally ill, deranged, demented, disturbed, unhinged, insane, mad; informal crazy.
2 *a most unbalanced article:* biased,

prejudiced, one-sided, partisan,
inequitable, unjust, unfair.
OPPOSITES: stable, unbiased.

unbearable adjective *the heat and
the smell were unbearable:* intolerable,
insufferable, insupportable, unendurable,
more than flesh and blood can stand,
overpowering; informal too much.
OPPOSITES: bearable, tolerable.

unbeatable adjective *she has been
in unbeatable form since her World
Championship triumph:* invincible,
unstoppable, unassailable, unsurpassable,
matchless, peerless, unrivalled; supreme.

unbecoming adjective
1 *a stout woman in an unbecoming striped
sundress:* unflattering, unattractive,
unsightly, ugly; unsuitable.
2 *he was suspended for conduct unbecoming
to an officer:* inappropriate, unfitting,
unsuitable, unsuited, out of keeping,
untoward, incorrect, unacceptable;
unworthy, improper, unseemly,
undignified.
OPPOSITES: flattering, appropriate.

unbelievable adjective *the whole story
is of course completely unbelievable:*
incredible, beyond belief, inconceivable,
unthinkable, unimaginable; unconvincing,
far-fetched, implausible, unlikely,
improbable; informal hard to swallow.
OPPOSITES: credible.

unbend verb *he could be fun if he'd only
unbend a little:* relax, unwind, loosen up,
let yourself go; informal let your hair down.

unbending adjective *he was an
unbending man with firm convictions:*
uncompromising, inflexible, unyielding,
unrelenting, intransigent, immovable;
strict, tough, unfriendly, austere, formal,
stiff, reserved, forbidding.

unbiased adjective *unbiased professional
advice:* impartial, unprejudiced,
independent, neutral, non-partisan,
disinterested, dispassionate, objective,
open-minded, equitable, even-handed, fair.
OPPOSITES: biased, prejudiced.

unblemished adjective *he had an
unblemished record as a law-abiding
citizen:* impeccable, flawless, faultless,
perfect, pure, whiter than white, clean,
spotless, unsullied, unspoilt, undefiled,
untarnished; guiltless, sinless, innocent,
blameless.
OPPOSITES: flawed.

unbounded adjective *his unbounded
enthusiasm for his work | the possibilities
are unbounded:* unlimited, boundless,
limitless, unrestricted; untold,
immeasurable, endless, unending, infinite,
inexhaustible; literary illimitable.
OPPOSITES: limited.

unbreakable adjective *a new type of*
unbreakable plastic bottle: shatterproof,
indestructible, durable, long-lasting;
toughened, sturdy, stout, hard-wearing,
heavy-duty.
OPPOSITES: breakable, fragile.

unbridled adjective *his unbridled
enthusiasm | their unbridled greed for
profit:* unrestrained, unconstrained,
uncontrolled, uninhibited, unrestricted,
unchecked, rampant, irrepressible,
unstoppable; intemperate, immoderate.
OPPOSITES: restrained.

unbroken adjective
1 *the last unbroken glass:* undamaged,
unharmed, unscathed, sound, intact,
whole, perfect.
2 *an unbroken chain of victories:*
uninterrupted, continuous.
3 *his record is still unbroken:* unbeaten,
undefeated, unsurpassed; unrivalled,
unmatched, unequalled.

unburden verb *she had a sudden wish to
unburden herself to him:* open your heart,
confess, tell all; informal come clean.

uncalled adjective
□ **uncalled for**
I'm ignoring that uncalled-for remark:
gratuitous, unnecessary, needless;
undeserved, unmerited, unwarranted,
unjustified, unreasonable, unfair,
inappropriate; unasked, unsolicited,
unprompted, unprovoked.

uncanny adjective
1 *the silence was uncanny:* eerie,
unnatural, unearthly, strange, odd, weird,
mysterious, unsettling; informal creepy,
spooky.
2 *there was an uncanny resemblance
between the two pictures:* striking,
remarkable, extraordinary, incredible.

unceasing adjective *an unceasing barrage
of rockets and mortar shells:* incessant,
ceaseless, constant, continual, unabating,
endless, unending, never-ending,
continuous, non-stop, uninterrupted,
unbroken, unremitting, persistent,
relentless, unrelenting, unrelieved,
sustained.
OPPOSITES: intermittent.

unceremonious adjective *her
unceremonious dismissal:* abrupt, sudden,
hasty, hurried, summary, perfunctory,
undignified; rude, discourteous, impolite.

uncertain adjective
1 *what happens next is uncertain | an
uncertain future:* unknown, indefinite,
undecided, undetermined, debatable,
open to question, in doubt, unsure, in
the balance, up in the air; unpredictable,
unforeseeable.
2 *uncertain weather conditions:*
changeable, variable, unpredictable,
unreliable, unsettled, erratic, fluctuating.
3 *I was uncertain how to proceed:* unsure,

u

undecided, unconvinced, irresolute, hesitant, ambivalent, in two minds, doubtful, dubious.
4 *an uncertain smile:* hesitant, tentative, faltering, unsure.
OPPOSITES: predictable, certain.

unchangeable adjective *our values are unchangeable, but policies are open to change:* unalterable, immutable, changeless; permanent, enduring, abiding, lasting, indestructible, ineradicable, irreversible, fixed, hard and fast, set in stone.

unchanging adjective *the unchanging routine of shipboard life:* unvarying, invariable, predictable, regular, consistent, fixed, changeless, permanent, set in stone, abiding, enduring, lasting.

uncharitable adjective *I regretted all the uncharitable things I had thought or said:* mean, mean-spirited, unkind, inconsiderate, thoughtless, insensitive, unfriendly, unsympathetic, uncaring, ungracious, unfair, selfish.

uncharted adjective *a foray into uncharted territory:* unexplored, unmapped, untravelled, unfamiliar, unknown.

uncivilized adjective *such uncivilized behaviour has no part in our society:* uncouth, ill-mannered, coarse, rough, boorish, vulgar, ill-bred, thuggish, loutish, antisocial; philistine, uneducated, uncultured, unsophisticated, benighted.

unclean adjective
1 *the firm was fined for operating in unclean premises:* dirty, filthy, grubby, soiled, unwashed; polluted, contaminated, insanitary, unhygienic.
2 *he confessed to unclean thoughts:* sinful, immoral, impure, bad, wicked.
OPPOSITES: clean, pure.

unclear adjective
1 *the motive for this killing is unclear | their future remains unclear:* uncertain, undetermined, unsure, up in the air, debatable, open to question, in doubt, doubtful, unsettled; ambiguous, indefinite, mysterious, obscure.
2 *people were unclear about what was expected of them:* uncertain, unsure, in doubt, vague, hazy.
OPPOSITES: clear, obvious.

uncomfortable adjective
1 *the accommodation was uncomfortable and noisy | a pair of very uncomfortable shoes:* cramped, confined, poky; tight, ill-fitting.
2 *I felt uncomfortable in her presence | an uncomfortable silence:* uneasy, awkward, nervous, tense, edgy, embarrassed; strained, fraught; informal twitchy.

uncommon adjective
1 *disputes between writers and directors are not uncommon in the film industry:* unusual, out of the ordinary, abnormal, atypical, strange, odd, exceptional; rare, scarce, few and far between, isolated, infrequent.
2 *she displays an uncommon capacity for hard work:* remarkable, extraordinary, exceptional, singular, unparalleled, prodigious, phenomenal, enormous, great.

uncommunicative adjective *he had always been uncommunicative and moody and he had few friends:* taciturn, quiet, unforthcoming, reserved, reticent, tight-lipped; guarded, secretive, close, private; distant, withdrawn, unsociable; informal stand-offish.
OPPOSITES: talkative.

uncomplicated adjective *installing the software was a fairly uncomplicated procedure:* simple, straightforward, clear, undemanding, trouble-free, painless, effortless, easy, elementary; accessible, user-friendly; informal a piece of cake, child's play, a cinch, a doddle, a breeze.
OPPOSITES: complicated, complex.

uncompromising adjective *her uncompromising attitude led to clashes with the governor:* inflexible, unbending, unyielding, unshakeable, rigid, hard-line, immovable, intractable, firm, resolute, determined, iron-willed, obstinate, stubborn, obdurate, intransigent, pig-headed; Brit. informal bloody-minded.
OPPOSITES: flexible.

unconcerned adjective *they are entirely unconcerned about what others think of them:* indifferent, unmoved, unaffected, uninterested, incurious, untroubled, unworried, relaxed, unruffled; nonchalant, blasé, insouciant.
OPPOSITES: interested, concerned.

unconditional adjective *he knew he could count on the unconditional support of the president:* unqualified, unquestioning, unequivocal, unreserved, unlimited, unrestricted, wholehearted; complete, total, full, absolute.

unconnected adjective
1 *the earth wire was unconnected:* detached, disconnected, loose.
2 *a series of seemingly unconnected events:* unrelated, independent, separate, distinct.

unconscious adjective
1 *the victim was still unconscious:* insensible, comatose, knocked out; informal out cold.
2 *an unconscious desire for recognition | an unconscious gesture of annoyance:* subconscious, latent, suppressed, subliminal; unintentional, unthinking, unwitting, inadvertent.
3 *he ranted on, unconscious of the danger:* oblivious to, impervious to, unconcerned by, indifferent to, heedless of; unaware of.
OPPOSITES: conscious, voluntary.

uncontrollable adjective

1 *an uncontrollable child:* unmanageable, out of control, wild, unruly, undisciplined, ungovernable, disorderly.
2 *his father flew into an uncontrollable rage:* wild, violent, frenzied, furious, hysterical, passionate.
3 *I had an uncontrollable urge to laugh:* irrepressible, overpowering, overwhelming, uncontainable.

unconventional adjective *contemporary art employs unconventional techniques and materials:* unusual, unorthodox, unfamiliar, out of the ordinary, atypical, alternative, different; new, original, novel, experimental, innovative; eccentric, idiosyncratic, quirky, odd, strange, bizarre, offbeat, outlandish, far out, curious, extraordinary; nonconformist, bohemian, avant-garde; informal edgy, way out, weird.
OPPOSITES: conventional, orthodox.

unconvincing adjective *she felt his story was unconvincing:* improbable, unlikely, implausible, incredible, unbelievable, far-fetched, questionable, dubious, doubtful; feeble, weak, lame.
OPPOSITES: convincing, persuasive.

uncooperative adjective *the authorities were inclined to be uncooperative:* unhelpful, awkward, disobliging, recalcitrant, perverse, contrary, obstructive, difficult; stubborn, obstinate, wilful, stiff-necked, unyielding, unbending, inflexible; obstreperous, disobedient; Brit. informal bloody-minded.
OPPOSITES: cooperative, obliging.

uncoordinated adjective *her movements were jerky and uncoordinated:* clumsy, awkward, disjointed, lumbering, flat-footed, heavy-handed, graceless, gawky, ungainly; inept, unskilful, inexpert, maladroit; informal cack-handed, ham-fisted.
OPPOSITES: dexterous.

uncouth adjective *he was uncouth and socially immature:* coarse, uncivilized, unrefined, unsophisticated, rough, crude, loutish, boorish, oafish, ill-bred; churlish, rude, bad-mannered, impolite, discourteous, disrespectful, vulgar, crass, indelicate; Brit. informal yobbish.
OPPOSITES: refined.

uncover verb

1 *he uncovered the face of the dead man:* expose, reveal; unveil.
2 *they uncovered a money-laundering plot:* detect, discover, stumble on, chance on, find, turn up, unearth, dig up; expose, bring to light, unmask, unveil, reveal, lay bare.
OPPOSITES: cover, conceal.

unctuous adjective *he lay underneath the palm trees, waiting for the unctuous waiter to bring him a drink:* sycophantic, ingratiating, obsequious, fawning, servile, grovelling; Brit. informal smarmy.

undaunted adjective *despite an inauspicious start to the holiday, travellers were undaunted:* undeterred, unbowed, resolute, determined, indefatigable.

undecided adjective

1 *I was undecided as to what to do next:* uncertain, unsure, irresolute, in two minds, indecisive, doubtful, dubious.
2 *his father's fate was still undecided:* unresolved, uncertain, unsure, unclear, unsettled, indefinite, undetermined, unknown, in the balance, up in the air.
OPPOSITES: certain.

undemonstrative adjective *my grandmother was an undemonstrative woman:* reserved, reticent, uncommunicative, unforthcoming, stiff, aloof, distant, detached, remote, withdrawn, unemotional, cold, unresponsive; informal stand-offish.

undeniable adjective *the force of his theory is undeniable:* indisputable, unquestionable, beyond doubt, beyond question, indubitable, incontrovertible, incontestable, irrefutable, unassailable; certain, sure, obvious, unmistakable, self-evident.
OPPOSITES: questionable.

under preposition

1 *they hid under a bush:* beneath, below, underneath.
2 *the rent is under £250:* less than, below.
3 *branch managers are under the retail director:* subordinate to, junior to, inferior to, answerable to, responsible to.
OPPOSITES: above, over.

undercover adjective *they were arrested after a three-year undercover investigation:* covert, secret, underground; clandestine, cloak-and-dagger, hidden, concealed; informal hush-hush.
OPPOSITES: overt.

undercurrent noun *there was an undercurrent of despair in his words:* undertone, overtone, suggestion, intimation, hint, trace, suspicion, tinge, sense, feeling, atmosphere, aura.

undercut verb

1 *the firm undercut their rivals:* charge less than, undersell.
2 *his authority was being undercut:* undermine, weaken, impair, threaten, destabilize.

underestimate verb *his political opponents underestimated his capabilities:* underrate, undervalue, do an injustice to, be wrong about, sell short, play down, understate; minimize, underemphasize, diminish, downgrade, gloss over, trivialize; miscalculate, misjudge.
OPPOSITES: exaggerate, overestimate.

u

undergo verb *she had to undergo a ferocious and lengthy cross-examination:* go through, experience, face, submit to, be subjected to, come in for, receive, sustain, endure, brave, bear, tolerate, stand, withstand, weather.

underground adjective
1 *an underground cave:* subterranean, buried.
2 *underground organizations:* clandestine, secret, covert, undercover, cloak-and-dagger; subversive; informal hush-hush.
3 *the underground art scene:* alternative, radical, unconventional, unorthodox, avant-garde, experimental.
▷ noun *information from the French underground:* resistance; partisans, freedom fighters.

undergrowth noun *she groped her way through the thick undergrowth:* shrubbery, vegetation, greenery, ground cover, brushwood, brush, scrub, bushes, plants.

underhand adjective *he was accused of employing underhand tactics:* dishonest, deceitful, dishonourable, unethical, unscrupulous, unfair; devious, artful, crafty, conniving, scheming, sly; secret, sneaky, covert, cloak-and-dagger; informal shady.
OPPOSITES: honest.

underline verb
1 *she underlined a phrase:* underscore, mark, pick out, emphasize, highlight.
2 *the report underlined the importance of getting children into sport at a young age:* emphasize, stress, highlight, accentuate, accent, focus on, spotlight, point up.

underling noun *he dished out orders to his underlings:* subordinate, inferior, junior; henchman, factotum, minion, lackey, flunkey, retainer, hireling, servant; informal dogsbody, gofer; Brit. informal skivvy.

underlying adjective *the underlying assumption that economic growth is synonymous with progress:* implicit, inherent, intrinsic, essential; fundamental, basic, primary, central.

undermine verb *the findings of the inquiry further undermined the prime minister's authority:* weaken, threaten, compromise, erode, diminish, reduce, lessen, damage; subvert.
OPPOSITES: strengthen, support.

underprivileged adjective *the charity arranges holidays for underprivileged children:* needy, deprived, disadvantaged, poor, destitute, in straitened circumstances, impoverished, poverty-stricken, indigent; Brit. on the breadline.
OPPOSITES: privileged, wealthy.

underrate verb *most of us have a tendency to underrate our own skills:* undervalue, underestimate, do an injustice to, sell short, play down, understate, minimize, diminish, downgrade, trivialize.
OPPOSITES: overrate, exaggerate.

understand verb
1 *at last, she understood what he was saying:* comprehend, grasp, take in, see, follow, perceive, make sense of, fathom; unravel, decipher, interpret; formal apprehend; informal work out, figure out, make head or tail of, get your head around, take on board, get the drift of, get; Brit. informal twig.
2 *I understand how hard you've worked:* appreciate, recognize, realize, acknowledge, know, be aware of, be conscious of.
3 *I understand that you wish to leave:* believe, gather, take it; conclude, infer, assume, surmise.

understandable adjective
1 *he explains these complex issues in understandable, simple language:* comprehensible, intelligible, coherent, clear, unambiguous, transparent, plain, straightforward, digestible, user-friendly.
2 *such fears are understandable | it is understandable that mistakes occur sometimes:* unsurprising, predictable, inevitable; reasonable, normal, natural; justifiable, defensible, excusable, pardonable, forgivable.

understanding noun
1 *test your understanding of the language | war memorials are vital to our understanding of the past:* comprehension, apprehension, grasp, mastery; knowledge, awareness, insight, appreciation, perception.
2 *we had a tacit understanding:* agreement, arrangement, deal, bargain, pact.
3 *he always treated me with understanding:* compassion, sympathy, feeling, concern, consideration, kindness, sensitivity, humanity, charity, mercy, tolerance, forbearance.
4 *it was my understanding that this was free:* belief, perception, view, conviction, opinion, judgement, feeling, impression, assumption, supposition.
5 *a child of sufficient age and understanding to make an informed decision:* intellect, intelligence; judgement, discernment, insight, intuition, acumen, wit.
OPPOSITES: ignorance, indifference.
▷ adjective *an understanding friend:* compassionate, sympathetic, sensitive, considerate, kind, thoughtful, tolerant, patient, forbearing, forgiving, merciful.

understate verb *we have been guilty of understating the size of the problem:* play down, downplay, underrate, underplay, trivialize, sell short, minimize, diminish, downgrade, brush aside, gloss over; informal soft-pedal.
OPPOSITES: overstate, exaggerate.

u

undertake verb
1 *the team were asked to undertake a further project:* take on, handle, manage, deal with, tackle, be responsible for, commit yourself to; embark on, begin, engage in, set about, get down to, get to grips with.
2 *they undertook to keep prices to a minimum:* promise, pledge, guarantee; agree.

undertaking noun
1 *a risky undertaking:* enterprise, venture, project, scheme, plan, operation, endeavour, campaign, effort, task, business, procedure; mission, quest.
2 *he gave an undertaking that customers would not be charged:* pledge, promise, commitment, guarantee, assurance; oath, covenant, vow.

undertone noun
1 *he said something in an undertone:* low voice, murmur, whisper.
2 *the story's dark undertones:* undercurrent, overtone, suggestion, implication, connotation, nuance, vein, atmosphere, aura, tenor, flavour.

undervalue verb *I do not wish to undervalue the role or expertise of my colleagues:* underrate, underestimate, play down, understate, underemphasize, diminish, minimize, trivialize, sell short, belittle.

underwater adjective *there are some underwater caves nearby:* submerged, sunken; undersea, submarine.

underworld noun
1 *the violent underworld of New York:* criminal world, gangland, underbelly; criminals, gangsters.
2 *Osiris, god of the underworld:* the netherworld, the nether regions, hell; Hades.

underwrite verb *the company which underwrote the deal has crashed:* finance, fund, pay for; support, back, guarantee, indemnify, subsidize; informal bankroll.

undesirable adjective
1 *a mix of medicines may result in undesirable side effects:* unpleasant, disagreeable, nasty, unwelcome, unwanted, unfortunate.
2 *some very undesirable people:* unpleasant, disagreeable, obnoxious, objectionable, distasteful, unsavoury.
OPPOSITES: pleasant, agreeable.

undignified adjective *an undignified brawl broke out after the minister was splattered with an egg:* unseemly, indecorous, unbecoming, demeaning, ignominious, shameful, inglorious, degrading, discreditable; ungentlemanly, unladylike; informal infra dig.

undisciplined adjective *he was lazy and undisciplined:* unruly, disorderly, disobedient, badly behaved, recalcitrant, wilful, wayward, rebellious, insubordinate, disruptive, out of control, uncontrollable, wild, anarchic; disorganized, unsystematic, unmethodical.

undisguised adjective *he regarded her with undisguised contempt:* obvious, evident, patent, manifest, transparent, overt, unconcealed, unmistakable, undeniable, plain, clear, naked, visible; blatant, flagrant, glaring; informal standing/sticking out a mile.

undisputed adjective *his military preeminence was undisputed:* undoubted, uncontested, incontestable, unchallenged, incontrovertible, undeniable, indubitable, irrefutable, unmistakable; accepted, acknowledged, recognized.
OPPOSITES: doubtful.

undistinguished adjective *the two goals were the only moments of quality in an otherwise undistinguished game:* unexceptional, indifferent, run-of-the-mill, ordinary, average, commonplace, humdrum, lacklustre, forgettable, uninspired, uneventful, unremarkable, inconsequential, featureless, nondescript, mediocre, middling, moderate; informal nothing to write home about, OK, so-so.

undivided adjective *they need the undivided attention of a sympathetic listener:* complete, full, total, whole, entire, absolute, unqualified, unreserved, unbroken, consistent, exclusive, dedicated.

undo verb
1 *he struggled to undo his belt:* unfasten, unbutton, unhook, untie, unlace; unlock, unbolt; loosen, disentangle, extricate, release, detach, free, open; disconnect, disengage.
2 *this error of judgement served to undo much of the party's work:* cancel out, reverse, invalidate, negate, nullify, overturn; ruin, undermine, spoil, destroy, wreck; Brit. informal scupper.

undoing noun
1 *she plotted the king's undoing:* downfall, defeat, ruin, ruination, end, failure.
2 *their complacency was their undoing:* fatal flaw, Achilles' heel, weakness, weak point, failing.

undone adjective *some work was left undone:* unfinished, incomplete, half-done; neglected, disregarded, ignored; remaining, outstanding, deferred, pending; informal on the back burner.
OPPOSITES: finished.

undoubted adjective *her undoubted natural talent could have been put to better use:* undisputed, unchallenged, unquestioned, indubitable, incontrovertible, irrefutable, incontestable, certain, unmistakable; accepted, acknowledged, recognized.

u

undoubtedly adverb *there is undoubtedly a great deal of work still to be done:* doubtless, indubitably, no doubt, without doubt; unquestionably, indisputably, undeniably, incontrovertibly, certainly, definitely, of course.

undress verb *he undressed and got into bed:* strip, strip off, take off your clothes, disrobe.

undue adjective *make sure that you can afford the repayments without putting undue strain on your finances:* excessive, inordinate, immoderate, disproportionate; unnecessary, unwarranted, unjustified, unreasonable; inappropriate.

undulate verb *the surface of the water undulated:* rise and fall, ripple, surge, swell.

undying adjective *his undying devotion to the club:* abiding, lasting, enduring, permanent, constant; unceasing, perpetual, ceaseless, unending, never-ending; immortal, eternal, deathless.

unearth verb
1 *workmen unearthed an artillery shell:* dig up, excavate, exhume, disinter.
2 *I unearthed an interesting fact:* discover, uncover, find, come across, hit on, bring to light, expose, turn up, root out.

unearthly adjective
1 *there was an unearthly chill in the air:* other-worldly, supernatural, preternatural, alien; ghostly, spectral, mysterious; uncanny, eerie, strange, weird, unnatural; informal spooky, creepy, scary.
2 (informal) *they rose at some unearthly hour:* unreasonable, preposterous, extraordinary, absurd, ridiculous; informal ungodly, unholy.

uneasy adjective
1 *she felt distinctly uneasy about the journey:* worried, anxious, agitated, concerned, nervous, tense, edgy, apprehensive, restless, perturbed, fearful, troubled, uncomfortable, unsettled; informal jittery, nervy.
2 *she had an uneasy feeling that she was being watched:* worrying, disturbing, troubling, disquieting, unsettling, disconcerting.
3 *the victory ensured an uneasy peace:* tense, awkward, strained, edgy, fraught; precarious, unstable, insecure.
OPPOSITES: calm, stable.

uneconomic, uneconomical adjective *it was uneconomic for landlords to maintain rent-controlled housing:* unprofitable, uncommercial, non-viable, loss-making; wasteful, inefficient.

uneducated adjective *the workforce remains largely uneducated and unskilled:* untaught, unschooled, untutored; illiterate, ignorant, ill-informed, uninformed; unsophisticated, uncultured, unenlightened, philistine, benighted.

unemotional adjective *the unemotional way she dealt with her political opponents | a flat, unemotional voice:* detached, dispassionate, reserved, impassive, phlegmatic, stolid, undemonstrative; cold, cool, unfeeling, unsentimental, clinical, impersonal, matter-of-fact, businesslike; emotionless, expressionless, blank.

unemployed adjective *he lost his job in February and is still unemployed:* jobless, out of work, between jobs, unwaged, redundant, laid off; on benefit; Brit. signing on; Brit. informal on the dole, resting.

unending adjective *a seemingly unending series of radio, television, and press interviews:* endless, never-ending, perpetual, eternal, ceaseless, incessant, unceasing, non-stop, uninterrupted, continuous, continual, constant, persistent, unbroken, unabating, unremitting, relentless, interminable.

unendurable adjective *the heat of the stoves made the kitchen almost unendurable:* intolerable, unbearable, insufferable, insupportable, more than flesh and blood can stand.

unenthusiastic adjective *the play opened to unenthusiastic reviews and empty seats:* indifferent, apathetic, half-hearted, lukewarm, cool, unmoved.

unenviable adjective *he is faced with the unenviable task of turning around a business that is both loss-making and heavily in debt:* disagreeable, unpleasant, unwelcome, undesirable, thankless.

unequal adjective
1 *they are unequal in length:* different, dissimilar, disparate, uneven, irregular, varying.
2 *the unequal distribution of wealth:* unfair, unjust, inequitable, disproportionate.
3 *an unequal contest:* one-sided, uneven, unfair, ill-matched, unbalanced.
4 *she felt unequal to the task before her:* incapable of, unqualified for, unsuited to, not up to, inadequate for.
OPPOSITES: equal, fair.

unequalled adjective *an unequalled record of five World Cup victories:* unbeaten, unmatched, unrivalled, unsurpassed, unparalleled, peerless, matchless, incomparable, inimitable, second to none, unique.

unequivocal adjective *the report's advice was unequivocal:* unambiguous, clear, clear-cut, plain, explicit, definite, categorical, emphatic.
OPPOSITES: ambiguous.

unerring adjective *he has an unerring sense of direction:* unfailing, infallible, perfect, faultless, impeccable, flawless; sure, assured.

unethical adjective *it would be impractical and unethical to test this drug on very sick patients:* immoral, amoral, unprincipled, unscrupulous, dishonourable, dishonest, wrong; unprofessional, improper.

uneven adjective
1 *they stumbled over the uneven ground:* bumpy, rough, lumpy, stony, rocky, potholed, rutted, pitted, jagged.
2 *his teeth were yellow and uneven:* irregular, lopsided, crooked, asymmetrical.
3 *the sound quality is uneven:* inconsistent, variable, irregular, erratic, patchy, fitful.
4 *an uneven contest:* one-sided, unequal, unfair, unjust, inequitable, ill-matched, unbalanced.
OPPOSITES: even, regular, equal.

uneventful adjective *his uneventful life was turned upside down by Connie's death:* uninteresting, dull, monotonous, boring, tedious, humdrum, routine, unvaried, ordinary, run-of-the-mill, pedestrian, mundane, predictable.
OPPOSITES: eventful, exciting.

unexceptional adjective *an adequate but unexceptional hotel:* ordinary, average, undistinguished, unremarkable, unmemorable, nondescript, everyday, run-of-the-mill, routine; informal OK, so-so, no great shakes, fair-to-middling.

unexpected adjective *he received an unexpected invitation from Professor Dobson:* unforeseen, unanticipated, unpredicted, unlooked for, without warning; sudden, abrupt, surprising, out of the blue.

unfailing adjective *his mother had always been an unfailing source of reassurance | the unfailing generosity he has shown to people in need:* constant, reliable, dependable, steadfast, steady; endless, inexhaustible, limitless, boundless, infinite.

unfair adjective
1 *the trial was unfair:* unjust, inequitable, prejudiced, biased, discriminatory; one-sided, unequal, uneven, unbalanced, partisan.
2 *his comments were unfair:* undeserved, unmerited, uncalled for, unreasonable, unjustified, unwarranted; Brit. informal out of order.
3 *he was sent off for unfair play:* unsporting, unsportsmanlike, dirty, below the belt, dishonourable.
OPPOSITES: fair, just, justified.

unfaithful adjective
1 *her unfaithful husband:* adulterous, faithless, inconstant; informal cheating, two-timing.
2 *an unfaithful friend:* disloyal, treacherous, traitorous, untrustworthy, unreliable, undependable, two-faced, double-crossing, deceitful, duplicitous; literary false.
OPPOSITES: faithful, loyal.

unfaltering adjective *Emma's unfaltering belief in his writing talent helped him carry on:* steady, resolute, resolved, firm, steadfast, unswerving, unwavering, unflagging, tireless, indefatigable.

unfamiliar adjective
1 *an unfamiliar part of the city:* unknown, new, strange, foreign, alien.
2 *a yellow taxicab was an unfamiliar sight on these roads:* unusual, uncommon, uncharacteristic, novel, out of the ordinary, unexpected.
3 *investors unfamiliar with the stock market:* unacquainted with, unused to, unaccustomed to, inexperienced in, uninformed about, ignorant of, new to, a stranger to.

unfashionable adjective *I had to wear all my sister's unfashionable cast-off clothes:* out of fashion, outdated, old-fashioned, outmoded, dated, passé, démodé; dowdy, frumpy; informal uncool, square, mumsy.

unfasten verb undo, untie, unbutton, unzip, loosen, free; unlock, unbolt, open.

unfathomable adjective *the lyrics are completely unfathomable:* incomprehensible, impenetrable, indecipherable, obscure; inscrutable, enigmatic, mysterious, mystifying, deep, profound.

unfavourable adjective
1 *single mothers are often the target of unfavourable press attention:* critical, hostile, adverse, unfriendly, unsympathetic, negative; discouraging, disapproving, uncomplimentary, unflattering.
2 *the unfavourable economic climate:* adverse, disadvantageous, inauspicious, unpropitious, unpromising, gloomy; unsuitable, inappropriate.
OPPOSITES: favourable, positive.

unfeeling adjective *my mother was a cold, unfeeling woman:* uncaring, unsympathetic, unemotional, uncharitable; heartless, hard-hearted, hard, harsh, austere, cold, cold-hearted, callous.
OPPOSITES: compassionate.

unfeigned adjective *he looked at his wife with unfeigned admiration:* sincere, genuine, real, true, honest, unaffected, unforced, heartfelt, wholehearted.
OPPOSITES: insincere.

unfinished adjective *an unfinished essay:* incomplete, uncompleted; partial, half-done; sketchy, fragmentary, rough, draft.

u

unfit adjective
1 *the film is unfit for children:* unsuitable, unsuited, inappropriate.
2 *he's terribly unfit:* out of condition/ shape, in poor condition/shape, unhealthy.
OPPOSITES: fit, suitable.

unflagging adjective *an unflagging commitment to the ideals of peace:* tireless, persistent, dogged, tenacious, determined, resolute, staunch, single-minded, unrelenting, unfaltering, unfailing.
OPPOSITES: inconstant.

unflappable adjective (informal)
I prided myself on being unflappable even in the most chaotic circumstances: imperturbable, cool, calm, {cool, calm, and collected}, self-controlled, cool-headed, level-headed; informal laid-back.
OPPOSITES: excitable.

unflattering adjective
1 *an unflattering review of his new book:* unfavourable, uncomplimentary, harsh, unsympathetic, critical, hostile, scathing.
2 *an unflattering dress:* unattractive, unbecoming, unsightly, ugly, plain, ill-fitting.
OPPOSITES: complimentary, flattering.

unflinching adjective *he has shown unflinching determination throughout the campaign:* resolute, determined, single-minded, dogged, firm, committed, steady, unwavering, unflagging, unswerving, unfaltering, untiring, undaunted, fearless.

unfold verb
1 *Rajiv unfolded the map:* open out, spread out, straighten out, unroll.
2 *I watched the events unfold:* develop, evolve, happen, take place, occur, progress.

unforeseen adjective *the event had unforeseen consequences:* unexpected, unpredicted, unanticipated, unlooked for; surprising.

unforgettable adjective *a visit to Morocco is a truly unforgettable experience:* memorable, not/never to be forgotten; impressive, outstanding, extraordinary, exceptional.
OPPOSITES: unexceptional.

unforgivable adjective *he had committed the unforgivable sin—he had informed on his friends:* inexcusable, unpardonable, unjustifiable, indefensible; Christianity mortal.

unfortunate adjective
1 *it was some time before the unfortunate girl was rescued:* unlucky, hapless, out of luck, luckless, ill-fated, poor.
2 *the delay was an unfortunate start to our holiday:* inauspicious, unpromising, unfavourable, inopportune, unpropitious, unwelcome.
3 *an unfortunate remark:* regrettable,

inappropriate, unsuitable, infelicitous, injudicious, tactless.
OPPOSITES: fortunate, lucky, auspicious.

unfortunately adverb *unfortunately, she was unable to attend the opening night:* sadly, regrettably, unhappily, alas, sad to say; informal worse luck.

unfounded adjective *the article was a piece of unfounded speculation:* groundless, baseless, unsubstantiated, unproven, unsupported, uncorroborated, unconfirmed, unverified, unattested, without basis, without foundation, speculative, conjectural.
OPPOSITES: proven.

unfriendly adjective *'What do you want?' he asked in an unfriendly tone:* hostile, antagonistic, aggressive; unpleasant, disagreeable, surly, sour, inhospitable, unwelcoming, unsympathetic; unsociable, antisocial; aloof, cold, cool, frosty, distant, unapproachable; informal stand-offish, starchy.
OPPOSITES: friendly, amiable.

ungainly adjective *an uncouth man with an ungainly walk:* awkward, clumsy, ungraceful, graceless, inelegant, gawky, gauche, uncoordinated.
OPPOSITES: graceful.

ungovernable adjective *the country had become ungovernable:* uncontrollable, unmanageable, anarchic; unruly, disorderly, rebellious, riotous, wild, mutinous, undisciplined.

ungracious adjective *it was ungracious not to thank them:* rude, impolite, discourteous, ill-mannered, bad-mannered, churlish, disrespectful, uncouth; informal ignorant.
OPPOSITES: gracious, polite.

unguarded adjective
1 *an unguarded frontier:* undefended, unprotected, unfortified; vulnerable, insecure, open to attack.
2 *an unguarded remark:* careless, ill-considered, incautious, thoughtless, rash, foolish, indiscreet, imprudent, injudicious, ill-judged, insensitive.

unhappiness noun sadness, sorrow, dejection, depression, misery, despondency, despair, desolation, wretchedness, glumness, gloom, gloominess, dolefulness; melancholy, low spirits, mournfulness, woe, heartache, distress, grief, pain; informal the blues.

unhappy adjective
1 *Millie looked very unhappy:* sad, miserable, sorrowful, dejected, despondent, disconsolate, heartbroken, down, downcast, dispirited, downhearted, depressed, melancholy, mournful, gloomy, glum, despairing, doleful, forlorn, woebegone, woeful, long-faced, joyless, cheerless; informal down in the mouth/ dumps, fed up, blue.

u

2 *an unhappy coincidence:* unfortunate, unlucky, luckless; ill-starred, ill-fated.
3 *I was unhappy with the service I received:* dissatisfied, displeased, discontented, disappointed, disgruntled.
OPPOSITES: happy, cheerful, fortunate.

unharmed adjective
1 *they released the hostage unharmed:* uninjured, unhurt, unscathed, safe, safe and sound, alive and well, in one piece, without a scratch.
2 *the tomb was unharmed:* undamaged, unbroken, unmarred, unspoiled, unsullied, unmarked; sound, intact, perfect, unblemished, pristine.
OPPOSITES: injured, damaged.

unhealthy adjective
1 *he looked pale and unhealthy:* unwell, ill, in poor health, ailing, sick, sickly, poorly, run-down; Brit. peaky.
2 *an unhealthy diet | an unhealthy working environment:* harmful, detrimental, injurious, destructive, damaging, insalubrious.
OPPOSITES: healthy, well.

unheard of adjective
1 *the company offered its workers wages and benefits that were unheard of in the industry:* unprecedented, exceptional, extraordinary, out of the ordinary, unthought of, undreamed of, unbelievable, inconceivable, unimaginable, unthinkable.
2 *a game unheard of in the UK:* unknown, unfamiliar, new.
OPPOSITES: common, well known.

unheeded adjective *my protests went unheeded:* disregarded, ignored, overlooked.

unholy adjective
1 *an unholy act:* sinful, wicked, evil, corrupt; ungodly, irreligious, impious, blasphemous, sacrilegious, profane.
2 *an unholy alliance between the Fascists and Communists:* unnatural, unusual, improbable, made in hell.
3 (informal) *she was making an unholy noise:* shocking, dreadful, appalling, terrible, horrendous.

unhurried adjective *he began opening the drawers of his desk in an unhurried way:* leisurely, relaxed, slow, deliberate, measured, calm, easy, easy-going.
OPPOSITES: hasty.

unhygienic adjective *the animals are kept in cramped and often unhygienic conditions:* insanitary, unsanitary, dirty, filthy, contaminated, unhealthy, unwholesome, insalubrious, polluted, foul.
OPPOSITES: hygienic, sanitary.

unidentified adjective *the following day he received a message from an unidentified caller:* unknown, unnamed; anonymous, incognito, nameless.

unification noun *the costs of German unification:* union, integration, merger, amalgamation, coalition, combination, confederation, federation, synthesis.

uniform adjective
1 *a uniform temperature of between 18 and 21 degrees:* constant, consistent, steady, invariable, unvarying, unchanging, stable, static, regular, even.
2 *cut the vegetables into pieces of uniform size:* identical, matching, similar, equal; same, like, homogeneous, consistent.
OPPOSITES: variable.
▷noun *an officer in uniform:* costume, livery, regalia, outfit.

uniformity noun
1 *the constitution is not an attempt to impose uniformity on European diversity:* consistency, conformity, regularity, homogeneity, homogeneousness, equality.
2 *there was a drab uniformity about the place:* monotony, tedium, tediousness, dullness, dreariness.
OPPOSITES: variation, variety.

unify verb *he unified the confederacy into a powerful entity:* unite, bring together, join, integrate, amalgamate, consolidate, coalesce, combine, merge, fuse, blend, mix, bind.
OPPOSITES: divide, separate.

unimaginable adjective *despite his almost unimaginable wealth, he has retained his hunger for the business:* unthinkable, inconceivable, incredible, unbelievable, unheard of, unthought of, untold, undreamed of, beyond your wildest dreams.

unimaginative adjective *the production was plodding and unimaginative:* uninspired, uninventive, unoriginal, pedestrian, prosaic, mundane, ordinary, routine, humdrum, workaday, run-of-the-mill, dull, uninteresting, hackneyed, trite, derivative.
OPPOSITES: imaginative, creative.

unimpeachable adjective *this was information obtained from an unimpeachable source:* trustworthy, reliable, dependable, above suspicion, irreproachable.
OPPOSITES: unreliable.

unimpeded adjective *he had an unimpeded view of them:* unrestricted, clear, unhindered, unhampered, free.

unimportant adjective *the details are unimportant:* insignificant, inconsequential, of little/no importance, of little/no consequence, of no account, trivial, minor, trifling, irrelevant, immaterial, peripheral, extraneous, petty.

uninhabited adjective
1 *much of this land was uninhabited:* unpopulated, unpeopled, unsettled.

u

2 *an uninhabited hut:* vacant, empty, unoccupied, untenanted, to let.

uninhibited adjective
1 *uninhibited dancing:* unrestrained, unconstrained, abandoned, wild, reckless.
2 *I'm pretty uninhibited in company:* unreserved, unselfconscious, free and easy, relaxed, informal, open, spontaneous, outgoing, extrovert, outspoken, frank, forthright; informal upfront.
OPPOSITES: repressed.

uninspired adjective *an album full of uninspired love songs:* unimaginative, uninventive, pedestrian, prosaic, mundane, unoriginal, commonplace, ordinary, routine, humdrum, run-of-the-mill, hackneyed, trite; spiritless, passionless.

uninspiring adjective *they remained a weak and uninspiring political force:* boring, dull, dreary, unexciting, unstimulating; dry, colourless, bland, lacklustre, tedious, humdrum, run-of-the-mill.

unintelligent adjective *a good-natured but unintelligent girl:* obtuse, dull-witted, stupid, slow, vacuous, vapid; informal thick, dim, dense, dumb, dopey.

unintelligible adjective *the dialogue is often unintelligible:* incomprehensible, mumbled, indistinct, unclear, inarticulate, incoherent; baffling, confusing, unfathomable, obscure, opaque, cryptic.
OPPOSITES: intelligible, comprehensible.

unintentional adjective *I assure you, the insult was unintentional:* unintended, accidental, inadvertent, unwitting, unthinking, unpremeditated, unconscious.
OPPOSITES: intentional, deliberate.

uninterested adjective *Dilip was uninterested in politics:* indifferent to, unconcerned about, apathetic about, unenthusiastic about, lukewarm about; bored by.

USAGE

It is best to avoid using **disinterested** to mean the same as **uninterested** in formal writing. Strictly speaking, it should only be used to mean 'impartial' (*the judgements of disinterested outsiders are likely to be more useful*). Although **disinterested** is often used to mean 'not interested' (e.g. *he seemed disinterested in the conversation*), this is not accepted by everyone.

uninteresting adjective *an uninteresting book:* boring, dull, tedious, dreary, uninspiring, unexciting, tiresome, wearisome, lifeless, pedestrian, prosaic, humdrum, colourless, bland, insipid, banal, dry; informal samey.
OPPOSITES: interesting, exciting.

uninterrupted adjective *ten hours of uninterrupted sleep:* unbroken,

continuous, continual, undisturbed, sustained; consecutive.
OPPOSITES: intermittent.

uninvited adjective
1 *an uninvited guest:* unasked, unexpected; unwelcome, unwanted.
2 *uninvited suggestions:* unsolicited, unrequested, unsought.

uninviting adjective *the house looked dark and uninviting:* unappealing, unattractive, off-putting, unappetizing; bleak, cheerless, dreary, dismal, depressing, inhospitable, grim.
OPPOSITES: inviting, tempting.

union noun
1 *political and economic union:* unification, integration, uniting, joining, merger, amalgamation, coalition, combination, synthesis, fusion.
2 *the Students' Union:* association, society, league, confederation, federation.
OPPOSITES: separation, division.

unique adjective
1 *each design is unique:* distinctive, individual, special; exclusive, unrepeated; informal one-off.
2 *a unique insight into the history of this region:* remarkable, special, singular, extraordinary; unequalled, unparalleled, unmatched, unsurpassed, incomparable.
3 *species unique to the island:* peculiar, specific.

unison noun
□ in unison
1 *they lifted their arms in unison:* simultaneously, at the same time, at once, together.
2 *we are in complete unison:* in agreement, in accord, in harmony, of the same mind, as one.

unit noun
1 *the family is the fundamental unit of society | each course consists of three units plus an exam:* component, element, constituent, subdivision; module, section, segment, part.
2 *a unit of currency:* quantity, measure, denomination.
3 *a guerrilla unit:* detachment, contingent, division, company, squadron, corps, regiment, brigade, platoon, battalion; cell, faction.

unite verb
1 *his work unites theory and practice:* unify, combine, integrate, join, link, connect, amalgamate, bring together, knit together, fuse, synthesize.
2 *environmentalists and activists united:* join together, join forces, combine, band together, ally, cooperate, collaborate, work together, pull together, team up.
OPPOSITES: divide.

united adjective
1 *a united Germany:* unified, integrated,

amalgamated, merged; federal, confederate.
2 *the community must join together in a united effort to address the situation:* common, shared, joint, combined, cooperative, collective, collaborative.
3 *they were united in their views:* in agreement, agreed, in unison, of the same mind/opinion, like-minded, as one, in accord, in harmony.

unity noun
1 *European unity:* union, unification, integration, amalgamation; coalition, federation, confederation.
2 *unity between opposing factions:* harmony, accord, cooperation, collaboration, agreement, consensus, solidarity.
3 *the organic unity of the universe:* oneness, wholeness, singleness, uniformity, homogeneity.
OPPOSITES: division, discord.

universal adjective *state-provided education has emerged as a universal feature of developed countries | the show owes much of its success to its universal appeal:* general, common, widespread, ubiquitous; global, worldwide, international; all-inclusive, comprehensive.

universally adverb *progress is not always universally welcomed:* invariably, always, without exception, in all cases; everywhere, worldwide, globally, internationally; widely, commonly, generally.

universe noun
1 *the physical universe:* cosmos, macrocosm; infinity.
2 *in 2002, Sydney became the centre of the sporting universe:* world, sphere, domain, realm.

> WORD LINKS
> **cosmic** relating to the universe
> **astronomy** the branch of science which deals with the universe
> **cosmology** the study of the origin and development of the universe

university noun college, academy, institute; N. Amer. school.

unjust adjective *the unjust treatment of prisoners:* wrongful, unfair, unjustified, undeserved, unwarranted, uncalled for, unreasonable, unjustifiable, indefensible; inequitable, discriminatory.
OPPOSITES: just, fair.

unjustifiable adjective
1 *an unjustifiable extravagance:* indefensible, inexcusable, unforgivable, unpardonable, uncalled for, without justification, unwarrantable; excessive, immoderate.
2 *an unjustifiable slur on his character:* groundless, unfounded, baseless.
OPPOSITES: justifiable, reasonable.

unkempt adjective *a rough-looking youth with long unkempt hair:* untidy, messy, scruffy, disordered, dishevelled, rumpled, bedraggled, in a mess, messed up; tousled, uncombed; N. Amer. informal mussed up.
OPPOSITES: tidy, well groomed.

unkind adjective uncharitable, inconsiderate, unpleasant, harsh, nasty, mean-spirited, callous, unsympathetic, unfeeling, uncaring, hurtful, hard-hearted, cold-hearted; cruel, vicious, spiteful, malicious; informal bitchy, catty.
OPPOSITES: kind, considerate.

unknown adjective
1 *the memo was leaked by an unknown source in the White House:* unidentified, unnamed, nameless, anonymous; undisclosed, unspecified.
2 *an exploration into unknown territory:* unfamiliar, new, unexplored, uncharted, unmapped, untravelled.
3 *many of the paintings are by relatively unknown artists:* obscure, unheard of, unsung; minor, undistinguished.
OPPOSITES: familiar.

unlawful adjective *the unlawful use, production, or supply of a Class A controlled drug:* illegal, against the law, illicit, illegitimate; criminal, prohibited, banned, outlawed, proscribed, forbidden.
OPPOSITES: legal, lawful.

unleash verb *we unleashed the dog:* let loose, release, free, set free, unloose, untie, untether, unchain.

unlike preposition
1 *his latest work is unlike anything he has written before:* different from, dissimilar to.
2 *unlike Elena, he wasn't superstitious:* in contrast to, as opposed to.
OPPOSITES: similar to.

unlikely adjective
1 *it is unlikely they will ever recover:* improbable, doubtful, dubious.
2 *an unlikely story:* implausible, improbable, questionable, suspect, unconvincing, far-fetched, unrealistic, incredible, unbelievable, inconceivable.
OPPOSITES: probable, likely.

unlimited adjective
1 *offshore reserves of gas and oil are not unlimited:* inexhaustible, limitless, infinite, endless, boundless; literary illimitable.
2 *the unit will be given unlimited power to curb all environmentally destructive activities:* unrestricted, unqualified, unconditional.
OPPOSITES: finite, limited.

unload verb
1 *we unloaded the van:* unpack, empty.
2 *they unloaded the cases from the lorry:* remove, offload.
3 *he unloaded his stock before news of the*

u

company's precarious health was made public: sell, offload, get rid of, discard, dispose of, jettison; palm something off on someone, foist something on someone, fob something off on someone; informal dump.

unlock verb *I unlocked the door and led the way in:* open, unbolt, unlatch, unfasten.

unlooked-for adjective *the unlooked-for publicity made his work more saleable:* unexpected, unforeseen, unanticipated, unsought, unpredicted, undreamed of; fortuitous, chance, serendipitous.

unloved adjective *she felt lonely and unloved:* uncared for, unwanted, friendless, unvalued; rejected, unwelcome, spurned, neglected, abandoned.

unlucky adjective
1 *the unlucky passengers are being forced to wait until Friday before they can leave:* unfortunate, luckless, out of luck, hapless, ill-fated; informal down on your luck.
2 *an unlucky number:* unfavourable, inauspicious, unpropitious, ominous, ill-fated, ill-starred, ill-omened, disadvantageous.
OPPOSITES: lucky, fortunate, favourable.

unmanageable adjective *his behaviour was increasingly unmanageable:* uncontrollable, ungovernable, unruly, disorderly, out of control, undisciplined, disruptive, difficult, wayward.

unmanly adjective *he was on the verge of tears but did not wish to appear unmanly:* effeminate, effete; weak, soft; informal wimpish, wimpy.
OPPOSITES: virile.

unmarried adjective *an unmarried woman:* single, unwed; spinster, bachelor; unattached, available, eligible, free.

unmatched adjective
1 *a talent for publicity unmatched by any other politician:* unequalled, unrivalled, unparalleled, unsurpassed.
2 *they have captured all the subtleties of Beethoven with unmatched clarity and balance:* peerless, matchless, without equal, without parallel, incomparable, inimitable, superlative, second to none, in a class of its own.

unmistakable adjective *there was the unmistakable odour of whisky on his breath:* distinctive, distinct, telltale; clear, definite, obvious, evident, patent, indisputable, unambiguous, unequivocal, as plain as the nose on your face.

unmitigated adjective *the raid was an unmitigated disaster:* absolute, unqualified, categorical, complete, total, downright, outright, utter, out-and-out, unadulterated, unequivocal, veritable, perfect, consummate, pure, sheer.

unmoved adjective
1 *he was unmoved by her outburst:*

unaffected, untouched, unimpressed, undismayed, unworried; aloof, cool, unconcerned, indifferent, impassive, impervious.
2 *he remained unmoved on the crucial issues:* steadfast, firm, unwavering, unswerving, resolute, decided, resolved, inflexible, unbending, implacable, adamant.

unnatural adjective
1 *his left leg was bent at an unnatural angle* | *wanting to help other people is not unnatural:* abnormal, unusual, strange, odd, irregular, untypical.
2 *an unnatural colour:* artificial, man-made, synthetic, manufactured.
3 *her voice sounded unnatural:* affected, self-conscious, artificial, stilted, forced, strained, false, insincere.
OPPOSITES: normal, natural, genuine.

unnecessary adjective
1 *many people feel that holiday insurance is unnecessary:* unneeded, inessential, not required, uncalled for, unwarranted, unimportant, optional, dispensable, expendable, disposable, redundant, pointless.
2 *good construction is essential to avoid unnecessary waste:* needless, unwanted, excessive, superfluous.
OPPOSITES: necessary, essential.

unnerve verb *the bleakness of his gaze unnerved her:* demoralize, discourage, dishearten, dispirit, daunt, dismay, disconcert, perturb, discomfit, take aback, unsettle, fluster, agitate, shake, ruffle, throw off balance, alarm; informal rattle; Brit. informal put the wind up.
OPPOSITES: hearten.

unobtrusive adjective *the cinematography is quiet and unobtrusive, never once overshadowing the story:* inconspicuous, unnoticeable, low-key, discreet, low-profile, subtle, understated, unostentatious.
OPPOSITES: obtrusive, conspicuous.

unoccupied adjective
1 *an unoccupied house:* vacant, empty, uninhabited; free, available.
2 *many young people were unoccupied:* at leisure, idle, free, with time on your hands, at a loose end.

unofficial adjective
1 *unofficial figures put the death toll at over 300:* unconfirmed, uncorroborated, unsubstantiated, unauthenticated, off the record.
2 *an unofficial strike:* unauthorized, unsanctioned; unlawful.

unorthodox adjective *he frequently upset other scholars with his unorthodox views:* unconventional, unusual, radical, nonconformist; avant-garde, offbeat, idiosyncratic, eccentric; informal off the wall.
OPPOSITES: orthodox, conventional.

unpaid adjective
1 *unpaid bills:* unsettled, outstanding, due, overdue, owing, owed, payable, undischarged.
2 *unpaid charity work:* voluntary, honorary, unsalaried, pro bono.

unpalatable adjective
1 *unpalatable food:* unappetizing, unappealing, unsavoury; inedible, tasteless, flavourless.
2 *the unpalatable truth:* disagreeable, unacceptable, unpleasant, unwelcome, hard to take.
OPPOSITES: palatable, pleasant.

unparalleled adjective *an unparalleled investment opportunity | a work of unparalleled genius:* exceptional, unique, singular, rare, unequalled, unprecedented, without parallel, without equal; matchless, peerless, unrivalled, unsurpassed, incomparable, second to none.

unperturbed adjective *Daniel was unperturbed by the news:* untroubled, undisturbed, unworried, unconcerned, unmoved, unflustered, unruffled, undismayed, unbothered; informal unfazed.

unpleasant adjective
1 *the side effects can be unpleasant:* disagreeable, distressing, nasty, horrible, distasteful, invidious.
2 *when drunk, he became very unpleasant:* objectionable, obnoxious, disagreeable, nasty, rude, offensive.
3 *an unpleasant smell:* distasteful, unpalatable, unsavoury, uninviting, unappealing; offensive, obnoxious, disgusting, revolting, nauseating, sickening, repugnant, repulsive, repellent.
OPPOSITES: pleasant, agreeable, likeable.

unpopular adjective *he was unpopular at school:* disliked, friendless, unloved; ignored, rejected, shunned, spurned; unwelcome, unwanted.

unprecedented adjective *the scale of the development is unprecedented:* exceptional, extraordinary, unparalleled, unequalled, unmatched, unrivalled, without parallel, without equal, singular, remarkable, unique; unheard of, unknown, new, revolutionary.

unpredictable adjective *the weather in Scotland is notoriously unpredictable | she has a reputation for unpredictable behaviour:* changeable, variable, unreliable, erratic; volatile, unstable, capricious, temperamental, mercurial; unforeseeable, uncertain.

unprejudiced adjective
1 *science must start with unprejudiced observation:* objective, impartial, unbiased, neutral, non-partisan, detached, disinterested.
2 *unprejudiced attitudes:* unbiased, tolerant, non-discriminatory, liberal, broad-minded.
OPPOSITES: prejudiced, partisan.

unpremeditated adjective *this was not an unpremeditated attack:* unplanned, spontaneous, spur-of-the-moment; random.
OPPOSITES: premeditated, planned.

unprepared adjective
1 *she was unprepared for the financial consequences of her decision:* unready, off guard, surprised, taken aback; ill-equipped; informal caught napping, caught on the hop.
2 *they are unprepared to support the reforms:* unwilling, disinclined, loath, reluctant; resistant, opposed.
OPPOSITES: ready, willing.

unpretentious adjective
1 *he was thoroughly unpretentious:* unaffected, modest, unassuming, without airs; natural, straightforward, open, honest, sincere.
2 *an unpretentious hotel:* simple, plain, modest, humble, unostentatious, unsophisticated; Brit. homely.

unprincipled adjective *he is an unprincipled opportunist:* immoral, unethical, unscrupulous, dishonourable, dishonest, devious, deceitful.

unproductive adjective
1 *unproductive soil:* sterile, barren, infertile, poor.
2 *too much time and energy is expended on unproductive activities:* unprofitable, profitless, fruitless, futile, useless, pointless, worthless, ineffective, unrewarding.
OPPOSITES: productive, fruitful.

unprofessional adjective
1 *she was reprimanded for unprofessional conduct:* improper, dishonourable, unethical, unscrupulous, unprincipled, unseemly.
2 *complaints are mounting about the unprofessional job the contractors are doing:* amateurish, unskilled, unskilful, inexpert, incompetent, second-rate, inefficient, unsatisfactory, substandard, poor, shoddy, slipshod.

unpromising adjective *they were not deterred by this unpromising start:* inauspicious, discouraging, unfavourable, disheartening, unpropitious, ominous, ill-omened, bleak.
OPPOSITES: promising, auspicious.

unqualified adjective
1 *an unqualified accountant:* uncertificated, unlicensed; untrained, inexperienced.
2 *those unqualified to look after children:* unsuitable, unfit, ineligible, incompetent, unable, incapable.
3 *the chairman gave the manager his unqualified support:* unconditional, unreserved, unlimited, without

u

reservations, categorical, unequivocal, unambiguous, wholehearted; complete, absolute, downright, undivided, total, utter, unmitigated.

unquestionable adjective *the sincerity of his beliefs is unquestionable:* incontrovertible, indisputable, undeniable, irrefutable, incontestable, undoubted, beyond question, beyond doubt, indubitable, unequivocal; certain, sure, definite, self-evident, evident, manifest, obvious, apparent, patent.

unravel verb
1 *he unravelled the strands:* untangle, disentangle, separate out, unwind, untwist.
2 *detectives are trying to unravel the mystery:* solve, resolve, clear up, puzzle out, get to the bottom of, explain, clarify; informal figure out, suss out, make head or tail of.
OPPOSITES: entangle.

unreadable adjective
1 *the writing was smudged and unreadable:* illegible, hard to read, indecipherable, unintelligible.
2 *heavy, unreadable novels:* dull, tedious, boring, uninteresting, dry, stodgy, heavy going.
OPPOSITES: legible.

unreal adjective *the unreal world of art:* imaginary, fictitious, make-believe, false, artificial; illusory, fanciful.

unrealistic adjective *it is unrealistic to expect changes overnight:* impractical, impracticable, unfeasible, non-viable, unworkable; unreasonable, silly, foolish, fanciful, idealistic, romantic, starry-eyed.
OPPOSITES: realistic, pragmatic.

unreasonable adjective
1 *an unreasonable woman:* uncooperative, unhelpful, disobliging, obstructive, unaccommodating, awkward, contrary, difficult, perverse; obstinate, obdurate, wilful, headstrong, pig-headed, intractable, intransigent, inflexible; irrational, illogical.
2 *unreasonable demands:* unacceptable, unfair, unjust, unjustified, unwarranted; preposterous, outrageous, excessive, immoderate, disproportionate, undue, inordinate, uncalled for.

unrefined adjective
1 *unrefined vegetable oil:* unprocessed, untreated, crude, raw, natural.
2 *he was tough, brave, and polite, though slightly unrefined:* uncultured, uncultivated, uncivilized, uneducated, unsophisticated; boorish, coarse, uncouth.

unrelated adjective *the men had been arrested in two unrelated incidents:* separate, unconnected, independent, unassociated; distinct, discrete.

unrelenting adjective
1 *the unrelenting heat:* continual, constant, continuous, relentless, remorseless, unremitting, unabating, unrelieved, incessant, unceasing, endless, unending, persistent, interminable, merciless.
2 *an unrelenting opponent:* implacable, unyielding, unbending, relentless, determined, dogged, tireless, unflagging, unshakeable, unswerving, unwavering, inflexible, uncompromising.
OPPOSITES: intermittent.

unreliable adjective
1 *he's lazy and unreliable:* undependable, untrustworthy, irresponsible, unpredictable, inconsistent, erratic; fickle, inconstant, faithless.
2 *unemployment can be an unreliable indicator of the tightness of labour markets:* misleading, deceptive, inaccurate, false; questionable, open to doubt, doubtful, dubious, suspect, fallible.
OPPOSITES: reliable, dependable.

unremitting adjective *their lives were little more than unremitting toil:* relentless, unrelenting, continual, constant, continuous, unabating, unrelieved, sustained, unceasing, ceaseless, endless, unending, persistent, perpetual, interminable.

unrepentant adjective *he was unrepentant, claiming that his comments were completely accurate:* unapologetic, unashamed, unabashed, impenitent, unrepenting, shameless.
OPPOSITES: repentant, contrite.

unreserved adjective
1 *the Prime Minister has had the unreserved support of the Opposition:* unconditional, unqualified, without reservations, unlimited, categorical, unequivocal, unambiguous; absolute, complete, thorough, wholehearted, total, utter, undivided.
2 *an unreserved young man:* uninhibited, extrovert, outgoing, open, unconstrained, unselfconscious, outspoken, frank, candid.
3 *unreserved seats:* unbooked, unallocated, unoccupied, free, empty, vacant.
OPPOSITES: qualified, reticent, reserved.

unresolved adjective *some questions remained unresolved:* undecided, unsettled, undetermined, uncertain, open, pending, open to debate/question, in doubt, up in the air.

unrest noun *the government was clearly fearful of social unrest:* disturbance, disorder, agitation, disruption, trouble, turmoil, chaos, anarchy; discord, dissension, dissent, strife, protest, rebellion, uprising, rioting, insurrection.
OPPOSITES: peace.

unrestrained adjective *a period of unrestrained economic growth:*

uncontrolled, unconstrained, unrestricted, unchecked, unbridled, unlimited, unfettered, uninhibited, unbounded.

unrestricted adjective *employees have unrestricted access to all corporate records:* unlimited, open, free, clear, unhindered, unimpeded, unhampered, unrestrained, unconstrained, unconditional, unqualified. OPPOSITES: restricted, limited.

unripe adjective *unripe fruit:* immature, unready, green, sour.

unrivalled adjective *an unrivalled collection of rare coins:* unequalled, without equal, unparalleled, without parallel, unsurpassed, incomparable, beyond compare, inimitable, second to none, matchless, unmatched.

unruffled adjective
1 *he sat smoking a cigarette, looking totally unruffled:* calm, composed, self-possessed, self-controlled, untroubled, unperturbed, unflustered, at ease, relaxed, serene, cool, {cool, calm, and collected}, cool-headed, poised; informal unfazed, laid-back.
2 *the unruffled waters of the lake:* tranquil, calm, smooth, still, flat, motionless, like a millpond.

unruly adjective *the unruly behaviour of a large number of fans caused disturbance and noise in the area:* disorderly, rowdy, wild, unmanageable, uncontrollable, disobedient, disruptive, undisciplined, wayward, wilful, headstrong, irrepressible, obstreperous, difficult, intractable, out of hand, recalcitrant; boisterous, lively. OPPOSITES: orderly, disciplined.

unsafe adjective
1 *there was so much political unrest it was unsafe to remain in the country:* dangerous, hazardous, risky, perilous, life-threatening, high-risk; treacherous, insecure, unsound.
2 *the verdict was unsafe:* unreliable, insecure, unsound, questionable, open to question/doubt, doubtful, dubious, suspect.
OPPOSITES: safe, secure.

unsaid adjective *you've made me say things much better left unsaid:* unspoken, unuttered, unstated, unexpressed, unvoiced, untalked-of; tacit, implicit, understood, not spelled out, taken as read, implied.

unsanitary adjective *the houses are over-crowded and unsanitary:* unhygienic, insanitary, dirty, filthy, unclean, contaminated, unhealthy, germ-ridden, disease-ridden, infested, insalubrious, polluted.
OPPOSITES: hygienic.

unsatisfactory adjective *the decision was taken as a result of the unsatisfactory performance of some of the schools:* disappointing, dissatisfying, displeasing; inadequate, unacceptable, poor, bad, substandard, weak, mediocre, not good enough, not up to par, defective, deficient, imperfect, inferior; informal leaving a lot to be desired.

unsavoury adjective *an unsavoury character:* disreputable, unpleasant, distasteful, disagreeable; dishonourable, immoral, dishonest, unprincipled, unscrupulous; informal shady.

unscathed adjective *his wife and son were fortunate to escape unscathed:* unharmed, unhurt, uninjured, undamaged, in one piece, intact, safe, safe and sound, unmarked, untouched, without a scratch.
OPPOSITES: harmed, injured.

unscrupulous adjective *elderly people are particularly vulnerable to unscrupulous traders:* unprincipled, unethical, corrupt, dishonest, exploitative, dishonourable, immoral, amoral.

unseat verb *an attempt to unseat the president:* depose, oust, remove from office, topple, overthrow, bring down, dislodge, supplant, usurp, eject.

unseemly adjective *an unseemly squabble broke out between the candidates:* indecorous, unbecoming, undignified, discreditable, inappropriate, improper, indelicate, ungentlemanly, unladylike; embarrassing.
OPPOSITES: seemly, decorous.

unseen adjective *an unseen sniper:* hidden, concealed, camouflaged, out of sight; unnoticed, unobserved.

unselfish adjective *he always acted from unselfish motives:* altruistic, selfless, self-sacrificing, self-denying; philanthropic, public-spirited, charitable, generous, magnanimous, noble, benevolent, caring, kind, considerate.

unsettle verb *all this talk of death had unsettled him:* unnerve, disturb, perturb, discomfit, disconcert, upset, alarm, dismay, trouble, bother, agitate, fluster, ruffle, shake, throw, unbalance, destabilize; informal rattle, faze.

unsettled adjective
1 *I began to feel unsettled:* restless, restive, fidgety, anxious, worried, troubled, fretful; agitated, uneasy, unnerved, ill at ease, edgy, on edge, tense, nervous, apprehensive, disturbed, perturbed; informal rattled.
2 *the unsettled weather is expected to continue this week:* changeable, unpredictable, changing, variable, varying, inconsistent, erratic, unreliable.
3 *one question remains unsettled:* undecided, to be decided, unresolved, undetermined, uncertain, up in the air.
4 *the debt is still unsettled:* unpaid,

u

payable, outstanding, owing, owed, to be paid, due.

unshakeable adjective *he has an unshakeable confidence in the team's ability:* steadfast, resolute, staunch, firm, determined, unswerving, unwavering; indefatigable, tireless, unflagging, unyielding, dogged, obstinate, persistent.

unsightly adjective *the community was concerned that the unsightly industrial buildings would discourage tourists:* ugly, unattractive, unprepossessing, disagreeable, unpleasant; hideous, horrible, grotesque.
OPPOSITES: attractive.

unskilful adjective *the furniture had been repaired by an unskilful hand:* inexpert, incompetent, inept, unskilled, amateurish, unprofessional, inexperienced, untrained, unpractised; informal ham-fisted, ham-handed, cack-handed.

unskilled adjective *unskilled manual workers:* untrained, unqualified; manual, blue-collar.

unsociable adjective *he was grumpy and unsociable:* unfriendly, unapproachable, aloof, distant, remote, detached, uncommunicative, taciturn, reticent, reserved, withdrawn, introverted, reclusive; informal stand-offish.
OPPOSITES: sociable, friendly.

unsolicited adjective *he did not take easily to unsolicited advice:* uninvited, unsought, unasked for, unrequested.

unsophisticated adjective
1 *she seemed terribly unsophisticated:* unworldly, naive, innocent, ignorant, green, immature, callow, inexperienced; childlike, artless, guileless, ingenuous, natural, unaffected, unassuming, unpretentious.
2 *unsophisticated software:* simple, crude, basic, rudimentary, rough and ready; straightforward, uncomplicated, uninvolved.

unsound adjective
1 *the building is structurally unsound:* unsafe, unstable, dangerous, in poor condition; weak, rickety.
2 *she was mentally unsound:* disordered, disturbed, unstable, unbalanced.
3 *this line of argument is unsound:* untenable, flawed, ill-founded, flimsy, unreliable, questionable, dubious, tenuous, suspect.
OPPOSITES: sound, strong, cogent.

unspeakable adjective *an unspeakable crime:* dreadful, awful, appalling, horrific, horrifying, horrendous, abominable, shocking, ghastly, gruesome, monstrous, heinous, egregious, deplorable, despicable, execrable, vile.

unspecified adjective *he proposed to*

resign at an unspecified date: unnamed, unstated, unidentified, undefined, unfixed, undecided, undetermined, uncertain, unknown, indefinite, indeterminate.

unspectacular adjective *he had a steady, unspectacular career:* unremarkable, unexceptional, undistinguished, unmemorable; ordinary, average, run-of-the-mill.

unspoilt adjective *large areas of unspoilt countryside:* undamaged, unharmed, untouched, unmarked, unblemished, untainted, unsullied, undefiled; undeveloped, unchanged, in its natural state.

unspoken adjective *there was an unspoken agreement between them:* unstated, unexpressed, unuttered, unsaid, unvoiced, unarticulated, undeclared, not spelled out; tacit, implicit, implied, understood, taken as read.
OPPOSITES: explicit.

unstable adjective
1 *the spectacular but unstable cliffs:* unsteady, unsafe, insecure, precarious, dangerous.
2 *unstable coffee prices:* changeable, volatile, variable, fluctuating, erratic, unpredictable.
3 *he was mentally unstable:* unbalanced, of unsound mind, disturbed.
OPPOSITES: stable, steady.

unsteady adjective
1 *she was unsteady on her feet:* unstable, rocky, wobbly, rickety, shaky, tottery, doddery, insecure.
2 *an unsteady flow:* irregular, uneven, varying, variable, erratic, spasmodic, changeable, changing, fluctuating, inconstant, intermittent, fitful.
OPPOSITES: stable, steady, regular.

unstinting, **unstinted** adjective *the winner thanked her staff and gave unstinting praise to other nominees:* lavish, liberal, generous, open-handed, ungrudging, unsparing, willingly given, ready, profuse, abundant, ample.

unstudied adjective *she had an unstudied grace:* natural, easy, unaffected, unforced, uncontrived, unstilted, unpretentious, without airs, artless.

unsubstantiated adjective *there were unsubstantiated allegations of serious misbehaviour:* unconfirmed, uncorroborated, unsupported, unverified, unattested, unproven; unfounded, groundless, baseless, without foundation.

unsuccessful adjective
1 *an unsuccessful attempt:* failed, without success, abortive, ineffective, fruitless, profitless, unproductive; vain, futile, useless, pointless, worthless.
2 *an unsuccessful business:* unprofitable, loss-making.

u

unsuitable adjective
1 *local residents claim the area is a totally unsuitable site for development:* inappropriate, unsuited, ill-suited, inapt, inapposite, unacceptable, unfitting, ill-chosen, ill-judged, out of place/keeping.
2 *her comment came at an unsuitable moment:* inopportune, infelicitous, untimely.
OPPOSITES: suitable, appropriate.

unsullied adjective *an unsullied reputation:* spotless, untarnished, unblemished, unspoilt, untainted, impeccable, undamaged, stainless, immaculate.
OPPOSITES: tarnished.

unsung adjective *one of the finest unsung heroes of the last war:* unacknowledged, uncelebrated, unhailed; neglected, unrecognized, overlooked, forgotten.
OPPOSITES: celebrated.

unsure adjective
1 *she felt very nervous and unsure of herself:* unconfident, insecure, hesitant, diffident.
2 *he was unsure about accepting the offer:* undecided, in two minds, in a quandary; dubious, doubtful, sceptical, uncertain, unconvinced.
OPPOSITES: sure, confident.

unsurpassed adjective *inside, the quality of the workmanship is unsurpassed:* unmatched, unrivalled, unparalleled, unequalled, matchless, peerless, without equal, inimitable, incomparable, unsurpassable.

unsurprising adjective *his failure to win the leadership of the party was unsurprising:* predictable, foreseeable, to be expected, foreseen, anticipated, inevitable; informal on the cards.

unsuspecting adjective *Roy moved in with Rita and her unsuspecting husband:* unsuspicious, unwary, unwitting; trusting, gullible, credulous.
OPPOSITES: wary.

unswerving adjective *he was unswerving in his devotion:* unwavering, unfaltering, steadfast, unshakeable, staunch, firm, resolute, stalwart, dedicated, committed, constant, single-minded, dogged, indefatigable, unyielding, unbending, indomitable.

unsympathetic adjective
1 *I'm not being unsympathetic but I can't see why you put up with him:* uncaring, unfeeling, unconcerned, insensitive, unkind, heartless, hard-hearted.
2 *the government was unsympathetic to these views:* opposed to, against, antagonistic towards, ill-disposed towards; informal anti.
3 *an unsympathetic character:* unlikeable, disagreeable, unpleasant, objectionable,

unsavoury; uncongenial, unfriendly.
OPPOSITES: sympathetic, caring.

unsystematic adjective *the government is throwing money at the problems in a totally unsystematic way:* unmethodical, disorganized, haphazard, unstructured, unplanned, uncoordinated; indiscriminate, random, inconsistent, irregular, erratic, casual, chaotic.

untamed adjective *the untamed wildlife which proliferates in the region:* wild, feral, undomesticated.

untangle verb
1 *fishermen untangled their nets:* disentangle, unravel, straighten out, untwist, unknot.
2 *the FBI is trying to untangle the mystery:* solve, find the/an answer to, resolve, puzzle out, fathom, clear up, clarify, get to the bottom of; informal figure out.

untarnished adjective *the reputation of the school was untarnished:* untainted, unblemished, unsullied, undamaged, unspoilt, unimpaired; impeccable, spotless, stainless.

untenable adjective *the Government's position is untenable:* indefensible, undefendable, insupportable, unsustainable, unjustified, unjustifiable; flimsy, weak, shaky.

unthinkable adjective *it was unthinkable that John could be dead:* unimaginable, inconceivable, unbelievable, incredible, beyond belief.

unthinking adjective *an unthinking response:* automatic, mechanical, knee-jerk; thoughtless, unconsidered.
OPPOSITES: considered.

untidy adjective
1 *her long dark hair looked damp and untidy:* scruffy, tousled, dishevelled, unkempt, messy, disordered, disarranged, messed up, rumpled, bedraggled, uncombed, ungroomed, straggly, ruffled, tangled, matted, wind-blown.
2 *the room was very untidy:* disordered, messy, in a mess, disorderly, disorganized, in disorder, cluttered, in a muddle, muddled, in chaos, chaotic, topsy-turvy, in disarray, at sixes and sevens; informal higgledy-piggledy.
OPPOSITES: tidy, neat, orderly.

untie verb undo, unfasten, loosen, unknot, unlace, untether, unhitch; loose, free, set free, release, let go.

untimely adjective
1 *an untimely interruption:* ill-timed, badly timed, mistimed; inopportune, inappropriate; inconvenient, unwelcome, infelicitous.
2 *his untimely death:* premature, early, too soon, before time.
OPPOSITES: timely, opportune.

u

untiring adjective *an untiring advocate of political and economic reform:* vigorous, energetic, determined, resolute, enthusiastic, keen, zealous, spirited, dogged, tenacious, persistent, persevering, staunch; tireless, unflagging, unfailing, unfaltering, unwavering, indefatigable, unrelenting, unswerving.

untold adjective
1 *the markets surged ahead, generating untold wealth for some people:* incalculable, immeasurable, inestimable, boundless, limitless.
2 *untold billions have been poured into research:* countless, innumerable, endless, limitless, an infinite number of, without number, uncountable; numerous, many; literary numberless.
3 *the untold story:* unreported, unrevealed, undisclosed, undivulged, unpublished.

untoward adjective *both of them tried to behave as if nothing untoward had happened:* unexpected, unanticipated, unforeseen, unpredicted, surprising, unusual; inappropriate, unwelcome, unfortunate, inconvenient.

untrained adjective *the system can be utilized quickly by untrained users:* unskilled, inexperienced, unpractised; unqualified, unlicensed, amateur, non-professional; untaught, unschooled, untutored.

untried adjective *dealers used their clients as guinea pigs for their untried techniques:* untested, new, experimental, trial, test, pilot.

untroubled adjective *a man untroubled by a guilty conscience:* unworried, unperturbed, unconcerned, unruffled, undismayed, unbothered, unflustered; carefree, serene, relaxed, at ease, happy-go-lucky; insouciant, nonchalant, blasé; informal laid-back.

untrue adjective *these suggestions are totally untrue:* false, untruthful, fabricated, made up, invented, concocted, trumped up; erroneous, wrong, incorrect, inaccurate, mistaken; fallacious, unsound, unfounded, misguided.
OPPOSITES: true, correct, faithful.

untrustworthy adjective *the clubs are vulnerable to untrustworthy treasurers:* dishonest, deceitful, double-dealing, treacherous, traitorous, two-faced, duplicitous, dishonourable, unprincipled, unscrupulous, corrupt; unreliable, undependable.
OPPOSITES: trustworthy, reliable.

untruth noun *the emails contained many untruths:* lie, falsehood, fib, fabrication, invention, falsification, exaggeration; story, myth, piece of fiction; informal tall story, cock and bull story, fairy tale, whopper; Brit. informal porky pie.

untruthful adjective
1 *the answers may be untruthful:* false, untrue, fabricated, made up, invented, trumped up; incorrect, inaccurate, fallacious, fictitious.
2 *an untruthful person:* lying, mendacious, dishonest, deceitful, duplicitous, false, double-dealing, two-faced.
OPPOSITES: truthful, honest.

untutored adjective *to the untrained eye, the symbols look like a series of uninspiring lines and dots:* untrained, untaught, inexperienced, inexpert, unpractised; amateur, unqualified.

unused adjective *she was unused to this kind of work:* unaccustomed to, new to, a stranger to, unfamiliar with, unacquainted with, unconversant with.
OPPOSITES: used, accustomed.

unusual adjective
1 *the unusual sight of a golden eagle flying over Regents Park:* uncommon, unfamiliar, rare, abnormal, atypical, exceptional, unexpected, surprising; strange, odd, curious, out of the ordinary, extraordinary, unorthodox, unconventional, offbeat, outlandish, peculiar, bizarre; informal weird.
2 *a man of unusual talent:* remarkable, extraordinary, exceptional, singular, particular, outstanding, notable, noteworthy, distinctive, striking, significant, special, unique, unparalleled, prodigious.
OPPOSITES: common, usual.

unutterable adjective *moments of unutterable grief:* indescribable, beyond description, inexpressible, unspeakable, undefinable, inconceivable; extreme, great, overwhelming, dreadful, awful, appalling, terrible.

unvarnished adjective *the unvarnished truth:* straightforward, plain, simple, stark; candid, honest, frank, forthright, direct, blunt, straight from the shoulder.

unveil verb *the club has unveiled plans for a new 1600-seat stand:* reveal, announce, present, publish, release, bring out; display, show, exhibit, put on display.

unwanted adjective
1 *an unwanted development:* unwelcome, undesirable, undesired, unlooked for, unfortunate, unlucky, untoward; unpleasant, disagreeable, displeasing, regrettable.
2 *an unwanted guest | unwanted junk mail:* uninvited, unbidden, unasked for, unrequested, unsolicited.
3 *she felt alone and unwanted:* unloved, rejected; superfluous, useless, redundant.
OPPOSITES: welcome.

unwarranted adjective *the criticism is unwarranted:* unjustified, uncalled for, unnecessary, unreasonable, unjust, unfair, undeserved; unjustifiable, indefensible.
OPPOSITES: justified, warranted.

unwary adjective *accidents can happen to the unwary traveller:* incautious, careless, heedless, inattentive, off your guard.

unwavering adjective *their unwavering commitment to their faith:* steady, resolute, firm, steadfast, staunch, unswerving, unfaltering, untiring, tireless, indefatigable, unflinching, uncompromising, sustained, unceasing, enduring, abiding, constant, continuing.

unwelcome adjective
1 *I was made to feel unwelcome:* unwanted, uninvited, excluded.
2 *even a small price increase is unwelcome:* undesirable, undesired, unwanted, disagreeable, displeasing, regrettable, unfortunate.

unwell adjective *he had been feeling unwell for some time:* ill, sick, poorly, indisposed, ailing, not very well, not yourself, under/below par, out of sorts; queasy, nauseous; Brit. off colour, peaky; informal under the weather, lousy, rough; Brit. informal grotty.

unwieldy adjective *he was lugging an overstuffed suitcase and an unwieldy garment bag:* cumbersome, unmanageable; awkward, ungainly, clumsy, large, bulky, heavy, weighty.
OPPOSITES: manageable.

unwilling adjective
1 *the men they are fighting are mostly unwilling conscripts:* reluctant, unenthusiastic, grudging; involuntary, forced.
2 *he was unwilling to take on that responsibility:* disinclined, reluctant, averse, loath
▫ **be unwilling to do something** baulk at, demur at, hesitate to, shy away from, flinch from, shrink from, have qualms about, have misgivings about, have reservations about, have doubts about, not have the heart to.
OPPOSITES: keen, willing.

unwillingness adjective disinclination, reluctance, hesitation, resistance, objection, opposition, doubts, second thoughts, scruples, qualms, misgivings.

unwind verb *the cafe is a perfect place to unwind after work:* relax, ease up, slow down, unbend, rest, put your feet up, take it easy, loosen up; informal chill out, wind down, de-stress; N. Amer. informal hang loose.

unwise adjective *it would have been unwise to argue:* ill-advised, imprudent, foolish, silly, inadvisable, impolitic, injudicious, misguided, foolhardy, irresponsible, rash, hasty, overhasty, reckless.
OPPOSITES: wise, sensible.

unwitting adjective
1 *an unwitting accomplice:* unknowing,

unconscious, unsuspecting, unaware; innocent.
2 *an unwitting mistake:* unintentional, unintended, inadvertent, involuntary, unconscious, accidental.
OPPOSITES: conscious.

unworldly adjective
1 *she was a shy, unworldly girl:* naive, inexperienced, innocent, immature, unsophisticated, ingenuous, artless, guileless, childlike.
2 *an almost unworldly silence:* unearthly, other-worldly, ethereal, ghostly.

unworthy adjective
1 *he was unworthy of trust:* undeserving, unfit.
2 *your behaviour was unworthy of the position you held:* unbecoming, unbefitting, unsuitable, inappropriate, unfitting, unseemly, improper, unacceptable; discreditable, shameful, dishonourable, reprehensible, ignoble, contemptible, despicable.
OPPOSITES: deserving, fitting, worthy.

unwritten adjective *there are unwritten rules about what is acceptable:* tacit, implicit, unvoiced, taken for granted, accepted, recognized, understood; traditional, customary, conventional; oral, verbal, spoken, word-of-mouth.

unyielding adjective *his unyielding defence of traditional Vatican doctrines:* resolute, steadfast, staunch, unwavering, unshakeable, immovable, firm, determined, adamant, uncompromising, unbending, dogged, tenacious; intractable, intransigent, inflexible, rigid, obstinate, stubborn, obdurate, implacable, single-minded.

up-and-coming adjective *up-and-coming young players:* promising, budding, rising, on the up and up, with potential; talented, gifted.

upbraid verb *she had upbraided him firmly for his deception:* reprimand, rebuke, admonish, chastise, chide, reprove, reproach, scold, berate, take to task, give someone a piece of your mind, lecture, lambaste; informal tell off, haul over the coals, rap over the knuckles, bawl out, lay into; Brit. informal tick off, tear off a strip, give someone a rocket/rollicking.

upbringing noun *her upbringing had not prepared her for this | he had a Catholic upbringing:* childhood, early life, formative years; education, teaching, training, instruction.

update verb
1 *security measures are continually updated:* modernize, upgrade, bring up to date, improve, overhaul.
2 *I'll update him on today's developments:* brief, bring up to date, inform, fill in, tell, notify of, apprise of, keep posted; informal

u

clue in, put in the picture, bring/keep up to speed.

upgrade verb

1 *there are plans to upgrade the rail system:* improve, modernize, update, bring up to date, enhance; recondition, refurbish, renovate; reform, rehabilitate.
2 *he was upgraded to a seat in the Cabinet:* promote, give promotion to, elevate, move up, raise.
OPPOSITES: downgrade, demote.

upheaval noun *a period of political upheaval:* disruption, disturbance, turbulence, disorder, confusion, trouble, turmoil, chaos; revolution, change.

uphill adjective *we are facing an uphill task:* arduous, difficult, hard, tough, taxing, demanding, exacting, stiff, formidable, exhausting, tiring, wearisome, laborious, gruelling, back-breaking, punishing, burdensome, onerous, Herculean; informal killing.

uphold verb

1 *the court upheld his claim for damages:* confirm, sustain, endorse, approve, support, back, defend.
2 *they've a tradition to uphold:* maintain, sustain, continue, preserve, protect, keep, hold to, keep alive, keep going.
OPPOSITES: overturn, oppose.

upkeep noun

1 *the upkeep of the road:* maintenance, repair, service, servicing, care, preservation, conservation; running.
2 *the child's upkeep:* financial support, maintenance, keep, subsistence, care.

uplifting adjective *it's an uplifting tale of talent triumphing over prejudice:* inspiring, stirring, inspirational, life-affirming, rousing, moving, touching, affecting, heartening, heart-warming.

upper adjective

1 *the upper floor:* higher, superior; top.
2 *the upper echelons of the party:* senior, superior, higher-level, higher-ranking, top.
OPPOSITES: lower.
□ **the upper hand**
an advantage, the edge, the whip hand, a lead, a head start; ascendancy, superiority, supremacy, control, power, mastery, dominance, command.

upper-class adjective *an upper-class family:* aristocratic, noble, of noble birth, patrician, titled, blue-blooded, high-born, born with a silver spoon in your mouth; informal upper-crust, top-drawer; Brit. informal posh.

uppermost adjective

1 *the uppermost branches:* highest, top, topmost.
2 *his uppermost concern was his wife even though he was ill himself:* predominant, of greatest importance, to the fore,
foremost, dominant, principal, chief, main, paramount, major.

upright adjective

1 *an upright position:* vertical, erect, perpendicular, bolt upright, on end, plumb; Heraldry rampant.
2 *an upright member of the community:* honest, honourable, upstanding, respectable, reputable, law-abiding, right-minded, worthy, moral, ethical, righteous, decent, good, virtuous, principled, noble, incorruptible, trustworthy.
OPPOSITES: horizontal, dishonourable.

uprising noun *the uprising was put down by the police and the army:* rebellion, revolt, insurrection, mutiny, insurgence, rioting, riot; civil disobedience, unrest, anarchy, fighting in the streets; revolution, coup, coup d'état, putsch.

uproar noun

1 *the uproar in the kitchen continued for some time:* turmoil, disorder, confusion, chaos, commotion, disturbance, tumult, mayhem, pandemonium, bedlam, noise, din, clamour, hubbub, racket; shouting, yelling, babel; Brit. row; Brit. informal hullabaloo.
2 *there was an uproar when he was dismissed:* outcry, furore, howl of protest; fuss, commotion, rumpus, hue and cry, brouhaha; informal ructions.
OPPOSITES: calm.

uproarious adjective *an uproarious party:* riotous, rowdy, noisy, loud, wild, unrestrained, unruly, rip-roaring, boisterous; Brit. informal rumbustious.
OPPOSITES: quiet.

uproot verb

1 *other members of her family had been uprooted from their homeland:* move, displace.
2 *all these movements were concerned with uprooting authoritarianism:* eradicate, get rid of, eliminate, root out, destroy, put an end to, do away with, wipe out, stamp out.

upset verb

1 *the accusation upset her:* distress, trouble, worry, dismay, disturb, unsettle, disconcert, agitate, fluster, unnerve, shake; hurt, sadden, grieve.
2 *he upset a tureen of soup:* knock over, overturn, upend, tip over, topple over; spill.
3 *the dam will upset the ecological balance:* disrupt, interfere with, disturb, throw out, turn topsy-turvy, mess up.
▷ **noun**
1 *a legal dispute will cause worry and upset:* distress, trouble, dismay, disquiet, worry, agitation; hurt, grief.
2 *a stomach upset:* disorder, complaint, ailment, illness, sickness; informal bug; Brit. informal lurgy.
▷ **adjective**
1 *she looked pale and upset:* distressed,

troubled, worried, anxious, dismayed, disturbed, unsettled, disconcerted, agitated, flustered, unnerved, shaken; hurt, saddened, grieved; informal cut up, choked; Brit. informal gutted.
2 *an upset stomach:* disturbed, unsettled, queasy, bad; informal gippy.
OPPOSITES: unperturbed, calm.

upshot noun *the upshot of this conflict of interests was a compromise:* result, end result, consequence, outcome, conclusion; effect, repercussion, ramification, reverberations.
OPPOSITES: cause.

upside down adjective
1 *an upside-down canoe:* upturned, upended, overturned, inverted.
2 *they left the flat upside down:* in disarray, in disorder, jumbled up, in a muddle, untidy, disorganized, chaotic, all over the place, in chaos, in confusion, topsy-turvy, at sixes and sevens; informal higgledy-piggledy.

upstanding adjective *an upstanding member of the community:* honest, honourable, upright, respectable, high-minded, law-abiding, right-minded, worthy, moral, ethical, righteous, decent, good, virtuous, principled, noble, incorruptible.
OPPOSITES: dishonourable.

upstart noun *these upstarts, they don't know their place:* parvenu, arriviste, nouveau riche, vulgarian; social climber.

up to date adjective
1 *up-to-date equipment:* modern, contemporary, the latest, state-of-the-art, cutting-edge, new, present-day, up to the minute; advanced.
2 *the journal will keep you up to date with all the important news and events:* informed, in the picture, in touch, au fait, conversant, familiar, acquainted, aware; formal au courant; informal up to speed.
OPPOSITES: out of date, old-fashioned.

upturn noun *an upturn in the economy:* improvement, upswing, upward trend; recovery, revival, rally, resurgence, increase, rise, jump, leap, upsurge, boost.
OPPOSITES: fall, slump.

upward adjective *an upward trend:* rising, on the rise, ascending.
▷ **adverb** *the smoke drifted upward:* up, upwards, uphill; to the top.
OPPOSITES: downward.

upwards adverb *he inched his way upwards:* up, upward, uphill; to the top.
OPPOSITES: downward.
□ **upwards of**
the event usually attracts upwards of 25,000 spectators: more than, above, over, in excess of, exceeding, beyond.

urban adjective *crime rates are significantly higher in urban areas:* town, city, municipal, metropolitan, inner-city, built-up, suburban.
OPPOSITES: rural.

urbane adjective *the urbane and scholarly former information minister:* suave, sophisticated, debonair, worldly, cultivated, cultured, civilized; smooth, polished, refined, self-possessed; courteous, polite, civil, well mannered, mannerly, charming, gentlemanly, gallant.
OPPOSITES: uncouth, unsophisticated.

urchin noun ragamuffin, waif, stray.

urge verb
1 *she urged him to try again:* encourage, exhort, press, entreat, implore, call on, appeal to, beg, plead with, beseech; egg on, spur, push, pressure, pressurize; formal enjoin.
2 *she urged her horse down the lane:* spur on, force, drive, impel.
3 *I urge caution in interpreting these results:* advise, counsel, advocate, recommend.
▷ **noun** *his urge to travel:* desire, wish, need, compulsion, longing, yen, eagerness, yearning, hankering, craving, appetite, hunger, thirst; fancy, impulse; informal itch.

urgent adjective
1 *the urgent need for more funding:* acute, immediate, pressing, dire, desperate, critical, serious, grave, burning, compelling, extreme, high-priority, top-priority; life-and-death.
2 *an urgent whisper:* insistent, importunate, persistent, earnest, pleading, begging.

usable adjective *an old but usable computer:* ready/fit for use, able to be used, at someone's disposal; working, in working order, functioning, functional, serviceable, operational.

usage noun
1 *energy usage:* use, consumption, utilization.
2 *the usage of equipment:* use, utilization, operation, manipulation, running.
3 *the intricacies of English usage:* phraseology, parlance, idiom, way of speaking/writing, mode of expression; idiolect.
4 *the usages of polite society:* custom, practice, habit, tradition, convention, rule, observance; way, procedure, form; mores.

use verb
1 *police used tear gas and water cannons to disperse the protesters | he'd never used a digital camera before:* utilize, make use of, avail yourself of, employ, deploy, wield, ply, apply, put to use, press into service; work, operate.
2 *the court will use its discretion in making an order:* exercise, employ, bring into play, practise, apply.
3 *use your troops well and they will not*

u

let you down: manage, handle, treat, deal with, behave/act towards, conduct yourself towards.
4 *I couldn't help feeling that she was using me:* take advantage of, exploit, manipulate, take liberties with, impose on, abuse; capitalize on, profit from, trade on, milk; informal cash in on, walk all over.
5 *we have used all the available funds:* consume, get/go through, exhaust, deplete, expend, spend; waste, fritter away, squander, dissipate.
▷ **noun**
1 *the use of such weapons:* utilization, usage, application, employment, deployment, operation.
2 *his use of other people for his own ends:* exploitation, manipulation; abuse.
3 *what is the use of complaining—it won't change anything:* advantage, benefit, service, utility, usefulness, help, good, gain, avail, profit, value, worth, point, object, purpose, sense, reason.
4 *composers have not found much use for the device:* need, necessity, call, demand, requirement.

used adjective *a used car:* second-hand, pre-owned, old; worn, hand-me-down, handed-down, cast-off.
OPPOSITES: new.
□ **used to**
as a scientist, he was used to working with vast amounts of data: accustomed to, no stranger to, familiar with, at home with, in the habit of, experienced in, versed in, conversant with, acquainted with.

useful adjective
1 *a useful multi-purpose tool:* functional, practical, handy, convenient, utilitarian, serviceable; informal nifty.
2 *a useful experience:* beneficial, advantageous, helpful, worthwhile, profitable, rewarding, productive, constructive, valuable, fruitful.
3 (informal) *they had some very useful players:* competent, capable, able, skilful, skilled, talented, proficient, accomplished, good, handy.
OPPOSITES: useless, unhelpful, incompetent.

useless adjective
1 *it was useless to try | a piece of useless knowledge:* futile, to no avail, in vain, vain, pointless, to no purpose, unavailing, hopeless, ineffectual, ineffective, to no effect, fruitless, unprofitable, profitless, unproductive.
2 (informal) *he was useless at his job:* incompetent, inept, ineffective, incapable, inadequate, bad; informal pathetic, a dead loss; Brit. informal hopeless.
OPPOSITES: useful, beneficial, competent.

usher verb *she ushered him to a window seat:* escort, accompany, take, show, see, lead, conduct, guide, steer, shepherd.
□ **usher something in**
the railways ushered in an era of cheap

mass travel: herald, mark the start of, signal, set the scene for, pave the way for; start, begin, introduce, open the door to, get going, set in motion, get under way, kick off, launch.

usual adjective *his usual route to work:* habitual, customary, accustomed, normal, routine, regular, standard, typical, established, set, settled, stock, conventional, traditional, expected, predictable, familiar; average, general, ordinary, everyday; literary wonted.
OPPOSITES: unusual, exceptional.

usually adverb *he usually arrived home about 1 o'clock:* normally, generally, habitually, customarily, routinely, typically, ordinarily, commonly, conventionally, traditionally; as a rule, in general, more often than not, in the main, mainly, mostly, for the most part.
OPPOSITES: seldom.

usurp verb
1 *Richard usurped the throne:* seize, take over, take possession of, take, commandeer, assume.
2 *the Hanoverian dynasty had usurped the Stuarts:* oust, overthrow, remove, topple, unseat, depose, dethrone; supplant, replace.

utensil noun *an array of kitchen utensils:* implement, tool, instrument, device, apparatus, gadget, appliance, contraption, aid; informal gizmo.

utilitarian adjective *coal-burning fires have been replaced with utilitarian heaters and radiators:* practical, functional, serviceable, useful, sensible, efficient, utility; workaday, plain, unadorned.
OPPOSITES: decorative.

utility noun *a study that looks at the utility of using sled dogs rather than snowmobiles:* usefulness, use, benefit, value, advantage, advantageousness, profitability, practicality, effectiveness, service, help, helpfulness.

utilize verb *police are utilizing modern technology to assist in criminal investigations:* use, make use of, put to use, employ, avail yourself of, bring/press into service, bring into play, deploy, draw on, exploit.

utmost adjective
1 *a matter of the utmost importance:* greatest, highest, maximum, most, uttermost; extreme, supreme, paramount.
2 *the utmost tip of Shetland:* furthest, farthest, furthermost, farthermost, extreme, very, outermost, endmost.
▷ **noun** *a plot that stretches credulity to the utmost:* uttermost, maximum, limit.

Utopia noun *it may be your idea of Utopia, but it's not mine:* paradise, heaven, heaven on earth, Garden of Eden, Shangri-La; idyll, nirvana, ideal place; literary Elysium.

u

utopian adjective *a utopian vision of global democracy:* idealistic, visionary, romantic, starry-eyed, unrealistic; ideal, perfect, idyllic; literary Elysian.

utter[1] adjective *that's utter nonsense:* complete, total, absolute, thorough, perfect, downright, out-and-out, outright, sheer, arrant, positive, rank, pure, real, veritable, consummate, categorical, unmitigated, unqualified, unadulterated, unalloyed.

utter[2] verb
1 *he uttered an exasperated snort:* emit, let out, give, produce.
2 *he hardly uttered a word:* say, speak, voice, express, articulate, pronounce, enunciate, verbalize, vocalize.

utterance noun *the victory was soured by the jingoistic utterances of the commentators:* remark, comment, statement, observation, declaration, pronouncement, word.

utterly adverb *he was utterly convinced that he had the right man for the job:* completely, totally, absolutely, entirely, wholly, thoroughly, quite, altogether, one hundred per cent, perfectly, really, downright, outright.

uttermost adjective & noun. See UTMOST.

U-turn noun *a complete U-turn in economic policy:* volte-face, turnaround, about-face, reversal, shift, change of heart, change of mind, backtracking, change of plan; Brit. about-turn.

u

Vv

vacancy noun

1 *there are vacancies for computer technicians:* opening, position, situation vacant, post, job, opportunity, place.
2 *the arid vacancy of the desert:* empty space, emptiness, void.

vacant adjective

1 *40 per cent of the offices are still vacant:* empty, unoccupied, available, not in use, free, unfilled.
2 *a vacant look:* blank, expressionless, glazed, glassy, unresponsive, emotionless, impassive, uninterested; vacuous, empty-headed.
OPPOSITES: full, occupied, expressive.

vacate verb

1 *he was forced to vacate the premises:* leave, move out of, evacuate, quit, depart from; abandon, desert.
2 *he will be vacating his post next year:* resign from, leave, stand down from, give up, bow out of, relinquish, retire from; informal quit.
OPPOSITES: occupy, take up.

vacation noun

1 (N. Amer.) *a summer vacation:* holiday, trip, tour, break, mini-break; leave, time off; recess; Military furlough.
2 *the squatters' vacation of the occupied land:* departure from, evacuation of, abandonment of.

vacillate verb *I vacillated between teaching and journalism:* dither, be indecisive, be undecided, waver, hesitate, be in two minds, blow hot and cold, keep changing your mind; Brit. haver, hum and haw; informal dilly-dally, shilly-shally.

vacillating adjective *the campaign sought to portray him as a vacillating liberal:* irresolute, indecisive, dithering, undecided, hesitant, wavering, ambivalent, uncertain, in two minds, blowing hot and cold; informal dilly-dallying, shilly-shallying.
OPPOSITES: resolute.

vacuous adjective *a vacuous smile:* silly, inane, unintelligent, foolish, stupid, fatuous, idiotic, mindless, brainless, witless, vapid, vacant, empty-headed; Brit. informal gormless.
OPPOSITES: intelligent.

vacuum noun

1 *people longing to fill the spiritual vacuum in their lives:* emptiness, void, nothingness.
2 *the political vacuum left by the Emperor's death:* gap, space, lacuna, void.

vagabond noun. See VAGRANT noun.

vagary noun *the vagaries of the British weather:* change, fluctuation, variation, unpredictability, caprice, foible, whim; quirk, peculiarity, oddity.

vagrant noun *a temporary home for vagrants:* tramp, drifter, down-and-out, derelict, itinerant, wanderer, vagabond, transient, homeless person, beggar; N. Amer. hobo; N. Amer. informal bum.
▷ adjective *vagrant beggars:* homeless, drifting, roving, roaming, itinerant, wandering, vagabond, rootless, of no fixed address/abode.

vague adjective

1 *she saw a vague shape in the distance:* indistinct, indefinite, indeterminate, ill-defined; hazy, fuzzy, misty, blurred, blurry, out of focus, faint, shadowy, dim, obscure, nebulous, amorphous.
2 *a vague description:* imprecise, rough, approximate, inexact, non-specific, generalized, ambiguous, hazy, woolly.
3 *they had only vague plans:* hazy, uncertain, undecided, unsure, unclear, unsettled, indefinite, indeterminate, unconfirmed, up in the air, speculative.
4 *she was so vague in everyday life:* absent-minded, forgetful, dreamy, abstracted, with your head in the clouds; informal not with it; Brit. informal scatty.
OPPOSITES: clear, precise, certain.

vaguely adverb

1 *she looks vaguely familiar:* slightly, a little, a bit, somewhat, rather, in a way; faintly, obscurely; informal sort of, kind of.
2 *he fired his rifle vaguely in our direction:* roughly, more or less, approximately.
3 *he smiled vaguely:* absent-mindedly, abstractedly, vacantly.

vain adjective

1 *their flattery made him vain:* conceited, narcissistic, self-loving, in love with

yourself, self-admiring, self-regarding, egotistic, egotistical; proud, arrogant, boastful, cocky, immodest, swaggering; informal big-headed.
2 *a vain attempt to find a solution:* futile, useless, pointless, to no purpose, in vain; ineffective, ineffectual, unavailing, to no avail, fruitless, profitless, unproductive, unsuccessful, failed, abortive, for nothing; thwarted, frustrated, foiled.
OPPOSITES: modest, successful.
☐ in vain
1 *firefighters tried in vain to save him:* unsuccessfully, without success, to no avail, to no purpose, fruitlessly.
2 *his efforts were in vain.* See **VAIN** sense 2.

USAGE

Do not confuse **vain** with **vein** or **vane**. **Vain** means 'having an excessively high opinion of yourself' or 'unsuccessful'; **vein** means 'a tube that carries blood around the body' or 'a particular way, style, or quality' (e.g. *he continued in a more serious vein*); **vane** means 'a broad blade forming part of a windmill, propeller, or turbine'.

valiant adjective *a valiant warrior | neighbours and firefighters made valiant attempts to save her:* brave, courageous, plucky, valorous, intrepid, heroic, gallant, lionhearted, bold, fearless, daring; unflinching, unshrinking, unafraid, dauntless, undaunted, doughty, indomitable, mettlesome, stout-hearted, spirited; informal gutsy, spunky.
OPPOSITES: cowardly.

valid adjective
1 *a valid criticism | they had valid reasons for leaving:* well founded, sound, reasonable, rational, logical, justifiable, defensible, viable, bona fide; cogent, effective, powerful, convincing, credible, forceful, strong, weighty.
2 *a valid contract | all visitors require a valid passport:* legally binding, lawful, legal, official, signed and sealed, contractual; in force, in effect, effective, up to date, current.
OPPOSITES: invalid, spurious.

validate verb
1 *clinical trials now exist to validate this claim:* prove, substantiate, corroborate, verify, support, back up, bear out, confirm, justify, vindicate, authenticate.
2 *over 250 course proposals were validated:* endorse, approve, agree to, accept, authorize, license, certify; ratify, legalize, legitimize.
OPPOSITES: invalidate, disprove.

valley noun dale, vale; hollow, gully, gorge, ravine, canyon; Brit. combe, dene; Scottish glen, strath.

valour noun *the troops fought with great valour:* bravery, courage, pluck, intrepidity, daring, fearlessness, boldness,

dauntlessness, stout-heartedness, heroism; informal guts, spunk.
OPPOSITES: cowardice.

valuable adjective
1 *a valuable piece of jewellery | valuable antiques:* precious, costly, expensive; worth its weight in gold, worth a king's ransom, priceless.
2 *a valuable contribution:* useful, helpful, beneficial, invaluable, productive, constructive, effective, worthwhile, worthy, important.
OPPOSITES: cheap, worthless, useless.

valuables plural noun *valuables may be left in the hotel safe:* precious items, costly items, prized possessions, personal effects, treasures.

value noun
1 *instances of homelessness have increased as a result of rising property values:* price, cost, worth; market price, monetary value, face value.
2 *the value of adequate preparation cannot be understated | the research will be of great value to our industry:* importance, benefit, worth, usefulness, advantage, profit, help, helpfulness; significance.
3 *society's values are passed on to us as children:* principles, standards, beliefs; code of behaviour, moral code, morals, ethics.
▷ verb
1 *his estate was valued at £45,000:* assess, estimate the value of, price, put/set a price on.
2 *she valued his opinion:* think highly of, have a high opinion of, hold in high regard, rate highly, set great store by, appreciate, respect; prize, cherish, treasure.

valued adjective *a valued friend:* cherished, treasured, dear, prized; esteemed, respected, highly regarded.

valueless adjective *cherished but valueless possessions | their efforts were valueless:* worthless, of no value; useless, to no purpose, of no use, profitless, futile, pointless, vain, in vain, to no avail, to no effect, fruitless, unproductive, ineffective, unavailing.

vanguard noun
1 *the experimental spirit of the modernist vanguard:* leaders, founders, founding fathers, pioneers, trailblazers, trendsetters.
2 *this album underscores their position in the vanguard of new Scottish music:* forefront, front, front line, fore, cutting edge.
OPPOSITES: rearguard, rear.

vanish verb
1 *he vanished into the darkness:* disappear, be lost to sight/view, become invisible, vanish into thin air, recede from view.
2 *all hope of freedom vanished:* fade,

V

evaporate, melt away, come to an end, end, cease to exist.
OPPOSITES: appear, materialize.

vanity noun
1 *she had none of the vanity often associated with beautiful women:* conceit, narcissism, self-love, self-admiration, self-regard, egotism; pride, arrogance, boastfulness, cockiness, swagger; informal big-headedness.
2 *the vanity of all human wishes:* futility, uselessness, pointlessness, worthlessness, fruitlessness.
OPPOSITES: modesty.

vanquish verb *he successfully vanquished his rival:* conquer, defeat, beat, triumph over, be victorious over, get the better of, worst; overcome, overwhelm, overpower, overthrow, subdue, subjugate, quell, quash, crush, bring someone to their knees, trounce, rout.

vapid adjective *a vapid musical comedy:* insipid, bland, trite, uninspired, colourless, uninteresting, feeble, flat, dull, boring, tedious, tired, unexciting, uninspiring, unimaginative, lifeless, tame, vacuous.
OPPOSITES: lively, colourful.

vapour noun haze, mist, steam, condensation; fumes, exhalation, fog, smog, smoke; literary miasma.

variable adjective *the wind was variable in direction and strength:* changeable, changing, varying, shifting, fluctuating, irregular, inconstant, inconsistent, unsettled, unpredictable, unreliable, liable to change.
OPPOSITES: constant.

variance noun *minute variances in temperature in the surrounding environment:* difference, variation, change.
□ at variance
1 *his recollections were at variance with documentary evidence:* inconsistent, at odds, not in keeping, out of keeping, out of line, out of step, in conflict, in disagreement; different, differing, divergent, discrepant, dissimilar, contrary, incompatible, contradictory, irreconcilable.
2 *they were at variance with their previous allies:* in disagreement, at odds, at cross purposes, at loggerheads, in conflict, in dispute, quarrelling.

variant noun *there are a number of variants of the same idea:* form, version, variation, permutation; adaptation, alteration, modification.
▷ adjective *a variant spelling:* alternative, other, different.

variation noun
1 *regional variations in house prices | there was little variation in daytime temperatures during April:* change, difference, variance, fluctuation.

2 *about a quarter of the patients show some kind of variation from the norm:* divergence, deviation, departure.
3 *hurling is an Irish variation of hockey:* form, version, variant, permutation; adaptation, alteration, modification.

varied adjective *a varied selection of produce was on offer | he's had a long and varied career:* diverse, assorted, miscellaneous, mixed, sundry, heterogeneous, wide-ranging, multifarious; eclectic, multifaceted; disparate, motley.

variety noun
1 *I enjoy the variety that my current job affords me:* diversity, variation, diversification; many-sidedness.
2 *a wide variety of flowers and shrubs:* assortment, miscellany, range, array, collection, selection, mixture, medley, multiplicity; mixed bag, motley collection, potpourri.
3 *fifty varieties of pasta:* sort, kind, type; class, category, style, form.
OPPOSITES: uniformity.

various adjective *dresses of various colours:* diverse, different, differing, varied, varying, a variety of, assorted, mixed, sundry, miscellaneous, heterogeneous, disparate, motley.
OPPOSITES: uniform.

vary verb
1 *estimates of the probable cost vary:* differ, be different, be dissimilar.
2 *rates of interest vary over time:* fluctuate, rise and fall, go up and down, change, alter, shift, swing.
3 *the diaphragm is used for varying the aperture of the lens | 60 per cent of employers say they let staff vary their hours:* modify, change, alter, adjust; diversify.

vast adjective *a vast area of land | vast amounts of money:* huge, enormous, extensive, expansive, broad, wide; immense, great, massive, colossal, tremendous, mighty, prodigious, gigantic, gargantuan, mammoth, monumental; giant, towering, mountainous, titanic; literary Brobdingnagian; informal whopping, humongous, astronomical; Brit. informal ginormous.
OPPOSITES: tiny.

vat noun *a vat of hot tar:* tub, tank, cistern, barrel, butt, cask, drum, basin; vessel, receptacle, container.

vault[1] noun
1 *the jewels are kept in the vault of a Swiss bank:* strongroom.
2 *he was buried in the family vault in the church at Bawdsey:* crypt, undercroft, catacomb, burial chamber; tomb, mausoleum.
3 *the highest Gothic vault in Europe:* arched roof, dome, arch.

V

vault² verb *he vaulted over the gate:* jump over, leap over, spring over, bound over; hurdle, clear.

vaunt verb *the centre has been vaunted as the new Eden project:* boast about, brag about, make much of, parade; acclaim, praise, extol, celebrate.

veer verb *the car veered to the left and crashed into a van:* turn, swerve, swing, sheer, skew, career; change direction/course, go off course.

vegetate verb *I don't want to sit and vegetate in front of the television:* do nothing, idle, languish, laze, lounge, loll; moulder, stagnate; informal veg out.

vegetation noun plants, greenery, foliage; technical flora; literary verdure.

vehemence noun *she was taken aback by the vehemence of the reactions:* passion, force, forcefulness, ardour, fervour, violence, urgency, strength, vigour, intensity, keenness, enthusiasm, zeal.

vehement adjective *a vehement attack on the government's economic policies | a vehement opponent of capital punishment:* passionate, forceful, ardent, impassioned, heated, spirited, urgent, fervent, violent, fierce, strong, forcible, powerful, emphatic, vigorous, intense, earnest, keen, enthusiastic, zealous.
OPPOSITES: mild, apathetic.

vehicle noun
1 *vehicles are not permitted in this area:* motor vehicle.
2 *music provides a vehicle for the expression of emotional unrest:* channel, medium, means of expression, agency, agent, instrument, mechanism.

> WORD LINKS
> **automotive** relating to motor vehicles

veil noun *a thin veil of high cloud made the sun hazy:* covering, cover, screen, curtain, mantle, cloak, mask, blanket, shroud, canopy, cloud, pall.
▷ verb *the peak was veiled in mist:* envelop, surround, swathe, enfold, cover, conceal, hide, screen, shield, cloak, blanket, shroud; obscure.

veiled adjective *veiled threats | a veiled reference to his past:* indirect, implicit, implied, inexplicit, oblique, cryptic, elliptical.
OPPOSITES: overt.

vein noun
1 *a vein in his neck pulsed:* blood vessel.
2 *the mineral veins in the rock:* layer, lode, seam, stratum, stratification, deposit.
3 *white marble with grey veins:* streak, marking, mark, line, stripe, strip, band, striation.
4 *he closes the article in a humorous vein:* mood, humour, frame of mind, temper,

attitude, tenor, tone, key, spirit; manner, way, style.

> WORD LINKS
> **vascular**, **venous** relating to a vein or veins
> **phlebotomy** the surgical opening or incision of a vein

> USAGE
>
> Do not confuse **vein** with **vain** or **vane**. The chief meanings of **vein** are 'a tube that carries blood around the body' and 'a particular way, style, or quality'. **Vain** means 'having too high an opinion of yourself' (*their flattery made him vain*) or 'unsuccessful' (*a vain attempt to find a solution*); **vane** means 'a broad blade forming part of a windmill, propeller, or turbine'.

velocity noun
1 (technical) *light travels at a constant velocity:* speed.
2 (in general use) *the velocity of globalization is not in doubt:* speed, rate, pace, tempo, momentum; swiftness, rapidity.

venal adjective *local customs officers are notoriously venal:* corrupt, corruptible, susceptible to bribery; dishonest, untrustworthy, unscrupulous, unprincipled, dishonourable; informal bent.
OPPOSITES: honest.

> USAGE
>
> **Venal** and **venial** are sometimes confused. **Venal** means 'prepared to do dishonest or immoral things in return for money', whereas **venial** is used to refer to a sin or fault that is minor and able to be forgiven.

vendetta noun *the victim of a political vendetta | certain sections of the press were conducting a vendetta against him:* feud, quarrel, argument, dispute; campaign, fight, war.

vendor noun
1 *ice-cream vendors were doing a brisk trade:* seller, trader, stallholder; huckster, pedlar, hawker.
2 *independent software vendors:* seller, dealer, merchant, supplier; formal purveyor.

veneer noun
1 *American cherry wood with a maple veneer:* surface, lamination, layer, overlay, facing, covering, finish, exterior.
2 *a veneer of sophistication:* facade, front, false front, show, outward display, appearance, impression, semblance, guise, disguise, mask, masquerade, pretence, camouflage.

venerable adjective *he was a venerable older statesman:* respected, venerated, revered, honoured, esteemed, hallowed, august, distinguished, eminent, great.

venerate verb *Duchamp was venerated as a grand old man of the pre-war avant-garde:*

V

revere, hold in high esteem/regard, look up to, honour, respect, esteem; worship, adore, pay homage to.

veneration noun *Verdi's lifelong veneration for Shakespeare:* reverence, admiration, high regard, honour, respect, esteem; worship, adoration.

vengeance noun *he sought vengeance for the murder of his father:* revenge, retribution, retaliation, reprisal, satisfaction, an eye for an eye (and a tooth for a tooth).
□ **with a vengeance**
I set to work with a vengeance: vigorously, strenuously, energetically, with a will, with all the stops out, for all you are worth, all out, flat out.

vengeful adjective *Whistler's vengeful creditors were determined to ruin him:* vindictive, revengeful, out for revenge, unforgiving, grudge-bearing.
OPPOSITES: forgiving.

venial adjective *a venial sin | venial faults:* forgivable, pardonable, excusable; slight, minor, unimportant, insignificant.
OPPOSITES: mortal, unforgivable.

> USAGE
>
> Do not confuse **venial** with **venal**. **Venial** is used to refer to a sin or fault that is minor and able to be forgiven, while **venial** means 'prepared to do dishonest or immoral things in return for money' (*a self-serving, venal politician*).

venom noun
1 *snake venom:* poison, toxin.
2 *his voice was full of venom:* malice, spite, bitterness, vindictiveness, maliciousness, ill will, rancour, vitriol, bile, hostility, animosity, animus, acrimony, hate, hatred, malevolence.

venomous adjective
1 *a venomous snake | the spider's venomous bite:* poisonous, toxic; dangerous, deadly, lethal, fatal, mortal.
2 *each of his statements was more provocative and venomous than the one before:* vicious, malicious, spiteful, bitter, vitriolic, vindictive, poisonous, rancorous, acrimonious, antagonistic, hostile, malevolent; informal bitchy, catty.
OPPOSITES: harmless, benevolent.

vent noun *an air vent:* outlet, inlet, opening, aperture, hole, gap, orifice, space; duct, flue, shaft, well, passage, airway.
▷ **verb** *demonstrators vented their anger over the military strikes:* let out, give vent to, give free rein to, release, pour out, express, give expression to, air, voice, give voice to, ventilate.

ventilate verb
1 *the greenhouse must be properly ventilated:* air, aerate, oxygenate, air-condition; freshen, cool.

2 *workers ventilated their discontent:* express, give expression to, air, bring into the open, communicate, voice, give voice to, discuss.

venture noun *a business venture:* enterprise, undertaking, project, scheme, operation, endeavour; speculation, gamble, experiment.
▷ **verb**
1 *we ventured across the moor:* set out, go, travel, journey.
2 *he ventured the opinion that the team could only improve:* put forward, advance, offer, suggest, moot; risk.
3 *may I venture to add a few comments?* dare, make so bold as, presume; take the liberty of; informal stick your neck out, go out on a limb.

verbal adjective *he was given a verbal assurance that his application would be approved:* oral, spoken; unwritten.

verbatim adverb *their stories were taped and then transcribed verbatim:* word for word, letter for letter, line for line, to the letter, literally, exactly, precisely, faithfully.

verbose adjective *his prose is often annoyingly verbose:* wordy, long-winded, lengthy, prolix, tautological, periphrastic, circumlocutory, circuitous, diffuse, digressive, rambling; Brit. informal waffly.
OPPOSITES: succinct.

verbosity noun *the Internet is no place for verbosity:* wordiness, long-windedness, verbiage, prolixity, tautology, circumlocution; Brit. informal waffle.

verdant adjective *the verdant forests of southern Vermont:* green, leafy, grassy; lush, rich.

verdict noun *the coroner recorded a verdict of death by misadventure:* judgement, adjudication, decision, finding, ruling, resolution, pronouncement, conclusion, opinion.

verge noun
1 *the verge of the lake:* edge, border, margin, side, brink, rim, lip; fringe, boundary, perimeter.
2 *Spain was on the verge of an economic crisis:* brink, threshold, edge, point.
▷ **verb** *a degree of caution that verged on the obsessive:* approach, border on, be close/ near to, be tantamount to; tend towards, approximate to, resemble.

verification noun *there has been no independent scientific verification of her claim:* confirmation, substantiation, proof, corroboration, support, attestation, validation, authentication, endorsement.

verify verb *reports of the massacre could not be verified | his conclusions have been verified by later experiments:* substantiate, confirm, prove, corroborate, back up, bear

out, justify, support, uphold, attest to, testify to, validate, authenticate, endorse, certify.
OPPOSITES: refute.

vernacular noun *he wrote in the vernacular to reach a wider audience:* everyday language, colloquial language, conversational language, common parlance; dialect, regional language, regionalisms, patois.

versatile adjective
1 *a versatile player who can play in a number of positions:* adaptable, flexible, multitalented, all-round; resourceful.
2 *a versatile tool:* multi-purpose, adjustable, all-purpose

verse noun
1 *Elizabethan verse:* poetry, poems, versification, balladry.
2 *a poem with sixty verses:* stanza, canto, couplet.
OPPOSITES: prose.

version noun
1 *his version of events:* account, report, description, record, story, rendering, interpretation, explanation, understanding, reading, impression; side.
2 *the English version will be published next year:* edition, translation, impression.
3 *they have replaced coal-burning fires with gas versions:* form, sort, kind, type, variety, model.

vertex noun *a line was drawn from the vertex of the figure to the middle of the base:* apex, peak, tip, top.

vertical adjective *the manhole lid conceals a vertical shaft:* perpendicular, upright, erect, plumb, straight up and down, on end, standing, bolt upright, upended.
OPPOSITES: horizontal.

vertigo noun dizziness, giddiness, light-headedness.

verve noun *he performed with verve and panache:* enthusiasm, vigour, energy, dynamism, elan, vitality, vivacity, buoyancy, liveliness, animation, zest, sparkle, spirit, ebullience, life, brio, gusto, eagerness, keenness, passion, zeal, relish, feeling, ardour, fire.

very adverb *that's very kind of you | I'm very sorry:* extremely, exceedingly, exceptionally, extraordinarily, tremendously, immensely, deeply, intensely, acutely, abundantly, singularly, decidedly, particularly, supremely, highly, remarkably, really, truly, terribly, most; informal awfully, dreadfully, seriously, mega, ultra; Brit. informal ever so, well, dead, jolly.
OPPOSITES: slightly.
▷ adjective
1 *those were his very words:* exact, actual, precise.
2 *the very thought of food made her feel ill:* mere, simple, pure; sheer.

vessel noun
1 *a fishing vessel:* boat, ship, craft.
2 *pour the mixture into a heatproof vessel:* container, receptacle, holder; basin, bowl, pan, pot; cask, barrel, drum, butt, vat, urn.

vest verb *executive power is vested in the President:* confer on, entrust to, invest in, bestow on, grant to, give to; endow, lodge, lay, place.

vestibule noun *we sat in a high vestibule between the street and the courtyard:* entrance hall, hall, hallway, entrance, porch, portico, foyer, lobby, anteroom, antechamber, waiting room.

vestige noun
1 *the last vestiges of colonialism:* remnant, fragment, relic, echo, indication, sign, trace, mark, legacy, reminder; remains.
2 *she showed no vestige of emotion:* bit, touch, hint, suggestion, suspicion, shadow, scrap, tinge, speck, shred, jot, iota, whit, scintilla, glimmer; informal smidgen.

vestigial adjective
1 *vestigial limbs:* rudimentary, undeveloped; non-functional.
2 *he felt a vestigial flicker of anger from last night:* remaining, surviving, residual, leftover, lingering.

vet verb *press releases are vetted by an executive council:* check, examine, scrutinize, inspect, look over, screen, investigate; assess, evaluate, appraise; informal check out.

veteran noun *a veteran of 16 political campaigns:* old hand, past master, doyen; informal old-timer, old warhorse.
OPPOSITES: novice.
▷ adjective *a veteran diplomat:* long-serving, seasoned, old, hardened; adept, expert, well trained, practised, experienced; informal battle-scarred.

veto noun
1 *Britain would maintain its veto on the EU's tax policies:* right to reject.
2 *the Pope's veto on abortions:* ban, prohibition, embargo, interdiction.
OPPOSITES: approval.
▷ verb *the council vetoed plans to build a new housing development on the land:* reject, turn down, throw out, refuse to accept, dismiss, rule out; forbid, prohibit, embargo, ban; informal put the kibosh on, give the thumbs down to.
OPPOSITES: approve.

vex verb *Alice was vexed by his remarks:* annoy, irritate, anger, infuriate, exasperate, irk, gall, pique, put out, antagonize, get on someone's nerves, make someone's hackles rise, rankle; Brit. rub up the wrong way; informal aggravate, rile, nettle, needle, get to, bug, hack off, get someone's back up; Brit. informal wind up, nark.

V

vexation noun *she stamped her foot in vexation:* annoyance, irritation, exasperation, indignation, anger, displeasure, pique, disgruntlement; informal aggravation.

vexatious adjective *this is yet another vexatious regulation:* annoying, irritating, infuriating, tiresome, troublesome, irksome, vexing, frustrating; informal aggravating.

vexed adjective
1 *the vexed issue of border controls:* contentious, controversial, in dispute, disputed, debated, at issue; problematic, difficult, knotty, thorny.
2 *a vexed expression:* annoyed, irritated, cross, angry, infuriated, exasperated, irked, piqued, displeased, put out, disgruntled; informal aggravated, peeved, nettled, miffed, riled, hacked off; Brit. informal narked.

viable adjective *the committee came forward with the only viable solution:* feasible, workable, practicable, practical, possible, realistic, achievable, attainable; informal doable.
OPPOSITES: impracticable.

vibrant adjective
1 *a vibrant and passionate woman:* spirited, lively, full of life, energetic, vigorous, vital, animated, vivacious, dynamic, stimulating, exciting, passionate.
2 *a huge room decorated in vibrant blues and greens:* vivid, bright, striking, brilliant, strong, rich.
3 *his vibrant voice:* resonant, sonorous, reverberant, resounding, ringing, echoing; strong, rich, full.
4 *she was vibrant with anger:* quivering, trembling, shaking, pulsating.
OPPOSITES: lifeless, pale.

vibrate verb
1 *the floor beneath them vibrated:* quiver, shake, tremble, shiver, shudder, judder, throb, pulsate; oscillate.
2 *a low rumbling sound began to vibrate through the car:* reverberate, resonate, resound, ring, echo.

vibration noun tremor, shaking, quivering, quaking, judder, juddering, shuddering, throb, throbbing, pulsation.

vicar noun minister, rector, priest, parson, clergyman, clergywoman, cleric, ecclesiastic, pastor, father, man/woman of the cloth, curate, chaplain; informal reverend, padre.

vice noun
1 *a seedy world of drugs and vice:* immorality, corruption, wickedness, evil, iniquity, villainy, crime; depravity, degeneracy; sin.
2 *smoking is her only vice:* shortcoming, failing, flaw, fault, defect, weakness, foible, frailty.
OPPOSITES: virtue.

vicinity noun *people living in the vicinity are strongly opposed to the scheme:* neighbourhood, surrounding area, locality, locale, area, district, region, zone; environs, surroundings; informal neck of the woods.
□ **in the vicinity of**
the budget's going to be in the vicinity of $11 million: around, about, nearly, circa, approaching, roughly, something like, more or less; in the region of, near to, close to; Brit. getting on for.

vicious adjective
1 *a vicious killer:* brutal, ferocious, savage, violent, dangerous, ruthless, remorseless, merciless, heartless, callous, cruel, harsh, cold-blooded, inhuman, fierce, barbarous, barbaric, brutish, bloodthirsty, fiendish, sadistic, monstrous, murderous, homicidal.
2 *the paper has waged an astonishingly vicious campaign against her:* malicious, malevolent, spiteful, vindictive, venomous, poisonous, rancorous, mean, cruel, bitter, acrimonious, hostile; defamatory, slanderous.
OPPOSITES: gentle, kindly.

vicissitude noun *he maintains his sunny disposition despite life's vicissitudes:* change, alteration, shift, reversal, downturn; fluctuation, instability, uncertainty, unpredictability, variability, changeability; ups and downs.

victim noun
1 *a victim of domestic violence | earthquake victims:* sufferer, injured party, casualty; fatality, loss.
2 *the victim of a confidence trick:* dupe, target, prey, quarry, object, subject; informal stooge, sucker, fall guy; N. Amer. informal patsy.
3 *a sacrificial victim:* sacrifice, offering.
□ **fall victim to**
at the age of five she fell victim to smallpox: fall ill with, be stricken with, catch, develop, contract, pick up; succumb to, die from; informal go down with.

victimize verb *she was being victimized by her violent ex-husband:* persecute, pick on, intimidate, bully, abuse, terrorize, torment, harass, ill-treat, mistreat, maltreat; discriminate against.

victor verb winner, champion, conqueror, hero.
OPPOSITES: loser.

victorious adjective *the victorious British team brought the trophy back from Paris:* triumphant, conquering, winning, champion, successful, top, first; undefeated, unbeaten.

victory noun *they had won a tremendous victory:* success, triumph, conquest, win, coup; landslide.
OPPOSITES: defeat.

vie verb *restaurants vied with each other to attract custom:* compete, contend, contest, struggle, fight, battle, jockey, jostle.

V

view noun

1 *he has strong political views:* opinion, point of view, viewpoint, belief, conviction, persuasion, attitude, judgement, thinking, notion, idea, concept, hypothesis, theory; stance, standpoint, approach; feeling, sentiment.
2 *the view from her flat:* outlook, vista, prospect, panorama, scene, aspect, perspective, spectacle, sight; scenery, landscape.
3 *the church came into view:* sight, perspective, vision, visibility.

▷ **verb**
1 *free admission allows people to drop in to the gallery to view their favourite works:* look at, eye, observe, gaze at, stare at, contemplate, regard, scan, survey, inspect, scrutinize; informal check out.
2 *25 years ago, the organic movement was viewed as a joke:* consider, regard as, look on as, see as, perceive as, judge to be, deem, reckon to be.

□ **in view of**
in view of the controversy, we had expected the planning bid to be discussed in public: considering, bearing in mind, taking into account, on account of, in the light of, owing to, because of, as a result of.

□ **on view**
a collection of early Impressionist work is currently on view: on display, on exhibition, on show.

viewer noun *the new series has been a smash hit with viewers:* watcher, spectator; (**viewers**) audience, crowd.

viewpoint noun *as a newspaper, we must present different viewpoints whether we agree with them or not:* opinion, view, point of view, belief, attitude, feeling, sentiment, thinking; position, perspective, stance, standpoint, outlook.

vigilant adjective *there had been a rash of petty thefts and we were warned to be vigilant:* watchful, observant, attentive, alert, on the lookout, on your toes, eagle-eyed, hawk-eyed; wide awake, on your guard, cautious, wary, circumspect; informal beady-eyed.
OPPOSITES: inattentive.

vigorous adjective
1 *try to have 20 minutes vigorous exercise at least three times a week:* strenuous, energetic, brisk.
2 *the president's vigorous defence of his foreign policy:* energetic, strenuous, spirited, determined, powerful, strong, passionate, fervent, vehement; aggressive, hard-hitting.
3 *a tall, vigorous man:* robust, healthy, hale and hearty, strong, sturdy, hardy, tough, fit, athletic; energetic, active, lively, vibrant, dynamic.
OPPOSITES: weak, feeble.

vigour noun *they set about the task with renewed vigour:* energy, vitality, zest, verve, spirit, eagerness, enthusiasm, determination, dynamism; zeal, passion, fervour.
OPPOSITES: lethargy.

vile adjective
1 *a vile smell:* foul, nasty, disgusting, offensive, obnoxious, revolting, repulsive, horrible, dreadful, awful, terrible, appalling, abominable, atrocious, odious, nauseating, sickening, execrable; informal gross.
2 *a vile crime:* wicked, evil, iniquitous, appalling, shocking, heinous, abhorrent, monstrous, repugnant, deplorable, loathsome, hateful, contemptible, despicable.
OPPOSITES: pleasant.

vilify verb *he was regularly vilified in the tabloid press:* revile, condemn, abuse, malign, denigrate, defame, run down, disparage, criticize; informal pull apart, lay into, slam, bad-mouth; Brit. informal rubbish.
OPPOSITES: praise.

villain noun criminal, offender, felon, miscreant, wrongdoer; rogue, scoundrel; formal malefactor; informal crook.

villainous adjective wicked, evil, iniquitous, sinful, nefarious, vile, foul, monstrous, outrageous, atrocious, abominable, reprehensible, hateful, odious, contemptible, horrible, heinous, egregious, diabolical, fiendish, vicious, murderous; criminal, illegal, illicit, unlawful, lawless; immoral, corrupt, dishonourable, dishonest, unscrupulous, unprincipled; informal crooked, bent.
OPPOSITES: virtuous.

villainy noun wickedness, evil, iniquity, wrongdoing, dishonesty, corruption; crime, vice, criminality, lawlessness, lawbreaking.

vindicate verb
1 *he was vindicated by the jury:* acquit, clear, absolve, exonerate; informal let off.
2 *these figures vindicate claims that the government has consistently underestimated treasury receipts:* justify, show to be justified, show to be correct, uphold, support, defend, warrant; substantiate, corroborate, verify, confirm, prove.

vindictive adjective *the criticism was both vindictive and personalized:* vengeful, resentful, bitter, rancorous, baleful; spiteful, malicious, poisonous, venomous, malevolent, cruel.
OPPOSITES: forgiving.

violate verb
1 *they have violated the terms of the ceasefire:* contravene, breach, infringe, break, disobey, defy, flout; disregard, ignore.
2 *the tomb was violated:* desecrate, profane, defile; damage, vandalize, deface, destroy.
OPPOSITES: comply with, respect.

V

violation noun *the violation of UN resolutions:* contravention, breach, infringement, infraction, defiance.

violence noun
1 *accusations of police violence:* brutality, brute force, savagery, cruelty, barbarity.
2 *the violence of the blow:* forcefulness, force, power, strength, might, savagery, ferocity, brutality.
3 *the violence of her own feelings:* intensity, strength, force, vehemence, power.

violent adjective
1 *a violent criminal:* brutal, vicious, savage, rough, aggressive, fierce, wild, ferocious; cruel, thuggish, barbarous, barbaric; homicidal, murderous, dangerous.
2 *a violent blow to the back of his head:* powerful, forceful, hard, sharp, strong, vigorous, hefty, mighty; savage, ferocious, brutal, vicious.
3 *violent hatred:* strong, powerful, intense, vehement, extreme, acute; uncontrollable, ungovernable.
4 *a violent earthquake:* strong, powerful, devastating, destructive.
OPPOSITES: gentle, weak, mild.

virgin adjective *acres of virgin forest:* untouched, unspoilt, untainted, unsullied, unpolluted, undefiled, in its natural state; unexplored, uncharted, unmapped.

virginal adjective *a virginal young girl:* chaste, pure, uncorrupted, undefiled, unsullied, innocent.

virile adjective *he was dressed in a tight white T-shirt and looked fantastically virile:* manly, masculine; strong, tough, vigorous, robust, muscular, muscly, brawny, rugged, sturdy, husky; red-blooded, potent; informal macho, hunky.
OPPOSITES: effeminate.

virtual adjective *it was difficult to get arms and ammunition through despite the virtual absence of border controls:* effective, in effect, near, essential, to all intents and purposes.

virtually adverb *the huge building was virtually empty:* almost, effectively, in effect, all but, more or less, practically, nearly, close to, verging on, just about, as good as, essentially, to all intents and purposes; informal pretty much, pretty well.

V | **virtue** noun
1 *he dedicated himself to a life of virtue:* virtuousness, righteousness, morality, integrity, rectitude, honour, decency, respectability, nobility, worthiness, purity.
2 *punctuality was not one of her virtues:* good point, good quality, strong point, asset, forte, attribute, strength, talent.
3 *I can see no virtue in suffering in silence:* merit, advantage, benefit, usefulness, efficacy.
OPPOSITES: vice, failing, disadvantage.

□ **by virtue of**
they achieved pre-eminence by virtue of their superior military strength: because of, on account of, by dint of, by means of, as a result of, as a consequence of, on the strength of, owing to, thanks to, due to.

virtuosity noun *the playing combined breathtaking technical virtuosity with spontaneity and passion:* skill, skilfulness, mastery, expertise, prowess, proficiency, ability, aptitude; excellence, brilliance, talent, genius, artistry, flair, panache, finesse, wizardry; informal know-how.

virtuoso noun *the pianist is clearly a virtuoso:* genius, expert, past master, maestro, artist, prodigy, marvel; informal hotshot, wizard, ace.
▷ adjective *a virtuoso violinist:* skilful, expert, accomplished, masterly, master, consummate, proficient, talented, gifted, adept; impressive, outstanding, superb, exceptional, magnificent, supreme, first-rate, brilliant, excellent; informal mean, ace.

virtuous adjective *they were entirely virtuous in their endeavours:* righteous, good, moral, ethical, upright, upstanding, high-minded, principled, exemplary; law-abiding, irreproachable, blameless, guiltless, unimpeachable, honest, honourable, reputable, decent, respectable, noble, worthy; pure, whiter than white, saintly, angelic; informal squeaky clean.

virulent adjective
1 *a particularly virulent strain of the disease:* severe, harmful, pernicious, damaging, destructive; poisonous, toxic, deadly, lethal; infectious, infective, contagious, transmissible.
2 *a virulent attack on liberalism:* vitriolic, venomous, vicious, bitter, hostile, acrimonious, rancorous, scathing, caustic, withering, savage, harsh, vindictive, malicious, spiteful.

viscous adjective *viscous liquid had started to ooze across the floor:* sticky, thick, glutinous, gelatinous, viscid, mucilaginous; informal gooey.

visible adjective
1 *light from the fires was visible for many miles:* perceptible, discernible, observable, noticeable, detectable; in sight, in/on view, on display.
2 *visible signs of distress:* evident, apparent, manifest, transparent, plain, clear, conspicuous, obvious, distinct, unmistakable, prominent, striking, glaring.

vision noun
1 *her vision was blurred by tears:* eyesight, sight, observation, visual perception; view, perspective.
2 *his speech lacked vision:* imagination, inspiration, perception, insight, foresight, far-sightedness.

3 *visions of a better future:* dream, daydream, hope; plan, mental image, construct.
4 *nightmarish visions of the dead:* apparition, manifestation; hallucination, illusion, mirage.
5 *Melissa was a vision in lilac:* beautiful sight, feast for the eyes, pleasure to behold, delight, dream, beauty, picture, joy, marvel, sensation; informal sight for sore eyes, stunner, knockout.

> WORD LINKS
> **visual**, **optical** relating to vision
> **optics** the branch of science concerned with vision

visionary adjective *a visionary leader:* inspired, imaginative, insightful, far-sighted, perceptive, discerning, shrewd, wise; idealistic, quixotic; informal starry-eyed.

visit verb
1 *I came to visit my grandmother:* call on, pay a visit to, go to see, look in on; stay with; stop by, drop by; N. Amer. visit with; informal pop in on, drop in on, look up.
2 *Alex was visiting America:* stay in, stop over in, spend time in, holiday in; tour, explore; N. Amer. vacation in.
3 *in the last year of her life she was visited with a severe bipolar disorder:* afflict, beset, trouble, torment, bedevil.
▷ **noun**
1 *she paid a visit to her mother:* call, social call.
2 *a short visit to Paris:* trip, tour; stopover, stay; holiday, break; N. Amer. vacation.

visitation noun
1 *the bishop's pastoral visitations:* official visit, tour of inspection, survey.
2 *a supernatural visitation:* apparition, vision, appearance, manifestation.

visitor noun
1 *I'm expecting a visitor:* guest, caller; company.
2 *foreign visitors poured into the city each summer:* tourist, traveller, day tripper, tripper, sightseer; pilgrim; Brit. holidaymaker; N. Amer. vacationer.

vista noun *there's a marvellous vista from the hotel balcony:* view, prospect, panorama, aspect, perspective, spectacle, sight; scenery, landscape.

visual adjective *visual defects:* optical, optic, ocular, eye; vision, sight.

visualize verb *I visualized what the place might have looked like in its prime:* envisage, envision, conjure up, picture, call to mind, see in your mind's eye, imagine, evoke.

vital adjective
1 *it is vital that the system is regularly maintained* | *the mining industry plays a vital role in the country's economy:* essential, of the essence, fundamental, critical, crucial, indispensable, all-important, imperative.
2 *the vital organs:* major, main, chief; essential, necessary.
3 *she is young and vital:* lively, energetic, spirited, vivacious, exuberant, bouncy, enthusiastic, vibrant, dynamic, vigorous, zestful; sprightly, spry; informal full of beans, bright-eyed and bushy-tailed.
OPPOSITES: unimportant, minor, listless.

vitality noun *sparkling with renewed vitality, she was nearly her old self:* energy, liveliness, spirit, vivacity, animation, exuberance, buoyancy, bounce, verve, brio, zest, dynamism, passion, fire, vigour, drive; informal get-up-and-go.
OPPOSITES: lethargy.

vitriolic adjective *he launched a vitriolic attack on the government:* acrimonious, rancorous, bitter, scathing, withering, caustic, mordant, acerbic, trenchant, virulent, savage, venomous, poisonous, malicious, spiteful, splenetic; harsh, vindictive, barbed, sharp, cutting.

vivacious adjective *she was a pretty and vivacious brunette:* lively, animated, spirited, bubbly, ebullient, irrepressible, vibrant, vital, zestful, energetic, dynamic, full of life, buoyant, bouncy, sparkling, light-hearted, jaunty, merry, happy, jolly, full of fun, cheery, cheerful, perky, sunny, enthusiastic, upbeat.
OPPOSITES: dull.

vivid adjective
1 *vivid descriptions of life in small-town America in the 1950s:* graphic, clear, detailed, striking, arresting, impressive, colourful, rich, dramatic, lively, stimulating, interesting, fascinating; memorable, powerful, evocative, stirring, moving, haunting; realistic, lifelike.
2 *the vivid red of the bird's plumage:* bright, colourful, brilliant, radiant, vibrant, strong, bold, deep, intense, rich, warm.
OPPOSITES: vague, dull.

viz. adverb *Article 1 sets out the purpose of the Charter, viz. to ensure the continuation of farming:* namely, that is to say, in other words, to wit, specifically.

vocabulary noun
1 *she has an extensive vocabulary* | *the Sanskrit vocabulary:* lexicon; technical lexis.
2 *difficult terms are listed in the vocabulary at the end of each chapter:* glossary, word list, dictionary.

vocal adjective
1 *vocal sounds:* vocalized, voiced, articulated, oral; spoken.
2 *a vocal critic of the government:* vociferous, outspoken, forthright, plain-spoken, blunt, frank, candid, open; vehement, vigorous, emphatic, insistent, forceful, zealous.

V

vocation noun *his vocation as a clergyman was not eclipsed by his scientific career:* calling, life's work, mission, purpose, function; profession, occupation, career, job, employment, métier, business, work, trade, craft.

vociferous adjective. See **VOCAL** sense 2.

vogue noun *the current vogue for vintage trainers:* fashion, trend, fad, craze, enthusiasm, passion, obsession, mania; popularity.
□ **in vogue**
a fashionista colleague assures me that miniskirts are in vogue this season: fashionable, chic, stylish, all the rage, popular, in favour, in demand, sought-after; informal trendy, hip, cool, big, in, flavour of the month.

voice noun
1 *she's lost her voice:* power of speech.
2 *the new government must not ignore the voice of the electorate:* opinion, view, feeling, wish, desire; vote.
3 *a powerful voice for conservation:* mouthpiece, representative, spokesperson; forum, vehicle, instrument, channel, organ, agent.
▷ **verb** *there should be greater scope for employees to voice their opinions:* express, air, communicate, declare, state, reveal, give voice to, give vent to; utter, say, speak, articulate, vocalize, put into words; informal come out with.

void adjective
1 *the contract was void:* invalid, null and void, not legally binding; worthless, useless.
2 *the tundra is seemingly void of life:* devoid of, empty of, bereft of, free from; lacking, wanting, without.
3 *vast void spaces:* empty, blank, unfilled.
OPPOSITES: valid, full.
▷ **noun** *the black void of space:* vacuum, emptiness, nothingness, blankness; empty space, chasm, abyss.
▷ **verb**
1 *the Supreme Court voided the statute:* invalidate, annul, nullify; cancel, countermand, repeal, revoke, rescind, withdraw, reverse.
2 *they voided their bladders:* evacuate, empty, drain, clear.
3 *bacteria are voided in the urine:* eject, expel, emit, discharge, pass, excrete, eliminate.
OPPOSITES: validate, fill.

volatile adjective
1 *the political situation was becoming more volatile:* unpredictable, unstable, changeable, fluctuating; tense, strained, fraught, uneasy, uncomfortable; highly charged, explosive, turbulent.
2 *a volatile personality:* temperamental, highly strung, excitable, emotional, fiery, moody, tempestuous, changeable,

inconstant, inconsistent, unpredictable, erratic, unstable, blowing hot and cold, mutable; mercurial, capricious, fickle; technical labile.
OPPOSITES: stable, calm.

volition noun
□ **of your own volition**
they chose to leave early of their own volition: of your own free will, of your own accord, by choice, by preference; voluntarily, willingly, readily, freely; gladly, with pleasure.

volley noun
1 *he fired off a volley of shots from his semi-automatic rifle:* barrage, cannonade, battery, bombardment, salvo, fusillade; storm, hail, shower, torrent; historical broadside.
2 *he unleashed a volley of angry questions:* succession, series, barrage, salvo; stream, flood, torrent, storm.

voluble adjective *Mrs Maddox was as voluble as her husband was silent:* talkative, loquacious, garrulous, verbose, wordy, chatty, gossipy, effusive, gushing, forthcoming, conversational, communicative, expansive; articulate, fluent.
OPPOSITES: taciturn.

volume noun
1 *the library holds some 125,000 volumes:* book, publication, title; humorous tome.
2 *a glass syringe of known volume:* capacity, cubic measure, size, magnitude, mass, extent; dimensions, measurements, proportions.
3 *a huge volume of water | the database must be able to handle an incredible volume of data:* quantity, amount, body, mass, bulk.
4 *she turned the volume down:* sound, loudness, amplification.

voluminous adjective *he folded his arms into the voluminous sleeves of his robe:* capacious, roomy, spacious, ample, full, big, large, generous; billowing, baggy, loose-fitting.

voluntarily adverb *they signed a paper agreeing to leave the country voluntarily:* of your own free will, of your own accord, of your own volition, by choice, by preference; willingly, readily, freely; gladly, with pleasure.

voluntary adjective
1 *attendance is voluntary:* optional, discretionary, elective, non-compulsory, volitional.
2 *voluntary work:* unpaid, unsalaried, without charge, for nothing; honorary, volunteer; informal for free.
OPPOSITES: compulsory, paid.

volunteer verb
1 *he volunteered as a driver:* offer your services, present yourself, make yourself available, step forward, show willing.

2 *I volunteered my services* | *it never paid to volunteer information:* offer, make something available, proffer, put forward.

▷ **noun** *each volunteer was tested three times:* subject, participant; informal guinea pig.

voluptuous adjective *a tall, voluptuous woman:* curvaceous, shapely, ample, buxom, full-figured, Junoesque, Rubenesque; sexually attractive, seductive, sexy; informal curvy.

vomit verb
1 *the stench made him want to vomit:* be sick, spew; heave, retch, gag; N. Amer. get sick; informal throw up, puke, chunder, hurl; N. Amer. informal barf, upchuck.
2 *he vomited up his breakfast:* regurgitate, bring up, spew up; informal chuck up, throw up, puke; Brit. informal sick up.

voracious adjective *a voracious appetite:* insatiable, unquenchable, prodigious, gluttonous, greedy, rapacious, ravenous, hungry; avid, enthusiastic, eager, keen.

vortex noun
1 *a whirling vortex of water:* whirlpool, maelstrom, eddy; whirlwind.
2 *he was swept into the vortex of the civil war:* maelstrom, chaos, upheaval, turbulence, disorder, tumult, confusion.

vote noun
1 *protesters claim that the vote was rigged:* ballot, poll, election, referendum, plebiscite; show of hands.
2 *in 1918 women got the vote:* suffrage, voting rights, franchise, enfranchisement.

▷ **verb**
1 *only 36 per cent of voters aged 18 to 24 voted in the last election:* go to the polls, cast your vote.
2 (informal) *I vote that we stay here:* suggest, propose, recommend, move.

▢ **vote someone in**
those who voted him in continue to wait for his promised social reforms: elect, vote for, return, nominate, choose, pick.

> WORD LINKS
> **psephology** the statistical study of elections and trends in voting

vouch verb
▢ **vouch for**
I can vouch for the veracity of his story: attest to, confirm, verify, swear to, testify to, bear out, back up, support, corroborate,

substantiate, guarantee, prove, give credence to, endorse.

voucher noun *a free travel voucher:* coupon, token, ticket, licence, permit, pass; chit, slip, stub, docket; Brit. informal chitty.

vouchsafe verb
1 *the grace which God had vouchsafed him:* grant, give, accord; confer on, bestow on, favour with.
2 *you never vouchsafed that information before:* disclose, reveal, divulge, impart, give away, make known, broadcast, air.

vow noun *a vow of silence:* oath, pledge, promise, bond, covenant, commitment, profession, assurance, guarantee; word, word of honour.

▷ **verb** *I vowed to do better:* swear, pledge, promise, undertake, engage, make a commitment, give your word, guarantee.

voyage noun *a long sea voyage:* journey, trip, expedition, passage, crossing; pilgrimage, quest, crusade, odyssey; cruise, excursion, tour.

▷ **verb** *he voyaged along the South African coast:* travel, journey; sail, steam, cruise.

vulgar adjective
1 *a vulgar joke:* rude, indecent, indelicate, offensive, distasteful, off colour, coarse, crude, obscene, lewd, salacious, smutty, dirty, filthy, pornographic; ribald, risqué, naughty, suggestive, racy, earthy, bawdy; euphemistic adult; informal raunchy, saucy, blue.
2 *the decor was lavish but vulgar:* tasteless, ostentatious, overdone, showy, gaudy, garish, brassy, kitsch, loud.
3 *it was considered vulgar for a woman to whistle:* coarse, ill-mannered, indecorous, unseemly, ill-bred, boorish, uncouth, crude; unsophisticated, unrefined; Brit. common.
OPPOSITES: tasteful.

vulnerable adjective
1 *thousands of civilians were moved from vulnerable areas into villages that could be more easily defended:* in danger, in jeopardy, at risk, endangered, unsafe, unprotected, unguarded; open to attack, exposed; undefended, unarmed, defenceless, helpless.
2 *these fish swim near the surface and are vulnerable to attack from predators below:* open to, an easy target for, at risk of, exposed to.
OPPOSITES: invulnerable, resilient.

v

Ww

wacky adjective (informal). See ZANY.

wad noun
1 *a wad of cotton wool:* lump, mass, plug, pad, ball; bit, piece.
2 *a wad of dollar bills:* bundle, roll.

waddle verb *he waddled forward to greet her:* toddle, totter, wobble, shuffle, dodder.

waffle verb (Brit. informal) *he waffled on about his problems:* prattle, chatter, babble, ramble, jabber, gabble; informal blather; Brit. informal rabbit, witter, natter.

waft verb
1 *smoke wafted through the air:* drift, float, glide, whirl, travel.
2 *a breeze wafted the smell towards us:* convey, carry, transport, bear; blow, puff.

wag verb
1 *the dog's tail wagged frantically:* swing, swish, switch, sway, twitch; informal waggle.
2 *he wagged his stick at them:* shake, wave, flourish, brandish.

wage noun
1 *the new five-year deal will see his wages rise to over £50,000 a week:* pay, payment, remuneration, salary, stipend; earnings.
2 *the wages of sin is death:* reward, recompense, retribution; returns, deserts.
▷ **verb** *they waged war on the guerrillas:* engage in, carry on, conduct, pursue, prosecute, proceed with.

wager noun *a wager of £100:* bet, gamble; stake,; Brit. informal flutter, punt.
▷ **verb** *I'll wager a fiver on the home team:* bet, gamble, put money on; stake, risk, venture, hazard, chance; Brit. informal punt.

waif noun ragamuffin, urchin; foundling, orphan, stray; derogatory guttersnipe.

wail noun *a wail of anguish:* howl, cry, moan, groan; shriek, scream, yelp, yowl.
▷ **verb** *the children began to wail:* howl, weep, cry, sob, bawl, shriek, scream; Scottish greet.

wait verb
1 *he waited for over an hour, but no one turned up:* stay, stay put, remain, linger, delay; hold back, bide your time, hang fire, mark time, kill time, waste time, kick your heels, twiddle your thumbs; literary tarry; informal stick around, hang around, sit tight, hold your horses; Brit. informal stop.
2 *that job will have to wait:* be postponed, be delayed, be put off, be deferred; informal be put on the back burner, be put on ice.
▷ **noun** *there is likely to be a long wait before the scheme is operational:* delay, hold-up, interval, interlude; interruption, hiatus, gap.
□ **wait on someone**
the men ate in silence, waited on by the two girls: serve, attend to; minister to, take care of, look after.

waive verb *he will waive all rights to the money:* forgo, give up, relinquish, renounce, abandon, surrender, sacrifice.

> **USAGE**
>
> Do not confuse **waive** with **wave**. **Waive** means 'to choose not to insist on or demand a right or claim'; as a verb **wave** means 'to move to and fro' (*thousands of fans waved flags and banners*).

wake[1] verb
1 *he woke up at 4.30 a.m.:* awake, awaken, rouse yourself, stir, come to, come round, bestir yourself; get up, get out of bed.
2 *she woke her husband:* rouse, arouse, waken; Brit. informal knock up.
3 *they woke up to what we were saying:* realize, become aware of, take in, understand, comprehend, grasp.
4 *the name woke an old memory:* evoke, conjure up, rouse, stir, revive, awaken, rekindle, stimulate.
OPPOSITES: sleep.

wake[2] noun *the cruiser's wake:* backwash, wash, slipstream, turbulence.
□ **in the wake of**
an advisory group was set up in the wake of the inquiry: after, subsequent to, following, as a result of, as a consequence of.

waken verb. See WAKE[1] sense 2.

walk verb
1 *they walked along the road:* stroll, . saunter, amble, meander, wander, roam, promenade; march, stride; trudge, plod, tramp, traipse; hike, ramble, trek; troop; informal mosey.

2 *he walked her home:* accompany, escort, guide, show, see, usher, take, chaperone, steer, shepherd.

▷ **noun**
1 *a walk in the country:* stroll, saunter, amble, promenade; ramble, hike; turn, airing.
2 *her elegant walk:* gait, step, stride, tread.
3 *street lamps illuminated the riverside walk:* pathway, path, footpath, track, walkway, promenade.
□ **walk all over someone** (informal) *be firm or they'll walk all over you:* take advantage of, impose on, exploit, use, abuse, misuse, manipulate, take liberties with; informal take for a ride, runs rings around.
□ **walk off/away with**
he walked off with four awards: win, gain, receive, secure, collect, pick up, attain, earn, acquire; informal bag.
□ **walk out**
1 *he walked out in a temper:* leave, depart, storm off/out, flounce out; informal take off.
2 *teachers walked out in protest:* go on strike, strike, stop work; Brit. informal down tools.
□ **walk out on someone**
he walked out on his pregnant girlfriend: desert, abandon, leave, throw over, jilt, run out on; informal chuck, dump, ditch.

walker noun hiker, rambler; pedestrian; literary wayfarer.

walkout noun *a one-day walkout by 200 workers:* strike, stoppage, industrial action; withdrawal of labour.

walkover noun *It won't be a walkover—Wigan have won their last 11 games:* easy victory, rout, landslide; informal piece of cake, whitewash.

wall noun
1 *a glass wall divides the study from the bathroom:* barrier, partition; screen, panel.
2 *an ancient city wall:* fortification, rampart, barricade, bulwark, stockade.
▷ **verb**
1 *parts of the area had been walled off with concrete barricades:* enclose, encircle, confine, close in, shut in, fence in.
2 *the doorway had been walled up:* block, seal, close, brick up.

wallet noun purse; N. Amer. billfold, pocketbook.

wallow verb
1 *buffalo wallowed in the lake:* roll about, lie, splash about.
2 *a ship wallowing in stormy seas:* roll, lurch, toss, plunge, reel, rock, keel, list.
3 *she seems to wallow in self-pity* | *he wallowed in the media's adoration:* luxuriate, bask, take pleasure, take satisfaction, indulge yourself, delight, revel, glory; enjoy, like, love, relish, savour; informal get a kick out of, get a buzz from.

wan adjective
1 *she looked so wan and frail:* pale, pallid, ashen, white, grey; anaemic, colourless, bloodless, waxen, chalky, pasty, sickly, washed out, drained, drawn; Brit. peaky.
2 *the wan light of the moon:* dim, faint, weak, feeble, pale, watery, ghostly.
OPPOSITES: flushed, bright.

wander verb
1 *I wandered around the estate:* stroll, amble, saunter, walk, potter, ramble, meander; roam, rove, range, drift, prowl; informal mosey; Brit. informal mooch.
2 *the child wandered off:* get lost, lose your way, go astray, drift off, stray.
3 *the road wanders along the shore:* meander, wind, twist, curve, zigzag, bend, snake.

wane verb *public confidence in his leadership is waning:* decline, diminish, decrease, dwindle, shrink, ebb, fade, melt away, lessen, peter out, fall off, recede, slump, flag, weaken, wither, evaporate, die out.
OPPOSITES: grow.
□ **on the wane**
their popularity is on the wane: declining, decreasing, diminishing, dwindling, shrinking, subsiding, ebbing, fading, petering out, flagging, melting away, evaporating.

want verb *do you want a drink?* | *she'd always wanted a big, glamorous wedding:* desire, wish for, hope for, care for, like; long for, yearn for, crave, hanker after, have a yen for, hunger for, thirst for, covet; informal be dying for; Brit. informal fancy.
▷ **noun**
1 *the case collapsed for want of evidence:* lack, absence, non-existence; dearth, deficiency, inadequacy, insufficiency, paucity, shortage, scarcity.
2 *a time of want:* need, austerity, privation, deprivation, poverty, impoverishment, penury, destitution.
3 *all her wants would be taken care of:* wish, desire, demand, longing, yearning, fancy, craving, hankering; need, requirement.

wanting adjective
1 *the squad are not wanting in confidence* | *some of the transport operators were found to be wanting:* deficient, lacking; inadequate, unacceptable, substandard, insufficient, imperfect, flawed, defective.
2 *mandibles are wanting in many of these insects:* absent, missing, lacking, non-existent.
OPPOSITES: sufficient, present.

wanton adjective
1 *all across the region, there's evidence of this wanton destruction:* deliberate, wilful, gratuitous, unprovoked, motiveless, arbitrary, unjustifiable, needless, unnecessary, uncalled for, senseless, pointless, meaningless.

W

2 *a wanton seductress:* promiscuous, immoral, immodest, shameless, abandoned, lustful, lascivious.
OPPOSITES: justifiable, chaste.

war noun
1 *the Napoleonic Wars | the long and costly war ended in a stalemate:* conflict, warfare, combat, fighting, military action, struggle; battle, fight, clash, engagement, encounter; offensive, attack, campaign; hostilities; crusade.
2 *the war against drugs:* campaign, crusade, battle, fight, struggle, offensive, movement, drive.
OPPOSITES: peace.
▷ verb *rival emperors warred against each other:* fight, battle, wage war, take up arms; feud, quarrel, struggle, contend, cross swords; attack, engage, take on, skirmish with.

WORD LINKS
belligerent engaged in a war or conflict
martial relating to war

warble verb *larks warbled in the sky:* trill, sing, chirp, chirrup, cheep, twitter, tweet, chatter, peep.

ward noun
1 *the surgical ward:* room, department, unit, area.
2 *the most marginal ward in Westminster:* district, constituency, division.
3 *the boy is my ward:* dependant, charge.
□ **ward someone off**
Kelly held out a hand to ward him off: fend off, repel, beat back, chase away; informal send packing.
□ **ward something off**
1 *she warded off the blow:* parry, avert, deflect, block; evade, avoid, dodge.
2 *garlic is worn to ward off evil spirits:* keep at bay, drive away/off, fend off, stave off, resist, prevent, obstruct, foil, frustrate, thwart, check, stop.

warden noun
1 *the flats have a resident warden:* superintendent, caretaker, janitor, porter, custodian, watchman, concierge, doorman.
2 *a game warden:* ranger, keeper, protector.
3 *he was handcuffed to a warden:* prison officer, guard, jailer, warder; informal screw.

warder noun. See **WARDEN** sense 3.

wardrobe noun
1 *she opened the wardrobe:* cupboard; N. Amer. closet.
2 *her wardrobe is extensive:* collection of clothes, range of clothing; clothes, garments, outfits; formal attire.

warehouse noun *a furniture warehouse:* storeroom, storehouse, store, depot, depository; stockroom; informal lock-up.

wares plural noun *traders in the street markets displayed their wares:*

merchandise, goods, products, produce, stock, commodities.

warfare noun *the reality of modern warfare:* fighting, war, combat, conflict, military action, hostilities; bloodshed, battles.

warlike adjective *a warlike ruler:* aggressive, hostile, belligerent, warring, bellicose, pugnacious, combative, sabre-rattling; militaristic, militant; informal gung-ho.

warm adjective
1 *she felt herself shiver even though it was very warm in the bar:* hot, cosy, snug; informal toasty.
2 *a warm and sunny day:* balmy, summery, hot.
3 *wash thoroughly with soap and warm water:* heated, tepid, lukewarm.
4 *a warm sweater:* thick, chunky, woolly.
5 *he was touched by the warm welcome he received | she has a very warm personality:* friendly, cordial, amiable, genial, warm-hearted, kind, affectionate; welcoming, hospitable; sincere, genuine, wholehearted, heartfelt, enthusiastic, hearty.
OPPOSITES: cold, chilly.
▷ verb *warm the soup in that pan:* heat, heat up, cook; thaw.
OPPOSITES: chill.
□ **warm to/towards**
1 *everyone warmed to him:* like, take to, get on well with, hit it off with.
2 *he couldn't warm to the notion:* get enthusiastic about, be supportive of, get excited about, get interested in.
□ **warm up**
if you don't warm up first you can easily pull a muscle: limber up, loosen up, stretch; prepare.

warm-hearted adjective *she's a very warm-hearted person:* kind, kindly, warm, tender-hearted, tender, loving, caring, unselfish, selfless, good-natured; friendly, sympathetic, understanding, compassionate, considerate, thoughtful, charitable, generous.

warmth noun
1 *the warmth of the fire:* heat, warmness; cosiness.
2 *she smiled with real warmth:* friendliness, amiability, geniality, cordiality, kindness, affection; enthusiasm, eagerness.

warn verb
1 *the doctors warned us that his condition was serious:* alert, inform, notify, tell, make someone aware, forewarn; informal tip off, put wise.
2 *police warned people not to keep large amounts of cash in their homes:* advise, caution, counsel; exhort, urge.

warning noun
1 *she had only four days warning | police*

received a warning there would be explosions at those offices: advance notice, notice, notification, forewarning, alert, hint; informal a tip-off.
2 *a word of warning—don't leave your car there overnight:* caution, advice, information.
3 *his sentence is a warning to other drunk-drivers:* example, deterrent, lesson, caution, message, moral.
4 *a warning of things to come:* omen, portent, presage, signal, sign, token.

warp verb
1 *timber which is too dry will warp:* buckle, twist, bend, become distorted, become misshapen.
2 *he warped the mind of her child:* corrupt, twist, pervert, deprave.
OPPOSITES: straighten.

warrant noun *a warrant for his arrest:* authorization, order, permit; document.
▷ verb
1 *the employees feel that industrial action is warranted | the situation warrants further investigation:* justify, call for, need, necessitate; deserve, merit, qualify for, rate, be worthy of, be deserving of.
2 *the vendor warrants the accuracy of the report:* guarantee, affirm, swear to, attest to; vouch for, testify to, bear witness to.

warranty noun *a three-year warranty:* guarantee, assurance, promise, commitment.

warring adjective *envoys for peace are trying to bring the warring factions together:* opposing, conflicting, at war, fighting, battling, quarrelling; competing, hostile, rival.

wary adjective
1 *he was trained to be wary:* cautious, careful, circumspect, on your guard, chary, alert, on the lookout, on your toes, on the qui vive; attentive, heedful, watchful, vigilant, observant.
2 *we are wary of strangers:* suspicious, chary, distrustful, mistrustful; informal leery.
OPPOSITES: unwary, trustful.

wash verb
1 *she washed her hands | he washed down all the woodwork in the kitchen:* clean, cleanse, rinse, sponge, scrub, wipe, scour, mop; swab, disinfect, sluice down, hose down.
2 *she washed off the blood:* remove, sponge off, scrub off, wipe off, rinse off.
3 *her clothes had been washed and ironed:* launder, clean, rinse.
4 *waves washed against the hull:* splash, lap, splosh, dash, break, beat, surge, ripple, roll.
5 *the wreckage was washed downstream:* sweep, carry, convey, transport; deposit.
6 *a deep feeling of sadness washed over her:* course through, rush through, surge through, flood over, flow over.
OPPOSITES: dirty, soil.

▷ noun
1 *he needs a good wash and a haircut:* clean, shower, bath, soak.
2 *that shirt should go in the wash:* laundry, washing.
3 *the wash of a motor boat:* backwash, wake, trail.
4 *the wash of the waves on the beach:* surge, flow, swell, sweep, rise and fall, roll, splash.
□ **wash your hands of**
her father had washed his hands of her: disown, reject, give up on, turn your back on, cast aside, have nothing more to do with, abandon; formal forswear.

waspish adjective *she sounded waspish and impatient:* irritable, touchy, testy, cross, cantankerous, short-tempered, bad-tempered, crotchety, crabby; informal snappy.

waste verb
1 *he wasted his money on drink, fast cars, and women:* squander, misuse, fritter away, throw away, lavish, dissipate, throw around; informal blow, splurge.
2 *kids are wasting away in the streets:* grow weak, grow thin, become emaciated, wither away.
OPPOSITES: conserve.
▷ adjective
1 *ensure that waste materials are disposed of responsibly:* unwanted, excess, superfluous, left over, discarded, scrap, unusable.
2 *a patch of waste ground:* uncultivated, empty, undeveloped, unused; wild.
▷ noun
1 *the waste of precious resources | they had learned to avoid waste:* misuse, squandering, dissipation; extravagance, wastefulness, prodigality, lavishness.
2 *household waste:* rubbish, refuse, detritus, litter, debris, junk, scrap; effluent; N. Amer. garbage, trash.
3 *the frozen wastes of the South Pole:* desert, wasteland, wilderness, emptiness, wilds.

wasted adjective
1 *the real scandal of the whole saga—apart from the wasted time—is the wasted money:* squandered, misspent, misdirected, misused.
2 *a wasted opportunity:* missed, lost, forfeited, neglected, squandered; informal down the drain.
3 *I'm wasted in this job:* underemployed, underused.
4 *his wasted legs:* emaciated, withered, shrivelled, weak, frail, shrunken, wizened, atrophied.

wasteful adjective *the wasteful use of natural resources:* prodigal, uneconomical, extravagant, lavish, profligate, excessive, imprudent, improvident; thriftless, spendthrift; needless, useless.
OPPOSITES: frugal.

w

wasteland noun wilderness, desert, wastes, wilds; badlands.

watch verb
1 *I watched him as he got into his car and drove off:* observe, view, look at, eye, gaze at, stare at, gape at, peer at; contemplate, survey, keep an eye on; inspect, scrutinize, scan, examine, study, regard; ogle; informal check out, eyeball.
2 *he was being watched by the police:* keep under surveillance, monitor, keep in sight, track, survey, follow, spy on; informal keep tabs on, stake out.
3 *will you watch the kids?* look after, mind, keep an eye on, take care of, supervise, tend, attend to.
4 *the building is watched over by security guards:* guard, protect, defend, safeguard; cover, patrol, police.
5 *you should watch what you say:* be careful, mind, be aware of, pay attention to, consider, pay heed to.
OPPOSITES: ignore, neglect.
▷ noun
1 *Bill looked at his watch:* timepiece, chronometer; wristwatch, stopwatch.
2 *we kept watch on the yacht:* guard, vigil, lookout, an eye; observation, surveillance.
□ watch out
credit-card fraud is on the increase so watch out: be careful, be watchful, be on your guard, beware, be wary, be cautious, mind out, look out, pay attention, take heed, take care, keep an eye open/out, keep your eyes peeled, be vigilant.

watchful adjective *her mother kept a watchful eye on her:* observant, alert, vigilant, attentive, heedful, sharp-eyed; on the lookout, wary, cautious, careful.
OPPOSITES: inattentive.

watchword noun *efficiency in all things was the watchword:* guiding principle, motto, slogan, maxim, mantra, catchword, byword; informal buzzword.

water noun *a house down by the water:* sea, ocean; lake, river.
▷ verb *my mouth watered:* moisten, salivate.
□ hold water
this argument just does not hold water: be tenable, ring true, bear scrutiny, make sense, stand up, hold up, be convincing, be plausible, be sound.
□ water something down
1 *staff at the club had been watering down the drinks:* dilute, water, thin, weaken; adulterate; informal cut.
2 *the original proposals have been watered down:* moderate, tone down, soften, tame, weaken, dilute.

WORD LINKS
aqueous relating to or containing water
aqua-, hydro- forming words meaning 'relating to water', such as *aqualung* ('an apparatus enabling divers to breathe under water') or *hydroelectric* ('relating to the generation of electricity using flowing water')

waterfall noun cascade, cataract, falls, rapids; N. English force.

waterproof adjective *a waterproof jacket:* watertight, water-repellent, water-resistant, damp-proof; impermeable, impervious; rubberized, waxed.

watertight adjective
1 *a watertight container:* impermeable, impervious, sealed, hermetically sealed; waterproof, water-repellent, water-resistant, damp-proof.
2 *a watertight alibi:* indisputable, unquestionable, irrefutable, unassailable, impregnable, airtight, perfect, flawless.
OPPOSITES: leaky.

watery adjective
1 *a watery discharge:* liquid, fluid, aqueous.
2 *the watery ground:* wet, damp, moist, sodden, soggy, squelchy, soft; saturated, waterlogged; boggy, marshy, swampy, muddy.
3 *a bowl of watery porridge:* thin, runny, weak, dilute, diluted; tasteless, flavourless, insipid, bland.
4 *the watery morning light:* pale, weak, faint, wan, feeble.
5 *her eyes were red and watery:* tearful, teary, weepy, moist, rheumy.

wave verb
1 *he waved his flag furiously:* move up and down, move to and fro, wag, shake, swish, swing, brandish, flourish, wield; flick, flutter; informal waggle.
2 *the flags waved in the breeze:* ripple, flutter, undulate, stir, flap, sway, shake, quiver, move.
3 *the waiter waved them over:* gesture, gesticulate, signal, beckon, motion.
▷ noun
1 *waves crashed on the shore:* breaker, roller, ripple, white horse; (waves) swell, surf, white horses.
2 *a wave of strikes paralysed the government:* series, succession, spate; flood, stream, tide, deluge.
3 *a wave of excitement swept through her:* surge, rush, upsurge; thrill, frisson; feeling.
4 *his hair grew in thick waves:* curl, kink, corkscrew, twist, ringlet.
5 *electromagnetic waves:* vibration, oscillation, ripple.
6 *she gave him a friendly wave:* gesture, gesticulation; signal, sign, motion.
□ wave something aside
he waved aside her protest: dismiss, reject, brush aside, shrug off, disregard, ignore, discount, play down; informal pooh-pooh.
□ wave someone/something down
he waved down a taxi and drove off: flag down, hail, stop, summon, call.

W

waver verb
1 *the candlelight wavered in the draught:*
flicker, quiver.
2 *his voice wavered:* falter, wobble,
tremble, quaver, become unsteady.
3 *he wavered between the choices:* be
undecided, be irresolute, hesitate, dither,
equivocate, vacillate, fluctuate; think
twice, change your mind, blow hot and
cold; Brit. haver, hum and haw; informal shilly-
shally, sit on the fence.

wavy adjective *her long wavy hair | a wavy
line:* curly, curling, undulating, rippling;
curved, winding, sinuous.
OPPOSITES: straight.

waxen adjective *the gash on his cheek
was a startling contrast against his waxen
skin:* pale, pallid, wan, ashen, colourless,
anaemic, bloodless, washed out, white,
grey, drained, sickly.
OPPOSITES: ruddy.

way noun
1 *a way of reducing the damage:*
method, means, procedure, technique,
system, process; plan, strategy, scheme;
mechanism, approach, tack, avenue; modus
operandi, MO.
2 *she kissed him in her brisk way:* manner,
style, fashion, mode.
3 *I've changed my ways | he was showing off,
as is the way with adolescent boys:* practice,
habit, custom, convention, routine, modus
vivendi; trait, attribute, peculiarity,
idiosyncrasy; conduct, behaviour, manner,
style, nature, personality, temperament,
disposition, character; formal wont.
4 *in some ways, he may be better off:*
respect, regard, aspect, facet, sense; detail,
point, particular.
5 *the country is in a bad way:* state,
condition, situation, circumstances,
position; predicament, plight; informal shape.
6 *can you tell me the way to Leicester
Square?* route, course, direction; road,
street, track, path.
7 *they still had a long way ahead of them:*
distance, journey; time, period.
□ **by the way**
*by the way, Sharon rang while you were
out:* incidentally, by the by, in passing, en
passant.
□ **give way**
1 *the government gave way and passed
the bill:* yield, back down, surrender,
concede defeat, give in, submit, succumb;
acquiesce, agree, assent; informal throw in
the towel, cave in.
2 *the door gave way:* collapse, give, cave

in, fall in, come apart, crumple.
3 *grief gave way to guilt:* be replaced
by, be succeeded by, be followed by, be
supplanted by.
□ **on the way**
there's more snow on the way: coming,
imminent, forthcoming, approaching,
impending, close, near.

waylay verb *he waylaid me on the stairs:*
stop, intercept, accost, detain, take aside,
pounce on, interrupt; informal buttonhole.

wayward adjective *a wayward child:*
wilful, self-willed, headstrong, stubborn,
obstinate, perverse, contrary, disobedient,
insubordinate, undisciplined; rebellious,
defiant, uncooperative, recalcitrant,
unruly, wild, unmanageable, erratic;
difficult.
OPPOSITES: docile, cooperative.

weak adjective
1 *they are too weak to move:* frail,
feeble, delicate, fragile; infirm, sick,
sickly, debilitated, incapacitated, ailing,
indisposed; tired, exhausted, fatigued,
enervated.
2 *the argument is extremely weak | the
film's weak plot:* unconvincing, untenable,
tenuous, implausible, unsatisfactory, poor,
inadequate, feeble, flimsy, lame; informal
pathetic.
3 *a weak structure, vulnerable to heavy
rain:* flimsy, fragile, rickety, unsafe,
unsound.
4 *opinion polls show that the government
is in a weak position:* vulnerable, exposed,
unprotected, defenceless; dangerous
5 *he was too weak to be a rebel:* timid,
timorous, craven, cowardly, pusillanimous,
spineless; irresolute, indecisive, weak-
willed, ineffectual, meek, ineffective,
impotent, faint-hearted, effete; informal
weak-kneed, gutless.
6 *a weak light:* dim, pale, wan, faint, feeble,
muted.
7 *a cup of weak coffee:* watery, diluted,
dilute, watered down, thin, tasteless,
flavourless, bland, insipid, wishy-washy.
8 *we heard a weak voice from upstairs:*
indistinct, muffled, muted, hushed, faint,
low.
9 *she managed a weak smile:*
unenthusiastic, feeble, half-hearted; tired,
exhausted.
OPPOSITES: strong, powerful, resolute.

weaken verb
1 *the virus weakened him terribly:*
enfeeble, debilitate, incapacitate, sap,
enervate, tire, exhaust, wear out.
2 *his resistance weakened:* decrease,
dwindle, diminish, ebb, decline, falter.
3 *the move weakened her authority:* impair,
undermine, erode, compromise, reduce,
decrease, lessen; emasculate.

weakness noun
1 *with old age came weakness:* frailty,

w

feebleness, enfeeblement, fragility, delicacy; infirmity, sickness, debility.
2 *a company must evaluate both its strengths and weaknesses:* **fault**, flaw, defect, deficiency, weak point, failing, shortcoming, imperfection, Achilles' heel.
3 *she had a weakness for champagne:* **fondness**, liking, partiality, preference, love, penchant, soft spot, predilection, inclination, taste, eye; enthusiasm, appetite.
4 *the President was accused of weakness:* **timidity**, cowardliness; irresolution, ineffectuality, powerlessness, ineffectiveness, impotence.
OPPOSITES: strength.

wealth noun
1 *a gentleman of considerable wealth:* **affluence**, prosperity, riches, means, substance, fortune; money, cash, capital, finance; assets, possessions, resources, funds; property, stock, reserves, securities, holdings; informal wherewithal, dough, bread.
2 *the book contains a wealth of information on the subject:* **abundance**, profusion, plethora, mine, store, treasury, cornucopia; informal load, heap, mass, mountain.
OPPOSITES: poverty, dearth.

wealthy adjective *his aunt was a wealthy woman who showered him with gifts:* **rich**, affluent, moneyed, well off, well-to-do, prosperous, propertied; of substance; informal well heeled, rolling in it, in the money, made of money, loaded, quids in.
OPPOSITES: poor.

wear verb
1 *he was wearing a dark suit and a striped tie:* **be dressed in**, be clothed in, have on, sport.
2 *the nurse wore her usual grim expression:* **display**, exhibit, present, show; give, assume.
3 *the bricks have been worn down:* **erode**, abrade, rub away, grind away, wash away, wear down; corrode, eat away, dissolve.
4 *the tyres are wearing well:* **last**, endure, hold up, bear up, prove durable, stand the test of time.
▷ noun
1 *a velvet jacket that works well with jeans and evening wear:* **clothes**, clothing, garments, dress, garb, wardrobe; formal attire; informal get-up, gear, togs; Brit. informal kit, clobber.
2 *you won't get much wear out of that:* **use**, service, value; informal mileage.
3 *on inspection, the spark plugs showed signs of wear:* **damage**, friction, erosion, abrasion.
☐ **wear off**
the novelty soon wore off: **fade**, diminish, lessen, dwindle, decrease, wane, ebb, peter out, fizzle out, pall, disappear.
☐ **wear on**
the afternoon wore on: **pass**, elapse,

proceed, advance, progress, go by, roll by, march on, slip by/away, fly by/past.
☐ **wear out**
the stair carpet has worn out: **become worn**, wear thin, fray, become threadbare, go into holes, wear through.
☐ **wear someone out**
eventually her exertions wore her out: **exhaust**, tire out, weary, fatigue, drain, sap, enervate, debilitate, prostrate; informal knacker.

wearing adjective *it had been a rather wearing day:* **tiring**, exhausting, wearying, wearisome, fatiguing, enervating, draining; demanding, exacting, taxing, arduous, gruelling, difficult, hard, tough, laborious.

wearisome adjective *the night was long and wearisome:* **tiring**, wearying, enervating, fatiguing, exhausting; tiresome, trying, irksome, tedious, boring, dull, uninteresting, dreary.
OPPOSITES: exciting, interesting.

weary adjective
1 *she'd been up all night with the children, so morning found her heavy-eyed and weary:* **tired**, worn out, exhausted, fatigued, spent, drained, enervated; informal all in, done in, dead beat, ready to drop, bushed, shattered; Brit. informal knackered, whacked; N. Amer. informal pooped, tuckered out.
2 *she was weary of the arguments:* **tired of**, bored by, sick of; informal fed up with.
3 *a long and weary trip:* **tiring**, exhausting, wearying, fatiguing, enervating, draining, wearing, demanding, taxing, arduous, gruelling, difficult, hard, tough.
▷ verb
1 *she was wearied by her illness:* **tire**, fatigue, wear out, overtire, exhaust, drain, sap, enervate, debilitate, enfeeble, prostrate; informal shatter, do in; Brit. informal knacker.
2 *don't risk wearying the reader:* **bore**, tire; irk, irritate.
3 *he wearied of the struggle:* **tire of**, become bored by, sicken of; have had enough of; informal become fed up with.
OPPOSITES: refresh, interest.

weather noun *what's the weather like?* **forecast**, outlook; meteorological conditions, climate, temperature; the elements.
▷ verb *the industry has weathered the recession:* **survive**, come through, ride out, pull through; withstand, endure, rise above, surmount, overcome, resist; informal stick out.

weathered adjective *the weathered face of a true countryman:* **weather-beaten**, worn; lined, creased, wrinkled, gnarled.

weave[1] verb
1 *flowers were woven into their hair:* **entwine**, lace, twist, knit, intertwine, braid, plait.

2 *he weaves colourful plots:* invent, make up, construct, create, contrive, fabricate, spin; tell, recount, relate.

weave² verb *he had to weave his way through the crowds:* thread, wind, wend; dodge, zigzag.

web noun
1 *a spider's web:* mesh, net, lattice, latticework, lacework, webbing; gossamer.
2 *a web of friendships:* network, nexus, complex, set, chain.

wed verb
1 *they are old enough to wed:* marry, get married, become husband and wife; informal tie the knot, get hitched; Brit. informal get spliced.
2 *he wed his long-term girlfriend in Dublin last week:* marry, take as your wife/husband; informal make an honest woman of.
3 *she wedded the two forms of spirituality:* unite, unify, join, combine, amalgamate, fuse, integrate, merge.
OPPOSITES: divorce, separate.

wedded adjective
1 *25 years of wedded bliss:* married, marital, conjugal, nuptial.
2 *he is wedded to his work:* dedicated to, devoted to, attached to, fixated on, single-minded about.

wedding noun marriage, nuptials, union.

wedge noun *a wedge of cheese:* piece, segment, slice; chunk, lump, slab, hunk, block.
▷ **verb** *she wedged her case between two bags:* squeeze, cram, jam, ram, force, push, shove; informal stuff.

weed verb
□ **weed something/someone out**
a good agency will weed out those unsuitable candidates: remove, eliminate, get rid of, separate out, sift out, winnow out, filter out, sort out.

weedy adjective (informal) *a weedy little man:* puny, feeble, weak, undersized, slight, skinny.

weep verb *she buried her face in her hands and began to weep:* cry, shed tears, sob, wail, bawl, snivel, whimper, whine, keen; Scottish greet; informal blub, blubber.

weepy adjective *she was weepy and nervous, anxious about the baby:* tearful, close to tears, upset, distressed, sad, unhappy; in tears, crying, weeping, snivelling; informal teary.

weigh verb
1 *she weighed the vegetables:* measure the weight of, put on the scales.
2 *he weighs 118 kg:* have a weight of, tip the scales at.
3 *the situation weighed heavily on him.* See WEIGH SOMEONE DOWN sense 2.
4 *he has to weigh up the possibilities:* consider, think about, contemplate, mull over, chew over, reflect on, ruminate about, muse on; assess, evaluate, appraise, analyse, investigate, examine, review, explore, take stock of.
5 *they need to weigh benefit against risk:* balance, evaluate, compare, juxtapose, contrast.
□ **weigh someone down**
1 *my fishing gear weighed me down:* burden, overburden, encumber, hamper, handicap.
2 *the constant pressure was weighing me down:* oppress, depress, lie heavy on, burden, cast down, hang over, gnaw at, prey on your mind; trouble, worry, bother, disturb, upset.

weight noun
1 *bathroom floors are built to bear the weight of a standard bath not whirlpool spa baths:* heaviness, mass, load, burden, force; poundage, tonnage.
2 *his recommendation will carry great weight:* influence, force, leverage, sway, pull, importance, significance, consequence, value, substance, power, authority; informal clout.
3 *individuals differ in the weight they attach to various aspects of a job:* importance, significance, value.

weighty adjective
1 *a weighty tome:* heavy, hefty, thick, bulky, cumbersome.
2 *a weighty subject:* important, significant, momentous, major, vital, critical, crucial; serious, grave.
3 *a weighty responsibility:* burdensome, onerous, heavy, oppressive, taxing.
4 *weighty arguments:* compelling, cogent, strong, forceful, powerful, potent, effective, sound, telling; impressive, persuasive, convincing, influential, authoritative.
OPPOSITES: light, trivial, weak.

weird adjective
1 *a man passing the church at night heard weird sounds coming from the graveyard:* uncanny, eerie, unnatural, unearthly, other-worldly, ghostly, mysterious, strange, abnormal; Scottish eldritch; informal creepy, spooky.
2 (informal) *a weird sense of humour:* bizarre, quirky, outlandish, eccentric, offbeat, unconventional, unorthodox, unusual, idiosyncratic, surreal, crazy, peculiar, odd, strange, queer, freakish, zany, madcap, outré; informal wacky, way-out, off the wall.
OPPOSITES: normal, conventional.

welcome noun *we received a warm welcome from our hosts:* greeting, salutation; reception, hospitality; the red carpet.
▷ **verb**
1 *hotels should try to welcome guests in their own language:* greet, salute, receive, meet, usher in.

w

2 *we welcomed their decision:* be pleased by, be glad about, approve of, appreciate, salute; informal give the thumbs up to.
▷ **adjective** *this is welcome news for consumers:* pleasing, gratifying, encouraging, good, heartening, promising, favourable, pleasant; gladly received, appreciated.
OPPOSITES: unwelcome.

weld verb *they welded the sheets of metal together:* fuse, solder, bond, stick, join, attach, seal.

welfare noun
1 *the welfare of the children is paramount:* well-being, good, health, comfort, security, safety, protection, happiness; interests.
2 *we cannot claim welfare:* social security, state benefit, public assistance, support; sick pay, unemployment benefit; Brit. informal the dole.

well[1] adverb
1 *he behaved well:* satisfactorily, correctly, properly, appropriately, suitably, fittingly.
2 *they get on well together:* harmoniously, happily, amicably, amiably; informal famously.
3 *he plays the piano well:* skilfully, ably, competently, proficiently, adeptly, deftly, expertly, admirably, excellently.
4 *treat your employees well:* decently, fairly, kindly, generously, honestly.
5 *mix the ingredients well:* thoroughly, fully, completely.
6 *I know her very well:* intimately, closely.
7 *they studied the car market well:* carefully, closely, attentively, in depth, exhaustively, in detail, meticulously, scrupulously, conscientiously, methodically, comprehensively, fully, extensively, rigorously.
8 *they speak well of him:* admiringly, highly, approvingly, favourably, appreciatively, warmly, enthusiastically, in glowing terms.
9 *she makes enough money to live well:* comfortably, in (the lap of) luxury, in prosperity.
10 *he is well over forty:* considerably, very much, a great deal, substantially, significantly.
11 *she could well afford it:* easily, comfortably, readily.
12 *this litigation may well be followed by further claims:* very probably, in all likelihood, quite possibly.
OPPOSITES: badly, poorly, disparagingly, barely.
▷ **adjective**
1 *she was completely well again:* healthy, fit, robust, strong, vigorous, blooming, thriving, hale and hearty, in good shape, in good condition, in good trim, in fine fettle; informal in the pink.
2 *I do hope all is well:* satisfactory, all right, fine, in order, as it should be, acceptable; informal OK, hunky-dory.

3 *it would be well to tell us in advance:* advisable, sensible, prudent, politic, wise, judicious, expedient, advantageous, beneficial, desirable; a good idea.
OPPOSITES: unwell, unsatisfactory, inadvisable.
□ as well
the museum provides hours of fun and a few surprises as well: too, also, in addition, additionally, into the bargain, besides, furthermore, moreover, to boot.
□ as well as
the bars sell tea and coffee as well as alcohol: together with, along with, besides, and, with, on top of, not to mention, to say nothing of, let alone; informal plus.

well[2] noun *she drew water from the well:* borehole, bore, spring, waterhole.
▷ **verb** *tears welled from her eyes:* flow, spill, stream, run, rush, gush, roll, cascade, flood, spout; seep, trickle; burst, issue.

well advised adjective *you would be well advised to obtain legal advice:* wise, prudent, sensible.

well balanced adjective *children brought up in a loving family environment have more chance to develop into well-balanced individuals:* stable, steady, sensible, level-headed, down-to-earth, mature, having both feet on the ground, calm, self-possessed.

well behaved adjective *the pupils are very well behaved:* well mannered, polite, civil, courteous, respectful; obedient, compliant, cooperative, orderly, disciplined, peaceable, controlled, restrained.
OPPOSITES: naughty.

well-being noun. See WELFARE sense 1.

well bred adjective *she is too well bred to say anything:* well brought up, polite, well mannered, courteous; ladylike, gentlemanly, genteel, cultivated, urbane, refined, polished, well behaved.

well built adjective *he was about six feet tall and well built:* sturdy, strapping, brawny, burly, hefty, muscular, muscly, strong, rugged, lusty, Herculean; informal hunky, beefy, hulking.
OPPOSITES: puny.

well dressed adjective *she was always well dressed, regardless of the time of day:* smart, fashionable, stylish, chic, modish, elegant, neat, spruce, trim, dapper.
OPPOSITES: scruffy.

well founded adjective *they have a well-founded fear of persecution if they are deported:* justifiable, justified, warranted, legitimate, defensible, valid, admissible, allowable, understandable, acceptable, reasonable, sensible, sound.
OPPOSITES: groundless.

W

well known adjective
1 *a well-known fact:* familiar, widely known, established.
2 *a well-known family of architects:* famous, famed, prominent, notable, renowned, distinguished, eminent, illustrious, celebrated, acclaimed, important.
OPPOSITES: obscure.

well mannered adjective *they were well mannered and eager to please:* polite, courteous, civil, well bred, respectful, mannerly, decorous, refined, polished, civilized, urbane.

well-nigh adverb *policing the coastline all the time was well-nigh impossible:* almost, nearly, just about, more or less, practically, virtually, all but, as good as, nearing, approaching; informal pretty much.

well off adjective
1 *her family's very well off:* wealthy, rich, affluent, well-to-do, prosperous, moneyed, comfortable, propertied; informal rolling in it, in the money, loaded, well heeled, flush, made of money, quids in, worth a packet.
2 *the prisoners were relatively well off:* fortunate, lucky, comfortable.
3 *most of the clubs I've been at have been well off for strikers:* well supplied with, well stocked with, well furnished with, well equipped with.

well read adjective *he was very well read in this field:* knowledgeable, well informed, well versed, erudite, scholarly, literate, educated, cultured; bookish, studious.
OPPOSITES: ignorant.

wend verb *they wended their way across the city:* meander, wind your way, wander, amble, stroll, saunter, drift, roam, walk; journey, travel.

western adjective *the western coast of Scotland:* west, westerly; literary occidental.

wet adjective
1 *she took off her wet clothes | I slipped on the wet grass:* damp, moist, soaked, sodden, drenched, saturated, sopping, dripping, soggy; waterlogged, boggy, squelchy.
2 *it was cold and wet:* rainy, raining, pouring, teeming, showery, drizzly, drizzling; damp.
3 *the paint is still wet:* sticky, tacky; fresh.
4 *a wet mortar mix:* aqueous, watery, sloppy.
OPPOSITES: dry, fine.
▷ verb *he found a cloth and wetted it with lukewarm water:* dampen, damp, moisten; sprinkle, spray; soak, saturate, douse, souse, drench.
OPPOSITES: dry.

wharf noun quay, pier, dock, berth, landing, jetty; harbour, dockyard, marina.

wheedle verb *he wheedled a local banker*

into lending him the $40,000 he needed: coax, cajole, inveigle, induce, entice, charm, tempt, beguile, flatter, persuade, influence, win someone over, bring someone round, convince, prevail on, get round; informal sweet-talk, soft-soap.

wheel verb
1 *she wheeled the trolley away:* push, trundle, roll.
2 *gulls wheeled against the leaden sky:* turn, go round, circle, orbit.

wheeze verb *the illness often leaves her wheezing:* breathe noisily, gasp, rasp, croak, pant, puff, cough.

whereabouts noun *the whereabouts of the safe house is unknown:* location, position, site, place, situation; address.

wherewithal noun *she had the wherewithal to buy anything which took her fancy:* money, cash, capital, finances, funds; resources, means, ability, capability.

whet verb
1 *the trailer is just enough to whet an audience's appetite without giving away the entire movie:* stimulate, excite, arouse, awaken, rouse, kindle, trigger, spark, quicken, stir, inspire, fire.
2 *he whetted his knife on a stone:* sharpen, hone, strop, grind, file.
OPPOSITES: blunt.

whiff noun
1 *I caught a whiff of perfume:* faint smell, trace, sniff, scent, odour, aroma.
2 *the faintest whiff of scandal:* trace, hint, suggestion, impression, suspicion, soupçon, nuance, intimation, tinge, vein, shred, whisper, air, element, overtone.
3 *whiffs of smoke from the boiler:* puff, gust, flurry, breath, draught, waft.

while noun *he worked in America for a while:* time, spell, stretch, stint, span, interval, period; duration, phase; Brit. informal patch.
▷ verb *tennis helped to while away the time:* pass, spend, occupy, use up, kill.

whim noun *he seems determined to give away his family fortune by indulging various silly whims:* impulse, urge, vagary, inclination, notion, fancy, foible, caprice.

whimper verb *he was whimpering in pain:* whine, cry, sob, moan, snivel, wail, groan; Brit. informal grizzle.
▷ noun *she gave a whimper of protest:* whine, cry, sob, moan, bleat, wail, groan.

whimsical adjective
1 *a whimsical sense of humour:* fanciful, playful, mischievous, waggish, quaint, curious, droll; eccentric, quirky, idiosyncratic, unconventional, offbeat.
2 *a society ruled by law, not by whimsical personal likes or dislikes:* capricious, arbitrary, fickle, changeable, unpredictable, variable, erratic, mercurial, inconstant, volatile.

w

whine verb
1 *a small child was whining piteously:* wail, whimper, cry, mewl, howl, yowl.
2 *she began to whine about how hard she had been forced to work:* complain, grouse, grumble, moan, carp, mutter; informal gripe, grouch, bellyache, whinge.
▷ **noun**
1 *the dog gave a small whine:* whimper, cry, mewl, howl, yowl.
2 *a constant whine about the quality of public services:* complaint, grouse, grumble; informal gripe, moan, grouch, whinge, bellyache, beef.

whinge verb (informal) *they whinged about the weather.* See COMPLAIN.

whip verb
1 *they whipped him until he was unconscious:* flog, lash, thrash, beat, flagellate, tan someone's hide.
2 *he whipped his listeners into a frenzy:* rouse, stir up, excite, galvanize, electrify, stimulate, inspire, fire up, get someone going, inflame, agitate, goad, provoke.
3 *whip the cream until if forms stiff peaks:* whisk, beat.

whirl verb
1 *leaves whirled in eddies of wind:* swirl, twirl, spin, circle, wheel, turn, revolve, rotate, gyrate, pirouette.
2 *his mind was whirling:* spin, reel, swim.
▷ **noun**
1 *a whirl of dust:* swirl, flurry, eddy.
2 *the mad social whirl:* hurly-burly, activity, bustle, rush, flurry, fuss, turmoil, merry-go-round; informal to-do.
3 *Laura's mind was in a whirl:* spin, daze, stupor, muddle, jumble; state of confusion.

whirlwind noun
1 *the building was hit by a whirlwind:* tornado, hurricane, cyclone; N. Amer. twister.
2 *a whirlwind of activity:* tumult, mayhem, hurly-burly, commotion.
▷ **adjective** *a whirlwind tour of North America | their whirlwind romance:* rapid, lightning, breakneck, swift, fast, quick, speedy; sudden.

whisk verb
1 *the cable car will whisk you to the top:* speed, sweep, hurry, rush.
2 *she whisked the cloth away:* pull, snatch, pluck, tug, jerk; informal whip, yank.
3 *whisk the eggs and sugar for about a minute:* whip, beat, mix.

whisper verb *Ali whispered in his ear:* murmur, mutter, mumble, speak softly, speak sotto voce.
▷ **noun**
1 *she spoke in a whisper:* murmur, mutter, mumble, low voice, undertone.
2 *there are whispers of a blossoming romance between them:* rumour, story, report, speculation, suggestion, hint.

whit noun *no amount of talking will make a whit of difference:* scrap, bit, speck, iota, jot, atom, crumb, shred, grain, mite, touch, trace, shadow, suggestion, scintilla; informal smidgen.

white adjective
1 *a sheet of white paper:* colourless, bleached; snowy, snow-white, milky, chalky, ivory.
2 *her face was white with fear:* pale, ashen, bloodless, waxen, chalky; pallid, wan, washed out, drained, drawn.
3 *an old man with white hair and a white beard:* snowy, grey, silver, silvery, hoary, grizzled.
OPPOSITES: black, florid.

whitewash noun
1 *opposition parties claimed the report was a whitewash of the truth:* cover-up, camouflage.
2 (informal) *a four-match whitewash:* walkover, rout, landslide; informal pushover.
OPPOSITES: exposé.
▷ **verb** *this is just an attempt to whitewash the problem:* cover up, sweep under the carpet, hush up, suppress, draw a veil over, conceal, veil, keep secret; gloss over, downplay, soft-pedal.
OPPOSITES: expose.

whittle verb
1 *his powers were whittled away:* erode, wear away, eat away, reduce, diminish, undermine, weaken.
2 *the shortlist of fifteen was whittled down to five:* reduce, cut down, prune, trim, slim down, pare down, scale down.

whole adjective
1 *they refused to publish the whole report:* entire, complete, full; unabridged, unexpurgated, uncut.
2 *they discovered a whole marble mantelpiece:* intact, in one piece, unbroken; undamaged, unscathed.
OPPOSITES: incomplete.
▷ **noun**
1 *the two movements had been fused into a single whole:* entity, unit, body, discrete item.
2 *the whole of the year:* all, every part, the sum total.
□ **on the whole**
on the whole it was a very good speech: overall, all in all, all things considered, for the most part, in the main, in general, generally speaking, by and large.

wholehearted adjective
1 *he was praised for his wholehearted commitment to the club:* complete, full, total, absolute; unqualified, unreserved, without reservations, unconditional, unequivocal.
2 *they were wholehearted supporters of her economic strategy:* committed, devoted, dedicated, enthusiastic, unshakeable, unswerving.
OPPOSITES: half-hearted.

W

wholesale adverb *cultural treasures and temples were destroyed wholesale:* **extensively**, on a large scale, comprehensively; indiscriminately.
OPPOSITES: selectively.
▷**adjective** *the wholesale destruction of the natural habitat:* **extensive**, widespread, large-scale, comprehensive, total, mass; indiscriminate.
OPPOSITES: partial.

wholesome adjective
1 *the food is plentiful and wholesome:* **healthy**, health-giving, healthful, good for you, nutritious, nourishing; natural, organic.
2 *an evening to remember, providing wholesome fun and entertainment for the entire family:* **innocent**, decent, moral, virtuous; improving, edifying.

wholly adverb
1 *the measures were wholly inadequate:* **completely**, totally, absolutely, entirely, fully, thoroughly, utterly, quite, perfectly, downright, in every respect, in all respects; informal one hundred per cent.
2 *they rely wholly on you:* **exclusively**, only, solely, purely, alone.

whoop noun & verb *whoops of delight | he whooped for joy:* **shout**, cry, call, yell, roar, scream, shriek, screech, cheer; informal holler.

whopping adjective (informal). See HUGE.

whorl noun *elegant whorls of wrought iron:* **loop**, coil, hoop, ring, curl, twirl, twist, spiral, helix.

wicked adjective
1 *he will be punished for his wicked deeds | the kidnappers are wicked men:* **evil**, sinful, immoral, morally wrong, wrongful, bad, iniquitous, corrupt, base, depraved; villainous, nefarious, foul, vile, monstrous, shocking, atrocious, abominable, despicable, odious, contemptible, heinous, egregious, execrable, fiendish, vicious, murderous, barbarous; criminal, illicit, unlawful, illegal, unscrupulous; informal crooked.
2 *he has a wicked sense of humour:* **mischievous**, playful, naughty, devilish, impish, roguish, arch, puckish, cheeky.
OPPOSITES: virtuous.

wickedness noun **evil-doing**, evil, sin, sinfulness, iniquity, enormity, wrongdoing, unscrupulousness, villainy, viciousness, depravity, immorality, vice, corruption; formal turpitude.

wide adjective
1 *a wide river | wide, high-ceilinged rooms:* **broad**, extensive, spacious, vast.
2 *a wide range of opinion | a wide knowledge of classical music:* **comprehensive**, broad, extensive, large, wide-ranging, all-inclusive, all-embracing; encyclopedic, catholic.
3 *his shot was wide:* **off target**, off the mark, wide of the mark/target, inaccurate.
OPPOSITES: narrow.
▷**adverb**
1 *he opened his eyes wide:* **fully**, completely, to the fullest/furthest extent, as far/much as possible.
2 *he shot wide:* **off target**, wide of the mark/target, inaccurately.

wide-eyed adjective
1 *the whole class was wide-eyed:* **staring in amazement**, open-mouthed, dumbstruck, amazed, surprised, astonished, astounded, stunned, staggered; informal flabbergasted; Brit. informal gobsmacked.
2 *a wide-eyed country boy:* **innocent**, inexperienced, naive, impressionable, ingenuous, credulous, trusting, gullible.

widen verb
1 *a proposal to widen the motorway:* **broaden**, make/become wider, open up/out, expand, extend, enlarge.
2 *the company has widened its product range:* **extend**, broaden, increase, enlarge, augment, add to, diversify.

widespread adjective
1 *the idea has widespread support:* **general**, extensive, universal, common, global, worldwide, international, across the board.
2 *drug use is widespread in the area:* **prevalent**, rife, rampant, pervasive, endemic; ubiquitous, omnipresent.
OPPOSITES: limited.

width noun
1 *the width of his shoulders:* **breadth**, broadness; thickness, span, diameter, girth.
2 *the astounding width of his knowledge:* **range**, breadth, compass, scope, scale, extent, extensiveness, comprehensiveness.
OPPOSITES: length, narrowness.

wield verb
1 *he was wielding a sword:* **brandish**, flourish, wave, swing; use, employ, handle.
2 *he wielded enormous influence within the party:* **exercise**, exert, hold, maintain, command, control, have, possess.

wife noun **spouse**, partner, mate, consort, woman, bride; literary helpmate, helpmeet; informal old lady, missus.

> WORD LINKS
> **uxorial** relating to a wife
> **uxorious** very fond of your wife

wiggle verb *she wiggled her toes | Kelly came in, wiggling her hips as she walked:* **wriggle**, jiggle, twitch, wag; shake, shimmy; informal waggle.

wild adjective
1 *wild animals in their natural habitat:* **untamed**, undomesticated, feral; fierce, ferocious, savage.
2 *wild flowers:* **uncultivated**; native, indigenous.
3 *an expanse of wild moorland:*

W

uninhabited, uncultivated; rugged, rough, inhospitable, desolate, barren.
4 *a wild and bitterly cold night:* stormy, blustery, rough, squally, tempestuous, turbulent.
5 *the wall was built by the Romans to keep out the wild Caledonian tribes from the North:* primitive, uncivilized; savage, barbarous, barbaric.
6 *much of his money was wasted on wild schemes that will never prove profitable:* impractical, impracticable, unworkable, ill-considered, extravagant; madcap, ridiculous, ludicrous, foolish, stupid, foolhardy, idiotic, absurd, silly; informal crazy.
7 *her wild black hair:* dishevelled, tousled, tangled, windswept, untidy, unkempt.
8 *wild parties were never my scene:* disorderly, riotous, unrestrained, out of control, undisciplined, uncontrolled, unruly, rowdy.
9 *a wild guess:* random, arbitrary, haphazard, uninformed.
10 *his free kick sent the home fans wild with delight:* in a frenzy, frenzied, delirious, hysterical, beside yourself, berserk; informal mad, crazy.
OPPOSITES: tame, cultivated, calm, sensible, restrained.
□ **run wild**
1 *the garden had run wild:* grow unchecked, grow profusely, run riot.
2 *the children are running wild:* run amok, run riot, get out of control, be undisciplined.

wilderness noun
1 *the Siberian wilderness:* wilds, wastes, inhospitable region; desert.
2 *a litter-strewn wilderness:* wasteland.

wildlife noun animals, wild animals, fauna.

wilds plural noun *he spent a year in the wilds of Canada:* remote areas, wilderness; backwoods; N. Amer. backcountry; Austral./NZ outback, bush.

wiles plural noun *Rena plans to use her feminine wiles to get him to change his mind:* tricks, ruses, ploys, schemes, stratagems, manoeuvres, subterfuges; guile, artfulness, cunning, craftiness.

wilful adjective
1 *the wilful destruction of this historic building:* deliberate, intentional, done on purpose, premeditated, planned, calculated, conscious.
2 *a wilful child:* headstrong, self-willed, strong-willed, obstinate, stubborn, recalcitrant, uncooperative, obstreperous, unmanageable; formal refractory; Brit. informal bloody-minded.
OPPOSITES: accidental, amenable.

will¹ verb *accidents will happen:* have a tendency to, are bound to, do.

will² noun
1 *she has the will to succeed:*

determination, will power, strength of character, resolution, resolve, resoluteness, single-mindedness, purposefulness, drive, commitment, dedication, doggedness, tenacity, tenaciousness, staying power.
2 *they stayed against their will:* desire, wish, inclination, intention, intent.
3 *he believes it was God's will that he survived:* wish, desire, decision, choice; decree, command.
4 *his late father's will:* last will and testament.
▷ **verb**
1 *do what you will:* want, wish, please, see/think fit, think best, like, choose, prefer.
2 *they believed they were victorious because God willed it:* ordain, decree, order, command.
3 *she willed the money to her husband:* bequeath, leave, hand down, pass on, settle on.
□ **at will**
he seemed to think he could walk in and out of her life at will: as you please, as you think fit, to suit yourself, at whim.

willing adjective
1 *I'm willing to give it a try:* ready, prepared, disposed, inclined, of a mind, minded; happy, glad, pleased, agreeable, amenable; informal game.
2 *he thanked his staff for their willing help and support:* readily given, willingly given, ungrudging, enthusiastic.
OPPOSITES: unwilling, reluctant.

willingly adverb *Joe had gone with her willingly:* voluntarily, of your own free will, of your own accord; readily, without reluctance, ungrudgingly, cheerfully, happily, gladly, with pleasure.

willingness noun *many people have expressed a willingness to help:* readiness, inclination, will, wish, desire.

willowy adjective *a willowy blonde woman approached him:* tall, slim, slender, svelte, lissom, sylphlike, long-limbed, graceful, lithe; informal slinky.

will power noun. See **WILL²** noun sense 1.

willy-nilly adverb *cars were parked willy-nilly:* haphazardly, at random, randomly.

wilt verb
1 *the roses had begun to wilt:* droop, sag, become limp, flop; wither, shrivel.
2 *the girls were wilting in the heat:* languish, flag, droop, become listless.
3 *Shelley's happy mood wilted:* fade, ebb, wane, evaporate, melt away.
OPPOSITES: flourish.

wily adjective *he's a wily politician with more than one trick up his sleeve:* shrewd, clever, sharp, sharp-witted, astute, canny, crafty, cunning, artful, sly, foxy, scheming, calculating, devious; informal smart.
OPPOSITES: naive.

W

win verb

1 *Steve won the race:* be the victor in, be the winner of, come first in, take first prize in, triumph in, be successful in.
2 *she was determined to win:* come first, be the winner, be victorious, carry/win the day, come out on top, succeed, triumph, prevail.
3 *he won a cash prize:* secure, gain, collect, pick up, walk away/off with, carry off; informal land, net, bag, scoop.
4 *Ilona won his heart:* captivate, steal.
OPPOSITES: lose.
▷**noun** *a 3–0 win:* victory, success, triumph, conquest.
OPPOSITES: defeat.
☐ **win someone round/over**
Daisy made heroic efforts to win him round: persuade, talk round, convince, sway, prevail on.

wince verb *he winced at the pain:* grimace, pull a face, flinch, blench, start.

wind¹ noun *the trees were swaying in the wind:* breeze, current of air; gale, hurricane.

wind² verb

1 *the road winds up the mountain:* twist and turn, bend, curve, loop, zigzag, weave, meander, snake.
2 *she wound a scarf around her neck:* wrap, furl, loop, entwine, tie.
3 *Anne wound the wool into a ball:* coil, roll, twist, twine.
☐ **wind down**
the campaign was winding down: draw to a close, come to an end, tail off, slacken off, slow down.
☐ **wind someone up**
David was winding him up on purpose: annoy, anger, irritate, exasperate, get on someone's nerves, provoke, goad; Brit. rub up the wrong way; informal aggravate, rile, bug, put someone's back up, hack off; Brit. informal nark.
☐ **wind something up**
1 *Richard wound up the meeting:* conclude, bring to an end/close, end, terminate; informal wrap up.
2 *the company has been wound up:* close down, close, dissolve, put into liquidation.

winded adjective *he lay there for a moment, winded:* out of breath, breathless, gasping for breath, panting, puffing, puffed out; informal out of puff.

windfall noun *a £43,000 windfall:* bonanza, jackpot, pennies from heaven.

winding adjective *the winding country roads:* twisting and turning, meandering, serpentine, sinuous, curving, zigzag.
OPPOSITES: straight.

windpipe noun trachea, pharynx; throat.

windswept adjective

1 *the windswept moors:* exposed, bleak, bare, desolate.
2 *his windswept hair:* dishevelled, tousled, unkempt, wind-blown, untidy; N. Amer. informal mussed up.

windy adjective

1 *a windy day:* breezy, blowy, fresh, blustery, gusty; wild, stormy, squally, tempestuous.
2 *a windy hillside:* windswept, exposed, bare, bleak.
OPPOSITES: still, sheltered.

wing noun

1 *the east wing of the house:* part, section, side; annexe, extension.
2 *the radical wing of the party:* faction, camp, caucus, arm, branch, group, section; set, coterie, cabal.
▷**verb** *a seagull winged its way over the sea:* fly, glide, soar.

wink verb

1 *he winked an eye at her:* blink, flutter, bat.
2 *the diamond winked in the moonlight:* sparkle, shine, glint, glitter, gleam, glimmer, twinkle, flash.
☐ **wink at**
the authorities winked at their illegal trade: turn a blind eye to, close your eyes to, ignore, overlook, disregard; connive at, condone, tolerate.

winner noun victor, champion, conqueror; medallist; Brit. victor ludorum; informal champ, top dog.
OPPOSITES: loser.

winning adjective

1 *the winning team:* victorious, successful, triumphant, vanquishing, conquering; first, top.
2 *a winning smile:* engaging, charming, appealing, endearing, disarming, sweet, cute, winsome, attractive, pretty, fetching, lovely, adorable, delightful, captivating.

winnings plural noun *Sanchez collected his winnings:* prize money, gains, prize, booty, spoils; proceeds, profits, takings, purse.

winnow verb *the dust and chaff is winnowed from the grain:* separate, sift, filter out; isolate, find, identify; remove, get rid of.

winsome adjective. See WINNING sense 2.

wintry adjective

1 *a spell of wintry weather:* bleak, cold, chilly, chill, frosty, freezing, icy, snowy, arctic, glacial, bitter, raw; informal nippy; Brit. informal parky.
2 *a wintry smile:* unfriendly, unwelcoming, cool, cold, frosty, frigid.
OPPOSITES: summery, warm.

wipe verb

1 *Beth wiped the table with a paper towel:* rub, sponge, mop, swab; clean, dry, polish.
2 *he wiped the marks off the window:* rub

W

off, clean off, remove, get rid of, take off, erase, efface.
3 *she wiped the memory from her mind:* obliterate, expunge, erase, blot out, blank out.
□ **wipe someone/something out** *soldiers wiped out an entire village:* destroy, annihilate, eradicate, eliminate; slaughter, massacre, kill, exterminate; demolish, raze to the ground, obliterate.

wire noun cable, lead; Brit. flex.

wiry adjective
1 *a small, wiry man:* sinewy, strong, tough; lean, spare, thin, skinny.
2 *her wiry grey hair:* coarse, rough, strong; curly, wavy.

wisdom noun
1 *we questioned the wisdom of the decision:* sagacity, intelligence, sense, good sense, common sense, shrewdness, astuteness, judiciousness, judgement, prudence; logic, rationale, advisability.
2 *the wisdom of the East:* knowledge, learning, erudition, scholarship, philosophy; lore.
OPPOSITES: folly.

wise adjective *a wise old man | a wise decision:* sage, sagacious, intelligent, clever, learned, knowledgeable; astute, shrewd, sharp-witted, canny; sensible, prudent, judicious, discerning, perceptive, insightful, perspicacious; rational, logical, sound, well advised; informal smart.
OPPOSITES: unwise, foolish.

wish verb
1 *they wished for power:* desire, want, hope for, covet, dream of, long for, yearn for, crave, hunger for, lust after; aspire to, set your heart on, seek, hanker after, have a yen for; informal itch for.
2 *they can do as they wish:* want, desire, feel inclined, feel like, care; choose, please, think fit.
3 *I wish you to send them a message:* want, desire, require.
▷ noun
1 *his parents were very supportive of his wish to become a pilot:* desire, longing, yearning, urge, whim, craving, hunger; hope, aspiration, aim, ambition, dream; informal hankering, itch.
2 *she must carry out her father's wishes:* request, requirement, bidding, instruction, direction, demand, order, command; want, desire, will.

wishy-washy adjective
1 *their attitude to child-rearing makes the Jesuits look like wishy-washy liberals:* feeble, ineffectual, weak, vapid, effete, namby-pamby, insipid.
2 *wishy-washy soup:* watery, weak, thin; tasteless, flavourless.
3 *a wishy-washy colour:* pale, insipid, pallid, muted.

wisp noun *a stray wisp of hair:* strand, tendril, lock; scrap, shred, thread.

wispy adjective *her wispy blonde hair:* thin, fine, feathery, flyaway.

wistful adjective *he gazed out of the window with a wistful expression:* sad, regretful, plaintive, forlorn, rueful, melancholy, mournful; nostalgic, yearning, longing; pensive, reflective, contemplative.

wit noun
1 *he needed all his wits to escape:* intelligence, shrewdness, astuteness, common sense, wisdom, sagacity, judgement, acumen, insight; brains; informal nous, gumption, savvy, horse sense.
2 *I wanted to bowl him over with my sparkling wit:* wittiness, humour, drollery; repartee, badinage, banter, wordplay; jokes, witticisms, quips, puns.

witch noun sorceress, enchantress.

witchcraft noun sorcery, magic, black magic, witchery, wizardry, spells, incantations; rare thaumaturgy.

witch doctor noun medicine man, shaman, healer.

with preposition *she's gone out with her boyfriend and some of his mates:* accompanied by, escorted by; alongside, in addition to, as well as.

withdraw verb
1 *she withdrew her hand from his:* remove, extract, pull out, take out; take back.
2 *troops have withdrawn from the city:* leave, pull out of, evacuate, quit, retreat from.
3 *his partner withdrew from the project:* pull out of, back out of, bow out of; get cold feet.
4 *the ban on advertising was withdrawn:* discontinue, lift, set aside, end, stop, remove, cancel; reverse, revoke, rescind, repeal.
5 *she withdrew the allegation:* retract, take back, go back on; back down, climb down, backtrack, back-pedal, do a U-turn, eat your words.
6 *they withdrew to their rooms:* retire, retreat, adjourn, decamp; leave, depart, absent yourself.
OPPOSITES: insert, enter.

withdrawal noun
1 *the withdrawal of subsidies:* removal, discontinuation, cancellation.
2 *the withdrawal of the troops:* departure, pull-out, exit, exodus, evacuation, retreat.

withdrawn adjective *over the last few months he had become very withdrawn:* introverted, unsociable, inhibited, uncommunicative, unforthcoming, quiet, reticent, reserved, retiring, reclusive; shy, timid.
OPPOSITES: outgoing.

w

wither verb

1 *the flowers withered in the sun:* shrivel, dry up; wilt, droop, become limp, fade, perish.
2 *the muscles in his leg withered:* waste away, atrophy, shrivel, shrink.
OPPOSITES: thrive.

withering adjective *he launched a withering attack on his critics:* scornful, contemptuous, scathing, stinging, devastating; humiliating, mortifying.
OPPOSITES: admiring.

withhold verb

1 *he withheld the information:* hold back, keep back, refuse to give; retain, hold on to; hide, conceal, keep secret; informal sit on.
2 *she could not withhold her tears:* suppress, repress, hold back, fight back, choke back, control, check, restrain, contain.

within preposition

1 *within the prison walls:* inside, in, enclosed by, surrounded by; within the bounds of, within the confines of.
2 *within a few hours:* in less than, in under, in no more than, after only.
OPPOSITES: outside.

without preposition

1 *thousands were without food:* lacking, short of, deprived of, in need of, wanting, needing, requiring.
2 *I don't want to go without you:* unaccompanied by, unescorted by; in the absence of.

withstand verb *the company was able to withstand the rigours of the recession:* resist, weather, survive, endure, cope with, stand, tolerate, bear, defy, brave, hold out against, bear up against; stand up to, face, confront.

witness noun

1 *witnesses claimed that he started the fight:* observer, onlooker, eyewitness, spectator, viewer, watcher; bystander, passer-by.
2 *a whisky bottle was the only witness of his mood:* evidence, indication, proof, testimony.
▷ verb
1 *who witnessed the incident?* see, observe, watch, view, notice, spot; be present at, attend.
2 *the will is correctly witnessed:* countersign, sign, endorse, validate; N. Amer. notarize.
3 *his writings witness an inner toughness:* attest to, testify to, bear witness to, confirm, evidence, prove, verify, corroborate, substantiate; show, demonstrate, indicate, reveal; formal bespeak.

witter verb (Brit. informal). See JABBER verb.

witticism noun joke, quip, jest, pun, play

on words, bon mot; informal one-liner, gag, funny, crack, wisecrack.

witty adjective *his witty conversation:* humorous, amusing, droll, funny, comic, comical; jocular, facetious, waggish; sparkling, scintillating, entertaining; clever, quick-witted.

wizard noun

1 *the wizard cast a spell over them:* sorcerer, warlock, magus, enchanter.
2 *a financial wizard:* genius, expert, master, virtuoso, maestro, marvel; informal hotshot, demon, whizz-kid.

wizened adjective *the old man's wizened face:* wrinkled, lined, creased, shrivelled, withered, weather-beaten, shrunken, gnarled.

wobble verb

1 *the table wobbled:* rock, teeter, jiggle, sway, see-saw, shake.
2 *he wobbled across to the door:* teeter, totter, stagger, lurch, move unsteadily.
3 *her voice wobbled:* tremble, shake, quiver, quaver, waver.

wobbly adjective

1 *a wobbly table:* unsteady, unstable, shaky, rocky, rickety; precarious; uneven, unbalanced; informal wonky.
2 *her legs were a bit wobbly:* shaky, quivery, weak, unsteady; informal trembly, like jelly.
3 *she still felt a bit wobbly:* faint, dizzy, light-headed, giddy, weak, groggy.
OPPOSITES: stable.

woe noun

1 *a tale of woe:* misery, sorrow, distress, wretchedness, sadness, unhappiness, heartache, heartbreak, despondency, despair, depression, gloom, melancholy; adversity, misfortune, disaster, suffering, hardship.
2 *he attributes most of the company's financial woes to the sluggish economy:* trouble, difficulty, problem, trial, tribulation, misfortune, setback, reverse.
OPPOSITES: joy.

woebegone adjective *her woebegone expression:* sad, unhappy, miserable, dejected, disconsolate, forlorn, crestfallen, downcast, glum, gloomy, doleful, downhearted, despondent, melancholy, sorrowful, mournful, woeful, depressed, wretched, desolate; informal down in the mouth, down in the dumps, blue.
OPPOSITES: cheerful.

woeful adjective

1 *her face was woeful.* See WOEBEGONE.
2 *a woeful tale:* tragic, sad, miserable, gloomy, sorry, pitiful, pathetic, depressing, heartbreaking, heart-rending.
3 *the team's woeful performance:* dreadful, awful, terrible, atrocious, abysmal, appalling, disgraceful, deplorable, shameful, lamentable; informal rotten, pathetic, pitiful, lousy,

dire; Brit. informal chronic, hopeless, rubbish.
OPPOSITES: cheerful, excellent.

wolf verb *he wolfed down his breakfast:*
devour, gobble, guzzle, gulp down, bolt;
informal put away, demolish, shovel down,
scoff; N. Amer. informal scarf.

> WORD LINKS
> **lupine** relating to or like a wolf

woman noun
1 *two women got out of the car:* lady, girl,
female; Scottish & N. English lass, lassie; Irish
colleen; N. Amer. informal dame, broad; Austral./
NZ informal sheila.
2 *he's found himself a new woman:*
girlfriend, partner, significant other, lover,
sweetheart; fiancée; wife; informal bird;
N. Amer. informal squeeze.

> WORD LINKS
> **female**, **feminine** relating to women
> **gynaecology** the branch of medicine
> concerned with conditions specific to
> women and girls
> **misogyny** hatred of women

womanhood noun
1 *she was on the brink of womanhood:*
adulthood, maturity, sexual maturity.
2 *she was perceived as an ideal of
womanhood:* womanliness, femininity.

womanizer noun *he had a reputation
as a womanizer:* philanderer, Casanova,
Don Juan, Romeo, Lothario, ladies' man,
playboy; rake, roué, libertine; informal
ladykiller.

womankind noun women, woman, the
female sex, womanhood, womenfolk.

womanly adjective
1 *womanly virtues:* feminine, female.
2 *her womanly figure:* voluptuous,
curvaceous, shapely, ample, Junoesque,
buxom, full-figured; informal curvy.
OPPOSITES: masculine, boyish.

wonder noun
1 *she was speechless with wonder:* awe,
admiration, wonderment, fascination;
surprise, astonishment, amazement.
2 *the wonders of nature:* marvel, miracle,
phenomenon, sensation, spectacle, beauty;
curiosity.
> verb
1 *I wondered what was on her mind:*
speculate about, be curious about, ask
yourself, think about, reflect on, muse on,
ponder.
2 *I wonder you were so patient:* be
surprised, find it surprising.
3 *people wondered at such bravery:* marvel
at, be amazed by, be astonished by, stand
in awe of, be dumbfounded by.

wonderful adjective *I've had a wonderful
evening:* marvellous, magnificent, superb,
glorious, sublime, lovely, delightful; informal
great, fantastic, terrific, tremendous,

sensational, incredible, fabulous, super,
awesome, magic, ace, wicked, far out; Brit.
informal smashing, brilliant.
OPPOSITES: awful.

wont adjective *he was wont to arise at 5.30:*
accustomed, used, given, inclined; in the
habit of.
> noun *Paul drove fast, as was his wont:*
custom, habit, way, practice.

wonted adjective *Aldrich looked up
with his wonted patience and nodded
mildly:* customary, habitual, usual,
accustomed, characteristic, familiar,
normal, routine.

woo verb
1 *he had wooed her with romantic gestures
and words:* pay court to, pursue.
2 *political parties are making a conscious
effort to woo women voters:* seek the
support of, pursue, curry favour with, try
to win, try to attract, try to cultivate.
3 *an attempt to woo him out of retirement:*
entice, tempt, coax, persuade; informal
sweet-talk.

wood noun
1 *the walls and the floor were all made
of wood:* timber, planks, planking; logs;
N. Amer. lumber.
2 *a thick hedge divided the woods from
the field:* forest, woodland, trees; copse,
coppice, grove; Brit. spinney.

> WORD LINKS
> **ligneous** consisting of or resembling wood

wooded adjective *a wooded valley:*
forested, tree-covered, woody; literary
sylvan.

wooden adjective
1 *a wooden floor:* wood, timber, woody;
ligneous.
2 *part of the film's problem is the wooden
performances by the the two male leads:*
stilted, stiff, awkward, leaden; dry, flat,
lifeless, soulless.
3 *her face was wooden:* expressionless,
impassive, poker-faced, emotionless,
blank, vacant, unresponsive.

woodland noun *1000 acres of natural
woodland:* woods, wood, forest, trees.

woodwork noun carpentry, joinery.

wool noun
1 *lanolin is found naturally on sheep's wool:*
fleece, coat.
2 *a sweater made of cream wool:* yarn.

woolly adjective
1 *a woolly hat:* woollen, wool, fleecy.
2 *a sheep's woolly coat:* fleecy, shaggy.
3 *woolly generalizations:* vague, ill-defined,
unfocused, hazy, unclear, fuzzy, nebulous,
imprecise, inexact, indefinite; confused,
muddled.

woozy adjective (informal). See **GROGGY**.

W

word noun

1 *it's said that the Inuit have a hundred words for snow:* term, name, expression, designation; formal locution.

2 *his words were meant kindly:* remark, comment, observation, statement, pronouncement, utterance.

3 *everything will be taken care of—you have my word:* promise, word of honour, assurance, guarantee, undertaking; pledge, vow, oath, bond.

4 *I'm waiting for the word from HQ:* instruction, order, command; signal, prompt, cue; informal go-ahead.

5 *there's still no word from the hospital:* news, information, communication, intelligence; message, report, communiqué, dispatch, bulletin; literary tidings.

6 *I've got three weeks to learn the words:* script, lyrics, libretto.

7 *word has it he's turned over a new leaf:* rumour, hearsay, talk, gossip; informal the grapevine, the word on the street.

▷ **verb** *she had to be careful how she worded the question:* phrase, express, put, couch, frame, formulate, style; say, utter.

□ **have a word with**
could I have word with you later? speak to, talk to, have a chat with, have a conversation with, discuss something with.

□ **have words**
they'd had words the night before, after he got home late: quarrel, argue, squabble, bicker, fight, wrangle, disagree, dispute, fall out, clash; Brit. row.

□ **in a word**
the acting is, in a word, terrible: to be brief, in short, briefly, in a nutshell, to come to the point, to cut a long story short, not to put too fine a point on it; to sum up, to summarize, in summary.

□ **word for word**
1 *they took down the speeches word for word:* verbatim, letter for letter, to the letter; exactly, faithfully.

2 *a word-for-word translation:* verbatim, literal, exact, direct, accurate, faithful; unabridged.

> WORD LINKS
> **verbal**, **lexical** relating to words

wording noun *the wording of the question was ambiguous:* phrasing, choice of words, phraseology, language, expression, terminology.

wordplay noun punning, puns, play on words; wit, witticisms, repartee.

wordy adjective *a wordy speech:* long-winded, verbose, prolix, lengthy, protracted, long-drawn-out; rambling, circumlocutory, periphrastic; Brit. informal waffly.
OPPOSITES: succinct.

work noun

1 *he was tired after a day's work in the fields:* labour, toil, drudgery, exertion, effort, industry, service; informal slog, grind, sweat, elbow grease; Brit. informal graft, fag.

2 *I'm looking for work:* employment, a job, a post, a position, a situation; occupation, profession, career.

3 *haven't you got any work to do?* tasks, jobs, duties, assignments, projects; chores.

4 *works of literature:* composition, piece, creation; opus, oeuvre.

5 *this is the work of a radical faction:* handiwork, doing, act, deed.

6 *a lifetime spent doing good works:* deeds, acts, actions.

7 *the complete works of Shakespeare:* writings, oeuvre, canon, output.

8 *a car works:* factory, plant, mill, foundry, yard, workshop, shop.

9 *the works of a clock:* mechanism, machinery, workings, parts, movement, action; informal insides.
OPPOSITES: leisure.

▷ **verb**

1 *staff worked late into the night:* toil, labour, exert yourself; keep at it; informal slave away, slog away, beaver away, plug away, keep your nose to the grindstone, put your back into it, knock yourself out, sweat blood; Brit. informal graft.

2 *he worked in education for years:* be employed, have a job, earn your living, do business.

3 *farmers worked the land:* cultivate, farm, till, plough.

4 *his car was working perfectly:* function, go, run, operate; informal behave.

5 *how do I work this machine?* operate, use, handle, control, manipulate, run.

6 *their ploy worked:* succeed, be successful, work out, turn out well, go as planned, get results, be effective; informal come off, pay off, do the trick.

7 *blusher can work miracles:* bring about, accomplish, achieve, produce, perform, create, contrive, effect.

8 *he worked the crowd into a frenzy:* stir, stir up, excite, drive, move, rouse, fire, galvanize; whip up, agitate.

9 *work the mixture into a paste:* knead, squeeze, form; mix, stir, blend.

10 *he worked the blade into the padlock:* manoeuvre, manipulate, guide, edge.

11 *her mouth worked furiously:* twitch, quiver, convulse.

12 *he worked his way through the crowd:* manoeuvre, make, thread, wind, weave, wend.
OPPOSITES: rest, fail.

□ **work on someone**
leave him to me—I'll work on him: persuade, manipulate, influence; coax, cajole, wheedle, soften up; informal twist someone's arm, lean on.

□ **work out**
1 *the bill works out at £50:* amount to, add up to, come to, total; Brit. tot up to.

2 *my idea didn't work out.* See **WORK** verb sense 6.

w

3 *things didn't work out the way she planned:* end up, turn out, go, come out, develop; happen, occur; informal pan out.
4 *he works out at the local gym:* exercise, train.

□ **work something out**
1 *work out what you can afford:* calculate, compute, reckon up, determine.
2 *I'm trying to work out what she meant:* understand, comprehend, puzzle out, sort out, make sense of, get to the bottom of, unravel, decipher, decode; informal figure out, make head or tail of; Brit. informal suss out.
3 *they worked out a plan:* devise, formulate, draw up, put together, develop, construct, arrange, organize, contrive, concoct; hammer out, negotiate.

□ **work something up**
he couldn't seem to work up any enthusiasm: stimulate, stir up, rouse, raise, arouse, awaken, excite.

workable adjective *a workable solution to the problem:* practicable, feasible, viable, possible, achievable; realistic, reasonable, sensible, practical; informal doable.
OPPOSITES: unworkable, impracticable.

workaday adjective *they look like they might play dull workaday pop-rock, but the reality is quite different:* ordinary, average, run-of-the-mill, middle-of-the-road, conventional, unremarkable, unexceptional, undistinguished, commonplace, mundane, pedestrian, humdrum; routine, everyday, day-to-day; informal bog-standard; Brit. informal common or garden.
OPPOSITES: exceptional.

worker noun *a strike by 500 factory workers:* employee, member of staff; workman, labourer, hand, operative.

workforce noun *the company has a 9000-strong workforce:* staff, employees, personnel, workers, labour force, manpower; human resources; informal liveware.

working adjective
1 *working parents could soon receive more help towards childcare costs:* employed, in employment, in work, waged.
2 *the mill still has a working waterwheel:* functioning, operating, running, active, operational, functional, serviceable; informal up and running.
3 *they have a working knowledge of contract law:* sufficient, adequate, viable; useful, effective.
OPPOSITES: unemployed, faulty.

▷ **noun**
1 *the working of a carburettor:* functioning, operation, running, action, performance.
2 *the workings of a watch:* mechanism, machinery, parts, movement, action, works; informal insides.

workman noun worker, manual worker, labourer, hand, operative; employee; journeyman.

workmanlike adjective *the team put up a solid, workmanlike performance:* efficient, competent, professional, decent, acceptable, satisfactory, adequate.

workmanship noun *the pieces demonstrate a very high standard of workmanship:* craftsmanship, artistry, craft, art, artisanship, handiwork; skill, expertise, technique.

workshop noun
1 *a car repair workshop:* factory, works, plant; garage.
2 *he abandoned painting after a fire destroyed his workshop:* workroom, studio, atelier.
3 *a workshop on combating stress:* study group, discussion group, seminar, class.

world noun
1 *he's doing his bit to save the world:* earth, globe, planet.
2 *the academic world | the world of British theatre:* sphere, arena, milieu, province, domain, orbit, preserve, realm, field, discipline.
3 *she felt as though the eyes of the world were watching her:* everyone, everybody, people, mankind, humankind, humanity, the public, the general public, the populace, all and sundry.
4 *she renounced the world:* society, secular interests, temporal concerns, earthly concerns.

□ **on top of the world** (informal). See OVERJOYED.
□ **out of this world** (informal). See WONDERFUL.

worldly adjective
1 *his youth was wasted on worldly pursuits:* earthly, temporal, mundane, terrestrial; mortal, human, material, materialistic, physical, carnal, fleshly, bodily, corporeal, sensual.
2 *a worldly man:* sophisticated, experienced, worldly-wise, knowledgeable, knowing, enlightened, shrewd, mature, seasoned, cosmopolitan, urbane, cultivated, cultured.
OPPOSITES: spiritual, naive.

worldwide adjective *a worldwide effort to stop the spread of Aids | credit-card fraud is a worldwide problem:* global, international, intercontinental, universal; extensive, widespread, ubiquitous, far-reaching.
OPPOSITES: local.

worn adjective
1 *his jacket was old and worn:* shabby, worn out, threadbare, tattered, in tatters, falling to pieces, ragged, frayed, moth-eaten, scruffy, having seen better days; informal tatty, the worse for wear.
2 *her face looked worn:* exhausted, fatigued, tired, weary, drained, drawn,

careworn, haggard, hollow-eyed, pinched, pale, wan.

worn out adjective
1 *after about an hour they were worn out:* exhausted, tired out, fatigued, weary, drained; informal all in, done in, dog-tired, dead beat, shattered; Brit. informal knackered.
2 *a pair of worn-out shoes.* See **worn** sense 1.
3 *he portrayed them as the party of worn-out ideas:* old, stale, hackneyed, trite, overused, overworked, clichéd, unoriginal; informal played out, old hat.

worried adjective *you've been gone for nearly four and a half hours—I've been so worried:* anxious, perturbed, troubled, bothered, concerned, upset, distressed, distraught, disquieted, uneasy, fretful, agitated, nervous, edgy, on edge, tense, overwrought, worked up, keyed up, jumpy, stressed; apprehensive, fearful, afraid, frightened, scared; informal uptight, a bundle of nerves, on tenterhooks, jittery, twitchy.

worry verb
1 *she worries about his health:* fret, be concerned, be anxious; agonize, panic, lose sleep, get worked up; informal torment yourself.
2 *is something worrying you?* trouble, bother, concern, make anxious, perturb, disturb, distress, agitate, upset, unsettle, stress; torment, prey on your mind, weigh down, gnaw at.
3 *a dog worried the sheep:* attack, savage, maul.
▷ noun
1 *I'm beside myself with worry:* anxiety, concern, perturbation, distress, uneasiness, unease, disquiet, fretfulness, agitation, edginess, tension, stress; apprehension, fear, dread, trepidation, misgiving.
2 *the pound's strength is a worry for exporters:* problem, difficulty, trouble, concern; cause for concern; informal headache.

worrying adjective *the worrying rise in the number of firearms offences:* disturbing, giving cause for concern, alarming, disquieting, perturbing, distressing, worrisome, unsettling.

worsen verb
1 *insomnia can worsen a patient's distress:* aggravate, exacerbate, compound, add to, intensify, increase, magnify, heighten, inflame, augment.
2 *her condition worsened during the flight:* deteriorate, degenerate, decline; informal go downhill.
OPPOSITES: improve.

worship noun
1 *the worship of saints:* reverence, veneration, adoration, glorification, glory, exaltation.
2 *Sunday morning worship begins at 10.30:* service, religious rite, religious observance; devotion, prayer, praise, thanksgiving.
3 *for all her worship of Madonna, the 21-year-old exhibits none of her appetite for controversy:* admiration for, adulation of, idolization of; hero-worship.
▷ verb
1 *they worshipped pagan gods:* revere, venerate, reverence, pay homage to, honour, adore, pray to, glorify, exalt, praise, extol.
2 *her sons worship her:* adore, be devoted to, dote on, treasure, idolize, revere, hero-worship; informal put on a pedestal

worth noun
1 *he knew the painting's worth and refused to sell it for less:* value, price, selling price, cost.
2 *the intrinsic worth of education:* benefit, advantage, use, value, merit, virtue, utility, service; desirability.
3 *a sense of personal worth:* worthiness, merit, value, calibre, quality, stature, consequence, importance, significance.

worthless adjective
1 *the item was worthless:* valueless, of no value; useless, of no use.
2 *the president's pledge to provide $1 billion for the fight against Aids proved worthless:* useless, ineffective, ineffectual, fruitless, unproductive, unavailing, valueless, inadequate, meaningless, empty, hollow; formal nugatory.
3 *she had been deserted by her worthless husband:* good-for-nothing, ne'er-do-well, useless, shiftless, feckless; despicable, contemptible; informal no-good.
OPPOSITES: valuable, useful.

worthwhile adjective *everyone felt that the campaign had been worthwhile:* valuable, useful, of use, of service, beneficial, rewarding, advantageous, positive, helpful, profitable, gainful, fruitful, productive, constructive, effective, meaningful, worthy.
OPPOSITES: useless.

worthy adjective *a worthy citizen | a worthy objective:* virtuous, righteous, good, moral, upright, upstanding, high-minded, principled, exemplary, honest, honourable, reputable, decent, respectable; noble, meritorious, admirable, praiseworthy, laudable, commendable, creditable.
OPPOSITES: unworthy, disreputable.
▷ noun *portraits of local worthies:* dignitary, personage, grandee, VIP, pillar of society, luminary, leading light, big name; informal bigwig.
OPPOSITES: nobody.
□ **be worthy of**
these issues are worthy of further consideration: deserve, merit, warrant, rate, justify, earn, be entitled to, qualify for.

w

would-be adjective *persistence is the secret weapon for would-be entrepreneurs:* aspiring, eager, ambitious, hopeful; prospective, potential; budding, promising; informal wannabe.

wound noun
1 *a chest wound:* injury, lesion, cut, gash, laceration, tear, slash; graze, scratch, abrasion; bruise, contusion; Medicine trauma.
2 *that interview reopened old wounds and he started drinking heavily:* pain, distress, grief, trauma, anguish, torment; injury, hurt.
▷ verb
1 *he was critically wounded:* injure, hurt, harm; maim, mutilate; lacerate, cut, graze, gash, stab, slash.
2 *her words had wounded him:* hurt, upset, distress, grieve, sadden, pain, sting; offend, affront; injure; scar, damage.

wrangle noun *he left the team after a bitter financial wrangle:* argument, dispute, disagreement, quarrel, war of words, shouting match; Brit. row.
▷ verb *we wrangled over the details:* argue, quarrel, bicker, squabble, fall out, have words, disagree, be at odds, fight, battle, feud, clash; Brit. row.

wrap verb
1 *she wrapped herself in a towel:* swathe, swaddle, enfold, envelop, cover; wind.
2 *I wrapped the vase carefully:* parcel up, package, pack; gift-wrap.
▷ noun *he put a wrap round her shoulders:* shawl, stole, cloak, cape, mantle, scarf, pashmina.

wrath noun *he hadn't the nerve to face his mother's wrath:* anger, rage, fury, outrage, spleen, vexation, displeasure, annoyance; literary ire.

wreak verb *torrential rain wreaked havoc yesterday:* cause, result in, bring about, create; inflict, unleash.
□ wreak havoc on
these policies would wreak havoc on the British economy: damage, devastate, ravage, ruin, wreck.

wreath noun *a delicate wreath of roses:* garland, circlet, festoon; ring, loop, circle.

wreathe verb
1 *a pulpit wreathed in holly:* festoon, garland, drape, cover, bedeck, deck, decorate, ornament; adorn.
2 *blue smoke wreathed upwards:* spiral, coil, loop, wind, curl, twist, snake, curve.

wreck verb
1 *he had wrecked her car:* demolish, crash, smash up, damage, destroy; vandalize, deface, write off; N. Amer. informal trash, total.
2 *his ship was wrecked:* shipwreck, sink, capsize, run aground, break up.
3 *the injury wrecked his chances of a professional career:* ruin, spoil, put a stop to, frustrate, blight, crush, dash, destroy, undo, shatter, devastate, sabotage; informal mess up, screw up, foul up, put paid to, stymie, put the kibosh on; Brit. informal scupper.
▷ noun
1 *salvage teams landed on the wreck:* shipwreck, sunken ship.
2 *the wreck of a stolen car:* wreckage, debris, remainder, ruins, remains.

wrench noun
1 *with an almighty wrench she pulled her legs free:* tug, pull, jerk, heave; informal yank.
2 *it will be a real wrench to leave after so long:* painful experience, traumatic experience, trauma.
▷ verb
1 *he wrenched the gun from her hand:* tug, pull, jerk, wrest, heave, twist, grab, seize, snatch, force, prise; informal yank.
2 *she wrenched her ankle:* sprain, twist, turn, strain, rick, crick, pull; injure, hurt.

wrest verb *he tried to wrest the weapon from her grasp:* wrench, snatch, seize, grab, prise, tug, pull, jerk, dislodge; informal yank.

wrestle verb *as police wrestled with the gunman, a shot rang out:* grapple, fight, struggle, contend, vie, battle; scuffle, tussle, brawl; informal scrap.

wretched adjective
1 *I felt so wretched without you:* miserable, unhappy, sad, heartbroken, grief-stricken, sorrowful, distressed, desolate, devastated, despairing, disconsolate, downcast, dejected, crestfallen, depressed, melancholy, gloomy, doleful, forlorn, woebegone; informal blue.
2 *I feel wretched:* ill, unwell, poorly, sick.
3 *their living conditions are wretched:* harsh, hard, grim; terrible, awful, dire, atrocious, appalling, dreadful, bad, poor, lamentable, deplorable; pitiful, pathetic, miserable; Brit. informal grotty.
4 *the wretched inhabitants of a Soviet penal colony:* unfortunate, unlucky, luckless, ill-starred, hapless, poor.
OPPOSITES: cheerful.

wriggle verb
1 *she kicked and wriggled but he held her firmly | I wriggled my way into the sleeping bag:* squirm, writhe, wiggle, jiggle, jerk, thresh about, flail, twitch, twist and turn; worm.
2 *he tried to wriggle out of his responsibilities:* avoid, shirk, dodge, evade, elude, sidestep; escape from; informal duck.

wring verb
1 *he wrung out the cloth in the sink:* twist, squeeze, screw up, scrunch up.
2 *the company has found a way to wring more money out of its customer base:* extract, squeeze, wrest, wrench, force, exact.
3 *his expression wrung her heart:* stab, pierce, tear at, wound, rend.

W

wrinkle noun *the wrinkles around her eyes:* crease, fold, pucker, line, crinkle, furrow, ridge, groove; informal crow's feet.

▷ **verb** *he wrinkled his brow in puzzlement:* crease, furrow, crinkle, scrunch up; crumple, rumple, ruck up.

wrinkled adjective
1 *the wrinkled sheets:* creased, crumpled, rumpled, rucked up, crinkled.
2 *her wrinkled skin:* lined, creased, wrinkly, furrowed, wizened.
OPPOSITES: smooth.

writ noun *they were served with a High Court writ:* summons, subpoena, court order.

write verb
1 *he wrote her name in the book:* put in writing, write down, put down, jot down, make a note of, note down, take down, record, register, log, list, transcribe; inscribe, sign, scribble, scrawl, pencil.
2 *she wrote a letter to her mother:* compose, compile, draft, pen, dash off.
3 *he took her address and promised to write:* correspond, write a letter, communicate, get in touch, keep in contact; informal drop someone a line.

□ **write someone/something off**
1 *he urged the bank to write off the debt:* forget about, disregard, cancel, wipe out.
2 *he wrote off his new car:* wreck, smash up, crash, destroy, demolish, ruin; N. Amer. informal total.
3 *they were written off as a bunch of no-hopers:* disregard, dismiss.

writer noun author, wordsmith, man/woman of letters, penman; novelist, essayist, biographer; journalist, columnist, correspondent; scriptwriter, playwright, dramatist, dramaturge, tragedian; poet; informal, often humorous scribe; informal scribbler, pen-pusher, hack.

writhe verb *she writhed about on the floor in agony:* squirm, wriggle, thrash, thresh, flail, toss, toss and turn, twist, twist and turn, struggle.

writing noun
1 *I can't read his writing:* handwriting, hand, script; penmanship, calligraphy; informal scribble, scrawl.
2 *the writings of Gertrude Stein:* works, compositions, books, publications, oeuvre; papers, articles, essays.

WORD LINKS
graphology the study of handwriting

wrong adjective
1 *the wrong answer | I'm afraid I was wrong:* incorrect, mistaken, in error, erroneous, inaccurate, inexact, wide of the mark; informal off beam, out.
2 *he knew he had said the wrong thing:* inappropriate, unsuitable, inapt, inapposite, undesirable; ill-advised,

ill-considered, ill-judged, impolitic, injudicious, infelicitous, unfitting, out of keeping, improper; informal out of order.
3 *I've done nothing wrong:* illegal, unlawful, illicit, criminal, dishonest, dishonourable, corrupt; unethical, blameworthy, reprehensible, immoral, bad, wicked, sinful, iniquitous, nefarious; informal crooked.
4 *there's something wrong with the engine:* amiss, awry, out of order, not right, faulty, defective.
OPPOSITES: right, correct.

▷ **adverb** *she guessed wrong:* incorrectly, wrongly, inaccurately, erroneously, mistakenly.

▷ **noun**
1 *the difference between right and wrong:* immorality, sin, sinfulness, wickedness, evil; unlawfulness, crime, corruption, villainy, dishonesty, injustice, wrongdoing, misconduct, transgression.
2 *an attempt to make up for past wrongs:* misdeed, offence, injury, crime, transgression, peccadillo, sin; injustice, outrage, atrocity.
OPPOSITES: right.

▷ **verb**
1 *she was determined to forget the man who had wronged her:* ill-use, mistreat, do an injustice to, do wrong to, ill-treat, abuse, harm, hurt, injure; informal do the dirty on.
2 *perhaps I am wronging him:* malign, misrepresent, do a disservice to; defame, slander, libel.

□ **get someone/something wrong** misunderstand, misinterpret, misconstrue, mistake, misread; get the wrong idea/impression; informal get the wrong end of the stick, be barking up the wrong tree.

□ **go wrong**
1 *I've gone wrong somewhere:* make a mistake, make an error, make a blunder, miscalculate, trip up; informal slip up, screw up.
2 *their plans went wrong:* go awry, go amiss, go off course, fail, be unsuccessful, fall through, come to nothing; backfire, misfire, rebound; informal come to grief, come a cropper, go up in smoke; Brit. informal go adrift.
3 *the radio's gone wrong:* break down, malfunction, fail, stop working, crash, give out; informal be on the blink, conk out, go kaput; Brit. informal play up, pack up.

□ **in the wrong**
the hospital refused to admit that it was in the wrong: to blame, blameworthy, at fault, reprehensible, responsible, culpable, answerable, guilty.

wrongdoer noun offender, lawbreaker, criminal, felon, delinquent, villain, culprit; sinner, transgressor, miscreant, rogue, scoundrel; formal malefactor; informal crook.

wrongdoing noun
1 *good journalism can expose wrongdoing:*

w

crime, criminality, lawbreaking, lawlessness, misconduct, misbehaviour, malpractice, corruption, vice, immorality, sin, wickedness, evil, iniquity, villainy.
2 *their alleged wrongdoings:* offence, wrong, misdeed, misdemeanour, fault, transgression, peccadillo; crime, felony

wrongful adjective *she's suing her former employer for wrongful dismissal:* unjustified, unfair, unjust, unwarranted, undeserved, unreasonable, groundless, indefensible, inappropriate, improper, unlawful, illegal, illegitimate.
OPPOSITES: rightful.

wry adjective
1 *his wry humour:* ironic, sardonic, mocking; dry, droll, witty, humorous.
2 *he sipped the coffee and pulled a wry face:* unimpressed, disgruntled, disappointed, dissatisfied; annoyed, irritated, vexed, piqued; informal peeved.

W

xenophobic adjective (derogatory)
chauvinistic, jingoistic, excessively
patriotic, excessively nationalistic.

X-ray noun radiograph, X-ray image/
picture/photograph, roentgenogram.

> WORD LINKS
>
> **radiography** the medical process of taking
> X-rays
> **radiology** the science of X-rays and similar
> radiation

Yy

yank verb (informal) *he yanked open the door:* jerk, pull, tug, wrench, rip; snatch, seize.

yardstick noun *league tables are not the only yardstick of a school's performance:* standard, measure, gauge, scale, guide, guideline, indicator, test, touchstone, barometer, criterion, benchmark, point of reference, model.

yarn noun *you need to use a fine yarn:* thread, cotton, wool, fibre, filament; ply.

yawning adjective
1 *there was a yawning hole where the door had been wrenched off:* gaping, wide open, wide, cavernous, deep.
2 *the yawning gap between expenditure and resources:* wide, huge, great, enormous.

yearly adjective *a yearly payment:* annual.
▷ adverb *the guide is published yearly:* annually, once a year, every year, each year, per annum, by the year.

yearn verb *she yearned to be with him:* long, pine, ache, desire, want, wish, hanker, crave, hunger, thirst, eat your heart out, have your heart set on.

yearning noun *they sometimes feel a yearning for the mountains and the sea:* longing, craving, desire, wish, hankering, yen, urge, hunger, thirst.

yell verb *he yelled in agony:* cry out, call out, call at the top of your voice, shout, howl, wail, scream, shriek, screech, yelp, squeal, yowl; roar, bawl; informal holler.

yellow adjective golden, gold, blonde, fair; lemon, primrose, mustard; literary flaxen.

yelp verb *he yelped in pain:* squeal, shriek, howl, yowl, yell, cry, shout.

yen noun *he had a yen for foreign travel:* hankering, yearning, longing, craving, urge, desire, wish, hunger, thirst, lust, appetite; fancy, inclination; informal itch.

yes adverb all right, very well, of course, by all means, sure, certainly, absolutely, indeed, affirmative, agreed; roger; Scottish, N. English, & old use aye; informal yeah, yep, okay, OK.
OPPOSITES: no.

yet adverb
1 *he hasn't made up his mind yet:* so far, as yet, up till/to now, until now; formal thus far.
2 *don't celebrate just yet:* now, right now, at this time; already, so soon.
3 *he was doing nothing, yet he appeared purposeful:* nevertheless, nonetheless, even so, but, however, still, notwithstanding, despite that, in spite of that, for all that, all the same, just the same, at the same time, be that as it may.
4 *he supplied yet more unsolicited advice:* even, still, further, in addition, additionally, besides, into the bargain, to boot.

yield verb
1 *too many projects yield poor returns:* produce, bear, give, supply, provide, afford, return, bring in, earn, realize, generate, deliver, pay out.
2 *the nobility had yielded power to the new capitalist class:* relinquish, surrender, cede, part with, hand over; make over, bequeath, leave.
3 *the army was forced to yield:* surrender, capitulate, submit, relent, admit defeat, back down, climb down, give in, give up the struggle, lay down your arms, raise/show the white flag, throw in the towel.
4 *he yielded to her demands:* give in to, give way to, submit to, bow down to, comply with, agree to, consent to, go along with; grant, permit, allow; formal accede to; informal cave in to.
5 *the floorboards yielded underfoot:* bend, give, give way.
OPPOSITES: withhold, resist.
▷ noun *risky investments usually have higher yields:* profit, gain, return, dividend, earnings.

yob, yobbo noun (Brit. informal). See **HOOLIGAN**.

yoke noun
1 *the horses were loosened from the yoke:* harness, collar, coupling.
2 *countries struggling under the yoke of imperialism:* tyranny, oppression, domination, dominance, hegemony; bonds, chains, fetters, shackles.
▷ verb
1 *a pair of oxen were yoked together:* harness, hitch, couple, tether, fasten, attach, join.

y

2 *their aim of yoking biology and mechanics:* unite, join, link, connect, tie.

yokel noun rustic, bumpkin, peasant, provincial, country cousin, countryman/ woman; N. Amer. informal hillbilly, hick.

young adjective
1 *young people:* youthful, juvenile; adolescent, teenage; in the springtime of life, in your salad days.
2 *she's very young for her age:* immature, childish, inexperienced, unsophisticated, naive, unworldly; informal wet behind the ears.
3 *the young microbrewery industry:* fledgling, developing, budding, in its infancy, emerging.
OPPOSITES: old, elderly, mature.
▷ **noun**
1 *a robin feeding its young:* offspring, progeny, family, babies.
2 *the young are amazingly resilient:* young people, children, youngsters, youth, the younger generation, juveniles; informal kids.

youngster noun child, teenager, adolescent, youth, juvenile, minor, junior; Scottish & N. English lass, lassie; informal lad, kid, teen.

youth noun
1 *he was a keen sportsman in his youth:* early years, young days, teens, teenage years, adolescence, boyhood, girlhood, childhood; minority.
2 *she had kept her youth and beauty:* youthfulness, freshness, bloom, vigour, energy.
3 *a group of local youths:* young man, boy; informal lad.
4 *the youth of the nation:* young people, young, younger generation, next generation; informal kids.
OPPOSITES: adulthood, old age.

youthful adjective *he had remained remarkably youthful:* young-looking, well preserved, spry, sprightly, active, energetic; young, boyish, girlish; fresh-faced, in the springtime of life, in your salad days.
OPPOSITES: old, elderly.

y

Zz

zany adjective *the film has a zany plot and some peculiar characters:* eccentric, unconventional, quirky, idiosyncratic, funny, mad, crazy, madcap; bizarre, peculiar, odd, strange; informal weird, wacky, oddball, off the wall.
OPPOSITES: conventional, sensible.

zeal noun *he displayed an almost missionary zeal when talking about the artist's importance:* passion, ardour, fervour, fire, avidity, devotion, enthusiasm, eagerness, keenness, appetite, relish, gusto, vigour, energy, intensity, vehemence; fanaticism.
OPPOSITES: apathy.

zealot noun *reforming zealots destroyed a vast collection of papers:* fanatic, extremist, enthusiast, radical, activist, militant; sectarian, partisan.

zealous adjective *zealous supporters of his presidential campaign:* ardent, fervent, fervid, passionate, impassioned, devoted, committed, dedicated, enthusiastic, eager, keen, avid, vigorous, energetic, intense, vehement, fierce, fanatical.
OPPOSITES: apathetic.

zenith noun *the king was at the zenith of his power:* highest point, high point, crowning point, height, top, summit, peak, pinnacle, apex, acme, apogee; climax, culmination.
OPPOSITES: nadir.

zero noun
1 *you've left off a zero:* nought, o; Computing null character.
2 *I rated my chances as zero:* nothing at all, nil; informal zilch.
□ **zero in on**
different scientists chose to zero in on different diseases: focus on, focus attention on, concentrate on, home in on, fix on, pinpoint, highlight, spotlight; informal zoom in on.

zero hour noun *as zero hour approached, thirty ships swung into position:* the appointed time, the critical moment, the moment of truth, the point/moment of decision; informal the crunch.

zest noun
1 *she had a great zest for life:* enthusiasm, gusto, relish, appetite, enjoyment, eagerness, keenness, avidity, zeal, passion; verve, vigour, liveliness, fire, animation, vitality, dynamism, energy, spirit, exuberance, high spirits, brio; informal get-up-and-go.
2 *I used to try to beat past records to add zest to my monotonous job | flavoured vinegars can add zest to your meals:* piquancy, excitement, interest, an edge; tang, flavour, savour, taste, spice, relish, bite; informal kick.
3 *the zest of an orange:* rind, peel, skin.
OPPOSITES: apathy.

zigzag adjective *I steered a zigzag course between the trees:* twisting, full of twists and turns, serpentine, meandering, snaking, winding, crooked.
OPPOSITES: straight.

zone noun *the demilitarized zone between North and South Korea:* area, sector, section, belt, stretch, region, territory; district, quarter, locality, neighbourhood, province.

zoom verb (informal) *cars zoomed past:* speed, rush, race, career, charge, shoot, hurtle; informal whizz, tear.